Who Was Who in America®

Who Was Who in America®
with world notables

2014-2016
Volume XXVI

MARQUIS
Who'sWho®

430 Mountain Avenue, Suite 400
New Providence, NJ 07974 U.S.A.
www.marquiswhoswho.com

Who Was Who in America®
Marquis Who's Who

Published by Marquis Who's Who LLC. Copyright © 2016 by Marquis Who's Who LLC. All rights reserved.

For information, contact: Marquis Who's Who, 430 Mountain Avenue, Suite 400
New Providence, New Jersey 07974
1-800-473-7020; www.marquiswhoswho.com

WHO WAS WHO IN AMERICA® is a registered trademark of Marquis Who's Who LLC.

International Standard Book Number	978-0-8379-0303-3	(28-Volume Set)
	978-0-8379-0301-9	(Volume XXVI)
	978-0-8379-0300-2	(Index Volume)
	978-0-8379-0302-6	(Volume XXVI & Index Volume)
International Standard Serial Number	0146-8081	

Table of Contents

Preface

Marquis Who's Who is proud to present the 2014-2016 Edition of *Who Was Who in America*. This 26th edition features over 3,400 profiles of individuals who had previously been profiled in *Who's Who in America* and other Marquis Who's Who publications, whose deaths we are recognizing since the publication of the last edition of *Who Was Who in America*.

Of course, not every person profiled in this volume is a household name. These pages include the profiles of individuals in the fields of education, law, medicine, government, business, religion, science, broadcasting, publishing, technology, sports, literary and cultural arts, entertainment, among others.

The biographical information included in the profiles that follow was gathered in a variety of manners. In most cases, those listed had submitted their personal biographical details during their lifetime. In many cases, though, the information was collected independently by our research and editorial staffs, which use a wide assortment of tools to gather complete, accurate, and up-to-date information.

All of the profiles featured in *Who Was Who in America* are available through a subscription on www.marquiswhoswho.com. At the present time, subscribers to *Marquis Biographies Online* have access to all of the names included in all of the Marquis Who's Who publications, as well as many new biographies that will appear in upcoming publications.

The following notable individuals profiled in this volume had an enormous impact during their lifetime, and their influence is certain to live on. It has been an honor to compose this edition of *Who Was Who in America*.

Medicine, Science & Technology

Deborah Susan Asnis
Endre Alexander Balazs
Forrest Bird
Frederic Brandt
Eugenie Clark
Norman Farberow
Sherwood Fawcett
Alfred Gilman
Howard W. Jones, Jr.
James Jude
John Knauss
Edward Lammer
Frederick Li
John Millar
Marvin Minsky
John Nash, Jr.
Beny Primm
Dana Raphael
Irwin Rose
Oliver Sacks
Louis Sokoloff
Ernest Sternglass
Stanley Stookey
John Marks Templeton, Jr.
Richard Von Herzen
John Willke

Broadcasting & Publishing

Michael Brick
Stanton Cook
John Burr Fairchild
Arthur Twining Hadley, II
Charles Harbutt
Vicki Johnson
Acel Moore
Bud Paxson
Marlene Sanders
Gaylord Shaw
Bob Simon
Frederick Stickel
Phyllis Alexander Tickle

Literature

Jackie Collins
Alice Denham
E.L. Doctorow
Umberto Eco
René Girard
P.D. James
Harper Lee
John Leggett
Sir Terry Pratchett
Ann Rule

Sports

Alger Arbour
Ernie Banks
Yogi Berra
Walter Byers
Billy Casper
Arthur "Bud" Collins, Jr.
Nelson Doubleday, Jr.
Mel Farr
Raymond Gandolf
Frank Gifford
Bill Guthridge
Lindy Infante
Meadowlark Lemon
Moses Malone
Ted Marchibroda
Anthony George Douglas Mason
Calvin Peete
Hank Peters
Keith Anthony Phillips (Tony Phillips)
Pat Quinn
Ramon Rameriz
Albert Rosen
Flip Saunders
Jerry Tarkanian
Mario Vázquez-Raña
Bobby Wanzer

Entertainment

Lynn Anderson
Paul Bley
David Bowie
Joe Cocker
Natalie Cole
Wes Craven
Oscar de la Renta
Gina DePalma
Everett Firth
Glenn Frey
Coleen Gray
Daniel (Pat) Harrington, Jr.
Daniel Hicks
George Kennedy Jr.
B.B. King
Ben King
Sir Christopher Lee
Robert Loggia
Marjorie Lord
Anne Meara
Leonard Nimoy
Maureen O'Hara
Gary Owens
Paul Prudhomme
Alan Rickman
Wayne Rogers
Ettore Scola
Omar Sharif
Kerry Simon
Percy Sledge
Douglas Slocombe
Dick Van Patten
Abe Vigoda
Maurice White
Phil Woods
Alan "Bud" Yorkin
Gail Zappa

Academics

Stephen W. Bosworth
Owen Chadwick
Ray Farabee
Edward Foote, II
Elizabeth Garrett
Abraham Gitlow
Beverly Hall
John Lo Schiavo
Robert Spitzer
Charles Townes

Politics, Law, Military, Public Affairs & Foreign Leaders

Roger Adelman
Abdallah bin Abd al-Aziz Al-Saud
Jacqueline Berrien
Beau Biden
William McCormick Blair, Jr.
Julian Bond
Boutros Boutros-Ghali
Richard Cardamone
Miriam Cedarbaum
Ahmad Chalabi
Barbara M. Clark
Robert Del Tufo
Robin Chandler Duke
George Elsey
Francisco Guillermo Flores Pérez
John Fraser
Marie Garibaldi
Alan S. Gordon
Helen Holt
Avul Pakir Jainulabdeen Abdul Kalam
Judith Smith Kaye
Jerome Kohlberg, Jr.
Andrew Kohut
Yitzhak Navon
Nancy Reagan
Margaretta "Happy" Rockefeller
Antonin Scalia
William Schaap
Louis Stokes
Fred Thompson
Leo Tindemans
Edgar Whitcomb

Religion

Marcus Joel Borg
Malcom Boyd
Edward Michael Egan
William Friend
Francis Eugene George
Joseph Girzone
Theodore Hesburgh
Richard McBrien
Everett C. Parker
Robert Schuller
Harold Schulweis
Bernice Tannenbaum
Elio Toaff
Jean-Claude Turcotte

Performing & Cultural Arts

Van Alexander
Lennart Anderson
Leslie Raymond Bassett
Pierre Boulez
Bryony Brind
Eldzier Cortor
Robert Craft
Mattiwilda Dobbs
John C. Eaton
Charles Garabedian
Nikolaus Harnoncourt
James Horner
Ellsworth Kelly
William King
Ezra Laderman
Paul Laffoley, Jr.
Marvin Levy
Marvin Bentley Lipofsky
Kurt Masur
William McKinley
Charles Simonton Moffett, Jr.
George Ortman
Fred Otnes, Jr.
Richard Frank Sapper
Gunther Schuller
Aaron Shikler
Violette Verdy

Business

Gene Myron Amdahl
Robert Benmosche
John Correnti
Fred DeLuca
Donald G. Drapkin
Michele Ferrero
Curtis Gans
Walter Gerken
Leon A. Gorman
Charles S. Hallac
Michael David Hammond
Alan Hirschfield
Michael Jaharis
Harry Jay Katz
Michael King
Aubrey McClendon
Ralph J. Roberts
Ronald Rogers
Arthur Robert Taylor
Barbara Carlson Travaglini
Lillian Vernon

Key to Information

[1] **LINDELL, JAMES ELLIOT,** [2] literature educator; [3] b. Jacksonville, Fla., Sept. 27, 1969; [4] s. Elliot Walter and Tamara Lindell; [5] m. Colleen Marie, Apr. 28, 1993; [6] children: Richard, Matthew, Lucas, Samantha. [7] BA in English, Temple U., 1991, MA in English, 1993; PhD in English Lit., U. Chgo., 1996. [8] Cert. ESL 1992. [9] Assoc. prof. English U. Chgo., 1995-2004, prof. 2004-09, English dept. head 2009-11; [10] mem. ESL Coalition, Teach for Tomorrow; bd. dir., Chgo. HS Scholarship Assn. [11] Contbr. articles to profl. jours. [12] vol. Red Cross, 2000-10. [13] Served to USMC, 1992-94. [14] Recipient Outstanding Tchr. award U. Chgo., 2008; grantee Teach for Tomorrow, 2012. [15] Fellow Assn. Tchrs. for ESL; mem. MADD, Am. Soc. ESL Tchrs. [16] Democrat. [17] Roman Catholic. [18] Achievements include the expansion of teaching English as a second language to European countries. [19] Avocations: swimming, reading, traveling. [20] Home: Chicago, Ill. [21] Died May 23, 2014.

KEY

[1]	Name
[2]	Occupation
[3]	Vital statistics
[4]	Parents
[5]	Marriage
[6]	Children
[7]	Education
[8]	Professional certifications
[9]	Career
[10]	Career-related
[11]	Writings and creative works
[12]	Civic and political activities
[13]	Military
[14]	Awards and fellowships
[15]	Professional and association memberships, clubs and lodges
[16]	Political affiliation
[17]	Religion
[18]	Achievements
[19]	Avocations
[20]	Home address
[21]	Death

Table of Abbreviations

The following is a list of some of the most frequently used Marquis abbreviations:

A

A Associate (used with academic degrees)
AA Associate in Arts
AAAL American Academy of Arts and Letters
AAAS American Association for the Advancement of Science
AACD American Association for Counseling and Development
AACN American Association of Critical Care Nurses
AAHA American Academy of Health Administrators
AAHP American Association of Hospital Planners
AAHPERD American Alliance for Health, Physical Education, Recreation, and Dance
AAS Associate of Applied Science
AASL American Association of School Librarians
AASPA American Association of School Personnel Administrators
AAU Amateur Athletic Union
AAUP American Association of University Professors
AAUW American Association of University Women
AB Arts, Bachelor of
AB Alberta
ABA American Bar Association
AC Air Corps
acad. academy
acct. accountant
acctg. accounting
ACDA Arms Control and Disarmament Agency
ACHA American College of Hospital Administrators
ACLS Advanced Cardiac Life Support
ACLU American Civil Liberties Union
ACOG American College of Ob-Gyn
ACP American College of Physicians
ACS American College of Surgeons
ADA American Dental Association
adj. adjunct, adjutant
adm. admiral
adminstr. administrator
adminstrn. administration
adminstrv. administrative

ADN Associate's Degree in Nursing
ADP Automatic Data Processing
adv. advocate, advisory
advt. advertising
AE Agricultural Engineer
AEC Atomic Energy Commission
aero. aeronautical, aeronautic
aerodyn. aerodynamic
AFB Air Force Base
AFTRA American Federation of Television and Radio Artists
agr. agriculture
agrl. agricultural
agt. agent
AGVA American Guild of Variety Artists
agy. agency
A&I Agricultural and Industrial
AIA American Institute of Architects
AIAA American Institute of Aeronautics and Astronautics
AIChE American Institute of Chemical Engineers
AICPA American Institute of Certified Public Accountants
AID Agency for International Development
AIDS Acquired Immune Deficiency Syndrome
AIEE American Institute of Electrical Engineers
AIME American Institute of Mining, Metallurgy, and Petroleum Engineers
AK Alaska
AL Alabama
ALA American Library Association
Ala. Alabama
alt. alternate
Alta. Alberta
A&M Agricultural and Mechanical
AM Arts, Master of
Am. American, America
AMA American Medical Association
amb. ambassador
AME African Methodist Episcopal
Amtrak National Railroad Passenger Corporation
AMVETS American Veterans
ANA American Nurses Association
anat. anatomical
ANCC American Nurses Credentialing Center

ann. annual
anthrop. anthropological
AP Associated Press
APA American Psychological Association
APHA American Public Health Association
APO Army Post Office
apptd. appointed
Apr. April
apt. apartment
AR Arkansas
ARC American Red Cross
arch. architect
archeol. archeological
archtl. architectural
Ariz. Arizona
Ark. Arkansas
ArtsD Arts, Doctor of
arty. artillery
AS Associate in Science, American Samoa
ASCAP American Society of Composers, Authors and Publishers
ASCD Association for Supervision and Curriculum Development
ASCE American Society of Civil Engineers
ASME American Society of Mechanical Engineers
ASPA American Society for Public Administration
ASPCA American Society for the Prevention of Cruelty to Animals
assn. association
assoc. associate
asst. assistant
ASTD American Society for Training and Development
ASTM American Society for Testing and Materials
astron. astronomical
astrophys. astrophysical
ATLA Association of Trial Lawyers of America
ATSC Air Technical Service Command
atty. attorney
Aug. August
aux. auxiliary
Ave. Avenue
AVMA American Veterinary Medical Association
AZ Arizona

B

B Bachelor
b. born
BA Bachelor of Arts
BAgr Bachelor of Agriculture
Balt. Baltimore
Bapt. Baptist
BArch Bachelor of Architecture
BAS Bachelor of Agricultural Science
BBA Bachelor of Business Administration
BBB Better Business Bureau
BC British Columbia
BCE Bachelor of Civil Engineering
BChir Bachelor of Surgery
BCL Bachelor of Civil Law
BCS Bachelor of Commercial Science
BD Bachelor of Divinity
bd. board
BE Bachelor of Education
BEE Bachelor of Electrical Engineering
BFA Bachelor of Fine Arts
bibl. biblical
bibliog. bibliographical
biog. biographical
biol. biological
BJ Bachelor of Journalism
Bklyn. Brooklyn
BL Bachelor of Letters
bldg. building
BLS Bachelor of Library Science
Blvd. Boulevard
BMI Broadcast Music, Inc.
bn. battalion
bot. botanical
BPE Bachelor of Physical Education
BPhil Bachelor of Philosophy
br. branch
BRE Bachelor of Religious Education
brig. gen. brigadier general
Brit. British
Bros. Brothers
BS Bachelor of Science
BSA Bachelor of Agricultural Science
BSBA Bachelor of Science in Business Administration
BSChemE Bachelor of Science in Chemical Engineering
BSD Bachelor of Didactic Science
BSEE Bachelor of Science in Electrical Engineering
BSN Bachelor of Science in Nursing
BST Bachelor of Sacred Theology
BTh Bachelor of Theology
bull. bulletin

bur. bureau
bus. business
BWI British West Indies

C

CA California
CAD-CAM Computer Aided Design–Computer Aided Model
Calif. California
Can. Canada, Canadian
CAP Civil Air Patrol
capt. captain
cardiol. cardiological
cardiovasc. cardiovascular
Cath. Catholic
cav. cavalry
CBI China, Burma, India Theatre of Operations
CC Community College
CCC Commodity Credit Corporation
CCNY City College of New York
CCRN Critical Care Registered Nurse
CCU Cardiac Care Unit
CD Civil Defense
CE Corps of Engineers, Civil Engineer
CEN Certified Emergency Nurse
CENTO Central Treaty Organization
CEO Chief Executive Officer
CERN European Organization of Nuclear Research
cert. certificate, certification, certified
CETA Comprehensive Employment Training Act
CFA Chartered Financial Analyst
CFL Canadian Football League
CFO Chief Financial Officer
CFP Certified Financial Planner
ch. church
ChD Doctor of Chemistry
chem. chemical
ChemE Chemical Engineer
ChFC Chartered Financial Consultant
Chgo. Chicago
chirurg., der surgeon
chmn. chairman
chpt. chapter
CIA Central Intelligence Agency
Cin. Cincinnati
cir. circle, circuit
CLE Continuing Legal Education
Cleve. Cleveland
climatol. climatological
clin. clinical
clk. clerk
CLU Chartered Life Underwriter
CM Master in Surgery
cmty. community

CO Colorado
Co. Company
COF Catholic Order of Foresters
C. of C. Chamber of Commerce
col. colonel
coll. college
Colo. Colorado
com. committee
comd. commanded
comdg. commanding
comdr. commander
comdt. commandant
comm. communications
commd. commissioned
comml. commercial
commn. commission
commr. commissioner
compt. comptroller
condr. conductor
conf. Conference
Congl. Congregational, Congressional
Conglist. Congregationalist
Conn. Connecticut
cons. consultant, consulting
consol. consolidated
constl. constitutional
constn. constitution
constrn. construction
contbd. contributed
contbg. contributing
contbn. contribution
contbr. contributor
contr. controller
Conv. Convention
COO Chief Operating Officer
coop. cooperative
coord. coordinator
corp. corporation, corporate
corr. correspondent, corresponding, correspondence
coun. council
CPA Certified Public Accountant
CPCU Chartered Property and Casualty Underwriter
CPH Certificate of Public Health
cpl. corporal
CPR Cardio-Pulmonary Resuscitation
CS Christian Science
CSB Bachelor of Christian Science
CT Connecticut
ct. court
ctr. center
ctrl. central

D

D Doctor
d. daughter of
DAgr Doctor of Agriculture
DAR Daughters of the American Revolution
dau. daughter

DAV Disabled American Veterans
DC District of Columbia
DCL Doctor of Civil Law
DCS Doctor of Commercial Science
DD Doctor of Divinity
DDS Doctor of Dental Surgery
DE Delaware
Dec. December
dec. deceased
def. defense
Del. Delaware
del. delegate, delegation
Dem. Democrat, Democratic
DEng Doctor of Engineering
denom. denomination, denominational
dep. deputy
dept. department
dermatol. dermatological
desc. descendant
devel. development, developmental
DFA Doctor of Fine Arts
DHL Doctor of Hebrew Literature
dir. director
dist. district
distbg. distributing
distbn. distribution
distbr. distributor
disting. distinguished
div. division, divinity, divorce
divsn. division
DLitt Doctor of Literature
DMD Doctor of Dental Medicine
DMS Doctor of Medical Science
DO Doctor of Osteopathy
docs. documents
DON Director of Nursing
DPH Diploma in Public Health
DPhil Doctor of Philosophy
DR Daughters of the Revolution
Dr. Drive, Doctor
DRE Doctor of Religious Education
DrPH Doctor of Public Health
DSc Doctor of Science
DSChemE Doctor of Science in Chemical Engineering
DSM Distinguished Service Medal
DST Doctor of Sacred Theology
DTM Doctor of Tropical Medicine
DVM Doctor of Veterinary Medicine
DVS Doctor of Veterinary Surgery

E

E East
ea. eastern
Eccles. Ecclesiastical

ecol. ecological
econ. economic
ECOSOC United Nations Economic and Social Council
ED Doctor of Engineering
ed. educated
EdB Bachelor of Education
EdD Doctor of Education
edit. edition
editl. editorial
EdM Master of Education
edn. education
ednl. educational
EDP Electronic Data Processing
EdS Specialist in Education
EE Electrical Engineer
EEC European Economic Community
EEG Electroencephalogram
EEO Equal Employment Opportunity
EEOC Equal Employment Opportunity Commission
EKG electrocardiogram
elec. electrical
electrochem. electrochemical
electrophys. electrophysical
elem. elementary
EM Engineer of Mines
EMT Emergency Medical Technician
ency. encyclopedia
Eng. England
engr. engineer
engring. engineering
entomol. entomological
environ. environmental
EPA Environmental Protection Agency
epidemiol. epidemiological
Episc. Episcopalian
ERA Equal Rights Amendment
ERDA Energy Research and Development Administration
ESEA Elementary and Secondary Education Act
ESL English as Second Language
ESSA Environmental Science Services Administration
ethnol. ethnological
ETO European Theatre of Operations
EU European Union
Evang. Evangelical
exam. examination, examining
Exch. Exchange
exec. executive
exhbn. exhibition
expdn. expedition
expn. exposition
expt. experiment
exptl. experimental

Expy. Expressway
Ext. Extension

F

FAA Federal Aviation Administration
FAO UN Food and Agriculture Organization
FBA Federal Bar Association
FBI Federal Bureau of Investigation
FCA Farm Credit Administration
FCC Federal Communications Commission
FCDA Federal Civil Defense Administration
FDA Food and Drug Administration
FDIA Federal Deposit Insurance Administration
FDIC Federal Deposit Insurance Corporation
FEA Federal Energy Administration
Feb. February
fed. federal
fedn. federation
FERC Federal Energy Regulatory Commission
fgn. foreign
FHA Federal Housing Administration
fin. financial, finance
FL Florida
Fl. Floor
Fla. Florida
FMC Federal Maritime Commission
FNP Family Nurse Practitioner
FOA Foreign Operations Administration
found. foundation
FPC Federal Power Commission
FPO Fleet Post Office
frat. fraternity
FRS Federal Reserve System
FSA Federal Security Agency
Ft. Fort
FTC Federal Trade Commission
Fwy. Freeway

G

GA, Ga. Georgia
GAO General Accounting Office
gastroent. gastroenterological
GATT General Agreement on Tariffs and Trade
GE General Electric Company
gen. general
geneal. genealogical
geog. geographic, geographical
geol. geological
geophys. geophysical

geriat. geriatrics
gerontol. gerontological
GHQ General Headquarters
gov. governor
govt. government
govtl. governmental
GPO Government Printing Office
grad. graduate, graduated
GSA General Services
Administration
Gt. Great
GU Guam
gynecol. gynecological

H

hdqs. headquarters
HEW Department of Health,
Education and Welfare
HHD Doctor of Humanities
HHFA Housing and Home Finance
Agency
HHS Department of Health and
Human Services
HI Hawaii
hist. historical, historic
HM Master of Humanities
homeo. homeopathic
hon. honorary, honorable
House of Dels. House of
Delegates
House of Reps. House of
Representatives
hort. horticultural
hosp. hospital
HS High School
HUD Department of Housing and
Urban Development
Hwy. Highway
hydrog. hydrographic

I

IA Iowa
IAEA International Atomic Energy
Agency
IBRD International Bank for
Reconstruction and
Development
ICA International Cooperation
Administration
ICC Interstate Commerce
Commission
ICCE International Council for
Computers in Education
ICU Intensive Care Unit
ID Idaho
IEEE Institute of Electrical and
Electronics Engineers
IFC International Finance
Corporation
IL, Ill. Illinois
illus. illustrated
ILO International Labor
Organization

IMF International Monetary Fund
IN Indiana
Inc. Incorporated
Ind. Indiana
ind. independent
Indpls. Indianapolis
indsl. industrial
inf. infantry
info. information
ins. insurance
insp. inspector
inst. institute
instl. institutional
instn. institution
instr. instructor
instrn. instruction
instrnl. instructional
internat. international
intro. introduction
IRE Institute of Radio Engineers
IRS Internal Revenue Service

J

JAG Judge Advocate General
JAGC Judge Advocate General
Corps
Jan. January
Jaycees Junior Chamber of
Commerce
JB Jurum Baccalaureus
JCB Juris Canoni Baccalaureus
JCD Juris Canonici Doctor, Juris
Civilis Doctor
JCL Juris Canonici Licentiatus
JD Juris Doctor
jg. junior grade
jour. journal
jr. junior
JSD Juris Scientiae Doctor
JUD Juris Utriusque Doctor
jud. judicial

K

Kans. Kansas
KC Knights of Columbus
KS Kansas
KY, Ky. Kentucky

L

LA, La. Louisiana
LA Los Angeles
lab. laboratory
L.Am. Latin America
lang. language
laryngol. laryngological
LB Labrador
LDS Latter Day Saints
lectr. lecturer
legis. legislation, legislative
LHD Doctor of Humane Letters
LI Long Island
libr. librarian, library
lic. licensed, license

lit. literature
litig. litigation
LittB Bachelor of Letters
LittD Doctor of Letters
LLB Bachelor of Laws
LLD Doctor of Laws
LLM Master of Laws
Ln. Lane
LPGA Ladies Professional Golf
Association
LPN Licensed Practical Nurse
lt. lieutenant
Ltd. Limited
Luth. Lutheran
LWV League of Women Voters

M

M Master
m. married
MA Master of Arts
MA Massachusetts
MADD Mothers Against Drunk
Driving
mag. magazine
MAgr Master of Agriculture
maj. major
Man. Manitoba
Mar. March
MArch Master in Architecture
Mass. Massachusetts
math. mathematics, mathematical
MB Bachelor of Medicine,
Manitoba
MBA Master of Business
Administration
MC Medical Corps
MCE Master of Civil Engineering
mcht. merchant
mcpl. municipal
MCS Master of Commercial
Science
MD Doctor of Medicine
MD, Md. Maryland
MDiv Master of Divinity
MDip Master in Diplomacy
mdse. merchandise
MDV Doctor of Veterinary
Medicine
ME Mechanical Engineer
ME Maine
M.E.Ch. Methodist Episcopal
Church
mech. mechanical
MEd. Master of Education
med. medical
MEE Master of Electrical
Engineering
mem. member
meml. memorial
merc. mercantile
met. metropolitan
metall. metallurgical
MetE Metallurgical Engineer

meteorol. meteorological
Meth. Methodist
Mex. Mexico
MF Master of Forestry
MFA Master of Fine Arts
mfg. manufacturing
mfr. manufacturer
mgmt. management
mgr. manager
MHA Master of Hospital
Administration
MI Military Intelligence, Michigan
Mich. Michigan
micros. microscopic
mid. middle
mil. military
Milw. Milwaukee
Min. Minister
mineral. mineralogical
Minn. Minnesota
MIS Management Information
Systems
Miss. Mississippi
MIT Massachusetts Institute of
Technology
mktg. marketing
ML Master of Laws
MLA Modern Language
Association
MLitt Master of Literature,
Master of Letters
MLS Master of Library Science
MME Master of Mechanical
Engineering
MN Minnesota
mng. managing
MO, Mo. Missouri
moblzn. mobilization
Mont. Montana
MP Member of Parliament
MPA Master of Public
Administration
MPE Master of Physical Education
MPH Master of Public Health
MPhil Master of Philosophy
MPL Master of Patent Law
Mpls. Minneapolis
MRE Master of Religious
Education
MRI Magnetic Resonance
Imaging
MS Master of Science
MSc Master of Science
MSChemE Master of Science in
Chemical Engineering
MSEE Master of Science in
Electrical Engineering
MSF Master of Science of
Forestry
MSN Master of Science in Nursing
MST Master of Sacred Theology
MSW Master of Social Work
MT Montana

Mt. Mount
mus. museum, musical
MusB Bachelor of Music
MusD Doctor of Music
MusM Master of Music
mut. mutual
MVP Most Valuable Player
mycol. mycological

N

N North
NAACOG Nurses Association of
the American College of
Obstetricians and Gynecologists
NAACP National Association for the
Advancement of Colored People
NACA National Advisory
Committee for Aeronautics
NACDL National Association of
Criminal Defense Lawyers
NACU National Association of
Colleges and Universities
NAD National Academy of Design
NAE National Academy of
Engineering, National Association
of Educators
NAESP National Association of
Elementary School Principals
NAFE National Association of
Female Executives
N.Am. North America
NAM National Association of
Manufacturers
NAMH National Association for
Mental Health
NAPA National Association of
Performing Artists
NARAS National Academy of
Recording Arts and Sciences
NAREB National Association of
Real Estate Boards
NARS National Archives and
Record Service
NAS National Academy of
Sciences
NASA National Aeronautics and
Space Administration
NASP National Association of
School Psychologists
NASW National Association of
Social Workers
nat. national
NATAS National Academy of
Television Arts and Sciences
NATO North Atlantic Treaty
Organization
NB New Brunswick
NBA National Basketball
Association
NC North Carolina
NCAA National College Athletic
Association

NCCJ National Conference of
Christians and Jews
ND North Dakota
NDEA National Defense
Education Act
NE Nebraska
NE Northeast
NEA National Education
Association
Nebr. Nebraska
NEH National Endowment for
Humanities
neurol. neurological
Nev. Nevada
NF Newfoundland
NFL National Football League
Nfld. Newfoundland
NG National Guard
NH New Hampshire
NHL National Hockey League
NIH National Institutes of Health
NIMH National Institute of
Mental Health
NJ New Jersey
NLRB National Labor Relations
Board
NM, N.Mex. New Mexico
No. Northern
NOAA National Oceanographic
and Atmospheric Administration
NORAD North America Air
Defense
Nov. November
NOW National Organization for
Women
nr. near
NRA National Rifle Association
NRC National Research Council
NS Nova Scotia
NSC National Security Council
NSF National Science Foundation
NSTA National Science Teachers
Association
NSW New South Wales
nuc. nuclear
numis. numismatic
NV Nevada
NW Northwest
NWT Northwest Territories
NY New York
NYC New York City
NYU New York University
NZ New Zealand

O

ob-gyn obstetrics-gynecology
obs. observatory
obstet. obstetrical
occupl. occupational
oceanog. oceanographic
Oct. October
OD Doctor of Optometry

OECD Organization for Economic Cooperation and Development
OEEC Organization of European Economic Cooperation
OEO Office of Economic Opportunity
ofcl. official
OH Ohio
OK, Okla. Oklahoma
ON, Ont. Ontario
oper. operating
ophthal. ophthalmological
ops. operations
OR Oregon
orch. orchestra
Oreg. Oregon
orgn. organization
orgnl. organizational
ornithol. ornithological
orthop. orthopedic
OSHA Occupational Safety and Health Administration
OSRD Office of Scientific Research and Development
OSS Office of Strategic Services
osteo. osteopathic
otol. otological
otolaryn. otolaryngological

P

PA, Pa. Pennsylvania
paleontol. paleontological
path. pathological
pediat. pediatrics
PEI Prince Edward Island
PEN Poets, Playwrights, Editors, Essayists and Novelists
penol. penological
pers. personnel
PGA Professional Golfers' Association of America
PHA Public Housing Administration
pharm. pharmaceutical
PharmD Doctor of Pharmacy
PharmM Master of Pharmacy
PhB Bachelor of Philosophy
PhD Doctor of Philosophy
PhDChemE Doctor of Science in Chemical Engineering
PhM Master of Philosophy
Phila. Philadelphia
philharm. philharmonic
philol. philological
philos. philosophical
photog. photographic
phys. physical
physiol. physiological
Pitts. Pittsburgh
Pk. Park
Pky. Parkway
Pl. Place
Plz. Plaza

PO Post Office
polit. political
poly. polytechnic, polytechnical
PQ Province of Quebec
PR Puerto Rico
prep. preparatory
pres. president
Presbyn. Presbyterian
presdl. presidential
prin. principal
procs. proceedings
prod. produced
prodn. production
prodr. producer
prof. professor
profl. professional
prog. progressive
propr. proprietor
pros. prosecuting
pro tem. pro tempore
psychiat. psychiatric
psychol. psychological
PTA Parent-Teachers Association
ptnr. partner
PTO Pacific Theatre of Operations, Parent Teacher Organization
pub. publisher, publishing, published, public
publ. publication
pvt. private

Q

quar. quarterly
qm. quartermaster
Que. Quebec

R

radiol. radiological
RAF Royal Air Force
RCA Radio Corporation of America
RCAF Royal Canadian Air Force
Rd. Road
R&D Research & Development
REA Rural Electrification Administration
rec. recording
ref. reformed
regt. regiment
regtl. regimental
rehab. rehabilitation
rels. relations
Rep. Republican
rep. representative
Res. Reserve
ret. retired
Rev. Reverend
rev. review, revised
RFC Reconstruction Finance Corporation
RI Rhode Island
Rlwy. Railway

Rm. Room
RN Registered Nurse
roentgenol. roentgenological
ROTC Reserve Officers Training Corps
RR rural route, railroad
rsch. research
rschr. researcher
Rt. Route

S

S South
s. son
SAC Strategic Air Command
SAG Screen Actors Guild
S.Am. South America
san. sanitary
SAR Sons of the American Revolution
Sask. Saskatchewan
savs. savings
SB Bachelor of Science
SBA Small Business Administration
SC South Carolina
ScB Bachelor of Science
SCD Doctor of Commercial Science
ScD Doctor of Science
sch. school
sci. science, scientific
SCV Sons of Confederate Veterans
SD South Dakota
SE Southeast
SEC Securities and Exchange Commission
sec. secretary
sect. section
seismol. seismological
sem. seminary
Sept. September
s.g. senior grade
sgt. sergeant
SI Staten Island
SJ Society of Jesus
SJD Scientiae Juridicae Doctor
SK Saskatchewan
SM Master of Science
SNP Society of Nursing Professionals
So. Southern
soc. society
sociol. sociological
spkr. speaker
spl. special
splty. specialty
Sq. Square
SR Sons of the Revolution
sr. senior
SS Steamship
St. Saint, Street
sta. station

stats. statistics
statis. statistical
STB Bachelor of Sacred Theology
stblzn. stabilization
STD Doctor of Sacred Theology
std. standard
Ste. Suite
subs. subsidiary
SUNY State University of New York
supr. supervisor
supt. superintendent
surg. surgical
svc. service
SW Southwest
sys. system

T

Tb. tuberculosis
tchg. teaching
tchr. teacher
tech. technical, technology
technol. technological
tel. telephone
telecom. telecommunications
temp. temporary
Tenn. Tennessee
TESOL Teachers of English to Speakers of Other Languages
Tex. Texas
ThD Doctor of Theology
theol. theological
ThM Master of Theology
TN Tennessee
tng. training
topog. topographical
trans. transaction, transferred
transl. translation, translated
transp. transportation
treas. treasurer
TV television
twp. township
TX Texas
typog. typographical

U

U. University
UAW United Auto Workers

UCLA University of California at Los Angeles
UK United Kingdom
UN United Nations
UNESCO United Nations Educational, Scientific and Cultural Organization
UNICEF United Nations International Children's Emergency Fund
univ. university
UNRRA United Nations Relief and Rehabilitation Administration
UPI United Press International
urol. urological
US, USA United States of America
USAAF United States Army Air Force
USAF United States Air Force
USAFR United States Air Force Reserve
USAR United States Army Reserve
USCG United States Coast Guard
USCGR United States Coast Guard Reserve
USES United States Employment Service
USIA United States Information Agency
USMC United States Marine Corps
USMCR United States Marine Corps Reserve
USN United States Navy
USNG United States National Guard
USNR United States Naval Reserve
USO United Service Organizations
USPHS United States Public Health Service
USS United States Ship
USSR Union of the Soviet Socialist Republics
USTA United States Tennis Association
UT Utah

V

VA Veterans Administration
VA, Va. Virginia
vet. veteran, veterinary
VFW Veterans of Foreign Wars
VI Virgin Islands
vis. visiting
VISTA Volunteers in Service to America
vocat. vocational
vol. volunteer, volume
v.p. vice president
vs. versus
VT, Vt. Vermont

W

W West
WA, Wash. Washington (state)
WAC Women's Army Corps
WAVES Women's Reserve, US Naval Reserve
WCTU Women's Christian Temperance Union
we. western
WHO World Health Organization
WI Wisconsin, West Indies
Wis. Wisconsin
WV, W.Va. West Virginia
WY, Wyo. Wyoming

X, Y, Z

YK Yukon Territory
YMCA Young Men's Christian Association
YMHA Young Men's Hebrew Association
YM & YWHA Young Men's and Young Women's Hebrew Association
yr. year
YT Yukon Territory
YWCA Young Women's Christian Association

Alphabetical Practices

Names are arranged alphabetically according to the surnames, and under identical surnames according to the first given name. If both surname and first given name are identical, names are arranged alphabetically according to the second given name.

Surnames beginning with De, Des, Du, however capitalized or spaced, are recorded with the prefix preceding the surname and arranged alphabetically under the letter D.

Surnames beginning with Mac and Mc are arranged alphabetically under M.

Surnames beginning with Saint or St. appear after names that begin Sains, and are arranged according to the second part of the name, e.g., St. Clair before Saint Dennis.

Surnames beginning with Van, Von, or von are arranged alphabetically under the letter V.

Compound surnames are arranged according to the first member of the compound.

Many hyphenated Arabic names begin Al-, El-, or al-. These names are alphabetized according to each biographee's designation of last name. Thus Al-Bahar, Neta may be listed either under Al- or under Bahar, depending on the preference of the listee.

Also, Arabic names have a variety of possible spellings when transposed to English. Spelling of these names is always based on the practice of the biographee. Some biographees use a Western form of word order, while others prefer the Arabic word sequence.

Similarly, Asian names may have no comma between family and given names, but some biographees have chosen to add the comma. In each case, punctuation follows the preference of the biographee.

Parentheses used in connection with a name indicate which part of the full name is usually omitted in common usage. Hence, Chambers, E(lizabeth) Anne indicates that the first name, Elizabeth, is generally recorded as an initial. In such a case, the parentheses are ignored in alphabetizing and the name would be arranged as Chambers, Elizabeth Anne.

However, if the entire first name appears in parentheses, for example, Chambers, (Elizabeth) Anne, the first name is not commonly used, and the alphabetizing is therefore arranged as though the name were Chambers, Anne.

If the entire middle name is in parentheses, it is still used in alphabetical sorting. Hence, Belamy, Katherine (Lucille) would sort as Belamy, Katherine Lucille. The same occurs if the entire last name is in parentheses, e.g., (Brandenberg), Howard Keith would sort as Brandenberg, Howard Keith.

For visual clarification:

Smith, H(enry) George: Sorts as Smith, Henry George
Smith, (Henry) George: Sorts as Smith, George
Smith, Henry (George): Sorts as Smith, Henry George
(Smith), Henry George: Sorts as Smith, Henry George

Who Was Who in America®

ABBOTT, JOHN COPE, forensic research administrator; b. Quincy, Mass., Nov. 23, 1946; s. John Tucker and Anne Elisabeth (Skelly) A. BA in Premed. Biology, Gordon Coll., 1973; MS in Forensic Chemistry, Northeastern U., 1978. Sr. instr. Carnegie Inst., Boston, 1972-77; lab. scientist Mich. Dept. State Police, Bridgeport, 1978-79; forensic serologist Mass. Dept. Pub. Safety, Boston, 1979-81; lectr. forensic techniques convs., colls. and seminars, Mass., 1980-87; forensic serologist, mgr. Serological Rsch. Inst., Burlington, Mass., 1982-85, forensic serologist, owner Bedford, Mass., 1985-88; supr. toxicology Boston City Hosp., 1986-87, mgr. hematology and biochemistry lab., 1987-88; chief cons., owner Forensic Consultations, Bedford, from 1988; tech. mgr. Jewish Meml. Hosp. and Rehab. Ctr., Boston, 1989-98, lab. dir., 1998-99; lab. mgr. Dorchester (Mass.) House Multi-Svc. Ctr., from 2001. Editor (newsletter) Mass. Soc. Am. Med. Technologists, 1982-83, Piscataqua Pioneers Ancestors. Del. diocesan conv. Episcopal Diocese Mass., Boston, 1990. Recipient Silver Good Citizenship medal Nat. Soc. SAR, Louisville, 1978, Meritorious Svc. medal, 1987, Disting. Svc. award Am. Med. Technologists, 1987, Exceptional Merit award, 1991. Fellow Soc. Antiquaries (Scotland), Internat. Assn. Tartan Studies (life, sec. 1998—), Scottish Tartans Authority (life); mem. Am. Med. Technologists, Assn. Profls. in Infection Control, Am. Cons. League, Am. Soc. Clin. Lab. Sci., Nat. Assn. Desktop Publs., Midwestern Assn. Forensic Scientists, Clin. Lab. Mgmt. Assn., Internat. Assn. Bloodstain Pattern Analysts, Coll. Am. Pathologists, Scottish-Am. Mil. Soc. (life, nat. councillor 1993—), Nat. Soc. Descendants Colonial Clergy (life), Descendents Old Plymouth Colony (life, pres. gen. 1996-99), Clan Bell Soc. Internat. (pres. 1995—), Founders and Patriots Am. (life). Avocations: scientific reading, history, European travel, classical music, art. Died Mar. 18, 2007.

ABDUL, CORINNA GAY, software engineer, consultant, educator; b. Honolulu, Aug. 10, 1961; d. Daniel Lawrence and Katherine Yoshie (Kanada) A. BS in Computer Sci., U. Hawaii, 1984. Programmer, analyst, adminstrv. and fiscal svcs. U. Hawaii, Honolulu, 1982-84, software engr. libr. of divsn. of planetary geoscis., 1984; sys. software engr. II, test systems and software engr. dept space and tech. TRW Inc., Redondo Beach, Calif., 1985-89; systems software engr. II, Sierra On-Line, Inc., Oakhurst, Calif., 1989-90; sr. programmer, analyst Decision Rsch. Corp., Honolulu, 1990-92; ind. computer cons. Honolulu and Guam, from 1992; computer cons. Wailuku, Hawaii, from 1994; instr. Maui C.C., Kahului, Hawaii, from 1999; computer cons. QuizServer, U. Hawaii, from 2002; cluster specialist Nat. Ctr. Excellence for High Performance Computer Tech., Kihei, Hawaii, from 2002. Instr. cmty. coll. Kahului, Hawaii, 1999—; computer cons. Interactive Content Engines, LLC, Honolulu, 2002—. Recipient The 20th Century award for achievement, 1994. Avocations: traditional chinese medicine herbalist, practice japanese meridian therapy. Home: Wailuku, Hawaii. Died May 15, 2007.

ABEL, CHARLES GERALD, management, sales consultant; b. Monroe, Iowa, Dec. 19, 1920; s. Robert Carl and Margaret (Dotts) A.; m. Lucie W. Morris, June 4, 1963; children: Margaret, Steve, Tamara, Bryan. V.p. Brickell Inst., Memphis, 1950-58; exec. v.p. Nat. Investors Life Ins., Little Rock, 1958-71; pres. Charles G. Abel, Inc., Jonesboro, Ark., from 1971. Lectr. various univs. Author: Profitable Prospecting, 1985, How to Work Payroll Accounts, 1979. Past vice chmn. Pioneer dist. Boy Scouts Am.; past mem. exec. bd. Quapaw Area council Boy Scouts Am.; past dir. Ark. Arthritis Found.; former tng. chmn. United Fund. Served to capt. USAF, 1942-46. Mem. Assn. Life Underwriters Speakers Bur., Sales and Mktg. Exec. Clubs Speakers Bur. Clubs: Rotary. Republican. Methodist. Home: Jonesboro, Ark. Died Apr. 14, 2007.

ABEL, MICHAEL L., marketing executive; b. New London, Wis., Jan. 15, 1952; s. William A. and Delores R. (Shuey) A.; m. Monica L. Miller, Dec. 18, 1971; children: Richard M., David M. AAS, Joliet Jr. Coll., Ill., 1975; BA in Bus. Adminstrn., Lewis U., 1977, MBA, 1979. Lab. technician No. Petrochem. Co., Morris, Ill., 1975-76, tech. specialist, 1976-80, nat. account rep. Des Plaines, Ill., 1980-82; product mgr. Enron Chem. Co., Omaha, 1982-85, mktg. mgr., 1985-87; sr. account exec. Quantum Chem. Co., Rancho Mirage, Calif., 1987-89; sr. v.p. N.Am. ops. Intac Automotive Products, Inc., Lemont, Ill., from 1989; pres., chief exec. officer Desert Leisure Devel. Corp., Palm Springs, from 1991, bd. dirs. Bd. dirs. Palm Cts. Assn., Rancho Mirage, 1988-97, The Kids Business, Inc., Rancho Mirage, 1996—. Patentee in chem. engrng. field. Pres. Palm Ct. Owners Assn., Rancho Mirage, 1988-97; mem. Rep. Presdl. Task Force, 1990—. Mem. ASTM, Soc. Automotive Engrs., Nat. Assn. Corrosion Engrs. (sec. 1981-82), Internat. Platform Assn. Republican. Lutheran. Home: Rancho Mirage, Calif. Died Dec. 19, 2006.

ABLES, NOTA D., retired medical, surgical and geriatrics nurse; b. East Prairie, Mo., Sept. 27, 1920; d. John Wesley and Byrd (Cooper) Dover; m. Cline Ables, July 27, 1946; children: Marilyn Y. Ables Boyce, Don Wesley Ables. Diploma in nursing, St. Louis City Hosp., 1941. Scrub nurse St. Louis City Hosp.; charge nurse, tchr. CNA program M.D. Med. Ctr., Sikeston; ret. ARC nurse. Mem. ANA. Home: Sikeston, Mo. Died Jan. 26, 2007.

ABRAMOWITZ, JONATHAN, cellist; b. Greenbelt, Md., Mar. 15, 1947; s. Benjamin and Ruth (Rosen) A.; m. Lauree Nelson, Dec. 2, 1983. MusB, Juilliard Sch. Music, 1969, MS, 1970, D in Mus. Arts, 1972. Ind. cellist, recitalist, soloist with orchs. worldwide, from 1965; artist-in-residence various univs. Calif., Ariz., Utah. Recipient Unanimous Medal Geneva Internat. Competition, 1965, 1st prize Nat. Soc. Arts and Letters, 1961, 1st prize Young Concert Artists Internat. Competition, 1966, 1st prize Friday Morning Nat. Competition, 1966. Died Jan. 23, 2007.

ABRAMS, HERBERT LEROY, radiologist, educator; b. NYC, Aug. 16, 1920; s. Morris and Freda (Sugarman) Abrams; m. Marilyn Spitz, Mar. 23, 1943; children: Nancy, John. BA, Cornell U., 1941; MD, Downstate Med. Ctr., NYC, 1946. Diplomate Am. Bd. Radiology. Intern L.I. Coll. Hosp., 1946—47; resident in internal medicine Montefiore Hosp., Bronx, NY, 1947—48; resident in radiology Stanford U. Hosp., Calif., 1948—51; practice medicine specializing in radiology Stanford U., Calif., 1951—67, mem. faculty Sch. Medicine, 1951—67, dir. divsn. diagnostic roentgenology Sch. Medicine, 1961—67, prof. radiology Sch. Medicine, 1962—67; Philip H. Cook prof. radiology Harvard U., 1967—85, now prof. emeritus, chmn. dept. radiology, 1967—80; prof. radiology Stanford U. Sch. Medicine, 1985—90, prof. emeritus, 1990—2016; clin. prof. U. Calif. Sch. Medicine, San Francisco, 1986. Radiologist-in-chief Peter Bent Brigham Hosp., Boston, 1967—80; chmn. dept. radiology Brigham and Women's Hosp., Boston, 1981—85; radiologist-in-chief Sidney Farber Cancer Inst., Boston, 1974—85; R.H. Nimmo vis. prof. U. Adelaide, Australia; mem.-in-residence Ctr. for Internat. Security and Cooperation, Stanford U., from 1985; mem. radiation study sect. NIH, 1962—66; sr. fellow Stanford's Freeman Spogli Inst. for Internat. Studies; dir. Physicians for Social Responsibility; cons. to hosps., profl. socs. Author (with others): Angiocardiography in Congenital Heart Disease, 1956, Congenital Heart Disease, 1965, Coronary Arteriography: A Practical Approach, 1983, Brigham Guide to Diagnostic Imaging, 1986, Assessment of Diagnostic Technology in Health Care; editor: Abrams' Angiography, 3d edit., 1983; author: The President Has Been Shot: Confusion, Disability and the 25th Amendment, 1992, 1994, The History of Cardiac Radiology, 1996; mem. editl. bd.: Investigative Radiology, editor-in-chief, founder: Cardiovasc. and Interventional Radiology, 1978—88, Postgrad. Radiology, 1983—99. Named David M. Gould Meml. lectr., Johns Hopkins, 1964, William R. Whitman Meml. lectr., 1968, Leo G. Rigler lectr., Tel Aviv U., 1969, Holmes lectr., New Eng. Roentgen Ray Soc., Boston, 1970, Ross Golden lectr., N.Y. Roentgen Ray Soc., N.Y.C., 1971, Stauffer Meml. lectr., Phila. Roentgen Ray Soc., 1971, J.M.T. Finney Fund lectr., Md. Radiol. Soc., Ocean City, 1972, Aubrey Hampton lectr., Mass. Gen. Hosp., Boston, 1974, Kirklin-Weber lectr., Mayo Clinic, 1974, Crookshank lectr., Royal Coll. Radiology, 1980, Alpha Omega Alpha lectr., vis. prof., U. Calif. Med. Sch., San Francisco, 1961—65, W.H. Herbert lectr., U. Calif., Caldwell lectr., Am. Roentgen Ray Soc., 1982, Percy lectr., McMaster Med. Sch., 1983, Charles Dotter lectr., Soc. Cardiovasc. and Interventional Radiology, 1988, Philip Hodes lectr., Jefferson Med. Coll., 1988, David Gould Meml. lectr., Johns Hopkins U., 1991, Hymer Friedell lectr., Western Res. Sch. Medicine, 1993, Felix Fheischner Meml. lectr., Harvard Med. Sch., 1997, Charles Dotter Meml. lectr., Am. Heart Assn., 1998; fellow, Nat. Cancer Inst., 1950, Spl. Rsch. fellow, Nat. Heart Inst., 1960, 1973—74, Henry J. Kaiser sr. fellow, Ctr. for Advanced Study in Behavioral Sci., 1980—81. Fellow: Am. Coll. Cardiology, Am. Coll. Radiology, Royal Coll. Radiology (Gt. Britain) (hon.), Royal Coll. Surgery (Ireland) (hon.); mem.: NIH (working group on disability of U.S. pres. 1995—98, internat. blue ribbon panel radiation effects rsch. found. Hiroshima 1996, chmn. consensus panel on MRI), NAS (com. biol. effects of low-level ionizing radiation BEIR VII 1999—2005), Nat. Coun. Health Tech. Assessment, Soc. Chmn. Acad. Radiology Depts. (pres. 1970—71), Soc. Cardiovasc. Radiology (Gold medal 2000), Internat. Physicians for Prevention of Nuc. War (founding v.p., participant Nobel Peace prize 1985), N.Am. Soc. Cardiac Radiology (pres. 1979—80), Radiol. Soc. N.Am. (Gold medal 1995), Am. Soc. Nephrology, Am. Heart Assn., Inst. Medicine, Assn. Univ. Radiologists (Gold medal 1984), Alpha Omega Alpha, Phi Beta Kappa. Achievements include naming of Abrams conference room in radiology and Women's Hospital; development of Herbert L. Abrams annual lectures of Harvard Medical School. Home: Palo Alto, Calif. Died Jan. 20, 2016.

ABRAMS, MEYER HOWARD, language educator; b. Long Branch, NJ, July 23, 1912; s. Joseph and Sarah (Shanes) A.; m. Ruth Gaynes, Sept. 1, 1937; children: Jane Brennan, Judith Abrams. AB, Harvard U., 1934, MA, 1937, PhD, 1940; postgrad. (Henry fellow), Cambridge U., Eng., 1934-35; DHL (hon.), U. Rochester, 1978, Northwestern U., 1981, U. Chgo., 1982, Western Md. Coll., 1985, Le Moyne Coll., 1993, Carleton Coll., 2003, Yale U., 2007. Instr. Harvard, 1938-42; research asso. psycho-acoustic lab. Harvard U., 1942-45; asst. prof. English, Cornell U., Ithaca, NY, 1945-47, asso. prof., 1947-53, prof., 1953-60, Frederic J. Whiton prof. English, 1960-73, Class of 1916 prof. English, 1973-83, prof. emeritus, from 1983. Adv. editor W.W. Norton & Co., Inc., 1961—; bd. editors various Cornell publs. Hon. sr. fellow Sch. Criticism and Theory, Cornell U., Fulbright lectr. Royal U. Malta, Cambridge U., 1953; Roache lectr. U. Ind., 1963; Alexander lectr. U. Toronto, 1964; Ewing lectures UCLA, 1975; Cecil Green lectr. U B.C., 1980; Lamont lectures Union Coll., 1995; Mem. founders group Nat. Humanities Ctr.; mem. coun. of scholars Libr. of Congress, 1980-94, chmn. coun. of scholars, 1984-94. Author: The Milk of Paradise, 1934, 2d edit., 1970, The Mirror and the Lamp: Romantic Theory and the Critical Tradition, 1953, A Glossary of Literary Terms, 1957, 10th edit., 2010, Natural Supernaturalism: Tradition and Revolution in Romantic Literature, 1971, The Correspondent Breeze: Essays on English Romanticism, 1984, Doing Things with Texts: Essays in Criticism and Critical Theory, 1989, also publs. on mil. communications; editor: The Poetry of Pope, 1954; Editor: Literature and Belief, 1958, The Romantic Poets: Modern Essays in Criticism, 1960, rev. edit., 1975, The Norton Anthology of English Literature, 1962, 7th edit., 1999, Wordsworth: A Collection of Critical Essays, 1972, (with others) Wordsworth's Prelude: Norton Critical Edition, 1979 Recipient Christian Gauss prize Phi Beta Kappa, 1954, James Russell Lowell prize, 1971, Am. Acad. award humanistic studies, 1984, Disting. Scholar award Keats-Shelley Assn., 1987, Am. Acad. and Inst. Arts and Letters award for lit., 1990, Nat. Endowment for the Humanities medal, 2013; Rockefeller fellow, 1946; Ford fellow, 1952; Guggenheim fellow, 1958, 60-61; fellow Center for Advanced Study in the Behavioral Scis., Palo Alto, Calif., 1967-68; vis. fellow All Soul's Coll., Oxford, 1977. Mem. AAUP, MLA (exec. council 1961-64), Am. Acad. Arts and Scis., Am. Acad. Arts and Letters, Am. Philos. Soc., Brit. Acad. (corr. fellow), Phi Beta Kappa, Sigma Xi. Home: Ithaca, NY. Died Apr. 21, 2015.

ABSHIRE, DAVID MANKER, policy and research organization executive, retired ambassador; b. Chattanooga, Apr. 11, 1926; s. James Ernest and Phyllis (Patten) A.; m. Carolyn Lamar Sample, Sept. 7, 1957; children: Lupton Patten, Anna Lamra Abshire Bowman, Mary Lee Sample Abshire Jensvold, Phyllis Anderson Abshire d'Hoop, Carolyn Abshire Hall. Student, U. Chattanooga, 1945; BS, U.S. Mil. Acad., 1951; PhD in History, Georgetown U., 1959; DHL (hon.), Va. Theol. Sem., 1992; DCL (hon.), U. of the South, 1994; DHL (hon.), Georgetown U., 2006; LittD (hon.), Washington Coll., 2006. Minority staff member US House of Representatives, 1958-60; dir. spl. projects American Enterprise Inst. (AEI), Washington, 1961-62; from exec. dir. to pres. and co-founder Center Strategic & Internat. Studies (CSIS) Georgetown U., 1962-99, vice chmn., from 1999; asst. sec. for congressional rels. US Dept. State, Washington, 1970—73, US permanent rep. to NATO Brussels, 1983-87; spl. counsellor to Pres. The White House, The White House, 1987; pres. Ctr. for the Study of the Presidency & Congress (CSPC), Washington, 1999—2012, Richard Lounsbery Found., 2002—14. Presdl. appointee Congressional Commn. on Orgn. of Govt. for Conduct of Fgn. Policy, 1973-75; chmn. US Bd. for Internat. Broadcasting, 1974-77; dir. nat. security group Transition Office of Pres.-Elect Ronald Reagan, 1980-81; mem. Preident's Fgn. Intelligence Advisory Bd.,1981-83, President's Task Force on US Govt. Internat. Broadcasting, 1991; bd. dirs. Ogden Corp., 1987-96; adj. prof. Georgetown U., 1973-83. Author: The South Rejects a Prophet: The Life of Senator D.M. Key, 1967, International Broadcasting: A New Dimension of Western Diplomacy, 1976, Foreign Policy Makers: President vs. Congress, 1979, The Growing Power of Congress, 1981, Preventing World War III: A Realistic Grand Strategy, 1988, The Global Economy, 1990, Saving The Reagan Presidency: Trust Is The Coin Of The Realm, 2005, A Call to Greatness: Challenging Our Next President, 2008; co-author: Putting America's House in Order, 1996; editor: National Security, 1963, Portuguese Africa, 1969, Research Resources for the Seventies, 1971, Triumphs and Tragedies of the Modern Presidency: Seventy-Six Case Studies in Presidential Leadership, 2001; co-editor Washington Quar., 1977-83; contributing editor: Detente: Cold War Strategies in Transition, 1964, Vietnam Legacy, 1976, The Global Economy, 1990; editor-in-chief: Report to the President-elect 2000: Triumphs and Tragedies of the Modern Presidency, 2000, Saving the Reagan Presidency, 2005. Mem. advisory bd. Naval War Coll., 1975-79; vice-chmn. bd. Youth for Understanding, 1979-80; bd. dirs. Spaak Found.,

Brussels; trustee George W. Marshall Found. With AUS, 1945-46; 1st lt. 1951-56; capt. Res. ret. Decorated Bronze Star with oak leaf cluster, with V for Valor, V commendation ribbon with metal pendant; Order of Crown, comdr. Order of Leopold (Belgium); grand ofcl. Order of Republic of Italy; recipient Medal of Pres. of Italian Republic, Senate, Parliament and Govt. and of Pio Manzu Ctr.; recipient John Carroll award, US Dept. Def. disting. Public Svc. Medal, 1988, Presdl. Citizens medal, 1989, Medal of Diplomatic Merit Republic of Korea, 1993; First Class Order of The Lion of Finland insignia of the Comdr., 1994, US Military Acad. Castle award, 1994, Order of the Liberator, Argentina, 1999, Order of Sacred Treasure Gold and Silver Star, Japan, 2001. Mem. Coun. American Ambassadors, Coun. on Competitiveness, Coun. Fgn. Rels., Inst. Strategic Studies, Trinity Nat. Leadership Roundtable (co-founder), Gold Key Soc., Alfalfa Club, Met. Club, Cosmos Club, Alibi Club, Phi Alpha Theta. Republican. Episcopalian. Home: Alexandria, Va. Died Oct. 31, 2014.

ACKERMAN, RUDY SCHLEGEL, artist, educator; b. Allentown, Pa., Mar. 30, 1933; s. Harvey J. and Alma (Schlegel) A.; m. Rosemarie Ercolani, 1953; children: Sally Ann, Ann Marie. BS in Art Edn., Kutztown U., 1958; MS in Edn., Temple U., 1961; EdD in Art Edn., Pa. State U., 1967. Art specialist So. Lehigh State U., Coopersburg, Pa., 1958-63; prof., chmn. dept. art Moravian Coll., Bethlehem, Pa., 1963-2000, prof. arts and humanities, from 1990; exec. dir. Baum Sch. of Art, Allentown, Pa., from 1965. Commd. works include sculpture installations at Lehigh U., Pa. State U., Bethlehem Sculpture Garden, Moravian Coll., various pvt. collections; lectr. in field. Pres. Allentown Arts Commn., 1992—. With U.S. Army, 1953-55. Mem. Coll. Art Assn., Nat. Guild of Schs. of the Arts. Home: Allentown, Pa. Died May 21, 2015.

ADAIR, JACQUELINE PRITNER, psychotherapist, hypnotherapist; b. Whittington, Tex., Jan. 14, 1936; d. Ural Dick and Ina Alene (Singleton) Adair; m. Calvin L. Pritner, Sept. 3, 1954 (div. Mar. 1983); children: Christopher P., Juliet P. BS, Ill. State U., 1972, MS, 1978. Sec. to office mgr. P&G, Kansas City, Kans., 1957-59; rsch. asst. Nat. Assn. County Officers, Washington, 1960; tchr. English Univ. High Sch., Normal, Ill., 1972-73; clin. program mgr. McLean County Ctr. for Human Svcs., Bloomington, 1978-83; tchr. English Cen. Cath. High Sch., Bloomington, Ill., 1974-75; clin. psychologist Perth (W, Australia) Psychiat. Clinic, 1984-87, Victoria Health Dept., Ballarat, Victoria, Australia, 1987-88; staff counselor Ill. State U., Normal, Ill., 1990-93; psychotherapist pvt. practice Normal, from 1990. Cons. Dept. Children and Family Svcs., Bloomington, Ill., 1990-94. Bd. dirs. Am. Cancer Soc., Mc Lean County, Ill., 1993-94. Mem. Am. Psychol. Assn. (assoc.), Am. Acad. Psychotherapists. Avocations: tennis, horseback riding, walking/hiking, aerobics. Died Aug. 29, 2007.

ADAMS, ALVIN PHILIP, JR., diplomat; b. NYC, Aug. 29, 1942; s. Alvin P. Adams and Elizabeth Miller; m. Mai-Anh Nguyen (div.); children Lex N., Tung Thanh (dec. 1989) BA, Yale Coll., 1964; JD, Vanderbilt Law Sch., 1967; LittD (hon.), Conn. Coll., 1994. Bar: N.Y. 1967, D.C. 1977. Amb. to Djibouti U.S. Dept. State, 1983-85, dep. dir. office counter terrorism, 1986-89, amb. to Haiti, 1989-92, amb. to Peru, 1993-96; pres., CEO UN Assn. U.S., NYC, 1996-98. Mem. Yale Club N.Y.C. Home: Honolulu, Hawaii. Died Oct. 10, 2015.

ADAMS, ARLIN MARVIN, lawyer, retired judge, arbitrator, mediator; b. Phila., Apr. 16, 1921; s. Aaron M. and Mathilda (Landau) A.; m. Neysa Cristol, Nov. 10, 1942; children: Carol (Mrs. Howard Kirshner), Judith A., Jane C. BS in Econs. with highest honors, Temple U., 1941; LLB with honors, U. Pa., 1947, MA in Econs., 1950; DHL (hon.), Temple U., 1964; DSc (hon.), Phila. Coll., 1965, LLD (hon.), 1966, Susquehanna U., 1985, Muhlenberg Coll., 1986, Villanova U., 1987, U. Pa., 1998. Bar: Pa. 1947; U.S. Ct. Appeals (3rd cir.), 1947. Law clk., Chief Justice Horace Stern Pa. Supreme Ct., 1947; assoc. firm Schnader, Harrison, Segal & Lewis, Phila., 1947-50, sr. ptnr., 1950-63, 66-69; sec. pub. welfare Commonwealth of Pa., Phila., 1963-66; judge U.S. Ct. Appeals (3d cir.), Phila., 1969-87; counsel Schnader, Harrison, Segal & Lewis, Phila., 1987—2012. Apptd. ind. counsel to investigate Dept. HUD, 1990-95; apptd. chmn. commn. to investigate prison br.; apptd. spl. counsel Pa. Commn. of Police, 1994-95; instr. Am. Inst. Banking, Phila., 1949-52; lectr. fed. practice Law Sch., U. Pa., Phila., 1952-56, lectr. constl. law, 1972-97; endowed chair Arlin M. Adams Professorship Constl. Law, U. Pa. Law Sch., 2004. Author: Law and Religion, 2 vols., 1991, A Nation Dedicated to Religious Liberty, 1990; Editor-in-chief Law Review U. Penn., 1947; contbr. articles to profl. jours. Pres. Annenberg Inst., 1988—91; chmn. bd. dirs. Moss Rehab. Hosp., Phila., 1962—63; trustee U. Pa., from 1985; chmn. U.S. Supreme Ct. Jud. Fellows Commn., 1987—93, Fels Inst. Govt., Phila., 1967—77, Sch. of Social Work, Bryn Mawr (Pa.) Coll., 1967—78, Diagnostic and Rehab. Ctr., Phila., 1971—72; chmn. overseers U. Pa. Law Sch., 1985—92; trustee Med. Coll. of Pa., 1974—80, hon. trustee, 1981—98; trustee German Marshall Meml. Fund, 1972—84, Lewis H. Stevens Trust, Bryn Mawr Coll., 1972—78, Columbia U. Ctr. for Law and Econ. Studies, U. Pa. Inst. for Law and Econs., William Penn Found.; hon. trustee Phila. Mus. Art, from 1998; mem. Cardinal's Commn. re Abuse of Children, 2002. With USNR, 1942—45, North Pacific. Recipient Disting. Service award U. Pa. Law Sch., 1981, Justice award Am. Jud. Soc., 1982, John Courtney Murray award DePaul U., 1987, Cresset award Rosemont Coll., 1988, Gold Medallion award Chapel of Four Chaplains, Founders award Temple U., 1997, Phila. award, 1997. Mem. ABA (del. ho. of dels. 1966-67, 75-77, chmn. trade assn. com.), Am. Law Inst., Am. Bar Found., Pa. Bar Assn. (pres. jr. bar 1950, ho. of dels. 1967-71, pres.'s award 2005), Phila. Bar Assn. (chancellor 1967, Gold Medal award 1999), Am. Judicature Soc. (pres. 1975-77, Justice award), Am. Philos. Soc. (sec. 1980-83, v.p. 1987-92, pres. 1993-99), Am. Acad. Arts and Scis., Arlin Adams Law and Soc. Inst., Phila. Club, Union League, Sun. Breakfast Club, Legal Club (pres. 1986-91), Jr. Legal Club, Order of Coif, Beta Gamma Sigma. Home: Elkins Park, Pa. Died Dec. 22, 2015.

ADAMS, CHARLES SIEGEL, university program director, researcher; b. Lawrence, Mass., May 16, 1936; s. Claude Everman and Lorena (Siegel) A.; m. Maurianne Schifren, June 11, 1961 (div. May, 1978); m. Patricia Ann Harrison, Apr. 21, 1984. BA, Haverford Coll., 1958; MA, Ind. U., 1968, PhD, 1972. Lectr. Marlboro (Vt.) Coll., 1960-61; teaching asst. Ind. U., Bloomington, 1961-64; instr. U. Mass., Amherst, 1964-70, asst. prof., 1970-76, dir., from 1972, dir. higher edn., from 1988. Cons. N.J. Dept. Higher Edn., 1985, 89, 90, USAID, Malawi, 1988, 89. U.S.-Scandinavian Found. fellow, 1959, Ford Found. fellow, 1962. Mem. Am. Assn. for Higher Edn., Am. Assn. for Study of Higher Edn., Am. Ednl. Rsch. Assn., Am. Folklore Soc. Avocations: trans-atlantic sailing, outdoors activities, collecting art and antiques. Home: Shelburne Falls, Mass. Died Mar. 27, 2007.

ADAMS, J. MACK, computer science educator; b. Marfa, Tex., Aug. 14, 1933; s. Glen Wayne and Albene Angie (Hughes) A.; m. Joe Ann Davis, Mar. 31, 1952; children: Mack Lane, Mark Wayne. BS, U. Tex., El Paso, 1954; MS, N.Mex. State U., 1960, PhD, 1963. Assoc. scientist Westinghouse Electric Corp., Pitts., 1954-56; supervising mathematician Flight Simulation Lab., White Sands Missile Range, N.Mex., 1956-60; dir. computer directorate Electronics R&D Activity, White Sands Missile Range, N.Mex., 1963-64; assoc. prof. U. Tex., El Paso, 1964-65; dir. computer ctr. N.Mex. State U., Las Cruces, 1965-70, prof., 1970-93, prof. emeritus, from 1993, assoc. dean Coll. Arts and Scis., 1990-93. Sr. Fulbright lectr., Cath. U., Santiago, Chile, 1972; vis. fellow Wolfson Coll., Oxford, England, 1978. Author: (with others) Introduction to Computer Science, 1970, Computers: Appreciation, Application, Implications, 1973, Social Effects of Computer Use and Misuse, 1976, An Introduction to Computer Science with Modula-2, 1988; contbr. articles to profl. jours. Univ. fellow N.Mex. State U., Las Cruces, 1960. Mem. Assn. Computing Machinery, Math. Assn. Am. Home: Las Cruces, N.Mex. Died Dec. 17, 2006.

ADAMS, JEANNE CLARE, computer scientist; b. Utica, NY, June 15, 1921; d. Charles W. and Rose C. (Struve) Clare; children: Clare, Douglas, Samuel. BA, U. Mich., 1943; MA, U. Colo., 1979. With Nat. Ctr. for Atmospher Rsch., Boulder, Colo., 1960-82, various mgnt. positions, 1960-75, mgr. user svcs. and planning, 1975-82, mem. computational support group, from 1985; CYBER 205 project coord., mgr. sys. Inst. for Computational Studies, Colo. State U., 1982-84. Chair and convenor Internat. Fortran Experts under ISO, 1977-85; chair fortran stds. com. X3J3 Am. NAt. Stds. Orgn., 1977-92. Author: Programmers Guide to Fortran 90, 1990, Fortran 90 Handbook, 1992, Fortran Top 90, 1994, Fortran 95 Handbook, 1997; mem. editorial bd. Computer Standards and Interfaces; contbr. numerous articles to profl. jours. Mem. Assn. for Computing Machinery, Am. Nat. Stds. Orgn., Internat. Stds. Orgn. Home: Boulder, Colo. Died Apr. 21, 2007.

ADAMS, JOHN DAVID VESSOT, manufacturing executive; b. Ottawa, Ont., Can., Jan. 7, 1934; s. Albert Oliver and Estelle Priscilla (Vessot) A.; m. Dorothy Marion Blyth, June 27, 1959; children: Nancy, Joel, Louis Student, Carleton U., 1950—51; B Engring., McGill U., 1955; MBA, U. We. Ont., 1958. Registered profl. engr., Ont. Project engr. Abitibi Paper Co., Toronto, 1962—63, Cockshutt Farm Equipment Co. Ltd., Brantford, Ont., 1958—62, Can. Industries Ltd., Kingston, Ont., 1955—58; mgr. fin. analysis and planning Rio Tinto Zinc Group, London, 1963—66; mgr. adminstrn. and planning Can. Gypsum Co. Ltd., Toronto, 1966—72; mgr. logistics and fin. Massey Ferguson Co. Ltd., Toronto, 1972—79; pres. Can. Spool & Bobbin Co. Ltd., Walkerton, Ont., 1979—88, Quality Performance Engring., Inc., Hanover, Ont., 1988—2006, Maple Leaf Engring. Corp., Hanover, from 2006. Cons. mfg., Hanover, Ont.; cons. Lean Mfg. Mem.: Gideons. Home: Hanover, Canada. Died Nov. 4, 2006.

ADAMS, JOHN HILLARY, trust company executive, lawyer; b. Montreal, Quebec, Aug. 28, 1941; s. Leyland John and Barbara Stell (Hillary) Adams; m. Helene Gravel, July 30, 1977; children: David J., Michelle J. BA, Mount Allison U. N.B., Can., 1964; LL.L., U. Laval, Quebec, 1968. Bar: Quebec 1970. Lawyer McCarthy & Monet, Montreal, Canada, 1971—75, Martineau, Walker, Montreal, 1975—77; sec., legal counsel Avon Canada Inc., Montreal, 1977—82; v.p., lawyer, sec. Morgan Trust., Montreal, 1982. Dir. Boys and Girls Club of Can., Montreal, 1976—77, West Island Vol. Bur., Pointe-Claire, 1977; legal adv. St. James United Ch., Montreal, from 1976. Mem.: Assn. des Chefs de Conteutieux, Can. Bar Assn., Que. Bar Assn. Progressive. Anglican. Home: Beaconsfield, Canada. Died Dec. 13, 2006.

ADAMS, LAURIE MARIE, art historian, educator; b. NYC, Sept. 29, 1941; d. Daniel Edward and Helen Louise (Nelson) Schneider; m. John Brettz Adams, July 24, 1970; children: Alexa, Caroline. BA, Tulane U., 1962; MA in Psychology & Art History, Columbia U., 1963, PhD in Art History, 1967. Prof. art history John Jay Coll. and Grad. Ctr., CUNY, from 1966. Vis. asst. prof. U. Fla., Gainesville, 1967, Sarah Lawrence Coll., Bronxville, NY, 1967, Mt. Holyoke Coll., 1972; lectr. Columbia U., NYC, 1968; instr. Sch. Visual Arts, NYC, 1976; pvt. psychoanalytic practice, NYC, from 1978. Editor: Giotto in Perspective, 1974, Source: Notes in the History of Art; author: Art Cop, 1974, Art on Trial, 1976, A History of Western Art, 1993, Art and Psychoanalysis, 1993; contbr. articles to profl. jours. Summer Travel grant, 1967—68, Columbia Summer Travel grant, 1967, 1986. Mem.: PEN, NY Ctr. Psychoanalytic Tng., Coll. Art Assn., Mystery Writers America, Am. Psychol. Assn. (assoc.). Home: New York, NY. Died June 19, 2015.

ADAMS, MARVIN LEE, nuclear engineer, researcher; b. Seattle, Jan. 23, 1959; s. Alton Lee Adams and Charlotte Eloise (Breazeale) Nowell; m. Jennifer Lee Pearson, June 14, 1980; children: David Carlton, Michael Pearson, John Bell. BS in Nuclear Engring., Miss. State U., 1981; MSE in Nuclear Engring., U. Mich., 1984; postgrad. student, Los Alamos (N.Mex.) Nat. Lab., summer 1984; PhD in Nuclear Engring., U. Mich., 1986. Nuclear engr. TVA, Chattanooga, 1982; physicist Lawrence Livermore (Calif.) Nat. Lab., 1986-91; from asst. prof. to assoc. head dept. nuclear engring. Tex. A&M U., College Station, from 1992, assoc. v.p. rsch., from 2005. Mem. advanced sci. computing non-nuclear rev. panel U.S. Dept. Energy, from 2000, mem. predictive sci. panel, from 2004; mem. rev. com. applied physics divsn. Los Alamos Nat. Lab., from 1998. Author profl. articles, papers and computational methods. Inst. Nuclear Power Ops. fellow, 1981, Montague Ctr. for Tchg. Excellence scholar, 1995, Univ. Faculty fellow, 2000, Tex. Engring. Experiment Sta. fellow, 2003; recipient Tenneco Meritorious Tchg. award, 1997. Fellow Am. Nuclear Soc. (mem. exec. com. math. and computations divsn. 1990-99, chair, 1997-98, mem. tech. program com. various meetings, named Most Outstanding U.S. Undergrad. Nuclear Engring. Student 1981); mem. Phi Kappa Phi, Tau Beta Pi, Alpha Nu Sigma. Home: College Station, Tex. Died Apr. 17, 2007.

ADAMS, ROBERT JAY, technical training manager; b. Wheelersburg, Ohio, June 8, 1935; s. John Benton and Phoebe Jane (Kraft) A.; m. Alice Ann Boyer, Apr. 10, 1961; children: Michael Jay, Cheryl Ann. AA magna cum laude, Hillsborough Community Coll., 1977; student indsl. tech., U. of South Fla., 1977-79. Cert. secondary tchr. Enlist USN, 1953, advanced through ranks to warrant officer, 1967, commd. ensign, 1969, advanced through grades to lt., 1971, retired, 1973; service mgr. Ohdt-Waring Corp., Tampa, Fla., 1973-79; supr. instrumentation Goodyear Atomic Corp., Piketon, Ohio, 1980-82; tchr. electronics Telemedia Corp., Jubail, Saudi Arabia, 1982-84; tng. mgr. Liebert Corp., Columbus, Ohio, from 1984. Pres. Western Australia Kindergarten Assn., Exmouth, West Australia, 1969-71, Minford (Ohio) Band Boosters Assn., 1979-82; trustee Tanglewood Home Owners Assn., Wheelersburg, 1980-82. Mem. Ohio Edn. Assn., Assn. Field Service Mgrs. Lodges: Rotary. Republican. Avocations: woodworking, fishing. Home: Columbus, Ohio. Died Apr. 19, 2007.

ADAMS, ROBERT SCOTT, education association executive; b. Salt Lake City, Aug. 16, 1949; s. Glen Everett and Etta (Gygi) A.; m. Julie Sieverts, June 2, 1982; children: Nichole, Trenton, Scott Rowdy. BS, U. Utah, 1986; postgrad., U. Nevada. Cert. adminstrv. law judge, 1982. Mktg. dir. Salt Lake City C. of C., 1973-74; pers. mgr. U.P.R.R., Cheyenne, Wyo., 1976-78, sr. mgr. Salt Lake City, 1978-85; chief negotiator Salt Lake City Mayor's Office, 1986-88; exec. dir. Wasatch Uniserv, Salt Lake City, from 1987. Chmn. Civil Svc. Commn., Salt Lake City, 1980—; hearing officer State-County Merit Commn., Salt Lake City, 1980—. Contbr. articles to Summer Cowboys mag., 1985-86. Chmn. Govs. Commn. on Veterans, 1983—; bd. dirs. Community Svcs. Coun., Salt Lake City, 1986. Recipient Lions Regional award, 1973; named Outstanding Young Man of Am., Hispanic Community, 1977, named Top Ten Outstanding Vietnam Vet., 1980. Mem. Utah Assn. Civil Servants Commn. (pres. 1980), Amer. Arbitration Assn. (arbitrator nat. panel 1987—, dir. 1988—), Utah Advt. Assn; arbitrator Nat. Panel-A.A.A. Democrat. Mem. Lds Ch. Avocations: rodeo, bull riding, skiing, bicycling. Home: Salt Lake City, Utah. Died June 11, 2007.

ADELMAN, ROGER MARK, lawyer, educator; b. Norristown, Pa., June 25, 1941; s. Lewis D. and Mary A. (Butz). BA, Dartmouth Coll., 1963; LLB, U. Pa., 1966. Bar: DC 1967, Pa. 1969. Asst. atty., prosecutor US Atty. DC, 1969—87; ptnr. Kirkpatrick & Lockhart, Washington, Calif., 1988—97; private practice, 1997—2015. Adj. prof. Georgetown U. Law Ctr., Washington, 1975—98. With US Army, 1967—68. Recipient Justice Potter Stewart award, Coun. for Court Excellence, 2015. Mem.: Assn. Bar DC. Home: Washington, DC. Died Sept. 12, 2015.

ADELSON, MERV LEE (MERVYN LEE ADELSON), entertainment and communication industry executive; b. Los Angeles, Oct. 23, 1929; s. Nathan and Pearl (Schwarzman) A.;m. Barbara Walters 1986, (div. 1992); m. Thea Nesis, May 25, 1993; 1 child, Lexi Rose; children from previous marriage: Ellen, Gary, Andrew Student, Menlo Park Jr. Coll. Pres. Markettown Supermarket and Builders Emporium, Las Vegas, 1953-63; mng. ptnr. Paradise Devel., Las Vegas, from 1958; pres. Realty Holdings, from 1962, La Costa, Inc., 1963-87; co-founder, chmn. bd. dirs. Lorimar Inc., Culver City, Calif., 1969-86; chmn. bd. dirs., chief exec. officer Lorimar Telepictures Corp., Culver City, 1986-89; vice chmn. Warner Communications, from 1989; chmn. East-West Capital Assocs., Inc. (now East-West Capital Venture Group), from 1989; bd. dirs. Time-Warner Inc. (now Warner EMI). Co-founder Nathan Adelson Hospice Found. Recipient Sherill Corwin Human Relations award Am. Jewish Com., 1987. Mem. Am. Film Inst. (trustee), Am. Mus. of Moving Images (trustee), Entertainment Industries Council (trustee), Acad. Motion Pictures Arts and

Scis., Acad. TV Arts and Sciences, Nat. Acad. Cable Programming, Alliance for Capital Access (bd. dirs.), Com. Publicly Owned Cos. (bd. dirs.). Died Sept. 8, 2015.

ADKINS, HARVEY JOHN, naval officer, microbiologist; b. Oklahoma City, Apr. 22, 1948; s. George Bernice and Mary Frances (McKelvey) A.; m. Paula Gail North, Jan. 6, 1973; children: Christopher North, Emily Gayle. BS in Microbiology, U. Okla., 1971, MS in Microbiology, 1978, PhD in Microbiology, 1982. Commd. ensign USN, 1971, advanced through grades to comdr.; gunnery officer USS Bigelow, 1971-72, ASW officer, 1972-73; head dept. of ops. U.S. Naval Facility, Barbados, W.I., 1974-75; head dept. microbiology U.S. Naval Hosp., Oakland, Calif., 1982-83; head dept. bacteriology Naval Med. Rsch. Unit 2, Manila, 1983-86; head microbiology br. U.S. Naval Hosp., Bethesda, Md., 1986-88; head dept. parasitology Bethesda detachment Naval Sch. Health Scis., San Juan, P.R., from 1988. Mem. Am. Soc. for Microbiology (specilist microbiologist in clin. and pub. health microbiology), Assn. Mil. Surgeons of the U.S. Avocation: tennis. Home: Levittown, PR. Died June 23, 2007.

ADLERCREUTZ, HERMAN CARL THOMAS, retired clinical chemist, endocrinologist; b. Helsinki, Finland, Apr. 10, 1932; s. Erik Alfred Herman and Elisabeth Hedvig Catharina Adlercreutz; m. Sirkka Tellervo Neva, Nov. 26, 1976; m. Marie-Louise Eleonore Gräsbeck, 1956; children: Gustav Carl Herman, Erica Elisabeth Maria, Gabriella Eva Maria. MD, U. Helsinki, 1958, PhD, 1963. Cert. in clin. chemistry Finnish State, 1966, diplomate internal medicine Finnish State, 1965, endocrinological lab. methods Finnish State, 1979. Rsch. fellow Karolinska Hosp., Stockholm, 1958—61; resident internal medicine U. Helsinki, 1961—64, acting asst. prof. internal medicine, 1964—65, assoc. prof. clin. chemistry, 1965—69, acting prof. clin. chemistry, 1967—69, prof. clin. chemistry, 1969—97; head ctrl. lab. Helsinki U. Ctrl. Hosp., 1965—69, chief physician, ctrl. lab., 1965—97; rsch. prof. Finnish Acad., Helsinki, 1983—88; dir. Folkhälsan Rsch. Ctr. Samfundet Folkhälsan, Helsinki, 1996—2002, 2013, dir. Inst. Preventive Medicine, Nutrition Cancer, from 1996. Assoc. editor Jour. Steroid Biochemistry and Molecular Biology, Paris, 1967—95; editor Scandinavian Jour. Clin. and Lab. Investigations, Oslo, 1976—86; co-editor Internat. Jour. Sports Medicine, 1978—80; cons. Med. Commn. Finnish Olympic Com., Helsinki, 1985—92; mem. Commn. Health and Sci. European Nat. Olympic Coms., 1985—93. Contbr. articles to numerous sci. publs. Recipient Schoeller-Junkmann Preis, German Soc. Endocrinology, 1972, I Class Decoration Finnish White Rose Order Knighthood, Finnish State, 1983, Tenth D.R. Edwards medal, Tenovus Inst. Cancer Rsch., 1987, Cross Merit Promoters Sport Culture Finland, Ministry Edn., 1988, Anniversary medal, Finnish Soc. Sports Medicine, 1989, Silver medal, U. Helsinki, 1992, Egon Diczfalusy Lecture medal, Karolinska Inst., 2001. Mem.: Finnish Soc. Clin. Chemistry, Finnish Soc. Endocrinology, Royal Norwegian Soc. Sci. Letters, Assn. Finnish Chem. Soc. (pres., sect. mass spectrometry 1980—84), Finnish Sports Assn. (pres. Finnish Sport Rsch. Found 1978—82), Scandinavian Soc. Clin. Chemistry Clin. Physiology (sec. 1967—69), Soc. Scientarium Fennica Societas Scientarium Fennica, Finnish Soc. Clin. Chemistry Clin. Physilogy (pres. 1969—73), Finnish Soc. Gastroenterology (v.p. 1966—69), Samfundet Folkhälsan (bd. chmn. 1993—98, Ossian Shauman medal 2002), Finnish Assn. Physicians (J.W. Runeberg award 1991), Finnish Soc. Nutrition Rsch (pres. 1985—87), Finnish Soc. Endocrinology (sec. 1965—68, v.p. 1971—73), Polish Soc. Lab. Diagnostics (hon.). Home: Helsinki, Finland. Died Oct. 26, 2014.

ADOMAVICIUS, JONAS, gastroenterologist, writer; b. Pernarava, Lithuania, Dec. 15, 1911; arrived in U.S., 1949; s. Anupras Adomavcius and Marija (Rimkute) Adomavicius. MD, Vytautes the Great U., Kaunes, Lithuania, 1938. Radio health show host (in Lithuanian); med. columnist in Lithuanian Lang. Weekly Newspaper. Author: 10 books; contbr. columns in newspapers Dienovydis (Lithuanian Lang. Newspaper), Draugas Lithuanian lang. daily Chgo., Lietuvill (bi-weekly), Ameikos Lietuviy Balsas (Lithuanian lang. weekly); author: Die Medizinische Fakultat der Eberhard-Karls-Universitat zu Tübingen der Grad enes Doctors der Medizin, Kvieslys Sveikaton. Mem.: Am. Gastroenterology Soc. Died Dec. 20, 2006.

AGARWALLA, CHAMAN LALL, import-export company executive; b. Calcutta, India, Sept. 14, 1924; came to U.S., 1983; s. Krishna Lall Agarwalla and Sundari Agarwalla; widowed; children: Arun, Asok, Anchala, Anjana. B of Commerce, City Coll, Calcutta, 1948. Pres., chief exec. officer Chaman Industries Ltd., Calcutta, 1946-84, Ashoke Internat. Ltd., Calcutta, 1954-84, Star Oil Co., Glendale, Calif., from 1985, Ichiman Inc., Santa Monica, from 1983; pres. Axil Global Trades, Glendale, from 1991. Cons. in field to gas stations. Avocation: spiritual and religious activities. Home: Glendale, Calif. Died Mar. 21, 2007.

AGLI, STEPHEN MICHAEL, literature and language educator; b. Yonkers, NY, Feb. 11, 1942; s. Michael Joseph and Pauline Joanna (Perrone) A. AB summa cum laude, Fordham Coll., 1965; AM, Harvard U., 1968, EdM, 1972; PhD, CUNY, 2005. Cert. secondary sch. English tchr., N.Y. Resident tutor Quincy House, Harvard Coll., Cambridge, Mass., 1968-73; instr. humanities Berklee Coll. Music, Boston, 1971-73; mem. curriculum devel. com., teaching fellow in expository writing Harvard U., Cambridge, 1973-77, tutor in expository writing Bur. of Study Counsel, 1977-81; tchr., chmn. English dept. Jewish H.S. South Fla., North Miami Beach, 1982-83, St. Sergius H.S., NYC, 1983-84; tchr. secondary sch. English Columbia Grammar and Prep. Sch., NYC, 1984-85; coll. counselor, ednl. adminstr. St. Sergius Acad., 1994-95. Bd. Freshman advisers Harvard Coll., 1970-77; counselor, ednl. cons., Cambridge, Mass., N.Y.C., 1977-82; ednl. rsch. and cons., N.Y.C., 1985—; adj. instr. English N.J. Inst. Tech., Newark, 1987-88, CUNY, 1992-2003; conf. session chmn. Soc. for Textual Scholarship, 1993; presenter rsch. papers Rockhurst Coll., Kansas City, Mo., 1989, St. Louis U., Gerard Manley Hopkins Centennial Celebration, 1989, Malone Soc. Centennial Conf., Stratford-upon-Avon, Eng., 1990; spkr. St. Sergius H.S. commencement, 1992-93; lectr. Gerard Manley Hopkins lecture series, various locations, U.S., 1999—. Alumni rep. Harvard U., 1982-90. Recipient Woodrow Wilson fellowship Woodrow Wilson Found. to Harvard U., 1965-66, CUNY travel and rsch. awards to confs. and librs. in U.S. and Europe, 1988-90, 95; fellow NDEA Dept. Celtic Langs. and Lit., Harvard U., 1967-70, CUNY, 1986-90, N.E. MLA, London and Oxford, 1990. Mem. MLA, N.E. MLA, Celtic Studies Assn. N. Am. (speaker annual meeting 1989), Phi Beta Kappa. Home: Moorestown, NJ. Died Jan. 8, 2007.

AHEDO, ALEJANDRO, electronics executive; b. El Paso, Tex., July 9, 1929; divorced; six children. Grad. high sch., La Mesa, N.M. Owner Alex Electronics, El Paso, from 1933. Died Mar. 26, 2007.

AHLEM, LLOYD HAROLD, psychologist; b. Moose Lake, Minn., Nov. 7, 1929; s. Harold Edward and Agnes (Carlson) A.; m. Anne T. Jensen, Dec. 29, 1952; children: Ted, Dan, Mary Jo, Carol, Aileen. AA, North Park Coll., 1948; AB, San Jose State Coll., 1952, MA, 1955; Ed.D., U. So. Calif., 1962. Tchr. retarded children Fresno County (Calif.) Pub. Schs., 1953-54; psychologist Baldwin Park (Calif.) Sch. Dist., 1955-62; prof. psychology Calif. State U., Stanislaus (formerly Stanislaus State Coll.), Turlock, Calif., 1962-70; pres. North Park U., Chgo., 1970-79, dir., 1966-70; exec. dir. Covenant Village Retirement Center, Turlock, 1979-89; dir. spl. projects Covenant Retirement Communities, Chgo., 1989-93; dir. Emanuel Med. Ctr., Turlock, Calif., 1984-99, Merced Mut. Ins. Co., Atwater, Calif., 1993—2005; chmn. Capital Corp. of West, Merced, Calif., 1995—2002; ret. Author: Do I Have To Be Me, 1974, How to Cope: Managing Change, Crisis and Conflict, 1978, Help for the Families of the Mentally Ill, 1983, Living and Growing in Later Years, 1992; columnist Covenant Companion, 1972-90. Decorated comdr. Order of Polar Star Sweden, 1976. Mem.: Delta Mu Delta, Sigma Delta Epsilon, PsyChi. Mem. Covenant Ch. Club: Rotary (Paul Harris fellow 1987). Home: Turlock, Calif. Died Sept. 29, 2013.

AIGLER, WILLIAM FRANK, lawyer; b. Bellewe, Ohio, July 20, 1916; s. Allan Garfield and Magdalene Louise Aigler; m. Nancy B. Aigler (dec.); children: Mark, Thomas; m. Marjorie B. Aigler, Apr. 8, 1989. BA, U. Mich., Ann Arbor, 1938, JD, 1943; HLLD (hon.), Heidelberg Coll., Tiffin, Ohio, 1994. Bar: Ohio 1943. Atty. Garfield, Baldwin, Cleve., 1943—52, Aigler Law Office, Bellevue, Ohio, from 1952. Mem. bd. trustees Heidelberg Coll., 1972—96, emeritus trustee, from 1996, vice chair bd., 1979—89, chair bd., 1989—94. Bd. dirs. homeland ministry United Ch. of Christ, vice chmn. bd. homeland ministry, 1977—87, chmn. bd. homeland ministry, 1985—87. Mem.: ABA, Ohio State Bar Assn. Republican. Avocation: sailing. Home: Bellevue, Ohio. Died Nov. 19, 2014.

AIKAWA, JERRY KAZUO, internist, educator; b. Stockton, Calif., Aug. 24, 1921; s. Genmatsu and Shizuko (Yamamoto) A.; m. Chitose Aihara, Sept. 20, 1944; 1 son, Ronald K. AB, U. Calif., 1942; MD, Wake Forest Coll., 1945. Intern, asst. resident N.C. Baptist Hosp., 1945-47; NRC fellow in med. scis. U. Calif. Med. Sch., 1947-48; NRC, AEC postdoctoral fellow in med. scis. Bowman Gray Sch. Medicine, 1948-50, instr. internal medicine, 1950-53, asst. prof., 1953; established investigator Am. Heart Assn., 1952-58; exec. officer lab. service Univ. Hosps., 1958-61, dir. lab. services, 1961-83, dir. allied health program, from 1969, assoc. dean allied health program, from 1983, pres. med. bd.; assoc. dean clin. affairs asst. prof. U. Colo. Sch. Medicine, 1953- 60, asso. prof. medicine, 1960-67, prof., from 1967, prof. biometrics, from 1974, assoc. dean clin. affairs, from 1974. Pres. Med. bd. Univ. Hosps. Fellow ACP, Am. Coll. Nutrition; mem. Western Soc. Clin. Research, So. Soc. Clin. Research, Soc. Exptl. Biology and Medicine, Am. Fedn. Clin. Research, AAAS, Central Soc. Clin. Research, AMA, Assn. Am. Med. Colls., Phi Beta Kappa, Sigma Xi, Alpha Omega Alpha Home: Phoenix, Ariz. Died Dec. 31, 2006.

AKERS, JOHN MCCORKLE, trucking company executive; b. Maysville, Ky., Apr. 5, 1907; s. William Wirt and Elizabeth (Scott) A.; m. Dorothy Amanda Dozier, Feb. 14, 1945; children— Mildred Elizabeth, Dorothy Joanne, Mary Kathleen. AB in Econs, Davidson Coll., 1928, LL.D. (hon.), 1978; MA in Econs, U. N.C. at Chapel Hill, 1932; grad. student, Duke, 1933, Princeton, 1934. Asst. dir. WPA, Washington, 1935-37; v.p., gen. mgr. Akers Motor Lines, Inc., Gastonia, N.C., 1937-55, pres., 1955-72, A. & W. Realty Co., Gastonia, 1949-78, Akers Realty & Sales Co., Inc., Atlanta, 1950-72, Akers Center Hardware & Supply, Inc., Gastonia, 1955-79, A&W Rentals, Inc., Gastonia, 1958-69; mng. partner A. and W. Investment Co., from 1977; partner Akers Sales Co., Gastonia, N.C., 1948-72; mem. N.C. adv. bd. Liberty Mut. Ins. Co., Charlotte, from 1961. Mem. N.C. Bd. Conservation and Devel., 1960-68; pres. N.C. Indsl. Devel. Found., 1962, bd. dirs., 1963-65; chmn. Davidson Coll. Alumni Fund, 1955-57; Pres. Akers Found., 1955— ; adv. bd. Transp. Center, Northwestern U., 1961-66; bd. visitors Davidson Coll., 1957— ; trustee Queens Coll., Charlotte, 1947— ; bd. dirs. N.C. Citizens Assn., 1961-77. Mem. Am. Trucking Assn. (bd. govs. regular common carrier conf. 1959-75, v.p. N.C. 1945-54, chmn. indsl. relations com. 1962-63, mem. exec. com. 1945— , nat. treas. 1954-62, 1st v.p. 1962-63, pres. 1963-64, chmn. bd. 1964-65), N.C. Motors Carriers Assn. (bd. mem. 1940— , pres. 1962-63), Transp. Assn. Am. (bd. dirs. 1962-72), Carolina Transp. Assn. (pres. 1940-60), Davidson Coll. Alumni Assn. (pres. 1957-58), U.S., Gastonia chambers commerce, Phi Beta Kappa, Pi Kappa Alpha. Presbyn. (chmn. deacons 1962, elder 1968—). Clubs: Gaston Country; Ponte Vedra (Fla.); Masons, Shriner. Home: Gastonia, NC. Died Oct. 22, 2010.

ALATALO, FRANCES ELINOR, retired psychologist; b. South Range, Mich., Sept. 20, 1917; d. Herman and Jenni (Niemi) A. BA, Wayne State U., 1949, MA, 1959. Social worker, supr. Detroit Welfare Dept., 1949-59; psychologist Pontiac (Mich.) State Hosp., 1959-71, Newberry (Mich.) Regional Mental Health Ctr., 1971-81; ret., 1981. Co-editor: (book of poems) North by Choice, 1991; contbr. poetry to various publs. With WAC, U.S. Army, 1943-46. Mem. APA (assoc.), Assn. for Humanistic Psychology, Assn. for Transpersonal Psychology, Psychologists for Social Responsibility, Inst. for Noetic Scis., Planetary Soc., Nature Conservancy, Sierra Club. Avocations: gardening, writing and reading poetry. Home: Newberry, Mich. Died Mar. 6, 2007.

ALAUPOVIC, PETAR, biochemist, educator; b. Prague, Czech Republic, Aug. 3, 1923; arrived in US, 1957; married, 1947; 1 child. ChemE, U. Zagreb, 1948, PhD in Chemistry, 1956; DHC (hon.), U. Lille, France, 1987, U. Buenos Aires, 1994, U. Goteborg, 1999. Rschr. pharms. rsch. lab. Chem Corp, Prague, 1948-49; rschr. organic lab. Inst. Indsl. Rsch., Yugoslavia, 1949-50; asst. agrl. faculty U. Zagreb, 1951-54, asst. chem. inst. med. faculty, 1954-56; rsch. biochemist U. Ill., 1957-60; with cardiovascular sect. Okla. Med. Rsch. Found., Oklahoma City, from 1960, head lipoprotein lab., 1972-92, also head Lipid and Lipoprotein Lab. Prof. rsch. biochemistry, sch. med. U. Okla., 1960—. Assoc. editor Lipids, 1974-78. Named Disting. Career Scientist Okla. Med. Rsch. Fund, 1990; NIH grantee, 1961-95. Mem. AAAS, Am. Soc. Biol. Chemists, Am. Chem. Soc., Am. Heart Assn. (Spl. Recognition award 1994), Am. Oil Chemistry Soc. Achievements include research in chemistry of naturally occuring macromolecular lipid compounds such as serum and tissue lipoproteins and bacterial endotoxins, biochemistry of red cell membranes isolation and characterization of tissue lipases. Home: Oklahoma City, Okla. Died Jan. 30, 2014.

ALBOSTA, DONALD JOSEPH, former United States Representative fom Michigan; b. Saginaw, Mich., Dec. 5, 1925; s. Paul Albosta and Laura A. Bennett; m. Dorothy Ankoviak, Feb. 10, 1951; children: Christine, Paul. Township trustee Saginaw County, commr., 1970—74; mem. Dist 86 Mich. House of Reps., 1974—76; mem. US Congress from 10th Mich. Dist., Washington, 1979—85. Named Outstanding Young Farmer of Yr., 1960. Mem.: Saginaw Co. Soil Conserve, Lions, Nat Beet Growers Assoc. Democrat. Died Dec. 18, 2014.

ALBRECHT, ERNST CARL JULIUS, former German government official; b. Heidelberg, Germany, June 29, 1930; s. Carl and Adda (Berg) A.; m. Heidi Adele Stromeyer, Mar. 7, 1953; children: Harald Ernst, Lorenz Berthold, Ursula Gertrud, Eva Benita, Hans Holger, Barthold Immanuel, Gerhard Donatus. BA, Cornell U., 1950; postgrad., U. Tübingen, 1951-53; diploma in Econs., U. Bonn., 1953. Attache coun. ministers European Coal and Steel Community, Luxemburg, 1954-56; head common market sect., chief exec. officer EEC, Brussels, 1958-67, dir. gen. for competition, 1967-70; finance dir. Bahlsens Keksfabrik, Hanover, 1970-76; prime min. Lower Saxony, 1976-90. Author: The State Idea and Reality, 1976. Vice chmn. Christlich Demokratische Union, Fed. Republic Geramany, 1979. Evangelical lutheran. Home: Burgdorf OT Beinhorn, Germany. Died Dec. 13, 2014.

ALBRECHT, IRENE DOROTHY, musician, educator; b. Storm Lake, Iowa, June 18, 1917; d. Frank August and Johanna (Bregas) A. BA, Buena Vista U., 1938; student, Chgo. Conservatory, 1943. Cert. tchr., Calif. Vocal coach Ind. State U., Terre Haute, 1964-66, Calif. Western U., San Diego, 1966-70; pvt. practise San Diego, from 1970; opera class U. San Diego, La Jolla, 1985; pvt. practise Chgo., 1947-66. Ch. organist Chula Vista (Calif.) Congl. Ch., 1967-83; ch. organist, minister music Lemon Grove (Calif.) Congl. Ch., 1985—. Keyboardist with San Diego Opera, 1967-76; (concerts) Chgo. Symphony, Theatre Men Tours, 1962-65; accompanist for soprano Maria Kurenko, bass Nicole Muscona, other artists. Mem. San Diego Community Concert Assn. (pres. 1965-67, 1988—, bd. dirs. 1966—), San Diego Nat. Assn. Tchrs. of Singing, Chgo. Musicians Union (life), San Diego Opera Guild. Avocations: travel, reading. Died Mar. 16, 2007.

ALBRECHT, MARY DICKSON, sculptor, designer, art company executive; b. Dothan, Ala., June 4, 1930; d. Leon Lowe and Luella (James) Dickson; m. Robert Louis Albrecht, Aug. 16, 1960; children: Kathleen, Gregory, Scheel, Channa. Student, U. Houston, 1947-50; BS, Tex. Woman's U., 1970. Owner/founder Albrecht Studio, Dallas, from 1968; pres, chief exec. officer PLIP, Inc., Tyler, Tex., from 1986, Albrecht Originals, Inc., Tyler, from 1986. Author newspaper column Albrecht on Art, 1977-79. Printmaker (serigraph) Image of Man, 1971; sculpture A Moment in..., 1986. Mem. Artists Coalition of Tex. (pres. 1977-79), Tex. Fine Arts Assn. (region II dir. 1971-72). Died Mar. 24, 2007.

ALDERSON, THOMAS, retired chemist; b. NYC, Aug. 18, 1917; s. Thomas Broker and Florence Amelia (Perry) A.; m. Ruthmary Mason, June 23, 1942; children: Thomas V, James Mason, Susan Elizabeth. BA, Ripon Coll., 1939; MA, Ohio State U., 1941, PhD, 1947. Rsch. chemist DuPont Co., Wilmington, Del., 1947-61, rsch. assoc., 1961-82; ret.,

1982. Pvt. practice cons., Wilmington, 1982—. Contbr. articles to profl. publs.; patentee in field. Mem. vestry Calvary Episcopal Ch., Wilmington. Maj. U.S. Army, 1941-45, ETO. Mem. Am. Chem. Soc., Phi Beta Kappa. Avocations: woodworking, reading, bridge, travel. Home: Clearwater, Fla. Died Mar. 21, 2007.

ALDISERT, RUGGERO JOHN, federal judge; b. Carnegie, Pa., Nov. 10, 1919; s. John S. and Elizabeth (Magnacca) Aldisert; m. Agatha Maria DeLacio, Oct. 4, 1952; children: Lisa Maria, Robert, Gregory. BA, U. Pitts., 1941, JD, 1947. Bar: Pa. 1947. Gen. practice law, Pitts., 1947—61; judge Ct. Common Pleas, Allegheny County, 1961—68, US Ct. Appeals (3d cir.), Pitts., 1968—84, chief judge, 1984—87, sr. judge Pitts., Santa Barbara, Calif., 1987—2014. Adj. prof. law U. Pitts. Sch. Law, 1964—87; faculty Appellate Judges Seminar, NYU, 1971—85, assoc. dir., 1979—85; chmn. Fed. Appellate Judges Seminar, 1972—78; mem. Pa. Civil Procedural Rules Com., 1965—84, Jud. Conf. Com. on Adminstrn. Criminal Law, 1971—77; chmn. adv. com. on bankruptcy rules Jud. Conf. U.S., 1979—84; vis. prof. univs. in U.S. and abroad, 1965—99; intensive lectures at univs in , Italy, Germany, France, Poland, Croatia and Serbia. Author: Il Ritorno al Paese, 1966—67, The Judicial Process, Readings, Materials and Cases, 1996, 2d edit., 1996, Logic for Lawyers: A Guide to Clear Legal Thinking, 1997, 3d edit., 1997, Opinion Writing, 1990, 2nd edit., 2009, Winning on Appeal, 2003, Road to the Robes: A Federal Judge Recollects Young Years and Early Times, 2005; contbr. over 50 articles to profl. publs. Allegheny dist. chmn. Multiple Sclerosis Soc., 1961—68; pres. ISDA, Cultural Heritage Found., 1965—68; chmn. Pitts. Sch. Law, 1969—99. Maj. USMC, 1942—46, with USMC, 1946—51. Recipient Outstanding Merit award, Allegheny County Acad. Trial Lawyers, 1964, Disting. Appellate Jurist award, 2005, Disting. Citizen of Carnegia Borough award, 2005, Golden Pen award, Legal Writing Inst., 2008, Disting. All Alumni Fellow award, U. Pitts., 2009. Mem.: ABA, American Law Inst., Italian Sons & Daughters American Fraternal Assn. (nat. pres. 1954—68), Omicron Delta Kappa, Phi Alpha Delta, Phi Beta Kappa. Democrat. Roman Catholic. Home: Santa Barbara, Calif. Died Dec. 28, 2014.

ALDRICH, LESTER KYLE, II, health physicist; b. Columbus, Ohio, Dec. 1, 1936; s. H. Lamar and Thora Belle (Campbell) A.; m. Shirley Elizabeth Melton, Oct. 18, 1956; children: Robert Charles, Elizabeth Ann, Diane Lynn, Linda Carol. BS in Nuclear Engring., N.C. State U., 1967, MS in Nuclear Engring., 1973. Cert. health physicist, cert. mgr. Supr. radiol. surveillance program N.C. Dept. Human Resources, Raleigh, 1971-74; sr. rsch. engr. Allied Chem. Co., Idaho Falls, Idaho, 1975-78, safety analysis supr., 1978-79; staff engr. Rockwell Hanford Ops., Richland, Wash., 1979-86; mgr. facility & radiol. support Westinghouse Hanford Co., Richland, 1986-88, prin. health physicist, 1988-90, mgr. radiol. support group, 1991-93; sr. prin. health physicist Fluor Daniel Hanford Inc., Richland, from 1993. Mem. Blue Mountain coun. Boy Scouts Am. With U.S. Army, 1955-70. Mem. ASTM (subcom. E10.04, sect. leader 1993—), Am. Acad. Health Physics (mem. continuing edn. com. 1993—, chair, 1997—, mem. nominating com. 1986-88), Health Physics Soc. (coun. mem. Columbia chpt. 1991-93), Am. Bd. Health Physics (mem. comprehensive panel of examiners 1987-90, Part I panel 95—), Tri-Cities Tech. Coun. (treas. 1989-91), Mensa, Elks. Republican. Avocations: bluegrass gospel music group, guitar, banjo, gardening. Home: Richland, Wash. Died Dec. 29, 2006.

ALEXANDER, CARL ALBERT, materials engineer, educator; b. Chillicothe, Ohio, Nov. 22, 1928; s. Carl B. and Helen E. Alexander; m. Dolores J. Hertenstein, Sept. 4, 1954; children: Carla C., David A. BS, Ohio U., 1953, MS, 1956; PhD, Ohio State U., 1961. Mem. staff Battelle Columbus Labs., from 1956, rsch. leader, from 1974, mgr. physico-chem. systems, from 1976; mem. faculty Ohio State U., from 1963, prof. ceramic and nuc. engrig., from 1977. Sr. rsch. leader, chmn. tech. coun. of Biol. and Chem. Scis. Directorate, 1987—, chief scientist, 1987; prof. materials sci. and engring., 1988—. Author; patentee in field. Served to lt. (j.g.) USNR, 1951-54. Recipient Merit award NASA, 1971, IR-100 award, 1987, R & D-100 award, 1988; citations Dept. Energy, citations AEC, citations ERDA. Mem. Am. Soc. Mass Spectrometry, Keramos, Sigma Xi Home: Grove City, Ohio. Died Dec. 27, 2013.

ALEXANDER, FAITH DOROTHY, retired training services executive; b. NYC, Aug. 1, 1933; d. Howard Phillip and Ruth Dorothy Rubinow; m. Fred John Dunne (dec.); children: John Dunne, Robert Dunne, Laurie Martin, Bonnie Hunter; m. Daniel Lee Alexander, Apr. 27, 2000. BA, MA, Columbia U. Sales promotion mgr. Aseptic Thermo Indicator Co., N. Hollywood, Calif., 1956—57; v.p. Dunne, Rogers, Dunne Advt. and Pub. Rels., LA, 1958—79, NYC, 1958—79; records supr., training officer Newport Beach Police Dept., Calif., 1980—86; records, info. svcs. command Riverside County Calif. Sheriff Dept., Calif., 1987—2000; cert. instr. Ben Clark Training Acad., 0187—1990; instr. Regional Training Ctr., San Diego, 1996—2003, Calif. Peace Officer Assn., Sacramento, 1996—2003; ret., 2000. Author: Early Childhood Education, Coast Guard Prodecures, 2003; co-editor: Calif. Police Recorder Mag. Pres. Barrance Elem. Sch. PTA, Covina, Calif., 1972—74; sec. Covina Valley PTA, 1974—75; pres. Sierra Vista Intermediate Sch. PTA, 1974—75; mem. Lake Elsinore Grand Prix Races, Calif., 1986; vol. Helmet Images, Riverside, Calif., 1988—2005; sec., mem. exec. bd. Urban League Formation Com., 1989—90; bd. dirs. Greater Riverside Area Urban League, 1990—93; commr. Riverside County Commn. Women, 1995—97; mem. vol. Homeland Security Dept., from 2003; mem. LA Rep. Ctrl. Com., 1974, Rep. Presdl. Task Force, 1981, 1989, 2003; chair Larry Smith for Sheriff of Riverside County, 1993, co-chair, 1998; chair Del Norte County Bush/Cheny Campaign, 2003; mem. vol. Del Norte County Elections Bd., 2003; life mem. Nat. Rep. Senatorial Com., from 2006; registrar of voters Del Norte County, 2006; vol. Faith EV Luth. Ch., Medford, Oreg., 2004—05; hon. chair House Majority Trust, 2006. Recipient 2000 Women of Achievement award, 1961, 1971, Wall of Tolerance award, 2003, Riverside Calif. Pub. Svc. award, 1999, Nat. Rep. Party Gold medal, 1992, 2004, Rep. Yr., 2003. Mem.: Crescent city Coast Guard Aux., Del Norte County Rep. Women, Calif. Dept. Edn. Task Force, Campfire Girls (bd. mem., vice chair 1972—74), Nat. PTA (Hon. Svc. 1961), Am. Records Mgmt. Assn., Calif. Peace Officer's Assn., Calif. Law Enforcement Assn. of Record Suprs. (life; state conf. chair 1978, pres. So. Chpt. 1988—90, state conf. dir. 1989, founder, pres. Inland chpt. 1992—95, state exec. bd. 1992—95, Hon. Svc. award 1991, 1996), Nat. Rep. Senatorial Com. (life). Republican. Avocations: theater, music, art, writing, travel. Home: Mira Loma, Calif. Died Nov. 26, 2006.

ALEXANDER, MARIE BAILEY, consulting editor, family economist; b. Chattanooga, Sept. 2, 1913; d. Claude Esmond and Elsie Blanche (Peterson) Bailey; m. Theron Alexander, Aug. 29, 1936; children: Thomas T., Mary E. BS, Maryville Coll., Tenn., 1935; postgrad., Fla. State U., 1950-51. Mktg. cons. Gas & Electric Co., Chattanooga, 1935; tchr. North High Sch., Chattanooga, 1935-36; cons. editor Iowa City, Iowa, 1957-65, Phila., 1966-86, Menlo Park, Calif., 1987-95, Atherton, Calif., from 1995. Deacon, Valley Presbyn. Ch., Portola Valley, Calif., 1989-90. Mem. AAUW (co-chmn. internat. rels. sect. Menlo-Atherton br. 1987-89, chmn. 1989—, mem. lit. group 1986-97, bd. dirs. 1987—), P.E.O. (del. regional bd. Calif. 1988-89, pres. Iowa chpt. E 1979-81). Democrat. Avocations: gardening, stitchery. Home: Redwood City, Calif. Died Dec. 19, 2006.

ALEXANDER, VAN (ALEXANDER VAN VLIET FELDMAN), composer, arranger, conductor; b. Harlem, May 2, 1915; s. Jack and Mildred (Van Vliet) Feldman; m. Beth Baremore, Sept. 22, 1938 (dec. 2011); children; Lynn Tobias, Joyce Harris. Student, Columbia U. Composer, LA, 1950-70. Composer: (soundtrack) several films, 1950-70; (TV music) hundreds of segments. co-composer (with Ella Fitzgerald) A Tisket-A-Tasket, 1938 (Grammy Hall of Fame 1986); author: (text for arrangers) First Chart, 1962. Three time Emmy nominee, 1969, 71, 72. Mem. Nat. Acad. of Recording Arts and Scis. (pres. 1962-64), Am. Soc. Music Arrangers (pres. 1984-86), ASCAP (Lifetime Achievement award, 2002), Acad. Motion Picture Arts and Scis. (music br.), Pacific Pioneer Broadcasters, Song Writers Guild. Home: Los Angeles, Calif. Died July 19, 2015.

ALEXEEV, VLADIMIR LEONIDOVICH (VLADIMIR LEONIDOVICH ALEKSEEV), chemist; b. Kemerovo, Russia, Mar. 30, 1959; s. Leonid Ivanovich and Raisa Vasilyevna Schakuro; stepmother Alexeeva Nina Andreyevna (Ivanova) A.; m. Irina Pavlovna Kulgashova, Aug. 5, 1989; 1 child, Serguei. MSc in Biochemistry, Petersburg U., 1981; PhD in Chemistry, Ukrainian Acad. Scis., Kiev, 1987. Jr. rschr. Petersburg Nuclear Physics Inst., Gatchina, Russia, 1984-98, sr. rschr., from 1998. Contbr. articles to profl. jours. CEN-Saclay fellow, 1994. Mem. Neutron Scattering Soc. U.S., Neutron Scattering Soc. Switzerland. Home: Saint Petersburg, Russia. Died Jan. 23, 2007.

ALEXEFF, IGOR, retired electrical engineering educator; b. Pitts., Jan. 5, 1931; s. Alexander and Tamara (Tchirkow) A.; m. Anne I. Fabina, Feb. 4, 1954; children: Alexander, Helen. BA with honors, Harvard U., 1952; MS, U. Wis., 1955, PhD, 1959. Registered profl. engr., Tenn. Research engr. Westinghouse Corp., Pitts., 1952-53; NSF postdoctoral fellow U. Zurich, Switzerland, 1959-60; group leader controlled thermonuclear fusion Oak Ridge Nat. Lab., 1960-71; prof. elec. engring. U. Tenn., 1971-96, prof. emeritus, from 1996; chief scientist Haleakala R&D Corp., Del., from 2004. Vis. prof. Inst. Plasma Physics, Nagoya, Japan, 1973, Phys. Rsch. Lab., Ahmedabad, India, 1975, physics dept. U. Natal, Durban, South Africa, 1976, U. Fed. Fluminense Niteroi, Brazil, 1978, Birla Inst. Tech., Ranchi, India, 1991; organizer Plasma Physics Workshop, U.S. and India, 1976; chmn. Gordon Rsch. Conf. on Plasma Physics, 1974; pres. So. Appalachian Sci. and Engring. Far, 1985-86. Co-author: High Power Microwave Sources, 1987; contbr. articles to profl. jours. Chancellor's rsch. scholar U. Tenn., 1984; recipient Advanced Tech. award Internat. Hall of Fame, 1989, 91, (with others) R&D 100 award R&D Mag., 1989, 91; named Most Outstanding Tchr. of Yr., U. Tenn. Elec. Engring. Dept., 1992. Fellow IEEE (assoc. editor Trans. on Plasma Sci., organizer 1st Internat. Conf. on Plasma Sci. 1974, former pres. Oak Ridge sect., Centennial medal 1987, Outstanding Engr. in S.E. award 1987), Am. Phys. Soc. (past sec.-treas. div. plasma physics); mem. ASI (co-founder), Tech. Corp., Tenn. Inventors Assn. (founding pres., Inventor of Yr. award 1988), Nuclear and Plasma Scis. Soc. of IEEE (chmn. plasma sect. 1983-84, v.p. 1998, pres. 1999-2000, Shea award for outstanding svc., Plasma Scis. and Applications award 2002). Achievements include 19 issued patents; discovery of propagating ion acoustic waves; ions acoustic waves in plasma. Home: Oak Ridge, Tenn. Deceased.

ALFONSO-FAUS, ANTONIO, aerospace engineer, physicist; b. Onteniente, Valencia, Spain, Jan. 9, 1939; s. Alfredo and Maria Faus. m. Maria Cecilia Estefan Arbelaez, March 29, 2003; children: Antonio, Javier, Miguel, Alicia. MSc in Physics, U. Minn., 1967, PhD in Physics, 1968; degree in aero. engring., Escuela Tecnica Superior Ingenieros Aeronautica, Madrid, 1964; PhD in Aero. Engring., Escuela U. De Ingenieria Tecnica Aeronautica, Madrid, 1969; Diploma in Space Sci., Univ. Coll., 1965. Prin. investigator Instituto Nacional de Tecnica Aeroespacial, Madrid, 1968-73; engring. coord. Iberia Airlines, 1973-78, plant engr., 1978-81, devel. engr. chief, 1981-87, total quality dir., 1988-91, devel. dir., 1991-94; engring. educator U. Poly. Madrid, 1974—2010, prof., 1995—2010; hon. prof. Madrid Tech. U., 2010, emeritus prof., from 2011. Contbr. articles to profl. jours. Fellow European Space Rsch. Orgn., 1964, NASA-European Space Rsch. Orgn., 1965. Mem.: Spanish Soc. Gen. Relativity. Roman Catholic. Avocations: piano, music. Home: Madrid, Spain. Died Apr. 2015.

ALGER, BRUCE REYNOLDS, former United States Representative from Texas, real estate broker; b. Dallas, Tex., June 12, 1918; s. David Bruce and Clare (Freeman) Alger; 1 child, Jill stepchildren: Robert Jones, Laura Jones. BA, Princeton U., 1940. Field rep. RCA Victor Mfg. Co., 1940—41; real estate and land developer Dallas; mem. US Congress from 5th Tex. Dist., 1955—65. Former pres. White Rock C. of C. Capt. US Army, 1941—45. Decorated Disting. Flying Cross. Republican. Home: The Villages, Fla. Died Apr. 13, 2015.

ALLEN, FRANCES MICHAEL, publisher; b. Charlotte, NC, Apr. 7, 1939; d. Thomas Wilcox and Lola Frances (Horne) A.; m. Joseph Taylor Lisenbee, Feb. 24, 1955 (div. 1957); 1 child, Leslie Autice., Abilene Christian U., Tex., 1954-56, Chico State U., Calif, 1957-59. Art dir. B&E Publs., LA, 1963-65, editor, 1969-70; art dir. Tiburon Corp., Chgo., 1970-75; founder, editor Boxers, Internat., LA, 1970-76; editor The Hound's Tale, 1974, Saints, Incorp., 1974-76; founder, editor Setters, Incorp., Costa Mesa, Calif., 1975-85; founder, owner Michael Enterprises, Midway City, Calif., from 1976; editor Am. Cocker Rev., Midway City, 1980-81; editor, pub. Am. Cocker Mag., 1981-99; editor, co-pub. Sporting Life, 1991; editor, pub. The Royal Spaniels, from 1995. Author: The American Cocker Book, 1989; editor, pub. The Royal Spaniels, 1995— (Dogs Writer's Assn. awards 1995, 96, 99); illustrator: The First Five Years, 1970, The Aftercare of the Ear, 1975, The Shenn Simplicity Collection, 1976, The Miniature Pinscher, 1967; prin. works include mag. and book covers for USA, most widely published show dog artist world wide, past 30 yrs. Recipient Dog World Award Top Producer, 5 times, 1966-88, 10-time winner and nominee Dog Writers Assn. Am., winner best breed publ. World Congress Pet Publs., Ukraine, 1995, winner Kirk Paper Co. award of excellence. Mem. Dog Writers Assn. Am. (life), Am. Spaniel Club (life). Republican. Mem. Ch. of Christ. Avocations: dog exhibiting, ballooning, photography, art. Died Nov. 17, 2006.

ALLEN, GREGORY SCOTT, bank executive; b. Rupert, Idaho, Aug. 17, 1955; s. Marion Calkins and Bessie Bee (Champion) A.; m. Bethanne Larsen, Dec. 18, 1976; children: Amanda Beth, Ian Gregory. Student, Rick's Coll., 1973-74, U. Phoenix, 1991. Br. mgr. Capital Fin. Svcs., Rexburg, Idaho, 1976-80; v.p., cashier Avco Craig (Colo.) Indsl. Bank, 1981-87; pres. Great West, Fed. Savs. Bank, Craig, from 1987. Bd. dirs. Moffat County Human Svc. Vols., Craig, 1988—, Moffat County Youth Care Ctr., Craig, 1989—; bishop LDS Ch., Craig, 1985-91; chartered orgn. rep. Boy Scouts Am. Mem. Craig C. of C. (bd. dirs. 1985-86, treas. 1986), Lions (treas. 1988-91). Republican. Avocations: reading, fishing, bicycling, camping. Home: Edmond, Okla. Died Dec. 9, 2006.

ALLEN, STEPHEN D(EAN), pathologist, microbiologist; b. Linton, Ind., Sept. 8, 1943; s. Wilburn and Betty Allen; m. Vally C. Autrey, June 17, 1964; children: Christopher D., Amy C. BA, Ind. U., 1965, MA, 1967; MD, Ind. U., Indpls., 1970. Diplomate Am. Bd. Pathology Anatomic and Clin. Pathology and Med. Microbiology. Intern in pathology Vanderbilt U. Hosp., Nashville, 1970-71, resident in pathology, 1971-74; clin. asst. prof. pathology Emory U., Atlanta, 1974-77; asst. prof. clin. pathology Ind. U., Indpls., 1977-79, asst. prof. pathology, 1979-81, assoc. prof. pathology, 1981-86, prof. pathology, 1986-92, prof. pathology and lab. medicine, from 1992, James Warren Smith prof. clin. microbiology, from 2006, assoc. dir. div. clin. microbiology, dept. pathology, 1977-92, dir. grad. progam pathology, from 1986, sr. assoc. chmn. dept. pathology, 1990-91, dir. divsn. clin. microbiology dept. pathology/lab. medicine, 1992-98, assoc. chair dept. pathology and lab. medicine & dir. labs., 1996-99; dir. disease control lab. divsn. Ind. State Dept. Health, Indpls., 1994—2004; dir. divsn. clin. microbiology dept. pathology/lab. medicine Clarian-Meth.-Ind U.-Riley Hosps., from 1998. Mem. residency rev. com. for pathology Accreditation Coun. for Grad. Med. Edn., 1996—2004, mem. residency rev. com. for molecular genetic pathology, 1999—2004, vice chmn., 2003—04, mem. molecular genetic pathology policy com., from 1999; trustee Am. Bd. Pathology, 1995—2006, life trustee, from 2007, chmn. microbiology test devel. and adv. com., 1995—2006, sec. bd., 2001—02, v.p., 2002, pres., 2003, immediate past pres., 2004. Co-author: Introduction to Diagnostic Microbology, 1994, Color Atlas and Textbook of Diagnostic Microbiology, 1997, 2006, Direct Smear Atlas, A Monograph of Gram-Stained Smear Preparations of Clinical Specimens, 2001, (CD-ROM) Direct Smear Atlas, 1998, Parasitology Image Atlas, 2003, Mycology Image Atlas, 2004, Bacteriology I Image Atlas, 2005; contbr. With USPHS, 1974—77. Fellow: Binford-Dammin Soc. Infectious Disease Pathologists, Infectious Diseases Soc. Am., Am. Acad. Microbiology, Coll. Am. Pathologists; mem.: Anaerobe Soc. Ams. (mem. coun. 1994—2002, pres. 2002—04), Am. Soc. Clin. Pathologists (coun. microbiology 1983—89), Masons (32d deg.), Shriners, Sigma Xi. Avocations: musicial instruments, fly fishing. Home: Indianapolis, Ind. Deceased.

ALLEN, WILLIAM DOUGLAS, physicist; b. Mussooree, India, July 27, 1914; s. John Howard and Clara Helen (Padman) A.; m. Gwendoline Genevieve Thomspn, Noc. 15, 1939; children: Catherine Elspeth, Margaret Gillian, David

Douglas, James Richard Alexander. BS, Adelaide U., Australia, 1932, BSc in Physics, 1935; DPhil in Physics, Oxford U., England, 1940. Jr. sci. officer, sci. officer, sr. sci. officer Min. Aircraft Prodn., Malvern, England, 1939-44; sr. sci. officer Uranium Isotope Separation Tube Alloys, Berkeley, Calif., 1944-45; rsch. officer Electron Acceleration, Sydney, Australia, 1945-46, prin. sci. officer, 1946-61; sr. prin. sci. officer Electrostatic Acceleration, Harwell, England, 1946-61; dep. chief sci. officer Chilton, 1961-77; prof. dept. elec. engring. Reading, 1976-78, Southampton, 1979-81. Author: Neutron Detection, 1949. Chmn. N. Berks Music Festival, 1960-683 Mem. England Phys. Soc., Probus Club. Avocation: gardening. Home: Abingdon, England. Died May 18, 2007.

ALMADA, MANUEL, advertising agency executive, sales executive; b. New Bedford, MA, Feb. 10, 1912; s. Manuel Salles and Mary (Medeiros) A. Student, U. Mass., 1965. Advt. writer C.F. Wing Dept. Stores, New Bedford, 1936-42, advt. dir., 1946-64; pres. 7 Services Advt. Agy., New Bedford, 1964-65; advt. salesman New Bedford Standard-Times, 1966-74; pres. Alma Day Sales WGH, New Bedford, from 1974; v.p. Jacques Advt. Agy., Inc. and MAISA, New Bedford, 1974-87, owner, pres., from 1993. Treas. Evco Corp. Windo-Inserted Staging, New Bedford, 1966. Author 509 articles, reports, poems, songs, religious radio plays, booklets, etc. Precinct warden Civil Def., New Bedford, 1942, shelter mgr., 1964; mem. Mayor's Auditorium Com., New Bedford, 1963; trustee New Bedford Indsl. Found. unitl 1964; mem. Citizen Com. on Planning and /Urban Renewal, New Bedford, 1962-64, Downtown Improvement Com., New Bedford, 1962-64. Sgt. USAF, 1942-45, ETO. Mem. New Bedford C. of C., Am. Legion. Avocations: writing, poetry, songwriting, publishing, sales. Home: New Bedford, Mass. Died Mar. 5, 2007.

ALMOND, PAUL (DAVID PAUL MACPHERSON ALMOND), film director and producer, scriptwriter, novelist; b. Montreal, Que., Can., Apr. 26, 1931; s. Eric and Irene Clarice Almond; m. Angela Leigh, 1957 (div. 1964); m. Genevieve Bujold, 1967 (div. 1973); 1 child, Matthew James ; m. Joan Almond, Sept. 11, 1976. Student, McGill U., Montreal, 1948—49; BA, Balliol Coll., Oxford, 1952, MA, 1954. Pres. Quest Films, Montreal, 1967—2002. Writer, prodr., dir. (TV films) The Dark Did Not Conquer, 1963, Journey to the Centre, 1963, (films) Isabel, 1968, Act of the Heart, 1970, Journey, 1972, Ups & Downs, 1982, The Dance Goes On, 1992, prodr., dir. (documentaries) Seven Up!, 1964; dir.: (films) Captive Hearts, 1984; (TV films) Every Person Is Guilty, 1979; author: La Vengeance des Dieux, 1999; author: (with M Ballantyne) High Hopes: Coming of Age in the mid-Century, 1999; author: (The Alford Saga) The Deserter, 2010, The Survivor, 2011, The Pioneer, 2012, The Pilgrim, 2012, Le Déserteur, 2013, The Chaplain, 2013, Le Défricheur, 2013, The Gunner, 2014, Les Batisseurs, 2014, The Hero, 2014, The Inheritor, 2015. Decorated officer Order of Can. Mem.: Writers Union of Can., Royal Can. Acad. Arts, Dirs. Guild Am., Dirs. Guild Can. (hon.; life mem., DGC Lifetime Achievement award). Anglican. Home: Malibu, Calif. Died Apr. 9, 2015.

ALONS, DWAYNE ARLAN, state legislator; b. Hull, Iowa, Oct. 30, 1946; m. Clarice Alons; children: Kevin, Kyle, Kristin, Karena. BS in Mathematics, Northwestern Coll., 1968; MS in Mgmt., U. Ark., 1974; Grad., Air Command & Staff Coll., 1984. Farmer; mem. Dist. 5 Iowa House of Reps., 1999—2002, mem. Dist. 4, 2003—14. Republican. Christian. Died Nov. 29, 2014.

ALPERN, MILTON, civil engineer, consultant; b. NYC, June 25, 1925; s. Nathan and Rae (Kraft) A.; m. Beverly Katzman, May 30, 1946; children: Warren Deems, Barbara Lynn. BSCE, Cooper Union, 1945; MSCE, Columbia U., 1951; postgrad., Poly. Inst. Bklyn., 1957-63. Registered profl. engr., N.Y., N.J., Pa., Conn., Mass., Ill., Tex., Ky., Mo., Fla., Okla., Colo., N.C.; also nat. certification. Test engr. Edo Aircraft Co., Flushing, N.Y., 1945; design engr. Frederick Snare Corp., NYC, 1947-49; asst. prof. civil engring. Cooper Union, NYC, 1948-60; prin. Milton Alpern cons. engr., Wantagh, N.Y., 1960-71, Alpern & Soifer, cons. engrs., Massapequa, N.Y., 1971-83, Bellmore, N.Y., 1983-92; mgr. spl. projects div. Shah Assocs., P.C., Bellmore, N.Y., from 1992. Mem. N.Y. State Bd. Engring. and Land Surveying, 1978-87, chmn., 1984-86; vis. prof. civil engring. N.Y. Inst. Tech., 1977-78, Pratt Inst., 1986-92, Polytech U., 1993—. Contbr. articles to profl. jours. Chmn. bldg. com. Union Free Sch. Dist. 5, Nassau County, 1955-56; pres. Wantagh Oaks Civic Assn., 1957; mem. steering com. Am. Cancer Soc. Theatre Party, 1968-76. Served with C.E., AUS, 1945-47. Recipient Engr. of Yr. award Nassau County Profl. Engring. Soc., 1972, Lincoln Arc Welding Design awards, , 1961, 69. Fellow ASCE (life, Engr. of Yr. award L.I. chpt. 1974); mem. ASTM, Am. Arbitration Assn., Soc. Am. Mil. Engrs., Am. Welding Soc., Nat. Acad. Forensic Engrs., Am. Concrete Inst., N.Y. State Soc. Profl. Engrs. (pres. 1972-73), Nat. Soc. Profl. Engrs. (dir. 1967-77), Prestressed Concrete Inst., Constrn. Specifications Inst., N.Y. Cons. Engrs. Coun. (pres. L.I. chpt. 1970-71, chmn. edn., long range planning, ethics coms. 1965-74), Internat. Assn. Bridge and Structural Engrs., Nat. Acad. Forensic Engrs., Nat. Coun. Engring. Examiners (cert., chmn. ABET com. 1981-83, dir. accreditation bd. for engring. and tech. 1981-83, dir. engring. manpower commn. 1978-79), Chi Epsilon, Tau Beta Pi. Home: Massapequa, NY. Died Apr. 8, 2007.

AL-SAUD, KING ABDALLAH BIN ABD AL-AZIZ, King of Saudi Arabia; b. Riyadh, Saudi Arabia, Aug. 1, 1924; s. Abdul Aziz Al Saud and Fahda. Student in Religion, Chivalry and Politics. First dep. min. def. Kingdom of Saudi Arabia, Riyadh, 1962-63, comdr. Nat. Guard, 1963—2010, second dep. prime min., 1975—82, crown prince, 1982—2005, dep. prime min., 1982—2005, assumed the throne upon the death of his brother King Fahd bin Abdul Aziz Al-Saud on Aug. 1, 2005, king, 2005—15, prime min., 2005—15. Mem. Saudi dels. to Arab/Islamic Summit Confs., state visits and UN Gen. Assembly sessions; chmn. Supreme Com. Adminstrv. Reform; v.p. Supreme Council Higher Edn. Named one of The 100 Most Influential People in the World, TIME mag., 2007, The Global Elite, Newsweek mag., 2008, The World's Most Powerful People, Forbes mag., 2009—14. Islam. Died Jan. 23, 2015.

ALSOP, REESE FELL, medical educator; b. NYC, Feb. 24, 1913; s. Reese Denny and Julia Chapin Alsop; m. Elise Coates, Nov. 7, 1947; children: Brooke, Elise, Jane, Anne, Penn. BA, Harvard U., 1936; MD, Columbia U., 1944. Diplomate Am. Bd. Internal Medicine. Resident Mary Imogene Bassett Hosp., Cooperstown, NY, 1944—45, Bellevue Hosp., NYC, 1947—48, Bronx VA Hosp., 1948—50; asst. prof. medicine NYU, NYC, 1950—60; chmn. dept. medicine Huntington Hosp., NY, 1968—98; clin. prof. medicine SUNY, Stonybrook, from 1990. Cons. in medicine Northport VA Hosp., NY, from 1990. Articles editor New Eng. Jour. Medicine, from 1952; author: (poetry) Back Talk, from, George and His Horse Bill, 1948, Miss Polly Chromasia's Husband, Joseph and the Goat, from 1943; contbr. articles and poems to Harvard Mag., N.E. Jour. Medicine. Reader Episcopal Ch., Cold Spring Harbor, NY, from 1970. Capt. Med. Corps US Army, 1942—47. Mem.: Century Assn. (hon.). Achievements include patents for an audiocatheter; examining glove; return envelope; invention of medicalendar. Avocations: reading, tennis, writing. Home: Huntington, NY. Died Dec. 19, 2006.

ALTMAN, GARY See OWENS, GARY

ALTMAN, PATRICIA MICHAELS, emergency medical service volunteer; b. Bklyn., May 31, 1942; d. Robert W. and Estelle (Rodale) Michaels; m. Richard M. Altman, Oct. 17, 1964; children: Elizabeth Jane, Michael Jay. BS, Cornell U., 1964; BSN, Cornell U.-N.Y. Hosp., NYC, 1976; MBA, Sacred Heart U., Bridgeport, Conn., 1986. RN, Conn.; cert. EMT, Conn., MAST-EGTA. Vol. Weston (Conn.) Emergency Med. Svc. Participant alumni-in-residence program Cornell U., 1989. Trustee, vice chmn. Wilbraham and Monson Acad., Mass. Mem. Cornell U. Coun. (past pres.), Cornell U.-N.Y. Hosp. Sch. Nursing Alumni Assn., N.Y.S. Coll. Human Ecology Alumni Assn. (bd. dirs.), Sigma Theta Tau. Home: Weston, Conn. Died Feb. 8, 2007.

ALYEA, BERTHA C., retired pediatrics and home health care nurse; b. Swift County, Mo., Jan. 8, 1927; d. Alfred and Anna Helen (Anderson) Christensen; m. James O. Alyea, Aug. 10, 1950; children: Kristin, James, Daniel, Eric. Diploma, Ancker Hosp., St. Paul, 1947; BSN cum laude, S.E. Mo. State U., 1972; MSN, U. Mo., 1978. Cert. gerontol. nurse. Head nurse Lawrence (Kans.) Meml. Hosp.; instr. dept. nursing edn. S.E. Mo. State U., Cape Girardeau; asst. patient care coord., educator Vis. Nurses Assn., Columbia, Mo.; staff nurse Option Home Health Care, Columbia. Contbr. articles to profl. jours. Mem. ANA, Mo. Nurses Assn. (bd. dirs. 7th Dist.), Sigma Theta Tau. Home: Columbia, Mo. Died Nov. 1, 2006.

AMANN, CHARLES ALBERT, mechanical engineer, researcher; b. Thief River Falls, Minn., Apr. 21, 1926; s. Charles Alois and Bertha Ann (Oetting) Amann; m. Marilynn Ann Reis, Aug. 26, 1950; children: Richard, Barbara, Nancy, Julie. BS, U. Minn., 1946, MSME, 1948. Instr. U. Minn., Mpls., 1946-49; rsch. engr. GM Rsch. Labs., Detroit, 1949-54, supervisory rsch. engr. Warren, Mich., 1954-71, asst. dept. head, 1971-73, dept. head, 1973-89, rsch. fellow & dir. engring. rsch. coun., 1989-91; prin. engr. KAB Engring., from 1991. Spl. instr. Wayne State U., Detroit, 1952—55; guest lectr. Mich. State U., 1980—2006; outside prof. U. Ariz., 1983; mem. adv. com. Gas Rsch. Inst., 1992—98, Oak Ridge Nat. Lab., 1996—98; invited lectr. Inst. Advanced Engring., Seoul, Republic of Korea, 1994. Author (with others): Automotive Engine Alternatives, 1986, Advanced Diesel Engineering and Operations, 1988, Marks' Standard Handbook for Mechanical Engineers, 2007; co-editor: Combustion Modeling in Reciprocating Engines, 1980. Lt. (j.g.) USNR, 1944—56. Recipient James Clayton prize, Inst. Mech. Engrs., 1975, Oustanding Achievement award, U. Minn., 1991. Fellow: Soc. Automotive Engrs. (Arch T. Colwell merit award 1972, Disting. Spkr. award 1981, Arch T. Colwell merit award 1984, Disting. Spkr. award 1991, Forest R. McFarland award 2001); mem.: ASME (Richard S. Woodbury award 1989, Soichiro Honda lectr. 1992, Spkr. award Internal Combustion Engine Divsn. 1997, Internal Combustion Engine award 2000, Disting. lectr. 2002—04), NAE, Tau Beta Pi, Tau Omega, Sigma Xi. Presbyterian. Achievements include patents in field. Avocation: music. Died Mar. 10, 2015.

AMAYO, JOSE G., physician; b. Trujillo, Peru, Oct. 11, 1939; s. I. Napoleon and M. Rosario (Zevallos) A.; divorced. MD, Trujillo Med. Sch., 1967. Diplomate Am. Bd. Phys. Medicine and Rehab., Am. Bd. Electrodiagnostic Medicine. Pvt. practice, Pitts., from 1985; chief occup. health, chief head injury program Harmonville Rehab. Ctr., Pitts., 1973-85. Mem. Am. Acad. Phys. Medicine and Rehab., Am. Assn. Electrodiagnostic Medicine. Home: Blawnox, Pa. Died Feb. 7, 2007.

AMBS, MARVIN NELLIS, band director, musician, educator; b. New Albany, Ind., Aug. 15, 1924; s. Nellis Andrew and Normah Pearl (Hollowell) A.; m. Jo Ann Gruber, May 12, 1949; children: Marvin Kevin, Steven William, Keith Andrew, Karen Leigh Davis. BS in Music Edn., U. Louisville, 1951, MS in Music Edn., 1961. Band dir., tchr. Taylorsville (Ky.) High Sch., 1951; band dir. Silver Creek Twp. Schs., Sellersburg, Ind., 1951-63; mem. Kosair Shrine Band, 1951-56; band dir. Jefferson County Pub. Schs., Louisville, 1963-85; tchr. music Jefferson Community Coll., Louisville, 1968-70. Concert and marching bands adjudicator, Ky., Ind., Ohio, Tenn., 1988. Dir. Westport High Sch. Band and Drill Team European Tour, Belgium, Eng., France, West Germany, Switzerland, Holland., 1971. Chmn. Sousa Meml. Found.; staff mem. John Philip Sousa Honors Band, Purdue U. Summer Band Camp, N.Am. Band Dirs. Coordinating Coun.; mem. Band Assoc. Fgn. Travel Com., Ky. Commn. on Secondary Schs.; chmn. bd. dirs. Shawnee Christian Ch., 1965-67; asst. chmn. Band Coordinating and Selection Com. of the Ky. Derby Festival; apptd. U. Louisville Alumni Welcome Ctr. Com., 1991—. Served with USN, 1943-46. Named to Hon. Order Ky. Cols., Ky. Adms., Hon. Col. Ky. State Police, Hon. Lt. Col. State of Ga., Disting. Citizen Louisville, Ky.; commd. Hon. Capt. Steamship Belle of Louisville, 1988. Mem. VFW, DAV, Internat. Platform Assn., Nat. Band Assn. (chmn. so. div., Citation of Exellence), Am. Legion, Musicians Union local 11-637, Music Educators Nat. Conf., Ind. Music Educators Assn., Ky. Music Educators Assn. (co-chmn. state conv. 1971, Dist. Svc. award 1983), Ky. Educators Assn., Jefferson County Tchrs. Assn., Jefferson Dist. XII Music Educators Assn. (pres. 1983, named Tchr. of Yr. 1985), Jefferson County Ret. Tchrs. Assn. (area membership chmn. 1990—). Lodges: Masons, Shriners. Home: Louisville, Ky. Died Nov. 9, 2006.

AMDAHL, GENE MYRON, computer company executive; b. Flandreau, SD, Nov. 16, 1922; s. Anton E. and Inga (Brendsel) A.; m. Marian Quissell, June 23, 1946; children: Carlton Gene, Beth Delaine, Andrea Leigh. BS in Engring. Physics, SD State U., 1948, DEng (hon.), 1974; PhD in Theoretical Physics, U. Wis., 1952, DSc (hon.), 1979; D.Sc. (hon.), Luther Coll., 1980, Augustana Coll., 1984. Project mgr. IBM Corp., Poughkeepsie, NY, 1952-55; group head Ramo-Wooldridge Corp., LA, 1956; mgr. systems design Aeronutronics, LA, 1956-60; mgr. systems design advanced data processing systems IBM Corp., NYC, Los Gatos, Calif., Menlo Park, Calif., 1960-70; founder, chmn. Amdahl Corp., Sunnyvale, Calif., 1970—79, chmn. emeritus, cons., 1979, ret., 1980; founder, chief exec. officer Trilogy Systems Corp., Cupertino, Calif., 1980-87; chmn. bd. Elxsi (name changed from Trilogy Systems Corp.), San Jose, Calif., 1987-89; founder, pres., CEO Andor Internat. Ltd., Cupertino, 1987—94, also bd. dirs.; founder, chmn. Comml. Data Servers, Mountain View, Calif., 1994—98, ret., 1998. Bd. advisors Massively Parallel Technologies. Patentee in field. With USN, 1942-44. Recipient Disting. Alumnus award SD State U., 1973, Centennial Alumnus award, 1987; Man of Yr. award Data Processing Mgmt. Assn., 1976, Disting. Svc. citation U. Wis., 1976, Michelson-Morley award Case Western Res. U., 1977; Harry Goode Meml. award for outstanding contbns. to design and manufacture of large, high-performance computers Am. Fedn. Info. Processing Socs., 1983, Eckert-Mauchly award 1987; Good Samaritan award City Team Ministries, San Jose, 1991, Man of Yr. Achievement award Computer Weekly mag., 1991; named to Info. Processing Hall of Fame, 1985; named One of 1000 Makers of 20th Century, London Times, 1991; laureate Jr. Achievement Bus. Hall of Fame, 1995; recipient Legend award Computer and Comm. Industry Assn., 1995; IBM fellow, 1965. Fellow IEEE, Brit. Computer Soc. (disting.), Computer Mus., NAE; mem. IEEE (profl. group W.W. McDowell award 1976, Assn. Computing Machinery/IEEE Eckert-Mauchly award, 1987, IEEE Computer Entrepreneur award, 1989), Quadrato della Radio, Pontecchio Marcon, Eta Kappa Nu (eminent mem.). Presbyterian. Home: Palo Alto, Calif. Died Nov. 3, 2015.

AMLIE, JAN P., physician, educator; b. V. Toten, Norway, Sept. 23, 1940; s. Magnus and Bjørnhild Amlie; m. May L. Amlie, Nov. 16, 1963; children: Lars Peder, Lise Katrine, Julie Mathilde. Med. Sch., U. Oslo, 1965, MD, 1980. Med. authorization, 1969. Med. doctor Rikshospitalet, Oslo, from 1973, prof., 1990. Contbr. over 140 articles to profl. jours. Maj. Army, 1967. Fellow European Soc. Cardiology; mem. Norwegian Soc. Cardiology (pres. 1987-91), Union European Med. Specialists (pres. cardiology sect. 2002—06, mem. coun. 2006-12). Home: Oslo, Norway. Died May 2014.

ANDERSEN, LEONARD CHRISTIAN, former state legislator, real estate investor; b. Waukegan, Ill., May 30, 1911; s. Lauritz Frederick and Meta Marie (Jacobsen) A.; m. Charlotte O. Ritland, June 30, 1937; children: Karen Schneider, Paul R., Charlene Olsson, Mark Luther. BA, Huron Coll., SD, 1933; MA, U. S.D., 1937. Tchr. Onida H.S., SD, 1934—35; dir. bus. tng. Waldorf Coll., Forest City, Iowa, 1935—39; ins. salesman, 1939—41; tchrs. econs., current history Morningside Coll., Sioux City, Iowa, 1941—43; ins., real estate investor Sioux City, 1943—76. Mem. Iowa Ho. of Reps., Woodbury County, 1961-64, 66-71; mem. Iowa Senate, 26th Dist., 1972-76, chmn. rules and adminstrn. com.; former mem. Iowa Commn. on Aging; former mem. investment adv. bd. IPERS; former mem. ctrl. com. Woodbury County Reps., del. county, dist. and state convs., 1998, 2000; former mem. Simpco Projects Rev. Com.; former pres., chmn. bd. Siouxland Rental Assn.; past mem. Sioux City Housing Appeals Bd., Siouxland Com. on Alcoholism; bd. regents Augustana Coll., Sioux Falls, S.D., mem. Augustana Fellows, 2003—; mem. fin. com. Morningside Luth. Ch., co-chair call com. 2003—; bd. dirs. Human Rights Commn., Sioux City, 1997-2003 Del. Evang. Luth. Ch. Conv., 1999, 2000, 01, 02, promoter Wordalone movement; apptd. anti-violence com. Siouxland Area; mem. fin. com. Morningside Luth. Ch., 2006—. Mem. Lions. Home: Sioux City, Iowa. Died Dec. 28, 2014.

ANDERSON, ARVID, arbitrator; b. Hammond, Ind., July 18, 1921; s. Carl and Alma (Hagstrom) Anderson; m. Avis M. Larrat, May 27, 1944; children: Susan Dean, Steven,

Kristin, Linda Hoard. BA in Labor Economics, U. Wis., 1946, LLB, 1948. Bar: Wis. 1948. Exec. sec. Wis. Employment Rels. Commn., 1948—60; commr., 1960—67; chmn. Office Collective bargaining, NYC, 1967—87; adj. prof. U. Wis.; Labor and Indsl. Rels. prof. State Sch. Labor and Indsl. Rels., Cornell U., NY; labor arbitrator, 1950; mem. Task force on Excellence, State and Local Govt. Through Labor Mgmt. Cooperation; sec. labor, 1994—95. Contbr. articles legal rev. 1st lt. USAF, 1943—45. Decorated Air medal, Purple Heart, Disting. Svc. award Am. Arbitration Assn. Mem.: ABA, Nat. Acad. Arbitrators (pres. 1987—88). Home: Minneapolis, Minn. Died July 22, 2015.

ANDERSON, BENEDICT RICHARD O'GORMAN, political science educator; b. Kunming, Yunnan, China, Aug. 26, 1936; came to U.S., 1967, permanent resident. s. James Carew O'Gorman and Veronica Beatrice Mary (Bigham) A.; 2 adopted sons BA in Classics, Cambridge U., Eng., 1957; PhD in Polit. Sc., Cornell U., 1967. Asst. prof. Cornell U., Ithaca, N.Y., 1967-72, assoc. prof., 1972-77, prof., 1972-88, Aaron L. Binenkorb prof. internat. studies to emeritus, 1988—2002, dir. S.E. Asia program, 1984-88, dir. Modern Indonesia Program, 1988. Author: Java in a Time of Revolution, 1972, Imagined Communities: Reflections on the Origin and Spread of Nationalism, 1983, rev. edit., 1991, In the Mirror, 1985, Language and Power, 1990; editor jour. Indonesia, 1966-84. Henry Luce Found. fellow, 1977-78, Guggenheim Found. fellow, 1982-83, Fulbright-Hays fellow, 1989-90, Social Sci. Rsch. Coun. fellow, 1989-90. Mem. Am. Acad. Arts and Scis., Assn. for Asian Studies. Home: Freeville, NY. Died Dec. 12, 2015.

ANDERSON, BRADLEY JAY, cartoonist; b. Jamestown, NY, May 14, 1924; s. Perle J. and Jennie (Solomonson) A.; m. Barbara Marie Jones, Sept. 8, 1945; children: Christine Dorothy (Mrs. Richard Potchernick), Craig Bradley, Paul Richard, Mark Stephen. B.F.A., Syracuse U., 1951. Art dir. audio visual dept. Syracuse U., 1950-51; free-lance mag. cartoonist, 1950—2015; art dir. Ball & Grier (pub. relations), Utica, NY, 1952-53. Syndicated cartoonist: Marmaduke, 1954—2015, Grandpa's Boy, 1954—2015, exhbns. include, San Diego Fair Fine Arts and Cartoons, 1966, Punch mag. exhbn., 1954, Selected Cartoons of 14 Sat. Eve. Post Cartoonists, 1958, Americana Overseas exhbn., 1957, Burchfield Center, State U. Coll. at Buffalo, 1976, San Francisco Mus. Fine Arts, 1978, Joe and Emily Lowe Art Gallery, Syracuse, N.Y., 1993, Smithsonian Exptl. Mus., 1993; represented in permanent collections, Albert T. Reid Coll., William Allen White Found., Syracuse U. Manuscripts Library.; Author: Marmaduke, 1955, More Marmaduke, 1958, 1973, Marmaduke, 1966, Marmaduke Rides Again, 1968, Marmaduke . . . Again?, 1976, Down Marmaduke!, 1978, Marmaduke Digs In, 1978, The Marmaduke Treasury, 1978, Marmaduke on the Loose, 1980, Marmaduke Super Dog, 1983, Meet Marmaduke, 1983, Marmaduke Mystery Puzzles, 1983, Marmaduke Large and Lovable, 1983, Marmaduke, Take 2, 1984, Ever Lovin' Marmaduke, 1985, Marmaduke Sounds Off, 1985, Encore, Marmaduke! Encore, 1985, Marmaduke Sounds Off, 1985, Sitting Pretty Marmaduke, 1986, Go For It Marmaduke, 1986, Tuned In Marmaduke, 1986, Marmaduke Hams It Up, 1986, Tuned in Marmaduke, 1986, It's a Dog's Life, 1989,Marmaduke Laps It Up, 1989, Marmaduke You Dog You, 1989. Served with USNR, 1943-46, 50-54. Mem. Newspaper Comics Council, Nat. Cartoonists Soc. (named Best Syndicated Panel Cartoonist, 1978), Sigma Delta Chi. Lodges: Masons. Home: Montgomery, Tex. Died Aug. 30, 2015.

ANDERSON, DAVID ROBERT, cardiac surgeon, consultant; b. Dungannon, Northern Ireland, Feb. 16, 1954; s. Robert William and Dorothy (Bradshaw) A.; m. Alison Christine Dore, June 14, 1986; children: Roisin, Colleen, Tara. BChir, Cambridge U., 1979, MA with hons., 1980. Reg. med. practitioner, specialist cardiac surgeon. Sr. house officer Frimley Park Hosp., 1981-82; registrar Southampton Gen. Hosp., 1982-84, Guys Hosp., London, 1984-86; rsch. fellow U. Pa., from 1988, Wayne State, Mich., 1989; sr. registrar Birmingham Children's Hosp., 1990-91; cons. Guys Hosp., London, from 1991. Hon. sr. lectr. United Med. & Dental Sch., 1991—; Hunterian prof. RCS London, 1991. Mem. British Cardiac Soc., British Med. Assn., Soc. Cardiothoracic Surgeons of Great Britain and Ireland. Home: London, England. Died Dec. 15, 2006.

ANDERSON, FLETCHER NEAL, chemical executive; b. Kansas City, Mo., Nov. 5, 1930; s. Chester Gustav and Astrid Cecilia (Crone) A.; m. Marilyn Lucille Henke; children: Karl C., Keith F., Susan L. BSChemE, U. Mo., 1951; MSChemE, Washington U., St. Louis, 1956; grad. exec. program, Stanford U., 1972. Registered profl. engr., Mo., Pa. With Mallinckrodt, Inc., St. Louis, 1951-81, group v.p. food, drug and cosmetic chems. group, 1974-76, group v.p. chem. group, 1976-78, sr. v.p. chem. group, 1978-81, also dir.; pres., dir. Chomerics, Inc., Woburn, Mass., 1981-85; pres., chief exec. officer, dir. Chemtech Industries, St. Louis, 1986-89; interim pres., CEO Brulin Corp., Indpls., 1990, bd. dirs., 1990-93; exec. v.p., COO, dir. F&C Internat., Cin., 1992-93, pres., CEO, 1993, also bd. dirs. Bd. dirs. Cytogen Corp., Princeton, N.J., 1987-95, Sepracor Inc., Malborough, Mass., 1993-95; chmn. bd. Med. Materials, Inc., Camarillo, Calif., 1992-93; mem. adv. coun. U. Mo. Engring. Sch. Columbia, 1978-89. Mem. Florissant (Mo.) Charter Commn., 1961-63. Recipient Disting. Service to Engring. award U. Mo., Columbia, 1978 Mem. Am. Inst. Chem. Engrs., Algonquin Golf Club. Lutheran. Died Dec. 1, 2006.

ANDERSON, JANE ELLSWORTH, retired secondary school educator; b. Chillicothe, Ohio, Mar. 30, 1943; d. Henry Branch and Beatrice Clara (Trainer) Ellsworth: m. George Leonard Anderson, Jr., Sept. 9, 1964; children: Doug, Jeff, Michele. BS in Edn., Ohio State U., 1983, MS in Edn., 1994. Cert. tchr. grades 7-12, Ohio. Long distance operator Ohio Bell Telephone Co., Dayton, 1962-64; real estate agt. Donna Vaughn Realtors, Dayton, 1965-67; sales rep., mgr. Tupperware Dayton Party Sales, 1972-74; tchr. Westerville (Ohio) City Schs., 1984—2003; ret. Advisor Westerville H.S. Yearbook, Golden Warrior, 1986 (1st pl. award), 1987 (1st pl. award). Various positions Englewood Hills Elem. Sch. PTA, Englewood, Ohio, 1971—76; phone counselor Bridge Counseling Ctr., Columbus, 1980—81; mem. Dem. Nat. Campaign, Dem. Congl. Campaign Com., Dem. Senators Campaign Com., Dem. Congl. Com.; active John Kerry for Pres.; youth dir. Unity Ch., Columbus, Ohio, 1978—80. Mem.: Natural Resources, Am. Diabetes Assn., Am. Cancer Soc., St. Labre Indian Sch., Am. Indian Youth, St. Joseph's Indian Sch., Nat. Parks Conservation, Habitat for Humanity, Eastern Paralyzed Veterans, Emily's List, So. Poverty Law Ctr., U.S. Holocaust Meml. Mus. Avocations: writing, reading, biking, photography. Home: Columbus, Ohio. Died Apr. 9, 2007.

ANDERSON, JERRY WILLIAM, JR., diversified financial services company executive, educator; b. Stow, Mass., Jan. 14, 1926; s. Jerry William and Heda Charlotte (Petersen) A. ; m. Joan Hukill Balyeat, Sept. 13, 1947; children: Katheleen, Diane. BS in Physics, U. Cin., 1949, PhD in Econs., 1976; MBA, Xavier U., 1959. Rsch. and test project engr. Wright-Patterson AFB, Ohio, 1949-53; project engr., electronics divsn. AVCO Corp., Cin., 1953-70, program mgr., 1970-73; program dir. Cin. Electronics Corp., 1973-78; pres. Anderson Industries Unltd., from 1978. Chmn. dept. mgmt. and mgmt. info. svcs. Xavier U., 1980-89, prof. mgmt., 1989-94, prof. emeritus, 1994—; lectr. No. Ky. U., 1977-78; tech. adviser Cin. Tech. Coll., 1971-80; co-founder, exec. v.p. Loving God Complete Bible Christian Ministries, 1988—. Contbr. articles on radars, lasers, infrared detection equipment, air pollution to govt. pubs. and prof. jours.; author: 3 books in field; reviewer, referee: Internat. Jour. Energy Sys., 1985—86. Mem. Madeira City Planning Commn., Ohio, 1962-80; founder, pres. Grassroots, Inc., 1964; active United Appeal, Heart Fund, Multiple Sclerosis Fund. With USNR, 1943-46. Named Man of Yr., City of Madeira, 1964. Mem. MADD, VFW (life), Am. Mgmt. Assn., Assn. Energy Engrs. (charter), Internat. Acad. Mgmt. and Mktg., Nat. Right to Life, Assn. Cogeneration Engrs. (charter), Assn. Environ. Engrs. (charter), Am. Legion (past comdr.), Acad. Mgmt., Madeira Civic Assn. (past v.p.), Cin. Art Mus., Cin. Zoo, Colonial Williamsburg Found., Omicron Delta Epsilon. Republican. Home: Rutland, Ohio. Died Jan. 27, 2014.

ANDERSON, JOHN EDWARD, information operations executive; b. Rapid City, SD, July 22, 1943; s. John H. and Ruth E. (Darling) A.; m. Jane A. Oyler, June 5, 1962 (div. 1982); children: Candice, Cadence. BA in Math., Ariz. State U., 1968, MS in Math., 1970. Programmer Brroughs (UNISYS), LA, 1970-72, U.S. Customs Svc., San Diego, 1972-75, mgr., 1975-80; instr., then dir. West Coast U., San Diego, 1974-80; dir. infosystems Nat. Libr. Medicine, Bethesda, Md., 1980-91; exec. v.p. BIOSIS, Phila., 1991-93, pres., from 1993. Steering com. Carnegie-Mellon Sr. Exec. Program, Pitts., 1985—. Recipient Merit award NIH, 1985. Mem. AAAS, Med. Libr. Assn. (Rogers award 1990), Coun. Biology Editors, Am. Inst. Biol. Scis. Home: Philadelphia, Pa. Died Feb. 21, 2007.

ANDERSON, KATHERINE DOSTER, retired library director; b. Mishawaka, Ind., Mar. 21, 1932; d. Howard George and Edith Katherine (Ratts) Doster; m. George Hamilton Anderson, Sept. 13, 1958; children: Howard H., Gordon L. BA, Wellesley Coll., 1953; MS, Palmer Grad. Libr. Sch., L.I., Greenvale, NY, 1972. Actuarial asst. George B. Buck, Cons. Actuary, NYC, 1953-63; libr. media specialist Herricks Pub. Schs., New Hyde Park, N.Y., 1972-92. Contb. articles to sch. newsletter. Bd. Wheatley Scholarship Fund, 1964-68, mem. budget adv. com. Wheatley Bd. Edn., Old Westbury, N.Y., 1968; docent Telfair Art Mus.; guide Hist. Savannah Assn.; elder Cmty. Ch., treas. World Svc., 1988, East Williston, N.Y. Mem. Nassau Suffolk Sch. Libr. Assn., Beta Phi Mu. Republican. Avocations: golf, tennis, sailing, platform tennis, bridge. Home: Savannah, Ga. Died July 21, 2007.

ANDERSON, LENNART, artist; b. Detroit, Aug. 22, 1928; m. Barbara Stenglein-Anderson (dec. 2002); children: Jeanette Wallace, Eliza, Orrin. B.F.A., Art Inst. Chgo., 1950; M.F.A., Cranbrook Acad. Art Mich., 1952. Instr. art Chatham Coll., Pitts., 1961-62, Pratt Inst., NYC, 1962-69, Skowhegan Sch., 1965, 67, Art Students League, NY, Yale U., 1967, Finch Coll., NYC, Columbia U.; prof. painting and drawing Bklyn. Coll., 1974—2004. One man shows include Tanager Gallery, NYC, 1962, Graham Gallery, 1963, 67, 69, 70, Davis & Long Co., 1976, Davis & Langdale Co., 1981, 84, 85, 91, 92, William Crapo Gallery, New Bedford, Mass., 1982, Darien Libr., Darien, Conn., 1984, Delaware Art Mus., Wilmington, 1992, Salander-O'Reilly Galleries, 1995, 97, 99, 2002, Rider Univ. Gallery, Lawrenceville, NJ, 2000, others; group shows include March Gallery, NYC, 1957, 58, Palazzo dell'Esposizione, Rome, 1958, 59, 60, Kans. City Art Inst., 1962, Carnegie Internat., Pitts., 1964, 67, Am. Fedn. Arts, NYC, 1965, Yale Univ., 1967, Cleve. Mus. Art, Ohio, 1972, Mus. Fine Arts, Boston, 1975, 1982-83, Art Inst. Chgo., 1976, Harold Reed Gallery, NYC, 1978, Pa. Acad. Fine Arts, Phila., 1981 Robert Schoelkopf Gallery, 1984, 85, Nat. Acad. Design, NYC, 1988, Meml. Art Gallery, Rochester, NY, 1989, Oglethorpe Univ. Art Gallery, Atlanta, 1990, Gerald Peters Gallery, Santa Fe, N.Mex., 1993, Salander-O'Reilly Galleries, Inc., NYC, 1994, 95, Aspen Art Mus., Aspen, Colo., 1996, Art Inst. So. Calif., Laguna Beach, Calif., 1999, Bates Coll. Mus. Art, 2000, Widener Gallery Trinity Coll., Hartford, Conn., 2003, others; represented in permanent collections, Whitney Mus. Am. Art, Bklyn. Mus., Hirschorn Mus., Washington, Mus. Fine Arts, Boston, Cleve., Yale Univ., New Haven, Conn., Delaware Art Mus., Wilmington, Mellon Bank, Pitts., Bklyn. Mus., NY, others. Recipient Prix de Rome, 1958-60; Raymond A. Speiser Meml. prize Pa. Acad. Fine Arts, 1966; Nat. Council on Arts prize, 1966, Academician NAD 1982,Emil & Dines Carlson award NAD, 1988, Benjamin Altman prize, 2005; Mus. Tiffany Found. grantee, 1957, 61, Guggenheim fellow, 1986; grantee Nat. Endowment for Arts, Tiffany Found. Am. Acad. and Inst. Arts and Letters; assoc. Am. Acad. Design. Home: Brooklyn, NY. Died Oct. 15, 2015.

ANDERSON, LYNN RENE (RENE ANDERSON), singer; b. Grand Forks, ND, Sept. 26, 1947; d. Casey and Liz Anderson; m. Glenn Sutton (div.); 1 child, Lisa Sutton; m. Harold Stream III (div.); children: Gray Stream, Melissa Stream Hempel. Singer, rec. artist, from 1966; appeared on Lynn Anderson Spls. Appearances on Lawrence Welk Show, 1967-70, Grand Old Opry, 1967, Ed Sullivan Show, Bob Hope Spls., Starsky and Hutch, (NBC Movie of the Week); singer 1971-97; TV guest appearances L. Frank Baum's The Marvelous Land of Oz, 1981, Country Gold, 1982, Law and Order, 1991, XXX's and OOO's, 1994, Babylon 5, 1994; rec. artist: (songs) I Never Promised You a Rose Garden, That's a No No, Promises, Promises, I've Been Everywhere, How Can I Unlove You, Keep Me in Mind, What a Man My Man Is, Cry, Fool Me, Listen to a Country Song, Your're My Man, Top of the World, Rocky Top, (albums) Encore, Under the Boardwalk, Greatest Hits, Rose Garden, What She Does Best, 1988, (duet with Gary Morris) You're Welcome to Tonight, 1983, What She Does Best, 1988, Country Spotlight, 1991, (with Emmylou Harris and Marty Stuart) Cowboys' Sweetheart, 1992; discs include Latest and Greatest, 1998, Anthology: The Columbia Years, 1999, Anthology: The Chart Years, 1999, Live at Billy Bob's Texas, 2000, Christmas, 2002, Pure Country, 2004, The Bluegrass Sessions, 2004, Heart Songs, 2004, Bridges, 2015 Recipient Grammy award; named Female Artist of the Decade by Record World, 1971, Best Female Vocalist, CMA Awards, Most Promising, Best Female Vocalist, Acad. Country Music Awards, Best Country Performance-Female, People's Choice awards. Achievements include first female country snger to sell out Madison Square Garden in New York in 1974. Died July 30, 2015.

ANDERSON, MARTIN CARL, economist; b. Lowell, Mass., Aug. 5, 1936; s. Ralph and Evelyn (Anderson) A.; m. Annelise Graebner, Sept. 25, 1965 AB summa cum laude, Dartmouth Coll., 1957, MS in Engring., MSBA; PhD in Indsl. Mgmt., MIT Sloan Sch. Mgmt., 1962. Asst. to dean, instr. engring. Thayer Sch. Engring. Dartmouth Coll., Hanover, NH, 1959; research fellow Joint Ctr. for Urban Studies MIT and Harvard U., Cambridge, 1961-62; asst. prof. finance Columbia U. Graduate Sch. Bus., NYC, 1962-65, assoc. prof. bus., 1965-68; spl. asst. to Pres. Richard Nixon The White House, Washington, 1969-70, spl. cons. for systems analysis, 1970-71, asst. for policy devel., 1981-82; sr. fellow Stanford U. Hoover Instn., Calif., 1971—2015, Keith and Jan Hurlbut sr. fellow, 1998—2015. Public interest dir. Fed. Home Loan Bank San Francisco, 1972-79; mem. Commn. on Crucial Choices for Americas, 1973-75, Def. Manpower Commn., 1975-76, Com. on the Present Danger, 1977-91, President's Fgn. Intelligence Advisory Bd., 1982-85, President's Econ. Policy Adv. Bd., 1982-88, President' Gen. Advisory Com. on Arms Control & Disarmament, 1987-93. Author: The Federal Bulldozer: A Critical Analysis of Urban Renewal, 1949-62, 1964, Conscription: A Select and Annotated Bibliography, 1976, Welfare: The Political Economy of Welfare Reform in the U.S., 1978, Registration and the Draft, 1982, The Military Draft, 1982, Revolution, 1988, Impostors in the Temple, 1992, Reagan in his Own Hand: The Writings of Ronald Reagan That Reveal His Revolutionary Vision For America, 2001, Reagan: A Life in Letters, 2003, Reagan's Path to Victory, 2004, Ronald Regan: Decisions of Greatness, 2015; columnist Scripps-Howard News Svc., 1993-94. Dir. rsch. Nixon Presdl. Campaign, 1968; policy adviser Ronald Reagan Presdl. Campaign, 1976, 80; del. Republican Nat. Conv., 1992-2000; policy adviser Dole Presdl. Campaign, 1996; sr. adviser George W. Bush Presdl. Campaign, 1998-2000; trustee Ronald Reagan Presdl. Found., 1985-92; mem. Calif. Governor's Coun. Econ. Advisors, 1993-98, chmn. Congressional Policy Advisory Bd., 1998-2001. 2d lt. AUS, 1958-59. Mem. Mont Pelerin Soc., Phi Beta Kappa. Clubs: Bohemian. Home: Portola Valley, Calif. Died Jan. 3, 2015.

ANDERSON, ROBERT EMRA, chemical executive; b. Mentone, Ind., Jan. 6, 1924; s. Emra D. and Lenna (Coplen) A.; m. Wilma Rae Hanna, Jan. 13, 1945; children: Kenneth R., Keith R. BS in Chemistry, Ind. U., 1949, MA in Inorganic Chemistry, 1951. Phys. chemist Dow Chem. Co., Midland, Mich., 1951-56, group leader, 1956-68, Diamond Shamrock Corp., Redwood City, Calif., 1968-78, sr. research scientist, 1978-82; cons. Sunnyvale, Calif., from 1982. Chmn. Gordon Research Conf. on ion exchange, 1971. Served with U.S. Army, 1943-46. Mem. Am. Chem. Soc., Sunnyvale Stamp Soc. (pres. 1974-75, 86). Presbyterian. Avocation: stamp collecting/philately. Died July 9, 2007.

ANDERSON, ROY EVERETT, retired electrical engineer; b. Batavia, Ill., Oct. 30, 1918; s. Elof and Nellie Amanda Anderson; m. Gladys Marie Nelson, Aug. 22, 1943; children: Paul V., David L., Barbara J. Anderson Wald, Dorothy M. Anderson Presser. BA in Physics, Augustana Coll., Rock Island, Ill., 1943; MSEE, Union Coll., Schenectady, 1952. Instr. physics Augustana Coll., 1943-44, 46-47; cons. engr. GE, Schenectady, 1947-83; co-founder, v.p. Mobile Satellite Corp., Malvern, Pa., 1983-88; owner, mgr., cons. Anderson Assocs., Glenville, NY, 1988—99;

pres. Rega Assocs., Glenville, 1993—2000; ret., 2000. Cons. Am. Mobile Satellite Corp., Washington, 1988-91; participant nat. and internat. regulatory and tech. orgns. leading to establishment generic mobile satellite svc. Contbr. over 125 articles to profl. jours.; patentee indsl. electronic measurement and quality control instruments, tone code ranging technique for position surveillance using satellites; developer Doppler radio direction finder. Trustee Dudley Obs., Schenectady, 1975-83, 90-2002, chmn. bd. trustees, 1980-83, 90. With USN, 1944-46. GE Coolidge fellow, 1970. Fellow IEEE, AAAS, Radio Club Am., Inst. Navigation; mem. AIAA. Home: Schenectady, NY. Died Dec. 7, 2011.

ANDERSON, VALERIE B., actress, writer; b. Boston, Jan. 4, 1961; d. Kittridge Anderson and Pamela Evelyn Booth; m. Remington Morris Patrick Murphy, Sept. 26, 1999. Cheerleader Phila. Eagles, 1980; model Reinhard Modelling Agy., Phila., 1980; comml. actress Sears, Phila., 1980; TV spokesperson Arpeggio's Restaurant, Phila., 1980; artist art-exchange. com, Inc., Hot Springs, Ark., 2006—07; with Writing Contest OC Christian Writers Conf. Subject of articles, radio program; spkr. in field; appearances on TV programs. Musician: (single) My Love Rolls Over, 1982, Dolly is a Swinger, 1984; author: (pen name Christina Alexandra) Five Lost Years: A Personal Exploration of Schizophrenia, 2000, The Witness Book: Sensitive Stories of Christian Outreach (Top Thirty Finalist award); author: (illustrator) Reflections on the Word in Black and White, 2002; illustrator: book cover; exhibitions include Main Line Art Ctr., 2004—05, drawing, Self-Portrait, art-exchange.com., Inc., 2006, multimedia slide show, Birds, Art-Exchange cafe, 2007, Heart, NY Art Expo, 2007, Warrior Princess, Jacob K. Javits Convention Center, 2007, exhibitions include 11th Annual Faces Internat. Juried Online Art Exhbn., Upstream People Gallery, 2009; author: (book) The Witness Book: Sensitive Stories of Christian Outreach, 2011, Dream Dynamo Tailspin, 2013, The Dream of Emerald Blue, 2014. Recipient Annual award Edn., Nat. Alliance for the Mentally Ill., Chester County, Pa., 2007, Citation award, Pa. State Senate, 2008, Spl. Recognition award, 14th Ann. Faces Juried; flute scholar, Jenkintown Music Sch. Mem.: Internat. Biog. Ctr. (Eng.), Nat. Alliance for the Mentally Ill, Mensa, Am. Assn. People with Disabilities. Avocations: travel, piano. Home: Abington, Pa. Died Feb. 3, 2015.

ANDERSON, WARREN M., retired chemical company executive; b. Bklyn., Nov. 29, 1921; s. John M. and Ida M. (Peterson) A.; m. Lillian K. Christensen, Feb. 22, 1947. AB in Chemistry, Colgate U., 1942; LL.B., Western Res. U., 1956. Chem. sales rep. Union Carbide Co., NYC, 1945, v.p. sales and mktg., Olefins div., 1962, pres. process chemicals divsn., 1967-69, v.p., 1969-73, exec. v.p., 1973-77, pres., 1977-82, chmn., CEO, 1982-86. Served in USNR, 1943-45. Mem. American Chem. Soc., Soc. Chem. Industry, ABA Died Sept. 29, 2014.

ANDREWS, PAULANN, community health nursing consultant; b. Detroit, May 7, 1931; d. Paul and Ann (Muir) A. BSN, Coll. St. Rose, Albany, NY, 1953; MA in Nursing Edn., Columbia U., 1955. Supervising nurse N.Y. State Dept. Health, Albany; dept. head nursing svc. Essex County Nursing Svc., Elizabethtown, N.Y.; dir. patient svcs. Rensselaer County, Troy, N.Y.; nurse cons. Mich. Dept. Pub. Health, Lansing. Mem. ANA, N.Y. State Nurse Assn., Assn. Bus. and Profl. Women. Home: Saranac Lake, NY. Died Apr. 30, 2007.

ANGEL, MICHAEL GONZALEZ, cultural organization administrator; b. Seattle, Dec. 21, 1960; s. Jose Vincente Gonzalez and Maria (del Carmen Romero de Villa) A.; m. Leni Alcantara Alonzo, May 1, 1992; 1 child, Catherine Isabella. BS in Bus. Adminstrn. magna cum laude, Creighton U., 1981; MBA, Harvard Bus. Sch., 1983. Project mgr. Harvard Group Devel., Manchester, NH, 1984-85, sales, leasing and mktg. mgr., 1986-87, gen. mgr., 1988-90; export product line mgr. Otto GmbH and Gebr. Otto KG, Cologne, Germany, 1991-92; export sales mgr. Latin Am. Otto Industries, Inc., Charlotte, NC, 1991-95; dir. N.Am. mktg. and sales Hyundai, San Diego, 1995-96; dir. wireless sales and internet applications Digital Sound Corp., Santa Barbara, CA, 1996-97; v.p. internat. bus. devel. and sales Messer/Hoechst AG, LA, 1998-2000; v.p. technology devel. and investment Verizon Comms., NYC, 2000-01; pres., CEO Nat. Assn. Advancement Hispanic People, from 2001. Mem. Harvard Club (N.Y. and Boston). Republican. Roman Catholic. Died Dec. 15, 2006.

ANGELINI, FIORENZO CARDINAL, cardinal; b. Rome, Aug. 1, 1916; Ordained priest of Rome, Italy, 1940; nat. ecclesiastical asst. Men's Cath. Action, 1945—47; master pontifical ceremonies Rome, 1947—54; official Roman Curia, 1956—77; appointed Titular Bishop of Messene, 1956, ordained, 1956, appointed Titular Archbishop, 1985; aux. bishop of Rome, Italy, 1977—85; pro-president Pontifical Commission for the Pastoral Assistance to Health Care Workers (renamed Pontifical Council for the Pastoral Assistance to Health Care Workers), Rome, 1985—89, pres., 1989—96; pres. emeritus Pontifical Council for Pastoral Assistance to Health Care Workers (renamed Pontifical Council for Health Pastoral Care), Rome, 1996—2014; elevated to cardinal, 1991; cardinal-deacon of Santo Spirito in Sassia (Holy Spirit in Sassia), 1991—2002, cardinal-priest, 2002—14. Participant of many international conferences regarding a variety of health issues. Author of many written works. Roman Catholic. Died Nov. 22, 2014.

ANGELO, JOHN MICHAEL, investment banking company executive; b. Manhattan, June 3, 1941; m. Judy Hart Angelo; children: Jack, Kate, Jesse. Grad., St. Lawrence U., 1963. Ptnr. L.F. Rothschild Unterberg Towbin Holdings, Inc., vice chmn., bd. mem. NYC, 1985; founder, CEO Angelo, Gordon & Co., NY, 1988—2016. Dir. Sotheby's, 2007. Co-writer of the song, Where Everybody Knows Your Name, theme for TV series Cheers. Served in US Army. Died Jan. 1, 2016.

ANGERMUELLER, HANS H., banker; b. Neudorf, Oct. 7, 1924; m. Katherine L. (Alberti) (dec. Dec. 21, 2013); children Hans Paul, Katherine Knetzger, Marianne Lynner, Victor, Susan Twombly BA, Harvard U., 1946, MS in Engring., 1947, LLB, 1950. Assoc. Shearman & Sterling, NYC, 1950—59, ptnr., 1959—73, of counsel, 1990—2015; with Citicorp, NYC, 1973—90, sr. v.p., gen. counsel, then sr. exec. v.p., then vice chmn., 1973—90, bd. dirs.; vice chmn., bd. dirs. Citibank N.A., NYC. Served with USN. Home: Westerly, RI. Died July 11, 2015.

ANSLOW, DAVID REESE, advertising and marketing executive; b. Cin., June 2, 1948; s. Benjamin and Margaret (Brown) A. BA in English, U. Cin., 1973. With client services dept., creative dir. Ben Anslow Advt., Bucyrus, Ohio, 1980-84; creative dir. Richardson & Assocs., Cin., 1984-85; freelance advt. cons. Cin., 1985-86; dir. advt. and mktg. Peabody Galion (Ohio), from 1986. Mem. Mktg. Club North Cen. Ohio. Died Nov. 20, 2006.

ANTER, ELAINE THERESA, oncology nurse; b. Pawtucket, RI, Feb. 16, 1950; d. Fernand N. and Mary E. (Miller) Malouin; m. Daniel Anter, May 17, 1969; children: Lori A., Daniel A. ADN, R.I. Jr. Coll., 1974. RN, R.I., Mass.; cert. oncology nurse. Staff nurse Roger Williams Hosp., Providence, 1975-87, asst. clin. nurse mgr., 1987-89, oncology nurse clinician, 1989-91, clin. nurse mgr. bone marrow transplant/med. oncology unit, from 1991. Mem. Oncology Nursing Soc. R.I. and S.E. Mass., Nat. Marrow Donor Program, VFW Aux. Avocations: tropical fish, cockatiels, cocker spaniels, crossword puzzles. Home: Smithfield, RI. Died July 14, 2007.

ANTHOINE, ROBERT, lawyer, educator; b. Portland, Maine, June 5, 1921; s. Edward S and Sara B (Pinkham) Anthoine; m. Margarita M. Hamilton, Dec. 12, 2006; children from previous marriage: Alison, Robert Neal, Nelson, Nina. AB, Duke U., 1942; JD, Columbia U., 1949. Bar: NY 1949, US Ct Appeals (2d cir) 1956, US Supreme Ct 1970. Rsch. assoc. Am. Law Inst. fed. income tax project Columbia U., NYC, 1949—50; assoc. Cleary, Gottlieb, Friendly and Cox, 1950—52; assoc. prof. law Columbia U., 1952—56, prof. law, 1956—64, adj. prof., 1964—94; ptnr. Winthrop, Stimson, Putnam and Roberts, 1963—86, sr. counsel, 1987—2000, in charge London office, 1972—76; sr. counsel Pillsbury Winthrop Shaw Pittman LLP, NYC, from 2001. Vis. prof. Law Sch. Ind. U., Bloomington, Ind., 1986; vis. prof. Law Sch. U. Tex., Austin, 1988; vis. prof. Law Sch. U. NC, Chapel Hill, 1991, U. Pa., Philadelphia, 1996, Seattle U., 1997. Author, editor: survey Tax Incentives for Investment in Developing Countries, 1979; contbr. articles to profl jours. Trustee Sevenarts, Ltd., London, from 1994; hon. gov. Royal Shakespeare Theatre, Stratford-upon-Avon, England, from 1977; chmn. emeritus Aperture Found., bd. dirs., 1978—2010; active Coun Fgn. Rels., 1982—2010; trustee, dir. Grosvenor Gallery (Fine Arts) Ltd., London, from 1994; pres. S K Yee Found., from 1983; hon. dir. Hazen Polsky Found., from 2000; bd. dirs., v.p. Morris Graves Found., from 2000; chmn. Lucid Art Found., 2005—11; bd. dirs. emeritus Eric and Salome Estorick Found, Vol. Lawyers Art. Lt. USN, 1942—46. Mem.: ABA, Asn Litèraire et Artistique Int (US), Int. Fiscal Assn., Assn. Bar City NY, Am. Law Inst. (life), Hurlingham Club (London), Century Assn. Club. Democrat. Died Jan. 23, 2015.

ANTON, BARBARA, writer; b. Pocono Pines, Pa., Apr. 3, 1926; d. Walter B. and Emma Agnes (Hess) Miller; m. Albert Anton, June 23, 1949. Grad. Gemologist, Gemol. Inst. of Am., 1964. Fashion and design editor Nat. Jeweler Mag., NYC, 1956-58; freelance writer novels/plays, from 1956; staff writer Writer's Guidelines and News Mag.; instr. sr. divsn. U. South Fla. , from 2000. Writing instr. Sr. Acad./Elderhostel U. South Fla., from 1999. Contbr. articles to numerous nat. mags. including Cosmopolitan, Family Circle, Bride's Mag., Saturday Evening Post, Thera Lit. Mag.;, author plays, (novels) Egrets to the Flames (Top Ten/Fla. Writers Festival, 1995), short stories, 13 plays produced off-Broadway, 1995—2003. Recipient First Prize Humor, Manatee Writers Contest, 2000—01, 1st prize, Father's Hall of Fame Contest, 2000—01, over 100 awards for various writings, 14 awards, Fla. Studio Theatre Shorts Contest. Mem. Dramatists Guild. Home: Sarasota, Fla. Died May 20, 2007.

ARAUJO, ROBERT JOHN, law educator; b. Dighton, Mass., Oct. 30, 1948; s. Caesar and Agnes Araujo. AB, Georgetown U., Washington, 1970, JD, 1973; JSD, LLM, Columbia U., NYC, 1992; MDiv, STL, Weston Sch. Theology, Cambridge, Mass., 1993; BCL, Oxford U., Eng., 1994. Trial atty., US dept. interior Office Solicitor, Washington, 1947—79; atty. Std. Oil Co., Cleve., 1979—85; mem. SJ, 1986—2009; prof. law Gonzaga U., Spokane, Wash., 1994—2005; ordinary prof. Pontifical Gregorian U., Rome, 2005—07; vis. prof. law Boston Coll., Chestnut Hill, 2008—09; John Courtney Murray prof. Loyola U. Chgo., Chgo., 2009—14, John Courtney Murray prof. emeritus, from 2014. Legal advisor The Holy See, Rome, 1997—2007. First lt. US Army, 1974, Ft. Lee, Va. Home: Weston, Mass. Died Oct. 21, 2015.

ARBOUR, ALGER, retired professional hockey coach; b. Sudury, Ont., Can., Nov. 1, 1932; m. Claire Arbour; children: Julie, Janice, Jo-Anne, Jay. Defenseman Detroit Red Wings, Chgo. Black Hawks, Toronto Maple Leafs, St. Louis Blues of Nat. Hockey League, 1953-71; coach St. Louis Blues, 1970, 71-72, asst. gen. mgr., 1971; coach N.Y. Islanders, Uniondale, 1973-86, 1988-94, v.p. hockey ops., 1995—97. Mem. 4 Stanley Cup championships teams, including Detroit Red Wings, 1954, Chgo. Black Hawks, 1961, Toronto Maple Leafs, 1964, 62; coach 4 Stanley Cup championship teams, 1980-83. Recipient Jack Adams Trophy, 1979, Lester Patrick Trophy, 1992; named to Hockey Hall of Fame, 1996. Died Aug. 28, 2015.

ARDEN, SHERRY W., publishing executive; b. NYC, Oct. 18, 1923; d. Abraham and Rose (Bellak) Waretnick; m. Hal Marc Arden (div. 1974); children: Doren (dec. 1981), Cathy; m. George Bellak, Oct. 20, 1979 (dec. 2002) Student, Columbia U. Publicity dir. Coward-McCann, NYC, 1965-67; producer Allan Foshko Assoc., ABC-TV, NYC, 1967-68; sr. v.p., pub. William Morrow & Co., NYC, 1968-85, pres., pub., 1985-89; owner Sherry W. Arden Lit. Agy., from 1990. Mem. Assn. American Pubs. (dir.) Clubs: Pubs. Lunch. Home: Santa Monica, Calif. Died Jan. 27, 2015.

ARGUE, JOHN SOMERS, telecommunications company executive, physician; b. Manchester, NH, Aug. 18, 1927; s. Forrest Birkley and Mary Evelyn (Sullivan) A.; m. Mary Elliott Peck, Sept. 1951; children: Catherine, John, Thomas, James, Daniel, David, Peter, Michael, Rosemary, Maureen, Christopher, Timothy. BS, U. Notre Dame, 1950; MD, Georgetown U., 1954. Lic. physician, N.Y., 1955. Phys., pres. Pittsfield (N.H.) Medicine and Surgery, 1960-86; med. dir. HealthSource Inc., Concord, N.H., 1985-90; pres. Granite Hills Telecomms. Co., Pittsfield, from 1992. Mem. editorial bd. Manchester Union Leader, 1965-82, Health Learning Sys., 1990—; mem. editorial adv. bd. Primary Cardiology,1975-89; mem. med. adv. bd. Physician News Network, 1990—. V.p. N.H. Republican Party, 1973-75; trustee Concord Hosp., 1985—, Concord Regional Vis. Nurse Assn., 1994—. Recipient A.H. Robins Cmty. Svc. award N.H. Med. Soc., 1977, Spl. Svc. citation Greater Concord C. of C., 1977; named N.H. Family Physician of Yr., N.H. Acad. Family Practice, Pittsfield Citizen of Yr., 1972. Fellow Am. Acad. Family Practice; mem. AMA, Merrimack County Med. Assn., Pittsfield Rotary Club. Roman Catholic. Home: Gilmanton Iron Works, NH. Died Feb. 4, 2007.

ARMSTRONG, DAVID BRADLEY, artist, photographer; b. Arlington, Mass., May 24, 1954; s. Robert William and Irma Frances (Hutchison) A. Diploma, Boston Mus. Sch., 1977, Fifth Yr. Cert., 1980; BFA, Tufts U., 1989. Co-author: (photo books) A Double Life, 1994, Fashion: Photography of the Nineties, 1996; author: (photo books) The Silver Cord, 1997, All Day Every Day, 2002, 615 Jefferson Ave, 2011 Avocations: antiques, classical music, horticulture. Home: Brooklyn, NY. Died Oct. 26, 2014.

ARNELL, WALTER JAMES WILLIAM, engineering educator, consultant; b. Farnborough, Eng., Jan. 9, 1924; arrived in U.S., 1953, naturalized, 1960; s. James Albert and Daisy (Payne) Arnell; m. Patricia Catherine Cannon, Nov. 12, 1955; children: Sean Paul, Victoria Clare, Sarah Michele. Aero. Engr., Royal Aircraft Establishment, 1946; BSc, U. London, 1953, PhD, 1967; MA, Occidental Coll., LA, 1956; MS, U. So. Calif., 1958. Lectr. Poly. and Northampton Coll. Advance Tech., London, 1948-53; instr. U. So. Calif., LA, 1954-59; asst. prof. mech. engring. Calif. State U., Long Beach, 1959-62, assoc. prof., 1962-66, prof., 1966—69, chmn. dept. mech. engring., 1964-65, acting chmn. divsn. engring., 1964-66, dean engring., 1967-69, rschr.; grad. affiliate faculty dept. ocean engring. U. Hawaii, 1970-74; adj. prof. systems and insdl. engring. U. Ariz., 1981—91; pres. Lenra Assocs. Ltd., from 1973; chmn., project mgr. Hawaii Environ. Simulation Lab., 1971-72. Contbr. articles to profl. jours. Trustee Rehab. Hosp. of the Pacific, 1975—78. Fellow: Inst. Ergonomics & Human Factors; mem.: Human Factors and Ergonomics Soc., Soc. Engring. Psychology sect., Am. Psychol. Assn. Soc., Royal Aero. Soc., Pi Tau Sigma, Phi Kappa Phi, Tau Beta Pi, Alpha Pi Mu, Psi Chi. Home: Tucson, Ariz. Deceased.

ARNOLD, GAYLE EDWARD, lawyer; b. Celina, Ohio, June 24, 1950; s. William Floyd and Mary Ellen (Fast) A.; m. Rebecca Gentile, Aug. 9, 1975 (div. Feb. 1989); m. Sue Anne Cannell, Oct. 27, 1989; children: Leah, Joshua, Elissa, Natalie, Katie, Cameron. BS, Taylor U., 1972; MS, Ball State U., 1975; JD, U. Notre Dame, 1980. Bar: Ohio 1980, U.S. Dist. Ct. (so. dist.) Ohio 1980, U.S. Ct. Appeals (6th cir.) 1987, U.S. Dist. Ct. (no. dist.) Ohio 1993. Tchr. Connersville (Ind.) Pub. Schs., 1972-73; residence hall dir., football coach Taylor U., Upland, Ind., 1973-76; tchr. Eastbrook Pub. Schs., Marion, Ind., 1974-76; assoc. Lane, Alton & Horst, Columbus, Ohio, 1980-85, Jacobson, Maynard, Tuschman & Kalur, Columbus, 1985-87, mng. ptnr., 1988-97, Arnola & Assocs. Co. LPA, from 1997. Home: Dublin, Ohio. Died July 25, 2007.

ARNOLD, JAMES ELLSWORTH, lawyer, military officer; b. Harve de Grace, Md., Oct. 11, 1956; s. James Henry and Georgia Etta (Owens) A.; m. Julia Louise Thompson, Aug. 24, 1985. BS, USAF Acad., 1978; JD with honors, George Washington U., 1985. Bar: Ill. 1985, U.S. Ct. Mil. Appeals 1987. Commd. 2d lt. USAF, 1978, advanced through grades to major, 1989, computer ops. officer Edwards AFB, Calif., 1979-81, judge adv. Chanute AFB Rantoul, Ill., 1985-88, Edwards AFB, Calif., 1988-91; judge adv., chief mil. law and affairs HQ 17th Air Force, Sembach, Germany, from 1991. Mem. ABA, Ill. Bar Assn., Air Force Assn. Republican. Avocations: mil. history, automobiles, war games. Home: APO, . Died Mar. 1, 2007.

ARNOTT, JACOB WILLARD, retired administrator; b. Rensselaer, Ind., Sept. 6, 1918; s. Fred E. and Mary Irene (Lutz) A.; m. Mary Louise McGee, Oct. 25, 1942; 1 child, Marilyn Sue. Student, Ball State U., 1938-39. Chmn. USAF

Chapel Bd., Yakota, Japan, 1954-56, Trinity Meth. Ch. Bd., Austin, Tex., 1962-64; bus. adminstr. University United Meth. Ch., Austin, Tex., 1964-74; chmn. Air Force Village Protestant Ch., San Antonio, 1985-86, Air Force Village II High Flight Chapel Policy Com., Air Force Village II Protestant Ch., San Antonio, 1987-88. Lt. col. USAF, 1939-63, WWII, Korea. Republican. Home: San Antonio, Tex. Died Nov. 15, 2006.

ARONSON, DAVID, artist, retired educator; b. Shilova, Lithuania, Oct. 28, 1923; came to U.S., 1929, naturalized, 1931; s. Peisach Leib and Gertrude (Shapiro) A.; m. Georgianna B. Nyman, June 10, 1956; children: Judith, Benjamin, Abigail. Certificate, Boston Mus. Sch., 1946; LHD (hon.), Hebrew Coll., 1993; DFA (hon.), Boston U., 2005. Instr. painting Boston Mus. Sch., 1943—55; prof. art Boston U., 1962-89, founder College of Fine Arts, 1955, establish Art Gallery, 1958, chmn. div., 1955—63, chmn. painting dept., 1963—89, prof. emeritus, 1989—2015. Artist David Aronson: Paintings, Drawings, Sculpture, 2005, Real & Unreal:The Double Nature of Art, Fourteen Americans, Dorothy Miller Mus. Modern Art, 1946; contbr. articles to profl. jours.; one man shows include Niveau Gallery, N.Y.C., 1945, 56, Mus. Modern Art, N.Y.C., 1946, Boris Mirski Gallery, Boston, 1951, 59, 64, 69, Downtown Gallery, N.Y.C., 1953, Nordness Gallery, N.Y.C., 1960, 63, 69, Rex Evans Gallery, L.A., 1961, Long Beach (Calif.) Mus., 1961, Westhampton (N.Y.) Gallery, 1961, J. Thomas Gallery, Provincetown, Mass., 1964, Zora Gallery, LA, 1965, Hunter Gallery, Chattanooga, 1965, Kovler Gallery, Chgo., 1966, Bernard Danenberg Galleries, N.Y.C., 1969, 72, Pucker Gallery, Boston, 1976, 78, 86, 90, 94, 99, 2005, 09, Phila. Mus. Judaica, 1990, Louis Newman Gallery, LA, 1977, 81, 84, 86, 89, 92, Sadye Bronfman Art Ctr., Montreal, Que., Can., 1982, Horwitch Newman Gallery, Scottsdale, Ariz., 1995, 96, MB Modern Gallery, N.Y., 1997, Alter & Gil Gallery, L.A., 1999, Sp. Galerie Yoram GIL, L.A., 2002, 04, David Findlay Jr. Fine Art NY, 2011; group shows include N.Y. World's Fair, 1964-65, Bridgestone Gallery, Tokyo, Royal Acad. London, Mus. Modern Art, Paris, Palazzo Venezia, Rome, Congresse Halle, Berlin, Charlottenborg, Copenhagen, Palais Des Beaux Arts, Brussels, Smithsonian Instn., 1965, retrospective exhbns. include Rose Mus., Brandeis U., Waltham, Mass., 1978, Jewish Mus., N.Y.C., 1979, Nat. Mus. Am. Jewish History, Phila., 1979, So. Middlesex U., South Dartmouth, Mass., 1983, Mickelson Gallery, Washington, 1985, Boston U., 2005; represented in permanent collections Art Inst. Chgo., Va. Mus. Fine Arts, Richmond, Bryn Mawr Coll., Brandeis U., Tupperware Mus., Orlando, Fla., Decordova Mus., Lincoln, Mass., Mus. Modern Art, Atlanta U., Atlanta Art Assn., U. Nebr., Krannert Art Mus. U. Ill., Whitney Mus. Am. Art, Colby Coll., U. N.H., Portland Mus. Art, Maine, Corcoran Gallery Art, Washington, Munson Williams Proctor Art Inst., Ithaca, N.Y., Boston Mus. Fine Arts, Smithsonian Instn., Washington, Milw. Art Inst., Pa. Acad. Fine Arts, Johnson Found., Racine, Wis., Worcester (Mass.) Art Mus., Colorado SPrings Fine Arts Ctr., Brockton (Mass.) Mus. Art, Longy Sch. Music, Cambridge, Mass., Boston U., Jewish Community Ctr., Boston, Nat. Acad. Design, N.Y., Joseph Hirschorn Collection, Hebrew Coll., Newton, Mass., David and Alfred Smart Mus., U. Ill., Chgo., Two-Ten Found., Boston, Pa. State U. Mus. Art, Syracuse (N.Y.) U., Beth Israel Hosp., Boston Mass. Guilford Coll. U. N.C., Greensboro Campus, U. Judaism, L.A., Fine Arts Ctr., Cheekville, Tenn., Danforth Mus., Framingham, Mass., Skirball Mus., L.A., Herbert F. Johnson Mus. Art, Cornell U., Museo Sefardi, Toledo, Spain, Flint Inst. Arts, Mich., Colo. Springs Fine Arts Ctr., Colo., Dayton Art Inst., Ohio, Danforth Mus. Art, Framingham, Mass., others; sculpture commns. Container Corp. Am., 1963, 65, Reform Jewish Appeal, 1980, Combined Jewish Philanthropies, 1981, Temple Beth Elohim, Wellesley, Mass., 1982, Brandeis U. Libr., Waltham, Mass., 1983, Brandeis U. Berlin Chapel, 1996. Recipient 1st Judges prize Inst. Modern Art, Boston, 1944, 1st Popular prize, 1944; Choice Friends of Art Art Inst. Chgo., 1946; Purchase prize Va. Mus. Fine Arts, 1946; Travelling fellow Boston Mus. Sch., 1946; Grand prize Boston Arts Festival, 1952, 54; 2d prize, 1953; 1st prize Tupperware Art Fund, 1954, cert. of merit for sculpture NAD, 1990; grantee in art Nat. Inst. Arts and Letters, 1958; Purchase prize, 1961, 62, 63; purchase prize Pa. Acad. Fine Arts, also other purchase prizes; Samuel F.B. Morse Gold medal NAD, 1973; Isaac N. Maynard prize NAD, 1975; Joseph S. Isidor gold medal NAD, 1976; Guggenheim fellow, 1960; Adolph and Clara Obrig prize NAD, 1968, Academician NAD, 1970. Home: Sudbury, Mass. Died July 2, 2015.

ARRONGE, STEVEN WILLIAM, lawyer; b. San Antonio, Mar. 14, 1947; s. Kurt H. and Margot H. (Koppell) A.; m. Rosalinda Camacho, Jan. 25, 1975; children: Lisa Michelle, Deborah Marie. BA, U. Tex., 1969, JD, 1972. Bar: Tex. 1972, U.S. Ct. Appeals (5th cir.) 1977, U.S. Dist. Ct. (we. dist.) Tex. 1979, U.S. Ct. Appeals (11th cir.) 1981, U.S. Supreme Ct. 1983. Dep. city atty. City of San Antonio, from 1972. Mem. ABA, Tex. Bar Assn. Home: San Antonio, Tex. Died Jan. 14, 2007.

ARSENIAN, JOHN, psychologist; b. Boston, Aug. 20, 1917; s. Aaron and Josephine (Dukmedjian) A.; m. Jean Martha MacDonald, May 27, 1942; children: John Toby, Michael Aaron. BS, Boston U., 1959; MA, Harvard U., 1940, PhD, 1945. Instr. psychology Smith Coll., Northampton, Mass., 1942-43; asst. prof. psychology Clark Y., Worcester, Mass., 1943-44; rsch. assoc. group dynamics MAT, Cambridge, Mass., 1944-45; instr. Boston U., 1945-47; head psychologist Boston State Hosp., Dorchester, Mass., 1948-56; asst. prof. clin. psychology Boston U. Grad. Sch., 1956-69; cons. clin. psychology VA, Boston, 1960-79. Lectr. social rels. Harvard U., Cambridge, 1960-65; dir. psychol. rsch. Boston State Hosp., 1956-77 Contbr. articles to profl. jours. Fellow Am. Psychol. Assn. Avocations: reading, gardening. Home: Rockport, Mass. Died Jan. 31, 2007.

ARTHER, RICHARD OBERLIN, polygraphist, educator; b. Pitts., May 20, 1928; s. William Churchill Sr. and Florence Lind (Oberlin) A.; m. Mary-Esther Wuensch, Sept. 12, 1951; children: Catherine, Linda, William III. BS, Mich. State U., 1951; MA, Columbia U., 1960. Chief assoc. John E. Reid and Assocs., Chgo., 1951-53, dir. NYC, 1953-58; pres. Sci. Lie Detection, Inc., NYC, 1958—2003, chmn., from 2003; pres. Nat. Tng. Ctr. Polygraph Sci., NYC, from 1958. Author: Interrogation for Investigators, 1958, The Scientific Investigator, 1964, 7th edit., Arther Polygraph Reference Guide, 1964-, 8th edit.; editor Jour. Polygraph Sci., 1966-. Fellow Acad. Cert. Polygraphists (exec. dir. 1962—), Am. Polygraph Assn. (founding mem.), Am. Assn. Police Polygraphists (founding mem., Polygraphist of Yr. 1980), N.Y. State Polygraphists (founder), N.J. Polygraphists (founder). Died July 5, 2007.

ARTHUR, CHARLES BURTON, retired education educator, researcher; b. Walpole, Mass., Aug. 22, 1911; s. David Sinclair and Elizabeth Blackburn (Daniels) A.; m. Lucy Elizabeth Sellman, July 14, 1946; children: Diane Jean, Catherine Charlotte, Charlene Elizabeth, Katherine Virginia. BA, Dartmouth Coll., 1934; MA, Harvard U., 1942, PhD, 1966. Head social sci. dept. Hebron (Maine) Acad., 1935-39; asst. to pres. Darmouth Coll., Hanover, N.H., 1943-46, mem. history dept. staff, 1943-46, Princeton (N.J) U., 1946; mgr. Can. and export products Kyanize Paints, Everett, Mass., 1947-64; dir. paint sales tng. New Eng. Paint Assn., Boston, 1950-63; head social sci. dept. Arlington (Mass.) High Sch., 1964-83; lectr. on western history Middlesex Community Coll., Bedford, Mass., 1973-77. Author: The Remaking of the English Navy by Admiral St. Vincent-Key to the Victory Over Napoleon-The Great Unclaimed Naval Revolution, 1985. Mem.: Elks. Republican. Episcopalian. Avocation: golf. Home: Pt Charlotte, Fla. Died July 20, 2007.

ARTHUR, GARY DAVID, agronomist; b. Ottawa, Ill., Apr. 29, 1950; s. Joseph Lawrence and Margaret Blanch (Thorson) A.; m. Kathy Louise Blase, Nov. 9, 1974; children: Brian Allen, Julie Diane. Student, U. Mont., 1969; BA in Biol. Sci., So. Ill. U., 1972, MS in Plant and Soil Sci., 1975. Corn breeder F.S. Svcs., Inc., Piper City, Ill., 1974-75; plant breeder Holden's Foun. Seeds, Inc., Williamsburg, Iowa, 1975-81; sales mgr. Stauffer Seeds, Inc., Springfield, Ill., 1982, rsch. dir., 1983; plant breeder Holden's Foundn. Seeds, Inc., Franklin, Ind., from 1984. Mem. Hoosiers for Better Schs., Ind., 1987. Mem. Ind. Crop Improvement Assn. (ex-officio bd. dirs. 1986-87, bd. dirs. 1991—, mem. exec. com. 1992—, pres. 1994), Ind. Seed Trade Assn. (bd. dirs. 1984-88, pres. 1987), Crop Sci. Soc. Am., Am. Seed Trade Assn., Phi Eta Sigma, Phi Kappa Phi. Home: Iowa City, Iowa. Died Dec. 26, 2006.

ASANO, MAKISHIGE, medical educator; b. Gunma, Japan, Aug. 1, 1928; s. Harusuke and Shima (Amagawa) A.; m. Tetsuko Sakai, Dec. 3, 1957. MB, Tokyo Med. and Dental U., 1955, MD, 1962. From rschr. to prof. emeritus Nat. Inst. of Pub. Health, Japan, 1956—98, prof. emeritus, from 1998, hon. rschr., 1990—2005, guest rschr., from 2005; prof. Tokyo Med. and Dental U., 1990-94, dean Sch. Allied Health Scis., 1993-94; prof. Japan Women's U., Tokyo, 1994-97; adviser Promotion Com. for Healthy Cities, from 2006. Author: Circulatory Physiology, 1976, Health Science of Smoking, 1985. Chmn. Promotion Com. for Healthy Cities, Tokyo, 1999—2006. Grantee, WHO, 1968. Fellow: Internat. Coll. Angiology; mem.: Japanese Soc. Biorheology (dir. 1975—2010, hon. advisor from 2010, OKA Syoten. prize 2006), NY Acad. Scis., Japanese Soc. Microcirculation (hon.), Internat. Soc. Biorheology. Avocations: fishing, reading. Home: Tokyo, Japan. Died Nov. 4, 2014.

ASHLAND, STEPHEN ROYAL, advertising executive; b. East Derry, NH, Apr. 7, 1942; s. Carroll Alexis and Jessica Kathryn (Friech) A.; m. Linda Diane Aubrey, Apr. 14, 1984; children: Christopher, Mark, Matthew. Grad. high sch., Derry, NH. Editor and pub. The Record Carrier, Derry, 1957-60; sales rep. Sta. WSMN, Nashua, N.H., 1960-61; photographer, reporter The Derry News, 1961-63; mgr. advt. The Derry Star, 1967; editor and pub. The Raymond (N.H.) Transcript/Candia Planet, 1963-66; advt. coord. WONS Newspaper Group, Jaffrey, N.H., 1968-69; account exec., local sales mgr. Sta. WMUR-TV, Manchester, N.H., 1969-83; nat. sales mgr. Sta. WNDS-TV, Derry, 1983-86, gen. sales mgr., 1987-88; advt. coord. United Cable Advt. N.H. divsn. United Broadcasting Co. N.H., Manchester, 1988-94; sr. account exec. Continental Cable Advt., Bedford, N.H., 1995-96; with Media One Advt. Svcs., Manchester, N.H., 1997-98, Comcast Advt. Svcs., Manchester, from 1999. Badge counselor Boy Scouts Am., Manchester, 1984-88, cubmaster pack 405, 1994-96; tchr. Ch. of Jesus Christ of Latter-day Saints, 1984-87, music dir., 1989-92; 1st counselor Elders quorum Presidency, 1992-95; tchr. CTR3, 1996—; fund-raiser Salvation Army, 1963-66. Mem. New Eng. Broadcasting Assn., N.H. Advt. Club. Republican. Mem. Lds Ch. Avocations: camping, tennis, photography, singing, dance. Home: Manchester, NH. Died Dec. 25, 2006.

ASHLEY, MARJORIE, retired secondary school educator; b. Schenectady, NY, Feb. 16, 1917; d. Richard J. and Margaret Middleton; m. John Edward Ashley, Aug. 20, 1940 (dec.); children: Richard M.(dec.) , John E. Jr., Willard Bishop. BA cum laude, SUNY, Albany, 1955, MA, 1958; cert. in French, Goucher Coll., 1959. Tchr. Burnt Hills-Ballston Lake H.S., Burnt Hills, NY, 1956, Roger B. Taney Jr. High Sch., Camp Springs, Md., Oxon Hill (Md.) Sr. H.S. Contbr. commentaries Kerrville Times. Sec. AAUW, Kerrville, Tex., 1976—80, pres., 1980—82; chmn., patron Kerrville Performing Arts Soc., 1980—2001; active Point Theatre, Schreiner U. Recipient Lifetime Achievement award, Hill Country Arts Found., 2003. Mem.: LWV, Animal Welfare Soc. Kerr County, Hill Country Arts Found. Unitarian Universalist. Home: Kerrville, Tex. Died June 22, 2007.

ASHLEY, ROBERT PAUL, JR., English literature educator; b. Balt., Apr. 15, 1915; s. Robert Paul and Ethel (Rice) A.; m. Virginia Woods, June 24, 1939; children: June Ashley Hager, Dianne, Cynthia, Robert Paul, Jacquelyne. AB, Bowdoin Coll., 1936; MA, Harvard U., 1937, PhD, 1949. Tennis coach and instr. English Portland (Maine) Jr. Coll., 1938-39; instr. English Colby Jr. Coll., 1939- 43; tng. instr. Boston Q.M. Depot, 1944; teaching fellow English Harvard U., 1946-48, coach tennis, 1946; asst. prof. English, asst. dean, coach tennis Washington and Jefferson Coll., 1948-51; asst. prof. English U.S. Mil. Acad., 1951-55; prof. English Ripon Coll., 1955-85, dean of coll., 1955-74, tennis coach, 1955-64, acting pres., 1966, v.p., 1968-74, chmn. English dept., 1977-80. Vis. prof. U.S. Naval Acad. 2d Sem., 1968-69; dir. news and records Midwest Athletic Conf., 1956-61, v.p., 1957-58, pres., 1958-59, 80-81, commr., 1960-66, acting commr., 1977-78; examiner, cons. North Central Assn., 1963-79; mem. Commn. on Colls. and Univs., 1968-72, Wis. Commn. Higher Ednl. Aids, 1964-67, chmn., 1965-66; chmn. Nat. Summer Conf. Acad. Deans, 1968 Author: Wilkie Collins, Understanding the Novel; (juvenile works) The Stolen Train, Rebel Raiders; co-author: The Bible as Literature, Ripon College: A History; editor: Civil War Poetry; co-editor: Elizabeth Fiction, The Short Stories of Wilkie Collins, Faulkner at West Point; contbr. articles to profl. jours. Served as lt. (j.g.) USNR, 1944-46; maj. U.S. Army Res., 1951-55; now col. (ret.). Mem. Wilkie Collins Soc., Phi Beta Kappa, Zeta Psi. Home: Ripon, Wis. Died Nov. 22, 2006.

ASHMORE, CARRIE MAE, educator; b. Springfield, Tenn., Mar. 5, 1923; d. James Dean and Vera Louvenia Barbee Osborne; m. Edward Travis Ashmore Ashmore, July 23, 1945; children: Travis Dean, Edward Lane, Juanita Sherri, Angela Jean, Angelo Gene, Andre Bernard. Student, Tenn. State U., 1943; BS, Wilberforce U., 1946; postgrad, Atlanta U., 1960, Chgo. State U., 1971, Roosevelt U., 1973. Tchr. Bransford High Sch., Springfield, Tenn., 1946—48, Atlanta Pub. Schs., 1960—62, Gary (Ind.) Pub. Schs., 1962—64, Wendell Phillips High Sch., Chgo., 1964—68, Hyde Pk. Career Acad., Chgo., from 1969, mem. tchr. corps project, Roosevelt U.; sec. Murrays Superior Products, Chgo., 1948—49; adminstrv. asst. Atlanta U., 1949—60. Recipient Am. Legion medal, 1941. Mem.: Chgo. Assn. Mentally Retarded, Zeta Sigma Pi, Lambda Eta Sigma. Home: Chicago, Ill. Died Nov. 6, 2006.

ASNIS, DEBORAH SUSAN, internist, infectious disease specialist, educator; b. July 17, 1956; d. Myron and Ruth (Kornblum) Asnis; m. Hal Kazdin; children: Joshua, Mathew. MD, Northwestern U., Evanston, Ill., 1981. Lic. NY, 1982, Fla., 1991, diplomate Am. Bd. Internal Medicine, 1985, Am. Bd. Internal Medicine-infectious disease, 1988. Resident ophthalmology LI Jewish Hosp., NY, 1982—83, resident internal medicine NY, 1983—85, fellow infectious disease, 1985—87; asst. clin. prof. of medicine Weill Cornell Med. Coll. Cornell Univ.; hosp. affiliations include: Flushing Hosp. Med. Ctr., Franklin Hosp., NYU Langone Med. Ctr., NY Cmty. Hosp., Peninsula Hosp. Ctr.; physician NY Hosp. Queens. Dir. infectious disease Flushing Hosp. Medical Ctr.; clinical researcher in H.I.V. infection. Died Sept. 12, 2015.

ATKERSON, TERESA SUSAN, newspaper editor; b. McAlester, Okla., Dec. 30, 1955; d. Virgil Riley and Joanne Ruth (Gill) A. BA, U. Sci. and Arts Okla., Chickasha, 1976, postgrad., 1980-83. Social worker I, Dept Human Svcs., McAlester, 1978-80; co-owner Sooner Constrn., McAlester, 1984-89; family, ch. and entertainment editor McAlester News Capital & Dem., from 1987. Bd. dirs. March of Dimes, McAlester Pub. Sch. Found., Adult and Cmty. Edn., Friends of Libr. of McAlester, Women in Safe Homes, Kiamichi Actors Studio Theatre; mem. Teenage Pregnancy Prevention Task Force; mem. planning com. Red Ribbon Week; mem. awareness com. Dist. III Okla. Cultural Coalition; active United Way McAlester, Soc. for Creative Anachronism, McAlester Pub. Schs. Parent U., MPS Learn and Serve, Parent's Club's Parents as Tchrs. adv. com. Recipient young careerist award Noon Bus. and Profl. Women's Club, 1990, McAlester Bus. and Profl. Women's Club, 1991, 3d place awrd for internat. pressbook competition Epsilon Sigma Alpha, 1990, Outstanding Media Person for Okla., Am. Heart Assn., 1991, 92; Actress of Yr. awrd Kiamichi Actors Studio Theatre, 1991, 94, Prodn. Mgr. of Yr. award 1994, 96, Supporting Actress of Yr. award, 1995, 96, Actress of Yr., 1997. Republican. Baptist. Avocations: playing piano, reenacting the middle ages, collecting music boxes nd elephants, reading. Home: Mcalester, Okla. Died Aug. 20, 2007.

ATOJI, MASAO, physical chemist; b. Osaka, Japan, Dec. 21, 1925; came to U.S., 1951; naturalized U.S. citizen, 1961; s. Yoshinori and Kiyo (Matsushima) A.; m. Iris Noma, May 18, 1957; children: Naomi Jean, Cynthia Ann, David Masao. BS, Osaka U., 1948, PhD, 1956. Rsch. assoc. U. Minn., Mpls., 1951-56; asst. prof. Iowa State U., Ames, 1956-60; assoc. chemist Argonne (Ill.) Nat. Lab., 1960-69, sr. chemist, 1969-81; sr. staff chemist Litton Systems Inc., Morris Plains, N.J., 1981-83; sr. staff scientist Motorola, Schaumburg, Ill., 1984-87; rsch. scientist Northwestern U., Evanston, Ill., 1988-90; assoc. editor Chem. Abstracts Svc., Columbus, Ohio, from 1990. Contbr. over 200 articles to

Jour. Chem. Physics, Acta Crystallographica, Solid State Communications, others. Fellow Am. Phys. Soc. (life); mem. AAAS, Am. Chem. Soc., Am. Crystallographic Assn., Am. Assn. for Crystal Growth, Soc. for Applied Spectroscopy, Phys. Soc. Japan (life), Am. Translators Assn., Sigma Xi (life). Achievements include rsch. in materials sci., neutron and x-ray diffraction, crystal and magnetic structures, semiconductor crystal growth and fabrications, metallurgy, cryogenics, high temperature instrumentation, spectroscopes, thermal analysis. Home: Downers Grove, Ill. Died Nov. 20, 2006.

AUGUSTYN, WALTER HENRY, physicist; b. Portland, Conn., Feb. 4, 1938; s. Walter Henry and Stella Margaret (Pietras) A.; m. Dolores Anne Ludka, May 21, 1960; children: Lori Anne, Eric Paul, Kristen Anne. AB, Dartmouth Coll., 1959; postgrad., U. Bridgeport, 1966, Fordham U., 1967. Staff scientist Perkin-Elmer Corp., Norwalk, Conn., 1959-77; tech. product line mgr. Zygo Corp., Middlefield, Conn., 1977-81; founder, v.p. CMX Systems, Inc., Wallingford, Conn., from 1981. Contbr. articles to profl. jours.; patentee in field. Mem. bd. fin., Monroe Conn., 1966. Avocations: swimming, painting, camping. Died Feb. 6, 2007.

AULIE, RICHARD PAUL, science history educator; b. Chgo., May 17, 1926; s. Henry Martin and Thora Willa (Döderlein) A. Med. student, U. Ill., Chgo., 1945-46; BS, Wheaton Coll., 1948; MS, U. Minn., 1953; PhD, Yale U., 1968. Biology educator Northwestern Coll., Mpls., 1949-52, Habibia Coll., Kabul, Afghanistan, 1953, Am. Univ. at Cairo, Egypt, 1954-55, Bloom Twp. High Sch., Chicago Heights, Ill., 1955-61, Evanston (Ill.) Twp. High Sch., 1961-62; biology expert UNESCO U. Liberia, Monrovia, 1962-64; asst. prof. Chgo. State Coll., 1968-71; editor, writer Encyclopedia Brittanica, Chgo., 1971-72; educator natural sci. Loyola U., Chgo., 1972-76; sci. instr. Montay Coll., Chgo., from 1992. Program chmn. Nat. Assn. Biology Tchrs., Chgo., 1971; organizer Creationism and Am. Culture Symposium, Chgo., 1982, Aids in Am. Soc., The Future of Food Prodn., 1988; mem. accreditation com. N. Ctrl. Assn., 1985; lectr. Am. Sci. Affiliation Conv., Wheaton, 1991. Contbr. articles to profl. jours. Vol. AIDS Com. Fourth Presbyn. Ch., Chgo., 1988-90; vol. meal deliverer Open Hand, 1989; participant NEH seminar on Islam and the sci. tradition in the Middle Ages, Columbia U., 1993. With USNR, 1943-45. USPHS fellow Yale U., 1964-68. Mem. Soc. for History of Discoveries, Soc. for History of Medicine in Chgo. Republican. Presbyterian. Died Dec. 11, 2006.

AVERS, MAX R., accountant, educator; b. Okmulgee, Okla., Feb. 19, 1945; s. Ralph Harvey and Edna Deane (Evans) A.; m. Judy Hafer, June 3, 1966; children: Michael Alan, Lori Kay. BBA, U. Okla., 1967, MBA, 1977. CPA, Okla., ACA accredited in Fed. Taxation. Capt. USAF, various, 1967-74; dir. fin. acctg. T.G. & Y. Stores Co., Inc., Oklahoma City, 1974-82; prof. of acctg. Oklahoma City Community Coll., from 1982. Pvt. practice acctg. Oklahoma City, 1982—. Capt. USAF, 1967-74, Vietnam. Mem. Am Inst. CPAs, Okla. Soc. CPAs, Nat. Assn. Accts., Am. Assn. Accts., Nat. Soc. Pub. Accts., Pi Kappa Alpha. Home: Edmond, Okla. Died July 14, 2007.

AVERY, EMERSON ROY, JR., judge; b. Cortland, NY, Mar. 28, 1954; s. Emerson Roy, Sr. and Phyllis Marie (Unold) A.; m. Marilyn Joan Weiss, July 17, 1977; children: Emerson Roy III, Michael Aaron. AB, Syracuse U., 1976; JD, Widener U., 1980. Bar: N.Y. 1981. Assoc. Emerson R. Avery Law Offices, Cortland, 1981-87; asst. pub. def. Cortland County Pub. Def. Office, Cortland, 1982-83, pub. def., 1983-84; asst. dist. atty. Cortland County Dist. Atty. Office, Cortland, 1984-86; corp. counsel dept. law City of Cortland, Cortland, 1988-91; ptnr. Avery & Avery Law Offices, Cortland, 1988-96; asst. dist. atty. Cortland County Dist. Atty.'s Office, 1992-96; judge Cortland County Family and Surrogate Ct., from 1996. Adj. prof. bus. law SUNY, Cortland, 1991-96. Bd. dirs. Coop. Extension Cortland County, v.p., 1980-84; bd. dirs. 1879 Houst Mus., Cortland, 1984-86, 93—, United Fund Cortland, 1986-87. Mem. ABA, ATLA, N.Y. State Bar Assn., Cortland County Bar Assn. (past pres.), N.Y. State Trial Lawyers Assn. Republican. Presbyterian. Avocations: reading, coin and stamp collecting, downhill skiing, water-skiing, scuba diving. Home: Cortland, NY. Died Feb. 25, 2007.

AVNER, YEHUDA, ambassador; b. Manchester, Eng., Dec. 30, 1928; m. Miriam Cailingold, 2015 (dec.); 4 children. PhD (hon.), Yeshiva U., 2012. Editor publs. Jewish Agy., Jerusalem, 1956—64; ministry fgn. affairs, editor polit. publs. & asst. to prime min. Levi Eshkol, 1964—67; counsul Israel NY, 1967—68; 1st sec. & counsellor Embassy Israel, Washington, 1968—72; ministry Jerusalem, asst. to prime min. Golda Meir, 1972—74; adviser to prime min. Yitzhak Rabin, 1974—77; adviser to prime min. Menachem Begin, 1977—83; amb.to Britain and Nonresident amb. to the Republic of Ireland, 1983—88; returned to Israel, 1988; amb. to Australia, 1992—95. Author: The Young Inheritors A Portrait of Israeli Youth, 1983, The Prime Ministers: An Intimate Narrative of Israeli Leadership, 2010. Home: London W8, England. Died Mar. 25, 2015.

AYOUB, JUDITH LORENE, retired nursing educator; b. Lima, Ohio, Nov. 14, 1941; d. Clarence William and Marjorie Avenell Croft; m. Waheeb Fahmy Ayoub (dec.). Nursing diploma, Miami Valley Hosp., Dayton, Ohio, 1963; BSN, Wright State U., Dayton, 1977; MSN, U. Cin., 1982; PhD, U. Ariz., Tucson, 1997. Staff nurse Miami Valley Hosp., Dayton, 1963—64, 1973—77, USAF, Maxwell AFB, Ala., 1964—66; nurse educator Lima Meml. Hosp. Sch. Nursing, Ohio, 1967—68; head nurse Ohio State U. Hosps., Columbus, 1969—72; nurse educator Lima Tech. Coll., 1977—81, Huron Rd. Hosp., Cleve., 1982—85, U. Ariz., Tucson, 1985—99, Mercy Coll. NW Ohio, Toledo, 1999—2006; ret., 2006. Bd. mem., treas. Ohio League for Nursing, Ohio, 2002—06. Co-editor: (on-line jour.) Jour. Undergrad. Scholarship, 1999—2006. Bd. mem. Am. Inst. Archeology, Toledo, 2002—06. Capt. USAF. Mem.: Nat. League Nursing (articulation task force 2003—04), Sigma Theta Tau. Republican. Presbyterian. Avocations: travel, singing. Home: Toledo, Ohio. Died Mar. 10, 2007.

AZIZ, TARIQ, former deputy prime minister of Iraq; b. Baghdad, Iraq, Apr. 28, 1936; Student, Coll. of Arts, Baghdad U. Mem. of staff Al'Jumhuriyah, 1958; chief editor Al'Jamahiir, 1963; with Baath Press, Syria; chief editor Al-Thawra Pub. House; mem. Revolutionary Command Coun. Gen. Affairs Bur., 1972; res. mem. Arab Baath Socialist Party Leadership, 1974-77; elected mem. Baath Regional Leadership, 1977; min. culture and info. Govt. of Iraq, 1974-78, dep. prime min., 1981—2003, min. fgn. affairs, 1983-91. Christian. Died June 5, 2015.

BACHMANN, ALBERT EDWARD, engineering educator; b. La Porte, Ind., Dec. 16, 1917; s. Albert W. and Margaret L. (Peterson) B.; m. Lois June Kopplow, Oct. 19, 1946. BSME, Purdue U., 1941; MBA, Harvard U., 1955; PhD in Engring. Mgmt., Clemson U., 1975. R&D engr. U.S. Naval Ordnance Lab., Washington, London, 1941-44; head joint British and U.S. intelligence task force USN, England, France, Germany, 1944-45; spl. products sales mgr. Collins Radio Co., Cedar Rapids, Iowa, 1945-48; chief mechanisms br. U.S. Naval Ordnance Lab., White Oak, Md., 1949-51; pres. BLEN Corp., Cambridge, Mass., 1951-53; gen. mgr. Bolt Beranek and Newman, Cambridge, Mass., 1952-54; chief product rsch. Simmonds Aerocessories, Inc., Tarrytown, N.Y., 1955-56; pvt. practice Coral Gables, Fla., 1956-77; assoc. prof. sch. bus. U. Miami, Coral Gables, 1957-81; chmn. grad. engring. mgmt. programs sch. bus. Fla. Inst. Tech., Melbourne, 1982-92; dir. The Innovation Ctr. of Brevard, Melbourne, 1982-92. Cons. State of Fla., Miami, 1966-68, Ea. Airlines, Miami, 1965-66, U.S. Dept. Def., Washington, 1953-58, NAS, Washington, 1952; adj. prof. Advanced Tech. Ctr., Brevard C.C., Palm Bay, Fla., 1993—, The High Performance Orgn., Webster U., 1998—. Inventor aircraft radio bandswitching digital display. Active Planning and Zoning Bd., Indialantic, Fla., 1986-91. Mem. IEEE, Am. Soc. Engring. Mgmt. (bd. dirs. 1985-87), Melbourne Yacht Club (treas. 1992), Elks, Moose. Republican. Lutheran. Avocations: gardening, music, golf. Home: Indialantic, Fla. Died Aug. 13, 2007.

BACHORIK, RICHARD JOHN, mechanical construction company executive; b. NYC, Dec. 12, 1931; s. John and Teresa (Rezek) B.; m. Marjorie Hammen, July 11, 1955 (div. Oct. 1976); children: Teresa Bachorik Wise, Richard J.; m. Gail Blenda Carlson, Nov. 24, 1977. Student bldg. constrn., Pratt Inst., 1955. Registered profl. engr., Mass., Ariz. Project engr. Myers-Laine Corp., Utica, N.Y., 1955-60, Limbach Co., Boston, 1960-65, v.p. Pitts., 1965-77, Columbus, Ohio, from 1988, Pizzagalli Constrn. Co., Burlington, Vt., 1977-85; exec. v.p. Phoenix Contractors Inc., Grand Rapids, Mich., 1985; pres. S.I. Industries, Phoenix, 1985-87; part owner, mgr. Conwest Inc., Phoenix, 1987-88. Mem. Mech. Contractors Assn. (v.p., bd. dirs. 1988—). Avocations: jogging, tennis, skiing, boating, horseback riding. Home: Powell, Ohio. Died Aug. 2, 2007.

BACKE, JOHN DAVID, communications corporation executive; b. Akron, Ohio, July 5, 1932; s. John A. and Ella A. (Enyedy) B.; m. Katherine A. Elliott, Oct. 22, 1955 (dec. 2014); children: Kimberly Marr, John. BSBA, Miami U., Oxford, Ohio, 1954; MBA, Xavier U., 1961; LLD (hon.), Miami U., Oxford, Ohio, 1977, Xavier U., 1978. Various managerial positions in engring., fin. and mktg. functions GE, 1957-66; v.p., dir. mktg. Silver Burdett Co. div. Gen. Learning Corp., 1966-68, pres., 1968-69; exec. v.p. Gen. Learning Corp., Morristown, N.J., 1969, pres., chief exec. officer, 1969-73; pres. CBS Pub. Group, 1973-76; v.p., dir. CBS, Inc., 1973-80, pres., chief exec. officer, mem. fin. com., dir., 1976-80; chmn. Cinema Products, 1992. Pres., CEO Tomorrow Entertainment, Inc., 1981-84, chmn., 1984-; chmn., CEO Backe Group Inc., 1984—; chmn. Gulfshore Comm. Co., Naples, Fla., 1986—, Sta. KDKY-TV, Lexington, Ky., 1985-93, Gulfstream Newspapers, Pompano, Fla., 1987-93, Andrews Comm., Inc., Westtown, Pa., 1987—, Atlantic Pubs., Accomac, Va., 1989—, Dorchester Pub. Co., N.Y.C., 1994—; purchased Sta. WRGB, 1983; bd. dirs. Bus. Mktg. Corp., N.Y.C. Trustee Salk Inst., United Fund Morris County, 1971-73; mem. campaign cabinet goals for enrichment program Miami U., 1979-81; mem. N.Y. State Alliance to Save Energy, Bus. Com. for Arts, 1977-80; mem. nat. adv. com. for U. Ill. Inst. for Aviation.; spl. del. to UNESCO Conf. on publishing for Arabic-speaking countries, 1972—. 1st lt. USAF, 1954-57. Recipient cable Ace award for ednl. instrnl. series. Mem. Assn. Am. Pubs. (bd. dir.). Home: Princeton, NJ. Died Oct. 22, 2015.

BACKER, TERRANCE E., state legislator; b. Stamford, Conn., Aug. 3, 1954; s. Henry and Catherine (Lagana); m. Mary Backer (div.); children: Jacob, Luke. Exec. dir. Soundkeeper Inc., Norwalk, Conn.; mem. Dist. 121 Conn. House of Reps., 1993—2015, asst. majority whip, mem. environment com., energy & tech. com., appropriations com. Mem. Conn. Coun. Environ. Quality, 1991—92, LI Sound Adv. Coun., Stratford Local Shellfish Commn.; v.p. Waterkeeper Alliance. Lic. master USCG. Democrat. Died Dec. 14, 2015.

BACKMAN, JEAN ADELE, real estate executive; b. NYC, Mar. 3, 1931; d. Seraphin Michael and Helen Elma (Matthews) Millon; m. Frank F. Backman, Sept. 27, 1953; children: Carl Eric, Adam Andrew. BA, Hunter Coll., 1954; degree in real estate mgmt., Am. U., 1980. Sales assoc. Ted Lingo Realty, Potomac, Md., 1970-73; sales mgr. House and Home Real Estate, Potomac, 1973-74; dist. mgr. Panorama Real Estate, Md., 1975-78, v.p., dir. mktg., sales Tysons Corner, Va., 1978-82; sr. v.p., regional sales mgr. Coldwell Banker Real Estate, Vienna, Va., 1983-88, sr. v.p., regional dir. orgnl. devel. and tng. Balt. and Washington, 1988-89; sr. v.p. Coldwell Banker Stevens REaltors, Vienna, Va., 1989-95, mgmt. cons., from 1996. Cons. Reston Pub. Co., Reston, Va., 1979-82, Panorama Condominiums, Tysons Corner, 1979-82. Mem. Realtors for Pol. Action, Falls Church, Va., 1985, profl. stds. com., 1989. Mem. Am. Mgmt. Assn., Nat. Assn. REaltors, Va. Assn. Realtors, No. Va. Bd. Realtors, Va. C. of C., Potomac C. of C., Grad. Realtors Inst., Cert. Residential Brokerage Mgr. Republican. Presbyterian. Avocations: swimming, reading, travel, paperweight collecting. Home: Potomac, Md. Died Jan. 15, 2007.

BADGLEY, JOHN ROY, architect; b. Huntington, W.Va., July 10, 1922; s. Roy Joseph and Fannie Myrtle (Limbaugh) B.; m. Janice Atwell, July 10, 1975; 1 child, Adam; children by previous marriage: Dan, Lisa, Holly, Marcus, Michael AB, Occidental Coll., LA, 1943; MArch, Harvard U., Cambridge, Mass., 1949; postgrad., Internat. Ctr., Vincenza, Italy, 1959. Lic. Calif. Pvt. practice, San Luis Obispo, Calif., 1952—65; chief arch., planner Crocker Land Co., San Francisco, 1965—80; v.p. Cushman & Wakefield Inc., San Francisco, 1980—84; pvt. practice San Rafael, Calif., 1984—2001. Prof. Calif. State U., San Luis Obispo, 1952—65. Bd. dirs. Ft. Mason Ctr., Angel Island Assn. With USCGR, 1942-54 Mem. AIA (emeritus), Am. Arbitration Assn., Golden Gate Wine Soc Home: Laguna Woods, Calif. Died Nov. 5, 2014.

BADILLO, HERMAN, former United States Representative from New York; b. Caguas, PR, Aug. 21, 1929; s. Francisco and Carmen (Rivera) Badillo; m. Norma Lit, 1949 (div. 1960); 1 child, David; m. Irma Deutsch Liebling, 1961 (dec. 1996); m. Gail Roberts, Aug. 17, 1996. Commr. housing relocation NYC, 1963—66; borough pres. Bronx, NY, 1966—70; chmn. NY State Constn. Conv. Com. on Health, Housing & Social Svc., 1967; delegate Democratic Nat. Conv., 1968—78; mem. Democratic Nomination Mayor NY, 1969, 1973, 1977, US Congress from 22nd NY Dist., Washington, 1971—73, US Congress from 21st NY Dist., Washington, 1973—77; delegate Democratic Nat. Mid-Term Conf., 1974, 1978, Democratic Nat. Conv., 1980; dep. mayor for policy NYC, 1978—79, spl. counsel for fiscal oversight of edn. to Mayor Rudolph W. Giuliani, 1994—96; spl. counsel Ferro, Berdon & Co. CPA, 1951—55; atty. Permut & Badillo, 1955—62, Stroock & Stroock & Lavan, NYC, 1970—74; ptnr. Fischbein, Olivieri, Rozenholc & Badillo, 1981—86; chmn. NY State Mortgage Agy., 1983—86; ptnr. Fischbein, Badillo, Wagner, & Harding, 1987—2005; of counsel Sullivan, Papain, Block, McGrath & Cannavo, 2005—06; sr. fellow Manhattan Inst. for Policy Rsch., 2006—11; sr. counsel Parker Waichman Alonso, 2011—14. Adj. prof. Fordham U. Sch. Urban Edn., 1970—80; trustee CCUNY, 1991—2001; chmn. bd. trustees CCNY, 1999—2001. Author: A Bill of No Rights: Attica and the American Prison System, 1972, One Nation, One Standard: An Ex-Liberal on How Hispanics Can Succeed Just Like Other Immigrant Groups, 2006. Republican. Protestant. Died Dec. 3, 2014.

BADR, GAMAL MOURSI, legal consultant; b. Helwan, Egypt, Feb. 8, 1924; came to U.S., 1970; s. Ahmad Moursi and Aisha Morshida (Al-Ailaly) B.; m. Fatima al-Zahraa Barakat, June 18, 1950; children: Hefni, Hussein. LLB, U. Alexandria, Arab Republic of Egypt, 1944, LLD summa cum laude, 1954; diploma in econs., U. Cairo, 1945, diploma in pvt. law, 1946. Asst. dist. atty. Mixed Cts. Egypt, Alexandria, 1945-49; from assoc. to ptnr. Vatimbella, Catzeflis, Garrana & Badr, Alexandria, 1949-63; legal advisor UN Congo Operation, Kinshasa, Congo, 1963-64; justice Supreme Ct. Algeria, Algiers, 1965-69; from mem. to dep. dir. legal dept. UN Secretariat, NYC, 1970-84; legal advisor Mission of Qatar to UN, NYC, 1984-94; advisor Mission of Saudi Arabia to UN, NYC, from 1998. Permanent bur. mem. Pan-Arab Lawyers' Fedn., Cairo, 1959-61; adj. prof. law NYU, 1982-98; lectr. The Hague Acad. Internat. Law, 1984. Author: Agency, 1980, State Immunity, 1984; gen. editor Commercial Law of the Middle East; contbr. articles to profl. jours. Mem. Internat. Law Assn. (London), Am. Soc. Internat. Law, Am. Arbitration Assn. (panel of arbitrators), Am. Fgn. Law Assn. (v.p. 1985-87, 89-92), Egyptian-Am. Assn. (pres. 1987-90), Rotary (pres. Alexandria Club 1962-63). Muslim. Home: Mooresville, NC. Died Feb. 20, 2007.

BAER, JOHN RICHARD FREDERICK, lawyer; b. Melrose Park, Ill., Jan. 9, 1941; s. John Richard and Zena Edith (Ostreyko) B.; m. Linda Gail Chapman, Aug. 31, 1963; children: Brett Scott, Deborah Jill. BA, U. Ill., Champaign, 1963, JD, 1966. Bar: Ill. 1966, US Dist. Ct. (no. dist.) Ill. 1967, US Ct. Appeals (7th cir.) 1969, US Ct. Appeals (DC cir.) 1975, US Ct. Appeals (9th cir.) 1979, US Supreme Ct. 1975. Assoc. Keck, Mahin & Cate, Chgo., 1966-73, ptnr., 1974-97; of counsel Sonnenschein Nath & Rosenthal LLP, Chgo., 1997-99, ptnr., 2000—10; officer Greensfelder, Hemker & Gale, P.C., from 2010. Mem. Ill. Atty. Gen.'s Franchise adv. bd., 1992-94, 96-2012, chair 1996-2012. Editor Commerce Clearing House Sales Representative Law Guide, 1998—2011; mem editl. bd. U. Ill. Law Forum, 1964-65, asst. editor, 1965-66; contbg. editor: Commercial Liability Risk Management and Insurance, 1978, editor-in-chief, ABA Forum on Franchising The Franchise Lawyer, 1999-2002; co-editor Internat. Jour. Franchising Law, 2011-; contbr. articles to profl. jours. Mem. Plan Commn., Village of Deerfield, Ill., 1976-79, chmn., 1978-79, mem. Home Rule Study Commn., 1974-75, mem. home rule implementation com., 1975-76. Recipient Lewis G. Rudnick award, ABA, 2009. Mem.: ABA (topics and articles editor Franchise Law jour. 1995—96, assoc. editor 1996—99, editor-in-chief The Franchise Lawyer 1999—2002, governing com. Forum on Franchising 2003—06), ICC Commn. Comml. Law and Practice (task force master franchise agreement 2011—14), N.Am. Securities Adminstrs. Assn. Franchise Project Group (mem. industry adv. com. 2007—10), Internat. Bar Assn. (officer franchising com. 2006, sec. franchising com. 2007—08, vice chair 2008—10, chair 2011—12), Ill. State Bar Assn. (competition dir. Region 8 nat. moot ct. 1974, profl. ethics com. 1977—84, spl. com. on individual lawyers advt. 1981—83, chmn. 1982—83, profl. responsibility com. 1983—84, standing com. on liaison with atty. registration and discplinary commn 1989—93, ISBA/CBA com. on ethics 2000 1999—2008, standing com. profl. conduct 2008—10, standing com., franchising and distbn. law 2008—11), Internat. Franchise Assn. (legal-legis. com. 1990—2012). Died Jan. 29, 2015.

BAER, RALPH HENRY, video game developer, engineering consultant; b. Germany, Mar. 8, 1922; arrived in US, 1938, naturalized; m. Dena Whinston, 1952; children: James Whinston, Mark Whinston, Nancy Doris. BS in TV Engring., Am. TV Inst. Tech., Chgo., 1949. Cert. radio svc. technician Nat. Radio Inst., Washington, 1940. Chief engr. Wappler, Inc., NYC, 1949—50; sr. engr. Loral Electronics, Bronx, NY, 1951—52; v.p., chief engr. Transitron, Inc., NYC, 1952—56; staff engr., mgr. equipment design divsn. Sanders Assocs., Inc., Nashua, NH, 1956—57, mgr. electronic design dept., equipment design divsn., 1957—58, divisn mgr., chief engineer equipment design, 1958—70, mgr. flexprint divsn. Manchester, NH, 1970—71, chief engr. Electro-optics divsn., 1971—73, engring. fellow, 1974—87, cons., 1987—90; founder, pres. R.H. Baer Consultants, 1975—2014. Cons. Marvin Glass & Assocs., Chgo., 1975—82. Author: Video Games: In the Beginning, 2005; contbr. article to profl. jours. Svc. with mil. intelligence US Army, 1943—46, London. Recipient Father of Video Game award, Gametronics Conf., San Francisco, 1973, Inventor of Yr. award, NY Patent Law Assn., 1979, State of NH, 1980, Someone Spl. award, sta. WKBR Manchester, NH, 1980, Nat. Medal Tech., The White House, 2004, Legend award, G-Phoria Video Game Awrads, 2005, Pioneer award, Game Developers Choice Awards, 2008; named to Am. Computer Mus., Bozeman, Mont., 2002, Nat. Inventors Hall of Fame, 2010. Mem.: IEEE (sr. life, Masaru Ibuka Consumer Electronics award 2008). Achievements include development of the 'Brown Box' console video game system and several other prototypes for playing games using a home TV set, licensed then renamed Magnavox Odyssey, the console was released to the public in 1972; invention of the first peripheral for a video game console, a light gun and game for home television use; an electronic pattern-matching game called Simon; pioneering microprocessor-controlled, VCR-based interactive video game methods; invention of picture frames that enable sound and voice to be recorded to match the photos, talking door mats and bicycle speedometers, as well as a line of talking tools, books and toys for companies such as Hasbro, Milton Bradley and Kenner; patents in field. Home: Manchester, NH. Died June 6, 2014.

BAGATELLE, WARREN DENIS, investment banker; b. Mt. Vernon, NY, Aug. 19, 1938; s. S. Jerry and Rose (Firestone) B.; m. Hedy Schwartz, Nov. 22, 1962; children: David S., Tracy L., Adrien G. BA in Econs., Union Coll., 1960; MBA in Fin., Rutgers U., 1961. CPA N.Y. Audit mgr. Arthur Andersen & Co., NYC, 1962-69; v.p. fin. & adminstrn. Ilex Optical Co., Inc., Rochester, N.Y., 1969-73; CEO Meson Electronics Inc., Rochester, N.Y., 1973-74; v.p. fin. Cross River Products, Inc., Rochester, N.Y., 1974-77; exec. v.p. Univ. Soc., Inc., Mahwah, N.J., 1977-81; v.p. corp. fin. Josephthal Lyon & Ross Inc., NYC, 1981-84, chmn. chief exec. officer, 1984-87; mng. dir. Loeb Ptnrs. Corp., NYC, from 1987. Bd. dirs. Fuel Cell Energy, Inc., Danbury, Conn., Electro Energy, Inc., Danbury; chmn. bd. dirs. Virtual Scopics LLC, Rochester, NY, from 2002; ptnr. HSB Capital, from 1984. With USCG, 1961-62. Mem.: AICPAs, Antique and Classic Boat Soc. (dir. 1993—97, treas. 1997—2002), Am. Legion. Avocation: antiques. Home: Wayne, NJ. Died May 31, 2007.

BAGLEY, GARY J., priest; b. Buffalo, Dec. 16, 1946; s. Howard Henry and Beatrice Elizabeth (Westfield) B. BA, St. John Vianney Sem., East Aurora, NY, 1966, MDiv, 1972; postgrad., Fordham U., 1968; MRE, Notre Dame Sem., New Orleans, 1975. Ordained priest Roman Cath. Ch., 1972. Assoc. pastor St. Christopher's Ch., Tonawanda, N.Y., 1972-76; tchr. Bishop Turner High Sch., Buffalo, 1976; assoc. dir. Youth Dept., Diocese of Buffalo, 1976-86, dir. dept., from 1986. Chaplain Sacred Heart Acad., Buffalo, 1977—, Franciscan Missionary Sisters, Williamsville, N.Y., 1979—. Contbr. articles to religious jours. Active Ellicott Creek Vol. Fire Co., Amherst, N.Y., 1972-76; bd. dirs. Our Lady of Victory Infant Home, Lackawanna, N.Y., 1980-86, Hopevale Inc., Hamburg, N.Y., 1989—. Mem. Nat. Fedn. for Cath. Youth (chairperson com.). Democrat. Home: Buffalo, NY. Died Nov. 14, 2006.

BAILEY, HOWLAND HASKELL, physicist, consultant; b. Boston, Apr. 5, 1912; s. William Henry and Edith Stone (Haskell) B.; m. Anne Margaret Becchetti, Aug. 30, 1941; children: Bernadine Oberst, Barbara Ruth Kernochan. AB, Haverford Coll., 1932; student, Duke U., 1932-34; PhD, Calif. Inst. Tech., 1941. Tchr. Am. Coll., Tarsus, Turkey, 1934-36; grad. asst. Calif. Inst. Tech., Pasadena, 1936-40; asst. prof. U. Wyo., Laramie, 1940-41, U. Okla., Norman, 1941-43; staff mem., group leader Radiation Lab. MIT, Cambridge, 1943-45; mem. tech. staff Bell Telephone Labs., Whippany, N.J., 1945-53; mem. tech. staff, group leader Rand Corp., Santa Monica, Calif., 1953-87, cons., 1987-91. Cons. Sci. Applications, Inc., La Jolla, Calif., 1977-81, Northrop Corp., Anahaeim, Calif., 1978-80, Pacific Sierra Rsch., Santa Monica, 1983. Contbr. articles to profl. jours. Mem. several Air Force Sci. Adv. Bd. Coms. Fellow Explorers Club; mem. Sierra Club (chpt. treas. 1980-82), Phi Beta Kappa. Avocations: hiking, music appreciation, travel. Home: Santa Monica, Calif. Died Dec. 26, 2006.

BAILEY, WILLIAM JAMES, JR., (BAILEY JIMMEY), transportation executive; b. Bonifay, Fla., Jan. 8, 1947; s. William James and Helen Julia (Adkins) B.; m. Glenda Joyce Bruner, Feb. 17, 1968; children: Catherine Julynne, Raegan Jaynelle. BS in Journalism, U. Fla., 1970; BS in Geography, Troy State U., 1974; MS in Adminstrn. and Supervision, U. of West Fla., 1984. Editor Gainesville (Fla.) Independent, 1968-70; news dir. Sta. WGVL-Radio, Gainesville, 1970; editor Milton (Fla.) Times, 1970-71; info. specialist Fla. Dept. Transp., Chipley, 1971-75, environ. specialist, 1975, dist. environ. coordinator, from 1975. Sec.-treas. Tri-County Airport Authority, Chipley, 1982-84. Author, editor environ. studies for various highway transp. projects 1971-87. Campaign mgr. Rep. Congrl. campaign; coach, umpire Youth Recreational Leagues, Chipley, 1974-84; chmn. Polit. Action Com., Chipley, 1981; bd. dirs. Washington County Taxpayers League, Chipley, 1981-84. Mem. Nat. Assn. Environ. Profls. Democrat. Avocation: reading. Home: Chipley, Fla. Died Mar. 8, 2007.

BAKER, GEORGE RICHARD, nuclear medicine physician, internist; b. Tacoma, June 16, 1923; s. George William Baker and Evla B. Hopkins; m. Betty Pallard, June 27, 1947; children: Delwyn, Carl, Bruce, Nancy. BS, U. Wash., 1945; MD, U. Oreg., 1948. Diplomate Am. Bd. Nuclear Medicine. Intern Ancker Hosp., St. Paul, 1948-49; resident in internal medicine VA Hosp., Denver, 1949-51, 53-54; thyroid disease cons., pvt. practice nuclear medicine Boise, Idaho, 1957-95; ret., 1996. Physician St. Lukes Hosp., Boise, 1957-95. Contbr. articles to profl. jours. Capt. USAF, 1951-53. Fellow Soc. Nuclear Medicine; mem. ACP. Avocations: skiing, hiking, photography, computers. Home: Boise, Idaho. Died May 9, 2007.

BAKER, GLADYS ELIZABETH, retired microbiologist, educator; b. Iowa City, Iowa, July 22, 1908; d. Richard Philip and Katherine (Riedelbauch) B. BA, U. Iowa, 1930, MS, 1932; PhD, Washington U., St. Louis, 1935. Biology instr. Hunter Coll., NYC, 1936-40; instr., then asst. prof. Vassar Coll., Poughkeepsie, N.Y., 1940-45, assoc. prof., then prof., chmn. dept. plant scis., 1945-61; prof. botany U. Hawaii, Honolulu, 1961-73. Acting chmn. botany dept., U. Hawaii, 1965. Illustrator: The Myxomycetes, 1934; contbr. articles on mycology to profl., sci. jours. Recipient 3 research grants NSF, 1952-60, others. Fellow AAAS; mem. Mycol. Soc. Am., British Mycol. Soc., Med. Mycol. Soc. of the Ams. (charter). Episcopalian. Home: Larkspur, Calif. Died July 27, 2007.

BAKER, RICHARD EARL, business management educator; b. Inglewood, Calif., Sept. 22, 1928; s. Glyn Maynard and Ruth Elizabeth (Norton) B.; m. Dorotha Jean (Mayo); children: Mary K. Walton, Thomas P., Kimberlee S. Tillman, Scott R. BS, U. So. Calif., 1951, MBA, 1956; post grad., U. Calif., Berkeley, 1958-60. Various mgmt. positions AT and T Co., Calif., 1952-76; cons. Graves and Campbell, LA, 1974-79; prof. U. Calif., LaVerne, Calif., 1976-79, Calif. State Poly. U., Pomona, Calif., 1976-80; cons. Kingman, Ariz., from 1980; instr. Mohave Cmty. Coll., Kingman, Ariz., from 1980. Bd. dir. profl. sales Gen. Motors Dealership, Kingman, 1987; adj. prof., Prescott Coll., Ariz., 1982—; sr. cons. Roberts & Heck Assocs., L.A., 1974-78; cons. Svc. Corps of Retired Execs. SBA, 1980—. Editor: Stress/Assertiveness, 1981; contbtg. articles to profl. jour. Foster parent, Foster Parent Assn., L.A., 1965-78; counselor Teenage Drug Rehab., L.A. 1970-78; coun. commr. Boy Scouts Am., L.A., 1975, scoutmaster, 1965-74; coord. Vocat. Adv. Coun., 1980-90. Lt. comdr. USN, 1945-48, PTO, 1950-52. Mem. Kingman C. of C., Kiwanis, Beta Gamma Sigma. Republican. Avocations: photography, marksmenship-gun collecting, landscaping, electronics. Died Aug. 6, 2007.

BAKER, WALTER WRAY, JR., lawyer; b. Raleigh, NC, July 27, 1942; s. Walter Wray and Maggie Lee (Holland) B.; m. Jane Marlyn Green, June 14, 1964; children: Susan, Valerie, Walter. AA, Campbell Coll., 1962; AB, U. N.C., 1964, JD, 1966. Bar: N.C. 1966, U.S. Dist. Ct. (ea. and mid. dists.) N.C., U.S. Supreme Ct. 1974. Rsch. asst. to chief justice N.C. State Supreme Ct., Raleigh, 1966-67; pvt. practice High Point, from 1967. Writer, lectr. continuing legal edn. personal injury & ethics; adj. prof. trial advocacy Wake Forest Sch. Law. Named among legal elite in litigation in N.C., Bus. N.C. Mag., 2002. Mem. N.C. Acad. Trial Lawyers (pres. 1985-86), High Point Bar Assn. (pres. 1985), N.C. State Bar (councillor 18th jud. dist.), Am. Bd. Trial Advocates, Joseph Br. Inn of Ct., Million Dollar Advocates Forum. Democrat. Mem. Wesleyan Ch. Home: High Point, NC. Died Mar. 4, 2007.

BALADI, ANDRÉ, international financier; b. Heliopolis, Egypt, Mar. 11, 1934; Swiss citizen. s. Albert and Laura-Elena (Ventura) B.; m. Adrienne-Sylvia Barben, 1958; children: Viviane, Sibyl, Alex. Student, English Sch., Jesuit Coll., French Lycée, Cairo, 1939-52; grad., Geneva U., Switzerland; postgrad., Geneva Inst. Internat. Studies, Brit. Inst. Mgmt., London, Inst. Mgmt. Devel., Switzerland, Mgmt. Ctr. Europe, Brussels. UN accredited journalist, Geneva, 1955-57; internat. exec. Nestlé Co., Europe, Asia and U.S., 1958-72; corp. devel. dir. Lesieur, Paris, 1973-74; exec. v.p., bd. dirs. Interfinexa, Co. Internat. pour le Dével. founded by BNP/Banexi, SFE and Smith Barney, Geneva, 1974-77; dir. SGS Soc. Gen. de Surveillance, Geneva, 1977-79; founder Baladi & Co. Internat. Devel. Group, Geneva, from 1980. Chmn. Geneva's Internat. Dispute Resolution Orgn. ARICI, 1989-; hon. participant Coun. Instnl. Investors CII, Washington; corp. gov. advisor to UN Group Accounting Experts, Geneva. Co-author: Globalization and the Reform of the International Banking and Monetary System, 2009. Mem. Internat. Corp. Govenance Network (co-founder, award Excellence in Corp. Governance, 2007), Internat. Adv. Bd. Paris Bourse, Euronext, NYSE Euronext Stock Exch., OECD Corp. Governance Adv. Bd., Assn. Swiss Fin. Analysts, Am. Internat. Club, Internat. Fin. Mgmt. Assn. (Geneva), Cercle de l'Union Interalliée (Paris), Died June 2015.

BALAM, BAXISH SINGH, chemistry educator; b. Kukar Pind, Punjab, India, Aug. 16, 1930; came to U.S. 1962; s. Ram Singh and Rajinder (Hothi) Boparai; m. Marilyn Kay Cogswell, Mar. 20, 1964; children: Elisabeth, Gabrielle, Bryan. BSc, Punjab U., 1951, MSc, 1953; PhD, Ohio State U., 1965. Asst. prof. chemistry Punjab (India) Agrl. U., 1953-60, assoc. prof., 1960-66; advisor IAEA of UN, Vienna, 1966-68; prof. chemistry Miss. Valley State U., Itta Bena, from 1968. Cons. D&R Corp., Sacramento, 1977-78; rsch. assoc. Argonne Nat. Lab., 1972-73. Contbr. articles to profl. jours. Mem. Am. Chem. Soc., Am. Soc. Agronomy, Sigma Xi. Achievements include partial acidulation of rock phosphate for use as a fertilizer; processing of Montmorillonite clay colloids for use as secondary barrier for radioactive waste disposal. Home: Greenwood, Miss. Died Feb. 8, 2007.

BALAZS, ENDRE ALEXANDER, physician, educator, researcher; b. Budapest, Hungary, Jan. 10, 1920; naturalized, 1956; s. Endre and Vilma (Bonta) B.; m. Eva Tomes (div.); children: Marianne, Andre; m. Janet Logan Denlinger, Oct. 7, 1977. MD, U. Budapest, 1942; MD (hon.), U. Uppsala, 1967. Rsch. Karolinska Inst., 1942—51; assoc. dir. Retina Found., Boston, 1951-61, pres., 1961-63; research dir. dept. connective tissue research Inst. Biol. and Med. Sciences, 1961-69; founder, pres. Boston Biomed. Research Inst., 1968—75, research dir. dept. connective tissue research, 1971-75, also trustee; dir. opthalmic rsch. Columbia-Presbyterian Med. Ctr., 1975—82; Malcolm P. Aldrich prof. ophthalmology Coll. Physicians and Surgeons, Columbia U., NYC, 1975—87, Malcolm P. Aldrich emeritus prof. ophthalmology, 1987—2015; co-founder, pres. Matrix Biology Inst., Ridgefield, 1982; co-founder, CEO, chief sci. officer Biomatrix, Inc. (sold to Genzyme in 2000), Ridgefield, 1981—2000. Lectr. dept. ophthalmology Harvard U. Med. Sch., 1957-76. Co-editor-in-chief Exptl. Eye Rsch., 1961-92; editor: The Amino Sugars: The Chemistry and Biology of Compounds Containing Amino Sugars, 1965-69, The Chemistry and Molecular Biology of the Intercellular Matrix, 1970. Recipient Friedenwald award Assn. for Research in Ophthalmology, 1963; Guggenheim fellow, 1968 Fellow Gerontol. Soc.; mem. Am. Soc. Biol. Chemists, Soc. Exptl. Biology and Medicine, Biochemical Soc., Internat. Soc. Eye Research (founder, pres. 1978), Internat. Soc. for Hyaluronan Sciences (founder) Died Aug. 29, 2015.

BALDWIN, JEFFREY KENTON, lawyer, educator, writer; b. Palestine, Ill., Aug. 8, 1954; s. Howard Keith and Annabelle Lee (Kirts) B.; m. Patricia Ann Mathews, Aug. 23, 1975; children: Matthew, Katy, Timothy, Philip R. BS summa cum laude, Ball State U., 1976; JD cum laude, Ind. U., 1979. Bar: Ind. 1979, U.S. Dist. Ct. (so. dist.) Ind. 1979, U.S. Ct. Appeals (7th cir.) 1979, U.S. Dist. Ct. (no. dist.) Ind. 1984. Majority leader's staff Ind. Senate, Indpls., 1976; instr. Beer Sch. Real Estate, Indpls., 1977-78, Am. Inst. Paralegal Studies, Indpls., from 1987; dep. Office Atty. Gen., Indpls., 1979-81; mng. ptnr. Baldwin & Baldwin, Danville, Ind., from 1979. Agt. Nat. Attys. Title Assurance Fund, Vevay, Ind., 1983—; officer, bd. dirs. Baldwin Realty, Inc., Danville; conf. participant White House Conf. on Small Bus. (Ind. meeting 1994), congl. appointee, 1995; bd. dirs. Small Bus. Coun. Author: (book) Danville, Ind. Bd. dirs. Hendricks Civic Theatre, Inc.; organizer, Hendricks County Young Republicans, 1972; sec. Hendricks County Rep. Com., 1978-84; bd. dirs. Hendricks County Assn. for Retarded Citizens, Danville, 1982-86; cons. Hendricks County Right to Life, Brownsburg, Ind., 1984—; mem. philanthropy adv. com. Ball State U., Muncie, Ind., 1987—; judge Hendricks County unit Am. Cancer Soc., 1987; coordinator region 2 Young Leaders for Mutz, Indpls., 1987-88; cubmaster WaPaPh dist. Boy Scouts Am., 1988, S.M.E. chmn., 1988-89; steering com. Ind. Lawyers Bush/Quayle; founder, chmn. Christians for Positive Reform; candidate for Congress 7th Congl. Dist. of Ind.; del. to Annual Conf. South Ind. Conf. of United Meth. Ch., 1993, 95-98, 2000; host com. Midwest Rep. Leadership Conf., 1997; dist. coord. Hoosier Famiies for John Price for U.S. Senate; advisor John Price for Gov., 1999-2000; v.p. Danville Little League Baseball, 1998—2002; pres. Hendricks County Mus., 2007-10; mem., bd. dirs. Hendricks County Mus., 2010-; mem. adv. coun. Cmty. Theatre, 2010-; mem., bd. Govs., Soc. Ind. Pioneers, 2010-; mem., Downtown Danville Partnership, 2010-. Recipient Presdl. award of honor Danville Jaycees, 1980; named hon. sec. State Ind., 1980. Mem. ABA, Ind. Bar Assn., Hendricks County Bar Assn., Indpls. Bar Assn., Internat. Platform Assn., Nat. Assn. Realtors, Ind. Assn. Realtors, Met. Indpls. Bd. Realtors (Hendricks County div.), Federalist Soc., Ind. Farm Bur., Nat. Fedn. Ind. Bus., Ind. C. of C., Danville C. of C. (sec. 1986), Moot Ct. Soc., Blue Key, Phi Soc., Circus Hist. Soc., Ind. Large Scale Railroaders, Civil War Roundtable West-Ctrl. Ind. Republican. Methodist. Home: Danville, Ind. Died Jan. 16, 2015.

BALDWIN, ROBERT HAYES BURNS, business executive; b. East Orange, NJ, July 9, 1920; s. John Frank and Anna (Burns) B.; children: Janet Kimball, Deborah Gay Baldwin Fall, Robert Hayes Burns Jr., Whitney Hayes, Elizabeth Brooks; m. Dorothy Tobin Ayres, Dec. 26, 1981; stepchildren: W. Dillaway Ayres, Mary Ayres Hack. AB, Princeton U., 1942. Chmn., mng. gen. ptnr. Morgan Stanley

& Co., NYC, 1946-88, gen. ptnr., 1958-65, 67-75, ltd. ptnr., 1965-67, pres., 1973-82, chmn., 1982—83; chmn. adv. bd. Morgan Stanley Group, Inc., NYC, 1984-88; with Lodestar Group, NYC, 1989. Served as under sec. Dept. Navy, 1965-67; mem. coun. on fgn. rels.; chmn. Cities in Schs., Inc.; bd. dirs. Arthur J. Gallagher and Co., Network Equipment Techs., Orgn. Resources Counselor. Vice chmn. bd. trustees Presbyn. Hosp., N.Y.C.; chmn., trustee Geraldine Rockefeller Dodge Found., com. econ. devel. Served to lt. USNR, 1942-46. Mem. Phi Beta Kappa Clubs: Links (N.Y.C.); Chevy Chase (Md.); Met. (Washington); Maidstone (East Hampton, N.Y.); Bridgehampton (N.Y.); Augusta Nat. Golf (Ga.), Seminole Golf (N. Palm Beach, Fla.). Republican. Episcopalian. Died Jan. 3, 2016.

BALISH, RUTH REITZ, retired community health nurse; b. Palmerton, Pa., Oct. 1, 1919; d. Chas. B. and Minnie E. Reitz; m. George F. Balish, Nov. 5, 1949; children: Deidre B. Talarico, Vicki B. DelMonte, Lori S. Hedges. Student, Moravian Coll., 1937-38; diploma in nursing, Grandview Hosp. Sch. Nursing, 1942; BSN, Temple U., 1944; cert., New England Hosp. Women, 1943; diploma in med. tech., Sacred Heart Hosp. Sch., Allentown, Pa., 1945. Chief med. technician Morris County Chest Clinic, Morris Place, N.J.; pub. health nurse City of Summit, N.J., 1968-73; chief rsch. histologist Merck Co., Rahway, NJ, 1947—50; pvt. duty nurse Clearwater, Fla., 1987-91, Lakeland, Fla., 1991-99; ret., 2000. Vol. nurse ARC Disaster Shelter, Boca Raton, Waynesville, N.C., Pinellas County, Fla., Lakeland Fla., 1978-82; co-owner, med. technologist North Summit Med. Lab., Summit, 1951-64. Vol. nurse Lakeland Regional Ctr., Morton Plant Hosp., Clearwater; adv. bd. J. Haley Vets. Hosp., Tampa, 1991-95, Bay Pines Vets. Hosp., St. Petersburg, Fla., VA Vol. Svc.; active Sr. Olympics, Lakeland, 1992-2002 Mem. DAR (officer 1961—, bd. dirs. to 2001-05, area chmn. commemorative WWII 50th anniversary Lakeland chpt. 1992-95, Excellence in Lakeland Cmty. Svc. award 1995), Am. Soc. Clin. Pathologists, Am. Chem. Soc., Daus. Am. Colonists, Order Ea. Star Avocation: ping pong/table tennis. Home: North Plainfield, NJ. Died Nov. 30, 2015.

BALKIND, BENJAMIN HART, lawyer; b. Bronx, Apr. 22, 1931; s. Max Z. and Katherine Jeanette Balkind; m. Mary Josephine Lee; children: Sarah Kershaw, Benjamin Lee, Jonathan Buck. BA, Harvard U., 1953; JD, Yale U., 1957. Ptnr. Curtis Mallet Prevost et at, NYC, from 1959. Judge Laurel Hollow Village. Home: Syosset, NY. Died July 12, 2007.

BALTZ, LEWIS, photographer; b. Newport Beach, Calif., Sept. 12, 1945; s. Charles Lewis and Lola Berenice (Anderson) B.; 1 child, Monica Diane. B.F.A., San Francisco Art Inst., 1969; M.F.A., Claremont Grad. Sch., 1971. Mem. individual grants panel Nat. Endowment Arts, 1977; mem. visiting com. George Eastman House, 1978-80 One-man shows: Leo Castelli Gallery, N.Y.C., 1971, 73, 75, 78, 81, 83, 85, Corcoran Gallery Art, Washington, 1974-76, George Eastman House, 1972, Balt. Mus. Art, 1976, Mus. Fine Arts, Houston, 1976, La Jolla Mus. Contemporary Art, 1976, Otis Art Inst., Los Angeles, 1981, San Francisco Mus. Modern Art, 1981, Victoria and Albert Mus., London, 1985, Tokyo Polytechnic Inst.; over 150 group exhbns.; represented in permanent collections 56 mus. in U.S., Europe, Australia, Can., U.S.; Photog. monographs include New Industrial Parks, Near Irvine, Calif., 1975, Md., 1976, Nev., 1978, Park City, 1981, San Quentin Point, 1986. Guggenheim fellow, 1976; U.S.-U.K. exchange fellow, 1979 Died Nov. 23, 2014.

BANCIK, STEVEN CHARLES, information specialist, researcher; b. Cleve., Apr. 23, 1958; s. Paul Milan and Geraldine (Everstine) B. BA in Sociology, Psychology, Anthropology, Kent State U., Ohio, 1994, MA in History and Pub. History, 1999, M in Libr. & Info. Sci., 2000. Asst. mgr. Waldenbooks, Akron, Ohio, 1983-88, mgr. without portfolio Northern, Ohio, 1988, mgr. divsn. reader's mkt. Akron, Ohio, 1988-90; scheduling advisor Dept. Undergrad. Studies Kent State U., computer lab. mgr., 1994-97; CEO, owner Lionheart Antiquities, Ltd., from 1998; tchg. asst. dept. history Kent State U., 1999; owner, CEO Lionheart Antiquities, Ltd., from 1998. Bd. trustees Kent State U., 1996-98, mem. commemoration com., program coord. sub-com.; senator rep. The Sch. of Libr. and Info. Sci. in Grad Student Senate; tchg. asst. Kent State U., 1999. Tech. design cons. Kent State Historian, 1998-99. Mem. Am. Libr. Assn. (rep. Kent State U. 1996, exec. officer student chpt. 1995-96), Libr. Adminstrn. Mgmt. Assn., Assoc. Libr. Student Svc. Orgn. (treas. 1996, newsletter cartoonist 1994-97). Republican. Avocations: museum studies, ancient antiquities, rare books, applied CD-ROM technologies, commercial art. E-mail: sbancik@ wordlnet.att.net. Home: Kent, Ohio. Died July 19, 2007.

BANDER, THOMAS SAMUEL, retired dentist; b. Grand Rapids, Mich., Mar. 3, 1924; s. Samuel and Jennie (David) B.; m. DoLores Abraham, Sept. 7, 1947; children: Samuel T., Jacquelyn Marie. AS, Grand Rapids Jr. Coll., 1944; DDS, U. Mich., 1948. Pvt. practice dentistry, Grand Rapids, Mich., 1948-2000; ret., 2000. Pres. St. Nicholas Orthodox Ch., Grand Rapids, 1965. Served with U.S. Army, 1941-44, to capt. USAF, 1955-57. Fellow Am. Coll. Dentists, Internat. Coll. of Dentists, ADA, Acad. Operative Dentistry; mem. West Mich. Dental Soc. (pres. 1978), Mich. Dental Assn. (chmn. sci. program 1977-78), Kent County Dental Soc. (pres. 1965), Cascade Hills Country Club. Republican. Eastern Orthodox. Avocations: golf, travel, tennis. Home: Grand Rapids, Mich. Died July 21, 2007.

BANGHAM, ROBERT ARTHUR, orthotist; b. San Antonio, Sept. 12, 1942; s. Robert Dave and Marguerite C. (Wyckoff) B. Student, Northwestern U., 1965, 71, 76, NYU, 1969, Washtenaw C.C., Ann Arbor, Mich., 1971; misc. courses in field, various hosps., and med. orgns. Cert. orthotist; ordained to ministry Jehovah's Witness Ch., 1957. Orthotic resident J. R. Reets, Ann Arbor, Mich., 1960-65; orthotist Dreher-Jouett, Inc., Chgo., 1965-68; cert. orthotist U. Mich., 1968-75, Wright & Filipis, Inc., Alpena, Mich., 1975-78; orthotist, mgr. Hittenbergers, Concord, Calif., 1978-81, 81-90, mgr., cert. orthotist Oakland, Calif., 1981-90, Concord, Oakland, 1988-90; mktg. mgr. western region Nat. Orthotic Labs., Winter Haven, Fla., 1990; CEO Mobile Orthotic & Prosthetic Assocs., Antioch, Calif., 1990-95, Oakland, Calif., 1990-95; practitioner Lakeshore Orthotics & Prosthetics, Muskegon, Mich., 1995-96; mgr., practitioner Hanger Orthopedic Group, Dothan, Ala., 1996-97; mgr. Hangar Orthop. Group, Gadsden, Ala., 1997-98; dir. mktg. Fourroux Orthotics and Prosthetics, Huntsville, Ala., from 1998. Orthotics cons. Benchmark Med. Group, 1992—; cons. Health Careers Profl. Assn., Calif. State Dept. Edn., 1992—; presenter papers in field to profl. assns., hosps., govtl. bodies Contbr. articles to profl. jours. Fellow Am. Back Soc. (internat. profl. rels. com., co-chair orthotics divsn., vice chair orthotics com., AAOP liaison rep. to ABS), Am. Acad. Neurological and Orthopedic Surgeons (head dept. orthotics); mem. Am. Prosthetic Assn., Am. Acad. Orthotics and Prosthetists (nat. dir. 1988-91, pres. Calif. chpt. 1986-87, chpt. dir. 1989-91, sci. com. chmn., societies com., charter chmn. Spinal Orthotics Soc. 1991, 92, sec. lower extremity orthotics soc., bd. dirs. No. Calif. chpt., past pres. No. Calif. chpt., rep. Calif. coalition Allied Health Profls. No. Calif. chpt., co-chmn. sci. edn. com. No. Calif. chpt.), Am. Orthotics and Prosthetics Assn. (bd. dirs., chair NSF program), Internat. Soc. Orthotists and Prosthetists, Calif. Coalition Allied Health Professions (pres. 1989-90). Avocations: ministry, lecturing. Home: Donna, Tex. Died Jan. 18, 2007.

BANKS, ERNIE (ERNEST BANKS), retired professional baseball player; b. Dallas, Jan. 31, 1931; s. Eddie & Essie B.; m. Mollye Banks, 1953 (div. 1959); m. Eloyce Banks (div. 1981); 1 child, Eloyce m. Marjorie Banks, 1984 (div. 1997); m. Liz Ellzey, 1997; 1 adopted child, Alyna; 2 children from previous marriages, Joey, Jerry Student, Northwestern U. Shortstop Kansas City Monarchs (Negro American League), 1950-51, 53, Chgo. Cubs, 1953-71, coach, 1971—73; minor-league instr., 1974—76; spokesperson New World Van Lines, from 1984. Co-owner, v.p. Bob Nelson-Ernie Banks Ford, Inc., Chgo.; with Associated Films Promotions, L.A., 1982-84; corp. spokesman, founder Live Above & Beyond Found. Author: (with Jim Enright) Mr. Cub. Bd. mem. Chgo. Transit Authority; active Boy Scouts America, YMCA. Served with AUS, 1951-53, Europe. Named to The Nat. League All-Star Team, 1955-62, '65, '67, 69; named Nat. League Most Valuable Player, 1958, 59; recipient Gold Glove award, 1960, Lou Gehrig Meml. award, 1968, Awards from Fans, 1969, Award from Press Club, 1969, Award from Jr. Chamber of Commerce, 1971, Presdl. Medal of Freedom, The White House, 2013; inducted into The Tex. Sports Hall Fame, 1971, The Baseball Hall of Fame, 1977 Died Jan. 23, 2015.

BARBER, MARGOT WEBBE, civic worker; b. Chgo., Sept. 28, 1919; d. Albion Scotson and Margaret (White) Webbe; m. Albert Harris Barber, May 25, 1946 (dec. June 1989); children: Gail Hathaway Sykes, Bruce Webbe. BA, Smith Coll., 1940. With U.S. Naval Tng. Sta., Great Lakes, Ill., 1941-43, Time, NYC, 1943-45, Life, Chgo., 1945-46. Bd. dirs. U. Chgo.-Know Your chgo., Chgo. Symphony Orch. Women, North Shore Country Day Sch., Winnetka, Ill.; pres., mem. Planned Parent Orgn., Ill. Children's Aid, ARC; precinct capt. Winnetka Rep. Com.; election judge; mem. Winnetka Village Caucus. Mem. Indian Hill Club, Univ. Club, Dairymen's Country Club, Winnetka Fortnightly Club, Contemporary Club of Chgo. (exec. com.). Avocations: golf, tennis, reading, volunteering. Died Dec. 25, 2007.

BARDELL, EUNICE BONOW, pharmaceutical educator; b. Milw., Feb. 8, 1915; d. Eric A. and Alma Helen (Stark) Bonow; m. Ross Bardell, Nov. 23, 1972. BS in Pharmacy, U. Wis., 1938, MS, 1949, PhD, 1952. Registered pharmacist, Wis.; registered microbiologist. Pharmacist ED Schuster & Co., Milw., 1940-42, Kremers Urban Co., Milw., 1942-44; instr., pharmacy U. of Wis., Milw., 1948-51, asst. prof., 1952-59, assoc. prof., 1960-72, prof., 1972-73; emerita prof. U. Wis., Milw., from 1973. Adj. prof. pharmacy U. Ky., Lexington, 1982-91. Author: The Wisconsin Showglobe, 1984; contbr. articles to profl. jours. Recipient Cert. of Merit, Milw. County Hist. Soc., 1981, Disting. Alumna Award, U. Wis. Pharmacy Alumni Assn., 1989. Fellow Am. Found. Pharm. Edn.; mem. Wis. Pharmacist Assn., Am. Pharm. Assn., Am. Inst. History of Pharmacy, Am. Guild Organists. Methodist. Avocation: music - organ. Home: Milwaukee, Wis. Died Jan. 24, 2007.

BARKAN, JOEL DAVID, political science professor, consultant; s. Manuel and Toby (Wolfe) B.; m. Sandra Lynn Hackman, Sept. 9, 1962; children: Bronwyn Michelle, Joshua Manuel. AB, Cornell U., 1963; MA, UCLA, 1965, PhD, 1970. Asst. prof. polit. sci. U. Calif., Irvine, 1969-72; asst. prof. polit. sci. U. Iowa, Iowa City, 1972-76, assoc. prof., 1976-81, prof., 1981—2005, prof. emeritus, from 2005; sr. assoc. Africa Program, Ctr. Strategic and Internat. Studies, Washington, from 2009. Vis. rsch. fellow Makerere U., Uganda, 1966—67, U. Dar es Salaam, Tanzania, 1973—74, Fondation Nat. des Scis. Politiques, Paris, 1978—79, U. Nairobi, Kenya, 1979—80, Ctr. Study of Developing Socs., New Delhi, 1984, Cornell U., 1990, US Inst. Peace, 1997—98, Woodrow Wilson Internat. Ctr., 2001—02, U. Cape Town, from 2004, Nat. Endowment for Democracy, 2000, 2005—06; regional governance advisor for Ea. and So. Africa USAID, 1992—94; sr. cons. on governance World Bank, 2000—08; vis. lectr. Princeton U., 2006; lectr. Johns Hopkins Sch. Advanced Internat. Studies, 2010—11. Co-author, editor: Politics and Public Policy in Kenya and Tanzania, 1979, rev. edit., 1984, Beyond Capitalism Versus Socialism in Kenya and Tanzania, 1994, Legislative Power in Emerging African Democracies, 2009; co-author: The Legislative Connection, 1984; author: An African Dilemma, 1975; contbr. articles to profl. jours. Pres. Iowa City Fgn. Rels. Coun., 1989—90. Grantee, Rockefeller Found., 1973—74, USAID, 1978—81, Ford Found., 1992—99; fellow, Social Sci. Rsch. Coun., 1966—68, Fulbright, 1978—79; Indo-Am. fellow, 1984, Randolph fellow, 1997—98, Woodrow Wilson fellow, 2001—02, Reagan-Fascell fellow, 2005—06. Mem. Am. Polit. Sci. Assn., African Studies Assn. (bd. dirs. 1990-93, treas. 2005—2007), Coun. Fgn. Rels. Died Jan. 10, 2014.

BARKER, CHARLES ANSON, lawyer; b. Trenton, NJ, Feb. 25, 1928; s. Anson and Millicent (Ringsdorf) B.; m. Sigrid Barbara Meisse, June 12, 1953; children: Louis Anson, Anne Stevens Barker McCoy, Abby Sagel. BA, Amherst Coll., 1950; JD, Columbia U., 1956. Bar: N.Y., 1957. With Moore-McCormack Lines, NYC, 1952-53, Appleton, Rice and Perrin, Albany, Gen. Mut. Ins. Co., NYC, Fireman's Fund Ins. Co., NYC; assoc. Law Offices of Julien Cornell, Central Valley, N.Y., 1960; sole practice Central Valley, from 1963. Capt., Fire Polics Squad, Woodbury Fire Dept., Highland Mills, N.Y. Served to staff sgt. USMC, 1950-52. Republican. Episcopalian. Avocation: bagpiper. Home: Central Vly, NY. Died Aug. 14, 2007.

BARKER, JOHN ARTHUR, protective services official; b. Pitts., Apr. 6, 1947; s. Charles Henry and Edith May (Arlinger) B.; children: Gwendolyn Elizabeth Clinton, Colin Clinton. AA, Palomar Community Coll.; student, U. Calif., Santa Cruz. Service mgr. Kawasaki Escondido, Calif., 1972-74; campus guard U. Calif., Santa Cruz, 1977-79; police officer Cabrillo Coll., Aptos, Calif., 1979-80, chief police, from 1980. Youth com. mem. United Way, Santa Cruz, 1983. Served with USN, 1966-70. Recipient Community Coll. Social Sci. award Bank of Am., 1973. Mem. Calif. Community Coll. Police Chiefs Assn. (pres. 1984-85), Calif. Peace Officers Assn. (mem. campus law enforcement com. 1986—), Santa Cruz County Law Enfrocement Chief Assn. (chmn. 1989), Assn. Calif. Community Coll. Adminstrs., Santa Cruz Peace Officers Assn. (bd. dirs. 1984-87). Democrat. Avocations: bicycling, Aikido, camping. Home: Watsonville, Calif. Died Apr. 30, 2007.

BARKER, LLOYDEANE A., nursing administrator; b. Borger, Tex., Nov. 8, 1955; d. Andrew J. and Bobbie (Lane) Melton; m. Daniel R. Baker, Aug. 2, 1974; children: Jennifer, James, Joel. RN, N.W. Tex. Hosp., Amarillo, 1977; BSN, W. Tex. State U., Canyon, 1987. Neonatal ICU charge nurse Women and Children's Hosp., Odessa, Tex.; asst. head nurse maternity floor Palo Pinto Gen. Hosp., Mineral Wells, Tex.; dir. infection control Coronado Hosp., Pampa, Tex. Mem. Panhandle Assn. Infection Control Nurses (pres. 1988, v.p. 1990). Home: Pampa, Tex. Died May 19, 2007.

BARNARD, EDWARD TOWNSEND, genealogist, volunteer; b. New Rochelle, NY, Oct. 10, 1910; s. Everett Larkin and Therina (Townsend) B.; m. Charlotte Taintor Williams, Sept. 13, 1935 (dec. 1979); children: Sara Williams Barnard Edwards, David Williams, Jeanette Townsend; m. Jeanette Tenney Poore, May 13, 1980. AB, Yale U., 1933; diploma, Air War Coll., Ala., 1964. Cert. geneal. records specialist. Editor, fgn. dept. UP, NYC, 1935-42; intelligence officer CIA, Washington, 1947-70; coord. projects Town of Guilford, Conn., 1971-73; prof. genealogist in pvt. practice North Branford, Conn., from 1973. Lt. col. with USAAC, 1942-46, ETO. Mem. New Eng. Hist. Geneal. Soc., Maine Hist. Soc., N.H. Hist. Soc., Conn. Soc. Genealogists, Conn. Coun. Profl. Genealogists, Yale Club, Baronial Order Magna Charta. Avocation: colonial U.S. history. Home: North Branford, Conn. Died Feb. 19, 2007.

BARNARD, KATHRYN ELAINE, nursing educator, researcher; b. Omaha, Apr. 16, 1938; d. Paul and Elsa Elizabeth (Anderson) B. BS in Nursing, U. Nebr., Omaha, 1960, DSc (hon.), 1990; MS in Nursing, Boston U., 1962; PhD, U. Wash., Seattle, 1972. Acting instr. U. Nebr., Omaha, 1960-61, U. Wash., Seattle, 1963-65, asst. prof., 1965-69, prof. nursing, 1972, prof. nursing emeritus, assoc. dean, 1987-92, founding dir. Ctr. on Infant Mental Health and Devel., 2001—15, Charles and Gerda Spence Endowed Prof. in Nursing, 2002—15, adj. emeritus prof. psychology. Bd. dirs. Nat. Ctr. for Clin. Infant Programs, Washington, 1980-2015; bd. mem. Zero to Three, Found. for Early Learning Chmn. rsch. com. Bur. of Community Health Svcs., MCH, 1987-89; commissioner King County Commission on Children and Families; mem. Nat. Alliance of Children's Trust and Prevention Funds' Nat. Working Group; Governor's appointee to Washington Coun. for Prevention of Child Abuse & Neglect Bd. Mem., Ctr. for Infant Mental Health and Development U. of Wash. Recipient Lucille Petry Leone teaching award Nat. League for Nursing, 1968, M. Scott award for Contributions to Nursing Sci. Edn. and Svc., Martha Mae Eliot award for Leadership in Maternal-Child Health, Am. Assn. Pub. Health, 1983, Nurse Scientist of Yr. award, Professorship award U. Wash., 1985, Gustav O. Leinhard award, Inst. of Medicine, 2002, Episteme award and Living Legend award, American Acad. of Nursing, 2006 Fellow Am. Acad. Nursing (bd. dirs. 1980-82); mem. Inst. Medicine (Gustav O. Leinhard Award, 2002); mem. Am. Nurses Assn. (chmn. com. 1980-82, Jessie Scott award 1982, Nurse of Yr. award 1984), Soc. Research in Child Devel. (bd. dirs. 1981-87), Sigma Theta Tau (founders award in research 1987, Episteme Award, 2003). Democrat. Presbyterian. Home: Seattle, Wash. Died June 27, 2015.

BARNESS, LEWIS ABRAHAM, retired physician; b. Atlantic City, July 31, 1921; s. Joseph and Mary (Silverstein) B.; m. Elaine Berger, June 14, 1953 (dec. Jan. 1985); children: Carol, Laura, Joseph; m. Enid May Fischer Gilbert, July 5, 1987; stepchildren: Mary, Elizabeth, Jennifer, Rebecca. AB, Harvard U., 1941, MD, 1944; MA (hon.), U. Pa., 1971; DS U. Wis. (hon.), 2002. Intern Phila. Gen. Hosp., 1944-45; resident Boston Children's Hosp., 1947-50; asst. chief, then chief dept. pediatrics Phila. Gen. Hosp., 1951-72; vis. physician U. Pa. Hosp., 1952-57, acting chief, then chief, 1957-72. Mem. faculty U. Pa. Sch. Medicine, 1951-72, prof. pediat., 1964-72; chmn. dept. U. So. Fla. Med. Sch., Tampa, 1972-88, prof. pediat., 1988—, Disting. Univ. prof., 2000—; vis. prof. Univ. Wis., 1987-92, prof. emeritus, 1993—. Author: Pediatric Physical Diagnosis Yearbook, edits. 1-6, 1957—; editor: Advances in Pediatrics, 1976-2004, Pediatric Nutrition Handbook, 3d edit., 1991; asst. editor Pediatric Gastroenterology and Nutrition, 1981-91; editl. bd. Cons., 1960-84, Pediatrics, 1978-83, Core Jour. Pediatrics, 1980-96, Contemporary Pediatrics, 1984—, Jour. Clin. Medicine and Nutrition, 1985-95, Nutrition Rev., 1985-87. Served to capt. AUS, 1945-46. Recipient Lindback Teaching award U. Pa., 1963; Borden award nutrition, 1972; Noer Disting. Prof. award, 1980, Joseph B. Goldberger award in clin. nutrition, 1984, Joseph St. Geme Leadership award 7 pediatric socs., 1991, U. So. Fla. Svc. award, 1997, President's Award, U. So. Fla., 2000, Distinguished Prof. award, 2000; inductee Phila. Pediat. Soc. Hall of Fame, 1996. Fellow Am. Inst. Nutrition; mem. AAAS, Am. Pediatric Soc. (recorder-editor 1964-75, pres. 1985-86, John Howland award 1993), Soc. Pediatric Rsch., Am. Acad. Pediatrics (chmn. com. on nutrition 1974-81), Abraham Jacobi award 1991, Hon. Internat. disting. fellow pediatric soc. Thailand, 2004, Med. Edn. Lifetime Achievement award, 1995, Sigma Xi, Alpha Omega Alpha. Home: Minneapolis, Minn. *Most people, when given the opportunity, try to be unselfish and prefer to do good. The human brain is a fantastic instrument, which when exercised, can solve most problems.* Died Nov. 18, 2013.

BARNET, SYLVAN SAUL, English literature educator; b. Bklyn., Dec. 11, 1926; s. Philip and Esther (Katz) B.; life partner William C. Burto (dec. 2013) AB, NYU, 1948; AM, Harvard U., Cambridge, Mass., 1950, PhD, 1954. Tchg. fellow Harvard U., 1951—54; faculty Tufts U., 1954—84, chmn. dept. English, 1962—67, 1980—82, Fletcher prof. English, 1963—84. Author: A Short Guide to Writing About Literature, 12th edit., 2012, (with W. Cain) Literature: Thinking Reading and Writing, 1997, Current issues and Enduring Questions, 10th edit., 2013, (with Hugo Bedau) Critical Thinking, Reading, and Writing, 1996, 5th edit., 2005, (with P. Bellanca and M. Stubbs) A Short Guide to College Writing, 4th edit., 2012, (with M. Berman, W. Burto and W. Cain) Introduction to Literature, 16th edit., 2011, A Dictionary of Literary, Dramatic and Cinematic Terms, 2d edit., 1971, A Short Guide to Shakespeare, 1974, A Short Guide to Writing About Art, 10th edit., 2011, (with W. Burto) Zen Ink Painting, 1982, (with Marcia Stubbs) Barnet and Stubbs's Practical Guide to Writing, 7th edit., 1995, (with Merry White) Comparing Cultures, 1995, (with W. Burto and W. Cain) A Little Literature, 2006; also essays; editor: (with M. Berman and W. Burto) Tragedy and Comedy, 1967, Nine Modern Classics, 1973, Types of Drama, 8th edit., 2001, also other anthologies; gen. editor: Signet Shakespeare, 1963-69, 2d rev. edit., 1998. Served with AUS, 1945-46. Mem. MLA. Home: Cambridge, Mass. Died Jan. 11, 2016.

BARNETT, RICHARD ALLEN, lawyer; b. Akron, Ohio, Dec. 26, 1949; s. James Joseph and Beverly Muriel (Gergel) B.; m. Nadeen Miller, June 21, 1992. BS in Econs.(magna cum laude), U. Pa., 1971; JD, Harvard U., 1975. Bar: Calif. 1975, Fla. 1978. Law clk. to presiding justice U.S. Dist Ct. Calif., San Diego, 1975-76; assoc. Krupnick & Campbell, Ft. Lauderdale, Fla., 1978-81; sole practice Hollywood, Fla., 1981-87; ptnr. Barnett and Hammer, Hollywood, 1987-93; pvt. practice Hollywood, Fla., from 1993. Author: Tort Trend Newsletter, 1984-87. Bd. dirs. Liberia Econ. and Social Devel. Inc., Hollywood, Fla., 1979—, pres. 1987—, Jewish Fedn. South Broward, chmn. community relations com. 1984-86, attys. and accts. campaign div. 1987-88, bd. dirs. 1984-91. With U.S. Army, 1970-72. Mem. ATLA, Calif. Bar Assn., Fla. Bar Assn. (bd. cert. civil trial lawyer, appellate rules com. 1990-93), Acad. Fla. Trial Lawyers (Amicus Curiae com. 1985—, chmn. 1989-91, bd. dirs. 1996—, chmn.-elect appellate practice sect.), Broward County Trial Lawyers (bd. govs. 1992—), Fed. Bar Assn. (pres. Broward county chpt. 1986-87, exec. com. 1987-93), Rotary Club of Hollywood, Depressive and manice Depressive Assn. Am. (founder Gold Coast chpt.). Avocations: golf, tennis, fishing, reading, travel. Home: Hollywood, Fla. Died Nov. 27, 2006.

BARNEY, JAMES EARL, research executive, chemist; b. Rossville, Kans., Sept. 1, 1926; s. James Earl and Irene (Franz) B.; m. Patricia Leonard, Oct. 4, 1946; children: Alan Earl, Anne Louise. BS in Chemistry, U. Kans., 1946, PhD in Chemistry, 1950. Group leader Standard Oil Co. (Ind.), Whiting, 1950-60; sr. scientist Spencer Chem. Co., Merriam, Kans., 1960-62; sect. mgr. Midwest Research Inst., Kansas City, Mo., 1962-69; dept. head Stauffer Cehm. Co., Richmond, Calif., 1969-78, mgr. Farmington, Conn., 1978-87, ICI Americas Inc., Farmington, 1987-88, Ciba-Geigy Corp., Farmington, from 1988. Contbr. articles to profl. jours. Pres. Farmington C. of C., 1983-85; chairperson Tunxis Com. Coll. Regional Adv. Coun., Farmington, 1988—. Mem. Am. Chem. Soc. (chmn. Kansas City sect. 1965), Rotary (sec. 1983-85, pres. 1987-88 Farmington chpt.). Home: Carson City, Nev. Died Feb. 20, 2007.

BARNEY, SUSAN LESLIE, academic administrator; b. Quantico, Va., Oct. 7, 1945; d. Duane Edwin and Joan Clarice (Long) B. BA, Ohio State U., 1972; JD, Capital U., 1977. Bar: Ohio 1979. With acctg. dept. Golden Gate U., San Francisco, 1977-80, dir. acctg., 1980-83, v.p. adminstrn., 1983-94, emerita v.p. adminstrn., from 1994. Asst. sec. bd. trustees Golden Gate U., 1983-94. Mem. ABA. Methodist. Home: Cleveland, Ohio. Died Apr. 6, 2007.

BARNHART, ROBERT KNOX, writer, editor; b. Chgo., Oct. 17, 1933; s. Clarence L. and Frances (Knox) B.; m. Cynthia Ann Rogers, Sept. 16, 1955; children: Michael, John, David, Rebecca, Katherine. BA, U. of the South, 1956. Editor Clarence L. Barnhart, Bronxville, N.Y., 1956-75, editor-in-chief, 1976-79; pres. Clarence L. Barnhart, Inc., Bronxville and Briarcliff, N.Y., 1979-92; pres., editor-in-chief Rogers Knox & Barnhart, Garrison, N.Y., from 1992. Author: Chambers Dictionary of Etymology, 1988, Barnhart Dictionary of New English, I, 1973, II, 1980, III, 1990, Dictionary of Science, 1986, The College Dictionary, The Barhart Abbreviations Dictionary, 1995, The Barnhart Concise Dictionary of Etymology, 1995; co-author: Let's Read, 1960-66, World Book Dictionary, 1976-99; contbr. World Book Ency., Dictionaries, Internat. Ency. of Lexicography. Owner Homehill Farm. Recipient Outstanding Book in Art, Lit., and Lang. award Assn. Am. Pubs., 1988. Mem. MLA, Am. Dialect Soc., Dictionary Soc. N.Am. Home: Garrison, NY. Died Apr. 9, 2007.

BARRETT, BETTY ANNE, small business owner, interior designer; b. Antofagasta, Chile, Sept. 4, 1936; came to U.S., 1954; d. Oscar Garvens and Baxter (Gaines) Berger; m. John G. Barrett, Aug. 11, 1956 (div. Dec. 1977); children: John, Mark, Kevin, Jennifer, Gregory. Student, Santiago U., Chile, 1954. Asst. Mario Buatta, Inc., NYC, 1968-78; asst. to pres., office mgr. John F. Saladino, Inc., NYC, 1978-82; pres., owner Betty Barrett Inc., NYC, from 1982. Mem. Interior Design Network, Nat. Assn. Female Execs. Clubs: Vertical (N.Y.C.). Roman Catholic. Avocation: travel. Died July 17, 2007.

BARRON, LINDSEY HAND, real estate broker; b. Greenville, SC, Dec. 16, 1923; s. Zeddie Pleasant and Opal Carolyn (Hand) B.; m. Genet Louise Heery, May 22, 1948; children: Thomas W., Frank H. BBA, Emory U., 1944; grad., Northweston USN Midshipman Sch., 1944. Owner, pres. Coweta Developers, Inc., Newnan, 1962-79, with, from 1979; salesman Proctor & Gamble, Atlanta, 1947-48; owner, pres. Lindsey's, Inc., Newnan, Ga., 1948-79, chmn., from 1979. Bd. dirs. Newnan Hosp., 1969-79, Residential Care for Elderly of Coweta County, Newnan, 1996—, Wesley Woods Found., Atlanta, 1995—; pres. Newnan-Coweta United Way, 1979. Lt. USN, 1944-47, PTO. Named Coweta County Citizen of Yr., Optimist Club, Newnan, 1965. Mem. Newnan-Coweta Realtors Assn. (pres. 1968), Newnan Mchts. Assn. (pres. 1955), Newnan-Coweta C. of C. (pres. 1967, 75, Citizen of Yr. award 1996), Kiwanis (pres. Newnan 1948, George F. Hixson award 1995, Man of Half Century award 1975). Baptist. Avocations: reading, travel, spectator sports. Home: Newnan, Ga. Died June 16, 2007.

BARRY, MARION SHEPILOV, JR., city councilman, former mayor; b. Itta Bena, Miss., Mar. 6, 1936; s. Marion S. and Mattie Barry; m. Blantie Evans, 1962 (div. 1964); m. Mary M. Treadwell, 1972 (div. 1977); m. Effi Slaughter, 1978 (div. 1992); 1 son, Marion Christopher; m. Cora Lavonne Masters, 1994 (div.) BS in Chemistry, LeMoyne Owen Coll., 1958; MS, Fisk U., 1960; postgrad., U. Kans., 1960-61, U. Tenn., 1961-64. Dir. ops. Pride Inc., Washington, from 1967; co-founder, chmn., dir. Pride Econ. Enterprises Inc., Washington, 1968; mem. Washington DC Sch. Bd., 1971-74; councilman-at-large DC City Coun., Washington, 1974-78, 1992—94, councilman, Ward 8, 2005—14; mayor Washington, 1979—91, 1995—99. Appeared in (documentaries) The Nine Lives of Marion Barry, 2009; author (with Omar Tyree): Mayor for Life: The Incredible Story of Marion Barry, Jr., 2014. First nat. chmn. Student Nonviolent Coordinating Com. (SNCC); mem. 3d World Coalition Against the War. Mem.: Alpha Phi Alpha. Democrat. *If there is a single ideal which has guided and inspired me in both my private and public life it is the quest for the uniquely American principle of justice and fair play for all men and women. The promise of this elusive goal took me, as a young man, away from my doctoral studies and has since been a major force in the direction my life has taken.* Died Nov. 23, 2014.

BARRY, THOMAS WAYNE, program administrator; b. Jefferson City, Mo., May 17, 1950; s. Paul and Margaret Eleanor (Roche) B.; children: Jonathan, Claire, Matthew. BS in Bus. Adminstrn., Cen. Mo. State U., 1972; postgrad., U. Okla., 1986-88. Personnel dir. DeLong's Inc., Jefferson City, Mo., 1966-83; project mgr. advanced tech. sect. Mo. Dept. Econ. Devel., Jefferson City, 1985, project mgr. small bus. programs, 1985-87, coord. high tech. programs, 1987-92, mgr. Mo. tech. programs, from 1992. Bd. dirs. Jefferson City Coun. Arts, 1977-79, Jefferson City Area United Way, 1977-85; treas., v.p., pres. Lincoln U. Found., 1977-82; mem. Mayor's Adv. Commn. of Jefferson City, 1979; mem. Jefferson City Police Pers. Bd., 1979-82; mem. Jefferson City Planning and Zoning Commn., 1983-87; trustee Mo. Jr. Acad. Sci., 1988, Mo. Inventors Assn., 1988, Jefferson City Libr., 1991, Thomas Jefferson Regional Libr., 1991; mem. Jefferson City Indsl. Devel. Authority, 1988; mem. Mo. Indsl. Devel. Coun. Named one of Outstanding Young Men Am., 1979, 81; recipient citation for svc. SBA, 1986, Flying Eagle award Mo. Acad. Sci., 1989. Roman Catholic. Home: Overland Park, Kans. Died Apr. 19, 2007.

BARTA, MARIE LAURA, music educator, church organist; b. Manly, Iowa, Oct. 4, 1917; d. Edward Francis and Katherine (Koci) B. Student, Drake U., 1957-60. state and nationally certified through Music Tchrs. Nat. Assn. Music tchr. pub. schs., Fertile, Iowa, 1936-61, Hanlontown, Iowa, 1936-60, Grafton, Iowa, 1959-63; tchr. music ind. studio Mason City, Iowa, 1960-88, Manly, 1988-97. Recipient Disting. Service award Nat. Guild Piano Tchrs., 1988; inducted into Nat. Piano Guild Hall of fame, 1991. Mem. Am. Coll. Musicians (adjudicator Austin, Tex. 1970-90, del. to Europe and USSR, 1976), Music Tchrs. North Iowa (sec.-treas. 1980—), Iowa Music Tchrs. Assn. (corresponding sec. 1985-88, historian 1988-90), Music Tchrs. Nat. Assn. (cert. local and nat. chpts.). Clubs: Pilot (Mason City) (pres. 1971-73, 1975-76), Women's Internat. Service. Lutheran. Avocations: knitting, reading. Home: Mason City, Iowa. Died July 25, 2007.

BARTH, ERNEST A.T., sociologist, educator; b. NYC, June 30, 1924; s. Ernest Albert and Jeanette Elvira (Thomson) B.; m. Grace Leone Williams (div. 1972); children: William Thomson, Georgia Jean, Donna, Joseph; m. Dorlous Schatz, 1993. BS in Psychology, U. Rochester, 1950; MA in Sociology, U. N.C., 1949, PhD in Sociology, 1953. From instr. to prof. sociology U. Wash., Seattle, 1950-88, prof. emeritus, from 1988. Author: Sandy's Gift, 1996, Grandpa Tom Tells Stories of Robin, 1996. Democrat. Home: Seattle, Wash. Died Feb. 22, 2007.

BARTHELMAS, NED KELTON, brokerage house and real estate executive; b. Circleville, Ohio, Oct. 22, 1927; s. Arthur and Mary Bernice (Riffel) B.; m. Marjorie Jane Livezey, May 23, 1953; children: Brooke Ann, Richard Thomas. BS in Bus. Adminstrn., Ohio State U., 1950. Stockbroker Ohio Co., Columbus, 1953-58; pres. First Columbus Securities Corp., from 1958; pres., dir. Ohio Fin. Corp., Columbus, from 1960; pres. Thwirs, Inc., Columbus, from 1986. Trustee, chmn. Am. Guardian Fin., Republic Fin.; bd. dirs. Nat. Foods, Midwest Capital Corp., Capital Equity Corp., Midwest Nat. Corp., 1st Columbus Realty Corp., Dublin Nat. Corp. (all Columbus); former mem. bd. dirs. adviser to Wonthington Industries, Banc One Corp, Lancaster Colony, Nationwide Ins., Easter Bancorp., Republic Industries, Medex Corp. Buckeye Steel Corp, Marzetti Foods, Liebert Corp., Eastern Bancorp, Medex Corp, Nat. Foods, White Castle Systems, and more. Served with Adj. Gen.'s Dept., AUS, 1944-47. Recipient Merit award, State of Ohio, 2001. Mem. Nat. Assn. Securities Dealers (past vice chmn. dist. bd. govs.), Investment Bankers Assn. (exec. com. 1973), Investment Dealers Ohio (sec., treas. 1956-72, pres. 1973), Nat. Stock Traders Assn., Young Pres.'s Orgn. (pres. 1971), World Bus. Coun., Columbus Pres.'s Assn., Nat. Investment Bankers (pres. 1973), Internat. Real Estate Inst., Columbus Jr. C. of C. (pres. 1956), World's Pres.'s Assn. (Exec. Hall of Fame award 1993), Columbus Area C. of C. (dir. 1956, named an Outstanding Young Man of Columbus 1962), Newcomen Soc., Coun. for Ethics in Econs., Coun. of Orgn. of Am. States, Winston Churchill's Wisdom Hall of Fame, Internat. Soc. Financiers, Oxford Club, Nat. Assn. Appraisers, Execs. Club, Pres.' Club (Ohio State U.), Internat. Platform Assn., Stock and Bond Club (past pres.), named top 25 corp. Dirs. (1984-90), Founders Club, World War II Meml. Mus., Columbus Club, Scioto Country Club, Crystal Downs Country Club, Ohio State U. Faculty Club, Wrigley Mansion Club (Ariz.), Kiwanis (legion of honor 1992), Am. Legion, Columbus Admirals Club, Alpha Kappa Psi, Phi Delta Theta (Golden Legion award). Home: Columbus, Ohio. Died May 16, 2015.

BARTHOLOMEW, CARROLL EUGENE, minister; b. Brookford, NC, Feb. 10, 1935; s. Gerald Fredrick and Clarissa (Cloninger) B.; m. Jane Harriet Young, June 25, 1961; children: Gerald Lee, Nathaniel Thomas. BS in Physics and Math., Lenoir-Rhyne Coll., 1960; BD (with honors), Lancaster Theol. Sem., 1963, MDiv, 1975, D of Ministry, 1982. Ordained to ministry United Ch. of Christ, 1963. Pastor Brick United Ch. of Christ, Whitsett, N.C., 1963-66; commd. lt. (j.g.) USN, 1966, advanced through grades to comdr., 1978; detailed to Field Med. Sch., USMC Base, Camp Pendleton, Calif., 1966, 3d Marine Div., Republic of Vietnam, 1966-67, Naval Air Sta., Cecil Field, Fla., 1967-69; various assignments, 1969-1977; detailed to 2d Marine Div., Camp Lejeune, N.C., 1977-79, Naval Dist. Washington, 1979-81, Naval Mil. Personnel Command, 1981-83; served on USS Mt. Whitney, 1983-85; detailed to Naval Air Sta., Oceana, Virginia Beach, Va., 1985-87, 88-90, COMSERVGRU 2, 1987-88; ret., 1990; pastor St. Luke's United Ch. of Christ, Salisbury, N.C., from 1990. Mem. So. Conf. United Ch. of Christ Christian Edn. Commn.; bd. dirs. Franklinton Ctr. at Bricks Inc. Author: A Program of Training and a Training Manual for Religious Lay Leaders Within the United States Marine Corps, 1982. Vol. chaplain Rowan Meml. Hosp. Sgt. USMC, 1953-56. Decorated Vietnam Svc. Medal with Bronze Star, Combat Action Ribbon; Gallantry Cross (Republic of Vietnam). Mem. Rowan Ministerium, Salisbury Rowan Ministerium, Civitan. Democrat. Home: Newton, NC. Died Mar. 10, 2007.

BARTLETT, RICHARD JAMES, retired lawyer; b. Glens Falls, NY, Feb. 15, 1926; s. George Willard and Kathryn M. (McCarthy) Bartlett; m. Claire E. Kennedy, Aug. 18, 1951 (dec. Apr. 9, 2010); children: Michael, Amy. BS, Georgetown U., 1945; LLB, Harvard U., 1949; LLD (hon.), Union Coll., 1974; ScD (hon.), Albany Med. Coll., 1986. Bar: N.Y. 1949. Pvt. practice, Glens Falls, 1949-73; mem. NY Assembly, 1959—66, Clark Bartlett & Caffry, 1962—73; justice NY State Supreme Ct., 1973-79; chief adminstr. judge NY State, 1974-79; dean Albany Law Sch., Union U., 1979-86; principal Bartlett, Pontiff, Stewart, & Rhodes P.C., Glens Falls, 1986—2010. Chair NY Penal

Law Commn., 1961—70; mem. NY Bd. Law Examiners, 1986—2001, chair, 1998—2001; chmn. NY Jud. Commn. Justice for Children, 1988—90; trustee Nat. Conf. Bd. Examiners, 1987—97, chair, 1996; dir. Nat. Conf. Bar Founds., 2001—03; del. NY Constl. Conv., 1967; dir. Arrow Fin. Corp and Glen Falls Nat. Bank and Trust Co., 1967—73, 1979—96. Trustee Hyde Collection, Glens Falls, 1967—98. Capt. USAF, 1951—53. Recipient Herbert Harley award, American Judicature Soc., 1995, Judge Duane award, Northern Dist. of NY Fed. Ct. Bar Assn., 2004, William Nelson Cromwell award, NY County Lawyers Assn., 2006; co-recipient Good Scout award, Boy Scouts, 2006. Fellow: Am. Bar Found.; mem.: ABA (ho. dels. 1997—2001), NY State Bar Assn. (ho. dels. 2002—06, Gold medal 2004), NY Bar Found. (bd. dirs. 1989—2006, pres. 2000—03), American Law Inst. (life), Warren County Bar (Charles Evans Hughes award 2002). Republican. Roman Catholic. Died May 6, 2015.

BARTLEY, DEE GRAY, information technology executive; b. Lytle, Tex. d. William McMurrian Gray and Velma Gladys McNiel; m. William Call Bartley, July 14, 1956; children: Carol Sue Bartley-Gourlas, Gregory William, Christopher Gray. MusB, San Antonio Coll., 1955; student, Mich. State U., East Lansing, 1960. Adminstrv. asst. procurement 17th Air Force, Tripoli, Libya, 1956—58; adminstrv. asst. to dir. Office Naval Intelligence, Dallas, 1960—63; asst. to pres. Grad. Rsch. Ctr., U. Tex., Richardson, 1963—66; personal asst. Senator A. Bible, U.S. Senate, Washington, 1967—74; appointments asst. Senator H. Jackson, U.S. Senate, Washington, 1975—82; protocol asst. to U.S. rep. UN/U.S. Mission, Geneva, 1982—88; protocol coord. Dept. State Arms Control U.S. Mission, Geneva, 1984—87; profl. staff Spkr. House Reps., 1989, Senate Majority Leader, Washington, 1990—93; assoc. Bartley Technologies Inc., Bandera, Tex., 1995—2009. Coord. U.S. Mex. Inter-Parliamentary Group, U.S. Senate Leadership, San Antonio, Boston, Cabo San Lucas, 1990—93; coord. nat. hist. site Tor House U.S. Senate Interior Com., Carmel, Calif., 1972—73; coord. land acquisition Einstein sculpture Nat. Acad. Sci., Washington, 1975—76. Editor: Science in Space, 1967. Fundraising coord. Internat. Red Cross Hdqrs., Geneva, 1987; fundraiser Bandera H.S. Chorale Group, 2005; mem. exec. com., bd. trustees, sec. Frontier Times Mus., 1998—2007; mem., fundraiser chair Friends Kronkosky Libr. Bandera County, from 2001; chair Bishop's Visits & Luncheons, 2004—11; chair and construction project dir. Ch. Interior Renovation, 2008—09; co-organizer music fund St. Christopher's Episc. Ch., Bandera, 2005, chair spl. events, 2007—11, chair culinary and kitchen planning com., 2008—09; mem. Altar Guild St. Christopher's Parish, 1999—2010; chair ch. Cemetery Com., 2009—11; chair St. Chris Meml. Garden Com.; dir. Construction of New Courtvard Project, 2010—11. Recipient Cert. of Appreciation for svc. 1984-86, U.S. Dept. State, 1986, Grateful Recognition honors, U.S. Senate, 1979, Outstanding Svc. award, U. Tex. System, 1966. Mem.: Bandera Fine Arts Club (nominating com. 1996). Episcopalian. Avocations: gardening, music. Home: Bandera, Tex. Died May 13, 2014.

BARTON, GAIL BARBARA, elementary and secondary education educator; b. Rockville Centre, NY, Dec. 23, 1950; d. John Charles and Winifred (Klinck) Jansen; m. David J. Barton, Nov. 23, 1974 (div. Nov. 4, 1988); children: Timothy D., Cori E.; m. Richard C. Girnius, July 13, 1991; stepchildren: Tracy, Jason. BS in Edn. in Phys. Edn., SUNY, Cortland, 1973; MA in Health Edn., Adelphi U., 1977; SDA/SAS in Adminstrn., C.W. Post Ctr., L.I. U., 1992. Cert. phys. and health edn., N.Y. Tchr. phys. edn. and health, girls' basketball coach Union Free Sch. Dist. 6, Port Jefferson, N.Y., from 1973. Advisor student govt.; supr. rewriting sch. constn. and restructuring student activities program, 1986-90, 94-95; mem. dist. drug free schs. com.; tchr. math. and phys. edn., dir. athletics, 1994-95; asst. prin., athletic dir. Port Jefferson Middle Sch., 1993-94. Tchr., supt. Sunday sch. 1st United Meth. Ch., Port Jefferson, 1978-80; coach Port Jefferson Soccer League, 1986; basketball coach Police Athletic League, Port Jefferson, 1984—; supr. basketball program PAL, 1990-91. Named C.W. Post-L.I. U. scholar, 1990-91; recipient several coaching awards, 1990-93. Mem. ASCD, AAHPERD, N.Y. State Assn. Health, Phys. Edn., Recreation and Dance (v.p.-elect secondary edn. Suffolk zone 1994-95), Human Understanding and Growth Seminars (adult asst. 1991). Avocations: hiking, basketball, gardening. Home: East Patchogue, NY. Died June 19, 2007.

BARTON, HUGH PERRY, bank executive; b. Modesto, Calif., Apr. 6, 1932; s. Robert Paul and Alice B.; m. Sheila Grieve, Dec. 29, 1954; children: Elizabeth, James. BS, U. Calif., Berkeley, 1954. Pres., CEO R.P. Barton & Co., Escalon, Calif., 1955-91; chair bd. Modesto (Calif.) Banking Co., 1977-94, Barton McLean & Waters, San Francisco, 1992-97; dir. Bank of Los Altos, Calif., from 1994, Heritage Commerce Corp., San Jose, Calif., 2000—02; chmn., dir. Pvt. Bank of the Peninsula, Palo Alto, Calif., from 2003. Recipient Salvation Army Order of Disting. Aux. award, 2005. Mem. Carmel Valley Ranch Golf Club, Pebble Beach Tennis Club, Old Capitol Club. Republican. Episcopalian. Home: Monterey, Calif. Died Nov. 20, 2013.

BARTOSZEWSKI, WLADYSLAW, former Polish government official; b. Feb. 19, 1922; m. Antonina Mijal (div.); m. Zofia Bartoszewski, 1967; 1 child, Wladyslaw Teofil. Ambassador to Austria, Poland, 1990—95; min. fgn. affairs Govt. of Poland, Warsaw, 1995—2002; chmn. Internat. Auscwitz Council; pres. Polish Pen Club, 2002. Died Apr. 24, 2015.

BASE, STEVE RICHARD, soil scientist; b. Gooding, Idaho, Apr. 24, 1939; s. Stephen and Lucille (Lewis) B.; m. Barbara Lee Anderson, July 1, 1980. BS, U. Idaho, 1962, MS, 1969. Soil scientist Soil Conservation Svc. USDA, Idaho Falls, Idaho, 1962-64, St. Anthony, Idaho, 1964-66, Moscow, Idaho, 1966-68, party leader, 1968-70, Grangeville, Idaho, 1970-73, soil scientist Bismarck, N.D., 1973-77, Lincoln, Nebr., from 1977. With U.S. Army, 1957-58. Scholar Pacific NW Plant Food Assn., 1961, Union Pacific, 1959. Mem. Soil Sci. Soc. Am., Alpha Zeta. Home: Lincoln, Nebr. Died Apr. 30, 2007.

BASKIN, ARNOLD M., urologist, educator; b. Albany, NY, Jan. 15, 1927; m. Myrna Fenn, Mar. 20, 1956; children: Suzanne, Nancy. BS, Union Coll.; MD, Albany Med. Coll.; postgrad., Yale U. Diplomate Am. Bd. Urology. Intern Yale-New Haven Hosp., 1952-53, resident in surgery, 1953-55, asst. resident in urology, 1955-56, chief resident urology, 1956-57, fellow in urology, faculty, 1957-58, asst. clin. prof. urology, mem. attending staff; attending surgeon urology Hosp. St. Raphael, New Haven. Mem. life sci. com. NASA. Contbr. articles to profl. jours. Fellow Sloan Kettering Meml. Hosp. Fellow ACS; mem. AMA, Am. Urology Assn. North Ea. Sect., N.Y. Yacht Club. Avocation: boating. Home: North Haven, Conn. Died Jan. 10, 2007.

BASSETT, LESLIE RAYMOND, composer, educator; b. Hanford, Calif., Jan. 22, 1923; s. Archibald Leslie and Vera (Starr) B.; m. Anita Elizabeth Denniston, Aug. 21, 1949; children Wendy Lynn (Mrs. Lee Bratton), Noel Leslie, Ralph (dec.). BA in Music, Fresno State Coll., 1947; M.Music in Composition, U. Mich., 1949, A.Mus.D., 1956; student, Ecole Normale de Musique, Paris, France, 1950-51; DFA (hon.), Calif. State U., Fresno, 2009. Tchr. music pub. schs., Fresno, 1951-52; mem. faculty U. Mich., from 1952, prof. music, from 1965, Albert A. Stanley disting univ. prof., 1977—92, Albert A. Stanley disting univ. prof. emeritus, 1992—2016, chmn. composition dept., 1970, Henry Russel lectr., 1984. Guest composer Berkshire Music Center, Tanglewood, Mass., 1973 Served with AUS, 1942- 46. Fulbright fellow, 1950-51; recipient Rome prize Am. Acad. in Rome, 1961-63; grantee Soc. Pub. Am. Music, 1960, Nat. Inst. Arts and Letters, 1964, Nat. Council Arts, 1966; Guggenheim fellow, 1973-74, 80-81; recipient Pulitzer prize in music for Variations for Orch., 1966; citation U. Mich. regents, 1966; Walter Naumburg Found. rec. award for Sextet, 1974; Disting. Alumnus award Calif. State U., Fresno, 1978; Disting. Artist award Mich. Council Arts, 1981; Citation of Merit, U. Mich. Sch. Music Alumni, 1980 Mem. Am. Composers Alliance, Mich. Soc. Fellows, Am. Acad. of Arts and Letters, Pi Kappa Lambda, Phi Kappa Phi, Phi Mu Alpha. Methodist. Home: Flowery Branch, Ga. Died Feb. 4, 2016.

BATES, ROBERT EDWARD, JR., personnel director; b. St. Louis, July 13, 1947; s. Robert Edward and Ann Shaw (Liggett) B.; m. Susan Elizabeth Spear, Dec. 19, 1970 (div. Aug. 1984); children: Robert E. III, Andrew Thomas; m. Sandra Jeanette Leith, Sept. 15, 1984. BS, U. Mich., 1969, MBA, 1971. Auditor Peat, Marwick, Mitchell & Co., Albany, N.Y., 1971-72; field sales mgr. Ford Motor Co., Dearborn, Mich., 1972-81; staff asst. to pres. Cars of Concepts Inc., Brighton, Mich., 1981-84; dir. adminstrn. ADP Network Services, Ann Arbor, Mich., from 1984. Instr. Dale Carnegie Assn., Southfield, Mich., 1978-83. Asst. chmn. United Way, Livingston County, Mich., 1983. Republican. Presbyterian. Avocations: world war ii aircraft, sports, travel. Home: Brighton, Mich. Died Jan. 8, 2007.

BATES, ROGER GORDON, chemist, educator; b. Cummington, Mass., May 20, 1912; s. Rollin Elder and Nellie Reid (Robbins) B.; m. Jo Jones, Sept. 9, 1941; 1 child, May Joan Bates Daw. BS, U. Mass., 1934; MA, Duke U., 1936, PhD, 1937. Sterling rsch. fellow Yale U., New Haven, 1937-39; rsch. chemist Nat. Bur. Standards, Washington, 1939-56, chief electrochem. analysis sect., 1956-69; prof. chemistry U. Fla., Gainesville, 1969-79, prof. emeritus, from 1979. USPHS fellow, U. Zurich, Switzerland, 1953-54. Author: Electrometric ph Determinations, 1954, Determination of ph, Theory and Practice, 1964, 2nd edit., 1973; contbr. over 275 articles to profl. jours. Recipient Hillebrand award, Am. Chem. Soc., 1955, Analytical Chemistry award, 1969, Exceptional Svc. award, U.S. Dept. Commerce, 1957, Anachem award, 1983. Fellow AAAS, Am. Inst. Chemists. Republican. Episcopalian. Died Aug. 20, 2007.

BATESON, MARION, entrepreneur, interior designer; b. Dallas, Aug. 6, 1935; d. Joseph Weldon and Marion (Monroe) B.; m. John Gibbert Rowe, May 24, 1955 (dec. 1967); children: Candy Ward, Cathy Rowe, Amy Folse. Grad., Design Inst. of San Diego, 1978-79. Owner Marion Bateson Interior Design, La Jolla, Calif., from 1980. Bd. dirs. San Diego Opera, 1987-90, Salvation Army, 1987-90, Door of Hope, 1987-90. Mem. La Jolla Beach and Tennis Club. Republican. Presbyterian. Avocations: bridge, walking, theater, travel, opera, symphony. Home: La Jolla, Calif. Died Feb. 26, 2007.

BATT, MILES GIRARD, artist; b. Nazareth, Pa., Oct. 12, 1933; s. Miles Edward and Phyllis (Thalia) B.; m. Irene Evangeline Charles Batt, June 15, 1951; children: Miles G. Jr., Bradford. Grad., Allentown (Pa.) High Sch., 1951. Pvt. practice, Ft. Lauderdale, Fla., from 1957. Author: Com Guide Creative Watercolor, 1988. Recipient 6 awards Hortt Meml. Ft. Lauderdale Mus., 1971-91, 5 awards Soc. of Four Arts, 1972-91, 6 awards Watercolor U.S.A. Honor Soc., 1981-98. Mem. Nat. Watercolor Soc. (11 awards 1970-98), So. Watercolor Soc. (9 awards 1977-91), Rocky Mountain Nat. Watercolor Soc. (7 awards 1977-96), Am. Watercolor Soc., Fla. Watercolor Soc. (11 awards 1972-98), Ga. Watercolor Soc. (86 additional nat. awards). Avocations: travel, sailing, collecting art books. Home: Fort Lauderdale, Fla. Died Nov. 20, 2015.

BATTJES, CARL ROBERT, electrical engineer; b. Grand Rapids, Mich., Dec. 30, 1929; s. Harold A. and Helen (Bolt) B.; m. Grace Lydia Battjes, Apr. 5, 1953 (div. 1979). BSEE, U. Mich., 1958; MSEE, Stanford U., 1960. Registered profl. engr., Oreg. Sr. engr. Sylvania Mt. View (Calif.) Labs., 1958-61; prin. engr. Tektronix, Inc., Beaverton, Oreg., 1961-83; pvt. practice Portland, Oreg., from 1983. Vis. prof. U. Calif., Berkeley, 1974. Contbr. articles to profl. jours.; patentee in field. 1st lt. USAF, 1950-55. Died Apr. 28, 2007.

BAUERLE, JAMES ERNEST, oral surgeon; b. Hamilton Pool, Tex., Sept. 24, 1923; s. Ernest and Nancy Ima Bauerle; m. Frances Irene Tankers, June 25, 1945 (div. Sept. 1979); children: Frances Diane, Nancy Lea, Janet Elizabeth; m. Charlotte Margaret Ehlers, May 27, 1983. BS in Pharmacy, U. Tex., 1943; DDS, St. Louis U., 1946; MS in Oral Surgery, U. Pitts., 1950; LLD, U. Tex., 1969. Regent U. Tex. System, Austin, 1973—79, chmn. bldg. & grounds, 1975—79; clin. prof. oral surgery U. Tex. Health Sci. Ctr., San Antonio, from 1979; Bauelre prof. U. Tex. Coll. Pharmacy, Austin, 1982. Capt. US Army, 1950—52. Recipient Alumni Merit award, St. Louis U., 1973. Fellow: Am. Coll. Dental & Maxilofacial Surgeons, Internat. Coll. Dentists, Am. Coll. Dentists, Royal Soc. Health (life); mem.: San Antonio Assn. Oral and Maxillofacial Surgeons, Soc. Advancement Gen. Anesthesia in Dentustry (life), Tex. Dental Assn. (life), Fedn. Dentaire Internat. (life), Tex. Pharm. Assn. (hon.), Am. Assn. Oral and Maxillofacial Surgeons, Tex. State Bd. Dental Examiners, San Antonio Breakfast Club (pres. 1968—2003), Scottish Rite, Masons, Rho Chi, Delta Sigma Delta. Republican. Prsbyterian. Avocation: ranching. Home: San Antonio, Tex. Died Feb. 6, 2007.

BAUMAN, DAVID BENJAMIN, minister; b. Angol, Araucania, Chile, Aug. 28, 1919; (parents Am. citizens); s. Ezra and Florence (Carhart) B.; m. Faith Erma Weber, Dec. 9, 1955; children: Mark Stephen, Philip David. AB, U. Denver, 1941; STB, Boston U., 1945. Ordained deacon United Meth. Ch., 1945, elder, 1947. Pastor United Meth. Ch., Gardiner, Oreg., 1944-49; missionary Bd. Global Ministries, served in tchr. children's Christian edn., dir. summer camps, dist. supt. Gujarat Conf. Meth. Ch. in India, 1951-86; pastor Zion United Meth. Ch., Elyria, Ohio, from 1987. Del. Gen. Conf. Meth. Ch. in India. Mem. Grange, Sr. Fellowship Club. Home: Lorain, Ohio. Died May 23, 2007.

BAUMHOVER, ALFRED HENRY, entomologist, researcher; b. Carroll, Iowa, June 17, 1921; s. Anthony Henry and Josephine Mary Baumhover; children: Judith B. Belch, Janiece B. Bladen. BS in Zoology and Entomology, Iowa State U., 1949. Area supr. grasshopper control USDA, Great Falls, Mont., 1949—50, rsch. entomologist insects-man and animals Orlando, Fla., 1951—57, field ops. entomologist screwworm eradication Sebring, Fla., 1958—59, rsch. entomologist fruits and vegetables Honolulu, 1960, rsch. entomologist man and animals Kerrville, Tex., 1961, rsch. leader screwworm eradication Mission, Tex., 1962—65, investigations leader tobacco insects Oxford, NC, 1966—84; ret., 1984. Contbr. articles to profl. jours. Avocations: gourmet cooking, gardening, photography. Home: Carrboro, NC. Died Feb. 18, 2007.

BAUS, RUTH BRUMME, stockbroker; b. NYC, Aug. 20, 1917; d. Richard Paul and Emilie (Waller) Brumme; m. Herbert M. Baus, July 11, 1937 (div. 1951). Student, UCLA, 1935-37. Stockbroker Walston & Co., LA, 1960-74, Crowell Weedon & Co., LA, from 1974. Author: Who's Running This Expedition, 1957. Founding mem. UCLA Friends of Archeology, L.A., 1966; pres. com. profl. women L.A. Philharm., 1972—. Avocations: travel, photography, gourmet cooking, music. Home: Los Angeles, Calif. Died Feb. 1, 2007.

BAXTER, RONALD STEPHEN, pharmacist; b. Jacksonville, Fla., Aug. 24, 1950; s. Thomas Jackson and Mary Louise (Walker) B.; m. Terry Ann Glisson, Dec. 31, 1954; 1 child, William Blair. BS in Pharmacy, Northeast La. U., 1977. Pharmacist, mgr. Pearson #3, Alexandria, La., from 1978. Served with USN, 1969-73, Vietnam. Republican. Baptist. Home: Pineville, La. Died Aug. 8, 2007.

BEAL, MERRILL DAVID, conservationist, museum director; b. Richfield, Utah, June 26, 1926; s. Merrill Dee and Bessy (Neill) B.; m. Jean Lorraine Wood, Feb. 24, 1947; children: John David, James Merrill. BA, Idaho State Coll., 1950; MS, Utah State U., 1952. Park ranger, naturalist Yellowstone Nat. Park, 1953-60; chief park naturalist Grand Canyon Nat. Park, 1960-69; asst. supt. Great Smoky Mountains Nat. Park, Gatlinburg, Tenn., 1969-72; assoc. regional dir. Midwest region Nat. Park Service, Omaha, 1972-75, regional dir., 1975-78; supt. Gt. Smoky Mountains Nat. Park, Gatlinburg, Tenn., 1978-83; asst. dir. Ariz.-Sonora Desert Mus., Tucson, 1983-91. Author: Grand Canyon, the Story Behind the Scenery, 1967. Mem. bd. Grand Canyon Sch., 1964-69. Served with USN, 1944-46. Recipient Meritorious Svc. award US Dept. Interior, 1975. Mem. Wildlife Soc., Gt. Smoky Mountains Natural History Assn. (bd. dirs. 1993-95), S.W. Parks and Monument Assn., Ea. Nat. Park and Monument Assn. (bd. dirs. 1989-95), Sigma Xi. Home: Eugene, Oreg. Died Sept. 21, 2010; Grand Canyon, Pioneer Cemetery.

BEAL, WINONA ROARK, retired church administrator; b. Birchwood, Tenn., Aug. 11, 1924; d. Thomas Jefferson and Minnie Belle (Price) Roark; m. Charles Hugh Beal, Aug. 6, 1949; children: Jeremy Lawrence, Eric David. BSBA, Tenn. Tech. U., 1948; postgrad., So. Bapt. Theol. Sem., 1950-54, U. Louisville, 1951-53, Manatee C.C., 1958-60. Tchr. Washington (Ga.) H.S., 1948-50; asst. to treas. So. Bapt. Theol. Sem., Louisville, Ky., 1951-54; asst. to bus. mgr. Agnes Scott Coll., Decatur, Ga., 1968-71;

religious edn. dir. Bay Haven Bapt. Ch., Sarasota, Fla., 1976-84, office program dir., 1985-89; ret., 1989. Spiritual guide, dir. Bay Haven Elem. Sch., Sarasota, 1965-68; mem. Sapphire Stores-Indian Beach Assn., Sarasota, 1985-2000, State Bd. Missions, Fla. Bapt. Conv., 1993-95, re-elected 96-99, mem. program com., 1993-94. 94-95, 98-99, loans com. 1995-98, state bd. missions. Past pres. Tech Christian Assn.; past pres. chorus Tenn. Tech. U., past v.p. associated student body, past v.p., treas., capt. basketball team bus. club, past v.p. Bapt. student union, past v.p. student coun., past mem. staff publs. Oracle, Eagle. Mem. S.W. Fla. Bapt. Assn. (dir. 4 world missions confs. 1976, 81, 88, 92, mem. exec. com. 1976-99, dir. Vacation Bible Sch. 1976-89, student work 1976-80, clk. 1994-98), S.W. Manatee Assn. (pres. of Metochai), Pastors Wives of S.W. Fla. Assn. (pres. 1972, 80, 84-89), Fla. Pastors' Wives Conf. (v.p. 1975, program chair 1979, sec.-treas. 1983, conf. historian 1983), Pi Omega Pi (past pres.). Democrat. *I believe that the greatest profanity is not of the lips but of the life.* Died Jan. 5, 2007.

BEARD, PATRICIA CLAIRE, minister, apparel designer; b. Commerce, Tex., Jan. 27, 1944; d. Herbert Alton and Laura Helen Stanford; m. Wayne Forrest Beard, Jr., Sept. 14, 1963; 1 adopted child, Trina Lynn Anderson (dec.). Student, Bus. Computer Sys., 1968; AA in Practical Theology, Christ for the Nations Inst., 1978. 25 mastered competition pieces level Nat. Piano Competition. Keypunch oper. and supr. various maj. oil and banking cos., Dallas and Houston, 1968—76; min. Full Gospel Chs. and Min. Internat., Dallas, from 1978; owner, designer Cana Creations Design Co., Lake Dallas, Tex., from 1980. Costumer, head costumer Scarborough Renaissance Faire, Waxahachie, Tex., 1995—2000; lifestyle and family counselor Cana Creations, Dallas and Lake Dallas, from 1980. Precinct del. Dallas County Dem. Conv., 1988; alternate state del. Dallas County Rep. State Conv., Dallas, 1988; entertainer, singer USO, Dallas, 1960—62. Scholar, East Tex. State U., 1962—63. Republican. Avocations: needlecrafts, painting. Home: Lake Dallas, Tex. Died Mar. 2, 2007.

BEASLEY, TROY DANIEL, secondary education educator; b. Whitestone, Ga., Dec. 5, 1942; s. Amos Daniel and Imogene (Duckett) B.; m. Debbie L. Jones, Feb. 23, 1985; children: Flannery Meghan, Annalise Sarah, Ammelia Katherine. BA, Ga. State U., 1973, MA, 1981. Cert. tchr., Ga. Tchr. English, drama and theatre Murray County H.S., Chatsworth, Ga., from 1973; tchr. Rinehardt Coll., Waleska, Ga., 1975-96. Del. Gov. Ga. Conf. on Edn., Atlanta, 1993. Staff sgt. USAF, 1963-68. Recipient Star Tchr. award Ga. C. of C., 1976, 77, 82, 85, 86, 94. Mem. Nat. Assn. Educators, Nat. Coun. Tchrs. English, Ga. Assn. Educators, Ga. Coun. Tchrs. English, Murray Assn. Educators (pres. 1983-85). Democrat. Roman Catholic. Avocations: theater, reading, swimming, movies. Home: Chatsworth, Ga. Died Mar. 19, 2007.

BEAVER, CARL R., marine scientist, educator, consultant; s. Robert and Phyllis Beaver; m. Robinn Crawford, Mar. 23, 2001; 1 child, Jennifer. BS, Corpus Christi State U.; MS, Tex. A&M U., Corpus Christi; D of Wildlife and Fisheries Sci., Tex. A&M U., College Station. Rsch. assoc. Ctr. for Coastal Studies, Corpus Christi, 1993—2000; prof. Our Lady of Corpus Christi Coll., 2001—03; postdoctoral rsch. assoc. Harte Rsch. Inst. for Gulf of Mex. Sci., Corpus Christi, 2002—03; assoc. rsch. scientist Fish & Wildlife Rsch. Inst., St. Petersburg, Fla., from 2003. Chief scientist Eco-Tones, Riverview, Fla., from 1999. Author: State of the Coral Reefs of the World, Fisheries, Reefs and Offshore Development. Mem. Sci. Diving Control Bd., Tex. State Aquarium, Corpus Christi, 2000—04. Mem.: Am. Fisheries Soc. (assoc.), Am. Assn. Underwater Scientists (assoc.). Home: Riverview, Fla. Died Dec. 18, 2006.

BECK, ANATOLE, mathematician, educator; b. Bronx, NY, Mar. 19, 1930; s. Morris and Minnie (Rosenblum) B.; m. Evelyn Torton, Apr. 10, 1954 (div.); children— Nina Rachel, Micah Daniel; m. Eve-Lynn Siegel, Nov. 30, 2003. BA, Bklyn. Coll., 1951; MS, Yale U., 1953, PhD, 1956. Instr. math. Williams Coll., Williamstown, Mass., 1955-56; Office Naval Rsch. rsch. assoc. Tulane U., New Orleans, 1956-57; traveling fellow Yale U., 1957—58; from asst. to assoc. prof. U. Wis., Madison, 1958—66, prof. math., from 1966; chair of math. London Sch. Econ./U. London, 1973—75. Vis. prof. Cornell U., 1960, Hebrew U., Jerusalem, 1964-65, U. Göttingen, Fed. Republic Germany, 1965, U. Warwick, 1968, Imperial Coll., U. London, 1969, U. Erlangen, Fed. Republic Germany, 1969, U. Md., 1971, Tech. U. Munich, Fed. Republic Germany, 1973, London Sch. Econs. and Univ. Coll., U. London, 1985, 91-92, 94-97, 99—; v.p. Wis. Fedn. Tchrs., 1975-83; co-founder Wis. U. Union, 1984, pres., 1988-91. Author: Continuous Flows in the Plane, 1974, (with M.N. Bleicher and D.W. Crowe) Excursions into Mathematics, 1969, 2d edit., 2000, The Knowledge Business, 1997; contbr. articles to profl. jours. Recipient Disting. Alumnus award, Bklyn. Coll., 1976. Mem. Am. Math. Soc. (council 1973-75), Math. Assn. Am., AAUP, Sigma Xi, Phi Beta Kappa, Pi Mu Epsilon. Home: Madison, Wis. Died Dec. 21, 2014.

BECK, BERNARD ODELL, retired physics laboratory apparatus designer; b. Manilla, Iowa, Feb. 17, 1914; s. Theron O. and Effie (Flint) B.; m. Adalene Lacey, Feb. 15, 1943; children: Dennis, Barbara, William. AB, Yankton Coll., SD, 1937. Supr. devel. of tech. equipment Air Corps Tech. Sch., Amarillo, Tex., 1942-45; lab. and rsch. designer, physics dept. U. Tex., Arlington, 1959-67; owner Bernard O. Beck & Co., Arlington, from 1965. Sgt. USAAC, 1940-45. Mem. Am. Assn. Physics Tchrs. Achievements include design of a ballistic pendulum and other apparatus for basic mechanics physics laboratories. Home: Arlington, Tex. Died June 17, 2007.

BECKER, BRUCE D., lawyer; b. Cleve., Feb. 12, 1954; s. Benjamin F. Becker and Marilyn (Winograd) Blaushild; m. Melinda S. Greenberg, Aug. 19, 1984; children: Julie, Adam. BA, Yale U., 1976; JD, Harvard U., 1979. Assoc. Isham Lincoln & Beale, Chgo., 1979-84; counsel Allnet Comms., Chgo., 1984-86; gen. atty. United Air Lines, Chgo., 1986-88; counsel Ameritech Corp., Chgo., from 1988. Mem. ABA, Am. Corp. Counsel Assn. (pres. Chgo. chpt. 1992-93, nat. bd. dirs.), Chgo. Bar Assn. (Maurice Weigel award 1983, vice chmn. young lawyers sect. 1986), Chgo. Bar Found. (pres. 1997—). Democrat. Jewish. Avocation: exercise. Home: Portland, Oreg. Died Feb. 3, 2007.

BECKER, ELEANOR LOUISE HALEY, real estate executive; b. Attleboro, Mass., Nov. 26, 1929; d. James Robert and Mary Hazel (White) Haley; m. Donald H. Perry (dec. 1964); children: Calvin J., Ronald M.; m. Robert Ivan Becker; stepchildren: Bradford, Don. BE, Boston U., 1964. Lic. tchr. Mass. Tchr. spl. edn. Paxton (Mass.) pub. Schs., 1964-68; tutor in hosps., instns., pvt. homes, Worcester, Mass., 1968-77; real estate assoc. Robert B. Love Co., Paxton, 1985-87; owner, mgr. Paxton Area properties, Ltd., Inc., Paxton, from 1987. Mem. Nat. Assn. Realtors, Mass. Assn. Realtors, Greater Worcester Bd. Realtors, Women's Council Realtors, Women in Sales, Women's Networking, Am. Bus. Women Assn., Sales Execs. Club, Kurlan's Sandler Sales Assn., Paxton Women's Club, Worcester Bus. and Profl. Women, Nat. Assn. Rep. Women., Mass. Assn. Rep. Women, Worcester C. of C., Better Bus. Bur., Boston U. Alumni Assn. Congregationalist. Avocations: herbs, travel, reading, camping, painting. Died Feb. 16, 2007.

BECKER, JEANIE LYNN, nursing consultant, critical care nurse; b. La Crosse, Wis., Dec. 11, 1960; d. Henry M. and Elaine A. Becker. BS in Nursing, Viterbo Coll., La Crosse, 1983. RN, Minn., Wash.; cert. in advanced cardiac life support. Neurology-neurosurgery staff nurse Mayo Clinic and St. Marys Hosp., Rochester, Minn.; ICU-CCU staff nurse U. Wash. Hosp., Seattle; ind. nursing cons., Seattle. Mem. Am. Assn. Critical Care Nurses. Home: Seattle, Wash. Died June 24, 2007.

BECKMAN, EARL L., pharmacist; b. Jamestown, ND, Dec. 21, 1944; s. Herman and Clara (Domek) B.; m. Peggy Schulz, May 29, 1971; children: Joan , Karen. BS, N.D. State U., 1967. Pharmacist White Drug, Jamestown, from 1967. Recipient Customer Svc. award Jamestown C. of C., 1986. Mem. N.D. Pharm. Assn., Lions (bd. dirs. Jamestown chpt. 1986-88), Elks, Eagles. Avocations: golf, restoring antiques. Home: Jamestown, ND. Died June 24, 2007.

BEDFORD, BRIAN, actor; b. Morley, Yorkshire, Eng., Feb. 16, 1935; s. Arthur and Ellen (O'Donnell) B.;life partner Tim MacDonald, 2013 Student, Royal Acad. Dramatic Art, London. Actor: (plays) A View From the Bridge, 1958, Five Finger Exercise, 1959, The Tempest, 1959, Write Me A Murder, 1962, Lord Pengo, 1962, The Doctor's Dilemma, 1963, The Private Ear, 1963, The Knack, 1964, The Unknown Soldier and His Wife, 1967, 73, Astrakhan Coat, 1967, The Cocktail Party, 1968, The Seven Descents of Myrtle, 1968, Hamlet, 1969, Private Lives, 1969, Three Sisters, 1969, Blithe Spirit, 1970, The Tavern, 1970, School for Wives, 1971 (Tony award for Best Actor 1971), Jumpers, 1972, Butley, 1973, Measure for Measure, 1975, Twelfth Night, 1975, Equus, 1976, Richard III, 1977, The Guardsman, 1977, As You Like It, 1977, The Winter's Tale, 1978, Uncle Vanya, 1978, Death Trap, 1979, The Seagull, 1980, Much Ado About Nothing, 1980, Whose Life Is It Anyway?, 1980, The Misanthrope, 1981, Arms and the Man, 1982, Blithe Spirit, 1982, Tartuffe, 1983, Richard II, 1983, 86, A Midsummer Night's Dream, 1984, Waiting for Godot, 1984, The Real Thing, 1985, The Tempest, 1985, Private Lives, 1986, Opera Comique, 1987, No Time for Comedy, 1987, The Merchant of Venice, 1988, Educating Rita, 1988, The Relapse, 1989, The Merchant of Venice, 1989, The Lunatic, The Lover and The Poet, 1989, Macbeth, 1990, Julius Caesar, 1990, Timon of Athens, 1991, Much Ado About Nothing, 1991, School for Wives, 1991, Two Shakespearean Actors, 1991, 92 (Tony award nominee for Lead Actor in a Play 1992), Measure for Measure, 1992, Timon of Athens, 1993, 94 (Tony award nominee for Lead Actor in a Play 1994), Twelfth Night, 1994, The Molière Comedies, 1994, 95, (Tony award nominee for Lead Actor in a Play 1995), Amadeus, 1995, 96, The Little Foxes, 1996, London Assurance, 1997 (Tony award nominee for Lead Actor 1997), Equus, 1997, Much Ado About Nothing, 1998, A Midsummer Night's Dream, 1999, The School for Scandal, 1999, As You Like It, 2005, and many others; (films) Man of the Moment, 1955, Miracle in Soho, 1957, The Angry Silence, 1960, Number Six, 1961, The Pad and How to Use It, 1966, Grand Prix, 1966, Robin Hood, 1973, Nixon, 1995, others; also numerous TV appearances; dir.: (plays) Titus Andronicus, 1978, The Rivals, 1981, Coriolanus, 1981, Blithe Spirit, 1982, Phaedra, 1990, Othello, 1994, Waiting for Godot, 1996, 98, Equus, 1997, The Winter's Tale, 1998. Inducted into Theatre Hall of Fame, 1996. Died Jan. 13, 2016.

BEEMAN, KENNETH EUGENE, finance company executive; b. Dec. 4, 1939; s. Doyle D. and Margarette (McCollough) B.; m. C. Rennee (div.); 1 child, Roxane Jo Robbins. DD (hon.), ULC Christian Ch., 1978. Ordained min. ULC Christian Ch., 1978. Commd. USAF, 1957, advanced through grades to capt., 1973; pres., chmn. bd. dirs. SEOCO, Internat. Properties Corp., Allied Tel. Co.; mgr. fact photo divsn. Chromoloy Am. Corp.; regional mgr. U.S. Life Ins. Co.; v.p., dir. life ins. RCA Ins. Co.; v.p. ops., dir., co-owner Victory Fin. Svcs. LLC, 1996, cons. corp. legal dept., from 1996; founder Living Faith Network (now Liberty Fin. Network), Mattoon, Ill., from 1997. Adv. oil, gas and energy Pres. U.S.; mem. adv. bd. U.S. Cogress, U.S. Security Coun. Found.; cons. Prairie State 2000 Authority, Ill.; co-owner KRB Enterprises. Author: Finding Oil and Gas Yesterday and Tomorrow, 1976. Mem. Moose (past gov., individual, state and team ritual champion). Avocations: pool, golf, fishing. Home: Charleston, Ill. Died Jan. 20, 2007.

BEKENSTEIN, JACOB DAVID, physicist; b. Mexico City, May 1, 1947; s. Joseph and Esther (Wladyslawovsky) B.; m. Bilha Surek, Jan. 18, 1978; children: Yehonadav, Uriyah, Rivka. BS, MS, Polytech. Inst., Bklyn., 1969, Princeton U., 1971, PhD, 1972. Postdoctoral fellow, Ctr. for Relativity U. Tex., Austin, 1972-74; sr. lectr. physics dept. Ben Gurion Univ., Beersheva, Israel, 1974-76, assoc. prof. physics dept., 1976-78, prof. physics dept., 1978-90; Robert and Jean Arnow Chair Astrophysics Ben Gurion Univs., Beersheva, Israel, 1983-90; prof., Racah Inst. of Physics Hebrew U., Jerusalem, from 1990, Michael Polak Chair of Theoretical Physics to Michael Polak Chair of Theoretical Physics emeritus, 1993—2015. Mem. Israel Acad. of Sciences Com. on Astrophysics, Jerusalem, 1989-90, Rothschild Prizes Found., Jerusalem, 1993-97, Coun. of the Basic Rsch. Found., Israel, 1989-92, Wolf Prizes Physics Com., Herzelya, Israel, 1994-97, Internat. Com. for General Relativity and Gravitation, 1983-92, 1997-2007, Council of the Israeli Space Agency, 2001-, Israel Acad. of Sciences Vis. Com. on Astronomy, 2002; chair Landau prize in Astrophysics Com., 2009, Israel prize in Physics Com., 2009; several visiting professorships, scientist positions. Contbg. author: To Fulfill a Vision, 1981, The Prism of Science, 1986, Quantum Theory of Gravity, 1984; mem. editl. bd. Entropy on-line open access journal, 2008- Recipient Ernst David Bergmann prize for Sci., Israel, 1977, Landau prize in Physics, Mifal Hapais, Israel, 1981, Rothschild prize in Physical Sci., Rothschild Found., Israel, 1988, Israel Nat. prize in Physics, 2005, Weizmann prize in the Exact Sciences of the Tel-Aviv Municipality, 2011, Wolf Found. prize in Physics, Israel, 2012; named Outstanding of NY-Polytechnic Univ., 1996. Mem. Israel Acad. Sciences and Humanities, Internat. Soc. for General Relativity and Gravitation, Internat. Astronomical Union, World Jewish Acad. of Sciences Achievements include co-discovery (with Stephen Hawking) of black hole thermodynamics. Home: Jerusalem, Israel. Died Aug. 23, 2015.

BELCHER, DONALD WILLIAM, engineering consultant; b. NYC, July 13, 1922; s. Donald Ray and Mary Carver (Williams) B.; m. Dariel Keith, Mar. 23, 1946; children: Dariel Jean Belcher Sellers, Donald Richard, Susan Keith Belcher Penedos, David Todd, Jonathan Rockwood. BE in Chem. Engring., Yale U., 1943. Registered profl. engr., N.J., La. Chem. supr. muriatic acid dept. E.I. DuPont de Nemours & Co., Inc., Grasselli, N.J., 1946, asst. dept. supt. silicate dept., 1946-48; project design engr. Bowen Engring. Inc., North Branch (now Columbia, Md.), N.J., 1948-51, mgr. functional design North Branch, N.J., 1951-57, v.p., chief engr., 1957-72, v.p., tech. dir., 1972-76, exec. v.p., dir., 1976-78, pres., dir., 1978-79, exec. v.p., dir., 1979-81; pres. Belcher Engring., Inc., from 1982, Drytec Coffee Inc., 1983-88. Bd. dirs. YMCA, Westfield, N.J., 1959-64. With USNR, 1943-46. Mem. AIChE, Nat. Soc. Profl. Engrs., Air and Waste Mgmt. Assn., Assn. Cons. Chemists and Chem. Engrs. Died Nov. 9, 2006.

BELDOCK, MYRON, lawyer; b. NYC, Mar. 27, 1929; s. George J. and Irene (Goldstein) B.; m. Elizabeth G. Pease, June 28, 1953 (div. 1969); children: David, Jennifer Fogarty, Hannah Beldock, Benjamin, Adam Schmalholz; m. Karen L. Dippold, June 19, 1986. BA, Hamilton Coll., 1950; LLB, Harvard U., 1958. Bar: (N.Y.) 1958, N.Y. (U.S. Dist. Ct. (ea. and so. dists.)) 1960, (U.S. Ct. Appeals (2d cir.)) 1960, (U.S. Supreme Ct.) 1973. Asst. U.S. Atty. U.S. Atty's Office, Eastern Dist., NY, 1958-60; assoc. Geist, Netter & Marx, NYC, 1960-62; sole practice NYC, 1962-64; ptnr. Beldock Levine & Hoffman LLP, NYC, from 1964. Bd. dirs., v.p Brotherhood-In-Action, N.Y.C., 1972-2006; bd. dirs. Brookdale Revolving Fund., N.Y.C., 1973-76. Served with U.S. Army, 1951-54. Recipient Milton S. Gould award for outstanding oral advocacy, Office of Appellate Defender, 2004. Mem. NY State Bar Assn. (award 2002), Assn. Bar City NY (spl. com. penology 1974-80, com. judiciary 2000-03, com. criminal justice, 2005-10), NY County Lawyers Assn., Bklyn. Bar Assn., Kings County Criminal Bar Assn. (Humanitarian of Yr. 1989), NY County Criminal Bar Assn. (award Excellence 2000), NY State Assn. Criminal Def. Lawyers (Pres.'s commendation 2004, Outstanding Svc. award, 2005), Nat. Assn. Criminal Def. Lawyers, Nat. Lawyers Guild (Peoples Lwyers award, NYC Chpt. 2010). Home: New York, NY. Died Feb. 1, 2016.

BELKE, GENEVIEVE ORTAGGIO, accountant, tax preparer; b. Chgo., Oct. 13, 1923; d. Samuel and Rella Irene (Grappy) Ortaggio; m. Arnold Harold Belke, Sept. 29, 1956; children: Denise A., John A. BA in Acctg., Gov.'s State U., 1985. Contr. Boodell, Sears, etal, Chgo., 1957-68, Allied Leasing Co., Inc., Northfield, Ill., 1968-73, R.J. MacDonald Internat., Inc., Elk Grove Village, 1979-80; real estate agt. Arlington Heights, Ill., 1973-80; asst. contr. CBS Mus. Instruments Inc., Deerfield, Ill., 1980-82; pres. No. Ind. Bus. Svcs., Inc., Elkhart, Ind., from 1984. Life mem. Inst. Mgmt. Acctg. (emeritus, chpt. pres. 1979-80, nat. com. 1980-83). Home: Elkhart, Ind. Died Jan. 5, 2007.

BELL, LEO S., retired physician; b. Newark, Nov. 7, 1913; s. Alexander M. and Marie (Saxon) B.; m. Edith Lewis, July 3, 1938; children; Jewyl Linn, David Alden. AB, Syracuse U., 1934, MD, 1938. Diplomate Am. Bd. Pediatrics. Intern N.Y.C. Hosp., 1938, Bklyn. Hosp., 1939-40; resident Sea View Hosp., NYC, 1940-41, N.Y.C. Hosp., 1941-42; pediatrician pvt. practice, San Mateo, Calif., 1946-84. Staff mem. Mills Meml. Hosp., San Mateo, Peninsula Hosp. & Med. Ctr., Burlingame, Children's Hosp., San Francisco; assoc. clin. prof. pediatrics U. Calif. Med. Sch., San Francisco;

prof. clin. emeritus Stanford Med. Sch., Palo Alto; mem. curriculum & ednl. affairs com. U. San Francisco Med. Sch., adminstrv. coun. Columnist San Mateo Times; contbr. articles to profl. jours. Bd. dirs. Mills Hosp. Found., San Mateo, U. Calif. San Francisco Hosp., San Mateo County Heart Assn., Hillsborough Schs. Found. (Calif.), 1980-83. Capt. USAAF, 1942-46. Recipient bronze and silver medals Am. Heart Assn. Fellow Am. Acad. Pediatrics, Am. Pub. Health Assn.; mem. AMA (alt. del. to ho. of dels), U. Calif. San Francisco Clin. Faculty Assn. (pres.), Calif. Fedn. Pediatric Socs. (pres.), Am. Fedn. Pediatric Socs. (pres.), Calif. Med. Assn., Am. Pub. Health Assn., Air Force Assn., Calif. Med. Assn. (ho. of dels.), San Mateo County Med. Assn. (vice chmn. quality assurance com. San Mateo county health plan), Internat. Snuff Bottle Soc., Hong Kong Snuff Bottle Soc., San Francisco Gem and Mineral Soc., World Affairs Coun. San Francisco, U. San Francisco Med. Sch. Clin. Faculty Assn. (coun., pres.), Peninsula Golf & Country Club, Commonwealth Club. Home: Burlingame, Calif. Died May 1, 2007.

BELL, MARY SUTTON, retired school counselor; b. Wilmington, NC, Jan. 24, 1932; d. Ivey J. and Annie May (Hobbs) Sutton; m. Guy W. Rawls, Jr., Feb. 2, 1952 (div. Oct. 1976); children: Guy W. III, Jane Rawls Simon, Charles R.; m. Herbert Patterson Bell, Jr., Oct. 22, 1976. MEd in Sch. Counseling, N.C. State U., 1970; EdD, Nova U., 1985. Adminstrv. cert. East Carolina U., 1987. Counselor Ravenscroft Sch., Raleigh, N.C., 1959-62, tchr., 1962-76; sch. counselor New Hanover Pub. Schs., Wilmington, N.C., 1976-97; ret., 1997. Teaching Fellows group leader, Raleigh, N.C., 1993-94. Trustee Cape Fear Cmty. Coll., Wilmington, 1980-98, S.E. Ctr. for Mental Health, 1978—; Pender Dem. Precinct and County v.p. and sec., Burgaw, N.C., 1985-98. Recipient Best Educator award, Channel 3 TV, Wilmington, 1990. Mem. Phi Delta Kappa, Delta Kappa Gamma-Theta (v.p., pres., 1980-84). Democrat. Episcopalian. Avocations: gardening, walking, reading. Home: Charlotte, NC. Died Apr. 1, 2007.

BELL, PEGGY DEANE HALL, credit bureau executive; b. Hartsville, Tenn., Apr. 27, 1919; d. M. Burnly and Prudie (Stubblefield) Hall; m. Charlie Berkeley Bell, June 23, 1943 (dec. May 1962); children: C. Berkeley Jr., William Hall, Hayden Darragh, Prudence. LLB, Cumberland U., 1941. Bar: Tenn. 1946. Owner Credit Bureau Greenville, Tenn., from 1948. Mem. Greenville Bar Assn., Assn. Credit Bureau. Democrat. Episcopalian. Avocations: sewing, dance. Died Mar. 17, 2007.

BELLALTA, ESMÉE CROMIE, landscape architect, retired educator; b. London, Oct. 6, 1927; came to U.S., 1976; d. Bernard Patrick and Irene Maud (Belcher) Cromie; m. Jaime Juan José; children: Esmée, Alexandra, Barbara, Antoniou, Angela, Josephine, Maria, Jaime, Diego, Felipe. BA, Harvard U., 1951, M in Landscape Architecture, 1952. Registered cert. landscape architect, Ind. Assoc. prof. Sch. Architecture U. Notre Dame, Notre Dame, Ind., 1976-95, assoc. prof. emerita, 1995; coord., faculty Justice Edn. Program St. Mary's Coll., Notre Dame, 1981-97. Vis. prof. Pontifica Univ. Cath. Chile, 1997, Harvard U. Grad. Sch. Design, 1993-94, Ball State U. Coll. Architecture & Planning, Landscape Dept., 1978-93; prof. landscape architecture U. Chile, 1974-76; prof. environ. design Coll. Architecture Cath. U. Chile, Santiago, 1973-76; tchr. Centro Nat. Familia, Chile, 1968-75, counselor, 1967-75; tchr. Calvert Sch., 1968-70; tchr. art Santiago Coll., 1955-75; co-dir. Inst. R&D Holistic Design Divsn. Ecology, Evanston, Ill., 1972—; cons. in field; rschr. in field. Contbr. articles to profl. jours. Mem Diocesan Liturgical Art & Environment Com., Ft. Wayne, South Bend, Ind., 1985-91; mem. cons. com. disabled U. Notre Dame, 1985-91; counselor Cath. Marriage Adv. Coun., Gt. Britain, 1964-67; apptd. Diocesan Liturgical Commn., 1989. Lily grantee St. Mary's Coll., 1989, 90; Environic Found. Internat. grantee, 1985, Kellogg Seed Money grantee Helen Kellogg Inst. Internat. Studies, 1984. Mem. Am. Soc. Landscape Archs. (elected mem.-at-large Ind. chpt. 1985-88, Merit award 1981, spl. award 1980), Royal Horticulture Soc., Amnesty Internat. Roman Catholic. Home: South Bend, Ind. Died Feb. 15, 2007.

BELLIS, ARTHUR ALBERT, financial executive, government official; b. Worcester, Mass., June 16, 1928; s. Frank Clayton and Ruth Porter (Gordon) B.; m. Barbara Swift, Feb. 22, 1952 (div. 1969); children: Bradford, Susan; m. E. Deborah Shea, May 28, 1972 (div. 1997); children: Cynthia, Michael. BSBA, Boston U., 1952. Asst. credit mgr. Procter & Gamble, NYC, 1955-56; asst. supr. capital budget Western Union, NYC, 1956-58; corp. budget analyst CBS, NYC, 1958-64; account exec. Edwards & Hanley, NYC, 1964-66, Spencer Trask, Worcester, 1966-70; sr. securities compliance examiner SEC, Boston, 1970-90; retired, 1990; treas., CFO, chief compliance officer Burlington Securities Corp., Chatham, Mass., 1993-97. Advisor Explorer program Mohegan council Boy Scouts Am., 1966-70; mem. Worcester Rep. Com., 1952-53, Rep. Presdl. Task Force, 1984-85; mem. fin. com. Town of Yarmouth, 1982-86; v.p. Sheriff's Cmty. Patrol, 1997—; extraordinary min. of Holy Communion, Roman Cath. Ch., 2004. Recipient Superior Performance award SEC, 1976, 1986; Medal of Merit, Pres. of U.S., 1985. Mem. Masons (treas. Howard lodge 1988-91, trustee 1992-97), Pine Run High Twelve Club (sec. 2003, leader cmty. emergency response team, 2003-2004), Ea. Star (warder). Roman Catholic. Avocations: flying, hiking, camping, keyboard, painting. Died Nov. 17, 2006.

BELLOCCHI, NATALE H., retired ambassador; b. Little Falls, NY, July 5, 1926; m. Sujr Lilan Liu; 2 children BS, Ga. Inst. Tech., 1948; MA, Georgetown U., 1954. Indsl. engr. Burlington Mills Corp., 1948-50; joined US Dept. State, 1955, diplomatic courier, 1955-60, adminstrv. asst. Hong Kong, 1960-61, gen. services officer Vientiane, Laos, 1961-63; asst. comml. attache US Embassy, Taipei, Taiwan, 1964-68, chief comml. unit Hong Kong, 1968-69, comml. attache Saigon, Vietnam, 1971-72, comml. counselor Tokyo, 1973-74; spl. asst. to asst. sec. for internat. affairs US Dept. Treasury, 1975-79; econ. counselor US Embassy, New Delhi, dep. prin. officer Hong Kong, 1979-81; dep. asst. sec. for current analysis, Bur. Intelligence & Rsch. US Dept. State, 1981-85, US amb. to Botswana Gaborone, 1985-88; internat. affairs advisor Indsl. Coll. Armed Forces, Ft. McNair, Washington, 1988—90; chmn. American Inst. Taiwan, 1990—95. Served with U.S. Army, 1950-53 Died Nov. 17, 2014.

BENDER, PEGGY WALLACE, charitable gift planning consultant; b. Athens, Ohio, Apr. 29, 1957; d. Allen Riley and Carol Jean (Jago) Wallace; children: Meghan Elizabeth, Erin Michelle. AS, Ohio U., 1986, BA, 1988. Cert. Fund Raising Exec., 1988. Asst. to dean Ohio U. Col. Bus. Admin., Athens, 1981-86; asst. dir. planned giving U. Cin. Found., 1986—88; dir. planned/major gifts Western Md. Col., Westminster, 1988-89; dir. planned giving Am. Red Cross, Cleve., 1991-93; pres. Strategies for Planned Giving, Cleve., from 1993. Bd. dirs. Nat. Com. Planned Giving, Indpls. Bd. dirs. Nat. Com. Planned Giving, 1998-2000. Named Outstanding Fund Raising Exec. No. Ohio Planned Giving Coun./NSFRE Cleve./Ohio Coun. Fundraising Execs., 1997. Mem. Northern Ohio Planned Giving Council (pres., 1993-96, bd. dirs.), Assn. Fundraising Profls. (v.p., 1992), Ohio Council Fund Raising Execs., Ohio Assn. Healthcare Philanthropy. Avocations: reading, travel, horses. Home: Columbia Station, Ohio. Died July 15, 2007.

BENDHEIM, LEONORE CAROLINE, psychotherapist; b. Amsterdam, The Netherlands, Oct. 26, 1921; came to the U.S., 1943; d. Martin and Alice Sofia (Mayer) B. B in Art Edn. and Art Therapy, Kans. U., 1970; B in Social Work, Washburn U., 1972; MS in Clin. Counseling/Art Therapy, Emporia State U., 1974; MS in Clin. Gerontology, Kans. State U., 1983. Interior designer Mehagians, Phoenix, 1950-59; pvt. practice interior design Phoenix, 1959-63; rsch. vol. Menninger Rsch., Topeka, 1963-66; art therapy vol. Topeka State Hosp., 1966; vol. vocat. rehab. Ctr. for the Blind, Topeka, 1967; psychiat. evaluation team mem. Kans. Psychiat. Diagnostic Ctr., Topeka, 1970-73; counseling in psychotherapy Colmery-O'Neil VA Med. Ctr., Topeka, 1973-83, Phoenix South Mental Health, 1987-89; pvt. practice psychotherapist Scottsdale, Ariz., 1989-93. Edn. coord. Ashram Assn., Topeka, 1970-73; pres. Unitarian-Universalist Fellowship, Topeka, 1973-75, program chmn., 1975-78, chmn. bd. dirs., 1978-80. Died Feb. 15, 2007.

BENJAMIN, DONALD JULIAN, health, safety and environment consultant; b. Chatswood, NSW, Australia, Sept. 21, 1936; s. Lawrence Raymond and Hazel Kathleen (Weaver) B.; m. Nora Marie Flahavin, Feb. 15, 1958 (div. 1987); children: Jeffrey Jon, Toni, Tanya; m. Sandra Jean Dale, Apr. 8, 1990. M Engring. Sci. in Indsl. Safety, Instn. Elec. Engrs., London, 1968. Assoc. mem. Instn. Elec. Engrs.; M engring. sci. (indsl. safety), 1992. Student apprentice GE, Salford, Eng., 1957-58; electronics technician Tel. and Elec. Industries, Sydney, 1959-60; tech. officer Sydney County Coun., 1960-62; engr. Statensprovningsanstalt, Stockholm, 1963-64; exptl. scientist Commonwealth Sci. and Indsl. Rsch. Orgn., Sydney, 1965-89, health, safety and environ. advisor, from 1989. Editor: (book) Australia Party Principles & Policies, 1972; editor: Cancer Info. & Support Soc. Newsletter, 1981—; contbr. articles to profl. jours. Pres. Secular Edn. Soc., Sydney, 1962; nat. policy coord. Australia Party, Sydney, 1970-77, Australian Dems., Sydney, 1977-80; convenor Cancer Info. & Support Soc., 1981—. Mem. Instn. Elec. Engrs. (assoc.). Avocations: volleyball, tennis, golf, piano. Home: Crows Nest, Australia. Died July 17, 2007.

BENJAMIN, JAMES WILLIAM, lawyer; b. Kansas City, Mo., Apr. 14, 1926; s. William S. and Nelle Marie (Cottingham) B.; m. Norma H. Carter, Dec. 26, 1965; children: Lynn Marie Williams, Steven J. Student, Park Coll., Parkville, Mo., 1944-45; BS in Liberal Arts, Northwestern U., 1946; JD, U. Mo., Kansas City, 1949. Bar: Mo. 1949, U.S. Dist. Ct. (we. dist.) Mo. 1949, U.S. Ct. Appeals (8th cir.) 1949, U.S. Supreme Ct. 1956. Dir. Field, Gentry & Benjamin, Kansas City, from 1950. Mem. rules com. Mo. Supreme Ct., 1975-80; lectr. in field. Contbr. articles to profl. publs. Bd. govs. Citizens Assn., Kansas City. Lt. USNR, 1944-52. Recipient Law Achievement award U. Mo., 1973. Fellow Am. Bar Found., Internat. Soc. Barristers; mem. Kansas City Bar Assn. (pres. 1968), Mo. Bar Assn. (pres. award 1970), Internat. Assn. Def. Counsel, Shriners, Masons, Sertoma Club Kans. City (past pres.), Phi Delta Phi. Mem. Christian Ch. (Disciples of Christ). Mem. Christian Ch. (Disciples Of Christ). Avocations: fishing, swimming, golf. Home: Kansas City, Mo. Died July 15, 2007.

BENMOSCHE, ROBERT HERMAN (BOB BENMOSCHE), retired insurance company executive; b. Brooklyn, NY, May 29, 1944; m. Denise Benmosche; children: Nehama, Beth, Ari. BA in Math., Alfred U., 1966. Staff cons. Arthur D. Little, 1969—75; with Chase Manhattan Bank, 1976—79, v.p. technology, 1979—82; with Paine Webber, 1982—95, sr. v.p. mktg., 1984-86, CFO retail bus., 1986-87, exec. v.p., dir. securities ops., 1989—95; exec. v.p. individual bus. dept. Metropolitan Life Insurance Co. (subs. MetLife, Inc.), 1995—97, pres., CEO, 1997—98, chmn., CEO, 1998—2000, MetLife, Inc., 2000—06; pres., CEO American International Group, Inc. (AIG), NYC, 2009—14. Bd. dirs. Met. Life Ins. Co., 1997—2005, Credit Suisse Group, 2002—13, American Internat. Group, Inc. (AIG), 2009—14. Bd. dirs. N.Y. Philharm. Lt. U.S. Army Signal Corps, 1966-68. Named one of Bus. People of Yr., Fortune mag., 2010. Mem. Life Ins. Mktg. & Rsch. Assn. (bd. trustees). Died Feb. 27, 2015.

BENNETT, HARVE (HARVE FISCHMAN), television and film producer, writer; b. Chgo., Aug. 17, 1930; m. Jani Bennett. Student, U. Calif. at Los Angeles. Asso.producer CBS-TV, then free-lance TV writer; program v.p. ABC-TV, Hollywood, Calif., to 1968. Performer: radio show Quiz Kids; newspaper columnist radio show, drama critic, free-lance writer; producer spl. events, CBS-TV; dir. TV film commls.; producer: TV show Mod Squad, 1968, (TV series) Time Trax, 1993; creator-writer: TV show The Young Rebels, 1970; exec. producer: TV show The Six Million Dollar Man, 1973; TV movie Guilty or Innocent: The Sam Sheppard Murder Case, 1975; TV series The Invisible Man, 1975-76, The Bionic Woman, 1976; TV miniseries Rich Man, Poor Man, 1976, Gemini Man, 1976, American Girls, 1978, From Here to Eternity; mini-series, 1979; A Woman Called Golda, 1982 (Emmy award 1982); mini-series The Jesse Owens Story, 1984; series Salvage I, 1978; film Star Trek II: The Wrath of Khan, 1982; producer and author film Star Trek III: The Search for Spock, 1984, Star Trek IV: The Voyage Home, 1986; producer, co-writer film Star Trek V: The Final Frontier, 1988. Died Feb. 25, 2015.

BENNETT, KENNETH ALAN, retired biological anthropologist; b. Butler, Okla., Oct. 3, 1935; s. Kenneth Francis and Lillian Imogene (McDaniel) B.; m. Helen Lucille Maze, Sept. 6, 1959; children: Letitia Arlene, Cheri Lynn. AS, Odessa Coll., 1956; BA, U. Tex., 1961; MA, U. Ariz., 1966, PhD, 1967. Asst. prof. anthropology U. Oreg., 1967-70; assoc. prof. U. Wis., Madison, 1970-75, prof., 1975-97, ret., 1997. Forensic anthropology cons. to Wis. law enforcement agys. and Wis. state crime lab., 1970—98. Author: The Indians of Point of Pines, Arizona, 1973, Fundamentals of Biological Anthropology, 1979, Skeletal Remains from Mesa Verde National Park, 1975, A Field Guide for Human Skeletal Identification, 1987, 2nd edit., 1993; editor Yearbook of Phys. Anthropology, 1976-81; contbg. editor Social Biology, 1981-87; mem. editl. com. Ann. Revs. in Anthropology, 1987-91; editor, reviewer Human Biology, 1981-87; contbr. articles to profl. jours. Mem. Wis. Burial Sites Preservation Bd., 1988. With U.S. Army, 1956-58. NIH fellow, 1964-67 Mem. Am. Assn. Phys. Anthropologists, Am. Soc. Naturalists, Human Biology Council, Soc. for Study Evolution, Am. Acad. Forensic Scis., Soc. for Study Human Biology, Soc. Systematic Zoology, Am. Assn. Physical Anthropologists (exec. com. 1976-81), Sigma Xi. Home: Madison, Wis. Died Feb. 6, 2014.

BENNETT, LISA, artist; b. Eng., Aug. 3, 1922; came to U.S., 1927; d. Reuben and Hannah Dora (Hacker) Bernstein. BA, Goddard Coll., MA, 1976. Instrl. coord. Walnut Creek (Calif.) Civic Arts, 1964-76; critic, art reviewer, essayist, reporter West Art, 1964-79, San Francisco Territorial News, 1962, 63; freelance writer Washington, 1980-81; adminstrn. coord. Gesell Inst., New Haven, 1982-84; owner, lectr. bur. Bennett Programs, San Francisco, 1985-86, freelance bus. writer, 1987-89; arts lectr. Oxford U., 1990-93; spl. editor Oxford U. Press, 1990-91; adj. lectr. Hunter Coll., NYC, 1992. Freelance lectr. San Francisco State U., 1974-79, U. Calif., Dominican Coll., St. Mary's Coll., San Quentin Prison (Coll. of Marin), Hayward State Coll. One-woman shows include Lincoln Gallery, 1960, Firehouse Gallery, Cowell, Calif., 1966, Womens Resource Ctr., Sarasota, 1995, Sheraton Hotel, Boston, 1995, U.S. Garage, Sarasota, 1996, Am. Inst. Arch. Hdqs. Gallery, Washington, 1998, Barret Ho., Va. Found. Arch., Richmond, 1999, Flat Iron Gallery, Peekskill, N.Y., 2000, Temple Israel, Croton, N.Y., 2001; exhibited in group shows at Art Students League, 1955, Golden Gate Gallery, San Francisco, 1961, Civic Arts, Walnut Creek, 1966, St. Edwards Art Gallery, Oxford, 1991, U.S. Garage, Sarasota, 1993, Sarasota Visual Art Ctr., 1994, Sur-la-Mer Gallery, Sarasota, 1995, Francesca Armijo Presents Gallery, 1996, Fulton-Burt Gallery, Sarasota, 1997, Gallery-at-Crystal Bay, Peekskill, 1997, Bedford Gallery, Dean Lesher Regional Ctr. Arts, Walnut Creek, Calif., 1998, Paramount Ctr. Arts, Peekskill, 1999, Peekskill Art Supply Gallery, 1999, Westchester C.C., Valhalla, N.Y., 2000, Katonah Mus. Artists' Assn., North Westchester Ctr. Arts, Mt. Kisco, N.Y., 2000, Westchester Arts Coun., White Plains, N.Y., 2001, Smithtown Twp. Arts Coun., St. James, N.Y., 2002, Hendrick Hudson Free Libr., Montrose, N.Y., 2002, Ceres Gallery, N.Y.C., 2002, 2003, Chapel H ill Estates, Peekskill, 2002; pub. and pvt. collections include Bryn Mawr (Pa.) Coll. Study Collection, Am. Inst. Archs. Found., Metromedia Fiber Networks, White Plains, Ginsburg Devel. Arch., Hawthorne, NY. Recipient Spl. Opportunity stipend, State of N.Y., 1998, Artists' Showcase award, Manhattan Arts Internat., 1999, Internat. Grant award, Pollock-Krasner Found., N.Y., 2000. Mem. Nat. Mus. for Women in the Arts, Mus. Archives, Artists Equity. Died Nov. 2, 2006.

BENNETT, ROBERT THOMAS (BOB BENNETT), lawyer, former political organization administrator, accountant; b. Columbus, Ohio, Feb. 8, 1939; s. Francis Edmund and Mary Catherine (Weiland) Bennett; m. Ruth Ann Dooley, May 30, 1959; children: Robert Thomas, Rose Marie. BS, Ohio State U., 1960; JD, Cleve. Marshall Law. Sch., 1967. Bar: Ohio 1967. CPA Ernst & Ernst, Cleve., 1963—63; tax asessing dept. Cuyahoga County Auditor's Office, Ohio, 1963—70; ptnr. Bartunek, Bennett, Garofoli & Hill, 1975—79, Bennett & Klonowski, 1979—83, Bennett & Harbarger, 1983—88. Contbr. articles to profl. pubs. Chmn. Ohio Republican Party, 1988—2009; vice chmn. Cuyahoga Republican. Orgn., 1974—88; chair Midwestern State Chmn.'s Assn.; bd. dirs. U. Hosp. Cleve./Southwest Gen. Health Ctr. Mem.: ABA, Capital Hill Club Washington, Citizens League Club, Ohio Soc. CPA, American Inst. CPA, American Soc. Atty.-CPA. Republican. Roman Catholic. Home: Cleveland, Ohio. Died Dec. 6, 2014.

BENNINGTON, DONALD LEE, general contractor; b. Martin's Ferry, Ohio, Nov. 26, 1942; s. Wesley Alonzo and Loucille Marjorie (Brown) B.; m. Brenda Sharon Parrish, Mar. 7, 1964; children: Brian Lee, Tawny Lynn Student, Kent State U., 1961-64. Prin. Donald L. Bennington Contractors, Massillion, Ohio. Mem.: Masons. Democrat. Presbyterian. Avocation: flying. Home: Massillon, Ohio. Died Jan. 20, 2007.

BENSON, PETER H., energy and environmental company executive, consultant; b. Martinez, Calif., Aug. 25, 1935; s. Howard Lucius and Alberta Clara (Bothe) B.; m. Lois Johanna Lee, May 23, 1958 (dec. 1962); 1 child, Scott Conrad; m. Judith Ellen Patterson, June 6, 1964; 1 child, Cydney Voss. BA, U. Calif., Berkeley, 1958; MA, San Francisco State Coll., 1960; PhD, U. So. Calif., LA, 1973. Instr. UCLA, 1966-68; scientist, dir. Lockheed Marine Biology Lab., San Diego, Calif., 1968-76; gen. mgr., chief scientist Lockheed Ctr. for Marine Rsch., Carlsbad, Calif., 1976-78; environ. scientist Argonne (Ill.) Nat. Lab., 1978-81; asst. dir. Gas Rsch. Inst., Chgo., 1981-86; pres. Renewable Energy Systems, Inc., Palos Park, Ill., from 1986. Plankton specialist Cooperative Study of the Koroshio, Antarctic Oceanology Prog., L.A., 1965-68. Editor Jour. Applied Phycology, 1989; co-editor: Seaweed Cultivation for Renewable Resources,1987; contbr. articles to profl. jours. Allan Hancock Found. fellow, 1965-68 Died July 16, 2007.

BERARD, PAUL MICHAEL, electrical engineer; b. Portsmouth, NH, Feb. 10, 1946; s. Paul Emile and Stella Marie (Gosselin) B.; m. Donna May Hill, Nov. 6, 1968; children: Brian Paul, Christine Marie. Assoc. in Engring., N.H. Tech. Inst., 1970; B of Engring. Tech., Northeastern U., 1978, BSEE, 1980; MSEE, U. N.H., 1982. Tech. assoc. Bell Labs., Holmdel, N.J., 1970-72, North Andover, Mass., 1972-80, mem. tech. staff, 1980-82, GTE Communication Systems, Phoenix, 1982-85, mgr. Siemems Transmission Systems, 1985-89; mgr. Poynting Systems div. Reliance Comm/Tec, Phoenix, from 1989. Patentee in field. Mem. Tau Beta Pi, Eta Kappa Nu. Died Feb. 28, 2007.

BERCOVITCH, SACVAN, English language professional, educator; b. Montreal, Que., Can., Oct. 4, 1933; s. Alexander and Brytha (Avrutick) B.; m. Susan L. Mizruchi; children: Eytan, Alexander. BA, Sir George William Coll., 1961; MA, Claremont Grad. Sch., Calif., 1963, PhD in American Studies, 1964; LittD (hon.), Concordia U., 1993; DHL (hon.), Claremont U., 2005. Asst. prof. English and American lit. Brandeis U., 1966-68; assoc. prof. U. Calif., San Diego, 1968-70; prof. English & American Lit. Columbia U., NYC, 1970-83; Powell M. Cabot rsch. prof. American lit. Harvard U., Cambridge, 1983—2001. Lectr., Kyoto, Tokyo, Shanghai, Beijing, Amsterdam, Frankfurt, Konstanz, Lisbon, Jerusalem, Tel Aviv, Salzburg, Coimbra, Montreal, Rome, Budapest, Paris, Venice, Bologna, Toronto, Oxford, Berlin, Moscow, Prague, Olomouc, Ostrava, Brno, Yale U., Princeton U., U. Pa., U. Calif., Berkeley, LA, San Diego, Irvine, Cornell U., Dartmouth Coll., Concordia U., Claremont Grad. U., many others; exec. com. American studies MLA, 1976-1978; exec. com. American Studies Assn. 1980-1982, pres. 1982-84; advisor, cons. in field. Author: Typology and Early American Literature, 1972, The American Puritan Imagination, 1974, The Puritan Origins of the American Self, 1975, new edit., 2011, The American Jeremiad, 1978, centenary edit., 2012, Reconstructing American Literary History, 1986, Ideology and Classic American Literature, 1986, The Office of the Scarlet Letter, 1991, centenary edit., 2013, The Rites of Assent: Transformations in the Symbolic Construction of America, 1992; editor The Art of Sylvia Ary, 2007; gen. editor: Cambridge History of American Literature (8 vols.); author more than 100 essays, many revs.; trans. Yiddish lit. 1884-2004. American Philos. Soc. fellow, 1968-69, Guggenheim fellow, 1969-70, American Coun. Learned Socs. fellow, 1971-72, Nat. Humanities Inst. fellow, 1975-76, Ctr. for Advanced Study in Behavioral Scis. fellow, 1978-79, NEH fellow, 1978-79, 86-87, Woodrow Wilson Ctr. fellow, 1990-91, Time-Life fellow Huntington Libr., 1994-2014, Cabot fellow for achievement in humanities, Mellon Emeritus fellow, 2004—14; recipient James Russell Lowell prize for scholarship, 1992, Disting. Scholar award for Extraordinary Lifetime contbns. in Early American Lit., 2003, Award for Excellency in Tchg., Jay B. Hubbell award for Lifetime Achievement in American lit. studies, MLA, 2004, Bode Pearson prize for Lifetime Achievement in American studies, 2007. Fellow American Acad. Arts & Sciences; mem. English Inst. Home: Brookline, Mass. Died Dec. 9, 2014.

BERG, DONALD W., investment company executive; b. Mpls., July 29, 1930; BS, U. Minn., Mpls., 1954. Dist. mgr. Am. Greeting, Grand Rapids, Mich., 1955-67; broker mgr. E. F. Hutton, Grand Rapids, 1967-76; broker Payne Webb, Grand Rapids, 1976-80; br. mgr., v.p. First of Mich. Corp., Grand Rapids, from 1980. Mem. Better Bus. Bur. Avocations: golf, fishing, travel. Home: Caledonia, Mich. Died Jan. 20, 2007.

BERGAU, FRANK CONRAD, real estate, commercial and investment properties executive; b. NYC, Sept. 17, 1926; s. Frank Conrad and Mary Elizabeth (Davie) B.; m. Rita I. Korotkin; children: Mary, Rita, Francis, Theresa, Veronica. BA in English, St. Francis Coll., Loretto, Pa., 1950; MS in Edn. and English, Potsdam State U., NY, 1969. Cert. tchr., supr., adminstr., NY; cert. comml. investment mem. Tchr. English, Gouverneur Schs., NY, 1962-81, dir. continuing edn., 1968-81, summer prin., 1974-80; project dir. St. Lawrence County Bd. Co-op Ednl. Svcs., Canton, NY, 1974; pres. Irenicon Assocs., Clermont, Fla. Bd. dirs. St. Lawrence County Assn. Retarded Children, 1965—; pres. bd. dirs. Gouverneur Libr.; mem. Family Care Coun., Fla. Dist. 13. Mem.: KC (fin. sec. coun. 13240), NEA, NY Assn. Continuing Edn. (dir.), South Lake County Devel. Coun. (pres.), Lake County Bd. Realtors, Nat. Assn. Realtors, Gouverneur C. of C. (bd. dirs. 1963—66), Kiwanis (creator Terrific Kids award 1985), Gouverneur Luncheon Club. Home: Clermont, Fla. Died Dec. 12, 2015.

BERGER, SANDY (SAMUEL RICHARD BERGER), financial consulting firm executive, former national security advisor; b. Sharon, Conn., Oct. 28, 1945; m. Susan Harrison; children: Deborah Berger Fox, Sara Berger Sandelius, Alexander. AB, Cornell U., 1967; JD cum laude, Harvard U., 1971. Bar: D.C. 1971. Legis. asst. to Senator Harold E. Hughes US Senate, Washington, 1971-72; spl. asst. to Mayor John V. Lindsay City of NY, 1972; dep. dir. policy planning staff US Dept. State, Washington, 1977-80; ptnr. Hogan & Hartson LLP, Washington, 1973—77, 1981—92, internat. strategic advisor; asst. dir. nat. security Presdl. Transition Team, 1992; dep. asst. to the Pres. for nat. security affairs NSC, Washington, 1993—97, asst. to the Pres. for nat. security affairs, 1997—2000; co-chmn., co-founder Stonebridge Internat. LLC, Washington, 2001—15; fgn. policy advisor to Senator Hillary Clinton US Senate, Washington, 2007—09. Author: Dollar Harvest, 1971, (with others) Manual of Foreign Investment in the United States, 1984. Recipient Global Humanitarian award, World Food Program U.S.A., 2015. Mem. ABA. Democrat. Died Dec. 2, 2015.

BERGMANN, BARBARA ROSE, economics professor; b. NYC, July 20, 1927; d. Martin and Nellie Berman; m. Fred H. Bergmann, July 16, 1965 (dec. 2011); children: Sarah Nellie, David Martin. BA, Cornell U., 1948; MA in Economics, Harvard U., 1955, PhD in Economics, 1959; PhD (hon.), De Montford U., 1996, Muhlenberg Coll., 2000. Economist U.S. Bur. Labor Stats., NYC, 1949-53; sr. staff ecomomist, cons. Council Econ. Advisors, Washington, 1961-62; sr. staff Brookings Inst., Washington, 1963-65; sr. econ. advisor AID, Washington, 1966-67; assoc. prof. U. Md., College Park, 1965-71, prof. econs., 1971-88; disting. prof. econs. American U., Washington, 1988-97, prof. emeritus, 1997—2015. Author: (with Chinitz and Hoover) Projection of a Metropolis, 1961; (with George W. Wilson) Impact of Highway Investment on Development, 1966; (with David E. Kaun) Structural Unemployment in the U.S., 1967; (with Robert Bennett) A Microsimulated Transactions Model of the United States Economy, 1985, Saving Our Children from Poverty: What the United States Can Learn from France, 1996, In Defense of Affirmative Action, 1996, Is Social Security Broke? A Cartoon Guide to the Issues, 1999, (with Suzanne W. Helburn) America's Child Care Problem: The Way Out, 2002, The Economic Emergence of Women, 1986, 2d edit., 2005; mem. editl. bd. Am. Econ. Rev., 1970-73, Challenge, 1978, Signs, 1978-85; columnist econ. affairs N.Y. Times, 1981-82. Mem. Economists for McGovern, 1977; mem. panel econ. advisors Congl. Budget Office, Washington, 1977-87; mem. price adv. com. U.S. council on Wage and Price Stability, 1979-80. Fellow: Nat. Acad. Polit. and Social Sci.; mem.: AAUP (coun. 1980—83, pres. 1990—92), Stanford U. Ctr. Poverty & Inequality (assoc. from 2007), American Sociol. Assn., Soc. Advancement Socio-Econs. (pres. 1995—96), Internat. Assn. Feminist Econs. (pres. 1999, co-founder), Ea. Econ. Assn. (pres. 1974), Am. Econ. Assn. (v.p. 1976, adv. com. to US Census Bur. 1977—82). Democrat. Home: Bethesda, Md. Died Apr. 5, 2015.

BERGQUIST, GENE ALFRED, farmer, rancher, retired commissioner; b. Paynesville, Minn., Aug. 5, 1927; s. Albin and Viola (Heinrich) B.; m. Ann Dorothy Corwin, Aug. 2, 1958; children: Wayne A., Viola M. Self-employed farmer-rancher, Rhame, from 1948; Slope County commr. Amidon, ND, 1982—2003; ret., 2003. Bd. dirs. Rhame, N.D. Cenex, 1970-82; bd. dirs. Harper Twp. Rhame; com. mem. Slope County Agrl. Stabilization and Conservation Svc.-USDA Commn., Amidon, 1968-84. Bd. dirs. Rhame Rural Fire Dept., 1976—, Bowman-Slope Social Svc. Bd., Bowman, N.D., 1991—, Deep Creek Twp., 1958-64, Richland Center Twp. Bd., 1952-57; elder Lyle Presbyn. Ch.; youth leader 4-H Slope County, 1950-57; mem. Bowman-Slope Revolving Loan Fund Com., 1998-2003; mem. job devel. bd. Slope and Bowman Counties, 1999—. Presbyterian. Avocations: reading, painting, fishing, riding, gardening. Home: Rhame, ND. Died May 23, 2007.

BERGSAGEL, DANIEL EGIL, hematologist, oncologist; b. Outlook, Can., Apr. 25, 1925; s. Knut and Josephine (Anderson) B.; m. Carol Joyce Sigurdson Bergsagel; children: Karen, Paul, Daniel, Leif. MD, U. Manitoba Med. Coll., Winnepeg, Can., 1949; PhD, Oxford U., UK, 1955. Diplomate Am. Bd. Internal Medicine. Asst. internist U. Tex. MD Anderson and Tumor Inst., Houston, 1955-57; assoc. internist, 1957-63; assoc. prof. Medicine U. Tex. Grad. Sch. Biomedical Scis., Houston, 1963-64; chief of medicine Ontario Cancer Inst. Princess Margaret Hosp., Toronto, Can., 1965-90; assoc. prof. medicine U. Toronto, Can., 1965-68; prof. medicine, from 1968. Exec. com. Am. Soc. Hematology, 1969-74; bd. dirs. Am. Soc. Clin. Oncology, 1979-81. Editor: Myeloma: Biology and Management, 1995, 2nd edit., 1998; contbr. numerous articles to profl. jours. Chmn. Med. Review Com., Gairdner Found., Toronto, Ont., 1984-92. Recipient Rsch. Career award Nat. Cancer Inst., Bethesda, Md., 1962, Waldenstrom award Myeloma Rsch. Internat. Myeloma Workshop Com., 1989; named Mem. of the Order of Can., Ottawa, 1989. Avocations: cyber investing, choral singing. Home: Toronto, Canada. Died Oct. 20, 2007.

BERKMAN, WILLIAM ROGER, lawyer, retired major general army; b. Chisholm, Minn., Mar. 29, 1928; s. Carl Emil and Millie (Mikkelson) B.; m. Betty Ann Klamt, Dec. 17, 1950. AB, U. Calif., Berkeley, 1950, JD, 1957. Bar: Calif. 1957, D.C. Ct. Appeals 1957, D.C. 1957. Law clk. to judge James Alger Fee, U.S. Ct. Appeals 9th cir., 1957-58; assoc. Morrison & Foerster, San Francisco, 1958-67, mem. firm, 1967-79; comdg. gen. 351st Civil Affairs Command, Mountain View, Calif., 1975-79; chief Army Res., Dept. of Army, Washington, 1979-86; mil. exec., Res. Forces Policy Bd., Office Sec. Def. Dept. of Def., Washington, 1986-92. Mng. editor: Calif. Law Rev, 1956-57. Pres. Sausalito (Calif.) Bd. Libr. Trustees, 1976-78; pres. Civil Affairs Assn., 1979-80, 93-99; bd. dirs. Army Distaff Found., 1988-92; dir. Sausalito-Marin City Sanitary Dist., pres., 2002—. Maj. gen. U.S. Army, 1979—. Decorated DSM with oak leaf cluster, Def. DSM , Def. Superior Svc. medal , S. Order of Calif., U.S. Spl. Ops. command medal U.S. Army, USN, C.G., Legion of Merit medal, Army Commendation medal; recipient Meritorious Svc. medal, Army Outstanding Civilian Svc. medal; named to Hall of Fame Sr. Army Res. Comdrs. Assn. Mem.: ABA (chmn. standing com. on lawyers in armed svcs. 1988—91), U.S. Army Civil Affairs Corps. (hon. chief civil affairs), Civil Affairs Assn. (pres. 1992—99, pres. emeritus from 1999), Res. Officers Assn., Assn. U.S. Army, Army and Navy Club (licentiate), Lions (dir. Sausalito Marin City san. dist., past pres.). Died Jan. 15, 2014.

BERLYNE, GEOFFREY MERTON, nephrologist, researcher; b. Manchester, Eng., May 11, 1931; came to U.S., 1976, naturalized, 1981; s. Charles Solomon and Miriam Hannah (Rosenthal) B.; m. Ruth Selbourne, June 7, 1969; children: Jonathan, Benjamin, Suzannah. B of Medicine and Surgery with honors, Manchester U., 1954, MD, 1966. Lectr. in medicine U. Manchester, 1961-62, sr. lectr., 1964-68, reader, 1969-70; prof. medicine and life scis. Negev (Israel) U., 1970-79; prof. medicine SUNY, Bklyn., from 1976; chief nephrology sect. Bklyn. VA Med. Center, 1976-96. Adj. prof. medicine Ben Gurion U. of Negev Faculty of Health Scis., Beer Sheter, Israel, 1995—. Author courses sci. topics, including renal diseases, 1966, electrolytes and body fluids, 1981; editor: Nephron; contbr. articles to profl. jours. Pres. area synagogue, 1982-90. Fellow Am. Coll. Nutrition; mem. Japanese Nephrology Soc. (named Disting Nephrologist 1979), Assn. Physicians Gt. Britain, Am. Fedn. Clin. Rsch. Jewish (chmn. 1970-74, pres. synagogue 1982-90). Home: Omer, Israel. Died May 19, 2007.

BERNABIE, CARMEN RALPH, food products executive; b. Midland, Pa., Nov. 3, 1942; s. Ralph Joseph and Jean Louise (Mosticone) B.; m. Linda Kay Smith, June 4, 1966; 1 child, Gina Marie. BSBA, Butler U., 1974. Tng. and devel. specialist Burger Chef System, Indpls., 1968-78; dir. tng. and personnel Clancy's Inc., Noblesville, Ind., 1978-81; mgr. field tng. Taco Bell Inc., Irvine, Calif., 1981-83; v.p. The Good Taco Inc., Pompano Beach, Fla., 1983-85; dist. mgr. Beuno Foods Inc., San Antonio, 1985-87; dir. tng. Steak N Shake Inc., Indpls., from 1987. Bd. dirs. Waycross Camp & Conf. Ctr., Indpls. Bd. dirs. United Episcopal Charities. With USAF, 1962-66. Mem. Coun. of Hotel and Restaurant Trainers, ASTD. Republican. Episcopal. Avocations: sports, reading. Home: Hilliard, Ohio. Died Nov. 6, 2006.

BERNARD, DAVID EDWIN, artist; b. Sheridan, Ill., Aug. 8, 1913; s. Edwin Louis and Cecile Louise Bernard; m. Vivian Lanfear Bernard, Aug. 21, 1948; 1 child, Joy Bernard Wieter. BFA, U. Ill., 1939; MFA, U. Iowa, 1949. Graphic artist K.B. Butler & Assocs., Mendota, Ill., 1941—42; instr. art Maryville Coll., Tenn., 1946—48; asst. prof., prof. Wichita State U., 1949—83, prof. emeritus, 1983; artist St. Cloud, Fla., 1983. Numerous print exhbns. Mem.: Oscola Ctr. Arts, Wichita Art Mus., Soc. Am. Graphic Artists. Avocations: travel, gardening, crafts, history, sculpting, woodcarving. Home: Saint Cloud, Fla. Died Dec. 21, 2006.

BERNHARDT, MELVIN, theater director; b. Buffalo; s. Max and Kate (Benatovich) B.; m. Jeff Woodman, 2011 BFA, U. Buffalo, 1952; MFA, Yale U. Sch. Drama, 1955. Asst. prof. Goodman Theatre Sch. Drama, Chgo., 1958-63. Dir. plays including Cop-Out, 1969, The Effect of Gamma Rays on Man-in-the-Moon Marigolds, off-Broadway, 1970 (OBIE award 1970), Early Morning, N.Y.C., 1970, And Miss Reardon Drinks a Little, Broadway, 1971, Other Voices, Other Rooms, Buffalo Studio Arena Theatre, 1973, Children (OBIE award 1976), Manhattan Theatre Club, Da (Tony award 1978, Drama Desk award 1978), Hide and Seek, Broadway, 1980, Crimes of the Heart (OBIE award 1980, Tony nominee, 1982, Pulitzer Prize winner), 1980, Life After High School?, Hartford Stage Co., 1981, What I Did Last Summer, summer tour, 1982, Bedrock, Hartman Theatre, 1983, Dancing in the End Zone, Braodway, 1985, The Beach House, Circle Repertory 1985, Harry and Thelma in the Woods, Mayfair Theatre, Santa Monica, Calif., 1987, Harvey, Cleve. Playhouse, 1991, Breaking the Code, Berkshire Theater Festival, 1993, Breaking the Silence, Berkshire Theatre Festival, 1994, The Gingerbread Lady, Am. Stage Festival, 1995, The Blues are Running, Manhattan Theater Club, 1996 (T.V.) The Rich Brother, Trinity Playhouse, 1990, The Widow's Mite (Emmy award 1992), Trinity Playhouse, 1991, daytime TV Another World, NBC-TV, 1974-82, 86-90, One Life to Live, ABC-TV, 1985; Mister Roberts, NBC-TV, 1984; author (stage play) Pied Piper of Hamelin, 1963. Died Sept. 12, 2015.

BERNS, WALTER FRED, political scientist, educator; b. Chgo., May 3, 1919; s. Walter Fred and Agnes (Westergard) B.; m. Irene Sibley Lyons, June 16, 1951; children: Elizabeth, Emily, Christopher. B.Sc., U. Iowa, 1941; postgrad., Reed Coll., 1948-49, London Sch. Economics & Polit. Sci., 1949-50; PhD, U. Chgo., 1953. Asst. prof. govt. La. State U., 1953-56; asst. prof. polit. sci. Yale U., 1956-59; mem. faculty Cornell U., 1959-69, prof. govt., chmn. dept., 1963-68; prof. polit. sci. U. Toronto, Ont., Can., 1970-79; resident scholar American Enterprise Inst., 1979—86, adj.

scholar, 1986-94; John M. Olin Univ. prof. Georgetown U., Washington, 1986-94. Mem. Salzburg (Austria) Seminar on American Studies, 1959. Author: Freedom, Virtue and the First Amendment, 1957, Constitutional Cases in American Government, 1963, The First Amendment and the Future of American Democracy, 1976, For Capital Punishment: Crime and the Morality of the Death Penalty, 1979; In Defense of Liberal Democracy, 1984, Taking the Constitution Seriously, 1987, Making Patriots, 2001, Democracy and the Constitution, 2006 ; co-author: Essays on the Scientific Study of Politics, 1963; editor: After the People Vote, 1992. Alt. U.S. rep. UN Commn. on Human Rights. Served with USNR, 1941-45. Recipient Nat. Humanities medal, The White House, 2005. Mem. American Polit. Sci. Assn., Nat. Council on Humanities Episcopalian. Died Jan. 10, 2015.

BERNSTEIN, STEPHEN LOUIS, lawyer; b. NYC, Nov. 22, 1933; s. Jack and Gertrude (Kalz) B.; m. Phyllis Goldberg, Jan. 16, 1960; children: Kenneth, Gail, Jeffrey. BA, Columbia Coll., 1955; LLB, Harvard U., 1958. Pvt. practice, NYC, 1958-67; gen. counsel The First Republic Corp. of Am., NYC, from 1994. Home: Woodmere, NY. Died Jan. 3, 2007.

BERNSTROM, RICHARD SVEN, investment banker, consultant; b. Paris, Sept. 27, 1941; came to the U.S., 1968; s. Sven Bror and Margareta Agaht (DeGeer) B.; div. Jan. 1986; 1 child, Erik. Grad., Lundsburgs Skola, 1961; M in Polit. Sci., Lund U., Sweden, 1967; MBA, INSEAD, Fontainbleau, France, 1968. Investment officer Citiban, NYC, 1968-71, Warburg-Paribas Becker, NYC, 1971-78; exec. dir. Bank of Am. Internat., London, 1978-86; mng. dir. Prudential Bache Securities, London, 1986-92; cons. Price Waterhouse-Ctrl., Tashkent, Republic of Uzbekistan, 1993-94; pres., CEO Ctrl. Asian-Am. Enterprise Fund, Washington, 1994-98; independent cons., from 1999. Sgt. Swedish Infantry, 1961-62. Home: London, England. Died Nov. 27, 2006.

BERRA, YOGI (LAWRENCE PETER BERRA), retired professional baseball player, retired professional baseball coach; b. St. Louis, May 12, 1925; s. Peter and Pauline (Longsoni) B.; m. Carmen Short, Jan. 26, 1949; children: Lawrence A., Timothy Thomas, Dale Anthony. PhD (hon.), Montclair State U., 1996. Catcher, outfielder Newark Bears, 1946, NY Yankees, 1946-63, mgr., 1964, 1984-85, coach, 1975-84, NY Mets, 1965-72, mgr., 1972-75; coach Houston Astros, 1986-89; former v.p. without portfolio Yoo-Hoo Chocolate Beverage Co., Carlstadt, NJ; ex-officio mem. bd. trustees Yogi Berra Mus. & Learning Ctr., Little Falls, NJ. Author: (with Ed Fitzgerald) Yogi Berra: The Autobiography of a Professional Baseball Player, 1961, (with Tom Horton): It Ain't Over ..., 1989, The Yogi Book: I Really Didn't Say Everything I Said, 1998, (with Dave Kaplan) When You Come to a Fork in the Road, Take It, 2001, 10 Rings-My Championship Seasons, 2003. Served with USNR, 1943-46. Named Am. League MVP, 1951, 54, 55; named to American League All-Star Team, 1948-62, Baseball Hall of Fame, 1972, NJ Hall of Fame, 2008; recipient Golden Plate award, Acad. Achievement, 2005. Mem.: Lions, Elks and Moose Clubs. Achievements include member of World Series championship winning New York Yankees, 1947, 1949-53, 1956, 1958, 1961, 1962; leading the American League in: stolen bases, 1949, 1952. Died Sept. 22, 2015.

BERRETT, LAMAR CECIL, religion educator; b. Riveron, Utah, Mar. 28, 1926; s. John Harold and Stella (Wright) B.; m. Darlene Hamilton, Aug. 3, 1950; children: Marla, Kim, Michael, Susan, LeAnn, Nathan, Evan, Ellen, Jared. BS, U. Utah, 1952; MS, Brigham Young U., 1960, EdD, 1963. Prof. religion Brigham Young U., Provo, chmn. dept. religion, 1968-76, dir. Religious Study Ctr., 1976-82. Dir. worldwide tours. Author: The Wilford Wood Collection Vol. 1, 1971, Discovering the World of the Bible, 1973; (family genealogy) Down Berrett Lane 2 Vols., 1980. Served with U.S. Army, 1944-46. Mem. Utah Hist. Soc. (pres. Utah Valley chpt. 1971-72), Sons of Utah Pioneers, Mormon History Assn. Republican. Mem. Lds Ch. Avocations: racquetball, pigeon raising, orchardist. Home: Orem, Utah. Died Aug. 25, 2007.

BERRIEN, JACQUELINE ANN, former federal commissioner; b. Nov. 28, 1961; d. Clifford and Anna Belle (Smith); m. Peter M. Williams. BA in Govt. & English, Oberlin Coll., 1983; JD, Harvard Law Sch., 1986. Bar: NY 1987. Law clk. to Hon. U.W. Clemon US Dist. Ct. (northern dist.) Ala., Birmingham, Ala., 1986—87; atty. Voting Rights Project, Lawyers' Com. Civil Rights, Washington, 1987—94; asst. counsel NAACP Legal Def. Fund (LDF), 1994—2001, assoc. dir.-counsel, 2004—10; prog. officer governance & civil soc. unit Ford Foundation Peace & Social Justice Program, 2001—04; chair US Equal Employment Opportunity Commn. (EEOC), Washington, 2010—14. Adj. prof. NYU Law Sch., from 1995, Harvard Law Sch. Contbr. articles to prof. legal jours. Died Nov. 9, 2015.

BERRY, MICHELLE, minister; b. Virgin Island, Md., May 30, 1932; d. George and Cora (Bakerville) Day; m. Noel J. Berry, Aug. 20, 1989; children: Emmanuel Day, Desline Day, Victoria Michelle Berry. BS, St. Augustine Bay Coll., St. Louis, Miss., 1953; MA, U. Md., Balt., 1964; BD, Chaplain Assoc. Coll. of D.C., 1979; PhD, Grace Christian Coll., Phila., 1985. Chief adminstr. Psychology Assocs., Inc., Bklyn.; asst. gen. supr. Faith Restoration Ctr., Inc., Bklyn. Bishop N.Y. and The Philippines Dist. Col. WAC, 1950-53. Recipient Psychologist Achievement award, Nat. Chaplains Merit award, Nat. U.S. Chaplains Promotion Honor award, Pres.'s award for svc. beyond the call of duty, African Merit award, Blackglama award. Mem. World Wide Spiritual Ministers Assn., Internat. Clergy Assn., U.S. Chaplains Assn., Am. Guild Hypnotherapists, Religious Sci. Doctrine Inst., Writers, Students and Truth-seekers Assn., Personal Counseling Svc., Inc. Home: Brooklyn, NY. Died Mar. 29, 2007.

BERRY, ROBERTA MILDRED, civic worker; b. Feb. 27, 1926; d. Judson Stewart and Anna Doretha (Neddermyer) Lawrence; m. Moses Berry, June 29, 1948; children: Scott, Mark. MusB, Cornell Coll., 1948. Choir dir. Presbyn., Meth. chs., Cedar Rapids, Iowa, 1949-71; tchr. assoc. Cedar Rapids Comty. Schs., 1963-73; dir. Pioneer Village, Cedar Rapids, 1982-83, Linn Comty. Food Bank, Cedar Rapids, from 1983. Pres. Chs. United, Cedar Rapids, 1984-85, v.p. Iowa state bd., 1994-97, 2000—; orginator Grade Sch. Picture Lady Program, Cedar Rapids, 1968-69; pres. Seminole Valley Farm, Cedar Rapids, 1980-81; pres. Ch. Women United, Cedar Rapids, 1985-86, also bd. dirs., editor newsletter for Iowa State. Bd. dirs. YWCA, Cedar Rapids, 1970-72, Cedar Rapids Symphony Guild, 1983-88, Iowa Rails to Trails, Cedar Rapids, 1983-88; pers. Methwick Manor Aux., Cedar Rapids, 1985; sec. Coun. on Aging, Cedar Rapids, 1984-85; rep. Civic Newcomers, 1986-93; pres. Cedar Rapids Area Peace Network Guide, Guide Brucemore Hist. Home, 1982—. Recipient Valiant Woman award, 1998. Mem. UN Assn. (Iowa state bd. 1993—, Linn County pres. 1996-99), Garst Leadership award 1999), Beethoven Club (pres. 1964-65), Coll. Club (pres. 1965-66), PEO (pres. 1982-83), Demolay Mothers Aux. (pres. 1974-75), Postal Workers Aux. (pres. 1974-75). Avocations: painting, needlecrafts, tennis, biking. Home: Cedar Rapids, Iowa. Died Nov. 14, 2006.

BERTHOT, JAKE (JOHN ALEX BERTHOT), artist, educator; b. Niagara Falls, NY, Mar. 30, 1939; 1 child, John. Student, New Sch. Social Rsch., 1960-61, Pratt Inst., 1960-62. Mem. faculty Cooper Union, 1960-62, Yale U., New Haven, 1982-90, Sch. Visual Arts, NYC, 1992—2014. Artist in residence Dartmouth U., 1995. One-man shows include O. K. Harris Gallery, N.Y.C., 1970, 1972, 1975, Portland (Oreg.) Ctr. Visual Arts, 1973, Galerie de Gestlo, Hamburg, Germany, 1973, 1977, David McKee Gallery, N.Y.C., 1976, 1978, 1982, 1983, 1986, 1988, 1989, 1991, 1995—2004, Nina Nielsen Gallery, Boston, 1979, 1984, 1992, 1995, 1996, 2000—02, Nigel Greenwood Gallery, London, 1979, 1991, U. Calif. Berkeley, 1984, Galleri Olsson, Stockholm, 1987, 1990, 1996, Nat. Art Gallery, Washington, 1989, Cork Gallery Lincoln Ctr., N.Y.C., 1991, Jaffe-Friede and Strauss Gallery, Hanover, N.H., 1995, The Phillips Collection, Washington, 1996, Cooper Union, N.Y.C., 1999, Marist Coll., 2005, Betty Cunningham Gallery, 2005, Kleiner/James Art Ctr., Woodstock, NY, 2006, exhibited in group shows at Whitney Mus. Art, N.Y.C., 1969, McKee Gallery, 2000, 2003, Randolph-Macon Woman's Coll., 2003, Whitney Mus. Art, N.Y.C., 1972, 1974, 1978, Art Inst. Chgo., 1971, Mus. Modern Art, N.Y.C., 1977, 1981, 1983—85, Meadows Art Gallery, Dallas, 1985, others, Represented in permanent collections Australian Nat. Gallery, Balt. Mus. Art, U. Calif. Berkeley Mus., Dallas Mus. Fine Arts, Fogg Mus. Harvard U., Guggenheim Mus., Mus. Modern Art, Whitney Mus. Art, others. Recipient Acad. Inst. award, American Acad. Arts & Letters, 1994; grantee, The Elizabeth Found., 1995—96; Guggenheim fellow, 1981. Died Dec. 30, 2014.

BERTLES, JOHN FRANCIS, physician, educator; b. Spokane, Wash., June 8, 1925; s. John Francis and Henrita Swart (Brown) B.; m. Jeannette Winans, 1948 (div. 1978); children: Mark Dwight, Jacquelyn Eve, John Francis; m. Lila Rodriguez, 1981. BS, Yale U., 1945; MD, Harvard U., 1952. Diplomate Am. Bd. Internal Medicine. Intern Presbyterian Hosp., NYC, 1952-53, asst. resident in medicine, 1953-55; research fellow in hematology U. Rochester and Strong Meml. Hosp., 1955-56; research fellow in immunohematology Harvard U. Med. Sch. and Mass. Gen. Hosp., Boston, 1956-58, research fellow in hematology, 1958-59; instr. in medicine Harvard U. Med. Sch. at Mass. Gen. Hosp., 1959-61; dir. hematology-oncology div. St. Luke's Hosp. Center, NYC, 1962-95, asst. attending physician, 1962-64, assoc. attending physician, 1964-71, attending physician, 1971-95; dir. transfusion services St. Luke's Roosevelt Hosp. Ctr., 1981-95; sr. research asso. dept. biol. scis. Columbia U., 1970-71, asst. clin. prof. medicine, 1962-67, assoc. clin. prof., 1967-71, assoc. prof., 1971-74, prof., 1974-95, prof. emeritus of medicine, from 1995; attending physician Montefiore Med. Ctr., NYC, 1995-97; clin. prof. medicine Albert Einstein Coll. Medicine, NYC, 1995-97. Vis. prof. medicine Nuffield dept. clin. medicine Radcliffe Infirmary, U. Oxford, Eng., 1977-78; cons. to various govt. agys., including hematology study sect. NIH, 1972-76, 82-84, blood rsch. rev. group, 1978-82; mem. dirs. coun. N.Y. Heart Assn., 1974-90; mem. basic rsch. adv. com. Nat. Found. March of Dimes, 1977-80. Contbr. articles to profl. publs. Ensign USNR, 1945-46. Fellow ACP; mem. Am. Soc. Clin. Investigation, Am. Physiol. Soc., Am. Soc. Hematology, Am. Fedn. Clin. Rsch., Am. Chem. Soc., Alpha Omega Alpha. Died Apr. 6, 2014.

BESSMAN, SAMUEL PAUL, pediatrician, educator, biochemist; b. Newark, Feb. 3, 1921; m. Alice Neuman, July 3, 1945; children: Joel David, Ellen. Student, Coll. William and Mary, 1938-41; MD, Washington U., St. Louis, 1944. Intern, asst. resident St. Louis Children's Hosp., 1944-45; asst. prof. pediatrics George Washington U., 1947-54; dir. research Children's Hosp., Washington, 1947-54; asso. prof. pediatrics U. Md., 1954-59, prof. pediatric research, 1959-68, prof. biochemistry, 1962-68; prof., chmn. dept. pharmacology and nutrition U. So. Calif., 1968-91, prof. pediatrics, 1969-91, prof. emeritus, from 1991. Dir. research Rosewood State Hosp., Md., 1962-68, Jewish Home for Retarded Children, Washington, 1962-68 Founding editor Biochem. Medicine; mem. editorial bd. Analytical Biochemistry. Pres. First Dist. Cmty. Coun., Balt., 1965; trustee Robert Lindner Found.; pres. Molly Towell Found., Alsam Found. Served with USPHS, 1945-47. Recipient Crawford Long award U. Ga., 1963, Creative Scholar award U. So. Calif., 1978, Maimonides award Technion, 1979, Disting. Sci. Achievement award Am. Heart Assn., 1984, Inst. for Advanced Studies award Louis Pasteur Libr. and Sci. Found., 1986, Alumni Achievement award Washington U. Med. Sch., 1994. Fellow AAAS, Am. Acad. Pediat.; mem. Am. Soc. Biol. Chemists, Soc. Pediat. Rsch., Am. Inst. Nutrition, Am. Soc. Pharmacology and Exptl. Therapeutics, Sigma Xi, Alpha Omega Alpha. Achievements include introduction of EDTA treatment of lead poisoning, theoretical basis of hepatic coma, mechanism of insulin action chemistry mental retardation, genetic basis of malnutrition, artificial implantable pancreas, creatine phosphate energy shuttle. Home: Los Angeles, Calif. Deceased.

BEST, BARBARA, retired personal manager, publicist; b. San Diego, Dec. 2, 1921; d. Charles Lewis and Leila Harrison (Sanders) B. BA in Journalism, U. So. Calif., Los Angeles, 1943. Unit publicist 20th Century Fox Co., Los Angeles, 1943-50; reporter San Diego Jour., 1950; asst. to publicity dir. Stanley Kramer Co., Los Angeles, 1950-53; owner, mgr. Barbara Best & Assocs., Los Angeles, 1953-66; ptnr. Freeman and Best Pub. Rels., Los Angeles, 1967-75; owner, pres. Barbara Best, Inc., Pub. Relations, Los Angeles, 1975-87; personal mgr. Barbara Best Mgmt., Los Angeles, 1987-98; ret. Exec. v.p. Maribar Prodns., Hollywood, Calif., 1986--. Co-founder, exec. dir. Vikki Carr Scholarship Found., Hollywood, 1971-82; pres. Publicists Fed. Credit Union, Hollywood, 1976-85. Mem. Hollywood Womens Press Club (past pres., bd. dirs.), Women in Film. Democrat. Episcopalian. Died Feb. 22, 2007.

BETENSKY, ROSE HART, artist; b. NYC, Sept. 6, 1923; d. Jacob and Clara Shainess; m. Seymour Betensky, July 11, 1943; children: Joel Benay, Richard Benay. Studied painting with Josef Presser, NYC. Pres. N.Y. Soc. Women Artists, NYC, 1970, Am. Soc. Contemporary Artists, NYC, 1972—74. Exhibitions include Nat. Acad. Galleries, Royal Acad. Edinburgh, Scotland, Norfolk (Va.) Mus. Arts and Scis., Cultural Inst., Guadalajara, Mex., Palazzo Vecchio, Florence, Italy, La Napoule, France, collections, Jane Voorhees Zimmerli Art Mus. of Rutgers U. Recipient Windsor and Newton award, Grumbacher award, Bee Paper Co. award, Nat. Assn. Women Artists award, Am. Soc. Contemporary Artists awards. Mem.: Nat. Assn. Women Artists (pres. 1970—72). Home: Port Washington, NY. Died Aug. 7, 2007.

BETTS, AUSTIN WORTHAM, retired research company executive; b. Westwood, NJ, Nov. 22, 1912; s. Irving Wilcox and Bessie Harris (Boardman) B.; m. Edna Jane Paterson, Dec. 8, 1934 (dec. Apr. 1992); children: Jerry W., Lee W., Lynn P.; m. Roberta Brungardt Wool, Nov. 1992. BS, U.S. Mil. Acad., 1934; MS, Mass. Inst. Tech., 1938; postgrad., Indsl. Coll. Armed Forces, 1955. Commd. 2d lt. U.S. Army, 1934, advanced through grades to lt. gen., 1966; dist. engr. Bermuda Dist., U.S. Engr. Dept., 1942-43; engr. 14th Air Force, 1944-45; assoc. dir. Los Alamos Sci. Lab., 1946-48; chief atomic energy br. G-4, Dept. Army, 1949-52; exec. to chief research and devel. Dept. Army, 1952-54; mil. exec. to spl. asst. for guided missiles Office Sec. Def., 1957-59; dir. Advanced Research Projects Agy., Office Sec. Def., 1959-61; dir. mil. application AEC, 1961-64; dep. chief research and devel. Dept. Army, 1964-66, chief research and devel., 1966-70; retired, 1970; sr. v.p. S.W. Research Inst., San Antonio, 1971-83. Exec. sec. Nat. Conf. on Advancement of Rsch., 1987-2000. Fellow AIAA (assoc.), Inst. Environ. Scis., Soc. Am. Mil. Engrs.; mem. Assn. U.S. Army, Nat. Def. Security Indsl. Assn. Lodges: Masons, Rotary (pres. San Antonio 1985-86). Presbyterian. Home: San Antonio, Tex. *Early in my life I was impressed by an autobiographical sketch of a great leader who commented that his goal in life was simply to leave tracks. I took that guidance for my own and have since tried to orient all my major activities toward service, those services to be of such nature that I can look back with pride at the tracks I have left behind me.* Died Nov. 26, 2006.

BETTS, BERT A., retired treasurer, accountant; b. San Diego, Aug. 16, 1923; s. Bert A. and Alma (Jorgenson) B.; m. Barbara Lang; children: Terry Lou, Linda Sue, Sara Ellen, Bert Alan, Randy Wayne, LeAnn, John Chauncey, Frederick P., Roby F., Bruce H. BBA, Calif. Western U., 1950. CPA, Calif., cert. pub. accountant. Accountant John R. Gillette, 1946-48; ptnr. Gillette & Betts, 1949-50; pvt. accounting practice, 1951-54; ptnr. Betts & Munden, Lemon Grove, Calif., 1954-57; sr. ptnr. Bert A. Betts & Co., 1958-59; treas. State of Calif., 1959-67; prin. Bert A. Betts & Assos., 1967-77; ret., 1977. CEO Internat. Prodn. Assocs., 1970-87; dir. Lifetime Cmtys. Inc.; gen. ptnr. Sacramento Met. Airport Properties 4, Ltd., 1970-02. Author (with Barbara Lang Betts): A Citizen Answers. Mem. Lemon Grove Sch. Bd., 1954-57; Calif. chmn. Max Baer Heart Fund; state employees chmn. Am. Cancer Sco., 1962-64, bd. dirs. county br., 1963-69, Sacramento County campaign chmn., mem. exec. com., 1965, pres. Sacramento chpt., 1967-68; sponsor All Am. B-24 Liberator Collings Found. Served as 1st lt. USAAF, 1942-45. Decorated D.F.C., Air medal with four clusters; recipient Louisville award Municipal Finance Officers Assn. U.S. and Can., 1963; honored by Calif. Mcpl. Treas.'s Assn., 1964; inductee Hoover H.S. Hall of Fame, San Diego, 1998, Grossmont Health Dist. Gallery of Honor, 2002. Mem. Nat. Assn. State Auditors, Comptrs. and Treas's Mcpl. Forum N.Y., Calif. Soc. CPAs, San Diego Squadron Air Force Assn. (past vice comdr.), Am. Legion, 2d Air Div. Assn., 8th Air Force Hist. Soc., VFW, Commemorative Air Force (col.), Native Sons. Golden West, Internat. B-24 Liberator Club, Foresters, Masons, Calif. Scholarship Fedn. (life),

DFC Soc., Nat. Rifle Assn., Sigma Phi Epsilon, Beta Alpha Psi (hon.), Alpha Kappa Psi (hon.). Clubs: Eagles; Men's (Lemon Grove) (pres.), Lions (Lemon Grove) (treas.); Commonwealth. Presbyterian. Home: Sacramento, Calif. Died May 28, 2014.

BETTS, RAYMOND FREDERICK, history educator, researcher; b. Bloomfield, NJ, Dec. 23, 1925; s. James William and Cora Anna (Banta) B.; m. Irene Elizabeth Donahue, June 25, 1957; children: Kenneth, James, Susan. AB, Rutgers U., 1949; MA, Columbia U., 1950, PhD, 1958; D, U. Grenoble, 1955. Asst. prof. Bryn Mawr (Pa.) Coll., 1956-61; assoc. prof., then prof. Grinnell (Iowa) Coll., 1961-71; prof. U. Ky., Lexington, from 1971, dir. honors program, 1978-90, dir. Gaines Ctr., 1983-98. Mem. Nat. Humanities and Liberal Arts faculty, 1980—; chmn. Ky. Humanities Coun., 1982-83; bd. dirs. Diedrich Ednl. Trust, Ashland, Ky., 1985—; faculty participant Leadership Lexington, 1987-91, 94—, Elderhostel, Lexington, 1987-97; presenter Ednl. Leadership Lexington, 1987-96. Author: Assimilation and Association in French Colonial Theory, 1961, Europe Overseas, 1968, The False Dawn, 1978, Decolonization, 1998; contbg. editor Britannia Com., 1999—; mem. editl. bd. French Hist. Studies, 1974-77. Trustee Carnegie Ctr., Lexington, 1998—. With U.S. Army, 1944-46, 50-51. Recipient Acorn award Advocates of Higher Edn., Ky., 1992. Avocations: writing, photography. Home: Lexington, Ky. Died Feb. 2, 2007.

BEUSSE, JACQUELINE A., writer, marketing professional; b. Albany, NY; d. H. A. and Christina M. (Collins) Beusse. Bus. degree, The Wood Sch., NYC, 1956; student mgmt. program for women, Pa. State U.; BA magna cum laude, Caldwell Coll., 1974; MA magna cum laude, N.Y. Inst. Tech., 1978. Sr. ct. stenographer Middlesex County Prosecutors Office, New Brunswick, N.J., 1955-57; adminstrv. asst. to Sen. John A. Lynch, Sr. Summer Stock Address Singer, New Brunswick, 1957-61; adminstrv. asst. to Judge John J. Rafferty New Brunswick, 1957-61; legitimate theatre actress, singer; product mgr. Johnson & Johnson, New Brunswick, 1961-73; dir. devel. and pub. rels. Caldwell (N.J.) Coll., 1974-76; pres., writer, mktg. cons. Mktg. by Objectives, Inc., Caldwell, from 1978; cons. Fleet Week NYC, Crosby Golf Tournament, NC. Cons. Gucci, Inc., Fraunces Tavern, Constn. Hall, JFK Ctr., Washington, D.C., 6 Frank Sinatra concerts, Am. Ballet Co., St. Luke's-Roosevelt Hosp., Hosp. for Spl. Surgery, Navy League, Fleet Week cons., USO, N.J. State Opera Ball; cons., pub. N.Y. Cornell Med. Ctr. Concert Series; cons., prodr., pub. Urban League, Lincoln Ctr. Concerts, editor and chair, Opera Ball Jour., NY Landmarks Conservancy, exec. pres. Frank Patterson in Concert; lectr. in field. Prodr. Dramatic Reading of The Letters of John and Abigail Adams, N.Y.C., 1986; exec. prodr., prodr., dir. Carnegie Hall Concert--Carmel Quinn and Friends, 1987; journalist Irish Echo, N.Y. Times, Star Ledger, Newark Metro Mag., Cath. Advocate, Omni Mag., Garden St. Woman, The Progress, exec. prodr., Dramatization Letters Abigail & John Adams NY, NJ(Starring Acad. award winner Celeste Holm), chmn., prodr., USO Salute to Peace, 50th Anniversary V.E. Day Victory in Europe, 1945-95, Rockefeller Ctr., NYC; cons., prodr. Bicential The US Constitution Kennedy Ctr. Performing Arts, Washington; contbr. articles to mags. and newspapers. County chair Independents for Kennedy Presdl. Campaign, 1960; chair Gov. Richard Hughes campaigns, 1960-61, 65; chmn. Theater on the Hill; bd. dirs. John F. Kennedy Trust, 1991, 92; NJ state commr. Motion Picture and TV, 1979-93; chmn. Grover Cleveland Sesquicentennial Celebration-Presdl. Tribute, 1987; media co-chair NJ State Dem. Com.; publicity chair Garden State Arts Ctr.-Irish Festival and Found.; cons. Meml. Sloan Kettering Cancer Ctr., Expo 2000; cons. prodr. 4 Bob Hope concerts for charity; prodr., cons. Am. Cancer Soc., NY Cornel U. Med. Ctr. Hosp.; v.p. Ellis Island Restoration Commn., 1975—, v.p., exec. com. Recipient Journalistic Excellence award Irish Am. Unity Conf., 1985, 86, West of Ireland Devel. and Ednl. award, 1987, CAMA Video award for documentary A Summer to Savor, Disting. Am. award, 1990-91, ASTRA 1st prize award for TV documentary We Are the Music Makers, 1991, 92; named Honoree Ellis Island Ceremony, 2000. Mem. USO (bd. dir.), AAUW (bd. dir.), N.J. Soc. to Prevent Blindness (bd. dir.), West Essex C. of C. (v.p., mem. exec. com.), Kappa Gamma Pi Honor Soc. (cons.). Democrat. Roman Catholic. Avocations: art, music, literature, historical research. Home: Essex Fells, NJ. Died July 3, 2014.

BEYER, GEORGE A., educator; b. Mar. 31, 1934; BA, UCLA, 1957. Tchr. Anaheim (Calif.) Schs., 1958-61; tchr. psychology Kalispell (Mont.) Schs., 1961-96; vol. Swan River Sch., Bigfork, Mont., from 1996. Home: Bigfork, Mont. Died Jan. 14, 2007.

BEYSTER, JOHN ROBERT, retired engineering company executive; b. Detroit, July 26, 1924; m. Betty Beyster; 3 children. BS in Engring., U. Mich., 1945, MS, 1948, PhD, 1950. Registered profl. engr., Calif. Mem. staff Los Alamos Sci. Lab., 1951—56; chmn. dept. accel. physics Gulf Gen. Atomic Co., San Diego, 1957—69; founder, pres., CEO, chmn. bd. Sci. Applications, Inc., La Jolla, Calif., 1969—2003; mem. Joint Strategic Target Planning Staff, Sci. Adv. Group, Omaha, 1978; panel mem. Nat. Measurement Lab. Evaluation panel for Radiation Research, Washington, 1983. Founder Found. for Enterprise Devel., La Jolla, Calif., 1986. Co-author: Slow Neutron Scattering and Thermalization, 1970. With USN, 1943—46. Fellow: American Phys. Soc., American Nuclear Soc.; mem.: NAE. Republican. Roman Catholic. Avocation: sailing. Home: La Jolla, Calif. Died Dec. 22, 2014.

BEZY, EMMA LOUISE, alternative medicine educator, psychotherapist; b. Denver, June 9, 1948; d. Edwin Byron and Elisabeth Marie Bezy. BA in Lit., Seattle U., 1969; MSW in Psychiatric Social Work, U. Wash., 1973. Cert. social worker Assn. Cert. Social Workers, Wash. State Assn. Cert. Social Workers, mediator Nat. Ctr. Dispute Resolution. Ct. liaison; drug and alcohol counseling specialist Project Escape, Kent, Wash., 1973—75; exec. dir., dir. couns., cmty. edn. specialist Kent Valley Youth and Family Svcs., Kent, Wash., 1975—80; faculty, MA in Whole Systems Design Antioch U., Seattle, 1982—85; faculty, human svcs. program We. Wash. U., Seattle, 1988—90; faculty, thesis advisor Leadership Inst. Seattle/Bastyr U., 1990—94; pvt. practice in psychotherapy and orgnl. devel. consulting Seattle-Tacoma, from 1980; chair dept. spirituality, health and medicine, mem. planning task force Bastyr U., Kenmore, Wash., 1997—2002. Bd. dirs., steering com. Pacific N.W. Orgnl. Devel. Network, Seattle, 1980—83, Pacific N.W. Pers. Mgrs. Assn., Bellevue, Wash., 1985—87; founder, steering com. N.W. Relationship-Centered Care Network/Fetzer Inst., Seattle, from 1999; newsletter editor N.W. Women's Inst., Seattle, 1996—98. Co-deisgner (coll. brochure) Spirituality, Health & Medicine, 1999—2000 (Outstanding Coll. Brochure, 1999, 2000). Founder, organizer Women's Network for World Survival, Seattle, 1980—81; facilitator, vol. instr. Whidbey Inst./Chinook Learning Ctr., Clinton, Wash., 1982—85; tutor for youth CARITAS, Seattle U., 1966—68; rsch. asst., writer Seattle Crisis Clinic, 1966—68. Fellow, NIH, 1971—73. Mem.: NASW, Inst. Noetic Scis. Died June 21, 2007.

BHAKTIPRANA, PRAVRAJIKA See **THOMAS, GWENDOLYN JEANNE**

BIAGGI, MARIO, former congressman; b. NYC, Oct. 26, 1917; s. Salvatore and Mary (Campari) B.; m. Marie Wassil, Apr.20, 1941 (dec. 1997); children: Jacqueline, Barbara, Richard, Mario II. LL.B., N.Y. Law Sch., 1963; DL (hon.), Fordham U. Bar: NY 1963. Detective lt. NYC Police Dept., 1942-65; community relations specialist NYC, 1961-63; asst. sec. state NY, 1966; mem. 91st-100th Congresses from 19th Dist. N.Y., 1969-88; also chmn. subcom. on Coast Guard and navigation 91st-100th Congresses from 10th Dist. N.Y.; resigned, 1988. Mem. edn. and labor com., mcht. marine and fisheries com., chmn. subcom. on human services of select com. on aging, ex-officio mem. select com. on narcotics abuse and control, Past 1st v.p., acting pres. Patrolmen's Benevolent Assn.; past bd. dirs. Police Widows Relief Fund, Police Recreation Center, Police Pension Fund, Municipal Credit Union. Recipient medal of honor NYC Police, 1967; decorated Star of Solidarity Italy, 1961, Cavaliere Order of Merit, 1965; recipient Pub. Service award Greek Orthodox Archdiocese of N. and S.Am., Am. Mcht. Marines Achievement award, 1983; named Grandparent of Yr., 1983; nominated for Nobel Peace Prize, 1982. Mem. ABA Bronx County Bar Assn., Trial Lawyers Assn., NAACP (life), Navy League, Columbia Assns. in Civil Service (pres. nat. council) Democrat. Home: Bronx, NY. Died June 24, 2015.

BIALLA, ROWLEY, lawyer; b. NYC, Aug. 13, 1914; s. Edward and Amy (Rowley) B.; m. Marian L. Dunham, Mar. 23, 1945 (div. Mar. 1951); children: Margaret L., Jean B. Murphy; m. Mary S. Wilson, Aug. 21, 1954; 1 child, Nancy R. AB, Dartmouth Coll., 1937; LLB, Yale U., 1940. Bar: N.Y. 1940; U.S. Supreme Ct. 1945. Assoc. White & Case, NYC, 1940-41, 46-51; house counsel Guggenheim Interests, NYC, 1952-79; pvt. practice, Northport, NY, 1979—2002. Sec. Daniel and Florence Guggenheim Found., N.Y.C., 1979-2002; sec., bd. dirs. Lavanburg Found., N.Y.C., 1981-2002. Capt. U.S. Army, 1941-45. Mem. ABA. Avocations: history, genealogy. Died Oct. 2, 2007.

BICKEL, MINNETTE DUFFY, artist; b. New Bern, NC, June 24, 1921; d. Richard Nixon and Minnette (Chapman) Duffy; m. William Croft, Jan. 3, 1947; children: Minnette B. Boesel, Susan B. Scioli. One-woman shows include, N.C., statewide portrait exhbns., (two 1st place awards), regional juried shows, (winner three internat. awards); portraits include Gen. Claude Larkin, Tyrone Power, Thomas Graham, James Beckwith, Arthur Rolander, Frederick E. Fox, Senator Jesse Helms, Rachel Carson, R. Bud Dwyer, William Genge, Allison Williams, Dennis O'Connor, Frank Cahouet, Dr. Robert Edwards, Robert Wilburn, Henry L. Hillman. Mem. Am. Soc. Portrait Artists (affiliated), Stroke of Genius Gallery, Washington Soc. Portrait Artists and Portrait Inst., Portrait Soc. Am. Republican. Home: Pittsburgh, Pa. Died Mar. 31, 2007.

BICKER, DANIEL WAYNE, travel agency executive; b. Pasadena, Jan. 17, 1953; s. Robert Paul and Beverly June (Wessel) B.; m. Susan Lowell Ilsley, Mar. 20, 1976; children: Kimberly, Elizabeth, Jonathan, Phillip. BA in Polit. Sci., Calif. State Poly. U., 1976. With United Airlines, Chgo., Denver, 1974-84; v.p. mktg. Destination Travel, Inc., Denver, 1984-87; pres. Assn. World Travel, Inc., Denver, from 1988; ptnr. Trinity Group Cons., Denver, from 1987. Mem. Am. Soc. Assn. Execs., Profl. Conv. Mgmt. Assn. (adv. bd. Convene mag. 1986--). Republican. Presbyterian. Avocations: flying, mountain climbing. Home: Littleton, Colo. Died May 21, 2007.

BIDEN, BEAU (JOSEPH ROBINETTE BIDEN III), former state attorney general; b. Wilmington, Del., Feb. 3, 1969; s. Joseph Robinette Biden and Neilia Hunter; m. Hallie Biden; children: Natalie, Hunter. BA in European Hist., U. Pa., 1991; JD, Syracuse U. Coll. Law, NY, 1994. Bar: Del., Md., US Dist. Ct. Del. Law clk. to hon. Steven J. McAuliffe US Dist. Ct. NH, 1994—95; counsel Office Policy Devel., US Dept. Justice, Washington, 1995—97, fed. prosecutor (ea. dist.) Pa. Phila., 1997—2002, interim legal advisor Kosovo, 2001; civil litig. atty. Monzack & Monaco, Wilmington, Del., 2002—04; ptnr. Bifferato, Gentilotti, Biden & Balick LLC, Wilmington; atty. gen. State of Del., Dover, 2007—15. Bd. dirs. Met. Wilmington Urban League, Wilmington Housing Partnership, World Affairs Coun. Wilmington. Capt., Del. Army Nat. Guard, mem. 261st Signal Brigade JAGC, Smyrna, Del. Decorated Bronze Star. Mem.: Richard Rodney Inn of Ct. Democrat. Home: Wilmington, Del. Died May 30, 2015.

BIELUCH, WILLIAM CHARLES, retired judge; b. Nov. 12, 1918; AB magna cum laude, Brown U., 1939; JD, Yale U., 1942. Bar: Conn. 1942. Assoc. Covington, Burling, Rublee, Acheson & Shorb, Washington, 1942-43; ptnr. Bieluch, Barry & Ramenda and predecessors, Hartford, 1946-68; judge Cir. Ct. Conn., 1968-73, Ct. Common Pleas Conn., 1973-76, Superior Ct. Conn., 1976-85, Appellate Session, 1979-83, Appellate Ct. Conn., 1985-88; ret., 1988; judge trial referee, 1988—2010; ret., 2010. Trustee emeritus S. S. Cyril and Methodius Roman Cath. Ch., Hartford. Lt. (j.g.) USCG, WWII. Decorated Knight St. Gregory, Pope Paul VI, 1972; recipient Merit award Polish Legion Am. Vets., 1952, Man of Yr. award United Polish Socs., 1968, Archdiocesan medal of appreciation Archbishop John F. Whealon, 1970, Disting. Grad. award Nat. Cath. Elem. Sch., 1995. Mem. Conn. Bar Assn. (chmn. Jr. Bar Sect. 1948-49), Hartford County Bar Assn., KC, Phi Beta Kappa. Republican. Home: West Hartford, Conn. Died Dec. 16, 2012.

BIGOS, JOHN PETER, pulmonologist; b. Springfield, Mass., Nov. 20, 1955; s. Stanley Anthony and Patricia (Collins) B. BA, Bowdoin Coll., 1977; MD, U. Conn., 1982; MPH, Harvard U., 1986. Diplomate Am. Bd. Internal Medicine, Nat. Bd. Med. Examiners, Am. Subspeciality Bd. Pulmonary Diseases. Med. intern Hartford (Conn.) Hosp., 1982-83; resident in internal medicine Danbury (Conn.) Hosp./Yale U. Sch. Medicine, 1983-85, fellow in pulmonary medicine, 1987-89; pvt. practice pulmonology New London, Conn., from 1989. Speaker, lectr. in field; co-chmn. carrier adv. com. Travelers Medicare, 1992—; attending physician chief grade internal medicine Boston VA/Boston U., 1986-87; vis. pulmonary fellow U. Conn. Health Ctr., 1988, Brompton Hosp., London, 1988; mem. U.S. Senate Labor Human Resources Com., 1982. Contbr. articles to profl. publs. Kellogg Found. fellow Harvard U., 1985-86; James Bowdoin scholar, 1976-77. Fellow Am. Coll. Chest Physicians; mem. AMA (caucus chmn. Conn. hosp. med. staff sect. 1991—, ad hoc health task force Conn. 1992), Am. Cancer Soc. (pres.-elect Conn. divsn., chmn. publ. issues com. 1992—, bd. dirs., exec. com. 1992—), Am. Thoracic Soc. and Lung Assn. (bd. dirs. Conn. divsn. 1988-90, fin. steering com. 1988, rsch. awards com. 1988), Conn. Thoracic Soc., Conn. State med. Soc. (assoc. councilor 1993-95, sec. 1995—), Am. Aging Assn., Am. Coll. Chest Physicians, Mass. Med. Soc., Phi Beta Kappa. Democrat. Roman Catholic. Home: Niantic, Conn. Died Dec. 9, 2006.

BIHLER, FREDERICK HENRY, electronics company executive; b. NYC, Sept. 8, 1926; s. Frederick H. and Isabelle A. (Ziegler) B.; m. Ruth M. Hinck, Sept. 18, 1948 (dec. July 1973); children: Barbara Bihler Schmidt, Douglas, Carol Bihler De Loriea, Susan Bihler Bandman; m. Nancy E. Woodruff, Feb. 22, 1975. BSEE, NYU, 1950. Nat. sales mgr. Furnas Electric Co., Batavia, Ill., 1962-69; v.p. sales and mktg. Clare div. Gen. Instrument Corp., Chgo., 1969-76; sr. v.p. Fujitsu Am. Inc., San Jose, Calif., 1976-85; pres. Advantest Am., Inc., Lincolnshire, Ill., from 1985. Mgmt. cons., Lake Forest, Ill., 1976, 85. Inventor dairy automation control system, 1960. Served with USN, 1944-46, PTO. Mem. IEEE. Avocations: horseback riding, photography, stamp collecting/philately, sailing. Home: Lake Forest, Ill. Died Feb. 19, 2007.

BIKEL, THEODORE MEIR, actor, singer; b. Vienna, May 2, 1924; came to U.S., 1954, naturalized, 1961; s. Josef and Miriam (Riegler) B.; m. Ofra Ichilov (div.) m. Rita Weinberg Call, 1967 (div.); m. Tamara Brooks (dec. 2012); m. Aimee Ginsburg; children Robert, Daniel; stepchildren Zeev and Noam Ginsburg Student, U. London; grad., Royal Acad. Dramatic Art, London, 1948; DFA (hon.), U. Hartford, 1992; LHD, Seton Hall U., 2003; DFH, Hebrew Union Coll., 2005. Apprentice with Habimah Theatre, Tel Aviv, 1942-44, a founder, Israel Cameri, 1944-46; theatrical prodns. include A Streetcar Named Desire, London, 1950, The Love of Four Colonels, London, 1950-52, Tonight in Samarkand, N.Y.C., 1954, The Lark, N.Y.C., 1955-56, Rope Dancers, N.Y.C., 1957-58, Sound of Music, N.Y.C., 1959-61, Fiddler on the Roof, various cities, 1968-72, 74, 77, 79, 80, 82-83, 85, 87-96, 98, 00, 01, 02, The Rothschilds (nat. co.), 1972, Jacques Brel is Alive and Well and Living in Paris, various cities, 1974-75, The Good Doctor, various cities, 1975, Zorba, various cities, 1976, 78, Inspector Gen., N.Y.C., 1978, Threepenny Opera, Mpls., 1983, My Fair Lady, Phoenix, 1988-89, She Loves Me, various cities, 1989-90, Sholom Aleichem Lives, 1997, The Disputation, Miami, 1999, Washington, 2005, The Gathering, N.Y.C., Miami, 1999, The Chosen, Miami and N.J., 2004; opera prodns. include La Gazza Ladra, Phila., 1990, Abduction from the Seraglio, Cleve., 1992, Ariadne auf Naxos, L.A. Opera, 1992, Sholem Aleichem: Laughter Through Tears, 2008; motion pictures include African Queen, 1951, The Little Kidnappers, 1951, Moulin Rouge, 1953, The Enemy Below, 1957, I Want to Live, 1958, The Defiant Ones, 1958 (Academy award nomination), Blue Angel, 1959, My Fair Lady, 1964, Sands of the Kalahari, 1965, The Russians are Coming, 1966, Sweet November, 1967, My Side of the Mountain, 1969, Darker Than Amber, 1970, The Little Ark, 1971, See You in the Morning, 1989, Shattered, 1991, My Family Treasure, 1993, Crime and Punishment, 1993, Shadow Conspiracy, 1995, Second Chances, 1997; also numerous TV appearances, 1954-2015; host, TV prodns. The Eternal Light, 1958, Look Up and Live, 1958-60; host-editor: TV prodn. Directions 61, 1961; weekly radio program At Home with Theodore Bikel, 1958-63; concert folk singer, 1955-2015, rec. artist for, Elektra and Reprise; albums include Israeli Folk Songs, 1955, Songs of Russia Old & New, 1960, A Taste of Passover, 1998, A Taste of Hanukkah, 2000, In My Own Lifetime: 12 Musical Theater Classics, 2006; reader books on tape including The Hope (Herman Wouk), The Glory (Herman Wouk), The Name of the Rose (Umberto Eco); Author: Folksongs and Footnotes, 1960, (autobiography) Theo, 1994, rev. editions., 2002, 2014 Mem. Nat. Coun. for Arts, 1977-82; founder arts chpt. Am. Jewish Congress, 1961-63, nat. v.p., 1963-70, chmn. governing coun., 1970-80, sr. v.p., 1980-2002; del. Democratic Nat. Conv., 1968; founder Newport Folk Festival Recipient Emmy award, 1988, Lifetime Achievement award Nat. Found. for Jewish Culture, 1997. Mem. AFTRA, SAG, AGMA, Acad. TV Arts and Scis. (gov. 1961-65), AEA (councillor 1961-64, 1st v.p. 1964-73, pres. 1973-82, pres. emeritus 1982-2015), Am. Coun. Arts (bd. dirs. 1970-80), Internat. Fedn. Actors (v.p. 1981-91), Associated Actors and Artists of Am. (pres. 1989), Acad. Motion Picture Arts and Scis., Am. Fedn. Musicians. *If I am a universalist-and I believe myself to be one-I derive my general standard of humanity from a particularist experience. For, above all and before all else, I am a Jew. That, to me, means a heightened awareness of the human condition and the sad-sweet knowledge that where we stand someone has stood before. It means a mode of living and a method of survival. Spiritually and culturally to be a Jew is to be a man on the road from Jerusalem to Jerusalem. I am an American; this is my home and my daily solace. Jerusalem, however, is my hope and my inspiration.* Died July 21, 2015.

BILKER, MINDY SUE, secretary; b. Phila., July 16, 1952; d. Stanley Burton and Beatrice (Weiner) Bloom; m. David Alan Bilker, June 20, 1976; 1 child, Stefanie. AAS, Community Coll. of Phila., 1971; cert. in med. lab. tech., Dobbins Tech. Sch., 1972. Med. technician U.S. VA Hosp., Phila., 1978-82; records analysis clk. Social Security Adminstrn., Phila. and Washington, 1983-89; med. technician Nat. Naval Med. Ctr., Bethesda, Md., 1989-91; med. technician, sec., from 1991. Parent advocate Easter Seal Soc., Phila., 1985-87. Mem. Am. Soc. Med. Technologists. Democrat. Avocation: cooking. Home: Rockville, Md. Died May 17, 2007.

BIRD, FORREST MORTON, retired medical inventor; b. Stoughton, Mass., June 9, 1921; s. Morton Forrest and Jane Bird; m. Mary Moran, 1945 (dec.); 1 child, Catherine Natoni; m. Dominique Deckers, 1988 (div. 1998); m. Pamela Riddle; 1 stepchild, Brandon Riddle; 1 stepchild, Rachel Schwam. PhD in Aeronautics, Northrop U., Inglewood, 1977; MD, Pontifical Catholic U. of Campinas, Brazil, 1979. Cert. Pilot. Technical air tng. officer Army Air Corps; founder Bird Corp., Bird Space Tech. Corp., Sandpoint, Idaho. Trustee emeritus Am. Respiratory Care Found. Inventor Bird Universal Medical Respirator for acute or chronic cardiopulmonary care, 1958, "Babybird" respirator, 1970. Inductee Nat. Inventors Hall of Fame, 1995; recipient Presidential Citizens medal, 2008, Nat. Medal Technology and Innovation, 2009. Avocations: collector & pilot of 18 vintage flying aircraft., travel. Died Aug. 2, 2015.

BIRDSALL, NORTON PHILO, retired sales and marketing professional; b. Margretsville, NY, Jan. 8, 1910; s. Ralph N. and Ruby (Norton) B.; m. Gertrude Clark, May 29, 1933; children: Cheryl C., David Norton. AS, Pratt Inst., 1931. Sales clk. Am. Machine & Foundry Co., New Haven, 1931-37, salesman, 1944-52; with tech. sales dept. Corbin Screw Corp., New Britain, Conn., 1937-44, Anaconda/Atlantic Richfield Co., 1951-74; cons. in pub. rels. and sales F. and S. Oil Co., Waterbury, Conn., 1975-93. Instr. engring. sci., mgmt. in war tng. U. Conn., Hartford, 1934-44. Mem. Masons. Congregationalist. Avocations: travel, photography. Home: Cheshire, Conn. Died Aug. 7, 2007.

BIRMINGHAM, STEPHEN GARDNER, writer; b. Andover, Conn., May 28, 1929; s. Thomas J. and Editha (Gardner) B.; m. Janet Tillson, Jan. 5, 1951 (div.); children: Mark, Harriet, Carey; partner Edward Lahniers BA in English (cum laude), Williams Coll., 1950; postgrad., Univ. Coll., Oxford U., Eng., 1951. Advt. copywriter Needham, Harper & Steers, Inc., NY, 1953-67. Taught creative writing U. Cincinnati. Author: Young Mr. Keefe, 1958, Barbara Greer, 1959, The Towers of Love, 1961, Those Harper Women, 1963, Fast Start, Fast Finish, 1966, Our Crowd: The Great Jewish Families of New York, 1967, The Right People: A Portrait of the American Social Establishment, 1968, Heart Toubles, 1968, The Grandees: America's Sephardic Elite, 1971, The Late John Marquand, 1972, The Right Places, 1973, Real Lace: America's Irish Rich, 1973, Certain People: America's Black Elite, 1977, The Golden Dream: Suburbia in the 1970's, 1978, Jacqueline Bouvier Kennedy Onassis, 1978, Life at the Dakota: new York's Most Unusual Address, 1979, California Rich, 1980, Duchess, 1981, The Grandes Dames, 1982, The Auerbach Will, 1983; The Rest of Us:The Rise of America's Eastern European Jews, 1984, The LeBaron Secret, 1986, Americas Secret Aristocracy, 1987, Shades of Fortune, 1989, The Rothman Scandal, 1991, Carriage Trade, 1993, The Wrong Kind of Money, 1997; contbr. numerous articles to numerous periodicals. Served with AUS, 1951-53. Mem. New Eng. Soc. City NY, Players Club (NYC), Queen City Club (Cin.), Nat. Arts Club (NYC), Phi Beta Kappa. Democrat. Episcopalian. Home: New York, NY. Died Nov. 15, 2015.

BISHOP, CHRISTY B., lawyer; b. Akron, Ohio, Mar. 10, 1960; m. Dennis R. Thompson. BA in Rhetoric, U. Akron, 1985, MA in Rhetoric, 1991, JD cum laude, 2002. Bar: Ohio 2003, US Dist. Ct. (no. dist.) Ohio 2003, US Dist. Ct. (so. dist.) Ohio 2006, US Supreme Ct. 2006, cert.: Ohio State Bar Assn. (labor and employment attorney) 2008, Ohio State Bar Assn. (in labor and employment law) 2008. Journalist Village Views, Akron, 1982—85; mng. editor Great Lakes Sailor Mag., Akron, 1986—89; prof. U. Akron, 1991—94, adj. faculty, sr. faculty, sch. comm., 2013; law clk. Thompson Law Office, Akron, 1992—2002; ptnr. Thompson & Bishop, Akron, from 2002. Mem. Tchg. Tolerance Campaign So. Poverty Law Ctr., from 2003; mem. leadership coun. Poverty Law Ctr.; mem. Democratic Nat. Campaign Com., from 1992, Leadership Coun. Southern Poverty Law Ctr. Recipient Westlaw Excellence award, 1998, Anderson Book award, 2001, Hon. Arthur Goldberg prize Constitutional Law, 2002; named Ohio Super Lawyer, 2008—11. Mem.: Nat. Employment Lawyers Assn. (mem. comm. com. from 2003), Ohio Employment Lawyers Assn. (mem. amicus brief com. from 2002, chmn. Akron chpt. from 2002, mem. judiciary com. from 2004). Democrat. Episcopalian. Avocations: writing, music, boating, hiking. Home: Akron, Ohio. Died Dec. 2, 2015.

BITTNER, JAMES ANTHONY, entertainment consultant; b. New Albany, Ind., Nov. 21, 1911; s. John and Anna Esther (Magness) B. Student pub. sch., Louisville, Ky. Singer radio program Sta. WHAS, Louisville, 1928-30; actor Brown Theatre, Louisville, 1929-31, Nat. Theatre, Louisville, 1932-33; master of ceremonies Log Cabin and Greyhound Night Clubs, New Albany, 1929-33, Coliseum and Arcadia Gardens, Chgo., 1934-41, Hawthorne Derby Show, Calif., 1935; entertainer, from 1935; disk jockey Sta. WGRC, 1945. Cons. Hon. Order Ky. Cols., Louisville, 1955—. Author: From Here to There, 1991. Recipient Golden Camel award, Kosair Temple, 1975, Fez award, 1977, Potentate Jewel award, 1979, Potentate's award, 1982. Mem. Masons, York Rite (Red Cap award 1975, White Cap award, 1991, Blue Cap award, 1994), Knights Kadosh (comdr. 1980-81), Downtown Hi-12 Club (pres. 1971-73), 32 Club (pres. 1972-74, 89-91) Republican. United Methodist. Home: Clarksville, Ind. Died May 16, 2007.

BLACKADAR, ALFRED KIMBALL, meteorologist, educator; b. Newburyport, Mass., July 6, 1920; s. Walter Lloyd and Harriett (White) B.; m. Beatrice J. Fenner, Mar. 23, 1946; children: Bruce Evan, Russell Lloyd, Thomas Alan. AB, Princeton U., 1942; PhD, NYU, 1950. From instr. to asso. prof. NYU, 1946-56; lectr. climatology Columbia U., 1953-55; mem. faculty Pa. State U., 1956—85, prof. meteorology, 1961—85, prof. emeritus, from 1985, head dept., 1967-81. Mem. exec. com. Univ. Corp. Atmospheric Rsch., 1965-68; mem. exec. com. divsn. earth scis. NRC, 1966-69; mem. Internat. Commn. on Dynamical Meteorology, 1978-94, chair working group A, 1978-85; vis. prof. Christian-Albrechts U., Kiel, Germany, 1985-95. Editor: Meteorological Research Revs., 1957; exec. editor: Weatherwise, 1981-95. Sec. Univ. Christian Assn., 1964-68. Served to maj. USAAF, 1942-46. Recipient Sr. Scientist award Alexander von Humboldt Found. Fellow AAAS, Am. Geophys. Union, Am. Meteorol. Soc. (sec. 1965-69, pres. 1971-72, editor monographs, Charles F. Brooks award 1969, Cleveland Abbe award 1986, award for outstanding contbns. to the advance of applied meteorology 2002, chmn. publs. commn. 1978-84, chair com. on awards 1989-90, elected hon. mem. 2008), Deutsche Meteorologische Gesellschaft (fgn. mem.), North Plainfield HS (NJ) Hall of Fame. Baptist. Home: State College, Pa. Died Jan. 17, 2015.

BLACKWELL, F. ORIS, environmental scientist, educator; b. Feb. 27, 1925; s. Floyd Weaver and Mary Olive Blackwell; m. Eleanor Louise Edwards, May 5, 1951; children: Susan, Betsy, Mary Ruth, Stephen. BS in Bacteriology and Pub. Health, Wash. State U., Pullman, 1950; MS in Bacteriology and Pub. Health, U. Mass., 1954; MPH in Environ. Health Adminstrn., U. Calif., Berkeley, 1965, DPh in Health Adminstrn., 1967. Rsch. scientist Calif. Gen. sanitarian Benton-Franklin Dist. Health Dept., Pasco, Wash., 1950—53; health and sanitation advisor USAID Program, Peshawar, Pakistan, 1954—56, sr. sanitation advisor Dacca, East Pakistan, 1957—59; asst. prof., acting chair dept. environ. health S.P.H. Am. U. Beirut, 1967—71; assoc. prof. environ. health Rutgers U., New Brunswick, NJ, 1967—71; assoc. prof. environ. health Sch. Medicine U. Vt., 1971—74; prof. environ. health East Carolina U., Greenville, NC, 1974—82; prof., chair dept. environ. health sci. Ea. Ky. U., Richmond, 1982—90; ret., 1990. Mem. gov. coun. USPHA, Washington, 1984—88; mem. various site visits accreditation Nat. Coun. Environ. Curriculum, Ind. State U., Ferris State U., others, 1977—78; curriculum cons. dept. bacteriology Wash. State U., Pullman, 1977; cons. water supply devel. USAID-MetaMetrics Inc., Sri Lanka, 1980; leader pub. health del. People to People Program to People's Republic of China, 1987. Editor: (book revision) Health and Safety in the School Environment, 1978. Apptd. Citizen's Task Force on Chem. Weapons Disposal, Ky., 1984—90. With USNR, 1943—46. Recipient Walter Mangold award, Nat. Environ. Assn., 1989; named a Ky. Col., Gov. W. Wilkerson, 1988. Mem.: Am. Acad. Sanitarians (bd. dirs. 1972—77, bd. cert. diplomate, Laureate diplomate 1977), Nat. Enivron. Health Assn. (life; pres. 1975—77). Democrat. Mem. Soc. Of Friends. Avocations: gardening, nature studies, conservation. Died Nov. 4, 2006.

BLAIR, CHARLES MELVIN, manufacturing company executive, scientist; b. Vernon, Tex., Oct. 24, 1910; s. Charles Melvin and Sallie (Gilliland) B.; m. Catherine E. Stone, June 12, 1936; children: Charles Melvin III, Sally. BA, Rice U., 1931, MA, 1932; PhD, Calif. Inst. Tech., 1935. Research chemist Petrolite Corp., St. Louis, 1935-43, research dir. for corp., 1943-52, pres., 1952-64; vice chancellor Washington U., St. Louis, 1964-67; v.p. Magna Corp., Santa Fe Springs, Calif., 1967-72, pres., 1972-76; chmn. bd. successor Baker Performance Chems. Inc., 1977-86; pres. Blair Petroleum Co., Fullerton, Calif., from 1986. Author articles on sci. and cultural subjects; patentee in field. Recipient Disting. Alumni award Rice U., 1992. Mem. AAAS, Am. Chem. Soc., Soc. Petroleum Engrs., Phi Beta Kappa, Sigma Xi, Phi Lambda Upsilon. Pioneer in applications of surface chemistry to solution of problems in petroleum and pharm. industries. Died Dec. 26, 2006.

BLAIR, FREDERICK DAVID, interior designer; b. Denver, June 15, 1946; s. Frederick Edward and Margaret (Whitely) Blair. BA, U. Colo., 1969; postgrad., U. Denver, 1981—82. Interior designer The Denver, 1969-76, store mgr., 1976-80; v.p. Hartley Ho. Interiors, Ltd., Denver, 1980-83; pvt. practice Denver, from 1983. Com. mem. Ice Ho. Design Ctr., Denver, 1985—86, Design Directory Western Region, Denver, 1986; mem. edn. com. ASID Nat. Conf., Denver, 1991; coord. Amb. Vol. Program Denver Internat. Airport, from 2000; mgr. concierge & visitors ctr. Cherry Creek Shopping Ctr., Denver, 2003; prog. dir. Pub. Rels. & Mkg. Denver Internat. Airport. Designs shown in various mags. Bd. dirs. One Day, Very Spl. Arts, 1993, Supporters Children, from 1996, mem. steering com., 1994, pres.-elect, 1996—97, pres., bd. dirs., from 1999; mem. Denver Art Mus., Nat. Trust Hist. Preservation, Hist. Denver. Recipient Aviation Ace Award, DIA, 2001. Mem.: Am. Soc. Interior Designers (co-chmn. com. profl. registration 1986, mem. edn. com. nat. conf. 1991, bd. dirs. Colo. chpt. from 1990, Humanist award 1997). Christian Scientist. Avocations: skiing, painting, tennis. Home: Denver, Colo. Deceased.

BLAIR, ROSEMARY MILES, retired art educator, environmentalist; d. George Bernard and Kathryn Gannon Miles; m. David William Blair, Jan. 30, 1954; children: Karen, Barbara, Maria, Amanda, David Belmont, Rachel. BA, Coll. New Rochelle, 1951; MA, Columbia U. Tchrs. Coll., 1969; post grad., Princeton U., 1975. Cert. adminstrn. N.J., 1973, N.Y., 1973, art instr. K-12 N.J., N.Y., prin. NJ, 1973. Art tchr., coord. and supr. Princeton Regional Schs., NJ, 1965—96; spl. cons. tchr. preparation program Princeton U.; ret., 1996. Chair 12th dist. U.S. Congressional Art Competition. One woman and group shows, US and Can., work in corp. and pvt. collections. Founding parent, vol. Stuart County Day Sch., Princeton, from 1963; cmty. activist Princeton Cmty. Dem. Org., from 1979; lector Aquinas Found. Princeton U.; bd. trustees St. Saviour Sch., Bklyn., 1990—95; founding pres. and chmn. bd. Friends Princeton Open Space, 1979—89; mem. alumni coun. Coll. New Rochelle, NY, 1983—87; pres. Del. & Raritan Canal Coalition, 1985—2012; founder, trustee Del. Raritan Greenway Land Trust, Princeton, from 1989; mem. Princeton Environ. Commn., 1998—2006. Mem.: Consortium Arts Edn. (exec. dir. 1983—93), Art Educators NJ (conf. chmn. 1981, pres. 1982), Nova Scotia Nature Trust. Democrat. Avocation: painting. Home: Princeton, NJ. Died July 2, 2015.

BLAIR, WILLIAM MCCORMICK, JR., lawyer; b. Chgo., Oct. 24, 1916; s. William McCormick and Helen (Bowen) B.; m. Catherine Gerlach, Sept. 9, 1961; 1 son, William McCormick III (dec.). AB, Stanford U., 1940; LL.B., U. Va., 1947. Bar: Ill. 1947, D.C. 1972. Assoc. firm Wilson & McIlvaine, Chgo., 1947-50; adminstrv. asst. to Gov. Adlai E. Stevenson of Ill., 1950-52; ptnr. firm Stevenson, Rifkind & Wirtz, Chgo., 1955-61, Paul, Weiss, Rifkind, Wharton & Garrison, NYC, 1957-61; U.S. ambassador to Denmark, 1961-64, to Philippines, 1964-67; gen. dir. John F. Kennedy Ctr., 1968-72; ptnr. firm Surrey & Morse, Washington, 1978-84, of counsel, 1984-86. Bd. dirs. Am.-Scandinavian Found., N.Y.C.; v.p. bd. dirs. Albert and Mary Lasker Found., N.Y.C., 1968-98. Capt. USAAF, 1942-46. Decorated Bronze Star U.S.; officer Order of Crown, Belgium; Order of Sikatuna, Philippines; comdr. cross Order of Dannebrog 1st class, Denmark). Mem. Am. Coun. Ambs. (vice chmn., pres. 1985-89), River Club (N.Y.C.), Phi Delta Phi. Died Aug. 29, 2015.

BLAKE, MICHAEL, writer; b. Fort Bragg, NC, July 5, 1945; m. Marianne Mortensen, 1993; 3 children. Student, U. N.Mex., Albuquerque, Eastern N.Mex. U., Portales. Screenwriter: Stacy's Knights, 1983, Dances with Wolves, 1990 (Golden Globe award for Best Screenplay-Motion Picture, 1991, Academy award for Best Adapted Screenplay, 1991, Writer's Guild award for Best Adapted Screenplay, 1991); dir.: (TV films) Laughing Horse, 1986; prodr.: (documentaries) The American West: On the Road with Michael Blake, 2008; featured in numerous documentaries; author: Dances with Wolves, 1988, (with Kevin Costner and Jim Wilson) Dances with Wolves: The Illustrated Story of the Epic Film, 1990, Airman Mortensen, 1991, Marching to Valhalla, 1996, The Holy Road, 2001, 2011, Indian Yell, 2006, Twelve the King, 2009, Into the Stars, 2011, (autobiography) Like a Running Dog, 2002. Served USAF, 1964-68. Mem. Acad. of Motion Picture Arts and Sciences. Died May 2, 2015.

BLAKE, ROBERT WADE, retired insurance company executive; b. Houston, Apr. 8, 1920; s. William Mark and Marion (Rowland) Blake; children: Sharon, Nan. Student, Okla. U., Tex. Tech. U. Oil, gas operator, Lubbock, Tex.; dir. Citizens Nat. Bank, Lubbock, Muleshoe (Tex.) State Bank, Harv Queen Mill & Elevator Co., Plainview, Tex., Caprock Investment Co., Lubbock, Arnett Benson life Ins. Co., Lubbock. Author: (autobiography) My Life: In War - In Business - In Politics, 2002. Co-chmn. Fund-Raiser for Pres. Gerald Ford, Lubbock, 1976, George Bush for Pres. Campaign, Lubbock, 1979—80, George Bush for Pres. Com., 1987—88; dir. Lubbock Fed. Housing Authority, 1952. First lt., navigator Army Air Corps, 1942—45, China. Decorated Silver Star Army Air Corps, Dist. Flying Crosses, Air medal with Clusters, Purple Heart, Dist. Svc. medal Rep. China. Mem.: The Flying Tigers, 14th Air Force Assn. (life), Nat. Football Found. and Hall of Fame (life). Republican. Meth. Avocations: hunting, fishing. Home: Lubbock, Tex. Died Mar. 28, 2007.

BLANKFORT, LOWELL ARNOLD, newspaper and book publisher; b. NYC, Apr. 29, 1926; s. Herbert and Gertrude (Butler) B.; m. April Pemberton; 1 child, Jonathan. BA in History and Polit. Sci., Rutgers U., 1946. Reporter, copy editor LI Star-Jour., NY, 1947—49; columnist London Daily Mail, Paris, 1949—50; copy editor The Stars & Stripes, Darmstadt, Germany, 1950—51, Wall St. Jour., NYC, 1951; bus., labor editor Cowles Mags., NYC, 1951—53; pub. Pacifica Tribune, Calif., 1954—59; freelance writer Europe, Asia, 1959—61; co-pub., editor Chula Vista Star-News, Calif., 1961—78; co-owner Paradise Post, Calif., 1977—2003. Co-owner Monte Vista Jour., Colo., Ctr. Post-Dispatch, Colo., Del Norte Prospector, Colo., 1978—93, Plainview News, Minn., St. Charles Press, Minn., Lewiston Jour., Minn., 1980—98, Summit Sentinel, Colo., New Richmond News, Wis., 1981—87, Yuba City Valley Herald, 1982—85, TV Views, Monterey, Calif., 1982—87, Summit County Jour., 1982—87, Alpine Sun, Calif., 1987—93, Bassics Mag., from 1998, Fingerstyle Guitar Mag., 1999. Columnist, contbr. articles on fgn. affairs to newspapers. Active Calif. Dem. Ctrl. Com., 1963. Recipient Best Editl. in Calif., non-dailies, 1st or 2d place seven consecutive yrs., Calif. Newspaper Pub. Assn., Best Editl. in US, Nat. Newspaper Assn., Best Editl. US Suburban Newspapers, Suburban Pubs. Newspapers Am., John Swett award, Calif. Edn. Assn., Spl. Media award for articles on S.Am., Nat. Conference Christians and Jews; named Citizen of Yr., Sweetwater Edn. Assn., Outstanding Layman of Yr., 1966, Citizen of Yr., City of Chula Vista, 1976, Headliner of Yr., San Diego Press Club, 1980. Mem.: ACLU (pres. San Diego chpt. 1970—71), World Affair Coun. Am. (dir. 2001—07, 2009—11), Soc. Profl. Journalists, Calif. Newspaper Pubs. Assn., East Meets West Found. (nat. v.p. 1992—98), World Federalist Assn. (pres. San Diego chpt. 1984—86, nat. bd. 1992—2000), UN Assn. (pres. San Diego chpt. 1991—93, nat. coun. 1992—97, nat. bd. 1997—2001, chpt. bd. from 1999), Internat. Ctr. Devel. Policy (nat. bd. 1985—90), Ctr. Internat. Policy (bd. dirs. from 1991), World Affairs Coun. San Diego (pres. 1996—99, v.p. 2005—06, dir. from 2009), Inst. of the Ams. (assoc.; internat. coun. from 1994). Achievements include interviewing many heads of state including Fidel Castro in Cuba, Li Peng and Li Ziannin in China, Benazir Bhutto in Pakistan, Kim Dae Jung in Korea, Paul Kagame in Rwanda. Home: San Diego, Calif. Died Mar. 8, 2015.

BLEDSOE, CHARLES WESLEY, industrial supply company executive; b. Ellensburg, Wash., Feb. 26, 1912; s. Howard Franklin and Vera (De Weese) B.; m. Marion McKenzie, Feb. 7, 1942; children: Charles Scott, James Barry. BA in Econs. and Bus., U. Wash., 1939. Mgr. men's dept. Roosevelt St. Store Sears, Roebuck & Co., Seattle, 1945-46; chief ground instr. Northern Aircraft Co., Seattle, 1946-49; sales rep. ITT Grinnel Co., Seattle, 1949-50; chmn. bd. Canal Indsl. Supply Co., Seattle, 1950-85. Trustee Northwest Theological Union, 1985—; elder United Presbyn. Ch., Seattle, 1952-79. Served as officer USAAF, WWII. Mem. Instrument Soc. Am. (lifetime), Nat. Assn. Corrosion Engrs., Soc. Port Engrs., Assn. Gen. Gen. Contractors, ASHREA, Sierra Club, Aircraft Owners and Pilots Assn., Common Cause (charter), World Without War Council of Greater Seattle, Seattle C. of C., Seattle Lincoln Hi Alumni Assn. (pres. 1982-83. Clubs: Seattle City, Swedish (Seattle). Lodges: Ballard Kiwanis (pres. 1956). Home: Seattle, Wash. Died Feb. 16, 2007.

BLEMKER, MARGARET RUTH, educator, world mission executive; b. New Bremen, Ohio, Apr. 2, 1915; d. Rudolf William and Lillian (Kohl) B. BA, Heidelberg Coll., Tiffin, Ohio, 1936, LHD (hon.), 1958; MEd, Syracuse U., 1942. Tchr. North Canton (Ohio) High Sch., 1936-39, Timken Voc. High Sch., Canton, 1939-40, Amerikan Kiz Koleji, Izmir, Turkey, 1945-48; dir. residences Univ. Hosps., Cleve., 1942-45; Near East exec. United Ch. Bd. for World Ministries, Boston, NYC, 1949-80. Mem. AAUW, LWV. Democrat. Mem. United Church of Christ. Home: Claremont, Calif. Died Jan. 7, 2007.

BLEY, PAUL (HYMAN PAUL BLEY), jazz pianist, composer, producer; b. Montreal, Que., Can., Nov. 10, 1932; s. Joseph and Betty Bley; m. Carla Bley 1957, (div. 1968); m. Carol Goss; children Vanessa Bley, Angelica Palmer, Solo Peacock Studied violin and piano, jr. diploma McGill Conservatory at age 11; studied composition, conducting at, Juilliard Sch. Music, 1950-52. Pres. Improvising Artists, Inc., 1975, v.p. Started musical career as leader of high sch. band; organizer: (quartet) Chalet Hotel, Montreal, 1945-48; with Ozzie Roberts, Clarence Joines; played at Alberta Lounge, 1949-50; weekly TV show Jazz Workshop, Montreal, 1952; with weekly TV show, Stan Kenton; in movie short dealing with jazz history; played N.Y.C. clubs, midwestern colls., 1955, nightclubs, Los Angeles, 1956-58, also group shows with Ornette Coleman and, Don Cherry, 1958, coll. concert, Calif., 1957-59; with Charlie Mingus, 1960, Jimmy Guiffre, 1960-61; toured Fed. Republic of Germany, 1961; performer coll. concerts including Town Hall and Lincoln Ctr., 1962-63; mem. Sonny Rollins' quartet, 1963; tours in U.S. and Europe; appearances onnetwork show Sta. WNDT-TV; concert tour of Japan and RCA Victor Recs., 1964; formed: trio for Bard Coll. concert, 1964; trio recorded for E.S.P. Records, 1965, toured Europe, 1965-67, tour Eastern U.S. colls., 1967; recs. for Mercury-Limelight Records, Milestone Records, Douglas Internat. Records (solo piano album), ECM Records; commd. to write and to play for Norddeutcher Rundfunk, Hamburg, Fed. Republic of Germany, 1969; solo pianist European tour, 1970-74; toured with Gary Peacock and Barry Altschul, Japan, 1976, Europe, 1976-77; numerous TV appearances; albums include Closer, Ballads, Open to Love, Alone Again, Quiet Song, Turning Point, Sonor, Tango Palace, Tears, Fragments, 1986, The Paul Bley Quartet, 1988. Recipient Composition award Nat. Endowment for Arts, 1977. Introduced new keyboard instrument Synthesizer at Philharmonic Hall, 1969. *As a pianist, it is my goal to compose as well as I can improvise.* Died Jan. 3, 2016.

BLISS, BILLIE SWINDELL, medical/surgical and community health nurse; b. Tex., May 4, 1930; d. Jesse Dee and Lucy Pauline (Northcut) Swindell; m. Lloyd V. Bliss, July 13, 1956; children: L. Charles, Jennifer, Howard W. AA, Cen. Wash. Deaconess Hosp., Wenatchee, 1951; student, South Seattle Community Coll., 1974. Cert. emergency rm. nurse, ACLS. Charge nurse, emergency Providence Hosp., Anchorage; supervising nurse, emergency Ballard Hosp., Seattle; gen. duty staff nurse Swedish Hosp. Med. Ctr., Seattle; home care nurse for neurologically disabled Mill Creek, Wash. Nurse instr. USPHS. Mem. ANA, Wash. State Nurses Assn. Died Feb. 28, 2007.

BLITZ, MORRIS E., education educator; b. Boston, Mass., May 7, 1914; s. Eliazer Louis and Esther (Goldstein) B.; m. Evelyn Silverman; children: Robert D., Phillip L. BA, Boston Coll., 1937; MA, Wahsington U., 1951. Cert. tchr., learning disabilities, psychol. examiner, Mo. Tchr. Normandy Sch. Dist., St. Louis, Mo., 1946-72, 1955-60, dir. personnel svcs., 1960-67, supt., 1967-72; test cons. U. Mo. St. Louis, from 1972. Football, wrestling coach, Normandy Sch. Dist., 1947-60; chmn. Normandy Tchrs. Assn. Founder U. Mo. St. Louis, 1958-61; sec. commn. on discipline of judges, Mo., 1987-93. 1st Lt. U.S. Army, 1941-46. Recipient Outstanding Alumni award, Boston Coll., 1967; named Outstanding Educator Mo. House of Reps. for Wayne Goode Resolution, 1977, Mo. Senate for Harriet Woods Resolution, 1977; named to Mo. H.S. Wrestling Hall of Fame. Mem. Am. Counselor Assn. (chmn. 1960-61). Avocations: reading, exercise, crossword puzzles. Home: Saint Louis, Mo. Died June 8, 2007.

BLOEDE, VICTOR CARL, lawyer, consultant, director; b. Woodwardville, Md., July 17, 1917; s. Carl Schon and Eleanor (Eck) B.; m. Ellen Louise Miller, May 9, 1947; children: Karl Abbott, Pamela Elena. AB, Dartmouth Coll., 1940; JD cum laude, U. Md., Balt., 1950; LLM in Pub. Law, Georgetown U., 1967. Bar: Md. 1950, Fed. Hawaii 1958, U.S. Supreme Ct. 1971. Pvt. practice, Balt., 1950-64; mem. Goldman & Bloede, Balt., 1959-64; counsel Seven-Up Bottling Co., Balt., 1958-64; dep. atty. gen. Pacific Trust Ter., Honolulu, 1952-53; asst. solicitor for ters. Office of Solicitor, U.S. Dept. Interior, Washington, 1953-54; atty. U.S. Justice, Honolulu, 1955-58; assoc. gen. counsel Dept. Navy, Washington, 1960-61, 63-64; spl. legal cons. Md. Legislature, Legis. Coun., 1963-64, 66-67; assoc. prof. U. Hawaii, 1961-63, dir. property mgmt., 1964-67; house counsel, dir. contracts and grants U. Hawaii Sys., 1967-82; house counsel U. Hawaii Rsch. Corp., 1970-82; legal counsel Law of Sea Inst., 1978-82; legal cons. Rsch. Corp. and grad. rsch. divsn. U. Hawaii, 1982—92; spl. legal cons. 1st Unitarian Ch. Honolulu, from 1992. Spl. counsel to Holifield Congl. Commn. on Govt. Procurement, 1970—73. Author: Hawaii Legislative Manual, 1962, Maori Affairs, New Zealand, 1964, Oceanographic Research Vessel Operations, and Liabilities, 1972, Hawaiian Archipelago, Legal Effects of a 200 Mile Territorial Sea, 1973, Copyright-Guidelines to the 1976 Act, 1977, Forms Manual, Inventions: Policy, Law and Procedure, 1982; writer, contbr. Coll. Law Digest and other publs. on legis. and pub. law. Mem. Gov.'s Task Force Hawaii and The Sea, 1969, Citizens Housing Com. Balt., 1952-64; bd. govs. Balt. Cmty. YMCA, 1954-64; bd. dirs. U. Hawaii Press, 1964-66, Coll. Housing Found., 1968-80; apptd. to internat. rev. commn. Can.-France Hawaii Telescope Corp., 1973-82, chmn., 1973, 82; co-founder, incorporator First Unitarian Ch. Honolulu. Served to lt. comdr. USNR, 1942-45, PTO. Grantee ocean law studies, NSF and NOAA, 1970—80. Mem.: ABA, Fed. Bar Assn., Am. Soc. Internat. Law, Nat. Assn. Univ. Attys. (founder & 1st chmn. patents & copyrights sect. 1974—76), Balt. Bar Assn. Home: Honolulu, Hawaii. Died Apr. 19, 2015.

BLOSSOM, BEVERLY, retired choreographer; b. Chgo., Aug. 28, 1926; d. Theodore and Florence (Pfeiffer) Schmidt; m. Roberts Blossom, 1966 (div.); 1 child, Michael. BA, Roosevelt U., 1950; MA, Sarah Lawrence, 1953. Dancer Alwin Nikolais Co., NYC, 1952-62; instr. Adelphi U., Long Island, NY, 1964-66; prof. dance U. Ill., Urbana, 1967-90. Choreographer Festival Theatre, Krannert Ctr., Black Traveler, 1961, Poem for the Theater #6, 1963, Brides, 1981, Urbana, Radio Show, 1985, Quick-Step, 1985, Heartbeat, 1985, Interlude from Veranda, 1985; choreographer: Rehearsal for a Class Act, 1983, You Are Still With Me, Fred, 1983, Dad's Ties, 1983, Ordinary Heartbreak, 1984, Egg, 1984, Weatherwatch, 1986, Potpourri, 1986, Eye of the Beholder, 1986, Russian Tea Room, 1986, Entitled, 1987, Grass Widow, 1987, Inch, 1987, Castles in Spain, 1988, Swansong, 1989, ...Exit, 1990, The Cloak, 1990, Onward, 1991, Shards, 1993, Dead Monkey, 1996, Cynicism, 1996, Cello Lessons, 2003, The Incomplete Lament of an Old Dancer, 2005, others. Choreography grantee Nat. Endowment for the Arts, 1986-90, 92-95, Ill. Arts Coun. Choreography grantee, 1980-82; recipient Bessie award, 1993, Martha Hill Lifetime Achievement award, 2009. Mem.: American Guild of Musical Artists (cert.), Screen Actors Guild (cert.), Union Profl. Employees (cert.). Home: Chicago, Ill. Died Nov. 1, 2014.

BLUMMER, KATHLEEN ANN, retired counselor; b. Iowa Falls, Iowa, Apr. 17, 1945; d. Arthur G. and Julia C. (Ericson) Thorsbakken; m. Terry L. Blummer, Feb. 13, 1971 (dec. 1980); 1 child, Emily Erica. AA, Ellsworth Coll., Iowa Falls, 1965; BA, U. Iowa, Iowa City, 1967; postgrad., Northeastern Ill. U., Chgo., 1969-70, U. N.Mex., Albuquerque, from 1980; MA, Western N.Mex. U., Silver City, 1973. Asst. buyer Marshall Field & Co., Chgo., 1967-68; social worker Cook County Dept. Pub. Aid, Chgo., 1968-69; tchr. Chgo. Pub. Schs., 1968-69; student fin. aid counselor Western N.Mex. U., Silver City, 1971-72; family social worker, counselor Southwestern N.Mex. Svcs. to Handicapped Children and Adults, Silver City, 1972-74; career edn. program specialist Galluo McKinley County Schs., N.Mex., 1974-76; dir. summer sch. Loving Mcpl. Schs., N.Mex., 1977; counselor, dept. chmn. Carlsbad Pub. Schs., N.Mex., 1977-82; counselor Albuquerque Pub. Schs., 1982—2003; ret., 2003. Mem. AAUW (topic chmn. Carlsbad chpt., v.p. Albuquerque chpt.), N.Mex. Personnel and Guidance Assn., Theos Club, Highpoint Swim and Racquet Club (Albuquerque), Elks. Democrat. Lutheran. Home: Albuquerque, N.Mex. Died Aug. 8, 2007.

BOEHM, GEORGE EDGAR, manufacturing and distributing executive; b. Dayton, Ohio, Aug. 18, 1931; s. Irwin Geroge Boehm and Martha B. (Mynes) Baldridge; m. Margaret Ann Chervenka, Oct. 15, 1959; children: Lynn Marie Boehm Jordan, Julie Ann Boehm Bonner. BBA in Acctg., Ohio State U., 1959. Sr. auditor Deloitte, Haskins & Sells, Milw., 1959-66; v.p. Aetna Bus. Credit Co., High Point, N.C., 1966-70; pres. Water Bonnet Inc., Coburn Industries Inc. and Advance Finishing Inc. all subs. Equity Nat. Industries Inc., Atlanta, 1970-74; exec. v.p. Cunningham Art Products Inc., Stone Mountain, Ga., 1974-75; cons. Stone Mountain, 1975; exec. v.p. Plaid Enterprises Inc., Norcross, Ga., from 1975. Mem. AICPA, Nat. Assn. Accts., Wis. Inst. CPA's, Atlanta Athletic Club, Masons, Pi Kappa Alpha Alumni Assn. Home: Duluth, Ga. Died May 18, 2007.

BOK, JOHN FAIRFIELD, retired lawyer; b. Boston, Aug. 30, 1930; AB magna cum laude, Harvard U., 1952, LLB magna cum laude, 1955. Bar: Mass. 1955, N.Y. 1982, Pa. 1984. Assoc. firm Ropes & Gray, Boston, 1957-62, 64-69; counsel to devel. adminstr. Boston Redevelopment Authority, 1962-64; ptnr. firm Csaplar & Bok, Boston, 1969-90, Gaston & Snow, Boston, 1990-91; of counsel Foley, Hoag & Eliot, Boston, 1991-2000. Instr. law Boston Coll. Law Sch., part-time 1974-75; lectr. Practicing Law Inst., 1974, New Eng. Law Inst., 1973 Editor Harvard Law Rev., 1954-55. Pres. Cambridge St. Cmty. Devel. Corp., 1972-75, Citizens Housing and Planning Assn., 1968-70, Met. Cultural Alliance, 1973-75, Beacon Hill Civic Assn., 1959-61, Beacon Hill Nursery Sch., 1964-65, Peddock's Island Trust, 1982-85, Mus. Wharf, 1989-94, Boston Ballet, 1991-94, Peter Faneuil Devel. Group, Inc., 1992—2004, Mass. Hort. Soc., 1995-98; v.p. The Cmty. Builders, Inc., 1969-97, pres. or chmn., 1998—2004; chmn. Boston Children's Mus., 1976-78, Mass. Housing Partnership, 1985-92, Social Policy Rsch. Group Inc., 1985-92, Boston Mcpl. Rsch. Bur., 1979-81, bd. dirs. and/or officer Boston Neighborhood Housing Svcs., 1974-76, Boston Waterfront Devel. Corp., 1970-85, Archtl. Conservation Trust for Mass., 1978-92, Wheelock Coll., 1980-95, Strawberry Banke, Inc., 1981-86, Met. Boston Housing Partnership, Inc., 1984-95, Cambridge Coll., 1984-95, Boston Housing Authority monitoring com., 1984-90, The Boston Harbor Assn., 1984-92, Back Bay Assn., 1988-92, Hist. Mass., 1989—, African Am. Meeting House, 1993—2005; mem. Boston Archives and Records Advt. Commn., 1988-95, Cmty. Music Ctr., 1995—, Island Alliance, 1995—, Light Boston!, 1995—. Fulbright-Hays scholar, 1976 Mem. ABA, Mass. Bar Assn., Boston Bar Assn. (chmn. land use com. 1971-74), Phi Beta Kappa. Home: Boston, Mass. Died Sept. 27, 2014.

BOLANDE, ROBERT PAUL, pathologist, scientist, educator; b. Chgo., Apr. 16, 1926; s. Herman Asher and Florence (Levy) B.; children: Deborah, Jennifer, Miriame, Hyam Asher. BS, Northwestern U., 1948, MS, MD, Northwestern U., 1952. Intern Chgo.-Wesley Meml. Hosp., 1952-53; resident in pathology Children's Meml. Hosp., Chgo., 1953-54; resident Inst. Pathology, Case Western Res. U., Cleve., 1954-56, chief pediatric pathology, 1956-66, assoc. prof. pathology, 1960-72; dir. labs. Akron Children's Hosp., Ohio, 1966-72; dir. pathology Montreal Children's Hosp.; prof. pathology McGill U., Montreal, 1972-83, also prof. pediatrics and cancer research, 1975-83; prof. pathology East Carolina U. Sch. Medicine, Greenville, N.C., 1983-95, prof. emeritus, from 1995. Cons. Nobel Prize Com. in Medicine and Physiology, 1982; Sidney Farber Meml. lectr. in pediatric pathology, Toronto, 1985 Author: Cellular Aspects of Development Pathology, 1967; editor Perspectives in Pediatric Pathology, 1973-80, Human Pathology, 1979; contbr. articles to profl. jours., also monograph. Served with USNR, 1944-46. Mem. Am. Assn. Pathologists, Internat. Acad. Pathology, Soc. for Pediatric Pathology (Spl. Disting. Colleague award 1990). Died Dec. 9, 2006.

BOLAÑOS, ALVARO FÉLIX, educator; b. Cartago, Valle, Colombia, Nov. 5, 1955; s. Alejandro Félix and Maria Omaira (Cardenas) B.; m. Katherine Robinson Keller, Sept. 12, 1987. BA, U. Del Valle, Cali, 1978; MA, U. Ky., 1984, PhD, 1988. Asst. prof. Tulane U., New Orleans, from 1988. Rsch. grant U. Ky. and Newberry Libr., 1984, Mellon-Tinker Found., 1989; summer stipend Nat. Endowment for the Humanities, 1991. Mem. MLA, Assn. Internat. de Hispanistas, Latin Am. Studies Assn., Assn. Colombiahistas Norteamericanos. Home: New Orleans, La. Died May 14, 2007.

BOLDA, ROBERT ANTHONY, personnel executive; b. Detroit, June 6, 1931; s. Floyd J. and Cecelia M. (Sokolowski) B.; m. Elizabeth J. Kalwinski, Feb. 20, 1954; children: Susan M., Robert A., Beth A., Carl J. BBA, Gen. Motors Inst., 1954; MS, Purdue U., 1956, PhD, 1958. Dir. personnel research Gen. Motors Corp., Detroit, from 1974. Vis. prof. Oakland U., Rochester, Mich., 1982-85. Contbr. articles to profl. jours. Mem. Am. Psychol. Assn., Mich.

Assn. Indsl. Psychologists, Soc. Psychologists in Mgmt. (exec. bd. 1986—). Avocation: amateur radio. Home: Rochester Hls, Mich. Died Jan. 28, 2007.

BOLES, JOHN PATRICK, bishop emeritus; b. Boston, Jan. 21, 1930; EdM, EdD, Boston Coll. Ordained priest Archdiocese of Boston, 1955, ordained bishop, 1992, aux. bishop, 1992—2006, aux. bishop emeritus, 2006—14. Roman Catholic. Died Oct. 9, 2014.

BOLES, LENORE UTAL, nurse psychotherapist, educator; b. NYC, July 3, 1929; d. Joseph Leo and Dorothy (Grosby) Utal; m. Morton Schloss, Dec. 17, 1955 (div. May 1961); 1 child, Howard Alan Schloss; m. Sam Boles, May 24, 1962; children: Anne Leslie, Laurence Utal; stepchildren: Harlan Arnold, Robert Gerald. Diploma in nursing, Beth Israel Hosp. Sch. Nursing, 1951; BSN, Columbia U., 1964; MSN, U. Conn., 1977. Bd. cert. clin. specialist in adult psychiatry/ mental health nursing, advanced practice registered nurse. Staff nurse Beth Israel Hosp., NYC, 1951, Kingsbridge VA Hosp., Bronx, N.Y., 1951-55; night supr. Gracie Square Hosp., NYC, 1959-60; head nurse Elmhurst City Hosp., Queens, N.Y., 1960-62; nursing instr. Norwalk (Conn.) Hosp., 1966-74; asst. prof. U. Bridgeport, Conn., 1976-78; nurse psychotherapist Nurse Counseling Group, Ltd., Norwalk, 1979—2003, Changing Perspectives, LLP, Westport, 2003; nursing faculty Western Conn. State U., Danbury, 1978-80. Adj. asst. prof. Sacred Heart U., Bridgeport, Conn., 1983-89; adj. faculty Western Conn. State U., Danbury, 1994, 96-2000; lectr. Yale U. Sch. Nursing, 2000-02; nurse cons. Bradley Meml. Hosp., Southington, Conn., 1982, Lea Manor Nursing Home, Norwalk, 1982, St. Vincent's Hosp., Bridgeport, 1982-92; staff devel. nurse Silver Hill Hosp., New Canaan, Conn., 1980-86, 94; cons. in field, 1980—. Author: (book chpt.) Nursing Diagnoses for Psychiatric Nursing Practice, 1994. V.p. Sisterhood Beth El, Norwalk, 1969-71; bd. dirs. religious sch. Congregation Beth El, Norwalk, 1971-75, 79-80, rec. sec. bd. trustees, 1975-77, v.p. congregation, 1977-80, bd. trustees, 1980-83. Named Speaker of Yr., So. Fairfield County chpt. Am. Cancer Soc., 1976. Mem. ANA, Northeastern Nursing Diagnosis Assn. (chair N.E. region conf. 1985, chair planning com. 1984-85, chair nominating com. 1989-91), N.Am. Nursing Diagnosis Assn., Coun. Psychiat./Mental Health Clin. Specialists, Conn. Nurses Assn. (Del. to convs. 1975-2000, legis. com. dist. 3 1984-86, nominating com. 1988-90, Florence Wald award 1984, Conn. Nursing Diagnosis Conf. Group 1980-87), Conn. Soc. Nurse Psychotherapists (founding mem.). Democrat. Jewish. Avocations: travel, reading, gardening, spending time with grandchildren. Home: Norwalk, Conn. Died Aug. 2, 2007.

BOLTON, THYRZA LAVERNE WILCOX, psychologist, counselor; b. Miami, Sept. 14, 1927; d. Herbert Hammond and Reva Ellen (Buell) W.; m. William Horton Bolton, (div. 1973); children: William Wayne, Bruce Henry, Janeen LaVerne. BS in Psychology, Fla. State U., 1949, MS in Edn., 1969, MS in Counseling, 1979. Cert. specialist in psychology, counseling, testing and evaluation, behavorial specialist. Social worker Dist. Welfare Bd., Live Oak, Fla., 1949-50; co-owner, operator Restaurant-Motel, Perry, Fla., 1955-65; psychol. evaluator Taylor County Bd. Pub. Instrn., Perry, 1967-69; guidance counselor Taylor County Jr. High Sch., Perry, 1968-69, resource tchr., 1969-70; sch. psychologist Tri-County Sch. Dist., Nashville, Ga., 1970-71; staff psychologist Children's Ctr. Glynn County, Brunswick, Ga., 1971-72; dist. sch. psychologist Taylor County Sch. Bd., Perry, 1973-77, counselor, 1978-89; ret., 1989. Mem. Fla. task force Children's and Youth Svcs., 1970-75; emergency svcs. crisis counselor Community Mental Health Svc., Tallahassee and Perry, 1979-83; pvt. practice, Perry, 1983-89. Author: Subliminal Audio Processes, 1969, Infant-Child Stimulation Project, 1973. Officer Taylor County Hist. Society, 1972-84; contbr. artifacts to LaMoyne Art Found. and Tallahassee Jr. Mus., 1969. Mem. AACD, Fla. Psychol. Assn. (charter), Fla. Assn. Sch. Psychologists, Fla. Asssn. Counseling and Devel., Ga. Psychol. Assn., Early Settlers of Fla., Order Eastern Star, United Daus. of Confederacy. Methodist. Avocations: photography, art, music, travel. Home: Perry, Fla. Died Feb. 21, 2007.

BOND, ALAN, land developer, yacht racing syndicate executive; s. Frank and Kathleen Bond; m. Eileen Hughes Bond, 1955 (div. 1992); children: John, Craig, Susanne(dec.) , Jody; m. Diane Bliss, 1995 (dec. 2012). Exec. chmn., dir. Bond Corp. Holdings Ltd., 1969—90. Founder Bond U. Decorated officer Order of Australia; recipient winner of 1983 America's Cup. Mem.: South Fremantle Football, Fremantle Sailing, Claremont Yacht Club, Cruising Yacht Club, Royal Perth Yacht. Home: Cottesloe, Australia. Died June 5, 2015.

BOND, JULIAN (HORACE JULIAN BOND), history professor, civil rights activist; b. Nashville, Jan. 14, 1940; s. Horace Mann and Julia Agnes (Washington) Bond; m. Pamela Sue Horowitz, Mar. 17, 1990; children from previous marriage: Phyllis Jane Bond McMillan, Horace Mann, Michael, Jeffrey, Julia Louise. BA, Morehouse Coll., 1971; LLD (hon.), Dalhousie U., 1969, U. Bridgeport, 1969, Wesleyan U., Conn., 1969, U. Oreg., 1969, Syracuse U., 1970, Eastern Mich. U., 1971, Tuskegee Inst., 1971, Howard U., 1971, Morgan State U., 1971, Wilberforce U., 1971, Patterson State Coll., 1972, NH Coll., 1973, Detroit Inst. Tech., 1973; DCL (hon.), Lincoln U., Pa., 1970, Bates Coll., 1998, Northeastern U., 1999, Edward Waters Coll., 1995, Gonzaga Sch. Law, 1997, Calif. State U., Monterey Bay, 1998, Washington U., 2000; LLD (hon.), Audrey Cohen Coll., New York, 2001, Williams Coll., 2005, U. Ill., 2006, Loyola U., New Orleans, 2007, George Washington U., 2008, Va. State U., 2009, Wagner Coll., 2014. Founder Com. Appeal for Human Rights, 1960, Student Nonviolent Coordinating Com., 1960, comm. dir., 1961-66; reporter, feature writer Atlanta Inquirer, 1960-61, mng. editor, 1963; mem. Ga. House of Reps., from Fulton County, 1965-75, Ga. State Senate, 1975-87; Disting. prof. in-Residence American U., Washington, 1991—2015; prof. history U. Va., Charlottesville, Va., 1998—2011; chmn. NAACP, Baltimore, Md., 1998—2010. Vis. prof. history Drexel U., 1988—89; Arnold Bernhard vis. prof. polit. sci. Williams Coll., 1992; taught at Harvard U., U. Pa. So. corr.: Reporting Racial Equality Wars; narrator Eyes on the Prize, Part 1, Part 2; author: (Book of Essays) A Time to Speak, a Time to Act, 1972; contributed works to The Nation, Negro Digest and Playboy. Mem. adv. bd. Harvard Bus. Sch., Initiative Social Enterprise; bd. dirs. So. Conf. Edn. Fund, Coun. for a Liveable World; co-founder, bd. dirs. So. Poverty Law Ctr., 1971—2015, pres., 1971—79, pres. emeritus, 1979—2015. Recipient Nat. Freedom award, 2002, Spingarm medal, NAACP, 2009, Living Legend award, Library of Congress, 2008; named to Power 150, Ebony mag., 2008. Died Aug. 15, 2015.

BONN, EVA LOUISE, recording and publishing company executive; b. Jasper, Mo., July 28, 1927; d. Troy Clayton and Rubye Thelma (Sebeck) Stephenson; m. Stanley Eils Bonn; children: De Dona, Clayton Eils. Grad. high sch., San Bernardino, Calif. Pres. ESB Records, Huntington Beach, Calif., from 1987, Bonnfire Pub. and Gather 'Round Music, Huntington Beach, from 1987. Mem. The Harry Fox Agy., Inc. Songwriter, producer: (records) Toe Tappin Country Man, 1991—, Don't Throw Stones, 1992 (artist John P. Swisshelm), The Sounds of the Universe, Star Child, 1993, Gather Round My Children, 1994 (artist Bobby Lee Caldwell), Doin' Without (artist Bobby Lee Caldwell), 1997, 2nd Wind (artist John Swisshelm), 1997, I Never Thought I'd Ever Feel This Good (artist Jeff Ashbaker), 1997, Everyone's In Love But Me (artist Rob Lynn), 1997, (artist Bobby Lee Caldwell) Highway 44, 1999. Mem. ASCAP, Broadcast Music, Inc., Calif. Country Music Assn., Country Music Assn. of Am., Greater So. Country Music Assn., European Country Music Assn., Internat. Country Music Assn. (Germany), Dutch and Danish Country DJ Assns. Republican. Died Apr. 9, 2007.

BOODY, FREDERICK PARKER, JR., nuclear engineer, optical engineer; b. Oak Ridge, Tenn., Feb. 23, 1949; s. Frederick Parker and Ruth (Rich) B. BS, Rensselaer Poly. Inst., 1971, MS, 1973; PhD, U. Mo., 1991. Engr. Knolls Atomic Power Lab., Schenectady, N.Y., 1972-74; sr. devel. engr. Combustion Engring., Inc., Windsor, Conn., 1974-76; rsch. asst. U. Ill., Urbana, 1976-80; diagnostic physicist Princeton (N.J.) Plasma Physics Lab., 1980-86; rsch. scientist U. Mo., Columbia, 1986-91; pres. Ion Light Corp. (formerly Nuclear-Pumped Laser Corp.), Huntsville, Ala., from 1981. Program com. Conf. on Physics of Nuclear-Pumped Lasers, Obninsk, Russia, 1991, 92; first western visitor Nuclear Weapons Insts, Arzamas-16 and Chelyabinsk-70, USSR, 1991; vis. prof. Fachhochschule Regensburg, Germany, 1993. Contbr. articles to profl. publs. Recipient Invention award Westinghouse Electric Corp., 1970. Mem. IEEE, Am. Nuclear Soc., Am. Phys. Soc., Optical Soc. Am., Sigma Xi, Tau Beta Pi. Achievements include co-development of photon intermediate direct energy conversion process for converting nuclear energy to light, electricity or useful chemicals. Home: Huntsville, Ala. Died Apr. 12, 2007.

BOOKER, TERRI JO, b. Tuscumbia, Ala., Apr. 1, 1953; d. Bobby Jo and Emma Frances (Curtis) Booker; m. Carl Edward Booker, Oct. 21, 1969; children: Chris, Carla, Brad. LPN, Northeast Miss. Jr. Coll., 1975; emergency med. tech., Muscles Shoals Tech. Coll., 1982; intermediate emergency med. tech., Northwest Ala. Jr. Coll., 1983; postgrad., U. NY State, 1987, from 1987. Registered emergency med. tech. Miss. Circuit clk. Tisomingo County Ct. House, Iuka, Miss., 1971—72; nurse Tishomingo County Hosp., Iuka, 1975—77; teamster Peter Kewiet Co., Paden, Miss., 1978—79; ceramic instr. Basement Ceramics, Iuka, 1979—82; florist Country Cottage Flowers, Iuka, 1980—82; nurse Pickwick Manor Nursing Home, Iuka, 1981—82; emergency room nurse Tishomingo County Hosp., 1982—84; with Metro Ambulance, Florence, Ala., 1984—86, Pickwick Manor Nursing Home, Iuka, from 1986; owner Designs Unltd., from 1984. Leader Girl Scouts USA, Iuka, 1978—82, CPR; first aid instr. ARC, Iuka; active Band Boosters, Iuka High Sch., from 1982; mem. Iuka Elem. and High Sch. PTA, from 1977. Mem.: Eastport Homemakers (Iuka), Order Eastern Star (Star Point). Democrat. Baptist. Home: Iuka, Miss. Died Nov. 15, 2006.

BOOTH, JOAN THORNLEY, interior design executive, real estate developer, landscape designer; b. Providence, July 15, 1933; BFA in Interior Architecture, R.I. Sch. Design, 1955. Archtl. draftsman Leland Larson, Bradly Hibbard, Boston, 1955-56, Castellucci Galli, Providence, 1962; interior designer Roitman Furniture Co., Providence, 1963-68; pres., designer Joan Booth Interiors, Inc., Barrington, R.I., from 1968. Designer Hist. Map of Barrington, 1968. Bd. dirs. Tockwotton in Barrington, 1986-87, Tockwotton Home Bd., Providence, 1985-87. Mem.: Providence Art, Barrington Garden. Avocations: landscaping, refurbishing old houses. Home: Warwick, RI. Died Feb. 25, 2007.

BORCHERDING, THOMAS EARL, economist; b. Cin., Feb. 18, 1939; s. Earl Schaff and Vivian Joan B.; m. Rhoda Larson, Nov. 23, 1968; children: Matthew, Benjamin. BA, U. Cin., 1961; PhD, Duke U., 1966. Asst. prof. U. Wash., Seattle, 1966-71; assoc. prof. Va. Polytech Inst., Blacksburg, 1971-73; prof. econs. Simon Fraser U., 1973-83; prof. law and econs. U. Toronto (Ont., Can.), 1978-79; prof. econs. Claremont (Calif.) Grad. U., from 1983. Editl. bd. CATO Jour., Washington. Author: The Egg Board: The Social Cost of Monopoly, 1981; contbr. articles to profl. jours. NDEA fellow Duke U., 1961-64, postdoctoral fellow U. Va., 1965-66, Hoover Instn., Stanford U., 1974-75, Avery fellow Claremont U. Ctr., 1988-97. Mem. Am. Econ. Assn., Western Econ. Assn. (editor 1980-97), Can. Econ. Assn., Pub. Choice Soc., Mont Pelerin Soc., Phi Beta Kappa, Omicron Delta Epsilon, Phi Delta Theta. Home: Claremont, Calif. Died Feb. 12, 2014.

BORDEN, MORTON, professor of history; b. Newark, Nov. 23, 1925; s. Samuel and Flora (Pistriech) B.; m. Estelle Schachter, Dec. 24, 1954 (dec. 1966); children: Jess, Sally, Lucy, Kate; m. Penn Ann Torgenrud, Jan. 16, 1970. BS, CCNY, 1948; MA, NYU, 1949; PhD, Columbia U., 1953. Instr. CCNY, 1950-53, Ohio State U., Columbus, Ohio, 1953-57; assoc. prof. U. Mont., Missoula, 1957-63; prof. U. Madrid, Spain, 1963-65, U. Calif., Santa Barbara, from 1965. Author: Jews, Turks and Infidels, 1984, Parties and Politics in the Early Republic, 1967, The Antifederalist Papers, 1965, The Federalism of James Bayard, 1955. With USAAF, 1944-46. Democrat. Avocations: tennis, single malt scotch. Home: Santa Barbara, Calif. Died June 21, 2007.

BORELL, MARY PUTNAM, language educator, playwright; d. Max Clyde and Elizabeth Maynard Putnam; m. Melvin George Borell, Sept. 9, 1979 (dec.); m. Ronald Reiner Wempen (div.); children: Rex Reiner, Eric Putnam. BA in English, Wellesley Coll., Mass., 1961; MA in Am. Studies, U. So. Calif., LA, 1968, MA in Profl. Writing, 2004; PhD in Ednl. Adminstrn., Northwestern U., Ill., 1974. Cert. tchr., adminstr. Instr. English San Antonio USD, San Antonio, 1968—69, Barat Coll., Lake Forest, Ill., 1970—73; asst. prof. English Calif. State U., LA, 1975—78; assoc. prof. English LA Southwest Coll., 1979—81, dean of instrn., 1981—92; dir. econ. devel. LA CC, 1992—98; prof. English LA Harbor Coll., Wilmington, Calif., from 1998. Edn. bd. mem. Pvt. Industry Council, LA, 1992—98, Rebuild LA, 1993—95. Author: (plays) In the Nude, 2002, Murder Ahoy, 2004, Not Status Quo, 2006. V.p. Nat. Women's Polit. Caucus, South Bay, Calif., Palos Verdes Rep. Women's Club, Calif. Recipient Chancellor's award, LA CC Dist., 1994, Mayor of LA award, City of LA, 1996, 1998. Mem.: Rotary (past pres.), Calif. CC Adminstrs., AAUW. Home: San Pedro, Calif. Died July 26, 2007.

BORG, MARCUS JOEL, theologian, theology educator; b. Fergus Falls, Minn., Mar. 11, 1942; s. Glenn F. and Esther (Stortroen) B.; m. Marianne Wells, Aug. 24, 1985; children: Dane, Julie. BA, Concordia Coll., Moorhead, Minn., 1964; diploma in Theology, U. Oxford, Eng., 1966; D.Phil., U. Oxford, 1972; postgrad., Union Theol. Sem., U. Tübingen, Fed. Republic Germany. With Concordia Coll., Minn., 1966—69, 1972—74, South Dakota State U., Brookings, 1975—76; prof. religion Carleton Coll., Northfield, Minn., 1976-79; prof. religion and culture to Dist. Prof. religion and culture Oreg. State U., Corvallis, 1979—2007, chair religious studies dept., 1988—92, Hundere Endowed chair of religious studies, 1992—2007. Disting. vis. prof. U. Puget Sound, Tacoma, Wash., 1986-87; vis. prof. N.T. Pacific Sch. Religion, Berkeley, Calif., 1989-91. Author: Year of Luke, 1976, Conflict and Social Change, 1971, Conflict, Holiness and Politics in the Teaching of Jesus, 1984, Jesus: A New Vision, 1987, Meeting Jesus Again for the First Time, 1994, Jesus in Contemporary Scholarship, 1994, The God We Never Knew, 1997 (named one of the 10 Best Books in Religion in 1997, Publisher's Weekly), Jesus and Buddha, 1997, Reading the Bible Again for the First Time, 2001 (named one of the 10 Best Books in Religion, Publisher's Weekly), The Heart of Christianity, 2003 (named one of the 10 Best Books in Religion, Publisher's Weekly), Jesus: Uncovering the Life, Teachings and Relevance of a Religious Revolutionary (New York Times Bestseller), 2006, Conversations with Scripture: Mark, 2009, (novel) Putting Away Childish Things, 2010, Speaking Christian, 2011, Evolution of the Word, 2012, (memoir) Convictions: How I Learned What Mattes Most, 2014; co-author The Meaning of Jesus: Two Visions, 1998, 2007 (Best General Interes Book of 1999, Assn. of Theological Bookseller), The Last Week, 2006, The First Christmas, 2007, The First Paul, 2009; contbr. articles to religious jours.; televised symposia Jesus at 2000, 1996, God at 2000, 2000; featured on PBS, NPR, National Geographic, ABC World News and the Today Show Canon, theologian Trinity Episcopal Cathedral, Portland, Oreg., 2009. Recipient Burlington-No. Teaching award Oreg. State U., 1986, Faculty Excellence award Oreg. State Legislature, 1987; vis. scholar, Plymouth Congregational United Church of Christ, Fort Collins, Colo. Fellow The Jesus Sem.; mem. Soc. Bibl. Lit.(nat. chair historical Jesus sect., co-chair Internat. New Testament Program Com.), Cath. Bibl. Assn., American Acad. Religion, Angelican Assn. of Biblical Scholars (pres.) Home: Portland, Oreg. Died Jan. 21, 2015.

BORNELL, DONALD GUSTAVE, movement education specialist; b. Chgo., May 4, 1930; s. Stanley Charles and Evelyn Marie (Caspersen) B.; m. Cecil Jean Headrick, Jan. 1, 1953; 1 child, Gaynet Lee. BS, Ill. State U., 1952; MS, UCLA, 1962, EdD, 1970. Cert. tchr., phys. edn. and adaptive phys. edn. tchr., adminstr., Calif. Tchr. phys. edn. Van Nuys (Calif.) Jr. High Sch., 1955-59; chmn. dept. phys. edn. Millikan Jr. High Sch., Sherman Oaks, Calif., 1960-62; instr. health, phys. edn. Los Angeles Valley Coll., Sherman Oaks, 1962-64; cons. phys. edn., environment Los Angeles County Schs. Office, LA, 1964-71, 72-73; edn. specialist Community Coll. Am. Samoa, Pago Pago, 1971-72; dir. fed. project H.E.L.P. (Health Edn. Liaison Project) Santa Barbara, Calif., 1973-76; coord. health and adaptive phys. edn. Santa Barbara County Schs. Office, 1976-78, specialist adaptive phys. edn. Santa Barbara, Calif., 1978-90; cons., movement edn. specialist Santa Ynez, Calif., from 1990; ptnr. MII/Funfitness, Santa Ynez, from 1990. Asst. prof. Calif. State U., Northridge, Ventura, 1980-81; co-chair V.D. Edn. Coalition, Santa Barbara, 1973-78; health dir. 15th

Dist. PTA, Santa Barbara, 1973-78; mem. Planned Parenthood Edn. Project, Santa Barbara, 1973-78; rsch. vol. Earthwatch; presenter wellness workshops, seminars. Co-author: Movement is Individuality, 1978, Stretch and Strengthen for Rehabilitation and Development, 1984, Body Friendly, 1989, Tap Dancing the Body's Beat, 1989; designer 10 pieces of movement edn. equipment, 1978; inventor strap-on taps, 1981. Exec. bd. Am. Lung Assn., Santa Barbara, 1975-80; violinist Allan Hancock Coll. Chamber Ensemble; mem. UNESCO internat. symposium on phys. edn. and sport programs for handicapped, 1982; advisor S. Coast Spl. Olympics Bd., Calif. Mem. AAHPERD, Calif. Assn. Health, Phys. Edn., Recreation and Dance, Internat. Tap Assn. Avocations: banjo, tap dance, swing dance, furniture making, cabinet making. Died Feb. 18, 2007.

BOROWSKY, IRVIN J., retired publishing executive; b. Phila., Nov. 23, 1924; children: Scott, Gwen, Ned, Ted. D (hon.), Drexel U., 2014. Founder TV Digest (now TV Guide), 1948; founder, pres. North American Publishing Co. (pubs. N.Y. Custom House Guide, Yacht Racing/Cruising, Business Forms and Systems, Am. Sch. and Univ., World Wide Printer, Zip Tark, Phila., from 1958; founder Nat. Library Mus., 2000. Lectr., seminar leader, writer and editor. Founder Am. Inst. for Study of Racial and Religious Cooperation Home: Philadelphia, Pa. Died Nov. 25, 2014.

BORTON, ALAN WAYNE, electrical engineer; b. Richland Center, Wis., Oct. 26, 1962; s. Edward Wayne and Barbara Ann (Gillingham) B.; m. Kelly Dawn Felton, May 25, 1985; children: Benjamin E., Zackary A. BSEE, U. Wis., Platteville, 1987. Elec. engr. Kornacki & Assocs., Inc., New Berlin, Wis., 1987-94, v.p. engring., from 1994. Mem. IEEE. Avocations: hunting, fishing, reading. Home: Waukesha, Wis. Died Nov. 5, 2006.

BOSCAK, VLADIMIR GUSTAV, chemical engineer, consultant; b. Zagreb, Croatia, Mar. 21, 1941; s. Gustav and Maria (Zupancic) B.; m. Harriet; children: Alexis, Sarah; m. Gyda Skat Nielsen. Diploma in Engring., U. Zagreb, 1964; MS in Chemistry, 1971; MSChemE, N.Y.U, 1969; PhD in Chem. Engring., U. Belgrade, Yogoslavia, 1972. Assoc. scientist PLIVA, Zagreb, Croatia, 1964-72; R&D mgr. PCS-Hormel, Mpls., 1972-74; sr. project mgr. TRC-Environ. Cons., Hartford, Conn., 1975-79; R&D mgr. G.E. Environ. Serv., Lebanon, Pa., 1979-87; sr. assoc. Buohicore Cashman Assn., Amherst, N.H., 1987-89; sr. tech. cons. Volund Ecology Sys., Brondby, Denmark, 1989-92; sr. researcher FLS Miljo, Valby, Denmark, from 1992. Invited speaker U.S. Info. Agy., Turkey, Yugoslavia, Czechoslovakia, 1987-89. Author and co-author 4 EPA reports on various environ. assessments and over 60 articles. Mem. AIChE, Air Pollution Control Assn., Dansk Ingeniorforening. Home: Horsholm, Denmark. Died Oct. 17, 2007.

BOSCH, RICHARD LAWRENCE, manaufacturing company executive; b. Bklyn., Sept. 21, 1956; s. Francis Lorenzo and Elly (Bobbe) B.; m. Stacy McLoughlin, Jan. 6, 1984. BS in Biology, Chile U., S.Am., 1978; BS in Chemistry, BS in Computer Sci., Adelphi U., 1982; BS in Chem. Engring., Calif. State Long Beach, 1986. Molecular research asst. Adelphi U., Garden City, N.Y., 1979-81; nuclear reactor supr. engr. Mich. State U., East Lansing, 1982-83; staff engr. thermodynamic div. RotoFlow Corp., Santa Monica, Calif., 1983-84; asst. product mgr. Fuller Co., Compton, Calif., from 1984. Mem. Am. Chem. Soc., Am. Inst. Chem. Engrs., Am. Mgmt. Assn. Democrat. Avocations: water-skiing, wind surfing, hang gliding. Died Dec. 16, 2006.

BOSTICK, TRUDY ANN, mathematics and computer science educator, consultant; b. Portsmouth, Ohio, Oct. 3, 1951; d. Floyd Kenneth and Mary Alice (Jackson) B. BS in Math. and Computers cum laude, Ohio U., 1972; postgrad., Ohio State U., 1977; MS in Math. and Computers cum laude, Wright State U., Dayton, Ohio, 1977; postgrad., Ohio U., 1982-83; postgrad. in computer sci. edn., Nova U., Ft. Lauderdale, Fla., from 1983. Cert. elem. and secondary tchr., Ohio. Math. instr. Northwest Local Schs., Lucasville, Ohio, 1972-82; math. instr. for blind and handicapped Wright State U., 1976-77; math. and data processing instr. Shawnee State U., Portsmouth, Ohio, from 1977; math., computer sci. and math edn. instr. Ohio U., from 1983. Computer sci. instr. for the gifted Continuing Edn., Shawnee State U., 1981—; software critical advisor various orgns., 1982—; pres., chief programmer, statis. cons. Scioto Software Systems, Inc., South Webster, Ohio, 1983—; computer sci. educator Community Action Orgn., Portsmouth, 1983—. Author: (novel) The Oval Mirror, 1982; (computer programs) The Inventory Wizard, 1983, The Questionnaire, 1985; contbr. articles on math. and computers to mags. Mem., jr. leader Scioto County 4-H Club, 1959-69, leader, mem. bd., officer, 1969—. Recipient numerous Ednl. Excellence awards Gov. of Ohio, 1977, Automobile Assn. Am. of So. Ohio, 1973-83, Ohio Ho. of Reps., 1981, 82, U.S. Congress, 1982. Mem. NEA, Ohio Edn. Assn., Scioto County Edn. Assn., Nat. Council Tchrs. Math., Ohio Council Tchrs. Math., Am. Math. Assn., Math. Assn. Am., Ednl. Computer Consortium of Ohio, Ohio's Women's Caucus, AAUW, Bus. and Profl. Women, Bloom Local Alumni Assn. (electronic media sec. 1969—), Internat. Platform Assn. Democrat. Methodist. Avocations: writing, graphic art, literature, gourmet cooking, playing jeopardy. Home: South Webster, Ohio. Died June 17, 2007.

BOSTICK, WILLIAM ALLISON, museum administrator; b. Marengo, Ill., Feb. 21, 1913; s. William Frederick and Alice Mabellian (Johnson) B.; m. Mary Jane Moore Barbey, June 14, 1942; children: Beatrice Annette, Christopher. BS in Graphic Comm. Mgmt., Carnegie Inst. Tech., 1934; MA in Graphic Arts History, Wayne State U., 1954. Field rep. NRA Graphic Arts Code Authority, Detroit, 1934-35; typographer Detroit Typesetting Co., 1935-36; advt. designer Evans, Winter, Hebb, Inc., Detroit, 1936-38; prop. Comml. Art Studio, Detroit, 1939-40; city supr. printing City of Detroit, 1940-41, 46; adminstr., sec. Detroit Inst. Arts, 1946-76; prop. La Stampa Calligrafica, Bingham Farms, Mich., from 1970. Bd. trustees mem. Detroit Inst. Arts Founders Soc., 1988-95, exec. sec., 1946-58, chmn. antiquaries, 1988-95. Author: A Guide to the Guarding of Cultural Property, 1977; author, illustrator: England Under GI's Reign, 1946, Calligraphy for Kids, 1991, Back to the Second Basic R—'Ritin', 1996; co-author: The Amphibious Sketch, 1944; designer, illustrator: The Mysteries of Blair House, 1948; exhibited paintings in numerous shows and pvt. collections. Lt. USNR, 1942-45; designed landing chart/maps for invasions of Sicily and Normandy. Mem. Scarab Club Detroit (bd. dirs., pres. 1962-63, Gold medal 1963, 68, 80), Internat. Torch Club Detroit and Windsor (pres. 1956-57), L'Alliance Francaise de Detroit (pres. 1972-73, bd. dirs.), Prismatic Club Detroit, Antiquaries of Detroit Inst. Arts (chmn. 1988-95), Skyline Club, Mich. Water Color Soc. (pres. 1946-47), Mich. Assn. Calligraphers, Order of Star of Italian Solidarity (knight), French Order Arts and Letters (chevalier), Delta Tau Delta. Republican. Avocations: painting, printmaking, calligraphy, foreign languages, teaching. Home: Bingham Farms, Mich. Died Aug. 15, 2007.

BOSWORTH, STEPHEN WARREN, retired dean; b. Grand Rapids, Mich., Dec. 4, 1939; s. Warren Charles and Mina (Phillips) B.; m. Christine Holmes, June 7, 1984; children: Andrew, Allison, Stacey and William Rutledge A.B., Dartmouth Coll., 1961; LLD (hon.), Darmouth Coll., 1986. Vice consul US Embassy, Panama City, Panama, 1962—63, prin. officer Colon, 1963—64; Panama desk officer US Dept. State, Washington, 1964—66; econ. officer US Embassy, Madrid, 1967—71, Paris, 1971—74; dep. asst. sec. US Dept. State, 1976-79, US amb. to Tunisia Tunis, 1979-81, dep. asst. sec. for Inter-American affairs, 1981-82, dir. policy planning staff coun. Washington, 1983-84, US amb. to the Philippines Manila, Philippines, 1984-87; pres. US-Japan Found., 1988-96; exec. dir. Korean Energy Devel. Orgn. (KEDO), 1995-97; US amb. to Republic of Korea US Dept. State, Seoul, 1997-2001; dean Tufts U. Fletcher Sch. Law & Diplomacy, Medford, Mass., 2001—13; spl. rep. for North Korea policy US Dept. State, Washington, 2009—11. Adj. prof. Columbia U. Sch. Internat. & Pub. Affairs, 1990-94. Co-author: Chasing the Sun, Rethinking East Asian Policy, 2006. Trustee Dartmouth Coll., 1992-2002, chmn. bd. trustees, 1996-99. Recipient Disting. Honor award, US Dept. State, 1976, 86, Arthur S. Flemming award, 1976, Disting. Svc. award, US Dept. Energy, 1979, Order of the Rising Sun, Gold & Silver Star, Govt. of Japan, 2005; named Diplomat of Yr., American Acad. Diplomacy, 1986 Died Jan. 4, 2016.

BOUGHTON, WILLIAM HART, microbiologist; b. Cleve., Apr. 2, 1937; s. Ralph H. Boughton and Eloise C. (Graul) deWolfe; 1 child, Cindy. BS, Oreg. Stae U., 1964; MS, U. Ariz., 1965, PhD, 1969. Dir. microbiology San Diego Inst. of Pathology, 1972-74, 1983-84; dir. microbiology and immuniology Pathology Assoc. Med. Lab., Honolulu, 1974-75, Kapiolani Children's Med. Ctr., Honolulu, 1975-81; co-dir. Anitbiotic Rsch. Lab., Honolulu, 1976-83; clin. lab. educator, vis. prof. Project Hope and USAID, Belize, Cen. Am., 1984-86; supr. microbiology Eisenhower Med. Ctr., Rancho Mirage, Calif., 1986-89; microbiologist Washoe Med. Ctr., Reno, from 1990. Cons. Lab. Techniques, Rancho Mirage, 1986-89. Contbr. 20 articles to sci. jours. Mem. Am. Soc. for Microbiology, Sigma Xi. Home: Reno, Nev. Died Apr. 3, 2007.

BOULEZ, PIERRE, composer, conductor; b. Montbrison, France, Mar. 26, 1925; s. Leon and Marcelle (Calabre) Boulez. Studied with Olivier Messiaen, Paris Conservatory; pvt. studies with René Leibowitz. Apptd. music dir. Jean-Louis Barrault's Theater Co., 1948; founder Concert du Petit Marigny, 1953—54; musical adv. Cleve. Symphony Orch., 1970—72; chief condr. BBC Symphony Orch., 1971—75; music dir. NY Philharm., 1971—77; dir., condr. Institut de Recherche et de Coordination Acoustique/Musique, France, 1976—91; prin. guest condr. Chgo. Symphony Orch., 1995—2006, Helen Regenstein condr. emeritus, 2006—16. Vis. prof. Harvard U., 1962—63; prof. Coll. de France, 1976; pres. Ensemble InterContemporain, 1976—97. Composer: toured Europe, N.Am., S.Am.; conducting appearances include: Edinburgh Festival, Bayreuth Festival, Salzburg Festival, Lucerne Festival; composer: Sonatina for flute and piano, 1946, Three Piano Sonatas, 1946, 1950, 1957, Le Soleil des eaux for voice and orchestra, 1947, Structures, 1952, Le Marteau sans maître, 1955, Deux improvisations sur Mallarmé, 1957, Tombeau (on text of Mallarmé), 1959, Pli selon pli, 1960, Structures II, 1962, Eclat, 1964, Domaines, 1968, Eclat/Multiples, 1970, cummings ist der dichter, 1970, explosante-fixe, 1973, Rituel, 1975, Messagesquisse, 1976, Notations I-IV, 1980, Répons, 1981, Dialogue de l'ombre double, 1986, Mémoriale, 1985, Visage nuptial, 1989, Dérive I, 1985, Anthèmes pour violin solo, 1992, explosante-fixe for large ensemble and electronics, 1993, Anthèmes for Violin Solo and Electronics, 1997, sur Incises, 1998, Notations VII, 1999, Déreive 2, 2002; author: Relevés d'apprenti, 1966, Points de Repère, 1981, le pays fertile-Paule Klee, 1989, Jalon-10 ans d'enseignement au Collège de France, 1989; musical criticism and analysis including: Penser la musique aujourd'hui, 1963. Recipient Siemens Found. prize, 1979, Sonning award, Léonie Sonning Music Found., Denmark, 1985, Praemium Imperiale, Japan Art Assn., 1989, Polar Music prize, Sweden, 1996, Wolf prize in arts (music), Wolf Found., Israel, 2000, Grawemeyer award, 2001, Glenn Gould prize, Canada, 2002, Kyoto prize, Inamori Found., Japan, 2009, Sanford medal, Yale U., BBVA Found. Frontiers of Knowledge award, 2013. Died Jan. 5, 2016.

BOURGUIGNON, ERIKA EICHHORN, anthropologist, educator; b. Vienna, Feb. 18, 1924; d. Leopold H. and Charlotte (Rosenbaum) Eichhorn; m. Paul H. Bourguignon, Sept. 29, 1950. BA, Queens Coll., 1945; grad. study, U. Conn., 1945; PhD, Northwestern U., 1951; DHL, Queens Coll., CUNY, 2000. Field work Chippewa Indians, Wis., summer 1946; field work Haiti; anthropologist Northwestern U., 1947-48; instr. Ohio State U., 1949-56, asst. prof., 1956-60, assoc. prof., 1960-66, prof., 1966-90, acting chmn. dept. anthropology, 1971-72, chmn. dept., 1972-76, prof. emeritus, from 1990; dir. Cross-Cultural Study of Dissociational States, 1963-68; chair Coun. Acad. excellence for Women, 1972—76; bd.dir. Soc. Psychol. Anthropology, 1991—93; exec.com. Anthropology Religion Sec., Am.Anthropological Asssoc., 1990—98; ed.bd. J.of Haitian Studies, from 2000; ed. bd. ethos, 1996—2014; jr. faculty women Ohio State U. Lectr. in Anthropology, Psychiatric Residents' Training Program. Columbus State Hosp., 1962-63; bd. dirs. Human Relations Area Files, Inc., 1976-79; P-H.Bourguignon Photoarchives:Haiti 1947-48, Peru 1949 Author: Possession, 1976, rev. edit., 1991, Psychological Anthropology, 1979, Italian transl., 1983; editor, co-author: Religion, Altered States of Consciousness and Social Change, 1973, A World of Women, 1980; co-author: Diversity and Homogeneity in World Societies, 1973; adv. editor: Behavior Sci. Rsch., 1976-79; assoc. editor Jour. Psychoanalytic Anthropology, 1977-87; mem. editl. bd. Ethos, 1979-89, 97—2012, Jour. Haitian Studies, 2000—, Anthropology of Consciousness, 2002—; editor: Margaret Mead: The Anthropologist in America—, Occasional Papers in Anthropology, No. 2, Ohio State U. Dept. Anthropology, 1986; (with Barbara Rigney) Exile: A Memoir of 1939 by Bronka Schneider, 1998; contbr. articles to profl. jours. Recipient Lifetime Achievement award, Soc. Psychol. Anthropology, 1999; named Disting. Lectr., Ctrl. States Anthropol. Soc., 1987. Fellow Am. Anthrop. Assn.; mem. Ctrl. State Anthrop. Soc. (treas. 1953-56, exec. com. 1995-98), Ohio Acad Sci., World Psychiat. Assn. (transcultural psychiatry sect.), Am. Ethnol. Soc., Current Anthropology (assoc.), Soc. for Psychol. Anthropology (nominations com. 1981-82, bd. dirs. 1991-93, lifetime achievement award 1999), Soc. for the Anthropology of Religion, Phi Beta Kappa, Sigma Xi. Home: Columbus, Ohio. *It is more important to enjoy doing what you do, and to be able to do what you want to do, than to be successful. Success, if it comes, is only a by-product, nothing more.* Died Feb. 15, 2015.

BOURN, PATRICIA MCANULTY, secondary school educator; b. Shelbina, Mo., Apr. 19, 1929; d. Clarence A. and Fannie E. (Sharp) Bourn; m. Benjamin Wayne Bourn, Apr. 22, 1951; 1 child, Peter Bradley. BS, NE Mo. State U., 1951, MA, 1968; postgrad., U. Mo., 1970—78. Sec. Hort. div. U. Mo., Colombia, 1949, Carter Oil Co., Tulsa, 1949—50; tchr. bus. edn. New London (Mo.) High Sch., 1952—56; instr. bus. edn. Hannibal (Mo.) High Sch. and Hannibal Area Vocat.-Tech. Schs., from 1955; mem. Hannibal Arts Council, from 1979, Mo. Adv. Council Vocat. Edn., from 1983. Recipient Outstanding Bus. Edn. award, Mo. Bus. Edn. Assn., 1977. Mem.: Hannibal Edn. Assn., Mo. Vocat. Assn., Am. Vocat. Assn., Nat. Bus. Edn. Assn. Christian Ch. Home: Hannibal, Mo. Died Dec. 27, 2006.

BOUTROS-GHALI, BOUTROS, former United Nations secretary general; b. Cairo, Nov. 14, 1922; LLD, Cairo U., 1946; Diploma in Higher Studies in Pub. Law, Paris U., 1947, Diploma of Higher Studies in Econs., 1948, Diploma of Polit. Sci. Ins., 1949, PhD in Internat. Law, 1949; dr. h.c., René Descartes U., Paris, 1980, Uppsala U., Sweden, 1986. Prof. internat. law, internat. rels., head dept. polit. scis. Cairo U., 1949-77; min. state Fgn. Affairs, Egypt, 1977-91, dep. prime min., 1991; sec.-gen. UN, NYC, 1992-96, La Francophonie Org., 1997—2002; chmn. South Centre, 2003—06; dir. Egyptian Nat. Coun. Human Rights, 2003. Assoc. dir. First Dag Hammarskjold Seminar, Netherland, 1963; dir. Ctr. Rsch. The Hague Acad. Internat. Law, 1963-64, mem. study group, 1965-66, mem. external program group, 1968-71, mem. curatorium adminstrv. coun., 1978-; vis. prof. faculty of law Paris U., 1967-68; co-dir. first session external program Acad. Internat. Law, Rabat, 1969; dir. first session of the sr. diplomats Union of the Abu Dhabi, 1973; lectr. internat. law, internat. rels. various univs. Author: (books) Contribution à l'Etude des Ententes Régionales, 1949, Cours de Diplomatie et de Droit Diplomatique et Consulaire, 1951, (with Youssef Chlala) Le Problème de Suez, 1957, Egypt and the United Nations: Carnegie Endowment for International Peace, 1957, Le Principe d'Egalité des Etats et les Organisations Internationales, 1961, Contribution à une Théorie Générale des Alliances, 1963, L'Organisation de l'Unité Africaine, 1969, Le Mouvement Afro-Asiatique, 1969, Les Difficultés Institutionelles du Panafricanisme, 1979, La Ligue des Etats Arabes, 1972, Les Conflits de Frontières en Afrique, 1973, (memoirs) Egypt's Road to Jerusalem, 1997, Unvanquished: A U.S.-UN Saga, 1999; co-author: Foreign Policies in a World of Change, 1983, Will We Survive?, 1989; founder, editor Al Ahram Al-Iktisadi, 1960-75, Al Siyassa Ad-Dawliya; mem. editl. bd. Egyptian Rev. Internat. Law, Yearbook of the Assn. of the Attenders, Alumni of the Hague Acad. of Internat. Law. Mem. Com. application of convs. and recommendations Internat. Labour Orgn., 1971-79; mem. cen. com. Polit. Bur. of the Arab Socialist Union, 1974-77; pres. Ctr. for Polit. and Strategic Studies, Al-Ahram, 1975—; mem. Internat. Commn. Jurist, Geneva, 1975-77; mem. Commn. Internat. Law of the UN, 1979-91; mem. secretariat Nat. Dem. Party, 1980-91. Decorated

Order of the Nile (Egypt), Grand Croix de l'Ordre de la Couronne (Belgium), Cavaliere di Gran Croce (Italy), Gran Cruz de la Orden de Boyaca (Colombia), Gran Cruz de la Orden de Antonio José de Irisarri (Guatemala), Grand Croix de la Légion d'Honneur (France), Gran Cruz de la Orden Nacional Al Merito (Ecuador), Gran Cruz de la Orden del Liberation San Martin (Argentina), Tishakti Patta (Nepal), Grand Croix de l'Ordre du Mérite du Niger, Grand Officer de l'Ordre du Mérite du Mali, La Condecoracion De Agulia Azteca (Mex.), Grand Croix de l'Ordre Pro Merito Melitensi de l'Ordre Souverain Militaire et Hospitalier de St. Jean de Jerusalem de Rhodes de Malte, Grand Cordon de l'Ordre du Phoenix de Grèce, Grand Cordon du Mérite du Chili, Order of the Crown of Brunei, Grand Cross of the Order of Merit (Germany), Gran Cruz del Sol del Peru, comdr. de l'Ordre du Mérite Nat. de la Côte d'Ivoire, Grand Croix de l'Ordre du Danebrog, Grand Officer Cross of the Order of the Polar Star (Sweden), The Order of Diplomatic Svc. Merit (Gwanghwa, Korea); Fulbright Rsch. scholar Columbia U., 1954-55. Mem. African Soc. Polit. Studies (pres. 1980), Egyptian Soc. Internat. Law (v.p. 1965), Inst. Pub. Internat. Law and Internat. Rels. Thessaloniki (curatorium 1976), Acad. des Scis. morales et politiques (assoc. 1989), Inst. Internat. Law (pres. 1985-87), Inst. Affari Internazionali (assoc. 1979), Acad. Mondiale pour la Paix (sci. com. 1975), Internat. Inst Human Rights (mem. coun., exec. com. 1975), Assn. Colombiana de Estudios de Politica Internacional Y Diplomacia (hon. 1980), Malgache Acad., Academia Mexicana de Dir. Internacional. Home: Cairo, Egypt. Died Feb. 16, 2016.

BOUTWELL, HARVEY BUNKER, traffic engineer; b. Concord, NH, May 16, 1924; s. Harley and Helen Louise (Bunker) B.; m. Margaret Ann Hindinger; children: Margaret Helen Boutwell Kolaya, William Bruce. B Engring., Yale U., 1946; cert. in hwy. safety, NYU, 1962. Registered profl. engr., N.H., Mass., Conn., Calif.; cert. traffic engr., Bur. Hwy. Traffic. Embalmer Boutwell Mortuary, Concord, 1946-54; traffic rsch. engr. N.H. Pub. Works and Hwys., Concord, 1954-64; rsch. assoc. Bur. Hwy. Traffic Yale U., New Haven, 1964-68; profl. traffic engr. Kaehrle Traffic Assoc., West Hartford, Conn., 1968-71; owner Hwy. Traffic Cons., Cheshire, Conn., from 1971. Chmn. Cheshire Town Safety Com., 1976-80, Cheshire Housing Authority, 1989—. Lt. (s.g.) USNR ret. Mem. VFW, Inst. Transp. Engrs. (pres. N.E. sect. 1970, internat. bd. dirs. 1974-76, chmn. dist. 1 1977, Disting. Svc. award N.E. sect. 1977, dist. 1 1990, Burton W. Marsh award 1994), Bur. Hwy Traffic Alumni Assn. (clk. 1985—), Masons (past master, 32 degree), Shriners, N.H. Good Rds., Exch. Club of Cheshire, Am. Legion. Republican. Died Nov. 20, 2006.

BOWER, MARK VICTOR, mechanical engineer, educator; b. Detroit, Nov. 26, 1953; s. M. Victor and Marjorie Rose (Osburn) B.; m. Peggy Joyce Harris, June 24, 1989; children: Renae Dawn, Amber Michelle, Elizabeth Victoria, Matthew Victor. BSE, U. Mich., 1978, MSE, 1979, PhD, 1985. Registered profl. engr., Mich. Developmental engr. Kelsey-Hayes Co., Ann Arbor, Mich., 1978-79, product engr., 1979-80; grad. teaching asst. U. Mich., Ann Arbor, 1980-84; asst. prof. U. Ala., Huntsville, 1984-95, assoc. prof., from 1995, mem. faculty senate, 1985-98, faculty rep. bd. trustees, 1995-98, asst. dean engring., 1999—2003, chair dept. mech. and aero. engring., from 2003. Cons. in field. Contbr. articles to profl. jours. With USN, 1975-77. NASA/Am. Soc. Engring. Edn. summer fellow, 1985, 86, 87, 92, 93; U. Mich. fellow, 1983-84; recipient Human Powered Vehicle World Record for transcontinental ride, 1988. Mem.: AIAA, ASEE, ASME, Accrediting Bd. Engring. and Tech. (evaluator), Order of Engr., Soc. Advancement Materials and Process Engring., Sigma Gamma Tau, Tau Beta Pi, Phi Kappa Phi, Omicron Delta Kappa, Pi Tau Sigma. Avocation: music. Home: Huntsville, Ala. Died Apr. 16, 2007.

BOWERS, DOUGLAS EDWARD, insurance executive; b. Royston, Ga., Dec. 18, 1947; s. Waco and Betty Frances (Thompson) B.; m. Sabra Elaine Slater, May 1, 1969; 1 child, Dana Lorraine. Student, Ga. State U., 1973-74; AA, DeKalb Community Coll., Clarkston, Ga., 1973. Credit rep. Gulf Oil Corp., Atlanta, 1968-70; credit mgr. Ga.-Pacific, Inc., Atlanta, 1970-72; credit rep. Moore Handley, Inc., Pelham, Ala., 1972-73, ctr. store mgr., 1973-75; ins. agt. Equitable Life, Atlanta, 1975-78, 82-85, dist. mgr., 1978-82; bus. cons., owner Bowers & Assocs., Duluth, Ga., from 1983; pres., owner, founder BAF Systems, Inc., from 1988. Named Rookie of Yr. Gen. Agts. and Mgrs. Assn., 1976, Equitable Life, 1976-78. Mem. Am. Soc. CLU's, Atlanta Assn. Life Underwriters, Million Dollar Round Table, Gwinnett County C. of C., Atlanta Jaycees (sec. 1978). Lodges: Optimists (pres. Duluth chpt. 1988-89). Avocations: golf, tennis. Home: Duluth, Ga. Died Jan. 21, 2007.

BOWIE, DAVID (DAVID ROBERT JONES), singer; b. London, Jan. 8, 1947; s. Hayward Stenton Jones and Margaret Mary Burns; m. Mary Angela Barnett, March 19, 1970 (div. February 8, 1980); 1 child, Duncan Haywood Zowie; m. Iman Abdul Majid, June 6, 1992; 1 child, Alexandria Zahra Jones. Ph.D (hon.), Berklee College of Music. Solo artist, from 1966; lead singer Tin Machine, 1989—91; founder Bowieart.com. Singer: (albums) David Bowie, 1967, Space Oddity, 1969, The Man Who Sold the World, 1970, Hunky Dory, 1971, The Rise and Fall of Ziggy Stardust and the Spiders from Mars, 1972, Aladdin Sane, 1973, Pin-ups, 1973, Diamond Dogs, 1974, David Live, 1974, Young Americans, 1975, Station to Station, 1976, ChangesOneBowie, 1976, Low, 1977, Heroes, 1977, Stage, 1978, Lodger, 1979, Scary Monsters(and Super Creeps), 1980, ChangesTwoBowie, 1981, Let's Dance, 1983, Tonight, 1984, Never Let Me Down, 1987, Sound + Vision, 1989, Changesbowie, 1990, Black Tie, White Noise, 1993, The Singles 1969-1993, 1993, Outside, 1995, The Deram Anthology 1966—1968, 1997, Earthling, 1997, The Best of David Bowie 1969/1974, 1997, The Best of David Bowie 1974/1979, 1998, hours..., 1999, Bowie at the Beeb, 2000, Heathen, 2002, Best of Bowie, 2002, Reality, 2003, The Collection, 2005, The Best of David Bowie 1980-1987, 2007, Live Santa Monica '72, 2008, Glass Spider Live, 2008, A Reality Tour, 2009, The Next Day, 2013, Blackstar, 2016; (soundtracks) Christiane F., 1981, Ziggy Stardust and the Spiders from Mars: The Motion Picture, 1983, Labyrinth, 1986, The Buddha of Suburbia, 1993; (with Tin Machine) Tin Machine, 1989, Tin Machine II, 1991, Tin Machine Live: Oy Vey, Baby, 1992; actor: (films) The Image, 1967, The Virgin Soldiers, 1969, The Man Who Fell to Earth, 1976, Just a Gigolo, 1978, Wir Kinder Von Bahnhof, 1981, (voice) The Snowman, 1982, The Hunger, 1983, Merry Christmas, Mr. Lawrence, 1983, Into the Night, 1985, Labyrinth, 1986, Absolute Beginners, 1986, The Last Temptation of Christ, 1988, The Linguini Incident, 1992, Twin Peaks: Fire Walk with Me, 1992, Basquiat, 1996, Mio West, II, 1998, Everybody Loves Sunshine, 1999, Mr. Rice's Secret, 2000, Zoolander, 2001, The Prestige, 2006, (voice) Arthur and the Invisibles, 2006, August, 2008, Bandslam, 2009; (TV films) Baal, 1976; (TV appearances) Theatre 625, 1968, Dream On, 1991, The Hunger, 1999, 2000, SpongeBob SquarePants, 2007; (plays) The Elephant Man, Booth Theatre, NYC, 1980; appeared in (concert films) Ziggy Stardust and the Spiders from Mars: The Motion Picture, 1983, Serious Moonlight, 1983, The Glass Spider, 1987, A Reality Tour, 1994; (documentaries) Cracked Actor: A Film About David Bowie, 1975, Mayor of the Sunset Strip, 2003, David Bowie: Five Years, 2014; prodr.: (albums by Lou Reed) Transformer, 1973, (albums by Mott the Hoople) All the Young Dudes, 1973; (albums by Iggy and the Stooges) Raw Power, 1973; (albums by Iggy Pop) The Idiot, 1977 Lust for Life, 1977, TV Eye Live 1977, 1977; collaborator (broadway musical) Lazarus Recipient Grammy award for best short-form video, 1984, British Phonographic Industry Award for British Male Solo Artist, 1984, Silver Clef award for Outstanding Achievement, 1987, Ivor Novello award for Outstanding Contribution to British Music, 1990, BRIT award for Outstanding Contribution to Music, 1996, Webby Lifetime Achievement award, 2007; inducted into The Rock and Roll Hall of Fame, 1996; named one of The 100 Greatest Artists of All Time, Rolling Stone mag., 2004 Died Jan. 10, 2016.

BOWLER, LEWIS J., communications executive; b. St. George, Utah, Sept. 8, 1930; s. Charles E. and Mary (Riding) B.; m. Dorcus Nower, Sept. 23, 1955; children: LuAnn, Mary Alice, Nancy, Scott L. Student, So. Utah State Coll., 1975, Dixie Coll., St. George, 1992. Lineman Mountain Bell Tel. Co., Salt Lake City, 1949-53, constrn. foreman, 1954-58, PBX and key technician St. George, 1958-60, ctrl. office technician, 1960-64, network mgr., 1964-79; owner Bowler's C Com, St. George, from 1980. Chmn. bd. dirs. Vocat. Adv. Bd., St. George, 1976-78; bd. dirs. So. Utah Alcohol Recovery, Cedar City, 1961-80; leader Boy Scouts Am., St. George, 1956—; mem. adv. bd. Washington County Sch. Dist., St. George, 1976-78; homeless adv. So. Utah Social Svc., St. George, 1981-85. With Signal Corps, U.S. Army, 1951-55. Recipient Svc. award Boy Scouts Am., 1988. Mem. Lions Internat. (club pres. 1991-92, lt. gov. 1992-93, zone chmn. 1992-93, dist. gov. 1994-95, past dist. gov. 1995—, 100% Pres. award 1992, Lion of Yr. 1993, 96, Gov. award 1993, Excel award 1995). Home: Saint George, Utah. Died Jan. 23, 2007.

BOWLES, JESSE GROOVER, lawyer; b. Baconton, Ga., Aug. 24, 1921; s. Jesse Groover Sr. and Bartow (Swann) B.; m. Ruth Florence Bowles, Aug. 31, 1945 (div. 1981); children: Jesse Groover III, Elizabeth Bowles Chastain; m. Jane Parkman, June 26, 1981. JD, U. Ga., 1946. Bar: Ga. 1946, U.S. Dist. Ct. (mid. dist.) Ga. 1946, U.S. Ct. Appeals (5th cir.) 1946, U.S. Supreme Ct. 1960. Justice Ga. Supreme Ct., Atlanta, 1977-81; ptnr. Bowles & Bowles, Cuthbert, Ga., from 1981. Pres. Randolph County Fed. Savs. & Loan Assn., 1965-85; mem. State Bd. Bar Examiners, 1972-76. Trustee Andrew Coll., 1997—, Randolph County Hosp. Authority, 1969—. With U.S. Army, 1942-43. Mem. Am. Coll. Trial Lawyers, Pataula Cir. Bar Assn. (pres.), Ga. Bar Assn. (bd. dirs.). Baptist. Avocations: golf, forestry, farming, construction, banking. Died Jan. 28, 2007.

BOWMAN, EUGENE WILLIAM, retired mathematics professor; b. North Powder, Oreg., Mar. 28, 1910; s. Albert Franklin and Helen (Groves) Bowman; m. Ida Jones (dec. 1995); children: Eugene William, Virginia. BS, U. Idaho, Moscow, 1935, MS, 1936. HS prin. cert. Wash., supt. credential Wash. Tchr. pub. schs., Forest Grove, Oreg., 1931—34; instr. Coeur d'Alene Jr. Coll., Idaho, 1936—38; supt. Rockford Pub. Schs., Wash., 1941—46; prof. math. So. Oreg. Coll., Ashland, 1949—75; ret., 1975. Contbr. articles to profl. jours. Fgn. svc. officer US Govt., Quito, Ecuador, 1960—62. Lt. comdr. USN, 1946—49. Mem.: Rotary, Masons, Phi Delta Kappa. Avocations: hunting, boating, fishing. Home: Sunnyvale, Calif. Died Aug. 10, 2007.

BOYCE, THOMAS KENNETH, psychiatrist; b. Middletown, NY, Apr. 26, 1923; s. Thomas A. and Lillian (Hackett) B. Reg. profl. nurse, Middletown State Hosp., 1947; AB, Marietta Coll., Ohio, 1951; MA, Tchrs. Coll. Columbia U., NYC, 1953; MD, Cath. U. Leuven, Belgium, 1961. Diplomate Am. Bd. Psychiatry and Neurology. From supervisory psychiatrist to unit chief of svc. Middletown Psychiat. Ctr., 1966-82, chmn. hosp. forensic and spl. release com., 1980-83 and from 84. Cons. psychiatrist Mercy Cmty. Hosp., Port Jarvis, N.Y., 1966—, Social Security Bur. Disability Determination, Albany, N.Y., 1967—, St. Anthony's Cmty. Hosp., Warwick, N.Y., 1970—. Pharmacists mate USNR, 1943-46. Fellow Am. Coll. Phys.; mem. AMA, Am. Psychiat. Assn., Orange County Med. Soc. (chmn. mental health com. 1979-91). Roman Catholic. Avocation: photography. Died Mar. 4, 2007.

BOYD, JERRY WAYNE, school system administrator; b. Odessa, Tex., June 22, 1945; s. Jack Ralston and Hazel Omer (Galloway) B.; m. Sally Louise Featherston, Jan. 18, 1967; children: Eric, Gretchen, Jason, Jerry Jr. BS, Sam Houston State U., 1967, MEd, 1980. Sales engr. Calgon Corp., Birmingham, Ala., 1967-70; dist. mgr. Mogul Chem. Co., Houston, 1975-76, Drew Chem. Co., Corpus Christi, Tex., 1977-78; nat. sales mgr. Keystone Labs., Decatur, Ala., 1978; tchr., coach various schs., 1978-81; prin. Neches (Tex.) Ind. Sch. Dist., 1981-83, Westwood Ind. Sch. Dist., Palestine, Tex., 1983-86, Miami (Tex.) Ind. Sch. Dist., 1986-87, Grapeland (Tex.) Ind. Sch. Dist., from 1987, Gustine Ind. Sch. Dist., from 1991. Pilot mem. Tex. Sch. Improvement Initiative, Austin, Tex., 1985—; bd. dirs. Baylor U. Prins. Ctr., Waco, Tex., 1983—, Region VII Prins. Acad., Kilgore, Tex., 1983-85. Contbr. articles to profl. jours. and popular newspapers. Chmn., del. Dem. Conv., San Antonio, 1980; bd. dirs. ARC, Palestine, 1982-87, Crimestoppers; pres. Youth Football League, Palestine. Mem. Tex. Elem. Prins. and Supts. Assn., Tex. Assn. Secondary Sch. Prins., Nat. Assn. for Edn. Young Children, Lions. Home: Bullard, Tex. Died Feb. 21, 2007.

BOYD, MALCOLM, minister, writer; b. Buffalo, June 8, 1923; s. Melville and Beatrice (Lowrie) B.; life ptnr. Mark Thompson. BA, U. Ariz., 1944; B.D., Ch. Div. Sch. Pacific, 1954; postgrad., Oxford U., Eng., 1955; S.T.M., Union Theol. Sem., NYC, 1956; DD (hon.), Ch. Div. Sch. of Pacific, 1995; PhD (hon.), Episcopal Div. Sch., Cambridge, Mass., 2014. Ordained to ministry Episcopal Ch., 1955. V.p., gen. mgr. Pickford, Rogers & Boyd, 1949-51; rector in Indpls., 1957-59; chaplain Colo. State U., 1959-61, Wayne State U., 1961-65; nat. field rep. Episcopal Soc. Cultural and Racial Unity, 1965-68; resident fellow Calhoun Coll., Yale U., 1968-71, assoc. fellow, from 1971; writer-priest in residence St. Augustine-by-the Sea Episcopal Ch., 1982-95. Lectr. World Council Chs., Switzerland, 1955, 64; columnist Pitts. Courier, 1962-65; resident guest Mishkenot Sha'ananim, Jerusalem, 1974; chaplain AIDS Commn. Episcopal Diocese L.A., 1989-2015; writer-in-residence Episcopal Diocese LA, 1996-2015, hon. canon, 2002; mem. adv. bd. White Crane Inst., 2007. Host (TV) Sex in the Seventies, LA, 1975; author: Crisis in Communication, 1957, Christ and Celebrity Gods, 1958, Focus, 1960, rev. edit., 2001, If I Go Down to Hell, 1962, The Hunger, The Thirst, 1964, Are You Running with Me, Jesus?, 1965, rev. edit., 1990, 40th anniv. rev. edit., 2006, Free to Live, Free to Die, 1967, Book of Days, 1968, As I Live and Breathe: Stages of an Autobiography, 1969, The Fantasy Worlds of Peter Stone, 1969, rev. edit., 2008, My Fellow Americans, 1970, Human Like Me, Jesus, 1971, The Lover, 1972, When in the Course of Human Events, 1973, The Runner, 1974, The Alleluia Affair, 1975, Christian, 1975, Am I Running with You, God?, 1977, Take Off the Masks, 1978, rev. edit. 2007, Look Back in Joy, 1981, rev. edit., 2007, Half Laughing, Half Crying, 1986, Gay Priest: An Inner Journey, 1986, Edges, Boundaries and Connections, 1992, Rich with Years, 1993, Go Gentle Into That Good Night, 1998, Running with Jesus: The Prayers of Malcolm Boyd, 2000, Simple Grace: A Mentor's Guide to Growing Older, 2001, rev. edit., 2014, Prayers for the Later Years, 2002, Wisdom for the Aging: Practical Advice for Living the Best Yeavs of Your Life Right Now, 2009; plays Boy, 1961, Study in Color, 1962, The Community, 1964, others; editor: On the Battle Lines, 1964, The Underground Church, 1968, (with Nancy L. Wilson) Amazing Grace: Stories of Gay and Lesbian Faith, 1991; (with Chester Talton) Race and Prayer: Collected Voices, Many Dreams, 2003, (with J. Jon Bruno) In Times Like These--How We Pray, 2005, A Prophet in His Own Land: A Malcolm Boyd Reader, 2008; book reviewer: LA Times, 1979-85; contbg. editor, columnist Episcopal News; columnist Modern Maturity, 1990-2000; contbr. articles to popular mags. including Newsday, Parade, The Advocate, also newspapers. Active voter registration, Miss., Ala., 1963, 64; mem. Los Angeles City/County AIDS Task Force. Malcolm Boyd Collection and Archives established Boston U., 1973; recipient Integrity Internat. award, 1978, Union Am. Hebrew Congregations award, 1980, Lazarus Project award, 2002, Louie Crew award for svc. to gay and lesbian people, 2003, Giants of Justice award Clergy and Laity United for Econ. Justice, 2004, Unitas award, Union Theol. Sem., NYC., 2005, Lambda Lit. Found. Life Achievement award, 2008, Rainbow Key award, Lesbian & Gay Cmty. West Hollywood, 2009. Mem. Nat. Council Chs. (film awards com. 1965), P.E.N. (pres. PEN Ctr. U.S. West 1984-87), Am. Center, Authors Guild, Integrity, Nat. Gay Task Force, Clergy and Laity Concerned (nat. bd.), NAACP, Amnesty Internat., Episc. Peace Fellowship, Fellowship of Reconciliation (nat. com.). Episcopalian. Home: Los Angeles, Calif. *The years have taught me the cost of getting involved in life. It is all a risk. One is on stage in an ever-new set without a script. The floor may give way without warning, the walls abruptly cave in. One may die at the hand of an assassin acting on blind impulse. Security, for which men sell their souls, is one of the few real jests in life. Yet the cost of not getting involved in life is higher; one has merely died prematurely. When one has stripped power of its mystique, its robes and artifices, it becomes vulnerable. When you stand up to power, you stand up to one or more individuals. Look an individual, then, in the eye, laugh, if you feel like it. This may be rightly received as a much-needed expression of human solidarity.* Died Feb. 27, 2015.

BOYE, FREDERICK CHARLES, organic research and development chemist; b. Buffalo, May 30, 1923; s. Fred Frederick and Emma Anna Rose (Schneider) B.; m. Virginia

Alice Kroll, July 17, 1951; children: Suzanne Renee, Frederick C., Jr., Christopher Karl. BA, U. Buffalo, 1949, MA, 1951, PhD, 1952. Rsch. chemist Cornell Aero. Lab., Inc., Cheektowaga, N.Y., 1951-52; R&D chemist Allied Chem. Co., Buffalo, 1952-67; sr. rsch. chemist Stauffer Ea. Rsch. Ctr., Dobbs Ferry, N.Y., 1967-70; sr. sci. Am. Can Tech. Ctr., Neenah, Wis., 1971-78; regulatory dir. coatings div. M&T Chem., Menasha, Wis., 1978-80; tech. bibliographer Inst. Paper Chemisty, Appleton, Wis., 1981-89; environ. scientist Banta Corp., Menasha, from 1986. Cons. in field. Editor: Reclaimed Fibers, 1983, Utilization of Lignins and Lignin Derivatives, vols. 1-3, 1984, 85, Closed Systems, 1985, Nonwoven Fabrics, vols. 1-4, 1986; bibliographer, editor: Air Pollution in Pulp and Paper Industry, 1987. With USNR, 1942-45. Fellow Am. Inst. Chemists (accredited). Achievements include patents in gelling agents for jet fuels, water insoluble dyes and precursors, arene sulfonic acid catalysts for methylenebis-(2-chloroaniline), fabric conditioner in compressed form for use in dryers; research in Nadic 200 epoxy curing agent, rigid refractory polyurethane/polyester foams for radome assemblies, psuedocumidine special by unique rearrangement of methylated xylidines, 2-oxy-1-naphthoic acid for dry-charge batteries. Home: Appleton, Wis. Died Mar. 8, 2007.

BOYER, TYRIE ALVIS, lawyer; b. Williston, Fla., Sept. 10, 1924; s. Alton Gordon and Mary Ethel (Strickland) B.; m. Elizabeth Everett Gale, June 9, 1945; children: Carol, Tyrie, Kennedy, Lee. BA, U. Fla., 1953, LLB, JD, 1954. Bar: Fla. Atty. Crawford, May & Boyer, Jacksonville, Fla., 1954-58, Boyer Law Offices, Jacksonville, 1958-60; judge Civil Ct. of Record, Jacksonville, 1960-63; cir. judge 4th Jud. Cir. of Fla., Jacksonville, 1963-67; atty. Dawson, Galant, Maddox, Boyer, Sulik & Nichols, Jacksonville, 1967-73; appellate judge 1st Dist. Ct. Appeal, Tallahassee, 1973-79; chief judge 1st Dist. Ct. Appeals, Tallahassee, 1975-76; atty. Boyer, Tanzler, Blackburn & Boyer, Jacksonville, 1979-84, Boyer, Tanzler & Sussman, Jacksonville, from 1984. Adj. prof. Fla. Coastal Sch. Law, Jacksonville, from 1996, U. North Fla., from 1998; chmn. Supreme Ct. Com. on Standard Conduct Governing Judges, Tallahassee, 1976—79. Contbr. articles to profl. jours. Chmn. Duval County Hosp. Authority, Jacksonville, 1970-73, Jacksonville Bldg. Fin. Authority, 1980-81; pres. Jacksonville Legal Aid Assn., 1954-61; bd. dirs. Jones Coll., Jacksonville, 1978-85; bd. advs. Fla. Coastal Sch. Law, 1996—; adj. prof. U. North Fla., 1998—. With USN, 1942—45, PTO. Mem. Am. Judicature Soc., Fla. Bar, Jacksonville Bar Assn., Am. Bd. Trial Advs., SCV (comdr.), Mil. Order Stars and Bars (comdr.), Masons, dir., Safari Club Internat., Fla. Blue Key, Order of Coif, Phi Beta Kappa, Phi Kappa Phi. Methodist. Home: Jacksonville, Fla. Deceased.

BOYLE, THOMAS FRANCIS, educational administrator; b. Coaldale, Pa., Apr. 18, 1947; s. Francis Dennis Boyle and Kathleen (Sheehan) Frankowski; m. Diane Lee Cannizzaro, June 20, 1970; children: Kristen C., Kellie E., Tiffany A. BA, William Paterson Coll., 1969; computer cert., St. Peter's Coll., Jersey City, 1976; Cert. Tax Assessor, Rutgers U., 1978; MA, Kean Coll., 1995; EdD, Nova Southeastern U., 2003. Cert. tchr., N.J.; cert. tax assessor, N.J.; cert. real estate appraiser Nat. Assn. Real Estate Appraisers, Phoenix; cert. prof. assessor Soc. Profl. Assessors; cert. supr., sch. bus. adminstr. Computer coord. Warren (N.J.) Middle Sch., 1986-97; supt. Somerset County Ednl. Svcs. Commn., Raritan, N.J., from 1997. Councilman Borough of Dunellen, N.J., 1978; committeeman Dem. Orgn., So. Plainfield, N.J., 1990. With U.S. Army, 1970-80. Mem. Warren Twp. Edn. Assn. (pres. 1976-78), Somerset County Edn. Assn. (1st v.p. 1980-82, treas. 1982-92), KC, Phi Kappa Phi. Roman Catholic. Home: South Plainfield, NJ. Died Aug. 25, 2007.

BOYLES, PATRICIA ANN, real estate executive; b. Cleve., Mar. 7, 1951; d. Charles William and Ann Marie (Galla) B. Student, Douglass Coll., 1969-72, Camden County Coll., 1976-77, Temple U., 1978. Mgr. advt., dir. pub. relations W.T. Grant Co., Somerset, N.J., 1972-73; staff announcer Sta. WGAY, Washington, 1973; freelance in broadcast prodn. Phila., 1973-75; dir. administrn. Houser Demolition Inc., Camden, 1975-76; exec. coordinator Capp Realty Co., Lindenwold, N.J., 1977-80; rep. sales Ryland Group Inc., Cherry Hill, N.J., 1980-87; corp. sec. Security Mortgage and Investment Co., 1977-80; dir. field sales Ryland Group Inc., Marlton, 1987-88, mgr. div. sales, from 1988. Mem. Nat. Assn. Female Execs., Nat. Assn. Realtors, N.J. Assn. Realtors, Camden County Bd. Realtors, Am. Soc. Notaries, Am. Soc. Profl. and Exec. Women, Kings Grant Civic Assn. Home: Marlton, NJ. Died Aug. 2, 2007.

BOYM, SVETLANA (SVETLANA GOLDBERG), literature educator, writer; b. Leningrad, Russia, Apr. 29, 1959; came to U.S., 1981; d. Yury Isaevich and Musa (Davidovna) Goldberg; Constantin Boym (div.); m. Dana Villa BA in Hispanic Languages and Literatures, Herzen State Pedagogical Inst., Leningrad, 1980; MA in Hispanic Languages, Boston U., 1983; PhD in Comparative Lit., Harvard U., 1988. Instr. lang. Boston U., 1981-83; instr. Harvard U., Cambridge, Mass., 1984—88, asst. prof., 1988—93, assoc. prof. to Curt Hugo Reisinger prof. of Slavic languages and lit. and comparative lit. Cambridge, 1993—2015. Author: (books) Death in Quotation Marks: Cultural Myths of the Modern Poet, 1991, Common Places: Mythologies of Everyday Life in Russia, 1994, The Future of Nostalgia, 2001, Kosmos: A Portrait of the Russian Space Age, 2001, Ninochka, 2003, Another Freedom: The Alternative History of an Idea, 2010; (short stories) The Club of TV Travellers, 1993, Mixed Salad with Russian Dressing, 1993, We Made Love Like..., 1989; (scriptwriter) Flirting with Liberty, 1989 (New Eng. Film and Video Festival Hon. Mention 1990), (playwright) The Woman Who Shot Lenin, 1988 (Boston Film and Video Found. award 1992, ARTLink Film award 1993), dir. with Nancy Dalzer film version; film editor Slavic Rev., 1992; contbr. articles to Boston Review, Slavic Review, New Formations, Yale Journal of Criticism. Grantee IREX, 1989, 92; fellow Harvard for Grad. Women, 1987, Jack Levine in Comparative Lit., 1986, Guggenheim Fellow, 1998; recipient Clark Fund Harvard U., 1993, MLA Travel award, 1993. Mem. MLA (chair exec. com. Div. Slavic and Ea. European Lits.), European U. of St. Petersburg Adv. Bd., Harvard Faculty Coun. Home: Cambridge, Mass. Died Aug. 5, 2015.

BRADLEE, BEN (BENJAMIN CROWNINSHIELD BRADLEE), publishing executive, retired editor-in-chief; b. Boston, Aug. 26, 1921; s. Frederick Josiah and Josephine (deGersdorff) Bradlee; m. Jean Saltonstall, Aug. 8, 1942 (div. 1955); 1 child, Benjamin Jr.; m. Antoinette Pinchot, July 6, 1956 (div.); children: Dominic, Marina; m. Sally Quinn, Oct. 20, 1978; 1 child, Josiah Quinn Crowninshield. AB, Harvard U., 1943; LHD (hon.), Georgetown U., 2006. Founder, reporter NH Sunday News, Manchester, 1946- 48; reporter Washington Post Co., 1948-51; asst. to press attachè US Embassy, Paris, 1951-53; European corr. Newsweek mag., Paris, 1953-57, reporter Washington bur., 1957-61, sr. editor, chief bur., 1961-65; dep. mng. editor for nat. & internat. affairs Washington Post Co., 1965, mng. editor, 1965-68, v.p., exec. editor, 1968-91, v.p. at large, 1991—2014. Author: Kennedy: That Special Grace, 1964, Conversations with Kennedy, 1974, A Good Life--Newspapering and Other Adventures, 1995. Chmn. St. Mary's City Commn., Md., 1991—2003; bd. trustees St. Mary's Coll., 2003—11. Served in USN, 1942—45. Decorated Knight of the Nat. Order of the Légion d'honneur France; recipient Presdl. Medal of Freedom, The White House, 2013. Home: Washington, DC. Died Oct. 21, 2014.

BRADLEY, CHARLES MACARTHUR, retired architect; b. Chgo., Sept. 26, 1918; s. Harold Smith and Helen Francis (MacArthur) B.; m. Joan Marie Daane, July 27, 1946 (dec.);children: Mary Barbara, Nancy Ann, Sally Joan, William Charles (dec.); m. Letricia L. Bradley, June 29, 2007, (div. June, 2014) BS in Architecture, U. Ill., 1940. With Holabird & Root, architects, Chgo., 1940-41, Giffels & Vallet, architects and engrs., Detroit, 1941-44; ptnr., corp. pres. Bradley & Bradley, architects and engrs., Rockford, Ill., 1947-2001; ret., 2001. Pres. Bradley Bldg. Corp., 1962—. Prin. works include North Sheboygan HS and addition, Wis., 1960-68, J.F. Kennedy Middle Sch., Rockford, 1968, Singer Health Clinic, Rockford, 1964, Jacobs HS, Algonquin, Ill., 1976, Atwood plant, Rockford, 1977, Admiral Home, Chgo., 1978, Bushnell Jr. HS, Ill., 1980, Bloom HS, 1983, Evenglow Lodge, 1984, East Aurora HS addition, 1992, Erie HS, 1994; author papers on life cycling old schs., roofing procedures. Active Blackhawk coun. Boy Scouts Am. Served with C.E., US Army, 1945-46. Recipient Meritorious Svc. award Ill. Assn. Sch. Bds., 1976. Mem. AIA (pres. No. Ill. chpt. 1962, treas. Ill. coun. 1973-74), Ill. Soc. Architects (pres. 1974), Edn. Facilities Planners Inst., Ill. Assn. Sch. Bd. Officers, Rotary, Union League, Univ. Club, Lauderdale Lakes Sailing Club, Meridian Club. Republican. Congregationalist. Died Oct. 16, 2014.

BRADLEY, JOAN CALLAN, perioperative nurse; b. Loretta, Pa., Feb. 28, 1928; d. Henry and Gertrude (Conrad) Callan; m. Walter J. Bradley, July 11, 1953; children: Kevin, Debora, Cynthia, Jon, Brian. Diploma, Mercy Hosp., 1948; BSN, U. Del., 1981; cert., Del. County Community Coll., 1987. RN, Del., Pa.; CNOR. Staff nurse oper. rm. Kent Gen. Hosp., Dover, Del., staff nurse; coll. nurse Wesley Coll., Dover; clin. instr. Jefferson Med. Ctr., Phila. 1st lt. USANC, 1951-53. Mem. Assn. Operating Room Nurses Del-A-Mar (past sec., v.p., program chmn.). Home: Dover, Del. Died Aug. 8, 2007.

BRADLEY, VINCENT GERARD, judge; b. Kingston, NY, Oct. 3, 1939; s. Vincent and Mary (McGowan) Bradley; m. Dorothy Maureen Roach, Jan. 4, 1964; children: Brigid, Vincent, Barney, Meghan, Rian, Caitlin. BS, NY State Maritime Coll., 1962; JD, Fordham U., 1967. Bar: NY. Ptnr. Ryan, Bradley, Kerr, Dall Vechia & Roach P.C., Kingston, 1967—81; justice State NY Supreme Ct., Kingston, from 1981. Mem.: Ulster County Bar Assn., NY Assn. Supreme Ct. Justices, NY State Bar Assn. Democrat. Roman Catholic. Home: Kingston, NY. Died Nov. 24, 2006.

BRADSHAW, PHYLLIS BOWMAN, historian, historic site staff member; b. Cumberland, Ky., June 19, 1929; d. Lawrence David and Ann Rees Bowman; m. Glenn Lewis Bradshaw, June 30, 1949 (dec. Feb. 2000)); children: Charles Lewis, David Bowman. Student, Ctr. Coll., Danville, Ky., 1947-50, N.Y Sch. Speed Writing, 1967. Sec. to dir. and asst. dir. Shakertown, Pleasant Hill, Ky., 1967-68, asst. food dir., 1968-70, mus. dir. dept. interpretation, 1970-72; mus. hist. interpreter Old Fort Harrod State Pk., Harrodsburg, Ky., 1993-98. Rschr.: book Beyond Shenandoah, 2001. Mem. Harrodsburg Hist. Soc., Ky. Hist. Soc., Girl Scouts Am., Nat. Trust, Libr. Congress, Washington; tchr. Sunday sch. Harrodsburg Presbyn. Ch.; life mem. Women's Soc., Burgin Meth. Ch., bd. dirs., tchr./leader H.S. group; pres., sec. Burgin PTA; den mother cub scouts Boy Scouts Am.; life mem. Ky. PTA, Shakertown at Pleasant Hill; founding mem. Harlan (Ky.) Musettes; active Mercer County Blood Bank; assisted in creation of The Ky. Classic Sauces-Bluegrass Trade Assn. Mem. DAR (Jane McAfee chpt.), Lewis and Clark Assn., N.W. Territory Assn., Hite Family Assn., Ky. History Tchrs. Assn., Colonial Dames Ct. of Honor (Ky. chpt.), Ctr. Coll. Alumni Assn., Lions Club. mem. Va. Hist. Soc., 2002. Home: Harrodsburg, Ky. Died Apr. 26, 2007.

BRADY, JULES MALACHI, philosopher, educator, priest; b. St. Louis, Mo., Feb. 17, 1919; s. Jules Musik and Laura Catherine Brady. BA, St. Louis U., 1939, PhD, 1949. Ordained Jesuit, 53. Prof. philosophy Rockhurst Univ., Kansas City, Mo., 1955—2000; retired, 2000. Roman Catholic. Home: Saint Louis, Mo. Died Jan. 21, 2007.

BRADY, SARAH, gun control activist; b. Kirksville, Mo., Feb. 6, 1942; m. James Brady, 1973; 1 child, James Brady Jr. BA in Edn., Coll. of William and Mary. Former tchr.; asst. campaign dir. Nat. Rep. Congressional Com., 1968-70; adminstrv. aide to Reps. Mike McKevitt, Joseph J. Maraziti, 1970-74; dir. adminstr., coord. field svcs. Rep. Nat. Com., 1974-78; lobbyist, then chmn. Handgun Control Inc.; chairwoman Brady Campaign to Prevent Gun Violence and Brady Ctr. to Prevent Gun Violence, 2000—15. Died Apr. 3, 2015.

BRAITHWAITE, WILFRED JOHN, retired physics professor; b. Ferndale, Wash., Apr. 11, 1940; s. John Alfred and Joyce Elinor (Gunderson) B.; m. Wanda Pearl Chism, June 3, 1961 (div. 1975). BS in Physics with honors, Seattle Pacific U., 1962; MS in Physics, U. Wash., 1965, PhD in Physics, 1971; postgrad, Sci. Edn. U. Tex., 1988—89. Instr. physics Princeton U., NJ, 1970-72; asst. prof. physics U. Tex., Austin, 1972-79, rsch. scientist faculty, 1979-81; tech. and sci. cons. Austin, 1981-89; assoc. prof. physics U. Ark., Little Rock, 1989-95, prof. physics, 1995—2007, prof. emeritus, from 2007. Vis. staff mem. Los Alamos Nat. Lab., N.Mex., 1975-76, 78-79; vis. scientist Ind. U., Bloomington, 1990-96; affiliate prof. physics U. Wash., Seattle, 1991-96; sci. assoc. PPE divsn. CERN, Geneva, Switzerland, 1992-2007; guest scientist Brookhaven Nat. Lab., Upton, NY, 1992-2007; grant referee Ark. Sci. and Tech. Authority, 1990-2007; cons. for GE Corp. R&D, 2002-07; lectr. in field. Numerous unedited contbns.; jour. referee Phys. Rev. C and Phys. Rev. Letters, 1970-2007, Found. Physics, Assoc. Ed. Ark. Acad. Sci., 2000-07. U.S. Dept. Energy rsch. grantee, 1992-95, 99-2007, Ark. Sci. and Tech. Authority rsch. grantee, 1993-94, 96-98; numerous grants from NSF, Dept. of Energy, Robert A Welch Found. Mem. IEEE, Am. Phys. Soc., Nat. Assn. for Rsch. in Sci. Teaching, N.Y. Acad. Sci., Ark. Acad. Sci. Achievements include rsch. on time reversal invariance; high excitation neutron particle-hole states; charge-dependent matrix elements in light nuclei; method for determining rotational symmetries of nuclear states using heavy ions; multiply-excited atomic states in helium-like and lithium-like oxygen; strength of the 3-alpha process in stellar helium burning; method for identifying antimatter stars; large isospin mixing in light nuclei via scattering comparisons of positive and negative pions near the pion-nucleon resonance, microwave refrigeration; measurement limits on source sizes formed in symmetric collisions of ultra-relativistic heavy nuclei; method for separating charged kaons and pions in Time Projection Chambers via in-flight decays using their known isotropic emissions in both COM frames; instrument design for high-energy nuclear physics, examining models to slow aging. Home: Little Rock, Ark. Died Dec. 22, 2013.

BRAND, EDWARD CABELL, retail executive; b. Salem, Va., Apr. 11, 1923; s. William F. and Ruth (Cabell) B.; m. Shirley Hurt, June 20, 1964; children: Sylvia, Miriam, Liza, Richie (dec.), John, Edward (dec.), Marshall (dec.), Caroline. Grad., Va. Mil. Inst., 1944; HHD (hon.), Roanoke Coll., 1997, Washington and Lee U., 1999, Ferrum Coll., 2005, Va. Western Coll., 2005. Dept. of State econ. analyst, intelligence office Berlin Mil. Govt., 1947-49; v.p. Ortho-Vent Shoe Co., 1949-62; pres. Brand Edmonds Assocs. Advertising, 1962-66, chmn. bd., 1962-81; founder, pres. Stuart McGuire Co., Salem, Va., 1962-85, chmn. bd., chief exec. officer, 1973-85; chmn. emeritus, cons. Stuart McGuire Co. (merged with Home Shopping (TV) Network), 1985-86; pres. Recovery Systems, Inc., Salem, Va., 1986—2005, Brand-Edmonds Assoc. Advertising, 1956—66, chmn. bd., 1962—81. Rsch. assoc., former instr. bus. adminstrn. and sales mgmt. Roanoke Coll., 1986-2005 Author: If Not Me Then Who, 2008. Chmn. Va. State Bd. Health, 1989-93; pres., founder, chmn. Cabell Brand Ctr. for Internat. Poverty and Resource Studies, 1988-; former dir. Southeast Rural Assistance Project Inn; cons. Rainwater Mgmt. Solutions; former mem. Bus. Leadership Adv. Coun-cil.; founder, pres. Total Action Against Poverty, Roanoke Valley, 1965-95; pres. Pvt. Sector Commn. Va. Community Action Agys., 1986-88; mem. Gov.'s Commn. on Fed. Funding of State Domestic Program, 1986-88; trustee Council on Religion and Internat. Affairs, Ethics Resource Ctr., Heinz Ctr. Sci., Econs. and Environ.; bd. dirs. Roanoke Coun. Cmty. Svcs., Woodlands Conf. divsn. Woodlands Ctr. for Future Research and the Houston Area Research Ctr., Global Water, Washington, Va. Health Care Found., Richmond, Va., 1993-2000, Va. Found. for the Humanities and Pub. Policy, Charlottesville, 1993-99, Blue Ridge Pub. TV, Roanoke, Va., 1993—2006, Action Alliance for Va. Children and Youth, Richmond, 1994-2000, Va. Conservation Network, Richmond, 1996—2009; bd. trustees Western Va. Land Trust, Roanoke, Va., 1995-2000; assoc. World Resources Inst., Washington, 1985., dir. Found. Alternative & Intrative medicine, 2005-, advisor to pres. Lynchburg, 2010-, Served from pvt. to capt. AUS, 1942-46, ETO. Decorated Bronze Star. Named Businessman in U.S. who has done most to help disadvantaged people, Vista, 1980; recipient LBJ Humanitarian nat. award, 1989, Outstanding Citizen Rotary Club, 1999, Lifetime Achivement award Salem Rocule County C. od C., 2010, John W Hancoch award, 1996, medal Nat. Soc. Daughters Am. Revolution, 2010, Heros award Am. Red Cross, 2010 Mem. NAS (coun., pres. cir.), Social Venture Network, Direct Selling Assn. (past dir., chmn. named to Hall of Fame), U.S. C. of C., Conf. Bd. (exec. coun.), World Pres. Assn. (past dir., chmn. Argentina Conf. 1988), Roanoke Touchdown Club (past pres.), Valley Torch Club (past pres.), Roanoke Sales Execs. (past dir.), Rotary (past. pres. Salem), US Assn. Club Rome, Roanoke Valley Hist. Soc, Home: Salem, Va. *In* *addition to trying to do the best job I could— whether in school, business, public service, or in my family— I have felt a continuing need to improve our system and society. This has led to extensive study, travels, and a variety of extra-curricular activities. Today I have great confidence in the future of the United States and the world, but see urgent need for dramatic changes in our value systems, and need for long range planning. Our Center focuses on inter-relationship between poverty and resource limitation for sustainable development with specific focus on water problems locally and globally and peace issues. Our major focus today is on peace and conflect resolution as explained in the last chapter of my book "If Not me, Then Who?".* Died Jan. 13, 2015.

BRANDT, FREDERIC SHELDON, dermatologist; b. Newark, June 26, 1949; BA, Rutgers U., 1971; MD, Hahnemann Med. Coll., 1975. Diplomate Am. Bd. Internal Medicine, Am. Bd. Dermatology, lic. physician N.Y., 1979, Fla., 1982, Calif., 1982. Intern NYU, NYC, 1975—76, resident in internal medicine, 1976—78; resident in dermatology U. Miami, Fla., 1978—81; pvt. practice dermatology Miami, Fla., 1982, NY, 1998. Clin. assoc. prof. dept. dermatology U. Miami, Fla.; clin. rsch. investigator Collagen Corp., from 2003; lectr. in field; mfr. Dr. Brandt Skin Care Products; cancer rschr. Sloan-Kettering; cons. and prin. investigator Medicis Aesthetics, Mentor Biologics, Dermik ColBar, Contura, Revance, Isolagen, Merz, Lumenis, Cutera, Palomar, Johnson & Johnson, Stiefel-GSK, & Allergan. Contbr. articles to profl. jours.; author: Age-Less: The Definitive Guide to Botox, Collagen, Lasers, Peels, and Other Solutions for Flawless Skin, 2002, 10 Minutes/10 Years: Your Definitive Guide to a Beautiful and Youthful Appearance, 2007; co-host Ask Dr. Brandt on Sirius XM radio. Mem.: AMA, Miami Soc. for Dermatology and Cutaneous Surgery, Internat. Soc. Cosmetic Laser Surgeons, Internat. Soc. for Dermatologic Surgery, Fla. Soc. Dermatology, Fla. Med. Assn., Dermatology Found. Leaders Soc., Dade County Med. Assn., Am. Soc. Dermatologic Surgeons, Am. Acad. Dermatology, Phi Beta Kappa. Died Apr. 6, 2015.

BRANDT, JEFFREY L., lawyer; b. Phila., Oct. 26, 1954; m. Dyane Lee MacDaniel, May 25, 1985; 1 child, Carson Fincham. BSEE, Lafayette Coll., Easton, Pa., 1976; JD, U. Balt., 1981. Bar: Maryland 1981. Elec. engr. Nat. Security Agy., Ft. G.G. Meade, Maryland, 1976-85; atty. G.E., Schenectady, N.Y., 1985-86, Eastman Kodak, Rochester, N.Y., 1986-87; counsel IBM, Fishkill, N.Y., 1987-96; counsel IP and licensing Walker Digital Corp., Stamford, Conn., from 1996. Mem. Licensing Exec. Soc. (pres. 1996—). Avocations: classical guitar, fencing. Home: Ridgefield, Conn. Died May 30, 2007.

BRANNIGAN, JOSEPH C., retired state legislator; b. Portland, Maine, July 16, 1931; m. Claire Brannigan; 1 child. Exec. dir. Shalom House; mem. Dist. 21 Maine House of Reps., 1978—80, mem. Dist. 117, 2003—06; mem. Dist. 29 Maine State Senate, 1980—94, mem. Dist. 35, 2001—02, mem. Dist. 9, 2006—12. Democrat. Roman Catholic. Died Jan. 17, 2015.

BRANNON, BRIAN RAY, financial advisor, lawyer, writer; b. New Hampton, Iowa, Mar. 5, 1944; s. Raymond Phillip and Andrea Yvonne (Robinson) B.; m. Jo Helen Kent, June 21, 1973; children: Shannon Christine, Douglas Brian. BA, U. Iowa, 1966, JD, 1973. Bar: Iowa 1973, Colo. 1986. V.p., trust officer Iowa State Bank & Trust, Iowa City, 1973-76; sr. v.p., mgr. trust dept. 1st Nat. Bank Dubuque, Iowa, 1976-78, U.S. Bank, Grand Junction, Colo., 1978-81; cons., advisor, writer, Grand Junction, from 1981. Bd. dirs. Kent News Co., Scottsbluff, Nebr., Adams Co., House Assit Corp.; tchr. courses on Fed. Res. Sys. and trust subjects Am. Inst. Banking. Mem., lector Immaculate Heart of Mary Parish Coun.; v.p. bd. dirs., chmn. fin. com. C.S.I.; mem. spl. events com., planned giving com. Mesa County chpt. Am. Cancer Soc.; active Pomona Sch. PTO, Holy Family Sch. PTO, Greenmeadows Homeowners Assn. Capt. U.S. Army, 1966-70, Vietnam; USAR, 1971-75. Decorated Bronze Star; Cross of Gallantry (Vietnam). Mem. ABA, AARP, Iowa Bar Assn., Colo. Bar Assn., Mesa County Bar Assn., Am. Mgmt. Assn., Internat. Platform Assn., Epilepsy Found. U.S.S., Epilepsy Found. Colo., DAV, Am. Legion, Vietnam Vets. Am., Grand Junction C. of C., U.S. Tennis Assn., U. Iowa Alumni Assn., Loras Coll. Alumni Assn., Bookcliff Country Club, Rotary (bd. dirs. Grand Junction 1991-92, editor 1987—), Phi Delta Phi. Republican. Roman Catholic (parish coun.). Avocations: investments, politics, tennis, skiing, conquering epilepsy disabilities. Died Dec. 28, 2006.

BRANSTNER, KARL CHRISTIAN, automobile manufacturing executive; b. Davison, Mich., Dec. 6, 1931; s. Bruno Karl and Anna Margaret (Stuetzer) B.; m. Nancy Helen Taylor, Nov. 8, 1952; children: Susan Kay, Steven Taylor, Kathleen Ann, Scott Walter. BBA, U. Detroit, 1962. First class lic. FCC. Labor rels. exec. PTO staff Chrysler Corp., Highland Park, Mich., 1961-64, pers. mgr. foundry Detroit, 1964-68, pers. mgr. New Stanton (Pa.) Assembly, 1968-70, pers. exec. car assembly div. Hamtramck, Mich., 1970-71, pers. mgr. Detroit trim ops., 1971-75, pers. mgr. Trenton (Mich.) engine div., 1975-86, power train ops. staff Highland Park, 1986-87, union rels. exec., 1987-88; staff exec. UAW-Chrysler Nat. Tng. Ctr. Bd. dirs. So. Wayne County C. of C., 1975-86. With USN, 1951-55. Mem. Soc. Human Resource Mgmt., U. Detroit Pers. Profls. Assn., Am. Legion. Republican. Methodist. Avocations: electronic servicing, golf, boating. Home: Auburn Hills, Mich. Died Dec. 10, 2006.

BRASIER, MARTIN DAVID, palaeobiologist, geologist, writer, educator; b. Wimbledon, Eng., Apr. 12, 1947; s. Tom and Violette Brasier; m. Cecilia Joyce Clement, July 7, 1975; children: Matthew, Alexander, Zoë. BS in Geology with honors, London U., 1969, PhD, 1973; MA, Oxford U., 1988. Micropalaeontologist Brit. Geol. Survey, Leeds, England, 1972—73; lectr. geology Reading U., Berkshire, England, 1973—74; from. lectr. geology to reader in paleobiology Hull U., England, 1974—88; lectr., fellow Oxford U., England, 1988—96, reader in geology, 1996—2002, prof. paleobiology, 2002—14; adj. prof. Meml. U. Newfoundland, 2006—14. Chmn. Cambrian subcommn. UNESCO, Paris, 1990—94, project leader, 1988—92; chmn. earth scis. subfaculty Oxford U., 2002—04; chmn. examiners earth scis. faculty, 1995, 1999, 2006; appointment bd. mem. Ruskin Professorship Oxford, 2001; senior tutor St Edmund Hall, 2001. Author: Microfossils, 1980, 2004; editor: Precambrian-Cambrian Boundary, 1989, Darwin's Lost World: The Hidden History of Animal Life, 2009, Secret Chambers: The Inside Story of Cells and Complex Life, 2012; contbr. several articles to profl. journals. Cons. Newfoundland and UNESCO World Heritage ite status, 2012. With HMS Fawn Royal Navy, 1970. Recipient Lyell medal, 2014. Fellow: Linnean Soc. London, St. Edmund Hall Oxford, Geol. Soc. London. Achievements include scientific and philosophical approaches needed for research into the origins of life, earliest cells, origins of plants and animals and the Cambrian explosion; definition and subdivision of Ediacaran system and of Cambrian system and of Precambrian-Cambrian boundary. Avocations: archaeology, numismatics, piano, harpsichords, jazz piano. Home: Oxford, England. Died Dec. 16, 2014.

BRATMAN, MARTIN D., communications sales company executive; b. NYC, Mar. 21, 1940; s. Irving and Irene (Solomon) B.; m. Elizabeth Jeanne Milch; children: Lawrence, Jamie. Student, Hofstra U., 1957-59. Buyer McCann, Erickson Internat., NYC, 1960-65; group supr. Grey Co., NYC, 1965-70; mgr., buyer T. Bates Co., NYC, 1970-71; account exec. PGW, NYC, 1979-76, Tel. Rep. Co., NYC, 1976-81; v.p., sales mgr. Blair Communications, NYC, from 1981. Ind. cons., N.Y.C. Served with USCG, 1960-66. Mem. Nat. Assn. Ind. TV Producers & Distbrs. Assn. (rep. adv. bd.). Avocations: reading, music, gardening. Home: Wayne, NJ. Died Aug. 15, 2007.

BRATZ, ROBERT DAVIS, retired biology educator; b. Sherman, Tex., Dec. 14, 1920; s. Lee Harrison and Gladys Claudius (Lisenby) B.; m. Dorothy Arleen Davis, Sept. 5, 1947; children: Barbara Lee, Cynthia Lin, Kenneth Gordon. BS, Sam Houston State Coll., 1941; postgrad., Manchester Coll., 1943; MS, Oreg. State U., 1950, PhD, 1952. Asst. prof. biology The Coll. Idaho, Caldwell, 1953-58, assoc. prof., 1958-63, prof., 1963-85, emeritus, from 1985. Plant survey of Reynolds Watershed Agrl. Research Service USDA, Boise, Idaho, 1964-74; with expeditions in U.S. and Mex., 1955-80. Fellow AAAS; mem. Idaho Acad. Sci. (life, Nat. Assn. Acad. of Sci. rep. 1970-82), Danforth Assocs. N.W. Inc. (hon.), Danforth Found. (assoc. N.W. region). Home: Caldwell, Idaho. Died Aug. 9, 2007.

BREHM, WARREN GAMALIEL HARDING, protective services official; s. Frank Lawrence and Alma Onedia (Shewbridge) Brehm; m. Dorothy Nettie Hutcheson, Aug. 22, 1947; children: Terry, Donna, Sharon. Cert. law enforcement instr. Md., instr. NRA. Hand trucker Cellanese, Cumberland, Md.; patrolman City Police, Cumberland, Md., 1949—62, sgt., 1962—71, lt., 1971—82. Chief instr. City Police, Cumberland, Md.; v.p. Police and Firemans Welfare Assn., Cumberland, Md. Photographer Cumberland Housing, 1986. Chief instr. Ft. Cumberland Rifle Club, Cumberland, Md., 1964. Served with USN, 1942—46. Recipient Policeman of Yr., Kiwanis Club, 1970. Mem.: 75th Seebee Constrn. Batallion (life), Destroyer Escourt Sailers Assn. (life; commander from 1994), Fraternal Order Police (life), Scottish Rite. Republican. Lutheran. Avocations: photography, bowling, swimming, aerobics, computers. Home: Cumberland, Md. Died Oct. 13, 2007.

BREITROSE, HENRY S., communications educator; b. Bklyn., July 22, 1936; s. Charles and Ruth (Leib) B.; m. Prudence Elaine Martin, Oct. 11, 1968; children: Charles Daniel, Rebecca Marjorie. BS, U. Wis., 1958; MA, Northwestern U., 1959; PhD, Stanford U., 1966. Writer Internat. Film Bur., 1958; mgr. Midwest office Contemporary Films Co., 1959; mem. faculty Stanford (Calif.) U., 1959—65, prof. communication, 1975—2005, chmn. dept. communication, 1976-82, prof. emeritus, 2005—14. Vis. prof. London Sch. Economics, 1976-77; ednl. adv. com. American Film Inst., 1974; v.p. for rsch. & publications Ctr. Internat. des Liasions des Ecoles du Cinema et du TV; Christensen vis. rsch. fellow St. Catherine's Coll., Oxford, 1996. Gen. editor: Cambridge Studies in Film; mem. editorial bd. Calif. Lawyer, 1980-86; author articles, chpts. in books. Bd. dirs. Sta. KQED, San Francisco, 1985-90, vice chmn. 1988; mem. advisory bd. Sta. KCSM. Grantee Rockefeller Found., 1965-66; Lilly Endowment, 1976-77; Stanford U. fellow, 1972-74, Christensen fellow Oxford U., 1996. Mem.: Internat. Assn. Film & Television Schools (v.p. rsch. & publications 1995—2008), Univ. Film Assn. (exec. v.p. 1987—89). Home: Stanford, Calif. Died Oct. 2, 2014.

BRELAND, HUNTER MANSFIELD, psychologist; b. Mobile, Ala., Aug. 11, 1933; s. Robert Milton and Cora (Peirce); m. Nancy Schact, Aug. 17, 1968; children: Alison, Julia. BS, U. Ala., 1955; MS, U. Tex., 1961; PhD, SUNY, Buffalo, 1972. Propulsion engr. Gen. Dynamics, Ft. Worth, 1955-59; astronautics engr. LTV, Inc., Dallas, 1960-61; mgmt. cons. Harbridge House, Inc., Boston, 1967-68; sr. rsch. scientist Ednl. Testing Svc., Princeton, N.J., from 1972. Cons. editor Revista InterAm. de Psicologia, 1983-86. Author: Population Validity, 1979, Assessing Student Characteristics, 1981, Personal Qualities and College Admission, 1982, Assessing Writing Skill, 1987; mem. editl. bd. Written Commn., 1983—. Fellow Am. Psychol. Assn. (chmn. membership com. 1983-85). Home: Pennington, NJ. Died June 6, 2007.

BREMSER, ALBERT HEINRICH, ceramics engineer; b. Sidney, NY, Oct. 29, 1937; s. Albert Theodore and Elly Karola (Karnatz) B.; m. Shirley Mae Weiss, June 23, 1962; children: Albert Weiss, Michael David. BS in Ceramic Engring., Alfred U., 1962; MS in Ceramic Engring., U. Ill., 1964, Phd in Ceramic Engring., 1967. Process planner Bendix Corp., Sidney, 1962-63; prin. engr. Babcock & Wilcox Co., Lynchburg, Va., 1966-71, rsch. specialist, 1971-94, sr. prin. engr., from 1994. Mem. Am. Ceramic Soc., Soc. Mfg. Engrs., Keramos, Sigma Xi. Avocations: gardening, outdoor activities. Home: Lynchburg, Va. Died June 21, 2007.

BRENNER, LAWRENCE, medical librarian, consultant; b. Lynn, Mass., Sept. 19, 1939; m. Ruth Ida Winer. BS in Edn., Northeastern U., 1962; cert. profl. libr., Boston State U./U. Mass., 1965; registered records adminstr., Northeastern U., 1976, MPA, 1981. Registered health info. adminstr. Sr. med. libr. Boston City Hosp., 1962-94; med. record cons. ind. co. Swampscott, Mass., 1994-95; med. record cons., coord. Vencor Corp., Boston, 1995—2004; ret., 2004. Contbr. articles to profl. jours. Recipient Nat. Scholastic Art award, Nat. Scholastic/Boston Globe, 1957. Mem.: ALA, Mass. Health Info. Mgmt. Assn. (contbg. writer Bookshelf and Consultants' Corner columns, Spl. award 1997), Am. Health Info. Mgmt. Assn., Masons (past master 1987, 1999—2000). Avocations: coins, stamps, china, gardening, government. Home: Swampscott, Mass. Died Jan. 27, 2007.

BRENTLINGER, PAUL SMITH, venture capital executive; b. Dayton, Ohio, Apr. 3, 1927; s. Arthur and Welthy Otello (Smith) B.; m. Marilyn E. Hunt, June 23, 1951; children: Paula, David, Sara. BA, U. Mich., 1950, MBA, 1951. With Harris Corp., Melbourne, Fla., 1951-84, v.p. corp. devel., 1969-75, v.p. fin., 1975-82, sr. v.p. fin., 1982-84; ptnr. Morgenthaler Ventures, Cleve., 1984—2013. Former chmn., bd. dirs. Hypres, Inc., Elmsford, NY; former chmn., bd. trustees Cleve. Inst. Art, 1992—98; mem., pres.'s visiting com. Case Western Res. U.; mem., adv. bd. Zell-Lurie Inst. Entrepreneurial Studies, U. Mich. Mem. Union Club, Phi Beta Kappa. Home: Chagrin Falls, Ohio. Died Dec. 22, 2014.

BRETOI, REMUS NICOLAE, aerospace engineer; b. St. Paul, Apr. 9, 1925; s. Nicolae and Elena (Puscas) B.; m. Yvonne Zumbusch, Dec. 28, 1953; children: Christopher Lee, Stephen Nicolae, Kim Ferdinand, Anita Elena. B Aero. Engring., U. Minn., 1945, MS in Aero. Engring., 1946; MBA, Golden Gate U., 1979. Registered profl. engr., Minn., Calif. Rsch. analyst N.Am. Aviation, Inc., El Segundo, Calif., 1946-48; flight control rsch. engr., then supr. Honeywell, Inc., Mpls., 1948-58, mil. products group planning staff, 1958-61; mgr. R & D Honeywell GmbH, Doernigheim, Fed. Republic Germany, 1961-63; sect. head guidance and control Honeywell Inc., Mpls., 1963-67; chief spl. projects office, control lab. NASA Elec. Rsch. Ctr., Cambridge, Mass., 1967-70; chief STOL experiments office, chief avionics rsch. br., staff asst. programs, rsch. engr./scientist NASA-Ames Rsch. Ctr., Moffett Field, Calif., from 1970, now, asst. chief extravehicular systems br., from 1990. Patentee aircraft control devices. Bd. dirs. Internat. Inst. Minn., St. Paul, 1959-67; pres. Casa Romana & Capela, Oakland, 1989-91; pres. parish coun. Holy Resurrection Romanian Orthodox parish, Oakland, 1984-88. Named Boss of Yr., Peninsula chpt. Am. Bus. Women's Assn., Palo Alto, Calif., 1972; named to Otto Bremer South St. Paul (Minn.) Hall of Excellence, 1987. Mem. AIAA, NSPE, Theta Tau, Sigma Gamma Tau. Avocations: photography, reading, hiking. Home: Palo Alto, Calif. Died Dec. 28, 2006.

BREWER, JAMES ROBERT, plant engineer, designer; b. Jefferson City, Tenn., Nov. 7, 1948; s. Robert Lee and Ruth Margaret (Eller) B.; m. Juanita Price, Jan 12, 1969; children: Tiffany Renee, Philip Craig. Cert. in mech. design, State Area Vocat. Tech., 1972; AS in Mfg. Tech., Walter State Community Coll., Morristown, Tenn., 1977. Machine operator Berkline Corp., Morristown, 1965-71; tool engr. Jeffrey Mfg., Morristown, 1972-77; indsl. technician Jeffrey Chain div. Dresser Industries, Morristown, 1977-78, sr. indsl. engr., 1978-80, supr. indsl. engr., 1980-84; plant engr. Jeffrey Chain Corp., Morristown, from 1984. Served with U.S. Army, 1969-71, Vietnam. Mem. Nat. Street Rod Assn. Repubican. Baptist. Lodge: Masons. Home: Russellville, Tenn. Died Feb. 11, 2007.

BRICK, MICHAEL (CHRISTOPHER MICHAEL BRICK), journalist; b. Cheverly, Md., June 21, 1974; m. Stacy Brick; children: John-Henry, Celia; 1 child from previous marriage, Sadie Aasletten. Attended, U. Tex., Austin. With The Corpus Christi Caller-Times; with thestreet.com; speechwriter for a Tex. Representative; researcher on the 2001 book The Informant; bus. desk reporter New York Times, 2001—05, Bklyn. Bur. reporter, 2005—08, columnist, Pushing the Limit, 2008—09; sr. writer The Houston Chronicle, 2014—16. Author: (articles) Permit Denial for Central Park Adds to Push for Protests There, 2004, Returning to Neighborhoods that are no Longer Homes, 2005, Saving the School: The True Story of a Principal, a Teacher, a Coach, a Bunch of Kids, and a Year in the Crosshairs of Education Reform, 2012, (Kindle Single e-book) The Big Race, 2013. Died Feb. 8, 2016.

BRIDGERS, JOHN DAVID, retired pediatrician; b. Greenville, NC, July 4, 1920; s. Samuel Leon and Essie Sutton (Whichard) B.; m. Edith Holland Hamrick, Aug. 29,

1945 (dec. Aug. 2000); children: John D. Jr., Sam L. II, Carl H., Raymond S., Barbara Jean, Ellen Holland. AB, E. Carolina U., 1940; MD, Duke U., 1950. Diplomate Am. Bd. Pediatrics. Intern USN Hosp., Chelsea, 1950; flight surgeon, aviator U.S. NAS, Atlantic City, N.J., 1952-54; resident pediatrician Children's Hosp. Phila., 1954-56, dir. Out Patient Dept., 1956-62; pvt. practice High Point, N.C., 1962-85; physician field rep. Joint Commn. for Accreditation of Healthcare Orgns., Chgo., 1985-88; med. dir. Burnette Tomlin Meml. Hosp., Cape May Court House, N.J., 1988-93; ret., 1994. Asst. prof. U. Pa., Phila., 1956-62. Comdr. USNR, 1941-60. Fellow Am. Acad. Pediatrics; mem. AMA, Am. Acad. Med. Execs. Democrat. Avocations: investments, writing, reading. Home: Alpharetta, Ga. Died May 12, 2007.

BRIDGMAN, LUTHER HARRY, insurance company executive; b. Ann Arbor, Mich., Apr. 4, 1919; s. Lewis Henry and Annie (Wright) B.; m. Elizabeth Pierce, Mar. 14, 1945; children: Charles Torrey, Sara M., Banjamin P. BA, Princeton U., 1941. CLU. Sports editor Paramount Newsreel, NYC, 1946-48; TV producer Kudner Advt. Agy., NYC, 1948-49, William Esty Advt. Agy., NYC, 1950-51; chmn. Brown Bridgman & Co. Inc., Burlington, Vt., from 1955. Lt. USNR, 1942-46. Mem. Million Dollar Round Table (life), Princeton Club (N.Y.C.). Democrat. Avocations: skiing, sailing. Home: Charlotte, Vt. Died Nov. 8, 2006.

BRIDWELL, NORMAN RAY, author, artist; b. Kokomo, Ind., Feb. 15, 1928; s. Vern Ray and Mary Leona (Koontz) Bridwell; m. Norma Ellen Howard, June 13, 1958; children: Emily Elizabeth, Timothy Howard. Student, John Herron Art Inst., 1945—49. Artist Flexo-Lettering, NYC, 1949—50, Raxon Fabrics, NYC, 1950—53, hd Rose Co., 1953—55. Author (illustrator): Clifford, the Big Red Dog, 1963, Zany Zoo, 1963, Bird in the Hat, 1964, Clifford Gets a Job, 1965, The Witch Next Door, 1965, Clifford Takes a Trip, 1966, Clifford's Halloween, 1966, 1968, The Country Cat, 1969, What Do They Do When It Rains?, 1969, Clifford's Tricks, 1969, How to Care for Your Monster, 1970, The Witch's Christmas, 1970, Merton the Monkey Mouse, 1973, The Dog Frog Book, 1973, Clifford's Riddles, 1974, Monster Holidays, 1974, Clifford's Good Deeds, 1975, My Pet the Rock, 1975, Boy on the Ceiling, 1976, The Big Water Fight, 1977, Clifford at the Circus, 1977, Kangaroo Stew, 1978, The Witch Grows Up, 1979, Clifford Goes to Hollywood, 1980, Clifford's ABC Book, 1983, Clifford's Story Hour, 1983, Clifford's Family, 1984, Clifford's Grouchy Neighbors, 1985, Clifford's Pals, 1985, Clifford's Manners, 1987, Clifford's Birthday Party, 1988, Clifford's Puppy Days, 1989, Where is Clifford?, 1989. Mem.: Vineyard Resident Writers Group, Authors Guild. Unitarian Universalist. Died Dec. 12, 2014.

BRIERLEY, RICHARD GREER, business consultant; b. Kearney, NJ, July 1, 1915; s. Josiah Richards and Castella Sophia (Parker) B.; m. Margaret Jean LaLone, Aug. 24, 1940; children: Linda, Sandra, Martha, Ann. AB, Dartmouth Coll., 1936; MBA, Tuck Sch., 1937; AMP, Harvard U., 1952. Salesman Armstrong Cork Co., Lancaster, Pa., 1937-40; with Archer-Daniels-Midland Co., Mpls., 1940-64; exec. v.p. Arcaer-Daniels-Midland Co., Mpls., 1979-61, Drackett Co., Cin., 1961-66; pres., chief exec. officer Bristol Myers Can., Toronto, Ont., 1966-68; v.p. corp. planning Bristol Myers Co., NYC, 1968-70; pres., chief exec. officer Stearns & Foster, Cin., 1970-75, chmn. bd. dirs., 1975-76; pres., chmn. bd. dirs. Brierley Assocs., Carefree, Ariz., from 1976. Bd. dirs. Transcapital Fin. Corp., Cleve., Galleon Beach Club, Antiqua, W.I. Avocations: tennis, golf, travel. Home: Carefree, Ariz. Died May 6, 2007.

BRIGGS, WILLIAM BENAJAH, retired aerospace engineer; b. Okmulgee, Okla., Dec. 13, 1922; s. Eugene Stephen and Mary Betty (Gentry) B.; m. Lorraine Hood, June 6, 1944; children— Eugene Stephen II, Cynthia Anne, Julia Louise, Spencer Gentry. BA in Physics, Phillips U., 1943, DSc (hon.), 1977; MSME, Ga. Inst. Tech., 1947. Aero. scientist NACA, Cleve., 1948-52; propulsion engr. Regulus II, Scout l.v., Dynasoar, Washington rep. Chance Vought Aircraft/LTV, Dallas, 1952-64; mgr. advanced planning Marsviking, Jupiter probe McDonnell Douglas Co., St. Louis, 1964-80, dir. program devel. fusion energy, 1980-87. Planetary quarantine adv. panel NASA. Contbr. articles on aero. engring. and energy to profl. jours.; patentee in field Chmn. Disciples Coun. Greater St. Louis, 1969-73; chmn. bd. Christian Bd. Publs., St. Louis, 1974-91; bd. dirs. Joint Cmty. Ministries, 1987-92, Emergency Childrens Home, 1994-2000; chmn. arrangements gen. assembly/synod Disciples of Christ/United Ch. of Christ, 1993; trustee Phillips U., Enid, Okla., 1996— . With USNR, 1943-46, Atlantic and West Pacific. Recipient Svc. award, Emergency Childrens Home, 2003. Assoc. fellow AIAA (dir. region 5 1974-77, v.p. mem. svcs. 1978-79); mem. VFW, Am. Nuclear Soc., Navy League. Mem. Disciples of Christ Ch. Home: Ballwin, Mo. *Facing a problem, size up the situation, determine what needs to be done, then take action. Steadfastly working your plan does produce results; just give serendipity a chance to happen.* Died Oct. 14, 2014.

BRILLHART, JAMES RICHARD, gynecological surgeon; b. Indpls., Mar. 28, 1929; s. Claud Ischmael and Velma Lorraine (Roberts) B.; m. Jean Iris Sawyer, June 3, 1948 (div. Mar. 1969); children: J.H., Richard Mark, David Michael, Susan Kay; m. Kathryn Norann Dowden, Mar. 8, 1980. BS, Butler U., 1949; MD, Loma Linda U., 1955. Diplomate Am. Bd. Ob-Gyn. Resident Ind. U. Med. Ctr., Indpls., 1956-60; practice medicine specializing in gynecol. surgery Indpls., from 1960. Asst. clin. prof. dept. family practice Ind. U. Sch. Medicine, Indpls., 1975-84, asst. clin. prof. dept. ob-gyn, 1985—; bd. dirs. Ind. Asphalt Paving Co., Indpls., Med. Scis., Indpls.; dir. ob-gyn tng. Community Hosp., Indpls., 1975-84; med. advisor Planned Parenthood, Indpls., 1986—. Judge Am. Kennel Club, N.Y.C., 1968—; sec.-treas. Indpls. Womens Ctr., 1975-86. Fellow Am. Coll. Ob-Gyn; mem. AMA, Ind. State Med. Assn., Marion County Med. Soc., Am. Fertility Soc., Brit. Royal Soc. Medicine, Am. Inst. Ultrasound in Medicine, Siberian Husky Club Am. Clubs: Pointe Country. Democrat. Adventist. Avocations: sports cars, dogs, diving. Home: Indianapolis, Ind. Died Nov. 23, 2006.

BRIMMER, CLARENCE ADDISON, retired federal judge; b. Rawlins, Wyo., July 11, 1922; s. Clarence Addison and Geraldine (Zingsheim) B.; m. Emily O. Docken, Aug. 2, 1953; children: Geraldine Ann, Philip Andrew, Andrew Howard, Elizabeth Ann. BA, U. Mich., 1944, JD, 1947. Bar: Wyo. 1948. Pvt. practice law, Rawlins, 1948-71; mcpl. judge, 1948-54; U.S. commr., magistrate, 1963-71; atty. gen. State of Wyo., Cheyenne, 1971-74; US atty. Dist. Wyo. US Dept. Justice, 1975; judge US Dist. Ct. Wyo., Cheyenne, 1975—2006, chief judge, 1986—92, sr. judge, 2006—13. Mem. panel multi-dist. litigation, 1992-2000; mem. Jud. Conf. U.S., 1994-97, exec., 1995-97. Sec. Rawlins Bd. Pub. Utilities, 1954-66; Republican gubernatorial candidate, 1974; trustee Rocky Mountain Mineral Law Found., 1963-75; served in USAAF, 1945-46. Mem. ABA, Wyo. Bar Assn., Laramie County Bar Assn., Carbon County Bar Assn., American Judicature Soc., Masons, Shriners, Rotary. Episcopalian. Home: Cheyenne, Wyo. Died Oct. 24, 2014.

BRIND, BRYONY, ballerina; b. Plymouth, Devon, Eng., May 27, 1960; d. Roger Michael Atchley and Jenifer Mary St. John (Grey) Brind; m. Ian McCorquodale. Student, Royal Ballet Sch., 1976—78. Mem. corps de ballet Royal Ballet Co., London, 1978, soloist, 1981—84, prin. ballerina, 1984—2015. Recipient Prix de Lausanne award, 1977, Benson & Hedges award, 1981. Avocations: music, art. Home: London, England. Died Dec. 2, 2015.

BRINK, ANDRÉ PHILIPPUS, author, educator; b. Vrede, South Africa, May 29, 1935; s. Daniel and Aletta (Wolmarans) B.; m. Estelle Naude, Oct. 3, 1959 (div.); 1 child, Anton; m. Salomi Louw, Nov. 28, 1965 (div.); 1 child, Gustav; m. Sophia Albertina Miller, July 17, 1970 (div.); children: Danie, Sonja; m. Marèsa de Beer, Nov. 16, 1990 (div.). BA, Potchefstroom U., 1955, MA, 1958, MA, 1959; DLitt, Rhodes U., 1975, Witwatersrand U., 1985; DLitt (hon.), Orange Free State U., 1997; PhD (hon.), Univ. Montpellier; DLitt (hon.), Rhodes U., 2001; DLitt (hon.), U. Pretoria, 2003. Lectr. Rhodes U., Grahamstown, 1961-73, sr. lectr., 1973-75, asst. prof., 1976-79, prof., 1980-90, U. Cape Town, from 1991. Author: Brandy in South Africa, 1973, Dessert Wine in South Africa, 1974, Die wyn van bowe, 1974, Die klap van die meul, 1974, Die fees van dies malles: 'n keur uit die humor, 1981, Mapmakers: Writing in a State of Siege, 1983, oom Kootjie Emmer en die nuwe bedeling, 1983, The Essence of the Grape, 1993; (fiction) Eindelose Weë, 1960, Lobola vir die lewe, 1962, Die Ambassadeur (File on a Diplomat), 1963, Orgie, 1965, Miskien nooit, 1967, A Portrait of Woman as a Young Girl, 1973, Kennis van die aand (Looking on Darkness), 1973, Die Geskiedenis van oom Kootjie Emmer van Witgatworteldraai, 1973, 'n Oomblik in die wind (An Instant in the Wind), 1975, Gerugte van Reën (Rumours of Rain), 1978, (Central News Agy. awrd for English Lit., 1978), 'n Droë wit seisoen (A Dry White Season), 1979 (Martin Luther King Meml. prize 1980, Prix Médicis étranger 1980), Houd-den-bek (A Chain of Voices, Ctrl. News Agy. award for English Lit.), 1982; (essays) Die Muur van die pes (The Wall of the Plague), 1984, Loopdoppies: Nog dopstories, 1984, States of Emergency, 1988, An Act of Terror, 1991, Cape of Storms, 1993, On the Contrary, 1993, Imaginings of Sand, 1996 (Premio Mondello 1997), Reinventing a Continent, 1996, Destabilising Shakespeare, 1996, Devil's Valley, 1998, The Rights of Desire, 2000 (Hertzog Prize 2001), The Other Side of Silence, 2002 (Commonwealth prize Africa, 2002, Sunday Times Fiction award 2002), (plays) Caesar, 1961, Bagasie: Triptiek vir die toneel, 1964, Elders mooiweer en warm, 1965, Die Rebelle: Betoogstuk in nege episodes, 1970, Die Verhoor: Verhoogstuk in drie bedrywe, 1970, Kinkels innie kabel: 'n verhoogstuk in elf episodes, 1971, Afrikaners is plesierig, 1973, Pavane, 1974, Die hamer die hekse, 1976, Die jogger, 1997 (Hertzog prize 2000); (criticism) Orde en chaos: 'n studie oor Germanicus ed die tragedies van Shakespeare, 1962, Aspekte van die nuwe prosa, 1967, Die Poësie van Breyten Breytenbach, 1971, Aspekte van die nuwe drama, 1974, Voorlopige rapport: Beskouings oor die Afrikaanse literatuur van Sewentig, 1976, Tweede voorlopige rapport: Nog beskouings oor die Afrikaanse literatuur van sewentig, 1980, Waarom literatuur?, 1985, Literatuur in die strydperk, 1985, Vertelkunde: 'n inleiding tot die lees van verhalende tekste, 1987, The Novel: Language and Narrative from Cervantes to Calvino, 1998; (travelogues) Pot-pourri: Sketse uit Parys, 1962, Sempre diritto: Italiaanse reisjoernaal, 1963, Olé: Reisboek oor Spanje, 1965 (Central News Agency award for Afrikaans literature 1965), Midi: Op reis deur Suid-Frankryk, 1969, Fado: 'n reis deur Noord-Portugal, 1970, Latynse Reise, 1991; translator: Lewis Carroll's Alice Through the Looking Glass (So. African Acad. Prose Translation prize 1970), others. Decorated Chevalier de Legion d'honneur, France, Commandeur de L'Ordre des arts et des lettres (France); recipient Reina Geerligs prize, 1964. Home: Cape Town, South Africa. Died Feb. 6, 2015.

BRINKMAN, CARL ALEXANDER, retired neurosurgeon; b. Resht, Iran, June 17, 1932; (parents Am. citizens); s. Harry and Adrianna (Van Lopik) B.;m. Diane Butler Sharon Valerie, June 1951(dec. July 1993); m. Jacqueline Carlisle, Sept. 30, 1995; children: Sharon, Valerie. AB cum laude, Bowdoin Coll., 1953; MD, Yale U., 1957. Intern U. Mich., Ann Arbor, 1957-58, resident, 1958-63; former dir. dept. neurosurgery Maine Med. Ctr., Portland; now ret. Mem. ACS, AMA, Frederick A. Coller Surg. Soc., New Eng. Neurosurg. Soc., Maine Neurosurg. Soc., So. Maine Neurosurg. Assn. (founder), Portland/Bermuda Golf (pres.). Republican. Congregationalist. Home: Okatie, SC. Died July 26, 2014.

BRINKWORTH, JEAN, mental health nurse; b. Columbus, Ohio, May 25, 1929; d. John and Christine (Brunton) Brinkworth; children: Patrice, Tim, Ellen, Peter, John. BSN, Coll. of Mt. St. Vincent, Riverdale, NY, 1950; MS, Columbia U., 1977, MEd, 1980. In-svc. dir. St. Vincent Hosp., Harrison, N.Y.; supr. New Rochelle Guidence Ctr., N.Y.; asst. prof. New Rochelle Sch. Nursing; asst. prof. nursing Coll. of Mt. St. Vincent, NYC. Mem. AAUP, Network of Psychiatric Clin. Specialists of N.Y., Am. Nurses Assn. Died Jan. 7, 2007.

BRINSMADE, AKBAR FAIRCHILD, chemical engineering consultant; b. Puebla, Mex., May 31, 1917; s. Robert Bruce and Helen Steenbock Brinsmade; m. Juanita Phillips, June 16, 1944; children: Anne Hudson Brinsmade, Robert Bruce P., Charlotte Lynn Brinsmade. BS in Chemistry, U. Wis., Madison, 1939; MSChemE, MIT, Cambridge, 1942; postgrad., Poly. Inst. Bklyn., 1945—46, NYU, 1947—49, Tulane U., New Orleans, 1967—73. Registered profl. engr., N.C., La. Gen. mgr. Cia. Minera SnFrancisco y Anex., San Luis Potosi, Mexico, 1939—40; sr. rsch. engr. Shell Oil Co. Inc., Houston and NYC, 1942—48; project mgr. Internat. Indsl. Cons., NYC and Caracas, 1949—50; mng. dir. Promotora Nacional de Indsl., Caracas, 1952—57; R&D engr. Hercules Powder Co., Rocket Center, W.Va., 1959—64; rsch. engring. specialist Chrysler Space Divsn., New Orleans, 1966—69; chem. engring. cons. to maj. U.S. and fgn. corps., from 1969. Author: Travel to the Stars, 1996, The Expanding of the Universe Revisited, 2000, The Origin of and a Cure for Cancer a Theory, 2009, The Center of Intelligent Life in the Universe and an Early Warning about Humanity's Extinction, 2013; contbr. chapters to books. Chmn. Citizens for Goldwater, Allegany County, Md., 1964. Fellow Am. Inst. Chemists; mem. NSPE, AIChE, Am. Chem. Soc., La. Engring. Soc. (profl. engr.), Phi Eta Sigma, Phi Lambda Upsilon, Sigma Alpha Epsilon. Republican. Lutheran. Achievements include patents for Gravity Module. Avocations: history, travel, tennis, reading, languages. Home: Biloxi, Miss. Died Dec. 28, 2014; Biloxi, Miss..

BRISCOE, JACK CLAYTON, lawyer; b. July 23, 1920; s. Park Harry and Elsie Gertrude (Woodward) B.; m. Dorothy Lillian Shaw, Sept. 3, 1949; children: Jacqueline Kamp, Jeffrey S., Ryd Joan. BS in Econs., U. Pa., 1943; LLB, Harvard U., 1948. Bar: Pa. 1950. Assoc. Robert C. Duffy, Phila., 1966—85; ptnr. Briscoe, Haggerty & Howard, Phila., 1966—85, Briscoe & Howard, Phila., 1986—90, Jack C. Briscoe & Assocs., Phila., from 1990. Instr. U. Pa., 1950—56; bd. dirs. Prime Inc.; chmn. bd. dirs. Master's Plan Fin. Svcs., Inc., Zoe Consulting Inc., Cmty. Capital Adivsors Inc.; chmn. Elder United Presbyn. Ch. Manoa; active Fellowship Christian Athletes; mem. Rep. Presdl. Task Force; dir., pres. emeritus Pa. Bible Soc.; mem. bd. dirs., chmn. bd. Faith Theol. Sem.; mem., bd. dirs., sec. People for People, Inc.; bd. dirs. Prime, Inc., Urban Youth Racing Sch., Inc. With USAF, 1943—46. Recipient Branch Ricky Assocs. award, Cert. Achievement award, Compulsory Arbitration Divsn. Phila. County Ct., John Burns award, Pa. Bible Soc. Fellow: Harry S. Truman Libr. Inst.; mem.: ABA, Chapel of Four Chaplains (legion hon. mem.), World Affairs Coun., Gideons Internat., Friendly Sons of St. Patrick, Pa. Soc. Harvard Law Sch. Assn., Phila. Bar Assn., Pa. Bar Assn., Emeritus Club Harvard Law Sch., Union League Club, Lawyers Club, Harvard Club. Home: Drexel Hill, Pa. Died Dec. 1, 2014.

BROADBENT, ROBERT RAYMOND, retail company executive; b. Lisbon, Ohio, May 25, 1921; s. Raymond and Ruth Edna (Schoonover) B.; m. Mary; 1 son, William Stuart. BBA, U. Akron, Ohio, 1946. Personal asst. to Cyrus S. Eaton, Cleve., 1946-49; various positions in retailing, 1949-58; exec. v.p., dir. Higbee Co., Cleve., 1958-73, pres., vice chmn. bd., 1979-84, chmn. bd., 1984-89; also dir.; chmn. bd., chief exec. officer Gimbel's, NYC, 1973-76; pres., chief exec. officer Liberty House-Mainland, San Francisco, 1976-79. Dir. Huntington Bank N.E. Ohio, D.H. Homes Co. Ltd., New Orleans, LISC, N.Y.C. Bd. dirs., exec. com. Greater Cleve. Growth Assn.; bd. dirs. Kent State Found., Cleve. Tomorrow, Cleve. 500 Found.; trustee Kent State U. Served with USAAF, 1943-45, ETO. Decorated D.F.C., Air medal with 4 oak leaf clusters. Mem. Am. Retail Fedn. (bd. dirs.). Clubs: Cleve. Racquet (Cleve.), Cleve. Country (Cleve.), Union (Cleve.); Union League (N.Y.C.). Achievements include being instrumental in the construction of Rock and Roll Hall of Fame in Cleveland; also help create Kent State University's Fashion School and Museum. Died July 13, 2015.

BRONK, J(OHN) RAMSEY, biochemistry educator; b. Phila., Dec. 20, 1929; s. Detlev Wulf and Helen (Ramsey) B.; m. Sylvia Smith, June 6, 1955; children: Richard Anthony Charles, Christopher Ramsey. AB, Princeton U., 1952; DPhil, Oxford U., 1955. Scientist USPHS, Bethesda, Md., 1956-58; asst. prof. zoology Columbia U., NYC, 1958-60, assoc. prof., 1960-65, prof., 1965-66; prof. biochemistry U. York (Eng.), 1966-97, emeritus prof., from 1997. Author: Chemical Biology, 1973, Membrane Adenosine Triphosphatases and Transport Processes, 1974, Human Metabolism, 1999; chmn. European editorial com. Physiol. Revs., 1980-85; editor Clin. Sci., 1987-91; contbr. numerous articles to profl. jours. Rhodes scholar, 1952-55; Guggenheim fellow, 1964-65. Fellow AAAS; mem. Biochem. Soc. (com. mem. 1977-81), Am. Soc. for Biochemistry and Molecular Biology, Physiol. Soc. (editor 1971-78). Avocation: sailing. Home: York, England. Died Dec. 31, 2007.

BRONSTEIN, ALVIN J., lawyer; b. Bklyn., June 8, 1928; s. Louis and Lillian (Spielman) Bronstein; m. Jan Elvin; children: Lisa Snitzer, Susie Renner, Laura Zatta, Sarah, Benjamin. LLD, NY Law Sch., 1951, LLD (hon.), 1990. Bar: NY 1952, Miss. 1967, La. 1971, US Ct. Appeals (DC, 1st, 2d, 3d, 4th, 5th, 9th, 10th and 11th cirs.), US Supreme Ct. 1961. Ptnr. Bronstein & Bronstein, Bklyn., 1952-63; pvt. practice Elizabethtown, NY, 1963-64; chief staff counsel Lawyers Constl. Def. Com., Jackson, Miss., 1964-68; fellow Inst. Politics, Kennedy Sch. Govt. Harvard U., Cambridge, Mass., 1968-69, assoc. dir. Inst. Politics, Kennedy Sch. Govt., 1969-71; ptnr. Elie, Bronstein, Strickler & Dennis, New Orleans, 1971-72; exec. dir. Nat. Prison Project, Nat. Prison Project ACLU Found., Washington, 1972-96, cons. nat. legal dept., 1996—2015. Cons., trial counsel CORE, NAACP, NAACP Legal Def. Fund, SCLC, SNCC, Miss. Freedom Dem. Party, Black Panther Party, Nat. Inst. for Edn. in Law and Poverty, and others; guest lectr. various law schs., 1964-2015; cons. various state corrections depts., 1972-2015; adj. prof. Am. U. Law Sch., 1973; expert witness in various prison litigs., 1978-2015; apptd. mem. Fed. Jud. Ctr. Adv. Com. on Experimentation in the Law, 1978-81. Contbg. author: The Evolution of Criminal Justice, 1978, Prisoners' Rights Sourcebook, Vol. II, 1980, Confinement in Maximum Custody, 1980, Sage Criminal Justice Annual, Vol. 14, 1980, Readings in the Justice Model, 1980, Our Endangered Rights, 1984, Prisoners and the Courts: The American Experience, 1985; author: (with Rudovsky and Koren) The Rights of Prisoners, 1988; author, editor: Representing Prisoners, 1981; editor: Prisoners' Self-Help Litigation Manual, 1977; contbr. articles to profl. jours. MacArthur Found. fellow, 1989; named one of the 100 Most Influential Lawyers in America, Nat. Law Jour., 1985, 88, 91, 94; recipient Roscoe Pound award Nat. Coun. on Crime and Delinquency, 1981, Karl Menninger award Fortune Soc., 1982, Pa. Prison Soc. award, 1991. Home: Chestertown, Md. Died Oct. 24, 2015.

BROOK, ROBERT HERBERT, electrical engineer consultant; b. NY, Apr. 16, 1929; s. Leo and Evelyn (Abrams) B.; m. Barbara Sheffer, Sept. 14, 1952; children: Eric, Carolyn, Elinor. BSEE, U. Conn., 1951. Engr. Sylvania Elec., Emporium, Pa., 1951-53; project engr. Filtron Co., Flushing, N.Y., 1953-59; specialist engr. Republic Aviation, Farmingdale, N.Y., 1959-66; sect. head EMC Eaton Corp. AIL, Deerpark, N.Y., 1986-93; pres. Brook Electro Magnetics Inc., Plainview, N.Y., from 1993. Contbr. article to profl. jours. Recipient Cert. Appreciation IEEE EMC/S, Washington, 1983, Appreciation award SUNY Maritime Acad., 1985. Mem. IEEE (Founder's award 1983), Elect. Engr. Soc.(vice chair, sec/treas. 1968—), EMC Soc., Soc. Social Implication of Tech., EMC Electromagnetic Compatibility Soc. (v.p., sec.). Avocations: boating, photography, music, bridge. Home: Plainview, NY. Died Jan. 16, 2007.

BROOKE, EDWARD WILLIAM, III, lawyer, former United States Senator from Massachusetts; b. Washington, Oct. 26, 1919; s. Edward William and Helen (Seldon) Brooke; m. Remigia Ferrari-Scacco, 1947 (div. 1978); children: Remy Cynthia, Edwina Helene; m. Anne Fleming, 1979; 1 child, Eric. BS, Howard U., 1940; LLB, Boston U., 1948, LLM, 1949; LLD, Howard U., 1967, George Wash. U., 1967; DSc, Lowell Tech. Inst., 1967; LLD, Boston U., 1968, Skidmore Coll., 1969, U. Mass., 1971, Amherst Coll., 1972. Bar: Mass. 1948, DC Ct. Appeals 1979, DC Dist. Ct. 1982, US Supreme Ct. 1962. Chmn. Boston Fin. Com., 1961-62; atty. gen. State of Mass., Boston, 1963-66; US Senator from Mass., 1967-79; chmn. Nat. Low-Income Housing Coalition; ptnr. O'Connor & Hannan, Washington; of counsel Csaplar & Bok, Boston, 1979—90. Author: The Challenge of Change: Crisis in Our Two-Party System, 1966, Bridging the Divide: My Life, 2007. Chmn. Boston Opera Co.; former commr. Pres.'s Commns. on Housing and of Wartime Relocation and Internment of Civilians; bd. dirs. Washington Performing Arts Soc. Served as capt. inf. AUS, World War II, ETO, 1941-46 Decorated Combat Infantryman's Badge, Bronze star; recipient Disting. Svc. award Amvets, 1952, Charles Evans Hughes award NCCJ, 1967, Springarn medal, NAACP, 1967, Presdl. Medal of Freedom, The White House, 2004, Congressoinal Gold medal, US Congress, 2009 Fellow ABA, American Acad. Arts & Sciences Republican. Achievements include being the first African American elected to the US Senate by popular vote, 1966. Home: Coral Gables, Fla. Died Jan. 3, 2015.

BROOKS, ANDREW PATTRICK, fluvial geomorphologist, researcher; b. Sydney, Mar. 6, 1964; s. George Peter Brooks and Mary Louise Abrahams; life ptnr. Petria Anne Wallace, Aug. 28, 1985; children: Thomas Peter Brooks-Wallace, Rose Jean Brooks-Wallace. BSc with honors, Macquarie U., 1994, PhD, 1999. Rsch. fellow Macquarie U., Sydney, 1999—2002; sr. rsch. fellow Ctr. for Riverine Landscapes, Griffith U., Nathan, Australia, from 2002. Mem. exec. com. Upper Hunter River Rehab. Initiative, Australia, 2002—05. Grantee Gen. Call Grant, Land & Water Australia, 2000—03, ARC Linkage Grant on Complex adaptive systems in rivers, Australian Rsch. Coun.; fellow Smart State Fellowship (1 of 4 in state), Dept State Devel., from 2004. Mem.: Australian & NZ Geomorphology Group, Am. Geophys. Union, Am. Fisheries Soc. (hon.). Achievements include reevaluating the extent of human impacts on Australian Rivers; development of a novel approach to restoring rivers based on emulating natural river processes. Avocations: swimming, cycling. Home: Alderley, Brisbane, Australia. Died Oct. 14, 2007.

BROOKS, JEFFERSON DAVIS, III, small business owner; b. Washington, Aug. 28, 1926; s. Jefferson Davis and Civella (Adams) B.; m. Inez Predia Stutts, Sept. 20, 1952; 1 child, Sharon Elizabeth. Student, George Washington U.; B equivalent, N.C. State U., 1966; student, U. Ala., Huntsville. Engr., asst. treas. Geodesics Inc., Raleigh, N.C., 1954-60; instr. tech. drafting Wake Tech. C.C., Raleigh, 1966-89; owner Geo-Matrixes Unltd., Raleigh, from 1989. Cons. radio engr. A.D. Ring and Assoc., Washington. Contbr. articles to profl. jours. Dir. cmty. planning Oxford/Granville County. Mem. Wake Tech. Retirees Assn. (pres.), EAA 506 Exptl. Aircraft Assn., Sons of Confed. Vets. Republican. Achievements include patent on arctic shelter-raft; discovery of Xindaheddron (geometric construction); theoretical electron paths; discovery of new graphic perspecive technique for 3-D construction. Home: Raleigh, NC. Died Feb. 12, 2007.

BROUMAS, JOHN GEORGE, retired banker, retired theatre owner; b. Youngstown, Ohio, Oct. 12, 1917; s. George Elias Broumas and Evelyn Vaveris; m. Ruth Darr, Sept. 16, 1944; children: Carole Ann, Sue Ann. Chem. warfare officer, Officer Candidate Sch., Edgewood Arsenal, Md., 1944; mem. class 1954 (hon.), West Point (N.Y.) Mil. Acad., 1975. Gen. mgr. Roth Theatres, Washington, 1946-54; chmn., pres. Broumas Showcase Theatres, Washington, 1954-83; dir. McLean and Madison Bank Va., 1975-91, chmn. of bd., 1983-91; chmn. of bd., pres. Madison Nat. Bank Va., 1986-91; actor, model motion pictures, commercials, from 1992. Dir. asst. to pres. Theatre Owners of Am., 1958-68; dir. v.p. Nat. Assn. of Theatre Owners, 1968-82; chmn., pres., dir. Md. Theatre Owners Assn.; v.p., dir. Va. Theatre Owners Assn.; dir. Washington D.C. Theatre Owners Assn., 1966-80, Ohio Theatre Owners Assn., 1966-80; chmn. bd. dirs. Grey Eagle, Ltd., 1992—; chmn. Caledonia Assocs.; lectr. motion pictures and film making Georgetown U., 1972-78; chmn. exec. com Madison Nat. Bank Va., 1987-91; dir. James Madison Ltd., Washington, 1987-90; dir. Potomac Fin. Group, 1991—; chmn. Hellenic studies Md. U., 1989-90. Appeared in films: Karate Kid IV, Dave, In the Line of Fire, Guarding Tess, The Firm, The Pelican Brief, True Lies, Major League II, Op Center, Clear and Present Danger, Korea Gate, Snow, G.I. Jane, Mars Attacks, Deep Impact. Trustee Leukemia Soc. Am., 1988, Edn. and Tng. Found. Ptnrs. Am. Vocat. Edn., 1991—; dir. USO, 1956-80, Found. Religious Action, 1965-76, Washington chpt. Coll. Football Hall of Fame, 1989 (appreciation award 1989); adv. coun., chmn. D.C. area Will Rogers Hosp., 1968-78; exec. com. East Coast div. Child Help U.S.A., 1989; vol. Am. Cancer Soc., Kidney Found., United Way, Salvation Army, Boy Scouts Am., others. Maj. U.S. Army, 1941-46. Recipient Presdl. Disting. Svc. medal Cath. U., 1989, Ahepa Achievement of Excellence award, 1981, Gold Reel award 50 Yrs. Motion Picture Industry, 1978, Outstanding Svc. award, 1978, Gold medal, 1978, Fairfax County, Va. Sch. Patrol Appreciation award, 1977, Good Guy award Motion Picture Industry, 1974, Humanitarian award Local Area Motion Picture Industry, 1972, Muscular Dystrophy Appreciation award Jerry Lewis Telethon, 1972, and others; named to Order of St. Andrew, Greek Orthodox Ch., 1987. Mem. SAG, Res. Officers Assn. (life), Fightin Frogs (hon. mem. 4th regiment 1992), Variety Club Internat. (Variety medal 1985, Life Liner award 1985, Humanitarian award 1965-66, 78-79), The Motion Picture Pioneers (dir. 1953-86), Touchdown Club, Georgetown Club, West Point Soc. D.C. (mem. leadership coun. 1994), West Point Alumni Assn. Republican. Avocations: sports, writing, travel, charity work, movies. Home: Washington, DC. Died July 21, 2007.

BROWER, WILLIAM B., JR., retired aeronautical and mechanical engineer; b. Jersey City, Oct. 29, 1922; s. William Bartley and Maude M. (Van Saun) B.; m. Yolanda E. Ebel, July 13, 1925; children: Patricia E., William B. III, Leslie A. B Aero. Engring., Rensselaer Polytech. Inst., Troy, NY, 1950, M Aero. Engring., 1951, PhD, 1961. Registered profl. engr., N.Y. Rsch. engr. N.Am. Aviation, Inc., Downey, Calif., 1951-52, Rensselaer Polytech. Inst., 1952-57, asst. prof., 1957-61, assoc. prof., 1961-89. Author 2 books in field. Lt. j.g. USN, 1943-47, PTO. Mem. ASME. Democrat. Achievements include patent for flowmeter. Home: Troy, NY. Died Jan. 15, 2007.

BROWN, AARON DONALD, environmental scientist; b. Binghamton, NY, Sept. 29, 1954; s. Donald F. and Patricia Brown. BA, Oberlin Coll., 1976; MSc, U. Mich., 1977; PhD, Utah State U., 1985. Cert. profl. soil scientist. Researcher, instr. Chiang Mai (Thailand) U., 1977-79; rsch. and teaching asst. Utah State U., Logan, 1980-84; rsch. soil scientist U. Calif., Riverside, 1984-91, asst. rsch. environ. chemist Santa Barbara, from 1991; chemistry instr. Ventura (Calif.) Coll., from 1995. Contbr. articles to profl. jours. Mem. AAAS (Klauber award 1983), Am. Geophys. Union, Internat. Soc. Soil Sci., Soil Sci. Soc. Am., Phi Kappa Phi. Achievements include contributions to specific mechanism of pyrite oxidation, integration of soil chemistry and watershed hydrology, geochemistry of alpine watersheds, uranium chemistry in soils. Home: Santa Barbara, Calif. Died May 14, 2007.

BROWN, ALBERT JACK, optometrists; b. Phila., July 26, 1941; s. Albert Joseph and Mildred Laverne (Mohler) B.; m. Rosalie Joan Carles, Sept. 16, 1959; children: Diane, Susan, Jacqueline. BS cum laude, Pa. State U., 1963; D Optometry cum laude, So. Coll. of Optometry, Memphis, 1966; ThD, Acad. Sch. of Theology, Harrisburg, Pa., 1979; D Ocular Medicine, Am. Coll. Optometric Physician, Memphis, 1987. Cert. eye laser physician N.E. State U./Phila. Light and Laser Inst. Rsch. asst. So. Coll. of Optometry, Memphis, 1964-65; pvt. practice Eye and Ear Aid Clinic, Andrews, N.C., 1966-68, Philipsburg, Pa., from 1968; theology tchr. Pa. State U., State College, 1972-76; dir., tchr. Acad. Sch. Theology, Harrisburg, 1977-79; TV co-host Rev. Dr. Brown Ministries, Harrisburg, from 1985; tchr. laser eye surgery Am. Coll. Optometric Physicians, North Miami Beach, Fla., from 1994, also bd. dirs. Fellow Am. Coll. Optometric Physicians (bd. dirs. 1987-96, award 1994); mem. Am. Pub. Health Assn., Pa. State U. Alumni Assn., Beta Sigma Kappa (hon. mem.), Sigma Alpha Sigma (hon.). Republican. Mem. Ch. of the Brethren. Avocations: hiking, woodworking, piano, art. Home: Philipsburg, Pa. Died Apr. 1, 2007.

BROWN, CARL HENRY, associate dean; b. Loup City, Nebr., Aug. 27, 1932; s. Cornel Hoblin and Victoria (Zaruba) B.; m. Mershonne J. Knecht, Sept. 14, 1953; children: Julie, Cathy, Peggy. BA, U. No. Colo., 1954; MA, Kearney State U., 1971. Math. instr. Hot Springs County High Sch., Thermopolis, Wyo., 1956-58; chemist Empire State Oil Co., Thermopolis, 1958-67; electronics instr. Cen. Community Coll., Hastings, Nebr., 1967-72, chmn., 1972-80, assoc. dean, from 1980; interim dean instrn., 1992-93. With U.S. Army, 1954-56. Mem. Nat. Assn. Ind. Tech., Am. Vocat. Assn., Nebr. Vocat. Assn., Electronic Tech. Assn., South Cen. Sports Club (pres.), Kiwanis. Avocations: tennis, fly fishing. Home: Hastings, Nebr. Died May 11, 2007.

BROWN, CHARLES DURWARD, aerospace engineer; b. Santa Fe, July 23, 1930; s. Charles Edward and Lila Mae (Turk) B.; m. Lawana Jane VanDall, Apr. 13, 1952; children: John, Lawana, Kelsey. BSME, U. Okla., 1952; MSME, So. Meth. U., 1961. With Martin Marietta, Denver, 1958-90; worked on Mariner '71, Viking Orbiter, 1971-77; mgr. Magellan program Martin Marietta, Denver, to 1990; ret., 1990. Lectr. in spacecraft design, Colo. U., Boulder, 1981-91. Author: Spacecraft Mission Design, AIAA, 1992; assoc. editor: Rocket Propellant and Pressurization Systems, 1964; editor: Spacecraft Design, 1982. Recipient NASA Pub. Svc. medal for Viking Orbiter, 1977, NASA award of Merit for Magellan, 1987, Jefferson Cup award Martin Marietta, 1971, 90, Silver Snoopy award Astronaut Corps, 1989, Outstanding Engring. Achievement award NSPE, 1989, Dr. Robert H. Goddard Meml. Trophy for leadership of Magellan program, 1992, NASA Pub. Svc. award for Magellan, 1992. Mem. Tau Beta Pi. Achievements include co-design of Magellan, the first planetary spacecraft to fly on shuttle and propulsion for Mariner 9, the first spacecraft to orbit another planet. Home: Castle Rock, Colo. Died Jan. 20, 2007.

BROWN, CHARLES EDWARD, physician; b. Locust Grove, Ga., Oct. 14, 1910; s. Joel Wyatt and Caroline Elder B.; m. Lorenna Ross, Mar. 21, 1953; children: Charles E. Jr., Lloyd Ross. BA, Emory U., 1932, MA, 1933, MD, 1943. Diplomate Am. Bd. Internal Medicine. Intern, resident Grady Hosp., Atlanta, 1943-45, Pratt Diagnostic Hosp., Boston, 1947-48; pvt. practice Atlanta, 1948-94; ret., 1994. Pres. of staff Ga. Bapt. Hosp., Atlanta, 1983. Clin. vol. instr. to prof. emeritus, Emory U. Sch. Medicine; pres. Atlanta Diabetes Assn., Diabetes Assn. of Ga. Capt. U.S. Army Med. Corps, 1945-47, Germany. Mem. AMA, Med. Assn. Atlanta, Am. Diabetes Assn., Am. Heart Assn. Methodist. Avocations: music, sports, reading. Home: Atlanta, Ga. Died Feb. 26, 2007.

BROWN, EDWARD JAMES, SR., utilities executive; b. Ft. Wayne, Ind., Sept. 30, 1937; s. William Theodore and Jane Elizabeth (Dix) Brown; m. Margaret Bessey, June 17, 1989; children: Edward James Jr., Elena Emily. BA, Yale U., New Haven, 1959; MA, Fordham U., NYC, 1962. CFA. Fin. writer E.F. Hutton & Co., NYC, 1970-71; economist N.Y. Power Authority, NYC, 1971-74, prin. economist, 1974-80, mgr., customer svcs., 1980-83, mgr. spl. projects, 1983-86, dir. strategic planning, 1986-93, dir. new bus., 1993-94. Mem. mgmt. com. Iroquois Gas Transmission Sys., 1989—94. Pres. Park Ave. Meth. Trust, NYC, from 1981; dir. Friends of Shakers, Inc., Sabathday Lake, Maine, 1980—2005, pres., 1982—84, treas., 1995—2005; trustee United Soc. Shakers, Sabathday Lake, 1982—84, from 1995, John St. Meth. Episcopal Trust Soc., NYC, from 1982; bd. dirs. Meth. Ch. Home for Aged, Riverdale, NY, 1995—2001, from 2003, mem. investment com., from 1983, co-chmn., 1994—2003, treas., 1996—2001, pres., 2003—10, v.p., from 2013; pres. Meth. Ch. Home Fund, 1996—99; bd. dirs., treas. John Wesley Towers, 1999—2010; bd. dirs. Yorkville Emergency Alliance, NYC, 1982—88; mem. internat. adv. coun. Mus. Am. Folk Art, NYC, 1988—2001; dir., chmn. investment com. United Meth. City Soc., NYC, from 1999, chartered fin. analyst. Home: New York, NY. Died May 23, 2015.

BROWN, JAMES, political scientist; b. Boston, May 1, 1934; 1 child, Shannon Sophia. BA, Tex. Christian U., 1960, MA, 1963, SUNY, Buffalo, 1969, PhD, 1971. Instr. polit. sci. So. Meth. U., Dallas, 1969-70, asst. prof., 1970-74, assoc. prof., 1974-81, prof. Dedman Coll. Humanities and Scis., from 1981, Ora Nixon Arnold rsch. fellow Am. Statesmanship & Diplomacy, from 1990, chair dept. polit. sci., 1992-93, dir. John G. Tower Ctr. for Polit. Studies, 1993-95; prof. nat. security affairs Air U., Air Command and Staff Coll., Maxwell AFB, Ala., 1979-80; spl. asst. to dep. under sec. def. for planning & resources Dept. Def., Washington, 1987-88; spl. asst. to dir. fgn. affairs specialist U.S. Arms Control and Disarmament Agy., Washington, 1991. Vis. lectr. Air Command and Staff Coll., Maxwell AFB, Ala., Air War Coll., Maxwell AFB, Bogazici U., Istanbul, Turkey, U. Erlangen-Nurnberg, Germany, U. Istanbul, U. Cologne, Germany, Naval War Coll., Newport, R.I., Panteos Sch. Polit. Sci., Athens, Greece; mem. adv. bd. Am.-Turkish Friendship Coun., Washington, 1991—; cons. U.S. Arms Control and Disarmament Agy., Air Force Tech. Applications Ctr., Pacific-Sierra Rsch. Corp., Ctr. Naval Analyses, Battelle Sci. Svcs. Author: Military Ethics and Professionalism: A Collection of Essays, 1981, Delicately Poised Allies: Greece and Turkey, 1991, Challenges in Arms Control for the 1990s, 1992; co-author: The Art of Politics: Electoral Strategies and Campaign Management, 1976; co-editor: Changing Military Manpower Realities, 1982, The Regionalization of Warfare: The Falkland Islands,

Lebanese, and Iran-Iraq Conflicts, 1985, The Reagan Administration's Defense Policies: An Assessment, 1988, Verfication: The Key to Arms Control in the 1990s, 1991, Challenges in Arms Control for the 1990s, 1993, others. S.W. area mgr. News Election Svc., 1972—. Sr. Fulbright scholar faculty polit. sci. U. Ankara (Miltiye), Turkey, 1985; grantee NSF and Arnold Found., 1973, 81, NASA Ames Lab., 1974-78, Dept. Def., 1987, Battelle, Columbus divsn., 1989, Arms Control and Disarmament Agy., 1991, Def. Advanced Rsch. Projects Agy., 1991-92, 93, 94, Los Alamos Nat. Lab., 1992, Lawrence Livermore Nat. Lab., 1992, Def. Nuclear Agy., 1992; recipient Cert. of Appreciation U.S. Arms Control and Disarmament Agy., 1991. Mem. Internat. Inst. Strategic Studies, Dallas Com. on Fgn. Rels., Am. Polit. Sci. Assn., Royal United Svcs. Inst.Def. Studies, Pi Sigma Alpha. Home: Dallas, Tex. Died Nov. 2, 2006.

BROWN, JANE BEVERLY, pianist, educator; b. Galion, Ohio, Mar. 12, 1934; d. Lester Webster and Florence Lillian (Rhoads) Metz; m. William E. Brown, May 29, 1957 (dec. Jan. 1994); children: Deborah Lynn, Jay Edward. BS, U. Findlay, 1957. Cert. piano instr., Ohio. Tchr. 5th grade, Findlay, Ohio, 1957; tchr. 6th grade, 1958; tchr. 5th and 6th grades Ontario, Ohio, 1959; tchr. 1st grade Galion, Ohio, 1960-70; piano tchr. Ontario, from 1963; tchr. kindergarten, 1969; tchr. 3d grade, 1971-79; substitute tchr., 1980-89. Active organist, pianist, vocalist various chs., Ontario, Galion, 1950—; vol. Renaissance Theatre, Mansfield, Ohio, 1984—. Mem. Ohio Music Tchr's Assn. (chmn. backeye auditions ctrl. dist. 1980's, historian, treas., 1990—), Music Tchrs. Nat. Assn. Avocations: reading, gardening, travel, writing. Home: Mansfield, Ohio. Died Feb. 10, 2007.

BROWN, KAREN LUCILLE, elementary school educator; b. Breese, Ill., Sept. 6, 1951; d. Edward William and Mary Ann (Haar) Ford; m. James Kevin Brown, June 30, 1973; children: James, Mark, Ann. BS, So. Ill. U., Edwardsville, 1973. Cert. tchr., Ill. Tchr. Wesclin Community Unit 3, Trenton, Ill., 1973-90; tchr. kindergarten Trenton Elem. Sch., from 1991. Mem. NEA, Ill. Edn. Assn., Wesclin Edn. Assn., St. Mary's Altar Sodality, St. Mary's Cath. Ch. Democrat. Roman Catholic. Avocations: painting, crafts, reading, piano. Died Dec. 6, 2006.

BROWN, LARRY JACK, funeral director; b. Dothan, Ala., Aug. 13, 1951; s. Jack Wilbur Brown and Mildred Pauline (Dunlap) Lyles; m. Jackie Valinda Ellis. Grad. high sch., Ozark, Ala. Assoc. Searcy Funeral Home, Enterprise, Ala., 1970-72; dir., embalmer Norris Funeral Home, Bay Minette, Ala., from 1973. Vol. North Baldwin United Fund, Bay Minette, 1985. Mem. Jaycees (Jaycee of Yr. Bay Minette 1983, Outstanding Pres. 4th Quarter Dist. 53 1985, Pres. Month Region Five 1986), Bay Minette Masonic Lodge (worshipful master 1993-94). Home: Bay Minette, Ala. Died June 30, 2007.

BROWN, MARCIA JOAN, author, artist, photographer; b. Rochester, NY, July 13, 1918; d. Clarence Edward and Adelaide Elizabeth (Zimber) B.; companion Janet Loranger Student, Woodstock Sch. Painting, summers 1938, 39; student painting, New Sch. Social Research, Art Students League; BA, NY State Coll. Tchrs., 1940; student Chinese calligraphy, painting, Zhejiang Acad. Fine Arts, Hangzhou, Peoples Republic China, 1985-87; studied painting with Judson Smith, Stuart Davis, Yasuo Kuniyoshi, Julian Levi; LHD (hon.), SUNY, Albany, 1996. Tchr. English, dramatics Cornwall HS, NY, 1940-43; library asst. NY Pub. Library, 1943-49; tchr. puppetry extra-mural dept. U. Coll. West Indies, Jamaica, B.W.I., 1953. Tchr. workshop on picture book U. Minn.-Split Rock Arts Program, Duluth, 1986, workshop on Chinese brush painting Oriental Brush Artists Guild, 1988; sponsor Chinese landscape painting workshops with Zhuo HeJun, 1988-89; sponsored workshops Chinese caligraphy with A. Wang Dong Ling, 1989-90, 92; invited speaker exhbn. illustrations, Japan, 1990, 94. Illustrator: The Trail of Courage (Virginia Watson), 1948, The Steadfast Tin Soldier (Hans Christian Andersen), 1953 (Caldecott Honor Book award), Anansi (Philip Sherlock), 1954, The Three Billy Goats Gruff (Asbjornsen and Moe), 1957, Peter Piper's Alphabet, 1959, The Wild Swans (Hans Christian Andersen), 1963, Giselle (Théophile Gautier), 1970, The Snow Queen (Hans Christian Andersen), 1972, Shadow (Blaise Cendrars), 1982 (Caldecott award 1983), How the Ostrich Got His Long Neck (Aardema, Mainichi Japan Picture Book award 1997, Translation Winner' prize Mainichi Newspapers and Sch. Libr. Assn. 1997), 1995, (with others) Sing a Song of Popcorn, 1988, Of Swans, Sugar Plums and Satin Slippers (Violette Verdy); author, illustrator: The Little Carousel, 1946, Stone Soup, 1947 (Caldecott Honor Book award), Henry Fisherman, 1949 (Caldecott Honor Book award), Dick Whittington and His Cat (retold), 1950 (Caldecott Honor Book award), Skipper John's Cook, 1951 (Caldecott Honor Book award), The Flying Carpet (retold), 1956, Felice, 1958, Tamarindo, 1960, Once a Mouse (retold), 1961 (Caldecott award), Backbone of the King, 1966, The Neighbors, 1967, The Bun (retold), 1972, All Butterflies, 1974 (Boston Globe Honor Book, Horn Book), The Blue Jackal (retold), 1977, Walk Through Your Eyes, 1979, (with photographs) Touch Will Tell, 1979; (with photographs) Listen to a Shape, 1979, Lotus Seeds; Children, Pictures and Books, 1985; (with others) From Sea to Shining Sea, 1993; translator, illustrator: Puss in Boots, 1952 (Caldecott Honor Book award), Cinderella (Charles Perrault), 1954 (Caldecott award 1955), How, Hippo!, 1969 (honor book Book World Spring Book Festival); author, photographer: film strip The Crystal Cavern, 1974; exhibited at Bklyn. Mus., Peridot Gallery, Hacker Gallery, Library Congress, Carnegie Inst., Phila. Print Club, Hammond Mus., North Salem, NY, 1988; one-woman show include: U. Albany, SUNY, 1997; represented in permanent collections Library of Congress, NY Pub. Library, Mazza Gallery Findlay (Ohio) Coll.; pvt. collections. Recipient Disting. Svc. to Children's Lit. award, U. So. Miss., 1972, Regina medal Cath. Libr. Assn., 1977, Disting. Alumnus medal SUNY, 1969, Laura Ingalls Wilder award, 1992; US nominee Internat. Hans Andersen award illustration, 1966, 76; career rsch. material in spl. libr. collection, SUNY, Albany, de Grummond Collection, U. So. Miss., Hattiesburg, Kerlan Collection, U. Minn.; named Marcia Brown Rsch. Rm. in her honor SUNY, Albany, 2001. Fellow Internat. Inst. Arts and Letters (life); mem. Author's Guild, Print Coun. Am., Art Students League, Oriental Brush Artists Guild, Sumi-e Soc. Am, Am. Artists of Chinese Brush Painting. Home: Laguna Woods, Calif. Died Apr. 28, 2015.

BROWN, MARY EVELYN, insurance agent; b. Hammond, Ind., Dec. 25, 1915; d. Frank and Mary Ann (Fuderich) Maglish; m. James Ward Brown, June 21, 1941. Grad. H.S., Griffith, Ind. Sec. Spitz & Miller Ins., Griffith, 1935-55; underwriter Spitz & Miller Ins. Inc., Griffith, 1955-75, sec., mgr., from 1975. Vol. Am. Cancer Soc., Griffith, 1986—. Recipient Ins. Woman of Yr. award Hammond Assn. Ins. Women, 1975. Mem. Nat. Assn. Ins. Women (regional dir. 1954-55, nat. rec. sec. 1955-56), Nat. Cath. Soc. Foresters, Ins. Women of Lake County (past pres. 1978, 86), Ind. Ins. Agts., Am. Legion. Republican. Roman Catholic. Avocations: classical music, golf, reading, cooking. Home: Griffith, Ind. Died Mar. 15, 2007.

BROWN, ROBERT JOSEPH, lawyer; b. Little Rock, Mar. 17, 1938; s. Robert James and Lizbeth (Ring) B.; m. Nan Selz, Sept. 7, 1960 (div.); children: Micah Harley, Jacob Selz; m. Terrell Brock, July 6, 1995 (div.); m. Ruth Ann Jefferies, Feb. 14, 1998. BA, Yale U., 1960; LLB, U. Ark., 1967. Bar: Ark. 1967, U.S. Dist. Ct. Ark. 1967, U.S. Ct. Appeals (8th cir.) 1968, U.S. Supreme Ct. 1970. Assoc. Rose Law Firm, Little Rock, 1967-70; chief dep. pros. atty. 6th Jud. Dist. Ark., Pulaski and Perry County, 1970-72; exec. v.p. Block Mortgage Co., Little Cork, 1972-75; ptnr. Crock & Brown PLLC, Little Rock, from 1975. Patentee voting booth. Pres. Ark. Mortgage Bankers Assn., 1975, Unitarian Universalist Ch. of Little Rock, 1995; bd. dirs. S.W. Dist. Unitarian Universalist Ch., 1995-96. Capt. USMC, 1960-63, res. Home: Little Rock, Ark. Died June 6, 2007.

BROWN, RUTH PRICE, association administrator; b. Stoneville, NC, Sept. 27, 1933; d. C.L. and Mary O. (Roland) Price; m. G.C. Triplett, Mar. 16, 1956 (div. Jan. 1974); 1 child, David; m. Russell G. Brown, Aug. 29, 1975 (dec. Nov. 1988). Grad. high sch., Stoneville. Office mgr. Assocs. Discount Corp., Winston Salem and Greensboro, N.C., 1953-64; broker Triplett Realty, Kernersville, N.C., 1965-71; exec. dir. Kernersville C. of C., from 1973. Treas. Our Town, Kernersville, 1976. Vice chmn. Kernersville Precinct, 1972-87, chmn., 1987—; del. to Rep. county, dist. and state convs., 1974—; mem. Friends of Libr., 1980—. Mem. Bus. and Profls. Woman's Club (pre 1976-77, Club Woman of Yr. 1976), Arts and Crafts Guild (hon. 1983-84), Capitol Hill Club (Washington), Kernersville Little Theatre (adv. bd. 1989-93, bd. dirs. 1993—). Methodist. Home: Kernersville, NC. Died Apr. 13, 2007.

BROWNROUT, HARVEY MURRAY, lawyer; b. Buffalo, Sept. 6, 1935; s. Abe and Lillian (Hager) B.; m. Sunny Sunshine, June 21, 1959; children: Todd, Jill, Melanie. SB, MIT, 1956; JD, Harvard U., 1960. Bar: U.S. Dist. Ct. (so. and ea. dists.) N.Y., 1971, Conn. 1988. Assoc. Davis, Hoxie, Faithful & Hapgood, NYC, 1960-65, Darby & Darby, NYC, 1965-68, Jacobs, Persinger & Parker, NYC, 1968-71; dir. software licensing Xerox Corp., Stamford, Conn., from 1971. 2d lt. U.S. Army, 1956-57. Mem. ABA, Am. Intellectual Property Law Assn., Computer and Bus. Equipment Mfg. Assn. (chmn. proprietary rights com. 1981-86). Home: Sarasota, Fla. Died July 23, 2007.

BRUBAKER, JANICE ALEEDA, historian; b. Springfield, Ohio, Oct. 5, 1930; d. French Garnet and Gertrude Ethel (Hull) Tipton; m. Angus Bonner Brubaker, Mar. 18, 1949; children: Mark Joseph, John Angus. Student, U. N.Mex., 1952, Berlitz Sch., Madrid, 1965; grad. in Libr. Sci., Wittenberg U., 1971; degree with hons. in religion, The Mayans, 1986. Mem. staff bookkeeping dept. Nat. Supply Co., Springfield, 1948-49; proofreader News and Sun newspapers, Springfield, 1954; newspaper columnist South Charleston Sentinel, London, Ohio, 1974-77; head Houston br. Clark County Pub. Librs., South Charleston, Ohio, 1971-91; recorder oral history Heritage Commn. Mus., South Charleston, 1974—2005; newspaper indexer South Charleston, from 1991. Exhibitions include Springfield YWCA, 1970; columnist Now and Then, 1974-77 Trustee, reporter Bicentennial Com., South Charleston, 1974-77, Heritage Commn. Corp., South Charleston, 1981—; mem. ARC, Springfield, 1980—. Recipient Family Svcs. Vol. award Torrejon Base, 1967, Cmty. Svc. award, 2005.; named Citizen of Month, South Charleston, 1980. Mem. Friends of Libr. Soc., Literary Club, The Mayans (10th deg.).[,] Masons. Democrat. Astarian. Avocations: writing, reading, singing, travel, painting. Home: South Charleston, Ohio. Died Aug. 16, 2007.

BRUCK, EVA DOMAN, design company executive; b. Budapest, Hungary, Apr. 29, 1950; came to U.S., 1957; d. Zoltan and Clara (Biro) Doman; m. Stuart A. Bruck, May 4, 1980; children: Spencer B. Doman, Natalie J. Claire. BA with honors, Northeastern U., 1972; postgrad., Boston U., 1973-75; BS in Urban Landscape Architecture, CCNY, 1978. Adminstrv. asst. Sargent Coll. Boston U., 1972-75; asst. to chmn. Internat. Design Conf. in Aspen, NYC, 1975-76; asst. to pres. Milton Glaser, Inc., NYC, 1977-83, bus. mgr., 1983-90, dir. mktg., 1991-92; account dir. Landor Assocs., NYC, 1990-91; tchr. Sch. of Visual Arts, NYC, from 1983. Design mgmt. cons. N.Y.C., 1985-92; bus. mgr. Diefenbach Elkins, 1992—. Author: (with Tad Crawford) Business and Legal Forms for Graphic Designers, 1990; contbr. articles to profl. jours. Mem. Internat. Coun. Graphic Design Assn. (mem. design com.), Am. Inst. Graphic Arts, Am. Notary Assn. Home: New York, NY. Died May 4, 2007.

BRUEGGEMAN, CHARLES JOSEPH, information systems consultant, retired; b. NYC, Mar. 22, 1931; s. Charles Herman and Edith (Katrina) B.; m. Joan Terace Shepherd (div. Jan. 1989); 1 child, Theresa Ann. BBA, CCNY, 1953, MBA, 1961. Cert. systems profl. Specialist clk. Brinton and Co., NYC, 1955-56; systems analyst S.H. Kress and Co., NYC, 1956-59; mgr. documents control McGraw-Hill, Inc., NYC, 1959, mgr. scheduling and control, mgr. electronic acctg. machines Highstown, N.Y., dir. product svcs. NYC; info. systems cons., Red Bank, N.J. Dir. Dodge Constrn. Info. Svcs. Product Svcs., 1988, Dodge Constrn. Info. Svcs. Database Integrity, 1992. Developer constrn. stats. Dodge Local, 1986 (New Product Devel. award), constrn. analysis system, 1983 (New Product Devel. award). Cpl. U.S. Army, 1952-53, Korea. Mem. Assn. Systems Mgmt. (pres. N.Y. chpt. 1961—, Achievement award 1980, Outstanding Svc. award 1971-72). Avocation: tennis. Home: Sun City Center, Fla. Died Nov. 25, 2006.

BRUMBACH, VIRGINIA WHITCOMB, English educator; b. Harlan, Ky., Sept. 11, 1922; d. Frederick Benjamin and Alice Louisa (Hoe) Whitcomb; m. Orin Lee Brumbach, Dec. 21, 1945 (dec. July 1991); children: Margaret Brumbach Bolding, Mary Alice. AA, Cumberland Coll., 1942; BA, Western Ky. U., 1944; MA, Baylor U., 1945; EdD, U. North Tex., 1970. Tchr. English and reading Birdville H.S., Ft. Worth, Tex., 1955-65; prof. English and Edn. U. Mary Hardin Baylor, Belton, Tex., 1965-70; con. in learning processes Region XI Edn. Svc. Ctr., Ft. Worth, 1970-71; prof. English Eastfield Coll., Mesquite, Tex., from 1971. Chair Eastfield Coll., Mesquite, 1980—, chair Literacy Festival, 1989—; student devel. chair So. Assn. Accreditation, Mesquite, 1989-91. Mem. AAUW (pres., program chair Garland br. 1980—), ABWA (pres. Tex. Star chpt. 1988, Woman of Yr. 1989). Avocations: reading, raising australian shepherd and maine coon cat. Home: Garland, Tex. Died Jan. 7, 2007.

BRUNNER, JAMES ALBERTUS, marketing educator; b. June 28, 1923; BA, Ohio State U., 1946, BSc Bus. Adminstrn., 1946, MBA, 1947, PhD, 1955. Grad. asst. Ohio State U., Columbus, 1947; asst. prof. Otterbein Coll., Westerville, Ohio, 1947-51; prof. mktg. U. Toledo, Ohio, 1961-92, chmn. dept. mktg. Ohio, 1951-76, prof. emeritus Ohio, from 1992. Bd. dirs. Lake Park, Sylvania, Ohio, 1974-88, Flower Hosp., Sylvania, 1988-96, Toledo Hosp., 1996—. Home: Toledo, Ohio. Died Feb. 3, 2007.

BRUNS, ROBERT EUGENE, auditor; b. Pipestone, Minn., July 10, 1952; s. Melvin Fred and Dorothy Jane (Hanson) Wiedow; m. Judith Ann Staley, June 15, 1973; children: Nathan, Matthew, Patricia. BS in Acctg., Mankato Tech. Inst., 1973. Dep. auditor Nicollet County, St. Peter, Minn., 1973-85, auditor, from 1985. Mem. Assn. Minn. Counties, Minn. Counties Computer Coop. (del. 1983—, tax adv. bd. 1987—), Minn. Assn. Cpounty Officers, Region 3 County Auditors (chmn. 1988—), St. Peter Jaycees (sec. 1981-82, nominated Outstanding Businessman, 1984), Kiwanis (pres. St. Peter club 1985-86). Home: Saint Peter, Minn. Died Jan. 8, 2007.

BRUUN, PER MOLLER, civil engineer, consultant; b. Skagen, Denmark, Feb. 28, 1917; arrived in U.S., 1952; s. Niels Bruun and Marie Moller; m. Elizabeth Bruun, Sept. 29, 1943; children: Brita, Niels. MSCE, Tech. U. Denmark, 1941, DSc, 1954; D (hon.), U. Santander, 1978, U. Iceland, 1996. Coastal engr. Ministry of Pub. Works, Denmark, 1941—49, Ministry Edn., Denmark, 1949—54; chmn. coastal engrs. U. Fla., Gainesville, 1954—67; chmn. port engrs. Tech. U. Norway, Trondheim, 1967—78; cons. Hilton Head, SC, from 1978. Author: Coast Stability, 1954, Port Engineering, 1973, 4th edit., 1990, Design and Construction of Mounds for Breakwaters and Coastal Protection, 1985, Tidal Inlets and Littoral Drift, 1960, 3d edit., 1978; assoc. editor: Jour. Coastal Rsch., from 1976; contbr. articles to profl. jours. Artilleryman Danish Armed Forces, 1941—42, artilleryman Danish Armed Forces, 1945—46. Recipient Coastal award, Internat. Orgn. Coastal Dynamics, 2001, Internat. Coastal Conf. award, ASCE, 2002, Medal of Honor, Fla. Shore and Beach Preservation Assn., 1992; named Knight of Icelandic Falcon, 1994. Fellow: ASCE (life); mem.: Norwegian Acad. Tech. Scis., Danish Acad. Tech. Scis., Danish Assn. Hydraulic Rsch. (hon.), Fla. Shore Protection Assn. (hon.). Avocation: writing. Home: Hilton Head Island, SC. Died Nov. 8, 2006.

BUCHHOLZ, LLOYD ARTON, industrial relations specialist; b. Chgo., Mar. 22, 1939; s. Grinnell William and Elvera Carlina (Arton) B.; m. Virginia Jean Salzman, July 11, 1959; children: Jamie Lynn Heier, Dana Marie Parrault, Michelle Lee. Data processing mgr. Imperial-Eastman, Niles, Ill., 1964-67, A.B. Dick Co., Niles, 1967-77; mng. dir. Applied Info. Devel., Oakbrook, Ill., 1977-84; salesman Software Internat., Itasca, Ill., 1984-85, McCormack & Dodge, Schaumburg, Ill., 1985-86; owner, operator Ican Cons., Glenview, Ill., from 1986. Mem. Am. Prodn. and Inventory Control Soc. (cert. practitioner inventory mgmt., mem. cert. com. 1981). Republican. Methodist. Avocations: fishing, racquetball, photography. Home: Glenview, Ill. Died June 24, 2007.

BUCHTA, EDMUND, engineering executive; b. Wostitz, Nikolsburg, Czechoslovakia, May 11, 1928; came to U.S., 1979; Kaufmann, Deutsche Wirtschaftoberschule, Bruenn, Czechoslovakia, 1942-45. Shop foreman Messerklinger,

Ernsting, Austria, 1949-51; constrn. foreman Hinteregger, U.S. Mil. Project, Salzburg, Siezenheim, Austria, 1951-52, Auserehl Constrn. Corp., NYC, 1963; pres. Grout Concrete Constrn. Ltd., Edmonton, Alta., Can., 1966-73; pioneer & explorer Canol Project Parcel B and Land Ownership N.W. Can., from 1968; pres. Barbarosa Enterprises Ltd., Yellowknife, Can., from 1971. Owner (with Barbarosa Enterprises Ltd.) Canol Project Parcel B, 1968—. Mem. Dem. Senatorial Campaign Com. With German Mil., 1943-45. Named Emperor of the North, McLean Mag., Can., 1976. Mem. Internat. Platform Assn., Dem. Senatorial Campaign Com. Home: Redondo Beach, Calif. Died May 14, 2007.

BUCKALEW, ROBERT JOSEPH, psychologist, consultant; b. Eustis, Fla., Mar. 24, 1924; s. Alfred Henry and Jessie Olive (Bowron) B.; m. Flora Jean Kissinger, Aug. 16, 1959; children: Flora C., Faye R. BS, West Chester U., Pa., 1948; MEd, Temple U., 1949, EdD, 1962. Cert. sch. psychologist, Pa. Group living tchr. N.J. Reformatory for Boys, Bordentown, 1948-49; social studies tchr., high sch. guidance counselor Milford (Del.) Spl. Sch. Dist., 1949-52, elem. guidance counselor, reading clinic, 1952-53; psychologist Del. Colony for the Feebleminded, Stockley, Del., 1953; guidance counselor, sr. high sch. tchr. sci., social studies Lord Balt. Cons. Schs., Millville, Del., 1953-55; spl. edn. tchr. Delhaas Sch. System, Bristol, Pa., 1955-57; asst. county supr. spl. edn. Carbon County Sch. Bd., Jim Thorpe, Pa., 1957-62; dir. rsch. and curriculum Kutztown (Pa.) U., 1962-70, prof., 1962-89; cons., past pres., mem. exec. com. Assn. of Pa. State Colls. and Univ. Ret. Faculties, Inc., from 1990. Bd. dirs. Tarsus Manor, Inc., Fleetwood, Pa., 1989-97. Maj. USAF, 1943-45. Decorated Air Medal with 2 oak leaf clusters. Mem. NEA, Am. Psychol. Assn., Pa. Psychol. Assn. (Outstanding Psychologist 1978), Berks County Psychol. Assn. (pres. 1978-79), Berks County Res. Officers Assn. (pres. 1980-83, 96—), SAR (pres. 1983-85, Silver Citizenship medal 1991), Am. Legion, Phi Delta Kappa. Republican. Avocations: history, genealogy, politics. Home: Fleetwood, Pa. Died Mar. 17, 2007.

BUCKLEY, FREDERICK JEAN, retired lawyer; b. Wilmington, Ohio, Nov. 5, 1923; s. William Millard and Martha (Bright) B.; m. Josephine K. Buckley, Dec. 4, 1945; children: Daniel J., Fredrica Buckley Elder, Matthew J. Student, Wilmington Coll., 1941-42, Ohio State U., 1942-43; AB, U. Mich., 1948, LLB, 1949; LLD (hon.), Wilmington Coll., 2004. Bar: Ohio 1950, U.S. Dist. Ct. (so. dist.) Ohio 1952, U.S. Supreme Ct. 1978, U.S. Ct. Appeals (6th cir.) 1981, Fla. 1982, U.S. Dist. Ct. (mid. dist.) Fla. 1991; cert. cir. ct. mediator, Fla. Assoc. G.L. Schilling, Sr., Wilmington, 1951-52; ptnr. Schilling & Buckley, Wilmington, 1953-56; sole practice Wilmington, 1956-62; sr. ptnr. Buckley, Miller & Wright, Wilmington, 1962—2002. Chmn. The Wilmington Savs. Bank, 1971—2003; solicitor City of Wilmington, 1954-63. Contbr. articles in field. With AUS, 1943-46, ETO. Joint program Mich. Inst. Pub. Adminstrn. fellow, 1948. Fellow Am. Coll. Trial Lawyers; mem. ABA, Am. Arbitration Assn. (comml. panel), Ohio State Bar Assn., Clinton County Bar Assn., Fla. Bar Assn. (Collier County), Ohio State Bar Found. Republican. Methodist. Home: Miami, Fla. Died Apr. 2, 2012.

BUCKSBAUM, MELVA JANE, foundation administrator; b. Wash., Apr. 5, 1933; d. William Venezky and Millie Ruth (Bronstein); m. Martin Bucksbaum (dec. 1995); children: Mary Bucksbaum Scanlan, Gene, Glenn; m. Robert I. Goldman (dec. 1998); m. Raymond J. Learsy; stepchildren: Bill Lese, Peter Lese, Olexa Mandelbaum. Attended, U. Md. Bd. pres. Des Moines Art Ctr., Iowa; mgr. Martin Bucksbaum Family Found., 1995—2015; dir. Robert I. Goldman Found., 1996—2015; bd. mem. American Friends of Israel Mus., The Jewish Mus., NY, Hirshhorn Mus. & Sculpture Garden, Washington, Save Venice, New York & Venice, Aspen Inst., Drawing Ctr., NYC, Woodrow Wilson Internat. Ctr. for Scholars, Washington; Internat. com. mem. Internat Com., Tate Gallery, London; visiting com. Grad. Sch. Design, Harvard U.; vice chairwoman Whitney Mus. of American Art. Recipient Gertrude Vanderbilt Whitney Award for outstanding arts patronage & philanthropy, 2004; named one of Top 200 Collectors (with Raymond Learsy), ARTnews Mag., 2004—13. Mem.: Whitney Mus. Am. Art (trustee from 1996, vice chmn. from 2004), Tate Gallery (Internat. Com.). Avocation: collector of contemporary art. Home: Sharon, Conn. Died Aug. 16, 2015.

BUDD, ISABELLE AMELIA, publisher; b. Feb. 8, 1923; AB, Shippensburg State U., 1977; MDiv, Gettysburg Theol. Sem., 1981. Instr, counselor Bordentown Tng. Sch., NJ, 1967—68; asst. dir. cottage life Skillman, NJ, 1968—69; adminstr. & therapist, pub. relations ofcl. Kinsman Hall Jacksman, Maine, 1969—75, Kinsman Hall Jacksman NP, 1970—75; mem. Liturg. Conf., Washington, 1981—84. Mem.: Internat. Acad. Poets. Home: Durham, NC. Died Dec. 23, 2006.

BUGLIOSI, VINCENT T., lawyer, writer; b. Hibbing, Minn., Aug. 18, 1934; s. Vincent and Ida (Valerie) B.; m. Gail Margaret Talluto, July 21, 1956; children: Wendy Suzanna, Vincent John. BBA, U. Miami, Fla., 1956; LLB, UCLA, 1964. Bar: Calif. 1964. Dep. dist. atty., Los Angeles County, 1964-72; pvt. practice law Beverly Hills, Calif., from 1972. Prof. criminal law Beverly Sch. Law, Los Angeles, 1968-74 Author: Outrage: The Five Reasons Why O.J. Simpson Got Away with Murder, 1996, The Phoenix Solution: Gettin Serious About Winning America's Drug War, 1996, No Island of Sanity: Paula Jones v. Bill Clinton-The Supreme Court on Trial, 1998, The Betrayal of America: How the Supreme Court Undermined the Constitution and Chose Our President, 2001, Reclaiming History: The Assassination of President John F. Kennedy, 2007 (Edgar award for best fact crime book 2008), The Prosecution of George W. Bush for Murder, 2008, Divinity of Doubt: The God Question, 2011; co-author: (with Curt Gentry) Helter-Skelter: The True Story of the Manson Murders, 1974 (Edgar award for best fact crime book 1975), (with Ken Hurwitz) Till Death Us Do Part: A True Murder Mystery, 1978 (Edgar award for best fact crime book 1979), (with Bruce B. Henderson) And the Sea Will Tell, 1991. Candidate for dist. atty., Los Angeles County, 1972, Dem. candidate Calif. atty. gen., 1974. Served to capt. AUS, 1957. Died June 6, 2015.

BUICAN, TUDOR NICOLAE, biophysicist, consultant; b. Bucharest, Romania, Apr. 6, 1949; s. Alexandru and Constanta Buican; 1 child, Matthew Alexander. BSc, King's Coll. U. London, 1972; PhD in Biophysics, U. BC, Vancouver, Canada, 1984. Asst. prof. biophysics U. Bucharest, Faculty Biology, Romania, 1972—78; postdoc. fellow Los Alamos Nat. Lab., N.Mex., 1984—86, prin. investigator & tech. staff mem., 1986—91; tech. founder, sr. v.p. r&d, cto, chmn. bd. Cell Robotics Inc., Albuqerque, N.Mex., 1988—93; pres. Biotechnology Inst., Albuqerque, 1993—96; mng. mem. Semiotic Engring. Associates LLC, Albuquerque, from 1996; v.p. tech. Digilab LLC, Randolph, Mass., 2001—02. Contbr. articles to profl. jours. Named Most Significant Innovations of Yr., 1988—89. Mem.: AAAS, Soc. Applied Spectroscopy, Optical Soc. America. Achievements include first to multiplex fluorescence labeling flow cytometry-use of abstract n-dimensional tomographic reconstruction and multiplex immunofluorescent labeling to overcome detection hardware limitations in flow; research in multiphysics modeling and simulation of VSPA PEMs using high-performance computer systems; patents for covering PEM-based FT spectrometry and applications; invention of PEM-based FT spectrometry-photoelastic modulator-based interferometry for ultra-high-speed FT spectrometry in the UV, visible and IR; floating amplitude technique -high-performance driving of stacks of PEMs for high spectral resolution PEM-based FT spectrometry, computer-controlled microrobotic manipulation using light pressure; virtual stack/phased array photoelastic modulators for ultra-high-performance FT spectrometry-a novel dedicated PEM design for ultra-high-performance FT spectrometry; patents for high retardation-amplitude photoelastic modulator covering VSPA PEM technology. Avocations: bicycling, literature, history, classical music. Home: Albuquerque, N.Mex. Died June 2014.

BULL, FRANK JAMES, retired architect; b. Chattanooga, June 25, 1922; s. Louis H. and Augusta (Clausius) B.; m. Betty Frances Graham, May 7, 1949; 1 child, Birney O'Brian. BS in Architecture, Ga. Inst. Tech., Atlanta, 1948, BArch, 1949. Registered architect, Ga., 1951; cert. Nat. Coun. Archtl. Registration Bds. Pilot Pan Am. World Airways, NY, Fla., 1942—46; arch. Aeck Assocs. Architects, Atlanta, 1948-57; ptnr. Bull & Kenney Architects, Atlanta, 1957-88, Bull, Brown & Kilgo, Architects, Atlanta, 1988—2003; ret., 2003. Cons. Fed. Republic of Germany Embassy, Washington, 1986-93; archtl. cons. for golf clubhouse Quinta do Peru, Sesimbra, Portugal and Palheiro Golfe, Funchal, Madeira Island, Portugal, 1991; lectr. in field. Co-author: Asbestos Abatement: Vol. 5 The Sourcebook on Asbestos Diseases, 1991; contbr. articles to profl. jours.; prin. works include Sanctuary for Holy Innocents Episc. Ch., Atlanta, Atlanta Speech Sch. and Clin., Hummel Hall Episc. H.S., Alexandria, Va., Jekyll Island Golf Clubhouse, McLarty Hall, Tull Hall, Turner Gymnasium, Westminster Schs., Atlanta, Dunwoody Country Club, Atlanta, East Lake Golf Clubhouse Restoration, Atlanta, others. Charter trustee Holy Innocents Episcopal Sch., Atlanta, 1962-68, chmn., 1966; founder Galloway Schs., Atlanta, 1969-75. Recipient Rambusch prize, Ecole de Beaux Arts, 1940, Lifetime Achievement award, Nat. Environ. Info. Assn., 2009. Mem. AIA (mem. emeritus, treas. Atlanta chpt. 1976-78, bd. dirs. Ga. assn. 1971-74), Am. Arbitration Assn. (mem. nat. panel constrn. industry arbitrators 1977-2002), Nat. Asbestos Coun. (founder, charter v.p., bd. dirs. 1983-86, 89-90, treas. 1987, exec. com. 1983-87), Cherokee Town and Country Club (charter, bd. govs. 1976-79, chmn. capital appropriations com., chmn. green com.), Omicron Delta Kappa, Tau Beta Pi, Phi Kappa Phi, Phi Eta Sigma, ANAK, Beta Theta Pi. Republican. Episcopalian. Avocations: golf, writing. Died Oct. 9, 2014.

BUMGARDNER, JAMES ARLISS, artist, educator; b. Winston-Salem, NC, Mar. 25, 1935; s. Edgar E. and Alma Faye (Preston) B.; m. Judith Joy, May 28, 1960; 1 child, Rhea Maya. BFA, Va. Commonwealth U., 1957. Prof. Va. Commonwealth U., Richmond, from 1958. Recipient Spl. award in painting N.C. Mus., 1958, 59, 60, 62, Cert. of Distinction, Va. Mus. Fine Art, 1959, 61, 63, 77, Purchase prize Southeastern Ctr. Contemporary Art, 1977, Purchase prize N.C. Mus., 1957. Died June 22, 2015.

BUMP, HERBERT DEWITT, state agency administrator; b. Gainesville, Tex., Mar. 23, 1932; s. Emery Dewitt and Rose Zella (Kreager) B.; m. Martha Jo Denmark, Mar. 30, 1974. AA in Mech. Engring., Sacramento City Coll., 1958; student, Okla. A & M U., 1951-52. Technician Aero Jet Gen. Corp., Sacramento, 1959-67; lab. supr. Norris Industries, Riverbank, Calif., 1967-69; lead technician Olin Chem. Corp., St. Marks, Fla., 1970-75; conservation lab. supr. Dept. of State, Tallahassee, Fla., from 1976; pres. Internat. Artifact Conservation and Rsch. Lab., Inc., Belle Chasse, La., from 1988. Presenter Can. Conservation Lab., Am. Soc. Metals. Contbr. articles to profl. jours. With USAF, 1952-56. Mem. Internat. Nautical Archeology, Internat. Inst. for Conservation Hist. and Artistic Works, Nat. Assn. Corrosion Engrs. (subcom. on conservation artistic and hist. works, subcom. on corrosion and sci. tech., subcom. on marine vessel corrosion, adv. panel on corrosion control, presenter Internat. Conf. Corrosion Engrs., 1986). Republican. Home: Tallahassee, Fla. Died Apr. 25, 2007.

BUMPERS, DALE LEON, former senator, governor, lawyer; b. Charleston, Ark., Aug. 12, 1925; s. William Rufus and Lattie (Jones) B.; m. Betty Lou Flanagan, Sept. 4, 1949; children: Dale Brent, William Mark, Margaret Brooke. Student, U. Ark., 1943, 46-48; JD, Northwestern U., 1951. Bar: Ark. 1952. Pres. Charleston Hardware and Furniture Co., 1951—66; city atty. Charleston, Ark., 1952-70; spl. justice Ark. Supreme Ct., 1968; operator Angus cattle farm, 1966-70; gov. State of Ark., Little Rock, 1971—75; US Senator from Ark., 1975—99; atty. Arent Fox Kintner Plotkin & Kahn (now Arent Fox LLP), Washington, 2000—16; dir. Ctr. for Def. Info., 1999. Mem. appropriations com., energy and natural resources com., small bus. com., senate Dem. policy com. Pres. Charleston Sch. Bd., 1969-70, C of C, Charleston. Sgt. USMC, 1943—46. Mem. Charleston C. of C. (pres.) Democrat. Methodist. Home: Little Rock, Ark. Died Jan. 1, 2016.

BUNN, ANN, artist, educator; BFA, U. Colo., 1954; post-grad., U. Denver, 1955, U. St. Thomas, Houston, 1982-83; MA in Edn., Calif. State Poly. U., Pomona, 1990. Cert. art tchr., Tex. Art instr. Port Arthur (Tex.) Ind. Sch. Dist., 1955-57, Contemporary Arts Mus., Houston, 1964-69, curator of edn., 1970-81; pvt. practice cons. visual arts edn. Houston, 1981-83, Glendora, Calif., 1983-93, Evergreen, Colo., from 1993; edn. coord. Univ. Art Mus. Calif. State U., Long Beach, 1990-93, asst. prof., lectr. art edn. LA, 1991-93; artist Shadow Mountain Gallery Artist's Coop., Evergreen. Contbr. articles to profl. jours., chpt. to book; author mus. guide: Art on View: Handbook for Educators, 1990; two-person show at Eleanor Bliss Ctr. Arts, Steamboat Springs, Colo., 2002 Recipient Outstanding Mus. Educator award Calif. Art Edn. Assn., 1991, Cert. of Appreciation, Calif. Art Edn. Assn., 1993. Mem. Nat. Art Edn. Assn., Colo. Art Edn. Assn., Evergreen Artists Assn., Nat. Collage Soc. (signature mem.), Soc. Layerists in Multimedia. Avocations: duplicate bridge, computers, travel, cross country skiing. Died July 17, 2007.

BUNN, DUMONT C., academic library director, educator, consultant; s. Cyril Hugh and Hazel (Kitching) Bunn, adopted s. John Wilson and Hattie Estelle (Hall) Bunn, s. Estelle (Jones) Bunn (Stepmother); m. Christine Adele Cooper, Aug. 1, 1964; 1 child, Kimberly Adele Elliott. BA, U. Ga., Athens, 1959; MLn, Emory U., Atlanta, 1961; PhD, Fla. State U., Tallahassee, 1989. Comml. pilot's lic. FAA, 1967. Classification supr. US Dept Agr., Macon, Ga., 1995—2003; dir. libr. svcs. Mid. Ga. Tech. Coll., Warner Robins, from 2003. Dir. u. libr. Mercer U., Ga., 1983—87, asst. prof., 1983—87. Organizer and founding pres. Ingleside Neighborhood Assn., Macon, 1983—86. Grant, NEH, 1979—80. Mem.: ALA, Tech. Coll. Sys. Ga. Libr. Coun., Southeastern Libr. Assn., Ga. Libr. Assn. Achievements include design of building programs for new libraries at Mercer University and at Middle Georgia Technical College and worked as consultant. Avocations: flying, sailing, photography, genealogy. Home: Macon, Ga. Died Oct. 31, 2015.

BUNN, EDWARD TED, marketing educator; b. Johnstown, Pa., Apr. 16, 1928; s. Walter J. and Erma K. (Rose) B.; m. D. Louise Petrikin, Feb. 7, 1950; 1 child, E ric S. BA, U. Pitts., 1950. Promotion mgr. WJAC, Inc., Johnstown, Pa., 1950-54; copywriter Cen. Advt. Agy., Lima, Ohio, 1954-57, account exec., 1957-64; advt. mgr. Dinner Bell Foods, Inc., Defiance, Ohio, 1964, mktg. mgr., 1967-73; dir. communications Celina (Ohio) Fin. Corp., from 1973; ret., 1992. Ind. cons. Lima, Ohio, 1981—, mktg., lectr. Lima Tech. Coll., 1978-85, mktg. intr. Wright State U., Celina, Ohio,1987—, English lectr. U. Pitts., Johnstown, 1950-54. Trustee and officer Amil Tellers of Dramatics, Inc., Lima, Ohio 1984-87, active in community theatre. Home: Lima, Ohio. Died Nov. 25, 2006.

BURDEN, CHRIS, artist; b. Boston, Apr. 11, 1946; m. Barbara Burden (div.); m. Nancy Rubins. B.F.A., Pomona Coll., 1969; M.F.A., U. Calif., Irvine, 1971. Vis. artist Fresno State U., Calif., 1974; faculty mem. UCLA Works in broadcast TV and live performances; one-person shows, Riko Mizuno Gallery, Los Angeles, 1972, 74, 75, Ronald Feldman Fine Arts, N.Y., 1974, 75, 83, Hansen Fuller Gallery, 1974, Alessandra Castelli Gallery, 1975, Rosamund Felsen Gallery, Los Angeles, 1982, 84, Chris Burden: Extreme Measures New Mus. in Manhattan, 2013, 2014; represented in permanent collections, Mus. Modern Art, N.Y.C., Long Beach (Calif.) Arts Mus.; creative works Shoot, 1971, Trans-Fixed, 1974; performances include Through the Night Softly, 1973, Doorway to Heaven, 1973, Velvet Water, 1974, Kunst Kick, 1974, White Light/White Heat, 1975; sculptural installations Ghost Ship, 2005, Urban, 2008, What My Dad Gave Me, 2008 Recipient New Talent award Los Angeles County Mus. Art, 1973; Nat. Endowment Arts grantee, 1974 Died May 10, 2015.

BURDNO, RICHARD FRANCIS, media specialist; b. Sault Ste. Marie, Mich., June 19, 1941; s. Richard Wilson and Betty (Sliger) B.; m. Joyce Ann Burdno, Feb. 19, 1966; children: Bridget Mary, Beth Ann, Brett Richard. BS in Edn., Kent State U., 1965; MS in Edn., Wis. State U., LaCrosse, 1969. Cert. secondary tchr., Ohio. Secondary tchr. La Cross City Schs., 1966-69; asst. dir. media ctr. Cuyahoga C.C./Metro Campus, Cleve., 1969-73; dir. learning materials ctr. Wooster (Ohio) High Sch., from 1973. Pres. Wooster Media Svcs., 1985—. Sch. spokesperson United Way of Ohio, Wooster, 1975. Mem. Nat. Tchrs. Assn., Ohio State Edn. Assn., Wooster Edn. Assn. Democrat. Roman Catholic. Avocations: photography, fishing, hunting, sailing. Home: Wooster, Ohio. Died Jan. 10, 2007.

BURGESS, ROBERT SARGENT, retired human services consultant; b. Providence, Oct. 19, 1916; s. Alexander Manlius and Abby (bullock) B.; m. Ruth Elizabeth Carter,

Sept. 21, 1940 (dec.); children: Joan Chesebro, Marjorie Waite, Robert S. Jr., David Dyer; m. Mary Lou Hemmerling, June 4, 1999. BA, Brown U., 1938; MA, U. Chgo., 1943. Cert. social worker. Field sec. Am. Friends Svc. Com., midwest area, 1938-41; asst. dir. Ill. Bd. Welfare Commrs., Chgo., 1942-43; asst. warden RI Correctional Instns., Cranston, RI, 1943-46; sr. supr. RI Divsn. Pub. Assistance, Providence, 1946-50; exec. dir. RI Heart Assn., Providence, 1950-57; planning dir. Health & Welfare Assn., Pitts., 1957—64; exec. dir. RI Coun. Cmty. Svcs., Providence, 1964-74; ret. Spl. del. Internat. Conf. Social Welfare, The Hague, Nairobi and San Juan, 1972-75; cons. Conservation Commn., Hanover, NH, 1991-99. Author: (book) "To Try the Bloody Law" the story of Mary Dyer. Pres. RIConsumers Coop., Providence, 1947-51; 1st male mem., bd. dirs. Planned Parenthood of RI, Providence, 1968-71; chmn. RI State Coun. on Aging, Providence, 1969-71, Mass. Bd. Pub. Welfare, Boston, 1973-78, chmn., 1975-78; chmn. Providence Model Cities Coun., 1973. Mem. NASW (nat. bd. dirs. 1971-74, Robert S. Burgess Comty Svc. award), Am. Friends Svc. Com., Democratic Socialist Am., Conservation Law Found., Adult Chamber Music Players, Assn. for Statewide Health and Welfare (nat. pres. 1972-73). Socialist. Avocations: tennis, squash, writing, orchestra and quartet playing. Home: Hanover, NH. Died Dec. 25, 2006.

BURKDOLL, FRANCIS BURCH, aircraft design engineer, consultant; b. Monson, Calif., July 31, 1923; s. Benjamin Harrison and Betty Mae (Burch) B.; m. Barbara Langdon, June 1947 (dec. Oct. 1974); children: Wayne, Karen, Diana; m. Joan Ellen Williams. BSME, U. Calif., Berkeley, 1955. Research engr. Caterpillar Tractor Co., Peoria, Ill., 1955-56, FMC Corp., San Jose, Calif., 1956-57, Stanford Research Inst., Menlo Park, Calif., 1957-59, test mgr., 1959-61; engr. mgr. Explosive Tech. Inc., Fairfield, Calif., 1961-67, pres., 1967-86, Burkdoll Design, Vacaville, Calif., from 1986. Inventor aircraft escape systems and devices. Mem. Am. Defense Preparedness Soc. (bd. dirs. 1982—). Republican. Avocations: photography, classic automobiles. Home: Vacaville, Calif. Died Aug. 8, 2007.

BURKE, NANCY VAN VLECK, residential specialist; b. NYC, July 27, 1920; d. Charles Edward Jr. and Natalie Dalton (Johnson) Van Vleck; m. Edwin Marston Burke, Mar. 21, 1942 (Oct. 1980); children: Natalie Marston, Edwin M. Jr., Stephen Johnson, Kevin Walker. Diploma, Ethel Walker Sch., Simsbury, Conn., 1937. Cert. residential specialist. Multi-engine and instruments flight instr. Trained Flight Safety, Inc. of Guardia Airport, Flushing, N.Y., 1964-70; residential specialist Nat. Assn. Realtors, Chgo., from 1985. Com. woman Rep. Party of Somerset County, Somerville, N.J., 1964-66. Mem. Nat. Assn. Realtors, N.J. State Bd. Realtors, Somerset County Bd. Realtors, Morris County Bd. Realtors, Hunterdon County Bd. Realtors, Grad. Realtors Inst., Fedn. Internat. des Professions Immobilieres-U.S.A. (edn. com.). Clubs: Colony (N.Y.C.); Somerset Hills Country (Bernardsville, N.J.). Episcopalian. Died Jan. 28, 2007.

BURKERT, WALTER, classicist, educator, historian; b. Neuendettelsau, Germany, Feb. 2, 1931; arrived in Switzerland, 1969; s. Adolf and Luise (Grossmann) B.; m. Maria Bosch, Aug. 1, 1957; children: Reinhard, Andrea, Cornelius. PhD, U. Erlangen, Fed. Republic Germany, 1955; LLD, U. Toronto, 1988; PhD (hon.), U. Fribourg, Switzerland, 1989, Oxford U., Eng., 1996, U. Chgo., 2001. Dozent U. Erlangen, 1961-65; jr. fellow Ctr. Hellenic Studies, Washington, 1965-66; prof. Tech. U. Berlin, 1966-69, U. Zürich, Switzerland, 1969-96. Sather prof. U. Calif., Berkeley, 1977. Author: Lore and Science in Ancient Pythagoreanism, 1972, Homo Necans, 1983, Greek Religion, 1985, Greek Mystery Cults, 1987, The Orientalizing Revolution, 1992, Creation of the Sacred, 1996; contbr. numerous articles to scholarly publs. Decorated Orden Pour le Mérite; recipient C.F. Gauss medal Braunschweigische Wissenschaftliche Gesellschaft, 1982, Balzan prize, 1990, Ingersoll prize, 1992. Mem. Heidelberger Akademie der Wissenschaften, Bayerische Akademie der Wissenschaften, Oesterreichische Akademie der Wissenschaften, Berlin-Brandenburgische Akademie der Wissenschaften, Brit. Acad., Am. Philos. Soc., Am. Acad. Arts and Scis. Home: Uster, Switzerland. Died Mar. 11, 2015.

BURKHOLZ, ROBERT CONRAD, lawyer; b. Benton Harbor, Mich., Dec. 4, 1956; s. Roland James and Zoe Emma (Shaffer) B.; m. Barbara Lynn Graham, June 22, 1991; children: Michael Sean, Alexander James. BA, U. Mich., 1979; JD, U. Detroit, 1982. Bar: Mich. 1982, U.S. Dist. Ct. (we. dist.) Mich. 1983, U.S. Ct. Appeals (6th cir.) 1983, U.S. Supreme Ct. 1987. Atty. Bennett and LaParl P.C., Kalamazoo, Mich., 1982-88, Bennett, LaParl & Burkholz P.C., Kalamazoo, Mich., 1989, Plunkett & Cooney P.C., Kalamazoo, Mich., from 1989. Mediator, Kalamazoo County Bar Assn., 1987—, Berrien County (Mich.) Bar Assn., 1987—, Van Buren County (Mich.) Bar Assn., 1988—, Cass County (Mich.) Bar Assn., 1988—. Contbr. Guide to Mich. Statutes of Limitations, 1988. Vol. Irvin S. Gilmore Internat. Keyboard Festival, Kalamazoo, 1994. Mem. Kalamazoo County Bar Assn. (chmn. libr. com. 1985-86, v.p. young lawyers sect. 1986-87). Republican. Methodist. Avocations: sailing, golf. Home: Portage, Mich. Died May 24, 2007.

BURNES, DONALD EDWARD, minister; b. Forsyth, Mont., Sept. 18, 1926; s. Ira Calvin Burnes and Mary Ann (Bell) Rask; m. Hilda Jean Koch, June 5, 1952; children: Christel Jean, Donald Edward Jr., Linda Annalesa, Deborah Lynn. AS, Altus Jr. Coll., 1973; BS, U. Md., 1984; postgrad., Nazarene Theol. Sem., Kansas City, Mo., 1984, So. Nazarene U., 1985. Ordained to ministry Ch. of the Nazarene, 1973. Pastor Ch. of the Nazarene, various U.S. cities, 1959-81, missionary Japan, 1981-85, pastor Eldorado, Okla., 1985-86, Kaiserslautern, Fed. Republic Germany, 1986-90, evangelist Altus, Okla., from 1990, min. outreach, from 1991. Asst. missionary Ch. of the Nazarene, The Philippines, 1966-68; tchr. religion, Topeka, 1971-72; CLT dir. La. Dist. Ch. of the Nazarene, 1962-63. With USAF, 1945-74; Vietnam. Democrat. Died Mar. 2, 2007.

BURNETTE, JOE EDWARD, clergyman; b. Denison, Tex., Dec. 27, 1918; s. Joe Stevenson and Lula Viola (Sisk) B.; m. Betty Ann Huguley, Oct. 8, 1954; 1 child, Joann. BA, Carson-Newman Coll., 1942; MRE, Southwestern Sem., 1946. Ordained to ministry, Bapt. Ch. Minister of edn. Immanuel Bapt. Ch., Tulsa, 1946-50, First Bapt. Ch., Baton Rouge, 1950-52, Columbia, S.C., 1952-61; adminstr. Bapt. Home for Aging, Florence, S.C., 1961-63; assoc. pastor First Bapt. Ch., Charlotte, N.C., 1963-93, ret., 1993. Mem. Nat. Alumni Assn. Southwestern Sem. (pres. 1977), So. Bapt. Religious Edn. Assn. (pres. 1972), Gator Bowl Assn., Rotary (pres. Charlotte chpt. 1985-86; Paul Harris fellow). Democrat. Avocations: sports, travel, history, reading. Home: Charlotte, NC. Died Aug. 10, 2007.

BURNETTE, MARK C., librarian; b. Chgo., Sept. 2, 1947; s. Wells D. and Cora C. Burnette. BA, Brandeis U., Waltham, MA, 1969; MA in Medieval History, SUNY, Binghamton, NY, 1978; MLA, U. Wis., Madison, 1987. Actor, writer Caravan Theatre, Cambridge, Mass., 1970—71; grad. tchg. & rsch. asst. SUNY, Binghamton, 1972—78; paralegal Fried, Frank, Harris, Shriver & Jacobson, NYC, 1978—82, Brynelson, Herrick, Gehl & Bucaida, Madison, Wis., 1983—85; archivist Evanston Hist. Soc., Ill., 1990—96; archives & spl. collection libr. Nat. Louis U., Chgo., from 1998. Contbr. chapters to books. Mem. NE Evanston Hist. Dist. Assn., 1987. Mem.: ALA, Chgo. Area Archivists, Midwest Archives Conf., Soc. Am. Archivists. Died Nov. 28, 2012.

BURNS, LAWRENCE COLE, manufacturing executive; b. NYC, Oct. 15, 1944; s. John Edmond and Evelyn (Cole) B.; m. Susan Cotting Gildersleeve, Sept. 13, 1969; 1 child, Tracy Livingston. Diploma in Criminal Psychology, N.Y. Corrections, 1966; BA, Providence Coll., 1967. Div. supr. Allstate Ins., Harrison, N.Y., 1980-83; asst. sec. Gen Reinsurance, Greenwich, Conn., 1973-83; gen. ptnr. Landstadt Co., Greenwich, from 1980; pres. Deflect Away Corp., Greenwich, from 1983; chief exec. officer Weather-All, Inc., Westbrook, Madison, Conn., from 1983. Instr., emergency med. technician ARC, Greenwich, 1974-83. Republican. Roman Catholic. Avocations: reading, golf, tennis, flying. Home: Old Saybrook, Conn. Died Feb. 5, 2007.

BURNS, PAUL YODER, forester, educator; b. Tulsa, Okla., July 4, 1920; s. Paul Patchin and Mary Emily (Knowles) B.; m. Kathleen Iola Chase, Dec. 4, 1942; children: Virginia B. Belland, Margaret B. Feierabend, Nancy B. McNeill. BS, U. Tulsa, 1941; M in Forestry, Yale U., 1946, PhD, 1949. Asst., assoc. prof. U. Mo., Columbia, 1948-55; prof. forestry La. State U., Baton Rouge, 1955-86, prof. emeritus of forestry, from 1986. Dir. sch. forestry La. State U., Baton Rouge, 1955-76; commr. La. Forestry Commn., Baton Rouge, 1955-76. Editor: Forest Management in Plan & Practice, 1956, Southern Forest Soils, 1959; co-editor: Southern Forestry in Practice, 1977, Christmas Tree Production & Marketing, 1983. Pres. bd. dirs. La. State U. YMCA-YWCA, Baton Rouge, 1957-59; mem. La. Conf. Ch. Bd., Baton Rouge, 1967-73; pres. La. Coun. Human Rels., Baton Rouge, 1987-89; chair bd. dirs. The FISH Good Samaritans, Baton Rouge, 1996. Recipient Disting. Alumnus award U. Tulsa, 1974, Humanitarian award Baton Rouge Coun. Human Rels., 1984, Peacemaking award, Bienville House Ctr. for Peace, Baton Rouge, 1991, Vol. Activist award Baton Rouge, La., 1992, Brotherhood award Baton Rouge chpt. NCCJ, 1995. Fellow Soc. Am. Foresters, La. Soc. Am. Foresters (chmn. 1990, Disting Svc. to Forestry 1989), Phi Kappa Phi, Sigma Xi, Xi Sigma Pi. Presbyterian. Achievements include inductee Hall of Fame, La. State University School of Renewable Natural Resources. Avocations: tennis, piano. Home: Bristol, Tenn. Deceased.

BURRI, RENÉ, photographer, filmmaker; b. Zurich, Switzerland, Apr. 9, 1933; s. Rudolphe and Berta (Haas) B.; m. Rosellina H. Bischof, Dec. 18, 1963 (dec. 1986); children: Yasmine, Oliver. Diploma, Kunstgewerbeschule, Zurich. Free-lance photojournalist for various publs. including Life, Look, Paris, Match, Stern, Fortune, Epoca, Geo; pres. Europe Magnum Photos, Paris, NYC. One-man shows include Galene Form, 1965, Art Inst. Chgo., 1967, Galene Rencontre, Paris, 1971, Raffi Photo Gallery, N.Y.C., 1972, Galleria Diaframina, Milan, Italy, 1972, Mus. Folkwang, Essen, Germany, 1980, Galerie Kicken, Cologne, Germany, 1981, Stedelijk Mus., Amsterdam, The Netherlands, 1982, Kunsthaus, Zurich, 1984, Musée d'Art Modern, Paris, 1984; represented in permanent collections Mus. Modern Art, N.Y.C., Kunsthaus, Zurich, Art Inst. Chgo., Folkwang Mus., Essen, Bibliothèque Nationale, Paris, Internat. Ctr. Photography, Rochester, N.Y.; films include: Zurich Art School, 1953, The Two Faces of China, 1965, After the Six-Day War, 1967, Braccia Si-uomini no!, 1967, What's it all About, 1967, The Great Team, 1967, Indian Summer, 1971, French Wine, 1973. Recipient Internat. Film and TV Festival award, N.Y., 1967. Home: Zürich, Switzerland. Died Oct. 20, 2014.

BURROWS, EVA EVELYN (EVANGELINE EVELYN BURROWS), religious organization administrator; b. Newcastle, Australia, Sept. 15, 1929; d. Robert John and Ella Maria (Watson) B. BA, Queensland U., 1950; postgrad. cert. in edn., U. London, 1952; MEd, Sydney U., Australia, 1959; PhD (hon.), EWHA Woman's U., Seoul, Korea, 1988; LLD (hon.), Asbury Coll., U.S.A., 1988. Missionary educator Howard Inst., Zimbabwe, 1952-67; prin. Usher Inst., Zimbabwe, 1967-69; vice prin. Internat. Coll. for Officers, London, 1970-73, prin., 1974-75; leader Women's Social Services of Great Britain and Ireland, 1975-77; territorial comdr. Salvation Army, Sri Lanka, 1977-79, Scotland, 1979-82, Australia, 1982-86; gen. (internat. leader) The Salvation Army, London, 1986—93, ret., 1993. Named Officer Order of Australia, 1986. Mem.: Internat. Bible Soc. (bd. dirs.). Home: London, England. Died Mar. 20, 2015.

BURRY-STOCK, JUDITH ANNE, education educator; b. Cleve., July 19, 1942; d. Harry Alice (Bayne) Mesnick; m. June 1, 1968 (div. Apr. 1977); children: Steven, Christine, Heidi; m. Carl William Stock, July 1993. BS in English and Elem. Edn., Bowling Green State U., 1964; EdM in Literacy, SUNY, Buffalo, 1968; EdS in Ednl. Psychology, U. No. Colo., 1984, PhD in Applied Stats. and Rsch. Methods, 1984. Tchr. South Euclid-Lyndhurst Pub. Schs., Ohio, 1964-66, jr. high sch. reading cons. Ohio, 1966-67; instr. SUNY, Buffalo, 1967—69; ednl. cons., reading cons. Buffalo, 1969—78; internship program U. No. Colo., Greeley, 1978-81, rsch. asst., 1981-84; asst. prof., rsch. assoc. U. Kans., Lawrence, 1984—88; prof. program coord. stats., measurement, evaluation/assessment U. Ala., Tuscaloosa, 1988—2008, prof. emerita, 2008. Cons. on tchrs.and adminstr. assessment States of Colo., Kans., Fla., SD, Iowa, Tenn., Ala., Conn., NJ and internationally, also Ednl. Testing Svc.; conf. presenter, 1983-. Contbr. articles to profl. jours. Project dir. Ctr. for Rsch. on Ednl. Accountability & Tchr. Evaluation, 1990—95. Recipient Acad. Excellence award Capstone Coll. Edn., U. Ala., 1993, Recognition award Nat. Ednl. Testing Svc. and Nat. Coun. on Measurement and Edn., 2002; grantee tchr. evaluation Office Edn. Rsch. and Improvement, Kans. Dept. Edn., 1985-88, Rsch. grant, Traditional Ctr. Ednl. Statis., 1997, 2004, Dwight D. Eisenhower, 1993; fellow Ednl. Testing Svc., Student fellowship, 2003-05, Travel grant Nat. Rsch. Coun., 1995, VIP Humanitarian award, 2010, Lifetime Achievement award, 2010. Mem. APA, Am. Ednl. Rsch. Assn., Am. Evaluation Assn. Am. Statis. Assn., Nat. Coun. on Measurement in Edn., Phi Delta Phi, Phi Delta Kappa, Phi Lambda Theta. Unitarian Universalist. Avocations: reading, piano, music, art, yoga. Home: Conifer, Colo. Died May 29, 2015.

BURTON, ROBERT VAN, business development manager; b. Richmond, Ill., Sept. 21, 1924; m. Norma Jean Schroder, Jan. 3, 1947; children: David S., Marc N. BSME, U. Minn., 1948. Design engr. Honeywell, Inc., Mpls., 1948-54, sr. devel. engr., 1954-60, prin. devel. engr., 1960-67, project engr., bus. devel. mgr., 1967-81, bus. devel. mgr., 1981-87, Sundstrand-Sauer Co., Mpls., from 1987. Author tech. papers, articles, govt. contract reports; patentee in field of hydraulic, fluidic, electrohydraulic components. Bd. dirs. Mpls. YMCA, 1958-75. Served to 2d lt. inf. U.S. Army, 1943-45, ETO. Mem. Fluid Power Soc. Mem. United Ch. of Christ. Avocations: golf, fishing, bicycling, reading, writing. Home: Minneapolis, Minn. Died July 7, 2007.

BUSFIELD, ROGER MELVIL, JR., retired trade association executive, educator; b. Ft. Worth, Feb. 4, 1926; s. Roger Melvil and Julia Mabel (Clark) B.; m. Jean Wilson, Mar. 26, 1948 (div. Oct. 1960); children: Terry Jean, Roger Melvil III, Timothy Clark; m. Virginia Bailey, Dec. 1, 1962 (dec. July 1991); 1 child, Julia Lucille; m. Addie Howard Davis, June 17, 1995. Student, U. Tex., 1943, student, 1946; BA, Southwestern U., 1947, MA, 1948; PhD, Fla. State U., 1954. Asst. prof. Southwestern U., 1947-49; instr. U. Ala., 1949-50, Fla. State U., 1950-54; asst. prof. speech Mich. State U., 1954-60; editl. svcs. specialist Oldsmobile divsn. Gen. Motors Corp., Lansing, Mich., 1960; gen. publs. supr. Consumers Power Co., Jackson, Mich., 1960-61; assoc. dir. Mich. Hosp. Assn., Lansing, 1961-73; exec. dir. Ark. Hosp. Assn., Little Rock, 1973-81, pres., 1981-94, pres. emeritus, from 1994. Adj. prof. health svcs. mgmt. Webster U., 1979-97. Author: The Playwright's Art, 1958, Arabic transl., 1964, (with others) The Children's Theatre, 1960; editor Theatre Arts Bibliography, 1964; contbr. articles to profl. jours.; author profl. motion picture scenarios. Trustee Ctrl. Mich. U., 1967-73, chmn., 1970; mem. Mich. Gov.'s Commn. on Higher Edn., 1972-74; mem. Ark. Gov.'s Emergency Med. Svcs. Adv. Coun., 1975-94, chmn., 1978-84; mem. Ark. Gov.'s Task Force on Rural Hosps., 1988-89, Ark. Dept. of Health Long Range Planning Com., 1988-89; chmn. AIDS adv. com. Ark. Dept. Health, 1990-97; mem. Ark. Gov.'s Task Force Health Care Reform, 1993-96; chmn. Health Data Task Force, Ark. Resources Comm., 1994-95; mem. adv. bd. Ark. Pediat. Facility, 1995-96. Served with USMC, 1943-46. Named Tex. Outstanding Author, Theta Sigma Phi, 1958; recipient Disting. Alumnus award Southwestern U., 1971, Senate-House Concurrent Resolution of Tribute, Mich. Legis., 1973, Bd. Trustees award Am. Hosp. Assn., 1994, Merit award Ark. Hosp. Assn., 1994. Mem. Am. Soc. Assn. Execs., Ark. Soc. Assn. Execs. (pres. 1981-82), Pub. Rels. Assn. Mich. (pres. 1966), Speech Comm. Assn., Am. Coll. Health Care Execs., State Hosp. Assn. Exec. Forum (sec., treas. 1989, pres. 1991), Am. Hosp. Assn. (coun. legis. 1975-77, coun. allied and govtl. rels. 1983-86), San Gabriel Writers League (pres. 2000-01), Rotary (Little Rock). Methodist. Home: Georgetown, Tex. Died May 4, 2015.

BUSH, JAMES WILLIAM, JR., oil company executive; b. Summerfield, La., July 21, 1931; s. James William and Pearl Lillian (Revel) B.; m. Florence Lorraine, Dec. 30, 1952; children: James R., Lillian Lorene, Gerald Wayne. BS, Roosevelt U., 1973; MBA, DePaul U., 1977. CPA, Ill, Tex.; cert. mgmt. acct. Mgr. Amoco Corp., Chgo., 1963-78, dir. results mgmt., 1978-83; controller Amoco Pipeline Co., Oak Brook, Ill., 1983-92; instr. Coll. of DuPage, Glen Ellyn, Ill., 1978-92, Univ. North Tex., San Antonio, from 1992. Bd. dirs. Wyco Pipeline, Chgo., Chicap Pipeline, Van, Tex.; instr. Ill. Benedictine U., Lisle, 1993-94. Bd. dirs. Calvary Temple, Naperville, Ill., 1980-92. Mem. Assn. Oil Pipelines (chmn. taxes 1988—), Ill. CPA Soc., Am. Acctg. Assn., Inst. Mgmt. Acctg. (cert. mgmt. acct.). Republican. Avocations: golf, fishing, geneaology. Died Feb. 14, 2007.

BUSH, MARJORIE ANN, broadcasting executive; b. Cleve., Sept. 13, 1925; d. Frank Victor and Helen (Stepnik) Dabkowski; m. John S. Bush, Nov. 13, 1948; children: Cynthia Bush Haynes, Victoria Bush Humpal. Grad. high sch., Cleve. Sec. Cleve. Rec. Co., 1943-50; with Sta. WIXY (formerly Sta. WDOK), Cleve., 1950-76, pub. svc. dir., 1969-74, music dir., 1970-76; adminstrv. asst., placement dir. Ohio Sch. Broadcast Technique, Cleve., 1976-90. Music coord. Globetrotter Communications, Inc., 1975—; sec. Ednl. Broadcast Svcs., Inc., 1976—. Bd. dirs. Bill Gavin Conv. ans Awards Com., Bill Gavin Report in San Francisco, 1974. Recipient Kal Rudman's Froday Morning Quarterback in Phila., 1975, Bobby Poe's Music Survey in Washington, 1975. Roman Catholic. Home: Cleveland, Ohio. Died Mar. 29, 2007.

BUSH, STANLEY GILTNER, secondary school educator; b. Kansas City, Mo., Nov. 4, 1928; s. Dean Thomas and Sallie Giltner (Hoagland) B.; m. Barbara Snow Adams, May 23, 1975 (dec. Mar. 1994); stepchildren: Deborah Gayle Duclon, Douglas Bruce Adams. BA, U. Colo., 1949, MA, 1959, postgrad., 1971, U. Denver, 1980, 85, 90. Tchr. Gering (Nebr.) Pub. Schs., 1949-51, 54-57, Littleton (Colo.) Pub. Schs., 1957-91. Emergency plan dir. City of Littleton, 1961—; safety officer Littleton Pub. Schs., 1968—; founder, chief Arapahoe Rescue Patrol, Inc., Littleton, 1957-92, search mission coord., 1975—; pres. Arapahoe Rescue Patrol, Inc., 1957—, Expedition, Inc., Littleton, 1973-2004; owner Emergency Rsch. Cons., 1990—. Contbr. chpts. to Boy Scout Field Book, 1984; co-author: Managing Search Function, 1987; contbr. articles to profl. jours. Safety advisor South Suburban Parks Dist., Littleton, 1985—; advisor ARC, Littleton, 1987—, Emergency Planning Com., Arapahoe County, Colo., 1987—; coord. search and rescue Office of Gov., Colo., 1978-82; state judge Odyssey of the Mind, 1996-97; steering com. on homeland security Metro Denver Mayors Office, 2002—; grand marshal Littleton We. Welcome Week, 2004. Sgt. U.S. Army, 1951-54. Shell Oil Co. fellow, 1964; recipient Silver Beaver award Boy Scouts Am., 1966, Vigil Order of Arrow, 1966, Award of excellence Masons, 1990, Service to Mankind award Arapahoe Sertoma, 1999, Dry Creek Sertoma, Ctrl. Colo. Dist., 2004. Mem. Nat. Assn. for Search and Rescue (life, Hall Foss award 1978), Colo. Search and Rescue Bd., NEA (life). Methodist. Avocations: mountain climbing, wilderness emergency care, emergency services. Home: Centennial, Colo. Died Apr. 30, 2007.

BUTLER, ELIZABETH MARIE, critical care nurse; b. Chester, Pa., July 23, 1955; d. Joseph J. and Elizabeth R. (O'Brien) Ciliberto; children: Jeffrey, Joshua. BSN, Our Lady of Angels, Aston, Pa., 1977. RN, Pa., Tex. Staff nurse Thomas Jefferson U. Hosp., Phila.; nurse mgr. critical care unit Humana Hosp., San Antonio. With U.S. Army; capt. USAF, 1978-84. Mem. AACN. Home: San Antonio, Tex. Died Mar. 13, 2007.

BUTLER-NALIN, KAY, secondary school educator; b. Kalamazoo, Mich., Nov. 25, 1948; d. Donald Thomas and Barbara (Little) Butler; m. Paul M. Nalin, Aug. 28, 1971; children: Alethea Lauren, Amelia Meagan. BA, Ctrl. Coll., 1971; MA, Stanford U., 1978, PhD, 1985. Compensatory reading project facilitator Ednl. Testing Svc., Princeton, 1972-78; assoc. rschr. Stanford (Calif.) U., 1985-88; asst. prof. composition Coll. San Mateo, Calif., 1988-90; asst. prof. English edn. U. No. Iowa, Cedar Falls, 1990—97, 1999—2003; rschr. grad. sch. edn. U. Calif., Santa Barbara, 1999—2001. Rschr. The Pangaea Network. Author poems, revs.; contbr. articles to profl. jours. and chpts. to books. Avocations: swimming, gardening, moonlore, technology. Died Nov. 13, 2006.

BUTTRICK, HAROLD, architect; b. Bryn Mawr, Pa., Jan. 2, 1931; s. Charles Edgar and Constance (La Boiteaux) B.; m. Ann Octavia White, Sept. 3, 1955; children: John Ward, Jerome Chanler, Mary Constance, Sarah Elizabeth, Catherine. Student, The Sorbonne, Paris, 1950-51; AB, Harvard U., 1953, MArch, 1959. Cert. NCRB. With Harold Buttrick & Assocs., NYC, 1963-75; prin. Smotrich Platt & Buttrick, NYC, 1975-76, Buttrick White & Burtis, NYC, 1976-97, Murphy Burnham & Buttrick, NYC, from 1998. Prin archtl. works include Corpus Christi Monastery, Nairobi, Kenya, 1967, Green Vale Sch., Iselin Ctr., Glen Head, N.Y., 1971, Trans World Airlines 747 Hangar, John F. Kennedy Airport, 1971, Carter Giraffe House, Bronx Zoo, 1981, 42 Tower Records Stores, 1982-94, St. Thomas Choir Sch., N.Y.C., 1987, Central Park projects, Loeb Boathouse, 1986, Ballplayers Refreshment Stand, 1990, restoration of the Pulitzer Fountain and Grand Army Plz., 1990, The Charles A. Dana Discovery Ctr., 1993, Performance Stage, Bushnell Park, Hartford, Conn., 1995, Battery Park City Authority Offices, 1996, Trinity Mid. Sch., NYC, 1998, St. Bartholomew's Ch., Master Plan, NYC, 2004. Bd. dirs. N.Y. Soc. Libr., 1989-93. Recipient Preservation League of N.Y. State awards, 1990-91, 96, City Club of N.Y. Bard awards Loeb Boathouse, 1986, St. Thomas Choir Sch., 1990, Ballplayers Refreshment Stand, 1992, St. Patrick's Cathedral Master Plan, 2006. Fellow AIA (Brick in Architecture award 1991, 95), NY State Assn. Archs.; mem. Century Assn., New Yorkers for Parks. Home: New York, NY. Deceased.

BUTTRICK, JOHN ARTHUR, economist, educator; b. Rutland, Vt., Sept. 12, 1919; s. George Arthur and Agnes (Gardner) B.; m. Ann Tatlow, July 24, 1958; children—Peter M., Hilary J., Michael S. BS, Haverford Coll., 1941; MA, Yale, 1947, PhD, 1950. Asst. prof. econs. Northwestern U., 1949-53; faculty U. Minn., Mpls., 1953-75, prof. econs., 1958-75, chmn. dept., 1960-63, dir. grad. studies, 1967-69; prof. econs. York U., Toronto, Ont., Can., from 1975, dir. grad. studies, 1979-83. Coord. Cerlac Program, 1986-88, 92—; vis. prof. U. Calif., Berkeley, 1957-59, U. Tokyo, 1963-64, U. de los Andes, Colombia, 1964-66, H.U.S.T., Wuhan, People's Republic China, 1990-91, U. West Indies, 1992, North-South U. Bangladesh, 1994; summer vis. prof. Vanderbilt U., Stanford, Harvard, Singapore; vis. lectr., Govt. Pakistan, 1961. Co-author: Economic Development, 1954, Spanish and Japanese edit., 1958, Theories of Economic Growth, 1960, Spanish edit., 1964, Consumer, Producer and Social Choice, 1968, Who Goes to University from Toronto, 1977, Educational Problems and Some Policy Options, 1977, Two Views of Aid and Development, 1979, Economic Discrimination in Toronto, 1987. Sec., treas. Black Creek Found., Blumenfeld Found.; mem. Planning Adv. Com. City of Toronto. Ont. Council Econs. fellow, 1976-77; fellow Fund for Advancement Edn., 1952-53; Ford Found. fellow, 1959-60; Fulbright fellow Japan, Singapore, 1963-64; research fellow NYU and Columbia U., 1983-84 Mem. Am. Econ. Assn., Can. Economic Assn., Can. Civil Liberties Assn., Sci. for Peace. Home: Toronto, Canada. Died July 15, 2007.

BYERS, WALTER, former athletic association executive; b. Kansas City, Mo., Mar. 13, 1922; s. Ward and Lucille (Hebard) B.; children: Ward, Ellen, Frederick. Student, Rice U., 1939-40, U. Iowa, 1940-43. News reporter United Press Assn. (later U.P.I.), St. Louis, 1944, U.P.I., Madison, Wis., 1945, sports editor Chgo., 1945, asst. sports editor NYC, 1946-47; also fgn. sports editor; dir. Big Ten Conf. Service Bur., Chgo., 1947-51; exec. asst. NCAA, Chgo., 1947-51, exec. dir., 1951-52, Kansas City, Mo., 1952-73, Shawnee Mission, Kans., 1973-87, exec. dir. emeritus, 1988-90. Pres. Byers Seven Cross Ranch, Inc., Emmett, Kans., 1974—, Ironwood Seven Cross Ranch, Inc., Hatfield, Mo., 1992-2002, Volland, Kans., 2002-06, Byers Land and Cattle Co., Emmett, 1996—; mgr. Byers Ranches, Limited Liability Co., Emmett, 1997-. With M.C. AUS, 1944. Named to Nat. Collegiate Basketball Hall of Fame, 2009. Died May 26, 2015.

BYRD, BENJAMIN FRANKLIN, JR., surgeon, educator; b. Nashville, May 18, 1918; s. Benjamin Franklin and Ida (Brister) B.; m. Allison Caldwell, Feb. 6, 1950; children: Benjamin Franklin, Barney Duncan, Damon Winston, Andrew Wayne, Evelyn Hope, John W. Thomas. AB, Vanderbilt U., 1938, MD, 1941. Intern, Nashville Gen. Hosp., 1941-42, asst. resident, 1942, Vanderbilt U. Hosp., 1945-47, resident, 1947-48; practice medicine, specializing in surgery Nashville, from 1948; chief surgery St. Thomas Hosp., 1964-70, pres. staff, 1977-79; mem. staff Baptist Hosp.; instr. surgery Vanderbilt U., Nashville, 1947-54, assoc. clin. prof. surgery, 1954-71, clin. prof. surgery, 1971-99; chmn. bd. of overseers Vanderbilt U. Cancer Ctr., from 1993; assoc. clin. prof. surgery Meharry Med. Coll., Nashville, 1951-69, prof. clin. surgery, from 1969, clin. prof. surgery emeritus, from 1999. Dir., mem. trust bd. Commerce Union Bank, 1974-80, 82-91; dir. NLT Corp. Pres. Tenn. divsn. Am. Cancer Soc., 1963, nat. bd. dirs., 1965—, nat. exec. com., 1970-80, chmn. med. and sci. exec. com., 1973—&, nat. pres., 1975-76; pres., mem. exec. bd. Tenn. Bot. Gardens and Fine Arts Ctr., 1971-73; trustee Sr. Citizens, Hermitage Assn.; bd. dirs. Cumberland Mus., Univ. Sch., 1985-91. Lt. col. M.C., AUS, 1941-45. Decorated Bronze Star with 2 oak leaf clusters, Silver Star, Purple Heart; named Nashvillian of Yr., Nashville Kiwanis, 1986; recipient Human Rels. award Nat. Fellow ACS (gov. 1973-79, chmn. commn. on cancer); mem. Am. Surg. Assn., So. Surg. Assn., Nashville Surg. Soc. (pres. 1962-63), Soc. Surg. Oncology, Tenn. Med. Assn. (mem. council, Disting. Service award, Physician of Yr. 1986), So. Med. Assn. (mem. council), Société International de Chirurgie, Southeastern Surg. Congress (mem. council, pres. 1968-69, Disting. Service award 1977), Nashville Acad. Medicine (pres. 1980, chmn. 1981), Nashville C. of C. (bd. govs. 1967-70, 82—, pres. 1985), Vanderbilt U. Med. Alumni (pres. 1979-81), Sigma Xi. Clubs: Nashville Exchange. Home: Nashville, Tenn. Died Dec. 7, 2006.

BYRNE, ARTHUR DILLARD, lawyer; b. Gainesboro, Tenn., Aug. 27, 1918; s. Arthur D. and Esther (Neeley) B.; m. Jean Currier White, Sept. 26, 1942; children: Jean Laurie, Ann Terrell. BA, Maryville Coll., 1939; JD, U. Tenn., 1942; cert. in meteorology, USAF Meteorol. Sch., Chanute Field, Ill., 1943; grad. as intelligence officer, Air Combat Intelligence Sch., Harrisburg, Pa., 1944. Bar: Tenn. 1942, U.S. Dist. Ct. (ea. dist.) Tenn. 1942, U.S. Ct. Appeals (6th cir.) 1942. Assoc. Poore, Cox, Baker, Ray & Byrne and predecessor firms, Knoxville, Tenn., 1942-62, ptnr., from 1962. Chmn. standing com. on admission to practice U.S. Dist. Ct. (no. dist.) Tenn., 1987—. Editor U. Tenn. Law Rev., 1941-42; contbr. chpt.: Fetal-Maternal Medicine, 1989; contbr. articles to profl. jours. Active Tenn. Hist. Soc.; bd. dirs. Knoxville Symphony Soc., 1963-80, pres., 1965-66. Capt. USAF, 1943-46, PTO. Fellow Am. Coll. Trial Lawyers, Am. Coll. Legal Medicine, Internat. Acad. Trial Lawyers (adminstrn. justice com.); mem. ABA, Tenn. Bar Assn. (v.p. 1964-65), Knoxville Bar Assn. (pres. 1962-63), Fedn. Ins. Counsel (chair publicity com.), Inns of Ct. (master of bench 1989—), Order of Coif, Masons, Phi Delta Phi, Phi Kappa Phi. Avocations: reading, sports, woodworking, painting. Home: Maryville, Tenn. Died June 26, 2007.

BYRNE, JANE MARGARET BURKE, former mayor; b. Chgo., May 24, 1934; d. William and Katherine (Nolan) Burke; m. William Patrick Byrne, Dec. 31, 1956 (dec. May 1959); 1 child, Katherine; m. Jay McMullen, Mar. 17, 1978 (dec. Mar. 18, 1992). BA, Barat Coll. With Chgo. Anti-Poverty Agy., 1964—68; commr. Chgo. Dept. Consumers Sales, Weights and Measures, 1968—77; mayor City of Chgo., 1979—83. Author: My Chicago, 1992. Sec.-treas. Chgo. Hdqs. John F. Kennedy Presdl. Campaign, 1960; chmn. resolutions com. Democratic Nat. Com.; co-chmn. Cook County Democratic Ctrl. Com., 1975—76. Democrat. Roman Catholic. Achievements include being the first female to be elected mayor of Chicago, 1979. Home: Chicago, Ill. Died Nov. 14, 2014.

BYRNE, JOHANNA ALBERTA, copyeditor; b. Voorburg, The Netherlands, Sept. 21, 1947; came to the U.S., 1970; d. Johannes Franciscus Andriessen and Jansje Bonefaas; m. Dennis John Byrne, Sept. 30, 1995. MA in Libr. and Info. Sci., Rosary Coll., 1991. Venture partnerships coord. Am. Health Care Sys., Lincolnshire, Ill., 1984-85; pres. US/Access, Inc., Deerfield, Ill., 1985-91; dir. rsch. exec. search Ernst & Young, Chgo., 1990-91; rsch. mgr. Real Estate Analysis Corp., Chgo., 1991-94; owner Info-Pros, Mineral Point, Wis., 1994-99; chief copyeditor Lands' End Inc., Dodgeville, Wis., from 1999. Author of numerous rsch. studies. Mem. Dictionary Soc. N.Am., Mineral Point C. of C. (chair econ. devel. 1995-98, sec./bd. mem. 1998—2000, Vol. of Yr. 1998). Avocations: quilting, gardening, reading. Home: Mineral Point, Wis. Died Jan. 21, 2007.

CADOW, WILLIAM SCHUYLER, JR., engineering company executive; b. Iowa City, Nov. 17, 1936; s. William Schuyler and Mary Elizabeth (Aust) C.; m. Alice Freeze, July 10, 1964 (div. Sept. 1986); children: William S. III, Lani C. BBA, U. Miss., 1959; MSA, George Washington U., 1980. Registered profl. engr., Calif. Commd. ensign USN, 1959, advanced through grades to capt., 1980, comdg. officer EOD Tech. Ctr. Indian Head, Md., 1976-79, comdr. explosive ordnance disposal group Ewa Beach, Hawaii, 1980-83, dir. ammo systems Naval Sea Systems Command Washington, 1983-86, ret., 1986; program mgr. Hercules Aerospace Co., Washington, 1986-95; v.p. tech. Lectro-Tech., Inc., Arlington, Va., from 1995. Decorated Legion of Merit. Mem. Inst. Indsl. Engrs., Internat. Assn. Bomb Tech. and Investigators, Navy League of the U.S. Presbyterian. Avocations: scuba diving, sailing. Died Jan. 26, 2007.

CAHILL, HARRY AMORY, diplomat, educator; b. NYC, Jan. 10, 1930; s. Harry Amory and Elaine Olga (Loumena) C.; m. Angelica Margarita Ravazzoli, Dec. 12, 1956; children— Alan, Daniel, Sylvia, Irene, Madeleine, Steven BA, Manhattan Coll., NYC, 1951; postgrad., Johns Hopkins U., 1964-65; MS, George Washington U., Washington, 1972. Sales exec. Johns Manville Corp., NY, 1954-56; fgn. service officer U.S. Dept. of State, Washington, 1956-59, Oslo, 1959-61, Warsaw, 1961-64, Belgrade, Yugoslavia, 1965-68, Montevideo, Uruguay, 1968-71, Lagos, Nigeria, 1975-78, Colombo, Sri Lanka, 1979-81; dir. comml. service U.S. Dept. Commerce, 1982-83; U.S. consul gen. Dept. of State, Bombay, 1983-87; U.S. Mission to UN, dep. U.S. rep. UN Econ. and Social Coun., NYC, 1987-89; pres. Amory Assoc., Inc., McLean, Va., from 1990, World of Film Found., NYC. Prof. Pepperdine U., from 1992, Georgetown U., 1995; cons. U.S. Dept. State, from 1991, U.S. Dept. Def., from 1999. Author: The China Trade and U.S. Tariffs, 1973. Pres. Hinduja Found., NYC, 1993—2002. Woodrow Wilson Nat. Fellowship found. fellow, 1990-93. Mem. Am. Fgn. Svc. Assn. Roman Catholic. Avocation: photography. Died Apr. 8, 2015.

CAHN, ROBERT WOLFGANG, physical metallurgist; b. Fuerth, Germany, Sept. 9, 1924; s. Martin Max and Else (Heinemann) C.; m. Patricia Lois Hanson, Aug. 9, 1947; children: Martin, Andrew, Judith, Alison. BA, Cambridge U., Eng., 1945, PhD, 1950, ScD, 1963. Sr. rsch. officer Atomic Energy Rsch., Harwell, Eng., 1947-51; lectr., sr. lectr., reader Birmingham (Eng.) U., 1951-62; prof. material tech. Univ. Coll. North Wales, Bangor, 1962—64; prof. material sci. Sussex U., Brighton, 1965-81; prof. metallurgy U. Paris-Sud, Orsay, 1981-83; vis. rsch. fellow GE, Schenectady, N.Y., 1985; Fairchild disting. fellow Calif. Inst. Tech., Pasadena, 1985-86; disting. rsch. fellow dept. materials sci. Cambridge U., from 1986. Material sci. corr. Nature jour., 1967—. Author: The Coming of Materials Science, 2001, The Art of Belonging--A Memoir, 2005; series editor-in-chief: Materials Science and Technology, 1987-99; editor: Physical Metallurgy, 1965, 4th edit., 1996; exec. editor Advances in Materials Sci. and Engring., 1986-92; sr. editor Cambridge Solid State Sci., 1972-92; editor Pergamon Materials Series, 1993—; joint editor-in-chief Ency. of Materials, 1998-2001; contbr. articles to profl. jours. Recipient A.A. Griffith medal, Materials Sci. Club, London, 1983, Medaille Ste. Claire-Deville, French Metall. Soc., 1975, Heyn medal German Materials Soc., 1996, Luigi Losana Gold medal Assn. Italiana di Metallurgia, 2001, Acta Materialia Gold medal, 2002; recipient numerous research grants. Fellow Royal Soc. of London, Am. Soc. Materials Internat., Inst. Metals London (v.p. 1975-77), Inst. Physics London, Indian Nat. Sci. Acad. (fgn.), The Minerals, Metals and Materials Soc.; mem. Acad. Arts and Scis. Göttingen, Royal Acad. Exact Sci. (Madrid), Chinese Acad. Sci., Indian Nat. Sci. Acad. Conservative. Jewish. Avocations: music, mountain climbing, alpine plants, theater, literature. Home: Cambridge, England. Died Apr. 9, 2007.

CALAMARI, ANDREW M., lawyer; b. NYC, Jan. 23, 1918; s. Frank and Caterina Calamari; m. Madeline Redmond, Aug. 1, 1959; children: Andrew, Michael, Joseph, David. BA, CCNY, 1939; JD cum laude, Fordham U., 1942. Bar: N.Y. 1942, U.S. Dist. Ct. (so. dist.) N.Y. 1948, U.S. Dist. Ct. (ea. dist.) N.Y. 1950, U.S. Ct. Appeals (2d cir.) 1964, U.S. Supreme Ct. 1973. Assoc. McLanahan, Merritt & Ingraham, NYC, 1946-59, Buell, Clifton & Turner, NYC, 1959-68; ptnr. Manning, Nakasian & Carey, NYC, 1968-83, Calamari & Calamari, NYC, from 1983. Sgt. U.S. Army, 1943-46. Mem. ABA, N.Y. State Bar Assn., Am. Arbitration Assn. (nat. panel arbitrators 1957—), Fordham Law Rev. Assn. (editorial bd. 1941-42), KC. Democrat. Roman Catholic. Home: Bronx, NY. Died Jan. 2, 2007.

CALDERON, JOSEPH, lawyer; b. NYC, Dec. 24, 1915; m. Dorothy Calderon, Nov. 28, 1940; children: Peter J., Phyllis Jacobson. BA, U. S.C., 1936; LLB, Columbia U., 1940. Bar: N.Y. 1941, U.S. Dist. Ct. (so. dist.) N.Y. 1947, U.S. Dist. Ct. (ea. dist.) N.Y. 1948, U.S. Ct. Appeals (2d cir.) 1951, U.S. Supreme Ct. 1958. Counsel Deutsch, Klagsbrun & Blasband (formerly Linden & Deutsch), from 1970. Counsel Internat. Radio and TV Found., Inc., N.Y.C., 1965-95; arbitrator Am. Arbitration Assn., 1965—. Sgt. U.S. Army, 1943-45, ETO. Home: Roslyn Heights, NY. Died Dec. 18, 2006.

CALHOUN, LARRY DARRYL, art educator; b. Revere, Mo., Oct. 9, 1937; s. Adren Kieth and Neva Isabel (Parker) C.; m. Marilyn Gail Walker, June 9, 1959; children: Eric, Rachael, Robin. BA in Art, Iowa Wesleyan, 1959; MA in Art, U. Iowa, 1961. Art instr. Westmar Coll., LeMars, Iowa, 1961-63; assoc. prof. art Millikin U., Decatur, Ill., 1963-70; assoc. prof. ceramics U. Akron, 1970-76; artist in residence Ill. Arts Coun., Decatur, Ill., 1977; chair, dept. art MacMurray Coll., Jacksonville, from 1978. Owner Village Arts, Jacksonville, 1978—; painter, 1989—; ceramist pottery and sculpture, 1961-89. Woodrow Wilson fellowship U. Iowa, 1960-61. Mem. NAACP, AAUP (pres. 1992—). Avocations: tennis, canoeing, exploring. Home: Jacksonville, Ill. Died Mar. 28, 2015.

CALLAHAN, JOHN MARTIN, theater educator; b. St. Louis, Oct. 19, 1943; s. Andrew Joseph and Dorothy (Rednour) C.; m. Patricia Ann Pisel, Aug. 26, 1967; 1 child, Kerry Kathleen. AB in Theatre magna cum laude, St. Louis U., 1965; MA in Theatre, So. Ill. U., 1967; PhD in Am. Theatre History, Kent State U., 1974. Instr. Coll. of Steubenville (Ohio), 1967-69, St. Louis Community Coll. at Meramac, 1971-74; prodn. coord. Communico, Inc., Fenton, Mo., 1974-75; assoc. prof. U. Tex., Tyler, 1975-80; prof. Kutztown (Pa.) U., from 1980. Dir. more than 40 full-length plays in ednl. theatre Coll. of Steubenville, St. Louis Community Coll. at Meramac, U. Tex., Tyler, Kutztown U. Author: Barron's Simplified Approach to Eugene O'Neill: Mourning Becomes Electra, 1970; contbr. articles to profl. jours. Emergency med. technician, 1985-88, Paramedic Dept. of Health Div. of Emergency Health Svcs., Commonwealth of Pa., 1988—. 2d lt. USAF, 1965. Mem. Actors' Equity Assn., Am. Soc. for Theatre Rsch., Soc. Am. Fight Dirs. Democrat. Roman Catholic. Avocations: paramedic work, reading theatre biographies. Home: Fleetwood, Pa. Died Aug. 24, 2007.

CALLAHAN, SUSAN LANE, mathematics professor; b. Kansas City, Aug. 27, 1956; d. Carter and Dora (Lane) Callahan. BS in Math., U. Mo.-Rolla, 1978, MS in Applied Math., 1980. Grad. tchg. asst. U. Mo., Rolla, 1978—80; faculty mem. math. Cottey Coll., Nevada, Mo., 1980—85, asst. prof. math., 1985—93, assoc. prof. math., from 1993, divsn. chair, from 2007. Recipient Gov.'s award for Excellence in Tchg., Coordinating Bd. Higher Edn., Mo., 2002. Mem.: Assn. Women in Math., Nat. Coun. Tchrs. Math., Am. Math. Assn. Two-Year Colls., Math. Assn. Am. (Mo. sect. sec./treas. 1998—2004, chair of com. to revise the Bylaws 2009—11, bd. govs. from 2012), Soroptimist Internat. Club (treas., v.p., pres., dir. 1998—2004, dir. 2007—08, treas. 2011—13, Nevada, Mo.), Phi Kappa Phi. Avocations: horseback riding, playing clarinet, walking, hiking. Home: Nevada, Mo. Died Apr. 20, 2015.

CALVIN, DONALD LEE, stock exchange official; b. Mount Olive, Ill., Nov. 10, 1931; m. Louise Elinor Peterson, Mar. 28, 1952; children: Jane Calvin Palasek, Sally Anne Calvin Salvaterra. Student, Ea. Ill. U., 1950-54, LLD, 1990; LLB, U. Ill., 1956. Bar: Ill. 1956. Atty. Office Sec. of State of Ill., Springfield, 1957-58, securities commr., 1959-62; syndicate mgr. A.C. Allyn & Co., Chgo., 1962-63; atty. F.I. DuPont & Co., Chgo., 1963-64; exec. asst. civic and govt. affairs NY Stock Exch., NYC, 1964-65, v.p., 1966-77, sr. v.p., 1977—86, exec. v.p., 1986—87; chmn. Internat. Bus. Enterprises, Inc., NYC, from 1987. Advisor to chmn. Chgo. Bd. Options Exch., Geneva Stock Exch., 1987—96; advisor to pres. Fedn. Internat. des Bourses de Valeurs, Paris, 1989—98, Kuala Lampur Stock Exch., 1991—2000, São Paulo (Brazil) Stock Exch., 1993—98, Stock Exch. of Hong Kong, 1995—98, Egypt: An Exch., from 1997, Nat. Stock Exch., Chgo., from 2002; chmn. and CEO Internat. Stock Exch. Execs. Emeriti, from 2008. With USMCR, 1951-56. Mem. ABA, Internat. Bar Assn., Ill. State Bar Assn., Chgo. Bar Assn., Am. Law Inst., Met. Club NYC, Manhasset Bay Yacht Club (Port Washington, NY). Home: Shelter Island Heights, NY. Died July 9, 2015.

CAMBEL, ALI B., engineering educator; b. Merano, Italy, Apr. 9, 1923; came to U.S., 1943, naturalized, 1951; s. H. Cemil and Remziye (Hakki) C.; m. Marion dePaar, Dec. 20, 1946; children: Metin, Emel, Leyla, Sarah. BS, Robert Coll., Istanbul, Turkey, 1942; postgrad., U. Istanbul, 1942-43, MIT, 1943-45; MS, Calif. Inst. Tech., 1946; PhD, U. Iowa, 1950. Registered profl. engr. Instr. U. Iowa, 1947-50, asst. prof., 1950-53; from assoc. prof. to prof. mech. engring. Northwestern U., 1953-61, Walter P. Murphy disting. prof., 1961-68, dir. gas dynamics lab., 1955-66, chmn. dept. mech. engring. and astronautical scis., 1957-66; from dir. research and engring. support divsn. to v.p. rsch. IDA, 1966-68; dean Coll. Engring., Wayne State U., Detroit, 1968-70; exec. v.p. for acad. affairs Wayne State U., 1970-72; v.p., dir. system rsch. divsn. Gen. Rsch. Corp., 1972-74; dep. asst. dir. for sci. and tech. NSF, 1974-75; prof. engring. & applied sci. George Washington U., Washington, 1975-88, prof. emeritus, 1988—2014, chmn. dept. civil, mech. and environ. engring., 1978-80, dir. energy programs, 1976-88. Cons. in field; staff dir. President's Interdeptl. Energy Study, 1963-64; engring. scis. advisory com. USAF Office Sci. Research, 1961-63; mem. Commn. Engring. Edn., 1966-68, Army Sci. Advisory Panel, 1966-72; nat. lectr. Sigma Xi, 1961-62. Author: Plasma Physics and Magnetofluidmechanics, 1963, Applied Chaos Theory: A Paradigm for Complexity, 1993; co-author: Gas Dynamics, 1958, Real Gases, 1963, Plasma Physics, 1965; co-editor: Transport Properties in Gases, 1958, The Dynamics of Conducting Gases, 1960, Magnetohydrodynamics, 1962, Second Law Analysis of Energy Devices and Processes, 1980, Dissipative Structures in Integrated Systems, 1989; co-editor AIAA Jour., Jet Propulsion, 1955-60, Energy, The Internat. Jour., 1975-95; mem. editl. bd. Energy, Environment, Economics, 1991; contbr. articles to profl. jours. Bd. dirs. YMCA. Recipient citation for solar satellite power system evaluation US Dept. Energy/NASA, 1981, Immigrant Achievement award Immigration Law Found., 2005; cert. for patriotic service Sec. of Army; award for excellence NSF/RANN; award for contbns. to sci. and edn. U.S. Immigrants League.; Washburn scholar, 1938. Fellow AIAA (J. Edward Pendray award 1959, nat. dir.), 1996, American Soc. Engring. Edn. (Curtis McGraw award 1960, George Westinghouse award 1966, chmn. engring. and public policy divsn. 1986-87), ASME (founding chmn. energy systems analysis tech. com. 1980-82), American Immigration Law Found. (Achievement award 2005), Cosmos Club (Washington), Sigma Xi, Pi Tau Sigma, Tau Beta Pi. Mem. Soc. Of Friends. Home: Mc Lean, Va. Died Oct. 7, 2014.

CAMERON, DWAYNE, secondary school educator; b. Middleboro, Mass., Feb. 23, 1947; m. Regina Pulminskas, Aug. 22, 1970; children: Erik, Allison, Jessica, Cameron. BA in Math., Ottawa U., Kans., 1969; MS in Tchg. in Math., U. N.H., 1979. Math. tchr. Old Rochester Regional Sch. Dist., Mattapoisett, Mass., from 1969. Math team coach Old Rochester Regional Sch. Dist., 1976—, chess team coach, 1983-86, 94, Varsity golf coach, 1972-85. Recipient Presdl. Excellence in Tchg. Math award NSF, 1989; Tandy Tech. scholar Tandy, Inc., 1991; Woodrow Wilson fellow Woodrow Wilson Nat. Fellowship Found, 1984. Mem. Nat. Coun. Tchrs. of Math. (com. mem., regional svcs. com. 1993, adv. panel 1991, yearbook 1989-91), Math. Assn. Am., Assn. Tchrs. of Math. in Mass. (bd. dirs., pres. 1999-2001), Mass. Assn. Math Leagues (pres. 1986-87, 99-2000, contest dir. 1985-86, 98-99), Assn. Tchrs. Math. New Eng. (pres. 1996-98). Avocations: chess, golf, skiing, travel. Home: Middleboro, Mass. Died July 16, 2007.

CAMP, WILLIAM W., environmental and architectural engineer; b. Wilmington, Del., Aug. 17, 1939; s. George Hayward and Frances (Ellison) C.; m. Dorothy Camp (div. June, 1968); children: Kathleen, Tammy M., William W. Jr.; m. Elizabeth L. Boyd, June 28, 1969; 1 child, David G. BS in Mech. Engring., Widener U., 1966. Registered profl. engr., Pa., Del., Ga., Ind., Ala., Fla, Tenn., Calif., R.I., Mass., S.C., N.C., Md., Va. Group v.p. Roy F. Weston, West Chester, Pa., 1967-77; v.p. Smith, Hinchman and Grylls, Detroit, Atlanta, 1977-79; pres. McCrary Engring. Corp., Atlanta, 1979-87; prin. YWC S.E. Inc., Atlanta, from 1985, YWC, Inc., Monroe, Conn., from 1989. Pres. Camp and Assocs., Inc., 1979—; chief exec. officer Ad + Soil, Inc., Kennett Sq., Pa., 1989-91. Author: (booklet) How to Select a Consulting Engineer, 1977. Mem. Zoning Bd. E. Caln Twp., Donningtown, Pa., 1976. Mem. Tech. Assn. of Pulp and Paper Industry, Water Pollution Control Fed. (program com.), Am. Wire Assn., Am. Assn. Energy Engrs. Achievements include patent disclosure of fluid bed encapsulation of high energy oxidizers. Died Dec. 20, 2006.

CAMPBELL, HENRY MORRIS, computer systems development professional; b. Beckley, W.Va., July 14, 1944; s. William Henry and Gloria Quail (Ward) C.; m. Andrea Welman Gray, June 25, 1977 (div. Dec. 1983); children: Shawn William, Colin Morris, Sally Jean, Sarah Muriel. AA in English, Beckley Coll., 1964; BA in Journalism, SUNY, Buffalo, 1979. Cert. Norell network adminstr. Tchr. Clay (W.Va.) County Schs., 1965-67; writer WCHS-TV, Charleston, W.Va., 1967-68; social worker Erie County Social Svcs., Buffalo, 1968-74; child abuse and neglect investigator Erie County, Buffalo, N.Y., 1974-78; sys. mgr. Niagara County, Niagara Falls, N.Y., 1980-85, Norfolk City, Va., from 1985. Mem. sys. devel. adv. bd. Va. Dept. Social Svcs., Richmond, 1988—. Contbr. articles to profl. jours. Recipient Pub. Tech. Incentive awards Pub. Tech., Inc., San Francisco, 1996, 97. Avocation: automobile restoration. Home: Norfolk, Va. Died Nov. 29, 2006.

CAMPBELL, HUGH BROWN, JR., judge; b. Charlotte, NC, Feb. 19, 1937; s. Hugh Brown and Thelma Louise (Welles) C.; m. Mary Irving Carlyle, Nov. 3, 1962; children: Hugh B. III, Irving Carlyle, Thomas Lenoir. AB, Davidson Coll., NC, 1959; JD, Harvard U., Cambridge, Mass., 1962. Atty. Craighill, Rendleman, Charlotte, 1964-77, Weinstein, Sturges, Charlotte, 1977-94, Cansler, Lockhart, Charlotte, 1994—2000; judge NC Ct. Appeals, Raleigh, 2000—02, 26th Jud. Dist. Ct., Charlotte, from 2003. Chmn. Jury Commn., Mecklenburg County, NC, 1985-97; exec. com. County Bar Assn., Mecklenburg County, 1989-92, civil cts. com. chair, 1990-92. Rep. NC House Reps., Raleigh, 1968-72; legis. liaison Charlotte/Mecklenburg County, Raleigh, 1971-72; state chmn. NC Zoo Bond Campaign, 1972; chmn. Carolinas Med. Ctr. Bond Campaign, 1976. Col. JAG US Army, 1962-64, Res., 1964-92. Decorated Legion of Merit, Meritorious Svc. medal (2); Honored Order of Hornet, Mecklenburg County, 1976. Mem. NC Bar Coun. (exec. com., chair ethics 1981-90), Planned Parenthood Charlotte (bd. dirs., chmn. 1980-81), YMCA Charlotte (adv. bd. 1992—), Rotary Club East Charlotte (pres. 1976-77), Robert Burns Soc.(pres. 1995-96), St. Andrew Soc. Carolinas (pres. 1999-2000), Mecklenberg County (chmn.). Democrat. Episcopalian. Avocations: tennis, swimming, hiking, reading, politics. Home: Charlotte, NC. Died Sept. 11, 2015.

CAMPBELL, JOHN ROBERT, management executive; b. Windsor, Ont., Can., Aug. 23, 1915; s. Arthur Benedict and Florence (Fugate) C.; m. Grace Ethel Mansfield, Sept. 21, 1940; children: Laurie Graham, Jane Lyons, Gail Schilly, Donald Bruce. Student, Lawrence Inst. Tech., Detroit, 1932-33. Rsch. tech. Automobile Mfrs. Assn., Detroit, 1941-43; asst. exec. dir. Automotive Electric Assn., Detroit, 1946-55; controller Knorr-Maynard Co., Detroit, 1955-60; boat show dir. Outboard Boating Club, Chgo., 1960-64; conv. dir. Nat. Sch. Bds. Assn., Chgo., 1964-78, Assn. Sch. Bus. Officials, Chgo., 1978-82; pres. CMS Assocs., Cape Coral, Fla., from 1982. Major U.S. Army, 1943-46. Mem. Nat. Assn. Exposition Mgrs. (emeritus). Avocations: golf, wood carving. Home: Cape Coral, Fla. Died Apr. 13, 2007.

CAMPBELL, MICHAEL JOHN, accountant; b. Johannesburg, Republic South Africa, Nov. 23, 1954; s. Henry Laughlan and Lily Maud (Ferris) C. B in Commerce, U. Witwatersrand, Republic South Africa, 1976, Hon. Diploma Acctg., 1978. Articled clk. Peat, Marwick and Mitchell, Johannesburg, 1977-80; mgmt. trainee Anglo Am. Corp. of South Africa, Johannesburg, 1980-84; gin. dir. Nat. Dairy Equipment, Johannesburg, 1984-85, group mng. dir., from 1985. With South African Army, 1973. Mem. South African Inst. Chartered Accts., Inst. Internal Auditors of South Africa. Mem. Anglican Ch. Avocations: photography, squash, tennis. Died Mar. 2, 2007.

CAMPBELL, MILDRED CORUM, business owner, nurse; b. Warfield, Va., Feb. 24, 1934; d. Oliver Lee and Hazel King (Young) Corum; m. Hugh Stuart Campbell, Dec. 2, 1972. BSN, U. Va., Charlottesville, 1956. Head nurse plastic surgery U. Va. Med. Ctr., Charlottesville, 1956-58, head nurse cardio-surg., 1958-61; staff nurse oper. rm. NIH Heart Inst., Bethesda, Md., 1961-62; supr. oper. and recovery rms. Med. Univ. of S.C., Charleston, 1962-64; head nurse cardio operating rms. Meth. Hosp., Tex. Med. Ctr., Houston, 1964-67; supr. oper. and recovery rms. Cedars of Lebanon Med. Ctr., LA, 1967-68; product-nurse cons. Ethicon, Inc., Somerville, N.J., 1968-69; nurse cons. Johnson & Johnson, New Brunswick, N.J., 1969-70; gen. mgr. Ariz. Heart Inst., Phoenix, 1970-72, oversaw plans, construction and startup ops.; owner, pres., bd. dirs. Highland Packaging Labs., Inc., Somerville, 1983—2002; ret., 2002. Mem., moderator Nat. Ass. Operating Rm. Nurses, Denver, 1963-76; pres. Aux. Orgn., Muhlenberg Hosp., Plainfield, N.J., 1979-80; chmn. Assn. for Retarded Citizens Fund Raising Ball, Somerset County, N.J., 1982. Mem.: Inst. Packaging Profls. Avocations: interior decorating, gardening, travel, sports, cooking. Home: Princeton, NJ. Died Mar. 17, 2015.

CAMPBELL, ROBERT ALLEN, pediatrician; b. Toledo, Dec. 21, 1924; s. Glenn Harold and Harriet Mae (Kintzley) C.; m. Mary Christine Muchka, Sept. 21, 1949; children: Robert Perry, Mary Ellen, Catherine Anne. BA, U. Calif., Berkeley, 1954; MD, U. Calif., San Francisco, 1958. Rsch. asst. dept. zoology U. Calif., Berkeley, 1950-54, intern. resident San Francisco, 1954-58; instr. pediatrics U. Oreg. Med. Sch., Portland, 1961-63, asst. prof., 1963-67, assoc. prof., 1967-72, prof., 1972-91, prof. emeritus, from 1991. Dir. pediat. renal-metabolic rsch. lab. OHSU, Portland, 1963—. Editor: Advances in Polyamine Research, 1978; contbr. articles to profl. jours., chpts. to books. Mem. World Coun., Portland, 1988—, Am. Chinese Orgn., Portland, 1988—; trustee, dir. Cystic Fibrosis Soc. Oreg., Kidney Assn. Oreg., Kerr Ctr. for Children, Portland. USPHS fellow U. Oreg. Med. Sch., 1961-63, Am. Pediat. Soc., Wyeth fellow, 1960-61. Fellow Am. Acad. Pediatrics, Am. Pediatric Soc., Am. Soc. Nephrology, Am. Soc. Pediat. Nephrology, Internat. Soc. Nephrology, Internat. Pediat. Nephrology Assn. Avocations: gardening, community service, dogs. Home: Portland, Oreg. Died Apr. 7, 2007.

CAMPBELL, TERI, executive director; b. Denver, Feb. 4, 1951; d. Leonard M. and Dot Jo (Baker) C. BBA, Loyola U., LA, 1973; MS in judicial, law office adminstrn., U. Denver, 1974. Dep. cir. exec. 10th Cir. Fed. Ct., Denver, 1974-93; exec. dir. Moorall, Sperling, Roehl, Harris & Sisk, Albuquerque, from 1994. Adj. instr. U. Denver Sch. Law, 1987-92. Vol. Families First, Denver; vol. Handicapped Ski program, Winter Park, Colo. Mem. ABA (law mgmt. com.), Assn. Legal Adminstrs. (pres. N. Mex. 1998), Albuquerque C. of C. Avocations: skiing, hiking, travel. Home: Denver, Colo. Died Dec. 4, 2006.

CAMPISE, JAMES ANTHONY, management consultant; b. Bryan, Tex., June 20, 1924; s. Anthony Charles and Mary (Cangelosi) C.; m. Constance Ficker, Dec. 26, 1946; children: Maureen Olivia Campise Davidson, Antoinette Marie Campise Broussard. BEE, Rice U., 1950; MS in Indsl. Engring., U. Houston, 1961. Registered profl. engr., Tex.; cert. data processor. Field tech. rep. IBM Corp., Houston, 1950-55; mgr. ops. and research Hughes Tool Co., Houston, 1955-64; mgr. Tex. ops. Computer Scis. Corp., Houston, 1964-68; instr. Rice U., Houston, 1969-79; pvt. practice as mgmt. cons. Houston, from 1968. Bd. dirs. Tel-Tex Inc., Houston, Trio Software, Inc., Albuquerque, Sureline Systems, Inc., Corpus Christi, Tex. Editor jour. of data mgmt., 1960—. Served with USAF, 1943-45. Mem. Data Processing Mgmt. Assn. (life) (Spl. Recognition award, 1978, Individual Performance award, 1977, cert. of appreciation, 1972), Assn. for Computing Machinery. Avocations: coins, first day covers, computer programming. Died Mar. 13, 2007.

CANFIELD, ELIZABETH FRANCES, retired lawyer; b. Fairport, Mo., Aug. 19, 1913; d. James Arthur and Bertha Mae (Ashley) Foard; m. Robert Roe Canfield, May 7, 1933 (dec. Sept. 1994); children: James Robert, Philip Roe. LLB, LaSalle Law Sch., 1949. Bar: Ill. 1950. Pvt. practice, Rockford, Ill., 1950-97; spl. asst. atty. gen. State of Ill.,

1974-84; ret. Rockford, Ill., 1997. Asst. atty. gen. State Ill., 1974-84; lectr. in field of women's rights and wills and probate. Women's divsn. chmn. United Fund Dri., Rockford, 1951; bd. trustees Ct. St. United Meth. Ch.; bd. dirs. Family Consultation Svc. Rockford; mem. blue ribbon adv. com. to Mayor of Rockford; elected mem. Dist. 58 Sch. Bd.; bd. dirs. Wesley Willows Retirement Home; bd. trustees North Rockford Convalescent home, Willows Health Ctr. Mem. AAUW, LWV (hon. life, Rockford pres. 1946-48), Winnebago County Bar Assn. (chmn. com. 1950—), Quota Internat. Exec. Women's Svc. (Rockford pres. 1980-82, mem. internat. by-laws and dist. gov.), PEO. Republican. Methodist. Avocations: writing, reading, swimming, travel, opera, theater. Died Dec. 28, 2006.

CANHAM, PRUELLA CROMARTIE NIVER, music educator; b. Statesboro, Ga., Dec. 4, 1924; d. Esten Graham and Mary Lee (Jones) Cromartie; m. Robert G. Niver June 4, 1946 (div. 1965) m. David L. Canham July 26, 1985; 1 child, Peddy Niver Hayhurst Moran. BS in Bus. and Music, Ga. So. U., 1944; postgrad., various univs. tchr. voice, piano, chorus and bus. career maths. North Ft. Myers H.S., Fla.; former sec. Statesboro Air Base, Ga., Warner Robbins Air Base, Macon, Ga.; former tchr. Westside Sch., Bulloch County, Ga., Southside Sch., Opelika, Ala. Mem. Singers Club of L.I.; guest spkr., panelist various cultural orgns. in Fla. and so. states; soloist various chs. and schs.; music cons. local theater groups; mem. Fla. State Secondary Music Instructional Materials Coun. Nominee Gannett Found. Heart of Gold Humanatarian award, 1981; named Vocal Solo. Lit. Music Specialist State of Florida, Lee County Florida Tchr. of the Year, 1987, nominee Nat. Tchr. Hall of Fame, 1998; recipient Nat. Libr. Poet's Editor's Choice award, 1994; cert. Appreciation Nat. Park Trust, 1995, Lee County Sch. Dist. Fla., 1991, numerous awards in 2002, including: ABI Hall of Fame, Poet of Year, Internat. Poet Merit and Honored Mem., Living Legions, Worlds Lifetime Achievement award, Companion of Honor, Internat. Peace Prize, Am. Medal of Honor; Nobel Prize for Oustanding Achievement and Contbr. to Humanity, 2002; recipient Congl. Medal of Excellence, 2004. Mem. AAAS, Am. Ch. Dirs. Assn., Fla. Music Educator Assns., Music Educators Nat. Conf., Lee County Alliance of the Arts (charter), Fla. Vocal Assn. (past coord., state bd.), Nat. Assn. of Tchrs. of Singing in Am. and Cand., So. Fla. Symphony and Chorus Assn., Am. Guild of Organists, Fla. League of the Arts (past pres. and bd. dirs., hon. life, 1998—), Lee County Ret. Tchrs. Assn., Fla. Vocal Assn., Am. Choral Assn., Internat. Soc. Poets (disting. mem. 1994, merit award, 1995), Profl. Women's Adv. Bd., others. Home: Fort Myers, Fla. Died Aug. 14, 2007.

CANNON, DOUGLAS A., retail merchandising educator; b. Sioux City, Iowa, July 5, 1948; s. Virginia L. Bose; m. Linda D. Cannon, Apr. 7, 1969; 2 children , Stephanie L. Barron. MBA, Lindenwood U., St. Charles, Mo., 1987. Bus. unit mgr. Boeing Corp., St. Louis, 1985—2003; prodn. control mgr. Monsanto Electronics Materials Co., St. Peters. Adj. prof. Sterling Coll., Kans., 1987—88. Firefighter, capt., & pub. info. officer O'Fallon Fire Protection Dist., Mo., 1989—94. Mem.: Delta Epsilon Chi (sponsor from 2008). Independent. Home: O Fallon, Mo. Died Nov. 30, 2014.

CANTOR, ARNOLD, labor relations official; b. Rochester, NY, Jan. 4, 1927; s. Samuel Abraham and Bessie (Brightman) Cantor; m. Meriam Renee Teichner; children: Nadine, Duane, Paul, Glenn, Erica. BMusic, U. Rochester, NYC, 1949; M in Music, U. Rochester, 1953; MA in Sociology, CCNY, 1995; PhD in Sociology, CUNY, 1997. Cert. clarinet performer Eastman Sch. of Music. Tchr. instrumental music Rochester Pub, Schs., NY, 1949—57, dean of students, 1957—62, v. prin. h.s., 1962—68, prin., 1968—70; exec. dir. Profl. Staff Congress CUNY, 1970—95. Adj. asst. prof. Baruch Coll. CUNY, from 1996. Conductor Rochester Veteran's Park Band, 1965—70. Mem.: AAUP (mem. exec. com. from 1969), NY State United Tchrs. (bd. dirs. 1961—70, pres. Rochester tchrs. assn 1963—65), Am. Fedn. Tchrs. (Disting. Svc. award 1994). Democrat. Jewish. Achievements include leading Rochester Tchrs. Assn. to the first collective bargaining contract agreement in New York state outside of New York City. Avocations: music, photography. Home: Silver Lake, Ohio. Died Dec. 22, 2014.

CANTRELL, SHARRON CAULK, principal; b. Columbia, Tenn., Oct. 2, 1947; d. Tom English and Beulah (Goodin) Caulk; m. William Terry Cantrell, Mar. 18, 1989; 1 child, Jordan; children from previous marriage: Christopher, George English, Steffenee Copley. BA, George Peabody Coll. Tchrs., 1970; MS, Vanderbilt U., 1980; EdS, Mid. Tenn. State U., 1986. Tchr. Ft. Campbell Jr. High Sch., Columbia, Tenn., 1970-71, Whitthorne Jr. High Sch., Columbia, Tenn., 1977-86, Spring Hill (Tenn.) High Sch., 1986—2000. Mem. NEA, AAUW (pres. Tenn. divsn. 1983-85), Maury County Edn. Assn. (pres. 1983-84), Tenn. Edn. Assn., Assn. Preservation Tenn. Antiquities, Maury Alliance, Friends of Children's Hosp., Rotary (bd. dirs.), Phi Delta Kappa. Mem. Ch. of Christ. Home: Spring Hill, Tenn. Died Jan. 17, 2015.

CANTU, HOMARO, chef, entrepreneur; b. Tacoma, Wash., Sept. 23, 1976; m. Katie McGowan, 2013; 2 children. Degree, Le Cordon Bleu, Portland. Sous chef Charlie Trotter's, Chgo., 1999—2004; exec. chef Moto Restaurant, Chgo., 2004—15; chmn., founder Cantu Designs Firm, Chgo. TV appearances include Unwrapped, 2007, Dinner: Impossible, 2007, At the Table with..., 2008, Roadtrip Nation, 2009, Future Food, 2010, Iron Chef America Countdown, 2012, Iron Chef America: The Series, 2007, 2013, Hell's Kitchen, 2011, 2013, featured in numerous culinary mags.; co-author: The Miracle Berry Diet Cookbook, 2012. Died Apr. 14, 2015.

CARAMIA, PHILIP DOMINICK, government official; b. Fairfield, Calif., May 7, 1955; s. Dominick Joseph and Genevieve Marie Caramia; m. Penney Marie Harwell, Sept. 30, 1989. BA in Polit. Sci., La. State U., 1984; MPA, North Tex. State U., 1987. Cert. govt. fin. mgr. Salesman Gibsons, Shreveport, La., 1973-74; shipping mgr. J.C. Penney, Shreveport, 1974-84; sr. evaluator GAO, Dallas, from 1985. Editor newsletter Countdown to Fountain Place, 1988. Del. Tex. Dem. Primary Conv., Dallas, 1988. Recipient leadership giving award Combined Fed. Campaign, 1998; Hatton Sumners fellow North Tex. State U., 1984. Mem. ASPA, Nature Conservancy, Am. Automobile Assn., World Ski Assn., CF/JM Homeowners Assn. Avocations: golf, travel writing, corporate correspondence, pruning. E-mail: c. Home: Dallas, Tex. Died July 14, 2007.

CARDAMONE, RICHARD JOSEPH, retired federal judge; b. Utica, NY, Oct. 10, 1925; s. Joseph J. and Josephine (Scala) Cardamone; m. Catherine Baker Clarke, Aug. 28, 1946; children: William, Richard, Roderick, Josephine, Catherine, Cecelia, Mary Brian, Ann, Margaret, Amy. BA, Harvard U., 1948; LLB, Syracuse U., 1952. Bar: NY 1952. Pvt. practice, Utica, 1952—62; judge NY State Supreme Ct., 1963—71, judge appellate divsn. 4th dept., 1971—81; judge US Ct. Appeals (2nd cir.), Utica, 1981—93, sr. judge, 1993—2008. Pres. NY State Assn. Supreme Ct. Justices, 1977—78. Lt. (j.g.) USNR, 1943—46. Mem.: Oneida County Bar Assn., NY State Bar Assn., Am. Law Inst. Roman Catholic. Died Oct. 16, 2015.

CARDOZA, MARVIN EDMUND, lawyer, retired banker; b. Half Moon Bay, Calif., Aug. 25, 1913; s. Manuel Edmund and Valda Malvina (Oleson) C.; m. Mafalda Cecelia Angelini, Aug. 16, 1936; children: Michael, Jill M., Jack. AA, San Mateo Jr. Coll., Calif., 1933; cert., Am. Inst. Banking, 1941; LLB, U. San Francisco, 1946. Bar: Calif. 1947. From various corp. titles to v.p. Bank of Am., San Francisco, 1934-78; atty. Brit. Motor Car Distbrs., San Francisco, from 1978. Mem. Calif. State Fair Bd., Sacramento, 1962-69, Calif. mem. exec. com., 1967-69; gov. USO, Washington, 1967-80; dir. J.A.C.S., Washington, 1980-89. Commr. Pub. Utilities Commn., San Francisco, 1970-72, pres. 1972, San Francisco Police Commn., 1972-76, pres. 1975; pres. U. San Francisco Alumni Assn., 1965-66; regent St. Mary's Cathedral, San Francisco, 1990, v.p. bd. regents; foreman San Francisco Civil Grand Jury, 1982-83. With USN, 1942-45. Named Humanitarian of the Yr., Met. YMCA, 1979; recipient Cert. of Appreciation, USO, 1986. Mem. Bankers Club of San Francisco (hon., asst. sec. 1970-78), World Trade Club of San Francisco, The Olympic Club (treas. 1980-81). Roman Catholic. Avocations: hunting, golf, farming. Home: San Francisco, Calif. Died Nov. 21, 2006.

CAREY, FRANCIS JAMES, retired lawyer and investment banker; b. Balt., Mar. 24, 1926; s. Francis James and Marjorie (Armstrong) C.; m. Mary Crozer Page, 1947 (dec.); children: Francis James III, Elizabeth Page; m. Emily Norris Large, June 8, 1956 (dec. Apr. 1997); children: Henry Augustus, Emily Norris, Frances Corey MacMaster. Student, Princeton, 1944; AB, U. Pa., 1945, JD, 1949. Comdr. U. Pa. Yacht Club, 1944—45; mem., faculty U. Pa., 1946—47, Bar: Pa., 1950; Law sec. to justice Supreme Ct. Pa., 1950-51; with law firm Townsend, Elliott & Munson and successor, Reed Smith Shaw & McClay, ptnr., mem. exec. com. Pitts., 1984—87, counsel Phila., 1987-92; bd. dir., 1973—97, 2000—12; pres. W.P. Carey & Co., Inc., 1987—97, 2000—12, chmn., from 2012; chmn., CEO, bd. dir. Carey Diversified LLC NYSE CDC, 1997—2000; vice chmn., 2000—05; chmn. exec. com., chief ethics officer, bd. dir. W.P. Carey & Co. LLC and successor W. P. Carey Inc. NYSE WPC, 2005—14, trustee emeritus, from 2014, trustee, pres., 1990—2012, chmn., from 2012; dir. Allergy Techs. LLC, from 2012. Bd. mgrs., mem. exec. com. Western Savs. Bank, 1970-82; mem. bus. adv. com. Bus. Coun. for UN, 1994—2002; trustee exec. com. Investment Program Assn., 1990-2000, chmn., 1998-2000 Mem. Com. of Seventy, Phila., 1957-58; mem. Lower Gwynedd Twp. (Pa.) Planning Commn., 1962-75, sec., 1962-65; trustee Germantown Acad., Fort Washington, Pa., 1961—, pres., 1966-72; overseer Sch. Arts and Scis., U. Pa., 1983-90; mgr. Law Alumni Soc., U. Pa., 1962-66; jr. warden St. Martin's in the Field, Biddeford Pool, Maine, 2003-04, chmn., sr. warden, 2004-07, warden-at-large, 2007-; life trustee Gilman Sch., Balt., 2002-; bd. trustees Md. Hist. Soc., 2002-12, v.p., mem. exec. com., 2007-11; Served to lt. USNR, 1943-46. Mem. ABA, Pa. Bar Assn. (chmn. real property, probate and trust law sect. 1966-67, chmn. conf. group to cooperate with Pa. Land Title Assn. 1970-77), Phila. Bar Assn. (chmn. com. on civil legis. 1962), Soc. Mayflower Descs. in State of N.Y., Fourth Street Club, St. Anthony Club (Phila.), Sunnybrook Golf Club (Plymouth Meeting, Pa.), Abenakee Club, Biddeford Pool Yacht Club (Biddeford Pool, Maine), Md. Club (Balt.). Republican. Episcopalian. Home: Ambler, Pa. Deceased.

CARLL, PAUL LOUDON, chemical company executive; b. Elgin, Kans., July 1, 1920; s. James Lawrence and Ora Lee (Louden) Carll; m. Marian Elizabeth Heckathorne, June 6, 1944; children: Thomas Paul, Peggy Lee Carll Keene, William Floyd. BS in Chem. Engring, Case Inst. Tech., 1949. Gen. mgr. plants Lubrizol Corp., Houston, 1967—69, v.p. mfg., 1969—75, v.p. purchasing and distbns., 1975—83, v.p. adminstrn. asst. to the pres. Wickliffe, Ohio, 1983—86, dir., 1973—76. Served to capt. USAAF, 1941—46. Mem.: AIChE, Am. Chem. Soc., Masons Lodge (32 deg.), Alpha Chi Sigma. Republican. Home: Cleveland, Ohio. Died Nov. 16, 2006.

CARLSON, A. BRUCE, engineering educator; b. Cleve., Jan. 31, 1937; s. Albin John and Mildred Elizabeth Carlson; m. Patricia Ann Carlson, Aug. 16, 1959; children: Kendra Leigh, Kyle Lehman, Kristen Lizbeth. AB, Dartmouth Coll., 1958; MS, Stanford U., 1960, PhD, 1964. Mem. tech. staff Bell Tel. Labs., Holmdel, N.J., 1967-68; asst. prof. Rensselaer Poly. Inst., Troy, N.Y., 1963-68, assoc. prof., 1968-93, prof., from 1993. Curriculum chair elec., computer and sys. engring., Rensselaer Poly. Inst., 1989—; telecom. cons. N.Y. State Dept. Health, Albany, 1965-67; ednl. cons. IBM Corp., Kingston, N.Y., 1973. Author: (textbooks) Communication Systems, 1968, Circuits, 1996; (with others) Linear Systems in Communication and Control, 1971, Electrical Engineering: Concepts and Applications, 1981. Chairperson Rensselaer County CROP Walk, Troy, 1990-94; bd. dirs. Troy Area United Ministries, 1994—; trustee Presbytery of Albany, Watervliet, N.Y., 1985-91. Fellow Am. Soc. for Engring. Edn. (ERM chair 1993-95, Western Electric Fund award 1974); mem. IEEE (sr., ABET evaluator 1996—, McGraw-Hill/Millman award 1994). Democrat. Home: Troy, NY. Died Mar. 18, 2007.

CARLSON, SYLVIA, nurse educator, consultant; b. Bklyn., Apr. 5, 1925; d. Louis and Nettie (Rosen) C. RN, Columbia Presbyn. Sch. Nursing, 1947; BSN, Columbia U., 1947; MSN, Adelphi U., 1967; PhD in Nursing Rsch., NYU, 1984. Staff nurse rehab. Queens Hosp. Ctr., Jamaica, N.Y., 1947-48; delivery room nurse Cath. Med. Ctr., Mary Immaculate Hosp., Jamaica, 1948-49; pvt. duty nurse Jamaica Hosp., 1949-50; office nurse otolaryngology Jamaica, 1950-54; nursing care coord. med. unit L.I. Jewish Hosp., 1954-56; sch. nurse, tchr. Plainedge Sch. Dist., Nassau County, 1956-62; clin. instr. Nassau County Med. Ctr., East Meadow, N.Y., 1962-66; asst. dir. nursing Insvc. Edn., 1966-71; assoc. dir. nursing Jewish Hillside Med. Ctr., New Hyde Park, N.Y., 1971-83; assoc. dir. nursing edn. N.Y.C. Health and Hosps. Corp. (Corp. Nursing Svc.), 1986-90, ret., 1990. Cons., lectr. in field, 1990—; del., speaker People to People Program on Rehab., People's Republic China, 1981; speaker Intercounty Soc. Nursing Insvc. Educators, 1982, numerous other hosps., univs. and assns. in field; adj. clin. prof. Boston U.; asst. prof. adult health Stony Brook (N.Y.) U.; asst. clin. prof. Adelphi U.; part-time instr. C.W. Post, 1972, 73; evening instr. med.-surg. nursing Adelphi U., 1968-69, instr. continuing edn., 1973. Contbr. articles to profl. publs. Organizer, originator Nurses for Polit. Action, 1980. Fellow Am. Sch. Health Assn.; mem. ANA, Gerontol. Soc., Am. Soc. Tng. Dirs., Nat. Acad. Insvc. Edn., Am. Acad. Polit. and Social Sci., Am. Heart Assn., Nat. League Nursing, N.Y. State Assn. Gerontol. Educators, Northeastern Gerontol. Soc., Columbia U. Alumni Assn. (Disting. Lectr. award 1981, Disting. Alumni award 1992), Sigma Theta Tau. Home: New Rochelle, NY. Died Dec. 21, 2006.

CARMELI, MOSHE, theoretical physicist; b. Baghdad, Iraq, June 15, 1933; arrived in Israel, 1951; naturalized US citizen, 1973; s. Eliaho and Neomi Carmeli-Chitayat; m. Elisheva Cohen, Aug. 17, 1961; children: Eli, Dorith, Yair. MSc, Hebrew U., Jerusalem, 1960; DSc, Technion-Israel Inst. Tech., Haifa, 1964. Rsch. assoc. Lehigh U., Bethlehem, Pa., 1964-65, Temple U., Phila., 1964-65, U. Md., Coll. Pk., Md., 1965-67, asst. prof., 1967-68; rsch. physicist USAF Lab., Dayton, Ohio, 1967-72; assoc. prof. Ben Gurion U., Beer Sheva, 1972-74, head physics dept., 1973-77, prof. physics, from 1974, Albert Einstein prof. physics, 1979—2004, emeritus prof. theoretical physics, from 2004, head Theoretical Physics Ctr., 1980-89. Vis. prof. Inst. for Theoretical Physics, SUNY, Stony Brook, 1977-78, 81, U. Md., Coll. Pk., 1985-86, Inst. Henri Poincaré, Paris, 1975, Internat. Ctr. for Theoretical Physics, Trieste, 1977, 78, 79, 80, 81, 82, 85, 87, 88, Max-Planck Inst., Munich, 1980, U. Mass., Amherst, 1985, Colgate U., Hamilton, NY, 1987, Queen Mary Coll., U. London, 1988, State U. Campinas, São Paulo, Brazil, 1998, Churchill Coll. U Cambridge, 2000, Inst. of Astrophysics U. Cambridge, 2000. Author: Group Theory and General Relativity, 1977, Classical Fields: General Relativity and Gauge Theory, 1982, Statistical Theory and Random Matrices, 1983, Cosmological Special Relativity: The Large-Scale Structure of Space, Time and Velocity, 1997, 2d edit., 2002, Cosmological RElativity: The Special and General Theories for the Structure of the Universe, 2006; co-author: Representations of the Rotation and Lorentz Groups, 1976, Gauge Fields: Classification and Equations of Motion, 1989, Gravitation: SL (2,C) Gauge Theory and Conservation Laws, 1990, Theory of Spinors, 2000; co-editor: Relativity, 1970; mem. editl. bd. Weizmann Sci. Press, 1978-80; referee Phys. Rev., Phys. Rev. Latt., Found. Phys., Gen. Relativity Gravitation, Jour. Math. Phys., Internat. Jour. Theoretical Physics, Nuovo Cimanto, Classical Quantatum Gravity, NSF, NRC, US-Israel Binat. Sci. Found. Rev.; reviewer Math. Reviews; contbr. more than 100 articles to profl. jours. Fellow AAAS, Am. Phys. Soc. (jour. referee); mem. Israel Phys. Soc. (pres. 1982-85), Internat. Soc. for Gen. Relativity and Gravitation, NY Acad. Sci., Sigma Xi. Home: Omer, Israel. Died Sept. 27, 2007.

CARMICHAEL, PAUL LOUIS, ophthalmic surgeon; b. July 8, 1927; s. Louis and Christina Ciamaichela; m. Pauline Cecilia Lipsmire, Oct. 28, 1950; children: Paul Louis, Mary Catherine, John Michael, Kevin Anthony, Joseph William, Patricia Ann, Robert, Christopher. BS in Biology, Villanova U., 1945; MD, St. Louis U., 1949; MS in Medicine, U. Pa., 1954. Diplomate Am. Bd. Ophthalmology; cert. isotope methodology Hahnemann Med. Coll. Rotating intern St. Joseph's Hosp., Phila., 1949-50; resident in ophthalmology Phila. Gen. Hosp., 1952-54; asst. prof. ophthalmology Hahnemann Med. Coll., Phila., 1960-66, clin. assoc. prof. nuclear medicine, 1974-90. With radioactive isotope dept. Wills Eye Hosp., Phila., 1956-61, sr. asst. surgeon, 1961-65, assoc. surgeon, 1966-72, assoc. surgeon retinal svc., 1972-90; attending ophthalmologist Holy Redeemer Hosp., Meadowbrook, Pa., 1963-65; assoc. ophthalmologist Grand View Hosp., Sellersville, Pa., 1958-75; instr. opthalmology

Grad. Sch. Medicine, U. Pa., Phila., 1956-63; clin. assoc. prof. ophthalmology Temple U., Phila., 1967-72; clin. assoc. prof. ophthalmology Thomas Jefferson U. Sch. Medicine, Phila., 1971-90; chief ophthalmology North Pa. Hosp., Lansdale, 1959-90, pres. staff, 1959; pres. Ophthalmic Assocs., Lansdale, 1969-90. Co-author: Nuclear Ophthalmology, 1976; contbr. chpts. to books, papers to profl. confs., articles to publs. in field. Pres. bd. dirs. North Pa. Symphony, 1976-78. Capt. M.C., U.S. Army, 1950-51. Named Outstanding Young Man of Yr., Lansdale Jaycees, 1959, Outstanding Young Man, State of Pa. Jaycees, 1960. Fellow ACS, Internat. Coll. Surgeons, Coll. Physicians Phila.; mem. AMA, Montgomery County Med. Soc., Pa. Med. Soc., Am. Acad. Ophthalmology, Pa. Acad. Ophthalmology, Assn. Rsch. in Ophthalmology, Inter-County Ophthalmol. Soc. (co-founder, pres. 1975-78), Ophthalmic Club Phila. (pres. 1964), Delaware Valley Ophthalmic Soc. (pres. 1985-89). Roman Catholic. Home: Park City, Utah. Died Dec. 26, 2006.

CARPENTER, BETTY O., writer; b. Montreal, June 1, 1926; d. Harry and Dorothy (Schacher) Shmerling; m. David G. Ostroff, Apr. 6, 1946 (div. 1972); children: Jack Ostroff, Lucy Ostroff Harrow; m. Russell William Carpenter, Jr., Oct. 2, 1976 (dec.); stepchildren: Annette Marie Carpenter Freedman, Cynthia Carpenter Jefferson, Lori Carpenter Bembry. BA in Edn., Bklyn. Coll., 1947, MA in Edn., 1953; PhD in Adminstrn., NYU, 1973. Cert. sch. supt., prin., N.J., guidance counselor, elem. tchr., N.Y. Tchr. elem. grades N.Y.C. Pub. Schs. 54 and 139, Bklyn., 1946-54, 62; asst. prin. Pub. Sch. 139, Bklyn., 1962-67; pres. asst. prin. assoc. Ctrl. Office Bd. of Edn., NYC, 1967-68, v.p. coun. suprs. and adminstrs., 1968-69, adminstrv. asst. pers., 1968-70; asst. supt. Plainfield (N.J.) Pub. Schs., 1970-74; supt. schs. Glen Rock (N.J.) Pub. Schs., 1974-84; ret. Author: Curriculum Handbook for Parents and Teachers, 1991, Tutoring for Pay, 1991, Musing, 1994, (book of poetry) The Brosh (Bionic Replacement of Species Humanoid), 1998, Lady of the Lake, 1999, Inherit the Rainbow, 2000, Art and Craftiness, 2001, Crystal Slopes, 2002, A Style of Their Own, 2002, Make Way for Pugsley, 2002. Trustee Glen Rock Libr. Bd., 1974-80, United Fund Bd., Glen Rock, 1975-77; vice chmn. Iredell County Bd. of Adjustment N.C., 1990-95; fellow mem. Lake Owners Gathered in Concern, N.C., 1985-88. Recipient Founders Day award NYU, 1973, Adminstrv. Leadership award NACEL, 1984. Mem. Soc. Children's Book Writers and Illustrators, Romance Writers Am., Nat. Writers Assn., Bergen County Supts. Assn. (pres.-elect), Nat. Scrabble Assn., Am. Contract Bridge League, Ariz. Writers Assn. Avocations: sculpture, golf, water aerobics, computers, bridge. Home: Scottsdale, Ariz. Died Aug. 29, 2007.

CARPENTER, CLARK GILBERT, manufacturing executive; b. Omaha, Ill., Mar. 20, 1936; s. Gilbert Eric and Lourene (Cahoon) C. BS, U. Nebr., 1958. Audit mgr. Ernst & Whinney, Chgo., Ill., 1958-72; v.p., treas. Elkay Mfg. Co., Oak Brook, from 1972-. With U.S. Army, 1959-61. Mem. Am. Inst. of CPA's., Ill. Soc. of CPAs. La Grange Country Club (Ill., treas. 1984--). Avocation: golf. Home: Willowbrook, Ill. Died Mar. 19, 2007.

CARR, DAVID MICHAEL, columnist, writer; b. Mpls., Sept. 8, 1956; s. John Lawrence and Joan (O'Neill) C.; m. Jill Rooney, Sept. 17, 1994; children: Erin and Meagan (twins), Madeline. BFA, U. Minn., 1981. Writer Twin Cities Reader, Mpls., 1981-84; editor Corp. Report Minn., Mpls., 1986-87, Minn. Lawyer, Mpls., 1990-93, Twin Cities Reader, Mpls., 1993-95, Washington City Paper, 1995; media writer Inside.com; contributing writer The Atlantic Monthly, New York Mag.; bus. reporter to columnist, The Media Equation New York Times, 2002—15. Mem. alumni selectin com. journalism dept. U. Minn., Mpls., 1985; comm. cons., Mpls., 1990-93; com. mem. Assn. Alternative Newspapers, Washington, 1995; columnist Family Times Mag., Mpls., 1995; spkr. addiction and recovery various orgns., Mpls. and Washington, 1988-96; featured in documentary about the New York Times, Page One: Inside The New York Times, 2011; Lack Prof. of Media Studies, Boston U., 2014-2015 Author: (memoir) The Night of the Gun, 2008. Recipient Page One award Soc. Profl. Journalists, Mpls., 1983-86, 93, 94, 95, Nat. Victory award, Washington, 1991, award Assn. Alternative Newspaper Columnist, Assn. Alternative Newspapers Media Column award, 1997; named Alumni of Distinction, U. Minn., Mpls., 1995. Home: Montclair, NJ. Died Feb. 12, 2015.

CARR, JACQUELYN B., psychologist, educator; b. Oakland, Calif., Feb. 22, 1923; d. Frank G. and Betty (Kreiss) Corker; children: Terry, John, Richard, Linda, Michael, David. BA, U. Calif., Berkeley, 1958; MA, Stanford U., 1961; PhD, U. So. Calif., 1973. Lic. psychologist, Calif; lic. secondary tchr., Calif. Tchr. Hillsdale High Sch., San Mateo, Calif., 1958-69, Foothill Coll., Los Altos Hills, Calif., from 1969. Cons. Silicon Valley Companies, U.S. Air Force, Interpersonal Support Network, Santa Clara County Child Abuse Council, San Mateo County Suicide Prevention Inc.,Parental Stress Hotline, Hotel/Motel Owners Assn.; co-dir. Individual Study Ctr.; supr. Tchr. Edn.; adminstr. Peer Counseling Ctr.; led numerous workshops and confs. in field. Author: Learning is Living, 1970, Equal Partners: The Art of Creative Marriage, 1986, The Crisis in Intimacy, 1988, Communicating and Relating, 1984, 3d edit., 1991, Communicating with Myself: A Journal, 1984, 3d edit., 1991; contbr. articles to profl. jours. Vol. US Peace Corps., Sri Lanka, 1997. Mem. Mensa. Clubs: Commonwealth. Home: Napa, Calif. Died May 6, 2007.

CARR, ROBERT LEROY, secondary school educator; b. Zeigler, Ill., Sept. 10, 1929; s. Alfred Carroll and Sarah Ann (Gurley) C.; m. Nancy Ann Plewes, Dec. 28, 1964 (div. 1974). BS in Edn., So. Ill. U., 1952, MS in Edn., 1955; postgrad., U. Mich., 1956-69. Cert. travel agt. Tchr. Thompsonville (Ill.) High Sch., 1954-55, Ann Arbor (Mich.) Pub. Schs., 1955-57, 59-90; guidance dir. USAF Def. Sch., Burtonwood, Eng., 1957-58; acad. counselor, tchr. Washtenaw Community Coll., Ann Arbor, from 1990. Pub. speaker, cons. in field. Bd. dirs. Am. Cancer Soc., Washtenaw County, 1986; mem. adv. coun. Juvenile Ct., Washtenaw County, 1990—; mem. Ann Arbor Civic Theatre, 1975—. With U.S. Army, 1952-53. Mem. NEA, Mich. Edn. Assn., Ann Arbor Edn. Assn., Kiwanis (pres. 1980-81). Republican. Methodist. Avocations: world travel, fine arts, theater, politics. Home: Ann Arbor, Mich. Died Nov. 19, 2006.

CARRERA, MARIANNE, nurse consultant; b. Jersey City, Feb. 6, 1932; d. Richard J. and Anna R. (Ulinski) Makowski; m. Ivan Carrera, Oct. 30, 1965. BSN, Niagara U., 1954; MA in Community Health, Columbia U., 1974; cert. in clin. counseling, Post-Grad. Ctr. Mental Health, NYC, 1987; MPH, Columbia U., 1988. RN; cert. clin. specialist in adult mental health ANA. Staff nurse operating rm. N.Y. Hosp., NYC, 1955-57; charge nurse neuro surg. suite operating rm. Mass. Gen. Hsop., Boston, 1957-59; instr. Sch. Nursing Flower & Fifth Ave. Hosp., NYC, 1959-60, asst. supr. operating rm., 1960-62, researcher surg., 1962-63, nursing coord. opern heart team, 1963-64; from asst. supr. insvc. edn. to admistrv. supr. operating rm Lenox Hill Hosp., NYC, 1965-70; asst. instr. med.-surg. nursing St. Luke's Hosp. Sch. Nursing, NYC, 1971-72, instr. med.-surg. nursing, 1972-74; hosp. nursing svcs. cons. OHSM N.Y. State Dept. Health, NYC, from 1975. Mem. Am. Pub. Health Assn., ANA. Home: New York, NY. Died Mar. 8, 2007.

CARRIKER, MELBOURNE ROMAINE, retired marine biologist; b. Santa Marta, Colombia, Feb. 25, 1915; s. Melbourne Armstrong Jr. Carriker and Carmela Myrtle Flye; m. Meriel Roosevelt McAllister, Oct. 17, 1943; children: Eric Berkeley, Bruce Leaycraft, Neal Armstrong, Robert Romaine. BA, Rutgers U., 1939; PhD, U. Wis., Madison, 1943; degree of sci. (hon.), Beloit Coll., Wis., 1968. From instr. to asst. prof. zoology Rutgers U., New Brunswick, NJ, 1946—54; assoc. prof. zoology U. N.C., Chapel Hill, 1954—61; supervisory fishery rsch. biologist, chief shellfish mortality program Biol. Lab. U.S. Bur. Comml. Fisheries, Oxford, 1961—62; dir. systematics-ecology program Marine Biol. Lab., Woods Hole, Mass., 1962—72, ind. investigator, 1972—73; prof. marine studies U. Del., Lewes, 1973—85, prof. emeritus, from 1985. Numerous adj. professorships, rsch. fellowships in field. Author: Vista Nieve, Adventures of an Early 20th Century Naturalist and His Family in Colombia, S. A., 2001, Spanish edit., 2002, Taming of the Oyster, A History of Evolving Shellfisheries and the National Shellfisheries Association, 2004; co-editor: Experiences of an Ornithologist Along the Highways and Byways of Bolivia, 2006, The Bird Call of the Rio Beni, Ornithological Adventures of a Father and Son, 2006; contbr. more than 100 articles to profl. publs. Pres. Ptnrs. of the Americas, Del.-Panama. Lt.(j.g.) USNR, 1943—45, PTO. Mem.: Am. Malacological Soc. (pres. 1985—87), Atlantic Estuarine Rsch. Soc. (pres. 1961—62), Nat. Shellfisheries Assn. (pres. 1955—57). Home: Lewes, Del. Died Feb. 25, 2007.

CARROCCIO, DOMONIC ANTHONY, carpet company executive; b. Cleve., Feb. 26, 1939; s. John Anthony and Emma (Mahoney) C.; m. Patricia Ann O'Neil, Sept. 2, 1961; children: Joan Marie Hall, Nickolas Anthony, Selene Marie. Grad. high sch., Cleve. Driver, salesman Pepsi-Cola Bottling Co., Cleve., 1960-64; driver Mattlack and others, Cleve., 1964-69; carpet installer Magic Carpet and Allen's Carpet, Cleve., 1969-74; propr. Great No. Carpet Co., Cleve., from 1974; pres. Carousel Concessions Equipment & Supply Co., Cleve., from 1988. Mem. Greater Cleve. Growth Assn. Died Jan. 19, 2007.

CARROLL, JOHN SAWYER, educator, former newspaper editor; b. NYC, Jan. 23, 1942; s. John Wallace and Margaret (Sawyer) C.; m. Kathleen Kirk, May 1, 1971 (div. Sept. 1982) children: Kathleen (Katita) Louise Strathmann, Margaret Adriane Vaughan; m. Lee Huston Powell, Nov. 1985; stepchildren Huston Powell, Griggs Powell, Caroline Powell BA in English lit., Haverford Coll., 1963. Reporter Providence Jour.-Bull., 1963-64, Balt. Sun, 1966-72, fgn. corr. Vietnam, 1967-69, fgn. corr. Mid. East, 1969, reporter Washington, 1969-72; city editor, met. editor Phila. Inquirer, 1973-79; exec. v.p., editor Lexington Herald-Leader, Ky., 1979-91; editor, sr. v.p. Balt. Sun, 1991—2000; v.p. Times Mirror Co., 1998—2000; editor LA Times, 2000—05, exec. v.p., 2000—05; Knight Vis. Lectr., Shorenstein Ctr. on Press, Politics and Public Policy JFK Sch. Govt., Harvard Univ., 2006. Pulitzer Prize juror, 1987, 89, 94; mem. Pulitzer Prize Bd., 1994-2003, chmn., 2002. Served with U.S. Army, 1964-66 Recipient Leadership Award Am. Soc. Newspaper Editors, 2004, Burton Benjamin Meml. Award Com. to Protect Journalists, 2004; named Nat. Press Found. Editor of Yr., 1998; Nieman Fellow Harvard U., 1971-72; vis. journalist fellow Queen Elizbeth House, U. Oxford, 1988. Fellow: Am. Acad. Arts & Sciences. Home: Lexington, Ky. Died June 14, 2015.

CARSON, JEAN HOPKINS KESSEL, civic worker; b. Dayton, Ohio, Sept. 24, 1929; d. Arthur Vincent and Mary Helen (Hopkins) Kessel; m. John Gregg Carson, Feb. 1, 1951; children: James G., Elizabeth M., David R., Mary C. BS, Purdue U., 1952; diploma, Diocesan Theol. Sch., 1994. Trustee Episcopal Cmty. Svcs. Found., 1996—2003, Highland County Domestic Violence Task Force, 1991—2002; mem. Scott House Com., 1990—96; founder, chmn. bd. trustees Samaritan Outreach Svcs. of Highland County, 1988—95; bus. mgr. Hillsboro chpt. Girl Scouts U.S., 1972—82; mem. Highland County Health Planning Coun., 1970—75; various activities with Scioto-Paint Valley Mental Health Ctr., Hillsboro Human Rels. Group, Ctrl. Ohio chpt. Am. Heart Assn., Highland County Mental Health Assn., St. Mary's Episcopal Ch., Hillsboro; mem. So. State C.C. Found. Bd.; various activities with Highland Dist. Hosp. Women's Aux., Episcopal Diocese of So. Ohio. Home: Hillsboro, Ohio. Died May 19, 2007.

CARSON, JOHN GREGG, priest; b. Cin., June 12, 1925; s. William Carson and Elizabeth Leslie Williams; m. Jean Hopkins, Feb. 1, 1951; children: James, Elizabeth York, David, Mary. BS, Purdue U., 1951; MDiv, Bexley Hall, Rochester, NY, 1954. Priest-in-charge St. Andrew's Episcopal Ch., Washington C.H., Ohio, 1954—56; adminstr. Highland County Mental Retardation Program, Hillsboro, Ohio, 1970—75; priest-in-charge St. Anthony's Episcopal Ch., Wilmington, Ohio, 1965—91; rector St. Mary's Episcopal Ch., Hillsboro, 1956—91, rector emeritus, from 1991. Various positions on coms. and commns. Episcopal Diocese of So. Ohio; mem. exec. com. Rural Workers Network; bd. trustees Episcopal Retirement Homes; vol. chaplain Clinton Meml. Hosp., Autumn Yrs. Nursing Home. Co-founder, bd. trustees, treas., fin. com. chmn., vol. Samaritan Outreach Svcs., mem. endowment com., 2005; co-founder, treas., coach Little League; mem. hosp. assn., levy campaign com., chmn. gift fund com., adv. com. on gift fund use, vol. chaplain Highland Dist. Hosp.; adv. com. Health Initiative of Cin. Recipient Disting. Svc. award, Hillsboro Jaycees, 1962, Appreciation Plaque, Heart Assn., 1981, Citizen of Month award, City of Hillsboro, 1985, Cmty. Svc. award, Grand Lodge of Free and Accepted Masons, 1995, Gov.'s Humanitarian award, Gov. Ohio, 1998, Good Samaritan award, Samaritan Outreach Svcs., 2002, Commendation, Ohio Ho. of Reps., 1998, Appreciation Plaque, Samaritan Outreach Svcs., 1998. Mem.: Highland County Mental Health Assn. (founder, pres.), Clinton County Ministerial Assn., Highland County Ministerial Assn. (pres.), Hillsboro Ministerial Assn. (pres.), Clergy Assn. So. Ohio (exec. com.), Hillsboro Rotary Club (pres., Appreciation Plaque 1960). Home: Hillsboro, Ohio. Died July 29, 2007.

CARSON, RICHARD MCKEE, chemical engineer; b. Dayton, Ohio, June 6, 1912; s. George E. and Gertrude (Barthelemy) C.; children: Joan Roderer, Linda McCartan. BS in Chem. Engring., U. Dayton, Ohio, 1934. Registered profl. engr., Ohio. Rsch. chemist Dayton Mall Iron Co., 1934-45; pres. Carson-Saeks, Inc., Dayton, 1945-80, Carson & Saeks Cons. Assocs. Inc., Dayton, from 1980; sec.-treas. Cecile Baird, Inc., Hillsboro, Ohio. Mem. AAAS, Am. Chem. Soc. Achievements include 6 patents for clinical test procedures, reagents, and closet accessories. Home: Dayton, Ohio. Died Dec. 3, 2006.

CARTER, BOBBY (ROBERT ESTIL CARTER), retired state legislator; b. Scott County, Va., Oct. 7, 1939; s. Robert Todd and Estelle (Pippin) C.; m. Pauline Taber, May 15, 1942; children: Genny Lee, Russell Todd. BS in Edn., U. Tenn., Knoxville, 1962; MS in Edn., U. Tenn., 1963. Coach, tchr. Beaver Area High Sch., Beaver, Pa., 1963-65, Humboldt High Sch., Humboldt, Tenn., 1965-67, Union U., Jackson, Tenn., 1967-68; v.p. sales sec. Coca-Cola Bottling Co., Jackson, 1967-82, exec. vp., sec., 1982-90; mem. Dist. 27 Tenn. State Senate, Nashville, 1995—2002. Gen. chmn. Unied Way of West Tenn., Jackson, 1983, pres., 1985; pres. Jackson Exch. Club, 1982; campaign chmn. Jim Wilder for State Senate, Jackson, 1982; candidate State Senate, Republican party, Jackson, 1986, 90; exec. com. Madison County Rep party, Jackson, 1987-88; pastor Gardner's Chapel Primitive Bapt. Ch. Named Jackon Man of Yr., 1986; recipient United Negro Coll. Fund leadership award Lane Coll., 1984-86. Republican. Baptist. Home: Jackson, Tenn. Died Jan. 5, 2015.

CARTER, DOUGLAS ALAN, lawyer; b. Syracuse, NY, Mar. 12, 1950; BA in History, Western Ky. U., 1971; JD, U. Okla., 1984. Pvt. practice, 1987-89; atty. Office of Hearings and Appeals Social Security Adminstrn., Oklahoma City. N.Y. State Regents Coll. scholar, 1967, Syracuse Homebuilders Coll. scholar, 1967. Mem. ABA (adminstrv. law sect., incomes apportionment com. 1993—), Okla. Bar Assn. (legal svcs. com. 1987—). Died May 15, 2007.

CARTER, JON MICHAEL, facilities management executive, consultant; b. Dayton, Ohio, Dec. 6, 1945; s. Gerald F. and Delores (Krebs) C.; m. Irene Antoniw; 1 child, Kristyn Michelle. Student, Wis. State U., 1967-70; BSME, Newark Coll. Engring., 1972. Registered profl. engr.; cert. plant engr. Engr. various cos., 1972-76; facility mgr. Johnson & Johnson, Skillman, N.J., 1976-80, A.E.L., Inc., Lansdale, Pa., 1980-84, dir. corp. facilities/environ. services, 1984-88; dir. facilities mgmt. GTE Data Svcs., Inc., Tampa, Fla., from 1988. Co-inventor disc brakes fail safe system. Mem. Victorians Villa Victoria Acad., Trenton, N.J., 1986—. Mem. ASME, Water Resources Assn. Del River Basin, Assn. Profl. Energy Mgrs., Am. Inst. Plant Engrs., Internat. Facilities Mgmt. Assn., Nat. Mgmt. Assn., Am. Assn. Airport Execs. Avocations: aircraft, autos, home rehab. Home: Tampa, Fla. Died Dec. 11, 2006.

CARTO, WILLIS ALLISON, publishing executive; b. Ft. Wayne, Ind., July 17, 1926; s. Willis Frank and Dorothy Louise (Allison) C.; m. Elisabeth Waltraud Oldemeier. Student, Denison U., 1947-49. Treas., chief executive officer Liberty Lobby, Washington, from 1955; pub. The Spotlight, Washington, 1975—2001, The Barnes Rev., Washington, 1994—2001, The American Free Press, 2001. Cons. The Noontide Press, Torrance, Calif., 1960-, The Nat. Investor, 1996. Founder: Jour. Hist. Rev., 1980; editor, author: Profiles in Populism, 1982, Conspiracy Against Freedom, 1986, Populism vs. Plutocracy, The Universal Struggle, 1996; contbr. articles to profl. jours. Founder, organizer Liberty Lobby, Washington, 1955, United Reps.

Am., Washington, 1965, Inst. for Hist. Rev., Costa Mesa, Calif., 1979, Populist Party, Pitts., 1984, Populist Action Com., 1991; pres. Liberty Trust Mint, 1973. Cpl. U.S. Army, 1944-46. Decorated Purple Heart, Combat Infantry Badge. Populist. Methodist. Died Oct. 25, 2015.

CARTWRIGHT, MARIAN KATHRYN, dietitian, therapist, director; b. Milw., Apr. 5, 1919; d. John and Kathryn (Fritz) Swedish; m. Guilbert Wayne Meier, June 14, 1947 (dec. Oct. 1973); children: Gregory Guilbert, Cathryn Sue Meier Dunning; m. Cecil Donald Cartwright, May 2, 1981. BS in Nutrition and Dietetics, Mount Mary Coll., 1941. Registered dietitian, Wis. Intern Michael Reese Hosp., Chgo., 1941-42; dietitian Milw. Hosp., 1942-43; therapeutic dietitian Wis. Gen. Hosp., Madison, 1943-48, Wesley Med. Ctr., Wichita, Kans., 1962-67; clin. dietitian Bapt. Med. Ctr., Oklahoma City, from 1967, also assoc. dir. Mem. Am. Dietetic Assn., Okla. Dietetic Assn., Oklahoma City Dist. Dietetic Assn. (pres. 1978-79). Republican. Roman Catholic. Avocations: gardening, gourmet cooking, dance, travel, reading. Home: Oklahoma City, Okla. Died Aug. 15, 2007.

CASANOVA, ALDO JOHN, sculptor; b. San Francisco, Feb. 8, 1929; s. Felice and Teresa (Papini) C.; children: Aviva, Liana, Anabelle. BA, San Francisco State U., 1950, MA, 1951; PhD, Ohio State U., 1957. Asst. prof. art San Francisco State U., 1951-53; asst. prof. Antioch (Ohio) Coll., 1956-58; asst. prof. art Tyler Sch. Art, Temple U., Phila., 1961-64, Tyler Sch. Art, Temple U. (Italy campus), Rome, 1968-70; prof. art Scripps Coll., Claremont, Calif., from 1966, chmn. art dept., 1971-73; vis. prof. SUNY, 1981; faculty mem. Skowhegan Sch. Painting and Sculpture, Maine, summers 1973-74. One-man shows include Esther Robles Gallery, L.A., 1967, Santa Barbara (Calif.) Mus., 1967, Calif. Inst. Tech., 1972, Carl Schlosberg Fine Arts, L.A., 1977, SUNY, 1981, Casanova Retrospective Williamson Galleries, Claremont Colls., Calif. 2002; represented in permanent collections Whitney Mus., San Francisco Mus. Art, San Diego Mus. Sculpture Garden, Hirshhorn Collection, Cornell U., Columbus (Ohio) Mus., UCLA Sculpture Garden, Calif. Inst. Tech., Pasadena, Univ. Judaism, L.A., Air and Space Mus., Washington, Collection of Nat. Acad. of Design, N.Y.C., 1993, Robert Feldmuth Meml. Commn., W.M. Keck Sci. Ctr., Claremont, Calif., 1995, Orange County Mus., Calif., 1996, Rancho Santa Ana Botanic Gardens, Claremont, Calif., Palm Springs Mus., Calif., Brookgreen Gardens, Pawley's Island, SC. Recipient Prix-de-Rome Am. Acad. in Rome, 1958-61; Louis Comfort Tiffany award, 1970, Annual Gold medal, Calif. Art Club, Pasadena, Silver medal, Nat. Sculpture Soc., NY. Fellow: Am. Acad. in Rome; mem.: NAD, Nat. Sculpture Soc. Democrat. Roman Catholic. Home: Claremont, Calif. Died Sept. 10, 2014.

CÁSAREZ-LEVISON, ROSA, psychologist; b. LA, Jan. 30, 1951; d. Juan Garcia and Felicitas (Najera) Cásarez; m. Philip M. Levison, Nov. 6, 1983 (div. Dec. 1990). BA, Pitzer Coll., 1973; MA, Claremont Grad. Sch., 1977; PhD, Stanford U., 1991. Tchr. Compton (Calif.) Unifed Sch. Dist., 1973-75; instr. San Jose (Calif.) State U., 1976-80, 82-83; rsch. asst. Stanford (Calif.) U., 1982-83; asst. prof. San Jose State U., 1991-92, Santa Clara U., from 1992; dir. student life U. Calif., Santa Cruz, 1992-93; asst. prof. San Francisco State U., from 1993; pres., founder Casarez & Assocs., Palo Alto, Calif., from 1985. Expert psychologist media/TV; presenter, cons. in field; adv. mem. L.A. Piensalo Drug Prevention Campaign, 1990-91. Contbr. articles, short stories, poems to profl. publs., chpt. to book. Mem. exec. bd. San Francisco Sch. Vols., 1990-93; vol. ARC; bd. dirs. YWCA, Palo Alto, 1987-88. Digital Power grantee, 1984, Pitzer Coll. grantee, 1971-73; fellow Ford Found., 1979-81, Irvine Found., 1989. Mem. APA, Am. Coll. Forensic Examiners, Am. Ednl. Assn., Nat. Assn. Victim Assistance, Nat. Soc. Study of Edn., Nat. Assn. Gifted Children, Internat. Soc. Arts and Tech. (exec. bd. dirs. 1987—). Democrat. Roman Catholic. Avocations: sewing, painting, writing, singing, handwriting analysis. Home: Palo Alto, Calif. Died Feb. 1, 2007.

CASEY, JOHN P., special education educator; b. Pitts., May 26, 1920; s. Patrick F. C.; m. Eileen; children: Charles, Carol. BA, Bethany Coll., W.Va., 1949; M.Ed., U. Pitts., 1950; Ed.D. in Secondary Edn., Ind. U., 1963. Cert. tchr., Ill., Ohio. Tchr. Columbus (Ohio) Public Schs., 1950-59; asst. prof. Ill. State U., Normal, 1959-63; div. chmn. dept. social studies Northwestern Coll., Orange City, Iowa, 1963-64; asst. prof. So. Ill. U., Carbondale, 1964-69, assoc. prof. dept. spl. edn. and profl. ednl. experiences, 1969-73, prof. curriculum and spl. edn., 1973-83, prof. emeritus, from 1983, dir. Talent Retrieval and Devel. Edn. Project (TRADE), 1965-83. Co-author: Roles in Off-Campus Student Teaching, 1967; contbr. articles to profl. jours. Bd. dirs. Hospicecare, Carbondale, 1987. With U.S. Army. Research in supervision, research and teaching of gifted children. Home: Tucson, Ariz. Died Nov. 11, 2006.

CASEY, PAUL ARNOLD, writer, producer, photographer, composer, director; b. Inglewood, Calif., Dec. 10, 1934; s. Paul Franklyn and Orilee Corinne (Gray) C. AA, BA, UCLA. Pres., genetics cons. CSCA Internat., Sun Valley, Calif.; pres., tech. advisor Solenz Corp., Wilmington, Del. Dramaturg L.A. Playwrights Group, 1996; dir., CEO L.A. Playwrights Group. Author: Open the Coffin, 2005, (poetry) Songs of Youth, 1951; writer TV show Lassie, 1969; photographer wildlife: Girl Scouts Calendar, 1995; developer breed of cat: Calif. Spangled, 1971-86; inventor power lens, 1967; prodr. (theatrical) Original Sins; dir.: (film and theatrical prodn.) Smoke Screen; playwright: Anna & Ylenna; playwright Jewel Box Theatre Ctr. for Performing Arts, 1998-02. With USN, 1953-54. Recipient Nat. Humane Soc. award, 1965, Meritorious Achievement award Contbn. to Sci., 1998; scholar U.S. Govt. scholar, 1954. Mem. L.A. Playwrights Group (gen. sec. 1995-96, bd. dirs. 1998-2006). Achievements include invention of wind driven desalination and water purification plant. Avocations: wildlife photography, astronomy, archaeology, natural power systems technology. Home: North Hollywood, Calif. Died Apr. 23, 2007.

CASPER, BILLY (WILLIAM EARL CASPER, JR.), golf professional; b. San Diego, June 24, 1931; m. Shirley Franklin; children: Linda, Billy, Robert, Byron, Judi and Jeni (twins), Charles, David, Julia, Sarah, Tommy. Joined PGA Tour, 1955, joined Sr. PGA Tour, 1981. Named champion New Orleans Open, 1975, Sammy Davis Jr.-Greater Hartford Open, 1973, We. Open, 1965, 66, 73, Kaiser, 1971, Masters, 1970, Can. Open, 1967, U.S. Open, Mamaroneck, N.Y., 1959, San Francisco, 1966, Shootout at Jeremy Ranch, 1982, Merrill Lynch/Pro-Am, 1982, USGA St. Open, 1983. Legends Golf, 1984, Sr. PGA Tour Roundup, 1984, Greater Grand Rapids Open, 1987, Del Webb Ariz. Classic, 1987, Vantage Tour, 1988, Masda Sr. TPC, 1988, Transam. Open, 1989, Japan Urbanet Championship, 1989. Died Feb. 7, 2015.

CASPER, JR., WILLIAM EARL See CASPER, BILLY

CASSIDY, DWANE ROY, insulation contracting co. exec. b. Bedford, Ind., Oct. 20, 1915; s. Leo Clayton and Lilly Fay (Robbins) Cassidy; m. Mary Catherine Shrout, Aug. 28, 1937; children: Gail Everling, Cheryl, Duane, Nina McAnulty. Student, Roscoe Turner's Sch. Aviation, 1944. With L. C. Cassidy & Son, Inc., Indpls., from 1934, v.p. Fla., from 1963. Served with USN, 1944—45, PTO. Mem.: Gideons Internat., Optimists. Methodist. Home: Plainfield, Ind. Died Mar. 29, 2007.

CAST, PATRICIA WYNNE, writer, former nun, executive secretary; b. London, July 2, 1931; came to U.S., 1952; d. Albert James and Norah (Wynne) C. BA in Modern Lang. with honors, Birmingham U., 1952. Sec. Exec. Office of Sec. Gen., UN, NYC, 1953-57; novice mistress Carmelite Monastery, NYC, 1957-70; personnel dir. Knutsen Cos., Inc., Mpls., 1973-74; mgr. Working Horse Trust, Sussex, Eng., 1988-91; ret., 1993. Author: Trees for the Forest, 1978, Diptych, 1993, Writings of the Sun, 1994, Arts of Decay, 1995, Shadows of the Moon, 1996; translator: Life of Céline Martin, 1962; contbr. articles to mags. Organizer UNICEF, Robertsbridge, Sussex, 1987. Mem. Assn. Contemplative Sisters (founder). Roman Catholic. Avocations: photography, history, music, ballet, embroidery. Home: Santa Fe, N.Mex. Died Feb. 1, 2007.

CASTEL, NICO, tenor, educator; b. Lisbon, Portugal, Aug. 1, 1935; s. Felix and Margalitt (Castel) Kalinhoff; m. Carol Bayard (div.); m. Nancy Benfield (div.); m. Carol Cates; 1 child BA, Temple U., 1952. Artist in residence Mannes Coll. of Music, NYC, from 1980. Instr. diction and langs. Mannes Coll. Music, Queens Coll., Boston U., Juilliard Sch. Music, Internat. Vocal Arts Inst., Tel Aviv, Finnish Nat. Opera, Helsinki, Aspen Festival, Colo.; diction coach Met. Opera; stage dir. opera; adj. faculty Boston U.; founder N.Y. Opera Studio summer program Vassar Coll. Author: The Nico Castel Book of Ladino Songs, A Singers' Manual of Spanish Lyric Diction, The Complete Puccini, Verdi, Mozart and Wagner Libretti with phonetics and translation; Debuts include, N.Y. City Opera, 1965, Metropolitan Opera, 1970; permanent artist, Metropolitan Opera; extensive concert tours, U.S., S.Am., Europe; tchr. master classes in multilingual diction and style; trans. over 123 operas With U.S. Army, 1952-54. Recipient Joy In Singing award, 1958. Mem. Am. Guild Mus. Artists. Democrat. Jewish. Home: New York, NY. Died May 31, 2015.

CASTRO, RAUL HECTOR, lawyer, former Governor of Arizona, retired ambassador; b. Cananea, Mexico, June 12, 1916; arrived in US, 1926, naturalized, 1939; s. Francisco D. and Rosario (Acosta) C.; m. Patricia M. Norris, Nov. 13, 1954; children: Mary Pat, Beth. BA, Ariz. State Coll., 1939; JD, U. Ariz., 1949; LL.D. (hon.), No. Ariz. U., 1966, Ariz. State U., 1972, U. Autonoma de Guadalajara, Mex. Bar: Ariz. 1949. Fgn. service clk. US Dept. State, Agua Prieta, Mexico, 1941-46; instr. Spanish U. Ariz., 1946-49; sr. ptnr. Castro & Wolfe, Tucson, 1949-51; dep. county atty. Pima County, Ariz., 1951-54; county atty., 1954-58; judge Pima County Superior Ct., Tucson, 1958-64, Tucson Juvenile Ct., Tucson, 1961-64; US amb. to El Salvador US Dept. State, San Salvador, 1964—68, US amb. to Bolivia La Paz, Bolivia, 1968—69, US amb. to Argentina Buenos Aires, 1977-80; pvt. law practice Tucson, 1969-74, Phoenix, from 1980; gov. State of Ariz., Phoenix, 1975-77; sr. ptnr. Castro, Zipf & Rogers, 1982—92, Castro & Zipf, 1992—2015. Operator Castro Pony Farm, 1954—64. Pres. Pima County Tb & Health Assn., Tucson Youth Bd., Ariz. Horseman's Assn.; Bd. dirs. Tucson chpt. A.R.C., Tucson council Boy Scouts America, Tucson YMCA, Nat. Council Christians & Jews, YWCA Camp; Bd. Mem. Ariz. N.G., 1935-39. Recipient Outstanding Naturalized Citizen award Pima County Bar Assn., 1964, Outstanding Am. Citizen award DAR, 1964, Pub. Service award U. Ariz., 1966, John F. Kennedy medal Kennedy U., Buenos Aires, Disting. Citizens award, 1977, Matias Delgado award, Govt. of El Salvador. Mem. American Fgn. Service Assn., American Judicature Soc., Inter-American Bar Assn., Ariz. Bar Assn., Pima County Bar Assn., Nat. Council Crime and Delinquency (bd. dirs.), Assn. Trial Lawyers America, Council American Ambassadors, Nat. Assn. Trial Judges, Nat. Council Juvenile Ct. Judges, Fed. Bar Assn., Nat. Lawyers Club, Phi Alpha Delta, Phi Sigma Delta. Clubs: Rotarian. Democrat. Roman Catholic. Achievements include being Arizona's first and only Hispanic governor and an American ambassador to three Lating American countries. Died Apr. 10, 2015.

CATCHING, J(EROME) P(ETER), film director, stunt specialist; b. San Antonio, June 19, 1926; s. Ben H. and Norma Belle (Clifton) C.; divorced; children: Cara, Robin, Trudy. Student, Philips Bus. Coll., Van Nuys, Calif., 1947. Actor/stuntman various TV programs and motion pictures, Hollywood, Calif., 1946-88; stuntman actor Cisco Kid, 1949-54; stunt coord. various TV programs and motion pictures, Hollywood, Calif., 1953-88, 2nd unit dir., 1965-88. 2d unit dir. Moon Over Parador. Mem. Yuma (Ariz.) C. of C. (mem. film commn.), Kiwanis (Yuma club), Elks, Sherriff's Posse. Republican. Avocation: outdoor activities. Died Aug. 24, 2007.

CATTELINO, CRAIG ALAN, mechanical engineer; b. Pitts., Nov. 14, 1958; s. John Joseph and Loretto Ann (Boelens) C.; m. Liane DeMar, Oct. 19, 1991. BSME, Kans. State U., 1983; MBA in Fin. and Internat. Bus., Regis U., 1991. Registered profl. engr., Colo. Asst. engr. Allied/Bendix Aerospace, Kansas City, Mo., 1984-86; rsch. asst. Purdue U., West Lafayette, Ind., 1986-87; staff mech. engr. Burns & McDonnell, Denver, 1987-92; sr. project engr. Engring. Econs. Inc., Golden, Colo., from 1992. Contbr. articles to profl. jours. Vol. Denver Food Bank, 1992—. Mem. ASHRAE, NSPE, Tau Beta Pi, Pi Tau Sigma. Republican. Avocations: reading, hiking, bicycling, sailing, volunteer work. Home: Littleton, Colo. Died July 3, 2007.

CAULKINS, DIANA KAY, computer programmer; b. Pekin, Ill., June 13, 1948; d. Leo John and Leola Mae (Moldenhauer) Pfeiffer; m. Lloyd Howard Caulkins, Apr. 25, 1969; children: James Allen, Clifton Lynn. Student, Western Ill. U., 1966-67, Canton Coll., 1967-68. Accounts payable Ben Schwartz, Peoria, Ill., 1968-70; bookkeeper, rental agt. Barnett Real Estate, Killeen, Tex., 1974-76; owner, mgr. Grandma's Fried Chicken, Temple, Tex., 1976-80, Village Market and Cafe, Forest City, Ill., from 1980; office mgr. Pfeiffer Grain Farm, Forest City, 1980-91; computer set up S.E.M. Inc., Pekin, from 1991. Active St. John's Luth. Ch., pres. Ladies Guild, 1982. Mem. Manito Area C. of C. (v.p., pres.). Home: Forest City, Ill. Died May 25, 2007.

CAUTLEY, PATRICIA WOODWARD, psychologist; b. Wilkinsburg, Pa., Jan. 16, 1914; d. Walter Roy and Martha Ellen (Patrick) Woodward; m. Randolph Cautley, May 22, 1948 (dec.); children: Eleanor Kingsman, Daniel Woodward. AB, U. Mich., 1935, MA, 1936; postgrad., U. Pitts., 1937-38; PhD, U. Pa., 1942. Psychologist Children's Aid Soc. and Cath. Charities, Pitts., 1940-43; assoc. exec. sec. Com. on Food Habits, Nat. Rsch. Coun., Washington, 1943-45; study dir. div. program surveys USDA, Washington, 1945-48; lectr. in psychology U. Cin., 1948-52; acting chief psychologist Columbus (Ohio) State Sch., 1957-60; project assoc. NIMH grant U. Wis., Madison, 1961-64; project dir. HEW grant Wis. Dept. Welfare, Wis. Dept. Health and Social Svcs., Madison, 1964-66, 68-73; co-investigator NICHD grant U. Wis., Madison, 1971-74, project dir. HEW, HSS grants, 1976-78, 80-83; sec.-gen. Internat. Coun. Psychologists, Madison, 1983-90. Author: New Foster Parents: The First Experience, 1980; contbg. author foster parent placement manuals. Mem. LWV, Am. Psychol. Assn., Wis. Psychol. Assn., UN Assn. (pres. Madison chpt. 1991). Democrat. Unitarian Universalist. Avocations: water colors, gardening, hiking. Home: Madison, Wis. Died Jan. 26, 2007.

CAVANAUGH, JOHN RICHARD, English language educator, priest; b. Rochester, NY, June 10, 1929; s. William and Helen Louise (Kavanaugh) C. BA, U. Western Ont., London, Can., 1952; STB, U. St. Michael's, Toronto, Ont., Can., 1955; MA, U. Toronto, 1956; PhD, St. Louis U., 1969. Joined Congregation of St. Basil, Roman Cath. Ch., 1946, ordained priest, 1955. Instr. English, St. John Fisher Coll., Rochester, 1956-59, asst. prof., 1962-64, assoc. prof., 1965-69, prof., from 1970, chmn. dept., 1964-69, 72-80, trustee, from 1986. Trustee emeritus Aquinas Inst., Rochester; bd. dirs. Friends Rochester Pub. Libr., 1983-88, Sister City Com. Waterford and Rochester, 1986—; chmn. Rochester chpt. Irish Am. Cultural Inst., 1989—. Mem. MLA, Renaissance Soc. Am., Am. Conf. for Irish Studies, Delta Epsilon Sigma. Democrat. Avocations: cooking, foreign travel. Home: Rochester, NY. Died July 26, 2007.

CAVE, YVONNE S., retired librarian; m. Richard K. Cave, Oct. 27, 1951 (dec.). Student, Cleve. State U., 1943—44; BS in Edn., Bowling Green State U., Ky., 1944—48; student, The Coll. of Wooster, Ohio, 1950; MA, Union Theol. Seminary, Tchrs. Coll.-Columbia U., 1950—51. HS libr., Willoughby, Ohio, 1948—50; mission rsch. libr. Union Theol. Seminary, NYC, 1950—51; libr., children's rm./reference Bentley Pub. Libr., Columbus, Ohio, 1955—57; libr. Kent State U., North Canton; part-time libr., law libr. Stark County Libr., Alliance, 1967—68. Active Panel Am. Women, Canton, Human Rels. Coun. Greater Canton. Mem.: AAUW. Independent. Presbyterian. Avocations: reading, gardening, stamp collecting/philately, history, biography. Home: Canton, Ohio. Died Feb. 19, 2007.

CAVENAGH, DESMOND WARING, JR., (TIM CAVENAGH), quality assurance professional; b. Watertown, NY, Dec. 24, 1937; s. Desmond Waring and Margaret Agatha (Moscoe) C.; m. Jackie Marie Baumer, Dec. 14, 1963 (div. Oct. 1972); m. Martha Schaller Heavner, Feb. 11, 1977; stepchildren: Emily Suzanne, Ronald Stewart. AAS, SUNY, Farmingdale, 1958; police acad. cert., Allan Hancock Coll., 1970; BS, Sussex Coll., London, 1981. Electronic technician GE, Syracuse, N.Y., 1958-60, field technician Clear, Alaska, 1960-61, Sacramento, 1961-62, Vandenberg AFB, Calif., 1962-77, radar system specialist, 1977-89; leader quality assurance Martin Marietta, Vandenberg AFB, Calif., from 1989. Capt. Sheriff's Dept. Res. Forces, Santa Maria, Calif., 1966—. Mem. Am. Soc. Quality Control (vice chmn.

Calif. ctrl. coast div. 1992), Peace Officers Rsch. Assn., Am. soc. Indsl. Security (outstanding officer of yr. 1993), AIAA (sr.), Elks. Republican. Avocations: amateur radio operator with call letters wa6htg, rebuilding sports cars. Home: Santa Maria, Calif. Died Dec. 3, 2006.

CAWLEY, CHARLES M., retired bank executive; married; children: C. Michael III, Maureen C. Rhodes. Grad., Georgetown U. With Md. Nat. Bank, 1972; founder, exec. v.p. Md. Bank N.A. (now MBNA), 1982, pres., 1985—2002; CEO MBNA Am. Bank, N.A., 1990—2002; pres., dir. MBNA Corp., Del., 1991—2003, chmn., CEO Wilmington, Del., 2002—03; ret., 2003. Bd. dirs. MasterCard Internat. Exec. com. bd. dirs. Am. Quality Found.; bd. regents Georgetown U. Died Nov. 18, 2015.

CEDARBAUM, MIRIAM GOLDMAN, federal judge; b. Brooklyn, Sept. 16, 1929; d. Louis Albert and Sarah (Shapiro) Goldman; m. Bernard Cedarbaum, 1957 (dec. 2006); children: Jonathan, Robert Ehrenbard. BA, Barnard Coll., 1950; LLB, Columbia U., 1953. Bar: N.Y. 1954, U.S. Dist. Ct. (so. dist.) N.Y. 1956, U.S. Ct. Appeals (2d cir.) 1956, U.S. Ct. Claims 1958, U.S. Supreme Ct. 1958, U.S. Dist. Ct. (ea. dist.) N.Y. 1980, U.S. Ct. Appeals (5th and 11th cirs.) 1981, Southern Dist. NY. Law clk. to Judge Edward Jordan Dimock US Dist. Ct. (so. dist.), 1953-54, asst. US atty., 1954—57, judge, 1986-98, sr. judge, 1998—2016; atty. Dept. Justice, Washington, 1958-59; part-time cons. to law firms in litig. matters, 1959-62; 1st asst. counsel N.Y. State Moreland Act Commn., 1963-64; assoc. counsel Mus. Modern Art, NYC, 1965-79; assoc. litig. dept. Davis Polk & Wardwell, Manhattan, 1979—83, sr. atty. NYC, 1983—86; acting village justice Village of Scarsdale, NY, 1978—82, village justice, 1982-86. Trustee emerita Barnard Coll.; com. defender svcs. Jud. Conf. U.S., 1993—99; mem. emerita bd. visitors Columbia Law Sch., chmn. NY state selection com. for Rhodes scholar, 2003, chmn. NY state selection com. for Rhodes scholarship, 2004. Mem. bd. revising editors Columbia Law Rev.; contbr. articles to profl. jours. James Kent scholar, Columbia Law Sch.; recipient Jane Marx Murphy prize, Medal of Distinction Barnard Coll., 1991, Riot Relief Fund Medal of Honor, 2010, Myra Bradwell Disting. Alumna award, Columbia Law Women's Assn., 2012. Mem. ABA (chmn. com. on pictorial graphic sculptural and choreographic works 1979-81, copyright com. fed. practice and procedure 1983-84), Am. Law Inst., Fed. Bar Coun., Copyright Soc. U.S.A. (trustee, exec. com. 1979-82), Supreme Ct. Hist. Soc., Am. Judicature Soc Jewish. Died Feb. 5, 2016.

CHADWICK, OWEN (WILLIAM OWEN CHADWICK), academic administrator, historian, educator; b. Bromley, Kent, Eng., May 20, 1916; s. John and Edith (Horrocks) C.; m. Ruth Hallward, Dec. 28, 1949 (dec. 2014); children: Charles, Stephen, Helen, Andre. BA, Cambridge U., Eng., 1939, LittD (hon.); LittD (hon.), Bristol U.; LittD (hon.), London U., Columbia U., East Anglia U., U. Kent, Eng., Leeds U.; DD (hon.), Oxford U., St. Andrews U., Wales U.; LLD (hon.), Aberdeen U. Ordained priest to Ch. of Eng. Chapel dean Trinity Hall, Cambridge, 1947; master of Selwyn Coll. Cambridge U., 1956-83, Dixie prof. ecclesiastical history, 1958-68, Regius prof. modern history, 1968-83, vice chancellor, 1969-71; chancellor U. East Anglia, 1985—94; fellow Brit. Acad., 1962, pres. London, 1981-85. Author: John Cassian: A Study in Primitive Monasticism, 1950, Victorian Miniature, 1961, The Reformation, 1964, The Victorian Church, 2 vols., 1966, 1971, The Secularization of the European Mind in the Nineteenth Century, 1976, The Popes and European Revolution, 1981, The Christian Church in the Cold War, 1993, A History of Christianity, 1995, History of the Popes 1830-1914, 1998, Acton on History, 1998, The Early Reformation on the Continent, 2001. Created knight, 1982; decorated Order of Merit (England), 1983; recipient Wolfson prize for historical writing, 1981. Home: Cambridge, England. Died July 17, 2015.

CHALABI, AHMED ABDEL HADI, former Iraqi government official; b. Baghdad, Iraq, Oct. 30, 1944; married; 4 children. Grad. in Math., M in Math., MIT; PhD in Math., U. Chgo., 1969. Prof. math. American U., Beirut; founder Petra Bank, Jordan, 1977, chmn., 1977—90; founder Iraqi Nat. Congress (INC), 1992, chair exec. coun., 1992—99; dep. prime min. Republic of Iraq, Baghdad, 2005—06, interim min. oil, 2005—06. Publsihed several mathematical papers. Died Nov. 3, 2015.

CHALMERS, JAMES FERGUSON, aerospace engineer, consultant; b. Ft. Madison, Iowa, Mar. 31, 1922; s. James Ferguson and Annie White (Rodgers) C.; m. Nancy McClellan, Oct. 27, 1945; children: Constance Chalmers Binst, Harleigh Chalmers Kehoe. BSME, BSCE, Calif. Inst. Tech., 1947; MBA, Harvard Bus. Sch., 1949. Jr. engr. Consolidated Aircraft Co., San Diego, summer 1942; tech. adminstr. Hughes Aircraft Co., El Segundo, Calif., 1950-52; program scheduler Ramo-Wooldridge Corp., El Segundo, Calif., 1952-55; asst. to v.p. Space Tech. Labs., El Segundo, Calif., 1955-60; dir. tech. adminstrn. The Aerospace Corp., El Segundo and Washington, 1960-85; sr. cons. Energetics, Inc., Columbia, Md., 1985-87, 88-89. Capt. USAF, 1942-45. Decorated Disting. Flying Cross, Air medal with 3 oak leaf clusters. Mem. East India Club London, Harvard Bus. Sch. Club Washington (chmn. membership 1979-80), St. Andrew's Soc. Washington, Ends of the Earth Club N.Y.C. Republican. Episcopalian. Avocations: marine painting, carpentry, travel, writing (adventure novles and short stories). Home: Naples, Fla. Died Dec. 11, 2006.

CHAMBERS, CURTIS ALLEN, clergyman, church administrator; b. Damascus, Ohio, Sept. 24, 1924; s. Binford Vincent and Margaret Esther (Patterson) C.; m. Anna June Winn, Aug. 26, 1946; children: David Lloyd, Curtis Allen II, Deborah Ann, Charles Cloyde. Th.B., Malone U., 1946; AB, Ind. Wesleyan U., 1947; B.D., Asbury Theol. Sem., 1950; postgrad., Oberlin Grad. Sch. Theology, 1951-53; S.T.M., Temple U., 1955, S.T.D., 1960; D.D. (hon.), Lebanon Valley Coll., 1967. Ordained to ministry Evang. United Brethren Ch., 1954. Pastor 1st Ch., Cleve., 1951-53, Rockville Ch., Harrisburg, Pa., 1953-59; editor adult publs. Evang. United Brethren Ch., 1959-65; assoc. editor Ch. and Home mag., Dayton, Ohio, 1963-66, editor, 1967-69; asst. editorial dir. Together and Christian Advocate, Meth. Pub. House, Park Ridge, Ill., 1969; editor Together mag., 1969-73; acting editorial dir. gen. periodicals United Meth. Ch., 1971-72, editorial dir., 1972-73; gen. sec. United Meth. Communications, 1973-84; gen. mgr. Alternate View Network, 1984-85; minister edn. and communication First United Meth. Ch., Shreveport, La., 1985-87, minister pastoral care and communication, 1987-88; minister program and communication St. Paul's United Meth. Ch., Monroe, La., 1988-90; religious communication cons. Nashville, from 1990; assoc. pastor Andrew Price United Meth. Ch., Nashville, 1991-94. Book editor Evang. United Brethren Ch., 1965-68; co-editor Plan of Union, United Meth. Ch., 1965-68, Plan of Union, United Meth. Ch. (Book of Discipline), 1968, chmn. staff com. long range planning, 1969-72, mem. commn. on ch. union, 1965-68; dir. radio-TV relations gen. confs. Evang. United Brethren Ch., 1958, 62, 66, United Meth. Ch., 1966, 68; Chmn. commn. on ednl. media Nat. Council Chs., 1965-66, chmn. com. on audio visual and broadcast edn., 1962-65, exec. com. broadcasting and film commn., chmn. communications commn., 1975-78, v.p., 1975-78; chmn. Religious Communications Congress, 1980; named 1 of 12 editors sent to Middle East on fact-finding trip, 1969 Contbr. articles to religious lit. Served as capt. (chaplain) CAP, 1960-65. Recipient Distinguished Alumni award Malone Coll., 1967, 92, Alumni of Year, 1978, Distinguished Alumni award Goshen High Sch. Alumni Assn., 1992; named to Communicators Hall of Fame United Meth. Assn. Communicators, 1992. Mem. Aircraft Owners and Pilots Assn., United Meth. Assn. Communicators (v.p. 1968-72, Communicators' Hall of Fame 1992), World Assn. Christian Communications (central com., chmn. Jour. editorial bd. 1975-82, chmn. periodical devel. com., exec. com., sec. 1978-82), Asso. Ch. Press (hon. life), Religious Pub. Relations Council. Clubs: Chgo. Press (Dayton), Torch (Dayton). Home: Terre Haute, Ind. *When I was young I thought that anything was possible for me and that I had a long, long time to achieve it. With maturity I have come to a recognition of mortality, finitude, a limitation of time and opportunity. Thus my life has taught me three things: 1) Choose the best. Life is too precious to squander it on the second rate. 2) Live for others. The quality of one's life is enhanced rather than diminished as one shares himself/herself with others. 3) Fulfill your dreams. Tomorrow may never come; act now so that life's opportunities may not be lost forever.* Died Jan. 3, 2015.

CHAMBERS, EDWARD THOMAS, foundation executive; b. Clarion, Iowa, Apr. 2, 1930; s. Thomas J. and Hazella Mae (Downing) C.; m. Ann L. Martin, 1974; children: Eve, Mae, Joseph, Lily, William. BA in Philosophy and Classics, U. St. John's, Collegeville, Minn., 1953. With Indsl. Areas Found., Chgo., NYC, from 1940, exec. dir., 1972—2009, trustee, 1972—2009. Author: Roots for Radicals: Organizing for Power, Action, and Justice, 2003. Home: Garden City, NY. Died Apr. 26, 2015.

CHAMBERS, FLOYD ALLEN, counselor; b. Shreve, Ohio, Oct. 3, 1928; s. Roscoe Coral and Myra Elizabeth (Wright) C.; m. Lyndall Lee Wooley, Feb. 1, 1953; children: Mark Allen, Debra Lynn, Norman Kent, Sheryl Yvonne, Jon Scott. BA, Coll. Wooster, 1950; MDiv, McCormick Seminary, Chgo., 1953; MEd, Coll. William and Mary, 1980, EdD, 1986. Lic. profl. counselor, Va. Min. Presbyn. Ch., Ky., Canada, 1953-56; chaplain, 1st lt. USAF, 1956, advanced through grades to lt. col., 1971, ret., 1978; pastoral counselor Tidewater Pastoral Counseling Svcs., Norfolk, Va., from 1979. Fellow Am. Assn. Pastoral Counselors; mem. Am. Assn. for Marriage and Family Therapy (clin.). Home: Hampton, Va. Died May 11, 2007.

CHAMPION, KENNETH STANLEY WARNER, physicist; b. Sydney, NSW, Australia, Dec. 7, 1923; s. Cecil Alexander Buckingham and Ellen Catherine (Moxham) C.; m. Mavis Audrey Hinckley, Nov. 27, 1948; children: Annette, Gwendalyn, Geoffrey, Sandra. BS, U. Sydney, 1945; PhD, U. Birmingham, Eng., 1951. Asst. lectr. physics U. Queensland, Australia, 1946-49; rsch. fellow Australian Nat. U., 1949-52; rsch. assoc. MIT, Cambridge, Mass., 1952-54; asst. prof. physics Tufts U., Medford, Mass., 1954-59; rsch. scientist, sr. scientist Atmospheric Physics/Br. Chief, 1959-64; sr. exec. AF Cambridge Rsch. Labs./Phillips Lab., 1964-94. Brit. Coun. Rsch. scholar, 1947-49; vis. prof. U. Adelaide, Australia, 1964; presenter in field in 21 countries. Contbr. articles to 6 internat. profl. jours. Co-pres. PTA, Lexington, Mass., 1965-75. Fellow Phys. Soc. of London; mem. AIAA (assoc. fellow), N.Y. Acad. Scis., Am. Phys. Soc., Am. Geophys. Union, Am. Meteorol. Soc., Sigma Xi. Episcopalian. Achievements include being a pioneer in early plasma fusion oriented rsch.; pioneer in space rsch. with rocket and satellite measurements and development of internationally accepted atmospheric models. Home: Vero Beach, Fla. Died Aug. 7, 2007.

CHAMPLIN, CHARLES DAVENPORT, television personality, critic, writer; b. Hammondsport, NY, Mar. 23, 1926; s. Francis Malburn and Katherine Marietta (Masson) C.; m. Margaret Frances Derby, Sept. 11, 1948; children: Charles Jr., Katherine, John, Judith, Susan, Nancy. AB cum laude, Harvard U., 1947. Reporter Life mag., NYC, 1948-49, corr. Chgo., 1949-52, Denver, 1952-54; asst. editor Life mag., NYC, 1954—59; corr. Time mag., LA, 1959-62, London, 1962-65; arts editor, columnist L.A. Times, 1965-91, prin. film critic, 1967-80, book critic, 1981-82. Host-commentator Ste. KCET-TV, L.A., ETV Network, Z Channel Cable TV, Bravo Channel, 1969-96; adj. prof. Loyola-Marymount U., L.A., 1969-86; adj. prof. U. So. Calif., 1986-96. Author: (with C. Sava) How to Swim Well, 1960, The Flicks, 1977, The Movies Grow Up, 1981, Back There Where the Past Was: a Small-Town Boyhood, 1989, George Lucas: The Creative Impulse, 1992, enlarged, 1997, John Frankenheimer: A Conversation, 1995, Woody Allen at Work, 1995, Hollywood's Revolutionary Decade, 1998, Tony's World, 1999, My Friend, You Are Legally Blind: A Writer Struggles with Macular Degeneration, 2001, A Life in Writing, 2006; contbr. numerous articles to mags. and publs. Trustee L.A. Film Tchrs. Assn.; served in U.S. Army, 1944-46, ETO. Decorated Purple Heart; recipient Order Arts and Letters, France, 1977 Mem. PEN, L.A. Film Critics Assn., Authors Guild. Democrat. Home: Los Angeles, Calif. Died Nov. 16, 2014.

CHANCE, TRUETT LAMAR, retired secondary school educator; b. Liberty Hill, Tex., Aug. 23, 1913; s. Edgar Lee and Edith Alma Chance; 1 child, Trudy Jo Kinnison. BS, Southwest Tex. State Tchrs. Coll., 1936; MEd, U. Tex., 1942, PhD, 1970. Tchr., supr. various schs., 1945—92; ret., 1992. With US Army. Democrat. Avocation: gardening. Home: San Antonio, Tex. Died Jan. 19, 2007.

CHANDLER, WILLIAM HENRY, lawyer; b. Heminway, SC, May 5, 1948; s. William Jackson and Margaret Eloise (Nelson) C.; m. Ann Rodgers Tomlinson, July 31, 1982; children: Jared Witherspoon Nelson, Martha Elizabeth Hartman, Ann Paisley Snowden. AB, U. S.C., Columbia, 1970, JD, 1973. Bar: S.C. 1973, U.S. Dist. Ct. (we. dist.) La. 1975, U.S. Dist. Ct. S.C. 1973, U.S. Ct. Mil. Appeals 1974. Ptnr. Chandler & Ruffin, Hemingway, S.C., 1978-84, Askins, Chandler, Ruffin & Askins, Hemingway, S.C., from 1984. Instr. bus. law Williamsburg Tech. Coll., Kingstree, SC, 1978—79, instr. state and local govt., 2002. Vice chmn. Williamsburg County Bd. Trustees, 1979—84, Williamsburg County Devel. Bd.; chmn. The Continuum of Care for Emotionally Disturbed Children, Williamsburg County Planning Commn., from 2001; mem. State Hist. Records Adv. Bd.; pres. Williamsburg Co. Forest Landowners Assn.; chmn. Williamsburg Co. Planning Commn.; supt. ch. sch. First Presbyn. Ch., Bossier City, La., 1975—77; lay spkr. Presbytery of the Pines Presbyn. Ch. U.S., Bossier City, 1976—77; ruling elder Indiantown Presbyn. Ch., Hemingway, from 1980; moderator, counsel, mem. judiciary com. The Presbytery of New Harmony; bd. dirs. Francis Marion Coll. Found., Williamsburg County Farm Bur.; vice chmn. Pee Dee Heritage Found.; bd. dirs. Williamsburg Regional Hosp. Found., Lake City Mus., Pee Dee Land Trust; atty. Town of Stuckey, SC, from 1979. Lt. col. USAF Ret., 1970—99. Mem. ABA, SAR, Am. Legion, SC Geneal. Soc., SC Libr. Soc., French Higuenot Soc., SC Hist. Soc., Williamsburg County Bar Assn. (pres. 2005—), Francis Marian Trail Commn., Williamsburg County Hist. Soc. (pres.), Three Rivers Hist. Soc. (pres.), St. Andrews Soc. City of Columbia, Charleston Preservation Soc., Lions, Masons (Hemingway), Williamsburg Hometown C.C. (bd. dirs.), SC Hall Fame (trustee), Hog Crawl Hunting Club, Wilson Lake Fishing Club, Phi Eta Sigma, Omicron Delta Kappa, Phi Delta Phi Home: Hemingway, SC. Died Dec. 15, 2006.

CHANEY, ROBERT GALEN, religious organization executive; b. LaPorte, Ind., Oct. 27, 1913; s. Clyde Galen and Maree (Francis) C.; m. Earlyne Cantrell, Oct. 4, 1947; 1 child, Sita. Student, Miami U., Ohio, 1931-33; DD, Coll. Universal Truth, 1954. Ordained to non-denominational ministry, 1939. Pastor various parishes, Eaton Rapids and Lansing, Mich., 1938-50; founder, pres. Astara, LA, 1951—76, Upland, Calif., from 1976. Author: The Inner Way, 1962, Adventures in ESP, 1975, Mysticism: The Journey Within, 1979, The Power of Your Own Medicine, 1995, Visits to the Manger, 1996. Mem. Masons, Kiwanis. Democrat. Died Dec. 20, 2006.

CHANEY, VICTOR HARVEY, secondary education educator, historical dramatist; b. Chgo., Nov. 11, 1940; s. Charles and Libby (Siegel) C.; m. Meta Bowman, July 14, 1973; 1 child, Dana; stepchildren: Gary (dec.), Rick, Randy. BA in Polit. Sci., UCLA, 1963; MEd, Calif. State U., Northridge, 1973. Tchr. Simi Valley (Calif.) Unified Sch. Dist., 1972-89, Beaverton (Oreg.) Sch., from 1989. Author: (poetry volume) Passing Through, 1984, Random Thoughts; (novel) The Bernstein Projections, 1991; creator and actor of one man plays and guest speaker presentations. Mem. Oreg. Tchrs. Assn., Nat. Audubon Soc., Nature Conservancy. Avocations: writing poetry and limericks, humorist articles. Home: Beaverton, Oreg. Died Aug. 24, 2007.

CHAPMAN, EDWARD ARNOLD, JR., marketing professional; b. Ann Arbor, Mich., Apr. 20, 1933; s. Edward A. and Mary Alice (Moore) C.; m. Mary Tewksbury, Sept. 13, 1957 (div. 1979); children: Mary, Edward. BA, Dartmouth Coll., 1955. Various positions with N.Y. Telephone, NYC, 1958-81; exhibit mktg. supr. AT&T, NYC, 1981-86; pres. Sextant Communications, NYC, from 1987. Author: The Candidates Guide, 1974, Exhibit Marketing, 1987. Mem. Internat. Exhibitors Assn., Health Care Exhibitors Assn., Nat. Assn. Exposition Mgrs., Trade Show Bur. Clubs: Richmond County Yacht. Republican. Episcopalian. Avocation: sailing. Died Jan. 19, 2007.

CHAPMAN, REID GILLIS, former broadcasting company executive; b. Indpls., July 27, 1920; s. Arthur Reid and Esther Mary (Gillis) C.; m. Janet K. Passwater, Oct. 20, 1942 (dec.); children: Arthur II, Martha Chapman Shull, Mark, Rosalie Chapman Hanefeld, James; m. Mary A. Ayers, June 17, 1977 (div.). Student, Butler U., 1938-40.

With radio sta. WAOV, Vincennes, Ind., 1943; with WISH, WISH-TV, Indpls., 1943-56; mgr. WANE Radio, Ft. Wayne, Ind., 1956-58; v.p., gen. mgr. WANE-TV, 1958-82; v.p., dir. Ind. Broadcasting Corp., Ft. Wayne, 1959-84, Summit Bank, Ft. Wayne. Exec. dir. Northeast Ind. Radio Reading Svc. Hon. chmn. Cancer Crusade Month, 1971; mem. Com. of 24, 1967— ; Bd. dirs. United Way, Conv. Bur., Parkview Meml. Hosp., Martin Luther King Meml. Fund, Asso. Chs. Ft. Wayne, YMCA, Legal Aid Soc., Ft. Wayne Art Mus.; bd. dirs. Jr. Achievement, Ft. Wayne, 1958— , pres., 1962-64; bd. dirs., v.p. Better Bus. Bur., 1962-65; bd. dirs. Goodwill Industries, 1959-65, v.p., 1964-65; adv. bd. Ind. U.-Ft. Wayne. Named to Ind. Broadcast Pioneer Hall of Fame; Paul Harris fellow Rotary Internat.; recipient Sagamore of Wabash award Gov. Evan Bayh of Ind., 1994. Mem. Ft. Wayne Advt. Club (past pres., Silver medal award 1971, hon.), Ft. Wayne Press Club (past pres., roastmaster and chmn. Gridiron Show), Ft. Wayne C. of C. (past v.p., dir.), Nat. Assn. Broadcasters (dir.), Ind. Broadcasters Assn. (past pres.), Broadcast Pioneers (pres.) Presbyterian (elder). Clubs: Summit (Ft. Wayne), Ft. Wayne Country (Ft. Wayne), Quest (Ft. Wayne). Lodges: Masons, Shriners, Scottish Rite, Rotary (hon.) Home: New Haven, Ind. Died Nov. 29, 2006.

CHAPMAN, WILLIAM B., lawyer; b. NYC, Feb. 7, 1935; s. Bruce Woodallen and Edna Mae (Coleman) C.; m. Judith B. Skillman, Sept. 22, 1956 (div. 1970); children: William, David; m. Mary L. Hudson, May 29, 1971. BS, Swarthmore Coll., 1956; JD, Stanford U., 1979. Bar: Calif. 1979, U.S. Dist. Ct. (ctrl. and no. dists.) Calif. 1979, U.S. Dist. Ct. (so. and ea. dists.) Calif. 1983, U.S. Ct. Appeals (9th cir.) 1982, U.S. Supreme Ct. 1984. Engr. Bell Tel. Co. Pa., Phila., 1958-59; creative dir. The Ullman Orgn., Phila., 1960-64; exec. dir. Am. Inst. Archs., Phila., 1965-69; asst. v.p., dir. planning, v.p. U. Hawaii, Honolulu, 1970-76; atty. Pettit & Martin, San Francisco, 1979; ptnr. Rogers, Joseph, O'Donnell & Quinn, San Francisco, 1980-93; founding ptnr. Chapman, Popik & White, San Francisco, 1993—2012. Adj. prof. Hastings Coll. Law, San Francisco, 1992-2000. Co-author: Our Man-made Environment, 1969. Fellow: Am. Bar Found.; mem.: ABA, Am. Bd. Trial Advs. Avocations: reading, skiing, trout fishing, squash, golf. Home: Sausalito, Calif. Died July 21, 2015.

CHARLES, ANDREW VALENTINE, psychiatrist; b. Chgo., Nov. 5, 1939; s. George and Carol Claire (Goettel) C.. BA cum laude, U. Mich., 1961; MD, U. Ill., 1965. Diplomate Am. Bd. Psychiatry and Neurology. Rotating intern Ill. Masonic Hosp., Chgo., 1965—66; psychiatry resident Presbyn. St. Luke's Hosp., Chgo., 1966—69; practice medicine specializing psychiatry Chgo., from 1969; instr. psychiatry Rush Med. Sch., Chgo., from 1970; psychiatrist Chgo. Bd. Edn., 1970—77; clin. dir. Exec. Assessment Corp., 1976—78. Pres., chief exec. officer contbg. editor Desmodus Pub. Corp. Contbr. articles to profl. jours. Mem.: AMA, Am. Assn. Utilization Rev. Physicians, Am. Acad. Med. Dirs., Chgo. Med. Soc., Ill. psychiat. Assns., Am. Group Psychotherapy Assn., Phi Rho Sigma. Home: Piedmont, Calif. Died Nov. 27, 2006.

CHARNEY, DAVID H., advertising executive, writer; b. NYC, July 30, 1923; s. Boris and Frances C.; m. Louse Verrette, Apr. 30, 1965; children: Beth, Steven, Kenneth. BFA, Cooper Union, 1977. V.p., sr. art dir. Ehrlich & Neuwirth, NYC, 1951-56; sr. art dir. Daniel & Charles, NYC, 1956-61; sr. v.p., creative dir. Robert A. Becker, NYC, 1961-92. Adj. instr. Fashion Inst. Tech., N.Y.C., 1980-99. Author: Magic, The Great Illusions, 1975, Sensei, 1983, Sword Master, 1984. 1st lt. USAAF, 1942-45, PTO. Home: Tuckahoe, NY. Died Dec. 12, 2006.

CHARREN, PEGGY, consumer activist; b. NYC, Mar. 9, 1928; d. Maxwell and Ruth (Rosenthal) Walzer; m. Stanley Charren, June 17, 1951; children: Deborah, Claudia. BA, Conn. Coll., 1949; LLD (hon.), Regis Coll., 1978; DHL (hon.), Emerson Coll., 1984; EdD (hon.), Bank St. Coll. Edn., 1985; DHL (hon.), Tufts U., 1988; EdD (hon.), Wheelock Coll., 1990. Founder, owner Art Prints, Inc., Providence, 1951-53, Quality Book Fairs, Newton, Mass., 1960-65; dir. Creative Arts Council, Newton, 1966-68; founder, pres. Action for Children's T.V., Inc., Cambridge, Mass., 1968—90; mem. Carnegie Commn. on Future of Public Broadcasting, 1977-79; mem. task panel on public attitudes and use of media for promotion of health President's Commn. on Mental Health, 1977-80; mem. Mass. Council on Arts and Humanities, 1980-87. Vis. scholar in edn. Harvard Grad. Sch. Edn., 1987—; mem. adv. bd. project on TV advt. and children NSF; mem. adv. bd. project on devel. of programs for children with spl. needs Am. Inst. Research; bd. dirs. Child Devel. Consortium, Media Access Project. Co-author: Changing Channels: Living Sensibly with Television, 1983, The TV-Smart Book for Kids, 1986; Television, Children and the Constitutional Bicentennial, 1986; contbr. articles to profl. publs. Bd. dirs. Women's Campaign Fund., Young Audiences of Mass.; mem. adv. bd. Am. Repertory Theater. Recipient Disting. Public Info. Service award Am. Acad. Pediatrics, hon. award Motion Picture Assn., Disting. Service award Mass. Radio and TV Assn., 1974, hon. medal Conn. Coll., 1974, Helen Homans Gilbert award Radcliffe Coll., Trustees' award NATAS, 1989, Presidential Medal of Freedom, 1995; named Humanist of Yr. Ethical Soc. of Boston, 1988. Democrat. Avocations: literature, theater, arts, politics. Home: Cambridge, Mass. Died Jan. 22, 2015.

CHARTOFF, ROBERT IRWIN, film producer; b. NYC, Aug. 26, 1933; s. William and Bessie Chartoff; 2 marriages ending in divorce; m: Jenny Weyman, 1991; children: Jenifer, William, Julie, Charley, Miranda. AB, Union Coll., 1955; LLB, Columbia U., 1958. Producer: numerous films including Double Trouble, 1967, Point Blank, 1967, The Split, 1968, Leo the Last, 1969, They Shoot Horses Don't They, 1969, The Strawberry Statement, 1970, The Gang That Couldn't Shoot Straight, 1971, The New Centurions, 1972, The Mechanic, 1972, Up the Sandbox, 1972, Busting, 1974, The Gambler, 1974, Peeper, 1975, Rocky, 1976 (Acad. award for best picture), Nickelodeon, 1976, New York, New York, 1977, Valentino, 1977, Comes A Horseman, 1978, Uncle Joe Shannon, 1978, Rocky II, 1979, Raging Bull, 1980, True Confessions, 1981, Rocky III, 1982, The Right Stuff, 1983, Rocky IV, 1985, Beer, 1986, Rocky V, 1990, Straight Talk, 1992, In My Country, 2004, Rocky Balboa, 2006, Tempest, 2010, Ender Game, 2013 Died June 10, 2015.

CHASE, CHARLENE ANN, social services executive; b. Long Beach, Calif., Dec. 30, 1941; d. Ernest Leo and Ruth Sultana (Cole) Miles; m. Amos J. Chase, Dec. 22, 1968 (dec. Apr. 1994); children: Amos John II, Joshua Miles. BA, L.A. Pacific, 1965; MA, Sierra U., 1989. Cert. social worker. Social worker L.A. County Social Svcs., Southgate, Calif., 1968-70, supr. LA, 1970-72, staff developer, 1972-77, adminstr. El Monte, Calif., 1977-82; dep. dir. Santa Barbara (Calif.) Social Svcs., 1982-88, dir., from 1988. Instr. Hancock C.C., Santa Maria, Calif., 1984-87; 1st v.p. Calif. Child Welfare Strategic Planning, 1990-91; bd. dirs. Santa Barbara Regional Health Initiative, 1989—, Area Agy. on Aging, Santa Barbara, 1990—. Mem. bd. ARC, Santa Barbara, 1982-89. Mem. Calif. County Welfare Dirs. Assn. (pres. 1991-92). Mem. Unity Ch. Avocations: playing organ, golf, walking by the sea, teaching. Home: Santa Maria, Calif. Died Feb. 3, 2007.

CHASE, RICHARD LEE, educational administrator, consultant; b. St. Augustine, Fla., Oct. 20, 1946; s. Lee and Jane (Duncan) C.; children: Allison, Christopher, Melinda. BA, U. Fla., 1975. Tchr. Clay County Schs., Green Cove Springs, Fla.; organizer Fla. Teaching Profession/NEA, Tallahassee, exec. dir., field svc. cons. Home: Jacksonville, Fla. Died July 27, 2007.

CHATTERJEE, ANIL KUMAR, mechanical engineer, consultant; b. Calcutta, India, May 27, 1923; came to U.S., 1951; s. Narayan Chandra and Indu (Banerjee) C.; m. Maya Mukherjee, Dec. 14, 1958; children: Bikash K., Pallab R. BME, U. Jadavpur, Calcutta, 1948; MS, Va. Poly. Inst., 1952; postgrad, U. Minn., 1952-56. Registered profl. engr., Calif., N.Y. Sr. staff engr. Ellerbe & Co., 1956-58; asst. prof. U. Akron, Ohio, 1958-61; engring. specialist Valve div. TRW, Cleve., 1961-66; sr. staff engr. Union Carbide, Tonawanda, N.Y., 1966-67, Torrax div. Carborundum Co., Niagara Falls, N.Y., 1967-74; engring. specialist, sr. staff engr. Acres Am. Inc., Buffalo, 1974-77; sr. rsch. engr. SRI Internat., Menlo Park, Calif., 1978-80; pres. Chatterjee & Assocs. Inc., Newark, Calif., from 1980. Engring. cons. World Bank, UNIDO, U.S. AID, Caribbean Community SECRTT, Asian Devel. Bank. Co-author: Biomass Conversion Processes for Energy and Fuels, 1981; contbr. articles to profl. jours.; patentee in field. Fulbright scholar New Delhi, 1951; recipient 1st prize for paper Am. Soc. Engring. Edn., 1960. Mem. ASME (bd. dirs. 1961-66), AIChE. Democrat. Hindu. Avocations: photography, tennis, hiking, writing, reading. Home: Newark, Calif. Died Feb. 17, 2007.

CHAUVIN, YVES, chemist; b. Menen, Belgium, Oct. 10, 1930; 2 children. MS, Lyon Sch. Chemistry, Physics & Engring. (CPE Lyon), France, 1954. Rscr. French Inst. Petroleum, Rueil-Malmaison, France, 1960—91, rsch. dir., 1991—95, ret., hon. rsch. dir., 1995. Recipient Carl Engler medal, German Sci. Soc. Coal & Petroleum Rsch.(DGMK), 1994, Nobel prize in chemistry, 2005. Mem.: French Acad. Scis. (corr. Clavel-Lespiau prize 1990). Achievements include co-developement of the metathesis method in organic synthesis, which has led to more efficient production and a major reduction in potentially hazardous waste products. Died Jan. 28, 2015.

CHEADLE, LOUISE, music educator, musician; b. Donora, Pa., July 4, 1935; d. Max Raphael and Helen Louise Busto; m. William George Cheadle, Feb. 12, 1959 (dec. Dec. 1993); children: William Robert, Amy Louise Fleming. BMusic, The Juilliard Sch., 1959. Founder, dir. Westminster Conservatory of Music/Rider U., Princeton, NJ, 1972—82; head piano dept. Amherst Summer Music Ctr., Raymond, Maine, 1971—72; adj. instr. music Bucks County C.C., Newtown, Pa., 1982-85; nationwide concert tours and workshops, various mgmts. and agys., throughout U.S., 1980s; nat. adjudicator Nat. Guild Piano Tchrs., Austin, Tex., from 1999; freelance recitals, workshops and pvt. tchg. includes Lincoln Ctr., Carnegie Hall, N.Y.C., from 1980. Debut recital with Pitts. Concert Soc., 1954; contbg. author: Teaching Piano, 1981; CD release Virtuoso Piano Music by Cecile Chaminate and Fanny Mendelssohn-Hensel, 2002. Bd. dirs., chair Cmty. Outreach. Juilliard Sch. scholar, 1956-59. Mem. Music Tchrs. Nat. Assn., N.J. Music Educators Assn. (bd. dirs., v.p.), N.J. Music Tchrs. Assn. (chair Young Artist Competition 1999, 2000, chair Master Class Competition 1999, 2000), Rossmoor (N.J.) Music Assn. (bd. dirs.), Piano Tchrs. Congress N.Y., Music Club of Princeton. Avocations: writing, reading, cooking, cultural events. Died Dec. 4, 2006.

CHEUSE, ALAN STUART, writer, journalist, educator; b. Perth Amboy, NJ, Jan. 23, 1940; s. Philip K. and Matilda (Diamond) C.; m. Mary Ethel Agan, Sept. 12, 1965 (div. Mar. 1974); 1 child, Joshua; m. Marjorie Pryse, June 12, 1976 (div. Jan. 1984); children: Emma, Sonya; m. Kristin Mitchell O'Shee, Aug. 17, 1991. BA, Rutgers U., 1961, PhD, 1974. NJ Turnpike toll collector, travel in Europe, welfare case worker, asst. fur-page editor, Women's Wear Daily Page, and a high school teacher in Mexico; faculty mem. Bennington Coll., Vt., The University of South, University of Virginia, University of Michigan; book critic, All Things Considered Nat. Pub. Radio, Washington, 1982—2015, host, The Sound of Writing; mem. writing faculty George Mason U., Fairfax, Va., 1987—2015. Leads fiction workshops Squaw Valley Community of Writers. Author: (short stories) Fishing for Coyotes, 1979, (novels) The Bohemians, 1982, The Grandmothers' Club, 1986, The Light Possessed, 1990, (memoirs) Fall Out of Heaven, 1987, Prayers for the Living, 2015; editor: (with Caroline Marshall) The Sound of Writing, 1992, Listening to Ourselves, 1994, (with Nicholas Delbanco) Talking Horse: Bernard Malamud on Life and Work, 1996. Fiction fellow NEA, 1979-80. Home: Washington, DC. Died July 31, 2015.

CHEVES, VERA LOUISA, retired librarian; b. Rockport, Mass., Nov. 13, 1908; d. Andrew Gustaf and Olga Amanda (Silen) Cederstrom; m. Robert Cheves, dec.; children: Robert (dec.), Constance. BS in Edn., Boston U., 1930; MLS, Simmons Coll., 1963. Libr. asst. Sawyer Free Libr., Gloucester, Mass., 1932-33; libr. Boston Pub. Libr., 1950-73; med. libr. Addison Gilbert Hosp., Gloucester, Mass., 1984-92. Organist Lanesville Congl. Ch., Gloucester, 1972—93. Home: Gloucester, Mass. Died June 24, 2007.

CHILDRESS, DUDLEY STEPHEN, biomedical engineer, educator; b. Cass Co., Mo., Sept. 25, 1934; m., 1959; two children. BS, U. Mo., Columbia, 1957; MS, U. Mo., 1958; PhD in Elec. Engring., Northwestern U., 1967. From instr. to asst. prof. Elec. Engring. U. Mo., Columbia, 1959-63; rsch. asst. Physiology Control Sys. Lab. Northwestern U., Evanston, Ill., 1964-66, from asst. prof. to assoc. prof. Elec. Engring., Ortho. Sur., 1972-77, co-dir. Rehab. Engring. prog., 1972-85, prof. Elec. Engring., Tech. Inst., 1977-86, prof. biomed. engring., 1986—2005; prof. Orthopedic Surgery Northwestern Med. Sch., 1977-97, dir. Prosthetics Rsch. Lab., 1971—2005, dir. Rehab. Engring. prog., 1985—2005; prof. phys. medicine rehab. Northwestrn Med. Sch., 1997—2005; ret., 2005. Elected to Inst. Med. Nat. Acad. Sci., 1995; mem. Com. Prosthetics Rsch. and Devel., Nat. Acad. Sci. Nat. Rsch. Coun., 1969-72. Recipient Nat. Inst. Gen. Med. Sci. rsch. career devel. award, 1970-75, Goldenson award, United Cerebral Palsy Found., Paul Magnuson award Va. RR&D Svc., 2002, DaVinci Lifetime award Mich. chpt. Nat. Multiple Sclerosis Soc. Mem. AAAS, Applied Physiology and Bioengring. Study Sec., NIH, 1974-78, Biomed. Engring. Soc., Rehab. Engring. Soc. N. Am., Inst. Soc. Prosthetics and Orthotics, Sigma Xi. Home: Wilmette, Ill. Died Aug. 6, 2014.

CHILTON, STEPHEN PRESLER, political science educator; b. Phila., Oct. 31, 1946; s. Arthur Bounds Jr. and Charlotte Ann (Presler) C.; m. Mary Constance Hannigan, Mar. 7, 1970 (div. Apr. 1980); children: Catherine Mary Chilton Blood. BS in Applied Math., Brown U., 1968; PhD in Polit. Sci., MIT, 1977. Assoc. dir. N.J. Poll Eagleton Inst. Politics, New Brunswick, 1974-75, dir. N.J. Poll, 1975-76; analyst in social legis. Congl. Rsch. Svc., Washington, 1977-81; asst. prof. polit. sci. N.Mex. State U., Las Cruces, 1981-86, U. Minn., Duluth, 1986-92, assoc. prof. polit. sci., from 1992. Author: Defining Political Development, 1988, Grounding Political Development, 1991; co-author: (with others) Political Reasoning and Cognition: A Piagetian Approach, 1988; mem. editorial bd. Comparative Political Studies, 1989—; contbr. articles to profl. jours. Mem., bd. dirs. Franklin Twp. (N.J.) Pub. Libr., 1971; precinct committeeman Dem. Party Mcpl. Com. Piscataway, N.J., 1972-73; del. Dem. Party County Conv., Duluth, Minn., 1988, 90, 92; del. Dem. Party State Conv., Duluth, 1992. Mem. Am. Polit. Sci. Assn., Midwest Polit. Sci. Assn., Minn. Polit. Sci. Assn., Assn. for Moral Edn., Morality and Social Action Interdisciplinary Colloquium, Unv. Edn. Assn. (bargaining team 1988-94, pres. elect 1992-94, pres. 1994-96). Avocations: politics, literature. Home: Duluth, Minn. Died Mar. 28, 2007.

CHING, ERIC SAN HING, health care and insurance administrator; b. Honolulu, Aug. 13, 1951; s. Anthony D.K. and Amy K.C. (Chong) C. BS, Stanford U., 1973, MS, MBA, 1977. Fin. analyst Mid Peninsula Health Service, Palo Alto, Calif., 1977; acting dep. exec. dir. Santa Clara County Health Systems Agy., San Jose, Calif., 1977-78; program officer Henry J. Kaiser Family Found., Menlo Park, Calif., 1978-84; dir. strategic planning Lifeguard Health Maintenance Orgn., Milpitas, Calif., 1984-90; v.p. strategic planning and dir. ops. Found. Life Ins. Co., Milpitas, 1986-90; sr. planning analyst Kaiser Found. Health Plan, Oakland, Calif., 1990-94, coord. product and competition analysis, 1994-95, mgr. ins. ops. and competitive intelligence cons., 1995-97, nat. product leader, from 1997. Adj. faculty Am. Pistol Inst., 1991-94. Mem. vol. staff Los Angeles Olympic Organizing Com., 1984; mem. panel United Way of Santa Clara County, 1985, panel chmn., 1986-87, mem. com. priorities and community problem solving, 1987-90, Project Blueprint, 1988-90. Mem. NRA, Law Enforcement Alliance of Am., Am. Soc. Law Enforcement Trainers, Internat. Assn. Law Enforcement Firearms Instrs., Stanford Alumni Assn., Stanford Bus. Sch. Alumni Assn., Stanford Swordmasters (pres. 1980-89), Safari Club Internat. Avocations: hunting, photography, travel, musical theater, reading. Home: Mountain View, Calif. Died July 28, 2007.

CHIODO, JACK RUSSELL, advertising executive; b. San Antonio, Nov. 16, 1955; s. Vincent Russell and Cleo Mable (Wilmeth) C.; m. Elizabeth Kay Hughes; children: Kari Leann, Tyler Russell, Kelly Sha. BFA, Tex. Tech. U., 1979. Advt. artist Handy Andy Supermarket, San Antonio, 1978; art dir. Mark VII Prodns., San Antonio, 1979-80; ptnr., owner Stout Advt. Agy., San Antonio, 1980-84; prin. Chiodo Advt. Agy., San Antonio, from 1984, also bd. dirs. Cons. advt. various polit. campaigns, San Antonio, 1982-86. Artist paintings, 1983. Recipient Addy award Advt. Fedn.

San Antonio, 1984; named one of Outstanding Young Men Am., 1985. Mem. San Antonio C. of C., Tau Kappa Epsilon (sec. 1976). Clubs: University (San Antonio), Plaza (San Antonio). Republican. Presbyterian. Avocations: sports, painting, hunting, fishing. Home: San Antonio, Tex. Died Feb. 26, 2007.

CHRISMAN, WILLIAM HERRING, tax specialist, consultant; b. Evanston, Ill., June 28, 1932; s. Roswell Herring and Virginia Ruth (Haynes) C.; m. Margaret Baker Craig, Apr. 17, 1989; children: Katherine Anne, Emily Louise. AB, Harvard U., 1955. Media buyer Leo Burnett Co., Chgo., 1958-60; account exec. Lennen & Newell Inc., NYC, 1960-63; subsidiary pres. Clairol Inc., NYC, 1963-72; exec. v.p. Metalware Corp., Chandler, Ariz., 1973-75; pres. Chrisman Farms, Inc., Scottsdale, Ariz., 1975-80, E. Allen Mgmt. Corp., Phoenix, 1980-85; gen. mgr. Oasis Family Water Park, Phoenix, 1985; asset mgr. Evans Withycombe Inc., Phoenix, 1985-87; prin. Real Estate Valuation Cons., Phoenix, 1987—2002; ret., from 2002. Advt. instr. Katherine Gibbs Sch., N.Y.C., 1963-65. 1st lt. U.S. Army, 1955-57. Mem. Christmas Cove Improvement Assn., Spa at Camelback Inn. Democrat. Methodist. Home: Paradise Valley, Ariz. Died Jan. 24, 2007.

CHRIST, EARLE L., lawyer; b. Racine, Wis., Aug. 8, 1915; s. Thomas Christ and Martha Peterson; m. Agnes Barabra Meurer, Dec. 4, 1943; children: Joellyn K. Keleske, Thomas E. LLB, JD, Marquette U., 1948. Pvt. practic, Racine. Maj. USAFR, 1942-64. Mem. Wis. State Bar Assn., Racine County Bar Assn. Republican. Roman Catholic. Avocations: camping, flying. Home: Largo, Fla. Died June 28, 2007.

CHRISTIAN, JAMES WAYNE, economist, writer; b. Ft. Worth, Oct. 7, 1934; s. Nap B. and Daphne (Wright) Christian; m. Jo June Maples, June 5, 1952; children: Amy Joella, Nicole Denise. BA, U. Tex., Austin, 1962, MA, 1964, PhD, 1965. Dir. internat. div. Fed. Home Loan Bank Bd., Washington, 1972—74; sr. v.p., chief economist Nat. Savs. and Loan League, Washington, 1974—80, U.S. League Savs. Inst., Chgo., 1980—91; pres. James Christian Assocs., Fair Oaks Ranch, Tex., 1991; dir. Real Estate Ctr. at Tex. A & M Univ., 1993—95. Prof. econs. Iowa State U., 1965—74; dir. Nat. Housing Conf., 1980—84; cons. 26 developing country govts., 1970—2001. Contbr. articles to profl. jour. Mem. Dem. Nat. Com. With USN, 1952—55, with USAF, 1955—59. Recipient Am. Legion award, 1949; univ. fellow, 1964, NSF fellow, 1965, Social Sci. Rsch. Coun. grant, 1968—69. Mem.: Cosmos, Phi Kappa Phi, Pi Sigma Alpha, Omicron Delta Epsilon, Phi Beta Kappa. Democrat. Methodist. Avocation: birdwatching. Died Mar. 31, 2015.

CHRISTOPHER, ROBERT, literature and language professor, researcher; b. NYC, Jan. 4, 1937; s. Constantine and Constance Christopher; m. Frima Yarmus Christopher; children: Nina, Noam. BA, City Coll. NY, 1960; MA, San Francisco State U., 1961; PhD, U. Calif., Berkeley, 1974. Instr. English U. Calif., Berkeley, 1967—69; asst. prof. English Pa. State U., University Park, 1969—74; prof. lit. Ramapo Coll., Mahwah, NJ, from 1974. Editl. bd. Jour. Basic Writing, NYC, 1993—99, Assn. Grad. Liberal Studies, from 1999. Author: Robert O Francel Flaherty: A Documentary UFO, 1883-1922, 2005. Recipient Outstanding Faculty Mem., Assn. Grad. Liberal Studies, 2001. Mem.: Assn. Intergraduate Studies, Assn. Can. Studies US. Avocation: art. Home: New York, NY. Died Dec. 16, 2006.

CHRISTY, NICHOLAS PIERSON, physician; b. Morristown, NJ, June 18, 1923; s. Leroy and Elizabeth (Baker) C.; m. Beverly Vairin Morris, June 21, 1947 (dec. Mar. 1997); children: Nicholas Pierson, Martha Vairin; m. Caroline P. Adams, June 26, 1999. AB, Yale, 1945; MD, Columbia, 1951. Diplomate: Am. Bd. Internal Medicine. Intern, asst. resident medicine, 1951—54; asst. vis. physician Delafield Hosp., NYC, 1955-66, vis. physician, 1966-75; asst. vis. physician 1st med. div. Bellevue Hosp., NYC, 1958-66; assoc. attending physician Presbyn. Hosp., NYC, 1962-78, attending physician, 1978-93. Dir. med. svc. Roosevelt Hosp., NYC, 1965-79; faculty Columbia Coll. Phys. and Surg., NYC, 1956—, assoc. prof. medicine, 1962-65, assoc. clin. prof., 1965-67, clin. prof. medicine, 1967-71, prof. medicine, 1971-79, lectr. in medicine, 1979-88, sr. lectr. medicine, 1988-93, spl. lectr. in medicine, 1993—; mem. Columbia U. Health Scis. adv. coun., 1993—; prof. medicine, assoc. dean vets. affairs Health Sci. Ctr. at Bklyn., SUNY, 1979-88, prof. emeritus, 1988—; chief staff Bklyn. VA Med. Ctr., 1979-88; writer-in-residence, alumni writer Coll. Physicians and Surgeons, Columbia U., 1988—; assoc. Nat. Humanities Ctr., Research Triangle Park, NC, 1979; cons. FDA, 1966, Bd. of Health, NYC, 1965—, NIH Nat. Inst. Diabetes, Digestive and Kidney Diseases tng. grants divsn., 1969-72, endocrinology study sect., 1975-79; cons., bd. dirs. Royal Soc. Medicine Found., 1984-93. Editor, co-author: The Human Adrenal Cortex, 1971; editor-in-chief: Jour. Clin. Endocrinology and Metabolism, 1963-67; assoc. editor: Beeson-McDermott Textbook of Medicine, 1968-75; cons. editor, 1975-79; cons. Med. Dictionary (Dorland), 1988; adv. editor and contbr. Internat. Dictionary of Medicine and Biology (Endocrinology), 1986; mem. adv. bd.: Am. Jour. Medicine, 1971-88; contbr. numerous papers to profl. publs. Served to lt. (j.g.) USNR, 1943-46, PTO. Recipient Borden award, Joseph Mather Smith prize Columbia; John and Mary R. Markle scholar; NIH tng. grantee, 1959-65, endocrinology study sect. grantee, 1958-69; honoree St. Luke's Roosevelt Hosp. Alumni Assn., 2000. Fellow Am. Med. Writers Assn. (hon., Swanberg award 1989); mem. Harvey Soc., AAAS, Soc. Exptl. Biology and Medicine, Am. Soc. Clin. Investigation, Assn. Am. Physicians, Am. Fedn. Clin. Rsch., A.C.P., NY Acad. Medicine, Laurentian Hormone Conf., Am. Physiol. Soc., NY State Med. Soc., NY County Med. Soc., Am. Clin. and Climatol. Assn. (recorder 1977-88, pres. 1990), Am. Assn. Study Liver Diseases, Endocrine Soc. (sec.-treas. 1978-89, Ayerst award 1986), NY Clin. Soc., NY Med. and Surg. Soc., Assn. Am. Physicians, Interurban Clin. Club, Hosp. Grads. Club, Peripatetic Soc., Practitioners Soc., Elizabethan (Yale), Colony (Yale), Century Assn. (pres. 1987-90, hon. 1995—). Home: Westerly, RI. Died Apr. 26, 2014.

CIANCI, VINCENT ALBERT, JR., (BUDDY CIANCI), former mayor; b. Providence, Apr. 30, 1941; s. Vincent Albert and Esther (Capobianco) C.; m. Sheila Bently McKenna (div. 1983); children Nicole Cianci (dec. 2012) Grad., Moses Brown Sch., Providence, 1958; BS, Fairfield U., Conn., 1962; MA in Polit. Sci, Villanova U., 1965; JD, Marquette U., 1966; D Pub. Service (hon.), Fairfield U., Conn., 1978; LLD (hon.), Roger Williams Coll.; D (hon.), Johnson & Wales Coll. Bar: R.I. bar 1967. Spl. asst. atty. gen. State of RI, Providence, 1969-73, prosecutor organized crime unit, 1973-74; mayor Providence, 1975—84, 1991—2001; candidate for mayor, 2014. Host Sta. WHJJ-Radio, Providence, 1984-90; polit. commentator Sta. WJAR-TV, 1987, Sta. WLNE-TV (CBS), 1988-90; radio host WPRO, 2007-2016; chief polit. analyst, contributing editor WLNE-TV ABC6, Your Attention Please, renamed Buddy TV, then The World According to Buddy; 2007-2016; co-host, On the Record with Buddy Cianci, 2008-2011, host, 2011-2016; lectr. in govt. Bryant Coll., Providence, 1969-74. Author (with David Fisher): Politics and Pasta: How I Prosecuted Mobsters, Rebuilt a Dying City, Dined with Sinatra, Spent Five Years in a Federally Funded Gated Community, and Lived to Tell the Tale, 2011. Trustee R.I. Hosp., Womens & Infants Hosp., Providence Pub. Library, Greater Providence Chamber of Commerce; Served to 1st lt. U.S. Army, 1966-69. Decorated Order Merit Italy); recipient Guardian Peace award State Israel Bonds, City Livability award U.S. Conf. Mayors, Vol. Fundraiser of Yr. award Northeast region ARC. Mem. Italian Am. War Vets. U.S., R.I. Bar Assn., Bar U.S. Ct. Mil. Appeals, Bar U.S. Dist. Ct., Nat. Dist. Attys. Assn., Am. Judicature Soc., R.I. Hist. Soc., Justinian Law Soc. R.I., Phi Delta Phi. Clubs: Brown Faculty, Aurora, Providence Art, Italo-Am. (Providence); K.C. Died Jan. 28, 2016.

CLANCY, LYNN ROGER, JR., retired principal, retired elementary school educator; b. Niagara Falls, NY, June 7, 1929; s. Lynn Roger Clancy and Jennie Marie Anderson; m. Doris Elizabeth Mathews, May 14, 1951 (div. May 1980); m. Sandra Virginia Nichols, June 20, 1987; children: Stephen Lynn, Kathleen Elizabeth Clancy Ellis. AB magna cum laude, Niagara U., 1957; MA, San Fernando Valley State U., 1960; PhD, UCLA, 1971. Cert. adminstr., tchr. K-14, Calif. Acting dir. Simi Valley (Calif.) Sch. Dist., 1973, prin., 1968-79, tchr., 1979-94, ret., 1994. Lectr., ednl. adminstrn. Calif. Luth. Coll., Thousand Oaks, 1969-73; tchr. Simi Valley Sch. Dist., 1966-68, LA Sch. Dist., 1957-66; cons. in field. Author: History of the American Federation of Teachers in Los Angeles, 1919-1969, 1971. Pres. Simi Valley PTA Coun., 1978-79; officer Boy Scouts Am., 1961-65. With USN, 1948-52. Named hon. citizen Boy's Town, Nebr. Mem. AARP, Nat. Wildlife Fedn., Wolf Edn. and Rsch. Ctr., Nat. Geographic Soc., Mensa, Delta Epsilon Sigma, Phi Delta Kappa. Democrat. Baptist. Avocations: photography, hiking, travel, woodworking, reading. Home: Prescott, Ariz. Died Feb. 15, 2007.

CLARK, A. JAMES (ALFRED JAMES CLARK), engineer, entrepreneur, construction executive, real estate and venture capital executive; b. Richmond, Va., Dec. 2, 1927; s. Woodruff and Salley (Wray); m. Alice Bratton; children: Paul, A. James Jr., Courtney Clark Pastrick. BS in Civil Engring., U. Md., 1950; PhD in Engring. (hon.), George Washington U., 2010. Joined George Hyman Construction Co., 1950, pres., 1969—77; founder Omni Construction (merged with Hyman to form Clark Construction), 1977—96; CEO Clark Enterprises, Inc., chmn. Former bd. dirs. CarrAmerica Realty Corp., Geico Corp., PEPCO Holdings, Inc., Martin Merietta (now Lockheed Martin). Bd. trustee George Washington U., 1988—93; hon. trustee U. Md. Coll. Park Found.; emeritus trustee John Hopkins U., John Hopkins Medicine; adv. bd. mem. PGA Tour Golf Course Properties. Named in his honor: A. James Clark Sch. Engring., U. Md.; named one of Forbes 400: Richest Americans, 2009; laureate, Washington Bus. Hall of Fame. Mem.: NAE. Died Mar. 20, 2015.

CLARK, BARBARA M., state legislator; b. Beckley, W.Va., June 12, 1939; d. Ada DeBerry; m. Thomas Clark; children: Jan, Crystal, Thomas III, Brian. Active mem. various NYC pub. sch. Parent-Teacher Associations; mem. Dist. 33 NY State Assembly, 1987—2016, dep. majority whip. Former mem. human services com. Nat. Conf. State Legislators, former vice chair; vice chair Edn. Commn. of States, 2008—10. Recipient Leadership award, Svc. NYC, Coun. Sr. Ctrs. Democrat. Died Feb. 22, 2016.

CLARK, CHARLES T(ALIFERRO), retired statistician; b. Danville, Ill., Mar. 18, 1917; s. Charles A. and Kathryn S. C.; m. Pearl W. DuBose, Oct. 6, 1943; children: Charles A., Mary D., Robert S. BBA, U. Tex., 1938, MBA, 1939, PhD, 1956. Asst. mgr. Austin C. of C., Tex., 1940-41; dir. personnel U. Tex., Austin, 1946-59, asst. prof. bus. stats., 1959-60, assoc. prof., 1961-79, prof., 1979-91, Mary Lee Harkins Sweeney Centennial prof. emeritus in bus., from 1991. Bd. dirs. Tex. Student Publs., Austin, 1964-69, Tex. Union, Austin, 1969-83, Univ. Fed. Credit Union, Austin, 1976-84 , Univ. Coop. Soc., Austin, 1980-84. Author numerous text books; (with L.L. Schkade) textbooks Statistical Analysis for Adminstrative Decision, 1969, 4th edit., 1983, (with John R. Stockton) Introduction to Business and Economic Statistics, 1971, 3d edit., 1980; contbr. articles to profl. jours. Served to 2d lt. USAAC, 1941-46, PTO. Recipient 11 teaching awards U. Tex., 1960-80 Mem. Coll. and Univ. Personnel Assn. (pres. 1959), Austin Personnel Assn. (pres. 1950), Austin Stat. Assn. (pres. 1975) Home: Austin, Tex. Died Nov. 25, 2014.

CLARK, EUGENIE, marine biologist, educator; b. NYC, May 4, 1922; m. Hideo Umaki, 1942; m. Ilias Konstantinou, 1949; 4 children ; m. Chandler Brossard, 1966; m. Igor Klatzo, 1969; m. Henry Yoshinobu Kon, 1997. BA, Hunter Coll., 1942; MA, NYU, 1946, PhD, 1950; DSc (hon.), U. Mass., Dartmouth, 1990, U. Guelph, 1995, U. South Hampton, 1995. Rsch. asst. ichthyology Scripps Instn. Oceanography, 1946-47; with NY Zool. Soc., 1947-48; rsch. asst. animal behavior Am. Mus. Nat. Hist., NYC, 1948-49, rsch. assoc., 1950-80; instr. Hunter Coll., 1954; exec. dir. Cape Haze Marine Lab., Sarasota, Fla., 1955-67; assoc. prof. biology CUNY, 1966-67; assoc. prof. zoology U. Md., 1968-73, prof. zoology, 1973-92, prof. emerita, sr. rsch. scientist, from 1992. Vis. prof. Hebrew U., 1972; sr. rsch. scientist, trustee emerita Mote Marine Lab., Sarasota, Fla., from 1999; sci. advisor Save Our Seas Found., from 2010. Author: Lady with a Spear, 1953, The Lady and the Sharks, 1969, Desert Beneath the Sea, 1991; subject of biographies Shark Lady (Ann McGovern), 1978, Adventures of the Shark Lady (Ann McGovern), 1998, Eugenie Clark, Adventures of a Shark Scientist (Ellen R. Butts, Joyce R. Schwartz), 2000, Fish Watching with Eugenie Clark (Michael E. Ross), 2000, America's Shark Lady (Ann McGovern), 2004, Eugenie Clark, Marine Biologist (Ronald A. Reis) 2005, Dr. Eugenie Clark Swimming with Sharks (Lisa Rao), 2006. Recipient Myrtle Wreath award in sci. Hadassah, 1964, Nogi award in art Underwater Soc. Am., 1965, Dugan award in aquatic sci. Am. Littoral Soc., 1969, Diver of Yr. award Boston Sea Rovers, 1978, David Stone medal, 1984, Stoneman Conservation award, 1982, Gov. of S. Sinai medal, 1985, Lowell Thomas award Explorers Club, 1986, Wildscreen Internat. Film Festival award, 1986, medal Gov. Red Sea, Egypt, 1988, Nogi award in Sci., 1988, Women's Hall of Fame award State of Md., 1989, Women Educators award, 1990, Alumnae award, Franklin Burr award Nat. Geog. Soc., 1993, Wyland Icon award, 2005, Henry Luce III Lifetime Achievement award, Wings WorldQuest Women of Discovery Awards, 2006, Conservation medal of Costa Rica, 2007, Sci. Diving Lifetime Achievement award, Am. Acad. Underwater Scis., 2007, Sci. Diving Lifetime medal of the Explorers Club, 2008, Bonaire's Lifetime Achievement award, 2010, Lifetime Making a Difference award, Nat. Marine Educators Assn., 2010, Nat. Coun. Jewish Woman award, 2010, Grand Cayman Internat. Scuba Diving Hall of Fame award, 2010, Beneath the Sea Women Divers Hall of Fame, 2010, Fla. Governor's award: Induction to Womens Hall of Fame, 2010; named to Hunter Coll. Hall of Fame, 1990, Diver's Equipment Mfg. Assn. Hall of Fame, 1993, Bermuda Underwater Explorers Inst. Hall of Fame, 2004, Hall of Fame Cmty. Video Archives, 2007, Fla. Women's Hall of Fame, 2010, Internat. Scuba Diving Hall of Fame, 2010, Beneath The Sea's Pioneer Diver of Yr., 2010; Fellow AEC, 1950; Saxton fellow, 1952; Breadloaf Writer's fellow; Fulbright scholar Egypt, 1951. Fellow: AAAS; mem.: Am. Elasmobranch Soc. (disting. fellow 1999), Am. Littoral Soc. (v.p. 1970—89), Nat. Pks. and Conservation Assn. (vice chmn. 1976), Internat. Soc. Profl. Diving Scientists, Soc. Woman Geographers (Gold medal 1975, U. Md. Pres.'s medal 1993), Israeli Zool. Soc. (hon.), Am. Soc. Ichthyology and Herpetology (life). Achievements include research in ecology and behavior of tropical sand and coral reef fishes; morphology and taxonomy marine fish; isolating mechanisms of poecillid fish; behavior of coral reef and deep sea sharks. Home: Sarasota, Fla. Died Feb. 25, 2015.

CLARK, JOHN PETER, III, engineer, consultant; b. Phila., May 6, 1942; s. John Peter Jr. and Victoria Mary (McQuaide) C.; m. Nancy Ann Lapin, June 22, 1968; children: Shannon John, Hannah Marie. BSChemE in Chem. Engring. cum laude, Notre Dame U., 1960—64; PhD in Chem. Engring., U. Calif., Berkeley, 1964—68. Registered profl. engr., Va., Ill.; cert. food scientist. Rsch. engr. Agrl. Rsch. Svc., USDA, Berkeley and Washington, 1968-72; from asst. to assoc. prof. Va. Poly. Inst. and State U., Blacksburg, 1972-78; dir. R & D, ITT Continental Baking, Rye, NY, 1978-81; pres. Epstein Process Engring. Inc., Chgo., 1981-94; pvt. practice, engring. cons., Oak Park, Ill., 1994-95; v.p. tech. Fluor Daniel, Inc., 1995-98; engring. cons. Oak Pk., from 1998. Author: Practical Design, Construction and Operation of Food Facilities, 2009, Case Studies in Food Engineering: Learning From Experience, 2009; co-author: Food Processing Operations and Scale-up, 1991; editor: Practical Ethics for Food Professionals, 2013, Exercises in Process Simulation, 1977; contbg. editor Food Tech.; contbr. articles to profl. jours.; patentee (with C.J. King) in field for sys. for freeze drying. Pres., bd. dirs. Oak Pk. River Forest Food Pantry, from 2011. Recipient Ernest W. Thiele award, AIChE, 2010, Life Achievement award, Internat. Assn. Engring. Food, 2011, Food, Pharm. Bioengring. Divsn. award, AIChE, 1998; fellow, 1992, Inst. Food Technologists, 2010. Mem.: Am. Assn. Cereal Chemists, Inst. Thermal Processing Specialists. Roman Catholic. Avocations: reading, folk music, Indian art. Died June 2015.

CLARKE, MARGUERITE EVELYN, retired secondary school educator; b. Bloomington, Ill., Nov. 23, 1916; d. Frank Raymond and Ella Ruth (Teske) Dobson; m. Harold Davison Clarke, June 9, 1940 (div. 1972); children: Jeannine Ruth Clarke Dodels, Laurel Jane Clarke Mozlin. BS, Ill. Wesleyan U., 1940; postgrad., Ill. State U., 1965-72. Cert. tchr.:. Tchr. lang. arts Saybrook-Arrowsmith (Ill.) Jr. High Sch., 1962-63; tchr. various schs., Whittier, Calif., 1963-64, Evanston, Ill., 1965-66, substitute tchr. Bloomington and Normal, 1967-87; ret., 1987. Researcher on World War II, Bloomington, 1975--. Author: Want to Know Your

Blooming Town?, 1971, Back Here: 1941 to 1945 A Nation at War, 1980, Tales and Details fof World War II, Plus a Few Reflections, 1985, rev. edit., 1989; contbr. articles on World War II to newspapers. Active McLean County Hist. Soc.; vol. Law and Justice Ctr. Mem. AAUW (chairperson hospitality com. 1986—), Am. Assn. Retired Persons (sec. 1982-91, bd. dirs.). Republican. United Methodist. Avocations: collect campaign buttons, elephants, world war ii memorabilia, tennis. Home: Chicago, Ill. Died Dec. 21, 2007.

CLEGG, ALBERT LAWRENCE, minister, religious organization administrator; b. Crystal Springs, Miss., Feb. 16, 1931; s. Cecil Grey and Winnie (Gardner) C.; m. Dorothy Ann Beckman, Feb. 11, 1956; children: Lauranne, Lawrence, Ronald, David. AA, Jones County Jr. Coll., 1951; BA, Miss. Coll., 1953; BD, New Orleans Bapt. Theol. Sem., 1956, ThD, 1958. Ordained to ministry So. Bapt. Conv., 1953. Pastor Coyt Bapt. Ch., Waynesboro, Miss., 1955-57, Silver Creek Bapt. Ch., McComb, Miss., 1957-59, 1st Bapt. Ch., Greensburg, La., 1959-61, Ponchatoula, La., 1961-80; dir. Associational Missions for S.E. La., La. Bapt. Conv., Hammond, from 1980; sec. So. Bapt. Conv. Dirs. of Associational Missions Conf., 1987-91. V.p. La. Bapt. Conv., 1974-75, chmn. missions com., 1968-72, mem. exec. bd., 1966-72; pres. Dist. 11 Bapt. Conv., 1963-65; pres. Dist. Bapt. Pastor's Conf., 1961-63, 66-68. Mem. Ponchatoula C. of C. Home: Ponchatoula, La. *Years ago I determined that I would look for the best in everything that happened. This meant that I would look for the best part of the good things and for something good in the bad. This has made a tremendous difference in my outlook on life and on my ability to accomplish in life.* Died May 7, 2007.

CLELAND, W(ILLIAM) WALLACE, biochemistry educator; b. Balt., Jan. 6, 1930; s. Ralph E. and Elizabeth P. (Shoyer) C.; m. Joan K. Hookanson, June 18, 1967 (div. Mar. 1999); children: Elsa Eleanor, Erica Elizabeth. AB summa cum laude, Oberlin Coll., 1950; MS, U. Wis., 1953, PhD, 1955. Postdoctoral fellow U. Chgo., 1957-59; asst. prof. U. Wis., Madison, 1959-62, assoc. prof., 1962-66, prof., from 1966, M.J. Johnson prof. biochemistry, from 1978, Steenbock prof. chem. sci., 1982—2002. Contbr. articles to profl. biochem. and chem. jours. Served with U.S. Army, 1957-59. Grantee NIH, 1960—, NSF, 1960-94; recipient Stein and Moore award Protein Soc., 1999. Mem. NAS, Am. Acad. Arts and Scis., Am. Soc. Biochemistry and Molecular Biology (Merck award 1990), Am. Chem. Soc. (Alfred R. Bader Bioinorganic or Bioorganic Chem. award 1993, Repligen award 1995). Achievements include development of dithiothreitol (Cleland's Reagent) as reducing agent for thiol groups; development of application of kinetic methods for determining enzyme mechanism. Died Mar. 6, 2013.

CLEMENCE, BARBARA ANN, retired nursing educator; b. Littleton, NH, May 24, 1927; d. Percy G. and Mary Edith (Mandiago) C. AA, North Park Coll., 1951; BS, U. Minn., 1959; MA, NYU, 1964; D of Nursing Sci., Boston U., 1973. Staff nurse New England Deaconess Hosp., Boston, 1948-49, 56, 57, Blackfeet Indian Hosp., Browning, 1951-53; pub. health nurse Glacier County, Cut Bank, Mont., 1953-55; sch. nurse Acton (Mass.) Sch. Dept., 1957-60; pub. health nurse Nashoba Bd. Health, Ayer, Mass., 1960-62; nurse educator Adelphi U., Garden City, N.Y., 1964-67, U. Ibadan, Nigeria, 1967-69, UCLA, 1973-79; nurse educator, assoc. dean U. Wis., Madison, 1979-85; nurse educator, pres./dean Rsch. Coll. Nursing, Kansas City, Mo., 1985-93. Pres., treas., chair Collegiate Nurse Educators, Kansas City, 1987-90; cons. North Cen. Assn. Coll. and Schs., Chgo., 1989-92, Rswch. Coll. Nursing, Kansas City, 1995, Cox Coll., Springfield, Mo., 1990-95. Author: (with others) Mental Health/Psych Nursing, 1984; contbr. articles to profl. jours. Grantee USPHS, 1962-64, 68-72, NIMH, UCLA, 1975-78, UCLA and U. Wis., 1973-83. Mem. ANA, Nat. League for Nursing (site visitor 1981-83), Midwest Alliance in Nursing (chmn. bylaws com. 1983), Sigma Theta Tau (pres. Beta Eta chpt. 1983-85). Avocations: sailing, golf, walking, reading, writing. Home: Reeds Spring, Mo. Died Apr. 13, 2007.

CLEMENT, KATHERINE ROBINSON, retired social worker; b. Balt., Dec. 19, 1918; d. Alphonso Pitts and Sue Seymour (Ashby) Robinson; m. Harry George Clement, 1941 (div. 1948). BA, Coll. Wooster, 1940; MSW, Smith Coll., 1953; post grad., Washington Sch. of Psychiatry, 1951. LCSW Calif. Social worker Family Svc., Cin., 1953-55, Hamilton, Ohio, 1955-57, Family Svc. Orange County, Calif., 1957-60; pvt. practice counselor Fullerton, Calif., 1959-63; social worker Family Svc., Long Beach, Calif., 1961-1963; child welfare worker San Mateo (Calif.) County Welfare Dept., 1963-1967; supr. child protection Yolo County Dept. Social Svcs., Woodland, Calif., 1967-79; pvt. practice Woodland, Calif., 1980-91; cons. psychiat. social svc. State Dept. Social Svcs., Sacramento, 1984—2001; ret., 2001. Pres., bd. dirs. Yolo Family Svc. Agy., 1977. Mem. Yolo County Health Coun.; active Yolo County Dem. Ctrl. Com.; founding bd. dirs. Yolo County Ct. Apptd. Spl. Advs. Mem.: AAUW, LWV, NOW, NASW, Mensa, Sorpotimists. Unitarian Universalist. Avocation: Rosarian. Home: Woodland, Calif. Died Apr. 28, 2007.

CLEMMER, EDITH, artist; b. Phila., Dec. 6, 1920; d. George Henry and Regina (Donnelly) Hoopes; m. Elwood Gregg Clemmer, Jan. 22, 1943; children: Peter Laird, Leonore, Philip, Mary Regina, Edith Ellen. Student, Dobbins Comml. Art Sch., Phila., 1938-39. Freelance artist, Oreg., from 1978. Exhibited in group shows at Oreg. Watercolor Co. Ann. Show, 1990, 92; represented in permanent collection Clemmer's Furniture Store, 1990—. Recipient Best of Show and Best of Category awards Gladstone (Oreg.) Art Guild, 1992, Best of Category and outstanding award Clackamas County, Canby, Oreg., 1992, Best of Show award, 1994. Mem. Watercolor Soc. Oreg., Brush and Palette Art Assn. Avocations: walking, outdoor sketching. Home: Boring, Oreg. Died Feb. 6, 2007.

CLEVER, RICHARD FLOYD, hospital official; b. West Homestead, Pa., Dec. 14, 1932; s. Stanley Ernest and Margaret Elizabeth (Bennett) C.; m. Jean Rosalie Uddenberg, Aug. 29, 1953 (dec. Nov. 1987); children: Richard Floyd Jr., Melanie D. Clever Jewell, Michael Stanley. Grad. high sch., Munhall, Pa. Enlisted man USN, 1950, hosp. corpsman, 1950-70, chief hosp. corpsman, 1962; ret., 1970; personnel asst. Youngstown (Ohio) Hosp. Assn. (now Western Res. Care System), 1970-74, personnel dir., 1974-85, dir. personnel and payroll, from 1985. Chmn. Diversified Health Occupation Adv. Com., Youngstown, 1975—; mem. Youngstown Adult Vocat. Edn. Com., 1986. Mem. Ohio Soc. for Hosp. Human Resource Adminstrs., Ohio Hosp. Assn. Republican. Home: Youngstown, Ohio. Died Dec. 19, 2006.

CLIFF, JOHNNIE MARIE, mathematics and chemistry professor; b. Lamkin, Miss., May 10, 1935; d. John and Modest Alma (Lewis) Walton; m. William Henry Cliff, Apr. 1, 1961 (dec. 1983); 1 child, Karen Marie. BA in Chemistry, Math., U. Indpls., 1956; postgrad., NSF Inst., Butler U., 1960; MA in Chemistry, Ind. U., 1964; MS in Math., U. Notre Dame, 1980; postgrad., Martin U., 2000. Cert. tchr. Ind. Rsch. chemist Ind. U. Med. Ctr., Indpls., 1956-59; tchr. sci. and math. Indpls. Pub. Schs., 1960-88; tchr. chemistry, math. Martin U., Indpls., from 1989, chmn. math. dept., from 1990, divsn. chmn. depts. sci. and math., from 1993. Adj. instr. math. U. Indpls., 1991, Ivy Tech State Coll., Indpls., 2002. Contbr. scientific papers. Grantee NSF, 1961-64, 73-76, 78-79, Woodrow Wilson Found., 1987-88; scholarship U. Indpls., 1952-56, NSF Inst. Reed Coll., 1961, C. of C., 1963. Mem. AAUW, NAACP, NEA, Assn. Women in Sci., Urban League, NY Acad. Scis., Am. Chem. Soc., Nat. Coun. Math. Tchrs., Am. Assn. Physics Tchrs., Nat. Sci. Tchrs. Assn., Am. Statis. Assn., Am. Assn. Ret. Persons, Neal-Marshall-Ind. U. Alumni Assn., U. Indpls. Alumni Assn., U. Notre Dame Alumni Assn., Ind. U. Chemist Assn., Notre Dame Club Indpls., Kappa Delta Pi, Delta Sigma Theta. Democrat. Baptist. Avocations: gardening, sewing. Home: Indianapolis, Ind. Died May 13, 2015.

CLIFF, RUTH SCHABACKER, foreign language educator; b. Dormont, Pa., Aug. 12, 1915; d. Horace Martin and Ethel May (Shreiner) Schabacker; m. David Leigh Cliff. BA, Dickinson Coll., 1937; diploma, U. Toulouse, France, 1938; MA, Middlebury U., 1950. Lang. tchr. Rehoboth (Del.) H.S., 1938-42, Abington Friends Sch., Jenkintown, Pa., 1942-43, 46-56, Summit (N.J.) H.S., 1956-77; ret., 1977. English tchr. lycée, Beauvais, France, 1952-53. Lt. USN, 1943-46. NDEA grantee, Ellensburg, Wash., 1957, Tours, France, 1958, Arcachon, France, 1959. Mem. AAUW, Phi Beta Kappa, Delta Kappa Gamma. Republican. Mem. Society Of Friends. Avocations: reading, bridge. Home: Sun City Center, Fla. Died Mar. 21, 2007.

CLIFFORD, CHERYL KUCHTA, Christian education administrator; b. Winsted, Conn., July 30, 1947; d. George Henry and Gertrude Marie (Weaving) Kuchta; m. Steven Dale Clifford, July 22, 1989; children: Ruth Marie, Paul Arthur, Heidi Lynn, Robert Steven (quadruplets). BS in Elem. Edn., U. Hartford, 1970; MS in Remedial Reading, Ctrl. Conn. State U., 1978; MDiv, Gordon-Conwell Theol. Sem., 1986. Ordained to ministry United Ch. of Christ, 1988; cert. tchr., Conn. Tchr. East Hartland (Conn.) Elem. Sch., 1970-81; assoc. pastor St. John's United Ch. of Christ, Massillon, Ohio, 1988-91; interim pastor Emmanual United Ch. of Christ, Akron, Ohio, 1992; dir. Christian edn. First United Ch. of Christ, Canton, Ohio, 1994—99; co-owner tax acctg. firm Clifford & Assocs., Canton, from 1991. Editor newsletter The Witness of Ohio, 1990-93. Recipient Cory Meml. Scholarship award for excellence in Christian edn. Scripture Press Ministries, 1986. Mem. Nat. Assn. Evangelicals. Republican. Avocations: downhill skiing, crafts, letterwriting. Home: Canton, Ohio. Died June 18, 2007.

CLIFFORD, HAROLD JOSEPH, retired oil and gas company executive; b. San Francisco, May 10, 1924; s. Michael Joseph and Margaret (King) C.; m. Caroline L. Roy, Aug. 1946 (div. 1973); children: Christine N., Paul C., Peter S., Marc J.; m. C. Jeanne Elliott, July 11, 1975. BS, U. Utah, 1951; postgrad., U. Calif., Berkeley, 1952. Registered geologist, Calif. Sr. geologist Shell Oil Co., Los Angeles, 1952-74; chief geologist Ageco, Benghazi, Libya, 1975-79; exploration mgr. Natural Gas Corp Calif., San Francisco, 1979-86; pvt. practice cons. geologist Vista, from 1986. Scout leader Boy Scouts Am., Bakersfield, Calif., 1960-62. Served as sgt. U.S. Army, 1943-46. Mem. AAAS, Am. Assn. Petroleum Geologists. Clubs: Commonwealth (San Francisco). Republican. Roman Catholic. Avocations: photography, music, reading. Home: College Place, Wash. Died Nov. 11, 2006.

CLIFFORD, ROBERT L., retired state supreme court justice; b. Passaic, NJ, Dec. 17, 1924; s. John P. and Elizabeth E. Clifford; m. Joan Sieben, Oct. 20, 1951 (div.); children: Robert L., John P. II, Michael A.; m. Ruth Clifford BA, Lehigh U., 1947; LLB, Duke U., 1950. Bar: N.J. 1950. Law sec. to Hon. William A. Wachenfeld N.J. Supreme Ct., 1953-54; pvt. practice law Newark, 1954-62, Morristown, N.J., 1962-70; commr. of banking and ins. State of N.J., 1970-72; commr. of instns. and agys. State of N.J., 1972-73; assoc. justice N.J. Supreme Ct., from 1973. With USNR, 1943-46. Recipient Trial Bar award Trial Attys. N.J., 1970 Fellow American Coll. Trial Lawyers, American Bar Found.; mem. American Judicature Soc., Morris County Bar Assn., N.J. State Bar Assn. (officer 1968-70), ABA. Democrat. Episcopalian. Died Nov. 29, 2014.

CLINE, FRANKIE KAY, social worker; b. Monongalia County, W.Va., Jan. 14, 1952; d. Wayne Franklin and Mary Kathleen (Parker) C. BSW cum laude, W.Va. U., 1974, MSW, 1986. Lic. social worker, W.Va., Pa.; cert. practitioner gerontology, W.Va. Geriat. social worker Family Svc. Assn., Morgantown, W.Va., 1976-80; social svc. dir. Sr. Monongalians, Inc., Morgantown, 1980-88; social worker, discharge planner Greene County Meml. Hosp., Waynesburg, Pa., 1988-92; case mgr. Mountainview Regional Rehab. Hosp., 1992-95; home health social worker Monongalia Gen. Hosp., Morgantown, 1995-97; dir. social svcs., admissions coord. Mon Pointe Cont. Care Ctr., Morgantown, from 1997. Cons. Franklin Care Ctr., Albert Gallatin Home Health, 1997—; govs. task force on long-term care, W.Va.; bd. dirs. Am. Cancer Soc.; co-facilitator Cancer Support Group; mem. Greene County Health and Welfare Coun.; adv. bd. Southwestern Home Health Agy., Inc., Waynesburg, 1995; field faculty W.Va. U. Sch. Social Work, 1980-95, 97-98, 2002-03. Bd. dirs. Meals on Wheels, 1988. Mem. NASW, Monongalia County Coun. Social Agys., Am. Acad. Cert. Social Workers, Nat. Assn. Case Mgrs. Home: Maidsville, W.Va. Died Mar. 29, 2007.

CLOSE, MICHAEL JOHN, property manager, lawyer; b. Sandusky, Ohio, Jan. 24, 1943; s. Robert J. and Mary Lee (Graefe) C.; m. Nancy L. Schelp, June 18, 1995; children: Christina C., Karen L. AB in History, Lafayette Coll., Easton, Pa., 1965; JD cum laude, U. Mich., 1968. Assoc. Dewey, Ballantine, Bushby, Palmer & Wood, NYC, 1968-76; ptnr. Dewey Ballantine, NYC, 1976-96; pres., CEO Balmer Parc LLC, NYC, from 2003. Chmn. Tax Rev., N.Y.C. Author: Tax Aspects of Oil and Gas Drilling Funds, 1972, Drilling Funds: The 1977 Perspective, 1977, Special Allocations in Oil and Gas Ventures, 1982, The Final Section 704 (b) Regulations: Special Allocations Reach New Heights of Complexity, 1986, Fringe Benefit Regulation and the New York Law Firm Culture: A New Era, 1989, Off Balance Sheet Financings, 1994; contbr. articles to profl. jours. Bd. dirs., adminstrv. vice-chmn. Conn. Swimming, Inc., 1992-99; chmn. ad-hoc com. on by-laws USA Swimming, Inc., 1995-96; bd. dirs. Sharks Swim Team, Inc., 1991-94, pres., 1992-94; trustee Asolo Theatre Repertory Endowment Fund, 2005—; bd. dirs. Asolo Repertory Theatre, Inc., 2006—, mem. exec. com., 2006-, mem. corp. governance com., 2007-, dir. emeritus, First Citizens Banc Corp., Sandusky, Ohio, 2011- Mem. ABA , Assn. of Bar of City of N.Y., N.Y. Law Inst. (life mem.), N.Y. State Bar Assn. , Ohio State Bar Assn., Real Estate Bd. N.Y.(assoc.), India House (N.Y.C.), Burning Tree Country Club (Greenwich, Conn.), Meadows Country Club (Sarasota, Fla.), Phi Delta Phi, Theta Chi. Republican. Home: Sarasota, Fla. Died 2013.

CLOUD, JACK L., psychotherapist, communication consultant; b. Detroit, Oct. 9, 1951; m. Bobbie Young, Apr. 9, 1977; children: Jaclyn, Ryan. BA, Oakland U., Rochester, Mich., 1972, MA, 1975, postgrad., 1976-89, Wayne State U., 1976-89. Lic. profl. counselor, med. psychotherapist, Mich.; cert. social worker, Mich.; nat. cert. counselor. With spl. projects dept. Troy (Mich.) Sch. Dist., 1973-75; coord. Midwest Mental Health, Troy, 1975-83; exec. dir. Gateway Counseling Ctr., Madison Heights, Mich., 1978-85; counselor Lakeside Family Counseling, Clinton Twp., Mich., from 1983. Cons. Lakeside Tng. and Devel., Clinton Twp., 1984—; ptnr. Mich. Supervision Inst., 1995; mem. exec. com. Health Occupations Bd., Lansing, Mich., 1990-93. Author: (tng. manual) Communication Essentials, 1990, (workbook) Personality Patterns, 1991, (audio tape series) Communication Patterns, 1991; also articles. Bd. dirs. Oakland Hills Subdiv., Bloomfield Hills, Mich., 1986-93. Named Alumnus of Yr., Oakland U., 1988, Counselor of Yr., Mich. Mental Health Assn., 1989. Mem. Am. Counseling Assn. (Contbns. to Profession and Svc. award 1993), Mich. Counseling Assn. (chmn. counselor licensure 1990—, polit. action com. 1991—). Home: Bloomfield Hills, Mich. Died Mar. 24, 2007.

CLYNE, ROSEMARIE BLACKSTONE, technical services librarian; b. Utica, NY, May 16, 1926; d. Arthur C. and Mary C. (Hofsass) Blackstone; m. Robert F. Clyne, Sr., Aug. 6, 1947; children: Robert Jr., Judi, James, Jeanne, Richard, Jeffrey, Cynthia, Debra, Lisa. AA, AS with honors, Polk Community Coll., 1970; BA magna cum laude, U. South Fla., 1972, MA magna cum laude, 1978. Cert. librarian. Ins. clk. Utica Mut. Ins. Co., 1943-46; clk. libr. Polk C.C., Winter Haven, Fla., 1971-73; libr. asst. Polk Community Coll., Winter Haven, Fla., 1973-78; libr. tech. svcs. Polk C.C., Winter Haven, Fla., 1978-91, libr. coord., 1989-91, prof. emeritus, from 1991. Sec. collection devel. com. U. South Fla. and related librs., 1990. Mem. Fla. Assn. Community Colls. (2nd v.p., chair learning resources com. 1990). Avocations: camping, needlecrafts, miniatures, dolls. Home: Lakeland, Fla. Died Mar. 3, 2007.

COATS, ARTHUR WILLIAM, clergyman; b. Froid, Mont., Jan. 18, 1930; s. Arthur Henry and Severine Austrid (Scott) C.; m. Virginia Irene Morgan, June 5, 1952; children: Vicki Irene, David Arthur. Diploma Bible, Multnomah Sch. of Bible, 1953; BS in Edn., Lewis and Clark Coll., 1955; MS in Edn., Western Mont. Coll., 1966. Cert. guidance counselor and tchr.; ordained to ministry Bapt. Ch., 1955. Pastor Bethel Bapt. Ch., Lewistown, Mont., 1955-60, First Bapt. Ch., Dillon, Mont., 1960-67, Nyssa (Oreg.) Conservative Bapt. Ch., 1969-73, Prior Lake (Minn.) Bapt. Ch., 1974-80, Lakeview Bapt. Ch., Orr, Minn., 1980-85, First Bapt. Ch., Milltown, Wis., from 1985. Adminstr. Heritage Christian Sch., Ft. Collins, Colo., 1973-74; founder Prior lake (Minn.) Christian Sch., 1977-80, Lakeview Bapt. Sch., Orr, Minn., 1984-85; trustee N.T. Assn. Ind. Bapt. Chs., Lakewood, Colo., 1986—. Author: Sunday School Commentary of Gospel of John, 1978, Sunday School Commentary on Book of Isaiah, 1979,

Sunday School Commentary on Book of Judges, 1983. Precinct coord. Rep. party, Prior Lake and Orr, 1979, 83; pres. Milltown Manor, Inc., 1991. *Serving the Supreme Being is supreme service. Serving the Savior (Jesus Christ) He sent to die for our sins is no sacrifice. Serving the people the Savior came to save is a privilege.* Died Mar. 9, 2007.

COBLE, JOHN HOWARD, retired United States Representative from North Carolina, lawyer; b. Greensboro, NC, Mar. 18, 1931; s. Joseph Howard and Johnnie (Holt) Coble Student, Appalachian State U., Boone, NC, 1949-50; BA in Hist., Guilford Coll., Greensboro, NC, 1958; JD, U. NC Sch. Law, Chapel Hill, 1962. Bar: NC 1966. Field claim rep., supt. State Farm Mut. Automobile Ins. Co., 1961-67; asst. county atty. Guilford County, NC, 1967-69; asst. US atty. Mid. Dist. NC, 1969—73; mem. NC House of Representatives, 1969, 1979—84; sec. NC Dept. Revenue, 1973—77; atty. Turner, Enochs & Sparrow, Greensboro, NC, 1979—83; mem. US Congress from 6th NC dist., 1985—2015, mem. transp. and infrastructure com., mem. judiciary com., ranking mem. cts. the Internet and intellectual property subcommittee. Served to capt. USCG, 1952-56, commdg. officer USCGR. Mem. NC Bar Assn., Greensboro Bar Assn., Masons (33 degree; master Mason), Am. Legion, VFW, Lions, SAR. Republican. Presbyterian. Home: Washington, DC. Died Nov. 3, 2015.

COBURN, RONALD MURRAY, ophthalmologist, surgeon; b. Detroit, Aug. 25, 1943; s. Sidney and Jean (Goldberg) C.; m. Barbara Joan Levy, Feb. 21, 1969; children: Nicholas Scott, Lauren Joy. BS, Wayne State U., 1965, MD, 1969; postgrad., Kresge Eye Inst., 1971—74. Diplomate Am. Bd. Ophthalmology, Am. Bd. Eye Surgery (surg. examiner). Dir. The Coburn Clinic, Dearborn, Mich., from 1976; chief ophthalmology Straith Hosp. for Spl. Surgery, Southfield, Mich., 1985—2000; dir. Cataract Specialty Surgery Ctr., Berkley, Mich., from 2003. Cons. CooperVision, Inc., Bellevue, Wash., 1985-88, Alcon Surg., Inc., Ft. Worth, 1988—. Co-author: Lens-Stat Intraocular Lens Modeling System; editorial advisor Phaco and Foldables, 1990. Trustee Straith Hosp. for Spl. Surgery, 1986—. Capt. Mich. N.G., 1969-76. Fellow: Rsch. Prevent Blindness, Soc. Excellence Eyecare, Soc. Eye Surgeons, Royal Soc. Medicine (London), Internat. Coll. Surgeons, Am. Coll. Surgeons; mem.: Leadership Soc., Internat. Glaucoma Congress, Soc. Geriatric Ophthalmology, Internat. Eye Found., Internat. Assn. Ocular Sci., NY Acad. Sci., Wayne County Medical Soc., Michigan Ophthalmological Soc., Am. Diabetes Assn., Am. Soc. Cataract and Refractive Surgery, Am. Assn. Advancement Scis., Phi Beta Kappa. Achievements include design of Am. Med. Optics PC19LB intraocular lens, CILCO CPLU CP20 intraocular lenses, CooperVision CP10BG posterior chamber intraocular lens, Alcon CZ20BD intraocular lens. Home: Bloomfield Hills, Mich. Died May 5, 2015.

COCHRAC, GERALD JOSEPH, chemist and lubrication engineer; b. Cleve., Jan. 29, 1940; s. Joseph George and Helen Hattie (Konopinski) C.; m. Janice Ann Dawes, Oct. 17, 1959; children: Geriann, Gail, Judith. BS in Chemistry, John Carroll U., Cleve., 1966. Lab technician Lubrizol, Wickliffe, Ohio, 1960-65, chemist, 1965-68, lab. mgr., 1968-86, tech. mgr., 1986-92, product mgr., from 1992. Mem. ASTM (chmn. subcom. D.02.09 1987—), Soc. Tribologists and Lubrication Engrs. (cert., pres. Cleve. sect. 1990-92, bd. dirs. 1986—, past chmn.), Am. Petroleum Inst., Am. Chem. Soc. Achievements include knowledge of lubrication principles, applications and chemistry. Died Aug. 13, 2007.

COCHRAN, ADA, writer; b. Lost Creek, Ky., Dec. 21, 1933; d. Shade and Doshie (Combs) Fugate; m. Alan Cochran, Oct. 1, 1956; children: Debra, Gail, Evangeline, Cheryl, William, Edward. AA, Charles County C.C., 1975; BA, U. Mo. Free-lance writer, Waldorf, Mo., from 1982; pub. Cochran's Corner, Waldorf, Mo., from 1982; realtor Manning Realty, Inc., Waldorf, Mo., from 1993. Author: Grey Wolf Lost, 1987. Mem. Nat. Assn. Exec. Women, Women's Writing Guild, Charles County Commerce Women, Internat. Toastmasters (pres. 1987-88). Democrat. Baptist. Avocations: music, growing roses, writing song lyrics, poetry. Died Dec. 4, 2006.

COCHRAN, TIM DANIEL, mathematician, educator; b. Phila., Apr. 7, 1955; BS, Mass. Inst. Tech., 1977; MA, U. Calif., Berkeley, 1979, PhD, 1982. Moore instr. Mass. Inst. Tech., Cambridge, 1982-84; rsch. fellow Math. Scis. Rsch. inst., Berkeley, 1984-85; vis. asst. prof. U. Calif., Berkeley, 1987-88, Northwestern U., Evanston, Ill., 1989-90; assoc. prof. math. Rice U., Houston, 1990—98, prof., 1998—2014. Author: Derivatives of Links, 1989. Rsch. fellow Math. Scis. Rsch. Inst., Berkeley, 1984; Math. Scis. Postdoctoral fellow NSF, 1985-87. Mem. American Math. Soc. Home: Houston, Tex. Died Dec. 16, 2014.

COCKER, JOE (JOHN ROBERT COCKER), singer; b. Sheffield, Eng., May 20, 1944; s. Harold and Madge Cocker; m. Pam Baker, Oct. 11, 1987. Singer: (albums) With a Little Help from My Friends, 1969, Joe Cocker!, 1970, Mad Dogs and Englishmen, 1971, I Can Stand a Little Rain, 1974, Jamaica Say You Will, 1975, Stingray, 1976, Luxury You Can Afford, 1978, Sheffield Steel, 1982, Civilized Man, 1984, Cocker, 1986, Unchain My Heart, 1987, Joe Cocker Live, 1990, One Night of Sin, 1989, Night Calls, 1992, Best of Joe Cocker, 1993, Have a Little Faith, 1994, Organic, 1996, Across from Midnight, 1998, Yance Arnold & the Average 1963, 2000, No Ordinary World, 2000, Respect Yourself, 2000, Heart & Soul, 2004, Sweet Forgiveness, 2006, Hymn for My Soul, 2008, Hard Knocks, 2008, Fire It Up, 2012 Recipient Order of the Brit. Empire (OBE), Her Majesty Queen Elizabeth II, 2007; named to The Sheffield Hall of Fame, 2007. Died Dec. 22, 2014.

COCKRILL, SHERNA, artist; b. Chgo., Dec. 19, 1936; d. Glenn Wesley and Ruby Jean Will; m. J. Mitchell Jr., Mar. 23, 1963; 1 child, Ashley. BA, U. Ark., 1958, MA, 1966. Represented by Boswell Gallery, Little Rock, Selby Pictures Ltd., London, Rocky Creek Gallery, Fayetteville, Ark., River Market Art, Little Rock. One-woman shows include KPMG Pete Marwick & Assocs. Collection, Little Rock, Ark., 1997, Arts Ctr. of Ozarks, 1997—98, Walton Art Ctr., Fayetteville, Ark., 1997, 1998, 2000, Sager Creek Art Ctr., Siloam Springs, Ark., 2000, Walton Art Ctr., Fayetteville, Ark., 2001, 2002, exhibited in group shows at Philbrook Art Ctr., 1968—69, Tulsa Regional 5-State Exhbn., 1968, Ark. Arts Festival, 1968—70, 1972—73, Okla. Mus. Art, 1970—71 (1st prize in oils, 1970), Artists N.W. Ark., 1969—72, Ft. Smith Art Ctr., 1972—74 (Grand prize, 1973), Greater New Orleans Nat. Exhbn., 1973, Ark. Arts Ctr., 1973—75, Little Rock Arts Fair, 1973 (1st prize in painting, 1973), Tex. Fine Arts Assn. Ann., 1973—74, S.E. Ark. Arts and Sci. Ctr., 1973, Ark. Festival Arts Invitational, 1974—76, Ark. Arts, Crafts and Design Fair, 1975—76, Gov.'s Disting. Artists Exhibit, 1976, U. Ark., 1979—86 (2d prize, 1981, 1984), Laguna Gloria Mus., Austin, Tex., 1984, 1986, Art Ctr. of Ozarks, 1999 (Pres. award, 2000), Walton Arts Ctr., Fayetteville, Ark., 2000—01, Represented in permanent collections Smithsonian Archives Am. Art, D.C., Mid Am. Mus., 1st Nat. Bank, Little Rock, Smithsonian Collection in Mid. Am. Mus., Hot Springs, Ark., WRMC Found., Butler Ctr., Little Rock, Ctrl. Ark. Libr. Sys., others, exhibitions include Arts Ctr. of Ozarks, 1998, 2000, Walton Art Ctr., 2001, 2002, Butler Ctr. for Ark. Studies, Little Rock, Ctrl. Ark. Libr., 2000, Nat. Mus. of Women in the Arts Archives, Washington, exhibitions include one-woman show Stephen Selby Pictures, Ltd./London, 2003, exhibitions include Nat. Mus. of Women in Art, Washington, D.C., 1998, Represented in permanent collections WRMC Found., Butler Ctr. Ark. Studies, Little Rock, Ctrl. Ark. Libr. Sys., Boswell Gallery, Little Rock, Rocky Creek Gallery, Fayetteville, River Market Art, Little Rock, Selby Pictures Ltd., London. Recipient 1st and 2d prizes Ozark Artist's Ann., 1972, Grand prize Ark. State Festival Art, 1973, 1st prize Ark. Arts, Crafts and Design Fair (8-State), 1974, 2d prize Greater New Orleans Nat., 1986, Gov.'s Collection, State of Ark., 1994, KPMG Collection 1995, Ark. Artists Registry Invitational, 1996, Sen. Pryor's Wash. Exhibit 1996, Arts Ctr. of the Ozark's one-woman exhibit, 1997, Walton Arts Ctr. one-woman exhibit, 1997, Arts Ctr. of the Ozark's Competitive Regional Pres.'s award for excellance in oils. Democrat. Episcopalian. Avocation: travel. Home: Fayetteville, Ark. Died Dec. 28, 2006.

CODY, ALDUS MORRILL, retired editor, journalist, typographer; b. Somerville, Mass., Jan. 11, 1915; s. Luther Morrill and Josephine Belle (Morrill) C.; m. Dorothy Gifford, Dec. 25, 1936; 1 child, Raymond Gifford; m. Bertha Hood Carnahan, June 1, 2002 (dec Sept. 2005). BA in Journalism, U. Fla., 1936. Editor Suwannee Dem., Live Oak, Fla., 1936-37, Williamson County News, Franklin, Tenn., 1937, Marion County News, Ocala, Fla., 1938-39, Kissimmee (Fla.) Gazette, 1939-41, Share Your Knowledge Rev. (later Rev. Graphic Arts), Cin., 1970-80, The High Twelvian, St. Louis, 1989-95; mng. editor Ocala Morning Banner, 1937-38; editor, pub. The Fla. Cattleman, Kissimmee, 1940-45; founder, CEO, Cody Publs., Kissimmee, 1946-77; editor News of Masonic Cmty., Kissimmee, 1989-96; ret., 1996; editor The Quadrangle, Good Samaritan Retirement Village, Kissimmee, 1996—2000. Author: (with Robert Cody) Osceola County—First 100 Years, 1996; editor The Connector, 1st United Meth. Ch., 2001—. Former commr. and mayor City of Kissimmee. Mem. Internat. Assn. Printing House Craftsmen (dist. gov. 1968-70, nat. editor 1970-80), Fla. Assn. Square Dancers (founder, pres.), Masons (past master), Shriners, Rotary (past pres. Kissimmee). Democrat. Methodist. Avocation: genealogy. Died Nov. 30, 2006.

COE, MARGARET LOUISE SHAW, community service volunteer; b. Cody, Wyo., Dec. 25, 1917; d. Ernest Francis and Effie Victoria (Abrahamson) Shaw; m. Henry Huttleston Rogers Coe, Oct. 8, 1943 (dec. Aug. 1966); children: Anne Rogers Hayes, Henry H.R., Jr., Robert Douglas II. AA, Stephens Coll., 1937; BA, U. Wyo., 1939. Asst. to editor The Cody Enterprise, 1939-42, editor, 1968-71. Bd. trustees Buffalo Bill Historical Ctr., 1966—, chmn., 1974-98, chmn. emeritus, 1998—; trustee emeritus Ctrl. City Opera House Assn., Millicent Rogers Found.; commr. Wyo. Centenniel Commn., Cheyenne, 1986-91. Recipient The Westerner award Old West Trails Found., 1980, Gold Medallion award Nat. Assn. Sec. of State, 1982, disting alumni award U. Wyo., 1984, exemplary alumni award, 1994, Gov.'s award for arts, 1988; inducted Nat. Cowgirl Hall of Fame, 1983. Mem. P.E.O., Delta Delta Delta. Republican. Episcopalian. Avocation: duplicate bridge. Home: Cody, Wyo. Died Nov. 15, 2006.

COHEN, ARMOND E., rabbi; b. Canton, Ohio, June 5, 1909; s. Samuel and Rebecca (Lipkowitz) C.; m. Anne Lederman; children: Rebecca Long, Deborah (dec.), Samuel. BA, NYU, 1931; rabbi, Jewish Theol Sem. Am., 1934, M Hebrew Lit., 1945, DD (hon.), 1966; LLD (hon.), Cleve. State U., 1969; LHD (hon.), Baldwin-Wallace Coll., 1989. Ordained rabbi, 1934. Rabbi Pk. Synagogue, Cleve., from 1934. Adj. prof. psychiatry Jewish Theol. Sem. Am., N.Y.C., 1970-75; bd. dirs. Inst. Religion and Health, N.Y.C. Author: All God's Children, Selected Readings on Zionism, Outline of Jewish History, Readings in Medieval Jewish Literature; mem. editorial bd. Jour. Religion and Health, 1943-67; contbr. articles to profl. jours. Bd. govs. Hebrew U., Jerusalem; trustee Am. Friends of Hebrew U., 1969—; bd. dirs. consumers League Ohio, Cleve., Jewish Community Fedn., Cleve., Coun. World Affairs, Cleve.; hon. v.p. Zionist Orgn. Am. Named Humanitarian of the Yr., Internat. Red Cross, 2002. Mem. Rabbinical Assembly Am., Cleve. Bd. Rabbis (founder), Lotos Club (N.Y.C.), Oakwood Club (Cleve.), Union Club (Cleve.). Home: Cleveland, Ohio. *Anyone can struggle through life without faith but everyone needs faith if he would confront life's inevitable challenges and sorrows and stand erect. It is easier to go through this life with faith than without it.* Died June 4, 2007.

COHEN, JOSEPH, English literature educator, writer, business owner; b. Central City, Ky., Apr. 27, 1926; m. Gloria A. Plitman, 1952 (dec. 1980); three children: m. Ruth S. Samuels, 1987 (dec. 1994); m. Thedora F. Sternberg, 1995. Student, Austin Peay State Coll., 1943-45, U. Minn., 1945-46; BA, Vanderbilt U., 1949, MA, 1951; postgrad., U. Wis., 1951, U. Cin., 1951-52; PhD, U. Tex., 1955. Instr. English Tulane U., New Orleans, 1955-58, asst. dean Coll. Arts & Sciences, 1957-58, from asst. prof. to prof., 1958-91, prof. emeritus, from 1991, prof.-in-charge Tulane-Newcomb Jr. Yr. Abroad, 1959-60, acting dir. Tulane-Newcomb Jr. Yr. Abroad, 1960-61, acad. asst. to dean Newcomb Coll., 1961-67, dir. Tulane Scholars and Fellows program, 1965-76, assoc. dean Newcomb Coll., 1967-76, dir. Jewish Studies, 1981-87, chmn. spl. projects on Jewish studies, 1987-91; owner, mgr. Gt. Acquisitions Books, New Orleans, 1992—2014. Mem. exec. bd. Nat. Coll. Honors Coun., 1967-72, pres., 1970-71; chmn. region 12 selection com. Woodrow Wilson Nat. Fellowship Found., 1970-73; dir. dissertations; mem. numerous PhD coms.; speaker to more than 100 profl. and civic orgns. Author: Journey to the Trenches: The Life of Isaac Rosenberg, 1890-1918, 1975, reissued 1992, Voices of Israel: Essays on and Interviews with Yehuda Amichai, A.B. Yehoshua, T. Carmi, Aharon Appelfeld and Amos Oz, 1990; editor: The Poetry of Dannie Abse: Critical Essays and Reminiscences, 1983, Proceedings of the Southern Honors Symposium, 1968, (jour.) Shirenu Bull. of the Jewish Studies Program, 1983-87; mem editorial bd. English Literature in Transition, 1964-70, contbg. editor Jour. Higher Edn., 1968-71; editorial cons. Style mag., No. Ill. U., 1985; columnist numerous Jewish newspapers and jours.; contbr. more than 200 articles to profl. jours. and newspapers; reviewer numerous books and articles. Mem. nat. adv. com. on Jewish coll. youth Nat. Jewish Welfare Bd., 1969-71; treas. La. Jewish Hist. Soc., 1981; bd. trustees Southern Jewish Hist. Soc., 1982-86, New Orleans Jewish Welfare Fedn., 1982-86, Friends of Tulane Library, 1982-89. Served with U.S. Army, 1945-46. Taft fellow U. Cin., 1951-52, Dolley fellow U. Tex., 1952-53. Mem. MLA (bus. mgr. South-Cen. div. 1956-59, founding chmn. contemporary lit. sect. South-Cen. div. 1957), Assn. Jewish Studies Conf. (chmn. Modern American Jewish Lit. sect. 1982). Home: New Orleans, La. Died Sept. 25, 2014.

COHEN, MILLARD STUART, diversified manufacturing company executive; b. Chgo., Jan. 17, 1939; s. Lawrence Irmas and Myra Paula (Littmann) C.; m. Judith E. Michel, Aug. 2, 1970 (dec. Dec. 1995); children: Amy Rose, Michele Lauren. BSEE, Purdue U., 1960. Design engr. GTE Automatic Electric Labs., Northlake, Ill., 1960-66; chief elec. engr. Nixdorff Krein Industries, St. Louis, 1966-68, dir. data processing, 1968-72, treas., from 1970, v.p., 1980-85, pres., from 1985, exec. v.p. Nixdorff Chain, 1972-76, pres. Grape Expectations, 1976, also bd. dirs. Mem. Mo. Wine Adv. Bd., 1980—, vice chmn., 1983, 93; mem. St. Louis County Restaurant Commn., 1979—, Augusta (Mo.) Wine Bd., 1981—. Dist. commr. Boy Scouts Am., 1968-72; judge Mo. State Fair; trustee Congl. Temple Israel. Recipient award of merit French Wine Commn., 1972. Mem. IEEE, Assn. for Computing Machinery, Internat. Wine and Food Soc. (gov. Ams. 1985—), Mensa, Les Amis du Vin, Chaine des Rotisseurs, Commanderie de Bordeaux, St. Louis Club. Home: Saint Louis, Mo. Died Oct. 23, 2006.

COHEN-SABBAN, NESSIM, auditor, accountant; b. Cairo, Aug. 4, 1930; came to U.S., 1984; s. Haim and Zakia (Baredes) C.-S.; m. Klemy Rodriguez, Apr. 7, 1960 (div. Mar. 1988); children: Haim, Nava, Shimon; m. Liliane Mann-Khasky, Sept. 8, 1988; children: Toufik, Elie, May. Grad., Cairo U., 1956, Tel Aviv U., 1964; postgrad., Touro Coll., 1991-92. CPA. Chief acct. David Ades & Son, Cairo, 1950-57; acct. Lodzia, Holon, Israel, 1957-61, Bank Leumi, Jaffa, Israel, 1961-64; internal auditor Head Office, Bank Le Melakha, Tel Aviv, 1964-78; auditor, acct. 1st Internat. Bank Israel, Tel Aviv, 1979-84, Greatway Co., NYC, 1985, 88; internal auditor Play Knits Inc., NYC, from 1988. Mem. Rabbinical of Bat-Yam, Israel, 1980-84; judge Bat-Yam City Ct., 1982-84. Officer Israel Army, 1961-84. Avocations: reading poems in english, french, hebrew and arabic, helping weak and poor people. Home: Brooklyn, NY. Died Mar. 10, 2007.

COHN, ISIDORE, JR., surgeon, educator; b. New Orleans, Sept. 25, 1921; s. Isidore and Elsie (Waldhorn) C.; m. Jacqueline Heymann, July 4, 1944 (div. Aug. 1971); children: Ian Jeffrey, Lauren Kerry; m. Marianne Winter Miller, Jan. 3, 1976. BS in Chemistry with honors, Tulane U., New Orleans, 1942; MD, U. Pa., Phila., 1945; M.Med. Sci. in Surgery, U. Pa., 1952, DMS in Surgery, 1955; LHD (hon.), U. SC, 1995. Diplomate Am. Bd. Surgery (bd. dirs. 1969-75). Intern Grad. Hosp. U. Pa., 1945-46, resident in surgery, 1949-52; fellow dept. surg. rsch. U. Pa., 1947-48; vis. surgeon Charity Hosp., New Orleans, 1952-62, sr. vis. surgeon, 1962-2000, hon. sr. vis. surgeon, from 2000; surgeon in chief La. State U. Svc., Charity Hosp., New Orleans, 1962-89; prof. surgery La. State U. Sch. Medicine, New Orleans, 1959-2000, emeritus chmn., emeritus prof. surgery, from 2000. Cons. surgeon VA Hosp., New Orleans, Touro Infirmary, New Orleans; instr. surgery La. State U. Sch. Medicine, New Orleans, 1952-53, asst. prof., 1953-56, assoc. prof., 1956-59, prof., 1959-2000, chmn. dept. surgery, 1962-89; mem. surg. rsch. rev. com. VA, Washington, 1967-68; dir. Nat. Pancreatic Cancer Project, 1975-84;

mem. Soc. Surg. Chairmen, 1962-89. Mem. editl. bd. Am. Surgeon, 1963-87, Current Surgery, 1964-90, Am. Jour. Surgery, 1968-96, emeritus, 1997—, Digestive Diseases and Scis., 1978-82, Surg. Gastroenterology, 1982—, Cancer, 1992—2002, Digestive Surgery, 1995—. Bd. dirs. New Orleans Met. Conv. and Visitors Bur., 1998-2000, New Orleans Mus. Art, 2004-2009, hon. life mem., 2010-, Jewish Endowment Found., 2006-2012. Served to capt. M.C., AUS, 1946-47. Isidore Cohn, Jr. Professorship named in his honor at La. State U., 1987, Isidore Cohn, Jr., M.D. Student Learning Ctr. at La. State U. Health Sci. Ctr. Sch. Medicine dedicated in his honor, 2002, Spirit of Charity award Med. Ctr. La., 2003; named Outstanding Alumnus, Isidore Newman Sch., New Orleans, La., 2003, Role Model, Young Leadership Coun. New Orleans, 2006, Tzedakah award, Jewish Endowment Found, 2009, Isaac Delgado Meml. award, New Orleans Mus. Art, 2012, Chmn.'s award Arts Coun. New Orleans, 2012, Chmn. award, Arts Coun. New Orleans (jt. mem. 2012). Fellow ACS (exec. com., bd. govs. 1987-91, vice-chmn. 1989-90, chmn. 1990-91, 1st v.p. 1993-94), Southern Surg. Assn. (1st v.p. 1979-80, treas.-recorder 1981-82, pres. 1982-83, hon. mem. 2009-); mem. AMA, Am. Surg. Assn., La. Surg. Assn. (pres. 1968), So. Med. Assn., La., Orleans Parish med. socs., Soc. Univ. Surgeons, Southeastern Surg. Congress (chmn. forum on progress in surgery 1967-69, councillor for La. 1967-73, pres. 1972), Surg. Biology Club II, Assn. Acad. Surgery, Isidore Cohn, Jr.-James D. Rives Surg. Soc., Internat. Surg. Soc., Am. Gastroenterol. Assn., Bockus Soc. Gastroenterology, Soc. Surgery Alimentary Tract (trustee 1969-80, recorder 1973-76, pres. 1976-77, chmn. bd. 1977-78, Founders medal 2004), Am. Soc. Microbiologists, Soc. Surg. Oncology, NY Acad. Scis., Am. Assn. Cancer Research, Southeastern Cancer Research Assn. (pres. 1975), Collegium Internationale Chirurgiae Digestivae, Am. Cancer Soc. (vice chmn. clin. investigation adv. com. 1969, chmn. clin. investigation adv. com. 1969-73), Tex. Surg. Soc. (hon.), Sigma Xi, Phi Beta Kappa, Alpha Omega Alpha, Omicron Delta Kappa, Home: Metairie, La. Died Oct. 14, 2015.

COKER, LINDA LOU, nurse; b. Ft. Wayne, Ind., Sept. 23, 1940; d. Clifton Eugene and Marlowe Maxine (Copeland) C. BSN, Coll. Saint Teresa, 1980; MA, Saint Mary's Coll., 1988. RN, Minn. Lic. practical nurse Parkview Hosp., Ft. Wayne, 1966-73, Saint Marys Hosp., Rochester, Minn., 1973-80, staff nurse, 1980-82; supr. orientation and continuing edn. Saint Mary's Hosp., Rochester, from 1982, coord. perioperative nursing program, from 1984. Mem. Reformed Ch. Women, Rochester, 1988, Rochester Symphony, 1976-89. Mem. Assn. Operating Room Nurses (pres. 1988-89). Avocations: stamp collecting/philately, reading, golf. Home: Bloomington, Ind. Died Feb. 4, 2007.

COLBOURN, TREVOR, retired academic administrator, historian; b. Armidale, NSW, Australia, Feb. 24, 1927; came to U.S., 1948; s. Harold Arthur and Ella Mary (Henderson) C.; m. Beryl Richards Evans, Jan. 10, 1949; children: Katherine Elizabeth, Lisa Sian Elinor. BA with honors, U. London, 1948; MA, Coll. William and Mary, 1949, Johns Hopkins, 1951, PhD, 1953. From instr. to asst. prof. Pa. State U., 1952-59; from asst. prof. to prof. Am. history Ind. U., 1959-67; dean Grad. Sch., prof. history U. N.H., 1967-73; v.p. for acad. affairs San Diego State U., 1973-77, acting pres., 1977-78; pres. U. Central Fla., Orlando, 1978-89. Author: The Lamp of Experience, 1965, 2d edit., 1998, The Colonial Experience, 1966, (with others) The Americans: A Brief History, 1972, 4th edit., 1985; co-editor: (with others) The American Past in Perspective, 1970; editor: (with others) Fame and the Founding Fathers, 1974, 2d edit., 1998. Mem. Orgn. American Historians, American Assn. State Colleges & Universities Home: Winter Park, Fla. Died Jan. 13, 2015.

COLE, NATALIE MARIA, singer; b. LA, Feb. 6, 1950; d. Nathaniel Adam and Maria (Harkins) Cole; m. Marvin J. Yancy, July 31, 1976 (div. 1980); 1 child, Robert Adam ; m. Andre Fischer, Sept. 16, 1989 (div. 1995); m. Rev. Kenneth Dupree, Oct. 12, 2001 (div. 2004). BA in Child Psychology, U. Mass., Amherst, 1972. Rec. singles and albums, 1975-2015; albums: Inseperable, 1975, Natalie, 1976, Unpredictable, 1977, Thankful, 1977, I Love You So, 1979, We're the Best of Friends (with Peabo Bryson), 1979, Don't Look Back, 1980, Happy Love, 1981, I'm Ready, 1983, Dangerous, 1985, Everlasting, 1987, The Natalie Cole Collection, 1987, Good To Be Back, 1989, Unforgettable...with Love, 1991 (Grammy award for Album of Yr., 1992), Too Much Weekend, 1992, I'm Ready, 1992, I've Got Love On My Mind, 1992, Take A Look, 1993, Holly and Ivy, 1994, Stardust, 1996, Magic of Christmas, 1999, Snowfall on the Sahara, 1999, Greatest Hits, 2000, Ask a Woman Who Knows, 2002, Leavin', 2006, Still Unforgettable, 2008 (Grammy award for Best Traditional Pop Vocal Album, 2009), Caroling, Caroling: Christmas with Natalie Cole, 2008, Natalie Cole en Español, 2013 (NAACP Image award for Outstanding World Music Album, 2014); songs: This Will Be, 1975, (Grammy award for Best R&B Vocal Performance, Female, 1976), Sophisticated Lady, 1976 (Grammy award for Best R&B Vocal Performance, Female, 1976), Unforgettable (wth Nat King Cole), 1991 (Grammy awards for Record of Yr., Best Traditional Pop Performance, 1992); actress: (TV appearances) Big Break (host), 1990, Touched by an Angel, 1995, Grey's Anatomy, 2006; (TV films) Lily in Winter, 1994, The Wizard of Oz in Concert, 1995, Always Outnumbered, 1998, Freak City, 1999, Livin' for Love: The Natalie Cole Story, 2000; co-author: Angel on My Shoulder, 2000, Love Brought Me Back, 2010; composer Easter Egg Escapade, 2005. Recipient Grammy award for Best New Artist, 1975, American Music awards for Favorite Female Artist - Soul/Rhythm & Blues, 1977, 1978, Favorite Artist - Adult Contemporary, 1991, George and Ira Gershwin award for Lifetime Musical Achievement, 1993, NAACP Image award for Best Jazz Artist, 2002, 2009. Mem.: Nat. Assn. Rec. Arts & Scis., AFTRA, Delta Sigma Delta. Baptist. Home: Los Angeles, Calif. Died Dec. 31, 2015.

COLEMAN, ALLEN MARKLEY, automotive executive; b. Wash., Jan. 3, 1949; s. Arrell and Nola Ragsdale (Markley) C.; 1 child, Monica Anita. BA, Howard U., 1971; MA, Ea. Mich. U., 1977; postgrad., Harvard Bus. Sch., Boston, 1984. Plant mgr. Hydramatic div. GM, Willow Run, Mich., 1977-85, mfg. mgr., 1985-87, plant mgr. Three Rivers, Mich., 1987-89, Warren, Mich., from 1989. Pres., dir. Ann Arbor Community Ctr., 1980. With U.S. Army, 1971-74. Decorated Nat. Def. medal, Army Commendation medal. Mem. Three Rivers C. of C. (bd. dirs. 1987). Republican. Baptist. Avocation: stamp collecting/philately. Died July 1, 2007.

COLEMAN, JOSEPH DALE, architect; b. Sarasota, Fla., Apr. 1, 1939; s. Joseph Paul and Frances Corinne (Stockstill) How; m. Rosemary Peduzzi, Nov. 24, 1965 (div. Feb. 1978); children: Lisa Anne, Laura Frances, Anna Elizabeth; m. Feay Shellman, Dec. 27, 1986; 1 child, Weslie Selena. BA, U. Miss., 1961; postgrad., Claremont Grad. Sch., 1961-62, U. Calif., Berkeley, 1968-69; BArch, Tulane U., 1974; MA in History, U. South Fla., 1992; PhD, U. Fla., 1998. Registered architect, Ga., NCARB. Archtl. draftsman Leo S. Wou and Assocs., Honolulu, 1969-69, Ray Bergeron and Assocs., New Orleans, 1974-76; planner Wolf/Kirkman Assocs., Albany, N.Y., 1970-72; architect N. Grant Nicklas and Assocs., Altoona, Pa., 1976-77, Maddox and Assocs., Savannah, Ga., 1977-80; pvt. practice architecture Savannah, 1980-88, Tampa, Fla., 1988—2000. Instr. drafting and design Pasco-Hernando C.C., New Port Richey, Fla., 1998-2000; asst. prof. Coll. Applied Sci., U. Cin., 2000—; judge Nat. Coun. Archtl. Registration Bds., Archtl. Record Exam., Ft. Lauderdale, Fla., 1985. Author: Construction Documents and Contracting, 2003; prin. works include pvt. residences. Mem. adv. bd. Hillsborough County Libr., 1989-92. With USN, 1962-67, Vietnam. U. Miss. scholar, 1958-61; Claremont Coll. fellow, 1961-62. Mem. AIA, Assn. for Preservation Tech., Icomos, Phi Eta Sigma, Phi Kappa Phi. Democrat. Roman Catholic. Avocation: travel. Home: Cincinnati, Ohio. Died Dec. 18, 2006.

COLEMAN, ORNETTE (RANDOLPH DENARD ORNETTE COLEMAN), jazz musician; b. Ft. Worth, Mar. 9, 1930; s. Randolph and Rosa C.; 1954; m. Jayne Cortez, 1954 (div. 1964); 1 child, Denardo. Doctorate (hon.), U. Pa., Bard Coll., New Sch. Social Rsch., Berklee Sch. Music. Founder Sound Grammar music label, NYC, 2004. Player alto and tenor saxophone, trumpet, violin, bassoon; toured with Clarence Samuels, 1949, with Pee Wee Crayton, 1950; led quartet with Don Cherry, Eddie Blackwell and Charlie Haden; appeared in numerous major festivals throughout the world including JVC Jazz Festival, NYC, 1991; toured Japan, Europe, and Africa; recs. for small jazz ensemble include Something Else, 1958, The Shape of Jazz to Come, 1959, Art of the Improvisors, 1959-61, Free Jazz, 1960, Chappaque Suite, 1965, Live at the Tivoli, 1965, Paris Concert-Nov. 4, 1965, Empty Foxhole, 1966, Live in Milano, 1968, Love Call, 1968, New York is Now, 1968, Dancing in Your Head, 1976, Fashion Faces, 1979, Of Human Feelings, 1979, (with Pat Metheny) Song X, 1985, At the Golden Circle, Stockholm, Vol. I, 1987, Vol. II, 1987, Naked Lunch, 1992, (with Jerry Garcia) Virgin Beauty, 1988, Beauty is a Rare Thing, 1993, Languages, 1993, Tone Dialing, 1995, Sound Museum: Hidden Man, 1996, Sound Museum: Three Women, 1996, Rock the Clock, 2006, Sound Grammar, 2006; others include Broken Shadows, Change of the Century, Dedication to Poets and Writers, Ornette on Tenor, Tomorrow is the Question, Town Hall Concert; played with own group, Prime Time; over 100 compositions for small jazz group and larger ensembles including Music of Ornette Coleman containing his works for string quartet and woodwind quintet recorded by London Symphony Orch.; composer symphony Skies of America; appeared in film Ornette: Made in America, 1986. Guggenheim Found. fellow, 1967, 1974; recipient Poses Creative arts award Brandeis U., 1985, Letter of Distinction, Am. Music Ctr., 1987, Genius award, MacArthur Found., 1994, Dorothy & Lillian Gish prize, 2004, NY State Gov. Arts award, Grammy Lifetime Achievement award, 2007, Pulitzer Prize for Music, 2007; named Jazz Man of Yr. by Jazz and Pop 3d Ann. Readers Poll, 1968; inducted to Downbeat Hall of Fame, Big Band & Jazz Hall of Fame, 1989, Am. Acad. Arts & Sciences, 1997. Mem.: ASCAP. Achievements include developing musical theory concept called Harmoldic theory for composers and players. Died June 11, 2015.

COLLIAS, ELSIE COLE, zoologist; b. Tiffin, Ohio, Mar. 24, 1920; d. Heath Kirk and Dora Della (Dunn) Cole; m. Nicholas Elias Collias, Dec. 21, 1948; 1 child, Karen Joyce. BA, Heidelberg Coll., Tiffin, Ohio, 1942; MS, U. Wis., 1944, PhD, 1948. Teaching asst. Heidelberg Coll., Tiffin, 1941-42, U. Wis., Madison, 1942-46; entomologist CDC, Savannah, Ga., 1946-47; rsch. asst. U. Wis. Dept. entomology, 1947-48; asst. prof. Heidelberg Coll., 1948-49; instr. zoology U. Wis., 1950; assoc. prof. biology Ill. Coll., Jacksonville, 1953-57; rsch. assoc. L.A. County Mus. Natural History, from 1963, UCLA, from 1960. Co-author: Nest Building and Bird Behavior, 1984, Evolution of Nest Building in the Weaverbirds, 1964; co-editor: External Construction by Animals, 1976; contbr. articles to profl. jours. Recipient world 1st breeding award Am. Fedn. Aviculture, 1977. Fellow Am. Ornithologists Union (Elliott Coues award 1980), Animal Behavior Soc. (founder, Jack Ward Film prize 1989), Cooper Ornithological Soc. (hon. mem.), Wilson Ornithological Soc. (Margaret Morse Nice award 1997). Avocations: bird watching, travel. Home: Van Nuys, Calif. Died Dec. 17, 2006.

COLLINS, ARTHUR WORTH, JR., (BUD COLLINS), sports columnist and commentator; b. Berea, Ohio; m. Palmer Collins (div.); children Suzanna Mathews; m. Mary Lou Barnum (dec. 1990); stepchildren Betsy Bartelt, Kristen Hunt, Sharon McMillan, Gretchen West; Judy Lacy (companion)(dec.); children Rob Lacy; m. Anita Ruthling Klaussen, Sept. 17, 1994; stepchildren Danielle and Karl Klaussen Grad., Baldwin-Wallace Coll.; M in Public Relations, Boston U., 2009. Sportswriter Boston Herald, 1955-63; tennis coach Brandeis U., 1959-63; sports columnist Boston Globe, 1963—2016, travel columnist, 1977—2016; sports commentator PBS, 1963-88, NBC, 1964, 1972—83, analyst, interviewer, 1983—2007; sports commentator CBS, 1968—72. Commentator various times for CBS, ESPN, USA, CBN, MSG, HBO, Tennis Channel Author: (with Rod Laver) The Education of a Tennis Player, 1971, (with Evonne Goolagong) Evonne, 1974, Bud Collins Tennis Encyclopedia, 1977, (autobiography) My Life with the Pros, 1989, The Bud Collins Modern Encyclopedia of Tennis, 1993; writer, sr. editor World Tennis Magazine With U.S. Army Named Best Announcer, Best Writer Tennis mag., 1987; recipient Ron Bookman award U.S. Tennis Writers Assn., Best Pro Match Interview award Tennis mag., 1989; inducted into Internat. Tennis Hall of Fame, 1994; name one of Top 50 Sportscasters Am. Sportscasters Assn., 2009. Died Mar. 4, 2016.

COLLINS, HERBERT MAXWELL, chemist; b. Conway, SC, Mar. 8, 1946; s. Francis Stokes and Mary Louise (Staats) C.; m. Patricia Hamilton, Aug. 8, 1967; children: Herbert Jr., Robert, Rebecca. BS in Chemistry, Coll. of Charleston, SC, 1974. Chemist WestVaco, Charleston, 1974-77, lab. supr. Winder, Ga., 1977-83, lab. mgr., 1983-85, Stepan Co., Winder, from 1985. Scoutmaster Boy Scouts Am., Winder, 1978-86; mem. Meth. Men's Club, Winder. Mem. Am. Chem. Soc., ASTM (subcom. chmn. 1984—). Clubs: Pine Shore (Winder) (pres. 1984-86). Republican. Home: Winder, Ga. Died July 28, 2007.

COLLINS, JACKIE (JACQUELINE JILL COLLINS), writer; b. London, Oct. 4, 1937; m. Wallace Austin 1959 (div.); 1 child: Tracy; m. Oscar Lerman, June 15, 1966 (dec. 1992); children: Tiffany, Rory. Author: The World Is Full of Married Men, 1968, The Stud, 1969, Sunday Simmons and Charlie Brick, 1971 (pub. as The Hollywood Zoo, 1975), Lovehead, 1974 (pub. as The Love Killers, 1977), The World Is Full of Divorced Women, 1975, Lovers and Gamblers, 1977, The Bitch, 1979, Chances, 1981, Hollywood Wives, 1983, Sinners, 1984, Lucky, 1985, Hollywood Husbands, 1986, Rock Star, 1987, Lady Boss, 1989, American Star, 1993, Hollywood Kids, 1994, Vendetta: Lucky's Revenge, 19, Thrill, 1998, L.A. Connections, 1998, Dangerous Kiss, 1999, Lethal Seduction, 2000, Hollywood Wives: The Next Generation, 2001, Deadly Embrace, 2002, Hollywood Divorces, 2003, Lovers & Players, 2005, Drop Dead Beautiful, 2007, Married Lovers, 2008, Poor Little Bitch Girl, 2010, Goddess of Vengeance, 2011, The Power Trip, 2012, Confessions of a Wild Child, 2014, The Santangelos, 2015; author (cookbook) The Lucky Santangelo Cookbook, 2014 Avocations: music, photography, travel. Died Sept. 19, 2015.

COLLINS, MARSHALL DAVIS, retired civil engineer; b. Huntington Park, Calif., Aug. 6, 1922; s. Albert Bernhardt and Marion Ida (Davis) C.; m. Rose Lytton, Nov. 1, 1943 (div. Oct. 1965); children: Marsha Leigh, Linda Rae (dec.); m. V. Mildred Collins, Oct. 20, 1966; stepchildren: Robert Hathaway, Craig Hathaway, Howard Hathaway. Student, U. So. Calif., 1940-41. Estimator, draftsman Owens Ill. Glass Co., LA, 1947-50; asst. field engr. Bethlem Steel Co. Mill, LA, 1950-51; steel detailing-design Ctrl. Indsl. Engring., South Gate, Calif., 1951-60; project mgr. So. Engring. & Constrn., Long Beach, Calif., 1960-63; constrn. mgr. Quinton Engrs., LA, 1963-71, VTN, Inc., Irvine, Calif., 1971-82; pvt. practice Crestline, Calif., 1982-90; ret., from 1990. Cons. in field. Contbr. articles to profl. jours. With USN, 1942-46. Mem. ASCE (life), Rotary (sec. Crestline chpt., pres-elect). Republican. Presbyterian. Avocation: machine shop work. Home: Crestline, Calif. Died July 28, 2007.

COLLINS, MARVA DELOISE NETTLES, secondary school educator; b. Monroeville, Ala., Aug. 31, 1936; d. Alex L. and Bessie Maye (Knight) Nettles; m. Clarence Collins, Sept. 2, 1960 (dec. 1995); children: Patrick, Eric, Cynthia; m. George R. Franklin BA, Clark Coll., 1957; BA (hon.), Howard U., 1980; D.H.L. (hon.), Wilberforce U., 1980, Chgo. State U., 1981; D.Hum. (hon.), Dartmouth Coll., 1981. Substitute teacher for 14 years, Chgo.; founder, dir. Westside Prep. Sch., Chgo., 1975—2008. Subject of numerous publs. including Marva Collins' Way, 1982; subject of feature film Welcome to Success: The Marva Collins Story, 1981; author Ordinary' Children, Extraordinary Teachers Mem. Pres.'s Commn. on White House Fellowships, from 1981. Recipient numerous awards including: Reading Found. Am. award, 1979, Sojourner Truth Nat. award, 1980, Tchr. of Yr. award Phi Delta Kappa, 1980, American Public Service award American Inst. for Public Service, 1981, Endow a Dream award, 1980, Educator of Yr. award Chgo. Urban League, 1980,Jefferson Nat. award, 1981, Nat. Humanities medal, 2004 Mem. Alpha Kappa Alpha. Clubs: Executive. Baptist. Home: Chicago, Ill. *A positive attitude is perhaps one of the richest aspects of my life. I find that I will go out of my way to be surrounded by people who are filled with the art of living, loving, and caring, and not because it is a duty, but because we all feel better when we have made the lives of others better through caring.* Died June 24, 2015.

COLLINS, STEVE ANTHONY, oil industry executive; b. Houma, La., May 18, 1973; s. Frankie P. and Hilda E. Collins. Grad., South Lafourche HS, Galliano, La., 1991. Gen. laborer Tidewater Dock, Golden Meadow, La., 1992—94; owner, operator Better Bodies Health Club, Larose, La., 1994—99; v.p. Global Contractors, Lockport, La., 1998—2000; owner, pres. So. Oilfield Svcs., Cut Off, La., 2000—03, Universal Svcs. LLC, Cut Off, from 2003; co-owner Better Bod Smoothies, Houma, La., from 2006. Cons., owner Internat. Labor Cons., Chennai, India, from 2002. Bd. dirs. Larose Civic Ctr., 2000—02. Mem.: Larose C. of C. Republican. Roman Catholic. Achievements include patents pending for solar powered devices. Avocations: fishing, exercise, investing. Home: Cut Off, La. Died May 6, 2007.

COLMANO, GERMILLE, physiology educator, biophysics researcher; b. Pola, Istria, Italy, Aug. 22, 1921; s. Giovanni and Elena (Bolmarchich) C.; m. Miranda Sobol, Jan. 12, 1947 (dec. Nov. 1994); children: Marino, Helen Elizabeth Sutton, Charles Riccardo. BA in Edn., Classic Lyceum "G. Carducci", Pola, Italy, 1942; DVM with honors, U. Bologna, Italy, 1949, PhD in Physiology and Biochemistry, 1950; MS, U. Wis., 1952. Lic. veterinarian, Italy, Ark. Instr. physiology U. Bologna, 1949-50, asst. prof. physiology, biochemistry, 1950-51; asst. vet. Phillips Vet. Hosp., Denver, 1951-52; rsch asst. physiology dept. vet. scis. U. Wis., Madison, 1952-53; project asst. Enzyme Biochem. Inst. Enzyme Rsch. U. Wis., Madison, 1954-56; scientist, biophysicist Rsch. Inst. Advanced Study, Balt., 1956-61; prof. physiology dept. vet. sci. Va. Poly. Inst. & State U., Blacksburg, Va., 1962-78, prof. physiology, biophysics Md./Va. Regional Coll. Vet. Med, 1978-92; advisor biomed. engring. Va. Poly. Inst. and State U., Blacksburg, 1980-84, affiliate Ctr. for Study of Sci. in Soc., 1981-92, prof. emeritus biomed. scis., from 1992. Rsch. vis. prof. Lab. of Cybernetics, Arco Felice, Naples Italy, summer 1970; pres. BioSpectra Co., Blacksburg, 1992-94, Germille, Inc., Blacksburg, 1996—. Inventor patent on isolation and purification of chlorophyll, intellectual property on salmonella detection. Nominated mem. Pratt Animal Nutrition Faculty, Va. Polytech Inst. and State U., Blacksburg, 1978; named Stoner postdoctoral vis. fellow U. Pitts. Sch. Med., 1961-62; recipient Horsley Rsch. award, Va. Acad. Sci., 1984. Fellow Royal Soc. Health; mem. Biophys. Soc. (emeritus), N.Y. Acad. Scis. (emeritus), Va. Acad. Sci. (emeritus). Avocations: philosophy, music, clogging, folk dancing, square dancing. Home: Blacksburg, Va. Died Nov. 16, 2006.

COLVIN, RICK F., medical organization executive; b. Rochester, Minn., June 17, 1944; s. Paul S. and Margaret M. Colvin; m. Irene J. Devine, Jan. 21, 1967; children: Susan, Lisa. BA, Drake U., 1966; JD, U. Minn., 1969. Spl. agt. FBI, Houston, New Orleans, 1969-72; atty. in pvt. practice Rochester, Minn., 1977-85; of counsel Mayo Found., Rochester, 1977-85; exec. dir. Mayo Med. Ventures, Rochester, from 1986. Bd. dirs. Aesgen Inc., Princeton, N.J. Episcopal. Avocation: boating. Home: Rochester, Minn. Died June 16, 2007.

COMEAU, PETER RAY, engineer; b. Iron Mountain, Mich., Dec. 14, 1957; s. James R. and Patricia L. Comeau; m. Marie M. Manfre; 1 child, Austin Keane. AS in Pollution Prevention, Broward C.C., 1980; BS in Bus., Nova U., 1983, MPA, 1987, MBA, 1991. Cert. drinking water treatment lic. class A. Divsn. head water City of Cape Coral, Fla., 1983-85; dir. utilities Charlotte County, Pt. Charlotte, Fla., 1985-87; pres., founder PCMC Mgmt. Cons., Cape Coral, 1987-90; area engr. reg. supr. mgmt. dist. South Fla. Water, Ft. Myers, 1989-91; stormwater utility mgr. Collier County, Naples, Fla., from 1991. Mem. Inst. Mgmt. Accts. Home: Tampa, Fla. Died Mar. 26, 2007.

COMFORT, PATRICK CONNELL, lawyer; b. Tacoma, Sept. 21, 1930; s. Arthur Blaine and Claire Gertrude (Connell) Comfort; m. Elena P. Comfort; children: Christopher, Erin, Sean, Kathleen, Maureen. AB, Gonzaga U., 1952; LLB, NYU, 1955. Bar: Wash. 1955, US Dist. Ct. (Western dist.) 1958, US Ct. Appeals (9th cir.) 1966, US Supreme Ct. 1973. Ptnr. Comfort & Comfort, Tacoma, 1958—60, Comfort Dolack Hansler Billett Hulscher Rosenow & Burrows, Tacoma, 1960—76, Comfort & Smith, Tacoma, from 1988, real estate developer; sole practice Fircrest, Wash., 1976—88. Chmn. Heart Fund Dr. Pierce County; chmn. cabinet Bellarmine Devel. Fund Dr.; co-chmn. St. Joseph's Psychiat. Unit Fund Dr.; rep. 26th Dist. House State of Wash., 1960—64; atty. City of Fircrest, from 1977; bd. visitors U. Puget Sound Sch. Law; mem. Found. Bd. Tacoma CC, 1990—93. With US Army, 1955—57. Named Outstanding Young Man America, US Jaycees, 1964. Mem.: ABA (del. 1987—93), Tacoma-Pierce County Bar Assn. (trustee 1971—74, pres. 1980), Wash. State Bar Assn. (gov. 6th dist. 1981—84, pres. 1985—86, chmn. lawyers assistance program 1988—93, spl. award honor 1984), Fircrest Golf Club (pres. 1974). Republican. Roman Catholic. Avocations: golf, bowling. Home: Tacoma, Wash. Died Dec. 9, 2006.

COMPOSTO, DENNIS MICHAEL, political science, law, finance educator; b. Chgo., July 3, 1940; s. Mario S. and Clare T. (Miceli) C.; m. Marie Montalbano, Oct. 28, 1963; 1 child, Dennis V. BA in Polit. Sci., Loyola U., Chgo., 1979, MEd, 1990; BA in Modern Langs., Loyola U., 1992, PhD in Edn., 1996; MA in Pub. Adminstrn., Northeastern Ill. U., 1992, EdD, from 1997. From work study dir. to bus. mgr. Niles Coll. of Loyola, Chgo., 1969-90, comptr., from 1990; asst. prof. Sch. Law and Sch. Fin., rschr. St. Joseph Coll. of Loyola, Chgo., from 1989. Died Mar. 12, 2007.

CONCANNON, GEORGE ROBERT, business educator; b. Berkeley, Calif., June 2, 1919; s. Robert Lawrence and Hilda (Morgan) C. AB, postgrad., Stanford U.; MBA, Harvard U.; postgrad., U. Calif., Berkeley, Hudson Inst., US Fgn. Svc. Inst., US Nat. War Coll., US Indsl. Coll. Armed Forces. Sales exec. Marchant Calculators, Inc.; U.S. govt. v.p. Holiday Airlines; corp. v.p. Kaiser Industries; pres., CEO Concannon Wine Co., Concannon Co.; prof. bus. U. Calif., Berkeley; ret. Vis. prof. Webster U., Austria, Ecole Superieure Commerce Tours, France, U. Wollongong, Australia, Urals Electromech. Inst., Russia, Estonian Bus. Sch., Concordia Internat. U. Estonia; mgmt. cons. US Govt., Bulgaria, Pvt. Industry, others; tchr. mktg. and mgmt. in field; tech. advisor State Calif. Econ. Devel. Agy. Contbr. articles to profl. jours. Bd. dirs. Stanford Camp Assn.; vol. chaplain damage unit and ICU Palo Alta VA Hosp. Lt. comdr. USN. Recipient Service to Country award Internat. Exec. S.C. Mem. Urban Land Inst., Am. Indsl. Devel. Coun., Dun's Rev. Indsl. Roundtable, World Affairs Coun. Home: Woodside, Calif. Died Nov. 16, 2006.

CONGDON, PAUL UBERT, retired educator, consumer credit counselor; b. Fitchburg, Mass., Aug. 24, 1922; s. James Leonard and Margaret Louise (Parmenter) C.; m. Phyllis Irene Young; children: James Leonard, Karen Elizabeth. BS, Springfield Coll., Mass., 1943; MA in Edn., Ariz. State U., 1948; EdD, Boston U., 1961. Cert. tchr., Mass. Tchr., coach Lumenburg (Mass.) Pub. Schs., 1947, 49-52, Townsend (Mass.) Pub. Schs., 1948-49; tchr., prin. South Fitchburg (Mass.) Sch., 1952-54; prin. Ashby (Mass.) Schs., 1954-57, Littleton (Mass.) Jr. and Sr. High Sch., 1957-59; teaching fellow, instr. Boston U., 1959-61; assoc. prof. Springfield Coll., 1961-63, dean of students, 1964-66, acad. dean, 1966-86, disting. Springfield prof. of humanics, 1987-88; consumer credit counselor, Wilbraham, Mass., from 1990. Chair task force Partnership in Excellence, Springfield, 1984-86. With USNR, 1941-47. Recipient Disting. Svc. award Dist. 789 Rotary, 1977, Svc. award Mass. Assn. Supervision and Curriculum Devel., 1986. Mem. Mass. Assn. Supervision and Curriculum Devel. (pres. 1979, 80), Rotary (dist. gov. 1980-81). Avocations: reading, theater, walking. Home: Wilbraham, Mass. Died June 18, 2007.

CONLEY, JERRY LYNN, protective services official; b. Dayton, Ohio, Sept. 9, 1946; s. Charles and Carol Juanita (Howey) C.; m. Norma Lee England, Dec. 3, 1966 (div. 1977); children: Carol Grace, Sarah Elizabeth, Rebekah Ruth; m. Patricia Ann Bryndza, Aug. 18, 1980; stepchildren: Jason Scott McIlhaney, Michelle Rose McIlhaney Gallier, Gwendolyn Marie Dubrevic. BS in Occupational Edn., Wayland Bapt. U., 1990. Cert. master peace officer, Tex. Dep. sheriff El Paso (Tex.) County Sheriff's Office, 1972-73; patrolman Amarillo (Tex.) Police Dept., 1974-80, detective, 1980-84, identification sgt., 1984-87, mem. accreditation com., 1987-88, auto theft detective, 1988-92, field supr., 1992-94, detective, from 1994. Mem. exec. bd., v.p. Panhandle chpt. Muscular Dystrophy Assn., 1982-84; mem. Amarillo Civic Chorus, Rep. Nat. Com. With U.S. Army, 1963-65. Named Nat. Champion, Am. Hot Rod Assn., 1967. Mem. NRA, Intertel, Tex. Assn. Vehicle Theft Investigators, Internat. Assn. Auto Theft Investigators, Am. Hot Rod Assn. (nat. champion 1967), Amarillo Police Officer's Assn. (past mem. exec. bd.), Mensa (pres. local chpt. 1985-87), KC (dep. grand knight coun. 1450). Roman Catholic. Avocations: auto brochures, singing, reading, video, marksmanship. Home: Amarillo, Tex. Died Jan. 11, 2007.

CONNER, GENE PATRICK, consultant; b. Morgantown, W.Va., Apr. 20, 1940; s. Gilbert Lionel and Esther Ruth (Mayfield) C.; m. Amy Elizabeth Evans, June 6, 1970. BS in Bus., Mountain State Coll., 1967. Pres. Conner Farm's, Columbus, Ohio, from 1968, BARCode Data Systems, Columbus, Ohio, from 1984, Data Acquisition Technology, Columbus, Ohio, from 1986. Cons. Automation Identification Systems Inc., Indpls., 1986—, dir. health and med. div., 1987—; cons. Conat, Inc., Stuart, Fla., 1984—. Designer: (software) BDS-BARCode Systems, 1984; 10 mil. amp Date Decoder, 1984, Executive Decoder, 1985. Mem.: Central Ohio 4WD (Columbus) (pres. 1974-76), East Coast 4WD (regional chmn. 1975-76). Avocations: reading, music. Home: Columbus, Ohio. Died Jan. 15, 2007.

CONNER, JAMES EDWARD, printing company executive; b. Catonsville, Md., Sept. 24, 1927; s. Robert Malcolm and Laura Virginia (Lehnert) C.; m. Lucille Thelma Springer, June 24, 1950; 1 child, Dianne Gay Poynor. Ph.B., Loyola Coll., Balt., 1949. Printing sales v.p. Garamond/Pridemark Press, Balt., 1954-82, v.p. sales, 1980-82, sr. v.p., from 1982. Bd. dirs. Catonsville Hist. Soc., Balt., 1986—, past pres. Young Dems. Howard County, Ellicott City, Md., 1966; vestryman St. John's Episcopal Ch. Mem. Balt. Bibiophiles, Patmos Lodge, Boumi Temple Shrine, Masons (32 degree). Avocation: magic. Home: Ellicott City, Md. Died Dec. 3, 2006.

CONNOR, LEO EDWARD, special education services professional; b. Phila., Sept. 5, 1922; s. Leo A. and Margaret (McMahon) C.; m. Frances Partridge, June 7, 1952. BA, LaSalle U., 1945; MA, U. Pitts., 1949; EdD, Columbia U., 1955. Cert. tchr. spl. edn., adminstr., audiologist. Tchr. Pitts. and Phila. schs., 1945-49; elem. prin., dir. elem. edn. Clarkstown Cen. Sch. Dist., New City, NY, 1950-57; ednl. dir. Lexington Sch. for the Deaf, NYC, 1957-68, exec. dir., 1968-85, Lexington Ctr. for Hearing Impaired, NYC, 1985-88. Chmn. N.Y. Schs. for Deaf and Blind, Albany, N.Y., 1968-83, Coun. on Edn. of Deaf, Washington, 1976-78, Nat. Adv. Com. on Media for Handicapped, Washington, 1978-80; adj. prof. edn. Columbia U., N.Y.C.; instr. NYU, N.Y.C. Author: Administration of Special Education, 1960, History of Research, 1978, History of the Lexington School for the Deaf, 1988, Review of Oral Education, 1980; editor: Speech for the Deaf Child, 1971, Lexington Education Series, 1965-80; contbr. articles to profl. jours. Chmn. Bd. Zoning Adjustment, Borough of Spring Lake, N.J., 1989-96, chmn. lake com., 1990-95; trustee New Rochelle (N.Y.) Coll.; mem. parish coun. St. Catherine's Ch. Recipient annual award N.Y. Coun. Exceptional Children, Albany, 1988. Fellow Am. Speech/Hearing/Lang. Assn. (clin. cert. competency and honors of the assoc.); mem. Alexander Graham Bell Assn. (Honors of the Assn. award 1986, pres. 1970-72), Coun. for Exceptional Children (pres. 1968-69). Roman Catholic. Home: Boca Raton, Fla. Died Aug. 2, 2007.

CONQUEST, ROBERT (GEORGE ROBERT ACWORTH CONQUEST), writer, historian, poet; b. Malvern, Worcestershire, Eng., July 15, 1917; s. Robert Folger Westcott and Rosamund Alys (Acworth) C.; m. Joan Watkins, 1942 (dis. 1948); children: John, Richard; m. Tatiana Mihailova, 1948 (div. 1963); m. Caroleen Macfarlane, 1964 (dis. 1978); m. Elizabeth Neece, Dec. 1, 1979; stepchild Helen Beasley Student, Winchester Coll., Eng., 1931-35, U. Grenoble, France, 1935-36, U. Oxford, 1936-39; MA, U. Oxford, Eng., 1972; DLitt, U. Oxford, 1975. First sec. H.M. Fgn. Svc., Sofia, Bulgaria, U.N., London, 1946-56; rsch. fellow London Sch. Econs., 1956-58; vis. poet U. Buffalo, NY, 1959-60; lit. editor The Spectator, London, 1962-63; sr. fellow Russian Inst. Columbia U., NYC, 1964-65; fellow Woodrow Wilson Internat. Ctr., Washington, 1976-77; sr. rsch. fellow Hoover Inst., Stanford (Calif.) U., 1977—79, 1981—2015. Disting. vis. scholar Heritage Found., Washington, 1980-81; adv. bd. Freedom House, N.Y.C., 1980-2015; rsch. assoc. Ukrainian Rsch. Inst. Harvard U., Cambridge, Mass., 1983-2015; adj. fellow Washington Ctr. Strategic Studies., 1984-2015. Author: Poems, 1955, A World of Difference, 1955, Common Sense About Russia, 1960, Power and Policy in the USSR, 1961, The Pasternak Affair, 1962, Between Mars and Venus, 1962, (with Kingsley Amis) The Egyptologists, 1965, Russia after Khrushchev, 1965, Industrial Workers in the USSR, 1967, The Great Terror, 1968, Arias from a Love Opera, 1969, The Nation Killers: The Soviet Deportation of Nationalities, 1970, Where Marx Went Wrong, 1970, V I Lenin, 1972, Kolyma: The Arctic Death Camps, 1978, Coming Across, 1978, The Abomination of Moab, 1979, Forays, 1979, Present Danger: Towards a Foreign Policy, 1979, We and They: Civic and Despotic Cultures, 1980, (with Jon M. White) What to do When the Russians Come, 1984, Inside Stalin's Secret Police: NKVD Politics 1936-39, 1985, The Harvest of Sorrow: Soviet Collectivization and the Terror-Famine, 1986, New and Collected Poems, 1988, Stalin and the Kirov Murder, 1988, Tyrants and Typewriters, 1989, The Great Terror:A Reassessment, 1990, Stalin: Breaker of Nations, 1991, Demons Don't, 1999, Reflections on a Ravaged Century, 1999, The Dragons of Expectation: Reality and Delusion in the Course of History, 2005. Capt. inf. Brit. Army, 1939-46, ETO. Decorated officer Order Brit. Empire, companion Order St. Michael and St. George; recipient Alexis de Tocqueville award, 1992, Light Verse award Acad. Arts and Letters, 1997, Presdl. Medal of Freedom, The White House, 2005; Jefferson Lecture Humanities, Washington, 1993, Richard M. Weaver prize for scholarly letters, 1999; Royal Soc. Lit. fellow, 1972. Fellow Brit. Acad., Brit. Interplanetary Soc., AAAL-Michael Braude Award Light Verse, Royal Soc. Lit., Am. Acad. Arts & Sci., Soc. Promotion Roman Studies; Mem. Literary Soc.; Clubs: Travellers (London). Home: Stanford, Calif. Died Aug. 3, 2015.

CONRAD, JOSEPH HENRY, animal nutrition educator; b. Cass County, Ind., Dec. 7, 1926; s. Ferdinand M. and Marie E. (Hubenthal) C.; m. Frances Ash, June 18, 1950; children: Kenneth A., Leonard J., Carol Ann, Joseph C. BS, Purdue U., 1950, MS, 1954, PhD, 1958; prof. (hon.), Fed. U. Viçosa, Brazil, 1965. Asst. prof. Purdue U., West Lafayette, Ind., 1958-63, assoc. prof., 1963-68, prof., 1968-71; animal scientist Fed. U. Viçosa, 1961-65; prof., coord. tropical animal sci. programs U. Fla., Gainesville, 1971-95. Co-author: Swine Production, 1982; contbr. monographs and numerous articles on animal nutrition and tropical animal prodn. to profl. jours. Served with USN, 1944-46. Recipient Disting. Nutritional award Distillers Feed Rsch. Coun., 1964; Moorman fellow, 1989. Fellow Am. Soc. Animal Sci. (Internat. Animal Agrl. award 1985, Bohstedt award 1987, Internat. Mktg. award 1989); mem. World Assn. Animal Prodn. (v.p.), Latin Am. Soc. Animal Prodn., Sociedade Brasileira de Zootecnia, Purdue U. Alumni Assn. (life, pres.'s coun.), Sigma Xi, Gamma Sigma Delta. Republican. Lutheran. Home: Gainesville, Fla. Died Aug. 12, 2015.

CONRATH, BARNEY JAY, astrophysicist; b. Quincy, Ill., June 23, 1935; s. Frederick Barney and Jayme Wilson (Cason) C.; m. Marjorie Ann Hilder, Sept. 3, 1962; children: Ann, Frederick, Susan. BA, Culver-Stockton Coll., Canton, Mo., 1957; MA, U. Iowa, 1959; PhD, U. N.H., 1966. Astrophysicist Goddard Space Flight Ctr., NASA, Greenbelt, Md., 1960-90, sr. fellow, 1990-95; vis. sr. scientist Ctr. Radiophysics Space Rsch., Cornell U., Ithaca, NY, from 1995. Co-author: Exploration of the Solar System by Infrared Remote Sensing, 1991, Exploration of the Solar System by Infrared Remote Sensing, 2d edit., 2003. Recipient Exceptional Sci. Achievement medal NASA, 1982, 90. Mem. Am. Astron. Soc. (Gerard P. Kuiper prize 1996), Am. Geophys. Union, Sigma Xi. Achievements include serving as principal investigator of Voyager infrared spectroscopy experiment which determined helium abundance, thermal structure, energy balance, and atmospheric composition of Jupiter, Saturn, Uranus and Neptune. Home: Charlottesville, Va. Died Apr. 23, 2014.

CONROY, PAT (DONALD PATRICK CONROY), writer; b. Atlanta, Oct. 26, 1945; s. Donald and Frances Dorothy (Peck) Conroy; m. Barbara Bolling, Oct. 10, 1969 (div. 1977); 1 child, Megan stepchildren: Jessica, Melissa;

m. Lenore Fleischer, 1981 (div. Oct. 25, 1995); 1 child, Susannah Ansley stepchildren: Gregory Fleischer, Emily; m. Cassandra King, 1997; stepchildren: Jake Ray, James Ray, Jason Ray. BA in English, The Citadel, Charleston, SC, 1967, LittD (hon.), 2000. Former English tchr., Beaufort, SC, Daufuskie Island, SC. Author: (novels) The Boo, 1970, The Water Is Wide, 1972 (Anisfield-Wolf Book award, Cleve. Found., 1972), The Great Santini, 1976, The Lords of Discipline, 1980 (Lillian Smith Book award, So. Regional Coun./U. Ga., 1981), The Prince of Tides, 1986, Beach Music, 1995, South of Broad, 2009 (#1 Publishers Weekly bestseller), The Death of Santini: The Story of a Father and His Son, 2013, (nonfiction) The Pat Conroy Cookbook: Recipes of My Life, 1999, My Losing Season, 2002, My Reading Life, 2010, (screenplays) Conrack, 1974, The Great Santini, 1979, The Lords of Discipline, 1983, Invictus, 1988, The Water Is Wide, 2006; co-author (with Becky Johnston) The Prince of Tides, 1991. Recipient Achievement in Edn. award, NEA, 1974, Governor's award for Arts, State of Ga., 1978, Golden Plate award, American Acad. Achievement, 1992, Lit. award, U. SC Thomas Cooper Libr. Soc., 1995, Gov.'s award in the Humanities for disting. achievement, State of SC, 1996, Humanitarian award, Ga. Commn. on Holocaust, 1996, Medal of Merit for outstanding lit. achievement, Lotos Club NYC, 1996; named to The SC Hall of Fame, 2009; grantee Ford Found., 1971. Mem.: PEN, Writers Guild, Authors Guild America. Democrat. Home: Atlanta, Ga. Died Mar. 4, 2016.

CONSTANTINE, THOMAS ARTHUR, federal agency administrator; b. Buffalo, Dec. 23, 1938; m. Ruth Cryan; children Thomas, Kevin, Patty Gatta, Lisa Reale, Kathy Constantine, Laura Jeczyk BS, SUNY, Buffalo; MS, SUNY, Albany. Dep. Erie County (N.Y.) Sheriff's Dept., 1960-62; uniform trooper N.Y. State Police, 1962, narcotics and maj. crime investigator, sgt., lt. in chg. recruiting, capt. of statewide organized crime task force, maj., troop comdr., staff inspector, asst. dep. supt., supt., 1986-94; adminstr. U.S. Drug Enforcement Agy., Washington, 1994-98. Faculty mem. State Univ. at Albany, Rockefeller Coll. of Public Affairs and Policy; sr. advisor to the dir. of the US Office of Nat. Intelligence, 2007. Recipient Gov.'s Law Enforcement Exec. of Yr. award State of N.Y., 1994. Mem. Internat. Assn. Chiefs of Police (bd. officers 1992-94, exec. com. and chmn. narcotics and dangerous drugs com. to date). Died May 3, 2015.

CONTOS, PAUL ANTHONY, engineer, investment consultant; b. Chgo., Mar. 18, 1926; s. Anthony Dimitrios and Panagiota (Kostopoulos) C.; m. Lilian Katie Kalkines, June 19, 1955 (dec. Apr. 1985); children: Leslie, Claudia, Paula, Anthony. Student, Am. TV Inst., Chgo., 1946-48, U. Ill., 1949-52, 53-56, Ill. Inst. Tech., 1952-53, U. So. Calif., 1956-57. Engr. J.C. Deagan Co., Inc., Chgo., 1951-53, Lockheed Missile and Space Co., Inc., Sunnyvale, Calif., 1956-62, engring. supr., 1962-65, dept. mgr., 1963—66, mgr. spl. classified program, 1964—84, staff engr. Sunnyvale, 1965-88; genealogy rsch. San Jose, Calif., from 1970; pres. PAC Investments, Saratoga, Calif., 1984-88, San Jose, Calif., from 1988, also advisor, cons., from 1984; program mgr. sci., from 1962. Author memoirs & short stories, Rain of Teror in the Sunshine, 2009, Coming Home, 2014. Mem. Pres. Coun. U. Ill., 1994—, vol. coach, Computer Learning Ctr. With U.S. Army, 1944-46, ETO. Decorated Purple Heart, Bronze Star medal, Combat Infantryman badge, African Mid. Ea. Campaign medal with 2 bronze stars, WWII Victory medal, Army of Occupation medal with Germany clasp, Good Conduct medal, Honorable Svc. Lapel Button WWII, Meritorious Unit citation, Sharp Shooter Badge with Rifle Bar. Mem. DAV (life, comdr. Chgo. unit 1948-51, Ill. state dept. exec. committeeman and fin. officer, 1953, 1954), VFW (life), Pi Sigma Phi (pres. 1951-53), Am. Legion. Republican. Greek Orthodox. Avocations: genealogy, reading, writing. Died May 19, 2015.

CONVERSE, PHILIP ERNEST, retired social sciences educator; b. Concord, NH, Nov. 17, 1928; s. Ernest Luther and Evelyn (Eaton) C.; m. Jean Gilmore McDonnell, Aug. 25, 1951; children: Peter Everett, Timothy McDonnell. BA in English, Denison U., 1949; MA in English Lit., State U. Iowa, 1950; cert., U. Paris, 1954; MA in Sociology, U. Mich., 1956, PhD in Sociology, 1958; DHL (hon.), Denison U., 1974, U. Chgo., 1979; LLD (hon.), Harvard U., 2006; DSc (hon.), U. Mich., 2007. Asst. prof. sociology U. Mich., 1960-65, prof. sociology & polit. sci., 1965-89, Robert C. Angell Disting. prof., 1975-89; ret., 1989. Asst. study dir. Inst. Social Rsch. U. Mich., 1956-58, study dir., 1958-65, program dir., 1965-82, dir. Ctr. for Polit. Studies, 1982-86, dir. Inst. Social Rsch., 1986-89; dir. Ctr. Advanced Study in Behavioral Scis., 1989-94; trustee Ctr. Advanced Study in Behavioral Scis., 1980-86, 94-2000, Russell Sage Found., 1982-92. Co-author: The American Voter, 1960, Elections and the Political Order, 1966, The Human Meaning of Social Change, 1972, The Quality of American Life, 1976, Political Representation in France, 1986; contbr. articles to profl. jours. Served with U.S. Army, 1950-52. Recipient Disting. Faculty Achievement award U. Mich., 1973; Fulbright fellow, 1959-60; NSF fellow, 1967-68; Guggenheim fellow, 1975-76; Ctr. Advanced Study in Behavioral Scis. fellow, 1979-80 Mem. AAAS, American Sociol. Assn., American Polit. Sci. Assn. (pres. 1983-84), Internat. Soc. Polit. Psychology (pres. 1980-81), Nat. Acad. Sciences, American Acad. Arts & Sciences, American Philos. Soc. Home: Ann Arbor, Mich. Died Dec. 30, 2014.

CONWAY, EDMUND VIRGIL, financial consultant, lawyer; b. Southhampton, NY, Aug. 2, 1929; s. Edmund Virgil Conway, II and Dorothy (Brandes) m. Elaine Wingate, June 28, 1969; children: Allison Worthington, Sarah Conway, (stepchildren) William Gay, John Gay BA Philosophy and Religion magna cum laude, Colgate U., 1951; LLB cum laude, Yale U., 1956; LLD (hon.), Pace U., 1990; LHD (hon.), SUNY, Stony Brook, 1998; LLD (hon.), Colgate U., 2002. Bar: N.Y. 1956. Assoc. Debevoise & Plimpton, NYC, 1956—64; supt. 1st dept. Banks of State N.Y., 1964—67; exec. v.p. Manhattan Savings Bank, NYC, 1967—68; pres., chmn., CEO The Seamen's Bank for Savings, NY, 1969—88; chmn. Rittenhouse Advisors, LLC, 2001—15. Bd. dirs. Union Pacific Corp., chmn. exec. compensation com., mem. exec. com. 1978-2002; bd. dirs. J.P. Stevens & Co., Inc., 1974-88 ; trustee, mem. exec. com., chmn. audit com. mut. funds managed by Phoenix Funds, 1990-2007; dir., mem. audit com. of mut. funds managed by Phoenix Duff & Phelps Funds, 1990-2006; trustee, mem. exec. com., chmn. exec. devel. & comp. Atlantic Mut. Ins. Co., 1974-2002; trustee, mem. exec., chmn. exec. pers. and pension coms. Consol. Edison Co. NY, 1970-2002; trustee, chmn. compensation com., mem. exec. com. Urstadt Biddle Property Co., 1989—; mem. bd. adv. dir. Blackrock BFM, Freddie Mac Securities Mortgage Fund, 1988-2001; NY rep. Conf. of State Bank Suprs., 1970-77, mem. adv. coun., 1973-74, mem. adv. com. to NY State Supt. Banks, 1967-70; chmn. Fin. Acct. Stds. Adv. Coun., 1992-1995; adv. dir. Fund Directions; dir. chmn. comp. com. Trism, Inc., 1995-2001; dir., mem. exec. com., audit com., chmn. stock option com. Accuhealth, Inc., 1995-2002; sec, NY State Banking Bd., 1964-67; vice chmn., bd. dirs. Seaman's Corp., 1986-89 Editor: Yale Law Jour Mem. Metropolitan Transportation Authority, audit and real estate coms., mem. Metro North LI RR and NYC Transit coms., 1992-95; chmn. Metropolitan Transportation Authority, LI RR, Metro North, Transit Authority of City of NY, Triborough Bridge and Tunnel Authority, 1995-2001; mem. NY State Thruway Authority, chmn. audit and fin. com., 2006, bd. mem.; chmn. Temporary State Commn. on Water Supply Needs of Southeastern NY, 1970-75; mem. Audit Com. NYC, 1981-1996, chmn., 1990-1996; Mayor's Mgmt. Adv. Bd., NYC, 1975-77; mem., chmn. meml. design com. NYC Korean Vets. Meml. Commn., 1981-83; del. Rep. State Conv. NY, 1962, 66; pres. NY Young Rep. Club, 1962-63,, vice chmn., Acad. Political Sci., 90-2015; mem. adv. bd. NYU Real Estate Inst., 1975-80; bd. dirs. Realty Found. NY, bd. dirs., 1975-2015; chmn. audit, fin., exec. coms. Josiah Macy, Jr. Found., 1974-2005; mem. bd. dirs. Transp. Learning Ctr. 2004, Urstadt Biddle Properties; bd. dirs. Adv. Bd. Columbia Pres. Hosp. Eye & Heart Divsns. 2005-; trustee, former vice chmn., mem. exec. com. Citizens Budget Commn., 1970-77; life trustee NYC Police Found., Pace U., NYC, Colgate U.; trustee NY coun. Boy Scouts Am.; hon. life trustee South St. Seaport Mus.; bd. govs., pres. Fed. Hall Meml. Assocs., Inc., 1981-84; bd. dirs., vice chmn, treas., mem. audit and fin., compensation, project planning and pub. policy com., NYC Partnership, Inc., 1980-91, hon. ptnr., 1991-2015; elder Reformed Ch. of Bronxville; mem., chnm. audit com. Westchester Indl. Devel. Agy., 1991-2009 Recipient Humanitarian award Jewish Hosp. and Rsch. Ctr., Denver, 1977, Montauk Playhouse Cmty. Ctr., 2005, Good Scout award Greater N.Y. couns. Boy Scouts Am., 1980, Eagle Scout award, 1988, Silver Beaver award, 1989, Spl. Recognition award NAACP, 1980, Disting. Svc. to Higher Edn. medal Brandeis U., 1976, Urban Leadership award NYU, 1981, Hundred Yr. Assn. Gold Medal award, 1986, Alexander Hamilton award Bowling Green Assn., Disting. Svc. award Bklyn. Bur. Cmty. Svc., 1995, Family of Yr. award Family Svc. Westchester, Inc., 1996, Norman Vincent Peale award, Insts. Religion and Health, 1998, Ellis Island medal of honor, Nat. Ethnic Coalition, 1998; Gov.'s Parks and Preservation award, 1999, March of Dimes Svc. to Humanity award, 2000, Urban Visionaries award, Cooper Union, 2002, Hudson Valley Hero's award, Historic Hudson Valley, 1998; named Man of Yr. Realty Found. N.Y., 1978, Brian Little Disting. Allumnus award, Colgate U., 2011. Mem. ABA, N.Y. State Bar Assn., Assn. of Bar of City of N.Y., Nat. Assn. Mut. Savs. Banks (past dir.), Savings Banks Assn. N.Y. State (pres. 1978-79, past dir. and chmn. legis.), N.Y. C. of C. and Industry (bd. dirs., exec. com., sec.-treas. 1974-91, chmn. mission rev. com. 1985), Real Estate Bd. N.Y. (bd. govs. 1976-79), Econ. Club N.Y., Knights of St. Patrick (bd. dirs., emeritus chmn.), Friendly Sons. of St. Patrick, Union League Club, Links Club, Siwanoy Country Club, Hillsboro Club, Mory's Assoc., Mont. Lake Club, Phi Beta Kappa. Home: Bronxville, NY. Died Oct. 21, 2015.

CONWELL, ESTHER MARLY, physicist, researcher; b. NYC, May 23, 1922; d. Charles and Ida (Korn) C.; m. Abraham A. Rothberg, Sept. 30, 1945; 1 son, Lewis J. BA, Bklyn. Coll., 1942, DSc, 1992, SUNY, Geneseo, 2009; MS, U. Rochester, NYC, 1945; PhD, U. Chgo., 1948; DSc, U. Rochester, 2011. Lectr. Bklyn. Coll., 1946-51; mem. tech. staff Bell Tel. Labs., 1951-52; physicist GTE Labs., Bayside, NY, 1952-61, mgr. physics dept., 1961-72; vis. prof. U. Paris, 1962-63; Abby Rockefeller Mauze prof. MIT, Cambridge, 1972; prin. scientist Xerox Corp., Webster, NY, 1972-80, rsch. fellow, 1981-98. Adj. prof. U. Rochester, 1990—2001, prof., 2001—14; cons., mem. advisory com. engring. NSF, 1978—81. Author: High Field Transport in Semiconductors, 1967, also rsch. papers; mem. editl. bd. Jour. Applied Physics, Proc. of IEEE, patentee in field. Recipient Nat. Medal Sci., The White Høuse, 2010. Fellow IEEE (Edison medal 1997), American Phys. Soc. (sec.-treas. divsn. condensed matter physics 1977-82); mem. AAAS, NAS, NAE, Soc. Women Engineers (Achievement award 1960, Susan B. Anthony Lifetime Achievement award 2006). Home: Rochester, NY. Died Nov. 16, 2014.

CONWELL, VIRGINIA DONLEY, librarian; b. Carlsbad, N.Mex., Jan. 3, 1921; d. William Guy and Frances Acree (Guthrie) Donley; m. Robert E.M. Conwell, Aug. 8, 1943 (dec. 1958); children: Elizabeth Conwell Shapiro, Virginia Conwell Hall. AB, U. N.Mex., 1944; degree in Libr. Credential, U. Southern Calif., 1962. Libr. Unified Sch. Dist., Montebello, Calif., 1982—86. Files chmn. Downey Alumnae Panhellenic, from 1978; del. Calif. Dem. Cen. Com., from 1986. Mem.: AARP, Assistance League Downey, Mortarboard, Downey Alumnae Panhellenic Club, Phi Alpha Theta, Chi Omega (LA coord. coun.). Democrat. Episcopalian. Died Dec. 15, 2006.

COOK, DONALD EUGENE, retired orthopedist; b. Cromwell, Ala., Oct. 19, 1935; s. Frances Aubrey and Ethie Francis (Nicholson) C.; m. Myrna Nell Shadow, June 20, 1959; children: Janet Lynn, Donald Scott. Student, U. Miss., 1959, MD, 1963. Extern Miss. State Hosp., Whitfield, 1962-63; intern Mobile Gen. Hosp., Ala., 1963-64; resident U. Miss. Med. Ctr., Jackson, 1964-68, chief resident, 1967-68; cons. physician Miss. Crippled Children's Svc., Meridian, 1968-72; staff Riley Meml. Hosp., Meridian, 1968-76, Meridian Regional Hosp., 1968-89, Anderson Med. Ctr., Meridian, 1968-99; pres. East. Ctrl. Orthops., Ltd., Meridian, 1982-99; ret., 2000. CEO Astro Devel. Co., Meridian, 1986—92; pres., CEO Planetary Products, Inc., 1986—93. Patentee. Mem. bd. dirs. ARC, Meridian, 1978-80; team physician Meridian Boxing Club, 1980-95. With U.S. Army, 1954-57. Mem.: AMA, Miss. State Med. Assn., Shriners, Masons (32 degree). Baptist. Home: Meridian, Miss. Died Feb. 8, 2007.

COOK, JAMES HERMAN, estate management consultant, financial advisor; b. Valley, Ala., Oct. 13, 1927; s. James W. and Lola S. Cook; m. Minnie Brown, Oct. 1, 1953; children: James M., Debra M., George M. BS in Bus. Adminstrn., Auburn U., 1950; MS in Bus. Mgmt., Columbus Coll., 1978. Commd. 2d lt. U.S. Army, 1951, advanced through grades to col.; ret., 1976; estate mgr., fin. cons., pvt. practice Valley, Ala., from 1976, Columbus, Ga., from 1976. Decorated Air medals, Legion of Merit, Bronze Star, and others. Mem. Ret. Officers Assn., 31st Dixie Divsn. Assn., Valley Srs. Golf Assn. Protestant. Avocations: geneology, coins. Died Dec. 8, 2006.

COOK, MARLOW WEBSTER, former United States Senator from Kentucky, lawyer; b. Akron, NY, July 27, 1926; m. Nancy Remmers; children: Christy, Nancy Spade, Louise Reed, Webster. BA in History, U. Louisville, 1948, JD, 1950. Atty., Louisville, 1950—57; mem. Ky. House or Reps., 1957—61; judge-exec. Jefferson County, Ky., 1961—68; US Senator from Ky., 1968—74; atty. Washington, 1974—89; ret., 1989. Served in USN. Mem.: Ky. Bar Assn. Republican. Roman Catholic. Home: Sarasota, Fla. Died Feb. 4, 2016.

COOK, STANTON RUFUS, media company executive; b. Chgo., July 3, 1925; s. Rufus Merrill and Thelma Maria (Borgerson) C.; m. Barbara Wilson, Sept. 23, 1950 (dec. Nov. 1994); children Douglas, Scott, David, Nancy Cook, Sarah Shumway BS in Mech. Engring., Northwestern U., 1949. With Shell Oil Co., 1949-51, Chgo. Tribune Co., 1951-81, v.p., 1967-70, exec. v.p. and gen. mgr., 1970-72, pres., 1972-74, pub., 1973-90, CEO, 1974-76, chmn., 1974-81; dir. Tribune Co., 1972-96, v.p., 1972-74, pres., 1974-88, chmn., 1989—93, CEO, 1974-90; chmn. Chgo. Nat. League Ball Club, Inc., 1990-94. Bd. dirs. AP, 1975-84, 2d vice chmn., 1979-84; bd. dirs. Newspaper Adv. Bur., 1973-92, Am. Newspaper Pubs. Assn., 1974-82; dep. chmn., bd. dirs. Fed. Res. Bank Chgo., 1980-83, chmn., 1984-85; bd. dirs. Robert R. McCormick Tribune Found., 1990-2001; former chmn. Chgo. Cubs Trustee Robert R. McCormick Trust, 1972-90, Savs. and Profit Sharing Fund of Sears Employees, 1991-94, U. Chgo., 1973-87, Mus. Sci. and Industry, Chgo., 1973, Field Mus. Natural History, Chgo., 1973, Gen. Douglas MacArthur Found., 1979, Northwestern U., 1987, Shedd Aquarium Soc., 1987, Am. Newspaper Pubs. Assn. Found., 1973-82. Mem. Newspaper Assn. Am. (bd. govs. 1992), Chgo. Coun. Fgn. Rels. (bd. dirs. 1973-93), Comml. Club (past pres.), Econ. Club (life, past pres.), Glen Lake Assn. (pres. 2001-04). Home: Kenilworth, Ill. Died Sept. 3, 2015.

COOKE, R(ICHARD) CASWELL, JR., architect; b. Richmond, Va., Dec. 19, 1935; s. Richard Caswell and Caroline (Kellock) C.; m. Mary Gibson, June 6, 1962; children: Richard, Frederick, Gordon, Molly. BArch, U. Va., 1962; MArch, Yale U., 1967. Registered architect, Mass., Conn., Va., N.J., Pa. Project mgr. Clinch Crimp Brown & Fischer, Boston, 1962-64, Paul Rudolph Arch., New Haven, 1964-65; prin., dir. Geotactics, Inc., New Haven, 1965-82; gen. mgr. Gulf Consult Archs., Al Khobar, Saudi Arabia, 1982-86; prin. Fellows, Read, Leoncavallo & Cooke, Princeton, N.J., 1986-89; v.p., dir. arch. Washington Group (formerly Raytheon Engrs. & Constructors), London, 1989—2000; pres. Washington Archs. LLC, Princeton, 2000—03, London, 2000—03; propr. Caswell Cooke Architect, Trenton, NJ, 2003—05; prin. C+C Architecture, LLC, Lawrenceville, NJ, from 2005. Lectr. Quinnipiac Coll., New Haven, St. Paul's Ch., Kiwanis Club; juried design Yale U. Prin. works include design of Petromin Corp. Bldg., Riyadh, Saudi Arabia, Baxter Health Care Facility, Calif., Roche Carolina Campus, SC, Can. Red Cross Facility, NS, Derby (Conn.) Elderly Housing, The Mus. at Ft. Bliss, El Paso, Tex., The Wireworks, Trenton, NJ, Indiantown (Fla.) Gateway. Chmn. New Haven Harbor Commn., 1976, Conn. Regional Planning Com., 1976; bd. dirs. Am. Businessmen's assn., Saudi Arabia, 1986; pres. Yale Alumni Assn. Sch. Architecture, 1978; past bd. dirs. Conn. Soc. Architects. Recipient Christchurch Sch. Alumni award, 1975, first design award Milford Yacht Club, 1977, Alpha Rho Chi award U. Va., 1962. Mem.: AIA, Episc. Diocesan Archtl. Commn., Am. Soc. Landscape Archs., Illuminating Engrs. Soc., Constrn. Specification Inst., Nat. Coun. Archtl. Registration Bds., NJ Soc. Archs., Henry Found. for Bot. Rsch., Sons of the Revolution (NJ bd. dirs., pres.), Assn. Yale Alumni, Trenton Symposium, Nassau Club (ho. com.), Yale Club of Princeton (past pres.). Episcopalian. Home: Lawrenceville, NJ. Died June 11, 2007.

COONTS, VIOLET GADD, retired business educator, retired art educator, artist; b. Charleston, W. Va., Sept. 23, 1913; d. Lundy John and Luvada (Cart) Gadd; m. Gilbert Gray Coonts, July 15, 1941; children: Stephen Paul, John Jacob. BS, W. Va. U., 1940; student, Mason Coll. Music and Fine Art, 1942-45. Bus. instr. East Bank (W. Va.) H.S., 1940-45, Charleston (W. Va.) H.S., 1945-46; bus. and art instr. Buckhannon-Upshur H.S., Buckhannon, W. Va., 1952-72. Instr. journalism Buckhannon-Upshur H.S., 1959-69, art W.Va. Wesleyan Coll., Buckhannon, 1972-75, oil painting Upshur-County Adult Edn., 1980-82. Author: The Western Waters, 1991; group exhbns. include Hunington (W.Va.) Gallery, 1964, Hackett Gallery, Charleston, W.Va., 1965, Parkers Art Studio, Parkersburg, W.Va., 1967, Clarksburg (W.Va.) Art Ctr., 1993-95, Art Co. of Davis, W.Va., 1994; designed mural Ctrl. Nat. Bank, 1978. Mem. United Methodist Ch. Mem. NEA (life), Barbour County Hist. Soc. (life), Order of the Ea. Star, Literary Club, Nat. Mus. Women in the Arts (charter). Methodist. Avocations: reading, giving programs, painting, writing, playing bridge. Home: Fulton, Md. Died Jan. 18, 2007.

COOPER, CAROL ELLEN, social worker; b. Los Angeles, Jan. 19, 1940; d. Harry and Barbara (Prupis) C. BA, U. Calif., Berkeley, 1962; diploma, Calif. Acupuncture Sch., 1984; MSW, Calif. State U., 1972. Diplomate Nat. Commn. Cert. Acupuncturists. Psychiat. social worker II Los Angeles County Forensic Unit, from 1973; pvt. practice psychotherapy Los Angeles, from 1975. Mem. Am. Fellowship Ch. Healing Arts (minister 1979—). Died Apr. 15, 2007.

COOPER, FLORA A., elementary school educator; b. Lawton, Okla., Aug. 19, 1924; d. Edd Ray and Nancy Sarah (Greenwood) Adkins; m. Floyd Willis Cooper (dec.), June 28, 1948; children: Deborah Joy Cooper Beaver, Floyd William Cooper. Student, Okla. Coll. for Women, Chickasha, Landmark Missionary Bapt. Coll, Sacramento; BA, So. Oreg. Coll., Ashland, 1970; postgrad., San Francisco State U. Tchr. Robla Sch. Dist., Sacramento, Salinas (Calif.) Elem. Schs., Richmond (Calif.) Elem. Sch. Dist., Christian Sch., Sacramento. Mem. NEA, Calif. State Tchrs. Assn., Robla Dist. Tchrs. Assn., Robla PTA. Home: Sacramento, Calif. Died Dec. 3, 2006.

COOPER, HOWARD PAYNE, psychologist; b. Washington, Oct. 7, 1930; s. Howard Perkins and Carol Jean C.; m. Shirley Cole Cooper, Dec. 24, 1951. BS, Pa. State U., 1951; MEd, Our Lady of the Lake U., 1975. Lic. profl. counselor, Tex. Served to lt. col. USAF, 1951-71; tchr., coach, counselor Holy Cross H.S., San Antonio, Tex., 1972-88; test adminstr. St. Philip's Coll., San Antonio, 1989-92. Adj. instr. Park Coll., 1992-96; adminstrv. bd. Holy Cross H.S., 1980-87. Ofcl. Spl. Olympics, San Antonio, 1986-87. Decorated Bronze Star, USAF, Air medal with two oak leafs, Air Commendation medal, Meritorious Svc. medal. Mem. Air Force Navigators Assn., Retired Officers Assn., Pa. State Alumni Assn. Republican. Avocations: racquetball, walking, chess. Home: San Antonio, Tex. Died Nov. 17, 2007.

COOPER, RICHARD FRANCIS, computer company executive; b. Rouses Point, NY, May 27, 1946; s. Richard Charles and Bernice (Traynor) C.; m. Cheryl Jones, Aug. 9, 1975. Student, Albany Bus. Coll., 1965, Plattsburgh State U., 1966-67. Coding clk., asst. data processing F.W Myers, Inc., Rouses Point, N.Y., 1965-67; operator, programmer No. Data Processing, Plattsburgh, N.Y., 1967; data processing supr. Au Sable Valley Telephone Co., Keeseville, N.Y., 1967-69; data processing mgr. John H. McGaulley CPA, Plattsburgh, 1969-71; owner Computer Bus. Systems, Plattsburgh, from 1971; mgr. Roctest, Inc., Plattsburgh, 1977-85; sales assoc. Met. Life Ins., Plattsburgh, 1976; chmn. of bd. Four-Star Heritage Group, Plattsburgh, from 1999. Pres. Am. RR Transpn. Co., Plattsburgh, 1980—; v.p. No. Sports & Recreation, Plattsburgh, 1982—; CEO Computer Bus. Systems, Plattsburgh, 1985—; v.p. Ardcom Satellite Comm. Svcs., Plattsburgh, 1992—. Dir. Camp Brandon for Boys, 1998—; active Big Buddy/Little Buddy Program. Episcopalian. Avocations: model rr, hiking, camping, rail travel. Home: Plattsburgh, NY. Died May 21, 2007.

COOPER, RICKEY EUGENE, writer, educator; b. Stockton, Calif., May 27, 1946; s. Robert Evertt and Barbara Louise Cooper. AA in Physics, San Joaquin Delta Jr. Coll., 1970; student, Calif. State U., Fresno, 1973. File and unit clk. Stockton (Calif.) State Hosp., 1974-75; billing unit supr. Divsn. Substance Abuse, Sacramento, 1976-78; bus. mgr. Nat. Socialist White People's Party, Arlington, Va., 1978-80; med. transcriptionist Georgetown U. Hosp., Washington, 1980-82, Silas B. Hays Army Cmty. Hosp., Ft. Ord, Calif., 1983-85, Hood River (Oreg.) Meml. Hosp., 1985-87, Columbia Gorge Orthopedics, Hood River, Oreg., 1986-88, Emanuel Hosp., Portland, Oreg., 1988-98, Webb & Assocs., Portland, Oreg., 98-99, Rodeer Sys., Portland, Oreg., 1999-2000, N.W. Mediscript, Kennewick, Wash., 2000—01. Spokesperson Nat. Socialist Vanguard. Sgt. USAF, 1964-68. Home: Goldendale, Wash. Died Nov. 26, 2006.

COPELAND, WILMA T., secondary school educator; b. Newton, Mass., Dec. 8, 1940; d. Willie Clifford and Lillie (Johnson) Thompson; m. James William Copeland, Sept. 14, 1963 (div. Oct. 1983); 1 child, James Kevin. BS, Alcorn State, 1963; MA, U. Cin., 1970. Tchr. Yalobusha County Schs., Coffeeville, Miss., 1963-65, Cin. Pub. Schs., from 1965. Membership capt. Cin. Art Mus., 1988-89; campaign chmn. Cin. Fine Arts Fund, Cin., 1990. Mem. Chums, Inc. (pres. Cin. chpt. 1982-86), Delta Kappa Gamma (corresponding sec. 1984-86), Delta Sigma Theta (chaplain 1987-89). Baptist. Avocations: travel, sewing, reading, cooking new recipes. Home: Cincinnati, Ohio. Died Apr. 14, 2007.

CORE, ORVILLE BEN, retired lawyer; b. Aug. 23, 1924; s. Opal Arch and Elizabeth (Ming) C.; m. Polly Anna Williams, Apr. 8, 1951; children: Michelle Eileen, Grady Bruce, Patrick Keith, Kathleen. BS in Pub. Adminstrn. with honors, U. Ark., 1949, LLB with honors, 1951. Bar: Ark. 1951, U.S. Dist. Ct. Ark. 1951, U.S. Supreme Ct. 1971. City atty. City of DeQueen, Ark., 1956-60; pros. atty. 9th Jud. Cir. Ark., 1961—63; city atty. City of Ft. Smith, Ark., 1966-70; ptnr. Daily & Woods, Ft. Smith, 1964—2001, Daily & Woods P.L.L.C. (and predecessor firm), Ft. Smith, from 1970, mng. ptnr., 1992—2001, ret., 2001, with, from 2002. Bd. dirs., sec. Ark. Inst. for Continuing Legal Edn., 1990-92. Contbr. articles to profl. jours. Mem. Ark. Bar Assn. (ho. of dels.), Ark. Assn. Def. Coun. (pres. 1982-83), Def. Rsch. Inst. (state chmn. 1979-92), Rotary (pres. Ft. Smith 1968-69). Home: Fort Smith, Ark. Died Aug. 15, 2007.

CORLISS, RICHARD NELSON, critic, magazine editor; b. Phila., Mar. 6, 1944; s. Paul William Corliss and Elizabeth (McCluskey) Corliss Brown; m. Mary Elizabeth Yushak, Aug. 31, 1969 BS, St. Joseph's Coll., Phila., 1965; M.F.A., Columbia U., 1967. Film critic Nat. Review mag., NYC, 1966-70; mem. staff film dept. Mus. Modern Art, NYC, 1968-70; editor Film Comment mag., NYC, 1970-89; film critic New Times mag., NYC, 1975-78, Soho Weekly News, NYC, 1980; assoc. editor Time mag., NYC, 1980-85, sr. writer, 1985—2015. Mem. selection com. N.Y. Film Festival, N.Y.C., 1971-87. Author: Talking Pictures: Screenwriters in the American Cinema, 1927-73, 1974, Greta Garbo, 1974, Lolita, 1974, Mom in the Movies: The Iconic Screen Mothers You Love and a Few You Love to Hate, 2014; editor: The Hollywood Screenwriters, 1972 Mem. N.Y. Film Critics, Nat. Soc. Film Critics Avocations: crossword puzzles; baseball statistics; songwriting. Died Apr. 23, 2015.

CORREA, CHARLES M., architect; b. Hyderabad, India, Sept. 1, 1930; m. Monika Sequeira, 1961; children: Nondita Correa-Mehrotra, Nakul. BArch, U. Mich., 1953; MArch MIT, 1955; D (hon.), U. Mich., 1980. Pvt. practice architecture, from 1958; chief arch. New Bombay, India, 1971—74; A. Farwell Bemis prof. MIT, from 2000. Chmn. Nat. Commn. Urbanization Govt. of India, 1985—88, Delhi Urban Arts Commn.; chmn. bd. Housing Urban Renewal Ecology, 1975—94; mem. steering com. Aga Khan Award for Architects, 1977—86, Padma Shri, Pres. of India, 1972. Prin. works include Mahatma Gandhi Meml. Mus., Sabarmati Ashram, Ahmedabad, Kanchanjunga apts., Bombay, Hotel Cidade de Goa, Brit. Coun. Hdqs., Delhi Nat. Crafts Mus., Delhi, State Assembly for Madhya Pradesh Govt., Bhopal, Jawahar Kala Kendra Mus., Jaipur, Delhi, Previ low-income housing, Peru; scriptwriter, dir. (documentaries) City on the Water, Govt. India, 1976, scriptwriter (audio-visual) VISTARA: The Architecture of India, 1986, scriptwriter, dir. (films) The Blessings of the Sky, 1995. Recipient Gold medal, RIBA, 1984, Indian Inst. Architects, 1987, Internat. Union Architects, 1990, Praemium Imperiale, Japan Art Soc., 1994, Aga Khan award, 1998. Fellow: AAAS (hon.), AIA (hon.); mem.: Indian Inst. Architects, Finnish Assn. Architects, Internat. Acad. Architects, French Acad. Architecture, Am. Acad. Arts Letters (hon.), UAP (hon.). Died June 16, 2015.

CORRENTI, JOHN DAVID, steel company executive; b. Rochester, NY, Apr. 1, 1947; s. Nicholas William and Sara Rita (Annalora) C.; m. Dawn Jane Major, Nov. 22, 1980; 1 child, Nicholas John. BCE, Clarkson U., 1969. Supr. of contrn. U.S. Steel, Pitts., 1969-80; v.p., gen. mgr. Nucor Corp., Plymouth, Utah, 1980-87, Nucor/Yamato Steel Co., Blytheville, Ark., 1987-91; pres., vice chmn., CEO Nucor Corp., Charlotte, NC, 1996—99; CEO Birmingham Steel (sold to Nucor Steel), Ala., 1999—2003; founder, pres., CEO Severstal Columbus Steel Co., 2005—08; founder, CEO Big River Steel, 2014—15. Bd. dirs. Navistar. Died Aug. 18, 2015.

CORTEGUERA, HOMERO JOSEPH, psychiatrist; b. Sancti Spiritus, Cuba, June 28, 1930; came to U.S., 1957; s. Joseph Maria and Natalia (Jimenez) C.; m. Sarah Dominga Villalon, Sept. 18, 1955; children: Rosemarie, Joseph Richard, Charles. MD, Havana U., Cuba, 1954. Diplomate Am. Bd. Psychiatry and Neurology. Postgrad. fellow Menninger Clinic, Topeka, 1964-66; asst. clin. dir. Menatl Health Ctr., West Palm Beach, Fla., 1966-67; staff psychiatrist Henderson Clinic, Ft. Lauderdale, Fla., 1967-68, Sheppard-Enoch Pratt Hosp., Balt., 1968-69; chief psychiatrist North Chicago VAH, Downey, Ill., 1969-72; clin. dir. Coral Ridge Psychiat. Hosp., Ft. Lauderdale, 1972-77, South Fla. State Hosp., Hollywood, 1977-78, sr. psychiatrist, 1978-93; dir. psychiatry 19th St. CRISIS, Ft. Lauderdale, from 1993. Clin. prof. psychiatry dept. Northwestern U. Med. Sch., Chgo., 1969-72, U. Miami (Fla.) Med. Sch., 1978—. Scholar U. Havana, 1956. Mem. AMA, Am. Psychiat. Assn., Fla. Med. Soc., Fla. Psychiat. Soc., N.Y. Acad. Scis., Broward County Med. Soc., Broward County Psychiat. Soc., Menninger Alumni Assn. Roman Catholic. Avocations: playing piano, classical music, theater, bicycling, ping pong/table tennis. Home: Fort Lauderdale, Fla. Died Nov. 4, 2006.

CORTOR, ELDZIER, artist, printmaker; b. Richmond, Va., Jan. 10, 1916; s. John and Ophelia (Twisdale) C.; m. Sophia Schmidt, Aug. 20, 1951; children: Michael, Mercedes, Stephen, Miriam. Student, Art Inst. Chgo., 1936-41, Inst. Design, 1942, 43, 47, Columbia U., 1946. Painting instr. Centre D'Art, Port au Prince, Haiti, 1949-51; printmaker Pratt Inst., Bklyn., 1972-74. One-man shows include Le Museè de Peuple Haitien, Port-au-Prince, Haiti, 1950, Ctr. d'Art, Port-au-Prince, 1950, Elizabeth Nelson Gallery, Chgo., 1951, James Whyte Gallery, Washington, 1953, exhibited in group shows at Met. Mus. Art, N.Y.C., 1950, Studio Mus. Harlem, 1973, 1982, Boston Mus. Fine Arts, 1975, Museo de Arte Moderno La Pertulia, Cali, Colombia, 1976, Columbia Mus. Art, S.C., 1980, Kenkeleba Gallery, N.Y.C., 1988, Taipei Fine Arts Mus., 1988, San Antonio Mus. Art, 1994, Michael Rosenfeld Gallery, N.Y.C., 1995, 1996, 1997, 1998, 1999, Mus. Contemporary Art, Chgo., 1996—97, M. Rosenfeld Gallery, 1998—2003, Schomburg Ctr., N.Y.C., 1998, Flint (Mich.) Inst. Arts, 1999, Kenkeleba Gallery, N.Y.C., 2000, Boston (Mass.) U., 2005, Rosenfeld Gallery, 2006, Ind. U., 2006, Represented in permanent collections Smithsonian Inst., Washington, Am. Fedn. Art, N.Y.C., Mus. Modern Art, IBM Corp., Portland (Oreg.) Art Mus., Art Inst. Chgo., Mus. Fine Arts, Boston. Recipient Bertha A. Florsheim award Art Inst. Chgo., 1945; recipient William H. Bartels award, 1946, Carnegie Inst. award, 1947; Julius Rosenwald fellow, Chgo., 1945-47; John Simon Guggenheim fellow, N.Y.C., 1949-50. Home: New York, NY. Died Nov. 26, 2015.

COTIER, RALPH, psychotherapist; b. NYC, Jan. 20, 1936; s. Richard Joseph and Alida (Dubé) C.; children: Vance Richard, Yvonne, Yvette. BS, St. John's U., 1962; MS, L.I.U., 1986. Nat. cert. counselor. Alcoholism counselor South Oaks Psychiat. Hosp., Amityville, N.Y., 1980-81; alcoholism counselor Mercy Hosp. New Hope, Garden City, N.Y., 1981; cons. L.I. Ctr., Huntington Station, N.Y., 1981-86; alcoholism group counselor leader Plainview (N.Y.) Rehab. Ctr., 1981-85; dir. Dorothy Young Recovery House, Plainview, 1985-92; evaluator, evaluator/supr., clin. supr. West Ctrl. Fla. Driver Improvement Inc., from 1993. Coord. alcoholism counselor tng. Queensborough Community Coll., Bayside, N.Y., 1986-89, lectr., 1986-92; lectr. Hofstra U., Hempstead, N.Y., 1990, 92, Adelphi U., 1992, Nassau Community Coll., Garden City, N.Y., 1990, Queens Coll., 1990-92, South Oaks Inst. Alcohol Studies, Amityville, 1987; mem. L.I. Counsel on Alcoholism, 1992; instr. defensive driving, Nat. Safety Coun., Attitudinal Dynamics of Driving, State of Fla. Hwy. Safety and Motor Vehicle Dept., 1997—. Contbr. articles to profl. jours. including a column in N.Y. Fedn. Alcoholism and Chem. Dependency Counselors' newsletter. With U.S. Army, 1955-58. Mem. N.Y. Fedn. Alcoholism and Chem. Dependency Counselors (bd. dirs. 1986-91, sec. 1988-89, v.p. 1989-90), L.I. Alcoholism and Chem. Dependency Counselors Assn. (regional rep. 1986-91, v.p. 1984-85, pres. 1985-86, Yev Gardiner award for outstanding achievement 1990). Home: Inverness, Fla. Died May 14, 2007.

COUCH, JESSE WADSWORTH, retired insurance company executive; b. Atlanta, Mar. 2, 1921; s. Jesse Newton and Laura (Day) W.; m. Charlotte Lucretia Collins, Jan. 13, 1945 (dec.); children: Robert Collins (dec.), Laura W.; m. Charlotte H. Gran, Oct. 17, 1997. AB, Princeton, 1947. With 1st Nat. Bank Houston, 1947-51; assoc. Wray Assocs., Houston, 1951-60; ptnr. Wray, Couch & Elder, Houston, 1960-69; v.p. Marsh & McLennan, Inc., 1969-83; pvt. cons., 1983-95. Mem. exec. bd. Episcopal Diocese of Tex., 1965-67, 68-71; trustee St. Luke's Episcopal Hosp., 1971-76; bd. dirs. Houston-Harris County YMCA, 1969-74, Houston Soc. Prevention Cruelty to Animals, 1974—2004; Bd. dirs. Tex. divsn. Am. Cancer Soc., mem. exec. com., 1982-91; chmn. Am. Cancer Soc. Greater Houston, 1981-83; trustee Mus. Fine Arts, Houston, 1970-74. Served to capt. USAAF, 1943-46. Mem.: Houston C. of C. (aviation com. 1965—75), Allegro Club, Bayou Club, Houston Country Club, Rod & Gun Club, Eagle Lake. Home: Houston, Tex. Died Mar. 4, 2015.

COUCH, THOMAS EMMETT, marketing executive; b. Hackensack, NJ, Aug. 28, 1938; s. Dean Arden and Margaret (Arnold) C.; m. Marilyn Boyce, Oct. 11, 1969; children: Heather Lynn, Michelle Anne. BS in Indsl. Mgmt., Ohio State U., 1961; MDiv., Gordon-Conwell Theol. Sem., 1968. Cert. Fin. Planner. Salesman Aluminum Co. of Am., Pitts., 1962-66; pastor Mt. Lebanon Presbyn. Ch., Pitts., 1968-72; sr. v.p. Ligonier (Pa.) Valley Study Ctr., 1972-84; v.p. Mktg. Chesapeake Fin. Group Inc., Balt., from 1984. Bd. dirs. C.S. Lewis Inst., Washington. Author (book) Video & Your Church, 1981; contbr. articles to Tabletalk mag. Active Nat. Right to Life, Search Ministries. With U.S. Army, 1961-62. Mem. Internat. Assn. Fin. Planners, Internat. Coun. of Fin. Planners, Registry of Cert. Fin. Planners, Balt. Assn. Fin. Planners. Episcoplian. Home: Ligonier, Pa. Died Aug. 8, 2007.

COULSON, JACK RICHARD, entomologist; b. Manhattan, Kans., Jan. 31, 1931; s. Emery Jack and Esther Marie (George) C.; married 1955 (div. 1959); 1 child, Susan Jane Rowland; m. Ursula E. M. Cobb, July 2, 1964; 1 child, Andrew McKenzie. BS in Zoology, Iowa State U., 1952. Entomologist Agr. Rsch. Svc. USDA, Paris and Moorestown, N.J., 1963-67, asst. to chief and rsch. leader Agr. Rsch. Svc. Beltsville, Md., 1968-85, dir. Agr. Rsch. Svcs. Biol. Control Documentation Ctr., from 1982. Contbr. book chpts. and over 50 articles to profl. jours. Sgt. USMC, 1952-56. Mem. Internat. Orgn. Biol. Control (pres. nearctic regional sect. 1987-88, pres. global body 1988-92), Entomol. Soc. Am., Entomol. Soc. Washington. Home: Bluemont, Va. Died Jan. 13, 2007.

COUREY, EDWARD GEORGE, retired insurance agent; b. Lennox, SD, Jan. 23, 1919; s. Samuel T. and Mabel Barbara Courey; m. Jean Mary Corbett, Feb. 14, 1946; children: Edward G., Taylor D., Cinderita Marie, Melinda J. Attended, Md. U. Staff intelligence U.S. Air Force, Montgomery, Ala.; insurance broker various companies, Silver Springs, 1954—84; ret., 1984. Founder One Kidney Clubs of Am., 1960; chmn. Jimmy Jabara Meml. Found., from 1996. Chmn. Lincoln Day Dinner, 1966; precinct ctrl. command Rep. Party, Md., 1958—80. Home: Silver Spring, Md. Died May 25, 2007.

COURREGES, ANDRÉ, fashion designer; b. Pau, Basses-Pyrenees, France, Mar. 9, 1923; s. Lucien and Celine (Coupe) Courreges; m. Coqueline Barrière Courreges, Sept. 17, 1966; 1 child, Marie. Degree in Civil Engring. and Constrn., Ecole des Travaux Pubs. et du Batiment. Couturier with Balenciaga, 1950—60; mgr. Soc. Andre Courreges Co., 1961—66; pres., gen. mgr. Soc. Andre Courreges Co. (Sold Brand in 2011 to Jacques Bungert and Frederic Tortoling), 1966—2011; mgr. Courreges-Parfums, 1966; reappeared on the Paris Fashion Week Runway under creative directors, Sebastien Meyer and Arnaund Vaillant, 2015. Mem.: Racing Club (France). Home: , France. Died Jan. 7, 2016.

COWAN, CASPAR FRANK, retired lawyer; b. Calais, Maine, May 7, 1915; s. Frank Irving and Helen Anna (Caspar) C.; m. Nancy Hopkinson Linnell, Oct. 19, 1946; children; Joanna Cowan Allen, Seth W., June Cowan Roelle. AB, Bowdoin Coll., 1936; JD, Harvard U., 1940. Bar: Maine 1940, U.S. Dist. Ct. Maine 1941, U.S. Ct. Appeals (1st cir.) 1946. Assoc. Cowan and Cowan, Portland, Maine, 1940-48, Perkins, Thompson, Hinckley & Keddy, Portland, Maine, 1948-51, ptnr., 1951-91, ret., 2004. Author: Maine Real Estate Law and Practice. Chmn. Portland Renewal Authority, 1952-64; chmn. Portland Housing Authority, 1958-59. Lt. U.S. Army, 1942-46. Decorated Bronze Star. Mem. ABA, Maine State Bar Assn. (econs. practice law com., life stds. com.), Cumberland County Bar Assn., 10th Mt. Divsn. Alumni Assn., Maine Charitable Mechanics Assn., Woodfords Club, Junto Club. Died Dec. 23, 2006.

COWHERD, YELVERTON, judge; b. Birmingham, Ala., Jan. 30, 1932; s. Yelverton and Lucille (Stephens) C.; m. Carolyn Purdy Baker, Feb. 2, 1952 (div. Sept. 1978); children: Diane C. Golfetto, James Y. Cowherd, Scott B. Cowherd, Andrew A. Cowherd; m. Libby Alexander, Mar. 7, 1981. BS, U. Md., 1956; LLB, George Washington U., 1963. Bar: Md. 1963, D.C. 1964, S.C. 1970, Tenn. 1974, U.S. Dist. Ct. D.C. 1964, U.S. Dist. Ct. Tenn. 1974, U.S. Dist. Ct. S.C. 1970, U.S. Ct. Appeals (4th, 5th and 6th cirs.). Atty. NLRB, Washington, Winston/Salem, N.C., 1963-69, Smith & Smith, Columbia, S.C., 1969-73, Jackson & Yeiser, Memphis, 1973-86; atty., house counsel Reynolds Electric & Constrn. Co., Las Vegas, 1987-90; judge U.S. Office of Hearing and Appeals, Alexandria, La., from 1990. With USN, 1950-52. Mem. Fed. Adminstrv. Law Judges Conf., Assn. Adminstrv. Law Judges. Avocations: camping, wildlife photography, golf. Home: Alexandria, La. Died Dec. 29, 2006.

COX, ALBERT REGINALD, retired dean, retired cardiologist; b. Victoria, BC, Can., Apr. 18, 1928; s. Reginald Herbert and Marie Christina (Fraser) C.; m. Margaret Dobson, May, 1954; children: Susan Margaret, David John (dec.), Steven Fraser. BA, U. B.C., 1950, MD, 1954. Intern Vancouver Gen. Hosp., 1954-55, resident, 1955-59; fellow in cardiology U. Wash., 1959-61; asst. prof. medicine U. B.C., 1962-65, assoc. prof., 1966-69; prof., chmn. medicine Meml. U., St. John's, Nfld., Canada, 1969-74, dean medicine, 1974-87, v.p. Health Scis. and Profl. Sch., 1988-90, v.p. acad., pro-vice chancellor, 1990-91; ret., 1991. Decorated mem. Order of Can. Fellow ACP, Royal Coll. Physicians and Surgeons Can., Am. Coll. Cardiology; mem. Nfld. Med. Assn., Can. Med. Assn., Can. Soc. Clin. Investigation, Assn. Can. Med. Colls. (pres. 1980-81), Coun. of Royal Coll. Physicians and Surgeons (v.p. medicine 1990-91), Alpha Omega Alpha. United Ch. Home: Cobble Hill, Canada. Died Oct. 14, 2015.

COX, LAWRENCE KOSSUTH, II, dentist; b. Mar. 12, 1936; BA in Chemistry and Biology, Albion Coll., 1959; DDS, U. Detroit, 1963. Pvt. practice dentistry, Adrian, Mich., from 1965. Health occupations adv. Lenawee County Vocat. Tech. Inst., 1968—, chmn., instr. dental div. 1968-75; sec./treas. Bixby Hosp. Dental Staff, 1969-72, chief, 1973-74; instr. U.S. Dental Inst., 1977—. Dentist rep. planning com. Mid-Mich. South Health System Agy., 1982-83; chmn. Adrian Election com., 1978—. Served to capt. USAF, 1963-65. Mem. ADA, Mich. Dental Assn. (ho. dels. 1985—), Jackson County Dental Soc., Detroit Dist. Dental Soc., Am. Soc. of Dentistry for Children, Pierre Fauchard Acad., Internat. Assn. Orthodontists, Am. Assn. Dental Research, Vietnam Vets. Am., Fedn. Orthodontic Assn., Am. Acad. Head Facial and Neck Pain and TMJ Orthopedics (bd. dirs. 1987—), Mich. Assn. Professions, Acad. Stress and Chronic Disease, Sutherland Cranial Found., U. Detroit Alumni Assn. (treas. 1969-71, pres. 1973-74), Am. Legion, Voiture 997, Gran Medicin, Lenawee Country Club (bd. dirs. 1981-84), Kiwanis (pres. Adrian 1907-71), Circle K (chmn. Mich. dist. 1972-75), Psi Omega, Alpha Tau Omega. Home: Adrian, Mich. Died May 7, 2007.

COX, MARJORIE MILHAM, marketing manager; b. Hamlet, NC, June 11, 1960; d. Seth Thomas and Claudia Ann (Milham) C. BS in Psychology, Duke U., 1981; MBA in Mktg., Vanderbilt U., 1985. Adminstr. Stanley H. Kaplan Edn. Ctr., Nashville, 1984-85; brand mgr. Procter & Gamble, Cin., 1985-87, Planters Lifesavers, Winston-Salem, NC, 1987-90; promotions mgr. Holly Farms, Wilkesboro, NC, 1990; product mgr. Oscar Mayer, Madison, Wis., 1990-92; mktg. mgr. Hanes Hosiery Div. of Sara Lee Corp., Winston-Salem, 1992-93; brand marketer British Am. Tobacco, Ho Chi Minh City, 1994—2003; founder, pres. Dimarxx Consulting, from 2003. Democrat. Episcopalian. Avocations: water-skiing, reading, travel, water-skiing, gardening. Died Nov. 8, 2006.

COX, TIMOTHY C., service executive; b. Kingstree, SC, July 11, 1946; s. Theron C. and Ora Lee (Tanner) C.; m. Elizabeth Motte, Dec. 25, 1984; 1 child, Angelia Dian. AA, Palmer Coll., Columbia, SC, 1969; BS, Francis Marion Coll., Florence, SC, 1982. Programmer Infitronics, Charlotte, N.C., 1969-71; programmer, operator Santee Electric Coop., Kingstree, 1971-72; sr. programmer S.C. Dept. Social Services, Columbia, 1972-75; host, coordinator Sta. WKSP-Radio, Kingstree, 1979-80; instr. Florence-Darlington Tech. Coll., 1983-85; owner, pres. Exec. Services of the Pee Dee, Florence, from 1986. Bd. dirs. Crimestoppers of the Pee Dee, Florence, 1987—. Recipient Mayor's Trophy for Handicapped Citizen of Yr., Florence, S.C. Handicapped Citizen of Yr. award, 1988. Mem. Am. Diabetes Assn., Carolina Transplant Found. (founder), Jaycees (named Outstanding Jaycee S.C. chpt. 1978). Republican. Home: Florence, SC. Died Dec. 15, 2006.

COYLE, WILLIAM, educator; b. Edinboro, Pa., Nov. 8, 1917; s. William and Vere (Steadman) C.; m. Charlotte Bliley, July 27, 1940; children— Mary Jo, Daniel, Barbara. BS, Edinboro State Coll., 1938; M.Litt., U. Pitts., 1940, MA, 1942; PhD, Western Res. U., 1948. Instr. English U. Pitts., 1939-42, 45-46, Western Res. U., 1946-48; mem. faculty Wittenberg Coll., 1948-68, prof. English, 1956-68, chmn. dept., 1964-68; prof. English Fla. Atlantic U., Boca Raton, 1968-95, prof. emeritus, from 1995, chmn. dept., 1969-79. Fulbright lectr., Sao Paulo, Brazil, 1962-63 Author: Research Papers, 1959, 11th edit., 1998, Ohio Authors and Their Books, 1960, The Young Man in American Literature, 1969, Aspects of Fantasy, 1986, Macmillan Guide to Research Papers, 1989, others; also articles and revs. Served with USMCR, 1942-45. Mem. MLA, So. Atlantic MLA, Popular Culture Assn., Coll. English Assn. Democrat. Home: Delray Beach, Fla. Died Dec. 17, 2006.

CRABILL, ROBERT LOUIS, city planner; b. Alexandria, Va., Sept. 24, 1937; s. Louis Milton and Caroline Catherine (Laing) C.; m. Patricia Louise Hudson; children: David Louis, Charles Fredric, Joseph Milton. Cert. in bus., U. Va., 1967; AS in Gen. Studies, North Va. Community Coll., 1979. Engring. asst. Va. Power, Alexandria, 1957-62; with City of Alexandria, from 1962, acting dir. of planning, 1984-85, chief spl. projects dept. planning and community devel., from 1981. Bd. dirs. City of Alexandria Employees Credit Union, 1986-90. Author: (with wife) How We Came to Be...A History of the Crabill Family, 1983. Coach Braddock Rd. Youth Club, Fairfax, Va., 1968-78; v.p. Turnpike Baseball League, Annandale, Va., 1976; pres. Greater Annandale Babe Ruth Baseball League, 1978; bd. dirs. W.T. Woodson High Sch. Boosters Club, Fairfax, 1984-88. With Va. N.G., 1954-55. Mem. Masons (master 1985), Scottish Rite (Venerable Master 1991), Shriner. Methodist. Avocations: music, genealogy. Home: Annandale, Va. Died July 23, 2007.

CRAFT, ROBERT LAWSON, conductor, writer; b. Kingston, NY, Oct. 20, 1923; s. Raymond and Arpha (Lawson) C.; m. Rita Christian (div.); m. Alva BA, Juilliard Sch. Music, 1946. Spl. seminar lectr., Dartington, Eng., 1957, Princeton U., 1959; Lucas lectr. Carleton Coll., 1981-82 Condr. orchs. in, Europe, Am. and Japan, 1952—2015; made world tour, 1961-62; condr. recs. including complete music Arnold Schoenberg, Alban Berg, Anton Webern, Edgar Varese; Co-author: Conversations with Igor Stravinsky, 1959, Memories and Commentaries, 1960, Expositions and Developments, 1962, Dialogues and a Diary, 1963, Table Talk, 1965, Themes and Episodes, 1966, (with Arnold Newman) Bravo Stravinsky, 1967, Retrospections and Conclusions, 1969, Stravinsky: The Chronicle of a Friendship, 1972, Themes and Conclusions, 1972, Prejudices in Disguise, 1974, Current Convictions: Views and Reviews, 1977, (with Vera Stravinsky) Stravinsky in Pictures and Documents, 1978, Stravinsky: Selected Correspondence, Vol. 1 1981, Vol. 2, 1984, Small Craft Advisories, 1989, Places: A Travel Companion for Music and Art Lovers, 2000, (memoir) An Improbable Life, 2002; editor of several volumes of Stravinsky's correspondence Served with AUS, 1943. Died Nov. 10, 2015.

CRAHAN, ELIZABETH SCHMIDT, librarian; b. Cleve., Oct. 6, 1913; d. Edward and Margaret (Adams) Schmidt; m. Kenneth Acker, 1938 (div. 1968); children: Margaret Miller, John Acker, Steven Acker, Charles Acker; m. Marcus E. Crahan, Dec. 16, 1968. Student, Wellesley Coll., Mass., 1931—32; BArch, U. So. Calif., 1937, MLS, 1960. Reference libr. Los Angeles County Med. Assn., LA, 1960—61, head reference libr., 1961—67, asst. libr., 1967—78, dir. libr. svcs., 1978—90. Mem.: Am. Assn. History Medicine, George Dock Soc. History of Medicine, Friends of the UCLA Libr. (pres. 1977—79, sec. 1978—97), Zamorano Club. Home: Elk, Calif. Deceased.

CRANE, KATHLEEN DOROTHY, psychiatric social worker; b. Oklahoma City, Mar. 23, 1918; d. Russell Sage and Lake (Smith) Grissom; widowed; children: Sharon Crane Stein,Michael L. BA in Psychology, U. So. Colo., 1966; MSW, U. Tex., Arlington, 1974. Cert. social svcs. adminstr. Tex.; cert. social psychotherapist, Tex. Psychotherapist Spanish Peaks Mental Health Ctr., Pueblo, Colo., 1966-68; supr. child abuse program Dallas County Child Welfare, Dallas, 1969-83. Group leader for incest victims Tex. Dept. Human Resources, Dallas, 1975-77; expert witness in child abuse cases; trainer in child abuse awareness Denver area Episcopal chs. Vol. Kempe Children's Found., Denver, 1991-92, Arapahoe Mental Health Ctr., 1974, 1994-95. Mem. AAUW, Sigma Kappa. Avocations: painting, sculpture, bridge, pottery. Home: Aurora, Colo. Died Jan. 11, 2007.

CRANE, PHILIP MILLER, former United States Representative from Illinois; b. Chgo., Nov. 3, 1930; s. George Washington III & Cora Ellen (Miller) C.; m. Arlene Catherine Johnson, Feb. 14, 1959 (dec. 2012); children: Catherine Anne, Susanna Marie, Jennifer Elizabeth, Rebekah Caroline, George Washington V, Rachel Ellen (dec. 1997), Sarah Emma, Carrie Esther. Student, DePauw U., 1948-50; BA, Hillsdale Coll., 1952; postgrad., U. Mich., 1952-54, U. Vienna, Austria, 1953-56; MA, Ind. U., 1961, PhD, 1963; LLD (hon.), Grove City Coll., 1973, Nat. Coll. Edn., 1987; D en Ciencias Politicas (hon.), Francisco Marroquin U., 1979. Advt. mgr. Hopkins Syndicate, Inc., Chgo., 1956-58; tchg. asst. Ind. U., Bloomington, 1959-62; asst. prof. history Bradley U., Peoria, Ill., 1963-67; dir. schools Westminster Acad., Northbrook, Ill., 1967-68; mem. US Congress from 13th Ill. Dist., Washington, 1969—73, US Congress from 12th Ill. Dist., 1973—93, US Congress from 8th Ill. Dist., 1993—2005. Author: Democrat's Dilemma, 1964, The Sum of Good Government, 1976, Surrender In Panama: The Case Against the Treaty, 1978; contbr.: Continuity in Crisis, 1974, Crisis in Confidence, 1974, Case Against the Reckless Congress, 1976, Can You Afford This House?, 1978, View from the Capitol Dome (Looking Right), 1980, Liberal Cliches and Conservative Solutions, 1984. Dir. rsch. Ill. Goldwater Orgn., 1964; mem. nat. advisory bd. Young Americans for Freedom; bd. dirs. American Conservative Union, 1965-82, chmn., 1976; bd. dirs., chmn. Intercollegiate Studies Inst.; bd. advisors Ashbrook Ctr., Ashland U., univ. trustee, 1988-93; founder Republican Study Com., 1972, chmn., 1984; commr. Commn. on Bicentennial U.S. Constn., 1986-91; trustee Hillsdale Coll. Recipient Distinguished Alumnus award Hillsdale Coll., 1968, Independence award, 1974, William McGovern award Chgo. Soc., 1969, Freedoms Found. award, 1973; named Ill. Statesman's Father Yr., 1979. Mem. ASCAP, VFW (award 1978), American Hist. Assn., Orgn. American Historians, Acad. Polit. Sci., American Acad. Polit. & Social Sciences, American Legion, Phila. Soc., B'nai B'rith (award 1978), Phi Alpha Theta, Pi Gamma Mu. Republican. Protestant. Home: Leesburg, Va. Died Nov. 8, 2014.

CRAVEN, WES EARL, film director; b. Cleve., Aug. 2, 1939; m. Bonnie Broecker, 1964 (div. 1969); children: Jonathan, Jessica; m. Mimi Craven, July 25, 1982 (div. 1987); m. Iya Labunka, Nov. 27, 2004. B, Wheaton; M in Philosophy, John Hopkins U. Co-owner prodn. co. Craven/Maddalena Films; prof. in Pa. and NY. Writer, editor, dir. (films) Last House on the Left, 1972, The Hills Have Eyes, 1977; 2d editor You've Got To Walk It Like You Talk It or You'll Loose That Beat, 1973; dir. (films) Deadly Friend, 1986, The Serpent and the Rainbow, 1988, Vampire in Brooklyn, 1995, Music of the Heart, 1999, Cursed, 2005, Red Eye, 2005, Scream 4, 2011, (TV films) A Stranger in Our House, 1978, Invitation to Hell, 1984, Chiller, 1985; actor: (films) The Fear, 1995, The Cutting Edge: The Magic of Movie Editing, 2004, (voice) Diary of the Dead, 2008, (TV films) Shadow Zone: The Undead Express, 1996; actor, dir.: (films) Scream, 1996, Scream 2, 1997, Scream 3, 2000; writer: (films) A Nightmare on Elm Street 2: Freddy's Revenge, 1985, A Nightmare on Elm Street 4: The Dream Master, 1988, A Nightmare on Elm Street: The Dream Child, 1989, Freddy's Dead: The Final Nightmare, 1991, Freddy vs. Jason, 2003, Pulse, 2006; writer, dir. (films) Deadly Blessing, 1981, Swamp Thing, 1982, A Nightmare on Elm Street, 1984; writer, prodr.: (films) The Hills Have Eyes II, 2007; writer, prodr., dir. (films) My Soul to Take, 2009; exec. prodr. (films) A Nightmare on Elm Street 3: Dream Warriors, 1987, Shocker, 1989, Night Visions, 1990, The People Under the Stairs, 1991, New Nightmare, 1994, The Outpost, 1995, Wishmaster, 1997, Carnival of Souls, 1998, Dracula 2000, Feast, 2005, (TV films) Laurel Canyon, 1993, Don't Look Down, 1998, They Shoot Divas, Don't They?, 2002, (TV series) Nightmare Cafe, 1992, Hollyweird, 1998, author: (novel) The Fountain Society. Mem. Dirs. Guild Am. Avocation: birdwatching. Died Aug. 30, 2015.

CRAWFORD, B., lawyer; b. Tulsa, June 29, 1922; s. Burnett Hayden and Margaret Sara (Stevenson) C.; m. Carolyn McCann, June 5, 1946 (div.); m. Virginia Baker, July 23, 1970 (dec. June 1994); m. Melanie Crowley, Dec. 24, 1994; children: Margaret Louise Crawford Brucks, Robert Hayden. BA, U. Mich., 1944, JD, 1949. Bar: Okla. 1949, U.S. Dist. Ct. (no. dist.) Okla. 1949, U.S. Supreme Ct. 1954, U.S. Ct. Appeals (10th cir.) 1954, U.S. Dist. Ct. (so. dist.) Ill. 1959, U.S. Ct. Mil. Appeals 1959, U.S. Ct. Appeals (fed. cir.) 1959, U.S. Dist. Ct. (we. and ea. dists.) Okla. 1960, U.S. Tax Ct. 1967. Law clk. to chief judge U.S. Dist. Ct. (no. dist.) Okla., 1950-51; asst. city prosecuter City of Tulsa, 1951-52, alt. mcpl. judge, 1952-54; U.S. atty. No. Dist. Okla., 1954-58; asst. dep. atty. gen. U.S. Dept. Justice, 1958-60; sole practice Tulsa, 1960-77; sr. ptnr. Crawford Crowne and Bainbridge, Tulsa, 1981-96, The Law Office of B. Hayden Crawford, Tulsa, from 1996. Lectr. in field. Rep. nominee U.S. Senate from Okla., 1960, 62; Okla. mem. adv. com. U.S. Ct. of Appeals (10th circuit); active civic and mil. orgns. Served to Rear Adm. USNR, 1942-78. Decorated Legion of Merit, Purple Heart, Disting. Pub. Svc. medal, Dept. Def. Disting. Svc. award; recipient Okla. Minute Man award 1974. Fellow Am. Assn. Matrimonial Lawyers; mem. ABA, Okla. Bar Assn., Tulsa County Bar Assn., Assn. Trial Lawyers Am., Okla. Trial Lawyers Assn., U.S. Res. Officers Assn. (nat. pres. 1973-74), Phi Delta Theta, Phi Delta Phi, Tula Summit Club, Army and Navy Club (Washington), Garden of Gods Club (Colorado Springs, Colo.), So. Hills Country Club (Tulsa), Masons, Kiwanis (pres. 1969). Presbyterian. Home: Tulsa, Okla. Died Dec. 18, 2006.

CRAWFORD, DANIEL JOHN, engineering consultant, systems analyst; b. Boston, Apr. 17, 1935; s. James Joseph and Bertile Gertrude (Nelligan) C. BS in Physics, U. Mass., 1961; MSEE in Automatic Control Theory, George Washington U., 1975; BS in Computer Sci., Christopher Newport U., 1996. Engr. NASA, Langley Rsch. Ctr., Hampton, Va., 1962-90, Lockheed, Hampton, 1992-93, Diversified Internat. Scis. Corp., Hampton, 1990-92; cons. engr. NASA Langley Rsch. Ctr., Hampton, 1996; with dept. engring. Norfolk State U., from 1996. Cons. engr. Lockheed, Hampton, 1994, NSI, Mantech., Sunnyvale, Calif., Fairfax, Va., 1994. Contbr. articles to profl. jours. Fellow AIAA (assoc.). Democrat. Roman Catholic. Avocations: stock market, cryptology. Home: Hampton, Va. Died Jan. 30, 2007.

CRAWFORD, FELIX CONKLING, retired dentist; b. Jan. 11, 1938; DDS, U. Tex. Dental Br., Houston, 1963. Pvt. practice, Plainview, Tex.; ret. Pres. Rotary, Plainview, 1971-72, Plainview Country Club, 1973-74, Plainview C. of C., 1984; chmn. Tex. Dental Found., 1990-92. Named Outstanding Alumnus, U. Tex. Dental Br., 1996. Fellow: Internat. Coll. Dentists; mem.: ADA (chmn. ADPac 1994—95, vice chmn. coun. govt. affairs 1999—2000, 2d v.p. 2001—02), Tex. Dental Assn. (chmn. DenPac 1982—85, pres. 1988, Pres. award 1991, Disting. Svc. award 1994), Am. Coll. Dentists (chmn. Tex. sect. 1994), Acad. Gen. Dentistry. Home: Plainview, Tex. Died Jan. 23, 2007.

CRAWFORD, MARVIN LEONARD, SR., retired school system administrator; b. LA, Mar. 12, 1926; s. James and Emily Georgia (Gough) Crawford; m. Ethel Mae Goodwin, Aug. 21, 1948; children: Carmen Crawford Wadley, Marvin Leonard Crawford Edd. Student, LA City Coll., 1944; BA, Humboldt State Tchrs. Coll., 1950; MA, Long Beach State Coll., 1958; postgrad., UCLA, from 1954, U SC, from 1964, Nova U., 1975. Tchr. Willobrook Dist. schs., 1950—51, Enterprise Dist. schs., 1951—54, prin., 1954—65, asst. supt., 1965—68, dist. supt., 1968—70; adminstrv. analyst Compton Unified Sch. Dist., LA, 1970—72, adminstr., 1972—74, asst. supt. elem. schs., 1974—76, disability leave of absence, 1976—86; ret., 1986. Guidance conf. cons. Sch. Edn., 1969, Tuskegee Inst., Ala., 1969; visitor sch. dists. around the world, 1961—62. Mem. purchasing adv. com. County Los Angeles, 1968—70. Sgt. maj. USAAC, 1944—46, PTO. Mem.: NEA, ASCD, PTA (life), Assn. Compton Unified Sch. Adminstrs., Compton Ednl. Assn., Calif. Assn. Sch. Adminstrs., Los Angeles County Sch. Adminstrs. and Suprs. Assn., Calif. Elem. Sch. Adminstrs. Assn., Am. Assn. Sch. Adminstrs., Calif. Tchrs. Assn., Dept. Elem. Sch. Prins., Enterprise Tchr. Assn., Phi Delta Kappa. Home: Van Nuys, Calif. Deceased.

CRESS, CECILE COLLEEN, retired librarian; b. Colorado Springs, Colo., Feb. 26, 1914; d. John Leo and Elizabeth Veronica (Rouse) Haley; m. Arthur Henry Cress, May 8, 1937 (div. 1960); children: Ronnie Lou Kordick, Dan, Elaine. BA, Adams State Coll., 1936; MA in English, Colo. Coll., 1964; MLS, Denver U., 1970. 5th grade tchr. Westcliffe (Colo.) Elem., 1953-56; English tchr. Penrose (Colo.) H.S., 1956-59; English-social studies tchr. Excelsior Jr. H.S. Dist. 70, Pueblo, Colo., 1959-64; libr. Pueblo County H.S. Dist. 70, Pueblo, 1964-80, Nat. Coll./Pueblo Br., 1980-91; cataloger in libr. Pueblo C.C., 1992-95. Tutor adult literacy program South Cen. Bd. Coop. Svcs., 1991. Recipient Ace of Clubs award Am. Contract Bridge League, 1988, 89. Mem. Pueblo Ret. Sch. Employees (v.p. 1990-92, pres. 1982-84, state bd. 1982-86, sec. 1995-97), Colo. Libr. Assn., Unit 367 Am. Contract Bridge Assn., Irish Club Pueblo (pres. 1995-96), Welsh Terrier Club Colo., Alpha Delta Kappa (Pueblo chpt., pres. 1976-78, state historian 1980-82, state bd. 1980-82, rec. sec. 1994-98), Am. Contract Bridge League (v.p. unit 367 1998-2000). Democrat. Roman Catholic. Avocations: duplicate bridge, welsh terriers, travel. Home: Athens, Ga. Died Feb. 6, 2007.

CRICHTON, JOHN HAYES, investment banker; b. Minden, La., July 21, 1920; s. Thomas and Bernard Moore (Hayes) C.; children by previous marriage: Kate, Bunnie, Lili, John Hayes; m. Flora Atherton, June 2, 1989. BS, Davidson Coll., 1942; JD, La. State U., 1949; exec. program, Stanford U., 1970. Bar: La. 1949. Assoc. Smitherman, Smitherman & Purcell, 1949-51; mng. dir. Better Hotels of La., Shreveport, 1951-61; exec. v.p., asst. to pres. Allied Properties, San Francisco, 1961-62; pres. Guaranteed Reservations Inc., Palm Beach, Fla., from 1962; also bd. dirs. Golden Rim Investment Corp., Palm Beach, Fla., from 1989. Pres., dir. Computer Controls Corp., 1967-70; chmn. bd. dirs. Commonwealth Group Inc.; bd. dirs. H & K Corp. Downtown Real Estate Inc., Lee Hardware Co., 1st Nat. Bank Sheveport. Maj., inf. AUS, 1942-46. Decorated Bronze star with oak leaf cluster. Mem. ABA, La. Bar Assn., Bath and Tennis Club (Palm Beach), Sigma Alpha Epsilon, Phi Delta Phi. Republican. Presbyterian. Home: San Antonio, Tex. Died May 16, 2007.

CRIM, ELEANOR C., obstetrician, gynecologist; b. Bangalore, India, Apr. 13, 1935; MD, U. Wash., Seattle, 1961. Intern King Co. Hosp.-Harborview, Seattle, 1961-62; resident in ob-gyn. Swedish Hosp. Med. Ctr., Seattle, 1962-66; chief ob-gyn LBJ Med. Ctr., Pago Pago, Am. Samoa, 1969-75; med. exec. com. Castle Med. Ctr., Kailua, Hawaii, 1992-95, staff sec.-treas., 1995-97, chief-elect staff, 1997-99, chief of staff, trustee, mem. fin. com., 1999-2001, bd. trustees, mem. fin. com., 1999-2001, chair ob-gyn. and pediats., from 2003; ob-gyn. pvt. practice, Kailua, Hawaii, 1975—2001. Mem. med. exec. com. Castle Med. Ctr., 2001—, dir. new physician orientation, 2002—. Mem. ACOG, Alpha Omega Alpha. Home: Kailua, Hawaii. Died June 13, 2007.

CRIST, THERESA MARIE, home health nurse; b. Chgo., Mar. 11, 1944; d. Luther F. and Marian (Snyder) Cree; m. Joseph T. Crist, June 23, 1984; children: Adam, Justin. BSN, U. Ill., Chgo., 1966; MSN, DePaul U., Chgo., 1983. V.p. home health Parkside Home Health, Park Ridge, Ill., 1985-87; adminstr. Franciscan Home Health, Geneva, Ill., 1987-88; gen. mgr. Hospice Care/Chicagoland, Lincolnwood, Ill., 1988-89; v.p. ops. Am. Nursing Care, Cin., from 1989. Mem. Ky. Home Health Assn., Ind. Assn. Home Health Agencies, Ohio Coun. for Home Care, Sigma Theta Tau. Died June 12, 2007.

CROFT, NELLIE JUNE, nursing administrator; b. Pomona, Calif., Feb. 11, 1919; d. Ray H. and Maude M. (Vipond) Miller; m. John T. Croft, Nov. 26, 1942; children: Nancy June Laird, Bette Ann Fields. Diploma, Loma Linda(Calif) Sch. Nursing, 1941; BS in Nursing, Adelphi U., Garden City, NY, 1970; MPH, Loma Linda Sch. Health, 1984. Office nurse Butka Med. Bldg., Pomona, Calif., 1941-42; dir. nurses Bates Meml. Hosp., Yonkers, N.Y.; staff duty nurse L.I. Coll. Hosp., Bklyn., 1943-46; dir. Adventist Nurse Svc. Agy. Greater N.Y. Conf. of Seventh Day Adventists, NYC, 1970-91. Mem. Sigma Theta Tau (life). Home: Jamaica, NY. Died July 1, 2007.

CROMER, ROBERT JOHN, lawyer, finance company executive; b. Bonne Terre, Mo., Dec. 27, 1949; s. Charles Felix and Sybil May (Rodbourn) C.; m. Judith Lee Wiser, June 20, 1970; children: Rebecca Lee, John Benjamin, Michael Robert. BA summa cum laude, U. Pitts., 1974, JD, 1977. Bar: Pa. 1977, U.S. Dist. (we. dist.) Pa. 1977. Assoc. Jones, Talland & Bailey, Murrysville, Pa., 1977-80; staff atty. Dollar Bank, F.S.B., Pitts., 1980-83, counsel, 1984-88, sr. counsel, 1988-90; sec., counsel, dir. Dollar Fin., Inc., Wilmington, Del., 1985-90; ptnr. Karlowitz & Cromer, Pltts., from 1990. Bd. dirs. Security Savs., Mortgage Corp., Canton, Ohio. Treas. DOLPAC, Pitts., 1984-90; bd. dirs. United Meth. Found., Pitts., 1985—; chmn. Trafford (Pa.) Zoning Bd., 1985-88; solicitor Trafford Borough, 1989-92. Mem. Pa. Bar Assn., Ohio Bar Assn., Allegheny County Bar Assn., Rotary (pres. Penn-Trafford chpt. 1987-88), Elks (presiding justice Norwin chpt. 1987—). Republican. Methodist. Avocations: fishing, hiking. Home: Trafford, Pa. Died June 28, 2007.

CRON, THEODORE OSCAR, writer, editor, educator; b. Newton, Mass., June 20, 1930; s. Jacob and Anna Ruth (Siegel) C.; m. Rosalie Heilpern, Jan. 17, 1954 (dec. Dec. 1998); children: Elizabeth Daryl Koozmin, Adam David; m. Suzanne Harris, Feb. 11, 2005. AB, Harvard U., 1952, MAT, 1954. Asst. commr. FDA, Washington, 1965—68; cons., writer Cron Comm., Chevy Chase, Md., 1969—77, from 1991; dir. info. FTC, Washington, 1977—79; speech writer Office of Surgeon Gen., Washington, 1979—89; dir. info. Nat. Assn. Elem. Sch. Prins., Alexandria, Va., 1989—91; editor Better Ways to Health, Chevy Chase, 1995—96; co-founder Magnificent Pub., Bethesda, Md., 2005. Adj. prof. journalism George Washington U., Washington, 1979-96; writer, editor NIH, Bethesda, Md., 1991—, Nat. Health Svc. Corps, Bethesda, 1992—, NSF, Washington, 1993—, Cardiology Rsch. Found., Washington, 1995—, NAS, 1996— Author: Portrait of Carnegie Hall, 1966, Assignment: Istanbul, A Jerry Stern--World Bank Adventure, 2005; contbr. articles to profl. jours. Chmn. bd. dirs. Edn. Study Ctr., Washington, 1968-73; trustee Intermet, Washington, 1971-75; bd. dirs. Nat. Coalition Consumer Edn., Madison, N.J., 1989-94. Recipient Spl. award Assn. Am. Indian Physicians, 1985, Freedom Found. at Valley Forge award 1989. Mem. Washington Ind. Writers, D.C. Sci. Writers Assn., N.Y. Acad. Sci. Avocation: watercolor painting. Home: Chevy Chase, Md. Died Dec. 20, 2006.

CRONE, PATRICIA, historian, educator; b. Kyndelose, Hyllinge, Denmark, Mar. 28, 1945; d. Thomas Georg Lonborg and Vibeke (Scheel-Richter) C. BA, Sch. Oriental/African Studies, London, 1969; PhD, Sch. of Oriental/African Study, London, 1974. Sr. rsch. fellow Warburg Inst., London, 1974-77; univ. lectr. U. Oxford, England, 1977-90, U. Cambridge, England, 1990-94, reader in Islamic history, 1994—97; prof. Inst. for Advanced Study, Princeton, NJ, 1997—2014. Author: Meccan Trade and The Rise of Islam, 1987, Pre-industrial Societies, 1989, Slaves on Horses, 1980, God's Rule: Government and Islam: Six Centuries of Medieval Islamic Political Thought, 2004, The Nativist Prophets of Early Islamic Iran, 2012; co-author: Hagarism: The Making of the Islamic World, 1977; mem. editorial bd. Internat. History Rev., 1990, Arabica, 1993, Islamic Law and Soc. Jour., 1993, Studies in Human History, 1990. Avocations: gardening, puppeteering. Home: Cambridge, England. Died July 11, 2015.

CROSON, CHARLOTTE JOANNE, retired language educator; b. Cleve., Mar. 15, 1938; d. Stanley John and Marie Croson. BE cum laude, Kent State U., 1960, MA in English cum laude, 1976. English tchr. New Carlisle Sch. Dist., Ohio, 1960—62, Hayward Unified Sch. Dist., Calif., 1962—68, Monrovia Unified Sch. Dist., Calif., 1968, Glendale Unified Sch. Dist., Calif., 1968—97; ret., 1997. English dept. chair Wilson Jr. HS, Glendale Sch. Dist., 1972—92; mem. curriculum study com. Glendale Unified Sch. Dist., 1972—92. Recipient Outstanding Svc. award, So. Council Tchrs. English, 1974, Increasing Membership award, Calif. Retired Tchrs. Assn., 2003. Mem.: Calif. Retired Tchrs. Assn. (officer from 1998), Inst. Survival Through Design (officer from 1980), Lambda Iota Tau, Gamma Phi Beta (chair, pres. 1959—60). Avocations: travel, reading, piano, hiking. Home: Los Angeles, Calif. Died July 17, 2007.

CROSTON, ARTHUR MICHAEL, pollution control engineer; b. Salford, Lancashire, Eng., Sept. 18, 1942; came to U.S. 1988; s. Arthur and Lydia (Preston) C.; m. Andrea Marina Morris, Dec. 21, 1974 (div. 1989); children: Faye Lizabeth, Joanna Elise; m. Sherrin Louise Wismer, July 28, 1991. Student, U. Manchester, Eng., 1968-70; Mech. Engr., U. Salford, Eng., 1972. Works mgr. John Hamilton & Sons, Manchester, 1965-72; design engr. Ames Crosta Mills, Toronto, Ont., Can., 1972-73, U.S. Filters, Toronto, Ont., Can., 1973-74; owner/designer CMS Rotordisk Inc., Toronto, Ont., Can., 1973-88, Amicros Inc., Toronto, Ont., Can., from 1985, East Aurora, N.Y., from 1989. Cons. Region of Peel, Mississauga, Can., 1985-87. Achievements include patents on rotordisk W.W.T. pollution control device, recirc/attenuation devise, upflow filtration devise. Died Sept. 16, 2014.

CROUCH, ANDRAE EDWARD, singer, composer; b. Los Angeles, CA, July 1, 1942; s. Benjamin Jerome and Catherine Dorthea (Hodnett) C. Student, Life Bible Coll., Los Angeles. Organizer, leader, The Disciples, gospel group, 1968—2015 ; rec. artist 10 albums including: Just Andrae (Nat. Acad. Rec. Arts and Scis. Grammy nominee), 1973, At Carnegie Hall, 1973, Take Me Back (Grammy award 1976), 1974, This Is Another Day (Dove award 1978), 1976, Live in London (Grammy award 1978, also Dove award), 1978, Don't Give Up (Grammy award 1981), 1981, Andrae Crouch - More of the Best, 1982, Finally, 1982, No Time to Lose, 1984, The Journey, 2011; appeared at White House, 1979; also on numerous TV spls. and talk shows.; film & TV composer: "Shine on Me" (theme from Amen, NBC), The Color Purple, 1986; producer record albums; author: Through It All, 1974 Recipient Gold Record for song Jesus Is the Answer; named Soul Gospel Artist of 1975 and 1977, Billboard mag.; Grammy award for I'll Be Thinking of You 1979; Daviticus awards 1979; Grammy award for best soul gospel performance, 1984. Died Jan. 8, 2015.

CROWELL, DAVID HARRISON, clinical professor pediatrics, retired biomedical researcher; b. Trenton, NJ, July 5, 1919; m. Doris Collins; children: Michael David, Sandra Crowell, Shannon Kathleen DeMaster, Megan Crowell Sheridan. Ph. D., State U. of Iowa, Iowa City, Iowa, 1946—50. Internship-fellowship U. Iowa 49;Yale 66, Scientist Commd. Corps,USPHS, 1954. Rsch. cons. Straub Clinic and Hosp., Honolulu, Hawaii, from 1983; prin. investigator Kapiolani Med. Crnter, Honolulu, 1991—2002; rsch. cons. Nat'l Inst. Health, Washington, DC, 1973—89; prof. emeritus U. of Hawaii, Honolulu. Author: (scientific articles) Psychophysiology; dir.(researcher): (experimental studies) Scientific Articles (Continuing Grants, 1963). Grantee Clin Home Infant, Clin. Study, Nichd, Nih, 1999-2000. Fellow: Amer Psychol. Assn., Amer Assn Adv Sci. (life); mem.: Population Assoc Am. (assoc.), Hawn Acad Sci. (assoc.; pres. 1953—54), Soc Rsch Child Devel (assoc.), Amer Acad Sleep Med (assoc.), Amer Clin Neurophysiology Soc (assoc.), Sigma Xi (assoc.). Home: Honolulu, Hawaii. Died Aug. 23, 2014.

CROWSON, DAVID LEE, lawyer, educator; b. San Juan, Tex., Jan. 15, 1954; s. Charles Felton and Vivian (Cates) C.; m. Jane Ann Whitley, Dec. 13, 1980; children: Luke, Drew, Cara. BBA in Acctg., Baylor U., 1976, JD, 1979. Bar: Tex. 1979. Assoc. Smead & Anderson, Longview, Tex., 1979-81; ptnr. Smead Anderson & Crowson, Longview, 1981-84; assoc. Kenley Boyland & Coghlan, Longview, 1984-86; ptnr. Coghlan Crowson, Longview, from 1986. Adj. prof. LeTourneau U., Longview, 1980—. Chmn. of deacons First Bapt. Ch., Longview, 1993; chmn. east Tex. chpt. ARC, Longview, 1995; sec. United Way, Longview, 1998. Southern Baptist. Home: Longview, Tex. Died Feb. 27, 2007.

CRUMP, ANN, artist; b. Cleve., June 13, 1939; d. Philip Chandler Hintz and Bessie Ann Leckie; m. Walter Gray Crump III, Dec. 28, 1968; children: Sarah Crump Collins, Walter Gray IV. BA, Skidmore Coll., 1961. Sys. engr. IBM, Detroit, Chgo., San Jose, San Francisco, 1961-68. Pvt. collections include St. Francis Yacht Club, San Francisco, Pier 39 San Francisco. Mem. Nat. Watercolor Soc. (signature mem.), Calif. Watercolor Assn. (signature mem.). Home: Belvedere, Calif. Died June 29, 2007.

CUCCI, ANTHONY RICHARD, former mayor; b. Jersey City, Aug. 8, 1922; s. Anthony and Mary (Priori) Cucci; m. Ann Homiak Buccolo Cucci. BA (hon.), Seton Hall U. Former sch. tchr. in NJ and NY; councilman Jersey City, 1977—81; former mayor, 1985—89. With USMC. Decorated Purple Heart. Roman Catholic. Died Feb. 26, 2015.

CULLINAN, BERNICE ELLINGER, education educator; b. Hamilton, Ohio, Oct. 12, 1926; d. Lee Alexander and Hazel (Berry) Dees; m. George W. Ellinger, June 5, 1948 (div. 1966); children: Susan Jane Ellinger, James Webb Ellinger; m. Paul Anthony Cullinan, June 9, 1967 (div. 1994); m. Kenneth Seeman Giniger, Apr. 13, 2002. BS, Ohio State U., 1948, MA, 1951, PhD, 1964. Cert. elem. educator Ohio, NY. Tchr. Maple Pk. Elem. Sch., Middletown, Ohio, 1944-46, Trotwood Elem. Sch., Ohio, 1946-47, Columbus Pub. Schs., Ohio, 1948-50, Upper Arlington Pub. Schs., Ohio, 1950-52; instr. Ohio State U., Columbus, 1959-64, asst. prof., 1964-67, Ohio State U./Charlotte Huck prof. children's lit., 1997; assoc. prof. NYU, NYC, 1967-72, prof. reading, 1972-97, prof. emeritus, from 1998; editor-in-chief Wordsong Books, Honesdale, Pa., 1990—2004. Chair selection com. Ezra Jack Keats New Writer award, 1984—2000; exec. sec. English Stds. Project, 1993—94. Author (with Lee Galda): Literature and the Child, 1989, 7th edit., 2010; author: Children's Literature in the Classroom: Weaving Charlotte's Web, 1989, 2d edit., 1994, Read to Me: Raising Kids Who Love to Read, 1992, 3d edit., 2006, Let's Read About: Finding Books They'll Love to Read, 1993; author: (with Brod Bagert) Helping Your Child Learn to Read, 1993; author: (with Dorothy Strickland and Lee Galda) Language Arts: Learning and Tchg., 2003; author: (with L. Galda and D. Strickland) Language, Literacy and the Child, 1993; author: 3d edit., 2002; author: (with Marilyn Scala and Virginia Schroder) Three Voices: Invitation to Poetry Across the Curriculum, 1995; author: 75 Authors and Illustrators Everyone Should Know, 1994; author: (with David Harrison) Poetry Lessons That Dazzle and Delight, 1999; editor: Children's Literature in the Reading Program, 1987, Invitation to Read: More Children's Literature in the Reading Program, 1992, Black Dialects and Reading, 1974, Fact and Fiction: Literature Across the Curriculum, 1993, Children's Voices, 1993, Pen in Hand, 1993, A Jar of Tiny Stars, 1996; editor: (with Diane Person) The Continuum Encyclopedia of Children's Literature, 2003; editor: (with Bonnie L. Kunzel and Deborah A.

Wooten) The Continuum Encyclopedia of Young Adult Literature, 2005; author (with M. Jerry Weiss): Books I Read When I Was Young, 1980; author: (with Carolyn Carmichael) Literature and Young Children, 1977; author: Children's Literature in the Classroom: Extending Charlotte's Web, 1993; mem. editl. bd. Nat. Coun. Tchrs. English, Champaign, Ill., 1973—76; contbr. articles to profl. jours. Adv. bd. Reading Rainbow, 1979—89; mem. selection com. Caldecott award ALA, Chgo., 1982—83; trustee Highlights Children Found., 1993—2004. Recipient Ind. U. Citation for outstanding contbn. to literacy, 1995; named Outstanding Educator in Lang. Arts, Nat. Coun. Tchrs. English, 2003; named to Ohio State U. Coll. Edn. Hall of Fame, 1995. Mem.: Reading Hall of Fame (pres. 1998—99, inducted 1989), Internat. Reading Found. (trustee 1984—91, Jeremiah Ludington award 1992), Internat. Reading Assn. (bd. dirs. 1979—84, pres. 1984—85, chair Tchrs. Choices 1988—91, chair spl. svc. award selection com. 2005—07, Arbuthnot award for outstanding tchr. children's lit. 1989), Alpha Chi Omega. Home: New York, NY. Died Feb. 5, 2015.

CULVER, IRENE, poet, writer; b. Sayre, Okla., Jan. 11, 1933; d. Joseph Carl and Thelma Veryl (Kirksey) C.; m. Allen L. Wray, Sept. 1, 1952 (div. 1974); children: Randall, Timothy, Christopher, Michelle. BA in English, Calif. State U., Sacramento, 1987. Poet, freelance writer, Sacramento, from 1968. Pub. relations cons. several non-profit orgns., Sacramento and Stockton, Calif., 1970-76. Contbr. numerous poems to lit. jours., articles to various publs. Avocations: running, bicycling. Home: Rocklin, Calif. Died May 11, 2007.

CULVER, JAMES OLIVER, SR., engineering analyst; b. Kewanee, Ill., Oct. 12, 1938; s. Oliver Tolson and Theodosia (Markham) C.; m. Dannie Elaine Powell, Aug. 28, 1965; children: James O. Jr., Jeffery O. BBA, St. Leo Coll., 1977; MS in Systems Mgmt., Fla. Inst. Tech., 1985. Enlisted U.S. Army, 1966, co. comdr., staff officer, pilot Ft. Fustis, Va., Ft. Story, Va., advanced through grades to capt., resigned active duty, 1975; 1st line supr. John Deere Harvester Works, East Moline, Ill., 1977-78, sr. engring. analyst, from 1978. Research and devel. cons. U.S. Army, The Pentagon, Washington, 1984—. Mem. City Planning Commn., Kewanee, Ill., 1984-85. Served to col. USAR. Decorated Air medal, Bronze Star. Mem. Assn. MBA Execs., Res. Officers Assn. Lodges: Order Eastern Star. Democrat. Methodist. Avocations: tennis, woodworking. Home: Kewanee, Ill. Died Feb. 22, 2007.

CUMFER, DONALD ALONZO, paper products executive; b. Oak Park, Ill., Jan. 31, 1924; s. Donald Alonzo and Ruth (Shannon) C.; m. Mary Katherine Sullivan (div. 1974); 1 child, Donald Alonzo; m. Wincy Johnson; children: Cynthia D., Neil J., Shawn J., Eric M. B.Chem. Engring., Vanderbilt U., 1949. With Mead Corp., 1951-60; gen. mgr. Daring & Bicking Paper Mills, Downingtown, Pa., 1960-61, Dura-Containers, Inc., Clarksville, Tenn., 1961-68; mgr. product devel. Mead Packaging div. Mead Corp., Atlanta, 1965-68; v.p. mfg. Hamilton Mfg. Co., Richmond, Va., 1968-76; mktg. mgr. James River Paper Converters, Richmond, 1976-79; exec. v.p. Hamilton Hybar Inc., Richmond, from 1979; pres. Vapacon Inc., Ashland, Va., from 1986. Editor part of series of books: Pulp and Paper Technology, 1989; patentee in field. Vice chmn. Ashland Bd. Zoning Appeals, 1984-87; chmn. Planning Commn., Ashland, 1971-75, Ashland Christian Emergency Svc., 1969-84. Decorated DFC, Air medals (2). Mem. ACS, TAPPI, Soc. Plastics Engrs., ASTM, AAAS, Hump Pilots Assn., Downtown Club. Avocation: golf. Home: Cookeville, Tenn. Died Jan. 5, 2007.

CUNNEEN, WALLACE VINCENT, JR., marketing executive; b. York, Pa., Sept. 18, 1922; m. Joan Eleanor Frederick, Jan. 8, 1955; children: Wallace, Mary, James. Student, U.S. Naval Acad., 1941—44, U. Pa., 1947, Naval Aviator, 1945—47. Sales rep. Diebold, Inc., Canton, Ohio, 1947—49; v.p. The Cunneen Co., Phila., 1949—57, Welton Becket & Assoc., LA, 1957—64; v.p., dir. John Carl Warnecke Assoc., San Francisco, 1964—69; v.p. programs devel. Hoover Assocs., Palo Alto, Calif., 1972—74; owner mktg./cons. practice Los Altos Hills, Calif., from 1974. Founder San Jose Nat. Bank, 1982. Author: Essential Element. Coun. pres., nat. bd. dirs. Navy League, 1979—81; mem. adv. com. AIA Rsch. Corp.; chmn. Santa Clara County, United Fund Los Altos, 1958—62; exec. bd. Stanford Area coun. Boy Scouts Am., 1977—78; pres. Los Altos PTA, 1961; chmn., Navy Moffett Field 50th Anniversary Celebration Hangar I Dinner. Mem.: Fremont Hills Club, St. Claire Club, Commonwealth Club. Republican. Roman Catholic. Died Oct. 31, 2006.

CUNNINGHAM, MICHAEL EUGENE, surgeon; b. Tel Aviv, May 18, 1958; arrived in U.S., 1959; s. Allen Hamilton and Nina (Gertzovsky) C. Student, Adelphi U., 1978, Harvard U., 1979-80, Columbia U., 1980-81; MD, U. St. Lucia, 1992. Fellow of surgery Yale U. Sch. Medicine, New Haven, Conn., from 1992. Mgr. Yale Surgical Immunology Rsch. Lab., New Haven, 1992—, Vascular Rsch. Labs.; rsch. in inflammatory bowel disease, gestational infection, and fetal surgery. Author: (with others) American College of Surgeons Clinical Congress Forum Book, 1993, 94, Am. Assn. Oral and Maxillofacial Surgeons; contbr. articles to profl. jours. Bd. dirs. Univ. Towers, New Haven, 1993—. With USN/Marines, 1975-77. Mem. AAAS, Am. Soc. Cell Biology, Fedn. Am. Soc. for Experimental Biology, N.Y. Acad. Scis., Conn. Soc. Parenteral and Enteral Nutrition (founding mem.). Avocations: working with physically challenged children and senior citizens, writing short stories, teaching. Died Dec. 5, 2006.

CUOMO, MARIO MATTHEW, lawyer, former Governor of New York; b. Queens County, NY, June 15, 1932; s. Andrea and Immaculata (Giordano) Cuomo; m. Matilda Raffa, June 5, 1954; children: Margaret Cuomo Maier, Andrew, Maria Cuomo Cole, Madeline Cuomo O'Donoghue, Christopher. BA summa cum laude, St. John's Coll., 1953; LLB cum laude, St. John's U., 1956, LLD (hon.), 1975, Yeshiva U., 1983, Coll. Holy Cross, 1984, U. Rochester, 1985, Fordham U., 1985, NYU, 1985, Syracuse U., 1986. Bar: NY 1956, US Dist. Ct. (northern dist.) NY 1957, US Dist. Ct. (southern dist.) NY 1998, US Supreme Ct. 1960, US Dist. Ct. (eastern dist.) NY 1962, US Ct. Appeals (2nd Cir.) 1967. Confidential legal asst. to Hon. Adrian P. Burke, NY State Ct. Appeals, 1956—58; assoc. Corner, Weisbrod, Froeb and Charles, Bklyn., 1958—63; ptnr. Corner, Cuomo & Charles, 1963—75; sec. of state State of NY, Albany, 1975—79, lt. gov., 1979—83, gov., 1983—94; of counsel Wilkie Farr & Gallagher LLP, NYC, 1995—2014. Mem. faculty St. John's U. Sch. Law, 1963—73; counsel to cmty. groups, including Corona Homeowners, 1966—72; charter mem. First Ecumenical Commn. of Christians and Jews for Bklyn. and Queens, NY. Author: Forest Hills Diary: The Crisis of Low-Income Housing, 1974, Diaries of Mario M. Cuomo, The Campaign for Governor, 1982, More Than Words: The Speeches of Mario Cuomo, 1993, The New York Idea: An Experiment in Democracy, 1994, Reason to Believe: A Keen Assessment of Who We Are: An Inspiring Vision of What We Could Be, 1995; co-author: The Blue Spruce, 1999; co-author: (with Harold Holzer) Why Lincoln Matters: Today More Than Ever, 2004; co-editor: Lincoln on Democracy, 1990; contbr. articles to legal publs. Spkr. keynote address Dem. Nat. Conv., San Francisco, 1984, nominating address Dem. Nat. Conv., NYC, 1992. Recipient Humanitarian award, Long Beach Lodge B'nai B'rith, 1975, Rapallo award, Columbia Lawyers Assn., 1976, Dante medal, Italian Govt.-American Assn. Teachers Italian, 1976, Silver medallion, Columbia Coalition, 1976, Public Adminstr. award, C.W. Post Coll., 1977, Human Svc. award, NY Regional Bd. Anti-Defamation League, 1981, Golden Cross, Archbishop Afxentios of Greece, 1981, Golden Lion award, Order Sons of Italy in America, 1983, Solitary Freedom award, Anti-Communist Confederation Polish Freedom Fighters, 1983, United Cerebral Palsy Humanitarian award, 1983, Theodore Roosevelt award, Internat. Platform Assn., 1984, Martin Luther King Leadership award, 1985, Robert F. Kennedy award, NY State Labor Religion Coalition, 1985. Mem.: ABA, American Judicature Soc., Assn. of Bar of City of NY, Queens County Bar Assn., Nassau Bar Assn., Bklyn. Bar Assn., NY State Bar Assn., Columbia Lawyers Assn., Cath. Lawyers Guild of Queens County (pres. 1966—67), St. John's U. Alumni Fedn. (chmn. bd. 1970—72), Skull & Circle, Delta Theta Pi, Pi Alpha Sigma. Democrat. Roman Catholic. Home: New York, NY. Died Jan. 1, 2015.

CUSHNY, THEODORUS VAN WYCK, trust company executive; b. NYC, May 19, 1932; s. Alexander Ogilvie and Katrina (Van Wyck) Cushny; m. Cora Cavanagh Cushny, June 10, 1955; children: Theodorus Van Wyck, Lillian Burns Jr., Michael B., Coralie. BA, Yale U., 1954; LLB, Columbia U., 1957. Cert. chartered fin. analyst. Atty. Wickes, Riddell, Morgan, Lewis & Bockius, NYC, 1957—65; analyst Fahnestock & Co., NYC, 1965—67; ptnr., v.p. J. & W. Seligman & Co., NYC, 1967—83; sr. v.p. J. & W. Seligman Trust Co., NYC, from 1983. Chmn. Zoning Bd. Appeals, Matinecock Village, Locust Valley, NY, 1966—70; trustee Nat. Horse Show Found., 1982—89; organist St. John's Ch., Rock Hall, Md., from 1986. Mem.: Nat. Horse Show Assn. America (bd. dirs. 1970—89, past pres.), St. Nicholas Soc. Republican. Roman Catholic. Home: Rock Hall, Md. Died Dec. 29, 2006.

CUSTER, CARYL BLANK, nurse, director of nursing; b. Bridgeport, Conn., Dec. 13, 1933; d. Abraham and Lillian Blank; m. Keith Custer, Apr. 14, 1961; children: Andy, Marni. BS in Nursing, U. Bridgeport, 1959; MS, Nova U., 1982. Head nurse Bridgeport Hosp., 1960-63; office nurse Dr. Keith Custer, Bridgeport, 1963-72; inservice dir. Colonial Manor Nursing Home, Youngstown, Ohio, 1974-76; instr. pharmacology Ft. Lauderdale (Fla.) Bd. Edn., 1976-83; dir. of nursing Hollywood Hills Nursing Home, Hollywood, Fla., 1982-88; pers. risk mgr., dir. staff devel. Coral Ridge Hosp., Ft. Lauderdale, Fla., from 1988. Instr. pharmacology Lic. Practicle Nurse's Assn., Youngstown, 1974-76; adv. bd. allied health Ft. Lauderdale Bd. Edn., 1982—. Author: Pharmacology for Senior Citizens, 1982. Mem. Fla. Nurses Assn., Dirs. of Nursing Assn. (pres. Ft. Lauderdale sect. 1983-88). Avocations: reading, cooking, fishing, antiques. Home: Hollywood, Fla. Died Dec. 30, 2006.

CUSUMANO, JOANN DESIMONE, retail manager; b. Bklyn., Feb. 5, 1936; d. Joseph and Lee A. (Giardelli) DeSimone; m. Charles L. Cusumano, Aug. 16, 1958; children: David, Barbara, Jeanne, Mark. BS, Marymount Coll., 1957. Chemist Rockefeller Inst., NYC, 1957-59, NIH, Washington, 1959-62; artist, potter JoAnn's Ceramics, Gainesville, Fla., 1968-79; bus. mgr. Chas. Cusumano, M.D., PA, Gainesville, from 1979; retail mgr. Four Seasons, Gainesville, from 1983. Contbr. articles to art publs. Bd. trustees Hippodrome Theater, Gainesville, 1972-80, Mus. Natural History, Gainesville, 1982-85; docent U. Fla. Mus. Natural History, Gainesville, 1979-85, 93—; active Alachua County Med. Aux. Roman Catholic. Avocations: ceramics, travel, cooking. Home: Gainesville, Fla. Died Aug. 10, 2007.

CUTLER, ARNOLD LLOYD, secondary education educator, consultant; b. Princeton, Minn., Oct. 15, 1938; s. Erving Ernest and Clara Adelade (Schlesner) C.; m. Janice Elaine Norman, June 11, 1961; children: Sheri Lynn Cutler Smith, Mark Christopher. BS, St. Cloud State U., Minn., 1960; MA, Coll. St. Thomas, St. Paul, 1968; postgrad., U. Minn., from 1987. Cert. life 7-12 math. and K-12 music tchr., Minn. Tchr. music Stewart (Minn.) Pub. Schs., 1960-62; tchr. math. Mounds View Sch. Dist., St. Paul, 1962-94, coord. math. curriculum, 1991-94; co-prin. investigator project U. Minn., from 1997. Tchr., curriculum revisor talented youth in math. program U. Minn., Mpls., 1988—; instr. summer math. inst. Macalester Coll., St. Paul, 1990—, mem. adv. bd. NSF calculus project, 1992—; vis. master tchr., medtronic fellow St. Olaf Coll., Northfield, Minn., 1990-91; head coach Minn. All-Star High Sch. Math. Team, St. Paul, 1988-90; K-12 cons. The Geometry Ctr., Mpls., 1991-98; mem. governing bd. Minn. Math. Moblzn., Mpls., 1992-98; bd. dirs. Minn. High Sch. Math. League, St. Paul, 1989—. Recipient Gov.'s commendation for coaching math. team, State of Minn., 1990, Disting. Educator award, 1993; grantee Medtronic Found., 1991-92. Mem. ASCD, NEA, Am. Math. Soc., Math. Assn. Am., Nat. Coun. Tchrs. Math., Minn. Coun. Tchrs. Math. (v.p. for high sch. 1987-90, pres.-elect 1992-93, pres. 1993-95). Democrat. Lutheran. Avocations: music, downhill skiing, camping, reading. Home: New Brighton, Minn. Died Apr. 19, 2007.

CUTLER, ETHEL ROSE, artist, designer; b. NYC, Mar. 13, 1915; d. Samuel and Sophie (Petrushinsky) C. BA in Fine Arts, CUNY, 1936; MA in Fine Arts, Columbia U., 1937; postgrad., U. Mo., 1951-52, Ill. Inst. Tech., 1953-55, NYU, 1958-68; PhD, Walden U., 1980. Instr., head arts program Highland Manor Sch. and Jr. Coll., West Long Branch, N.J., 1942-43; instr. design U. N.C., Greensboro, 1943-47; instr. drawing and design Adelphi Coll., Garden City, N.Y., 1947-50; asst. prof., head design dept. U. Mo., Columbia, 1950-55; asst. prof. fabric design, dept. head R.I. Sch. Design, Providence, 1955-59; freelance artist, designer, cons. and educator, from 1959. Art agt. Daniel E. Lewitt Fine Art, N.Y.C.; cons. in field. Exhbns. in group shows at Macy's Gallery, U. Mo., Ill. Inst. Tech., Lynn Kottler Galleries, N.Y.C. Ctr. Gallery, Daniel Lewitt Fine Arts Gallery; represented in permanent collections Grey Art Gallery, NYU, Jewish Mus. Am. Artists Sch. scholar, 1939-40, art scholar Met. Mus., 1968-69; Walden U. grantee, 1980. Mem. Art Dirs. Club, Artist Equity, Coll. Arts Assn., Nat. Soc. Interior Designers. Died Mar. 31, 2007.

CUTLER, KENNETH BURNETT, lawyer, investment company executive; b. Muskegon Heights, Mich., June 19, 1932; s. Stanley and Lucile (Miles) C.; m. Cecelia Bilsly, Mar. 9, 1967; children: Kenneth Burnett, Randall Miles, Cynthia Bilsly, Robert Appleby, Jeffrey Lamont Derrick. BBA, U. Mich., 1954, JD, 1957. Bar: Mich. 1957, NY 1960. Assoc. Dewey Ballantine, Bushby, Palmer & Wood, NYC, 1957-66; v.p., gen. counsel The Lord Abbett Managed Funds, NYC, 1966—97; ptnr., gen. counsel Lord, Abbett & Co., NYC, 1972-97. Mem.: NASD (arbitration bd. from 1976), Bronxville Field Club, Met. Club, Phi Delta Phi, Delta Tau Delta. Avocations: golf, tennis, skiing. Home: Bronxville, NY. Died Aug. 4, 2015.

CWIK, MARGARET ELIZABETH, health care insurance broker, nurse; b. Chgo., Aug. 18, 1946; d. John Gilbert and Dorothy Marie (Andersen) Springer; m. William Stanley Cwik, Sept. 11, 1971 (div. Jan. 1988). Diploma, St. Elizabeth's Hosp., Chgo., 1967; B in Health Care Adminstrn., Roosevelt U., 1986. RN, Ill.; assoc. in risk mgmt. Nurse Children's Meml. Hosp., Chgo., 1967-74, N.W. Community Hosp., Arlington Heights, Ill., 1975-78; health care risk mgmt. cons. Alexsis Risk Mgmt., Chgo., 1979-86; v.p. risk mgmt. Glen Nyman & Assocs., Rosemont, Ill., 1986-87; health care cons. Continental Ins., Chgo., 1987-88; health care svcs. mgr. St. Paul Ins., St. Paul, 1988-89; mgr. health care Alexander & Alexander, Chgo., from 1989. Mem. Metro Chgo. Health Care Risk Mgmt. Soc. (program com. 1990-91). Lutheran. Home: Schaumburg, Ill. Died Jan. 6, 2007.

CYPHERS, JAMES MICHAEL, construction executive; b. Pitts., Oct. 28, 1949; s. Francis Regis Jr. and Eleanor Ann (Grupp) C.; m. Sharon Louise Law, Apr. 3, 1971; children: Lynn Anne, Jennifer Marie, James Francis Patrick, Amy Elizabeth, Meaghan Colleen. BS, U. Dayton, 1971; student, U. Mich., 1971-72. Mgr. Old Allegheny Restaurant, Pitts., 1979-80, Colonnade Restaurant, Pitts., 1980-81, Burger King Corp., No. Va., 1985-86, Popeye's, Bethesda, Md., 1986-87, Pizza Hut, Inc., Burke, Va., 1987, Dale City, Va., from 1987; pres. Dessert Factory, Inc., Pitts., 1981-85, Camelot Builders, Inc., Dale City, Va., from 1988; mgr. Little Caesars East, Inc., Farmington Hills, Mich., 1988-89. Cons. in field. Budget adv. com. Keystone Oaks Sch. Dist., Pitts., 1981; coun. mem. St. Pius X Ch., 1983-85; bd. dirs. Cath. Hist. Soc. W. Pa., 1984-85. Pres.'s scholar U. Dayton, 1967; grad. fellow U. Mich., 1971. Mem. W. Pa. Geneal. Soc. (pres. 1981-82), SAR, Md. Hist. Soc. Democrat. Roman Catholic. Avocations: genealogy, family activities. Died May 20, 2007.

CYSARZ, JANUSZ MARIAN, textile company executive; b. Lwow, Poland, May 17, 1931; came to U.S. 1984; s. Edward Zenon and Julia Michalina (Sigmund) C.; m. Rosemary Mason Thomas, Aug. 20, 1960; children: Elisabeth, Richard. Dipl. in Textile Design, Scottish Coll. Textiles, UK, 1951. Chartered textile technologist diplomate. Textile mill mgr. J. Auty & Sons Ltd., Batley, Eng., 1951-52; textile designer/mgr. R.R. Buck & Sons Ltd., Carlisle, Eng., 1952-55; export exec. John Knox & Sons Ltd., Silsden, Eng., 1955-56; sr. devel. exec. Courtaulds Ltd., Manchester/Bradford, Eng., 1956-68; sr. exec. Coventry, Eng., 1968-84; dir. devel. Guilford Industries, Inc., Maine, 1984-86; sales exec. R. Parks Gallery, Bangor, Maine, 1986-87; sr. exec. Laurel Indsl. Textiles, Inc., Skowhegan, Maine, 1987-90; sr. sales exec. Pittsfield (N.H.) Weavin Co. Inc., from 1990. Cons. in field; lectr. in field. Contbr. articles to profl. jours. Recipient Bronze medal, Boras Filatelistforening for Internat. Philatelic Collection

Exhibit 6, Boras, Sweden, 1974. Fellow Textile Inst. Internat. Eng., Kiwanis (bd. dirs. 1987-88). Roman Catholic. Avocations: stamp collecting/philately, photography, music. Home: Guilford, Maine. Died Dec. 9, 2006.

DADE, NORMA THOMPSON, retired literature educator, writer; b. Torrington, Conn., July 30, 1911; d. James Richard and Norma Thompson; m. Hugh Risely Dade Widowed: Jun 06, 1993, Feb. 24, 1990; m. Harold Watts Richardson, June 3, 1936 (div. Feb. 6, 1952); 1 child, James Adrian Richardson. MA, Teacher's Coll. Columbia U., New York, New York, 1939; BA, NJ State Teacher's Coll., Montclair, New Jersey, 1933. Educator Cardozo H.S., Washington, 1952—78, Terrell Jr. H.S., Washington, 1951—52, Dunbar H.S., Washington, 1948—50, Terrell Jr. H.S., Washington, 1944—98; printer Bur. of Engraving, Washington, 1942—44; educator Armstrong H.S., Washington, 1941—42, Selma U., Selma, Ala., 1934—36. Author: (novels) They Shall Mount Up. Mem.: Zica Creative Arts & Literacy Guild, Third Order of Mary, Sigma Gamma Rho. D-Liberal. Roman Catholic. Avocations: gardening, sewing, writing. Home: Atlanta, Ga. Died Feb. 21, 2007.

DALEY, ROYSTON TUTTLE, architect; b. Boston, Jan. 12, 1929; s. Joseph Wheeler and Marion Jeannette (Tuttle) D.; m. Lillian Mary Stuart, July 8, 1961 (div. 1976); children: Christopher, Jennifer, Stephanie, Elizabeth; m. Nancy Gay Powell, May 24, 1986. BA magna cum laude, Williams Coll., 1951; BArch, MArch, Harvard U., 1956. Registered architect, Mass., Conn., Vt., N.H., N.Y. Jr. architect, designer Shepley, Bullfinch, Richardson & Abbott, Boston, 1955-58; with Steffian, Steffian & Bradley, Boston, 1958-64, The Architects Collaborative, Cambridge, Mass., 1964-90, v.p., 1979-82, prin., 1982-90, also bd. dirs.; prin. Linea 5, Inc., Cambridge, 1990-93; with Tsoi/Kobus & Assocs, Cambridge, 1993-96, PAPA Programming and Planning for Arch., Concord, from 1997. Chmn. Design Adv. Group, Lexington, Mass., 1970-72; ex officio mem. Lexington Planning Bd., 1971-72. Fellow Am. Acad. in Rome (Prix de Rome in Architecture 1960-62); mem. AIA, Boston Soc. Architects, Phi Beta Kappa. Democrat. Avocations: hiking, model trains, sketching. Home: Concord, Mass. Died Nov. 14, 2006.

DALIS, IRENE, mezzo soprano, performing arts association administrator; b. San Jose, Calif., Oct. 8, 1925; d. Peter Nicholas and Mamie Rose (Boitano) D.; m. George Loinaz, July 16, 1957 (dec. 1990); 1 child, Alida Mercedes. AB, San Jose State Coll., 1946; MA in Teaching, Columbia U., 1947; MMus (hon.), San Jose State U., 1957; studied voice with, Edyth Walker, NYC, 1947-50, Paul Althouse, 1950-51, Dr. Otto Mueller, Milan, Italy, 1952-72; MusD (hon.), Santa Clara U., 1987; DFA (hon.), Calif. State U., 1999. Prin. artist Berlin Opera, 1955-65, Met. Opera, NYC, 1957-77, San Francisco Opera, 1958-73, Hamburg (Fed. Republic Germany) Staatsoper, 1966-71; prof. music San Jose State U., Calif., 1977—2004; founder, gen. dir. Opera San Jose, 1984—2014. Dir. Met. Opera Nat. Auditions, San Jose dist., 1980-88. Operatic debut as dramatic mezzo-soprano Oldenburgisches Staatstheater, 1953, Berlin Staedtische Opera, 1955; debut Met. Opera, N.Y.C., 1957, 1st American-born singer, Kundry Bayreuth Festival, 1961, opened, Bayreuth Festival, Parsifal, 1963; commemorative Wagner 150th Birth Anniversary; opened 1963 Met. Opera Season in Aida; premiered: Dello Joio's Blood Moon, 1961, Henderson's Medea, 1972; rec. artist Parsifal, 1964 (Grand Prix du Disque award); contbg. editor Opera Quar., 1983. Recipient Fulbright award for study in Italy, 1951, Woman of Achievement award Commn. on Status of Women, 1983, President's award Nat. Italian American Found., 1985, award of merit People of San Francisco, 1985, San Jose Renaissance award for sustained and outstanding artistic contbn., 1987, Medal of Achievement Acad. Vocal Arts, 1988, Lifetime Achievement award Arts Coun. Silicon Valley, 2009; named Honored Citizen City of San Jose, 1986; inducted into The Calif. Public Edn. Hall of Fame, 1985, others. Mem. Beethoven Soc., San Jose Arts Round Table, San Jose Opera Guild, American Soc. Univ. Women, Arts Edn. Week Consortium, Phi Kappa Phi, Mu Phi Epsilon. Home: San Jose, Calif. Died Dec. 14, 2014.

DALTON, PATRICK DALY, JR., biology educator; b. Salt Lake City, Oct. 11, 1922; s. Patrick Daly and Ora (Johnson) D.; m. Lela Jesperson, Dec. 20, 1948; children: Tanya, Erin Colleen, Mark Edward. BS, Ariz. State U., 1949; MS, Utah State U., 1951; PhD, U. Ariz., 1961. Reporter, printer Mesa (Ariz.) Jour. Tribune, 1939-42, L.A. Times, 1942, Sta.'s Corp., Los Angeles, 1942; lab. and teaching asst. Ariz. State U., Tempe, 1945-49; rsch. and teaching asst. Utah State U., Logan, 1949-51; range mgr., adminstrn., rsch. and instrn. Soil Conservation Svc. USDA, Tooele, Utah, 1951-52; range mgr., adminstrn. and instrn. Bur. Land Mgmt. U.S. Dept. Interior, Price, Utah, 1952; instr. math., phys. and biol. scis., agrl. and indsl. arts, supt. bldgs. and grounds, assoc. plantation mgr. Tongan Mission Liahona High Sch., Nuku'alofa, Tonga, 1953-55; pres. Tongan Mission, Nuku'alofa, Tonga, 1963-66; asst. prof., dir. farm ops. Depts. Agrl. and Phys. Sci. Ch. Coll. Hawaii, Laie, 1955-58, assoc. prof. biol. scis., 1966-70; prof. biol. scis. Ch. Coll. Hawaii now Brigham Young U. Hawaii, Laie, 1970-88; research and teaching assoc. Dept. Plant Sci. U. Ariz., Tucson, 1958-61; asst. prof. range mgmt. U. Nevada, Reno, 1961-62; dir. forest and range research and rehab. UNESCO, Seoul, Rep. of Korea, 1962-63. Prof. emeritus Brigham Young U., Hawaii, 1988. Contbr. articles to profl. jours. Dist. commr. Aloha council Boy Scouts Am., Ko'olau dist., 1980-89; mem. Laie Elem. Sch. PTA, Kahuku (Hawaii) High Sch. PTA; sci. fair judge State of Hawaii High Schs., 1965-88; pres. LDS Nuku'alofa, Tonga Temple, 1989-92, master M man. With USNR, 1942-45, 49-52. NSF fellow 1959-60; recipient Eagle Scout medal with Bronze, Gold and Silver palms, Silver Beaver award, Gold Service medal Boy Scouts Am., Scouter's award Boy Scouts Am., Order of Merit award Boy Scouts Am., Order of Arrow award Boy Scouts Am., Arrowhead award, Wood Badge award. Mem. AAAS, Am. Inst. Biol. Sci., Ecol. Soc. Am., Am. Soc. Range Mgmt., Nat. Geographic Soc., Hawaiian Acad. Sci., Hawaiian Bot. Soc., Sons Utah Pioneer, U.S. Mormon Battalion Inc., Army West, Blue Key, Sigma Xi, Alpha Gamma Rho, Alpha Phi Omega, Lambda Delta Sigma, Alpha Zeta, Beta Beta Beta, Xi Sigma Pi, Delta Sigma Pi. Mem. Lds Ch. Home: Salt Lake City, Utah. Died Dec. 12, 2006.

DANAHER, FRANK ERWIN, transportation technologist; b. Montclair, NJ, Mar. 5, 1936; s. Frank E. and Mildred (Acquino) D.; m. Joan Marie Donovan, Apr. 12, 1986; children: Maria (dec.), Frank, Heather (dec.). BA in Math., Rutgers U., 1961; MBA, Fairleigh Dickinson, 1982. Supr. programming ITT, Paramus, N.J., 1961-66; mgr. systems Lummus, Bloomfield, N.J., 1966-83; rsch. specialist Dun & Bradstreet, Basking Ridge, N.J., 1983-87; technologist Met. Transp. Auth., NYC, from 1987. Cons. in field. Contbr. articles to profl. publs. Area gov. Toastmasters, N.Y.C., 1984-85, chpt. pres., 1993; pres. Fairleigh Early Birds, 1982, 94; spkr. in field. With U.S. Army, 1959. Urban Mass Transit Authority grantee, 1988, 90. Mem.: Info. Tech. Mgrs. Soc., Radio User Group Met. Transp. Authority, Tech. Mgrs. N.Y., User Group Met. Transp. Authority (chmn. 1990—2003), Computer Aided Design and Drafting, Geog. Info. Sys. Users (chmn. 1990—2003), Rock Spring Country Club, Delta Mu Delta. Republican. Roman Catholic. Home: Hamburg, NJ. Died Nov. 1, 2006.

DANIERO, JOSEPH JAMES, financial executive; b. Smock, Pa., Oct. 31, 1938; s. Joseph and Sophia Ann (Spiranac) D.; m. Virginia Marie Coney, June 6, 1978; children: James Joseph, Christine Marie. BS in Econs., U. Pa., 1963. Computer programmer Provident Mut. Ins. Co., Phila., 1964-65; systems analyst Richardson-Merrell Inc., Phila., 1965-66; systems cons. Levin-Townsend Svc. Co., Phila., 1966-68; systems mgr. Delaware Mgmt. Co., Phila., 1968-74, computer svcs. officer, 1974-78, asst. v.p. EDP, 1978-81, v.p. EDP, 1981-85, exec. v.p., 1985-88, pres., from 1988. Cons. Micromation Scis. Corp., Phila. Mem. Internat. Assn. Fin. Planning, Am. Mgmt. Assn., Inst. Cert. Computer Profls., Data Processing Mgmt. Assn. Republican. Roman Catholic. Avocation: breeding thoroughbred race horses. Home: Cherry Hill, NJ. Died May 28, 2007.

DANNER, DEAN JAY, geneticist; b. Milw., Sept. 26, 1941; s. Julius Alexis and Evalyn Anna (Pautz) D.; m. Susan Melissa Reddin, Aug. 25, 1968; children: Mark Jay, Kirstin Melissa. BS in Chemistry/Biology, Lakeland Coll., 1963; PhD in Biochemistry, U. N.D., 1968. Postdoctoral fellow St. Jude Children's Rsch. Hosp., Memphis, 1968-70; asst. prof. Northwestern State U., Natchitoches, La., 1970-73, Emory U., Atlanta, 1973-78, assoc. prof., 1978-89, prof., 1989-97, chmn. dept. genetics, 1997—2001, vice chair Human Genetics, from 2001, acting chair Biochemistry, from 2001. Mem. NIH Study Sect. Med. Biochemistry, Bethesda, Md., 1989-93. Presbyterian. Home: Decatur, Ga. Died Jan. 2, 2007.

DANNHAUSEN, WILLIAM O., publishing executive; b. Oak Park, Ill., Nov. 11, 1921; s. Emil Gustav and Anna Barbara (Heil) D. Student, Northwestern U., 1940-42, 46-48. Sales records clk. McGraw-Hill Pub. Co., Chgo., 1940-42; regional sales mgr. Huebner Pub. Tooling and Prodn. Mag., Chgo., 1949-52, Gas Mag. and Butane Propane News, Chgo., 1952-56; founder, pres., pub. E & A News, Inc., Park Ridge, Ill., from 1956; owner Better Roads mag., Park Ridge, from 1964. Mem. citizen's bd. Ill. Masonic Hosp. Assn., Chgo. 1987. Chief warrant officer AUS 1943-46, PTO. Mem. Guild Ancient Supplers (hon. knight 1985), Chgo. Yacht Club, Masons (32 degree), Shriners. Republican. Lutheran. Home: Lk In The Hls, Ill. Died Feb. 25, 2007.

DARK, ALVIN RALPH, retired professional baseball manager; b. Comanche, Okla., Jan. 7, 1922; m. Jackie Dark; children: Allison, Gene, Eve, Margaret, Laura, Rusty. Student, La. State U., Southwestern La. Inst. Shortstop Boston Braves, 1946—49, NY Giants, 1950—56, St. Louis Cardinals, 1956—58, Chgo. Cubs, 1958—59, Phila. Phillies, 1960, Milw. Braves, 1960; mgr. San Francisco Giants, 1961-64, Kansas City Athletics, 1966-67, Cleve. Indians, 1968-71, Oakland Athletics, 1974, 75, San Diego Padres, 1977; coach Chgo. Cubs, 1965, spl. scout, 1983; dir. pub. rels. Smithfield's, Easley, S.C. Co-author (with John Underwood): When in Doubt: Fire the Manager, 1980. Served with USMCR. Named Rookie of Yr., Major League Baseball, 1948; mem. Nat. League All-Star Team 1951, 52, 54, The Sporting News All-Star Major Team, 1954; All-American football player Southwestern La. Inst.; played in three World Series; managed two World Series; won pennants in both leagues; won World Championship with Oakland A's, 1974. Died Nov. 13, 2014.

DARKES, ETHEL MAY, lay church worker; b. Lebanon, Pa., Apr. 24, 1912; d. Harry Stonewall and Emma Jane (Swope) Hower; m. Clarence George Darkes, June 20, 1937; 1 child, Anetta Jane. BA cum laude, Lebanon Valley Coll., Annville, Pa., 1931; MEd, Temple U., 1955. Cert. tchr., Pa. Tchr. Drumore Twp. High Sch., Chestnut Level, Pa., 1931-32, Lebanon High Sch., 1939-55, counselor, 1955-64, Kennard-Dale High Sch., Fawn Grove, Pa., 1964—77; ret. Author of the Washington Letter "Union Signal," Woman's Christian Temperance Union Mag., 1991—. Pres. Cleona-Lebanon Woman's Christian Temperance Union, 1941—; mem. Pa. Women's Christian Temperance Union, pres., 1978-83, Woman's Christian Temperance Union. Mem. AAUW (pres. 1982-86), Am. Assn. Ret. Persons (pres. 1987-89, com. coord.), Woman's Club of Lebanon (treas. 1986-90), Delta Kappa Gamma (pres. 1970-72). Democrat. Methodist. Avocations: music, word puzzles, reading, church work. Home: Cleona, Pa. Died May 29, 2007.

DAUGHERTY, WALTER EMORY, lawyer; b. Washington, May 7, 1926; s. Walter Emory and Juanita Lingle (Stanley) D.; m. Georgette Haigh, May 21, 1953 (div.); children: Mileva, Woodland, Valory; m. Yvonne Bigio. AB, Harvard U., 1949; LLB, U. Miami, 1953. Bar: Fla., U.S. Fed. Dist. Ct. 1953, U.S. Ct. Appeals (D.C. cir.) 1965, U.S. Supreme Ct. 1981. Atty. law firm, Miami, 1953-55; pvt. practice Miami, Havana, Cuba, 1955-59, Miami, 1971, Boca Raton, Fla., 1983-96, Deerfield Beach, Fla., from 1996. With USN, 1944-46. Mem. Masons. Democrat. Congregationalist. Avocation: jazz drums. Died Mar. 1, 2007.

DAVENPORT, BETTY JOAN, communications specialist; b. Boise, Idaho, Sept. 26, 1954; d. Delmer Clyde and Mary Elizabeth (Petrie) D.; children: Phillip, Steven, Laura. Grad. high sch., Henderson, Nev. With social svcs. dept. Econ. Opportunity Bd., Las Vegas, Nev., 1974-76; communications specialist Met. Police Dept., Las Vegas, from 1981. Contbr. poetry and short stories to various publs. Mem. Writer's Group Nev. (co-founder). Avocations: reading, drawing, biking. Died June 27, 2007.

DAVENPORT, WILLIAM WEEKS, retired pilot, retired military officer; b. Jacksonville, Fla., Apr. 2, 1926; s. Boswell Utz and Pauline Genereaux Davenport; m. Ada Lee Byrd (div.); children: Carroll Ann, Virginia Lee; m. Candy Jeanie Rivera, Aug. 19, 1984; 1 child, James William. AA, Princeton U., 1948. Commd. ens. USN, 1944, advanced through grades to lt. comdr., ret.; capt., flight mgr., chief pilot Am. Airlines, Washington, ret.; ops. inspector FAA, Washington, ret. Author: Foleyisms, 1982. Recipient Commendation for sailboat rescue, USCG, 1984. Master: Masons (32d degree); mem.: Washington D.C. Hangar. Republican. Episcopalian. Home: Reston, Va. Died Aug. 2, 2007.

DAVEY, PATRICIA AILEEN, poet, artist, writer; b. Portland, Oreg., Nov. 21, 1933; d. James Lewis and Jean K. (Dick) Watson; widowed; 1 child, Georgia Aileen Davey; m. Maurice R. Jones (div.). Student, Lewis and Clark Coll., 1951-54, U. Wash., 1964-66, Portland State U., 1966-67. Various office jobs, Portland and Seattle, 1954-66; poet, artist and writer, from 1968. Exhibited in group shows at Eloise's Contemporary Gallery, many others; contbr. poems to mags. and anthologies. Mem. Astara. Avocations: photography, ufo research. Home: Roswell, N.Mex. Died Nov. 3, 2006.

DAVIDOFF, HOWARD, investment banker, venture capitalist; b. Bklyn., June 8, 1956; s. Robert George and Esther Sarah (Schneier) D.; m. Lisa Jane Klein, Apr. 5, 1987; children: Melanie Marissa, Owen Maxwell, Gabrielle Lynn. BBA, Boston U., 1978; MBA, NYU, 1980. Corp. loan officer Chase Manhattan Bank, NYC, 1981-82, asst. treas., 1982-83, 2d v.p., 1983-85, v.p., 1985-86, Carl, Marks & Co. N.Y., NYC, from 1986. Bd. dirs. Uniflex Corp. Inc., SMF Systems Inc., Samuel Aaron Inc., Mid-Way Inst. Corp., Mejn Win Internat. Mem. Assn. for Corp. Growth, N.Y. Venture Capital Assn., Beta Gamma Sigma. Republican. Jewish. Home: Port Washington, NY. Died Nov. 14, 2006.

DAVIDSON, NORMAN DOUGLAS, writer, lecturer; b. Edinburgh, Scotland, U.K., Jan. 12, 1933; came to U.S., 1986; s. Alfred and Isobel (Nairn) D.; m. Edythe Kemp, Jan. 9, 1954 (div. May 1963); children: Douglas, Fiona, Ruth; m. Annelies Guldemond, July 26, 1969. LLD, Internat. Coll., 1987. Journalist, U.K., 1953-63; worked with disadvantaged children & adults, 1966-69; sch. tchr., 1970-86; dir. tchr. tng. Waldorf Inst. Sunbridge Coll., Spring Valley, N.Y., 1986-98. Author: Astronomy and the Imagination, 1985, Sky Phenomena, 1993. Served in Royal Air Force, 1950-52, Egypt. Mem. Br. Astronomical Assn., Royal Astronomical Soc. Can., Astronomical Soc. Pacific. Avocations: astronomy, mathematics, writing, birdwatching, walking. Died Apr. 14, 2007.

DAVIS, ALFRED CARL, retail executive, consultant; b. Cleve., June 28, 1941; s. Alfred James and Anna Marie (Nemeshansky) D.; m. Carol Ann Brown, Feb. 18, 1961; children: David Scott, Donald Brent. Diploma, Police Acad., Cleve., 1967, State of Ohio, 1967. Police officer City of Cleve., 1967-79; chief of security Bishop Complex, Willoughby, Ohio, 1980-84; mgr. Cir. K Corp., Ft. Myers, Fla., 1985-89; pres. Tamiami Arms, Ft. Myers, from 1989. Police tng. officer, Police Dept., Cleve., 1967-79, police firearms instr., 1972-74; tng. NCO, NG, Painsville, Ohio, 1970-84; firearms instr. Boy Scouts Am., Police Dept. Civic Orgn., Cleve., 1970-84. Author: Federation Beginning, 1968; editor: (monthly newspaper) C.O.P. Beat, 1967. Founder Am. Security Coun., Washington, 1977. Staff Sgt. U.S. Army, 1960-66. Decorated Silver Star, two Bronze Stars, two Purple Hearts. Mem. N.Am. Gun Pro Assn., Christian Patriots Def. League, NRA, Amvets, Ft. Myers C. of C., Jaycees (Richfield, Ohio) (pres. 1975-76), Elks. Republican. Avocations: camping, fishing, hunting, shooting sports, reading. Home: N Fort Myers, Fla. Died June 22, 2007.

DAVIS, ALICE BERNICE STORLIE, physical therapist; b. Whalen, Minn., Jan. 21, 1921; d. Arthur Edwin Storlie and Ingeborg Bellah Hanson Zehren; m. Ronald Chester Davis, July 15, 1944 (div. Dec. 1981); children: Kent Loren and Scot Colin (twins), Daniel Bruce, Ronald Clark. Student, Winona State U., Minn., 1940; Cert. in Phys. Therapy, Mayo Clinic, Rochester, Minn., 1943. Registered phys. therapist, Minn.; lic. cosmetologist. Phys. therapist St. Vincent's Hosp., Billings, Mont., 1944-45, Mpls. Curative Workshop, 1946-51, St. Joseph's Hosp., St. Paul, 1968-73, Regency Manor, St. Paul, 1974-89, Midway Manor, St.

Paul, 1974-89; dir. and supr. phys. therapy M.J. Hellman Nursing Home, Richfield, Minn., 1973-88; ret. Sec. WELCA, Highview Christian Luth. Ch., Farmington, Minn., 1993-95; rep. Northfield Retirement Aux., 1990. Named Miss Winona (Minn.), 1939. Mem. Am. Phys. Therapy Assn. (life), Afternoon Cir. (leader Bible study 1992-95), Sons of Norway (refreshment coord. 1992-99), Order Ea. Star. Republican. Lutheran. Avocations: swimming, card playing. Home: Minneapolis, Minn. Died Apr. 25, 2007.

DAVIS, ALICE VIRGINIA GUNN, piano educator; b. Daingerfield, Tex., July 24, 1918; d. Walter Harrison and Lena Belle (Porter) Gunn; m. Joseph Marion Davis, Dec. 25, 1938; children: Joe Lane, Jerrol Porter. Student, Daingerfield. Pvt. instr. piano, Omaha, Tex., from 1962; organist Meth. Ch., from 1965; dir. children's music, tchr. Sunday Sch., Bible Study Leader. Contbr. articles to newspapers. Mem.: NE Tex. Music Tchrs. Assn. Am. Assn. Ret. Persons (program chmn. local chpt.), Nat. Music Tchrs. Assn. (officer), Nat. Guild Piano Tchrs. (sr. collegiate diploma, hall of fame). Died Nov. 4, 2006.

DAVIS, CAROLYN LEIGH, priest, psychotherapist; b. Houston, Mar. 18, 1936; d. William Harvey Speight and Veral Audra Speight (Nunn) Poole; m. John C. Rogers, June 22, 1957 (div. Nov. 1970); children: Elizabeth Leigh Porterfield, Rena Kathleen Stephan; m. L. B. Davis, Sept. 14, 1972 (dec. Feb. 1994). Diploma in nursing, U. Houston, 1956; MSW, U. Denver, 1981; MDiv, Iliff Sch. Theology, 1990; cert. individual theol. studies, Episcopal Theol. Sem. S.W., 1990. Cert. alcohol, drug counselor Colo.; RN Tex., Colo.; ordained as deacon Episcopal Ch., 1990, ordained to priesthood Episcopal Ch., 1990; LCSW Colo. Therapist Bethesda Mental Health Ctr., Denver, 1972-73; supr. emergency alcoholism services Denver Gen. Hosp., 1973-74; dir. alcoholism services Jefferson County Health Dept., Lakewood, Colo., 1974-78; pvt. practice psychotherapy Lakewood, 1981-93; curate St. Joseph's Episc. Ch., Lakewood, 1991, interim rector, 1991-92, rector, 1992-99; vicar St. Luke's Episcopal Ch., Livingston, Tex., 1999—2002; rector St. Luke's Episcopal Parish, Livingston, from 2002. Author: The Most Important Nine Months of Your Child's Life: Fetal Alcohol Syndrome. Mem.: NASW. Democrat. Avocations: bridge, music. Home: Center, Tex. Died Aug. 15, 2007.

DAVIS, CHARLES ARTHUR, psychiatrist; b. Greensboro, NC, Nov. 14, 1921; s. Charles Arthur and Ann Ethel D. BS, Columbia Union Coll., Takoma Park, Md., 1950; MD, Loma Linda U., 1953. Diplomate Am. Bd. Psychiatry and Neurology, Am. Bd. Forensic Psychiatry. Chief addiction svc. USPHS Hosp., Ft. Worth, Tex., 1956-58; med. dir. Kings View Hosp., Reedley, Calif., 1958-73; clin. dir. Kings View Corp., Fresno, Calif., 1970-75; exec. dir. Kings County Mental Health, Hanford, Calif., 1975-91; lectr. U. Calif., San Francisco, from 1980; program adminstr. Calif. State Prison, Corcoran, from 1992; ct.'s examiner Superior Cts. of Fresno, Madera, Tulare & King Counties, from 1960. Vis. prof. U. Guadalajara, Mexico, 1979-81. Pres. Fresno County Mental Health Adv. Bd., 1986-88. Lt. comdr. USPHS, 1955-58. Fellow Am. Psychiat. Assn. (life, Gold award 1970); mem. AMA, Cen. Calif., Psychiat. Soc. (pres. 1970), Calif. Med. Assn. (del. 1985-86), Kings County Med. Soc. (governing bd. 1981-87, pres. 1985), Calif. Conf. Local Mental Health Dirs., Am. Acad., Psychiatry and Law. Died Dec. 23, 2006.

DAVIS, DORIS ROSENBAUM (DEE DAVIS), artist, writer; b. NYC, Nov. 7, 1919; d. Lewis Newman and Bella (Wretnikow) Rosenbaum; m. Lewis F. Davis, Aug. 13, 1940 (div. Dec. 1989); children: Laurie, Peter. BA, Sarah Lawrence Coll., 1941. Crafts instr. Cooper Hewitt Mus., NYC, 1977-87, Pratt Inst., NYC, 1988-92, Am. Craft Mus., NYC, 1996—2004, Adventures in Crafts, NYC, 1971—2006. Represented in permanent collections Cooper-Hewitt Mus., Am. Craft Mus., Mus. City of N.Y., Gracie Mansion, Sarah Lawrence Coll.; author: Découpage, 1995, Decoupage, A Practical Guide, 2000; co-author: Step by Step Découpage, 1976, The Découpage Gallery, 2001, The Victorian Scrap Gallery, 2003; contbr. articles on découpage, faux finishes, gilding to craft mags.; appeared in (TV series) Our Home, 1997—98, HGTV, 2001. Democrat. Jewish. Avocations: traveling abroad, visiting museums, galleries, reading, classical music. Home: New York, NY. Died June 14, 2007.

DAVIS, DWIGHT D., financial advisor; b. Tulane, Calif., July 29, 1947; s. Delbert H. and Dorothy J. (Bell) D.; m. Celia Lynn, Nov. 24, 1973; children: Brionne Dee, Chance Del. BBA, East Tex. State U., 1973. Salesman Dwight Davis Fin. Svc., Paris, Tex., from 1972. Pres. Paris Bd. Realtors, 1990. Active Dwight Davis MDA Jail N Bail, Paris, 1988-92. With U.S. Army, 1969-72. Mem. Nat. Assn. Life UN, Tex. Real Estate Tchrs. Assn. (cert. real estate instr. 1994-98). Democrat. Avocation: athletics. Died May 23, 2007.

DAVIS, GERALDINE SAMPSON, special education educator; b. Tacoma, Wash., Aug. 18, 1919; d. Philip and Merta M. (Thomas) Sampson; m. John Allen Davis, Nov. 26 1942 (div. 1971); children: Denise, Karin, Glen (dec.), Grant (dec.), Page, Gail (dec.). BS with distinction, U. Minn., 1941; MEd, San Francisco State U., 1971. Cert. tchr., Calif., cert. adminstr., Calif. Art and English instr. White Bear Lake (Minn.) Jr. and Sr. High Sch., 1941-43; Am. club mobile operator ARC, Eng. and Europe, 1944-45, exec. dir. Lincoln County chpt. Newport, Oreg., 1947-48; substitute tchr. Santa Cruz (Calif.) County Dept. Edn., 1964-67; learning disabled instr. Live Oak Dist. Schs., Santa Cruz, 1967-89. Peer tutor developer Live Oak Schs., 1970-73, reading program mgr., 1973-76; evaluation team mem. County of Santa Cruz, 1980-84. Exhibited paintings in numerous galleries shows including Los Gatos Art Cooperative, 1961-65, Santa Cruz Art Festival, 1962, San Juan Bautista Art Fair, 1963, Santa Cruz County Fair, 1965; paintings represented in several pvt. collections. Chpt. sec. March of Dimes, Lincoln County, 1949-51, Santa Cruz County; vol. tutor Vols. of Santa Cruz, 1978-83; fundraiser Boulder Creek (Calif.) Schs., 1963; scenic and prop designer Santa Cruz County Schs., 1964, Boulder Creek Theater Group, 1965. Mem. Calif. Assn. Neurol. Handicapped Children (chair 1964-66, scholarships 1968-71), Women's Dem. Club, AAUW (com. chair for women's issues 1990—), Reproductive Rights Network, Santa Cruz Reading Assn. (sec. 1980, rep. Asilomar reading conf. bd. 1981-82, Chpt. and Internat. Reading Assns. award 1985), Calif. Ret. Tchrs. Assn. (nominating com. 1985—), Assn. Ret. Persons, Sr. Citizens Santa Cruz County, Pub. Citizens, Pub. Broadcasting Network, Conservation of Am, Amnesty, Delta Phi Delta (life, pres. Mpls. chpt. 1939-41), Pi Lambda Theta (life). Avocations: swimming, travel, animals, politics, cross generational communication. Home: Santa Cruz, Calif. Died Apr. 2, 2007.

DAVIS, HUMPHREY DENNY, publisher; b. Fayette, Mo., May 8, 1927; s. Lionel Winchester and Sarah Elizabeth (Denny) D.; m. Barbara Ellen Hartsgrove, June 6, 1954; 1 child, Thomas Shackelford. Student, Central Meth. Coll., Fayette, 1944-45, 46-47; BJ, U. Mo., 1949. Reporter, wire editor S.E. Missourian, Cape Girardeau, 1949-54; corr. UPI, Oklahoma City, Tulsa, Denver, 1954-55, exec. Albuquerque, 1955-56, bur. mgr. Lima, Peru, 1955-58, mgr. for Brazil Rio de Janeiro, 1958-68; mgr. no. div. Latin Am. Mexico City, 1968-75; regional exec. Charlotte, N.C., 1975-78; founder, owner pub. Wood Creek Corp., Fayette, from 1978; editor Fayette Advertiser and Democrat-Leader, Fayette, 1984—2001. Author profl. manual; contbr. articles to mags. and newspapers. Chmn. Fayette Planning and Zoning Commn., 1980-87; chmn. Howard County Rep. Cen. Com., Fayette, 1982-98; pres. Franklin or Bust, Inc., Fayette, 1988-2000; mem. Santa Fe Trail Nat. Hist. Trail Nat. Adv. Coun., 1991-97. With USN, 1945-46, 50-51. Mem. NRA, Santa Fe Trail Assn., Fayette Area Heritage Assn. (v.p. 1989-91), Am. Legion. Republican. Episcopalian. Avocation: local history. Home: Fayette, Mo. Died Dec. 30, 2006.

DAVIS, JAMES CLARK, manufacturing executive; b. Dresden, Ohio, July 11, 1935; s. James Howard and Helen Elizabeth (Longstreth) D.; m. Lorilee Ann Griggs, June 25, 1960. Degree mech. engring., Ohio State U., 1957; student, U. Colo. Grad. Sch. Banking, 1971-74; student bank mgmt., Columbia U., 1975-76. Mech. engr. Steel Ceilings, Inc., Coshocton, Ohio, 1957-60; indsl. engr. Cyclops Steel Corp., Coshocton, 1960-68; gen. mgr. Hathaway Engring., Colorado City, Colo., 1968-70; sr. v.p. Republic Nat. Bank, Pueblo, Colo., 1970-77; pres. Do-Ray Lamp Co., Inc., Colorado City, from 1977, also bd. dirs. Bd. dirs. Intrawest Bank, Pueblo, First Total Systems, Denver. Pres. Pueblo County Bldg. Authority, 1976; vice chmn. Pueblo County Retirement Bd., 1978. Mem.: Pueblo Country, Elks. Republican. Avocations: golf, fishing. Home: Denver, Colo. Died Apr. 3, 2007.

DAVIS, JOHN EDWARD, chemical engineer; b. Somerville, Mass., July 17, 1931; s. John Edward and Helen V. (Conroy) D.; m. Betty Louise Curier, Sept. 9, 1951; children: John J., James E., Joanne M., Joseph E., Jeanne M., Jayne M., John M. AS, Lincoln Coll., 1958; BBA, Northeastern U., 1960, MBA, 1964. Registered profl. engr., Mass. Technician bldg. mtcs lab. MIT, Cambridge, 1951-52; rsch. technician Wasco Chem. Co., Cambridge, Mass., 1954-55; chem. engr. Artisan Industries Inc., Waltham, Mass., 1955-71, Polaroid Corp., Waltham, from 1971. Guest lectr. MIT, Cambridge, 1970. Mem. Gov.'s Alliance Com., North Reading, Mass., 1985—, Sch. Reorgn. Com., North Reading, 1990; coach, pres. North Reading Pony League Baseball, 1970-80. With U.S. Army. Recipient Appreciation award (with wife) North Reading Sch. Com., 1992. Mem. AIChe (student chpts. com., Boston chpt. chmn.), Sigma Epsilon Rho (pres.). Achievements include patent on wiped film processing apparatus for evaporating and concentrating viscous material. Home: North Reading, Mass. Died Apr. 9, 2007.

DAVIS, KATHRYN IRENE JENNINGS, school nurse; b. Vance, Miss., June 4, 1934; d. Thomas Arthur and Opal Kathryn (Tabb) Jennings; widow; 1 child, Monique I. Davis. Diploma, Kings Daus. Sch. Nursing, Greenville, Miss., 1955. Staff nurse Tuomey Hosp., Sumter, S.C., 1973-74, Shaw Air Force Base, Sumter, S.C., 1975; head nurse recovery rm. NW Miss. Regional Med. Ctr., Clarksdale, 1975-82; chpt. I sch. nurse State of Miss. Coahoma County Sch., Clarksdale, from 1983; staff nurse Kings Daus. Hosp., Greenville, 1955, The Gen. Hosp., Greenville, 1955-58, Greenville Air Force Base, 1958-64, Blytheville (Ark.) Air Force Base, 1964-70, U.S. Naval Hosp., Guam, Mariana Islands, 1970-72. Mem. Am. Sch. Health Assn. Home: Vance, Miss. Died Feb. 3, 2007.

DAVIS, MARK HEZEKIAH, JR., electrical engineer; b. Knoxville, Tenn., Oct. 5, 1948; s. Mark Hezekiah and Grace Carson (Owens) D.; m. Susan Nakamura, July 14, 1977; children: Michell Grace, Kelli Michelle, John Micheal. BSEE, U. Tenn., 1972, MS, 1973. Devel. engr. Westinghouse Electric Corp. - U.S. ACE, Pitts. and Oakridge, 1969-76; sr. rsch. engr. N.L. Petroleum Svc., Houston, 1977-79; mgr. rsch. and devel. Advanced Ocean Systems divsn. Hydril Corp., Houston, 1980-81; engring. mgr. Schlumberger Corp., Sugarland, Tex., 1981-82; dir. electronics devel. Tech. for Energy Corp., Knoxville, 1982-84; mgr. digital signal processing N.E.C. Electronics, Mountain View, Calif., 1984-88; dir. comm. Executon Info. Systems, Stamford, Conn., 1988-93; dir., v.p. engring. C.S.I. Telecom, Palm Springs, Calif., from 1993. Pres. N.W. Houston United Civic Assn., 1980-82. Robert Miller scholar, 1971; U. Tenn. Nat. Alumni scholar, 1972; U.S. AEC grantee, 1973. Mem. IEEE (sr.), Am. Soc. Engring. Edn., Optical Soc. Am., Electro-Chem. Soc., Marine Tech. Soc., Soc. Photo-Optical Instrumentation Engrs. Achievements include: current work in fiber optic sensors and comm. systems and high temperature electronics in geosci.; subspecialties: ocean engineering; fiber optics. Home: Houston, Tex. Died Dec. 8, 2006.

DAVIS, PATRICIA W., medical/surgical nurse; b. Grayson County, Va., June 20, 1942; d. Elmer T. and Vada Louise (Anders) Williams; m. Sidney S. Davis, Aug. 16, 1984; 3 children. ADN, Wytheville Community Coll., Va., 1989; Deg. Bus. Mgmt., Wytheville Community Coll., 1990; student, Patrick Henry Community Coll., Martinsville, Va., 1975, U. Va., 1977-79. Sec./deputy Henry County Sheriff's Dept., Martinsville; technician So. W.Va. Tng. Ctr., Hillsville, Va.; family counselor Family Resource Ctr., Wytheville; med./surg. nurse Wythe County Community Hosp., Wytheville, from 1989. Nurse-patient educator Wythe County Community Hosp. Chmn. United Way; clk. Jubilee Bapt. Ch. Mem. Nat. League for Nursing, Va. Soc. Social Welfare, AAUW, Phi Beta Lambda, Phi Theta Kappa. Home: Fries, Va. Died Nov. 28, 2006.

DAVIS, ROBERT JOCELYN, engineering executive; b. Johannesburg, May 28, 1951; came to U.S., 1982; s. Louis and Albertine (Lambert) D.; m. Cecile Robyn Mosselson, Oct. 31,1976; children: Chantelle, Justin. BSME, U. Natal, 1973; MS in Aero. Engring., U. Witwatersrand, 1975. Project engr. Airtec Davidson, Johannesburg, 1976-79, mgr. blower dept., 1979-81; tech. and comml. dir. Berry Davidson, Lille, France, 1981-82; v.p. sales and engring. Am. Davidson Co., Dearborn, Mich., 1982-84, v.p. mktg. and engring. Hyde Park, Mass., 1985-88; v.p. mktg. Air Purator Corp., Boston, 1988-90, pres., 1991-92, Pollution Control Tech., Inc., Boston, 1992-95; exec. v.p. TRC Process Engring. Inc., Braintree, Mass., 1995-97; v.p. Rizzo Assocs., Inc., Natick, Mass., 1997—2000; pres. Refinity Corp., 2000—04; v.p., bus. devel. Thermatrix, Inc.; dir. indsl. rels. Coll. Engring. Northeastern U., from 2005. Inventor nolubrication inlet vanes; contbr. articles to profl. jours. Mem. AIAA, ASME, ASTM, AIChE, Am. Mktg. Assn., Internat. Soc. Pharm. Engrs. Avocations: golf, music, nautilus. Home: Salem, Mass. Died Dec. 1, 2006.

DAVIS, ROLAND HAYES, university official; b. Cleve., Feb. 9, 1927; s. Sylvester Sanford Sr. and Amaza (Weaver) D.; m. Jean Alston, Aug. 26, 1951 (div. Oct. 1979); children: Jeffrey Hayes, Leslie Suzanne, Kurt Bradley. Student, Case Western Res. U., 1945-46, Hofstra Coll., 1955-58; BA, L.I. U., 1961; MSW, Adelphi U., 1969. Social worker Nassau County (N.Y.) Dept. Social Svcs., 1966-79; ret., 1979; univ. adminstr. Hofstra U., Hempstead, N.Y., 1979-92. Cons. to pres. Hofstra U., Hempstead, 1992—; bd. dirs. Vanguard/Guardian Bank, Hempstead, 1975-89, chmn. 1975-85. Past pres. Assn. Minority Enterprises Inc. of N.Y., 1980-85. Lt. U.S. Army, 1946-66. Recipient Unispan award Hofstra U., 1979, Bus. Leadership award L.I. Bus. Community, 1981, Legis. citation Legislature of State of N.Y., 1983, Community Svc. Recognition award Pres. of U.S., 1984, Man of Yr. Hempstead C. of C., 1986. Mem. NAACP (life), The Edges Group, Inc. (treas. 1990—), Legal Aid Soc. Nassau County (bd. dirs. 1993—), Health and Welfare Coun. Nassau County (bd. dirs. 1982-91), Hempstead Gen. Hosp. Adv. Bd., 100 Black Men, NAssau/Suffolk, Inc. (pres. 1980-85). Avocations: golf, bowling. Died Apr. 30, 2007.

DAVISON, LUELLA MAY, organization executive, retired writer; b. Woonsocket, SD, Apr. 26, 1922; d. Milton Israel and Blanche Lyda (Dilley) Brady; m. Kenneth Earl Davison, Oct. 10, 1940; children: Suzanne, Pamela. Grad. high sch., Pontiac, Mich. Freelance writer Inter-Lake News, Mich., 1965-72. Vol., mem. youth, recruiting and escort coms. Pontiac Gen. Hosp., 1984-89; founder Grandparents Anonymous, Sylvan Lake, Mich., 1976, Mich. Grandparents and Grandchildrenns Day, Mich., 1985. Recipient Nat. Grandparent of Yr. award The Nat. Coun. for Observance of Grandparents' Day, 1982, Michiganian of Yr. award Mich. mag. Detroit News, 1982, award Waterford Village Sch., 1984. Avocations: working with youth, snare drum, reading, gardening, keeping scrapbooks. Home: Waterford, Mich. Died Dec. 2, 2006.

DAWSON, ALICE SHANKLE, b. San Antonio, Oct. 6, 1938; d. Perry and Alice (Stratton) Dawson; m. Joseph Meadows Dawson, Sept. 10, 1960; children: Leslie Elizabeth, Susan Phillips; m. Harlan Kelly, Nov. 5, 1999. BA, U. Tex., 1960; student, Stanford U., 1982. Cert. travel counselor Inst., Travel Agts. Tchr. St. Mary's Hall, San Antonio, 1960—70, 1971—73, Alamo Heights High Sch., San Antonio, 1969—70; office mgr. Bexar Insulation Co., San Antonio, 1970—74; mgr. Travel Boutique, San Antonio, 1975—78; travel counselor Sanborn's, San Antonio, 1979—80; sec. Perry Shankle Co., San Antonio, 1980—81, v.p., 1981—84; mgr. Travel Design, San Antonio, 1987—90; leisure sales mgr. Chaparral Travel Svcs., San Antonio, 1990—95; pres. Jillita's Savories, San Antonio, 1992—95. V.p., dir. Bexar Insulation Co., San Antonio, 1969—84, South Tex. Insulation Co., San Antonio, 1970—84, Polar Bear Insulation, San Marcos, Tex., 1975—84; bd. dirs. Fiesta San Antonio Commn., 1979—85, San Antonio Charity Ball Assn., 1982—89, Friends San Antonio Pub. Library, 1986—90; adv. bd. Sch. Bus. U. Tex., San Antonio, from 1985; v.p. Battle Flowers Assn., 1983—84, Univ. Roundtable, 1986—88, pres., 1988—89; dir. Friends Shakespeare U. Tex. San Antonio, 1989—91; mem. adv. bd. Jr. League San Antonio, 1989—92. Named one of 100 Best Travel Agents, Travel & Leisure, 2002,

2003. Mem.: SW Assn. Indian Arts, Greater San Antonio C. of C. (task force free enterprise), Inst. Cert. Travel Agents (life), Friends Folk Art. Republican. Presbyn. Home: San Antonio, Tex. Died Dec. 11, 2006.

DEADERICK, LUCILE, retired librarian; b. Knoxville, June 22, 1914; d. Paul Stuart and Josephine Lee (Galyon) D. BA, U. Tenn., 1934; BLS, U. Ill., 1937. Catalog asst. Lawson McGhee Libr., Knoxville, 1929-41; editor bull. ALA, Chgo., 1941-47; libr. Ft. Loudoun Regional Libr., Lenoir City, Tenn., 1947-51, Knox County Schs., Knoxville, 1951-68; assoc. prof. Libr. Sch. U. Tenn., Knoxville, 1968-69; dir. Knoxville-Knox County Pub. Libr., 1970-78. Editor: Heart of the Valley: A History of Knoxville, Tennessee, 1976. Pres., bd. dirs. Mabry-Hazen Mus., Knoxville, 1992-95; bd. dirs., sec. ARC, Knoxville, 1980-95. Mem. Assn. for Preservation of Tenn. Antiquities, East Tenn. Hist. Soc. (treas., pres.). Democrat. Roman Catholic. Avocations: reading, bridge, genealogy. Home: Knoxville, Tenn. Died Nov. 8, 2006.

DEAHL, WARREN ANTHONY, lawyer; b. South Bend, Ind., Sept. 18, 1918; s. Floyd Anthony and Sarah Talitha (Rosenbury) D.; m. Marjorie Katherine Sears, Nov. 29, 1941; children: Floyd R., John O. Student, U. Mich., 1937-38, U. Notre Dame, 1938-41; BA in Econs., U. Notre Dame, Ind., 1941; JD, U. Notre Dame, 1944. Bar: Ind. 1944, U.S. Dist. Ct. (no. dist.) Ind. 1946, U.S. Ct. Appeals (7th cir.) 1947, U.S. Supreme Ct. 1971. From assoc. to ptnr. Oare, Thornburg, McGill & Deahl (and predecessor firms), South Bend, 1946-64, Thornburg, McGill, Deahl, Harman, Carey & Murray, South Bend, 1964-82; ptnr. Barnes & Thornburg, South Bend, 1982-85, of counsel, from 1985. Pres. Bus. Devel. Corp., South Bend, 1982, mem. exec. com. and bd. dirs.; instr. law U. Notre Dame, Ind., 1948, 69; instr. bus. law Ind. U., South Bend, 1947-50; past v.p. New Bus. Facilities, Inc., South Bend. Vestryman St. Michael's Episcopal Ch., South Bend, 1984-85; solicitor Kiwanis Crippled Children's Fund, Snite Mus., Notre Dame, 1990, South Bend Symphony, 1988-93; trustee YMCA, South Bend, 1964-65; bd. dirs. Project Future, South Bend, 1985. Sgt. U.S. Army, 1943-46, ETO. Deocrated Bronze Star. Fellow Am. Bar Found., Ind. Bar Found.; mem. ABA, Ind. Bar Assn., St. Joseph County Bar Assn. (bd. govs., pres. 1972-73), Am. Arbitration Assn. (cert.), St. Joseph County C. of C., Inc. (bd. dirs., pres. emeritus 1964, disting. bus. leader award 1988). Avocations: boating, golf, computers, photography. Home: South Bend, Ind. Died Nov. 7, 2006.

DEAHL, WILLIAM EVANS, JR., minister; b. Twin Falls, Idaho, Apr. 21, 1945; s. William Evans Deahl Sr. and Cora Elizabeth Hardberger; m. Diane Elizabeth Davis, June 4, 1967. BS, Nebr. Wesleyan U., Lincoln, 1966; MA, No. Ill. U., DeKalb, 1968; MDiv., MST, Iliff Sch. Theology, Denver, 1970-81; PhD, So. Ill. U., Carbondale, 1974. Ordained to ministry United Meth. Ch., 1969. Instr. speech and theatre Nebr. Wesleyan U., Lincoln, 1970-71, 82-84; chmn. speech and theatre Va. Intermont Coll., Bristol, 1972-74; instr. speech and theatre Ea. Mont. Coll., Billings, 1974-76; chmn. speech and theatre Midland Luth. Coll., Fremont, Nebr., 1976-82; min. Nebr. Wesleyan U., Lincoln, 1984-92; instr. speech S.E. C.C., 1993-95; min. 1st United Meth. Ch., Kearney, Nebr., 1995-98, Calvary United Meth. Ch., Fremont, from 1998. Minister United Meth. Ch., Ryegate, Mont., 1975-76, Rising City, Nebr., 1976-82, First United Meth. Ch., Springfield, Nebr., 1982-83, Grace United Meth. Ch., Lincoln, 1983-95. Co-author: Speech Liberal Arts Context, 1981; contbr. articles to profl. jours. Recipient Bishop Baker Grad. award United Meth. Ch., 1989. Mem. Am. Acad. Religion, Assn. for Religion and Intelligent Life, Assn. Coll. and Univ. Chaplains, Order of St. Luke, Levinas Soc. Nebr., Abraham Heschel Soc., Order of DeMolay, Johann Baptist Metz Group for Study of Justice. *The unceasing quest for excellence and beauty in life, especially in relationship to the divine, community, and friendship, is necessary to escape the constant lure of conformity and mediocrity so rampant in our culture.* Died Dec. 10, 2006.

DEAN, ROBERT BERRIDGE, editor; b. San Francisco, Feb. 20, 1913; arrived in Denmark, 1977; s. Thomas Berridge and Margaret Beatrice (Postlethwaite) D.; m. Kirsten M. Jalmer, Apr. 4, 1939 (dec. 1975); children: Eric, Karen, Peter, Carl; m. Ebba Lund, June 8, 1978 (dec. 1999). BA, U. Calif., Berkeley, 1935; PhD, Cambridge U., Eng., 1938. Rsch. assoc. Cambridge U., England, 1938-39; rsch. asst. physiology U. Rochester, NY, 1939-40; tchg. asst. physiology U. Minn., Mpls., 1940-41; rsch. assoc. chemistry Stanford U., Calif., 1941-44; asst. prof. chemistry U. Hawaii, Honolulu, 1944-47, U. Oreg., Eugene, 1947-52; mgr. sales devel. lab. Borden Chem. Co., Bainbridge, NY, 1952-64; chief ultimate disposal EPA, Cin., 1964-75; jour. founding editor Waste Mgmt. & Rsch., Copenhagen, from 1982. Cons. WHO, Copenhagen, 1975-85. Author: Modern Colloids, 1948, Ebba Lund: The Girl With the Red Hat, 2006; co-author: Water Reuse, 1981; editor: Incineration of Mcpl. Waste, 1988. Recipient Food Packaging Regulations Recognition award Adhesive Mfrs. Assn., 1960. Mem. AAAS. Avocations: gardening, woodworking, fixing things. Home: Copenhagen, Denmark. Died Dec. 30, 2007.

DEAN, ROBERT GEORGE, oceanographic engineering educator; b. Laramie, Wyo., Nov. 1, 1930; s. George Horton and Harriet Maud (Blevins) D.; m. Phyllis Leone Thomas, Sept. 12, 1954; children: Julie, Timothy. AA, Long Beach City Coll., 1952; BSCE, U. Calif., Berkeley, 1954; MS in Phys. Oceanography, Tex. A&M U., 1956; ScD in Civil Engring., MIT, 1959. Asst. prof. civil engring MIT, Cambridge, Mass., 1959-60; sr. rsch. engr. Chevron Rsch. Corp., La Habra, Calif., 1960-65; acting assoc. prof. oceanography U. Wash., Seattle, 1965-66; prof. coastal oceanographic engring. U. Fla., Gainesville, 1966-75, chmn. dept. coastal oceanographic engring., 1966-72 and from 92, grad. rsch. prof. coastal and oceanographic engring., from 1982, prof. emeritus coastal oceanographic engring., 2003—15; Unidel prof. civil engring./marine studies U. Del., Newark, 1975-82; dir. divsn. beaches and shores Fla. Dept. Natural Resources, Tallahassee, 1985-87. Mem. Coastal Engring. Rsch. Bd., Vicksburg, Miss., 1968-80, 93—. Co-author: Water Wave Mechanics, also numerous papers in field. Recipient award Nat. Acad. Engring., 1980, Outstanding Civilian Svc. medal Dept. of Army, 1981, Internat. Coastal Engring. award ASCE, 1983. Mem. NAE. Achievements include patent for directional wave gage; development of highly nonlinear water wave theory, of methodology for engineering application of equilibrium beach profiles. Home: Gainesville, Fla. Died Feb. 28, 2015.

DEAR, JOSEPH ALBERT, pension fund administrator; b. 1951; married; 2 children. BA in Polit. Economy, Evergreen State Coll., Olympia, Wash., 1976; grad. Program for Sr. Execs. in Govt., Harvard U., 1986. Founder, exec. dir. People for Fair Taxes, 1977—81; rsch. dir. Wash. State Labor Coun., 1981-85; dir. Wash. Dept. Labor & Industries, 1987—93; asst. sec. Occupl. Health & Safety Adminstrn. US Dept. Labor, 1993—97; chief of staff to Gov. State of Washington, Olympia, 1997—2001; govt. rels. officer Frank Russell Co., 2001—02; exec. dir. The Washington State Investment Bd. (WSIB), 2002—09; chief investment officer The Calif. Public Employees' Retirement Sys. (CalPERS), 2009—14. Bd. trustees Washington State Investment Bd., 1987—92, chmn., 1989—91. Mem. Nat. Assn. Govtl. Labor Ofcls. (pres. 1990-91), Occupl. Safety & Health State Plan Assn. (bd. dirs. 1989-93). Died Feb. 27, 2014.

DEASY, DONALD WAYNE, real estate broker; b. Yakima, Wash., Dec. 27, 1938; s. Wayne Delbert and Louise Anita (Nocchi) D.; m. E. Jane England, Sept. 23, 1961; children: Kimberly, Deanne, Matthew, Joseph. BA, U. Wash., 1961. Salesman IBM, Seattle, L.A., 1963-66; v.p. Pacific Nat. Bank of Wash., Seattle, 1966-77; sales assoc. Windermere Real Estate Co., Seattle, 1977-80; pres. Windermere Real Estate/East Inc., Bellevue, Wash., from 1980. Cons. Windermere Svcs. Co., Seattle, 1983—. Pres. Bellevue (Wash.) Breakfast Rotary, 1989-90. 1st lt. U.S. Army, 1961-63. Mem. Rotary Internat. (Paul Harris fellow 1990), Bellevue Athletic Club, Lakes Club. Home: Bellevue, Wash. Died Jan. 30, 2007.

DE BORCHGRAVE, ARNAUD, editor, writer, lecturer; b. Brussels, Oct. 26, 1926; s. Count Baudouin and Audrey (Townshend) de B.; m. Dorothy Solon, Apr. 1950; 1 child, Arnaud; m. Eileen Ritschel, Mar. 31, 1959; 1 child, Trisha; m. Alexandra D. Villard, May 10, 1969 Student, Maredsous, Belgium, 1936—39, King's Sch., Canterbury, Eng., 1940—42. Free-lance writer, Ea. Europe, 1946—47; staff United Press, We. Europe, 1947—51; mgr. Benelux Countries, 1949—51; European Corr. Newsweek, Paris, North Africa, Mid. East, Indo-China, 1951—54, fgn. editor, sr. editor, 1955—59, chief fgn. corr., 1959—62, mng. editor internat. edits., 1962—63, chief Newsweek Corr., 1964—80; columnist, TV host; sr. assoc. Ctr. for Strategic and Internat. Studies, 1981—85; editor in chief The Washington Times and Insight Mag., 1985—91; dir. Transnat. Threats Initiative, sr. advisor Ctr. for Strategic and Internat. Studies, Washington, from 1991; pres., CEO UPI, Washington, 1999—2001. Editor-at-large, Washington Times and UPI, 2001— Served with Brit. Royal Navy, 1942-46 Decorated French Legion of Honor, 2014, commandeur de l'Ordre de Leopold II, commandeur de l'Ordre de Couronne, Medaille Maritime Belge; recipient Medal of Honor Def. Coun., 1980, Medal of Honor World Bus. Coun., 1981, Lifetime Achievement award Phillips Found., Washington Dateline award Soc. Profl. Journalists, also numerous awards for fgn. reporting Mem. Am. Soc. Newspaper Editors, Internat. Press Inst., Inter-Am. Press Assn., Coun. Fgn. Rels., Racquet and Tennis Club, Met. Club, Econ. Club Washington, Nat. Press Club Home: Washington, DC. Died Feb. 15, 2015.

DECKELMAN, ARTHUR D., lawyer, film producer; b. Balt., Apr. 21, 1929; s. Ruben and Ida (Havelock) D.; m. Wilma Schoenbuch, June 1961 (dec. Aug. 1974); 1 child, Daniel J.; m. Jennifer Hull, Nov. 5, 1977; children: Jennette, Erica. BBA in Acctg., U. Miami, 1953, LLB/JD, 1957; LLM, NYU, 1961; MBA in Taxes, Golden Gate U., 1982. Bar: Fla. 1953, N.Y. 1961, Calif. 1977, U.S. Dist. Ct. (so. dist.) Fla. 1964, U.S. Dist. Ct. (mid. dist.) Fla. 1982, U.S. Dist. Ct. (ctrl. dist.) Calif. 1977, U.S. Ct. Appeals (5th and 9th cirs.), U.S. Supreme Ct. 1964. Auditor Coopers Lybrandt, NYC, 1957-61; assoc. atty. Hammer Rothblatt, NYC, 1961, Walters, Moore & Costanzo, Miami, 1961-68; sole practitioner Miami, 1968-76; ptnr. Hillsinger & Costanzo, LA, 1977-82, Hillsinger, Costanzo, Deckelman & Mason, Clearwater, Fla., 1982-84; sole practitioner Palm Harbor, Fla., from 1984. Bd. dirs. New Focus Films, Inc., Orlando, Fla. Contbg. author: Criminal Law of New York, 1960, Successful Techniques for Criminal Trials, 1961, Art of Cross Examination, 1971, Fundamentals of Criminal Advocacy, 1974, others. Bd. dirs. Suncoast YMCA, Clearwater, 1983; mem. adv. bd. Salvation Army, Clearwater. With JAGC, U.S. Army, 1953-55, Japan. Mem. ABA, ATLA, Clearwater Bar Assn., Rotary Internat. (pres. Clearwater 1997, Paul Harris fellow 1985). Democrat. Died Feb. 23, 2007.

DECRAENE, SANDRA IRENE, retired elementary school educator; b. Mishawaka, Ind., Jan. 18, 1940; d. George Thomas and Ida Marie (Foreman) Baughman; m. Richard Paul DeCraene, June 30, 1962; children: Richard, Kevin. BS, Ball State U., 1962; MS, Ind. U., South Bend, 1977. Lic. tchr., Ind. Tchr. grade 3 New Castle (Ind.) Schs., 1962-64, Mishawaka Sch. City, 1964-65, tchr. grade 1, 1970-71, 77-78, tchr. grade 4, 5, 6 music and art, 1978-80, tchr. grade 1, 1980—2002. Student tchr. adv. bd. Ind. U., South Bend, 1990-92. Mem. Svc. Guild, South Bend, 1974-76. Mem. ASCD, NEA (bldg. rep. 1986-89), Internat. Reading Assn., Panhellenic Assn., Four Lakes Country Club, Univ. Club of Notre Dame, Pi Beta Phi Alumnae Assn., Delta Kappa Gamma. Avocations: reading, music, painting, swimming, walking. Home: Granger, Ind. Died May 17, 2007.

DEEB, ANN MARIE, purchasing manager; b. Meadville, Pa., Feb. 10, 1929; d. Nigab and Emilene (Ezor) D.; 1 child, Virginia Jane. BA, Allegheny Coll., 1951. Cert. purchasing mgr. (life). Order clk. Mameco Internat. (formerly named Master Mechs. Co.), Cleve., 1956-68, supr. customer rels., 1968-69; office mgr. Isonetics, Cleve., 1969-73; asst. purchasing agt. Electro-Gen. Plastics, Cleve., 1973-76, purchasing agt., 1976-90; purchasing mgr. Plastivax, Inc., Mentor, 1990-94; ret. Mem. Nat. Assn. Purchasing Mgmt., Purchasing Mgmt. Assn. Cleve. (hon. 1996) Roman Catholic. Avocations: reading, walking, collecting antiques, mysteries. Home: Lakewood, Ohio. Died June 25, 2007.

DEFFNER, JOHN FREDERICK, research chemist; b. Pitts., Aug. 7, 1932; s. Joseph J. and Mary M. (Snyder) D.; m. Mary T. Bonner, June 28, 1958; children: Mary P. Patterson, Cecile M., Margaret M. Mullen, Joseph J. BS in Chemistry, Duquesne U., 1954, MS in Organic Chemistry, 1956. Chemist E.I. DuPont de Nemours, Wilmington, Del., 1956-57; research chemist Gulf Oil, Pitts., 1957-75, sr. research chemist, 1975-80, research assoc., 1980-85; sr. research chemist Chevron Research Co., Richmond, Calif., from 1985. Patentee in field. Pres. Parent Tchrs. Guild, Vincentian High Sch., Pitts., 1979-80; treas. St. Bonaventure Sch., Pitts., 1973-74. Mem. Am. Petroleum Inst. (chmn. task force 1980-85), Soc. Automotive Engrs. (sect. chmn. Pitts. 1984-85, Outstanding Sect. award 1985), Am. Chem. Soc. Lodges: Elks. Avocations: jogging, gardening. Home: Pittsburgh, Pa. Died Nov. 10, 2006.

DEFRANCO, BUDDY (BONIFACE FERDINAND LEONARD DEFRANCO), jazz clarinetist, bandleader; b. Camden, NJ, Feb. 17, 1923; s. Ferdinand Leonard & Louise (Giordano) D.; m. Mitchell Vanston (div.); 1 child, Christopher (dec. 2001); m. Joyce O. Yount, 1975; 1 child, Charles Lee. Student, Mastbaum Music Sch., Phila. Alto saxophonist, solo clarinetist Johnny Scat Davis Band, on tour, 1939, Gene Krupa Orch., on tour, 1941-42, Charlie Barnett Orch., on tour, 1943; solo clarinet Tommy Dorsey Orch., on tour, 1944-48, Count Basie Septet, on tour, 1950; bandleader Buddy DeFranco Orch., 1951; featured clarinetist Jazz at the Philharm. All Star Tours, worldwide, 1952-54; condr. Glenn Miller Orch., 1966-74; leader, guest artist The Buddy DeFranco Group, Panama City, Fla. Performer, clinician Yamaha Music Corp., Grand Rapids, Mich.; clinician, judge various univs. Author: Buddy DeFranco Hand in Hand with Hanon, 1996, Buddy DeFranco on Jazz Improvisation, 1973, Mel Bay Presents Modern Jazz Compositions and Studies for the Clarinet, 1983; rec. artist numerous albums including Hark: Buddy DeFranco Meets the Oscar Peterson Quartet, 1994, Chip Off the Old Bop, 1994, You Must Believe in Swing, & Nobody Else But Me, with Metropole Orch., 1997, Flying Fingers of Art Tatum and Buddy DeFranco, Cross Country Suite with Nelson Riddle (Grammy award 1956), Mr. Lucky, Mood Indigo, Chicago Fire with Buddy DeFranco and Terry Gibbs, George Gershwin Songbook with Oscar Peterson, Buddy DeFranco/Dave McKenna: Do Nothing 'Till You Hear From Us, 1999, Buddy DeFranco: Cookin' the Books w/ John Pizzarelli Trio & Butch Miles, 2004 Named #1 Jazz Clarinetist over 45 times Downbeat mag., Metronome mag., Playboy Mag. All Stars-All Stars, Ency. Jazz Musicians poll; named 2006 Jazz Master, Nat. Endowment for Arts. Fellow Nat. Assn. Jazz Educators; mem. ClariNetwork, ASCAP. Died Dec. 24, 2014.

DE GROOTE, ROBERT DAVID, general and vascular surgeon; b. Hackensack, NJ, Aug. 30, 1951; s. Emiel and Filomena Lillian (Candio) De G. BS in Biology, Fordham U., 1973; MD, Autonomous U. Guadalajara, 1978. Diplomate Am. Bd. of Surgery. Resident gen. surgery U. Medicine and Dentistry N.J. Med. Sch., Newark, 1979—84, fellow critical care medicine, 1981—82, fellow vascular surgery, 1984—86; fifth pathway St. Joseph's Hosp., Paterson, NJ, 1978—79; attending surgeon Hackensack Med. Ctr., Hackensack, NJ, from 1986. Contbr. articles to Surgery, Stroke, Archives of Surgery, Annals of Vascular Surgery. Named Man of Yr., Lyndhurst, N.J. chpt. Italian-Am. Nat. Svc. Orgn., 1993, Top Doctor in New York, New York Mag., Top Doctor in N.J., N.J. Monthly. Fellow ACS; mem. AMA, Internat. Soc. for Cardiovascular Surgery, Soc. for Critical Care Medicine, Ea. Vascular Soc. Roman Catholic. Home: Bay Head, NJ. Died Apr. 17, 2007.

DEIMLING, PAULA KAY, writer; b. Cin., Dec. 11, 1952; d. Paul Henry and Ruth Patricia (Koehler) D.; m. Mark W. Harlow, Mar. 23, 1991. BA in English Lit., U. Cin., 1976; MS in Journalism, Ohio U., 1987. Reporter, assoc. editor Milford (Ohio) Advertiser, 1976-77, editor, 1977-81; grad. tchg. asst. Ohio U., Athens, 1981-82; editl. asst. Writer's Digest, Cin., 1982-83; gen. markets asst. Writer's Digest Books, Cin., 1983-84, editor, 1984-86; markets editor Writer's Digest Mag., Cin., 1984-86; instr. writing and editing U. Cin., 1988-97. Contbg. author: The Writer's Essential Desk Reference, 1991, 2d edit., 1996; editor: Writer's Market, 1985, 86. Mem. Soc. Profl. Journalists, Romance Writers Am., Cin. Editors Assn. Avocation: genealogy research. Home: Loveland, Ohio. Died June 18, 2007.

DEITS, MARY PATRICIA, counseling therapist, stress mastery consultant; b. Redlands, Calif., Jan. 9, 1936; d. Erbert Junior and Helen Enid (Denslow) Powell; m. Frank Lewis Deits, Mar. 22, 1959; children: Patricia Ann Deits Gardiner, John Alan. BA, Whittier Coll., Calif., 1957;

student, U. Calif., Santa Barbara, 1969-72; M in Counseling, Idaho State U., 1978. Nat. cert. counselor; Ariz. cert. counselor. Substitute tchr. Sierra Sands Sch. Dist., Ridgecrest, Calif., 1969-74; real estate sales United Farm Agy., Willows, Calif., 1974-76; group facilitator nurses jr. clin. program Idaho State U., Pocatello, 1979-80; psychology instr., assoc. faculty Pima Community Coll., Tucson, 1984-86; self employed Growth Oriented Counseling, Tucson, Pocatello, from 1976, Mind Body Prodns., Tucson, from 1989. Cons./therapist Bannock House, Pocatello, 1980-81; adv. bd. mem. S.E. Idaho Mental Health, Pocatello, 1980-81; dir. biofeedback Canyon Ranch Resort and Spa, Tucson, 1986-90; cons. to biofeedback profls., 1992— Author: (relaxation tapes) At Ease, 1990, A Quiet Place, 1991; co-developer biofeedback equipment Model F1000 Focused Technology, 1986—. Youth counselor Meth. Ch., Ridgecrest, 1959-62, 65-69, Alamogordo, N.Mex., 1962-65; hot-line worker Indian Wells Valley Mental Health, Ridgecrest, 1969-71; adv. bd. mem. YMCA, Tucson, 1982-83. Mem. Ariz. Counselors Assn., Biofeedback Soc. Ariz. (so. rep. 1989-90, study group facilitator 1990-91, v.p., editor newsletter and program chmn. 1991-95). Avocations: camping, swimming, organic gardening. Home: Ridgecrest, Calif. Died Apr. 17, 2007.

DEKOKER, RICHARD CARROLL, television screenwriter, travel cinematographer; b. Chgo., Dec. 15, 1929; s. Richard and Estelle (Carroll) D.; m. Louise Rosalie Rubin, Oct. 3, 1954. BS, U. Wis., 1952; MBA, Temple U., 1960. Passenger svc. mgr. Pan Am. World Airways, Chgo. and Phila., 54-69; pres., chief exec. officer Richard Dekoker, P.A., Tampa, Fla., from 1969. Author screenplay, Gangster Chronicles, 1960; author, producer motion pictures: Gangster Wars, 1965, Juggernaught, 1968. Capt. U.S. Army, 1952-54, Korea. Mem. Screen Writers Guild, Masons. Republican. Methodist. Avocation: travel. Died Aug. 30, 2007.

DE KRUIF, WILLIAM RAYMOND, electronics executive, electrical engineer; b. Oak Park, Ill., Apr. 22, 1960; s. Willard Rice and Joan (Singley) D.; m. Vivian Everosk, July 12, 1986; children: Paul, Karena, Erik. BS, Colo. State U., 1983; BSEE, U. Colo., 1989; MBA in Mgmt., Northwestern U., 1994. Bus. dir. Motorola Inc., Chgo., from 1989. Mem. IEEE. Republican. Avocations: stamp collecting/philately, reading, collecting first editions of books, sailing. Home: Regency Park, Singapore. Died Nov. 24, 2006.

DE LA RENTA, OSCAR (OSCAR ARISTIDES DE LA RENTA FIALLO), fashion designer; b. Santo Domingo, Dominican Republic, July 22, 1936; s. Oscar and Maria Antonia (deFiallo) de la Renta; m. Francoise de Langlade, Oct. 31, 1967 (dec. 1983); m. Annette Reed, Dec. 26, 1989; 1 adopted child, Moises. Student, Acad. San Fernando, Madrid; D (hon.), Hamilton Coll., Clinton, NY, 2013. Couture asst. Lanvin, Paris; designer custom clothing Elizabeth Arden, NYC, 1963—65; designer Oscar de la Renta for Jane Derby, 1965—66, Oscar de la Renta, Ltd., from 1966, chmn. bd. dirs., chief designer, 1974—2014; designer Pierre Balmain, Paris, 1993—2002, Tortuga Bay hotel, 2006. Launched signature fragrance Oscar, 1977, fragrance for men, Pour Lui, 1980, Oscar for men, 1995, Intrusion, 2002. Bd. dirs. La Casa del Nino Orphanage & Sch., Santo Domingo, Met. Opera, NYC, NY Opera House, Carnegie Hall, sta-WNET, New Yorkers for Children, America's Soc., Queen Sofia Spanish Inst., NYC. Decorated Gold Medal of Bellas Artes King of Spain, 2000, Order al Mérito de Juan Pablo Duarte, Order of Cristóbal Colón Dominican Republic; recipient Coty award, 1967, 1968, Golden Tiberius award, 1968, Neiman-Marcus award, 1968, Lifetime Achievement award, Coun. Fashion Designers of America, 1990, Perennial Success award, Fragrance Found., 1991, Living Legend award, American Soc. Perfumers, 1995, Lifetime Achievement award, Hispanic Heritage Soc., 1996, Super Star award, Night of Stars, 2009, Founder's award, Coun. Fashion Designers of America, 2013; named The Grand Marshall of NY Hispanic Day Parade, 2000, Designer of Yr., Coun. Fashion Designers of America, 2000, 2007; named to The American Fashion Critic's Hall of Fame, 1973, The Internat. Best Dressed List Hall of Fame, 1973. Mem.: Coun. Fashion Designers of America (pres. 1973—76, 1986—88, Lifetime Achievement award 1990, Womenswear Designer of Yr. award 2000, 2007). Achievements include helping to build two schools incorporating orphanages and day-care centers in La Romana and Punta Cana, Dominican Republic. Died Oct. 20, 2014.

DEL BUONO, DEBORAH, community health nurse; b. Phila., Sept. 11, 1957; d. Domenick and Rita (Viggiano) Volpe; m. Gregory Del Buono, Aug. 27, 1983; 1 child, Michael. Diploma, St. Agnes Med. Ctr., Phila., 1979. Cert. intravenous nurse, CPR. Nurse, head nurse St. Agnes Med. Ctr., Phila., 1979-87; home health nurse Ind. Health Care, Phila., 1987-89, IAMA, Inc., Phila., from 1989. Home: Philadelphia, Pa. Died June 29, 2007.

DEL DUCA, RITA, language educator; b. NYC, Apr. 1, 1933; d. Joseph and Ermelinda (Buonaguro) Ferraro; m. Joseph Anthony Del Duca, Oct. 29, 1955; children: Lynn, Susan, Paul, Andrea. BA, CUNY, 1955. Elem. tchr. Yonkers (N.Y.) Pub. Schs., 1955-57; tchr. kindergarten Sacred Heart Sch., Yonkers, 1962-64; tchr. piano, Scarsdale, N.Y., 1973-79; asst. office mgr. Foot Clinic, Hartsdale, N.Y., 1977-85; tchr. ESL, Linguarama Exec. Sch., White Plains, N.Y., 1985-89; ESL tutor, Scarsdale, from 1989. Dist. leader Greenburgh (N.Y.) Rep. Com., 1991-92. Mem.: ASCAP. Avocations: painting, piano teaching, tennis, theatre arts. Died Apr. 13, 2007.

DELEAR, RICHARD HENRY, personnel consultant; b. Wichita, Kans., Dec. 19, 1927; s. Ernest C. Delear and Clara M. Boberg; m. Helen J. Clark, Jan. 8, 1950 (dec. Mar. 1994); children: Cherie, Cindy, Kimberly, Kirkland, Dianne, Michelle. Student, Hiedleburg U., Germany, 1946-47, San Jose St. U., 1959-60. Cert. hypnotherapist. Enlisted U.S. Army, 1944, advanced through grades to m/sgt., 1952, ret., 1959; entrepreneur Calif., 1960-74; human resources cons. Success Thru Humaneering, Scotts Valley, Calif., from 1974. Lectr. in field. Author: Leadership Strategies, 1988. Pres. Exchange club, Scotts Valley, 1978-79. Decorated two Bronze Stars, two Purple Hearts, Silver Star. Republican. Roman Catholic. Home: Scotts Valley, Calif. Died Aug. 22, 2007.

DEL TUFO, ROBERT J., retired lawyer, former state attorney general, former US attorney; b. Newark, Nov. 18, 1933; s. Raymond and Mary (Pellecchia) Del T.; m. Katherine Nouri Hughes; children: Barbara, Ann Jackopin, Robert Jr., David; stepchildren Caitlin Hughes, Johanna Hunsbedt BA in English, cum laude, Princeton U., 1955; JD, Yale U., 1958. Bar: NJ 1959. Law sec. to chief justice NJ Supreme Ct., 1958-60; assoc. firm Dillon, Bitar & Luther, Morristown, NJ, 1960-62, ptnr., 1962-74; asst. prosecutor Morris County, NJ, 1963-65; 1st asst. prosecutor, 1965-67; 1st asst. atty. gen. NJ, 1974-77; dir. criminal justice, 1976-77; US atty. Dist. of NJ, Newark, 1977-80; prof. Rutgers U. Sch. Criminal Justice, 1979-81; ptnr. firm Stryker, Tams & Dill, 1980-86, Hannoch Weisman, 1986-90; atty. gen. State of NJ, 1990—94; ptnr. Skadden, Arps, Slate, Meagher & Flom, NYC and Newark, 1993—2004, of counsel, 2004—14; commr. NJ State Commn. of Investigation, 1981-84. Instr. bus. law Fairleigh-Dickinson U., 1964; mem. NJ State Bd. Bar Examiners, 1967-74; mem. criminal law drafting com. Nat. Conf. Bar Examiners, 1972-2002; bd. dirs. Nat. Ctr. for Victims of Crime, 1995-2003, Nat. Italian Am. Found., 1995-2003, Integrity Inc., 1995—, John Cabot U. in Rome, 1997—, Legal Svcs. NJ, 2000-; adv. bd. Yale Law Jour., 2003-05, IOLTA, 1994-99, NJ Pub. Interest Law Ctr., 1996-99, Daytop Village Found., 1998—, Planned Parenthood, 1998-99; mem. com. on character NJ Supreme Ct., 1982-84; mem. lawyers' adv. com. NJ Fed. Dist. Ct., 1998—; mem. adv. com. of former attys. gen. NJ Atty. Gen. 2000-; spl. master, fed. jail onvercrowding litigation, Essex County, 1989-90; NE regional trustee Boys and Girls Clubs of Am., 2000-05, Lawyers' Fund for Client Security, NJ, 2000-05, chmn. bd. trustees U. Med. & Dentistry NJ, 2006-2011, mem. bd. 2011-12; mem. bd. regents Nat. Coll. Dist. Attys., 2005—2008, mem. book bd. Criminal Justice Sect. Am. Bar. Assn., 2009- Bd. editors Yale U. Law Jour.; mem. editl. bd.: NJ Lawyers, from 2008; contbr. articles to profl. jours. Mem. law enforcement adv. com. County Coll. of Morris, 1970-85; mem. Morris County Ethics Com., 1968-71, Morris County Jud. Selection Com., 1970-72, Essex County Jud. Selection Com., 1982-84; v.p., mem. exec. com. United Fund of Morris County, 1966-70; chmn. Morris Twp. Juvenile Conf. Com., 1963-74; bd. dirs. Nat. Found. March of Dimes, 1966-68, Vis. Nurse Assn. Morris County, 1963-70, Morristown YMCA, 1970-74; trustee Atty.'s Fund for Client Protection, 1999-2005; trustee Newark Acad., 1976-95, 97—2002, pres. bd. dirs. 1983-87; bd. regents St. Peter's Coll., 1979-85; mem. bd .trustees PAX, 2008-12. Fellow Am. Bar Found.; mem. Am., NJ Bar Assns., Nat. Dist. Attys. Assn., Soc. Former Attys. Gen., Nat. Assn. Former US Attys., Order of Coif. Home: Princeton, NJ. Died Mar. 2, 2016.

DELUCA, FRED, food service executive; b. Oct. 3, 1947; s. Salvatore and Carmela (Ombres) DeLuca; m. Elisabeth DeLuca, 1966; 1 child. Grad., U. Bridgeport, Doctorate (hon.), 2002. Co-founder, CEO Subway Restaurants, Milford, Conn., 1965—2015; founder Micro Investment Lending Enterprise (MILE), 1996. Co-author: Start Small, Finish Big: 15 Key Lessons to Start--and Run--Your Own Successful Business, 2000. Named one of Forbes 400: Richest Americans, from 2006. Died Sept. 14, 2015.

DELUCCA, ROBERT KENNETH, adult education educator, writer, translator; b. Pitts., Oct. 14, 1957; s. Michael and Catherine Delucca; m. Roberta Ricci, May 11, 1998. BA, Columbia U., 1982; MA, Johns Hopkins U., 1995, PhD, 1998. Freelance writer, translator, from 1984; vis. lectr. Johns Hopkins U., Balt., 1991-95, Duke U., Durham, N.C., 1997-99. Contbr. articles to profl. jours. Fullbright fellow, 1997; Mellon fellow, 1997. Mem. MLA, Am. Assn. Italian Studies. Avocation: writing. Died July 6, 2007.

DEL VALLE, JUAN, paper company executive; b. Colon, Republic of Panama, Mar. 4, 1933; s. William A. and Vina (Saunders) del V.; m. Wendy Hobart, Sept. 4, 1954; children: Cristina Cross, Tracy Saunders. BS, Yale U., 1953; MBA, Harvard U., 1958. Engr. Weyerhauser Co., Longview, Wash., 1958-62; various positions Boise Cascade Corp., 1962-81; pres. Port Townsend Paper Corp., Bainbridge Island, Wash., from 1983. Served to lt. (j.g.) USN, 1953-56. Home: Bainbridge Is, Wash. Died July 15, 2007.

DEMAREE, DAVID HARRY, utilities executive; b. Chgo., Oct. 17, 1939; s. Harry Stambough and Alve (Barnes) D.; m. Brenda Faye Locke, Mar. 2, 1962; children: David Christopher, Dawn Claire. BS in Math., Ga. State U., 1965; grad., U. Wis., 1972; diploma, Grad. Sch. Banking. Audit officer Continental Ill. Bank & Trust Co., Chgo., 1966-73; v.p. Utilities, Inc., Northbrook, Ill., 1973-85, v.p. ops., sec., 1985-94, sr. v.p., sec., from 1994. Cons. USAF, Chgo., 1984; expert witness 11 state utility commns. water and sewer utilities. Speaker on disaster planning Nat. Assn. of Regulatory Utility Commrs. Mem. Am. Water Works Assn., Nat. Assn. Water Cos., Lake Barrington Shores Country Club, Mission Hills Country Club, N. Suburban YMCA, Navy League, Ducks Unltd., Phi Kappa Tau Alumni Assn. (Chgo. chpt. pres. 1968-73), Phi Kappa Tau (bd. govs. 1963-64). Republican. Episcopalian (vestry). Avocations: sailing, golf, tennis, fishing. Home: Barrington, Ill. Died June 22, 2007.

DE MARGERIE, CHRISTOPHE, oil industry executive; b. Mareuil-sur-Lay, France, Aug. 6, 1951; Degree, Ecole Supérieure de Commerce. Joined financial divsn. TOTAL SA, Courbevoie, France, 1974, financial mgr. exploration and prodn. subsidiaries, group treas., 1987, finance dir. then v.p Middle East, pres. Middle East to sr. v.p. Trading and Middle East divsn., 1990—92, mem. mgmt. com., 1992, pres. exploration and prodn. Totalfina, 1995, mem. exec. com., 1999—2014, sr. v.p. exploration and prodn. TotalfinaElf, 2000—02, pres. exploration and prodn. TotalFinaElf (became Total in 2003), 2002—07, chmn. exec. com., CEO, 2007—10, chmn., CEO, 2010—14. Bd. dirs. TOTAL SA, 2006—14, BNP Paribas, 2013—14. Died Oct. 21, 2014.

DEMIRAY, TANEL, computer company executive consultant; b. Istanbul, Turkey, Nov. 30, 1946; came to U.S., 1979; s. Ibrahim and Nermin (Baydargil) D. BS, Liverpool U., Eng., 1970; MSc, Aberystwyth U., Wales, 1972. Asst. prof. Aberdeen Computer Ctr., Scotland, 1974-75, computer cons., 1976-76; founder, dept. head BIMSA Operational Rsch. Dept., Istanbul, Turkey, 1976-79; pres. Tanel Electronics, Inc., New Hyde Park, N.Y., from 1980, Tanel Computer Consultants, New Hyde Park, from 1980. Author: How to Use BMD Program, 1975, How to Use SPSS Program, 1976. Mem. Am. Friends of Turkey, New Hyde Park Lions Club, The World Trade Club N.Y. Died Dec. 11, 2006.

DEMIREL, SÜLEYMAN, former president of Turkey; b. Isparta, Turkey, Nov. 1, 1924; m. Nazmiye Demirel, 1948 (dec. 2013). Grad. civil engr., Istanbu Tech. U., 1948; postgrad., U.S. Registered profl. engr. Worker, U.S.A., 1949-51, 54-55; with Dir. Gen. Elec. Studies, Ankara, Turkey, 1950-52; engr. in charge building various hydroelectric schemes, 1952-54; head Dept. of Dams, dir. gen. water control, 1954-55; dir. State Hydraulics Adminstrn., 1955-60; teacher English Middle East Tech. U., 1960-64; pvt. practice, cons. to Morrison-Knudsen, 1961-65; dep. prime min., leader Justice Party Ankara, 1964—81; leader True Path Party, 1987—93; prime min. Republic of Turkey, Ankara, 1965-71, 75-77, 1979-80, 91-93, pres., 1993—2000. Author books, political essays, articles. Chmn. True Path Party, 1987. D.W. Eisenhower fellow, U.S., 1955. Died June 17, 2015.

DEMPSEY, JAMES RAYMON, manufacturing executive; b. Red Bay, Ala., Oct. 4, 1921; s. Newman W. and Maude (Berry) D.; m. Dolores Barnes, Jan. 19, 1943 (dec. Sept. 1997); children: Susan, David Barnes, Anne. Student, U. Ala., 1937—39; BS, U.S. Mil. Acad., 1943; MS, U. Mich., 1947, D (hon.) of Engring., 1964. Commd. 2d lt. U.S. Army, 1943; advanced through grades to lt. col. USAF, 1951; with photo reconnaissance squadron Eng., France, World War II; squadron comdr., 1945; guided missiles project officer, then chief guided missile projects (Research and Devel. Directorate, Air Force Hdqrs.), 1948- 49; exec. officer to (Dep. Chief Staff for Devel.), 1950-51; chief project sect. (Air Force Missile Test Center), Patrick AFB, Fla., then operations officer missile test range, 1951-53, resigned, 1953; asst. to v.p. planning Convair div. Gen. Dynamics Corp., 1953-54; dir. Gen. Dynamics Corp. (Atlas program), 1954-57; mgr. Gen. Dynamics Corp. (Convair-Astronautics div.), 1957-58; v.p. Gen. Dynamics Corp. (Convair div.), 1958-61; sr. v.p. Gen. Dynamics Corp.; pres. Gen. Dynamics Astronautics, 1961-65, Gen. Dynamics Convair, 1965-66; v.p. missiles, space and electronics group Avco Corp., 1966-68, v.p., group exec. govt. products group, 1968-75; pres. Digital Broadcasting Corp., 1978-79; mng. partner J.J. Finnigan Industries, Duluth, Ga., 1978-85; pres. Southeastern Rail Car Co., 1986-89; pvt. investor, from 1990. Trustee Phoenix Series Fund, 1968-91, Big Edge Series Fund, 1985-91, Phoenix Multi-Portfolio Fund, 1989-91, Precious Metal Holdings, 1980-93, Keystone Internat., 1987-93; chmn. bd. Transatlantic Capital Corp., Transatlantic Investment Corp., 1984-86; spl. com. on space tech. NASA Decorated Air medal with clusters, D.F.C.; Croix de Guerre (France); recipient Disting. Grad. award U.S. Mil. Acad., 2002 Fellow AIAA, Am. Astronaut. Soc.; mem. Air Force Assn. (bd. dirs. 1958-59), Burning Tree Club, Congl. Country Club. Home: Potomac, Md. Died Apr. 15, 2014.

DEMPSEY, JERRY (JEROME RICHARD DEMPSEY), retired state legislator; b. Henderson, Minn., Apr. 21, 1933; s. Mark & Mabel Dempsey; m. Joanne T. Mangan, June 13, 1959 (dec.); children: Nicholas, Mark, Catherine, Patrick BA in Edn., U. St. Thomas, 1955; MA in Edn., U. Wis., River Falls, 1976; Specialist degree in Edn. Adminstrn., Winona State U., 1976. Social studies tchr. Hastings Sr. High Sch., 1960—74; asst. prin. Hastings Jr. High Sch., 1974—93; mem. Dist. 29A Minn. House of Reps., 1993—2006. Served in US Army, 1955—57. Republican. Home: Hastings, Minn. Died Jan. 14, 2015.

DEMUN, TAYLOR K., military officer; b. Shreveport, La., Dec. 13, 1929; s. John Russel and Audrey May (Taylor) DeM.; m. LaVolla Mae Light, Mar. 13, 1953; children: Kory, Warren, Eric, Nancy. BS, Oreg. State U., 1952; MBA, U. Puget Sound, 1980. Commd. ensign U.S. Navy, 1952, advanced through grades to capt., 1972, comdg. officer USS Andrew Jackson Charleston, S.C., 1966-70, ret., 1978; exhbn. mgr. Seattle Trade Ctr., from 1978. Mem. King County Fair Bd., 1985-86; bd. dirs. Seattle Sea Fair, 1987. Mem. Navy League of U.S. (pres. Seattle Council 1986, outstanding Council award 1986, nat. bd. dirs. 1987—), Submarine League, Nat. Assn. Exhbn. Mgrs., Sigma Alpha Epsilon (pres. Oreg. State U. chpt. 1951-52). Home: Mercer Island, Wash. Died Aug. 28, 2007.

DENG, LIQUN (XIAPING DENG), Chinese government official; b. Guidong County, Hunan Province, China, 1914; m. Luo Liyun (dec.); children: Yingtao Ding(dec.) , Luo

Xiaoyun; 2 children from previous marriage. Mem. Chinese Communist Party (CCP), from 1936; dir. Edn. Marxism-Leninism Inst., Propaganda Dept. CCP Jibei Prefecture Com., Policy Rsch. Office of CCP Liaoning Provincial Com., Propaganda Dept. of Xinjiang Bur. under CCP Ctrl. Com., Policy Rsch. Section under CCP Ctrl. Com., 1981, CCP Ctrl. Com. Propaganda Dept., 1982—85; dep. dir. Gen. Office of Fin. and Econ. Commn. of N.E. China; chmn. Cultural and Edn. Com. of Xinjiang Regional People's Com. after the founding of People's Republic of China in 1949; editor and dep. editor-in-chief Red Flag; v.p. Acad. of Social Sciences, 1978; adv. Soc. for Study of Econ. of Minority Areas, 1981, Soc. of Labor Sci., 1982, Soc. for Study of Workers' Polit. and Ideological Work; mem. 12th CCP Ctrl. Com., 1982, Secretariat, 1982—87; vice-chmn. Nat. Com. for Promoting Socialist Ethics, 1983; head CCP Ctrl. Leading Grp. for Edn. of Cadres, 1985; mem. CCP Ctrl. Adv. Commn., 1987; dep. head CCP Ctrl. Com. Party Bldg. Group, from 1990, CCP Ctrl. Com. Leading Grp. for Party History Work, from 1994; hon. pres. Soc. for Studies on Party Members, from 1991. Died Feb. 10, 2015.

DENHAM, ALICE, writer; b. Jacksonville, Fla., Jan. 21, 1927; d. T.B. Simkins and Leila Meggs Denham; first marriage ended in a divorce; m. John Mueller. Grad., U. NC, 1949; Master's Degree in English, U. Rochester. Author: My Darling from the Lions, 1967-68, Coming Together, 1969-70, AMO, 1974-75, (memoir) Sleeping With Bad Boys: A Juicy Tell-All of Literary New York in the Fifties and Sixties, 2006, Secrets of San Miguel, 2013; contbr. articles and short stories various pubs. Home: New York, NY. Died Jan. 27, 2016.

DENISON, GILBERT WALTER, chemical engineer, administrator; b. Oklahoma City, Okla., Oct. 7, 1929; s. Henry Clark and Mary Ella (McBride) D.; m. Agatha Lorena Bitsche, Nov. 23, 1956; children: Brian, Gregory, Alice, Ronald. BS in Chem. Engring., U. Okla., 1957, MS in Chem. Engring., 1958, PhD, 1962. Registered profl. engr., Okla. Rsch. engr. Esso Rsch. & Engring., Linden, N.J., 1962-65; lab. mgr. J.M. Huber, Borger, Tex., 1965-66; sr. devel. engr. Continental Oil, Ponca City, Okla., 1966-69; R&D mgr. Dart Industries, Inc., Paramus, N.J., 1969-72; bus. cons. Raymond Chem. Co., Toledo, Ohio, 1972-73; various rsch. and engring. positons Chemical and Engring. Cos., Cleve., 1973-87; cons. in chem. engring. Cleve., also Okla., 1987-95; v.p. ops. and devel. Fed. Recycling Techs., Inc., Norman, Okla., from 1995. Inventor: formula for specialty adhesive for supporting mining roofs; co-inventor process for EPDM rubber, process method and system for recovering valuable products from scrap tires. With USMC, 1944-46, 50-52, PTO. Monsanto scholar, 1956-57, NSF fellow, 1957-59, NSF grantee, 1959-62. Mem. AIChE, Am. Chem. Soc. Republican. Achievements include development and design of process for manufacturing flame retardant; refinement, engineering and formulation of manufacturing process for ABS polymer; development of equipment and field test procedures for pipeline sealing process. Died Aug. 21, 2007.

DENNIS, BARBARA ANN, lawyer, criminal justice educator; b. Newark, July 28, 1950; d. Chandler Malcolm and Lois Venice (Brown) D. BA, Upsala Coll., East Orange, NJ, 1972; JD, Villanova U., 1976. Bar: Pa. 1976, N.J. 1978, U.S. Dist. Ct. N.J. 1978. Instr. criminal justice Trenton (N.J.) State Coll., 1976-78; spl. agt. FBI, NYC, 1978-89; pvt. practice East Orange and West Orange, N.J., from 1981; asst. prof. criminal justice County Coll. Morris, Randolph, N.J., from 1989. Mem. legal edn. and bar admission com. Pa. Bar, 1976-83. Contbr. articles to profl. jours. Speaker County Coll. Morris Speaker Bur., 1989—; mentor East Orange Entrepreneur Club, 1989—. Mem. NAFE, Greater Newark C. of C. (speaker 1990—), Order Eastern Star. Avocations: computers, calligraphy, drawing, music, writing. Died Apr. 25, 2007.

DENNISON, STANLEY SCOTT, retired forest products company executive, consultant; b. Mitchelville, Md., Sept. 1, 1920; s. Ralph Stanford and Cora Adeline (Scott) D.; m. Sharon Lee Johnson, June 1, 1983; 1 stepchild, Whitney C. Maddox; children by previous marriage: Judith Dennison Tucci (dec.), Joan Dennison Daffron, Joyce Dennison Bischoff. Ed., Columbia Union Coll., 1938; BS, Calif. We. U., 1976, MS, 1979, PhD, 1983. Operative builder Dennison Co., 1939-43; traffic rep. U.P. R.R., 1943-49; v.p. Arlington Millwork, Va., 1949-52, Internat. Filling Machine Co., Petersburg, Va., 1952-57, Atlanta Oak Flooring Co., 1957-62; regional mgr. Ga.-Pacific Corp., Portland, Oreg., 1962-70, v.p., 1970-78, sr. v.p., 1978-82, exec. v.p., 1982-85; exec. mgmt. cons., from 1985. Past trustee Stonehill Coll., U. Portland, Calif. Western U.; bd. dirs. Aquinas Ctr. Theology at Emory U., Atlanta. Mem. Capital City Club (Atlanta), Commerce Club (Atlanta), Alpha Kappa Psi. Democrat. Roman Catholic. Home: Norfolk, Va. Died Dec. 21, 2006.

DENTON, WILLIAM LEWIS, performing arts company administrator; b. San Diego, July 25, 1932; s. D. Lewis and Ruth Virginia (Goodbody) D. BA, San Diego State U., 1957. Mng. dir. Atlanta Symphony, 1968-70, Nat. Symphony, Washington, 1970-77; exec. dir. Ill. Arts Coun., 1977-78; gen. mgr. San Diego Symphony, 1964-68, 80-82; exec. dir. Midsummer Mozart Festival, San Francisco, from 1986. Adj. prof. Gov's. State U., Springfield, Ill., 1976-78. With USAF, 1950-54. Fisher fellow, N.Y., 1971-75. Mem. Am. Symphony League (treas. 1972-74), Marines Meml. Democrat. Avocation: reading. Home: Palm Springs, Calif. Died July 4, 2007.

DEPALMA, GINA, chef; b. NY; BA in Polit. Sci., Coll. New Rochelle. Apprentice Chanterelle; pastry cook Gramercy Park Hotel; pastry chef The Cub Room, Babbo, NYC, 1998—2013. Wrote a dessert chapter, Babbo Cookbook, 2002; author: Dolce Italiano, Desserts From the Babbo Kitchen, 2007; writer (weekly column) Seriously Italian for the website Serious Eats; contbr. Recipient Outstanding Pastry Chef award, James Beard Found., 2009; named Chef of Yr., Bon Appetit Mag., 2008; named one of Ten Best Pastry Chefs in America, Pastry Art & Design Mag., 2005. Died Dec. 27, 2015.

DEPEW, CAROL ANN, pharmaceutical sales representative; b. Kalamazoo, Mar. 2, 1962; d. Norman Sylvester and Margaret Ann (Mitscher) D. BA, U. Tenn., Knoxville, Tenn., 1986; MEd, U. Va., 1988. Nat. cert. counselor. Transition resource specialist Project PERT, Woodrow Wilson Rehab. Ctr., Fishersville, Va., 1989-1991; social worker Victor C. Newman Sch., Chgo., 1992-93; marriage and family couns. Community Svcs. Bd., Appomattor, VA, 1993-94; sales rep. Eli Lilly Co., 1994-98, Hoffman LaRoche, from 1999. Home: Lynchburg, Va. Died May 13, 2007.

DEROO, HENRY VALERE, dentist; b. Regina, Sask., Can., Dec. 13, 1928; came to U.S., 1964; s. Valere Cornelius and Lydia (Sapergia) D.; m. Llewella Pearl Roberts, Sept. 2, 1951; children: Carol Marie, Lynelle Fay. BSc, 1955, DDS, 1960. Med. technician Chinese Hosp., San Francisco, 1957-60; pvt. practice dentistry Williamshake, B.W.I., Can., 1960-64, Lancaster, Calif., from 1964. Mem. ADA, Calif. Dental Assn., Acad. Gen. Dentistry. Seventh-day Adventist. Avocations: making and decorating european style wedding cakes, woodworking, flying. Died Jan. 23, 2007.

DERTHICK, MARTHA ANN, political science educator; b. Cleve., June 20, 1933; d. Everest Plum and Mabel Esther (Carmichael) D. BA, Hiram Coll., 1954; MA, Radcliffe Coll., 1956, PhD, 1962. Historian Joint Chiefs of Staff, Washington, 1957-58; lectr. Dartmouth Coll., Hanover, N.H., 1963, Stanford U., Palo Alto, Calif., 1963-64; from instr. to asst. prof. Harvard U., Cambridge, Mass., 1964-70; assoc. prof. Boston Coll., Chestnut Hill, Mass., 1970-71; sr. fellow Brookings Inst., Washington, 1971-83, dir. govtl. studies, 1978-83; Julia Allen Cooper prof. govt. and fgn. affairs U. Va., Charlottesville, 1983—99. Mem. Congl. Panel on Social Security Orgn., Washington, 1984; mem. Pres. Commn. on Campus Unrest, Washington, 1970; mem. Adminstrv. Conf. of U.S. Author: Between State and Nation, 1974, Uncontrollable Spending for Social Services Grants, 1975, Policymaking for Social Security, 1979 (Brownlow award 1980), (with others) Politics of Deregulation, 1985 (Brownlow award 1986), Agency under Stress, 1990 Trustee Hiram (Ohio) Coll., 1979—. Guggenheim fellow, 1981-82, fellow Ctr. Advanced Study in Behavioral Scis., Palo Alto, 1981-82. Mem. Am. Polit. Sci. Assn. (v.p. 1979, Kammerer prize 1980, Gaus award 1992), Nat. Acad. Social Ins., Am. Acad. Arts and Scis. Home: Charlottesville, Va. Died Jan. 12, 2015.

DE SANTIS, MARY ANN THERESA, nurse; b. Phila., Mar. 23, 1938; d. Americus Anthony and Mary Theresa (McCann) De S.; (div.); 1 child, Christopher. BS, St. Joseph's Coll., 1960; RN, St. Francis Coll., 1963; MS, U. Pa., 1980, PhD, 1988. RN, N.J., Pa. Tchr. Phila. Diocese, 1955-60; RN Burdette Tomlin Hosp., Cape May Court House, N.J., 1963-68; tchr. Cape May County Vocat. Sch., Cape May Court House, 1968-70; head nurse VA Hosp., Lyons, N.J., 1970-71; instr. Union County Coll., Scotch Plains, N.J., 1971-75, Cape May County Vocat. Sch., 1975-80, 84-86; sch. nurse St. Ann's Sch., Wildwood, N.J., 1980-84; nurse mgr. Burdette Tomlin Hosp., 1986-89; dir. nurses Cape May Care Ctr., Cape May Court House, 1989-91; dir. residential svcs., geriatric wellness Harvest Village, Atco, N.J., from 1991; dir. nurisng Park Pleasant Health Care Facility, Phila. Bd. Mem. Cape May County Mental Health, 1984-88. Mem. Am. Nurses Assn., Oncology Assn., Gerontology Assn. N.J., N.J. Nurses Assn., Moose. Republican. Roman Catholic. Home: Laurel Spgs, NJ. Died Feb. 5, 2007.

DESOER, CHARLES AUGUSTE, electrical engineer; b. Ixelles, Belgium, Jan. 11, 1926; came to U.S., 1949, naturalized, 1958; s. Jean Charles and Yvonne Louise (Peltzer) D.; m. Jacqueline K. Johnson, July 21, 1966; children: Marc J., Michele M., Craig M. Ingenieur Radio-Electricien, U. Liege, 1949, DSc (hon.), 1976; DSc in Elec. Engring, MIT, 1953. Rsch. asst. MIT, Cambridge, 1951—53; mem. tech. staff Bell Telephone Labs., Murray Hill, NJ, 1953—58; assoc. prof. elec. engring. and computer scis. U. Calif., Berkeley, 1958—62, prof., 1962—91, prof. emeritus, from 1991, Miller rsch. prof., 1970—71. Author: (with L. A. Zadeh) Linear System Theory, 1963, (with E. S. Kuh) Basic Circuit Theory, 1969, (with M. Vidyasagar) Feedback Systems: Input Output Properties, 1973, Notes for a Second Course on Linear Systems, 1970, (with F. M. Callier) Multivariable Feedback Systems, 1982, (with L.O. Chua and E.S. Kuh) Linear and Nonlinear Circuits, 1987, (with A.N. Gündes) Algebraic Theory of Linear Feedback Systems with Full and Decentralized Compensation, 1990, (with F.M. Callier) Linear System Theory, 1991; contbr. numerous articles on systems and circuits to profl. jours. Served with Belgian Arty., 1944-45. Decorated Vol.'s medal; recipient Best Paper prize 2d Joint Automatic Control Conf., 1962, medal U. Liège, 1976, Disting. Tchg. award U. Calif., Berkeley, 1971, Prix Montefiore Inst. Montefiore, 1975; Field award in control sci. and engring., 1986, Am. Automatic Control Coun. Edn. award, 1983, Berkeley Citation, 1992; Guggenheim fellow, 1970-71. Fellow IEEE (Edn. medal 1975, Outstanding Paper award 1979), AAAS.; mem. IEEE Control Sys. Soc., IEEE Circuits and Systems Soc. (Mac Van Valkenburg award 1996), Nat. Acad. Engring., Am. Math. Soc. Died Nov. 1, 2010.

DE SOTO, ERNEST FRANK, artist, writer; b. Tucson, Oct. 26, 1923; s. Robert Carlos and Artemisa Ortiz Soto; m. Rosalind Braun, Dec. 15, 1950 (div. June 1962); m. Josephine Mary Panyk, Aug. 6, 1962. Cert., Chouniard Art Sch., LA, 1942—43, WWII Camoflege Tech., 1943—46, Chouniard Art Sch., 1946—47; BFA, U. Ill., 1961. Owner, dir. Ernest F. de Soto Workshop, San Francisco, 1978-93; master printer Edits. Press, San Francisco, 1972-76, Collectors Press, San Francisco, 1967-72. Pub.: (graphics) Limited Editions, 1978-93; book illustrator: Robin Crusoe, Folk Tales of Mexico, 1957-58; collections: South Pacific Theatre War. Bd. trustees Mex. Mus., San Francisco, 1987-93; art instr. Western Res. U., Cleve., 1952-53, U. Ill., Urbana, 1954-62. Sgt. USAF, 1943-46, PTO. Recipient Award of Honor, San Francisco Arts Commn., Bank of Am., 1982; rsch. tech. lithography grantee Ford Found., U. Ill., 1958, Master Printer Ford Found. grantee Tamarind Lithography Workshop, 1965-67. Avocations: art, painting, graphics. Home: Tucson, Ariz. Died Dec. 29, 2014.

D'ESPAGNAT, BERNARD, theoretical physicist, science philosopher; b. Fourmagnac, France, Aug. 22, 1921; s. Georges and Marguerite (de Genestet) d'Espagnat; m. May de Schoutheete de Tervant, 1950 (dec. 2012); children: Isabelle Mersier, Anne Bachy. PhD in Physics, Ecole Polytechnique and the Institut Henri Poincaré, 1950. Researcher Centre National de Recherche Scientifique (CNRS), 1947—57; worked with Enrico Fermi Chgo., 1951—52; worked with Niels Bohr Inst. in Copenhagen, 1953—54; with Centre d'Etudes de Recherches Nucleaires (CERN), Geneva; theoretical physicist European Organization for Nuclear Rsch., 1954—59; sr. lectr., faculty of sci. U. Paris (now known as U. Paris-Sud), Orsay, 1959—87, emeritus prof., 1987—2015. Dir., lab. theoretical physics and elementary particles U. Paris XI, Orsay, 1980—87; vis. prof. U. Tex., Austin, 1977, U. Calif., Santa Barbara, 1984. Author: Conceptual Foundations of Quantum Mechanics, 1971, Nonseparability and the Tentative Descriptions of Reality, 1974, On Physics and Philosophy, 2006; author of several other books. Recipient Templeton prize, 2009. Mem.: French Acad. Moral and Polit. Sciences, Brussels Internat. Acad. (Philosopher of Sci.). Died Aug. 1, 2015.

DESTEPHANO, ARTHUR JOHN, human resources executive; b. Chgo., Feb. 3, 1939; s. Anthony Paul and Marie (Fraveletti) D.; m. Carmylle Stelter, Mar. 29, 1963 (div. July 1974); 1 child, Deanne; m. Ruth P. Destephano, Nov. 20, 1983; children: Amanda, Anthony. BS in Adminstrn., Lewis U., 1961; MS, Loyola U., Chgo., 1977. Personnel mgr. S&C Electric Co., Chgo., 1966-72; dir. employee relations Consolidated Packaging, Chgo., 1972-77; dir. human resources Thomas Internat., Niles, Ill., 1977-79; dir. employee rels. TRW Niehoff, Chgo., 1979-84; v.p. human resources John Crane, Inc., Morton Grove, Ill., 1984-88; pres. H.R. Cons., Inc., Crystal Lake, Ill., from 1988. Dir. Niles Twp. Sheltered Workshop, Niles, Ill., 1984-87. Campaign chmn. Skokie Valley Indsl. Assn., 1984—. 2d lt. U.S. Army, 1961-63. Mem. Midwest Personnel Mgmt. Assn. (mem. bd. 1985, pres. 1988). Avocations: farming, harness racing. Home: Schaumburg, Ill. Died Apr. 18, 2007.

DEVINE, PATRICK CAMPBELL, urologist, educator; b. Norfolk, Va., June 7, 1925; s. Charles Joseph and Julia Campbell Devine; m. Linda Marie Dofflemoyer, June 13, 1953; children: Catherine, Patrick Jr., Michael, William. BA, Washington and Lee U., 1948; MD, U. Va., 1953. Diplomate Am. Bd. Urology. Intern surgery U. Va. Hosp., Charlottesville, 1953-54, resident urology, 1954-57; prof. dept. urology Ea. Va. Med. Sch., from 1975. Cons. Lake Taylor City Hosp., Norfolk, Va., U.S. Navy Med. Ctr., Portsmouth, Va., VA Ctr., Hampton, Va.; active staff Med. Ctr. Hosps., Inc., DePau Hosp., Children's Hosp. of the King's Daughters; vis. prof. and presenter in field. Contbr. chpts. to books and articles to profl. jours. With U.S. Army, 1944-46. Fellow ACS, Am. Soc. Plastic and Reconstructive Surgeons, Inc. (assoc.), Am. Acad. Pediat.; mem. AAAS, AMA, Am. Assn. Clin. Urologists, Assn. Am. Med. Colls., Am. Urol. Assn. (pres. Mid-Atlantic sect. 1973-74, hon. mem. Southeastern sect.), Med. Soc. Va., Va. Urol. Soc., Norfolk Acad. Medicine, Tidewater Urol. Assn., Soc. Internat. D'Urologie, Confedn. Am. de Urologia, Soc. for Pediat. Urology, Soc. Univ. Urologists, So. Soc. Urologic Surgeons, So. Med. Assn., Seaboard Med. Assn., Norfolk Yacht and Country Club, Harbor Club, Norfolk C. of C., Norfolk German Soc., Princess Anne Country Club. Roman Catholic. Avocations: golf, hunting. Home: Virginia Beach, Va. Died Apr. 12, 2007.

DEW, ALVIN GLEN, salesperson; b. Polo, Ill., Aug. 4, 1920; s. Byron Elmer and Maybelle Elizabeth (Coursey) D.; m. Helen Elizabeth O'Brien, Feb. 22, 1943; children: Gary Allan, Bradley James. Student, No. Ill. U., 1953-55. Sales clk. A&P Foods, Oregon, Ill., 1934-38, Fischer's Book Store, Oregon, 1938-40; with DeKalb (Ill.) Ogle Telephone Co., 1940-42, installer, repairman, 1946-50; carpet installer DeLano Floor Corp., DeKalb, 1952-64; salesperson, installer Glen Dew Floor Corp., DeKalb, 1965-80. Salesperson Electrolux Corp., Elgin, Ill., 1955—. Mem. Pres.'s Task Force, Washington, 1983-90. Staff sgt. USAF, 1942-46, 50-51. Recipient Lions Internat. Highest award, 1991; Melvin Jones fellow. Mem. Lions (pres. DeKalb chpt. 1984-85, bd. dirs. 1985—, Lion of the Yr. 1984-85, 86-87, 88-89, Sales award 1986-90, Pres.'s Citation 1981-82). Republican. Mem. Christian Ch. Avocations: antique autos, parades. Home: Saint Charles, Ill. Died Nov. 3, 2006.

DEZURKO, EDWARD ROBERT, art educator; b. NYC, Mar. 25, 1913; s. Edward and Hattie (Lehman) DeZ.; m. Madith Smith, July 30, 1938 (div. 1962); children: Robin Klein, Sandra Krchnak; m. Grace Crump, Sept. 5, 1964. BS in Edn., U. Ill., 1939, BS in Arch., 1940; MS in Arch., Columbia U., 1942; PhD, NYU, 1954. former registered arch. Tchr. Champaign (Ill.) H.S., 1941; tchr. arch. Kans. State Coll., Manhattan, 1942-47, Rice U., Houston, 1947-62; head dept. art Austin Coll., Sherman, Tex., 1962-66; prof. art, grad. coord. U. Ga., Athens, 1966-79, emeritus prof. art, from 1979. Draftsman, illustrator U.S. Naval Ordnance Lab., Washington, 1943-44. Author: Early Kansas Churches, 1949, Origins of Functionalist Theory, 1957, Vistas and Mazes, 1997, Through Cracks in the Wall, 2001; co-author: Man and the Cultural World, 1947; contbr. articles to profl. jours. Recipient Ga. Poet of Yr. award Nat. League Am. Pen Women, 1997, Internat. Order of Merit award. Mem. AIA, Ga. Poetry Soc., Author's Club Athens, Pi Delta Phi, Zeta Zeta. Avocations: poetry, gardening, travel. Home: Fayetteville, NY. Died July 15, 2007.

DIAMANDOPOULOS, PETER, philosophy professor, academic executive, consultant; b. Herakleion, Crete, Greece, Sept. 1, 1928; came to U.S., 1948, naturalized, 1964; s. Theodore George and Rita (Mouzenides) D.; m. Maria Stanton, 1949 (div. 1980); children: Theodoros, Cybele, Ariadne, Mary (stepchild) Diploma with honors, Athens Coll., 1947; AB cum laude, Harvard Coll., 1951, MA, 1956; PhD, Harvard U., 1957; LHD (hon.), Am. Internat. Coll., 1988. Instr. philosophy Bates Coll., 1958; instr., then asst. prof. philosophy U. Md., 1958-62; mem. faculty Brandeis U., 1962-77, prof. philosophy, 1964-77, dean faculty, 1965-71, chmn. dept. philosophy and history of ideas, 1972-76, faculty mem. bd. trustees, 1974-77; pres. Calif. State U.-Sonoma, 1977-83, pres. emeritus, from 1983; univ. trustees' prof. Calif. State U., San Francisco, 1983-85; pres., trustee Adelphi U., Garden City, NY, 1985—97; prof. philosophy and humanities, spl. asst. to pres. Boston U., 1998—2008. Dir. internat. studies Adlai Stevenson Inst., Chgo., 1969-74; cons. history of Sci. Smithsonian Inst., 1959-62; bd. dirs. Atlantic Bank of NY; lectr. to profl., learned socs., acad. instns., Art Gallery IKAROS Inc., NYC Contbr. articles to profl. jours. Trustee Adelphi Acad., Athens Coll., 1987—2013; chmn., bd. advisers US Command and Gen. Staff Coll., 1987. Recipient Cum Laude Soc. award Am. Internat. Coll., 1988,; named Outstanding Tchr., Confucius Inst. Am., 1983; Teschemacher fellow in classics and philosophy Harvard U., 1954-57; sr. fellow Adlai Stevenson Inst. for Internat. Studies, 1969-74. Mem. Am. Philol. Assn., Am. Philos. Assn., MIND Assn., Aristotelian Soc., Hellenic Soc., Assn. Am. Colls., Soc. for Promotion Hellenic Studies (London), Assn. Governing Bds. Univs. and Colls., NY Acad. Scis., Nat. Assn. Scholars (bd. Advisors), The Links, Harvard Club of NYC, Art Gallery, Ikaros, Inc. (NYC & Athens, Elounda, Crete) (pres.), The Links, Union League Club NYC, Harvard Club NYC. Avocations: art appraising, trading, collecting. Died Apr. 1, 2015.

DIAZ-CRUZ, MARIO, III, lawyer; b. Havana, Cuba, 1946; BBA cum laude, U. Miami, 1967; JD, Harvard U., 1970. Bar: NY 1971. Ptnr., corp. dept., past mem. policy com., chair, L.Am. practice group, chair benefit investment com. Dorsey & Whitney LLP, NYC, from 1995. Trustee Cath. Charities Archdiocese NY; chmn. emeritus Spain-US C. of C. Mem.: ABA, Assn. Bar City NY, NY State Bar Assn. Died Sept. 21, 2015.

DICKINSON, PETER (PETER MALCOLM DE BRISSAC DICKINSON), author; b. Livingstone, England, Dec. 16, 1927; m. Mary Rose Barnard (dec. 1988); children: Philippa, Polly, John, James; m. Robin McKinley. B in English, King's Coll., Cambridge, 1951. Asst. editor Punch mag., London, 1952-69. Author: Skin Deep, 1968, The Weathermonger, 1968, A Pride of Heroes, 1969, Heartsease, 1969, The Seals, 1970, The Devil's Children, 1970, Sleep and His Brother, 1971, Emma Tupper's Diary, 1971, The Lizard in the Cup, 1972, The Dancing Bear, 1972, The Green Gene, 1973, The Gift, 1973, The Iron Lion, 1973, The Poison Oracle, 1974, Chance, Luck and Destiny, 1975, The Lively Dead, 1975, The Blue Hawk, 1976, King and Joker, 1976, Annerton Pit, 1977, Waling Dead, 1977, Hepzibah, 1978, One Foot in the Grave, 1979, Tulku, 1979, The Flight of the Dragons, 1979, City of Gold, 1980 (Carnegie Medal), A Summer in the Twenties, 1981, The Last House-Party, 1982, Healer, 1983, Hindsight, 1983, Death of a Unicorn, 1984, A Box of Nothing, 1985, Tefuga, 1986, Perfect Fallows, 1988, Merlin Dreams, 1988, Eva, 1988, Skeleton-in-Waiting, 1989, Some Deaths Before Dying, 1999 Mem. Soc. Authors (chmn. 1979-80). Died Dec. 16, 2015.

DICKSON, NANCY STARR, retired elementary school educator; b. Frankfort, Ind., Apr. 3, 1936; d. Harley Ledger and Olivia (Starr) F., (stepmother) Geneve (Daugherty) F.; m. Sam W. Dickson, Aug. 23, 1959; 1 child, Hal S. BS, Ball State U., Muncie, Ind., 1958, MA, 1964, cert. reading specialist, 1972. Cert. elem. tchr., Ind. Tchr. Edgelea Elem. Sch., Lafayette, Ind., 1958-59, McKinley Elem. Sch., Muncie, Ind., 1959-65; tchr. spl. reading Garfield Elem. Sch., Muncie, Ind., 1967-78, reading specialist, 1996-98, Garfield Elem., Muncie, Ind., 1978-96; reading supr., tutor trainer 4 elem. schs., Muncie, Ind., 1978—96; ret., 1998. Author (tchr.'s edition textbook): Our Language Today- Grade 3, 1966, Our Language Today- Grade 4, 1966. Mem. NEA (life), Internat. Reading Assn. (literacy award 1986), Ind. Reading Assn. (pres. 1996-97, coord. 6 couns. 1975—, outstanding svc. award 1986, 89), Muncie Area Reading Coun. (membership dir. 1974-96, past pres.), Ind. Tchrs. Assn., Muncie Tchrs. Assn., Ball State U. Women, Pi Lambda Theta (pres. 1988-90), Delta Kappa Gamma (pres. 1990-92), Alpha Sigma Alpha (pres. alumnae 1986-87, advisor 1986-95). Democrat. Methodist. Avocations: reading, sewing, swimming. Home: Muncie, Ind. Died Feb. 20, 2007.

DIEPHOLZ, DANIEL R., real estate consultant, accountant; b. Calif., Aug. 25, 1964; s. Eugene L. and Ruby J. (Forsch) D. BSBA in Acctg., Valparaiso U., 1985; MS in Real Estate with acad. honors, NYU, 1990. CPA, Calif.; lic. real estate broker, Calif. Auditor Blue Cross Calif., Woodland Hills, 1986-87; corp. fin. assoc., v.p. Bateman Eichler, Hill Richards Inc., L.A., NYC, 1987-89; real estate cons. Price Waterhouse, LA, 1990-96; founder Diepholz & Co., Indian Wells, Calif., from 1996. Chmn. bd. Taos Palms Inc., L.A., 1990—. Mem. ABA, Inst. of Mgmt. Accts., Nat. Assn. Accts. (bd. dirs. 1990-95). Democrat. Avocations: tennis, golf, sailing, swimming. Died Feb. 9, 2007.

DIESING, DONALD CARL, real estate broker; b. Manistee, Mich., Feb. 22, 1923; s. Otto Carl and Julia Alvina (Stevenson) D.; m. Wilma Regina Widing, July 23, 1945; children: David Alan, Daryl Lee. Student, Mich. State U., 1944; grad., U. Mich., 1956. Auctioneer, Scottville, Mich., 1940-44 and from 46; with Strout Realty, Diesing Realty, Scottville, from 1949. Pres. Manistee County Jr. Farm Bur., 1942-43; sec. Manistee Twp. Community Farm Bur., 1942-44; active Manistee County Planning Commn., 1944; various positions City of Scottville, 1958-62; active Mason County Cen. Sch. Found. Commn., Scottville, 1990. Tech. Sgt. U.S. Army, 1944-46. Mem. Mason-Oceana-Manistee Bd. Realtors (pres., Realtor of Yr. 1959, 79), Mich. Assn. Realtors, Nat. Assn. Realtors, Scottville C. of C. (bd. dirs.), Mich. State Auctioneers Assn. (pres. 1980), Nat. Auctioneers Assn., Rotary (Paul Harris fellow Scottville chpt. 1989). Republican. Lutheran. Avocations: travel, forestry, gardening, social games. Home: Scottville, Mich. Died Apr. 8, 2007.

DIETER-CONKLIN, NAN, retired astronomer; b. Springfield, Ill., June 10, 1926; BA, Gaucher coll., 1948; PhD, Harvard, 1958. Rsch. astronomer UC Berkeley, 1965—77. Author: Two Paths To Heaven's Gate, 2006. Recipient Women Air Force V.Glass award, USAF; Obs. fellow, Maria Mitchell Found., Grad. Study fellow, Harvard U., Astronomy Rsch. fellow, NSF. Died Nov. 16, 2014.

DIGGLE, RAYMOND HERBERT, JR., financial executive; b. Washington, Jan. 18, 1943; s. Raymond and Lucille (Lamb) D.; m. Martha Anne Rucker, June 25, 1966; children: Laura, Jennifer, Douglas. BBA, U. Mich., 1965, MBA, 1966; PhD, Ohio State U., 1971. CFA. CEO First Security Investment Mgmt., Salt Lake City, 1985-87; portfolio mgr. United Mgmt., Indpls., 1987-88; dir. rsch. Raffensperger Hughes, Indpls., 1988-92; v.p. rsch. R.W. Baird & Co., Indpls., 1992-94; dir. rsch. First of Mich. Corp., Detroit, from 1994. Bd. dirs. South Ind. Meth. Found., Indpls., 1992-94, Indpls. Ballet, 1991-94. Republican. Avocations: gardening, boating. Home: Ormond Beach, Fla. Died Apr. 21, 2007.

DIGGS, BEATRICE M., retired research assistant; b. Rochester, NY, Apr. 10, 1904; d. Alfred Mark and Agnes (Pettengill) Moshier; m. L. W. Diggs, Nov. 30, 1929 (dec.); children: Walter, Alice, John, Margaret. A, Wellesley Coll., 1926. Rsch. asst. U. Rochester, 1926—29, U. Tenn., Memphis, 1929—95; ret., 1995. Med. editor U. Tenn., Memphis, 1929—95. Mem.: AAUW (pres. 1942—43). Republican. Unitarian Universalist. Avocation: gardening. Home: Cordova, Tenn. Died Apr. 12, 2007.

DILLON, SALLY PIERSON, nursing educator; b. St. Joseph, Mich., Oct. 4, 1959; d. Donald Richard and Elizabeth Louise (Collins) Pierson; m. Bruce Arthur Dillon, Nov. 28, 1979; children: Donald Bruce, Michael Charles. AS, So. Missionary Coll., 1979; BS in Health Care Adminstrn., Columbia Union Coll., 1990. RN, Ill.; CCRN. Float nurse Mercy Med. Ctr., Chgo.; staff nurse critical care unit Meth. Med. Ctr., Peoria, Ill.; staff nurse-open heart Washington Adventist Hosp., Takoma Park, Md., asst. head nurse coronary care, critical care instr., 1992; asst. v.p. nursing Shenandoah County Meml. Hosp., Woodstock, Va., 1994; pres. BSJ Assocs., Timberville, Va. Freelance writer; instr., instr. trainer ARC; field supr. Pvt. Nurses Registry, Wilmette, Ill. Mem. AACN, Nat. Nurses Staff Devel. Orgn. (pres. Blue Ridge chpt.). Died Jan. 6, 2007.

DILLON, WILLIAM JOSEPH, small business owner; b. NYC, Oct. 21, 1938; s. William Joseph and Irene Jenny (Boyd) D.; m. Nadine Haskins, June 19, 1965. BSBA, Syracuse U., NY, 1960. Copywriter Popular Club Plan, Passaic, N.J., 1962-65, J.C. Penney, NYC, 1965-66; agy. liaison copy chief Consol. Edison, NYC, 1966-73; copywriter Fletcher Walker Gessell, Ridgewood, N.J., 1973-74; owner, mgr. Boyce Travel Svc., Ridgewood, from 1975. Pres. Fish of Ridgewood and vicinity, 1971, 73. Author: Moosings, 1977; playwrite, screenwriter lyrics Valhalla, 1992. Sch. dir. Upper Ridgewood Community Ch., 1973; bd. dirs. Community Chest of Ridgewood and vicinity, 1966-70, YMCA, Ridgewood, 1967-72. Capt. U.S. Army, 1960-66, ETO. Mem. Am. Soc. Travel Agys. Republican. Avocations: tennis, golf, sailing, bowling. Home: Ridgewood, NJ. Died Mar. 5, 2007.

DILLON, WILTON STERLING, anthropologist, foundation administrator; b. Yale, Okla., July 13, 1923; s. Earl Henry and Edith Holland (Canfield) D.; m. Virginia Leigh Harris, Jan. 20, 1956; 1 child, James Harris BA, U. Calif. Berkeley, 1951; postgrad., Inst. Ethnology, U. Paris, U. Leyden, 1951—52; PhD, Columbia U., 1961. News reporter Holdenville Daily News, Okla., 1936—41; info. specialist, civilian mem. Civil Info. and Edn. Sect. SCAP, Tokyo, 1946—49; vis. lectr. sociology and anthropology Hobart and William Smith Colls., Geneva, NY, 1953—54; staff anthropologist Japan Soc. N.Y.; also lectr. Japanese studies Fordham U., 1954; dir. Clearinghouse for Rsch. in Human Orgn., Soc. Applied Anthropology, NYC, 1954—56; exec. sec., dir. rsch. Phelps-Stokes Fund N.Y.; dir. rsch. project on higher edn. and African nationhood U. Ghana, 1957—63; vis. lectr. Columbia U., New Sch. Social Rsch., 1957—63; staff dir. Nat. Acad. Scis., 1963—69; dir. symposia and seminars Smithsonian Instn., Washington, 1969—85, dir. interdisciplinary studies, 1986—90, sr. scholar, from 1990; sr. scholar emeritus. Dir. internat. commemoration of 250th anniversary of birth of Thomas Jefferson, 1992—; adj. prof. U. Ala., 1971—; chmn. Oxford U.-Smithsonian Seminars, 1985 Author: Gifts and Nations, 1968, Smithsonian Stories: Chronicle of A Golden Age 1964-1984, 2015; editor: (with John F. Eisenberg) Man and Beast: Comparative Social Behavior, 1971, The Cultural Drama, 1974, (with Neil G. Kotler) The Statue of Liberty Revisited: Making a Universal Symbol, 1993; contbr. articles to profl. jours.; editl. bd. Ala. Heritage Del. internat. confs. including UNESCO, Pugwash; adv. coun. Africa Dept. State, 1964-68; hon. commr. Internat. Year of Child, 1979-80; pres. bd. dirs. Inst. Intercultural Studies, NYC; trustee emeritus Phelps-Stokes Fund, 1985—2013; sec.-treas., bd. dirs. Inst. Psychiatry and Fgn. Affairs; bd. visitors Wake Forest U., 1978-81; adv. com. Hubert Humphrey Inst. for Pub. Affairs, 1988-94; bd. dirs. Delta Rsch. and Ednl. Found., 1987-95; trustee Friends of Raoul Wallenberg Found., 1995-97, Lives and Legacies Inc., 1995—2009; advisor Nation's Capital Bicentennial Celebration 1999-2000, Margaret Mead Centenary 2001, Claude Levi-Strauss Centenary, 2008, Historic Mt. Vernon 1999, Benjamin Franklin Creativity Found., 2002; lay reader NY Episc. Diocese, 1958-60. Served with USAAF, 1943—46, Philippines and Japan. Decorated Chevalier de l'ordre des arts et lettres; Woodrow Wilson Internat. Center for Scholars guest scholar, 1970. Fellow AAAS, Am. Anthrop. Assn., Royal Soc. Arts; mem. NY Acad. Scis., Lit. Soc. Washington (pres. 1990), Anthrop. Soc. Washington, Cosmos Club Washington. Avocation: writing. Home: Alexandria, Va. Died Aug. 22, 2015.

DISANDRO, LINDA ANITA, counselor; b. Phila., Aug. 23, 1950; d. Anthony and Frances Helen (Lopinski) D. BA, Holy Family Coll., 1972. Exec. sec. dept. radiology Episcopal Hosp., Phila., 1972-77; sr. sec. dept. radiology Hosp. U. Pa., Phila., 1977-89; faculty Cheltenham Township Adult Evening Sch., Wyncote, Pa., 1982-84; admissions counselor Holy Family Coll., Phila., 1989-96, assoc. dir. admissions, 1996-98; dir. coll. counseling St. Basil Acad., Fox Chase Manor, Pa., from 1998. Mem. AAUW, Nat. Assn. Coll. Admission Counselling (co-chair Phila. Nat. Coll. Fair 1995-97), Pa. Assn. Secondary Sch. and Coll. Admissions Counselors, Pa. Assn. Cath. Colls. Admission Officers (adv. bd. 1991-98), Phila. Area Cath. Colls. (adv. bd./transp. coord., 1991-98), Polish Am. Congress, Assoc. Polish Home Phila. Democrat. Roman Catholic. Avocations: arts and crafts, travel, theater. Home: Philadelphia, Pa. Died Nov. 23, 2006.

DITTMAN, ROBERT ALLAN, retired music educator; b. Springfield, Ohio, Aug. 25, 1933; s. Charles Thomas Dittman and Helen Louise Watkins; m. Mina Marie Gilliland, Dec. 20, 1959; children: James Michael, Lee Patrick, Daniel Dale, Gary Allan. MusB, Sherwood Music Sch., 1955; MEd, Miami U., Oxford, Ohio, 1956. Cert. tchr. Ohio State Bd. Edn., Fla. State Bd. Edn. Band dir. Kennard Jr. H.S., Cleve., 1956—57; vocal dir. Manatee H.S., Bradenton, Fla., 1957—61, West Carrollton H.S., Ohio, 1961—70, Palmetto H.S., Fla., 1970—87, Lincoln Mid. Sch., Palmetto, 1987—95; ret., 1995. Composer: Fla. Vocal Assn. Sight Reading Music, 1977—2005, Christmas Cantata, 1991, 1992. Lutheran. Avocation: antiques. Home: Blairsville, Ga. Died Feb. 8, 2007.

DJERASSI, CARL, writer, retired chemistry professor; b. Vienna, Oct. 29, 1923; s. Samuel and Alice (Friedmann) Djerassi; m. Virginia Jeremiah (div. 1950); m. Norma Lundholm (div. 1976); children: Dale, Pamela(dec.) ; m. Diane W. Middlebrook, 1985 (dec. 2007); 1 stepchild, Leah Middlebrook. AB summa cum laude, Kenyon Coll., 1942, DSc (hon.), 1959; PhD, U. Wis., 1945, DSc (hon.), 1995, Nat. U. Mex., 1953, Fed. U., Rio de Janeiro, 1969, Worcester Poly. Inst., 1972, Wayne State U., 1974, Columbia U., 1975, Uppsala U., 1977, Coe Coll., 1978, U. Geneva, 1978, U. Ghent, 1985, U. Man., 1985, Adelphi U., 1993, U. S.C., 1995, Swiss Fed. Inst. Tech., 1995, U. Md.- Balt. County, 1997, Bulgarian Acad. Scis., 1998, U. Aberdeen, 2000, Polytechnic U., 2001, Cambridge U., 2005, Tech. U. Dortmund, 2009. Rsch. chemist Ciba Pharm. Products, Inc., Summit, NJ, 1942—43, 1945—49; assoc. dir. rsch. Syntex, Mexico City, 1949—52, rsch. v.p., 1957—60; v.p. Syntex Labs., Palo Alto, Calif., 1960—62, Syntex Rsch., 1962—68, pres., 1968—72; founder, pres. Zoecon Corp., 1968—83, chmn. bd. dirs., 1968—86; prof. chemistry Wayne State U., 1952—59, Stanford (Calif.) U., 1959—2002; ret., 2002. Founder Djerassi Resident Artists Program, Woodside, Calif. Author: The Futurist and Other Stories, 1988, In Retrospect: From the Pill to the Pen, 2014; author: (novels) Cantor's Dilemma, 1989, The Bourbaki Gambit, 1994, Marx Deceased, 1996, Menachem's Seed, 1997, NO, 1998; author: (poetry) The Clock Runs Backward, 1991; author: (plays) An Immaculate Misconception, 1998, BBC World Svc. Play of Week, 2000, ICSI--a pedagogic wordplay for 2 voices, 2002, Calculus, 2003, (musical version) Music Werner Schulze, 2005, Ego, 2003, Three on a Couch, 2004, Taboos, 2006, Phallacy, 2007, Four Jews on Parnassus, 2008; author: (with Roald Hoffmann) Oxygen, 2001, BBC World Svc.Play of Week, 2001; author: (with Pierre Laszlo) NO--a pedagogic wordplay for 3 voices, 2003; author: (autobiography) The Pill, Pygmy Chimps and Degas' Horse, 1992; author: (memoir) This Man's Pill, 2001; author: (with D. Pinner) Newton's Darkness: Two Dramatic Views, 2004; author: 9 other books; mem. editl. bd. Jour. Organic Chemistry, 1955—59, Tetrahedron, 1958—92, Steroids, 1963—2001, Procs. NAS, 1964—70, Jour. Am. Chem. Soc., 1966—75, Organic Mass

Spectrometry, 1968—91, contbr. numerous articles to profl. jours., poems, memoirs and short stories to lit. publs. Decorated Austrian Cross of Honor 1st class, sci. & art, Great Cross of Merit Germany, Silver Cross of Honor Austria; recipient Intrasci. Rsch. Found. award, 1969, Freedman Patent award, Am. Inst. Chemists, 1970, Chem. Pioneer award, 1973, Nat. medal of Sci. for first synthesis of oral contraceptive, 1973, Wolf prize in chemistry, Israel, 1978, John and Samuel Bard award in Sci. and Medicine, 1983, Roussel prize, Paris, 1988, Discovers award, Pharm. Mfg. Assn., 1988, Nat. medal Tech. for new approaches to insect control, 1991, Nev. medal, 1992, Thomson medal, Internat. Soc. Mass Spectroscopy, 1994, Prince Mahidol award, Thailand, 1995, Sovereign Fund award, 1996, Othmer Gold medal, Chem. Heritage Found., 2000, Author's prize, German Chem. Soc., 2001, Erasmus medal, Acad. Europeae, 2003, Gold medal, Am. Inst. Chemists, 2004, Serono prize fiction, Rome, 2005, Lichtenberg medal, Göttingen Acad., 2005; named to Nat. Inventors Hall of Fame. Fellow: Royal Soc. London (fgn. mem.); mem.: NAS (Indsl. Application of Sci. award 1990), Acad. Europeae, Bulgarian Acad. Scis. (fgn. mem.), Mex. Acad. Scis., Brazilian Acad. Scis., Royal Swedish Acad. Engring. (fgn. mem.), Royal Swedish Acad. Scis. (fgn. mem.), Am. Acad. Pharm. Scis. (hon.), German Acad. Leopoldina, Am. Acad. Arts and Scis., Royal Soc. Chemistry (hon. fellow, Centenary lectr. 1964), Am. Chem. Soc. (award pure chemistry 1958, Baekeland medal 1959, Fritzsche award 1960, award for creative invention 1973, award in chemistry of contemporary tech. problems 1983, Esselen award 1989, Priestley medal 1992, Gibbs medal 1997), NAS Inst. Medicine, Sigma Xi (Proctor prize for sci. achievement 1998), Phi Beta Kappa, Phi Lambda Upsilon (hon.). Home: San Francisco, Calif. Died Jan. 30, 2015.

DOAR, JOHN MICHAEL, lawyer; b. Mpls., Dec. 3, 1921; s. William and Mae Doar; m. Anne Leffingwell (div. 1973); children: Gael, Michael, Robert, John Burke; m. Patty Ferguson Conroy, 1984 (div. 1996). AB, Princeton U., NJ, 1944; LLB, U. Calif. Boalt Hall Sch. Law, Berkely, 1949. Bar: Calif. 1950, Wis. 1950, US Supreme Ct. 1963, NY 1975, US Dist. Ct. (southern & eastern districts) NY 1979, US Ct. Appeals (11th cir.) 1983, US Ct. Appeals (DC dist.) 1984, US Ct. Appeals (2nd cir.) 1985. First asst. atty. gen., Civil Rights Divsn. US Dept. Justice, Washington, 1960—65, asst. atty. gen., 1965—67; pres. Bedford-Stuyvesant D & S Corp., Bklyn., 1968—73; spl. counsel US House Judiciary Com., Washington, 1973—74; sr. counsel Doar Rieck Kaley & Mack, NYC, 1979—2014. Counsel, mem. investigating com. Judicial Coun. of 11th US Cir. Ct. Appeals, 1983—88; mem. adv. com. on criminal rules Judicial Conf. of US, 1987—93. Recipient NCAA Inspiration award, 2006, Lifetime Achievement award, The American Lawyer mag., 2008, Presdl. Medal of Freedom, The White House, 2012. Mem.: ABA, Assn. Bar City of NY, State Bar Wis., State Bar Calif., NY State Bar Assn. Died Nov. 11, 2014.

DOBBS, MATTIWILDA (MATTIE WILDA SYKES), opera and concert singer, coloratura soprano; b. Atlanta, Georgia; d. John Wesley and Irene Ophelia (Thompson) D.; m. Luis Rodriguez Garcia de la Piedra, Apr. 4, 1953 (dec. June 26, 1954); m. Bengt Janzon, Dec. 23, 1957 (dec. 1997). BA with honors, Spelman Coll., Atlanta, 1946, DMus (hon.), 1979; MA, Tchrs. Coll. Columbia, 1948; studied voice with, Mme. Lotte Leonard, NYC, 1946-50; student, Mannes Music Coll., 1948-49, Berkshire Music Festival, 1949; studied French music with, Pierre Bernac, Paris, 1950-52. Performing prof. voice U. Tex., Austin, 1973-74, also Spelman Coll., Howard U. Washington Appeared: Dutch Opera, Holland Festival, 1952, also recitals, Holland, Paris, Stockholm; appeared: LaScala Opera, Milan, Italy, 1953, also concerts, Eng., France, Italy, Scandinavia, Austria, Belgium, command performance, Covent Garden, London, 1954, concert tours, U.S., 1954—2015, Australia, 1955, 59, 72, Israel, 1957, 59, USSR, opera and concerts, 1959, Hamburg State Opera, 1961-62, Am. opera debut, San Francisco Opera, 1955, debut, Met. Opera, N.Y.C., 1956, recitals, orchestral concerts in, N.Y.C., Phila., Va., Tex., Kan., N.C., Fla., Ala., Ga., La., midwest, 1972, 73, 74, 75; artist-in-residence, Spelman Coll., 1974-75 (Recipient 2d prize Marian Anderson awards 1947), (1st prize Internat. Competition Mus. Performers, Geneva Conservatory Music 1951); recordings include Mozrt's The Abduction From the Seraglio, Bizet's The Pearl Fishers and Offenbach's Tales of Hoffmann John Hay Whitney fellow Paris, 1950 Congregationalist. Died Dec. 8, 2015.

DOBYNS, EDWARD ROBERT, retired mechanical engineer, storyteller; b. Muskegon, Mich., June 15, 1935; s. Alonzo Edward and Evelyn Mae (Schram) D.; m. Betty Lou Scroggs, Mar. 17, 1956 (div. Jan. 1962); children: Patrick Edward, John Timothy; m. Cheryl Joan Kirwer, Feb. 15, 1966; children: Elizabeth Lee, Samantha Grace, Kathryn Ann. BSME, La. State U., 1959. Registered profl. engr., Calif., Ill. Divsn. mgr. nuc. products divsn. Paul Munroe Hydraulics, Anaheim, Calif., 1972-74; mgr. R&D, engring. product line mgr. hanger divsn. ITT Grinnell, Providence, 1975-76; self-employed cons. engr. New Eng. Techs., Inc., North Kingstown, R.I., 1976-81; contract design engr., 1981-84; engr. So. Calif. Edison Co., San Onofre Nuc. Power Sta., 1984-94; sales staff Sales Solutions Inc., San Clemente, Calif., 1997-98; ret. Cons. New Eng. Techs., North Kingstown, R.I., Edward Dobyns & Assocs., L.A. Author: The Ballad of Moby Dick, 1990 (also casette album 1991). With USAF, 1952-56. Mem. Tau Beta Pi, Pi Tau Sigma. Republican. Avocations: reading, chess. Died Jan. 26, 2007.

DOCTOROW, E.L. (EDGAR LAWRENCE DOCTOROW), writer, English educator; b. Bronx, NY, Jan. 6, 1931; s. David Richard and Rose (Levine) Doctorow; m. Helen Esther Setzer, Aug. 20, 1954; children: Jenny, Caroline, Richard. AB in Philosophy, with honors, Kenyon Coll., Gambier, Ohio, 1952, LHD (hon.), 1976, Brandeis U., Waltham, Mass., 1989; LittD (hon.), Hobart & William Smith Coll., Geneva, NY, 1979. Script reader Columbia Pictures, Inc., NYC; assoc. editor to sr. editor New Am. Libr., NYC, 1959-64; editor-in-chief Dial Press, NYC, 1964-69, v.p., pub., 1968-69; vis. writer U. Calif., Irvine, 1969—70; mem. faculty Sarah Lawrence Coll., Bronxville, NY, 1971-78; creative writing fellow Sch. Drama Yale Sch. Drama, New Haven, 1974-75; Loretta & Lewis Glucksman prof. English and American Letters NYU, from 1982, prof. English. Vis. prof. U. Utah, 1975; vis. sr. fellow Coun. on Humanities, Princeton U., NJ, 1980. Author: (novels) Welcome to Hard Times, 1960, Big As Life, 1966, The Book of Daniel, 1971 (Nat. Book award nomiee), Ragtime, 1975 (Nat. Book Critics Cir. award for fiction, 1975), Loon Lake, 1980 (Nat. Book award nomiee), World's Fair, 1985 (Nat. Book award, 1986), Billy Bathgate, 1989 (Nat. Book Critics Cir. award for fiction, 1989, AAAL's William Dean Howells medal, PEN/Faulkner award, Pulitzer prize finalist), The Waterworks, 1994, City of God, 2000, The March, 2005 (Nat. Book Critics Cir. award for fiction, 2005, PEN/Faulkner award, Pulitzer prize finalist, Nat. Book award nomiee), Homer & Langley, 2009, Andrew's Brain, 2014, (short stories and collections) The Songs of Billy Bathgate, 1968, Lives of the Poets: Six Stories and a Novella, 1984, Sweet Land Stories, 2004 (NY Times Notable Book), Wakefield, 2008, All The Time in the World, 2009, (essay collections) Jack London, Hemingway, and the Constitution: Selected Essays 1977-92, 1993, Reporting the Universe, 2003, Creationists: Selected Essays 1993-2006, 2006, (plays) Drinks Before Dinner, 1979. Cpl. signal corps US Army, 1954—55, Germany. Recipient Am. Acad. & Nat. Inst. Art award, 1976, Nat. Humanities medal, The White House, 1998, Commonwealth award for Outstanding Achievement in Lit., 2000, Medal for Disting. Contribution to American Letters, National Book Foundation, 2013; fellow John Simon Guggenheim Meml. Found., 1973. Fellow: AAAL, American Philisophical Soc., American Acad. Arts & Sciences; mem.: PEN, Authors Guild, Writers Guild America, Century Assn. Died July 21, 2015.

DODGE, GEORGE ALAN, marketing executive; b. Hayward, Calif., Mar. 9, 1957; s. Alan Couch and Roxie F. (Lewis) D.; m. Stephanie Lynn Warne, Aug. 2, 1986; children: Joshua M., David K., Gary D. AS, Modesto Jr. Coll., Calif., 1977; BS, U. Calif., Fresno, 1979; M of Bible Studies, Tyndale Inst., 1997; MBA, Trinity So., 2003. Mgr. purchasing Mandrel Industries, Geosource, Modesto, 1981-82; mgr. product line ESD Geosource, Modesto, 1982-83; regional mgr. PSO Geosource, Modesto, 1984-85; mgr. nat. sales ESM Geosource, Houston, 1985-87; mktg. mgr. ESM Internat., Inc., Houston, from 1987; pres. Ctrl. Mach., 1995; dir. SRC Vision, 1997-2000; v.p. Woodside Electronics Corp., from 2000. Mem. Nat. Peanut Coun. Atlanta, 1986-87; bd. dirs. Ironfish and Co., Houston, Salad Manfg. Assn., Internat. Mktg. Svcs.; pres. Xeltron U.S. Contbr. chpts. to books and articles to profl. jours. Mem. Food Processor and Suppliers Assn. (mem. export task force 1985-87, cons. 1987), Soc. Mech. Engrs., Ergonomics Assn., Refridgerated Foods Assn. (bd. dirs., pres. south cen. machinery), Food Processing Mech. Supply Assn. (bd. dirs.), IEFP (Internat. Export Food Processors com.). Republican. Avocations: flying, scuba diving, skiing, auto racing, piano. Home: Medford, Oreg. Died Apr. 23, 2007.

DOIG, IVAN, writer; b. White Sulphur Springs, Mont., June 27, 1939; s. Charles Campbell and Berneta (Ringer) D.; m. Carol Dean Muller, Apr. 17, 1965. BJ, Northwestern U., 1961, MS in Journalism, 1962; PhD in History, U. Wash., 1969; LittD (hon.), Montana State U., 1984, Lewis and Clark Coll., 1987. Editorial writer Lindsay-Schaub Newspapers, Decatur, Ill., 1963-64; asst. editor The Rotarian, Evanston, Ill., 1964-66. Author: (memoir) This House of Sky, 1978, Heart Earth, 1993, (non-fiction) Winter Brothers, 1980; (novels) The Sea Runners, 1982, English Creek, 1984, Dancing at the Rascal Fair, 1987, Ride With Me, Mariah Montana, 1990, Bucking the Sun, 1996, Mountain Time, 1999, The Whistling Season, 2006, The Bartenders Tale, 2012 Sgt. USAFR, 1962-69. Recipient Gov.'s Writers Day Disting. Achievement award, 1979, 81, 85, 88, award for lit. excellence Pacific N.W. Booksellers, 1979, 81, 83, 85, 88, 94, Disting. Achievement award Western Lit. Assn., 1989, Evans Biography award, 1992, Wallace Stegner award, 2007; fellow Nat. Endowment for Arts, 1985. Mem. Authors Guild, PEN Am. Ctr. Died Apr. 9, 2015.

DONAHUE, VERONICA A., geriatrics nurse, women's health nurse; b. Emmett, Mich., Apr. 8, 1923; d. Frank J. and Anne M. (Mackey) Grace; m. Michael J. Donahue, Aug. 28, 1948; children: Michael, David, Dianne, Brigid. Diploma, St. Joseph Hosp. Sch. Nursing, Mt. Clemens, Mich., 1944, Midland (Mich.) Hosp. Insvcs. Charge nurse, gen. post-op. Bon Secour Hosp., Grosse Point, Mich.; head nurse, labor and delivery Midland Hosp. Assocs.; head nurse, oper. room St. Joseph Hosp., Mt. Clemens, Mich.; charge nurse Stratgord Pines Nursing Home, Midland. Nurse cadet, 1943-45. Mem. ANA, Mich. Nurses Assn. Home: Midland, Mich. Died Dec. 1, 2006.

DONOHOE, ROBERT JAMES, spectroscopist; b. Phoenix, Dec. 3, 1956; s. Thomas Aquinas and Lillian Julia (Doerr) D.; m. Anne Reynolds, Apr. 14, 1985; children: Sean, Patrick. PhD, N.C. State U., 1985. Fellow Carnegie-Mellon U., Pitts., 1985-88, Los Alamos (N.Mex.) Nat. Lab., 1988-91, staff mem., from 1991. Contbr. articles to profl. jours. Fellow NIH, 1987. Mem. Phi Lambda Upsilon. Achievements include discovering indirect communication of localized chromophores via coulombic and backbonding effects; first accurate description of vibrational modes in chlorophyll and bacteriochlorophyll; researched vibrational characteristics of defect states and defect mobilization in low-dimensional materials, vibrational characteristics of groundstates in low-dimensional materials under pressure. Home: Los Alamos, N.Mex. Died Apr. 26, 2007.

DOOLEY, JOHN MICHAEL, government agency administrator; b. Fargo, ND, May 27, 1941; s. Kiaran Leonard and Katharine Mary (McDonald) D. AA, Bismarck Jr. Coll., ND, 1961; BSCE, N.D. State U., 1964. Rotation engr. Pacific N.W. U.S. Bur. Reclamation, Boise, Idaho, 1965-66, hydraulic engr. Snake River Devel. Office, 1966-74, hydraulic engr. Upper Mo. Region Billings, Mont., 1974-82, regional hydrologist Mo. Region, 1982-84, hydraulic engr. flood hydrology sect. Denver, 1985-88, chief ops. maintenance Minidoka Project Burley, Idaho, 1988-90, project supt. Minidoka Project, 1990-93, mgr. Columbia River sys. ops. Portland, Oreg., 1993-95, program mgr. Native Am. Affairs Pacific N.W. Regional Office Boise, from 1995. Hydraulic engr. U.S. Bur. Reclamation, Brasilia, Brazil, 1987; mng. spl. project to internat. Conf., Durham, South Africa, 1994. Roman Catholic. Avocations: hiking, biking, golf, music. Died Mar. 17, 2007.

DORNER, IRENE MARIE-THERESE, medical technologist; b. LA, Jan. 6, 1934; d. Otto Urban and Erna Johanna (Schule) Wilhelm; m. Robert W. Dorner, June 27, 1954 (div. 1977); children: Samuel Robert, Jessica Anne. BA in Bacteriology, UCLA, 1957. Lic. med. technologist Calif. Med. technologist Riverside Community Hosp. (Calif.), 1957—58; sr. med. technologist hematology San Bernardino Cmty. Hosp. (Calif.), 1958—62; supr. blood bank Jewish Hosp., St. Louis, 1962—64, Barnes Hosp., St. Louis, 1965—79; instr. Sch. Anesthesiology, 1970—79; instr. blood bank specialist program Washington U. Med. Ctr., St. Louis, 1968—79; clin. instr. dept. allied health svcs. St. Louis U., 1968. Contbr. articles to profl. publs. Cub master St. Louis Coun. Boy Scouts America, St. Louis, 1978—79; mem. Soc. Preservation Health, St. Louis. Recipient L. Jean Stubbins award, South Ctrl. Assn. Blood Banks, 1975. Mem.: ARC (med. adv. bd. 1973—79, tech. adv. bd. 1974—79), Clin. Lab. Mgmt. Assn., Heart America Assn. Blood Banks (pres. 1969—70, v.p. 1982—83), American Assn. Blood Banks (insp. 1975—80), American Assn. Clin. Pathologists. Republican. Roman Catholic. Home: Saint Louis, Mo. Died Jan. 26, 2013.

DORSEY, DENNIS BASIL, health care management consultant; b. Braymer, Mo., Mar. 3, 1912; s. Claude Purdue and Mary Alice (Lankford) D.; m. Hazel Louise Overley, Mar. 11, 1939; children: Alice Louise Dorsey Smith, Carol Ann Dorsey Bristol, David C. AB, Baker U., Baldwin City, Kans., 1933; MD, Kans. U., 1937. Diplomate Am. Bd. Pathology. Postgrad. surgery tng. Augustana Hosp., Chgo., 1937-42, resident in pathology, 1947-50; pvt. practice Lawrence, Kans., 1946-47; dir. dept. of pathology Lakeview Meml. Hosp., Danville, Ill., 1950-64, Cen. DuPage Hosp., Winfield, Ill., 1964-77; pres. Dorsey of Boca Grande, Fla., from 1980. Chmn. med. exec. com. MDS Health Group Inc., Amherst, N.Y., 1979-84; chmn. health adv. com. MDS Health Group Ltd., 1984—; co-chmn. med. adv. bd. MDS Labs., Etobicoke, Ont., Can., 1984-93: mem. med. adv. bd. MDS-Hudson Valley Labs., Poughkeepsie, N.Y., 1988—; cons. dept. pathology VA, Washington, 1975-83; bd. dirs., v.p., pres. Boca Grande Health Clinic, Inc., 1984-87, 88-91; Brindley vis. prof. U. Tex. Med. Br., Galveston, 1984. Author, editor: Administration in the Pathology Lab, 1962; contbr. articles to profl. jours.; inventor camera exposure controls, child safe bottle caps. Bd. dirs. Gasparilla Island Conservation and Improvement Assn., Boca Grande, 1983-86. Major U.S. Army, 1942-46. Fellow Am. Soc. Clin. Pathologists (emeritus, Joint Disting. Svc. award 1986), Coll. Am. Pathologists (life, pres. 1975-77, Pathologist of Yr. award 1969, Presdl. honors 1982); mem. AMA, Nat. Reference Sys. in Clin. Chemistry Coun. (chmn. 1983-84, Presdl. citation 1985), Gasparilla Island Golf Club, Alpha Omega Alpha. Republican. Episcopalian. Avocations: golf, watercolor painting, photography, international travel. Died June 12, 2007.

DOUBLEDAY, NELSON, JR., former professional baseball team executive; b. Oyster Bay, July 20, 1933; Graduating with degree in Economics, Princeton, 1955. With Doubleday & Co. Inc., NYC, 1954—56, former pres., chief exec. officer, chmn. bd. dirs.; chmn. bd., majority owner N.Y. Mets Baseball Team, 1980—2002. Served with USAF, 1956-59. Died June 17, 2015.

DOUGLASS, RAMONA ELIZABETH, medical sales professional; b. NYC, Aug. 15, 1949; d. Howard William and Lena Verona (Belle) D. Student, Colo. Sch. Mines, 1966-68; BS in Physical Sci., Colo. State U., 1970. Adminstrv. asst. S.E. Queens Community Corp., Queens, N.Y., 1970-71; research editor Encyclopedia Britannica, Chgo., 1971-73; sales rep. Scott Foresman Co., Glenview, Ill., 1973-75, Am. Sci. Products, McGaw Park, Ill., 1975-78; mgr. New Eng. territory Hollister, Inc., Libertyville, Ill., 1978-81; mgr. midwest region Precision Dynamics Corp., San Fernando, Calif., 1981-95, mgr. Western region, bar code specialist, from 1995, mng. editor sales and mktg. newsletter, from 1998. Ptnr. Douglass/Sherod-Winter Assocs., Chgo., 1986-88, DMB Group, Internat., 1990-91; mem. Nat. Network Women in Sales, 1986-93, v.p. corp. rels., 1989-90; co-founder Healthy Concepts, Inc., 1993, mktg. v.p., cons., 1998—; apptd. to Fed. 2000 Census Adv. Com., 1995—, mem. Fed. Working Group on Racial and Ethnic Tabulations, 1997—; lectr., spkr. in field; appearances on radio and TV programs, including Oprah Winfrey Show, Jerry Springer Show, Mark Walberg Show, CBS Sunday Morning, Aaron Freeman Show, others. Contbr. poetry Great Am. Poetry Anthology, 1987; subject in The Rainbow Effect: Interracial Families, 1987, Heroes of Conscience: A Biographical Dictionary, 1996; contbg. author:

The Multiracial Experience: Racial Borders as the New Frontier, 1995. Founding mem. The Nat. Alliance Against Racist & Polit. Repression, Chgo., 1972; bd. dirs., chair publicity The Biracial Family Network, Chgo., 1987-90, v.p., 1990-92, pres., 1992-93; v.p. pub. rels. Assn. Multi-Ethnic Ams., 1988-90, v.p. midwest region, 1991-94, pres., 1994—. Recipient Pioneer award for outstanding contbn. to multiracial issues U. Calif., Berkeley, 1997, Building Bridges award Racial Harmony award Multiracial Ams. of so. Calif., 1996. Mem. NAFE. Democrat. Avocations: creative writing, music, gourmet cooking, sailing. Died May 29, 2007.

DOW, IRVING APGAR, JR., minister, consultant; b. Elizabeth, NJ, Sept. 8, 1920; s. Irving Apgar Sr. and Freda Anna (Schenk) D.; m. Barbara Alice Davidson, Oct. 16, 1943; children: Mark I., Matthew A. BA, Columbia Union Coll., 1950; M In Religious Edn., Tenn. Christian U., 1974, PhD in Sacred Theology and Philosophy, 1975; MDiv, Shaw U., 1977. Ordained minister, 1950, ordained minister, Calvary Grace Christian Church of Faith, Fort Lauderdale, FL., 1973, ordained minister, North Jersey Baptist Assoc., Newark, NJ., 1980. Pastor N.J. Conf. Seventh Day Adventists, Trenton, 1950-54; pres. Dow Home Builders, Inc., Alexandria, Va., 1956-60; cons., lectr. pastoral, clin. counseling in psycho-theology Elizabeth, from 1975. Patentee oil saving device used in oil burning boilers. With USAAC, 1943-45; lt. col. USAR, 1975-98. Republican. Avocations: church restoring, wood carving. *Living in a frightening and unprecedented period in human history, we are faced with new, overwhelming, destructive perplexities and anxieties. The, heretofore, stabilizing influence of love is now, itself, misunderstood and faith seems futile. With hope crushed beneath the load, I have verified to scientists and countless others, there is an answer to human despair. "Peace is what I leave with you...I do not give as the world does. Do not be worried and upset: Do not be afraid" (Good News Bible, Jn. 14:27). God, the spokesman, is there and does care!.* Died Apr. 21, 2007.

DOYLE, WILLIAM RANDALL, health educator, researcher; b. Stilwell, Okla., Aug. 22, 1954; s. Heral Ray Doyle and Mary Louise (Spicer) Shaffer; m. Martha Ann Denison, May 20, 1989; children: Aaron, Jared Spencer, Derrick, Patrick, Lilith. BA, U. Ark., 1990; D of Naturopathy, Trinity U., 1995; PhD, Summit U., 1996. Dir. Ozark Wellness Ctr., Fayetteville, Ark., 1989-90, Summit Home Retreat, Winslow, Ark., 1995-96; founder and dir. Earth Acad. Natural Scis., 1997. Author: Naturopathy Wellness and You, 1996, Essential Principals of Naturopathy, 1996; editor: The Nature Path, 1996. With USMC, 1972-79, Vietnam. Mem. Am. Naturopathic Med. Assn., Nat. Health Fedn., Am. Naturopathic Practitioners (pres. 1995—), Am. Massage Therapists Assn., Hummingbird Med. Soc. (chmn. 1984—). Achievements include development of Cellular Level Emotional Access and Release Protocol (CLEAR trademark). Home: Winter Spgs, Fla. Died July 10, 2007.

DRAKE, ERVIN MAURICE, composer, author; b. NYC, Apr. 3, 1919; s. Max and Pearl Edith (Cohen) D.; m. Ada Sax, May 28, 1947 (dec. Mar. 1975); children: Linda Shifra, Betsy Jennifer; m. Edith Bein Berman, Nov. 19, 1982. BS in Social Sci., CCNY, 1940; studies with Tibor Serly, Jacob Druckman; D in Mus. (hon.), Five Towns Coll., 1998. Composer: I Believe, 1998, It Was a Very Good Year, 1999 (recorded by Robbie Williams 2001), Tico Tico, Perdido, Al Di Là, A Room Without Windows, Good Morning Heartache, 1999, Come to the Mardi Gras, The Rickety Rickshaw Man, Across the Wide Missouri, My Friend, Father of Girls, Quando Quando Quando, Sonata, Made for Each Other, Cherry, One God, Now That I Have Everything, Just For Today, There Are No Restricted Signs in Heaven, Marilyn; composer music and lyrics Leslie Uggams CD Painted Mem'ries, 1995, From John Gabriel With Love CD, 1997, One God (recorded by Barbra Streisand), Who Are These Strangers (recorded by Michael Feinstein), 2003; lyricist, co-librettist, composer Florence of Arabia, 1985; composer, lyricist, co-librettist Songs in Sophisticated Ladies, 1983, 84, Shades of Harlem, 1985, Lady Day, 1987; composer, lyracist Broadway musical What Makes Sammy Run?, 1964-65; composer, lyricist, librettist Her First Roman, 1968 Recipient Honor, Friars Club, 2002, Soc. Singers, 2003; named to The Songwriters Hall of Fame, 1983. Mem.: American Guild Authors & Composers (pres. 1973—82), Players Club, Lotos Club, Dutch Treat Club. Died Jan. 15, 2015.

DRAKE, PHYLLIS, realtor, writer; b. Oakland, Calif., Mar. 21, 1922; d. William Edward and Ruth (Andrew) Gunby; m. Charles Bernard Drake, Aug. 26, 1944; children: Douglas S., Linda MacDonald. Student, Fullerton Jr. Coll., 1939-41, U. Calif., 1941-44. Mgr. Century 21 Stalcup, Scottsdale, Ariz., 1973-74, with, 1987—2003; owner Century 21 Aquarius, Phoenix, 1974-80; ret., 2003. Lectr. State Real Estate Dept., 1982; guest on radio talk shows, Ktar, KLff, 1982-87. Author: How to Succeed in Selling Reals Estate, 1982, A Matter of Choice, 2002. Avocation: writing fiction. Home: Scottsdale, Ariz. Died Aug. 16, 2007.

DRAPKIN, DONALD G., venture capitalist; m. Ellen Drapkin (div.); 1 child, Matthew Adam ; m. Bernice Drapkin; children: Dana Gabrielle, Nicole, Dustin, David, Amanda. Grad., Brandeis U., 1968; LLB, Columbia U., 1971. Assoc. Cravath, Swaine & Moore, 1971—77; mergers ptnr. Skadden, Arps, Slate, Meagher & Flom, 1977; vice chmn., dir. MacAndrews & Forbes Holdings Inc., NYC, 1987—2007; vice chmn., chmn. investment com. Lazard, Ltd., 2007—10; co-founder Casablanca Capitol, LP, 2010—16. Bd. dirs. SIGA, from 2001, chmn., 2001—07; bd. dirs. Anthracite Capital, Inc., Playboy Enterprises, Inc., Revlon Consumer Products Corp., Revlon Inc., Nephros, Inc., from 1997, PharmaCore, Inc., TransTech Pharma, Inc. Bd. dirs. Brandeis U., Lincoln Ctr. Theatre, Phoenix House Found. Inc.; bd. visitors Columbia Law Sch. Died Feb. 22, 2016.

DRAUDEN, GAIL, psychologist, consultant; b. Joliet, Ill., Jan. 13, 1948; d. Floyd and Marian (Krieger) D. BA, U. Iowa, 1968; PhD, U. Minn., 1980. Psychologist test validation ctr. State of Minn., St. Paul, 1973-76; sr. researcher employee relations Honeywell Corp., Mpls., 1979-82; prin. cons. Gail Drauden & Assocs., Mpls., from 1983. Mem. Am. Psychol. Assn., Soc. Indsl. Orgnl. Psychologists. Home: Minneapolis, Minn. Died Jan. 7, 2007.

DREW, FRASER BRAGG ROBERT, language educator; b. Randolph, Vt., June 23, 1913; s. George Albie and Hazel (Fraser) Drew. AB magna cum laude, U. Vt., 1933; MA, Duke U., 1935; PhD, U. Buffalo, 1952. Instr. Latin Green Mt. Coll., Poultney, Vt., 1936-39; grad. asst. English Syracuse U., 1939-41; instr. English Buffalo State Coll., 1945-47, asst. prof., 1947-52, prof., 1952-73, Disting. Tchg. prof., 1973-83. Author: (books) John Masefield's England, 1973; author: (with Hank Nuwer) One Long Wild Conversation, 2009; contbr. articles to profl. jours. Chmn. St. Patrick Scholarship Fund, Buffalo, 1969—79. Recipient Disting. Alumnus award, U. Vt., 1968, Irishman of the Yr. award, United Irish Socs. Western NY, 1970; grantee, SUNY Rsch. Found., 1960, 1967; St. Patrick scholar, 1967. Mem.: Robinson Jeffers Tor Ho. Found., Hemingway Soc., Boulder Soc., Wilbur Soc., Ira Allen Soc., John Masefield Soc., Housman Soc., Green Mountain Cir., Friends Duke U. Chapel, Duke U. Heritage Soc., Friends Bailey/Howe Libr., Friends Hemingway Collection John F. Kennedy Libr., Iron Dukes, Washington Duke Club, Phi Beta Kappa, Lambda Iota. Died June 24, 2013.

DREWS, JOSEPH HARVEY, administrator; b. Milw., July 9, 1939; s. Joseph Frank and Hazel Julia D.; divorced; children: Shane, Jason, Aaron. BS, Ariz. State U., 1977. Chem. analyst Hella Mining Co., Casa Grande, Ariz., 1977; prodn. mgr. Rsch. Labs., Globe, Ariz., 1977-79; plant, prodn. mgr. Naturalife Labs., Torrance, Calif., 1979-82; mfg. mgr. Vita-Fresh Vitamin Co., Garden Grove, Calif., 1982-84; plant mgr. Gen. Rsch. Labs., Northridge, Calif., 1984-85; plant mgr., prodn. mgr. Naturalife Labs., Torrance, from 1985. Avocation: computer spreadsheet programs. Home: Redondo Beach, Calif. Died Dec. 18, 2006.

DREYER, WARREN MORSE, SR., (MICHAEL DREYER), medical technician, educator; b. Milw., Sept. 16, 1935; s. Donald C. Dreyer and Charlotte F. (Clark) Krajweski; m. Sandra Lee Eder, Sept. 17, 1954 (div. Apr. 1982); m. Joyce Adele Barbieri, Apr. 24, 1982; children: Donald, Warren, Bobby, John, Kathy, Fred, Terri, Theodore, David, Russell, Stephan. AA, Phoenix Coll., 1978; BS, U. Phoenix, 1984, MA in Mgmt. Human Rels. and Orgnl. Behavior, 1986. Cert. emergency med. technician. Gen. mgr. Emergency Medics, Inc., Phoenix, 1983—84; ambulance driver Profl. Med. Transport, Phoenix, 1983—84, dispatcher, 1983—84; asst. dir. health safety ARC, Phoenix, 1982—83; dir. disaster svcs. Wichita Falls, Tex., 1979—81; pres. M & J Dreyer Enterprises, Phoenix, from 1982; field supr. Glendale Ambulance Co., 1984—85; gen. mgr. Metrocare Ambulance, 1986—87; educator Scottsdale Meml. Health Sys., Inc., 1988. Author: Emergency Action Procedures: First Aid and CPR Made Simple, 1980. Instr. trainer ARC, from 1950, Am. Heart Assn., from 1978; loaned exec. United Way, Mesa, Ariz., 1982; pct. committeeman Rep. Party. Recipient Vol. award, ARC, 1978, 30-Yr. Pin, 1980, Lifesaving award, CAP, 1974. Mem.: Ariz. Emergency Med. Technicians Assn. (v.p. edn. 1984—85), Assn. Safety Engrs. Ariz. (1st v.p. 1984—85, treas. 1983—84), Commodore Longfellow Soc. Republican. Home: Phoenix, Ariz. Died Dec. 31, 2006.

DRIES, COLLEEN PATRICIA, adult education educator; b. Lansing, Mich., Apr. 15, 1948; d. Peter C. and Mary Alice (Campion) D. BA, St. Louis U., 1971; postgrad., U. Ill.; MA, Bradley U., 1996. Cert. elem. edn., secondary edn., ESL edn., gen. adminstrn. Elem., mid. and jr. high sch. tchr. Holy Family Grade Sch., Peoria, Ill., 1973—76; tchr. Peoria Pub. Schs., from 1977, ESL tchr., GED tchr.; prin. Adult Edn. & Family Literacy Ctr., from 2002. Tchr. adult basic edn., mem. Peoria Pub. Schs. Adult Edn. Task Force; mem. Commn. on Adult Basic Edn., region 4 rep., 1994-96, nominations and elections com., 1996. Mem. Gov.'s Parent Sch. Initiative Region 12 Adv. Com., 1993; Ill. rep. to Dept. Edn.'s Nat. Forum on Adult Edn. and Literacy, 1998. Named Ill. Adult Edn. Tchr. of Yr., 1989. Mem.: ASCD, Ill. Adult and Continuing Educators Assn. (regional dir. 1987—91, conf. chair 1991—92, conf. com. 1991—2002, pres. 1992—93, nomination and elections chair 1993—94, membership chair 1994—98, legis. chair from 1994, Ill. adult edn. adv. com. 1997—99, com. to advance adult edn. funding 2000—02, legis co-chair from 2003, Pres. award outstanding contbns. to adult edn. in Ill. 1995), Ctrl. Ill. Addv. Edn. Svc. Ctr. (GED adv. com.), Nat. Coun. Tchrs. English, Am. Assn. Adult and Continuing Edn. (nominations and elections com. 1996, mem. adult basic edn.), Internat. Reading Assn. Home: East Peoria, Ill. Died Dec. 28, 2006.

DRIGGS, JOHN D., retired bank executive; b. Douglas, Ariz., June 16, 1927; m. Gayle Driggs; 5 children. AB, Stanford U., 1952, MBA, 1954. Chmn. Western Savings & Loan Assn., Phoenix, 1976—89; mayor City of Phoenix, 1970—74. Served in USN, 1945—46. Lds Church. Died Dec. 11, 2014.

DRUMHELLER, KIRK, retired engineering company executive; b. Walla Walla, Wash., Jan. 14, 1925; s. William Lewis and Elsie McIver Drumheller; m. Betty Vaara, June 17, 1950; children: Karen, Susan, Ellen, Michael. BS, MIT, 1945; postgrad., Harvard U., 1947—48. Engr. and design mgr., projects mgr. GE, Richland, Wash., 1951—65; R&D mgr. Battelle, Richland, 1965—69, mgr. Jrsey nuc. project, 1969—70, lab. solar program coord., 1970—84, mgr. industry rels. and industry programs Seattle, 1984—89; pres. Heliostats, Inc., Seattle, 1989—2003; ret., 2003. Prin. investigator Foresight Sci. and Tech., New Bedford, 1998—2001. Contbr. book Reactor Technology, Selected Reviews-196, 1965, book Radiosotope Engineering, 1972. Mem., chmn. Wash. State Solar Adv. Group, Olympia, 1979—83. Apprentice seaman US Navy, 1942, Lt. (j.g.) USN, 1945—46. Recipient Fin. Assistance award, U.S. Dept. Commerce, 1994-1995. Mem.: Am. Solar Energy Soc. Achievements include patents for process of forming an isotopic heat source; child proof latches; heliostat components. Avocations: jogging, skiing, travel, conservation and energy education of the public. Home: Renton, Wash. Died Mar. 12, 2015.

DRUMKE, RONALD ALFRED, lawyer; b. Chgo., June 17, 1941; s. Alfred Conrad and Olga Mary (Piskorski) D.; m. Sandra Drumke, Aug. 26, 1963; children: Michael William, David John, Michelle Lynn, Danielle Anne. BA, Northwestern U., Chgo., 1963, JD, 1966. Bar: Ill. 1966, U.S. Dist. Ct. (no. dist.) Ill. 1967. Assoc. Taylor Miller Sprowl, Chgo., 1966-70, Louis G. Davidson & Assocs., Chgo., 1970-82; ptnr. Drumke & Patterson, Chgo., 1982-93; prin. Ronald A. Drumke & Assocs., Ltd., Chgo., from 1993. Mem. ABA, Am. Trial Lawyers Assn., Soc. Trial Lawyers, Ill. State Trial Lawyers, Ill. State Bar Assn., Chgo. Bar Assn. Democrat. Avocation: saxophone. Home: Evanston, Ill. Died July 30, 2007.

DUBASKY, MAYO RUTH, library clerk; b. Palco, Kans., Oct. 27, 1923; d. Rixey Jewell and Daisy Clarice (Pickinpaugh) Griggs; m. Francis Charles Pfanneschlag, Sept. 18, 1943 (div. May 1947); m. Alexander Cosmo, June 7, 1947; children: Valentina, Phillip, Ariadne, Richard, Evan. Libr. clk., receptionist Congl. Rsch. Svc., Libr. of Congress, Washington, 1975-95; congl. rsch. receptionist Libr. of Congress, Washington, 1995. Editor: The Gist of Mencken, 1990; contbr. articles to mags. Legis. chmn. PTA, Washington, 1963-72. Avocations: books, photography. Home: Hoxie, Kans. Died Aug. 21, 2007.

DUBOV, D. LESTER, mechanical engineer; b. Bklyn., Aug. 18, 1920; s. Simon and Ella Grace (Goldberg) D.; m. Selma Rita Soskil, Jan. 27, 1950; children: Gail, Helene. BSME, Poly. U., 1950. Pres. Dura Plastron Co., NYC, 1946-66; engr., sales mgr. Machine Components Corp., Plainview, N.Y., from 1966. Editor: Company Catalogs and Technical References, 1966—. Sgt. U.S. Army, 1942-46. Home: Boynton Beach, Fla. Died June 7, 2007.

DUDDY, JOAN FRANCES, retired performing arts administrator, dancer; b. Waltham, Mass., June 26, 1937; d. Walter Francis and Gladys Rita (Wallace) D.; m. Isaac Schambelan, Sept. 1980 (dec.). Studied, Alicia Langford Sch. of Ballet, 1957-59, Boston Conservatory of Music, 1956-58, Joffrey Ballet Sch., 1959-65, Am. Ballet Ctr.-Richard Thomas, 1965-74. Sec. dept. physiology Sch. Pub. Health, Harvard U., 1957-58; sec. to exec. v.p. Monrovia Pt. Mgmt. Co., Ltd., 1963-66; exec. sec., office mgr. Simat, Helliesen & Eichner, Inc., 1966-72; adminstrv. asst. to dir. Coun. on Environ. City of N.Y., 1972-74; exec. sec. E.D. Rosenfeld Assocs., 1974-75; asst. to pres., editor tech. reports Bedford Health Assocs., Katonah, N.Y., 1975-83; dance program adminstr., asst. to exec. dir. Dia Ctr. for the Arts, NYC, 1983-96; dance program adminstr. for Joyce SoHo Joyce Theatre, NYC, 1996—2004; ret., 2004. Dance tchr. Alicia Langford Sch. Ballet, 1957-59, pvt. instr., N.Y.C., 1972-73, Children's History Theatre, Woodstock, N.Y., 1981-83; bd. dirs. Ralph Lemon Co., Momenta Found., New Dance Alliance, Muna Tseng Dance Projects, Theater By The Blind; mem. selection com. Yard Choreographer's Colony, Martha's Vineyard, Mass., 1992-93, Manhattan Cmty. Arts Fund, 1994; founder, co-dir. Dance Across Borders, First Internat. Symposium on Coop. Exch. in Dance, N.Y.C., 1995; co-curator Dia Salon Project, 1987-96. Dancer Alicia Langford Boston Ballet Co., 1957-59, Boston-New Eng. Opera Co., 1958, Myra Kinch Dancers, 1959, Robert Joffrey Ballet, 1959-62; choreographer Green Room Players NYU, 1973, Children's History Theatre, 1981-82, Lincoln Ctr. Libr., N.Y.C., 1982. Recipient N.Y. Dance and Performance Bessie award for sustained svc. to dance cmty. Dance Theatre Workshop, 1993. Home: New York, NY. Died Nov. 27, 2015.

DUDELHEIM, HANS RUDOLF, communications executive; b. Berlin, Fed. Republic of Germany, June 17, 1927; s. Alfred and Agnes (Ebinger) D.; children: Wendy, Karen. Student, Sch. of Photography, 1946, New Sch. of N.Y., 1959. Film editor ABC-TV, NYC, 1951-66; producer, dir., editor Cinema Arts Assn., NYC, from 1966, pres., from 1987. Founder Cinema Arts Film Soc., N.Y.C., 1961. Editor (documentaries) Saga of Western Man (Emmy award, 1963), Comrade Student (Hillman award, 1964); producer, editor (short film) Sublimated Birth (Bronze award, 1965); editor, assoc. producer (documentary) Kent State 1970 (Cine Golden Eagle, 1975); recent films include Sigmund Freud, IBM Motivation Project, The Forgotten Pioneers of Hollywood, Painting With Love. Campaigner Adlai Stevenson for Pres., 1952. Served as cpl. with U.S. Army, 1947-50. Recipient Bronze medal Internat. Film Festival of N.Y., 1973, Silver medal, 1976. Avocations: sailing, tennis, swimming. Home: New York, NY. Died Jan. 6, 2007.

DUDLEY, EVERETT HASKELL, JR., lawyer; b. Fitchburg, Mass., June 2, 1930; s. Everett H. Sr. and Marguerite I. (Connors) D.; m. Joyce Pettapiece, Aug. 23, 1952; children: Everett H. III, Lisa R.Rentz. AA, Boston U., 1950,

BS, 1954; JD, U. Miami, 1960. Bar: Mass. 1961, Fla. 1960, U.S. Dist. Ct. (so. dist.) Fla. 1961, U.S. Supreme Ct. 1964. Assoc. Sams, Anderson, Alper, Meadows & Spencer, Miami, Fla., 1960-61; ptnr. Stamey, Kravitz & Dudley, Hialeah, Fla., 1961-63, Kravitz, Dudley & Dean, Hialeah, Fla., 1963-69, Kravitz, Dudley & Duckworth, Hialeah, Fla., 1972-79, Weinbtraub, Weintraub, Seiden, Dudley & Press, Miami, Fla., 1979-85; judge Dade County Criminal Ct. of Record, Miami, Fla., 1969-71, City of Miami Springs, Fla., 1971-73; pres., prin. Everett H. Dudley Jr., P.A., Ft. Lauderdale, Fla., 1985-89; ptnr. Keeley, Hayes, Dudley, Johnson, Roberts, Keeley, Hayes & Dudley, Boca Raton, Fla., 1989-95, Keeley, Hayes, Dudley, Garrett & Mahle, Boca Raton, from 1995. Founder, pres. Coun. on Drug Edn., Miami, 1970-72; chmn. Nat. Cancer Cytology Ctr., 1961-79, Miami Springs Charter Bd., 1974, Miami Springs Code Rev. Bd., 1975; cons. Dade County Drug Abuse Adv. Bd., 1971-75; mem. Dade County Secretariat on Crime and Law Enforcement, 1971-72; bd. dirs. Dade County Crime Commn., 1971-81. With USMC, 1953-56. Recipient Citizen of Yr. award Op. Self-Help, 1970, Disting. Svc. award City of Miami Springs, 1974; commd. Ky. Col., Commonwealth of Ky., 1990. Mem. ABA, Assn. Trial Lawyers Am., Am. Judicature Soc., Mass. Bar Assn., Fla. Bar Assn., Am. Arbitration Assn., Navy League of U.S. (judge adv. Delray Beach coun. 1990—), Am. Legion, Masons, Shriners, Delta Theta Phi, Sigma Alpha Epsilon. Home: Boca Raton, Fla. Died Feb. 16, 2007.

DUFFEY, DICK, nuclear engineer, educator; b. Wabash County, Ind., Aug. 26, 1917; s. Glen and Kate (Parker) D. BS, Purdue U., 1939; MS, U. Iowa, 1940; PhD, U. Md., 1956. Registered profl. engr., D.C., Md. Engr. Union Carbide, Buffalo, 1940-42, U.S. AEC, Washington, 1946-54, MIT, Cambridge, 1954; prof. engring. U. Md., College Park, from 1954. Contbr. over 100 articles to profl. jours. With U.S. Army, 1942-46. Grantee AEC. Achievements include 5 patents in field. Died Nov. 10, 2006.

DUFFY, ROBERT ALOYSIUS, aeronautical engineer; b. Buck Run, Pa., Sept. 9, 1921; s. Joseph Albert and Jane Veronica (Archer) D.; m. Elizabeth Reed Orr, Aug. 19, 1945 (dec.); children: Michael Gordon, Barclay Robert (dec.), Marian Orr (dec.), Judith Elizabeth Parsons, Patricia Archer; m. Jenifer Williams Pickett, Nov. 28, 1992. BS in Aero. Engring., Ga. Inst. Tech., 1951. Commd. 2d lt. U.S. Army, 1942; commd. U.S. Air Force, advanced through grades to brig. gen., 1967; vice comdr. USAF Space and Missile Systems Orgn., LA, 1970-71; ret., 1971; v.p., dir. Draper Lab. div. MIT, Cambridge, Mass., 1971-73; pres., chief exec. officer Charles Stark Draper Lab., Inc., 1973-87, dir., 1973-91, dir. emeritus, from 1991. Contbr. articles to profl. jours. Decorated Disting. Svc. medal, Legion of Merit; recipient Thomas D. White award Nat. Geog. Soc., 1970; named to Ga. Tech. Engring. Hall of Fame, 1994. Fellow AIAA; mem. NAE, Internat. Acad. Astronautics, Inst. Navigation (Thurlow award 1964, pres. 1976-77), Air Force Assn., Tau Beta Pi. Home: Naples, Fla. Died Feb. 4, 2015.

DUKE, ROBIN CHANDLER (GRACE ESTER TIPPETT), retired public relations executive, former ambassador; b. Balt., Oct. 13, 1923; d. Richard Edgar and Esther (Chandler) Tippett; m. Jeffrey Lynn (div. 1958); children: Jeffrey R. Lynn, Letitia Lynn; m. Angier Biddle Duke, May 1962 (dec. 1995); children Angier Biddle Duke Jr. Fashion editor N.Y. Jour. Am., NYC, 1944-46; freelance writer NYC, 1946-50; broker Orvis Bros., NYC, 1953-58; v.p. pub. rels. Pepsi Cola Co., Internat., NYC, 1958-62; US amb. to UNESCO US Dept. State, Belgrade, 1980, US amb. to Norway Oslo, 2000—01. Bd. dirs. Am. Home Products, NYC, Internat. Flavors & Fragrances, NYC, East River Bank, New Rochelle, NY; dir. Rockwell Corp., 1977—95; dir. emeritus Inst. Internat. Edn. Co-chmn. Population Action Internat., N.Y.C., 1975-96; Met. Club Washington; bd. dirs. David and Lucile Packard Found., U.S. Japan Found. (also co-founder), World Childhood Found., Charles A. and Anne Morrow Lindbergh Found.; trustee Inst. of Internat. Edn.; overseer , Internat. Rescue Com. Recipient Albert and Mary Lasker Social Svc. award, 1991, Margaret Sanger Woman of Yr. Valor award, 1995. Mem. Coun. on Fgn. Rels., Acad. Arts & Scis., World Affairs Coun. L.I. (co-chmn.), Colony Club, River Club. Democrat. Avocations: skiing, swimming. Home: Charleston, SC. Died Feb. 6, 2016.

DUKES, BILL, former state legislator; b. Tarma, Ky., Aug. 26, 1927; m. Juanita Jean Willoughby; 4 children. AB, Bowling Green State U.; grad., U. Miss. Adminstrv. asst. Ky. Tuberculosis Assn.; adminstrv. asst. to mayor City of Decatur, mayor; educator, bus. mgr. NW Miss. Jr. Coll.; mem. Dist. 8 Ala. House of Reps, Montgomery, 1994—2011. Served with US Army. Mem.: Decatur Jaycees, American Legion. Democrat. Died Dec. 18, 2014.

DUNHAM, JOHN HANDY, II, real estate developer and broker; b. Chgo., Sept. 29, 1925; s. John H. and Lee (Yerger) D.; divorced; children: John H. III, James U. BS, Purdue U., 1950. Salesman Workman Mfg., Chgo., 1950-58, Wallace Press, Chgo., 1958-66; exec. v.p., owner tech. sales Datafold Inc., Chgo., 1967-79; co-founder, owner Datafold Inc. (merger Am. Brands), 1979; owner, CEO, founder Span, Inc., Vail, Colo., from 1980; real estate developer and broker, from 1980. Internat. chair R&D, Computer Supplies Industry Worldwide, 1970-79. Developer of test equipment; patentee in field. Active for more than 55 yrs. Boy Scouts Am., dir. transp. for 2 nat. jamborees and 1 world jamboree, 1995; bd. dirs. Bravo Guild/Music Festival of Vail, 1994-97. With USN, WWII, PTO, 1942-46. Decorated 13 battle stars; recipient Vigil, Scouters Key, Scout Masters Key, Dist. award of Merit, Silver Beaver award and Silver Antelope award Boy Scouts Am., 1956—. Avocations: swimming, scuba, sailing, hunting, fishing. Home: Delavan, Ill. Died June 26, 2007.

DUNN, FLOYD, biophysics and biomedical engineering professor; b. Kansas City, Mo., Apr. 14, 1924; s. Louis and Ida (Leibtag) Dunn; m. Elsa Tanya Levine, June 11, 1950; children: Andrea Susan, Louis Brook. Student, Kans. City Jr. Coll., 1941-42, Tex. A&M U., College Station, 1943; BS, U. Ill., Urbana, 1949, MS, 1951, PhD, 1956. Rsch. assoc. elec. engring. U. Ill., Urbana, 1954-57, rsch. asst. prof. elec. engring., 1957-61, assoc. prof. elec. engring. and biophysics, 1961-65, prof., 1965—95, prof. elec. engring., biophysics and bioengring., 1972-95, faculty mem. Beckman Inst. Advanced Sci. and Tech., prof. emeritus, from 1995, dir. bioacoustics rsch. lab., 1976-95, chmn. bioengring. faculty, 1978-82. Vis. prof. U. Coll., Cardiff, Wales, 1968—69, Inst. Chest Diseases and Cancer, Tohoku U., Sendai, Japan, 1989—90, U. Nanjing, China, 1983; mem. bioengring., radiation, diagnostic radiology and NIBIB study sects. NIH, 1970—81, 2008; steering com. workshop interaction ultrasound and biol. tissues NSF, 1971—72; vis. sr. scientist Inst. Cancer Rsch., Sutton, Surrey, England, 1975—76, Sutton, 1982—83, Sutton, 1990; chmn. working group health aspects exposure to ultrasound radiation WHO, London, 1976; mem. tech.-elec. products radiation stds. com. FDA, 1974—76; vis. prof. radiation oncology U. Ariz., Tucson, 1996—2008, rsch. prof., radiology dept., 2008—14; mem. Nat. Coun. Radiation Protection and Measurement, 1980—2003, fellow, from 2003; treas. Interscience Rsch. Inst., Champaign, Ill., 1957—58; mem. sci. adv. bd. Resonant Med. Inc., Montreal, 2005—09. Mem. editl. bd. Jour. Acoustical Soc. Am., 1968—2009, Ultrasound Medicine and Biology, from 1981, Ultrasonics, 1981—2003, Encyclopedia of Acoustics, 1981—97, Encyclopedia of Applied Physics, 1981—91, Am. Inst. Physics Series Modern Acoustics and Signal Processing, 1990—97; contbr. articles to profl. jours.; cons. Piezo Energy Technologies LLC, from 2007. Trustee Hensley Twp., Ill., 1980—81. With AUS, 1943—46. Recipient Spl. Merit medal, Acoustical Soc. Japan, 1988, History Med. Ultrasound Pioneer award, AIUM/WFUMB, 1988; Spl. Rsch. fellow, NIH, 1968—69, Eleanor Roosevelt-Internat. Cancer fellow, Am. Cancer Soc., 1975—76, 1982—83, Fulbright fellow, 1982—83, Japan Soc. Promotion Sci. fellow, 1982, 1996, Fogarty Internat. fellow, 1990. Fellow: AAAS, IEEE (life), Inst. Acoustics (U.K.), Am. Inst. Ultrasound in Medicine (William J. Fry meml. award 1984, Joseph H. Holmes Basic Sci. Pioneer award 1990), Acoustical Soc. Am. (assoc. editor Jour. 1968-2009, exec. coun. 1977-80, v.p. 1980-81, pres. 1985-86, chmn. pub. policy com. 1994-2005, Silver medal 1989, Gold medal 1998), Am. Inst. Med. Biol. Engring. (IEEE Engring. Medicine and Biology Soc. Career Achievement award 1995, Edison medal 1996, William J. & Francis J. Fry award 2008), Internat. Acad. Med. Biol. Engring.; mem.: NAE, NAS, Biophys. Soc., Rochester Soc. Biomed. Ultrasound (hon.), Japan Soc. Ultrasound in Medicine (hon.), Am. Inst. Physics (mem. editl. bd. series in modern acoustics and signal processing 1990—97, publs. policy com. 1992—2000), NCRP Alumni Assn., NIH Alumni Assn., Sigma Xi, Phi Sigma Phi, Phi Sigma, Pi Mu Epsilon, Tau Beta Pi, Eta Kappa Nu, Sigma Tau. Home: Tucson, Ariz. *Excellent, dedicated and understanding teachers, bright and energetic students, and a single-mindedness to see a problem to solution are the ingredients for a modest success.* Died Jan. 24, 2015.

DUNN, JACK NEWTON, urologist; s. Isaac Newton and Geraldine K. Dunn; m. Helen F. Snelling; children: Diane, Jack Jr., Sharon. BA, The Citadel, Charleston, SC, 1951, BS, 1955; MD, Med. Coll. SC, Charleston, 1960. Intern Charity Hosp., New Orleans; urology resident Tulane U., 1963—67; founder Western Carolina Urology, Hendersonville, NC, 1967—91. With US Pub. Health Svcs., Alaska, 1961—63. Col. USAR, with US Army, 1951—55, Korean War. Fellow: Am. Coll. Surgeons, Internat. Coll. Surgeons, AMA; mem.: Am. Urol. Assn. (southeastern sect.), Western Carolina African Med. Mission, NC Med. Soc. Avocations: flying, genealogy, photography, travel. Home: Hendersonville, NC. Died Nov. 20, 2015.

DUNNING, DAVID MICHAEL, history educator; b. Buffalo, Feb. 18, 1945; s. Francis S. and Marion P. Dunning; m. Judith A. Dunning. BA, Occidental Coll., 1966; PhD, U. Ill., 1995. Instr. Honolulu (Hawaii) C.C., 1988-91; assoc. faculty Seattle Ctrl. C.C., 1991-93, Mohave C.C., Lake Hausu City, Ariz., 1993-96, West Shore C.C., Ludington, Mich., 1996-97, Grand Valley State U., Allendale, Mich., 1997; asst. prof. history U. Alaska Southeast, Ketchikan, Alaska, from 1997. Adv. bd. Tongass Hist. Mus., Ketchikan, 1998—; bd. dirs. Ketchikon Hist. Com., 1998—; bd. dirs., treas. Hist. Ketchikan, 1998—; apptd. mem. Kaneohe Bay Task Force, Kaneohe, 1990-91; del., platform com. Dem. Party State Conv., Honolulu, 1990; dist. 3 rep., vice chair Kahuluu Neighbor Bd. #29, Kahaluu, 1987-91. Wilson grantee U. Alaska S.E., 1998, 99, Ketchikan Centennial Planning grantee Alaska Humanities Forum, 1998; postdoctoral fellowship Lilly Found., 1996. Mem. Tongass Hist. Soc. (pres.), Mining History Assn., Gastineau Channel Hist. Soc., Alaska History Soc., Western History Assn. Home: Ketchikan, Alaska. Died Apr. 27, 2007.

DURANT, GRAHAM JOHN, medicinal chemist, drug researcher; b. Newport, Gwent, U.K., Mar. 14, 1934; s. Edgar Counsell and Florence (Pocock) D.; m. Rosemary Margaret Towle, Apr. 14, 1962; children: Julian Clive, Adrian Charles. BSc in Chemistry with honors, U. Birmingham, UK, 1955, PhD, 1958; postdoctoral study, State U. Iowa, Iowa City, 1958-59. Sr. rsch. officer Smith Kline & French Rsch., Welwyn Garden City, Hertfordshire, U.K., 1960-75, head dept. medicinal chemistry, 1975-85, head rsch. adminstrn., 1985-86; Disting. prof. medicinal chemistry Coll. Pharmacy, U. Toledo, Ohio, 1987-92, dir. Ctr. for Drug Design and Devel. Ohio, 1987-92; sr. dir. chemistry Cambridge (Mass.) Neurosci., Inc., 1992-98; pharm. cons., from 1998. Contbr. articles to profl. jours.; co-holder over 100 patents. Trustee Inventure Place, Akron, Ohio, 1990-98. Inducted into Nat. Inventors Hall of Fame, 1990. Fellow Royal Soc. Chemistry (Medicinal Chemistry award 1983, mem. fine chems. group com. 1985-87). Avocations: genealogy, travel. Died Mar. 2009.

DURANTE, JAMES PETER, lawyer; b. NYC, July 17, 1914; s. Salvatore and Grace (Rocco) D.; m. Joan Marilyn Durante (dec.). LLB, St. John's U., Queens, NY, 1938. Bar: N.Y. 1939, U.S. Dist. Ct. (so. dist.) N.Y. 1947, U.S. Supreme Ct. 1956. Ptnr. Reavis & McGrath, 1962-80, Fulbright & Jaworski, NYC, from 1990. Mediator Citizen Dispute Settlement Program, Sarasota, Fla., 1983—; arbitrator Better Business Coun., Sarasota, Fla.; testified as a labor arbitrator, mediation expert U.S. Congress Judiciary Com. Author: Law of Sports, 1950. With USMC, 1942-43. Mem. ABA (labor arbitration com.). Died Feb. 8, 2007.

DYER, WAYNE WALTER, psychologist, writer, radio and television personality; b. Detroit, May 10, 1940; s. Melvin Lyle and Hazel Irene (Vollick) Dyer; m. Marcelene Louise Dyer (separated); children: Shane, Stephanie, Skye, Sommer, Serena, Sands, Saje; 1 child from previous marriage, Tracy. BS, Wayne State U., Detroit, 1965, MS in Counseling and Ednl. Psychology, 1966, EdD in Counseling and Psychology, 1970. Tchr., counselor Pershing HS, Detroit, 1965-67; dir. guidance/counseling Mercy HS, Farmington, Mich., 1967-71; instr. counselor edn. Wayne State U., 1970—73; staff cons. Herman Kiefer Hosp., Detroit, 1974-75; staff cons., instr. guidance and sch. psychol. pers. Half Hollow Sch. Dist., Huntington, NY, 1973-75; mem. tchg. faculty North Shore U. Hosp., Cornell U. Med. Coll., Manhasset, NY, 1974-75; asst. prof. counselor edn. St. John's U., Jamaica, NY, 1971-74, assoc. prof., 1974-77. Author: Counseling Techniques That Work, 1975, Your Erroneous Zones, 1976, Pulling Your Own Strings, 1978, Group Counseling for Personal Mastery, 1980, The Sky's the Limit, 1980, Gifts from Eykis : A Story of Self-Discovery, 1983, What Do You Really Want for Your Children, 1985, Happy Holidays!, 1986, Real Magic: Creating Miracles in Everyday Life, 1992, Everyday Wisdom, 1993, How to Be a No-Limit Person, 1994, You'll See It When You Believe It: The Way to Your Personal Transformation, 1995, Your Sacred Self: Making the Decision to Be Free, 1995, A Promise Is a Promise: An Almost Unbelievable Story of a Mother's Unconditional Love and What It Can Teach Us, 1996, Manifest Your Destiny: The Nine Spiritual Principles for Getting Everything You Want, 1997, Wisdom of the Ages, 1998, There's a Spiritual Solution to Every Problem, 2001, 10 Secrets For Success And Inner Peace, 2002, It's Never Crowded Along the Extra Mile, 2002, Getting in the Gap: Making Conscious Contact With God Through Meditation, 2002, The Caroline Myss & Wayne Dyer Seminar, 2003, The Power of Intention: Learning to Co-Create Your World Your Way, 2004, Staying on the Path, 2004, Incredible You!, 2005, Inspiration: Your Ultimate Calling, 2006, Being in Balance: 9 Principles for Creating habits to Match Your Desires, 2006, Everyday Wisdom for Success, 2006, Making Your Thoughts Work for You, 2007, Change Your Thoughts - Change Your Life: Living the Wisdom of the Tao, 2007, Living The Wisdom Of The Tao: The Complete Tao Te Ching and Affirmations, 2008, Excuses Begone!, 2009, The Shift: Taking Your Life from Ambition to Meaning, 2010, Wishes Fulfilled: Mastering the Art of Manifesting, 2012, (memoir) I Can See Clearly Now, 2014, (ebook) A New Way of Thinking, A New Way of Being, 2010; co-author: Co-creating as Its Best: A Conversation Between Master Teachers, 2014, Memories of Heaven: Children's Astounding Recollections of the Time Before They Came to Earth, 2015; author: (children's books) No Excuses! How What You Say Can Get Get In Your Way, 2009, I Am: Why Two Little Words Means So Much, 2012, Good-bye Bumps! Talking to What's Bugging You, 2014; several appearances on TV/radio programs including Phil Donohue Show, Tonight Show, Dinah Shore Show, Merv Griffin Show, Mike Douglas Show, Good Morning America, Canada AM, Oprah Winfrey Show, others; contbr. numerous articles to profl. jours.; host (weekly radio show) HayHouseRadio.com, produced several DVD, Compact Discs, videos and cassettes. Served with USN, 1958—62. Recipient Disting. Alumni of Yr., Wayne State U., 1980, Golden Gavel award, Internat. Toastmasters, 1987. Home: Fort Lauderdale, Fla. Died Aug. 30, 2015.

DYKES, MARY JANE MCLIN, educational administrator; b. Clinton, Okla., Feb. 16, 1932; d. Thomas William and Willie Darcus (Reeder) McL.; m. John Hugh Dykes, Feb. 17, 1951; children: Lora Louise Biddy, John Leslie. BS in Edn. summa cum laude, Midwestern U., Wichita Falls, Tex., 1966; MEd, North Tex. State U., 1972; EdD, Tex. Woman's U., 1983. Cert. in spl. edn., reading, mid-adminstrn., Tex. Dir. outside funds Arlington (Tex.) Ind. Sch. Dist. Mem. Internat. Reading Assn., Nat. Coun. Tchrs. English, Tex. Elem. Prins. and Suprs. Assn., Alpha Chi, Phi Delta Kappa. Home: Weatherford, Tex. Died Apr. 19, 2007.

DYNKIN, EUGENE BORISOVICH, mathematics professor; b. Leningrad, USSR, May 11, 1924; came to U.S., 1977, naturalized, 1983; s. Boris and Rebecca (Sheindlin) D.; m. Irene Pakshver, June 2, 1959; 1 child, Olga. BA, Moscow U., 1945, PhD, 1948, D.Sc., 1951; D Honoris Causa, U. Pierre and Marie Curie, Paris, 1997, Ind. Moscow U., U. Warwick, UK, 2003. Asst. prof. Moscow U., 1948-49, assoc. prof., 1949-54, prof., 1954-68; sr. research scholar Central Inst. Math. Econ. Acad. Sci., Moscow, 1968-76; prof. math. Cornell U., Ithaca, NY, 1977—2014. Author: Theory of Markov Processes, 1960, Mathematical Conversations, 1963, Markov Processes, 1965, Mathematicl

Problems, 1969, Markov Processes-Theorems and Problems, 1969, Controlled Markov Processes, 1979, Markov Processes and Related Problems of Analysis, 1982, An Introduction to Branching Measure-Valued Processes, 1994, Biography and Bibliography in the Dynkin Festschrift, Markov Processes and Their Applications, 1994, Selected Papers of E.B. Dynkin, 2000, Diffusion, Superdiffusions and Partial Differential Equations, 2002, Superdiffusions and Positive Solutions of Nonlinear Partial Differentiae Equations, 2004. Fellow: AAAS, Inst. Math. Stats.; mem.: NAS, Bernoulli Soc. Math. Stats. and Probability, Moscow Math. Soc. (hon. prize 1951), American Math. Soc. (Leroy P. Steele prize 1993). Home: Ithaca, NY. Died Nov. 14, 2014.

DYSART, RICHARD ALLEN, actor; b. Brighton, Mass., Mar. 30, 1929; m. Kathryn Jacobi. BS, Emerson Coll., 1956, MS, 1983, LLD (hon.), 1988; PhD (hon.), U. Maine, 1992. Actor appeared off Broadway in Our Town, Six Characters in Search of an Author; on Broadway in A Man for All Seasons, The Little Foxes, A Place Without Doors, That Championship Season, Another Part of the Forest,(films) Petulia, 1968, The Lost Man, 1969, The Sporting Club, 1971, The Hospital, 1971, The Terminal Man, 1974, The Crazy World of Julius Vrooder, 1974, The Day of the Locust, 1975, The Hindenberg, 1975, Prophecy, 1979, Meteor, 1979, Being There, 1979, An Enemy of the People, 1978, The Thing, 1982, The Falcon and the Snowman, 1985, Mask, 1985 Pale Rider, 1985, Warning Sign, 1985, Wall Street, 1987, Back to the Future Part III, 1990, Panther, 1995, Hard Rain, 1998, (TV films) The Autobiography of Miss Jane Pittman, 1974, Guess Who's Coming to Dinner, 1975, Riding With Death, 1976, The Court Martial of George Armstrong Custer, 1977, It Happened One Christmas, 1977, First You Cry, 1978, Bogie, 1980, The Ordeal of Dr. Mudd, 1980, Churchill and the Generals, 1981, Sandburg's Lincoln, People Vs. Jean Harris, 1981, Norma Rae, 1981, Bitter Harvest, 1981, The Seal, 1981, Missing Children: A Mother's Story, 1982, Malice in Wonderland, 1985, Blood & Orchids, 1986, Last Days of Patton, 1986, Six Against the Rock, 1987, Moving Target, 1988, Mickey's 60th Birthday, 1988, Day One, 1989, Mystery of the Keys, 1991, Marilyn and Bobby: Her Final Affair, 1993, Truman, 1995, A Child Is Missing, 1995, L.A. Law Reunion Movie, 2002, (TV series) You Are There, 1953, East Side/West Side, 1963, Mr. Broadway, 1964, The Doctors and the Nurses, 1964, The Defenders, 1965, CBS Playhouse, 1969, NET Playhouse, 1966-72, All in the Family, 1972, Baretta, 1975, Maude, 1975, Doc, 1975, Doctors' Hospital, 1975, Cannon, 1976, Sara, 1976, The Andros Targets, 1977, Columbo, 1978, Vision, 1978, Lou Grant, 1980, American Playhouse, 1984, Insight, 1984, Challenge of the GoBots, 1984, L.A. Law, 1986-94 (Supporting Actor TV-Series Emmy award 1992), Batman: The Animated Series, 1992-94, My Secret Summer, 1995, Spawn, 1997-99, (PBS spl.) Concealed Enemies; (mini-series) Lincoln, 1975-76, Gemini Man, 1976, War and Remembrance, 1989 Trustee Gallaudet U., Washington, 1990-2003, trustee emeritus, 2004-2015, Gould Acad., Bethel, Maine; founding mem. Am. Conservatory Theatre, San Francisco; active Native Am. Rights Fund, 1978-2015. Sgt. USAF, 1951—55. Mem.: Am. Judicature Soc. (bd. dirs., nat. exec. com. from 1998). Died Apr. 5, 2015.

EATON, JOHN C., composer, educator; b. Bryn Mawr, Pa., Mar. 30, 1935; s. Harold C. and Fannie E. (Geer) E.; m. Nelda E. Nelson, May 31, 1973; children: Elizabeth Estela, Julian R.P. AB, Princeton U., NJ, 1957, MFA, 1959. Performing artist Columbia Artists, NYC, 1961-65; prof. music Ind. U., Bloomington, from 1970, U. Chgo., 1991—2001. Composer-in-residence Am. Acad., Rome, Italy, 1975-76; lectr. Salzburg Seminar in Am. Studies, Austria, 1976; honored guest Soviet Composers Soc., 1977 Composer numerous operas, most recently: Myshkin, 1972 (Peabody award 1972), Danton and Robespierre, 1978, The Cry of Clytaemnestra, 1980, The Tempest, 1985 (Santa Fe Commn.), The Reverend Jim Jones, 1988, Peer Gynt, 1989, Let's Get This Show on the Road, 1993, Don Quixote, 1994, Golk, 1995, Travelling with Gulliver, 1997, Antigone, 1999, ...inasmuch, 2002, Pinocchio, 2003, The Curious Case of Benjamin Button, 2010, numerous chamber orchs. and elec. comps.; featured in numerous articles in profl. jours. Recipient Prix de Rome, Am. Acad., Rome, 1959-62; citation Am. Inst. Arts and Letters, 1972; plaque Ind. Arts Council, 1975; MacArthur "Genius" Fellow award, 1990; Guggenheim fellow, 1962, 65 Achievements include being called the most interesting opera composer writing in America today. Died Dec. 2, 2015.

EBBELS, BRUCE JEFFERY, retired physician, health facility administrator; b. NYC, Dec. 26, 1924; s. Walter Jeffery and Mildred Christiana (Bruce) E.; m. Shirley Marie Cooley, July 3, 1950; children: Bruce Jeffery Jr., Cynthia, Stephanie, Leslie, David. Student, Colgate U., 1943-44; MD, N.Y. Med. Coll., 1948. Intern Hurley Med. Ctr., Flint, Mich., 1948-49; staff Mercy Hosp., Watertown, NY, 1954—88, House of the Good Samaritan, Watertown, 1954—88; resident in internal medicine VA Hosp., Richmond, Va., 1951—54; pvt. practice gastroenterology and internal medicine Watertown, N.Y., 1954-90; med. dir. N.Y. Air Brake Co., Watertown, 1992-94; med. coord. VA Clinic, Watertown, N.Y., 1994-97; staff Genesis Healthcare, Watertown, NY, 1998-99; med. advisor Credo Cmty. Ctr. Addictions, Carthage, NY, from 1992. Chief medicine Mercy Hosp., Watertown, N.Y., 1975-78, House of the Good Samaritan Hosp., Watertown, 1978-83, pres. med. staff, 1978; cons. in internal medicine E.J. Noble Hosp., 1960-88, Lewis County Gen. Hosp., 1960-88, Carthage Area Hosp., 1966-88; cons. in field. Contbr. chapters to books. Pres. Jefferson County Assn. for Mental Health, Watertown, 1969-70; bd. trustees Watertown (N.Y.) Savs. Bank, 1971—; bd. vestry Trinity Ch., Watertown, 1972-78, 2000—; med. advisor Credo-Cmty. Ctr. for Addicitons, 1992—. Capt. USNR, 1979—. Recipient John Philips Rice Svc. award Jefferson County Assn. for Mental Health, Watertown, 1970, Disting. Svc. award Jefferson County divsn. Am. Heart Assn. Fellow ACP (life), Am. Coll. Gastroenterology (sr.); mem. AMA (life), Med. Soc. State N.Y. (life), Med. Soc. Jefferson County (life; pres. 1979-80), Staplin Creek Soc. (past pres.). Republican. Episcopalian. Avocations: aquatic sports, scuba diving, writing, lecturing. Home: Watertown, NY. Died Mar. 22, 2007.

EBERL, JAMES JOSEPH, physical chemist, consultant; b. Dunkirk, NY, Oct. 7, 1916; s. George M. and Florence S. (Stedler) E.; m. Donna Davis, July 18, 1996. BA, U. Buffalo, NYC, 1938, PhD, 1941; AMP, Harvard U., Cambridge, Mass., 1955. Asst. prof. chemistry U. Del., Newark, 1941-42; mgr. rsch. Paper Chem. Divsn. Hercules Inc., Wilmington, Del., 1942-43; sr. fellow Mellon Inst. Indsl. Rsch., Pitts., 1943-44; dir. spl. prodn. rsch. Johnson and Johnson, New Brunswick, N.J., 1944-48; asst. corp. v.p. Scott Paper Co., Chester, Pa., 1948-70; pres., CEO Newbold Inc., Phila., 1970-72; cons. Moylan, Pa., 1972-2000; pres., CEO Eberl Group, from 2000, Ebersytes, LLC, from 2002. Contbr. articles to profl. jours. Trustee The Franklin Inst., Phila., 1960—, mem. sci. and arts com., 1987—; chmn. bd. dirs. rsch. fund Phila. Gen. Hosp., 1963-76; mem. adv. coun. Pa. Tech. Assistance program Pa. State U., 1965-71; mem. dean's adv. coun. U. Buffalo Coll. Arts and Scis., 2000—. Receipent Disting. Alumni award, U. Buffalo, 1999. Mem. Am. Chem. Soc., Am. Inst. Chem. Engrs., N.Y. Acad. Scis., Empire State Paper Rsch. Assn. (pres. 1965-71), Sigma Xi. Achievements include 50 patents for dusting powder for surgical rubber gloves that does not produce abdominal adhesions, single crystal whisker fibers, process for making hard coated plaster of Paris bandages, process for making high strength plaster of Paris, polystyrene foam sheet process, making soybean protein, bleaching process for groundwood pulp; for new chemical sterilization of microbes with epoxides, hemostatic agents, synthetic paper pulp fiberous extenders; process for the manufacture of Viva paper towel; novel dermal formulations; Dermatological Compositions Using Bio-Activating Organocatalysts. Home: Hilton Head Island, SC. Died June 6, 2015.

EBERTS, ROBERT EUGENE, chemist; b. Columbus, Ohio, May 30, 1931; s. Robert Eugene and Anna (Buechner) E.; m. Louise Cresentia Berner, Sept. 5, 1953; children: Patricia M., Margaret A., Eberts Lind, Robert J., William G., Colleen L. Eberts Mangeot. BS in Chemistry, U. Dayton, 1953; PhD in Phys. Chemistry, Iowa State U., 1957. Sr. devel. chemist pigments divsn. The Mearl Corp., Peekskill, N.Y., 1971-73, group leader pigments divsn., 1973-84, corp. eviron. and reg. affairs pigments divsn., 1984-90, dept. head pigments divsn., 1987-89, asst. plant mgr. pigments divsn., 1989-94, plant mgr. pigments divsn, 1994-96; retired, 1996. Bd. dirs. N.Y. State Chem. Alliance, Albany, 1982-96. Contbr. articles to profl. jours. 1st lt. U.S. Army, 1958. Fellow Am. Inst. Chemists; mem. Am. Chem. Soc. Roman Catholic. Achievements include 6 patents in field. Home: Cincinnati, Ohio. Died Feb. 5, 2007.

EBINGER, LINDA ANN, retired nurse; b. North Attleboro, Mass., Apr. 6, 1944; d. Donat Leo Deshetres and Muriel Francis Mumford; m. Carl R. Ebinger, Jr. (dec. Apr. 1994); children: Carl R. III, Eric Edward. Diploma in practical nursing, Lindsay Hopkins Nursing Sch., Miami, 1978. LPN, Fla.; cert. LPN IV therapy. ECG technician Sturdy Meml. Hosp., Attleboro, Mass., 1962-65, with radiology dept., 1968-69; stewardess TWA, 1965; clin. lab. technician Wrentham State Sch., Mass., 1965-71, EKG dept. mgr. Mass., 1965-70; rental property owner, mgr., from 1973; orthop./med.-surg. unit nurse Bapt. Hosp. Miami, 1978-81, oncology unit nurse, 1981-82, ob-gyn. unit, 1982—84, with Joslin Diabetes Care Ctr., 1984-93, orthop./neurol. nurse, 1993-99, nurse short stay overnight unit, 1999—2001, ret., 1961. Vol. Domestic Violence Abuse Ctr., Punta Gorda, Fla., from 2002; mem. Team Punta Gorda. Mem. LWV (sec. Dade County 1995-98, bd. dirs. 1998-2001, pres. Port Charlotte, Fla. chpt. 2004-), Freeman House Soc. (sec. 2002-05), Punta Gorda Isles Yacht Club (co-chair hospitality com.). Republican. Roman Catholic. Home: Port Charlotte, Fla. Died Jan. 2, 2007.

EBISUZAKI, YUKIKO, retired chemistry professor; b. Mission City, BC, Can., July 25, 1930; came to U.S., 1957; d. Masuzo and Shige (Kusumoto) E. BS with honors, U. Western Ont., London, Can., 1956, MS, 1957; PhD, Ind. U., 1962. Postdoctoral U. Pa., Phila., 1962-63; faculty rsch. assoc. Ariz. State U., Tempe, 1963-67; acting asst. prof. UCLA, 1967-75; assoc. prof. N.C. State U., Raleigh, 1975-99, assoc. prof. emeritus, from 1999. Contbr. articles to profl. jours. Ont. Rsch. Found. fellow Ont. Rsch. Coun., 1957-60, Gerry fellow Sigma Delta Epsilon, 1977-78. Mem. Am. Chem. Soc., Sigma Xi. Home: Raleigh, NC. Died May 27, 2007.

ECKER, ARTHUR DAVID, neurologist; b. NYC, Jan. 29, 1913; s. Murray and Olga (Edelstein) E.; m. Marcia Schlesinger, Sept. 15, 1935; children: Sandra Ecker Kaplan, Jonathan Ecker. AB, Dartmouth Coll., 1931; MD, Johns Hopkins, 1934; MS in Neurology, PhD in Neurology, U. Minn., 1938. Diplomate Am. Bd. Neurol. Surgery, Am. Bd. Psychiat. and Neurology. Intern Mary Hitchcock Meml. Hosp., Hanover, N.H., 1934-35; fellow neurology and neurosurgery Mayo Clinic, Rochester, Minn., 1935-39; pvt. practice Syracuse, N.Y., 1939-88; ret., 1988; sr. attending neurosurgeon Community Gen. Hosp., Crouse-Irving Meml. Hosp., Syracuse, 1955-57. Founder Dept. Neurosurgery Med. Sch., Syracuse U., 1939; clin. prof. neurosurgery SUNY, 1955-57. Author: Normal Cerebral Angiography, 1951; (with others) Angiographic Localization of Cerebral Masses, 1955; contbr. over 115 articles to profl. jours. and publs. Major U.S. Army, 1942-45. Fellow ACS, Am. Acad. Neurology, Am. Assn. of Neurol. Surgeons, Assn. of Mil. Surgeons, N.Y. Acad. of Medicine. Avocation: research on etiopathogenesis of trigeminal neuralia. Home: Jamesville, NY. Died Dec. 5, 2006.

ECKSTEIN, ARTHUR, graphic designer, consultant; b. NYC, Aug. 16, 1923; s. Ernest and Bertha (Gross) E.; m. Edith Wiener, Aug. 25, 1946; children: Karen Eve, Mark Ernest, Eric Neil. BA, Bklyn. Coll., 1946. Designer, photographer Ernest Eckstein Studios, NYC, 1946-50; advt. mgr. Delta Brush Mfg. Corp., NYC, 1950-55; pres. Eckstein-Stone Inc., NYC, 1955-70, Arthur Eckstein & Assocs. Inc., NYC, 1970-84; owner, mgr. Arthur Eckstein & Assocs., Roslyn Heights, N.Y., from 1984; managing dir. Exeter Assocs. Inc., Providence and Roslyn Hts, 1990-97. Mem. faculty Poly. Inst. Bklyn., 1959, Assn. for Graphic Arts, N.Y.C., 1974-89, Hofstra U., Hempstead, N.Y., 1985-87; cons. Gorham Co. div. Textron, Providence, 1985-87, Devlin Video Svc., N.Y.C., 1975-90, Paul Kagan Group, Carmel, Calif., 1969—; lectr. gen. mgmt. program McGraw-Hill, N.Y.C., 1988; guest lectr., speaker N.Y. Inst. Tech., LaGuardia Community Coll., Chgo. Art Dirs. Club, Package Designers Coun., Young Printing Exec. Club, Women in Design, Graphic Arts Assn., Am. Mktg. Assn. Co-author: Preparing Art for Printing, 1965, rev., 1983; patentee graphic arts color tool, skier's exercise device. Bd. dirs. Sea Cliff (N.Y.) Chamber Players, Inc., 1987-95, v.p., 1990-95. Recipient numerous awards for graphic design from various orgns., including Type Dirs. Club, Soc. Typog. Arts, Printing Industries Assn., N.Y. Internat. Film and TV Festival, Packaging Inst., Chgo. Internat. Film Festival, San Francisco Internat. Fil Festival, Soc. Illustrators, CLIO Awards, Art Dirs. Club N.Y., Am. Inst. Graphic Arts, Print Desi Awards. Mem. Am. Inst. Graphic Arts. Jewish. Avocations: skiing, tennis, horseback riding, painting, woodworking. Died Jan. 26, 2007.

ECO, UMBERTO, semiotics educator, author; b. Alessandria, Italy, Jan. 5, 1932; s. Giulio and Giovanna (Bisio) Eco; m. Renate Ramge, Sept. 24, 1962; children: Stefano, Carlotta. Laurea in Philosophy, U. Torino, 1954; Libero Docente in Aesthetics, 1961; Ordinario di Semiotica, U. Bologna, 1975; several honorary degrees from international and domestic universities (hon.). Lectr. aesthetics U. Turin, Milan Poly., 1956—64; assoc. prof. visual comm. U. Florence, 1966—69; assoc. prof. semiotics Milan Poly., 1969—71, U. Bologna, 1971—75, prof. semiotics, 1975—2008, prof. emeritas, from 2008. Dir. Instituto di Discipline della Communicazione e dello Spettacolo U. Bologna, 1976—77, 1980—83, dir. Instituto di Discipline della Communicazione, 1983—88, dir. semiotics PhD program, 1986, 2002, pres. Scuola Superiore di Studi Umanistici, from 1999; mem. exec. sci. com. U. San Marino, 1989—95, pres. Internat. Ctr. Semiotics & Cognitive Studies, from 1989; pres. Consiglio Scientifico Inst. Italiano di Scienze Umane, 2002—05, pres. Comitato dei Garanti, from 2006; vis. prof. NYU, 1969—70, 1976, Northwestern U., 1972, U. Calif. San Diego, 1975, Yale U., 1977, 1980, 1981, Columbia U., 1978, 1984, Collège de France, Paris, 1992—93, École Normale Superiore, Paris, 1996; vis. Fellow, Italian Acad. Columbia U., 1996; Tanner lectr. Cambridge U., 1990; Norton lectr. Harvard U., 1992, 1993; Goggio lectr. U. Toronto, 2002; Weidenfeld lectr. Oxford U., 2002; chair, Corso di Laurea, Scienze della Communicazione U. Bologna, 1993—98. Editor cultural programs RAI Italian Radio-TV, Milan, 1954—59, sr. non-fiction editor Casa Editrice Bompiani Pub. House, 1959—75, columnist Il giorno, La stampa, Corriere della Sera, La Repubblica, L'Espresso, Il Manifesto, from 1962, cofounder Marcatré rev., 1961, Quindici rev., 1967; editor: Versus, from 1971; mem. editorial bd. Semiotica, Poetics Today, Degrès, Structuralist Rev., Text, Communication, Problemi dell'informazione, Word & Images, Alfabeta; author: (fiction works include) The Name of the Rose, 1983 (Premio Strega, 1981, Premio Anghiari, 1981, Prix Medicis best fgn. novel, 1982, LA Times fiction prize nom., 1983), Foucault's Pendulum, 1989, The Island of the Day Before, 1994, Baudolino, 2002, The Mysterious Flame of Queen Loana, 2005, On Ugliness, 2007, Turning Back the Clock, 2008, The Infinity of Listss, 2009, The Prague Cemetary, 2011, Numero Zero, 2015, (non-fiction works include) A Theory of Semiotics, 1977, The Role of the Reader, 1979, Postscript to The Name of the Rose, 1984, Semiotics & the Philosophy of Language, 1984, Art & Beauty in the Middle Ages, 1985, Travels in Hyperreality, 1986, The Aesthetics of Thomas Aquinas, 1988, The Open Work, 1989, The Middle Ages of James Joyce, 1989, The Limits of Interpretation, 1990, Interpretation & Overinterpretation, 1992, Misreadings, 1993, Apocalypse Postponed, 1994, How to Travel with a Salmon, 1994, Six Walks in the Fictional Woods, 1994, The Search for the Perfect Language, 1995, Talking of Joyce, 1998, Serendipities: Language & Lunacy, 1999, Belief or Nonbelief?, 2000, Kant & the Platypus, 2000, Experiences in Translation, 2000, Five Moral Pieces, 2001, Mouse or Rat?: Translation as Negotiation, 2004; editor: History of Beauty, 2004; co-editor: The Picture History of Inventions, 1963, Il caso Bond (The Bond Affair), 1965, A Portrait of Italy, 1967, A Semiotic Landscape, 1979, The Sign of Three: Pierce, Holmes, Dupin, 1983, Carnival!, 1984, Meaning & Mental Representations, 1988, On the Medieval Theory of Signs, 1989, Conversations About the End of Time, 1999; author of several philosophy books; author: (children's books) The Bomb and the General, 1966, The Three Astronauts, 1966, Gli gnomi di Gru, 1992. Recipient Prix Medicis Etranger, France, 1892, Columbus award, Rotary Club, Florence, 1983, Marshall McLuhan award, Unesco Canada & Teleglobe, 1985, Golden Cross of the Dodecannese, Greece, 1995, Orden pour le Merite für Wissenschaften und Künst, Germany, 1999, Crystal award,

World Economic Forum, 1999, Austrian State award for European Literature, 2002, Prix Mediterranée Etranger, France, 2002, Kenyon Review award, 2005, Prize from City of Budapest, 2007, McKim medal, American Acad. of Rome, 2007; named Commandeur de l'Ordre des Arts et des Lettres, France, 1985, Cavaliere di Gran Croce al Merito, Italy, 1996, Chevalier de la Legion d'Honneur, France, 2003, Gran Gagliaudo d'Oro della Citta di Alessandria, 2004. Fellow: St. Anne's Coll., Oxford (hon.), Kellogg Coll., Oxford (hon.); mem.: Polish Acad. of Arts & Sciences (fgn. mem.), Am. Acad. Arts & Letters (hon.), James Joyce Assn. (hon. trustee), Internat. Acad. Philosophy & Art, Coun. Advisors Bibliotheca Alexandrina, Acad. Europea de Yuste, Acad. Sci. Bologna, Acad. Sci. Bologna, Acad. Universelle des Cultures, Internat. Assn. Semiotic Studies (sec. gen. 1972—79, vice pres. 1979—83, hon. pres. from 1994). Died Feb. 19, 2016.

EDDLEMAN, FLOYD EUGENE, retired language educator; b. Mena, Ark., Dec. 3, 1930; s. Floyd Newton and Ruby Kate (Cannon) E. BSE, U. Cen. Ark., 1951; MA, U. Ark., 1955, PhD, 1961. Teaching asst. English U. Ark., Fayetteville, 1953-55, 56-58; instr. English & Speech U. Colo., Boulder, 1955-56; instr. English Tex. Tech U., Lubbock, 1958-62, asst. prof., 1962-65, assoc. prof., 1965-75, prof., 1975-90, prof. emeritus, from 1991. Author: American Drama Criticism, 1976, 79, 84, 89, 92; co-editor: Almayer's Folly in the Cambridge Edit. of the Works of Joseph Conrad, 1994; contbr. articles to profl. jours. Sgt. US Army, 1951—53. Democrat. Avocation: genealogy. Home: Mena, Ark. Died Jan. 13, 2015.

EDDY, ELSBETH MARIE, retired government official, statistician; b. Buffalo, Apr. 8, 1934; d. Willy and Wilhelmine (Hartman) Gnueg; m. Leonard John Eddy, Feb. 5, 1956; children: John, Bruce, Lisa. Student, Schs. in Md., Va., DC; spl. courses, U.S. Dept. Agriculture Grad. Sch.; cert. in mgmt., Prince Georges Coll., 1976. With fgn. trade div. U.S. Bur. Census, Washington, 1967-90, chief metals and minerals, 1980-90. Recipient Cert. of Appreciation, USAF, 1973. Republican. Avocations: swimming, gardening, growing orchids, painting, mineral and gem collecting. Home: Sebastian, Fla. Died Feb. 13, 2014.

EDELMAN, JUDITH HOCHBERG, architect; b. Bklyn., Sept. 16, 1923; d. Abraham and Frances (Israel) Hochberg; m. Harold Edelman, Dec. 26, 1947 (dec. 1999); children: Marc, Joshua. Student, Conn. Coll., 1940—41, NYU, 1941—42; BArch, Columbia U., 1946. Designer, drafter Huson Jackson, NYC, 1948-58; Schermerhorn traveling fellow, 1950; pvt. practice, 1958-60; ptnr. Edelman & Salzman, NYC, 1960-79, Edelman Partnership, NYC, 1979—2002, Edelman, Sultan, Knox, Wood /Architects LLP, NYC, 2002—14. Adj. prof. Sch. Architecture CUNY, 1972-76, vis. lectr. grad. program in environ. psychology, 1977, 77; vis. lectr. Washington U., St. Louis, 1974, U. Oreg., 1974, MIT, 1975, Pa. State U., 1977, Rensselaer Poly. Inst., 1977, Columbia U., 1979; First Claire Watson Forrest Meml. lectr. U. Oreg., U. Calif., Berkeley, U. So. Calif., 1982. Prin. works include Restoration of St. Mark's Ch. in the Bowery, N.Y.C., 1970-82, Two Bridges Urban Renewal Area Housing, 1970-2008, Jennings Hall Sr. Citizens Housing, Bklyn., 1980, Goddard Riverside Elderly Housing and Cmty. Ctr., N.Y.C., 1983, Columbus Green Apartments, N.Y.C., 1987, Chung Pak Bldg., N.Y.C., 1992, Child Care Ctr., Queens, N.Y., 1999. Mem. Charles B. Wang Cmty. Health Ctr., 2000, New Heights Acad. Charter Sch., 2009. Recipient Bard 1st honor award City Club N.Y., 1969, Bard award of merit, 1975, 82, award for design excellence US Dept. Housing & Urban Devel. (HUD), 1970, 1st prize Nat. Trust for Hist. Preservation, 1983, award of merit Mcpl. Art Soc. N.Y., 1983, Public Svc. award Settlement Housing Fund, 1983, Women of Vision award NOW, 1989, 1st prize for Design Excellence Chamber of Commerce, Borough of Queens, N.Y., 1989, Best in Srs.' Housing award Nat. Assn. Home Builders, 1993, Hamilton-Madison House Cmty. Svc. award, 1997, Preservation League award NYS, 2009. Fellow AIA (dir. N.Y. chpt., chmn. commn. on archtl. edn. 1971-73, chmn. nat. task force on women in architecture 1974-75, v.p. N.Y. chpt. 1975-77, chmn. ethics com. 1975-77, Residential Design award 1969, Pioneer in Housing award 1990, N.Y. State Assn. Archs.-AIA Honor award 1975, Design Merit award N.Y. chpt. 2005, NY State Citation award, 2001, Interior Design Merit award NY chpt., 2005); mem. Alliance of Women in Architecture (founding, mem. steering com. 1972-74), Archs. for Social Responsibility (mem. exec. com. 1982-85), Columbia Archtl. Alumni Assn. (bd. dirs. 1968-71). Home: New York, NY. Died Oct. 4, 2014.

EDER, RICHARD GRAY, retired newspaper critic; b. Washington, Aug. 16, 1932; s. George Jackson and Marceline (Gray) E.; m. Esther Garcia Aguirre, Apr. 21, 1955; children: Maria, Ann, Claire, Michael, Luke, Benjamin, James. BA, Harvard U., 1954. Fgn. corr. N.Y. Times, various countries in Europe and Latin Am., 1962-77, 80-82, theater critic, 1977-79; book critic L.A. Times, 1982-99, L.A. Times and Newsday, 1992-99. Vis. lectr. Bard Coll., 1983, Boston U., 1986-87; lectr. MIT, 1997. Ferris Fellow Princeton U., 1984-85, 95-96; recipient Pulitzer Prize for Criticism, 1987. Mem. Nat. Book Critics Circle (citation for reviewing 1987). Roman Catholic. Died Nov. 21, 2014.

EDMONDS, FRANKLIN SPICER, paper manufacturing executive; b. Richmond, Va., June 5, 1931; s. John W. Jr. and Katherine (Spicer) E.; m. Mary Ellen Sample, Mar. 30, 1968; children: Franklin Jr., J. Rice. BS in Bus., U. Richmond, 1952. Sales rep. converter sales Union Camp Corp., Franklin, VA., 1958-63; assoc. pub. Peninsula Enterprises, Accomac, Va., 1964; mktg. mgr. paper div. Weyerhaeuser Co., NYC, 1965-68; asst. to mgr. converter sales Union Camp Corp., Franklin, Va., 1968-69, western regional mgr. converter sales Chgo., 1969-70, asst. mgr. converter sales Franklin, 1970-80, mgr. converter sales Chgo., from 1980. Served to lt. USNR, 1953-55. Mem.: Cypress Cove Country. Episcopalian. Home: Franklin, Va. Died Apr. 19, 2007.

EDMONDSON, GEORGE ALAN, JR., program director; b. Orange, NJ, Mar. 16, 1955; s. George Alan and Helen (Kruk) E. BA in Recreation Adminstrn., Kean Coll. N.J., 1980; MS in Sports Adminstrn., St. Thomas U., 1984. Recreation leader S. Orange (N.J.) Recreation Dept., 1972-80; sports info. dir. Kean Coll. N.J., Union, 1980-83; asst. dir. student activities St. Thomas U., Miami, Fla., 1984-85, dir. student activities, 1985-87, dean student affairs, 1987-89, dir. alumni affairs, from 1989. Adj. instr. St. Thomas U., Miami, 1985—. Mem. The Miami Coalition, 1988—; bd. dirs. YMCA-N.W. Br., Miami, 1990—. Pres. scholar Kean Coll. N.J., 1978. Mem. Coun. for Advancement and Support of Edn., Nat. Soc. Fund Raising Execs., U.S. Golf Assn. Republican. Roman Catholic. Avocations: writing, poster art, golf, softball, island travel. Home: Hollywood, Fla. Died Apr. 2, 2007.

EDWARDS, ANTHONY, academic program coordinator; b. Denmark, SC, Nov. 11, 1956; s. Melvin and Annie Mae (Crum) E. BS, U. S.C., Columbia, 1987. Documents contr. U. S.C.-Grad. Sch. Office, Columbia, 1983-84, data control specialist, 1984-86; spl. svcs. coord. U. S.C.-Dean's Office, Columbia, 1986-88, rsch. and data mgr., 1988-91; program coord. U. S.C.-Grad. Sch., Columbia, from 1991. Mem. ASCD, Assn. Instnl. Rschrs., Nat. Assn. Grad. Admissions Profls., Nat. Assn. Student Employment Adminstrs., Assn. for the Study Higher Edn., U. S.C. System Data Adminstrn. Democrat. Baptist. Avocations: reading, travel, writing, sports. Died Apr. 4, 2007.

EDWARDS, DON (WILLIAM DONLON EDWARDS), former congressman; b. San Jose, Calif., Jan. 6, 1915; s. Leonard P. and Clara (Donlon) E.; first two marriages ended in divorces; m. Edith B. Wilkie (dec. 2011); c. Leonard Perry (II), Samuel Dyer, Bruce Haven, Thomas Charles, William Don. AB, Stanford, 1936; student, Law Sch., 1936-38. Bar: Calif. Agt. FBI, 1940-41; mem. US Congress from 10th Calif. Dist., 1963—94, mem. Judiciary Com. & ranking majority mem, Vet. Affairs Com.; owner Valley Title Ins. Co., 1951. Nat. chmn. Americans for Democratic Action, from 1965. Served to lt. USNR, 1941-45. Recipient Appreciation award, Santa Clara County Head Start Program, Computer & Bus. Equipment Mfg. Assn., Hubert H Humphrey award, Leadership Coun. Civil Rights, Friend of Labor award, Clara County Ctrl. Labor Coun., Founder's award, Save San Francisco Bay Assn., 1988, Philip Hart Svc. award, Consumer Fedn. America. Democrat. Unitarian Universalist. Home: Carmel, Calif. Died Oct. 1, 2015.

EDWARDS, JAMES BURROWS (JIM EDWARDS), retired academic administrator, former Governor of South Carolina, United States Secretary of Energy; b. Hawthorne, Fla., June 24, 1927; s. O.M. and Bertie R. (Hieronymus) E.; m. Ann Norris Darlington, Sept. 1, 1951; children: James Burrows Jr., Catharine Edwards Wingate. BS, Coll. of Charleston, 1950, LittD, 1975; DMD, U. Louisville, 1955, D Social Sci., 1982; postgrad. advanced correlated clin. scis., U. Pa. Grad. Med. Sch., 1957-58; LittD (hon.), Coll. Charleston, 1975; LLD (hon.), U. SC, 1975, Bob Jones U., 1976, The Citadel, 1977, Newberry Coll., 1986; HHD (hon.), Francis Marion Coll., 1978, Bapt. Coll. Charleston, 1981; DS (hon.), Erskine Coll., 1982, Georgetown U., 1982; D of Social Sci. (hon.), U. Louisville, 1982; others. Diplomate American Bd. Oral & Maxillofacial Surgery, 1963. Deck officer Alcoa Steamship Co., 1950—51; resident in oral surgery Henry Ford Hosp., Detroit, 1958-60; practice dentistry specializing in oral and maxillofacial surgery Charleston, SC, 1960—70; clin. assoc. Med. U. SC Coll. Dental Medicine, Charleston, 1970—77, clin. asst. prof., 1977—82, prof., 1982—99, pres., 1982-99, pres. emeritus, from 2000; mem. Dist. 13 SC State Senate, Columbia, 1972—74; gov. State of SC, Columbia, 1975-79; sec. US Dept. Energy, Washington, 1981—82. Bd. dirs. Nat. Data Corp., Atlanta, GS Industries, Inc., Charlotte, NC; mem. advisory bd. Norfolk-Southern Corp., Va. Past bd. dirs. Coastal Carolina coun. Boy Scouts America; past trustee Charleston County Hosp., Greater Charleston YMCA, Coll. Preparatory Sch., Charleston, Baker Meml. Hosp., Charleston; chmn. Charleston County Rep. Party, 1964-69; del. to Nat. Republican Conventions, 1968, 72, 76, 80, 84, 88, 92, chmn. 1st Congressional Dist. Republican Com., 1970-71; chmn. subcommittee on nuclear energy Nat. Governors Assn., 1978; chmn. Southern Governos Conf., 1978; founder, charter mem., chmn. bd. dirs. Oral Surgery Polit. Action Com., 1971-73; bd. dirs. Harry Frank Guggenheim Found., NYC, Gaylord and Dorothy Donnelley Found., Chgo. Served in US Maritime Svc., 1944—47 USNR, 1947—49. Recipient Periclean award, 1976, Thomas P. Hinman Disting. Svc. medal, 1977, Humanities award, Fr. Soc. Bienfaisance, 1984, Founder's medal, Coll. Charleston, 1985, Lawrence-Grever award, U. Louisville, 1987, Alumni Fellow award, 1990, Tree of Life award, Jewish Nat. Fund, 1990, Alfred C. Fones Meml. medal, Conn. State Dental Assn., 1990, Good Citizenship silver medal, Nat. Soc. Sons of American Revolution, 1990, Order of Palmetto, Gov. of SC, 1994, Sgt. William Jasper Freedom award, SC Chamber of Commerce, 1994, Fauchard Gold medal, Pierre Fauchard Acad., 1998; named to The SC Hall of Fame, 1997. Fellow Internat. Coll. Dentists, American Coll. Dentists; mem. ADA (Disting. Svc. award, 1994), SC Dental Soc. (George Hoffman award, 1995), Coastal Dist. Dental Soc. (past pres.), Chalmers J. Lyons Acad. Oral Surgery, Southeastern Soc. Oral & Maxillofacial Surgeons, American Soc. Oral & Maxillofacial Surgeons, Brit. Assn. Oral & Maxillofacial Surgeons, Internat. Soc. Oral & Maxillofacial Surgeons, Fedn. Dentaire Internat., SC Soc. Oral & Maxillofacial Surgeons (founder, charter mem., past pres.), Oral Surgery Polit. Action Com. (founder, charter mem., chmn. bd. dirs. 1971-73), SC Acad. Sci., American Dental Soc. Anesthesiologists, Soc. Cin., Navy League US, American Hellenic Ednl. Progressive Assn., AHEPA (Plato chpt. # 4), Rotary, Masons, Pi Kappa Phi, Delta Sigma Delta, Omicron Delta Kappa. Republican. Episcopalian. Home: Mount Pleasant, SC. Died Dec. 26, 2014.

EDWARDS, WALLACE WINFIELD, retired automotive executive; b. Pontiac, Mich., May 9, 1922; s. David W. and Ruby M. (Nutting) E.; m. Jean Austin Wolfe, Aug. 24, 1944; children: Ronald W., Gary R., Ann E. BS in Mech. Engring. Gen. Motors Inst., 1949; MBA, Mich. State U., 1966. With GMC Truck & Coach div. Gen. Motors Corp., Pontiac, Mich., 1940-78, truck service mgr., 1961-62, head engine design, 1962-64, dir. reliability, 1964-66, dir. prodn. control and purchasing, 1966-70, dir. engring., 1970-78; dir. Worldwide Truck Project Center, Warren, Mich., 1978-80; gen. dir. Worldwide Truck and Transp. Sys. Center, 1980-81; v.p. G.M.O.D.C., 1980-81; group mgr. small and light truck and van ops. Truck and Bus. Group, Gen. Motors Corp., 1981-82, mgr. internat. staff, 1982-84, gen. dir. mil. vehicle ops. Power Products and Def. Group, 1984-86. Bd. dirs. Crystal Mountain Resort, Thompsonville, Mich., 1991-2003. Past pres., mem. exec. com. Clinton Valley coun. Boy Scouts Am.; dir. Grand Traverse Regional Land Conservancy, 1991-2003, chmn. 1996-98; regent Nat. Eagle Scout Assn. (life). Served with USNR, 1944-46. Mem. Soc. Automotive Engrs., U.S. Navy League, Tau Beta Pi, Beta Gamma Sigma. Died Nov. 7, 2014.

EGAN, EDWARD MICHAEL CARDINAL, cardinal, archbishop emeritus; b. Oak Park, Ill., Apr. 2, 1932; s. Thomas J. and Genevieve (Costello) Egan. PhB, Saint Mary of Lake, Mudelein, Ill., 1954; Seminary Studies, Pontifical North American College, Vatican City; LTh, Pontifical Gregorian U., 1958, JCD, 1964; PhD (hon.), Saint John's U., Thomas More Coll., New Hampshire, Western Conn. State U., Fordham U., Manhattan Coll., U. Lublin, Cardinal Wyszynski U., Warsaw, Coll. New Rochelle, Iona Coll., NY Med. Coll., Ave Maria Sch. Law, Naples, Fla. Ordained priest of Chgo., Ill., 1957, asst. chancellor, sec. to Albert Cardinal Meyer, 1958—60, vice-chancellor, 1964—68, sec. to John Cardinal Cody, 1966—68, co-chancellor, sec. of the Archdiocesan Commissions on Ecumenism and Human Relations, 1968—72; asst. vice-rector Pontifical North American Coll., Vatican City, 1960—65; judge Tribunal of the Sacred Roman Rota, Vatican City, 1971—85; appointed Titular Bishop of Allegheny, 1985, ordained, 1985; aux. bishop, vicar for edn. of New York, 1985—88, archbishop, 2000—09, archbishop emeritus, 2009—15; bishop of Bridgeport, Conn., 1988—2000; elevated to cardinal, 2001; cardinal-priest Santi Giovanni e Paulo (Saints John and Paul on the Caelian Hill in Rome), 2001—15. Prof. of Civil and Criminal Procedure Studium Rotale; prof. Canon Law Pontifical Gregorian U.; commissioner Congregation for the Sacraments and Divine Worship; consultor Congregation for the Clergy; chmn. bd. govs., Pontifical N.Am. Coll. Rome National Conference of Catholic Bishops, 1991—95, chmn. com. Pontifica N.Am. Coll. Rome, mem. Committee on Canonical Affairs, mem., Committee on Education, mem., Committee on National Collections, mem., Committee on Nominations, mem. administrative bd.; chmn. bd. Bishop Curtis Homes, Fairfield County, Conn., 1988—2000, New York State Cath. Conf., from 2000, North East Hispanic Conf., from 2001; chmn. bd. trustees Saint John Neumann Seminary Residence and Hall, Dunwoodie, NY; mem. bd. trustees National Shrine of Immaculate Conception, Washington, 2000—09; adminstrv. bd. United States Cath. Conf., 1991—94, 1996—99; relator general 10th Ordinary General Assembly of the Synod of Bishops, 2001; mem. Pontifical Coun. for the Family, from 2000, Pontifical Coun. for Finance and Adminstrv. Affairs of the Holy See, from 2000, Supreme Tribunal of the Apostolic Signatura, from 2001, Prefecture of the Econ. Affairs of the Holy See, from 2001, Pontifical Commn. for the Cultural Goods of the Church, from 2001, Council of Cardinals for the Study of the Organizational and Economic Concerns of the Holy See, from 2001, Pontifical Council for the Family, from 2001, Coun. Orgnl. and Econ. Affairs Holy See, from 2001, Congregation for the Oriental Churches, from 2005, Permanent Commission for the Protection of the Historic and Artistic Patrimony of the Holy See. Chmn. bd. trustees Saint Joseph Med. Ctr., Stamford, Conn., 1988—96, Sacred Heart U., Fairfield, Conn., 1988—2000, Catholic Near East Welfare Assn., 2000—15, Catholic Charities of New York, Archdiocesan Healthcare of New York (ArchCare); chmn. Inner-City Found. for Edn. and Charity, Fairfield County, Conn., 1992—2000, North East Hispanic Catholic Ctr., Inc., 2000—15; bd. trustees Thomas More Coll., Merrimack, NH, 1995—2015, Richard Tucker Music Found., NYC, 1998—2015, Ratisbonne Inst., Jerusalem, 2000—15, Cath. U. America, Washington, 2000—15, Whitehead Sch. Diplomacy and International Relations, Seton Hall U., 2009—15, Ave Maria School of Law, Naples, Fla., Center for Labor and Employment Law of the Law School of Saint John's U., Queens, NY; Principal Chaplain, Bailiff Grand Cross of Honor and Devotion American Association of the Sovereign Military Order of Malta, 2000—10; president Bureau of Black and Indians Mission Office, Washington, 2007—09. Named one of New York's Influentials, New York Mag., 2006, Grand Prior, Association of Knight and Ladies of the Equestrian Order of the Holy Sepulchre of Jerusalem, 2000—09. Roman Catholic. Died Mar. 5, 2015.

EHRLICH, MARGARETE, physicist, researcher; b. Vienna, Sept. 28, 1915; arrived in U.S., 1939; d. Josef and Charlotte (Kobak) Ehrlich. Grad., U. Vienna, 1938; PhD, Cath. U., Washington, 1955. Chief x-ray technician Grady Meml. Hosp., Atlanta, 1942—48; physicist Nat. Bur. Stds.,

NIST, Gaithersburg, 1948—85, guest worker, 1985—87; ret., 1985. Physicist Internat. Atomic Energy Commn., Vienna, 1960—61; mem. Com. Radiol. Units, 1982—87. Contbr. articles to profl. jours. Recipient Bronze medal, U.S. Dept. Commerce, 1972, Gold medal, 1977. Mem.: AAAS, Health Physics Soc. Home: Chevy Chase, Md. Died Aug. 1, 2007.

EIBEN, ROBERT MICHAEL, pediatric neurologist, educator; b. Cleve., July 12, 1922; s. Michael Albert and Frances Carlysle (Gedeon) E.; m. Anne F. Eiben; children: Daniel F., Christopher J., Thomas M., Mary, Charles G., Elizabeth A. BS, Western Res. U., 1944, MD, 1946. Diplomate Am. Bd. Pediatrics. Intern medicine Univ. Hosp., Cleve., 1946-47; asst. resident pediatrics and contagious diseases City Hosp., Cleve., 1947; asst. resident pediatrics Babies and Children's Hosp., Cleve., 1948, clin. fellow pediatrics, 1948-49; clin. instr. pediatrics Western Res. U., 1949-50; asst. med. dir. div. contagious diseases City Hosp., 1949-50, visitant in pediatrics, 1949-50; practice medicine specializing in pediatrics Cleve., 1949-90; acting dir. dept. pediatrics and contagious diseases City Hosp., 1950-52; asst. dir. dept. pediatrics and contagious diseases Cleve. Met. Gen. Hosp., 1952-60; med. dir. Respiratory Care and Rehab. Center, 1954-60, pres. med. staff, 1958-60; USPHS fellow in neurology U. Wash., 1960-63; pediatric neurologist Cleve. (Ohio) Met. Gen. Hosp., 1963—90, acting med. dir. comprehensive care program, 1966-67, med. dir., 1968-73, mem. med. exec. com., 1974-76; acting chief, sect. on clin. investigations and therapeutics Developmental and Metabolic Neurology br. Nat. Inst. Neurol. and Communicative Disorders and Strokes, NIH, Bethesda, Md., 1976-77; acting dir. dept. pediatrics Metro Health Med. Ctr., 1979-80; from instr. pediatrics to prof. emeritus Western Res. U., from 1950, prof. emeritus pediatric neurology, from 1991; vis. lectr. pediat. neurology Case Western Res. U., 2008. Cons., project site visitor Nat. Found. Birth Defects Center Programs, 1961-66; mem. adv. com. on grants to train dentists to care for handicapped Robert Wood Johnson Found., 1975-80; emeritus faculty marshall Case Western Res. U., 1992-2007, mem. regional leadership coun., 2003-. Mem. coun. Bratenahl Village-County of Cuyahoga, 1982-98. Recipient Presdl. award Internat. Poliomyelitis Congress, Geneva, 1957, Clifford J. Vogt Alumni Svc. award Case Western Res. U., Cleve., 1985, Robert M. Eiben, MD established annual endowed lectureship, 2009, Lifetime Commitment Recognition award, Case Western Res. U. Sch. Medicine, 2011; established Annual Robert M. Eiben, MD. vis. professorship in child neurology MetroHealth Med. Ctr. Dept. Pediat., 1991. Mem.: Child Neurology Soc. (chmn. tng. program com. 1976—77, sec.-treas. 1978—81, pres. 1983—85, Lifetime Career Achievement award 2005), Innominatum Soc., No. Ohio Pediat. Soc., Am. Epilepsy Soc., Am. Pediat. Soc., Am. Soc. Human Genetics, Am. Acad. Neurology (chmn. residence exam. com. 1989—93), Am. Acad. Pediat., Case Western Res. U. Med. Alumni Assn. (pres. 1979, bd. of trustees from 2002), Pasteur Club. Home: Lakewood, Ohio. Died Dec. 28, 2013.

EICHER, ROMA JEAN, performing arts association administrator; b. Harper, Kans., Nov. 21, 1942; d. John Albert and Emily Fern (Detweiler) Diller; m. Christian Samuel Eicher, June 14, 1963; children: Marisa, Dani, Jaqui. AA, Hesston Coll., 1963. Sch. accompanist Oregon State U., Corvallis, 1963-64; pvt. instr. Albany, Oreg., 1963-86; instr. Price Sch., Albany, 1971-74, Yamaha Music Sch., Albany, 1975-78; founder, adminstr., owner Conservatory for Music Edn., Albany, from 1986. Mem. budget com. Greater Albany Pub. Sch. Bd., 1982-85, chair, 1983-85, bd. mem., 1991; mem. Western Mennonite H.S. Bd., Salem, Oreg., 1992-94, sec., 1982-84, com. mem. 1982-84, vice chmn., 1984-86, chmn., 1986-88, chair fin. com., 1993-94, chair jubilee celebration, 1994-96; co-mgr. Linn County Fair, Albany, 1976; regional dir. Hesston (Kans.) Coll., 1978-84; co-chair Nat. Mennonite Ch. Gen. Assembly and Conv., 1991; music dir. Lebanon Mennonite Ch., 1993—; del. Pacific Coast Conf., 1993—. Mem. Oreg. Music Tchrs. Assn. (state cert., pres. Linn Benton dist., state v.p. 1987-89, chair student auditions 1991-94, state syllabus chair 1994-96, state convention chair 1996—), Music Tchrs. Nat. Assn. (nat. cert., chair N.W. divsn. Yamaha H.S. auditions 1991-95, nat. competition com. 1995, ad hoc com. to study nat. competitions 1995—). Republican. Mennonite. Home: Albany, Oreg. Died Dec. 9, 2006.

EICK, ELIZABETH M., medical/surgical nurse; b. Coshcton, Ohio, Aug. 18, 1930; d. William Clyde and Amanda Marie (Klein) Warren; m. Richard L. Eick, Apr. 25, 1953; children: William L., Kevin E., June Eick Lauvray, Sherrie Eick Sampsel. Diploma, Good Samaritan Hosp., 1951. RN, Ohio. Float staff nurse Good Samaritan Hosp., Zanesville, Ohio; charge nurse med./surg. unit Coshocton Meml. Hosp., charge nurse ICU, staff nurse post anesthesia. Mem. ANA, Ohio Nurses' Assn. (bd. dirs. Muskingum Valley dist.), Coshocton RN Assn. (pres.). Home: Coshocton, Ohio. Died June 26, 2007.

EIGEL, JOHN ROHAN, investment consultant, political activist; b. St. Louis, Feb. 26, 1944; s. Edwin George and Catherine Christina (Rohan) E.; m. Sue Ellen Walker, Feb. 6, 1970; 1 child, John Rohan Jr. BA, St. Louis U., 1966. Pension adminstr. Marsh & McLennan, Inc., St. Louis, 1969-72, pension cons., 1973-77; pension mgr. Consolidated Aluminum Corp., St. Louis, 1977-80; pres., owner JRE Investors, St. Louis, 1980-82, Meramec Fin. Services, Inc., St. Louis, from 1982. State adv. U.S. Congl. Adv. Bd., Washington, 1984. Author: The American Eigels, 1984, The Am. Rohans, 1985. Mem. Rep. Presdl. Task Force, Washington, 1984—, Nat. Rep. Congl. Com., Washington, 1984—. Served to sgt. USAF, 1966-69. Mem. Am. Assoc. Individual Investors, Nat. Assn. Investors Corp., Am. Security Council Found., Permanently and Totally DAV, St. Louis Geneal. Assn., Nat. Rifle Assn. Republican. Roman Catholic. Avocations: genealogy, numismathist. Died Apr. 25, 2007.

EIKENBERRY, ARTHUR RAYMOND, writer, service executive, researcher; b. Sebring, Fla., June 5, 1920; s. Leroy Albertus and Vernie Cordelia (Griffin) E.; m. Carol Jean Parrott, June 10, 1955; children: Robin Rene, Shari LaVon, Jan Rochelle, Karyn LaRae, Kelli Yvette. Student, Pasadena CC, Calif., 1939, Kunming U., China, 1944-45. MSgt. Army Air Corps, 1941-45, re-enlisted in grade of TSgt., 1947; advanced through grades to SMSgt. USAF; ret., 1973; mgmt., pers., adminstrv. and security insp.; mgr. property control, real estate agent TR Devel. Co., Englewood, Colo., 1973-74; real estate agt. The Pinery, Parker, Colo., 1974-75; mgr., patient acctg. dept. Univ. Colo. Health Scis. Ctr., Denver, 1975-89; ret., 1989. Author: Investment Strategies for the Clever Investor, 1989, LOTTO GURU (Omni-Personal Selection Systems & Strategies), 1989. Charter mem. U.S. Congl. Adv. Bd. Fellow Internat. Biog. Ctr. (hon. life patron, dep. dir. gen.); mem. Am. Biog. Inst. (life, dep. gov., nat. adviser), World Inst. of Achievement (disting.), Masons, Eastern Star, Royal Order of the Amaranth. Died July 12, 2007.

EISENBRAUN, ERIC CHARLES, lawyer; b. Quinn, SD, Dec. 26, 1955; s. Emmanuel Edward and Glenda Mae (Cleveland) E.; m. Sharon Patricia Connolly, Jan. 29, 1977; children: Quinn, Alec, Erika, Sarah. BS with honors, Augustana Coll., 1978; JD, So. Meth. U., 1981. Bar: Tex. 1981, U.S. Dist. Ct. (no., so., ea. and we. dists.) Tex. 1981, U.S. Ct. Appeals (5th cir.) 1985. Assoc. Coke & Coke, Dallas, 1981-84, Gibson, Dunn & Crutcher, Dallas, 1984-89, Morgan & Weisbrod, Dallas, 1989-91; pvt. practice Law Offices of Eric Eisenbraun, Dallas, from 1991. Contbr. articles to profl. jours. East Dallas chmn. Assn. for Retarded Citizens, 1982; vol. advisor East Dallas Legal Clinic, 1986—. Named one of Outstanding Young Men Am. U.S. Jaycees, 1984. Mem. ABA, Tex. Bar Assn., Assn. Trial Lawyers Am., Tex. Trial Lawyers Assn., Dallas Trial Lawyers Assn., Dallas Bar Assn., Coll. State Bar Tex. Democrat. Avocations: reading, constrn./carpentry, animal husbandry, fishing, racquetball. Home: Rockwall, Tex. Died Dec. 30, 2006.

EISENSTEIN, ELIZABETH ANN LEWISOHN, historian, educator; b. NYC, Oct. 11, 1923; d. Sam A. and Margaret V. (Seligman) Lewisohn; m. Julian Calvert Eisenstein, May 30, 1948; children: Margaret Eisenstein DeLacy, John Calvert (dec., 1974), Edward Lewisohn; another son died at birth (1949). AB, Vassar Coll., 1944; MA, Radcliffe Coll., 1947, PhD, 1953; LittD (hon.), Mt. Holyoke Coll., 1979; LHD (hon.), U. Mich., 2004. From lectr. to adj. prof history American U., Washington, 1959-74; Alice Freeman Palmer prof. history U. Mich., Ann Arbor, 1975-88, prof. emerita, 1988—2016. Scholar-in-residence Rockefeller Found. Ctr., Bellagio, Italy, June 1977; mem. vis. com. dept. history Harvard U., 1975-81, vice-chmn., 1979-81; dir. Ecole des Hautes Etudes en Sciences Sociales, Paris, 1982; guest spkr., participant confs. and seminars; I. Beam vis. prof. U. Iowa, 1980; Mead-Swing lectr. Oberlin Coll., 1980; Stone lectr. U. Glasgow, 1984; Van Leer lectr. Van Leer Fedn., Jerusalem, 1984; Hanes lectr. U. N.C., Chapel Hill, 1985 first resident cons. Ctr. for the Book, Libr. of Congress, Washington, 1979; mem. Coun. Scholars, 1980-88; pres.'s disting. visitor Vassar Coll., 1988; Pforzheimer lectr. N.Y. Pub. Libr., 1989, Lyell lectr. Bodleian Libr., Oxford, 1990, Merle Curti lectr. U. Wis., Madison, 1992, Jantz lectr. Oberlin Coll., 1995, Clifford lectr. Austin, Tex., 1996; vis. fellow Wolfson Coll., Oxford, 1990; sem. dir. Folger Inst., 1999. Author: The First Professional Revolutionist: F. M. Buonarroti, 1959, The Printing Press as an Agent of Change, 1979, 2 vols. paperback edit., 1980 (Phi Beta Kappa Ralph Waldo Emerson prize 1980), The Printing Revolution in Early Modern Europe, 1983 (reissued as Canto Book, 1993), 2d edit., 2005, Grub Street Abroad: Aspects of the French Cosmopolitan Press From the Age of Louis XIV to the French Revolution, 1992, Divine Art, Infernal Machine, 2011; mem. editorial bd. Jour. Modern History, 1973-76, 83-86, Revs. in European History, 1973-86, Jour. Library History, 1979-82, Eighteenth Century Studies, 1981-84; contbr. articles to profl. jours., chpts. to books. Bd. dirs. Folger Shakespeare Libr., 2000-08. Belle Skinner fellow Vassar Coll., NEH fellow, 1977, Guggenheim fellow, 1982, fellow Ctr. Advanced Studies in Behavioral Scis., 1982-83, 92-93, Humanities Rsch. Ctr. fellow Australian Nat. U., 1988; recipient Gutenberg award, Internat. Gutenberg Soc., 2012 Fellow Am. Acad. Arts and Scis., Royal Hist. Soc.; mem. Soc. French Hist. Studies (v.p. 1970, program com. 1974), Am. Soc. 18th Century Studies (nominating com. 1971), Soc. 16th Century Studies, Am. Hist. Assn. (com. on coms. 1970-72, chmn. Modern European sect. 1981, coun. 1982-85, Scholarly Distinction award 2003), Renaissance Soc. Am. (coun. 1973-76, pres. 1986), Am. Antiquarian Soc. (exec. com., adv. bd. 1984-87), Phi Beta Kappa. Home: Washington, DC. Died Jan. 31, 2016.

EISENTHAL, ROBERT, biochemist; b. London, Feb. 5, 1936; s. Henry Eisenthal and Hilda Lewis; m. Janet Anne Pryke, Feb. 12, 1983; 1 child, Anne; m. Mary Ross (div.); children: Deborah, David, Naomi, Daniel. BA, Amherst Coll., 1956; PhD, U. NC, 1960. Rsch. instr. U. Wash., 1961—62; sr. rsch. assoc. U. East Anglia, 1964; rsch. asst. U. Coll., 1965—67; from lectr. to prof. U. Bath, from 1967. Editor: Enzyme Assays: A Practical Approach, 2002; contbr. articles to profl. jours. Fellow Rsch. fellow, NIH, 1963. Mem.: British Soc. Parasitology (coun. 1992—95), Biochem. Soc. (coun. 1992—95, exec. 1993—95). Achievements include research in enzyme kinetics. Avocations: car restoration, bridge, jazz. Home: Bath, England. Died Oct. 16, 2007.

ELDER, ROBERT EARNEST, construction executive, consultant; b. Richard, Tex., Jan. 25, 1934; s. Robert and Virneice (Manning) E.; m. Albertina Brenda Harris, May 25, 1958; children: Kenneth Earl, Derrick Wayne. BS, Tex. So. U., 1953, Tuskegee Inst., Ala., 1957, Air Command and Staff Coll., 1973; postgrad., Air War Coll., 1977. Commd. 2d lt. USAF, 1957, ret., 1978; constrn. engr., mgr. McDonald's Corp., Houston, 1978-87; owner Pt. Arthur (Tex.) Constrn. Co., from 1987. Mem. Jersey Village Land Bd., Houston, 1983, Urban League, Houston, 1986; v.p. Jersey Civic Club, Houston, 1980; chmn. Japan Dist. Boy Scouts Am., 1975-78; century mem. Far East coun. Boy Scouts Am., 1975. Recipient Good Deed medal Japanese Govt., 1978. Mem. Soc. Am. Mil. Engrs., Am. Inst. Plant Engrs., Far East Soc. Architects and Engrs., NAACP, Optimists, McDonald's Black Network (chmn. 1983-87), Prince Hall Macons, Alpha Phi Alpha (dean of pledges 1954-57). Democrat. Baptist. Home: Houston, Tex. Died May 27, 2007.

ELDRIDGE, THOMAS ENGLE, restaurant executive; b. Oak Park, Ill., Sept. 5, 1937; s. Leslie and Sherley E.; m. Betty Lee Polite, Mar. 15, 1963; children: Jody, Kimberly, Michael, Daniel. Student, U. Colo., 1955-58. Owner Tom's Tavern, Boulder, Colo., from 1959. Councilman City of Boulder, from 1997; bd. dirs. Downtown Boulder, Inc., from 1999. Avocations: scuba diving, travel. Home: Boulder, Colo. Died May 13, 2007.

ELLIOTT, CLARE W., osteopath, educator; b. Cortland, Ohio, Dec. 24, 1925; s. Ural S. and Nellie M. (Everitt) E.; children: Jeri, James, John, William, Robert; m. Cheryl Christine Curry, Feb. 14, 1975; children; Jeffrey, Meghan, Lori, Brian. Student, Kent State U., 1943-44, St. Mary's Coll., Winona, Minn., 1944-45; BS, U. Minn., 1946; DO, Phila. Coll. Osteo. Medicine, 1950. Diplomate Am. Bd. Osteo. Surgery. Intern Grandview Osteo. Med. Ctr., Dayton, Ohio, 1950-51, resident in gen. surgery, 1951-54, mem. staff, sr. attending surgeon, 1954-76; past chmn. dept. surgery and div. gen. surgery Dayton, 1954; pvt. practice, 1954-76, Largo, Fla., from 1976. Assoc. clin. prof. Wright State U., 1975-76; assoc. prof. clin. Ohio U. Sch. Osteo. Medicine, 1976; clin. asst. prof. W.Va. Sch. Osteo. Medicine, 1984—; clin. assoc. prof. Kirksville (Mo.) Coll. Osteo. Medicine, 1989—; mem. staff Sun Coast Hosp., Largo; clin. prof. surgery Nova Southeastern U., 1994—, chmn. dept. surgery, lectr. profl. orgns., dir. Gen. Surg. Rsch. Program. Trustee, sec. St. Paul's Episcopal Sch. Lt. (j.g.) USN, 1944-46, mem. Res. ret. Recipient Disting. Svc. award Grandview Hosp., 1990. Fellow Am. Coll. Osteo. Surgery (bd. govs. 1973-82, v.p. 1979, pres. 1980-81, residency evaluating com., Disting. Osteo. Surgeon award 1984, Orel F. Martin award 1990); mem. Am. Osteo. Assn. (past mem. editorial adv. bd., cons. surgery residency programs), Ohio Osteo. Assn. (past mem. ho. of dels.), Tex. Surg. Soc. (hon.), Airplane Owners and Pilots Assn., Phi Sigma Gamma. Avocations: flying, photography, travel. Died Mar. 13, 2007.

ELLIOTT, CLARK ALBERT, archivist, librarian, historian; b. Ware, Mass., Jan. 22, 1941; s. Leroy and Bertha Lyons Elliott; m. Priscilla Alden Jordan, 1965; children: Andrew, Glenn. AB, Marietta Coll., Marietta, Ohio, 1963; MSLS, Case Western Reserve U., 1965, MA, 1968, PhD, 1970. Asst. prof. Sch. of Libr. Sci., Simmons Coll., Boston, 1969—71; asst. curator Harvard Univ. Arch., 1971—74, assoc. curator, 1974—97; librarian Burndy Libr., Dibner Inst. for History of Sci. and Tech., Cambridge, Mass., 1997—2000; cons. Am. Acad. Arts and Sci., 2000—05. Author: Biographical Dictionary of American Science: The Seventeenth Through the Nineteenth Centuries, 1979, History of Science in the United States: A Chronology and Research Guide, 1996, Thaddeus William Harris (1795-1856): Nature, Science, and Society in the Life of an American Naturalist, 2008; co-editor (with Margaret W. Rossiter): Science at Harvard University: Historical Perspectives, 1992; co-editor: (with Pnina Abir-Am) Commemorative Practices in Science: Historical Perspectives on the Politics of Collective Memory, 1999; contbr. articles to profl. jours. Mem.: History Sci. Soc. Congregationalist. Died Feb. 1, 2014.

ELLIOTT, GEORGE ARMSTRONG, III, artist, journalist; b. Wilmington, Del., July 24, 1929; s. George Armstrong Elliott Jr. and Amy Lewis (Rupert) Thomas; m. Shirley Barbara Henin, Oct. 16, 1965. BA, Colgate U., 1951; cert. in journalism, Columbia U., NYC, 1964. Reporter, copy editor, corr. Local and Nat. Newspapers and News Agys., 1946—66, Wilmington Jour. Every Evening, 1946—47, Bethlehem Globe Times, 1954—55, Balt. Sun, 1955-62, N.Y. Herald Tribune, 1964, New York Daily News, 1965-66; adminstrv. asst./press sec. Spiro T. Agnew, Baltimore County Exec., Towson, Md., 1962-65, campaign press mgr., 1962; campaign press sec., speechwriter Spiro T. Agnew, Gov. of Md., 1966; writer Md. Gov. Theodore R. McKeldin Mayor, Balt., 1963; writer numerous congl. and local polit. campaigns, 1962—63; pub. affairs dir. Md. State Rds. Commn., Balt., 1967-69; legis. asst. U.S. Congresswoman from Mass. Margaret M. Heckler, Washington, 1969-71; spl. asst. U.S. Sec. of Commerce Peter G. Peterson, Washington, 1972; campaign writer John H. Chafee for U.S. Senator, Providence, 1972; speechwriter Chmn. of FTC Lewis Engman, Washington, 1973; dir. nat. campaign for 55 m.p.h. speed limit U.S. Dept. Transp., Washington, 1976-77; speechwriter campaign spokesman 55 m.p.h. Lt. Gen. Benjamin O. Davis, Jr., 1976—77; spl. asst., speechwriter U.S. Congressman from Minn. Albert H. Quie, Washington and Mpls.-St. Paul, 1978; campaign speechwriter Albert H. Quie, Gov. Minn., 1978; press sec. Rep. Margaret M. Heckler, Washington, 1979-81; prin. writer Nat. Alcohol Fuels Commn., Washington, 1980; writer Nat. Commn. on Air Quality, Washington, 1980-81; internat. pub. rels. counsel A. F. Sabo Assocs., Washington, 1981; Washington and

East Coast corr. Jet Cargo News, Washington, 1984-93; profl. Chinese brush painting artist, from 1993. Exhibitions include M-Pac Fine Arts Shows, Sugarloaf Mt. Works Shows, Towson, Md., Invitational Art Exhibit, Waterford, Va., Art Mart and Garden tour, Wilmington, Brandywine Arts Festival, Bethesda, Bethesda Row Arts Festival, Sydney (NSW, Australia) Internat. Art Soc., 1996, Internat. Salon de Haute-Loire, Puy-en-Velay, France, 1997, 99, 7th St. Internat., Washington, 1997, 99, Lalit Kala Nat. Acad. Art, New Delhi, 1998, 1999-2000, 2002, Forte Cup 20th Century Asian Pacific Art Competition, 1999, Overseas Chinese Culture and Art Festival, Wash., 2000, Internat. Cultural Union, Haifa, 2000-2001, Cooper Street Gallery, Memphis Tenn. 2000, Balt. City Hall Courtyard Galleries, 2000, Marlboro Gallery, , Largo, Md., 2000, Mus. Contemporary Art, Wash., 1996, 2001, 03, 08, Russian Cultural Centre, Wash., 2002, 04, Acad. Arts and Design, Tsinghua U., Beijing and Capital Normal U., Beijing, 2002, The Warehouse, Washington, 2003, Gorohavaya 6 EGO Gallery, St. Petersburg, Russia, 2003, All India Fine Arts and Crafts Soc. Galleries, New Delhi, 2004,09, Vision Gallery, Washington, 2005, Al-Ahram Galleries, Cairo, Grand Gallery of Faculty Fine Arts, Luxor, Egypt, 2005, U.S. Capitol Rayburn Office Bldg., Wash., 2006, Mus. Americas, Doral, Fla. 2006, Chinese Artists Assn. Greater Wash. DC, 2006, 09, 10, 11, Asian Fusion Gallery, NY, 2006, Florence Biennale, 2007, Artexpo NY, 2008, Artexpo Las Vegas, 2008, Sumi-e Soc. Am. Juried Exhibition, Bethesda, Md., 2008, Art Dubai, 2009, VisArts at Rockville Rockville, Md., 2011. With U.S. Army, 1951-54. Ford Found. fellow in advanced internat. reporting Grad. Sch. Journalism, Columbia U., 1963-64, recipient Lorenzo il Magnifico Art Career prize, Florence Biennale, 2007. Mem. Nat. Assn. Govt. Communicators, Overseas Press Club Am., Washington Ind. Writers, Montgomery County Art Assn., Internat. Artists Support Group (pres. 1999-2001, 2008-), Sumi-e Soc. Am., Harmonious Art Group. Died Jan. 28, 2015.

ELLIOTT, RAY ANDREW, JR., retired surgeon, consultant; b. Milw., Nov. 6, 1926; s. Ray Andrew and Irene (Jacobs) E.; m. Elisabeth Bartlett, Sept. 2, 1950 (div. 1989); children: David Wayne, Daonald Warren, Ray Andrew III. BA, Drew U., 1948; MD, Union U., Albany, NY, 1951. Diplomate Am. Bd. Surgery, Am. Bd. Plastic Surgery. Intern Albany (N.Y.) Med. Ctr., 1951-53, resident in plastic surgery; resident in gen. surgery Ind. U. Med. Ctr., Indpls., 1953-56; fellow in hand surgery Calif. Hosp., LA; fellow in head and neck cancer Roswell Park, Buffalo; clin. prof. gen. surgery (plastic) Albany Med. Ctr., prof. orthopedic surgery (hand). V.p. Plastic Surgery Edn. Found., 1976-77. Contbr. over 100 articles to med. jours., chpts. to books. Pres. Northeastern N.Y. Speech Ctr., Albany, 1967-68; bd. dirs. Vis. Nurse Assn., Albany, 1970-73, Sedona Cultural Park Bd., 2000—; charter mem. Albany County Airport Authority, 1994-98, vice chmn., 1994-95; maj. CAP, 1993—; col. N.Y. N.U.G., 1995—, N.Y.G. State surgeon, 1998—. Recipient awards Drew U., 1948-98. Fellow ACS; mem. AMA (ho. dels. 1972-94), Am. Assn. for Hand Surgery (pres. 1973-74), Am. Soc. Plastic and Reconstructive Surgery, Am. Soc. Aesthetic Plastic Surgeons, Internat. Soc. Aesthetic Plastic Surgeons (sec. gen. 1989-92, hon. citation 1992). Avocations: private, commercial and instrument pilot. Home: East Berne, NY. Died Feb. 9, 2007.

ELLISON, JAMES OLIVER, federal judge; b. St. Louis, Jan. 11, 1929; s. Jack and Mary (Patton) E.; m. Joan Roberts Ellison, June 7, 1950; 1 son, Scott. Student, U. Mo., Columbia, 1946-48; BA, LL.B., U. Okla., 1951. Bar: Okla. Pvt. practice law, Red Fork, Okla., 1953-55; ptnr. Boone, Ellison & Smith, Davis & Minter, 1955-79; judge US Dist. Ct. (northern dist.) Okla., Tulsa, 1979—94, chief justice, 1992—94, sr. judge, 1994—2014. Trustee Hillcrest Med. Center, Institution Programs, Inc.; elder Southminster Presbyterian Ch. Served to capt., inf. AUS, 1951-53. Mem. ABA, Okla. Bar Assn., Tulsa County Bar Assn., Alpha Tau Omega. Died Nov. 22, 2014.

ELLISON, JOHN VOGELSANGER, retired engineer; b. Cape Girardeau, Mo., Aug. 7, 1919; s. Floyd Anderson and Clara (Vogelsanger) Ellison; m. Louise Ruby Day, Dec. 15, 1949; children: Elizabeth Louise Marks, Barbara Henley Stalker; m. Virginia Klutz Ellison, June 1940 (div. July 1949); children: Andrea Lee Keebler(dec.) , Victoria Sue. BA, S.E. Mo. State U., 1940; grad. study, State U. Iowa, Ill. Inst. Tech., Mass. Inst. Tech. Registered profl. engr., DC, 1952, electrical engr./electronics, DC, 1959. Tchr. physics and biology Fornfelt Mo. Pub. Sch., 1939—40, Sikeston Mo. Pub. Sch., 1940—41; grad. asst. Ill. Inst. Tech., Chgo., 1941; dean of instrs. Am. TV Labs., Chgo., 1941—43; staff mem. divsn. of war rsch. Columbia U., New London, Conn., 1943—45; staff mem. radiation lab. Mass. Inst. Tech., Cambridge, Mass., 1945; scientist U.S. Naval Rsch. Lab., Washington, 1945—59; mgr. reconnaissance lab, McDonnell Aircraft Co. McDonnell Douglas Corp., St. Louis, 1959—83. Mem.: OBP (sec., v.p., pres. 1966—71), Am. Radio Relay League, 10-10 Internat. (head, Gateway chpt. 1975—84), Acoustical Soc. of Am. Episcopalian. Achievements include invention of underwater telephone for submarines; mine and torpedo detectors; design of sonar displays; patents in field. Avocations: amateur radio, photography. Home: Mesquite, Tex. Died Feb. 7, 2007.

ELLSWORTH, JOSEPHINE MILDRED STAATS, special education educator, author; b. Wilmington, Del., June 13, 1911; d. John Perkins Staats, Jr. and Margaret Ann Welch; m. Ivan James Ellsworth, Aug. 5, 1932; 1 child, Nadene June. BA in Biology, U. Del., 1933; MSEd, SUNY, 1955. Cert. tchr. elem. reading, secondary biology, Del., N.Y., Ky., S.C., Va., Tenn. Corr. tchr. Calvert Sch. and Willis (Va.) Pub. Sch., Floyd County, Va., 1946-47; tchr. Schuylerville Sch. Sys., Saratoga County, N.Y., 1947-52, Greenwich Ctl. Sch. Sys., N.Y., 1952-64, Hardin County Pub. Schs., Counce, Tenn., 1965-67, Chesterfield Reading Resource, Richmond, Va., 1967-68, Chicahominay Acad., 1968-69; tchr. 6th grade Harlan Sch., Wilmington, Del., 1969-71; tchr. reading study ctr. U. Del., Newark, 1971-72; tutor disabilities Ednl. Svc., Inc., Wilmington, Del., 1971-93. Author: The STAATS Family, 1992; contbr. articles and poems to profl. mags.; corrs. Savannah Courier, Tenn. Mem. AAUW (chairperson 1965-67), Nat. Soc. DAR, Hist, Soc. Del., Geneal. Soc. Del., Acad. Lifelong Learning, Historical N.P. Stillwater Nat. Park (southeast regional chairperson), Shiloh Nat. Mil. Park, Richmond N. Battlefield Park, Young Women's Christian Assn., N.Y. State Fedn. of Women's Club, DAR, numerous others. Died Sept. 6, 2007.

ELSEY, GEORGE MCKEE, retired foundation administrator; b. Palo Alto, Calif., Feb. 5, 1918; s. Howard McKee and Ethel May (Daniels) E.; m. Sally Phelps Bradley, Dec. 15, 1951 (dec. 2004); children: Anne Kranz, Howard McKee. AB, Princeton U., 1939; A.M., Harvard U., 1940; L.H.D., Am. Internat. Coll., 1982. Asst. to spl. counsel to Pres. The White House, 1947—49, adminstrv. asst. to Pres., 1949—51; asst. to dir. Mutual Security Agy., 1951—53; with ARC, 1953-61, v.p., 1958-61; with various divs. Pullman Inc., 1961-65, asst. to chmn. and pres., 1966-70; pres. Am. Nat. Red Cross, 1970-82, pres. emeritus, 1983—2015. Mem. Washington adv. bd. MNC Fin., 1991-93; bd. dirs. The White House Hist. Assn., pres., 1990-95, dir. emeritus 1995-2015 Author: An Unplanned Life: A Memoir, 2005 Pres. Meridian House Internat., Washington, 1961-66, vice chmn., 1967-68, counselor, 1971—; trustee Brookings Instn., 1971-83, George C. Marshall Rsch. Found., 1973-83, Harry S. Truman Libr. Inst., 1973-95, hon. trustee, 1996-, PCC Charitable Found., 1997-2005; mem. Nat. Archives Adv. Coun., 1974-79, mem. com. on presdl. libs., 1988-95; trustee emeritus Nat. Trust Hist. Preservation, 1976—; fin. chmn. League Red Cross and Red Crescent Socs., Geneva, 1977-87; mem. adv. bd. Nature's Best Found., 1999—; bd. dirs. U.S. Capitol Hist. Soc., 1993-95. Comdr. USNR, 1941-47. Decorated Legion of Merit, Order Brit. Empire, medals from Red Cross Socs. Finland, Korea, Greece, Netherlands, Fed. Republic Germany, Can. and Magen David Adom (Israel); recipient Disting. Pub. Svc. medal Dept. Def. Internat. Humanitarian award Am. Red Mogen David for Israel, Henry Dunant medal Internat. Red Cross and Red Crescent, 1989. Mem. Smithsonian Instn. (Paul Peck award, 2004), Nat. Geog. Soc. (trustee 1977-93), Met. Club (Washington), City Tavern Club (Washington), White House Mil. Aides Assn. (hon. chmn. 1998—), Phi Beta Kappa. Presbyterian. Home: Irvine, Calif. Died Dec. 30, 2015.

ELY, JACK BROWN, musician, singer; b. Portland, Oreg., Sept. 11, 1943; s. Kenneth Ely and Helen Cherie (Brown) Nelson, stepfather: Robley W. Nelson; children: Robert Sterling, Sean Nelson, Sierra Lead singer The Kingsmen, Portland, 1957-63; with The Squires, The Courtmen. Singer popular song "Louie Louie"; (solo album) Love is All Around You Now, 2011 Died Apr. 28, 2015.

EMERSON, CLAUDIA, poet, language professor; b. Chatham, Va., Jan. 13, 1957; d. Claude and Mollie E.; m. Kent Ippolito, 2000. BA in English, U. Va., 1979; MFA in Creative Writing, U. NC, Greensboro, 1991. Acad. dean Chatham Hall, Chatham, Va., 1996—98; assoc. prof. English U. Mary Washington, Fredericksburg, Va., 1998—2008; Siragusa Found. poet-in-residence Chatham Hall, 2008—13; creative writing faculty Va. Commonwealth U., 2013—14. Bd. trustees Chatham Hall, Chatham, Va., 1998—2004. Contbg. adv. editor Shenandoah, guest editor Visions Internat.; author: (poetry collections) Pharaoh, Pharaoh, 1997, Pinion, An Elegy, 2002, Late Wife, 2005 (Pulitzer Prize for Poetry, 2006), Figure Studies, 2008, Secure the Shadow, 2012. Recipient Associated Writing Program's Intro award, 1991, Acad. of American Poets Prize, 1991, Mary Washington Coll. Alumni Assn. Outstanding Young Faculty award, 2003; named Poet Laureate of Va., Gov. Tim Kaine, 2008—10; grantee Nat. Endowment for Arts fellowship, 1994, Va. Commn. for Arts Individual Artist Fellowship in Poetry, 1995, 2002, Witter Bynner Found. Fellowship in Poetry, Libr. of Congress, 2005, Guggehein Fellowship, 2011. Home: Fredericksburg, Va. Died Dec. 4, 2014.

EMERY, LARRY C., financial executive; b. Poplar Bluff, Mo., June 15, 1939; BA, Washington U., St. Louis, 1961. Investment cons. Merrill Lynch, Kansas City, Mo., 1968-78, Smith Barney, Kansas City, Mo., 1978-90, Kidd Peabody, Kansas City, Mo., 1990-94; account v.p. Paine Webber, Kansas City, Mo., from 1995. Contbr. articles to newspapers. Mem. Optimist Club (Optimist of Yr. 1979-80), Optimist Youth Club. Republican. Lutheran. Avocations: spectator sports, travel. Died May 14, 2007.

EMERY, MARGARET ROSS, elementary school educator; b. Columbus, Ohio, May 21, 1923; d. Galen Starr and Stella May (Albright) Ross; m. Richard Clayton Emery, Oct. 27, 1943 (dec. June 1988); children: Richard C. Jr., Margaret Elizabeth Chapman. BA in Edn., U. Mich., 1944; MS in Elem. Guidance, U. Notre Dame, 1967. Life lic. in edn., Ind. 1st grade tchr. Grosse Ile (Mich.) Schs., 1944-45; 2nd grade tchr. Rumson (N.J.) Pub. Schs., 1945-46; homebound tutor Schenectady (N.Y.) Pub. Schs., 1946-48; tutor Hinsdale (Ill.) Pub. Schs., 1948-50; substitute tchr. South Bend (Ind.) Pub. Schs., 1951-53 and from 93; head lower sch., guidance couns., 1st grade tchr. The Stanley Clark Sch., South Bend, 1958-88. Mem. St. Joseph County Rep. Women, South Bend, 1958-96; election day clk. Election Bd., South Bend, 1986-96; docent No. Ind. Hist. Soc., South Bend, 1990—. Mem. AAUW, Panhellenic Assn. (pres. South Bend Mishawaka 1993-95), Zonta Internat. (historian, bd. mem. 1994—), Delta Kappa Gamma (pres. Nu chpt. 1992-94). Republican. Presbyterian. Avocations: reading, needlecrafts, golf, volunteer tutoring, bridge. Home: Mishawaka, Ind. Died Apr. 23, 2007.

EMOTO, MASARU, publishing executive, researcher; b. Yokohama, Kanagawa, Japan, July 22, 1943; s. Hiroshi and Kazu Emoto; m. Kazuko Kanemitsu, Nov. 16, 1968; children: Yoko Yamamoto, Kentaro, Hiromasa. BA in Internat. Rels., Yokohama Mcpl. U., Kanagawa, 1965; D in Alternative Medicine, Open U. Sri Lanka, 1992. Regional mgr. Chubu Yomiuri Newspaper Co., Nagoya, Japan, 1973—80; pres. I.H.M Co., Ltd, Tokyo, 1986—2007, Office Masaru Emoto LLC, 2008. Hado cons. I.H.M Co., Ltd, Tokyo, 1987—92; hon. dir. Japan Assn. of Subtle Energy, from 2002; top advisor Japan Assn. of Vibrational-Medicine, 2005—06; pres. emeritus Internat. Water for Life Found., Oklahoma City, from 2005; chmn. Emoto Peace Project, 2011; spkr. in field. Author: (books) The Hidden Messages in Water (NY Times Best Seller list, 2004), The True Power of Water (NY Times Best Seller list, 2005). Achievements include captured frozen water crystals in photographs; proved the existence of Hado, subtle energy and spread the development of its application. Avocations: sports, music. Home: Urayasu, Japan. Died Oct. 17, 2014.

ENELOW, MICHAEL RALPH, marketing executive; b. Greensburg, Pa., July 19, 1932; s. William and Goldye (Ruben) E.; m. Nancy Leber; children: Wendy Cindy, Michelle, Jenny. BA, Pa. State U., 1954. Chief exec. officer Enelow Shoe Enterprises, Greensburg, 1955-67, Comml. Distbrs., Irwin, Pa., 1967-80, EMS, Irwin, 1970-80, Comml. Beverage Dispensing Systems, Miami, Fla., 1975-80, Century 21 Flagship Realty, Fla., 1980-85, M.R.E. Inn Room Bartender, Miami, 1982-85, Barnacle Bill's Seafood, Greensburg, 1968-72; treas. Sheraton Motor Inns., Daboise, Pa., 1972-80; nat. dir. mktg. and sales Salcus Computer Corp., Greensburg, from 1986; pres., ptnr. Enelow & Leber Ltd.; exec. v.p. Computerized Maintainance & Security; pres. Titan Software Corp., 1990. Named Man of Yr. B'nai Brith, 1960. Mem. Rep. Inner Circle. Home: Monroeville, Pa. Died Apr. 9, 2007.

ENG, JOAN LOUISE LOUISE, retired special education educator; b. Yakima, Wash., July 29, 1934; d. Vernon Ross and Vivian Thelma (Rust) Dent; children: Andrew, Jane, William, June, Vern, Eric, Fred BEd English and Social Studies, Seattle U., 1961; MEd Exceptional Children, Ctrl. Wash. U., 1965; postgrad., U. Wash., 1962, LeVerne U., 1972—73, Ea. Wash. U., 1975—76, Seattle Pacific U., 1976, Yakima Valley Coll., 1977, U. South Sch. Theology, 1997. Cert. tchr., elem. prin., Wash. Tchr. English Selah H.S., Wash., 1962—65, Yakima Valley Coll., 1965—66; tchr. Adams Elem. Sch., Yakima, 1966—71, McKinley Elem. Sch., Yakima, 1971—72, Stanton Elem. Sch., Yakima, 1972—77, Franklin Jr. H.S., Yakima, 1977—82, John F. Kennedy H.S., Seattle, 1984—85, Artz-Fox Elem. Sch., Mabton, Wash., 1988—98; ret., 1998. Supt. ch. sch. St. Timothy's Episcopal Ch., Yakima; cons. Tonnemaker Corp., Seattle, life vowed Sister-Cmty. Paraclete; ordained deacon Diocese of Spokane Episcopal Ch., 2003; long term care ombudsman, Wash., 2000-04 Editor Yakima Deanry Newsletter, 1998—, Paracletian Focus, 1998-2000 Asst. min., guardian St. Stephen's Priory, 1992-96, Seattle; chpt. guardian Spirit-In-Life, 1996—, Yakima, 1994-97; coord. Sunday worship team Heritage Garden Nursing Home, 1998—; coord. ann. retreat Cmty. of Paraclete, 1999—, mem. pastoral care team, 1996—; tchr. St. Michael's Sunday Sch., 1998—; vestry mem. St. Michael's, 1998-2001; del. Diocesan Conv. 1998, 99, 2001; mem. com. on handicapped, confined and chonically ill Diocese of Spokane, WA, 1998-2001; hospice vol., 1999—; vol. Annie Tran Grief and Loss Ctr., 1999-2001 Mem. NEA, Mabton Edn. Assn., Wash. Edn. Assn., Ret. Tchrs. Yakima, Washington State Ret. Tchrs. Avocations: knitting, crocheting. Home: Yakima, Wash. Died July 31, 2007.

ENGLAND, BRENDA, transportation financial executive; b. Pine Bluff, Ark., May 24, 1940; d. W.D. and Hortense (Jones) E.; m. Joseph N. Norris, Sept. 1980; children: Billy, Sharon, Kthy, Ken, Benjy, J.J., Kellye. Student, U. Ark., 1969, Stephen Coll., 1977, La. State U., 1988. Owner The Parsons Co., Pine Bluff, 1970-74, Nat. Tax Svc., Ft. Smith, Ark., 1974-80, Palace Grocery, Alexandria, La., 1980-82; CFO La. Air Freight Corp., Alexandria, 1982-91; corp. officer Magnolia Distbn., Inc., from 1991. Founded, owned and operated several businesses. Recipient Youth award, 1965. Mem. Mental Health Assn., Local, State Women's Info. and Networking Group (originator, nat. bd. dirs.), Soroptimists (pres. 1977). Home: Baton Rouge, La. Died Apr. 21, 2007.

ENGLEHART, EDWIN THOMAS, metals company executive; b. Johnstown, Pa., Aug. 7, 1921; s. Edwin T. and Genevieve (Conley) E.; m. Genevieve Whittaker, May 26, 1951; 1 child, Daria. BS, Pa. State U., 1943; postgrad., U. Pitts., 1946-49. Corrosion engr. Alcoa Rsch. Labs., New Kensington, Pa., 1943-59, asst. chief ehem. metals div., 1959-77; sect. head corrosion alloy tech. div. Alcoa Tech. Ctr., Alcoa Ctr., Pa., 1977-83. Advisor, com. mem. ASTM, Am. Welding Soc., Nat. Assn. of Corrosion Engrs. Author: Aluminum Updated, 1983, Vol. III, 1967; contbr. over 20 articles to profl. jours. Mem. K.C., Lions, Sigma Xi. Republican. Home: Gibsonia, Pa. Died Dec. 13, 2006.

ENGLISH, MILDRED OSWALT, retired nurse supervisor; b. Moberly, Mo., May 28, 1916; d. Oscar and Lulu (Street) Oswalt; m. Deaver English, Apr. 9, 1955. RN, Jewish Hosp. St. Louis Sch. Nursing, 1942; BS, U. N.C., 1952. RN, Tex. Pub. health nurse supr. Mo. Div. Health, Jefferson City, Mo., 1946-56; supervising pub. health nurse L.A. County Health Dept., 1957-67; sch. nurse Bonita Unified Sch. Dist., San Dimas, Calif., 1967-72; quality assurance coord. Moberly (Mo.) Regional Med. ctr., 1973-83; ret., 1983. Cmdr. Nurse Corps, USNR Ret., active duty 1943-46. Home: Arlington, Tex. Died July 5, 2007.

ENGLISH, WILLIAM RUSSELL, retired insurance company executive, lawyer; b. Little Rock, Nov. 14, 1918; s. Carl Russell and Mabel Therese (Casey) E.; m. Mary Louise Harden, Aug. 31, 1948; children: Jan Ellen English Leary, William David. JD, U. Mo., 1950. Bar: Mo. 1950. Fire underwriter Pacific Nat. Fire Ins. Co., Chgo., 1938-41; mgr. personal lines Gen. Ins. Co., Seattle, 1950-58; exec. dir. fire and inland marine Wolverine Ins. Co., Battle Creek, Mich., 1958-65; sr. v.p. Utica Mut. Ins. Co., New Hartford, N.Y., 1965-83, bd. dirs., 1976-83; pres. IRM Ins., White Plains, N.Y., 1984-85; arbitrator Am. Arbitration Assn., Syracuse, N.Y., from 1985. With AUS, 1941-46, ETO; maj. U.S. Army, 1951-52. Mem. Sadaquada Golf Club (New Hartford), Yahnundasis Golf Club (New Hartford), Englewood Golf Club (Fla.). Home: Clinton, NY. Died Nov. 2, 2006.

ENGWALL, GREGORY BOND, lawyer; b. Sioux City, Iowa, May 23, 1950; s. Glen Leslie and Maxine Lillian (Bond) E.; m. Jeanne Ann Van Drasek, July 22, 1977; children: Thomas Gregory, Daniel Henry, Laura Ann. BA, Gustavus Adolphus Coll., 1972; JD, U. Minn., 1975. Bar: Minn. 1975. Assoc. Larson Law Office, Winthrop, Minn., 1975-94; sole practitioner Engwall Law Office, Winthrop, from 1995. Mem. Minn. State Bar Assn., Guild of St. Ansgar, K.C., Mensa, Iota Delta Gamma. Republican. Roman Catholic. Home: Hutchinson, Minn. Died Apr. 16, 2007.

ENLOW, DONALD HUGH, retired anatomist, dean; b. Mosquero, N.Mex., Jan. 22, 1927; s. Donald Carter and Martie Blairene (Albertson) E.; m. Martha Ruth McKnight, Sept. 3, 1945; 1 child, Sharon Lynn. BS, U. Houston, 1949, MS, 1951; PhD, Tex. A&M U., 1955. Instr. biology U. Houston, 1949-51; asst. prof. biology West Tex. State U., 1955-56; instr. anatomy Med. Coll. S.C., 1956-57; asst. prof. U. Mich. Med. Sch., Ann Arbor, 1957-62, assoc. prof., 1962-67, prof. anatomy, 1969-72; dir. phys. growth program Center for Human Growth and Devel., 1966-72; prof., chmn. dept. anatomy W.Va. U. Sch. Medicine, Morgantown, 1972-77; Thomas Hill disting. prof., chmn. dept. orthodontics Case Western Res. Sch. Dentistry, Cleve., 1977-89, prof. emeritus, from 1989, asst. dean for rsch. and grad. studies, 1977-85, acting dean, 1983-86. Adj. prof. U. NC, from 1992; lectr. in field in 32 fgn. countries. Author: Principles of Bone Remodeling, 1963, The Human Face, 1968, Handbook of Facial Growth, 1975, 3d edit., 1990, Essentials of Facial Growth, 2nd edit., 2008; contbr. chpts. to 30 books, numerous articles to profl. jours. Served with reserves USCG, 1945—46. Recipient Outstanding Research award Tex. Acad. Sci., 1952, Dewel award, 2006, Thomas Graber award, 2006. Fellow Royal Soc. Medicine, Am. Assn. Anatomists, Internat. Assn. Dental Research; hon. mem. Am. Assn. Orthodontists (Mershon Meml. lectr. 1968, Spl. Merit award 1969, award for outstanding contbns. to orthodontia, 1984, Thomas Grober award 2003), Gt. Lakes Orthodontic Soc., Cleve. Dental Soc., Cleve. Orthodontic Soc., Omicron Kappa Upsilon. Republican. Methodist. Home: Milton, Wis. Died July 5, 2014.

EPPLER, JAMES DALE, retail executive; b. Carnegie, Okla., Nov. 5, 1926; s. James Alex and Alma Gertrude (Bethel) E.; m. Robena Lee Dalgety, June 27, 1948; children: James Alan, David Dale, Kimberly Ann, Thomas Edward. Student, U. Wash., 1945; BS in Bus., Okla. CityU., 1949; MS in Retailing, NYU, 1950. Assoc. dir. Bur. Bus. Rsch. Oklahoma City U., 1948-49; sect. mgr. B. Altman & Co., NYC, 1949-50; asst. gen. merchandise mgr. Goldwaters Inc., Phoenix, 1950; sr. merchandiser Montgomery Ward & Co., Mail Order House, Ft Worth, Tex., 1952-54; gen. merchandise mgr. Ft. Bliss Army & Air Force Exchange Svc., El Paso, Tex., 1954-58; div. merchandise mgr. The White House Dept. Store, El Paso, Tex., 1958-62; gen. merchandise mgr. Hemphill-Wells Co. Dept. Store, Lubbock and San Angelo, Tex., 1962-86; corp. dir., economist Hemphill-Wells Corp., Lubbock and San Angelo, Tex., 1980-85; pres., owner Eppler's Ladies Specialty Store, Lubbock, from 1986. Chmn. bus. and industry liaison Dirs. Adv. Com., Wayland Bapt. U., Lubbock, 1989-91, adj. faculty in retailing, 1989—. Author: A Ten Year Analysis of Lubbock Economic Indicators, 1977. Pres. Singing Plainsmen Barber Shoppers, Soc. for the Preservation and Encouragement of Barbershop Quartet Singing in Am., Lubbock, El Paso, 1962-65; pres., trustee Tex. Tech U. Dads Assn., 1980; chmn. complete count com. U.S. Census Bur., Lubbock, 1990. 1st lt. U.S. Army, 1945-47, 50-52. Recipient Hero's award, Lubbock Visitors & Conv. Bur., 1986, Speakers award, Lubbock Econ. Outlook Seminar, Lubbock Econ. Coun., 1985, 86, 89. Mem. Nat. Assn. Bus. Economists (chpt. coord. 1967-86), Lubbock Econs. Coun. (pres. 1976-77), S. Plains Better Bus. Bur (dir., pres. 1973-76), Lubbock Sales Execs. Assn., Lubbock C. of C. (chmn. retail merchants com. 1989-90), Round Table Investments Club (v.p. 1967-85), Lions (Chairman's award 1980). Republican. Methodist. Avocations: barbershop harmony, gardening, stockmarket. Home: Lubbock, Tex. Died Jan. 20, 2007.

ERDAL, BRUCE ROBERT, environmental company executive; b. Albuquerque, June 15, 1939; s. Selmer Clifford and Louise Marion (Hubbell) E.; m. Jean Elizabeth Davis, June 25, 1970. Student, U. N.Mex., Albuquerque, 1961; PhD, Washington U., St. Louis, 1966. Rsch. assoc. Brookhaven Nat. Lab., LI, 1967-69; vis. scientist CERN, Geneva, 1970-71; asst. physicist Ames (Iowa) Lab., 1971-72; mem. staff Los Alamos (N.Mex.) Nat. Lab., 1972-80, dep. group leader, 1980-82, project officer, 1980-82, assoc. div. leader, 1982-87, program mgr. environ. techs., from 1987. NSF fellow, 1969-70. Fellow Am. Inst. Chemists; mem. AAAS, Am. Chem. Soc. (sec. div. nuclear chem. tech. 1983-86, chmn. 1991—), Am. Geophys. Union, Materials Rsch. Soc., Phi Kappa Phi, Sigma Xi. Avocation: music. Home: Los Alamos, N.Mex. Died May 23, 2007.

ERICKSON, SUZANNE JEAN, health facility administrator; b. Lansing, Mich., Mar. 6, 1930; d. Victor Fredrick and Elvera Christine (Anderson) Marquardt; m. Dennis W. Erickson, Nov. 26, 1952; children: Craig, Cindy, Michael. Diploma, Mercy Cen. Sch. Nursing, 1951. Charge nurse John Day Hosp. and Clinic, Oreg., 1952-53, St. Elizabeth Hosp., Baker, Oreg., 1964-72, dir. home health, 1972-89; quality assurance dir. Hospice of Wexford-Missaukee, Cadillac, Mich., 1989-95; retired. Mem. Oreg. League for Nursing (bd. dirs. 1984), Oreg. State Nurses Assn. (pres. 1978-80), Eastern Oreg. Health Sys. Agy. (pres. 1984-86), Cadillac Rotary Club (bd. dirs. 1993—, sec. 1993—), Mich. Hosp. Nurses Assn. (bd. dirs. 1995-97). Home: Tustin, Mich. Died Dec. 26, 2006.

ERKFRITZ, DONALD SPENCER, mechanical engineer; b. Highland Park, Mich., Mar. 16, 1925; s. Clarence Frederick and Dorothy N. (Spencer) E.; m. Marjorie Alethea Isard, Dec. 24, 1948; children: Jeannette, D. Michael, Lisa. Student, Henry Ford Trade Sch., 1938-42; lic. mechanic & ground sch. instr., A&E Mechanics Sch., Chillicothe, Ohio, 1945. Cert. mfg. engr. Design engr. Beaver Tool & Engring., Big Beaver, Mich., 1950-52; chief engr. Delman Co. Labs., Detroit, 1952-60, Futurmill, Inc., Farmington, Mich., 1960-68; R&D engr. Ingersoll Milling Machine Co., Rockford, Ill., 1968-72, Southfield, Mich., 1974-78; chief engr. Valenite div. Valeron Corp., Troy, Mich., 1972-74; milling programs mgr. Carboloy div. Gen. Electric, Warren, Mich., 1978-85; metalworking cons. Dba Rsch., Etc., Clarkston, Mich., from 1985. Cons. Gen. Motors Tech. Ctr., Warren, 1985-88, Focus Hope, Detroit, 1990-92; devel. engr. Ingersoll Milling Machine Corp., Rockford, 1988-90; exptl. machinist AP Products, Auburn Hills, Mich., 1994-95; tooling engr. spl. projects Dijet, Inc., Plymouth, Mich., 1997-98; engring. cons. Wolverine Cutting Tool Inc., Oxford, Mich., 1998—; v.p. Laser Ink Corp.; adj. tchr. Oakland C.C., Auburn Hills, Mich., 1997-98. Patentee in field. Instr. first aid ARC, Pontiac, 1958-68; co-chair High Fever Follies PGH Aux., Pontiac, Mich., 1962; host family Youth for Understanding Fgn. Exch. Student Program, 1967-68; mem. Pontiac Police Res., 1959-63. Mem. Henry Ford Trade Sch. Alumni Assn, Descs. and Founders Ancient Windsor, Mayflower Soc., Found. Geneal. and Hist. Rsch., Huntley Nat. Assn., Spencer Family Assn., Geneal. Soc. Vt., Ont. Geneal. Soc., Elder William Brewster Soc. Avocations: genealogy, music, woodcrafts, piano technician, machinist. Died Nov. 27, 2006.

ETHEREDGE, KENNETH R., securities trader; b. Dallas, Jan. 3, 1943; s. Ralph B. and Juanita (Redford) E.; m. Cheryl Dianne Willis, Aug. 30, 1969; children: Elliott K., Meagan Ann. BBA, U. Okla., 1964. V.p. Kidder Peabody & Co., Inc., Dallas, 1974-79; v.p., ptnr. Schaenen Fellerman Peck & Co., Dallas, 1979-82, Schaenen, Jacobs, Etheredge & Co., Dallas, 1982-85; pres. M.S. Etheredge & Co., Inc., Dallas, from 1985. Bd. dirs. Episc. Sch. of Dallas, 1986—. Served 1st lt. Spl. Forces, U.S. Army, 1964-68, Vietnam. Decorated Bronze Star; Air medal. Mem. Nat. Assn. Securities Dealers, Dallas Securities Dealers Assn. Republican. Methodist. Home: Dallas, Tex. Died Nov. 8, 2006.

ETTL, DOROTHY ANNE, home economist, retired educator; b. Marysville, Calif., Apr. 19, 1943; d. Walter Joseph and Celia Marie (Hill) E. BS, U. Calif., Davis, 1964; MS in Home Econs., Tex. Tech. U., 1969; postgrad., U. Hawaii, summer 1970; PhD in Home Econs., U. Minn., 1976. Cert. spl. vocat. tchr., Tex., standard secondary tchr., Calif. County extension home economist Agrl. Extension Service, U. Wyo., Lusk, Wyo., 1964-67; teaching and rsch. asst. Tex. Tech. U., Lubbock, 1968-69; asst. prof. home econs. Calif. State U., Chico, 1969-73; rsch. asst. U. Minn., St. Paul, 1973-76; assoc. prof. Wash. State U., Pullman, 1976-89, mem. faculty senate, 1980-84. Substitute tchr. Yuba Community Coll., 1991. Contbr. numerous articles to extension publs.; author audio-visual ednl. materials; columnist Info. Kettle, 1964-67. Mus. aide Community Meml. Mus., Sutter County, 1992—; vol. tchr. Yuba City Parks and Recreation Dept., 1991-92; bd. dirs. Friends Mus. Art, Wash. State U., 1985-88. Mem. AAUW (chair pub. policy, br. treas.), Am. Home Econs. Assn. (life; cert.), Assn. Coll. Profls. Textiles and Clothing (exec. bd. 1979-82), Nat. Assn. Extension Home Economists, Coop. Extension Assembly (v.p. 1985-88), Photog. Soc. Am., Assn. Faculty Women Wash. State U. (treas. 1987-89), Whitman County Hist. Soc. (life), Sutter County Hist. Soc., Colusi Hist. Soc., Epsilon Sigma Phi (sec. Beta chpt. 1986-88). Avocations: travel, photography, gardening, needle arts, walking. Home: Yuba City, Calif. Died Jan. 13, 2007.

EUBANKS, EDWIN E., radiation oncologist; b. Canton, Ohio, Sept. 22, 1952; s. Edwin E. and Merle F. Eubanks; m. Deborah Naomi Euganks; children: Jemma, Emily. AB summa cum laude, Princeton U., 1974; MA with honors, Oxford U., Eng., 1977; MB BChir with distinction, Cambridge U., Eng., 1985. Diplomate Am. Bd. Radiology, Am. Bd. Internal Medicine. Resident, chief resident in radiation oncology Stanford U. Med. Ctr., Palo Alto, Calif., 1992-95, clin. tchg. faculty in radiation oncology, 1999; staff physician Redwood Regional Oncology Group, Santa Rosa, Calif., from 1996. Recipient Ray Hively Humanitarian award Kaiser Found. Hosp., 1991. Mem. AMA, Am. Soc. for Therapeutic Radiation Oncology, Am. Coll. Radiology, Calif. Med. Assn. Died July 6, 2007.

EUFINGER, ROSALIE RIGG, public relations executive; b. St. Louis, Jan. 10, 1940; d. Dean and Helen Katherine (Grothe) Rigg; m. R. J. Eufinger Jr., Sept. 25, 1963 (dec. Jan. 1987). AB, Washington U., St. Louis, 1963. Corp. mag. editor, pub. rels. writer Oakite Products, Berkeley Heights, N.J., 1967-74; asst. advt. and pub. rels. mgr. Fleetwood Enterprises, Riverside, Calif., 1975-78; mgr. corp. news bur. Tymshare, Cupertino, Calif., 1979-83; v.p. editl. svcs. Mathews & Clark Comms., Sunnyvale, Calif., from 1983. Mng. editor: Channel, 1991—. Avocations: hiking, cooking, theater, travel, music. Home: Cupertino, Calif. Died Dec. 8, 2006.

EUSTACHE, DANIEL LEE, secondary school educator; b. Troy, Ohio, July 4, 1943; s. Floyd Richard and Jeanette Elizabeth (Steinke) E.; m. Jeanette Lois Vagi, June 12, 1965. BSc, Ohio State U., 1965; MEd, Cleve. State U., 1973; postgrad., Western Wash. State Coll., Bellingham, 1973, U. Wyo., Debois, 1982. Tchr. vocat. agrl. Bradford (Ohio) H.S., 1965-66, No. Balt. (Ohio) H.S., 1966-67; tchr. sci., asst. prin. Cory-Rawson H.S., Cory, Ohio, 1967-68; tchr. sci. Parma City Schs., Parma, Ohio, from 1968; sci. dept. head Parma H.S., Parma, Ohio, from 1973. Sci. curriculum devel., Parma city schs., 1973-95; owner, operator D.L. Builders, Hinckley, Ohio, 1976-87; facilator Regional Sci. Olympiad, Lorin, Ohio, 1989-94; presentor Ohio Acad. Sci. Symposium, 1971, State Sci. Conf., 1991. Author: DOE/SECO Workshop, 1991. Adv. bd. mem. CEI Energy, Cleveland, 1985-93. Jennings Found. Environ. grant, 1991; recipient Tchr. Achievement award, Parma PTA 1988, 90; named Outstanding Sci. Olympiad Coach, Lorain Ohio, 1991-94. Mem. NEA, N.E. Ohio Ed. Assn., Ohio Ed. Assn., Parma Edn. Assn. (rep. 1969-72). Avocations: hiking, biking, whitewater rafting, bridge, theater. Home: Northfield, Ohio. Died Aug. 17, 2007.

EVANS, ALBERT PIERCE, dancer; b. Atlanta, Ga., Dec. 29, 1968; Student, Patsy Bromleys Terpsichore Expressions, Sch. Am. Ballet, 1986. Mem. corps de ballet NYC Ballet, 1988—91, soloist, 1991—95, prin., 1995—2010, ballet master, 2010—15. Dancer (ballets) Agon, Danses Concertantes, A Midsummer Nights Dream, The Nutcracker, Stravinsky Violin Concerto, Symphony in Three Movements, Gershwin Concerto, Ash, The Beethoven Seventh, Jeu de Cartes, Swan Lake, The Beethoven Seventh, The Sleeping Beauty, Appalachia Waltz, Steel and Rain, Open Strings, Swerve Poems, Duke!. Died June 22, 2015.

EVANS, ELIZABETH CARPENTER, retired social worker and family counselor; b. Glens Falls, NY, Jan. 3, 1911; d. William Morton and Beulah (Mason) Carpenter; m. John E. Evans, Jr., Aug. 28, 1933 (dec. Oct. 1982); children: John Edgar III, Claire Louise. AB, Radcliffe Coll., 1932; MSW, U. Pitts., 1964. Dir. family counseling Cath. Social Svc., Pitts., 1964-76; ret., 1976. Sec. Southwestern Pa. coun. Girl Scouts U.S.A., 1975-76, v.p. 1976-82, bd. dirs., 1982-85. Mem. Nat. Assn. Social Workers, Zonta (pres. Pitts. 1975-76), Pitts. Coll. Club (bd. dirs.). Republican. Methodist. Avocations: travel, needlecrafts, photography. Home: Eau Claire, Wis. Died Jan. 30, 2007.

EVANS, ELIZABETH HENDRICK CAUSEY, public relations specialist; b. Bowling Green, Ky., June 15, 1920; d. Henry Lee and Jocelyn Nimrod (Price) Hendrick; m. William W. Causey, Apr. 1, 1939 (div. 1946); 1 child, Norman Michael; m. Gillespie Stevenson Evans, Sept. 3, 1961 (dec. Sept. 1964). BA in Communication, Am. U., 1957, MA in Internat. Rels. & Orgn., 1960. Sec. G-3 War Dept., Gen. Staff, The Pentagon, Washington, 1945-47; mem. newsroom staff ABC, Washington, 1947-49; writer, editor Dept. State, U.S. Inf. Agy., Washington, 1950-61; assoc. editor Paradise Mag., Honolulu, 1961-63; co-editor jour. George Washington U., Washington, 1963-64; pub. affairs officer U.S. Govt. HEW Offices Higher Edn. and Health Stats. HUD, Washington, 1964-67, 68-78; faculty Western Ky. U., Bowling Green, 1967-68; founder, dir. Spanish-Am. Club, Majorca, Spain, 1975-78. Author: USSR and Eastern Europe after Khruschev, 1960; contbr. articles to miscellaneous jours. Pres. Rep. Women's Club Federated, 1987-92. Mem. AAUW, Ptnrs. Of Ams. (bd. regents Fla. chpt. 1980—), UN Assn. (past pres. Southwest chpt.), Geneology Soc., Nat. Assn. Ret. Fed. Employees, Conversational Spanish Roundtable. Republican. Avocations: reading, walking, travel, rsch. geneology, real estate. Home: Lehigh Acres, Fla. Died Dec. 2, 2006.

EVANS, JAMES HURLBURT, retired transportation and natural resources executive; b. Lansing, Mich., June 26, 1920; s. James L. and Marie (Hurlburt) E.; m. Mary Johnston Head, 1984(dec. 2014); children by previous marriage: Eric B. (dec. 1996), Carol E. Jepperson, Joan E. Madsen. AB, Centre Coll., 1943, DHL (hon.), 1987; JD, U. Chgo., 1948; LLD (hon.), Millikin U., 1978. Bar: Ill. 1949. Atty., loan officer Harris Trust & Savs. Bank, Chgo., 1948-56; sec.-treas. Reuben H. Donnelley Corp., Chgo., 1956-57; v.p., dir. Reuben H. Donnelley Corp. (merged with Dun & Bradstreet 1961), NYC, 1957-62; v.p. fin. Dun & Bradstreet, 1962-65, also bd. dirs.; pres. Seamen's Bank for Savs., NYC, 1965-68, chmn. bd., 1968, trustee, 1965-78; pres. Union Pacific Corp., NYC, 1969-77, chmn., CEO, 1977-85. Ret. dir. AT&T, GM Corp., Citicorp/Citibank, Met. Life Ins. Co., Bristol-Myers, Dun & Bradstreet, Anaconda Corp. Bd. govs. ARC, 1970-76, nat. fund chmn. 1974-76; hon. trustee, former vice chmn. John F. Kennedy Ctr. for Performing Arts; life trustee Nat. Recreation Found., pres. 1971-75, U. Chgo., Ctr. Coll. Ky., Ctrl. Park Conservancy; founding mem. Citizens Adv. Com. on Environ. Quality, 1966-70. Served to lt. USNR, 1943-46; life trustee N.Y. Presbyn. Hosp. Mem. ABA, Phi Beta Kappa, Omicron Delta Kappa, Delta Kappa Epsilon. Clubs: Racquet and Tennis, Knickerbocker (N.Y.C.); Metropolitan, Alfalfa (Washington); Maidstone (East Hampton). Presbyterian. Died May 11, 2015.

EVANS, LANE ALLEN, former United States Representative from Illinois; b. Rock Island, Ill., Aug. 4, 1951; s. Lee Herbert and Joycelene (Saylor) E. BA, Augustana Coll., 1974; JD, Georgetown U., 1978. Bar: Ill. 1978. Mng. atty. Western Ill. Legal Assistance Found., Rock Island, 1978-79; mem. nat. staff Edward M. Kennedy for Pres., Washington, 1978-80; atty., ptnr. Community Legal Clinic, Rock Island, Ill., 1981-82; mem. US Congress from 17th Ill. Dist., Washington, 1983—2007. Served in USMC, 1969-71. Mem. AmVets, American Legion, Marine Corps League, Vietnam Vets Ill. Democrat. Roman Catholic. Died Nov. 5, 2014.

EVANS, MEDFORD STANTON, newspaper editor; b. Kingsville, Tex., July 20, 1934; s. Medford Bryan and Alice Josephine (Stanton) E.; m. Sue Ellen Moore, Apr. 14, 1962 (div. 1974) BA, Yale, 1955; postgrad., NYU, 1955. Asst. editor Freeman, 1955; editorial staff Nat. Rev., 1955-56, asso. editor, 1960-68; mng. editor Human Events, 1956-59, contbg. editor, from 1968. Publs. dir. Intercollegiate Soc. Individualists, 1956-59, trustee, 1960; chief editorial writer Indpls. News, 1959-60, editor, 1960-1974; chmn. American Conservative Union, 1971-77; taught journalism, Troy U., Alabama, 1974-2004; led National Journalism Ctr., Washington, 1977-2002 Broadcaster: Spectrum series, CBS Radio, from 1971, also National Public Radio and Voice of America; Author: Revolt on the Campus, 1961, The Fringe on Top, 1962, The Liberal Establishment, 1965, The Politics of Surrenders, 1966, The Lawbreakers, 1968, The Future of Conservatism, 1968, Assassination of Joe McCarthy, 1970, Blacklisted by History: The Untold Story of Senator Joe McCarthy and His Fight Against America's Enemies, 2007 Recipient Freedoms Found. awards for editorial writing, 1959, 60, 65, 66; award for outstanding editorial pages Nat. Headliners Club, 1960 Mem. Am. Soc. Newspaper Editors, Nat. Headliners Club, Indpls. C. of C., Phi Beta Kappa, Sigma Delta Chi. Clubs: Capitol Hill (Washington); Elizabethan (Yale); Indpls. Press, Indpls. Athletic, Yale of Ind. Republican. Methodist. Died Mar. 3, 2015.

EVANS, WALTER REED, retired engineering executive, consultant; b. El Paso, Tex., Oct. 25, 1921; s. Charles Reed and Ruby Estelle (Simpson-Rountree) E.; m. Frances Adelaide Lounsbury, Jan. 15, 1942 (dec. 1975); children: Sandra Frances, Roger Reed, Sharon Adelaide; m. Dorothy May Cuthbertson, 1975; stepchildren: Jack W., William D., Charles T. Rogers. BS in Mech. Engring., U. Tex. Registered profl. engr. La., Tex. Engring. and mech. supr. Celanese and Exxon Corps., Tex. and Venezuela, 1948-57; plant mgr., pres. Falcon Chem. Corp., Lake Charles, La., 1957-59; refining coord., Stanvac divsn. Exxon-Mobil, White Plains, NY, 1959—60; cons. SIP, Inc., Houston, 1960-62; instrument engr. Exxon, Aruba, 1963, mech.supt. Malaga, Spain, 1964—65, chief engr. Pakistan, 1966—71, divsn. head Sriracha, Thailand, 1972; project mgr. S & B, Inc., Houston, 1973-79; mech. mgr. Arabian Am. Oil Co., Ras Tanura, Saudi Arabia, 1979-81; pvt. practice mech. engring. cons., 1982-88; Tex. state coord., lobbyist ASME, Austin, 1988-94; prof., competency monitor Tex. State Bd. Engring. Registration, 1995-99. Founder, v.p. Structural Metals, Inc. divsn. Comml. Metals, Inc., Seguin, Tex., 1947-48; trustee Teal Petroleum Co. divsn. W.R. Grace Co., 1975-79; apprentice mechanic, aircraft engine, Kelly Field, Tex., 1939; owner's rep. Himont, Inc. divsn. Dupont, 1984-85. Author: Aircraft Engine Overhaul, 1942. Enlisted Tex. N.G., 1938; lt. USAAF, 1942-44, ETO. Fellow ASME (life); mem. NSPE (life), NRA, Squires Bus. Men's Orgn., Austin Amateur Radio, Men's Garden Club, Austin Rifle Club. Republican. Episcopalian. Avocations: hunting, fishing, stamp/coin collecting, gardening, reading. Died July 18, 2007.

EVREN, KENAN, former president of Turkey; b. Manisa, Turkey, July 17, 1917; married; 3 children. Grad., War Acad. Turkey, 1938. Commd. 3rd lt. Turkish Army, 1938, advanced through grades to gen., 1964, battery comdr., 1940-46, arty. bn. comdr., 1949-57; asst. chief ops. 1st Army, 1957-58; chief of staff Turkish Brigade, Korea, 1958-59; comdg. Inf. Regt., 1961-62; chief of staff Army Corps, 1962-63, chief tng. br., 1963-67, comdg. gen. div., 1967-68, army chief of staff, 1968-70; chief insp. bd. and chief of staff Turkish Land Forces Command, 1972-75; dep. chief Turkish Gen. Staff, 1975-76; comdr. Aegean Army and Turkish Land Forces, 1976-78; chief Turkish Gen. Staff, 1978-80; chmn. Nat. Security Council and head of state Republic of Turkey, 1980-82, pres., 1982-89. Died May 9, 2015.

EWALD, WILLIAM BRAGG, JR., writer, consultant; b. Chgo., Dec. 8, 1925; s. William Bragg and Mary Ann (Niccolls) E.; m. Mary Cecilia Thedieck, Dec. 6, 1947 (dec. Feb. 1997); children: William Bragg, Charles Ross, Thomas Hart Benton. AB, Washington U., St. Louis, 1946; MA, Harvard U., 1947, PhD, 1951. Instr. English, humanities Harvard U., Cambridge, 1951-54; spl. asst. on White House staff, asst. to Sec. Interior Washington, 1954-61; with IBM, Armonk, 1961-88. Author: The Masks of Jonathan Swift, 1954, The Newsmen of Queen Anne, 1956, Eisenhower the President:Crucial Days, 1951-1960, 1981, Who Killed Joe McCarthy?, 1984, McCarthyism and Consensus, 1987, Trammell Crow: A Legacy of Real Estate Bus. Innovation, 2005; asst. to former Pres. Eisenhower in preparation of 2-vol. memoirs, White House Years: Mandate for Change, 1953-1956 and White House Years: Waging Peace, 1956-1961 Pres. Bruce Mus. Assocs., Greenwich, 1972-73; vestry mem. Christ Ch., Greenwich, 1986-89; bd. dirs. Eisenhower World Affairs Inst., 1984-91. Grantee Am. Philos. Soc., 1952, Harvard Found. Advanced Study and Research, 1952-53; Eisenhower Exchange fellow, 1960. Mem. Judson Welliver Soc., Phi Beta Kappa. Clubs: Cosmos (Washington); Round Hill (Greenwich). Republican. Episcopalian. Home: Greenwich, Conn. Died Mar. 16, 2015.

EZELL, HOWARD LEE, retail executive; b. Lavinia, Tenn., June 26, 1928; s. Finis Howard and Carrye Barton (Strayhorn) E.; m. Jackie Charmane Jackson, Dec. 27, 1949 (div. 1956); 1 child, Melanie Zann; m. Katrina Lewis, Sept. 26, 1975. BS, Memphis State U., 1953. With sales Proctor & Gamble, Memphis, 1953-56; dept. head Sears Roebuck & Co., Columbus, Ga., 1956-58; dist. mgr. Litton Industries, various locations, 1958-75; pres. Ezell's Office Products, Greensboro, N.C., from 1976. Pres. Greensboro/Guilford Crime Stoppers, 1987; bd. dirs. Greensboro Better Bus. Bur., 1986—. Served with U.S. Army, 1946-48. Recipient award of Excellence, Greensboro Better Bus. Bur., 1986. Mem. Carolinas Office Products Assn. (treas. 1978-80), Adminstrv. Mgmt. Soc. (pres. 1983-84). Lodges: Rotary (pres. Summit club, Greensboro, 1982). Republican. Avocations: golf, travel. Home: Milan, Tenn. Died Mar. 20, 2007.

EZZAT, HAZEM AHMED, research and business executive; BSc, U. Cairo, 1963; MS, U. Wis., 1967, PhD, 1971. Project engr. Suez Canal Authority, Egypt, 1963-65; instr. faculty engring. Cairo U., 1965-66; rsch. asst. U. Wis., Madison, 1966-70; with Gen. Motors Rsch. Labs., Warren, Mich., 1970—2005, asst. head engring. mechanics dept., 1981-84, head power sys. rsch. dept., 1984-95, head mfg. and design sys., 1995-98, dir. thermal and energy sys. lab., 1998—2001, dir. powertrain sys. rsch., 2001—05; chief scientist GM Europe, 2000—02; founding v.p. rsch. Nile U., Cairo, 2007—10; CEO Optumatics LLC, from 2009, co-founder. Contbr. articles to profl. and management jours. Mem. ASME (Henry Hess Best Paper award 1973), Soc. Automotive Engrs., Internat. Assn. Mgmt. Tech., Sigma Xi. Achievements include patents for surgical equipment. Home: Needham, Mass. Died Jan. 2015.

FAHRINGER, HERALD PRICE, lawyer; b. Lewisburg, Pa., Nov. 6, 1927; s. Herald Price and Pauline A. (Dyer) F.; m. Barbara Falk (div.) BA, Pa. State U., 1950, MA, 1951; LLB, U. Buffalo, 1956, JD, 1968. Bar: N.Y. Ptnr. Lipsitz, Green, Fahringer, Roll, Schuller & James, Buffalo. Spkr. Continuing Legal Edn courses; invited lectr. in field. Guest appearances Good Morning America, Good Day New York, American Journal, Inside Edition, The Crier Report, American Justice, The Phil Donahue Show, The News Hour with Jim Lehrer, The Merv Griffin Show and the David Susskind Show, legal commentator CNN, subject of feature articles in The New York Times, London Times, New York Daily News, New York Law Journal, The National Law Journal, and other national newspapers. With U.S. Army, 1946-48, Korea. Recipient award for Legal Defense of Freedom of Press, N.Y. Press Club, 1979, NY Criminal Bar Assn. award, Thurgood Marshall award, NY State Assn. of Criminal Defense Lawyers, Outstanding Profl. Achievement award, SUNY Buffalo-Sch. of Law, Disting. Alumni award, Pa. State U., Disting. Alumni award. SUNY-Buffalo Sch. of Law, Lifetime Achievement award, Lawline.com Fellow American Coll. Trial Lawyers, Internat. Soc. Barristers, American Acad. of Appellate Lawyers, American Bd. of Criminal Lawyers; mem. ABA (Edward R. Finch award), NY State Bar Assn. (Outstanding Practitioner award criminal law sect. 1974, Charles F. Crimi Meml. award, criminal justice sect.), First Amendment Lawyers Assn. (gen. counsel), Nat. Assn. Criminal Defense Lawyers, NY Coun. of Defense Lawyers, Died Feb. 12, 2015.

FAIRCHILD, JOHN BURR, publishing executive; b. Newark, Mar. 6, 1927; s. Louis W. and Margaret (Day) F.; m. Jill Lipsky, June 8, 1950; children: John Longin, James Burr, Jill and Stephen L. (twins). BA, Princeton U., 1950. Mem. rsch. dept. J.L. Hudson Co., Detroit, 1950-51; with Fairchild Publs., Inc., NYC, from 1951; pub. Women's Wear Daily, Daily News Record, from 1960, editor-in-chief corp. publs., 1964-65, pub. dir., 1965-66, pres., 1966-70, chmn. bd., CEO corp. publs., 1970-97, ret., 1997. Exec. v.p., dir. Capital Cities/ABC, Inc., exec. v.p. Author: The Moonflower Couple, The Fashionable Savages, Chic Savages; editor-at-large W Mag., Women's Wear Daily, 1997. Served with AUS, 1947-48. Decorated chevalier de L'Ordre National de Merite, France; grade de chevalier de la Légion d'Honneur, France, officier des Arts et Lettres, France. Mem.: Travellers (Paris, France), Tir aux Pigeons (Paris, France); Century (N.Y.C.). Died Feb. 27, 2015.

FALLON, PATRICK ROBERT, advertising executive; b. Columbus, Ohio, Sept. 7, 1945; s. Jerome and Katherine Fallon; children: Kevin, Megan, Duffy, Reilly, Tressa. Degree in Philosophy, U. Minn. With Leo Burnett, Chgo., 1967-69, Stevson & Assocs., Mpls., 1969-76, Martin/Williams Advt., Mpls., 1976-81; founder, chmn., CEO Fallon McElligott Rice (now Fallon Worldwide), Mpls., 1981—2007; chmn. Fallon Worldwide, 2007, chmn. emeritus, 2008—15. Co-author (with Fred Senn): Juicing the Orange: How to Turn Creativity into a Powerful Business Advantage, 2006. Commr. Minn. Combative Sports Commn., from 2008; bd. dirs. Children's Def. Fund, Washington, from 2008, Guthrie Theater, Mpls., Minn. Zoo, Minn. Orch. Named to Advt. Hall of Fame, American Advt. Fedn., 2010. Died Nov. 13, 2015.

FANGOR, VOY (WOJCIECH FANGOR), painter; b. Warsaw, Nov. 15, 1922; came to U.S., 1966; s. Konrad and Wanda Fangor; m. Magdalena Shummer. MFA, Acad. of Fine Arts, Warsaw, 1946. Asst. prof. Warsaw Acad. Art, 1953-61; tchr. Fairleigh Dickinson U., Madison, N.J., 1966-83. Participant internat. artist seminar Fairleigh Dickinson U., Madison, 1965; vis. lectr. Bath Acad. Art Corsham, Wiltshire, Eng., 1965-66; vis. critic arch. Grad. Sch. Design, Harvard U., Cambridge, Mass., 1967-68; set designer Martha Graham Dance Co., 1970. One-man shows include Study of Space, New Culture Salon, Warsaw, 1958, Inst. Contemporary Art, Washington, 1962, Galerie Lambert, Paris, 1963, Galerie Falazik, Bochum, Germany, 1964, Dom Galerie, Cologne, Germany, 1966, Galerie Chalette, N.Y.C., 1967, 69, 70, Solomon R. Guggenheim Mus., N.Y.C., 1970, Univ. Art Mus., Berkeley, Calif., 1971, Fort Worth Art Mus., Tex., 1971, Hokin Gallery, Chgo., 1974, Walter Kelly Gallery, Chgo., 1978, Bodley Gallery, N.Y.C., 1983, Zacheta Gallery, Warsaw, 1990, Mitchell Algus Gallery, N.Y.C., 1993, retrospective exhib. Nat. Mus., Krakow, 2012, Color, Light, Space, gallery 3 Grafton Street, London, 2014, survey show of installations and sculptures, Ctr. for Polish Sculpture, Oronsko, 2015; group shows include Stedlijk Mus., Amsterdam, 1959, Mus. Modern Art, N.Y.C., 1961, 65, Guggenheim Mus., N.Y.C., 1964, 67, 80, Riverside Mus., N.Y.C., 1965, Carnegie Inst., Pitts., 1967, 70, Newark Mus., 1969, Cin. Art Mus., 1969, Thorp Gallery, N.Y.C., 1980, Harm Bouckaert Gallery, N.Y.C., 1984, Gallery 53, Cooperstown, N.Y., 1988; represented in permanent collections Guggenheim Mus., N.Y.C., Mus. Modern Art, N.Y.C., San Antonio Mus. Art, Phillips Collection, Washington, Newark Mus., State Mus., Trenton, N.J., Aldrich Mus. Contemporary Art, Ridgefield, Conn., Rose Art Mus., Waltham, Mass., Carnegie Mus. Art, Pitts., Hirshhorn Mus., Smithsonian Inst., Washington, Power Gallery Art, Sidney, Australia, Muzeum Sztuki, Lodz, Poland, Muzuem Narodowe, Poznan and Warsaw, Poland, Stedelijk Mus., Amsterdam, Schloss Morsbroich Mus., Leverkusen, Germany, Mus. des XX Jahrhunderts, Berlin, Aachen (Germany) Mus. Art, Mus. Art, Munich, Milw. Mus. Art, Harlem Mus., N.Y.C. Recipient Alfred Jurzykowski Found. award, 1978; fellow Inst. Contemporary Art, 1962; Ford Found. grantee, 1964-65. Home: Santa Fe, N.Mex. Died Oct. 25, 2015.

FANNING, DANA BRIAN, actor; b. Wakefield, RI, Feb. 3, 1951; s. Howard Earl and Yvonne Marie (Morin) F. Assoc. in Fine Arts, Community Coll. of R.I., 1984. Actor, singer Theatre By The Sea, Matunuck, R.I., 1983, technician, 1982-86; guest artist State Ballet of R.I., Lincoln, 1986-91; actor, singer, dancer RAM III Prodns., New Hope, Pa., 1987. Actor: (summer stock mus.) Showboat, 1983, 42d Street, 1987, My One and Only, 1987; mime (ballet) Coppelia, 1986, 88, 89, 90; dancer Giselle, 1990 (State Ballet R.I.), Americana, 1991; dancer/actor Phantomgreen, 1990-91. With USN, 1971-74. Avocations: percussionist, surfer, basketball. Home: Kingston, RI. Died May 14, 2007.

FARABEE, RAY (KENNETH RAY FARABEE), retired academic administrator; b. Wichita Falls, Tex., Nov. 22, 1932; s. David Farabee; m. Helen Jane Farabee, 1958 (dec. July 28, 1988); children: Steven R., David Lee; m. Mary Margaret Albright, 1991. Student, Midwestern U.; BBA, U. Tex.; LLB. Admitted Tex. Bar; mem. Dist. 30 Tex. State Senate, 1975—88, pres. pro tempore, 1985; vice chancellor, gen. counsel U. Tex. System, 1988—2000, exec. asst. to chancellor, 2000—02. Author: Ray Farabee: Making It Through the Night and Beyond: A Memoir, 2009. Co-recipient Clara Driscoll Arts award, 2009. Democrat. Home: Austin, Tex. Died Nov. 20, 2014.

FARBER, LILLIAN, retired photography equipment company executive; b. NYC, Aug. 4, 1920; d. Louis and Fannie (Disraeli) Bachrach; m. Leonard L. Farber, Nov. 3, 1940 (div. 1975); children: Lindy Linder, Robert D. (dec.), Peggy, Felicia Gervais. BA, NYU, 1940; MA, Sarah Lawrence Coll., 1966. Co-dir. Upward Bound Sarah Lawrence Coll., Bronxville, N.Y., 1966-70, dean student svcs., 1973-76; v.p., owner Zone VI Studios, Inc., Newfane, Vt., 1976-90, ret., 1990. One-woman photography shows include, Vt., N.Y. V.p. Greenburgh LWV, Hartsdale, NY, 1955—63; family adv. Westchester Coun. Social Agys., White Plains, NY, 1970—73; pres. bd. trustees Free Libr., Newfane, 1977—97; trustee Marlboro (Vt.) Coll., from 1982, chmn. bd. trustees, 1982—97; trustee Vt. Coun. on the Arts, 1992—96; mem. Vt. Bicentennial Commn., 1990—91; state committeewoman N.Y. State Dem. Com., 1968—70. Mem.: ACLU. Avocation: photography. Home: Brattleboro, Vt. Died July 23, 2007.

FARBEROW, NORMAN LOUIS, psychologist; b. Pitts., Feb. 12, 1918; s. Louis and Minnie (Cohen) F.; m. Pearl Ross, Mar. 16, 1947 (dec. 2008); children: L. David, Hilary Farberow-Stuart. BA in Psychology, U. Pitts., 1938, MSc in Psychology, 1940; PhD in Psychology, UCLA, 1950. Cert. Am. Bd. Examiners in Profl. Psychology. Psychologist VA, LA, 1949-81; co-dir. L.A. Suicide Prevention Ctr., 1958—2015. Emeritus adj. prof. U. So. Calif. Sch. Medicine, L.A., 1960-2015; founder Internat. Assn. for Suicide Prevention Author: (with David K. Reynolds) Suicide Inside and Out, 1961, (with Dr. Shneidman and Dr. Litman) Taboo Topics, 1963, The Psychology of Sucide, 1970, (with Glen Evans) The Encyclopedia of Suicide, 1988; editor: Family Shadow, 1980, Many Faces of Suicide, 1981; contbr. to several articles Capt. USAAF, 1941-45, ETO. Fellow Am. Psychol. Assn. (Harold M. Hildreth award div. 18, 1972, Disting. Sci. Contbn. award 1977); mem. Internat. Assn. Suicidology (past pres.), Am. Assn. Suicidology (past pres., Louis I. Dublin award 1973), Soc. for Personality Assessment, So. Calif. Psychol. Assn. (Disting. Sci. Contbn. award 1974, Disting. Humanitarian award 1981). Jewish. Home: Los Angeles, Calif. Died Sept. 10, 2015.

FARBSTEIN, SOL, entertainer; b. Phila., June 29, 1927; s. Hyman and Edith (Gordon) F.; m. Rhoda Clark Coverman, June 2, 1951; children: Cathy Miller, Scott. A in Bus., Temple U., 1950. Entertainer USO, Phila., 1946-48; dir. Temple U., Phila., 1948-50, U. Vienna, Austria, 1949. Actor various night clubs, Phila., 1947-53, TV shows, 1947-60. Actor (plays) Seven Year Itch, 1953, Girl Crazy, 1954; dir. variety shows; producer (recording) Dovells, 1980. Pres. Blackwood (N.J.) Bus. Assn., 1959; dir. Blackwood Christmas Parade, 1956-60. Mem. Jewish War Vets., Rising Star Lodge. Home: Scottsdale, Ariz. Died Jan. 1, 2007.

FAREWELL, JOHN PHILIP, chemist; b. Worcester, Mass., May 29, 1942; s. George Franklin and Madeline Eva (Hartwell) F.; m. Judith Anne Malady, Feb. 24, 1968; children: Jean Marie, Joanna Margaret. BS in Edn., SUNY, Plattsburgh, 1964; PhD in Chemistry, U. Buffalo, 1969. Sr. rsch. chemist R & D div. Union Camp Corp., Princeton, N.J., 1968-72, sr. process engr. Blch div. Franklin, Va., 1972-76; sr. rsch. chemist Am. Cyanamid Corp., Stamford, Conn., 1976-88; applications chemist A.E. Staley Mfg. Co., Decatur, Ill., 1988-92; with Sequa Chemical Corp., Chester, S.C., from 1992. Patentee emulsion stabilizers; editor: Papermaking Additives, 1990. Deacon Union Meml. Ch., Stamford, 1984-86. Mem. TAPPI (chmn. tech. trends com. 1991-92), Am. Wargaming Assn. (pres. 1985). Avocations: writing, mathematics, wargaming, game design and collecting. Home: Rock Hill, SC. Died Apr. 8, 2007.

FARHA, ZACK, food company executive; b. Kansas City, Mo., Oct. 9, 1928; s. Zack Abraham and Jennie M. (Monsour) F.; m. Jeannette Leilah Naifeh, Feb. 11, 1961; children: Vincent, Christopher. BS in Mktg., U. Kans., 1951. Gen. mgr. Pioneer Foods Co., Hutchinson, Kans., 1951-56; owner Pioneer Sales Co., Wichita, Kans., 1956-59; co-founder, exec. v.p. Swiss Chalet Food Products, Wichita, 1970-73, sales cons., from 1974, owner, from 1981. Chmn. bd. dirs. Pioneer Properties, Inc., Wichita and Toronto, Can. Contbr.: (textbook) Dynamics in Marketing, 1951. Active local Boy Scouts Am.; bd. dirs. St. Jude's Hosp., Memphis, Aid to Lukemia Stricken Am. Children. Served with AUS, 1951-53. Mem. Kans. U. Alumni Assn., Sigma Phi Epsilon, Order St. Ignatius. Lodges: Masons, Shriners, Elks, Lions (past internat. bd. dirs.). Republican. Eastern Orthodox. Home: Wichita, Kans. Died Feb. 25, 2007.

FARMER, CLARA ANN, secondary school educator; b. Sanford, Fla., Feb. 1, 1948; d. Zeke and Juanita (Brown) Southward; children: Talisa Tarzette, latasha Lajourn, Walter Erie II, TaMira LaVette. AA, Seminole Jr. Coll., Sanford, 1968; BS in Math. Edn., U. Cen. Fla., 1970. Tchr. math. Orange County Schs., Orlando, Fla., 1970-71, Winter Garden, Fla., 1974-86, Seminole County Schs., Altomonte, Fla., 1971-74; dir., owner Walter E. Farmer Learning Ctr., Orlando, from 1985. Democrat. Home: Orlando, Fla. Died Apr. 18, 2007.

FARNUM, NANCY ALYSON, communications executive; b. Birmingham, Ala., Mar. 2, 1949; d. Leon Vernon and Martha Reeves (McGahee) F. BA, Rockford Coll., 1971; MSLS, Case We. Reserve U., 1972. cert. health information profl. Information specialist Merrell-Nat. Lab. Pharm. Co., Cin., 1973-78; dir. and comptroller U.S. ops. Applied Human Cybernetics, London, 1975-78; asst. prof. and online search analyst Coll. Medicine E. Tenn. State U., Johnson City, Tenn., 1982-84; assoc. dir. N.W. Area Health Edn. Ctr., Salisbury, N.C., 1984-88; asst. prof. Bowman Gray Sch. Medicine, Winston Salem, 1984-88; coord. multimedia svcs. U. Ala., Birmingham, 1989-92; cons. MRM Communications, LA, from 1988. Cons. St. George's (Grenada) U. Sch. Medicine, 1989; chmn. K-12 devel. U. of the World, La Jolla, Calif., 1989—; mem. Gov.'s Tech. Task Force on Edn. Reform, Montgomery, Ala., 1993—. Coord. Global Awareness Seminar Birmingham Pub. Schs., 1988-93, World Peace Day Friends of the City of Birmingham, 1988—. Recipient Grad. endowment Nat. Inst. Health, Bethesda, Md., 1971-72; scholarship Sch. Theology at Claremont (Calif.), 1993, Fuller Theol. Sem., Pasadena, Calif., 1996-97. Mem. NAFE, Med. Libr. Assn., Network Birmingham, Acad. Health Info. Profls. Episcopalian. Died Feb. 5, 2007.

FARR, MEL, automotive sales executive, former professional football player; b. Beaumont, Tex., Nov. 2, 1944; BS, UCLA. CEO Mel Farr Automotive Group, Mich., Ohio, Tex. and Md.; prin. Triple M Fin. Co. With Detroit Lions, 1967-73; mem. NFL Players Adv. Bd., 1990-92. Named to UCLA Sports Hall of Fame, 1988, NFL Rookie of Yr., 1967, Most Valuable Offensive Player, 1967, Most Valuable Offensive Player, 1968. Died Aug. 3, 2015.

FARRAR, HARRY, IV, nuclear physicist; b. London, Dec. 31, 1935; came to U.S., 1962; s. Harry III and Betty (Crickmay) F.; m. Sharon Marie Mitchelmore, May 26, 1962; children: Harry V, Bruce. BA with honors in Math. & Physics, U. Toronto, 1958; MSc in Nuclear Physics, McMaster U., Hamilton, Ont., Can., 1959, PhD in Nuclear Physics, 1962. Doctoral and postdoctoral rschr. on fission yields McMaster U., Hamilton, 1959-62; mgr. applied nuclear tech. Rockwell Internat., Atomics Internat., Canoga Park, Calif., 1962-91; leader expert missions on food irradiation Internat. Atomic Energy Agy., Vienna, from 1993. Contbr. articles to profl. jours. Recipient IR 100 award Indsl. Rsch. Mag., Chgo., 1978. Fellow ASTM (chmn. subcom. E10.01 1984—, chmn. com. E-IO, 1997—, award of merit 1991); mem. Internat. Orgn. Standardization (convenor ISO/TC85/WG3 1997—). Achievements include development of the helium accumulation fluence monitor to measure neutron flux; led international group of experts to develop 25 standards on dosimetry for radiation processing. Home: Bell Canyon, Calif. Died Apr. 12, 2007.

FASTABEND, GLORIA J., secondary school educator; b. San Diego, Calif., June 7, 1951; d. Arthur George and Faith June (Davis) F. BA, Boise State U., 1973; MEd, Coll. of Idaho, 1987. Advanced secondary teaching cert., Idaho; lic. profl. counselor, Idaho; cert. clin. hypnotherapist. Right-hand man Hoffman's Greenhouse & Nursery, Nampa, Idaho, 1965-84; social studies tchr. South Jr. High, Nampa, 1973-87; tchr. govt. and psychology, advisor Associated Student Body Nampa Sr. High Sch., from 1987, coach ski team, 1987-95; mental health counselor, pvt. practice Nampa and Caldwell, Idaho, from 1987; trainer Nat. Diffusion Network IPLE, from 1991. Bd. dirs. Mercy House, Nampa, 1987-91. Mem. NEA, Am. Mental Health Counselors Assn., Am. Sch. Counselors Assn., Am. Counseling Assn., Idaho Mental Health Counselors Assn. (bd. dirs.), Idaho Sch. Counselors Assn., Idaho Edn. Assn., Nampa Edn. Assn. (bldg. rep. 1974-77), Nat. Coun. Social Studies, others. Avocations: skiing, sailing, tennis. Home: Caldwell, Idaho. Died July 25, 2007.

FATZINGER, JAMES A. S., construction educator, estimator; b. Bethlehem, Pa., Jan. 27, 1926; Student, Pa. State Coll., 1943-44, Moravian Coll., 1957-58, Fullerton Jr. Coll., 1972-73. Journeyman various cos., 1951-72; supr. 3M Co., Montpelier, Ohio, 1966-67; journeyman Endicott Brass Co., Montpelier, 1967; substation operator Pub. Svc. Elec. and Gas Co., Newark, 1959-65; constrn. estimator various cos., from 1972; contractor Calif., Ariz., 1980-85; constrn. instr. Mesa (Ariz.) CC, Rio Salado CC, Mesa, 1974-78, CC So. Nev., Las Vegas, 1978-97, U. Nev., Las Vegas, 1992-97. Pres., owner Basic Estimating Ltd., Las Vegas, 1978—99. Author: Basic Estimating for Construction, 1996, Blueprint Reading for Construction, 1997; : 2d rev. edit., 2003. Scoutmaster Boy Scouts Am., Bethlehem, 1950—60, commr. Huntington Beach, Calif., 1976—77; trustee Fullerton Jr. Coll., 1986—92. 1st sgt. US Army, 1944—46, ETO. Mem.: Am. Soc. Profl. Estimators (cert., emeritus). Republican. Avocations: motor home travel, music. Home: Las Vegas, Nev. Died Nov. 18, 2006.

FAUDREE, RALPH JASPER, retired academic administrator, mathematician, educator; b. Durant, Okla., Aug. 23, 1939; s. Ralph J. Faudree Sr. and Vinita Faudree; m. Patricia Lee Newsom; children: Paja, Jill. BS in Math. & Physics, Okla. Bapt. U., Shawnee, 1961; MS in Math., Purdue U., 1962, PhD in Math., 1964. Instr. math. U. Calif., Berkeley, 1964—66; asst. prof. math. U. Ill., Urbana, 1966—71; assoc. prof. math. Memphis State U., 1971—76, prof. math., 1976—2012, chmn. dept. math., 1983—94, dean Coll. Arts & Sciences, 1995—2000, interim pres. Tenn., 2000—01, provost, 2001—12. Recipient Emminent Faculty award, Bd. Visitors - U. Memphis, 1994, Euler medal, Inst. Comvinatorics and Applications, 2005. Mem.: APLU, SIAM, Math. Assn. America, Am. Math. Soc. Home: Memphis, Tenn. Died Jan. 13, 2015.

FAULK, MIKE (MICHAEL ANTHONY FAULK), state legislator, lawyer; b. Kingsport, Tenn., Sept. 10, 1953; s. Loy Glade and Rosella E. (Dykes) F.; children: Katherine Lea, Andrew McLain. BS, U. Tenn., 1975; M in Pub. Adminstrn., Memphis State U., 1978, JD, 1979. Bar: US Dist. Ct. (western dist.) Tenn. 1980, US Dist. Ct. (eastern dist.) Tenn. 1985, US Supreme Ct., 1998; cert. civil trial specialist, Nat. Bd. Trial Advocacy. Dep. clk. to presiding justice Shelby County Chancery Ct., Memphis, 1977-79; assoc. Weintraub & Dehart, Memphis, 1980-82; ptnr. Frazier & Faulk, Church Hill, Tenn., 1982-83; sole practice Church Hill, 1983-93; ptnr. Law Offices of Faulk, May & Coup, Church Hill, Tenn., 1993-96; sole practice Church Hill, 1996—2014; mem. Dist. 4 Tenn. State Senate, 2009—12. Commr. Tenn. Human Rights Commn., Nashville, 1985-92, vice chmn. 1988-92; referee Hawkins County Juvenile Ct., Rogersville, Tenn., 1985-96; bd. commrs. Hawkins County, 1998-2002; bd. dirs. Legal Services Inc., Johnson City, Tenn. Bd. dirs. Upper East Tenn. divsn. American Heart Assn., Blountville, 1984-86. Named one of Outstanding Young Men in America U.S. Jaycees, 1977, American Leading Lawyers, 1993, Super Lawyer of Mid. South, 2007. Mem. ABA, Hawkins County Bar Assn. (pres. 1987-88), Assn. Trial Lawyers America, Ducks Unltd. (chmn. Holston River chpt. 1984-98). Lodges: Moose. Republican. Baptist. Avocation: outdoors. Home: Kingsport, Tenn. Died Nov. 12, 2014.

FAULKNER, ROBERT LLOYD, advertising executive, graphics designer; b. Chgo., Nov. 8, 1934; s. L. Lester and Agnes Elizabeth (Irons) F.; m. Elizabeth Alice Thomas, June 14, 1958; children: Anne Elizabeth, Lynn Marie, Thomas Robert. BFA in Advt. Design, U. Ill., 1958. Account exec. Brad Sebstad Advt., Chgo., 1966—67; sr. account exec. D'Arcy Advt. Co., Chgo., 1967—70; v.p. Wm. A. Robinson Inc., Northbrook, Ill., 1970—71; nat. mdse. and promotion mgr. James B. Beam Distilling Co., Chgo., 1971—73; v.p. Coord. Advt., Chgo., 1973—77, Grant/Jacoby Inc., Chgo., 1977—79, Kennedy Advt., Chgo., 1979—86; exec. v.p. Kamen/Faulkner Inc., Chgo., 1986—89; pres., owner Bob Faulkner Corporation, Westchester, Ill., from 1989. Course coord., advt. lectr. grad. level advt. courses Northwestern U. and Roosevelt U., Chgo., 1980-85; computer instr. SeniorNet. Author: Learn to Cross Country Ski, 1976; co-author: Cross-Country Skiing for Everybody, 1975. Dir. Western Springs Hist. Soc., 1992-95; mem. Illegitimate Theatre of Western Springs; pres. Indian Prarie Computer Club, 2007—. Recipient numerous advt. awards. Mem. Bus. Mktg. Assn. (Cert. Bus. Communicator), Nat. Ski Patrol (life), Model T Ford Owners Assn., Sports Car Club Am., Portage Lake Yacht Club. Episcopalian. Avocation: fine art painting. Died June 17, 2007.

FAWCETT, SHERWOOD LUTHER, lab administrator; b. Youngstown, Ohio, Dec. 25, 1919; s. Luther T. and Clara (Sherwood) F. BS, Ohio State U., 1941, PhD (hon.); MS, Case Inst. Tech., 1948, PhD, 1950; PhD (hon.), Gonzaga U., Whitman Coll., Otterbein Coll., Detroit Inst. Tech., Ohio Dominican Coll. Registered profl. engr., Ohio. Mem. staff Columbus (Ohio) Labs. Battelle Meml. Inst., 1950-64, mgr. physics dept., 1959-64; dir. Pacific Northwest Labs., Richland, Wash., 1964-67; trustee Battelle Meml. Inst., Columbus, 1968-92, exec. v.p., 1967-68, CEO, 1968-84, pres., 1968-80, chmn., 1981-84, chmn. bd. trustees, 1985-87, assoc. trustee, 1987-94. Emeritus chmn. bd. dirs. Transmet Corp. With USNR, 1941-46. Decorated Bronze Star; recipient Washington award Western Soc. Engrs., 1989. Mem. AIME, NSPE, Am. Nuc. Soc., Am. Phys. Soc., Sigma Xi, Tau Beta Pi, Delta Chi, Sigma Pi Sigma. Home: Columbus, Ohio. Died Feb. 3, 2015.

FAY, PETER CARLYLE, mechanical engineer; b. Pitts., Nov. 2, 1958; s. Carlyle Waldie and Marjorie Ann (Sundquist) F.; m. Laura Elizabeth Coerper, Nov. 27, 1981. BSME, U. Wis., 1981; MBA, Keller Grad. Sch. Mgmt., 1992, M Human Resources Mgmt., 1994, postgrad., 1995. Registered profl. engr., Wis., Ill. Field engr. Schlumberger Wells Svcs., Laurel, Miss., 1981-83; tech. engr. Commonwealth Edison, Braidwood, Ill., 1983-84, startup test engr., 1984-85, hot functional dir., 1985-86, fuel load coord., 1986, startup test coord., 1986-88, supr. maintenance staff Zion, Ill., 1988-92, integrated assessment adminstr. Downers Grove, Ill., 1992-98, Inst. of Nuclear Power Ops. APOC, from 1998. Mem. ASME, Am. Nuclear Soc. Republican. Lutheran. Avocations: airplane and balloon flying, home restoration. Home: Mundelein, Ill. Died Nov. 2, 2006.

FAZEKAS, KALMAN, electrical engineer, educator; b. Budapest, Hungary, Nov. 4, 1938; s. Kalman and Gabriella (Kadas) F.; m. Elizabeth Ruppert, Feb. 23, 1970. MSEE, Tech. U., Budapest, 1962, MS in Tchr. Engring., 1968, PhD in Elec. Engring., 2004. Cert. in engring. Asst. prof. dept. comms. Tech. U., Budapest, 1962-66, prof. dept.broadband infocomm. systems, from 1967; with IWSSIP, 1994. Lectr. Mil. Coll., Budapest, 1968-74; Hungarian mem. COST Tech. Com. Telecomms. Info., Sci. and Tech.; mem. mgmt. com. COST 229, COST 254, COST 276, and COST 292 Actions; expert COST DC, reviewer jours. Author, co-author: (textbook series) Impulsetechnique, 1980-86 (prize of rector of univ. 1986), Expert of Cost DC; contbr. articles to profl. jours.; guest editor: Jour. Comms., 1991, reviewer sci. articles Recipient decoration, Ministry of Def., 1975, prize Ministry of Edn., 1981, Best Paper award Pollak-Virag award 1988, 93, 2002. Mem. IEEE (sr.), Eurasip, Euromicro, N.Y. Acad. Sci. Roman Catholic. Home: Budapest, Hungary. Deceased.

FEIGENBAUM, ARMAND VALLIN, systems engineer, information technology executive; b. NYC, Apr. 6, 1920; s. S. Frederick and Hilda (Vallin) F. BS, Union Coll., 1942, DSc (hon.), 1992; MS, MIT, 1948, PhD, 1951; LHD (hon.), U. Mass., 1996; DSc (hon.), Mass. Coll. Liberal Arts, 2003. Engr. test program GE, Schenectady, 1942-45, factory tng. course, 1945-47, sales engr., 1947-48, supr. tng. mfg. personnel Lynn, Mass., 1948-50, asst. to gen. mgr. aircraft gas turbine divsn. Cin., 1950-52, mgr. aircraft nuclear propulsion dept. NYC, 1952, co. mgr. quality control, 1956, co.-wide mgr. mfg. ops. and quality control, 1958-68; pres., CEO Gen. Systems Co., Inc., Pittsfield, Mass., from 1968; Nat. Acad. Engring. U.S., from 1992. Bd. overseers Malcolm Baldrige Nat. Quality Program, Washington, 1988-91; founding chmn. global quality body Internat. Acad. Quality, pres., 1966-79, chmn. bd. dirs., 1979—; adv. group US Army, 1966—; lectr. MIT, U. Cin., Union Coll., U. Pa.; spkr. in field. Author: Quality Control-Principles and Practice, 1951, Total Quality Control-Engineering and Management, 1961, Management Programming, 1980, The Organization Process, 1980, Total Quality Control, 3d edit., 1983, Total Quality Control, 40th Anniversary edit., 1991, The Power of Management Capital (translation in Japanese, Chinese, Brazilian Portuguese, Taiwanese, Arabic, others), 2003, The Power of Management Innovation, 2009; contbr. articles to profl. jours. Chmn. inst. adminstrn., mgmt. coun. Union Coll., 1963—. Recipient Founders medal, 1977, medaille Georges Borel, Republic of France, 1988, Disting. Svc. award Nat. Inst. for Engring., Mgmt. and Sys., 1991, Disting. Leadership award Quality and Productivity Mgmt. Assn., 1993, Ishikawa/Harrington medal Asia-Pacific Quality Orgn., 1996; Armand V. Feigenbaum Mass. Quality award established by Gov. Mass., 1992, Singapore's Ngee Ann Polytechnic inaugurated the ann. Dr. A.V. Feigenbaum Gold medal award for outstanding quality assurance engring. grad., 1994, Mass. Gov.'s proclamation on 50th anniversary of book, 2001, Feigenbaum Leadership Excellence award, Dubai, UAE, 2005, Six Sigma Grand Master medal Walter L. Hurd Found., 2006, 2007, Nat. Medal Technology and Innovation, US Pres., Washington, 2007; fellow World Acad. Productivity Sci., 1993; Armand V. and Donald S. Feigenbaum Hall named in his honor Union Coll., 1996, Armand and Donald Feigenbaum Disting. Professorship named in his honor U. Mass. Med. Sch., 1998; recognized with the Outstanding Engring. Alumnus award, 2003, Nat. Medal Tech. and Innovation, US Pres. Wash., 2007 Fellow Am. Soc. Quality Control (pres. 1961-63, chmn. bd. 1963-64, Edwards medal 1966, Lancaster medal 1982, hon. mem. 1986, Feigenbaum award established 1999), World Acad. Productivity Sci.; mem. IEEE (life), NSPE (Disting. Svc. award 1991), ASME (life), AAAS (hon.), Nat. Security Indsl. Assn. (nat. award merit 1965), Inst. Math. Stats., Acad. Polit. and Social Scis., Am. Econ. Assn., Soc. Advancement Mgmt., Indsl. Rels. Rsch. Soc., Coun. Internat. Progress in Mgmt. (chmn. bd. 1968-70), China Assn. Quality Control (hon. advisor), Argentine Inst. Quality (hon.), Philippines Soc. for Quality Control (hon.), NAE. Home: Pittsfield, Mass. Died Mar. 13, 2014.

FELDMAN, ALEXANDER VAN VLIET See ALEXANDER, VAN

FELDMAN, RUTH DUSKIN, writer, editor, website designer, ceremonial officiant; b. Chgo., June 13, 1934; d. Boris and Rita (Schayer) Duskin; m. Gilbert Feldman, June 14, 1953; children:Steven Jeffrey (Jal), Laurie Nadine, Heidi Carolyn. BS, Northwestern U., Evanston, 1954. Cert. ceremonial leader Internat. Inst. Secular Humanistic Judaism, HS tchr. Ill. Tchr. Nichols Sch., Evanston, Ill., 1954-55, U.S. Army, Ft. Sheridan, Ill., 1964; tchr. and curriculum coord. Congregation Beth Or, Deerfield, Ill., 1970-80; corr.

and staff writer Lerner Newspapers, Highland Park, Ill., 1973-81; creative editor Humanistic Judaism, Farmington Hills, Mich., 1983—2015; contract author Psychology, McGraw-Hill Higher Edn., from 1987. Panel mem. Quiz Kids Radio & TV Program, Chgo., 1941-50; quizmistress Chgo. Sun-Times Quizdown, 1947-50; guest editor Mademoiselle mag. coll. bd., N.Y.C., 1952; freelance writer for mags. and newspapers, 1974-2015. Author: Chemi the Magician, 1947, Whatever Happened to the Quiz Kids, 1982, 2000 (Ind. Writers Chgo. award 1983), 2nd edit., 2014; co-author: Rematch, 1989, Communicoding, 1989, 91, Experience Human Development, 1984-2015, 12th edit., 2012, Adult Development and Aging, 1996, 3d edit. 2007, A Child's World, 1999, 13th edit, 2014, Child Development, 2003. Mem., League Women Voters; website adminatr., Moraine Twp. Democratic Orgn., Tenth Congressional District Democrats; mem., mktg. com., membership com., Kol Hadash Humanistic Congregation, Lincolnshire, Ill. Named James Alton James scholar, Northwestern U., Evanston, 1953-54; recipient Benjamin Fine award for outstanding editl. writing, Nat. Assn. Secondary Sch. Prins., 1983, Lowell Thomas award (runner-up), Soc. Am. Travel Writers, 1986. Mem.: Am. Soc. Journalists and Authors, Authors Guild, Nat. Writers Union, PEN-USA, Soc. for Humanistic Judaism (Sherwin T. Wine Lifetime Achievement award, 2014), Leadership Conf. Secular & Humanistic Jews, Kol Hadash Humanistic Congregation, Phi Beta Kappa. Democrat. Jewish. Avocations: music, theater, crossword puzzles, photography. Died May 18, 2015.

FELLHAUER, JUDITH ANN, gerontology nurse; b. NJ, Aug. 19, 1937; d. Arthur Lorenz and Hazel Violet (Messimore) Fahringer; children: Ardyth Ann, Andrew C., Adam E. Diploma, Toledo Hosp. Sch. Nursing, 1958; BSN, Lourdes Coll., 1991. RN, Ohio. Staff nurse The Toledo (Ohio) Hosp., 1958-60; office nurse Drs. Smith and Houk, Toledo, 1960-61; indsl. nurse Textile Leather, Div. Gen. Tire & Rubber Co., Toledo; office nurse Dr. Marker and Huffman, Toledo, 1965-69, Drs. Smith, Houk, and Lloyd, Toledo, 1974-77; day nurse Heartland of Perrysburg, Ohio, 1977-80, asst. dir. nursing, 1980-89, Found. Park Care Ctr., Toledo, 1989-91; asst. DON Lake Park Care Ctr., Sylvania, Ohio, 1991-93; with Don Lake Park, 1993-94; gerontol. nurse Don Swan Creek Health Care Ctr., Toledo, from 1995. Home: Toledo, Ohio. Died July 1, 2007.

FELLIN, OCTAVIA ANTOINETTE, retired librarian, historical researcher; b. Santa Monica, Calif. d. Otto P. and Librada (Montoya) F. Student, U. N.Mex., 1937—39; BA, U. Denver, 1941; BS in L.S., Dominican U., River Forest, Ill., 1942. Asst. libr. instr., libr. sci. St. Mary-of-Woods Coll., Terre Haute, Ind., 1942-44; libr. U.S. Army, Bruns Gen. Hosp., Santa Fe, 1944-46, Gallup (N.Mex.) Pub. Libr., 1947-90; post libr. Camp McQuaide, Calif., 1947; freelance writer, from 1950; chmn. Gallup Mus. Ind. Arts & Crafts. Libr. cons.; N.Mex. del. White House Pre-conf. on Librs. & Inof. Svcs., 1978; dir. Nat. Libr. week for N.Mex., 1959, v.p., N.Mex. Libr. Assn., 1957. Author: Yahweh the Voice that Beautifies the Land, 1975; A Chronicle of Mileposts a Brief History of the University of New Mexico, Gallup Campus, 1968-1993. Chmn. Gallup St. Naming Com., 1958—59; organizer Gt. Decision Discussion groups, 1963—85; chmn. Aging Com., 1964—68, Gallup Mus. Indian Arts and Crafts, 1964—78, Gallup Sr. Citizens Ctr., 1965—68; publicity com. Gallup Inter-Tribal Indian Ceremonial Assn., 1966—68; active Gov.'s Com. 100 on Aging, 1967—70; bd. dirs., sec., co-organizer Gallup Area Arts Coun., 1970—78; bd. dirs. Gallup Opera Guild, 1970—74; chmn. adv. bd. Gallup Sr. Citizens, 1971—73; active N.Mex. Libr. Adv. Coun., 1971—75, vice chmn., 1974—75; mem. Eccles. Conciliation and Arbitration Bd., Province of Santa Fe, 1973—74; chmn. pledge campaign Rancho del Nino San Huberto Empalme, Mexico, 1975—80; chmn. hist. com. Gallup Diocese Bicentennial, 1975, steering com., 1975—78; active Cathedral Parish Coun., 1980—83, v.p., 1981; cmty. edn. adv. coun. U. N.Mex., Gallup, 1981—82; pres. Rehoboth McKinley Christian Hosp. Aux., 1983; chmn. Red Mrsa Art Ctr., 1984—88; Diocese of Gallup rep. to nat. convocation on laity concerns with Pope John Paul II, San Francisco, 1987; pres. Gallup Area Arts Coun., 1988; century com. Western Health Found., 1988; cultural bd. Gallup Multi-Model Cultural Com., 1988—95; chmn. aux. scholarship com. Rehoboth McKinley Christian Hosp. Aux., from 1989; co-organizer, v.p. chair fund raising com. Gallup Pub. Radio com., 1989—95; active McKinley County Recycling Com., from 1990; local art selection com. N.Mex. Art Dirs., 1990; N.Mex. organizing chmn. Rehoboth McKinley Christian Hosp. Aux., chmn. cmty. edn. loan selection com., from 1990; com. mem. Rio Grande Hist. Collection, NMSU, 1991—96; bd. dirs., corr. sec. Rehoboth McKinley Christian Hosp. Aux., 1991—94; chmn. Trick or Treat for UNICEF, Gallup, 1972-77, Artists Coop, 1985-89; active Network: Nat. Cath. Social Justice Lobby; mem. N.Mex. Humanities Coun., 1979, Gallup Centennial Com., 1980-81; 35th anniversary com. U. N.Mex., Gallup, 2001—02; mem. mural project Gallup, N.Mex., 2005—06; mem. coalition to repeal death penalty Gallup (N.Mex.) Group, 2001—09; fund devel. cons. Cath. Indian Ctr., 2001—03; mem. Gallup Area Resource Coun., 1980—83, Cathedral Guild, 1970—80, Diocesan Gallup Liturgical Commn., 1970—80; v.p., sec. pastoral coun. Diocese of Gallup, 1973—76, mem. liturgical commn., 1980—83; active N.Mex. ACLU, from 2001; mem. adv. coun. to U.S. Cath. Bishops, 1969—74; chmn. Gallup (N.Mex.) Sr. Citizen Ctr., 1974—77. Recipient Dorothy Canfield Fisher Libr. award, 1961, Outstanding Cmty. Svc. award Gallup C. of C., 1968, 70, Outstanding Citizen award, 1974, Benemerenti medal Pope Paul VI, 1977, Celibrate Literacy award Gallup Internat. Reading Assn., 1983-84, Woman of Distinction award Soroptimists, 1985, N.Mex. Disting. Pub. Svc. award, 1987, Edgar L. Hewitt award Hist. Soc. N.Mex., 1992, Gov.'s award as Outstanding N.Mex. Woman, 1988, Cmty. Svc. award U. N.Mex., 1993, Co-organizer award, McKunlee Area Recycling Coun., 1980, McKinley Area award, 2006; Octavia Fellin Pub. Libr. named in her honor, 1990, 20th Anniversary award Gallup Area Arts Coun., 1995, NM Citizen's award Gallup Campus, 1995; named one of Auxiliar of the Yr. RMCH Aux., 2006; named Vol. of Yr., N.Mex. Hosp. Assn., 2007. Mem.: NOW, NAACP, AAUW (co-organizer Gallup br. 1969—94, v.p. co-organizer Gallup br., chmn. com. on women), LWV (v.p. 1953—56), ALA, Local Art Selection Com (N.Mex. Arts Divsn.), Gallup Cmty. Couns. Assn. (bd. mem. & campaign chair 1953—85), N.Mex. Gallup Film Soc. (v.p. 1950—58, co-corgnizer), N.Mex. Mcpl. League (pres. libr.'s divsn. 1979), Gallup C. of C. (organizing chmn. women's div. 1972, v.p. 1972—73), N.Mex Archtl. Found., Plateau Scis. Soc., N.Mex. Libr. Assn. (hon.; chmn. hist. materials com. 1964—66, pres. 1965—66, chmn. com. to extend libr. svcs. 1969—73, chmn. local and regional history roundtable 1978, v.p., sec., salary and tenure com., nat. coord. N.Mex. Legis. com., hon. mem., Libr. of Yr. award 1975, Cmty. Achievement award 1983, Hon. Lifetime Membership award 1994), Nat. New Deal Preservation Assn. (bd. mem. N.Mex. chpt. from 2005), Call to Action Nat. Ca. Renewal Org., Pax Christi U.S.A., Hist. Soc. N.Mex. (bd. dirs. 1980—83), Gallup Hist. Soc., Women's Ordination Conf., N.Mex. Women's Polit. Caucus, N.Mex. Foklore Soc. (pres. 1958), Habitat for Humanity, NMLA (life), Alpha Delta Kappa (hon.). Roman Catholic. Died Jan. 9, 2015.

FENTON, DONALD MASON, retired oil company executive; b. LA, May 23, 1929; s. Charles Youdan and Dorothy (Mason) F.; m. Margaret M. Keehler, Apr. 24, 1953; children: James Michael, Douglas Charles. BS, U. Calif., LA, 1952, PhD, 1958. Chemist Rohm and Haas Co., Phila., 1958-61; sr. rsch. chemist Union Oil Co., Brea, Calif., 1962-67, rsch. assoc., 1967-72, sr. rsch. assoc., 1972-82, mgr. planning and devel., 1982-85; mgr. new tech. devel. Unocal, Brea, 1985-92. Cons. AMSCO, 1967-73; co-founder, 1st chmn. Petroleum Environ. Rsch. Forum; chmn. bd. dirs. Calif. Engring. Found., 1991-92. With U.S. Army, 1953-55. Inventor in field. Fellow Am. Inst. Chemists, Alpha Chi Sigma; mem. Am. Chem. Soc. Achievements include more than 100 patents in field; co-invention of unisulf process. Home: Merritt Island, Fla. Died Jan. 30, 2007.

FERGUSON, BILLY LEE, pediatrician; b. Haw River, NC, Mar. 10, 1933; s. Bertram Lindsay and Ellen Flora (McCaskill) F.; m. Odessa Maxine Dale, Sept. 15, 1957; children: William Lee, Ann Michele Bishop; m. Sandra Helen Ritter, May 23, 1995. BS, Guilford Coll., 1954; MS in Pub. Health, U. N.C., 1955; MD, Bowman Gray Sch. Medicine, 1959. Diplomate Am. Bd. Pediat. Intern USAF Hosp., San Antonio, 1960-64; resident in pediat. N.C. Bapt. Hosp., Winston-Salem, 1964-66; commd. 2d lt. USAF, 1959, advanced through grades to maj., 1969; pvt. practice Greensboro, N.C., from 1969. Avocations: duplicate bridge, ping pong/table tennis. Died June 7, 2007.

FERGUSON, PATRICIA ANN, clinical psychologist; b. Washington, May 30, 1953; d. James Hilburn and Ann Marie (Keefe) F.; m. Timothy Francis Ferris, June 8, 1974 (div. May 1978); m. Ron G. Sisson, Aug. 7, 1986; children: Nicole, Elliot. AA in Social Scis. with honors, Lake Tahoe C.C., 1984; BS, San Diego State U., 1986; D in Psychology, Nova Southeastern U., 1992. Lic. clin. psychologist, Calif. Psychologist asst. Lorraine Wincor, PsyD., Ft. Lauderdale, Fla., 1984-90, Family Violence Program, Ft. Lauderdale, Fla., 1989-90, Dr. Marilyn Wooley, Redding, Calif., 1991-93; asst. prof. U. Calif.-Davis, Redding, 1994-96; clin. psychologist Far No. Regional Ctr., Redding, 1994-98; pvt. practice Redding, from 1993. Contbr. articles to profl. jours. Vol. Big Sister, San Diego, 1985-86; domestic violence counselor Women's Ctr., Lake Tahoe, Calif., 1983-84. Recipient scholarship Nova Southeastern U., 1986-88. Mem. NOW, Redding C. of C., Phi Beta Kappa. Democrat. Avocations: writing, painting, skiing, spending time with children. Home: Redding, Calif. Died Jan. 10, 2007.

FERGUSON, ROBERT P. (H-BOMB FERGUSON), musician, songwriter; b. Charleston, SC, May 9, 1929; s. Lorenzo and Irene (Thomas) F.; m. Christine Marie Busemeyer, Sept. 24, 1988; 1 child, Robert Hamilton. Mem. Joe Liggins and the Honeydrippers; performer The Baby Grand Club, NYC; mem. Charlie Singleton and Orch., H-Bomb Ferguson and His Mad Lads, The Medicine Men. Rec. artist with Derby Records, Atlas, Savoy Records, Earwig Music; musician, comedian at various clubs, N.Y.C., Cin., including Cotton Club, Apollo Theatre, others, at Chgo. Blues Fest, 1992, Mississippi Valley Blues Fest, Davenport, Iowa, 1994, numerous other blues music festivals. Composer various blues songs, including Slowly Goin' Crazy, My Brown Frame Baby, Bookies Blues, Tortured Love, Midnight Ramblin' Tonight, Mary Little Mary, Leavin You Tomorrow. Appeared in benefit concerts for musical colls. and sr. citizen groups, Cin. Recipient W.C. Handy award Nat. Blues Found., 1986, 89. Died Nov. 26, 2006.

FERREIRA, PENELOPE ANNE SIMOES, lawyer, association executive; b. Capetown, South Africa, Jan. 22, 1939; came to U.S. 1975; d. Edgar George Sandler and Jocelyn Mary Cox Cockshutt; m. Jose Pedro Simoes Ferreria, Oct. 13, 1962; children: Gabriela, Margarida, Jose Paulo. BA, U. Witwatersrand, South Africa, 1960; LLB, U. London, 1970; LLM in Internat. Law, Cambridge U., Eng., 1973; JD, Duquesne U., 1978. Bar: Pa. 1986. Assoc. prof. Duquesne U., 1975-78; rsch. assoc. Nossaman Krueger & Marsh, 1978-80; cons. U. Va., Charlottesville, 1980-82; assoc. divsn. dir. ABA, Washington, from 1982. Contbr. articles to profl. jours. Mem. ABA, Am. Soc. Internat. Law. Avocations: painting, swimming, gardening, reading. Home: Pittsburgh, Pa. Died Aug. 15, 2007.

FERRERO, MICHELE, chocolate products executive; b. Apr. 26, 1925; s. Pietro Ferrero and Piera (Cillario); m. Maria Franca Fissolo; children: Pietro, Giovanni. Owner Ferrero SpA, Italy. Named one of World's Richest People, Forbes Mag., from 2001. Achievements include best known as richest candyman in the world; richest man in Italy; led Ferrero SpA from 1949 until the 1990's. Died Feb. 14, 2015.

FESMIRE, FRANCIS MILLER, emergency medicine physician; b. Atlanta, Nov. 16, 1959; s. Francis Miller Fesmire Sr. and Mary Carolyn (Block) Pierce; m. Connie Elizabeth Bowling; children: Forrest, Hunter. BA magna cum laude, Harvard U., 1981; MD, Vanderbilt U., Nashville, 1985. Lic. physician, Tenn. Resident emergency medicine U. Fla., Jacksonville, 1985-88; attending emergency physician Meml. Hosp., Chattanooga, 1988-91, Erlanger Med. Ctr., Chattanooga, 1991—2014; asst. prof. to full prof. U. Tenn. Coll. Medicine, Chattanooga, 1992—2014. Contbr. articles to profl. jours. Recipient Ig Nobel award for Medicine, 2006, Hero of Emergency Medicine, American Coll. Emergency Physicians, 2008. Fellow American Coll. Emergency Physicians (Young Investigator award 1996). Avocations: golf, skiing, civil war relic collecting, astronomy. Home: Chattanooga, Tenn. Died Jan. 31, 2014.

FESSLER, RAYMOND R., metallurgical engineering consultant; b. St. Nazianz, Wis., May 6, 1939; BS, Carnegie Inst. Tech., 1961; PhD in Metallurgy, MIT, 1965. Staff mem. Battelle Columbus Divsn., 1965-68, assoc. mgr. ferrous metallurgy sect., 1968-77, mgr. phys. metallurgy sect., 1977-82, assoc. dir. programs corp. tech. devel., 1982-83, mgr. transp. and structure dept., 1983-85, mgr. advanced materials dept., 1985-86; dir. basic indsl. rsch. lab. Northwestern U., Evanston, Ill., 1987-96; prin. cons. BIZTEK Cons., Inc., Evanston, Ill., from 1997. Fellow Am. Soc. Metals Internat. Achievements include research in physical metallurgy of steels, high temperature alloys and nonferrous metals; fracture toughness; metal physics; optical and electron metallography; advanced ceramics; process and physical metallurgy; polymers; corrosion; electrochemistry; mechanics. Died Dec. 2014.

FIDLER, ALAN BANDELIN, retired physician; b. West Allis, Wis., June 30, 1922; s. Clarence Celester and Marie Rose (Bandelin) F.; m. Betty Mae Meyer, May 24, 1947; children: Susan Lynn Fidler Watson, Jahn Alan, Paul Robert. BS, U. Wis., 1944, MD, 1946. Diplomate Am. Bd. Radiology. Inern, resident Evangelical Deaconess Hosp., Milw., 1946-48, resident in gen. practice, 1950-51; resident in radiology Kansas City (Kans.) Rsch. Hosp., 1951-53; radiology practice Habbe, Wright, Schmidt & Fidler, Milw., 1953-57; with Milw. Radiologists, S.C., 1967-77, Radiation Oncology Assocs., S.C., Milw., 1977-88. Capt. U.S. Army, 1943-51. Fellow Am. Coll. Radiology; mem. AMA, Wis. State Med. Soc., Milwaukee County Med. Soc., Radiol. Soc. N.Am., Milw. Roentgen Ray Soc. (past pres.), Wis. Radiol. Soc., Nuclear Medicine Soc., Milw. Acad. Medicine. Avocations: music, photography, computers, reading, home workshop. Home: East Troy, Wis. Died Feb. 25, 2007.

FIELDS, DARREL REX, engineering consultant; b. Poplar Bluff, Mo., Dec. 14, 1925; s. Roy Dean and Estella Iona (Ball) F.; m. Mary Evelyn Payne, July 2, 1948 (div. Dec. 1979); children: Rhonda Sue, Denise Gay; m. Bette Jane Neuenfeldt, Mar. 24, 1980. BS in Naval Tech., U. Minn., 1946; BSME, U. Ark., 1949; MS in Econs., Baylor U., 1969; MA in Pub. Adminstrn., U. N.Mex., 1987. Registered profl. engr., Calif., N.Mex.; cert. quality engr. Mech. engr. J.C. Lewis Co., Little Rock, 1948; commd. 2d lt. U.S. Army, 1950, advanced through grades to lt. col., 1950, civil engr. U.S. Army Corps Engrs. Little Rock, 1949-50, nuclear weapons officer, 1950-68; sr. nuclear weapons engr. U.S. Naval Weapons Evaluation Facility, Albuquerque, 1968-87; ret., 1968; ret. Civil Svc., 1987; cons. engr. Fields Cons. Co., from 1987. Quality engr. Sperry-Honeywell, Albuquerque, 1987, EG&G, Albuquerque, 1988, GE Aircraft Engines, Albuquerque, 1988—. Col. N.Mex. State Def. Force, Albuquerque, 1981—; air pollution cons. City of Albuquerque. Lt. (j.g.) USN, 1943-47, PTO. Mem. Sys. Safety Soc., Am. Soc. Quality Control (vice chmn., chmn. Albuquerque sect. 1971-72), Ret. Officers Assn. (life), Res. Officers Assn. (life), Nat. Assn. Uniformed Svcs. (life), Assn. U.S. Army, State Fef. Force Assn. U.S., Nat. Assn. Ret. Fed. Employees, Kirtland AFB Officers Club, Pi Alpha Alpha. Democrat. Lutheran. Avocations: stamps, vcr recording, travel. Died July 16, 2007.

FIERING, SUSANNAH, art therapist, educator; b. NYC, Mar. 18, 1934; d. Stephen and May (Cavin) Leeman; m. Alvin Fiering, Jan. 27, 1957 (div. 1984); children: Gina, Wendy, Chloe. BA, Bard Coll., 1955; MFA, Inst. Allende, Guanajuato, Mex., 1973; MEd, Lesley Coll., 1980. Registered art therapist. Instr. art, art history, art edn. Lesley Coll., Bunker Hill C.C., Stonehill Coll., Cambridge, Charleston, No. Easton, Mass., 1975-78; art therapist, intake specialist, case mgr. New Ctr. for Psychotherapies, Boston, 1977-81; instr. art therapy Lesley Coll. Grad. Sch., Cambridge, 1982; chairperson acad. coun. Beacon Coll., Boston, 1983-84; instr. psychology, art prison edn. project Curry Coll., Lancaster, Mass., 1983, 85; instr. art therapy Salve Regina U., Newport, R.I., 1985-92; expressive therapist Phase, Taunton, Mass., 1986-88, Waltham (Mass.)/Weston Hosp., 1988-91; pvt. practice art therapy, counseling, from 1980. Art therapist Charter Hosp. Austin, 1991-92; art and child therapist House of the Morning Star, Austin, 1993, St. Mary's Hosp., Tucson; workshop leader, staff devel. trainer numerous orgns., 1987—. Executed mural for Charter

Hosp. Austin, 1992; sculptures reproduced in Woman Poets #3, 1974; woodcut prints reproduced in Magical Blend mag., 1993; exhibited in group shows at De Cordova Mus., 1986 and numerous others. Active Save our Springs, Austin, 1991-93. Mem. Am. Art Therapy Assn. Avocations: reading, music, swimming, canoeing, kayaking. Home: Richmond, Calif. Died June 8, 2007.

FIETE, RICHARD WAYNE, minister; b. Chariton, Iowa, May 21, 1938; s. Claude Dean Fiete and Viola Catherine (Watkins) Brechwald; m. Kathryn Tucker, Nov. 25, 1961; children: Stephen C., Tamara L. BA, Buena Vista Coll., 1960; BD, Princeton Theol. Sem., 1966; D Ministry, McCormick Theol. Sem., Chgo., 1985. Ordained to ministry Presbyn. Ch. (U.S.A.), 1966. Pastor Trinity Presbyn. Ch., Scotia, N.Y., 1966-74; assoc. pastor 1st Presbyn. Ch., Albany, N.Y., 1974-78, pastor Morgantown, W.Va., from 1978. Moderator Presbytery of W.Va. Presbyn. Ch. (U.S.A.), 1987-88, chair theology and worship unit, 1989-91. Trustee Davis & Elkins Coll., Elkins, W.Va., 1982-88. Mem. Rotary. Home: Morgantown, W.Va. Died Feb. 19, 2007.

FIGUEROA, JOSÉ MANUEL See SEBASTIAN, JOAN

FILIP, HENRY (HENRY PETRZILKA), physicist; b. Chgo., Mar. 29, 1920; s. Joseph and Aloisie (Filip) Petrzilka; m. Marie Louise Krajcovic, Sept. 17, 1957; children: Henry Jr., Frederick, Marie Louise; 1 stepchild, Jan Janecka. BS, Ill. Wesleyan U., 1944. Tech. asst. Fermi Pile, Manhattan Project U. Chgo., 1944; rsch. asst. atom bomb external trigger system Los Alamos (N.Mex.) Nat. Lab., 1944-49, rsch. asst. internal neutron source for atom bomb, 1949-56, exptl. researcher Rover program Flyable Nuclear Reactor, 1956-72, exptl. researcher isotope separation program, 1972-84, exptl. physicist x-ray analysis of atomic explosions, 1984-85; exptl. physicist Western Rsch. Corp., San Diego, 1985; exptl. physicist Star Wars Laser System Jan Bec Corp., San Diego, 1985-88. Cons. x-ray analysis Los Alamos Nat. Lab., 1984-85, Western Rsch. Corp., San Diego, 1984-85. Mem. Pierottis Clowns. Mem. Palisade Lions (bd. mem. 1989-92), Los Alamos Rotary (pres. 1983-87), Los Alamos Kiwanis (hon.). Democrat. Avocations: woodworking, golf, skiing. Home: Palisade, Colo. Died Jan. 23, 2007.

FILLOY, BEVERLEE ANN HOWE, clinical social worker; b. Ogden, Utah, Mar. 11, 1926; d. Albert Herman Howe and Bernice Anna (Ewing) Howe Routt; m. Jose Antonio Filloy-Alvarez, Feb. 4, 1945 (dec. 1988); children: Richard Anthony (dec.), Emily Ann. BA with honors, U. Calif., Berkeley, 1947, MSW, 1954; PhD, Calif. Inst. Clin. Social Work, Berkeley, 1980. Bd. cert. diplomate clin. social work, sex therapist, clin. supr.; diplomate Am. Bd. Sexology. Social caseworker Family Svc. Agy., Sacramento, 1959-63; cons. Stanford Lathrop Meml. Home, Sacramento, 1964-69; cons., supr. Arnold Homes for Children, Sacramento, 1968-71; pvt. practice social work Sacramento, from 1963; faculty Calif. Soc. Clin. Social Work, Sacramento, 1979—2004, Calif. State U., Sacramento, 1956-58, 90. Sec. Nat. Registry Providers of Health Care in Clin. Social Work, 1983-85, bd. dirs., 1980-86, treas. Nat. Fedn. for Socs. for Clin. Social Work, 1981-86. Founder, bd. Planned Parenthood of Sacramento, 1964. Fellow Calif. Soc. for Clin. Social Work (pres. 1983-85, bd. dirs. 1969-87, Mem. of Yr. award 1990), Calif. Inst. for Clin. Social Worker (bd. trustees, sec.-treas. 1976-88, v.p. 1989-94); mem. ACLU, Soc. for Sci. Study Sex, Amnesty Internat., Older Women's League (pres. Sacramento chpt.), Phi Beta Kappa. Democrat. Avocations: travel, swimming, gardening, theater, entertaining. Home: Sacramento, Calif. Died May 20, 2007.

FINKEL, GILBERT, food scientist, researcher; b. Bklyn., Dec. 12, 1935; s. Reuben and Sarah (Shadovitz) F.; m. Millicent Heft, Sept. 7, 1958; children: Richard Howard, Lynn Finkel Lutz. BSc, Delaware Valley Coll., Doylestown, Pa., 1957; MBA, Fairleigh Dickinson U., 1973. Rsch. chemist Standard Brands, Inc., Stamford, Conn., 1957-59; group leader DCA Food Industries, Inc., NYC, 1959-67; sr. scientist Lever Bros. Co., Edgewater, N.J., 1967-68; mgr. product devel. M & M/Mars, Hackettstown, N.J., 1968-72; pres. Food-Tek, Inc., Morris Plains, N.J., from 1972. Contbr. articles to profl. jours.; patentee in field. With U.S. Army, 1959. Avocations: flying, tennis. Home: Morristown, NJ. Died Jan. 5, 2007.

FINKS, ROBERT MELVIN, paleontologist, educator; b. Portland, Maine, May 12, 1927; s. Abraham Joseph and Sarah (Bendette) F. BS magna cum laude in Biology, Queens Coll., 1947; MA in Geology, Columbia U., 1954, PhD in Geology, 1959. Lectr. Bklyn. Coll., 1955-58, instr., 1959-61; lectr. Queens Coll., CUNY, 1961-62, asst. prof., 1962-65, acting chmn., 1963-64, assoc. prof. geology, 1966-70, prof., 1971—2002, prof. emeritus, from 2002; geologist U.S. Geol. Survey, 1952-54 and from 63; rsch. assoc. Am. Mus. Natural History, 1961—77, Smithsonian Instn., from 1968; rsch. assoc. in paleontology N.Y. State Mus.; rsch. prof. dept. geology Union Coll., Schenectady, NY. Doctoral faculty CUNY, 1983—; cons. in field. Author: Late Paleozoic Sponge Faunas of the Texas Region, 1960; co-author: Treatise on Invertebrate Paleontology, Part E, Porifera, vol. 2, 2003, vol. 3, 2004, (poems) Sonatas and Other Music, 2010; editor: Guidebook to Field Excursions, 1968; contbr. articles profl. jours. Queens Coll. Scholar, 1947. Fellow AAAS, Geol. Soc. Am., Explorers Club; mem. AAUP, Paleontol. Soc. (vice chmn. Northeastern sect. 1977-78, chmn. 1978-79), Paleontol. Assn. Britain, Soc. Econ. Paleontologists and Mineralogists Soc. for Sedimentary Geology, Internat. Palaeontol. Assn., Geol. Soc. Vt. (charter mem.), Planetary Soc. (charter), Phi Beta Kappa (v.p. Sigma chpt. NY 1993-95, pres. 1995-99), Golden Key (hon.), Sigma Xi (exec. sec. Queens Coll. chpt. 1982-85; treas. Union Coll. chpt. 2006—). Home: Flushing, NY. *Be humble in studying nature.* Died Mar. 25, 2014.

FINNERTY, PETER JOSEPH, water transportation executive; b. Petersburg, Va., Sept. 9, 1942; s. Peter Francis and Alice P.F.; m. Tory Boone, Aug. 23, 1969; children: Peter, Will, Kate, Michael. BS, N.Y. Maritime Coll., 1964; MBA, U. Pa., 1966; JD, Georgetown U., 1972. Bar. D.C. 1973. Asst. to pres. Am. Merchant Marine Inst., NYC, 1966-68; dep. dir. Am. Assn. Port Author, Washington, 1968-69; mgr. adminstrn. Sea-Land Svc., Washington, 1970-71, dir. govt. sales, 1971-73; v.p. CSX Corp., Washington, from 1987; dir. regulatory affairs Sea-Land Svc., Edison, N.J., 1974, v.p. pub. affairs, from 1977. Chmn. Maritime Inst. for Rsch. and Indsl. Devel., Washington, 1988-97; trustee U.S. Coun. on Internat. Bus., N.Y.C., 1985-88, 95—. Bd. dirs., mem. exec. com., v.p. USCG Found., Stonington, Conn., 1991—; bd. dirs. Bryce Harlow Found., Naval War Coll. Found.; chmn. Chamber of Shipping of Am., 1996. Lt. (j.g.) USNR, 1964-70. Mem. Maritime Adminstrn. Bar Assn., India House, Georgetown Club, City Club, 116 Club, Propeller Club of U.S. (nat. pres. 1995-96). Roman Catholic. Home: Washington, DC. Died Feb. 8, 2007.

FIRTH, EVERETT JOSEPH, tympanist; b. Winchester, Mass., June 2, 1930; s. Everett Emanuel and Rosemary (Scandura) F.; m. Olga Kwasniak, June 22, 1960; children—Kelly Victoria DeChristopher, Tracy Kimberly Firth. Mus.B. with distinction, 1952. Faculty head, percussion dept. New Eng. Conservatory, 1950—2015; mem. faculty Berkshire Music Center, 1956—2015. Pres., CEO Vic Firth Inc. (mfr. and distbr. worldwide drum sticks and mallets); CEO Vic Firth Mfg., Newport, Maine; mem. Percussive Arts Soc. Hall of Fame Solo tympanist, Boston Symphony Orch., 1952—1956, prin. tympanist, 1956-2002 Boston Pops Orch., 1952—2002, Boston Symphony Chamber Players; Recs. with RCA Victor, Mercury, Columbia, Cambridge, Deutsche Grammophon. Mem. ASCAP, Phi Kappa Lambda, Phi Mu Alpha Sinfonia. Home: Dover, Mass. Died July 26, 2015.

FISCHMAN, HARVE See BENNETT, HARVE

FISHER, JOSEPH STEWART, management consultant; b. Athens, Pa., Mar. 3, 1933; s. Samuel Royer and Agnes Corinne (Smith) F.; m. Anita Ann Coyle, May 15, 1954; 1 child, Samuel Royer. BS in Tech. Mgmt., Regis U., 1981; postgrad., U. Colo., 1986-87, Iliff Sch. Theology, 1988-89. With IBM Corp., Kingston, Syracuse & Endicott, N.Y., 1956-60, Boulder, 1960-87; cons., sole propr. Fisher Enterprises, Boulder, from 1975. Bd. dirs. Vervcraft Inc., Loveland, Colo. Leadership devel. Boy Scouts Am., 1975—, chmn. long range planning, 1982-86, chaplain, 1991—; bd. dirs. Longs Peak Coun., 1983-87, Colo. Crime Stoppers, 1983-88; exec. dir. Caring About People, Inc., Colo., 1990—; v.p. Helplink, Inc., Boulder, 1991—. With USN, 1952-56, Korea. Recipient Silver Beaver award Boy Scouts Am., Boulder, 1978, God and Svc. award Boy Scouts Am. and United Meth. Ch., 1991, OES Rose award 1994; James E. West fellow Boy Scouts Am., 1997, Masonic Scouter's award, 2002. Mem. Am. Soc. Indsl. Security (cert. CPP, lifetime CPP status 2000, treas. 1985), Colo. Crime Prevention Assn. (cert. CPS), Mason (treas. Columbia lodge #14 1969-85, 1990-2001), Royal Arch. Masons, Commandery Knights Templar of York Rite, Scottish Rite (32nd degree), Shriners. Republican. Methodist. Avocations: scouting, church and masonic. Died July 17, 2007.

FISHER, MARCIA ANN, real estate executive; b. Geneva, Ill., Feb. 28, 1957; d. Robert L. and Beverly J. (Hopp) F. Student, Moser Bus. Sch., 1975; student, U. Ill., 1975-76; BS, U. Iowa, 1978, BS in Indsl. Relations, 1980. Paralegal Rate, Nolan, Moen & Parsons, Iowa City, 1980-82, legal adminstr., 1982-94; dir. risk mgmt. real estate devel. Nat. Propane, L.P., Cedar Rapids, Iowa, 1994-99; dir. contracts/real estate devel. Columbia Propane, L.P., Richmond, Va., from 1999. Appointed Iowa State Foster Care Review Bd., 1987; del. Citizen Ambassador Program to People's Republic of China, 1988, to USSR, 1990. Rotary scholar, 1975. Mem. Nat. Assn. Legal Adminstrs., Iowa Assn. Legal Adminstrs., Iowa Assn. Legal Assts. (treas. 1984), Iowa Risk and Insurance Mgmt. Soc., Nat. Risk and Insurance Mgmt. Soc., Propane Gas Defense Assn. Avocations: gourmet cooking, tennis, photography, swimming, reading. Died July 22, 2007.

FISHER, MARION LEROY, JR., retired school superintendent, real estate broker; b. Detroit, Nov. 20, 1925; s. Marion LeRoy Sr. and Clela Mae (Smith) F.; m. Mary-Frances Allsbrook, Dec. 16, 1973. BA, Defiance Coll., Ohio, 1947; MDiv, Duke U., 1950; MEd, Bowling Green State U., Ohio, 1959; EdD, Nova U., 1981. Cert. tchr., N.C., S.C. Minister Meth. Ch., Harmony, N.C., 1950-52; tchr. high sch. Holgate Local Schs., Ohio, 1952-60, prin., tchr. high sch. Ohio, 1958-60; prin. Poynor Jr. High Sch., Florence, S.C., 1960-67; dir. adult edn. and dir. fed. programs Florence Sch. Dist. 1, 1967-68; asst. supt. Weldon City Schs., SC, 1968-69, supt. SC, 1969-89; salesman Wilkie Real Estate, Inc., Roanoke Rapids, N.C., 1990, broker, 1990-92, Ginger Hale Real Estate, from 1993; ednl. rschr. Luton (Eng.) Indsl. Coll., from 1993; broker Ginger Hale Real Estate, from 1993. Instr. driver's edn. and religion U. S.C., Florence, 1966-68; cons. human rels St. Augustine's Coll., Raleigh, N.C., 1968-72; instr. psychology, social sci. Halifax Community Coll., Weldon, 1969—92 interim nat. dir. Indsl. and Comml. Ministries, Harrisonburg, Va., 1991. Chaplain Roanoke Rapids (N.C.) Fire Dept., 1989-93; mem. bd. trustees Lakeland Cultural Arts Ctr., Littleton, N.C., 1987-92. Gen. Electric Co. fellow, 1956; named Sci. Tchr. of the Yr., N.W. Ohio Edn. Region, 1960, Outstanding Adminstr. of the Yr., Edn. Region 3, 1979. Mem. NEA, Am. Assn. Sch. Adminstrs., Rotary, Masons, Phi Delta Kappa. Methodist. Avocations: landscaping, boating, fishing. Home: Roanoke Rapids, NC. Died Feb. 19, 2007.

FISHER, THOMAS MICHAEL, secondary education educator; b. Jersey City, NY, Mar. 17, 1934; s. Harold Wilburn and Sara Cecilia (Kelly) F.; m. Dorothy Anne Roberts, Apr. 8, 1959; children: Michael Vincent, Karen Cecilia. AA, St. Bernard's Coll., 1954; AB, St. Bonaventure U., 1956; MS, Syracuse U., 1963. Cert. secondary edn. tchr., N.Y. Tchr. Elmira (N.Y.) Schs., 1959-89; sanitary chemist City of Elmira, 1963-73; rsch. dir. Canine Eye, San Francisco, 1969-82; adj. instr. Corning (N.Y.) C.C., 1972-79; sci. cons., computer specialist St. Mary Our Mother Sch., HHorseheads, N.Y., from 1984; facilitator nat. sci. support East Tenn. State U., Johnson City, 1988. Bibliographical specialist McGraw Hill, Charlottesville, Va., N.Y.C. Contbr. over 140 articles to profl. jours. Dir. Elmira Symphony Soc., 1986-89; mem., treas. Campus Ministry Corning C.C., 1989-92; eucharistic min. St. Mary Our Mother Ch., Horseheads, 1988—. Mem. Libr. of Congress. Roman Catholic. Avocations: composing poetry, classical music, travel. Home: Horseheads, NY. Died June 25, 2007.

FITCH, DONALD EVERETT, librarian; b. Miles City, Mont., Apr. 9, 1928; s. Everett Willis and Teresa Helen (Sagaser) F.; m. Dorothy Ann Lamb, June 19, 1954; children: Stephen, Charles, Robert, Jane, Alan, Hugh. BA in English, Gonzaga U., 1953; MA in English, UCLA, 1954; MLS, U. Calif., Berkeley, 1959. Tchr. Coeur d'Alene (Idaho) High Sch., 1954-56, Santa Monica (Calif.) Coll., 1958; libr. U. Calif., Santa Barbara, from 1959, head reference dept., 1963-84, asst. coll. devel. officer, from 1984. Author: Blake Set to Music, 1990; composer choral works include Ye Sons and Daughters, 1991; editor: Soundings Jour., 1969—; contbr. articles to profl. jours. Home: Santa Barbara, Calif. Died Jan. 23, 2007.

FITCH, VAL LOGSDON, nuclear physicist; b. Merriman, Nebr., Mar. 10, 1923; s. Fred B. and Frances Marion (Logsdon) Fitch; m. Elise Cunningham Fitch, June 11, 1949 (dec. 1972); children: John Craig(dec.) , Alan Peter; m. Daisy Harper Sharp, Aug. 14, 1976. BSEE, McGill U., Montreal, Que., Can., 1948; PhD in Physics, Columbia U., NYC, 1954. Instr. Columbia U., 1953; instr. physics Princeton U., NJ, 1954—56, asst. prof., 1956—59, assoc. prof., 1959—60, prof., 1960—94, Class 1909 prof. physics, 1968—76, Cyrus Fogg Bracket prof. physics, 1977—84, James S. McDonnell Distinguished Univ. prof. physics, 1984—94, prof. emeritus, 1994—2015. Mem. Pres.'s Sci. Adv. Com., 1970—73. Svc. with US Army, 1943—46. Recipient Rsch. Corp. award, 1967, E.O. Lawrence award, US Dept. Energy, 1968, John Price Wetherill medal, Franklin Inst., 1976, Nobel prize in physics, 1980, Grad. Alumnus award, Am. Assn. State Colleges & Universities, 1984, Disting. Alumnus award, Columbia U., 1985, Nat. Medal Sci., 1993; fellow Alfred P. Sloan Found., 1960. Fellow: AAAS, American Phys. Soc. (pres. 1987—88, 1988—89); mem.: NAS, American Philos. Soc., American Acad. Arts & Sciences. Died Feb. 5, 2015.

FITTON, HARVEY NELSON, JR., former government official; b. Washington; s. Harvey Nelson and Ada Hortense (Marshall) F.; m. Bernice Jeanette Sutton, Jan. 8, 1946 (dec. Sept. 1998); m. Judith Ann Knauss, Dec. 11, 2004 Student, Nat. Acad. Theater, 1940; degree in Am. Studies, George Washington U., 1949, MA in Am. Lit. and Cultural History, 1956; postgrad., Am. U., 1963. Editor, rsch. asst. Nat. Acad. Scis., Nat. Rsch. Coun., Washington, 1949-56; med. writer and editor NIH, Bethesda, Md., 1956-58; info. specialist farmer cooperative svc. USDA, Washington, 1958-61, publs. editor office of info., 1961-63, chief editorial br. office of info., 1963-66, head pub. divsn. office govtl. and pub. affairs, 1966-84, dep. dir. of info., office govt. and pub. affairs, 1984. Instr. USDA Grad. Sch., Washington, 1962-92, chmn. editl. adv. com., 1976-85, mem. comm. skills adv. com., 1986-97. Author (book) Musings, 2009; editor, rsch. asst. Atlas of Tumor Pathology, 1949-56; editor NIH Record, 1956-58; author. Musings; contbr. articles to profl. jours. Pres. Clermont Woods Community Assn., Fairfax County, Va., 1968, No. Va. Family Svc., Falls Church, 1972-73; elder local Presbyn. Ch. With USN, 1942-45. Recipient Horace Hart award Edn. Coun. of Graphic Arts Industry, 1980; inductee Internat. Poetry Hall of Fame, 1996. Fellow Soc. for Tech. Comm. (pres. Washington chpt. 1972-73, asst. to pres. for recognition programs 1976-77); mem. Acad. Am. Poets, Internat. Soc. Poets, Haiku Soc. Am., Agrl. Communicators in Edn. (pres. Washington chpt. 1968, Spl. Achievement award 1986), Nat. Assn. Govt. Communicators (pres. Washington chpt. 1979, nat. pres. 1980, mem. editl. bd. Govt. Comm., 1994—, Communicator of Yr. 1984), St. Andrews Soc., Nat. Assn. Scholars, Assn. Lit. Scholars and Critics, Toastmasters (pres. Alexandria chpt. 1959-60), SAR. Avocations: gardening, singing, book collecting, poetry, tap dancing. Died Jan. 22, 2015.

FITZGERALD, JAMES GORDON RICHARD, retired rental company executive; b. Winnipeg, Man., Can., June 26, 1928; s. Gordon Wesley and Sarah Thomas (McFadyen) F. V.p. Fasco Rentals Ltd., Edmonton, Alta., Can., 1953-63, pres., CEO, 1963-96; ret., 1996. Senator U. Alberta, 1986-89. Col. Can. Mil. Police Res. (ret.). Fellow Augustan Soc., Can. Guild Authors; Soc. Antiquaries (Scotland), Mil. Vehicle Preservation Assn. (pres. 1986-89), 15th Svc. Battalion. Assn. (senator), Royal Humane Soc. (gov.). Conservative. Avocation: automobile and military vehicle collecting (antique). Home: Edmonton, Canada. Died Apr. 21, 2007.

FITZGERALD, ROBERT JAMES, microbiologist, oral biologist; b. NYC, Nov. 3, 1918; s. Maurice Edward and Anna Marie (Ledogar) F.; m. Dorothea Babbitt, June 20, 1945. BS, Fordham U., 1939; MS, Va. Tech. U., 1941; PhD, Duke U., 1948. Microbiologist Am. Cyanamid Corp., Stamford, Conn., 1941-45; sanitarian, ensign USPHS, Kansas City, Kans., 1945-46, lt. (j.g.), 1948, advanced through grades to capt., 1963; rsch. microbiologist USPHS NIH, Bethesda, Md., 1948-69; ret. USPHS, 1969; rsch. career scientist U.S. Dept. Vets. Affairs, Miami, Fla., 1969-94. Prof. microbiology Sch. Medicine U. Miami, 1969-88; rsch. prof. dentistry U. Fla., Gainesville, 1971-94; cons., advisor USPHS, Bethesda, 1970-94, Navy Dental Rsch. Inst., Great Lakes, Ill., 1972-94; cons. Merck Rsch., South Fla. Vets. Affairs Rsch. Found., 1994—. Contbr. 7 book chpts., 130 papers to scholarly and profl. books and jours. Recipient rsch. award Chgo. Dental Soc., 1968, Dental Rsch. prize Fedn. Dentaire Internat., Cologne, Fed. Republic of Germany, 1970, Sci. award Internat. Assn. Dental Rsch., Copenhagen, 1977, Undersec. for Health Honor award, 1994, Sec. of Vets. Affairs Exceptional Svc. award, 1994, Nat. Inst. Dental Rsch. Disting. Svc. award NIH. Fellow AAAS, Am. Soc. Microbiology. Achievements include proof that mutans streptococci cause dental caries. Home: Miami, Fla. Died Jan. 18, 2007.

FITZSIMONS, MAUREEN See O'HARA, MAUREEN

FLANAGAN, JAMES LOTON, electrical engineer, educator, researcher; b. Aug. 26, 1925; s. Hanks and Wilhelmina (Barnes) Flanagan; m. Mildred Bell; children: Stephen, James, Aubrey. BSEE, Miss. State U., 1948; SMEE, MIT, 1950, ScDEE, 1955; PhD (hon.), U. Madrid, 1992, U. Paris, 1996. Elec. engring. faculty Miss. State U., 1950-52; tech. staff Bell Labs., Murray Hill, N.J., 1957-61, head dept. speech and auditory rsch., 1961-67, head dept. acoustics rsch., 1967-85, dir. info. prins. rsch. lab., 1985-90; dir. ctr. for advanced info. processing Rutgers U., Piscataway, NJ, 1990—2005, v.p. for rsch., 1993—2005, prof. emertius. Evaluation panel Nat. Bur. Standards/NRC, 1972—77; adv. panel on White House tapes U.S. Dist. Ct. for D.C., 1973—74; sci. adv. bd. Callier Center, U. Tex., Dallas, 1974—76; sci. adv. panel on voice comm. Nat. Security Agy., 1975—77. Author: Speech Analysis, Synthesis and Perception, 1972; contbr. articles to profl. jours. Recipient Disting. Svc. award in sci., Am. Speech and Hearing Assn., 1977, L.M. Ericsson Internat. prize in telecomms., 1985, Nat. Medal Sci., Nat. Medal Sci. Com., Pres. Clinton, 1996, N.J. R&D Coun. Sci. and Tech. medal, 2000; fellow, Marconi Internat., 1992. Fellow: IEEE (selection com. 1979—81, Edison medal 1986, Honor medal 2005), Am. Acad. Arts and Scis., Acoustical Soc. Am. (assoc. editor Speech Comm. 1959—62, exec. coun. 1970—73, v.p. 1976—77, pres. 1978—79, Gold medal 1986); mem.: NAS (chmn. engring. sect. 1996—99), NAE, Acoustics, Speech and Signal Processing Soc. (v.p. 1967—68, pres. 1969—70, Achievement award 1970, Soc. award 1976), Eta Kappa Nu. Achievements include patents in field. Died Aug. 25, 2015.

FLASTER, DONALD J., retired pharmaceutical executive; s. Murray J. and Theresa Flaster; m. Susan J. Alexander, Dec. 16, 1988. AB in Biol. Scis., Johns Hopkins U., Balt., 1953; MD, U. Naples, Italy, 1959. Intern Meyer Meml./Erie County Hosp., Buffalo; resident Millard Fillmore Hosp., Buffalo, Emergency Hosp., Buffalo; pvt. practice physician Valley Cottage, NY, 1961—67; assoc. med. dir. Pfizer Labs., NYC, 1967—69; dir. clin. rsch. USV Pharm., NYC, 1969—72; assoc. dir. clin. rsch. Sandoz Inc., East Hanover, NJ, 1972—74; pres., CEO SRS Inc., Morristown, NJ, 1974—90; ret., 1990. Cons. SRS Inc., Morristown, 1974—90. Author: Malpractice: A Guide to the Legal Rights of Patients and Doctors, 1983—84. Recipient Outstanding Contbn. award, NY State Acad. Family Physicians, 25 Yrs. Comprehensive Svc. award. Fellow: Am. Acad. Family Physicians (life); mem.: NJ Med. Soc. (emeritus). Avocation: music. Home: Eustis, Fla. Died Nov. 24, 2014.

FLEEGAL, TIM LEE, computer company executive; b. Harrisburg, Pa., July 28, 1945; s. Leo West and Hilda L. (Coleman) F.; m. Cheryl Lynn Brown, June 26, 1978; 1 child, Ginger Lee. BA, Lehigh U., 1967. Owner/operator F-Penn-L Personnel, Harrisburg, Pa., 1967-73; forms sales rep. Profl. Bus. Services, Harrisburg, 1973-74; with Olivetti Corp. Am., Harrisburg, 1974-76; cons. in data processing Harrisburg, 1976-77; data processing mgr. Speed Mail Services, Harrisburg, 1977-78; with R.T. Becker Assocs., Reading, Pa., 1978; asst. data processing mgr. Stabler Cos., Harrisburg, 1978-83; computer support exec. Growing Concerns Computer Support, Harrisburg, from 1981. Cons. Community Gen. Osteopathic Hosp., Harrisburg, 1986—. Contbr. articles to profl. jours. Initiator City Island Youth Clean-up, Harrisburg, 1974; instr. Dauphin County Children & Youth, Harrisburg, 1986-87. Mem. Cen. Pa. IBM Users Group. Clubs: Harrisburg Camera (instr. 1986-87). Lodges: Sertoma (v.p. sponsorship 1987-88). Republican. Lutheran. Avocation: photography. Died Apr. 27, 2007.

FLEISCHER, ALBERT GEORG, health facility administrator; b. Mineral Wells, Tex., Sept. 26, 1940; s. Albert Georg and Lilith Martesia (Boyd) F. AB, Austin Coll., 1962; MD, U. Tex., 1966. Fellow in spinal cord injuries Rusk Inst., NYC, 1968, asst. prof., 1968-80; dir. rehab. medicine S.I. (N.Y.) Hosp., 1980-89; chair rehab. medicine S.I. U. Hosp., 1989-93; chmn. St. Vincent's Med. Ctr., SI, from 1993, Bayley Seton Hosp., SI, from 1993. Asst. prof. Downstate Med. Ctr., Bklyn., 1985-95; assoc. clin. prof. phys. therapy divsn. Coll. S.I., 1991—; dir. rehab. medicine Luth. Med. Ctr., Bklyn., 1985-93. Mem. Mayor's Com. for Disabled, N.Y.C., 1980—, chairperson, 1990—; chair Borough Pres. Com. for Disabled, S.I., 1989—; med. dir. United Cerebral Palsy, N.Y.C., 1991—; pres. Tibetan Mus. Bd., 1993—; bd. dirs. Staten Island Ctr. for Ind. Living, 1983—; mem. N.Y. State Ind. Living Coun., N.J. State Brain Injury Coun., 1993—, N.Y. State Occupl.Therapy Licensure bd., 1990. Paul Harris fellow, 1989; named Humanitarian of Yr., N.Y. State Ctrs. for Ind. Living, 1993, Person of Yr., Salvation Army, S.I., 1994; recipient Nat. Spinal Cord Injury award 1996; torch bearer for 1996 Olympics. Mem. AMA, Am. Congress Rehab. Medicine, N.Y. Assn. Phys. Medicine and Rehab., Am. Assn. Phys. Medicine and Rehab., Am. Acad. Cerebral Palsy and Devel. Disabilties. Republican. Presbyterian. Avocations: cooking, reading. Home: New York, NY. Died July 10, 2007.

FLEMING, JAMES DONALD, professional photographer; b. Spartanburg, SC, Feb. 7, 1935; s. James Clarence and Clara (Robinette) F.; m. Anne Howell Jones, June 29, 1963; children: Rebecca Anne, Donald Robinette. Student, Clemson U., 1953-56. Field engr. IBM Corp., Atlanta, 1963-65; dealer Loyd Jones Chevrolet, Demopolis, Ala., 1965-80; prin., photographer Fleming Photography Studio, Demopolis, from 1980. Photos exhibited 1985 (Merit, Court of Honor awards). Bd. dirs. Marengo County Hist. Soc., Demopolis, 1977-80, Demopolis C. of C., 1977-79; city councilman, mayor pro tempore City of Demopolis, 1976-80. Served with USAF, 1958-62. Mem. Profl. Photographers Am., Profl. Photographers Miss. and Ala., Southeast Profl. Photographers Assn. Lodges: Kiwanis. Home: Demopolis, Ala. Died Nov. 18, 2006.

FLETCHER, WILLIAM ADRIN, minister; b. Graham, Tex., Apr. 22, 1948; s. Henry Jesse and Frances Merle (Thigpen) F.; m. Terri Lynn Hoch, June 19, 1970; children: Colin, Scott. BS, Abilene Christian U., 1970, MS, 1997. Minister Eliasville (Tex.) Ch. of Christ, 1967-70; missionary, minister Sighthill Ch. of Christ, Edinburgh, Scotland, 1970-75; minister West 34th St./Brookhollow Ch. of Christ, Houston, 1975-83, Murray St. Ch. of Christ, Rockdale, Tex., 1983-99, Munday Ch. of Christ, Munday, Tex., from 2002. Part-time chaplain Vista Care/Family Hospice, 1997—99. Contbr. articles Munday Courier. Bd. dirs. Cen. Tex. Area Mus., Salado, 1980—, v.p., 1983-85, 2000-, pres. 1986-98; bd. dirs., pres. NW Christian Sch., Houston, 1983; bd. dirs. South Milam County United Way, 1988-90, pres., 1988-89; bd. dirs. Richards Meml. Hosp., Rockdale, 1989-99; registrar Knox County Relay for Life; vol. Hospice of Wichita Falls, mem. Munday City Coun. Named one of Outstanding Young Men Am., Jaycees, 1978. Mem.: Am. Assn. Christian Counselors, Lions Club (Munday chpt.) (sec.-treas. from 2003). Avocations: photography, swimming, reading. Home: Pflugerville, Tex. Deceased.

FLICK, DONALD ROBERT, broadcast executive; b. Cin., July 29, 1949; s. William and Louise (Brown) F. Student, U. Cin., 1971. Registered profl. engr., Ohio. Announcer Sta. WCVL, Crawfordsville, Ind., 1971-72; program dir. Sta. WAAM, Ann Arbor, Mich., 1972-74, salesman, 1974-76; prin., v.p. Sta. WQTC-FM, Two Rivers, Wis., 1976-80, Sta. WRTR, Two Rivers, 1980-83; mgr. Sta. WKTT-FM, Cleveland, Wis., from 1983. Freelance writer, announcer, Wis., 1983—. Mem. Manitowoc County C. of C., Sheboygan C. of C. Lodges: Rotary. Republican. Died Dec. 31, 2006.

FLITCRAFT, RICHARD KIRBY, II, former chemical company executive; b. Woodstown, NJ, Sept. 5, 1920; s. H. Milton and Edna (Crispin) F.; m. Bertha LeSturgeon Hitchner, Nov. 14, 1942; children: Alyce, Anne, Elizabeth, Richard. BS, Rutgers U., 1942; MS, Washington U., 1948. With Monsanto Co., St. Louis, from 1942, dir. inorganic rsch., 1960-65, dir. mgmt. info. and systems dept., 1965-67, asst. to pres., 1967-68, group mgr. electronics enterprises, 1968-69, gen. mgr. electronic products div., 1969-71; v.p. Monsanto Rsch. Corp., 1971-75; dir. Mound Lab., 1971-75, v.p. ops., 1975-76; pres. Monsanto Resh. Corp., Dayton, 1976-82, ret., 1982. Past chmn., bd. dirs. United Way, Dayton; bd. dirs. City-Wide Devel. Corp.; former trustee and chmn. bd. Miami Valley Hosp.; past bd. dirs. Pvt. Industry Coun., Srs., Inc.; chmn. bd. Headstart program Miami Valley Child Devel., Inc., bd. mem., pres. Dayton Montogomery County Scholarship Program. Mem. AAAS, AICE, Am. Chem. Soc., Am. Inst. Chemists, Am. Mgmt. Assn., N.Y. Acad. Scis., Ohio Acad. Scis. (past exec. com.), Dayton C. of C. (past bd. dirs., chmn. small bus. adv. bd., mil. affairs com.), Engrs. Club of Dayton (past bd. dirs.), Engrs. Club Dayton Found. (bd. trustees, chmn.), Moraine Country Club, Dayton Racquet Club, mound Sci. & Energy mus.(bd. mem., pres.) Presbyterian. Home: Dayton, Ohio. Died Dec. 16, 2014.

FLOM, ROBERT MICHAEL, interior designer; b. Grand Forks, ND, Oct. 27, 1952; s. John Nicholai and Irene Magdaline (Miller) F.; m. Holly Suzanne Schue, July 20, 1975 (div. June 1986); m. Margaret Elizabeth Moon, Oct. 15, 1988; children: Amy Michelle Moon, Jamie Bryant Moon. Student, Western Tech., 1970-71, U. N.D., 1980-83, LaSalle U., 1994-95, Century U., from 1996. Asst. food and beverage mgr. Holiday Inn/Topeka Inns, Denver, 1970-71; interior designer, fl. mgr. Crossroads Furniture, Grand Forks, 1972-85; store mgr. Greenbaums, Tacoma, 1986-88, interior designer, from 1986. Tng. advisor Greenbaums, Bellevue, Wash., 1988—. Mem. Am. Soc. Interior Designers (allied mem.), Autism Soc. Tacoma-Pierce County (treas. 1991—96). Avocations: reading, bicycling, cross country skiing, hiking, woodworking. Home: University Place, Wash. Died Dec. 12, 2006.

FLOOD, MARTIN WILLIAM, primary school educator; b. Dallas, Mar. 29, 1956; s. Martin G. and Lois A. (Ritter) F. Cert., Eastfield C.C., Mesquite, Tex., 1983-84, AA in Child Devel., 1984, AA in Child Care Adminstrn., 1986. Toddler tchr. First Meth. Ch., Dallas, 1981, substitute tchr., 1984; substitute tchr. aide Meth. Hosp. Child Ctr., Dallas, 1982; tchr. East Grand Bapt. Ch., Dallas, 1985; home caregiver Dallas, 1985-86; substitute tchr. Emanuel Luth. Ch., Dallas, 1987; resource, asst. tchr. Cradle to Crayon Child Devel., Dallas, 1988-95; subt. tchr. childcare Dallas Svc., Employment, Devel. Jobs for Progress, 1995; asst. lead tchr. Svc., Employment, Devel., Child Devel. Ctr., Dallas, 1996-98, from 1998. Day camp supr. Eastfield C.C., Mesquite, summer 1984. Recipient Outstanding Vol. award Downtown Dallas Family Shelter, 1988, Team Svc. award Corp. Child Care Mag., 1993. Mem. Dallas Assn. for the Edn. of Young Children. Avocations: coin collecting/numismatics, stamp collecting/philately, metal detecting, reading, gem collecting. Home: Dallas, Tex. Died July 8, 2007.

FLOREA, WALTER GRAYDON, JR., (TED FLOREA), internal revenue service agent, poet; b. Broken Bow, Nebr., Aug. 22, 1954; s. Walter G. Sr. and Melva D. (Bristol) F.; m. Beverly R. Hromas, Dec. 22, 1973; children: Paul M., Elizabeth A. BA in English and History, Kearney State Coll., 1975, MA in History and English, 1978. English tchr. Medicine Valley High Sch., Curtis, Nebr., 1975-79; examiner IRS, Omaha, from 1979. Author: (poetry) Platte Valley Rev., Plainsongs, Whole Notes, The Scrivener, 1979—. Deacon Ch. of Christ, North Platte, Nebr., 1984. Recipient Nebraskaland Days Poetry award, 1979, 80, 81, 82, 83. Mem. Nat. Treas. Employees Union. Democrat. Avocations: hunting, fishing, gardening, photography, reading. Home: North Platte, Nebr. Died Dec. 7, 2006.

FLORES PÉREZ, FRANCISCO GUILLERMO, former president of El Salvador; b. Santa Ana, Oct. 17, 1959; m. Lourdes Rodriguez; children: Juan Marco, Gabriela. BA in Political sci., Amherst Coll., 1981; studied at Harvard U. and Trinity Coll. at Oxford U. Instr. philosophy and mgr. irrigation project for a community of 300 families, 1983—90; various ministerial and advisory positions for Pres. Cristiani and Pres. Armando Calderon Sol Govt. El Salvador, 1989—92, mem., Nat. Assembly, 1992—99, pres. Nat. Assembly, 1994—97, pres., 1999—2004. Died Jan. 30, 2016.

FLYNN, BARBARA SKWIRUT, elementary school educator; b. Newark, July 14, 1945; d. Stanley John and Aniela Josephine (Krzyzewska) Skwirut; m. David Michael Flynn, May 27, 1972; 1 child, Lauren. BA, Montclair State Coll., 1967. Cert. tchr., N.J. Clk. Hillside (N.J.) Pub. Libr., 1960-67, tchr., 1967-81, Westfield (N.J.) H.S., from 1985. Recipient Hillsboro Bd. Edn. mini-grant, 1981. Mem. NEA, N.J. Edn. Assn., Nat. Art Educators Assn., Art Educators N.J., Westfield Edn. Assn. (treas. 1993—), Alpha Delta Kappa (pres. 1975-78). Roman Catholic. Avocations: photography, calligraphy, desktop publishing. Home: Westfield, NJ. Died Jan. 9, 2007.

FLYNN, GEORGE RICHARD, poet; b. Bklyn., Aug. 14, 1926; s. Francis Joseph and Mary Josephine Flynn; m. Catherine Mary Regan, Oct. 31, 1945 (div. 1975); children: Margaret, Christine, William. BS English Edn., NYU, 1951. Ins. claims adjuster Gt. Am. Ins. Co., NYC, 1951—59; poet, 1959—72. Author: Selected Poems, 1965, The High Ground: New Poems, 1972, Zingers: 25 Poems, 1978. With USN, 1943—45. Avocations: physical therapy, softball, swimming, films, theater. Home: New York, NY. Died July 2, 2007.

FLYNN, MARGARET ALBERI, nutritionist, dietitian; b. Hurley, Wis., Nov. 22, 1915; d. Bernard and Anna (Chiado) Alberi; m. May 31, 1938 (dec. 1960); children: Phoebe, Timothy. BS, Coll. St. Caterine, St. Paul, 1937; MS, U. Iowa, 1938; PhD, U. Mo., 1960. Registered dietitian, diplomate Am. Bd. Nutrition, lic. dietitian Mo. Instr. Coll. St. Catherine, St. Paul, 1937-38; rsch. asst. pediatrics U. Iowa, Iowa City, 1939-40; instr. dietetics Levi Meml. Hosp., Hot Springs, Ark., 1942-46; teaching dietitian Holy Name Hosp., Teaneck, N.J., 1950-54; rsch. asst. pediatrics U. Mo., Columbia, 1961-63, asst. prof. nutrition and dietetics, 1966-69, assoc. prof. medicine, 1969-75, prof. medicine, 1975-86, prof. emeritus medicine, from 1986. Contbr. articles to profl. jours. Nat. Cancer Inst. grantee, 1977; Nat. Meat Bd./Wallace Genetic Found. grantee, 1978—; named Sesquicentennial Prof. U. Mo., 1989, Disting. Faculty awardee, 1988, Faculty Alumni award, 1976. Fellow Am. Coll. Nutrition; mem. Am. Soc. Clin. Nutrition, Am. Inst. Nutrition. Home: Cary, NC. Died July 20, 2007.

FLYNN, RAYMOND REGIS, press company executive; b. Steubenville, Ohio, July 2, 1921; BA in Econs., Notre Dame U., 1943. Rep. MacDonald Fluid Power, Rochester Hills, Mich., 1969-84, Burton Press Co., Inc., Rochester Hills, 1969-84, pres., from 1984, MacDonald Fluid Power, Rochester Hills, from 1984. With U.S. Army Infantry ETO, 1943-45. Decorated Bronze Star and other mil. awards. Mem. Soc. Mfg. Engrs., Am. LEgion, Saturday Club. Avocation: collecting antique automobiles. Home: Bloomfield Hills, Mich. Died May 16, 2007.

FOK, THOMAS DSO YUN, civil engineer; b. Canton, China, July 1, 1921; came to U.S., 1947, naturalized, 1956; s D. H. and C. (Tse) F.; m. Maria M.L. Liang, Sept. 18, 1949. B.Eng., Nat. Tung-Chi U., Szechuan, China, 1945; MS, U. Ill., 1948; MBA Dr. Nadler Money Marketeer scholar, NYU, 1950; PhD, Carnegie-Mellon U., 1956. Registered profl. engr., N.Y., Pa., Ohio, Ill., Ky., W.Va., Ind., Md., Fla. Structural designer Lummus Co., NYC, 1951-53; design engr. Richardson, Gordon & Assocs., cons. engrs., Pitts., 1956-58; assoc. prof. engring. Youngstown U., Ohio, 1958-67, dir. computing ctr. Ohio, 1963-67; ptnr. Cernica, Fok & Assocs., cons. engrs., Youngstown, Ohio, 1958-64; prin. Thomas Fok & Assocs., cons. engrs., Youngstown, Ohio, 1964-65; ptnr. Mosure-Fok & Syrakis Co., Ltd., cons. Engrs., Youngstown, Ohio, 1965-76; cons. engr. to Mahoning County Engr. Ohio, 1960-65; pres. Computing Systems & Tech., Youngstown, Ohio, 1967-72; chmn. Thomas Fok and Assocs., Ltd., cons. engrs., Youngstown, Ohio, from 1977. Contbr. articles to profl. jours. Trustee Pub. Libr. of Youngstown and Mahoning County, 1973—; trustee Youngstown State U., 1975-84, chmn., 1981-83; mem. Ohio State Bd. Registration for Profl. Engrs. and Surveyors, 1992-96. Recipient Walter E. and Caroline H. Watson Found. Disting. Prof.'s award Youngstown U., 1966, Outstanding Person award Mahoning Valley Tech. Socs. Council, 1987. Fellow ASCE; mem. Am. Concrete Inst., Internat. Assn. for Bridge and Structural Engring., Am. Soc. Engring. Edn., Nat. Soc. Profl. Engrs., AAAS, Soc. Am. Mil. Engrs., Ohio Acad. Sci., N.Y. Acad. Sci., Sigma Xi, Beta Gamma Sigma, Sigma Tau, Delta Pi Sigma Lodges: Rotary. Achievements include development of a design method by computer for a solid-ribbed tied, through arch Ft. Duquesne Bridge; development of Analysis of Continuous Truss by Digital Computer. Home: Youngstown, Ohio. Died Aug. 24, 2013.

FOLGER, WILLIAM MONTRAVILLE (BILL FOLGER), actor, journalist; b. Lockport, NY, May 13, 1916; s. Wayne Harrison and MayBelle Alzina (Upson) F.; widowed; children: Valerie Ely, W. Earl Folger (dec.). BS in gen. bus., U. Ill., 1938; MA in pol. sci., Syracuse U., 1975. News writer, reporter, editor National Broadcasting Co., Washington, 1944-46; news writer, newscaster Washington Post, Washington, 1946-48; news commentator Radio Station WISH, Indpls., 1950-51; pub. rels. dir. Coe Coll., Cedar Rapids, Iowa, 1952-53; trans. writer, columnist Courier-Express, Buffalo, N.Y., 1955, religion writer, columnist, 1959-73; journalism lectr. Syracuse (N.Y.) U., 1973-75; journalism prof. U. Northern Colo., Greeley, 1975-81; freelance actor Denver, from 1981. Precinet chmn. Dem. Party, Greeley, 1975-77, state conv. del., 1988; spokesman Am. Civil Liberties Union, Greeley, 1978-80; editor Colo. Environ. Coalition, 1990-97. Recipient Fine Reporting award Newspaper Guild, Buffalo, 1960, Interpretive Reporting award, 1961-62, Best Theatre Ensemble award Westword, Denver, 1988, Am. Scene award Am. Fedn. TV and Radio Artists, Denver, 1988; named to Colo. Journalism Hall of Fame, 1995. Mem. Soc. Profl. Journalists (Colo. chpt. pres. 1977-78), Colo. Audubon Soc. (sec. 1985-88), Colo. Environ. Coalition (sec. 1983-85, editor 1990-97), Religion Writers' Assn. of U.S. and Can. (pres. 1970-74). Presbyterian. Avocations: travel, music. Home: Ponte Vedra, Fla. Died Nov. 4, 2006.

FOOTE, EDWARD THADDEUS, II, former academic administrator, lawyer; b. Milw., Dec. 15, 1937; s. William Hamilton and Julia Stevenson (Hardin) F.; m. Roberta Waugh Fulbright, Apr. 18, 1964 (dec. May, 2015); children: Julia Foote LeStage, William, Thaddeus. BA, Yale U., 1959; LLB, Georgetown U., 1966; LLD (hon.), Washington U., St. Louis, 1981, Barry U., 1991; degree (hon.), Tokai U., Tokyo, 1984; LLD (hon.), Barry U., 1991. Bar: Mo. 1966. Reporter Washington Star, 1963-64, Washington Daily News, 1964-65; exec. asst. to chmn. Pa. Ave. Commn., Washington, 1965-66; assoc. Bryan, Cave, McPheeters & McRoberts, St. Louis, 1966-70; vice chancellor, gen. counsel, sec. to bd. trustees Washington U., St. Louis, 1970-73, dean Sch. Law, 1973-80, spl. adv. to chancellor and bd. trustees, 1980-81; pres. U. Miami, Coral Gables, Fla., 1981—2001. Mem. exec. com., bd. dirs. Am. Coun. Edn., 1986-88; chmn. citizens com. for sch. desegregation, St. Louis, 1980; chmn. desegregation monitoring and adv. com., St. Louis, 1980-81. Author: An Educational Plan for Voluntary Cooperation Desegregation of School in the St. Louis Met. area, 1981 Mem. Coun. on Fgn. Rels.; founding pres. bd. New City Sch., St. Louis, 1967-73; mem. gov.'s task force on reorganization State of Mo., 1973-74, steering com., chmn. governance com. Mo. Gov.'s Conf. on Edn., UN Assn. Greater St. Louis chpt., 1977-79, adv. com. Naval War Coll., 1979-82, Fla. Coun. of 100, Southern Fla. Metro-Miami Action Plan, exec. com. Miami Citizens Against Crime; founding chmn. Miami Coalition for a Drug Free Community, 1988—. Recipient Order of Sun (Peru). Democrat. Died Feb. 15, 2016.

FORD, MICHAEL P., management consultant; b. Chgo., Sept. 29, 1953; s. Henry B. and Mildred C. (Davis) F.; m. Holly M. Duescher, Oct. 18, 1988; children: Hannah M., Andrew H. BS, Elmhurst Coll., 1976; MBA, Chgo. U., 1985. Sales and mktg. exec. Humane Mfg., Baraboo, Wis., 1977-86; mktg. mgr. Medalist Forming, Madison, Wis., 1986-90; bus. cons. Ford Mktg., Baraboo, from 1990. Died Oct. 30, 2006.

FORD, SAMUEL GEORGE, sales executive; b. Newton, Iowa, Jan. 22, 1927; s. Samuel Hall and Marie (Miner) F.; m. Pauline VanAuken, Oct. 20, 1951; children: James M., Paul N., Janet L. BS in Mech. Engring., Iowa State U., 1951. Design engr. B-O-P div. Gen. Motors Corp., Kansas City, Kans., 1951-52, Detroit Transp. div. Gen. Motors Corp., 1952-54; design engr. sales Eagle Iron Works, Des Moines, Iowa, from 1954. Served with USAF, 1945. Mem. Nat. Sand and Gravel Assn. (engring. com. 1973—, chmn. mfrs. div. 1973-74), Nat. Stone Assn. (chmn. mfrs. div. 1985-87), Assn. Equipment Distbrs. (industry round table). Republican. Mem. Christian Ch. Avocations: church choir, golf, racquetball, auto racing, travel. Home: Des Moines, Iowa. Died Apr. 26, 2007.

FORD, WENDELL HAMPTON, former United States Senator from Kentucky; b. Owensboro, Ky., Sept. 8, 1924; s. Ernest M. and Irene (Schenk) F.; m. Jean Neel, Sept. 18, 1943; children: Shirley Jean (Mrs. Dexter), Steven. Student, U. Ky., 1942-43. Past ptnr. Gen. Ins. Agy., Owensboro; chief asst. to Gov. Bert T. Combs State of Ky., 1959-61, lt. gov., 1967-71, gov., 1971-74; mem. Ky. State Senate, 1966-67; US Senator from Ky., 1974-99; Democratic whip, 1991-99. Past chmn. Dem. Senatorial Campaign Com., Nat. Dem. Gov.'s Caucus; chmn. Dem. Nat. Campaign Com., 1976; ranking minority mem. Commerce, Sci. and Transp. Subcom. on Aviation, Rules and Adminstrn. Com.; mem. Energy and Natural Resources Com., Joint Com. on Printing, Senate Dem. Policy Com., Senate Dem. Steering and Coordination Com., Senate Dem. Tech. and Comm. Com.; cons. Dickstein Shapiro Served with AUS, 1944-46, Ky. N.G., 1949-62. Disting. fellow Martin Sch. Pub. Policy and Adminstr. U. Ky., 1999—. Mem.: Elk, Jaycees. Democrat. Baptist. Home: Owensboro, Ky. Died Jan. 22, 2015.

FORRESTER, STAN, retired mechanical engineer, writer; b. Carlisle, Eng., Oct. 21, 1931; came to U.S., 1963; s. Robert Edward and Annie (Farish) F.; m. Ann Judith Round, Apr. 21, 1951 (dec. Sept. 1984); m. Linda Jean Lidgett, Apr. 15, 1991. BS in Mech. Engring., Glasgow U., Scotland, 1953. Profl. engr., N.J. Cons. paper mill, 1962-94, ret. Author, pub.: (novels) Fool Circle, 1993, Fool Square, 1994, Fool Triangle, 1995, Fool Deck, 1997, Freedom on Choice, 1998. Mem. Masons. Avocations: bridge, sailing. Home: Clatskanie, Oreg. Died Mar. 27, 2007.

FORSTER, HARRIET HERTA, retired physicist; b. Vienna, June 20, 1917; d. Karl Samuel and Olga (Frankfurter) F.; m. Kurt Engelberg, Jan. 22, 1942 (div. 1952); m. George Frederick John Garlick, Jan. 6, 1977. Student, U. Vienna, 1936-38; MA, U. Calif., Berkeley, 1947, PhD, 1948. From instr. to prof. physics U. Southern Calif., LA, 1948—64, prof. physics, 1964—88, prof. emeritus LA, 1988—2014, chair dept. physics, 1962-64. Dep. chief investigator Nuclear Physics Lab., U. Southern Calif. Contbr. articles to profl. jours. Recipient Woman of Achievement award, 1981, Faculty Lifetime Achievement award, U. Southern Calif., 1988; grantee fellow, American Assn. Univ. Women, 1956—57. Fellow American Phys. Soc. Home: Los Angeles, Calif. Died Sept. 28, 2014.

FORSYTH, RAYMOND ARTHUR, civil engineer, consultant; b. Reno, Mar. 13, 1928; s. Harold Raymond and Fay Exona (Highfill) F.; m. Mary Ellen Wagner, July 9, 1950; children: Lynne, Gail, Alison, Ellen; m. Adeline Skog, Nov. 15, 1996. BS, Calif. State U., San Jose, 1952; MCE, Auburn U., 1958. Jr. engr., asst. engr. Calif. Divsn. Hwys., San Francisco, 1952-54; assoc. engr., sr. supervising, prin. engr. Calif. Dept. Transp., Sacramento, 1961-83, chief geotech. br., 1972-79, chief soil mechanics and pavement br., 1979-83; chief Transp. Lab., Sacramento, 1983-89. Cons., lectr. in field; geotech. engr. cons., 1989—. Contbr. articles to profl. jours. Served with USAF, 1954-56. Fellow ASCE (pres. Sacramento sect., chmn. Calif. coun. 1980-81); mem. Transp. Rsch. Bd. (chmn. embankments and earth slopes com. 1976-82, chmn. soil mechanics sect. 1982-88, chmn. group 2 coun. 1988-91), ASTM. Home: Sacramento, Calif. Died Mar. 11, 2013.

FORTENBERRY, ROBERT EARL, mechanical engineer; b. Brookhaven, Miss., Dec. 3, 1926; s. Fred S. and Bessie L. (Burch) F.; m. Gloria A. McCoy, Nov. 25, 1953; children: Robert E. Jr., Patricia, Cheryl. BE, Miss. State U., 1948; BME, La. State U., 1959. Registered profl. engr., La. Instr. agriculture Marion-Walthall High Sch., Darbun, Miss., 1948-49, Collins (Miss.) High Sch., 1949-51; lab. technician Exxon USA, Baton Rouge, 1952-59; sales and dist. engr. Mobil Oil Corp., New Orleans, Cleve, St. Louis, 1959-69; v.p. Sample Bros., Inc., New Orleans, 1969-76, pres. St. Louis, 1977-83, Refco Sales, Inc., St. Louis, from 1983, also bd. dirs. Sgt. U.S. Army, 1951-52. Mem. ASME, Soc. Naval Architects and Marine Engrs. (assoc.), St. Louis Propeller Club, East Side Rivermans Club, Shriners. Avocation: golf. Died Aug. 11, 2007.

FORZAGLIA, FRANK EUGENE, poet, publishing executive; b. NYC, July 7, 1940; s. Frank and Ada (Debenedetto) F.; m. Gloria Margrita Santos, Sept. 4, 1965; children: Ada, Gloria, Christopher. Pub. Oddjobs Pub., St. Petersburg, Fla., from 1992. Author of poetry. Home: New Prt Rchy, Fla. Died July 9, 2007.

FOSTER, LESLIE DONLEY, English educator, poet; b. Chgo., Oct. 19, 1930; s. Hollis Donley F. and Esther May (Lundy) Grim; m. Geraldine Pearl Raddatz, Jan. 27, 1968 (div. 1976); 1 child, Katharine Quinn. AB in Liberal Arts, U. Chgo., 1954, MA in English, 1960; postgrad., U. Toronto, 1962-63; PhD in English, U. Notre Dame, 1973. Instr. English Valparaiso (Ind.) U., 1959-62, 63-64, No. Mich. U., Marquette, 1967-71, asst. prof. English, 1971-75, assoc. prof. English, 1975-82, prof. English, from 1982. Vis. prof. English Njala U. Coll. U. Sierra Leone, West Africa, 1982-84, Birzeit U., Israel, 1975-77; panelist conf. on tenure Danforth Found., Ohio, 1973, Mich Conf. AAUP, 1973. Author: (poetry) Myths for Dorothy, 1992, also some 200 published poems; contbr. articles to profl. and lit. publs. and chpts. to books. Active ACLU, Mich., Ill., 1956—, del. upper peninsula, 1970-75. With USAF, 1951-53. Mem. AAUP (nat. coun. 1978-79, past pres. local chpt., bargainer, numerous state conf. and local offices, spl. com. non-tenured faculty 1972-75), Poetry Soc. Am. Democrat. Episcopalian. Avocation: poetry. Home: Marquette, Mich. Died June 13, 2007.

FOSTER, WALTER HERBERT, JR., real estate company executive; b. Belmont, Mass., Nov. 2, 1919; s. Walter Herbert and Gertrude (Sullivan) F.; m. Hazel Campbell, Aug. 7, 1942 (div. July 1979); children: Katherine D., Walter H. III, Stephen C., Banton T.; m. Nedra Ann Thompson, July 3, 1981; 1 child, Timothy John. Student, Harvard U., 1937-38; BS, U. Maine, 1947; grad. in real estate, Tri-State Inst., 1968-70. Cert. gen. appraiser, Maine. Owner, mgr. Foster Bros., Lyndeborough, N.H., 1947-56; ter. sales mgr. Beacon Milling Co., Oakland, Maine, 1956-64; v.p. Sherwood & Foster, Inc., Old Town, Maine, 1964-67; sales rep. Bangor (Maine) Real Estate, 1967-73; chief appraiser James W. Sewall Co., Old Town, 1970-73; mgr. J.F. Singleton Co., Bangor, 1973-80; pres. Coldwell Banker Am. Heritage, Bangor, from 1980. Dean Tri-State Inst., 1981; mem. Maine Real Estate Commn., 1987-93, chmn. 1991. Active Rep. Nat. Com., Washington, 1980; assessment bd. appeals Old Town, Maine, Holden Assessment Bd. of Appeals; bd. dirs. Penobscot Theatre, 1987-92, treas., 1989, mem. Maine State Bd. Property Rev., 1998—. Capt. USAF, 1941-46, USAFR ret., 1966. Mem. Nat. Assn. Realtors (bd. dirs. 1980-81), Maine Assn. Realtors (life, bd. dirs. 1976-80, pres. 1980, Realtor of Yr. 1984), Bangor Bd. Realtors (bd. dirs. 1973-74, pres. 1976, Realtor of Yr. 1976, 84), Maine Real Estate Commn. (chmn. 1991-92), Maine State Bd. Property Tax Review, Commn. to Study Real Estate Appraiser Cert. and Licensing, Nat. Assn. Rev. Appraisers, Am. Assn. Cert. Appraisers, Res. Officers Assn., Appraisal Inst. (assoc.), Nat. Assn. Ind. Fee Appraisers (sr.), Harvard Club of Ea. Maine (treas.), Rotary (bd. dirs. local club, Paul Harris fellow 2005), Am. Legion., Ret. Offices Assn., Mil. Officers Assn. Am. Episcopalian. Avocations: woodworking, gardening. Home: Holden, Maine. Died Mar. 20, 2007.

FOSTER, WILLIAM, instrument manufacturing company executive; b. Wimbledon, Surrey, July 13, 1947; s. Edward Waddington and Doris (Pearson) Foster; m. Geraldine Marion Bailey, Sept. 25, 1971; children: Janet, Clare, Christopher. BSEE, Imperial Coll. Sci. and Tech., U. London, 1969; ME in Microwave Engring., U. Sheffield, 1972. Chartered engr. & applications engr. Plessey Rsch., Caswell, Northern Ireland, 1972—75; applications mgr. Plessey Memories, Irvine, Calif., 1975—76; mktg. mgr. Europe Plessey Opto and Microwave, Towcester, Northern Ireland, 1976—78; product devel. mgr., 1978—80; comml. mgr. Marconi Instruments, Stevenage, Hertfordshire, England, 1980—83; mktg. mgr. St. Albans, Hertfordshire, from 1983. Contbr. articles to profl. jours. Vol. svcs. overseas Hardy Sr. Tech. Inst., Ceylon, Sri Lanka, 1970—71. Mem.: Instn. Elec. Engrs. Home: Bygrave SJ7 5DX, England. Died Jan. 4, 2007.

FOUKAL, DONALD CHARLES, electronics manufacturing executive; b. Cleve., Mar. 6, 1926; s. James A. and Leona M. (Kirchner) F.; m. Lois Mae Bell, June 25, 1955; children: Laura H., Diana H., Donald C. Jr. AB, Dartmouth Coll., 1946, MBA, 1949. Sales rep. Dunn & McCarthy Inc., Auburn, N.Y., 1950-61; gen. mgr. Fasson Div. Avery Products, Pasadena, Calif., 1961-72; pres., chief exec. officer Floyd Bell Inc., Columbus, Ohio, from 1972. Lt. USN, 1944-47. Republican. Home: Westerville, Ohio. Died Feb. 9, 2007.

FOURNIER, WALTER FRANK, real estate executive; b. Northampton, Mass., Feb. 26, 1912; s. Frank Napoleon and Marie Ann F.; m. Ella Mae Karrey, May 16, 1938; children: Margaret Irene, Walter Karrey. BS in Mktg., Boston U., 1939; postgrad., Anchorage Community Coll., 1963-64, Alaska Pacific U., 1964-65. Coin sales supt. Coca Cola Co., Springfield, Mass., 1946-48; sales coord. for pre-fabricated homes Sears Roebuck & Co., Western Mass., 1948-49; wholesale sales rep. Carl Wiseman Steel and Aluminum Co., Great Falls, Mont., 1949-51; supt. City Electric Co., Anchorage, 1951-52; owner, adminstr. Acme Electric Co., Anchorage, 1953-64; appraiser Gebhart & Peterson, Anchorage, 1964-68; broker, owner Walter F. Fournier & Assocs., Anchorage, from 1968. Pres. Alaska Mortgage Cons., Anchorage, 1968-69; owner Alaska Venture Capital, 1981—. Pres. Fairview Community Council, Anchorage, 1980-81. Served with U.S. Army, 1928-31, with USN, 1944-45, PTO. Recipient Spl. Recognition award HUD, 1967. Mem. Review Mortgage Underwriters, Inst. Bus. Appraisers, Internat. Soc. Financiers, Soc. Exchange Counselors (rep. 1970), Alaska Creative Real Estate Assn. (pres. 1978, Gold Pan award 1988), Alaska Million Plus Soc. (pres. 1983). Lodges: KC. Roman Catholic. Avocations: weightlifting, flying, fishing. Died Nov. 15, 2006.

FOUTZ, DEVIN JON, recording engineer; b. Farmington, N.Mex., May 29, 1970; s. E.J. and Ruth Marie (Marshall) F. Student, N.Mex. State U., 1988-89; degree in recording arts, Full Sail Ctr. Recording Arts, Orlando, Fla., 1990. Intern in promotion Island Records, LA, from 1990; intern in artist and repertoire I.R.S. Records, Universal City, Calif., from 1990; with One on One Recording Studios, North Hollywood, Calif., from 1990, Summa Music Group, LA, from 1991, Record Plant, Hollywood, Calif., from 1991. Home: Farmington, N.Mex. Died Feb. 1, 2007.

FOWLER, DAVID COVINGTON, language educator; b. Louisville, Jan. 3, 1921; s. Earle Broadus and Susan Amelia (Covington) F.; m. Mary Gene Stith, Jan. 28, 1943 (dec., July 22, 2005); children: Sandra Fowler Berryman (dec.), Caroline F. Aaron. BA in English, U. Fla., 1942; MA in English, U. Chgo., 1947, PhD in English, 1949. Prof. English U. Wash., Seattle, 1952-92, prof. emeritus, from 1992. Author: The Bible in Early English Literature, 1976, The Bible in Middle English Literature, 1984, John Trevisa, 1993, The Life and Times of John Trevisa, 1995, The Governance of Kings and Princes: John Trevisa's Middle English Translation of the De Regimine Principum of Aegidius Romanus, 1997; contbr. articles to profl. jours. Lt. (s.g.) USNR, 1942-46. ACLS scholar U. Pa., 1951-52; Guggenheim fellow, 1962-63, 75-76. Mem. AAR/SBL N.W. (pres. 1974), Medieval Assn. of Pacific (pres. 1980-82), Modern Lang. Assn., UW Folklore Rsch. Group (chmn. 1981-87), Calif. Folklore Soc. Home: Seattle, Wash. Died Apr. 30, 2007.

FOWLES, DEBORAH MARIE, controller; b. Rockland, Maine, Apr. 4, 1954; d. Donald Clyde and Cora M. (Rowling) F. BS in Youth Leadership, Brigham Young U., 1976; BS in Mgmt. Studies, U. Md., 1990. Corp. adminstr.

Program Resources, Inc., Rockville and Annapolis, Md., 1976-83; mgr. acctg. and adminstrn. Pathology Assocs., Inc., Frederick, Md., 1983-89, contr., 1989-95, also officer and bd. dirs.; contr., officer Pathology Assocs. Internat., Frederick, Md., from 1995. Mem. NAFE, Inst. Mgmt. Accts., U. Md. Alumni Assn. (vol. mentor 1992—). Republican. Avocations: writing, travel, ornithology. Home: Georgetown, Maine. Died Feb. 23, 2007.

FOX, RAYMOND CHARLES, film exhibitor; b. NYC, July 6, 1930; s. Walter Donald and Viola Virginia (Bradley) F.; m. Lucille Marie Saccocio, June 4, 1955; children: Lynn Marie, Laura Jeanne, John Raymond, Joanne Mary, Judi Ann, Carol Jane. BS in Econs., Villanova U., 1952; MBA, NYU, 1957. Sr. v.p., dir. Plitt Theatres, Inc., LA, 1974-85, Snowscan Corp., LA, 1985-94, PEG, LA, from 1985; pres., dir. Plitt Amusement Co., LA, from 1990. Cons. in field. Trustee Plitt So. Theatres Employee Trust, L.A., 1982—. Cpl. U.S. Army, 1953-55, Korea. Mem. Variety Club, Motion Picture Pioneers, Will Rogers Fund. Avocations: golf, carpentry, bowling, tennis. Home: Palos Verdes Peninsula, Calif. Died July 12, 2007.

FRADKIN, DAVID MILTON, physicist, researcher; b. Los Angeles, Apr. 20, 1931; s. Aaron and Annie (Gordon) F.; m. Dorothea Edna Fairweather, Nov. 25, 1959; children: Lee, Mark, Steven. BS, U. Calif., Berkeley, 1954; PhD, Iowa State U., 1963. Exploitation engr. Shell Oil Co., Los Angeles, 1954-56; research assoc. Iowa State U. and Ames Lab., Ames, Iowa, 1963-64; NATO postdoctoral fellow U. Rome, 1964-65; asst. prof. physics Wayne State U., Detroit, 1965-69, assoc. prof., 1969-75, prof., 1975-94, chmn. dept. physics, 1981-91; prof. emeritus, from 1994. Del. Argonne (Ill.) Univs. Assn., 1981-83; vis. fellow U. Durham, Eng., 1991-92. Contbr. articles to profl. jours. Vice chmn. adv. bd. Detroit pub. schs., 1972-73; trustee Detroit Sci. Ctr., 1986-94. Recipient award Probus Club, 1973; sr. postdoctoral fellow U. Edinburgh, Scotland, 1977-78. Mem. Am. Phys. Soc., Sigma Xi. Avocations: tennis, fishing, golf, genealogy. Home: Portland, Oreg. Died July 23, 2014.

FRANK, CLAUDE, pianist; b. Nürnberg, Fed. Republic of Germany, Dec. 24, 1925; came to U.S., 1941; Louis and Irma (Ehrlich) F.; m. Lilian Margaret Kallir, Aug. 29, 1959 (dec. 2004); 1 child, Pamela. Grad., Columbia U., 1948. Prof. music Bennington (Vt.) Coll., 1948-55; instr. piano Mannes Coll. Music, NYC, from 1963; prof. piano Yale U., New Haven, 1971—88; instr. Curtis Inst. Music, Phila. Vis. prof. music Kans. U., Lawrence Soloist most maj. symphony orchs.; recitalist six continents; appearanced at most music festivals including Aspen, Tanglewood, Marlboro; recs. include piano sonatas with Pamela Frank, by Beethoven for RCA, several piano concertos by Mozart, chamber music by Mozart, Schubert, Brahms.; co-author: (with Hawley Roddick) The Music That Saved My Life: From Hitler's Germany to the World's Concert Stages Served to sgt. inf. U.S. Army, 1944-46, ETO, PTO. Mem.: Century Assn. (N.Y.). Jewish. Home: New York, NY. Died Dec. 27, 2014.

FRANKEL, JAMES BURTON, retired lawyer; b. Chgo., Feb. 25, 1924; s. Louis and Thelma (Cohn) F.; m. Louise Untermyer, Jan. 22, 1956; children: Nina, Sara, Simon. Student, U. Chgo., 1940-42; BS, U.S. Naval Acad., 1945; LLB, Yale U., 1952; MPA, Harvard U., 1990. Bar: Calif. 1953. Mem. Steinhart, Goldberg, Feigenbaum & Ladar, San Francisco, 1954-72; of counsel Cooper, White & Cooper, San Francisco, 1972-97; ret., 2000. Sr. fellow, lectr. in law Yale U., 1971—72; lectr. Stanford U. Law Sch., 1973—75; vis. prof. U. Calif. Law Sch., 1975—76, lectr., 1992—2000, U. San Francisco Law Sch., 1994—2000; adj. asst. prof. Hastings Coll. Law, 1996—2000. Pres. Coun. Civic Unity of San Francisco Bay Area, 1964-66; chmn. San Francisco Citizens Charter Revision Com., 1968-70; mem. San Francisco Pub. Schs. Commn., 1975-76; trustee Natural Resources Def. Coun., 1972-77, 79-92, staff atty., 1977-79, hon. trustee, 1992—; chmn. San Francisco Citizens Energy Policy Adv. Com., 1981-82. Mem. ABA, Calif. Bar Assn. Died Feb. 2, 2015.

FRANKLIN, BERNICE ANNETTE See TANNENBAUM, BERNICE

FRANKLIN, WAYNE LEONARD, telecommunications executive; b. Wichita, Kans., June 7, 1955; s. Earl L. and Barbara (Walker) F.; m. Ethel Mae Peppers, Sept. 12, 1981; children: Wayne Michael, James Nathaniel BS in Polit. Sci., Kans. State U., 1978. Asst. mgr. customer svcs. Southwestern Bell Telephone Co., Mission, Kans., 1978-81, asst. mgr. community rels. Salina, Kans., 1981-83, staff specialist Topeka, 1983-84, constituency rels. area mgr., 1984-90, area mgr. pub. affairs, 1990-92, area mgr. external affairs Manhattan, Kans., from 1992. Bd. chmn. Topeka Met. Transit Authority, Topeka, 1986-92; sch. bd. mem. Topeka Sch. Bd. #501, 1991-92. Mem. Sunset Optimist Club. Democrat. Home: Olathe, Kans. Died Apr. 13, 2007.

FRANKS, DAVID A., computer engineer; b. Washington, June 24, 1929; s. David Ransom and Lela Becton (Duncan) F.; m. Erta Mae Williford, June 20, 1953; children: David Bryan, Kathleen Elva. BS in Math., Howard U., 1951, MS in Math., 1952; postgrad., U. Ill., 1953-54. 1st lt. U.S. Army, 1953-57; various engring. positions Westinghouse Electric Corp., Balt., 1957-92, mgr. applications software, 1968-91; cons. Dafer Enterprises, Columbia, Md., from 1992. Mem. Assn. for Computing Machinery, Data Processing Mgmt. Assn., Balt. Computer Users Group, Capital Computer Users Group. Home: Columbia, Md. Died Feb. 8, 2007.

FRANZ, MARIAN CLAASSEN, elementary school educator; b. Newton, Kans., Oct. 12, 1930; d. Ernest G. and Justine (Wiebe) Claassen; m. Delton W. Franz, Dec. 12, 1932; children: Gregory, Gayle, Coretta. BA, Bethel Coll., Newton, 1954; M Religious Edn., Mennonite Bibl. Sem., Chgo., 1957. Elem. sch. tchr., Whitewater, Kans., 1951-52, Hillsboro, Kans., 1954-55; ch. sch. supr. Ch. Fedn. Greater Chgo., 1957-63; dir. Dunamis, Washington, 1970-80. Exec. dir. Nat. Campaign for a Peace Tax Fund; vice chair Conscience and Peace Tax Internat. Author: Questions That Refuse to Go Away, 1991; contbr. chpts. to books, 1990—. Mennonite. Avocations: swimming, walking. Home: Washington, DC. Died Nov. 17, 2006.

FRASER, JOHN MALCOLM, former Australian Prime Minister; b. Melbourne, Vic, Australia, May 21, 1930; s. John Neville and Una Arnold (Woolf) F.; m. Tamara Sandford Beggs, Feb. 12, 1956; children: Mark, Angela, Hugh, Phoebe. MA, fellow, Magdalen Coll., Oxford, UK, 1982; LLD (hon.), U. S.C., 1981; LittD (hon.), Deakin U., 1989. Min. Army Fed. Govt., Australia, 1966-68, min. for edn. and sci., 1968-69, min. for def., 1969-71, min. for edn., 1971-72; prime min. Australia, 1975-83; parliamentary Leader of Liberal Party, Australia, 1975-83; chmn. Care, Australia, from 1987; pres. Care Internat., 1990-95, v.p., 1995-99. Co-chmn. Commonwealth Eminent Persons Group on South Africa, 1986; chmn. UN Sec.-Gen.'s expert group on African Commodity Problems, 1989-90, Interaction Coun. of Former Heads of Govt., 1996-2015. Named Appointed Mem. of Privy Coun., 1976, Companion of Honour, 1977, Hon. v.p. Oxford Soc., 1983, sr. adj. fellow CSIS, 1983, Ctr. for Internat. Affairs, Harvard U., 1985, Hon. V.P. Royal Commonwealth Soc., 1983, Companion of the Order of Australia, 1988; recipient B'Nai B'rith Pres.'s Gold medal for Humanitarian Svc., 1980. Mem. Melbourne Club. Died Mar. 20, 2015.

FREBERG, STAN(LEY) VICTOR (VICTOR FREBERG), satirist; b. Los Angeles, Calif., Aug. 7, 1926; s. Victor Richard and Evelyn Dorothy (Conner) F.; m. Donna Andresen(dec. 2000); children: Donna Jean, Donavan Stanley. Recording artist Capitol Records, Hollywood, Rhino Records; pres. Freberg Ltd., 1958. Author: It Only Hurts When I Laugh, 1988; comedy albums include Stan Freberg Presents The U.S.A., Child's Garden of Freberg, St. George and the Dragonet, Stan Freberg, 1990, Greater Hits, 1993, The Stan Freberg Show, 1994, Stan Freberg Presents The U.S.A. Vol.II (nom. Grammy 1996); actor, writer; children's TV show Time for Beany (Winner 3 Emmys); creator, The Stan Freberg Show, CBS, 1957, The New Stan Freberg Show!, Nat. Public Radio, 1991; works located in Ctr. for Advertising Hist. Nat. Mus. of Am. Hist., Washington and Mus. of TV and Radio, N.Y.C. Mem. founding bd. of govs. Nat. Acad. of Recording Arts and Scis. Recipient Best Written Comedy Radio Show, CBS, 1957, Grammy award 1958, Gold Medal N.Y. Art Dirs., 21 Clios, Cannes Film Festival, Grand Prize, Venice Film Festival; star Hollywood Walk of Fame; named to Radio Hall of Fame, Chgo. Mus. Broadcasting, 1995. Mem. ASCAP, Songwriters Hall of Fame, Soc. Composers and Lyricists, Writers Guild of Am., Dirs. Guild of Am. Home: Los Angeles, Calif. Died Apr. 7, 2015.

FREDERICK, ROBERT MELVIN, retired farm organization executive; b. Wadsworth, Ohio, Feb. 1, 1923; s. Llewellyn Rorthrock and Golda May (Joycox) F.; m. Rosemary Rothgary, Feb. 14, 1955; children: Pamela Sue, Mark Llewllyn. BA, Ohio State U., 1948. Horticulturist family farm, Wadsworth, 1948-56; ext. horticulturist Purdue U., Vincennes, Ind., 1957-59; exec. sec. Am. Vegetable Growers Assn., Washington, 1959-61; gen. mgr. Fla. Flower Assn., Ft. Myers, 1961-63, Fla. Growers Coop., Ft. Myers, 1963-66; pres. Ruke Transport, Ft. Myers, 1966-67; sales mgr. Green Thumb Products, Toledo, 1967-68; legis. dir. Nat. Grange, Washington, 1968-96, dir. adminstrn., from 1996. Mem. agr. policies adv. com. USDA/U.S. Trade Rep., Washington, 1970-80, mem. fruit and vegetable com., 1970-84; mem. agr. census adv. com. Dept. Commerce, Washington, 1971-85. Mem. Medina County (Ohio) Rep. Com., 1956. Sgt. USMCR, 1942-45, PTO. Recipient Alumni Disting. Svc. award Ohio State U., 1995, Agr. Frat. Centennial hon. Alpha Zeta, 1997. Mem. Nat. Planning Assn. (food and agr. com.), Nat. Grange (7th degree, past master, ec., exec. com. Potomac chpt.). Avocation: gardening. Home: Arlington, Va. Died Feb. 1, 2007.

FREEDMAN, MARVIN IRVING, mathematics educator; b. Boston, Oct. 4, 1939; s. Maurice and Rose (Kane) F.; m. Corey E. Langberg, Apr. 24, 1966; children: Emily M., Nicole L. BS, MIT, 1960; MA, Brandeis U., 1962, PhD, 1964. Instr. math. U. Calif., Berkeley, 1964-66; scientist NASA, Cambridge, Mass., 1967-70; assoc. prof. math. then prof. Boston U., from 1970, chmn. dept. math., from 1991. Vis. prof. math. Brown U., Providence, R.I., 1968-69. Mem. Am. Math. Soc., Math. Assn. Am., Soc. Indsl. and Applied Math. Democrat. Jewish. Home: Wellesley, Mass. Died Apr. 26, 2007.

FREEDMAN, MONROE HENRY, lawyer, educator; b. Mt. Vernon, NY, Apr. 10, 1928; s. Chauncey and Dorothea (Kornblum) F.; m. Audrey Willock, Sept. 24, 1950 (dec. 1998); children: Alice Freedman Korngold, Sarah Freedman Izquierdo (dec. 2014), Caleb (dec. 1998), Judah. AB cum laude, Harvard U., 1951, LLB, 1954, LLM, 1956. Bar: Mass. 1954, Pa. 1957, D.C. 1960, U.S. Dist. Ct. (ea. dist. N.Y.), U.S. Ct. Appeals (D.C. cir.) 1960, U.S. Supreme Ct. 1960, U.S. Ct. Appeals (2d cir.) 1968, N.Y. 1978, U.S. Ct. Appeals (9th cir.) 1982, U.S. Ct. Appeals (11th cir.) 1986, U.S. Ct. Appeals (Fed. cir.) 1987. Assoc. Wolf, Block, Schorr & Solis-Cohen, Phila., 1956-58; ptnr. Freedman & Temple, Washington, 1969-73; dir. Stern Community Law Firm, Washington, 1970-71; prof. law George Washington U., 1958-73; dean Hofstra Law Sch., Hempstead, NY, 1973-77, prof. law, 1973—2015, Howard Lichtenstein Disting. prof. legal ethics, 1989—2003; Drinko-Baker & Hostetler chair in law Cleve. State U., 1992; CFO Olive Tree Mktg. Internat., 1998—2004; vis. prof. Georgetown U. Law Ctr., 2007—12, Judges & Lawyers Conf., Toronto, Canada, 2010. Faculty asst. Harvard U. Law Sch., 1954-56, instr. trial advocacy and legal ethics, 1978-2010; lectr. on lawyers' ethics; exec. dir. U.S. Holocaust Meml. Coun., 1980-82, gen. counsel, 1982-83, sr. adviser to chmn., 1982-87; cons. US Commn. on Civil Rights, 1960-64, Neighborhood Legal Services Program, 1970; legis. cons. to Senator John L. McClellan, 1959; spl. com. on courtroom conduct NYC Bar Assn., 1972; exec. dir. Criminal Trial Inst., 1965-66; expert witness on legal ethics state and fed. ct. proceedings, US Senate and House Coms., US Dept. Justice, FDIC; spl. investigator Rochester Inst. Tech., 1991; reporter Am. Lawyer's Code of Conduct, 1979-81; mem. Arbitration panel US Dist. Ct. (ea. dist.) NY, 1986—; Inaugural Wickwire lectr. Dalhousie Law Sch., N.S., 1992; lectr. SC Bar Found., 1993, numerous profl. confs; adv. subgroup on ethics U.S. Dist. Ct. (ea. dist.) NY, 1994-96. Author: Contracts, 1973, Lawyers' Ethics in an Adversary System, 1975 (ABA gavel award, cert. of merit 1976), Teacher's Manual Contracts, 1978, American Lawyer's Code of Conduct, Public Discussion Draft, 1980, Understanding Lawyers' Ethics, 1990, (with Abbe Smith)4th ed., 2010, (with Eric Freedman) Group Defamation and Freedom of Speech-The Relationship Between Language and Violence, 1995, (with Abbe Smith) How Can You Represent Those People, 2012; columnist Cases and Controversies, Am. Lawyer Media, 1990-96, mem. panel acad. contbrs. Black's Law Dictionary, 2002-03; television appearances include Donohue, CNN Money Line, CBS 60 Minutes, CNN Late Edition, Court TV, C-SPAN, O'Reilly Factor, Hannity and Colmes, Fox News Powerplay, and others; contbr. articles to profl. jours. Pro bono cons. in death penalty and Guantanamo cases. With USN, 1946—48. Recipient Martin Luther King Jr. Humanitarian award, 1987, The Lehman-LaGuardia award for Civic Achievement, 1996, Alumni Outstanding Prof. award Hofstra Law Sch., 2006, David Diamond award, 2010 Fellow Am. Bar Found.; mem. ABA (ethics adv. to chair criminal justice sect. 1993-95, ethics and profl. responsibility com. 2005, Michael Franck award 1998), ACLU (nat. bd. dir. 1970-80, nat. adv. coun. 1980—, spl. litigation counsel 1971-73), Am. Law Inst. (consultative group on the law governing lawyers, 1990-99, consultative group on Uniform Comml. Code art. 2 1990-2002), Soc. Am. Law Tchrs. (mem. governing bd. 1974-79, exec. com. 1976-79, chmn. com. on profl. responsibility 1974-79, 87-90), ABA (vice chmn. ethical considerations com. criminal justice sect. 1989-90, ethics advisor to chmn. criminal justice sect., 1993-96), N.Y. State Bar Assn. (com. on legal edn. and admission to bar 1988-92, criminal justice sect. com. on profl. responsibility, 1990-92, award for Dedication to Scholarship and pub. svc. 1997, Sanford D. Levy award for scholarship on profl. ethics 2005, award for edn. in criminal justice 2006), Assn. Bar City N.Y. (com. on profl. responsibility 1987-90, com. on profl. and jud. ethics 1991-92), Fed. Bar Assn. (chmn. com. on profl. disciplinary standards and procedures 1970-71), Am. Soc. Writers on Legal Subjects (mem. com. on constitution and bylaws 1999-2000), Am. Jewish Congress (nat. governing coun. 1984-86), Am. Arbitration Assn. (arbitrator, nat. panel arbitrators 1964—, cert. svc. award 1986), Nat. Network on Right to Counsel (exec. bd., exec. com. 1986-90), Nat. Right to Counsel Com., Nat. Prison Project (steering com. 1970-90), Nat. Assn. Criminal Def. Lawyers (vice chmn. ethics adv. com. 1991-93, co-chmn., 1994), Am. Bd. Criminal Lawyers (hon., Special Tribute award, 2011). Democrat. Jewish. Died Feb. 26, 2015.

FREITAG, CAROL WILMA, political scientist; Diploma in Dental Hygiene, Northwestern U., 1959; BA, Purdue U., Hammond, Ind., 1988. Registered dental hygienist, Ill. Pvt. practice dental hygiene Henry W. Freitag, D.D.S., Homewood, Ill., 1959-85; mem. group practice Chgo., 1970; faculty, interim dir. dental hygiene Prairie State Coll., Chgo. Heights, Ill., 1971-72; pvt. practice James J. Kreuz, D.D.S., Homewood, 1985-90. Contbr. articles to profl. jour. Chair US Constn. Bicentennial Commn., Village of Matteson, Ill., 1986-89; pres. Matteson Hist. Soc., 1987-89; panel spkr. South Suburban Heritage Assn., Homewood, 1990. Calumet rep. Bicentennial Com. Purdue U., 1988; vis. com. Northwestern Dental Sch., 1997-98; mem. centennial celebration com. Bloom Twp. HS, 2000; program chair, class 50th reunion mem. Hist. Columbia SC Found. 2003-08. Recipient Key to City, Village of Matteson, 1990, Svc. award Northwestern U., 1980, Good Neighbor award Village of Matteson, Ill., 1990, Outstanding Alumni 1950's Decade award Bloom Twp. H.S., 2000. Mem. Am. Dental Hygienists' Assn. (chair Ann. Session Program 1975), Ill. Dental Hygienists Assn. (pres. 1968-69, bd. dirs., Merit award 1979), G.V. Black Soc. (leader, pres. 1997-2001), Evelyn E. Maas Soc. (pres. 1989-90, bd. dirs., Merit award 1993), Northwestern Dental Sch. Alumni Assn. (bd. dirs. 1969-2001, pres. 1977-78, v.p. 1976-77, 90-93), Acad. Polit. Sci., First Presbyn. Ch., Chgo. Heights (deacon 2008-10), Daughters Am. Revolution (Dewalt Mehlin Chapt. Sec. 2012-2013), Homewood Historical Soc. (sec. 2011-2013, bd. dirs. 2010-2013), Sigma Phi Alpha, Alpha Chi. Avocation: travel. Home: Tinley Park, Ill. Died June 15, 2014.

FRENCH, LARRY L., counseling center director; b. San Angelo, Tex., Oct. 2, 1948; s. Lester L. and Ann (Newton) F.; m. Beverly J. Brink, Nov. 20, 1976; children: Robin, Jennifer, Leah, David. BA, U. N.C., Charlotte, 1973; MA, Azusa Pacific U., Calif., 1978. Lic. profl. counselor. Co-dir. Reach Out Counseling Ctr., Brandon, Fla., 1974-76; prin. Reach Out Sch., Brandon, 1975-76; co-dir. Arcadia (Calif.) Christian Counseling Ctr., 1977-79; dir. Growing Edge Counseling Ctr., Arcadia, 1979-84; dir., marriage, family and child counselor Va. Ctr. for Family Rels., Charlottesville, from 1986. Cons. pvt. schs., Arcadia, 1976-91, employee asst. programs, Pasadena, Calif. and Va., 1979-91;

writer newspaper column Dope on Drugs; tchr., lectr. workshops, classes, seminars. Cons. Parent Alert, Arcadia, 1983, Charlottesville Pregnancy Ctr., 1991. With USCG, 1966-70. Mem. Am. Assn. for Marriage Family Therapy (clin., approved supr.), Va. Clin. Counselor Assn. (clin., area rep. 1989-90), Christian Assn. for Psychol. Studies. Avocations: guitar, camping, tennis, sports. Home: Charlottesville, Va. Died June 13, 2007.

FRENZEL, BILL (WILLIAM ELDRIDGE FRENZEL), former United States Representative from Minnesota; b. St. Paul, July 31, 1928; s. Paul and Paula (Schlegel) F.; m. Ruth Purdy, June 9, 1951; children: Deborah, Pamela, Melissa. BA, Dartmouth, 1950, MBA, 1951; LLD (hon.), Hamline U., 2002. Mem. exec. com. Hennepin County, Minn., 1966—67; pres. Mpls. Terminal Warehouse Co., 1966-70, Northern Waterway Terminals Corp., 1965-70; mem. Minn. House of Reps., 1962-70, US Congress from 3rd Dist. Minn., Washington, 1971—91. Apptd. Nat. Econ. Commn., 1988; Lt. USNR, 1951-54, Korea. Recipient Order of the Rising Sun, Govt. of Japan, 2000; named a Friend of Sci., Nat. Coalition of Sci. & Technology, 1984. Mem. US Capitol Hist. Soc. (exec. bd.); Clubs: Rotarian, Minneapolis Republican. Home: Mc Lean, Va. Died Nov. 17, 2014.

FRENZEL, FRANCES JOHNSON, nurse, educator, real estate broker, poet; b. Bedford, Va., Feb. 2, 1911; d. J. James and Willie Calpernia (Markham) Johnson; m. Paul H. Frenzel, Dec. 21, 1933 (dec. 1990). RN, Wash. Adventist Hosp., Takoma Park, Md., 1932; BS, Columbia Union Coll., 1933; real estate license, Glendale CC, Calif., 1968. Cert. real estate broker. RN supr. Glendale (Calif.) Adventist Med. Ctr., 1933-34; instr. various flower show schs., Nat. Coun. State Garden Clubs, U.S. & Mex., 1951-98; flower design instr. Edinburg (Tex.) Coll., 1953. Founder, chmn. World Flower Festival L.A. Garden Club and Greater L.A. Dist. Calif. Garden Clubs, Inc., 1962-98; lectr. in many states including Hawaii. Author: Arrangements on Parade, 1950; contbr. poems to books and nat. and state mags.; contbr. photographs of flower arrangements to profl. jours. Mem. City of Glendale Beautification adv. council, from 1974, L.A. County Med. Auxiliary Glendale, from 1956, pres., 1968—69; founder The Golden Garden Angel fund, 1998; election precinct officer L.A. County, Glendale, 1956—2000. Recipient numerous Garden Club awards, 1962—, Editor's Choice award, 1999, Lifetime Beautification Achievement award, City of Glendale and Com. for a Clean and Beautiful Glendale, 2001, various other awards from organizations and Los Angeles County; named Guardian Angel, Staff Golden Gardens Mag., 2001; grantee Proton Treatment Ctr., Loma Linda (Calif.) Med. Ctr. Mem.: Internat. Soc. Poetry, L.A. County Med. Assn. Alliance (pres. Dist. IV 1968—69), L.A. Garden Club (pres. 1960—62), Judges Coun. Orange County, Judges Coun. So. Calif. (chmn. 1978—80), Internat. Soc. Poets, Ikebana Internat. (L.A. chpt.), Greater L.A. Dist. Calif. Gardens Club (dir. 1962—64), Nat. Coun. State Garden Clubs Inc. (life), Calif. Garden Clubs Inc. (life; pub. rels. chmn. from 1999, founder golden gardens angel fund for bd. from 1999, bd. dirs., Woman of Yr. 2002). Avocations: flower arranging, gardening, gourmet cooking, interior decorating. Died Nov. 28, 2006.

FREY, GLENN (GLENN LEWIS FREY), songwriter, vocalist, guitarist; b. Detroit, Nov. 6, 1948; s. Edward Frey; m. Cindy Frey; children: Taylor, Deacon, Otis. Former band mem. The Mushrooms, Four of Us, The Subterraneans, Heavy Metal Kids; founding mem., guitarist, keyboardist, vocalist The Eagles, 1971—2016; co-founder Mission Records. Musician: (albums) (with Eagles) Eagles, 1972, Desperado, 1973, On the Border, 1974, One of These Nights, 1975, Hotel California, 1976 (VH1's 100 Greatest Albums, 2001), The Long Run, 1979, Eagles Live, 1980, Hell Freezes Over, 1994 (Am. Music award, Favorite Rock Album, 1996), Long Road Out of Eden, 2007, (solo albums) No Fun Aloud, 1982, The Allnighter, 1984, Soul Searchin', 1988, Strange Weather, 1992, Glen Frey Live, 1993, Solo Collection, 1995, After Hours, 2012, (songs) (with Eagles) Lyin' Eyes, 1975 (Grammy award for Best Group Pop Vocal Performance, 1976), Hotel California, 1976 (Grammy award for Record of Yr., 1978, VH1's 100 Greatest Rock Songs, 2000, Rolling Stone & MTV's 100 Greatest Pop Songs, 2000), New Kid in Town, 1976 (Grammy award for New Kid in Town, 1978), Heartache Tonight, 1979 (Grammy award for Best Group Rock Vocal Performance, 1980), How Long, 2007 (Grammy award for Best Group Vocal Country Performance, 2008), I Dreamed There Was No War, 2007 (Grammy award for Best Pop Instrumental Performance, 2009); composer (theme song): (TV series) Miami Vice, Body by Jake, 1988; actor: (TV series) Wiseguy, 1988, South of Sunset, 1993; (films) Let's Get Harry, 1986, Jerry Maguire, 1996. Recipient Favorite Rock Group award, Am. Music Awards, 1981, 1996, Favorite Adult Contemporary Artist award, 1996, Favorite Rock Album award, 1996, Kennedy Ctr. Honors (as mem. of The Eagles), John F. Kennedy Ctr. Performing Arts, Washington, 2015; named one of Greatest Artists of Rock & Roll, VH1, 1998, The Immortals: The 100 Greatest Artists of All Time, Rolling Stone, 2004; named to Rock and Roll Hall of Fame (with Eagles), 1998. Died Jan. 18, 2016.

FRI, ROBERT WHEELER, retired museum director; b. Kansas City, Kans., Nov. 16, 1935; s. Homer O. and Cora Ruth (Wheeler) F.; m. Jean Landon, Jan. 16, 1965; children: Perry, Sean, Kirk. BA, Rice U., 1957; MBA, Harvard Bus. Sch., 1959. Assoc. McKinsey & Co., Washington, 1963-68, prin., 1968-71, 73-75; dep. adminstr. EPA, Washington, 1971-73, acting adminstr., 1973; dep. adminstr. for energy devel. Energy Rsch. & Development Adminstrn. (ERDA), Washington, 1975-77, acting adminstr., 1977; head U.S. del. to IAEA, Washington, 1977; pres. Energy Transition Corp., 1978-86; pres., sr. fellow Resources for the Future, 1986-95; dir. Nat. Mus. Natural History, 1996-2001. Mem. Sec. Energy Advisory Bd., 1990—95, President's Commn. on Environmental Quality, 1991—92, Nat. Petroleum Coun., 1994—2014; bd. dirs. American Electric Power Co., 1995—2008, Electric Power Rsch. Inst., 2003—07; bd. govs. U. Chgo. Argonne Nat. Lab, 1995—2001; vis. scholar Resources for the Future, 2001—14; mem. advisory council Electric Power Rsch. Inst., 2007—14. Lt. USNR, 1959-62. Baker scholar. Fellow American Acad. Arts & Scis.; mem. Phi Beta Kappa, Sigma Xi. Democrat. Presbyterian. Home: Bethesda, Md. Died Oct. 10, 2014.

FRIEDMAN, ESTELLE RAPPORT, psychologist; b. NYC, Aug. 4, 1926; d. Nathan and Leah (Rosensweig) Rapport; widowed; children: Howard, Michael, Daniel, Leona, Gerald. BA, Queens Coll., 1945; MS, Columbia U., 1946; PhD, Queens Coll., 1975. Diplomate Am. Bd. Med. Psychotherapists, fellow; lic. psychologists, Conn. Clin. psychologists Utica (N.Y.) State Hosp., 1948-49; rsch. assoc. Greystone project Columbia U., N.Y., N.J., 1949; clin. psychologist Southbury (Conn.) Tng. Sch., 1957-64, Conn. Dept. Health, Hartford, 1964-82, Norwich (Conn.) Hosp., 1982-89; rsch. assoc. dept. psychiatry Yale U., New Haven, from 1989. Adj. prof. Quinnipac Coll., Hamden, Conn., 1989—. Book reviewer Psychiat. Quar., Utica, 1948-68, Am. Jour. Mental Deficiency, N.Y., 1975-82. Mem. adv. bd. New Haven Assn. for Retarded Citizens, 1980-81. Mem. Conn. Psychol. Assn. (program chair, sec. 1981-85), Am. Psychol. Assn., Am. Psychol. Soc. (charter), Ea. Psychol. Assn., New Eng. Psychol. Assn. (sec. 1996-98). Avocation: folk musician. Home: Sharon, Mass. Died Jan. 30, 2007.

FRIEDMAN, LYMAN GUETTEL, lawyer; b. Chgo., May 13, 1918; s. Mitchell M. and Sophie (Guettel) F.; m. Elaine Pickus, Mar. 29, 1949; children: James N., Sally F. Sowell. AB, Washburn U., 1941, LLB, 1943. Bar: Mo. 1943, D.C. 1958, U.S. Dist. Ct. D.C. 1958, U.S. Ct. Appeals (2nd, 6th and fed. cirs.), U.S. Tax Ct., U.S. Ct. Claims, U.S. Supreme Ct. Sole practice, Kansas City, Mo., 1943-50; spl. atty. office of chief counsel IRS, Cin., 1950-58; atty. Wenchel, Schulman, Manning, Washington, 1958-62, ptnr., 1962-78; of counsel Williams & Connolly, Washington, from 1978. Home: Bethesda, Md. Died Dec. 12, 2006.

FRIEDMAN, SYDNEY M., anatomist, educator, medical researcher; b. Montreal, Que., Can., Feb. 17, 1916; s. Jacob and Minnie (Signer) F.; m. Constance Livingstone, Sept. 23, 1940. B.Sc., McGill U., Montreal, Can., 1938, MD, C.M., 1940, M.Sc., 1941, PhD, 1946. Med. licentiate, Que. Teaching fellow anatomy McGill U., Montreal, Que., Can., 1940-42, asst. prof. anatomy, 1944-48, assoc. prof. anatomy, 1948-50; prof., head dept. anatomy U. B.C., Vancouver, Can., 1950-81, prof. anatomy, 1981-85, prof. emeritus, from 1985. Mem. panel on shock Def. Research Bd., Ottawa, Can., 1955-57; sci. subcom. Can. Heart Found., 1962-66, Am. Heart Assn., 1966-68, B.C. Heart Found., Vancouver, founding mem. Author: Visual Anatomy, 1950, 2d edit., 1970; contbr. more than 200 articles to profl. publs. Served as flight lt. RCAF, 1943-44. Recipient Premier award for rsch. in aging CIBA Found., 1955, Outstanding Svc. award Heart Found. Can., 1981, Disting. Achievement award Can. Hypertension Soc., 1987; Commemorative medal 125th Anniversary Can. Confedn.; Pfizer travel fellow Clin. Rsch. Inst., Montreal, 1971. Fellow AAAS, Royal Soc. Can., Coun. High Blood Pressure Rsch.; mem. Am. Anatomical Assn. (exec. com. 1970-74), Can. Assn. Anatomists (pres. 1965-66, J.C.B. Grant award 1982), Internat. Soc. Hypertension, Am. Physiol. Soc., Royal Vancouver Yacht Club, Alpha Omega Alpha. Avocation: painting. Home: Vancouver, Canada. Died Feb. 16, 2015.

FRIEL, BRIAN (BERNARD PATRICK FRIEL), playwright; b. Omagh, County Tyrone, No. Ireland, Jan. 9, 1929; s. Patrick and Christina (MacLoone) F.; m. Anne Morrison, Dec. 27, 1955; children: Paddy, Mary, Judy, Sally, David. Student, St. Columb's Coll., 1941-46; BA, St. Patrick's Coll., Maynooth, Ireland, 1948; postgrad., St. Joseph's Tchrs. Tng. Coll., Belfast, Ireland, 1949-50; Litt.D. (hon.), Dominican Coll., Chgo., Nat. U. Ireland, New U. Ulster, Trinity Coll., Dublin, Ireland, Georgetown U. Tchr. various schs., Derry City, 1950-60; freelance writer, 1960—2015; with Tyrone Guthrie Theatre, 1963; co-founder Field Day Theatre Co., Derry, No. Ireland, 1980; opened Brian Friel Theater and Ctr. for Theater Rsch., Queen's U., Belfast, 2009. Author: (short stories) A Saucer of Larks, 1964, The Gold in the Sea, 1966, The Diviner: Brian Friel's Best Short Stories, 1983, (plays) This Doubtful Paradise, 1960, The Enemy Within, 1962, The Blind Mice, 1963, Philadelphia, Here I Come!, 1964, The Loves of Cass McGuire, 1966, Lovers, 1967, Crystal and Fox, 1968, The Mundy Scheme, 1969, The Gentle Island, 1971, The Freedom of the City, 1972, Volunteers, 1975, Living Quarters, 1977, Faith Healer, 1979, Aristocrats, 1979 (London Evening Standard Best Play award 1988, Best Fgn. Play award N.Y. Drama Critics Circle 1989), Translations, 1980 (Christopher Ewart-Biggs Meml. prize Brit. Theatre Assn. 1981, Plays and Players Best New Play award 1981), American Welcome, 1980, The Communication Cord, 1982, Making History, 1988, Dancing at Lughnasa, 1990 (Tony Best Play award 1992), Wonderful Tennessee, 1993, Molly Sweeney, 1994, Give Me Your Answer, Do!, 1997, The Yalta Game, 2001, Two Plays After, 2002; translator: Three Sisters (Anton Chekhov), 1981, Uncle Vanya, 1998, Two Plays After, 2002, Performances, 2003, Fathers and Sons (Ivan Turgenev), The Home Place, 2005, Hedda Gabler (IBSEN), 2008; (screenplay) Philadelphia, Here I Come!, 1970; (version) A Month in the Country; editor: The Last of the Name; contbr. short stories to New Yorker. Mem. Irish Senate, 1987. Recipient Macauley fellow Irish Arts Coun., 1963, Ulysses medal, U. Coll. Dublin, 2010; hon. fellow U. Coll., Dublin; named to Theatre Hall of Fame, 2007; named one of Ireland's seven Saoi of Aosdana, or Wise Man of the People of Art, 2006 Companion to Royal Soc. Literature; mem. Nat. Assn. Irish Artists, Am. Acad. Arts and Letters. Died Oct. 2, 2015.

FRIEND, WILLIAM BENEDICT, bishop emeritus; b. Miami, Oct. 22, 1931; s. William Eugene and Elizabeth Friend. Student, U. Miami, 1949—52; degree, St. Mary's Coll., St. Mary, Ky., 1955, Mt. St. Mary's Sem., Emmittsburg, Md., 1959; MA in Edn., Cath. U. Am., 1965; LLD, St. Leo Coll., 1986. Ordained priest Diocese Mobile-Birmingham, Ala., 1959; parish priest, educator, counselor, adminstr. Diocese of Mobile, 1959—68, vicar for edn., supt. schs. Ala., 1971—76, chancellor adminstrn., vicar for edn., 1976—79; ednl. rsch. adminstr. U. Notre Dame, Ind., 1968—71; ordained bishop, 1979; aux. bishop Diocese of Alexandria-Shreveport, Shreveport, La., 1979—83, bishop, 1983—86, Diocese of Shreveport, Shreveport, La., 1986—2006, bishop emeritus, from 2007. Mem. Nat. Conf. Cath. Bishops, 1979; chmn. Campaign for Human Devel., 1980—93; mem. sci. and human values com. Commn. of Bishops and Scholars, Com. Sci. & Human Values, 1983; chmn. Commn. of Bishops and Scholars, 1986—92, cons., 1993—2006, sec., USCCB, 2000—04; mem. Pontifical Coun. for Culture, 1993—2008. Editor (with Ford and Daues): Evangelizing the Cultures in A.D. 2000, 1990; co-editor (with J. Anderson): The Culture of Bible Belt Catholics, 1995; contbr. articles on Cath. edn., Cath. ch. leadership and mgmt. and theol. reflections to profl. publs. Bd. dirs., v.p. S.E. Regional Hispanic Ctr., Miami, 1986—2008; trustee Notre Dame Sem., 1976—2006, St. Joseph Coll. Sem., New Orleans, 1979—2006; bd. councillors Cmty. Renewal Internat.; chmn. bd. Ctr. for Applied Rsch. in the Apostolate, 1997—2004; mem. adv. bd. The John J. Reilly Ctr. Sci., Tech. and Values U. Notre Dame, 2000—04; bd. dirs. La. Interchurch Conf., La. Catholic Conf., 1979—2006. Decorated Order of Fleur de Lis K.C., knight comdr. with star Knights of Holy Sepulchre of Jerusalem; recipient Presdl. award, Nat. Cath. Ednl. Assn., 1978, O'Neil D'Amour award, Nat. Assn. Bds. Edn., 1982, NCCJ Brotherhood and Humanitarian award, 1987, Human Rels. Coun. award, 2000, Harry Blake award, 2004, Cordinal Cushing medal, Ctr. Applied Rsch. Georgetown U., Wash., 2010. Mem.: World Futures Soc., NY Acad. Scis., Cath. Acad. Sci. USA, KC (former state chaplain La. coun.). Roman Catholic. Avocations: hiking, art, music, reading. Home: Coral Springs, Fla. Deceased.

FRISCH, MORTON JEROME, political scientist, educator; b. Chgo., Jan. 26, 1923; s. Harry Isadore and Gertrude Frisch; m. Joelyn Alice Saltzman, Feb. 20, 1949; children: Hollis, Mark, Seth. BA, Roosevelt U., 1949; MA, U. Chgo., 1949; PhD, Pa. State U., 1953. Asst. prof., assoc. prof. Govt. Coll. William and Mary, Williamsburg, Va., 1953—64; assoc. prof., prof. Polit. Sci. No. Ill. U., DeKalb, 1964—91, prof. emeritus, from 1992. Vis. prof. Polit. Sci. U. Minn., Mpls., 1957—58; Fulbright prof. Statskunskap U. Stockholm, 1963—64; sr. scholar in resident U. Va., Charlottesville, 1977—78; Fulbright Disting. prof. Korea U., Seoul, 1992; tutor U. Coll., Oxford, England, 1984. Author: A. Hamilton and the Political Order, 1991; editor: Selected Writings and Speeches of A. Hamilton, 1985; co-editor: American Political Thought, 1971. T/5 US Army, 1943—46. Grantee, Earhart Found., 1981, 1985, 1988, 1989; Rsch. fellow in polit. ideology, Rockefeller Found., 1956, NEH Bicentennial Challenge grant, Am. Enterprise Inst., 1981—82. Mem.: Am. Polit. Sci. Assn. Home: Dekalb, Ill. Died Dec. 24, 2006.

FRISCH, ROSE E., population sciences researcher; b. NYC, July 7, 1918; d. Louis and Stella Epstein; m. David H. Frisch; children: Henry J., Ruth Frisch Dealy. BA, Smith Coll., 1939; MA in Zoology, Columbia U., 1940; PhD in Genetics, U. Wis., Madison, 1943. Rsch. fellow biology dept. Harvard U., Cambridge, Mass., 1953—54, assoc. prof. population sciences, mem. Harvard Ctr. for Population and Develop. Studies, 1984-92, assoc. prof. population sciences emerita, 1992—2015; sr. rsch. asst. Harvard Ctr. for Population Studies, Cambridge, Mass., 1965—67; rsch. assoc. children's Hosp. Med. Ctr., Boston, 1974—80. Lectr. population sciences, mem. Harvard Ctr. for Population and Develop. Studies, 1975—84; cons. Food and Climate Panel, Aspen Humanistic Inst., 1977—78. Author: Female Fertility and the Body Fat Connection, 2002, paperback edit., 2004, (children's book) Plants That Feed the World; contbr. articles to profl. jours. Recipient Rsch. Grant award, Nat. Inst. of Child Health and Human Develop., 1988—91, Rally Day medal for Med. Rsch. and Reproductive Health, Smith Coll., North Hampton, Mass., 2003, Disting. Prof. Emeritus Merit award, Harvard Sch. Pub. Health, 2005; fellow Bunting Inst., Cambridge, Mass., 1993—94; John Simon Guggenheim Meml. fellow, 1975—76, Sr. Fellow, East-West Population Inst., Honolulu, HI, 1976. Fellow: American Acad. Arts and Sciences; mem.: AAAS, Endocrine Soc., Soc. for the Study of Fertility, Soc. for the Study of Reproduction, Population Assn. of America, Phi Beta Kappa, Sigma Xi (nat. lectr. 1988—90). Home: Cambridge, Mass. Died Jan. 30, 2015.

FRITZ, EUNICE M., county superintendent of schools; b. Bladen, Nebr., Jan. 14, 1909; d. Charles and Martha May (Phillips) Hanson; m. Karl F. Fritz, July 13, 1938 (dec.). AB, U. Nebr.; MA, Kearney Coll. Elem. edn. educator Webster County, Nebr., 1928-42, Red Cloud (Nebr.) Schs., 1942-52, high sch. tchr., 1952-74; supt. schs. Webster County, from 1974. Home: Bladen, Nebr. Died Dec. 3, 2006.

FROELICH, HELEN LOUISE See HOLT, HELEN

FRUCHTMAN, SHIRLEY MILLSTEIN, accountant; b. Newark, Sept. 8, 1922; d. Harry M. and Regina (Kalmuk) Millstein; m. Harvey L. Fruchtman; children: Lois D. Pierce, Debra J. Fruchtman Rigberg, Amy M. AA in Acctg.,

Essex County Coll., Newark, 1976; BS in Acctg., Stockton State Coll., Pomona, NJ, 1979. Substitute tchr. So. Regional High, Manahawkin, N.J., 1977-89; vol. tax counselor for elderly Solono County, Calif., 1986, 87, 89, Ocean County, N.J., 1990. Vol. fundraising South Ocean County Hosp., 1986. Mem. AAUW (treas. 1986-89). Avocations: walking, tax aid, art, keeping the beaches clean. Home: Delray Beach, Fla. Died Nov. 4, 2006.

FUCHS, MURRAY LOUIS See LOUIS, MURRAY

FUERTES, CARLOS, banker; b. Veguellina, Leon, Spain, July 11, 1929; came to U.S. 1955; s. Manuel F. and Araceli (Garcia) de la Fuente; m. Dolores M. Muniz, Jan. 13, 1962. Student, Colegio Castilla, La Coruna, Spain, 1935-42; BBA, Santiago U., 1945, MBA, 1951. CPA, Spain; prof. mercantil. Loan mgr. GAC Finance/Gen. Acceptance Corp., Allentown, Pa., 1955-60; auditor Gen. Acceptance Corp., Allentown, 1960-66, auditor supr., 1966-68; account exec. Gen. Rediscount Corp. (GAC), Allentown, 1968-76; mgr. sales and mktg. GECC (purchased GRC 1976), Allentown, 1976-86; v.p. The Phila. Nat. Bank Rediscount Financing, Phila., 1987-92; cons. ind. consumer fin. cos., from 1992. Treas. Pa. Playhouse, Bethlehem, 1957-62; mem. GAC Finance Spkrs. Bur., Allentown, 1955-74. Recipient Caligrafy, Spanish Govt., Spain, 1942. Mem. State Assn. of the Loan Industry (Ga., S.C., N.C., Fla., La., Miss., Ky., Pa., Va.), Nat. Assn. Am. Financial Svcs. Assn. Republican. Roman Catholic. Avocation: golf. Home: Bethlehem, Pa. Died July 28, 2007.

FULLER, MIRIAM A., nursing educator, medical-surgical nurse; b. NYC, Apr. 14, 1939; d. Ira Bernard and Muriel (Cozier) Nesbitt; m. Charles H. Fuller, Jr., Aug. 4, 1962; children: Charles H. 3d, David Ira. Diploma, Phila. Gen. Hosp. Sch. Nursing, 1960; BS in Edn., Temple U., 1974. RN, Pa. Staff pub. health nurse City of Phila.; instr. practical nursing Phila. Bd. Edn.; asst. profject dir. Early and Periodic Screening Diagnosis and Treatment; instr. student nurse aides Phila. Bd. Edn. Lectr. in field. Vol. ARC, work with homeless women and children. Recipient award Health Occupations Student Am. Mem. ANA, Ethnic Nurses of Color. Roman Catholic. Home: Philadelphia, Pa. Died Dec. 21, 2006.

FUNK, ARTHUR LAYTON, history educator, author; b. Bklyn., May 10, 1914; s. Merton Layton and Marion Anna (Thompson) F.; m. Genevieve Standard, June 10, 1944 (div. 1981); children: Alexander, James; m. Elaine Carson, May 30, 1987. AB, Dartmouth Coll., 1936; MA, U. Chgo., 1937, PhD, 1940. Instr. St. Petersburg (Fla.) Jr. Coll., 1940-42; asst. prof. Drake U., Des Moines, 1945-46; assoc. prof. U. Fla., Gainesville, 1946-56, prof., 1962-83, ret., 1983; cultural attache U.S. Fgn. Svc., Damascus, Madras and Tananarive, 1956-62. Author: Charles De Gaulle: The Crucial Years, 1943-44, 1959, The Politics of Torch, 1974, De Yalta a Potsdam, 1982, Hidden Ally, 1992. Lt. comdr. U.S. Navy, 1942-45. Guggenheim Found. fellow, 1954. Mem. Am. Com. on the History of the Second World War (chmn. 1975-90), Internat. Com. of the History of the Second World War (v.p. 1975-90), Am. Hist. Assn., Spl. Forces Club. Democrat. Avocation: tennis. Home: Gainesville, Fla. Died June 17, 2007.

FURMAN, WALTER LAURIE, priest; b. Charlotte, NC, Nov. 30, 1913; s. Henry Sylvester and Edna Earl (Jenkins). BS, The Citadel, 1933; MS, U. Fla., 1941, PhD, 1961. Instr. Springhill Coll., Mobile, Ala., 1943-46, 51-53; instr. U. Fla., Gainesville, 1953-57; prof. Springhill Coll., Mobile, 1957-79; Roman Catholic priest Soc. Jesus, from 1950. Mem. Am. Math. Soc. Democrat. *God controls everything.* Died July 23, 2007.

FURUYA, DANIEL KENSHO, aikido instructor, priest; b. LA, Apr. 25, 1948; s. Tetsuo and Kimiye (Kuromiya) F. BA, U. So. Calif., 1970. Ordained priest. Soto Zen Buddhism. Master instr. Aikido, Iaido Japanese Swordsmanship Aikido Ctr L.A. Resident chief instr., dir. Aikido Ctr. of L.A., 1974—; presenter demonstrations and workshops in field. Author (video series): Art of Aikido, 1996, author (book): KODO: Ancient Ways-Lessons in the Spiritual Life of the Warrior-Martial Artist, 1997, contbr. articles on martial arts. Served three terms grant com. panel City of L.A. Multi-Cultural Grants Com.; pres. L.A. Japanese Sword Soc., So. Calif. Yamanashi Prefectural Assn., bd. dirs. U.S. Japanese Sword Soc., Greater Little Tokyo Anti-Crime Assn., Little Tokyo Community Gymnasium, So. Calif. Japan Prefectional Assn.; mem. Community Adv. Bd. Da Camera Soc., Exec. Com. Civilian Martial Artist Adv. Panel L.A. Police Dept. Grantee Brody Multi-Cultural Arts,1990-93, Nat. Def. Act Carnegie project grant, Harvard U., 1969. Mem. Nisei Week Festival Com., Soto Zen Internat. Dept. Zen Buddhist. Home: Los Angeles, Calif. Died Mar. 6, 2007.

FUSSICHEN, KENNETH, computer scientist; b. Bklyn., Aug. 3, 1950; s. Lorenzo Anthony and Sue (Treppiedi) F.; m. Bobbie J. Ezra, May 18, 1974; children: Matthew, David, Vanessa, Natalie, Adam, Michael. AS in Data Processing, San Antonio Coll., 1975; BS in Bus., Ind. U., Indpls., 1980; MS in Mgmt., Ind. Wesleyan U., 1991. Programmer, analyst Computer Mgmt. Sys., Indpls., 1976-81; sr. programmer, analyst Jefferson Nat. Life, Indpls., 1981-84; project leader Healthcare Adminstrv. Sys., Inc., Indpls., 1984-87; sr. computer scientist Computer Scis. Corp., Indpls., 1987-96; computer scientist Data Networks Corp., Dayton, Ohio, 1996; with Adecco Tech. Svcs., Cin., from 1997. Assoc. prof. computer scis. Ind. U.-Purdue U., Indpls., 1981-88; tech. advisor U.S. del. Internat. Stds. Orgn. on Ada 95 and Info. Systems, 1992-94. Info. Systems mgr. Cerebral Palsy Support Group, Indpls., 1987-89; computer cons. United Cerebral Palsy Ctrl. Ind., 1984-85; participant Ada 95 Lang. Rev., 1990-95 Mem. IEEE, Assn. Computing Machinery, Indpls. Computer Soc. (pres. 1989-90). Home: Xenia, Ohio. Died Feb. 4, 2007.

FUTCH, JOAN WILLIAMS, health facility administrator; b. Cook County, Ga., Aug. 18, 1943; d. Lory E. and Bessie F. (Ethridge) Williams; m. H. Eschol Futch, Aug. 20, 1966; children: Roger, Sandra, Pamela, Peggy. Diploma, Ga. Bapt. Hosp. Sch. Nursing, 1964; BSN, Armstrong State Coll., 1978; MS in Nursing, Med. Coll. Ga., 1981. RN, Ga. Nursing supr. Glynn Brunswick (Ga.) Meml. Hosp.; dir. nursing Sylvan Grove Hosp., Jackson, Ga., Upson County Hosp., Thomaston, Ga.; asst. adminstr. nursing S. Ga. med. Ctr., Valdosta; v.p. patient care svcs. St. Jude Med. Ctr., Kennan, La., 1990-91; dir. nursing Goodlark Med. Ctr., Dickson, Tenn., 1991-92, Dekalb Gen. Hosp., Smithville, Tenn., from 1992. Recipient Woman of Achievement, BPW, 1984. Mem. Am. Orgn. Nurse Execs., Nat. League Nursing, Ga. Nurses' Assn., ANA, Ga. Orgn. Nurse Execs. Died Apr. 7, 2007.

FYFE, WILLIAM SEFTON, geochemist, educator; b. New Zealand, June 4, 1927; s. Colin Alexander and Isabella Fyfe; m. Patricia Walker, Feb. 27, 1981; children: Christopher, Catherine, Stefan. BSc, U. Otago, New Zealand, 1948, MS, 1949, PhD, 1952; DSc (hon.), Meml. U., Lisbon, Portugal, 1989-90, Lakehead U., 1992, Guelph U., 1994, St. Mary's U., Otago, New Zealand, 1994, Otago U., New Zealand, 1995, U. Western Ont., 1995. Prof. chemistry in, N.Z., 1955-58; prof. geology U. Calif., Berkeley, 1958-66; research prof. Manchester U. and Imperial Coll., London, 1966-72; chmn. dept. geology Western Ont. U., 1972-84, prof. dept. geology, 1984-92, prof. emeritus dept. earth sci., from 1992, dean faculty sci., 1986-90. Decorated companion Order of Can.; Commemorative medal (New Zealand), Commemorative medal (Canada); recipient Logan medal Geol. Assn. Can., Arthur Holmes medal European Union of Geoscis., Can. Gold medal for Sci. and Engring., 1991; Guggenheim fellow, 1964, 83; named hon. prof. U. Beijing. Fellow Geol. Soc. London (hon.; Wollaston medal 2000), Royal Soc. London, Geol. Soc. Am. (hon. life, Day medal), Mineral Soc. Am. (Roebling medal); mem. AAAS (chmn. geology geography sect. 2000—), Internat. Union Geoscis. (pres. 1992-96, Grand Cross Ordem Nacional do Merito Cientifico, Brazil, 1996), Nat. Sci. and Engring. Rsch. Coun. Can., Royal Soc. Can., Acad. Sci. Brazil, Brit. Chem. Soc., Russian Acad. Sci., Indian Acad. Sci., Chinese Acad. Sci. Home: London, Canada. Died Nov. 11, 2013.

GABLE, EDWARD BRENNAN, JR., lawyer; b. Shamokin, Pa., Mar. 15, 1929; s. Edward Brennan and Kathleen (Welsh) Gable; m. Judy Lipshy Gable, July 17, 1981; stepchildren: Steven H., Karen Sue, Scott Michael- ;children from previous marriage: Karen Lynn, Kimberly Ann, Katherine Rebel. BS, Villanova U., 1953; JD, Georgetown U., 1957. Bar: DC 1957, US Dist. Ct. DC 1957, US Ct. Appeals (D.C. cir.) 1957, US Ct. Customs and Patent Appeals 1969, US Customs Ct. 1961, US Ct. Mil. Appeals 1966, US Supreme Ct. 1967, US Ct. Appeals (fed. cir.) 1982. With US Customs Svc., Treasury Dept., Washington, 1958—88, chief documentation br., 1965—66, chief carrier rulings br., 1966—76, chief penalties br., 1976—78; spl. asst. to asst. commr. Office of Regulations and Rulings, 1978—82, dir. carriers, drawback and bonds div., 1983—88, legal cons. in martime law Washington, from 1988; pres. Griffin Unit Owners' Assn., from 1999. Pres. Customs Fed. Credit Union, 1967—69; mem. U.S. del. Intergovtl. Maritime Cons. Orgn., London, 1972—75; U.S. rep., inter-sessional meeting Hamburg, Fed. Rep. Germany, 1973; dir. Foggy Bottom Assn., from 1992. Recipient Superior Performance award, Treasury Dept., 1962, commendation cert., Customs Outstanding Performance award, 1983, Customs Cash Performance award, 1984—85. Mem.: Elks Club, United Seamen's Svc. (coun. of trustees 1986—88), Propeller Club US, Fed. Bar Assn., Customs Lawyers Assn. (pres. 1965—66), Nat. Lawyers Club, Delta Theta Phi, Delta Pi Epsilon. Roman Catholic. Died Mar. 26, 2012.

GABLE, FREDERICK W., theater company executive; b. Reading, Pa., July 2, 1947; s. Joseph E. and Dorothy (Wagner) G.; m. Jamie Sue Guensch, Jan. 9, 1971; children: Heather Lynn, Brian Philip. BA, Albright Coll., 1970; student, Millersville State U., 1977-78. Dist. supr. Ogden Food Svc., Phila., 1978-80; v.p. Budco Theatres, Doylestown, Pa., 1980-87, Loews Theatres, Secaucus, N.J., from 1987. Co-chmn. concession com., Variety, N.Y.C., 1987—. Mem. Nat. Assn. Concessionaires. Democrat. Avocations: classical piano, painting, baseball, football. Home: Clinton, NJ. Died Jan. 8, 2007.

GABLEHOUSE, CHARLES JOHN, retired aviation executive, state agency administrator; b. NYC, Apr. 16, 1928; s. Charles Henry and Elisabeth (Ochse) Giebelhaus; m. Marge Holman, June 21, 1964; 1 child, Stephanie. Student, NYU, 1952-53, Coll. of William and Mary, 1957, L.I. Agrl. and Tech. Inst., 1958-59, Fordham U., 1960, Acad. Aeronautics, LaGuardia Airport, NY, 1953-54. Lic. comml. airplane and seaplane pilot. Co. rep. to U.S. Army Test Ctr. DeLackner Helicopters, Mt. Vernon, N.Y., 1956-58; tech. editor, project leader Grumman Aircraft Engring Corp., Bethpage, L.I., N.Y., 1958-61; assoc. editor Bus./Comml. Aviation mag., NYC, 1961-62, aviation writer, 1961-68; with aviation dept. Port Authority of N.Y. and N.J., NYC, 1962-88, airport services analyst, 1968-88. Author: Helicopters and Autogiros, 1967 (Nat. Tech. Writing award); contbr. numerous articles to profl. jours. Dir. pub. relations Ethical Culture Soc., Bergen County, N.Y., 1975—; town rep. to N.Y. Motion Picture and TV Devel. Commn., Passaic, 1979—; commr. planning bd., Passaic, 1980-85; bd. dirs. Passaic Mental Health Clinic, Passaic, 1983-84. Served to sgt. U.S. Army, 1950-52, Korea. Decorated Bronze Star, 1951; recipient industry award Soc. Tech. Writers and Publs., 1963, vol. award Bergen Ctr. for Child Devel., 1986. Mem. Aviation/Space Writers Assn., Planning Assn. of North Jersey. Avocations: flying, community activity. Home: Athens, NY. Died Aug. 5, 2007.

GABRIEL, HOWARD WAYNE, III, publishing executive; b. Berkeley, Calif., Dec. 28, 1946; s. Howard Wayne Jr. and Lorraine Celia (Novak) G.; m. Mona Beth Prather; children: Anna, Howard IV. BA, Eastern Wash. U., 1969; MA, No. Mich. U., 1970; PhD, U. Utah, 1972. Instr. No. Mich. U., Marquette, 1969-70; research assoc. U. Utah Med. Ctr., Salt Lake City, 1970-72; assoc. dir. S. Cen. Kans. Health Council, Wichita, 1973-75; mgmt. cons. Gabriel Assocs., Sacramento, Calif., 1975-76; exec. dir. Southeast Alaska Health Systems, Ketchikan, 1976-82; propr. M&H Enterprises, Sacramento, from 1982. Preceptor U. Okla. Sch. Pub. Health, Norman, 1973-74. Author: Growing Up With Character, 1986, Loving Memories From Dog to Dog, 1987, Adventures with Shivers the Hamster, 1987, Natural Procreation Alternatives for Men with Low Sperm Counts--A Guide for Laypersons Under Medical Supervision and Consultation, 1987, Hypothermic Vectors as Etiological Factors in Oligospermia, 1972, Lost and Found in Alaska, The Mystery of Red Mountain, Timothy Befriends A Homeless, The Mystery of Old Dan, A Tale of Two Families, I Always Wondered Yet Always Knew, A Tale of Two Great Grandmothers, Move Right 21 AZ. Counselor Rancho San Antonia Boys Town, Chatsworth, Calif., 1966; chmn. Ketchika(Alaska) Health Council, 1982, Valley Park Sch. Parent Bd., Ketchika, 1982; bd. trainer United Way, Sacramento, Calif., 1985; bd. dirs. Am. River Little League, Cub Scout pack 634 Boy Scouts Am. Mem. AAAS, Internat. Soc. Edn. Health Scis. (charter), N.W. Health Assn. (pres. 1980-82), Am. Rural Health Assn. (mem. exec. adv. bd. mem. 1978-82), Am. Pub. Health Assn., Nat. Rural Health Assn., Calif. Pub. Health Assn. Avocations: sports, jogging, music, reading. Home: Galt, Calif. Died Nov. 15, 2006.

GADOLA, PAUL VICTOR, retired federal judge; b. Flint, Mich., July 21, 1929; AB, Mich. State U., 1951; JD, U. Mich., 1953. Diplomate Nat. Bd. Trial Advocacy; Bar: Mich. Atty. Hoffman & Rubenstein, Flint, Mich., 1955-60; pvt. practice Flint, 1960-88; judge US Dist. Ct. (eastern dist.) Mich., Detroit, 1988—2001, sr. judge, 2001—09. Bd. dirs. Mackinac Ctr. for Public Policy Rsch. Served in US Army, 1953-55. Fellow American Trial Lawyers Found. (life), Roscoe Pound Found. (life), Mich. State Bar Found.; mem. Mich. State Bar Assn., U. Mich. Alumni Assn., Mich. State U. Alumni Assn., Soc. Irish/American Lawyers (pres.), Hannah Soc. and Pres.'s Club of Mich. State U., Federalist Soc., Flint Coll. and Cultural Fund Committed of Sponsors, Phila. Soc., Econ. Club of Detroit. Died Dec. 26, 2014.

GAGNE, VERNE CLARENCE (LAVERNE CLARENCE GAGNE), professional wrestler; b. Mpls., Feb. 26, 1926; s. Clarence and Ellsie G.; m. Mary Ardith Marxen, 1949 (dec. 2002); children: Gregory, Kathleen, Elizabeth, Donna. Student, U. Minn., 1943-44, 47-49. Champion Nat. Collegiate U. Minn., Mpls., 1948-49, AAU nat. champion, 1949; wrestler Olympic Team Wrestling, 1948; big ten champion, 1944, 47-49; co-founder to owner Am. Wrestling Assn., Mpls., 1960—91, heavyweight champion, 1960-62, 67-75, 1980-81; producer All Star Wrestling, Mpls., 1985. Coach 1972 Olympics Wrestling Team, 1972. Producer and appeared in The Wrestler, 1969. With USMC, 1944-46. Named to World Wrestling Entertainment Hall of Fame, 2006. Mem. Mpls. Boxing and Wrestling, All Star Wrestling. Died Apr. 27, 2015.

GAGNON, JOHN HENRY, sociologist, educator; b. Fall River, Mass., Nov. 22, 1931; s. George and Mary (Murphy) G.; m. Patricia A. Orlikoff, Mar. 20, 1955 (div. Jan. 1979); children: André Giselle, Christopher Hans; m. Cathy Stein Greenblat, Dec. 1988; stepchildren: Leslie Heather Greenblat Shah, Kevin David. BA, U. Chgo., 1955, PhD, 1969. Adminstrv. asst. to sheriff Cook County, Ill., 1955-58; clin. asst. dept. neurology and psychiatry Northwestern U. Med. Sch., Chgo., 1958-59; lectr. Ind. U., Bloomington, 1959-67; trustee Inst. for Sex Research, 1959-68, sr. research sociologist, 1959-68; asso. prof. State U. N.Y., Stony Brook, 1968-70, prof. sociology, from 1970, prof. dept. psychology, from 1973, dir. lab. for social relations, 1968-70; dir. Center for Continuing Edn., 1970-72; prof. dept. psychiatry Health Sci. Center, 1972-74; sr. scientist Ctr. for Health and Policy Rsch., from 1997. Vis. scientist Inst. Criminology, U. Copenhagen, 1976, Walter Reed Army Inst. Rsch., 1990; vis. prof. Lab. Human Devel. Grad. Sch. Edn., Harvard U., 1978-80; vis. prof. dept. sociology U. Essex (Eng.), 1983-84, dept. sociology Princeton (N.J.) U., 1987-88; rsch. assoc. NORC U. Chgo., 1987—; cons. Global Program on AIDS WHO, Ctrs. for Disease Control, NIMH, Nat. Ctr. for Health Stats.; mem. com. on AIDS Rsch. and the Behavioral, Social, and Statis. Scis. NRC, 1987—; faculty assoc. Harris Sch. Pub. Policy Studies U. Chgo., 1992-93, rsch. assoc. Nat. Opinion Rsch. Ctr., 1987-91, vis. scholar dept. sociology, 1988; cons. in field.; mem. com. on AIDS Rsch. and Behavioral, Social and Statis. Scis. NRC, 1987-94; co-chair Social Sci. Rsch. Coun. Sexuality Fellowship Rsch. Program, 1996—; mem. sexuality working group Harvard AIDS and Reproductive Nealth Network, 1992-95. Author: Sex Offenders: An Analysis of Types, 1965, Sexual Deviance, 1967, The Sexual Scene, 1970, Sexuelle Aussenseiter, 1970, Sexual Conduct: The Social Sources of Human Sexuality, 1973, Human Sexualities, 1977, Life Designs: Individuals, Marriages and Families, 1978, Human Sexuality in Today's World, 1977; co-author: The Social Organization of Sexuality, 1994, Sex in America, 1994 (Dutch, German, Japanese and Chinese translations); co-editor: Conceiving Sexuality: Approaches to Sex Research in a

Post Modern Era, 1995, Encounters with AIDS: The Impace of the HIV/AIDS Epidemic on the Gay and Lesbian, In Changing Times: Gay Men and Lesbians Encounter HIV/AIDS, 1997 Communities, 1997. Recipient Spl. Achievement award Nat. Hemophilia Found., 1977, award for career contbn. to sex research Soc. for Sci. Study of Sex, 1980; Overseas fellow Churchill Coll. U. Cambridge, Eng., 1972-73; Spl fellow NIMH, 1972-73; grantee NIMH, Nat. Inst. Child Health and Human Devel., Office AIDS Rsch., Ford Found., Am. Found. AIDS Rsch., N.Y. Cmty. Trust, Robert Wood Johnson Found., John and Mary MacArthur Found., Albert Mellon Found., Rockefeller Found. Fellow AAAS, Internat. Acad. Sex Research (pres. 1987-88); mem. Am. Sociol. Assn., AAAS, Soc. for Study Social Problems, Sex Info. and Edn. Council U.S. (dir. 1967-70), Biol. Scis. Curriculum Study (steering com. 1969-72), Sociol. Rsch. Assn. Research in social and cultural change, environ. studies, social biology, human sexual conduct. Home: Nice, France. Died Feb. 11, 2016.

GAILEY, JOAN DALE, retired finance educator; b. Beaver Falls, Pa., May 10, 1940; d. Irvin D. and Elizabeth Jane (Hollander) Anderson; m. Ronald L. Gailey, Aug. 15, 1957; 1 child, Ronald. BSBA, Geneva Coll., 1975; MBA, Youngstown State U., 1980; PhD, U. Pitts., 1987. Libr. tech. Community Coll. Beaver County, Monaca, Pa., 1969-74; customer liaison, floor supr. LTV Steel, Aliquippa, Pa., 1975-79; instr. Youngstown (Ohio) State U., 1980-83; asst. prof. bus. mgmt. Kent State U., East Liverpool, Ohio, 1984-91, assoc. prof. bus. mgmt., from 1992, prof. bus. mgmt., from 1998, prof. Trumbull campus Warren, Ohio, 2001—02, prof. East Liverpool campus, 2003, prof. emeritus, 2003. Cons. in bus. mgmt., 1988—; dir. Kent State East Liverpool Bus. Resource Ctr. Abstract editor Interface, 1994, 95, 96, 97, proceedings editor, 1998; co-editor: Humanities and Technology Rev., 1999—; contbr. articles to profl. jours. Mem. Rochester (Pa.) Area Planning Commn., 1989, Rochester Area Mktg. Com., 1990; tutor Adult Lit. Coun., Monaca, 1984-91; mem. adv. bd. Ret. Sr. Vol. Program, Lisbon, Ohio, 1990, vice chair, 1993-2000, facilitator Columbiana County Mini-Loan Fund, 1994-96. Recipient Kent State Teaching Devel. award, 1990, Kent State Profl. Devel. award, 1992; tchg. coun. grantee Kent State U., 1997-98, Summer award Univ. Tchg. Coun., 1999. Mem. Am. Ednl. Rsch. Assn. (editor newsletter 1993-94, program chair 1992), Nat. Assn. Indsl. Tech., Midwest MLA, Ohio Bus. Tchrs. Assn., Humanities and Tech. Assn. (exec. bd. dirs. 1997—), Assn. for Bus. Comm., Alpha Mu (Outstanding Mktg. Tchr. 1983). Home: Rochester, Pa. Died Feb. 14, 2007.

GAISER, RICHARD EDWARD, lawyer; b. NYC, June 13, 1943; s. Charles H. and Winifred E. Gaiser; m. Ruth Ann Cavill, June 24, 1967; children: Kristin, Karin. BA cum laude, C.W. Post Coll., 1967; MA, Cen. Mich. U., 1982; JD, Woodrow Wilson Law Sch., 1980. Bar: Ga. 1981, U.S. Dist. Ct. (no. dist.) Ga. 1981, U.S. Ct. Appeals (11th cir.) 1981, U.S. Supreme Ct. Atty. FAA, Lilburn, Ga., from 1988. Contract administr. USAFR, Robins AFB, GA., 1983—. Served to lt. col. USAF, 1967-72, Vietnam. Decorated D.F.C., 1972. Mem. ABA, Air Force Assn. Clubs: Atlanta Navy Flying Club. Avocations: reading, jogging. Died Nov. 26, 2006.

GALEANO, EDUARDO HUGHES (EDUARDO GERMÁN MARIA HUGHES GALEANO), writer; b. Montevideo, Uruguay, Sept. 3, 1940; s. Eduardo Hughes Roosen and Licia Ester Galeano Muñoz; m. Silvia Brando; 1 child, Veronica; m. Graciela Berro; children: Florencia, Claudio; m. Helena Villagra. Author: Open Veins of Latin America, 1971, Days and Nights of Love and War, 1977; (trilogy) Memory of Fire, 1981-87 (American Book award, 1989), The Book of Embraces, 1990, Walking Words, 1994, Football in Sun and Shadow, 1995, Soccer in Light and Shadow, 1997, I Am Rich Potosi: The Mountain That Eats Men, 1999, Upside Down: A Primer for the Looking-Glass World, 2000, Voices of Time: A Life in Stories, 2004, Mirrors:Stories of Almost Everyone, 2009, Children of the Days: A Calendar of Human History, 2013 and several others Decorated with Order Rubén Darío, Govt. Nicaragua, 1989; recipient Casa de las Americas, 1975, 1978, Internat. Human Rights award, Global Exchange, 2006, Stig Dagerman prize, 2010 Home: Montevideo, Uruguay. Died Apr. 13, 2015.

GALES, EDWIN ALAN, economist, consultant; b. NYC, May 5, 1921; s. Emanuel and Shirley (Cowan) G.; m. Helen Bearman, July 7, 1957; 1 child, Karen Lynn. BS in Polit. Sci., Harvard U., 1948; postgrad., Stanford U., Palo Alto, Calif., 1948-49. Community devel. advisor Calif. Dept. Community Svcs., LA, 1950-58; fgn. svc. officer Agy. for Internat. Devel., Washington and, overseas, 1958-80, community devel. advisor South Korea, 1958-60, area ops. officer Eritrea, Ethiopia, 1961-63, desk officer Washington, 1963-66, program officer East African community, 1966-69, regional program officer so. Africa, 1969-71, Southern African affairs officer Washington, 1971-76, chief loan div. South Korea, 1976-79, regional devel. advisor Philippines, 1979-80. Cons. Philippine program U. Calif., Berkeley, 1981; cons. evaluations Agy. for Internat. Devel., Fiji, Tonga and Western Samoa, 1984, operational cons., Belize, 1986-87; operational cons. RCA, Belize Inst. Mgmt., 1988. Career guidance counselor Harvard U. for Fgn. Svcs. Applicants, 198090; lectr. U. Calif. Extension, San Diego, 1989—, Orient Lines, Singapore to East Africa, 1994. Capt. U.S. Army, 1942-46, ETO. Recipient Indsl. Advancement Adminstrn. award, Korea, 1979. Mem. World Affairs Coun., Archaeol. Inst. Am., Inst. for Continued Learning (bd. dirs. 1989-91), Harvard Club, Stanford Club. Avocations: travel, research, sports. Home: San Diego, Calif. Died Jan. 6, 2007.

GALLATIN, HARRY JUNIOR, retired basketball player; b. Roxana, Ill., Apr. 26, 1927; s. Harry E. and Cecile (Hartmann) Gallatin; m. Beverly Hull, 1949; children: Steve, Jim, Bill. BS, Northeast Mo. State Tchrs. Coll., 1948. With NY Knickerbockers, 1948-57, Detroit Pistons, 1957-58; coach So. Ill. U., Carbondale, 1958-62, St. Louis Hawks, 1962-65, NY Knicks, 1965-66. Basketball/golf coach So. Ill. U., Edwardsville, 1967-70, also tchr., dean of students Served in USN. Named NBA Coach of Yr., 1963, Naismith Memorial Basketball Hall of Fame, 1991. Achievements include member All-NBA first team, 1954, All-NBA second team, 1955, selection to All-Star game seven times, league leader in rebounding, 1954. Home: Edwardsville, Ill. Died Oct. 7, 2015.

GALLO, JON JOSEPH, lawyer; b. Santa Monica, Calif., Apr. 19, 1942; s. Philip S. and Josephine (Sarazan) G.; m. Jo Ann Broome, June 13, 1964 (div. 1984); children: Valerie Ann, Donald Philip; m. Eileen Florence, July 4, 1985; 1 child, Kevin Jon. BA, Occidental Coll., 1964; JD, UCLA, 1967. Bar: Calif. 1968, U.S. Ct. Appeals (9th cir.) 1968, U.S. Tax Ct. 1969. Assoc. Greenberg, Glusker, Fields, Claman & Machtinger, LA, 1967-75, ptnr., from 1975. Bd. dirs. USC Probate and Trust Conf., L.A., 1980—; bd. dirs. UCLA Estate Planning Inst., chmn. 1992—99. Contbr. articles to profl. jours. Fellow Am. Coll. Trust and Estate Counsel; mem. ABA (chair generation skipping taxation com. 1992-95, co-chair life ins. com. 1995-2000, chair psychol. and emotional issues of estate planning 2001—), Internat. Acad. Estate and Trust Law, Assn. for Advanced Life Underwriting (assoc.). Avocation: photography. Home: Santa Monica, Calif. Died June 2014.

GALVIN, JOHN ROGERS, retired army officer, law educator; b. Wakefield, Mass., May 13, 1929; s. John James and Mary Josephine (Rogers) G.; m. Virginia Lee Brennan, June 5, 1961; children: Mary Jo Schrade, Elizabeth Ann Galvn White, Kathleen Mary Galvin, Erin Elizabeth Scranton. BS, U.S. Mil. Acad., 1954; MA in English, Columbia U., 1962; postgrad., U. Pa., 1964-65; grad., Command and Gen. Staff Coll., 1966. Commd. 2d lt. U.S. Army, 1954, advanced through grades to gen.; mil. asst. to Supreme Allied Comdr. Europe, 1974-75; comdr. DISCOM, chief of staff 3d Infantry div., Germany, 1975-78; asst. div. comdr. 8th Infantry div., 1978-80; comdg. gen. 24th Infantry div., Ft. Stewart, Ga., 1981-83, also post comdr.; comdg. gen. VII U.S. Corps, Stuttgart, Fed. Republic Germany, 1983-85; comdr. in chief U.S. So. Command, Quarry Heights, Panama, 1985-87; supreme allied comdr. Europe, comdr.-in-chief U.S. European Command, 1987-92; ret., 1992; Olin disting. prof. nat. security studies U.S. Mil. Acad., West Point, NY, 1992-93; disting. vis. policy analyst The Mershon Ctr., Ohio State U., 1994-95; dean Fletcher Sch. Law and Diplomacy, Tufts U., Boston, 1995-2000; dean emeritus, 2000—15. Author: The Minute Men, 1967, Air Assault, 1969, Three Men of Boston, 1976, Fighting the Cold War: A Soldier's Memoir, 2015 Former bd. dirs. Wesleyan Coll. Fletcher Sch. of Law and Diplomacy fellow, 1972-73; decorated Silver Star, Legion of Merit, DFC, Bronze Star, Disting. Svc. Medal; named to US Army Ranger Hall of Fame Mem. Ctr. for Creative Leadership (past bd. govs.), Seligman (bd. dirs.), Am. Coun. on Germany (chmn. emeritus bd. dirs.), Inst. for Def. Analyses (trustee, 1995-2002). Roman Catholic. Home: Jonesboro, Ga. Died Sept. 25, 2015.

GAMBINO, RICHARD JOSEPH, materials engineer, educator; b. NYC, May 17, 1935; BA, U. Conn., 1957; MS, Polytech Inst. N.Y., 1976; DSc (hon.), Stony Brook U., 2012. Phys. sci. U.S. Army Signal Rsch. Lab., Ft. Monmouth, NJ, 1958—60; metallurgist Pratt & Whitney Aircraft divsn. United Aircraft Corp., 1960—61; rsch. staff mem. T.J. Watson Rsch. Ctr., IBM, Yorktown Heights, NY, 1961—93; prof., lab. dir. Stony Brook U., 1993—2009. Pres. MesoScribe Technologies, Inc., 2002—04, CTO, from 2004. Lt. Signal Corps. USAR, 1957—66. Recipient Nat. Medal of Tech., 1995. Fellow: IEEE (life); mem.: IEEE Magnetic Soc., Nat. Acad. Engring., Materials Rsch., Tau Beta Pi, Sigma Xi. Home: Port Jefferson, NY. Died Aug. 3, 2014.

GAME, DAVID AYLWARD, physician; b. Adelaide, Australia, Mar. 31, 1926; s. Tasman Aylward and Clarice Mary (Turner) G.; m. Patricia Jean Hamilton, Dec. 8, 1949; children: Ann, Philip, Timothy, Ruth. MB, BS, U. Adelaide, 1949. Resident Royal Adelaide Hosp., 1950, Outpatient Registrar, 1951; gen. practice medicine Adelaide, 1953-96. Chmn. Eastern Region Geriatric and Rehab. Adv. Com., 1976-83; chmn. Cen. Ea. Health Adv. Com., 1983-86. Mem., chmn. social welfare coun. Diocese of Adelaide; chmn. Anglican Cmty. Svcs. Coun., 1989-95; mem. standing com. Synod Diocese Adelaide, Australian Anglican Ch., 1966-79, 81-84. Decorated Officer Order of Australia, Knight of Grace Sovereign Order St. John of Jerusalem. Fellow Australian Med. Assn., Royal Australian Coll. Gen. Practitioners (chmn. fed. coun. 1969-72, pres. elec. 1972-74, pres. 1974-76, censor in chief, 1976-80), Royal Coll. Gen. Practitioners (fellow ad eudem), Hong Kong Coll. Gen. Pracitioners, Australian Postgrad. Fedn. in Medicine (life, gov., patron); mem. Coll. Family Physicians of Can., World Orgn. Nat. Colls. and Acads. and Academic Assns. Gen. Practitioners/Family Physicians (hon. sec. treas. 1972-80, pres. 1983-86), Australian Postgrad. Fedn. Medicine (coun.), Australian Med. Assn., Australian Geriatric Soc., Lorna Laffer Med. Dir. of South Australian, Postgrad. Mech. Edn. Assn., Adelaide Club. Died May 14, 2015.

GAMMANS, JAMES PATRICK, ceramic engineer; b. Atlanta, Sept. 18, 1952; s. Raymond Francis Jr. and Alice Jane (Rhodes) G.; m. Brenda Diane Klingenberg, Dec. 10, 1983; 1 child, John Patrick. BS magna cum laude, U. Ga., 1976; B Ceramic Engring. with highest honors, Ga. Inst. Tech., 1976; MBA, Ga. State U., 1985. Reg. profl. engr. Ceramic engr. Ga. Sanitary Pottery Inc., Atlanta, 1976-80, Universal Rundle Corp., Monroe, Ga., from 1980. TRI-FIRE scholar The Refractories Inst., Ga. Inst. Tech., 1975-76. Mem. Am. Ceramic Soc. (sec. S.E. sect. 1988-89, vice chair 1990, chair 1992). Roman Catholic. Home: Conyers, Ga. Died June 5, 2007.

GAMON, ADAM EDWARD, retired internist; b. Hillside, NJ, Sept. 6, 1918; s. Adam Edward and Mary (Yanick) G.; m. Lottie Irene Snyder, Sept. 8, 1939; children: Judith Diane, Robert Edward. BS, Alfred U., 1939; MD, Temple U., 1943. Diplomate Am. Bd. Internal Medicine. Intern N.Y.C. Hosp., 1944, resident in pathology, 1946, asst. med. resident, 1947-47, chief med. resident, 1948-49; resident internal medicine Saginaw (Mich.) Gen. Hosp., 1946-47; gen. practice internal medicine Saginaw, 1950-69; with Mich. State Disability Determination Service Lansing, 1969-71; med. dir. Malleable Iron div. Gen. Motors, Saginaw, 1971-73, Dow Corning Corp., Midland, Mich., 1973-88. Chief medicine St. Luke's Hosp., Saginaw, 1953-67; cons. St. Mary's Hosp., Gen. Hosp., St. Luke's Hosp., Saginaw Midland Hosp. Inventor disposable tracheotomy set, portable bed chair. Dep. coroner Saginaw County, 1973—; cons. Social Security Adminstrn., HEW, Saginaw, 1973-77. Served to capt., M.C., U.S. Army, 1944-46. Mem. ACP (life), Am. Coll. Angiology, Am. Soc. Internal Medicine, Mich., Midland County Med. Socs., AMA, Mich. Soc. Internal Medicine, Indsl. Med. Assn., Pan Am. Med. Assn., Am. Radio Relay League. Home: Brant, Mich. Died June 12, 2007.

GANDOLF, RAYMOND L., sportscaster; b. Norwalk, Ohio, Apr. 2, 1930; s. Raymond L. Gandolf and Rose (Brenner) Gandolf Neller; m. Blanche Haywood Cholet, Oct. 13, 1956; children—Alexandra, Jessica, Victoria, Amanda, Susanna BS in Speech, Northwestern U., 1951. Actor, 1951-62; writer, producer WCBS-TV, NYC, 1963-65; writer, corr. CBS News, NYC, 1965-82; corr. ABC News-Sports, NYC, 1982-92, host, Our World, 1986-87. Panel mem. Dictionary of Contemporary Usage, 1985 Recipient Peabody award U. Ga., 1980, Dupont award Columbia U., 1981, Emmy award, 1987. Mem. AFTRA, Writers Guild Am. Home: New York, NY. Died Dec. 2, 2015.

GANS, CURTIS BERNARD, think-tank executive; b. Manhattan, June 17, 1937; s. Kurt and Irene (Katz); m. Shelly Fidler (div.); m. Eugenia Grohman (div.); 1 child, Aaron. AB, U. N.C., 1959. Co-founder, dir., v.p. Com. for the Study of the Am. Electorate, 1977—2015; reporter Miami News, UPI. Cons. Woodrow Wilson Ctr. Internat. Scholars, Nat. Com. for Effective Congress. Contbr. articles to reviews including The Atlantic, Public Opinion, The Washington Monthly, The Nation, The New Republic, Social Policy, The N.Y. Times Book Rev., Book World, books and anthologies; guest Today, Good Morning Am., All Things Considered, The McNeil-Lehrer Report. Served with USMC Res. Avocation: baseball. Died Mar. 15, 2015.

GARABEDIAN, CHARLES, artist; b. Detroit, Dec. 29, 1923; m. Gwendolyn Garabedian, 1963; children: Claire, Sophia Octeau. Studied lit., U. Calif., Santa Barbara; degree in history, U. Southern Calif.; MFA, UCLA, 1961. Solo shows include LaJolla (Calif.) Mus. Art, 1966, CeJee Gallery, N.Y., 1966, 67, Eugenia Butler Gallery, L.A., 1970, Newspace Gallery, L.A., 1974, Whitney Mus. Am. Art, N.Y.C., 1976, Broxton Gallery, L.A., 1976, L.A. Louver Gallery, Venice, Calif., 1979, 83, 86, 89, 90, 92, 94, 96, 2004, LaJolla Mus. Contemporary Art, 1981, Ruth S. Schaffner Gallery, Santa Barbara, Calif., 1982, Rose Art Mus., Waltham, Mass., 1983, Hirschl & Adler Modern Mus., N.Y.C., 1984, Gallery Paule Anglim, San Francisco, 1985, 93, 98, numerous others; exhibited in group shows at numerous mus. including Rose Art Mus., The High Mus., Atlanta, 1980, Emanuel Walter Gallery, San Francisco, 1981, LaJolla Mus. Contemporary Art, 1981, Mizumo Gallery, L.A., 1981, Mandeville Art Gallery, San Diego, Oakland Mus. Art, 1981, Brooke Alexander Gallery, N.Y., 1982, Kunst Mus., Luzern, 1983, Fresno Art Ctr., 1983, Tibor de Nagy Gallery, N.Y.C., 1983, Hirshhorn Mus. and Sculpture Garden, Smithsonian Instn., Washington, 1984, Newport Harbor Art Mus., Calif., 1984, El Museo Rufino Tamayo, Mexico City, 1984, L.A. Mcpl. Art Gallery, 1984, L.A. Louver, Venice, 1985, Whitney Mus. Art, 1986, DiLaurenti Gallery, N.Y., 1986, R.C. Erpf Gallery, N.Y., 1987, N.Y. State Mus., Albany, 1987, Richard Green Gallery, 1988, Bklyn. Mus. Art, 1989, James Corcoran Gallery, 1991, Riva Yares Gallery, Scottsdale, Ariz., 1994, Hirschl & Adler Mus., 1996, Mcpl. Art Gallery L.A., 1997; pub. collections include Met. Mus. Art, N.Y.C., Whitney Mus. Am. Art, Mus. Contemporary Art, L.A., Rose Art Mus., San Diego Mus. Contemporary Art, L.A. County Mus. Art Staff sgt. USAF, 1942-45. Nat. Endowment for the Arts fellow, 1977, John Simon Guggenheim Meml. Found. fellow, 1980 Died Feb. 11, 2016.

GARBER, DOROTHY HELEN, rancher, artist; b. Fredricktown, Mo., Oct. 7, 1917; d. Chester Payton and Bessie Belle (Sykes) Brewington; m. H. Derwood Garber, 1933 (dec.); children: Patricia Kay, Marici Lea; m. Samuel T. Ramey, Sept. 1959 (div. Dec. 1971). Rancher Patty K. Ranch, Hotchkiss, Colo., from 1945. Bookkeeper, owner Garber Clo, Hotchkiss, 1954-56, co-owner, mgr., 1966-80; owner, mgr., buyer Dorothy's, Hotchkiss, 1956-66. Artist, judge, exhibitor, lectr. and demonstrator; retrospective art exhibit Gallery Connections Hotchkiss, Colo., 1997. One-woman shows include Western Colo. Ctr. for Arts, Grand Junction, Hotel Colorado Art Gallery, Glenwood Springs, Colo., Aristracrat, Paonia, Colo., Finishing Touch Gallery, Hotchkiss, Pavilion, Montrose, Colo., etc.; exhibited in group shows at Montrose Pavilion, Mitchell Mus., Trinidad,

Colo., Old Pass Gallery, Raton, N.Mex., Doherty Gallery, Delta, Colo., Castano Gallery, Denver, Rocky Mountain Nat. Watercolor Exhibition, Golden, Colo., San Diego Internat. Watercolor Soc. Exhibition, State Fair Fine Arts Gallery, Albuquerque, The Tubac Mus., Tubac, Ariz., Albuquerque Mus. Fine Arts, Western Colo. Ctr. for Arts, Grand Junction, Gallery Connections, Hotchkiss, Colo., 1997, Catherine Lorillard Wolf Art Club, N.Y.C., 1998, others. Mem. Western Fedn. Watercolor (signature mem.), N.Mex. Watercolor Soc., Western Colo. Watercolor Soc. (founder, past pres., adv. bd.), Hotchkiss Fine Arts (past pres., charter mem.), Delta Fine Art. Democrat. Baptist. Died Nov. 13, 2006.

GARCIA-BUÑUEL, LUIS, neurologist; b. Madrid, Feb. 24, 1931; came to U.S., 1955; s. Pedro Garcia and Concepcion Buñuel; m. Virginia May Hile, June 30, 1960. BA, BS, U. Zaragoza, Spain, 1949; MD, U. Zaragoza, 1955. Diplomate Am. Bd. Psychiatry and Neurology. Resident neurology Georgetown U., Washington, 1955-59; postdoctoral fellow Washington U., St. Louis, 1959-61; asst. prof. neurology Thomas Jefferson U., Phila., 1961-67; assoc. prof. U. N.Mex., Albuquerque, 1967-72, U. Oreg. Health Scis. Ctr., Portland, 1972-84; chief neurology svc. Portland VA Med. Ctr., 1972-84; pvt. practice, Phoenix, from 1984; chief staff Carl T. Hayden VA Med. Ctr., Phoenix, 1984-96. Contbr. articles to sci. jours., including Nature, Sci., Neurology, Jour. Neurol. Sci. Lt. Spanish Air Force, 1952-55. Fellow Am. Acad. Neurology (sr. mem.), Sigma Xi. Unitarian Universalist. Avocations: painting, computer art, steel-welded sculpture. Died Jan. 28, 2015.

GARDE, MICHAEL JAMES, business executive; b. NYC, Apr. 12, 1937; s. James Vincent Garde and Ruth Ann (Loar) Shearer; m. Evelyn Therese Simpson, Sept. 9, 1961; children: Mary Beth, Thomas, Michael F., James. AA, St. Joseph Sem., 1957; AB, Seton Hall U., 1961. Route salesman Coca-Cola Bottling Co. of N.Y., Paterson, N.J., 1961-62; regional mgr. Yoo-Hoo Beverage Co., Carlstadt, N.J., 1963-65; marine sales rep. Johns-Manville Corp., NYC, 1965-71; regional mgr. Sunday Pubs., Caldwell, N.J., 1972-76; pres. Bon Venture Svcs. Inc., Flanders, N.J., from 1976. Bd. dirs. Am. Cancer Soc., Monroe County, Pa., 1985—; patron Market St. Railway Co., San Francisco, 1983—. Mem. Boston St. Railway Assn., Pa. Trolley Mus., Washington Theol. Union (bd. trustees, devel. com.), Lions (bd. dirs. 1977-90). Roman Catholic. Avocation: street railways. Home: East Stroudsburg, Pa. Died Feb. 13, 2007.

GARDNER, GRACE DANIEL, company executive; b. Nashville, Oct. 15, 1911; d. John and Grace Olive (Knight) Daniel; m. Edwin Sumner Gardner, July 10, 1935; children: Gretchen, Patricia, Edwin Sumner. BA, Vanderbilt U., 1932. Tchr. Nashville pub. sch., 1932-33; dept. mgr. Tenn. Electric Power Co., Nashville, 1933-35; devel. officer Tenn. Performing Arts Found., Nashville, 1975-78, exec. dir., from 1978. Chmn. fund raising ARC, Nashville, 1947, active various other charitable orgns. Fellow: Nat. Soc. Fund Raising Execs., Centennial (dir. music com. chmn.). Episcopalian. Avocations: sewing, cooking, hiking. Home: Nashville, Tenn. Died Aug. 2, 2007.

GARDNER, WILLIAM F., lawyer; b. Birmingham, Ala., Apr. 24, 1934; s. Lucien D. and Amy Y. (Young) G.; m. Melanie Terrell, Oct. 20, 1961; children; John L., Robert T. BA, U. Ala., 1956; LLB, U. Va., 1959. Bar: Ala. 1959, U.S. Dist. Cts. (no., mid., so. dists.) Ala., U.S. Ct. Appeals (5th cir, 11th cir.); Supreme Ct. Ala. Assoc. Cabaniss Johnston, Birmingham, Ala., 1959-65; ptnr. Cabaniss, Johnston, Gardner, Dumas & O'Neal, Birmingham, from 1965. Chmn. Equal Employment Opportunity Com. Defense, Rsch. and Trial Lawyers Assn., 1974-75. Contbr. articles to legal jours. Fellow Am. Coll. Trial Lawyers. Episcopalian. Home: Birmingham, Ala. Died May 15, 2007.

GARFINKEL, BARBARA ANN, pianist, educator, musicologist; b. Elizabeth, NJ, Dec. 19, 1931; d. Irving and Lillian (Treister) Slavin; m. Burton Garfinkel, June 28, 1952; children: Steven, Joan Struss. BS in Edn., Boston U., 1953. Cert. vocal music instr., piano instr. Pvt. piano tchr., Millburn, N.J., 1949-52, Livingston, N.J., 1968-90; elem. sch. tchr. Nahant (Mass.) Pub. Schs., 1953-54, Maplewood (N.J.) Pub. Schs., 1954-56; profl. pianist, vocalist, from 1984. Music tchr. Downs Syndrome Children, Livingston, 1982-85; choir dir. Daughters of Miriam, Clifton, N.J., 1986, Cranford (N.J.) Home Continuing Care, 1990. Composer liturgical and show music; performer one woman shows vocal and piano. Vol. pianist Grotta Nursing Home, West Orange, N.J., 1988-93; judge teen piano finalists Garden State Art Ctr., Holmdel, N.J., 1985-95; local leader Dem. Party, Livingston, 1990—; v.p. Christ Hosp. Auxiliary, Jersey City, 1980-85; instrs. Russian, Israeli, Chinese immigrants, 1980-93; diplomat World Jewish Congress, 1995—. Mem. N.J. Music Tchrs. Assn., Schumann Music Study Club (program chair 1994-95), Pro Musica Hon. Music Club, Pi Lambda Theta. Avocations: swimming, boating, gardening, writing, movies. Home: West Orange, NJ. Died Dec. 4, 2006.

GARFINKEL, DAVID ABOT, investment company executive; b. NYC, Sept. 21, 1955; s. Barry Herbert and Patricia Zelda (Averbach) G.; m. Shelley Robin Spector, Apr. 17, 1986; 1 child, Pamela Rachel. BA, Hamilton Coll., 1978. Sales rep. Procter & Gamble, White Plains, N.Y., 1978-80; account exec. Drexel Burnham, NYC, 1980-82, v.p., 1982-84, 1st v.p., 1984-89; sr. v.p. Smith Barney, NYC, from 1989. Fundraiser United Jewish Appeal, N.Y.C., 1980—, March of Dimes, N.Y.C., 1982-84, Multiple Sclerosis Soc., N.Y.C., 1990—. Democrat. Avocations: family, skiing, football. Home: New Rochelle, NY. Died Jan. 24, 2007.

GARIBALDI, MARIE LOUISE, former state supreme court justice; b. Jersey City, Nov. 26, 1934; d. Louis J. and Marie (Serventi) G. BA, Conn. Coll., 1956; LLB, Columbia U., 1959; LLM in Tax. Law, NYU, 1963. Atty. Office of Regional Counsel, IRS, NYC, 1960-66; assoc. McCarter & English, Newark, 1966-69; ptnr. Riker, Danzig, Scherer, Hyland & Pernutti, Newark, 1969-82; assoc. justice N.J. Supreme Court, Newark, 1982-2000. Contbr. articles to profl. jours. Trustee St. Peter's Coll.; co-chmn. Thomas Kean's campaign for Gov. of N.J., 1981, mem. transition team, 1981; mem. Gov. Byrne's Commn. on Dept. of Commerce, 1981, bd. dirs, Crown Holdings, 2000-. Recipient Disting. Alumni award NYU Law Alumni of N.J., 1982; recipient Disting. Alumni award Columbia U., 1982 Fellow Am. Bar Found.; mem. N.J. Bar Assn. (pres. 1982), Columbia U. Sch. Law Alumni Assn. (bd. dirs.) Roman Catholic. Achievements include being the first woman to serve on the NJ Supreme Court; first woman to head the State Bar Association. Home: Weehawken, NJ. Died Jan. 15, 2016.

GARMAN, RAY FILLMORE, occupational physician, director; s. Wynona Hudson Garman; m. Eugenie (Gigi) Virginia Moravec, Aug. 16, 1958; children: Ray Fillmore III, Scott Clayton, Andrew Seitz. AB, Johns Hopkins U., Balt., 1957; MD, George Wash. U., Washington, DC, 1961; MPH, Med Coll. Wis., Milw., 1995. Cert. in internal medicine U. Penna Grad. Sch. Medicine, Phila., 1962, Am. Bd. Internal Medicine, 1968, in pulmonary diseasese Am. Bd. Internal Medicine, 1974, in occupl. medicine Am. Bd. Preventive Medicine, 1996. Pulmonary medicine physician Guthrie Clinc/Robert Packer Hosp., Sayre, Pa., 1972—81, chief pulmonary medicine, 1981—90, med. dir., 1991—95; chief occupl. medicine and environ. health Lexington Clinic, Ky., 1995—99; med. dir. Gen. Electric Appliance Divsn., Bloomington, Ind., 1999—2000; clin. med. dir. Toyota Motor Mfg., Georgetown, Ky., 2000—04; assoc. prof., dir. occupl. med. training U. Ky., Lexington, from 2004, vice chair, dept. preventive medicine & environ. health, dir., Occupl. Medicine Residency Program, from 2004; survey chair Lexington Forum, 1997—2005, bd. dirs., 2009—12; fellow, vice-chair Sect. Environ. Medicine, Am. Coll. Ocpl. Environ. Medicine. Sr. aviation med. examiner FAA, Lexington, from 1977; pres. Bradford County Med. Soc., Sayre, Pa., 1979—80; instr. quality process Quality Coll. (Crosby), Winter Park, Fla., 1989—90. Active Lexington Children's Mus., 1995—99; treas. Lex-Fayette Urban County Airport Bd., Lexington, 2003, sec., 2002, chmn., 2004—05; vice chair-med. Lexington Arts & Cultural Coun., 2000—04; pres. Lexington Opera Soc., 2005—07, bd. dirs., from 2009; pres. Lexington Kennel Club, 2002—05; chmn. Flight 5191 Meml. Commn., from 2006; commr. Ky. Airport Zoning Bd., from 2011; bd. dirs. Planned Parenthood of the Bluegrass, 2005—07, Aviation Mus. Ky., from 2006, chair bd., 2007—12. Capt. USAF, 1963—66, Brig Gen. Res., mobilization asst. to surgeon AF Material Command USAF, chief flight surgeon. Decorated Golden Cross of Royal Order of Phoenix King of Greece, Legion of Merit USAF. Mem.: Ky. Occupl. Med. and Environ. Health Assn. (v.p. 2007, pres. 2008), Ky. Dept. Aviation, Lexington Club, Delta Omega (Disting. Alumni Membership, MCW). Home: Lexington, Ky. Died Sept. 20, 2014.

GARNER, MILDRED ESLICK, poet; b. Danville, Ark., June 5, 1927; d. William Beaden and Fannie May (Nickless) Eslick; m. David Edmond Garner, June 11, 1944; children: Barbara Garner Harless, Beverly Garner Holzkamper, Brenda Garner Mitchell, Belinda Garner Bender, David, Ronnie. Ordained minister, 1983. V.p. Gen. Assembly Firstborn, Watts, Okla., 1980. Author, pub.: A Gift for a King, 1992, Poems of Sentiment and Inspiration, 1994; poems included in World Treasury of Great Poems, 1988, Golden Treasury of Great Poems, 1988, Great Poems of the Western World, 1989, World Treasury of Golden Poems, 1989, Poems that will Live Forever, 1989, Heaven in My Heart, 1990, Our World's Favorite Gold and Silver Poems, 1991, Great Poems of Our Times, 1991, Poetic Voices of America, 1992, On a Threshold of a Dream, 1992, Our World's Favorite Poems, 1992, Whispers in the Wind, 1993, Outstanding Poets of 1994, 1994. Co-founder, v.p., copastor Gen. Assembly of the Firstborn, Watts, Okla., 1983. Mem. Poets of the Roundtable, Writers Guild, Siloam Springs Writers (pres. 1995). Home: Watts, Okla. Died Jan. 29, 2007.

GARNETT, GRIFFIN TAYLOR, lawyer, writer; b. Washington, Aug. 15, 1914; s. Griffin Taylor and Susie Lee (Crump) G.; m. Harriet Waddy Brooke, Sept. 21, 1938; children: Griffin Taylor III, Thomas Brooke. BA, U. Richmond, 1936; LLB, Nat. U. Law Sch., 1940. Bar: Va. 1940, D.C. 1945. Asst. clk. U.S. Dist. Ct., Washington, 1939-41; ptnr. Radigan & Garnett PC, Arlington, Va., 1995—2002. Author: (short stories) Pleasant Living, 1993, (novel) The Sandscrapers, 1995, Taboo Avenged, 1997, Sam's Legacy, 2003. Past mem. retirement bd. Arlington (Va.) Pub. Utilities Commn. Sr. lt. U.S. Navy, 1943-46, PTO. Mem. Va. Bar Assn., Arlington Bar Assn. (pres. 1960), U.S. Landing Ships Medium Assn. (life), Washington Golf and Country Club (pres. 1971). Republican. Episcopalian. Avocations: golf, cruising, reading, creative writing, music. Home: Arlington, Va. Died June 15, 2007.

GARRETT, ELIZABETH, academic administrator, law educator; b. Oklahoma City, June 30, 1963; d. Robert D. and Jane (Thompson) Garrett. BA in History with Spl. Distinction, U. Okla., Norman, 1985; JD, U. Va., Charlottesville, 1988. Bar: Tex. 1988, DC 1989. Law clk. to Hon. Stephen Williams US Ct. Appeals, DC, Washington, 1988—89; law clk. to Hon. Thurgood Marshall US Supreme Ct., Washington, 1989—90; legal adviser to Hon. Howard M. Holtzman Iran-US Claims Tribunal, The Hague, Netherlands, 1990—91; legal counsel, tax counsel for Senator David L. Boren, Washington, 1991—93, legis. dir., tax counsel, 1993—94; asst. prof. U. Chgo. Law Sch., 1995—99, prof., 1999—2003, dep. dean academic affairs, 1999—2001; co-dir. USC-Caltech Ctr. Study Law & Politics U. Southern Calif., L.A., from 2003, vice provost acad. affairs, 2005—06, v.p. academic planning & budget, 2005—10, Frances R. & John J. Duggan prof. law, polit. sci. & public policy, interim provost, sr. v.p. academic affairs, 2010, provost, sr. v.p. academic affairs, 2010—14; pres. Cornell U., 2014—16. Vis. assoc. prof. U. Va., Charlottesville, 1994—95, vis. prof., 2001; vis. asst. prof. Harvard U., Cambridge, Mass., 1998; vis. prof. Ctrl. European U., Budapest, Hungary, 1999—2003, Interdisciplinary Ctr. Law Sch., Tel Aviv, 2001, Calif. Inst. Tech., Pasadena, 2004, U. So. Calif. Law Sch., LA, 2002; bd. dirs. Initiative & Referendum Inst., U. So. Calif.; mem. Adv. Panel on Fed. Tax Reform, 2005; commr. Fair Polit. Practices Commn., Calif., 2009—13. Co-author: Cases and Materials on Legislation: Statutes and Creation of Public Policy, 2007; co-editor: Fiscal Challenges: An Interdisciplinary Approach to Budget Policy, 2008, Statutory Interpretation Stories, 2011; mem. editl. bd. Election Law Jour.; contbr. articles to profl. jours. Vice chair nat. governing bd. Common Cause, from 2006. Recipient U. Va. Disting. Alumni award, 2016. Fellow: American Bar Found.; mem.: ABA, ALI, DC Bar Assn., Tex. Bar Assn., American Law Econ. Assn., Phi Beta Kappa, Mortar Bd., Order of Coif, Chi Omega. Achievements include the first female president for Cornell University. Died Mar. 6, 2016.

GARRETT, ROBERT, investment banking executive; b. Morristown, NJ, Feb. 27, 1937; s. Harrison and Grace Dodge (Rea) Garrett; m. Jacqueline E. Marlas, July 10, 1965; children: Robert Jr., Johnson. AB in History, Princeton U., NJ, 1959; MBA in Bus. & Fin., Harvard U., 1965. V.p. Smith Barney & Co., 1965-69, Robert Garrett & Sons, Inc., Balt./NYC, 1969-71, pres., from 1986; 1st v.p. Smith, Barney, Harris Upham & Co., 1972-78; sr. v.p. Smith Barney Real Estate Corp., 1978-84; exec. v.p. Security Capital Corp., 1979—85; founder, pres. AdMedia Ptnrs. Inc., 1990—2005, mng. dir., 2005—07, chmn., 2007—08; ptnr. Media Adv. Ptnrs., from 2010. Chmn. Penn Va. Corp., 2000—11, bd. dirs., 2011—12, PVG GP, LLC, 2006—10. Trustee Cleveland H. Dodge Found., Abell Found., NY Bot. Garden, Adirondack Coun. Svc. with US Army, 1959—63. Mem.: Univ. Club NY, Knickerbocker Club NY, Nantucket Yacht Club. Episcopalian. Home: New York, NY. Died Mar. 12, 2015.

GARRISON, RICHARD NEIL, artist; b. Ft. Bidwell, Calif., Nov. 26, 1912; s. John Henry and Vera Calista (Bell) G.; m. Ruth Geraldine George, Mar. 1, 1932 (div. Jul. 1968); m. Jeanne Trimble, Oct. 12, 1968. Student, Visalia (Calif.) Jr. Coll., 1930-32. Dir. Art League of Manatee Co., Bradenton, Fla., 1964-70. Author book of poetry, 1996, 95, 97. Mem. Art League of Manatee County, Longboat Key Art Ctr. Republican. Home: Bradenton, Fla. Died Apr. 24, 2007.

GARTH, DAVID, political and media consultant; b. Woodmere, NY, May 26, 1930; s. Leo and Beulah (Jagoda) Goldberg. BS in Mass Psychology, Washington & Jefferson U., 1952. Involved in election campaigns of Adlai Stevenson, Gov. Hugh Carey, Sen. John Tunney, Mayor Edward Koch, Sen. John Heinz, Gov. Jay Rockefeller, Sen. Arlen Specter, Mayor Tom Bradley; pres. Garth Group Inc., NYC, 1964—2014. Recipient Peabody awards for TV prodns., 1961-63. Democrat. Died Dec. 15, 2014.

GARVEY, JOANNE MARIE, lawyer; b. Oakland, Calif., Apr. 23, 1935; d. James M. and Marian A. (Dean) Garvey. AB with honors, U. Calif., Berkeley, 1956, MA, 1957, JD, 1961. Bar: Calif. 1962. Assoc. Cavaletto, Webster, Mullen & McCaughey, Santa Barbara, Calif., 1961-63, Jordan, Keeler & Seligman, San Francisco, 1963-67, ptnr., 1968-88, Heller, Ehrman, White & McAuliffe, San Francisco, 1988—2008, Sheppard Mullin Richter & Hampton, San Francisco, from 2008. Bd. dirs. Mex.-Am. Legal Def. and Ednl. Fund; chmn. Law in Free Soc., Continuing Edn. Bar; mem. bd. councillors U. So. Calif. Law Ctr. Recipient Paul Veazy award, YMCA, 1973, Internat. Women's Yr. award, Queen's Bench, 1975, honors, Advs. Women, 1978, CRLA award, Boalt Hall Citation award, 1998, Judge Lowell Jensen Cmty. Svc. award, 2001, Margaret Brent award, 2003, Latcham State and Local Disting. Svc. award, 2003, Lifetime Achievement award, The Am. Lawyer mag., 2006, Jim Pfeiffer award, CDCBA, 2008. Fellow: Am. Bar Found.; mem.: ABA (gov., state del., chmn. SCLAID, chmn.delivery legal svcs., chmn. 10LTA), Calif. Women Lawyers (founder), Am. Law Inst., San Francisco Bar Assn. (pres., pres. Barristers), Calif. State Bar (v.p., gov., tax sect., del., Jud Klein award, Joanne Garvey award), Phi Beta Kappa, Order of Coif. Democrat. Roman Catholic. Home: San Francisco, Calif. Deceased.

GASTWIRTH, DONALD EDWARD, lawyer, literary agent; b. NYC, Aug. 7, 1944; s. Paul and Tillie (Scheinert) G.; m. Joanne Martin, Sept. 25, 2011. BA, Yale U., 1966, JD, 1974. Bar: Conn. 1979, U.S. Dist. Ct. Conn. 1981. Mem. advt. staf New Yorker mag., NYC, 1967-68; v.p. Reader's Press, New Haven, 1968-74, dir., 1968-75; exec. v.p. Mainstream TV Studio, New Haven, 1974-77, dir., 1974-79; pres. Quasar Assocs., New Haven, 1979-89; account exec. Bache Halsey Stuart Shields Inc., New Haven, 1977-79; ptnr. Gastwirth, McMillan & Still, New Haven, 1981-84; pres. Don Gastwirth & Assocs. Literary Agy., New Haven, from 1984. Adj. prof. law Thomas Jefferson Sch. Law, 1996-99; lectr. in field; advisor fund raising, mem. benefit com. John Steinbeck Lit. Project, 1986-94; assoc. fellow Trumbull Coll., Yale U., 1991—. Assoc. prodr. Yankee Fishing (TV series, 1995-98); contbr. to Nat. Rev., Wall St. Jour., New Haven Register; mem. bd. advisors Yale Lit. Mag., 1987-94, Touchstone Mag., 1990-95, 98-99.

Trustee Yale Ctr. for Parliamentary History, 1995-2002; bd. dirs. Chancel Opera Co. Conn., 2003-06, New Haven Downtown Soup Kitchen, 2004-06; mem. bd. advisors Endowment for Middle East Truth, 2005—. Mem.: PEN Writers Assn., ABA, Federalist Soc., Writers Guild Am., Berzelius Soc., Lambs Club (NY), Yale Club (New Haven, NY), Elizabethan Club. Died Jan. 25, 2015.

GATES, CHARLES R., college administrator; b. Sanger, Calif., Mar. 12, 1943; s. Charles Elmer and Elizabeth A. (Senior) G.; m. Julie M. Gates, May 10, 1982; children: Darlene Canale, Ranell Bond. BS, Barclay Coll., Haviland, Kans., 1995. Regional sales mgr. Gulf Devel., Torrence, Calif., 1971-77; sales mgr. Lakeside Printing, Skaniatelas, N.Y., 1977-79; v.p. mktg. Century Pub., Post Falls, Idaho, 1979-81; classified dir. Coeur d'Alene (Idaho) Press, 1981-83; v.p. mktg. Better Homes, Ceour d'Alene, 1983-86; v.p. devel., coll. adminstr. Barclay Coll., Haviland, 1988-95; dir. stewardship Back to the Bible, Lincoln, Nebr., from 1995. Seminar presenter Barclay Coll., Haviland, 1988-95; fin. counsel Christian Fin. Concepts, Gainesville, Ga., 1982—. Writer news articles Kiowa County Signal, 1990-95; author, articles writer Barclay Progress, 1988-95. Chair fin. com. Mid-Am. Yearly Meeting of Friends, Wichita, Kans., 1992-95; mem. City Coun., Haviland, 1994, 95. Sgt. USMC, 1963-68. Mem. Christian Stewardship Assn. Republican. Avocations: golf, fly fishing. Home: Hayden, Idaho. Died Dec. 20, 2006.

GAY, PETER, historian, educator, writer; b. Berlin, June 20, 1923; came to U.S., 1941, naturalized, 1946; s. Morris Peter and Helga (Kohnke) G.; m. Ruth Slotkin, May 30, 1959 (dec., May 9, 2006); stepchildren: Sarah Khedouri, Sophie Glazer Cohen, Elizabeth Glazer. BA, U. Denver, 1946; MA, Columbia U., 1947, PhD, 1951; LHD (hon.), U. Denver, 1970, U. Md., 1979, Hebrew Union Coll., Cin., 1983, Clark U., 1985, Suffolk U., Boston, 1987, Tufts U., 1988; LHD (hon.), Tavistock Inst., 1999; LHD (hon.), U. Ill., 2003; HD Phil, Oldenburg U., 2008. Faculty Columbia U., NYC, 1947-69, prof. history, 1962-69, William R. Shepherd prof. history, 1967-69; prof. comparative European intellectual history Yale U., New Haven, from 1969, Durfee prof. history, 1970-84, Sterling prof., 1984-93, Sterling prof. emeritus, 1993—2015; dir. Ctr. for Scholars and Writers N.Y. Pub. Libr., from 1997. Author: The Dilemma of Democratic Socialism: Eduard Bernstein's Challenge to Marx, 1952, Voltaire's Politics: The Poet as Realist, 1959, The Party of Humanity: Essays in the French Enlightenment, 1964, A Loss of Mastery: Puritan Historians in Colonial America, 1966, The Enlightenment: An Interpretation, vol. I, The Rise of Modern Paganism, 1966, Weimar Culture: The Outsider as Insider, 1968, The Enlightenment, vol. II, The Science of Freedom, 1969, The Bridge of Criticism: Dialogues on the Enlightenment, 1970; author: (with R.K. Webb) Modern Europe, 1973; author: Style in History, 1974, Art and Act, 1976, Freud, Jews, and Other Germans, 1978, Education of the Senses, 1984, Freud for Historians, 1985, The Tender Passion, 1986, A Godless Jew: Freud, Atheism, and the Making of Psychoanalysis, 1987, Freud: A Life for Our Time, 1988, A Freud Reader, 1989, Reading Freud: Explorations and Entertainments, 1990, The Cultivation of Hatred, 1993, The Naked Heart, 1995, Pleasure Wars, 1998, My German Question: Growing Up in Nazi Berlin, 1998, Mozart, 1999, Schnitzler's Century: The Making of Middle-Class Culture, 1815-1914, 2001, Savage Reprisals, Bleak House, Madame Bovary, Buddenbrooks, 2002, Modernism, The Lure of Heresy; from Bandelaire to Beckett and Beyond, 2007. Fellow Am. Coun. Learned Soc., 1959-60, Ctr. Advanced Study Behavioral Scis., 1963-64; Guggenheim fellow, 1967-68, 77-78; Overseas fellow Churchill Coll., Cambridge, 1970-71; Rockefeller Found. fellow, 1979-80; Wissenschaftskolleg zu Berlin, 1984; recipient First Amsterdam prize in Hist. Sci., 1991. Mem. Am. Philos. Soc., Am. Inst. Arts and Letters (gold medal in history 1996), Ctr. for Scholars and Writers (dir. emeritus), N.Y. Pub. Libr., Phi Beta Kappa. Home: New York, NY. Died May 12, 2015.

GAYNOR, MITCHELL LEE, oncologist, consultant; b. Plainview, Tex., June 5, 1956; s. J. Irvin and Elaine (Shure) Gaynor; children: Eric, David. MD, U. Tex. Southwestern Med. Sch., Dallas. Cert. med. oncology, interntal medicine, hematology. Fellow in molecular biology Rockefeller U.; founder Gaynor Integrative Oncology; clinical prof. Cornell U. Weill-Med. Coll.; dir. med. oncology Weill-Cornell Ctr. for Integrative Medicine; cons. & former dir. med. oncology Strang Cancer Prevention Ctr. Adv. bd. Healthy Living Mag., Sass Med. Found.; ed. bd. Integrative Cancer Therapies. Author: Dr. Gaynor's Cancer Prevention Program, 1999, Sounds of Healing, 1999, Healing Essence, 2000, The Healing Power of Sound, 2002, Nurture Nature, Nurture Health, 2005, The Gene Therapy Plan, 2015; co-producer, record title Change Your Mind, 2013. Mem.: NY Acad. Sciences, Am. Coll. Physicians, Am. Soc. Clin. Oncology. Died Sept. 15, 2015.

GEARHART, JANE ANNETTE SIMPSON, retired lawyer; b. Seibert, Colo., Mar. 2, 1918; d. V.L. and Frances Louise (Taylor) Simpson; m. Richard C. Gearhart, July 6, 1946 (div. 1957); 1 child, Suzanne Gearhart Carroll. BA, U. Denver, 1939, LLB, 1942, LLD, 1970. Bar: Colo. 1942, Oreg. 1956. Staff atty. League of Oreg. Cities, Eugene, 1957-60; dep. legis. counsel Oreg. Legis., Salem, 1962-73; adminstrv. law judge Oreg. Employment Div., Eugene, 1977-84; cons. adminstrv. law Corp. Commr., Supt. of Banks, Salem, 1973-86. Trustee Christos Trust, Eugene, 1990. Lt. (j.g.) USNR, 1943-46. Avocations: amateur genealogy, writing, hiking, photography. Home: Eugene, Oreg. Died May 17, 2007.

GEDDES, CHARLES LYNN, retired history educator; b. Corvallis, Oreg., Jan. 3, 1928; s. James Edward and Dorothy Marie (Green) G. BS, U. Oreg., 1951; AM, U. Mich., 1954; PhD, U. London, 1959. Asst. prof. Am. U. Cairo, 1956-61, U. Colo., Boulder, 1961-65; Fulbright prof. Tribubhan U., Kathmandu, Nepal, 1965-66; prof. history U. Denver, 1967-92. Author: Guide to Reference Books for Islamic Studies, 1985, A Documentary History of the Arab-Israel Conflict, 1991. Pfc. U.S. Army, 1945-46. Fellow Mid. East Inst.; mem. Am. Oriental Soc., Mid. East Studies Assn., Am. Inst. Yemeni Studies, Am. Inst. Islamic Studies (resident dir. 1965). Avocations: gardening, cooking. Home: Denver, Colo. Died Dec. 23, 2006.

GEE, ROBERT LEROY, agriculturist, dairy farmer; b. Moorhead, Minn., May 25, 1926; s. Milton William and Hertha Elizabeth (Paschke) G.; m. Mae Valentine Erickson, June 18, 1953 BS in Agronomy, N.D. State U., 1951, postgrad., 1955, Colo. A&M U., 1954. Farm labor controller Minn. Extension Service, Clay County, 1944-45, county 4-H agt., 1951-57; rural mail carrier U.S. Postal Service, Moorhead, Minn., 1946-47; breeder registered shorthorn cattle and registered southdown sheep Moorhead, Minn., 1950-63; owner, operator Gee Dairy Farm (Oak Grove Farm), Moorhead, Minn., from 1957. Asst. prof. status U. Minn., 1951-57; bd. dirs. Red River Valley Devel. Assn., Crookston, Minn., v.p., 1992—; treas. Red River Milk Producers Pool, Minn., ND, 1968-78; chmn. bd. Cass Clay Creamery Inc., Fargo, ND, 1982-85, 92-95, v.p., 1990-91; mem. Nat. Dairy Promotion Bd., Washington, 1984-88. Treas. Oakport Twp., 1974-82, supr., 1986-2002, v.p., 1987-2002; mem. Clay County Planning and Zoning Commn., 1991-2000, vice chmn., 1992-96, chmn., 1996-2000; mem. Clay County Bd. Adjustment, 1995-2000, chmn., 1996-2000. With USN, 1945-46. Recipient Grand Champion Farm Flock award Man. Expn., 1960, Clay County's Outstanding Agriculturist award, 1996; named Clay County King Agassiz, Red River Valley Winter Shows, 1966, Grand Champion forage exhibit Red River Valley Winter Shows, 1979, 82, Fair Person of Yr., 2008; co-recipient Clay County Dairy Farm Family of Yr. award Red River Valley Dairymen's Assn., 1979. Mem. Minn. Milk Producers Assn. (bd. dirs. 1977-88, 93-97, sec. 1972-78, treas. 1977-87), Minn. Assn. Coops. (bd. dirs. 1984-96), State Coop. Assn. (dairy council 1975-96), Am. Farm Bur. Fedn., Nat. Farmers Union, Kragnes Farmers Elevator Assn., Red River Valley Livestock Assn., Am. Shorthorn Breeders Assn., Am. Southdown Breeders Assn., Holstein-Friesian Assn. Am. Republican. Mem. United Ch. of Christ. Club: Agassiz (v.p. 1979-81, pres. 1981-82) (Moorhead) Avocations: hunting, fishing, skiing. Home: Dilworth, Minn. Died Oct. 28, 2014.

GEHRING, FREDERICK WILLIAM, mathematician, educator; b. Ann Arbor, Mich., Aug. 7, 1925; s. Carl E. and Hester McNeal (Reed) G.; m. Lois Caroline Bigger, Aug. 29, 1953; children: Kalle Burgess, Peter Motz. BSE in Elec. Engring., U. Mich., 1946, MA in Math, 1949; PhD (Fulbright fellow) in Math, Cambridge U., Eng., 1952, ScD, 1976; PhD (hon.), U. Helsinki, Finland, 1977, U. Jyväskylä, 1990, Norwegian U. Sci. & Technology, 1997. Benjamin Peirce instr. Harvard U., Cambridge, Mass., 1952-55; instr. math. U. Mich., Ann Arbor, 1955-56, asst. prof., 1956-59, assoc. prof., 1959-62, prof., 1962-96, T.H. Hildebrandt prof. math., 1984-96, prof. emeritus, 1996, chmn. dept. math., 1973-75, 77-84, disting. univ. prof., from 1987; hon. prof. Hunan U., Changsha, People's Republic of China, 1987. Vis. prof. Harvard U., 1964-65, Stanford U., 1964, U. Minn., 1971, Inst. Mittag-Leffler, Sweden, 1972, Mittag-Leffler, Sweden, 1990; Lars Onsager prof. Norwegian Tech. Hochschule, Norway, 1995; chair program in Geo Function Theory, Math. Scis. Rsch. Inst., Berkeley, 1986. Editor Duke Math. Jour., 1963-80, D. Van Nostrand Pub. Co., 1963-70, North Holland Pub. Co., 1970-94, Springer-Verlag, 1974-2002; editl. bd. Procs. Am. Math. Soc., 1962-65, Ind. U. Math. Jour., 1967-75, Math. Revs., 1969-75, Bull. Am. Math. Soc., 1979-85, Complex Variables, 1981—, Mich. Math. Jour., 1989-98, Annales Academiae Scientiarum Fennicae, 1996—, Conformal Geometry and Dynamics, 1997—, Computational Methods and Function Theory, 2001—; contbr. numerous articles on rsch. in pure math. to sci. jours. With USNR, 1943-46. Decorated comdr. Finnish White Rose; NSF fellow, 1959-60; Fulbright fellow, 1958-59; Guggenheim fellow, 1958-59; Sci. Rsch. Coun. sr. fellow, 1981; Humboldt fellow, 1981-84; U. Auckland Found fellow, 1985; Finnish Acad. fellow U. Helsinki, 1989. Mem. NAS, Am. Acad. Arts and Scis., Assn. Women in Math., Math. Assn. Am., Am. Math. Soc. (coun. 1969-75, 80-83, trustee 1983-93, mem. editl. bd. 1997-98, Leroy P. Steele prize for Lifetime Achievement, 2006), Inst. for Math. and Its Applications (gov. 1981-84), Swiss Math. Soc., Finnish Math. Soc., London Math. Soc., Finnish Acad. Sci., Royal Norwegian Soc. Scis. and Letters. Died May 29, 2012.

GEISHEIMER, FRED, contractor; b. Cleve., Oct. 4, 1926; s. Fredric William and Elsie Marie Adeline (Gorges) G.; m. Rosemary Margaret Lipuma, Oct. 8, 1949; children: Kurt Fredrick, Karl Anthony, Kristine Marie, Kenneth Joseph. BEE, Case Inst. Tech., Cleve., 1951. Registered profl. engr., Ohio, N.Y., Ill. Engr. Dingle-Clark Co., Cleve., 1951-58, W.W. Clark Corp., Cleve., 1959-64, engring. mgr., 1965-71, chief engr., 1972-77, v.p., 1978-88, Forest Electric Corp. Ohio, Cleve., from 1989. Contbr. articles to profl. jours. With U.S. Army, 1945-46, ATO. Mem. Cleve. Engring. Soc., IEEE (sr.), Assn. Iron and Steel Engrs., Acacia Country Club, Mid-Day Club Cleve., Masons, Beta Theta Pi. Republican. Episcopalian. Avocations: flying, golf, bowling. Home: Cleveland, Ohio. Died May 28, 2007.

GENCSOY, HASAN TAHSIN, mechanical engineering educator; b. Balikesir, Turkey, July 4, 1924; came to U.S., 1945; s. Ahmet Sukru and Zumbule G.; m. Fatma Suheyla Akyurek, May 14, 1953; 1 child, S. Nilgun. BSME, U. Calif., Berkeley, 1949; MSME, W.Va. U., 1951. Registered profl. engr. Customer engr. IBM World Trade Corp., N.Y., 1951-52; mng. chief engr. Bakir Sanayi Turk Anonim Sirketi, Istanbul, Turkey, 1953-55; instr. to full prof. W.Va. Univ., Morgantown, 1955-85; prof. emeritus, self employed forensic tech. cons. Ft. Lauderdale, Fla., from 1985. Researcher, cons. various fed. govts., state govts. and pvt. industries, 1955-85. Contbr. articles to profl. jours. Lt. Turkish Army, 1952-53. Recipient Nat. Adams Meml. award Am. Welding Soc., 1966. Mem. ASME, Am. Soc. Engring. Edn., Sigma Xi, Pi Tau Sigma. Achievements include patent for Rotary Piston Coal Feeder, for Wear Compensating Seal Means for Rotary Piston Coal Feeder; patent for Automatic Coin Feeder for Parking Meters; research on measurement of residual stresses and acid rain purification of West Virginia streams. Died June 21, 2007.

GENTRY, BETTIJAINE, marketing company executive, consultant; b. Waltham, Mass., Sept. 14, 1946; d. John Elisha and Sally (Winogradski) G. BS in English, U. Mass., 1971; cert., Ulpan-Bat-Galim, Haifa, Israel, 1974; cert. Pub. Comms. Inst., Boston U., 1983. Instr. IDF, Haifa, 1975, U. Haifa, 1975-76, Technion U., Haifa, 1976-77; mktg. cons. Stoughton, Mass., 1978-86; founder, pres. Gentry Promotions, Inc., Phila., from 1986. Mktg. writer Mus. Modern Art, Haifa, 1977. Co-chair mentor program Am. Jewish Com., Boston, 1998; exec. bd. Black Jewish Econ. Roundtable, 1998-99. Mem. Boston C. of C. Avocations: sailing, tai chi, painting, watersports. Died Nov. 12, 2006.

GENTRY, DAPHNE SUE, historian; b. Danville, Va., Oct. 7, 1941; d. Arthur Merritt Jr. and Lucy Marguerite (Humphreys) G. BA, U. N.C., Greensboro, 1963, MA, 1964. Archivist Libr. Va., Richmond, 1964-79, historian, from 1979. Author: Dog Art: A Selection from the Dog Museum, 1996, The New West Highland White Terrier, 1998; asst. editor: Key to Survey Reports, 1990; editor Westie Imprint, 1991—, Mag. Va. Genealogy, 1993-96. Mem. West Highland White Terrier Club Am. (bd. dirs., v.p., pres. 1989-91, Pres.' award 1986, 94, 96), West Highland White Terrier Club Greater Wash. (sec.), West Highland White Terrier Club Ind., Va. Kennel Club (sec., pres., bd. dirs.). Avocations: breeding and showing west highland white terriers, needlecrafts. Home: Manakin Sabot, Va. Died Feb. 6, 2007.

GEORGE, DAVID B(RUCE), hotel executive; b. Wichita, Kans., Feb. 28, 1944; s. Harold R. and Helen V. (Gray) G.; m. Leslie A. Blake, Aug. 14, 1965 (div. Nov. 1980); children: David Blake, Alison Ann; m. Helen Angela Linn, Sept. 2, 1988. BSBA, Kans. State U., 1966. With Target Stores, Inc., 1966-74, personnel mgr. Houston, 1969-71, ops. mgr. Clinton, Iowa, 1971-74; pres., chief operating officer Local Loan Co., Wichita, 1974-81; gen. mgr. Residence Inn Co., Tulsa, 1981-85; v.p. ops. TMH Hotels, Inc., Wichita, from 1985. Bd. dirs., chmn. Local Loan Co., Wichita; gen. ptnr. DG Properties, L.P., Wichita, 1986—; mem. com. for operating stds. and procedures Residence Inn by Marriott, Bethesda, Md., 1988-2000. Co-chmn. United Way, Clinton, 1973. Mem. Nat. Pawnbrokers Assn., Tulsa Hotel and Motel Assn. (v.p. 1983), Jaycees (pres. Clinton chpt. 1974, Outstanding Pres. 1974), Optimists (v.p. Wichita chpt. 1977), Phi Delta Theta. Republican. Methodist. Home: Wichita, Kans. Died Apr. 27, 2007.

GEORGE, FRANCIS EUGENE CARDINAL, cardinal, archbishop emeritus; b. Chgo., Jan. 16, 1937; s. Francis J. and Julia R. (McCarthy) George. BTh, U. Ottawa, 1964, MA in Theology, 1971; MA in Philosophy, Cath. U. America, 1965; PhD in Philosophy, Tulane U., 1970; STD, Pontifical Urbaniana U., 1988; LLD (hon.), U. Portland, 1997, John Marshall Law Sch., 1998; DHL (hon.), Loyola U., Chgo., 1998; Doctorate of Pedagogy (hon.), Franciscan U., Steubenville, 2000; DHL (hon.), Barat Coll., 2000; LLD (hon.), Creighton U., 2001; DHL (hon.), Saint Xavier U., 2004. Joined Oblates of Mary Immaculate, 1957, ordained priest, 1963, provincial superior Midwest province Saint Paul, 1973—74, vicar gen. Rome, 1974—86; instr. in philos. Seminary of the Oblates, Pass Christian, Miss., 1964—69; tchg. fellow in philos. Tulane U., 1968—69; asst. prof. philosophy Creighton U., Omaha, 1969—73; coord. Circle of Fellows Cambridge Ctr. for Study of Faith and Culture, Mass., 1987—90; bishop of Yakima, Wash., 1990—96, ordained Wash., 1990; archbishop of Portland, Oreg., 1996—97, of Chgo., 1997—2014, archbishop emeritus, 2014—15; elevated to cardinal, 1998; cardinal-priest of San Bartolomeo all'Isola (Saint Bartholemew on Tiberina Island), 1998—2015. Vis. instr. in philosophy Our Lady of the Lake U., San Antonio, 1965; episcopal moderator, mem. Council of the Nat. Catholic Office for Persons with Disabilites, 1990—2008; episcopal moderator Cursillo Movement, 12th Region, 1990—97, Ministry of Transportation Chaplains, from 2003; vis. prof. religious studies Gonzaga U., 1993; bd. trustee Catholic U. of America, Washington, from 1993; mem. Council of Administration of the Oblate Media, Belleville, Ill., from 1988, Synod of Bishops on Consecrated Life, 1994, Council of Administration of the Pope John XXIII Ctr., Boston, from 1994; worked on the Com. on Religious Life and Ministry and the American Bd. of Catholic Missions within the Nat. Conference of Catholic Bishops (NCCB), 1994—97; consultor for the NCCB on the following commissions: Science and Human Values, 1994—97, Hispanic Affairs, 1994—97, Evangelization, 1991—93, African American Catholics, 1999—2002; mem. Commissions of the National Conference of Catholic Bishops in the United States of America, including Doctrine, 1991—94, 1996, Missions, 1991, Adhoc Com. on Shrines, 1992, The Church in Latin America, 1994, Adhoc Com. to Oversee the Use of the Catechism, 1995; mem. Council of Administration of the Catholic U. of America, from 1995; pres. Commn. for Bishops and Scholars NCCB, 1992—94, representative on the International

Commn. for English in the Liturgy, 1997—2006; chancellor Cath. Church Extension Soc., from 1997, U. Saint Mary of the Lake, from 1997; delegate, special secretary American Synod, 1997; mem. Basilica of the Nat. Shrine of the Immaculate Conception, from 1997; trustee Pontifical Foundation, from 1997; mem. Congregation Divine Worship and Discipline of the Sacraments, Rome, from 1998, Congregation for Institutes of Consecrated Life and Societies of Apostolic Life, Rome, from 1998, Pontifical Coun. Cor Unum, Rome, 1998, Pontifical Commn. for Cultural Heritage of the Church, Rome, from 1999, Congregation for the Evangelization of Peoples, Rome, from 1999, Congregation for Oriental Churches, Rome, from 2001, Pontifical Coun. for Culture, Rome, from 2004; v.p. United States Conf. Cath. Bishops, 2004—07, pres., 2007—10; mem. Catholic Commn. on Intellectual and Cultural Affairs, Council of Kohl McKornick Early Childhood Teaching awards, Com. Vox Clara, Council of Cardinals for the Study of Organizational and Economic Affairs of the Holy See, from 2010, Special Council for America of the General Secretariat of the Synod of Bishops, American Catholic Philosophical Assn., American Soc. Missiologists; council Catholic Church Extension Soc., Saint Mary of the Lake U., Mudelein, Ill.; honorary conventual chaplain Fed. Assn. of the Sovereign Military Order of Malta; grand prior North Central Lieutenancy of the United States for the Equestrian Order of the Holy Sepulchre of Jerusalem; bd. dirs. Nat. Catholic Bioethics Ctr., Philadelphia, Pa. Author (pastoral letter): Becoming an Evangelizing People, 1997, Dwell in My Love, 2001; author: Inculturation and Ecclesial Communion, 1990, The Difference God Makes: A Catholic Vision of Faith, Communion, and Culture, 2009, God in Action: How Faith in God Can Address the Challenges of the World, 2011; contbr. chapters to books, articles to theol. jours. Recipient Outstanding Educator of America award, 1972—73; Flannery Lecture, Gonzaga U., 1992, plenary address, American Catholic Philos. Assn. Convention, 1992. Roman Catholic. Died Apr. 17, 2015.

GEORGHIOU, MICHAEL, construction and development executive; b. Cyprus, Nov. 14, 1932; s. George and Ourania (Haralambous) G.; m. Helen P. Modenos, Aug. 15, 1961; 1 child, Christina. BS in Acctg. and Fin., London U., 1952. Comptroller, treas. James W. Elwell & Co., Inc., NYC, 1968-83; exec. v.p., treas. Theodore & Theodore Assocs., Inc., NYC, 1984-93. Bd. dirs. Broadway Corp., 1993—, Transteck Svc. Network, Inc., Evacutech. Safety Products LLC. Trustee St. Demetrios Greek Orthodox Ch., N.Y.C., 1969—; v.p. Am. Cyprus Congress, N.Y.C., 1984—. Recipient Humanitarian award Greek Orthodox Archdiocese, 1975, Govt. of Cyprus, 1975. Died May 20, 2007.

GERBERDING, WILLIAM PASSAVANT, retired academic administrator; b. Fargo, ND, Sept. 9, 1929; s. William Passavant and Esther Elizabeth Ann (Habighorst) G.; m. Ruth Alice Albrecht, Mar. 25, 1952; children: David Michael, Steven Henry, Elizabeth Ann, John Martin. BA, Macalester Coll., 1951; MA, U. Chgo., 1956, PhD, 1959. Congressoinal fellow American Polit. Sci. Assn., Washington, 1958-59; instr. Colgate U., Hamilton, N.Y., 1959-60; research asst. to Senator Eugene McCarthy US Senate, Washington, 1960-61; staff mem. to Rep. Frank Thompson, Jr. US House of Reps., Washington, 1961; faculty mem. UCLA, 1961-72, prof., chmn. dept. polit. sci., 1970-72, exec. vice chancellor, 1975-77; dean faculty, v.p. for acad. affairs Occidental Coll., Los Angeles, 1972-75; chancellor U. Ill., Urbana-Champaign, 1978-79; pres. U. Wash., Seattle, 1979-95. Cons. US Dept. Def., 1962, Calif. State Assembly, 1965. Author: United States Foreign Policy: Perspectives and Analysis, 1966; co-editor, contbg. author: The Radical Left: The Abuse of Discontent, 1970. Trustee Macalester Coll., 1980—83, 1996—2001, Gates Cambridge Trust, U. Cambridge, England, 2000—14. With USN, 1951—55. Recipient Distinguished Teaching award U. Calif., Los Angeles, 1966; Ford Found. grantee, 1967-68 Died Dec. 27, 2014.

GERKEN, WALTER BLAND, insurance company executive; b. NYC, Aug. 14, 1922; s. Walter Adam and Virginia (Bland) G.; m. Darlene Stolt, Sept. 6, 1952 (dec. 2009); children: Walter C., Ellen M., Beth L., Daniel J., Andrew P., David A. BA, Wesleyan U., 1948; MPA, Maxwell Sch. Citizenship and Pub. Affairs, Syracuse, 1958. Supr. budget and adminstrv. analysis, Wis., Madison, 1950-54; mgr. investments Northwestern Mut. Life Ins. Co., Milw., 1954-67; v.p. finance Pacific Mut. Life Ins. Co., LA, 1967-69, exec. v.p., 1969-72, pres., 1972-75, chmn., CEO, 1975—86, chmn. exec. com. Los Angeles, 1986—95, also dir.; ret. sr. advisor Boston Consulting Group. Bd. dirs. Mullin Cons., Inc.; vice-chmn. Global Fin. Group, 2000. Bd. dirs. Keck Found.; trustee emeritus Occidental Coll. L.A., Wesleyan U., Middletown, Conn.; bd. dirs. Nature Conservancy Calif.; mem. Calif. Citizens Budget Com., Calif. Commn. Campaign Fin. Reform, Calif. Commn. on Higher Edn.; bd. dirs., former chair Exec. Svc. Corps. So. Calif.; v.p. Orange County Cmty. Found.; mem. adv. bd. The Maxwell Sch. Citizenship and Pub. Affairs, Syracuse U. Decorated D.F.C., Air medal. Mem. Calif. Club, Dairymen's Country Club (Boulder Junction, Wis.), Automobile Club So. Calif. (bd. dirs.), Pauma Valley Country Club, Edison Internat., Times Mirror Co. Home: Corona Del Mar, Calif. Died Oct. 5, 2015.

GERMON, GEORGE, small business owner; b. White Plains, Apr. 1, 1945; m. Johanne Killeen. Degree, R.I. Sch. of Design; Dates in Culinary Arts (hon.), Johnson and Wales Univ., 2000. Chef, co-owner Al Forno Restaurant, Providence, 1975—2015. Appeared (TV series) Julia Child's Kitchen with Master Chefs, Baking with Julia, Martha Stewart Living, David Rosengarten's Grilling, Cooking Live Primetime (Sarah Moulton); co-author: CUCINA SIMPATICA:Robust Trattria Cooking. Actively involved Providence Pub. Libr., R.I. Food Bank, R.I. Projects Aids, R.I. Ballet. Recipient World's Restaurant for causal dining, Internat. Herald Tribune, Disting. Restaurants of North Am., Conde Nast Traveler's, 1992—2003, Hall of Fame award, Nations Restaurant News, Ivy award, James Beard award for being best chefs in the Northeast, 1994, Insegna del Ristorante Italiano, Italian Ministries of Agrl. and Foriegn Trade, 1999; named Rising Stars of Am., James Beard Found.; named one of The Ten Best Chefs in Am., Food and Wine. Died Oct. 27, 2015.

GESIORSKI, STANLEY LOUIS, accountant; b. Chgo., Sept. 10, 1951; s. Stanley and Katharine (Nowak) G.; m. Julie Graham, Sept. 24, 1983. BS in Acctg., U. Ill., Chgo., 1973. CPA., Ill. Revenue agt. IRS, Chgo., 1973-77; pvt. practice acctg. Addison, Ill., from 1978. Mem. Am. Inst. CPA's, Ill. CPA Soc. Roman Catholic. Avocations: sports, camping, travel. Home: Wood Dale, Ill. Died Nov. 20, 2006.

GESLER, DONNA MARIE, newsletter editor, consultant; b. Detroit, June 11, 1940; d. John Edward and Loretto Marie (Snyder) Kennedy; m. William G. Gesler, Aug. 1, 1959; children: Marvin, Alexander, William III, Rebecca. AA, Wayne County C.C.; BA, Ea. Mich. U., 1978; MBA, Mich. State U., 1984. CPIM. Sr. demand/supply specialist Unisys, Plymouth, Mich., 1989-91; sr. ops. specialist GE Med. Systems, Novi, Mich., 1991-94; cons. Gesler & Assocs., Northville, Mich., from 1994. Adj. faculty Ctrl. Mich. U., Troy, 1987—. Editor, cons. (newsletter) Productivity News. Dep. registrar of voters Twp. of Nankin, 1962. Mem. Am. Prodn. Inventory Control Soc., Soc. Logistics Engrs., Prodn. Ops. Mgmt. Soc., NAFE. Avocations: reading, gardening, computing. Home: Northville, Mich. Died Feb. 7, 2007.

GIBBLE, WALTER PAUL, oil and gas industry consultant; b. Atglen, Pa., July 26, 1916; s. Walter Paul and Mabel Teresa (Wise); m. Jeanne A. van Dyck, Dec. 31, 1960. BS, U. Pa., 1941; MS, U. Ariz., 1951, PhD, 1956. Dir. research Vegetable Oil Products, Wilmington, Calif., 1955-57, VA Hosp., Tucson, 1957-62; sr. chemist Hunt-Wesson Foods, Fullerton, Calif., 1962-76; tech. cons. Govt. of India, New Delhi, 1979-80; indsl. cons. Edible Oil Cos., from 1980. Cons. Hunt-Wesson Foods, Fullerton, Wilsey Food Inc., City of Industry, Calif., Surya Agroils Ltd., New Delhi, Modipon Ltd., Modingar, India. Contbr. articles to sci. jours.; patentee in field. Served to commdr. USN, 1942-49. Recipient Highest Merit award Hunt-Wesson Foods, Fullerton, 1971. Mem. Service Corps Retired Execs. (chmn. local satellite chpt. 1983—), Am. Chem. Soc., Am. Oil Chemists Soc., Sigma Xi. Lutheran. Avocations: fishing, photography. Died Apr. 18, 2007.

GIBBONS, JOHN HOWARD (JACK, JACK GIBBONS), federal official, physicist; b. Harrisonburg, Va., Jan. 15, 1929; s. Howard K. and Jessie Diana (Conrad) G.; m. Mary Ann Hobart, May 21, 1955; children: Virginia Neil Barber, Diana Conrad (dec. 2014), Mary Marshall Meyer. BS in Math. and Chemistry, Randolph-Macon Coll., 1949, ScD (hon.), 1977; PhD in Physics, Duke U., 1954, ScD (hon.), 1997; PhD in Humane Letters and Sci. (hon.), Ill. Inst. Tech., 1994; PhD in Sci. (hon.), Mt. Sinai Med. Sch., 1995; ScD (hon.), U. Delaware, 1996, U. Md., 1997. Physicist and group leader nuclear geophysics Oak Ridge Nat. Lab., 1954-69, dir. environ. program, 1969-73; first dir. Energy Conservation Office, Washington, 1973-74, Federal Energy Adminstr.; prof. physics, dir. Energy, Environ. and Resources Center, U. Tenn., Knoxville, 1974-79; dir. Office of Tech. Assessment, U.S. Congress, 1979—93; asst. to Pres. for sci. and tech. Exec. Office of the Pres., Washington, 1993-98; dir. of sci. and tech. policy Exec. Office of Pres., Washington, 1993-98; pres. Resource Strategies, from 1998; Karl T. Compton lectr. MIT, 1998-99; sr. fellow NAE, 1999-2000; sr. advisor U.S. Dept. State, 1999-2000. Adv. com. neutron cross sects. US Atomic Energy Commn., 1969—70; adv. com. nat. ctr. analysis energy sys. Brookhaven Nat. Lab., 1976—77; chmn. demand/conservation panel Com. Nuclear & Alternative Energy Sys., 1976—79; chmn. adv. com. energy and environ. sys. divsn. Argonne Nat. Lab., 1977—79; chmn. adv. com. nat. ctr. analysis energy sys. Brookhaven Nat. Lab., 1977; adv. bd. energy R&D US Dept. Energy, 1978—79; mem. Energy Rsch. Adv. Bd., 1978—79; mem. bd. sci. and tech. for internat. development Com. Nuclear & Alternative Energy Sys., 1979—87; energy and resources com. Aspen Inst., from 1979; sr. adv. panel Energy Modeling Forum Stanford U., 1980—92, mem. adv. com. Sch. Engring., 1984—87; bd. dirs. Resources for the Future, 1983—92; mem. steering com. Symposium Series Tech. & Soc., 1984—92; mem. adv. com. Electric Power Rsch. Inst., 1986—92; mem. exec. com. An Energy Agenda for 1990s, 1987—88; mem. Carnegie Corp. Sci., Tech. and Govt. Task Force on Long Term Goals and Priorities, 1990—92, Governor's Commn. Climate Change, Common Wealth Virginia, from 2008, Adv. Panel, EPCOT Walt Disney World, 1981—82; mem., bd. dirs. The Energy Found., 1990—92; bd. dirs. Dynamac Corp., from 1998; mem. coun. advisors Nat. Renewable Energy Lab., from 1998; mem. steering com. Nat. Climate Assessment, 1998—2001; bd. dirs. World Resource Inst., 1998—2003, chair program com., 1999—2000; bd. dirs. Interstate Waste Techs., LLP, from 1999, Black Rock Forest Consortium, from 1999, Action LLC; chair World Bank panel on millenium sci. initiatives, 2000—01, Com. Improving Effectiveness Environ. Non-Gov. Programs, Russia, 2000; mem. internat. adv. bd. com. on internat. programs Nat. Acads., 2001—06, divsn. advisor divsn. on phys. scis. and engring., from 2001; chief acad. advisor Shenglongda Co. Ltd., 2001—06; mem. strategic adv. com. Gas Tech. Inst., 2003—06; chmn. bd. Population Action Internat., 2003—06; mem. adv. bd. MIT Innovations Tech./Governance/Globalization Jour., from 2005; mem. Idaho Nat. Lab. Sci. and Tech. Com., from 2005; cons. Lawrence Livermore Nat. Lab., from 2002; adv. bd. Airlie Found., from 2006; bd. dirs. Scientists and Engrs. Am., from 2006; sr. adviser Global Environment and Tech. Found., 2006; mem. adv. bd. Ctr. Am. Progress Jour. Sci. Tech. and Human Values, from 2007; bd. dirs. Transition Energy, 2007; steering com. chair, Tech. and Peace Building Nat. Acad. Engring., 2001—08; cons. in field. Author: (with William U. Chandler) Energy: The Conservation Revolution, 1981, This Gifted Age: Science and Technology at the Millennium, 1997; contbr. articles to profl. jours. Trustee, Randolph-Macon Coll., Ashland, Va., 1977-79, chmn., bd. assocs. 1980-83; bd. dirs. World's Fair Enegy Expo, 1978-79, 1982, State Tenn. Energy Authority, 1977-1979; adv. com. Corp. Thomas Jefferson's Poplar Forest, 1983. Decorated comdr. Ordre des Palmes Academiques (France), 1994, officer's cross Order of Merit (Germany), 1991; recipient Disting. Svc. award Fed. Energy Adminstrn., 1974, Disting. Alumni award James Madison U., 1993, Disting. Pub. Svc. award, Nat. Scis. Found., 1998, Life Achievement in Sci. award Commonwealth of Va., 1995, First Seymour Cray High Performance Computing Industry Recognition award, 1997, Governor's Outstanding Tennessean award, 1997; Disting. Svc. medal NASA, 1998, Alumni Excellence award Va. Found. for Ind. Colls., 2002, Disting. Career in Sci. and Engring. award Washington Acad. Scis., 2005, First George Brown award Coop. R&D Found., 2005, Lifetime Achievement in Energy Efficiency award, Alliance to Save Energy, 2007, Alumni Disting. Alumnus award, Randalph-Macon Coll. Soc., 2008. Fellow: AAAS (bd. dirs. 1988—90, Philip Hauge Abelson prize 1993), Am. Assn. Engring. Socs. (chmn.'s award 1998), Am. Phys. Soc. (Leo Szilard award for physics in pub. interest 1991), Am. Acad. Arts and Scis., Assn. for Women in Sci.; mem.: Am. Philos. Soc., N.Y. Acad. Scis. (bd. govs. 1998—2002), Coun. Fgn. Rels., Nat. Acad. Engring. (chmn. steering com. 2007, Arthur Bueche award 1998), Cosmos Club, Sigma Pi Sigma, Pi Mu Epsilon, Omicron Delta Kappa, Pi Gamma Mu, Phi Beta Kappa, Sigma Xi (nat. Sigma lectr. 1978—79, pres. 2000—01, John P. McGovern Sci. and Soc. award and medal 1997). Episcopalian. Avocations: hiking, farming. Home: The Plains, Va. *My formal training in physics, backed by a liberal arts education, enabled me to drink deeply from the sweet spring of basic research for many years. When I took leave from disciplinary research and became immersed in analysis of sociotechnical issues, it was a most discomforting step. But having taken it, the new challenges were not only enlivening, but also surprisingly susceptible to the problem-solving approaches I had learned in science. The lessons: (1)Training in physics is an effective instrument to learn how to solve many kinds of problems; (2)A change in professional direction about every decade or so is a great tonic; (3)Attacking issues from fresh perspectives is a natural ingredient of creativity.* Died July 18, 2015.

GIBBS, JAMES CALVIN, editor, publisher, composer, educator, scientist; b. Asheville, NC, Mar. 28, 1924; s. Jeter Prichard and Inez Louise (Hilton) G.; m. Clara Camps, June 20, 1947 (dec. June 1973). BA in Human Rels., U. Miami, 1954; graduate, Inst. of Psychorientology, Laredo, Tex., 1973. Chief clk. U.S. Govt., Cherry Point, N.C., 1942; mgr. Pan Am Airways, Miami, 1946-79; tchr. Assoc. Schs., North Miami Beach, Fla., 1980-85; pub., editor Gibbs Pub. Co., North Miami Beach, 1956-99, Burnsville, N.C., from 1999. Contbr. articles on parapsychology to various mags. and primary publs. Sgt. USMC, 1943-46. Mem. Am. Parapsychol. Rsch. Found. (charter), Life Dynamics Fellowship (assoc.), Inst. of Cosmic Sci. (charter, Parapsychology award 1977), MENSA, Internat. Tesla Soc. Avocations: writing, publishing and teaching parapsychology, journalistic assignments. Died Apr. 4, 2007.

GICLAS, HENRY LEE, astronomer; b. Flagstaff, Ariz., Dec. 9, 1910; s. Eli and Hedwig Herminna (Leissling) G.; m. Bernice Francis Kent, May 23, 1936; 1 child, Henry Lee. BS, U. Ariz., 1937; postgrad., U. Calif., Berkeley, 1939-40; PhD with honors, No. Ariz. U., 1980. Research asst. Lowell Obs., Flagstaff, 1931-44, astronomer, 1944-79, exec. sec., 1952-75; adj. prof. Ohio State U., Columbus, 1968-79, No. Ariz. U., 1972-79. Mem. Flagstaff Freeholder's Com., 1959; exec. v.p. Raymond Ednl. Found., 1971-77, pres., 1977-91. Fellow AAAS; mem. Am. Astron. Soc., Ariz. Acad. Sci., Astron. Soc. Pacific (dir. 1959-61), No. Ariz. Pioneers Hist. Soc. (pres. 1972-80), Internat. Astron. Union. Clubs: Coconino Country (pres 1962), Continental Country (adv. bd. 1972-75). Lodges: Elks. Home: Flagstaff, Ariz. Died Apr. 2, 2007.

GIFFORD, FRANK NEWTON (FRANCIS NEWTON GIFFORD), former sportscaster, commentator, former professional football player; b. Santa Monica, Calif., Aug. 16, 1930; s. Weldon Wayne and Lola (Hawkins) G.; m. Maxine Ewart (div.); children: Jeffery, Kyle, Victoria; m. Astrid Naess, Mar. 1978 (div. 1986); m. Kathie Lee (Epstein), 1986; children: Cody Newton, Cassidy Erin. Student, Bakersfield Jr. Coll., 1948-49; BA, U. So. Calif., 1952. Mem. N.Y. Giants (profl. football team), 1952—64; sports reporter CBS Radio, NYC, 1957-59; Nat. Football League pre-game show host CBS-TV Network, NYC, 1959-62; sports reporter WCBS-TV, NYC, 1962-71; reporter ABC Radio Info., NYC, 1971-77; sports corr. ABC TV Network, NYC, 1971-1986; corr. Eyewitness News, NYC, 1971-1986; announcer ABC Monday Night Football, 1971-86, commentator, 1986-98, program show host, 1998. Host The Superstars Series.; dir. sports writers and broadcasters Spl. Olympics, 1972-75 Author: Frank Gifford's NFL-AFL Football Guide, 1968, rev. edits., 1969, 70, Frank Gifford's Football Guide Book, 1966, (with Charles Mangel) Gifford on Courage, 1976, (with Harry Waters, Jr.) Gifford: The Whole Ten Yards, 1993; guest co-host, Live with Regis and

Kathy Lee Bd. dirs. Nat. Soc. for Multiple Sclerosis, 1973-78; co-founder Cody House, Cassidy's Place, Children's Healthcare Facilities, N.Y. Named Collegiate All-Am., 1952, NFL MVP, 1956, Sportsman of Yr., Cath. Youth Orgn., 1964; elected to Nat. Football Found. Hall of Fame, 1976, Pro Football Hall of Fame, 1977, U. So. Calif. Athletic Hall of Fame, 1994; recipient Gil Hodges Meml. sports award Cath. Med. Center, 1976, Adam award Men's Fashion Assn. Am., 1976, Emmy award for outstanding sports personality, 1977, Christopher award, 1984, Founder's award Multiple Sclerosis Soc., N.Y., 1984, others. Died Aug. 9, 2015.

GILBERT, SIR MARTIN (JOHN), historian; b. London, Oct. 25, 1936; s. Peter and Miriam (Green) G.; m. Helen Robinson; 1 child, Natalie; m. Susan Sacher; children: David, Joshua; m. Ester Goldberg; stepchildren Shoshana Israel, Mirit Poznansky BA with honors, Oxford U., Eng., 1960; PhD (hon.), Oxford U., 1999. Fellow Merton Coll., Oxford, 1962—95, hon. fellow, 1995—2015; prof. history dept. U. Western Ontario, 2006—07; biographer of Sir. Winston Churchill, from 1968. Author: Winston S. Churchill, vols. 3-8, 1971-88, The Holocaust, The Fate of the Jews of Europe, 1933-45, 1983, Shcharansky, Hero of Our Time, 1986, A History pf the Jews of Europe During the Second World War, 1986, The Second World War, A Complete History, 1989, Churchill, A Life, 1991, The First World War, 2002 and several others; co-author The Appeasers, 1963 Recipient Wolfson prize Wolfson History Awards, 1987, Dr. Leopold Lucas prize, U. Tubingen, 2003; named comdr. of the Order of the Brit. Empire, 1990, Knighted, 1995; Disting. felloe, Hillsdale Coll., Mich., 2002, hon. fellow Churchill Coll., 2008 Fellow Royal Soc. of Lit. Avocation: drawing historical maps. Home: London, England. Died Feb. 3, 2015.

GILBERT, S. PARKER (SEYMOUR PARKER GILBERT, III), retired investment company executive; b. NYC, Nov. 15, 1933; m. Gail Gilbert; children: Lynn Tudor, S. Parker Jr., David Parker. BA, Yale U., 1956. With Morgan Stanley & Co. Inc., NYC, 1960—89, ptnr., 1969—70, mng. dir., 1970—89, mem. mgmt. com., 1974—89, pres., 1983—89, chmn. bd., 1984—89. Bd. dirs. NY Stock Exchange, 1986—90, Burlington Resources, 1990—2001, ITT Corp., 1991—95, Taubman Centers, Inc., 1992—2004, ITT Industries, 1995—99, Morgan Stanley Group, Inc., 1986—97, Bessemer Securities. Vice chmn. bd. trustees St. Luke's-Roosevelt Hosp. Ctr.; trustee Hotchkiss Sch., Lakeville, Conn., Metropolitan Mus. of Art, Alfred P. Sloan Found., Josiah Macy Jr. Found.; bd. dirs. Josiah Macy, Jr. Found.; head Pierpont Morgan Library and Mus., 1988-2001, also bd. dirs. Served in US Army, 1956—59. Died May 27, 2015.

GILBERT, III, SEYMOUR PARKER See GILBERT, S. PARKER

GILES, JIMMIE DREXAL, meteorologist; b. Hillsdale, Ind., Nov. 2, 1939; s. James Herbert and Nedra Olis (Thornton) G.; m. Hannelore Gudrun Schrank, Dec. 7, 1963; children: Andrea Gudrun, Angela Erika. BS in Sci., Math., Ball State U., 1961; student, U. Tex., 1961-62; MS in Meteorology, U. Okla., 1967; teaching cert., St. Mary's U., 1973; postgrad. in Meteorology, U. Tex., 1975-81. Commd. 2d lt. USAF, 1961, advanced through grades to capt., weather officer Socialist Republic of Vietnam, 1964-65, ret., 1970; tchr. sci. Holmes High Sch., San Antonio, 1973-75; teaching asst. U. Tex., Austin, 1975-80; weather forecaster Sta. KVET-KASE, Austin, 1977; assoc. prof. U. Tex., Austin, 1981; weekend weather anchorman Sta. KXAS-TV, Ft. Worth, 1980-81, Sta. WBAP-KCSC, Ft. Worth, 1980-81; weekday TV anchorman Sta. KTVV-TV, Austin, 1977-81; weekday weather forecaster Sta. KWEN-FM, Tulsa, from 1981; weekday weather anchorman Sta. KOTV-TV, Tulsa, from 1981. Adj. prof. U. Tulsa, 1983; pres. Giles Cons., Inc., Tulsa, 1985—. Contbr. articles to profl. jours. Organizer, pres. Forest Oaks Community Assn., Leon Valley, Tex., 1972-74; host Vol. Telethon, Tulsa, 1985—; spokesman Giles' Coats for Kids Salvation Army, Tulsa, 1986—; host Tulsa location Jerry Lewis Muscular Dystrophy Telethon, 1986—. Mem. Am. Meteorol. Soc. (pres. Cen. Tex. chpt. 1972-73, v.p. 1976-77). Clubs: German-American Soc. (Tulsa). Methodist. Avocations: fishing, camping, world travel. Home: Okmulgee, Okla. Died Dec. 20, 2006.

GILLIGAN, EDWARD PATRICK, finance company executive; b. Bklyn., July 13, 1959; m. Lisa Sneddon; children: Katie, Kevin, Shane, Meaghan. BS in Economics and Mgmt., NYU, 1982. Sr. v.p. bus. travel American Express Co., NYC, 1988—92, sr. v.p. comml. card & bus. travel, 1992—95, pres. corp. services, 1996—2000, group pres., internat. & global corp. services, 2005—07, group CEO bus. to bus., 2007—09, vice chmn., 2007—15, pres., 2013—15. Bd. dirs. Concur Technologies, Inc., from 2008. Died May 29, 2015.

GILMAN, ALFRED GOODMAN, pharmacologist, educator; b. New Haven, July 1, 1941; s. Alfred and Mabel (Schmidt) Gilman; m. Kathryn Hedlund, Sept. 21, 1963; children: Amy, Anne, Edward. BS, Yale U., New Haven, 1962; MD, PhD, Case Western Res. U., Cleve., 1969, DSc (hon.), 1995, U. Chgo., 1991, U. Miami, 1999; DMS (hon.), Yale U., 1997. Pharmacology rsch. assoc. NIH, Bethesda, Md., 1969—71; asst. prof., then assoc. prof. pharmacology U. Va., Charlottesville, 1971—77, prof., 1977—81, dir. med. sci. tng. program, 1979—81; prof. pharmacology, chmn. dept. U. Tex. Southwestern Med. Ctr., Dallas, 1981—2005, Raymond & Ellen Willie disting. chmn. molecular neuropharmacology, 1987—2009, regental prof. pharmacology emeritus, from 1994, interim dean Southwestern Med. Sch., 2004—05, dir. Cecil H. & Ida Green Comprehensive Ctr. Molecular Computational and Sys. Biol., 2004—09, provost, exec. v.p. acad. affairs, dean Southwestern Med. Sch., 2005—09; chief scientific officer Cancer Prevention Inst. Tex., 2007—10. Mem. pharmacology study sect. NIH, 1977—81, mem. nat. adv. gen. med. scis. coun., 1992—95; bd. sci. counselors Nat. Heart, Lung Blood & Inst., 1982—86; mem. sci. adv. com. Am. Cancer Soc., NYC, 1982—86; mem. sci. adv. bd. Huntsman Cancer Inst., U. Utah, 1995—2000, Ernest Gallo Clinic & Rsch. Ctr., U. Calif., San Francisco, 1996—2001, Lucille P. Markey Charitable Trust, Miami, 1984—96; mem. sci. rev. bd. Howard Hughes Med. Inst., Bethesda, 1986—93; dir. Regeneron Pharmaceutics, from 1989, Eli Lilly and Co., Inc., from 1995; mem. vis. com. Case Western Res. U. Sch. Medicine, 1995—99; chmn. steering com. Alliance Cellular Signaling, 2000—08. Editor The Pharmacological Basis of Therapeutics; contbr. articles to profl. jours. Recipient Poul Edvard Poulsson award, Norwegian Pharmacology Soc., 1982, Gairdner Found. Internat. award, 1984, Albert Lasker award for basic med. rsch., 1989, Passano Sr. award, Passano Found., 1990, Waterford Biomed. Sci. award, Scripps Clinic & Rsch. Found., 1990, Basic Sci. Rsch. prize, Am. Heart Assn., 1990, City of Medicine award, Durham, NC, 1991, Ciba-Geigy Drew award, 1991, Nobel prize in physiology/medicine, 1994, Disting. Alumnus award, Case Western Res. U., 1995, Am. Acad. Achievement award, 1995, Med. Honor Basic Rsch. award, Am. Cancer Soc., 1995; named to Tex. Hall of Fame, 2001. Mem.: NAS (Richard Lounsbery award 1987), Tex. Acad. Sci. Engring. & Medicine, Am. Acad. Arts & Scis., Inst. Medicine, Am. Soc. Biol. Chemistry, Am. Soc. Pharmacology & Exptl. Therapeutics (John J. Abel award in pharmacology 1975, Louis S. Goodman and Alfred Gilman award 1990, Torald Sollman award 1997). Home: Dallas, Tex. Died Dec. 23, 2015.

GILMARTIN, CLARA T., volunteer; b. East Stroudsburg, Pa., Jan. 23, 1922; d. Harry and Clarissa (Snearley) Treible; m. John Gilmartin, Jan. 18, 1945 (dec. Feb. 1956); children: Ronald, Donald; m. William Gilmartin, Sept. 8, 2002. BA, Rutgers U., 1961, MA, 1966. Elem. sch. tchr. Union Beach (N.J.) Pub. Sch., 1956-61; lang. arts tchr. Holmdel Village (N.J.) Intermediate Sch., 1961-82; Fulbright exch. tchr. New Zealand, 1973-74; mem. adv. bd. Juvenile Conf. Com., from 1986. Chair bd. trustees Grace Meth. Ch., Union Beach, 1997—. Mem. Monmouth County Ret. Educators Assn., Am. Legion (Post 321 Color Guard, scholarship com., trustee, chaplain), Triad. Democrat. Home: Union Beach, NJ. Died Dec. 26, 2006.

GILROY, FRANK DANIEL, playwright; b. NYC, Oct. 13, 1925; s. Frank B. and Bettina (Vasti) Gilroy; m. Ruth Dorothy Gaydos, Feb. 13, 1954; children: Anthony, John, Daniel. BA magna cum laude, Dartmouth Coll., 1950; postgrad., Yale Sch. Drama. Author became TV writer, (TV series) (originated) Burkes Law, (TV writer, scripts prod. on programs) Playhouse 90, U.S. Steel Hour, Omnibus, Kraft Theatre, Lux Video Theatre, Studio One, Westinghouse Studio; dir.(writer): 40 Gibbsville, 1975, The Doorbell Rang, 1977, Money Plays, 1997; author: (plays) Who'll Save the Plowboy? (presented off-Broadway, 1962), 1957, (completed) The Subject Was Roses, 1962, (presented on Broadway, 1964), 1962; presented (Broadway plays) That Summer-That Fall, 1967, The Only Game in Town, 1968, Last Licks, 1979, Any Given Day, 1993, (off Broadway plays) Contact With the Enemy, 1999, one-act (produced off-Broadway plays) The Next Contestant, 1978, Real to Reel, 1987, Match Point, 1990, A Way With Word, 1991, Give the Bishop My Faint Regards, 1992, Contact with the Enemy, 2000, Inspector Ohms, 2001, Piscary, 2008; prodr.(writer, dir.): (films) Desperate Characters, 1970 (best screenplay award Berlin Film Festival), From Noon Till Three, 1977, The Gig, 1985, Once in Paris (original screenplay), 1978; writer, dir. (films) The Luckiest Man in the World, 1989; author: Present Tense, prod. off-Broadway, 1972, (novels) Private, 1970, (with Ruth Gilroy) Little Ego, 1970, From Noon till Three, 1973, (non-fiction) I Wake Up Screening-Everything You Need to Know About Making Independent Films Including A Thousand Reasons Not To, 1993, Writing for Love and/or Money: Outtakes From a Life on Spec-The Early Years, 2007, (screenplays) (with Russell Rouse) The Fastest Gun Alive, 1956, (with Beirne Lay Jr.) Gallant Hours, 1960, Desperate Characters, 1971, The Subject was Roses, The Only Game in Town, From Noon till Three, Once in Paris. With US Army, 1943—46, ETO. Recipient Obie award for best Am. play, 1962, Outer Circle award, 1964, Drama Critics Circle award, 1964, N.Y. Theatre Club award, 1964—65, Antoinette Perry award, 1965, Pulitzer prize for drama, 1965; nominee Best Play N.Y. Drama Desk, 1999—2000. Mem.: Writers Guild Am., Dirs. Guild Am., Dramatists Guild (pres. 1969—71). Home: Monroe, NY. Died Sept. 12, 2015.

GIMBERLINE, JACQUELINE L., accountant, internal auditor; b. Akron, Iowa, Sept. 21, 1946; d. John W. and Amelia May (Lambert) Henrich; m. Donald Dean Gimberline, Oct. 30, 1993; children: Kimberly J. Bitz McCleary, Sandra L. Bitz. MB, Morningside Coll., 1988; MBA, U. S.D., 1993. CPA, Iowa. Asst. mgr. Midwest divsn. Prices Fine Chocolate, Sioux City, Iowa, 1980-84; adminstrv. asst. Morningside Coll., Sioux City, 1984-88; acct. Midwest Energy, Sioux City, 1988-89; investment analyst Midwest Capital Group, Sioux City, 1989-90, adminstr., 1990-91; mgr. internal audit Midwest Power Systems, Sioux City, from 1994; mgr. treasury InterCoast Energy Co., Des Moines, Iowa, from 1995. Treas. Sioux Land Youth Symphony, Sioux City, 1994; bd. dirs. curriculum adv. bd. We. Iowa Tech., Sioux City, 1992-94. Mem. AICPA, Inst. Mgmt. Accts. Home: Dubuque, Iowa. Died Jan. 26, 2007.

GIMBLE, JOHNNY (JOHN PAUL GIMBLE), country musician; b. May 30, 1926; m. Barbara Kemp (div.); children: Dick, Cyndy, Paula Gay Bullock. Played with Rhythmaires, Corpus Christi, 1948, Bob Willis and Texas Playboys, 1949. Musician: (albums) Fiddlin' Around, 1974, Johnny Gimble's Texas Dance Party, 1976, Johnny Gimble's Texas Honky Tonk Hits, Johnny Gimble & the Texas Swing Pioneers, 1980, Texas Fiddle Collection, 1981, Glorybound, 1987, Still Fiddlin' Around, 1988, Under the X of Texas, 1992, A Case of the Gimbles, 2005, Celebrating with Friends, 2010. Served US Army. Recipient Grammy award, 1994, Grammy award Best Country Instrumental Performance, 1995, of Nine-Best Fiddler awards, Academy of Country Music; named five times-Instrumentalist of the Yr., Country Music Assn.; Nat. Heritage Fellowship, Nat. Endowment for the Arts, 1994. Died May 9, 2015.

GINIGER, KENNETH SEEMAN, publisher; b. NYC, Feb. 18, 1919; s. Maurice Aaron and Pearl (Triester) G.; m. Carol Virginia Wilkins, Sept. 27, 1952 (dec. Aug. 1985); m. Bernice Dees Ellinger Cullinan, Apr. 13, 2002. Student, U. Va., 1935-39, N.Y. Law Sch., 1940-41. Ptnr. Signet Press, 1939-40; assoc. editor Arts and Decoration and The Spur, 1940-41; dir. pub. relations Prentice-Hall, Inc., 1946-49, editor-in-chief trade book div., 1949-52; v.p., gen. mgr. Hawthorn Books div., 1952-61; pres. Hawthorn Books, Inc., NYC, 1961-65, K.S. Giniger Co., Inc., NYC, from 1965, Consol. Book Pubs. div. Processing & Books, Inc., Chgo., 1969-74, Tradewinds Group div. IPC Ltd., Sydney, 1974-76; pub. Sports Medicine Fitness Report, 1981—83. Lectr. New Sch. Social Rsch., 1948—49, NYU, 1979—81, adj. asst. prof., 1981—83, adj. assoc. prof., 1983—85; asst. to dir. CIA, 1951—52. Author: The Compact Treasury of Inspiration, 1955 (NCCJ Brotherhood Week citation), America, America, America, 1957, A Treasury of Golden Memories, 1958, A Little Treasury of Hope, 1968, A Little Treasury of Comfort, 1966, A Little Treasury of Christmas, 1968, The Sayings of Jesus, 1968, The Family Advent Book, 1979, Pope John Paul II: Pilgrim of Faith, 1987; author: (with Walter Russell Bowie) What is Protestantism?, 1965; author: (with Will Yolen) Heroes for Our Times, 1969; author: (with Sir John Templeton) Spiritual Evolution, 1998; editor: Internat. Pub. News, 1983—91, European Bookseller Pub. World/Update Newsletter, 1991—92; mem. editl. bd. RAM Reports, 1977—83, Communications and the Law, 1978—94. Sec. Com. Collective Security, 1952—65; nat. adv. bd. Found. Religious Action, 1956—94; dir. Layman's Nat. Bible Com., 1957—2006, pres., 1963—71, chmn., 1987—94, chmn. emeritus, from 1994; mem. adv. bd. Templeton Found., 1992—2000, 2004—06, Am. Theater Wing, from 1999, Blanton-Peale Inst., from 2002. Pvt. to capt. US Army, 1941—52. Decorated French Legion of Honor; recipient Norman Vincent Peale award for Positive Thinking, Blanton-Peale Inst., 2006. Mem.: PEN, Church Club NYC, Dutch Treat Club, Army and Navy Club Washington, Garrick Club London, Yale Club NYC, Phi Delta Phi. Republican. Episcopalian. Home: New York, NY. Died Feb. 2015.

GIRARD, RENÉ NOEL, author, educator, philosopher; b. Avignon, France, Dec. 25, 1923; came to U.S., 1947; s. Joseph and Thérèse (Fabre) G.; m. Martha McCullough, June 18, 1951; children: Martin, Daniel, Mary Girard Brown. Archiviste-paléographe, Ecole des chartes, Paris, 1947; PhD, Ind. U., 1950. Tchr. Romance langs. Ind. U., 1947-52, Duke U., 1952-53, Bryn Mawr Coll., 1953-57; faculty Johns Hopkins U., 1957-68, prof. French lit., 1961-68, chmn. dept. Romance langs., 1966-68, James M. Beall prof. French and humanities, 1977-80; disting. faculty prof. arts and letters SUNY, Buffalo, 1971-77; Andrew B. Hammond prof. French and Comparative Lit., Stanford U., 1981-95; prof. emeritus, 1995—2015; with Achever Clausewitz, 2007, French Acad., 2005. Hon. chair Colloquium on Violence and Religion. Author: Mensonge romantique et vérité romanesque, 1961, 78, Marcel Proust: A Collection of Critical Essays, 1962, 77, Deceit, Desire and the Novel, 1967, 76, La Violence et le Sacré, 1972, English transl., 1977, Critique dans un souterrain, 1976, Des Choses cachées depuis la fondation du monde, 1978, To Double Business Bound, 1978, Le Bouc émissaire, 1982, La Route antique des hommes pervers, 1985, Things Hidden since the Foundation of the World, 1987, Job: the Victim of his People, 1987, Shakespeare: Les feux de l'envie, 1990, A Theater of Envy. William Shakespeare, 1991, Quand ces choses commenceront, 1994, The Girard Reader (ed. James Williams), 1996, Resurrection from the Underground: Feodor Dostoevsky (ed. James Williams), 1997, Je Vois Satan Tomber Comme L'Éclair, 1999, I see Satan fall like Lightning, 2001, Celui par qui le scandale arrive, 2001, La voix méconnue du réel, 2002, Les origines de la culture, 2004; contbr. articles to profl. jours. Guggenheim fellow, 1960, 67; recipient Prix Médicis Essai, 1990, Premio Nonino, 1998, Modern Language Assn. Lifetime Achievement award, 2009, Order of Isabella the Catholic, King of Spain, 2013 Mem. Acad. Arts and Scis., French Legion Honor, Acad. Francaise (Grand prix de philosophie 1996). Home: Stanford, Calif. Died Nov. 4, 2015.

GIRZONE, JOSEPH FRANCIS, retired priest, writer; b. Albany, NY, May 15, 1930; s. Peter Joseph and Margaret Rita (Campbell) G. BA in Biology, St. Bonaventure U., 1953; D Theology, Whitefriars Hall, 1955. Entered Carmelite Order, 1948; ordained Catholic priest, 1955; high sch. tchr. NY, 1955-64, Pa.; mem. faculty St. Albert's Seminary, Middletown, NY, 1960-61; pastor various chs., NY, 1964-81, Our Lady Mt. Carmel Ch., Amsterdam, NY, 1974-81; writer, 1981—2015. Bd. dirs. Schenectady Joint Commn. Christians and Jews; dir. Dominican 3d Order Religious Lay People, 1964-76; mem. N.Y. State Bishop's adv. comm. criminal justice; chmn. Schenectady County N.Y. Human Rights commn., 1973-74; vice chmn. Title III adv. bd. N.Y. State Office Aging, 1974-76. Author: Kara: The Lonely Falcon, 1979, Who Will Teach Me?, 1982, Gloria: Diary of a Teenage Girl, 1982, Joshua, 1983, Joshua and the Children: A Parable, 1989, The Shepherd, 1990, Joshua in the Holy Land, 1992, Never Alone: A Personal Way to God, 1994, Joshua and the City, 1995, A Portrait of Jesus, 1998, Joshua in a Troubled World, 2005 Pres. Amsterdam Community Concerts; co-owner Golden Age Sentinel. Recipient Liberty Bell award ABA, 1974, Citizen of Age Enlightenment award Soc. Creative Intelligence, 1976. Died Nov. 29, 2015.

GITLOW, ABRAHAM LEO, retired dean; b. NYC, Oct. 10, 1918; s. Samuel and Esther (Boolhack) G.; m. Beatrice Alpert, Dec. 12, 1940; children: Allan Michael, Howard Seth. BA, U. Pa., 1939; MA, Columbia U., 1940, PhD, 1947. Substitute instr. Bklyn. Coll., 1946-47; instr. NYU, NYC, 1947-50, asst. prof., 1950-54, assoc. prof., 1954-59, prof. econs., 1959-89, prof. emeritus, from 1989; acting dean NYU Coll. Bus. and Pub. Adminstrn., 1965-66, dean, 1966-85, dean emeritus, from 1989. Hon. dir. Bank Leumi USA; pres. bd. edn. Ramapo (N.Y.) Ctrl. Sch. Dist. 2, 1963-66. Author: Economics of the Mt. Hagen Tribes, New Guinea, 1947, Economics, 1962, Labor and Manpower Economics, 1971, Being the Boss: The Importance of Leadership and Power, 1992, NYU's Stern School: A Centennial Retrospective, 1995, Reflections on Higher Education: A Dean's View, 1995, Corruption in Corporate America, 2005, 2007; co-editor: General Economics: A Book of Readings, 1963, America's Research Universities: The Challenges Cehead, 2010; contbr. articles to profl. jours. Served to 1st lt. USAAF, 1943-46, PTO. Recipient Univ. medal Luigi Bocconi U., 1983. Mem. Am. Econ. Assn. Home: Miami Beach, Fla. Deceased.

GIUNTOLI, DAVID LAURENCE, research scientist; b. Cin., Feb. 2, 1966; s. Laurence John and Dorothy Marie (Beatty) G. BS, U. Cin., 1990, postgrad. Researcher sleep disorders Mercy Hosp., Cin., 1987-89; researcher molecular genetics U. Cin. Coll. Medicine, 1989-92, researcher pathobiology and molecular medicine, from 1992. Died July 28, 2007.

GLANZ, RUTH, audiovisual communications professional; b. NYC, Nov. 28, 1928; d. Joseph and Miriam (Greenfield) Ginsberg; m. Lawrence Goldstein, Feb. 22, 1951 (div. 1978); children: Beth Erica Goldstein McKee, Donna Lee Strugatz, Tina Cindy Goldstein; m. Spencer Glanz, June 11, 1989. BA, CUNY, 1949, MS, 1975. Asst. dir. audiovideo Equitable Life Assurance Soc., NYC, 1975-77; dir. audiovisual comms. Associated Merchandising Corp., NYC, 1977-92. Videographer, editor, adj. prof. Hunter Coll. CUNY, N.Y.C., 1969-75. Producer over 1000 multi-image and video programs. Pres. PTA, 1963-64; coord. Women Strike for Peace, Manhattan, 1967-69. Mem. Internat. TV Assn., Assn. for Multi-Image Internat., Fashion Group, Internat. Furnishings and Design Assn. Avocations: tennis, reading, theater, cinema, concerts. Died July 30, 2007.

GLASCOCK, RAY D., engineering services and furniture and equipment company executive; b. Auxausse, Mo., Apr. 1, 1922; s. Joseph Ewing and Mildred Hazel (Thomas) G.; m. Martha G. Greene, Nov. 18, 1977; children: Barbara Joan (Mrs. Jerry Bourland), Donald Ray. BS, U. Ill., 1949, MS, 1950. Group leader Norair div. Northrop Corp., Hawthorne, Calif., 1951-59; sect. leader communications div. Hughes Aircraft Co., Los Angeles, 1959-63; sect. head aeronutronic div. Philco Ford Corp., Newport Beach, Calif., 1964-65; owner, mgr. Engring. Corp. of Am.-Orange County, Anaheim, Calif., from 1966. Owner Glascock Enterprises, Anaheim, 1976—. Served with U.S. Maritime Service, 1943-46. Mem. IEEE, Gallups Island Radio Assn., Eta Kappa Nu. Home: Anaheim, Calif. Died Feb. 5, 2007.

GLASSER, SELMA G., writer, columnist; b. NYC, Jan. 2, 1920; d. Morris and Clara (Dlugash) Goldstein; widowed. Instr. Bklyn (N.Y.) Coll., until 1985, Valley Coll., 1985—, Van Nuys, Calif. Author: The Complete Guide to Prize Contests, Sweepstakes and How to Win Them, Prize Winning Recipes, The Complete Guide to Selling Fillers-Verse-Short Humor and Winning Contests, Your Secret Shortcut to Power Writing-Analogy Book of Related Words, Analogy Anthology, Rhyming Dictionary; contbr. articles to popular mags., including Good Housekeeping, Saturday Evening Post, Fun 'N Games, others. Pres. Bklyn. Contest Club. Recipient $4000 Cruise Prize 1997, $5000 1st place prize Aspen Essay Contest, 1997. Mem. Sr. Singles (treas. 1997-98). Avocations: bridge, lectures, hiking, speaking. Died Mar. 30, 2007.

GLENN, FRANCES BONDE, retired dentist; b. Tampa, Fla., Nov. 29, 1933; Student, U. Fla., 1951-52; DDS, U. Pa., 1956. Resident Children's Hosp., Washington, 1956-57; pvt. practice dentistry Miami, from 1957. Vis. lectr. U. Miami, 1959—, Miami Dade Sch. of Dental Hygiene, 1979; cons. D.C. Tng. Ctr. for the Retarded and Handicapped, 1956-57; lectr. Lindsey Hopkins Vocat. Sch., 1981, U.S. and other countries; bd. overseers U. Pa. Sch. Dental Medicine; rschr. Pediat. Dent. Ortho. Author: How to Have Children with Perfect Teeth, 2000, 2nd edit., 2005; contbr. articles to Lady's Home Jour., Parents Mag., Chicago Tribune Newspaper, Med. and Dent. Jour. Active Dade County Welfare and Planning Coun., 1959-61; vol. dentist Cerebral Palsy Clinic, 1959-63; advisor, cons. Crippled Children's Soc., 1976—; dental clinic staff mem. Coral Gables Jr. Women's Club, 1959-61. Recipient Alumni award merit U. Pa. Sch. Dental Medicine, 1984. Fellow Am. Acad. of Pedodontics; mem. Am. Orthodontic Soc. (diplomate of bd., Moore Disting. Svc. award 1994), Fla. Soc. Dentistry for Children, Am. Assn. Women Dentists. Achievements include discovering that children of expectant mothers who take sodium fluoride don't get cavities. Home: Vero Beach, Fla. Deceased.

GLENN, JOE DAVIS, JR., retired civil engineer, consultant; b. Fair Play, SC, Aug. 12, 1921; s. Joe Davis and Elise Glenn; m. Margaret Glenn, Feb. 21, 1946 (dec. Mar. 1986); children: Joe Davis III, William Harry, Diane Elizabeth, Mary Kathryn; m. Ruth Robinson, Mar. 21, 1987. BSCE, Clemson U., 1942; MSCE, U. Tenn., 1955. Asst. prof. civil engring. Clemson (S.C.) U., 1946-56; structural engr. Tidewater Constrn. Corp., Norfolk, Va., 1956-60; owner, pres. Joe D. Glenn Jr. & Assocs., Norfolk, 1960-76; pres. Glenn-Rollins & Assoc., Inc., Norfolk, 1976-82, Joe D. Glenn & Assoc., Inc., Norfolk, 1982-89, chmn., 1989-91, Glenn and Sadler Assoc. Inc., Norfolk, 1991-93; retired, 1993. Past elder Coleman Place Presbyn. Ch., Norfolk. Served with C.E. U.S. Army, 1942-46. Decorated Bronze Star. Mem. ASCE (life, Hardy Cross Hall of Fame 1991), NSPE (bd. dirs. 1976-80), Va. Soc. Profl. Engrs. (pres. 1975-76, Engr. of the Yr. 1976), Cons. Engrs. Coun. of Va., Hampton Rds. Engrs. Club (pres. 1974), Soc. Am. Mil. Engrs., Norfolk-Princess Anne Club, Kiwanis (pres. 1963). Home: Virginia Beach, Va. Died June 18, 2007.

GLONTI, OMAR ALEKSANDRES, mathematician, researcher; b. Gori, Georgia, USSR, Oct. 12, 1939; s. Alexander and Rusudan (Suskiashvili) G.; m. Ketevan Goderzishvili, June 24, 1971; children: Rusudan, Khatuna. D in Physical and Math. Scis., Tbilisi U., Georgia, 1962. Sci. rschr. Inst. Cybernetica, Tbilisi, 1962-65; postgrad. Tbilisi Math. Inst., 1965-68; sci. rschr. Inst. Applied Math., Tbilisi, 1968-73; dept. chief Inst. Econs. and Law, Tbilisi, 1973-83; sector chief Tbilisi Ramadze Math. Inst., 1983-90; lab. chief Tbilisi State U., from 1990. Prof. in probability theory and math. stats., Tbilisi State U., 1968—. Author: Investigations in the Theory of Conditionally Gaussian Processes, 1985; contbr. over 50 articles to profl. jours. dealing with probability theory and math. stats., 1968—. Mem. Am. Math. Soc., Internat. Statis. Inst. Avocations: reading, painting. Home: Tbilisi, Ga. Died 2015.

GLOSECKI, STEPHEN ORIN, English educator, folklorist; b. Springfield, Ill., Mar. 12, 1952; s. Andy Raymond and Edith Irene (Crossland) G.; m. Karen Anne Reynolds, Aug. 15, 1981; children: Dylan Matthew, Christopher Michael. BA in English and History, Beloit Coll., Wis., 1974; MA in English, U. Calif., Davis, 1978, PhD, 1980. Asst. prof. U. Ala., Birmingham, 1982-88, assoc. prof. dept. English, from 1988. Fulbright prof. U. Tromso, Norway, 1991-92; folklore cons. local TV, newspaper and radio, 1985—; folklore cons., prodr. Towers Prodns., Chgo., 1999. Author: Shamanism and Old English Poetry, 1989, (poem in Old English) With Saendendum, 1986 (Caedmon prize); contbg. author: Encyclopedia of Medieval Folklore, 1999, also articles. Recipient E.G. Ingalls award U. Ala. Birmingham, 1991; NEH travel grantee, 1990, Fulbright fellow, 1991-92; U. Ala. Birmingham rsch. grantee, 1994. Mem. MLA, Medieval Acad. Am. Avocations: calligraphy, watercolor, linocut, line drawing. Died Apr. 4, 2007.

GLOTZER, MORTIMER M., quality assurance consultant; b. Hartford, Conn., Jan. 14, 1930; s. Isidore and Sara J. (Saxe) G.; m. Arline I. Leichtman, Feb. 12, 1956; children: David L., Helen D. B in Mech. Engring., NYU, 1951. Project liaison engr. Combustion Engring., 1968-69, mgr. quality assurance engring. for nuclear fuel mfg., 1969-87, mgr. quality control, 1987-92, dir. quality assurance, 1992, dir. quality systems, 1992-94, quality sys. lead auditor; quality cons. pvt. practice, West Hartford, Conn., from 1994. Sec. ASME/Am. Nat. Standards Inst. N45-2.11, 1972-74. PTA pres. King Philip Elem. Sch., West Hartford, Conn., 1978-79; bd. dirs., pres. brotherhood Temple Beth Israel, West Hartford, 1985-86; mem. West Hartford Regents. Recipient Dist. award of merit Boy Scouts Am., Hartford, 1982, Silver Beaver award Boy Scouts Am., Hartford, 1986, Shofar award Jewish Com. on Scouting, Boy Scouts Am. Republican. Avocations: boy scouts, camping. Home: West Hartford, Conn. Died Jan. 27, 2007.

GLOVER, CLIFFORD BANKS, JR., textiles company executive, retired; b. Newnan, Ga., June 11, 1919; s. Clifford Banks and Ann Rebecca (Knight) G.; m. Ethel Inez Taylor, Apr. 28, 1945; children: Clifford B. III, S. Taylor, Peter L. Student, The Citadel, Charleston, SC, 1937—38, Ala. Poly. Inst., Auburn, 1939—40. Indsl. engr. Newnan (Ga.) Cotton Mills, 1945-57; in indsl. planning Mt. Vernon Mills, Newnan, 1957-60; in standards, quality control and safety West Point Pepperell, Newnan, 1960-84. Bailiff State Ct. Ga., Coweta County, 1989-94, chmn. deacons, mem. Ctr. Bapt. Ch., Newnan, 1989. Recipient Silver Beaver award Boy Scouts Am., 1980. Mem. Jolly Boys Assocs., Newnan-Coweta Hist. Soc. (pres. 1988), Coweta Pers. Assn. (hon.), Featherstone Fishing Club (pres. 1980-85), Elks. Avocations: gardening, bee keeping, fishing, hunting. Home: Newnan, Ga. Died June 18, 2007.

GODDARD, BURTON LESLIE, religion educator; b. Dodge Center, Minn., July 4, 1910; s. William Bliss and Myra Estella (Beckwith) G.; m. Esther Anna Hempel, July 16, 1940. Student, U. Minn., 1928-30; AB, UCLA, 1933; ThB, Westminster Theol. Sem., 1937; STM, Harvard U., 1938, ThD, 1943; SM, Simmons Coll., 1957; DD (hon.), Gordon-Conwell Theol. Sem., 1986. Pastor Carlisle (Mass.) Congl. Ch., 1937-41; asst. in Semitic langs. Harvard Divinity Sch., 1938-39, 40-41; instr. in bible and christian edn. Gordon Coll. and Divinity Sch., Wenham, Mass., 1941-44, prof. O.T., 1943-51, dean, 1944-51, Gordon-Conwell Theol. Sem., South Hamilton, Mass., 1951-61, prof. bibl. lang. and exegesis, 1951-75, libr. dir., 1961-73, libr. cons., 1973-75. Trustee Boston Theol. Inst., 1971-74. Author: (booklet) Animals in the Bible, 1963, The NIV Story, 1989, Meet Jeremiah, 1992; editor: Encyclopedia of Modern Christian Missions, 1967; joint editor, translator: The Holy Bible, New International Version, 1978; contbr. numerous articles to profl. jours. Mem. Am. Theol. Libr. Assn. (chmn. membership com. 1970-71), Soc. Bibl. Lit., Evang. Theol. Soc. (editor 1949-54, pres. 1964). Republican. Home: New Oxford, Pa. *I like the perspective of the Apostle Paul: "Although he longed to leave this life and enter the presence of God, he was willing rather to forego that if to stay here would bring joy to others".* Died July 22, 2007.

GODDARD, DEAN ALLEN, minister; b. Ft. Morgan, Colo., Feb. 19, 1942; s. Fay Fair and Dorothy Arvilla (Suttle) G.; m. Mary Lee Leonard, May 29, 1963; children: Rebekah, Matthew. BA, Bob Jones U., Greenville, SC, 1964; postgrad., Western Conservative Bapt.Sem., Portland, Oreg., 1964-65; DD, Maranatha Bapt. Coll., Watertown, Wis., 1980; DST, Berean Bapt. Sem., India, 1987. Ordained to ministry Bapt. Ch., 1965. Dean Pacific Coast Bapt. Coll., San Dimas, 1967-71; pastor Mid-Cities Bapt. Temple, Downey, Calif., 1971-77, Calvary Bapt. Ch., Casper, Wyo., 1977-81, Bethany Bapt. Ch., Cayce, S.C., 1981-84, Fairway Park Bapt. Ch., Hayward, Calif., from 1984. V.p. Bapt. Coll. of West, San Francisco, 1985-91; bd. dirs. Fellowship of Fundamental Bapt. of No. Calif., San Francisco, 1985—; trustee Lucerne Christian Conf. Ctr., 1985—. Mem. Wyo. Assn. Christian Schs. (pres. 1977-81). Home: Hayward, Calif. Died Apr. 17, 2007.

GODFREY, EUTHA MAREK, elementary school educator, consultant; b. Balt., Mar. 25, 1937; d. Louis Joseph and Estella Virginia (Stickels) Marek; m. Stanley I. Lewis (div. June 1970); children: Mark W. Lewis, Ronald A. Lewis, Kari S. Howard; m. Carl Godfrey Sr., Nov. 20, 1983 (dec. July 1993). BMus, Johns Hopkins U., 1959; postgrad., N.C. A & T State U., 1972—75, U. N.C., 1974—76. Cert. early childhood edn. Tchr. Murray County Schs., Chatsworth, Ga., 1959—60, Fulton County Schs., Roswell, Ga., 1960—62; tchr. music Balt. County Schs., 1962—63; tchr. band, chorus Guilford County Schs., Greensboro, NC, 1963—67, tchr. kindergarten, 1967—73; cons., early childhood State Dept. Pub. Instrn., Raleigh, NC, 1972—76; tchr. early childhood Peeler and Erwin Magnet Schs. Greensboro City Schs., 1973—91; cons. Reading divsn. State Dept. Pub. Instrn., Raleigh, 1976—82; dir. music Palm Coast United Meth. Ch., Fla., 1993—98; min. coord. St. John's United Meth. Ch., from 1999. Cons., presenter, Individually Guided Edn., St. Louis, 1977; workshop presenter, Greensboro City Assn. for Edn. of Young Children, 1980-90; accreditation team, Southern Assn. of Schs. and Colls. State of N.C., 1977-91. Bd. dirs. Family Life Ctr., Palm Coast, 1992-95; mem. exec. com. Dem. Party, Greensboro, N.C., 1975. Greensboro Pub. Sch. Fund grantee, 1987-88; Full Competative scholar Peabody Conservatory, 1955. Mem. N.C. Ret. State Employees, Fellowship of United Meth. in Music and Worship Arts, Royal Sch. Ch. Music, Am. Choral Dir.'s Assn., Mu Phi Epsilon. Avocations: music, writing, cooking. Home: Greensboro, NC. Died May 24, 2007.

GODFREY, GARLAND ALONZO, retired academic administrator; b. Booneville, Ark., Nov. 5, 1909; s. William Wylie and Lelia (Clay Coatney) G.; m. Merriam Jocille Morris, Nov. 4, 1933; children: Merriam Rose Godfrey Paul, Anna Lee Godfrey Reynolds, Joseph William, Jon Thomas. AA, Ark. Tech. U., 1931; BS, Okla. State U., 1933, MA, 1936, EdD, 1957. From tchr. to supt. schs. pubs. schs., Okla., 1933-60; pres. U. Ctrl. Okla., Edmond, 1960-75. Democrat. Avocations: fishing, travel, rock hounding. Home: Bella Vista, Ark. Died Feb. 14, 2007.

GODINEZ, MARYE H., anesthesiologist; b. Louisville, Aug. 19, 1945; d. Jerome and Hilda Marie Durbin; m. Rodolfo I. Godinez, June 28, 1969; children: Lucas, Peter, Paul, Adela, Sarah, Ruth. BS, Gonzaga U., Spokane, Wash., 1967; MD, St. Louis U. Sch. Medicine, 1971. Diplomate Am. Coll. Anesthesiologists, 1974. Dir. ENT, neuro and opthalmology anesthesia Barnes Hosp., St. Louis, 1974—77; dir. obstet. anesthesia Temple U. Hosp., Phila., 1978—79; rsch. assoc. Dept. Anesthesiology and Critical Care Children's Hosp., Phila., 1985—2011. Contbr. articles to sci. jours. Home: Bryn Mawr, Pa. Died May 29, 2014.

GOETZ, GEORGE ARTHUR, entrepreneur, educator; b. Milw., May 8, 1926; s. George Gustav and Mary Louise (Hall) G.; married, Nov. 24, 1954; children: G. Gilbert, Thomas H., Robert F. BME, Cornell U., 1950; MBA, Harvard U., 1952. CPCU. Mem. rsch. staff Nat. Rsch. Corp., Cambridge, Mass., 1952-54; chmn. Rollins Burdick Hunter, Milw., 1954-69; pres. Marden Electronics Inc., Burlington, Wis., from 1985, Berkeley Ptnrs., Ltd., Milw., from 1969; prof. entrepreneurship Bus. Sch., Cornell U., Ithaca, N.Y., 1981-83, Sch. Bus. Adminstrn., U. Wis., Milw., from 1983. Bd. dirs. Charter Mfg. Co., Milw., Motor Casting Co., Milw., Milw. Mut. Ins. Co., Century Fence Co., Waukesha, Wis., Acro Automation Systems, Milw.; mem. adv. com. Milw. Bus. Sch. U. Wis. Chmn. fund dr. United Way, Milw., 1977; pres. Child Care Ctrs., Milw., 1975, Day Care Svcs. for Children, Milw., 1976, Immanuel Presbyn. Ch., Milw., 1988. Mem. Engring. Coun. Cornell U., Engring. Coun. No. Ill. U., Rotary (bd. dirs. Milw. chpt. 1988—), Beta Gamma Sigma. Avocations: reading, rowing, bicycling, treking. Home: Milwaukee, Wis. Died July 16, 2007.

GOLDBERG, SVETLANA See BOYM, SVETLANA

GOLDBERGER, MARVIN LEONARD, physicist, researcher; b. Chgo., Oct. 22, 1922; s. Joseph and Mildred (Sedwitz) G.; m. Mildred Ginsburg, Nov. 25, 1945; children: Samuel M., Joel S. BS, Carnegie Inst. Tech., 1943; PhD, U. Chgo., 1948. Research assoc. Radiation Lab., U. Calif., 1948-49; research assoc. Mass. Inst. Tech., 1949-50; asst.-assoc. prof. U. Chgo., 1950-55, prof., 1955-57; Higgins prof. physics Princeton U., 1957-77, chmn. dept., 1970-76, Joseph Henry prof. physics, 1977-78; pres. Calif. Inst. Tech., Pasadena, 1978-87; dir. Inst. Advanced Study,

Princeton, N.J., 1987-91; prof. physics UCLA, 1991-93, U. Calif., San Diego, 1993-2000, dean divsn. natural scis., 1994-99, prof. emeritus, 2000—14. Mem. President's Sci. Advisory Com., 1965-69; chmn. Fedn. American Scientists, 1971-73. Fellow American Phys. Soc., American Acad. Arts & Sciences; mem. Nat. Acad. Scis., American Philos. Soc., Council on Fgn. Relations. Died Nov. 26, 2014.

GOLDGRABER, MOSHE BEER, physician; b. Zamosc, Lublin, Poland, July 7, 1913; arrived in Israel, 1939; s. Jacob Goldgraber and Haya-Yochevo Friedman; m. Dvora Epstein, Nov. 9, 1943; children: Hayim, Jacob, Rivka. MD, U. Padua, Italy, 1939; MS, U. Chgo., 1964. Asst. prof. dept. gastroenterology, rsch. assoc. U. Chgo., Chgo., 1952-64; sr. lectr. U. Jerusalem, from 1966. Contbr. articles to profl. jours. Mem. Allergy and Immunology Israeli Med. Orgn., Brit. Soc. Allergy and Clin. Immunology. Avocation: gardening. Home: Jerusalem, Israel. Died Nov. 26, 2007.

GOLDMAN, CHARLOTTE RUBENS, psychiatrist; b. Sept. 5, 1921; BA, Wellesley Coll., Mass., 1941; MA, Columbia U., 1948; MD, Harvard U., 1954. Resident in psychiatry Mass. Mental Health Ctr., Boston, 1955-58, McLean Hosp., Belmont, Mass., 1976-78; pvt. practice Psychiat. Med. Assocs., Chelmsford, Mass., from 1959; clin. instr. Harvard Med. Sch., Boston, 1978-88; attending psychiatrist McLean Hosp, Belmont, Mass., 1978-88, courtesy staff, from 1988. Died Mar. 23, 2007.

GOLDMAN, MORTON IRWIN, environmental and nuclear engineer; b. NYC, Nov. 29, 1926; s. Samuel Nathan and Sadie Ruth (Lapkin) G.; m. Marcia Janet Strunsky, May 27, 1950; children: Lee Alan, Lise Ann. BCE, NYU, 1948; MS in Sanitary Engring., MIT, 1950, MS in Nuclear Engring., 1958, ScD, 1960. Registered profl. engr. N.Y., Calif., D.C., Md., Ariz., S.C.; diplomate Am. Acad. Environ. Engrs. Various positions USPHS, 1950-61; with Halliburton NUS, Gaithersburg, Md., from 1961; engr. NUS Corp., Gaithersburg, Md., v.p. environ., sr. v.p. environ. group, sr. v.p. tech. dir. Vis. com. nuclear engring. dept. MIT, Cambridge, 1965-70; expert com. waste mgmt. chair IAEA, Vienna, 1968. Contbr. over 70 articles to profl. jours. With USNR, 1943-45. Mem. ASCE (life, State of Art award 1980), Am. Nuclear Soc., Am. Acad. Environ. Engrs. Home: Rockville, Md. Died Nov. 21, 2006.

GOLDSCHMID, HARVEY JEROME, law educator, former federal commissioner; b. NYC, May 6, 1940; s. Bernard and Rose G.; m. Mary Tait Seibert, Dec. 22, 1973; children: Charles Maxwell, Paul MacNeil, Joseph Tait. AB magna cum laude, Columbia U., NYC, 1962, JD magna cum laude, 1965. Bar: NY 1965, US Supreme Ct. 1970. Law clk. US Ct. Appeals (2nd cir.), NYC, 1965-66; assoc. Debevoise & Plimpton, NYC, 1966-70; asst. prof. law Columbia U., 1970-71, assoc. prof., 1971-73, prof., 1973-84, Dwight prof. law, 1984—2015, founding dir. Ctr. for Law and Econ. Studies, 1975-78; gen. counsel SEC, 1998-99, sr. adv. to chmn. Levitt, 2000, commr. Washington, 2002—05; sr. counsel Weil, Gotshal & Manges, NYC, 2000—02, 2005—15; co chair IASB FASB Fin. Crisis Adv. Gr., 2008—10; mem. Systemic Risk Coun., 2012—15. Mem. Bd. Govs. Fin. Industry Regulatory Authority (FINRA), 2007-2015, chair Regular Policy Com.;trustee Internat. Fin. Reporting Stds. Found, 2010-2015, adv. bd. Millstein Ctr. Corp. Governance and Performance, Yale U., 2005—12; cons. in field. Author: (with others) Cases and Materials on Trade Regulation, 1975, 6th edit., 2010; editor: (with others) Industrial Concentration: The New Learning, 1974, Business Disclosure: Government's Need to Know, 1979, The Impact of the Modern Corporation, 1984. Chmn. bd. advisors program on philanthropy and the law NYU Sch. Law, 1992-94; bd. dir. Nat. Ctr. on Philanthropy and the Law, 1996-2015; nat. coun. Washington U. Sch. of Law, 1999-2006; bd. dirs. Greenwall Found., 1996-2012, vice chair, 1999-2002, chair, 2006-12 Recipient Willis L.M. Reese award, Columbia U. Sch. Law, 1996, 1997, Chairman's award for excellence, SEC, 1999. Fellow Am. Bar Found. (life); mem. ABA (task force on lawyers polit. contbns. 1997-98), Am. Law Inst. (reporter part IV, duty of care and the bus. judgment rule, corp. governance project 1980-93), NY State Bar Assn., Assn. Bar City NY (v.p. 1985-86, chmn. exec. com. 1984-85, chmn. com. on antitrust and trade regulation 1971-74, com. on the 2d century, chmn. com. on securities regulation 1992-95, chmn. audit com. 1988-96, chmn. com. on corp. takeover legislation 1985-86, 88-92, treas., mem. exec. com. 1996-98, chmn. nominating com. 2000-01), Assn. Am. Law Schs. (chmn. sect. antitrust and econ. regulation 1976-78), Am. Assn. Internat. Commn. Jurists (sec.-treas., bd. dir. 1969-2002, 2005-2015), Ctr for Audit Quality (governing bd. mem. 2007-, vice chair 2011-), Transparency Internat. USA (bd. dir. 2001-02, 05-2015), Century Assn., Riverdale Yacht Club (bd. dir. 1987-90), Phi Beta Kappa. Home: New York, NY. Died Feb. 12, 2015.

GOLDSCHMIDT, CHARLES, advertising agency executive; b. NYC, June 15, 1921; s. Harry and Adele (Safir) G.; m. Patricia Nevins, Jan. 17, 1951; children: Richard Walter, Jane, Peter. BA, NYU, 1941. Advt. copywriter Warner Bros. Pictures Co., 1946-48, Buchanan & Co., NYC, 1948-49, Ray Austrian Assocs., NYC, 1949-52; founder, ptnr. Daniel & Charles Inc., NYC, 1952; chmn. bd. dirs. LCF&L, Inc., from 1980. Author fiction, play, articles. Served to lt. USNR, 1941-46. Mem. Beach Point Club, Phoenix Country Club. Democrat. Home: Mamaroneck, NY. Died Oct. 15, 2015.

GOLDSTEIN, CHARLES ARTHUR, lawyer; b. Perth Amboy, NJ, Nov. 20, 1936; s. Murray and Evelyn V. Goldstein; m. Judith Stein, Sept. 29, 1962 (div. 1982); 1 child, Deborah Ruth David; m. Carol Sager, Nov. 10, 1990 (div. 1995); stepchild Graham Spearman. AB, Columbia U., 1958; JD cum laude, Harvard U., 1961. Bar: N.Y. 1962. Law clk. U.S. Ct. Appeals (2d cir.), 1961-62; assoc. Fried, Frank, Harris, Shriver & Jacobson, NYC, 1962-69; ptnr. Schulte Roth & Zabel, NYC, 1969-79, Weil, Gotshal & Manges, NYC, 1979-83, counsel, 1983-85, Squire, Sanders & Dempsey, NYC, 1996—2001, Herrick Feinstein, NYC, 2001—15, Com. Art Recovery, 2001—15; ptnr. Shea & Gould, NYC, 1985-94, Sutherland, Asbill & Brennan, NYC, 1994-95; counsel to amb. Ronald S. Lauder, 2001—06. Lectr. Columbia U. Law Sch. Gen. counsel to Citizens Budget Commn., 1980-87; mem. Temp. Commn. on City Fins., 1975-77; mem. Gov.'s Task Force on World Trade Ctr. Home: New York, NY. Died July 30, 2015.

GOLDSTEIN, KENNETH B., lawyer; b. Bklyn., Sept. 16, 1949; s. Nathan and Isabella (Solow) G. BA, Tulane U., 1973, JD, 1974; postdoctoral, Fordham U., 1979. Bar: N.Y. 1977, U.S. Dist. Ct. (so. and ea. dist.) N.Y. 1980, U.S. Ct. Appeals (D.C. cir.) 1981. Gen. mgr., v.p. Middletown (N.Y.) Window Cleaning Co., Inc., 1974; tchr. various schs., Middletown and Chester, N.Y., 1975-77; asst. sr. v.p., dir. mktg. Saks Fifth Ave, NYC, 1977-79; sr. asst. dist. atty. Orange County, Goshen, N.Y., 1979-81; assoc. Zola & Zola, NYC, 1981-83, Freedman, Weisbein & Samuelson P.C., Garden City, N.Y., 1983-85, Jaffe & Asher, NYC, 1985-91, Raoul Lionel Felder P.C., NYC, from 1991. Bd. dirs. Middletown Window Cleaning Co., Inc. Bd. dirs. New Orleans Jazz and Heritage Found., 1972-74, Jewish Family Svcs. Orange County, 2000—. Named one of Outstanding Young Men in Am., 1980. Mem. ABA, N.Y. State Bar Assn., Middletown Bar Assn., Orange County Bar Assn., Order of DeMolay. Republican. Jewish. Avocations: swimming, art, dance, opera. Home: New York, NY. Died Nov. 14, 2006.

GOLDSTEIN, SIMEON HAI FISCHEL, real estate broker; b. NYC, Dec. 26, 1915; s. Herbert S. and Rebecca V. (Fischel) G.; n. Naomi R. Ginsburg, Aug. 27, 1942; children: Deborah J. Goldstein Stepelman, Seth M., Jonathan D. BA, Columbia Coll., 1936; MS, Columbia U., 1938. From bldg. mgr. to exec. dir. Harry & Jane Fischel Found. & affiliates, NYC, 1936-86; broker assoc. J. Clarence Davies Realty Co., Inc., NYC, 1986-89; real estate broker Simeon H.F. Goldstein, NYC, from 1989. Contbr. articles to profl. jours. Rep. nominee N.Y. State Legis., Bronx, 1946, 48, 50, 52, 54, 55; v.p. Citizens Housing & Planning Coun. of N.Y., 1989—; mem. community planning bd. Bronx, 1963-83, 1990—, chmn. Bd. #4 in past, currently chmn. econ. devel. com. of Bd. #11; pres. Pelham Pkwy. Rep. Club, Bronx, 1976-92; bd. dirs. Jewish Community Coun. of Pelham Pkwy., 1981—, Congregation Kehal Adas Yeshurun, Bronx, 1980—; del. Assn. Bronx Jewish Community Couns., 1989-91; exec. coun. Commn. on Synagogue Rels., UJA- Fedn. Jewish Philanthropies. Mem. Bronx County Hist. Soc. (charter). Avocations: politics, reading. Home: Bronx, NY. Died Dec. 18, 2006.

GOLDSTEIN, WILLIAM N., psychiatrist, psychoanalyst; b. Balt., Jan. 7, 1943; s. Edward H. and Gladys (Hack) G.; m. Karin Lynn Zinberg, Nov. 2, 1969; children: Matthew, Lauren. BA, Oberlin Coll., 1964; MD, U. Md., 1968. Diplomate Am. Bd. Psychiatry, Am. Bd. Psychoanalysis; bd. cert. in psychiatry and psychoanalysis. Intern Washington (D.C.) Hosp. Ctr., 1968-69; resident in psychiatry Downstate-Kings County Med. Ctr., Bklyn., 1969-72; staff psychiatrist Chestnut Lodge, Rockville, Md., 1972-75; asst. prof. psychiatry Georgetown U. Sch. Medicine, 1975-84; psychiat. cons. Oak Hill Youth Ctr., Laurel, Md., 1983-87; staff & chief psychiatrist, dep. & acting med. dir. D.C. Inst. for Mental Health, Washington, 1987-92; pvt. practice psychiatry, from 1972. Part-time psychiatrist Washington VA, 1975-83, St. Elizabeths Hosp., Washington, 1983-87; psychiat. cons. Washington & Washington Enterprises, Washington, 1984—; clin. asst. prof. psychiatry Howard U. Sch. Medicine, 1973-76; assoc. clin. prof. psychiatry & behavioral scis. George Washington U. Med. Ctr., 1984—; teaching analyst Balt.-Washington Inst. for Psychoanalysis, 1984—; assoc. clin. prof. psychiatry Georgetown U. Med. Ctr., 1989-92, clin. prof. psychiatry, 1992—. Author: An Introduction to Borderline Conditions, 1985; mem. editorial bd. Am. Jour. of Psychotherapy, 1988—; contbr. 30 articles to profl. jours. Co-dir. ext. divsn. Balt.-Washington Inst. for Psychoanalysis, 1985-92, dir. adult psychotherapy tng. program, 1985—. Fellow Washington Psychiat. Soc.; mem. Balt.-Washington Soc. for Psychoanalysis (officer 1981-93, pres. 1992-93). Home: Rockville, Md. Died Nov. 16, 2006.

GOLDWYN, SAMUEL JOHN, JR., film producer; b. Los Angeles, Sept. 7, 1926; s. Samuel John and Frances (Howard) G.; m. Jennifer Howard, Aug. 16, 1950 (div. Feb. 7, 1968); m. Peggy Elliott, Aug. 23, 1969 (div. 2005); children: Catherine, Francis, John, Anthony, Elizabeth, Peter; m. Patricia Strawn Attended, U. Va. Owner, CEO Samuel Goldwyn Co., Los Angeles, 1978—2015. Producer: (films) Cotton Comes to Harlem, 1970, Come Back Charleston Blue, 1972, The Golden Seal, 1983, Once Bitten, 1985, A Prayer for the Dying, 1987, Fatal Beauty, 1987, April Morning, 1987, Hollywood Shuffle, 1987, Mr. North, 1988, Mystic Pizza, 1988, Outback, 1989 Stella, 1990, The Program, 1993, The Preacher's Wife, 1996, Tortilla Soup, 2001, Master and Commander: The Far Side of the World, 2003, The Secret Life of Walter Mitty, 2013 Pres. Samuel Goldwyn Found.; Pres. trustees Fountain Valley Sch. Colorado. Served with AUS, 1944-46, 50-52. Mem. Acad. Motion Picture Arts & Scis. (bd. govs. 1999-2002), American Film Inst., Centre Theater Group Los Angeles Died Jan. 9, 2015.

GOLIN, CHARLES, lawyer; b. Phila., Mar. 3, 1924; s. Harry and Mazie Golin; m. Edith Grace Yoffe, June 18, 1950; children: Jonathan L., David W. BS in Bus. Adminstrn., Ohio State U., 1947; JD, Widener Coll., 1976. Bar: Pa., Fla. From gen. mgr. to pres. Lancaster (Pa.) Packing Co., 1947-80; ptnr. Golin, Haefner & Bacher, Lancaster, from 1972. With U.S. Army, 1943-46. Mem. Elks. Republican. Jewish. Avocation: boating. Died June 14, 2007.

GOLLANCE, ROBERT BARNETT, ophthalmologist; b. NYC, Oct. 25, 1937; s. Harvey and Sarah (Chinitz) G.; m. Carmen Cote Gollance, Nov. 8, 1969 (dec. Oct. 6, 2014); 1 child, Stephen Andrew. BA cum laude, Harvard Coll., 1958; MD, Columbia Coll., 1962. Diplomate Am. Bd. Ophthalmology, Nat. Bd. Med. Examiners. Intern in medicine NYU-Bellevue, 1962-63, resident and chief resident in ophthalmology, 1963-66; fellowship NIH, 1964-69; sec.-treas. Ophthalmology Assocs., Wayne, NJ, 1970-93; pres. Eye Assocs. of Wayne, from 1993; lectr. in ophthalmology Columbia U., NYC, 1998-2001; adv. bd. for devel. UMDNJ, 2002—10. Chmn. ophthalmology Chilton Meml. Hosp., Pompton Plains, NJ, 1987-89, pres. med. staff, 1991; great hands adv. com. Becton Dickinson Corp., Franklin Lakes, NJ, 1990—96; adv. com. Bausch & Lomb Corp., Rochester, NY, 1980-83; found. bd. Eye Inst. NJ Med.-Dental Sch., faculty cataract surgery and lens implantation; cons. Pharmacia Corp. Clin. Rsch. Glaucoma Medications, 2002-05. Contbr. articles to profl. jours. Chmn. parents fund raising Loomis Chaffee Sch., Windsor, Conn., 1989-90. Capt. U.S. Army, 1966-68. Recipient Letter of Appreciation Korean Opthalomology Soc., 1967, Cath. Med. Ctr., 1967. Fellow ACS, Am. Soc. Cataract and Refractive Surgery, Am. Acad. Ophthalmology, European Soc. Cataract and Refractice Surgery. Died Oct. 6, 2014.

GONCZ, ARPAD, president of Hungary, writer; b. Budapest, Hungary, Feb. 10, 1922; s. Lajos and Ilona (Heimann) G.; m. Zsuzsanna Maria Gonter, Jan. 11, 1947; children: Kinga, Benedek, Annamaria, Daniel. JD, U. Pázmány Péter, Budapest, 1944. Journalist, editor, 1945-48; iron worker, agrl. engr., 1948-56; prisoner for involvement in revolution, 1957; released with amnesty, 1963; freelance writer, lit. transl., from 1963; pres. Govt. of Hungary, 1990—2000. Transl.: The Sound and the Fury (William Faulkner), Ragtime (E.L. Doctorow), World's Fair (Doctorow), The Centaur (John Updike), The Witches of Eastwick (Updike). Mem. exec. com. Assn. of Free Dems., Budapest, 1988-90; v.p. Com. for Hist. Justice, Budapest, 1986—; exec. pres. League for Human Rights Budapest chpt., 1989-90. Mem. Union of Writers (pres. 1988-89), Assn. Hungarian Writers (pres. 1989-90), Hungarian PEN Club (v.p. 1989-94, hon. pres. 1994—). Roman Catholic. Died Oct. 2015.

GONG, EDMOND JOSEPH, lawyer; b. Miami, Fla., Oct. 7, 1930; s. Joe Fred and Fayline G.; m. Sophie Vlachos, July 25, 1957 (dec.); children: Frances Fayline, Peter Joseph (dec.), Madeleine, Joseph Fred, II, Edmond Joseph; m. Dana Leigh Clay, Dec. 7, 1988. AB cum laude, Harvard U., 1952, postgrad. in law, 1954-55; JD, U. Miami, 1960. Bar: Fla. 1960. Spl. writer Hong Kong Tiger Standard, 1955-56; staff writer Miami Herald, 1958-59; assoc. firm Helliwell, Melrose and DeWolf, 1960-61; asst. U.S. atty. So. Dist. Fla., 1961-62; mem. Fla. Ho. of Reps., 1963-66, Fla. Senate, 1966-72; trustee Fla. Gulf Realty Trust, 1974-80; pres. Inflahedge Resources Fund, from 1969, Pub. Policy Cons. Inc., from 1988. Sr. pub. policy analyst and legal counsel Everett Clay Assocs., Inc., 1988—; chmn. Fla. Land Sales Advisory Council, 1974-76; vice chmn. Bd. Bus. Regulation, State of Fla., 1976-77; fellow Inst. Politics John Fitzgerald Kennedy Sch. Govt., Harvard U., 1969-70, assoc. dir., 1971-72 Mem. Harvard 350th Commn., 1984-86; mem. com. on univ. resources, bd. overseers and pres. and fellows Harvard Coll., 1984-86; mem. North Key Largo Habitat Conservation Planning Study Com., 1984-88; regional chmn. Selection Com. for Anglo-Am. Conf., Johns Hopkins Sch. Advanced Internat. Studies, 1985; mem. Fairbanks Ctr. Com., Fairbank Ctr. for East Asian Research, Harvard U., 1987-90. Mem. ABA, Fla. Bar, Harvard U. Alumni Assn. (dir.-at-large), Fla. Audubon Soc. (bd. dirs. 1990-93), Coral Reef Yacht Club. Episcopalian. Home: Miami, Fla. Died May 19, 2015.

GONZALES, SYLVIA ALICIA, academic administrator, communications executive; b. Ft. Huachuca, Ariz., Dec. 16, 1943; d. Nazario Antonio and Aida (Lopez) G. BA, U. Ariz., 1965; EdD, U. Mass., 1974. Libr. clk. Tucson Pub. Libr., 1963-66; mem. congl. staff US House of Representatives, Washington, 1966-67; social scis. analyst U.S. Commn. Civil Rights, Washington, 1967-68; chief adminstrv. officer Interstate Rsch. Assocs., Washington, 1968-69; personnel mgmt. specialist Office Personnel Mgmt., Washington, 1969-70; dep. projects coord. City of Tucson, 1970-71; Robert Kennedy fellow Robert Kennedy Meml., Washington, 1971-72; Ford fellow exec. leadership Ford Found., Amherst, Mass., 1972-74; prof., chmn. dept. San Jose State U., 1974-82; acad. advisor Internat. Coll., LA, 1982-85; exec. dir., owner Ctr. Holistic Edn., San Jose, 1983-85; pvt. practice as internat. mgmt. cons. Tucson and Miami, Fla., 1985-93; divsn. dir. Gold Coast Media, Miami, from 1993. Author: La Chicana Piensa, 1974, Hispanic Am. Vol. Orgn., 1985, (chpt.) Social Science Jour., 1977; editor: Que Tal Anthology, 1975; contbr. chpt. to Comparative Perspective of Third World Women; contbr. poetry to Bay Area Women Poets, The Third Woman: Minority Women Writers in the United States. Bd. dirs. Nat. Congress Hispanic Am. Citizens, Washington, 1975-77, YWCA, Santa Clara County, 1980-81, Cath. Social Svcs., Women's Programs, United Way of Santa Clara County; acting exec. dir. Nat. Women's Studies Assn., San Jose, 1977-78; nat. com. chair NOW, Washington, 1971-72; project dir. Nat. Hispanic Feminist Conf., 1980-81. Recipient Women of Achievement award San Jose Mercury News, Santa Clara County, 1980; Pres. vis. scholar N.Mex. State U., Las Cruces, 1982. Mem. Hisp. Affairs Coun. (Outstanding Svc. award 1980). Avocations: music, reading, writing. Died Mar. 14, 2007.

GOODMAN, RONALD BURTON, supervising combustion engineer; b. Bklyn., July 2, 1932; s. Herbert Samuel and Rose (Shiller) G.; m. Hannah Indig, Nov. 19, 1960; children: Doreen Goodman Townley, Karen Goodman Ingamells. BSChemE, Bucknell U., 1954; postgrad. in engring., Columbia U., 1954-55; postgrad. in bus., NYU, 1957-60. Mgr. proposals and estimating Foster Wheeler Corp., Livingston, N.J., 1957-77; prin., combustion engr. C.F. Braun, Inc., Alhambra, Calif., 1977-87; pvt. practice cons. heat transfer equipment Northridge, Calif., 1987-88; supervising combustion engr. Brown & Root Braun, Alhambra, 1988-94; cons. Combustion Equipment, Northridge, Calif., from 1994. Real estate developer, 1988-93. Patentee in field. Pres. Troy Hills Civic Assn. Parsippany, N.J., 1965; treas. Chpt. F City of Hope, Northridge, 1983-85. 1st lt. U.S. Army, 1955-57. Mem. Am. Petroleum Inst. (mem. subcom. on fired heaters 1981—), Valley Socialites, Masons, Shriners. Democrat. Avocations: photography, square dancing, travel. Home: San Diego, Calif. Died Apr. 12, 2007.

GOODREAU, ROBERT CHARLES, surgeon; b. Wellsboro, Pa., Aug. 10, 1934; s. Charles William and Nellie Marie Goodreau; m. Stephanie Lynne Hauser, Sept. 10, 1958; 7 children. M in Psychiatry, Harvard U., 1958, PhD in Neuropsychiat. Surgery, 1969. Physician FBI, 1956—75, VA, from 1975. Inventor automatic gear shift, ball point and felt tip pens. Col. US Army, 1953—56, Korea. Methodist. Achievements include creator of the original blue prints for television camera and receiver. Avocation: reading. Died Apr. 25, 2007.

GORDON, ALAN S., lawyer, labor union administrator; b. NYC, Apr. 22, 1945; s. Murray and Lenore (Plotkin) G.; m. Susan E. H. Gordon, Sept, 1973; children: Jessica, Elizabeth Gordon Rosenfeld BA, CCNY, 1966; JD, Syracuse Univ., NY, 1969. Assoc. Apellate Div., N.Y. Supreme Ct., 1969-71; asst. gen. counsel Textile Workers Union, NYC, 1971-73; assoc. gen. counsel Dirs. Guild of Am., NYC, 1973-79, exec. sec., 1979; exec. dir., gen counsel Am. Guild Musical Artists, NYC. Home: Scarsdale, NY. Died Jan. 1, 2016.

GORDON, MELVIN JAY, food products executive; b. Boston, Nov. 26, 1919; s. Jacob S. and Sadye Z. (Lewis) G.; m. Ellen Rubin, June 25, 1950; children: Virginia Lynn, Karen Dale, Wendy Jean, Lisa Jo. BA, Harvard, 1941, MBA, 1943. V.p. Clear Weave Hosiery Stores, Inc., Boston, 1945—50, Tenn. Knitting Mills, Inc., Columbia, 1945—56; pres. P.R. Hosiery Mills, Inc., Arecibo, 1956—61; ptnr. Manchester Hosiery Mills, NH, 1964—69; pres. Hampshire Designers Inc., 1969—77; pres., bd. dirs. HDI Investment Corp., 1977; pres. MJG, Inc., 1981, Ellen Gordon Inc., 1984—88, Lisa Gordon, Inc., 1987, Wendy Gordon, Inc., 1989, Tootsie Roll Industries Inc., Chgo., 1968—69, CEO, 1962—2015, chmn. Chgo., 1962—2015. Adv. com. Mfrs. Hanover Bank, N.Y.C., 1967-88; bd. dirs. Sweets Company (now known as Tootsie Roll Industries, Inc.), 1952-2015 Author: Better Than Communism, 1958. Mem. Pres.'s Citizens Adv. com. Fitness Am. Youth, 1957-60, exec. com. 1959-60; del. White House Conf. Youth Fitness, 1962; co-chmn. Com. Support Psychol. Offensive, 1961-63; bd. dirs. mem. exec. com. Coun. World Tensions, N.Y.C., 1960-65; chmn. Mass. Gov.'s Com. Youth Fitness, 1958-64; bd. dirs. New Eng. Econ. Edn. Coun., 1960-63, N.H. Coun. on World Affairs, 1962-65; bd. dirs., chmn. exec. com. Citizen Exchange Corps., N.Y.C., 1964-66, hon. chmn. adv. coun. 1966-67; del. Prime Minister's Econ. Conf., Israel, 1968, 73; bd. overseers Harvard Coll., mem. vis. com. behavioral scis., 1967-71, vis. com. psychology, 1972; vis. com. Russian Rsch. Ctr., 1972-76; dir. Rensselaerville Inst., N.Y., 1966—; chmn. N.E. region m. Com. for Weizmann Inst. Sci. Rehovot, Israel, 1972-73; dir. Am. com., 1973-75; nat. trustee Nat. Symphony Orch., Washington, 1993—. Recipient Dean's award Nat. Candy Wholesalers Assn., 1978 Mem. Chief Execs. Orgn., World Bus. Coun., World Affairs Coun. Boston (treas., bd. dirs. 1966-67, v.p., bd. dirs. 1968-74), New Eng. Soc. N.Y.C., Harvard Varsity Club, Harvard Club (Boston). Clubs: Harvard (Boston); Varsity (Harvard). Died Jan. 21, 2015.

GORDON, SEYMOUR, cardiologist; b. Detroit, May 9, 1929; s. Morris and Minnie (Jamitz) G.; m. Marilynn R. Pensler, June 21, 1951; children: Nancy Elizabeth, Richard Eliot, Carol Ann. BA, U. Mich., 1951, MD, 1954. Intern Harper Hosp., 1954-55, resident, 1955-58, cardiovascular fellow, 1958-59; co-dir. cardiac lab. Children's Hosp. Mich., Detroit, 1961-67, Harper Hosp., Detroit, 1967-73; co-dir. div. cardiology William Beaumont Hosp., Royal Oak, Mich., 1967-87, dir. electrocardiology and cardiac rehab./exercise labs., from 1987. Editorial cons. Catheterization and Cardiovascular Intervention, Miami, Fla., 1986—. Co-author: Exercise in Modern Medicine, 1989, Ob-gyn. Clinics of North America, 1990, Sports Medicine, 1991, Rehabilitation of the Coronary Patient, 1992; editor: Exercise in Modern Medicine, 1987; contbr. 159 papers to profl. jours. Bd. dirs. United Way of Mich., Lansing, 1984—; cen. allocations com. mem. United Way of Southeastern Mich., Detroit, 1985—; del. Nat. Republican. Conv., New Orleans, 1988; nat. bd. mem. Am. Heart Assn., Dallas, 1987-88, regional v.p., Chgo., 1987-88. Recipient Horace E. Dodge award Am. Heart Assn./Mich., 1986, Dodrill award for excellence, 1994. Fellow Am. Coll. Cardiology, Am. Coll. Physicians, Coun. Clin. Cardiology-Am. Heart Assn., Coun. on Geriatric Cardiology (founding). Jewish. Achievements include advancements in cardiac pacemaker technology. Home: Franklin, Mich. Died July 29, 2007.

GORENBERG, NORMAN BERNARD, retired aeronautical engineer, consultant; b. St. Louis, May 18, 1923; s. Isadore and Ethel G.; m. Lucille Richmond, June 10, 1947; children: Judith Allyn Gorenberg Stein, Carol Ann Gorenberg, Gershom Gorenberg. BSME, Washington U., St. Louis, 1949. Registered profl. engr., Mo. Aero. engr. USAF Wright Air Devel. Ctr., Dayton, Ohio, 1949-51; aerodynamicist McDonnell Aircraft Corp., St. Louis, 1951-59; supervisory engr. Boeing Co., Vertol Div., Phila., 1959-62; R & D engr. Lockheed Corp., Burbank, Calif., 1962-89; vertical takeoff and landing aircraft cons. Dana Point, Calif., 1989-94; ret., 1994. Contbr. articles to profl. reports. With USAAF, 1943-46. Mem. AIAA, ASME, Am. Helicopter Soc. (chmn. St. Louis sect. 1955-56, nat. aerodyns. com. 1969-70, tech. dir. western region 1969-70), Nat. Mgmt. Assn. (life). Jewish. Died Mar. 12, 2007.

GORLITZ, SAMUEL J., real estate executive; b. Chgo., May 17, 1917; m. Grace Karasik, Mar. 30, 1941; children: Gail, Paula. AB, U. Chgo., 1938, postgrad., 1940-41. Adminstrv. asst. U.S. Forest Svc., Milw., 1938-40; economist War Prodn. Bd., Washington, 1941-43, U.S. Dept. Agr., Washington, 1946, U.S. Housing Agy., Washington, 1947; chief economist U.S. Dept. State, Washington, 1947-57; proprietor Investor Svc. Inc./Investor Svc. Securities, Inc., Washington, 1957-75; founder Fed. Realty Investment Trust, Chevy Chase, Md., 1962-79; pres. Gorlitz Assocs., Chevy Chase, from 1979. Trustee Fed. Realty Investment Trust, 1979—. Contbr. articles to profl. jours. Cons. Ctr. for Def. Info., Washington, 1980—. With U.S. Army, 1943-46. Mem. City Tavern Club. Home: Sarasota, Fla. Died Jan. 5, 2007.

GORMAN, CHARLES JOHNNY, training services executive, retired human resources specialist; s. Chuck Gorman and Elizabeth Ann Allen. AAS, Wallace State C.C., Hanceville, Ala., 1987; BS, Athens State Coll., Ala., 1987; cert. pub. mgr., Auburn U., Montgomery, Ala., 1994; M in Crimnal Justice Adminstrn., Northwestern U., Evastion, Ill., 1989; MPA, Sonata U., Louisville, 1998. Cert. fire officer 1 Ala., fire instr. 1 Ala., radiation instr. Dept. Energy, FEMA, DHS, WMD/Hazmat specialist FEMA, DOT, DHS, Ala. Fire Coll., incident command amd homeland security instr. Ala. fire Coll., NFA, FEMA, DHS, DOD, hazardous materials/WMD instr. FEMA, DHS, DOT, pub. safety diver instr. MDEA, PSDA, rescue technician Pro Bd., Fire Coll., incident command instr. FEMA,NFA, DHS, DOD, Pro Bd. Safety and health dir. Ala. Dept Transp., Montgomery, 1990—97; constable State of Ala., Elmore County, Wetumpka, from 2004. Dir. Southea. Tng. & Consulting Group, Montgomery, from 1989. Mem. Internat. Chem. Terrorism Coun., Atlanta, from 2002, Poseidon Handicapped Scuba Assoc, Palm Beach, Fla., from 2002; mem. adv. bd. Shelby State C.C., Memphis, 1990—94; mem. Gov.'s Traffic Safety Bd., Montgomery, from 2002, ARC, Montgomery, 1990—94. Served with USMC. Died May 8, 2007.

GORMAN, LEON ARTHUR, retired mail order company executive; b. Nashua, NH, Dec. 20, 1934; s. John and Barbara (Bean) Gorman; m. Lisa Davidson; children: Jeffrey, Ainslie Boroff, Jennifer Wilson stepchildren: Shimon Cohen, Nancy Cohen. Graduate, Bowdoin Coll., 1956. Mdse. trainee Filene's of Boston, 1956; with L.L. Bean, Inc., Freeport, Maine, 1961—2013, v.p., treas., 1961—67, pres., 1967—2001, chmn., 2001—13, chmn. emeritus, 2013—15. Dir. Ctrl. Maine Power Co., Depositors Corp., Carroll Reed Ski Shops. Author: (memoir) L.L. Bean: The Making of an American Icon, 2006. Mem. dir. C. of C. Greater Portland; alumni coun. Bowdoin Coll.; bd. dir. Pine Tree Coun. Boy Scouts Am.; trustee Hurrican Usland Outward Bound Sch.; adv. trustee Maine Audubon Soc. Lt. USNR, 1957—60. Recipient Navigator award for Entrepreneur of Yr., Maine C. of C and Bus. Alliance, 1997, Business Hall of Fame award for compassion, courage and commitment in bus. leadership, Maine C. of C., 2001; named to Direct Mktg. Assn. Hall of Fame, 1992. Died Sept. 3, 2015.

GORYAEVA, ELENA MIKHAILOVNA, retired research scientist; b. Leningrad, Russia, Nov. 11, 1944; d. Mikhail Danilovitch and Nadezgda Vladimirovna (Milstein) Zinin; m. Stanislav Mikhailovitch Lifshitch, May, 1966 (div. Oct. 1972); m. Mikhail Alexandrovitch Goryaev, Mar., 1976; 1 child, Olga. MS in Optico-Electronics, Leningrad Inst. Optics and Exact Mechanics, 1967. Engr. State Optical Inst., Leningrad, 1967-72, jr. rsch. specialist, 1972-82, rsch. specialist, 1982—2008; ret., 2008. Rsch. areas include photochemistry, liquid lasers, luminiscence spectroscopy, concentrating on proton transfer and non-radiative energy transfer. Contbr. articles to profl. jours.; inventor in field. Tech. informator State Optical Inst., 1974-80, trade union organizer, 1972-76; recruiter Bibliophilic Soc., Leningrad, 1980-86. Recipient Labour Vet. medal Leningrad City Coun. of People's Deps., 1988. Avocations: swimming, cycling, museum visiting, classical music concerts. Home: Saint Petersburg, Russia. Died Jan. 8, 2016.

GOSNELL, RICKY DALE, minister; b. Spartanburg, SC, June 4, 1958; s. Jessie James and Lillian (Spake) G.; m. Robin Ann Metts, June 11, 1983; children: Hannah Dale, Rebekah Metts. BA, Wofford Coll., 1980; MA, U. S.C., 1982; MDiv, So. Bapt. Theol. Seminary, Louisville, 1989, postgrad. Ordained to ministry Bapt. Ch., 1987. Pastor Buffalo Lick Bapt. Ch., Shelbyville, Ky., from 1987. Garrett fellow, dept. evangelism for Billy Graham/Prof. Evangelism, So. Bapt. Theol. Seminary, 1989—. Recipient full acad. scholarship Wofford Coll. via Spartan Mills, Spartanburg, S.C., 1976. Republican. Died Mar. 4, 2007.

GOSNELL, TOM (THOMAS CHARLES GOSNELL), former mayor; b. London, Ont., Can., Apr. 7, 1951; s. James Fredrick and Evelyn Winnifred (Head) G.; m. Laurel Joanne Strople, Apr. 17, 1986; children: Craig, Jennifer. BA in Polit. Sci. and History, U. Western Ont., 1974. Pres. Gosnell Paving Stone, Inc., London, 1978; alderman City of London, 1978-85, mayor, 1985-95; with Goswell Passmore & Co., London, Ont., Can., from 1995. Mem. diaster and emergency co-ordinating com., liaison com. City of London/Middlesex County; bd. dirs. London Pub. Library, Western Fair Assn., London; bd. govs. U. Western Ont., Can. Mem. Fedn. Can. Municipalities (big city mayor's caucus), Assn. Municipalities of Ont. Avocations: golf, football. Died Dec. 8, 2014.

GOSSLING, JENNIFER, microbiologist; b. Welwyn Garden City, England, July 25, 1934; came to U.S., 1962; d. Richard S. and Millicent E. (Hodson) Sayers; m. William Frank Gossling, Nov. 3, 1956. BA, Cambridge U., Eng., 1955; PhD, W.Va. U., 1973. Asst., instr. U. Manchester, Eng., 1966-69, W.Va. U. Med. Ctr., Morgantown, 1969-73, Med. Col. Ohio, Toledo, 1975; postdoctoral scholar Dental Rsch. Inst., U. Mich., Ann Arbor, 1978-79; mem. staff Indiana (Pa.) Hosp., 1979-80; med. technologist Jewish Hosp. of St. Louis, from 1980; asst. prof. Sch. of Dental Medicine, Washington U., St. Louis, 1981-91, St. Louis Coll. Pharmacy, 1993-95. Contbr. to Bergey's Manual of Systematic Bacteriology, Vol. 3, 1989. Home: Saint Louis, Mo. Died July 14, 2007.

GOUGH, CLARENCE RAY, retired designer, educator; b. Denton County, Tex, Dec. 7, 1919; s. Herman Lang and Gertrude (Page) G.; m. Georgia Belle Leach, Feb. 7, 1975. BS in Art, U. North Tex., Denton, 1940, MS in Art, 1941; BArch, Ill. Inst. Tech., 1950. Art tchr. Edinburg Ind. Sch. Dist., Tex., 1941; interior designer Contemporary House, Dallas, 1950; environ. designer Gough Assoc., Denton, 1951-90; prof. U. North Tex., Denton, 1951-88. Juror Nat. Coun. Interior Design Qualifications, 1983-88; chmn. accreditation com. Found. Interior Design Rsch., 1985-90. Illustrator Modern Dance for the Youth of Am., 1944, photographer (exhibitions) Visual Arts Ctr., Denton, 2001; exhibitions include photography No. Tex. area Art League Exhbn., 2003. Exhbn. chmn. U. North. Tex., Denton, 1950-63; curator exhbns. Greater Denton Arts Coun., 1997-98. Lt. USNR, 1942-46, PTO. Recipient Career Educator award Am. Soc. Interior Designers, 1993, Dallas, Svc. award Gov. Conf. on the Arts, Denton, 1990; Internat. Artist award, North Tex. Area Art League, 2003, Green Glory award, U. North Tex., 2004, Recognition award Gough Gallery Visual Arts Ctr., Denton, Tex. Avocations: photography, collecting art. Home: Denton, Tex. Died Apr. 12, 2015.

GOULD, LILIAN, writer; b. Phila., Apr. 19, 1920; d. Reuben Barr and Lilian Valentine (Scott) Seidel; m. Irving Gould, Nov. 16, 1944; children: Mark, Scott, Paul, John. Student, U. Pa., Charles Morris Price Sch. of Advt. and Journalism, Phila. Copywriter, mgr. advt. agys., Phila. Author: Our Living Past, 1969, Jeremy and the Gorillas, 1977 (award 1977); freelance journalist mags. and newspapers. Mem. Authors Guild, Phila. Children's Reading Roundtable, Phila. Writers Orgn., Soc. of Children's Book Writers and Illustrators. Home: Villanova, Pa. Died Nov. 7, 2006.

GRAHAM, LOIS, artist; b. Kewanee, Ill., Aug. 27, 1930; d. Emmons Lorenzen and Clara Marjorie Christina (Johnson) Gord; m. Gene Orloff Graham, Mar. 29, 1952; children: Douglas, Gareth, Andrew, Julia. BA magna cum laude, Knox Coll., 1952. Art tchr. Fairview Sch., St. Louis, 1952—56; visual artist self employed, St. Louis, 1952—56, Tacoma, 1956—62, Stuttgart, Germany, 1962—66, Denver, 1966—67, Bellevue, Wash., 1967—92, Seattle, from 1992. Artist adv. bd. Metro Transit Art Program, Seattle, 1986—91; visual arts chair exec. com. King County Arts Commn., Seattle, 1986—91; founder, adminstr. Union Art Co-op, Inc., Seattle. Represented in permanent collections Seattle Opera House. Recipient Honors award, Seattle Arts Commn., 1984, Outstanding Achievement in the Arts award, Bellevue Arts Commn., 1986. Mem.: Artist Trust (hon. chair 1995—98). Avocations: opera, classical music. Died Oct. 9, 2007.

GRAMLEY, LYLE ELDEN, economist, former federal official; b. Aurora, Ill., Jan. 14, 1927; s. Cook Gramley and Myrtle (Pflugfelde); m. Wachtel Evelyn Gramley, 1951 (dissolved 1981); children: Alan, Lynn Gramley Dawson; m. Sandra Royal, 1983 (div.); m. Marlys Fee Jensen, 1989; stepchildren: Michael Jensen, Kevin Jensen. BA, Beloit Coll., Wis., 1951; MA, Ind. U., 1952, PhD, 1956. Fin. economist Fed. Res. Bank Kans. City, 1955-62; asst. prof. economics U. Md., 1962-64; fin. economist Fed. Res. Bd., 1964-66, assoc. adviser, 1966-67, adviser, 1968-77; mem. Coun. Econ. Advisers, Exec. Office of the Pres., Washington, 1977-80; mem. bd. governors Fed. Res. Sys., Washington, 1980-85; chief economist Mortgage Bankers Assn. of America, Washington, 1985—2002; sr. econ. adviser Stanford Group Co., Washington, Potomac Rsch. Group, Washington, Del. Author: Scale Economics in Banking, 1962; co-author: Essays in Commercial Banking, 1962. Served in USN, 1944-47. Mem. Am. Econ. Assn., Am. Fin. Assn. Democrat. Home: Potomac, Md. Died Mar. 22, 2015.

GRANGER, CLIFFORD BILLINGS, pharmaceutical executive; b. Buenos Aires, Dec. 18, 1938; came to U.S., 1947; s. Gordon Fitzhugh G. and Eleanor Clarke Billings; m. Carolyn Francis Miller, Aug. 23, 1965 (div. Aug. 1984); m. Ginny Bailes, Aug. 27, 1986; children: David, Samantha, Sara, Jenny, Lucy, Sharon, Renee, Price. BA, Williams Coll., 1961; Sr. Exec., IMEDE, Lausanne, Switzerland, 1981. Mng. dir. CPC Internat., Nairobi, Kenya, 1975-81, Durban, South Africa, 1981-86, v.p. Asia Hong Kong, 1986-1987; mng. dir. Getz, Bangkok, 1987-91, Inca Plastics, Bangkok, 1991-92; gen. mgr. Asia F.H. Faulding & Co., Singapore, from 1992. Bd. dir. subs. With U.S. Army, 1962-63. Mem. Tanglin Club, Durban Country Club. Republican. Avocations: tennis, golf, scuba diving. Home: Singapore, Singapore. Died Aug. 24, 2007.

GRASS, GÜNTER WILHELM, writer, playwright; b. Danzig-Langfuhr (now Gdańsk), Poland, Oct. 16, 1927; s. Willy and Helene (Knoff) Grass; m. Anna Margareta Schwartz, 1954 (div. 1978); children: Franz, Raoul, Laura, Bruno; m. Ute Grunert, 1979. Attended, Düsseldorf Art Acad., Germany, Acad. Fine Arts, Berlin; D (hon.), Kenyon Coll., 1965, Harvard U., 1976. Worked as farm laborer & miner, Düsseldorf, Berlin; sculptor, graphic artist, writer Paris, Berlin, 1956—59. Author: (works translated in English) The Wicked Cooks, 1956, The Flood, 1957, The Tin Drum, 1959, Cat and Mouse, 1963, Dog Years, 1965, The Plebeians Rehearse the Uprising, 1966, Four Plays, 1967, Speak out! Speeches, Open Letters, Commentaries, 1969, Local Anaesthetic, 1970, Max, 1972, From the Diary of a Snail, 1973, In the Egg and Other Poems, 1977, The Flounder, 1978, The Meeting at Telgte, 1981, Headbirths, or, the Germans are Dying Out, 1982, The Rat, 1987, Show Your Tongue, 1989, Two States One Nation?, 1990, The Call of the Toad, 1992, My Century, 1999, Too Far Afield, 2000, Crabwalk, 2002, Peeling the Onion, 2007, Dummer August, 2007, Die Box, 2008, numerous other works, poetry and plays in German. Served with German Mil. Svc., 1944—46. Recipient Around South German Radio Poetry prize, 1955, Fgn. Book prize, France, 1962, Georg Büchner prize, Germany, 1965, Fontane prize for lit., City of Neuruppin, Germany, 1968, Internat. Lit. prize, City of Palermo, Italy, 1977, Carl von Ossiersky medal, 1977, Viareggio Lit. prize, Italy, 1978, Alexander-Majakowski Medal, Gdańsk, 1979, Antonio Feltrinelli prize, Lincean Acad., Italy, 1982, Great Lit. of Bavarian Acad. award, 1994, Nobel prize for lit., 1999. Fellow: Royal Soc. Lit. (hon.); mem.: Berlin Acad. Arts (pres. 1983—86). Died Apr. 13, 2015.

GRAVES, MICHAEL, architect, educator; b. Indpls., July 9, 1934; s. Thomas Browning and Erma Sanderson (Lowe) Graves; children from previous marriage: Sarah Browning, Adam Daimhin, Michael Sebastian Min. BS in Architecture, U. Cin., 1958; MArch, Harvard U., 1959; acad. fellow, Am. Acad. Rome, 1960—62; DFA (hon.), U. Cin., 1982; LHD (hon.), Boston U., 1984; HHD (hon.), Savannah Coll. Art and Design, 1986; DFA (hon.), RI Sch. Design, 1990, NJ Inst. Tech., 1991; LHD (hon.), Rutgers U., NJ, 1994, U. Colo., 1995; PhD (hon.), Internat. Fine Arts Coll., 1996, Pratt Inst., 1996, Drexel U., Phila., 2000. Lectr. architecture Princeton U., NJ, 1962—67, assoc. prof., 1967—72, Schirmer prof. architecture, 1972—2001, emeritus prof., 2001—15; pres. Michael Graves & Associates, Princeton, NYC, 1964—2015. Arch. in residence Am. Acad. Rome, 1979. Exhibited in group shows including Mus. Modern Art, NYC, 1967, 68, 75, 78, 79, 80, 81, 84, Cooper-Hewitt Mus., 1976, 78, 79, 80, 82, 85, 87, Triennale, Milan, Italy, 1973, 85, Roma Interrotta, Rome, 1978, Venice Biennale, Italy, 1980, Met. Mus. Art, 1985, 86, 87, Emory U. Mus. Art and Archaeology, Atlanta, 1985, Denver Art Mus., 2002; one-man shows include U. So. Calif., 1981, No. Ill. U., 1982, Inst. Architecture and Urban Studies, NYC, 1982, Colby Coll., Maine, 1982, Moore Coll. Art, Phila., 1983, Fla. Internat. U., Miami, 1983, Pa. State U., Univ. Pk., 1984, Royal Inst. Brit. Archs., Heinz Gallery, London, 1984, Wadsworth Athenaeum, Hartford, Conn., 1984, Carleton Coll., Northfield, Minn., 1986, W.Va. U., 1986, Hamilton Coll., Clinton, NY, 1987, Archivolto Gallery, Milan, Italy, 1987, U. Va., Charlottesville, 1987, U. Md., College Park, 1988, Duke U. Mus. Art, Durham, NC, 1988, Butler Inst. Art, Youngstown, Ohio, 1989, 1989, Deutsches Architekturmuseum, Frankfurt, German Dem. Republic, 1989, Washington Design Ctr., 1989, Syracuse U. Sch. Architecture, 1990, Kunstemes Hus, Oslo, 1990, Mikimoto Hall, Tokyo, 1992, Pitts. Cultural Trust, 1993, Richard Stockton Coll., 1993, Clark County Libr., 1994, Thessaloniki Design Mus., Greece, 1996, The Min. Bldg., Seoul, Korea, 1996, Princeton Arts Coun., 1996, 99, U. Conn. Aronoff Ctr. Design and Art, 1996, NJ Sch. Arch., NJ Inst. Tech., 2000; prin. works include Hanselmann House, 1967 (AIA Nat. Honor award, 1975), Newark Mus., 1968, Rockefeller House, 1969 (Progressive Architecture Design award, 1970), Gunwyn Ventures Office, 1971 (AIA Nat. Honor award, 1979), Snyderman House, 1972, Crooks House, 1976 (Progressive Architecture Design award, 1977), Schulman House, 1976, (AIA Nat. Honor award, 1982), Fargo-Moorhead Cultural Ctr., 1977-79 (Progressive Architecture Design award, 1978), Plocek House, 1978 (Progressive Architecture Design award, 1979), pvt. residence in Green Brook, NJ, 1978 (Progressive Architecture Design award, 1980), Sunar showrooms NYC, 1979, 81 (Interiors award, 1981), Chgo., 1979, Houston, 1980, LA, 1980, London, 1985, Loveladies Beach House, 1979 (Progressive Architecture Design award, 1979) Environ. Edn. Ctr., 1980 (Progressive Architecture award, 1983), Portland Bldg., 1980 (AIA Nat. Honor award, 1983), San Juan Capistrano Pub. Libr., Calif., 1980 (AIA Nat. Honor award, 1985), Newark Mus. Master Plan and Renovation, 1982 (AIA Nat. Honor award, 1992), Human Bldg., Louisville, 1982 (Interiors award, 1985, AIA NAt. Honor award, 1987), Emory U. Mus. Art and Archaeology, 1982 (Interiors award 1985, AIA Nat. Honor award, 1987), Riverbend Music Ctr., 1983, Whitney Mus. Am. Art, NYC, 1984, Diane Von Furstenburg Boutique, 1984, Clos Pegase Winery, Calif., 1984 (AIA Nat. Honor award, 1990), Sotheby's Tower, NYC, 1985, Warehouse Renovation (Graves House), 1985 (Progressive Architecture Design award, 1978), Aventine Devel., La Jolla, Calif., 1985, Shiseido Health Club, Tokyo, 1985, Disney Co. Corp. Office Bldg., Burbank, Calif., 1985, Crown Am. Hdqs., Johnston, Pa., 1985, Walt Disney World Dolphin and Walt Disney World Swan hotels, Fla., 1986 (Progressive Architecture award, 1989), Youngston (Ohio) Hist. Ctr. Industry and Labor, 1986 (Progressive Architecture Design award, 1987), 10 Peachtree Pl., Atlanta, 1987, Henry House, Rhinebeck, NY, 1987 (Progressive Architecture award, 1989), U. Va. Arts. and Scis. Bldg., Charlottesville, 1987, Portside Dist. Condominium Tower, Yokohama, Japan, 1987, Momochi Dist. Apt. Bldg., Fukuoka, Japan, 1987, Metropolis Master Plan LA, 1988, stores and galleries for Lenox, Tysons Corner, Va., 1988, Palm Beach, 1988, NYC, 1988, Mpls., 1988, Costa Mesa, 1989, Frankfurt, 1989, Phila., 1989, Nashville, 1989, Midousuji Minami Office Bldg., Osaka, 1988, Tajima Office Bldg., Tokyo, 1988, Hotel NY, 1988, Euro Disneyland, France, 1988, Inst. for Theoretical Physics, U. Calif., Santa Barbara, 1989, Detroit Inst. of Arts Master Plan, 1989, Indpls. Art Ctr., 1989, Emory U. Mus. Art and Archaeology Addition, 1989, Fukuoka Internat. Office Project, 1990, Kasumi Group Rsch. and Tng. Ctr., Tsukaba City, Japan, 1990, Clark County Libr., Las Vegas, 1990, U. Cin. Sci. and Engring. Rsch. Ctr., 1990, Richard Stockton Coll. Arts and Scis. Bldg., Pomona, NJ, 1991, Denver Ctrl. Libr., 1991 (AIA-NJ Design award, 1992, 95, AIA Nat. Honor award for Interior Architecture, 1998, AIA and Am. Libr. Assn. Excellence award, 2001), Astrid Park Plz. Hotel and Bus. Ctr., Antwerp, Belgium, 1992, Thomson Consumer Electronics Hdqs., Indpls., 1992 (AIA-NJ Design award, 1994), Rome Reborn Vatican Exhibit, Libr. Congress, 1992 (Casebook award Print Mag., 1993), Pitts. Cultural Trust Theater and Office Bldg., 1992, Taiwan Mus. Pre-History, Taipei, 1993 (AIA-NJ Design award, 1994), Archdiocesan Ctr., Newark, 1993, Internat. Fin. Corp. Hdqs., Washington, 1993 (AIA-NJ Design award, 1997), 1500 Ocean Dr. Condominiums, Miami, 1994, Del. River Port Authority Hdqs., Camden, NJ, 1994 (AIA-NJ Design award, 1998), St. Martin's Coll. Libr., Lacey, Wash., 1994, Topeka (Kans.) and Shawnee County Pub. Libr., 1995, Miramar Hotel, Egypt, 1995 (AIA-NJ Design award, 1996), NJ Inst. Tech. Residence Hall, 1995, Jiang-to Blvd. Master Plan, Xiamen, China, 1995, Alexandria (Va.) Ctrl. Libr., 1996, US Courthouse Annex, Washington, 1996, Life Mag. Dream House, 1996, Lake Hills country Club, Seoul, Korea, 1996, World Trade Exch., Manila, 1996, new residence Hall, Drexel U., Phila., 1997, Miele Appliances Americas Hdqs. Bldg., Princeton, 1997 (AIA-NJ Design award, 2002), NovaCare Sports Training Facility, 1997 (AIA-NJ Design award, 2002), El Gourna Golf Villas, Egypt, 1997 (AIA-NJ Design award, 2002), French Inst. Libr, NYC, 1997, Hyatt Regency Taba Heights Hotel, Egypt, 1997, St. Mary's Ch., Rockledge, Fla., 1998, Rice U. Master Plan, Houston, 1998, The Impala Bldg., NYC, 1998, Wash. Monument Restoration Scaffolding, 1998 (AIA-NJ Design award, 1998), Rolex Watch Technicum Tng. and Svc. Ctr., Lancaster County, Pa., 1999, Theater Square: Pitts. Cultural Trust Svc. Ctr., 1999, Mus. Shenandoah Valley, Winchester, Va., 1999, 425 Fifth Ave. Tower, NYC, 2000, Mahler IV Mixed-Use Bldg., Amsterdam, 2000, Fed. Res. Bank Dallas: Houston Br., 2000, Famille-Tsukishima Bldg., Tokyo, 2000, US Embassy, Seoul, 2000, Dept. Transp. Hdqs., Washington, 2001, Detroit Inst. Arts, 2001, St. Coletta's Sch., Washington, 2002, NJ City U. Arts and Scis. Bldg., 2002, Nat. Automobile Mus., The Netherlands, 2003, US Courthouse, Nashville, 2003; designer furniture, artifacts, textiles, and consumer products, V'Soske, 1979-80, Sunar, 1980-83, Alessi, 1981—Baldinger Archtl. Lighting, 1983—, Swid Powell, 1985—, Steuben, 1986—, Munari, 1986—Tajima, 1987-88, WMF, 1987—, Atelier Internat., 1987—Vorwerk, 1987—, Lenox Inc., 1988—, Markuse Corp., 1989—, Dunbar Furniture, 1989—, Arkitektura, 1989—, Moeller Internat. Design, 1992—, Target Stores, 1997—, Glen Eden Wool Carpet, 2002—, Delta Faucets, 2003—; monographs include: Five Architects, 1972, Michael Graves, Academy Editions, 1979, Michael Graves: Buildings and Projects 1966-1981, 1981, Michael Graves: Buildings and Projects 1982-1989, 1990, Michael Graves: Buildings and Projects 1990-1994, 1995, The Master Architect Series III: Michael Graves: Selected and Current Works, 1999, Michael Graves: Buildings and Projects 1995-2002, 2003. Recipient Arnold W. Brunner Meml. prize in Architecture, 1981, 61 awards, NJ Soc. Archs., Euster award, 1984, Ind. Arts award, 1984, Henry Hering Meml. medal, Am. Sculpture Soc., 1986, Nat. Medal Arts, Nat. Endowment Arts, 1999, Frank Annunzio award, 2001, AIA Gold medal, Sigma Tau Delta, 2003, Michael Graves Lifetime Achievement award, AIA-NJ, Topaz medallion, AIA and the Assn. Collegiate Schools Architecture, 2010; named Designer of Yr., Interiors, 1981; named one of Best Archs. and Designers Working Today, Archtl. Digest, 1990, 1995, 2000; named to NJ Hall of Fame. Fellow: AIA (Gold medal, 2001); mem.: NY Sch. Interior Design (bd. trustees), Mus. Arts and Design (bd. trustees), Am. Acad. Rome (bd. trustees, Rome prize 1960—62), Am. Acad. Arts and Letters. Home: Princeton, NJ. Died Mar. 12, 2015.

GRAY, COLEEN (DORIS BERNICE JENSEN), actress; b. Staplehurst, Nebr., Oct. 23, 1922; d. Arthur Ludwig and Anna (Thomsen) Jensen; m. Rodney Amateau, Aug. 10, 1945 (div. Mar. 1949); 1 child, Susan; m. William Clymer Bidlack, July 14, 1953 (dec. May 1978); 1 child, Bruce; m. Joseph Frederick Zeiser, May 19, 1979. BA summa cum laude, Hamline U., 1943. Independent actress, from 1947. Appeared in several films including Kiss of Death, 1947, Nightmare Alley, 1947, Red River, 1948, Fury at Furnance Creek, 1948, Sand, 1949, Riding High, 1949, Father Is a Bachelor, 1950, Riding High, 1950, The Sleeping City, 1950, Lucky Nick Cain, 1951, Apache Drums, 1951, Models Inc. 1952, Kansas City Confidential, 1952, The Vanished, 1953, Sabre Jet, 1953, The Fake, 1953, Arrow in the Dust, 1954, Las Vegas Shakedown, 1955, Tessessee's Partner, 1955, The Twinkle in God's Eye, 1955, The Wild Dakota, 1956, The Killing, 1956, Star in the Dust, 1956, Frontier Gambler, 1956, Death of a Scoundrel, 1956, The Black Whip, 1956, Destination 60,000, 1957, The Vampire, 1957, Copper Sky, 1957, Hell's Five Hours, 1958, Johnny Rocco, 1958, The Leech Woman, 1960, The Phantom Planet, 1961, Town Tamer, 1965, P.J., 1968, The Late Liz, 1971, Mother, 1978, Cry From the Mountain, 1985; several TV appearances including Pulitzer Prize Playhouse, 1950, Starlight Theatre, 1951, Danger, 1951, Armstrong Circle Theatre, 1951, Faith Baldwin Romance Theatre, 1951, Celanese Theatre, 1952, The Unexpected, 1952, Schlitz Playhouse, 1951-52, The Ford Television Theatre, 1953, Lux Video Theatre, 1951-54, Four Star Playhouse, 1955, The Millonaire, 1955, Damon Runyon Theter, 1955, Frontier, 1956, Climax!, 1956, Crossroads, 1956, Crusader, 1956, Matinee Theatre, 1957, Mike Hammer, 1958, Playhouse 90, 1958, Markham, 1959, Captain David Grief, 1959, Shotgun Slade, 1960, Tales of Wells Fargo, 1960, Walt Disney's Wonderful World of Color, 1960, The Deputy, 1960, Insight, 1960, General Electric Theater, 1960, Hong Kong, 1961, Lawman, 1961, Maverick, 1961, Coronado 9, 1961, The Tall Man, 1961, Have Gun-Will Travel, 1961, Bus Stop, 1961, Rawhide, 1962, Alfred Hitchcock Presents, 1962, Window on Main Street, 1962, Saints and Sinners, 1962, Wide Country, 1962, 77 Sunset Strip, 1961-62, Mister Ed, 1961-62, The Adventures of Ozzie & Harriet, 1963, The Dakotas, 1963, Kraft Suspense Theatre, 1964, Branded, 1965, Days of Our Lives, 1965, Perry Mason, 1960-66, The Virginian, 1966-67, My Three Sons, 1965-67, Run for Your Life, 1967, Bonanza, 1968, Family Affair, 1968, Judd for the Defense, 1968, Bright Promise, 1969, The Name of the Game, 1969, Adam-12, 1970, The F.B.I., 1971, The Bold Ones: The New Doctors, 1971, Mannix, 1971, The Sixth Sense, 1972, Ironside, 1968-75, Emergency!, 1972-76, McCloud, 1974-77, Whiz Kids, 1984, Tales from the Darkside, 1986; (TV films) Ellery Queen: Don't Look Behind You, 1971, The Best Place to Be, 1979 Pres. World Adoption Internat. Fund, Los Angeles, 1958. Republican. Presbyterian. Avocations: painting, hiking, choir singing, travel. Died Aug. 3, 2015.

GREEN, ERNESTINE CHURCHILL, retired elementary school educator; b. Natchez, Miss., Feb. 21, 1947; d. William and Emma (Johnson) Churchill; m. Alonzo Pete Green, May 31, 1969. BS, Alcorn A&M Coll., 1970; MA, Alcorn State U., 1977; AAA, U. So. Miss., Natchez, 1982; postgrad., U. So. Miss., Hattiesburg, from 1987. Tchr. Jefferson County Tchrs. Assn., Fayette, Miss., 1970—96, ret., 1996. Mem. Nat. Tchrs. Assn. Baptist. Home: Natchez, Miss. Died May 1, 2007.

GREEN, HOWARD, biologist, educator; b. Toronto, Ont., Can., Sept. 10, 1925; MD, U. Toronto, 1947; MS in Physiology, Northwestern U., 1950; DSc (hon.), State U. NY, Stony Brook, 1993; DSc, La.State U., 2008; DSc (hon.), U. Conn., 1985. Rsch. asst. dept. physiology Northwestern U. Sch. Medicine, Chgo., 1948—50; rsch. assoc., instr. biochemistry U. Chgo., Ill., 1951-53; instr. pharmacology NYU Sch. Medicine, NY, 1954-55, asst. prof. chem. pathology NY, 1956-59, assoc. prof. pathology NY, 1959-65, prof. NY, 1965-68, prof., chmn. cell biology dept. NY, 1968-70; prof. cell biology MIT, Cambridge, Mass., 1970-80; Higgins prof. cellular physiology Harvard U. Med. Sch., Boston, 1980-86, George Higginson prof. cellular physiology, 1980—93, chmn. dept. physiology and biophysics, 1986-88, chmn. dept. cellular and molecular physiology, 1988-93, George Higginson Prof. cell biology, from 1993. Lectr. in field Contbr. articles to profl. jours. Served as capt. M.C. USAR, 1955-56. Recipient Mr. And Mrs. J. N. Taub Internat. Meml. award, 1977, Selman A. Waksman award, 1978, Lewis S. Rosenstiel award, 1980, Lila Gruber Research award Am. Acad. Dermatology, 1980, Passano award, 1985, Noble Found. Rsch. Recognition award, 1992, Blaise Pascal medal, 2007, Warren Alpert Found. prize, 2010; co-recipient March of Dimes prize in Developmental Biology Mem. NAS, Am. Acad. Arts and Sci., Institut de France (Nat. Acad. of Sci.) Am. Soc. Cellular Biology, Soc. Investigative Dermatology, Inst.Curie (pres. sci. coun. 1999-2007), Chevalier de la Legion d'Honneur (hon.), Japanese Soc. Plastic & Reconstructive Surgery; fellow. Am. Acad. Microbiology. Home: Brookline, Mass. Died Oct. 31, 2015.

GREEN, ROBERTA HELEN, rancher, writer, historian; b. Challis, Idaho, Sept. 4, 1919; d. Robert Weir and Ethel Belle (Thompson) Philps; children: Joann, Judith, Ronald, Gary, Melissa. Cattle rancher, Idaho, from 1934; historian Custer County, Challis, Idaho, 1980. Author: (books) They Passed This Way, They Followed Their Dreams, The Glory Trail. Mem. Idaho Press Women (Communicator of Yr. Idaho 1997, nominated for Nat. Communicator of Yr., 1997), Cowboy Poets of Idaho. Republican. Mem. Congregational Ch. Avocations: painting, cowboy poetry. Home: Challis, Idaho. Died Dec. 5, 2006.

GREENE, GEORGE WILLIAM, lawyer; b. Mpls., Oct. 17, 1938; s. George William Greene and Verla (Clausen) Miller; m. Suzanne Elizabeth Selover, Aug. 5, 1961; children: Alison Jay, Robert Clausen, Andrew McKinnon. BA, U. Minn., 1960, LLB, 1965; postgrad., U. Tex.-Austin, 1962-63. Bar: Wis. 1965, U.S. Dist. Ct. (ea. and we. dists.) Wis. 1965, U.S. Supreme Ct. 1972, U.S. Ct. Appeals (7th cir.) 1987. Assoc. Borgelt, Powell, Peterson & Frauen, Milw., 1965-70, Prosser, Wiedabach & Quale, S.C., Milw., 1970-93; cir. ct. judge Milwaukee County, 1993-94, jud. ct. commr., from 1994. Sec., bd. dris. Rogers Meml. Hosp., Oconomowoc, Wis., 1972-98; pres. bd. dirs. Maple Dale-Indian Hill Sch. Dist., Fox Point, Wis., 1975-81; pres. The Gathering food program, Milw., 1982; trustee Village of Fox Point, 1985-91. Capt. U.S. Army, 1960-62. Recipient Spl. Service award Met. Milw. Civic Alliance, 1987, Layperson of Yr. award Episcopal Diocese Milw., 1988. Mem. ABA (tort and ins. practice sect.), State Bar Wis. (litigation sect., bd. govs.), Order of St. Andrew. Republican. Home: Milwaukee, Wis. Died Nov. 26, 2006.

GREENE, LOUIS LEON, dentist; b. NYC, Sept. 5, 1917; s. Morris and Anna Greene; m. Sarah Shenk Greene, Mar. 21, 1943; children: Judy, Diane, Steven. BS, Columbia,

1939, postgrad, 1954; DDS, Ohio State U., 1943. Pvt. practice, NYC, from 1946; dir. rsch. Greene Lab; v.p. Morris Plastic Co., NYC, 1959—60; vis. dental surgeon Harlem Hosp.; lectr. crown & bridge 1st Dist. Dental Soc., NY; postgrad. lectr. NY U. Sch. Dentistry. Designer comml. plastics, toys Sec. Saddle Rock P.T.A., 1959. Bd. dirs. Saddle Rock Estates Civic Assn., Saddle Rock Estates Pool Club. Served to capt. USAR, 1943—46. Recipient Interfaith award, 1966, award, Fedn. Jewish Philanthropies, 1966, Plaque N.Y. Oral Rehab. Study Group. Achievements include patents for indsl plastics, toys, dentistry. Home: Great Neck, NY. Died Dec. 6, 2006.

GREENHAUS, DONALD, artist; b. Bklyn., Dec. 17, 1941; s. Benjamin G. and Etta (Epstein) G. Photographer, painter, print maker, NYC. Lectr. in field; faculty New Sch. for Social Rsch., N.Y.C., 1974-87. Works represented in Bklyn. Mus., Mus. History and tech., Smithsonian Inst., Washington, Mus. City of N.Y. and pub. colletions in Spain and France. Home: New York, NY. Died Jan. 19, 2007.

GREENSPAN, EDWARD LEONARD (EDDIE GREENSPAN), lawyer; b. Niagara Falls, Ont., Can., Feb. 28, 1944; s. Joseph and Emma (Mercel) Greenspan; m. Suzy Greenspan, Aug. 18, 1968; children: Juliana, Sammantha. Grad., U. Toronto, 1965, Osgoode Hall Law Sch., 1970; doctorate (hon.), Law Soc. Upper Canada, 1999; Doctorate of Civil Laws (hon.), U. Windsor, 2002; LLD (hon.), Assumption U., 2004, Brock U., 2012. Received: Queen's Counsel 1982. Sr. ptnr. Greenspan, White. Lectr. criminal law U. Toronto Law Sch., 1972—99; lectr. criminal procedure York U., 1972—81, lectr. advanced evidence in criminal cases, 1987—89. Co-author (with George Jonas): (autobiography) Greenspan: The Case for the Defence, 1987; host (TV series) The Scales of Justice, 1982—94. Recipient G. Arthur Martin medal, 2001, Advocates' Soc. medal, 2009. Mem.: American Coll. Trial Lawyers, York County Law Assn., Internat. Assn. Jewish Lawyers and Jurists, Criminal Lawyers Assn., Canadian Bar Assn., Internat. Soc. Barristers, American Nat. Assn. Criminal Def. Lawyers, The Advocates' Soc., Canadian Civil Liberties Assn., Exec. for Soc. for Reform of Criminal Law. Jewish. Died Dec. 24, 2014.

GREENWOOD, JAMES GREGORY, fine arts educator, college dean; b. Duluth, Minn., Jan. 8, 1947; s. Byron Joseph and Patricia (Ehr) G. BA, No. Ill. U., 1968, MA, 1969; grad., Ohio State U., 1974. Dir. of debate Washington & Jefferson Coll., Washington, 1974-81; chmn. Sta. WLFC-FM Findlay (Ohio) Coll., from 1981, chmn. div. fine arts, from 1983, asst. dean dept., from 1986. Contbr. articles to Speech Monographs, Cen. States Speech Jour., Jour. of the Univ. Film Assn. Served with U.S. Army, 1969-71. Mem. Speech Communication Assn., Cen. States Speech Assn., Ohio Speech Communication Assn., Am. Forensic Assn., Soc. to Preserve and Encourage Radio Drama, Variety and Comedy, Phi Kappa Sigma. Avocations: gardening, old time radio, contemporary music. Home: Findlay, Ohio. Died May 30, 2007.

GREER, GAYLE, musician; b. Ft. Worth, Texas, Mar. 20, 1956; BMus., MMus., Rice U., 1981. Prin. violist Houston Ballet Orch., 1978-82; violist Tex. Chamber Orch., Houston, 1981-82; asst. prin. violist Boston ProArte Chamber Orch., 1983-85; violist Portland (Maine) Symphony Orch., 1983-85; solo violist Regensburg (Fed. Republic of Germany) Philharm. Orch., from 1986. Mem. faculty Am. Inst. of Mus. Studies, Graz, Austria and Dallas, Greater Boston Youth Symphony, 1984-85. Recipient Grad. Assistantship, Boston U., 1983, 1984, Scholarship Award, Civic Symphony of Boston, 1983-84. Died Mar. 31, 2007.

GREER, KAREN, medical/surgical nurse; b. Chgo., June 21, 1946; d. Thomas and Sophia (Pickley) Carlisle; m. Daniel Greer, Sept. 19, 1981; children: Laura Vanderipe, Christy Haines, Sam Haines. ADN, Purdue U., 1982; BA, Nat.-Louis U., 1984. Dir. nursing Countryside Place, Knox, Ind., 1985-86, Staffbuilders, Crown Point, Ind., 1986-88, Lake Holiday Manor, Demotte, Ind., 1988-89; instr. Sawyer Coll., Merrillville, Ind., from 1989. Mem. Am. Heart Assn. Home: Hebron, Ind. Died Apr. 26, 2007.

GREIF, EDWARD EARL, management consultant; b. Lexington, Ky., Feb. 12, 1939; s. Edward Gholson and Agnes Irene (Stith) G.; m. Helen Mae Grant, Nov. 10, 1958 (div. Dec. 1979); children: Carmen Lea, Grant Edward, Gregory Scott, Robert Smith; m. Phyllis Jane Hobbs, Feb. 20, 1982. BS in Pharmacy and Chemistry, U. Ky., 1961. Cert. mgmt. cons. Clin. pharmacist U. Ky. Med. Ctr., Lexington, 1960-64; asst. prof. U. Pa. Hosps., Phila., 1965-69, asst. dir. pharmacy and materials mgmt., 1965-69; clin. instr. Phila. Coll. pharmacy and Sci., Phila., 1965-69; dir. clin. rsch. Edward Weck & Co., Long Island City, N.Y., 1969-70; sales and mktg. exec. Picker Internat., Cleve., 1970-83; pres., CEO Ed Greif & Co. Inc., Wichita, from 1983. Author audio and video learning systems, 1986—; contbr. articles to profl. jours.; inventor med. devices. Mem. adv. bd. Boy Scouts Am., Doylestown, Pa., 1975-78. Recipient Silver award Explorer Scouting, Boy Scouts Am., 1955. Mem. Nat. Speakers Assn. (pres. 1988-89), Am. Soc. Hosp. Pharmacists (chpt. pres.), Am. Mktg. Assn., Inst. Mgmt. Cons. (chpt. officer), U. Ky. Alumni Assn. (life; chpt. officer), Nat. Eagle Scout Assn. (life). Republican. Roman Catholic. Home: Wichita, Kans. Died Apr. 13, 2007.

GRESTINI, MARIO HARRY, accountant; b. NYC, June 22, 1946; s. Amillio Mari and Anette Grestini; m. Cathy Diane Grestini, July 18, 1975; children: Craig, Kyle, Carley, Clint, Don. B in Bus., Western Mich. U., 1968. Income tax advisor City of Battle Creek, Mich., 1974-83, budget asst. Mich., 1983-95, income tax adminstr. Mich., from 1995. Mem. Notary Pub., Mich., 1974-79. With U.S. Army, 1968-70. Mem. Govt. Fin. Officers Assn. Avocations: stamp collecting/philately, sports. Home: Battle Creek, Mich. Died Feb. 21, 2007.

GRIFFIN, ROBERT PAUL, former United States Senator from Michigan; b. Detroit, Nov. 6, 1923; s. J.A. and Beulah M. G.; m. Marjorie J. Anderson, 1947; children Paul Robert, Richard Allen, James Anderson, Martha Jill. AB, BS, Central Mich. U., 1947, LLD, 1963; JD, U. Mich., 1950, LLD, 1973; LL.D., Eastern Mich. U., 1969, Albion Coll., 1970, Western Mich. U., 1971, Grand Valley State Coll., 1971, Detroit Coll. Bus., 1972, Detroit Coll. Law, 1973; L.H.D., Hillsdale Coll., Mich., 1970; J.C.D., Rollins Coll., 1970; Ed.D., No. Mich. U., 1970; D. Pub. Service, Detroit Inst. Tech., 1971. Bar: Mich. 1950. Pvt. practice, Traverse City, Mich., 1950-56; mem. US Congress from 9th Mich. Dist., Washington, 1957-66; US Senator from Mich. Washington, 1966-79; counsel Miller, Canfield, Paddock & Stone, Traverse City, 1979-86; assoc. justice Mich. Supreme Ct., Lansing, 1987-95. Trustee Gerald R. Ford Found. Served with inf. AUS, World War II, ETO. Named 1 of 10 Outstanding Young Men of Nation U.S. Jaycees, 1959 Mem. ABA, Mich. Bar Assn., D.C. Bar Assn., Kiwanis. Died Apr. 16, 2015.

GRIFFIS, CURTIS RAYMOND, religion educator; b. Paris, Tex., Oct. 20, 1935; s. Robert Eugene and Mary Maude (Bills) G.; m. Barbara Anne Sanders, June 7, 1957; children: Sarah Reneé, Robert Curtis, Amy Elizabeth. BA, Midwestern U., 1962; MRE, Southwestern Sem., 1965. Ordained to ministry Bapt. Ch., 1969. Min. of edn. Sans Souce Bapt. Ch., Greenville, S.C., 1965-67, Far Hills Bapt. Ch., Dayton, Ohio, 1967-68; dir. of religious edn. Greater Dayton Assn. Bapts., 1968-73; dir. ch. devel. Bapt. Gen. Assn. New Eng., Northboro, Mass., 1973-79; min. edn. Mid. River Bapt. Ch., Balt., 1979-82; metro evangelism assoc. Ill. Bapt. State Assn., Springfield, 1982-87; min. of edn. Cen. Bapt. Ch., Winchester, Ky., from 1987. Newspaper-pressman, stereotyper Duncan (Okla.) Banner, Wichita Falls News, Dallas News, 1953-65. Home: Englewood, Colo. Died July 24, 2007.

GRIFFITH, BARBARA E., social worker, political activist; b. Bklyn., Feb. 17, 1943; d. Carl and Ruth (Cramer) Horowitz; m. Richard Michael Griffith, Feb. 12, 1942; children: Kim Griffith McFadden, David Wark. BSW, Ohio State U., 1965; postgrad., Adelphi U., 1965-66. Social worker Columbus Home for Mentally Disturbed Children, Columbus, Ohio, 1965; case worker Nassau County Social Svcs., LI, N.Y., 1965-66, Red Bank (N.J.) Dept. Social Svcs., 1966-67, Dept. Social Svcs. Honolulu, 1967-69; asst. dir. nursery sch. Cleve., 1975-78; advt. mgr. mags. Toronto, Ont., Can., 1979-84; substitute tchr. West Windsor (N.J.) Plainsboro H.S., 1987-90; polit. activist Bus. & Profl. Women's Assn., N.J., 1989-93; owner R.M.G. Assocs., Inc., Princeton Junction, N.J., from 1993. V.p. mktg. and sales Thornhill Month Mag. Pub., 1985; real estate devel. cons., 1991—; owner Lady Limo of N.J., 1996—. Counselor for homeless people; active Clinton Presdl. Campaign, N.J.; dir. Hughes Congl. Campaign for U.S. Congress, 1992, N.J.; local town councilwoman, Can., 1982; participant Lobby Day, Washington, 1990-94. Mem. NOW, LWV (Princeton chpt. 1988—), N.J. Bus. & Profl. Women Assn. (chmn. N.J. legis. chpt. 1992-93), Women's Agenda (com. mem. N.J. law sect.) Avocations: travel, working with children, video projects, working with homeless. Home: Princeton Junction, NJ. Died Jan. 30, 2007.

GRIFFITH, PATRICIA ANN, county official, volunteer; b. Dallas, Nov. 21, 1949; d. E.J. and R. Jacquiline (Lacy) Sublett; m. J. Richard Griffith, June 12, 1970 (div. Oct. 1981); 1 child, Jennifer. Ins. underwriter various agencies, Denton, Tex., 1968-85; chief adminstr. to commr. Denton County, Denton, 1985-88, coord. indigent healthcare, from 1988. Bus. mgr. Lakes Cities United Meth. Ch., Lake Dallas, Tex., 1997—, adminstrv. coun. chair, 1995-96; bd. dirs. Flow Healthcare Found., Denton, 1996-97, Am. Cancer Soc., Denton, 1987-95; sec. bd. dirs. HelpNET of Greater Denton Area, 1999. Named Pub. Citizen of Yr. NASW, 1992. Methodist. Avocations: reading, volunteering. Home: Lake Dallas, Tex. Died July 20, 2007.

GRIMES, MARILYN JANE LARSEN, nursing administrator; b. Pierre, SD, July 28, 1933; d. Hans and Selma (Rappana) Larsen; m. Walter W. Grimes, June 5, 1955; children: Mark W., Christine E., Paul C. Diploma, Sioux Valley Hosp. Sch., Sioux Falls, SD, 1954; BS in Nursing, U. Ill., Chgo., 1971, MS in Nursing, 1973. Cert. clin. specialist psychiat./mental health. Supervisory nurse Ill. Psychiat. Inst., Chgo., 1973-78; assoc. adminstr. Ill. Nurses Assn., Chgo., 1978-81; clin. nurse cons. II U. Ill. Hosp., Chgo., from 1981. Vol. Human Rights Authority, Ill. Commn. Guardianship and Advocacy. Recipient Constituent Leadership award U. Ill. Alumni Assn., 1985. Mem. ANA, Midwest Nursing Rsch. Soc., Ill. Nurses Assn., Chgo. Nurses Assn., U. Ill. Coll. Nursing Alumni Assn. (pres., bd. dirs., loyalty award 1978), Nat. Assn. Perinatal Addiction Rsch. and Edn., Sigma Theta Tau. Home: Lombard, Ill. Died Dec. 16, 2006.

GROSSER, ELMER JOSEPH, priest; b. Dayton, Ky., Aug. 31, 1922; s. Albert J. and Rose Mary (Wiegand) G. BA, St. Gregory Sem., Cin., 1943; postgrad., St. Mary Sem., 1943-46; MA, U. Toronto, 1949, PhD in Philosophy, 1951. Ordained priest Roman Cath. Ch., 1946. Prof. philosophy Holy Cross Sem., La Crosse, Wis., 1951-53; rector, prof. philosophy Sem. of St. Pius X, Erlanger, Ky., 1953-73; pastor Blessed Sacrament Ch., Covington, Ky., 1973-81, St. Philip Ch., Covington, 1981-86, Holy Cross Ch., Covington, from 1987. Consultor to priests' senate, mem. fin. coun. Diocese of Covington, 1955—. Died Apr. 13, 2007.

GROTHENDIECK, ALEXANDRE, retired mathematician; b. Berlin, Mar. 28, 1928; s. Alexander Shapiro and Hanka Grothendieck. Student, Monpellier U., Ecole Normale Supérieur, Paris, 1948-49; PhD, U. Nancy; postgrad., U. San Paulo, 1953-55, U Kans., 1956. With Centre Nat. de la Recherche Scientifique, 1950-53, 56-59; chair Institut des Hautes Etudes Scientifique, 1959-70; vis. prof. Coll. France, 1970-72, Orsay, 1972-73; prof. U. Montpellier, 1973-84; dir. rsch. Centre Nat. de la Recherche Scientifique, 1984-88. Recipient Fields Medal, Internat. Math. Union Congress, 1966, Crafoord prize in Math., Royal Swedish Acad. Sciences, 1988. Achievements include fields of abstract algebra, category theory, algebraic geometry and logic. Died Nov. 13, 2014.

GRUBER, LOREN CHARLES, literature and language professor, writer; s. Maurice Deputy and Harriett Helen (Brynteson) G.; m. Irene Ellen Olson, Mar. 5, 1967 (div. 1980); children: Elizabeth Gruber Shinall, Stephen, Margaret; m. Meredith Adair Crellin, Jan. 22, 1983 (div. 1999). BA, Simpson Coll., 1963; MA, Western Res. U., Cleve., 1964; PhD, U. Denver, 1972. English instr. Grove City Coll., Pa., 1964-66, Simpson Coll., Indianola, Iowa, 1966-69; tchg. asst. U. Denver, 1968-69, tchg. fellow, 1969-70; from asst. to assoc. prof. Simpson Coll., Indianola, 1970-82; announcer, news writer Sta. KBAB-AM, Indianol, 1980—82; chief exec. cons. Stanley, Barber, Southard, Brown and Assocs., San Diego, 1982-83; account exec. Sta. KJEM-AM and K-95-FM, Bentonville, Ark., 1983-87; mgr., news dir. Sta. KQIS-FM, Clarinda, Iowa, 1987-89; asst. prof. English N.W. Mo. State U., Maryville, 1989-93, interim dir. composition, 1992-93; prof. English, mass comm. Mo. Valley Coll., Marshall, 1993—2013, prof. emeritus, from 2013, chair mass comm., 1995-98, chair English dept., 1996-98, dean divsn. arts and humanities, 1998—2004; pvt. practice Muskie Guide Svcs., 2005—09; profl. muskellunge fisherman and lure field tester. Reviewer Choice, Middletown, Conn., 1973-82; Muskie Prof., KMMO-FM and KMMO.COM 2005-; design cons., field tester, Jensen Jigs Musky Clatterbaits, Neenah,Wis., 2006-. Gen. editor In Geardagum Series, 1974-82, 91-92; editor-in-chief: (with Meredith Crellin Gruber and Gregory K. Jember) Essays on Old, Middle, Modern English and Old Icelandic, 1999; bibliographer Neuphilologische Mitteilungen, Helsinki, Finland, 1978-82; bus. mgr. Laurel Rev., 1989-93; assoc. editor Lyrical Iowa, 1999-2000; contbr. articles to profl. jours., poetry, short fiction to magazines. Founding pres. Indianola Writers Workshop, 1972; sec. Indianola Fine Arts Commn., 1973; state del. Iowa Rep. Party Conv., Des Moines, 1976, 80, 88; hon. mem. 4-H, Page County, Iowa, 1988; bd. dirs. Writers Hall of Fame, 1995-98; founder Mid-Mo. chpt. Writers' Hall of Fame, 1996-98; charter mem. Missouri Valley Coll. President's Soc. Recipient John McCallum Excellence in Tchg. award, Mo. Valley Coll., 2005, ADDY awards, KJEM-AM, Bentonville, Arkansas, 1984, Lt. Governor's spl. award, 1986, Silver Merit award, Kiwanis Internat. Club Pres, Missouri-Arkansas Kiwanis District Governor's award, 2013; Walter Zeller fellow, Kiwanis Internat., George F. Hixson fellow. Mem. Medieval Acad. Am. (life, mem. endowment campaign com. 1995-96), Soc. Advancement Scandinavian Studies (life), Soc. New Lang. Study (exec. sec. 1973-82, 91-92), Mo. Writers Guild (life) (bd. dirs. 1992—1996, editor News 1992-94, pres. 1995-96), Soc. Children's Book Writers and Illustrators (1996-present), Iowa Poetry Assn. (pres. 1980-82, 88-92), Bentonville/Bella Vista Ark. Kiwanis (pres. 1985-86, lt. gov.'s award 1986; Kiwanis InterNat. Club Pres.'s Silver Merit Award, 1986), Clarinda Iowa Rotary (pres. pro-tem 1989), Mo. Writers' Guild (Marshall chpt., charter), Kiwanis (bd. dirs. Marshall chpt. 1999-2001, pres. 2005-2006), Sigma Tau Delta (publs. and handbook com. 2000—2005), Trinity Episcopal Ch. Marshall, Mo., Vestry, Discernment Com, Muskies, Inc. (life), Sigma Alpha Epsilon (life), Missouri-Arkansas Kiwanis District, Region 1, Divsn.. 3 (lt. governor, 2012-14, Earl Collins trustee; Kiwanis InterNat. Convention Delegate, 2012, 2013, 2014; The Formula, Club Opener, Divsn. 3) Republican. Episcopalian. Avocations: fishing, hunting, ornithology, travel. Home: Marshall, Mo. Died Nov. 9, 2014.

GRUBIAK, MICHAEL ROBERT, chemist; b. Yonkers, NY, Aug. 1, 1934; s. Michael John and Ann (Fenyo) G.; m. Dorothy Ann Nylis, May 12, 1956 (div. Jan 1982); children: Lorraine, Linda, Robert, James, Jeffrey, Christopher; m. Lois Brenda Williamson, Aug. 21, 1982. Student, Bklyn. Community Coll., 1952, Columbia U., 1956-58, Fordham U., 1958-61. Sr. lab. technician Philips Labs., NYC, 1958-66; engring. specialist Ferruxcube Corp., NYC, 1966-84; sr. chemist Tempel Steel Corp., Chgo., from 1985. Served with USN, 1954-56. Mem. AAAS, Am. Chem. Soc., Am. Applied Scis. Lodges: Lions (sec. 1978-80, v.p. 1980-81). Democrat. Died Mar. 15, 2007.

GRUENBERG, ELLIOT LEWIS, electronics engineer and company executive; b. NYC, Mar. 16, 1918; s. Lewis and Sadie (Schoenbrun) G.; m. Ruth Frankel, Apr. 19, 1947. BEE, CCNY, 1938. Engr., inspector US Signal Corps Line Inspection, Newark, NJ, 1939-43; quality control mgr. Tech. Devices, Roseland, NJ, 1943-48; sr. engr. J.H. Bunnell, Bklyn., 1948-51, Freed Radio, NYC, 1951; sr. engr., mgr. W.L. Maxson, NYC, 1951-58; sr. engring. mgr. Fed. Systems div. IBM, Bethesda, Md., 1958-73; cons. West New York, NJ, 1974-79; chmn. BroadCom, Inc., Secaucus, NJ, 1979-88, also bd. dirs.; chmn., pres. CompFax Corp., West New York, NJ, 1988-92; pres. Digital Compression Tech., L.P., NYC, from 1993. Editor: Handbook of Telemetry and Remote Control, 1967; inventor SYNAPZ Microwave Comm., radar, electronic telecomm., telemetry, BGET Secure Comm., DTIC Digital Transmission Bandwidth Compression, Superresonant Digital Modulation and Filtering, Pulset Time Position Modulation; patentee in field; contbr.

articles to profl. jours. Fellow Am. Inst. Aeronautics and Astronautics (assoc.); mem. IEEE (sr. life mem. 1940—). Democrat. Mem. Ethical Culture. Avocations: puzzles, astronomy. Deceased.

GRUENEWALD, DORIS, psychologist; b. Mannheim, Germany, Oct. 22, 1916; came to U.S., 1937; d. Joseph C. and Anne (Winter) Wiener; m. Ernst Gruenewald, May 27, 1938 (dec. Aug. 1989); children: Hannah Neubauer, Ruth Skoglund. BA, Roosevelt U., 1956, MA, 1961; PhD, U. Chgo., 1966. Diplomate Am. Bd. Profl. Psychology, Am. Bd. Psychol. Hypnosis; lic. psychologist, Calif. Rsch. assoc. U. Chgo., 1967-76, clin. assoc. prof. psychiatry, 1976-88; dir. adult treatment program, sr. clin. psychologist Michael Reese Hosp. & Med. Ctr., Chgo., 1966-86. Author chpts. in books; contbr. numerous articles to profl. jours. Fellow APA, Am. Soc. Clin. Hypnosis, Soc. Clin. and Exptl. Hypnosis (chair ethics com. 1990-93), Psi Chi, Sigma Xi. Home: Bethlehem, Pa. Died May 6, 2007.

GRUETTER, RICHARD ALLEN, chemical company executive; b. Atlanta, Oct. 11, 1946; s. Walter and Betty Marie (Joseph) G.; m. Mary Louise Sanchez, Apr. 6, 1979. AA in Bus., Delta Jr. Coll., Stockton, Calif., 1966. Inventory control clk. Baker Commodities, LA, 1970-71; buyer Hehr Internat., LA, 1971-75; sr. buyer Paul-Monroe Hydraulics, Whittier, Calif., 1975-78; sr. project buyer Ralph M. Parsons, Pasadena, Calif., 1978-80; sr. buyer Occidental Engring., Irvine, Calif., 1980-82, Phone Mate, Inc., Torrance, Calif., 1983; purchasing supr. Centon Electronics, Irvine, 1983-84; sr. buyer Santa Fe/Braun Engrs., Alhambra, Calif., 1984-87; contract adminstr. U.S. Borax & Chemical Corp., LA, 1987-91; sr. project buyer Brown and Root Braun, Alhambra, Calif., from 1991. With U.S. Army, 1966-67, Vietnam. Mem. Mensa. Democrat. Avocations: reading, most sports. Died Dec. 4, 2006.

GRUNDISH, LEE ANNE, small business owner, writer; b. Kalamazoo, Mich., Apr. 13, 1959; d. Allen Grundish and Jeane Gratop. BA in Psychology, U. Toledo, 1984. Bus. owner, pres. Grafix Svcs./Achieve Success!, Toledo, from 1989. Bus. develp. mktg. cons., 1985—89. Lyricist (song) Love Is What We Need; writer: numerous resumes in resume guides including Expert Resumes for Baby-Boomers, Barron's Designing the Perfect Resume, Best Resumes and Letters for Ex-Offenders, others. Parent counselor Family and Child Abuse Prevention Ctr., Toledo, 1984, fundraising vol., 1998; youth mentor Big Bros. & Big Sisters, Toledo, 1990—91, fundraising vol., 1995—98, Arts Commn. of Greater Toledo, 1998; voters' rights vol. Nat. Voice, Toledo, 2004. Mem.: ASCAP, ACA, Nat. Resume Writers Assn., Nat. Employment Counselors Assn. Democrat. Avocations: poetry, politics. Home: Toledo, Ohio. Died Mar. 28, 2007.

GRZYLL, LAWRENCE ROBERT, chemical engineer, researcher; b. Milw., Oct. 21, 1961; s. Lawrence Robert and Caryl Ann (Vetter) G.; m. Deborah Jean Arnold, Mar. 18, 1989. BSChemE, Fla. Inst. Tech., 1984, MSChemE, 1986. Rsch. assoc. Fla. Inst. Tech., Melbourne, 1984-87; sr. chem. engr. Mainstream Engring. Corp., Rockledge, Fla., from 1987. Contbr. articles to profl. jours. Republican. Lutheran. Achievements include patents for micro-climate control vest and for supersonic compressor for thermally powered heat pumping applications; 4 patents pending. Home: Merritt Island, Fla. Died June 25, 2007.

GUIDRY, URSULA CROMMIE, internist, cardiologist; b. Houston, Dec. 21, 1965; d. Cliffie Andrew and Ethelyn Guidry. AB in Biology magna cum laude, Harvard U., 1988; MD, U. Calif., San Francisco, 1992. Diplomate Am. Bd. Internal Medicine with subspeciality in cardiovascular disease. Intern, resident Mass. Gen. Hosp., Boston, 1992-95; fellow in cardiology Brigham and Women's Hosp., Boston, 1995-98; fellow Framingham Heart Study, 1998-99; cardiologist Kaiser Permanente Med. Group, Oakland, Calif., from 1999. Avocation: west coast swing dancing. Home: Oakland, Calif. Died Apr. 3, 2007.

GUIHER, JAMES MORFORD, JR., publisher, writer; b. Clarksburg, W.Va., Feb. 21, 1927; s. James Morford and Ruth Holt (Souders) G.; m. Elizabeth Ewing Hart, Aug. 20, 1954; children: Catharine Brownfield, Deborah Hart. BA, Princeton U., 1951; postgrad., Harvard U., 1951-52, Boston Mus. Sch. Fine Arts, 1953-54. Editor coll. textbooks Prentice-Hall, Inc., Englewood Cliffs, NJ, 1954-66, exec. editor Ednl. Book div., 1966-68, editor-in-chief, 1968-74, v.p., gen. mgr., 1974-76; publishing cons. Author: How's Your Water Working? Some Significant Words in My Life, 2009, (plays) Candoo!, 2010, Aphrodite, 2010, (song) I'm In Love with You, 2010, (poem) Alone, 2012. Served with AUS, 1945-47. Home: Catonsville, Md. Died Dec. 17, 2014.

GUILLERM, NELLY ARMANDE See VERDY, VIOLETTE

GUILLERMIN, JOHN (YVON JEAN GUILLERMIN), film director; b. London, Nov. 11, 1925; s. Joseph and Genevieve Guillermin; m. Maureen Connell (div.); m. Mary Scarlett; children: Michael(dec.) , Michelle. Student, Cambridge U. Dir.: films Torment, 1949, Smart Alec, 1951, Two On The Tiles, 1951, Four Days, 1951, Bachelor in Paris, 1952, Miss Robin Hood, 1952. Operation Diplomat, 1953, Adventure In The Hopfields, 1954, The Crowded Day, 1954, Dust And Gold, 1955, Thunderstorm, 1955, Town On Trial, 1957, The Whole Truth, 1958, I Was Monty's Double, 1958, Tarzan's Great Adventure, 1959, The Day They Robbed The Bank of England, 1960, Never Let Go, 1960, The Waltz of the Toreadors, 1962, Tarzan Goes To India, 1962, Guns at Batasi, 1964, Rapture, 1965, The Blue Max, 1966, P.J., 1968, House of Cards, 1969, The Bridge at Remagen, 1969, El Condor, 1970, Skyjacked, 1972, Shaft in Africa, 1973, The Towering Inferno, 1974, King Kong, 1976, Death on the Nile, 1978, Mr. Patman, 1980, Sheena, 1984, King Kong Lives, 1986, The Tracker, 1988, The French Revolution, 1988. Served in Royal Air Force. Died Sept. 27, 2015.

GUIMOND, MICHEL, former Canadian legislator; b. Chicoutimi, Que., Can., Dec. 26, 1953; m. Mariette Langlois; children: Louis-Alexandre, Isabelle. BA in Labour Rels., U. Montreal, 1976; LLB, Laval U., 1988. M.P. for Beauport-Montmorency-Orléans House of Commons, 1993—2011, chmn. public accounts com., 1996—97. Alderman for Boischatel, 1989-93. Mem. Boischatel Optimist Club. Avocations: golf, theater, outdoors. Died Jan. 19, 2015.

GUION, ROBERT MORGAN, psychologist, educator; b. Indpls., Sept. 14, 1924; s. Leroy Herbert and Carolyn (Morgan) Guion; m. Mary Emily Firestone, June 8, 1947; children: David Michael, Diana Lynn, Keith Douglas, Pamela Sue, Judith Elaine. BA, State U. Iowa, 1948; MS, Purdue U., 1950, PhD, 1952. Vocat. counselor Purdue U., 1948-51, research fellow, 1951-52; mem. faculty Bowling Green (Ohio) State U., from 1952, prof. psychology, from 1964, univ. prof., 1983-85, univ. prof. emeritus, from 1985, chmn. dept., 1966-71. Vis. prof. U. Calif., Berkeley, 1963—64, U. N.Mex., 1965; tech. adviser Dept. Pers. Svcs., State of Hawaii, 1970; vis. rsch. psychologist Ednl. Testing Svc., 1971—72; cons. in field. Author: (book) Personnel Testing, 1965, Assessment, Measurement and Prediction for Personnel Decisions, 1998, 2nd edit., 2011; editor: Jour. Applied Psychology, 1983—88; co-author (with Scott Highhouse): Essentials of Personnel Assessment and Selection, 2006. With AUS, 1943—46. Recipient Stephen E. Bemis award, Internat. Pers. Mgmt. Assn., 2000. Mem.: APA (pres. divsn. 14 1972—73, pres. divsn. 5 1982—83, James McKeen Cattell award divsn. 14 1965, 1981, Disting. Sci. Contbn. award divsn. 14 1987, Disting. Svc. award divsn. 14 1993, Lifetime Contbn. award divsn. 5 1997), Assn. Psychol. Scis. (James McKeen Cattell award 2000). Methodist. Home: Bowling Green, Ohio. Died Oct. 23, 2012.

GULBRANSON, JAMES BERNHARD, retail executive; b. Glendale, Calif., June 28, 1942; s. Bernard Theodore and Frances (Slang) G.; m. Kathleen Berg, May 6, 1967; children: Kirsten, Erik, Ingrid. AA, Antelope Valley Jr. Coll., Lancaster, Calif., 1962; BA, Calif. Luth. U., 1964. Pres. San Fernando Valley Glass Co., Panorama City, Calif., from 1967, Van Nuys Glass Co. Inc., Panorama City, from 1979. Mem. nominating com. Mission District, Boy Scouts Am., 1972—; mem. San Fernando Valley Hist Soc., v.p. 1969, 83, pres. 1970, bd. dirs. 1983-85; bd. dirs. Heritage Mus. Fine Arts; commr. City of San Fernando hist. bldgs. and sites; active many historical groups and societies; mem. Los Angeles County Rep. Com. Served to 1st lt. U.S. Army, 1964-67, Vietnam. Decorated Silver Star, Air medal; recipient Disting. Service award San Fernando Jaycees, 1973. Mem. So. Calif. Glass Assn. (bd. dirs. 1987—), San Fernando Valley Internat. Soc. Interior Designers (bd. dirs. 1987—), San Fernando Valley Bus. and Profl. Assn., Calif. Luth. Coll. Alumni Assn. Lodges: Rotary (San Fernando) (treas. 1971-72, Paul Harris fellow, 1976). Lutheran. Avocations: photography, music, art collecting. Died June 5, 2007.

GUSHEA, HARRIET S., nurse, educator; b. North Bangor, NY, Mar. 22, 1941; d. Leo E. and Helen Collette Snyder; m. Stuart S. Gushea, Nov. 12, 1960; 1 child, Kimberly Ann. AAS, SUNY, Canton, 1977; BS, SUNY, Utica, 1987. RN, N.Y. Staff nurse, asst. charge nurse, relief charge nurse Massena (N.Y.) Meml. Hosp., staff devel. dir.; head nurse, supr. PHN, Potsdam, N.Y. Mem. N.Y. State Nurses Assn. (dist. 6), Far No. Dirs. Nursing and Staff Educators, Sigma Theta Tau. Home: Potsdam, NY. Died July 20, 2007.

GUTHRIDGE, BILL, university basketball coach; b. Parsons, Kans., July 27, 1937; m. Leesie Guthridge; children: Jamie, Stuart, Megan. BS in Math., Kans. State U., 1960, MEd, 1963. Coach Scott City H.S, Kans.; asst. football coach Kans. State U.; freshman basketball coach, co-asst. varsity coach U. NC, Chapel Hill, from 1973, asst. coach, 1968-97, head coach, 1997—2000. Coach Puerto Rican AAU Summer Leagues; coach Puerto Rican Olympic Team, 1968. Named Coach of Yr., Puerto Rican AAU, Nat. Coach of Yr., Nat. Assn. Basketball Coaches, Sporting News, CBS/Chevrolet, Columbus Touchdown Club, Atlantic Coast Conf., 1998; recipient Naismith award Atlanta Tipoff Club. Home: Chapel Hill, NC. Died May 12, 2015.

GUTIERREZ, LAURA L., director medical-surgery, oncology services; b. Columbus, Ohio, Nov. 30, 1954; d. Willis L. and Judith C. (Hymrod) K.; children: Elijah, Nathan, Willis, Andrew, Aaron. BSN, Mich. State U., 1976. Charge nurse Ingham County Med. Care Facility, Adrian, Mich.; charge nurse, chem. dependency Bixby Med. Ctr., Adrian, Mich., charge nurse, mental health, unit mgr., chem. dependency. Home: Adrian, Mich. Died Dec. 25, 2006.

GUTTENBERG, JOHN PAUL, JR., public relations consulting company executive; b. Rochester, NY, Nov. 23, 1936; s. John Paul and Carol Ruth (Sloman) G.; m. Diana Lee Swartz, Apr. 18, 1959; children: Karen Lee Guttenberg Greer, Jennifer Anne. BA in English Lit., Lafayette Coll., 1958. Spl. asst. to press sec. The White House, 1961; adminstrv. asst. to pres. Clark U., 1962-63; asst. to dir. pub. relations Xerox Corp., Rochester, 1963-65, mgr. communications services, 1967-68, mgr. civic affairs, spl. asst. to chmn., 1968-71; dir. pub. relations Univ. Microfilms Inc., Ann Arbor, Mich., 1965-66; v.p. pub. affairs Council Better Bus. Burs., Washington, 1971-72; v.p. corp. affairs Datran, Washington, 1972-76; ptnr. Drayne/Guttenberg, Washington, 1976-78; pres. Guttenberg & Co., Alexandria, Va., from 1978. Bd. dirs. Faxfair Corp., Ctr. for the New Leadership. Author: Edward Hicks, Historical Flasks. Pres., Genesee Valley Bottle Collectors Assn., Rochester, 1969-70, Mt. Vernon Civic Assn., 1977; chmn. Fedn. Hist. Bottle Clubs, Fairport, N.Y., 1970-71; bd. dirs. S.E. House, Washington, 1976-80, Studio Theatre, Washington, 1983—, Consonant Ltd., 1984-86, Young Audiences, Washington, 1984-87; trustee Green Mountain Coll., 1988—. Served to lt. USN, 1958-62. Mem. Pub. Relations Com., USIA, Pub. Relations Soc. Am., Internat. Assn. Bus. Communicators, Inst. Policy Studies (Johns Hopkins U.), Japan-Am. Soc., Meridian House Internat., Nat. Lafayette (Coll.) Council. Clubs: Econ. of Washington, Nat. Press, Fed. City, George Town, Capitol Hill, Nat. Democratic, Nat. Assn. Execs., St. Thomas (V.I.) Yacht, Royal Hamilton (Bermuda) Amateur Dinghy. Democrat. Home: Alexandria, Va. Died Nov. 11, 2006.

HABER, SANDRA K., speech-language pathologist; b. Newark, Aug. 19, 1940; d. Carl and Dora (Busch) Katcher; m. William Haber, May 15, 1960; children: Gary L., Lori L. BA, Newark State Coll., 1973; MA, Kean Coll., 1977. Lic. speech-lang. pathologist; cert. myofunctional therapist; cert. gen. elem. edn. tchr., learning disabilities tchr.-cons., adminstrv. supr., adminstrv. prin. Prin., dir., dialect coach Accent on Comm., Red Bank, N.J.; learning cons. spl. svcs. South Amboy (N.J.) Bd. Edn. Mem. Am. Speech-Lang.-Hearing Assn., N.J. Speech-Lang.-Hearing Assn., Myofunctional Therapy Assn. Am., Orton Dyslexia Soc., N.J. Assn. Learning Cons., N.J. Edn. Assn. Home: Long Branch, NJ. Died Apr. 8, 2007.

HAC, LUCILE ROSE, biochemistry educator; b. Lincoln, Nebr., May 18, 1909; d. Peter F. and Carrie E. (Orinsky) H. BA, U. Nebr., 1930, MSc, 1931; PhD, U. Minn., 1935. Microbiologist Md. State Health Dept., Balt., 1935-36; rsch. assoc. dept. Ob-gyn. U. Chgo., 1936-43; rsch. dir. Internat. Minerals & Chem., Chgo., Calif., Tex. and, Fla., 1943-61; assoc. prof. biochemistry Northwestern U. Med. Sch., Chgo., 1961-77, emeritus prof., from 1977; job counsellor North Shore Sr. Ctr., Northfield, Ill., 1978-98. Patentee in field; contbr. articles to profl. jours. Bd. dirs. LWV, Wilmette, Ill., 1980-84. Recipient Kuppenheimer grant U. Chgo., 1936-45, Claude Pepper Disting. Svc. award, 1990, Clyde Murray Older Worker award Operation Able Chgo., 1991; named to Sr. Citizen Hall of Fame, Chgo., 1985. Mem. Am. Chem. Soc. (dir., bd. dirs. 1940-45), AAUW, Zonta Internat., Phi Beta Kappa, Sigma Xi, Iota Sigma Pi, Sigma Delta Epsilon. Republican. Avocations: music, flowers. Home: Lincoln, Nebr. Died Dec. 27, 2006.

HACKETT, JOSEPH LEO, microbiologist, clinical pathologist; b. Springfield, Ohio, Jan. 11, 1937; s. John Roger and Alice Pearl (Parker) H.; m. Phyllis Ann Boice, Apr. 27, 1963; children: Amy, Ron, Beth, Susan. MS, Ohio State U., 1963, PhD, 1968. Rsch. asst. Ohio State U., Columbus, 1962-67; quality control mgr. Courtland Abbott Labs., Chgo., 1967-69, micro sect. head Reference Lab. North Hollywood, Calif., 1969-72; quality control supr. Pfizer Diagnostics, Maywood, N.J., 1972-74; staff microbiologist FDA, Rockville, Md., 1974-80, br. chief, 1980-91, assoc. div. dir., from 1991. Mem. microbiological area com. Nat. Com. Clin. Lab. Stds., Villanova, Pa., 1991—, susceptibility subcom., 1986-90. Contbr. articles to profl. jours. Mem. Am. Soc. for Microbiology. Home: Walkersville, Md. Died Feb. 2, 2007.

HACKLEY, BRENNIE ELIAS, JR., chemist; b. Roanoke, Va., July 29, 1924; s. Brennie Elias and Rowena Kathleen (Draper) H.; m. Ethel Battle, Dec. 24, 1948; children: Michele Hackley Johnson, Michael B., Brennie E. III. BS in Chemistry, Wilberforce U., 1946; MS in Chemistry, U. Del., 1954, PhD in Chemistry, 1957. Rsch. chemist Johns Hopkins U., Balt., 1950-52; asst. chief, chemotherapy br. Chem. Rsch. and Devel. Lab, Edgewood, Md., 1952-62; rsch. organic chemist Med. Rsch. Lab, Edgewood, 1962-71; sr. rsch. chemist USA Biomed. Lab., APG-EA, Md., 1971-80; scientific advisor USA Med. Rsch. Inst. of Chem. Def., APG-EA, Md., from 1980. Assoc. prof. chemistry U. Md., Balt., 1960-65. Patentee in field; contbr. articles to scientific publs. and books. Scout master Boy Scouts of Am., Joppa, Md., 1966-81; pres. Res. Officers' Assn., Edgewood, Md., 1963-65, Past PTA pres. Edgewood (Md.) High Sch., 1975-78; judge Internat. Sci. Fair, Columbus, Ohio, Albuquerque, 1983-84. Col. U.S. Army, 1950-81. Fellow Am. Inst. Chemists; mem. Am. Chem. Soc., Soc. Neurosci., Am. Soc. Neurochemistry, Sigma Xi. Avocations: golf, reading, travel. Home: Joppa, Md. Died Nov. 5, 2006.

HADEN, HUGH H., physician; b. Summit, Ala., July 31, 1924; s. Hugh H. and Pearle (Murray) H.; m. Ira Carmetta Craddock, Dec. 1, 1949; children: Courtney, Valerie, Conrad, Murray, Stanley, Bruce. BS in Pharmacy, Howard Coll., Birmingham, Ala., 1944; MD, Med. Coll. Ala., 1949. Pvt. practice, Birmingham, from 1955. Med. dir. Birmingham Alcoholism Clinic, 1968-75, Alcoholism Recovery Ctr., Birmingham, 1975—; cons. Eastside Mental Health Ctr., Birmingham, 1975-89. Contbr. numerous articles to med. jours. Mem. Med. Assn. State of Ala., Jefferson County Med. Soc., Mensa. Home: Birmingham, Ala. Died June 3, 2007.

HADIDIAN, CALVIN Y., retired surgeon; b. Beirut, Apr. 26, 1924; s. Yenovk and Helen (Koundakjian) H.; m. Betty Ann Myers, May 15, 1960 (div. 1989); children: Gwynne Ann, Jocelyn Kate. BA, Am. U., Beirut, 1943, MD, 1947. Diplomate Am. Bd. Surgery, Am. Bd. Thoracic Surgery. Asst. thoracic surgery U. Md. Sch. Medicine, Baltimore, 1955-56; thoracic-vascular surgery pvt. practice, Cumberland, Md., 1957-85; clin. asst. prof. U. Pitt., Pa., from 1995.

Contbr. articles to profl. jours. Mem. Soc. Thoracic Surgeons (founding). Independent. Avocations: tennis, singing, theater, writing. Home: East Haven, Conn. Died July 17, 2007.

HADLEY, ARTHUR TWINING, II, writer; b. NYC, June 24, 1924; s. Morris and Katherine (Blodgett) H.; m. Jane Byington Danish, Feb. 24, 1979 (dec.); children: Arthur T. III, Kate Hadley Baker, George M., Nicholas J., Elisabeth J. Wheeler, Caroline Theis. BA magna cum laude, Yale U., 1949. Def. dept. correspondent Newsweek, 1949-53, white house correspondent, 1953-55, persicope editor, 1955-56; asst. exec. editor N.Y. Herald Tribune, 1957-60; writer, journalist NYC and Washington, from 1960. Cons. in field. Author: Joy Wagon, 1958, Do I Make Myself Clear?, 1956, Power's Human Face, 1966, A Life in Order, 1970, The Invisible Primary, 1976, The Empty Polling Booth, 1978, The Straw Giant, 1986, and many more, (plays including) Winterkill, 1960, The Four Minute Mile, 1961; contbr. articles to profl. jours. including N.Y. Times Mag., Washington Post Mag., Washington Star, Newsday, Atlantic Monthly, Playboy. Maj. AUS, 1942. Decorated Purple Heart, Silver Star with one Oak Leaf Cluster; Am. Acad. of Arts and Scis. grantee, 1960. Mem. Century Assn., Phi Beta Kappa. Avocations: sailing, swimming, fly fishing. Home: New York, NY. Died Nov. 25, 2015.

HADLEY, ELEANOR MARTHA, economist, educator; b. Seattle, July 17, 1916; d. Homer More and Margaret Sarah (Floyd) H. BA, Mills Coll., 1938; MA, Radcliffe/Harvard U., 1943; PhD, Harvard U., 1949. Rsch. analyst Office Strategic Svcs., Washington, 1943-44; economist Dept. State, Washington, 1944-46, GHQ-SCAP, Tokyo, 1946-47; staff mem. Pres. Trumans Commn. Migratory Labor, Washington, 1950-51; assoc. prof. Smith Coll., Northampton, Mass., 1956-65; economist U.S. Tariff Commn., Washington, 1967-74; professorial lectr. George Washington U., Washington, 1972-84; group dir. internat. div. Gen. Acctg. Office, Washington, 1974-81; vis. scholar U. Washington, Seattle, 1986-94. Class dean Smith Coll., Northampton, 1958-62; participant Occupation of Japan series Brit. Broadcasting Co., London, 1989; participant Power in the Pacific KCET, L.A. and Australian Broadcasting Co., 1989. Author: Antitrust in Japan, 1970; contbg. author: Political Power of Economic Ideas, 1989; contbr. to Kodansha Ency. of Japan; author articles. Vol., bd. dirs. Seattle Pub. Libr. Found., 1987—, Blakemore Found., 1995-98. Recipient Sacred Treasure award Emperor of Japan, 1986; Fulbright rsch. scholar, Japan, 1962-64. Mem. Assn. for Asian Studies (regional coun. mem., dir. nat. orgn., bd. dirs., 1987-89, named Disting. Lectr. 1985, award for disting. contbns. to Asian studies 1997), U. Wash. Mortar Bd. (hon. mem.). Home: Seattle, Wash. Died June 1, 2007.

HAGAN, ROBERT WILLIAM, banker; b. Houston, Aug. 24, 1948; s. James Joseph and Lucille Elizabeth (Korge) H.; m. Peggy Ann Krailo, Nov. 22, 1972; children: Randy Christopher, Jennifer Earlene. Diploma in Functional Banking, Am. Inst. of Banking, Houston, 1985; BA, Houston Community Coll., 1986. Credit mgr. Gordon's Jewelry Corp., Houston, 1970-78, Fingers Furniture, Houston, 1978-80; owner Hagan & Hagan Adjustors, Houston, 1980-82; recovery mgr. Allied Bank of Tex., Houston, 1981-89; v.p. comml. workout Bank One, Houston, 1989-92; pvt. practice liquidation cons. to comml. bus., from 1992. Instr. Credit Rep. of Houston, 1970-88; speaker in field. Leader Boy Scouts Am., Houston, 1983—. Sgt. USAF, 1966-70, Vietnam. Mem. Vietnam Vets. Assn. (treas. Houston chpt. 1987—). Avocations: scouting, hunting, fishing. Died Aug. 1, 2007.

HAGEN, PAUL BEO, pharmacologist; b. Sydney, Feb. 15, 1920; emigrated to Can., 1959, naturalized, 1965; s. Conrad and Mary (McFadzean) von H.; m. Jean Himms, Sept. 29, 1956; children— Anna, Nina. M.B., BS, U. Sydney, 1945. Intern, resident New South Wales Dept. Health, Sydney, 1945-48; lectr. physiology U. Sydney, 1948-50; sr. lectr. physiology U. Queensland, 1950-52; research fellow Oxford U., 1952-54; asst. prof. pharmacology Yale U., 1954-56, Harvard U., 1956-59; head biochemistry dept. U. Man., 1959-64, Queens U., 1964-67; dir. NRC, Ottawa, Ont., 1967-68; dean grad. studies U. Ottawa, 1968-83, chmn. pharmacology dept., 1983-86. Mem. med. bd. Muscular Dystrophy Assn. Can., 1981-87, chmn., 1976-87, nat. pres., 1980-83; vice chmn. Med. Research Council, 1967; trustee Can. Inst. Particle Physics, 1971-79 Mem. Editorial bd. Biochem. Pharmacology, 1961-66, Jour. Pharmacology and Exptl. Therapeutics, 1960-64, Can. Jour. Biochemistry, 1963-67; contbr. to books and periodicals on physiol., biochem. and pharm. subjects. Chmn. Ont. Bd. Libr. Coordination, 1971-73; trustee Ottawa Gen. Hosp., 1984-94. Recipient Lederle Faculty award Yale U., 1956, Centennial medal Govt. of Can., 1967; Jubilee medal, 1977; C.J. Martin fellow Oxford U., 1952; J.H. Brown fellow Yale U., 1954; Fulbright fellow, 1954 Fellow Chem. Inst. Can. (v.p., pres. biochem. div. 1962-64); mem. Brit. Pharm. Soc., Am. Soc. Pharmacology. Home: Ottawa, Canada. Died Apr. 7, 2007.

HAGENSTEIN, WILLIAM DAVID, forester, consultant; b. Seattle, Mar. 8, 1915; s. Charles William and Janet (Finigan) H.; m. Ruth Helen Johnson, Sept. 2, 1940 (dec. 1979); m. Jean Kraemer Edson, June 16, 1980 (dec. 2000). BS in Forestry, U. Wash., Seattle, 1938; MForestry, Duke U., Durham, NC, 1941. Registered profl. engr., Wash., Oreg. Field aid in entomology U.S. Dept. Agr., Hat Creek, Calif., 1938; logging supt. and engr. Eagle Logging Co., Sedro-Woolley, Wash., 1939; tech. foreman U.S. Forest Svc., North Bend, Wash., 1940; forester West Coast Lumbermen's Assn., Seattle and Portland, Oreg., 1941-43, 45-49; sr. forester FEA, South and Central Pacific Theaters of War and Costa Rica, 1943-45; mgr. Indsl. Forestry Assn., Portland, 1949-80, exec. v.p., 1956-80, hon. dir., 1980-87; pres. W.D. Hagenstein and Assocs., Inc., Portland, 1980—2008. H.R. MacMillan lectr. forestry U. B.C., 1952, 77; Benson Meml. lectr. U. Mo., 1966; S.J. Hall lectr. indsl. forestry U. Calif. at Berkeley, 1973; cons. forest engr. USN, Philippines, 1952, Coop. Housing Found., Belize, 1986; mem. U.S. Forest Products Trade Mission, Japan, 1968; del. VII World Forestry Congress, Argentina, 1972, VIII Congress, Indonesia, 1978; mem. U.S. Forestry Study Team, West Germany, 1974; mem. sec. Interior's Oreg. and Calif. Multiple Use Adv. Bd., 1975-76; trustee Wash. State Forestry Conf., 1948-92, Keep Oreg. Green Assn., 1957—, v.p., 1970-71, pres., 1972-73; adv. trustee Keep Wash. Green Assn., 1957-95; co-founder World Forestry Ctr., dir., 1965-89, v.p., 1965-79, hon. dir. for life, 1990. Author: (with Wackerman and Michell) Harvesting Timber Crops, 1966, Corks & Suspenders, 2010; Assoc. editor: Jour. Forestry, 1946-53; columnist Wood Rev., 1978-82; contbr. numerous articles to profl. jours. Trustee Oreg. Mus. Sci. and Industry, 1968-73. Served with USNR, 1933-37. Recipient Hon. Alumnus award U. Wash. Foresters Alumni Assn., 1965, Dist. Svc. award, 2003, Forest Mgmt. award Nat. Forest Products Assn., 1968, Western Forestry award Western Forestry and Conservation Assn., 1972, 79, Gifford Pinchot medal for 50 yrs. Outstanding Svc., Soc. Am. Foresters, 1987, Charles W. Ralston award Duke Sch. Forestry, 1988, Lifetime Achievement award Oreg. Soc. Am. Foresters, 1995; honored as only surviving co-founder World Forestry Ctr., 2000, Centennial Resource Stewardship award, US Forest Svc., 2005; named Lumberman of Yr. Portland Wholesale Lumber Assn., 2005, Named Founding Father Am. Tree Farm System Am. Forest Found. 2008- Fellow Soc. Am. Foresters (mem. coun. 1958-63, pres. 1966-69, Golden Membership award 1989); mem. Am. Forestry Assn. (life, hon. v.p. 1966-69, 74-92, William B. Greeley Forestry award 1990), Commonwealth Forestry Assn. (life), Internat. Soc. Tropical Foresters, Portland C. of C. (forestry com. 1949-79, chmn. 1960-62), Nat. Forest Products Assn. (forestry adv. com. 1949-80, chmn. 1972-74, 78-80), West Coast Lumbermen's Assn. (v.p. 1969-79), Forest History Soc. (bd. dirs. 2001-04), David Douglas Soc. Western N. Am., Lang Syne Soc., Hoo Hoo Club, Xi Sigma Pi (outstanding alumnus Alpha chpt. 1973). Republican. Home: Portland, Oreg. Died Sept. 4, 2014.

HAGGERTY, MARY ELIZABETH, retired elementary school educator; b. Little Falls, NY, Jan. 15, 1948; d. Edward C. and Margaret (Dise) H. BA, Utica Coll., 1969; MS, Syracuse U., 1971. Cert. elem. tchr., N.Y. Tchr. Little Falls City Schs., Little Falls, 1969—2003, ret., 2003. Active Foothills Girl Scout Coun., Utica, ARC, Herkimer, N.Y.; bd. dirs. Greater Little Falls Community Ch., 1976—, Women's Christian Assn., Little Falls, 1984—. Mem. DAR (registrar 1980—), Little Falls Tchr.'s Assn. (treas. 1976-2003). Roman Catholic. Home: Little Falls, NY. Died Nov. 3, 2006.

HAGLER, MARTIN DAVID R., sales executive; b. Fuerth, Fed. Republic of Germany, Dec. 15, 1932; s. Martin Josef and Anna Wilhelmine (Menzel) H.; m. Marie-Luise Seyde (div. Nov. 1970); children: Dagmar Angelika, Martin Rainer. Student, Commerce and Trade Coll., Erlangen, Fed. Republic of Germany, 1947-49, Hebrew Union Coll., NYC, 1981-86. Trainee Quilling Shoe Co., Munich, 1949-51; asst. mgr. Hagler Shoe Co., Fuerth, 1952-59; pres., owner Hofer Shoe Co., Hagler Shoe Co., Ansbach, Fed. Republic of Germany, 1959-75; export rep. Lander & Co., NYC, 1975-76; v.p. Lorenzo Performance Ltd., NYC, 1976-80; sales mgr. Elsy Clothing Co., NYC, 1981-84; sales rep. Harper Motors Co., Bklyn., from 1984. Designer Hagler Sport Co., N.Y.C., 1982—. Author: The Greatest Lies Ever, 1981; contbr. articles to profl. jours. Pres. Orgn. for Release and Return of Temple Treasures, N.Y.C., 1982—, Orgn. Discovery Ancient Treasures, D.Z.R.K.D., N.Y.C., 1987; mem. Village Temple, 1979-82, Hopatcong Jewish Ctr. and Mt. Freedom Synagogue, 1988—. Avocations: swimming, car racing, skiing, history. Died Feb. 19, 2007.

HAHN, HENRY, metallurgical engineer, consultant; b. Brno, Czech Republic, Feb. 5, 1928; came to U.S., 1941; s. Oskar and Helene (Gottlieb) H.; m. Edythe Marilyn Shotz; children: Anita Caryl, Jeffrey Stuart. BS in Metallurgy, MIT, 1951; MMetE, Rensselaer Poly. Inst., 1953; Profl. Engring. Degree (PE), Columbia U., NYC, 1956. Registered profl. engr., Calif. From engr. to chief project engr. Curtiss-Wright Corp., Wood Ridge, N.J., 1956-63; mgr. materials lab. Melpar, Falls Church, Va., 1964-70; pres., chmn. bd. dirs. Artech Corp., Chantilly, Va., 1970-94; pres., legal cons. Henry Hahn Assocs., Fairfax, Va., from 1994. Contbr. over 30 articles to profl. publs. Chmn. North Pine Ridge Civic Assn., Fairfax, 1990—. Recipient Engring. and Sci. award Am. Soc. for Testing Materials, Phila., 1989; Crusade for Freedom scholar MIT, 1950. Fellow Am. Soc. Metals (chmn. Washington chpt. 1983-94); mem. Am. Welding Soc. (mem. tech. adv. com. 1992—), Internat. Stds. Orgn. (chmn. testing of welds 1996—). Achievements include 2 patents for porous coated surgical implants; 4 patents for composite materials. Died June 7, 2007.

HAIGH, ROBERT WILLIAM, business professor; b. Phila., Aug. 22, 1926; s. Harry E. and Mildred (Elliott) H.; m. Jane Stanton Sheble, June 19, 1948; children: Cynthia Jane, Anne Sheble, Robert William, Barbara Lynne. Student, Muhlenberg Coll., 1944-45; AB cum laude, Bucknell U., 1948; MBA with high distinction, Harvard U., 1950, DCS, 1953. Research and teaching faculty Harvard U. Grad Sch. Bus. Adminstrn., 1950-56, asst. prof., 1953-56; asst. to pres. Helmerich & Payne, Inc., Tulsa, 1956, controller and asst. to pres., 1956-57, fin. v.p., dir., 1957-61, White Eagle Internat. Oil Co., 1957-60; v.p. corp. planning and devel. Standard Oil Co. (Ohio), Cleve., 1963-66; pres. Sohio Chems. & Vistron Corp. Subs., 1966-67, Sohio Chemicals and Vistron Corp. Subs., 1966-67; group v.p., pres. edn. group, dir. Xerox Corp., Stamford, Conn., 1967-72; exec. v.p. Swedlow Corp., 1973-74, pres., chief exec. officer, dir., 1974; pres. Hillsboro Assocs., 1974-75; sr. v.p. Freeport Minerals Co., 1975-76; chmn. bd., chief exec. officer Photo Quest, Inc., Cognitrex, Inc., 1977-78; dir. Wharton Applied Rsch. Ctr., lectr. U. Pa., Phila., 1978-79; Disting. prof. bus. adminstrn., dean Darden Grad. Sch. Bus. U. Va. Tayloe Murphy Internat. Bus. Studies Ctr., 1979-95; prof. emeritus U. Va., from 1995. Author: (with John G. McLean) The Growth of Integrated Oil Companies, 1954, Leading Virginia Industries series: Textiles and Apparel, A Business Update, 1986, Wood and Paper Products, 1987, Investment Strategies and the Plant-Location Decision: Foreign Companies in the U.S., 1989, Global Markets for Pollution-Control Equipment: An Export Opportunity for Virginia Business, 1991, Medical Products Companies in Virginia: Export Status Report. Served with USNR, 1944-45. Mem. Phi Beta Kappa, Phi Lambda Theta. Home: Charlottesvle, Va. Died Dec. 26, 2006.

HAINES, JOE (JOSEPH E. HAINES), retired state legislator; b. Greene County, Ohio, Sept. 30, 1923; m. Joy Haines; children: Thomas, Thaddeus, Jonathan, Barbara. BS, Ohio State U., 1949. Commr. Greene County, 1968-76; mem. Dist. 75 Ohio House of Reps., 1981-92, mem. Dist. 74, 1993-99; dep. dir. Ohio Dept. Agrl., 1999—2003. Mem. Nat. Assn. County Commrs. (chmn.), SW Dist. County Commr. Assn. (chmn.), Ohio Shorthorn Breeders (past pres.), Farm Bur., Kiwanis (past pres.), YMCA (bd. dirs.). Republican. Home: Xenia, Ohio. Died Jan. 5, 2015.

HALL, ANITA G., nursing administrator and educator; b. Seattle, June 3, 1931; d. Ernest J.A. and Effie (Walker) Griffin; m. Lester Leroy Hall, June 4, 1956; children: Lesli Genstler, Mark N. BSN, Walla Walla Coll., 1953; MPH, Loma Linda U., Calif., 1979. Supr. Walla Walla (Wash.) Gen. Hosp.; nursing educator Walla Walla Community Coll. Mem. ASDAN. Home: Milton Freewater, Oreg. Died Jan. 11, 2007.

HALL, BEVERLY L., former school system administrator; b. Montego Bay, Jamaica; m. Luis Hall, Dec. 22, 1973; 1 child, Jason. BA in English, Bklyn. Coll., 1970, MA in Guidance & Counseling, 1973; PhD in Adminstrn., Fordham U., 1990. English tchr. Jr. H.S. 265, Bklyn., 1970—76; asst. prin. Satellite West Jr. H.S., Bklyn., 1977—83; prin. Pub. Sch. 282, Bklyn., 1983—87, Jr. H.S. 113, Bklyn., 1987—92; supt. Cmty. Sch. Dist. 27, Queens, NY, 1992—94; dep. chancellor for instrn. NYC Pub. Schools, 1994—95; supt. Newark City Schools, 1995—99, Atlanta Pub. Schools, 1999—2011. Died Mar. 2, 2015.

HALL, DON COURTNEY, construction company executive; b. Youngstown, Ohio, Apr. 13, 1937; s. Carl George and Geraldine Francis (Wilson) H.; m. Barbara Nell Brakeman, Sept. 22, 1962; children: Cathleen, Carl Douglas, Todd Courtney. BSCE, Ohio U., 1959. Registered profl. engr., Ohio, Pa., W.Va., Md., Ala., Tenn., Ky., Mass., Va., Ill.; registered surveyor W.Va. Engr. Copperweld Steel Co., Warren, Ohio, 1959-61; asst. chief engring. R.J. Schomer Co., Poland, Ohio, 1961-68; chief engr., v.p. Joseph Bucheit & Sons, Bucheit Internat., Youngstown, 1968-92; pres. Donco Constrn. Co., Canfield, Ohio, from 1985. V.p. Buttermilk Acres Stoneware, Inc., Canfield, Ohio, 1988—; registered fallout shelter analyst U.S. Govt., Ohio, 1962—. Bd. dirs. Boys Club of Youngstown, 1979—; dir. Boy Scouts Am., Mahoning County, 1980—; mem. County Cen. Rep. Com., Canfield Twp., Ohio, 1985—; mem. Mahoning County Bldg. Inspection Appeals Bd., 1978-96, Canfield Twp. Zoning Bd., 1973—; mem. bd. appeals Canfield Fire Dept., 1994—. Recipient Silver Beaver award Boy Scouts Am., 1992. Mem. Christian Ch. Club: Four Square (Youngstown) (past pres.). Lodge: Rotary (past pres. Boardman club, Paul Harris fellow 1979). Home: Canfield, Ohio. Died Mar. 11, 2007.

HALL, HARVEY DALE, dentist, rancher; b. Citra, Okla., July 26, 1925; s. George Dewey and Nettie Mae (Nickell) H.; m. Peggy Jo Duniver, June 14, 1946; children: Deborah Ann, Bruce Alan. BS, East Cen. U., 1949; DDS, Washington U., St. Louis, 1954. Pvt. practice, Ada, Okla., from 1954; rancher Arrowhead Ranch, Ada, from 1968. Preceptor sch. dentistry U. Okla., Oklahoma City, 1972—; tchr. implant tech., Ada. Author: (with others) Clinical Dentistry Volume 5; contbr. articles to profl. jours. Elder First Presbyn. Ch., Ada; mem. com. Pontotoc County Agri-Plex Supporters; past mem. adv. bd. Salvation Army. With USN, PTO. Mem. ADA, Am. Acad. Implant Dentistry (credentialized), Ark. Acad. Oral Implantology (cons.), Okla. Cen. Dist. Dental Soc., Okla. Dental Assn. (Seids Cup award, 35 Yr. Jade cert. 1991), Ada C. of C., Elks. Home: Ada, Okla. Died Mar. 3, 2007.

HALL, JAMES GRANVILLE, JR., history professor; b. Phila., Aug. 22, 1917; s. James Granville and Jane Margaret (Moorehead) H.; m. Eva Mae Woodruff, June 1946; 1 child, Evelyn Alison. AB, George Washington U., 1950; cert., Georgetown U., 1951; postgrad., U. Colo., Colorado Springs, 1965-67; MA, Va. State U., 1972. Commd. 2nd lt. U.S. Army, 1943; transferred to USAF, 1948, advanced through ranks to lt. col., 1961; aircraft controller U.S. Army, Panama, U.S., 1943-50; various assignments, 1950-64; comdr. dir. staff officer, weapons staff officer NORAD, 1964-67; comdr. MDC, King Salmon, 1968, Air Def. Sector, King Salmon, Alaska, 1967-68; dir. ops. 5th Tactical Control group, comdr. 605th Tactical Control Squadron, Clark Air Base, The Philippines, 1969-71; chief control & environ. 20th Air Div., Ft. Lee, Va., 1971-72; retired USAF, 1972; faculty history and govt. Austin (Tex.) C.C., Austin, 1973-93. Participant Mid. East Seminar, Fgn. Svc. Inst., U.S. Dept. State, Washington, 1953; lectr. civic and garden clubs, Tex., 1974—; organizer Okla. Chrysanthemum Soc.,

2005. Author: Men's Garden Club Show and Judges Handbook, 1980; contbr. articles to profl. jours. Polit. worker, Austin, 1974—2000; bd. dirs. Colorado Springs Opera Assn., 1967; organizer, leader Girl Scouts Am., Opheim, 1959—60; pres. Little League, Itazuke, Japan, 1961—63; mem. Austin Lyric Opera, 1987—90; guest expert TV and radio garden shows Austin, from 1976. Decorated Meritorious Svc. medal, Joint Svcs. Commendation medal, Air Force Commendation medal, Am. Campaign medal, World War II Victory medal, Nat. Def. Svc. medal with 1 Bronze Star, Vietnam Svc. medal with 1 Bronze Star, Armed Forces Expeditionary medal, Combat Readiness medal with 1 Bronze Oak Leaf Cluster, Air Force Reserve medal, Air Force Outstanding Unit Citation, Master Weapons Dir. Badge; recipient Philippine Presidential Unit Citation for Humanitarian Svc., 1970-71. Mem.: Heritage Found., Capitol Area Chrysanthemum Soc. (pres. 1975, 2000—03), S.W. Chrysanthemum Region Soc. (organizer, pres. 1981—82), Nat. Chrysanthemum Soc. (accredited judge 1976—85, awards chmn. 1986—91, master judge from 1986), VFW (life), Men's Garden Club of Am. (accredited judge from 1976, nat. schs. and judges chmn. 1979—81, judge emeritus from 2000), Men's Garden Club (pres. 1977, bd. dirs. from 2006). Republican. Anglican. Avocations: gardening, bridge, computers. Died Nov. 16, 2006.

HALL, MAUD CHRISTINE, educational administrator; b. Stockholm, Aug. 3, 1942; came to U.S., 1949; d. Holger and Kristina (Bjorndahl) Larson; m. George Daniel Hall, June 27, 1964 (dec. June 1987). BA, Augustana Coll., Rock Island, Ill., 1964; MA, NYU, 1968; PhD, Northwestern U., 1976. Cert. tchr., adminstr., Ill. Tchr. Spanish, Downers Grove (Ill.) North High Sch., 1964-65; tchr. Spanish and French, Ridgewood High Sch., Norridge, 1966-73; teaching asst. Northwestern U., Evanston, 1973-76, asst. to provost, 1976-77; curriculum dir. Sacred Heart Schs., Chgo., 1977-79, Sch. Dist. 96, Buffalo Grove, Ill., 1979-81; asst. dir. gen. edn. Sch. Dist. 200, Wheaton, Ill., 1981-83, dir. gen. edn., 1983-84, asst. supt., 1984-91; supt. Salt Creek Dist. 48, Villa Park, Ill., from 1991. Adj. instr. Nat. Coll. Edn., Evanston, Chgo., Lombard, Ill., 1981— Mem. Assn. for Supervision and Curriculum Instrn. (presenter ann. conf. 1986), Am. Ednl. Rsch. Assn., Am. Assn. Sch. Adminstrs., Ill. Assn. for Supervision and Curriculum Devel. (coord., chmn. for planning ann. conf. 1988), West Suburban Assn. for Supervision and Curriculum Devel. (pres.), Du Page County Curriculum Devel. Assn. (v.p. 1987-89, pres. 1989-91), Phi Delta Kappa (pres. elect 1989-90). Lutheran. Home: Chicago, Ill. Died Dec. 18, 2006.

HALL, NANCY ANNE WIRTANEN, academic lab coordinator; b. Palmer, Ark., June 15, 1943; d. Eino Wallace and Fannie Sofia (Leppanen) W.; m. Samuel Leon Hall, Sept. 23, 1968 (div. 1975). BS, U. Alaska, 1966; MS, U. Guam, 1984; PhD, U. Oreg., 1987. Cert. tchr., Alaska. Math. tchr. Taylor Jr. High Sch., Eielson AFB, Alaska, 1966-69, Amoan High Sch., Pago Pago, American Samoa, 1970-76, Untulan Middle Sch., Barrigada, Guam, 1976-81; resource tchr. Lang. Arts and Math. Program, Agana, Guam, 1981-86; prof. Guam Community Coll., Mangilao, Guam, 1986-93, acad. lab. coord., from 1991. Exec. coun. Guam Fedn. of Tchrs., Mangilao, 1989-93; chairperson Guam Community Coll. Accrediatation Com., 1988-89; curriculum writer Vocat. High Sch., Mangilao, 1990-91; presenter in field. Adv. mem. Guam Community Coll. Bd. of Trustees, 1989—; mem. Joint Bds. of Edn., Agana, Guam, 1991. Recipient Profl. Devel. Svc. award Guam Fedn. Tchrs., 1990, 91, 92. Mem. AAUW (editor 1988-91, treasurer 1985-87), Guam Coun. Internat. Reading Assn., Guam Libr. Assn., Phi Delta Kappa (editor 1988-93). Lutheran. Avocations: travel, reading, desktop publishing, adult edn. Home: Latte Heights, Guam. Died May 9, 2007.

HALL, VICTORIA ELLEN (VICKI HALL), human resource manager; b. Balt., Aug. 30, 1944; d. Robert G. and Della Vern (Chesshir) H.; m. Duane E. Sweatland, Feb. 2, 1963 (div. 1965); 1 child, Michael Gray. Student, Delta Coll., 1968, U. of Ark., Little Rock, 1979, U. Cen. Ark., 1980. Sec. U.S. Dept. Navy, Washington, 1965-68; bookkeeper Aero-Craft Boats, St. Charles, Mich., 1968-71; sec. Franklin Electric Co., Jacksonville, Ark., 1971-74, supr. employee relations, 1974-85; mgr. employee and community relations Brinkley (Ark.) Motor Products, 1985-89; human resources mgr. AMW Industries, Conway, Ark., 1989-90; human resource mgr. Ark. Aerospace, Inc., Little Rock, from 1990. Owner retail bus. Cabot Country, 1987. Recipient Recruiter award ARC, 1979. Mem. Ark. Personnel Assn., NAFE, Am. Entrepreneur Assn., Am. Soc. Personnel Adminstrs., Am. Soc. Safety Engrs., Beta Sigma Phi. Baptist. Avocations: freelance writing, reading. Home: Cabot, Ark. Died June 11, 2007.

HALLAC, CHARLES S., investment company executive; b. 1964; m. Sarah Hallac; children: David, Rebecca, A.J. BS in Economics & Computer Sci., Brandeis U., 1986. Various positions BlackRock Inc., 1988—2006, vice chmn., head BlackRock Solutions, 2006—09, COO, 2009—14, co-pres., 2014—15. Died Sept. 9, 2015.

HALLENBORG, BRUCE P., psychiatrist; b. NYC, Apr. 28, 1946; s. John and Henrietta (De La Guard) H. MD, U. Pitts., 1973. Diplomate Am. Bd. Psychiatry and Neurology. Pvt. practice psychiatry Brown & Hallenborg, Atlanta, 1977-95, pres., from 1992. Mem. Alpha Omega Alpha. Avocations: skiing, travel. Died Mar. 11, 2007.

HALLO, WILLIAM WOLFGANG, literature and language professor, writer; b. Kassel, Germany, Mar. 9, 1928; came to U.S., 1940, naturalized, 1946; s. Rudolf and Gertrude (Rubensohn) H.; m. Edith Sylvia Pinto, June 22, 1952 (dec. Oct. 10, 1994); children: Ralph Ethan, Jacqueline Louise; m. Nanette Stahl, Oct. 18, 1998. BA magna cum laude, Harvard U., 1950; candidatus Litterarum Semiticarum, U. Leiden, Netherlands, 1951; MA, U. Chgo., 1953, PhD, 1955; MA (hon.), Yale U., 1965; DHL (hon.), Hebrew Union Coll.-Jewish Inst. Religion, 1986. Rsch. asst. U. Chgo. Oriental Inst., 1954—56; from instr. to asst. prof. Bible and Semitic langs. Hebrew Union Coll.-Jewish Inst. Religion, Cin., 1956-62; asst. prof. Assyriology Yale U., 1962—65, prof. Assyriology, 1965-75, William M. Laffan prof. Assyriology and Babylonian lit., 1976—2002, prof. emeritus, from 2002; curator Babylonian collection, 1963-2001; master Morse Coll., 1982-87; chmn. dept. Near Eastern langs. and civilizations, 1975-82, 85-89. Chmn. Univ. (now adv.) com. on Judaic Studies, 1979-84, acting chmn., 1998; vis. prof. Mid. Eastern civilization Columbia U., 1970-71, 80, Jewish Theol. Sem., 1981, 82-83, 2002; Franz Rosenzweig guest prof. U. Kassel, Germany, 1991. Author: Early Mesopotamian Royal Titles, 1957, Sumerian Archival Texts, 1973, The Book of the People, 1991, Origins: The Ancient Near Eastern Background of Some Modern Western Institutions, 1996, The World's Oldest Literature Studies in Sumerian Better Letters, 2009; (with J.J.A. van Dijk) The Exaltation of Inanna, 1968; (with W.K. Simpson) The Ancient Near East: A History, 1971, 2d edit., 1998; (with Briggs Buchanan) Early Near Eastern Seals in the Yale Babylonian Collection, 1981; co-author: The Torah: A Modern Commentary, 1981, 2d edit., 2005, Heritage: Civilization and the Jews, 2 vols., 1984, The Tablets of Ebla, 1984; editor: Essays in Memory of E.A. Speiser, 1968; (with Carl D. Evans and John B. White) Scripture in Context: Essays on the Comparative Method, 1980; (with James C. Moyer and Leo G. Perdue) Scripture in Context II: More Essays on the Comparative Method, 1983; (with Bruce W. Jones and Gerald L. Mattingly) The Bible in Light of Cuneiform Literature: Scripture in Context III, 1990; (with K. Lawson Younger Jr. and Bernard F. Batto) The Biblical Canon in Comparative Perspective: Scripture in Context IV, 1991; (with K. Lawson Younger Jr.) The Context of Scripture, vol. I: Canonical Compositions from the Biblical World, 1997, Vol. II Monumental Inscriptions from the Biblical World, 2000, Vol. III Archival Documents from the Biblical World, 2002; (with Irene J. Winter) Seals and Seal Impressions, 2001; translator: The Star of Redemption, 1971; contbr. articles and book revs. to profl. jours.; mem. editl. bd. Yale Near Eastern Researches, 1967—2002; editor, 1970-2002; mem. editl. bd. Moment Mag., Bible Rev., Archaeology Odyssey, 1980-2003, Bibl. Archaeology Rev., 2004—. Mem. commn. Jewish edn. Union Am. Hebrew Congregations, 1967-71; co-founder, dir., mem. exec. com. Assn. Jewish Studies, 1970-71, v.p., 1972-74. Fulbright scholar, 1950-51; fellow Guggenheim, 1965-66, Inst. Advanced Studies, Hebrew U., Jerusalem, 1978-79, Nat. Humanities Inst., 1987-88, Shelby Cullom Davis Ctr. for Hist. Studies, Princeton U., 1996-97; honored by an anniversary volume: The Tablet and the Scroll: Near Eastern Studies in Honor of William W. Hallo, 1993. Mem. Am. Oriental Soc. (assoc. editor, 1965-71, chmn. Ancient Near East sect. 1971-78, v.p. 1987-88, pres. 1988-89), World Union Jewish Studies, Fulbright Assn. (v.p. Conn. chpt. 2002-), Harvard Club (So. Conn.), Yale Club (N.Y.C.), Phi Beta Kappa. Home: Hamden, Conn. Died Mar. 30, 2015.

HALLOCK, JOSEPH THEODORE (TED HALLOCK), electric conservation-planning council official; b. LA, Oct. 26, 1921; s. Joseph Homer and Mary Elizabeth (Peninger) H.; m. Phyllis Natwick, Jan. 1946 (div. Mar. 1968); children: Stephanie, Christopher, Leslie; m. Jacklyn Louise Goldsmith, Sept. 12, 1969. BS in Journalism, U. Oreg., 1948. Assoc. editor Down Beat mag., Chgo., 1947-48; program dir. Sta. KPOJ, Portland, Oreg., 1948-53; dir. pub. affairs J. Henry Helser & Co., Portland, 1953-58; state coord. Oreg. Centennial Commn., Portland, 1958-59; pres. Ted Hallock Inc., Portland, 1959-63, The Hallock Agy. Inc., Portland, 1981-88, corp. sec., from 1988; mem. Oreg. Senate, Salem, 1963-83; Oreg. mem. Pacific N.W. Power Coun., Portland, 1988-94. Trustee Portland Art Mus., 1987-88. Capt. USAAF, 1943-45, ETO. Decorated DFC, Air medal with three oak leaf clusters, Purple Heart with oak leaf cluster. Mem. AFTRA, Soc. Profl. Journalists. Democrat. Presbyterian. Died Dec. 16, 2006.

HALPERN, DONALD F., consulting scientist; b. NYC, May 9, 1936; s. Max C. Halpern; m. Karin Bjorck, Apr. 14, 1965 (div.); 1 child, Peter. BA, Queens Coll., 1959, MA, 1964; PhD, CUNY, 1971. Consulting sci. Anaquest divsn. BOC, Murray Hill, N.Y., 1975-93; ind. cons. organofluorine and pharm. chemistry Providence, N.J., from 1993. Author chpts. to books; holder 11 patents. Mem. Am. Chem. Soc., Assn. Consulting Chemists and Chem. Engrs., Scandiavian Collectors Club (pres. 1977-78). Avocation: scandiavian postal history. Home: Broomfield, Colo. Died Apr. 19, 2007.

HALPIN, PETER, information systems specialist, programmer; b. Orange, NJ, Jan. 28, 1938; s. Thomas A. and Ethel Rita (Matthews) H.; m. Joan Elizabeth Wu, Nov. 21, 1964; children: Eric Glenn, Gary Kevin. BSME, N.J. Inst. Tech., 1959. Engr. State of N.Y., Babylon, 1959-60, U.S. Army Engring. Rsch. and Devel. Lab., Ft. Belvoir, Va., 1961-62; vol. Peace Corps, Arecibo, P.R., Brattleboro, Vt., 1963; sci. bibliographer Libr. of Congress, Washington, 1964; phys. scientist U.S. Def. Tech. Info. Ctr., Alexandria, Va., 1965-66; tech. info. specialist U.S. EPA, Washington, 1966-69, Rsch. Triangle Park, N.C., 1969-78, U.S. Dept. Health and Human Svcs., Washington, 1978-84, program analyst, 1984-92, mgmt. analyst, 1992-93, computer specialist, from 1993; freelance programmer Washington, from 1990. Author: (with others) Air Pollution, 3d edit., 1977, (thesaurus) Standard Air Pollution Classification Network, 1978; contbr. articles to profl. jours. Vol. Homeless Children's Tutorial Project, Washington, 1990-92. With U.S. Army, 1960-62. Mem. Am. Soc. for Info. Sci. (chmn. Carolinas chpt. 1973-74), Mensa. Avocations: jazz music, photography. Home: Leesburg, Va. Died Jan. 27, 2007.

HALSEY, ALBERT HENRY (CHELLY HALSEY), retired sociologist; b. London, Apr. 13, 1923; s. William Thomas and Ada (Draper) H.; m. Gertrude Margaret Littler, Apr. 10, 1949 (dec. 2004); children: Ruth, Robert, Lisa, David, Mark. BSc, London Sch. Econs., U. London, 1950; PhD, U. London, 1954; MA, U. Oxford, Eng., 1962; D in Social Scis. (hon.), U. Birmingham, Eng., 1987; DLitt, Open U., Warwick, Leicester, Glamorgan, 1996, U. Northampton, 2006. Research assoc. U. Liverpool, Eng., 1952-54; lectr. U. Birmingham, 1954-62; prof. social & adminstrv. studies U. Oxford, 1962—90, prof. emeritus, 1990—2014; adv. to Edn. Sec. Anthony Crosland Govt. of United Kingdom, 1965—68. Editor: Traditions of Social Policy, 1976; co-author (with Jerome Karabel): Power and Ideology in Education, 1977; co-author: (with AF Heath & JM Ridge) Origins and Destinations: Family, Class and Education in Modern Britain, 1980; co-author: (with Norman Dennis) English Ethical Socialism: Thomas More to RH Tawney, 1988; co-author: (Josephine Webb) 20th Century British Social Trends, 2000; author: Decline of Donnish Dominion: The British Academic Professions in the Twentieth Century, 1992, No Discouragement, 1996, Changing Childhood, 2009. Fellow Brit. Acad.; mem. American Acad. Arts & Sciences Mem. Labour Party. Anglican. Avocation: gardening. Home: Oxford, England. Died Oct. 14, 2014.

HALSTED, ISABELLA, writer; b. Manchester-by-the-Sea, Mass., May 8, 1907; d. Charles Sydney and Elinor (Curtis) Hopkinson; married, Nov. 25, 1930; divorced, 1950; 4 children. Tchr. King-Coit Sch., NYC, 1929-30, Dedham (Mass.) Country Day Sch., 1942-48; exec. dir. Boston Ctr. for Internat. Visitors, 1961-68, bd. dirs., 1961-95. Author: The Aunts, 1992. Founder, Riverbend Park, Cambridge, Mass., 1975. Died Dec. 13, 2006.

HAMBLEY, DELBERT EUGENE, real estate developer; b. Allegan County, Mich., July 28, 1933; s. George Verne Sr. and Ruth Irene (Sharp) H.; m. Shirley Ann Garn, Dec. 20, 1952; children: Colleen Sue, Michael Eugene, Sharon Ann. BA, Greenville Coll., 1953; MEd, Western Mich. U., 1960. Tchr. Sheridan (Mich.) H.S., 1953-57, Plainwell (Mich.) Jr. H.S., 1957-59; prin. East Cooper Elem. Sch., Kalamazoo, 1959-61; tchr. Portage (Mich.) Pub. Schs., 1961-88; builder, apartment mgr. Kalamazoo, 1958-81; developer Hambley-Beyer Devel., Kalamazoo, 1993-2000. Plat com. mem., 1994—; chmn. land use plan com., Tex. Township, Kalamazoo, 1996-99. Republican. Mem. Free Methodist Ch. Avocations: collecting presidential biographies, reading, writing, music. Died Feb. 24, 2007.

HAMDANI, ZUBEDA A., elementary school educator; b. Bombay, Oct. 23, 1930; arrived in U.S., 1969, naturalized; d. Fazlehusen K. Lakdawala and Amtabai Bokha; m. Abbas H. Hamdani, June 4, 1961; children: Sumaiya, Amal(dec.). BA, U. Bombay, 1954; cert. modern math., Hamilton Coll., Clinton, NY, 1967; BS Elem. Edn., U. Wis. Milw., 1974, MS Elem. Edn., 1983. Cert. tchr. K-6, ESL Wis. Dept. Edn. Tchr. St. Josephs Convent Sch., Nagpur, India, 1954—56, Rajkumar Coll., Rajkot, India, 1956—61, Port Said Sch., Cairo, 1962—67, Cairo Am. Coll., 1967—69; substitute tchr. Milw. Pub. Schs., 1974—76, tchr., 1976—94; ret., 2001. Trainer new tchrs. Milw. Pub. Schs., 1976—94; vol. tchr. Adult Learning Ctr., Milw., 1974—76, Milw., 2001—06. Mem.: AAUW (corr. sec. Milw. br. 2001—09, Lake Sumter Branch mem. from 2010), Whitefish Bay Women's Club (scholarship com. Milw. br. 2001—09), Eustis Fla. Womens Club. Avocations: swimming, camping. Home: Mount Dora, Fla. Deceased.

HAMILTON, MAX CHESTER, farmer, writer; b. Mo., Dec. 29, 1918; s. Grady C. and Pearl (Layson) H.; m. Anna M. Pew, May 18, 1937; children: Larry, Ronald, Roger. Spl. courses, Mo. U.; JD, Blackstone Sch. Law, 1964. Lic. real estate broker and appraiser-councilor; cert. profl. real estate litigation mgr.; realty specialist. Electrification advisor Rural Electric Administrn., 1947-58; developer of working fish and wildlife rsch. farm, from 1950; dist. right of way agt. Inter State Hwy. Systems, 1958-64; real estate aquisitions U.S. Army C.E., 1970-83; real estate officer U.S. Postal Svc., 1983-86; freelance writer, outdoor writer, photographer, editor various mags., from 1948-. Real estate developer. Outdoor editor Constitution Tribune Daily Paper, Chillicothe, Mo., outdoor radio program, Sta. KEHI, Chillicothe; contbr. articles to profl. jours. and mags. on outdoor and environment. Dir. Rsch. Found., 1980--; pres. Nat. Wild Turkey Fedn., 1970-74. With USN, 1944-45, WWII. Recipient Pres.'s award Nat. Wild Turkey Fedn., 1978-79, Roger M. Lathom Sportsmen's Svc. award, 1983, C.B. McCloud Disting. Svc. award, 1990, Wild Turkey Conservation award Mo. Wild Turkey Fedn., 1993; named Conservationist of Yr., N.E. Mo. Wild Turkey Fedn., 1989, Conservationist of Yr., Wildlife Soc., 1991, Wildlife Conservationist, Conservation Fedn., 1992. Mem. Outdoor Writers Am., Ducks Unltd., Mo. Outdoor Writers Assn. (pres. 1951-53), Ruffed Grouse Soc. U.S., Pheasants Forever, Quail Unltd., Mo. Farm Bur., Nat. Tree Farmers Am., Catfish Farmers Am. (charter), Mo. Fish Farmers (charter). Avocations: outdoor recreation, hunting, fishing, bird watching, nature hikes. Home: Chillicothe, Mo. Died Nov. 12, 2006.

HAMILTON, THOMAS PERCY, preventive medicine physician, military officer; b. Buffalo, July 11, 1932; s. James Alexander and Charlot Clara (Krathwohl) H.; m. Elsie Marie Myers, Apr. 2, 1971; children: Stephen, Patricia, Beverly, Susan. BS, Case-Western Res. U., 1954; MD, SUNY, Buffalo, 1957; MPH, U. Mich., 1969. Diplomate Am. Bd. Preventive Medicine, Pub. Health Adminstrn.; lic.

MD, Calif., Ga., Mich., Nev., N.J., Pa. Internship U.S. Naval Hosp., Charleston, S.C., 1958; sr. med, officer, squadron flight surgeon U.S. Navy, various locations, S.C., N.J., 1958-61; regional flight surgeon FAA, Atlanta, 1961-62; family practitioner Levittown (Pa.) Med. Ctr., 1962-63; staff physician, asst. med. dir. Rutgers U., New Brunswick, N.J., 1963-64, 64-66; dir. health dept., cons. in local health adminstrn. various health depts., Adrian, Detroit, Lansing, Mich., 1966-71; dir. health and human svcs., health officer various counties, Santa Ana, Pasadena, L.A., Calif., 1971-84; dep. comdr. U.S. Army Aeromed., med. staff officer Health Svcs. Command, Ft. Rucker/Sam Houston, Ala., Tex., 1984-86, 88-89; chief preventive medicine svc., dep. comdr., comdr. Brooke Army Med. Ctr., Fort Sam Houston, 1989-90, 90-92; prof. and chief preventive medicine, ret. Army Med. Dept. Ctr. and Sch., Fort Sam Houston, 1992-93 and from 93. Assoc. clin. prof. community and environ-.medicine U. Calif., Irvine, 1972—; asst. clin. prof. dept. preventive medicine U. So. Calif., 1977—; asst. clin. prof. dept. family medicine Loma Linda U., 1983—; residency dir. preventive medicine L.A. and Riverside County Health Depts., 1979-84; acad. chair continuing med. edn. Health Officers Assn. of Calif., 1977-84. Contbr. numerous articles to profl. jours. Fellow Am. Coll. Preventive Medicine, Am. Pub. Health Assn.; mem. Am. Coll. Physician Execs., Assn. U.S. Army, Assn. Army Flight Surgeons, Calif. Med. Assn., Res. Officers Assn., Riverside County Med. Assn., The Ret. Officers Assn. Avocations: music, computing. Home: Las Vegas, Nev. Died May 3, 2007.

HAMILTON, WILLIAM JOSEPH, retired music educator; b. Massillon, Ohio, Oct. 15, 1930; s. Melvin Ray and Ann Elizabeth (Kutz) H.; m. Sally Ellen Bassett, June 20, 1954 (div. 1985); m. Nancy Rae Wolgamott, Jan. 4, 1986; children: Christine Ann, William Donald. MusB, Heidelberg Coll., 1952; M Music Edn., Kent State U., 1961. Cert. music tchr., Ohio. Dir. choral music Plain Local Schs., Canton, Ohio, 1956-69, dir. speech and drama, 1957-65; prof. music Kent State U., Canton, 1969-91, prof. emeritus, from 1991. Condr. Canton Civic Opera Co., 1969-90, various sch., coll., ch. and community choral orgns.; musical and stage dir. local musical theatrical prodns.; organizer, condr. The Greater Canton Men's Chorus, 1992. With USN, 1952-56. Mem. Am. Choral Conductors Assn. (state pres. 1972-74), Music Educators Nat. Conf., Masons. Avocations: travel, reading. Home: Massillon, Ohio. Died Jan. 15, 2007.

HAMMACK, GLADYS LORENE MANN, reading specialist, educator; b. Corsicana, Tex., Nov. 15, 1923; d. John Elisha and Maude (Kelly) Mann; m. Charles Joseph Hammack; Sept. 4, 1949;children: Charles Randall, Cynthia Lorain, Kelly Joseph. B in Journalism, U. Tex., 1953; elem. tchr. cert., U. Houston, 1970, MEd, 1974, cert. reading specialist, 1974. Cert. profl. reading specialist, Tex. Tchr. Zion Luth. Sch., Pasadena, Tex., 1964-68, Housman Elem. Sch., Houston, 1970-74, Pine Shadows Elem. Sch., Houston, 1975-76; reading lab. tchr. Spring Br. High Sch., Houston, 1976-82; tchr. St. Mark Luth. Sch., Houston, 1982-88, pvt. tutor and homework study hall tchr., from 1988. Mem. Spring Br. Ind. Sch. Dist. Textbook Selection Com., Houston, 1973; field rep. to. student tchrs., U. Houston, 1974; presenter reading workshop, U. Tex., Austin, 1983. Author: (guide) Evaluation of Textbooks, 1974. Del. Tex. Dem. Conv., Austin, 1960. Recipient scholarship, U. Tex. Sports Assn., Austin, 1947. Mem. Tex. State Tchrs. Assn., Tex. Ret. Tchrs. Assn. Lutheran. Avocations: collector shells, foreign dolls, travel, reading. Home: Houston, Tex. Died Jan. 13, 2007.

HAMMER, PETER L., mathematics professor, researcher; s. George and Elizabeth Hammer; m. Anca L. Ivanescu, Nov. 4, 1961; children: Maxim D., Alexander B. D in Math., Bucharest U., Romania, 1966; DSc Honoris Causa (hon.), Swiss Fed. Inst. Tech., Lausanne, 1986; Laurea Honoris Causa (hon.), La Sapienza, Rome, 1998; DSc Honoris Causa (hon.), U. Liege, Belgium, 1999. Sr. rsch. mathematician Inst. Math., Romanian Acad., Bucharest, 1958—67; assoc. prof. Technion, Haifa, Israel, 1967—70, U. Montreal, Canada, 1969—72; prof. U. Waterloo, Canada, 1972—83; dir. rutcor Rutgers U., Piscataway, NJ, from 1983. Author, editor 16 books, founder, editor-in-chief Annals Ops. Rsch., from 2004. Recipient George Tzitzeica prize, Romanian Acad., 1966. Fellow: Inst. of Combinatorics and its Applications (life Euler award 1999), AAAS (life). Achievements include initiated the use of Boolean methods in operations research, graph theory, data mining and biomedical informatics. Home: Princeton, NJ. Died Dec. 27, 2006.

HAMMERSCHMIDT, JOHN PAUL, former United States Representative, Arkansas, lumber company executive; b. Harrison, Ark., May 4, 1922; s. Arthur Paul and Junie (Taylor) H.; m. Virginia Sharp (dec. 2006); 1 child, John Arthur. Student, The Citadel, U. Ark., Okla. State U.; BS in Bus. Mgmt., Canbourne U., London, MA in Philosophy magna cum laude; PhD in Internat. Studies, Wallingham U., London; LLD (hon.), U. Ark., 2011. Ordained elder, deacon in Presbyn. Ch. Chmn. bd. Hammerschmidt Lumber Co., Harrison, 1946-84; mem. 90th-102d Congresses from 3d Ark. Dist., 1967-93. Mem. Pub. Works and Transp. Com., 1967-93, ranking mem., 1987-93; mem. V.A. Com., 1967-93, ranking mem., 1973-86; bd. dirs. 1st Fed. Bank of Ark.; sr. chmn. bd. 1st Fed. Bankshares of Ark.; chmn. emeritus N.W. Ark. Coun.; nat. committeman Ark. Citizen of Yr. Com.; mem. Presdl. Commn. on Aviation Security and Terrorism; mem. Pres.'s task force on Vets. Health Care; mem. Claude and Mildred Pepper Found., 1989-90 (PVA Speedy award), bd. Met. Washington Airports Authority; past chmn. bd., trustee Ark. State U., U. of the Ozarks; committeeman Nat. Rep. Party, 2002; bd. mem. Arks. Western Found., 2006-2010. Chmn. Ark. Republican Com., 1964-66; mem. Rep. Nat. Finance Com., 1960-64, nat. Rep. committeeman from, Ark., 1976-80; mem. Harrison City Coun., 1948, 60, 62. Served as pilot USAAF, World War II, CBI. Decorated Air medal with 4 oak leaf clusters, D.F.C. with 3 oak leaf clusters, 3 Battle Stars, The China War Meml. medal, Meritorious Svc. award VFW Congl. award, Silver Helmet award, Nat. Order Trenchrats Legis. Svc. award, Award for Life Svc. to Vets., Boy Scouts Golden Eagle award, 2012; named. Ark. Citizen of Yr., 1991, Ark. Aerospace Found. Hall of Fame, 1991. Mem. Ark. Lumber Dealers Assn. (past pres.), Midwest Lumbermens Assn. (past pres.), Harrison C. of C. (named Man of Yr. 1965), Am. Legion, Masons (33 degree-Grand Cross), Scottish Rite, Shriners, Jesters, Elks, Rotary (past pres. Harrison). Republican. Presbyterian. Home: Harrison, Ark. Died Apr. 1, 2015.

HAMMOND, MICHAEL DAVID, information technology executive; b. Des Moines, Nov. 28, 1961; m. Lisa Hunt, 2011 (dec. June 2015); children: Michael, Jessica. Co-founder Gateway, Sioux City, 1985, v.p. Asia-Pacific orgn., sr. v.p. global mfg., head bus. process simplication team, sr. v.p. ops. Poway, Calif., sold to Acer, 2007; founder Dakota Muscle, North Sioux City. Died Oct. 29, 2015.

HAMMOND, ROSS WILLIAM, management consultant; b. NYC, Mar. 20, 1918; s. Rene Ross and Elsie Glynn (Richards) H.; m. Betty Bennett, Apr. 28, 1990. BSEE, U. Tex., 1951, MS in Indsl. Engring., 1952. Area devel. engr. Tex. Electric Svc. Co., Ft. Worth, 1952-61; exec. dir. Am. Inst. Indsl. Engrs., NYC, 1961-63; dir., econ. devel. lab Ga. Inst. Tech., Atlanta, 1963-77, dir. internat. programs, 1977-79, dir. Asia office, 1979-81; pres. Applied Rsch. and Devel., Atlanta, from 1981. Cons. indsl. projects in developing countries, 1963—. Contbr. articles to profl. jours. 2nd lt. USAF, 1943-46. Fellow Inst. Indsl. Engrs. (past. nat. pres., exec. dir.); mem. Ga. Indsl. Devel. Assn. (pres. 1967), Kiwanis. Republican. Presbyterian. Home: Atlanta, Ga. Died Mar. 13, 2007.

HAMPFORD, JOHN EDWARD, chemical company executive, chemist; b. Pottsville, Pa., Feb. 1, 1932; s. James J. and Barbara (Nieder) H.; m. Clare M. Malarkey, Sept. 14, 1957; children: Clare, John, Anne, Martin, Timothy. BS in Chemistry, Pa. State U., 1954. With R&D Atlantic Refinery, Phila., 1954-58; with comml. devel. Pennsalt Chem., Phila., 1954-60; mgr. comml. devel. Connestoga Chem., Wilmington, Del., 1960-67; from v.p. to pres. Ware Chem., Stratford, Conn., 1967-79; pres. Synpro-Ware div. Dart Kraft, Stratford, 1979-83, Hampford Rsch., Inc., Stratford, from 1983. Adv. bd. Lafayette Bank & Trust, Bridgeport, Conn. Mem. alumni bd. Coll. of Sci., Pa. State U., University Park, 1985-88; mem. assoc. bd. Bridgeport (Conn.) Found., YMCA, Bridgeport, Boys Club Bridgeport; vol. United Way, Bridgeport, 1983. Alumni fellow Pa. State U., 1991. Mem. Comml. Devel. Assn., Chem. Mktg. and Resource Assn., ACS, Soc. Plastics Engrs., AAAS, Am. Mgmt. Assn., Synthetic Organic Chem. Mfrs. Assn., Chemists Club N.Y., Brooklawn Country Club, Jupiter Hills Club, Pres. Country Club, Algonquin Club, Alpha Chi Sigma. Achievements include co-development of the crosslinking agent which pioneered the development of the two piece golf ball. Home: Trumbull, Conn. Died Mar. 23, 2007.

HANCHETT, WILLIAM A. BARTON, mechanical engineer, designer; b. San Francisco, June 11, 1928; s. William A. Barton Sr. and Tempest Caroline (Wilder) W.; m. Jane Elizabeth Connell, Apr. 6, 1948; children: William A. Barton III, Barbara Lee, Marc Connell. BSBA, SUNY, 1976; BSME, Cath. U. Am., 1980, MSME, 1981. Cert. sr. safety engr. Commd. 2d lt. U.S. Army, 1952, advanced through grades to col., 1971, retired, 1975; dir. Hanchett Engring., Springfield, Va., 1975-81, Ojai, Calif., from 1981; program dir. Advanced Tech., Camarillo, Calif., 1982-88; dist. mgr. Am. Mgmt. Systems Inc., Port Hueneme, Calif., 1988-93. Named hon. mayor Bretten-Badden, Fed. Republic of Germany, 1964-66; decorated Legion of Merit (twice), Joint Svcs. Commendation medal, Army Commendation medal (three times), Vietnam medal of Valor (twice); recipient Engring. Recognition award Cath. U. Amer., 1980. Mem. ASME, ASTM, Soc. Am. Mil. Engrs. (bd. govs. 1986-89), Am. Soc. Safety Engrs., Systems Safety Soc., Am. Soc. Indsl. Security (vice-chmn. 1989-90, 95, chmn. 1996-97), Am. Soc. Naval Engrs. Republican. Avocations: woodworking, inventions, remodeling houses, german shepard show dogs. Died July 7, 2007.

HANCOCK, WILLIAM FRANK, JR., professor; b. Richmond, Va., Jan. 4, 1942; s. William Frank and Gladys Elizabeth (George) H.; m. Donna G. Hosmer, May 18, 1968 (div.), Joy T. Shelley, Dec. 14, 2010; children: Peter James, Jeffrey William, Jennifer Beth. BBA, U. Iowa, 1964; MBA, U. Pa., 1966; postgrad., Capella U. CPA, CLU, CPCU, CMA, CDP. Exec. asst. to exec. v.p. John Hancock Mut. Life Ins. Co., 1966-69; mgmt. cons. Keane Assocs., 1969-74, regional mgr., 1974-75; v.p., gen. mgr. comml. sys. SofTech, Inc., Waltham, Mass., 1975-79; dir. internat. sales and field ops. Nixdorf Computer Co., Burlington, Mass., 1979-80; mgr. mktg. Digital Equipment Corp., 1980-84, electronic commerce mgr., 1984-97; mgmt. cons. electronic commerce Grant Thornton LLP, 1997—98; mgmt. cons., nat. electronic commerce practice Ernst & Young, LLP, 1998—2000; prin. IBM Corp., 2000—02; mng. dir. 3 Rivers Assocs., Mills River, NC, from 2002. Adj. prof. acctg. and fin. Grad. Sch. Bus., Northeastern U., Boston, 1966—, sr. instr. acctg. Grad. Sch. Bus. Babson Coll., Wellesley, Mass, 1985—; assoc. dean and prof. Sch. Mgmt., Cambridge Coll., 2002—2008; prof. Jinan U., China, 2007, assoc. dean, acctg. and fin. prof. Hult Internat. Bus. Sch., 2008-, Cambridge, Mass.; bd. dirs. Ctrl. Cambridge Bus. Assn. Treas. Pilgrim Ch.; trustee Sherborn Libr.; chmn. Sherborn coun. Boy Scouts Am. With U.S. Army, 1967-72. Recipient Outstanding Teacher of Yr. Awd., Northeastern Univ., 1989, Prof. of Yr., Hult Internat. Bus. Sch., 2011. Mem. AICPA, Data Processing Mgmt., Nat. Assn. Accts., Assn. Computing Machinery, Boston C. of C., Exec. Club Boston, Wharton Alumni Club, U. Iowa Alumni Assn., Cambridge Bus. Assn. (bd. dirs. 2008-). Presbyterian. Died Nov. 7, 2014.

HANCOCK, WILLIAM MARVIN, computer security and network engineering executive; b. Portsmouth, Va., Feb. 10, 1957; s. William H. and Marjorie E. (Davis) H. BA in Computer Sci., Thomas A. Edison Sr. Coll., 1992; MS in Computer Sci., Greenwich U., 1993, PhD in Computer Sci., 1994. Cert. info. systems security profl., network expert. Programmer Tex. Instruments, Dallas, 1972-74; cons. Digital Equipment Corp., Dallas, 1979-82; div. analyst Standard Oil of Ohio, Dallas, 1982-84; v.p. engring. New Leaf Techs., Arlington, Tex., 1984-90, Network 1 Inc., Arlington, 1990-94; exec. v.p. and chief tech. officer Network 1, Boston, 1990-2000; sr. v.p. security, chief security officer Exodus Comm., Inc., Arlington, from 2000. U.S. network expert Am. Nat. Stds. Inst., N.Y.C., 1985-87; stds. editor Internat. Orgn. for Stds., Geneva, 1986-88; co-chair White House Com. on B2B Security. Author: Designing and Implementing Ethernet Networks, 1988, Network Concepts and Architectures, 1989, Issues and Problems in Computer Networks, 1990, Advanced Ethernet/802.3 Management and Performance, 1992, Computer Consulting is a Very Funny Business, 1993, Designing and Implementing ATM Networks, 1994, Applied Networking, 1996, Advanced Network Architecture, 1996, Everything You Wanted to Know About Networks But Were Afraid to Ask, 1998, Windows-NT Network Security, 1998, Networking Explained, 1999, Network Security Concepts, 2000, Practical Guide to Network Security, 2000, Computer Communications and Network Technologies, 2001; editor-in-chief Computers and Security Mag.; columnist Network Security Mag. With USN, 1974-79. Recipient Arnold Fletcher award, 1992. Mem. IEEE, NSOR, ANSI, Internat. Computer Security Assn., Digital Equipment Computer Users Soc. (Tech. Excellence award 1992), Assn. for Computing Machinery, Computer Security Inst. Achievements include design of over 4300 computer networks. Six-time world aikido champion. Home: Rhome, Tex. Died Jan. 1, 2007.

HANDELMAN, EILEEN TANNENBAUM, physics educator; b. Holyoke, Mass., Dec. 11, 1928; d. Samuel and Lena (Cohen) Tannenbaum; m. Robert B. Handelman, Feb. 22, 1959; 1 child, Audrey C. BA, Mt. Holyoke Coll., 1950, MA, 1952; PhD, U. Calif., 1955. Post-doctoral fellow U. Copenhagen, Denmark, 1955-56; mem. tech. staff Bell Telephone Lab., Murray Hill, N.J., 1956-66; acad. dean Simon's Rock Coll., Great Barrington, Mass., 1977-84, dean of coll., 1981-84, faculty in physics, from 1968. Contbr. articles to profl. jours.; patentee in field. Recipient Program Devel. grant NSF, 1972-75, Skinner fellowship Mt. Holyoke Coll., 1951-52, Shell fellowship U. Calif., 1953-54, Dow fellowship, 1954-55. Mem. Am. Assn. Physics Tchrs. Avocations: hybridizing daylilies, cross country skiing. Home: Hillsdale, NY. Died Aug. 16, 2007.

HANDLEY, RALPH WILLIAM, accountant; b. Oregon City, Oreg., Sept. 24, 1913; s. Charles and Amy Rose (Moore) H.; m. Ruth G. Snider, Sept. 5, 1937; children: Joan M. Handley Runyon, Barbara M. Handley McLean. BAA, Ohio U., 1938. CPA, Calif. Auditor Firestone Rubber, Akron, Ohio, 1938-43; acct. Bus. Mgmt., Beverly Hills, Calif., 1946-53; bus. mgr. motion picture and TV Studio City, Calif., 1953-78; ret., 1978. Author: Book of Family Records, 1975. Mgr., bd. dirs. Irene Ryan Found., Encino, Calif., 1978—. Lt. comdr. USNR, 1943-46, PTO. Mem. Rotary (various offices), Masons (line officer 1970-75). Presbyterian. Avocations: golf, bridge. Home: Palm Desert, Calif. Died May 10, 2007.

HANE, GUY ELLIOTT, producer, director; b. Mpls., Oct. 15, 1952; s. Carl Edward Sr. and Dorothea Velma Lang. Asst. mgr. Maritz Labs. Inc., 1976-79; photographer Badiyan Prodns., Inc., 1979-82, producer, dir., 1983-85; telecine colorist Tele-Edit Inc., 1982-83; co-founder E.A. Lowery & Co., Eden Prairie, Minn., 1983, producer, dir., 1985—90; computer and video graphics Guy Hane Prodns., from 1990. Freelance photographer. Served with U.S. Army, 1972-75. Recipient Gold award N.Y. Internat. Film Festival, 1984, Silver award N.Y. Internat. Film Festival, 1984, Bronze Cindy award Assn. Visual Communicators, 1985, award of Excellence Internat. TV Assn., 1987, Bronze Telly award, 1988, Bronze Telly award, 1990, Silver Telly award, 1990. Democrat. Home: Hopkins, Minn. Died Apr. 24, 2007.

HANNAHS, RAPHAEL, television engineer and consultant; b. Bridgeport, Ohio, Apr. 7, 1916; s. Otmer Wilson and Anna Earnestina (Klemmer) H.; m. Lucille Agnes Hayden, Nov. 15, 1944 (div. 1963); children: Roger (dec.), Michelle, Christine. BA, Ohio Wesleyan U., 1940; BS, Ohio State U., 1942; postgrad., Columbia U., 1955-59, Fairfield U., 1968. Engr. TV research lab. GTE/Sylvania, NYC, 1943-54; tech. dir. Automatic Prodn. Research, Riverside, Conn., 1954-68; staff assoc. Bell Labs. div. United Teletech, Holmdel, N.J., 1968-74; project engr. Dictograph, Florham Park, N.J., 1976-79; engr. CBS, NYC, 1979-86; cons. TV-A Assocs., Menlo Park, N.J., from 1987. Cons. editor McGraw Hill, N.Y.C., 1958-59; contbr. numerous articles to profl. jours.; patentee in field. Mem. Soc. Motion Picture and TV Engrs. (assoc.). Republican. Avocations: amateur radio, regional theater. Home: Washington, DC. Died Apr. 25, 2007.

HANNON, VIOLET MARIE, surgical nurse; b. Wayne, Mich., Sept. 11, 1943; d. John R. and Ethel L. (Goudy) Hines; children: Judith, Susan. Diploma, Grace Hosp. Sch. Nursing, Detroit, 1964; BS summa cum laude, U. Detroit, 1985; postgrad., Cen. Mich. U., from 1997. Cert. ACLS, CNOR. Staff nurse Grace Hosp., 1964-67, Sinai Hosp.,

Detroit, 1971-75, Oakwood Hosp., Dearborn, Mich., 1967-71, 1975-86; ophthalca svcs. nurse Henry Ford Hosp., 1987-93, HCIA, Inc., 1993-98, Eisenhower Hosp., from 1999. Mem. Assn. Operating Room Nurses. Home: Palm Desert, Calif. Died Aug. 11, 2007.

HANRETTA, ALLAN GENE, psychiatrist, pharmacist; b. Galveston, Tex., June 24, 1930; s. Aloysius Thomas and Genevieve M. (Feeney) H.; m. Carolyn Jean Jacobs, Sept. 4, 1954; children: Allan Thomas, Patrice M., Mark D. BS in Pharamcy, U. Tex., Austin, 1952, BA in Arts and Sci., 1957; MD, U. Tex., Galveston, 1959. Diplomate Am. Bd. Psychiatry and Neurology. Gen. rotating intern USPHS Hosp., San Francisco, 1959-60; resident in psychiatry U. Tex. Med. Br., Galveston, Tex., 1960-63; fellow in clin. electroencephalography Meth. Hosp.-Tex. Med. Ctr., Houston, 1963-64; pvt. practice, Santa Barbara, 1964-83. Chief staff Dani's Psychiat. Hosp., Santa Barbara, 1971-79; mem. med. staff Cottage Hosp., St. Francis Hosp., Goleta Valley Community Hosp., Camarillo State Hosp., 1964—. Lectr. Santa Barbara Pharm. Assn., 1975. Lt. (j.g.) USN, 1952-54. Recipient contbn. to pharmacy award Santa Barbara Pharm. Assn., 1975. Mem. AMA, Am. Psychiat. Assn., So. Calif. Psychiat. Assn., Santa Barbara Psychiat. Soc. (pres. 1977-79). Avocations: travel, chess, tennis, boating, flying. Home: Santa Barbara, Calif. Died Mar. 18, 2007.

HANSEN, GUNNAR, writer, publisher, actor; b. Reykjavik, Iceland, Mar. 4, 1947; s. Skuli Eggert Hansen and Sigrid Eva Saetersmoen; partner Betty Tower BA, U. Tex., 1970. Assoc. editor Maine Mag., Ellsworth, 1976-78; freelance writer Northeast Harbor, Maine, from 1977; pub. LoonBooks, Northeast Harbor, from 1980, Washington County Mag., Northeast Harbor, 1981-82; ptnr. Acadia Film, Northeast Harbor, from 1978. Adj. faculty Coll. of the Atlantic, Bar Harbor, Maine. Author: Bear Dancing on the Hill, 1979, Not a Common House, 1981, Islands at the Edge of Time, A Journey to America's Barrier Islands, 1993, Chain Saw Confidential, 2013; mng. editor The Yacht, 1986-87; actor (films) The Texas Chain Saw Massacre, 1974, The Demon Lover, 1977, Hollywood Chainsaw Hookers, 1988, Campfire Tales, 1991, Exploding Angel, 1995, Mosquito, 1995, Freakshow, 1995, Repligator, 1996, Hellblock 13, 1999, Hatred of a Minute, 2002, Witchunter, 2002, Rachel's Attic, 2002, Sinister, 2002, Next Victim, 2003, The Business, 2004, Chainsaw Sally, 2004, Murder-Set-Pieces, 2004, Aconite, 2005, Apocalypse and the Beauty Queen, 2005, Wolfsbayne, 2005, Swarm of the Snakehead, 2006, The Deepening, 2006, Brutal Massacre: A Comedy, 2007, Shudder, 2007, Gimme Skelter, 2007, Won Ton Baby!, 2009, It Came from Trafalgar, 2009, Reykjavik Whale Watching Massacre, 2009, Texas Chainsaw 3D, 2013; writer, prodr. (films) Death House, 2016; contbr. articles to Tex. Monthly, New Eng. Monthly, Yacht, Down East, Yankee, other mags. W.S. Davidson scholar U. Tex, Austin, 1965-67; recipient 2 planning grants Maine Council for Humanities, 1978, 2 book pub. grants Maine Writers and Pubs. Alliance, 1982, 85. Home: Northeast Harbor, Maine. Died Nov. 7, 2015.

HANSON, BRETT ALLEN, nuclear engineer; b. Kittery, Maine, Mar. 12, 1963; s. Dennis Wilfred and Joan Alberta (Patton) H.; m. Karen Anne Leahy, Aug. 24, 1989. MSEE, Fla. Inst. Tech., 1988, MS in Physics, 1990; postgrad., U. Va., from 1990. Rsch. asst. Fla. Inst. Tech., Melbourne, 1989-90; grad. rsch. asst. U. Va., Charlottesville, from 1990. Mem. IEEE, Soc. Physics Students, Am. Nuclear Soc., Dielectrics and Elec. Insulation Soc., Sigma Pi Sigma. Home: Skippack, Pa. Died Feb. 7, 2007.

HANSON, JAMES EDWARD, chemist; b. Wichita, Kans., Mar. 25, 1962; s. James Robert and Mary Jane (Laird) H. BS in Chemistry and Geology, Tex. Christian U., 1984; PhD in Chemistry, Calif. Inst. Tech., 1990. Postdoctoral mem. tech. staff AT&T Bell Labs., Murray Hill, N.J., 1989-91; asst. prof. Seton Hall U., South Orange, N.J., from 1991. Patentee in field; contbr. articles to profl. jours. Recipient Predoctoral fellowship NSF, 1985-88. Mem. Am. Chem. Soc., Sigma Xi. Avocations: sports, music. Home: Verona, NJ. Died July 30, 2007.

HARBUTT, CHARLES HENRY, photojournalist; b. Camden, NJ, July 29, 1935; s. Charles Henry and Catharine (McMahon) H.; m. Alberta Eleanor Steves, Aug. 8, 1958 (div.); children: Sarah, Charles, Damian; m. Joan Liftin, Dec. 22, 1978. BS, Marquette U., 1956. Assoc. editor Jubilee Mag., NYC, 1956-59; mem. Magnum Photos, NYC and Paris, 1963-81, Archive Pictures, NYC, 1981-89; pres. Actuality Inc., NYC, 1970—2015. Cons. N.Y.C. Planning Commn., 1968-70; taught photography Parsons Sch. of Design Author: Travelog, 1974 (Best Arles 1974), Departures and Arrivals, (monograph) I Grandi Photographi, 1983; Progreso, 1986; co-editor: America in Crisis, 1969; curator: exhibit American Pavilion, Salford, 1980; photographs appeared in Life, Look, Time, National Geographic, Paris-Match, New York Times Magazine, Newsweek and Fortune Home: Philmont, NY. Died June 30, 2015.

HARDIN, WILLIAM DOWNER, retired lawyer; b. Newark, Sept. 27, 1926; s. Charles R. and Emma (Downer) H.; m. Rosemarie Koellhoffer, Jan. 19, 1952 (dec. Mar. 21, 1996); m. Ruth M. Johnson, May 29, 1999; children: William Downer, Jr., David Gerth, Peter Roe. AB, Princeton, 1948; LL.B., Columbia, 1951. Bar: N.J. 1951. Law clk. N.J. Superior Ct., 1951-52; assoc. firm Pitney, Hardin, Kipp & Szuch, Newark and Morristown, 1952—57, mem. firm, 1957—96. Mem. N.J. Bd. Bar Examiners, 1964-68, chmn., 1968; mem. local draft bd. SSS, 1953-74, chmn., 1970-74; mem. Family Svc. Bur., Newark, 1953-75, pres., 1960-66; mem. Family Svc. Morris County, 1976-85, 87-98, pres., 1979-82, 95-97, v.p., 1992-95; mem. membership com. Family Svc. Assn. Am., 1965-78, dir., 1971-79, 89-95; mem. Nat. Budget and Consultation Com., 1966-71, Coun. on Accreditation Svcs. for Families and Children, 1978-80. Trustee Newark Acad., 1952-85, pres., 1969-72, chmn., 1976-78; mem. Legal Svcs. of N.J., 1983-2002, chmn., 1990-96; mem. Legal Aid Soc. of Morris County, N.J., 1984-93, pres., 1989-90. With USNR, 1944-46. Mem. ABA, Fed. Bar Assn., N.J. Bar Assn., Essex County Bar Assn., Morris County Bar Assn., Short Hills Club, Rockaway River Country Club. Episcopalian. Home: Stuart, Fla. Deceased.

HARDY, JOHN EDMISTON, JR., insurance agent; b. Jersey City, May 25, 1947; s. John Edmiston and Maureen Jane (McComb) H.; m. Pamela Jean Briggs, July 9, 1973; children: Brandon John, Shannon Leigh, Meghan Elizabeth. BS in Bus. Adminstrn., Northwestern U., 1969; MS in Fin. Svcs., Am. Coll., 1989. Chartered life underwriter, fin. cons. Mgr. data processing John O. Todd Orgn., Evanston, Ill., 1967-73, prin. Northfield, Ill., 1975-87; life ins. agent Northwestern Mutual Life, Evanston, Ill., from 1973; prin. and co-founder Compensation Resource Group, Northbrook, Ill., from 1987. Contbr. articles to profl. jours. Vestry St. James the Less Episcopal Ch., Northfield, 1981-84; coach Northbrook Soccer Club, 1981-89, adv. bd. Northbrook Park Dist., 1983-87. Mem. Nat. Assn. Life Underwriters, Am. Soc. Chartered Life Underwriters and Chartered Fin. Cons., Assn. for Advanced Life Underwriting, Million Dollar Round Table. Avocations: cylcing, swimming, woodworking. Died May 22, 2007.

HARDY, JULIA IRENE, elementary school educator; b. Montrose, Iowa, Aug. 11, 1917; d. Carl Alfred Peterson, Achsa Leah LaDuke; m. Francis William Hardy, Oct. 12, 1940; children: Judith (Jeudi) Kay Vitale Eblin, Bruce William. BS in Edn., We. Ill. U., 1965, MS in Edn., 1970; postgrad., Colo. State U., Nat. Coll. Edn., U.S. Internat. U., U. Hawaii. Cert. Permanent profl. cert. Iowa, 1976. Clk. - typist Burlington Ordnance Plant, Iowa, 1941—45; tchr., counselor, reading specialist Keokuk Cmty. Sch. Dist., Keokuk, Iowa, 1957—81. Tchr. Lee County Pub. Schs., Montrose, Iowa, 1936—48; grad. asst. We. Ill. U., Macomb, 1967—68; bd. dirs., chmn. credit com. Keokuk Cmty. Sch. Employees Credit Union, 1986—2001; pvt. tutor, Keokuk, Iowa, 1969—89; presenter poetry programs and readings Christvision, Keokuk, Iowa, 1993—98; presenter poetry symposiums and convs., 1985—2003. Author: Theatre of the Wind, 2003—04, Colours of the Heart, 2003—04, (inspirational poetry) The Wonder of It All, 1996; composer: poems set to music for Emerald Records, from 2000. Tchr. Bethel Bible, 1970. Mem.: Internat. Soc. Poets (life Internat. Poetry Hall of Fame 1997), Internat. Reading Assn. (life Outstanding Achievement in Poetry award), Am. Legion Aux., Order Ea. Star (past matron, Grand page 1952), Kappa Delta Pi, Delta Kappa Gamma (com. mem. Alpha Epsilon chpt., Scholarship 1960), Internat. Beta Sigma Phi. Democrat. Lutheran. Avocations: art, reading, poetry, dramatics, family. Home: Wever, Iowa. Died July 23, 2007.

HARKAVY, IRA BAER, retired supreme court justice; b. Bklyn., Apr. 13, 1931; s. Morris Abraham and Esther (Brown) Harkavy; m. Roberta Susan Firsty, Aug. 11, 1957; children: Steven Jeffrey, Daniel Joseph, Elliot Glenn. AB, Bklyn. Coll., 1951; JD, Columbia U., 1954. Bar: N.Y. 1954, U.S. Dist. Ct. (ea. and so. dists.) N.Y. 1957, U.S. Supreme Ct. 1960. From assoc. to ptnr. Harkavy, Tell & Mendelson, NYC, 1954-67; ptnr. Harkavy & Tell, NYC, 1967-70; sr. ptnr. Delson & Gordon, NYC, 1970-81; judge Civil Ct. N.Y.C., Kings County, 1982-92; acting justice Supreme Ct., Kings County, 1992-2000, justice, 2000—07, Judicial Hearing Offices, 2008—14. Chmn. bd. justices Supreme Ct. 2d Dist., 2006—07. Chmn. Planning Bd. 14, Bklyn., 1967—81; mem. Bklyn. Bicentennial Com., 1975—77, Bklyn. Borough Bd., 1976—81, Bklyn. Civic Coun., 1975—82; chmn. Anti-Defamation League of B'Nai B'Rith, Bklyn., 1966—70; mem. N.Y. Regional Bd., 1985—90; bd. dirs. Bklyn. Coll. Found., 1958—81, sec., 1959—64, 1971—81; 1st v.p. YM-YWHA, Kingsbay, 1975—76, pres., 1997—2001; trustee Bklyn. Coll. Hillel Found., 1975—2006, v.p., 1976—77, pres., 1977—81, chmn. bd., 1983—88, Midwood Devel. Corp., 1976—81; v.p. bd. judges Civil Ct., NYC, 1979—83, pres. bd. judges, 1993—96; bd. trustees Bklyn. Pub. Libr., 1975—2013; adv. bd. Am. Jewish Congress, 1972—75; pres. Madison Jewish Ctr., 1978—81, Jewish Cmty. Coun. Kings Bay, from 2001. Recipient Pres.'s medal, Bklyn. Coll., 1975, Cert. of Merit, Bklyn. Borough, 1976, 1981, award, N.Y. State Assn. Libr. Bds., 1991. Mem.: ALA (Trustee of Yr. 1995), Nat. Arbitration Mediation Assn. (mediator from 2008), N.Y. State Trial Lawyers Assn., Bklyn. Bar Assn., N.Y. State Bar Assn., Assn. of Bar of City of N.Y., Am. Judges Assn., Am. Arbitration Assn. (arbitrator 1968—81), Am. Libr. Trustee Assn. (sec. 1988—89, regional v.p. from 1989), B'nai B'rith (pres. King County Lodge 1965—67, pres. Bklyn. Unity Lodge 1985—89), Bklyn. Coll. Alumni Assn. (pres. 1973—83, bd. dirs.), ABA, Phi Alpha Delta. Avocation: Avocations: reading, golf, computers. Home: Somerset, NJ. Died May 17, 2015.

HARMAN, DENHAM, retired medical educator; b. San Francisco, Feb. 14, 1916; s. Leslie and Ruth (Wright) H.; m. Helen Cronbach; children: Douglas, David, Mark, Robin. BS, U. Calif., Berkeley, 1940; PhD, U. Calif., 1943; MD, Stanford U., 1954. Rsch. chemist Shell Devel. Co., Emeryville, Calif., 1943-49; rsch. assoc. Donner Lab. Med. Physics, Berkeley, 1954-56; from asst. prof. to prof. Coll. Medicine U. Nebr., Omaha, 1958-86, prof. emeritus, 1986—2014. Chmn. White House Conf. on Aging, Washington, 1981. Contbr. more than 70 articles to profl. jours.; holder 35 chem. patents. Mem. Mayor City of Omaha Commn. on Aging, 1970-74. Named Scientist of Yr. Sigma Xi, 1984. Fellow American Coll. Physicians, American Heart Assn., American Geriatric Soc., Gerontol. Soc. America, Radiation Rsch. Soc.; mem. American Aging Assn. Avocations: tennis, reading. Home: Plano, Tex. Died Nov. 25, 2014.

HARMS, PHYLLIS RAE MAHNKE, social services administrator; b. Milw., May 26, 1925; d. Louis William and Clara C.S. (Albrecht) Mahnke; m. Paul W.F. Harms, June 24, 1950; children: Steven P., Rae Antoinette, Claudia N., Nathan S., Caleb D., Seth S. BA, Valparaiso U., Ind., 1947; postgrad., Washington U., St. Louis, 1949. Sec. Immanuel Luth. Ch., Valparaiso, 1946-49; recorder Concordia Sem., St. Louis, 1949-50; tchr. Ashland (Oreg.) Schs., 1950-51; exec. asst. Ohio Nurses Assn., Columbus, 1977-85; adminstrv. asst. Luth. Social Services, Columbus, from 1985. Pres. Trinity Luth. Ch., Columbus, 1982-86; v.p. So. Ohio Synod Evang. Luth. Ch. in Am., 1987—. Mem. AAUW. Democrat. Avocation: church choir. Home: Columbus, Ohio. Died Jan. 9, 2007.

HARNEY, DIANA LARAYNE, civic worker; b. Anderson, Ind., Aug. 5, 1945; d. Adrian Earl Smith and Harriett Alice (Keesling) Robertson; m. Colin Douglas Harney, Oct. 20, 1963; children: Dawn Angela Harney Sargent, Donald Edwin Lane. Student, Anderson Coll., 1984-85. Mediator, vol. coord. Community Justice Ctr. of Madison County, Anderson, from 1990; art cons. Art Finds Internat., Anderson, from 1991. Pres. Epilepsy Found. Madison County, Ind., 1981-83, coord. support group, 1983-85; coord. Driving While Intoxicated Victim-Offender Encounter Group Program; mediator victim-offender restitution program Community Justice Ctr. Madison County, Anderson, 1991—. Mem. Toastmasters (parliamentarian Anderson 1984), Epsilon Sigma Alpha (editor Ind. coun. 1983-84, rec. sec. 1984-85, treas. 1985-86, v.p. 1986-88, pres. 1988-89, jr. pres. 1989-90, assoc. mem. coord. 1990-91, ednl. dir. Alpha Omega chpt. 1991—). Avocations: writing, walking, travel, photography, nature. Home: Daleville, Ind. Died July 10, 2007.

HARNONCOURT, NIKOLAUS, musician, conductor; b. Berlin, Dec. 6, 1929; s. Eberhard and Ladislaja (Meran) Harnoncourt; m. Alice Hoffelner, 1953; 3 children. Student, Matura Gymnasium, Graz, Acad. Music, Vienna; DMus. (hon.), U. Edinburgh, 1987. Cellist Vienna Symphony Orch., 1952—69; founder mem. Concentus Musicus Wien Ensemble, 1953—2016; concentus musicus Ensemble for Ancient Music, 1954; prof. Mozarteum U. Music and Dramatic Arts, Salzburg, 1973—93; founder Styriarte Festival, Graz, 1985; condr. Zurich Opera House, Amsterdam Concertgebouw Orkest, Chamber Orchestra of Europe, Vienna and Berlin Philharmonic. Numerous concerts Europe, Australia, Japan and USA; mem. Order Pour le Merite of the Sciences and the Arts, 2002; hon. mem. Vienna Concert House Soc., 1988; Gesellschaft der Musikfreunde, Vienna, 1992; mem. Vienna Philharmonic Orchestra, from 2004. Author: Musik als Klangrede--Wege zu einem neuen Musikverstandis, 1982, Der Musikalische Dialog, 1984. Recipient Erasmus prize, Netherlands, 1980, Grand Prix Mondiale, Grand Prix du Disque, Academie Charles Cros, France, 1992, Deutscher Schallplattenpreis, Polar Music prize, Royal Swedish Acad. Music, 1994, Hanseatic Goethe prize, Alfred Toepfer Stiftung FVS, Hamburg, Germany, 1995, Robert Schumann prize, City of Zwickau, Germany, 1997, Ernst von Siemens Music prize, Germany, 2002, Kyoto prize, Inamori Found., 2005. Died Mar. 5, 2016.

HARPER, JAMES WELDON, III, finance consultant; b. Frederick, Md., Mar. 3, 1937; s. James Weldon Jr. and Mildred Mary (Conaway) H. Student, Duke U. Coll. rep. Time, Inc., 1955-59; jr. exec. trainee Merrill Lynch Pierce Fenner and Smith, NYC, 1959-60; v.p. fin. planning Haight and Co., Inc., Washington, 1961-72; pres. fin. cons. Weldon Enterprises Ltd., Washington, 1973-95; founder, chmn., CEO emeritus Enviro Tek Corp. Internat., Waterford, Va., 1994—2003; founder, CEO emeritus Argicell.com, Inc., from 2000; v.p. corp. devel. Matrix Tech., Va., from 2003. Former pres. U.S. Energy Conservation Service, Inc.; cons. Aries Corp.; nat. coord. Nat. Planned Giving Assocs., Inc., 1983-92; bd. dirs. 6 cos., 1962-91; involved with 151 corps., 98 partnerships, 1960-; conservator Nat. Real Estate Trust for Health Care, Inc., 1987-92., svc., various bds., fin. planning 6, 1999-. Author 3 manuals. With U.S. Army, 1959. Methodist. Died Jan. 20, 2015.

HARRINGTON, (DANIEL) PAT(RICK), JR., actor; b. Astoria, NY, Aug. 13, 1929; s. Daniel Patrick and Anne Francis (Hunt) H.; m. Marjorie Gortner, Nov. 19, 1955 (div.); children: Patrick, Michael, Terry, Tresa Caitlin; m. Sally Cleaver BA in Polit. Philosophy, Fordham U., 1950, MA, 1952. Account exec. NBC-TV, NYC, 1954. Created character Guido Panzini on Jack Paar Show, 1958-60; appeared on Steve Allen Show, 1959-61, Danny Thomas Show, 1959-60, The Jack Paar Tonight Show, 1960; actor (TV series) Make Room for Daddy, 1959-60, Grindl, 1964, Kentucky Jones, 1964, The Littlest Hobo, 1964, Mr. Novak, 1965, The Lucy Show, 1965, The Munsters, 1964-65, The Man From U.N.C.L.E., 1965-67, Hank, 1966, McHale's Navy, 1966, F Troop, 1966, The Beverly Hillbillies, 1966, Insight, 1966-1976, Run for Your Life, 1967, Captain Nice, 1967, Journey to the Center of Earth, 1967, Good Morning, World, 1968, The Outsider, 1968-69, Mr. Deeds Goes to Town, 1969, Aquaman (voice) 1968-1969, The Pink Panther Show (voice), 1969, Here Come the Brides, 1970, The Flying Nun, 1970, The Most Deadly Game, 1970, The New Andy Griffith Show, 1971, The Interns, 1970-71, Marcus Welby, M.D., 1971, The Bold Ones: The Lawyers, 1971, Cade's County, 1971, Nanny and the Professor, 1971, The Courtship of Eddie's Father, 1972, Owen Marshall-Councilor at Law, 1971-74, The New Scooby-Doo Movies (voice), 1972, The New Temperature Rising Show, 1972, Circle of Fear, 1973, The Rookies, 1973, The Addams Family (voice) 1973, The Girl With Something Extra, 1973, Love, American Style, 1970-73, The Partridge Family, 1970-73, The New Perry Mason, 1973, Faraday and Company, 1973, Chase, 1974, The New Dick Van Dyke Show, 1974, Banacek, 1974, Columbo, 1974, Kolchak: The Night Stalker, 1975, Police Story, 1975, Police Woman, 1975, Fay, 1975, McMillan & Wife, 1974-75, Ellery Queen, 1975, The Invisible Man, 1975, Good Heavens, 1976, One Day at a Time, 1975-84 (Golden Globe award 1981, Emmy award 1984), Captain Caveman and the Teen Angels, 1977-80, The Love Boat, 1977-84, Glitter, 1984. Who's The Boss, 1985, Comedy Factory, 1985, Crazy Like a Fox, 1985, Hotel, 1986, Duet, 1989, The Ray Bradbury Theatre, 1989, Sydney, 1990, Murder, She Wrote, 1985-91, The Golden Girls, 1991, Yo Yogi! (voice), 1991, The Trials of Rosie O'Neill, 1992, Street Justice, 1992, Civil Wars, 1992, Yabba-Dabba Do! (voice), 1993, Duckman: Private Duck/Family Man, (voice), 1994, Silk Stalkings, 1994, The George Carlin Show, 1995, Burke's Law, 1995, Kirk, 1995, The Wayans Brothers, 1996, Aaahh!! Real Monsters (voice), 1994-97, Fantasy Island, 1999, Diagnosis Murder, 1999, As Told by Ginger (voice), 2000, Las Vegas, 2003, Curb Your Enthusiasm, 2005, The King of Queens, 2006, Hot In Cleveland, 2012; films include The Wheeler Dealers, 1963, Move Over Darling, 1963, Easy Come, Easy Go, 1967, The President's Analyst, 1967, 2000 Years Later, 1969, The Candidate, 1970, Every Little Crook and Nanny, 1972, Round Trip to Heaven, 1992, Ablaze, 2001; (TV films) A.P.O. 923, 1962, The Yellowbird, 1964, The Computer Wore Tennis Shoes, 1969, Wednesday Night Out, 1972, The Affair, 1973, Savage, 1973, The Healers, 1974, Let's Switch, 1975, Benny & Barney: Las Vegas Undercover, 1977, The New Love Boat, 1977, The Critical List, 1978, The Last Convertible (mini series), 1979, Between Two Brothers, 1982, Spring Fling!, 1995, These Old Broads, 2001; scriptwriter One Day at a Time. Served with USAF, 1952-54. Mem. Screen Actors Guild, AFTRA (v.p. Los Angeles local 1985-86). Clubs: Riviera Country. Democrat. Roman Catholic. Avocation: flying. Home: Los Angeles, Calif. Died Jan. 6, 2016.

HARRIS, BENJAMIN LOUIS, chemical engineer, consultant; b. Savannah, Ga., Aug. 1, 1917; s. Raymond Branson and Edith (Kontner) H.; m. Janet Diekmann, Oct. 4, 1942; children: Benjamin S., Stefanie Harris Hunt, Deborah Harris Kommalan, Penelope Harris Clifton, Rebecca Harris Gutin. BE, Johns Hopkins U., 1938, PhD, 1941; diploma, Indsl. Coll. Armed Forces, Washington, 1965. Registered profl. engr. Md. Asst. prof. Johns Hopkins U., Balt., 1946-53; with R & D Command U.S. Army, Edgewood Arsenal, Md., 1952-66; dep. asst. dir. def. R & D U.S. Office Sec. Def., Alexandria, Va., 1966-70; tech. dir. U.S. Army Chem. Rsch., Devel. and Engring. Ctr., Aberdeen, Md., 1970-81; pres. Engring. Rsch. Co. of Glenarm, Md., 1981-83. Cons. in field, 1981—; pres. Profl. Engrs. Bd., Md., 1987-88, v.p., 1988-98. Editor St. George Philatelic Soc. Newsletter, 1988-96; patentee in field, contbr. articles to profl. jours. Mem. Gov.'s Exec. Adv. Coun., Md., 1988-95; mem. exec. bd. Balt. Area coun. Boy Scouts Am., 1964—; mem. adv. com. USCG, NRC, Washington, 1967-77; mem. com. ethics and professionalism Nat. Coun. Examiners Engring. and Surveying. Maj. U.S. Army, 1941-46, Res., 1938-41, 46-77, ret. col., 1977. Recipient Silver Beaver award Boy Scouts Am., 1952, Silver Antelope award, 1987, Disting. Eagle award, 1976, Lamb award Luth. Ch., 1964, St. George award Cath. Ch., 1983; named Ky. Col. Fellow AAAS, AIChE; mem. SAR (past pres. Col. Nicholas Ruxton Moore chpt.), Am. Chem. Soc., Order Founders and Patriots Am. (gov. gen. 1996-98), Sons and Daus. of Pilgrims (gov. Md. br. 1996-98), Soc. Boonesborough, Nat. Congress Patriotic Orgns., Descendants of Ancient Planters, Sons of Confederate Vets., Soc. of Colonial Wars State of Md., Order of the Crown of Charlemgne USA, Huguenot Soc. Md., Order Honorable Arty. Co., St. George Soc. Balt., St. Andrews Soc. Balt., Ancient and Honorable Mech. Co. of Balt., Nat. Gavel Soc., Mil. Order World Wars (past comdr. Balt.-Devereaux chpt.), Ret. Officers Assn., Res. Officers Assn., Chem. Corps Regtl. Assn., Soc. of War of 1812 in State of Md., Corps. of the U.S. (charter mem., sr. exec., 1978), Democrat. Lutheran. Avocations: genealogy, stamp collecting/philately, crafts, gardening. Died Nov. 18, 2006.

HARRIS, CHARLES FREDERICK, publishing executive; b. Portsmouth, Va., Jan. 3, 1934; s. Ambrose Edward and Annie Eula (Lawson) H.; m. Sammie Lou Jackson, Dec. 8, 1956; children— Francis Charlton, Charles Frederick. Student, Norfolk State Coll., Va., 1951-53; BA, Va. State Coll., 1955; postgrad., NYU, 1957-63. Research analyst, editor Doubleday & Co., Inc., NYC, 1956-65; v.p., gen. mgr. subs. John Wiley & Sons, Inc., NYC, 1965-67; mng. editor, sr. editor adult trade div. Random House, Inc., NYC, 1967-71; exec. dir. Howard U. Press, Washington, 1971-86; pres., chief exec. officer Amistad Press, Inc. (sold to HarperCollins), NYC, 1986—99, editorial dir., 1999—2003. Formerly adj. prof. journalism Howard U. Co-editor: Amistad I and II, 1970. Served as 1st lt. inf. U.S. Army, 1956. Mem. Reading is Fundamental (bd.dirs.), Alpha Phi Alpha. Died Dec. 16, 2015.

HARRIS, DIXIE LEE, former corrections educator; b. Paragould, Ark., Feb. 22, 1926; d. Elmer Henderson and Alice (Cothern) H. BS in Math. and Chemistry, Ark. State U., 1946; MA in Sci. Tchg., Columbia U., 1955; PhD in Comparative Edn., Syracuse U., 1970; labor studies diploma, Cornell U., 1989. Cert. tchr. secondary scis. and math.; secondary supr./prin., N.Y. Qualitative analyst Tenn. Eastman Corp., Oak Ridge, 1946-47; chemist The Tex. Co.,

Beacon, 1947-55; tchr. math. and chemistry Bur. Indian Affairs, Mt. Edgecumbe, Alaska, 1957-60; corrections tchr. Matteawan State Hosp., Beacon, N.Y., 1967-91, Fishkill Correction Facility Pub. Employees Fedn., 1983-91. Internat. study in 65 countries, 1955-67. Author: Twenty (fictional) Stories of Bible Women, 1980. Elected union rep., steward, exec. bd. Pub. Employees Fedn., Albany, N.Y., 1983-91; bd. dirs., trails com. chair Environ. Planning Lobby (now named Environ. Advocates), Albany, 1967-83; mem. numerous environ. and civic orgns. Mem. ACLU, NOW, Americans United for Seperation of Ch. and State, Soc. Bib. Lit., Bib. Arch. Soc., Pub. Employees Fedn. Retirees, Am. Mensa, Am. Youth Hostels, Religious Coalition for Reproductive Choice, Scenic Hudson, N.Y. State Labor-Religion Coalition. Democrat. Methodist. Avocations: nature walks, rooftopping, shakespeare, art, history. Home: Beacon, NY. Died Dec. 20, 2006.

HARRIS, HERBERT EUGENE, II, former United States Representative from Virginia; b. Kansas City, Mo., Apr. 14, 1926; m. Nancy Fodell (dec. 2001); children: Herbert III, Frank, Susan, Sean(dec.) , Kevin. Attended, Mo. Valley Coll., 1944—45, U. Notre Dame, 1945—46; BA, Rockhurst Coll., 1948; JD, Georgetown U. Law Ctr., 1951. Ptnr. Harris & Ellsworth Law Firm, Washington; mem. Fairfax County Bd. Supervisors, 1968—74, vice chmn., 1971—74, chmn., 1972; commr. Northern Va. Transp. Authority, 1968—74; 1st vice chmn. Washington Metropolitan Area Transit Authority, 1971—74, 2nd vice chmn., 1973; pres. Fairfax County Fed. Citizens Assn.; mem. US Congress from 8th Va. Dist., Washington, 1975—81. Bd. dirs. Washington Metropolitan Area Transit Authority, 1970. Mem.: KofC, Mo. Bar Assn. (founding mem.), DC Bar Assn. (founding mem.). Democrat. Roman Catholic. Died Dec. 24, 2014.

HARRIS, JOHN BUNYAN, III, investment advisor; b. Greenwood, SC, Jan. 9, 1952; s. John Bunyan Jr. and Marian (Leake) H.; m. Eileen Dripchak; children: Emily, Ashley, John. BA, Clemson U., 1974; MA, John Hopkins U., 1977; MBA, George Washington U., 1980. Asst. mgr. Lillian-Morrison, Inc., Washington, 1975-78; researcher Internat. Bus. & Econ. Rsch. Corp., Washington, 1978-79; fin. analyst Overseas Pvt. Investment Corp., Washington, 1979-82; mgr. fin. U.S. Synthetic Fuels Corp., Washington, 1982-85; pres. Greenwood Rsch. Inc., Washington, from 1985. Mng. ptnr. Pinecrest Properties, 1988—; chmn. bd. dirs. Coal Gasification, Inc., Chgo. Mem. DeBordieu Club, Melrose Club, Kiawah Club. Home: Bethesda, Md. Died Dec. 11, 2006.

HARRIS, LUCILLE SAWYER, retired musician, educator; b. New Bern, NC, Aug. 26, 1926; d. James Henry and Ida Cahoon Sawyer; m. Carl Vernon Harris, Aug. 6, 1955. AA, Mars Hill Coll., NC, 1944; AB, Meredith Coll., Raleigh, NC, 1946, Mus B, 1947. Tchr. piano Mars Hill Coll., 1947—50, Gov. Morehead Sch. for Blind, Raleigh, NC, 1950—55, U. Wis., Platteville, 1956, Wake Forest U., Winston-Salem, NC, 1957—91, prof. emerita, from 1991. Organist Mars Hill Bapt. Ch., 1947—50, Fairmont Meth. Ch., Raleigh, 1950—52. Mem.: Am. Assn. Univ. Women, Music Tchrs. Nat. Assn., NC Music Tchrs. Assn., Alliance Bapts., Kappa Nu Sigma. Avocations: reading, music. Home: Winston Salem, NC. Died Aug. 2, 2014.

HARRIS, MARGARET T., school system administrator; b. Boston, Feb. 22, 1944; d. Michael Cotter and Margaret Murnane; m. James M. Harris Jr., May 28, 1966; children: Troy, Jason, Damien, Gillian. BSEd, U. Mass., Boston, 1966; MLS, Boston U., 1973; MSc, Syracuse U., 1989; EdD, U. Mass., Amherst, 2003. Cert. tchr. Nat. Bd. Edn., 2003. Tchr. Boston Schs., 1966—67; tchr. history and social studies Martha's Vineyard Schs., Oak Bluffs, Mass., 1976—2003, dir. curriculum and instrn. Tisbury, Mass., 2003—04, head history dept., 1980—2003, asst. supt. curriculum, from 2004. Contbr. articles to profl. publs. Mem. Martha's Vinehard Libr. Commn., Oak Bluffs 1977—80, Martha's Vineyard Conservation Commn., Oak Bluffs, 1978—82. Fulbright fellow, Brazil, 1993, Japan, 1997, South Africa, 2001. Mem.: AAUW, Orgn. Am. History (mem. various coms.), Phi Beta Kappa. Democrat. Avocations: dogs, music, dance, reading, knitting, walking. Died Nov. 13, 2006.

HARRIS, ROBERT DALTON, retired history professor, researcher, writer; b. Jamieson, Oreg., Dec. 24, 1921; s. Charles Sinclair and Dorothy (Cleveland) H.; m. Ethel Imus, June 26, 1971. BA, Whitman Coll., Walla Walla, Wash., 1951; MA, U. Calif., Berkeley, 1953, PhD, 1959. Tchg. asst. U. Calif., Berkeley, 1956-59; instr. history U. Idaho, Moscow, 1959-61, asst. prof., 1961-68, assoc. prof., 1968-74, prof. history, 1974-86, prof. emeritus, from 1986. Author: Necker, Reform Statesman of Ancient Regime, 1979, Necker & Revolution of 1789, 1986 1st lt., U.S. Army, 1942-46; Ballet Folk of Moscow, Idaho, (bd. dirs., 1971-73), Historian, First United Methodist Church, Moscow, Idaho, 1989—. Mem.: AAUP, Am. Hist. Assn. Democrat. Methodist. Avocations: social dancing, violinist. Home: Moscow, Idaho. Died Aug. 15, 2007.

HARRIS, SISTER TERESA L., state nursing administrator; b. Newark, Aug. 29, 1923; d. Carl Alvin and Agnes (Herring) H. Grad. RN, St. Mary's Hosp. Sch. Nursing, Passaic, NJ, 1944; BSN, Seton Hall U., 1958; MS, St. Louis U., 1963. V.p. nursing Hackensack (N.J.) Med. Ctr.; v.p. nursing, dir. Sch. of Nursing St. Elizabeth (N.J.) Hosp.; ret. exec. dir. Bd. of Nursing, State of N.J., Newark. Mem. ANA, N.J. State Nurses Assn. (practice com. chair, treas.), Nat. League for Nursing, Nat. Coun. State Bds. Nursing (nurse practice and edn. com., dir. Area IV), Sigma Theta Tau. Home: Elizabeth, NJ. Died Dec. 6, 2006.

HARRISON, DANIEL EDWARD, minister; b. Montgomery, Ala., Apr. 26, 1955; s. Charles Winford and Joyce Hilda (Gibbs) H.; m. Jeri Ann Baty, Sept. 8, 1979; children: Joy Elizabeth, Timothy Daniel. AS, Walker Coll., Jasper, Ala., 1978; BS, U. Ala., Tuscaloosa, 1980; MDiv, So. Bapt. Seminary, Louisville, 1983. Pastor Concord Bapt. Ch., Headland, Ala., 1983-88, 1st Bapt. Ch., Florala, Ala., 1988-90; chaplain U.S. Army, from 1990. Author: (newspaper column) Pastor's Pulpit, 1986-87. Mem. Henry County Humanitarian Resources Com., Abbeville, Ala., 1984-86. Mem. Judson Bapt. Assn. (pastor's conf., bd. dirs., royal amb.'s com. 1985—, vice moderator 1987—), Florala Area Ministerial Assn. (pres. 1988-90), Covington Bapt. Assn. (chmn. ch. minister rels. com.). Home: Fort Riley, Kans. Died July 27, 2007.

HARRISON, HELEN HERRE, writer, volunteer, advocate; b. Harrisburg, Pa., Aug. 23, 1946; d. Edward Albert Herre Jr. and Rebecca Irene (Allen) Webster; (stepfather) Donald Steele Webster; m. Alfred Craven Harrison Jr., Apr. 4, 1970; children: Edward Alfred, Amy Ruth Harrison Sanchez AB, U. Calif., Berkeley, 1968. Writer St. Martin's Press, from 1976. Author: The Premature Baby Book: A Parent's Guide for Coping and Caring in the First Years, 1983; edited: Parent to Parent Newsletter, 1978-80, Support Lines, 1984; contbg. column for Twins Mag., 1984-88; editorial adv. bd. Twins Mag., 1988—. Mem. Phi Beta Kappa. Home: Berkeley, Calif. Died July 4, 2015.

HART, ELDON CHARLES, educator; b. Plain City, Utah, Mar. 1, 1915; s. Charles Walter and Mildred (England) H.; m. Julina Smith, June 8, 1938; children: Eldon, Julina, Mildred, Lewis. BA, Brigham Young U., 1938; BS, U. Ill., 1939, MA, 1940, PhD, 1963. Cert. flight instr. FAA; cert. repairman FAA. Coll. adminstr. Ricks Coll., Rexburg, Idaho, 1940-80; physics libr. U. Ill., Urbana, 1961-64; pres., instr. Aero Technicians, Inc., Rexburg, from 1972. Adminstr. Authorized Prometric Tsting Ctr., FAA Airframe and Powerplant Mechanic & Avionics Technicians Sch.; fin. adminstr. Hart Enterprises and Aero Technicians, Inc. Mem. Rotary Internat. Republican. Mem. Lds Ch. Home: Rexburg, Idaho. Died Jan. 27, 2007.

HART, RICHARD WESLEY, religious organization administrator, pastor; b. Greensboro, NC, Feb. 21, 1933; s. Shelly Monroe and Virginia (Boaz) H.; m. 1954; (div. May 1969); children: Richard Wesley Jr., Larry Earl, Howard Clayton; m. Shirleen Atkins Chance, Aug. 16, 1997. BDiv, Toccoa Falls Coll., Ga., 1951; DDiv, Evang. Christian Sem., 1966. Regional dir. Am. Evang. Christian Chs., Fontana, Calif., 1958-66; pres. Evang. Christian Chs., San Bernardino, Calif., 1966-83; founder, dir. Reidsville (N.C.) Urban Ministry, from 1983. Mem. Rep. Nat. Com., Washington, 1991—; establisher AGAD Scholarship Fund, 1992. Mem. Am. Vets. Avocation: coin and old currency collector. My aim in life has always been to set specific goals and formulate a plan to reach those goals and to listen to others whose views may differ from mine-but from whose views I may be able to increase my own knowledge. Died Feb. 26, 2007.

HART, ROBERT L., data processing executive; b. Yreka, Calif., July 21, 1932; s. Victor W. Hart. BA, U. Calif., Berkeley, 1954. Sr. programmer Calif. Farm Ins. Co., Berkeley, 1958-60; mgr. data processing City of Oakland, Calif., 1960-61, Roseburg (Oreg.) Lumber Co., 1962-77, Cascade Wood Products, White City, Oreg., from 1978. Served to lt. USN, 1955-58. Mem. Assn. Systems Mgmt. Home: Roseburg, Oreg. Died May 22, 2007.

HARTMAN, ARTHUR ADAIR, international business consultant; b. Flushing, Queens, Mar. 12, 1926; s. Joel Hartman; m. Donna Van Dyke Ford, 1949; children: David, John, Ben, Sarah. AB, Harvard U., 1947; postgrad., Law Sch., 1947-48. Econ. officer ECA, Paris, 1948-52; mem. U.S. del. European Army Conf., Paris, 1952-54; polit.-mil. officer Paris/USRO, 1954-55, Saigon, 1956-58; internat. affairs officer Econ. Orgn. Affairs Sect., Bur. European Affairs, Dept. State, 1958-61, staff asst. to undersec. for econ. affairs, 1961-62, spl. asst., 1962-63; chief econ. sect. Am. Embassy, London, 1963-67; spl. asst. and staff dir. to undersec. Dept. State, 1967-69, dep. dir. for coordination, 1969-72; dep. chief of mission and minister counselor U.S. Mission to Common Market, Brussels, 1972-74; asst. sec. for European affairs Dept. State, Washington, 1974-77; U.S. ambassador to France Paris, 1977-81; U.S. ambassador to Soviet Union Moscow, 1981-87; cons. APCO Consulting Group, Washington, from 1989. Bd. dirs. ITT Hartford Ins. Co., Dreyfus Funds, Ford Meter Box Co., Lawter Internat.; chmn. Barings' First NIS Regional Investment Fund. Bd. dirs. French-Am. Found.; former pres. bd. overseers Harvard U. With U.S. Army Air Corp, 1944-46. Mem. French Legion of Honor (officer), Coun. on Fgn. Rels. Home: Washington, DC. Died Mar. 16, 2015.

HARTNETT, THOMAS D., psychiatrist; b. Chgo., Mar. 4, 1933; m. Anna E. Hartnett. BS, Loyola U., 1955; MD, U. Ottawa, Ont., Can., 1959. Diplomate Am. Bd. Psychiatry and Neurology. Acting chief, dept. psychiatry Cochran Vets. Hosp., St. Louis, 1965-67; instr. psychiatry St. Louis U., 1965-72; asst. dir. dept. of psychiatry Jewish Hosp., St. Louis, 1967-76; instr. psychiatry St. Louis U., 1965-72, asst. clin. prof. psychiatry, 1972-78, assoc. clin. prof. psychiatry, from 1978; pvt. practice St. Louis from 1965; asst. dir. dept. psychiatry Compton Heights Hosp., St. Louis from 1991. Attending physician Compton Heights Hosp., 1991—, Barnes Hosp., 1994—; St. Mary's Health Ctr., 1990—; cons. St. Louis U. Hosp., 1965—. Capt. U.S. Army, 1961-62. Mem. Am. Psychiat. Assn. (life), Am. Psychoanalytic Assn., St. Louis Psychoanalytic Soc. (pres.), Mo. State Med. Assn. Avocation: grandchildren. Died Jan. 15, 2007.

HARTWELL, DAVID GEDDES, publishing consultant, educator, writer, anthologist; b. Salem, Mass., July 10, 1941; s. Henry Geddes and Constance Elizabeth (Nash) H.; m Patricia Lee Wolcott, Aug. 30, 1969 (div. 1992); m. Kathryn E. Cramer, Mar. 29, 1997; children: Alison Wolcott Hartwell, Geoffrey Solan, Peter Henry Cramer Hartwell, Elizabeth Cramer Hartwell. BA, Williams Coll., 1963; MA with distinction, Colgate U., 1965; PhD in Comparative Medieval Lit., Columbia U., 1973. Ptnr. Dragon Press, 1973-78, propr., from 1978. Cons. sci. fiction editor New Am. Libr., 1971-73, Berkley Pub./G.P. Putnam & Sons, 1973-78, G.K. Hall & Co., 1975-86; cons. sci. fiction editor Tor Books, 1984-95, sr. editor, 1995-2016; editor-in-chief Berkley Sci. Fiction, 1978; instr. Stevens Inst. Tech., 1973-76, Clarion Sci. Fiction Writing Workshop, Seattle, 1984, 86, 90; vis. prof. Harvard U., 1987, 88, 89, 90, 91, 92, 93, NYU, spring 1993; dir. sci. fiction Pocket Books/Simon & Schuster, 1978-83, Arbor House, 1984-88, William Morrow, 1988-91; co-pub. Entwhistle Books, 1967-82; cons. Waldenbooks Otherworlds Club, 1983-84; cons. sci. fiction Book-of-the-Month Club, 1989; judge Readeroon Small Press Awards, 1989; adminstrv. cons. Turner Tomorrow Awards, 1990-91; with adminstrn. World Fantasy Awards, World Fantasy Conv., 1975—; with adminstrn. Philip K. Dick Awards, 1982-92, chmn., 1993—. Author: Age of Wonders, 1984, revised, expanded edit., 1996; editor: (with L.W. Currey) The Battle of the Monsters, 1977, The Dark Descent, 1987 (pub. as 3 vols. The Color of Evil, The Medusa in the Shield, A Fabulous Formless Darkness, 1991-92, World Fantasy Award Best Anthology 1988), The World Treasury of Science Fiction, 1988, (with Kathryn Cramer) Christmas Ghosts, 1988, The Spirits of Christmas, 1989, Ascent of Wonder, 1994, (with assistance of Kathryn Cramer) Masterpieces of Fantasy and Enchantment, 1988, Masterpieces of Fantasy and Wonder, 1989, Foundations of Fear, 1992 (pub. as 3 vols. Shadows of Fear, Visions of Fear, Worlds of Fear, 1994), Christmas Stars, 1992, Christmas Forever, 1993 (World Fantasy award nominee Best Anthology 1994), (with Glenn Grant) Northern Stars, 1994 (Aurora award nominee Best Other Work in English 1994), Christmas Magic, 1994, The Screaming Skull, 1994, (with Milton Wolf) Visions of Wonder, 1996, Years Best, SF 1996, Years Best SF #3, 1998, The Science Fiction Century, 1997, Year's Best SF #3, 1998, The Space Opera Renasissance, 2006; pub. N.Y. Review of Sci. Fiction, 1988-; sci. fiction reviewer, columnist Crawdaddy, 1968-74; sci. fiction reviewer Locus, 1971-73; editor Cosmos, 1977-78; editor, pub. The Little Mag., 1965-88; contbr. essays and revs. to lit. publs. Hugo award nominee for Best Sci. Fiction Editor, 1982, 83, 84, 87, 88, 89, 90, 98, for Best semi-Pro Mag. (The New York Rev. of Sci. Fiction), 1989, 90, 91, 92, 93, 94, 95, 96, 97, World Fantasy award nominee, Spl. award, 1977, 87, 88; Sci. Fiction Chronicle Poll winner for Best Editor Books, 1987, 88, 89, others. Mem. Internat. Assn. for the Fantastic in the Arts, Modern Lang. Assn., PEN Am. Ctr., Sci. Fiction Rsch. Assn., Coun. of Editors of Learned Jours., Internat. Assn. for Fantastic in the Arts. Unitarian Universalist. Avocations: folk guitar, book collecting. Died Jan. 20, 2016.

HARVEY, DENISE ELAINE, secondary school educator; b. Marceline, Mo., Aug. 26, 1959; d. Wayne Lee and Karen Beth (Jones) Drake; m. Timothy Edward Harvey, July 25, 1981; children: Joshua Timothy, Cierra Denise. BS in English Edn., N.E. Mo. State U., 1981, MA, 1986. Cert. tchr. and libr., Mo. Tchr. LaPlata (Mo.) High Sch., 1981-82, Macon (Mo.) R-I High Sch., 1982-98, Shelby County R-IV Schs., Shelbina, Mo., from 1998. Instr. Moberly Area (Mo.) C.C., 1992—; libr. Macon Elem. Sch., 1992, 94. Active tchr., youth sponsor Clarence (Mo.) Christian Ch., 1982—, dir. vacation Bible sch., 1990-91. Named one of Outstanding Young Women Am., 1984; recipient Tchr. Appreciation award Mo. Scholars Acad., 1994. Mem. Nat. Coun. Tchrs. English, Mo. Coun. Tchrs. English, Mo. State Tchrs. Assn., South Shelby Tchrs. Assn., Delta Kappa Gamma. Republican. Avocations: water-skiing, crafts, reading, writing. Home: Clarence, Mo. Died Dec. 30, 2006.

HARVEY, ROY SEARS, oil company executive; b. Iconium, Mo., Nov. 3, 1920; s. Roland Roy and Ruth Anna (Sears) H.; m. Eleanor L. Striegel, Sept. 4, 1949; children: Vance, Kala, Shane. BS, Kans. State U., 1948. Jr. clk. Stanolind Oil & Gas, Ulysses, Kans., 1948-51, Standard Oil & Gas, Hobbs, N.Mex., 1948-51; office mgr. B&M Svc. Co., Hobbs, 1951-69; sec.-treas. D.C. Well Svc., INc., Denver City, Tex., 1969-88, pres., from 1988. Mem. Lions, Elks, Masons, Shriners, Moose, Am. Legion, VFW. Republican. Presbyterian. Avocation: coin collecting/numismatics. Home: Hobbs, N.Mex. Died Dec. 5, 2006.

HASEN, IRWIN HANAN, cartoonist; b. NYC, July 8, 1918; s. Jack and Serena (Weinberg) H. Student, NAD, 1938-40, Art Student League, NYC, 1939-40. Creator: cartoon strip The Goldbergs; co-creator: cartoon strip Dondi, 1955—1986 Served with AUS, 1944-46. Mem. Nat. Cartoonist Soc., Comics Council. Jewish. Home: New York, NY. Died Mar. 13, 2015.

HASTEN, RALPH GERALD, minister, protective services official; b. Mineola, Tex., June 18, 1926; s. Judge Roberts and Rose Chap Hasten; m. Wynona Cauthen Hasten, Aug. 24, 1947; children: Deborah Ann Gagne, David Ward. BA, Southwestern U., 1951; ThM, So. Meth. U., 1954. Pastoral appts., Cen. and S.W. Tex., 1951—63; field rep. Presbyn. Min.'s Fund, Ft. Worth, 1963—66, Min.'s Life and Casualty Union, Houston, 1966—69; vocat. rehab. counselor Tex. Rehab. Commn., Houston, 1969—91; dep. sheriff Harris County Sheriff's Dept., Houston, 1991—97, sgt., from 1997. Part-time pastor United Meth. Ch., Houston, 1966—91. Author: (book) Grampoetry for Grandkids of All Ages, 1997, More Grampoetry for Grandkids of All Ages, 2000, JD's Joyful Jailhouse Jawings, 2001. Chaplain CAP, Houston, 1970—72, Goodwill Industries, Inc., Houston, 1978—81. Sgt. USMC, 1944—47. Mem.: Fraternal Order of Police (cert. mem.). Democrat. United Methodist. Avocations: horticulture, writing, hunting, fishing, family-centered activities. Home: Houston, Tex. Died May 20, 2007.

HASTINGS, CONSTANCE MOORE, editor, consultant; b. Chgo., July 12, 1941; d. James Edward and Edna (Ellis) Moore; m. Donald Winslow Hastings, Aug. 25, 1962; children: Peter Winslow, Laura Robinson. BA in English, U. Tenn., 1979. With JBF Assocs., Knoxville, Tenn., 1985, U. Tenn.-Energy Environ. and Resources Rsch. Ctr., Knoxville, Tenn., 1982-84. Ind. contr. various cos. including Dept. Energy, Martin Marietta Energy Systems, Inc., Oak Ridge Nat. Lab., Simon and Schuster, Halliburton Nus Environ. Corp., Bechtel Nat., Inc., Sci. Applications Internat. Corp., U. of Tenn. Press, Oak Ridge Assocs. Univs. Author: The SAVVY Cook, 1989. Mgr. Practical Conf. on Communication, Knoxville, 1982. LMem. Soc. for Tech. Communication (East Tenn. chpt., sr. mem., pres. 1989-90, v.p. 1988-89, program mgr. 1979-80, Disting. brochure category 1986, Chpt. Achievement award 1989). Avocations: corporate writing, gourmet cooking. Died Mar. 1, 2007.

HASTINGS, JACK BYRON, artist; b. Kennett, Mo., Nov. 16, 1925; m. Arlyn Ende; m. Dorothy Furlong (div.); 1 child, Dorian Hastings. Student, La. State U., 1947—49, Escuela Pintura y Escultura, Mex. City, 1949. One-man shows include Delgado Mus. Art., New Orleans, 1958, Barone Gallery, NYC, 1960, Fine Arts Ctr., Cheekwood, Nashville, 1974, exhibited in group shows at Orleans Gallery, New Orleans, 1957—59; founding mem. Orleans Gallery, New Orleans; Exhibited in group shows at Georg Jensen, NYC, 1962, Signature Shop and Galleries, Atlanta, 1979, executed sculpture, An Environmental Garden, Welcome Ctr., Chattanooga, 1983, sunscreen sculpture exterior, Free Med. U. West Berlin, 1960, bronze sculpture, Pub. Schs. NYC, 1961—63. With, carved cement fountain El Presidio Civic Plz. Tucson, 1970; with, fountain Vol. State Cmty. Coll., Gallatin, Tenn., 1982; atrium mobile sculpture TVA, 1986, metal sculpture watts bar facility, 1987. Mem.: Tenn. Artist Craftsmen's Assn. Died July 23, 2013.

HASTINGS, JOHN JACOB, writer, lyricist, consultant, activist; b. Walla Walla, Wash., Oct. 7, 1953; s. Frederic William and Margaret Mary (McElliggot) Hastings. AA, Walla Walla C.C., 1976; BFA, Ea. Wash. U., 1979. Mgr. Monroe Cigar Co., Chgo., 1980-83; prof. Harry Truman C.C., Chgo., 1981; farmer Touchet, Wash., 1986-99. Author: Four Score Seven, 1995; (poetry) Playing Possum, 1995, Back on the Stack, 1998, Linda's Lullaby in Heaven, 1998, Penultimate Glory, 1998, Excellent annus, 1998, Eiriecalm, 2000, Moods, Anew, 2001; lyricist: Hilltop Records, Hollywood, Calif., 1997-98. Moderate Nat. Orgn. Dems., 1975-2005; precinct com. mem. Walla Walla (Wash.) County Dem. Ctrl. Com., 1992-99, mem. Dem. Nat. Com., 1998, 2005, Dem. Senatorial Campaign, 1998, 2000, 01, 02, 05, Westchester County Dem. Party, 2000-2005; activist Peace Movement, Walla Walla and Bellingham, Wash., 1977-86; mem. MADD, ACLU. Recipient Man of the Yr., Am. Biog. Inst., 2006. Mem. Nat. Geographic Soc., Nat. Trust for Hist. Preservation, Walla Walla Pioneers Hist. Soc. (faculty mem.), Nat. Assn. Women in Arts (assoc.), Smithsonian Instn., Libr. Congress (assoc.), Ea. Wash. U. Alumni, Nat. Parks and Conservation Assn. Wilson Ctr., Handyman's Club Am., Nature Conservancy, Hastings Art Entertainment Ltd. (pres, C.L.O.), N.Y. Acad. Polit. Sci., N.Y. Acad. Sci., Metro. Registry, Manhattan Club. Roman Catholic. Avocations: conservationist, tree planter, advocate, writing. Died Mar. 12, 2007.

HAUGEN, JUANITA HARRIET, small business owner, school system administrator; b. San Francsico, Nov. 17, 1937; d. Harry and Louina Juanita Sakajian; m. Gilbert Russell, Nov. 22, 1961 (dec. 1990); children: Heather, Heidi, Hilary, Holly. BA, U. So. Calif., 1959. Tchg. asst. U. So. Calif., LA, 1960-61; vol. Palo Alto and Pleasanton Schs., 1961—81; probation officer L.A. County Probation Dept., 1981—82; intern Office Alameda County Supt. Schs., Hayward, Calif., 1982-83; owner Jewelry by Jonne', Pleasanton, Calif., from 1987. Trainer, presenter, cons. on parenting, 1991—; pres. Calif. Suburban Sch. Dists., 1991-93; apptd. to Calif. Commn. on Tchr. Credentialling, 1992-96; sch. trustee, 1979—; cons. civility responsibility svc. learning. Current lay reader St. Clare's Episcopal Ch.; bd. govs. YMCA, Pleasanton, 1988; edn. commn. State Commn. Calif., from 1998, steering com. Named 15th Dist. Woman of Yr., Calif. Assembly, 1989, Woman of Distinction Soroptomist Internat., 1990, Pleasanton Woman of Yr., 2005; recipient svc. award AAUW Edn. Found., 1990, Activist award Pleasanton C. of C., 2005. Mem. AAUW, Calif. Elected Women's Assn. for Edn. and Rsch. (pres. 2005-06), Assn. Bd. Dirs. (mem. nat. sch. bd. 1998—), Calif. Sch. Bd. Assn. (pres. 1997, mem. nat. assessment governing bd. 1998-2004), So. Calif. Alumni Assn. (scholarship chmn. East Bay Chpt. 1965-95), Alpha Omicron Pi (past pres. San Jose-Peninsula alumnae chpt., founder, 1st pres. Palo Alto chpt., Amador Valley Rose award 1967) Republican. Episcopalian. Avocations: music, reading, crafts. Home: Pleasanton, Calif. Died Mar. 5, 2007.

HAUGER, HAROLD KEITH, lawyer; b. Pitts., May 28, 1945; s. Harold N. and Ruth A. (Irwin) Hauger. BS, U. Pitts., 1968; JD, Duquesne U., 1973. Bar: Pa. 1973, Fla. 1977, U.S. Dist. Ct. (we. dist.) Pa. 1974, U.S. Supreme Ct. 1979, U.S. Patent Office 1982, U.S. Trademark Office 1982, Calif. 1986. Assoc. Martin and Finnegan, Monroeville, Pa., 1974-77; sole practice Pitts., from 1977. Agt. Lawyers Title Ins. Co. Past bd. dirs. Turtle Creek Valley Mental Health/Mental Retardation, Inc.; v.p. Greenridge Civic Assn.; active Greater Irwin Bd. Realtors. Mem. ABA (real estate, intellectual property, legal econs. sects.), Pa. Bar Assn. (intellectual property sect.), Fla. Bar Assn. (by-laws com.), Allegheny County Bar Assn., Westmoreland County Bar Assn. (chmn. unauthorized practice of law com.), Assn. Trial Lawyers Am., Pa. Trial Lawyers Assns., Patent Law Assn. Pitts., Calif. Bar Assn. (intellectual property sect.), Am. Patent Law Assn., Pitts. High Tech. Coun., ASME, Engrs. Soc. We. Pa., Rotary (past bd. dirs., coms.), Jaycees (pres. 1977-78, exhausted rooster), Pitts. Ski Club, We. Pa. Corvette Club, Delta Theta Phi. Home: Tampa, Fla. Died Dec. 23, 2006.

HAUGLAND, JOHN CLARENCE, emeritus university vice chancellor; b. Superior, Wis., Nov. 29, 1929; s. Christ R. and Molla (Haugen) H.; m. Joan C. Palm, Sept. 23, 1950; children— Debra Ann, Gregg John. BS, Wis. State U., Superior, 1954; postgrad., U. Wis., 1955; MA, U. Minn., 1958, PhD, 1961. Tchr. pub. schs., Manitowoc, Wis., 1954-56; with J.C. Penney Co., Sioux City, Ia., 1956-57; adminstrv. fellow, faculty U. Minn., 1957-61, tchr., asst. grad. dean, 1963-65; faculty Wis. State U., Superior, 1961-63, 66—, dean letters and sci., 1966-67, vice chancellor acad. affairs, dean of faculty, 1967-89, vice chancellor emeritus, from 1989. Postdoctoral acad. adminstrn. internship Am. Council Edn., U. Md., 1965-66 Contbr. articles profl. jours. Mem. Douglas County Overall Econ. Devel. Plan Com., 1968-70; Alderman Superior City Council, 1971-73; Bd. dirs. Wis. Community Devel. Inst., Superior YMCA, Catholic Charities Bur. Served with U.S. Army, 1948-50, 50-51. Recipient U. Minn. Grad. Sch. grant, 1960, Wis. State U.-Superior research grant, 1962 Mem. Superior C. of C. Home: Superior, Wis. Died Mar. 19, 2015.

HAUSER, RAYMOND JOSEPH, management consultant, investor, educator; b. Buffalo, Aug. 28, 1930; s. Leroy Joseph and Margaret Ellen (Joyce) H.; m. Marie F. Pfohl-Heimiller, Mar. 4, 1952; children: Donna Rae, Hauser Gordon. BS in Aerospace Engring., Northrop Univ., 1955; M in Engring. Edn., Chapman Coll., 1968; PhD, Calif. Western U., 1975; postgrad., various colls. Cert. instr. U.S. Govt.; cert. radiol. monitoring specialist. Project engr., engring. mgr., sr. research/devel. engr. various aerospace cos., 1954-69; prof. engring. Calif. Poly. U., San Luis Obispo, 1969-83; pvt. practice estate conservatorship, mgmt. Santa Maria, Calif., from 1980; prin. Tech. Analysis Services Cons., Santa Maria, from 1985. Regional agt. United Farm Real Estate Corp., Carmel, Calif., 1982-83; faculty group leader internat. edn. program Calif. State Univ. and Colls., Europe, 1974. Newspaper science columnist The Decatur (Ala.) Daily, 1964-66; contbr. approximately 50 aerospace reports and papers to profl. jours.; designed own residence, 1983-84. Trustee, charter mem. Presdl. Task Force, Washington, 1982—; mem. parish council various Cath. parishes, N.Y. and Ala., 1964-67. Served to 1st lt. U.S. Army, 1951-53, with Res., 1953-58. NSF fellow at U. Ill, 1978, at Stanford, 1979; NASA fellow, 1977; Lilly Found. fellow, 1975; others. Mem. Nat. Defense Preparedness Assn., Soc. for Indsl. and Applied Math., Nat. Soc. for the Study of Edn., Am. Soc. for Aeronautics and Astronautics, AAAS, N.Y. Acad. Scis., ASME, Am. Math. Assn., Am. Soc. Profl. Cons., Internat. Platform Assn., Nat. Writers Assn., Am. Legion. Lodges: Elks (membership chmn. Carmel club 1983), KC, Mil. Order World Wars (membership com. chmn. Carmel club 1983, adjutant exec. com. 1983). Roman Catholic. Avocations: technical reading, writing, travel, parachuting, swimming. Home: Santa Maria, Calif. Died Nov. 18, 2006.

HAVENS, CARL BRADFORD, retired research scientist; b. Hope, Mich., May 30, 1918; s. Boyd L. and Mary Ada (Gransden) H.; m. Grace Jeannette Cummins, Oct. 1, 1936 (div. Apr. 1990); children: David Carl, Sandra Jeanette, Paul Lewis. BS, U. Mich., 1944. Chem. engr. Dow Chem. Co., Midland, Mich., 1944-47, group leader, 1948-58, plant supt. Bay City, Mich., 1959-61, rsch. mgr. Cleve., 1961-65, Fresno, Calif., 1966-76, rsch. scientist Granville, Ohio, 1976-86. 55 U.S. patents and 100 fgn. patents in field; contbr. articles to profl. jours. Republican. Presbyterian. Avocations: skiing, swimming, fishing, chess, investing. Home: Palos Verdes Peninsula, Calif. Died June 23, 2007.

HAWK, CAROLINE WINN, manufacturing executive; b. Columbus, Ohio, Oct. 2, 1933; d. Thomas Parsons Winn and Gussie (Bailey) Raymond; m. David Nelson Hawk, June 13, 1954; children: Kathleen Ivy, Cynthia Beatrice Hawk Black. Student, Ohio State U., 1951-54. Owner, mgr. Hawk's Card & Hobby Shop, Canton, Ohio, 1958-67; asst. to v.p advt. Citizen's Savs. Assn., Canton, 1967-70; gift buyer Stern & Mann Co., Canton, 1970-72; sales rep. Mut. N.Y. Ins. Co., Akron, Ohio, 1972-75; pres., owner Timber Line Products, Inc., Sugarcreek, Ohio, from 1975; distbr. Lincoln Logs, Ltd. Log Homes, Sugarcreek, from 1979; pres. Dach Med. Claims Svc., Inc., Dover, Ohio, from 1992. Sec.-treas. Wood-B-Right Inc., Massillon, Ohio, 1991—. Arbitrator Better Bus. Bur. Mem. Am. Bus. Women's Assn. (treas., Boss of Yr. award 1978), Ohio C. of C., Tuscarawas County C. of C., Tuscarawas City Home Builders Assn. Lutheran. Home: Sugarcreek, Ohio. Died Nov. 3, 2006.

HAWKINS, DENIS FRANK, obstetrician, gynecologist, educator; b. London, Apr. 4, 1929; married. BSc, Univ. Coll., London, 1949; PhD, 1952; MBBS, U. Coll. Hosp. Med. Sch., 1955; MD, Boston U., 1967; DSc, U. London, 1967. Instr. pharmacology Harvard Med. Sch., Boston, 1957—59; sr. house officer, registrar in obstetrics and gynecology Hammersmith Hosp., 1959—61; lectr. obstetrics and gynecology Univ. Coll. Hosp. Med. Sch., 1961—65; prof., chmn. obstetrics and gynecology Boston U. Sch. Medicine, 1965—68; sr. lectr., reader obstetrics and gynecology Inst. Obstetrics and Gynecology, U. London, 1968—79; prof. obstetric therapeutics U. London, from 1979. Author: Human Fertility Control, 1979; editor: Obstetric Therapeutics, 1974, Gynaecological Therapeutics, 1981, Drugs and Pregnancy, 1983; mem. editorial bd. Brit. Jour. Pharmacology, 1970—76; contbr. articles to jours. Fellow: Am. Coll. Obstetricians and Gynecologists, Royal Coll. Obstetricians and Gynecologists; mem.: Savage Club (London), Hellenic Soc., Brit. Pharmacological Soc., Brit. Med. Assn. Avocations: archaeology, sculpting. Died Sept. 26, 2007.

HAWKINS, ELIZABETH ANNE, clergy; b. Peoria, Ill., Apr. 24, 1957; d. William Joseph and Carol (Harper) H. BA, Millikin U., 1979; MDiv., St. Paul Sch. of Theology, Kansas City, Mo., 1982; post grad., Baptist Med. Ctr., Kansas City, Mo., 1986. Ordained to ministry Presbyn. Ch., 1985. Dir. christian edn. Emerson Park Christian Ch., Kansas City, Kans., 1979-81; asst. minister Parkville Presbyn. Ch., Kansas City, 1981-86; chaplain resident St. Luke's Hosp., Kansas City, 1982-83, Baptist Med. Ctr., Kansas City, 1983-86; supr. pastoral tng. Allegheny Gen. Hosp., Pitts., 1986-89; interim min. Rennerdale Presbyn. Ch., Pitts., 1988-89; mgr., supr. pastoral care and edn. Allegheny Gen. Hosp., Pitts., from 1989. Adj. faculty Pitts. Theol. Sem., 1987-92; preceptor Duquesne U. Pastoral Min., Pitts., 1989-92; group facilitator Bethel Park Nursing Home, Pitts., 1989-93; adj. faculty Sts. Cyril & Methodius Byzantine Cath. Sem., 1994—. Mem. Internat. Assn. of Women Ministers (past pres.), Soc. of Chaplains (Pa.), Assn. Clin. Pastoral Edn. Democrat. Presbyterian. Avocations: cooking, needlecrafts, reading, attending cultural events. Home: Springfield, Ill. Died Dec. 27, 2006.

HAWKINS, FRANCES PAM, business educator; b. Woodland, Ala., Dec. 2, 1945; d. Lowell M. and Bernice E. Mcmanus; children: Scott Cummings, Veronica Lovvorn. AS in Bus., Southern Union C.C., 1989; BS in Bus. Edn., Auburn U., 1990, MEd, 1992. Ptnr. C & S Pharmacy, Roanoke, Ala., 1974—90; bus. office tech. instr. West Ga. Tech. Coll., Lagrange, Ga., from 1991. Bus. tech., divsn. chair West Ga. Tech. Coll., Lagrange, 1999—2003, bus. office tech. adv. com. mem., from 1992, chairperson libr. com., from 2001; mem. tech. in edn. com. Ga. Dept. Edn., Atlanta, from 2001. Team leader March of Dimes, LaGrange, from 1998. Mem.: Ga. Bus. Edn. Assn., So. Bus. Edn. Assn., Nat. Bus. Edn. Assn. (com. mem. 2001), Auburn Alumni Assn., Phi Beta Lambda (local advisor from 1992, sec. 1997—2001, pres. Ga. Found. Inc. from 1998, state advisor 1999—2005, nat. bd. dirs. future bus. leaders Am. from 2001, exec. dir. from 2005). Methodist. Home: Roanoke, Ala. Died Dec. 8, 2006.

HAWKINS, LIONEL ANTHONY, life insurance company executive; b. Jackson, Miss., June 20, 1933; s. Lionel A. and Ruth (Hanna) H.; m. Anne Giesecke, June 29, 1958; children: Lionel A. III, John Randall, Hollie A. Miezio. Student, U. Tex., Arlington, 1951-54, George Washington U., 1957-59. Ins. agt., asst. mgr. Mut. Ins. of N.Y., Washington, 1959-63; regional supr. and mgr., agy. mgr. Kansas City (Mo.) Life Ins., 1963-69, gen. agt., 1971-73; agy. dir. Jefferson Nat., Indpls., 1969-70, Allied Life Ins., Birmingham, Ala., 1970-71; agy. dir., regional v.p. Mut. Trust Life Ins., Oakbrook, Ill., 1973-87; field v.p., dir. agys. Am. Gen. Life Ins. Co., Oakbrook Terrace, Ill., 1987-92; regional v.p. Fidelity and Guaranty Life Ins. Co., Plano, Ill., 1993-94; ins. cons., from 1994. Mem. Merit Commn. Kendall County Sheriff's Dept., Ill., 1993-94, Marion County (Ark.) Dem. Com. 1st lt. U.S. Army, 1955-59. Mem. Nat. Assn. Life Underwriters, Gen. Agts. and Mgrs. Assn., Western Agy. Officers Assn. (bd. dirs. 1983-87), Flippin Area C. of C. (bd. dirs.). Democrat. Avocations: hunting, fishing. Died Apr. 25, 2007.

HAWS, ZADA M., retired elementary school educator, alcohol and drug abuse services professional; b. Colo., July 2, 1922; d. George J. and Nada V. McGill; m. Robert J. Haws, Jan. 26, 1944 (dec.); children: Nikki Lovell, Sidney Pennington, Leslie Rothbaum. BEd, Weber State U., 1964; EdS in Adminstrn., Bringham Young U., 1977, EDD, 1986. Tchr. Blytheville Schs., Blytheville, Ark., 1956—59; tchr., cmty. sch. dir. Ogden City Schs., Ogden, Utah, 1959—88; ret., 1988. Prevention specialist Dept. Human Svcs., Ogden, Utah, from 1988; presenter Crystal Crest Awards Weber State U., from 2000. Contbr. articles to profl. jours. Pres. Utah Assn. of Adult, Cmty. & Continuing Edn., from 1989; mem. Utah State Prevention Specialists, Utah Child Care Coalition, SW Reg. Ctr. Safe & Drug-Free Schs. Adv. Bd.; exec. bd. mem. United Way; sec. Utah Fedn. Youth Inc., from 1995; mem. bd. Children Aftersch. Resource Edn. Sv cs.; mem. Utah Foster Care Bd., Utah State U. Extension Adv. Bd Edn. & Health Lifestyles Com.; region II rep. Utah Assn. Cmty. Edn., 1975—90; past. chair., mem. Women's Coun. Stewart Rehab. Ctr., 1983—2005; mem. Weber Mental Health Youth Adv. Bd., Renaissance Adv. Bd., 1985, Weber Mentally Retarded/Developmentally Disadvantaged Coord. Coun., 1980, Weber County Resource Coord. Coun., 1990; mem. Continuing Edn. Adv. Bd. Weber State U., from 1995, mem. Families Alive Adv. Bd.; mem. YWCA Bd., McKay Dee Hosp. Found., 2001; chair Midtown Health Ctr. Bd., 1995—2003; mem. Cmty. Family Resource Bd.; com. co-chair Ogden Home for the Holidays, from 1999; mailing chair Women's Coun. Breast Cancer Conf.; pres. Altrusa Club Ogden, from 1990; mem. nat. coun. cmty. edn. State Assn. NC SCEA; mem. nat. conf. NASV; mem. Egyptian Found. Bd., Weber County Nutrition Bd., Weber Basin Job Corp. Adv. Bd., Mission 2000 Health & Welfare, Mission 2000 Edn.; chair Parent Connection, 1993—96; founder Weber Human Svcs. Found., from 1996; chair Coalition Ednl. Resources, from 1995; mem. Women Mgmt. Ogden C. of C.; mem. Ogden City Utilities Budget Adv. Bd., Ogden Police Budget Adv. Bd. Recipient Utah Adult Educator Yr., 1974, Utah Cmty. Edn. Profl. award, 1983, Jim Burgon Mem. award, Utah Assn. Adult Cmty. and Continuing Edn., 1986, Carnation Bowl award, Utah Commn. Vols., 1987, Mountain Plains Adult Edn. Assn. award, 1988, Woman Yr., Your Cmty. Connection, 1989, Cmty. Svc. award, Utah Assn. Adult, Cmty. & Continuing Edn., 1994. Mem.: Nat. Cmty. Edn. Assn., League Women Voters, Phi Delta Kappa, Alpha Delta Kappa (pres. from 1978). Home: Ogden, Utah. Died June 19, 2007.

HAY, JESS THOMAS, retired finance company executive; b. Forney, Tex., Jan. 22, 1931; s. George and Myrtle Hay; m. Betty Jo Peacock, l95l (dec. 2005); children: Deborah Hay Spradley, Patricia Hay. BBA, So. Meth. U., 1953, JD magna cum laude, 1955. Bar: Tex. Assoc. Locke, Purnell, Boren, Laney & Neely, 1955-61, partner, 1961-65; pres., chief exec. officer Lomas Fin. Corp., Dallas, 1965-69, chmn. bd., chief exec. officer, 1969-94; chmn. bd., chief exec. officer, trustee Lomas & Nettleton Mortgage Investors, 1969-92; chmn., CEO Capstead Mortgage Corp. (formerly Lomas Mortgage Corp.), 1985-91. Chmn. HCB Enterprises Inc, 1996-2007; bd. dirs. Hilltop Holding, Inc., Exxon Mobil Corp., AT&T (SBC Comm.) Trinity Industries Inc., M Corp., Republic Fin. Svcs., Allied Fin. Co., Money Gram Internat., bd. mem., Friends Nat. World War Meml., mem. adv. bds., Briscoe Ctr. Am. History Studies, U. Tex. Austin, U. Tex. Press, John Glenn Sch. Pub. Policy Ohio State U. Former mem., nat. fin. chmn. Dem. Nat. Com., bd. trustees, governing body Southern Meth. U., former chmn. bd. regents U. Tex. Sys.; former mem. Dallas Citizens Coun., Dallas Assembly; mem. Greater Dallas Planning Coun.; mem. WWII Meml. Adv. Bd.; bd. dirs. Tex. Rsch. League, North Tex. Food Bank, Child Care Partnership Dallas, Dallas County Hist. Found.; chmn. bd. Tex. Found. for Higher Edn.; trustee Southwestern Med. Found. Recipient Disting. Svc. award, Assn. Governing Bds. Univs. and Colls., 1987, Disting. Alumnus award, Southern Meth. U., 1977, Santa Rita award, U. Tex. Sys., 1991. Mem. ABA, Dallas Bar Assn., Tex. Bar Assn., Am. Judicature Soc., Newcomen Soc. N.Am., U.S. C. of C. Methodist. Home: Dallas, Tex. Died Apr. 5, 2015.

HAYES, MARY ESHBAUGH, editor, writer; b. Rochester, NY, Sept. 27, 1928; d. William Paul and Eleanor Maude (Sievert) Eshbaugh; m. James Leon Hayes, Apr. 18, 1953; children: Pauli, Eli, Lauri Le June, Clayton, Merri Jess Bates. BA in English and Journalism, Syracuse U., NYC, 1950. With Livingston County Republican, Geneseo, NY, summers, 1947-50, mng. editor, 1949-50; reporter Aurora Advocate, Colo., 1950—52; reporter-photographer Aspen Times, Colo., 1952-53, columnist, from 1956, reporter, 1972-77, assoc. editor, 1977-89, editor-in-chief, 1989-92, contbg. editor, from 1992. Instr. Colo. Mountain Coll., 1979; Aspen corr. Reuters, from 1997. Author, editor: The Story of Aspen, 1996 (1st prize, 1996); contbg. editor: Destinations Mag., 1994—97, Aspen Mag., from 1996, Aspen Sojourner Mag., from 2005; editor: Aspen Pot Pourri, 1968 (1st prize, 1990), rev. edit., 2002 (1st prize, 2002). Recipient Living Landmark award, Aspen Hist. Soc., 2002, Art award, 2013; named Photographer, Red Brick Ctr. Mem.: Colo. Press Women's Assn. (writing award 1974—75, 1978—85, sweepstakes award for writing 1977—78, 1984—85, 1991—2003, 2d pl. award 1976, 1979, 1982—83, 1994—95, Woman of Achievement 1986), Nat. Fedn. Press Women (1st prize in writing and editing 1976—80, 1st prize in adv. photography 1998). Home: Aspen, Colo. Died Jan. 22, 2015.

HAYES, ROSEMARY, geriatrics nurse, educator; b. Cliffside Park, NJ, Aug. 19, 1928; d. George and B. Marie (Rinn) Najar. Diploma, Jersey City Sch. Nursing, 1950; BS, McMaster U., 1971; BSN, Ea. Mennonite Coll., 1976; MEd, James Madison U., 1976. RN Va. Instr. Brantford (Ont., Can.) Sch. Nursing, 1971-72, Rockingham Meml. Hosp., Harrisonburg, Va., 1972-76; instr. nursing Ea. Mennonite Coll., Harrisonburg, Va., 1976-77; instr. U. Va., Charlottesville, 1977-81; sr. clinician Med. Ctr. U. Va., Charlottesville, 1981-87; ADON Eldercare Gardens NH, Charlottesville, 1988-90; asst. DON Cedars Nursing Home, 1987-88; acting DON Eldercare Gardens NH, Charlottesville, 1988-90; educator Third Age Inc., Charlottesville, 1990-95. CNA instr. Piedmont (Va.) C.C., 1990-94. Active Area Bd. on Aging. Home: Charlottesvle, Va. Died Nov. 4, 2006.

HAYWARD, RONALD HARRY, import/export professional; b. Portland, Maine, Sept. 6, 1944; s. Philip Artell and Viola May (Maddox) H.; m. Julie Nazarewicz, Apr. 24, 1965; children: Brian Scott, Stevan Eric, Michele Capri. Student, U. Akron, 1962-64. Export traffic coord. internat. div. B.F. Goodrich Co., Akron, Ohio, 1974-75, sr. export traffic coord., 1975-80, supr. export traffic internat. div., 1980-81, supr. export traffic various divs., 1981-88; supr. export, transport RJF Internat. Corp., Fairlawn, Ohio, from 1988. Baptist. Avocations: travel, reading. Home: Tallmadge, Ohio. Died Dec. 24, 2006.

HEALY, MARY (MRS. PETER LIND HAYES), singer, actress; b. New Orleans, Apr. 14, 1918; d. John Joseph and Viola (Armbruster) H.; m. Peter Lind Hayes, Dec. 19, 1940 (dec. Apr. 1998); children: Peter Michael, Cathy Lind. Degree (hon.), St. Bonaventure U. With 20th Century Fox, Hollywood, Calif. Author: Twenty-five Minutes from Broadway, 1961; pictures and others, 1937-40; Broadway prodns. Around the World, 1943-46; (with husband) TV series Inside U.S.A, 1949, Peter and Mary Show, Star of the Family, 1952, Peter Lind Hayes Radio show, CBS, 1954-57; Broadway prodn. Who Was That Lady I Saw You With?, 1957-58, Peter Lind Hayes show, ABC-TV, 1958-59, Peter and Mary, ABC-Radio, 1959—, Peter and Mary in Las Vegas; TV-film; Star (with husband) WOR radio show, 6 yrs; TV film series Fin. Planning for Women; (with husband) Film The 5000 Fingers of Dr. T, 1953; Appeared in: (with husband) Film Peter Loves Mary, 1960, When Television Was Live, 1975; films: Second Fiddle, 1939, You Ruined My Life, 1986, Looking To Get Out with Jon Voight, 1985. Mem. Pelham Country Club. Roman Catholic. Died Feb. 3, 2015.

HEARD, ETHEL JACKSON, medical/surgical, psychiatric-mental health nurse; b. White Springs, Fla., Aug. 13, 1930; d. J.D. and Novella (Gordon) Jackson; m. Arthur John Williams, Nov. 10, 1951 (dec. Jan. 1973); children: Harold Rosendor, Harriett Williams Davis, Arthurine Williams Flemons, Janice R.; m. Laron Novell Heard, Mar. 18, 1988. Diploma, Brewster Hosp. Sch. Nursing, Jacksonville, Fla., 1952; student, Fla. A&M Coll., 1952, Calif. State U., LA, 1964-65, SW Jr. Coll., 1975. RN, Fla., Calif. Supr. nursing svc. Cheshire Nursing Home, Jacksonville; charge nurse Duval Med. Ctr., Jacksonville, Brewster Hosp.; staff nurse gen. psychiatr. unit Brentwood div. West L.A. VA Med. Ctr.; also sr. nurse rep. Recipient awards for 10, 20 and 25 yrs. svc. Mem. ANA, Calif. Nurses Assn., Fla. Nurses Assn. Home: Hawthorne, Calif. Died Aug. 22, 2007.

HEBALD, MILTON ELTING, sculptor; b. NYC, May 24, 1917; s. Nathan and Eva (Elting) H.; m. Cecile Rosner, June 10, 1938 (dec. Feb. 1998); 1 child, Margo; m. Kathleen Arc, Feb. 12, 2000. Student, Art Students League, 1927-28, Nat. Acad. Design, 1931-32, Beaux Arts Inst. Design, 1932-35. Tchr. American Artist Sch., 1940-41, Cooper Union, 1945-53, Bklyn. Mus. Art Sch., 1946-52, Skowhegan Art Sch., summers 1950-52, U. Minn., 1949, Long Beach (Calif.) State, summer 1968. Recipient 2d prize Social Security Competition, U.S. Govt. relief in Post Office, Toms River, N.J. 1940, 2d prize Wings for Victory 1942, 1st prize Bklyn. Mus. 1950, 2d prize Pa. Acad. 1951, 1st prize N.Y.C. Dept. Pub. Works for East Bronx Tb Hosp. 1953, Prix de Rome in Sculpture 1955-58); Commns. include facade Equador Pavilion, N.Y. World's Fair, 1939; trophy, Rep. Aviation Co., 1942, Turtle Tent; play sculpture, Phila., 1954, Isla Verdi Aeroport, San Juan, P.R., 1954, 16 foot bronze group, East Bronx (N.Y.), Tb Hosp, 1954; portrait bust of Archibald MacLeish, Am. Acad. Arts and Letters, 1957; bronze relief Zodiac, Pan American Terminal, Kennedy Airport, 1957-58, Ackland Meml, U. N.C., 1961, James Joyce Monument, Zurich, Switzerland, 1966, Marshall Field Meml, Sun-Times Bldg., Chgo., 1966, Shakespeare Group, Central Park, N.Y.C., 1973; heroic head C.V. Starr, Tokyo, 1974; Shakespeare relief, Oslo, Norway, 1975, Joyce Portrait, Tower Mus., Dublin, 1975, Starr Portrait, Tokyo and Hong Kong, 1975, Dancing Family group, Delora Art Ctr., St. Charles, Ill., 1979, Richard Tucker Monument, N.Y.C., 1980, Romeo and Juliet bronze, Wilshire Blvd, Los Angeles, 1981, Olympics L.A. 1984 monument, 2 bronzes, Los Angeles YMCA sculpture garden, 1986, Dancing Family group, The Great Escape Park, Lake George, N.Y., 1988, others, one-man exhbns. include, ACA Gallery, N.Y.C., 1937, 40, Grand Central Moderns, N.Y.C., 1950, 54, Schneider Gallery, Rome, Italy, 1957, Nordness Gallery, N.Y.C., 1959-71, Cheekwood Center, Nashville, 1968, 78, Mickelson Gallery, Washington, 1972, 78, Aschehoug Gallery, Oslo, 1975, Sestiere Gallery, Rome, 1975, Yares Gallery, Scottsdale, Ariz., 1975, 78, Heritage Gallery, Los Angeles, 1978, Gilman Gallery, Chgo., 1978, Harmon Gallery, Naples, Fla., 1978, 81, 84, Randall Gallery, N.Y.C., 1978, Foster Harmon Gallery Am. Art, Sarasota, Fla., 1981, Bronze Plaque 100 Anni, Scuola Artiglieriadi Bracciano, 1988, Life Size Group, Ft. Wayne, Ind., 1988; group shows include, Arte Figurativo, Rome, Italy, 1964, 67, Carnegie Inst., Pitts., 1967, Va. Mus. Fine Arts; represented permanent collections, N.Y. Acad. Arts and Letters, Notre Dame U., N.J., Phila. Mus., Whitney Mus. American Art, Yale, U. Ariz., U. N.C., Brandeis U., Columbia (S.C.) Mus. Art, Ackland Meml., Tel Aviv Mus., Israel, Nat. Portrait Gallery, Smithsonian Instn., Washington, Joyce Mus., Dublin, Oslo U., Bergan, Norway, Privatbank, others. Fellow American Acad. in Rome; mem. Annual American Group. Subject of monograph by Frank Getlein, Milton Hebald: A Studio Book, 1971, also revs. and articles. Died Jan. 5, 2015.

HECK, RICHARD FRED, chemist, retired chemistry professor; b. Springfield, Mass., Aug. 15, 1931; m. Socorro Nardo (dec. 2012). BS, UCLA, 1952, PhD in Philosophy, 1954. Postdoctoral rsch. ETH, Zurich, Switzerland; with Hercules Co., Wilmington, Del., 1957—71; prof. chemistry & biochemistry U. Delaware, 1971—89, Willis F. Harrington prof. emeritus Dept. Chemistry and Biochemistry, 1989—2015. Adj. prof. De La Salle U., Manila, 1989—2015. Recipient Lectureship named in honor, U. Delaware, 2004, Herbert C. Brown award for Creative Rsch. in Synthesis Methods, 2006; co-recipient Nobel Prize in Chemistry, The Nobel Found., 2010. Achievements include research on palladium-catalyzed cross couplings in organic synthesis. Died Oct. 9, 2015.

HECKER, LAWRENCE HARRIS, industrial hygienist; b. Detroit, July 14, 1944; s. Joseph and Rose Vivian (Harris) H.; m. Phyllis Rosalind Cohen, June 29, 1966; children: Charles Aaron, David Alan. BA in Geography and Chemistry, Wayne State U., 1965, MS in Indsl. Hygiene, 1967; MS in Air Pollution, U. Mich., 1969, PhD of Indsl. Health, 1972. Cert. indsl. hygienist Am. Bd. Indsl. Hygiene. Asst. prof. indsl. and environ. health U. Mich., Ann Arbor, 1972-78; mgr., dir. corp. indsl. hygiene Abbott Labs., North Chgo., Ill., 1978-94, dir. corp. health and safety regulatory affairs, 1994—2003; sr. cons. corp. regulatory and quality sci. Abbott Labs, 2003—04; sr. cons. Hospira, Lake Forest, Ill., from 2004. Cons. Ann Arbor, 1970-78, Northbrook, Ill., 1996—; chief chemist, ind. hygienist Environ. Health Labs. Franklin, Mich., 1966-68; lab. technician Wayne State U., Detroit, 1964-66. Contbr. numerous articles to profl. jours.

Mem.: ASTM, AAAS, ASTM (internat. exec. com., ESS.91 chair com.), APHA, Internat. Com. E55, Nat. Assn. Mfrs. (chmn. safety com. from 1992, vice chair occupl. safety and health com. from 2002, occupl. safety and health com., ergonomics com.), Bus. Coun. on Indoor Air (bd. dirs.), Pharm. Safety Group, Pharm. Rsch. and Mfrs. Assn., Remote Sensing of Atmosphere, Orgns. Resource Councillors (respirator com., chmn. respiratory study task force, risk assessment task force, permissible exposure limti adv. com. task force, TB task force, chmn. latex rubber task force, PVC task force, ergonomics task force), Halogenated Solvents Industry Alliance, Ethylene Oxide Industry Coun. (vice chmn. bd. and exec. com. 1982—95, bd. dirs., ethylene glycol panel, phthalate ester panel), Am. Chemistry Coun. (bd. dirs., occupl. safety and health com., Ethylene Glycol panel, OSHA legis. group), Internat. Stds. Orgn. (chmn. tech. com. 194 biol. evaln. med. devices from 2001, U.S. del. Geneva, convener tech. com. 194, working group 11, working groups 1, 12, 14, 15, liaison ISO tech. com. 210 and 172 joint working group 4, ISO TC210 working group 4, liaison global harmonization task force study group 1), Assn. Advancement Med. Tech. (product safety working group, PVC working group, toxicology task group, proposition 65 working group, latex working group, chair med. device utilization study group), Assn. Advancement of Med. Instrumentation, Air Pollution Control Assn., Am. Indsl. Hygiene Assn. (bd. dirs. 1983—86), Am. Conf. Govtl. Indsl. Hygienists, Am. Chem. Soc., Advanced Am. Acad. Indsl. Hygiene, Sigma Xi. Died June 23, 2007.

HEDRICK, LINNEA S. (FKA DIETRICH), retired art historian; d. Frederic A. and Elsie S. Stonesifer; m. David R. Hedrick; 1 child, Richard Fredrick Dietrich. PhD, U. Del., Newark, 1973. Cert. prof. Ohio. Prof. art history U. South Fla., Tampa, Ohio, 1968—89, Miami U., Oxford, Ohio, 1989—2007, chair, art dept., 1989—2004. Contbr. articles to profl. jours. Pres. Common Cause, Tampa, 1985—86. Grant, Nat. Endowment Arts, 1977—78. Mem.: Midwest Art History Soc. (bd. mem. 2001—07), Coll. Art Assn. Liberal. Avocation: travel. Home: Tucson, Ariz. Died May 8, 2014.

HEICKSEN, MARTIN HENRY, retired archaeology and biblical literature educator; b. Columbus, Mont., Apr. 17, 1911; s. Henry Martin and Bertha Ann (Crawford) H.; m. Amanda Eldora Bolstad, July 18, 1938; children: Byron Homer, Gerald Eugene, Darlene Joyce. AB, San Francisco State U., 1955, MA, 1957. Life C.C. anthropology credential, Calif. Min., pastor 4 Assemblies of God chs., Mont., 1936-42; exec. sec.-treas. Mont. dist. coun. Assembly of God, 1942-47; instr. Ctrl. Bible Coll., Springfield, Mo., 1947-48; prof. bibl. lit. Bethany Coll., Santa Cruz, Calif., 1948-67; assoc. prof. archaeology Wheaton (Ill.) Coll., 1967-71; vis. prof. archaeology Cabrillo Coll., Aptos, Calif., 1974-76; prof. archaeology and O.T., Omega Tng. Ctr., San Jose, Calif., 1976-79, St. James Coll., Pacifica, Calif., 1980-90; ret., 1990. Field archaeologist San Francisco State U. and U. Calif., Berkeley, 1950-63; archaeologist, photographer Dothan (Jordan) Archaeol. Expdn., 1964; dir. Tekoa (Israel) Archaeol. Expdn., 1968-71; cons. archaeologist, Santa Cruz, 1971-76. Author: Settlement Patterns in Jordan, 1966, Tekoa: Excavations in 1968, 1969, Tekoa, Historical and Cultural Profile, 1970; author, photographer: Zondervan, Pictorial Ency.-Bible, 5 vols., 1975. Rsch. grantee Am. Philos. Soc., 1964. Mem. Near East Archaeol. Soc. (sec. 1969-94). Republican. Baptist. Avocations: photography, woodworking. Home: Sierra Vista, Ariz. Died Feb. 9, 2007.

HEIM, DIXIE SHARP, family practice nurse practitioner; b. Kansas City, Kans., Feb. 28, 1938; d. Glen Richard and Freda Helen (Milburn) Stanley; m. Theodore Eugene Sharp, Aug. 12, 1960 (dec. Apr., 1972); children: Diane Yvonne Price, Andrew Kirk, Bryan Scot; m. Roy Bernard Heim, June 14, 1979. Diploma nursing, St. Luke's Hosp. Sch. Nursing, Kansas City, Mo., 1959; family practice nurse clinician, Wichita State U., 1974. Cert. advanced registered nurse practitioner, Kans. Nurse surg. ICU Staff Kaiser Found. Hosp., San Francisco, 1959-61; oper. rm. supr. St. Luke's Hosp., Kansas City, Mo., 1962-63; emergency rm., oper. rm. supr. Lawrence (Kans.) Meml. Hosp., 1963-72; nurse clinician various doctors, Lawrence, 1973-81; nursing supr. spl. projects St. Francis Hosp. and Med. Ctr., Topeka, 1981-94; primary health care giver Health Care Access, Lawrence, 1992-94; nurse practitioner Dr. Glen Bair, Topeka, 1990-94; advanced registered nurse practitioner Dr. Jerry H. Feagan, Topeka, 1994, McLouth (Kans.) Med. Clinic, from 1994, Jefferson County Meml. Hosp., Winchester, Kans., 1995-96; family practice nurse practitioner Robert E. Jacoby II., M.D., Mathew Bohm M.D., Topeka, Kans., 1995-2000. Preceptor nurse practitioner program U. Kans., 1993-2001, registered nurse program Washburn U., 1996-2001; primary health care provider Jefferson County Law Enforcement Ctr., Oskaloosa, Kans., 1995-96. V.p. Am. Bus. Women. Assn. Lawrence chpt., 1969, sec. 1968; vol. Children's Hour, Lawrence, 1965-72, Comty. Resource for Career edn., 1975-76; adv. bd. E. Ctrl. Kans. Econs. Opportunity Corp., Lawrence, 1993-95; mem. Rep. Women Douglas County, Lawrence, 1994-2004. Recipient Nursing the Heart of Health Care award Kaiser Permanente, 1994. Mem. ANA, Am. Acad. Nurse Practitioners (cert.), Kans. State Nurses Assn. (v.p. 1958, chairperson fund raising campaign 1994, bd. dirs. 1996). Home: Lawrence, Kans. Died Nov. 27, 2006.

HEIR, KAL M., financial executive; b. Jersey City, Sept. 30, 1919; s. Michael and Bessie H.; m. Rosamond; children: Jeffrey, Marilyn, Brian. BS, N.J. State Tchrs. Coll., 1940. Mgr. Chun King Inc., Duluth, Minn., 1953-56; eastern sales mgr. Mead Johnson Co., Evansville, Ind., 1956-59; v.p. mktg. Technical Tape Inc., New Rochelle, N.Y., 1959-62; pres. Golden Fleece Sales, NYC, 1962-70, Evergreen Merchandising Inc., NYC, 1962-88; cons. to U.S. food and drug cos. NYC, from 1988. Dir. Evergreen Sales Internat., N.Y.C., 1988-89; philanthropist State of Israel-Hebrew Scholarship Endowment N.J. State Tchrs. Coll. Author: Creative Selling, 1960. Dist. Commr. Cub Scouts of Am. With U.S. Army, 1942-44. Recipient Presdl. medal N.J. State Tchrs. Coll., 1990. Mem. Jewish War Vet. (post comdr.), B'nai B'rith, Sales Exec. Club. Republican. Jewish. Avocation: collecting french impressionist paintings and contemporary art and sculpture. Home: Pompano Beach, Fla. Died May 13, 2007.

HEISS, RICHARD WALTER, retired bank executive, consultant, lawyer; b. Monroe, Mich., July 8, 1930; s. Walter and Lillian (Harpst) H.; m. Nancy J. Blum, June 21, 1952; children: Kurt Frederick, Karl Richard. BA, Mich. State U., 1952; LLB, Detroit Coll., 1963, LLD (hon.), 1982; LLM, Wayne State U., 1969; cert., Stanford U. Exec. Program, 1979. Bar: Mich. 1963, U.S. Dist. Ct. (federal dist.) Mich. 1963. Asst. trust officer Mfrs. Nat. Bank of Detroit, 1960-62, trust officer, 1962-66; v.p., trust officer Mfrs. Nat. Bank Detroit, 1966-68, v.p., sr. trust officer, 1968-75, 1st v.p., sr. trust officer, 1975-77, sr. v.p., 1977-89, exec. v.p., 1989-92; dir. Detroit Coll. Law Found., 1995—2007, vice chair, 1995—2001, chair, 2001—07, hon. lifetime dir., from 2008. Pres., CEO, Mfrs. Nat. Trust Co. Fla., 1984-88, chmn. bd., 1988-92; lectr. Inst. Continuing Legal Edn., Procknow Grad. Sch. Banking, U. Wis., Southwestern Grad. Sch. Bank, Am. Bankers Assn., Banking Sch. South; chmn. mem. exec. com. Trust Mgmt. Seminar, 1980; expert witness fiduciary law, 1993-2003. Mem. Legal-Fin. Network, Cmty. Found. S.E. Mich.; bd. dirs. Hist. Trinity, Inc., 1992-12; trustee Mich. State U. Coll. Law, 1972-2007, pres., 1983-94; pres. Mich. State U. Bus. Sch. Alumni Bd., 1983; mem. allocation and evaluation com. United Way S.E. Mich., 1989-92. 1st lt. AUS, 1952-57. Fellow State Bar Mich. Found.; emeritus mem. Mich. Bar Assn., Am. Bankers Assn. (pres. 1981, exec. com. trust divsn., pvt. banking com. 1984-89, investment adv. com. 1984-89), Mich. Bankers Assn. (chmn. trust divsn. exec. com. 1975), Detroit Golf Club (bd. dirs., pres. 1983), Mich. Srs. Golf Assn. (bd. govs. 1994-12, emeritus 2012-), Club at Seabrook Island (golf and green com.), Delta Chi, Sigma Nu Phi. Republican. Lutheran. Home: Novi, Mich. Died Jan. 23, 2015.

HELBING, EMIL GEORGE, textile executive; b. Wilmington, Del., Dec. 25, 1926; s. Emil and Martha Ellen (Doughten) H.; m. Joan Lorraine Bize, Oct. 6, 1956; children: Matthew, Joseph, Christine, Timothy, James, Thomas. BA in Bus. Adminstrn., Muhlenberg Coll., 1952. Acct. DuPont Co., Wilmington, Del., 1952-54; supr. acct. Jos. Bancroft, Inc., Wilmington, Del., 1954-64, Hewlett-Packard, Avondale, Pa., 1964-69; asst. controller Mannington Mills, Salem, N.J., 1969-71; treas., chief fin. officer Wellco Carpet Corp., Calhoun, Ga., from 1971, bd. dirs., from 1973. Avocations: gardening, golf, exercise. Home: Rome, Ga. Died Nov. 10, 2006.

HELLMERS, HENRY, retired plant physiology educator; b. Palmerton, Pa., Sept. 5, 1915; s. Henry B.C. and Mary Louise (Hofeditz) H.; m. Lou Ann Moynihan, Nov. 24, 1945; children: Rosemary, Carol Ann. BS in Forestry, Pa. State U., 1937, MS, 1939; PhD in Plant Physiology, U. Calif., Berkeley, 1950. Forester Pa. Turnpike Commn., Sommerset, 1940-41; rsch. plant physiologist U.S. Forest Svc./Calif. Inst. Tech., Pasadena, 1949-65; prof. plant physiology Duke U., Durham, N.C., 1965-83, prof. emeritus, from 1983. Dir. Phytotron Controlled Environ. Lab. for Plant Rsch., Duke U., 1968-80; vis. prof. Japan. Co-author: Controlled Cimate and Plant Research, 1946; contbr. over 65 articles to profl. publs. Comdr. USN, 1942-45, World War II. Sr. rsch. fellow New Zealand Govt. Mem. Am. Soc. Plant Physiologists, Soc. Am. Foresters (chmn. So. Calif. sect. 1950's). Avocation: motorhoming. Home: Steamboat Spr, Colo. Died June 4, 2007.

HEMENWAY, JOAN ELIZABETH, hospital pastoral educator, chaplain, counselor; b. Phila., Mar. 14, 1938; d. Seymour Harrison and Katherine Jayne (McKown) H. BA, Conn. Coll., 1960; MDiv, Union Theol. Sem., 1968; D of Ministry, Andover Newton Theol. Sch., 1994. Ordained to ministry Meth. Ch., 1974; cert. chaplain, 1978. Assoc. editor youth mag. United Ch. of Christ, Phila., 1962-5, 69-73; dir. promotion Luth. Ch. in Am., Phila., 1967-69; chaplain Presbyn. Hosp., Phila., 1974-78; dir. clin. pastoral edn. Healthcare Chaplaincy, NYC, 1978-84, Hartford (Conn.) Hosp., 1984-93; dir. pastoral care and clin. pastoral edn. Bridgeport (Conn.) Hosp., 1995—2000; dir. supervisory edn. program, dept. religious ministries Yale-New Haven Hosp., 2000—05. Assoc. min. 1st Meth. Ch. Germantown, Phila., 1976-78; pastoral counselor Manchester Counseling Ctr., Conn., 1988-94. Author: Inside the Circle: A Historical and Practical Inquiry Concerning Process Groups in CPE, 1997; contbr. articles to profl. jours. Co-founder Covenant House Health Ctr., Phila., 1964. Recipient Disting. Svc. award, Coll. Chaplains, 1985, Assn. Clin. Pastnel Edn. Disting. Svc. award, 2000. Fellow: Am. Assn. Pastoral Counselors; mem.: Assn. Clin. Pastoral Edn. (regional dir. 1983—90, bd. reps., cert. supr., pres.-elect 2005—06, pres. from 2006). Democrat. Avocations: reading, sailing, travel. Home: Guilford, Conn. Died Jan. 31, 2007.

HENDERSON, JAMES HAROLD, entrepreneur, financial planner; b. Knoxville, Tenn., June 18, 1948; s. Harold Alpheus and Joanna Elizabeth (McCammon) Henderson. BS in Mgmt. and Econs., U. North Ala., 1971; MS in Systems Mgmt., U. So. Calif., Los Angeles, 1981. Cert. fin. planner, registered investment advisor. Commd. U.S. Army, 1971, advanced through grades to capt., 1975, resigned, 1979; owner Worldwide Merchantile and Co., Clarksville, Tenn., Oscoda, Mich. and Cowley, Wyo., from 1979, Cowley, from 1979; freelance fin. planner, Clarksville, Tenn. and Oscoda, Mich., 1979-92; investment advisor James H. Henderson and Co., Oscoda, Mich., 1987-92; with ExxonMobil Pipeline Co., Houston, from 2007. Counselor Christian Fin. Concepts, Inc., 1985—89. Asst. army attache to India USAR, 1991—99; def. and army attache to Nepal, 1994; def. and army attache to Ethiopia, Eritrea, Djibuti, 1998. Lt. col., ret. USAR, 1971—99. Mem.: Civil Air Patrol (squadron comdr. 2001—03, group comdr. 2004—05, wing dir. homeland security 2005—07), Officer's Christian Fellowship (area cord. 1984—90), Inst. Cert. Fin. Planners (cert.), Nat. Eagle Scout Assn. Avocations: aviation, water sports, fly fishing, cross country skiing, travel. Home: Cowley, Wyo. Died Aug. 20, 2007.

HENDERSON, MARVIN L., lawyer; b. Lexington, Ky., Feb. 3, 1943; s. O.W. and Emma (Fowler) H. BA, U. Ky., 1963, JD, 1964. Bar: Ky. 1965; U.S. Dist. Ct. (ea. dist.) Ky., 1965; U.S. Ct. Appeals (6th cir.) 1971; U.S. Supreme Ct., 1970. Lawyer, Lexington, Ky., from 1965. Democrat. Avocations: golf, tennis. Died May 4, 2007.

HENDERSON, ROBERT MORTON, engineer, consultant; b. LA, Jan. 24, 1931; s. Ira Luther and Genevieve Grace (Morton) H.; m. Barbara Joyce McGlothlin, June 29, 1952; children: Vonda Dee Bixby, Mark Douglas, Coleen Renay Parker. BS, U. Calif., LA, 1959. Mem. tech. staff Space Tech. Lab., Hawthorne, Calif., 1959-61, TRW Systems Group, Redondo Beach, Calif., 1961-65; asst. mgr. Snow Irrigation Co., Fallbrook, Calif., 1965-75; owner, cons. Agrl. Irrigation Design, Inc., Fallbrook, 1975-82; irrigation designer S.W. Irrigation Co., Fallbrook, 1982-83; gen. mgr. A.G. Water Supply Co., Sebring, Fla., 1983-84; v.p. tech. ops. Hendry Irrigation Co., La Belle, Fla., 1984-88; specification mgr. Rainbird Sprinkler Mfg. Co., Glendora, Calif., 1988-89, Johnston Irrigation Co., La Belle, Fla., 1989-90; pvt. practice Ft. Meyers, Fla., from 1990. With USAF, 1949-53. Mem. Irrigation Assn., Fla. Irrigation Soc. (bd. dirs. 1990, agr. standards com. 1989-92), Am. Soc. Agrl. Engrs., Am. Soc. Agrl. Cons. Republican. Avocation: photography. Died Jan. 30, 2007.

HENDRICKSON, TOM ALLEN, engineering executive; b. LA, Dec. 25, 1935; s. Harold Martin and Josara Alberta (Whyers) H.; m. Helen Herron Bell, Nov. 28, 1964 (div. 1979); children: Andrew Edwin, Holly Marie (adopted), Anne Alfhild (adopted); m. Anne Marie Church, June 27, 1981. AB in Physics, Harvard U., 1957; MS in Physics, Georgetown U., 1962. Lic. profl. engr., N.Y., N.J. Div. dir. Naval Nuclear Propulsion Program, Washington, 1957-72; v.p. Burns and Roe, Inc., Oradell, N.J., 1972-85; pres., chief exec. officer Magnetic Bearings, Inc., Groton, Conn., 1985-90; prin. dep. asst. sec. Nuclear Energy U.S. Dept. Energy, Washington, 1990-91, dir. Office of New Prodn. Reactors, 1991-92, acting under sec., 1992; dir. nuclear waste tech. Raytheon Engrs. & Constructors, NYC, from 1993. Bd. dirs. Magnetic Bearings, Inc., Groton, 1983-85, SWUCO, Gaithersburg, Md., 1985-89, SISCO, Gaithersburg, 1988-89, Gen. Physics Corp., Columbia, Md., 1974-85. Mem. ASME, Am. Phys. Soc., Am. Nuclear Soc. Republican. Home: Midland Park, NJ. Died May 8, 2007.

HENRY, RENE PAUL, financial consultant; b. Dallas, Mar. 9, 1917; s. R.P. and Grace (Cowden) H.; m. Ernestine Ryan, Sept. 1, 1939; children: Ghristine Gruenholz, Mary Miller, Rene P. Jr. BA, Baylor U., 1937; JD, U. Tex., 1940; I.A., Harvard U., 1943. Bar: Tex. 1940, U.S. Supreme Ct. 1946, Okla. 1949. Acct. Haskin & Sells, Dallas, 1937; asst. dist. atty. Dallas County, Dallas, 1940; pvt. practice Dallas, 1941-42; atty. rev. div. Office of Chief Counsel, Bur. Internal Revenue, Washington, 1946-49; treas., tax counsel Mid-Continent Petroleum Corp., Tulsa, 1949-55; dir., fin. v.p., treas. Sunray Mid-Continent Oil Co., Tulsa, 1955-62; dir., sr. v.p. fin. and planning Sunray DX Oil Co., Tulsa, 1962-68; v.p., bd. dirs. Sunray DX Oil div. Sun Oil Co., Tulsa, 1968-70; dir., v.p. fin. planning and analysis Sun Oil Co., Phila., 1970-71; cons. corp. fin. Tulsa, from 1972. Bd. dirs., chmn. fin. and audit com. T.D. Williamson, Inc. Mem. exec. com. Indian Nations coun. Boy Scouts Am.; deacon, tchr. Bible 1st Bapt. Ch., Tulsa; mem. adv. coun. Southwestern Bapt. Theol. Sem., Ft. Worth. Lt. USN, 1943-46. Mem. Tulsa Club (past pres.). Home: Tulsa, Okla. Died Oct. 13, 2007.

HENSEL, ROBERT OTTO, theology educator; b. Zweibrücken, Pfalz, Germany, July 7, 1930; s. Karl and Frieda (Emmerich) H.; m. Hildegard Maurer, June 25, 1931; children: Martin, Andreas. ThD, U. Mainz, Germany, 1957. Lectr. theology Seminars of Revs., Landau, 1955-61; pastor Protestant Ch. of Palatinat, Dahn, Germany, 1961-65, dean Bad Bergzabern, Germany, 1965-83, prof. theology Speyer, Germany, 1983-91. Author books. Home: Pfalz, Germany. Died Apr. 21, 2007.

HENSON, JANE ELIZABETH, information management professional, adult education educator; b. Ft. Wayne, Ind., Dec. 1, 1946; d. Robert Eugene and Lucile Catherine (Feeney) Tucker; m. Phillip Likins Henson, Aug. 23, 1971; 1 child, Robert Likins. BS in Edn., Ind. U., 1970, MS in Edn., 1973, MLS, 1976. Tchr. pub. schs., Ft. Wayne, 1970-71, Nevada, Mo., 1971-72; libr., cataloger Ctrl. Conn. State U., New Britain, 1976-77; libr. numeric data U. Wis., Madison, 1978-80; adj. prof. libr. Navy Safety Sch. Ind. U., Bloomington, 1981-83, reference libr. Vocat. Edn. Project, 1984-86; asst. dir. ERIC Clearinghouse, Bloomington, 1988-95, assoc. dir., 1995-98, co-dir., 1999—2003; assoc. dir. Ctr. for Social Studies and Internat. Edn., Bloomington, 2004—08; coord. tchr. edn. assessment Sch. Edn., Ind. U., Bloomington, from 2008. Co-author: Rising Expectations: A Framework for ERIC's Future in the National Library of Education, 1997; editor: Libraries Link to Learning: Final

Report on the Indiana Governor's Conference on Libraries and Information Services, 1990. Chair ERIC tech. com. U.S. Dept. Edn. ERIC Program, Washington, 1990-2003, mem. ERIC exec. com., 1990-2003 Mem. Am. Soc. Info. Sci. (dept. dir. SIG cabinet 1993, chair behavioral and social sci. SIG 1994, cert. of appreciation 1993). Roman Catholic. Avocations: reading, travel. Home: Bloomington, Ind. Died May 10, 2015.

HENTZ, ANN LOUISE, English language educator; b. Phila., June 23, 1921; d. Robert Alexander and Elizabeth (Jones) H. BA with high honors, U. Rochester, 1950; MA, Ohio State U., Columbus, 1951, PhD, 1956. Instr. Lake Forest (Ill.) Coll., Ill., 1956-58, asst. prof., 1958-65, assoc. prof., 1965-81, prof., 1981-86, prof. emerita, from 1986. Contbr. articles to profl. jours. Mem. Phi Sigma Iota, Phi Beta Kappa. Democrat. Home: Lake Forest, Ill. Died Dec. 31, 2006.

HERBERT, LEROY JAMES, retired accounting firm executive; b. Long Branch, NJ, Aug. 3, 1923; s. LeRoy J. and Edna Hazel (Keller) H. BS, U. Md., 1950. CPA, N.J., N.Y., Ohio, Tenn., La., N.C., Va.; chartered acct. South Africa. Profl. staff mem. Ernst & Ernst, Balt., 1950-58, asst. mgr., 1958-60, mgr. internat. ops. NYC, 1960-63, ptnr., 1963-67; sr. U.S. ptnr. Whinney Murray Ernst & Ernst, London and Paris, 1967-70; ptnr. in charge internat. ops. NYC, 1970-78; internat. exec. ptnr. Ernst & Whinney Internat., NYC, 1979-83; ret., 1983. Bd. dirs., past chmn. Monmouth Med. Ctr., Long Branch; bd. dirs. Brookdale CC Found., U. Md. Found., St. Barnabas Health Care Sys., Ronald McDonald House, Long Branch, N.J., Monmouth Med. Ctr. Found. With U.S. Army, 1942-46. Recipient Disting. Alumnus award U. Md. Coll. Bus. and Mgmt., 1980, Disting. Acctg. Alumnus award, 1991; named to Long Branch H.S. Disting. Alumni Hall of Fame, 1996. Mem. AICPA, N.Y. Assn. CPAs, Ohio Assn. CPAs, Md. Assn. CPAs, Transvaal Soc. Accts. (South Africa), Deal Country Club, Harpoon and Needle Club, Pres.'s Club (U. Md.), Beta Alpha Psi Episcopalian. Died Nov. 22, 2012.

HERBERT-JONES, HUGO JARRETT, retired diplomat; b. London, Mar. 11, 1922; s. Hugh and Dora (Rowlands) H.-J.; m. Margaret Veall, May 20, 1954; children: Sarah Elsbeth, Nicholas David, Rebecca Sian. BA with honors, Worcester Coll., Oxford, Eng., 1941. Mem. Her Majesty's Fgn. Svc., Eng., 1947-79; dir. Confedn. Brit. Industry, Eng., 1979-87; mayor Aldeburgh, Suffolk, 2007—08. Chmn. The Aldeburgh Soc., 1988-93. Maj. Welsh Guards, 1946. Decorated Order Brit. Empire, 1963, Companion of Order of St. Michael & St. George, 1973. Mem. Garrick Club, Marylebone Cricket Club, London Welsh Rugby Football Club, Aldeburgh Yacht Club, Aldeburgh Golf Club. Anglican. Avocations: music, sailing, golf, shooting, spectator sports. Home: London, England. Died Nov. 19, 2014.

HERING, DORIS MINNIE, dance critic; b. NYC, Apr. 11, 1920; d. Harry and Anna Elizabeth (Schwenk) H. BA cum laude, Hunter Coll., 1941; MA in Romance Languages, Fordham U., 1985. Freelance dance writer, 1946-52; assoc. editor, prin. critic Dance mag., NYC, 1952-72; exec. dir. Nat. Assn. for Regional Ballet, NYC, 1972-87; adj. assoc. prof. dance history NYU, 1968-78; freelance dance writer, lectr., cons., 1987—2014. Dance panel NEA, 1972-75, cons., 1991-2014; dance panel NY State Coun. Arts, 1992-96, program auditor; bd. dirs. Walnut Hill Sch., Internat. Ballet Competition; hon. bd. dirs. Phila. Dance Alliance; cons. Regional Dance America; adj. assoc. prof. dance history NYU Grad. Sch. Edn. Author: 25 Years of American Dance, 1950, Dance in America, 1951, Wild Grass, 1965, Giselle and Albrecht, 1981; sr. editor Dance mag., from 1989. Howard D. Rothschild Rsch. fellow Harvard U., 1991-93; recipient 33d ann. Capezio Dance Found. award for Lifetime Svc., 1985, Award of Distinction Dance mag., 1987, Sage Cowles Land Grant chair in dance U. Minn., 1993, Sr. Critics tribute Dance Critics Assn., 2002, Annual award, Martha Hill Dance Fund, 2002; named to The Hunter Coll. Alumni Hall of Fame, 1986, award, ASIA Charritable Trust, 1999. Mem. Dance Critics Assn., Assn. Dance History Scholars, Phi Beta Kappa, Chi Tau Epsilon (hon.). Died Oct. 15, 2014.

HERRINGTON, ALEX P., stocks and bonds trader; b. Richmond, Ky., Aug. 30, 1907; s. Lewis Butler and Susan (Hume) H.; m. Diana Woods, June 1, 1936 (div. Mar. 1942); m. June 2, 1945; children: Alex P. Jr., Lewis Redmond. BA, U. Ky., 1929. Dist. mgr. Mich. Pub. Svc., Whitehall, 1929-33; lighting mgr. Ky. Utilities, Lexington, 1932-35; salesman W. L. Lyons, Lexington, 1935-42, mgr., 1946-66, Stein Brothers & Boyce, Lexington, 1966-68; assoc. mgr. Prudential Bache Securities, Lexington, from 1968-. With U.S. Army, 1942-45, PTO. Died Dec. 14, 2006.

HERRMANN, EDWARD KIRK, actor; b. Washington, July 21, 1943; s. John Anthony and Jean Eleanor (O'Connor) H; m. Leigh Curran, Sept. 9, 1978 (div. 1986); m. Star Hayner, 1993 BA, Bucknell U., 1965; postgrad. (Fulbright scholar), London Acad. Music and Dramatic Art, 1968-69. With Dallas Theater Center, 4 years. Appeared in numerous plays including Moonchildren, Mrs. Warren's Profession (Tony award for Best Supporting actor 1976), Journey's End, 1978, The Beach House, 1979-80, Hedda Gabler, The Front Page, 1981, Plenty, 1982 (Theater Guild medal), Uncle Vanya, 1984, Tom and Viv, 1985, Not About Heroes, 1985, Julius Caesar, 1988, A Walk in the Woods (London), 1988-89, Harvey, 1990, Candy is Dandy: An Evening with Odgen Nash, 1993, Life Sentences, 1993; (films) The Paper Chase, 1972, The Great Gatsby, 1973, Day of the Dolphin, 1973, The Great Waldo Pepper, 1974, The Betsy, 1977, The North Avenue Irregulars, 1977, The Brass Target, 1978, Take Down, 1978, Harry's War, 1979, Reds, 1981, Death Valley, 1982, A Little Sex, 1982, Annie, 1982, Mrs. Soffell, 1984, The Purple Rose of Cairo, 1985, The Man with One Red Shoe, 1985, Compromising Positions, 1985, The Lost Boys, 1987, Overboard, 1987, Big Business, 1988, Hero, 1992, Born Yesterday, 1993, My Boyfriend's Back, 1993, The Foreign Student, 1994, Richie Rich, 1994, Nixon, 1995, Critical Care, 1997, Better Living, 1998, Walking Across Egypt, 1999, Double Take, 2001, Down, 2001, The Cat's Meow, 2001, The Emperor's Club, 2002, Intolerable Cruelty, 2003, Welcome to Mooseport, 2004, The Aviator, 2004, Relative Strangers, 2006, The Pleasure of Your Company, 2006, Factory Girl, 2006, I Think I Love My Wife, 2007, Sherman's March, 2007, The States, 2007, The Skeptic, 2009, Bucky Larson: Born to be a Star, 2011; (TV films) Eleanor and Franklin: The White House Years (TV Critics Circle award as Best Actor 1977), A Love Affair: The Eleanor and Lou Gehrig Story, 1978, Freedom Road, 1978, Portrait of a Stripper, 1979, Sorrows of Gin, 1979, M.A.S.H, 1979, The Private History of a Campaign that Failed, 1980, Dear Liar, 1981, The Electric Grandmother, 1982, The Gift of Life, 1982, Concealed Enemies, 1984, (BBC) A Foreign Field, 1992, Don't Drink the Water, 1994, The Face on the Milk Carton, 1995, Here Come the Munsters, 1995, Soul of the Game, 1996, A Season in Purgatory, 1996, What Love Sees, 1996, Pandora's Clock, 1996, Saint Maybe, 1998, Atomic Train, 1999, Vendetta, 1999, James Dean, 2001, (voice) Isaac's Storm, 2003, Bereft, 2004, (narrator) Eighty Acres of Hell, 2006, Violent Earth: New England's Killer Hurricane 2006; TV series: Gilmore Girls, 2000-07; (host, cable TV) Our Century. Died Dec. 31, 2014.

HERSH, NADINE FERN MILLER, community health nurse; b. Bklyn., Mar. 13, 1945; d. Jack J. and Lillian K. (Markowitz) Miller; m. Eric M. Hersh, Oct. 9, 1977; children: Erica Nicole, Ric Tommy. Student, Franklin Square Hosp., Balt., 1965. RN, N.Y., Md., Fla.; cert. hosp. adminstr. Freelance sch. nurse, office nurse; staff RN Nassau County Med. Ctr., East Meadow, N.Y.; head RN ob-gyn, head RN pediatrics Long Beach (N.Y.) Meml. Hosp. Home: Tucson, Ariz. Died Jan. 16, 2007.

HERWIG, KARL ROBERT, physician; b. Phila., Nov. 12, 1935; s. Louis and Elizabeth Frances (Myers) H.; m. Barbara K. Bosscher, Oct. 26, 1963; children: Susan Elizabeth, K. Robert. BS, Ursinus Coll., 1957; MD, Jefferson Med. Coll., 1961. Diplomate Am. Bd. Urology. Intern U. Mich., Ann Arbor, 1961-62, resident gen. surgury, 1962-64; fellow Peter Sent Brigham Hosp., Boston, 1964; urology resident U. Mich., Ann Arbor, 1964-67; staff urologist U.S. Naval Medical Ctr., Bethesda, Md., 1967-69; urology faculty U. Mich., 1969-77; staff urologist Scripps Clinic, La Jolla, Calif., from 1977. Instr., assoc. prof. U. Mich., 1969-77; urology div. head Scripps Clinic, 1977-95, sr. cons., 1994; clinical assoc. prof. U. Calif., San Diego, 1977—. Contbr. articles to profl. jours. With U.S. Navy, 1967-69. Recipient Faculty Achievement award U. Mich., 1972. Fellow Am. Coll. Surgeons; mem. Am. Urological Assn., Cen. Surgical Soc., Am. Assn. Endocrine Surgeons, Collier Surgical Soc., Am. Med. Soc., Rotary. Republican. Presbyterian. Avocations: golf, history, financial areas. Home: Rancho Santa Fe, Calif. Died Nov. 30, 2006.

HERZSTEIN, ROBERT EDWIN, history professor; b. NYC, Sept. 26, 1940; s. Harold and Jean; m. Daphne Newman Stassin (div. 1975). BA, NYU, 1961, MA, 1963, PhD, 1964. Asst. prof. Carnegie-Mellon U., Pitts., 1964-65, MIT, Cambridge, Mass., 1966-72; assoc. to prof. U. SC, Columbia, 1972—2015, Carolina disting. prof. to emeritus, 1990—2015. Spl. aide to gov. Conn., Hartford Author: Waldheim: The Missing Years, 1988, Roosevelt & Hitler: Prelude to War, 1980, Henry R. Luce: A Political Portrait, 1994, The War that Hitler Won, 1978, Henry R. Luce, Time, and the American Crusade in Asia, 2005. Advisor, witness Govt. Reform subcom. U.S. Ho. of Reps., 1994-98; co-organizer Conf. on the legacy of Nuremberg trials, Columbia, 1997. Recipient Founders Day award NYU, 1965, Russell award U. S.C., 1978, Signing pen by Pres. Clinton upon signing Nazi War Crimes Disclosure Act, 1998. Mem. German Studies Assn., WWII Studies Assn., Soc. for Historians of Am. Fgn. Rels. Jewish. Died Jan. 24, 2015.

HESBURGH, THEODORE MARTIN, clergyman, former university president; b. Syracuse, NY, May 25, 1917; s. Theodore Bernard and Anne Marie (Murphy) H. Student, U. Notre Dame, 1934-37; PhB, Gregorian U., 1939; postgrad., Holy Cross Coll., Washington, 1940-43; STD, Cath. U. Am., 1945; 124 hon. degrees awarded between 1954-92. Joined Order of Congregation of Holy Cross, 1934, ordained priest Roman Cath. Ch., 1943. Chaplain Nat. Tng. Sch. for Boys, Washington, 1943-44; vets. chaplain U. Notre Dame, 1945-47, 138 hon. degrees awarded between 1954-98, 1948-49, exec. v.p., 1949-52, pres., 1952-87, pres. emeritus, 1987—2015, instr., asst. prof. religion, 1945-48, chmn. dept. religion, 1948-49. Fellow Am. Acad. Arts and Scis.; mem. Internat. Fedn. Cath. Univs., Commn. on Humanities, Inst. Internat. Edn. (pres., dir.), Cath. Theol. Soc., Chief Execs. Forum, Am. Philos. Soc., Nat. Acad. Edn., Coun. on Fgn. Rels. (trustee), Nat. Acad. Scis. (hon.), U.S. Inst. Peace (bd. dirs.). Author: Theology of Catholic Action, 1945, God and the World of Man, 1950, Patterns for Educational Growth, 1958, Thoughts for Our Times, 1962, More Thoughts for Our Times, 1965, Still More Thoughts for Our Times, 1966, Thoughts IV, 1968, Thoughts V, 1969, The Humane Imperative: A Challenge for the Year 2000, 1974, The Hesburgh Papers: Higher Values in Higher Education, 1979, God, Country, Notre Dame, 1990, Travels with Ted and Ned, 1992. Former dir. Woodrow Wilson Nat. Fellowship Corp.; mem. Civil Rights Commn., 1957-72; mem. of Carnegie Commn. on Future of Higher Edn.; chmn. U.S. Commn. on Civil Rights, 1969-72; mem. Commn. on an All-Volunteer Armed Force, 1970; chmn. with rank of ambassador U.S. delegation UN Conf. Sci. and Tech. for Devel., 1977-79 ; Bd. dirs. Am. Council Edn., Freedoms Found. Valley Forge, Adlai Stevenson Inst. Internat. Affairs; past trustee, chmn. Rockefeller Found.; trustee Carnegie Found. for Advancement Teaching, Woodrow Wilson Nat. Fellowship Found., Inst. Internat. Edn., Nutrition Found., United Negro Coll. Fund, others; chmn. Overseas Devel. Council; chmn. acad. council Ecumenical Inst. for Advanced Theol. Studies, Jerusalem. Decorated comdr. L'ordre des Arts et des Lettres. Recipient U.S. Navy's Disting. Pub. Service award, 1959; Presdl. Medal of Freedom, 1964, Gold medal Nat. Inst. Social Scis., 1969, Cardinal Gibbons medal Cath. U. Am., 1969, Bellarmine medal Bellarmine-Ursuline Coll., 1970; Meiklejohn award AAUP, 1970, Charles Evans Hughes award Nat. Conf. Christians and Jews, 1970; Merit award Nat. Cath. Ednl. Assn., 1971, Pres.' Cabinet award U. Detroit, 1971; Am. Liberties medallion Am. Jewish Com., 1971; Liberty Bell award Ind. State Bar Assn., 1971; Laetare medal Univ. Notre Dame, 1987, Pub. Welfare medal NAS, 1984; Pub. Svc. award Common Cause, 1984, Disting. Svc. award Assn. Cath. Colls. and Univs., 1982, Jefferson award Coun. Advancement and Support of Edn., 1982, Congl. Gold medal, 2000. Fellow Am. Acad. Arts and Scis.; mem. NAS (hon.), Internat. Fedn. Cath. Univs., Commn. on Humanities, Inst. Internat. Edn. (pres., bd. dirs.), Cath. Theol. Soc., Chief Execs. Forum, Am. Philos. Soc., Nat. Acad. Edn., Coun. on Fgn. Rels. (trustee). Died Feb. 26, 2015.

HESS, JOANNE DUKES, nursing educator; b. Greenville, SC, Apr. 21, 1948; m. Karl Hess IV, June 6, 1970. BSN, Georgetown U., 1970; cert. pediatric nurse practitioner, U. Va., 1973; MSN, U. Colo., 1981. RN, N.Mex., Va.; cert. pediatric nurse practitioner, Va. Staff nurse Children's Med. Ctr., Washington, 1970-71; RN, pediatric nurse practitioner Univ. Va., Charlottesville, 1971-74; instr. U. Va., Charlottesville, 1974-76; pediatric nurse practitioner H.E.S. Physicians, Washington, 1976-77; sch. nurse Poudre Sch. Dist., Ft. Collins, Colo., 1979-80; pediatric nurse practitioner Larimer County Health Dept., Ft. Collins, 1978-82, Ft. Collins (Colo.) Youth Clinic, 1977-79, 81-82; assoc. prof. N.Mex. State U., Las Cruces, from 1986. Expert witness N.Mex. Office of the Atty. Gen. for the N.Mex. Bd. Nursing, 1990—; ethics cons. Meml. Med. Ctr., Las Cruces, 1991—; mem. advanced directives com. Meml. Med. Ctr., Las Cruces, 1991—; liaison N.Mex. Nurses Assn. and ANA Ctr. for Ethics and Human Rights, 1991—. Recipient three Rsch. grants Coll. Human Community Svcs., Las Cruces, 1990, 91, Vol. award Project Head Start, Las Cruces, 1991. Mem. ANA, N.Mex. Nurses Assn. (treas. dist. 14 1987-89, chair scholarship and awards com. 1989—, bd. mem., Nurse Educator of Yr. award 1992), Sigma Theta Tau. Home: Charlottesvle, Va. Died Feb. 28, 2007.

HESS, RICHARD ALFRED, insurance executive, educator; b. NYC, Nov. 19, 1926; s. Bernard Hess and Rhea (Abrahams) Newman; m. Mary Ellen Andrews, Apr. 3, 1953 (div. June 1981); children: Robert A., Pamela A., John A.; m. Alice A. March, Nov. 21, 1992. BA, Columbia U., NYC, 1950, cert. CLU, 1959. CLU. V.p. John C. Paige & Co., NYC, 1955-65, Fred S. James, NYC, 1965-68, Schiff Terhune & Co., NYC, 1968-78, exec. v.p. LA, 1978-84, GNW Ins., LA, from 1984. Chmn. ins. com. Cedars Sinai Hosp., L.A., 1985-90, mem. exec. com., bd. govs., 1988—; adj. prof. ins. NYU, 1976-80; guest lectr. U. So. Calif. Extension, U. Calif., Berkeley. Capt. Larchmont (N.Y.) Fire Dept., 1976-78. With USN, 1945-47. Avocations: tennis, fishing, riding, golf, shooting. Home: Los Angeles, Calif. Died June 16, 2007.

HESTER, JAMES MCNAUGHTON, retired foundation administrator, retired academic administrator; b. Chester, Pa., Apr. 19, 1924; s. James Montgomery and Margaret (McNaughton) H.; m. Janet Rodes, May 23, 1953; children: Janet McN., Margaret, Martha. BA, Princeton U., 1945, LL.D. (honoris causa), 1962; BA (Rhodes scholar 1947-50), Oxford U., Eng., 1950, D.Phil., 1955; LL.D., Lafayette Coll., 1964, Morehouse Coll., 1967; L.H.D., Hartwick Coll., 1964; LHD (hon.), Pace U., 1971, U. Pitts., 1971, Colgate U., 1974; L.H.D., N.Y. U., 1977; DCL, Alfred U., 1965; LLD (hon.), Hofstra U., 1967, Hahnemann Med. Coll., 1967, Fordham U., 1971, Amherst Coll., 1975, New Sch. for Social Rsch., 1975, Union Coll., 1983. Civil information officer Fukuoka Mil. Govt. Team, Japan, 1946-47; asst. to American sec. to Rhodes Trustees, 1950; asst. to pres. Handy Associates, Inc. (mgmt. cons.), NYC, 1953-54; account supr. Gallup & Robinson, Inc., Princeton, NJ, 1954-57; provost Bklyn. Center Long Island U., 1957-60, v.p., 1958-60; prof. history, exec. dean arts and sci., dean NYU, 1960-61, pres., 1962-75; rector UN U., Tokyo, 1975-80; pres. NY Botanical Garden, 1980-89, The Harry Frank Guggenheim Found., NYC, 1989—2004. Trustee Lehman Found. Served with USMCR, 1943-46, 51-52. Mem. Assn. American Rhodes Scholars Clubs: Century Assn., University, Pretty Brook Tennis. Home: Princeton, NJ. Died Dec. 31, 2014.

HESTER, NELL LEATH, educator, biologist; b. Jamestown, Ala., Jan. 4, 1934; d. David Graves and Ruthie (Tucker) Leath; m. Pelham E. Hester, Jan. 1, 1956; children: Leatha, Kathy, William. BS, Auburn U., 1956; MEd, U. Tenn., Chattanooga, 1965. Therapeutic dietitian Erlanger Hosp., Chattanooga, 1957-61; tchr. biology Red Bank High Sch., Chattanooga, from 1961. Tchr. anatomy and physiology Chattanooga State Jr. Coll., 1980-81. Lyndhurst Found. grantee, 1982, 89. Mem. AAUW (sec. 1987-88, pres. 1990—), Hamilton County Edn. Assn. (mem. exec. bd, treas. 1980-81, mem. negotiating team 1981-82, Outstanding Tchr. of Yr. 1980). Episcopalian. Avocations: bridge, travel, gourmet cooking. Died Aug. 21, 2007.

HICKS, DANIEL IVAN, singer, musician, song writer; b. Little Rock, Dec. 9, 1941; s. Ivan L. and Evelyn (Kehl) E. H.; m. Clare; stepchildren Sara BA in Broadcasting, San Francisco State U., 1965. Composer, singer, performer (TV commls.) Levi's 501 Blues, 1986, McDonald's hamburgers, Ball Park Franks, (TV animations) Sesame Street, (radio) Bic Lighters; TV appearances include Flip Wilson, Johnny Carson, Dick Cavett, MTV spls.; singer (films) Revolution, 1968, Class Action, 1991; recorded 7 albums with musical groups Hot Licks and Acoustic Warriors; drummer, occassional singer, Charlatans, 1965-68 Died Feb. 6, 2016.

HICKS, HORACE ANDREW, secondary school educator; b. Memphis, Jan. 7, 1938; s. Shirley V. (Person) Hicks; m. Geraldine McCray, June 5, 1961; children: Kevin Andrew, William Daryl. BBA, Memphis State U., 1972, MEd, 1974. Materials handler Internat. Harvester Co., Memphis, 1962-72; tchr. Memphis City Schs., from 1972. Bd. dirs. Shelby Recreational and Vocat. Services, Memphis. Pres. N.E. Shelby County Polit. Action Com., Tenn., 1968-78. Mem. Alpha Phi Alpha, Delta Sigma Pi. Democrat. Avocations: reading, swimming, hunting. Home: Arlington, Tenn. Died July 30, 2007.

HICKS, JONATHAN PRUITT, journalist; b. St. Louis, Dec. 4, 1955; s. John H. and Minnie Hicks; m. Christy Deboe; 1 child, Lindsay. Reporter Ariz. Daily Star; bus. writer Cleveland Plain Dealer, 1982—85, New York Times, 1985—92, polit., metro. reporter, 1992—2009; sr. fellow Medgar Evers Coll. DuBois Bunche Ctr. for Public Policy, 2009—14; sr. corr. BET.com, 2011—14. Faculty mem. Century Inst., 1999. Author: (articles) Coors Mends Minority Fences, 1985. Mem.: Kappa Alpha Psi Frat. (past editor jour.). Died Oct. 27, 2014.

HIGANO, NORIO, retired internist; b. Seattle, May 6, 1921; s. Hanji and Ura (Kameta) H.; m. Dorothy Wright Taylor; children: Celestia, Priscilla, Stuart. BS, U. Wash., 1943; MD, St. Louis U., 1945. Diplomate Am. Bd. Internal Medicine, Am. Bd. Nuclear Medicine. Intern Boston City Hosp., 1945-46; resident pathology Mass. Meml. Hosp., 1947-48; resident medicine Mt. Auburn Hosp., 1948-49, Boston Lying-In Hosp., PBBH, 1950-51; fellow Thornike Meml. Lab. Harvard Med. Sch., 1951-52; mem. rsch. lab. The Meml. Hosp., Worcester, Mass., 1953-61, chief nuclear medicine lab., 1953-95, attending physician, 1952-99; ret. Fellow ACP, Am. Coll. Endocrinology; mem. AMA, Mass. Med. Soc., Worcester Dist. Med. Soc., Soc. of Nuclear Medicine (pres. New England chpt. 1975-76). Avocations: art, photography. Home: Westborough, Mass. Died June 16, 2007.

HIGH, (MARY) ELIZABETH HILLEY, retired art educator; b. Wilson, NC, Mar. 24, 1920; d. Howard Stevens Hilley and Maggie Tucker; m. Larry Allison High, May 12, 1940; children: Rebecca Elizabeth Tingen, Larry Allison, Robert Marshal, Margaret Almand Nowell. BA magna cum laude, Atlantic Christian Coll., 1939; MEd, East Carolina U., 1972. File clk. U.S. Army Depots, Richmond, Va., 1941—44, chief personnel; tchr. Nash County Schs., Rocky Mount, NC, 1966—82. Pres. Nash County Assn. Classroom Tchrs., Nashville, 1976—77; mem. NC State Sch. Accreditation Bd. Mem. Planning Bd., Nashville, 1964—66; former chmn. NC Assn. Educators, Secondary Divsn.; former pres. NC Art Edn. Assn.; mem. acquisitions com. Nash County Arts Coun., 2001—03. Recipient Painting prize, Rocky Mt. Ann. Art Exhibit. Mem.: NC Mus. Art, Womens' Soc. Christian Svc., Barton Soc., Friends Cooley Libr., Friends Braswell Libr., Kappa Delta Pi, Delta Kappa Gamma. Meth. Home: Nashville, NC. Died Nov. 29, 2007.

HIGUCHI, SHINPEI, clergyman; b. LA, Sept. 17, 1923; s. Shiro and Fuku (Saito) Higuchi; m. Fumiko Higuchi, Feb. 19, 1949; children: Nobuko, Mari, Naomi. MDiv, Fuller Theol. Sem., 1958. Pastor Fujimigaoka Ch., Tokyo, 1951—66, Makiki Christian Ch., Honolulu, 1966—74; tchr. Japan Christian Coll., Tokyo, 1958—66; prof., O.T. Tokyo Christian Coll., Tokyo, 1974—86, pres., 1975—86, bd. dirs. & trustee, 1975—86. Moderator Japan N.T. Ch., Tokyo, 1961—65; pres. Coun. Japanese Christian Chs., Honolulu, 1970—72; mem., exec. com. Asia Theol. Assn., Taipei, Taiwan, 1975—82. Translator: New Japanese Bible, 1966; author: Commentary, Book of Ruth, 1969, The Fruit of the Spirit, 1981, Paul's Letter of Love, 1990; editor: Ortho Peridocial; contbr. articles to profl. jours. Ordained to ministry Japan N.T. Ch., 1963. Recipient Tokinosuke Joshima award, Macedonian Soc., 1983. Died Mar. 10, 2007.

HILAS, MARY ELIZABETH (BETTY HILAS), civic volunteer; b. Polson, Mont., Oct. 31, 1918; d. Fredrick Thomas and Elizabeth (Patterson) Turner; m. Frank Lorenzo Brown, July 30, 1936 (div. 1954); children: Frank L. Jr., Thomas M., James D., Timothy L.; m. George Hilas, Mar. 29, 1975. AA, East L.A. Jr. Coll., 1963. Group supr. Calif. Youth Authority Reception Guidance Ctr., Norwalk, 1963-64; women's correctional supr. I Calif. Rehab. Ctr. for Drug Addicts, Corona, 1964-65, 66-71, Calif. Dept. Corrections Outpatient Ctrl. Testing clinic, LA, 1965-66; correctional officer Calif. Dept. Correctons, Soledad Prison, 1971-72, Calif. Med. Facility for Men, Vacaville, 1972-74, correctional program supr. I, 1974-76, ret., 1976. Staff rep. Calif. Med. Facility Equal Employment, Vacaville, 1974-76. Active affirmative action, Friends Outside; pres. East Montebello Coord. Coun., 1950; adv. com. L.A. County Fedn. Cmty. Coord. Couns., 1951; mem. Sr. Citizens, Georgetown, Calif., 1983—, LWV of the Divide, Garden Valley, 1991—. Mem. ACLU, PTA (life), Calif. State Retirees, VFW Aux., Ret. Officers Assn. Aux., Friends of the Libr. Democrat. Unitarian Universalist. Avocations: politics, reading, cards. Home: Garden Valley, Calif. Died Dec. 25, 2007.

HILDEBRAND, VERNA LEE, human ecology educator; b. Dodge City, Kans., Aug. 17, 1924; d. Carrell E. and Florence (Smyth) Butcher; m. John R. Hildebrand, June 23, 1946; children: Carol Ann, Steve Allen. BS, Kans. State U., 1945, MS, 1957; PhD, Tex. Women's U., 1970. Tchr. home econs. Dickinson County H.S., Chapman, Kans., 1945-46; tchr. early childhood Albany (Calif.) Pub. Schs., 1946-47; grad. asst. Inst. Child Welfare U. Calif., Berkeley, 1947-48; tchr. kindergarten Albany Pub. Schs., 1948-49; dietitian commons and hosp. U. Chgo., 1952-53; instr. Kans. State U., Manhattan, 1953-54, 59, Okla. State U., Stillwater, 1955-56; asst. prof. Tex. Tech U., Lubbock, 1962-67; from asst. prof. to prof. Mich. State U., East Lansing, 1967-97, prof. emeritus, from 1997. Legis. clk. Kans. Ho. of Reps., Topeka, 1955. Author: Introduction to Early Childhood Education, 1971, 6th edit., 1997, Guiding Young Children, 1975, 7th edit., 2004,8th edit., 2009, Parenting and Teaching Young Children, 1981, 1990, 2000, Management of Child Development Centers, 1984, 6th edit., 2007, 2011, Parenting: Rewards and Responsibilities, 1994, 7th edit., 2004, Guilding Young Children, 8th edit., 2008, tchrs. annotated edit., 2003; co-author: China's Families: Experiment in Societal Change, 1985, Knowing and Serving Diverse Families, 1996, 3rd edit., 2007, co-Author: Patricon Heacon Mem. Nat. Assn. for the Edn. Young Children (task force 1975-77), Am. Home Econs. Assn. (bd. dirs., Leader award 1990), Women in Internat. Devel., Nat. Assn. Early Childhood Tchr. Edn. (award for meritorious and profl. leadership 1995). Home: Denver, Colo. Died 2014.

HILL, C. THOMAS, JR., radiologist; b. Corinth, Miss., Oct. 23, 1919; s. C. Thomas Hill and Ruby Paris Bryant; widowed. BS, U. Miss., 1951; MD, U. Tenn., Memphis, 1952. Diplomate Am. Bd. Nuc. Medicine, Am. Bd. Radiology. Intern Bapt. Hosp., Knoxville, Tenn., 1952—53; resident Southwestern Med. Sch., Dallas VA Hosp., Baylor U. Hosp., Dallas, 1965—68; radiologist, 1958-96. Capt. USAF. Mem. Radiol. Soc. N.Am., Am. Coll. Radiology, Am. Roentgen Ray Soc. Home: Ponca City, Okla. Died July 29, 2007.

HILL, JOHN DAVID, executive; b. Rockport, Ind., July 5, 1920; s. David and Mary (McMillin) H.; m. Jane Mahoney, Apr. 9, 1947 (dec. Oct. 1997); children: Mary, James. BS, Ind. U., 1942. CEO, chmn. bd. Sioux City (Iowa) Brick & Tile, from 1991. Lt. col. U.S. Army, 1942-48. Republican. Methodist. Avocations: golf, gardening, reading. Home: Sioux City, Iowa. Died Dec. 30, 2006.

HILL, PAUL, JR., electrical engineer, educator; b. Opelika, Ala., May 28, 1947; s. Paul and Eliza (Lochart) H.; m. Mary Elizabeth Stewart, Apr. 21, 1969 (div. Apr., 1983); 1 child, Cynthia Denise. BS, Ala. A&M U., 1970; BSc in Elec. Engring., Howard U., Washington, 1993; postgrad. studies in Elec. Engring., Polytech. U., Bklyn., from 1993. Tech. staff mem. Rockwell Internat., Anaheim, Calif., 1970-73; rsch. asst. lab. Howard U., Washington, 1990-93. Mem. AAAS, IEEE, Optical Soc. Am. (vol.) Republican. Methodist. Avocation: volley ball. Died Dec. 5, 2006.

HILLMAN, ALAN L., internist, educator, researcher; b. NYC, July 12, 1956; s. Herman David and Edith (Geilich) H.; children: Jennifer, Abigail. BA cum laude, Cornell U., 1978, MD, 1981; MBA with distinction, U. Pa., 1986. Intern in internal medicine N.Y. Hosp., 1981-82, asst. resident in internal medicine, 1982-84; dir. clin. programs Hosps. of U. of Pa., Phila., 1986-90, med. dir. Health Pass, 1987-90; assoc. dir. med. group U. Pa., Phila., 1987-90, sr. scholar clin. epidemiology, from 1990, dir. Ctr. for Health Policy, 1990-98, mem. comprehensive cancer ctr., 1992—98; assoc. prof. health care Wharton Sch., U. Pa., Phila., 1993—96, prof. health care mgmt., from 1996; assoc. prof. medicine Sch. of Medicine, U. Pa., Phila., 1993—96, prof. medicine, from 1996; assoc. dean health svcs. rsch. U. Pa., Phila., 1995-98. Asst. instr. dept. medicine N.Y. Hosp.-Cornell Med. Ctr., 1981—84; mem. Inst. for Human Gene Therapy, U. Pa. Med. Ctr., Phila., 1995—96; mem. drug use effects com. Hosp. of U. Pa., 1990—91; mem. admissions and awards com. health care mgmt. dept. Wharton Sch., 1990—92; mem. exec. com. Leonard Davis Inst. Health Econs., from 1990, sr. fellow, from 1984; co-dir. Health of the Pub. program Sch. Medicine U. Pa., 1991—92, mem. com. on jud. ethics, 1993—99, mem. ctr. for bioethics adv. com., faculty senate Sch. Medicine, 1994—2000, mem. master's program in med. ethics adv. com. Coll. Arts and Scis., 1995—99, mem. com. on health svcs. rsch. Sch. Medicine, 1995—99, mem. com. on multiculturalism in rsch. Inst. on Aging, 1995—99, mem. info. sys. strategic planning steering com. Sch. Medicine, 1996; cons. Solvay Pharms., Marietta, Ga., U. Mo. Sch. Medicine, Columbia, 1994, UNISYS Corp., Blue Bell, Pa., 1993, Prudential Ins. Co., Atlanta, 1993—99, PACC Bd. Dirs., Clackamas, Oreg., 1993, Gate Pharms., Kulpsville, Pa., 1994—95, Exogen Co., Princeton, NJ, 1994—99, Forest Labs., NYC, 1994—99, VidaMed Corp., Palo Alto, Calif., 1993—95, Health Industry Mfrs. Assn., Washington, 1993—94, Procter & Gamble, Morris Plains, NJ, 1993, Syntex, from 1993, Eli Lilly Corp., Indpls., 1993—95, Amgen, Thousand Oaks, Calif., from 1993, Rhone-Poulenc Rorer, Antony Cedex, France, from 1992, Abbott Labs., Abbott Park, Ill., 1991—99, others; lectr. in field. Contbr. over 150 articles to profl. jours. and newspapers, chpts. to books. Recipient Article of the Year award Assn. for Health Svcs. Rsch., 1990, Young Investigator's award, 1993. Fellow ACP, Am. Bd. Internal Medicine; mem. Internat. Soc. Tech. Assessment in Health Care, Soc. Gen. Internal Medicine, Phila. Coll. Physicians, Internat. Soc. for Pharm. Outcome Rsch., Am. Fedn. for Clin. Rsch., Assn. for Health Svcs. Rsch., Physicians for Social Responsibility, Soc. Gen. Internal Medicine, Am. Soc. for Clin. Investigation, Alpha Omega Alpha, Gamma Beta Sigma. Home: Bala Cynwyd, Pa. Died May 24, 2007.

HILLMAN, ELSIE HILLIARD (MRS. HENRY LEA HILLMAN), political organization worker; b. Pitts., Dec. 9, 1925; d. Thomas Jones and Marianna (Talbott) Hilliard; m. Henry Lea Hillman, May 1945; children: Juliet Lea Hillman Simmonds, Audrey Hillman Fisher, Henry Lea Jr., William Talbott. Student, Westminister Choir Coll., 1944—45; student (hon.), Waynesburg Coll., 1978; student, Duquesne U., 1980. Mem. 14th ward Republican Com., 1956, chmn., 1964—70; mem. Rep. Fin. Com., 1963, Pa. State Adv. Com., from 1963; alt. del. Rep. Nat. Conv., 1964; del., 1968, 1984; dep. del., 1976; del.-at-large, 1980; chmn. Rep. Exec. Com. Allegheny County, 1976—77; co-chmn. Re-elect Nixon Dinner, 1971; mem. Rep. Nat. Com., from 1975; co-chmn. Pa. Reagan-Bush Com., 1984; worked for the election of Tom Ridge as Governor of Pa., 1994; advised and supported former Republican Governors of Pa. William W. Scanton and Dick Thornburgh, former senators John Heinz and Arlen Specter, Vice-President Nelson A. Rockefeller. Trustee Ellis Sch., Pitts., 1961—66; hon. bd. mem., from 1966; trustee Carlow Coll.; bd. dirs., v.p. WQED Pub. TV, Pitts. Oratorio Soc.; bd. dirs. Squirrel Hill Urban Coalition, 1972; v.p., from 1972; bd. dirs. Westminster Choir Coll. Recipient Women of Yr., Squirrel Hill Kiwanis, 1965, Pitts./Vectors award, 1982, Humanitarian award, Guardians of Greater Pitts., 1973, Nat. Brotherhood award, NCCJ, 1973, Pa. Disting. Rep. award, 1974, Disting. Dau. of Pa. award, 1975, Community Service award, Jaycees, 1979, Catherine Booth award, Salvation Army, 1987, Spirit of Israel award, Jewish Nat. Fund, 1988, St. Barnabas Hance award. Mem.: Urban League of Pitts. Episcopalian. Home: Pittsburgh, Pa. Died Aug. 4, 2015.

HILLS, RODERICK MALTMAN, lawyer; b. Seattle, Mar. 9, 1931; s. Kenneth Maltman and Sarah B. (Love) H.; m. Carla Helen Anderson, Sept. 27, 1958; children: Laura, Roderick Jr., Megan, Allison. BA in History, Stanford U., 1952, LLB, 1955. Bar: Calif. 1957, U.S. Supreme Ct. 1960, D.C. 1977. Law clk. to Justice Stanley F. Reed US Supreme Ct., 1955-57; assoc. Musick, Peeler & Garrett, LA, 1957-62; ptnr. Munger, Tolles & Hills, LA, 1962-75; chmn. Republic Corp., LA, 1971-75; counsel to Pres. The White House, 1975; chmn. SEC, 1975-77; chmn., CEO Peabody Coal Co., St. Louis and Washington, 1977-79; ptnr. Latham, Watkins & Hills, Washington, 1978-82; chmn. Sears World Trade, Inc., Washington, 1982-84; chmn., mng. dir. Hills Enterprises, Ltd. (formerly The Manchester Group, Ltd.), Washington, from 1984; mng. ptnr. Donovan, Leisure, Rogovin, Huge & Schiller, Washington, 1989-92; chmn. internat. practice group Shea & Gould, Washington, 1992-94; ptnr. Mudge Rose Guthrie Alexander & Ferdon, Washington, 1994-95, Hills Stern & Morley, Washington, 1995—2014. Vis. prof. law Harvard U., 1969—70; lectr. law Stanford U., 1960—69; Disting. faculty fellow in internat. finance Yale U. Sch. Mgmt., 1986—89; vice chmn. Oak Industries, 1990—2000, Feg. Mogul Corp., 1977—2003, chmn., 1996; bd. dirs. Chiquita Brands Internat., 2002—07; chmn. Hills Governance Program, Ctr. for Strategic & Internat. studies (CSIS), 2001—14, chmn. assoc. audit com., 2005—14. Bd. editors, comment editor: Stanford Law Rev, 1953-55. Trustee Com. Econ. Devel., co-chair, 2005-08; bd. dirs. U.S.-ASEAN Bus. Coun., Inc., chmn., 1986-90, vice chmn., 1990—2010, chmn. emeritus, 2010-14 Fellow American Bar Found.; mem. ABA, U.S. Supreme Ct. Bar Assn., L.A. County Bar Assn., State Bar Calif., Order of Coif, Chancery Club, Chevy Chase Club, Phi Delta Phi. Republican. Episcopalian. Avocations: tennis, golf, history. Home: Washington, DC. Died Oct. 29, 2014.

HINKLE, JAMES LISLE, oil company executive; b. Roswell, N.Mex., Aug. 12, 1931; s. Clarence E. and Lillian T. (Tannehill) H.; m. Elaine Shiflet, Jan. 3, 1965; children: Lawrence, Mark, Laurie. BA in Geology, Washington & Lee U., 1953, LLB, 1956. Sec., treas. Gen. Western Inc., Roswell, 1959-80, pres., from 1980; v.p. Hinkle Investments, Roswell, from 1959; pres. HHB, Inc., Monterey, Calif., from 1986. Mgr. Vina Madre Winery, Roswell, 1977—; ptnr. Five Oaks, Monterey, Calif., 1978—, Tannehill Oil Co., Taft, Calif., 1978—. Patentee structural stud system. Bd. dirs. Chaves County Hist. Mus., Roswell, 1981—, Eastern N.Mex. Med. Ctr., Roswell, 1982—. Served to capt. JAGC, U.S. Army, 1956-58. Mem. Am. Soc. for Enology and Viticulture. Lodges: Masons, Rotary. Home: Roswell, N.Mex. Died Aug. 13, 2007.

HINKLE, WILLIAM PAUL, mechanical and electrical engineer, consultant; b. Thomasville, NC, Sept. 24, 1921; s. William Alphus and Julia Ida (Snider) H.; m. Dora Nell Workman, July 15, 1950; children: Paula Yvonne, William Lynn. BS in mech. engring., N.C. State U., 1943; postgrad., Citadel Coll., Charleston, SC, 1944-45; postgrad. engring. cert., Western Electric Grad. Sch., Princeton, NJ, 1967-69. Registered profl. engr., N.C.; land surveyor, N.C.; pesticide applicator, N.C. Naval architect Charleston Navy Yard, 1943-46; mech. planning engr. AT&T Techs., Greensboro, N.C., 1946-75; profl. engr., cons. Thomasville (N.C.) Svc., from 1976; pres. Thomasville Golf Course, from 1976. Autor: "G" Factor Designs, 1960, Electical Shielding, 1963; inventor: magnetic trim strips, cabinet mounting frames. Instr. pub. speaking Boy Scouts Am., Winston-Salem, N.C., 1973. With USN, 1943-46. Mem. IEEE (sr. life mem., del. 1966-67, publicity chmn. 1965-70, Exec. Com. award 1968), ASME (life, Carolina chmn. 1971-72, Dist. Chmn. award 1972, Ann. Handbook award 1943), NSPE (exec. com. 1964-67, Exec. Com. award 1967), Am. Congress

Surveying and Mapping, Nat. Soc. Profl. Surveyors, Toastmasters Internat. (disting., club pres. 1965, 73, dist. area gov. 1967-68, Disting. Toastmaster award 1969, Gov. of Yr. 1968, Hall of Fame award 1968). Methodist. Avocations: collecting antique artware, stock car engine development, carpentry designs, golf, photography. Home: Thomasville, NC. Died June 16, 2007.

HIRSCH, ELISABETH SCHIFF, retired education educator; b. Szombathely, Hungary, June 14, 1918; d. Edmund and Hilda (Schlesinger) Schiff; m. Julius E. Hirsch, Dec. 4, 1939; children: Naomi, Susan BS, Columbia U., 1950; MA, New Sch. Social Rsch., 1954; PhD, NYU, 1967. Cert. early childhood edn. Tchr. Beth Hayeled Sch., NYC, 1948—51, Sch. for Young Profls., NYC, 1951—52; tchr., dir. Young Israel of Sunnyside, NYC, 1952—53, Jackson Heights Coop Nursery, NYC, 1953—57; dir. Montefiore Nursery Sch., NYC, 1957—59; tchr. Little Red Sch. House, NYC, 1959—68; asst. prof. H.H. Lehman Coll. CUNY, 1968—70, prof. City Coll., 1970—88, prof. emeritus City Coll., from 1988. Pres. Early Childhood Edn. Coun., N.Y.C., 1973-76; mem. Tchr. Edn. Conf. Bd., Albany, N.Y., 1973-75; participant Longitudinal In-Depth Study N.Y. Dept. Edn., Albany, 1976-81; dir. Comprehensive Day-Care Tng. Program, CCNY, 1977-81, part-time adj. prof., 1988-2001. Author, editor: The Block Book, 1974, 3d edit., 1996; author: Problems of Early Childhood, 1983, (pamphlet) Transition Periods, 1974; contbr. articles to profl. jours Bd. mem. Early Childhood Resource Ctr. N.Y. Pub. Libr., N.Y.C Mem. Nat. Assn. for Edn. Young Children, Assn. for Childhood Edn. Internat., Orgn. Mondiale pour l'Edn. Prescholaire. Jewish. Avocations: classical music, opera, reading, crossword puzzles. Home: Brooklyn, NY. Died Feb. 24, 2014.

HIRSCH, JULES, physician, researcher; b. NYC, Apr. 6, 1927; m. Helen Davidoff (dec. 2010); children: David, Joshua. Student, Rutgers U., 1943—45; MD, U. Tex., 1948; DSc (hon.), SUNY, 1988. Intern pathology and medicine Duke Hosp., NC, 1948—50; from asst. resident to resident coll. medicine SUNY, Syracuse, 1950—52; asst. prof., assoc. physician Rockefeller U., NYC, 1954—60, assoc. prof., physician, 1960—67, prof., 1967—98, sr. physician, 1967—92, physician-in-chief, 1992—96. Sherman Fairchild prof. Rockefeller U., 1988—98, emeritus, from 1998; sr. physician Rockefeller U. Hosp., from 1967, physician-in-chief, 1992—96, emeritus, from 1996. Recipient Robert H. Herman award, 1994, McCollum award, 1984. Fellow: ACP, Royal Coll. Physicians Edinburgh; mem.: Harvey Soc., Am. Fedn. Clin. Rsch., Assn. Am. Physicians, Am. Soc. Clin. Nutrition, Am. Soc. Clin. Investigation, Inst. of Medicine of NAS, AAAS, Assn. for Patient Oriented Rsch. (founding mem.). Achievements include research in obesity, human behavior, internal medicine, biochemistry and physiology of lipids, lipid metabolism and nutrition. Died July 23, 2015.

HIRSCH, LOIS CELESTE, retired librarian; b. Seattle, July 30, 1929; d. Albert Chester and Susan Milliken (Osborne) Heidenreich; m. Julius Hirsch, June 19, 1952; children: Steven Allan, David Stewart, Mark Edward. BS, Northwestern U., 1951; MLS, Rosary Coll., 1967. Libr. Sch. Dist. #68, Skokie, Ill., from 1967;, 1967-94. Mem. NEA, Ill. Edn. Assn. (treas. 1990—), Ill. Computing Educators, No. Ill. Apple Users Group, Ill. Quilters Guild, Dulcimer Soc. No. Ill. (pres. 1990—), Chgo. Zither Club. Avocations: tournament bridge, sewing, spinning, miniatures, zither. Home: Skokie, Ill. Died Feb. 16, 2007.

HIRSCHFIELD, ALAN JAMES, entrepreneur; m. Berte Schindelheim; children: Scott, Laura, Marc. BS, U. Okla.; MBA, Harvard U. V.p. Allen & Co., Inc., 1959-67; v.p. fin., dir. Warner Bros. Seven Arts, Inc., 1967-68; with Am. Diversified Enterprises, Inc., 1968-73; pres., CEO Columbia Pictures Industries, NYC, 1973-78; vice chmn., COO 20th Century-Fox Film Corp., LA, 1979-81, chmn. bd., CEO, 1981-85; cons., investor entertainment industries, LA, 1985-89; mng. dir. Wertheim Schroder & Co., LA, 1990-92; dir. Jackson Hole Ctr. for the Arts. Co-CEO, co-chair Data Broadcasting Corp., 1990-2000; bd. dirs. Cantel Med. Corp., Carmike Cinemas, Inc., Leucadia Nat. Corp. Bd. dirs. Cmty. Found. Jackson Hole; trustee Dana Farber Cancer Inst, 2002. Home: Wilson, Wyo. Died Jan. 15, 2015.

HISEY, LYDIA VEE, educational administrator; b. Memphis, Tex., July 10, 1951; d. Murray Wayne Latimer and Jane Kathryn (Grimsley) Webster; m. Gregory Lynn Hisey, Oct. 4, 1975; children: Kathryn Elizabeth, Jennifer Kay, Anna Elaine. BS in Edn., Tex. Tech U., 1974, MEd, 1990. Cert. tchr., mid-mgmt., Tex.x. Tchr. phys. edn. Lubbock (Tex.) Ind. Sch. Dist., 1975-79, tchr., 1982-91, asst. prin., 1991-95, prin., 1995-2000, assoc. H.S. prin., 2000. Recipient Way-To-Go award Lubbock Ind. Sch. Dist., 1989, Impact II grantee, 1991. Mem. Tex. Assn. Secondary Sch. Prins., Tex. Elem. Prins. and Suprs. Assn., Lubbock Elem. Prins. and Suprs. Assn. (v.p. 1997-98, pres. 1998-99), Delta Kappa Gamma, Phi Delta Kappa. Baptist. Avocation: gardening. Home: Lubbock, Tex. Died June 7, 2007.

HIXSON, ALLIE CORBIN, retired adult education educator, advocate; b. Columbia, Ky., May 28, 1924; d. Alfred B. Corbin and Emma Triplett-Corbin; m. William Forrest Hixson, Aug. 16, 1945; children: Mary Emma, Clarence Hervey, Walter Lawrence. BA in English, Okla. A&M Coll., 1949; MA in Humanities, U. Louisville, 1961, PhD in English, 1969. Sec.-bookkeeper Ky. Farm Bur., Louisville, 1942-45; tchr. English Pub. H.S., Stillwater, Okla., 1949, various secondary schs., Louisville, 1957-64, Ind. U. S.E., Jeffersonville, 1965-69, Bellarmine Coll., Louisville, 1970; head English dept. Collegiate Prep. Girls Sch., Louisville, 1970-74; tchr. Began All-Vol. Feminist Advocacy, 1975-95; ret., 1995. Spkr. in field. Author: A Critical Study of Edwin Muir, 1977, (with Riane Eisler) ERA Facts and Action Guide, 1986 (Sally Bingham award, grant 1986), (with Martha Grise) Survey of Rural Displaced Homemakers, 1980 (nat. funding AAUW, 1979). Lobbyist women's issues Ky. Women Advs., Frankfort, 1975-78; co-organizer, chmn. Ky. Pro-ERA Alliance-Statewide, 1975-95; chmn. coordinating com. Ky. Internat. Women's Year, 1977; co-chmn. Internat. Women's Yr. continuing com. Houston Conf., 1985-89; state rep. Nat. Women's Polit. Caucus, Louisville, 1978; charter mem., State and Nat. Older Women's Leagues, Louisville, 1980; founder, chmn. Nat. ERA Summit, Washington, 1991-97. Recipient ERA Advocacy award Ky. Pro ERA Alliance, 1996, Women's Equity Action League, 1997, Celebration of Svc. Women of Distinction award, 2003; named Feminist of Yr. Ky. NOW, 1999, One of Most Prominent Feminist leaders in Ky., 2001; named to Ky. Women Remembered permanent exhibit. Mem. AAUW (pres. Ky. Divsn. 1980-84, Predoctoral U. Louisville Coll. Faculty award 1964-65), Campbellsville Bus. and Profl. Women (past pres., nat. ERA chmn. 1975-76; Ky. Woman of Distinction 1991, 2001, 2003), Kappa Delta Gamma (hon.). Democrat. Unitarian Universalist. Avocations: reading, writing memoir, caring for pets, bird watching, taking walks. Home: Louisville, Ky. Died Oct. 30, 2007.

HLUBEK, JEFFRY JOSEPH, communications executive; b. Amboy, Ill., Jan. 31, 1946; s. Adolph Joseph and Regina Marie (Kuhn) H.; m. Sheila Anne Webb, Feb. 15, 1969. BA, U. Iowa, 1968, MA, 1972. Vice pres., sr. counselor Young & Rubicam, Cedar Rapids, Iowa, 1978-87; prin. Communication Specialties, Arcata, Calif., from 1987. With U.S. Army, 1968-70. Mem. Pub. Rels. Soc. Am. (counselors acad.), Ingomar Club. Home: Jacksonville, Ala. Died May 21, 2007.

HOAG, DAVID GARRATT, retired aerospace engineer; b. Boston, Oct. 11, 1925; s. Alden Bomer and Helen Lucy (Garratt) H.; m. Grace Edward Griffith, May 10, 1952; children— Rebecca Wilder, Peter Griffith, Jeffrey Taber, Nicholas Alden, Lucy Seymour. BS, MIT, 1946, MS, 1950. Staff engr. instrumentation lab. MIT, Cambridge, 1946-57; tech. dir. Polaris Missile Guidance, 1957-61; tech. dir., program mgr. Apollo Spacecraft Guidance, 1961-72; advanced system dept. head C.S. Draper Lab., Inc., Cambridge, 1972-86; ret., 1990. Mem. Open Space Com., Medway, Mass. With USN, World War II. Recipient Pub. Svc. award NASA, 1969, Spl. award Royal Inst. Navigation, Britain, 1970, Laurels, Aviation Week, 1970. Fellow AIAA (Louis W. Hill Space Transp. award 1972); mem. Nat. Acad. Engring., Inst. Navigation (Thurlow award 1969, pres. 1978-79), Internat. Acad. Astronautics (assoc. editor ACTA Astronautica 1973-79). Home: Medway, Mass. Died Jan. 19, 2015.

HOCHMAN, HARRY, mortgage broker; b. Butler Twp., Pa., July 19, 1925; s. Morris and Tillie (Morainess) H.; m. Lillian Blau, June 24, 1945 (dec. Oct. 1980); children: Michael J., David B., Randy H. Wells, Terry H. Marcus; m. Eileen Kessler, Apr. 9, 1981 (dec. Apr. 1984); m. Carol Ruth Kohn, Feb. 9, 1985. BSBA, Butler U., 1950. CPA, Ind. Acct. Geo S. Olive & Co., CPA's, Indpls., 1952-54; prin. Haddad-Hochman & Co., Pub. Accts., Cleve., 1955-59; v.p. Alvin Homes, Cleve., 1959-61, Met. Mgmt. Co., Cleve., 1961-67, Leader Mortgage Co., Cleve., 1967-69; v.p., CEO Mascom Co. mortgage investment advisor to U.S. Realty Invest, Cleve., 1969-71; sr. v.p. Leader Mortgage Co., Cleve., 1971-74; pvt. practice mortgage broker Cleve., from 1974. With U.S. Army, 1944-46. Mem. Cleve. Mortgage Bankers Assn. Jewish. Died Nov. 18, 2006.

HODGSON, PAUL EDMUND, surgeon, department chairman; b. Milw., Dec. 14, 1921; s. Howard Edmund and Ethel Marie (Niemi) H.; m. Barbara Jean Osborne, Apr. 22, 1945; children: Ann, Paul. BS summa cum laude, Beloit Coll., 1943; MD cum laude, U. Mich., 1945. Diplomate: Am. Bd. Surgery. Intern U. Mich. Hosp., 1945-46, resident in surgery, 1948-52; mem. faculty dept. surgery U. Mich., 1952-62, assoc. prof., 1956-62; prof. surgery U. Nebr. Coll. Medicine, Omaha, 1962-88, prof. emeritus, from 1988, asst. dean for curriculum, 1966-72, chmn. dept. surgery, 1972-84. Trustee Beloit Coll., 1977-80 Served to capt. M.C. U.S. Army, 1946-48. Mem. A.C.S., Frederick A. Coller Surg. Soc., Soc. Univ. Surgeons, Central Surg. Assn., Soc. Surgery Alimentary Tract, Am. Assn. Surgery Trauma, Western Surg. Assn., Am. Surg. Assn. Presbyterian. Home: Omaha, Nebr. Died Aug. 28, 2013.

HOEFLING, JUDY ELAINE, elementary school educator; b. Saginaw, Mich., Sept. 14, 1946; d. Sinclair George and Elaine (Duncan) H. BA, Cen. Mich. U., 1968, MA in Guidance and Counseling, 1969. Cert. elem. tchr. Tchr.'s aide Head Start, Riverdale, Mich., 1968; tchr. 2nd grade Owosso (Mich.) Pub. Schs., 1969-74, tchr. 3rd grade, 1975-78, tchr. 4th grade, from 1979. Sch. rep. comms. com. Owosso Pub. Schs., 1988-90, mem. health-social studies, libr. coms., 1978-90, sch. improvement com., 1991-94; cooperating tchr. edn. dept. Mich. State U., East Lansing, 1987-93. Vol. Coun. on Aging, Owosso, 1990, Owosso Meml. Healthcare Ctr., 1993-94; mem. cmty. outreach bd. United Meth. Ch., Owosso, 1993-94; bd. dirs. Noah's Ark Children's Ctr., Owosso, 1993-94. Mem. AAUW, Mich. Edn. Assn., Mich. Counseling Assn., Owosso Edn. Assn. Avocations: fiction writing, walking, drawing, music, line dancing instructor. Home: Christiansburg, Va. Died Aug. 6, 2007.

HOFFENBERG, MARVIN, retired political science professor; b. Buffalo, July 7, 1914; s. Harry and Jennie Pearl (Weiss) H.; m. Betty Eising Stern, July 20, 1947; children: David A., Peter H. Student, St. Bonaventure Coll., 1934—35; BSc, Ohio State U., 1939, MA, 1940, postgrad., 1941. Asst. chief divsn. interindustry econs. Bur. Labor Statistics, Dept. Labor, 1941-52; cons. U.S. Mut. Security Agy., Europe, 1952, Statistik Sentralbyra, Govt. Norway, Oslo, 1954; economist RAND Corp., 1952—56; dir. rsch., econ. cons. dept. deVegh & Co., 1956—58; staff economist Com. Econ. Devel., 1958-60; project chmn. Rsch. Analysis Corp. (formerly Johns Hopkins U. Ops. Rsch.), 1960-63; dir. cost analysis dept. Aerospace Corp., 1963-65; rsch. economist Inst. Govt. and Pub. Affairs, UCLA, 1965-67, prof.-in-residence polit. sci., 1967-85, prof. emeritus, from 1985; dir. pol. sci. dept., M.P.A. program, co-chmn. Interdepartmental Program in Comprehensive Health Planning UCLA, 1974-76. Author: (with Kenneth J. Arrow) A Time Series Analysis of Inter-Industry Demand, 1959; editor: (with Levine, Hardt and Kaplan) Mathematics and Computers in Soviet Economics, 1967, (with W.W. Leontief) The Economic Effects of Disarmament, 1961; contbr. articles to profl. jours., chpts. to books. Mem. bd. advisers Sidney Stern Meml. Trust; foreman L.A. County Grand Jury, 1990-91; commr. L.A. County Economy and Efficiency Commn., 1991-92. C.C. Stillman scholar Ohio State U., 1940, U. fellow, 1941; Littauer fellow Harvard U., 1946; recipient Disting. Svc. award Coll. Adminstrv. Scis., Ohio State U., 1971. Mem.: AAAS (life fellow 1957), LA Chpt. Am. Jewish Com. (bd. mem.), UCLA Hillel (trustee), Am. Jewish Com. Jewish. Home: Honolulu, Hawaii. Died Dec. 2012.

HOFFMAN, DONALD STUART, music director; b. San Francisco, June 11, 1931; s. Donald Stuart and Emma Coolidge (Painter) H. BA, Dartmouth Coll., 1953; MA, Harvard U., 1955. Collection mgr. Beneficial Finance Co., Boston, 1956-57; music instr. Am. Coll. for Girls, Istanbul, Turkey, 1957-63; asst. prof. music Robert Coll., Istanbul, 1965-73; instr. various schs., Istanbul, 1973-78; announcer Sta. WPFW, Washington, 1978-82; producer, announcer Sta. WYSU, Youngstown, Ohio, 1982-85; music dir. Prairie Pub. Radio, Bismarck, N.D., 1985-94; prodr. Community Access TV, Bismarck, from 1990. Music activities dir. Robert Coll., Istanbul, 1965-73, Dutch Chapel Choir, Istanbul, 1966-69. Author: (book) A Tree To Climb, 1967; composer, editor numerous works, 1957-73; contbr. articles to profl. jours. and mags., 1957-73. Bd. dirs. Dakota Stage Ltd., Bismarck, N.D., 1994—. Fulbright grantee, 1963. Avocations: reading, films. Home: Bismarck, ND. Died Oct. 31, 2006.

HOFFMAN, FRANK LLOYD, data processing executive; b. Aberdeen, Wash., July 11, 1956; s. Joseph and Grace Naomi (Wright) H. ATA in Electronic Tech., Centralia Coll., 1977. Cert. gen. radio/telephone FCC. Technician communications Cascade Loggers Supply, Chehalis, Wash., 1978-79; engr. computer Richmar Corp., Chehalis, 1979-82; technician, engr. software Pacific Sci., Chehalis, 1979-81; asst. technician communications Pacific Power and Light, Portland, Oreg., 1982-83; engr. computer Lloyd I/O Inc., Portland, from 1983. Cons. computer software Gaard Automation, Portland, 1983-84, TEC Am. Inc., Torrance, Calif., 1984-85, Edge Tech., Portland, 1987—. Author: (software user manuals) K-Basic, CRASMB, CRACKER, ED, PATCH, Search and Rescue, 1981—; contbr. articles profl. jours. Precinct person Multnomah County Cen. Republican Com., Portland. Mem. Chehalis Valley Amateur Radio Soc. (co-founder 1978-82). Avocations: amateur radio, model R.R., photography, recreational craft. Home: Beaverton, Oreg. Died Nov. 30, 2006.

HOFFMAN, GEORGE HENRY, JR., retired minister; b. Lebanon County, Pa., July 2, 1924; s. George Henry and Lillie May (Eberly) H.; m. Evelyn Mae Krall, Mar. 27, 1948; children: Bryan George, David Michael, Susan Marie, Rebecca Ann. Grad., Lancaster Theol. Sem., 1965. Ordained to ministry United Ch. of Christ, 1965. Mission pastor Twin Valley Charge United Ch. of Christ, Halifax, Pa., 1965-69; pastor The Valley United Ch. of Christ, Halifax, 1969-72, Emmanuel Reformed United Ch. of Christ, Export, Pa., 1972-90, pastor emeritus, from 1990. Bd. dirs. Penn West Conf. United Ch. of Christ, Greensburg, 1976-81, spl. asst. Appalachian affairs; cons. ch. affairs Bishop's Resource Team, Luth. Ch. in Am. Bd. dirs. St. Paul Homes, Greenville, 1981—. Mem. Alban Inst. Republican. Home: Lebanon, Pa. Died Feb. 11, 2007.

HOFFMAN, KARLA ANN, mathematics educator; b. Burlington, Vt., May 19, 1953; d. Donald Elwood and Lenora Mae (McElhiney) H. Student, W.Va. Wesleyan Coll., 1971-73; BS in Math., Towson State U., 1975; M Ednl. Adminstrn., U. Mass., 1986, cert. advanced grad. study, 1988. Tchr. math. Oxon Hill (Md.) High Sch., 1975-80; tchr. Harriet Tubman Mid. Sch., Portland, Oreg., 1980-84, chmn. dept., 1982-84; teaching and adminstrv. asst. grad. program ednl. adminstrn. U. Mass., Boston, 1984-88, instr. math. various programs, 1987-89; asst. prof. math. Calif. U. of Pa., from 1989. Vis. cons. for mid. and high sch. math. tchrs. Boston Area Pub. Schs., 1986-89; instr. basic math. Curry Coll., Milton, Mass., 1988-89. Recipient Disting. Scholar award U. Mass., 1986. Mem. ASCD, Nat. Coun. Tchrs. Math., Pa. Coun. Tchrs. Math. Avocations: sports, swimming, boating, reading. Home: Coal Center, Pa. Died Nov. 1, 2006.

HOFFMANN, STANLEY, political science educator; b. Vienna, Nov. 28, 1928; came to U.S., 1955; m. Inge Schneier Hoffmann, Oct. 3, 1963. AM in Govt., Harvard U., 1952; LLD, U. Paris, France, 1953. Instr. Govt. Harvard U., Cambridge, Mass., 1955-57, asst. prof. Govt., 1957-59, assoc. prof., 1959-63, prof., 1963—2015, chmn. Ctr. European Studies, 1969—2015, Douglas Dillon Prof. Civilization of France, 1969-95. Author: Le Mouvement Poujade, 1956, Decline or Renewal? France Since the 1930s, 1974, Janus and Minerva, 1986, The European Sisyphus: Essays on Europe, 1964-94; co-author: In Search of France, 1963, The New European Community, 1992; frequent contributor to journals like Foreign Policy, The New York Review of Books and The New Republic Mem. Coun. Fgn. Rels. (bd. dirs. 1984-92). Home: Cambridge, Mass. Died Sept. 2015.

HOGAN, JOSEPH MICHAEL, state legislator; b. Fort Dodge, Iowa, Aug. 10, 1937; m. Sandy S. Hogan; children: Kathleen, J. Michael, David J., J. Alan. BBA, U. Notre Dame; JD, Georgetown U. Mem. Dist. 10 Nev. State Assembly, Nev., 2004—14. Served with USN, 1959—62. Mem.: Nature Conservancy, Am. Civil Liberties Union, League Women Voters, Common Cause, Nat. Urban League. Democrat. Died Oct. 17, 2014.

HOGAN, JOSEPH PATRICK, advertising agency executive, real estate executive; b. Glen Ridge, NJ, Oct. 15, 1927; m. Marie S. Kelly, June 6, 1951. Student, Bethany Coll., W.Va., 1945, Swathmore Coll., Pa., 1945-46, Syracuse U., 1947-48; BBA, U. Tenn., 1950. Prodn. mgr. Lavidge & Davis Advt., Knoxville, Tenn., 1950-54; chief exec. officer, chmn. bd. J.P. Hogan & Co., Inc., Knoxville, from 1954; chmn. of the bd., chief exec. officer Horoco, Inc. Real Estate, Knoxville, from 1956. Bd. dirs. Knoxville Dogwood Arts Festival, 1958-61. Served with USNR, 1945-47. Mem. Mutual Advt. Agy. Network (pres. 1977), Knoxville C. of C., Knoxville Sales and Mktg. Execs., Knoxville Advt. Club. Clubs: Deane Hill Country. Republican. Roman Catholic. Home: Knoxville, Tenn. Died Oct. 30, 2006.

HOGAN, MICHAEL ARTHUR, pediatrician; b. Ft. Wayne, Ind., Nov. 18, 1931; s. Michael Thomas and Esther (Chapman) H.; m. Mary Ann Healy, June 15, 1957; children: James B., Michael T., John L., Matthew E. (dec.). Student, Purdue U., 1953; MD, Ind. U., 1957. Cert. Am. Bd. Pediatrics. Commd. ensign USN, 1957, advanced through grades to lt., intern San Diego, 1957-58, med. officer Camp Pendleton, Calif., 1958-60, resigned, 1960; resident pediatrics Ind. U. Med. Ctr., Indpls., 1960-62; pvt. practice pediatrics Indpls., from 1962; chmn. dept. pediatrics St. Vincent Hosp., Indpls., from 1983. Clin. prof. pediatrics Ind. U. Sch. Medicine, Indpls., 1989—. Mem. Am. Acad. Pediatrics (Ind. chpt., treas. 1975-81, v.p. 1981-84, pres. 1984-90, com. on hosp. care 1985—). Roman Catholic. Avocations: reading, gardening. Home: Indianapolis, Ind. Died May 24, 2007.

HOGAN, TERRENCE PATRICK, psychologist, university administrator; b. Dubuque, Iowa, May 10, 1937; s. Clement Joseph and Clarissa Elizabeth (Theis) H.; m. Elizabeth Anne Gonner, May 15, 1963 (dec. 1992); children: Maureen Anne, Timothy Patrick, Sean Michael; m. Jennie Thomas, July 7, 1994. BA, Loras Coll., 1959; MA, Cath. U. Am., 1961, PhD, 1963. Chief clin. psychologist VA Hosp., Clinton, Iowa, 1963-65; asst. prof. Bradley U., Peoria, Ill., 1965-67; pvt. practice psychology Marshfield, Wis., 1967-69; from asst. prof. to prof. psychology, dir. clin. tng. U. Man., Winnipeg, Can., 1969-77, asso. dean arts, prof. psychology, 1977-80, dean faculty grad. studies, prof. psychology/cmty. health, 1980-82, assoc. acad. v.p., 1982-91, v.p. rsch. and external programs, from 1991. Cons. Health Scis. Ctr., Winnipeg, Man. Telephone Svc., Winnipeg; active Social Sci. and Humanities Rsch. Coun. Can., 1983-86, Econ. Innovation and Tech. Coun., Man., 1993—; bd. dirs. Man. Health Rsch. Coun., 1992—, vice chair, 1994—; bd. dirs. TRLabs, Edmonton; mem. exec. com. HVDC Ctr., Winnipeg. Author: (with Richard I. Hartman and John T. Wholihan) Modern Business Administration: An Introduction, 1969, (with Gerald Erickson) Family Therapy: An Introduction to Theory and Techniques, 2d edit., 1981. Recipient several grants. Fellow Can. Psychol. Assn. (pres. 1982-83); mem. Am. Psychol. Assn., Social Sci. Fedn. Can. (dir.), Psychol. Assn. Man., Man. Psychol. Soc., Soc. Personality Assessment, Can. Soc. for the Study of Higher Edn. (bd. dirs., pres. 1991-92), Internat. Union Psychol. Scis. (exec. com.), Delta Epsilon Sigma, Sigma Xi, Psi Chi. Roman Catholic. Home: Winnipeg, Canada. Died Sept. 19, 2007.

HOGBERG, FRANK ALBERT, industrial sales engineer; b. Chgo., Sept. 11, 1939; s. Carl Seils and Frances (Harris) H.; m. Daveda Frances Nelson, Sept. 15, 1962; children: Eric David, Kristen Frances. BS in Mktg., Bowling Green State U., Ohio, 1961. Dept. mgr. Sears, Roebuck & Co., Chgo., 1964-67; sales rep. quad cities Hewitt Robbins, Litton Inc., Moline, Ill., 1967-70; v.p. Beaty Machine Works, Keokuk, Iowa, 1970-74; br. sales mgr. Berry Bearing, Ft. Madison, Iowa, 1974-76; sales engr., mgr. M.R.S. Indsl., Peoria, Ill., from 1976. Advisor Jr. Achievement, Chgo. 1964-66; merit badge counselor, Boy Scouts Am., Peoria, 1981—. Mem. Am. Assn. Lubrication Engrs., Am. Mgmt. Assn., Am. Mktg. Assn. Roman Catholic. Avocations: computer software applications, photography, reading. Home: Dunlap, Ill. Died Dec. 3, 2006.

HOKE, DONALD EDWIN, clergyman, educator; b. Chicago, June 18, 1919; s. Edwin Floyd and Edith Mary (Dingle) H.; m. Martha Cowan, July 20, 1945; children: Donald Edwin Jr., Steven T. BA, Wheaton Coll., 1941, MA, 1944, DD (hon.), 1959. Ordained ministry Presbyn. Ch., 1943. Founding pastor South Park Ch., Park Ridge, Ill., 1941-47; asst. to pres. Columbia (S.C.) Bible Coll. and Sem., 1947-52; missionary Evangelical Alliance Mission, Wheaton, Ill., 1952-73; founding pres. Tokyo Christian U., 1955-73; co-founder Japan Bible Sem., Tokyo, 1958-73; exec. dir. Internat. Congress for World Evangelization, Lausanne, Switzerland, 1973-74, Billy Graham Ctr., Wheaton, 1974-78; sr. pastor Cedar Springs Presbyn. Ch., Knoxville, Tenn., 1978-89. Treas. Lausanne Com. World Evangelization, Charlotte, N.C., 1975-89; trustee World Radio Missionary Fellowship, Quito, Ecuador, 1986—; bd. dirs. Mission to World Presbyn. Ch. Am., 1983-89. Author, editor: The Church in Asia, 1975; editor: Refugee, 1971, Evangelicals Face the Future, 1977; contbg. editor Christian Life, 1943-75. Trustee Columbia Bible Coll., 1986—, Spiritual Leadership Knoxville, 1987—; mem. adv. coun. Knoxville Juvenile Ctr., 1987-91. Mem. Evang. Theol. Soc. Republican. Avocations: travel, book collecting, reading. *In this day, when traditional values are being abandoned and society is adrift, now as never before we need to return to the Bible for truth, moral guidance, hope and eternal life.* Died Nov. 14, 2006.

HOKE, SHEILA WILDER, retired librarian; b. Greensboro, NC; d. Herbert Bruce Wilder and Virginia Dare (Caylor) Wilder-Dell; m. Robert Edward Hoke, Nov. 22, 1958 (dec.); children: Raymond Fellow, Philip Wilder. Student, Montclair Coll., 1948; BA in History, U. Kans., 1950, postgrad., 1951, BS in Edn., 1952; postgrad., John Hopkins U., 1955; MLS, U. Wis., 1955; MS in Edn., Southwestern Okla. State U., 1977; postgrad., Johns Hopkins U., Montclair State Coll. Tchr. history Fredonia (Kans.) High Sch., 1952-54; student asst. U. Wis., Madison, 1954-55; children's libr. BR Enoch Pratt Libr., Balt., 1955-58; libr. dir. U.S. Army Spl. Svcs., Bavaria, Fed. Republic Germany, 1958-59; libr. U.S. Army Dependent Schs., Straubing, Fed. Republic Germany, 1959-60; cataloger Southwestern Okla. State U. Libr., Weatherford, 1963-69, libr. dir., 1969-93; ret., 1993. Mem. spl. projects com. Okla. Dept. Edn., 1974, adv. com. Okla. State Regents Libr., 1975-77. Mem. Okla. State Regents for Higher Edn. Libr. Networking, 1989-93; vol. with children Agape Med. Clinic; reading tutor to 1st grade student Weatherford Pub. Schs.; vol. helper for home-bound; active sr. citizens groups., student asst. Med. Libr., U Wis. Named Vol. of Yr., Pioneer Citizens Weatherford Group, 2010. Mem. AAUW (pres., state bd. dirs. 1980, Weatherford br. 1981-83), Nat. Assn. Ret. Fed. Employees, Okla. Libr. Assn. (chmn. tech. svcs. divsn. 1969-70, chmn. coll. and univ. divsn. 1972-73, chmn. adminstrs. workshop 1973, chmn. libr. edn. divsn. 1975-76, chmn. recruitment com. 1978, archives com. 1980), Okla. Ret. Tchrs. Assn., Weatherford C. of C. (edn. com. 1974-75, cert. meritorious achievement from Gov. Nigh 1985), Custer County Hist. Soc., western Okla. Hist. Soc., Higher Edn. Alumni Coun. Okla., Delta Kappa Gamma (pres. Lambda chpt. 1980-82), Phi Alpha theta, Kappa Kappa Iota (pres. Lambda chpt. 1984-85, 2005-06). Republican. Baptist. Avocation: travel. Home: Weatherford, Okla. Died Oct. 2014.

HOLLAMON, ELIZABETH ERSKINE, educational consultant; b. Seguin, Tex., Aug. 9, 1930; d. Thomas Henry and Elizabeth Humphreys (Erskine) H.; m. Bert A. Perry, Jr., Aug. 7, 1954 (div.). BA, U. Tex., 1952; MS, Fla. State U., 1967; EdD, Kennedy We. U., 1989. Lic. elem. and secondary tchr., Tex. Headmistress Trinity Episc. Sch., Galveston, Tex., 1970-94; interim head Tex. Mil. Inst., 1994-95; ednl. cons., from 1995. Mem. bd. Nat. Assn. Episcopal Schs., 1976-81; life bd. mem. Southwestern Assn. Episcopal Schs., 1973—. Bd. dirs. William Temple Found., Galveston, 1981-86, Youth Orch., San Antonio; pres. bd. Salvation Army, Galveston, 1991. Grantee Fla. State U., 1966-67, NSF, 1966-67. Mem. Ind. Sch. Assn. S.W. (exec. com. 1987-89, treas. 1986-88), Philos. Soc. Tex., DAR, Daus. Republic Tex., Colonial Dames, Kappa Kappa Gamma. Home: Seguin, Tex. Died Mar. 6, 2007.

HOLLIDAY, PETER OSBORNE, JR., dentist; b. Macon, Ga., July 9, 1921; s. Peter Osborne and Martha Elizabeth (Riley) H.; m. Mary Lucille Dozier, Nov. 12, 1949; children: Peter III, Lucy, Lindsay, Mary. DDS, Emory U., 1945; postgrad., U. Mich., 1947-48. Pvt. practice dentistry, Macon, from 1947. Mem. Gov. Carter's Dental Adv. Com., Atlanta, 1972. Head dental div. United Givers Fund, Macon, 1956; mem. bicycle com. Macon-Bibb County Planning & Zoning Commn., 1995—. With USNR Dental Corps, 1945-47, China. Fellow Am. Coll. Dentists, Internat. Coll. Dentists (dep. regent for Ga. 1983-85); mem. ADA (alt. del. 1978), Ga. Dental Assn. (sec.-treas. 1971-76, v.p. 1977, pres. 1978-79), Ga. Acad. Dental Practice (charter), Hinman Dental Soc., Ctrl. Dist. Dental Soc. (pres. 1963, Dentist of Yr. 1962), Pierre Fauchard Acad., League of Am. Wheelmen. Democrat. Unitarian Universalist. Home: Macon, Ga. Died Jan. 20, 2007.

HOLLWEG, ARND, clergyman; b. Mar. 23, 1927; s. Ernst and Henriette (Voswinckel) Hollweg; m. Astrid Blomerius, Aug. 30, 1961; children: Heike, Uta, Karen. Student, U. Bonn, 1946—48, U. Goettingen, 1948—50, U. Tuebingen, 1952—53, U. So. Calif., 1953—54, U. Muenster, 1955—56; D of Theology, U. Bonn, 1967. Ordained to ministry United Chs. Rhineland, 1958. Tchr. religion Gymnasium and Berufsschule, Lobberich, Germany; asst. min. ch. Essen, Germany, 1955—57; lectr. Inst. Theology and Edn. of Rhineland Protestant Ch. (W.Ger.); regional pastor Rhineland Christian Edn., 1958—63; rschr. Ecumenical Inst., U. Bonn, 1964—65; pastor Bad Honnef, W.Ger., 1966—72; dept. head. hdqrs. diaconical relief ctr. German Protestant Ch., Stuttgart, 1973—76; pastor Ref. Bethlehemsgemeinde, Berlin, 1976—90; chmn. German Reformed Ch. of West Berlin, 1976—90; freelance writer and scientist, from 1991. Lectr. Free U., Berlin, 1978—79, Kirchliche Hochschule, Berlin, 1979—84. Author: Theologie und Empirie, 3d edit., 1974, Gruppe-Gesellschaft-Diakonie, 1976; author: (with others) Obdachlosenhilfe, 1981; author: (with Astrid Hollweg) Biblischer Glaube und neuzeitliches Bewusstsein, 1999; author: Die Glaubensbotschaft von Kurt Gerstein, 2002, Man in the Context of Life in his World, 2004, Ramifications of Globalizations, 2004, Basic Questions of Anthropological and Theological Cognition, 2005, Spirituality and Mysticism, 2006, Christian Faith, Philosophy and Science Against the Background of the Present Ecumenical Discussion, 2007, Contexts of the Global Economical Crisis in the Perspective of Empirical Theology, 2009, Work and Economy in Social Life Today, 2010, Theorie versus Lebenspraxis, 2010, The World Both As Gods Creation and Also as the Object of Science and Technology, 2012, Human Life-Nature-Technique in the Perspective of Agenda 21, 2013; editor: Innere Mission und Diakonie; contbr. numerous essays to profl. publs. With German Army, 1943—44, with German Inf., 1945. Mem.: Bibliotheque World Wide Soc. / IAPGS, Soc. Gestalt Theory and Its Applications, Soc. Protestant Educators (lectr. 1958—63), German Soc. Pastoral Psychology (founder dept. group dynamics and social Psychology). Achievements include discovery of theological scientific approach to social dynamics and theories of cognition and hist. of scis. in the dialogue between theology, interdisciplinary scis. and empirical thinking. Home: Berlin, Germany. *The knowledge of God, ourselves and reality, on which we live, belongs together in Jesus Christ. What does that mean for thinking and science today?.* Died Apr. 19, 2015.

HOLM, JOHN ALEXANDER, linguist, educator; b. Jackson, Mich., May 16, 1943; s. James P. and Leah (Reisbig) H.; m. Michael Pye BA in English, U. Mich., 1965; MA in Tchg. English as a Fgn. Lang., Columbia U., 1968; PhD in Linguistics, U. London, 1978. Tchr. English U. Los Andes, Bogotá, Colombia, 1965-66; tchr. English and German Detroit Inst. of Tech., 1971-73; tchr. of English Kollegium Sarnen, Switzerland, 1973-75; lectr. in linguistics Coll. of the Bahamas, Nassau, 1978-80; prof. English Hunter Coll., CUNY, 1980-98; prof. linguistics Grad. Ctr., CUNY, 1989-98; chair English linguistics U. Coimbra, Portugal, 1998—2015, dir. grad. program descriptive linguistics, 2002—15. Editor: (with F. Byrne) Atlantic Meets Pacific, 1993; editor: Central American English, 1983; author: (with A. Shilling) Dictionary of Bahamian English, 1982, Pidgins and Creoles, 1988-89 (2 volumes), Introduction to Pidgins and Creoles, 2000, Languages in Contact: The Partial Restructuring of Vernaculars, 2004, Comparative Creole Syntax: Parallel Outlines of 18 Creole Grammers, 2007 (co-editor); bd. editors Jour. of Pidgin and Creole Langs., Am. Speech, Creole Lang. Libr. Fulbright scholar U. Coimbra, Portugal, 1993-94, U. London, 1986-87, Excellence in scholarship Hunter Coll., 1988; rsch. grantee NEH, 1973-84; travel grantee U. Papua New Guinea, 1989, Brazilian Linguistics Assn., 1999, Linguistic Soc. So. Africa, 2000, Inst. Cervantes de Manila, 2000, U. Copenhagen, 2001, U. Puerto Rico, 2001, U. de la Reunion, 2002; Woodrow Wilson fellow, 1967-68. Mem. Soc. for Pidgin and Creole Linguistics (pres. 1993-95). Avocations: travel, languages. Home: Miranda do Corvo, Portugal. Died Dec. 28, 2015.

HOLMAN, DIXON WADE, retired judge; b. Harlingen, Tex., Oct. 17, 1933; s. Dixon James and Ruth Stovall Holman; m. Sharon Green Holman, Nov. 29, 1958; children: Dixon Ray, Mary Claire Holman Sullivan. BBA, U. Tex., Austin, 1955, JD, 1958. Bar: Tex., U.S. Ct. Appeals (5th cir.), U.S. Supreme Ct 1966, U.S. Dist. Ct. (no. dist.) Tex., U.S. Dist. Ct. (ea. dist.) Tex. Ho. counsel Allied Fin. Group, Dallas, 1960—71; ptnr. Cribbs, McFarland & Holman, Arlington, Tex., 1971—81; justice 2d Ct. Appeals State of Tex., Fort Worth, Tex., 1981—83; judge 141st Dist. Ct. State of Tex., 1988—90, 48th Dist. Ct. State of Tex., 1992—95; justice 2d Ct. Appeals State of Tex., 1995—2008. Bd. mem. North Ctrl. Tex. Coun. of Govts., 1979—81; mem. Tex. Joint Select Com. on Judiciary, 1987—88. Author: Consumer Credit Law in Texas, 1970. Coll. footbal referee; mem. Tex. Ho. Rep., Austin, Tex., 1957—59, Arlington City Coun., 1977—81; bd. mem. Tarrant County Coll. Sys., 1987. Recipient Silver Gavel award, Tarrant County Bar Assn., 2003. Mem.: Tarrant Bar Found., State Bar Tex. Found., N.Ctrl. Tex. Coun. Govt., Tarrant County Bar Assn. (Silver Gavel award 2003). Republican. Methodist. Died Sept. 26, 2015.

HOLMES, ALFRED, minister; b. Aiken, SC, Oct. 14, 1939; s. Bright Ridge and Glwillie (Corbitt) H.; m. Gladys Folks, Dec. 19, 1959; children: Catharine, Annette, Jeannette, Telford, Rebecca, Stephanie. BA in Bible, Bible Sem., Plymouth, Fla., 1985. Ordained to ministry, Bapt. Ch. Pastor Mt. Anna Bapt. Ch., Aiken, S.C., from 1978, Carey Hill Bapt. Ch., Edgefield, S.C., from 1978. Moderator Storm Br. Assn., Aiken, 1985—, Macedonia Assn., Barnwell, S.C., 1975-83; bd. dirs. ACT Clergy Bd., 1990—, mem. homeless com., 1990—; bd. dirs. Bapt. State Conv., Columbia, 1976—. Died Feb. 7, 2007.

HOLMES, DAVID GROVER, lawyer, military safety administrator; b. Troy, Ala., Aug. 21, 1938; s. Roy and Irene Holmes; children: David, Brent, Heather. BS, U. Ala., Tuscaloosa, 1959; MS in Systems Mgmt., U. So. Calif., 1973; JD, Jones Law Inst., 1982. Bar: Ala. 1982, U.S. Supreme Ct. 1992. Commd. ensign U.S. Navy, 1961, advanced through grades to lt. comdr., 1971, aviator, 1961-76, resigned, 1971; safety specialist Safety Ctr. U.S. Army, Ft. Rucker, Ala., 1971-82, safety mgr. Atlanta, 1982-91; pvt. practice of law Brundidge, Ala., from 1983. Life mem. Gideons; active Big Bros. Internat. Mem. Fellowship of Christian Farmers, Christian Legal Soc., Lawyers Christian Fellowship. Baptist. Avocation: cattle ranching. Home: Troy, Ala. Died May 9, 2007.

HOLMES, DOROTHY SPARHAWK, writer, retired nurse; b. Rowley, Alta., Can., Nov. 30, 1914; d. Lafayette Freemont and Bertha Emily (Whipp) Sparhawk; m. George F. Holmes, Apr. 13, 1936; children: Delores Jean, Ramone Joan, Debra Lee. GED, Ctrl. Oreg. C.C., 1964, LPN, 1967. Nurse St. Charles Hosp., Bend, Oreg., 1967-69, with admitting office, 1969; mem. staff Elzora Convalescent Home, Milton-Freewater, Oreg., 1969-70, Blue Mountain

Convalescent Ctr., 1970-73; ret., 1973. Author: Sir Chester Cricket, 1990, Songs of a Singing Heart, 1996. Avocations: writing, painting, drawing. Home: Yakima, Wash. Died Feb. 27, 2007.

HOLMES, JAMES HILL, III, lawyer; b. Birmingham, Ala., Sept. 10, 1935; s. Houston Eccleston and Celia Lindsey (Wearn) Holmes; m. Julia (Judy) Ryman, Aug. 17, 1963; children: James H. IV, Randell Ryman, Tucker Malone. BBA, So. Meth. U., 1957, LLB, 1959; grad, ROTC, USAF. Bar: Tex. 1959, U.S. Ct. Mil. Appeals 1960, U.S. Dist. Ct. (no. dist.) Tex. 1963, U.S. Dist. Ct. (ea. dist.) Tex. 1966, U.S. Dist. Ct. (we. dist.) Tex. 1979, U.S. Ct. Appeals (5th and 11th cirs.) 1981, U.S. Supreme Ct. 1974. Ptnr. Burford & Ryburn, Dallas, from 1962. Mock trial participant Tex. Nurses Assn., 1978—86; spkr. State Bar Tex. Profl. Devel. Program, 1987—2012; co-chair adv. com. professionalism Supreme Ct. Tex., 1989—90; law sch. rep. So. Meth. U., alumni assn. bd. dirs., 2005—08. Contbr. articles to profl. jours. Past mem. University Park (Tex.) Bd. Adjustment; chmn. University Park (Tex.) Planning and Zoning Commn., 1988—94; numerous other offices in civic orgns.; city councilman City of University Park, 1994—2000, 2002—04, mayor pro tem, 1998—2000, mayor, 2004—10; past dir. Child Guidance Clinic; past bd. dirs. Park Cities Town North YMCA; trustee Tex. Ctr. Legal Ethics & Professionalism, 2001—03; vice chmn. adminstrv. Tex. Ctr. Legal Ethics and Professionalism, 2001—03; past dir., past pres. All Sports Assn., Dallas, 1977; pres. University Park Cmty. League, 1987—88. Judge adv. gen. dept. USAF, 1959—62. Recipient Presdl. Citation, State Bar of Tex., 1995, Judge Sam Williams Local Bar Leadership award, 2001, Professionalism award, Coll. of the State Bar Tex., 1999, Morris Harrell Professionalism award, Dallas Bar Assn. and Tex. Ctr. for Ethics and Professionalism, 2000, Lola Wright Found. award, 2002, Jo Anna Moreland Outstanding Com. Chair award, DBA, 2002, 2003, Disting. Alumni award atty. in pvt. practice, So. Meth. U. Law Sch., 2004—05, award, City Univ. Pk., Holmes Aquatic Ctr., 2010, Disting. Alumni award, Southern Meth. U., 2012, Martindale-Hubbell AV Preeminent Rating, 2012, Disting. Alumni award, Highland Pk. HS, 2014; named Trial Legend, Dallas Bar Assn., Tort & Ins. Practice Sect., 2013; named one of Tex. Super Lawyers, Tex. Monthly, 2003—11, Texas Legal Legend, State Bar Tex., 2009, Inducted as Tex. Legal Legend, Litig. Coun. State Bar Tex., 2012. Fellow: Tex. Bar Found., Am. Coll. Trial Lawyers; mem.: Nat. ROTC Soc., Dallas Bar Found., Patrick E. Higginbotham Am. Inn of Ct. (master 1989—95), Am. Bd. Trial Advocates (pres. Dallas chpt. 2000, named Tex. and Dallas chpts. Trial Lawyer of Yr. 2004), Tex. Bar Assn., Dallas Bar Assn. (numerous coms.), Def. Rsch. Inst. (state chmn. 1994), Internat. Assn. Def. Counsel, Assn. Def. Trial Attys., Tex. Assn. Def. Counsel (pres. 1992—93, Founder's award 1997, Civil Justice Preservation award 2010), Dallas Assn. Def. Counsel (chmn. 1975), Blue Key, Phi Delta Theta, Phi Alpha Delta. Episcopalian. Avocations: fitness, spectator sports, outdoors. Home: Dallas, Tex. Died Oct. 8, 2014.

HOLMES, LOIS O., healthcare administrator; b. Ga., Aug. 25, 1930; d. James M. and Minnie L. (Zinnoman) Vann; m. William J. Holmes, Nov. 19, 1955; children: Gaie, William Jr., Rodney. Grad. lic. practical nurse, YWCA, NYC, 1952; AS, Bronx Community Coll., 1974. RN; cert. CPR. Homefield nurse Ellis Agy., White Plains, N.Y., 1975-76; head nurse Met. Hosp., NYC, 1953-81; supr. Jeff Davis Hosp., Hazlehurst, Ga., 1981-83; coord. King Harbor Care Ctr., Bronx, N.Y., from 1983. Home: Yonkers, NY. Died Feb. 8, 2007.

HOLT, HELEN F. (HELEN LOUISE FROELICH), former government official; b. Gridley, Ill., Aug. 16, 1913; d. William Edward and Edna (Gingerich) Froelich; m. Rush Dew Holt, June 19, 1941 (dec. Feb. 1955); children: Helen Jane Holt Seale (dec. 2008), Rush Dew Holt Jr. AA, Stephens Coll., Columbia, Mo., 1932; BA, Northwestern U., Evanston, Ill., 1934, MS, 1938; postgrad., U. Mo., Columbia, U. NC, Chapel Hill, George Washington U., Washington, Marine Biol. Lab., Woods Hole, Mass.; LHD (hon.), W.Va. U., 2013. Sci. librarian, instrl. asst. Stephens Coll., 1934—37; tchg. fellow Northwestern U., 1937—38; instr. biology Nat. Park Coll., Forest Glen, Md., 1938—41; instr. sci. Greenbrier Coll., W.Va., 1955—58; mem. W.Va. Ho. of Dels., 1955—57; sec. of state W.Va., 1957—59, asst. commr. pub. instns., 1959—60; spl. asst. to commr., dir. mortgage ins. program for constrn. long term care facilities FHA, 1960—70; asst. to sec., dir. elderly programs Dept. Housing and Urban Devel., 1970—84; mem. adv. bd. Small Bus. Adminstrn., 1986—90. Cons. in field. Contbr. articles to profl. jours. Del.-at-large, vice chmn. platform com. State of W.Va. Rep. Nat. Conv., 1958; sr. citizen vol. Rep. Nat. Com., 1984; elder local Presbyn. Ch., 1975—, bd. trustees 1968-74, 80-86, bd. deacons, 1988-94; bd. dirs. Thompson Markward Hall, Nat. Alliance Sr. Citizens, Nat. Safety Coun., exec. com. Women's div. 1975-87, chmn. 1987; pres. Exec. women in Govt., bd. mem. St. Andrews Estate NSF fellow, 1956; recipient Community Svc. Human Rights award, UN Assn., 1985, Stephens Coll. Alumnae award, TIAW World Difference award, 2009. Fellow Am. Coll. Health Care Adminstrs. (Community Svc. award 1978); mem. Am. Health Care Assn., Nat. League Am. PEN Women (br. pres., nat. chaplain), Washington Forum (pres.), Potomac Bus. and Profl. Women (pres. 1983, Woman of the Yr. 1978), Gen. Fedn. Women's Clubs (state v.p. 1989—, other offices), The Washington Club (mem. com.), Sigma Delta Epsilon, Sigma Xi, AAAS, Delta Delta Delta (dist. pres.), Zeta Mu Epsilon (life)(nat. pres.), Zonta (bd. dirs.). Democrat. Presbyterian. Home: Boca Raton, Fla. Died July 12, 2015.

HOLT, MARJORIE JENSEN, artist; b. Salt Lake City, Nov. 3, 1919; d. Peter Joseph and Artimesia (Snow) Jensen; m. Robet Lewis Holt, Oct. 3, 1942; children: Karen Anne, Katherine, Robert, Elida, Peter. BS, U. Utah, 1941. Tchr. art Granite Sch. Dist., Salt Lake City, 1967-68, 68-69; tchr. graphic design Salt Lake CC, Salt Lake City, 1991—99. Exhibitions include Spraglie Libr., 1995—96. Mem.: Utah Water Color Soc. (pres. 1993—94). Republican. Mem. Lds Ch. Home: Salt Lake City, Utah. Died Aug. 3, 2007.

HOLYFIELD, JAMES ROBERT, accountant, consultant; b. Highpoint, NC, May 17, 1940; s. Richard Graves Holyfield and Elouise Blanche (Barnett) Stephens; m. Lourdes Rivera, Sept. 13, 1969; children: Amy Elizabeth, Brian Arthur. BS, Fla. So. Coll., 1962. CPA, Fla. Acct. Ring, Mahoney and Arner, Miami, Fla., 1962-69; mgr. Lybrand, Ross Bros. and Montgomery, Miami, 1970-72; ptnr. Coopers and Lybrand, West Palm Beach, Fla., 1973-82; pres. Holyfield Assocs. P.A., West Palm Beach, from 1983. Lt. gov. Isaac Allerton Colony, Palm Beach, Fla. Mem. AICPAs, Fla. Soc. CPAs, Nat. Assn. Accts., Health Care Fin. Mgmt. Assn., Mcpl. Fin. Officers Assn., Soc. Mayflower Descendants, SAR (1st v.p. Palm Beach chpt.), Forum Club of the Palm Beaches, Governor's Yacht Club (Palm Beach), Exec. Club. Avocation: photography. Home: Lake Worth, Fla. Died Aug. 8, 2007.

HOLZSAGER, MEL, graphic and industrial designer; b. NYC, Aug. 1, 1921; s. Murray I. and Sophie Ida (Levine) H.; m. Miriam Sinofsky, July 30, 1944; children: Gary Lewis, Kathi B. Holzsager Packard, Frederic William. BFA, Cooper Union, 1977. Asst. art dir. United Advt., Newark, 1945-46; prin., art dir. Vision Art Studios, Paterson, N.J., 1946-49; designer Frank Gianninoto, NYC, 1949-52, Jim Nash Assocs., NYC, 1955-57; design dir. Alan Berni Assocs., NYC, 1952-54, 57-59; advt. and packaging dir. Levy & Fryer, NYC, 1954-55; exec. v.p., design dir. Design Directions, Inc., NYC, 1959-69; pres., advt. dir., design dir. Mel Holzsager/Assocs. Inc., NYC, from 1969. Flight officer, bombardier-navigator USAAF, 1943-45. Recipient 3 awards for packaging excellence Packaging Mag., 1967, Bravo award Graphics, USA, 1968. Mem. Package Designers Coun., Packaging Inst., Am. Inst. Graphic Arts (cert. of execellence 1961, 66), Publicity Club N.Y., B'nai B'rith (pres. Fair Lawn 1970, Palisades coun. dist. 3). Jewish. Died Apr. 3, 2007.

HONAN, PARK (LEONARD HOBART PARK HONAN), literature and language professor; b. Utica, NY, Sept. 17, 1928; s. William Francis and Annette (Neudecker) Honan; m. Jeannette Colin, Dec. 22, 1952 (dec. 2009); children: Corinna, Matthew, Natasha. MA, U. Chgo., 1951; PhD, U. London, 1959. Asst. prodn. mgr. Friendship Press; asst. NY Herald Tribune Book Review, 1951—52; instr. English Conn. Coll., 1959—62; asst. to assoc. prof. Brown U., 1963—68; lectr. to sr. lectr., reader English U. Birmingham, England, 1968—84; prof. English & American Lit. U. Leeds, England, 1984—93, prof. emeritus, 1993—2014. Co-author (with William Irvine): The Book, the Ring and the Poet, 1974; author: Matthew Arnold: A Life, 1981, Jane Austen: Her Life, 1988, Authors' Lives: On Literary Biography and the Arts of Languages, 1990, Shakespeare: A Life, 1998, Christopher Marlowe: A Poet and Spy, 2005; editor: The Beats: An Anthology of "Beat" Writing, 1987. Fellow: Royal Soc. Literature. Died Sept. 27, 2014.

HOOD, CAROL A., music educator; b. Axtell, Kans., Oct. 24, 1952; d. Melvin H. and Annalene A. Haverkamp; 1 child, Tonja Dawn Metcalf. MusB, U. Kans., Lawrence, 1974; MusM, Ft. Hays State U., Kans., 1988. 5- 12 instrumental music tchr. USD 212 No. Valley, Almena, Kans., 1974—76; substitute tchr. Usd 231, Morland, Kans., 1976—77; women's accessories merchandiser J. C. Penney's, Winfield, Kans., 1977—79, fine jewelry merchandiser Hays, Kans., 1980—85; 1-12 gen., vocal music tchr. Usd 462, Burden, Kans., 1979—80; grades 1-6 gen., vocal music Usd 457, Garden City, Kans., 1985—87; grades k-8 gen., vocal music Usd 332, Cunningham, Kans., 1988—91; grades k-6 gen., vocal music Usd 383, Manhattan, Kans., 1992—93; customer svc. mgr. J. C. Penney's, Salina, Kans., 1991—92; grades 7-12 instrumental, vocal music Usd 498, Blue Rapids, Kans., 1993—2010. Mid. level honor choir chair NC Dist. KMEA, Junction City, Kans., 2001—03, 2005—07, mid. level honor band chair, from 2005; profl. devel. chair USD 498 Valley Heights, 2004—07; negotiating team mem. Valley Heights Educators Assn., Blue Rapids, 2006—10. Dir.: (valley heights hs band) Cotton Bowl Classic Music Festival (5th Pl. Concert Band, 2001), National Festival States Wash., 2006, 2010; singer (asst. dir.): (Wamego Dutch Mill sweet adeline chorus) Harmony Classic Internat. Competition (2nd Pl. Small Chorus, 2005). Choir dir. United Presbyn. Ch., Blue Rapids, 2001—08, New Hope Evan. Presbyn. Ch., Blue Rapids, from 2008; bd. mem. Marshall County Arts Coop., Marysville, Kans., 2005—07; team capt. Marshall County Relay for Life, Waterville, Kans., from 2003; mem. clarinet player Marshall County Cmty. Band, Marysville, from 2004. Nominee Mid. Level Band Dir. of Yr., NC Dist. Kans. Music Educators, 2006—07. Mem.: Nat. Educators Assn., Kans. Music Educators Assn. Conservative. Presbyterian. Home: Waterville, Kans. Deceased.

HOOVER, LARRY ALLAN, data processing and telecommunications director; b. Statesville, NC, June 13, 1940; s. Robert Paul and Ruby (Kyles) H.; m. Gerlinde Kaspari, Apr. 26, 1997; 1 child, William Christopher; stepchildren: Christine, Jeffrey, Jason. BS, N.C. State U., 1965; MS, Am. U., 1979. Sys. analyst, project mgr. Synergistic Cybernetics Inc., Falls Church, Va., 1965-74; project mgr. Boeing Computer Svcs., Vienna, Va., 1974-80; pvt. practice cons. Sterling, Va., 1980-82; dep. dir. Planning Rsch. Corp., McLean, Va., 1982-85; mgr. MIS Dynamics Rsch. Corp., Andover, Mass., 1985-87; dir. Gaston County, Gastonia, N.C., 1987-96; pres. Strategic Solutions, Gastonia, 1996-97; dir. bus. devel. Gulf Computers, Inc., Washington, from 1997. Sec. Jaycees Altavista, Va., 1965-67; mem. Gaston Civitan Club, 1994—, United Way Fund Distbn., 1992—; mem. bus. adv. coun. Goodwill Industries, 1991—. Mem. Am. Mgmt. Assn., Data Processing Mgmt. Assn. (bd. dirs., v.p. 1980, 87-90), Assn. for Sci., Tech. and Innovation (membership chair 1978-79), Aircraft Owners and Pilots Assn., Wash. Acad. Scis. (policy chair 1982), Pi Alpha Alpha (local chpt. v.p. 1978-79). Republican. Avocations: flying, entertaining, golf, travel, astronomy. Home: Gastonia, NC. Died June 30, 2007.

HOPKINS, JAMES ROY, psychology educator; b. Fieldale, Va., Dec. 7, 1944; s. Luther Edwin and Vergie Emma (Spencer) H. BA with high honors, U. Va., 1968; PhD, Harvard U., 1974. Asst. prof. Vassar Coll., Poughkeepsie, N.Y., 1974-79; assoc. prof. St. Mary's Coll., St. Mary's City, Md., 1980-85, prof., from 1985, head human devel. divsn., 1993-96, assoc. provost, 1998—2002. Cons. Child and Family Resource Program, Poughkeepsie, Head Start, Poughkeepsie. Author: (textbook) Adolescence: The Transitional Years, 1986; co-author: (textbook) Psychology, 1987, 3d edit., 1994; book rev. editor: Jour. of Adolescence, 1993-98. Bd. dirs. Assn. Retarded Citizens, St. Mary's City, 1983-86, v.p., 1985-86. Fellow APA; mem. Soc. Rsch. in Child Devel., Soc. Rsch. in Adolescence, Soc. Psychol. Study of Social Issues, Phi Beta Kappa, Sigma Xi, Psi Chi. Home: Afton, Va. Died Dec. 11, 2006.

HOPKINS, JEAN HARKEY, nurse administrator; b. Santa Cruz, Calif., May 26, 1926; d. Wright Davis and Clara Belle (Gist) Harkey; m. Ira Hopkins, June 25, 1950; children: Wright Davis, Ira. Diploma, Charity Hosp. Sch. Nursing, 1950; BS, Miss. State U., 1948; postgrad., La. State U., 1955, Tulane U., 1974. Corp. pres. Tiny's Cleaning and Laundry Svc., Inc., Gretna, La.; profl. cons. Profl. Staffing, New Orleans; systems analyst West Jefferson Med. Ctr., Marrero, La.; sr. sys. analyst to med. info. sys.-database mgmt., 1991-95. Recipient numerous awards. Mem. ANA (pres.), La. Nurses Assn., Nursing Svc. Assn., La. League for Nurses. Home: Gretna, La. Died Mar. 23, 2007.

HOPKINS, MARK T., information technology executive; BS in Info. Sys. Mgmt., Univ. Md. Insurance sys. analyst; exec. dir. to v.p. adminstrn. Johns Hopkins Bayview Physicians, 2000—01; chief info. officer Univ. Pitts. Med Ctr.'s Presbyn. Hosp. and Shadyside Hosp., 2001, Univ. Pitts. Med. Ctr.'s Academic & Community Hospitals. Named one of Premier 100 IT Leaders, Computerworld, 2007. Died Nov. 13, 2007.

HORNER, JAMES ROY, composer; b. Aug. 14, 1953; s. Harry Horner and Joan Ruth (Frankel). B in Music, U. Southern Calif.; Masters Degree, doctorate, UCLA. Film scores include: The Drought, 1978, Fantasies, Gist and Evans, 1978, Landscapes, 1978, Just for a Laugh, 1978, The Watcher, 1978, Up From the Depths, 1978, The Lady in Red, 1979, Battle Beyond the Stars, 1980, Humanoids from the Deep, 1980, Deadly Blessing, 1981, The Hand, 1981, The Pursuit of D.B. Cooper, 1981, Wolfen, 1981, Star Trek II: The Wrath of Khan, 1982, 48 Hours, 1982, Brainstorm, 1983 (Best Music-Saturn award, 1983), The Dresser, 1983, Krull, 1983, Gorky Park, 1983, Something Wicked This Way Comes, 1983, Space Raiders, 1983, Testament, 1983, Uncommon Valor, 1983, The Stone Boy, 1984, Star Trek III: The Search for Spock, 1984, Commando, 1985, (with Chris Young) Barbarian Queen, 1985, Cocoon, 1985, Heaven Help Us, 1985, The Journey of Natty Gann, 1985, Volunteers, 1985, Wizard of the Lost Kingdom, 1985, In Her Own Time, 1985, Aliens, 1986, An American Tail, 1986, The Name of the Rose, 1986, Off Beat, 1986, Where the River Runs Black, 1986, *batteries not included, 1987, P.K. & the Kid, 1987, Project X, 1987, Cocoon: The Return, 1988, Red Heat, 1988, Vibes, 1988, Willow, 1988, The Land Before Time, 1988, Dad, 1989, Field of Dreams, 1989 (Grammy award-Best Album of Original Instrumental Background Score, 1990), Glory, 1989 (Grammy award Best Instrumental Composition written for a Motion Picture, 1991), Honey, I Shrunk the Kids, 1989, In Country, 1989, I Love You to Death, 1990, Another 48 Hours, 1990, (with Ernest Troost) Andy Colby's Incredibly Awesome Adventure, 1990, Class Action, 1991, My Heroes Have Always Been Cowboys, 1991, Once Around, 1991, The Rocketeer, 1991, An American Tail: Fievel Goes West, 1991, Patriot Games, 1992, Sneakers, 1992, Thunderheart, 1992, Unlawful Entry, 1992, House of Cards, 1993, Jack the Bear, 1993, Hocus Pocus, 1993, Swing Kids, 1993, A Far Off Place, 1993, Once Upon a Forest, 1993, Searching for Bobby Fischer, 1993, The Man Without a Face, 1993, Bopha!, 1993, We're Back!: A Dinosaur's Story, 1993, The Pelican Brief, 1993, The Pagemaster, 1994 (Grammy award-Whatever You Imagine-Best Song,1996), Clear and Present Danger, 1994, Legends of the Fall, 1994, Apollo 13, 1995, Braveheart, 1995, Casper, 1995, Jade, 1995, Jumanji, 1995, Balto, 1995, The Spitfire Grill, 1996, Ransom, 1996, The Devil's Own, 1997, Titanic, 1998 (Academy award for Best Original Dramatic Score, and Best Original Song-My Heart Will Go One, 1997, Chicago Film Critics Assn Best Original Score, 1997, Golden Globe Best Original Score and Song, 1997, Satellite awards Best Original Score and Song, 1997, Grammy award for My Heart Will Go On-Record of the Year, Song of the Year, Best Song written for Motion Picture, 1999), Mighty Joe Young, 1998, The Mask of Zorro, 1998, Deep Impact, 1998, Bicentennial Man, 1999, The Perfect Storm, 2000, How the Grinch Stole Christmas, 2000 (Saturn awards Best Music, 2000), Enemy at the Gates, 2001, Iris, A Beautiful Mind, 2001 (All Love Can Be-Satellite awards Best Original Song, 2001, Grammy award for Best Score Soundtrack

Album for Motion Picture, 2003), Windtalkers, 2002, The Four Feathers, 2002, Beyond Borders, 2003, Radio, 2003, The Missing, 2003, House of Sand and Fog, 2003, Bobby Jones: A Stroke of Genius, 2004, Troy, 2004, The Forgotten, 2004, The Chumscrubber, 2005, Flightplan, 2005, The Legend of Zorro, 2005, The New World, 2005, All the King's Men, 2006, Apocalypto, 2006, , The Life Before Her Eyes, 2007, The Spiderwick Chronicles, 2008, The Boy in the Striped Pajamas, 2008, Avatar, 2009 (Saturn award Best Music, 2009, Grammy award for Best Score Soundtrack Album for Motion Picture, 2011, I See You-Best Song written for Motion Picture, 2011), The Karate Kid, 2010, Day of the Falcon, 2011, Cristiada, 2012, The Amazing Spider-Man, 2012, Wolf Totem, 2015, One Day in Auschwitz, 2015, Living in the Age of Airplanes, 2015, The 33, 2015, Southpaw, 2015; TV scores include A Few Days in Weasel Creek, 1981, Angel Dusted, 1981, A Piano for Mrs. Cimino, 1982, Rascals and Robbers: The Secret Adventures of Tome Sawyer and Huck Finn, 1982, Between Friends, 1983, Amazing Stories, 1985, Surviving, 1985, Tales of theCrypt, 1989, Extreme Close-Uo, 1990, Fish Police, 1992, Michell Kwan Skates to Disney's Greatest Hits, 1999, Freedom Song, 2000; Short Films include Captain EO, 1986, Tummy Trouble, 1989, First in Flight, 2012. Recipient Max Steiner award at the Hollywood in Vienna Gala, 2013. Died June 22, 2015.

HORNER, WINIFRED BRYAN, humanities educator; b. St. Louis, Aug. 31, 1922; d. Walter Edwin and Winifred (Kinealy) Bryan; m. David Alan Horner, June 15, 1943; children: Winifred, Richard, Elizabeth, David. AB, Washington U., St. Louis, 1943; MA, U. Mo., 1961; PhD, U. Mich., 1975. Instr. English U. Mo., Columbia, 1966-75, asst. prof. English, 1975-80, chair lower divsn. studies, dir. composition program, 1974-80, assoc. prof., 1980-83, prof., 1984-85, prof. emerita, from 1985; prof. English, Radford chair rhetoric and composition Tex. Christian U., Ft. Worth, 1985-93, Cecil and Ida Green disting. prof. emerita, 1993-97. Disting. vis. prof. Tex. Woman's U. Editor: Historical Rhetoric: An Annotated Bibliography of Selected Sources in English, 1980, The Present State of Scholarship in Historical Rhetoric, 1983, Composition and Literature: Bridging the Gap, 1983, rev. edit., 1990, 2nd edit., 2010, Rhetoric and Pedagogy: Its History, Philosophy and Practice, 1995; author: Rhetoric in a Classical Mode, 1987, Nineteenth-Century Scottish Rhetoric: The American Connection, 1993, Life Writing, 1996; co-author Harbrace Coll. Hancbook, 11th edit., 1990, 12th edit., 1994, 14th edit., 1998. Named Disting. prof. Tex. Woman's U., 1999, Disting. Alumna, Washington U.; Inst. for the Humanities fellow U. Edinburgh, 1987, Rhetoric fellowship named in Winifred Homers honor U. Mo.; NEH grantee, 1976, 87; recipient Examplar award, Nat. Coun. Tchrs. English, 2003. Mem. Internat. Soc. for History Rhetoric (exec. coun. 1986), Rhetoric Soc. Am. (bd. dirs. 1981, pres. 1987), Nat. Coun. Writing Program Administrs. (v.p. 1977-85, pres. 1985-87), Coll. Conf. on Composition and Communication (exec. com.), Modern Lang. Assn. (mem. del. assembly 1981). Died Feb. 4, 2014.

HORNSBY, DAVID MCMILLAN, musician, music educator; b. Fort Worth, Tex., Nov. 14, 1928; s. David Franklin and Anna Estelle Hornsby; m. Lenda Ruth Jones, 1969 (div. 1973); m. Tamara Wilder Dower, 1963 (dec. 1964); 1 child, Michael David. Diploma, Ft. Worth Conservatory, 1945; MusB, Tex. Christian U., 1945—49; MA in Music and Music Edn., Columbia U., 1949—50; postgrad., U. Colo., 1949, postgrad., 1956, postgrad., 1978; studied with, Jeannette Tillett, Ernest von Dohnanyi, Edwin Hughes, Howard Waltz. Piano faculty mem. Ft. Worth Conservatory, 1946—49; ann. piano concerts Chautauqua, Boulder, Colo., 1951—63; music tchr. PR Pub. Schools, PR, 1953—55; music instr. Colordo Pub. Schools, 1955—58; piano instr. Pvt. Piano Studio, Boulder, Colo., 1956—78; music dir. Colegio Bolivar, Cali, Colombia, 1978—79; piano instr. Pvt. Piano Studio, San Antonio, from 1980; music dir. San Antonio Acad. of Tex., 1981—84. Condr., Christmas concert Gov. of PR, 1954; concert performance Polytechnic Inst., San German, PR, 1955; ann. judging tours Nat. Guild of Piano Teachers, from 1963; lectr. Music Teacher's Nat. Conv., Denver, 1975. Co-author: Bassetti Primer; author: (book of poetry) River Scattered Forest. Recipient Piano Guild Hall of Fame, Nat. Guild of Piano Teachers, 1971, Margie B. Boswell Prize for Best Alumni Poem, Tex. Christian U., 1952. Mem.: San Antonio Music Teachers Assn., Tex. Music Teachers Assn., Music Teachers Nat. Assn., The Leschetizky Assn., The Bohemians (N.Y. Musicians Club), Phi Mu Alpha Sinfonia (life). Died Feb. 21, 2007.

HOROWITZ, JAMES See SALTER, JAMES

HORTON, JOSEPH JULIAN, JR., economics and finance educator; b. Memphis, Tenn., Nov. 7, 1936; s. Joseph Julian and Nina (Williams) H.; m. Linda Anne Langley, May 30, 1964; children: Joseph Julian, Anne Adele, David Douglas. AA, Lon Morris Jr. Coll., 1955; BA, N.Mex. State U., 1958; MA, So. Meth. U., 1965, PhD, 1968; postgrad., Harvard U., 1970—71. Claims examiner Social Security Adminstrn., Kansas City, Mo., 1958-60, claims authorizer, 1960-61; with FDIC, Washington, 1967-71, fin. economist, 1967-69, coord. merger analysis, 1969-71; prof., chmn. dept. econs. and bus. Slippery Rock (Pa.) State Coll., 1971-81; vis. fin. economist Fed. Home Loan Bank Bd., Washington, 1978-79; prof., chmn. commerce divsn. Bellarmine (Ky.) Coll., 1981-82, dean W. Fielding Rubel Sch. Bus., 1982—86; dean Sch. Mgmt. U. Scranton, Pa., 1986-96; prof. Coll. Bus. Adminstrn. U. Ctrl. Ark., Conway, 1996—2001, prof. econ. and fin., from 2001. Asst. prof. George Washington U., Washington, 1968-69, U. Md., College Park, 1969-70; pres. Pa. Conf. Economists, Internat. Acad. Bus. Disciplines, Congress of Polit. Economists, U.S.A. Bd. editors Ea. Econ. Jour.; contbr. articles to profl. jours. Recipient Cokesbury award So. Meth. U., 1965; NSF Grad. fellow, 1964-66, Ford Found. Dissertation fellow, 1966-67, Harvard U. Rsch. fellow, 1970-71, Bank Adminstrn. Inst. Clarence Lichtfeldt fellow, 1981, Burk fellow. Mem. Am. Econ. Assn., Am. Fin. Assn., Internat. Acad. Bus. Disciplines (pres.), N.Am. Econs. and Fin. Assn. (bd. dirs., v.p., pres.), Ea. Econ. Assn. (v.p.). Home: Conway, Ark. Died Jan. 2015.

HORTON, LOUIS CHARLES, retired business products company executive, sales professional; b. Coos Bay, Oreg., Aug. 22, 1918; s. Louis Harrison and Myrl Irene (Cox) H.; m. Elizabeth Young, Nov. 10, 1942; children: Louis Charles Jr., David William. Student, San Francisco Jr. Coll., 1937-39. Sales mgr. Jumbo Ice Cream Co., Balt., 1946-47; ter. mgr. electronic cash registers Nat. Cash Register Co., Balt., 1948-73; retail systems sales mgr. electronic cash registers Victor Bus. Products, Balt., 1974-75, br. sales mgr., 1976, dist. retail systems sales mgr., 1977-78, retail systems br. mgr. electronic cash registers Balt. and Washington, 1979-80, dist. dealer sales mgr. Md., Va., W.Va., N.C., S.C., D.C., 1981-83; ret., 1983; salesman Cash Register Sales & Svc., Balt., from 1983. Pres. Calvary Luth. Ch. and Sch., Balt., 1964-65, v.p., 1985-89; organizer, pres. Sunny Gardens Improvement Assn., Balt., 1954-55. With U.S. Army, 1941-45. Recipient Disting. Salesman's award Sales Exec. Coun., 1961. Mem. Nat. Com. To Preserve Social Security and Medicare. Republican. Avocations: golf, church work. Home: Fallston, Md. Died Nov. 4, 2006.

HORTON, MICHAEL L., mortgage company and publishing executive; b. Pasadena, Calif., Oct. 19, 1961; s. Jerry S. and Mary L. Horton. BA in Bus. Econs., Claremont McKenna Coll., 1983. Lic. real estate broker. Gen. mgr. I.W.S., Pasadena, 1976-80; proprietor NBB Svcs. Orgn., Upland, Calif., 1980-85; regional mgr. Sycamore Fin. Group Inc., Rancho Cucamonga, Calif., 1984-87; CEO, pres. Boulder Fin. Corp., Rancho Cucamonga, from 1987, M.C.M. Pub. Corp., Rancho Cucamonga, from 1992; pres., CEO Sandstone Realty Group, Inc., from 1995; chm. C.H.A.M.P. Inc., from 1996. Author: A Real Estate Professional's Guide to Mortgage Finance, 1985; author Mortgage Fin. Newsletter, 1984—; author fin. workshop. Mem. Rep. State Ctrl. Com., Calif., 1980—, Bldg. and Industry Assn., Rancho Cucamonga, 1988—, Res Publica Soc., Claremont, Calif., 1986—; donor mem. L.A. World Affairs Coun., 1988—. Claremont McKenna Coll. scholar, 1981-83; recipient Dons D. Lepper Meml. award Exec. Women Internat., 1981, So. Calif. Edison Bus. Competition award, 1979, 81. Mem. Nat. Assn. Realtors, Inland Valley Bd. Realtors. Avocations: basketball, racquet sports, water sports. Died Apr. 20, 2007.

HORVATH, STEVEN MICHAEL, physiologist, biomedical engineer, educator; b. Cleve., Sept. 15, 1911; s. Steven Michael and Mary (Pinka) H.; m. Elizabeth Dill Sept. 2, 1940 (dec.); children: Aletha Mary Crowder, Steven Michael, Peter Joseph. Student, Oberlin Coll., 1930; BA in Chemistry and Phys. Edn., Miami U., Ohio, 1934, MS in Physiology, 1935; postgrad., Ohio State U., 1935-37; PhD in Physiology and Biology, Harvard U., 1942. Research asst. Woods Hole Biol. Lab., 1936; instr. Miami (Ohio) U., 1937-39; research asst. Harvard U. Fatigue Lab., Boston, 1939-42, tutor in biochem. scis., 1940-42; dir. physiol. research Met. State Hosp. for the Insane, Waltham, Mass., 1939-42; asst. prof. phys. medicine U. Pa., Phila., 1946-47, 1948-49; assoc. prof. physiology State U. Iowa, Iowa City, 1949-50, prof., 1951-58, acting dir. Inst. Gerontology, 1951-57; attendant in physiology VA Hosp., Des Moines, 1952-58; vis. prof. U. Copenhagen, 1958-59; dept. head physiology Lankenau Hosp., Phila., 1958-61; vis. prof. in physiology Jefferson Med. Coll., Phila., from 1959; prof. physiology and biomedical engring. U. Calif., Santa Barbara, 1962-96, prof. emeritus, from 1996, chmn. dept. ergonomics and occupational health scis., 1979-80; rschr. Sansum Med. Rsch. Found., Environ. Stress Lab, Santa Barbara, Calif., from 1995; eminent scientist in residence Sanrum Med. Rsch. Found., Environ. Stress Lab, Santa Barbara, Calif., from 1997. Cons. in field; com. mem. Dept. Energy Health Effects Working Group on Coal Techs., EPA, Gordon Conf. on the Chemistry of Aging (chmn.), Gov's. Com. on Aging (Iowa), Nat. Health Council (N.Y.), Nat. Inst. Occupational Safety and Health, NIH, Nat. Research Council, Nat. Social Welfare Assembly. Contbr. articles to profl. jours.; mem. editorial bd. Am. Jour. Physiology, Jour. Applied Physiology, Jour. Gerontology, Sci. and Medicine in Sports; reviewer for Am. Rev. Respiratory Disease, Climatic Change, Jour. Clin. Investigation, Jour. Neurophysiology, Jour. Occupational Medicine, Jour. of the Autonomic Nervous System Sci. Fellow AAAS, Am. Coll. Cardiology, Am. Coll. Sports Medicine, N.Y. Acad. Scis.; mem. AHA, Am. Physiol. Soc., Am. Pub. Health Assn., Gerontological Soc., Inst. Radio Engrs., Pan Am. Med. Assn., Phila. Physiol. Soc., Soc. Experimental Biology and Medicine, Undersea Med. Soc. Home: Buffalo, NY. Died Mar. 21, 2007.

HOSKYNS, SIR JOHN AUSTIN HUNGERFORD, business executive; b. Aug. 23, 1927; s. Chandos Benedict Arden and Joyce Austin H.; m. Miranda Jane Marie Mott, 1956; 3 children. Student, Winchester Coll.; DSC (hon.), Salford, 1985; DU, Essex, 1987. Capt. Rifle Brigade, 1945-57; with IBM U.K. Ltd., 1957-64; founder, chmn., mng. dir. John Hoskyns & Co. Ltd., 1964-75; policy adv. to shadow cabinet Govt. of United Kingdom, 1975—79, policy adv. to Prime Min. Margaret Thatcher London, 1979—82. Dir. gen. Inst. Dirs., 1984-89; bd. dirs. ICL plc, 1982-84, AGB Rsch. plc, 1983-89, McKechnie plc, 1983-93, Ferranti Internat. plc, 1986-94 Named a Knight Comdr. of the Most Excellent Order of the British Empire, Her Majesty Queen Elizabeth II, 1982. Avocations: opera, shooting. Died Oct. 20, 2014.

HOTCHKISS, HENRY WASHINGTON, real estate broker, financial consultant; b. Meshed, Iran, Oct. 31, 1937; s. Henry and Mary Bell (Clark) Hotchkiss. BA, Bowdoin Coll., 1958. French tchr. Choate Sch., Wallingford, Conn., 1959—62; v.p. Chem. Bank, NYC, 1962—80, Chem. Bank Internat., San Francisco, 1973—80; dir. corp. rels., mgr. Credit Suisse, San Francisco, 1980—87; fin. cons., from 1989; with Dan Mello Real Estate, 1994—2003, Mello & Hotchkiss Real Estate, from 2003. Bd. dirs. Calif. Coun. Internat. Trade, 1976—87; dir. Indonesia-U.S. Bus. Seminar, LA, 1979. Bd. dirs. Gordonstown Am. Found., 1986—2004, pres., 1986—99, trustee emeritus, from 2012; chmn. Capt. Joshua Slocum Centennial Com., Fairhaven, Mass., 1995—98; bd. dirs. Joshua Slocum Soc. Internat., Inc., 1998—2001; assoc. bd. regents L.I. Coll. Hosp., 1969—71, pres., 1971, bd. regents, 1971—73. Capt. USAR, 1958—69. Mem.: Soc. of the Cin., SAR, Mayflower Soc. Home: Fairhaven, Mass. Died Aug. 2, 2014.

HOUGAN, CAROLYN AILEEN, writer; b. New Iberia, La., Dec. 16, 1943; d. Samuel Arvid and Elisabeth (Case) Johnson; m. James Richard Hougan, Dec. 17, 1966; children: Daisy Case, Matthew Edwards. BA, U. Wis., Madison, 1966. Writer, from 1980. Author: Shooting in the Dark, 1984, The Romeo Flag, 1989, Blood Relative, 1992. Mem. Wash. Ind. Writers. Home: Silver Spring, Md. Died Feb. 25, 2007.

HOUNTRAS, PETER TIMOTHY, psychologist, educator; b. Memphis, Dec. 7, 1927; s. Timothy John and Ethel (Trakas) H.; m. Helen Madias, Nov. 21, 1954; children: John, Dean. BS cum laude, U. Toledo, 1946; MA, U. Mich., 1951, PhD, 1955. Instr. U. Mich., 1954-57; asst. prof. psychology and edn. U. Pitts., 1957-59, assoc. prof., 1959-61; assoc. prof. ednl. psychology, guidance and counseling Northwestern U., Evanston, Ill., 1961-66; prof. counseling and guidance, chmn. dept. U. N.D., Grand Forks, 1966-70; dean of counseling services Eastern Mich. U., Ypsilanti, 1970-76, adj. prof. psychology, 1972-76; cons. psychologist, from 1957. Regional counseling and testing cons. Bur. Employment Security, U.S. Dept. Labor, 1966— ; cons. to U.S. Office of Edn., 1967— Author: Mental Hygiene, 1961, Manifest Anxiety and Achievement, 1970; Contbr. articles profl. jours. Supr. psychologist Pine Rest Christian Hosp., 1989—. Recipient Distinguished Service Citation Gov. N.D., 1969 Fellow Am. Psychol. Assn.; mem. Am. Personnel and Guidance Assn., Ill., Midwestern psychol. assns., Assn. Counselor Educators and Suprs., Psychologists Interested in Advancement Psychotherapy, Am. Ednl. Research Assn., A.A.U.P., Mich. Psychol. Assn., Sigma Xi, Psi Chi, Phi Kappa Phi, Phi Delta Kappa, Kappa Delta Pi. Presbyn. (elder). Club: Rotarian. Home: Zeeland, Mich. Died Nov. 23, 2013.

HOUSEWRIGHT, ARTEMIS SKEVAKIS JEGART, artist, painter, sculptor; b. Tampa, Fla., July 18, 1927; d. Paul Herakles and Evelyn Dorothy (Marshman) Skevakis; m. Rudolf A. Jegart, Mar. 12, 1952 (div. 1968); children: Rudi Artemis, Nike Chrysanthe A.; m. Riley D. Housewright, Aug. 30, 1969. AB, Fla. State U., 1949, MA, 1952. One man shows include Lee Nordness Little Studio, Ltd., NYC, 1957, Washington Fed. Savs. & Loan, Miami Beach, Fla., 1957, 59, 62, 68, Valdosta State Coll., Ga., 1968, LeMoyne Art Ctr., Tallahassee, 1968, Cosmos Club, Washington, 1976, 98, Evelyn Walborsky Gallery, Tampa, 1979, Soc. Four Arts, Palm Beach (First prize, Purchase prize 1956, 57, 58), Tampa State Fair (First prize, Purchase prize 1955), Claude Pepper Gallery Tallahassee, Fl, 2003, others; exhibited in group shows at Mus. of Art, Sarasota, Fla., 1955, Butler Inst. Art, Youngstown, Ohio, 1956, 57, 60, Columbia Mus. Art, SC, 1957, Sarasota Art Assn., Fla., 1957, 59 (Purchase prize), Miss. Art Assn., Jackson, 1957 (Purchase prize), Nat. Mins. Harvard, Cuba (FSU, LSU), Atlanta Art Assn, Madison Sq. Garden, 1959, numerous others; executed cement and shell mosaic murals for Old Westbury Gardens, LI, NY, 1969, Washington Fed. Savs. and Loan, Hollywood, Fla., 1976, 2d Nat. Fed. Savs. Bank, Washington, DC, 1989, oil painted murals Ceresville (Md.) Mansion, 1990, Fla. State U., Tallahassee, Fla., 2001, 03, Vero Beach Mus. Art, 2003, 50th Retrospective Exhbn. Vero Beach Mus. of Fine Art, 2003, Lew Allen Gallery, Santa Fe, 2006, others. Episcopalian. Avocations: swimming, faux finishes. Died Aug. 9, 2015.

HOUSTON, ANITA FOUILHOUX, community volunteer; b. Portland, Oreg., Oct. 30, 1912; d. Jacques André and Jean (Clark) Fouilhoux; m. Isaac Hyne Houston, Apr. 22, 1940; children: André Fouilhoux, Katherine Houston Bradford., Jean C., Marianna Houston. Weber. BA, Bryn Mawr Coll., 1934. Nat. chmn. Resources Unltd., New Canaan, Conn., 1978-81, U.N. Study Group of Fairfield County, 1983-86; vice chmn. Internat. Commn. of Fairfield County (Conn.), Bryn Mawr Assn. of Fairfield County, 1983-86; bd. dirs. Conn. com. for Nuclear Disarmament, 1983-87, Internat. Div. ARC of Conn., Hartford, 1967—. Mem.: Cosmopolitan (N.Y.C.) (chair internat. com. 1984-86); New Canaan Country. Democrat. Roman Catholic. Avocations: politics, internat. relations, tennis, travel. Home: New Canaan, Conn. Died Mar. 17, 2007.

HOUX, MARY ANNE, investments executive; b. Kansas City, Mo., Aug. 16, 1933; d. Rial Richardson Oglevie and Geraldine Marie (McHale) Oglevie; m. Phillip Clark Houx, May 12, 1962 (dec. Dec. 1974); 1 child, Clark Oglevie. BS in Edn., U. Kans., 1954. Tchr. Kirkwood (Mo.) Pub. Schs., 1954-55, Kansas City (Kans.) Pub. Schs., 1955-57; asst. to v.p. Woolf Bros., Kansas City, Mo., 1957-59; Midwest dir. C.A.R.E., Inc., Kansas City, 1959-62; legal sec. Phillip C. Houx, Chico, Calif., 1962-74; owner Mary Anne Houx Investments, Chico, from 1974. Trustee Chico Unified Sch. Dist. Bd., 1977-90; coun. person City of Chico, 1990-91; 3rd dist. supr. County of Butte, Calif., 1991—. Named Woman of Yr., Calif. Assembly, 2001. Mem. Calif. Sch. Bds. Assn. (pres. 1987-88), Greater Chico C. of C. (Athena award 1993). Republican. Roman Catholic. Died Nov. 17, 2006.

HOVEY, JAMES E., psychiatric clinical nurse specialist; b. Milford, Mass., May 22, 1949; s. Harry D. and Claire A. (Thibeault) H.; m. Donna L. Marwell, May 18, 1973; children: Keith L., Cindy A. Student, UCLA, 1977-80; ASN, U. Maine, 1991; BSN magna cum laude, U. So. Maine, 1991; MSN in Psychiat. Nursing, Case Western Res. U., 1994. RN, Mass., Maine, Ohio. Rsch. assoc. NIMH/LEAA Neuro Rsch. Found., Boston, 1971-72, Boston State Hosp., Mattapan, Mass., 1972-75; program dir. med./psychiat. unit Deer Island House of Correction, Winthrop, Mass., 1973-74; co-founder, project dir. UCLA Neurobehavioral Clinic, Reed Neurol. Rsch. Ctr., 1977-80; mental health cons. Neurobehavioral Rsch. Found., Hermosa Beach, Calif., 1979-80; exec. dir. Neurobehavioral Diagnostics, Reading, Mass., 1980-81; pres. Ctr. for Behavioral Neurology Inc., NYC, 1981-83; staff relief charge nurse psychiat. ICU unit Jackson Brook Inst., South Portland, Maine, 1991-93; instr. psychiat. mental health nursing Ctrl. Maine Med. Ctr. Sch. Nursing, Lewiston, 1994; pvt. practice behavioral mgmt. resources, Plymouth, Maine, from 1994. Presenter in field. Contbr. articles to profl. jours. Mem. Am. Psychiat. Nurses Assn. (Maine rep. 1992-96, bd. dirs. New Eng. chpt. 1992-98, pres. 1995-97, inmed past pres. 1997-98, editor The Clinician Issues in Psychiat. Nursing 1996—, Native Son Trailblazer award 1994, Excellence in Writing award 1996, Grayce M. Sills Disting. Svc. award 1997), Internat. Assn. Forensic Nurses. Republican. Roman Catholic. Avocations: Karate, scuba diving, hunting. Home: Casco, Maine. Died Nov. 29, 2006.

HOVSEPIAN, LEON, artist, designer; b. Bloomsburg, Pa., Nov. 20, 1915; m. Mary Bedeian, Mar. 28, 1941; children: Leon II, Marlene Markarian. Cert., Worcester Art Mus., 1937; BFA, Yale U., 1941. Art instr. Bancroft Sch., Worcester, Mass., 1936-37, N.H. Womens Coll., New Haven, 1940-41, Worcester Art Mus. Sch., 1941-82; pres. TriArt Designers, Worcester, from 1941; art instr. Clark U., Worcester, 1982-83. Designer chapels in Archeveche de Papeete, Tahiti, 1983-84, chapels Oblates of Mary Immaculata, Haiti, 1977-78, stained glass windows Narthex-Ch. of Our Saviour, Worcester, 1988, baptismal font Ch. Our Saviour, Worcester, 1989; painting Baptism of Christ Ch. of Our Saviour, Worcester, 1989; one-man shows include Armenian Libr. and Mus. Am., Inc., 1991, Aurora Gallery, Worcester; represented in permanent collections City Hall, Manchester, England, Town Hall, Worcester, Eng., Mus. Modern Art, Erevan, USSR; represented in numerous pub. and pvt. collections. Scholar St. Wulstan, 1932-40, Alice Kimball English Travel, Yale U., 1941; Ford Found. grantee, 1979. Mem. Bohemian's Club, Pi Alpha. Avocations: travel, sketching, photography. Home: Worcester, Mass. Died Apr. 28, 2010.

HOWARD, ALAN MACKENZIE, actor; b. London, Aug. 5, 1937; s. Arthur John and Jean (Compton Mackenzie) Howard; m. Stephanie Hinchcliffe Davies, 1965 (div. 1976); m. Sally Beauman, 1976; 1 child. Student, Ardingley Coll. Stage hand, asst. stage mgr., actor Belgrade Theatre Coventry, 1958—60; debut London West End, Duke of York's Theatre In Roots, 1969, N.Y. debut, 1971; with Royal Shakespeare Co., from 1966; assoc. artist, from 1971. Actor: (plays) Twelfth Night, As You Like It, The Relapse, King Lear, Much Ado About Nothing, Dr. Faustus, Camlet, Midsummer Night's Dream, Man of Mode, The Balcony, The Bewitched, Henry IV parts 1 and 2, Henry V, Henry VI parts 1, 2, and 3, Anthony and Cleopatra, Children of the Sun, Richard II, Richard III, Breaking the Silence, 1985, The Silver King, 1990, Scenes from a Marriage, 1990, Pygmalion, 1990; (films) The Heroes of Telemark, Work is a Four Letter Word, The Return of the Musketeers; (TV series) The Way of the World, Comet Among the Stars, Coriolanus, The Holy Experiment, Poppyland, Sherlock Holmes, Evensong, THe Double Helix, 1986, A Perfect Spy, 1987, The Dog it was that Died, Hercule Poirot's Casebook, 1988, The Cook, The Thief, His Wife and Her Lover; voice of the Ring The Fellowship of the Ring, 2001, The Return of the King, 2003. With RAF, 1956—58. Recipient Plays and Players London Theatre Critics most promising actor award, 1969, Best Actor award, 1977, Soc. West End Theatre Mgrs. Best Actor in a Revival award, 1976, 1978, Evening Standard Drama award, 1978, Variety Club of Britain Best Actor award, 1980. Died Feb. 14, 2015.

HOWARD, CAROL HAMANN, artist; b. Cleve., Oct. 3, 1928; d. Carl F. and Constance (Kline) Hamann; div. 1975; children: Constance, Catherine, Virginia. Student, Skidmore Coll., 1946-48; BFA, Pratt Inst., 1951; postgrad., U. Wis., Mex. Art Workshop, Positano Art Workshop. Tchr. of ceramics and sculpture to blind at IHB; mem. women's com. Bklyn. Mus.; treas. Atlantic Gallery, N.Y.C., 1984-87, bd. dirs., 1987-89, 2000-2003. Solo exhbns. include: Salena Gallery, L.I. U., Bklyn., End of Main Gallery, Essex, Conn., Atlantic Gallery, N.Y.C., 1976, 78, 81, 83, 86, 88, 90, 93, 95, 98, 2001, Intown Club Gallery, Cleve., Chester (Conn.) Gallery, Citifin, Milan, 1987, La Galleria 9, Bologne, Italy, Galleria and Colonne, La Citifin, Florence, Italy, 1988, Citibank, Milan, 1989; group shows include: Nat. Acad. Design, World Trade Ctr., Bklyn. Mus., Cleve. Mus., Touchstone Gallery, Washington, Salamagundi Club; represented in corp. collections. Mem. N.Y. Artist Equity (bd. dirs.), Roebling Soc., Conn. Watercolor Soc., Nat. Painters of Casine and Acrylic, Audubon Artists, Essex Art Assn., Clinton Art Assn. Home: Brooklyn, NY. Died Dec. 26, 2006.

HOWARD, CLIFTON MERTON, psychiatrist; b. Quincy, Mass., Aug. 11, 1922; s. Clifton Merton and Ruth Gilkey (Henderson); m. Margaret Carroll, June 16, 1951 (div. Aug. 1964); children: Kristen, Lauren, Siri; m. Susan D. Krex., May 30, 1965; children: Michael Scott, Jonathan, Robert. SB, Harvard U., 1944, AM, 1947; MD, Columbia U., 1963. Diplomate Am. Bd. Med. Examiners. Rsch. physicist divsn. of Atomic Energy Com. Brookhaven Nat. Lab., 1947-48; founder Waveforms, Inc., 1951-53; pres., CEO Electronic Workshop Sales Corp., 1951-59, Sound Workshop, Inc. and E.W. Assocs., Inc., 1953-59; intern Mt. Sinai Hosp., NYC, 1963-64; resident in psychiatry Columbia-Presbyn. Med. Ctr., 1964-65, N.Y. State Psychiat. Inst., NYC, 1965-66; sr. psychiat. resident Drug Rsch. Svc., 1966-67; dir. evening Psychiat. Clinic, Mt. Carmel Guild, Union City, N.J., 1964-67; asst. attending psychiatrist Vanderbilt Clinic, Columbia Presbyn. Med. Ctr., 1969-75; cons. in psychiatry Columbia Presbyn. Med. Ctr., 1969-75, assoc. attending psychiatrist, psychiat. drug rsch. unit, 1971-75; pvt. practice NYC, 1967-98, N.J., from 1980. Instr. engring. dept., Harvard Coll., 1946; instr. physics dept. CCNY, 1948-50, NYU, 1948-54, instr. psychiatry dept. Columbia Coll. of P&S, 1967-71, assoc. in psychiatry dept., 1971-75. Staff writer APPLE computer mag., 1982-85; founder, pres., CEO S&H Software, Inc.; Apple computer cert. software developer lic. to Reader's Digest, D.C. Heath Co., John T. Wiley & Sons, and others. Lt. USNR, 1943-46, PTO. Mem. APA, Ams. of Armorial Ancestry, Ancient and Hon. Artillery Co. of Mass., Baronial Order of Magna Charta, Flagon and Trencher, Gen. Soc. Mayflower Descs. (surgeon gen. N.J. soc. 1978-84, 99), Jamestowne Soc., New Eng. Hist. and Geneal. Soc., Old Bridgewater Hist. Soc., Order Founders and Patriots of Am., Order of the Crown of Charlemagne, Soc. Descs. of Colonial Clergy, Soc. Ams. Royal Descent, Descs. of Illegitimate Sons and Daus. of Kings and Queens of England (aka Royal Bastard Soc.), Soc. Colonial Wars, Sons of Revolution, SAR. Avocations: genealogy, computers, medieval history, gardening. Died Mar. 3, 2007.

HOWARD, JAMES EDWARD, computer software development corporation executive; b. Los Angeles, July 18, 1942; s. John Andrew and Mary Alice (Vare) H.; m. Margaret Lynne Hornbeck, Sept. 5, 1964 (div. 1981); children: John, Cynthia, Cheryl, Christine. BS, UCLA, 1964, MS, 1965, PhD, 1969. Sr. staff engr. Hughes Aircraft Co., Culver City, Calif., 1964-77; sr. mem. corp. staff Mark Resources, Los Angeles, 1977-81; pres. Howard Soft, La Jolla, Calif., from 1981. Mem. IEEE. Avocations: jazz, swimming. Died Feb. 8, 2007.

HOWARD, RUFUS OLIVER, ophthalmologist; b. Knoxville, Tenn., June 30, 1929; s. Thomas Oliver and Mary Agnes (Smith) H.; m. Martha Grace Lang, Apr. 16, 1955; children: Amy, Thomas, Mary, Martha, Emily. BS, William and Mary Coll., 1949; SB, MIT, 1949, PhD, 1953; MD, Med. Coll. of Va., 1961. Diplomate Am. Bd. Ophthalmology. Researcher U.S. Army, Frederick, Md., 1952-54; rsch. chemist E.I. DuPont, Richmond, Va., 1954-57; student, intern Med. Coll. of Va., Richmond, 1957-62; resident ophthalmology Yale Med. Sch., New Haven, 1962-66, asst. prof., assoc. prof., 1967-74; ophthalmologist pvt. practice Grove Hill Med. Ctr., New Britain, Conn., from 1974; clin. prof. ophthalmologist Yale Med. Sch., New Haven, from 1977. Contbr. 75 articles to profl. jours. Mem. Am. Ophthal. Soc., Am. Acad. Ophthalmology, Conn. State Med. Soc., AMA. Presbyterian. Avocations: tennis, travel, genealogy. Home: Guilford, Conn. Died Aug. 22, 2007.

HOWE, LEE MARTIN, electronics marketing executive, army officer; b. Oakland, Calif., Nov. 7, 1952; s. Nate Houghton and Helen J. (Martin) H.; m. Donna G. Keuper, June 6, 1976; children: Christine Ann, Kenneth Martin. BA in Bus. and Pub. Adminstrn., U. San Francisco, 1974, MA in Mktg. and Internat. Rels., 1976; MA in Mil. Sci. and Strategy, Command and Gen. Staff Coll., 1988. Lic. comml. pilot. Storekeeper, buyer Officers Open Mess, Nas Alameda, Calif., 1968-70; computer systems operator Bank of Am., San Francisco, Calif., 1970-74; dist. salesman Clairol Corp., San Mateo, Calif., 1974-76; reconnaissance officer 2d Mil. Intelligence Bn., Europe, 1979-82; dist. sales mgr. Rockbestos Wire & Cable Co., New Haven, 1984-85; sr. govt. account mgr., regional specialist Gould Computer Systems, Santa Clara, Calif., 1985-86; mgr. internat. sales and mktg. Walkins-Johnson Co., Palo Alto, Calif., 1986-92; pres. ID. Internat. Mtkg., Redwood City, Calif., from 1992. Author: Aerial Reconnaissance Handbook, 1981; editor (area studies) Tech. Transfer into the Pacific Rim, 1988. Mem. spl. com. on youth employment City and County of San Francisco, 1974-75; mem. spl. com. Assn. Bay Area Govts., Berkeley, Calif., 1974-76; active U.S. Little League, Fremont, Calif., 1988—; spokesperson Nat. Crime Prevention Coun., San Francisco Bay Area, Calif., 1994; vol. World Cup Soccer USA, 1994. Lt. col. USAR, 1984—. Decorated 3 Army Commendation medals, 2 Meritorious Svc. medals, Presdl. Award Excellence. Mem. Assn. Old Crows (chpt. rep. 1986-88), Alumni Assn. U. San Francisco (chmn.), Animal Rescue Found., Nat. Crime Prevention Coun. (spokesperson 1994—). Avocations: horseback riding, sailing, mountain climbing, baseball. Home: Fremont, Calif. Died Dec. 27, 2006.

HOWTON, RONALD JEFFREY, banker; b. Bryan, Tex., June 25, 1955; s. Greeley Burtchell and Mary Laura (Corley) H.;; m. Deborah Marie Fuselier, Sept. 3, 1983; children: Robert Fuselier, Brian Daniel, Leslie Elise. BS in Commerce and Bus. Adminstrn., U. Ala., 1978; student, Nat. Installment Credit Sch., 1981, Nat. Sch. Real Estate Fin., 1986; MS with honors, Grad. Sch. Banking of South, 1989. Lic. real estate agt., La.; notary pub., La. Nat. bank examiner Office Comptroller of Currency, Washington, 1978-81; v.p. Bank of Lafayette (La.), 1981-85, State Nat. Bank of New Iberia (La.), 1985-88; v.p., loan rev. mgr. southwest region, corp. loan officer Premier Bank N.A., Lafayette, 1988-96; v.p., sr. credit officer Iberia Savings Bank, Lafayette, La., from 1996. Coach youth soccer, 1990-91, youth baseball, 1991-93; leader cub scouts Boy Scouts Am., 1992. Mem. Krewe of Bonaparte Mardi Gras Assn., Le Triomphe Golf and Country Club, U. Ala. Alumni Assn. Lodges: Sertoma (bd. dirs. Lafayette 1982, v.p. 1983, sec. 1984, Sertoma of Yr. award 1983). Republican. Avocations: family, reading, golf, outdoor sports. Home: Lafayette, La. Died Feb. 23, 2007.

HOYT, DARLENE E. T., nursing consultant, psychiatric nurse; b. Portland, Oreg., July 4, 1938; d. James Van and Christine (Von Lunstedt) Whisler; m. Robert A. Hoyt, Sept. 1969; 1 child, James Michael. BA in Sociology, U. Portland, 1975, BSN, 1976; MSN, U. Wash., 1980. RN, Oreg.; cert. nursing child assessment satellite tng. program. Nurse epidemiologist Seattle-King County Health Dept., 1976-81; dir. nursing edn. Dammasch State Hosp., Wilsonville, Oreg., 1982-87; dir. nursing Psychiat. Medicine Ctr., Salem (Oreg.) Hosp., 1987-89; pres., chief exec. officer Hoyt and Assocs., Ltd., psychiat.-mental health cons., Salem and Lake Oswego, Oreg., from 1989; teaching asst. in pub. health sci. and epidemiology U. Portland, 1975-76. Clin. preceptor community health nursing Seattle-Pacific U.; cons. nurse emergency room Group Health Coop. Puget Sound, Seattle; dir. jail health care Seattle-King County; mgr., clinician Maple Valley Community Clinic; mem. adj. faculty Clackamas Community Coll., Oregon City, Oreg.; pvt. practice individual and group psychotherapy, Lake Oswego, 1984-89; mem. nursing leadership com. mental health div. State of Oreg.; various positions Oreg. Bd. Nursing. Author: Psychopharmacology: A Self-Learning Model, 1986, The Administration of Medications for Nursing Assistants, 1987; contbr. articles to nursing jours. Scholar U. Portland, 1973-76, grantee, 1975; grantee NIMH, 1976-78. Mem. ANA (cert. community health nurse, psychiat.-mental health clin. specialist), Oreg. Nurses Assn. Nurse Practitioners Spl. Interest Group. Home: Lake Oswego, Oreg. Died Mar. 17, 2007.

HUBBARD, FRED LEONHARDT, lawyer; b. Carlinville, Ill., Apr. 14, 1940; s. David Fred and Frances Pauline (Leonhardt) H.; m. Sharon L. Woodyard, Nov. 13, 1964; 1 child, Glenn Edward. BS in Commerce, U. Ill., 1961, JD, 1963. Bar: Ill. 1963. Ptnr. Lowenstein and Hubbard, Danville, Ill., 1965-73, Lowenstein, Hubbard & Smith, Danville, Ill., 1973-88, Hubbard, Smith & Kagawa, Danville, Ill., 1989—92, Gunn & Hickman, P.C., Danville, Ill., 1992-97, Fred L. Hubbard Law Office, Danville, Ill., from 1997. Chmn. Vermilion County Am. Cancer Soc., 1982-83; pres. Plankeshaw coun. Boy Scouts Am., 1984-85. Served to sgt., U.S. Army, 1963-69. Recipient Silver Beaver award Boy Scouts Am., 1980, also Dist. award of Merit. Mem. Vermilion County Bar Assn. (pres. 1991-92), Ill. State Bar Assn., Vermilion County Hist. Soc., Masons (33d degree). Republican. Methodist. Avocations: music, woodworking, photography, model railroading, antiques. Home: Catlin, Ill. Died Dec. 18, 2006.

HUBER, NORMAN KING, geologist; b. Duluth, Minn., Jan. 14, 1926; s. Norman and Hedwig Marie (Graessner) H.; m. Martha Ann Barr, June 2, 1951; children: Steven K., Richard N. BS, Franklin and Marshall Coll., 1950; MS, Northwestern U., 1952, PhD, 1956. Registered geologist, Calif. Geologist U.S. Geol. Survey, Menlo Park, Calif., from 1954. Authority geology of Sierra Nev. Contbr. articles to profl. jours. With U.S. Army, 1944-46, Europe and Japan. S.F. Emmons fellow Soc. Econ. Geologists, 1953-54. Fellow Geol. Soc. Am. Home: Mountain View, Calif. Died Feb. 24, 2007.

HUBRED, GALE LEE, retired chemist consultant; b. Alexandria, Minn., Jan. 4, 1939; BSChemE, U. Minn., 1962; MS in Oceanography, U. Hawaii, 1970; PhD in Materials Sci., U. Calif., Berkeley, 1973. With Dow Chem., Midland, Mich., 1962-68, Kennecott Corp., Lexington, Mass., 1973-78, Occidental, Irvine, Calif., 1979; sr. chem. processing cons. Chevron, LaHabra, Calif., 1979-99; ret. Fellow Marine Tech. Soc. (v.p. 1985-90); mem. AIChE (life, chmn. ocean tech. 1980-90), Soc. Petroleum Engrs., The Metalurgical Soc. (hydrometallurgy), U. Calif. Alumni Assn. (life). Achievements include over 30 patents in field. Home: Brea, Calif. Died Aug. 4, 2007.

HUCKSTEP, RONALD LAWRIE, traumatic and orthopaedic surgery educator, consultant; b. Chefoo, China, July 22, 1926; (parents English citizens), arrived in Australia, 1972; s. Herbert George and Agnes (Lawrie-Smith) H.; m. Margaret Ann Macbeth, Jan. 2, 1960; children: Susan, Michael, Nigel. MA, MB BChir, Cambridge U., Eng., 1952, MD, 1957; MD (hon.), U. New South Wales, Australia, 1988. Chief asst. orthopaedic dept. St. Bartholomews Hosp., London, 1959-60; prof. orthopaedic surgery Makerere U., Kampala, Uganda, 1960-71; found. prof., head dept. traumatic and orthopaedic surgery U. New South Wales, Sydney, Australia, 1972-92, chmn. sch. surgery, 1972-92, emeritus prof., from 1993; dir. accident svcs., chmn. orthopaedic surgery Prince of Wales Hosp., Sydney, Australia, 1972-92. Hon. cons. orthopaedic surgeon Mulago and Mengo Hosps. and Round Table Polio Clinic, Kampala, 1960—72; hon. orthopaedic surgeon to all govt. and mission hosps., Uganda, 1960—72; hon. adviser to Rotary Internat., The Commonwealth Found., WHO, UN, from

1970; sr. med. disaster comdr., chmn. various disaster and emergency coms. Dept. Health, New South Wales, Australia, 1972; founder, hon. mem. World Orthopaedic Concern, 1973—2002; cons. orthopaedic surgeon Royal S. Sydney and Sutherland Hosps., Sydney, 1974—92; hon. prof. dept. surgery U. Sydney, from 1995; vis. prof. surgery Sydney U., from 1995. Author: (Book) Typhoid Fever and Other Salmonella Infections, 1962, A Simple Guide to Trauma, 5th edit., 1995, A Simple Guide to Trauma, Italian edit., 1978, A Simple Guide to Trauma, Japanese edit., 1982, Poliomyelitis Including Appliances and Rehabilitation, 1975, A Simple Guide to Orthopaedics, 1993, Picture Tests orthopaedics and Trauma, 1994; contbr. chapters to books Brit. Jour. Bone and Joint Surgery, 1965—72. Recipient Melsome Meml. prize, 1948, Raymond Horton Smith prize, 1957, Irving Geist award Internat. Soc. for Rehab. of Disabled, 1969, James Cook medal Royal Soc. New South Wales, 1984, Humanitarian award Orthopaedics Overseas, 1991, Centenary medal Australia, 2003, Eyre-Brook medal, World Orthop. Concern, 2009; Paul Harris fellow and medal Rotary Internat. and Rotary Found., 1987. Fellow Royal Coll. Surgeons Edinburgh, Royal Coll. Surgeons Eng., Royal Australasian Coll. Surgeons Australia, Australian Acad. Technol. Scis. and Engring. (K.L. Sutherland medal 1986), Australian Orthopaedic Assn. (v.p. 1982, Betts Meml. medal 1983), Brit. Orthopaedic Assn., Western Pacific Orthopaedic Assn. (hon.), Assn. Surgeons Uganda (hon.); mem. Coast Med. Assn. (pres. 1986), Med. Soc. U. New South Wales (patron), Australian Club. Achievements include invention of Huckstep locking nail and hip plus calipers and wheelchairs for developing countries. Died Apr. 10, 2015.

HUDAK, DOROTHY ANN, nurse educator; b. Donora, Pa., Aug. 10, 1944; d. Frank and Jessie (Opatkiewick) Palko; m. Thomas F. Hudak, July 27, 1963; children: Diana, Debra, Thomas. BSN, U. Pitts., 1983; postgrad., Calif. U. Pa., 1986; MSEd, Duquesne U., 1991. Cert. first aid, CPR, sch. nurse, Am. Nurses Credentialing Ctr. Staff nurse St. Clair Hosp., Pitts.; nurse secondary and elem. sch. Peters Twp. Sch. Dist., McMurray, Pa.; adolescent and family therapist Outreach South, Mt. Lebanon, Pa.; pvt. practice Mt. Lebanon. Named to Sigma Theta Tau. Mem. ACA, Nat. Assn. Sch. Nurses, Am. Sch. Health Assn., Washington-Greene County Sch. Nurses Assn., Pa. Counselors Assn. Home: Presto, Pa. Died Mar. 5, 2007.

HUDDLESTON, FOREST WILLIS, retired mental healing counselor; b. Kingsburg, Calif., Oct. 3, 1915; s. John Samuel and Myra Jennie (Beaver) H.; m. Allene Moore, June 3, 1944 (div. 1979); children: June M., Ralph Reed-,Virginia Marie; m. Jacqueline Louise Barber, Sept. 3, 1986. Student, Redley (Calif.) City Coll., 1934-36, U. Puget Sound, 1936-38, Fresno State Coll., 1940-41, 47-48. Ordained to ministry Universal Life Ch., 1978. Mem. sales staff various furniture stores, Sacramento, 1959-70; research dir. Allied Research and Counseling, Sacramento, 1970-76, Huddleston Claibourne Counseling Ctr., Sacramento, 1983-84; ret., 1984. Developer Huddleston Method treatment for mental illness. Asst. dir. Oak Park Youth Band, Sacramento, 1968-70; active various community service orgns., Sacramento, 1958--. Sgt. USAF, 1942-45. Nominated Nobel Peace Prize, 1992. Avocation: coin collecting/numismatics. Died Jan. 15, 2007.

HUDDLESTON, WAYNE ALLAN, electric utility executive; b. Salem, Oreg., Apr. 4, 1937; s. Glen Harry and Evelyn Delores (Arnold) H.; m. Leahnel Marie Johnson, Sept 23, 1967 (div. Jan. 1970); m. Judy Belle Smith, Dec. 14, 1975; 1 child, Andrew. BCE, Oreg. State U., 1959. Registered profl. engr., Oreg. Gen. mgr. power op. Gen. Electric Co., Portland, Oreg., 1975-82, v.p. adminstrv. services, 1982-84, v.p. operating services, 1984-87; sr. cons. Utility Resources, Inc., Portland, from 1987. Bd. dirs. Portland Rose Festival Assn. 1985-89. Served with USAR, 1960. Republican. Avocations: fishing, enology. Home: Portland, Oreg. Died Nov. 4, 2006.

HUDSON, YVONNE MORTON, retired elementary school educator; b. Cin., July 25, 1943; d. Eugene Benjamin and Eura Selenora (Williams) Morton; m. McKinley Hudson, Aug. 27, 1966; children: Shawna, McKinley Jr. BS in Primary Edn., U. Cin., 1965; MEd, Boston U., Mons, Belgium, 1988. Cert. tchr., Calif.; advanced profl. cert., Md. Tchr. Cin. Bd. Edn., 1965-66, 67-68, 71-73, Anne Arundel County Pub. Schs., Annapolis, Md., 1968-69, 73-76, Dept. Def. Dependents Schs., Kaiserslautern, Fed. Republic Germany, 1980-83, San Francisco Unified Sch. Dist., 1989-94, Montgomery County Pub. Schs., Rockville, Md., 1994—2008; ret., 2008. Mem. Sch. Adv. Bd., Kaiserslautern, 1981-83. Vice pres. PTO, Kaiserslautern, 1981-82, San Francisco, 1991, pres., Ft. McClellan, Ala., 1984-85; mem. Ft. McClellan Elem. Sch. Bd., 1984-85; troop leader Girl Scouts U.S.A., East Point, Ga., 1977-80, bd. dirs. North Atlantic coun., 1987-88. Recipient Patriotic Civilian Svc. award Dept. Army, 1988; named Parent of Yr. George Washington H.S., San Francisco, 1994. Mem. NEA, AAUW, Calif. Tchrs. Assn., United Educators San Francisco (rep. 1989-94, negotiating team 1989-94, ethnic leadership awareness com. 1989-94, exec. bd. dirs. 1992-94, tchr. ctr. policy bd. 1992), Montgomery County Edn. Assn. (bd. dirs., minority affairs com. 1998-2000, negotiating team 1999-2000, elected faculty rep., peer assistance and rev. panel, bd. dirs. 2008-, ret. dir. equity com., 2008-, profl. rights & responsibilities com. mem. 2010-), Nat. Coun. Negro Women, Presidio Officers Wives Club, Alpha Kappa Alpha (awards com. mem., scholarship com., social justice com., connections com.), League Women Voters of Montgomery County (bd. dirs. edn. com. 2009-13, county Budget Process Com. mem., 2010-11), Md. State Ednl. Assn. (leadership tng. convention arrangements 1998-), Wings Joys (bd. dirs. 2013-), Wings For Joy (treas., bd. dirs. 2013). Avocations: reading, travel, shopping, collecting. Home: Burtonsville, Md. Died Feb. 10, 2015.

HUDSPETH, HARVEY GRESHAM, history professor; b. Clarksdale, Miss., Oct. 17, 1955; s. Joseph MacDonald Hudspeth and Martha Lou Shelton. BA in History and Polit. Sci., U. Miss., 1978, JD, 1981, PhD in History, 1994. Bar: Miss. 1981, U.S. Dist. Ct. (no. dist.) Miss. 1981, U.S. Dist. Ct. (so. dist.) Miss. 1984, U.S. Ct. Appeals (5th cir.) 1985, Ill. 1989. Staff atty. Miss. Sec. of State, Jackson, 1981-83; pvt. practice Gulfport, Miss., 1983-85; land analyst Shell Oil Co., Houston, 1985-87; title examiner 1st Am. Title, Chgo., 1987-89; credit adminstr. Citicorp, Chgo., 1989-90; tchg. asst. U. Miss., University, 1991-94; history program coord., asst. prof. history Mississippi Valley State U., Itta Bena, Miss., 1994-2000, assoc. prof., 2000—05, U. Ark., Pine Bluff, 2005—06. Presenter in field. Contbr. to books: Tennessee Encyclopedia of History, 1998, Booker T. Washington: Essays, 1998, Encyclopedia of the Supreme Court, 2001, Encyclopedia of the Gilded Age, 2003, Franklin D. Roosevelt and the Transformation of the Supreme Court, 2003, Mississippi Encyclopedia of History, 2005; contbr. articles to profl. jours. Chmn. Com. to Elect Joe Hudspeth Pub. Svc. Commr., Miss., 1983. Recipient Miss. Humanities Coun. Tchr. of Yr. award, 2000, WTHS Marshall Wingfield award, 1998, EBHS Charles J. Kennedy award, 2005. Mem. Am. Hist. Assn., Orgn. Am. Historians, Miss. Hist. Assn., Gulf South Hist. Assn., So. Conf. on Afro-Am. Studies, Inc., Econ. and Bus. Hist. Soc. (trustee 2000-01. pres.-elect 2001-02, pres. 2002-03), Miss. Bar Assn., Ill. Bar Assn. Republican. Presbyterian. Avocations: travel, politics, reading. Home: Avondale Estates, Ga. Died Mar. 7, 2007.

HUEBL, HUBERT CARL, surgeon; b. Glendive, Mont., Sept. 12, 1932; s. Hubert Carl Huebl and Idamae Myers; m. Helen Katherine Sugrue, Feb. 23, 1963; children: John, Michael, Katherine Doyle, Carolyn. BA, U. Chgo., 1952; MD, Washington U., 1956. Bd. cert. gen. and thoracic surgery. Resident gen. surgery Bellevue Hosp., NYC, 1959—62, 1959—62; resident gen. and thoracic surgery Wayne State U., Detroit, 1962-67; clin. asst. prof. Wayne State U./Oakwood Hosp., from 2000; intern Mpls. Gen. Hosp.; thoracic surgeon Cardiothoracic Assocs., Malden, Mass., 1968-77; gen. surgeon Dearborn (Mich.) Surg. Assocs., 1977-2000. Lt. USNR, 1957-59. Mem. ACS, AMA, Soc. Thoracic Surgeons, Mich. State Med. Soc., Wayne County Med. Soc. Roman Catholic. Home: Dearborn, Mich. Died July 17, 2007.

HUFF, JOHN WESLEY, veterinary medicine educator; b. Weston, Tex., Feb. 23, 1927; s. James German Monroe and Loice (Culwell) H.; m. Mariam Jean Davis, Sept. 23, 1950; children: Julia Ann Huff Sookma, John Scott, Janet Lynne Huff Sweet. DVM, Tex. A&M U., 1958, BS, MS, Tex. A&M U., 1962. Instr., vet. microbioogy, asst. dept. head Vet. Pathobiology Tex. A&M U., College Station, 1958-62, asst. prof., 1962-66, assoc. prof., 1966-74, prof., from 1974. Officer St. Paul's United Meth. Ch., Bryan, Tex., 1958—, dist. officer, 1970—. Recipient Norden Teaching award Norden Labs., 1968, Faculty Disting. Teaching award Tex. A&M Student Assn., College Station, 1970. Mem. Masons. Home: Bryan, Tex. Died Nov. 9, 2006.

HUFFINE, VIRGINIA ELIZABETH, artistic director, dancer, choreographer; b. Cumberland, Md., June 2, 1922; d. Dudley Malcolm and Mary Virginia (Edson) Browne; m. Coy Lee Huffine, Mar. 31, 1951; children: Jeremy Bennett, Lucinda Jane. Cert., Chalif Sch. Ballet, NYC, 1943; studies with M. Hermann, NYC, 1942-44, studies with I. Torrup, 1944-45, studies with V. Grant, 1945-48. Dance faculty Ardsley Sch. for Girls, Ardsley on Hudson, N.Y., 1944-45; choreographer, soloist Gilbert and Sullivan Opera Co., Ridgewood, N.J., 1944-50; prin. dancer Raga Dancers, NYC, 1946-51; dir. sacred dance 1st Unitarian Ch., Winchester, Mass., 1961-68, Unitarian/Universalist Ch., Rochester, Minn., 1969-75; founder, dir. liturgical dance trio Seraphim III, Rochester, from 1983. Cons. liturgical dance various chs., 1969—; lectr. dance history secular and religious orgns., 1969—; dance panelist S.E. Minn. Regional Arts Council, 1975-76; leader dance therapy workshop Luth. Social Services, Minn., 1981—. Co-author: Barefoot in the Chancel, 1964; choreographer, performer: (dances) A Vernal Creed, 1967, The Messiah, 1983, Shaker Dances, 1985, Persephone, 1989, A Celebration of Angels, 1996, Healing Dances, 1997, Be Thou My Vision, 1998, Panis Angelicus, 1998; editor Arts Calendar Quar., 1985-77; producer, host (TV show) Kaleidoscope, 1977. Mem. Sacred Dance Guild, Inc. (regional dir., nat. sec. 1965-67), Daus. Brit. Empire (hon. 1945—). Home: Rochester, Minn. Died Dec. 23, 2006.

HUFNAGEL, ANNA BERNICE, English educator; b. Jasper, Ind., Jan. 7, 1935; d. Claude Matthew and Clara Catherine (Hagedorn) Miller; m. Linus J. Hufnagel, Aug. 17, 1957; children: Michelle Clare Wathen, John Joseph, Mary Anne. BS, Ind. U., 1957, MS, 1971; postgrad., Ind. State U., Terre Haute, 1965-82. Lic. tchr., Ind. English tchr. Sumner (Ill.) High Sch.; study skills instr., tutor Vincennes (Ind.) U., libr. Shake Libr., community coll. English tchr., asst. prof. community coll. Mem. LWV. Mem. AAUW, Nat. Coun. Tchrs. English, Pi Lambda Theta, Pi Lambda Theta. Home: Vincennes, Ind. Died Aug. 11, 2007.

HUGHES, GENE WYATT, construction company executive; b. Dayton, Ohio, Feb. 20, 1926; s. John Clayborne and Catherine (Wyatt) H.; Julie Clare Loeffel, May 22, 1964; children: Robert, Meredith, John. BA, Williams Coll., 1950; MS, Stanford U., 1960; MBA, U. San Francisco, 1970. Registered profl. engr., Ohio. Project engr. Hughes Simonson, Dayton, 1954-59; dept. mgr. Scott Co. of Calif., Oakland, 1960-67; project mgr. Swinerton-Walberg, San Francisco, 1967-70; v.p. Hughes Bechtol, Dayton, 1970-82, pres., chief exec. officer, 1982-84; pres. Frebco, Inc., Dayton, from 1984. Adv. com. Sinclair Community Coll., 1980—. Served with USNR, 1944-46, PTO. Mem. ASHRAE, (chpt. v.p. 1974-75), Internat. Exec. Service Corps, Mech Contractors Assn. (bd. dirs.), Am. Arbitration Assn. Clubs: Dayton Country. Lodges: Rotary (pres. Oakwood chpt. 1983-84). Republican. Presbyterian. Avocations: skiing, golf, running, exercise, music. Home: Prescott, Ariz. Died Nov. 3, 2006.

HUGHES, MARK EDWARD, financial services company executive; b. Dayton, Ohio, Mar. 14, 1949; s. Howard R. and Elsa Fredia (Ley) H.; m. Arlene Joyce Hornyak, Jan. 25, 1973; children: Diana Kaye, April Dawn. BA in Theology, Southwestern Union Coll., Keene, Tex., 1980. Ptnr. Outland Design Builders, Keene, 1981-83; regional sales mgr. Wyckoff Fund Raising, Vassar, Mich., 1983-84; area sales rep. Home Health Edn. Service, Berrien Springs, Mich., 1984-87; regional mgr. A.L. Williams, Flint, Mich., from 1987. Coordinator Bible Lab., Vassar, 1987—; div. leader Jr. Div. Vacation Bible Sch., Vassar, 1984-87. With USMC, 1968-70, Vietnam. Mem.: Pathfinders (Vassar) (dep. dir. 1985-88). Republican. Seventh Day Adventist. Avocations: raising dogs, scuba diving, camping, flying. Died June 14, 2007.

HUITT, JIMMIE L., rancher, oil and gas industry executive, real estate developer; b. Gurdon, Ark., Aug. 21, 1923; s. John Wesley and Almedia (Hatten) H.; m. Janis C. Mann, Oct. 30, 1945; children— Jimmie L., Jr., Allan Jerome BS in Chem. Engring., La. Tech. U., 1944; MS in Chem. Engring., U. Okla., 1948, PhD, 1951. Research engr. Mobil Oil Corp., Dallas, 1951-56, Gulf Research Co., Pitts., 1956-67; ops. coordinator Kuwait Oil Co., London, 1967-71; gen. mgr. Gulf Oil-Zaire, Kinshasa, 1971-74; mng. dir. Gulf Oil-Nigeria, Lagos, 1974-76; sr. v.p., exec. v.p. Gulf Oil Exploration and Prodn. Co., Houston, 1976-81, pres., CEO, 1981—85; rancher Four Jays Ranch, Industry, Tex., from 1986. Contbr. articles to profl. jours.; patentee in field Served to 1st lt. U.S. Army, 1944-47 Mem. Soc. Petroleum Engrs. (chmn. various coms. 1956—), Masons, Shriners. Republican. Home: Brenham, Tex. Died Oct. 4, 2014.

HUIZINGA, WILLIAM ARYS, III, insurance executive, business owner; b. Oak Park, Ill., Nov. 11, 1942; s. William Arys Sr. and Sylvia (De Graaf) H.; m. Jamie Anne Osgard, Apr. 6, 1968; children: Todd, Anne, Sarah. BS in Edn., U. Idaho, 1966, MS in Edn., 1967. Tchr., coach Everett (Wash.) Sch. Dist., 1967-73; from agt. to mgr. Northwestern Nat., Mpls., 1973-82; supt., dir. of edn. Life Ins. Co., 1982-83; v.p. sales No. Life Ins. Co., Seattle, 1983-89; regional sales dir. Western United Life, Tacoma, Wash., from 1989. Stewardship chmn. Christ Luth. Ch., Tacoma, 1986-87. Mem. Nat. Assn. Life Underwriters, Am. Soc. Chartered Life Underwriters, Lakewood Jr. Soccer Assn., Oakbrook Golf and Country Club (bd. dirs., pres. 1987—). Avocations: gardening, travel, golf. Home: Olympia, Wash. Died Jan. 7, 2007.

HULLAH, ANN MARIE, elementary school educator; b. Buffalo, Dec. 18, 1933; d. Paul and Ida (De Forest) Ronde; m. Eugene Henning, July 27, 1955 (dec. 1975); children: Anita Hasseler, Paul Henning, Karen Morris; m. Stanley Hullah, June 10, 1977; children: Stan Jr., Kris Kyle, Lynn Princl, Nocole Frances, Jacqueline, Les. BEd., Wis. State U., 1969; MST, U. Wis., Whitewater, 1981. Cert. elem. reading tchr., Wis. Tchr. Merrifield Sch., Milton, Wis., 1953-55, Crist Sch., Beloit, Wis., 1955-56, Turner Middle Sch., Beloit, 1970-91, reading specialist, from 1981; reading specialist, chpt. I Powers, Townview Schs., Beloit, 1991-95, ret., 1995. Team leader, reading curriculum writer Turner Middle Sch., Beloit, 1975—; lang. arts study group Turner Sch. Dist., Beloit, 1991-94. Organist Congregational Ch., Shopiere, Wis., 1960—. Recipient scholarshp Whitewater (Wis.) State Coll., 1951. Mem. ASCD, S. Kettle Moraine Reading Coun., Village and Valley Homemakers, Women of the Moose. Avocations: travel, music, golf, reading. Died Mar. 30, 2007.

HUNT, MARY REILLY, organization executive; b. NYC, Apr. 17, 1921; d. Philip R. and Mary C. (Harten) Reilly; m. Robert R. Hunt, Apr. 10, 1943,; children: Marianne Schram, Philip R., Robert R., Elise Hannah. Student, CCNY, 1939; DHL (hon.), Thomas More Coll., 2005. Tax investigator Ind. Dept. Revenue, 1970-80; pres. Ind. Right to Life, 1973-77; treas. Nat. Right to Life Com., Washington, 1974, 77, 78, mem. exec. com., 1974, 76-81, vice chmn., 1976, exec. dir., 1978, dir. devel., 1979-94, v.p. devel., 1994-97, hon. bd. mem., from 1983; v.p. devel. Nat. Life Ctr., Woodbury, from 1997; pres. Mary Reilly Hunt & Assoc., Inc., South Bend, Ind., from 1985. Bd. dirs., v.p. YWCA, 1968-73, bd. dirs. Mental Health Assn. St. Joseph Co., 1972-78; candidate for state legis., 1988; mem. St. Joseph County Rep. Women precinct com., South Bend, 1964-79, alt. del. to Nat. Rep. Conv., 1976, 84, 88, 92; mem. Coun. for Nat. Policy, 1988—, mem. exec. com., 2000-06. Recipient St. Patrick's medal St. Patrick's Coll. and Sem. (Ireland), 1996. Mem. Am. Soc. Sovereign Mil. Order of Malta, Coun. Nat. Policy. Republican. Roman Catholic. Avocations: gardening, antiques. Home: Granger, Ind. Died Mar. 10, 2014.

HUNT, NELSON BUNKER, retired oil industry executive; b. El Dorado, Ark., Feb. 22, 1926; s. Haroldson Lafayette & Lyda (Bunker) H.; m. Caroline Lewis, 1951; children: Elizabeth, Ellen, Mary, Houston Student, U. Tex.; Grad., Southern Meth. U. Chmn. Great Western United Corp., Dallas, 1974-78, Hunt Energy Corp., Dallas, Hunt Exploration & Mining Co.; owner Titan Resources Corp.

Mem. Park Cities Presbyterian Church, 1991. Served in USN. Recipient Eclipse award for Outstanding Breeder, 1976, 1985, 1987. Mem.: Coun. of the John Birch Soc., Tex. Bible Soc. Republican. Christian. Avocation: horse breeding. Died Oct. 21, 2014.

HUNT, WILLIAM JOSEPH, company executive; b. St. Paul, Aug. 15, 1925; s. William Joseph and Margaret Mary (Maguire) H.; m. Corinne Evelyn Bakke, June 19, 1948 (div. 1975); children: William, Robert, Thomas, Judith, Janice; m. Olga Irene Ismeir, Apr. 22, 1978. Student, U. Kans., 1943; BBA, U. Minn., 1949. Exec. v.p. White Farm Equip., Mpls., 1949-69; pres., chief exec. officer Larson Industries, Edina, Minn., 1970-73; chmn., chief exec. officer M11 Inc., Lincoln, Ill., from 1974. Bd. dirs., chmn. Meml. Med. Ctr., Springfield, Ill., 1986—, Ill. Polit. Action Com., Chgo., 1985-87; bd. dirs., v.p. Rail Charity Classic, Springfield, 1982-90. With U.S. Army, 1943-46. Mem. Ill. C. of C. (vice chmn. 1979-85), Elks. Republican. Roman Catholic. Avocations: golf, bridge. Home: Springfield, Ill. Died Apr. 26, 2007.

HUNTER, VALERIE JEAN DEXTER, real estate broker; b. Hackensack, NJ, Sept. 27, 1943; d. Perry and Vera May (Bates) D.; married, Sept. 5, 1965 (div. Mar. 1986); children: Kevin David, Keith Perry; m. William G. Hunter, Aug. 22, 1987. Grad. high sch., Lyndon Center, Ver. Dept. sec. U.S. C. of C., Washington, 1961-63; sec. The Cosmodyne Corp., Hawthorne, Calif., 1963; receptionist, pvt. sec. Sta. WTWN radio, St. Johnsbury, Ver., 1964-65; adminstrv. sec. Sanders Assocs., Inc., Nashua, N.H., 1967-72; co-owner, sec., bookkeeper Gallup Adjustment Service, Skowhegan, Maine, 1975-82; realtor Century 21 Whittemore's Real Estate, Skowhegan, 1981-87; realtor-broker Century 21 Nason Realty, Winslow, Maine, from 1987. Mem. Maine Assn. Realtors, No. Kennebec Valley Bd. Realtors, No. Kennebec Valley Multiple Listing Service, Lakewood Ladies Golf Assn. Died June 10, 2007.

HURLEY, FRANK THOMAS, JR., realtor; b. Washington, Oct. 18, 1924; s. Frank Thomas and Lucille (Trent) H.; m. Betty Guisinger, Aug. 9, 1997. AA, St. Petersburg Jr. Coll., 1948; BA, U. Fla., 1950. Reporter St. Petersburg Evening Independent, Fla., 1948-53; editor Arcadia Tribune, Calif., 1956-57; reporter Los Angeles Herald Express, 1957; v.p. Frank T. Hurley Assocs., Inc. Realtors, from 1958, pres., from 1964. Author: Surf, Sand and Post Card Sunsets, 1977, Pass-a-Grille Vignettes, 1999. Elected St. Petersburg Beach Bd. Commrs., 1965—69; chmn. Pinellas County Traffic Safety Coun., 1968—69; apptd. mem. Pinellas County Hist. Commn., from 1993, chmn., 2003; pres. Pass-A-Grille Cmty. Assn., 1963; mem. St. Petersburg Mus. Fine Arts, St. Pete Beach Aesthetic and Hist. Rev. Bd., chmn., 1994—96; apptd. mem. Pinellas County Sesquicentennial Coord. Com., 1995; pres. Gulf Beach Bd. Realtors, 1969; bd. govs. Palms of Pasadena Hosp., 1979—86. With USAAF, 1943—46. Recipient St. Petersburg Beach Vol. of Yr. award, 2006, Disting. Svc. award, Fla. Trust for Hist. Preservation, 2007; named Nat. Assn. Realtors. Mem.: Fla. Assn. Realtors (dir., dist. v.p. 1971), St. Petersburg Suncoast Assn. Realtors (life, Ambassadors award 1994), St. Petersburg Beach C. of C. (dir., pres. 1975-76, Citizen of Yr. award 1983), Fla. Hist. Soc., Ky. Col., Am. Legion, Pass-A-Grille Yacht Club (bd. govs.), Sigma Delta Chi, Sigma Tau Delta. Home: Saint Petersburg Beach, Fla. Died Feb. 28, 2014.

HURLEY, SUSAN LYNN, philosopher, educator; b. NYC, Sept. 16, 1954; d. Roy Thomas and Esther (Sarchian) H. AB summa cum laude, Princeton U., 1976; B Philosophy with distinction, Oxford U., Eng., 1979, MA, 1981, PhD, 1983; JD cum laude, Harvard U., 1988. Jr. research fellow All Souls Coll., Oxford, Eng., 1981-84; Brockhues fellow, lectr. philosophy St. Edmund Hall Oxford U., from 1985; prof. polit. and ethical theory U. Warwick, from 1998, prof. of philos. Coventry, England. Vis. prof. law U. Calif. Berkeley, 1984; Meyer vis. prof. program law, philosopy, social theory NYU, 1987; vis. lectr. Harvard U. Law Sch., Cambridge, Mass., 1987; vis. fellow in Coun. of the Humanities, Princeton, N.J., 1988; fellow All Souls Coll., Oxford, England, 2000; sr. rsch. reader British Acad., 1990-92. Author: Natural Reasons: Personality and Polity, 1989, Consciousness in Action, 1998; co-editor: Foundations of Decision Theory, 1991, On Human Rights, 1993; Perspectives on Imitation: From Neuroscience to Social Science, Rational Animals co-edited with Matthew Nudds. 2005, Active Perception and Perceiving Action: The Shared Circuits Hypothesis, T. Gendler and J. Hawthorne (eds.) Perceptual Experience, Oxford U. Press, contbr. articles on philos. and law to profl. jours. Grad. scholar St. Catherine's Coll., Oxford, 1977-80; Nuffield Found. Social Sci. Rsch. fellow 1997-98. Mem. Anmesty Internat. Avocation: photography. Died Aug. 7, 2007.

HURST, FRANCES ETHEL WEEKLEY, retired librarian; b. Birmingham, Ala., Feb. 27, 1919; d. Harold Hudson and Nota Leigh (Windham) Weekley; m. Henry Odessa Hurst, Sept. 8, 1947 (dec. 1962); children: Rosalind Frances Hurst Minderhout, Walter Henry; m. Kenneth Dean, 1983 (div. 1987). BA in Edn., U. Ala., 1941; BA in LS, Emory U., 1945. Tchr. pub. schs. of Ala., 1941-44, 50-52, 1957-62; librarian TVA, Wilson Dam, Ala., 1945-46, U. Ala., Tuscaloosa, 1946-50, 62-69; case worker Talladega County Dept. Pub. Welfare, Talladega, Ala., 1952-53; librarian Jefferson State Community Coll., Birmingham, 1969-87. Mem. AAUW, Ala. Edn. Assn., NEA, Ala. Ret. Tchrs. Assn., Capstone Coll. Edn. Soc., Nat. Alumni Asn. of U. Ala., Am. Assn. Ret. Persons, Kappa Delta Pi, Pi Tau Chi, Triangle. Methodist. Home: Birmingham, Ala. Died May 14, 2007.

HURWITZ, JOSHUA JACOB, physician; b. Boston, Nov. 24, 1921; s. Albert Hurwitz and Ada Godinski; m. Rose Kosofsky, Mar. 24, 1946; children: Joel, Deborah, Ruth, Charles. Student, Harvard Coll., 1943; MD, Harvard Med. Sch., 1946. Bd. cert. urology. Surg. intern Beth Israel Hosp., Boston, 1946-47; urology resident New Eng. Med. Ctr., 1990-93, physician Boston, 1951-65, Mass. Gen. Hosp., Boston, 1954-61, Waltham (Mass.) Hosp., 1951-95, Edith N. Rogers VA Hosp., Bedford, Mass. Capt. U.S. Army, 1943-46, 47-49, 49-50. Died Feb. 18, 2007.

HUTTON, JOHN EVANS, JR., surgeon, educator, retired military officer; b. NYC, Sept. 9, 1931; s. John Evans and Antoinette (Abbott) H.; m. Barbara Seward Joyce, Apr. 15, 1961; children: John III, Wendy, James, Elizabeth. BA, Wesleyan U., 1953; MD, George Washington U., 1963. Diplomate: Am. Bd. Surgery, Am. Bd. Med. Examiners. Commd. 2d lt. USMC, 1953, advanced through grades to capt., 1962; discharged USMCR; commd. capt. U.S. Army, 1963, advanced through grades to brig. gen., 1989, intern, resident in gen. surgery Walter Reed Army Med. Ctr. Washington, 1963-68, fellow vascular surgery, 1969-70, asst. chief vascular surgery, 1970-71, mem. staff gen. surgery svcs., 1969-71, chief dept. surgery, 1981-84, White House physician, 1984-86, physician to the Pres. Ronald Reagan, 1987—88, chief surgeon 91st Evacuation Hosp., Republic of Vietnam, 1968—69, chief vascular surgery, asst. chief gen. surgery Letterman Army Med. Ctr., 1971-74, chief gen. and vascular surgery, program dir., gen. surgery residency Letterman Army Med. Ctr. San Francisco, 1975-81; comdr. 47th Field Hosp., Honduras, 1984; commanding gen. Madigan Army Med. Ctr. U.S. Army, Tacoma, 1989-92; ret., 1992; prof. surgery, chief div. gen. surgery, dept. surg. Uniformed Svcs. U. Sch. Medicine, Bethesda, Md., from 1992, mem. faculty senate, 1996—99, mem. students promotion com., 1993-96, 2002—05, mem. instl. rev. bd., 1993-96, mem. com. appointments, promotion and tenure, 1998-99, pres. elect faculty senate, 1997; pres. faculty senate Uniformed Svcs. U. Health Scis., Bethesda, 1998. Assoc. clin. prof. surgery U. Calif., San Francisco, 1978-81, mem. dean's adv. group Uniformed Svc. U. Health Sci., 1998-99; assoc. prof. surgery, vice chmn. dept. surgery Uniformed Svcs. U. Health Scis., Bethesda, 1981-84, prof. surgery, 1985—; clin. prof. surgery Tulane U. Sch. Medicine, 1988—, George Washington Sch. Medicine, Washington, 1985—. Contbr. articles, photographs to profl. publs., chpts. to books. Mem. men and boys choir Grace Cathedral, San Francisco, 1971-75. Decorated D.S.M., Bronze Star, Meritorious Svcs. medal with oak leaf cluster, Army Commendation Medal, Navy Commendation Medal, Joint Svc. Commendation Medal, Vietnam Svc. medal with four bronze svc. stars, Nat. DSM with two bronze svc. stars, Naval Occupation medal, WWII, Vietnam Honor medal 1st class, Vietnam Cross of Gallantry; recipient Barron Dominique Larrey award for excellence in surgery, Disting. Svc. medal, Uniformed Svcs. U. Sch. Medicine, 2000. Fellow: ACS; mem.: Internat. Soc. Vascular Surgery, Soc. Vascular Surgery, Soc. Med. Cons. Armed Forces (councilor 1988—89, v.p. 2000, pres. 2001), Acad. Medicine Washington D.C., Chesapeake Vascular Soc., Soc. Mil. Vascular Surgery, Am. Assn. Surgery of Trauma, Soc. Clin. Vascular Surgery, Bay Surg. Soc. (hon.), U.S. Naval Acad. Sailing Squadron, Severn Sailing Assn., St. Francis Yacht Club (membership com. 1978—81). Republican. Episcopalian. Avocations: music, photography, sailing, sports. Home: Silver Spring, Md. Died Dec. 19, 2014.

HYMER, DONALD EUGENE, physical education educator; b. Shanondale, Ind., Jan. 30, 1931; s. Orion Oka and Bertha Racheal (Quigg) H. BA, Earlham Coll., 1954; MEd, Ill. State U., 1958; EdS, U. Ill., 1963. Tchr. sci. and phys. edn. Crystal High Schs., Crystal Lake, Ill., 1958-65, Turkey Run Schs., Marshal, Ind., 1965-67, Russellville (Ind.) Sch., 1967-70, tchr. sci., history and phys. edn., 1972-78, prin., 1975-76, Washington Jr. High Sch., Thornton, Ind., 1970-72; asst. prin. Roachdale (Ind.) Sch., 1978-79, tchr. sci., history and phys. edn., from 1978. Football and wrestling coach Crystal Lake (Ill.) High Sch., 1958-65, Turkey Run Sch., Marsal, Ind., 1966-67, Russellville & North Putnam, Roachdale, 1968-70, coach elem. sports, 1970-79. Contbr. articles to profl. jours. Insp. Election Bd., Franklin Twp., Ill., 1989-90; chmn. Just Say No Program, North Putnam Sch., 1988-90. Cpl. U.S. Army, 1954-56, Korea. Named Ind. South Dist. Sec. Disting., 1991-92; recipient Honor Shoot Roachdale Gym Club, 1991. Mem. Ind. Optimists (Disting. Sec. 1978-78, 80, 81, 82, lt. gov. 1982-83, chmn. 1986, essay chmn. 1987), Optimists Internat. (Disting. Sec. 1988-89), Roachdale Optimists (pres., sec. 1966-90), Masons (master 1979), Shriners, VFW (bd. trustees 1983-90), AAHPERD, Ind. Assn. Health, Phys. Edn., Recreation and Dance. Democrat. Mem. Soc. Of Friends. Avocation: trap shooting. Home: Roachdale, Ind. Died Dec. 21, 2006.

HYNES, JOHN THOMAS, food scientist, retired; b. Bklyn., Sept. 6, 1933; s. Patrick Joseph and Mary Ann (Greaney) H.; m. Elaine Marie Biers, Aug. 31, 1957; children: Karen, David, Teresa, Sean, Patricia, Christopher, Margaret. BS, Manhattan Coll., 1956. Scientist I Nat. Dairy Products Corp., Oakdale, N.Y., 1956-60, scientist II, 1960-65; rsch. scientist Kraft Gen. Foods, Glenview, Ill., 1965-70, group leader, 1970-74, sr. scientist I, 1974-79, sr. scientist II, 1979-84, sect. mgr., 1984-89, rsch. prin., 1989-93; ret., 1993; dairy rsch. and industry cons., from 193. Mem. Inst. Food Technologists, Am. Chem. Soc. Home: Glenview, Ill. Died Mar. 18, 2007.

HYSMITH, EVA MARIE, personnel specialist; b. Bethlehem, Pa., Feb. 22, 1941; d. Andrew George and Dorothy Clare (Fulton) Pieller; m. Thomas Eugene Hysmith, May 10, 1962; 1 child, James Andrew (dec.). AA, Manatee Community Coll., 1975. Adminstrv. sec. Manatee Community Coll., Bradenton, Fla., 1959-85, personnel specialist, Office Human Resources, from 1985. Vol. Am. Heart Assn., Bradenton, 1985—; div. leader United Way of Manatee County, 1985—; mem. Manatee Commn. on Status of Women, bd. dirs. 1986. Mem. Fla. Assn. Community Colls. (bd. dirs. 1960—), Women in Govt., Coll. and Univ. Personnel Assn. (assoc.), Sarasota Human Resources Assn. Fla. Women in Govt. Democrat. Episcopalian. Avocations: nascar winston cup racing, country crafts, reading, floral gardening. Home: Palmetto, Fla. Died Dec. 5, 2006.

IMANA, JORGE GARRON, artist; b. Sept. 20, 1930; came to US, 1964, naturalized, 1974. s. Juan S. and Lola (Garron) I.; m. Cristina Imana; children: George, Ivan. Grad. fine arts acad., U. San Francisco Xavier, 1950. cert. Nat. Sch. for Tchrs., Bolivia, 1952. Prof. art. Nat. Sch. Tchrs., Sucre, 1954-56; prof. biology Padilla Coll., Sucre, 1956-60; head dept. art Inst. Normal Simon Bolivar, La Paz, Bolivia, 1961-62; propr., mgr. The Artists Showroom, San Diego, from 1973. Over 100 one-man shows of paintings in US, S. Am., and Europe, 1952—, including: Gallery Banet, La Paz, 1965, Artists Showroom, San Diego, 1964, 66, 68, 74, 76, 77, San Diego Art Inst., 1966, 68, 72, 73, Univ. de Zulia, Maracaibo, Venezuela, 1969, Spanish Village Art Ctr., San Diego, 1974, 75, 76, La Jolla Art Assn. Gallery, 1969, 72-93, Internat. Gallery, Washington, 1976, Galeria de Arte L'Atelier, La Paz, 1977, Mus. Nat., La Paz, 1987, 88, Casa del Arte, La Jolla, Calif., 1987, Simon Patino Found., Bolivia, 1994; numerous group shows including: Fine Arts Gallery, San Diego, 1964, Mus. Modern Art, Paris, 1973; exhibits in galleries of Budapest, Hungary, 1975, Moscow, 1975, Warsaw, Poland, 1976, Galerias del Mar, Polo's Gallery, and Mcpl. Cultural Ctr., Rosarito, Baja Calif., Mex., Esquina de Bodegas, Ensenada, Mex. Others from 1990-2007; represented in permanent collections: Mus. Nat., La Paz, Mus. de la Univ. de Potosi, Bolivia, Mus. Nat. de Bogota, Colombia, S. Am. Ministerio de Edn., Managua, Nicaragua, Bolivian Embassy, Moscow and Washington, also pbt. collections in U.S., Europe and Latin Am.; executed many murals including; Colegio Padilla, Sucre, Bolivia, 1958, Colegio Junin, Sucre, Bolivia, 1959, Sindicato de Construccion Civil, Lima, Peru, 1960. Hon. consul of Bolivia, So. Calif., 1969-73. Served to lt. Bolivian Army, 1953. Recipient Mcpl. award Sucre, Bolivia, 1985, Gold medal, Bolivian Govt., 2003, Disting. Svc. Gold medal, Mariscal de Ayacucho, Bolivia, 2006. Mem. San Diego Art Inst., San Diego Watercolor Soc., Internat. Fine Arts Guild, La Jolla Art Assn. Home: La Jolla, Calif. Deceased.

INCIVILITO, DIANA, import and customs manager; b. Bklyn., June 1, 1953; d. Joseph Paul and Mary Jean (Maltese) I. BBA, Pace U., 1987. Import, customs mgr. Warnaco, Inc., NYC, 1979-89; pvt. cons. Scottsdale, Ariz., from 1989. Cons. K & K Sports, N.Y.C., 1986—. Mem. Nat. Assn. Female Execs., Am. Assn. Exporters and Importers. Roman Catholic. Avocation: color analysis. Died July 13, 2007.

INFANTE, LINDY (GELINDO INFANTE), professional football coach; b. Miami, Fla., May 27, 1940; s. Gelindo and Elizabeth (Nichols) I.; m. Stephanie Claire Kitchell; children: Brett, Brad. BPE, U. Fla., Gainesville, 1964. Backfield coach Miami Sr. High Sch., Fla., 1965; asst. football coach U. Fla., Gainesville, 1966-71; offensive coord. and asst. head coach Memphis State U., 1972-74; asst. coach Charlotte Hornets, N.C., 1975; offensive coord. Tulane U., New Orleans, 1976, 1979; asst. coach, receivers N.Y. Giants, NFL, 1977-78; offensive coordinator Cin. Bengals, NFL, 1980-82; head coach Jacksonville Bulls, USFL, Fla., 1983-85; offensive coord. Cleve. Browns, NFL, 1986-87; head coach Green Bay Packers, NFL, Wis., 1988—91, Indpls. Colts, 1996-97. Named NFL Coach of the Yr., 1989. Avocations: golf, sailing, racquetball, skiing. Home: Saint Augustine, Fla. Died Oct. 8, 2015.

INGELS, MARTY (MARTIN INGERMAN), agent, broadcast executive; b. Bklyn., Mar. 9, 1936; s. Jacob and Minnie (Crown) Ingerman; m. Jean Maire Frassinelli, Aug. 3, 1960 (div. 1969); m. Shirley Jones, 1977; stepchildren Shaun, Patrick, and Ryan Founder Ingels Inc., 1975—2015; formed Stoneypoint Prodns., 1981; TV and motion picture producer U.S. and Abroad; mgr. of Shirley Jones. Star: I'm Dickens and He's Fenster series, ABC-TV, 1962-63; co-star: Pruitts of Southampton, 1968-69; films include Armored Command, 1962, Wild and Wonderful, 1964, Horizontal Lieutenant, 1965, Busy Body, 1967, Ladies Man, 1966, Guide for a Married Man, 1968, If It's Tuesday This Must Be Belgium, 1969; numerous TV appearances, The Phil Silvers Show, The Aquanauts, The Dick Van Dyke Show, The Addams Family, The Phyllis Diller Show, Murder She Wrote, CSI and others Active various charity drives. Achievements include owning the world's largest celebrity brokerage service, 1974; widely noted as the Henry Kissinger of Madison Avenue. Died Oct. 21, 2015.

INGERMAN, MARTIN See INGELS, MARTY

INGHAM, NORMAN WILLIAM, literature educator, genealogist; b. Holyoke, Mass., Dec. 31, 1934; s. Earl Morris and Gladys May (Rust) I. AB in German and Russian cum laude, Middlebury Coll., 1957; postgrad. Slavic philology, Free U. Berlin, 1957—58; MA in Russian lang. and lit., U. Mich., 1959; postgrad. in Russian lang. and lit., Leningrad State U., 1961—62; PhD in Slavic langs. and lit., Harvard U., 1963. Postdoctoral rschr. Czechoslovak Acad. Scis., Prague, 1963—64; asst. prof. dept Slavic langs. and lits. Ind. U., Bloomington, 1964—65; asst. prof. Harvard U., Cambridge, Mass., 1965—70, lectr., 1970—71; assoc. prof. U. Chgo., 1971—82, prof., 1982—2006, chmn. dept., 1977—83, dir. Ea. Europe and USSR lang. and area ctr., 1978—91, prof. emeritus, from 2006. Mem. Am. Com. Slavists, 1977-83; mem. com. Slavic and Ea. European studies U. Chgo., 1979-91, chmn., 1982-91, also other coms.; dir. Ctr. for East European and Russian/Eurasian Studies, 1991-96; cert. genealogist, 1994—. Author: E.T.A. Hoffman's Reception in Russia, 1974; editor: Church and Culture in Old Russia, 1991; co-editor: (with Joachim T. Baer) Mnemozina: Studia litteraria russica in honorem Vsevolod Setchkarev; mem. editorial bd. Slavic and East European Jour., 1978-87, adv. bd., 1987-89; assoc. editor Byzantine Studies, 1973-81; contbg. editor The Am. Genealogist, 1995—; contbr. and translator articles and book revs. Fulbright fellow, 1957-58, vis. fellow Dumbarton Oaks Ctr. for Byzantine Studies, 1972-73. Mem. Am. Assn. Advancement Slavic Studies (rep. coun. on mem. instns. 1985-96, area rep. nat. adv. com. for Ea. European lang. programs 1985-96), Am. Assn. Tchrs. Slavic and East European Langs., Early Slavic Studies Assn. (v.p. 1993-95, pres. 1995-97), Chgo. Consortium for Slavic and East European Studies (v.p. 1982-84, 98, pres. 1984-86, 98-2000, exec. coun. 1992-94), Phi Beta Kappa. Home: Montague, Mass. Died Apr. 27, 2015.

INGRAM, CHARLES OWEN, priest, educator; b. Lee County, Miss., Oct. 23, 1929; s. Leonard Thaddeus and Elizabeth Owen Ingram; m. Frances Chick Hyde, Jan. 8, 1977 (dec.); m. Dorothy Ann Lott, Aug. 29, 1952 (dec.); 1 child, Charles Mark. BS, U. Memphis, 1950, MA, 1958; BD, Southwestern Theol. Sem., Ft. Worth, 1953; PhD, U. Ariz., Tucson, 1967. Ordained priest Bishop Kenneth Woollcombe of Christ Ch. Cathedral, Oxford, 1975. Missionary Sudan Interior Mission, Addis Ababa, Ethiopia, 1954—57; headmaster, chaplain Decamere Boys' Home, 1955—57; dir. U. Ariz. Learning Ctr., Tucson, 1962—87, asst. prof. psychology, 1967—72; deacon St. Stephan's House, Oxford, England, 1974—75; vicar St. Andrews Episcopal Ch., Tucson, 1975—81, rector, 1981—93. Pres. standing com. Diocese of Ariz., Phoenix, 1984, 1985, 1987; chmn. bd. Found. Campus Ministry, Tucson, 1982—88, A Place Apart, Ecumenical Retreat Ctr., Tucson, 1985—91. Founder New Start Program Acad. Assistance for Minority Students, U. Ariz., 1967, Frensdorff House for Persons with AIDS, Tucson, 1988—93, St. Andrew's Bach Soc., Tucson, from 1989; dep. Bicentennial Gen. Conv. of Episcopal Ch., LA, 1985. Mem.: Gibbs Soc., Soc. St. Mary (assoc.), Phi Alpha Theta. Democrat. Episcopalian. Avocations: art, travel. Home: Tucson, Ariz. Died Oct. 23, 2014.

INGRIM, ROBERT WILTON, management consultant; b. Detroit, Dec. 18, 1928; s. Charles Wilton and Rena Faye (Neuhardt) I.; m. Sigrid Susanne Moos, June 10, 1954; children: Cora, Erika, Roxana, Barbara. BS, U. Pitts., 1949; MBA, U. Pa., 1955. Mgr. employee and comty. rels. GE Co., Wiesbaden, Germany, 1961-63; mgr. human resources Rockwell Mfg. Co., Pitts., 1963-66; v.p. adminstrv. svcs. L. B. Foster Co., Pitts., 1966-82; pres., owner Robert W. Ingrim and Assocs., Pitts., from 1982. Mem. exec. bd., vice chmn. Smaller Mfr.'s Coun., Pitts., 1986-91; mem. adv. bd. U. Pitts. exec. programs, 1982-90. Staff sgt. U.S. Army, 1950-53, Germany. Republican. Presbyterian. Avocations: art songs, church music, backpacking, travel. Died July 30, 2007.

INTRILIGATOR, MARC STEVEN, lawyer; b. Oceanside, NY, July 14, 1952; s. Alan and Sally (Jacobs) I.; m. Roxann Kathleen Hoff, Aug. 28, 1977; children: Seth Adam, Joshua Ross, Daniel Benjamin. BA, SUNY, Binghamton, 1974; JD, Boston U., 1977. Bar: N.Y. 1978. Assoc. Dreyer and Traub, NYC, 1977-83, assoc. ptnr., 1984-85, sr. ptnr., 1985-96; of counsel Fischbein Badillo Wagner Harding, NYC, 1996—2005; shareholder Cozen O'Connor, NYC, from 2005. Projects editor: Boston U. law rev., 1976-77. Past pres. Croton Jewish Ctr., Highlands Country Club, pres. First Hebrew Congretion, 2013-15; 2nd v.p., First Hebrew Congregation, 2011-13, trustee, First Hebrew Congregation, 2010-11. Mem. Assn. Bar City N.Y., Trump Nat. Hudson Valley Golf Club, Barefoot Resort Golf Club, Tau Epsilon Phi. Home: Croton On Hudson, NY. Died Nov. 29, 2015.

IRVIN, MONTE (MONFORD MERRILL IRVIN), retired professional baseball player; b. Columbia, Ala., Feb. 25, 1919; s. Cupid Alexander and Mary Eliza Irvin; m. Dorinda Irvin (dec. 2008). Baseball player NY Giants, 1949-55, Chgo. Cubs, 1956; scout NY Mets, 1967-68. Named to Baseball Hall of Fame, 1973; mem. World Series Champions, 1954. Died Jan. 4, 2016.

ISAACS, ARNOLD See SCAASI, ARNOLD

ISAACS, S. TED, engineering and sales executive; b. Louisville, July 13, 1914; s. Max and Rose (Kaplan) Isaacs; m. Ann Fabe, June 7, 1939 (dec. 2001); children: Marjorie McKelvey Isaacs, Susan Freund Isaacs. ChE, U. Cin., 1936, AS, 1944. Registered profl. engr., Ohio, cert. sr. grade fluid power tech. Instrument engr. Std. Oil Co. Ohio, Latonia, Ky., 1936-41; instrumentation mgr. Wright Aero. Corp., Lockland (now Evendale), Ohio, 1941—45; sr. process engr. Drackett Co., Cin., 1945-48; engr. control sys. H. K. Ferguson Co., Cleve., 1948; pres. and field salesman Isaacs Co., Cin., 1948-86; mng. gen ptnr. and pres. artist mgmt. divsn. AFTI Sys., from 1986. V.p. sales, pres. Indsl. Engring. Corp., Louisville, 1951—55. Author: Executive Sweets, 1999, rev. edit., 2000, (poetry, illustration) Purple and Gold, 2002, A Guide to the Perplexed, 2002, numerous poems; columnist: B-Right-On, 1999—2001; contbr. articles to profl. jours., monthly column Jour. of Mfrs. Agt. Nat. Assn., 1978—85. Chmn. energy com. City Environ. Task Force, Cin., 1970—72; personal reader Cin. Radio Reading Svc., 1990—96; sponsor ann. tennis tournament Technion Israel Inst. Tech., Haifa, from 1999; sponsor ann. prize paper contest U. Cin. Coll. Engring. Mem.: Am. Technion Soc. (bd. dirs. Midwest region from 2003), Metric Assn. (v.p. 1962—65), Fluid Power Soc., Assn. Engrs. and Archs. Israel, Engring. Soc. Cin. (life; pres. jr. chpt. 1947—48), Instrument Soc. Am. (sr.; local bd. dirs. 1946—47), U. Cin. Baldwin Soc., Nat. Assn. R.R. Passengers, U. Cin. Herman Schneider Legacy Soc., Ohio Assn. R.R. Passengers, Sierra Club, Cin. Hatikva Investment Club (pres. 1991—93, v.p. rsch. 1994—99), Cephalo-Caudad Investment Club (pres. 1992—93). Democrat. Jewish. Avocations: swimming, bridge, spectator sports, music, art. Died Apr. 11, 2007.

IVY, DARSIE, nursing administrator; b. Benton County, Miss., Nov. 16, 1934; d. Ernest Raney and Ezera Gadd; m. Alvie Lacy Ivy, July 17, 1955; children: Deborah, Tommy. AA, Itawanba Coll., Tupelo, Miss. Cert. ACLS. DON, mgr. quality assurance infection control Meml. Hosp., Holly Springs, Miss., dir. patient svcs. Past pres. Ladies Aux. 1st Pentacostal Ch., Holly Springs. Home: Potts Camp, Miss. Died Nov. 7, 2006.

IWATA, SATORU, gaming company executive, software and game developer; b. Hokkaido Prefecture, Japan, Dec. 6, 1959; Grad. in Computer Sci., Tokyo Inst. Tech. Joined HAL Lab., Inc. (subsidiary of Nintendo), 1982, pres., 1993—2000, coord., software production, 1983—93, corres., 1993—2000; head, corp. planning divsn. Nintendo Co., Ltd., Kyoto, 2000—02, pres., bd. dirs., 2002—13, pres., CEO, Nintendo of Americas, 2013—15. Contbr. to the design Wii. Died July 11, 2015.

IYER, NATRAJ, product designer; b. Bombay, Dec. 26, 1975; permanent resident, 2006; s. Venkatachalam and Vatsala Iyer; m. Emily Marie Rynard, Apr. 19, 2005. B, U. Bombay, 1997; M, Purdue U., West Lafayette, Ind., 2000—00, D, 2005. Sr. design engr. Stryker Endoscopy, San Jose, Calif., 2005—06; product designer W.L. Gore and Assoc., Sunnyvale, Calif., from 2006. Contbr. scientific papers. Vis. scholar Innovation fellow, Purdue U., 2002—04. Mem.: ASME (assoc.). Hindu. Achievements include patents pending for shape based searching for 3D models; invention of 3D shape search engine; research in breaking down CAD models into shape descriptors; aluminum alloys for injection molding. Home: San Jose, Calif. Died Dec. 30, 2006.

IZZI, JOHN, mathematics educator, writer, actor, artist; b. Providence, Dec. 31, 1931; s. Joseph and Elizabeth (Kinney) I.; m. Barbara Ann Freethy, Dec. 18, 1954; children: Kathleen, Donna, James; m. Patricia Margaret Crowley, Aug. 27, 1979; children: John, Matthew, Jessica. BA, Providence Coll., 1953; MEd, RI Coll., 1965; postgrad., U. Vt., 1959, postgrad., 1960, postgrad., 1963, Seton Hall U., 1961, Yale U., 1966, Boston U., 1968—70. Tchr. LaSalle Acad., Providence, 1955-58, Warren HS, RI, 1958-60, Warwick Vets. HS, 1960-62, 2003—04; chmn. Brown U., Warren Math. Project; tchr. Pilgrim HS, Warwick, 1962—66, 1999—2001, head math. dept., 1968-72, Seekonk HS, Mass., 1966-67; state supr. math. Mass. Dept. Edn., 1967-68; head math. dept. Toll Gate HS, Warwick, 1972—88, 2001—02; coord. secondary sch. RI Hosp., 1988-89; tchr. math., sci. Westport HS, Mass., 1989-91, math. adviser, biology, sci. tchr.; adj. faculty Bristol CC, Mass., 1992-94; head dept. edn. mem., 1967—68. Dir. Prep. Inst., Warwick, Math. Edn. Svc., Providence, 1965-66, Toll Gate Metrication Project, Warwick, 1972-73; textbook reviewer AAAS, 1968-74; book reviewer Phi Delta Kappan, 1974-76; pres. Smallstate Co., Warwick, 1975—; prin. Warwick Adult Edn., 1987-88; ext. lectr. U. RI, 1976—: math. coach Toll Gate Acad. Decathlon State Champions, 1985, New Eng. Math. League Divsn. Champions, 1989-90; creator 1st federally funded sch. metrication project in US, 1972, Izzi Metric Slide Chart, 1974, Izzi Decimal Notation, 1974; dir. Smallstate Math. Inst., Warwick, 1989-90, Smallstate Scholarship Svc., Warwick, 1991-93; pres. Smallstate Pub., 1994-96; advisor Am. Security Coun., 1973-79; pres. P & J Izzi Assocs., Warwick, 1997-99; metrication cons. Nat. Coun. Tchrs. Math., 1973—, computer software reviewer, textbook reviewer, 1981-88; adj. faculty CC RI, 1981-85, Bristol CC, 1992-94; editl. adviser New England Mathematic Jour., 1982-85; metrication cons. State Depts. Edn., New Eng., Pa. and NY, 1977-80. Author (illustrator): Metrication, American Style, 1974, Looking at the Metric System, 1977, Adult Metric Guide, 1977, Basic Metric Competency Test, 1977, My Irish, Voices of America, 1991, In Lieu of Dying, 2011; actor: (TV) Brotherhood, 2004—06, Waterfront, 2004—06; contbr. articles to publs. Mem. Mass. Gov.'s Hwy. Safety Act Com., 1967-68. With US Army, 1953-55. NSF grantee 1959-61, 63, 66, 68-70; recipient Disting. Achievement award Ednl. Press Assn. Am., 1974; named Best Math. Tchr. Am., Ky. Ednl. TV, 1990, named a Nat. Leader Mass. Gov.'s Hwy. Safety Act Com. Mem. ASCD, NEA, Am. Fedn. Tchrs., Nat. Coun. Tchrs. Math., Am. Assn. Sch. Adminstrs. Metric Assn., Assn. Tchrs. Math. New Eng., New Eng. Regional Metric Assn. (edn. commr. 1976-80), Mass. Dept. Edn. Assn. (v.p. 1967-68). Died Aug. 3, 2013.

JABLONSKI, FRED FRANCIS, social worker; b. Buffalo, June 5, 1930; s. Anthony and Rose Jablonski; m. Irene E. Slon, Oct. 8, 1960; children: Cynthia, Peter. MSW, SUNY Buffalo, 1985. Med. technologist Lafayette Gen. Hosp., Buffalo; social worker Buffalo. Author: Dynamics of an East Buffalo Ethnic Neighborhood, 2001. Exec. bd. mem. Pastoral Coun. Boy Scouts Am., Buffalo, commr.; pres. Polish Philatelic Soc., Buffalo; vice chmn. 9th Zone Dem., Buffalo. Mem.: Holy Name Soc. (chmn.), Polish Am. Congress. Democrat. Roman Catholic. Avocation: Avocations: wine making, stamp collecting, growing roses. Home: Buffalo, NY. Died Nov. 29, 2006.

JACKLIN, ANNA, food products executive; b. Heidelberg, Baden, Fed. Republic of Germany, May 17, 1923; came to U.S., 1961; d. Karl Michael and Frieda (Jakob) G.; m. Duane Elsworth Jacklin, Jan. 11, 1958; children: Oskar, Crysta, Carmen, Thomas. BBA, Hoehere Handel Schule, Heidelberg, 1945. Pres. Jacklin's Corp., Clovis, N.Mex., from 1973, Siam Import Corp., Amarillo, Tex., from 1984. Mem. DAV (comdr. 1975-77, Comdr. of Yr. 1977), Am. Ex-prisoners of War. Lodges: Masons (pres. 1974-75), Demolay (Mother of Yr. 1976), Elks. Avocations: gardening, antiques, coins, art. Home: Clovis, N.Mex. Died Dec. 29, 2006.

JACKOBS, JOSEPH ALDEN, retired agronomist; b. Shell Lake, Wis., Oct. 23, 1917; s. Joseph Marcus and Edith (Sawyer) J.; m. Marian Elizabeth Caine, June 17, 1940; children: Carol (dec.), Meredith, James (dec.). BS, U. Wis., 1940, MS, 1944, PhD, 1947. Prof. crop prodn. U. Ill., 1951-86, ret., 1986. Soybean cons. FAO, Hanoi, Vietnam, 1984, Bangkok, 1988; crop prodn. cons., Jabalpur, India, 1967-69; edn. cons. Jogjakarta, Indonesia, 1973-75. Fellow AAAS, Am. Soc. Agronomy, Crop Sci. Soc. Am.; mem. Alpha Zeta, Sigma Xi. Methodist. Avocation: travel. Home: Urbana, Ill. Died Feb. 25, 2007.

JACKSON, JESSE LUTHER, III, pastor; b. Kinston, NC, Jan. 15, 1947; s. Jesse Luther Jr. and Iris Elizabeth (Cauley) J.; m. Carol Ann Vest, Aug. 24, 1968; children: Jesse Luther IV, James Joshua. BS in Aerospace Engring., N.C. State U., 1968; MME, U. So. Calif., LA, 1976; MDiv, Mid-Am. Bapt. Theol. Sem., Memphis, 1979. Ordained to ministry So. Bapt. Conv., 1979. Sr. sys. engr. Garrett AiResearch, Torrance, Calif., 1968-76; sem. asst. Bellevue Bapt. Ch., Memphis, 1976-79; sr. pastor Williston (Tenn.) Bapt. Ch., 1979-82, Marble City Bapt. Ch., Knoxville, Tenn., 1982-87, Westwood Hill Bapt. Ch., Virginia Beach, Va., from 1987. Pres. Fayette County Pastors' Conf., Somerville, Tenn., 1981-82; tchr., trainer Evangelism Explosion Internat., Ft. Lauderdale, Fla., 1987—. Recipient Hudgin's award Tenn. Bapt. Conv., Brentwood, 1981, Eagle award So. Bapt. Sunday Sch. Bd., Nashville, 1985, Top Ten in Evangelism Bapt. Gen. Assn. Va., Richmond, 1988-93. Avocations: golf, personal computers. Home: Virginia Beach, Va. *God forbid that I should glory, save in the cross of our Lord Jesus Christ (Galations 6:14).* Died June 7, 2007.

JACO, CHARLES MAPLES, JR., management and engineering consultant; b. Montgomery County, Miss., Jan. 28, 1924; s. Charles M. and Ada Marie (Dorris) J.; m. Jennie Erle Cox, June 12, 1946; children: Charles Erle. ChE, Miss. State U., 1943; BS, U.S. Mil. Acad., 1946; MChE, U. Del., 1956; postgrad., U.S. Staff & Command Coll., 1961. Cert. mgmt. cons. Mem. engring. faculty U.S. Mil. Acad., West Point, N.Y., 1956-60; mgr. corp. devel. Dravo Corp., Pitts., 1966-71; plant mgr. Midland-Ross, Cleve.; pres., gen. mgr. Georgetown Ferreduction Corp., Georgetown, S.C., 1972-73; pres. Midrex Corp., Charlotte, N.C., 1973-74; mng. cons. JCi Cons., 1975-95; cons. Inst. Mgmt. Cons., N.Y. Co-author engring. texts for U.S. Mil. Acad. Mem. AICE, Assn. Iron & Steel Engrs., Rotary, Char. City Club, River Hills Country Club. Methodist. Home: Lake Wylie, SC. Died Jan. 26, 2007.

JACOBS, EUGENE ROBERT, radiologist; b. NYC, Sept. 22, 1929; BA in Chemistry cum laude, Syracuse U., 1951; MD, SUNY, Syracuse, 1955. Diplomate American Bd. Radiology. Intern Temple U. Hosp., 1955-56, resident in radiology, 1956-59; radiologist George Washington U. Hosp., Washington, 1984—97, assoc. prof. emeritus, 1997—2014; dir. radiology Nat. Hosp. Orthopedics & Rehabilitation, 1961—84. Fellow American Coll. of Radiology, Assn. Univ. Radiologists, Radiol. Soc. North America; mem. AMA, American Coll. Physicians., Alpha Omega Alpha. Home: Spotsylvania, Va. Died Oct. 6, 2014.

JACOBS, ROLLY WARREN, judge; b. Nashville, Aug. 26, 1946; s. William Clinton Jr. and Eleanor Olive (Warren) J.; m. Karen Lee Ponist, Sept. 16, 1972; children: Collin Wayne, Tyler Warren. BA in Econs., Washington & Lee U., 1968; JD, U. S.C., 1974. Bar: SC 1975, US Dist. Ct. SC 1975. Assoc. Carl R. Reasonover, Camden, S.C., 1975-77; ptnr. Reasonover & Jacobs, Camden, S.C., 1977-80; pvt. practice law Camden, S.C., 1980-99; judge family ct. 5th Jud. Cir., S.C., from 1999. Asst. city judge Mcpl. Ct., Camden, 1976-77; master in equity S.C. Jud. Sys., Camden, 1978-99; mem. Jud. Coun. for S.C., Columbia, 1989-2000; mem. fee dispute panel S.C. Bar Assn., 1986-93. Bd. dirs. ARC, Camden, 1976-78, Am. Cancer Soc., Camden, 1976-78, United Way, Camden, 1978-82; active Boy Scouts Am., Camden, 1984-96. Capt. U.S. Army, 1968-72. Recipient Dist. Award of Merit Indian Waters Coun. Boy Scouts Am., 1991; named Scouting Family of Yr., 1990. Mem. ABA, VFW, S.C. Bar Assn., Am. Legion, Res. Officers Assn., Elks, DAV. Methodist. Home: Camden, SC. Died May 13, 2007.

JACOBSEN, ROBERT GAIL, investment specialist; b. Erie, Pa., Mar. 27, 1947; s. Kenneth Phillip and June (Burkett) J.; m. Karen Bostick, Feb. 21, 1969; 1 child, Kenneth Kristian. BBA, Wake Forest U., 1970; MBA, Ga. State U., 1972. Analyst Provident Life & Accident Ins. Co., Chattanooga, 1972-74; v.p. Atlantic Bank, N.A., Jacksonville, Fla., 1974-79, Sun Bank, N.A., Orlando, Fla., 1979-82; sr. v.p., prin. Stein Roe and Farnham, Ft. Lauderdale, Fla., from 1982. Capt. USAR, 1970-72. Fellow Inst. Chartered Fin. Analysts; mem. Chartered Investment Counselors Assn., Fin. Analysts Soc. Republican. Episcopalian. Home: Boca Raton, Fla. Died Aug. 21, 2007.

JACOBSON, ALAN P., lawyer; b. Chgo., May 8, 1953; s. George Harris Jacobson and Rachel (Perelman) Fisher; m. Jeanne Marie Jacobson; children: Lee, Grant, Stuart. BS,

So. Ill. U., 1976; JD, John Marshall U., 1989. Claims supr. The Travelers, Chgo., 1977-84; claims mgr. Chgo. Bd. Edn., 1984-87; sr. claim analyst CNA, Chgo., 1987-89; assoc. Clausen Miller Gorman & Caffrey, Chgo., from 1989. Contbr. articles to profl. jours. and hockey mags. Mem. Ill. Bar Assn., Washington D.C. Bar Assn., D.U. Internat., Blue Goose Intenat., Chgo. Claims Assn., Chgo. Bar Assn. Home: Chicago, Ill. Died Aug. 1, 2007.

JACOBSON, RALPH HENRY, retired science administrator, retired military officer; b. Salt Lake City, Dec. 31, 1931; m. Joan Mathews; children: Mary, Matthew, James. Student, U. Utah, 1950-52; BS, U.S. Naval Acad., 1956; MS in Astronautics, Air Force Inst. Tech., 1962; MS in Bus. Adminstrn., George Washington U., 1966; Grad., Air Command and Staff Coll., 1966, Indsl. Coll. Armed Forces, 1974, Naval War Coll., 1976. Commd. 2d lt. U.S. Air Force, 1956, advanced through grades to maj. gen., 1979; project officer Ballistics Systems Div., Norton AFB, Calif., 1962-65; action officer Directorate of Plans, Hdqrs. U.S. Air Force, Washington, 1966-69; wing ops. staff officer 14th Spl. Ops. Wing, Nha Trang Air Base, Republic of Vietnam, 1969-70; successively research and devel. project officer, div. chief and dep. dir. research Air Force Spl. Projects, Los Angeles Air Force Sta., 1970-75; comdr. Air Force Satellite Control Facility, Los Angeles Air Force Sta., 1976-79; asst. dep. chief of staff for space shuttle devel. and ops. Office of Dep. Chief of Staff for Research, Devel. and Acquisitions, Hdqrs. U.S. Air Force, Washington, 1979-80, dir. space systems and command, control and communications, 1980-81; vice dir. Office of Sec. of Air Force Spl. Projects, Los Angeles Air Force Sta., 1981-83, dir., 1983-87; pres., CEO, The Charles Stark Draper Lab., Inc., Cambridge, Mass., 1987-97. Decorated D.S.M. (Defense, Nat. Intelligence Community, Air Force), Legion of Merit with one oak leaf cluster, DFC. Fellow AIAA. Home: Park City, Utah. Died Nov. 1, 2014.

JACQUES, IMELDA DE GARCIA, psychiatric-mental health and rehabilitation nurse; b. Montrose, Colo., July 8, 1933; d. Epifanio and Eleanor (Garcia) J.; children: Sandra Hull Bowers, Suzanne Hull Trimble, Dianne Hull, Linda Hull, Robert Hull. AA in Nursing, Sacramento City Coll., 1957; BA in Health Sci. and Psychology, Calif. State U., Sacramento, 1968, MA in Health Sci. and Psychology, 1970; PhD in Psychology and Health Sci., Columbia Pacific U., San Rafael, Calif., 1981. RN, Calif., Alaska; cert. master hypnotist, secondary tchr. (life). Staff nurse labor and delivery room Mercy Hosp., 1957-60; head nurse pediatric unit Santa Clara County Hosp., 1961-65; staff nurse labor and delivery room, head nurse Kaiser Found. Hosp., Sacramento, 1966-70; asst. prof. nursing, pub. health Alaska Meth. U., 1971-74; safety compliance officer Alaska Dept. Labor, 1976-77; dir. nurses Alderson Convalescent Hosps., 1978-79; dir. profl. svcs. Vis. Nurses Assn., Stockton, Calif., 1979-81; clin. substitute, instr. Los Rios Community Colls., 1983-85; psychiat. nurse Sacramento Mental Health Ctr., Sacramento, 1985-88; coord. med. care Intracorp, Sacramento, 1988-92; pvt. practice rehab. cons., psychologist Sacramento, from 1992. Chmn. coms. U. Alaska Consortium Continuing Edn., 1972-74; relief nurse various med. ctrs., 1982-83; owner, mgr. health edn.-counseling svc., 1979—; mem. faculty Columbis Pacific U., 1981-92; faculty rep. Western Interstate Commn. on Health Edn.; workshops coord. Alaska Child Protection Task Force; chmn. edn. com. Alaska Health Manpower Corp., also dir. nursing coun. Named Tchr. of Yr. Mem. ANA, APHA, AAUP, Am. Assn. Safety Engrs., Calif. Nurses Assn., Alaska Pub. Health Assn., Alaska Nurses Assn. Home: Anchorage, Alaska. Died Aug. 20, 2007.

JAFFA, HARRY VICTOR, political philosophy educator emeritus; b. NYC, Oct. 7, 1918; s. Arthur Sol and Frances (Landau) J.; m. Marjorie Etta Butler, Apr. 25, 1942 (dec. 2010); children: Donald Alan, Philip Bertran, Karen Louise Jaffa McGoldrick. BA in English Literature, Yale U., 1939; PhD in Political Philosophy, summa cum laude, New Sch. for Social Rsch., 1951; LLD (hon.), Marietta Coll., 1979, Ripon Coll., 1987. Instr. Queens Coll., CCNY, New Sch. for Social Rsch., 1945-49, U. Chgo., 1949-51, Ohio State U., 1951-64; faculty Claremont (Calif.) McKenna Coll. and Claremont Grad. Sch., 1964-89, Henry Salvatori Rsch. prof. polit. philosophy, 1971-89, prof. emeritus, 1989—2015; Disting. fellow The Claremont Inst., 1989—2015. Author: Thomism and Aristotelianism: A Study of the Commentary by Thomas Aquinas on the Nicomachean Ethics, 1952, Crisis of the House Divided: An Interpretation of the Issues in the Lincoln-Douglas Debates, 1959, Equality and Liberty: Theory and Practice in American Politics, 1965, The Conditions of Freedom: Essays in Political Philosophy, 1975, How to Think About the American Revolution, 1978, American Conservatism and the American Founding, 1984, Original Intent and the Framers of the Constitution: A Disputed Question, 1994, Storm Over the Constitution, 1999, A New Birth of Freedom: Abraham Lincoln and the Coming of the Civil War, 2000; (with Allan Bloom) Shakespeare's Politics, 1964, Crisis of the Strauss Divided Essays on Leo Strauss as Political Philosoph, 2012; contbg. author: Shakespeare As Political Thinker, 1981; editor, contbg. author: Statesmanship: Essays in Honor of Sir Winston Churchill, 1982; co-editor: (with Robert Johannsen) In the Name of the People: Speeches and Writings of Lincoln and Douglas in the Ohio Campaign of 1859, 1959. Organizer/dir. Bicycle Racing Program, Claremont Coll., 1976-81. Fellow Ford, Rockefeller, Guggenheim, and Earhart founds. Fellow The Claremont Inst. Study of Statesmanship & Political Philosophy (disting.); mem. American Polit. Sci. Assn. Republican. Jewish. Home: Claremont, Calif. Died Jan. 10, 2015.

JAHARIS, MICHAEL (EMMANUEL MICHAEL JAHARIS), pharmaceutical executive; b. Evanston, Ill., July 16, 1928; s. Michael and Katerina Jaharis; married; children: Steven, Kathryn. BA, Carroll Coll.; law degree, DePaul U. V.p. Ethical Drug Divsn. Miles Laboratories, 1961—72; pres., CEO Key Pharmaceuticals, 1972—86; cons. Schering-Plough; dir. Triad Pharmaceuticals, Inc.; founder, chmn. of bd. Kos Pharmaceuticals, 1988—2006; chmn. Kos Investments, Kos Holdings; formed Vatera Healthcare Partners. Chmn. bd. overseers Tufts U. Sch. Medicine. Trustee Tufts U. Named one of Forbes 400: Richest Americans, from 2006. Died Feb. 17, 2016.

JAHIEL, RENE INO, physician; b. Boulogne, Seine, France, Mar. 29, 1928; s. Richard and Cecile (Lwovsky) J.; m. Deborah Berg, May 8, 1955; children: Abigail, Richard, Beth. BA, NYU, 1946; MD, SUNY, Bklyn., 1950; PhD, Columbia U., 1957. Intern Montefiore Hosp., NYC, 1950-51; resident Mt. Sinai Hosp., NYC, 1951—52, fellow in virology, 1952-55; exptl. immunologist Nat. Jewish Hosp., Denver, 1957-59; asst. attending pathologist, exptl. pathology Mt. Sinai Hosp., 1959-61; asst. prof. pub. health Cornell U. Med. Coll., NYC, 1961-66; rsch. assoc. prof. preventive medicine NYU, NYC, 1967-70, rsch. prof., 1970-76, rsch. prof. medicine, Sch. Medicine, 1976-88. Cons. health svcs. rsch., policy and planning, 1989—; adj. prof. health svcs., rsch. and policy New Sch. for Social Rsch., 1991-96; dean faculty of sci. and pub. health, Ecole Libre des Hautes Etudes of N.Y., 1991-94, v.p. scis., 1994—, acting pres., 2003-06, pres. 2006—; vis. prof. dept. cmty. medicine and healthcare U. Conn. Health Ctr., 1995-98, lectr., 1999—2010; pres. Internat. Health Policy Rsch. Corp., Hartford, Conn., 1995—; med. dir. Southbury (Conn.) Tng. Sch., 1993-95; med. cons. State of Conn. Dept. Mental Retardation, 1996-97; tchr. met. leadership program, U. Coll., NYU, 1969-73; physician Assn. for Help for Retarded Children, 1982-88, Young Adult Inst., 1984-89, Assn. for Children with Retarded Mental Devel., 1988-93; cons. Nat. Ctr. for Health Svcs. Rsch., 1983-85; bd. dirs. N.Y. Scientists Com. Pub. Info., 1974-79, Physicians Forum, 1975-84; cons. Yale U Primary Care Tng. Program at Waterbury (Conn.) Hosp., 2000-04. Editor: Homelessness: A Prevention-Oriented Approach, 1992; mem. editl. bd. European Jour. Disability Rsch., from 2007, Rehab. Process and Outcome, from 2011; contbr. articles to profl. jours. Mem. interferon adv. com. Am. Cancer Soc., 1984-93; mem. nat. bd. Com. for Nat. Health Svc., 1976-79, coalition, 1980-85. Lt. USNR, 1955-57. Recipient Daring to Dream award, U. Maine, 2005; grantee, USPHS, 1966—79. Mem.: APHA (chmn. com. health svcs. rsch. 1980—87, governing com. 1983—85, chmn. homelessness study group 1984—90, chmn. policy com. caucus on disablement 1989—92, founding chmn. caucus on homelessness 1990—91, chmn. membership com. spl. interest group on disability 1993—97, chair 1998—99, governing com. 1999—2007, edn. bd. 2000—01, pres. conf. emeritus mem. 2009—11, mem. ann. meeting program com. 2011—12, Med. Care sect. award 1985, Lifetime Achievement award disability sect. 2011), Am. Assn. Psychol. Rehab., Acad. Health (Disability Rsch. Interest Group award 2012), Internat. Soc. for Equity in Health (founding), World Assn. Psychosocial Rehab. (chmn. com. on mental handicaps 1992—94), Assn. Health Svcs. Rsch. (Spl. Recognition award 1986), Physicians for Social Responsibility, Internat. Assn. Health Policy (bd. dirs. 1998—2000). Achievements include research in tissue culture, virology, interferon, preventive medicine, health policy, health svcs. rsch., disability, homelessness, social epidemiology and sociology of knowledge. Died Mar. 14, 2014.

JAMAIL, JOSEPH DAHR, JR., lawyer; b. Houston, Oct. 19, 1925; s. Joseph Dahr and Marie (Anton) Jamail; m. Lillie Mae Hage, Aug. 28, 1949 (dec. 2007); children: Joseph Dahr III, Randall Hage, Robert Lee. BA, U. Tex., 1950; LLB, U. Tex. Sch. Law, 1953. Bar: Tex. 1952. Asst. dist. atty., Harris County, Tex., 1953—55; founder, owner Jamail & Kolius, Houston, 1953—2015. Author: (autobiography) Lawyer: My Trials and Jubilations, 2003; contbr. articles to profl. jours. Grand marshall Martin Luther King Day Parade, Houston, 1989; co-chair Tex. Access to Justice Commn. Recipient Jurisprudence award, Anti-Defamation League B'nai B'rith, 1989, Brotherhood award, Nat. Conf. Christians & Jews, 1993, War Horse award, Southern Trial Lawyers Assn., 1993, Outstanding Alumnus award, U. Tex. Sch. Law, 1996; named Trial Lawyer of Century, Calif. Trial Lawyers, 1999; named one of Forbes 400: Richest Americans, from 2006. Fellow: Internat. Acad. Trial Lawyers, Internat. Soc. Barristers, Internat. Acad. Law & Sci., Tex. Bar Found. (life); mem.: ABA, World Jurist Assn., World Assn. Lawyers, American Judicature Soc., Assn. Trial Lawyers America, Inner Circle Advocates (Outstanding Fifty Yr. Lawyer award 2003), State Bar Tex., Houston Bar Assn., American Coll. Trial Lawyers, U. Tex. Ex-Students' Assn. (life), Delta Theta Phi, Order of Barristers. Achievements include recognition as one of the country's leading trial lawyers; represented Pennzoil Co. in a lawsuit against Texaco Inc. in 1985, receiving the largest jury verdict upheld on appeal in legal history; has tried more than 500 jury and bench trials, which resulted in more than $13 billion in judgments for his clients; has given large donations to th University of Texas, having a swim-ming center, a law school pavilion and the foot-ball field named for him. Home: Houston, Tex. Died Dec. 23, 2015.

JAMES, JUSTICE HAROLD, pathologist; b. Paw Paw, Mich., May 10, 1925; s. Stanley James and Ruth Webb; m. Theresa H. Macalis, June 1, 1960; 1 child, Stanley. DO, Kirksville Coll., 1956. Intern Doctors Hosp., Columbus, Ohio, 1957; resident in pathology Phila., 1957-60; pathologist Chgo. Osteopathic Hosp., 1960-62, Phila. Osteopathic Hosp., 1963-70; resident in pathology L.A. County Osteopathic Hosp., 1970-72; pathologist Cherry Hill (N.J.) Med. Ctr., 1972-81, Lansing (Mich.) Hosp., 1981-83, Phila. Coll. Osteopathic Medicine, 1983-93, Selby Gen. Hosp., Marietta, Ohio, from 1993. Republican. Avocations: sports, gardening. Home: Barnegat, NJ. Died Dec. 27, 2006.

JAMES, P.D. (PHYLLIS DOROTHY JAMES WHITE, BARONESS JAMES OF HOLLAND PARK), author; b. Oxford, Eng., Aug. 3, 1920; d. Sidney Victor and Dorothy May Amelia (Hone) James; m. Connor Bantry White, 1941 (dec. 1964); children: Clare Bantry, Jane Bantry. LittD (hon.), U. Buckingham, 1992, U. Hertfordshire, 1994, U. Glasgow, 1995, Durham U., 1998, Portsmouth U., 1999; DLitt (hon.), U. London, 1993; D (hon.), U. Essex, 1996. Adminstr. Nat. Health Svc., England, 1949-68; apptd. prin. Civil Svc. Home Office, 1968; prin. Police Dept., 1968-72, Criminal Policy Dept., 1972-79; ret., 1979. Chmn. lit. adv. panel Arts Coun. Eng., 1988—92, Brit. Coun., 1988—93; bd. govs. BBC, 1988—93. Author: (novels) Cover Her Face, 1962, A Mind to Murder, 1963, Unnatural Causes, 1967, Shroud for a Nightingale, 1971 (Best Novel award, Mystery Writers America, 1971, Macallan Silver Dagger for fiction, Crime Writers' Assn., 1971), The Maul and the Pear Tree: The Ratcliffe Highway Murders, 1811, 1971, An Unsuitable Job for a Woman, 1972 (Best Novel award, Mystery Writers America, 1973), The Black Tower, 1975 (Macallan Silver Dagger for fiction, 1975), Death of an Expert Witness, 1977, Innocent Blood, 1980, The Skull Beneath the Skin, 1982, A Taste for Death, 1986 (Best Novel award, Mystery Writers America, 1986, Macallan Silver Dagger for fiction, 1986), Devices and Desires, 1989, The Children of Men, 1992 (Deo Gloria award, 1992), Original Sin, 1994, A Certain Justice, 1997, Death in Holy Orders, 2001, The Murder Room, 2003, The Lighthouse, 2005, The Private Patient, 2008, Talking About Detective Fiction, 2009, Death Comes to Pemberley, 2011, (autobiography) Time to Be in Earnest, 1999. Decorated Officer, Order of Brit. Empire, 1983, Life peer (Baroness) House of Lords, Parliament of UK, 1991; recipient Cartier Diamond Dagger (Lifetime Achievement award), Crime Writers' Assn., 1987, Grandmaster award, Mystery Writers America, 1999; named to Internat. Crime Writing Hall of Fame, 2008. Fellow: Royal Soc. Arts, Royal Soc. Lit.; mem.: Soc. Authors (chmn. 1984—86), Detection Club. Died Nov. 27, 2014.

JANDINSKI, JOHN JOSEPH, III, dentist, immunologist; b. Northampton, Mass., July 28, 1946; m. Mary McKenna, Sept. 18, 1951. BA, Case Western Res. U., 1968; DMD, Tufts U., 1972. Postdoctoral fellow Harvard Med. & Dental Sch., Boston, 1972-76, Duke U. Med. Ctr., Durham, N.C., 1976-79; rsch. assoc. in oral pathology Merck & Co., Rahway, N.J., 1979-81; rsch. assoc. Johnson & Johnson, New Brunswick, N.J., 1981-82; assoc. prof. NYU Dental Ctr., NYC, 1982-85; prof. dentistry, assoc. prof. pediat. medicine U. of Medicine & Dentistry of N.J., Newark, from 1985. Dental dir. Children's Hosp. AIDS program. Newark, 1989—; cons. Cistrin Biotech., Pinebrook, N.J., 1991—. Editor: Physical Diagnosis in Dentistry, 1974; contbr. articles to profl. jours. Mem. Light House Keepers, Watch Hill, R.I., 1988—. Recipient Bates Rsch. award Tufts U., 1971. Mem. AAUP (pres. 1992), Am. Assn. Immunology, Clin. Immunology Soc., Am. Acad. Oral Medicine, Soc. for Leukocyte Biology, Sigma Xi, Omicron Kappa Upsilon. Achievements include first demonstration of T cell subpopulations, first demonstration of role of cytokines in periodontal disease; patent pending for 1-hour diagnostic test for periodontal disease and for medications that inhibit Intevelerkin 1B prodn.; renowned consultant for oral diseases in pediatric AIDS. Home: Madison, NJ. Died Feb. 22, 2007.

JARVIS, JOHN CECIL, lawyer; b. Clarksburg, W.Va., May 11, 1949; s. James M. and Maud Lee (Duncan) J.; m. Rebecca Ann Ullom; children: Amy, Jennie, Brian. BS in Civil Engring., Lehigh U., 1971; JD, Vanderbilt U., 1975. Bar: W.Va. 1975. Ptnr. McNeer, Highland, McMunn and Varner L.C., Clarksburg, from 1975. Vice chmn., bd. dirs. W.Va. United Health Sys., Inc.; bd. dirs. One Valley Bank Inc. Democrat. Methodist. Home: Clarksburg, W.Va. Died May 22, 2007.

JENKINS, MILDRED NEVA, coomputer company executive; b. Meringo, Ind., June 1, 1928; d. John Herman and Georgia Nell (Summerland) Jungers; m. Robert E. Jenkins, Jan. 14, 1960 (dec. 1978); children: James Edward, George Alan, Deborah Marion, Robert Edison. Engraver, Tampa, Fla., 1968-70; tchr.'s aide East Elem. Sch., Ocean Springs, Miss., 1970-72; engraver CalWest Trophies, Chula Vista, Calf., 1972-75, Oceanside, Calif., 1976-77, Trophies and Awards, San Diego, 1975-76; sales mgr. Calco Computers, Oceanside, 1980-87, owner, from 1987. Pres. Commodore Users Group, Oceanside, 1980-85; pres. Palomer Ham Radio, Vista, Calif., 1978-79. Author 2 poems. Mem. Nat. Assn. for Female Execs., Am. Assn. Ret. Persons, Rancho Santa Margarita Gem Soc. (sec., editor), DAV Aux. Avocations: lapidary, amateur radio, writing poems, fishing, hunting. Home: San Diego, Calif. Died June 16, 2007.

JENNINGS, LOUIS BROWN, retired humanities educator; b. Lancaster, SC, May 5, 1917; s. Arthur Ewart and Selma Helms Jennings; m. Grace Irene Allen, May 24, 1943 (dec.); children: Carolyn Jennings Sautter, Sharon Jennings Moore. AB, Duke U., Durham, NC, 1938; BD, Crozer Theology Sem., Chester, Pa., 1945; grad. studies, U. Pa., Phila., 1942—45; PhD, U. Chgo., 1964. Ordained minister United Ch. of Christ, 1956. From instr. to prof. Marshall U., Huntington, W.Va., 1948—79; assoc. prof. Ohio U., Portsmouth, 1961—69, prof. Ironton, 1965—72. Dept chmn. Marshall U., 1948—79. Co-author: (Book) Biography of

Edgar Johnson Goodspeed, 1948; author: Biography of Shirley Jackson Case, 1949, The Function of Religion, 1978. Grantee Ford Found. for Advancement of Edn., 1951—52; fellow Crozer Theol. Sem., 1947—48, Univ. of Chgo., 1947—48. Democrat. United Ch.Of Christ. Avocation: walking. Home: Huntington, W.Va. Died Nov. 18, 2006.

JENSEN, DORIS BERNICE See GRAY, COLEEN

JENSEN, RICHARD CURRIE, lawyer; b. Flushing, NY, June 5, 1939; s. David T. and Isabel (Currie) J.; m. Leslie Dodge, Jan. 9, 1965; children: Tracy, Richard, David, Meredith, Lauren, Christopher. BS in Social Studies, Villanova U., 1961; JD, Fordham U., 1964. Bar: N.Y. 1965. Staff atty. Comml. Union Ins. Co., NYC, 1964—68; ptnr. Morris, Duffy, Ivone & Jensen, NYC, 1968—84, Ivone, Devine & Jensen, Lake Success, NY, 1985—2015. Mem. ABA, N.Y. State Bar Assn., Nassau County Bar Assn., Am. Soc. Law & Medicine, N.Y. State Med. Malpractice Def. Bar Assn. (bd. dirs.) Republican. Roman Catholic. Home: Glen Cove, NY. Died Sept. 27, 2015.

JERDE, JON ADAMS, architect; b. Alton, Ill. m. Janice Ambry; children: Jennifer Jerde Castor, Maggie Jerde Joyce, Kate Jerde Cole, Christopher, Oliver. Degree, U. So. Calif. Formerly with Charles Kober Assocs.; founder, chmn. The Jerde Partnership. Prin. works include Seventh Market Pl., L.A., Horton Pla., San Diego, Westside Pavilion, West Los Angeles, Fashion Island, Newport Beach, Calif., Mall of America, Minn., Universal City Walk Hollywood, Calif., Treasure Island Hotel and Casino, Nev., Fremont Street Experience, Nev., Canal City Hakata, Japan, Bellagio, Nev., Palms Casino Resort, Nev., Roppongi Hills, Japan, Wynn Las Vegas, Palms Phase II, Palms Place, Namba Parks, Santa Monica Place Recipient U. So. Calif. Sch. of Arch. Disting. Alumnus award, 1985. Fellow: American Inst. of Architects. Died Feb. 9, 2015.

JIBILIAN, GERALD ARSEN, lawyer, manufacturing corporation executive; b. Toledo, Mar. 30, 1938; s. Gary Sarkis and Rochelle M.; m. Jary Sue Ridout, Dec. 26, 1965; 1 child, John Frederick. AB, Duke U., 1960; JD, U. Mich., 1963. Bar: Ohio 1963. Assoc. Cobourn, Yager, Smith & Falvey, Toledo, 1963—65; chief prosecutor City of Toledo, 1965—69; gen. counsel and v.p. Ogden Foods, Inc., NYC, 1969—71; counsel and exec. v.p. Schrafft's div. Pet Inc., NYC, 1971—73; sr. atty. Wyeth (formerly Am. Home Products, Corp.), NYC, 1973—85; asst. gen. counsel Am. Home Products, Corp., 1985—86, assoc. gen. counsel, 1987—91, v.p. and assoc. gen. counsel, 1991—2002; bus. and legal cons.; iron duke Duke U. Lectr. Seton Hall U. Law Sch.; book reviewer NJ Pub. Libr. Mem.: ABA, Nat. Assn. Mfrs., Pharmaceutical Mfrs. Assn., Med. Device Assn. (legal com. 1972—2000), Grocery Mfrs. Assn. (legal com. 1972—2000), Takeda Chem. (Tokyo) (mem. bd. dirs.), Univ. (NYC), Burning Tree Country (Greenwich, Conn.), Panther Valley Country Club (NJ), Phi Delta Phi, Phi Delta Theta (pres.). Home: Chester, NJ. Died Sept. 12, 2014.

JILES, DAVID COLLINGWOOD, physicist, materials science educator; b. London, Sept. 28, 1953; s. Kenneth Gordon and Vera Ellen (Johnson) J.; m. Helen Elizabeth Graham, Oct. 29, 1979; children: Sarah Jane, Elizabeth Anne, Andrew John, Richard David. BSc, Exeter U., Eng., 1975; MSc, Birmingham U., Eng., 1976, DSc, 1990; PhD, Hull U., Eng., 1979. Registered profl. engr.; chartered engr. Postdoctoral fellow Victoria U., Wellington, New Zealand, 1979-81; rsch. assoc. Queens U., Kingston, Ont., Canada, 1981-84; rsch. fellow Iowa State U., Ames, 1984-86, assoc. physicist, 1986-88, physicist, 1988-90, assoc. prof., 1988-90, sr. physicist, from 1990, prof., from 1991, Anson Marston disting. prof., from 2003, Palmer Endowed chair, elec. & computer engring. dept., from 2010; prof. magnetics, dir. Wolfson Ctr. U. Cardiff, Wales, 2005—10, dir., Inst. for Advanced Materials and Energy Sys., 2006—10. Chmn. Conf. on Properties and Applications of Magnetic Materials, Chgo., 1985-2001; pres. Magnetics Tech. Inc., Ames, 1989—; dir. Magnetics Tech. U.K., Ltd., 2004—; cons. engr. State of Iowa, Des Moines, 1996; sci. advisor Brit. Admiralty, 1991-92, NATO, 1992-2000, U.S. NRC, 1996-97; vis. prof. U. Hull, Eng., 1991, 94, U. Saarland, Germany, 1992, 97, Tech. U. Vienna, 2000, 03, Cardiff (Wales) U., 2004; vis. scientist Czech Acad. Sci., 1999. Author: Introduction to Magnetism and Magnetic Materials, 1991, 2d edit., 1998, Introduction to Electronic Properties of Materials, 1994, 2d edit., 2001, Introduction to the Principles of Materials Evaluation, 2007; editor: IEEE Transactions on Magnetics, 1992—2004, editor-in-chief, 2004-11; editor Nondestructive Testing and Evaluation, 1988-2005, Jour. of Materials Sci. Materials in Electronics, 2002; contbr. more than 600 articles to profl. jours. Recipient Fed. Lab. Consortium award U.S. Dept. Energy, 1994, Magnetics Soc. Disting. Lectr. award, 1997; Royal Soc. rsch. fellow. Fellow IEEE, Inst. Elec. Engrs. UK, Inst. Physics, Am. Phys. Soc. (chair topical group on magnetism and its applications, 1997-99), Magnetics Soc. (adminstrv. com. 1995-2001, 03-), Inst. Math. and its Applications, Inst. Materials, UK, Japanese Soc. for Promotion Sci., Indian Soc. Nondestructive Testing (hon.); mem. AAAS. Achievements include 15 patents; developer of various models relating to non-linear effects and theory of ferromagnetic hysteresis. Home: Ames, Iowa. Deceased.

JOHNSON, BADRI NAHVI, social studies educator, real estate company owner; b. Tehran, Iran, Dec. 1, 1933; came to U.S., 1957; d. Ali Akbar and Monir Khazraii Nahvi; m. Floyd Milton Johnson, July 2, 1960; children: Rebecca, Shahla, Nancy, Robert. BS, U. Minn., 1967, MA, 1969, PhD, 2001. Stenographer Curtis 1000, Inc., St. Paul, 1958-62; lab. instr. U. Minn., Mpls., 1966-69, teaching asst., 1969-72; chief exec. officer Real Estate Investment and Mgmt. Enterprise, St. Paul, from 1969; prof. emeritus sociology Anoka-Ramsey C.C., Coon Rapids, Minn., 1973—2003. Pub. speaker, bd. dirs., sponsor pub. radio KFAI, Mpls., 1989-93; established an endowed scholarship for women Anoka Ramsey C.C., 1991. Radio talk show host KCW, Brookline Parks, Minn., 1993. Organizer Iranian earthquake disaster relief, 1990; bd. dirs. dist. 7 Cmty. Coun., 1996-98. Recipient Earthquake Relief Orgn. citation Iranian Royal Household, 1968, Islamic Republic of Iran citation for organizing earthquake disaster relief, 1990. Mem.: NEA, Sociologists of Minn., Minn. Edn. Assn., Women's Leadership Forum, Nat. Social Scis. Assn., U. Minn. Alumni Assn. Avocations: gardening, travel, reading. Home: Saint Paul, Minn. Died Feb. 20, 2015.

JOHNSON, CHARLES FOREMAN, architectural firm executive; b. Plainfield, NJ, May 28, 1929; s. Charles E. and E. Lucile Johnson; m. Beverly Jean Hinnendale, Feb. 19, 1961; children: Kevin, David; m. Susie Mills, 2005. Student, Union Jr. Coll., 1947-48; BArch, U. So. Calif., 1958; postgrad., UCLA, 1959-60. Draftsman Wigton-Abbott, P.C., Plainfield, 1945—52; arch., cons. graphic, interior and engring. sys. designer, from 1953; designer, draftsman H.W. Underhill, Arch., LA, 1953—55; tchg. asst. U. So. Calif., LA, 1954—55; designer with Carrington H. Lewis, Arch., Palos Verdes, Calif., 1955—56; grad. arch. Ramo-Wooldridge Corp., LA, 1956—58; tech. dir. Atlas Weapon Sys. Space Tech. Labs., LA, 1958—60; advanced planner and sys. engr. Minuteman Weapon Sys. TRW, LA, 1960—64, dir. staff ops. divsn., 1964—68; cons. N.Mex. Regional Med. Program and N.Mex. State Dept. Hosps., 1968—70; prin. Charles F. Johnson, arch., LA, 1953—68, Santa Fe, 1968—88, Carefree, Ariz., 1988—97, Carpenteria, Calif., 1998—2003, Green Valley, Ariz., 2003—09, Gold Canton Ariz., from 2009. Founder Keva West LLC, owner and operator Keva Juice Smoothie stores; freelance archtl. photographer, Santa Fe, 1971—; tchr. archtl. apprentice program, 1974—; program writer, workshop leader, keynote spkr. Mich. Archtl. Design Competition, 1993; keynote spkr. Mex. Inst. Tech. y de Estudios Superiores, 1993; lectr., spkr., judge III Bienal Arch. and Urbanism Costa Rica, 1996. Major archtl. works include: residential bldgs. in Calif., 1955-66; Bashein Bldg. at Los Lunas (N.Mex.) Hosp. and Tng. Sch., 1969, various residential bldgs., Santa Fe, 1973—, Kurtz Home, Dillon, Colo., 1981, Whispering Boulders Home, Carefree, 1981, Hedrick House, Santa Fe, 1983, Kole House, Green Valley, Ariz., 1984, Casa Largo, Santa Fe (used for film The Man Who Fell to Earth), 1974, Rubel House, Santa Fe, 1986, Smith House, Carefree, 1987, Klopfer House, Santa Fe, 1988, Janssen House, Carefree, 1988, Art Start Gallery, 1988, Dr. Okun's House, 1990, Luterback House, Carefree, 1992, Phillips House, Carefree, 1992, Balagura House, Santa Fe, 1993, Davis House and Guest House of Rio Rico, AZ, 2004; master plan cons. Sky Ranch devel., N.Mex.; subject mag. articles, projects in books, shown on TV; contbr. articles on facility planning and mgmt. to profl. publs.; contbr. archtl. photographs to mags. in U.S., Eng., France, Japan and Italy; contbr. articles on facility mgmt., planning info. sys. to profl. jours. Pres. Santa Fe Coalition for the Arts, 1977; set designer Santa Fe Fiesta Melodrama, 1969, 71, 74, 77, 78, 81, Ariz. Audiophile Soc., 1997; designer Jay Miller & Friends Fiesta float, 1970-88 (winner 20 awards); started Keva West LLC, owns and oper. Keva Juice smoothie stores. Named one of Top 100 Archs., Archtl. Digest mag., 1991. Mem. Ariz. Audiophile Soc. (bd. dirs.), Delta Sigma Phi. Avocations: music, photography, architecture. Home: Gold Canyon, Ariz. Died Jan. 14, 2014.

JOHNSON, CLIFFORD GILBERT, retired double bassist; b. Mpls., Nov. 20, 1921; s. Iver Theodore and Amy Olivea (Good) J.; m. Thelma Irene Larson; children: Gordon, James. Grad. high sch., Mpls. Double bassist Minn. Orch. (formerly Mpls. Symphony), Mpls., 1948-95, symphony piano technician, 1965-87; instr. piano tuning MacPhail Ctr., Mpls., 1958-75; ret., 1995. Ind. pipe carver, Mpls., 1941—, bow maker, Mpls., 1965—. Served as sgt. U.S. Army, 1942-45, ETO. Avocations: carving smoking pipes, making bows and chin rests, rebuilding pianos, tuning grand pianos. Home: Minneapolis, Minn. Died Feb. 17, 2007.

JOHNSON, DENIS P., physics educator; b. Kansas City, Mo., Oct. 27, 1941; s. Albert Burton and Maxine (Paige) J.; m. Alice Elizabeth Smith, Sept. 4, 1965; children: Brian, Eric, Lise. BS, U. Kans., Lawrence, 1963, PhD, 1971. Physicist Hanford Atomics Products Ops., Richland, Wash., 1963-64; postdoctoral rschr. La. State U., Baton Rouge, 1971-72; postdoctoral physicist U. Libre de Bruxelles, Brussels, Belgium, 1972-75; staff physicist Vrije U. Brussels, 1975-84, 85-87, asst. prof. physics Vesalius Coll., 1987-91, prof. physics, from 1991; mem. tech. staff AT&T Bell Labs., Holmdel, N.J., 1984-85. Contbr. over 135 articles to profl. jours. Predoctoral fellow Argonne (Ill.) Nat. Lab., 1967-71. Mem. Am. Phys. Soc. Avocations: tennis, travel. Home: Wezembeek-Oppem, Belgium. Died May 1, 2007.

JOHNSON, DONALD E., lawyer; b. Harrisburg, Pa., Sept. 25, 1946; s. Robert Gordon and Anne (O'Neill) J.; m. Margaret B., Nov. 22, 1969; children: Christopher, Philip, Meredith. BA, LaSalle Coll., 1968; JD, Villanova U., 1972. Bar: Pa. 1972, U.S. Ct. Appeals (3d cir.) 1979, Minn. 1985, U.S. Ct. Appeals (8th cir.) 1985. Prosecutor Dist. Atty.'s Office, City of Phila., 1972-73, Delaware County, Media, Pa., 1973-78, spl. prosecutor, 1978-80; sr. trial atty. Atty. Gen.'s Office, State of Pa., 1980-82; chief counsel Pa. Crime Commn., 1982-85; assoc. gen. counsel Burlington No. R.R., St. Paul, from 1985. Instr. Phila. Police Acad., 1972-73; mem. faculty Temple U., Phila., 1973-76; cons. Pa. State Police, 1973-84. Recipient Trial Advocacy award U. Chgo., 1981, cert. Rochester-influenced and Corrupt Orgns. div. Justice Dept., 1983; named Ky. col., 1983. Mem. ABA, Pa. Bar Assn., Minn. Bar Assn., Nat. Inst. Trial Advocacy (trial advocacy award 1985), Nat. R.R. Trial Lawyers Assn. Avocations: hunting, fishing, fly-tying, trap and skeet shooting. Died Dec. 5, 2006.

JOHNSON, DONALD ROSS, entomologist, consultant; b. Chgo., Feb. 9, 1920; s. George William and Grace Anna (Roos) J.; m. Beryl Lucille Edman, June 15, 1947; children: Gary R., Lynn Kay, Lee R., Laura Kay. BSc in Entomology, U. Ill., 1943; MSc in Entomology, U. Minn., 1950. Lab. asst. dept. entomology U. Ill., Urbana, 1939-41; sci. aide U.S. Dept. Agr., Urbana, 1941-43; pest control technician Illini Pest Control Co., Urbana, 1943; rsch. asst. dept. entomology U. Minn., St. Paul, 1946-48; asst. state entomologist State of Minn., St. Paul, 1948-51; malaria advisor, entomologist Fgn. Aid Program USPHS/ U.S. AID, Djakarta, Indonesia, 1951-53; dep. chief malaria control and eradication program USPHS/U.S. AID, Washington, 1953-64; chief spl. svcs., malaria programs CDC, Atlanta, 1964-73; pub. health entomologist, cons. Atlanta, from 1973. Contbr. numerous articles to sci. jours. mem. adv. bd. Pest Control mag., Cleve., 1980—. Lt. (j.g.) USN, 1943-46, New Guinea and Philippines; capt. USPHS. Recipient Meritorious Svc. citation U.S. Agy. Internat. Devel., Washington, 1963, Meritorious Svc. cert. U.S. Armed Forces Pest Control Bd., Washington, 1973. Mem. Am. Mosquito Control Assn. (Meritorious Svc. award 1974, 82), Soc. for Vector Ecology, Entomol. Soc. Am. (emeritus), Pi Chi Omega. Lutheran. Avocations: travel, genealogy, gardening. Home: Marietta, Ga. Died Mar. 24, 2007.

JOHNSON, DONNY RAY, banker; b. Loudon, Tenn., Nov. 16, 1951; s. James Clifford Sr. and Mildred Fay (Scott) J.; m. Nancy Sue Corbin, Apr. 14, 1972; children: Don Joshua, Seth Micah. M in Barber Sci., Molar Tri City Barber Coll., 1968; BS, U. Tenn., 1975. Real estate salesman Simco Real Estate, Knoxville, Tenn., 1972-73; sr. collector Hamilton Nat. Bank, Knoxville, 1975-77; jr. credit analyst United Am. Bank, Knoxville, 1977-78, sr. credit analyst, 1978-79, credit officer, 1979-81, loan review officer, 1981-83, First Tenn. Bank, Knoxville, 1983-85, comml. banking officer, 1985-87, v.p. comml. lending, 1987-90; v.p., credit adminstr. Union Planters Nat. Bank, Oak Ridge, Tenn., from 1990. Speaker in field; mem. adv. bd. Fairview Tech. Ctr. Host cable TV program Innovations. Fund raiser Jr. Achievement, Knoxville, 1985. Mem. Venture Exchange Forum, Robert Morris Assocs., Knoxville C. of C. (fund raiser 1986), Optomists Club. Republican. Avocations: woodworking, canoeing, clay sculpture, piano, guitar, golf, volleyball. Home: Knoxville, Tenn. Died June 23, 2007.

JOHNSON, DOROTHY CURFMAN, elementary school educator; b. Smithsburg, Md., Nov. 21, 1930; d. Paul Frank and Rhoda Pearl (Witmer) Curfman; m. Robert Nelson Johnson, Jan. 24, 1953 (div. Dec. 1965); children: Gregory Nelson, Eric Paul. Student, Gettysburg Coll., 1948-50, Waynesboro Bus. Coll., 1950, Broward C.C., Ft. Lauderdale, Fla., 1967; BS in Edn., Fla. Atlantic U., 1969, postgrad., 1975-76. Cert. tchr., Fla. Sec. to prodn. mgr. Westinghouse Elec. Corp., Sunbury, Pa., 1951-53; sec. to v.p., sales Metal Carbides Corp., Youngstown, Ohio, 1966; tchr. Sch. Bd. of Broward County, Ft. Lauderdale, Ohio, 1969-93, curriculum specialist, 1993-96. Masters in Edn. Prog., 1973-74, team coord. Sanders Park Elem., Pompano Beach, Fla., 1985-96; mem. North Area Adv. Bd., Pompano Beach, 1990-96; sec. Sanders Park PTA, Pompano Beach, 1994-96. Sec.-treas. Georgen Arms Bd. of Dirs., Pompano Beach, 1997—; dir. Georgen Arms Condo, Inc., Pompano Beach, 1974—; active Jr. League, Youngstown. Recipient Master Tchr. award State of Fla., 1981-82. Mem. Alpha Xi Delta. Lutheran. Home: Pompano Beach, Fla. Died June 1, 2007.

JOHNSON, DOUGLAS HERBERT, ophthalmologist; b. Rochester, Minn., Apr. 17, 1951; s. Herbert Wesley and Betty Lou (Hevle) J.; m. Nancy Lee Schilling, July 19, 1975; children: Emily, Valerie. BA summa cum laude, St. Olaf Coll., Northfield, Minn., 1973; MD, Mayo Med. Sch., 1977. Diplomate Am. Bd. Ophthalmology. Resident in ophthalmology Mayo Clinic, Rochester, 1977-81, cons. in ophthalmology, clin. investigator, from 1983; fellow in ophthalmology Harvard U., Boston, 1981-83, clin. instr. ophthalmology, 1981-83. Dir. Glaucoma Rsch. Lab., Mayo Clinic. Group leader Cmty. Bible Study, Rochester, 1990—. Mem. Phi Beta Kappa. Home: Rochester, Minn. Died July 26, 2007.

JOHNSON, ELIZABETH HILL, foundation administrator; b. Ft. Wayne, Ind., Aug. 21, 1913; d. Harry W. and Lydia (Buechner) Hill; m. Samuel Spencer Johnson, Oct. 7, 1944 (dec. 1984); children: Elizabeth Katharine, Patricia Caroline. BS summa cum laude, Miami U., Oxford, Ohio, 1935; MA in English Lit., Wellesley Coll., 1937; postgrad., U. Chgo., 1936. Cert. tchr., Ohio. Pres., co-founder S.S. Johnson Found., Calif. Corp., San Francisco, from 1947. Mem. Oreg. State Bd. Higher Edn., Eugene, 1962-75, Oreg. State Edn. Coord. Com., Salem, 1975-82, Assn. Governing Bds., Washington, 1970-80, chairperson, 1975-76; mem. Oreg. State Tchr. Standards and Practices Commn., Salem, 1982-89; bd. dirs. Lewis and Clark Coll., Portland, Oreg., 1985—, Pacific U., Forest Grove, Oreg., 1972-75, 1982-89, 1993-97, Sunriver Prep. Sch., 1983-92, Oreg. Hist. Soc., Portland, 1985-97, Cen. Oreg. Dist. Hosp., Redmond, 1982—, Oreg. High Desert Mus., 1984-97, Bend, Oreg., Health Decisions, 1986-92, Ctrl. Oreg. Coun. Aging, 1991-97; Deschutes County Hist. Soc., 1996—. Lt. USNR, 1943-46. Named Honoree March of Dimes White Rose Luncheon, 1984; recipient Aubrey Watzek award Lewis and

Clark Coll., 1984, Cen. Oreg. 1st Citizen award, Abrams award Emanuel Hosp., 1982, Pres. award Marylhurst Coll., 1991, Thomas Jefferson award Oregon Historical Soc., 1993, Glenn L. Jackson medallion, 1998, Pres.'s award Redmond C. of C., 1996. Mem. Am. Assn. Higher Edn., Am. Assn. Jr. Colls., ASCD, Soroptimists (hon.), Francisca Club, Town Club, Univ. Club, Waverley Club, Beta Sigma Phi, Phi Beta Kappa, Phi Delta Kappa, Delta Gamma. Republican. Lutheran. Home: Redmond, Oreg. Died Jan. 1, 2007.

JOHNSON, ELSPETH ANN, librarian; b. Cambridge, Mass., Aug. 12, 1934; d. Edwin Warren and Resda Clair (Murray) Conable; m. Walter Edwin Johnson, Jan 28, 1956; children: Debora Ann Johnson Refior, Steven Forrest (dec.). BS in Edn., No. Ill. U., 1956; MA, Nat. Coll. Edn., 1969, Adminstrn. cert., 1973; Media Cert., Northeastern Ill. U., 1973. Tchr. pub. schs. Northfield (Ill.) Sch. Dist., 1962-69; librarian, learning ctr. West Pub. Sch., Glencoe, Ill., 1969-74; IMC library Kodiak (Alaska) Island Sch., from 1974. Contbr. articles to profl. jours. Mem. Council Govs.' ESEA Title IV Adv. Council, Juneau, Alaska, 1978-83; Episcopal Women; vol. Kodiak Hist. Soc., active Kodiak Reps. Mem. Alaska Libr. Assn. (v.p. 1976-77, pres. 1977-78, 89-90), Kodiak Libr. Assn. (pres. 1976-77, 88-89), Alaska Edn. Assn., Kodiak Edn. Assn. (media com. 1979-80), AAUW (v.p. Kodiak chpt. 1982-83, pres. 1983, bd. dirs. 1984-85), Am. Orchid Soc., Alaska Orchid Soc., DAR (vice-regent Natalia Shelikof chpt. 1984-86, regent 1986-88), Kodiak Pub. Broadcasting Assn., Kodiak Retailer's Assn., Kodiak C. of C., Delta Kappa Gamma (v.p. 1990-91). Died Nov. 29, 2006.

JOHNSON, IRVING STANLEY, pharmaceutical executive, biomedical research consultant; b. Grand Junction, Colo., June 30, 1925; s. Walter Glenn and Frances Lucetta (Tuttle) J.; m. Alwyn Neville Ginther, Jan. 29, 1949; children: Rebecca Lyn, Bryan Glenn, Kirsten Shawn, Kevin Bruce. BS, Washburn U., Topeka, 1948; PhD in Devel. Biology, U. Kans., Lawrence, 1953; student, Cornell U., Duke U., Harvard U. With Lilly Rsch. Labs., Indpls., 1953-88, v.p. rsch., 1973-88; mem. profl. edn. com. Am. Cancer Soc., 1972-82. Rschr. cancer, virus, genetic engring.; mem. UCLA Symposia Bd., 1988-; bd. dirs. Allelix Biopharms., Ligand Pharms.; sci. adv. bd. Elan Corp., 1996-; cons., Swedish Govt. & European Pharma Co., trustee La Jolla Cancer Rsch. Found., 1990-93; advisor to biomed. rsch. cos., venture capital groups; mem. Recombinant Adv. Com., NIH; indep. biomedical rsch. cons. Editor: Biology and Medicine in the 21st Century, 2007; mem. sci. adv. bd. Biotech., 1986—; mem. editorial bd. Chemico-Biol. Interactions, 1968-73; contbr. articles to profl. publs.; patentee in field. Industry spkr. NAS Open Forum. With USNR, 1943—46. Named Ten Outstanding Young Men, US C.of C., 1960; recipient 1st ann. Congl. award for sci. and tech., 1984, Alumni Disting. Achievement award U. Kans., 2005, Disting. Svc. Citation award U. Kans., 2006, Recognition award, US Congress State Legis. Coms., Frint Amount Continuous award, Svc. & Tech., 1990, nominated award, Nat. Acad. Fellow AAAS; mem. Am. Assn. Cancer Rsch. (emeritus mem; Cain Meml. award for outstanding preclin. rsch. in cancer chemotherapy 1986), Am. Soc. Cell Biology (mem. pub. policy com.), Environ. Mutagen Soc., Internat. Soc. Chemotherapy, NY Acad. Scis., Soc. Exptl. Biology and Medicine, Am. Soc. Immunologists (mem. sci. adv. bd. biotech), Soc. for Neurosci., NSF (del. mem.), Sigma Xi, Phi Sigma. Episcopalian. Achievements include being widely acknowledged for leadership team which led to the production and approval of the first health care product manufactured by recombinant DNA/genetic engineering techniques, ie human insulin. Died July 10, 2014.

JOHNSON, JAMES MYRON, psychologist, educator; b. Sauk Centre, Minn., Aug. 4, 1927; s. Wilfred and Sophie Catherine (Koelzer) J.; m. Constance Mary Blodgett, Apr. 15, 1950; children: Kathryn, Peter, Donna, Daniel, Amy, Linda, Eric, Christian. BA, U. Minn., 1948; MA, Clark U., 1950; PhD, Columbia, 1958; ME (hon.), Stevens Inst. Tech., 1986. Staff psychologist Lever Bros. Co., 1955-64; Adj. prof. Grad. Sch. Indsl. Engring., N.Y.U., 1963-66; dep. dir. lab. psychol. studies Stevens Inst. Tech., 1964-67, dir., 1967-73, prof. mgmt. sci. and psychology, 1966-89, prof. emeritus, from 1989, assoc. dean acad. affairs, 1972-76, dir. tech. and soc. curriculum, 1972-75; dir. Center for Mgmt. of Organizational Resources, 1976-81; sr. partner Organizational Scis. Assocs., 1980-88; v.p. G. W. Fotis Assocs., Inc., 1982-88, head, dept. of mgmt., 1988-89. Cons. to industry. Prodr.: (film) The Man Who Revolutionized Management: Frederick Winslow Taylor; co-editor: Parish Life; editor: Lyme Cath. Observer. Pres. Darien (Conn.) Mental Health Assn., 1961-64, 68-70; mem. Darien Democratic Town Com.; bd. dirs. Gateway, Inc., 1979-86. Served with USNR, 1945-46. Mem. Am. Psychol. Soc., Met. N.Y. Assn. Applied Psychology (pres. 1963-64), Sigma Xi (treas. 1984-89), Old Lyme Country Club. Democrat. Roman Catholic. Home: Fiskdale, Mass. Died Apr. 25, 2011.

JOHNSON, KEITH JAMES, wholesale distribution executive; b. Racine, Wis., Feb. 3, 1934; s. Oliver Edwin and Julia (Taylor) J.; m. Nancy Dunn, Nov. 23, 1962; children: Denise, Lisa, Lydia. Student, Stetson U., 1956-57. Br. mgr., salesman Allied Screw div. Allied Products, Miami and St. Petersburg, Fla., 1961-70; S.E. regional mgr. Allmetal Screw Products Co., NY and Atlanta, 1970-71; pres. Johnson & Assocs., Marietta, Ga., 1971-78; sales rep. Atlanta Fasteners, Norcross, Ga., 1978-84; mgr. field sales Atlanta Hardware Splty. Co., Inc., Norcross, from 1984. Editor: Fastener Data Book, 1987. Lay speaker North Ga. Conf. United Meth. Ch., 1987—. Served with USN, 1951-54. Mem. Nat. Fastener Distributors Assn. (assoc.), Mana Mfrs. Agts. Nat. Assn. (assoc.). Republican. Avocations: golf, colonial woodcrafts, civil war history. Home: Marietta, Ga. Died Feb. 16, 2007.

JOHNSON, LENNART INGEMAR, materials engineering consultant; b. Mpls., Dec. 23, 1924; s. Sixten Richard Wilhem and Marie Augusta Johnson; m. Muriel Grant, Oct. 7, 1961; 1 child, Sandra Lee. BS in Chem. Engring., U. Minn., 1948. Petroleum engr. Northwestern Refining Co., New Brighton, Minn., 1948-49; sr. engr. Ordnance Div. Honeywell, Hopkins, Minn., 1949-67, prin. materials engr. Def. Sys. Div., 1967-69, supr. engring. Def. Sys. Div., 1969-87; staff engr. Armament Sys. Div. Honeywell Inc., Hopkins, Minn., 1987-88; cons. Soc. Automotive Engring., Warrandale, Pa., 1989-99. Cons. Ecubed Assocs., Inc., 1993-97; forum leader and presenter, U. Wis. Engring. Inst., Madison, 1965; presenter in field. Author: Handbook of Aerospace Composite Standards, 1992; contbr. numerous articles to profl. jours. Mem. credentials com. Hennepin County Rep. Conv., Minn., 1972, alt. del., 1974. Recipient Prize Paper award, IEEE, 1965. Fellow Am. Inst. Chemists (emeritus); mem. Soc. Automotive Engrs. (sec. aerospace composites com. 1986-87, chmn. 1987-89). Achievements include development of injection molding technology, urethane and epoxy casting resins, and urethane foaming resins. Died Apr. 4, 2012.

JOHNSON, MARIAN ILENE, education educator; b. Hawarden, Iowa, Oct. 3, 1929; d. Henry Richard and Wilhelmina Anna (Schmidt) Stoltenberg; m. Paul Irving Jones, June 14, 1958 (dec. Feb. 1985); m. William Andrew Johnson, Oct. 3, 1991. BA, U. La Verne, 1959; MA, Claremont Grad. Sch., 1962; PhD, Ariz. State U., 1971. Cert. tchr., Iowa, Calif. Elem. tchr. Cherokee Sch. Dist., Iowa, 1949-52, Sioux City Sch. Dist., Iowa, 1952-56, Ontario Pub. Schs., Calif., 1956-61, Reed Union Sch. Dist., Belvedere-Tiburon, Calif., 1962-65, Columbia Union Sch. Dist., Calif., 1965-68; prof. edn. Calif. State U., Chico, 1972-91. Avocation: travel. Home: Sun Lakes, Ariz. Died Oct. 24, 2006.

JOHNSON, OPAL BURTON, retired elementary school educator; b. Mercer County, W.Va., May 30, 1929; d. Martin Luther and Annie Elizabeth (Gentry) Burton; m. Eugene Hunter Johnson, Mar. 13, 1948; children: Eugene Hunter Jr., Nancy Gayle Johnson Canady. BA, King Coll., Bristol, Tenn., 1966; MA in Teaching, East Tenn. State U., 1977. Cert. elem. tchr., Va. Tchr. Bristol Sch. Sys., Va., 1966—95, ret., 1995. Mem. reading, math, spelling and social studies textbook adoption coms., individually guided end. unit leader, sch. handbook com. Bristol Sch. Sys., Va., tchr. evaluation com., drug edn. com. Development of: 2d grade curriculum in math, sci., health and social studies, grades 1-6 lang. art curriculum. Named Tchr. of Yr., Bristol (Tenn.-Va.) Rotary Club, 1989; nominated Va. Tchr. of Yr., 1990. Mem. NEA, So. Assn. Colls. and Schs. (chmn. self study steering com.), Va. Edn. Assn., Bristol Edn. Assn., Phi Kappa Phi, Phi Delta Kappa. Presbyterian. Avocations: rose gardening, crafts. Home: Bristol, Tenn. Died Jan. 5, 2015.

JOHNSON, OWEN H., retired state legislator; b. Mineola, NY, Dec. 3, 1929; m. Christel Grosswendt, 1966; children: Owen, Chirsten. BA in History, Polit. Sci., Hofstra Coll., NY, 1956; LLD (hon.), Hofstra U., NY, 1998. Committeeman Suffolk County Rep. Com., Long Island; pres. Johnson & Johnson Agy. Inc., West Babylon, NY; mem. Dist. 4 NY State Senate, 1973—2012. Mem. advisory coun. drug abuse edn. & prevention West Islip Public Sch., 1988. Recipient Outstanding Contributions award, Nat. Safety Coun., Disting. Achievement award, Long Island Regional Coun. Parents, Early Childhood Ctr. Plaque, Wyandanch Cmty. LaFrancis Hardiman, Recognition award, Nat. League Families America & Missing Prisoners SE Asia, Sr. Citizens award, United Srs. Babylon, Honor Roll award, United New Yorkers for Choice; named Estabrook award, Hofstra U., Legislator of Yr., NY State Conservation Coun., 1994, NY State Chiropractors Assn., 1996, Citizen of Yr., NY State Soc. Profl. Engineers, 1996. Mem.: Suffolk County Assn. Ins. Agents (former pres.), American Legislature Exch. Coun. (nat. chmn. 1987—88, nat. dir., Lifetime award 1995), American Red Cross (Babylon Town Chpt.), Salvation Army (former vice chmn.), Sunrise Rep. Club (former pres.), Shriners. Republican. Lutheran. Died Dec. 24, 2014.

JOHNSON, PATRICK MICHAEL, marketing professional; b. Phoenix, May 9, 1954; s. George Michael and Maryann (Gardulski) J.; m. Robin Hartiens; children: Lauren, Faith, Meredith. BS in Biology, U. San Diego, 1977; postgrad., La. State U., 1987. Sand control trainee Baker Sand Control Co., Lafayette, 1977-78, sand control specialist Ventura, Calif., 1978-79; field salesman Reed Tool Corp., Ventura, 1979-80, regional sales mgr. Shreveport; U.S. mktg. mgr. Sachs Dolmar Div., Shreveport, 1986-90; gen. mgr. Husquarna S.E., Charlotte, N.C., from 1990. Bd. dir. Masonary and Concrete Saw Mfg. Inst. Cleve., 1986--. Recipient Merit Scholarship Finalist Nat. Merit Found., 1972, Calif. State Scholarship, 1972-77, Bus. to Bus. Advt. award Arklatex. Mem. Direct Mktg. Assn., Masonary and Concrete SAW Mfg. Inst., PPEMA, Am. Petroleum Inst., Northwood Country Club, YMCA. Republican. Roman Catholic. Avocations: basketball, weightlifting, golf, jazz. Home: Lafayette, La. Died May 4, 2007.

JOHNSON, RAYMOND ARD, psychiatrist, educator; b. Lewistown, Pa., Nov. 22, 1942; s. Raymond Ard and Elsie Clara (Sowers) J.; m. Linda R. Johnson; 1 child, Hilary. BS in Speech Therapy, Bloomsburg State U., 1965; MD, Temple U., 1972. Diplomate Am. Bd. Psychiatry and Neurology. Speech therapist Montgomery County Sch. System, 1965-68; intern in internal medicine Hahnemann U., Phila., 1972-73, resident in psychiatry, 1977-80, now asst. clin. instr.; emergency room physician, adminstr. Atlanta Emergency Physicians Group, Riverdale, Fla., 1975-77; pvt. practice Penn Valley, Pa., from 1980; dir. chem. dependence unit The Willough, Naples, Fla., from 1995; med. dir. Ruth Cooper Ctr., Ft. Myers, Fla. Dir. addictive svcs. Guiffre Med. Ctr., Phila., 1980-81, program dir. substance abuse unit Fairmount Inst., Phila., 1981-87, Horsham Clinic, Ambler, Pa., 1987-89; med. dir. Malvern (Pa.) Inst., 1989-91; psychiat. cons. Impaired Physicians Com., Lemoyne, Pa., 1988-89, Camden (N.J.) Diocese, 1988-89; bd. dirs. Starting Point, Collingswood, N.J.; speaker in field; mem. complimentary med. staff Northwestern Psychiat. Inst.; exec. mem. Coun. for Compulsive Gambling; assoc. med. dir. addiction svcs. Northwestern Inst. Psychiatry., 1993; active med. staff Horsham Clinic. Contbr. articles to med. jours. Lt. comdr. M.C., USN, 1973-75. Mem. AMA, Am. Psychiat. Assn. (Falk fellow 1980), Am. Soc. Addictive Medicine (cert.), Fla. Psychiat. Assn. Republican. Avocations: music, great books. Died May 24, 2007.

JOHNSON, RICHARD THOMAS, machinery manufacturing company executive; b. Monticello, NY, Jan. 11, 1922; m. Eleanor H. Youngs, Feb. 12, 1949 BS, Syracuse U., 1952. A founder Stein, Inc., Sandusky, Ohio, 1955, pres., also bd. pres., 1985-87, bd. dirs., 1955-93. Patentee batter and breading machinery. With USN, 1940-46. Home: Sandusky, Ohio. Died Aug. 28, 2007.

JOHNSON, ROBERT LELAND, lawyer; b. Denver, May 1, 1933; m. Pamela Gay Stearns, June 6, 1964; children: Mary Morris (dec.), Anthony Morris. BA, Yale U., 1955; JD, U. Denver, 1958, BA in English, 1962. Bar: Colo. 1959, U.S. Dist. Ct. Colo. 1959, U.S. Ct. Appeals (10th cir.), 1959, U.S. Supreme Ct. 1959. Pvt. practice law, Denver, from 1962. Asst. regional svcs. counsel region 8 US Gen. Svcs. Adminstrn.; law clk. Colo. Supreme Ct.; lectr. U. Colo., 1978-83; Dem. candidate Colo. Atty. Gen. Author: The Newspaper Accounts of B.F. Wright, Esq., and Others of Louisa County, Iowa, 1967, Trial Handbook for Colorado Torts Lawyers, 1967, Matrimonial Practice in Colorado Courts, 1969, The American Heritage of James Norman Hall, 1970, Colorado Mechanic's Liens, 1970, A Genealogical Excursion Through Historic Philadelphia, 1976; (with Pamela Gay Johnson) A Mother's Love, 1977, Letters to Glenn Doman: A Story on Enriched and Accelerated Childhood Development, 1980, Super Babies, 1982, Super Kids & Their Parents, 1986, The Ancestry of Anthony Morris Johnson, vol. 1, 1989, vol. 11, 1989, Corriegenda Supplement to the Ancestry of Anthony Morris Johnson vol. 3, 1991, The King Arthur Book, 1991, In Memory of Colonel Edmund Scarborough II (Scarburgh) (1618-1671) and Anne Toft (1643-1687) of Accomack County, Virginia, 2003, A Good Gene Pool of the Eastern Shore of Virginia And Maryland, 2006. Parent connector MIT; interviewer Yale Alumni; mentor U. Denver, Sturm Coll. Law; mem. Duke of Gloucester Soc. of Colonial Williamsburg Found., Va.; Dem. committeeman, polit. adviser to Mitch Morrissey Denver Dist. Atty. Campaign, 2004. Mem. ABA, Am. Judicature Soc., Colo. Trial Lawyers Assn., Denver Bar Assn. (legal aid and pub. defender com., family law com., interprofl. com.). Democrat. Mem. Soc. Of Friends. Home: Denver, Colo. Died Feb. 26, 2007.

JOHNSON, VICKI, producer and talk show host; d. Rosario Caserta Raciti and Marianna Asprea; m. John Charles King, June 13, 2000; children from previous marriage: Joseph Surace, Lennerd W. Degree, LA City Coll., U. Calif., LA, U. Perugia, Italy. Tchr., Nat. King. Coll. Columbia Studios, LA, 1965, tchr.,Streisano, 1969, tchr., Tommy Boyce & Bobby Hart, 1970, tchr., Cat cast; radio talk show host KBU Radio, Malibu, Calif., 1980—85; TV talk show host Vicki Johnson Show, Santa Monica, Malibu, Calif., from 1985; time warner Charter Eagle Rock, Marina del Rey & San Fernando Valley, Adelphia Cable, Malibu, 1985—99; TV talk show host Dennis Weaver, 1985—95, Jerry Lewis Telethon, 1990, Barbara Sinatra, from 2010. Author: (book) Talking with the Stars, 2008, (translated to Italian) Shoes of the Fisher; contbr. articles to French, to mags.; host The Vicky Johnson Show; translator (host): Shoes of the Fisherman; movie, The Angles Cried. V.p. Malibu Garden Club, 1985; acting pres. Roundtable Pub., Malibu, 1992—2000. Recipient Miss San Diego Beauty Contest award, 1991, Miss Calver City award, 2003. Home: Wildomar, Calif. Deceased.

JOLLEY, BETTY CORNETTE, history educator; b. Taylors Valley, Va., Apr. 3, 1927; d. Benjamin Harrison and Joyce Joanne (Stamper) Cornette; m. Harley Edison Jolley, Dec. 24, 1949; children: Benjamin Joseph, Stuart Lynn. BS, Appalachian State U., 1949, MA, 1955; postgrad., U. N.C., Chapel Hill, U. London. Tchr. Haynes Sch., Winston Salem, N.C., 1949-50, Newton Elem. Sch., Asheville, N.C., 1950-52, Nathans Creek (N.C.) Sch., 1952-53; asst. librarian Mars Hill (N.C.) Coll., 1953-55, prof. history, from 1955-. Cons. various N.C. public schs., 1970--; supr. social studies tchrs., Mars Hill Coll., 1970--; prof. tchr. Continuing Edn. Program, Mars Hill Coll., 1970--; workshop leader, 1986; mem. Southern Assn. Accreditation Com., 1987, social studies tchr., edn. coord., Tchr. Evaluation Com., N.C. Edn. Assn.; chair Appalachian Consortium Regional coop. and Devel. Com., 1990--; advisor local coll. chpt. Phi Alpha Theta, 1982--. Co-author: (video) North Carolina: A Goodly Land and a Hardy People, 1985; contbr., advisor (workbook) Appalachian Studies. Precinct chmn. Madison County (N.C.) Constitutional Bicentennial Com., 1987-91, Dem. precinct chair, Mars Hill, 1986-89; judge Optimist Club, Buncombe County, N.C., 1984-89, N.C. Western dist. judge dist. oratorical/CCHI finals, 1993; speaker various N.C. churches, 1989—. Piedmont U. study/travel grantee,

London, Paris, 1966, faculty devel. grantee, 1991, NEH grantee, 1967, N.C. Humanities Media grantee, 1969, Nat. Humanities travel/study grantee, China, 1989; recipient Disting. Service and Mentor award Mars Hill Coll., 1985. Mem. Western N.C. Historical Assn., Hist. Preservation Orgn., Delta Kappa Gamma (pres. Alpha Phi chpt.). Baptist. Avocations: reading, travel, cooking, rockhounding, writing poems. Died July 23, 2007.

JOLLIE, SUSAN BARBARA, lawyer; b. Milw., May 23, 1950; d. Harry William and Dolores Eleanor (Schlueter) J. BA, Marquette U., Milw., 1972; JD, Georgetown U., Washington, DC, 1976. Bar: DC 1976; US Ct. Appeals (DC cir.) 1985, US Ct. Appeals (8th cir.) 1991, (9th cir.) 2008. From trial atty. to assoc. gen. counsel antitrust, litigation Civil Aeronautics Bd., Washington, 1977-83; gen. counsel SMC Internat., Washington, 1984-85; assoc. Galland, Kharasch, Morse & Garfinkle pc, Washington, 1985-87, ptnr., 1987—96; pvt. practice law Annandale, Va., from 1996. Rep. McLean Civic Assn., Va., 1991-92; pres. Nat. Women's History Mus., 2001-07. Mem. Wisc. State Soc. (v.p. 1980—), Hummer Woods Civic Assn. (v.p. 2006-07, pres. 2007-), Internat. Aviation Club, Aero Club. Home: Annandale, Va. Died Mar. 4, 2014.

JONER, BRUNO, aeronautical engineer; b. Oskarstrom, Sweden, Dec. 17, 1921; came to U.S., 1962, naturalized, 1967; s. Algot and Hanna (Erickson) J.; m. Ingrid Gustafsson, Oct. 3, 1953; children: Peter, Eva, David. BS in Aero. and Mech. Engring., Stockholm Inst. Tech., 1940. Tech. dir. Ostermans Aero AB, Stockholm, 1946-52; devel. engr. mgr. STAL Finspong, Sweden, 1952-57; mgr. aviation dept. Salen & Wicander, AB, Stockholm, 1957-62; project engr. Boeing Vertol Co., Phila., 1962-77, Boeing Marine Systems Co., Seattle, 1977-88, Boeing Huntsville (Ala.) Internat. Space Sta., 1988-96, Boeing Rotorcrafts, Phila., from 1997. Author papers in field; co-author: Feasibility Study of Modern Airships. With Swedish Air Force, 1942-43. Assoc. fellow AIAA; mem. U.S. Naval Inst., Nat. Assn. Unmanned Vehicle Systems (charter). Home: Saint Augustine, Fla. Died Jan. 30, 2007.

JONES, ANNE, librarian; b. St. Louis, Mo., July 29, 1934; d. Bernard Joseph and Mary Christina (DeRubertis) Muller-Thym. BA in English, CUNY, 1958. Libr. J.H. Whitney & Co., NYC, 1957-67; reference libr. Am. Mgmt. Assn., NYC, 1967-86, libr., database adminstr., 1986-89, mgr. info. resource ctr., from 1989. Author: Celebrate the Journey: History of the West End Presbyterian Church, 1988. Democrat. Presbyterian. Avocations: reading, poetry. Home: Bronx, NY. Died Mar. 3, 2007.

JONES, ANNIE WALTON, retired secondary school educator; b. Marshall, Tex., Nov. 3, 1952; d. Ollie and Obelia (Brown) Walton; m. Roger Lee Jones, Aug. 21, 1987; children: Ardis Delano Walton, Kristie Elease Walton Jones. BA, Wiley Coll., 1976; cert. in teaching, 1981; MEd Guidance, Counseling, Prairie View Med. Coll., 1984; cert. in mid-mgmt., F. Austin U., 1999. Respiratory technician Meml. Hosp., Marshall, 1974-76; rural housing asst. E-TEX.HUDCO, Marshall, 1977-78; housing adminstr. City of Marshall Housing Authority, 1978-79; from payroll clk. to adminstrv. asst. for devel. Wiley Coll., Marshall, 1979-81; tchr. Marshall Ind. Sch. Dist., 1982—2006, ret., 2006. Mem. Tex. State Tchrs., NEA, Tex. Vocat. Guidance Assn. (auction com. 1988-89), Nat. Assn. Curriculum Devel., Nat. Assn. Female Execs., Women's Softball Club, Delta Sigma Theta (life). Democrat. Baptist. Avocations: competing in softball, singing. Home: Marshall, Tex. Died Feb. 27, 2007.

JONES, DAVID ROBERT See BOWIE, DAVID

JONES, DEAN CARROLL, actor; b. Decatur, Ala., Jan. 25, 1931; s. Andrew Guy and Nolia Elizabeth (Wilhite) J.; m. Mae Inez Entwisle, Jan. 1, 1954 (div.); children: Caroline Elizabeth, Deanna Mae Demaree; m. Lory (Patrick) Basham Jones, June 2, 1973; 1 child, Michael David. Student, Asbury Coll. Blues singer, New Orleans; performances include: (Broadway) There Was A Little Girl, 1960, Under the Yum Yum Tree, 1961, Company, 1970, Into the Light, 1986; (films) The Opposite Sex, 1956, Tea and Sympathy, 1956, These Wilder Years, 1956, Somebody Up There Likes Me, 1956, The Great American Pastime, 1956, The Rack, 1956, Until They Sail, 1957, Jailhouse Rock, 1957, 10,000 Bedrooms, 1957, Designing Woman, 1957, Torpedo Run, 1958, Handle With Care, 1958, Imitation General, 1958, Never So Few, 1959, Night of the Quarter Moon, 1959, Under the Yum-Yum Tree, 1963, New Interns, 1964, That Darn Cat!, 1965, Two On a Guillotine, 1965, The Ugly Dachshund, 1966, Any Wednesday, 1966, Monkeys, Go Home!, 1967, The Horse in the Grey Flannel Suit, 1968, Blackbeard's Ghost, 1968, The Love Bug, 1969, Mr. Superinvisible, 1970, The $1,000,000 Duck, 1971, Snowball Express, 1972, The Shaggy D.A, 1976, Herbie Goes to Monte Carlo, 1977, Born Again, 1978, St. John in Exile, 1986, Other People's Money, 1991, Beethoven, 1992, Clear and Present Danger, 1994, Kickboxer 5, 1994, A spasso nel tempo, 1996, That Darn Cat, 1997, (voice) Batman & Mr. Freeze: SubZero, 1998, Mandie and the Secret Tunnel, 2009 (TV series) Ensign O'Toole, 1962-63, What's It All About, World?, 1969, Adventures from the Book of Virtues, 1998 (host), The Chicago Teddy Bears,1971, Herbie, The Love Bug, 1982, Beethoven (animated), 1994, (voice) Jonny Quest: The New Adventures, 1996; (TV movies) The Great Man's Whiskers, 1971, Guess Who's Been Sleeping in My Bed, 1973, Once Upon a Brothers Grimm, 1977, When Every Day Was the 4th of July, 1978, The Long Days of Summer, 1980, Fire and Rain, 1989, Saved By the Bell: Hawaiian Style, 1992, The Computer Wore Tennis Shoes, 1995, Special Report: Journey to Mars, 1995, The Love Bug, 1997, Scrooge and Marley, 2001; appeared on TV series Wagon Train, Murder She Wrote, Superman. With USN Air Corps, 1950-54. Mem. Acad. Motion Picture Arts and Scis., Acad. TV Arts and Scis., Acad. Rec. Arts and Scis. Home: Tarzana, Calif. Died Sept. 1, 2015.

JONES, HARVEY ROYDEN, JR., neurologist; b. Plainfield, NJ, Nov. 18, 1936; m. Mary Elizabeth Norman, Mar. 18, 1961; children: Roy, Kathryn, Frederick, David. BS, Tufts U., 1958; MD, Northwestern U., 1962. Diplomate in neurology, clin. neurophysiology and neuromuscular medicine Am. Bd. Psychiatry and Neurology, bd. dirs., 1997-2004 Am. Bd. Psychiatry and Neurology, diplomate Am. Bd. Electroencephalography, Am. Bd. Electrodiagnostic Medicine. Intern Phila. Gen. Hosp., 1962-63; resident in internal medicine Mayo Grad. Sch. Medicine, Rochester, Minn., 1963-65; resident in neurology Mayo Grad. Sch. medicine, Rochester, Minn., 1965-66; chief neurology svc. U.S. Army Hosp., Bad Cannstatt, Germany, 1966-70; resident in neurology/clin. neurophysiology Mayo Grad. Sch. medicine, Rochester, Minn., 1970-72; from clin. instr. to clin. prof. neurology Harvard Med. Sch., Boston, from 1973; staff neurologist, Jaime Ortiz-Patino chair neurology, chair divsn. of med. specialties, emeritus chair Lahey Clinic, Burlington, Mass., from 1972; assoc. in neurology, assoc. divsn. neurophysiology, dir. emeritus electromygraphy lab. Children's Hosp., Boston, from 1977; assoc. in neurology, assoc. divsn. neurophysiology Brigham Women's Hosp., Boston, 2001—09. Editor, author: CIBA Collection, Nervous System Part II, 1986, Pediatric Clinical Electromyography, 1996, Neuromuscular Disorders of Infancy, Childhood and Adolescence, A Clinician's Approach, 2003, Netter's Neurology, 2005, CLinical Neurophysiology of Infancy, Childhood & Adolscence, 2006; contbr. numerous articles to profl. jours. Fellow Am. Acad. Neurology; mem. Am. Neurol. Assn. Home: Wellesley, Mass. Died 2013.

JONES, HATTIE ELIZABETH RUSSELL, data processing educator; b. Laurel, Va., Feb. 18, 1932; d. Ervin Smith and Eula Burns (Puckett) Russell; m. Robert Noble Jones, May 27, 1972. BS, Concord Coll., 1957; MEd, Va. Poly. Inst. State U., 1964. Tchr. Bluestone (Va.) Sch., 1952-55, Tazewell (Va.) High Sch., 1957-65; prof. Chowan Coll., Murfreesboro, N.C., 1965-95; ret., 1995. Sec. 1st Nat. Bank, Bluefield, 1957, 58, 60. Democrat. Baptist. Avocations: piano, reading, computers, travel. Died Jan. 2, 2007.

JONES, HERMAN OTTO, JR., agricultural products executive; b. Jacksonville, Fla., Dec. 1, 1933; s. Herman Otto Sr. and Esther (Powell) J.; m. Marjorie Seaver, June 4, 1955 (dec. June 1996); two children (dec.); m. M. Beth Seaver, May 10, 1997. BSA, U. Fla., Gainesville, 1956. V.p. Oak Crest Hatcheries, Inc., Jacksonville, 1956-71; exec. v.p. Oak Crest Enterprises, Inc., Jacksonville, 1958-71; dir. sales Diversified Imports, Inc., Lakewood, N.J., 1971-73, BEC Ltd., Winchester, Eng., 1973-78; sales rep. Paul Revere Ins. Co., Jacksonville, 1978-81; v.p. Anitox Corp., Buford, Ga., 1981-85; pres. Gateway Suppliers, Inc., Jacksonville, 1986-98; v.p. Sales Agritek Bio Ingredients Corp., Montreal, Quebec, Can., 1993-97; pres. Gateway Bio-Nutrients, Inc., from 1998. Contbr. articles to profl. jours. Vice chmn. bd. deacons Riverside Bapt. Ch., 1988-89, deacon, 1991-94, sec. of deacons, 1991-92, dir. Sunday Sch., 1992-93; bd. dirs. South Shore Condos, 1998-2001, treas., 1998-2001, 2003, pres., 2001-03, 06; past pres. Duval Co. Farm Bur., 1964, Fla. Poultry Assn., 1964, Fla. Hatchery, 1964, Fla. Breeders Assn., 1965, Fla. Poultry Fedn., 1965; mem. Duval County Rep. Exec. Com., 2003. Named Outstanding Mem., Fla. Poultry Fedn., 1965, Southeastern Poultry and Egg Assn., 1963, State Outstanding Young Farmer, Fla. Jaycees, 1968; recipient Disting. Service award, Jacksonville Jaycees, 1970. Mem.: Fla. Feed Assn., U.S. Poultry and Egg Assn., Greater Jacksonville Agrl. Fair Assn. (bd. dirs. from 2002, vice chmn. 2004), Mandarin Mus. and Hist. Soc., Beaches Sea Turtle Patrol, Gainesville Quarterback Club, Order of DeMolay (Chevalier degree state master councilor state of Fla. 1953), Order Ea. Star (past patron), Jesters, Shriners, Masons (master), Rotary (bd. dirs. South Jacksonville 1989—91, Paul Harris fellow). Republican. Avocations: golf, travel. Home: Jacksonville, Fla. Died Mar. 1, 2007.

JONES, HOWARD WILBUR, JR., gynecologist; b. Balt., Dec. 30, 1910; s. Howard Wilbur and Ethel Ruth (Marling) J.; m. Georgeanna Emory Seegar, June 22, 1940 (dec. 2005); children—Howard Wilbur III, Georgeanna S. Jones Klingensmith, Lawrence M. AB, Amherst Coll., 1931; MD, Johns Hopkins U., 1935; Dr. Honoris Causa, Cordoba, 1968; D.Sc. honoris causa, Old Dominion U., 1986; D.Sc. Honoris Causa, Amherst Coll., 1986; Dr. Honoris Causa, Madrid, 1987; D.Sc. honoris causa, Ea. Va. Med. Sch., 1988. Intern, asst. resident, resident gynecology Johns Hopkins Hosp., 1935-37, 46-48; asst. resident, resident surgery Ch. Home and Hosp., Balt., 1937-40; practice medicine, specializing in obstetrics and gynecology Balt., 1948-79. Instr., asst. prof., assoc. prof., prof. gynecology and obstetrics Sch. Medicine Johns Hopkins, 1948-79, prof. emeritus, 1979-2015; prof. obstetrics and gynecology, reader, writer, attended lectures, Ea. Va. Med. Sch. (Jones Institute for Reproductive Medicine), 1978-2015 (stopped working with patients in 1990's); nat. cons. USAF, 1968-78. Author: (with W.W. Scott) Genital Anomalies and Related Endocrine Disorders, 1958, rev. edit., 1971, (with G.S. Jones) Textbook of Gynecology, 1965, 10th edit., 1981, (with R. Heller) Pediatric and Adolescent Gynecology, 1968, (with J.A. Rock) Reparative and Constructive Surgery of the Female Generative Tract, 1983, 2d edit., 1992; editor in chief: (with G.E.S. Jones) Obstetrical and Gynecological Survey, 1957-90; contbr. (with G.E.S. Jones) articles to profl. jours.; (self-published books) War and Love: A Surgeon's Memoir of Battlefield Medicine With Letters To and From Home, 2004, Personhood Revisited: Reproductive Technologies, Bioethics, Religion and the Law, 2013; author In Vitro Fertilization Comes to America: Memoir of a Medical Breakthrough, 2014 Served to maj. M.C. AUS, 1943-46. Decorated Bronze Star medal. Mem. AMA, Am. Assn. Cancer Research, Am. Cancer Soc. (dir. Md. div.), Am. Coll. Obstetrics and Gynecology, Soc. Pelvic Surgeons, Sociedad de Obstetricia Y Gynecologia die Buenos Aires, Sociedad Peruana de Obstetricia Y Ginecologia, Am. Fertility Soc. (past chmn.) Achievements include opening the first sex-change clinic in an American hospital, John Hopkins Gender Identity Clinic in 1965; helping achieve the first birth through in vitro fertilization in the US-"first test-tube baby" by cesarean section at 7:46 am, 12/28/81-Elizabeth Jordan Carr; co-founded with wife, the Jones Institute for Reproductive Medicine, Eastern Virginia in 1979. Doctors came to train there; only American gynecologists invited to the Vatican in 1984 to advise Pope John Paull II about reproductive technology. Home: Norfolk, Va. Died July 31, 2015.

JONES, KENSINGER, advertising executive, author, educator, conservationist; b. St. Louis, Oct. 18, 1919; s. Walter C. and Anna (Kensinger) Jones; m. Alice May Guseman, Oct. 7, 1944; children: Jeffrey, Janice A. Jones Geary. Student, Washington U., St. Louis, 1938-39. Lectr. radio writing Wash. U., 1947—52; TV writer, advt. agy. supr. Leo Burnett Co., 1952-57; exec. v.p., creative dir. Campbell-Ewald Co., Detroit, 1957-68; sr. v.p., creative dir. D.P. Brother & Co., Detroit, 1968-70; sr. v.p., exec. creative dir. Leo Burnett Co., Inc., Chgo., 1970-73; regional creative dir. Leo Burnett Pty. Ltd., Sydney, Australia, 1973-75, Leo Burnett, SE Asia, 1975-77; creative supr. Biggs/Gilmore, 1981-83; lectr. Mich. State U., 1982-95; emeritus, 1996. Vis. lectr., China, 1988, Taipei, Taiwan, Jakarta, Indonesia, 1990, Dalhousie U., N.S., 1992. Author: Enter Singapore, 1974, Looking for the Best, 1994; author: (as R. N. Lake) Not Guilty, Just Dead, 1999; co-author: Cable Advertising-New Ways to New Business, 1986, A Call From the Country, 1989, Love Poems of a Business Man, 1997, Case Histories in Co-operation, 1999; author: Various Verses, 2009, (radio series) Land We Live In, 1945—52, numerous poems; contbr. articles to profl. jours.; exhibitions include Detroit Hist. Mus., 2004, Represented in permanent collections Hartman Collection, Duke U. Bd. dir. World Med. Relief, Inc., 1961—92, dir. emeritus, 1993; mem. comm. com. Nat. Coun. Boy Scouts Am., 1966—92; mem. Econ. Devel. Action Group, 1988—96; chmn. Barry County Planning and Zoning Commn., Pks. and Recreation Commn.; county grants coord. Barry County, 1977—78, mem. futuring steering com., from 1988, mem. natural resources action team, 2002—08; mem. dean's cmty. coun. arts Mich. State U., 1993—96, mem. coop. ext. adv. coun., 1993—95. With US Army, 1940—44. Recipient Silver Beaver award, Boy Scouts Am., Silver salute, Mich. State U., 1982, award, Freedoms Found., 1984, Positive Action for Tomorrow award, Barry County, 1995; named Barry County Sr. Citizen of the Yr., 1999. Mem.: Adcraft Club Detroit, Circumnavigators Club, Players Club. Home: Hastings, Mich. *The opportunity to absorb, examine, synthesize and then utilize facts and experience is what makes creative endeavor fascinating. Somehow the individual mind finds new and meaningful relationships between previously unrelated data. An idea is born. It becomes an advertising campaign, a book or movie, a new product. Trying to find those new relationships makes life rewarding in so many ways. Dissatisfaction with the status quo is the prod toward all progress. Use your talents broadly. Not just to make a living, but to improve your life, your environment, your society. By doing so you'll improve your talents.* Died Mar. 10, 2015.

JONES, LISA GRANTZ, nutritionist; b. Louisville, Apr. 2, 1958; d. Raymond Kenneth and Julie (Eliott) Grantz; m. David L. Jones, Oct. 23, 1981; children: Jennifer, Kathleen. BS in Dietetics, Western Ky. U., 1981; MS in Food Svc. Adminstrn., U. Tenn., 1982. Registered dietitian/nutritionist. Clin. dietitian Jackson Hosp., Montgomery, Ala., 1982-83, Meth. Hosp., Hattiesburg, Mis., 1983-84, Ft. Sanders Med. Ctr., Knoxville, from 1988. Mem. pool com. New Harbour Recreation Assn., Knoxville, 1991; mem. Wood Harbor Recreation Assn. Mem. Am. Dietetic Assn., Knoxville Dist. Dietetic Assn. (fellowship chair 1991—), Moneychangers Club, Toastmasters. Democrat. Roman Catholic. Avocations: swimming, aerobics, sewing, crosstich. Home: Knoxville, Tenn. Died Feb. 21, 2007.

JONES, MARY LOUISE JORDAN, writer; b. Fredericksburg, Tex., May 10, 1916; d. Charles Jerome and Ima Lucille (Jackson) Jordan; m. Charles Ingram Jones, Aug. 16, 1941 (dec.). BA, Tex. Women's U., 1939; MA, Columbia U., 1946; PhD, Sorbonne Experimenting Colls. and Univs., 1983. Prin. local elem. sch., Aransas Pass, Tex., 1937-39; tchr. art Walter Noble Jr. High, Aransas Pass, 1939-43; tchr. govt. and history Aransas Pass High Sch., 1943-46; tchr. Robert E. Lee High Sch., Baytown, Tex., 1946-51; art counselor Am. Schs., Tripoli, Libya, 1961-62, Bitburg, Fed. Republic of Germany, 1962-63; tchr. Ross S. Sterling High Sch., Baytown, 1970-75; prof. art European campus U. Md., 1975-83; free-lance writer, cons. art Baytown, from 1983. Judge art shows, 1939-80. Author: Woody Watches the Masters, Books I, II, III, 1985, 86; (play) Jade, 1937; inventor ednl. game. Mem. dist. bd. Girl Scouts U.S., Beeville, Tex., 1946-51; pres. Art League, Baytown, 1971-72; life mem. Bay Area Heritage Soc., Baytown; mem. Friends of Sterling Mcpl. Library, Baytown, Lee Coll. Found., Lee Coll. Symphony, Jr. League Houston, patron. Named to Fine Arts Hall of Fame AAUW, 1959; Sorbonne scholar, 1967-68. Mem. Nat. Art Educators Assn., Tex. Art Educators Assn., AAUW, Houston Mus. Fine Arts, Young Women of Arts, Delta Kappa Gamma (life). Clubs: Bar Assn. Aux., East Harris County. Democrat. Episcopalian. Avocations: volunteer, swimming, horseback riding, travle, aerobics. Home: Baytown, Tex. Died June 14, 2007.

JONES, MICHAEL RICHARD, architect; b. Los Angeles, Nov. 14, 1944; s. Paul Jones and Charlene (Pritchard) Jennings; m. Sara Van Ammelrooy, June 10, 1972. BArch, Calif. Poly. State U., 1972; M in City Planning, San Diego State U., 1977. Registered architect, Calif., Oreg., Nev., Tex., Ariz., Hawaii. Designer Rick Engring., San Diego, 1972-73, Brian Paul, architect, San Diego, 1973-74; project architect Robert Ferris, San Diego, 1974-76; prin. Environ. Design Co., San Diego, 1976-78; pres. Michael Jones Architects, Inc., San Diego, from 1978. Pres. San Diego Land Devel. Co., 1979-84. Pres. Spl. Olympics, San Diego, 1985; served as cpl. USMC, 1962-66, Vietnam. Named Vol. of Yr. Spl. Olympics, San Diego, 1983. Mem. Soc. Am. Registered Architects (pres. 1985-86, service award 1985), AIA, Nat. Council Archtl. Registration Bds. Clubs: Toastmasters (pres. 4 clubs, 1974, 79, 84, area gov. 1984, Toastmaster of Yr. Hard Hats chpt. 1978). Lodges: Kiwanis (pres. San Diego chpt. 1978). Republican. Avocations: travel, racquetball, underwater photography, antique doorknobs. Home: San Diego, Calif. Died Nov. 8, 2006.

JONES, PHILIP NEWTON, internist, educator; b. Billings, Mont., May 27, 1924; s. Robert Newton and Edith (Woodbury) J.; m. Rebecca Ann Means, June 13, 1948; children: Robert Newton II, Rebecca Ann, Margaret Jane. Student, Stanford, 1942-43, U. Wis., 1944; MD, Washington U., St. Louis, 1948. Diplomate Am. Bd. Internal Medicine. Intern St. Luke's Hosp., Chgo., 1948-49, resident in internal medicine, 1949-51; rssch. fellow internal medicine Northwestern U., Chgo., 1953, clin. asst. medicine, 1954-57; practice medicine, specializing in internal medicine and hepatology Chgo., 1954-94; clin. asst. medicine U. Ill., Chgo., 1957-58, from clin. instr. to clin. assoc. prof. medicine, 1958-71; assoc. prof. medicine Rush Coll. Medicine Chgo., 1971-75, prof. medicine, 1975-94, prof. emeritus, from 1994. Sr. attending physician Presbyn.-St. Luke's Hosp., Chgo., 1954-94, treas. med. staff, 1960-62, mem. exec. com., med. staff, 1960-62, 72-77, sec. med. staff, 1972-73, pres. med. staff, 1973-75; mem. exec. bd. Rush-Presbyn.-St. Luke's Med. Ctr., Chgo., 1973-75, trustee, 1973-77. Contbr. articles to books and profl. jours. Mem. bd. edn., Kenilworth, Ill., 1962-68, pres., 1965; mem. Welfare Council Met., Chgo., 1965-66; bd. dirs. Presbyn. Home, Evanston, Ill., 1978-88, 93-2009. Served with AUS, 1943-46, to capt. USAF, 1951-53. Fellow Am. Coll. Physicians, Inst. Medicine Chgo.; mem. Am. Assn. Study Liver Disease, Chgo. Soc. Internal Medicine, Am. Fedn. Clin. Research, AMA, Ill. Med. Assn., Chgo. Med. Soc., Nu Sigma Nu. Republican. Congregationalist (pres. bd. trustees). Home: Lake Forest, Ill. Died Sept. 30, 2014.

JONES, RAYMOND MOYLAN, strategy and public policy educator; b. Phila., Dec. 28, 1942; s. Raymond and Elizabeth (Shaw) J.; m. Barbara Ann Donaghue, May 22, 1965; children: Andrea Marie, Audra Marie. BS, U.S. Mil. Acad., 1964; MBA, Harvard U., 1971; JD, U. Tex., 1973; PhD, U. Md., 1993. Bar: Tex. 1973, U.S. Supreme Ct. 1993. Commd. 2d lt. U.S. Army, 1964, advanced through grades to capt., 1966, ret., 1969; legal asst. to chmn. Occidental Petroleum Corp., LA, 1973-75; pres. Oxy Metal Industries Internat., Geneva, 1975-77, Occidental Resource Recovery Corp., Irvine, Calif., 1978-81; v.p. Hooker Chem. Corp., Houston, 1977-78; pvt. practice cons. Austin and Irvine, 1981-86; lectr. Calif. State U., Long Beach, 1986, U. Md., College Park, 1986-90, Loyola Coll., Balt., from 1990. Cons. to multinational and domestic orgns. Author: Strategic Management in a Hostile Environment: Lessons from the Tobacco Industry, 1998; contbr. articles, book rev. to profl. publs. Mem. Friends of Austin Symphony Orch.; mem. Ludwig Von Mises Inst., Burlingame, Calif., 1987—, Intercoll. Studies Inst., Bryn Mawr, Pa., 1987—; mgmt. con. ARC, Balt., 1988—. Grantee U. Md. 1987, Loyola Coll. 1993. Mem. Am. Econ. Assn., Acad. Internat. Bus., Strategic Mgmt. Soc., Acad. Mgmt., State Bar Tex., Harvard Club. Roman Catholic. Home: Baltimore, Md. Died Nov. 29, 2006.

JONES, ROBERT WAYNE, supply company executive; b. Memphis, Aug. 2, 1956; s. Robert Eugene Sr. and Helen Janece (Bridges) J.; m. Mary Patricia Bleuel, June 10, 1978; 1 child, Alicia Michelle. BBA in Mgmt., Lamar U., 1983, MBA, 1986. Shop hand Delta Indsl. Constrn. Co., Beaumont, Tex., 1974-75, toolroom foreman, 1975, shop foreman, 1975-76, equipment mgr., 1976-77, warehouse mgr., 1977-80; mgmt. trainee Drago Supply Co., Port Arthur, Tex., 1980-81, purchasing agt., 1981-83, salesman, 1983-85, inventory control mgr., from 1985; pres. AMJ Mfg. Co., Beaumont, from 1986. Cons. in field, Beaumont. Mem. Assn. MBA Execs. Inc., Lamar U. Cardinal Club, Lamar U. Alumni Assn., Pi Kappa Alpha Alumni. Lodges: Optimists. Republican. Avocations: hunting, scuba diving, auto repairing, camping, aerobics. Home: Beaumont, Tex. Died July 9, 2007.

JONES, RUSSELL WARD, optometrist; b. La Junta, Colo., Dec. 11, 1946; s. William Russell and Josephine Johnny (Mahill) J.; m. Daphne Sue Dean, Dec. 29, 1966; children: Ean Trent, Chian Alicia. BS, U. Colo., 1968; MS, U. Ariz., 1972; OD, Pacific U., Forest Grove, Oreg., 1976. Pvt. practice, Flagstaff, Ariz., from 1976. Dir. Big Bros. of Flagstaff, treas., 1988-94. Recipient Silver Medal award Pacific U., 1976. Mem. Am. Optometric Assn. (state lic. regulation com.), Ariz. Optometric Assn. (pres. 1986, Optometrist of the Yr. 1992), Rotary (pres. 1983), Beta Sigma Kappa. Avocations: skiing, travel. Home: Flagstaff, Ariz. Died Aug. 18, 2007.

JONES, STANTON WILLIAM, retired management consultant; b. New Orleans, May 24, 1939; s. Albert DeWitt and Clara Arimenta (Stanton) J.; m. Gladys Marina Caceres, Aug. 22, 1990; children: Hazel Nathalye, Albert Stanton, 1 child from a previous marriage, Ellen Marie. BS, Embry-Riddle Aero. U., Daytona Beach, Fla., 1973; MBA, Syracuse U., NY, 1977. Cert. internal auditor. Commd. 2d lt. U.S. Army, 1963, advanced through grades to lt. col., 1979, fixed wing pilot Ft. Rucker, Ala., 1965-72, rotary wing pilot, 1972; mgmt. cons. Stanton W. Jones & Assocs., San Francisco, from 1987. Joint venture ptnr. Budget Analyst to Bd. Suprs., San Francisco, 1988—. Decorated Meritorious Svc. medal. Mem. Alpha Phi Alpha (pres. 1988-90). Roman Catholic. Avocations: chess, reading, jogging. Home: Oakland, Calif. Died May 20, 2015.

JONES, THOMAS WILLIAM, priest; b. St. Paul, Oct. 27, 1955; s. William Trevor and Kathryn Cecelia (Garvey) J. BS, U. Minn., 1977; postgrad., Cath. U., 1978-81; MA in Religious Studies, Mt. St. Mary's, LA, 1991. Ordained to Roman Cath. Ch., 1982. Assoc. pastor St. Nicholas Cath. Ch., North Pole, Alaska, 1981-86; assoc. dir. U. Cath. Ctr. U. Calif., LA, 1986-88, dir., from 1988. Cons. Missionary Soc. of St. Paul the Apostle, N.Y.C., 1990—. Mem. Univ. Religious Conf. (pres. L.A. chpt. 1989-91). Democrat. Avocations: hockey referee, tennis, downhill skiing. Home: Los Angeles, Calif. Died Jan. 15, 2007.

JORDAHL, AUDREY HEXOM, retired securities and insurance representative; b. Dec. 17, 1922; m. Erling L. Jordahl, June 12, 1949 (dec. May 12, 2011); children: Jonathan, James. BA, Luther Coll., Decorah, Iowa, 1941, BA, 1948; degree, U. Iowa, Iowa City, 1949, NY Inst. Fin., 1965. Tchr. Rake Iowa HS, 1950—51, Tiffin HS, Iowa, 1958—59; stock broker White & Co., Iowa City, 1965—69. Chmn., call com. Christ The King Ch., 1991. State rep. candidate, Iowa City, 1984. Mem.: Mensa (life; proctor coord. 1970—2000), Waves Nat. (life; unit pres. 1994—96, regional rep. 1998—2002, nat. parliamentarian 2004). Avocations: bridge, politics, reading. Home: Ankeny, Iowa. Died July 4, 2014.

JORDAN, GERDA PETERSEN, foreign language educator; b. Hamburg, Ger., Nov. 14, 1927; d. Georg and Olga (Paschen) Petersen; 1 child, Francis H. Jordan. BA in German, U. S.C., 1964, MA in Linguistics, 1967, PhD in Comparative Lit., 1971. Instr. dept. lang. U. S.C., Columbia, 1967-72; asst. prof. dept. lang. Francis Marion Coll., Florence, S.C., 1972-73, U. S.C., Columbia, 1973-78, assoc. prof. dept. fgn. lang., from 1978, dir. prog. in comparative lit., 1979-92. Author: Max Frisch's Biedermann und Die Brandstifter, 1978, H.H. Jahnn's Thirteen Uncanny Stories, 1984, Deutsche Kultur in Epochen, 1992. Mem. Am. Comparative Lit. Assn., S. Atlantic Modern Lang. Assn. (exec. com. 1978-81), Phi Beta Kappa, Delta Phi Alpha. Avocations: opera, music, gardening, sewing, beachcombing. Home: Columbia, SC. Died May 27, 2007.

JORDAN, GREGORY WAYNE, aeronautical engineer; b. Chgo., Sept. 22, 1937; s. Robert John and Edythe Lydia (Applehans) J.; m. Judith Gay Narland, June 27, 1961; children: Rachel Anne, Catherine Jeanne, Elizabeth Rebecca. BS in Aeronautical Engring., U. Ill., 1960; MBA, U. Chgo., 1967. Internal cons. Lockheed Missile and Space, Sunnyvale, Calif., 1963-65, Hewlwtt-Packard, Palo Alto, Calif., 1967-68; project mgr. Rohr Industries, Chula Vista, Calif., 1968-73; program mgr. Booz, Allen and Hamilton, Cin., 1974; dir. internal bus. United Technologies, Hartford, Conn., 1974-82; dir., bus. analysis and planning Northrop Corp., LA, from 1982-. Advisor U.S. Dept. Comml. Spl. Trade Rep., Washington, 1976-84. Capt. USMC 1960-63. Mem. Planning Forum (steering com. 1989-90), Am. Inst. Astronautics and Aeronautic, Am. Defense Preparadness Assn., Sierra Club (sec., treas. 1988--). Home: Calabasas, Calif. Died Mar. 3, 2007.

JORDAN, JOHN EDWARD, dentist; b. Nashville, Nov. 17, 1930; s. John Edward Jordan and Mary Celess (Mar) Richardson; m. Dec. 26, 1958 (widowed); 1 child, John Edward III. AB in Biology, 1952, DDS, 1957, Meharry Med. Coll., 1957. Dentist Memphis Health Dept., Wellington Ctr., Head Start Program; pvt. practice Memphis. Editor Hyde Park Newsletter, 1991, 92. V.p. North Memphis Neighborhood Watch, 1990-92; v.p. trustees Middle Bapt. Ch., 1986-92; coord. sec. Memphis Bapt. Laymen, 1991-92; pres. Laymen Middle Bapt. Ch., 1983-99, Sanctuary Choir, 1989-92; pres. West Tenn. Bapt. Layman, 1992-99, West Tenn. Missionary and Edn. Assn., to 1996; pres. Austin St. Neighborhood Watch, 1988-91; exec. dir. Hollywood Block Club, pres., 1992; bd. dirs. Kennedy Dem. Club, Hyde Park Neighborhood Coalition, pres., 1993-98; del. to U.S. Presdl. Inaugural Celebration, 1993. Recipient Plaque, Colgate Dental Health Edn. Adv. Bd., 1990, Shanknon Hills Civic Club, 1991, Northside High Sch., 1991, 30 Year Participation in Dentistry plaque, Svc. cert. Middle Bapt. Ch., 1993; recipient Martin Luther King award for Civil Rights, 1992. Mem. Shelby County Dental Soc. (v.p. Memphis chpt., chmn. dental health month, Plaque 1986), Evergreen Optimist Club (v.p., sec., treas. 1987-90, v.p. 1992), Kappa Alpha Psi (Germantown Chpt.). Avocations: tennis, swimming, aerobics, weightlifting. Died Mar. 31, 2007.

JORDAN, JOHN MOYER, transportation executive; b. San Marino, Calif., Sept. 25, 1942; s. Fred Moyer Jordan and Elisabeth (Shuler) Jarecki; m. Christina Louise Holmes, June 21, 1969. BSEE, Stanford U., 1964, MSIE, 1967. Ops. rsch. analyst Ford Motor Co., Dearborn, Mich., 1967-69, supr. capital budgeting Ypsilanti, Mich., 1969-72; dir. operational planning IU Internat. Corp., Phila., 1972-76; sr. dir. planning Gotaas-Larsen, Inc., NYC, 1976-79; v.p. corp. planning Gotaas-Larsen Ltd., London, 1979-82; v.p. fin. Interpool Ltd., NYC, 1982-86; cons. Marine Med. Svcs., Inc., Solana Beach, Calif., 1986-87; dir. fin. planning and reporting Am. Pres. Cos., Ltd., Oakland, Calif., from 1988. Republican. Avocations: astronomy, tennis. Home: San Francisco, Calif. Died Mar. 28, 2007.

JORGENSEN, ERIK, forest pathologist, educator, consultant; b. Haderslev, Denmark, Oct. 28, 1921; emigrated to Can., 1955, naturalized, 1960; s. Johannes and Eva Bromberg (Hansen) J.; m. Grete Moller, June 13, 1946; children: Marianne, Birthe. M. Forestry, Royal Vet. and Agrl. Coll., Copenhagen, 1946. Forest pathologist Royal Vet. and Agrl. Coll., Copenhagen, 1948-55; forest pathologist sci. service Agr. Can., 1955-59; asst. prof. U. Toronto, 1959-63, assoc. prof., 1963-67, prof. forest pathology and urban forestry, 1967-73; chief urban forestry program Can. Forestry Service, Environ. Can., 1973-78; arboretum dir., prof. environ. biology U. Guelph, Ont., 1978-87; cons. in field, 1987-89. Author: The Development of an Urban Forestry Concept, 1967; contbr. articles to sci. jours. Served to 2d lt. Danish Army, 1946-48. Recipient Authors citation Internat. Shade Tree Conf., 1970; recipient Maple Leaf award Internat. Shade Tree Conf., 1975, Can. Patents and Devel. Ltd. Inventors cert., 1975, Trees for Tomorrow award Can. Forestry Assn., 1993. Fellow Can. Inst. Forestry; mem. Ont. Profl. Foresters Assn., Internat. Soc. Arboriculture, Ont. Shade Tree Council (life, Jaap Salm Meml. award 1975), Sigma Xi. Lutheran. Home: Guelph, Canada. *A dedication to the application of forest science to the service of mankind.* Died May 25, 2012.

JORGENSEN, JOYCE ORABELLE, artist, writer; b. Newell, Iowa, Feb. 26, 1928; d. James G. and Elsie C. (Haahr) Andersen; m. John G. Jorgensen, Apr. 27, 1949 (dec. Dec. 1958); children: Richard, Kirsten, John (dec.); m. L.A. Johnson, Jan. 1, 1965 (div. Jan. 1968); 1 child, Brian. Pvt. art study, Arthur Schweider, 1945-46. Co-pub. and editor Orleans (Nebr.) Chronicle, 1949-53, Ouray County Herald, 1954-56; operator Little Studio & Gallery, Ouray, Colo., 1954-56; pvt. sec., office mgr. Atty. Gen., Juneau, Alaska, 1957-58; freelance artist, instr., operator Jorgensen Studio and Gallery J, Ouray, 1959-68; editor Ouray County Plaindealer, 1967-70, pub., editor, 1970-90; established, pub., editor The Ridgway (Colo.) Sun, 1980-90. Sec. Ouray City Planning and Zoning Commn., 1969-70; chmn. Ouray Bd. of Zoning Appeals, 1971-75; bd. dirs., creator Ouray County Arts Coun. and Artists Alpine Holiday, 1961-62; originator, dir. Small Sch's. Art Program, 1963-64; originator, mem. com. to Restore Ouray City Hall Facade, 1974-78, 1987-88; Colo. Press Assoc. State Chmn. to Nat. Newspaper Assoc., 1978-79. Recipient Gov's award in Arts and Humanities, 1974, Outstanding Communicator award Denver Press Club for Bill Daniels Comm. Ctr., 1982, B.P.O.E. (Elks) Disting. Citizenship award, 1986; named Ouray County Woman of the Yr., 1974, Outstanding Communicator Sigma Delta Chi (Colo. chpt.), Soc. Prof. Journalists, 1974. Died Mar. 20, 2007.

JOSEPH, JAMES HERZ, author, columnist; b. Terre Haute, Ind., May 12, 1924; s. Lawrence Herz and Lucille (Liberman) J.; m. Marjorie Helen Waterman, Aug. 20, 1950 (div. 1971); children: Nancy Lee, James Jay. Student, Northwestern U., Evanston, Ill., 1942; BA, Stanford U., 1949. Freelance ind. contractor, from 1949; pres. James Joseph Corp., LA, 1992-96; editor-in-chief Kessler Assocs., LA, 1986-88; v.p., editl. dir. Am. Automotive Pub. Group, Simi Valley, Calif., 1996; dir. comm. Paisa,Inc., San Dimas, Calif., 1996. Syndicated columnist Quick Stops, 1986-91; author: You Fly It, 1965, Careers Outdoors, 1969, Here is Your Hobby: Snowmobiling, 1970, Annual Snowmobiling Guide, 1972, 73, 74, The Complete Out-of-Doors: Job, Business and Profession Guide, 1974, Beckman's Incredible Flying Circus, 1978, Chilton's Diesel Guide, 1980, The Car-Keeper's Guide, 1982, Chilton's Guide to Auto Detailing, 1993, Ashes, 1994, Driving Emergencies, 1994, Speaking With God, 1997, Road to Discovery in America, 1998, Big Speed: The Quest for Supersonic Speed on Land, 1999, others; co-author: (with William Divale) I Lived Inside the Campus Revoluution, 1970; contbr. articles to major mags. U.S. and abroad, chpts. to books. Fellow Am. Soc. Journalists and Authors (chmn. So. Calif. chpt. 1960—, Dial-a-Writer com. 1997—), Authors Guild Am. Avocations: sailing, fishing, camping. Died Feb. 22, 2007.

JOSLYN, WILLIAM, stained glasss craftsman, artist; b. Oneonta, NY, Feb. 6, 1950; s. Lynn Joslyn and Edith (Layman) Foote; m. Gail Anne Altmeyer, June 20, 1981. BA, SUNY, Oneonta, 1972. Instr. stained glass Wilmette (Ill.) Pk. Dist., from 1976; stained glass craftsman Botti Studios, Evanston, Ill., 1976-83, Mountain Light Glass, Highland Pk., Ill., from 1978; glass craftsman Crystal Cave, Wilmette, from 1983; wood crafter, art specialist U.S. Army, Ft. Sheridan, Ill., from 1987. Presbyterian. Died Apr. 12, 2007.

JOURDAN, LOUIS (LOUIS GENDRE), actor; b. Marseille, France, June 19, 1921; came to U.S., 1946; s. Henry Gendre and Yvonne J.; m. Berthe Frederique, Mar. 11, 1946; m. Micheline Prealel; 1 son, Louis Henry. Student pvt. schs. Profl. actor, from 1940. Appeared in French motion pictures, 1940-46; film debut in Le Corsaire, 1940; Am. motion picture appearances include: Her First Affair, 1947, No Minor Vices, 1948, The Paradise Case, 1948, Letter from an Unknown Woman, 1948, Madame Bovary, 1949, Bird of Paradise, 1951, Anne of the Indies, 1951, Three Coins in the Fountain, 1954, The Swan, 1956, Julie, 1956, Gigi, 1958, The Bride is Much Too Beautiful, 1958,

Dangerous Exile, 1958, Best of Everything, 1959, Can-Can, 1960, Leviathan, 1961, The Story of the Count of Monte Cristo, 1962, Mathias Sandorf, 1963, The V.I.P.'s, 1963, Disorder, 1964, Made in Paris, 1966, A Flea In Her Ear, 1968, Young Rebel, 1969, To Commit a Murder, 1970, The Count of Monte Cristo, 1976, Silver Bears, 1978, Double Deal, 1981, Swamp Thing, 1982, Octopussy, 1983, The Return of Swamp Thing, 1989, Counterforce, 1989, Year of the Comet, 1992; TV movies include: Run a Crooked Mile, 1969, Fear No Evil, 1969, Ritual of Evil, 1970, The Great American Beauty Contest, 1973, The Man in the Iron Mask, 1977, Dracula, 1978, The French Atlantic Affair, 1979, The First Olympics—Athens 1896, 1984, Beverly Hills Madam, 1986; TV series includes Paris Precinct, 1954-55; Broadway debut in The Immoralist, 1954; other theatre appearences include Tonight at Sammarkand, 1955, On a Clear Day You Can See Forever, 1965, 13 Rue de L'Amour, 1978. Died Feb. 14, 2015.

JOYNER, ALBERT LEWIS, JR., minister; b. Lexington, NC, Sept. 3, 1946; s. Albert Lewis Joyner and Myrtle (Hardy) Miller; m. Gaynelle Garwood, Apr. 27, 1969; children: Christi Michele, Chadwick Lewis. AB, Pfeiffer Coll., 1983; MDiv, Duke U., 1987. Mgmt. Burlington Industries, Greensboro, N.C., 1967-78, Springs Mills Corp., Lancaster, S.C., 1978-80; minister United Meth. Ch., Asheboro, N.C., from 1980. Mem. Phi Alpha Theta, Phi Delta Sigma. Lodges: Lions (pres. Franklinville, N.C. club 1985). Democrat. Methodist. Avocations: offshore fishing, golf. Home: Kannapolis, NC. Died Nov. 30, 2006.

JUDD, RICHARD MUNSON, retired American studies educator; b. Holyoke, Mass., Sept. 23, 1923; s. Clifford Kellogg Judd and Adah Lisette (Richard) Green; m. Suvia Edith Whittemore, Feb. 3, 1945; children: Suvia Thayer, Katharine Richard. BA cum laude, Williams Coll., 1947; PhD, Harvard U., 1960; LittD (hon.), Marlboro Coll., 1996. Am. studies tchr. Marlboro Coll., Vt., 1950-89, dean of students Vt., 1960-65, acting dean of faculty Vt., 1963-64, acting dean of the coll. Vt., 1968-69, trustee, prof. emeritus Vt., from 1989. Author: The New Deal in Vermont: Its Impact & Aftermath, 1979. Mem. Marlboro Town Sch. Bd., Vt., 1953-57, 59-67, chmn., 1969-80; moderator Marlboro Town, Vt., 1982—. Sgt. USAAF, 1943-46. Mem. Orgn. Am. Historians, Vt. Hist. Soc. (trustee 1977-78), Phi Beta Kappa. Democrat. Avocations: cross country skiing, woodcutting, vegetable gardening. Home: Marlboro, Vt. Died May 7, 2007.

JUDE, JAMES RODERICK, retired thoracic surgeon; b. Maple Lake, Minn., June 7, 1928; s. Bernard Benedict and Cecilia Mary (Leick) J.; m. Sallye Garrigan, Aug. 4, 1951; children Roderick, John, Cecilia Prahl, Victoria Steele, Peter, Robert, Chris. BS, Coll. St. Thomas, St. Paul, 1949; MD, U. Minn., 1953. Intern Johns Hopkins Hosp., 1953-54, resident in surgery, 1954-55, 58-61, fellow in cardiovascular research, 1955-56; instr. surgery Johns Hopkins U. and Med. Sch., 1961-62, asst. prof., 1962-64; prof. surgery, chief thoracic and cardiovascular surgery U. Miami Sch. Medicine and Jackson Meml. Hosp., 1964-71; clin. prof. U. Miami Sch. Medicine, from 1971; practice medicine specializing in cardiovascular surgery Miami, 1971—2000; ret., 2000. Scholar Johns Hopkins U., 1992; chmn. Mercy Med. Clinic, Miami, Fla., 1992-95, Primus Health Care Corp., 1995-2000. Author Closed Chest Cardiac Resuscitation: Methods, Indications, Limitation, 1966; co-suthor (with James O. Elam) Fundamentals of Cardiopulmonary Resuscitation, 1967, Coping with Heart Surgery and Bypassing Depression, 1991; contbr. articles to med. jours. Mem. Coral Gables (Fla.) Planning Bd., 1973-77. With USPHS, 1956-58. Named One of Ten Outstanding Young Ams., U.S. Jaycees, 1962. Fellow Am. Coll. Chest Physicians, Am. Coll. Cardiology, A.C.S.; mem. Am. Assn. Thoracic Surgery, Am. Surg. Assn., So. Surg. Assn., Soc. Vascular Surgery, Soc. Thoracic Surgeons, Am. Heart Assn., Soc. Univ. Surgeons. Democrat. Roman Catholic. Achievements include being co-developer cardiopulmonary resuscitation (CPR). Home: Miami, Fla. Died July 28, 2015.

JUDKINS, SYLVIA L. A., medical/surgical nurse; b. Memphis, Sept. 18, 1953; d. Frederick Sills and Patricia Darlene (Quinby) Anton; m. Randal D. Judkins; children: Miranda Leigh, Audrey Brooke. ADN, U. Ark., 1983. RN, Tenn. 1st asst. to pvt. surgeon, Memphis; staff nurse oncology St. Vincents Infirmary, Little Rock; DON Gulf Pines Hosp., Port St. Joe, Fla.; cmty. hea.th nurse Gulf County Pub. Health Unit, Port St. Joe, Fla. Died Feb. 3, 2007.

JULIAN, MARSHA ROANNE, counselor, educator; b. New Castle, Pa., Sept. 19, 1936; d. George Henry and Dora June (Atchison) Hicks; m. Vincent Julian, June 13, 1959. BA, Westminster Coll., 1958, MS, 1961; EdD, Nova U., 1976. Lic. profl. counselor, Ohio. Tchr. Beaty Jr. High Sch., Warren, Pa., 1958-59, Mohawk Jr. High Sch., Bessemer, Pa., 1959-62, Cleveland Hgts. (Ohio) High Sch., 1962-64; counselor Warrensville Hgts. (Ohio) High Sch., 1964-66, Cuyahoga Community Coll., Cleve., from 1966. Active Cancer Soc., Cleve., 1988-90, Heart Assn., Cleve., 1988-90, March of Dimes, Cleve., 1990. NDEA grantee, 1962; recipient Teaching Excellence award Nat. Inst. for Staff and Orgn. Devel., 1991, Outstanding Pub. Employee award City of Cleveland, 1991. Mem. AAUP, Met. Campus Faculty Senate. Democrat. Episcopalian. Avocations: travel, gardening, interior decorating, animals. Home: Cleveland, Ohio. Died June 20, 2007.

JUNG, RODNEY C., internist, academic administrator; b. New Orleans, Oct. 9, 1920; s. Frederick Charles and Clara (Cuevas) J. BS in Zoology with honors, Tulane U., 1941, MD, 1945, MS in Parasitology and Microbiology, 1950, PhD, 1953. Diplomate: Am. Bd. Internal Medicine. Intern Charity Hosp. La., New Orleans, 1945-46; dir. Hutchinson Meml. Clinic, 1948; asst. parasitology Tulane U., 1948-50, instr. tropical medicine, 1950-53, asst. prof., 1953-57, assoc. prof. tropical medicine, 1957-63, prof. tropical medicine, 1963-73, clin. prof. internal medicine, 1973-91, clin. prof. tropical medicine, 1983-92, prof. emeritus tropical medicine, from 1992, head div. tropical medicine, 1960-63; health dir. City of New Orleans, 1963-70, 79-82; internist in charge Ill. Central Hosp., New Orleans, 1956-70. Sr. vis. physician Charity Hosp., 1959— ; mem. study sect. on tropical medicine and parasitology Nat. Inst. Allergy and Infectious Disease, 1963-67; mem. Commn. on Parasitic Diseases Armed Forces Epidemiol. Bd., 1967-73; chief communicable disease control, City of New Orleans, 1978; sr. in internal medicine Touro Infirmary. Co-author: Animal Agents and Vectors of Disease and Clinical Parasitology; editl. bd. Am. Jour. Tropical Medicine and Hygiene, 1972-94; contbr. articles to profl. jours. Pres. Irish Cultural Soc. New Orleans, 1980-92, pres. emeritus 1992—; officer res. div. New Orleans Police Dept., 1977-84; chmn. New Orleans Mosquito and Termite Control Bd. John and Mary Markle Scholar in med. sci. Fellow ACP; hon. fellow Brazilian Soc. Tropical Medicine; mem. Am., Royal socs. tropical medicine and hygiene, Am. Soc. Parasitologists, La. State Med. Soc., Orleans Parish Med. Soc., Nat. Rifle Assn., Irish Georgian Soc., La. Mosquito and Termite Control Assn., La. Soc. Internal Medicine, Am. Soc. Internal Medicine, New Orleans Acad. Internal Medicine, Am. Def. Preparedness Assn., Irish-Am. Cultural Inst., Nat. Trust. Historic Preservation, La. Landmarks Soc., Naval Inst., New Orleans Mus. Art, New Orleans Opera Assn., La. Wildlife Fedn., Phi Beta Kappa, Sigma Xi, Delta Omega, Alpha Omega Alpha. Presbyterian. Home: New Orleans, La. Died Oct. 11, 2013.

JUSTI, CHRISTIAN LEROY, financial and engineering consultant; b. Kenosha, Wis., Jan. 4, 1928; s. Harald Christian and Gertrude Emma (Schulz) Justi; m. Rose Marie Leon, Feb. 14, 1982; children from previous marriage: Paul, Ann. BS in Engring., Johns Hopkins U., 1950; MS in Fin. and Econs., NYU, 1953, PhD, 1955. Engr. Johnson Corp. (acquired by Martin Marietta Corp.), Balt., 1946—50; pro-asst. cashier fgn. dept. Bank Am., Internat., NYC, 1950—55; petroleum and fin. engr. ARCO, LA; dir. adminstrn. Vehicle Research Corp., Pasadena, Calif., 1955—60; propr. Fin. Engring. Cons., West Covina, Calif., from 1960. Mem. adv. and youth bds. LA County Dist. Atty., from 1965; pres. West Covina Beautiful, 1965—67, 1981—82, Republican Assembly San Gabriel-Pomona Valley, 1971—73; advisor Nat. Commn. Youth Action, from 1976, Nat. Youth Commn., from 1981. Recipient numerous awards for civic contbns. Mem.: West Covina C. of C. (dir., Ambassador of Yr. 1980), Nat. Registry Engrs., Nat. Assn. Accountants, Am. Inst. Econ. Rsch. Roman Catholic. Home: West Covina, Calif. Died Nov. 3, 2006.

KABLE, KELVIN, physician; b. Corvallis, Oreg., Nov. 18, 1923; s. George Wallace and Florence Kopan Kable; m. Meriam June Oglesby; children: Sharon Diane, George Kristan, Kelvin Duane Jr., Pamela Gaines(dec.). BS in Biology, Va. Poly. Inst., 1954; MD, Wake Forest Coll., 1953; MPH, U. Calif., Berkeley, 1964. Cert. bd. cert. aerospace medicine/preventive medicine, lic. Va. Intern, resident in internal medicine Brooke Army Hosp., Ft. Sam Houston, Tex., 1953—57; resident in aerospace medicine USAF Sch. Aerospace Medicine, Brooks AFB, Tex., 1964—66; enlisted USAF, 1943, pilot B17 and others 23 missions over Europe, 1943—46; aerospace medicine physician USAF Med. Corps, 1953—59; staff officer aerospace medicine consultation svcs. USAF Sch. Aviation Medicine, Randolph AFB, Tex., 1957—59; chief flight medicine, chief med. adv. divsn Japanese Air Self-Def. Force, Fuchu AFS, Japan, 1959—62; chief med. intelligence HQ USAF, Washington, 1962—63; chief aerospace medicine br., chief aeromed. indoctrination br. USAF Sch. Aerospace Medicine, Brooks AFB, 1966—67; comdr. USAF Hosp. Edwards, Edwards AFB, Calif., 1967—71, USAF Regional Hosp., Fairchild AFB, Washington, 1974—76; chief cen. aeromed. svc., comdr. 4th med. svc. squadron HQ USAFE, Wiesbaden, Germany, 1971—74; chief edn. divsn. USAF Sch. Aerospace Medicine, 1976—78, aerospace medicine consultation svcs., 1978—79; staff physician Philip Morris, from 1979. Cons. aerospace medicine Japanese Air Self Def. Force, 1959—62; cons. in aerospace medicine USAFE, 1971—74; presenter and lectr. in field. Col. USAF, 1969—79. Decorated Legion of Merit, Meritorious Svc. medal, Air Force Commendation medal, Air Force medal with 2 bronze oak leaf clusters, Air Force Outstanding Unit award with 1 oak leaf cluster, Good Conduct medal, Am. Campaign medal, European-African-Mid. Ea. Campaign medal, WWII Victory medal, Army of Occupation medal with clasp, Nat. Def. Svc. medal with bronze svc. star, Vietnam Svc. medal, Air Force Longevity Svc. Award ribbon with 2 bronze oak leaf clusters, Armed Forces Res. medal, Small Arms Expert Marksmanship ribbon. Fellow: Am. Coll. Preventive Medicine, Aerospace Med. Assn. (assoc.; mem. edn. and tng. com.); mem.: AMA, Richmond Acad. Medicine, Med. Soc. Va., Am. Occupl. Med. Assn., Soc. USAF Flight Surgeons, Phi Kappa Phi, Phi Rho Sigma, Phi Sigma. Achievements include research in review of electrocardiographic findings in 67,375 asymptomatic active duty Air Force personnel; study of cardiovascular abnormalities and their significance in Air Force flying personnel. Avocations: hunting, fishing, camping, photography. Home: Concord, NC. Died Mar. 13, 2007.

KADANOFF, LEO PHILIP, physicist, educator; b. NYC, Jan. 14, 1937; s. Abraham and Celia (Kibrick) Kadanoff; m. Diane Gordon (div.); m. Ruth Kadanoff; children: Marcia, Felice, Betsy 1 stepchild, Michal Ditzian. AB, Harvard U., 1957, MA, 1958, PhD, 1960. Fellow Neils Bohr Inst., Copenhagen, 1960—61; from asst. prof. to prof. physics U. Ill., Urbana, 1961—69; prof. physics and engring., univ. prof. Brown U., Providence, 1969—78; prof. physics U. Chgo., 1978—82, John D. MacArthur Disting. Service prof., 1982—2004, prof. emeritus, 2004—15. Mem. tech. com. R.I. Planning Program, 1972—78, mem. human svcs. rev. com., 1977—78; pres. Urban Obs. R.I., 1972—78. Author: Electricity Magnetism and Heat, 1967; co-author: Quantum Statistical Mechanics, 1963; adv. bd. Sci. Year, 1975—79, editl. bd. Statis. Physics, 1972—79, Nuc. Physics, from 1980. Recipient Wolf prize in physics, Wolf Found., Israel, 1980, Boltzmann medal, Internat. Union Pure and Applied Physics, 1990, Grande Medaille d'Or, Acad. Scis. Inst. France, 1998, Nat. Medal Sci., 1999; fellow NSF, 1957—61, Sloan Found., 1963—67. Fellow: AAAS, Am. Acad. Arts and Scis., Am. Phys. Soc. (pres. 2007, Buckley prize 1977, Onsager prize 1998); mem.: NAS, Am. Philosophical Soc. Home: Chicago, Ill. Died Oct. 26, 2015.

KAEMPEN, CHARLES EDWARD, manufacturing executive; b. Quincy, Ill., Mar. 10, 1927; s. Charles Herman and Margo (Gochicoa) K.; m. Inger Margareta Nystrom, Aug. 5, 1951; children: Charles Robert, Donald Michael, Annette Earline, Laura Inger. BS in Aeron. Engring., U. Ill., Urbana, 1950; DSc in Astronautics, Internat. Acad. Astronautics, Paris, 1964. Registered profl. engr., Calif., Conn. Sr. designer Saab Aircraft Co., Linkôping, Sweden, 1950-52; design analyst Sikorsky Helicopter United Aircraft, Stratford, Conn., 1952-56; space mission analyst Missle div. N.Am. Rockwell, Downey, Calif., 1957-60; staff scientist Hughes Aircraft, Fullerton, Calif., 1961-63; lunar systems analyst Northrop Space Lab., Hawthorne, Calif., 1963-64; pres. Am. Space Transport Co., Tustin, Calif., 1964-66; transport systems analyst Dashaveyor Co., Venice, Calif., 1966-67; pres. Kaempen & Assocs., Orange, Calif., 1967-68; sr. rsch. engr. Baker Oil Tools Inc., LA, 1968-69; pres. Kaempen Industries, Inc., Santa Ana, Calif., 1969-82, Kaempen & Assocs., from 1982; pres., CEO Kaempen Composite Products, Inc., 1996-2000; pres. Kaempen Corp., Inc., from 2000. Author papers on fiberglass composites and filament winding; patentee in field. With U.S. Army, 1944-47. Fellow AIAA; mem. ASME, ASTM, NSPE, Soc. Aerospace Materials and Process Engring., Soc. Plastics Industry, Masons. Republican. Lutheran. Home: Orange, Calif. Died Feb. 10, 2007.

KAIDY, MITCHELL, retired journalist, legislative staff member, freelance writer; b. Bklyn., Mar. 23, 1925; s. Murad Abdallah and Asma Araman Kaldy; m. Jean Harris Kaldy; children: Kristen, Mark. Student, U. Miss., 1943—44, Clemson A&M Coll., SC, 1944; BS in Journalism, NYU, 1948. Cert. Army Special Training Program. Reporter, editor Monticello Evening News, NY, 1948—49, Middletown Times Herald, NY, 1949—50, Rochester Dem. & Chronicle, NY, 1950—65; legis. aide and speech writer NY State Legis., Albany, 1966—83; freelance TV comml. prodr. Rochester, 1983—90; freelance writer, from 1983; staff mem. NY State Constitutional Convention, 1969; founder Genesee Valley Chpt. NY Civil Liberties Union, 1954. Dir. rsch. NY State Joint Legis. Com. on Conservation, 1967; legis. aide NY State Senate Com. on Labor, Albany, 1966; pres., sec. Rochester Newspaper Guild, NY, 1953—60, NY State Newspaper Guild; legis. rep. Albany, Rochester, 1965—69. Manuscript editor Becoming American: The Early Arab Immigrant Experience, by Alixa Naff, 1985; contbr. columns in newspapers, articles to profl. jours. (Project Censored award, 1993), articles to series (Pulitzer Prize citation, 1963). Founder Peace and Justice Edn. Ctr., Rochester, 1962; founder, pres. Genesee Valley chpt. Vets. of Battle of the Bulge; founder Rochester chpt. Amnesty Internat.; historian 87th Inf. Divsn., from 1994; major contbr. 87th Inf. Divsn. website; lectr. US Army Historical Ctr., Carlisle Barracks, Pa., World War II; candidate Monroe County, 1963, NY Legis., 1968, Congress, 1982—84; founder Genesee Valley chpt. NY Civil Liberties Union, 1954. Cpl. US Army, 1943—45, ETO. Decorated Bronze Star medal, Combat Infantry Badge, European theater ribbon with three battle stars, Army of Occupation medal, Good Conduct medal, WWII Victory medal US Army, Comdr.'s award 87th Inf. Divsn.; named Journalist of Yr., Utica, NY, 1966; Am. Newspaper Guild fellow, Cornell U., 1963. Democrat. Achievements include design of and writing of four plaques in Belgium, commemorating 87th Infantry Divsn. engagements during Battle of the Bulge, 1995; ceremony and plaque in Oswego, NY honoring S/Sgt. Curtis F. Shoup, Medal of Honor winner, Battle of the Bulge; 87th Infantry division highway signs, I-390, South of Rochester, NY, 2002; freelance contributor NY times Christian Science Monitor, progressive populist. Avocations: travel, journalism, writing. Home: Rochester, NY. Died Jan. 10, 2013.

KAISER, HANS ELMAR, pathology educator, researcher; b. Prague, Czech Republic, Feb. 16, 1928; arrived in U.S., 1961. s. Rudolf and Charlotte (Thiel) K.; m. Charlotte (Moehring), Oct. 12, 1960. ScD, U. Tuebingen, Fed. Republic of Germany, 1958. Rsch. prof. U. Md., Balt., 1988; hon., sci. dir. Internat. Inst. Anticancer Rsch., Attiki, Greece. Hon. cons. Bulgarian Med. Acad., Sofia; vis. prof. Martin Luther U., Halle-Wittenberg, Fed. Republic of Germany, U. Vienna, Austria; pres. Internat. Soc. for Study of Comparative Oncology, German Soc. Comparative Oncology, Inc. Author: Das Abnorme in der Evolution, 1970; Morphology of Sirenia, 1972; Species Specific Potential of Invertebrates, 1980; editor, author: Neopolasms, Comparative, Pathology of Growth. . ., 1981; Cancer Growth and Progression, 10 vols., 1989; others; mem. editl. bd. Anticancer Rsch., in

Vivo. Mem.: Physikalisch Medizinische Societaet Erlangen (corr.), Turkish Kanseroloji ve Ekoloji Dernegi (hon.). Home: Gaithersburg, Md. Died July 18, 2007.

KAISER, KEITH E., lawyer; b. Stillwater, Okla., Sept. 9, 1943; s. Carl Joseph and Genevieve Ann (Smith) K.; m. Diann M. Bartek, Nov. 8, 1986; children: Peter Mark, Blair Wallace. BA, Tex. Tech. U., 1966; JD, St. Mary's U., San Antonio, 1972. Bar: Tex. 1972, U.S. Supreme Ct., U.S. Ct. Appeals (5th, 9th, 11th cir.), U.S. Dist. Ct. (no., so., we. dist.) Tex. Assoc. Cox & Smith Inc., San Antonio, from 1972. Adj. prof. fed. antitrust law St. Mary's U. Sch. Law, San Antonio, 1975-77. Contbr. articles to profl. jours. Bd. dirs. Jr. Achievement of S. Tex., 1987-90. Capt. U.S. Army, 1967-71. Fellow Am. Coll. Trial Lawyers, Tex. Bar Found.; mem. State Bar Tex. (governing counsel antitrust sect. 1981-86, chmn. 1984-85), St. Mary's Law Alumni Assn. (bd. dirs., pres. 1984-85). Home: San Antonio, Tex. Died Apr. 21, 2007.

KALAJIAN, JOHN LEO, city councilman, real estate investment company executive; b. Tubingen, Germany, Oct. 14, 1945; s. Paul Nubar and Araxi (Pashaian) K.; children: Jill, Matthew. Student, Northeastern U., U. Fla. Anesthetist Venice (Fla.) Hosp., 1974—81; pres. D.J.'s Paper Clip, Inc., Venice, 1982—83; v.p. The Loveland Ctr., Venice, 1983—84; pres., 1984—85; prin. Combined Capital Corp., Venice, from 1986. V.p. Exceptional Industries, 1981—82; mem. GTE Adv. Bd., 1986—88; mem. exec. com. Sarasota County (Fla.) Reps., from 1979; chmn. intergovtl. relations com. Fla. League Cities, Tallahassee, 1982—87; mem. Sarasota County Tourist Devel. Coun., 1987—88. With US Army, 1966—68. Recipient Outstanding Cmty. Svc. award, Venice Kiwanis Club, 1983. Mem.: Venice Jaycees (hon., Good Govt. award 1987), Pleasant Places Fla., Sertoma. Home: Venice, Fla. Died Dec. 27, 2006.

KALAM, AVUL PAKIR JAINULABDEEN ABDUL (A. P. J. ABDUL KALAM), former President of India; b. Rameswaram, Tamil Nadu, India, Oct. 15, 1931; BSc in Physics, St. Joseph Coll., Trichi, 1954; postgraduate student, Madras Inst. Tech., 1954—58; D (hon.), Indian Inst. Tech., 2000. Sr. sci. asst. DRDO, 1958—63; with ISRO (Indian Space Rsch. Orgn.), 1963—82, DRDO, 1982—92; sci. adv. to def. min. and sec. Dept. Def. Rsch. and Devel., 1992—99; cabinet min. Govt. of India, 1999—2001, pres., 2002—07. Vis. prof. Indian Inst. of Mgmt., Ahmedabad, Indore; prof. Anna U., Chennai; chancellor Indian Inst. of Space Sci. and Tech.; disting. prof. Indian Space Rsch. Orgn., 2000. Author (with Arun Tiwari): (book) Wings of Fire; author: (with Y.S. Rajan) India 2020: A Vision for the New Millenium; author: My Journey, Ignited Minds: Unleashing the Power Within India. Recipient Padma Bhushan, 1981, Padma Vibhushan, 1990, Bharat Ratna, 1997, Indira Gandhi award for Nat. Integration, 1997, Ramanujar, 2000, Internat. von Karman Wings award, Calif. Inst. of Tech., 2009, Hoover medal, ASME Found., 2009; named People's President, Missile Man of India. Mem.: IEEE (hon.). Achievements include development of ballistic missile and space rocket tech; India's first indigenous satellite launch vehicle; many missiles in India including Agni and Prithvi although the entire project has been criticised for being overrun and mismanaged; proposed a research program for developing bio-implants. Died July 27, 2015.

KALIL, DAVID THOMAS, lawyer; b. Detroit, Sept. 22, 1926; s. David A. and Rose Kalil; m. Helga A. Kalil, Nov. 1, 1958; children: David E., John T. BSE in Chem. Engring., U. Mich., 1948; LLB, Mich. State U., Detroit, 1951. Bar: Mich. 1951, Pa. 1989, U.S. Dist. Ct. (we. dist.) Pa. 1989, U.S. Dist. Ct. (ea. dist.) Mich. 1951. Examiner U.S. Patent Office, Washington, 1951-52; pvt. practice, Detroit, 1952-58; patent lawyer Internat. Nickel Co., Inc., NYC, 1959-63; gen. and patent lawyer Kaynar Mfg. Co., Inc., Fullerton, Calif., 1963-64; asst. dir. law dept. Amax, Inc., NYC, 1964-77; v.p., gen. counsel Jones & Laughlin Steel, Pitts., 1977-83; pvt. practice, Pitts., from 1989. Cons. D.E. Cummings, Inc., Bethlehem, Pa., 1985—; gen. mgr. Mindlin Co., Pitts., 1983-85. Cpl. USAAF, 1945-46, ETO. Roman Catholic. Avocations: golf, reading, lecturing, mentoring. Home: Pittsburgh, Pa. Died Aug. 2, 2007.

KALISH, ARTHUR, lawyer; b. Bklyn., Mar. 6, 1930; s. Jack and Rebecca (Biniamofsky) K.; m. Janet J. Wiener, Mar. 7, 1953; children: Philip, Pamela. BA, Cornell U., 1951; JD, Columbia U., 1956. Bar: N.Y. 1956, D.C. 1970. Assoc. Paul, Weiss, Rifkind, Wharton & Garrison, NYC, 1956-64, ptnr., 1965-95, of counsel, from 1996. Lectr. NYU Inst. Fed. Taxation, Hawaii Tax Inst., Law Jour. Seminars Contbr. articles to legal jours. Assoc. trustee L.I. Jewish Med. Ctr., New Hyde Park, N.Y., 1978-82, trustee, 1982-95, hon. trustee, 1995-97; trustee emeritus North Shore - L.I. Jewish Health Sys., 1997-98, life trustee, 1998-2003, exec. com., 2007-, trustee, 2003—, Lenox Hill Hosp., 2010-; trustee S.I. U. Hosp., 2004—, exec. com., 2008-; bd. dirs. Cmty. Health Program of Queens Nassau Inc., New Hyde Park, 1978-94, pres., 1981-89, chmn. emeritus, 1994-97; bd. dirs. Managed Health, Inc., New Hyde Park, 1990-98, chmn., 1994-95. Advanced from ensign to lt. (j.g.) USN, 1951—53. Fellow Am. Coll. Tax Counsel; mem. ABA, N.Y. State Bar Assn., Assn. Bar City N.Y., Columbia Law Sch. Assn. (bd. dirs. 1990-94). Home: Old Westbury, NY. Died Sept. 3, 2012.

KALNES, DONNA M. SIMONDET, retired principal, alcohol and drug abuse education program director; b. North Redwood, Minn., Jan. 24, 1934; d. Oscar Walter and Alma Mae Simondet; m. Rasmus B.A. Kalnes, Aug. 21, 1954; children: David Michael(dec.) , Stephanie Kae, Eric Peter. BA in Elem. Edn., Luther Coll., Decorah, Iowa, 1953; MS in Tchg., U. Wis., Whitewater, 1979; splty. degree in ednl. adminstrn., U. Wis., Madison, 1995. Tchr. 2d grade Jackson Sch. Dist., Minn., 1953—54; 1st and 2d grade tchr. Hayfield Sch. Disst., Minn., 1954—56, Nichols Sch. Dist., Monona, Wis., 1956—57, Madison Sch. Dist., 1961; tchg. grades 1-8 Mukwonego Sch. Dist., Wis., 1966—68; tchr. grades 4, 7, 8 Palmyra-Eagle Sch. Dist., Wis., 1968—83, prin., 1978—94. Alcohol and other drug abuse coun. dir. K-12 Palmyra-Eagle Sch. Dist., 1983—94; alcohol and other drug abuse program grant reader Wis. Dept. Pub. Instrn., 1985—94, alcohol and other drug abuse prrogram coun. mem., 1988—94; pres. Four Lakes Prins. Assn., 1991; presenter in field. Bd. dirs., bd. curators Wis. Hist. Soc., Madison, 1999—2001; adult leader 4-H, Eagle, 1967—93; cookbook com. Friends of Old World Wis., 1988; vol. holiday fair Waukesha County Hist. Soc., from 1990; edn. com. Eagle Hist. Soc., from 2005; state del. Rep. Party of Wis., Madison, from 1975; co-author 100-yr. history St. John's Luth. Ch., North Prairie, Wis., adult Bible study leader; edn. officer Luth. Brotherhood Prairie Br. # 8146, 1987—95; bd. dirs. Friends of Wis. Hist. Soc., Madison, from 1976, pres., 1999—2001; bd. dirs. Palmyra-Eagle Scholarship and Ednl. Found., from 2003. Recipient Disting. Svc. award, Luther Coll., 1988, US Mcht. Marine Acad., 1992, Assn. Wis. Sch. Adminstrs., 1998; named Mother of Yr. for Wis., Mother of the Yr. Program, 1980, Citizen of Yr., Eagle Lioness, 1986; named one of Outstanding Elem. Tchrs. of Am., 1974, 1975, 1976. Mem.: Assn. Wis. Sch. Adminstrs. (pres., chair exec. dir. search com. 1995, 1998, bd. dirs. 1991—97, region 2 dir. 1991—93, pub. rels. com. 1993—97, chair regional profl. conf. 1994—95, co-chair exec. dirs. retirement celebration 1995), Nat. Assn. Elem. Sch. Prins., Phi Delta Kappa (nat. fellows program 1989). Lutheran. Avocations: Bible study, rosemaling, gardening, piano, crossword puzzles. Home: Eagle, Wis. Died Jan. 12, 2007.

KAMINSKI, ISABELLE, pre-school educator, music educator; b. Trenton, NJ, Sept. 4, 1910; d. Francis and Elizabeth (Zielinski) Kaminski. BA, N.Y.U., NYC, 1958, MEd, 1962. Piano instr., owner Trenton Conservatory of Music, Trenton, NJ, 1960—2003; owner, tchr. Wee Sch./Ive Sch., Trenton, NJ, 1960—90. Guild judge Nat. Piano Guild, Houston, 1960—90. Mem.: Nat. Music Tchrs. Assn., Nat. Guild Piano Tchrs. Home: Trenton, NJ. Died Aug. 9, 2007.

KAMMERER, ANDREW HARMON, insurance underwriter; b. Oakland, Calif., June 7, 1956; s. Burleigh K. and Kathryn (Fitzpatrick) Sinnott; m. Elaine Victoria Kammerer, Oct. 3, 1987; 1 child, Phillip Robert. BA, San Francisco State U., 1985. Gen. contractor Kammerer Constrn., Berkeley, Calif., 1982-86; project mgr. Powelson Assocs., Berkeley, 1986-88; surety underwriter Chubb and Son Inc., San Francisco, from 1988. Mem. Commonwealth Club Calif., Assoc. Gen. Contractors Calif. (assoc.). Home: Alameda, Calif. Died Dec. 8, 2006.

KAMSLER, MILTON A., JR., internist; b. Phila., July 12, 1923; s. Milton A. and Mercia Marie Etta (Trenner) K.; m. Ruth M. Harris, Sept. 3, 1946; children: Scott, Susan, Kirk. BA, Amherst Coll., 1945; MD, U. Pa., 1947, postgrad. student, 1950-51. Diplomate Am. Bd. Internal Medicine. Intern Good Samaritan Hosp., Portland, Oreg., 1947-48; gen. practice Salem, Oreg., 1948-50; fellowship in internal medicine Cleve. Clinic, 1951-53; assoc. staff Henry Ford Hosp., Detroit, 1955-56; pvt. practice internal medicine Burlingame, Calif., 1956-83; staff internist VA Med. Ctr., Poplar Bluff, Mo., 1985-90; retired Brookfield, Wis., from 1990. Candidate for Rep. Congressional Nomination, Burlingame, Calif., 1978. Capt. U.S. Army Med. Corps, 1953-55. Mem. AMA, Am. Coll. Physicians. Avocations: writing: letters to the editor, political articles, a book. Home: Saint Augustine, Fla. Died Mar. 23, 2007.

KANE, DAVID FRANCIS, tax lawyer; b. Brockton, Mass., Oct. 7, 1952; s. Kenneth Francis and Margaret A. (Herlihy) K. BS in Acctg., Stonehill Coll., 1975; JD, Boston Coll., 1979. Bar: Mass. 1979; CPA, Mass. Assoc. Louison, Witt & Hensley, Brockton, Mass., 1980-81; tax specialist Peat, Marwick & Mitchell, Boston, 1982-85; tax atty. Textron, Inc., Providence, 1985-87, Gerald T. Reilly & Co., Boston, from 1987. Democrat. Roman Catholic. Home: North Easton, Mass. Died June 9, 2007.

KANTNER, PAUL LORIN, musician; b. San Francisco, Mar. 17, 1941; s. Paul S. and Cora Lee (Fortier) K.; children: Gareth, China, Alexander. Student, U. Santa Clara, 1959-61, San Jose State Coll., 1961-63. Mem. group: Jefferson Airplane, 1965-71, 89, Jefferson Starship, 1972-84, Planet Earth Rock and Roll Orch., 1984-85, Kantner Balin Casady Band, 1985-88; rec. artist: (with others) (album) KBC Band, 1986; albums with Jefferson Airplane include Jefferson Airplane Takes Off, 1966, Surrealistic Pillow, 1967, After Bathing at Baxters, 1967, Crown of Creation, 1968, Bless It's Pointed Little Head, 1969, Volunteers, 1969, Worst of Jefferson Airplane, 1970, Bark, 1971, Long John Silver, 1972, Thirty Seconds over Winterland, 1973, Early Flight, 1974, Jefferson Airplane's Flight Log 1966-76, 1977, 2400 Fulton Street-An Anthology, 1987, Jefferson Airplane, 1989, White Rabbit and Other Hits, 1990; albums with Jefferson Starship include Blows Against the Empire, 1970, Dragon Fly, 1974, Red Octopus, 1975, Spitfire, 1976, Earth, 1978, Gold, 1979, Freedom at Point Zero, 1979, Modern Times, 1981, Jefferson Starship At Their Best, 1993; (with Grace Slick) Sunfighter, 1971, (with Slick and David Freiberg) Baron von Tollbooth and the Chrome NSN, 1973; author: Nicaragua Diary: How I Spent My Summer Vacation, or , I Was a Commie Dupe for the Sanfinistas, 1988. Recipient Grammy Lifetime Achievement award (Jefferson Airplane), 2016; named to Rock and Roll Hall of Fame, 1996. Mem. Futant Soc., Hellfire Club. Died Jan. 2016.

KANWAL, RAM PRAKASH, mathematics educator; b. Jhang, Punjab, India, July 4, 1924; arrived in US, 1954, naturalized, 1973; s. Isher Dass and Bhagwan Bai (Nandi) Kanwal; m. Vimla Kanwal, June 16, 1954; children: Neeru Kiran, Neeraj Kumar. BA with honors, Punjab U., India, 1945, MA with honors, 1948; PhD, Ind. U., 1957. Rsch. assoc. Ind. U., Bloomington, 1954—57; asst. prof. U. Wis., Madison, 1957—59; assoc. prof. Pa. State U., University Pk., 1959—62, prof. math., 1962—91; prof. emeritus. Vis. prof. Denmark Inst. Tech., Copenhagen, 1965—66, Royal Inst. Tech., Stockholm, 1966—67; vis. scientist Oak Ridge Nat. Lab., 1957; assoc. editor Jour. Integral Equations, 1978—86. Author: (book) Linear Integral Equations, 1971, Generalized Functions, 1983; co-author (with R. Estrada): Asymptotic Analysis-Distributional Approach, 1993; contbr. articles to profl. jours. Mem.: Soc. Indsl. and Applied Math., Allahabad Math. Soc. Home: State College, Pa. Died Oct. 31, 2006.

KAPLAN, ALLEN STANFORD, rabbi; b. Chgo., Mar. 26, 1939; s. Nathan and Belle Sarah (Levin) K.; m. Jane Gruber, July 22, 1967; children: Walter H., Sarah N., David J. BA, U. Cin., 1960; BHL, MAHL, Hebrew U. Coll.-Jewish Inst. Religion, 1965; DD, NYC, 1990. Ordained rabbi, 1965. Rabbi Temple Beth Sholom, NYC, 1970-78; assoc. dir. N.Y. Bd. Rabbis, NYC, 1978-82, N.Y. Fedn. Reform Synagogues, NYC, 1982-91, dir., from 1991. V.p., bd. dirs. JACS Found., N.Y.C.; advisor on religious matters Gay Men's Health Crisis, N.Y.C., 1988—. Co-author: Drugs, Sex and Integrity, Vol. II; contbr. articles to profl. jours. Capt. USNR, 1980—. Mem. Cen. Conf. Am. Rabbis, Internat. Psychology Assn., Naval Res. Assn., Assn. N.Y. Reform Rabbis (treas. N.Y.C. chpt. 1987—, pres. 1993—). Avocation: photography. Home: New York, NY. Died June 22, 2007.

KAPLAN, HAROLD MORRIS, physiologist, educator; b. Boston, Sept. 4, 1908; s. Max and Mollie (Smith) K.; m. Bernice Stone, June 1935; children: Elaine Beth, Joyce M., Lee Allan. AB, Dartmouth Coll., 1930; A.M. (Jeffries Wyman scholar), Harvard U., 1931, PhD, 1933. Asst. instr. Harvard, 1933-34; prof. Middlesex Med. Sch., 1934-35, Middlesex Vet. Sch., 1945-47; writer Washington Inst. Medicine, 1946-49; asso. prof. U. Mass., 1947-48; prof. So. Ill. U., from 1948, vis. prof. Med. Sch., from 1974, chmn. emeritus, from 1992. Curriculum cons. Okla. Coll. Osteopathic Medicine and Surgery, 1981; Asso. editor Am. Assn. Lab Animal Sci., 1959, pres., 1966-67; chmn. editorial bd. Lab. Animal Scis., 1959-73; cons. Applied Research and Devel. Lab., Mt. Vernon, Ill. Fellow AAAS; mem. Am. Soc. Zoologists Ill. Acad. Sci. (pres. 1968-69, councilor 1969—), Ill. Soc. Med. Research (dir. 1966—), Inst. Lab. Animal Resources (past adv. council), Am. Physiol. Soc., Electron Microscope Soc. Am., Midwest Soc. Electron Microscopists, Am. Assn. Lab. Animal Sci. (pres., exec. bd. 1969-70), Sigma Xi, Phi Kappa Phi (pres. chpt. 1983), Phi Eta Sigma. Home: Carbondale, Ill. Died Nov. 28, 2006.

KAPLAN, PETER W., publishing executive; b. South Orange, NJ, Feb. 10, 1954; s. Robert E. and Roberta Wennik Kaplan; m. Audrey Mary Walker, June 24, 1984 (div.); 3 children. BA in American Studies, Harvard Coll., 1976. Desk asst. ABC Radio; editor NY Times Mag., Esquire; Style sect. corr. The Washington Post; cultural corr. The NY Times, 1984; exec. editor & editl. dir. Manhattan, Inc.; editor-in-chief NY Observer, 1994—2009; creative dir. Condé Nast Traveler, 2009—10; editl. dir. Fairchild Fashion Group, 2010—13. Exec. prodr.: (TV series) The Charlie Rose Show, 1993. Died Nov. 29, 2013.

KARAM, ERNEST, chief magistrate; b. Cleve., Apr. 3, 1909; s. Henry Harvey and Frieda K.; m. Lucille Himebaugh, Nov. 23, 1934 (dec. 1985). BS in Bus. Adminstrn., Ohio State U., 1933; LLB, Chase Coll. Law, Cin., 1947; JD, Chase Coll. Law, 1968. Bar: Ohio, U.S. Ct. Mil. Appeals, 1955, U.S. Tax Ct., 1976, U.S. Supreme Ct., 1955. Circulation exec. Cin. Post, 1933-74; referee Hamilton County Domestic Rels. Ct., Cin., 1976-77, chief referee, 1977-97, dir., 1978-97, chief magistrate, 1997—2006, ret., 2006. Spl. counsel Atty. Gen. Ohio, 1983. Lt. cmdr. U.S. Navy, 1943-46, USNR, 1947-74. Recipient Disting. Svc. award, No. Ky. U., Lifetime Achievement award, Solmon P. Chase Coll. Law; named Citizen of Day and Citizen of Decade, Radio WLW-700, Cin., 1968, Hon. Col., Office of Gov. Okla., from 1969; named to Ky. Col., from 1969; Ernest Karam Day named in his honor, Apr. 2, 1999, City of Cin. Fellow: Ohio State Bar Assn. Found. (hon.; life); mem.: ABA, Assn. Trial Lawyers Am., Ohio State Bar Assn., Cin. Bar Assn. Home: Cincinnati, Ohio. Died July 10, 2007.

KARAMI, OMAR ABDUL HAMID, former Prime Minister of Lebanon; b. Al Nouri, Tripoli, Lebanon, May 1, 1935; s. Abduhamid Karami; m. Mariam Koptam; 4 children. Student, American U., Beirut; BS of Laws, Cairo U., 1956. Min. edn. and the arts Govt. of Lebanon, Beirut, 1989—90, MP, from 1991, prime min., 1990—92, 2004—05, 2005. Founder Karama Welfare Dispensaries, 'Al-Manar University, 1991, Nat. Liberation Movement, Tripoli, 1992; honorary pres. Islamic Welfare & Relief Assn. Islam. Died Jan. 1, 2015.

KARMIN, BENNETT MICHAEL, computer company executive; b. NYC, Aug. 17, 1929; s. Alexander Stanley and Berte (Wolf) K.; m. Meta Louise, Sept. 20, 1964; children: Craig, Douglas. BS, NYU, 1951. Pub. rels. writer United Airlines, NYC, 1958-62; sr. pub. rels. rep. J.C. Penney Co., NYC, 1962-66; acct. exec. BBDO-ADV, NYC, 1966-68; program adminstr. IBM, San Jose, Calif., 1968-91. Contbr. articles to newspapers. Democrat. Avocations: reading, writing, hiking, boating. Home: San Jose, Calif. Died June 25, 2007.

KARPINSKI, HUBERTA, library board clerk; b. Cato, NY, Jan. 4, 1925; d. Alfred Raymond and Lena Margaret (Fuller) Tuxill; m. Edward Karpinski, Nov. 17, 1956; children: Susan Tanielian, Rebecca Hitch, Amy Jaward. Student, U. Mich., Ann Arbor, 1943—45, Wayne U., Detroit, 1949—50; grad., NY Art Acad. Design, Detroit, 1972. Operator to svc. observer supr. Mich. Bell Telephone Co., Detroit, 1946—57; tchr. art Birmingham (Mich.) Pub. Sch., 1977—87; libr. trustee Redford (Mich.) Twp. Dist. Libr., 1972—2009. Chmn. Lola Valley Civic Assn., Redford, 1960-70; vice chmn. Redford Twp. Coun. Civic Assn., 1967-71; bd. dirs. 17th Dist. Mich. Dem. Party, Redford, 1968-71. Mem. Nat. Mus. Women in arts (charter), Mich. Porcelain Artists, Internat. Porcelain Art Tchrs. Avocation: painting. Home: Redford, Mich. Died Sept. 27, 2014.

KASS, JEROME ALLAN, writer; s. Sidney J. and Celia (Gorman) K.; m. Artha Schwartz (div.); children Julie, Adam; m. Delia Ephron, May 21, 1982. BA, NYU, 1958, MA, 1959. Adj. prof. Film Sch. Colulmbia U. Playwright: Monopoly, 1965, Saturday Night, 1968, (mus.) Ballroom, 1978 (Tony nomination), (mus.) Norman's Ark, Montclair U., 2002, (TV) A Brand New Life, 1973, Queen of the Stardust Ballroom, 1975 (Writers Guild Am. award, Emmy nomination), My Old Man, 1979, The Fighter, 1982, Scorned and Swindled, 1984, Crossing to Freedom (aka Pied Piper), 1990, Last Wish, 1991, The Only Way Out, 1993, Secrets, 1995; screenwriter: The Black Stallion Returns, 1981, (miniseries) Evergreen, 1985; author: Four Short Plays by Jerome Kass, 1966, Saturday Night, 1969; adapted to concert form Finian's Rainbow, L.A., 1997, Pajama Game, L.A., 1998, Fiorello, L.A., 1999; musical version Queen of the Stardust Ballroom, Chgo., 1998, Norman's Ark, LA, 2008; published a collection of autobiographical short stories, Out of the Bronx: The Joel Sachs Stories, 2014 Mem. Dramatists Guild, Writers Guild Am., Actors Studio, Phi Beta Kappa. Home: New York, NY. Died Oct. 22, 2015.

KASTENMEIER, ROBERT WILLIAM, former Congressman; b. Beaver Dam, Wis., Jan. 24, 1924; s. Leo Henry and Lucille (Powers) K.; m. Dorothy Chambers, June 27, 1952; children: William, Andrew, Edward. B, Carleton Coll., Minn.; LL.B., U. Wis., 1952. Bar: Wis. 1952. Dir. br. office claims service War Dept., Philippines, 1946-48; practiced in Watertown, 1952-58; justice of the peace, 1955-58; mem. US Congress from 2nd Dist. Wis., 1959-91; mem. com. on judiciary, chmn. subcom. house jud. com.; mem. select com. on intelligence. Contbr. articles to law jours. Served from pvt. to 1st lt., inf. US Army, 1943-46. Recipient Rex Stout Award, Authors Guild Inc, 1977, Distinguished Serv Award, Nat. Ctr. for State Courts, 1985, Warren E. Burger Award, Inst. Court Mgmt., 1985, Justice Award, Am. Judicature Soc., 1988. Home: Arlington, Va. Died Mar. 20, 2015.

KATZ, ALAN MARTIN, secondary school educator; b. Bronx, NY, Apr. 14, 1945; s. Joseph and Alice (Laster) K.; m. Gale Idette Dubin, July 4, 1971; children: Lawrence, Elyse. BA, U. Bridgeport, 1966; MS, Fla. State U., 1968. Cert. tchr., N.Y. Tchr. sci. Commack (N.Y.) Pub. Schs., from 1968. Ednl. asst. Maldemar Med. Rsch. Found., Woodbury, N.Y., 1971-72, rsch. asst., 1973; instr. marine biology Bd. Coop. Ednl. Svcs. Inst. for Gifted and Talented, Dix Hills, N.Y., 1974-88; adj. instr. Suffolk County C.C., 1981-84; program dir. Babylon (N.Y.) Consortium for Marine Studies, 1987-90, Commack Summer Marine Sci. Program, 1990—; chairperson sci. dept. Commack H.S., 1995. Coauthor: Marine Science Curriculum for High School, 1989. Recipient Outstanding Tchr. award Tandy Corp., 1991-92, cert. of honor N.Y. Sci. Talent Search, 1992, cert. of honor Westinghouse Sci. Talent Search, 1991, 92. Mem. N.Y. State Sci. Tchrs. Assn., Suffolk County Sci. Tchrs. Assn., Pine Barrens Soc. Avocations: scuba diving, golf, sailing. Home: East Setauket, NY. Died Feb. 25, 2007.

KATZ, HARRY JAY, public relations consultant; b. NYC, Dec. 25, 1940; s. Lawrence and Selma (Green) Katz; m. Julia Mae Levin (div.); children: Susan Levin, David B.; m. Andrea Lull Diehl, Oct. 7, 1979 (div.); children: Jessica Mazzenga, Zachary; m. Tracey Birnhak (div.); m. Debra Renee Katz. BA, U. Pa., 1975. Chief exec. Campus Cakes, 1961—63; treas. Doris Investment Corp., Melrose Pk., Pa., 1963; oper. officer Allegheny Steel Corp. Chem. Divsn., Bryn Mawr, Pa., 1963—65; cons. to pres. Consol. Bottling Co., Phila., 1965—67; asst. to pres. Bala Industries and B.T. Babbit, Bala Cynwyd, Pa., 1965—67; franchisee Playboy Club Phila., 1967—71; commentator Sta. KYW-TV, Phila., 1970—71; franchise developer Penthouse Mag., 1971; exec. dir. Camden Too, 1971—73, Bicentennial Lang. Incentive Program, Camden, NJ, 1971—73; mktg. cons. MacAndrews & Forbes Co., Phila., 1972—79; operator, gen. mgr. Cafe Erlanger and The Erlanger Theatre, Phila., 1973—75; pvt. practice, pub. rels. cons., from 1976; with publicity, pub. rels. Bill Boggs' Midday Show, NYC, 1977; chief exec. Home Clone Corp., 1978; pub. ELECTRICity, Phila., 1979—83. Chief exec. Roddy Rod & Reel Co., 1967—70, S.S. United States Corp., 1973—80; guest lectr. Temple U., 1973—76, Wharton Sch. Bus. U. Pa., 1978, 1981; spl. cons. Dept. Edn. State NJ. Syndicated columnist The Drummer and The Daily Planet, weekly column: The Katz Meow, 1972—79. Bd. dirs. Phila. Civic Ballet; past bd. dirs. Assn. Retarded Citizens, Shackamaxon Soc. Old Ft. Mifflin; co-founder, free breakfast program Tasker Homes Project. With US Army, 1967. Recipient Key to City, Fredonia, Kans., 1971, award, Drexel U. Alumni Assn., Achievement awards, Kiwanis Club Phila., 1972, Rotary Club Pitman, NJ. Mem.: Pa. Soc., Locust Club Phila., Golden Slipper Square Club, Variety Club (past bd. dirs. Tent 13), Masons Lodge (32d degree). Died Feb. 23, 2016.

KAVCHOK, RONALD W., chemical engineer; b. Phila., Mar. 7, 1946; s. John and Mary (Makara) K.; m. Irene Loginow, Nov. 2, 1968; children: Kevin Andrew, Ronald Christopher, Steven William. BSChE, Drexel U., 1968. Staff rsch. engr. Goodyear Tire & Rubber, Akron, Ohio, 1968-76; lab. mgr. Diamond Shamrock, Morristown, N.J., 1976-81; project mgr. Ashland Chem., Boonton, N.J., 1981-85; sr. rsch. engr. Lonza Corp., Fairlawn, N.J., 1985-89; pilot plant mgr. Ausimont USA Inc., Morristown, 1989-95; plant mgr. Wm. Zinsser Co., Somerset, N.J., from 1995. Contbr. articles to profl. jours. Mem. AIChE, Am. Chem. Soc. (rubber divsn.). Achievements include 5 U.S. patents. Home: Hillsborough, NJ. Died July 20, 2007.

KAYE, JUDITH SMITH (JUDITH ANN SMITH), lawyer, retired state appeals court chief judge; b. Monticello, NY, Aug. 4, 1938; d. Benjamin and Lena (Cohen) Smith; m. Stephen Rackow Kaye, Feb. 11, 1964 (dec. Oct. 30, 2006); children: Luisa Marian, Jonathan Mackey, Gordon Bernard BA, Barnard Coll., 1958; LLB cum laude, NYU, 1962; LLD (hon.), St. Lawrence U., 1985, Union U., 1985, Pace U., 1985, Syracuse U., 1988, L.I. U., 1989. Bar: NY State 1963. Assoc. Sullivan & Cromwell LLP, NYC, 1962-64; staff atty. IBM Corp., Armonk, NY, 1964-65; asst. to dean NYU Sch. Law, 1965-68; ptnr. Olwine Connelly Chase O'Donnell & Weyher, NYC, 1969-83; assoc. judge NY State Ct. Appeals, Albany, 1983-93, chief judge, 1993—2008; of counsel Skadden, Arps, Slate, Meagher & Flom LLP, NYC, 2009—16. Pres., Conf. of Chief Justices; chair bd. dir., Nat. Ctr. for State Cts., 2002-03; bd. dir. Sterling Nat. Bank. Bd. editor, NY State Bar Journal; contbr. articles to profl. jours. Former bd. dirs. Legal Aid Soc.; chair, Permanent Jud. Commn. on Justice for Children; founding mem., hon. chair, Judges and Lawyers Breast Cancer Alert (JALBCA); trustee, William Nelson Cromwell Found. Recipient Vanderbilt medal NYU Sch. Law, 1983, Medal of Distinction, Barnard Coll, 1987, John Marshall award, ABA Justice Ctr., 2005, William H. Rehnquist award for Judicial Excellence, Adoption Excellence Award, US Dept. Health & Human Services, Margaret Brent Women Lawyers of Achievement award, ABA Commn. on Women in the Profession, Lifetime Achievement award The American Lawyer mag., 2010 Fellow Am. Bar Found.; mem. Am. Law Inst., Am. Coll. Trial Lawyers, Am. Judicature Soc. (bd. dirs. 1980-83), ABA (co-chair, Commn. on the Am. Jury, 2004-05). Democrat. Achievements include being the first women to serve on the New York State's Court of Appeals; being the first women to occupy the state judiciary's highest office, Chief Judge. Home: New York, NY. Died Jan. 7, 2016.

KEANE, GERALD JOSEPH, toy company executive; b. Detroit, Oct. 24, 1947; s. Bernard Patrick and Jovita Mary (Tolksdorf) K.; m. Margaret Ann Wray, May 8, 1970; children: Daniel, Patrick, Katherine, Dennis. BBA, U. Toledo, 1973; MBA, U. So. Calif., 1988. Sales rep. Procter & Gamble, Toledo, 1971-73, Louisville, 1973-74, M&M/Mars, Louisville, 1974-76, unit sales mgr. Cleve., 1976-78, bus. mgr. western div. Los Angeles, from 1984; sales mgr. western div. Kal Kan Foods, Los Angeles, 1978-81; bus. mgr. ea. div. Mars Broker div., Detroit, 1981-84; dir. nat. sales spl. market Mattel Toys co., Hawthorne, Calif., from 1988. Lectr. in field. Head coach Washington Jr. Football League, Toledo, 1968-72; coach Mission Viejo (Calif.) Little League, 1985, 86, NJB Basketball, 1988-89; athletic dir. Saddleback Valley Pop Warner, 1986, 87; v.p. Santa Margarita High Sch. Football Boosters Club; vice-chmn. St. Catherines Endowment Com., Laguna Beach, Calif., 1986—. Mem. Nat. Candy Wholesalers Assn. Republican. Roman Catholic. Avocations: football, baseball, basketball, golf. Home: Laguna Hills, Calif. Died July 2, 2007.

KEARBY, PAUL DOYLE, minister; b. Oklahoma City, Nov. 30, 1955; s. John C. and Elaine F. (Pollard) K.; m. Teresa A. Smith, Dec. 31, 1977; children: Laura Beth, Stephen Paul. BS in Bibl. Studies, Okla. Christian Coll., 1979. Assoc. minister Mayfair Ch. of Christ, Oklahoma City, 1978-79; minister Wayne (Okla.) Ch. of Christ, 1979-81, Ch. of Christ, Alva, Okla., 1981-82, Cherry Hill Ch. of Christ, Joliet, Ill., 1982-84; chaplain Joliet Correctional Ctr., 1982-84; minister Ch. of Christ, Valparaiso, Ind., from 1984; chaplain Westville (Ind.) Correctional Inst., 1985-86. Missionary work Austria, Hungary and Yugoslavia, 1977-78; tchr., co-dir. Lariet Creek Christian Camp, Okla., 1979-82; tchr, counselor Rockford (Ill.) Christian Camp, 1982—; teaching house parent Shults-Lewis Child and Family Care Agy., Valparaiso, 1984-86. Author: Historical Outlines of Old Testament Characters, 1979, Accepting God's Power, 1981, Detours, Dead Ends and Dry Holes, 1982, Marriage, Divorce and Remarriage, 1985; co-host radio program, 1981-82; featured columnist The Paul's Valley Dem., 1980, The Alva Rev. Courier, 1981-82. Named one of Outstanding Young Men of Am., 1982, 83. Mem.: Exchange (Joliet), Rotary (bd. dirs. Alva club 1982). Avocations: writing, golf, softball. Home: Gillette, Wyo. Died July 11, 2007.

KEARNEY, ANNETTE GAINES, school superintendent; b. Elizabeth, NJ, Mar. 30, 1939; d. Roosevelt and Rose Mary (Motley) Gaines; m. Phillip C. Kearney; children Phillip A., Lisa G., Larry. BA, Kean Coll., 1961, MA, 1970; PhD, Rutgers U., 1973. Cert. tchr., counselor, administr. Tchr. Elizabeth (N.J.) Pub. Schs., 1961-64, Rahway (N.J.) Pub. Schs., 1965-68, counselor, 1968-70; grad. asst. Rutgers U., 1971-72; asst. prof. Mich. State U., 1972-74; program dir. Kings County Hosp. Ctr., Bklyn., 1974-75; asst. supt. Newark Pub. Schs., 1975-78; program dir. Nat. Council Negro Women, NYC, 1979-83; various adminstrv. positions Plainfield (N.J.) Pub. Schs., 1983-87, supt., from 1987. V.p. Human Excellence Resourses Systems, Inc., Roselle, N.J., 1981—; cons. Univ. Md., 1979-81, Delaware State Coll., 1980-81, Social Sci. Edn. Consortium, Inc., 1967-69; cons./trainer: Somerset County Sch. Dist., Weaver High Sch., Hartford , Conn.; cons./psychologist: Douglas Coll., 1974, N.J. State Dept. Health, 1974, Newark State Coll., 1974. Author numerous papers, studies, presentations. Active in v.p.'s Task Force on Youth Unemployment, 1979; Roselle Bd. Edn., 1974-77, Nat. Task Force Consortium of Sci., 1975; bd. trustees, Mental Health Assn. Essex County, 1975-78; nat. program coordinator and exec. mem. Assn. for Non-white (Appreciation Award 1976). Recipient: Dorothy A. Early Award for excellence in piano, 1965, honors in vocal music, 1968, Community Svc. Award Roselle, N.J., 1971; honored in Core Mag. as successful female achiever 1975; featured in profiles in Black (biographical sketches of 100 living black unsung heroes) 1976. Mem. Nat. Council Negro Women (life mem. award 1967, edn. award 1974), Nat. Assn. Negro Bus. and Profl. Women's Club (Profl. Woman of the Year 1975), Internat. Dynamic Edn. Assn., Inc. (Ednl. Achievement Award 1975), Am. Personnel and Guidance Assn., Assn. for Non-White Concerns in Personnel and Guidance, Black Alliane on Grad. and Profl. Edn., Nat. Assn. Black Psychologists, Nat. Assn. Black Sch. Educators, Am. Psychological Assn., Kappa Delta Pi, Phi Delta Kappa, Alpha Kappa Alpha. Baptist. Home: N Brunswick, NJ. Died June 12, 2007.

KEARNEY, JOHN WALTER, sculptor, painter; b. Omaha, Aug. 31, 1924; m. Lynn Haigh, June 2, 1951; children: Daniel Raymond, Jill Ann. Student, Cranbrook Acad. Art, 1946—48. Tchr., from 1948; co-founder, 1949; since pres. Contemporary Art Workshop Chgo. Mem. adv. bd. Art Inst. Chgo., A.R.S.G., Fine Arts Work Ctr., Provincetown, Mass., Chgo. Coun. on Fine Arts; vis. artist Am. Acad. in Rome, 1985, 92, 98, 03—; mem. summer faculty Fine Arts Work Ctr., Provincetown, 1996. Numerous one-man shows including A.C.A. Gallery, NYC, (5 shows) 1964-79, 03-04, Ft. Wayne (Ind.) Mus., 1966, Galleria Schneider, Rome, 1969, Ill. Inst. Tech., 1976, 91, Ulrich Mus. Art, Wichita State U., 1976, Dirksen Fed. Bldg., Chgo., 1979, Cherrystone Gallery, Wellfleet, Mass., 1980, 92, Contemporary Art Workshop, 1981, 84, Goldman-Kraft Gallery, Chgo., 1985, others in NYC, 1964-79, Venice, 1964, Rome, 1964, 68, Chgo., 1966-85, Berta Walker Gallery, Provincetown, Mass., 1992, 93, 95, 97, 2005, Mitchell Mus., Mt. Vernon, Ill., 1994, Chgo. Cultural Ctr., 2006, Art in Pub. Pls., Stamford, Conn., 2006; sculpture show 1998, Thomas McCormick Fine Art, Chicago, 1998. 2-person show, Art Inst. Chgo., A.R.S.G., 1977, Contemporary Art Workshop Chgo., 2009; represented in permanent collections, Milw. Art Mus., Wis., Mus. Contemporary Art, Chgo., Standard Oil Bldg., Chgo., Lawrence U., Appleton, Wis., Interfirst Plaza, Dallas, Mundelein Coll., Chgo., Norfolk Art Mus., Va., Ulrich Mus. Art of Wichita State U., Canton Art Inst., Capitol Bldg. Complex State Ill., Springfield, 1993, Detroit Children's Mus., Ft. Wayne Art Mus., Minn. Mus., St. Paul, New Sch. Social Rsch., NYC, City of Chgo. Park Dist., Northwestern U., Roosevelt U., Chgo., U. Wyo. Art Mus., St. Lawrence U., Canton, NY, Wichita Art Mus., Youth Art Ctr., Fayetteville, Ark., Peace Mus., Chgo., Kans. Coliseum, Wichita, Fourth Fin. Ctr., Wichita, Kresge Collection, Troy, Mich., Ill. State Mus., Ill. Capitol Bldg. Mitchell Mus., Mt. Vernon, Ill., Cranbrook Acad. Art, Bloomfield Hills., Mich., Oakton Coll., Des Plaines, Ill., Oz Park, Chgo., Tin Man, Screcrow, Cowardly Lion, Dorothy and Toto, Goudy Sch., Chgo.; also pvt. collections including, John D. Rockefeller IV collection, Robert Mayer collection, spl. sculpture in bronze and silver, Sculpture Park (4 works) Munster Ind., 2000, steel bumpers sculpture, others. Trustee Ill. Com. for Handgun Control. Served with USN, World War II, PTO. Named Man of Year in Arts in Chgo., 1963; Fulbright grantee, 1963-64; Italian Govt. grantee, 1963-64; grantee Nat. Endowment Arts, 1968; Resolution Chgo. City Coun. in Honor of Sculpture, 2007 Mem. Provincetown Art Assn. (former v.p. and trustee) Died Aug. 10, 2014.

KEELEY, ROBERT VOSSLER, retired ambassador; b. Beirut, Sept. 4, 1929; s. James Hugh and Mathilde Julia (Vossler) K.; m. Louise Benedict Schoonmaker, June 23, 1951; children: Michal M., Christopher J. AB, Princeton U., 1951, postgrad., 1951-53; postgrad. (Princeton fellow in pub. affairs), 1970-71; postgrad. (Nat. Inst. Pub. Affairs fellow), Stanford U., 1965-66. With Fgn. Svc. US Dept. State, Washington, 1956—63, officer in charge Congo (Leopoldville) external affairs, 1963-64, officer-in-charge Congo (Brazzaville), Rwanda and Burundi affairs, 1964-65, polit. officer Greece, 1966-70; detailed Woodrow Wilson fellow Princeton U., 1970; dep. chief of mission US Embassy, Kampala, Uganda, 1971-73; alt. dir. East African affairs US Dept. State, Washington, 1974; dep. chief of mission US Embassy, Phnom Penh, Cambodia, 1974-75; dep. dir. Interagency Task Force for Indochina Refugees, 1975-76; US amb. to Mauritius US Dept. State, Port Louis, Mauritius, 1976-78, dep. asst. sec. for African Affairs Washington, 1978-80, US amb. to Zimbabwe Harare, 1980-84, US amb. to Greece Athens, 1985-89; sr. fellow Ctr. for Study Fgn. Affairs, Washington, 1984-85. Pres. Middle East Inst., Washington, 1990-95; founder Five and Ten Press, Inc., 1995-2015 Author: The Colonels' Coup and the American Embassy: A Diplomat's View of the Breakdown of Democracy in Cold War Greece, 2010; editor: First Line of Defense-Ambassadors, Embassies and American Interests Abroad, 2000 Lt. (j.g.) USCGR, 1953-55. Mem. American Fgn. Svc. Assn. (Christian Herter award), Washington Inst. Fgn. Affairs, American Acad. Diplomacy, Cosmos Club. Home: Washington, DC. Died Jan. 9, 2015.

KEENAN, TERRY MARIE (THERESA KEENAN), newscaster; b. Albany, NY, May 16, 1961; d. Joseph and Marie (Thibodeau) Keenan; m. Ronald R. Kass, Apr. 23, 1994; 1 child, Benjamin. BS in Math., Johns Hopkins U., 1983. Anchor bus. news programs CNBC; from segment prodr. to on-air corr. CNN Financial News, NYC, co-anchor Street Sweep, sr. corr. The Moneyline News Hour with Lou Dobbs; anchor, Cashin' In FOX News Channel, NYC, 2002—09; bus. columnist NY Post, 2009—14. Recipient Cable Ace award. Irish Catholic. Died Oct. 23, 2014.

KEENEY, WILLIAM ECHARD, educator, minister; b. Fayette County, Pa., July 17, 1922; s. William Leroy and Kathryn Olive (Echard) K.; m. Willadene Hartzler, Oct. 12, 1947; children: Lois Ruth Keeney Palmer, Carol Louise, William Leroy, Richard Lowell. AB, Bluffton Coll., 1948; BD, Bethany & Mennonite Bibl. Sem., 1953; STM, Hartford Theol. Sem., 1957, PhD, 1959. Ordained to ministry gen. conf. Mennonite Ch., 1953. Cmty. assoc. and acting dir. edn. divsn. Nat. Mental Health Found., Phila., 1946-47; relief worker in Germany Mennonite Ctrl. Com., 1948-49, dir. Netherlands program, 1949-50, rep. Netherlands, chair European Peace com., 1961-63, peace sect. study sec. Inst. Mennonite Studies fellow, 1973-74; asst. to pres., instr. Bible Bluffton (Ohio) Coll., 1953-56, asst. prof. Bible, 1958-59, assoc. prof. Bible, 1959-65, dir. publicity, 1958-61, 63-65, prof. Bible, 1965-68; acad. dean Bethel Coll., 1968-72, prof. Bible and religion, 1968-80, prof. peace studies, 1974-80, provost, 1972-73, dir. Mennonite Hist. Libr. and Archives, 1972-73, dir. experiential learning, 1974-78, dir. continuing edn., 1975-80, exec. dir. consortium on peace rsch., edn., and devel., 1978-84. Vis. asst. prof. integrative change Kent (Ohio) State U., 1980-86, asst. prof. peace and conflict studies, 1987-90, acting dir. Ctr. for Peaceful Change, 1987-89; asst. pastor Woodlawn Mennonite Ch., Chgo., 1952-53; pastor Nepaug (Conn.) Congl. Ch., 1956-57, Trinity Mennonite Ch., Hillsboro, Kans., 1976, First Mennonite Ch., Hillsboro, 1976-77, Mcpherson, Kans., 1977-78, Wadsworth, Ohio, 1983-84, Summit Mennonite Ch., Barberton, Ohio, 1984-86, among others. Author: The Development of Dutch Anabaptist Thought & Practice from 1539-1564, 1968, Lordship as Servanthood: The Biblical Basis of Peace, 1975; co-author, translator: The Writings of Dirk Philips, 1992, Preaching the Parables: Series II, Cycle A, 1995, Preaching the Parables: Series II, Cycle B, 1996, Preaching the Parables, Series II, Cycle C, 1997; cons. editor Mennonite Quar. Rev.; assoc. editor Fides et Historia, 1976-77. Chairperson Harvey County Edn. Action Coun., 1976-80; mem. adv. coun. self-directed profl. devel. program Prairie View Mental Health Ctr., 1976-80; mem. Delegation in Dialogue for Reconciliation to Teheran, 1980; co-chairperson Kent Ecumenical Peace Group, 1983-88, mem., 1988-91; mem. Gov.'s Commn. on Peace and Conflict Mgmt., 1988-89, co-chair task force on pub. edn., 1988-89; incorporator, bd. dirs. Franklin Mills Mediation Svc., Kent, 1988-90, sec., treas. bd. dirs., 1988-90; chairperson Peace and Change Exec. Com., 1985-87; mem. Et Cetera (Self Help and Thrift Shop), 1991-97, chair, 1991-97; mem. Ctrl. Dist. Conf. Hist. Com., 1992—, chair, 1992-97, sec., 1997-98; bd. dirs. Chgo. Mennonite Learning Ctr., 1992—, pres. bd. dirs., 1996—; bd. missions, peace and svc., First Mennonite Ch., Bluffton, 1992-95, vice-chair, 1992-95, moderator, 1995-97. Named Outstanding Alumni Bluffton Coll., 1988. Mem. Lions (bd. dirs. 1991-93, pres. 1997—). Avocations: jogging, leatherwork, computer work, writing. Home: Bluffton, Ohio. Died Nov. 12, 2006.

KEES, KENNETH LEWIS, research scientist; b. Highland Park, Mich., Jan. 17, 1950; s. Otis Francis and Georgette Marie (Vincent) K. BS in Chemistry, Wayne State U., 1973; PhD in Chemistry, U. Calif., Santa Cruz, 1979. Rsch. scientist Wyeth-Ayerst Rsch., from 1983. Postdoctoral rsch. assoc., vis. lectr., U. Calif. Berkeley, Santa Cruz, 1979-81; adj. lectr. U. Santa Clara, Calif., 1982-83; presenter in field. Contbr. articles to profl. jours.; patentee in field. Home: Glenmoore, Pa. Died Nov. 22, 2006.

KEEZER, DEBORAH ANN, elementary school educator; b. Rutland, Vt., July 10, 1952; d. Ross Lester and Patricia Margaret Roberts; m. Jerel Evan Keezer, June 24, 1977. BS in Edn., Castleton State Coll., Vt., 1975, MA in Edn., 1985; Ednl. Specialist, Simmons Coll., Boston, 2006. Tchr. Poultney Elem., Vt., from 1976, reading specialist, 2002—05. Trainer Am. Reads, Vt., 2005—06. Named Outstanding Tchr., Poultney Sch. Dist., 1995. Mem.: Poultney Tchrs. Assn. (negotiator 1988—2006). Democrat. Home: Poultney, Vt. Died May 17, 2007.

KEHOE, JAMES WOODWORTH, printing company executive; b. Detroit, Mar. 20, 1920; s. Arthur DeWitt and Evelyn (Woodworth) K.; m. Terry Benson, Oct. 16, 1943; children: Arthur, Robert, Margaret, Michael, Raymond, Evelyn. BSME, U. Mich., 1943; ME, Cornell U., 1944. Plant engr. Shelby (Ohio) Bus. Forms Inc., 1946-48, chief engr., 1948-63, plant mgr., v.p., 1963-76, v.p. mfg., 1976-79, pres., 1979-81; pres., chief exec. officer J.W. Kehoe Corp., Shelby, from 1988. Bd. dirs. lst Nat. Bank, Shelby. Bd. dirs. Shelby Meml. Hosp., 1964—, Richland County Found., Mansfield, Ohio, 1985—; trustee North Ctrl. Tech. Coll., Mansfield, 1973—; pres., trustee Shelby Found., 1986—, Shelby Little House Inc.-Girl Scouts U.S. Lt. (j.g.) USNR, 1943-46. Mem. Rotary (numerous offices Shelby 1968—). Home: Shelby, Ohio. Died Apr. 22, 2007.

KEIDAN, SARAH WEINER, lawyer, political science and business law educator; b. Detroit, July 2, 1938; d. Leonard H. and Josephine (Stern) Weiner; m. Fred H. Keidan, June 20, 1961 (div. 1973); children: Laura Ruth, Marian Rosalind. BA, U. Mich., 1959; MA, U. Chgo., 1960; JD, Detroit Coll. Law, 1985. Bar: Mich. 1985. Tchr. Berkeley (Mich.) Pub. Schs., 1960-64; prof. Oakland County Community Coll., Farmington Hills, Mich., from 1968. Co-author: A Realistic and Human Look at Political Systems, 1971; contbr. articles to profl. jours. State legis. chmn. Greater Detroit sect. Nat. Coun. Jewish Women, 1967-69; bd. dirs. Oakland Family Svcs., Pontiac, Mich., 1988—. Woodrow Wilson fellow, 1959-60. Mem. ABA, Acad. Polit. Sci., State Bar Mich., Oakland County Bar Assn., LWV (bull. editor Royal Oak, Mich. 1964-65), Phi Beta Kappa. Avocations: reading, travel, fitness activities. Died Mar. 17, 2007.

KEIL, CHARLES EMANUEL, corporation executive; b. NYC, Aug. 27, 1936; s. E. William and Marie Katherine (Diebold) K.; m. Patricia Ann O'Toole, Dec. 21, 1970; children: Brett, Morgan. AB, Bklyn. Coll., 1964, postgrad., 1964-65. Sales mgr. Columbian Bronze Corp., Freeport, N.Y., 1960-66; sr. v.p., group pub., mng. dir. Marine Engrng.-Log Group Simmons Boardman Pub. Co., NYC, 1966-78; sr. v.p. Thomas Internat. Pub. Co., NYC, 1978-82; gen. mgr. Tech. Pub. Co., Boca Raton, Fla., 1983-88; pub. Indsl. Computing, 1989-94; COO Ashlee Pub. Co., NYC, from 1995. V.p. internat. ops. The Maritime Group. With USNR, USMCR, 1956-58. Mem. Internat. Soc. Philos. Enquiry, Soc. Naval Archs. and Marine Engrs., Nat. Propeller Club, Navy League of U.S. Home: Boca Raton, Fla. Died Jan. 1, 2015.

KEITH, PAULINE MARY, artist, illustrator, writer; b. Fairfield, Nebr., July 21, 1924; d. Siebelt Ralph and Pauline Alethia (Garrison) Goldenstein; m. Everett B. Keith, Feb. 14, 1957; 1 child, Nathan Ralph. Student, George Fox Coll., 1947—48, Oreg. State U., 1955. Illustrator Merlin Press, San Jose, Calif., 1980-81; artist, illustrator, watercolorist Corvallis, Oreg., 1980-94. Author 6 chapbooks including Christmas Thoughts, Retelling the Story, 1985, Poems, 1999; editor: Four Generations of Verse, 1979; author numerous poems; contbr. articles to profl. jour; one-woman shows include Roger's Meml. Libr., Forest Grove, Oreg., 1959, Corvallis Art Ctr., 1960, 98-99, Human Resources Bldg., Corvallis, 1959-61, Corvallis Pastoral Counseling Ctr., 1992-94, 96, Hall Gallery, Sr. Ctr., 1993-03, Consumer Power, Philomath, Oreg., 1994, 02, 03, 04, 05, 07, Art, Etc., Newburg, Oreg., 1995-2002; exhibited in group shows at Hewlett-Packard Co., 1984-85, Corvallis Art Ctr., 1992, Chintimini Sr. Ctr., 1992, 94, 01-04, Art Vine show, 2006, 2007—. Co-elder First Christian Ch. (Disciples of Christ), Corvallis, 1988-89, co-deacon, 1980-83, elder, 1991-93; sec. Hostess Club of Chintimini Sr. Ctr., Corvallis, 1987, pres., 1988-89, v.p., 1992-94; active Luth. Ch. Coun., 1999-2000. Recipient Watercolor 1st price Benton County Fair, 1982-83, 88-89, 91, 2d prize, 1987, 91, 3d prize, 1984, 90, 92, 3d prize Newberg Festival, 2005. Mem. Oreg. Assn. Christian Writers, Internat. Assn. Women Mins., Am. Legion Aux. (post poet), ArtVine (Pres.'s Choice, 1999-2002, honorable mention, 2005, Newburg Annual Festival art show 3d prize 2006) Republican. Avocation: walking. Deceased.

KELLER, CHARLOTTE EVELYN, restaurant owner, consultant; b. Chgo., Feb. 26, 1932; d. Charles Spellman and Ethel Ruth (Ritchey) Greene; m. Ralph Joseph Keller, Sept. 12, 1953; children: Robert, Susan, Robin, David. Grad., High Sch., Hyde Park, Chgo., Ill., 1950. Sec. USAF, Chgo., 1950-53; civic worker Lansing, Mich., from 1953; owner, operator Charlotte's Web Gift Shop, Williamston, Mich., 1975-82, Keller's Restaurant and Ice Cream Parlor, Williamston, from 1982. Developer, owner Keller's Plaza, Williamston, 1982—. Author: Childrens Stories, 1949. Active Lansing Gen. Hosp., 1956—; organizer polit. campaign, Meridian Twp., Mich., 1978; chairperson Discover Williamston Day, 1981, 86, Mich. Sesquicentennial, Williamston, 1986-87. Republican. Roman Catholic. Avocations: profl. artist, photographer, swimming, sailing, flying. Home: Okemos, Mich. Died June 23, 2007.

KELLER, DANIEL SYLVESTER, director; s. Richard Sylvester and Virginia Lynn Keller; m. Bernice Marie Worthington, Oct. 29, 1966; children: Jason Douglas, Cynthia Lynnette Hilyer. BS, U. Ga., Athens, 1975—79; ThD, Andersonville Theol. Sem., Camilla, Ga., 1996—97; MEd, U. Phoenix, 2002—05. Cert. K-8 tchr. Tenn., 2005. Sr. pastor Assemblies God, White Pine, Tenn., 1982—2002. Sgt. e6 US Army, 1968—86, Ft. Campbell, Ky. Mem.: Assn. Christian Schs. Internat., Assn. Supervison & Curriculum Devel. Home: Dandridge, Tenn. Died Dec. 20, 2006.

KELLER, DOROTHY MARGARET MILLER, elementary school educator; b. Crafton, Pa., June 2, 1910; d. George Walter and Edna Lida (Daum) Miller; m. Frank Rugh Keller, Sept. 7, 1935; children: Marjorie Ann Hottel, Nancy Louise Wilson, David Frank. BS in Edn., U. Pitts., 1934. Cert. tchr. kindergarten through high sch. With H. C. Frick Sch. for Pitts. Tchrs., 1928-31; tchr. Shady Side Jr. Acad., Pitts., 1931-34; arts and crafts tchr. Pitts. (Pa.) Pub. Sch. Humboldt Sch., 1934-35. Tchr. in ch. sch. classes and depts. Coraopolis United Meth. Ch., 1935-48, Ravenna, Ohio, 1948-53, dept. supt., 1955-70. Editor: Historic Calendar, 1988, Original Pen and Ink Drawings Historic Landmarks 200th Ann. book of Moon Twp., Pa. Pres. Corapolis United Meth. Women's Soc., 1964-65; bd. dirs., sec. Moon Twp. Pks. and Recreation Bd., Coraopolis, 1963-70; organizer property given to Moon Twp., Robin Hill Pk. nature preserve and cultural ctr., 1971-79, West Area Conservation Coun., Pa., 1970; active PTA, Coraopolis and Ravenna, pres. 1949-51, 55-57, 61-63; mem. adminstrv. bd. United Meth. Ch., Coraopolis. Named Woman of Yr., Moon Twp. Jaycees, 1968, Western Br. Pitts. YWCA, 1965, Garden Club Dist. of Western Pa., Pitts., 1966-71, Woman of Yr. for Community Activities, 1971, Woman of Yr., Coraopolis-Sewickley AAUW, 1994; recipient State of Pa. Conservation award DAR, 1991. Mem. AAUW (hon. life), Am. Assn. Ret. Persons, We. Area Art League (Moon Twp., Coraopolis), Old Moon Twp. Hist. Soc. (co-editor Bicentennial History Book 1988), United Meth. Women, Garden Club of Moon Twp. Republican. Methodist. Avocations: arts, crafts, gardening, bridge, concerts and plays. Home: Gaithersburg, Md. Died Feb. 12, 2007.

KELLEY, GORDON EDWARD, health educator, dentist; b. Fairland, Ind., Aug. 5, 1934; m. Gail Ruth Gallinger, Aug. 2, 1958; children: Elizabeth, Pamela, Priscill, Marcella. BS, Ind. U., 1957; DDS, 1964; MSD, Ind. Sch. Dentistry, 1967. Med. lab. tech. Meml. Hosp., Mattoon, Ill., 1958—59; dir. Ind. Fluride Programs Ind. Univ. Sch. Dentistry, Indpl., 1965—71; asst. prof., 1967—71; dir. allied health programs Ind. State U., Evansville, 1971—78, chmn. div. allied health, 1978—88; head start cons. Dept. Health and Human Svc., Chgo., from 1976. Vice chmn. Met. Emergency Svc. Coun., Evansville, 1980—84; adv. com. Ind. Vocat.-Tech. Coll., Evansville, from 1982; assoc. dean health professions U. So. Ind., from 1988. Author: (book) Sherlock Holmes: On Screen and in Sound, 1994; contbr. articles to profl. jours.; auctioneer Pub. TV, Evansville, from 1976, auction prodr., weekend announcer, engr. Pub. Radio, Evansville, announcer old radio programs. 2nd lt. US Army, 1957—58. Mem.: ADA, Ohio Valley Writers Guild (treas. 1992—93), Kaypro Computer Users Group (editor 1985—90), Ind. Soc. Hosp. Edn. and Tng. (pres. 1976—77), Am. Soc. Allied Health Professions, Am. Assn. Dental Schs., Ind. Dental Assn., Tri-State Computer Club (pres. 1991—92). Avocations: flying, collecting old radios and programs, photography, computer programming. Home: Evansville, Ind. Died Oct. 23, 2006.

KELLY, ELLSWORTH, painter, sculptor; b. Newburgh, NY, May 31, 1923; s. Allan Howe and Florence Bithens Kelly. Student, Pratt Inst., 1941—43, Boston Mus. Fine Arts Sch., Ecole des Beaux-Arts, Paris, 1946-48; DFA (hon.), Pratt Inst., 1993, Bard Coll., 1996, Royal Coll. Art, London, 1997, Harvard U., 2003, Williams Coll., 2005, Brandeis U., 2013. Works exhibited: Salon de Realities Nouvelles, Paris, 1950, 1951, Carnegie Inst., 1958, 1961, 1964, 1967, 1985, Sao Paulo Biennial, 1961, Tokyo Internat., 1963, Documenta III, Germany, 1964, Documenta IV, 1968, Documenta IX, 1992, Venice Biennale, 1966, Guggenheim Internat., 1967, Corcoran Ann., Washington, 1979, others; one-man shows include Galerie Arnaud, Paris, 1951, Galerie Maeght, Paris, 1958, 1964, 1965, Sidney Janis Gallery, NYC, 1965, 1967, 1968, 1971, Betty Parsons Gallery, NYC, 1956, 1957, 1959, 1961, 1963, Tooth Gallery, London, 1962, Washington Gallery Modern Art, 1964, Inst. Contemporary Art, Boston, 1964, Dayton's Gallery 12, Mpls., 1971, Albright Art Gallery, 1972, Hans Mayer Gallery, Dusseldorf, Germany, 1972, Leo Castelli Gallery, NYC, 1973, 1977, 1979, 1981, 1982, 1984, 1985, 1986, 1988, 1989, 1992, Irving Blum Gallery, Los Angeles, 1965-68, 1973, Greenberg Gallery, St. Louis, 1973, 1989, Whitney Mus. Am. Art, NYC, 1982, St. Louis Mus. Art, 1983, NY Mus. Modern Art, 1973, Pasadena Mus. Modern Art, Calif., 1974, Walker Art Mus., Mpls., 1974, 1994, Detroit Inst. Fine Arts, 1974, Ace Gallery, Venice, Calif., 1975, Janie Lee Gallery, Houston, 1975, Blum/Helman Gallery, NYC, 1975, 1977, 1979, 1981, 1982, 1984, 1985, 1986, 1988, 1989, 1992, Met. Mus., NYC, 1979, Stedelijk Mus., Amsterdam, 1979, Hayward Gallery, London, 1980, Centre Georges Pompidou, Paris, 1980, Staatliche Kunsthalle, Baden Baden, 1980, Margo Leavin Gallery, LA, 1984, 1991, John Berggruen Gallery, 1991, Castelli Graphics, NY, 1988, BlumHelman Gallery, LA, 1988, Daniel Templon, Paris, 1989, 1992, Overholland Mus., Amsterdam, 1989, Susan Sheehan Gallery, NYC, 1990, 1992, 1995, 1996, Gallery Kasahara, Osaka, Japan, 1990, Portikus, Frankfurt, Fed. Rep. Germany, 1990, Matthew Marks Gallery, NYC, 1992, 1994, 1996, 1998, 1999, 2001, Anthony D'Offay, London, 1992, 1994, Paula Cooper Gallery, NYC, 1992, 1994, Modern Art Mus. Ft. Worth, 1987, Mus. Fine Arts, Boston, Art Gallery Ont., Toronto, Balt. Mus. Art, San Francisco Mus. Modern Art, Nelson-Atkins Mus. Art, Kansas City, Detroit Inst. Arts, 1987, Huntsville Mus. Art, Ala., Des Moines Art Ctr., Iowa, Neuberger Art Mus., Purchase, NY, LA County Mus. Art, U. Okla. Mus. Art, Berkshire Mus., Pittsfield, Mass., U. Art Mus., Berkeley, Calif., Hood Mus. Art, Hanover, NH, Ellsworth Kelly, The French Years, 1948-54, Galerie Nationale du Jeu de Paume, Paris, 1992, Westfalishes Landesmus, Munster, Germany, 1992, Nat. Gallery, Washington, 1993, Eli Broad Found., LA, 1994, Milw. Art Mus., 1994, Gugghenheim Mus., 1996, Mus. Contemporary Art, LA, 1997, Tate Gallery, 1998, Haus der Kunst, 1998, Met. Mus. Art, 1998, Fogg Art Mus., 1998, 1999, Boston U., 1998, New Brit. Mus. Am. Art, 1998, Newcomb Gallery Art, 1998, High Mus. Art, 1999, Art Inst. Chgo., 1999, Kunstmuseum Winterthur, 1999, Stadtische Galerie, 1999, Kunstmuseum Bonn, 1999, Del. Art Mus., 1999, Smithsonian, 2000, Whitney Mus. Am. Art Philip Morris, 2000, San Francisco MOMA, 2002, Phila. Mus. Art, 2007, MoMA, NY, 2007, Musee d'Orsay, 2008, Haus der Kunst, 2012, Mus. Wiesbaden, 2012, Nat. Gallery of Art, Wash DC, 2013; represented in permanent collections Mus. Modern Art, Met. Mus., Whitney Mus., Carnegie Inst., Albright Art Gallery, Buffalo, Chgo., Art Inst., Worcester Mus., Toronto Mus., Can., Tate Gallery, London, Walker Art Center, Mpls., Guggenheim Mus., NYC, LA County Mus., Centre Georges Pompidou, Paris, Stedlijk Mus., Amsterdam, Kroller-Mueller Mus., Otterlo, Holland, Munster Mus., Germany, UNESCO, Paris, Centro Reina Sofia, Madrid, Lenbachhaus, Munster, Balt. Mus. Art, Nat. Gallery, Washington, San Francisco Mus. Modern Art. sculpture: lobby, Transp. Bldg., Phila., 1956, Barcelona, Spain, 1985, Balt. Mus. Garden, 1988, Walker Art Ctr. Garden, 1988, Mus. Fine Arts, Houston, 1986, Myerson Symphony Ctr., Dallas, 1989,

Nestle S.A., Vevey, Switzerland, 1991, Carre d'Art, Museee d'Art Contemporain, Nimes, France, Holocaust Mus., Washington, 1993; curator Clark Art Inst., 2015. Mem. USAAF, 1943—45. Decorated chevalier Ordre Arts et Lettres, Legion of Honor, comdr. Arts et Lettres (France); recipient Brandeis painting award, 1963, Edn. Min. award Tokyo Internat., 1963, 4th prize Carnegie Inst., 1962, painting prize, 1964; painting prize Art Inst. Chgo., 1964, 74, Showhegan, 1981, medal Pratt Inst., Bklyn., 1993, medal for outstanding achievement Sch. Mus. Fine Arts, Boston, 1996, ann. tribute award Friends Art and Preservation in Embassies, US Dept. State, 1996, Govs. award NY Sate Coun. on Arts, 1998, Nat. Medal of Arts, Nat. Endowment for the Arts, 2012, James Smithson Bicentennial medal, 2015; named Friend of Barcelona and recipient medal Mayor of Barcelona, 1993. Fellow Acad. Arts and Scis.; mem. Nat. Acad. Arts and Letters, NAD (academician, 1994-2015). Died Dec. 27, 2015.

KELLY, GREGORY MAXWELL, mathematics professor; b. Sydney, New South Wales, Australia, June 5, 1930; s. Owen Stephen and Rita Margaret (McCauley) K.; m. Constance Imogen Datson, Nov. 5, 1960; children: Dominic John, Martin Paul, Catherine Louise, Simon Matthew. BSc, U. Sydney, 1951; BA, Cambridge U., Eng., 1953, PhD, 1957. Lectr. pure math. U. Sydney, 1957-60, sr. lectr., 1961-65, reader, 1965-66, prof., 1973-94, prof. emeritus, professorial fellow, from 1994; prof. U. New South Wales, Sydney, 1967-73. Author: An Introduction to Algebra and Vector Geometry, 1972, Basic Concepts of Enriched Category Theory, 1982; editor Jour. of Pure and Applied Algebra., 1971—, Applied Catagorical Structures. 1992—; contbr. over 80 articles to acad. jours. Fellow Australian Acad. Sci.; mem. Australian Math. Soc., Am. Math. Soc., Cambridge Philos. Soc. Avocations: bridge, music, swimming. Home: Pymble, Australia. Died Jan. 26, 2007.

KELLY, HENRY ALOYSIUS, safety engineer; b. Phila., Oct. 14, 1921; s. Harry Aloysius and Kathryn (Markey) K.; m. Mary Maxwell Marsh, Sept. 13, 1950 (dec. 1979); children: Marion, Kathryn, Harry III; m. Margaret Brown Hobbs. BS in Commerce, U. N.C., 1947. Prodn. mgr. Whitehall Knitting Mills, Inc., Mt. Holly, N.C., 1947-50; gen. mgr. Kelly Dyeing and Finishing Co., Inc., Charlotte, N.C., 1950-59; plant engr. Fleming Labs., Inc., Charlotte, 1959-73; sr. mech. engr. Catalytic, Inc., Charlotte, 1973-75; compliance safety officer N.C. Dept. Labor, Charlotte, 1975-90. Capt. USAF, 1942-45. Mem. Am. Soc. Safety Engrs. (cert. safety engr.). Republican. Roman Catholic. Home: Charlotte, NC. Died June 3, 2007.

KELLY, J. ROBERT, composer; b. Clarksburg, W.Va., Sept. 26, 1916; s. Dallas D. and Fannie M. (Robinson) K.; m. Mary E. Wilson, Dec. 25, 1942; children: John, Thomas, James. MusB, Curtis Inst. Music, 1942; MusM, Eastman Sch. Music, 1952. Prof. composition U. Ill., Urbana, 1946-76, prof. emeritus, from 1976. Composer: (opera) The White Gods, 1955, (symphony) Symphony #2, 1958, Emancipation Symphony, 1963, (choral instrumental) Walden Pond, 1975, (concertos) Concerto for Violin & Orchestra, 1968, Concerto for Cello & Orchestra, 1974, Concerto for Viola & Orchestra, 1976, Concerto for Violin, Viola and Orch., 1980, A Symphony of Rose Sonnets for voice and orch., 1993, Fifth Symphony, 1996. Recipient Commn. NEA, Washington, 1976. Fellow McDowell Colony; mem. Am. Composers Alliance, Broadcast Music Inc., Am. Music Ctr. Avocations: photography, hiking. Home: Urbana, Ill. Died July 4, 2007.

KELLY, JAMES JOSEPH, physicist; b. Amityville, NY, Mar. 4, 1955; s. James Joseph and Rita Ann (Steigerwald) K.; m. Melinda Forgues, Apr. 10, 1982; 1 child, Colleen Michele. BS, Calif. Inst. Tech., 1977; PhD, MIT, 1981. Rsch. assoc. MIT, Cambridge, 1981-83; J. Robert Oppenheimer fellow Los Alamos (N.Mex.) Nat. Lab., 1983-84; asst. prof. Dept. Physics U. Md., College Park, 1984-89, assoc. prof., from 1989. Chmn. Ind. U. Cyclotron Facility User's Group, Bloomington, 1989-90; mem. program com. Los Alamos Meson Physics Facility, 1989-91, mem. User Group; mem. Bates Users Group, Continuous Electron Beam Accelerator Facility Users Groups; referee Phys. Rev., Jour. of Physics. Contbr. 50 articles to profl. jours. Alice Patterson scholarship Newsday, Inc., 1973. Mem. Am. Phys. Soc. Achievements include rsch. on empirical effective interaction for nucleon-nucleus scattering, method for measuring neutron transition densities using proton inelastic scattering by nuclei, consistent analyses of electron and proton scattering nuclei. Home: Bladensburg, Md. Died Apr. 21, 2007.

KELLY, JOHN FRANCIS, lawyer, educator; b. Buffalo, Mar. 14, 1929; s. John James and Catherine McGeever Kelly; m. Louise Mary Heretick; children: Michael J., Catherine E. Cabell, Martin P., Theresa A. Poland, Timothy P., Mary L. Gressens, John F. Jr., Christopher D., Dawn M. Siedlecki. BA, U. Richmond, 1951, LLB, 1956; LLM, William and Mary, 1980. Bar: (Va.) 1956. From assoc. to mng. ptnr. Cohen, Cox & Kelly, Richmond, Va., 1956—70; ptnr., mng. ptnr. Hirschler Fleischer, Richmond, 1970—81; mgr. Kelly & Lewis, PC, Richmond, 1981—98; mgr., mem. Kelly & Kelly, PLC, Richmond, from 1998. Adj. prof. William and Mary Law Sch., Williamsburg, Va., 1986—95, U. Richmond Law Sch., 1996—2001. Cpl. US Army, 1951—53. Fellow: Am. Coll. Tax Counsel. Roman Catholic. Avocations: golf, sports. Home: Midlothian, Va. Died Feb. 27, 2007.

KELSEY, FRANCES OLDHAM, retired government official; b. Cobble Hill, Vancouver Island, Can., July 24, 1914; came to U.S., 1936, naturalized, 1956; d. Frank Trevor and Katherine (Stuart) Oldham; m. Fremont Ellis Kelsey, Dec. 6, 1943 (dec. 1966); children— Susan Elizabeth Duffield, Christine Ann. B.Sc., McGill U., 1934, M.Sc., 1935; PhD in Pharmocology, U. Chgo., 1938, MD, 1950. Instr., asst. prof. pharmacology U. Chgo., 1938-50; editorial assoc. AMA Journal, Chgo., 1950-52; assoc. prof. pharmacology U. S.D., 1954-57; med. officer FDA, Washington, 1960-63, chief investigational drug br., 1963-66, dir. divsn. oncology and radiopharm. drug products, 1966-67; dir. divsn. sci. investigations Office of Compliance, FDA, Rockville, Md., 1967-95, dep. for sci. and medicine Office of Compliance, 1995—2005; ret., 2005. Author: (with F.E. Kelsey, E.M.K. Geiling) Essentials of Pharmacology, 1960. Recipient Pres.'s award for Distinguished Fed. Civilian Service (refusal to approve coml. distbn. thalidomide in U.S.), 1962. National Women's Hall of Fame, 2000, Order of Canada, 2015 Mem. Am. Soc. Pharmacology and Exptl. Therapeutics, Am. Med. Writers Assn., Teratology Soc., Sigma Xi, Sigma Delta Epsilon. Home: Bethesda, Md. Died Aug. 7, 2015.

KELSEY, MAVIS PARROTT, SR., retired internist; b. Deport, Tex., Oct. 7, 1912; s. John Roger Kelsey, Sr. and Bonita Parrott Kelsey; m. Mary Randolph Wilson, Sept. 17, 1939 (dec. Oct. 1997); children: John Wilson, Thomas Randolph, Mavis Parrott Jr. BS, Tex. A&M U., 1932; MD, U. Tex., Galveston, 1936; MS in Medicine, U. Minn., 1946. Diplomate Am. Bd. Internal Medicine. Intern Bellevue Hosp., NYC, 1936—37; instr. pathology U. Tex. Med. Br., Galveston, 1937—38; jr. staff Scott & White Clinic, Temple, Tex., 1938—39; fellow medicine Mayo Clinic, Rochester, Minn., 1939—47, staff internal medicine, 1947—49; pvt. practice, chief Kelsey Seybold Clinic, Houston, 1949—86; ret., 1986. Chief endocrinology U. Tex. M.D. Anderson Cancer Ctr., Houston, 1949—65; acting dean U. Tex. Sch. Postgrad. Medicine, Houston, 1951—52; from instr. to prof. emeritus Baylor U. Coll. Medicine, Houston, 1949—2003. Editor in chief: Air Surgeon's Bull.-USAF, 1943—45 (Legion of Merit, 1945); author: Physiology of Flight, 1945, Winslow Homer Graphics, From the Mavis P. and Mary Wilson Kelsey Collection, Musem of Fine Arts Houston, 1977, Benjamin Parrott, 1795-1839 and Lewis Stover, 1781-1850/60 of Overton County, Tennessee and Their Descendants, 1979, The Family of John Massie, 1743-c1830, Revolutionary Patriot of Louisa County, Virginia, Including Early Immigrants to Kentucky and Texas and Related Families, 1979, Samuel Kelso/Kelsey, 1720-1796, Scotch-Irish Immigrant and Revolutionary Patriot of Chester County, South Carolina. His Origin, Descendants and Related Families, 1984, Robert Wilson, 1750-1826, of Blount County, Tennessee, Some of His Descendants and Related Families, 1987, James George Thompson, 1880-1879. Cherokee Trader-Texian-Secessionist. His Papers and Family History., 1988, Travel Journals of Mary Wilson Kelsey. Letters and Diaries from Some of Her Many Foreign Travels between 1922 and 1990, 1990, The Mitchell Family of Tipton County, Tennessee. Their Antecedents in Colonial Southside Virginia including Jones and Bishop Fanilies, 1990, The Courthouses of Texas, A Guide, 1993; contbr. articles to profl. jours.; author: The Making of a Doctor, Mavis Parrott Kelsey, Sr. Early Memoirs From 1912 to 1949, 1995, Doctor in Houston and My Story of the Kelsey-Seybold Clinic and Kelsey-Seybold Foundation, 1996, The Word from Mary, When Letter Writing was Still an Art, 1998, A Cookbook by the Kelsey Family and Friends, 1998, A Twentieth Century Doctor, 1999, The Ancestry, Related Families and Descendants of Mavis Parrott Kelsey, Sr. (1912-) and his wife Mary Randolph Wilson Kelsey (1910-1997), 2002, Engraved Prints of Texas, 1554-1900, 2004. Trustee Mus. Fine Arts, Houston, 1990—2001; mem. devel. bd. U. Tex. Med. Br., 1989—2000, mem. emeritus, 2000—14; mem. devel. coun. Tex. A&M U. Health Sci. Ctr., College Station; friend Cushing Libr.; mem. coun. Tex. A&M Inst. Biol. Tech., Houston. Lt. col. USAF, 1941—45. Named Disting. Alumnus, Tex. A&M U., U. Tex. Med. Br. Mem.: SAR, Am. Endocrine Soc., Am. Hist. Print Soc., Tex. Philos. Soc., Tex. State Hist. Soc., Alpha Omega Omega. Republican. Episcopalian. Achievements include research in radioiodine in diagnosis and treatment of thyroid disease. Avocation: collecting art and rare books. Home: Houston, Tex. Died Nov. 12, 2013.

KEMP, JAMES, inventor; b. St. Louis, Apr. 10, 1942; s. James and Mary Francis (Piercy) K.;m. Freda Ray, Mar. 10, 1965; children: Michelle Denise, James Michael. BA, U. So. Calif., 1964, MA, 1965; PhD, Met. Coll., London, 1980. Ind. inventor, cons. numerous orgns. Patentee multi chamber cushion, multi chamber insole, water purifier, child restraint systems; contbr. articles to profl. jours. Avocations: tennis, swimming, reading. Died Apr. 1, 2007.

KEMPER, WILLIAM ALEXANDER, physicist; b. Balt., Jan. 1, 1911; s. Julius and Carrie (Alexander) K.; m. Genevieve Haile, May 26, 1956 (div. Apr. 1973); m. Marcia Jeannette Berndt, Apr. 21, 1973. PhD, Johns Hopkins U., 1934. Chemist Gas and Electric Co., Balt., 1934-43; physicist Navy Surface Weapons Ctr., Dahlgren, Va., 1947-75; physics instr. Met. State Coll. and U. Colo., Denver, 1976-86; retired. Chmn. USN Aeroballistic Adv. Com., 1966-68; gunnery advisor USN Adv. Mission, Korea, 1968; sci. advisor Commander, Cruisers, Destroyers, Atlantic Fleet, Newport, R.I., 1972-73; U.S. del. The Tech. Cooperation Panel on Ballistics. Reviewer Sci. Books and Films mag. Served to lt. comdr., USN, 1943-46, capt. Res., 1954. Mem. AAAS, Am. Phys. Soc., Naval Inst., Am. Def. Preparedness Assn. (treas. Wyo. chpt. 1984—). Clubs: Balt. Ski (pres. 1939-42). Jewish. Avocations: skiing, bicycling, mountain walking. Home: Lakewood, Colo. Died Feb. 27, 2007.

KENDALL, ROBERT LOUIS, JR., lawyer; b. Rochester, NH, Oct. 13, 1930; s. Robert Louis and Marguerite (Thomas) K.; m. Patricia Ann Palmer, Aug. 13, 1955; children: Linda J., Cynthia J., Janet L. AB cum laude, Harvard U., Cambridge, Mass., 1952; JD cum laude, U. Pa., Phila., 1955; Diploma in Law, Oxford U., Eng., 1956. Bar: Pa. 1957, Ga. 1993. Assoc. Schnader, Harrison, Segal & Lewis, Phila., 1956—65, ptnr., 1966—96. Lectr. Temple U. Law Sch., Phila., 1976-77; spl. instr. U. Pa. Law Sch., 1959-62. Contbr. to Antitrust Law Developments, 2d edit. 1984 Bd. dirs. Mann Music Ctr., Inc., Phila., 1971-98, Phila. Settlement Music Sch. 1984—; Jr. C. of C., Phila., 1962-65; HS Turner Lectr. Com., 2008-13, Entertainment Com., 2005-. Mem. ABA, Pa. Bar Assn., Ga. Bar Assn., Phila. Bar Assn., Atlanta Bar Assn., U. Pa. Law Alumni Assn. (bd. mgrs.), Order of Coif (pres. 1979-80), Rotary Club Phila., Lawyers Club Atlanta, Harvard Club; Fellow Soc. Values in Higher Edn., 1985-, Welsh Soc. (Steward) Phila., Episopal Church Club Phila., 1990-; Dunwoody Village: 2005 Chair, Fire Safety com. 2005-11; HS Turner Lectr. Com., 2008-12, Editorial Board of Inside Dunwoody 2005-13, Entertainment Com. 2005-. Democrat. Episcopalian. Home: Newtown Square, Pa. Died Aug. 20, 2014.

KENDRICK, RICHARD LOFTON, university administrator, consultant; b. Washington, Nov. 19, 1944; s. Hilary Herbert and Blanche (Lofton) K.; m. Anne Ritchie, Mar. 5, 1966; children: Shawn Elizabeth, Christopher Robert. BS in Bus. and Mktg., Va. Poly. Inst., 1971; postgrad., U. Ky., 1978-80. Adminstr. U.S. Army Security Agy., Washington, 1965-69; with credit, sales and adminstrv. depts. U.S. Plywood-Champion Internat., Pa., N.C. and Va., 1971-77; purchasing dir. James Madison U., Harrisonburg, Va., 1977-78, fin. officer, 1978-85; cons. Systems and Computer Tech. Corp., Malvern, Pa., 1986; dir. fin. svcs. Hillsborough C.C. System, Tampa, Fla., 1986-87; agt. Mass Mut. Life Ins., Harrisonburg, 1987-88; asst. vice chancellor/treas. U. Ark., Fayetteville, 1988-92; dir. fin. svcs. Clinch Valley Coll. U. Va., Wise, 1992-97; cons. Computer Mgmt. and Devel. Systems, Harrisonburg, 1997-98; CFO RMC, Inc., Harrisonburg, 1998; fin. mgr. Massanetta Springs, Harrisonburg, 1998-99; dir. fin. and adminstrn. U. South Fla. Sarasota/New Coll., 1999—2002; v.p. bus. Luth. Theol. So. Sem., Columbia, SC, from 2002. Affirmative action, equal opportunity officer treas., CVC Found., affirmative action-equal opportunity officer; credit cons. to plywood and lumber industry; cons. to higher edn. Leader, treas. Boy Scouts Am., Harrisonburg, 1977-86; mem. Ashbury United Meth. Ch., 1975-77, Trinity United Meth. Ch., 1992-97. Served with Security Agy., U.S. Army, 1965-69. Recipient New Idea award U.S. Plywood-Champion Internat., 1972; named Profl. Pub. Buyer Nat. Inst. Govt. Purchasers, 1977. Mem. Am. Mktg. Assn., Nat. Assn. Accts., Nat. Assn. Coll. and Univ. Bus. Officers, Fin. Officers of State Colls. and Univs., So. Assn. Coll. and Univ. Bus. Officers, Internat. Platform Assn., Ark. Assn. of Univ. and Coll. Bus. Officers, Nat. Assn. Cash Mgrs., Exchange (Harrisonburg), Kiwanis. Avocations: home building, designing world war ii dioramas. Home: Harrisonburg, Va. Died Nov. 8, 2006.

KENDRO, ROBERT LOUIS, financial executive; b. Canton, Ohio, Sept. 5, 1934; s. Joseph F. and Anna M (Kvasnick) K.; m. Nancy A. Holeski, Dec. 28, 1963; children: Lisa, Stephen. BS, Kent State U., 1968. Asst. supt. Wickliffe (Ohio) City Schs., 1964-69; asst. to fin. dir. City of Newport Beach, Calif., 1969-71; dir. finance City of Upland, Calif., 1971-76, City of Reno, Nev., 1976-78; dir. property and fin. Airport Authority of Washoe County, Reno, 1978-84; controller EPCO, Reno, 1984-85; fin. mgr. Tucson Airport Authority, from 1986. Bus. adv. council mem. Tucson Unified Sch. Dist., 1988-89. Mem. Ariz. Airports Assn., Calif. Assn. Airport Execs., Airport Operations Council, Gov. Fin. Officers Assn., Catalina Rotary, Reno S. Rotary, Upland Rotary. Roman Catholic. Avocations: swimming, walking, hiking, gardening. Home: Tucson, Ariz. Died July 30, 2007.

KENNEDY, DONALD REID, engineer; b. San Diego, Dec. 7, 1922; s. James Royce and Berniece Estelle (McMakin) K.; m. Jacqueline Marie Harbarger, Aug. 1949 (div. 1965); children: Michael, Robert, Laurie, Paul; m. Wilma LaJune Relaford, Sept. 3, 1966; 1 child, Kathryn. BA in Gen. Engring. with hons., San Diego State U., 1948. Analyst missile flight test Convair, San Diego, 1948-49; scientific staff asst., ordnance engr. USN Ordnance Test Sta., China Lake, Calif., 1949-53; tech. specialist, tech. asst. to mgr. ordnance div. Aerojet Gen. Corp., Azusa, Downey, Glendale, Calif., 1953-65; sr. tech. specialist Def. Tech. Labs. FMC Corp., Santa Clara, Calif., 1965-75; sr. rsch. specialist Shock Hydrodynamics div. Whittaker Corp., Los Altos, Calif., 1975-76; ordnance engr., cons. Setter Assocs., Inc., Menlo Park, Calif., 1976-78; pres. D.R. Kennedy & Assocs., Inc., Los Altos, Calif., from 1978. Cons. terminal ballistician.; researcher in field. Contbr. articles to profl. jours.; patentee in ballistics. With U.S. Army, 1940-43, PTO. Named to Order of St. Barbara U.S. Army Artillery Ctr., 1983. Mem. Am. Def. Preparedness Assn. (life, recipient Bronze medal 1983, ADPA award 1989), U.S. Armor Assn. (winner tank design contest. 1962), Royal Philatelic Soc. (London), Pearl Harbor Survivors Assn., Am. Philatelic Soc., Friends of the Western Philatelic Library, Sigma Xi, Sigma Pi Sigma. Republican. Lutheran. Died Aug. 4, 2007.

KENNEDY, ELLEN WOODMAN, elementary and home economics educator; b. Laconia, NH, June 23, 1950; d. Arthur Stone and Rosemary (Jackson) Woodman; m. Thomas Daniel Kennedy, July 27, 1974 (dec. Aug. 1988); children: Susan Elaine, Margaret Ann. Student, Westbrook Coll., 1968-69; BEd, Keene State Coll., 1973; MS in Elem. Edn., So. Conn. State U., 1982, postgrad. in Nutrition Edn., from 1991. Cert. tchr., N.H. Tchr. home econs. Ctrl. H.S.,

Manchester, N.H., 1974-75, High and Mid. Schs., West Haven, Conn., 1975-83; adult edn. tchr. Derry (N.H.) Adult Edn., 1974, 92; devel. 1st grade instr. North Sch., Londonderry, N.H., from 1996. Author: New England Saturday Night Suppers, 1988. Republican. Congregationalist. Avocations: all hand embroidery, camping, genealogy. Died June 23, 2007.

KENNEDY, EUGENE CULLEN, psychology professor, writer; b. Syracuse, NY, Aug. 28, 1928; s. James Donald and Gertrude Veronica (Cullen) K.; m. Sara Connor Charles, Sept. 3, 1977. AB in Philosophy, Maryknoll Coll., 1950; STB, Maryknoll Sem., 1953, MRE, 1954; MA, Cath. U. Am., 1958, PhD, 1962; LHD (hon.), Barat Coll., 1990. Lic. psychologist Ill., 1961. Instr. psychology Maryknoll Sem., Clarks Summit, Pa., 1955-56, Cath. U., Washington, 1959-60; prof. psychology Maryknoll Coll., Glen Ellyn, Ill., 1960-69, Loyola U., Chgo., 1969-95, prof. emeritus, 1995—2015, dept. chmn. Cons. Menninger Found., 1965-67; mem. profl. adv. bd. Chgo. Dept. Mental Health; bd. dirs., cons. King Kullen Grocery Co., 1985-2015, mem. exec. com., 1994-; ptnr. Associated Growth Investors, 1992; bd. dirs. Crown Mktg. Group, Inc. Author of several books, including In the Spirit, in the Flesh, 1971, The Pain of Being Human, 1973, Believing, 1974, Himself! The Life and Times of Richard J. Daley, 1978 (Carl Sandburg award 1978), Father's Day, 1981 (Soc. of Midland Authors fiction award 1981, Friends of Lit. award 1981, Carl Sandburg award 1981), Queen Bee, 1982, The Now and Future Church, 1984, (with Sara Charles) Defendant, 1985, Bernardin: Life to the Full, 1987, Tomorrow's Catholics, Yesterday's Church, 1988, Fixes, 1989, Cardinal Bernardin, 1989, (with Sara Charles) On Becoming a Counselor, 1990, (with Sara Charles) Authority, 1996, This Man Bernadin, 1996, My Brother Joseph, 1997, The Unhealed Wound: The Church and Human Sexuality, 2001, Thou Art That, 2001, Meditations at the Center of the World, 2002, Cardinal Bernardin's Stations of the Cross, 2003, Blogging Toward Bethlehem, 2008, Believing, 2013 (Nat. Catholic Book award, 2014); author TV play: I Would Be Called John: Pope John XXIII, PBS, 1987; also articles, book revs.; columnist Religion News Svc., 1991-92, 97-2015, Chgo. Tribune, 1992-93; contbr. to editl. page, 1993-2015; columnist, Nat. Catholic Reporter Online, 2010-2015. Trustee U. Dayton, 1977—86. Recipient Thomas More medal, 1972, 78, Wilbur award Religious Pub. Relations Council. Fellow Am. Psychol. Assn. (div. pres. 1975-76); mem. Authors Guild. Roman Catholic. Home: Benton Harbor, Mich. *My principal goal in all my work is to try to understand and to try to help others understand what is so human about all of us.* Died June 3, 2015.

KENNEDY, FRANCIS BARRETT, priest; b. Cin., Aug. 10, 1915; s. Joseph James and Helen Marie (Taylor-Barrett) K. BA, Atheneum, Ohio, 1936; STL, Pontifical Gregorian U., Rome, 1940. Ordained priest Roman Cath. Ch., 1939, monsignor, 1957. Asst. pastor Archdiocese Cin., 1940-52; tchr., librarian Elder High Sch., Cin., 1946-52; asst. nat. sec. Cath. Nr. East Welfare Assn., NYC, 1952-57; asst. dir. Papal mission to Palestinians, Beirut, 1954-56; rector St. Peter in Chains Cathedral, Cin., 1957-70; pastor St. William Ch., Cin., 1970-90, emeritus, from 1990. Sec. Archdiocesan Priest Senate, 1966-72; dean St. Lawrence Deanery, Cin., 1972-75. Pres. HOPE Cin., 1967-72; chmn. trustees Sr. Chateau on the Hill, Cin., 1972—'; mem. West End Task Force, 1967, Cin. Restoration, 1974-76. Lt. comdr. USNR, 1944-57. Named domestic prelate by Pope Paul VI, 1967; decorated knight comdr. with star Order Knights Holy Sepulchre, 1957. Mem. KC. Democrat. Died Mar. 13, 2007.

KENNEDY, GEORGE HARRIS, JR., actor; b. NYC, Feb. 18, 1925; s. George and Helen Kennedy; m. Dorothy Gillooly, 1943 (div.); m. Norma (Revel) Wurman, June 23, 1959 (div. 1971), remarried Nov. 22, 1973 (div. Aug. 11, 1978); 2 children; m. Joan McCarthy, Aug. 24, 1978 (dec. 2015); 4 adopted children. Degree, Tarleton Agrl. Coll., Tex. Actor: (films) Little Shepard of Kingdom Come, 1961, Lonely Are The Brave, 1962, The Silent Witness, 1962, Charade, 1963, The Man from the Diners' Club, 1963, Hush...Hush, Sweet Charlotte, 1964, Straight-Jacket, 1964, Island of the Blue Dolphins, 1964, McHale's Navy, 1964, The Flight of the Phoenix, 1965, In Harm's Way, 1965, Mirage, 1965, The Son's of Katie Elder, 1965, Shenandoah, 1965, The Dirty Dozen, 1967, Hurry Sundown, 1967, Cool Hand Luke, 1967 (Acad. award for Best Supporting Actor, 1967), Bandolero!, 1968, The Boston Strangler, 1968, The Legend of Lylah Clare, 1968, The Pink Jungle, 1968, The Ballad of Josie, 1968, Guns of the Magnificent Seven, 1969, Gaily Gaily, 1969, The Good Guys and the Bad Guys, 1969, Airport, 1970, ...Tick...Tick...Tick, 1970, Zig Zag, 1970, Dirty Dingus Magee, 1970, Fool's Parade, 1971, Lost Horizon, 1973, Cahill, United States Marshall, 1973, Thunderbolt and Lightfoot, 1974, Earthquake, 1974, Airport 1975, 1975, The Eiger Sanction, 1975, The Human Factor, 1975, Airport '77, 1977, Death on the Nile, 1978, Brass Target, 1978, Mean Dog Blues, 1978, The Concord-Airport '79, 1979, The Double McGuffin, 1979, Death Ship, 1980, Just Before Dawn, 1980, Steel, 1980, Virus, 1980, Hotwire, 1980, Modern Romance, 1981, Search and Destroy, 1981, Striking Back, 1981, The Jupiter Menace, 1982, Wacko, 1983, Bolero, 1984, Chattanooga Choo Choo, 1984, A Race Breed, 1984, Savage Dawn, 1984, Rigged, 1985, The Delta Force, 1985, Radioactive Dreams, 1986, Creepshow 2, 1987, Born to Race, 1987, Private Road—No Tresspassing, 1987, Nightmare at Noon, 1988, Demonwarp, 1988, The Naked Gun, 1988, Brain Dead, 1989, Ministry of Vengeance, 1990, Naked Gun 2 1/2: The Smell of Fear, 1991, Driving Me Crazy, 1991, The Naked Gun 33 1/3: The Final Insult, 1994, Small Soldiers, 1998, Dennis the Menace Strikes Again, 1998, Men in White, 1998, also Counterforce, The Uninvited, The Terror Within, Esmerelda Bay, Hangfire, Distant Justice, (voice) Cats Don't Dance, 1997, Three Bad Men, 2005, Truce, 2005, Don't Come Knocking, 2005, The Man Who Came Back, 2008, Six Days in paradise, 2010, Mad Mad Wagon Party, 2010, Another Happy Day, 2011, The Gambler, 2014; (TV films) See How They Run, 1964, The Priest Killer, 1971, Sarge: The Badge or the Cross?, 1971, A Great American Tragedy, 1972, Deliver Us From Evil, 1973, A Cry in the Wilderness, 1974, The Blue Knight, 1975, Backstairs at the White House, 1979, The Archer-Fugitive from the Empire, 1981, The Jesse Owen's Story, 1984, International Airport, 1985, Liberty, 1986, Kenny Rogers as The Gambler II-The Legend Continues, 1987, What Price Victory, 1988, Good Cops, Bad Cops, 1990, Final Shot: The Hank Gathers Story, 1992, Dallas: J.R. Returns, 1996, Dallas: War of the Ewings, 1998, Men in White, 1998, Sands of Oblivion, 2007; (TV series) Sarge, 1971-72, The Blue Knight, 1975-76, Dallas, 1988-91, Young and the Restless, 2003, 2010; author: Murder On Location, 1983, (autobiography) Trust Me, 2011. Served with US Army, 16 years. Recipient Star, Hollywood Walk of Fame, 2007. Home: Star, Idaho. Died Feb. 28, 2016.

KENNEDY, JAMES HARRINGTON, editor, publisher; b. Lawrence, Mass., Feb. 20, 1924; s. James H. and Margaret Helen (Hyde) Kennedy; m. Sheila Conway, July 1, 1950; children: Kathleen, Brian, Kevin, Gail, Patricia, Maureen, Constance. BS, Lowell Textile Inst., 1948; MS, MIT, 1950. Mgmt. trainee Chicopee Mfg. Corp., Manchester, NH, 1950—51; mng. editor Textile World McGraw Hill Pub. Co., Greenville, SC, 1951—54; dir. comm. Bruce Payne & Assocs., Westport, Conn., 1954—58; pres. James H. Kennedy & Co., Westport, 1958—70; editor, pub. Cons. News, Fitzwilliam, NH, 1970—96, Exec. Recruiter News, 1980—96; incorporator Cheshire Health Found., Sharon Arts Ctr., from 1992. Founder Fitzwilliam Conservation Corp., pres., 1970—72; mem. Fitzwilliam Planning Bd., 1970—72; chmn. Fitzwilliam Sq. Dances, 1970—80; trustee Am. Liquid Trust, Greenwich, Conn., 1975—78; chmn. Fitzwilliam Indsl. and Comml. Devel. Commn., 1994—95. Served to capt., inf. US Army, 1942—46. Mem.: Nat. Press., NY Bus. Press Editors, Acad. Mgmt., Fitzwilliam Hist. Soc., Fitzwilliam Swimming (pres. 1978—84), Phi Psi. Republican. Roman Catholic. Died Nov. 3, 2006.

KENNEDY, JOHN ROBERT, plant engineer; b. Frederick, Md., Mar. 25, 1925; s. Francis Leo and Floranzo V. (Marsh) K.; m. Mary Ann E. Clery, Dec. 29, 1945; children: John R. Jr., Eileen M., Katherine A., Michael J. AA, Vincennes U., 1947; BS in Aero. Engring., Purdue U., 1949. Cert. plant engr. Aero. engr. U.S. Govt. Fort Detrick, Frederick, Md., 1949-58; super gen. engr. USDA Nat. Animal Disease Ctr., Ames, Iowa, 1958-79, chief engring. and plant mgmt., 1980; cons. Vincennes, Ind., from 1980. 1st Lt. USAF, 1943-45. Mem. Am. Ex-POWs, Elks, KC. Democrat. Roman Catholic. Avocations: golf, travel, video. Home: Jasper, Ind. Died Feb. 26, 2007.

KENNEDY, VIRGINIA FRANCES, retired education educator; b. Cleve., Oct. 1, 1925; d. William M. and Stephanie (Wing) K.; m. Nicholas Howard Kurko, Mar. 1947 (div. Mar. 1976); children: Jean, Kaye, Lee Ann and Paul Kurko (dec.). BA, Antioch Coll., 1949; MS, U. Tenn., Knoxville, 1969; EdD, Tex. A&M U., 1979. Cert. ednl. diagnostician, TEx. Tchr. Knoxville Pub. Sch. Sys., 1966-67; ednl. diagnostician Ft. Worth Ind. Sch. Dist., 1969-76; assoc. prof. Tarleton State U., Stephenville, Tex., 1976-98. Mem.: Tex. Learning Disabilities Assn. (pres. 1961—63), S.W. Unitarian Universalist Women (pres. 2001—03), Phi Delta Kappa (chpt. 2d v.p. from 1998). Democrat. Unitarian Universalist. Avocations: gardening, working with children with learning differences. Home: Stephenville, Tex. Died Mar. 12, 2007.

KEOUGH, DONALD RAYMOND, investment company executive; b. Maurice, Iowa, Sept. 4, 1926; s. Leo H. and Veronica (Henkels) K.; m. Marilyn Mulhall, Sept. 10, 1949; children: Kathleen Anne, Mary Shayla, Michael Leo, Patrick John, Eileen Tracey, Clarke Robert. BS, Creighton U., 1949, LLD (hon.), 1982, U. Notre Dame, 1985, Emory U., 1993, Trinity U., Dublin, Ireland, 1993, Clarke U., 1994. With Butter-Nut Foods Co., Omaha, 1950-61; with Duncan Foods Co., Houston, 1961-67; v.p., dir. mktg. foods divsn. The Coca-Cola Co., Atlanta, 1967-71, pres. foods divsn., 1971-73; exec. v.p. Coca-Cola USA, Atlanta, 1973-74, pres., 1974-76; exec. v.p. The Coca-Cola Co., Atlanta, 1976-79, sr. exec. v.p., 1980-81, pres., COO, 1981-93, advisor to bd., 1993-98; chmn. Coca-Cola Enterprises, Inc., Atlanta, 1986-93, Allen & Co., LLC, Atlanta, from 1993, DMK Internat. Bd. dirs. The Coca Cola Co., 1981-93, 2004-13, Interactive Corp. (IAC), 1998-, Convera Corp., 2002-08, Berkshire Hathaway Inc., 2003- Served in USNR, 1944-46. Named to The Advt. Hall of Fame, 2006, The Irish American Hall of Fame, 2010. Mem. American Acad. Arts & Sciences, Capital City Club, Piedmont Driving Club, Commerce Club, Peachtree Golf Club. Home: Atlanta, Ga. Died Feb. 24, 2015.

KERKORIAN, KIRK, investment company executive; b. Fresno, Calif., June 6, 1917; s. Ahron and Lily Kerkorian; m. Hilda Schmidt, Jan. 24, 1942 (div. Sept. 27, 1951); m. Jean Maree Hardy, Dec. 5, 1954 (div. 1983); children: Tracy, Linda; m. Lisa Bonder, Aug. 13, 1999 (div. 1999). Comml. airline pilot, 1940—47; owner L.A. Air Svc. (later Trans Internat. Airlines Corp.), 1948—68; founder Internat. Leisure Corp., 1968; co-chmn., pres., CEO Tracinda Corp., 1969—2015; controlling stockholder Western Airlines, 1970; CEO Metro-Goldwyn-Mayer, Inc., Culver City, Calif., 1973-74, chmn. exec. com., vice-chmn. bd., 1974-79. Bd. dirs. MGM Mirage, 2000—10, MGM Resorts Internat., 2010—11. Served as capt. Transport Command RAF, 1942—44. Named one of 50 Most Generous Philanthropists, Fortune Mag., 2005, World's Richest People, Forbes Mag., from 1999, Forbes 400: Richest Americans, from 1999. Died June 15, 2015.

KERKOVIUS, RUTH, artist; b. Berlin, June 9, 1921; raised in Riga, Latvia; came to U.S., 1949; m. Jay L. Johnson. Student, U. Munich, 1946-48, Pratt Graphic Art, 1958-62, Art Students League, 1951-53, 86-88; degree in textile engring. (hon.), Ga. Inst. Tech., 1955. Head mill designer Wamsutta Mills, New Bedford, Mass., 1949-52; car upholstery designer Chicopee Mills, Johnson & Johnson, N.Y. & Ga., 1953-58; printmaker etcher Assoc. Am. Artist, Weyhe, Main Galleries, NY, Ariz. and Chgo., 1962-85; painter, sculptor, from 1988. Represented in collections at IBM Gallery, Bell Telephone, Mobil, Exxon, Mayo Clinic, Mus. Fine Arts, Boston, Pa. Acad. Fine Arts, Phila., Mus. Western Art, Ft. Worth, U. Chgo., Cin. Art Mus., Pepsi-Cola, De Pauw U., Greencastle, Ind., also numerous pvt. collections. Died Jan. 23, 2007.

KERN, IRVING JOHN, retired food company executive; b. NYC, Feb. 10, 1914; s. John and Minnie (Weitzner) Kleinberger; m. Beatrice Rubenfeld, June 22, 1941; children: John Alan, Arthur Harry, and Robert Michael. BS in Math., NYU, 1934, student Grad. Sch. Art and Sci., 1960-65; DHL, Mercy Coll., Dobbs Ferry, NY, 1980. Asst. buyer Bloomingdale's Dept. Store, NYC, 1934-40; with Dellwood Foods, Inc., Yonkers, NY, 1945-82, pres., 1966-77, chmn. and chief exec. officer, 1977-82; cons., 1982—85. Dir. Scarsdale Nat. Bank; adj. prof. polit. sci., San Diego State U., 1989-95. Mem. County Mental Health Svcs. Bd. of Westchester County, 1954-59; mem. bd. dirs., sec. Westchester County Assn., 1950-57, 76-80; exec. bd. Westchester County Better Bus. Bur., 1970-73; bd. dirs. Westchester Coalition, 1972-80, Westchester Minority Bus. Assistance Orgn., 1973-75, Milk Industry Found., 1976-82, Nat. Dairy Coun., 1979-81; bd. dirs., vice chmn. Westchester Pvt. Industry Coun., 1979-82; mil. adv. coun. Ctr. for Def. Info., 1986-97. Lt. col. AUS, 1940-45. Decorated Bronze Star. Mem. N.Y. Milk Bottlers Fedn. (pres., dir.), Met. Dairy Inst. (exec. v.p., dir.), Phi Beta Kappa, Tau Epsilon Phi. Home: retired in San Francisco, Calif. Died Jan. 7, 2011.

KERRI, KENNETH DONALD, civil engineering educator; b. Napa, Calif., Apr. 25, 1934; s. Kenneth R. and Eunice E. (Beck) K.; m. Judith Reeves, Aug. 22, 1958; children: Christopher, Kathleen. BSCE, Oreg. State U., Corvallis, 1956, PhD of Civil Engring., 1965; MS in Sanitary Engring., U. Calif., Berkeley, 1959. Registered profl. engr., Calif.; diplomate Am. Acad. Environ. Engring., Am. Acad. Water Resources Engrs. Asst. sanitary engr. USPHS, San Francisco, 1956—58; asst. prof. Sacramento State U., 1959—63; assoc. prof. Calif. State U., Sacramento, 1963—68, project dir., 1965—99, prof., 1968—99. Cons. in field, Sacramento, 1960—. Author: Operation of Waste Water Treatment Plants, 1980, Water Treatment Plant Operation, 1983, Small Water System O&M, 1993. Fellow ASCE; mem. Nat. Environ. Tng. Assn. (pres. 1979-80, Trainer of Yr. 1982), Assn. Bds. Cert. (pres. 1983), Calif. Water Pollution Control Assn. (pres. 1983-84), Water Environment Fedn. (hon.). Home: Sacramento, Calif. Died Dec. 15, 2014.

KERSEY, JEROME, retired professional basketball player; b. June 26, 1962; m. Teri Folsom, 2013; 1 child, Kiara stepchildren: McKenzie, Brendan, Maddie. Student, Longwood Coll., 1980—84; grad., Longwood U., 2006. Forward Portland Trail Blazers, 1984—95, dir. players program, 2003—04, amb., 2015; forward Golden State Warriors, 1995—96, LA Lakers, 1996—97, Seattle Supersonics, 1997—98, San Antonio Spurs, 1999—2000, Milw. Bucks, 2000—01, asst. coach, 2004—05; ret., 2001; also after retirement worked in mortgage and auto wholesale businesses. Participant slam-dunk competition NBA All-Star Weekend, 1986-89. Active Boys and Girls Clubs; health coach, Take Shape for Life; dir. player develop. Kuri Productions, Inc. Recipient William Henry Ruffner Alumni award, Longwood U., 2015; named to Longwood U. Athletics Hall of Fame, 2005, Va. Sports Hall of Fame, 2008, Portland Sports Hall of Fame, 2008. Avocations: golf, riding horses, collecting classic automobiles and matches. Died Feb. 18, 2015.

KESSLER, SIDNEY H., history educator; b. NYC, Mar. 14, 1926; s. Benjamin I. and Bessie (Weber) K.; divorced; children: Perry Sean, Sybil Bess. BA cum laude, Montclair State Coll., 1948; MA in History, Columbia U., 1950; MLS, Pratt Inst., 1953; Cert. Judaic Studies, Gratz Coll., 1975. High sch. tchr. Logan County High Sch., Sterling, Colo., 1948-49; caseworker N.Y.C. Dept. Welfare, 1951-52; libr. Bklyn. Pub. Libr., 1953-54, Suffern (N.Y.) High Sch., 1954-55, The Rhodes Sch., NYC, 1955-57; instr. history Glassboro (N.J.) State Coll., 1958-63, asst. prof., 1963-65, assoc. prof., 1965-78, prof., 1978-91, prof. emeritus of history, 1991, chmn. dept., 1977-79. In-svc. tng. leader, Bridgeton (N.J.) Pub. Schs., 1972-73; adult edn. cons. Margate (N.J.) Jewish Ctr., 1973; tchr. adult inst. Temple Beth El, Cherry Hill, N.J., 1974; adj. prof. extension div. Gratz Coll., Phila., 1975. Contbr. articles to profl. jours. and books. With U.S. Army, 1944-46. Recipient N.Y. State War Svc. scholarship, 1957, Merit award Sch. Liberal Arts, Glassboro State Coll., 1985-86; named to Legion of Honor, Chapel of Four Chaplains, Phila, 1984; grantee Sch. Liberal Arts, Glassboro State Coll., 1979, 80, 87, 88. Mem. Nat. Coun. Holocaust Educators, Am. Legion, Phi Alpha Theta, Kappa Delta Pi. Jewish. Avocations: photography, classical music, poetry, english as second language, hiking. Home: Deptford, NJ. Died Aug. 10, 2007.

KEYES, IRWIN, actor; b. NYC, Mar. 16, 1952; s. Nathan and Geraldine (Goldstein) K. BA, SUNY, New Paltz, 1974. Appeared in TV shows: The Jeffersons, 1981-84, Police Squad, 1982, Laverne & Shirley, 1982, Moonlighting, 1985, Brothers, 1986, Walt Disney's Wonderful World of Color, 1987, Outlaws, 1987, Married with Children, 1987, Thirty-something, 1988, Sonny Spoon, 1988, Growing Pains, 1989, On The Air, 1992, Tales from the Crypt, 1992, Get Smart, 1995, EZ Streets, 1996, Black Scorpion, 2001, Dead Last, 2001, CSI: Crime Scene Investigaton, 2007, Eagle-heart, 2012, And You Know Who You Are, 2012, Pretty Little Liars, 2013; Films: Stardust Memories, 1977, The Prizefighter, 1977, The Private Eyes, 1978, Team-Mates, 1978, Manny's Orphans, 1978, The Warriors, 1979, Nocturna, 1979, Squeeze Play, 1979, The Prize Fighter, 1979, Bloodrage, 1979, The Private Eyes, 1980, The Exterminator, 1980, Stardust Memories, 1980, Lovely But Deadly, 1981, Zapped!, 1982, Chained Heat, 1983, Exterminator 2, 1984, Nice Girls Dont's Explode, 1987, Death Wish 4: The Crackdown, 1987, Kandyland, 1987, Frankenstein General Hospital, 1988, Kandyland, 1988, Down the Drain, 1990, Disturbed, 1990, Mob Boss, 1990, Guilty As Charged, 1991, Adventures in Dinosaur City, 1991, Motorama, 1991, Dream Lover, 1993, The Silence of the Hams, 1994, Oblivion, 1994, The Flintstones, 1994, Timemaster, 1995, Oblivion 2: Backlash, 1996, Asylum, 1997, The Godson, 1998, Tequila Body Shots, 1999, The Flintstones in Viva Rock Vegas, 2000, Perfect Fit, 2001, Legends of the Phantom Rider, 2002, House of 1000 Corpses, 2003, Intolerable Cruelty, 2003, Neighborhood Watch, 2005, ShadowBox, 2005, Wristcutters: A Love Story, 2006, El Mascarado Massacre, 2006, Careless, 2007, The Urn, 2008, Black Dynamite, 2009, Dahmer vs. Gacy, 2010, Evil Bong 3-D: THe Wrath of Bong, 2011, Dead Kansas, 2013, Catch of the Day, 2014; TV movies Here Come the Munsters, 1995, The Fallen Ones, 2005, Professor Creepy's Scream Party, 2013 Mem. bd. Acad. Sci. Fiction, Fantasy, and Horror. Mem. AFTRA, SAG, Actors Equity. Avocations: swimming, watercolor painting. Home: Santa Monica, Calif. Died July 8, 2015.

KEYTON, JAMES W., religious organization administrator; b. Thomasville, Ga., Mar. 10, 1932; s. James W. and Maude (Redding) K.; m. Katherine Hanna Keyton, Sept. 3, 1954; children: J. W. III, Ginger Keyton Palmer, Sandra Keyton Whalen, Kay Keyton Attaway. BA in Ind. Mgmt., Ga. Inst. Tech., 1955. Pres. Thomasville (Ga.) Ice & Mfg. Co., 1956-82, Colguitt Ice Co., Moultrie, Ga., 1956-66, West End Ice Co., Quitman, Ga., 1957-66; judge Small Claims Ct., Thomasville, Ga., 1964-82; pres. Lifeline Ministries, inc., Thomasville, from 1976. Pres. Lifeline Communicaitons Corp., Thomasville, 1984—, Lifeline Radio Corp., Albany, Ga., 1986—; treas. Keyton Assocs., Thomasville, 1990—. Author: The Master Plan. Mem. Thomasville Sch. Bd; bd. dirs. Vashti Sch. Mem. South Ga. Vols. in Missions (bd. dirs.), South Ga. Meth. Men (bd. dirs.), Moutrie C. of C. (pres.), Casa de Ninos Orphange (dir.), United Givers (pres.), Kiwanis. Avocations: golf, fishing, hunting, boating. Died Mar. 31, 2007.

KIDDER, CORBIN SHERWOOD, transit consumer advocate; b. Madison, Wis., May 8, 1922; s. Charles Joseph and Donna Mary (Kutchin) K.; m. Kathleen Kidder, Aug. 8, 1947 (div. June 1969); children: Paul, Deborah, Faith, Ellen, Jonathan; m. Ann Loring Woodworth Meissner, Oct. 28, 1979. BS, Pa. State U., 1950; postgrad., U. Minn., 1950-53. Data applications analyst Sperry Corp., St. Paul, 1960-64, quality engr., 1965-75, quality audit instr., 1976-81. Vice chair Adv. Com. Transit, Mpls., 1979-85; participant Urban Mass Transit Adminstrn. Consumer Affair Conf., Arlington, Va., 1980, Ann Arbor, Mich., 1982; dist. sec., mem. cen. com. Dem. Farm Labor Party-sec. Minn. SD 65. Served to 1st lt. U.S. Army, 1943-46, 1st lt. Res. 1946-81. Mem. Am. Soc. Quality Control, Nat. Assn. Transit Consumer Orgn. (bd. dirs. 1981—), Minn. Transp. Mus., Travelers Protective Assn. Avocations: computers, politics, photography, graphics. Died Mar. 11, 2007.

KIFFMEYER, WILLIAM WAVEL, high tech planning manager, economist; b. Peru, Ind., Aug. 9, 1936; s. Edward William and Evelyn Grace (Weller) K.; m. Barbara Scott Burkert, Dec. 7, 1961 (div. Jan. 1981); children: Fritz William, Wade Burkert, Jennifer Weller; m. Annette Marie Mulee, Mar. 16, 1981. BEE, Purdue U., 1959; MS in Econs., U. Wis., 1970, PhD in Econs., 1977. Devel. engr. Allen-Bradley, Milw., 1962-64, sr. project engr., 1964-71, product mgr., 1972-74, project mgr., 1974-77; mgr. corp. econs. Tektronix, Beaverton, Oreg., 1977-83, mgr. bus. planning Wilsonville, Oreg., 1983-87, mgr. market analysis Beaverton, Oreg., from 1987. Cons. local firms Portland, Oreg. 1977—; advisor to gov. State of Oreg., Salem, 1981—. Patentee in field (10). Served to first lt. USAR, 1960-61. State of Wis. fellow, 1971-73; State of Ind. scholar, 1954-55. Mem. Am. Econ. Assn., Nat. Assn. Bus. Economists., MENSA, Sigma Delta Chi, Kappa Delta Rho. Republican. Congregationalist. Avocations: music, tennis. Home: Portland, Oreg. Died Nov. 23, 2006.

KILLION, VIDA FRAZIER, minister, writer; b. Blue Ridge, Tex., Aug. 28, 1914; d. Charles Jesse Frazier and Mary Albino (Harris) Snow; m. Olen Trueman Killion, Mar. 3, 1933 (dec. June 12, 1996); 1 child, Dou Vena Charlene. Student, East Tex. State U. (formerly East Tex. State Tchr.'s Coll.), 1931. Lic. min. Assembly God, 1933, ordained min. Assembly God Ch., 1944. Co-pastor Assembly of God, Northridge, Calif., 1948—52, sectional dir. Texarkana, Ark., 1957—63, Abilene, Tex., 1966—75; tchr. Bible Assembly of God Ch., Houston, from 1989. Election clk. Harris County Elections, Houston, 1989, 2000, 2002, 2003, 2004. Recipient Golden Poet award, World of Poetry, 1988, Hon. award 50 Yrs. of Ministry, Assemblies of God, 1933—83. Mem.: Assembly of God Heritage Soc. (life Honor award for 50 yrs. svc. 1983), Cisco Writers Club (life; news reporter 1969—83, 1969—83, cert. achievement 1998). Avocations: reading, writing, music, crocheting, Scrabble. Died Mar. 22, 2007.

KILLORAN, CYNTHIA LOCKHART, retired elementary school educator; b. Collinsville, Ill., June 19, 1918; d. Hugh McLelland and Estelle (Jones) Lockhart; m. Timothy Thomas Killoran, Feb. 9, 1944 (dec. Mar. 1991); children: Margaret, Kathleen, Timothy P., Cynthia, Mary. BS, U. Ill., 1940, postgrad. Home econs. tchr. LaMoille HS, Ill., 1940-41; home supr. Farm Security, Dept. Agr., Pittsfield, Ill., 1941-42; civilian instr. radio operating procedure USAAC, Sioux Falls, S.D., 1942-44, Batavia, Ill., 1944-69; kindergarten tchr. Batavia Sch. Dist. # 101, 1967-93; ret., 1993. Methodist. Home: Batavia, Ill. Died July 8, 2007.

KILMER, JOYCE CARL, real estate company executive; b. Malmo, Minn., Aug. 29, 1924; s. Carl William and Anna Christine (Ostermann) Kilmer; m. Ione Bernice Hust, Jan. 3, 1953; children: Jeffrey, Jana Lee. Student, U. Minn., 1944—45, Colo. U., 1967—68. Cert. in real estate sales Regis Coll., 1981. Lineman Mountain Bell Tel. Co., Denver, 1947—50, recordman, 1950—53, right-of-way engr., 1953—55, right-of-way agent, 1955—83, real estate cons. Grand Junction, Colo., 1984; field supr. US Telecom., Kansas City, 1985—86; project supt. acquisitions Williams Telecom. Co., Tulsa, Okla., 1986; supr. United Tel. Co., Ohio, from 1986. Real estate cons. Butler Svc. Group, Durango, Colo., 1983—84, Orlando, Fla., 1983—84, Livingston, Mont., 1983—84, GTE-Sprint, Orlando, Fla., from 1984, Grand Junction, from 1984, Power Engrs., Inc., Portland and Klamath Falls, Oreg., 1991, NW Pipeline Co., 1991; right-of-way cons. US Telecom, Inc., 1985—86, Wiltel Inc., 1986, Henkels & McCoy, Inc., 1989—91, Baystar Comm. Inc., U.S. West Comm. Inc., Grand Junction; cons. and supr. United Tel. Co., Ohio, 1986; right-of-way sr. project engr. Ill. Bell Tel. Co., Peoria, 1988—91; right-of-way agent, 1991. Active Boy Scouts Am., Denever, 1954, 1961—78; vice comdr. USCG Aux., Grand Junction, 1975—76, flotilla comdr., 1976—78. Served US Army, 1943. Mem.: Am. Legion., Nat. Assn. Ind. Appraisers, Internat. Right-of-Way Assn. (sr. pres. Colo. West chpt. 70 1978—91, internat. dir. Rocky Mountain region 1979, regional chmn. 1982, Profl. of Yr. 1982, 1983, Frank C. Balfour award finalist 1983, 1985, recognition forty yr. mem. 1993). Republican. Methodist. Home: Las Vegas, Nev. Died Oct. 23, 2006.

KIM, CHARLES CHUL, banker; b. Seoul, Korea, Feb. 9, 1945; came to U.S., 1971; s. In Suk and Sung Sook (Chun) K.; m. Soomee Rhee, Jan. 19, 1971; 1 child, Alexander K. BA, Seoul Nat. U., 1971; MA in Internat. Studies, Johns Hopkins U., 1973. Loan officer Wells Fargo Bank, Pomona, Calif., 1974-76; asst. v.p. Calif. Korea Bank, LA, 1976-78; internat. fin. analyst Sunkist Growers, Inc., Van Nuys, Calif., 1978-80; chief fin. officer Hanmi Bank, LA, 1980-82, World Trade Bank, Beverly Hills, Calif., 1982-84; pres. Calif. Ctr. Bank, LA, from 1984. Home: Cypress, Calif. Died Mar. 11, 2007.

KIM, YOUNG-SAM, former president of Republic of Korea; b. Koje-gun, South Kyongsang Province, Republic of Korea, Dec. 20, 1927; s. Kim Hong-Jo and Park Bu-ryon; m. Myoung-Soon Sohn; 5 children. Student, Pusan U.; BA in Philosophy and Polit. Sci., Seoul Nat. U., 1952; PhD (hon.), Towson State U., 1974. Mem. Nat. Assembly, Korea, 1954-79, 88-92; founder, mem. Dem. Party, 1954-55, spokesman, fl. leader, 1967-70; pres. New Dem. Party, 1974-79; under house arrest, 1979-80; co-chair Coun. Promotion Democracy, 1984; organizer New Korea Dem. Party; founder, pres. Reunification Dem. Party, 1987-90; co-founder, exec. chair Dem. Liberal Party, from 1990, pres., 1992, Govt. of Republic of Korea, Seoul, 1993—98. Spkr. National Sun Yat-sen U., Kaohsiung. Author: There is No Hill We Can Depend On, Politics is Long and Political Power is Short, Standard-Bearer in his Forties, My Truth and My Country's Truth. Presdl. candidate Republic of Korea, 1987. Avocations: calligraphy, mountain climbing, jogging, swimming. Died Nov. 22, 2015.

KIMBALL, REID ROBERTS, psychiatrist; b. Draper, Utah, June 29, 1926; s. Crozier and Mary Lenore (Roberts) Kimball; m. Barbara Joy Radmore, Aug. 3, 1962; children: Valery, Michael, Pauline, Karen, Kay. BS, Brigham Young U., 1949; MD, U. Utah, 1951. Intern Thomas D. Dee Hosp., Ogden, Utah, 1951-52; resident Norristown (Pa.) State Hosp., 1952-53, Oreg. State Hosp., Salem, 1953-55, Palo Alto (Calif.) VA Hosp., 1956; practice medicine specializing in psychiatry Eugene, Oreg., 1957-60, Salem, 1960-72, Portland, Oreg., 1972-77; pvt. practice Eugene, 1957-60, Salem, 1960-72, Portland, 1972-77, Eugene, 1977-89; mem. staff Sacred Heart Hosp., Eugene; consultation/liaison psychiatry, 1977-90; locum teneas numerous locations, from 1990. Dir. Out-Patient Clinic Oreg. State Hosp., Salem, 1956—57, dir. med. edn., 1984; asst. prof. psychology U. Oreg., Eugene, 1957—65, prof., from 1977, asst. prof., Portland, 1965, adj. asst. prof., 1982—83, clin. prof., 1983—92. Mem. adv. bd. Lane County Cmty. Mental Health, 1980—81. With USN, 1943—45. Mem.: AMA, Lane County Psychiat. Assn. (pres. 1979—80), N. Pacific Psychiat. Assn. (pres. 1988—89), Am. Psychiat. Assn. (pres. Oreg. dist. br. 1973—74), Lane County Med. Soc., Oreg. Med. Assn. (chmn. psychiatry sect. 1973—74). Died Feb. 12, 2015.

KIM LIANG, TAN, engineer; b. Singapore, Nov. 6, 1977; s. Tan Keng Hai and Seow Aik Eng; m. Loke Christina, Oct. 7, 2006. MSc in Electronics Instrumentation Sys., U. Manchester, Eng., 2002. Project engr. Tat Lee Engring. Pte, Ltd., Singapore, 2003—04; product engr. Hewlett Packard Singapore Pte, Ltd., Singapore, from 2004. Home: Singapore, Singapore. Died Jan. 2015.

KING, B.B. (RILEY B. KING), musician, singer; b. Itta Bene, Miss., Sept. 16, 1925; s. Albert and Nora Ella King; 15 children. LHD (hon.), Tougaloo Coll., Miss., 1973; MusD (hon.), Yale U., 1977, Berklee Coll. of Music, 1982; D of Fine Arts, Rhodes Coll. of Memphis, 1990; PhD (hon.), U. Miss., 2004, Brown U., 2007. Began teaching self guitar, 1945, later studied Schillinger System, former disc jockey and singer Memphis radio station, WDIA (nicknamed-Beale Street Blues Boy, then Blues Boy King, eventually B.B. King), recs. RPM, Crown, Bullet, Kent, ABC Records, ABC/Dunhill Records, musician, singer (albums) Singin' the Blues, 1957, The Blues, 1958, B.B. King Wails, 1959, Sings Spirituals, 1960, King of Blues, 1960, The Great B.B. King, 1960, My Kind of Blues, 1961, More, 1961, Blues for Me, 1961, Easy Listening Blues, 1962, Twist with B.B. King, 1962, Blues in My Heart, 1962, A Heart Full of Blues, 1962, Swing Low, 1963, Mr. Blues, 1963, Rock Me Baby, 1964, Let Me Love You, 1965, Boss of the Blues, 1965, Live at the Regal, 1965, Live! B.B. King on Stage, 1965, Confession' the Blues, 1966, Turn on to B.B. King, 1966, The Original Sweet Sixteen, 1966, 9 x 9.5, 1966, R&B Soul, 1967, Blues Is King, 1967, Lucille, 1968, Blues on Top of Blues, 1968, Live & Well, 1969, The Feeling They Call the Blues, 1969, The Feeling They Call the Blues, Vol. 2, 1969, Completely Well, 1969, The Incredible Soul of B.B. King, 1970, Indianola Mississippi Seeds, 1970, Live in Cook County Jail, 1971, Live in Japan, 1971, BB in London, 1971, L.A. Midnight, 1972, Guess Who, 1972, To Know You Is to Love You, 1973, Friends, 1974, Together for the First Time and Live performance, 1974, Together Again-...Live, 1976, King Size, 1977, Midnight Believer, 1978, Take It Home, 1979, Rarest B.B. King, 1980, Live "Now Appearing" at Ole Miss, 1980, There Must Be a Better World Somewhere, 1981 (Grammy award for Best Ethnic or Traditional Recording, 1982), Love Me Tender, 1982, Blues 'n' Jazz, 1983 (Grammy award for Best Traditional Recording, 1984), Six Silver Strings, 1985, One Nighter Blues, 1987, Introducing B.B. King, 1987, Doing My Thing, Lord, 1988, Across the Tracks, 1988, Lucille Had a Baby, 1989, Blues is King, 1990, I Like to Live the Love, 1990, Live at the Apollo, 1990 (Grammy award for Best Traditional Blues Album, 1992), Live at San Quentin, 1991 (Grammy award for Best Traditional Blues Recording, 1991), Live at the Regal, 1991, There is Always One More Time, 1992, Better Than Ever, 1993, Blues Summit, 1993, B.B. King/Mayfield/Flack, 1994, Live in Kansas City, 1994, True Blue, 1994, Swing Low Sweet Chariot, 1995, Lucille & Friends, 1995, On the Road with B.B. King: An Interactive Autobiography, 1996, The Masters of the Blues, 1997, Paying the Cost to Be the Boss, 1997, Deuces Wild, 1997, King Biscuit Flower Hour Presents B.B. King, 1998, Blues on the Bayou, 1998 (Grammy award for Best Traditional Blues Album, 2000), Let the Good Times Roll: The Music of Louis Jordan, 1999, Makin' Love Is Good for You, 2000, (with Eric Clapton) Riding with the King, 2000 (Grammy award for Best Traditional Blues Album, 2001), A Night in Cannes, 2001, A Christmas Celebration of Hope, 2001 (Grammy award for Best Traditional Blues Album, 2003), Reflections, 2003, B.B. King & Friends: 80, 2005 (Grammy award for Best Traditional Blues Album, 2006), Blues d'Azur, 2006, Things Spiritual, 2006, Woke Up This Morning, 2006, A Night of Blues, 2006, Flyleaf, 2007, Live, 2008, One Kind Favor, 2008 (Grammy award for Best Traditional Blues Album, 2009), Live at the Royal Albert Hall, 2011, albums (guest appearance) Six Pack, 1993, guest artist with U2's Rattle and Hum, 1988, Deuces Wild, 1997, subject, collaborator B.B. King, The World's Greatest Living Blues Artist, Blues Guitar, A Method by B.B. King, 1973; performer: at closing ceremonies Summer Olympics, 1996; author (autobiography, with David Ritz): Blues All Around Me, 1996 (2d prize 8th Ann. Ralph J. Gleason Music Book awards); author: (with Dick Waterman) The B.B. King Treasures, 2005; appeared (films) When We Were Kings, 1996, Blues Brothers, 1998, 2000, appeared in commercials for One Touch Ultra, Toyota Camry with guitar Lucille, 2014. Co-founder Found. Advancement Inmate Rehab. and Recreation, from 1972; founding mem. Kennedy Performing Arts Ctr., 1971. Recipient Golden Mike award, NATRA, 1969, 1974, Image awards, NAACP, 1975, 1981, 1993, Grammy award Best Rhythm & Blues Vocal Performance, Male for The Thrill is Gone, 1971, Humanitarian award, Fed. Bur. Prisons, 1972, B'nai B'rith Music and Performance Lodge, N.Y.C., 1973, Gallery of Greats and Best Blues Guitarist, 1974, Artist of the Decade and Humanitarian award, Record World mag., 1974, W.C. Handy award Blues Found., 1983, 1985, 1987, 1988, 1991, Hall of Fame award Nat. Assn. for Campus Activities, 1986, Grammy award for Best Traditional Blues Recording for My Guitar Sings the Blues, 1986, Grammy Lifetime Achievement award, 1987, MTV Video Music award for Best Video from a Film, 1988—89, Presdl. medal of the Arts, 1990, Songwriter's Hall of Fame Lifetime Achievement award, 1991, Nat. award of distinction, U. Miss., 1992, Grammy award for Best Traditional Blues Album for Blues Summit, 1994, Kennedy Ctr. Honors, 1995, Lifetime Achievement award, 1997, Pioneer in Music award, Nat. Assn. Black Owned Broadcasters, 1997, Living Legend award Trumpet Awards, 1997, Grammy award for Best Pop Collarboration with Vocals for Is You or Is You Ain't (Baby), 2001, Grammy award for Best Pop Instrumental Performance for Auld Lang Syne, 2003, Polar Music prize, Royal Swedish Acad. Music, 2004, Golden Plate award, Acad. Achievement, 2004, Presdl. Medal of Freedom, 2006, Orville H. Gibson Lifetime Achievement award, Gibson Guitar Co.; co-recipient Grammy award for Best Rock Instrumental Performance, for SRV Shuffle, 1997; named

Best Blues Instrumentalist, Ebony Mag., 1974—75, Best Male Blues Singer, 1974—75, Blues Guitarist of Yr., Guitar Player Mag., 1970—74, Best Blues Singer Nat. Assn. TV and Radio Announcers, 1974, Blues Act of Yr., Performance Award Polls, 1985, Most Outstanding Blues Singer, Living Blues Mag., 1993—94, 1996—97, Blues Act of Yr., Performance Award Polls, 1987, 1988, Blues Artist of Yr., 1994; named to Hall of Fame and Best Blues Vocalist and Guitarist , Ebony mag., 1974, Blues Found. Hall of Fame, 1980, Rock and Roll Hall of Fame, 1987, Rock Walk, 1989, Amsterdam Walk of Fame, 1989, Hollywood Walk of Fame, 1989; Nat. Heritage fellow Nat. Endowment of the Arts, 1991. Fellow: Am. Acad. Arts & Scis. *I would say to all people, but maybe to young people especially— black and white or whatever color— follow your own feelings and trust them; find out what you want to do and do it, and then practice it and practice it every day of your life and keep becoming what you are, despite any hardships and obstacles you meet.* Died May 14, 2015.

KING, BEN E. (BENJAMIN EARL NELSON), singer; b. Henderson, NC, Sept. 28, 1938; m. Betty King, 1964; 3 children. Singer The Five Crowns, 1958, The Drifters, 1958—60. Singer: (solo albums) Spanish Harlem, 1961, Ben E. King Sings for Soulful Lovers, 1962, Don't Play that Song, 1962, Seven Letters, 1965, What is Soul?, 1967, Rough Edges, 1970, The Beginning of It All, 1971, Supernatural, 1975, I Had a Love, 1976, Benny and Us, 1977, Let Me Live In Your Life, 1978, Music Trance, 1980, Street Tough, 1981, Save the Last Dance for Me, 1988, What's Important to Me, 1992, Shades of Blue, 1999, I've Been Around, 2006, Love Is Gonna Get You, 2007, Heart & Soul, 2011, (albums with The Drifters) Save the Last Dance for Me, 1962, (songs) (with The Drifters) There Goes My Baby, 1959, This Magic Moment, 1960, Save the Last Dance for Me, 1960 (Grammy Hall of Fame award, 2001), I Count the Tears, 1960, (solo) Spanish Harlem, 1961 (Grammy Hall of Fame award, 2002), Stand By Me, 1961 (Grammy Hall of Fame award, 1998). Founder Stand By Me Found. Named to Rock and Roll Hall of Fame (with The Drifters), 1988, NC Music Hall of Fame, 2009. Died Apr. 30, 2015.

KING, FLORENCE, columnist; b. Washington, Jan. 5, 1936; d. Herbert Frederick and Louise Ruding King. BA, Am. U., 1957. Feature writer News and Observer, Raleigh, N.C., 1964-67; columnist National Review mag., NYC, 1990—2002. Author: Southern Ladies and Gentlemen, 1975, He: An Irreverent Look at the American Male, 1978; Confessions of a Failed Southern Lady, 1985, Reflections in a Jaundiced Eye, 1989, Lump It or Leave It, 1990, With Charity Toward None: A Fond Look at Misanthropy, 1992, (anthology) The Florence King Reader, 1995, others; (as Laura Buchanan) The Barbarian Princess, 1977; mem. usage panel Am. Heritage Dictionary, 1986 Home: Fredericksburg, Va. Died Jan. 6, 2016.

KING, JOHN (JACK), human services administrator; b. Chgo., Nov. 9, 1930; s. John Joseph and Catherine (Clifford) K.; m. Betty Jane King, Mar. 29, 1957; children: Katherine, Kelly, John, Patricia, Maureen, Colleen, Jeremiah, Eileen. Grad., Betty Ford Ctr. Profls., Plam Springs, Calif. Lic. recovery house Ill. Dept. Alcholoholism and Substance abuse; cert. counselor. Supr., rte. salesman Honey Crust Corp., Chgo., 1953-59; fire fighter City fo Chgo. Fired Dept., 1959-90; house mgr. Wayback Inn Halfway House, Maywood, Ill., 1982-83; founder, exec. dir. Guildhaus, Blue Island, Ill., from 1985, also past pres. bd. Lectr. in field. With USAF, 1949-53, Korea. Recipient First Annual Cmty. Svc. award South Suburban Coun. Alchoholism and Substance Abuse, 1993, City of Chgo. award Mayro Richard M. Daly and Commr. Raymond E. Orozco, Sertoma award, 1995. Mem. Ill. Addictions Counselors Assn., Ill. Alchoholism and Drug Dependent Assn., Ill. Assn. Residential Extended Care Facilites (v.p. 1992-94), Blue Island Cmty. Coun. (pres. 1991-93), Assn. Halfway House Alchoholism Programs, Internat. Assn. Fire Fighters (employee assistance program), Lions Internat., Am. Legion, Amvets, VFW. Roman Catholic. Avocations: carpentry, travel, dance, fishing. Home: Blue Island, Ill. Died Nov. 3, 2006.

KING, MARGARET ANN, communications educator; b. Marion, Ind., Feb. 27, 1936; d. Paul Milton and Janet Mary (Broderick) Burke; m. Charles Claude King, Aug. 25, 1956; children: C. Kevin, Elizabeth Ann, Paul S., Margaret C. Student, Ohio Dominican, 1953-56, U. Kans., 1980-81; BA in Communication, Purdue U., 1986, MA in Pub. Communication, 1990. Regional rep. Indpls. Juv. Justice Task Force, 1984-85; vis. instr. dept. communication Purdue U., West Lafayette, Ind., 1992-96; v.p. King Mktg. Cons., Inc., 1996—2002; adj. lectr. U. Cin., from 2002. Bd. dirs. Vis. Nurse Home Health Svcs.; adj. instr. U. Cin., from 2002. Contbr. chpt. to book. Grad. mem. Leadership Lafayette, 1983. Purdue U. fellow, 1986-87. Mem. AAUW, Ctrl. States Comm. Assn. (conf. presenter 1989), Golden Key, Phi Kappa Phi. Republican. Roman Catholic. Avocations: poetry writing, vocal and piano music. Home: West Chester, Ohio. *Personal philosophy: Ignorance is its own reward.* Died Jan. 8, 2015.

KING, MICHAEL, syndicated programs distributing company executive; s. Charles King; married; 4 children BA in Mktg., Fairleigh Dickinson U., 1971. Advt. salesman Sta. WORC, Worcester, Mass.; from sales mgr. to part owner Sta. WAAF-FM, Worcester; pres., CEO King World Prodns., NYC, 1977—2015. Died May 27, 2015.

KING, PHILIP GORDON, public relations counselor; b. Ely, Minn., Apr. 11, 1922; s. Herbert Sidney and Ruth Marie (Trimble) K.; m. Onriette Lebron, Feb. 23, 1957; children: Gordon Rivard, Philip David, Bernardine Victoria. A in Bus., Ely Jr. Coll., 1942; BS, Northwestern U., 1948, MA, 1950; postgrad., Columbia U., 1950-51. Tech. dir. Columbia U. Theater, 1950-51, Houston (Tex.) Playhouse, 1951-52, Civic Light Opera, Grand Rapids, Mich., 1952-54; editor/publicist CBS/TV Network, LA, 1954-60; v.p. Pat McDermott Co., NYC, 1960-62; pub. info. dir. Sta. WCBS-TV, NYC, 1962-65; pub. rels. cons. NEA, NYC, 1965-68; dir. press, radio and TV rels. Washington, 1968—83; pres. King Comms., Washington, 1983-88, Warren, Vt., from 1988; grad. lectr. CCNY, 1962-64. Civilian pers. dir. USO Camp Shows in Europe, 1945-46; pub. rels. cons. NEA, Washington, 1983-88, Prentice Hall Inc., Englewood Cliffs, N.J., 1984, Assn. Supervision and Curriculum Devel., 1984-88, Phi Delta Kappa Internat., 1984-89, Green Mountain Cultural Ctr., 1988—2006, Internat. TV and Film Festival N.Y., 1988—2005, League of Vt. Writers, 1989—2004, The Valley Reporter, 1994—2006. Capt. U.S. Army, 1942-46, ETO. Mem. NEA, Am. Assn. Pub. Rels. Execs., Edn. Writers Assn. Democrat. Presbyterian. Achievements include presiding over NEA media relations from 1965-85 during which the average teacher salary rose from $4,000 to $40,000 and black and white teachers associations merged in 17 southern and boarder states. Home: Port Republic, Md. Died Feb. 23, 2015.

KING, WILLIAM, sculptor; b. Jacksonville, Fla., Feb. 25, 1925; s. Walter and Florence (Dickey); m. Connie Fox; children from previous marriage: Eli, Amy stepchildren: Megan Chaskey, Brian Boyd. Student, U. Fla., 1942-44, Cooper Union Art Sch., 1945-48, Bklyn. Mus. Art Sch., 1949, Acad. dei Belle Arti, Rome, 1949-50, Ctrl. Sch., London, 1952. Art instr. Bklyn. Mus. Art Sch., 1952-55, U. Calif., Berkeley, 1956-66, Art Students' League, 1968-69, U. Pa., Phila., 1972-73. Artist in residence, SUNY at Fredonia, New Paltz, Jamestown, Oswego, Plattsburgh. One person art exhibitions include: Alan Gallery, N.Y.C., 1954, 55, 61, San Francisco Mus. Art, 1970, Santa Barbara Mus. Art, 1970, Ringling Mus., Sarasota, Fla., 1971, Dag Hammerskjold Pla., N.Y.C., 1971, Jacksonville (Fla.) Art Mus., 1972, Worcester (Mass.) Art Mus., 1972, Elvehjom Art Ctr., U. Wis., Eau Claire, 1973, William Benton Mus., U. Conn., 1973, U. Ga., Athens, 1973, Traveling Exhbn. SUNY, 1974, Benson Gallery, Bridgehampton, N.Y., 1976, Louise Himmelfarb Gallery, Water Mill, N.Y., 1980, Wingspread Gallery, N.E. Harbor, Maine, 1981, Alpha Gallery, Boston, 1971, 82, Hunter Mus., Chattanooga, 1987, David Heath Gallery, Atlanta, 1987, Marilyn Pearl Gallery, N.Y.C., 1988, Internat. Sculpture Ctr., Sothebys, 1989, Simmons Visual Arts Ctr., Brenau Coll., Gainesville, Ga., 1992, U. Pitts., 1995, Seacon Sq., Bangkok, Thailand, 1996, Terry Dintenfass Gallery, N.Y.C., 1962, 64-71, 73, 76, 80-84, 86, 89-92, 94, 97. and others; group exhibitions include: Mus. Modern Art, N.Y.C., 1955, Ann. Exhbn. Whitney Mus. Am. Art., 1952, 54, 56, 58, 60, 62, 64, 66, 68, Fogg Art Mus., Dartmouth Coll., Vassar Cool, Bowdoine Coll. (traveling exhbn. 1972-73), Art Gallery Budapest, Hungary, 1973, Weatherspoon Art Gallery, U. N.C., 1974, Galeria Tonay Schubert, Marbella, Spain, 1976, Grand Palais, Paris, 1976, Inst. Contemporary Art, Boston, Dayton Art Inst., 1982, Chgo. Internat. Art Exhbn., 1982, Am. Acad. Arts and Letters, 1995, White House, 1995, many others; collection Met. Mus. Art, N.Y.C., Guggenheim Mus., Whitney Mus., Nelson and John Rockefeller Collections, others; also commissions. Recipient Sculpture prize, Cooper Union Art Sch., 1948, Fulbright grant, 1949-50. Margaret Tiffany Blake fresco award, 1951, Augustus St. Gaudens medal, Cooper Union, 1964, Creative Artist Pub. Svc. award and grant, 1974, Hakone Open-Air Mus., Japan, Distinction prize, 1980, Nat Acad. Design gold medal, 1986, Am. Acad. Arts and Letters, Louise Nevelson award, 1995. Mem.: NAD (academician from 1991, past pres.), Am. Acad. Arts and Letters. Home: East Hampton, NY. Died Mar. 4, 2015.

KINNELL, GALWAY MILLS, poet, translator; b. Providence, Feb. 1, 1927; s. James Scott and Elizabeth (Mills) K.; m. Ines Delgado de Torres, 1965 (div. 1985); children: Maud, Fergus; m. Barbara Kammer Bristol, 1997 AB summa cum laude, Princeton U., 1948; MA, U. Rochester, 1949. Instr. English Alfred U., N.Y., 1949-51; dir. liberal arts program U. Chgo., 1951-55; American lectr. U. Grenoble, France, 1956-57; Fulbright lectr. U. Iran, Teheran, 1959-60; adj. assoc. prof. Columbia U., NYC, 1972, adj. prof., 1974, 76; Citizens' prof. U. Hawaii at Manoa, Honolulu, 1979-81; dir. writing program NYU, NYC, 1981-84, Samuel F.B. Morse prof. arts and scis., 1985-92, Erich Maria Remarque prof. creative writing, 1992—2014. Lectr. summer session U. Nice, France, 1957; vis. prof. Queens Coll. of CUNY, 1971, Pitts. Poetry Forum, 1971, Brandeis U., 1974, Skidmore Coll., 1975, U. Del., 1978; poet-in-residence Juniata Coll., 1964, Reed Coll., 1966-67, Colo. State U., 1968, U. Wash., 1968, U. Calif., Irvine, 1968-69, U. Iowa, 1978, Holy Cross Coll., 1977; vis. poet Sarah Lawrence Coll., 1972-78, Princeton U., 1976; resident writer Deya Inst., Mallorca, Spain, 1969-70; vis. writer Macquarie U., Sydney, Australia, 1979; poetry dir. Squaw Valley Cmty. of Writers Author: (poetry) What a Kingdom It Was, 1960, Flower Herding on Mount Monadnock, 1964, Body Rags, 1968, Poems of Night, 1968, The Hen Flower, 1969, First Poems: 1946-1954, 1970, The Shoes of Wandering, 1971, The Book of Nightmares, 1971, The Avenue Bearing the Initial of Christ into the New World: Poems 1946-1964, 1974, Mortal Acts, Mortal Words, 1980, Selected Poems, 1982 (Nat. Book award for poetry 1983, Pulitzer Prize for poetry 1983), The Fundamental Project of Technology, 1983, The Past, 1985, When One Has Lived a Long Time Alone, 1990, Imperfect Thirst, 1994, A New Selected Poems, 2000, Strong is Your Hold, 2006; (novels) Black Light, 1966; (children's) How the Alligator Missed Breakfast, 1982; (non-fiction) The Poetics of the Physical World, 1969, Walking Down the Stairs: Selections from Interviews, 1978, Thoughts Occasioned by the Most Insignificant of All Human Events, 1982, Remarks on Accepting the American Book Award, 1984; translator: Rene Hardy's Bitter Victory, 1956, Henri Lehmann's Pre-Columbian Ceramics, 1962, The Poems of Francois Villon, 1965, Yves Bonnefoy's On The Motion and Immobility of Douve, 1968 (Cecil Hemley Poetry prize Ohio U. Pr. 1968), Yvan Goll's The Lackawanna Elegy, 1970, Yves Bonnefoy's Early Poems, 1947-1959, 1990, The Essential Rilke, 1999; editor: The Essential Whitman, 1987. Fulbright scholar, 1955-56; Guggenheim fellow, 1961-62, 74-75; grantee Ford Found., 1955, Nat. Inst. Arts and Letters, 1962, Rockefeller Found., 1962-63, 68; Amy Lowell travelling fellow, 1969-70, MacArthur fellow, 1984; recipient Longview Found. award, 1962, Bess Hokin prize Poetry Mag., 1965, Eunice Tietjens prize Poetry Mag., 1966, Ingram Merrill Found. award, 1969, Brandeis U. Creative Arts award, 1969, Shelley prize Poetry Soc. America, 1974, Medal of Merit Nat. Inst. Arts and Letters, 1975, Landon Translation prize, 1979, Hutchinson medal U. Rochester, 2001, Frost medal Poetry Soc. America, 2002; named Vt. State Poet, 1989-93. Mem. Nat. Acad. & Inst. Arts & Letters, American Acad. Arts & Sci., Acad. American Poets (chancellor). Died Oct. 28, 2014.

KINNIER, EMILY P., artist; d. Nelson Palmore and Elizabeth Bott; m. Eugene Howard Kinnier, Feb. 4, 1939. Grad., Pan Am. Bus. Coll., Richmond, VA, 1935; Studied, Art Students League, NYC, 1953—70. Treas. patterson nj br. Nat. League of Am. Penwomen, Patterson, NJ, 1968—69; treas. Richmond br. Nat. League of Am. Pen Women (Hdgs.), Washington, 1977—78. Studied with Laura Glenn Douglas, Washington, 1950—50; studied with Vytlacil, Kantor, Hovannes, Ben Cunningham, Hale Art Students League, NYC, 1953—72; studied with Burgoyne Diller Studio Atlantic Highlands, Atlantic Highlands, NJ, 1960—64; studied with Laura Pahris Richmond Printmaking Workshop, Richmond, Va., 1980—82. One-woman shows include Middle St. Gallery, Wash., Va., 1996—98, exhibited in group shows, 2000, 2002, exhibitions include Juried Show, Newark Mus., 1964 (Second Prize in Watercolor), State Juried Show, Montclair Mus., 1964 (2nd prize on watercolor), Montclair Mus., N.J., 1964, Jersey City Mus., 1965, Festival of Arts, Monmouth Coll., N.J., 1966, Middle St. Gallery, Wash., Va., 1995, 1708 Gallery, Richmond, Va., 1996—2004, Nations Bank Gallery, 1998. Arts bd. St. Pauls Episc. Ch., Richmond, Va., 1982—84. Mem.: Nat. League of Am. Pen Women Richmond Br., Art Students League N.Y.C. (life). Avocations: travel, gardening. Home: Richmond, Va. Died Nov. 18, 2006.

KINZER, WILLIAM LUTHER, lawyer; b. Mifflintown, Pa., Jan. 25, 1929; s. John Raymond and Ethel Naomi (Sellers) K.; m. Ann Marie Rosato, May 3, 1958; children: Karen, Carolyn, Cynthia, Matthew, Mark. BA, Dickinson Coll., Carlisle, Pa., 1950; LLB, Temple U., 1956; LLM, Georgetown U., 1961. Bar: D.C. 1957, Ga. 1962. Atty. IRS, Washington, 1956-62; assoc. Powell, Goldstein, Frazer & Murphy, Atlanta, 1962-65, ptnr., 1965-2000, of counsel, 2000—04, Powell Goldstein LLP, from 2004. Author miscellaneous tax articles, 2 BNA Tax Portfolios. Capt. USAF, 1951-53. Mem. ABA (com. chmn. 1987-89), Fed. Bar Assn., Ga. Bar Assn., Atlanta Bar Assn., Atlanta Tax Forum (pres. 1980, trustee 1978-81), Cherokee Town and Country Club (Atlanta). Roman Catholic. Avocation: golf. Home: Woodstock, Ga. Deceased.

KIPLINGER, AUSTIN HUNTINGTON, editor, publisher; b. Washington, Sept. 19, 1918; s. Willard Monroe and Irene (Austin) K.; m. Mary Louise Cobb, Dec. 11, 1944; children: Todd Lawrence, Knight Austin. AB, Cornell U., 1939; postgrad., Harvard U., 1939-40; LLD (hon.), Union Coll., 1977; DAM (hon.), Embry Riddle Aero. U., 1980; DHL (hon.), Bryant Coll., 1982, St. Mary's Coll., 1986, Ohio State U., 1988. Reporter Kiplinger Washington Letter, 1939, San Francisco Chronicle, 1940-41; exec. editor Kiplinger mag., Changing Times, 1945-48; columnist Chgo. Jour. of Commerce, 1949-50; news commentator ABC, Chgo., 1951-55, NBC, Chgo., 1955-56; exec. v.p. The Kiplinger Washington Editors, 1956-59, pres., 1959-92, chmn., 1992—2015; editor Kiplinger Washington Letter, from 1961; pub. Changing Times Mag., 1959-79, editor in chief, 1979-83. Author: (with W. M. Kiplinger) Boom and Inflation Ahead, 1958, (with Knight A. Kiplinger) Washington Now, 1975, (with Arnold B. Barach) The Exciting '80s, 1979, (with Knight A. Kiplinger) America in the Global '90s, 1989. Pres. Juvenile Protective Assn. Chgo., 1955-56, Tudor Place Found., 1990-2015; chmn. Mayor's Adv. Com. on Youth Welfare, Chgo., 1956, Washington Internat. Horse Show, 1988—; vice chmn. Nat. Capital Health and Welfare Coun., 1960-67; chmn. Fed. City Coun., 1990-2015; trustee Landon Sch., 1960-63, Cornell U., 1960-89, trustee emeritus, 1989-2015, chmn. bd. trustees, 1984-89, chmn. univ. coun., 1965-68; trustee Greater Washington Edn. Telecomms. Assn., 1967-77, Washington Journalism Ctr., 1967-2015, Mt. Vernon Coll., 1990-91; pres. Nat. Symphony Orch. Assn., 1977-80. Mem. Telluride Assn., Assn. Radio and TV News Analysts, Soc. Prof. Journalists (Hall of Fame 1989), Phi Beta Kappa, Delta Upsilon. Clubs: Metropolitan, Nat. Press, Alibi, Alfalfa, Overseas Writers (Washington); Commonwealth (Chgo.); Cornell (N.Y.); Potomac Hunt, Chevy Chase. Unitarian Universalist. Home: Poolesville, Md. Died Nov. 20, 2015.

KIRBY, JOAN HEFLIN, graphics designer; b. Beckley, W.Va., July 25, 1935; d. John Frank and Margaret Ennis Heflin; m. Herbert Weldon Kirby, June 16, 1956; children: Mark Weldon, Caryn Leah, Lauren Lys. BA in Edn., BA in Comm. Arts, Mich. State U., 1956; student, U. of South Sch. of Theology, 1997. Secondary sch. tchr. Houston Pub. Sch., 1956-57; vol. coord. Morris Mus., Convent Station, N.J., 1981-82; art dir. Genesis Graphics, Mountain Lakes, N.J., from 1991. Dir. Challenge info. and referral agy., Kay

County, Okla., 1963, Respite Care of Morris County, 1983-84; 1st vol. Riverside Hospice, Morris County, 1974-85. Named Outstanding Vol. Voluntary Action Ctr., Morris County, 1981. Mem. AAUW (pres. Mountain Lakes, N.J., br. 1989-90; grant honoree 1997), Internat. Guild Miniature Artisans, Nat. Assn. Miniature Artisans, Soc. of Scribes. Episcopalian. Avocations: miniatures, calligraphy. Home: Mountain Lakes, NJ. Died Mar. 20, 2007.

KIRK, JAMES EDGAR, retired chemical engineer; b. Cranbrook, BC, Can., June 1, 1923; s. Henry Wilbert and Laura Orillia (Levere) K.; m. Eileen Beatrice Leverance, June 30, 1949; children: Kathleen Ann Kirk Kucera, Elisabeth Rae Kirk Ingerson, Margaret Louise Kirk Ettestad, Robert Bruce. BS in Chem. Engring., Queen's U., Kingston, Ont., Can., 1950. Registered profl. engr., Ont. Rsch. chemist Minn. & Ont. Paper Co., International Falls, Minn., 1947-57, prodn. supr., 1957-59, devel. engr., 1959-66, Insulite div. Boise Cascade Co., International Falls, 1966-87; ret., 1987. Flying officer, RCAF, 1943-46, CBI. Mem. U.S. Curling Assn. (bd. dirs. 1987-91), Minn. Curling Assn., Rotary, Masons. Republican. Mem. United Ch. of Christ. Avocations: flying, photography, curling. Home: International Falls, Minn. Died Nov. 10, 2006.

KIRKMAN, MONROE WAKEFIELD, lawyer; b. Sacramento, Calif., June 24, 1924; s. Lester Williams and Agnes (Monroe) K. AB, Stanford U., 1949, JD, 1952. Bar: Calif., U.S. Dist. Ct. (so. dist.) Calif., U.S. Ct. Appeals (9th cir.) 1953, U.S. Supreme Ct. 1972. Assoc. Luce, Forward, Kunzel & Scripps, San Diego, 1953-58; ptnr. Reed, Vaughn & Brockway, San Diego, 1958-60; pvt. practice San Diego, from 1960. Comdr. USNR, 1944-46, 50-51. Home: La Jolla, Calif. Died Mar. 14, 2007.

KIRKWOOD, CAROL ELAINE, lawyer; b. Edmonton, Alta., Can., Oct. 6, 1952; came to U.S., 1954; d. Dale and Bonnyle (Watts) Bowen; m. Mark Edgar Hammons, July 23, 1981 (div. July 6, 1989); children: Mark Edgar II, Kenneth Dale; m. Victor Lee Kirkwood, Mar. 29, 1991. BA, U. Okla., 1974; JD, Oklahoma City U., 1979. Bar: Okla. 1979, Tex. 1994, U.S. Dist. Ct. (no., ea. and we. dists.) Okla. 1980, U.S. Dist. Ct. (no. dist.) Tex. 1991, U.St. Ct. Appeals (1oth cir.) 1979, U.S. Ct. Appeals (5th cir.) 1994. Dep. chief fed. divsn. and asst. atty. gen. Atty. Gen.'s Office, State of Okla., Oklahoma City, 1978-81; ptnr. Hammons, Wolking and Hammons, Oklahoma City, 1981-89; sr. civil rights atty. Office for Civil Rights, Dept. of Edn., Dallas, from 1989. Pres. Canadian County Dem. Women, Oklahoma City, 1984-86. Named Outstanding Bus. Woman, Canadian County Bus. Assn., 1988. Mem. AAUW, Okla. Women's Lawyers Assn. (pres. 1983-84), Bus. and Profl. Women's Assn. (pres. 1985-88). Democrat. Baptist. Home: Plano, Tex. Died Dec. 12, 2006.

KIRN, FREDERICK SHELLY, reactor physicist, consultant; b. Kalamazoo, Mich., Apr. 17, 1922; s. Fred W. and Edna S. (Shelly) K.; m. June R. Hoffsommer, June 19, 1948; children: Frederick C., Douglas I., Deborah S., Rebekah S. BA, North Cen. Coll., Naperville, Ill., 1944; MA, U. Ill., 1948. Rsch. asst. Armour Rsch. Found., Chgo., 1944-45; physicist Nat. Bur. Standards, Washington, 1949-54; sr. scientist Argonne Nat. Lab., Idaho Falls, Idaho, 1954-88; ret., 1988. Author articles on fast reactor ops., physics and failed fuel identification. With U.S. Army, 1945-47. Fellow Am. Nuclear Soc. Methodist. Home: Idaho Falls, Idaho. Died Aug. 19, 2007.

KISER, LUTHER LEON, retired school administrator; b. El Dorado, Kans., Aug. 30, 1931; s. Luther Levi and Evelyne Leone (Cousland) K.; m. Naomi Curfman, Jan 1, 1954; children: Christina Ruth, Scott Nelson, Gregory Lynn, Martin Lee. BA, Southwestern Coll., Winfield, Kans., 1953; MS in Edn., U. Kans., 1961; EdD, U. Mo., 1970. Elem. tchr. to prin. Shawnee Mission Schs., Overland Park, Kans., 1955-68; grad. asst. to asst. dir. U. Mo. Lab. Sch., Columbia, 1968-70; asst. supt. C&I Ames (Iowa) Community Schs., 1970-87, interim supt., 1987-88, assoc. supt. C&I, 1987-92, assoc. supt. adminstrv. svcs., 1992-93. Vis. prof. U. Mo., Iowa State U., 1968-90; cons. Heartland Area Edn. Agy., Johnston, Iowa, 1989-90. Bd. dirs. Arts. Coun., Sr. Vols., Mayor's Long-range Planning Com., Mainstream Living, First Meth. Ch., Ames; mem. Iowa State U. Mus. Adv. bd. Svc. awards, Iowa Youth Conservation Corps, 1981, Vol. Bur., Story County, Iowa, 1985, Mainstream Living, Story County, 1987, Iowa State U. Track and Field Officials, 1989. Mem. ASCD (exec. coun. 1982-85, 88-91), Iowa Assn. for Supervision and Curriculum Devel., Am. Assn. Sch. Adminstrs., Sch. Adminstrs. of Iowa, Ames C. of C. (bd. dirs., svc. award), Ames Golf and Country Club, Phi Delta Kappa. Avocations: golf, reading, music. Died Jan. 20, 2007.

KISHEV, STEPHEN VASILEV, urologist; b. Ikhtiman, Bulgaria, Aug. 14, 1921; arrived in U.S., 1964; s. Vasil Nikolov Kishev and Nadezhda Parlapanova; m. Tanya Petrova Stanoeva-Kishev, Feb. 26, 1951. Degree in Premedicine, Med. U., Vienna, Austria, 1940; degree in Medicine, Med. U., Tuebingen, Germany, 1942, Med. U., Sofia, Bulgaria, 1946. Diplomate Am. Bd. Urology, 1972. Intern VA Med. Ctr., Orange, NJ, 1964—65, urologist, 1966—67, Manhattan, NY, 1965—66, chief Sect. Urology Asheville, NC, 1968—76; clin. assoc. prof. Diace Med. Ctr., Asheville, 1970—76; chief Sect. Urology VA Med. Ctr., Salisbury, NC, 1977—86. Attending urologist Pardee Hosp., Hendersonville, NC, 1969—74. Contbr. chapters to books, articles to profl. jours. Mem.: Am. Urol. Assn. Home: Salisbury, NC. Died Jan. 4, 2007.

KISSIN, EVA H., literature educator; b. NYC, Feb. 12, 1923; d. Samuel A. Hertz and Rose Harlam Rubenstein; m. Benjamin Kissin, July 1, 1950; 1 child, Ruth Helman. BA magna cum laude, Syracuse U., 1943; MA in English Edn., NYU, 1949, MA in Lit., 1973. Formerly tchr. Hunter Coll. High Sch., Ramaz Sch., Marymont Coll., NYC, to 1983; adj. asst. prof. lit. NYU, NYC, from 1983. Program chair for docents Bklyn. Mus., 1960-70, writer docent lectures. Mem. Cosmopolitan Club, Phi Beta Kappa. Avocations: literature, theater, art, travel. Home: New York, NY. Died Aug. 18, 2007.

KISSLINGER, CARL, geophysicist, educator; b. St. Louis, Aug. 30, 1926; s. Fred and Emma (Tobias) K.; m. Millicent Ann Thorson, Mar. 27, 1948; children: Susan, Karen, Ellen, Pamela, Jerome. BS, St. Louis U., 1947, MS, 1949, PhD in Geophysics, 1948—52. Faculty St. Louis U., 1949-72, prof. geophysics, geophys. engring., 1961-72, chmn. dept. earth and atmospheric scis., 1963-72; prof. geophysics U. Colo., Boulder, 1972-94; dir. Coop. Inst. for Rsch. in Environ. Sci., 1972-79, 93-94; emeritus U. Colo., Boulder, from 1994; UNESCO expert in seismology, chief tech. adviser Internat. Inst. Seismology and Earthquake Engring., Tokyo, 1966-67; chmn. com. seismology NRC-Nat. Acad. Scis., 1970-72. Mem. U.S. Geodynamics Com., 1975-78; U.S. nat. corr. Internat. Assn. Seismology and Physics of Earth's Interior, 1970-72; mem. Internat. Union Geodesy and Geophysics, bur., 1975-83, v.p., 1983-91; mem. Gov.'s Sci. Adv. Council, State of Colo., 1973-77, com. on scholarly communication with People's Republic of China, Nat. Acad. Scis., 1977-81, NRC/Nat. Acad. Scis. adv. com. to U.S. Geol. Survey, 1983-88; governing bd. Am. Inst. Physics, 1989-95; chair NRC/Nat. Acad. Scis. panel on seismic hazard evaluation, 1992-96. Editor: International Handbook of Earthquake and Engineering Seismology, 2003; co-author: CIRES pp. VIII+183, U. Colo., 2002; contbr. 85 Scientific papers, reports, books. With USN, 1944—46. Recipient Alumni Merit award St. Louis U., 1976, Alexander von Humboldt Found. Sr. U.S. Scientist award, 1979, U.S. Geol. Survey's John Wesley Powell award, 1992, Disting. Svc. award U. Colo., 1993, Commemorative medal USSR Acad. Scis., 1985. Fellow Am. Geophys. Union (bd. dirs. sect. seismology 1970-72, fgn. sec. 1974-84), Geol. Soc. Am., Assn. Exploration Geophysics (India), AAAS; mem. Soc. Exploration Geophysicists, Seismol. Soc. Am. (dir. 1968-74, pres. 1972-73), Austrian Acad. Sci. (corr.), Ret. Faculty Assn. U. Colo. (v.p./pres. elect 2001-02, pres. 2003-04), Phi Beta Kappa, Sigma Xi. Clubs: Cosmos. Democrat. Jewish. Avocations: photography, stamp collecting/philately, gardening, astronomy. Home: Kansas City, Mo. Died Dec. 31, 2008.

KISZCZAK, CZESLAW, retired army officer, politician; b. Roczyny, Poland, Oct. 19, 1925; s. Jan and Rozalia Kiszczak; m. Maria Teresa Korzonkiewicz, 1958; 2 children. Grad., Acad. Gen. Staff. With resistance movement during Nazi occupation Polish People's Army, 1945, chief mil. intelligence, dep. chief gen. staff, 1972-79, maj. gen., 1973, lt. gen., 1979, gen., from 1983; chief Mil Police of Ministry of Nat. Defence, 1979-81; under sec. of state, head Ministry of Internal Affairs, 1981; min. Internal Affairs, 1981-90; mem. Mil. Coun. of Nat. Salvation, 1981-83; dep. mem. cen. com. Polish United Workers Party, 1980-81, mem. cen. com., from 1981, alternate mem. polit. bur., 1982-86, mem. polit. bur., from 1986; dep. Seym Parliament, from 1985; retired from polit. life in the mid-1990's. Decorated Order of the Banner of Labor, Order of Cross Grunwald 3d class, Order of the Builders of People's Poland, 1984 and many other nat. and fgn. mil. decorations. Avocations: hunting, tourism. Died Nov. 5, 2015.

KLASS, ROSANNE TRAXLER, writer, editor, south Asia specialist; b. Cedar Rapids, Iowa, Mar. 29, 1929; d. Raymond N. and Ann (Traxler) K.; m. William K. Archer (div.) BA in Lit., U. Wis.; MA in Lit., CUNY. Asst. to concert publicist; instr. English Ministry of Edn., Kabul, Afghanistan, 1950s, Balanchine ballet " The Figure in the Carpet", NYC Ballet, 1960; freelance writer, editor, journalist, NYC, from 1961; contbg. editor Internat. Ency. Art, 1968-72; mem. editorial staff Woman's Day mag., NYC, 1972-77; arts editor The Trib, NYC, 1977-78; mem. editorial staff Week in Rev., The New York Times, 1978-79; writer, editor, NYC, from 1980; dir. Afghanistan Info. Ctr. and SW Asia Program Freedom House, NYC, 1980-91. Specialist in Afghanistan and S.W. Asia, 1960-2015; sec. Afghanistan coun. Asia Soc., N.Y.C., 1959-65; co-founder, sr. v.p. Afghanistan Relief Com., N.Y.C., 1979-96; script cons. MGM, 1968; lectr. in field. Author: Land of High Flags, 1964, 2007; co-author, editor: Afghanistan:The Great Game Revisited, 1988, revised edit., 1990; editor Opera Spotlight mag., 1980-82, contbr. chapters, articles to books, newspapers and mags. Founding mem. N.Y.C. Opera Guild, 1959-83; co-founder Soc. Asian Music, N.Y.C., 1960; mem. exec. com. Norman Treigle Meml. Fund, N.Y.C. and Cin., 1975-85; donor Met. Mus. Art, N.Y.C., 1976-77, Spl. Rosanne Klass Archives on Afghan Soviet War Eisenhower Libr. John Hopkins U.. Mem. Authors Guild Am., U.S. English Avocations: travel, history, musical theater. Died July 21, 2015.

KLEBE, DONALD FRED, consulting engineering company executive; b. Miami, Fla., Mar. 25, 1936; s. Fred and Anna Margaret (Herstein) K.; m. Carol JoAnn Jensen, Apr. 6, 1958 (div. Aug. 1986); children: Vickie Lynn Klebe Fisher, Daniel Fred; m. Elizabeth Jean Pecsok Dewey, Sept. 27, 1986. BSEE, Iowa State U., 1962. Registered profl. engr., Ariz., Colo., Ill., Iowa, Ky., Md., Mich., Minn., Mo., N.Y., N.D., Ohio, Pa., Wis. Instr. Iowa State U. Tech. Inst., Ames, 1961-62; engr. Stanley Cons., Muscatine, Iowa, 1962-68, project mgr., 1968-70, regional mgr. Cleve., 1970-74; mgr. elec. dept. R.E. Warner & Assocs., Lorain, Ohio, 1974-78, v.p., 1981-84, exec. v.p., 1984-87, Westlake, Ohio, 1987-90, pres., 1990-93, also bd. dirs.; v.p. Stanley Cons., Muscatine, Iowa, 1993-94, sr. v.p., bd. dirs., from 1994; pres. Stanley Cons. Power Devel., from 1994. Bd. dirs. Stanley Design-Build. Pres. Zion Luth. Ch., Muscatine, 1968-69, St Paul Luth. Ch., Berea, Ohio, 1972-73, Maison DuLac Condominium Assn., Rocky River, Ohio, 1991-93; v.p. Crystal Cove Condominium Assn., Vermilion, Ohio, 1984-85. With U.S. Army, 1954-57. Named Jaycee of Yr., Muscatine Jaycees, 1969, Engr. of Yr. Cleve. Nat. Engrs. Wk. Comm., 1992. Mem. IEEE, NSPE, Am. Cons. Engrs. Coun. (peer reviewer 1985—, nat. bd. dirs. 1987-89), Ohio Assn. Cons. Engrs. (pres. 1982-83, Pres.'s award 1980), Cleve. Cons. Engrs. Assn. (pres. 1978-80), Ohio Assn. Profl. Engrs., Cleve. Engring. Soc., Iowa Engring. Soc., Cons. Engrs. Coun. Iowa, Vermilion Power Squadron, Sandusky Yacht Club, Tau Beta Pi, Phi Kappa Phi, Eta Kappa Nu. Republican. Avocations: boating, reading, music, walking. Home: Avon, Ohio. Died Jan. 22, 2007.

KLEEMAN, JAMES ALLEN, psychiatrist; b. Cin., Feb. 22, 1922; s. Walter B. and Elsa (Morgenroth) K.; widowed; children: John, Thomas, David, Bettina, Merrick, Tammron; m. Myrna Briskin, Apr. 9, 1995. BS, MD, Yale U. Diplomate Am. Bd. Psychiatry and Neurology; cert. Am. Psychoanalytic Assn. Intern in pediatrics Yale/New Haven Hosp., 1946-47, fellow in pediatrics, 1947-48, resident in psychiatry, 1950-53; assoc. clin. prof. psychiatry Yale U., New Haven; attending in psychiatry Yale-New Haven Hosp.; mem. faculty We. New Eng. Inst. for Psychoanalysis. Contbr. chpt. to book, articles to profl. jours. Mem. Am. com. Weizmann Inst. Sci. Fellow Am. Psychiat. Assn. (life), Am. Orthopsychiat. Assn. (life), Am. Acad. Child and Adolescent Psychiatry; mem. AMA, Am. Psychoanalytic Assn. (life), Conn. State Med. Soc. (life), New Haven County Med. Assn. Died Mar. 30, 2007.

KLEIMAN, MACKLEN, manufacturing executive; b. Boston, Aug. 15, 1913; s. Samuel and Anna (Kaufman) K.; m. Ida Maletz Kleiman; children: Steven Lawrence, Terry Sue. BSEE, MIT, 1935. Pres., CEO Lynn (Mass.) Screw Corp., from 1950. 2d lt. U.S. Army. Mem. Rotary. Avocation: gardening. Home: Marblehead, Mass. Died Jan. 5, 2007.

KLEIN, ARNOLD WILLIAM, dermatologist; b. Mt. Clemens, Mich., Feb. 27, 1945; s. David Klein; m. Malvina Kraemer. BA, U. Pa., 1967, MD, 1971. Intern Cedars-Sinai Med. Ctr., LA, 1971—72; resident in dermatology Hosp. U. Pa., Phila., 1972—73, UCLA, 1973—75; pvt. practice Beverly Hills, Calif., 1975—2015. Prof. dermatology/medicine U. Calif. Ctr. Health Scis.; mem. med. staff Cedars-Sinai Med. Ctr.; asst. clin. prof. dermatology Stanford U., 1982—89; from asst. clin. prof. to prof. dermatology/medicine UCLA, trustee David Geffen Sch. Medicine, from 2003; mem. adv. bd. Botox, Allergan Inc.; retained cons., investigator Elan Pharms.; cons., investigator Inamed Aesthetics, Q-Med, Medicis, Skin-Medica, Ortho-Neutrogena; presenter seminars in field. Assoc. editor: Jour. Dermatologic Surgery and Oncology, reviewer: Jour. Sexually Transmitted Diseases, Jour. Am. Acad. Dermatology; mem. editl. bd. Men's Fitness mag., Shape mag., Archives Dermatology; contbr. articles to profl. jours. Mem. CAlif. State Adv. Com. Malpractice, 1983—89; med. adv. bd. Skin Cancer Found., Lupus Found. Am.; founder R. Tarlow/Dr. Arnold Klein Fund Breast Cancer Treatment. Mem.: AFTRA, AMA, Am. found. AIDS Rsch. (founder, bd. dirs.), Soc. Cosmetic Chemists, Am. Venereal Disease Assn., Jennifer Jones Simon Found. (trustee), Hereditary Disease Found. (bd. dirs.), Discovery Fund Eye Rsch. (bd. dirs.), Lupus Found., Internat. Psoriasis Rsch. Inst., Scleroderma Found., Dermatology Found., Am. Acad. Dermatology, Met. Dermatology Soc., Am. Coll. Chemosurgery, LA Med. Assn., Assn. Sci. Advisors, Am. Assn. Cosmetic Surgeons, Internat. Soc. Dermatologic Surgery, Am. Soc. Dermatologic Surgery, Calif. Med. Assn., Children's Mus. LA (founder), Dance Gallery LA (founder), LA Mus. Contemporary Art (founder), Friars Club, Delphos, Phi Beta Kappa, Sigma Tau Sigma. *The sincerest form of respect is trust. Being a Physician is all about serving this trust. Also, it is about dedication, observation, obsession and creative intelligence. Who and what I am...where I begin and where I end...is all about being a physician.* Died Oct. 22, 2015.

KLEIN, BERNARD, academic administrator, educator; b. Czechoslovakia, Oct. 15, 1928; came to U.S., 1948; m. Shirley Sonnenfeld, Jan. 23, 1961; children: Yaakov, Eleazer. BA magna cum laude, Bklyn. Coll., 1954; MA, Columbia U., 1956, PhD, 1962. Lectr. Bklyn. Coll., 1958-61, L.I. U., Bklyn., 1960-61, CCNY, NYC, 1965; prof. Kingsborough Community Coll., Bklyn., from 1965. Presenter in field. Author: New Developments in Jewish Curricula, 1965; contbr. articles to profl. jours. Mem. Phi Beta Kappa. Home: Brooklyn, NY. Died Aug. 12, 2007.

KLEIN, CATHY M., funeral director; b. BayShore, NY, Jan. 9, 1953; d. Harry and Marie Routledge; m. James Klein, May 20, 1979; children: Shannon, Chelsea. LPN, Hermann Hosp., 1980; AAS, Briarwood Coll., 1998. Funeral dir. Ch. & Allen Funeral Home, Norwich, Conn., 1998—2000, D'Esopo Funeral Home, Wethersfield, Conn., from 2003. Mem.: NFDA, CFDA, Columbia BOE. Home: Columbia, Conn. Died Mar. 31, 2007.

KLEIN, THOMAS FERDINAND, communications company executive; b. Seguin, Tex., Mar. 28, 1928; s. Rudolph William and Wanda M. (Kurre) K.; m. Irene Nell Bode, Apr. 14, 1948; children: Terri Lynn Klein Filipski, Donna Sue Biggs. Acctg. cert., Draughans Bus. Coll., San Antonio, 1947. Contr. Russ & Co., Inc., San Antonio, 1947-55, asst. v.p., 1955-63, v.p., 1963-73, adv. bd. dirs., 1970-73; v.p., contr. Clear Channel Communications, Inc., San Antonio, 1974-84, sr. v.p., chief fin. officer, from 1984. Treas. Prime

Time, Inc., San Antonio, 1975—; mgr. 222 Bldg. Joint Venture, San Antonio, 1977—. Republican. Lutheran. Avocations: hunting, fishing, gardening, travel. Died June 30, 2007.

KLEPERIS, JOHN VICTOR, aerospace executive; b. aunrauna, Latvia, June 19, 1935; arrived in US, 1950, naturalized, 1955; s. Otto and Elza Otilija (Zarins) K.; m. Margaret Dean, Dec. 28, 1957; children: John V. Jr., Richard W. BS in Math., U. Conn., 1957; MS in Materials Engring., Air Force Inst. Tech., 1964. Registered profl. engr., Ohio. Commd. 2d lt. US Air Force, 1957; advanced grades to col., 1977; dir. program mgmt. Andrews Air Force Base, Md., 1976—77; dir. simulator SPO Aeronautical Div., Wright Patterson Air Force Base, Ohio, 1977—79; dir. SPO cadres, 1979—80; dir. F-15 projects, 1980—82; ret., 1984; asst. v.p. Sci. Applications Internat. Corp., Dayton, Ohio, from 1984. Decorated Legion Merit award DFC, Bronze Star; recipient Air medal. Mem.: Soc. Old Crows, Am. Def. Preparedness Assn., Air Force Assn., Sigma Phi Epsilon, Tau Beta Pi. Republican. Avocation: cooking. Home: Dayton, Ohio. Died Dec. 29, 2006.

KLETT, SHIRLEY LOUISE, columnist, writer, critic, researcher; b. Bend, Oreg., Mar. 31, 1929; d. John Dickinson and Sylva Ethel (Woodard) Hertz; m. Carroll James Klett, Feb. 5, 1950; 1 child, John David. BS in Psychology, Wash. State U., 1950, MS in Psychology, 1953; PhD in Psychology, U. Wash., 1957. Analyst Boeing Aircraft Co., Seattle, 1951-52; rsch. assoc. U. Wash., Seattle, 1952-54; vis. psychology King County Schs., Seattle, 1953-54; rsch. psychologist VA Med. Ctr., Perry Point, Md., 1959-62, U.S. Army Human Engring. Lab., Aberdeen Proving Ground, Md., 1964-66, ops. rsch. analyst, 1966-67; columnist Jour. Internat. Assn. Jazz Record Collectors, Bel Air, Md., from 1979. Reviewer Cadence mag., 1978—. Mem. Internat. Assn. Jazz Record Collectors (v.p. 1985-87, pres. 1987-89, corr. sec. 1989—, Meritorious Svc. award 1989), Phi Beta Kappa, Sigma Xi, Phi Kappa Phi. Died Jan. 5, 2007.

KLIESCH, WILLIAM FRANK, retired physician; b. Franklinton, La., Nov. 4, 1928; s. Edward Granville and Elsie Jeni (Sylvest) K.; m. May Virginia Reid, Dec. 17, 1955; children: Thomas Karl, William August, John Francis. BS, La. State U., 1949, MD, 1953. Intern Valley Forge Hosp., Phoenixville, Pa., 1953—54; intern in med. rsch. Charity Hosp., New Orleans, 1956—57; resident, fellow in internal medicine Ochsner Found. Hosp., New Orleans, 1957—59; pvt. practice New Orleans, 1959—69, Jackson, Miss., 1969—99; dir. spinal injury svc. Miss. Meth. Rehab. Ctr., Jackson, 1980—99; ret., 1999. Capt. U.S Air Force, 1953-56. Fellow Am. Coll. Emergency Physicians; mem. Am. Spinal Injury Assn., Internat. Paraplegia Soc. Episcopalian. Avocations: gardening, farming. Home: Jackson, Miss. Died Mar. 2, 2007.

KLINE, GEORGE LOUIS, author, translator, retired philosophy and literature educator; b. Galesburg, Ill., Mar. 3, 1921; s. Allen Sides and Wahneta (Burner) K.; m. Virginia Harrington Hardy, Apr. 17, 1943 (dec. April 5, 2014); children: Brenda Marie, Jeffrey Allen, Christina Hardy (Mrs. Francis C. Hanak). Student, Boston U., 1938-41; AB with honors, Columbia Coll., 1947; MA, Columbia U., 1948, PhD, 1950. Instr. philosophy Columbia U., 1950-52, 53-54, asst. prof., 1954—59; vis. asst. prof. U. Chgo., 1952-53; vis. lectr. philosophy and Russian Bryn Mawr Coll., 1959—60, assoc. prof. philosophy and Russian, 1960-66, prof. philosophy, 1966-81, Milton C. Nahm prof. philosophy, 1981-91, chmn. dept., 1977-82, chmn. Dept. Russian, 1990-91, Milton C. Nahm prof. emeritus, 1991—2014, Katharine E. McBride prof. philosophy, 1992-93; adj. rsch. prof. history of ideas Clemson U., 2005—14. Lectr. Free U., West Berlin, Heidelberg U., Marburg U., Germany, London Sch. Economics & Polit. Sci., Mid East Tech. U., Ankara, Turkey, Oxford (Eng.) U., Queens U., Belfast, Trinity Coll., Dublin, U. Belgrade, U. Zagreb, Yugoslavia, U. P.R., Uppsala U., Sweden; internat. conf. participant, Austria, Can., Denmark, Eng., France, Germany, Italy, Mex., The Netherlands, Russia, Scotland. Author: Spinoza in Soviet Philosophy, 1952, 1981, partial German transl., 1971, Religious and Anti-Religious Thought in Russia, 1968 (nominated for the Emerson prize of the Phi Beta Kappa Soc., 1969); author: (with others) Continuity and Change in Russian and Soviet Thought, 1955, Marx and the Western World, 1967, Hegel and the Philosophy of Religion, 1970, Sartre: A Collection of Critical Essays, 1971, Hegel and the History of Philosophy, 1974, Dissent in the USSR: Politics, Ideology, and People, 1975, Speculum Spinozanum, 1977, Western Philosophical Systems in Russian Literature, 1979, Vico and Marx: Affinities and Contrasts, 1983, Nineteenth Century Religious Thought in the West, 1985, Spinoza nel 350 anniversario della nascita, 1985, Hegel and Whitehead: Contemporary Perspectives on Systematic Philosophy, 1986, George Lukács and His World: A Reassessment, 1987, Dictionary of Literary Biography Yearbook, 1987, 1988, Europa und die Folgen: Castelgandolfo-Gespräche, 1987, 1988, Hegel and His Critics, 1989, Brodsky's Poetics and Aesthetics, 1990, Spinoza: Issues and Directions, 1990, Histoire de la littérature russe, 1990, The Trotsky Reappraisal, 1992, Metaphysics as Foundation: Essays in Honor of Ivor Leclerc, 1993, Philosophical Imagination and Cultural Memory, 1993, Hryhorij Savyč Skovoroda: An Anthology of Critical Articles, 1994, Phenomenology and Skepticism: Essays in Honor of James M. Edie, 1996, Russian Religious Thought, 1996, Iosif Brodskii: Trudy i dni, 1998, A William Ernest Hocking Reader, 2004, Gustav Shpet's Contribution to Philosophy and Cultural Theory, 2009; translator: A History of Russian Philosophy (V.V. Zenkovsky) 2 Vols., 1953, 2003, Boris Pasternak: Seven Poems, 1969, 1972, Joseph Brodsky: Selected Poems, 1973; co-translator: A Part of Speech (Joseph Brodsky), 1980, To Urania (Joseph Brodsky), 1988; editor: Soviet Education, 1957, Portuguese transl., 1959, Alfred North Whitehead: Essays on his Philosophy, 1963, 1989; editor, contbr.: European Philosophy Today, 1965; co-editor: Iosif Brodskii: Ostanovka v pustyne, 1970, 2000; co-editor, contbr.: Russian Philosophy 3 Vols., 1965, 1969, 1976, 1984, Explorations in Whitehead's Philosophy, 1983, Philosophical Sovietology, 1988; co-editor: Jour. Philosophy, 1959—64; cons. editor:, 1964—78, Ency. Philosophy, 1962—67, Studies in Soviet Thought (now Studies in East European Thought), from 1962, Jour. Value Inquiry, from 1967, Process Studies, 1971—2007, Soviet Union, 1975—80, Philosophy Research Archives (now Jour. Philos. Rsch.), from 1975, Jour. History of Ideas, 1976—86, 1988—98, Slavic Review, 1977—79, Soviet Studies in Philosophy (now Russian Studies in Philosophy), from 1987, History of Philosophy Quar., 1990—93, Skepsis, from 1990, Symposion: A Journal of Russian Thought, from 1996, cons. editor philosophy: Current Digest of Soviet Press, 1961—64; contbr. articles to nat. and internat. jours.; works transl. into numerous fgn. languages. Served with USAAC, 1942-45. Decorated D.F.C, 1944; Cutting traveling fellow Paris, 1949-50; Fulbright fellow Paris, 1950, 79; Ford fellow Paris, 1954-55; Rockefeller fellow USSR and East Europe, 1960; Nat. Endowment for Humanities sr. fellow, 1970-71; Guggenheim fellow, 1978-79; recipient Disting. Career award, Needham HS, Mass., 1995. Mem.: Zenkovsky Soc. Historians of Russian Philosophy in Moscow (hon.), American Philos. Assn. (exec. com. eastern divsn. 1990-93), Metaphys. Soc. American (councillor 1969-71, 78-82, v.p. 1984-85, pres. 1985-86, del. to American Coun. Learned Socs., 1994-97), Philosophy Edn. Soc. (pub. Rev. Metaphys., dir. 1966-90), Soc. Phenomenology and Existential Philosophy, American Assn. Advancement Slavic Studies (now Assn. for Slavic, East European, and Eurasian Studies) (dir. 1972-75, award for Disting. Contbns. to Slavic Studies 1999), Hegel Soc. America (councillor 1968-70, 74-78, v.p. 1971-73, pres. 1984-86), Soc. Advancement America Philosophy, Phi Beta Kappa (nominated Emerson prize). Achievements include the Kline fellowships, which since 2004, have made it possible for 60 students and junior faculty members to spend a semester or more in Russia. Home: Anderson, SC. Died Oct. 23, 2014.

KLINE, JERRY ROBERT, retired administrative judge, ecologist; b. Mpls., May 20, 1932; s. Frederick Andrew and Margaret (Wicklund) K.; m. Alice Nell Reed, Sept. 4, 1954 (dec. 1999); children: Steven, Jennifer, Robert, Neil, Daniel. BS, U. Minn., 1957, MS, 1960, PhD, 1964. Postdoctoral rsch. assn. Argonne Nat. Lab., Ill., 1964-65, group leader rsch. Ill., 1968-74; scientist, dir. Rainforest Project P.R. Nuclear Ctr., 1965-68; sr. scientist Nuclear Regulatory Commn., Washington, 1974-80, adminstrv. judge, 1980—99. Contbr. articles to profl. jours., chpts. to books. Bd. dirs., chmn. Cedar Lane Unitarian Ch. Served with U.S. Army, 1950-53. Recipient NRC Spl. Achievement award, 1979. Mem. Nature Conservancy, Sigma Xi. Avocations: travel, gardening. Home: Silver Spring, Md. Died Oct. 29, 2015.

KLUCK, EDWARD PAUL, chief of police; b. Irvington, NJ, Oct. 8, 1946; s. Arthur and Dolores (Wesoloski) K.; m. Theresa Helen Moore, May 11, 1973. Grad., FBI Acad., Avantico, Va., 1979. Chief of police, Madison, N.J. Vol. Project Cmty. Aide, Madison, 1976—; mem. Madison Alliance Drug Use, 1990—. Staff sgt. USAF, 1965-69. Mem. Internat. Chiefs of Police Assn., N.J. Pub. Mgrs. Assn., FBI Nat. Graduates, Madison Golf Club. Died Nov. 23, 2006.

KLUTZOW, FRIEDRICH WILHELM, retired neuropathologist; b. Bandoeng, Dutch East Indies, Aug. 6, 1923; arrived in US, 1953; s. Rudolph F.W. and Pauline (Van Thiel) K.; m. Apr. 2, 1954; children: Judith A., Michael J.; m. Merlene Hutto Byars, Dec. 10, 1999. MD, U. Utrecht, Netherlands, 1951. Diplomate Am. Bd. Neuropathology and Anatomic Pathology., 1972. Chief of staff Cmty. Meml. Hosp., Oconto Falls, Wis., 1965-68; pathology resident U. Wis., Madison, 1968-71, Armed Forces Inst. Pathology, Washington, 1971—72; neuropathologist VA Hosp., Mpls., 1972-75, dir. pathology dept. Brockton, Mass., 1975-83, Wichita, Kans., 1983-87, chief of staff Bath, N.Y., 1987-90, ret. neuropathologist Bay Pines, Fla., 1991—2011; ret., 2011. Clin. assoc. prof. pathology U. Rochester (N.Y.) Sch. Medicine, U. South Fla., Tampa; cons. in neuropathology Minn. Bd. Med. Practice, 1998—2011, Internat. Biographical Ctr., 2007; invited spkr. Oxford U., England, 1997, Lisbon, Portugal, 1999, U. Cambridge, England, 2001. Prin. author: Neuropathology Manual: The Practical Approach, 1996; contbr. articles to profl. jours. Col. USAR, 1979-85. Recipient Paul Harris fellowship, Rotary Internat., Bath, NY, 1990, Outstanding Career award, Dept. Vet. Affairs, Washington, 1990; named to Hall Fame, Am. Biog. Inst., 2002. Fellow: Coll. Am. Pathologists; mem.: Internat. Soc. Neuropathology, Am. Assn. Neuropathologists. Republican. Achievements include research in persistent vegetative state; practical approach to lesions in neuropathology; the therapeutic potential of food, which can virtually cure any illness, including many cancers. Home: West Columbia, SC. Died Feb. 27, 2015.

KNAPP, DOROTHY TESTER, retired primary and elementary school educator; b. Nampa, Idaho, June 13, 1935; d. Walter Vernon and Dora Dorothy (Peters) Tester; children: David D., Mark E. BA, Kansas City Coll. and Bible Sch., Overland Park, Kans., 1958; BS in Edn., Lincoln U., 1965, MS in Guidance/Counseling, 1968. Cert. elem. sch. tchr., cert. elem. and secondary sch. guidance counselor, cert. elem. and secondary sch. psychol. examiner, Mo. Elem. tchr. Ft. Osage Sch. Dist., Blue Hills, Mo., 1959, Cole R-V Schs., Eugene, Mo., 1959-73, New Bloomfield (Mo.) Schs., 1970-74, Centertown (Mo.) Elem. Sch., 1973-74; high sch. counselor Sch. of the Osage, Lake Ozark, Mo., 1974-88, tchr. kindergarten, 1988-91, ret., 1991. Mem. Assn. Am. Ret. Persons, Assn. Nazarene Social Workers, Mo. State Tchrs. Assn. Mem. Ch. of the Nazarene. Avocations: music, gardening, reading. Home: Loveland, Colo. Died Dec. 30, 2006.

KNAUSS, JOHN ATKINSON, retired federal agency administrator, oceanographer, educator, retired dean; b. Detroit, Sept. 1, 1925; s. Karl Ernst and Loise (Atkinson) K.; m. Marilyn Mattson, Sept. 6, 1954 (dec. 2007); children: Karl, William. BS, MIT, 1946; MS, U. Mich., 1949; PhD, U. Calif., 1959; DSc (hon.), U R.I., 1992. Oceanographer Navy Electronics Lab, San Diego, 1947, Office Naval Rsch., 1949-51, Scripps Instn. Oceanography, 1951-52, 55-62; prof. Grad. Sch. Oceanography, U. R.I., Narragansett, 1962-90, dean, 1962-87, provost for marine affairs, 1969-82, v.p. marine programs, 1982-87, prof., dean emeritus, from 1990; undersecretary for oceans and atmosphere Dept. Commerce, Washington, 1989-93; adminstr. Nat. Oceanic and Atmospheric Adminstrn., Washington, 1989-93; U.S. commr. Internat. Whaling Commn., 1991-93; rsch. assoc. Scripps Inst. Oceanography U. Calif., San Diego, 1993—2004. Leader 10 oceanographic expdns. to study oceanic circulation, 1955-65; chair US phys.-chem. panel Internat. Indian Ocean Expdn., 1959-62; mem. Pres's. Commn. on Marine Scis., Engring. and Resources, 1967-68; mem. State Dept. Pub. Adv. Com. on Law of Sea, 1970-82; chair sr. adv. com. on environ. scis. Ctr. for Energy and Environ. Rsch., U. PR, 1977-80; mem. Nat. Adv. Com. on Oceans and Atmosphere, 1978-85, vice chair, 1979-81, chair 1981-85; chair bd. govs. Joint Oceanographic Instns., Inc., 1978-80; co-founder Law of Sea Inst., mem. exec. bd. 1965-76, 82-87; bd. dirs. Coun. for Ocean Law, 1983-89, 94-01; chair marine divsn. Nat. Assn. State U. and Land Grant Colls., 1984-85; chair Joint Oceanographic Instns. for Deep Earth Sampling, 1984-86; bd. dirs. Harbor Br. Oceanographic Instn., 1987-89; 1st vice chmn. Intergovernmental Oceanographic Commn., 1991-93; mem. bd. trustees Bermuda Biological Sta. Rsch., 1995-05, life trustee, 2005-; mem. ocean rsch. adv. panel Nat. Oceanographic Rsch. Leadership Coun., 1998-02, chair, 1998-02, Sea Grant adv. com., 2003-05. US Congress renamed its Sea Grant fellowship the Dean John A. Knauss Fellowship program in 1987. With USNR, 1943-46, 53-54. Named to RI Heritage Hall of Fame, 1983; recipient Albatross award Am. Miscellaneous Soc., 1959, Nat. Sea Grant award, 1974. Fellow AAAS (v.p. 1972-73), Am. Geophys. Union (pres. oceanography sect. 1965-67, pres-elect 1996-98, pres. 1998-2000, Ocean Sci. award 1988); mem. Am. Meteorol. Soc. (hon., coun. 1980-82). Home: Saunderstown, RI. Died Nov. 19, 2015.

KNAUST, CLARA DOSS, retired elementary school educator; b. Freistatt, Mo., Feb. 18, 1922; d. John Fredrick and Hedwig Louise (Brockschmidt) Doss; m. Donald Knaust, July 7, 1946 (dec.); children: Karen Louise, Ramona Elizabeth, Heidi Marie. BS in Edn., S.W. Mo. State U., 1969. Elem. tchr. Trinity Luth. Sch., Freistatt, 1942-46; tchr. kindergarten Trinity Luth Ch., Springfield, Mo., 1961-65, Redeemer Luth Ch., Springfield, 1962-63, 66-69, Springfield R-12 Sch. System, 1969-70, 73-84, elem. tchr., 1970-73; elem. and kindergarten tchr. Springfield Luth. Sch., 1984-88. Mem. planning bd. Early Childhood Conf., U. Mo., Columbia, 1977-80. Pres. Springfield Gen. Hosp. Guild, 1969-71; local and zone pres. Luth. Women's Missionary League, Springfield, 1986-94; historian Trinity Luth. Ch., 1985-94; chair bd. edn. Grace Luth. Ch., Tulsa. Mem. Assn. for Childhood Edn. Internat. (br. state pres. 1980-84, president's coun. 1983-85, Hall of Fame plaque 1988, state pres. 1989-93), Springfield Edn. Assn. (life), Springfield Luth. Sch. Assn. (pres. 1992-94), S.W. Dist. Kindergarten Assn. (pres. 1978-79), Alpha Delta Kappa. Avocations: painting, crafts, collecting, music. Home: Tulsa, Okla. Died Mar. 18, 2007.

KNIGHT, EDWARD R., judge, psychologist, law educator; b. Milw., Oct. 5, 1917; s. Harry and Lillian (Bachman) K.; m. Judith A. Weidberg, July 6, 1941; 1 child, Barbara Jane. AB, U. Wis., 1940, JD, 1941; AM, NYU, 1942, PhD, 1943. Bar: Wis. 1941, N.J. 1976; diplomate Am. Bd. Profl. Psychology. Master Oxford Acad., Pleasantville, NJ, 1941, psychologist, 1942, head psychologist, 1943, asst. headmaster, 1945-47, headmaster, 1947-73, emeritus, from 1973. U.S. magistrate judge, 1976—; judge Mcpl. Ct., Margate City, N.J., 1976-81; ptnr. Fox, Rothschild, Atlantic City, N.J., 1976—; dir. First Fidelity Bank, 1950-90. Pres., bd. govs. Atlantic City Med. Ctr., 1973-87, chmn. emeritus, 1987—; chmn. Master Planning Bd., Egg Harbor Twp., N.J., 1961-73; chmn. Atlantic County (N.J.) Charter Study Commn., 1973-74. Author: Self-Discipline and Academic Failure; mem. editl. bd. Parental Delinquency; contbr. articles on edn. and psychology to profl. jours. Capt., USAAF, 1943-45; personnel com., personnel div. ATSC, Wright Field. Named Trustee of Century, Atlantic City Med. Ctr., 1998. Fellow APA (sch. psychologists div.); mem. Ea. N.J. psychol. assns., Nat. Assn. Ind. Schs., N.J. Assn. Sch. Psychologists, Interam. Soc. Psychology, Boarding Sch. Headmasters Assn. Mid. States (pres. 1966-67), Wis. Alumni Assn., U. Wis. Mem. Union (life), Atlanticare Health Sys. (vice-chmn. bd.), Phi Delta Kappa, Kappa Delta Pi. Home: Margate City, NJ. Died Apr. 12, 2014.

KNIGHTS, PHYLLIS LOUISE, tax preparer, accountant; b. Hartford, Conn., Jan. 6, 1943; d. Harold Daniel and Louise Edith (Hart) Hall; m. Richard Lowe, Sept. 2, 1960 (div. Sept. 1995); children: Richard, James, Daniel, Charles, Debbie Sue, Penny Candy; m. Weldon G. Knights, Sept. 17, 1983; stepchildren: Lynn, Peter, Terry. BSA, Plymouth State Coll., 1984, MBA, 1986. Cert. accreditation Coun. Acctg.

Owner H & R Block Satellite, Bellows Falls, Vt., 1970-74, Littleton, N.H., 1975-80, Knights Tax Svc., Monroe, N.H., from 1983. Contbr. articles to newsletters. Bd. dirs. Littleton Self-Help Clinic, 1979-86; town chair Reps. for Wayne King, Monroe, 1988. Mem. VT-Woodsville (sec., Presdl. citation 1994), Rotary (past pres. Woodsville-Wells River Club, 1st woman to be admitted, 1st woman to hold office). Avocation: gardening. Home: Monroe, NH. Died June 19, 2007.

KNODT, HERMANN OTTO, hospital chaplain; b. Meinerzhayen, Germany, July 1, 1929; came to Can., 1954; s. Wilhelm and Gertrud (Hofmann) K.; m. Sarah Puett; children: David H., Grace Elizabeth. BS in Pharmacy, Ohio No. U., 1958; MDiv, Methesco, 1964. Lic. pharmacist; cert. hosp. chaplain. Dir. pastoral care Grant Riverside Hosp., Columbus, Ohio, 1972-94. Mem. YMCA. Fellow Coll. of Chaplains. United Methodist. Avocations: swimming, walking, reading, praying, counseling. Home: Worthington, Ohio. Died Dec. 30, 2006.

KNOLES, GEORGE HARMON, history educator; b. LA, Feb. 20, 1907; s. Tully Cleon and Emily (Walline) K.; m. Amandalee (Barker), June 12, 1930; children: Ann Barker (Nitzan), Alice Laurane (Simmons). AB (hon.), Coll. of Pacific, 1928, AM, 1930; PhD, Stanford U., 1939. Instr. history Union High Sch., Lodi, Calif., 1930-35; history asst. Stanford U., 1935-36, history instr., 1937-41, asst. prof., 1942-46, assoc. prof., 1946-51, prof. history, 1951-72, Margaret Byrne prof. history, 1968-72, chmn. history dept., 1968-72, prof. emeritus, 1972—2014. Dir. Inst. American History, 1956-72; prof. history; chmn. div. social sci. State Coll. Edn., Greeley, Colo., 1941-42; summer tchr. Central Wash. Coll. Edn., Ellensburg, 1939, State Coll., Flagstaff, Ariz, 1940, 1941, U. Calif. at Los Angeles, 1947; Stanford U., Tokyo U.; American Studies Seminars, Tokyo, 1950-52, 56, U. Wyo., 1955; cons. acad. history Hdq. USAF, 1950-52; dir. summer Inst. Tchrs. America, Alpach, Austria, 1965; Blazer lectr. U. Ky., 1961; Throchmorton lectr. Lewis & Clark Coll., 1965; Fulbright distinguished lectr., Japan, 1971 Author: The Presidential Campaign and Election of 1892, 1942; Readings in Western Civilization, (with Rixford K. Snyder), 1951; The Jazz Age Revisited, 1955, The New United States, 1959; Editor: The Crisis of The Union, 1860-61, 1965; Sources in American History, 10 vols, 1965-66, The Responsibilities of Power, 1900-1929, 1967; Essays and Assays: California History Reappraised, 1973; Contbg. articles to profl. jour. Lt., USNR, 1944-46. Mem. American Southern Hist. Assn.; Orgn. American Historians (exec. com. 1950-54, bd. editors rev. 1955-58); American Studies Assn. (council 1952-54); Soc. of American Historians. Clubs: Commonwealth. Methodist. Home: Palo Alto, Calif. Died Aug. 27, 2014.

KNORR, SUSAN MAISH, diabetes/endocrine clinical nurse specialist; b. Abington, Pa., June 30, 1950; d. William Wallace and Priscilla (Williams) Maish; m. Gerald Joseph Knorr, May 23, 1987. BA, Mt. Holyoke Coll., 1972; BSN, Columbia U., 1974; PNP, U. Va., 1982, MSN, 1983. Cert. diabetes educator. Staff nurse Children's Hosp. Med. Ctr., Boston, 1975, sr. staff nurse, 1975-80; project coord. Children's Hosp. of the King's Daughters, Norfolk, Va., 1983-84; nurse coord. Children's Specialty Svcs. Va. Dept. of Health, Norfolk, 1984-90; diabetes clin. nurse specialist Children's Hosp. of the King's Daus., Norfolk, Va., from 1990. Mem. Am. Diabetes Assn. (Tidewater chpt. bd. dirs.), Am. Assn. Diabetes Educators, Eastern Va. Assn. Diabetes Educators. Home: Chesapeake, Va. Died Nov. 18, 2006.

KNOWLES, HARROLD BROOK, physicist, consultant; b. Berkeley, Calif., July 28, 1925; s. Harrold Brook and Constance (Darrow) K.; m. Geraldine Lore, June 15, 1949; children: William Brook, Laura Elizabeth. BA in Physics, U. Calif., Berkeley, 1947, MA in Physics, 1951, PhD in Physics, 1957. Rsch. asst. in oceanography U. Wash., Seattle, 1948-50; rsch. asst in physics Lawrence Berkeley (Calif.) Lab., 1951-57; sr. exptl. physicist Lawrence Livermore (Calif.) Nat. Lab., 1957-61; rsch. assoc. in physics Yale U., New Haven, 1961-64; assoc. prof./prof. physics Wash. State U., Pullman, 1964-80; prin. staff mem. The BDM Corp., Albuquerque, 1980-83; cons. H.B. Knowles, Physics Cons., Albuquerque, 1983-84; mem. tech. staff VI Rocketdyne Divsn. Rockwell, Canoga Park, Calif., 1984-91; cons. H.B. Knowles, Physics. Cons., El Sobrante, Calif., from 1991. Cons. Los Alamos (N.Mex.) Nat. Lab., 1983-84, U. Calif., L.A., 1991-92, Lawrence Berkeley (Calif.) Lab., 1992-93, Mass. Gen. Hosp., Boston, 1995, Johns Hopkins U., 1996, 98, Dept. Energy, 1992, 99. Contbr. articles to profl. jours. Mem. Am. Phys. Soc., Health Physics Soc., Sigma Xi. Democrat. Achievements include discovery in magnetic optics; co-discovery of etch induction time in track detectors; first complete study of beam-weapons space platforms including cooling. Home: El Sobrante, Calif. Died Feb. 20, 2007.

KNOX, TRUDY, publisher, consultant, psychologist; b. Cape Girardeau, Mo., Aug. 11, 1926; d. Raymond Kenneth and Gertrude (McCann) K.; m. Joseph Russel Bagby, Feb. 14, 1962 (div. July 1969); children: Kenneth, Laurel, James. BS, Northwestern U., 1948; MA, U. Fla., 1951; EdD, U. Ark., 1973. Lic. psychologist, Ill. Psychologist Columbus State Sch. State of Ohio, 1952-57, Scioto Village State of Ohio, Delaware, 1957-62; psychologist, cons. Singer Zone Ctr., Rockford, Ill., 1962-67; psychologist Ohio Reformatory for Women, Marysville, 1987-90. Adj. faculty Ohio State U., Newark, Columbus, 1974-87; weekly columnist Community Booster, 2000-07. Pub. books and cassette programs The Music Is You by R. Perez, 1983, Turn Right at The Next Corner by Pat Vivo, 1991, Economics of Education by Martin Schoppmeyer, 1992, Sans Souci Spa Dining by Susanne Kircher, 1993, Where There's Hope by Hope Mihalap, 1994; contbr. articles to profl. jours. Cofounder Columbus Met. Club, 1975. Mem. APA, Am. Group Psychotherapy Assn., Ohio Speakers Forum (founder, charter pres. 1980-81, Trudy Knox award 1986), Funeral Consumers Alliance(pres. 1986-89). Home: Columbus, Ohio. Died June 25, 2014.

KNUTSON, WAYNE SHAFER, retired theater and English educator; b. Sisseton, SD, June 1, 1926; s. Edward and Julia (Sanden) K.; m. Esther Marie Johnstad, July 30, 1950; children: David Wayne, Jon Eric, Jane Marie. BA, Augustana Coll., 1950; MA, U. S.D., 1951; PhD, U. Denver, 1956. Purchasing agt. First Nat. Bank Black Hills, Rapid City, S.D., 1951-52; prof. speech and dramatic arts, also dir. Univ. Theater U. S.D., Vermillion, 1952-66, prof. English, 1966-73, chmn. dept., 1966-71, dean Coll. Fine Arts, 1972-80, v.p. acad. affairs, 1980-82, prof. theater and English, 1982-87, Univ. Disting. prof., 1987, Univ. Disting. prof., emeritus, from 1987. Assoc. dir., bus. mgr. Black Hills Playhouse, Inc., Custer, SD, 1952-63; assoc. dir. NSF Honors Inst., U. SD, summers 1964, 65, Harrington lectr., 1972; dir. merger activities U. SD, South State Coll., 1971; mem. SD Humanities Coun., 1985-91, chmn. 1989-91; mem. lit. com. SD Arts Coun., 1968-70, mem. coun., 1970-78, chmn. coun., 1971-78. Author: lyric dramas The Mirrored Maze, 1957, Dream Valley, 1959; drama: The Dakota Descendants of Ola Rue, 1985; opera Prosopa, 1964, Arabesque, 1967; readers theatre The Stavig Letters, 1996 (Regional Emmy award, SD Pub. Broadcasting TV, 2011); editor, contbr. to: Dramatics, 1964. Mem. lit. panel Nat. Endowment for Arts, 1975-77; trustee Shrine to Music Mus., Inc., 1975-80, 84-86, emeritus, 1987—; hon. bd. dirs. Black Hills Playhouse, Inc., 1977— . Served with U.S. Mcht. Marine, 1944-46; Served with AUS, 1946-47; Served with AUS, Korean occupation. Recipient Best Tchr. award U. SD, 1968, Disting. Svc. award Speech Comm. Assn. SD, 1985, SD Gov.'s Distinction award in Creative Achievement, 1986, Burlington No. Found. Faculty Achievement award U. SD, 1986, Alumni Achievement award Augustana Coll., 1992; named Alumnus of Yr. Sisseton HS, 1989; named to SD Hall of Fame, 2001; SD Arts Coun. Artist in Theatre fellow, 1987. Mem. Nat. Coll. Players, Eta Sigma Phi (hon.), Omicron Delta Kappa (hon.) Lutheran. Achievements include the main stage theater at the University of South Dakota being renamed in his honor, 1999. Home: Vermillion, SD. Died Dec. 7, 2015.

KOCH, MARGARET E., organist, piano educator; b. Checatah, Okla., Apr. 20, 1913; d. William Alvin and Mary M. (Pugh) Ellington; m. Rudolph Julius Koch, June 20, 1934; children: Rudy, William E., Mary Margaret Dornan, Carolyn Marinda Hutcherson. Student, Linden Wood Coll., St. Charles, Mo., Tulsa U. Piano tchr. Music Tchrs. Nat. Assn., Okla., from 1973; organist, pianist First Meth. Ch., from 1926. Author: (booklet) The Family Joke, 1998. Mem. PEO. Republican. Home: Checotah, Okla. Died July 20, 2007.

KOCI, BRUCE R., engineer; b. St. Paul, Jan. 10, 1943; s. Raymond E. and Hazel J. (Bauman) K.; m. Ann I. Guhman, Aug. 2, 1980. BA, U. Minn., 1966, MSc, 1975. Project engr. Rosemont Eng., Mpls., 1966-71; grad. student U. Minn., Wildlife Mgmt., St. Paul, 1971-75; research asst. U. Minn. Geology, Mpls., 1974-78; sr engr. Polar Ice Coring Office, Lincoln, Nebr., from 1978, engr., from 1995. Mem. AIAA, Ecol. Soc. Am., Internat. Glaciological Soc. Avocations: canoeing, backpacking, photography, swimming. Home: Middleton, Wis. Died Nov. 13, 2006.

KOELLE, MARY L., marketing professional; b. Chgo., Nov. 20, 1948; d. David L. Jr. and Helen R. (Salomon) Liebman; m. Kevin B. Wolcott, May 21, 1977 (div. 1979); m. John R. Koelle, Feb. 12, 1983. BA, Conn. Coll., 1970; MBA, Columbia U., 1972. Security analyst Bankers Trust Co., NYC, 1972; with Young & Rubicam, Chgo., 1979-82; acct. supr. Ogilvy & Mather, NYC, Chgo., 1976-79; v.p., mgmt. supr., sr. v.p. dir. client svcs. Jan Zwiren Agy., Zwiren & Wagner, Chgo., 1982-86; dir. advt. and promotion Hyatt Hotels Corp., Chgo., 1986-88; mgr. mktg. communications Xerox Corp., Rochester, N.Y., from 1988. Vice chmn. Pres.'s Coun. Mus. Sci. and Industry, Chgo., 1986-88. Avocations: gourmet cooking, travel, interior decorating. Home: Lake Forest, Ill. Died Dec. 17, 2006.

KOHLBERG, JEROME, JR., (JERRY KOHLBERG), venture capitalist, lawyer; b. NYC, July 10, 1925; s. Jerome Kohlberg, Sr. and Edith; m. Nancy Kohlberg; children: James, Karen, Pamela, Andrew. BA, Swarthmore Coll., 1946; MBA, Harvard Bus. Sch.; LLM, Columbia U. Sch. Law, 1950. Bar: NY. Formerly with Bear Stearns & Co., Inc., 1955—76; sr. founding ptnr. Kohlberg, Kravis, Roberts & Co., NYC, 1976-87; chmn. Houdaille Industries, Inc., Fort Lauderdale, Fla., exec. com.; chmn., co-founder Kohlberg & Co., Mt. Kisco, NY, 1987—94, spl. limited principal, 1994—2015. Bd. dirs. Sterndent Corp. Founder Kohlberg Found., Campaign for America, Campaign Reform Project; bd. managers Swarthmore Coll. Served USN. Named one of Forbes' Richest Americans, 2006; named to Private Equity Hall of Fame, 1994. Fellow: Am. Acad. Arts & Sciences. Achievements include forming the Campaign Reform project which was pivotal in passing The McCain-Feingold campaign finance reform bill. Died July 30, 2015.

KOHN, JEROME MILTON, life insurance agent; b. Far Rockaway, NY, Nov. 8, 1915; s. Jerome and Frieda (Quittner) K.; m. Betty Sanders, Mar. 16, 1941; children: Leslie Clemens, Sandra Kohn, Jay Kohn. BS, U. Va., 1936; JD, U. Mont., 1938. Chartered life underwriter. Pvt. practice in law, Billings, Mont., 1938-42; ptnr. Wholesale Distbn. Firm, Billings, 1944-55; agt. and gen. agt. Am. Nat. Ins. Co., Billings, from 1955. Exec. sec. LUPAC-Mont., Billings, 1982—. Lt. USNR, 1942-45. Mem. Optimist Internat., Elks. Democrat. Jewish. Avocations: stamp collecting/philately, puzzles, games, bridge. Home: Billings, Mont. Died Mar. 28, 2007.

KOHUT, ANDREW, retired research center executive; m. Diane Colasanto. AB, Seton Hall U., 1964; studied grad. sociology, Rutgers U., 1964—66. Pres. Gallup Orgn., 1979—89; founding dir. Princeton Survey Rsch. Associates, 1989; founding dir. surveys Pew Rsch. Center for The People and The Press (originally Times Mirror Ctr.), 1990—92, dir., 1993—2013; pres. Pew Rsch. Center, Washington, 2004—13; dir. Pew Global Attitudes Project. Former mem. Coun. Fgn. Rels.; pub. opinion cons., analyst Nat. Pub. Radio; writer RealClearPolitics.com. Co-author: The People, the Press, and Politics: The Times Mirror Study of the American Electorate, 1988, Estranged Friends? The Transatlantic Consequences of Societal Change, 1996, The Diminishing Divide: Religion's Changing Role in American Politics, 2000, What the World Thinks in 2002, 2003, America Against the World: How We Are Different and Why We Are Disliked, 2006. Named one of The 50 Most Powerful People in DC, GQ mag., 2007. Mem.: Market Rsch. Coun., Nat. Coun. Pub. Polls (pres. 2000—01), Am. Assn. Pub. Opinion Rsch. (pres. 1994—95, award for Exceptionally Disting. Achievement 2005, Innovators award, NY chapt. award for Outstanding Contbn. to Opinion Rsch. 2000). Died Sept. 8, 2015.

KOLIN, IRVING SEYMOUR, psychiatrist; b. Bklyn., Feb. 15, 1940; m. Rochelle Tinkelman, Sept. 4, 1966; children: Lawrence, Marc. BA in Psychology cum laude, U. Buffalo Sch. Arts and Scis., 1961; MD, SUNY, Sch. Medicine, Buffalo, 1965. Diplomate in forensic psychiatry Am. Bd. Psychiatry and Neurology, 1997, sr. disability analyst, diplomat Am. Bd. Disability Analysts, 1997, Am. Bd. Adolescent Psychiatry, Am. Bd. Addiction Medicine, 2009, Am. Bd. Quality Assurance and Utilization Review Physicians, 2013, Am. Acad. Pain Mgmt., 2013. Intern NY Presbyn. Hosp., NYC, 1965—66, resident, Payne Whitney Clinic, 1966—69, resident, child psychiatry, Payne Whitney Clinic, Cornell U. Med. Coll., 1968—69; pvt. practice psychiatry Winter Park, Fla., from 1971; prin. investigator Kolin Rsch. Group, from 1971; tchr., planning curriculum com. U. Ctrl. Fla., Coll. Medicine, Orlando, 2007—08, assoc. prof. psychiatry, dept. med. edn., from 2008; cons. psychiatrist U. Ctrl. Fla. Health Svcs., from 2012. Med. staff Orlando Regional Healthcare Sys., from 1971, Fla. Hosp., from 1984; courtesy clin. assoc. prof., dept. psychiatry U. Fla., Coll. Medicine, 1986—2011; prin. investigator Pfizer, from 1996, CeNeRx BioPharma, Inc., from 2009, Forest Rsch. Inst., from 2010, Boehringer-Ingelheim, 2010, PharmaNeuroBoost NV, from 2011, Shire, from 2011, Otsuka, from 2011; adj. clin. prof. psychiatry-neurology LECOM Bradenton, Coll. Osteopathic Medicine, Sch. Pharmacy, Bradenton, Fla., from 2011; spkr. in field; rschr. in field. Book cons.: Wild High and Tight (author Peter Golenbock), 1994, Been There, Done That (author Eddie Fisher), 1999, The Mickey Mantle Novel (author Peter Golenbock), 2008, The Little Rich Boy Who Built The Yankee Empire, 2009; contbr. scientific papers to numerous rsch. publs. Mem. Orange County Mental Health Assn., from 1973, pres., 1977—78; bd. mem. Lakeside Alternatives Mental Health Svcs., Orange County, 2002—05. Lt. comdr. Med. Corps. USN, 1969—70, comdr. Med. Corps. USN, 1970—71, Dept. Neuropsychiatry, Naval Hosp. Orlando, Fla. Named one of Best Drs. in America, from 1986, Top Drs. in America, from 1999. Fellow: Am. Coll. Psychiatrists, Am. Psychiatric Assn. (disting. life fellow from 2003); mem.: AMA, Am. Acad. Child and Adolescent Psychiatry. Home: Winter Park, Fla. Died Apr. 2014.

KOLOMIYSKY, ARKADIY NAUMOVICH, physicist, researcher, educator; b. Potsdam, Germany, July 26, 1947; arrived in Russia, 1950; arrived in US, 2001. s. Naum Veniaminovich Kolomiysky and Shuamis Zimelevna Lin. MS/Engr. in Physics, Moscow Inst. Physics & Tech., 1971; PhD in Physics and Math., I.V. Kurchatov Atomic Energy Inst., Moscow, 1981. Rsch. engr. I.V. Kurchatov Atomic Energy Inst., Moscow, 1971-73; rsch. scientist Br. I.V. Kurchatov Atomic Energy Inst., Troitsk, Moscow, Russia, 1973-83, group leader Troitsk/Moscow, 1983-87, sr. scientist Troitsk, 1987-90; lead scientist Troitsk Inst. Innovation and Fusion Rsch., Troitsk, 1990—2001; sr. scientist Altair Ctr., Shrewsbury, Mass., 2001—03; security officer Allegiance Security Corp., from 2004. Assoc. prof. Moscow Inst. Physics and Tech., 1978—. Contbr. articles to profl. jours. Avocations: literature, theater, travels. Home: Brooklyn, NY. Died Feb. 5, 2007.

KOMMRUSCH, JUDITH ANN, educational consultant; b. Milw., Jan. 15, 1942; d. Lawrence LeRoy Kumoier and Alice Elizabeth Kramer; m. Fredrick Gustav Kommrusch, Nov. 24, 1966. BS in Elem. Edn., U. Wis., Milw., 1964, MS in Elem. Edn., 1967, ED, 1971, LD, 1974. Elem. instr. Glendale Pub. Sch., Wis., 1964—68, St. Amelion Ct. Sch., Milw., 1971—72; instr. spl. edn. Shorewood Pub. Schs., Wis., 1972—74; office mgr. Milw. Jewish Newspaper, 1974—76; sr. editor Milw. Impression City Mag., 1976—83; edn. liasion dir. Marcus Student Incentive Program, Milw., 1985—2010; v.p. FGK Consulting, Glendale, from 1985. Lit. agent Daniel P. King Agy., Milw., 1976—86; corp. rep. Start Smart Milw., 1986—88; com. chmn. Marcus Turn Around Scholarship, Milw., 1997—2012. Mem. exec. bd. Books Kids, Next Door Found., Milw., from 1987; bd. mem. Friends Edn. Alumni, Milw., 2002—04; mem. scholarship com. NAACP, Waukesha, Wis., from 2011. Mem.: Am. Contract Bridge League (dir. from 1967), Phi Lamda Theata (Beta Epsilon chpt.). Died Apr. 29, 2015.

KONA, MARTHA MISTINA, retired librarian, information specialist; b. Banovce, Slovakia; came to U.S., 1950; d. Albert and Anna (Kubrican) Mistina; m. William Kona, Aug. 6, 1955 (dec. Dec. 1989); children: Olivia Kona, Lindy Kona. BA in Economics & German, Rosary Coll. Riverforest Ill.; MALS, Dominican U. (formerly Rosary Coll. Riverforest Ill.). Libr. U. Ill. Med. Libr., 1954—60; assoc. prof. U. Ill.; rsch. libr. Cen. Soya Chemurgy, Chgo.; asst. dir. Rush U. Libr., Chgo., 1979; pvt. practice cons., info. specialist Wilmette, Ill., 1980—85. Cons. liaison Matica Slovenska, Martin, Slovakia; rep. European-Am. Adv. Bd. Archdiocese Chgo., 1993—2005; chair Woman's Club Wilmette, Philanthropy, 1991—93; chair, lectr., author Slovak Conf. US. Author: Soybean Proteins, 1969, Multi Media Catalog, Health Science Librarians of Illinois, 1977-85, Slovak Americans and Canadians in American Catholic, 1985, Kona-Mistina Family In The USA, 1995; Co-Author, editor Archbishop Dr. Karol Kmetko, 1989. Decorated Grand Cross Sovereign Military Order Temple Jerusalem, Order of Merit, Order St. John Jerusalem, Dames of Order US; recipient Matica Slovenska medal Distinction, Stefan Moyses Soc. Mem. AAUW, AAUP (chair bylaws com. 1975-77), Slovak World Congress (chair heritage and culture com. 1990—), Slovak Cath. Falcon, Ill. Audio Visual Assn. (pres. 1975-77), Sovereign Mil. Order of Temple of Jerusalem (Grand Cross, 1975, Order of Merit in Grade and Rank of Grand Comdr., 1999—, Grand Magistral Liaison, 1989-96), Slovak Inst. (Rome) (2nd v.p.), Imperial Order of Constantine the Great and St. Helena (bd. dirs. 1977—), Order St. John Jerusalem, Woman's Club Wilmette Philanthropy (chair 1991-93), Med. Libr. Assn. (membership com.), Cath. Libr. Assn., Spl. Libr. Assn., Midwest Libr. Assn., Tri-state Hosp. Assembly, Health Scis. Libr. (hon., life mem.), Am. Assn. U. Profs. (com. mem. 1990), AAUW, AAUP(chair bylaws com.,1975-77), Jednota, Slovak Cath. Falcon & Slovak League of America(2nd. v.p.), Slovak Inst.(Rome), Orgn. Slovak Artists, Writers, and Cultural Reps. Outside Slovakia. Avocations: reading, travel, classical music, physical fitness, beachcombing. Home: Toledo, Ohio. Died Apr. 13, 2014.

KONSELMAN, LANCE MARCONNAY, non-profit organization executive; b. Garden City, NY, Apr. 1, 1947; s. Charles Bremer and Elenora Marcia (Jenkins-Rofe) K. BA in History, Yale U., 1969. Sr. trust officer Citibank, N.A., NYC, 1973-81, v.p. treasury, 1981-84; mng. dir. Weil Bros, Inc., NYC, 1984-87; dir. adminstrn. Project Return Found., NYC, 1988-92; mgr. field activities HIV Care Svcs., NYC, 1992-96; contr. Praxis Housing Initiatives, Inc., 1996-98; v.p. fin. and adminstrn. Staten Island (N.Y.) Botanical Garden, from 1998. Cons. in non-profit real estate, N.Y.C., 1988—. Trustee Found. for Treatment of Children with AIDS, N.Y.C., 1994—; committeeman N.Y. County Rep. Com., N.Y.C., 1980—; pres., bd. dirs. N.Y. Young Reps., N.Y.C., 1977-90; pres., chmn. bd. dirs. 84th St. Cooperative Corp., N.Y.C., 1984-88. With U.S. Army, 1969-72. Avocations: sailing, tennis, golf, bridge. Home: Staten Island, NY. Died July 29, 2007.

KOONTZ, ELDON RAY, management and financial consultant; b. Randolph County, Ind., Oct. 20, 1913; s. Irvin Delbert and Martha Caroline (Farmer) K.; m. Florence Gloria Gustus, Jan. 20, 1944; children: Rebecca Anne Koontz Stumm, Stephen Wickey Koontz. AB in Econs., Earlham Coll., 1938; Diploma in Bus. Adminstrn., Alexander Hamilton Inst., NYC, 1956. Chief cost acct. and spl. assignments, Crosley Div. Avco Mfg. Corp., Richmond, Ind.; asst. to pres. F.C. Russell Co., Cleve.; controller, asst. sec. Pacific Mercury Electronics, Joplin, Mo.; sr. mgmt. engr. Bell Aerosystems Co., Wheatfield, N.Y.; controller, asst. sec. Fleet of America, Inc., Buffalo, N.Y.; asst. to pres., acting gen. mgr. Tycodyne Industries, Inc./Lakeside Mfg. Co., Lackawanna and Honeoye, N.Y.; chmn., pres. E.R. Koontz & Assocs., Inc., Williamsville, N.Y., from 1970; mng. dir. Koontzco Internat. div. E.R. Koontz & Assocs., Inc., from 1990; exec. dir. Troika Sys. Engring. Group div. E.R. Koontz & Assocs., Inc., from 1993. Contbg. author: Mergers and Acquisitions Procedures, 1987. Treas. First English Luth. Ch., Richmond, Ind., 1950-55; v.p. Cen. Presbyn. Ch., Buffalo, N.Y., 1979-85; mem. The Chapel, Amherst, N.Y., 1986. Capt. U.S. Army, 1943-45. Mem. Richmond Accts. Assn. (pres. 1951-52), Nat. Assn. Cost Accts. (assoc. dir. for publs. Dayton, Ohio 1951-55), Nat. Assn. Mergers and Acquisitions Cons. (bd. dirs., sec. 1973-83), Internat. Assn. Mergers and Acquisitions Cons. (bd. dirs., sec. 1974-83), Am. Fin. Assn. (charter), Am Legion, Amherst C. of C., Rotary (Rotarian of Yr. North Amherst chpt. 1990). Republican. Avocations: golf, fishing. Home: Williamsville, NY. Died Nov. 23, 2006.

KOPP, STEPHEN JAMES, academic administrator; b. Panama, Mar. 28, 1951; m. Jane Kopp; children: Adam, Elizabeth. BS, U. Notre Dame, 1973; PhD in Physiology and Biophysics, U. Ill., Chgo., 1976. Postdoctoral fellow dept. physiology St. Louis U., 1976-77; rsch. assoc. dept. biol. chemistry U. Ill. Med. Ctr., Chgo., 1977-78, NIH postdoctral fellow, 1979-85; asst. dir. Magnetic Resonance Lab. Chgo. Coll. Ostepathic Medicine, 1979-85, acting dean Allied Health Programs Downers Grove, Ill., 1991-92, dean Coll. Allied Health Professions, 1992-97, chmn. dept. physiology, 1983-94; dean Herbert H. and Grace A. Dow Coll. Health Professions Ctrl. Mich. U., Mt. Pleasant, 1997; founding dean Coll. Allied Health Professions Midwestern U.; provost Ohio State U., Athens, 2002—04; spl, asst. to chancellor Ohio Bd. Regents; pres. Marshall U., Huntington, W.Va., 2005—14. Cons. MITRE Corp., McClean, Va., 1980-81. Contbr. articles to profl. jours. Named Outstanding Young American, 1980; Granite City Steel Rsch. fellow, 1975. Mem. American Osteopathic Assn. (evaluator 1996-98). Died Dec. 17, 2014.

KOPRIVICA, DOROTHY MARY, management consultant, insurance and real estate broker; b. St. Louis, May 27, 1921; d. Mitar and Fema (Guzina) K. BS, Washington U., St. Louis, 1962. cert. in def. inventory mgmt. Dept. Def., 1968. Mgmt. analyst Transp. Supply and Maintenance Command, St. Louis, 1954-57, Dept. Army Transp. Material Command, St. Louis, 1957-62; program analyst Dept. Army Aviation System Command, St. Louis, 1962-74, spl. asst. to comdr., 1974-78; ins. broker D. Koprivica, Ins., St. Louis, 1978-81; real estate broker St. Louis, 1978-81; ret., 2002. Mem. Bus. and Profl. Women (pres. 1974-75), Order Ea. Star. Eastern Orthodox. Home: Chesterfield, Mo. Died Nov. 14, 2006.

KOPRUCKI, MARK EDWARD, financial analyst; b. Blue Island, Ill., Sept. 12, 1955; s. Paul Vincent and Martha Germane (Van Gansbeke) K.; m. Patricia Jane Huffman, Dec. 26, 1976. BS in Fin., So. Ill. U., 1977; MBA, Xavier U., Cin., 1981. CFA. Analyst, portfolio mgr. Star Bank, Cin., 1978-83; rsch. dir. Gradison & Co., Cin., 1983-91, The Ohio Co., Columbus, from 1992. Mem. Assn. for Investment Mgmt. and Rsch., Columbus Fin. Analysts Soc. Home: Columbus, Ohio. Died Nov. 18, 2006.

KORAB, ARNOLD ALVA, engineering executive; b. Penns Grove, NJ, June 15, 1917; s. Harry Emil and Lydia Maria (Toykalla) K.; m. Evelyn Marr Stevens, June 16, 1939 (dec. Oct. 1972); children: William, Anne; m. Helen Norine Schlossnagel, Dec. 30, 1973. BSME, U. Md., 1938; degree in Aero Engrng., Calif. Inst. Tech., 1943. Registered profl. engr. Md., D.C. Engr. Office of James Posey, Balt., 1938-40, Pub. Bldg. Adminstrn., G.S.A., Washington, 1940-43; cons. engr. Redmile, Korab & Wood, Inc., Washington, 1946-57; chmn. Ellenco, Inc., Brentwood, Md., 1957-2000. Bd. dirs. Ellenco, Inc., Brentwood; ptnr. Korab Assocs., Brentwood, 1958-92. Lt. comdr. USN, 1943-46, PTO. Mem. NSPE, Nat. Fire Protection Assn., Mil. Order of World Wars, Rotary Internat., Masons, Shriners, Pi Tau Sigma. Episcopalian. Avocations: reading, investing, sailing, bridge. Home: Woodbine, Md. Died Oct. 31, 2006.

KOREN, JEROME QUENTIN, publishing executive; b. Cleve., Aug. 4, 1947; s. Joseph Thomas and Monica Fran (Groh) K. BA in History, U. Western Ontario, Can., 1970. Mgr. Book Fairs Ltd., Oakville, Ontario, Can., 1970-72; buyer T. Eaton & Co., Toronto, Ontario, Can., 1972-76; owner Book Gallery Ltd., Toronto, Ontario, Can., 1976-78; dir. Prometheus Books, Buffalo, 1978-82; dir. mktg. Loyola U. Press, Chgo., 1982-85; co-founder Campion Books, Chgo., 1982-85; pres. Madison Ave. Inc., Chgo., from 1985. Dir. edn. Chgo. Book Clinic, 1984-85. Avocations: reading, music, walking. Died July 9, 2007.

KOSOVAC, DOROTHY ANN, secondary school educator; b. Detroit, Oct. 16, 1923; d. Stanley George and Hazel Mary (KcKenney) Forsyth; m. Nicholas Kosovac, July 16, 1942; children: Margaret Wolf, Cynthia Mulligan. BS, Wayne State U., 1960, MS, 1962. Sec. Ferndale (Mich.) Pub. Schs., 1954-60, tchr., 1960-65, dir., 1965-88. Mem. adv. com. Eastern Mich. U. Ctr. for Community Edn., Ypsilanti, 1972-75, Ednl. Leadership, 1985—. Named to Mich. Edn. Hall of Fame. Mem. Mich. Assn. Adult and Continuing Edn. (pres.), Mich. Assn. Adult and Community Edn. (pres.), Exchange Club. (bd. dirs.). Democrat. Home: Sarasota, Fla. Died Jan. 23, 2007.

KOSSAK, HOWARD S., investment banker; b. Newark, July 28, 1940; s. Irving and Martha (Weiner) K.; m. Susan N. Kossak, Nov. 22, 1966; children: Adam D., Daniel J. BS in Indsl. Engring., Rutgers U., 1964; MBA, Harvard U., 1973. Branch mktg. mgr. IBM, Miami, 1963-79; v.p. sales SEL, Inc., Ft. Lauderdale, Fla., 1979-83; v.p. world wide sales Modcomp, Pompano Beach, Fla., 1983-85; pres. Dash Assocs., Coral Springs, Fla., 1985-91; sr. v.p. strategic devel. Servantis/Checkfree, Norcross, Ga., 1991-96; v.p. mergers and acquisitions Affinith Tech., Columbia, S.C., from 1996. Author: Ins, Outs, Ups of Venture Capital, 1986. Trustee Temple Emanuel, Atlanta, 1993-96. Mem. Masada Lodge, F. & A.M. Home: Atlanta, Ga. Died Dec. 28, 2006.

KÖTTER, ROLF, biomedical researcher, educator; Dr. med., U. Essen, 1990; Privatdozent, U. Düsseldorf, 2002. Specialist in anatomy U. Düsseldorf, 1995. Rsch. fellow U. Otago, Dunedin, New Zealand, 1991—94; rschr. U. Düsseldorf, 1994—97, staff, 1997—2006, prof., 2006; prof., chair neurophysiology and neuroinformatics dept. Radboud U. Med. Ctr., Nijmegen, Netherlands. Guest prof. E. China U. Sci. & Tech., Shanghai, 2006. Editor: (book) Neuroscience Databases. Achievements include development of CoCoMac database of primate brain connectivity and further neuroinformatics resources; research in the Limbic System; models of basal ganglia (mal-)function; development of flash photolysis of caged glutamate for mapping of connectivity in brain slices. Deceased.

KOUTAL, REUBEN KAMIAR, mechanical engineer; arrived in Israel, 1979; m. Miriam Cohantebb, Mar. 3, 1994. BS in Engring. Tech., Aircraft Maintenance, 1976; BS in Mech. Engring., Northrop U., 1978. Cert. CMC Ltd., Tel-Aviv, 1991, in design and inspection of elec. sys. Inst. Engring. Archs., Tel-Aviv, 1995, in computer aided design, auto cad R-12 Israel Inst. Productivity, Tel-Aviv, 1995, HP ME 10, 1992, HP ME 30; in electronic packaging engring., Israel Aircraft Industries, Ltd., 1989; airframe and powerplant mechanic FAA, 1976. Profl. mem., Arj Karaj Rd., 1978—79; mech. engr. Palbam Ein-Kharod Ikhoud, Israel, 1981, Kulso Ltd., Haifa, Israel, 1982—85, Bezek Israel Telecom. Co. Ltd., Tel-Aviv, 1986—98, Micromat Ltd., Misgav, Israel, 1998; unskilled worker Ben Dor Ltd., Israel, 1980—81; translator Express Tikshoret, Petakh-Tikva, 1999. Tech. writer Borochov, Korakh & Ptnrs., Tel-Aviv, 1999—2008; patent agt. Israel Patent & Trademark Office, 2004—10; reviewer in fields. Contbr. articles to jours. Mem.: ACS, AAAS (Societal Impacts Sci. & Engring., Sect. X, Math., Sect. A, profl. mem., Linguistics & Lang Scis. Sect. Z phys. chemistry divsn.), IEEE (sr.), Am. Soc. Mech. Engrs., Oceanic Engring. Soc., Control Sys. Soc., Minn. Pub. Radio (sustaining mem.). Avocations: literature, sports. Home: Tel Aviv, Israel. Died Aug. 2015.

KOVALESKI, DIANE MARIE, secondary school educator; b. Scranton, Pa., Aug. 17, 1973; d. Joseph Andrew and Mary Patricia Kovaleski. BA in English, Cedar Crest Coll., 1995; MS, Wilkes U., 2004. Cashier KMart, Pittston, Pa., 1989—95; prodn. asst. OCC Sports, LA, 1995; project mgr. Creative Graphics, Inc., Allentown, Pa., 1995—97; call specialist Notify MD/Ring Med., Moosic, 1997—99; substitute tchr. Pittston Area Sch. Dist., 1999; tchr. bus. Saucon Valley Sch. Dist., Hellertown, 1999—2000, Pen Argyl Area High Sch., from 2000. Mem.: NEA, Nat. Bus. Edn. Assn., Internat. Soc. Tech. Edn. Democrat. Roman Catholic. Avocations: reading, writing, music, scrapbooks. Home: Nazareth, Pa. Died Jan. 13, 2007.

KOZAK, ANDREW FRANK, economics professor; b. Phila., Nov. 11, 1950; s. John J. and Emma H. Kozak. MS, U. Notre Dame, 1981, PhD, 1983. Assoc. prof. St. Mary's Coll. Md., 1984—2014, chmn. Dept. Economics, 2004—09, St. Mary's Coll. Md, 2011—12. Dir. Honors Program/Paul Nitze Scholars Program St. Mary's Coll. Md, 1998—2003. Author: Critical Issues in Supply Side Economics; co-author (with Donald R. Stabile): Markets, Planning and the Moral Economy: Business Cycles in the Progressive Era and the New Deal, 2013. Commr. Housing Authority St. Mary's County, Leonardtown, 2002—09. With US Army, 1970—71, Fort Bragg, NC. Recipient Homer L. Dodge Excellence Tchg. Award, St. Mary's Coll. Md., 1988. Mem.: American Econ. Assn. Home: Saint Marys City, Md. Died Oct. 16, 2014.

KRAEMER, PAUL WILHELM, retired utilities executive; b. Mpls., Dec. 28, 1920; s. John C. and Rose (Schoenstuhl) K.; m. Doris Carter, Jan. 2, 1946 (dec. 2002); children: Bruce, Fred (dec. 1970) BS in Chem. Engring, U. Minn., 1942; BS in Law, William Mitchell Coll. Law, 1957. With Minn. Gas Co., 1947—58, v.p. ops., 1958-66, exec. v.p., 1966-67, pres., CEO, 1967-81. Contbr. articles to profl. jours. Served to lt. USNR, 1942-46. Recipient Operating award of merit American Gas Assn., 1959; named Engr. of Year Mpls. Engrs. Club, 1968 Mem. Engrs. Club, American Gas Assn., Clubs: Masons (Mpls.), Mpls. (Mpls.), Minikahda Country (Mpls.); Delray Dunes Country (Fla.). Home: Delray Beach, Fla. Died Oct. 30, 2014.

KRAMARSIC, ROMAN JOSEPH, engineering consultant; b. Mokronog, Slovenia, Feb. 15, 1926; came to U.S., 1957; s. Roman and Josipina (Bucar) K; m. Joanna B. Ruffo, Oct. 29, 1964; children: Joannine M., Roman III. Student, U. Bologna, Italy, 1947-48; B of Applied Sci. in Mech. Engring., U. Toronto, 1954, M of Applied Sci., 1956; PhD, U. So. Calif., 1973. Registered profl. engr., Ont. Rsch. engr. Chrysler Rsch., Detroit, 1957-58; chief design engr. Annin Corp., Montebello, Calif., 1959-60; mgr. Plasmadyne Corp., Santa Ana, Calif., 1960-62; sr. rsch. engr. NESCO, Pasadena, Calif., 1962-64; asst. prof. U. So. Calif., LA, 1971-77; mgr. engring. div. MERDI, Butte, Mont., 1977-78; sr. rsch. engr. RDA, Albuquerque, 1978-85; sr. staff mem. BDM, Albuquerque, 1985-90; owner Dr. R. J. Kramarsic's Engring. Svcs., Laguna Beach, Calif., from 1985. Cons. various tech. cos., So. Calif., 1964—; mem. various govt. coms. evaluating high power lasers. Author tech. presentations; contbr. articles to profl. jours. Violinist Albuquerque Civic Light Opera, 1980-85. Mem. ASME (life), AIAA (life; sr.), ASM Internat., Nat. Ski Patrol (aux. leader 1990-94). Roman Catholic. Avocations: classical music, violin, skiing. Home: Santa Clara, Calif. Died Mar. 6, 2007.

KRAMER, PATRICIA JO, lawyer; b. Oak Park, Ill., Feb. 20, 1964; d. Joseph Jack and Diane Sue (Jansen) K. BA, U. N.Mex., 1987; JD, St. Mary's U., San Antonio, 1993. Bar: Tex. 1993, Colo. 1993. Law clk. Law Office of Martha Fitzwater, San Antonio, 1990-93; pvt. practice Montrose, Colo., from 1994; exec. dir. Montrose Resource Ctr., from 1995. Bd. dirs. Colo. Rural Legal Svcs., Inc., 1995—, Law Alumni, San Antonio, 1993-95; mem. Libr. Yes Com., Montrose, 1994; sr. ptnr. Ptnrs. of Montrose, 1994—. Mem. ABA, Colo. State Bar Assn., Colo. Women's Bar Assn., 7th Jud. Dist. Assn., Altrusa of Montrose. Home: Montrose, Colo. Died Aug. 18, 2007.

KRANTZ, EJNAR SANFRID, composer, musician, educator; s. Sam Krantz and Hannah Victoria Carlson. MusB, Sherwood Music Sch., Chgo., 1939; MusM, Chgo. Musical Coll., 1943; DFA, Chgo. Musical Coll. Roosevelt U., 1954. Choral dir. Grace Luth. Ch., San Antonio, 1944—47; concert pianist U.S. and Europe, 1947—54; organist and dir. St. Matthew Luth. Ch., Washington, 1954—55; minister of music First Presbyn. Ch., Battle Creek, Mich., 1955—57; adj. faculty Ind. U. at South Bend, 1962—95; interim asst. prof. music Manchester Coll., 1960—62, Goshen Coll., 1963; minister of music First Presbyn. Ch., South Bend, 1957—60. Contbr. articles to profl. jours.; composer: (vocal solos) Israel's Lament, Restoration/Snow, The Highlands Sing, The Mesa Trail, Vocal Solos by Ejnar Krantz, (choral works) Come Unto Me, Hear My Cry, O God (Psalm 61), In Him Will I Trust (Psalm 91), Lo, I Am With You Alway, Psalm 100: Make a Joyful Noise Unto the Lord, Psalm 121: I Will Lift Up Mine Eyes, Radiance: The Thing Most Beautiful, (piano) All Kinds of Pieces for Little Fingers, An Approach to Fingering in Piano Playing, Two Tone Pictures-Melancholy and Capriccio, Four Little Mood Pictures, Sonorous Sketches from the Four Winds., Three Greetings, (organ) Four Offeratories, Preludes on Four Familiar Hymn

Tunes, Toccata Chromatica in A Minir. Recipient Chgo. Artists Assn. award, 1938; Rudolph Ganz scholar, Chgo. Musical Coll., 1942—43. Avocations: languages, sailing, swimming, reading. Home: South Bend, Ind. Died May 1, 2007.

KREBS, JOHN HANS, former United States Representative from California; b. Berlin, Dec. 17, 1926; arrived in US, 1946, naturalized, 1954; s. James L. and Elizabeth (Stern) Krebs; m. Hanna Jacobson, Sept. 9, 1956; children: Daniel Scott, Karen Barbara. BA, U. Calif., 1950; LLB, Hastings Coll. Law, San Francisco, 1957. Bar: Calif., 1957. Mem. Fresno County Planning Commn., 1965-69; mem. bd. supervisors Fresno County, 1970-74; mem. US Congress from 17th Calif. Dist., 1975—79; atty., pvt. practice, 1958-75, 79-92. Chmn. Fresno County Democratic Central Com., 1965-66. Served with US Army, 1952-54. Democrat. Jewish. Home: Fresno, Calif. Died Nov. 10, 2014.

KRIEGER, STANLEY LEONARD, manufacturing executive; b. Bklyn., Feb. 15, 1942; s. Hyman and Frances (Strolovitz) K.; children: Elyse, Stephanie. BBA, U. Miami, 1962. Vice pres. Ampco Products Inc., Hialeah, Fla., 1962-79, pres., from 1979. Mem. grievance com. Fla. Bar Assn., Miami, 1979-82. Mem. Decorative Laminate Products Assn. (pres. 1976-78). Home: Coconut Grove, Fla. Died June 11, 2007.

KRIGE, DANIEL GERHARDUS, mining engineer, consultant; b. Bothaville, South Africa, Aug. 26, 1919; s. Jacobus Joubert Krige and Magdalena Roux; m. Anna Maria Hendriks, Mar. 24, 1990; m. Anna Marie Esterhuysen (dec.); children: Tersia, Heleen, Annemarie, Jaco. BS in Engring., Witwatersrand U., 1938, MS in Engring., 1951, DS in Engring., 1963; D in Engring. (hon.), Pretoria U., 1981; DS in Engring. (hon.), U. South Africa, 1996; DS (hon.), Moscow State Mining U., 1997. Sect. surveyor Rand Leases Gold Mine, South Africa, 1939—45; dep. inspector mining leases State Dept. Mining, 1945—52; group fin. engr. Anglovaal Mining Group, 1952—81; prof. mineral econs. Witwatersrand U., 1981—91; independent cons., from 1991. Contbr. articles to profl. jours. Fellow: Royal Soc. South Africa; mem.: Nat. Acad. Engring. (fgn. assoc.), South African Statis. Assn. (life), South African Inst. Mining and Metallurgy (life). Avocations: travel, photography. Home: Constantia Kloof, South Africa. Died Mar. 3, 2013.

KROM, DONALD TEMPLETON, sales executive; b. Cornwall-on-Hudson, NY, Apr. 30, 1926; s. George R. and Helen (Templeton) K.; m. Stephanie W. Wahlers, June 17, 1950; children: Dietlind, Donald, Barbara. BS, NYU, 1950. Asst. treas. Windsor Bldg. Supplies Co., Inc., Poughkeepsie, N.Y., 1955-79, treas., 1979-80, pres., from 1980. Mem. New Hackensack Reform Ch., 1982—. Served with USN, 1944-46. Mem. Hudson Valley Homebuilders, Mid Hudson Lumber Dealers (pres. 1952—), Poughkeepsie C. of C. bd. dirs. 1950—). Lodges: Rotary (bd. dirs. Poughkeepsie chpt. 1980—). Republican. Avocations: golf, sailing. Home: Poughkeepsie, NY. Died Feb. 16, 2007.

KRUGER, FRED WALTER, mechanical engineering educator, university administrator; b. Chgo., Dec. 17, 1921; s. Fred and Magdalen (Lotz) K.; m. Esther Marie Foelber, Aug. 23, 1947; children— Paul Walter, John Robert, Thomas Herman. Student, Valparaiso U., 1940-42; BS in Elec. Engring, Purdue U., 1942-43, BS in Mech. Engring, 1947; MS in Mech Engring, Notre Dame U., 1954. Registered profl. engr., Ind. Mem. faculty Valparaiso U., from 1947, prof., from 1959, chmn. dept. mech. engring., 1955-65, dean Coll. Engring., 1965-72, v.p. bus. affairs, 1974-87, prof. emeritus, from 1987. Cons. McDonnell Aircraft Co., Caterpillar Tractor Co., Argonne Lab., No. Ill. Gas Co., Ind. Bd. Registration for Profl. Engrs. City councilman Valparaiso, 1972— ; mem. City Plan Commn., 1977-83. Served to lt. USNR, 1943-46. Mem. Am. Soc. M.E., Am. Soc. Engring. Edn., Tau Beta Pi. Lutheran. Home: Valparaiso, Ind. Died Dec. 25, 2006.

KRUM, JACK KERN, food products executive; b. Kansas City, Mo., Mar. 17, 1922; s. Charles Jean Krum and Clara Louise Struble; m. Miriam Emily Siebert; children: Mark, Meredith, Eric, Andrew. BA, Hope Coll., 1940—44; MA, Mich. State U., 1946—48; PhD, U. Mass., 1949—51. Prof. food tech. U. of Tenn., 1950—52; dir. quality control, rsch. food tech. Oscar Mayer Inc., Madison, Wis., 1952—55; rsch. food tech. Nat. Biscuit Co., NYC, 1955—57; tech. dir. Sterwin Chem., NYC, 1956—68; v.p. tech. dir. Rt. French Co., 1972—80. Pres. Techniques, Inc., Kans. City., from 1980. Mem. Heartland Art Guild. Lt. USN, 1944—52. Fellow: Inst. Food Tech. Avocations: woodcarving, watercolors. Home: Paola, Kans. Died Mar. 9, 2007.

KUBOTA, SHIGEKO, artist; b. Niigata, Japan, Aug. 2, 1937; BA in Sculpture, Tokyo U. Edn., 1960; postgrad., NYU, 1965-66, New Sch. for Social Rsch., 1966-67, Art Sch. Bklyn. Mus., 1967-68. Vice chmn. Fluxus Orgn., NYC, 1964; video curator anthology Film Archives, NYC, 1974-82; tchr. video art Sch. Visual Arts, NYC, 1978; video artist-in-residence Brown U., Providence, 1981. Video artist-in-residence Sch. Art Inst. Chgo., 1973, 81, 82, 84 Numerous one-woman shows, 1964-2015, including Sch. Art Inst. Chgo., 1973, Everson Mus. Art, Syracuse, N.Y., 1973, 75, 78, Art Gallery Ont., Toronto, Can., 1976, 77, Mus. Modern Art, N.Y.C., 1978, Mus. Contemporary Art, Chgo., 1981, D.A.A.D. Gallery, Berlin, 1981, Kunsthaus, Zurich, Switzerland, 1982, Am. Mus. Moving Image, Astoria, N.Y., 1991, Hara Mus. Contemporary Art, Tokyo, 1992, Stedelijk Mus., Amsterdam, The Netherlands, 1992, Kunstahlle in Kiel, Germany, 1993, Eric Fabre Gallery, Paris, 1996, Galerie de Paris, 1996, Whitney Mus. Am. Art, N.Y.C., 1996, Kamakura Gallery, Tokyo, 1998, Lance Fung Gallery, N.Y.C., 2000; exhibited in numerous group shows, 1962-2015, including Tokyo Mcpl. Mus., 1962, Mus. Modern Art, N.Y.C., 1974, 77, 88, Whitney Mus. Modern Art, 1975, 79, 83, 88, 95, Seibu Mus., Tokyo, 1981, Kennedy Ctr. for Performing Arts, Washington, 1982, Palais Beaux Art, Brussels, 1983, Stedelijk Mus., 1984, Tamayo Mus., Mexico City, 1985, Phila. Mus. Art, 1987, Houston Contemporary Art Mus., 1987, Aldrich Mus. Contemporary Art, Ridgefield, Conn., 1988, Art Space, Sydney, Australia, 1988, Nat. Mus. Art, Osaka, Japan, 1992, Walker Art Ctr., Mpls., 1993, Yokohoma (Japan) Mus., 1994, San Francisco Mus. Contemporary Art, 1995, Whitney Mus. Am. Art, 1995, Venice Biennale, 1995, Kwangju (Korea) Biennale, 1995, Jeu de Paume, Paris, 1996; work reviewed in numerous publs.; prodr. numerous videography, video sculpture and video installations. Recipient Indie award Assn. Ind. Video and Filmmakers, 1977, Maya Deren award Am. Film Inst., 1995; grantee Creative Artists Pub. Svc. Program, 1975, N.Y. Found. for Arts, 1985, visual arts grantee Nat. Endowment for Arts, 1988; fellow Nat. Endowment for Arts, 1975, 78, 80, Rockefeller fellow, 1979, German Acad. Exch. Svc., Berlin, 1979, Guggenheim fellow, 1987. Home: New York, NY. Died July 23, 2015.

KUEHN, LUCILLE M., retired humanities educator; b. NYC, May 26, 1924; d. David and Hilda Maisel; children: Susan, Robert, David. BA magna cum laude, U. Minn., Mpls., 1948; MA, U. Calif., Irvine, 1969. Instr. comparative culture Sch. Humanities U. Calif., Irvine, 1966—68; govtl. cons. Corona Del Mar, Calif., 1979—96. Lectr. Radcliffe Coll. Inst., 1972. Founding pres. LWV of Orange County, Newport Beach, 1961—63; bd. dirs. Orange County Grand Jury, Santa Ana, Calif., 1964—65, Orange County Juvenile Justice Commn., Santa Ana, 1965—66; mem. Orange County Mental Health Commn., Santa Ana, 1966—67, Newport Beach City Coun., 1974—78, Newport Harbor Art Mus., Newport Beach, 1974—87, South Coast Repertory Theatre, Costa Mesa, Calif., 1974—83, Town Hall of Calif., LA, 1975—85; pres. Town Hall Orange County Forum, 1981—84; co-chair Newport Beach Conservancy, 1987—90; pres. Town & Gown U. Calif., Irvine, 1989—90, mem. dean's coun. Sch. of the Arts, from 2000, mem. Humanities Assocs., 1995—2008; bd. dirs. Newport Beach Pub. Libr. Found., 1989—94, Newport Beach Pub. Libr. Bd., 1992—96; mem. Newport Beach Gen. Plan Com., Calif., 2002—06. Recipient Leadership in Bus. and Industry award, No. Orange County YWCA, 1982, Lauds and Laurels for Cmty. Svc. award, U. Calif., Irvine Alumni Assn., 1990, Award for Vision and Efforts, Newport Beach Pub. Libr., 1994, Outstanding Citizenship award, Women for Orange County, 1995; named Newport Beach Citizen of Yr., 1966, Newport Harbor C. of C., 1996; fellow, US Office of Edn., 1970. Jewish. Achievements include University of California Irvine named Lucille Kuehn Auditorium in her honor. Avocations: education, reading, gardening. Home: Newport Coast, Calif. Died Nov. 2013.

KUHLMANN, MARVIN EARL, minister; b. Chester, Nebr., Sept. 15, 1931; s. Walter Oscar and Hulda Katherine (Grabau) K.; m. Donna Mae Schneller, Oct. 17, 1954; children: Brent, Karen. AA, St. John's Coll., 1952; BA, Concordia Sem., 1954, BD, 1963, MDiv, 1972. Pastor St. Peter Luth. Ch., Westgage, Iowa, 1963-65, St. Stephen Luth. Ch., Liberty, Mo., 1965-71, St. Mark Luth. Ch., Flint, Mich., 1971-78, Holy Trinity Luth. Ch., Grandview, Mo., from 1978. Mem. spiritual life com. Ozanam Home for Boys, Kansas City, Mo., 1978-87. Mem. Clay County Home Com., Liberty, 1967. Home: Raymore, Mo. *If you strive to serve and search to give life will never disappoint you.* Died Apr. 19, 2007.

KUIVILA, ALLAN MATT, mechanical engineer; b. Painesville, Ohio, Oct. 7, 1957; s. Toivo Oswald and Alice (Clark) K. BME, Cleve. State U., 1987; AA, Lakeland Community Coll., 1983. Mfg. engr. Whitey Co., Cleve., 1983-86, project engr., from 1986. Mem. Exptl. Aircraft Assn. Home: Mentor, Ohio. Died Dec. 21, 2006.

KUMAR, NIRMAL, mechanical engineer; b. Dabro, Sindh, Pakistan, Apr. 14, 1941; came to U.S., 1975; d. Shyam and Leelawati Sunder; m. Leela Kumar, May 21, 1970; children: Leena, Naresh. BSME, Ranchi U., India, 1964; M. Engring. Adminstrn., U. Utah, 1989. Registered profl. engr. Kans., Utah. Engring. trainee Heavy Engring. Corp., Ranchi, 1964-66, engr., 1966-70, sr. engr., 1970-75; engr. EIMCO PEC, Salt Lake City, 1976-80, sr. engr., 1980-89, project engr., from 1989. V.p. South Cottonwood Lions, Salt Lake City, 1982-84. Mem. ASME (co-program chair 1990—), Am. Soc. Metals. Avocations: tennis, photography. Home: Midvale, Utah. Died Mar. 31, 2007.

KUMMERLE, HERMAN FREDERICK, retired environmental consulting firm executive; b. NYC, Apr. 25, 1936; s. Herman O. and Edyth K. (Osburg) K.; m. Joan D. Bell, June 1, 1957 (dec. July 1985); children: Anne R. Trachsel, Katherine L. Greenhill; m. Evelyn Hummon Holton, Mar. 1, 1986. BSChemE magna cum laude, NYU, 1957; MSChemE, U. Toledo, 1967. Registered profl. engr., Ohio, Mich., N.Y., Ind. Research engr. Union Carbide Corp., Niagra Falls, N.Y., 1957-61; process engr. Maumee Chem. Co., Toledo, 1962-65; sr. engr., group leader Owens Ill., Toledo, 1965-67, chief chem. engring., 1967-72, mgr. devel. and engring. services, 1972-76, adminstrn. mgr. corp. tech., 1976-79, mgr. energy tech., 1979-84; v.p. tech. and operating services Ann Arbor (Mich.) Cirs., 1985-88; v.p. Midwest Environ. Cons., Toledo, 1988-1999. Mem. tech. rev. team Ohio Dept. Energy, Columbus, 1977-80; mem. environ. and energy subcom. Toldeo Econ. Planning Council, 1979-81. Contbr. articles to profl. jours.; patentee in field. Chmn. bd. dirs. Toledo Met. Mission, 1977-78; mem. exec. com. Toledo Area Council of Chs., 1977-78; bd. dirs. Friendly Ctr., Inc., Toldeo, 1973-76, 80-82; chmn. bd. trustees Toledo dist. United Meth. Ch., 1980-82, lay mem. West Ohio conf., 1981—, chmn. coun. on fin. and adminstrn. West Ohio conf., 1992-97. Served to capt. U.S. Army, 1961-62. Mem. Am. Inst. Chem. Engrs. (various offices), Toledo Soc. Profl. Engrs., Gas Research Inst. (gas firing reseach task force 1982-83), Glass Packaging Inst. (chmn. energy task force 1976-83), Tau Beta Pi, Phi Kappa Phi, Phi Lambda Upsilon, Sigma Xi. Methodist. Avocations: photography, tennis, bridge. Home: Gahanna, Ohio. Died Jan. 15, 2007.

KURTZ, JEROME, lawyer, educator; b. Phila., May 19, 1931; s. Morris and Renee (Cooper) Kurtz; m. Elaine Etta, July 28, 1956 (dec. 2003); children: Madeleine, Nettie Kurtz Greenstein. BS with honors, Temple U., Phila., 1952; LLB magna cum laude, Harvard U., Cambridge, Mass., 1955. Bar: Pa. 1956, NY 1981, DC 1982; CPA, Pa. Assoc. Wolf, Block, Schorr & Solis-Cohen, Phila., 1955-56, 57-63, ptnr., 1963-66, 68-77; tax legis. counsel Dept. Treasury, Washington, 1966-68; commr. IRS, 1977-80; ptnr. Paul, Weiss, Rifkind, Wharton & Garrison, 1980-90; prof. law NYU, 1991-2001, dir. grad. tax program, 1995-98. Instr. Villanova Law Sch., 1964-65, U. Pa., 1969-74; vis. prof. law Harvard U., 1975-76; mem. adv. group to commr. IRS, 1976. Editor: Harvard Law Rev, 1953-55; contbr. numerous articles to profl. jours. Pres. Ctr. Inter-Am. Tax Adminstrn., 1980; bd. dirs. Common Cause, 1984-90, chmn. fin. com., 1985-88; bd. dirs. Nat. Capitol Area ACLU, 1990-91; mem. adv. bd. NYU Tax Inst., 1988-97, Little, Brown Tax Practice Series, 1994-96. Recipient Exceptional Service award Dept. Treasury, 1968, Alexander Hamilton award, 1980 Mem.: ABA (chmn. tax shelter com. 1982—84), Am. Coll. Tax Counsel, Am. Law Inst. (cons. fed. income tax project taxation of pass through entitites), Assn. Bar of City of NY (chmn. tax. coun. 1993—95), Phila. Bar Assn. (chmn. tax sect. 1975—76), Pa. Bar Assn., NY Bar Assn. (exec. com., tax sect. 1981—82), Beta Gamma Sigma. Home: New York, NY. Died Feb. 27, 2015.

KURTZMAN, RALPH HAROLD, JR., biochemist, researcher, consultant; b. Mpls., Feb. 21, 1933; s. Ralph Harold, Sr. and Susie Marie (Elwell) K.; m. Nancy Virginia (Leussler), Aug. 27, 1955; children: Steven Paul, Sue. BS, U. Minn., 1955; MS, U. Wis., 1958, PhD, 1959. Asst. prof. U. R.I., Kingston, 1959—62, U. Minn., Morris, 1962—65; biochemist USDA, Albany, Calif., 1965—97; ret., 1997. Instr. U. Calif., Berkeley, 1981-82; cons., spkr. Bliss Valley Farms, Twin Falls, Idaho, 1983-84, Kodik Farm, Lida, Belarus, 2003, Small Farms, Manazales, Colombia, 2004, VostokAgrabaza, Ust Kamenogorsk, Kazakhstan, 2004, Gusev Farm, Melenki, Russia 2005, Irzem Co. Batyrevo, Russia, 2005, CARE Farmers Assn., Upper Egypt, 2006-07, Assn. Mushroom Producers, Kiev, Ukraine, 2007, Mushroom Producers, Lutsk, Lviv & Kharkiv, Ukraine, 2008, Technol. U. Tajikstan, Chkalovsk, 2007, 08, Balm of Hope, Nakuru, Kenya, 2008, CLUSA Nampula Mozambique, 2009, John The Bapt. Enterprises, Hohoe, Ghana, 2010, Bemcom Youth Assn., Techiman, Ghana, 2012; pres. Santa Clara Valley Tex. Instrument PC Users' Group, 1991-92, editor, 1993-97, cons. CIBC, Kanungu, Uganda. Author: Oyster Mushroom Cultivation, 2004; editor Internat. Jour. Mushroom Sci., 1995-2000; co-editor Micologia Aplicada Internat., 2001—; editor, pub. Solliday/Sallade Family of Bucks County, Pa., 1999; mem. editl. bd. Pakistan Jour. Phytopathology, 2001—; inventor mushroom substrate (compost) preparation, decaffeination of beverages; contbr. articles to profl. jours. Chmn. Berkeley YMCA Camp Program Com., 1971-72; official Amateur Athletic Union (swimming), San Francisco, 1973-80; treas. Calif. Native Plant Soc., 1970; docent Oakland Mus. Calif., 2001-09. Mem. Am. Mushroom Inst., Mycological Soc. Am. (organizer symposium mushroom cultivation in Am. tropics 1998), Mycological Soc. Japan, Sigma Xi, Premium Mushroom Growers Assn. Avocations: computers, woodworking, photography, clock making. Died Oct. 20, 2015.

KUTLER, STANLEY IRA, historian, law educator; b. Cleve., Aug. 10, 1934; s. Robert P. and Zelda R. (Coffman) K.; m. Sandra J. Sachs, June 24, 1956; children: Jeffrey, David, Susan, Andrew. BA, Bowling Green State U., 1956; PhD, Ohio State U., 1960. Instr. history Pa. State U., State College, 1960-62; asst. prof. San Diego State U., 1962-64; from asst. prof. to prof. U. Wis., Madison, 1964-80, E. Gordon Fox prof. American Institutions, law and history, 1980—96; ret., 1996. Disting. exchange scholar to China Nat. Acad. Scis., 1982; Kenneth Keating lectr. Tel Aviv U., 1984; sr. Fulbright lectr. to Japan, 1977, to Israel, 1985, China, 1986; disting. vis. Fulbright scholar, Peru, 1987; Bicentennial prof. Tel Aviv U., 1985; cons. NEH, 1975, The Constitution Project, 1985; disting. chair Polit. Sci., U. Bologna, 1991; hist. cons. BBC/Discovery series Watergate, 1994. Author: Judicial Power and Reconstruction, 1968, Privilege and Creative Destruction, 1971, 2d edit., 1990, The American Inquisition, 1983, The Wars of Watergate: The Last Crisis of Richard Nixon, 1990, 92, Abuse of Power: The New Nixon Tapes, 1997; editor: Supreme Court and the Constitution, 1969, 3d edit., 1984, Looking for America, 1975, 80, The Encyclopedia of the Vietnam War, 1995, Encyclopedia of 20th Century America, 1995, American Perspectives: Historians on Historians, 1996, Watergate: The Fall of Richards Nixon, 1996, Dictionary of American History, 10 vols., 1996; founding editor Rev. in American History, 1972-97; mem. adv. editor Greenwood Pub., 1968-73, Johns Hopkins U. Press, 1982; play: I Nixon, 2008. Recipient Silver Gavel award ABA; fellow Sage Found., 1967-68, Emmy award, 1994, Peabody award, 1994, Best Reference Work award, Am. Assn. Pubs., 1996; fellow Guggenheim Found., 1971-72, Rockefeller Found., 1979-80. Jewish. Home: Madison, Wis. Died Apr. 7, 2015.

KUTLINA, JOSEPH WILLIAM, engineer; b. Niagara Falls, NY, July 24, 1923; s. Ludwig John and Mary Ann (Folga) K.; m. Frida Marlene Reumel, Feb. 21, 1948; children: Doris, Joseph, Ludwig, Paul, David, Emma, Mary, Paula. Diploma in indsl. chemistry, Trott Vocat. Sch., Niagara Falls, 1942; diploma in stationary engring., ICS. Lic. chief stationary engr. N.Y. Locomotive fireman/stationary engr. N.Y. Ctrl. R.R., Niagara Falls, 1941-53; stationary engineer Olin Corp., Niagara Falls, 1953-89, chief engr., 1990; stationary engr. Pure Carbonic Corp., Niagara Falls, 1963-64; chief engr. cons. Spallino Devel. Co., Niagara Falls, 1967-92; HVAC cons., chief engr. Niagara Falls Meml. Med. Ctr., 1993-97; trainer, cons. boiler ops. Goodyear Corp., Niagara Falls, from 1998. HVAC cons. Waldorf Motel, Niagara Falls, various govt. bldgs., fed., state and local bus., 1967-92. With U.S. Army, 1943-46. Decorated Bronze Star. Mem. YMCA. Achievements include pioneering of the operation of steam generators using hydrogen gas as a fuel in computer controlled furnaces. Home: Niagara Falls, NY. Died Mar. 15, 2007.

KUVIN, SEYMOUR FLEISHFARB, psychiatrist; b. Newark, Nov. 30, 1924; s. Jacob Fleishfarb and Frieda Kuvin; m. Judith Kate Saxe (dec.); children: June Volk, Joshua. BS, Pa. State U., 1948, MS, 1949; MB, Chgo. Med. Sch., 1953, MD, 1954. Diplomate Am. Bd. Pediatrics. Intern Morristown (N.J.) Meml. Hosp., 1953-54; resident in pediatrics St. Michael's Med. Ctr., Newark, 1954-56; resident in psychiatry Greystone Park Psychiat. Hosp., 1967-70; dir. psychiat. inst. Psychiat. Inst., Newark, 1970-90; sr. attending psychiatrist St. Michael's Med. Ctr., Newark, 1971-90, psychiatrist emeritus, from 1990; pvt. practice pediatrics Morristown, 1956-70. Med. dir. Morris County Sch. Emotionally Disabled, Morris Plains, N.J., 1961-67; clin. asst. prof. psychiatry U. Medicine and Dentistry of N.J., Newark, 1970-90; assoc. prof. psychiatry Seton Hall Grad. Sch. Medicine, 1988—; prin. psychiatrist N.J. Bell, Newark, 1971-90. Contbr. articles to profl. jours. Active Bd. Health, Morristown, 1965-69; docent Turtle Back Zoo, West Orange, 1982-90; post surgeon VFW, Livingston, N.J., 1986-90, sr. vice comdr., 1990-92, comdr., 1993-94. Cpl. U.S. Army, 1941-46. Fellow Am. Acad. Pediatrics, Am. Coll. Physicians, Falk fellow Am. Psychiat. Assn. Jewish. Home: Toms River, NJ. Died Jan. 31, 2007.

KYBURZ, LINDA M., family counselor; b. Fairbury, Ill., July 25, 1949; d. Viola M. (Kyburz) Flint. Cert. women's studies, U. Mo., St. Louis, 1992, MEd, 1996. Lic. social worker, Mo.; cert. substance abuse counselor, Mo. Substance abuse counselor Bridgeway Counseling, St. Charles, Mo., 1990-93; overnight supr. Life Skills, St. Louis, 1991-93; program coord. Grace Hill Neighborhood Svcs., St. Louis, 1993-95, family therapist, from 1995; family counselor Hyland Ctr., St. Louis, 1993-995; family therapist Family Resource Ctr., St. Louis, from 1995. Vol. Women's Ctr., St. Charles, 1994—. Democrat. Lutheran. Avocations: movies, reading, travel. Home: Winfield, Mo. Died Nov. 10, 2006.

LA CHAPELLE, DOLORES, environmentalist, writer; b. Louisville, July 4, 1926; d. John A. and Anna May (Kelly) Greenwell; divorced. BA, Denver U., 1947. Co-founder Deep Ecology; dir. Way of Mountain Learning Ctr., Silverton, Colo.; workshops leader, from 1981. Workshop presenter U. Utah, Salt Lake City, 1981-94, U. Wis., La Crosse, 1988-91, Notre Dame U., 1989, U. North Tex., Denton, 1990. Author: Earth Festivals, 1976, Earth Wisdom, 1978, rev. edit., 1984, also German translation, Sacred Land, Concerning Deep Ecology and Celebrating Life, rev. ed. 1992, also German translation, Deep Powder Snow, 1993, also Italian translation, D.H. Lawrence: Future Primitive, 1996. Mem. various environ. orgns., 1976—. Mem. Phi Beta Kappa. Avocations: teaching skiing, leading mountain climbing and outdoor rituals. Home: Silverton, Colo. Died Jan. 21, 2007.

LADA, SYLVESTER, company executive; b. West Warwick, RI, June 20, 1924; s. Walter and Alexandra (Peczynski) L.; m. Eleanore Kardynal, Jan. 18, 1947; children: Catherine, Sandra, Thomas, Gregory. Student, MaComb Community Coll., Warren, Mich., 1975-88, Wayne State U., 1985. With circulation dept. Detroit News, 1940-41; technologist Earle M. Jorgensen Co., 1951-84; ret. With USN, 1941-51. Mem. Soc. Mfg. Engrs. (Recipient Pres.'s award 1983), Robotics Internat. of Soc. Mfg. Engrs., Computer and Automated Systems Assn., Machine Vision Assn., Grosse Point Garden Club. Home: Roseville, Mich. Died May 30, 2007.

LADD, JOSEPH CARROLL, retired insurance company executive; b. Chgo., Jan. 26, 1927; s. Stephen C. and Laura (McBride) L.; m. Barbara Virginia Carter, June 5, 1965; children: Carroll, Joseph Carroll, Barbara, Virginia, William. BA, Ohio Wesleyan U., 1950; CLU, Am. Coll., Bryn Mawr; D in Bus. Adminstrn. (hon.), Spring Garden Coll., 1985. Agt. Conn. Gen. Life Ins. Co., Chgo., 1950-53, staff asst., 1953-54, mgr. Evanston (Ill.) br. office, 1954-60, dir. agys., 1960-62, mgr. Los Angeles br. office, 1963; v.p. sales Fidelity Mut. Life Ins. Co., Phila., 1964-67, sr. v.p. sales, 1968, exec. v.p., 1969-71, pres., chief exec. officer, dir., 1971-84, chmn., chief exec. officer, dir., 1984-89, chmn., dir., 1989-91; ret. Bd. dirs. Corestates Fin., Phila. Suburban Corp., Phila. Electric Co. Trustee Bryn Mawr Hosp.; trustee United Way of S.E. Pa.; trustee Phila. United Way, also gen. chmn. 1978 campaign; bd. dirs. Phila. YMCA. Served with USNR, 1945-46. Recipient Civic Achievement award Am. Jewish Com., 1978, Achiever's award WHEELS Med. and Specialized Transp., 1978, Ohio Wesleyan U. Life Achievement award Delta Tau Delta, 1982, William Penn award, Greater Phila. C. ofC. and PENJERDEL Coun., 1988, Robert Morris Citizenship award Valley Forge Coun. Boy Scouts Am., 1988; named YMCA Man of Yr., 1979, William Penn Found. Disting. Pennsylvanian, 1980. Mem. Greater Phila. C. of C. (dir., chmn. 1979, 83-84), Phila. Country Club, Union League Club (Phila.), Summer Beach (Fla.) Country Club. Home: Bryn Mawr, Pa. Died June 18, 2014.

LADD, MARY ISOBEL, secondary school educator; b. Redford, Mich., Dec. 31, 1916; d. Raphael and Stella Mary (Westlake) Mettetal; m. John Maxwell Ladd, Aug. 12, 1939 (dec. July 1984); children: Mary Gail, Sandra Joyce, Craig Geoffrey. BS, Mich. State U., 1938. Tchr. Big Rapids H.S., 1939-40. Pres. Roselle (Ill.) Garden Club; pres. Village Pines Golf Club; activeMeth. ch., women's socs. Mem. AAUW, Phi Kappa Phi. Republican. Avocations: crafts, civic activities, bridge. Home: Hot Springs National Park, Ark. Died Dec. 19, 2006.

LADERMAN, EZRA, composer, educator, college dean; b. Bklyn., June 29, 1924; life ptnr. Aimlee Laderman; children: Isaiah, Jacob, Rachel. BA, Bklyn. Coll., 1950; MA, Columbia U, 1952; studies with Stefan Wolpe, Otto Luening, Douglas Moore, & P. Lang, Columbia U. Dir. music program Nat. Endowment for Arts, 1979-82; pres. Nat. Music Coun., 1985-89; vis. composer Yale U., New Haven, 1988, dean Sch. Music, 1989-95, prof. to prof. emeritus, composition, 1996—2015. Chmn. Am. Composers Orch., 1987-90; taught at Sarah Lawrence Coll., SUNY-Purchase Compositions include several symphonies, string quartets, operas, compostions and recordings; (dramatic operas) Jacob and the Indians, 1954, Goodbye to the Clowns, 1956, The Hunting of the Snark, 1958, Sarah, 1959, Air Raid, 1965, Shadows Among Us, 1967, Galileo Galilei, 1978, Marilyn, 1993; (orchestral) Piano Concerto, 1939, Leipzig Symphony, 1945, Piano Concerto, 1957, 8 Symphonies, 1964-84, Flute Concerto, 1968, Viola Concerto, 1975, Violin Concerto, 1978, Piano Concerto No. 1, 1978, Concert for String Quartet and Orchestra, 1981, Cello Concerto, 1984, Clarinet Concerto, 1995; (vocal) oratorio The Eagle Stirred, 1961, oratorio The Trials of Galileo, 1967, Columbus, 1975, oratorio A Mass for Cain, 1983; (chamber) Wind Octet, 1957, Clarinet Sonata, 1958, 9 String Quartets, 1959-96, Double Helix for Flute, Oboe, and String Quartet, 1968, Partita for Violin, 1982, Double String Quartet, 1983; (film scores) The Charter, 1958, The Invisible Aton, 1958, The Question Tree, 1962, Odyssey, 1964, The Eleanor Roosevelt Story, 1965, The Black Fox, 1965, Magic Prison, 1966, The Meaning of Modern Art, 1967, Confrontation, 1968, Image of Love, 1968, The Bible as Literature, 1972, Burden of Mystery, 1972; (television movie scores) Herschel, 1959, Invisible City, 1961, The Voice of the Desert, 1962, Eltanin, 1962, Grand Canyon, 1964, The Forgotten Peninsula, 1967, Our Endangered Wildlife, 1967, California the Most, 1968, Before Cortez, 1970, In the Fall of 1844, 1971, Cave People of the Philippines, 1972, Lamp Unto My Feet, 1978. Radio operator Army, WWII. Guggenheim fellow 1955, 1958, 1964; recipient Rome prize, 1963; Kennedy Center Friedheim Award, 2nd place, 1981. Mem.: AAAL (pres. 2006—08). Died Feb. 28, 2015.

LAFFOLEY, PAUL GEORGE, JR., artist, architect; b. Cambridge, Mass., Aug. 14, 1935; s. Paul George and Mary Ellen (Lyons) L. BA, Brown U., Providence, RI, 1958; postgrad., Harvard U., 1958-62, MIT, 1964-65, Boston Archtl. Ctr., 1967-69. Registered architect, Mass. Apprentice in sculpture The Studio of Mirko Baseldella, Cambridge, 1961-62, The Studio of Frederick J. Kiesler, NYC, 1962-63; archtl. designer Emery Roth and Sons, Architects, NYC, 1963-64, Techbuilt Inc., North Dartmouth, Mass., 1964-66, James Lawrence Jr., Architect, Brookline, Mass., 1966-67; concept designer The Tufts New England Med. Ctr. Planning Office, Boston, 1967-70; pres. The Boston Visionary Cell, Inc., 1971—2015. Exhibiting mem. The Ward-Nasse Gallery, Boston and N.Y.C., 1970-84, Stux Gallery, Boston and N.Y.C., 1985-88, Kent Fine Art, Inc., 1989 and numerous one-person and group nat. and internat. exhibits, 1966-2015; author: The Phenomenology of Revelation, 1989; contbr. author and artworks various books, featured writer and artist: Alchemy: The Telenomic Process of the Universe, 1973, Black-White Hole: The Force of the History of the Universe to Produce Total Non-Existence, 1976, Sulfur 17: A Literary Tri-Quarterly of the Whole Art, 1986, The Pnenomenology of Revelation, 1989. Named finalist Fellowships of the Creative Artists' Svcs., U. Mass., 1976, Mass. Arts and Humanities Found., Boston U. Gallery, 1978; printing fellow Mass. Artists Found., 1989; grantee The Marie Walsh Sharpe Art Found., 1991-92. Mem. Inst. Contemporary Art (Englehard award 1985), Theosophical Soc., U.S. Psychotronics Assn., World Future Soc. (Boston-Cambridge chpt.), New England Soc. Psychic Sci. Researchers (earned recognition 1982), Faculty Club Harvard U. Avocations: yoga, raising birds. Home: Boston, Mass. Died Nov. 16, 2015.

LAIRD, ANNE MARIE, personnel director; b. Orange, NJ, June 23, 1941; d. Paul M. and Anne (Byrne) Kelly; m. Daniel A. Laird, Aug. 13, 1960; children: Daniel, Michael, Kelly, Paul. Student, Glassboro State Coll. Employment supr. Continental Can Co., Millville, N.J., 1976-78, human resrouces supr., 1978-81, Houston, Tex., 1981-85; complex human resources supr. Santa Ana, Calif., from 1985. Chair N.J. United Way, Millville, 1978, CEDA Program, 1979. Mem. Am. Soc. Personnel Mgrs., Personnel Indsl. Relations Assn., Internat. Mgmt. Council (pres. 1978). Died May 21, 2007.

LAKOFF, EVELYN, music association executive; b. Bklyn., Apr. 8, 1932; d. Boris and Ray (Feldman) Schleifer; m. Sanford Allan Lakoff, June 4, 1961. BA, Queens Coll., 1953; MA in Music Edn., Columbia U., 1955; MA in Musicology, Harvard U., 1963. Pres. San Diego (Calif.) Early Music Soc. Music tchr. N.Y.C. 1955-60, Northport, N.Y., 1965-67. Avocations: playing viola da gamba, singing in madrigal group, playing piano, collecting teddy bears. Home: San Diego, Calif. Died Nov. 25, 2006.

LAMBETH, STEVEN KEITH, engineer; b. Winston-Salem, NC, Oct. 14, 1952; s. Hoyle Alfred and Evelyn (Spainhour) L.; m. Rose Beardsley, June 25, 1977. Project engr. Carolina Med. Electronics, King, N.C., from 1977. Served with USN, 1971-77. Home: Winston Salem, NC. Died Aug. 9, 2007.

LAMFALUSSY, ALEXANDRE, federal agency administrator; b. Kapuvar, Hungary, Apr. 26, 1929; m. Anne-Marie Cochard, 1957; children Christophe, Isabelle, Laurence, Jérome Attended, U. Louvain, Nuffield Coll., Oxford. Economist, then econ. advisor Bank of Brussels, 1955-65, exec. dir., chmn. exec. bd., 1965-75, exec. dir. Lambert, 1975; econ. adv. head monetary and econ. dept. BIS, 1976-81, asst. gen. mgr., 1981-85, gen. mgr., 1985-93; pres. European Monetary Inst., 1994-97; with European Inst. Studies, Louvain-La-Neuve, Belgium, from 1997. Vis. lectr. Yale U., New Haven, 1961-62. Author: Investment and Growth in Mature Economies: The Case of Belgium, 1961, The U.K. and The Six: An Essay on Growth in Western Europe, 1963, Les Marchés financiers en Europe, 1968. Died May 9, 2015.

LAMICA, GEORGE EDWARD, SR., writer, importer; b. Watertown, NY, Feb. 22, 1930; s. James Alfred and Madeline Catherine (Glossl) L.; m. Louise Holden, Feb. 22, 1951 (div. Feb. 1969); children: George Edward, Mary Catherine. AA, Wilmington Coll., 1954; BSBA, U. S.C., 1955. Mgmt. trainer Belks, Wilmington, N.C., 1951-79, Columbia, S.C., West Palm Beach, Fla.; ptnr. Martha's Flower Shoppe, Wilmington, 1979-86; owner Lamica Flowers Internat., Wilmington, 1986-88, Lamica Ltd. Internat., Wilmington, 1988-91. Dir. New Hanover Workshop, Wilmington; cons. Liberty Furniture Co., Wilmington, Carribean Imports, Wilmington; mem. exec. com. New Hanover Spl. Olympics, Wilmington, 1984. Author: (book and screenplay) Day the Earth Cracked, 1992, The Odyssey of Herman, 1994, (book) Bride to Be Guide, 1993. Pres. Optimist Club, Wilmington, 1978—. With USMC, 1947-52, Korea. Mem. So. Writers Assn., Cape Fear Writers Assn. Avocations: chess, gardening. Home: Castle Hayne, NC. Died May 27, 2007.

LAMMER, EDWARD JAMES, geneticist; b. Dubuque, Feb. 26, 1953; s. Benedict and Anne (Lyons) Lammer; m. Dibsy Machta; children: Aaron, Ellie. B in Biology, Washington U., St. Louis, 1975; MD, U. Iowa, 1979. Worked for Epidemic Intelligence Svc., Centers for Disease Control and Prevention; prin. investigator Benioff Children's Hosp. Rsch. Inst., U. Calif., San Francisco; dir. med. genetics Children's Hosp., Oakland, Calif.; ret., 2016. Asst. prof. Stanford U. Died Feb. 20, 2016.

LAMMERS, NANCY ALICE, travel consultant; b. Hull, Iowa, Aug. 23, 1940; d. Bert Vande Stouwe and Fay (Thompson) Kooistra; m. Stan G. Lammers, May 1, 1959; children: Bret (dec.), Stanley Grant, Dana. BA, Northwestern U., Orange City, Iowa. Mgr. and founder Travel Assured Corp., Rock Valley, Iowa, from 1982. Bd. dirs. Area Edn. Bd. #4, Sioux Center, Iowa, 1982-88. Mem. Rock Valley C. of C. (bd. dirs. 1983-86). Home: Sioux Center, Iowa. Died Feb. 9, 2007.

LAMPHERE, LEIGH ANN, elementary school educator, music educator; b. Montpelier, Vt., Oct. 28, 1960; d. Robert Ivan Lamphere and Marjorie Louise Pillsbury; m. Brian Charles Allaire, July 7, 1990; children: Phillip Lamphere Allaire, Nathan Lamphere Allaire. MusB, SUNY, Potsdam, 1982; MEd, St. Michaels Coll., 1994. Tchr. music Union Elem. Sch., Montpelier, Vt., 1982—84, Morristown Elem. Sch., Morrisville, from 1985. Instr. Morrisville Ski Program, Stowe, 2001—05; bd. dirs. Lamoille County Mental Health, Lamoille Valley Mentoring Partnership. Mem.: NEA, Vt. Alliance Arts Edn. (Leadership Honoree 2007), Am. Choral Dirs. Assn., Vt. Music Educators Assn., Music Educators Nat. Conf. Democrat. Avocations: theater, reading, skiing. Home: Morrisville, Vt. Died June 21, 2007.

LAND, ALLAN HERBERT, broadcast executive; b. NYC, May 17, 1922; s. Harry J. and Theresa A. (Brown) L.; m. June Oster, Aug. 17, 1947; children: Eric, Michael, Myra. BS, St. John's U., 1947. Announcer Sta. WCNW, NYC, 1940-41; reporter Sta. WMRF, Lewistown, Pa., 1947; news dir. Sta. WHIZ-AM-FM-TV, Zanesville, Ohio, 1947-53, program dir., 1953-54, gen. mgr., 1954-69; v.p. T/R, Inc., Zanesville, 1969-76, S.E. Ohio Broadcasting System, Inc., Zanesville, from 1976. Chmn. Ohio Ednl. Broadcasting Network, Columbus, Ohio, 1981—, Zanesville/Musingam County Port Authority, 1986—. Sgt. U.S. Army, 1942-46, ETO. Decorated Bronze Star, Purple Heart, ETO ribbon; named Broadcaster of Yr. Miami U., Oxford, Ohio, 1977. Mem. Nat. Assn. Broadcasters (pres. 1976-78), Ohio Assn. Broadcasters (pres. 1972-76, Broadcaster of Yr. 1975), Rotary. Republican. Avocations: golf, aviation, music, theater. Home: Watchung, NJ. Died Nov. 16, 2007.

LANDAU, HERMAN, newspaperman retired; b. Louisville, Apr. 12, 1911; s. Oscar Hayim and Rebecca (Fuhrer) L.; m. Leah Seligman, Apr. 15, 1946 (dec. 1974); children: Kay Landau Miller, Rebecca Landau Greenfield; m. Helen Berman Landau, June 15, 1975; children: Margaret Berman Goldberg, Susan Berman Rogers, Joseph. B in Liberal Studies, U. Louisville, 1985. Makeup editor The Courier-Jour., Louisville, 1928-52, The Louisville Times, 1952-75; ret., 1975; founder, contbr. Cmty., Louisville, 1977-91, editor emeritus, from 1991. Author: (book) Adath Louisville, 1981. Bd. dirs. Jewish Cmty. Ctr., 1945-72, Jewish

Cmty. Fedn., 1970—, B'nai B'rith Louisville Lodge #14, 1937—, Jewish Edn. Assn., N.Y.C., 1980. Recipient Vol. of Yr. award Jewish Cmty. Ctr., Louisville, 1959, Jewish Cmty. Fedn., 1991, Outstanding Participation award, Bonds for Israel, 1981, Jewish Person of Yr. award B'nai B'rith, 1997. Democrat. Jewish. Home: Louisville, Ky. Died Dec. 28, 2006.

LANDMAN, LOUIS CHARLES, chemical company executive; b. St. Paul, Aug. 31, 1914; s. Philip Albert and Julia Florence (Smith) L.; m. Mae Catherine Claffey, Oct. 22, 1938; children: L. Charles Jr., Mary Louise Landman Nixon. BA, Coll. St. Thomas; LLD, St. Mary's Coll., Winona, Minn., 1969. Pres. Nat. Chems. Inc., Winona, 1949-79, sr. exec. officer, from 1979. Served to lt. USN, 1944-47. Republican. Roman Catholic. Avocation: golf. Home: Winona, Minn. Died Feb. 16, 2007.

LANDSTROM, ELSIE HAYES, retired editor; b. Kuling, Kiangsi, China, June 22, 1923; came to the U.S., 1935; d. Paul Goodman and Helen Mae (Wolf) Hayes; m. Victor Norman Landstrom, Jan. 21, 1953 (dec. Oct. 1989); children: Peter S., Ruth H. BA magna cum laude, Hamline U., 1945. Writer, editor adminstrv. staff Am. Friends Svc. Com., Phila., 1946-52, MIT, Cambridge, Mass., 1952-53; mem. editl. bd. Approach Mag., Phila. and Needham, 1947-67; sr. editor Word Guild, 1976-82; freelance writer and editor Conway, Mass., 1976-98; ret., 1998. Author: Closing the Circle-An American Family in China, 1998; (poetry) Lions Walk Around My Bed, 2007; editor: Propaganda and Aesthetics, 1979, Taoism and Chinese Religion, 1981, Hyla Doc in China 1924-1949, 1991, Hyla Doc in Africa 1950-1961, 1994; exhibits include Greenfield, Mass., 1996, Book Mill, Montague, Mass., 1997, Began to Paint age 70. Newsletter editor, draft resisters support com. Wellesley (Mass.) Friends Meeting; chair Fair Housing Com., Needham. Avocations: birding, reading, painting. Died Feb. 13, 2015.

LANG, BARBARA BRYANT, business association administrator; b. Jacksonville, Fla., Oct. 16, 1943; d. Chester A. and Margaret (Small) Bryant; m. Gerald B. Lang, Apr. 30, 1962; 1 child, Yalanda Maria. BS in Bus. Edn., Edward Waters Coll., Jacksonville, Fla., 1965; postgrad., Calif. Rsch. Lab., Sacramento, 1982. Adminstrn. mgr. IBM, Atlanta, 1976—78, mgr. secretarial svcs., 1980—84, sr. fin. mgr., 1984—85; pres. GYB Assocs., Atlanta, 1985—86; mgr. plans & controls IBM Corp. Asset Mgmt., Rockville, Md., 1986—88; corp. program mgr. govt. & external programs IBM Corp., 1988; pres. CEO DC C. of C., 2002—. Past chpt. pres. Jack and Jill Am., 1983; co-chair adv. com. Southside HS, Atlanta, 1985—86; mem. task force Just Us Theatre, Atlanta, 1986; chair polit. action com. Nat. Coalition 100 Black Women, 1988. Named one of 100 Most Powerful Women in DC, Washingtonian Mag., 2009. Mem.: The Profl. Woman (bd. dirs.), Atlanta C. of C. (womens workshop com. mem. 1985), Nat. Assn. Female Execs., Am. Soc. Tng. & Devel., Women Bus. Owners. Democrat. Presbyterian. Avocation: interior decorating. Home: 5300 Macarthur Blvd NW Washington DC 20016-2522 Office: DC C of C 1213 K St NW Washington DC 20005 Office Phone: 202-347-7201 ext. 239. Business E-Mail: president@dcchamber.org.

LANG, PAUL ANDREW, air compressor manufacturing company executive; b. Boston, Aug. 17, 1923; s. Stephen Christian and Margaret Florence (MacLeod) L.; m. Celia Alison Lindsay, July 20, 1945; children: Stephen Lindsay, Jenifer Madeleine, Gordon MacLeod. AB, Harvard Coll., 1946, MBA, 1950. Supr. Corning (N.Y.) Glass Works, 1950-56, plant mgr., 1956-63, Muskogee, Okla., 1963-69, Martinsburg, W.Va., 1969-73, mgr. mfg., 1973-85; chief exec. officer P.K. Lindsay Co., Deerfield, N.H., 1990, chmn. bd., from 1991, also bd. dirs. Cons. on mfg. practices, Wolfeboro, N.H., 1985—. Author: Cost Reduction Manual, 1985. Pres., life mem. Spencer Crest Nature Ctr., Corning, 1975-85; pres. No. Wolfeboro Area Assn., 1988-89, Wolfeboro Friends of Music, 1989-91, Corning Philharm., 1948-59; active N.H. Timberland Owners Assn., 1983—. With inf. AUS, 1942-45, ETO. Mem. Rotary (past bd. dirs.). Republican. Mem. United Ch. of Christ. Avocations: tree farming, woodworking, photography, music. Home: Wolfeboro, NH. Died May 3, 2007.

LANGE, LAWRENCE ROBERT, prosthetist, orthotist; b. Chgo., Nov. 22, 1955; s. Jacques Kenton and Lorraine Marie (Barland) L.; children: Amy, Lori, Ashley, Jeffrey; m. Kathleen Marie Morrelli, July 19, 1988. BA, UCLA, 1978, cert. in orthotics and prosthetics, 1979. Cert. Am. Bd. Orthotists and Prosthetists (mem.). Staff prosthetist, orthotist J.E. Hanger, Inc., Washington, 1979-83; dir. orthotics and prosthetics Shriners Hosp., Phila., 1983-88; asst. dir. orthotics and prosthetics Rusk Rehab. Inst., NYC, 1987; mgr., jr. ptnr. Hanger Orthopedics, Wheeling, W. Va., from 1988. Dir. Regional Acad. Orthotics Prosthetics, Phila., 1984-85; mem. editorial bd. Jour. of Prosthetics and Orthotics, Alexandria, Va., 1988. Editor Orthotics and Prosthetics, 1983-88; contbr. articles to profl. jours.; developed Lange silicone partial foot prosthesis. Recipient scholarships, Lions Club, Fremont, Calif. , 1973, Anaconda Reynolds Corp., Fremont, 1973. Fellow Am. Acad. Orthotists and Prosthetists. Avocations: flying, car collecting. Home: Friendswood, Tex. Died July 15, 2007.

LANGFIELD, RAYMOND LEE, real estate developer; b. Houtzdale, Pa., Jan. 31, 1921; s. Arthur H. and Sadie L. (Morris) L.; m. Helen Deborah Elion, Oct. 15, 1952; 1 child, Joanna Langfield Rose. BS in Indsl. Engring., Pa. State U., 1942. Registered profl. engr., Conn. Chief mgmt. engr. CIT Fin. Corp., NYC, 1947-50; v.p. Mosler Safe Co., NYC, 1950-60; pres. Spicer Fuel Co., Groton, Conn., 1960-86, United Fuel Corp., Groton, 1962-86, Spicer Gas Co., Groton, 1982-86, Conn. Hotel Corp., New London, 1986-94; real estate developer, from 1980. Bd. dirs. New London Fed. Savings and Loan, 1982—86; founder, bd. dirs. Bank of Mystic, 1987—90. Mem. Conn. Energy Adv. Bd., Hartford, 1985-87; pres. Grade Arts Ctr., New London, 1985-87. Lt. comdr. USNR, 1941-47. Mem. Southeast Conn. C. of C. (bd. dirs., chmn. bd. 1978-80), Ind. Conn. Petroleum Assn. (chmn. bd. 1973-74, Oil Man of Yr., 1975), New Eng. Fuel Inst. (bd. dirs. 1972-84), Navy League Conn. (bd. dirs. 1985-87). Jewish. Avocations: fresh-water fishing, electronics. Home: Boca Raton, Fla. Died July 10, 2007.

LANO, CHARLES JACK, retired financial executive; b. Port Clinton, Ohio, Apr. 17, 1922; s. Charles Herbin and Antoinette (Schmitt) L.; m. Beatrice Irene Spees, June 16, 1946 (dec. 1995); children: Douglas Cloyd, Charles Lewis. BS in Bus. Adminstrn. summa cum laude, Ohio State U., 1949. C.P.A., Okla. With U.S. Gypsum Co., 1941-46, Ottawa Paper Stock Co., 1946-47; accountant Arthur Young & Co. C.P.A.'s, Tulsa, 1949-51; controller Lima div. Ex-Cell-O Corp., 1951-59, electronics div. AVCO Corp., 1959-61, Servomation Corp., 1961; asst. comptroller Scovill Mfg. Co., Waterbury, Conn., 1961-62, comptroller, 1962-67; controller CF&I Steel Corp., Denver, 1967-69, v.p., controller, 1969-70; controller Pacific Lighting Corp., 1970-76; exec. v.p. Arts-Way Mfg. Co., Armstrong, Iowa, 1976-85; mgmt. auditor City of Anaheim, Calif., 1985-96; ret., 1996. Served with USMCR, 1942-45. Mem. Am. Inst. C.P.A.'s, Calif. Soc. C.P.A.'s, Inst. Internal Auditors. Home: Redondo Beach, Calif. Died Jan. 10, 2015.

LARGENT, MARGIE, retired architect; b. Adrian, Mo., Feb. 28, 1923; d. Arlie Everett Largent and Ruby Lacey Grosshart; m. Creighton A. Anderson, May 10, 1954; children: Michael Creig, Jon William Everett. Student, Capital Bus. Coll., 1942, Art Ctr. Sch. of Design, LA, 1944, 45, 46, Willamette U., 1946-47; BArch, U. Oreg., 1950. Registered arch., Wash., Oreg., Alaska. Sr. structural draftsman Stone & Webster Engrs., L.A. and Boston, 1950-52; prodn. coord. Jon Konigshofer, Carmel, Calif., 1953-54, Daniel-Mann-Johnson, Archs., LA, 1954-55, Gordon Cochran, Arch., Portland, Oreg., 1956-57, John Groom, Arch., Salem, Oreg., 1958-60; designer Largent & Anderson, Lake Oswego, Oreg., 1961-63; arch. Margie Largent, Lake Oswego, from 1964. Prin. works include Shon Tay Profl. Ctr., Lake Oswego, 1965-78, Jackson Residence, Warm Springs Reservation, Oreg., 1974, Crosby-Earth Shelter, San Juan Island, Wash., 1975, Anderson Tri-Plex, Cordova, Alaska, 1983. Active Land Use Com., Lake Oswego, 1970—, Park Adv. Bd., Clacksmas County, Oreg., 1975-79, Bldg. Bd. Appeals, Lake Oswego, 1978-98; pres. Associated C. of C., Clackamas County, 1970. Mem.: Constrn. Specifications Inst. (Portland chpt. pres. 1977, 1986, editor 1979, 1984, archivist 1980, Capital chpt. archivist 1995—2003). Home: Astoria, Oreg. Died July 31, 2007.

LARIMER, JAMES LYNN, biology educator, researcher; b. Jonesboro, Tenn., Jan. 7, 1932; children: Linda, Bret. BS, East Tenn. State U., 1953; MA, U. Va., 1954; PhD, Duke U., 1959. Asst. prof. zoology U. Tex., Austin, 1959, assoc. prof., 1964-68, prof., from 1968. Corr. editor Brain and Behavioral Sci.; mem. physiology study sect. NIH, marine sci. equipment com. NSF. Author: Animal Physiology, 1969, 74; contbr. over 90 articles to sci. jours. Recipient Jacob Javits award NIH, 1988-95; Guggenheim fellow, 1978, DuPont fellow, 1953-54. Fellow AAAS. Home: Austin, Tex. Died July 3, 2007.

LA ROSSA, JAMES MICHAEL, retired lawyer; b. Bklyn., Dec. 4, 1931; s. James Vincent and Marie Antoinette (Tronolone) La R.; m. Gayle Marino (div.) children: James M., Thomas, Nancy, Susan; m. Dominique Bazin-Thall, Aug. 11, 1998 (div.) BS, Fordham U., 1953; JD, Fordham U. Sch. Law, 1958. Bar: N.Y. 1958, U.S. Dist. Ct. N.Y. 1961, U.S. Supreme Ct. 1969. Pvt. practice law, NYC, 1958—62, 1967—74; asst. US atty. (eastern dist.) NY US Dept. Justice, Bklyn., 1962—65; ptnr. Lefkowitz & Brownstien, NYC, 1965-67, La Rossa, Shargel & Fishetti, NYC, 1974-76, La Rossa, Brownstein & Mitchell, NYC, 1980-82, La Rossa, Axenfeld & Mitchell, NYC, 1982-84, La Rossa, Cooper, Axenfeld, Mitchell & Bergman, NYC, 1984-85, 86-98, LaRossa, Mitchell & Ross, 1986—98, LaRossa & Ross, 1998—2001; founding ptnr. Law Offices of James M. LaRossa, 2001—14. Author: White Collar Crimes: Defense Strategies, 1977, Federal Rules of Evidence in Criminal Matters, 1977, White Collar Crimes, 1978. Served to 1st lt. USMC, 1953-55. Recipient Guardian of Freedom award B'nai B'rith, 1979, Career Achievement award N.Y. Coun. Def. Lawyers, 1996; Ann. honoree N.Y. Criminal Bar Assn., 1999. Mem. ABA, N.Y. State Bar Assn. (Criminal Law Practitioner of Yr. 1990), Fed. Bar Counsel, Assn. Bar City N.Y. Home: Manhattan Beach, Calif. Died Oct. 15, 2014.

LARROCA, RAYMOND G., lawyer; b. Jan. 5, 1930; s. Raymond Gil and Elsa Maria (Morales) L.; m. Barbara Jean Strand, June 21, 1952 (div. 1974); children: Denise Ann Sheehan, Gail Ellen, Raymond Gil, Mark Talbot, Jeffrey William. BSS, Georgetown U., 1952; JD, 1957. Bar: DC 1957, US Supreme Ct. 1960. Assoc. Kirkland, Fleming, Green, Martin & Ellis, Washington, 1957-64; ptnr. Kirkland, Ellis, Hodson, Chaffetz & Masters, Washington, 1964-67, Miller, Cassidy, Larroca & Lewin, Washington, 1967-2000, Baker Botts, Washington, from 2000. Served with arty. US Army, 1948-49, to 1st lt., inf., 1952-54. Mem. ABA, DC Bar, Bar Assn. DC, The Barristers. Republican. Roman Catholic. Club: Congl. Country (Potomac, Md.). Home: Washington, DC. Deceased.

LASALLE, BARBARA TULLOCH, nursing administrator; b. Milford, Mass., Dec. 29, 1932; d. William Wallace and Helen Lorraine (Platner) Tulloch; m. Conrad George LaSalle, Oct. 2, 1954; children: Lynne Marie Laughton, Brenda Lee Seamer. RN, Cen. Maine Gen. Hosp., Lewiston, Maine, 1954. Charge nurse Sacred Heart Hosp., Manchester, N.H., 1955-56; head nurse Elliott Hosp., Manchester, 1957-59; head nurse/supr. Edward H. White Hosp., St. Petersburg, Fla., 1978-87; infection control coord. HCA Oak Hill Hosp., Spring Hill, Fla., 1987-88, supr., from 1988. Home: Hernando, Fla. Died Dec. 19, 2006.

LATHROP, THOMAS ALBERT, language educator, publisher; b. LA, Apr. 18, 1941; s. Donald C. and Ethel M. (Challacombe) L.; m. Constance Ellen Cook, Aug. 30, 1969; 1 child, Aline. BA, UCLA, 1964, MA, 1965, PhD, 1970. Mem. faculty Spanish & Portuguese UCLA, 1964-66, U. Wyo., 1966-68, Transylvania U., 1973-76, Lafayette Coll., 1976-80; prof. Romance langs. U. Del., Newark, from 1980. Founding editor Juan de la Cuesta Hispanic Monographs, 1978—; co-editor The Cabrilho Press, 1974-89; pres. Linguatext, Ltd., 1989—; asst. editor Cervantes Bull. of the Cervantes Soc. Am., 1980-90, editor, 2008-10. Author: The Legend of the Siete Infantes de Lara, 1972; (with F. Jensen) The Syntax of the Old Spanish Subjunctive, 1973, La Vie Saint Eustace, 2000; Espanol--Lengua y cultura de hoy, 1974; The Evolution of Spanish, 1980; De Acuerdo! and Tanto Mejor, 1986; (with E Dias) Portugal, Lingua e Cultura, 1978, 2d edit., 1995, Curso de gramatica historica espanola, 1984, 89, (with E. Dias) Brasil: Lingua e Cultura, 2002, student edit. Don Quixote, 1997, Don Quixote translation, US, 2010, UK, 2011, Zola's Therese Raquin (student edition), 2007, Marcel Pagnol's La Gloire de mon pere (student edition) 2007, others; editor: European Classics, 2001-, Cervantes Soc. Bull, 2007-10. AID grantee, 1968; Nat. Endowment for Humanities grantee, 1976, 81; Gulbenkian Found. grantee, 1973; Del Amo Found. grantee, 1972. Decorated Order of Don Quijote by Nat. Spanish Honorary, 2006, Orden de Isabel la Catolica by the Casa Real de Espana, 2007. Mem. Cervantes Soc. Am., Internat. Assn. Hispanists. Home: Newark, Del. Died Feb. 17, 2014.

LAUER, HARRY CURTIS, retired civil engineer; b. Jersey City, Jan. 23, 1927; s. Harry Carl and Sarah Cecilia Lauer; divorced; children: Harry Curtis, Pamela Elizabeth, Eric Rivard. BSCE, Ind. Inst. Tech., 1950. Rodman Nickel Plate R.R., Ft. Wayne, Ind., 1950-51; with Lederle Labs/Am. Cynamid, Water Supply, Pearl River, N.Y., 1951-52; engr. DuPont/Atomic Energy Plant Constrn., Aiken, S.C., 1952; resident engr. Western Electric/AT&T, Winston-Salem, N.C., 1952-54; plant and project engr. Universal Atlas Cement div. U.S. Steel, various locations, 1955-70; sr. resident mgr. constrn. GE, Columbia, Md. and Research Triangle Park, N.C., 1970-73; project mgr. J. A. Jones Constrn. Co., Charlotte, N.C., 1974-75; project mgr., constrn. mgr. Bendy Engring. Co., Santa Cruz, Calif. and St. Louis, Mo., 1975-85; chief civil engr. Arab Swiss Engring. Co., Cairo, 1983; constrn. and plant engr. Fla. Crushed Stone, Brooksville, 1984—92. Engr., investigator Bahama Cement Co., Freeport, The Bahamas, 1967. Engr., investigator report Silo Failure Investigation (Commendation award 1967). Chief, founder YMCA Indian Guides, Columbia, Md., 1970; deacon Christian Ch., 1963, 68. With USN, 1944-46. Mem. Am. Inst. Plant Engr. (cert., del. to nat. conv. 1987), Ky. Cols., Am. Legion, Elks, Moose, Hernando Beach Yacht Club. Avocations: sailing, construction projects. Died Aug. 10, 2007.

LAURA, PATRICIO ADOLFO ANTONIO, applied scientist, researcher; b. Lincoln, Argentina, June 13, 1935; s. Lauro Olimpio Laura and Berta Elena Casas; m. Nelida Beatriz Gómez Villafane, Aug. 22, 1959; children: Patricio Carlos, Monica, Paul Alexander, Silvina, Diego. Civil engr. degree, U. Buenos Aires, 1959; PhD, Cath. U., 1964. From instr. to prof. Cath. U., Washington, 1961-69; prof. U. Nacional del Sur, Bahia Blanca, Argentina, from 1970; dir., rsch. scientist Inst. Applied Mechanics, Bahia Blanca, Argentina, 1975-99. Lectr. on Sci. and the Catholic Ch. Author 6 books; co-author: Conformal Mapping Methods and Applications, 1991; contbr. over 600 articles to profl. jour. Recipient First Nat. Engring. award, Argentina, 1985. Fellow: Am. Acad. Mechanics (founding mem.), Acoustical Soc. Am. (emeritus); mem.: Nat. Acad. Engring. (Buenos Aires), Nat. Acad. Sci. (Cordoba, Argentina). Achievements include contributions in conformal mapping applications to vibrations, buckling and unsteady diffusion problems; leadership in acoustic emission to monitor structural health of mechanical cables; develop. of anti-shock devices for nuc. applications; contributions in optimization of variational methods. Home: Bahia Blanca, Argentina. Died Nov. 6, 2006.

LAURENCE, ALFRED EDWARD, chemist, writer, educator; b. Breslau, Silesia, Fed. Republic of Germany, Dec. 12, 1910; came to U.S., 1941; arrived in Eng. 1952; s. Franz and Marie (Schonbeck) Lomnitz; m. Lotte Ilse Hadda, Mar. 19, 1949; children: Thomas Martin, Geoffrey Francis, Virginia Marie. LLD and Econs. degree, U. Breslau, Fed. Republic of Germany, 1933; Physique Chimie, Scis. Naturelles, U. Caen, France, 1935, Diploma in Chem. Engring., 1936. Rsch. chemist Shell Chem. Corp., Calif., U.S.A., 1937-52; European rsch. dir. 3Ms, Inc., St. Paul, Europe, Minn., 1954-63; vis. prof. U. Utah, Salt Lake City, 1969-70. Rsch. assoc. United Nations Spl. Fund, N.Y.C. 1962-68; mem. UNESCO. Contbr. articles profl. jours. Tchr. Adult Edn. Courses. 1st lt. U.S. Army, 1943-46. Recipient Battlefield Commn. U.S. Army, Germany, 1945. Mem. Am. Chem. Soc., Royal Soc. of Chemists, Am. Sociol. Assn., Am. Club. Unitarian Universalist. Avocation: genealogy. Home: Swanage Dorset, England. Died Dec. 28, 2006.

LAVENTHOL, DAVID ABRAM, newspaper editor; b. Phila., July 15, 1933; s. Jesse and Clare (Horwald) L.; m. Esther Coons, Mar. 8, 1958; children: Peter, Sarah. BA, Yale U., 1957; MA, U. Minn., 1960; LittD (hon.), Dowling Coll., 1979; LLD (hon.), Hofstra U., 1986. Reporter, news editor St. Petersburg Times, Fla., 1957-62; asst. editor, city editor N.Y. Herald-Tribune, 1963-66; asst. mng. editor Washington Post, 1966-69; from assoc. editor to pub., CEO Newsday, LI, NY, 1969-86; group v.p. newspapers Times Mirror Co., LA, 1981-86, sr. v.p., 1987-93, pres., 1987-93; pub., CEO L.A. Times, 1989-93; editor-at-large Times Mirror Co., LA, 1994-98; editor, pub. Columbia Journalism Rev., 1999—2003; chmn. Com. to Protect Journalists, from 2002. Mem. Pulitzer Prize Bd., 1982-91, chmn., 1988-89; vice-chmn. Internat. Press Inst., 1985-93. Bd. dirs. United Negro Coll. Fund, 1988, Mus. Contemporary Art, L.A., 1989-, chmn., 1993-97; bd. dirs. Associated Press, 1993-96, Columbia Journalism Sch., 1995—, Nat. Parkinson Found., 1995—, Saratoga Performing Arts Ctr., 1993-2002. Recipient Columbia Journalism award for Disting. Svc., 1994. Mem. Am. Soc. Newspaper Editors (chmn. writing awards bd. 1980-83), Council Fgn. Relations. Clubs: Century (N.Y.C.), Regency (L.A.). Died Apr. 8, 2015.

LAWRENCE, JOY ELIZABETH, music educator, organist; b. Cleve., Feb. 13, 1926; d. Wilbur Clyde and Annie Laurie Lawrence. MusB, Mt. Union Coll., 1948; MusM, Union Theol. Sem., 1951; PhD, Case Western Res. U., 1974. Cert. music tchr., Ohio. Tchr. choral and gen. edn. Strongsville (Ohio) Elem. Schs., 1955-56, Rocky River (Ohio) Elem. Schs., 1956-61, Horace Mann Jr. High Sch., Lakewood, Ohio, 1961-63, Roxboro Jr. High Sch., Cleveland Heights, Ohio, 1963-70, Monticello Jr. High Sch., Cleveland Heights, 1971-74; prof. music edn. and organ Kent (Ohio) State U., from 1974. Organist, dir. music Rocky River Meth. Ch., part-time 1951-55, assoc. organist, dir. youth choirs Ch. of the Covenent, Cleve., 1955-63; organist, dir. music Euclid Ave Christian Ch., Cleveland Heights, Ohio, 1963-79; organist Grace Luth. Ch., Cleveland Heights, 1979—; pageant dir. Cleveland Heights/Univ. Heights Bd. of Edn., 1981-82; workshop leader, clinician, nationwide. Author: (with William M. Anderson) Music and Related Arts for the Classroom, 1978, (with John A. Ferguson) The Musician's Guide to Church Music, 1981, (with William M. Anderson) Integrating Music into the Classroom, 1985, 2d edit., 1991, The Organist's Shortcut to Service Music, 1986, The Organist's Shortcut to Service Music Supplement # 1, 1988; contbr. articles to profl. jours. Mem. Music Educators Nat. Conf., Ohio Music Educators Assn., Am. Choral Dirs. Assn., Choristers Guild, Hymn Soc. Am., Soc. for Gen. Music Coun. for Rsch. in Music Edn., Am. Guild Organists (dean 1959-61, founder ch. music conf., exec. bd.). Republican. Lutheran. Avocations: travel, photography, reading. Died Jan. 27, 2007.

LAWRENCE, SIGMUND JOSEPH, chemical engineer; b. Chgo., May 20, 1918; m. Helen Agnes Shields (dec. 1964); children: Clifford, Keith, Claudia, Karen; m. Helen Asquith, July, 14, 1973 (div.); children: Joan, Mary. BS, Ill. Inst. Tech., 1939; MS, U. Iowa, 1942, PhD, 1943. Registered profl. engr., N.Y. With Shell Devel., 1943-46, GE, 1946-73; chem. engr. GE Hanford Works, 1946-48, Knolls Atomic Power Lab., 1948-51; rsch. assoc. GE Rsch. Lab., 1951-52; chem. engr. silicone prodn. dept. GE, Waterford, N.Y., 1953-57, chem. engr. Gen. Engring. lab. Schenectady, N.Y., 1957-59, systems engr. systems sales and engring. dept., 1959-67, mgr. sensor programs instrumentation dept. West Lynn, Mass., 1967-69, cons. instrumentation Re-entry divsn. Phila., 1969-73; process engr. Catalytic, Inc. United Engrs. and Constructors, Phila., 1974-91; cons., engr. All States Design, Trevose, Pa., 1992-93; pvt. cons. engr., 1991-92 and from 93. Lectr. in field. Citizens sch. bd., Schenectady, 1958; ops. chief Civil Def., Schenectady, 1955-67. Mem. AIChE (emeritus, treas. nat. meeting Lake Placid, N.Y. 1956, chmn. automation seminar Troy, N.Y. 1962, sect. chmn. 1965), Am. Chem. Soc. (emeritus). Republican. Unitarian Universalist. Achievements include patents for silicones production, fuel cells. Died Apr. 3, 2007.

LAWSON, ROSE MARY, history educator; b. Brooksville, Ky., Sept. 11, 1929; d. C.F. and Estelle (Blades) Haley; m. Fred Taylor Lawson, Oct. 28, 1951; children: Fred Haley, Thomas Taylor. AB, U. Ky., 1951; MA in Pub. History, Wright State U., 1977. Dir. edn. Montgomery County Hist. Soc., Dayton, Ohio, 1984-88; instr. history Sinclair Community Coll., Dayton, from 1990. Co-dir. Berkshire Shaker Seminar, 1986, 93. Contbr. articles to The Shaker Messenger, Miami Valley History; co-author paper doll book: Shaker Paper Dolls, 1981, reprint, 1993. Docent Dayton Art Inst., 1967—; tchr. Sunday sch. So. Bapt. Ch., Dayton. Mem. AAUW (br. pres. 1964-66), Am. Hist. Assn., Soc. Ohio Archivists, Communal Studies Assn., Phi Beta Kappa. Democrat. Baptist. Avocations: travel, reading, farming. Home: Sevierville, Tenn. Died Aug. 10, 2007.

LAWSON, WALTER REYNOLDS, retired manufacturing company executive; b. Amherst, NS, Can., Feb. 11, 1918; s. Gerald and Rose (Smith) L.; m. Harriet Senior, June 22, 1946; children: Cecily, Geoff, Tim, Heather. BS in Chem. Engring., Dalhousie U., Halifax, NS, 1940. Plant engr. Domtar Ltd., Toronto, Ont., 1945-47, project engr. Montreal, Que., 1952-54, gen. sales mgr., 1954-57, v.p., 1957-62, v.p. purchasing and traffic, 1966-70; v.p., gen. mgr. Domtar Packaging Co., 1970-76, pres., 1976-79; exec. v.p. Domtar Inc., 1979-82, ret., 1982; plant mgr. Sifto Salt Co., Sarnia, Ont., 1947-50, Manistee Salt Works, Mich., 1951-52. Bd. govs. Montreal Gen. Hosp., 1965-75. Served to maj. Can. Army, 1940-45. Mem. Can. Mfrs. Assn. (nat. pres. 1974-75, chmn. Que. div. 1964-65), Inst. Applied Econ. Research (bd. govs. 1975—) Clubs: Royal Montreal Golf (dir. 1964-67), Granite, St. James (dir. 1976-77). Home: Senneville, Canada. Died Jan. 1, 2007.

LAXMAN, R.K. (RASIPURAM KRISHNASWAMY IYER LAXMAN), cartoonist, writer; b. Mysore, Karnataka, India, Oct. 24, 1921; m. Kumari Kamala (div.); 1 child, Srinivas; m. Kamala Laxman. BA, U. Mysore; DLitt (hon.), U. Marathwada, U. Delhi. With Swarajya newspaper, Blitz newspaper, Gemini Studios, Madras; polit. cartoonist Swatantra newspaper, Free Press Jour., India, 1946; cartoonist Times of India, 1947—2015. Creator (comic strip) You Said It, 1951—2015, illustrator Laugh With Laxman, The Best of Laxman: The Common Man Stand in Queue, The Best of Laxman: The Common Man Goes to the Village, The Best of Laxman: The Common Man Balances His Budget, The Best of Laxman: The Common Man Takes a Stroll, The Best of Laxman: The Common Man Meets the Mantri, The Best of Laxman: The Common Man at Home, The Best of Laxman: Common Man Watches Cricket, The Best of Laxman: The Common Man in the New Millennium, The Common Man At Large, The Common Man Casts His Vote, Malgudi book series, Brushing Up the Years: A Cartoonist's History of India 1947-2004, 2005, The Eloquent Brush: A Selection of Cartoons from Nehru to Rajiv, 50 Years of Independence through the eyes of R.K. Laxman; author: Idle Hours, The Distorted Mirror, 2003, (novels) Hotel Riviera, 1988, The Messenger, 1993, Servants of India, (autobiography) The Tunnel of Time, 1998. Recipient B.D. award, Indian Express, Durga Ratan Gold medal, Hindustan Times, Padma Bhushan, Govt. India, Padma Vibhusban, 2005, Ramon Magsaysay award journalism, lit. and creative comm. arts, 1984. Hindu. Died Jan. 26, 2015.

LEAMAN, LEONARD S., JR., science educator; b. NYC, Nov. 30, 1945; s. Leonard S. and Elinore McNamee Leaman. BA, Holy Cross Coll., 1968; MFA, NYU, 1971. Camping and trip leader Camp Winaco, Sebago, Maine, 1970—92; sci. tchr. St. Hilda's and St. Hugh's Sch., NYC, 1976—80, Trinity Sch., NYC, from 1980, dean, 1993—99, from 2001. Writer, dir.: (film) Papa You're Crazy, 1971; writer, dir., photographer: (film) One Year's Spring, 1971; cameraman: (film) Eugene, 1971 (Cine Golden Eagle award 1971). Charles Bluhdorn fellow Trinity Sch., 1983, Earthwatch fellow, 1994. Mem. Assn. Tchrs. in Ind. Schs., Am. Mus. Natural History (assoc.), N.Y. Acad. Scis., Appalachian Mountain Club, Orion Soc., N.Y. Bot. Garden. Roman Catholic. Home: New York, NY. Died June 26, 2007.

LECHLEIDER, JOSEPH WILLIAM, computer engineer; b. Bklyn., Feb. 22, 1933; m. Marie; children Robert, Pamela BME, Cooper Union, 1954; MEE, Poly. Inst. Bklyn., 1957, PhD in Elec. Engring., 1965. Engr. Gen. Electric Co., 1954-55; mem. tech. staff Bell Telephone Labs., 1955-65, supr. transmission studies, outside plant/underwater sys., 1965-67, head loop transmission maintenance engring. dept., 1970-76, head software design dept., 1976—91. Bd. dirs. Bellcore. Named to Nat. Inventors Hall of Fame. Mem. IEEE (sr.); mem. Am. Math. Soc., Sigma Xi. Achievements include being best known as the Father of DSL (Digital Subscriber Line). Died Apr. 18, 2015.

LECHNER, GEORGE WILLIAM, surgeon; b. Denver, July 30, 1931; s. Frank Clifford and Hazel Mae (Elkins) L.; m. Betty Jane Baumbach, Aug. 3, 1952; children: Kathleen Ann, Elaine Marie, Carol Jean, Patricia Louise, James Richard. Student, U. N.Mex., 1948-49; BA, Pacific Union Coll., 1952; MD summa cum laude, Loma Linda U., 1956. Diplomate Am. Bd. Surgery. Intern Pontiac (Mich.) Gen. Hosp., 1956-57; resident in surgery Harper Hosp., Detroit, 1957-58, Wayne State U. Hosp., 1961-64; instr. surgery Wayne State U., 1963-64; practice medicine specializing in gen., vascular and bariatric surgery Kettering, Ohio, 1964-95. Mem. faculty and clin. staff Kettering Med. Ctr., Dayton, Ohio, 1967-95, also assoc. dir. gen. surgery residency, mem. active staff; clin. assoc. prof. surgery, assoc. dir. emergency medicine residency Wright State U., 1975-78; active staff Sycamore Hosp.; pres. Kettering Emergency Room Corp. Active Big Bros./Big Sisters; bd. elders Seventh-Day Adventist Ch., Kettering; trustee, mem. exec. com. Kettering Med. Ctr., 1971-74; pres. Spring Valley Acad. sch. bd., 1973-75, trustee 1973-78. Served with AUS, 1958-61, Japan. Recipient C.V. Mosby award for acad. excellence, 1956; ACS fellow. Mem. AMA, AAAS, ACS, Midwest Surg. Assn., Dayton Surg. Soc., Ohio and Montgomery County Med. Socs., Am. Soc. Bariatric Surgery, Am. Coll. Emergency Physicians, Soc. Tchrs. Emergency Medicine, Univ. Assn. Emergency Med. Services. Lodges: Rotary. Republican. Home: Dayton, Ohio. Died Apr. 24, 2007.

LECIEJEWICZ, JANUSZ TADEUSZ, retired physics professor; b. Poznan, Poland, Jan. 8, 1928; MS in Chemistry, Warsaw U. Tech., 1951; DSc, Inst. Nuc. Rsch., 1975. Asst. dept. inorganic chemistry Warsaw U. Tech., 1949—52; postgrad. fellowship Wroclaw U. Tech., 1952—55; sr. asst Inst. Nuc. Rsch., Swierk Rsch. Establishment, 1955—64, assoc. prof., 1964—78, head dept. solid physics, 1970—81, full prof., 1978—83; prof., dir. Inst. Nuc. Chemistry & Tech., Warszawa, Poland, 1983—91, part-time prof., from 1991. Recipient award, State Atomic Energy Agy. Mem.: Polish Nutron Scattering Soc., Polish Phys. Soc., Polish Soc. Crystallography. Avocation: history. Died Nov. 28, 2014.

LEE, SIR CHRISTOPHER FRANK CARANDINI, actor, writer, singer; b. London, May 27, 1922; s. Geoffrey Trollope and Estelle Marie (Carandini) L.; m. Birgit (Gitte) Kroencke, Mar. 17, 1961; 1 child, Christina Erika. Scholar, Eton Coll., Wellington Coll. With theatrical and film industry, from 1946; actor: (films) Corridor of Mirrors, 1947, One Night with You, 1948, A Song for Tomorrow, 1948, Penny and the Pownall Case, 1948, Scott of the Antarctic, 1948, The Gay Lady, 1949, They Were Not Divided, 1950, Prelude to Fame, 1950, Captain Horatio Hornblower R.N., 1951, Valley of the Eagles, 1951, The Crimson Pirate, 1952, Bombay Waterfront, 1952, Babes in Bagdad, 1952, Destination Milan, 1954, That Lady, 1955, Police Dog, 1955, The Cockleshell Heroes, 1955, Alias John Preston, 1955, Storm Over the Nile, 1955, Port Afrique, 1956, Pursuit of the Graf Spee, 1956, Beyond Mombasa, 1956, Night Ambush, 1957, The Accursed, 1957, She Played with Fire, 1957, The Curse of Frankenstein, 1957, Bitter Victory, 1957, The Truth About Women, 1957, A Tale of Two Cities, 1958, The Horror of Dracula, 1958, Missiles from Hell, 1958, Corridors of Blood, 1958, The Hound of the Baskervilles, 1959, The Man Who Could Cheat Death, 1959, Hot Money Girl, 1959, The Mummy, 1959, Uncle Was a Vampire, 1959, Playgirl After Dark, 1960, The Two Faces of Dr. Jekyll, 1960, The City of the Dead, 1960, Wild for Kicks, 1960, The Hands of Orlac, 1960, The Terror of the Tongs, 1961, Scream of Fear, 1961, The Devil's Daffodil, 1961, Hercules in the Haunted World, 1961, Secret of the Red Orchid, 1962, The Pirate of Blood River, 1962, The Devil's Agent, 1962, Sherlock Holmes and the Deadly Necklace, 1962, Stranglehold, 1962, Katarsis, 1963, Horror Castle, 1963, The Whip and the Body, 1963, The Devil-Ship Pirates, 1964, Crypt of the Vampire, 1964, Castle of the Living Dead, 1964, The Gorgon, 1964, Dr. Terror's House of Horrors, 1965, She, 1965, The Skull, 1965, The Face of Fu Manchu, 1965, Dracula:Prince of Darkness, 1966, Rasputin: The Mad Monk, 1966, Psycho-Circus, 1966, The Brides of Fu Manchu, 1966, Island of the Burning Damned, 1967, The Vengence of Fu Manchu, 1967, Blood Fiend, 1967, Five Golden Dragons, 1967, The Torture Chamber of Dr. Sadism, 1967, The Devil Rides Out, 1968, Eve, 1968, The Blood of Fu Manchu, 1968, Dracula Has Risen from the Grave, 1968, Curse of the Crimson Altar, 1968, Sax Rohmer's The Castle of Fu Manchu, 1969, The Oblong Box, 1969, The Magic Christian, 1969, Scream and Scream Again, 1970, The Bloody Judge, 1970, Eugenie...The Story of Her Journey Into Perversion, 1970, Count Dracula, 1970, Taste the Blood of Dracula, 1970, Julius Caesar, 1970, The Private Life of Sherlock Holmes, 1970, Scars of Dracula, 1970, Umracle, 1970, The House That Dripped Blood, 1971, I, Monster, 1971, Hannie Caulder, 1971, Dracula A.D., 1972, Horror Express, 1972, Nothing But the Night, 1973, Dark Places, 1973, The Creeping Flesh, 1973, The Satanic Rites of Dracula, 1973, The Wicker Man, 1973, The Three Musketeers, 1974, Raw Meat, 1973, The Four Musketeers: Milady's Revenge, 1974, The Man with the Golden Gun, 1974, The Butcher, the Star and the Orphan, 1975, Diagnosis: Murder, 1975, The Diamond Mercenaries, 1976, To the Devil a Daughter, 1976, The Night of the Askari, 1976, Dracula and Son, 1976, The Keeper, 1976, Meatcleaver Massacre, 1977, Airport 77, 1977, End of the World, 1977, Starship Invasions, 1977, Caravans, 1978, Return from Witch Mountain, 1978, Circle of Iron, 1979, The Passage, 1979, Arabian Adventure, 1979, Nutcracker Fantasy, 1979, Jaguar Lives!, 1979, Bear Island, 1979, 1941, 1979, Serial, 1980, The Salamander, 1981, An Eye for an Eye, 1981, Steigler and Steigler, 1981, Safari 3000, 1982, The Last Unicorn, 1982, House of the Long Shadows, 1983, The Return of Captain Invincible, 1983, The Rosebud Beach Hotel, 1984, Howling II:...Your Sister Is a Werewolf, 1985, Jocks, 1986, Mio in the Land of Faraway, 1987, Roadtrip, 1987, The Girl, 1987, Dark Mission: Evil Flowers, 1988, Olympus Force: The Key, 1988, Mask of Murder, 1988, House of the Long Shadows, 1989, La revolution francaise, 1989, Fall of the Eagles, 1989, Murder Story, 1989, L'avaro, 1990, The Rainbow Thief, 1990, Journey of Honor, 1991, The Return ofthe Musketeers, 1990, Gremlins II: The New Batch, 1990, Cyber Eden, 1992, Funny Man, 1994, Police Academy: Mission to Moscow, 1994, A Feast at Midnight, 1994, Tale of the Mummy, 1998, Jinnah, 1998, Sleepy Hollow, 1999, The Lord of the Rings: The Fellowship of the Ring, 2001, Star Wars, Episode II-Attack of the Clones, 2002, The Lord of the Rings: The Two Towers, 2002, The Lord of the Rings: The Return of the King, 2003, Crimson Rivers 2: Angels of the Apocalypse, 2004, Grey Friars Bobby, 2004, Star Wars Episode III: Revenge of the Sith, 2005, Greyfriars Bobby, 2005, Charlie and the Chocolate Factory, 2005, (voice) Corpse Bride, 2005, The Golden Compass, 2007, Triage, 2009, (films, voice) Star Wars The Clone Wars, 2008, Glorious'39, 2009, Boogie Woogie, 2009, The Heavy, 2010, Alice in Wonderland, 2010, Burke and Hare, 2010, The Wicker Tree, 2011, The Resident, 2011, Season of the Witch, 2011, Hugo, 2011, The Hunting of the Snark, 2012, Dark Shadows, 2012, Frankenweenie, 2012, The Hobbit: An Unexpected Journey, 2012, Night Train to Lisbon, 2013, The Girl from Nagasaki, 2013, The Hobbit: There and Back Again, 2013, The Hobbit: The Battle of the Five Armies, 2014; (TV miniseries) How the West Was Won, 1977-1978, Goliath Awaits, 1981, The Far Pavillions, 1984, Around the World in Eighty Days, 1989, Ivanhoe, 1997, Wyrd Sisters, 1997, Gormenghast, 2000, Ghost Stories for Christmas, 2000; (TV films) Poor Devil, 1973, The Pirate, 1978, Captain America II; Death Too Soon, 1979, Once Upon a Spy, 1980, Goliath Awaits, 1981, Massarati and the Brain, 1982, Charles and Diana: A Royal Love Story, 1982, The Disputation, 1986, Un Metier du Seigneur, 1986, Shaka Zulu, 1987, Around the World in 80 Days, 1989, Treasure Island, 1990, The Care of Time, 1990, Sherlock Holmes and the Leading Lady, 1991, Young Indy, 1992, Incident at Victoria Falls, 1992, Death Train, 1992, Double Vision, 1992, Detonator, 1993, Moses, 1995, Im Brunnen der Träume, 1996, Princess Alisea, 1996, The Many Faces of Christopher Lee, 1997, In the Beginning, 2000, Pope John Paul II, 2005, The Color of Magic, 2008;

(TV series) Kaleidoscope, 1946—47, Colonel March of Scotland Yard, 1954, The Vise, 1955, Tales of Hans Anderson, 1954—55, Moby Dick Rehearsed, 1955, Chevron Hall of Stars, 1956, The Scarlet Pimpernel, 1956, Rheingold Theatre, 1953—56, Aggie, 1956, Sailor of Fortune, 1956, The Errol Flynn Theatre, 1956-57, Assignment Foreign Legion, 1956-57, The Gay Cavalier, 1957, O.S.S., 1958, Ivanhoe, 1958, White Hunter, 1958, William Tell, 1959, Tales of the Vikings, 1959, Alcoa Presents: One Step Beyond, 1961, Alfred Hitcock Hour, 1964, The Avengers, 1967-69, Great Mysteries, 1973, Space:1999, 1975, Charlie's Angels, 1980, Faerie Tale Theatre, 1984, The Young Indiana Jones Chronicles, 1992, Chronicles The Tomorrow People, 1995, Street Gear, 1995, Tales of Mystery and Imagination, 1995, The New Adventures of Robin Hood, 1997-98, The Odyssey, 1997, Soul Music, 1997, Les redoutables, 2001; author: Archives of Terror, 1975, Tall Dark and Gruesome, 1977, rev. edit., 1999, The Great Villains, 1979, Lord of Misrule, 2004, Sir Christopher Lee, 2011, Night Train to Lisbon, 2012; (albums) Charlemagne: By the Sword and the Cross, 2010 (recipient Spirit of Metal award, Metal Hammer Golden Gods Ceremony, 2010), Charlemagne: The Omens of Death, 2012, Metal Knight, 2014, (christmas songs) A Heavy Metal Christmas, 2012, Heavy Metal Christmas Too, 2013. Served with RAF and Spl. Forces, 1941-46. Decorated Polonia Restituta (Poland); officer Arts, Lettres et Scis. (France); comdr. Order Brit. Empire, Order of St. John of Jerusalem; officier Arts Lettres (France), 2002, Knighted, 2009, Comdr. Artist award, 2011, Comdr. Arts Lettres (France), 2011. Mem. SAG, AFTRA, Brit. Actors Equity, Variety, Clubs Internat. Conservative, Hon. Company Edinburgh Golfers, Bucks's Club (London), Travellers Club (Paris), Pugs Club; fellow. BAFTA, BFI. Mem. Ch. Eng. Died June 7, 2015.

LEE, FRANCIS WILSON, educational association administrator; b. Boston, Aug. 16, 1927; s. Guy Hunter Lee and Simone (Pailley) Seznec; m. Susanne Slough, Dec. 10, 1980 (dec. 1981); children (by previous marriage): Thomas H., Alexandra, Katherine, Elizabeth, Nicholas. AB, Harvard U., 1948; MA, Johns Hopkins U., 1950. V.p. First Nat. Bank of Boston, 1955-66; asst. treas. Raytheon Co., Lexington, Mass., 1966-70; treas. J. Walter Thompson Co., NYC, 1970-72; v.p. fin. Internat. Basic Economy Corp., NYC, 1972-76; owner, operator Today's Restaurant, Washington, Conn., 1977-81; innkeeper Sherwood Inn, Skaneateles, N.Y., 1982-85; sr. mgmt. counselor Boston Coll., Chestnut Hill, Mass., from 1985; assoc. dir. Mass. Capital Formation Svc., Boston Coll., Chestnut Hill, from 1987. Cons., Westchester, N.Y., 1976-81. Lt. USN, 1945-46, 50-54, Panama. Avocations: microcomputers, handcrafts, classical music. Home: Arlington, Mass. Died Mar. 15, 2007.

LEE, HARPER (NELLE HARPER LEE), writer; b. Monroeville, Ala., Apr. 28, 1926; d. Amasa Coleman and Frances Cunningham (Finch) Lee. Attended, Huntingdon Coll., Montgomery, Ala., U. Ala., Tuscaloosa, Oxford U.; D (hon.), U. Ala., 1990, U. Notre Dame, 2006; LHD (hon.), Spring Hill. Coll., Mobile, Ala., 1997. Reservation clk. Eastern Airlines, NYC, 1950—58, Brit. Overseas Airline Corp., 1950—58. Apptd. mem. Nat. Coun. Arts, 1966—72. Author: (novels) To Kill a Mockingbird, 1960 (Pulitzer prize for fiction, 1961, Brotherhood award, Nat. Conf. Christians and Jews, 1961, Ala. Libr. Assn. award, 1961, Bestsellers Paperback of Yr. award, 1962, Best Novel of Century, Libr. Jour., 1999), The Mockingbird Next Door, 2014, Go Set a Watchman, 2015, (essays) Love-In Other Words, 1961, Christmas to Me, 1961, When Children Discover America, 1965, Romance and High Adventure, 1985. Recipient Ala. Humanities award, Ala. Humanities Found., 2002, ATTY award, Spector Gadon & Rosen Found., Phila., 2005, LA Pub. Libr. Lit. award, 2005, Presdl. Medal of Freedom, The White House, 2007, Nat. Medal of Arts, Nat. Endowment for the Arts, 2010. Mem.: AAAL. Avocation: golf. Died Feb. 19, 2016.

LEE, JAMES, social services administrator; b. Eutaw, Ala., Mar. 11, 1925; s. James Polk and Classie (Ryans) L.; m. Joann Jones, June 24, 1951; children: Hilary, Denise. BSW, Wayne State U., 1977, MSW, 1978. Lic. social worker, Mich. Juvenile group leader I Wayne County Youth Home, Detroit, 1969-76, juvenile group leader II, 1976-78, dept. mgr., from 1982; supr. juvenile group leaders D.J. Healy Children's Ctr., Detroit, 1978-82. Served with USN, 1943-46. Mem. Mich. Juvenile Detention Assn. (treas. 1973-77, Child Care Worker of Yr. 1975). Avocations: bowling, spectator sports. Home: Detroit, Mich. Died Apr. 26, 2007.

LEE, JAMES BAINBRIDGE, JR., diversified financial services company executive; b. NYC, Oct. 30, 1952; s. James Bainbridge and Marylou (Orteig) L.; m. Elizabeth B. Lee, Feb. 8, 1981; children: Alexandria, James B., Elizabeth G. BA in Economics & Art History, Williams Coll., Williamstown, Mass., 1975. With Chemical Bank, NYC, 1975-79, calling officer ASEAN, 1977-79, dep. rep. Sydney, 1979, rep., 1979-81; mng. dir. Merchant Bank, Melbourne, Australia, 1982-83; chief of staff Chem. Bank, NYC, 1983-85, v.p. syndications, 1985-87, mng. dir. structured fin., syndications and pvt. placements, 1987—94; vice chmn. JPMorgan Chase & Co., NYC, 1994—2015, co-chmn., investment banking North America, 2002—15. Pres. Berkshire Broadcasting Corp., Danbury, Conn. Pres. Norton Bay Property Owners Assn., Darien, Conn., 1987-89. Recipient Harvard Book award, 1971. Mem. Royal Prince Edward Yacht Club, Athaneum Club, Woodbury Country Club. Home: Darien, Conn. Died June 17, 2015.

LEE, JOSEPH ALLEN, JR., retired financial consultant; b. Evanston, Ill., Dec. 9, 1921; s. Joseph Allen and Barbara Thruston (Senseney) Lee; m. Barbara Clemens Burnham, Oct. 8, 1949; children: Donald P., Allen C., Linda H., Andrew S. Student, Yale U., 1939—42; MBA, Harvard U., 1948. Salesman Union Securities Corp., 1948—50; v.p., mgr. instnl. dept. Reynolds & Co., 1950—60; v.p., dep. dir. investment rsch. Bankers Trust Co., 1961—66; sr. investment advisor Rockefeller Family & Assocs., 1966—76; fin. cons. Carmel, Calif., 1977—86. Bd. dirs. Calif. Mut. Ins. Co., Monterey Fin. Corp., Am. Eagle Ins. Co. Trustee, v.p. Monterey Peninsula Found.; pres. Comty. Found; former trustee Greenwich Hosp., Whitby Sch., Brookridge Assn., Robinson Jeffers Tor House Found., Riverside Ch. Served to 1st lt. USAAF, 1943—45. Mem.: Fin. Analysts Soc., NY Soc. Security Analysts, Wailea Golf Club, Old Capital Monterey Peninsula Country Club, Pebble Beach and Tennis Club, Cypress Point Club. Republican. Episcopalian. Died Nov. 1, 2006.

LEE, RALPH DONALD, real estate developer; b. Terre Haute, Ind., Dec. 29, 1929; s. Arthur P. and Margaret Ann (Jones) L.; m. Pat Helen Ann Lee, June 19, 1949 (div. Dec., 1970); children: Ralph D. Lee II, Latona Jean Lee McKeigue; m. Betty Jane Smittkamp, Aug. 31, 1972; children: Elizabeth Lynn, Gwendolyn Sue Gosnell. BS in Acctg. and Bus. Adm, Ind. State U., 1958, MS in Bus. Mgmt., 1964. Prodn. recorder Stran Steel Corp., Terre Haute, 1958; cost acctg. supr. Anaconda Aluminum Co., Terre Haute, 1958-66; controller Terre Haute Chrysler Plymouth, 1966-68; dist. mgr. Federated Mut. Ins. Co., 1968-71; controller Lusterlite Corp. div. Eagle-Picher, Hinsdale, Ill., 1971-73, Ea. Express, Inc., Terre Haute, 1973-76; real estate salesman Branam Williams Assoc., Terre Haute, 1976-80; v.p., treas. Grand Atriums of Am., Inc., Terre Haute, from 1984; pres., fin. broker Century 21 Ralph Lee Agy., Terre Haute, from 1980. Rep. Century 21 Regional Brokers Congress, Indpls., 1984-87; pres. Century 21 Ind. Brokers Council, 1985-68, West Central Ind. Council, Terre Haute, 1982-89. Contbr. column to newspaper. Served as cpl. U.S. Army, 1952-54. Mem. Terre Haute C. of C., Multiple Listing Assn. (bd. dirs.), Masons, Shriners, Eagles. Democrat. Lutheran. Avocations: hunting, fishing, gardening. Former Nat. Collegiate Rifle Champion. Home: Terre Haute, Ind. Died Dec. 23, 2006.

LEE, ROBERT GUM HONG, chemical company executive; b. Montreal, Que., Can., May 22, 1924; s. Hai Chong Lee and Toy Kay Yip; m. Maude Toye; children: Peter, Patricia, Cathrine. BS in Engring., McGill U., Montreal, 1947. Research engr. Can. Liquid Air, Ltd., Montreal, from 1947. Co-inventor OBM/Q-BOP Oxygen Seel Refining Process, 1967. Bd. dirs. Montreal Chinese Hosp., 1975-82. Mem. Soc. for Crybiology, Can. Inst. of Mining and Metallurgy (Airey award 1974, Falconbridge Innovation awd., 1992), Am. Inst. of Mining and Metallurgy, Am. Chem. Soc. Home: Montreal, Canada. Died Oct. 31, 2006.

LEE, SIDNEY PHILLIP, chemical engineer, state senator; b. Pa., Apr. 20, 1926; s. Samuel L. and Mollie (Heller) L. B.Sc., U. Pa., 1939; McMullin fellow, Cornell U., 1939-40, then M.Ch.E. Chem. engr. Atlantic Richfield Co., 1938-42; sr. chem. engr., 1942-45; pres. Dallas Labs., from 1945, Asso. Labs., Dallas, from 1945, West Indies Investment Co., from 1957; chmn. exec. com. West Indies Bank & Trust Co. Dir., mem. exec. com. Am. Ship Bldg. Co.; prin. West Indies Investment Co., St. Croix, 1956— Writer of Lee Lets Loose column for local Carribean newspapers. Mem. V.I. Senate, 1976—, now v.p.; chmn. com. govt., chmn. com. on fin. ops. V.I. Govt. Dem. nat. committeeman for V.I., 1969—; mem. V.I. Bd. Edn., 1969-76; mem. Gov.'s Blue Ribbon Commn. for Econ. Devel., 1995—; commr. V.I. Port Authority, 1997—. Fellow Am. Inst. Chemists; mem. AIChE (sr.), AIME (sr.), AARP (chmn. legis. com. 1984—), St. Croix C. of C. (v.p. 1995), Rotary (pres. 1971-73), Lions (pres. 1960), Tau Beta Pi, Sigma Tau, Beta Sigma Rho. *In retrospect, elation from supposed triumphs or defeats is blurred in memory; and of greater importance is the quality of one's life or how one played the game.* Died June 19, 2008.

LEEDY, WALLACE CURTIS, former educator; b. Dinuba, Calif., Nov. 15, 1924; s. Walter Boston Leedy and Stella Eunace Fields; m. Barbara Mace, July 1, 1945 (dec. June 1999); 1 child, Dawn Caroline Leedy Guest. BA, Fresno State Coll., 1951; Tchr. Cert., 1952. Cert. tchr. secondary sch. Tchr. L.A. City Schs., 1952-56, N.Am. Aviation, 1956-85; ind. rschr., writer social behavioral sci. and biology. Mem. Social Sci. Honor Soc., Edn. Honor Soc., Arabian Horse Assn. of San Fernando Valley (past pres.). Avocation: Arabian horses. Died July 10, 2007.

LEEMON, JOHN ALLEN, lawyer; b. Hoopeston, Ill., Jan. 12, 1928; ss. Allen Wallace and Eva Carol (Merritt) L.; m. Sally Paul Pierce, July 14, 1951; children: John Paul, Lisa Ann Johnson. BS, U. Ill., 1950, LLB, 1952. Bar: Ill. 1952, U.S. Dist. Ct. (no. dist.) Ill. 1958, U.S. Tax Ct. 1985. Pvt. practice, Savanna, Ill., 1952-54, Mt. Carroll, Ill., 1969-95; ptnr. Eaton & Leemon, Mt. Carroll, Ill., 1954-55, Eaton, Leemon & Rapp, Mt. Carroll, Ill., 1966-69, Leemon, Weinstine, Shirk & Mellott PC, Mt. Carroll, Ill., 1995-97, Leemon & Kane, Mt. Carroll, Ill., from 1997. Spl. asst. atty. gen. Ill. Atty. Gen., 1969-76. Mem. Ill. State Bar Assn. (negligence coun. 1961-66, grievance com. inquiry divsn. 1967-70), Carroll County Bar Assn., Whiteside County Bar Assn. Avocations: golf, fishing, hunting. Home: Mount Carroll, Ill. Died Feb. 28, 2007.

LEFF, DAVID, lawyer; b. Dec. 19, 1933; s. Solomon and Anna (Schnitzer) L.; m. Barbara Kantrowitz, Dec. 23, 1954; children-Abbey, Jody. BA with honors, Rutgers U., 1955, LLB, 1958. Bar: N.J., 1958, U.S. Dist. Ct. N.J. 1958. Assoc. Eichenbaum, Kantrowitz & Eichenbaum, Jersey City, 1958-62; ptnr. Eichenbaum, Kantrowitz & Leff, Jersey City, 1962-87; sr. ptnr. Eichenbaum, Kantrowitz, Leff & Gulko, Jersey City, from 1987. Judge Mcpl. Ct. Jersey City, 1978-80; bd. dirs. Consumer Credit Dept. Counseling Service N.J., Provident Savings Bank, 1992—; bd. dirs. Rutgers Law Alumni Council; pres., exec. bd. Hudson County C. of C.; v.p. exec. bd., bd. dirs. Jewish Hosp., Jersey City and River Vale; bd. dirs. Goodwill Industries N.J., named Man of Yr.; bd. trustees Jersey City Med. Ctr. Found., Walter Head Found.; exec. bd. Bergen County United Jewish Appeal; bd. dirs. United Jewish Community Bergen County; bd. dirs. Tri-State United Way, Jersey City State Coll. Devel. Fund. Cert. consumer credit exec. Internat. Consumer Credit Assn., 1964. Bd. dirs. United Cmty. Fund Hudson County, 1972, pres., 1973; v.p. Hudson-Hamilton Coun. Boy Scouts Am., 1974, dir., 1970; pres., exec. bd. Hudson County C. of C.; bd. dirs. Temple Sholom, River Edge, N.J., 1975. Recipient Disting. Svc. award Jersey City State Coll., 1984/ Mem. ABA, N.J. Bar Assn., Hudson County Bar Assn. (trustee, pres. 1976), Am. Judicature Soc., Hudson County C. of C. (pres. 1980-82, chmn. bd. 1983-84), Kappa Alpha Tau (nat. pres. 1951). Club: Edgewood Country (River Vale) (dir., pres. 1982, 83). Lodge: Rotary (dir. pres. Jersey City club 1975). Avocation: golf. Died May 19, 2007.

LEFF, SANFORD LEONARD, electrical distributor executive; b. Cleve., Mar. 13, 1918; s. harry and Sarah Alta (Kohn) L.; m. Seena Sylvia Glaser, Dec. 1, 1942; children: Drew M., Deeda Leff-Shubert, Bruce E., Sanford L. Jr., Stuart E. BS, Western Res. U., 1940. Chief exec. officer, chmn. bd. H. Leff Electric Co., Cleve., 1932-40 and from 45. Lt. comdr. USN, 1940-45. Mem. Elec. League No. Ohio (pres. 1987-88), Beechmont Country Club (pres. 1981-82). Jewish. Avocations: golf, tennis. Died Jan. 22, 2007.

LEGGETT, JOHN WARD, writer; b. NYC, Nov. 11, 1917; s. Bleecker Noel and Dorothy (Mahar) L.; m. Mary Lee Fahnestock, Oct. 2, 1948 (div. 1986); children: Timothy, John, Anthony; m. Edwina Benington, Oct. 26, 1986. BA, Yale U., New Haven, Conn., 1942. Publicist, editor Houghton Mifflin Co., Boston, 1951-60; editor Harper & Row, NYC, 1960-69; dir. writers' workshop U. Iowa, Iowa City, 1969-87. Dir. Napa Valley Writers' Conf., Napa, Calif., 1987-2015 Author: Wilder Stone, 1960, Who Took the Gold Away, 1969, Gulliver House, 1979, Ross and Tom: Two American Tragedies, 1974, A Daring Young Man, 2002, others; editor: (textbook series) Elements of Literature, 1988. Lt. USN, 1943-45. Mem. Century Assn. Home: Napa, Calif. Died Jan. 25, 2015.

LEHRER, RUTH JEANNETTE, social work supervisor; b. NYC, Apr. 17, 1923; d. Samuel and Mollie Kinbar; widowed. BS, Hunter Coll., 1944; MSW, Columbia U., 1946. Med. social worker Jewish Hosp. of Bklyn., 1946; social worker N.Y. Assn. for New Ams., NYC, 1946-50; med. social worker Maimonides Hosp., Bklyn., 1950-51; social worker Jewish Family Svc. Assn., Essex County, N.J., 1951-58; med. social worker Mt. Sinai Hosp., NYC, 1958-59; social worker N.Y. Guild for Jewish Blind, NYC, 1959-61, Wiltwyck Sch. for Boys, NYC, 1961-64; sr. psychiat. social worker Lincoln Hosp. Cmty. Mental Health Ctr., Bronx, NY, 1964—67; instr. Albert Einstein Sch. Medicine, 1964-67; psychiat. social work supr. Maimonides Hosp. Cmty. Mental Health Ctr., Bklyn., 1967—97. Mem. NASW. Avocations: folk dancing, sketching, Scrabble, reading, ping-pong. Home: New York, NY. Died Aug. 8, 2007.

LEICHHARDT, JERRINE KAY, human resources consultant; b. Wichita, Kans., May 9, 1931; d.Gustave Adolphus Jr. and Birdie Jerrine (Gauntt) L. BS, Kans. State U., 1953. Home economist Culinary Arts Inst., Chgo., 1953-56; project dir. Nat. Cert. INTVS, Chgo., 1956-60; mktg. rsch. analyst The Quaker Oats Co., Chgo., 1960-62; rsch. asst. Community Action for Youth, Cleve., 1964-66; personnel mgr. The Higbee Co., Cleve., 1966-68; employment supr., mgr. employee rels., HRIS mgr. Diamond Shamrock Corp., Cleve., 1968-83; prin. Leichhardt Consulting Svc., Rocky River, Ohio, from 1983. Speaker Baldwin-Wallace Coll., Cleve. State U., Cleve. State U., Cuyahoga Community Coll., Kent State U. Editorial reviewer HR Mag. of Soc. for Human Resource Mgmt., 1987—; contbr. articles to profl. jours. Master gardener, vol. Cuyahoga County Coop. Extension Svc., Cleve., 1986—; mem. Kans. Organic Producers, 1987—. Mem. Human Resources Systems Profls. (program chmn. 1984, Most Valuable Chpt. Mem. 1985), Soc. for Human Resources Mgmt. (past membership com., sec.-treas.), NE Ohio PC Club (treas. 1984-85), Women's Computer Network (bd. dirs. 1985), Alpha Chi Omega. Avocations: gardening, culinary herbs, travel, music, computer bulletin boards. Home: Chagrin Falls, Ohio. Died Nov. 1, 2006.

LEIGH, GERALD GARRETT, research engineer; b. Burley, Idaho, Sept. 10, 1931; s. Wilbur Garrett and Iva Grace (Morehead) L.; m. Ruth Ann Kurtz, Dec. 28, 1957 (div. Feb. 1983); m. Ann Christen Galloway, March 5, 1983; children: Christi Leigh, Lauren Schieffer, Thomas Crawley (stepson). BS in Chem. Engr., U. Idaho, 1955; MS in Mechanical Engring., Ariz. State U., 1964, PhD in Engring. Mechanics, 1971. Commd. USAF, 1955, retired, 1976; sr. rsch. engr. N.Mex. Engring. Rsch. Inst., Albuquerque, 1976-93. Contbr. articles to profl. jours. Home: Albuquerque, N.Mex. Died Dec. 30, 2006.

LEIGHTON, ALEXANDER HAMILTON, psychiatry educator; b. Phila., July 17, 1908; s. Archibald Ogilvy and Gertrude Anne (Hamilton) L.; m. Dorothea Cross, Aug. 17 1937 (div. Oct. 1965); children: Dorothea Gertrude, Frederick Archibald; m. Jane Murphy, July 30, 1966. AB, Princeton U., 1932; MA, Cambridge U., Eng., 1934; MD, Johns Hopkins U., 1936; AM (hon.), Harvard U., 1966; DSc (hon.), Acadia U., Wolfville, NS, 1974, Laval U., Que., Can., 1991. Med. intern Johns Hopkins Hosp., 1936-37, house officer psychiatry, 1937-39, 40-41; Social Sci. Rsch. Coun. fellow Columbia U., 1939-40; former prof. sociology, anthropology and psychiatry Cornell U.; prof. social psychiatry, head dept. behavioral scis. Harvard Sch. Pub. Health, Boston, 1966-75, prof. emeritus, from 1975; prof. psychiatry, prof. comty. health & epidemiology Dalhousie U., Halifax, N.S., from 1975. Dir. Stirling County project; cons. WHO; mem. com effects herbicides in Vietnam, NAS, 1971-73. Author: The Governing of Men, 1946, Human Relations in a Changing World, 1949, My Name Is Legion, 1959, An Introduction to Social Psychiatry, 1960, Caring for Mentally Ill People, 1982, (novel) Come Near, 1971, also numerous articles; co-author: Navaho Door, 1944, People of Cove and Woodlot, 1960, Psychiatric Disorder Among the Yoruba, 1963, The Character of Danger, 1963; editor: (with others) Explorations in Social Psychiatry, 1957; co-editor: Approaches to Cross-Cultural Psychiatry, 1965; contbr., collaborator: Psychiatric Disorder and the Urban Environment, 1971. Developer, dir. rsch. unit to aid adminstrn. Japanese Relocation Ctr., Poston, Ariz., 1942-44; developer, dir. rsch. unit for analysis of current Japanese social and psychol. changes OWI, 1944-45; one of rsch. leaders moral divsn. U.S. Strategic Bombing Survey of Japan, 1945-46. With M.C., USNR, WWII, 1941. Recipient Human Rels. award Am. Assn. Advancement Mgmt., 1946, Lapouse award APHA, 1975, McAlpin award Nat. Assn. Mental Health, 1975, Malinowski award Soc. for Applied Anthropology, 1984; fellow Ctr. Advanced Study Behavioral Scis., 1957-58, Carnegie Reflective fellow, 1962-63, fellow (with Dorothea C. Leighton) Guggenheim Found., 1946-47; Thomas W. Salmon lectr. N.Y. Acad. Medicine, 1958. Fellow AAAS, ACP, Royal Coll. Psychiatrists (hon.), Am. Psychiat. Assn. (life, chmn. coun. nat. affairs and social issues 1970-72, coun. nat. affairs 1972-75), Am. Anthropol. Assn., Soc. de Psychopathologie et d'Hygiene Mentale de Dakar (corr.); mem. Sociol. Rsch. Assn. (hon.), Am. Philos. Soc., Am. Psychopath. Assn., Can. Acad. Psychiat. Epidemiology (pres. 1994—), Assn. Am. Indian Affairs (dir.), Phi Beta Kappa, Sigma Xi. Home: Smith Cove, Canada. Died Aug. 11, 2007.

LEIPZIG, ARTHUR, photographer, retired educator; b. Bklyn., Oct. 25, 1918; s. Julius M. and Esther Pearl (Rubin) L.; m. Mildred Levin, Mar. 21, 1942; children: Joel Myron, Judith Anne. Attended, Photo League Classes Sid Grossman, 1942—43, Photo League, 1942—49, Paul Strand Photo Workshop, 1946. Staff photographer PM newspaper, NYC, 1942-46, Internat. News Photos, NYC, 1946; freelance photographer Sea Cliff, NY, 1942—94; prof. art, dir. photography C.W. Post Coll., Long Island U., Greenvale, NY, 1968—90, prof. emeritus, 1991—2014. Contbr. photographs to Fortune, Look, Parade, Life, Natural History, Sunday Times, also indsl. mags.; guest editor Infinity Mag., NYC, 1970, mem. editorial bd., 1973-75; interview and photographs included Life Documentary Photo Book, NYC, 1972, 83; exhibited works Mus. Modern Art, 1946-51, 55-58, Met. Mus. Art, 1961, 62, Nassau Mus. Art, 1975, Queens Mus. Art, 1982, Transco Gallery, Houston, 1985, Daniel Wolf Gallery, NYC, Houston Foto Fest, 1986, Photo Find Gallery, Woodstock, Coll. Art Gallery, New Paltz, NY, Smithsonian Mus., Washington, 1987, Mus. of the City of NY, Children's Games, 1988, Photofind Gallery, NYC, 1990, ICP, Bklyn., 1992; one-man shows include Midtown Y Gallery, 1978, Henry St. Settlement, Arts for Living Ctr., 1986, Frumkin Adams Gallery, NYC, 1990, 92, Photofind Gallery, 1990, Howard Greenberg Gallery, 1991, 98, Salena Gallery, Bklyn., 1992, Port Washington Libr., 1994, Mus. of the City of NY, 1995, 96, Albin O. Kuhn Gallery, Balt., Md., Milw. Inst. Art & Design, 1998, Firehouse Gallery, Nassau CC, 2001, Arthur Leipzig: A Tribute to Influence, Columbus Mus. Art, 2005-06, Hillwood Mus., 2006, Stritch U., Milw., Wis., 2006, Suermondt-Ludwig Mus., Aachen, Germany, Arthur Leipzig- Next Stop, NYC, 2008, De Cordova Mus., Lincoln, Mass., 2008, Nat. Portrait Gallery, NYCI Internat. Perspectives, Russia, 2009-; group shows include Balt. Mus. Art, 1998, Whitney Mus. American Art, 1999, Am. Embassy, Copenhagen Art in Embassies, 1999, The Jewish Mus., The Changing Face of Family, 1999, NY: Capital of Photography, The Jewish Mus., 2002; represented in permanent collections Mus. Modern Art, Bklyn. Mus., Eastman House, Nat. Gallery Art, Nassau Mus. Art, Houston Mus. Fine Arts, Midtown Y Gallery, Visual Studies Workshop, Pablo Casals Mus., Internat. Ctr. Photography, Nat. Mus. Am. Art, Washington, Consol. Freightways, San Francisco, Bank of Am. Art Program, San Francisco, Bibliotheque Nationale, Paris, The Jewish Mus., NYC, Mus. Folkwang, Essen, Germany, Nat. Portrait Gallery, Washington, The Gilman Paper Co., Queens Coll., NY, Madison Art Ctr., Wis., U. Tex., Dallas, Dreyfus, NYC, Soho Grand Hotel, Columbus Mus. Art, Nassau CC, Kresge Mus. Art, East Lansing, Mich., Milbank Meml. Fund, Santa Barbara Mus. Art, Balt. Mus. Art, BB King Mus., Indianola, Miss., Beale St. Murals, 2008; retrospective exhbn. Hillwood Gallery, Brookville, NY, 1989, Musée De La Civilisation, Quebec City, 1990, Balt. Mus. Art, Reader's Digest Corporate Art Gallery; featured on World of Photography, Sta. WABC-TV; pub. Classic Photographs from the Brooklyn Museum Collection, 1987, Sarah's Daughters, 1988, Master Photographs Photography in Fine Arts Exhbt. Internat. Ctr. Photography, 1988, 92, The Nat. Portrait Gallery, 1992, High Mus., Altlanta, 1992, Mus. of the City of NY, 1995; Next Stop NY, 2008, photographer: (art books) Shari Lewis Puppet Book, Sarah's Daughter, 1987, Growing Up in NY, 1995, On Assignment with Arthur Leipzig, 2005; photos included in 2007 Women of Our Time, Faces of Photography, Encounters with 50 Master Photographers of the 20th Century. NY St. Games Film, 2008, Next Stop NY, 2008, The Family of Man, The Family of Children, Cityspaces: A History of New York in Images, Documentary Photography CTimes-Life Books, This was the Photo League, City Play, The Faces of Photography, Face to Face with Fifty Master Photographers, Sputnik, US Camera Annual Photography Year Books; exhibitions: NYC Internat. Perspective, 2009-2010, Auer Photo Found., Switzerland, 2011; contbr. to profl. publs. Adv. bd. Midtown Y Gallery, 1983; bd. dirs. Nassau Mus. Fine Art, 1973-75. Recipient Nat. Urban League award, 1962, ORT award, 1976, Nassau County Office Cultural Devel. award, 1982, Award for Scholarly Achievement, LI U. Trustees, 1983, 89, David Newton Excellence in Tchg. award, 1989, Lucie award for Fine Art Photography Awards, 2004. Mem. Am. Soc. Mag. Photographers (bd. govs., trustee 1960-65, treas. 1965), Assn. Internat. Photography Art Dealers (mem. photo leagues panel 2010). Home: Sea Cliff, NY. *My photography is very personal, my focus the human condition, exploring people, their humanity and inhumanity. I am not a cerebral photographer. My Images come as intuitive responses and they deal with my feelings about life. Through my work I have learned about myself and the world.* Died Dec. 5, 2014.

LEMBERG, LOUIS, cardiologist, educator; b. Chgo., Dec. 27, 1916; s. Morris and Frances Lemberg; m. Dorothy Feinstein, 1940 (dec. 1969); children: Gerald, Laura Bott, Paula Saltzman; m. Miriam Mayer, Jan. 29, 1971. BS, U. Ill., Chgo., 1938; MD, U. Ill., 1940. Intern Mt. Sinai Hosp., Chgo., 1940-41, resident, 1945-48, asst. prof. med., 1955-58, assoc. prof. med., 1958-70; prof. clin. cardiology U. Miami (Fla.) Sch. Medicine, from 1970, dir. coronary care unit, 1965-75. Chief cardiology Mercy Hosp., 1974-79; chief staff Nat. Children's Cardiac Hosp., 1959-66; cons. cardiology VA Hosp., Miami, 1953-64; dir. cardiology Dade County Hosp., 1953-64, dir. Heart Sta. and Electrocardiography, U. Miami Jackson Meml. Med. Ctr., 1952-75, program dir. Courses in Coronary Care for Practicing Physician, 1970-2003, Courses in Coronary Care for Nurses, 1970-90; Master Approach to Cardiovascular Problems, 1972-82, Cardiology Update for Intensive Care Nurses, Am. Coll. Cardiology, 1978-92, Cardiology Update, 1987-2002. Author: Vectorcardiography, 1969, 2d edit., 1975, Electrophysiology of Pacing and Cardioversion, 1969; editor-in-chief Current Concepts in Cardiovascular Disorders, 1984-86; contbr. to med. publs. Served to maj. AUS, 1941-55, ETO. Recipient U. St. Torres (Phillippines) Luis Guerrero hon. lectr. award, 1977, Recognition award U. Miami Sch. Medicine, Lifetime Achievement award Jackson Meml. Med. Ctr. U. Miami, 1997, Key to City of Miami Beach, Fla., Nurses Pioneering Spirit award Am. Assn. Critical Care, 2000, Physicians Recognition awards AMA. Fellow ACP, Am. Coll. Cardiology (editl. bd. jour.); mem. Heart Assn. Greater Miami (pres.), Fla. Heart Assn. (pres.), Am. Heart Assn. (fellow coun. clin. cardiology). Democrat. Jewish. Achievements include pioneer in development Demand Pacemaker, 1964, a chair in cardiology established at the U. Miami Sch. of Medicine entitled The Louis Lemberg Professor of Cardiology, 1990. Home: Miami, Fla. Died Jan. 1, 2012.

LEMMON, MARCIA HILARY, company executive; b. Flushing, NY, July 10, 1958; d. Martin Hurd and Sarah Gertrude (Schmittberger) L. BA magna cum laude, Queens Coll., London, 1980; MBA cum laude, NYU, 1982; LittD (hon.), Pacifica U., San Luis Obispo, Calif., 1987. V.p. ops. Interphoto Systems, Inc., Pitts., 1980-82; v.p. direct mail Spiratone, Inc., Flushing, N.Y., 1983-85; mng. dir. Direct-Mail Cons., Inc., NYC, from 1984; pres., chief exec. officer Lemmon & Co., Flushing, from 1986. Bd. dirs. Lemmon Love Found., Flushing; cons. T K R Systems Group, Inc., N.Y.C., 1984-89, JL Communications Corp., Netcong, N.J., 1984-85; bd. mem. Flushing Freewomen, 1980-81. Author: The Direct-Mail Maze, 1984, Mail Order Management, 1985, Self-Help Directory, 1986; inventor Tofu Sausages, 1989. Mem. Community Bd. 69, Queens, N.Y., 1988; advisor Met. Transit Authority, N.Y.C., 1989; observer Queens County Criminal Cts., Jamaica, N.Y., 1988. Recipient Svc. award Flushing Freewomen, 1988. Mem. Am. Soc. Female Inventors (Woman Inventor award 1989), Woodchuck Club, Inc. (Pres. Honors 1986), Thursday Lunch Club (pres. 1988—). Avocations: scuba diving, hang gliding, bicycling, travel. Died Dec. 2, 2006.

LEMON, MEADOWLARK (MEADOW LEMON III), retired professional basketball player; b. Wilmington, NC, Apr. 25, 1932; s. Meadow and Maime (Nesbitts) Lemon; m. Willie Maultsby (div.); m. Willye Lemon (div.); m. Cynthia Lemon, 1994; children: George, Beverly, Donna, Robin, Jonathan, Richard, Jamison, Angela, Crystal, Caleb. DD, Vision Internat. U., 1986. With Harlem Globetrotters, 1954—80, 1994; formed basketball group The Bucketeers, 1980—83, Meadowlark Lemon's Harlem All Stars, 1988; with Shooting Stars, 1984—87; co-owner Smoky Mountain Jam (American Basketball Assn.), 2009—15. Motivational spkr. Actor: (TV series) Harlem Globe Trotters (voice), 1970—71; (films) The Fish that Saved Pittsburgh, 1979; (TV films) Crash Island, 1981; featured in numerous TV commercials, recording artist (albums) My Kids, 1979. Founder Camp Meadowlark, 1989; co-founder Meadowlark Lemon Ministries, 1994. With US Army, 1952—54. Recipient John Bunn award for Lifetime Achievement, 2000, Internat. Clown Hall of Fame Lifetime Laughter award, 2000, Victor award, Acad. American Sports Awards, 2001, Star, NC Walk of Fame, 2006; named to NC Sports Hall of Fame, 1975, Naismith Meml. Basketball Hall of Fame, 2003. Achievements include having his #36 retired by the Harlem Globetrotters, 2001. Died Dec. 27, 2015.

LENA, PAUL JOSEPH, internist; b. New London, Conn., Feb. 11, 1929; s. Hugh F. and Helen (Gartland) L.; m. Joan R. Hadley, Apr. 23, 1955; children: Mark, Jay, Timothy, Patrick. AB, Dartmouth Coll., 1950, 2 yr. med. cert., 1951; MD, Harvard U., 1953. Diplomate Am. Bd. Internal Medicine. Intern Evanston (Ill.) Hosp., 1953-54; resident internal medicine Mary Hitchcock Hosp., Hanover, N.H., 1954-56, 58-59; practice medicine specializing in internal medicine and hematology Concord, N.H., from 1959; active med. staff Concord Hosp. Cons. physician N.H. State Hosp.; adj. clin. prof. medicine Dartmouth Med. Sch., 1968—; assoc. med. dir. Chubb Life Co., Concord. Lector, extraordinary minister St. John's Ch., Concord, 1978. Served to capt. M.C. U.S. Army, 1956-58. Fellow ACP (gov. for N.H. 1986); mem. Am. Soc. Internal Medicine, N.H. Med. Soc. Clubs: Bow Brook (Concord), Norford (Norwich, Vt.). Avocations: cross-country and downhill skiing, sailing, tennis, hunting. Home: Concord, NH. Died Jan. 30, 2007.

LENGYEL, ALFONZ, art history, archeology and museology educator; b. Godollo, Hungary, Oct. 21, 1921; arrived in US, 1957; s. Aurel and Margit (Furedy) Lengyel; m. Hongying Liu. Degree in mil. sci., Royal Mil. Lvdovika Acad., Budapest, 1944; degree in law and polit. sci., U. Budapest, 1948; MA, San Jose State Coll., 1959; PhD, U. Paris, 1964; LLD (hon.), London Inst. Applied Rsch., 1973. Asst. prof. San Jose State Coll., Calif., 1961-63; faculty U. Md. European Div., Paris and Heidelberg, Germany, 1963-68; intern museology Ecole du Louvre, Paris, 1965-66; prof. Wayne State U., Detroit, 1968-72, No. Ky. U., Highland Heights, 1972-77; dean, prof. Inst. Mediterranean Art and Archaeology, Cin., 1977-82; coord. art history Rosemont Coll., Pa., 1982-86; rsch. prof. art history, dir. Goebel's Print Collection, Ea. Coll., St. Davids, Pa., 1986—88; pres. Fudan Mus. Found., China, 1988—2008; dir. Sino-American, Sch. Archaeology, 1989—2009. Adj. curator Detroit Inst. Arts, 1968-72; cons. Paris Am. Acad., 1963—; dir. UPAO, Washington, 1983-87; adv. prof. Fudan U., Shanghai, People's Republic of China; cons. prof. Xian Jiaotong U., Xian, People's Republic of China, founder Sino-Am. Field Sch. Archaeology; mem. Sarasota County Arts Coun., Fla., 1995—. Author: Pub. Rels. for Mus., 1992, Archaeology for Museologists, 1993, Chinese Chronological History, 1993, Field Work in Archaeology, 2001, Chinese Chronological History, 2001; co-author: The Archaeology of Roman Pannonia, 1983; contbr. numerous articles to profl. jours. Bd. dirs. Hungarian-Am. Fedn., Cleve., 1983-91, exec. v.p., Ft. Lauderdale, Fla., 1991-2005; mem. Rep. Presdl. Task Force, Washington, 1982-86; mem. adv. bd. U.S. Dept. Interior Nat. Pk. Svc., 1987-91; bd. dirs. Mus. Asian Art, Sarasota, Fla., 2001-05, bd. dirs., US China Friendship Assn., 2008-; officer Cross of Honor, Hungarian Republic, 1992; bd. dirs. US-China Peoples Friendship Assn. Sarasota. Grantee Rockefeller Found., 1957, Govt. France, 1962-63, Smithsonian Instn., 1968, HEW, 1971.; S.H. Kress Found. lectureship Denison U., Ohio, 1967-68; Named Man of Yr., Am. Biog. Inst., 2006 Fellow: Internat. Acad. Sci. and Lettres, Oriental Sect. Arpad Acad. (pres. 1982—), Szechenyi Acad., Am. Assn. Swiss, German, Austrian Profs.; mem.: Internat. Coun. Mus., Renaissance Soc. Am., Coll. Art Assn. Am., Archaeol. Inst. Am., Nat. Fedn. Hungarian-Ams., Soc. Architectural Historians, NY Acad. Scis., Hungarian Acad. Scis., Mich. Acad. Scis. and Letters, Register of Profl. Archaeologists, Christopher Giest Hist. Soc., Detroit Classical Assn., Mich. Acad. Arts and Scis., Am. Assn. Mus., Manatee County Hist. Preservation Bd., Time Sifters Archaeological Assn. Sarasota Fla., 2012. Republican. Roman Catholic. Home: Sarasota, Fla. Died Jan. 24, 2016.

LENOX, CATHERINE CORNEAU, volunteer; b. Evanston, Ill., Sept. 16, 1920; d. Joseph Addison and Catherine Roberts Corneau; m. Lionel R. Lenox II, Dec. 9, 1945 (dec. Jan. 1994); children: Ruth Lenox Jones, Nancy, Catherine L., Elizabeth L. Howey. BA in English, Wellesley Coll., 1941; BA in Early Childhood Edn., Mills Coll., 1946; cert. in applied social gerontology, San Jose State U., 1983. Adult edn. credential San Jose State U. Tchrs. asst. Rivers Country Day Sch., Boston, 1941—42, Chestnut Hill Country Day Sch., Bethesda, Md., 1942—48; dir. Day Care Ctr., Springfield, Ill., 1943—44; tchr. Mills Coll. Childrens Sch., Oakland, Calif., 1944—45. Mem.: Sisters of Hiram (past pres., mem. sunshine com.). Republican. Baptist. Avocations: music, reading. Home: Santa Cruz, Calif. Died June 1, 2007.

LENSKI, MARY CAROLE See LITTLE, CAROLE

LENZ, SIEGFRIED, writer; b. Lyck, East Prussia, Germany, Mar. 17, 1926; Student, U. Hamburg, Germany. Reporter Die Welt, Hamburg, 1948-50, editor, 1950-51; freelance writer, from 1952. Mem. cultural bd. Die Welt, 1949-51; vis. lectr. U. Houston, 1969. Author: (novels) Es waren Habichte in der Luft, 1951, Duell mit dem Schatten, 1953, So zärtlich war Suleyken, 1955, Der Mann im Strom, 1957, Dasselbe, 1957, Jäger des Spotts, 1958 (pub. as Jäger des Spotts, und andere Erzählungen, 1965), Brot und Spiele, 1959, Das Feuerschiff, 1960, Das Wunder von Striegeldorf, 1961, Stimmungen der See, 1962, Stadtgespräch, 1963 (pub. as The Survivor, 1965), Der Hafen ist voller Geheimnisse: Ein Feature in Erzählungen und zwei masurische Geschichten, 1963, Lehmanns Erzählungen; oder, So schön war mein Markt: Aus den Bekenntnissen eines Schwarzhändlers, 1964, Der Spielverderber, 1965, Begegnung mit Tieren, 1966, Das Wrack, and Other Stories, 1967, Die Festung und andere Novellen, 1968, Deutschstunde, 1968 (pub. as The German Lesson, 1971), Hamilkar Schass aus Suleyken, 1970, Lukas, Sanftmütiger Knecht, 1970, Gesammelte Erzählungen, 1970, So war es mit dem Zirkus: Fünf Geschichten aus Suleyken, 1971, Erzählungen, 1972, Meistererzählungen, 1972, Das Vorbild, 1973 (pub. as An Exemplary Life, 1976), Ein Haus aus lauter Liebe, 1973, Der Geist der Mirabelle: Geschichten aus Bollerup, 1975, Einstein überquert die Elbe bei Hamburg, 1975, Die Kunstradfahrer und andere Geschichten, 1976, Heimatmuseum, 1978 (pub. as The Heritage, 1981), Der Verlust, 1981, Der Anfang von etwas, 1981, Ein Kriegsende, 1984, Exerzierplatz, 1985 (pub. as The Training Ground, 1991), Der Verzicht, 1985, Die Erzählungen: 1949-1984 (3 vols.), 1986, Das serbische Mädchen, 1987, Geschichten ut Bollerup, 1987, Motivsuche, 1988, Die Klangprobe, 1990; (plays) Das Schönste Fest der Welt, 1956, Zeit der Schuldlosen; Zeit der Schuldigen, 1961, Das Gesicht: Komödie, 1964, Haussuchung, 1967, Die Augenbinde; Schauspiel; Nicht alle Förster sind froh: Ein Dialog, 1970, Drei Strücke, 1980, Zeit der Schuldlosen und andere Stücke, 1988; (other) So leicht fängt man keine Katze, 1954, Der einsame Jäger, 1955, Das Kabinett der Konterbande, 1956, Flug über Land und Meer: Nordsee-Holstein-Nordsee, 1967 (pub. as Wo die Möwen schreien: Flug über Norddeutschlands Küsten und Länder, 1976), Leut von Hamburg: Satirische Porträts, 1968, Versäum nicht den Termin der Freude, 1970, Lotte soll nicht sterben, 1970 (pub. as Lotte macht alles mit, 1978), Beziehungen: Ansichten und Bekenntnisse zur Literatur, 1970, Die Herrschaftssprache der CDU, 1971, Verlorenes Langgewonnene Nachbarschaft: zur Ostpolitik der Bundesregierung, 1972, Der Amüsierdoktor, 1972, Der Leseteufel, 1972, Elfenbeinturm und Barrikade: Schriftsteller zwischen Literatur und Politik, 1976, Die Wracks von Hamburg: Hörfunk-Features, 1978, Himmel, Wolken, weites Lands: Flug über Meer, Marsch, Geest und Heide, 1979, Waldboden: Sechsunddreissig Farstuftzeichnungen, 1979, Gespräche mit Manès Sperber und Leszek Kołakowski, 1980, Über Phantasie: Siegfried Lenz, Gespräche mit Heinrich Bö, Günter Grass, Walter Kempowski, Pavel Kohout, 1982, Fast ein Triumph: aus einem Album, 1982, Elfenbeinturm und Barrikade: Erfahrungen am Schreibtisch, 1983, Manès Sperber, sein letztes Jahr, 1985, Etwas über Namen, 1985, Kleines Standgut, 1986, Am Rande des Friedens, 1989; editor: Wippchens charmante Scharmützel, 1960. Served with German Navy, 1943-45. Recipient Schickele prize, 1952, 62, Lessing prize, 1953, Gerhart Hauptmann prize, 1961, Mackensen prize, 1962, City of Bremen prize, 1962, State of Rhine-Westphalia arts prize, 1966, Gryphius prize, 1979, German Free Masons prize, 1979, Thomas Mann prize, 1984, Raabe prize, 1987, Fed. Booksellers peace prize, 1988, Galinsky Found. prize, 1989, Goethe prize, 1999 Mem. Free Acad. Arts Hamburg. Home: Hamburg, Germany. Died Oct. 7, 2014.

LEONARD, JOSEPH HOWARD, staff specialist; b. Cambridge, Md., Oct. 20, 1952; s. Joseph Francis and Catherine (Hill) L.; m. Jacquelyn Lee McCall, June 7, 1975 (div. Dec. 1981); m. Margaret Ann Shenton, June 26, 1982 (div. Dec. 2004); children: Stephanie Kristina, Jacquelyn Margaret. BA in Psychology, Salisbury State U., 1976; MA in Rehab. Counseling, Gallaudet U., 1979; postgrad., Washington Coll., 1984, Wasington Coll., 1988, U. Md., 1986—87, San Diego State U., 1996, Johns Hopkins U., 1998. Cert. profl. counselor, Md. Instr., program coord. Dorchester Devel. Unit, Inc., Cambridge, 1976—77; rehab. counselor Tex. Rehab. Commn., Austin, 1979; instr. Am. Sign Lang., develop. disabilities Chesapeake Coll., Wye Mills, Md., 1979—90; case mgr., coord. spl. programs Dorchester County Health Dept., Cambridge, 1979—90; ind. interpreter Am. Sign Lang. Md., from 1979; exec. dir. Deaf Ind. Living Assn., Inc., Salisbury, Md., 1990—2005; adj.faculty, interpreter tng. program Catonsville C.C., Md., 1995—2000; state coord. deaf svcs. divsn. Rehab. Svcs., Balt., from 2005. V.p., bd. dirs. Deaf Ind. Living Assn., Inc., Md., 1984-90; trustee Md. Sch. for the Deaf, 1985-02, pres., 1996-97; adv. bd. Devel. Disabilities program Chesapeake Coll., 1986-90; mem. Gov.'s Commn. on the Hearing Impaired, Md., 1984-90; surveyor Applied Rsch. and Evaluation U., U. Md., 1988-89; mental health adv. com. for deaf and hearing impaired, Md., 1986—; adv. coun. Office for the Deaf and Hard of Hearing, Md., 2001—, chair 2003—. Contbr. articles to profl. jours. Asst. scoutmaster Boy Scouts Am., Cambridge, 1973-78; v.p. bd. dirs. Dorchester County Family YWCA, 1985; pres. bd. dirs. Dorchester Assn. for Devel. Disabled, 1979-88; bd. dirs. Ea. Shore Ctr. Ind. Living, 1998-2005, v.p., 2003-04, Md. Assn. of Deaf, 1982-86; bd. dirs. Md. Assn. of Cmty. Svcs., 1992-02; pres. Trappe Little League Baseball and Softball Assn., 2000-02; . With USN, 1970-73, with USCGR, 1975-86. Recipient Founder's award Gallaudet U., 1993, Disting. Svc. award Md. Assn. of the Deaf, 1995, Agy. Innovation award Md. Assn. Cmty. Svcs., 1996. Mem. Am. Deafness and Rehab. Assn., Md. Rehab. Assn., Nat. Assn. Deaf, Registry of Interpreters for the Deaf (bd. dirs. Potomac chpt. 1996-2000), Chi Sigma Iota, Psi Chi, Rho Sigma Chi. Roman Catholic. Avocations: photography, boating, canoeing, sailing, woodcarving. Home: Easton, Md. Died Aug. 4, 2007.

LEONE, RICHARD CARL, foundation executive; b. Rochester, NY, Apr. 30, 1941; m. Anita Osper (div.); 1 child, Kate; m. Meg Cox; 1 child, Max. AB, U. Rochester, 1962; M in Pub. Affairs, Princeton U., 1965, PhD, 1969. Mem. faculty Princeton U., NJ, 1969-73, 78, 79; pres. Center for Analysis of Pub. Issues, 1970-73; treas. State of NJ, 1973-77; pres. NY Mercantile Exchange, 1980-82, Atlantic Commodities subs. Amerada-Hess, 1982-84; mng. dir. Dillon, Read and Co., Inc., NYC, 1985-89; pres. Twentieth Century Fund, NYC, 1989—2011; chmn. Port Authority of NY and NJ, 1990—94. Bd. dirs. Dreyfus Mut. Fund Bds., RAC Mortgage Investment Co. Contbr. articles on pub. policy and pub. fin. to profl. jours.; host weekly pub. affairs program WNET (Channel 13) and N.J. Pub. TV, 1979-83. Del. Dem. Nat. Conv., 1984; bd. dirs. N.J. Sports and Expo. Authority (Meadowlands), 1974-77, Circle Repertory Theatre, 1980-86, Pres.'s Commn. on Mgmt. Improvement in Fed. Govt., 1978-80. Died July 16, 2015.

LEPKOWSKI, FRANK (FRANCIS JOSEPH LEPKOWSKI), librarian; b. Erie, Pa., Oct. 24, 1955; BA in English, Cornell U., 1978; MLS, U. Mich., 1982; MA in English, Oakland U., 1992. Asst. libr. SUNY, Potsdam, 1982-85; from asst. prof. to assoc. prof. Oakland U., Rochester, Mich., 1985—2014. Contbr. poetry and articles to profl. jours. Fulbright fellow Coun. for Internat. Exch. Scholars, 1987-89. Mem. MLA, Mich. Libr. Assn., Nat. Coun. Tchrs. English, Phi Beta Kappa, Beta Phi Mu. Avocation: jazz music. Home: Royal Oak, Mich. Died Oct. 28, 2014.

LESLIE, LOTTIE LYLE, retired secondary education educator; b. Huntsville, Ala., Aug. 5, 1930; d. James Peter and Amanda Lacy Burns; children: Thomas E. Lyle Jr., Theodore Christopher Leslie, DeMarcus Miller Leslie. BS, Ala. A and M U., 1953, student, 1960-83; training cert., Learning Ctrs. of Am., 1985. Cert. secondary tchr. Social studies, English, Music. Tchr. Madison County Bd. Edn., Huntsville, Ala. Author: Teaching the Importance of Character Through Poetry, 1968-69, Ways to Teach Language Composition and Literature, Versatility Versus Violence, Families and Foreign Relationships, Musical Instruments of the World From K-12 and Undergraduate to Graduate; contbr. poetry to profl jours. Active St. Joseph's Cmty., 1959—; organist Antioch AME Zion Ch., 1995—; mem. Huntsville Lit. Assn. (poetry divsn.), 1997—; sponsor Arts Festival for Madison County Schs., 1966; dir. voters edn. Project for Youth, 1977; consulting sponsor Ednl. Expo, 2000. Recipient Miss Liberty trophy, 1986, Victory pin, 1987, Medal of Honor Commemorating Disting. Lifelong Achievements, 1993, cert. appreciation Indian Creek P.B. Ch., 1994. Mem. NEA, ASCD, NAACP, Ala. Edn. Assn., Madison County Music Edn. Assn., Internat. Black Writers and Artists, Inc., N.Y. Poetry Soc., Am. Poetry Assn. (vol. IV no. 2 summer 1985), Huntsville Literary Assn. (poetry divsn. 1997—). Home: Huntsville, Ala. Died June 21, 2007.

LETSINGER, RICHARD PHILLIPS, real estate brokerage company executive; b. Bloomfield, Ind., July 31, 1921; s. Reed Alexander and Leonia Etna (Phillips) L.; m. Patricia Rollins Edgeworth, Jan. 19, 1946; children: Richard Keith, Patricia Laurie Letsinger Schenck. AB in Polit. Sci., Ind. U., 1943. Dept. mgr. Sears Roebuck, Flint, Mich., 1944-49; sales mgr. Victor Oolitic Stone Co., Bloomington, Ind., 1949-54; owner, mgr. Letsinger Real Estate, Bloomington, from 1955; ptnr. Letsinger & Morrow, Bloomington, 1957-74; owner, CEO. Letsinger, Inc., Realtors, Singer Island, Fla., from 1974, also bd. dirs. V.p., bd. dirs. Letsinger Coal Co., Bloomfield; CEO, bd. dirs. Victor Buff Stone Co., Bloomington, 1985—, Number Fourteen Corp., Singer Island, 1985—. Chmn. Pub. Housing Adminstrn., Bloomington, 1964-68; formerly active for mayoral campaign coms., Bloomington. With U.S. Army, 1943-45, ETO. Decorated Bronze Star. Mem. Nat. Bd. Realtors, Fla. Bd. Realtors, Bloomington Bd. Realtors (pres. 1959), Am. Legion, Carriage Assn. Am., Masons, Shriners, Elks. Republican. Methodist. Avocations: writing, horseback riding, driving. Home: Riviera Beach, Fla. Died Aug. 1, 2007.

LEVEEN, PAULINE, emeritus government and history professor; b. NYC, Mar. 5, 1925; d. Aaron and Sophie (Karp) Ugelow; m. Seymour Leveen, Nov. 5, 1944; children: David Ian, Amy Frances, Adriane Beth. Student, Coll. City NY, 1944; BA, Elmira Coll., 1963, MS, 1965; postgrad., Cornell U., 1967, 71-72, Syracuse U., 1981-82. Cert. tchr. permanent secondary social studies. Substitute tchr. Elmira (N.Y.) Sch. Dist., 1960-65; prof. history and govt. Corning (N.Y.) C.C., 1965-92, prof. emeritus, from 1992, dir. paralegal program, 1975-93, chmn. div. social scis., 1984-91, liaison accelerated coll. edn., 1982—2006. Lectr. Elderhostel, Painted Post, N.Y., 1982—2000. Recipient Athena Internat. award, 2012. Mem. AAUW (chair Elmira-Corning br., 1989-1996, pres., 2003-06, chair edn. & econ. equity 2004—), Phi Alpha Theta (hon. edn. assocs.), Beta Chi/Delta Kappa Gamma Corning (profl. affairs 1968, 75, legis. 1989—, hon. edn. assocs.). Avocation: reading. Home: Bronx, NY. Died Nov. 10.

LEVEROCK, ALAN WINFIELD, computer programer; b. Bridgetown, Barbados, July 13, 1935; s. Edmund Wilfred and Lillian (Johnson) L. Programmer analyst Moodys Investors Service, NYC, 1973-79; project leader Brown Bros. Harriman, NYC, 1979-81; asst. cashier Algemene Bank, NYC, 1981-84; tech. officer Mfrs. Hanover Trust Co., NYC, 1984-89, retired, 1989; ptnr. Mandy Shipping Co. N.V., Saba N.A., 1989-92. Served in USN, 1954-58. Republican. Episcopalian. Avocation: gardening. Home: Palm Harbor, Fla. Died Mar. 8, 2007.

LEVINE, PHILIP, poet, educator; b. Detroit, Jan. 10, 1928; s. A. Harry and Esther Gertrude (Priscol) L.; m. Frances Artley, July 12, 1954; children: Mark, John, Teddy. BA, Wayne State U., 1950, A.M., 1955; M.F.A., U. Iowa, 1957, studied with John Berryman, 1954. Instr. U. Iowa, 1955-57; instr. Calif. State U., Fresno, 1958—69, prof. English, 1969-92, prof. English emeritus, 1992—2015; prof. English Tufts U.; tchr. Princeton U., Columbia U., U. Calif., Berkeley.; Elliston lectr. poetry U. Cin.; poet-in-residence Vassar Coll., Nat. U. Australia; instr. Am. Acad. Art and Letters, 1997, Am. Acad. Arts and Scis., 2002; disting. poet-in-residence NYU. Chmn. lit. panel Nat. Endowment Arts, 1985; adj. prof. NYU, Spring, 1984, Univ. prof. Brown U., spring 1985; tchr. NYU, U. Iowa, Vanderbilt U., U. Houston; part-time vis. prof. various universities; poet laureate 2011-12 Author: On the Edge, 1963, Silent in America: Vivas for Those Who Have Failed, 1965, Not This Pig, 1968, 5 Detroits, 1970, Thistles, 1970, Pili's Wall, 1971, Red Dust, 1971, They Feed They Lion, 1972, 1973, 1974, On The Edge & Over, 1976, The Names of the Lost, 1976 (Lenore Marshall award Best Am. Book Poems 1976), 7 Years from Somewhere, 1979 (Nat. Book Critics Circle prize 1979, Notable Book award Am. Libr. Assn. 1979), Ashes, 1979 (Nat. Book Critics Circle prize 1979, Nat. Book award 1979), Don't Ask, 1979, One for the Rose, 1981, Selected Poems, 1984, Sweet Will, 1985, A Walk with Tom Jefferson, 1988 (Bay Area Book Reviewers award), What Work Is, 1991 (L.A. Times Book Prize 1991, Nat. Book award for poetry, 1991), New Selected Poems, 1991, Earth, Stars, and Writers, 1992, The Bread of Time: Toward an Autobiography, 1994, Simple Truth, 1994 (Pulitzer Prize for poetry 1995), Unselected Poems, 1997, The Mercy, 1999, So Ask: Essays and Conversations, 2002, Breath, 2004; editor: (with Henri Coulette) Character and Crisis, 1966, (with E. Trejo) The Selected Poems of Jaime Sabines, (with Ada Long) Off the Map, The Selected Poems of Gloria Fuertes, 1984, (with D. Wojahn and B. Henderson) The Pushcart Prize XI, 1986, The Essential Keats, 1987, Poetry, 1998, Unselected Poems, 2000, So Ask, 2002. Active anti-Vietnam war movement. Recipient Joseph Henry Jackson award San Francisco Found., 1961, The Chaplebrook Found. award, 1968, Frank O'Hara Meml. prize, 1973; Amer. Academy of Arts and Letters Award of Merit, 1974; Levinson Prize, 1974; Harriet Monroe Meml. prize for poetry, 1976; Golden Rose award New Eng. Poetry Soc., 1985, Ruth Lilly Poetry Prize, Modern Poetry Assn. and Am. Council Arts, 1987, Elmer Bobst award NYU, 1990, Lit. Lion New York Public Library 1993; named outstanding lectr. Calif. State U., Fresno, 1971, outstanding prof. Calif. State U. System, 1972; Stanford U. poetry fellow, 1957, Nat. Inst. Arts and Letters grantee, 1973, Guggenheim fellow, 1973-74, 80; Nat. Endowment for Arts grantee, 1969, 76, 81, 87. Mem. AAAL, Acad. Am. Poets (chancellor 2000), Am. Acad. Arts and Scis. Home: Fresno, Calif. *My hope is to write poetry for people for whom there are no poems.* Died Feb. 14, 2015.

LEVITAN, STANLEY BERNARD, publishing executive; b. NYC, Aug. 14, 1926; m. Este Polsky; 1 child, Cheryl Stahl. BA, CUNY, 1948. Salesman Met. Tobacco Co., NYC, 1948-50; metro sales rep. Major Liguor Distbrs., Oyster Bay, N.Y., 1950-65; nat. sales mgr. Dare mag., NYC, 1965-68; metro sales mgr. Redbook mag., NYC, 1968-69; nat. sales mgr. Sci. and Tech. mag., NYC, 1969-70, Gernsback Pub., NYC, 1970-86; pres. Stan Levitan Assocs., NYC, from 1986. Mem. Nat. Assn. Publs. Reps., Electronics Industry Assn. Home: Boca Raton, Fla. Died Aug. 13, 2007.

LEVITT, RODNEY CHARLES, music company executive, composer; b. Portland, Oreg., Sept. 16, 1929; s. Samuel Jerome and Anne Ruth (Canter) L.; m. Jean Leah Mullenix, Apr. 1, 1962; 1 child, Barry. BA in Music, U. Wash., 1951. Trombonist Dizzy Gillespie, NYC, 1956-57, Radio City Music Hall Orch., NYC, 1957-63; rec. artist RCA Victor Records, NYC, 1963-66; music producer, composer Rod Levitt Enterprises, NYC, from 1966. Composer, arranger: (record albums) Dynamic Sound Patterns, 1963 (Grammy award 1964), Insight, 1964 (Grammy award 1965), Solid Ground, 1965, Forty-Second Street, 1966. Served to sgt. USAF, 1951-55. Recipient Clio award Benton and Bowles, 1965. Avocations: tennis, running. Home: Wardsboro, Vt. Died May 9, 2007.

LEVY, JULIUS, lawyer; b. NYC, Feb. 15, 1913; s. Samuel and Esther (Pashman) L.; m. Jane Frederick, Nov. 7, 1940; children: Frederick J., Douglas J. BA, U. Mo., 1934; LLB, Columbia U., 1936. Bar: N.Y. 1936, U.S. Dist. Ct. (so. and ea. dists.) N.Y. 1937, U.S. Ct. Appeals (2d, 8th and D.C. cirs.) 1945, U.S. Supreme Ct. 1946. Of counsel Pomerantz, Levy, Haudek, Block & Grossman, NYC, 1946-97, ret., 1997. Bd. dirs. Univ. Settlement House, N.Y.C. Served to lt. (j.g.) USNR, 1943-46. Mem. ABA, N.Y. County Lawyers Assn., Am. Arbitration Assn. (nat. panel). Lodges: B'nai B'rith. Jewish. Avocation: tennis. Home: New York, NY. Died Dec. 4, 2006.

LEVY, KENNETH ST. CLAIR, barrister, criminologist, psychologist, accountant; b. Brisbane, Australia, Dec. 23, 1949; s. Francis and Grace (Ferguson) Levy; m. Veronica Mary Forster, Jan. 7, 1978; children: Clare, Gregory. BA in Psychology, U. Queensland, Australia, 1978, BCom in Commerce, 1980, PhD, 1994; LLB, Queensland U. Tech., 1986. Registered Barrister at Law High Ct. Australia, Supreme Ct. Queensland, tax agt., chartered tax adviser. Numerous mgmt. and organizatioal positions, 1974—89; dep. dir. gen. Dept. Justice, 1989—2000, dir. gen., 2000—03, cons. psychologist and barrister, from 2004, sr. mem. adminstrv. appeals tribunal, from 2004, dir. acctg. profl. ethical stds. bd., 2006—09; clin. prof. Bond U. Law Faculty, 2007—13; acting chmn. Crime and Corruption Commn. Queensland, 2013—15. Mem. bd. mgmt. Australian Inst. Criminology, 1991—2003, mem. criminology rsch. coun., 1991—2003; chair Mgmt. Resource Solutions, 2007—08. Founding mem. Rental Bond Authority, 1989—90; pres. Alternative Dispute Resolution Coun., 1994—2000. Lt. col. Australian Army Res. Fulbright scholar, 1995; recipient Outstanding Law Alumni award Queensland U. Tech., 2002, Res. Force decoration, 1990, Centenary medal, Australia, 2003, Nat. Svc. medal, 2004, Australian Def. medal, 2006. Fellow: CPA Australia (v.p. prof. devel. 1996—97, dep. chair 1997, dep. pres. 1998, dep. chmn. disciplinary com. Queensland divsn. 1998—99, pres. 1999, chmn. Queensland divisional coun. 1999—2000, chair disciplinary com. Queensland divsn. 2000—01, nat. v.p. corp.gov. 2002, nat. dep. pres. 2003, nat. pres. 2004), Inst. Chartered Accts. Australia and New Zealand; mem.: APA, Chartered Tax Adviser, Coll. Forensic Psychology, Bar Assn. Queensland, Australian Psychol. Soc., United Svcs. Club. Avocations: music, reading, travel. Died Jan. 20, 2016.

LEVY, MARVIN DAVID, composer; b. Passaic, NJ, Aug. 2, 1932; s. Benjamin and Bertha (Tramberg) L. BA, N.Y. U., 1954; MA, Columbia U., 1956; pupil of, Philip James and Otto Luening. Asst. dir. Am. Opera Soc., 1952-61; music critic Mus. Am. Herald Tribune, 1952-58; assoc. prof. of music Bklyn. Coll., 1974-76. Former artistic dir. Fort Lauderdale Opera. Composer: orchestral Caramoor Festival Overture, 1958, Symphony, 1960, Kyros, 1961, One Person, 1962, Piano Concerto, 1970, Trialogus, 1972, In Memoriam: W.H. Auden, 1974, Canto de los Maranos, 1978, Pascua Florida, 1987, Arrows of Time, 1988; oratorios For The Time Being, 1959, Sacred Service, 1964, Masada (Nat. Symphony commn.); operas Mourning Becomes Electra (Met. Opera commn.), 1967, Escorial, 1958, Sotoba Komachi, 1957, The Tower, 1956; musical The Grand Balcony, 1990, 95; film theater scores; chamber music; artistic dir. Ft. Lauderdale Opera, 1989-94. Recipient Prix de Rome, 1962, 65, N.Y.C. Scroll award for Disting. and Exceptional Svc., 1967; Guggenheim grantee, 1960, 64, Ford Found. grantee, 1965, Damrosch grantee, 1961, NEA grantee, 1974, 78. Mem. ASCAP. Home: Fort Lauderdale, Fla. Died Feb. 9, 2015.

LEWIS, ANDREW LINDSAY, JR., (DREW LEWIS), former United States Secretary of Transportation; b. Phila., Nov. 3, 1931; s. Andrew Lindsay and Lucille L. (Bricker); m. Marilyn S. Stoughton, June 1, 1950; children: Karen Lewis Sacks, Russell Shepherd, Andrew Lindsay IV. BS, Haverford Coll., Pa., 1953; MBA, Harvard Bus. Sch., 1955; postgrad., MIT, 1968. Various positions Henkels & McCoy, Inc., Blue Bell, Pa., 1955-60; v.p. sales American Olean Tile Co., Inc., Lansdale, Pa., 1960-68; with Nat. Gypsum Co., Buffalo, 1960-70; chmn. Simplex Wire & Cable Co., Boston, 1970—72, chmn., CEO, 1972-74; pres., CEO Snelling & Snelling, Inc., Boston, 1972-74; financial & mgmt. cons. Lewis & Associates, Plymouth Meeting, Pa., 1974-81; sec. US Dept. Transp., Washington, 1981-83; chmn. Warner Amex Cable Communications Inc., NYC, 1983-86; chmn., CEO Union Pacific R.R., Omaha, 1986; pres. Union Pacific Corp., NYC, 1986-87, chmn., CEO Bethlehem, Pa., 1987-97. Bd. dirs. American Olean Tile Co., Inc., 1960—68, American Express Co., 1986—2000. Mem. Republican Nat. Com. (RNC), 1976—90, dep. chmn., 1980—81; Republican Candidate for Gov. of Pa., 1974; dep. polit. dir. Reagan-Bush Campaign Com., 1980; co-chmn. Nat. Econ. Commn., 1988—89; chmn. The Bus. Roundtable, 1990—99. Mem.: Loblolly Pines Golf Club (HobeSound, Fla.), Bohemian Club (San Francisco), Saucon Valley Country club (Bethlehem, Pa.), Sunnybrook Golf Club (Plymouth Meeting, Pa.), Phila. Club. Republican. Died Feb. 10, 2016.

LEWIS, DOROTHY LEI (PLOETNER), education educator; b. Louisville, June 24, 1923; d. Victor Michael, Jr. and Agnes Marie (Lynch) Ploetner; m. Norman Millard Lewis, Sr., May 17, 1946 (dec. Jan. 1978); children: Norman Millard, Jr., Julian Jerome. BS in Secondary Edn., Ind. U., 1949, MS in Elem. Edn., 1953; PhD in Rhetoric and Comp., U. Louisville, 1984. Lic. elem. and secondary English lang. tchr. Sec. E.I. du Pont, Charlestown, Ind., 1940-44; recruiter U.S. Coast Guard, New Orleans, 1944-46; student aide Sch. Edn. Ind. U., Bloomington, 1946-49; elem. tchr. Clarksville (Ind.) Community Schs., 1949-57, secondary tchr., 1957-86; prof. English dept. U. Louisville, 1985-87, adj. asst. prof. Sch. Edn., from 1987. Presenter Assn. Gifted Edn., St. Louis, 1982; participant Ind. Writing Project, Indpls., 1982; cons. Personal Lang. Arts Svcs., Bardstown, Ky., 1988-89, Carroll County, Ky, 1989-90. Contbr. articles to profl. jours. Lay eucharistic minister St. Paul's Episcopal Ch., Jeffersonville, Ind., 1987—; pres. So. Ind. Tourism Bur., Clarksville, 1991; sec. Clarksville Riverfront Found., 1987—; pres. Clarksville Community Sch. Bd. of Edn., 1990; mem. precinct com. # 34 Clark County Dem. Ctrl., Clarksville, 1985—. With USCG, 1944-46. Recipient Clark County Woman of Yr. award Evening News, 1986-87. Mem. NEA (life), Ky. Coun. Tchrs. English (editor newsletter 1987-89), Phi Kappa Phi, Delta Kappa Gamma (State Sch. award 1980-83, Internat. award 1981, pres. 1972-74), Phi Lambda Theta. Avocations: reading, bird watching, gardening, walking, volunteering. Home: Clarksville, Ind. Died May 11, 2007.

LEWIS, GEOFFREY, actor; b. San Diego, July 31, 1935; m. Glenis Batley, 1973 (div. 1975); m. Paula Hochhalter, 1976; children: Dierdre, Lightfield, Juliette, Brandy, Peter, Matthew. Actor (Films) The Fat Black Pussycat, 1963, Welcome Home, Soldier Boys, 1971, The Culpepper Cattle Co., 1972, Bad Company, 1972, High Plains Drifter, 1973, Dillinger, 1973, My Name is Nobody, 1973, Thunderbolt and Lightfoot, 1974, The Great Waldo Pepper, 1975, The Wind and the Lion, 1975, Smile, 1975, Lady Luck, 1975, The Return of the Man Called Horse, 1976, Shoot the Sun Down, 1978, They Died with Their Boots On, 1978, Every Which Way But Loose, 1978, Tilt, 1979, Human Experiments, 1979, Tom Horn, 1980, Bronco Billy, 1980, Heaven's Gate, 1980 Any Which Way You Can, 1980, I, the Jury, 1982, 10 to Midnight, 1983, Night of the Comet, 1984, Lust in the Dust, 1985, Stitches, 1985, Time Out, 1988, Out of the Dark, 1988, Fletch Lives, 1989, Pink Cadillac, 1989, Catch Me If You Can, 1989, Disturbed, 1990, Double Impact, 1991, The Lawnmower Man, 1992, Wishman, 1992, Point of No Return, 1993, Army of One, 1993, The Man Without a Face, 1993, Only the Strong, 1993, White Fang 2: Myth of the White Wolf, 1994, Maverick, 1994, The Dragon Gate, 1994, An Occasional Hell, 1996, American Perfekt, 1997, Midnight in the Garden of Good and Evil, 1997, Five Aces, 1999, The Prophet's Game, 2000, The Way of the Gun, 2000, Highway 395, 2000, Sunstorm, 2001, A Light of Darkness, 2002, The New Guy, 2002, Mind Games, 2003, Renegade, 2004, Social Guidance, 2005, Down in the Valley, 2005, The Devil's Rejects, 2005, Fingerprints, 2006, Wicked Little Things, 2006, Cold Ones, 2007, Chinaman's Chance: America's Other Slaves, 2008, Thomas Kinkade's Christmas Cottage, 2008, The Butcher, 2009, Pickin' & Grinnin', 2010, Miss Nobody, 2010, Mommy's Little Monster, 2012, Retreat!, 2012, (TV Films) Moon of the Wolf, 1972, Honky Tonk, 1974, The Gun and the Pulpit, 1974, The Great Ice Rip-Off, 1974, Attack on Terror: The FBI vs the Ku Klux Klan, 1975, The New Daughters of Joshua Cabe, 1976, The Great Houdini, 1976, The Deadly Triangle, 1977, The Hunted Lady, 1977, When Every Day Was the Fourth of July, 1978, The Jericho Mile, 1979, Samurai, 1979, Salem's Lot, 1979, Belle Starr, 1980, Skyward Christmas, 1981, The Shadow Riders, 1982, Life of the Party: The Story of Beatrice, 1982, The Return of the Man from U.N.C.L.E.: The Fifteen Years Later Affair, 1983, Travis McGee, 1983, September Gun, 1983, Stormin' Home, 1985, Dallas: The Early Years, 1986, Annihilator, 1986, Spot Marks the X, 1986, Desert Rats, 1988, Pancho Barnes, 1988, Desperado: The Outlaw Wars, 1989, Matters of the Heart, 1990, Gunsmoke: The Last Apache, 1990, Day of Reckoning, 1994, Gambler V; Playing for Keeps, 1994, When the Dark Man Calls, 1995, Kansas, 1995, Trilogy of Terror II, 1996, Rough Riders, 1997, The Underworld, 1997, A Painted House, 2003, My Life with Men, 2003, Plainsong, 2004, Patients, 2004, The Fallen Ones, 2005, Voodoo Moon, 2006, Wild Hearts, 2006, (TV mini series) Centennial, 1979; actor or guest appearances (TV series) Then Came Bronson, 1970, Bonanza, 1970, The High Chaparral, 1970, The Young Lawyers, 1970, The Name of the Game, 1971, Longstreet, 1971, Cade's County, 1971, Mannix, 1971-72, Alias Smith and Jones, 1971-72, Mission Impossible, 1972, Gunsmoke, 1972, Cannon, 1972, Mod Squad, 1973, Kung Fu, 1973, The Waltons, 1974, S.W.A.T., 1975, Starsky and Hutch, 1975, The Streets of San Francisco, 1975, Harry O, 1975, Bert D'Angelo/Superstar, 1976, The Rookies, 1976, City of Angels, 1976, Alice, 1976, McCloud, 1976, Police Woman, 1975-1976, Ark II, 1976, Laverne & Shirley, 1977, Hunter, 1977, The Six Million Dollar Man, 1977, Hawaii Five-O, 1977, Quark, 1978, Mork & Mindy, 1978, The Amazing Spider-Man, 1979, Hizzonner, 1979, A Man Called Sloan, 1979, Barnaby Jones, 1973-80, B.J. and the Bear, 1980, Lou Grant, 1977-80, Flo, 1980-81, Bret Maverick, 1982, Little House onf the Prairie, 1976-83, Gun Shy, 1983, Mama's Family, 1983, After MASH, 1983, Maximum Security, 1984, Blue Thunder, 1984, The Yellow Rose, 1984, Hot Pursuit, 1984, Falcon Crest, 1984, Highway to Heaven, 1984, Wildside, 1985, Spenser: For Hire, 1985, The Fall Guy, 1985, Scarecrow and Mrs. King, 1985, Shadow Chasers, 1985, The A-Team, 1984-85, Magnum, P.I., 1984-86, Amazing Stories, 1986, Sidekicks, 1986, MacGyver, 1986, Easy Street, 1987, Desiging Women, 1987, The Golden Girls, 1987, J.J. Starbuck, 1987, Matlock, 1988, CBS Summer Playhouse, 1988, Mathnet, 1988, Square One TV, 1988, Guns of Paradise, 1989, In the Heat of the Night, 1990, Walker, Texas Ranger, 1994, Murder She Wrote, 1987-96, Land's End, 1995-96, The X-Files, 1999, Pensacola: Wings of Gold, 2000, The Huntress, 2001, Thieves, 2001, The Guardian, 2003, Odyssey 5, 2002-03, Titus, 2001, Dawson's Creek, 2003, Nip/Tuck, 2003, Cold Case, 2004, Las Vegas, 2004, The Mountain, 2004, Law & Order: Criminal Intent, 2004, Fat Actress, 2005, My Name Is Earl, 2006, Criminal Minds, 2006, House M.D., 2007; (voice) The Haunted World of El Superbeasto, 2009; (shorts) Freedom, 1970, The Janitor, 1995, Old Man Music, 2005, Better Angels, 2011. Died Apr. 7, 2015.

LEWIS, HARTWELL ARTHUR, venture capitalist; b. Abbeville, La., Mar. 18, 1927; s. William Slaughter and Laura (Lee) L.; m. Mentor Pourciau, Feb. 14, 1952; children: Laura Lewis Millet, Hartwell A. Jr. BSBA, U. S.W. La., 1949. Salesman Burroughs Corp., New Orleans, 1949-54; mgr. C.R. Patterson Agy., Inc., Houma, La., 1954-68; v.p. Harlan of La., Inc., Houma, 1968-75, Bayly, Martin & Fay of La., Houma, 1975-83, pres., 1983-85; pres., owner Capital for Terrebonne, Inc., Houma, from 1985. Pres. La. Assn. Ins. Agts., Baton Rouge, 1963-64, Private Industry Coun., Houma, 1981-83; vice-chmn. Housing Authority Houma, 1966-85. Lay advisor to bd. dirs. Perkins Sch. Theology, 1986—; bd. dirs. United Way, 1988-94; treas. Alcohol and Drug Abuse Coun., 1990-91, pres., 1992-94; bd. commrs. Hosp. Svc. Dist. 1, Terrebonne Parish, La., 1994; chmn. 1st United Meth. Ch., Houma, 1989-90, mem. fin. com., 1985-91, treas., 1993—. With USNR, 1945-46. Mem. Bayou Bd. Realtors (pres. 1961-62, Terrebonne C. of C. (bd. dirs. 1958-94), Rotary (bd. dirs. 1986-91, past pres.). Avocation: stained glass. Home: Houma, La. Died Mar. 12, 2007.

LEWIS, JERRY M., psychiatrist, educator; b. Utica, NY, Aug. 18, 1924; s. Jerry M. and Margaret (Miller) L.; m. Patsy Ruth Price, Sept. 24, 1949; children: Jerry M., Cynthia Lewis-Reynolds, Nancy Minns, Tom. MD, Southwestern Med. Sch., Dallas, 1951. Diplomate Am. Bd. Psychiatry and Neurology. Staff psychiatrist Timberlawn Psychiat. Hosp., Dallas, 1957-63, chief women's svc., 1963-66, chief adolescent svcs., 1966-70, dir. profl. edn., 1970-79, psychiatrist-in-chief, 1979-88, dir. rsch., 1988-93. Dir. rsch. and tng. Timberlawn Psychiat. Rsch. Found., Dallas, 1967-88, sr. rsch. psychiatrist, 1988—; clin. prof. psychiatry, family practice and cmty. medicine Southwestern Med. Sch.; cons. in psychiatry Baylor U. Med. Ctr., Dallas. Author: No Single Thread, 1976, How's Your Family, 1978, To Be a Therapist, 1979, The Long Struggle, 1983, Swimming Upstream: Teaching Psychotherapy in a Biological Era, 1991, The Monkey-Rope, 1995, Marriage as a Search for Healing: Theory, Assessment & Therapy, 1997, (with John Gossett, Ph.D.) Disarming the Past: How an Intimate Relationship Can Heal Old Wounds, 1999, Reflections on the Good Life: A Psychotherapist Writes to His Grandchildren, 2005, Famous Marriages: What They Can Teach Us, 2006. Served with USN, 1943-45. Fellow Am. Coll. Psychiatrists (pres. 1985), Am. Psychiat. Assn., So. Psychiat. Assn. (pres. 1979); mem. Group for Advancement of Psychiatry (pres. 1987), Benjamin Rush Soc. (pres. 1994-95), AMA, Tex. Med. Assn. Died Aug. 5, 2012.

LEWIS, MICHAEL EDWIN, financial institution executive; b. Toledo, Ohio, Apr. 28, 1956; s. Edwin Neldon Lewis and Lois Blanche (Smith) Lewis Phalen: m. Lori Ann Brueshaber, Sept. 11, 1976; children: Michael Fredrick Jennifer Christine. Student, U. Toledo, 1974-81. Asst. bus mgr. Cosmos Broadcasting Corp., Toledo, 1976-81; bus. mgr., controller Heftel Broadcasting Corp., Indpls., 1981-83; comml. loan officer Firstmark Fin. Corp., Indpls., 1983-85, v.p. broadcast fin., 1985-86, sr. v.p., from 1986; v.p. Summit Bank Indpls., from 1988. Bd. dirs. Fishers (Ind.) Recreational League, 1987—. Mem. Nat. Assn. Broadcasters, Indpls. Mus. Art. Republican. Baptist. Avocations: sports, baseball cards, photography. Home: Fishers Ind. Died July 31, 2007.

LEWIS, OWEN DONALD, real estate broker; b. Winston-Salem, NC, Apr. 9, 1925; s. Andrew Bruce and Daisy Imogene (Owen) L.; m. Betty Caroline Felmet, July 17, 1965; children: Suzanne, Julius, Sarah, Owen Jr. BS, U. N.C., 1949; EdS, U. N.C., Greensboro, 1978; MS, N.C. A & T State U., 1973. Cert. tchr., prin., supt., N.C.; lic. real estate broker, ins. agt., N.C. Trainee Atlas Supply Co., Winston-Salem, 1949-51; mgr. Wachovia Bank and Trust Co., Winston-Salem, 1951-56, Piedmont Pub. Co., Winston-Salem, 1956-61; art gallery mgr. Winston-Salem, 1961-63; writer Greensboro Daily News, 1963-69; pub. info. dir. Greensboro Pub. Schs., 1969-76, tchr., 1976-90. Owner, operator real estate brokerage and property mgmt. firm, Greensboro, 1976—; pvt. practice as cons., Louisville, Winston-Salem, Greensboro, 1961—; exhibit dir. Salem Coll., Winston-Salem, 1967-70; vis. scholar N.C. Ctr. for Advancement of Tchg., 1987. Contbr. articles to newspapers (Sch. Bell award 1968-69, Arch. Writing award 1967, Internat. Reading Assn. award 1968, Religion Writing award 1966). Mem. planning bd. City of Greensboro, 1987-92, chmn., 1991-92; pres. Southeastern Ctr. for Contemporary Art, Winston-Salem, 1957-68; parliamentarian Eden (N.C.) Preservation Soc., Guilford County Dem. Exec. Com., Greensboro, 1980-90, 95—; mem. Guiford County Bd. of Adjustment, 1993—, Greensboro City Bd. of Adjustment, 1995—; bd. dirs. Exec. Club, 1989-95; pres. Greensboro/Guilford Ret. Sch. Pers., 1994—, Optimist Club Greensboro, 1972-73, pres. Breakfast club, 1979-80; lt. gov. N.C. Dist., 1973-74. With Merchant Marine, 1943-46. Mark Ethridge fellow Ford Found., 1966-67, N.C. Inst. Polit. Leadership, 1996. Mem. N.C. Assn. Educators (comm. com.), N.C. Sch. Pub. Rels. Assn. (pres. 1972-73), Rotary (editor, program chair, bd. dirs. Crescent Club), Elks (chmn. scholarship com. 1973—), Greensboro City Club, Forsyth Country Club, Twin City Club, Phi Delta Kappa (bd. dirs., advisor Triad chpt., pres. 1974-75, svc. key 1981, founder High Point U. chpt.), Kappa Delta Pi, Delta Pi Epsilon. Presbyterian. Home: Greensboro, NC. Died May 15, 2007.

LEWIS, RICHARD, SR., securities broker, consultant; b. Macon, Ga., Jan. 18, 1930; s. William Chapman and Florida (Zelius) L.; m. Iris Joy Clements, Sept. 10, 1949; children: Richard Jr., Linda Lee. Cert. pistol and rifle instr. State trooper Fla. Hwy. Patrol, various cities, 1951-72; pres. Gateway Shooters Supply, Inc., Jacksonville, Fla., 1973—79, Jacksonville Police Pistol Club, 1972—82, Bobcat Enterprises Inc., 1983-84; broker Global Investments Securities Inc., Miami, 1985-86, Investacorp, Inc., Miami Lakes, Fla., 1986-89. Lobbyist Fla. Assn. of State Troopers, Tallahassee, 1988-89. With U.S. Army, 1952-54, mem. Georgia Rep. Party, White County Rep. Party Recipient cert. of appreciation, State of Fla., Tallahassee, 1972; Demolay Cross of Honor, Internat. Coun., Kansas City, Mo., 1973; cert. of commendation, State of Fla., 1972, Svc. award, Masons Grand Lodge Fla.. Mem. NRA (life), SAR, SCV (life), Am. Assn. State Troopers, Ret. Troopers Assn., Fla. Assn. State Troopers (legis. chmn. retirees 1987), High Meadow Landowners Assn. (pres. 2001-07), VFW., Jacksonville Pistol Club (pres. 1968-72), Marion Dunn Masons (life), Elks, Mil. Order Stars and Bars (life), Fraternal Order Police, Scottish Rite, Nobles Mystic Shrine (life, amb.-at-large), (life)Am. Legion, VFW, Republican. Methodist. Avocations: fishing, photography. Home: Cleveland, Ga. Died May 13, 2014.

LI, FREDERICK PEI, medical educator; b. China, May 7, 1940; s. Han Hun Li and Chu Fang Wu; married, Elaine Shiang, 1975; children Andrew, Margaret, Irene BA, U. NY, Rochester, 1960; MD, U. NY, 1965; MA, Georgetown U., 1969, Harvard U. Epidemiologist Nat. Cancer Inst., 1967-80; prof. clin. epidemiology Harvard Sch. Pub. Health, 1980—2008, prof. medicine; med. officer, epidemiology Dana-Farber Cancer Inst., Boston. Recipient Charles S. Mott medal, 1995. Mem. Am. Soc. Clin. Oncology, Am. Assn. Cancer Rsch. Home: Boston, Mass. Died June 12, 2015.

LIBAVA, JERRY RONALD, franchise consultant; b. Cleve., Oct. 6, 1936; s. Sanford and Dora (Friedlander) L.; m. Judith Rosalie Hollender, May 30, 1958; children: Joel, Jonathan, Janet. Hairdresser Bonwit Teller, Cleve., 1957-60; make-up artist, sales Revlon, Cleve. & NYC, 1960-66; sales, sales mgr. Loreal-Lancome, Cleve., 1966-72; sales, regional mgr. Colonia, Inc., Stanford, Conn., 1981-83; dir. franchise devel. Physicians Weight Loss Ctrs., Akron, 1984-90; pres. Internat. Franchise Devel. LLC, Cleve., from 1990.

Spkr. in field. With U.S. Army, 1957. Mem. Franchise Network (vice-chmn. 1993—). Jewish. Avocations: bicycling, walking, golf. Died June 23, 2007.

LIEBERMAN, EVELYN S. (EVELYN MAY SIMONOWITZ), diplomat; b. NYC, July 9, 1944; d. Jack and Rose (Cohen) S.; m. Edward H. Lieberman. BS in English, SUNY, Buffalo, 1966; graduate in English Lit., St. John's U. Press sec. U.S. Senator Joseph R. Biden, Jr. (D-DE), 1988-93; asst. to chief of staff Office of First Lady The White House, 1993-94, dep. asst. to Pres., dep. press sec. for ops., 1994-95, asst. to Pres. and dep. chief of staff, 1996-97; dir. Voice of Am., Washington, 1997-99; under sec. of state for public diplomacy and public affairs Dept. of State, Washington, from 1999. Dir. pub. affairs, comms. dir. Children's Def. Fund, Nat. Urgan Coalition. Dir. public affairs Children's Defense Fund; comms. dir. Nat. Urban Coalition. Home: Washington, DC. Died Dec. 12, 2015.

LIEBMAN, PAUL ROBERT, vascular surgeon; b. Richmond, Va., Dec. 4, 1945; s. Morris and Helen (Neiman) L.; m. Patricia B. Sherin, Dec. 29, 1973; children: Joseph, Benjamin, Andrew. BS in Zoology, George Washington U., 1967; MD, Georgetown U., 1971; postgrad. in History, Fla. Atlantic U., from 2004. Diplomate Am. Bd. Surgery, Am. Bd. Vascular Surgery. Intern Boston U.-Boston City Hosp., 1971-72, resident in surgery, 1972-73, 77-80, rsch. fellow, 1975-77; vascular fellow Med. Coll. Va., Richmond, 1980-81; attending surgeon St. Mary' Hosp. and Good Samaritan Med. Ctr., West Palm Beach, Fla., from 1981; dir. surgery div. Good Samaritan Med. Ctr., West Palm Beach, 1987—92; ptnr. Surg. Specialists of the Palm Beaches, West Palm Beach. Mem. adv. bd. Palm Beach County Blood Bank, West Palm Beach, 1991-94, metabolic unit Good Samaritan Med. Ctr., West Palm Beach, 1991-92. Bd. dirs. Good Samaritan Med. Ctr. Found.; mem. bd. govs. Intracoastal Health Sys. Maj. USAF, 1973-75. Fellow ACS; mem. Internat. Soc. for Cardiovascular Surgery, Southeastern Surg. Congress, So. Assn. for Vascular Surgery, Fla. Vascular Soc. (founding, pres.), Alpha Omega Alpha. Avocations: antique car restoration, history. Home: West Palm Beach, Fla. Died Mar. 16, 2007.

LIEBSCHUTZ, ALAN MORTON, retired physicist; b. Chgo., Jan. 12, 1926; s. Morton Dunbar and Mirian Ruth (Libman) L.; m. Katherine C. Neel (dec. 1976); m. Betty Jo Kemmer (div. 1982); m. Mary Margaret Washburn, Sept. 28, 1983. BS in Physics, Purdue U., 1947, MS in Physics, 1949, PhD in Physics, 1953. Sect. head radiation effects Convair divsn. Gen. Dynamics, Fort Worth, Tex., 1953-55; program mgr., lab. scientist, sect. head Lockheed, Marietta, Ga., 1955-62; asst. dept. mgr. Hughes Aircraft Co., Fullerton, Calif., 1962-68, dept. mgr., program mgr. survivability dept.; program mgr. Autonetics Minute Man Divsn., 1968-69; dept. mgr. TRW, Redondo Beach, Calif., 1969-78. Instr. physics Purdue U., 1947-53; pvt. bus. cons. radiation effects, 1978-84; dept. mgr., program mgr. Hughes Space & Communications Divsn., El Segundo, Calif., 1984-92, program chmn. and dir. Orange Coast IBM PC User's Group, 1993-99. Contbr. articles to profl. jours. and chpts. to books. USN fellow, 1947-49, Signal Corps fellow, 1949-50, Atomic Energy Commn. fellow, 1950-53. Fellow IEEE (chmn. L.A. chpt.); mem. AIEE, Am. Phys. Soc., Am. Men of Sci., Orange Coast PC Users Group, Saddlebach Computer Club, Palmia Computer Club, Sigma Xi, Sigma Pi Sigma. Home: Plano, Tex. Died July 30, 2007.

LIETZ, JEREMY JON, educational administrator, writer; b. Milw., Oct. 4, 1933; s. John Norman and Dorothy B. (Drew) L.; m. Cora Fernandez, Feb. 24, 1983; children: Cheryl, Brian, Angela, Andrew, Christopher, Jennifer. BS, U. Wis., Milw., 1961; MS, U. Wis., Madison, 1971; EdD, Marquette U., 1980. Tchr. Milw. Pub. Schs., 1961-63, diagnostic counselor, 1968-71, sch. adminstr., 1971-95, hearing panel ombudsman, from 1999, acting student svcs. coord., 1999—2003; tchr. Madison Pub. Sch., Wis., 1964-65; rsch. assoc. U. Wis., Madison, 1965-67; instr. Marquette U., Milw., 1980-82, Milw. U. Sch., 2000—02. Lectr. HEW Conf. on Reading, Greeley, Colo., 1973, NAESP Conf. on Reading, St. Louis, 1974, various state and nat. orgns.; co-founder, bd. dirs., cons. Ednl. Leadership Inst., Shorewood, Wis., 1980—; dir. Religious Edn. Program, Cath. Elem. East, Milw., 1985-86. Author: The Elementary School Principal's Role in Special Education, 1982; contbr. numerous articles, chpts., tests, revs. to profl. jours. V.p. PTA, 1961-62. With U.S. Army, 1954-56, ETO. Recipient Cert. of Achievement award NAESP, 1974. Mem. AAAS, Assn. Wis. Sch. Adminstrs. (mem. state planning com. 1977-79, lectr. 1982), Adminstrs. and Suprs. Coun. (mem. exec. bd. dist. 1977-79, mem. contract negotiations com. 1991-95), Filipino Am. Assn. Wis., U. Wis. Alumni Assn. (Madison), Milw. Mcpl. Chess Assn., U.S. Chess Fedn., Phi Delta Kappa. Home: Thiensville, Wis. Died Apr. 1, 2007.

LIFE, LAWRENCE LELAND, director, choreographer, theatre educator; b. Muncie, Ind., Aug. 26, 1943; s. Hershel and Nixola Vernon (Scranton) L. BS, Ball State U., 1967, MA, 1969. Instr. Tex. A&I U., Kingsville, 1969-71; assoc. prof. Ind. U.-Purdue U., Ft. Wayne, from 1971. Artist-in-residence Wabash Coll., Crawfordsville, Ind., 1974-75, La. State U., Baton Rouge, 1976; guest choreographer Mo. Concert Ballet, St. Louis, 1976; guest dir. & choreographer Black Hills Playhouse, 1989-91, U. Nev., Las Vegas, 1991; dance adv. panel Ind. State Arts Commn., Indpls., 1977; panelist and workshop dir. Am. Coll. Theatre Festival, Washington, D.C., 1973—; lectr. in field. Dir., choreographer numerous stage prodns. including Luther, 1971, Dames At Sea, 1973, Hair, 1976. Mentor Northwest Allen County Schs., Ft. Wayne, 1988. Democrat. Roman Catholic. Home: Fort Wayne, Ind. Died Feb. 10, 2007.

LIGHTFOOT, ALBERT J., clergyman; b. Birmingham, Ala., July 2, 1926; s. Albert and Odessa Lightfoot; m. Catherine Kidd; children: Calvin, Cornelius, Reggie, Ronald, Phillip, Nedra, Phyllis. Student, U. Mich., 1960-62, Liberty Bible Coll., 1965-68, Union Bapt. Sem., 1975. Ordained to ministry Bapt. Ch., 1965. Organizer, pastor New Hope Bapt. Ch., Ann Arbor, Mich., from 1965, also gen. supt. Sunday sch., trustee clk., deacon, organizer Kangaroo Day Care Program. Moderator Huron Valley Dist. Assn., 1996; mem. Wolverine State Conv., Nat. Bapt. Conv. USA Inc. Mem. Ypsilanti-Ann Arbor Vicinity Ministerial Alliance (pres.). Home: Ann Arbor, Mich. Died Nov. 26, 2006.

LIMA, DONALD ROGER, retired computer programmer; b. San Luis Obispo, Calif., Jan. 9, 1935; s. Donald Joseph Lima and Vera Cora Moraga; m. Esther Hardin; 1 child, Gary. BA, Calif. State U., LA, 1995. Programmer analyst City of L.A., 1975-95; ret., 1995. Author: (book) A Piece Is Missing, 1998; appearance in Theater Americana of Altadena, 1988-90. With U.S. Army, 1953-56. Democrat. Methodist. Avocation: pinochle. Died May 6, 2007.

LINCOLN, ANNA, publishing executive, language educator; b. Warsaw, Dec. 13, 1932; came to U.S., 1948; d. Wigdor Aron and Genia Szpiro; m. Adrian Courtney Lincoln Jr., Sept. 22, 1951; children: Irene Anne, Sally Linda, Allen, Kirk. Student, U. Calif., Berkeley, 1949-50; BA in French and Russian with honors, NYU, 1965; student, Columbia Tchrs. Coll., 1966-67. Tchr. Waldwick (N.J.) H.S., 1966-69; chmn. Tuxedo Park (N.Y.) Red Cross, 1969-71; pres. Red Cross divsn. Vets. Hosp.; pres. China Pictures U.S.A. Inc., Princeton, NJ, from 1994; prof. fgn. rels. Fudan U., Shanghai, from 1994, prof. English and humanitarian studies, from 1996. Adv. bd. guidance dept. Waldwick (N.J.) H.S., 1966-69; hon. bd. dirs. Shanghai Fgn. Lang. Assn., 1994; hon. prof. Fudan U., Shanghai, 1994; leader seminars, China at top univs., 1996—; pub. spkr., human rels., China, 2003—. Author: Escape to China, 1940-48, 1985, Chinese transl., 1985, The Art of Peace, 1995, Anna Lincoln Views China, 2000; publ.: China Beyond the Year 2000 and the Nature of Love, 1997, Anna Lincoln Views China, 1999; co-dir. (TV docudrama) Escape to China 1941-48, 1998. Hon. U.S. Goodwill amb. for peace and friendship, China, 1984, 85, 86, 88; founder Princeton-Lincoln Found., Inc., 1985—. Named Woman of Yr. Am. Biog. Soc., 1993; recipient Peace Through the Arts prize Assn. Internat. Mujeres en las Artes, Madrid, 1993. Mem. AAUW, Women's Coll. Club (publicity chmn. 1991-96), Lit. Coll. Princeton, Present Day Club. Avocations: reading, swimming, bridge, seminars, ballroom dancing. Died Aug. 27, 2013.

LIND, ANITA DOROTHY, medical/surgical nurse; b. Caledonia, Minn., Apr. 18, 1933; d. A.W. and Nina C. (Onstad) Schroeder; m. Donald K. Lind, Aug. 3, 1958; children: Kari, Susan, Douglas, David, Daniel. Diploma, Fairview Sch. of Nursing, Mpls., 1955; student, Luther Coll., 1951-52. Dir. of nurses Green Lea Manor Nursing Home, Mabel, Minn.; charge nurse, dir. nursing Caledonia (Minn.) Community Hosp.; night supr. Community Meml. Hosp., Winona, Minn., staff and charge nurse. Luther Coll. scholar. Mem. Minn. Nursing Assn. (bargaining com.). Home: Rushford, Minn. Died May 15, 2007.

LINDENMANN, JEAN HENRI, immunology and virology educator, retired; b. Zagreb, Yugoslavia, Sept. 18, 1924; arrived in Switzerland, 1939; s. Jean Henri and Julienne Gabriele (VanDemberghe) L.; m. Ellen Ruth Buchler, Oct. 4, 1956 (dec. 2007); children: Christian, Jean-Michel. MD, U. Zurich, 1951. Asst. U. Zurich, Switzerland, 1952-56; postdoctoral staff Nat. Inst. for Med. Rsch., London, 1956-57; instr. U. Zurich, 1957-59; bacteriologist Swiss Fedn. Office of Pub. Health, Bern, Switzerland, 1960-61; vis. asst. prof. U. Fla., Gainesville, 1962-64; assoc. prof., Immunology and Virology U. Zurich, 1964-69, full prof., Immunology and Virology, 1969-92, emeritus prof., 1992—2015. Contbr. articles to profl. jours. Recipient Swiss Cancer awards Swiss Cancer Soc., 1964, 1987, Goetz prize Med. Faculty Zurich, 1969, Robert Koch prize Robert Koch Soc. Bonn., 1973, Marcel Benoist prize Swiss Fed. Govt. Bern, 1977. Home: Gockhausen, Switzerland. Died Jan. 15, 2015.

LINDSAY, RUSSELL CHARLES, mechanical and forensic engineer; b. Hickory, NC, Oct. 4, 1960; s. Charles Windell and Retta Jane Lindsay; m. Paula LeAnn Buss, June 25, 1983; children: Aaron, Christopher. BS in Mech. Engring., Va. Tech. U., 1982, MS, 1983. Registered profl. engr., Ga., Ind., Ky., Mich., N.C., Ohio, Pa., S.C., Tenn., Va., W.Va. Design engr. GE Aircraft Engines, Cin., 1983-89; forensic engr. P.A.C.E., Inc., Cin., 1989-93; owner, forensic engr. PARC Engring. Assocs., Asheville, N.C., from 1994. Forensic engring. cons. to numerous attys. and ins. cos., 1989—. With dist. com. Boy Scouts Am., 1991-92; den leader, cubmaster, tiger cub group coach pack 24 Daniel Boone coun., Asheville, 1994—. Mem. NSPE, SAE, Am. Soc. Mech. Engrs., ASCE. Achievements include co-development and qualification testing of proprietary system for advanced military aircraft engines. Home: Asheville, NC. Died Nov. 11, 2006.

LING, CHENG CHANG, mechanical engineering educator; b. Chia-Yi, Taiwan, Oct. 3, 1931; s. Wen Li and Hwang Shiau L.; m. Dai Li Xu, Aug. 1963; children: Katherine A., Enid A. BSME, Nat. Cheng-Kung U., Taiwan, 1957; MS, U. Cin., 1965, PhD, 1974. Chief engr. Am. Tool Inc., Cin., 1965-81; gen. mgr. Kingston Engring. Con., Cin., 1981-87; sr. engr. Pratt & Whitney Aircraft, 1987-91; engring. exec. Mech. Indsl. Rsch. Lab./Indsl. Tech. Rsch. Inst., Hsinchu, Taiwan, 1991-93; prof. Nat. Chung-Cheng U., Chia-Yi, from 1993. Tech. advisor Mech. Indsl. Rsch. Lab./Indsl. Tech. Rsch. inst., Hsinchu, 1993—; auditor Precision Machinery R&D Ctr., Taichung, 1993—; dir. Kaohsiung Divsn. of Chinese Soc. Mech. Engring., Kaohsiung, 1995-97. Contbr. articles to profl. jours.; inventor high speed spindle with built-in motor, automatic coolant through spindle hole, spindle positioning mechanism and the fuel nozzle swirler for combustor of the F-16 fighter engine for P&W Aircraft Co. Recipient Outstanding award for Engring. Profs. Chinese Soc. Mech. Engring., Taipei, 1996, Outstanding Tch. Rsch. award nat. Chung-Cheng U., 1996, outstanding award of Class A Rsch., Nat. Sci. Coun., Taipei, 1996. Mem. Chinese Soc. Automation, Nat. Chung-Cheng U. Golf Club. Achievements include specialization in design of CNC machine tools. Died Oct. 21, 2007.

LINKE, SIMPSON, electrical engineering educator; b. Jellico, Tenn., Aug. 10, 1917; s. Meyer Lion and Bella Yetta L.; m. Esther Silverman, Sept. 15, 1946; children: Martha Ellen, Laura Miriam. BS in Elec. Engring., U. Tenn., 1941; M in Elec. Engring., Cornell U., 1949. Instr. elec. engring. Cornell U., Ithaca, N.Y., 1946-49, asst. prof. elec. engring., 1949-53, assoc. prof., 1953-63, prof., 1963-86, prof. emeritus, from 1986. Cons. N.Mex. Pub. Svc. Commn., Santa Fe, 1981; mem. US Nat. Com. Conf. Internat. des Grands Réseaux Electriques a Haute Tension, 1964-80, Attwood assoc., 1988. Editor Connections, Cornell Elec. and Computing Engring. Newsletter, 1992—2005. Capt., U.S. Army, 1943-46. Recipient grants NSF, Office Naval Rsch., 1963-73; merit award Coun. Advancement and Support Edn., Ithaca, 1982. Fellow IEEE (life); mem. IEEE Power & Enrgy Soc., Sigma Xi, Eta Kappa Nu. Avocations: writing, music, theater, opera, walking. Home: Ithaca, NY. Died Dec. 27, 2013.

LINN, DIANA PATRICIA, retired elementary school educator; b. Perth, Western Australia, Dec. 31, 1943; arrived in US, 1946; d. Evan Andrew and Grace Henrietta (Springhall) Jarboe; m. Jim F. Erlandsen, July 9, 1966 (div. Mar. 1989); children: Rebecca Erlandsen Barrouk, Tim Erlandsen, Jenny Erlandsen Jones; m. Richard George Linn, Mar. 31, 1990; 1 stepchild, Cristal Linn Buckner. AA, Olympic Coll., 1963; BA in Elem. Edn., Western Wash. U., 1965; MA, U. Ariz., 1969. Cert. tchr. Wash. Tchr. Neomi B. Willmore Elem., Westminster, Calif., 1965—66; tchr. English, sci., & core program Sunnyside Jr. H.S., Tucson, 1966-70; tchr. kindergarten All Seasons Sch., Tucson, 1972-74; tchr. St. Cyril's Sch., Tucson, 1974-77; elem. tchr. Grace Christian Sch., Tucson, 1977-80; kindergarten and elem. tchr. Ridgeview Christian Ctr., Spokane, Wash., 1983-85, Spokane Christian Schs., 1985-87; dir. Ridgeview Christian Learning Ctr., Spokane, 1987-88; tchr. kindergarten Arlington Elem. Sch., Spokane, 1988-96, Grant Elem. Sch., Spokane, 1996—2005; ret. Spokane Sch. Dist. #81, 2006; coord. Childrens Ch. Spokane Dream Ctr., 2011—12. Mem. curriculum study com. Sunnyside Sch. Dist., Tucson, 1967—68; chmn. accreditation and sch. bd. St. Cyril's Sch., Tucson, 1976—77; chair faculty involvement group Arlington Elem., Spokane, 1992—93, chair staff devel, chair wellness com., 1988—96, sch. reporter, 1994—95, chair faculty involvement group, mem. strategic plan equity com., 1995—96; instr. reading readiness, reading presenter Family Learning Fair, Home Schooling Seminar, Spokane Falls CC, Spokane, 1986; chair, coord. pre-sch. coop. Arlington Elem. with Spokane Falls CC, 1992—93; chair faculty, equity team Grant Elem. Sch., 1996—2006, wellness chair, 1992—2001, site coun. faculty rep., 2001—04, primary team faculty rep., 2003—04. Brownie troop leader Willmore Elem., Westminster, 1965—66; ednl. restructuring rep. Spokane Sch. Dist. 81 Arlington Elem., 1992—93, mem. equity com., 1996—99, mem. early childhood com., 1996—2004, mem. strategic planning com., 1998—2003, wellness chmn., 1998—2000, mem. instrnl. team, 1999—2003; primary rep. site coun. Grant Elem., 2002, pres. site coun., 2003—04; prayer counselor Spokane Dream Ctr., 2005—12; tchr. Women's Discipleship; leader Home Group, 2009—12; dir. Children's Ch., 2011—12; co-leader Women's Group, 2010—12; advisor Spokane Valley Aglow, 2011—12; leader Valley Aglow, from 2011; coord. Christian edn. Valley Foursquare Ch., Spokane, 1982—87; coord. children's ch. Victory Faith Fellowship, Spokane, 1993—2003. Scholar, Naval Officer's Wives Club, 1961—62; Eisenhower grantee, 1990, 1994, 1996—97. Mem.: NEA, ASCD, Spokane Edn. Assn. (Arlington Elem. rep. 1991—93), Wash. Edn. Assn., CPA Wives Club (sec., ball chair 1983—84), Alpha Delta Kappa (membership chair 1994—95, corr. sec. 1996—99). Republican. Avocations: doll collecting, plate collecting, swimming, quilting. Home: Veradale, Wash. Died Feb. 11, 2015.

LIOY, PAUL JAMES, environmental health and exposure scientist; b. Passaic, NJ, May 27, 1947; s. Nicholas Paul and Jean Elizabeth (Licurse) L.; m. Mary Jean Yonone, June 13, 1971; 1 child, Jason. BA in Physics and Edn., Montclair State Coll., 1969; MS in Physics and Applied Math., Auburn U., 1971; MS in Environ. Sci., Rutgers U., 1973, PhD in Environ. Sci., 1975. Sr. engr. air pollution Interstate Sanitation Commn., NYC, 1975-78; asst. to assoc. prof. Inst. Environ. Medicine/NYU Med. Ctr., NYC, 1978-85, dep. dir. lab. of aerosol rsch., 1982-85; assoc. prof. to prof. Robert Wood Johnson Med. Sch. U. Medicine and Dentistry of NJ, Piscataway, NJ, Rutgers U., from 1985; vice chair, dept. environ. and occupl. medicine U. Medicine and Dentistry of NJ, Rutgers, from 2007; dir. sci. divsn. Environ. and Occupational Health Scis. Inst. (EOHSI), Piscataway, NJ, from 1986, dep. dir., from 1995, assoc. dir., 2001—03; mem. grad. faculty Rutgers U., from 1986, admissions chair in environ. scis., 1993—2006; prof. environmental and occupational health N.J. Sch. Pub. Health, Rutgers U., 2000—15; adj. prof. Sch. Pub. Health, U. Pitts., 2008—15; dir. Ctr. for Exposure and Risk Modeling N.J. Sch. Pub.

Health, U. Medicine and Dentistry N.J., 1999—2015; exec. com. U. Ctr. Disaster Preparedness Emergency Response, 2007—15; co-chair NJ U. Consortium for Homeland Security Rsch., 2006—15; mem. NJ Preparedness Coll., 2008—15. Dir. joint grad. program in human exposure access Rutgers U./U. Medicine and Dentistry N.J., 1994-96; mem. Cancer Inst. N.J., 1997-2015; cons. bd. environ. studies and toxicology NRC, NAS, Washington, 1989-92, mem. numerous coms., 1984—; chmn. Com. on Exposure Analysis for Air Pollution, 1987-90, co-chair Exposure Science in the 21st Century, 2010-2012; Clean Air Coun., N.J. Dept. Environ. Protection, Trenton, 1981-94; mem. Internat. Air Quality Bd., Internat. Joint Commn. U.S.-Can., 1992-2007; mem. sci. adv. bd. U.S. EPA, 1991—, chair subcom. on health and ecol. evaluation for Clean Air Act, mem. com. on homeland security, mem. com. asbestos; mem. European com. European Exposure Study-EXPOLIS, 1996-2003; acad. advisor State Legislature, N.J., 1998-2006; mem. dean's adv. bd. Coll. Sci. and Math. Auburn U., Ala., 1996-2008, mem. v.p., Rsch. Adv. Bd. Auburn U., Ala., 2010-2015; mem. deans adv. bd. coll. math, sci, Montclair State U., 2008-2015; adj. asst. prof. Bklyn. Coll., 1977-78; adj. prof. Med. U. S.C., 1996-2015; mem. sci. adv. com. Harvard U.; sci. and litigation cons. on environ. health, indoor air pollution, human exposure, and hazardous waste investigations and remediations; mem., v.p. Rsch. Com. Sci., 2009-2015; co-chmn. Com. Exposure Scis., 2010-2015, World Trade Ctr. Tech. Comm. USEPA & CEQ, co-chair, Com. Exposure Sci. 21st Century, 2010-2015. Author 280 sci. publs., 1975-2015, chpts. in 15 books; author: Toxic Air Pollution, 1987, Dust: The Inside Story of its Role in the September 11th Aftermath, 2010; co-editor: (with M.J. Yonone-Lioy) Air Sampling Instruments, 1985, (with Clifford P. Weisel) Exposure Science: Basic Principles and Applications, 2014; exec. editor emeritus: Atmospheric Environment Jour., 1989-94; assoc. editor: Environ. Rsch., 1995-2015, deputy editor in chief Jour. Exposure Sci. and Environ. Epidemiology, 2013-2015; reveiwer Aerosol Rsch. and Tech., 1990-93, Environ. Health Perspectives, 2004-2015, Jour. Exposure Sci. and Environ. Epidemiology, 2006-; editl. bd. Jour. Applied Environ. and Occupl. Hygiene, Internat., 1999-2015. Chair Cranford (NJ) Environ. Commn., 1978; treas. Cranford Little League, 1984-85; bd. mem. Cranford C. of C., 2006-2009, 2014. Rsch. grantee EPA, NIH, CDC, ATSDR, NJ Dept. Environ. Protection, API, DOE, HUD Indsl., 1978—, Frank Chamber award for outstanding achievement in the sci. and art of air pollution control, Air Waste Mgmt. Assn., 2003, R. Walter Schlisinger Mentoring award, 2006, Disting. Alumni award in Math., Phys. Scis. and Engring., Rutgers U. Grad. Sch., New Brunswick, NJ, 2008-2009; Nat. Conservation award Daughters Am. Revolution, 2009, Nat. Ellen Hanlin Walworth Patrotism medal., 2009. Fellow Collegium Ramazzini (Italy), 1999-; mem. Air Waste Mgmt. Assn. (chmn. editorial bd. 1978-80), Am. Conf. Gov. Indsl. Hygiene (chmn. air sample inst. com. 1984-87), Am. Assn. Aerosol. Rsch. (editorial bd. 1988-90), Internat. Soc. Environ. Epidemiology (bd. councilors 1988-89), Internat. Soc. Exposure Sci. (ISES) (founder, pres. 1993-94, treas. 1990-91, exec. com. 1989-95, Wesolowski Lifetime Achievement award 1998, Disting. Lectr. award 2008-11), Soc. of Risk Analysis, Assn. Profl. Indsl. Hygienists, Cranford C. of C. (bd. dirs. 2000-2005), Italian Am. Commn. NJ(program. adv 2006-09). Avocations: restoration of houses, tennis, automobiles. Home: Cranford, NJ. Died July 8, 2015.

LIPKIN, SEYMOUR AUSTEN, musician, conductor, educator; b. Detroit, May 14, 1927; s. Ezra and Leah (Vidaver) L.; m. Catherine Lee Bing, Dec. 27, 1961 (div. 1983); 1 son, Jonathan Michael; m. Ellen Werner, 2003; stepchildren Daniel Walker, Benjamin Walker, Sarah Hodges MusB, Curtis Inst. Music, 1947; studied piano with, David Saperton, 1938-41, Rudolf Serkin, Mieczyslaw Horszowski, 1941-47; conducting with, Serge Koussevitzky, Berkshire Music Center, 1946, 48-49. Piano tchr. Juilliard Sch. Music, NYC, from 1986. Faculty Manhattan Sch. Music, 1965-70, 72-86, NYU, 1980-86; piano faculty Curtis Inst. Music, 1969-, New Eng. Conservatory, 1984-86, faculty music dept. Marymount Coll., Tarrytown, N.Y., 1963-72, chmn. music dept., 1968-71. Condr. Bklyn. Coll. Orch., 1973-74; Ford Found. commn. to perform concerto by Harold Shapero, 1959; debut with Detroit Civic Orch., 1937; apprentice condr. to George Szell, Cleve. Orch., 1947-48; appearances as pianist other U.S. orchs. including Boston Symphony in Tanglewood; ann. tours including soloist, Buffalo and Nat. Symphony, soloist, asst. condr. N.Y. Philharm. tour, Europe and Russia, 1959; conducting debut Detroit Symphony, 1944; recitalist, 92d St YMHA, N.Y.C., 1981, 83, soloist N.Y. Philharm., N.Y.C., 1983, participant in chamber music, Spoleto Festivals, 1982, 83, co-condr. Curtis Inst. Orch., 1952-53, asst. condr. Goldovsky Opera Co. on tour, 1953, condr. N.Y.C. Opera Co., 1958, 1 of 3 asst. condrs. New York Philharm., 1959-60; mus. dir. Teaneck Symphony, N.J., 1961-70, L.I. Symphony, 1963-79, Scarboro Chamber Orch., N.Y., 1964-65, Joffrey Ballet, N.Y. City Center, 1966-68, 1972-79, prin. guest condr., 1968-72; artistic dir. Kneisel Hall Summer Chamber Music Sch. and Festival, 1987-2015,(performed cycle of 32 Beethoven Sonatas 1988-90, Gardner Mus., Boston, 1996-99, Beethoven Soc., N.Y., 1997-, 10 Beethoven Violin Sonatas with Andrew Dawes 1995, Uto Ughi, Santa Cecilia, Rome, 1995, 5 cello sonatas with David Soyer 1989, Laurence Lesser, 1996, 5 piano concertos with Santa Fe Symphony 1993, complete sonatas of Schubert at Kneisel Hall, Gardner Mus., Boston, Kaye Playhouse, N.Y.C.); appearances as opera condr. Curtis Inst., Teatro Petruzzelli, Bari, Italy, 1986-87; participant in chamber music Norfolk Fest., 1984-85, Marlboro Fest., 1986; recorded Stravinsky Piano Concerto and Capriccio with N.Y. Philharm., Bernstein, Grieg, Saint-Saens, Strauss sonatas with Aaron Rosand (violin), Grieg, Dohnanyi, Weiner sonatas with Oscar Shumsky (violin), Franck Sonata, Chausson Concerto with Rosand, Beethoven Sonatas op. 106 and 109, complete Schubert violin and piano works with Arnold Steinhardt (violin), 32 Beethoven piano sonatas, Complete Schubert piano Sonatas, Moments Musicaux and Wanderer Fantasy ; tour of China, recitals and master classes, 2004, 08; artistic dir. internat. piano festival and William Kapell competition U. Md., 1988-92. Recipient 1st prize Rachmaninoff Piano Competition, 1948. Home: New York, NY. Died Nov. 16, 2015.

LIPOFSKY, MARVIN BENTLEY, art educator; b. Elgin, Ill., Sept. 1, 1938; s. Henry and Mildred (Hyman) L.; 1 child, Lisa Beth Valenzuela; m. Ruth Okimoto, 1990 (div.) BFA in Indsl. Design, U. Ill., 1961; MS, MFA in Sculpture, U. Wis., 1964. Instr. design U. Wis., Madison, 1964; asst. prof. design U. Calif., Berkeley, 1964-72; prof., chmn. glass dept. Calif. Coll. Arts and Crafts, Oakland, 1967-87, pres. faculty assembly, 1984-87. Guest instr. Haystack Mountain Sch., Deer Isle, Maine, 1967, 73, 87, San Francisco Art Inst., 1968, Hunterdon Art Ctr., Clinton, N.J., 1973, Pilchuck Sch. Glass, Stanwood, Wash., 1974, 77, 81, 84, 88; vis. prof. Bazalel Acad. Art and Design, Jerusalem, 1971; pres. faculty assembly, 1984-87; founder studio-glass movement; started the Great Calif. Glass Symposium, 1967 One-man shows include Richmond (Calif.) Art Ctr., 1965, Anneberg Gallery, San Francisco, 1966, Crocker Art Gallery, Sacramento, 1967, San Francisco Mus. Art, 1967, Mus. Contemporary Crafts, N.Y.C., 1969, U. Ga., Athens, 1969, Utah Mus. Fine Arts, U. Utah, Salt Lake City, 1969, Calif. Coll. Arts and Crafts, 1970, Stedelijke Mus., Amsterdam, The Netherlands, 1970, Galerie de Enndt, Amsterdam, 1970, Baxter Art Gallery, Calif. Inst. Tech., Pasadena, 1974, Yaw Gallery, Birmingham, Mich., 1976, 78, Gallery Marionie, Kyoto, Japan, 1979, 87, U. Del., Newark, 1979, Greenwood Gallery, Washington, 1980, SM Gallerie, Frankfurt, Fed. Republic Germany, 1981, Galerie L. Hamburg, Fed. Republic Germany, 1981, Betsy Rosenfield Gallery, Chgo., 1982, Robert Kidd Gallery, Birmingham, Mich., 1984, Holsten Galleries, Palm Beach, Fla., Maurine Littleton Gallery, Washington, Union Bulgarian Artists, Sofia, 1991, Marvin Lipofsky: A World of Glass, 1994, Judah L. Magnes Mus., Berkeley, Calif., 1994, Marvin Lipofsky's World of Glass Show: A Hist. Retrospective, 1996, Kennedy Art Ctr. Gallery, 1996, Holy Names Coll., Oakland, Calif., 1996, Marvin Lipofsky: A Glass Odyssey, Retrospective, Oakland Mus. Calif., 2003, Fresno Art Mus., 2005-05, Calif. Poly. U., San Luis Obispo, 2006; vis. artist, critic Gerriet Rietveld Academie, Amsterdam; vis. artist Atheneium Sch. Art and Design, Helsinki, Finland, 1970, UCLA, 1973, Sommervail, Battle Mountain Glass Symposium, Vail, Colo., Miasa (Japan) Bunka Ctr., 1987, Internat. Glass Sumposium, Novy Bor, Czech Republic, 1982, 85, 88, 91. Trustee Calif. Coll. Arts and Crafts, Oakland, 1984-87. Named Calif. Living Treasure, 1985, Hon. Mem., Hungarian Glass Art Soc., 1996, Hon. Inspiration award Calif. Glass Exch., 2002; named to Coll. Fellows, Am. Craft Coun., 1991; NEA fellow, 1974, 76. Mem. Glass Art Soc. (hon. life, pres. 1978-80, jour. editor 1976-80, advisor 1980-), Am. Craft Coun. (trustee 1986-90, trustee emeritus 1998—), Bay Area Studio Art Glass (pres. 1993-). Died Jan. 15, 2016.

LIPPE, JANET SONYA See NORWOOD, JANET

LIPPMAA, ENDEL, science educator, researcher; b. Tartu, Estonia, Sept. 15, 1930; s. Teodor and Hilja-Helene L.; m. Helle Raam, July 20, 1960; children: Jaak, Mikk. Chem. Engr., Tallinn Tech. U, Estonia, 1953, PhD in Engring., 1956; DSc in Chem. Physics, Inst. Chem. Physics, Moscow, 1969. Lectr. Tallinn (Estonia) Tech. U., 1953-56, asst. prof., 1956-61; head dept. chem. physics Inst. Cybernetics, Tallinn, Estonia, 1961-80; prof. phys. chemistry and chem. physics Estonian Acad. Sci., Tallinn, from 1971; prof. Tartu (Estonia) U., from 1993. Divsn. head Estonian Acad. Scis., Tallinn, 1977-82, 99-2004; dir. Inst. Chem. Physics and Biophysics, Tallinn, 1980-2001; chmn. bd. Nat. Inst. Chemical Physics and Biophysics, Tallinn, 1999-2004; head Ctr. Excellence Analytical Spectrometry, 2001-. Patentee in field; contbr. articles to profl. jours. Rep. USSR Congress of Peoples' Deputies, Moscow, 1989-91; minister Eastern affairs Govt. Republic of Estonia, Tallinn, 1990-91, mem. Parliament, 1995-99, min. European affairs, 1995-96, Com. Elders, Estonian Def. League, 1994-2002. Decorated Order Nat. Coat of Arms; recipient R & D 100 award, 1989, Humboldt/Max-Planck Rsch. prize, 1992; named to Centenary Lectureship, Royal Soc. Chemistry, 1989; recipient Hon. Doctor degree Jyväskylä (Finland) U., 1975, Tallinn Tech. U., 1991, Tartu U., 1999, Nat. Sci. Prize Govt. of Rep. of Estonia, 2000. Fellow AAAS, Am. Chem. Soc., Am. Phys. Soc., IEEE, Electrochem. Soc., Internat. Soc. Magnetic Resonance, Groupement AMPERE (prize 1994), European Phys. Soc., German Phys. Soc.; mem. Estonian Acad. Sci., Finnish Acad. Sci., Royal Swedish Acad. Engring. Scis., Finnish Chem. Soc. Coalition. Lutheran. Achievements include initiated final denounciation of Soviet-German 1939 secret protocols dividing Europe. Home: Tallinn, Estonia. Died July 30, 2015.

LIPTON, JOAN ELAINE, advertising executive; b. NYC, July 12, 1927; 1 child, David Dean. BA, Barnard Coll., 1948. With Young & Rubicam, Inc., NYC, 1948-52, Robert W. Orr & Assocs., NYC, 1952-57, Benton & Bowles, Inc., NYC, 1957-64; asso. dir. Benton & Bowles, Ltd., London, 1964-68; with McCann-Erickson, Inc. (advt. agy.), NYC, 1968-85, v.p., 1970-79, sr. v.p., creative dir., 1979-85; pres. Martin & Lipton Advt. Inc., from 1985. Mem. Bus. Coun. UN Decade Women, 1977-78; bd. vis. PhD program bus. CUNY, 1986—. Recipient Honors award Ohio U. Sch. Journalism, 1976, Matrix award, 1979, YWCA award women achievers, 1979, Clio Classic award; named Woman Yr., Am. Advt. Fedn., 1974, Advt. Woman Yr., 1984; named Matrix Hall Fame, 1998. Mem. Advt. Women NY (1st v.p. 1975-76, v.p. Found. 1977-78), Women's Forum (bd. dirs. 1988-90), Women Comm. (pres. NY chpt. 1974-76, named Nat. Headliner 1976). Died Aug. 13, 2005.

LISTER, CAROL, anti-discrimination organization administrator; b. NYC, June 3, 1935; d. Jack and Esther (Freed) Orenstein; m. Martin Gunther Lister, June 30, 1957 (div. Nov. 1978); 1 child, Douglas Scott. BS, NYU, 1955. Copy chief Allen Christopher Advt., NYC, 1956-57; assoc. radio-TV dir. William D. Murdock Advt., Washington, 1957-60; writer, pub. rels. cons. Washington, 1960-66; news dir. mayoral campaign Balt., 1967; asst. dir. DC-Md. office Anti-Defamation League, Washington, 1968-75, regional dir. Columbus, Ohio, 1975-81, NYC, 1981-88, ea. area dir., 1986-88, assoc. dir. devel., from 1989. Bd. trustees Nat. B'nai B'rith Pension Plan, Washington, 1976-88; commr. N.Y.C. Commn. on Human Rights, 1988-90; acting chmn. N.Y. State Martin Luther King Inst., 1988-91; mem. Gov.'s Task Force on Bias Violence, N.Y., 1987-88; mem. adv. coun. N.Y. State Div. Human Rights, 1984-90. Died Mar. 17, 2007.

LISTON, TIMOTHY MICHAEL, advertising and public relations executive; b. NYC, Sept. 2, 1931; s. Timothy and Delia D. (Russell) L.; m. Rita R. Brunella, July 9, 1955; children: Timothy F., Matthew J., Martin J., Kenneth C. BBA, Manhattan Coll., 1953. Sr. acct. Price Waterhouse, NYC, 1953-59; asst. controller Ogilvy & Mather, Inc., NYC, 1960-70; v.p., treas. WCRS NA, NYC, 1970-87; v.p. fin. Rosenfeld, Sirowitz, Humphrey & Strauss, Inc., NYC, from 1988. Served with USNR, 1951-59. Mem. N.Y. Credit and Fin. Mgmt., Acct. Guild. Clubs: Auburndale Soccer (N.Y.C.) (chmn., pres. 1970-85). Lodges: KC. Democrat. Roman Catholic. Home: Flushing, NY. Died Apr. 5, 2007.

LITTELL, ROBERT EUGENE, retired state legislator; b. Orange, NJ, Jan. 9, 1936; s. Alfred Battie and Dorothy A. (Kershner) Littel; m. Virginia Newman; children: Alison, Luke. LLD, Centenary Coll., 1996; LHD (hon.), NJ Inst. Technology, 2001. Mem. Franklin Borough Coun., 1963—65; mem Dist. 24 NJ State Assembly, Trenton, NJ, 1968—90; del. Republican Nat. Conv., 1976; chmn. Monorail Legislature Comn., NJ, 1985—90; mem. Dist. 24 NJ State Senate, NJ, 1992—2008; pres. Littell Gas Svc. & Appliance Ctr. Recipient NJ Disting. Svc. award, 2001. Mem.: Sussex County Peace Officers Assn., American Legion Post 132. Republican. Home: Franklin, NJ. Died Nov. 14, 2014.

LITTLE, CAROLE (MARY CAROLE LENSKI), women's apparel company executive; b. Chgo., Sept. 27, 1934; m. Leonard Rabinowitz (div.); 1 child, Jennifer Heft. B in English, UCLA; studied fashion, LA Trade Technical Coll. Secretary Rose Marie Reid Co.; co-founder CL Cinema Line Films Corp., LA; co-founder, co-chmn. Calif. Fashion Industries, Inc., LA, 1974; co-founder CL Fashion, Studio CL, 2001—13. Guest design tchr. Parson's Sch. Design, N.Y.C., L.A.; contbg. designer Divine Design; sponsor many benefit fashion shows; guest designer Acad. Awards; costume designer feature film. Co-prodr. Anaconda, 1997. Mem. bds. Calif. Am. Women's Econ. Devel., Women Inc., The Trusteeship; hon. co-chair mus. Fashion Designers and Creators; mem. Pres. Circle, L.A. County Mus. Art; found. mem. Internat. House of Blues Found. Named One of Leading Women Entrepreneurs of World, Nat. Found. Women Bus. Owners, Paris, 1997. Died Sept. 19, 2015.

LITTON, MARTIN, conservationist; b. Feb. 13, 1917; m. Esther Litton. Travel editor Sunset mag., 1954—68. Bd. dirs. Sierra Club, 1964—73. Author: The Life and Death of Lake Mead, 1968. Recipient John Muir award Sierra Club, 1993. Died Nov. 30, 2014.

LIVERMORE, PETE (PETER L. LIVERMORE), state legislator; b. New Orleans, Mar. 22, 1941; m. Laurie Livermore; children: Richard, Sheri, Jackie. Ret. businessman; mem. Ward 3 Carson City Bd. Supervisors, Nev., 1998—2010; mayor pro tem Carson City, 2004—06; mem. Dist. 40 Nev. State Assembly, 2011—14. Served with USMC, 1958—62. Republican. Avocations: hunting, fishing, sports. Died Oct. 20, 2014.

LIVINGSTON, HOMER J., JR., retired stock exchange executive; b. River Forest, Ill., Aug. 24, 1935; s. Homer and Helen (Henderson) Livingston; m. Marge Wild; children: Liz, John. BA in Economics, Princeton U., 1957; JD, Chgo. Kent Coll. Law, 1966. Various positions including exec. v.p. corporate banking First Nat Bank Chgo., Chgo., 1963-79; chief investment bank Lehman Bros. Kuhn Loeb, Chgo., 1979-82; ptnr.-in-charge investment banking services for comml. customers William Blair & Co., Chgo., 1982-84; with Algemene Bank Nederland, Chgo., 1984-88, H. Livingston & Co., L.P., Chgo., 1988-92, Livingston Co. Southwest, L.P., Chgo., 1988-92; chmn. Chgo. Stock Exchange, Chgo., 1993—95, Midwest Bank & Trust Co., 2005—08. Served in USN, 1957—61, 1962—63. Died Dec. 22, 2014.

LOCKARD, WALTER JUNIOR, petroleum company executive; b. El Dorado, Kans., Dec. 6, 1926; s. Walter Allen and Ida May (Akright) L. BS in Bus., Emporia U., Kans., 1952. Pres. Lockard Petroleum Inc., Hamilton, Kans., from 1958. With USN, 1945-47. Mem. Soc. Vertebrate Paleontology, Paleontol. Soc., Kans. Acad. Sci. Achievements include discovering and collecting Hamilton Quarry fossils for Emporia State U. and other universities. Died Nov. 25, 2006.

LOCKHART, BECKY (REBECCA DAWN LOCKHART), state legislator; b. Reno, Nov. 20, 1968; m. Stan Lockhart; 3 children. Chairwoman Utah County Lincoln Day Dinner, 1998; mem. Dist. 64 Utah House of Reps., Utah, 1999—2015, spkr., 2011—15. Mem.: Utah County Rep. Women (co-chair). Republican. Home: Provo, Utah. Died Jan. 17, 2015.

LOCKHART, LILLIE WALKER, retired primary school educator; b. Anderson, SC, Mar. 19, 1931; d. Luther James and Katy Lee (Evans) Walker; m. Rufus Nelson Lockhart, Mar. 29, 1953. BA cum laude, Johnson C. Smith U., 1958; MA, Appalachian State U., 1981; Advanced MA, U. N.C., Charlotte, 1986. Cert. primary tchr., N.C. Prin. Airline Sch., Anderson, S.C., 1952-55; tchr. primary sch. Alexander St. Sch., Charlotte, N.C., 1956-60, First Ward, Charlotte, 1961-69, Lansdowne Sch., Charlotte, 1970-88; dir. music Rising Star Missionary Assn., 1988-92. Team leader, grade chmn., supr. student tchrs., com. chmn., tchr. Charlotte-Mechlenburg Sch. System, 1958-88. Active Nat. Sunday Sch. Congress Christian Edn. Nat. Bapt. Conv. USA, The Lott Carey Missionary Conv., Gen. Bapt. Conv., N.C., All Bapt. World Alliance; vol. March of Dimes, Multiple Sclerosis for N.W. Neighborhoods Svc. Ctr.; pres. Mountain and Catawba Missionary Women's Aux., 1960-64, supr., 1965-78; tchr. Fairview Heights Bapt. Ch., Salisbury, N.C., 1980-88; com. chair Womens Home and Fgn. Missionary Convention N.C., 1988-92, chair pres.'s address, 1990-93; pianist, supr., tchr. Sunday sch. Fairview Heights Bapt. Ch., Salisbury, 1978-92, program coord., 1986-93; tchr., pianist Rising Star Sunday Sch. Conv., Thomasville, N.C., 1989-92; tutor Enrichment Program of the Oaklawn Park and McCrocery Heights Cmty. Orgn., Charlotte, N.C. Recipient Svc. award Mountain and Catawba Women's Aux., 1964, Christ Call to Youth, 1970, Womens Home and Fgn. Missionary Conv., 1992, Fairview Heights Bapt. Ch., 1990-92, Recognition cert., 1990, Recognition cert. Time and Place, 1995; named N.C. Minister's Wife of Yr., N.C. Assn. Minister's Wives and Widows Interdenominational, Cert. of Appreciation Salisbury-Rowan County Missionary Union, 1996. Mem. NEA, Assn. Childhood Edn. Internat., Interdenominational Mins. Wives (pres., sec. 1966-76, chair budget com. 1992—, Silver Tray award 1988), Charlotte-Mecklenburg Assn. Educators (sch. rep. 1980-88), Charlotte Ret. Sch. Pers., Alumnae J.C. Smith and Appalachian State Univs., Dean St. Cmty. Club (sec. 1990-92), Order Eastern Star, Am. Diebetic Assn. Democrat. Home: Charlotte, NC. Died May 27, 2007.

LOCONTE, NICHOLAS A., lawyer; b. Bristol, Conn., Apr. 4, 1935; s. Angelo A. and Maria M. (Degruttola) L.; m. Phyllis LaPlante, Oct. 27, 1967; children: Anthony, Nicholas. BA, U. Conn., 1956; LLB, U. Conn., Hartford, 1959. Bar: Conn. 1960, U.S. Dist. Ct. Conn. 1961. Pvt. practice, Bristol. Small claims commr. City of Bristol; past sect. Dem. Town Com., Bristol; past chmn. Charter Rev. Commn., Bristol; atty. Bristol Housing Authority. Home: Bristol, Conn. Died Aug. 27, 2007.

LODDE, GORDON MAYNARD, retired health physics consultant; b. Lafayette, Ind., Aug. 19, 1933; s. Herman Morris and Eva Grace (Robinson) Lodde; m. Nancy Jean Caldwell, Aug. 21, 1955 (dec. Aug. 2006); children: Gordon A., Bruce C., Melissa J. BS, Purdue Univ., 1958; MS, Univ. Rochester, 1964. Health physist U.S. Army, 1959-79; health physics cons. Porter Cons., Ardmore, Pa., 1979-84; cons. engr. GPU Nuclear, Middletown, Pa., 1984-94; health physics cons. Mt. Joy, Pa., from 1994. Contbr. Handbook for Management of Radiation Protection Programs, 1992; contbg. author Ency. Occupl. Health and Safety, 1997. Scoutmaster Boy Scouts Am., White Sands, N.Mex., 1967—70, Edgewood, Md., 1975—79, post adv., 1976—80. With Med. Svc. Corp US Army, 1959—79. Decorated Commendation medal with two oak leaf clusters, , , Legion of Merit; recipient Merit award, Boy Scouts Am., 1976, Silver Beaver award, 1978. Fellow: Health Physics Soc.; mem.: Am. Conf. of Gov. Hygienists, Am. Nuc. Soc. Home: Knoxville, Tenn. Died Oct. 20, 2014.

LOEWENSTEIN, MARTHA J(OSEPHINE), retired financial executive; b. NYC, Mar. 8, 1913; d. Solomon and Frieda (Abelson) L. BA, Barnard Coll., 1933. Statistician Coun. Jewish Fedns. and Welfare Funds, NYC, 1938-40; adminstrv. asst. to exec. dir. Nat. Hadassah, 1940-41; exec. asst. to exec. dir. Jewish Welfare Bd., NYC, 1941-47; adminstr., contr., chief protocol Consulate Gen. of Israel and Israel Mission to UN, NYC, 1949-53; chief fiscal officer, sec. governing bodies Am. Com. for Weizmann Inst. Sci., NYC, 1953-78, bd. dirs., from 1978. Class pres. Barnard Coll., 1988-93, co-v.p., 1993—, co-chair fundraising, 1980-88. Mem. Am. Jewish Pub. Rels. Soc. (sec., exec. com. 1982—), Community Svc. Soc./Ret. Sr. Vol. Program (chmn. ret. profl. placement com. 1982-89, treas. N.Y.C. adv. bd. 1988—, sec. 1982-88, exec. com. 1985—), Friends of Ret. Sr. Vol. Program (bd. dirs. 1990—), Nat. Coun. Jewish Women (founder Norma Loewenstein Drabkin scholarship fund), Hadassah (life). Democrat. Avocations: travel, painting, ballet, theater, music. Home: New York, NY. Died June 4, 2007.

LOEWI, ANDREW WILLIAM, lawyer; b. NYC, May 15, 1950; s. Roger W. and Ruth C. (Chill) L.; m. Patricia Fotheringham Knous, Oct. 13, 1984; children: Kimberly Ann Knous, Samantha Michelle. BA, Grinnell Coll., 1971; JD, Harvard U., 1982. Bar: Colo. 1982, US Dist. Ct. Colo. 1982, US Ct. Appeals (10th cir.) 1982, US Ct. Appeals (2d cir.) 2000, US Supreme Ct. 2001. Legis. asst. to Senator Dick Clark, Washington, 1973-79; assoc. Sherman & Howard, Denver, 1982-83; dep. dist. atty. Denver Dist. Atty.'s Office, 1983-86; assoc. Brownstein Hyatt & Farber, Denver, 1986-88; ptnr. Brownstein, Hyatt, Farber & Schreck, Denver, from 1989. Counsel spl. com. on ethics U.S. Senate, Washington, 1977. Trustee Grinnell (Iowa) Coll., 1985—; bd. govs. Am. Jewish Com., 1996-98; nat. v.p. Muscular Dystrophy Assn., 1996—. Recipient Whitney M. Young Jr. award Urban League of Metro. Denver, 1993. Mem. Colo. Bar Assn. (coun. mem. criminal law sect. 1985-86), Denver Bar Asns. (co-chmn. criminal justice com. 1984-85), Denver C. of C. (Leadership Denver 1985), Leadership Denver Assn. (Outstanding Alumnus award 1993). Democrat. Jewish. Home: Denver, Colo. Died Apr. 8, 2007.

LOFTIS, JACK D., retired editor; b. Cheyenne, Wyo., Nov. 21, 1934; s. Allyne and Henry L.; m. Beverly Walker Blake. BBA, Baylor U., 1957. With Hillsboro Daily Mirror, 1955-62, editor, 1962-65; copy desk Houston Chronicle, 1965; editor Tex. Mag., 1970-72, features editor, 1972-74, asst. mng. editor features, 1974-79, asst. editor, 1979-87, v.p., editor, 1987-90, exec. v.p., editor, 1990—2002; assoc. publisher, editor Houston Chronicle, 1999—2002. Founding dir. Crime Stoppers Houston; v.p. Chronicle Goodfellows; past pres. Freedom Info. Found. Tex.; mem. Baylor Journalism Adv. Bd.; former dir. Houston READ Commn.; former mem. Clean Houston Commn.; mem. State Election Com.; mem. sesquicentennial coun. 150 Baylor U., 1993-95; hon. chmn. Tex. Inaugural Com., 1995; juror Pulitzer Prize, 1999. Recipient Disting. Alumnus award Baylor U., 1988, Media award, 1997, Jester award Newspaper Features Coun., 1992, Loving Hand award United Way, 1994, Lifetime Achievement award Headliners Found. Tex., 1994, Pulitzer Prize 1999 and 2000; inducted into Hall of Fame, Hillsboro Tex. Chamber of Commerce, 1988. Mem. American Assn. Sunday Feature Editors (past pres.), American Soc. Newspaper Editors, Newspaper Features Coun. (past pres.), Baylor Alumni Assn. (dir., bd. dirs.), Baylor Bear Found., Press Club Houston. Died Dec. 29, 2014.

LOGAN, ELISABETH ANN, information science educator; b. Ironwood, Mich., Apr. 22, 1935; d. Arthur Daniel and Doris Lee (Spencer) Lohr; m. David Gill Logan, Aug. 10, 1957 (div. 1973); chidren: Kathleen Spencer Rundquist, Keith Kellogg, Amy Logan Johnston; m. Edric Amory Weld Jr., Nov. 28, 1978. AB, Oberlin Coll., 1957; MLS, Case Western Res. U., 1971, PhD, 1989. Media specialist Cleve. Bd. Edn., 1973-80; asst. prof. info. sci. Fla. State U., Tallahassee, 1985-90, assoc. prof., from 1990, assoc. dean, from 1995. Cons. Fla. Dept. Edn., Tallahassee, 1988-91, Fla. Dept. Law Enforcement, Tallahassee, 1991-92, SW Ga. Regional Libr., Bainbridge, 1990-91. Contbr. numerous articles on bibliometrics and database user characteristics to profl. jours. Mem. Am. Soc. for Info. Sci. (chmn. student chpts. 1989-91, spl. interest group for edn. 1991-92, bd. dirs. 1993-96), Beta Phi Mu. Avocations: skiing, hiking, sailing, music. Home: Tallahassee, Fla. Died Jan. 31, 2007.

LOGGIA, ROBERT (SALVATORE LOGGIA), actor; b. Staten Island, NY, Jan. 3, 1930; s. Benjamin and Elena (Blandino) L.; m. Della Marjorie Sloan, 1954 (div. 1981); children: Tracey, John, Kristina, Cynthia Loggia Armstrong; m. Audrey Loggia, Dec. 27, 1982. Student, Wagner Coll., SI, 1947-49; B. Journalism, U. Mo., Columbia, 1951. Actor: (Broadway) Toys in the Attic, 1961, Three Sisters, 1964, Boom Boom Room, 1973-74; (TV series) T.H.E. Cat, 1968-69, The Nine Lives of Elfego Baca, 1958-59, Mancuso F.B.I., 1989-90, Sunday Dinner, 1991; (films) Somebody Up There Likes Me, 1956, The Garment Jungle, 1957, Cop Hater, The Lost Missile, 1958, Cattle King, 1963, Greatest Story Ever Told, 1965, Che!, 1969, First Love, 1977, Speed Trap, Revenge of the Pink Panther, 1978, The Ninth Configuration (Twinkle Twinkle Little Kane), S.O.B., 1981, An Officer and a Gentleman, 1982, Trail of the Pink Panther, 1982, Scarface, 1983, Psycho II, 1983, Curse of the Pink Panther, 1983, Prizzi's Honor, 1985, Jagged Edge, 1985, Armed and Dangerous, 1986, Over the Top, 1986, Hot Pursuit, 1986, That's Life, 1986, The Believers, Big, 1988, Oliver & Company (voice), 1988, Triumph of the Spirit, 1989, Gaby, 1989, Marrying Man, 1990, Opportunity Knocks, 1990, Necessary Roughness, 1991, Gladiator, 1992, Innocent Blood, 1992, Bad Girls, 1994, I Love Trouble, 1994, Mistrial, 1996, Independence Day, 1996, Smilla's Sense of Snow, 1996, Shakespeare's Sister, 1997, Flypaper, 1997, Lost Highway, 1997, Wide Awake, 1998, Holy Man, 1998, The Proposition, 1998, The Suburbans, 1999, I Dream of Africa, 1999, American Virgin, 1999, Return to Me, 2000, All Over Again, 2001, The Shipment, 2001, The Deal, 2005, Forget About It, 2006, Funny Money, 2006, Rain, 2006, Wild Seven, 2006, Her Morbid Desires, 2008, The Least of These, 2008, Shrink, 2009, HArvest, 2010, Fake, 2010, Obituary of the Sun, 2010, The Grand Theft, 2011, The Great Fight, 2011, The Life Zone, 2011, Tim and Eric's Billion Dollar Movie, 2012, The Diary of Preston Plummer, 2012, Margarine Wars, 2012,Real Gangsters, 2013, Snapshot, 2014, Scavenger Killers, 2014, An Evergreen Christmas, 2014, The Big Fat Stone, 2014, No Deposit, 2015, Bleeding Hearts, 2015, Sicilian Vampire, 2015, Angry Men and Women, 2015; (TV miniseries) Echoes in the Darkness, Favorite Son, 1989, Wild Palms, 1993; (TV films) Chicago Conspiracy Trial, 1988, Afterburn, 1992, Merry Christmas Baby, 1992, Nurses on the Line, 1993, Mercy Mission, 1993, White Mile, 1994, Lifepod, 1993, Between Love & Honor, 1995, Jake Lassiter, 1995, Pandora's Clock, 1996, Coldblooded, 1995, Man with a Gun, 1996, Fly Paper, 1997, Live Virgin, 1998, Mistrial, 1996, The Don's Analyst, 1997, Joe Torre: Curveballs Along the Way, 1997, Joan of Arc, 1999, Dodson's Journey, 2001, La Trattoria Sitcom, 2015; (TV appearances) The Guardian, 2001, Queens Supreme, 2003-07, Kojak, 2005, Men of a Certain Age, 2009-11, Family Guy, 2011-13. With US Army, 1951-53. Home: Los Angeles, Calif. Died Dec. 4, 2015.

LOGSDON, CHARLES ELDON, consultant; b. Mo., May 8, 1921; s. Millison and Mary Vivian (Reimenschneider) L.; m. Arloine Marie Schmidt, Aug. 20, 1948; children: Charles Louis, Onnalie Marie, John Calvert. BA, U. Kansas City, 1942; PhD, U. Minn., 1954. Rsch. assoc. U. Minn., St. Paul, 1947-50; rsch. aide U.S. Dept. Agrl., St. Paul, 1950-53, rsch. plant pathologist Palmer, Alaska, 1953-68; prof. plant pathologist U. Alaska, Palmer, 1954-78; assoc. dir. Agrl. Exp. Sta. U. Alaska, Palmer, 1970-78; owner Agresources, Palmer, 1978-85; sec., mgr. Alaska Crop Improvement Assn., Palmer, 1953-79; owner Pleasant Green North, Palmer, from 1986. Lobbyist Farmers & Stock Growers Assn., Alaska, 1984; seed analyst State of Alaska, 1987-89. Contbr. articles to profl. jours. Mem. city coun. City of Palmer, 1956-59, mayor, 1959-61; bd. trustees Valley Hosp., Palmer, 1962-70; bd. ethics MAT-SU Borough, Alaska, 1974-75; investment adv. bd. State of Alaska, 1976-78. 1st lt. U.S. Air Corps, 1940-45. Mem. Alaska Pioneers. Independent. Lutheran. Avocations: reading, writing letters, hiking, gardening, fishing. Home: Palmer, Alaska. Died Jan. 7, 2007.

LOHMANN, WOLFGANG HANS-JOACHIM, biophysics educator; b. Frankfurt, Germany, Aug. 1, 1930; s. Max and Gertrud (Klingenberg) L.; m. Christl Marie Margarete Nette, July 31, 1959; children: Birgit Marion, Chris Patrick. BS in Physics, U. Jena, German Dem. Republic, 1951, MS in Physics, 1954; PhD, U. Freiburg, Fed. Republic Germany, 1958. Asst. to assoc. prof. U. Ark., Little Rock, 1960-65; assoc. prof. U. Iowa, Iowa City, 1965-69; prof. Tech. U. Munich, 1969-74, U. Giessen, Fed. Republic Germany, from 1974. Author, editor: Biophysik, 1983, transl. to English, 1984. Recipient rsch. grants from several nat. and internat. founds. Mem. German Biophysical Soc., Radiol. Rsch. Soc. U.S., Sigma Xi. Home: Giessen, Germany. Died Mar. 22, 2007.

LOHRLI, ANNE, retired literature educator, writer; b. Bake Oven, Oreg., Feb. 9, 1906; d. Gottfried and Anna (Hüsser) L. BA, Occidental Coll., LA, 1927, MA, 1928, Columbia U., 1932; PhD, U. So. Calif., 1937. Tchr. L.A. city schs., 1937-45; prof. English N.Mex. Highlands U., Las Vegas, 1945-65. Vis. prof. U. Trieste, 1954. Compiler: Household Words, List of Contributors, etc., 1973; contbr. some 40 articles in Dickensian, Princeton U. Libr. Chronicle, Victorian Studies, Pacific Historian, others, 1963-94. Mem. Phi Beta Kappa, Phi Kappa Phi. Home: Talmage, Calif. Died Mar. 17, 2007.

LOMBARDI, NEIL, pediatric neurologist; b. Yonkers, NY, July 15, 1943; s. Neil and Angela Lombardi; m. Elizabeth C. Lombardi, July 2, 1966; children: Paul, Seth, Ethan. BA, MD, Boston U., 1967. Diplomate Am. Bd. Pediatrics, Am. Bd. Nat. Bd. of Med. Examiners, Am. Bd. Psychiatry and Neurology. Intern in pediatrics New England Med. Ctr. Hosps., 1967-68, resident in pediatrics, 1968-70; asst. attending pediatrician The Roosevelt Hosp., 1975-81; acting dir. developmental disabilities ctr. St. Lukes/Roosevelt Hosp. Ctr., 1977-78; cons. pediatrician neurology St. Lukes Roosevelt Hosp., 1976-81, cons. pediatrician child neurology, 1976-81, assoc. attending pediatrician and physician, 1981-98; cons. pediatric neurology St. Mary's Hosp. for Children, 1983-98, dir. neurology, 1986-90, dir. med. svcs., 1986-90, v.p. med. svcs., 1990-97; pediatric neurologist Children's Specialized Hosp., Mountainside, N.J., from 1997, pvt. practice Hudson Valley, N.J., 1997, Hudson Valley, 1997. Asst. attending physician pediatrics, 1978-98. Contbr. articles to profl. jours. Maj. USAF, 1970-72. Fellow Am. Acad. Pediatrics; mem. Am. Acad. of Neurology. Home: Teaneck, NJ. Died Feb. 15, 2007.

LONGHI, VINCENT J., lawyer; b. NYC, Apr. 16, 1916; s. Joseph and Rosa (Zitani) L.; m. Gabrielle Gold, Nov. 13, 1943; children: Jaime Gold, Gabrielle Jr. LLD, St. Lawrence U., 1946. Ptnr. Longhi & Loscalzo, NYC, 1952-80; prin. V.J. Longhi P.C., NYC, 1980-97; pres. V.J. Longhi Assoc., NYC, from 1997. Author: (plays) Two Fingers of Pride, 1955, Climb the Greased Pole, 1968, The Lincoln Mask, 1972, (book) Woody, Cisco and Me, 1997. Rep. candidate for congress, Bklyn. With Merchant Marine, 1943-45. Mem. N.Y. State Bar Assn., N.Y. State Trial Lawyers Assn., D.C. Bar Assn. Died Nov. 22, 2006.

LONNEMO, KURT ROLAND, hydraulic company executive; b. Söderbärke, Sweden, Dec. 24, 1936; came to U.S., 1967; s. Karl Georg and Elna Margareta (Stalhandske) L.; m. Margareta Siv Ingrid Lilja, Sept. 9, 1958; children: Mats Roland, Hans Anders, Klas Robert. MS in Mech. Engring., Royal Inst. Tech., Stockholm, 1961. Test engr. Royal Bd. Water Power, Stockholm, 1958-59; chief engr. AB Nordisk Vickers, Stockholm, 1963-67; engring. mgr. Sperry Vickers, Troy, Mich., 1968-73, planning mgr., 1973-76, product mgr., 1976-82; application market mgr. Vickers, Inc., Troy, Mich., from 1982. Cons. Swedish Water Power Assn., Stockholm, 1960-61; instr. Royal Sch. Navy, Nasby Park, Sweden, 1962; asst. prof. Royal Inst. Tech., 1964-67 Patentee in field; contbr. articles to profl. jours. Served to 2d lt. Swedish Army, 1962-63. Mem. Fluid Power Soc., Soc. Automotive Engrs. Republican. Lutheran. Avocations: woodworking, boating. Home: Searcy, Ark. Died Nov. 7, 2006.

LOOMIE, EDWARD RAPHAEL, lawyer; b. NYC, Aug. 18, 1918; s. Leo Stephen Loomie and Loretta F. Murphy; widowed; children: Christine, Paul. AB, Columbia U., 1940, JD, 1942. Pvt. practice. Pres. Internat. Copyrights Inc., Resources Plus Inc. Trustee Seventh Regiment Fund. Mem. 7th Regiment Vets. Assn. (v.p.). Home: Seaford, NY. Died Oct. 26, 2007.

LOONEY, THOMAS ALBERT, psychologist, educator; b. Dallas, Feb. 8, 1947; s. Billy Albert and Helen Dorothy

(Holland) L.; m. Margaret Ann Thomas, Aug., 1968 (div. 1982). BA, Tex. Tech. Coll., 1969; MS, Fla. State U., 1971, PhD, 1973. Instr. Northeastern U., Boston, 1973-75; asst. prof. Lynchburg (Va.) Coll., 1975-79, assoc. prof., 1979-86, prof., from 1986, chair dept. psychology, from 1987. Referee NSF. Contbr. articles to Jour. Comparative and Physiol. Psychology, Exptl. Analysis of Behavior, Bull. Psychonomic Soc., Worm Runner's Digest, Physiology and Behavior, Animal Learning and Behavior, Neurosci. and Biobehavioral Revs.; contbr. chpt. to book. Grantee NSF, HEW, NIMH, Gwathmey Trust; recipient Disting. Scholar award, 1986, Excellence in Tchg. award, 1992, Excellence in Citizenship award, 1994. Mem. Am. Psychol. Soc., Am. Psychol. Assn., Psychonomic Soc., Eastern Psychol. Assn., Southwestern Psychol. Assn., AAAS, Gold Key, Phi Kappa Phi, Psi Chi, Sigma Xi. Home: Lynchburg, Va. Died May 22, 2007.

LOPATA, MONTE LEE, accountant; b. St. Louis, Aug. 21, 1919; s. Charles and Minnie (Kligman) L.; m. Caroloyn Blumenfeld, Oct. 8, 1946; children: Lee, Loren, Heidi Ann. BSBA, Washington U., 1942; postgrad., U. Chgo., 1946. CPA, Mo. Treas. Frolic Footwear, Inc., Jonesboro, Ark., 1951-53, v.p., 1953-82, pres., 1982-87; chmn. Lopata, Lopata & Dubinsky, St. Louis, from 1987. Bd. dirs. A-I Mfg. Corp., St. Louis, Guild Craftsmen, St. Louis, Arion Products, St. Louis, C&M Products, St. Louis. Served to 1st lt. USAF, 1942-46. Mem. Am. Inst. CPA, Mo. CPA's. Clubs: Westwood Country, Whittemore (St. Louis). Avocations: photographer, golfer, bridge. Home: Saint Louis, Mo. Died Apr. 29, 2007.

LOPER, CARL RICHARD, JR., metallurgical engineer, educator; b. Wauwatosa, Wis., July 3, 1932; s. Carl Richard S. and Valberg (Sundby) Loper; m. Jane Louise Loehning, June 30, 1956; children: Cynthia Louise Loper Koch, Anne Elizabeth. BS in Metall. Engring., U. Wis., 1955, MS in Metall. Engring., 1958, PhD in Metall. Engring., 1961; postgrad., U. Mich., 1960. Metall. engr. Pelton Steel Casting Co., Milw., 1955-56; instr., rsch. assoc. U. Wis., Madison, 1956-61, asst. prof., 1961-64, assoc. prof., 1964-68, prof. metall. engring., 1968-88, prof. materials sci. and engring., 1988-2001, ret. prof. materials sci. and engring., 2001, assoc. chmn. dept. metall. and mineral engring., 1979-82; pres. CRL Corp., from 1979. Rsch. metallurgist Allis Chalmers, Milw., 1961; adj. prof. materials U. Wis., Milw., from 2002; cons., lectr. in field. Author: (book) Principles of Metal Casting, 1965; contbr. articles to profl. jours. Chmn. 25 Anniversary Ductile Iron Symposium, Montreal, Canada, 1973; pres. Ygdrasil Lit. Soc., 1989—90. Recipient Adams Meml. award, Am. Welding Soc., 1963, Howard F. Taylor award, 1967, Svc. citation, 1969, 1972, others, Silver medal award, Sci. Merit Portuguese Foundry Assn., 1978, medal, Chinese Foundrymen's Assn., 1989, E.J. Walsh Award, 2002, Merton Flemings award, Materials Processing Inst., 2006; fellow Foundry Ednl. Found., 1953—55, Wheelbrator Corp., 1960, Ford Found., 1960. Fellow: Am. Soc. Metals (chmn. 1969—70), Am. Inst. Mgmt.; mem.: Yedrasil-Norwegian-Am. Lit. Soc., Tau Beta Pi, Korean Inst. Metals and Materials (hon.), Foundry Ednl. Found. (E.J. Walsh award 2002), Am. Welding Soc., Am. Foundry Soc. (Wis. bd. dirs. 1967-70, 76-79, Foundry Ednl. Found. dirs. award 1994, Cast Iron Hon. Lecture 2006, Best Paper award 1966, 67, 85, John A. Penton gold medal 1972, Hoyt Meml. lectr. 1992, Aluminum Divsn. award sci. merit 1995), Blackhawk Country Club, Torske Klubben (bd. dirs., co-founder from 1978, Foundry Hall of Honor 2001), Gamma Alpha, Alpha Sigma Mu, Sigma Xi. Lutheran. Achievements include research in understanding the solidifcation and metallurgy of ferrous and non-ferrous alloys; solidification and cast iron metallurgy, education in metallurgy and materials science. Died Sept. 7, 2010.

LOPEZ, VITO JOSEPH, former state legislator; b. Bklyn., June 5, 1941; m. Joan Lopez (separated); children: Stacey Anne, Gina M. Lopez Summa. BS in Bus Adminstrn., LI U.; MSW, Yeshiva U., 1970. Adj. prof. human services LaGuardia CC; instr. Molloy Coll., Empire State Coll., Yeshiva U.; founder Ridgewood Bushwick Sr. Citizens Ctr., Bklyn.; mem. Dist. 53 NY State Assembly, NY, 1985—2013. Founder City-Wide Advocates for Seniors, North Bklyn. Sr. Citizens Coalition, Ridgewood Bushwick Sr. Citizens Coun., Inc. Democrat. Roman Catholic. Died Nov. 9, 2015.

LORD, MARJORIE (MARJORIE WOLLENBERG), actress; b. San Francisco, July 26, 1918; d. George Charles and Lillian Rosalie (Edgar) Wollenberg; m. John Archer, Dec. 30, 1941 (div. 1954); children: Gregg, Anne; m. Randolph M. Hale, May 26, 1958 (dec. Aug. 1974); m. Harry Joseph Volk, Aug. 14, 1976 (dec. 2000). Student high sch., San Francisco. Bd. dirs. The Joffrey Ballet, The Friends of the Library, U. So. Calif. Appeared in theater prodns. including The Old Maid, Anniversary Waltz on Broadway, Springtime for Henry, Signature, 1945, Little Brown Jug, 1946; more than 30 feature films including Johnny Come Lately; starred in Make Room for Daddy, 1957-64; countless TV shows including Love American Style, Sweet Surrender, 1987; TV film Side by Side, 1987; dir. and actress theater prodns.; dir. Sunday in New York, Black Comedy, The Tiger at Claremont College, Ginger in the Morning; author (memoir) A Dance & Hug, 2005; Author numerous books Bd. dirs. Hollywood Entertainment Mus., Friends of Libr. Home: Beverly Hills, Calif. Died Nov. 28, 2015.

LORFANO, PAULINE DAVIS, artist; b. Westbrook, Maine; d. Paul A. and Nellie R. (Robinson) Davis; m. Joseph James Lorfano, Apr. 18, 1952; children: Mary-Jo, Paula, Julie-Ann, Joseph III. Student, Westbrook Coll., 1946-48; Assoc. degree, Maine Coll. Art, 1950; BS, U. Maine, 1951; degree (hon.), Maine Coll. Art, 2000. Tchr. Riggs Sch., Gloucester, Mass., 1951-52; art tchr. Westbriar Elem., Vienna, Va., 1969-76, George Mason U., Fairfax, Va., 1976-80; art tchr., workshop instr. Va., from 1980; juror, lectr. art Va., from 1980. Illustrator: (book) Visiting Historic Vienna...A Child's Book to Color, 1995; one person shows include Summer Sch. Mus., 1988, Nat. Wildlife Fedn., 1989, Fisher Gallery, Schlesinger Art Ctr., No. Va. C.C., 2002, Dyn Corp. Gallery, Reston, Va., 2003, Result Gallery, Washington, 2005; group shows include Hilton Head Island Exhbn., Va. Watercolor Exhbn., Result Gallery, Wash., DC, 2005, alt. Watercolor Soc. Mid-Atlantic Regional, Maritime Mus. Concord, Calif., 2006, Result Gallery, Washington, 2006, Ventura Maritime Mus., Oxnard, Calif., 2006; works featured for mag. covers. Recipient Heritage Preservation award Historic Vienna, Inc., also awards for art. Mem. Vienna Arts Soc. Inc. (permanent, bd. dirs. 1990-98, pres. 1979-81, 88-90, 2004-05, Gold medal 1987, Stillwell award 1988, Treasury of Art 2004), Nat. League Am. PEN Women (juried-in mem., cons. art bd. 1994-96, chmn. art bd. 1982-84, art adv. 2004-06, 2d Pl. award Biennial Art Exhibit 1992), Va. Watercolor Soc. (co-pres. 2004, Richmond Region Watercolor award 2002), Internat. Soc. Marine Painters, Potomac Valley Watercolorists (juried, bd. dirs. 1990-98, pres. 1989-90, exec. bd. 2000—), Washington Watercolor Assn. (juried, exec. bd. chair 1996-97, newsletter editor 1997-2003, Am. Artist award), Arts Coun. Fairfax County, McLean Art Soc. Home: Vienna, Va. Died Aug. 8, 2014.

LORING, EMILIE, lawyer; b. Bklyn., May 29, 1923; d. Henry L. and Helen K. Smith; m. Len Loring, Mar. 24, 1948 (dec. Apr. 1991); children: Wendy Rightmire, Judith A. BA with high honors, Swarthmore Coll., 1944; MA with honors, U. Mont., 1963, JD with high honors, 1973. Bar: Mont., U.S. Dist. Ct. Mont., U.S. Ct. Appeals (D.C., 9th and 10th cirs.), U.S. Supreme Ct.; also Blackfeet Tribal Ct., Confederated Salish and Kootenai Tribal Ct., Tribal Ct. of Ft. Belknap Indian Cmty., Tribal Ct. of Chippewa Cree Tribe. Instr. U. Mont., Missoula, 1966-67, 69-70; legal intern NLRB, Seattle, 1972; ptnr. Hilley & Loring, Great Falls, Mont., 1973-92; sole practitioner Missoula, from 1992. Mem. state bd. dirs ACLU of Mont., 1988-94; mem. Mont. state adv. com. U.S. Commn. on Civil Rights, 1988-91; pub. mem. State Bd. Cosmetology, 1987-88. Mem. State Bar Mont., Western Mont. Bar Assn. (Disting. Atty. award 1995), Cascade County Bar Assn., Mont. Legal Svcs. Assn. (bd. dirs., pres. 1991-92, sec. 2002-03, v.p. 2003-04). Died June 16, 2007.

LO SCHIAVO, JOHN JOSEPH, academic administrator; b. San Francisco, Feb. 25, 1925; s. Joseph and Anne (Re) Lo S. AB, Gonzaga U., 1948, Ph.L. and MA, 1949; S.T.L., Alma Coll., 1962. Joined S.J., Roman Catholic Ch., 1942; tchr. St. Ignatius High Sch., San Francisco, 1949-50; instr. philosophy and theology U. San Francisco, 1950-52, 56-57, 61-62, dean of students, v.p. for student affairs, dean of students, 1962-68, pres., 1977-91, chancellor, 1991—2015, bd. trustee, rector. Pres. Bellarmine Coll. Prep. Sch., San Jose, 1968-75 Bd. dirs. Sch. of Sacred Heart, 1991-2000, St. Mary's Hosp., 1990-96, United Religion Initiative, 1999 Mem. Olympic Club, Bohemian Club, Univ. Club. Took a rare action in 1982 of suspending University of San Francisco's men's basketball program after repeated violations of the National Collegiate Athletic Association rules; reinstated the program back in 1983 for 1985-86 season. Home: San Francisco, Calif. Died May 15, 2015.

LOUER, THOMAS R., industrial hygienist, chemist, retired; b. Amsterdam, NY, May 4, 1939; s. Raymun W. and Anna (Jarosienski) L.; m. Felicia Ann Polischak; 1 child, Christopher. BS in Chemistry, U. Mass., 1961. Toxicologist, legal cons. DuPont, Wilmington, Del., rsch. mgr. Phila., mktg. mgr. Wilmington, product mgr., chemist Phila. Mem. Nat. Print and Varnish Assn. (chmn. labeling com.). Home: Newtown Sq, Pa. Died Feb. 25, 2007.

LOUIS, MURRAY (MURRAY LOUIS FUCHS), dancer, choreographer, dance teacher; b. NYC, Nov. 4, 1926; s. Aaron and Rose (Mintzer) Fuchs. BS, N.Y. U., 1951. Principal dancer Nikolais Dance Theatre, 1950-59; assoc. dir. dance div., Henry St. Playhouse, N.Y.C., 1953-70; artistic dir. Nikolais/Louis Found. Dance, N.Y.C., 1970-2016, Murray Louis Dance Co., 1953-; co-dir. Choreoarts, 1973-; choreographer numerous works, 1953—, including Porcelain Dialogues, 1974, Moments, 1975, Catalogue, 1975, Cleopatra, 1976, Ceremony, 1976, Deja Vu, 1976, Glances, 1976, Schubert, 1977, The Canarsie Venus, 1978, Figura, 1978, A Suite for Erik, 1979, Afternoon, 1979, The City, 1980, November Dances, 1980, Aperitif, 1982, A Stravinsky Montage, 1982, Repertoire, 1982, The After Boat, 1983, Frail Demons, 1984, Four Brubeck Pieces (with Dave Brubeck Quartet), 1984, Pug's Land, 1984, The Station, 1985, Revels, 1986, The Disenchantment of Pierrot, 1986, Black and White, 1987, Return to Go, 1987; choreographer: By George (music by George Gershwin for Cleve. Ballet), 1987, Act I (with Dave Brubeck Quartet), 1987, Bach II, 1987, Asides, 1987, Horizons, 1994, Alone, 1994, Tides, 1994, Homage to Swedish Ballet, 1995, Sinners All, 1996, Symphony, 1996, Tips, 1997, Venus, 1997, Millennium Loop, 1998; TV projects include Repertoire Workshop, CBS, N.Y.C., 1965, Proximities, Calligraph for Matyrs, ZDF-TV, Munich, 1974, Soundstage (with Dave Brubeck) PBS, Chgo., 1977, Studio Two, Polish Nat. TV, Warsaw, 1978, Murray Louis Dance Co., TeleFrance 1, Paris, 1982, video AT&T (with Dave Brubeck Quartet), 1988; 5 part film series Dance as an Art Form, 1974; choreographer for 23d, 27th Annual Coty Am. Fashion Critics awards; author: Inside Dance, 1980, On Dance, 1992, Letters to Nik from India; Nik and Murray (film by Christian Blackwood), 1986, Murray Louis on Dance, 1992. Chmn. U.S. chpt. Conseil Internat. de la Danse (UNESCO). Served with USNR, 1945-46. Guggenheim fellow, 1969, 73; grantee Rockefeller Found., 1974; Nat. Endowment Arts, 1968, 70, 72, 74-78, Mellon Found., 1976; recipient Critics award Internat. Festival Weisbaden, Ger., 1972, Dance Mag. award, 1977, Grand Medaille de la Ville de Paris, 1979; decorated knight Order of Arts and Letters, France, 1984, Citation from NYC Mayor, Edward L. Koch, 1989, Lucia Chase Fellow, 1998, Phi Beta Kappa Vis. Scholar, 1998. Mem. Am. Guild Mus. Artists, Assn. Am. Dance Cos., Asso. Council Arts, Dance Notation Bur. Jewish. Home: New York, NY. *An artisthas to discover the intuitive force within oneself, and then know how to utilize and trust its judgment, is essential for the creative artist. My aesthetics were achieved by this intuitive judgment.* Died Feb. 1, 2016.

LOVERN, TERRANCE LEE, production manager; b. Spokane, Oct. 8, 1945; s. Theodore and Tressa Clar (Adams) L. Grad. high sch., NYC. Prin. understudy Ice Capades, 1963-64; prin. skater, dancer Casa Carioca Ice Revue, Garmisch, Germany, 1964-66; prin. skater Holiday on Ice, U.S. & South Am., 1966; prin. skater, dancer Conrad Hilton Hotel Ice Revue, Chgo., 1966-68; dancer Tropicana Hotel, Las Vegas, 1968-72, Lido de Paris, Las Vegas, 1972-74; dancer, singer Bobbie Gentry Show, Las Vegas, 1974-76; prin. skater, dancer Flamingo Hilton, Las Vegas, 1976-81; dancer, singer Lido deParis Show, Stardust Hotel, Las Vegas, 1976-81; instr. ice skating Ice Land Ice Arena, Las Vegas, 1983-88; skater, dancer Flamingo Hilton, Las Vegas, 1986-89; co. mgr. Stardust Hotel, Las Vegas, 1989-91, prodn. mgr., 1991-2000; prodn. stage mgr. Wayne Newton Show, Stardust Resort & Casino, from 2000. Artistic dir. Civil Ballet, Las Vegas, 1988-95. Bd. dirs. Golden Rainbow Las Vegas, 1997. Recipient Can. Figure Skating Gold medal, Vancouver, B.C., 1963. Home: Las Vegas, Nev. Died Dec. 30, 2006.

LOW, JAMES A., physician; b. Toronto, Ont., Can., Sept. 22, 1925; s. Donald M. and Doris V. (Van Duzer) L.; m. Margery Una, Oct. 5, 1952; children: Donald E., Margeret P., Norman I. MD, U. Toronto, 1949. Intern Toronto Gen. Hosp., 1949-50; resident in ob-gyn U. Toronto, 1950-54; fellow ob/gyn Duke U., 1955; clin. instr. dept. ob-gyn U. Toronto, 1955-65; prof. and chmn. dept. ob-gyn Queens U., Kingston, Ont., Canada, 1965-85, prof., 1985—2011. Exec. dir. Mus. Health Care at Kingston, 1995—2011. Mem. editl. bd. Ob-Gyn., 1986-89, Am. Jour. Ob-Gyn., 1995-99. Served with Can. Navy, 1943-45. Recipient Pres. award, SOCG, 1985, Spl. Recognition award, Kingston Gen. Hosp., 1997, William B. Spaulding Cert. of Merit, AMS Found., 1999, Disting. Svc. award, Queen's U., 2006—07, First Capital Honorable Achievement award, Kingston, 2010, The Queen Elizabeth II Diamond Jubilee medal, 2012, Kingston Hist. award, 2012, Ptnrs. Ronald G. Calbourn Sci. Amb. award, 2013, Order of Can., 2014. Fellow: Royal Coll. Obstetricians and Gynecologists, Royal Coll. Physicians and Surgeons Can. (chmn. splty. com. 1976—82, chmn. manpower com. 1984—92); mem.: Can. Soc. Clin. Investigation, Soc. Obstetricians and Gynecologists Can., Soc. Gynecol. Investigation, Am. Gynecol. and Obstet. Soc., Assn. Profs. Ob-Gyn. Can. (sec.-treas. 1972—80, pres. 1983—84). Home: Kingston, Canada. Died Feb. 15, 2015.

LOWE, MARTHA JANE, piano teacher; b. North Wilkesboro, NC, Apr. 26, 1935; d. John Andrew and Dallie Arcos (Johnson) Johnston; m. John Samuel Lowe, Apr. 10, 1955; children: John, Jesse, James, Joseph, Debra. Student, Tulsa C.C., from 1983. Cert. in piano. Pvt. tchr. piano, Tulsa, from 1983. Pianist Born Again Believer Singers, Sapulpa, Okla., 1985—; pianist and organist at weedings, funerals and banquets, Sapula, 1960—. Pianist, substitute organist Forest Hills Bapt. Ch., Sapulpa, 1960—; vol. pianist at nursing homes, 1985—, also other chs.; vol. Am. Cancer Soc., 1990—; participant Love Run for Muscular Dystrophy. Mem. Music Tchrs. Nat. Assn., Am. Coll. Musician, Tulsa Accredited Music Tchrs. Assn. (rec. sec. 1993-95). Democrat. Avocations: camping, walking, jogging, fixing family dinners for 14 people, entertaining 7 grandchildren. Home: Sapulpa, Okla. Died Nov. 2, 2006.

LOWENFELD, ANDREAS FRANK, law educator; b. Berlin, May 30, 1930; s. Henry and Yela (Herschkowitsch) L.; m. Elena Machado, Aug. 11, 1962; children: Julian, Marianna. AB magna cum laude, Harvard U., 1951, LLB magna cum laude, 1955. Bar: NY 1955, US Supreme Ct. 1961. Assoc. Hyde and de Vries, NYC, 1957-61; spl. asst. legal adv. US State Dept., 1961-63, asst. legal adviser econ. affairs, 1963-65, dep. legal adviser, 1965-66; fellow John F. Kennedy Inst. Politics Harvard U., Cambridge, Mass., 1966-67; prof. law Sch. Law NYU, NYC, from 1967, Charles L. Denison prof. law, 1981-94, Herbert and Rose Rubin prof. internat. law, 1994—2009, emeritus, from 2009. Arbitrator internat. comml. panels Internat. C. of C., Am. Arbitration Assn., Internat. Ctr. Settlement Investment Disputes. Author (with Abram Chayes and Thomas Ehrlich): Internat. Legal Process, 1968—69; author: Aviation Law, Cases and Materials, 1972, 2d edit., 1981, Internat. Economic Law, vol.I, 1975, 3d edit., 1997, vol. II, 1976, 2d edit., 1982, vol. III, 1977, vol. IV, 1977, 2d edit., 1984, vol. VI, 1979; : 2d edit., 1983, Conflict of Laws, Fed., State and Internat. Perspectives, 1986, 2002, Internat. Litig. and Arbitration, 1993, 2d edit., 2002, 3d edit, 2006, Internat. Litig.: The Quest for Reasonableness, 1996, The Role of Govt. in Internat. Trade: Essays Over Three Decades, 2000, Internat. Econ. Law, 2002, 2nd edit., 2008, Lowenfeld on International Arbitration, 2005; editor, co-author Expropriation in the Americas: A Comparative Law Study, 1971; assoc. reporter: Am. Law Inst. Restatement on Foreign Relations Law, 1987; co-reporter Am. Law Inst. Project on Internat. Jurisdiction and Judgments, 2006; contbr. articles to profl. jours. Mem.: ABA, Internat. Acad. Comparative Law, Inst. de Droit Internat., Coun. Fgn. Rels., Am. Law Inst., Am. Arbitration Assn. (arbitrator), Am. Soc. Internat. Law (Manley O. Hudson medal 2007), Assn. Bar City NY. Home: Bronx, NY. Died June 9, 2014.

LOZIER, PAUL GEORGE, materials engineer; b. Poughkeepsie, NY, July 31, 1930; s. George Russell and Sopie Marie Lozier; m. Theresa Anne Quandt, Feb. 4, 1956; children: Kurt Thomas, Kim Tracey, Kelly Thomas. BAtMetE, Univ. Kans., Lawrence, Kans., 1956; MS in Mech. Tech., Univ. State N.Y., Alfred, NY, 1958. Supr. mgr. Knolls Atomic Power Lab., Niskayuma, NY, 1959—69, sr. metall. engr., from 1969. Chief of downhill course maintenance Winter Olympics, Lake Placid, NY, 1980; U.S. rep. Fed. Internat. Ski, 1984—96. Recipient Nova award, Lockheed Martin, Washington, 2002. Mem.: Am. Soc. Metals. Achievements include patents for. Avocations: pilot, experinmental aircraft construction, canoeing, skiing, sailing. Home: Ballston Lake, NY. Died Mar. 16, 2007.

LUNCE, STEPHEN EDWARD, information systems educator; b. Dallas, June 12, 1947; s. Carroll Edward and Lucille Jane (Seth) L.; m. Barbara Dale Booher, Dec. 30, 1969; 1 child, Stephen Edward II. Student, Tex. A&M U., 1965-67; BA in History, U. Dallas, 1977, MBA in Mgmt. Info. Systems, 1988; PhD in Bus. Adminstrn., U. Tex., Arlington, 1994. Cert. computing profl. 1994. Adminstrv. mgr. Airmotive Engring. Corp., Dallas, 1969-80; gen. mgr. Aircraft Cylinder Svc., Fort Worth, 1980-81; asst. gen. mgr. Tex. Aircraft & Engine, Fort Worth, 1981-84; info. systems specialist Standard T. Chem., Dallas, 1984-89; instr. U. Tex., Arlington, 1989-92; asst. prof. computer info. systems Tex. A&M Internat. U., Laredo, 1992-96, assoc. prof. info. systems, 1996—2001, prof. info. systems, from 2001; prof., chair MIS dept. Midwestern State U., 2004. Adj. prof. U. Dallas, Irving, 1991-92; sr. exec. cons. R&S Cons., Laredo, 1993—. Contbr. articles to profl. jours. Head baseball coach YMCA, Irving, 1985-92, asst. soccer coach, 1983-89. With U.S. Army, 1968-69. L.L. Schkade rsch. fellow U. Tex., 1992; recipient Senator Zafferini medal, 2001. Mem. Assn. Info. Systems, Assn. of Info. Tech. Profls., Planetary Soc., Assn. of Mgmt., Info. Resources Mgmt. Assn., Acad. of Internat. Bus., Inst. for Ops. Rsch. and Mgmt. Sci., Assn. Systems Mgmt., Decision Scis. Inst. (campus rep. 1989-97), Sigma Beta Delta, Beta Gamma Sigma, Alpha Iota Delta, Sigma Iota Epsilon, Phi Alpha Theta, Sigma Iota Epsilon. Republican. Avocations: golf, science fiction. Home: Wichita Falls, Tex. Died May 4, 2007.

LUND, FREDERICK HENRY, retired aerospace and electrical engineer; b. Seattle, June 2, 1929; s. Henry George and Minnie (Wilbern) L.; m. Joyce Pauline Mon Pleasure, Sept. 8, 1950; children: Frederick Bradley, Christopher Michael, Peter Andrew, Andrea Leslie. BSEE, U. Wash., Seattle, 1951; postgrad., U. Calif., LA, 1954-56, 57-59; MS in Aeros., MIT, 1957. Registered profl. engr., Fla. Electronics engr. U.S. Naval Air Missile Test Ctr., Point Mugu, Calif., 1951, 53-56; head systems employment br., aero. rsch. engr. U.S. Naval Missile Ctr., Point Mugu, 1957-61, head plans and analysis group, gen. engr., 1961-65; sr. rsch. engr. Stanford Rsch. Inst., Menlo Park, Calif., 1965-69; mem. profl. staff Martin Marietta Missile Systems, Orlando, Fla., 1969-93; P.E. cons., 1994—95; electronics engr. Naval Air Depot, Jacksonville, Fla., 1995—2012. Chmn. com. Ventura area Coun. Boy Scouts Am., Camarillo, Calif., 1962-65, asst. dist. commr., Stanford area coun., Los Altos, Calif., 1967-69, instnl. rep. Cen. Fla. counc., Orlando, 1972-74; mem. pres.'s coun. U. Fla., Gainesville, 1987—. 1st lt. C.E., USAR, 1951-53. USN Bur. Aeros. scholar, 1956-57. Mem. AIAA (sr., missile sys. tech. com. 1987-91), IEEE (life, sect. chmn. 1962-63), Aerospace and Electronics Systems Soc. of IEEE (chpt. chmn. 1972-73), Mil. Ops. Rsch. Soc. (dir. 1962-66), Assn. Old crows (sec. 1973, club dir. 1986-90), Adelphi (sub-chpt. pres. 1948-51), Wesley, Kiwanis, Sigma Xi. Died Dec. 21, 2013.

LUNDIN, MORRIS ALBIN, graphic artist; b. Warren, Minn., Aug. 3, 1932; s. Henry A. and Myrtle E. (Hanson) L.; m. Ginko Nagaoka, Jan. 21, 1957; children: Thomas A., Katherine M., Rhonda K. BA, U. Minn., 1954. Prodn. mgr. Burgess Pub. Co., Mpls., 1958-88; owner Mori Studio, Mpls., from 1962. Illustrator: Let's Say Poetry Together, 1964, Let's Say Poetry Together Vol. II, 1966; inventor ski storage rack; cartoons published in Stars & Stripes newspaper, 1955-56. Pres. Risers Breakfast Club, Mpls., 1973. Maj. U.S. Army, 1955-57, USAR, 1957-78. Mem. Midwest Ind. Pubs. Assn., Minn. Book Builders, Masons, Scottish Rite, Zuhrah Shriners, Am. Legion. Republican. Lutheran. Avocations: photography, video production, computers. Home: Fountain Hls, Ariz. Died Dec. 1, 2006.

LUNT, ALAN NICHOLAS, rehabilitation services professional; b. Pitts., Dec. 11, 1955; s. Harry Edward and Carmela Lunt. BA, Rutgers U., 1979; AS, U. Medicine and Dentistry N.J., 1995, MS, 2001. Peer adv. Mental Health Assn. of Morris Co., Madison, NJ, 1995—96, Bridgeway, Elizabeth, NJ, 1995—2003. Contbr. articles to profl. jours. Mem. USPRA, Nat. Alliance for Mentally Ill, Mental Health Assn. of Morris County, N.J. Psychiat. Rehab. Assn. (bd. dir. 1997-2003). Avocation: piano. Home: Boonton, NJ. Died Nov. 9, 2006.

LYLE, LAURA LOUISE, nursing educator; b. Bronx, NY, May 10, 1931; d. William George and Dorothy Louise (Hoyt) Knight; m. John Bruce Lyle Sr., Oct. 30, 1949; children: John Bruce Jr., Steven Robert, Robin Ann Lyle Miller. Diploma in practical nursing, Union County Tech. Inst., 1968; AAS in Nursing Edn., Middlesex County Coll., 1970; BSN, Rutgers U., 1976. Staff nurse Overlook Hosp., Summit, N.J.; dir. nursing Med. Pers. Pool, Morris Plains, N.J.; coordinating instr., ward clk., unit sec. Union County Tech. Inst., Scotch Plains, N.J.; asst. prof. practical nursing Union County Coll., Scotch Plains. Home: Roselle Park, NJ. Died July 22, 2007.

LYNCH, CHARLES STAFFORD, lawyer; b. Tulsa, Aug. 3, 1922; s. Hubert Walter and Girthel May (Ritchie) L.; m. Elizabeth Ann Schruth, Aug. 16, 1943; children: William Stafford, Nancy Elizabeth, Peter Michael Elliott. BS in Chem. Engring., Purdue U., 1943; LLB, George Washington U., 1956. Bar: Va. 1956, D.C. 1960, U.S. Supreme Ct. 1964. Chem. engr. Std. Oil Co., Baton Rouge, 1943-45, Phillips Petroleum Co., Bartlesville, Okla., 1945-53, patent agt. Arlington, Va., 1953-56, patent atty. Bartlesville, 1956-59; patent counsel Owens-Ill. Inc., Toledo, Ohio, 1959-66, asst. dir. patents, 1966-83; patent counsel Std. Oil Ohio and BP Am., Cleve., 1983-93; of counsel Renner, Otto, Boisselle and Sklar, Cleve., from 1993. Patentee in field. Mem. ABA, Am. Intellectual Property Law Assn. Home: Moreland Hls, Ohio. Died Feb. 28, 2007.

LYNCH, WILLIAM LEO, manufacturing executive; b. Rome, NY, Jan. 16, 1932; s. William L. and Anna (Keough) L.; m. Ann C. Peach. BS in Mech. Engring., U. Notre Dame, 1955; MBA, Dartmouth Coll., 1957. Pres., treas. Rome Turney Radiator Co. Bd. dirs. Rome Savings Bank, Indsl. Assn. of the Mohawk Valley, Associated Industries of N.Y. State, Ea. Adv. Bd. Marine Midland Bank - Cen., Blue-Cross-Blue Shield, Utica, N.Y. Bd. dirs. Iroquois Council Boy Scouts Am., Rome United Way; pres. bd. trustees Jervis Library Assn., Rome. Mem. NAM, ASME, ASHRAE, Am. Soc. Metals, U. of Notre Dame Alumni Assn., Dartmouth Alumni Assn., Rome C. of C. Clubs: Teugega Country, Rome (bd. dirs.), Lake Delta Yacht, Yahnundasis Golf, Key Biscayne Yacht. Lodges: Elks, Kiwanis. Home: Rome, NY. Died May 23, 2007.

LYTLE, ROBERT FRANK, lawyer; b. Oberlin, Kans., Nov. 27, 1931; s. Howard Ivan and Sylvia Gladys (Godfrey) L.; m. Shirley June Kurz, Aug. 14, 1954; children: Susan Elizabeth Stewart, Robert F. Jr. Student, U. Kansas City, 1949-52; BA, U. Kans., 1953, LLB, 1955. Bar: Kans., Mo., U.S. Dist. Ct. Mo., U.S. Dist. Ct. Kans., U.S. Ct. Mil. Appeals, U.S. Supreme Ct. Assoc. Mudge, Stern, Baldwin & Todd, NYC, 1955-56; ptnr. Bennett Lytle Wetzler Martin & Pishny and its predecessors, Prairie Village, Kans., from 1958. Coll. atty. Johnson County C.C., Overland Park, 1967—. Editor in chief Kans. Law Rev., 1954-55; contbr. articles to profl. jours. Lt. USAF, 1956-58. Mem. Order of Coif. Presbyterian. Home: Prairie Vlg, Kans. Died Apr. 28, 2007.

MAAS, BARBARA E., nurse, retired, volunteer; b. Milw., July 15, 1933; BSN, U. Wis., Milw., 1965. RN, Wis. Staff nurse Milw. Luth., 1954-58, head nurse, 1958-61, supr., 1961-71; supr. infection control Luth./Good Samaritan, Milw., 1971-80; infection control/discharge planning Good Samaritan, Milw., 1980-88; infection control/utilization review Sinai-Samaritan Med. Ctr., Milw., 1988-93. Editor (newsletter) Rose Hybridizers Assoc., 1985—, Petals and Thorns, 1990—. Mem. Wauwatosa (Wis.) Beautification Com., 1992—. Mem. AAUW, Am. Rose Soc. (dir. 1985—, Outstanding Consulting Rosarian 1981, Silver medal 1984). Lutheran. Avocations: rosarian, travel. Home: Wauwatosa, Wis. Died May 14, 2007.

MABEE, CARLETON, historian, educator; b. Shanghai, Dec. 25, 1914; s. Fred Carleton and Miriam (Bentley) M.; m. Norma Dierking, Dec. 20, 1945; children: Timothy I., Susan (Mrs. Paul Newhouse). AB, Bates Coll., 1936; MA (Perkins scholar), Columbia U., 1938, PhD, 1942. With Civilian Public Svc., 1941-45; instr. history Swarthmore (Pa.) Coll., 1944; tutor Olivet (Mich.) Coll., 1947-49; asst. prof. liberal studies Clarkson Coll. Tech., Potsdam, NY, 1949-51, assoc. prof., 1951-55, prof., 1955-61; dir. social studies divsn. Delta Coll., University Center, Mich., 1961-64; prof., chmn. dept. humanities and social scis. Rose Poly. Inst., Terre Haute, Ind., 1964-65; prof. history State U. Coll. at New Paltz, NY, 1965-80, prof. emeritus NY, 1980—2014. Participant in projects for American Friends Svc. Com., 1941-47, 53, 63; Fulbright prof. Keio U., Tokyo, 1953-54 Author: The American Leonardo, A Life of Samuel F.B. Morse, 1943, The Seaway Story, 1961, Black Freedom: The Nonviolent Abolitionists from 1830 through the Civil War, 1970, Black Education in New York State: From Colonial to Modern Times, 1979, (with Susan Mabee Newhouse) Sojourner Truth: Slave, Prophet, Legend, 1993, Listen to the Whistle: An Ancedotal History of the Wallkill Valley Railroad in Ulster and Orange Counties, N.Y., 1995; editor: (with James A. Fletcher) A Quaker Speaks from the Black Experience: The Life and Selected Writings of Barrington Dunbar, 1979, Bridging the Hudson: The Poughkeepsie Railroad Bridge and its Connecting Rail Lines, a Many-Faceted History, 2001, Gardiner and Lake Minnewaska, 2003, Promised Land: Father Divine's Interracial Cmtys. in Ulster County, NY, 2008, Gardiner Library: Its Beginning, Its Growing Energy, Its Struggle For Space, 2009; contbr. articles to profl. jours. Trustee Young-Morse Hist. Site, Poughkeepsie, N.Y., 1991-2002; ofcl. town historian, Gardiner, N.Y. Recipient Pulitzer Prize in Biography, 1944, Bergstein award for excellence in tchg. Delta Coll., 1963, Anisfield-Wolf award race rels., 1971, Gustavus Myers award for Outstanding Book on Human Rights, 1994, M. L. King award Ulster County Mins. Alliance, 2010; rsch. grantee Rsch. Found. SUNY, 1965, 67, 68, 80, American Philos. Soc., 1970, Nat. Inst. Edn., 1973-76, NSF, 1982-83. Mem. N.Y. State Hist. Assn., Phi Beta Kappa, Delta Sigma Rho. Methodist. Home: Gardiner, NY. Died Dec. 18, 2014.

MACAULEY, CHARLES CAMERON, media appraiser, consultant; b. Grand Rapids, Mich., Oct. 20, 1923; s. George William and Emma Ann (Hobart) M.; m. Marianne Shirley Johanson, June, 1951; children: Gavin Keith, Alison Jean. BA, Kenyon Coll., Gambier, Ohio, 1949; MS, U. Wis., 1958. Ptnr. Cameron-King Photographers, Gambier, 1946-49; film producer U. Wis., Madison, 1951-58, U. Calif., Berkeley, 1959-63, dir. statewide media ctr., 1964-83; pres. CCM Assocs., El Cerrito, Calif., from 1984. Prof. U. Wis., Calif., 1951-83; sr. founding cons. Media Appraisal Cons., El Cerrito, 1986—; instr. film seminar San Francisco Art Inst., 1959-60; awards juror numerous nat. and internat. film and video festivals, 1953—. West coast corr. The Appraiser; producer over 50 motion pictures; contbr. numerous articles, essays and fictional works to publs. With USN, 1943-46. NSF grantee, 1959-64, NEA grantee, 1974, 76, Maurice Falk Med. Fund grantee, 1970; recipient Gold Ribbon award Am. Film and Video Festival, 1991. Mem. Appraisers Assn. Am., Ednl. Film Libr. Assn. (pres. 1973-74), Am. Film and Video Assn. (life), Consortium Coll. and Univ. Media Ctrs. (life), Fossils, Inc., History of Photography Group, Square Riggers Club (historian 1989—, hon. 1989—). Avocations: genealogy, photographic history, writing, tv, reading. Home: El Cerrito, Calif. Died May 17, 2007.

MACDOUGALL, HARTLAND MOLSON, retired bank executive; b. Montreal, Que., Can., Jan. 28, 1931; s. Hartland Campbell and Dorothy (Molson) MacD.; m. Eve Gordon, Oct. 29, 1954; children: Cynthia, Wendy, Keith, Willa, Tania. Student, LeRosey, Switzerland, 1947-48, McGill U., 1949-53, Advanced Mgmt. Program, Harvard U., 1976. With Bank Montreal, various locations, 1953-84, dir., 1974, vice chmn., 1981; chmn., dir. Royal Trustco Ltd., Toronto, 1984-93. Dep. chmn. London Ins. Group, Inc., London Life Ins. Co., 1985-97; chmn. emeritus, dir. Robert T. Jones Jr. Can. Scholarship Found. Founding chmn. Heritage Can., St. Michael's Hosp. Found., The Japan Soc.; past chmn. Can.-Japan Bus. Com.; gov., past pres. Coun. Can. Unity; past pres. Royal Agrl. Winter Fair; advisor Can. Sports Hall of Fame; bd. govs. Can. Olympic Found.; sen. Stratford Shakespearean Found.; former chmn. The Duke of Edinburgh Awards Internat. Coun.; v.p., dir. The Macdonald Stewart Found. Decorated Order of Can., comdr. Royal Victorian Order, Order of the Rising Sun, Gold and Silver Star (Japan); recipient Gabrielle Leger medal, 1978. Avocations: golf, tennis. Home: Belfountain, Canada. Deceased.

MACK, ALICE D., investment advisor; b. Canton, China, Aug. 14, 1932; arrived in U.S., 1932; m. Robert Mack; children: Stephen, Phylis, Samsm, Fontaive. PhD, 1962. Chemistry Mt. Sinas Hosp., San Francisco; health Naval relief, from 1947. Died Apr. 10, 2007.

MACK, RICHARD G., mathematician, consultant; s. Emil and Rose Machacek; m. Dolores Prusinski, Dec. 27, 1958; children: Richard, Nancy Holder, Robert, Sharon. BS in Edn., U. Cin., 1957; MS in Edn., U. Akron, Ohio, 1970. Cert. assessment for learning facilitator Assessment Tng. Inst., instr. ratios Lesson Lab. Tchr. Cleve. City Schs., 1957—64, Independence Local Sch., Ohio, 1964—91; curriculum dir. Parma City Schs., Ohio, 1991—2005; math. cons. Smart Consortium, Cleve., from 2005. Workshop facilitator Ednl. Rsch. Coun. Am., Cleve., 1970—73. Author: Educational Research Council, 1971, Ohio Math Academy Program, 2004. Mem.: Ohio Coun. Tchrs. Math., Nat. Coun. Tchrs. Math. Died Aug. 4, 2007.

MACKAY, DONALD N., physician; b. Stonington, Maine, July 29, 1934; s. Gordon and Helen Lake (Noyes) MacK.; m. Sandra Jean Schon, Sept. 11, 1959; children: Nancy MacKay Green, Susan Schon, Sandra Noyes. AB magna cum laude, Dartmouth Coll., 1956; MD, Cornell U., 1960. Diplomate in internal medicine and infectious diseases Am. Bd. Internal Medicine. Intern N.Y. Hosp., 1960-61, resident, 1961-63, chief resident NYC, 1963-64; chief of infectious disease Dartmouth-Hitchcock Med. Ctr., Hanover, N.H., 1966-88; internist Stanford (Calif.) U. Med. Sch., 1988-98. Capt. U.S. Army, 1964-66. Fellow ACP (bd. govs. 1980-84). Democrat. Avocation: sailing. Died Apr. 28, 2007.

MACLEOD, ANGUS, retired internist; b. Romford, Essex, Eng., Apr. 24, 1943; came to U.S., 1967; s. Malcolm Macleod and Jean (Littlefair) McKean; m. Gwynne Louise Grellner, May 23, 1969 (div. Aug. 1987); children: Kenneth, Anne, Stephen; m. Betty Durante (Dees), Oct. 23, 2009. MB, ChB, Glasgow U., 1967. Diplomate Am. Bd. Internal Medicine. Intern Luth. Hosp., St. Louis, 1967—68; resident in internal medicine St. Louis U., 1969, 1971—73, fellow in cardiology, 1973—74; physician Grandel Med. Group, St. Louis, 1974—2000, ret., 2000. Instr., then asst. prof. medicine St. Louis U.; chmn. dept. medicine Lutheran Hosp., St. Louis; pres. Grandel Med. Group, St. Louis. Capt. U.S. Army, 1969-71. Decorated Bronze Star. Fellow: ACP; mem.: St. Louis Met. Med. Soc., Mo. State Med. Soc. Home: Poplar Bluff, Mo. Died Mar. 1, 2013.

MACNEE, (DANIEL) PATRICK, actor; b. London, Feb. 6, 1922; s. Daniel and Doratisea Mary (Henry) M.; m. Kate Woodwille, 1965 (div. 1969); m. Baba Majos de Nagyzsebyem Feb. 25, 1988 (dec. 2007); children: Rupert, Jenny Student, Webber Douglas Academy Dramatic Art, 1940. Appearances include (theatre) in Eng., 1939-42, 46-52, in Can. and U.S., 1952-60, (films) The Life and Death Colonel Blimp, 1945, Dead of Night, 1946, The Fatal Night, 1948, All Over The Town, 1949, Hour of Glory, 1949, The Fighting Pimpernel, 1950, The Girl Is Mine, 1950, Dick Barton At Bay, 1950, The Fighting Pimpernel, 1950, A Christmas Carol, 1951, Flesh and Blood, 1951, Three Cases of Murder, 1955, of the Graf Spee, 1956, Until They Sail, 1957, Les Girls, 1957, Pursuit Mission of Danger, 1959,

Incense for the Damned, 1970, King Solomon's Treasure, 1979, Dick Turpin, 1980, The Hot Touch, 1981, The Howling, 1981, The Sea Wolves, 1980, Young Doctors in Love, 1982, The Creature Wasn't Nice, 1983, Sweet Sixteen, 1983, This Is Spinal Tap, 1984, Shadey, 1985, A View to a Kill, 1985, For the Term of His Natural Life, 1985, Transformations, 1988, Waxwork, 1988, The Chill Factor, 1989, Lobster Man From Mars, 1989, Masque of the Red Death, 1989, Eye of the Widow, 1991, A Stroke of Luck, Incident at Victoria Falls, 1991, Waxwork II: Lost'n Time, 1992, King B: A Life in the Movies, 1993, The Avengers (voice), 1998, The Low Budget Time Machine, 2003 (TV series) The Avengers, 1961-69, The New Avengers, 1978-80, Battlestar Galactica, 1978-79, Gavilan, 1982-83, Empire. 1984, Lime Street, 1985, Tales from the Darkside, 1985, P.S.I. Luv U, 1991, Super Force 1990-92, Thunder in Paradise, 1994, (mini-series) The Veil, 1958, Around the World in 80 Days, 1989, (TV movies) Arms and the Man, 1946, A Month in the Country, 1947, The Brontes, 1947, Hamlet, 1947, Wuthering Heights, 1948, Macbeth, 1949, Myself a Stranger, 1949, Ten Minute Alibi, 1950, The Strange Case of Dr. Jekyll and Mr. Hyde, 1950, Nocturne in Scotland, 1951, The Affair at Assino, 1953, Shadow of a Pale Horse, 1960, The Hill, 1960, The Winter's Tale, 1962, Mister Jerico, 1970, The Women I Love, 1972, Sherlock Holmes in New York, 1976, Dead of Night, 1977, Evening in Byzantium, 1978, The Billion Dollar Threat, 1979, The Fantastic Seven, 1979, Comedy of Horrors, 1981, Rehearsal for Murder, 1982, Likely Stories, Vol. 2, 1983, The Return of the Man From U.N.C.L.E.: The Fifteen Years Later Affair, 1983, For the Term of His Natural Life, 1983, Club Med, 1986, Where There's a Will, 1989, Sorry, Wrong Number, 1989, Dick Francis: Blood Sport, 1989, Super Force, 1990, The Gambler Returns: The Luck of the Draw, 1991, Sherlock Holmes and the Leading Lady, 1991, Incident at Victoria Falls, 1992, The Hound of London, 1993, Nightman, 1997, Nancherrow, 1999; guest appearances Tales of Adventure, 1952-53, BBC Sunday-Night Theatre, 1950-53, Scope, 1955, CBC Summer Theatre, 1955, Producers' Showcase, 1956, Armstrong Circle Theatre, 1956, Star Tonight, 1956, Playwrights '56, 1956, The Alcoa Hour, 1956, Pacific 13, 1957, First Performances, 1957, Schlitz Playhouse, 1958, On Camera, 1955-58, Suspicion, 1958, Matinee Theatre, 1956-58, Kraft Theatre, 1956-58, Studio One in Hollywood, 1958, Northwest Passage, 1958, Alcoa Theatre, 1958, The United States Steel Hour, 1959, Black Saddle, 1959, Alcoa Presents: One Step Beyond, 1959, Folio, 1955-59, General Electric Theater, 1959, Markham, 1959, Alfred Hitchcock Presents, 1959, 1988, Walt Disney's Wonderful World of Color, 1959, Playhouse 90, 1959, Twilight Zone, 1959, Adventures in Paradise, 1959, The Unforeseen, 1960, Startime, 1960, Encounter, 1953-60, ITV Play of the Week, 1960, Thursday Theatre, 1964, Conflict, 1966, Love Story, 1964-66, Armchair Theatre, 1960-66, The Virginian, 1970, Alias Smith and Jones, 1971, Night Gallery, 1971, Diana, 1973, Great Mysteries, 1974, Dial M for Murder, 1974, Columbo, 1975, Kahn!, 1975, Caribe, 1975, Matt Helm, 1975, The Hardy Boys/Nancy Drew Mysteries, 1978, $weepstake$, 1979, The Littlest Hobo, 1980, Vega$, 1981, Dick Turpin, 1981, House Calls, 1981, Automan, 1983, Empire, 1984, Magnum P.I., 1984, Hart to Hart, 1984, The Love Boat, 1984, Hotel, 1985, Mary, 1986, Blacke's Magic, 1986, Lime Street, 1985-86, Murphy's Law,1988, War of the Worlds, 1989, The Ray Bradbury Theatre, 1990, DreamOn, 1992, Murder, She Wrote, 1985-92, Coach, 1992, Jack's Place, 1993, King Fu: The Legend Continues, 1993-94, Diagnosis Murder, 1997, Spy Game, 1997-98, Family Law, 2000, Frasier, 2001; author: (with Marie Cameron) Blind in One Ear, 1988. 1st lt. Brit. Navy, 1942-46. Recipient Variety Artist award of Gt. Britain, 1963. Mem. Actors Equity, AFTRA, Screen Actors Guild, Assn. Can. TV and Radio Artists. Home: Rancho Mirage, Calif. Died June 25, 2015.

MACRAE, DONALD ALEXANDER, astronomy educator; b. Halifax, Nova Scotia, Can., Feb. 19, 1916; s. Donald Alexander and Laura Geddes (Barnstead) M.; m. Margaret Elizabeth Malcolm, Aug. 25, 1939; children— David Malcolm, Charles Donald, Andrew Richard. BA, U. Toronto, Ont., Can., 1937; A.M., Harvard U., Cambridge, Mass., 1940, PhD, 1943. Research asst. U. Pa., Phila., 1941-42; lectr. Cornell U., Ithaca, N.Y., 1942-44; scientist Carbide & Carbon Chem. Corp., Oak Ridge, Tenn., 1944-46; asst. prof. Case Inst. Tech., Cleve., 1946-53; assoc. prof. to prof. astronomy, dir. David Dunlap Observatory, U. Toronto, 1953-78, prof. and dir. emeritus, from 1978. Trustee Univs. Space Research Assn., Lunar and Planetary Inst., Houston, 1969-76, Can.-France-Hawaii Telescope Corp., Kamuela, Hawaii, 1973-79, Cascatrust, 1991-94. Fellow Royal Soc. Can., Royal Astron. Soc. (London); mem. Can. Astron. Soc., Royal Astron. Soc. Can., Am. Astron. Soc. Home: Toronto, Canada. Died Dec. 6, 2006.

MACY, BRUCE WENDELL, research institute executive; b. Oskaloosa, Iowa, Oct. 16, 1930; s. Loring Kenneth and Juanita Louise (Holdsworth) M.; m. Elizabeth Ann Ross, July15, 1954; children: Janet Lynn, David Loring. Student, U. Md., College Park, 1948-50; BS, Iowa State U., 1952, MS, 1954. Rsch. assoc. Coll. Bus. U. Md., College Park, 1955-58; from assoc. economist ot dep. dir. Econs. and Mgmt. Scis. Midwest Rsch. Inst., Kansas City, Mo., 1958-80, dir. Ctr. for Technoecons., 1980-82, dir. Internat. Programs, from 1982. Contbr. numerous articles to profl. jours. Home: Shawnee Mission, Kans. Died May 23, 2007.

MADDOX, ROGER WAYNE, minister; b. Sayre, Okla., Apr. 22, 1950; s. Earnest Clifford and Wilma Nell (Walkup) M.; m. Judith Ellen Mann, Aug. 23, 1968; 1 child, Deidra. AA in Gen. Edn., Sayre Jr. Coll., 1970; BA in Comml. Art, Southwestern Okla. State U., 1972, MEd in Art Edn., 1982; MDiv, Southwestern Bapt. Theol. Sem., 1989, postgrad., from 1994. Ordained to ministry So. Bapt. Ch., 1989. Cert. tchr. Okla., 1979, Tex., 1987. Evangelist Wedgwood Bapt. Ch., Ft. Worth, 1984-86; Mardi Gras evangelist New Orleans, 1985-86; physical plant journeyman Southwestern Bapt. Theol. Sem., Ft. Worth, 1984-87; mission pastor Wedgwood Bapt. Ch. to Oak Park Chapel, Ft. Worth, 1985-86; pastor First Bapt. Ch., Arnett, Okla., 1989-93, Pleasant Glade Bapt. Ch., Colleyville, Tex., from 1994. Exhibited in jurored shows, 1982; represented in Shorney Art Gallery, 1981-97. Recipient Excellence in Teaching award Ft. Worth Ind. Sch. Dist., 1987-89; featured artist Art Gallery Mag., 1982. Mem. Am. Acad. Religion, Soc. Bibl. Lit., Inst. for Bibl. Rsch., Evang. Theol. Soc. Republican. Home: Fort Worth, Tex. Died Jan. 12, 2007.

MAGID, LEE, video and recording producer, manager, composer, lyricist; b. NYC, Apr. 6, 1926; s. Abraham and Clara Magid; divorced; children: Diane, Deborah, Adam, Andrea. Grad. high sch., Bronx, NY, 1944. Produced for Decca, Jubilee, RCA, ABC, Bluesway, Dawn, LMI, others, 1946-2000; artist, repetoire Nat. Records, NYC, 1947-49, Savoy Records, Newark, 1950-53; pres. Lee Magid Inc., Malibu, Calif., 1967-99. Theatrical mgr., N.Y.C. and Calif., 1952—; music bus. cons., L.A., 1963-97; video and record producer, N.Y.C., 1944-97; developer careers of Della Reese, Lou Rawls, O.C. Smith, Al Hibbler, Tramaine Hawkins, Earl Grant, others. Prodr.: (video) Tramaine Hawkins Live, 1990 (Grammy and Dove awards 1991), Joy That Floods My Soul (Grammy and Dove awards 1989), Sparrow Records, LMI, Grass Roots Records; author, prodr. (theatre play): I Sing Because I'm Happy, the Devil, The Blues and The Gospel Queen; prodr. film based on life of Mahalia Jackson; writer: Top 1953 R&B Song Hit, "I Played The Fool". Mem. ASCAP, BMI, SESAC. Died Mar. 31, 2007.

MAGLARAS, NICHOLAS GEORGE, lawyer; b. NYC, Apr. 21, 1951; s. George Nicholas and Angelica (Alexander) M. BA in Econs. cum laude, CUNY, Queens, 1973; JD, Fordham U., 1976. Bar: N.Y. 1977, U.S. Dist. Ct. (so. and ea. dists.) N.Y. 1977, U.S. Ct. Appeals (4th and 5th cirs.) 1983, U.S. Supreme Ct. 1985, U.S. Ct. Appeals (11th cir.) 1990, U.S. Ct. Appeals (2d cir.) 1991. Ptnr. Lambos & Junge, NYC, from 1976. Co-author: The Needs of the Growing Greek-American Community in the City of New York, 1973. Mem. ABA, N.Y. State Bar Assn., N.Y. County Lawyers Assn. Democrat. Greek Orthodox. Avocations: dance, softball, meteorology. Home: Astoria, NY. Died Dec. 30, 2006.

MAGUIRE, CHARLOTTE EDWARDS, retired pediatrician; b. Richmond, Ind., Sept. 1, 1918; d. Joel Blaine and Lydia (Betscher) Edwards; m. Raymer Francis Maguire, Sept. 1, 1948 (dec.); children: Barbara, Thomas Clair II (dec.). Student, Stetson U., 1936—38, U. Wichita, 1938—39; BS, Memphis Tchrs. Coll., 1940; MD, U. Ark., 1944; LHD (hon.), Fla. State U., 2002. Intern, resident Orange Meml. Hosp., Orlando, Fla., 1944—46, med. staff., 1944—69, instr. nurses, 1947—57; resident Bellevue Hosp. and Med. Ctr., NYU, NYC, 1954—55; staff mem. Fla. Santarium and Hosp., Orlando, 1946—56, Holiday House and Hosp., Orlando, 1950—62; mem. courtesy and cons. staff West Orange Meml. Hosp., Winter Garden, Fla., 1952—67; active staff, chief dept. pediat. Mercy Hosp., Orlando, 1965—68; med. dir. childrens med. svcs., asst. sec. Fla. Dept. Health and Rehab. Svcs., 1969—71, med. dir. med. svcs. and basic care, 1975—84; med. exec. dir., med. svcs. divsn. worker's compensation Fla. Dept. Labor, Tallahassee, 1984—87; chief of staff physicians and dentists Ctrl. Fla. divsn. Children's Home Soc. Fla., 1947—56; dir. Orlando Child Health Clinic, 1949—58; pvt. practice Orlando, 1946—68; asst. regional dir. HEW, 1970—72; ret., 1987. Asst. dir. health and sci. affairs Dept. Health Edn. & Welfare, Atlanta, 1971-72, Washington, 1972-75; pediat. cons. Fla. Crippled Children's Commn., 1952-70, dir., 1968-70; med. dir. Office Med. Svcs. and Basic Care, sr. physician Office of Asst. Sec. Ops., Fla. Dept. Health and Rehab. Svcs.; clin. prof. dept. pediat. U. Fla. Coll. Medicine, Gainesville, 1980-87; mem. Fla. Drug Utilization Rev., 1983-87; real estate salesperson Investors Realty, 1982-2003; bd. dirs. Stavros Econ. Ctr. Fla. State U., Tallahassee; pres.'s coun. Fla. State U., U. Fla., Gainesville; Charlotte Edwards Maguire eminent scholar chair and scholarships for qualified students, 1999. Mem. profl. adv. com. Fla. Ctr. for Clin. Svcs. at U. Fla., 1952-60; del. to Mid-century White House Conf. on Children and Youth, 1950; U.S. del from Nat. Soc. for Crippled Children to World Congress for Welfare of Cripples, Inc., London, 1957; pres. of corp. Eccleston-Callahan Hosp. for Colored Crippled Children, 1956-58; sec. Fla. chpt. Nat. Doctor's Com. for Improved Med. Svcs., 1951-52; med. adv. com. Gateway Sch. for Mentally Retarded, 1959-62; bd. dirs. Forest Park Sch. for Spl. Edn. Crippled Children, 1949-54, mem. med. adv. com., 1955-68, chmn., 1957-68; mem. Fla. Adv. Coun. for Mentally Retarded, 1965-70; dir. ctrl. Fla. poison control Orange Meml. Hosp.; mem. orgn. com., chmn. com. for admissions and selection policies Camp Challenge; participant 12th session Fed. Exec. Inst., 1971; del. White House Conf. on Aging, 1980; dir. Stavros Econ. Ctr. Fla. State U.; trustee Fla. State U. Found., 1998—, mem. campaign com. Charlotte Edwards Maguire Eminent Scholarship named in her honor Fla. State U., Charlotte Edwards Maguire MLS Med. Libr., Fla. State U. Coll. Medicine named in her honor, 2005; named Outstanding Woman in Our Cmty. AAUW, Tallahassee, 2002; recipient David M. Solomon Disting. Pub. Svc. award Am. Geriatric Soc., 2005, Torch award Fla. State U., 2005. Mem. AMA (life), Nat. Rehab. Assn., Am. Congress Phys. Medicine and Rehab., Fla. Soc. Crippled Children and Adults, Ctrl. Fla. Soc. Crippled Children and Adults (dir. 1949-58, pres. 1956-57), Am. Assn. Cleft Palate, Fla. Soc. Crippled Children (trustee 1951-57, v.p. 1956-57, profl. adv. com. 1957-68), Mental Health Assn. Orange County (charter mem.; pres. 1949-50, dir. 1947-52, chmn. exec. com. 1950-52, dir. 1963-65), Fla. Orange County Heart Assn., Am. Med. Women's Assn., Am. Acad. Med. Dirs., Fla. Med. Assn. (life, chmn. com. on mental retardation), Orange County Med. Assn., Orange Med. Soc. (life), Fla. Pediat. Soc. (pres. 1952-53), Fla. Cleft Palate Assn. (counselor-at-large, sec.), Nat. Inst. Geneal. Rsch., Nat. Geneal. Soc., Assn. Profl. Genealogists, Tallahassee Geneal. Soc., Fla. State U. Found. Inc. (bd. dirs. Stavoris Ctr. for Econ. Edn.), Capital City Tiger Bay Club, Fla. Econs. Club, Francis Eppes Soc. Fla. State U., Econ. Club Fla., Governors Club. Deceased.

MAGUIRE, JOSEPH FRANCIS, bishop emeritus; b. Boston, Sept. 4, 1919; Student, Boston Coll., St. John's Sem., Boston. Ordained priest Archdiocese of Boston, 1945; ordained monsignor, 1964; asst. pastor St. Joseph Ch., Lynn, Mass., St. Anne Ch., Readville, Mass., Blessed Sacrament Ch., Jamaica Plain, Mass., St. Mary Ch., Milton, Mass.; sec. to Cardinal Cushing Boston, 1962-70; sec. to Archbishop Medeiros, 1970-71; ordained bishop, 1972; aux. bishop Diocese of Boston, 1972—76; coadjutor bishop Diocese of Springfield, Mass., 1976-77, bishop, 1977-91, bishop emeritus, 1991—2014. Roman Catholic. Home: Springfield, Mass. Died Nov. 23, 2014.

MAHON, KATHERINE A. (KIT MAHON), public relations executive, writer; d. Thomas Patrick Mahon and Winifred Marie Collins. BA, Hunter Coll., NYC; postgrad., Columbia U., NYU. Dir. fundraising and pub. rels. Girl Scout Coun. Greater NY, NYC, 1956—69; dir. comm. Girls Club Am., NYC, 1968—77; supr. Campbell Soup Co., Camden, NJ, 1977—91. Dir. pubs. rels. Fedn. Protestant Welfare Agys., NYC, 1959—66. Mem.: Women Execs. Pub. Rels., Pub. Rels. Soc. Am. (NY chpt. publicity com.). Home: Maple Shade, NJ. Died Feb. 12, 2007.

MAIERHAUSER, JOSEPH GEORGE, entrepreneur; b. Yankton, SD, Mar. 23, 1927; s. Joseph and Angela M. (Jung) M.; m. Reta Mae Brockelsby, Nov. 25, 1948 (div. 1965); 1 child, Joe; m. Martha Helen Kuehn, Dec. 10, 1965. Student, U. S.D., Vermillion, 1946, S.D. Sch. Mines and Tech., Rapid City, 1947. Sales mgr. Black Hills Reptile Gardens, Rapid City, S.D., 1949-54; operator Colossal Cave Park, Vail, Ariz., from 1956; ptnr. Sta. KRNR, Roseburg, Oreg., from 1961. Mem. adv. bd. Salvation Army, Tucson, 1979-86; govs. appointee San Pedro Rparian Nat. Cons. Area Adv. Com., 1989—; past pres. So. Ariz. Internat. Livestock Assn., 1987-88; bd. dirs. Friends of Western Art., Tucson; co-founder Pima County Parklands Found. With U.S. Navy Air Corps., 1944-45. Mem. Mountain Oyster Club (pres. 1989-91, bd. dirs. 1980-83). Republican. Avocation: conservation. Home: Vail, Ariz. Died Mar. 7, 2007.

MAJOROS, FERENC, food service specialist; b. Felsőgagy, Hungary, Aug. 19, 1941; came to U.S., 1968; s. Béla and Rozália (Pálinkás) M.; m. Maria Solc, Feb. 17, 1977; 1 child, Frank. Grad., Elelmiszer Ipari, Zemplén, Hungary, 1958. Meat cutter Heinens, Mentor, Ohio, from 1969. With Hungarian Army, 1960-65. Roman Catholic. Avocation: soccer. Home: Mentor, Ohio. Died Dec. 5, 2006.

MAKI, JOHN MCGILVREY, educator; b. Tacoma, Wash., Nov. 19, 1909; s. Alexander and Amanda (Bradley) McGilvrey; m. Mary Mariko Yasumura, Oct. 18, 1936 (dec. 1990); children: John Alexander, James Perry. BA, U. Wash., Seattle, 1932; MA, U. Wash., 1936; PhD, Harvard U., 1948; LLD, Hokkaido U., Japan, 1976. Assoc. U. Wash., Seattle, 1939-42; propaganda analyst FCC, Washington, 1942-43; with Office of War Info., Washington, 1943-45; civilian cons. Gen. Hdqrs. Supreme Comdr. for Allied Powers, Tokyo, 1946; from asst. prof. to prof. U. Wash., Seattle, 1948-66; prof. U. Mass., Amherst, 1966-80, vice dean arts and scis., 1967-71, prof. emeritus, from 1980. Author: Japanese Militarism: Cause and Cure, 1945, Government and Politics in Japan, 1962; editor/translator: Court and Constitution in Japan, 1964, Japan's Commission on the Constitution: The Final Report, 1980. Bd. dirs. Hampshire Community United Way, Northampton, Mass., 1981-90. Decorated Order of the Sacred Treasure (Japan). Mem. AAUP, New Eng. Conf. of Assn. for Asian Studies (pres. 1975-76), Assn. for Asian Studies. Home: Amherst, Mass. Died Dec. 7, 2006.

MAKOWSKI, ROBERT JOHN, human services executive, lawyer; b. Milw., Mar. 29, 1926; s. John J. and Rose Clara (Rozga) M.; m. Arleen Lois Jeka, Aug. 25, 1956; children: Robert J., Mary Lois. BPh cum laude, Marquette U., 1949, JD, 1950. Bar: Wis. 1950, U.S. Dist. Ct. (ea. dist.) Wis. 1950. Assoc. Foley & Lardner, Milw., 1950-53; sec. Miller Brewing Co., Milw., 1953-66; asst. prof. Sch. of Law Marquette U., Milw., 1966-68; exec. v.p. John Conway Ascos., Inc., Milw., 1968-80; pres., sponsor svcs. Wheaton (Ill.) Franciscan Svcs., Inc., from 1980. Sec., bd. dirs. Assisi Homes of Wis., Inc., Milw., 1988—; treas., bd. dirs. Franciscan Ministries, Inc., Wheaton, 1983—; v.p., bd. dirs. Wheaton Franciscan Svcs., Inc., 1983—; chair, bd. dirs. Clara Pfaender Fund, Inc., Wheaton, 1989—. Contbr. articles to profl. jours. Friend Milw. Art Mus., 1990—, Mils. Mus., 1990—, Performing Arts Ctr., Milw., 1990—; mem. com. Milw. Neighborhood Partnership, Inc., 1990—. Me. Wis. Bar Assn. Roman Catholic. Home: New Berlin, Wis. Died Oct. 24, 2006.

MALINA, JUDITH, actress, director, producer, writer; b. Kiel, Germany, June 4, 1926; came to U.S., 1945; d. Max and Rosel (Zamora) M.; m. Julian Beck, Oct. 30, 1948 (dec.); m. Hanon Reznikov, May 6, 1988; children—Garrick Maxwell, Isha Manna. Graduate, Dramatic Workshop, New Sch. Social Research, 1945-47. Adj. prof. Columbia U. Co-founder with husband Julian Beck, producer, actress, dir. The Living Theatre, 1947-2015; dir., actress: The Thirteenth God, Childish Jokes, Ladies Voices, He Who Says Yes and He Who Says No, The Dialogue of the Mannequin and the Young Man, 1951, Man Is Man, 1962, Mysteries and Smaller Pieces, 1964, Antigone, 1965, Paradise Now, 1968, The Legacy of Cain (including Seven Meditations on Political Sadomasochism), 1970-77, Strike Support Oratorium, 1974, Six Public Acts, The Money Tower, 1975, Prometheus, 1978, Masse Mensch, 1980, The Living Theatre Retrospectacle, 1986, The Zero Method, 1991; dir.: Doctor Faustus Lights the Lights, 1951, Desire Trapped by the Tail, Faustina, Sweeney Agonistes, The Heroes, Ubu the King, 1952, The Age of Anxiety, The Spook Sonata, Orpheus, 1954, The Connection, 1959, In the Jungle of Cities, 1960, The Apple, 1961, The Mountain Giants 1962, The Brig, 1963, The Maids, Frankenstein, 1965, The Archeology of Sleep, 1983, Kassandra, 1987, Us, 1987, VKTMS, 1988, I and I, 1989, German Requiem, 1990, Not in My Name, 1994; actress: The Idiot King, 1954, Tonight We Improvise, Phedre, The Young Disciple, 1955, Many Loves, The Cave at Machpelah, 1959, Women of Trachis, 1960, The Yellow Methuselah, 1982, Poland/1931, 1988, Anarchia, 1993; appeared in films: Flaming Creatures, 1962, Amore, Amore, 1966, Wheel of Ashes, 1967, Le Compromise, 1968, Etre Libre, 1968, Paradise Now, 1969, Dog Day Afternoon, 1974, Signals Through the Flames, 1983, Radio Days, 1986, China Girl, 1987, Lost Paradise, 1988, Enemies, A Love Story, 1989, Awakenings, 1990, The Addams Family, 1991, Household Saints, 1993, Men Lie, 1994, Looking for Richard, 1996; author: Paradise Now, 1971, The Enormous Despair, 1972, The Legacy of Cain (3 pilot projects), 1973, Seven Meditations on Political Sadomasochism, 1977, Living Means Theater, 1978, Theatre Diaries: Brazil and Bologna, 1978, Poems of a Wandering Jewess, 1983, The Diaries of Judith Malina 1947-57, 1984, The Piscator Notebook, 2012; translator: Antigone (B. Brecht), 1990. Vice chmn. U.S. Com. for Justice to Latin Am. Polit. Prisoners, 1973-74; sponsor Am. Friends of Brazil, 1973; mem. exec. coun. War Resisters League. Recipient Lola D'Annunzio award, 1959, Page One award Newspaper Guild, 1960, Obie awards, 1960, 1964, 1969, 1975, 87, 89, Grand Prix de Theatre des Nations, 1961, Paris Critics Circle medallion, 1961, Prix de l'Universite Paris, 1961, New Eng. Theatre Conf. award, 1962, Olympio prize Italy, 1967, 9th Centennial medal U. Bologna, Italy, 1988; named Humanist of the Yr., 1984; Guggenheim fellow, 1985. Died Apr. 10, 2015.

MALOHN, DONALD A., manufacturing executive, retired; b. South Bend, Ind., Mar. 26, 1928; s. Harry A. and Opal (Baker) M.; m Myla Claire Lockwood, Feb. 9, 1948; 1 child, Chris. BSEE, Tri-State U., Angola, Ind., 1952. Engr. jet engine div. Studebaker Corp., South Bend, Ind., 1952-54; prodn. rsch. engr. Ford Motor Co., Dearborn, Mich., 1954-61; sr. analytical engr. Solar, San Diego, 1961-62; dept. mgr. Sundstrand Aviation, Denver, 1962-66; asst. dir. engring. Ai Rsch. Mfg. Co., Phoenix, 1966-78; exec. v.p. Tiernay Turbines, Phoenix, 1978-94. Inventor: five patents, 1963; contbr. tech. jours. Mem. ASME, Am.Soc. Metals, Soc. Automotive Engrs., Life Mem. Soc. Republican. Avocations: reading, woodcraft. Home: Scottsdale, Ariz. Died June 5, 2007.

MALONE, MOSES EUGENE, retired professional basketball player; b. Petersburg, Va., Mar. 23, 1955; m. Alfreda Malone (div. 1992); 2 children. Mem. Utah Stars, American Basketball Assn., 1974-75, St. Louis Spirits, American Basketball Assn., 1975-76, Buffalo Braves, 1976, Houston Rockets, Nat. Basketball Assn., 1976-82, Phila. 76ers, 1982—86, 1993—94, Washington Bullets, 1986-88, Atlanta Hawks, 1988-91, Milw. Bucks, 1991—93, San Antonio Spurs, 1994—95. Named to ABA All-Rookie Team, 1975, All NBA First Team, 1979, 82, 83, 85, NBA All-Def. First Team, 1983, NBA MVP, 1979, 82, 83, NBA Finals MVP, 1983, All-Star Team, 1978-88, Basketball Hall of Fame, 2001 Died Sept. 13, 2015.

MALONEY, PAUL KEATING, urologist; b. Bklyn., Oct. 24, 1934; s. Paul Keating and Mary Veronica (Shanahan) M.; m. Maureen Christie Murphy, Dec. 5, 1964; children: Jennifer Maloney Seka, Paula, Edward. BS in Biology, Coll. of Holy Cross, Worcester, Mass., 1956; MD, Georgetown U., 1960. Intern, resident in surgery St. Vincent's Hosp., NYC, 1960-62; resident in urology Columbia Presbyn. Med. Ctr., NYC, 1962-65, fellow in pediat. urology Babies Hosp., 1967; attending physician Norwalk (Conn.) Hosp., from 1967, chief of staff. Lectr. urology U. Madrid Med. Sch., 1966; chief urology Norwalk Hosp., 1987-95, asst. chief of staff, 1995-97; bd. dirs. Precision Closure Co. Mem. bd. Mayor's Commn., Norwalk, 1994-95; pres. Shorehaven Rd. Assocs., Norwalk, 1985; pres., co-founder Frank J. Scallon Med. Found., Norwalk, 1980—; trustee Norwalk Hosp., 1995—. Capt. USAF, 1965-67, Spain. Fellow ACS; mem. AMA, Am. Urol. Assn. (New England sect.), Norwalk Med. Soc. (pres. 1985-86), Fairfield County Med. Assn. (pres. 1994-96). Roman Catholic. Avocations: golf, sailing, skiing, tennis, dance. Home: Fairfield, Conn. Died July 1, 2007.

MANDAL, ROBERT PARKASH, microelectronic engineering manager; b. Ahmedgarh, Punjab, India, June 24, 1935; came to U.S., 1935; s. Tulsi Ram and Elenora Louisa Wilhelmina (Koch) M.; m. Barbara Anne Brandys, June 27, 1974; children: Robert Walter, Richard Brandys, Stephanie Anne. BS, Calif. State U., Fresno, 1957; PhD, U. Calif., Berkeley, 1962; MBA, Century U., 1982. Teaching asst. U. Calif., Berkeley, 1957-59, rsch. assoc., 1959-61; mgr. applied R&D Aerojet ElectroSystems Co., Azusa, Calif., 1962-70; mgr. microsystems engring. Applied Technology, Sunnyvale, Calif., 1971-77; group leader Lockheed Missiles & Space Co., Sunnyvale, 1977-81; mgr. solid state Litton Systems Electron Devices, San Carlos, Calif., 1981-85; dir. Teledyne Monolithic Microwave, Mountain View, Calif., 1985-93; prin. technologist Silicon Valley Group, San Jose, Calif., 1994-96; mgr. dielectric dept. Applied Materials, Santa Clara, Calif., from 1996. Chmn. tech. program Internat. Microelectronics Symposium, 1973, Semiconductor Microlithograpy Symposium, 1976. Mem. IEEE (organizing and tech. program com. Gallium Arsenide Integrated Cir. Symposium 1981, 88, 89, 90), Am. Vacuum Soc., SPIE Soc. for Optical Engring., Sigma Xi, Phi Kappa Phi. Republican. Home: Saratoga, Calif. Died June 23, 2007.

MANDEL, LESLIE ANN, investment advisor, writer; b. Washington, July 29, 1945; d. Seymour and Marjorie (Syble) Mandel; m. Arthur Herzog III, Oct. 27, 1999. BA in Art History, U. Minn., 1967; cert., N.Y. Sch. Interior Design, 1969. Cert. Braillest Libr. Congress, 1966. Pres. Leslie Mandel Enterprises, Inc., NYC, from 1968; sr. v.p. Maximum Entertainment Network, L.A. and NYC, 1988-90; pres. Rich List Co., from 1968; pres., CEO Mandel Airplane Funding and Leasing Corp., NYC, Hong Kong, China and Mongolia, from 1990; CEO Mandel-Khan Inc., Ulaanbaatar, Mongolia, from 1994, Travel Safe: keep hers, keep his, from 2002; internat. sales dir. FTL Solar Cells Fabric, from 2010, bd. advisors, from 2015. Fin. advisor Osmed, Inc., Mpls., from 1986, Devine Comm./Allen & Co., NY, Del., Utah, N.Mex., NY, N.Y. WUWV, Utah KBER, WKTC-AM-FM, 1984—89, Am. Kefir Corp., NYC, 1983—89, Shore Group (Internat., Guyana), Flight Internat., from 1991, bd. advisor, from 2015; owner The Rich List Co., 150 internat. catalogs, mags. and fundraising lists; joint venture Mongolian Ind. Broadcasting Channel, Ulaanbaatar, 1995; pres., owner Mandel Airplane Funding and Leasing Corp.; rep. Israeli Govt. IAI Satellite, China, Romania, Costa Rica, Mongolia, Amos Satellite Network, China, from 1992; advisor rep. Gt. Wall Corp., Long March Corp., China, from 1992, Chinese Silk, from 1993, Am. Oil Refinery, from 1993; bd. dirs. Coastal Equipment Co., Bristol Airlines; cons. Exclusive Miat Airlines, Mongolia; purchasing agt. People's Republic of China-Aircraft; advisor Aeropostalis, Mexico, 1994—95; photographer; lectr. UN Internat. Direct Mail; advisor Aruba Airlines, Mexicana Airlines; aircraft agt., bd. dirs. Lazorlines Landing Equipment, from 1997; lease Estafada Airlines 757-200-C, from 2000, Chile Airlines 757-200C, 2002; advisor Guyana 2000 Airlines; ptnr. Laserline/Vulcan Power Plant, China, 2005, Greece, from 2005, Nicaragua, from 2005, Trinidad and Tobago, from 2005, Pakistan, from 2005, Turkmenistan, from 2005, Hungary, from 2005; bd. advisors FTL Global-.Net, from 2014. Photographer: Vogue, 1978, New Earth Times, 1995, Fortune mag.; Braille transcriber: The Prophet (Kalil Gibran), 1967, Getting Ready for Battle (R. Prawe Jhabuala), 1967; exec. prodr. film: Hospital Audiences, 1975 (Cannes award 1976); author: Hungry at the Watering Hole, Gardiners Island, 1636-1990, 1989, Expedition: In the Steps of Ghengis Kahn, 1994; advisor Port Libertè Ptnrs., 1988-94; contbr. articles to profl. jours. Fin. advisor Correctional Assn., Osborn Soc., 1977—; founder, treas. Prisoners Family Transportation and Assistance Fund, N.Y., 1972-77; judge Emmy awards of Acad. TV Arts and Scis., N.Y.C., 1970; bd. dirs. Prisoners Assn., 1990; chmn. U.S.A. com. Violeta B. de Chamarro for Pres. of Nicaragua Campaign. Recipient Inst. for the Creative and Performing Arts fellowship, N.Y.C., 1966, Appreciation cert. Presdl. Inaugural Com., Washington, 1981. Fellow: NY Women in Real Estate, Explorers Club (lectr. on Mongolia, fin. com., housing, student membership com., hospitality and Lowell Thomas coms., reciprocity com., legacy com.); mem.: Com. on Am. and Internat. Fgn. Affairs, Lawyers Com. on Internat. Human Rels., Bus. Exec. Nat. Security, Venture Capital Breakfast Club, The Coffee Club House, Sigma Delta Tau, Sigma Epsilon Sigma. Democrat. Avocations: painting, writing, fishing, canoeing, horseback riding. Home: New York, NY. Died June 23, 2015.

MANGOLD, WENDI LEIGH, mathematician, educator; b. Huntington, W.Va., June 28, 1971; d. Charles Philip and Glenia Dianna (Withrow) Bloss; m. David Gerald Mangold, June 7, 1997. BEd, U. Fla., 1993, MEd, 1994. Cert. tchr. math., Fla. Tchr. reading Lakeland (Fla.) Highlands Mid. Sch., 1994-95, tchr. math., 1995-97, George Jenkins H.S., Lakeland, from 1997. Instr. math. Hillsborough C.C., Tampa, Fla., 1996—. Mem. ASCD, Nat. Tchrs. Math., Fla. Tchrs. Math., Polk County Tchrs. Math. Republican. Methodist. Avocations: scuba diving, rollerblading. Home: Brandon, Fla. Died Mar. 25, 2007.

MANIGAT, LESLIE FRANCOIS, former president of Haiti; b. Port-Au-Prince, Haiti, Aug. 16, 1930; s. Francois and Haydee (Augustin) Manigat; m. Mirlande Hippolyte, 1970; 1 child, Beatrice; children: Mary Lucia, Marie-Dominique, Vivian, Jesse, Roberte, Sabine. Grad., U. Paris, 1949. With Ministry Fgn. Affairs, Haiti, 1953-60; prof., co-founder ctr. secondary studies U. Haiti, 1953-63, prof. law, 1953-57; prof. internat. relations U. Simon Bolivar, Caracas, Venezuela, 1978-86; acad. assessor Inst. Higher Studies Nat. Def., Caracas, 1983-84; pres. Republic of Haiti, 1988; polit. sci. prof. Wilson Ctr., Washington, 1988—90; co-founder Patriotic Union Party, 2002. Died June 27, 2014.

MANKIEWICZ, FRANK FABIAN, journalist, writer; b. NYC, May 16, 1924; s. Herman J. and Sara (Aaronson) M.; m. Holly Jolley, 1952 (div.); children: Joshua, Benjamin; m. Patricia O'Brien, 1988. AB in Journalism, UCLA, 1947; MS, Columbia U., 1948; LLB, U. Calif.-Berkeley, 1955. Bar: Calif. 1955, D.C. 1985. Engaged in journalism, Washington and Los Angeles, 1948-52; practice law Beverly Hills, 1955-61; dir. Peace Corps, Lima, Peru, 1962-64, Latin American regional dir. Washington, 1964-66; press sec. to Senator Robert F. Kennedy US Senate, 1966-68; syndicated columnist and TV news commentator, 1968-71; nat. polit. dir. Senator George McGovern's Presdl. Campaign, 1971-72; columnist The Washington Post, 1976-77; pres. Nat. Public Radio, 1977-83; vice-chmn. Hill & Knowlton (formerly Gray and Co.), 1983—2014. Author: Perfectly Clear: Nixon from Whittier to Watergate, 1973, U.S. v. Richard M. Nixon: The Final Crisis, 1974, With Fidel: A Portrait of Castro and Cuba, 1975, Remote Control: Television and the Manipulation of American Life, 1977; contbr. articles to newspapers and mags. Served with inf. AUS, 1943-46 Democrat. Died Oct. 23, 2014.

MANLEY, LARRY PAUL, investment banker; b. Houston, Aug. 22, 1947; s. James Olaf and Jaynelle (Christian) M. BBA in Fin., U. Tex., 1969, JD with honors, 1973. Bar: Tex. 1973. Assoc. Vinson & Elkins, Houston, 1973-79; shareholder, dir. Ross, Griggs & Harrison, Houston, 1979-87, dir. Austin, Tex., 1985-87; cons., acting gen. counsel Franklin Fed. Bancorp, Austin, Tex., 1987-89; ptnr. Hughes & Luce, Dallas and Austin, 1989-91; chmn., CEO The Manley Companies, Austin, Tex., from 1991; prin. Larry Paul Manley P.C., from 1991. Exec. dir. Tex. Dept. Housing and Cmty. Affairs, Austin, 1995—; pres. Tex. State Affordable Housing Corp., 1995—; adj. prof. U. Tex. Sch. Law, 1989—; speaker in field. Assoc. editor Tex. Law Rev., 1972-73. Bd. dirs. Nat. Housing Conf., Coun. of State Cmty. Devel. Agys.; chair Cmty. Devel. Block Grant Program Com.; bd. dirs. Tex. Bus. Hall of Fame Found. With USNG, 1969-75. Recipient Dist. Speaker award Houston Bar Assn., 1984. Mem. ABA (bus. law sect.), Tex. State Bar, Houston Young Lawyers Assn. (bd. dirs. 1975-76), Houston C. of C. (life, Golden Key award 1974), Travis County Bar Assn., Order of Coif, Texas Law Review (life member), Met. Club. Avocations: athletic activities, hunting, travel, reading. Home: Austin, Tex. Died Aug. 11, 2007.

MANN, GERALD LOUIS, pastor; b. Sturgeon Bay, Wis., Oct. 28, 1944; s. Wallace Howard and Eileen Amelia (Grosse) M.; m. Elaine Gail Fox, Aug. 2, 1969; children: Heidi, Janet. BA, Macalester Coll., 1966; ThM, Boston U., 1969. Pastor Butler (Wis.) United Meth. Ch., 1969-71; assoc. pastor Bay View United Meth. Ch., Milw., 1972-76; pastor Bethel-LaGrange United Meth. Ch., Elkhorn, Wis., 1976-83, Zion United Meth.Ch., Chippewa Falls, Wis., 1984-86; chaplain Lakeside Nursing and Rehab., Chippewa Falls, Wis., from 1987. Bd. dirs. health and welfare com. Wis. Ctr. Conf., United Meth. Ch., 1994—; pipe major Chippewa Falls Pipes and Drums, 1996—; bd. dirs. Chippewa Valley Cultural Assn., 1995—; pres. Chippewa Valley Cmty. Chorus, 1994—; elder Wis. Conf. United Meth. Ch., 1970—. Mem. Kiwanis (sec. 1992-96). Avocations: scottish bagpipes, biking, gardening, singing, photography. Home: Chippewa Falls, Wis. Died June 5, 2007.

MANNING, FERDINAND LARUE, lighting consultant; b. Cambridge, Mass., Oct. 1, 1925; s. George Charles and Blanche Marie (Larue) M.; m. Jean Alexander-Williams, Nov. 10, 1951 (dec. Sept. 1978); children: Jill Alexander Manning Stockman, Patricia Larue, James Williams; m. Kathryn Eleanore Reimers, Dec. 12, 1987; children: Ryan Edwin Farrell, Nicholas Farrell. BA, Tulane U., 1948; MFA, Yale, 1951. Lighting dir. CBS-TV, NYC, 1951-62; head lighting dept. Ednl. Broadcasting Co., NYC, 1962-63; lighting dir. Videotape Ctr., NYC, 1963-68; pres., lighting cons. Acad. Lighting Cons., East NYC, 1968-70; pres., founder, lighting cons. Lyteman Inc., NYC, from 1970. Dir. Martha Stuart Comm. Inc., Inst. Grad. Sch. Edn. Fairfield U., 1969, Am. Theatre Wing, 1956-57; lectr. New Sch. Social Rsch., N.Y.C.; lighting cons. to (Nixon) White House and Rep. Nat. Com., 1972-73, to Jimmy Carter Presdl. Campaign, 1976. Tech. dir. Nashes Barn Theatre, 1963, dir. Wilton Playshop, Westport Comm. Theatre, 1973-76, contbr. editor Lighting Dimensions, 1980-83. Served with AUS, 1944-45, USNR, 1945-46. Winner Emmy award for Kirov Ballet for PBS (mem. of prodn). Mem. Soc. Lighting Dirs. (charter), Internat. Assn. of Lighting Designers, Illuminating Engring. Soc. Died Feb. 21, 2007.

MANSK, SHARON SUE, graphic designer, writer; b. Elmhurst, Ill., Apr. 9, 1948; d. Robert William and Violet (Stamos) Conklin; m. Kenneth M. Mansk, Oct. 11, 1969; children: Jeffrey, Amanda, Bridget. Student, Elmhurst Coll., Ill., 1990, U. Ill., from 1991. Customer rep. Ill. Bell Tel., Elmhurst, 1964-67; collection correspondent Xerox Corp., Oak Brook, Ill., 1967-69; graphics technician Elmhurst Coll., Ill., 1984-91; graphic designer S.M. Graphics, Elmhurst, from 1991. V.p. York High Sch. Choral Parents Assn., 1989-92, pres., 1992-83; creator, editor newsletter YMPA. Recipient Supreme Patriotism Essay award Internat. Order of Job's Daughters, 1966. Mem. Newcomers Club Elmhurst (Publicity Mgr. 1973-74), Young Women's Ch. Group Club Elmhurst (Pres. 1980). Lutheran. Avocations: writing, computers, reading, painting. Died Feb. 12, 2007.

MANZ, MICHAEL PAUL, child psychiatrist; b. Mpls., Jan. 8, 1948; s. Paul Otto and Ruth Marie (Mueller) M.; m. Patricia Sue Stanwood, June 19, 1971; children: Erik, David, Rachael. BS, Augsburg Coll., 1970; MD, Baylor U., 1973. Resident in adult psychiatry Pacific Med. Ctr., San Francisco, 1974-76; fellow in child psychiatry U. Oreg. Health Sci. Ctr., Portland, 1977-79; staff child psychiatrist Cmty. Mental Health Ctr., Spokane, Wash., 1980-85; pvt. practice Spokane, from 1980. Med. dir. Sacred Heart Med. Ctr., Spokane, 1985—; owner, winemaker Mountain Dome Winery, Spokane. Lutheran. Home: Spokane, Wash. Died Nov. 1, 2006.

MARAMES, WILLIAM ETHEME, lawyer; b. NYC, Dec. 26, 1955; s. Gregory and Stella (Popescu) M. BA, Queens Coll., Flushing, NY, 1977; JD, Fordham U., 1980. Bar: N.Y. 1981, U.S. Dist. Ct. (so. and ea. dists.) N.Y. 1982. Assoc. Wyatt, Gerber, Shoup, Scobey and Badie, NYC, 1981-87, Kane, Dalsimer, Sullivan, Kurucz, Levy, Eisele & Richard, NYC, 1987-97; of counsel Howrey & Simon, Washington, from 1997. Asst. editor Ann Pubs. J. Geist Law fellow Queen's Coll., 1977. Mem. ABA (patent, trademark and copyright law sect., vice-chmn. com. on publs. 1985-87, 90-93, chmn. com. on possible new publs. and reorganization of existing publs. 1987-89, sports and entertainment sect.), N.Y. State Bar Assn., Phi Beta Kappa. Died Dec. 7, 2006.

MARCADIS, ELIZABETH, human services administrator; b. Racine, Wis., Feb. 3, 1936; d. Robert R. and M. Lucille (Stoddard) Yontz; m. Isaac Marcadis, June 28, 1959; children: Rebecca, Deborah, Miriam. BSN, Duke U., 1958. Cert. child and adolescent nurse ANA. Mgr. pediatrics J.F.K. Med. Ctr., Atlantis, Fla.; dir. svcs. Coun. on Child Abuse, West Palm Beach, Fla., Connor's Nursery, Residented Home for Infants with AIDS. Named Child Advocate of Yr., 1985. Home: West Palm Beach, Fla. Died June 3, 2007.

MARCHIBRODA, TED (THEODORE JOSEPH MARCHIBRODA), former professional football coach; b. Franklin, Pa., Mar. 15, 1931; m. Henrietta Marchibroda; children: Jodi, Teddy, Lonni, Robert. Student, St. Bonaventure Coll., 1950-51, U. Detroit, 1952. Football player Pitts. Steelers, 1953-54, 55-56, Chgo. Cardinals, 1957-58; asst. coach Washington Redskins, 1961-65, offensive coord., 1971-74; asst. coach L.A. Rams, 1966-70; head coach Balt. Colts, 1975-79; offensive coord., quarterbacks coach Chgo. Bears, 1981; offensive coord. Detroit Lions, 1982-83; offensive coord., quarterbacks coach Phila. Eagles, 1984-85; quarterbacks coach Buffalo Bills, 1987-88, offensive coord., 1989-92; head coach Indpls. Colts, 1992-95, Balt. Ravens, 1996-1998. Analyst for Indianapolis Colts radio broadcasts, 1999—2006. Served with U.S. Army, 1954-55. Died Jan. 16, 2016.

MARCHMAN, RICHARD KEITH, cable television executive; b. Clayton, Ga., Feb. 21, 1955; s. Charles Robert Sr. and Margaret Roberta (Nicholson) M.; m. Jill Marie Tate, July 28, 1985; children: Grant Vincent, Ryan Keith. BA in Polit. Sci. cum laude, Elon Coll., 1977. Forest worker U.S. Forest Service, Clayton, Ga., 1974-76; pres., chmn. bd. Mountain View Enterprises, Inc., Clayton, from 1978. Dem. campaign worker, Burlington, N.C., 1976. Recipient Gear award Rotary Internat., 1973. Mem. Sigma Pi, Pi Gamma Mu. Baptist. Avocations: white water canoeing, jogging, camping, wood carving. Home: Clayton, Ga. Died Jan. 28, 2007.

MARCUS, JAMES STEWART, investment banker; b. NYC, Dec. 15, 1929; s. Bernard Kent and Libby (Phillips) M.; m. Barbara Ellen Silver, July 18, 1962 (dec. Nov. 1970); m. Ellen Mary Friedman, June 21, 1974. AB magna cum laude, Harvard U., 1951, MBA with distinction, 1953. Assoc. Goldman, Sachs and Co., NYC, 1956-64, gen. ptnr., 1964-82, ltd. ptnr., 1982. Bd. dirs. Kellwood Co., St. Louis, Am. Bilrite Inc., Wellesley, Mass.; co-founder ARIA awards Bd. dirs. Met. Opera Assn., N.Y.C., 1973-2015, mng. dir., 1976-86, chmn., 1986-93, hon. dir., 1997, Met. Opera Guild, 1993-2015, Met. Opera Club; mem. exec. com. Lincoln Ctr. for the Performing Arts, N.Y.C., 1982-93; hon. trustee Lenox Hill Hosp., N.Y.C., 1985-2015, chmn. to chmn. emeritus, 1993-2015; bd. trustee Guild Hall, East Hampton, N.Y., 1977-2015 (mem. exec. com. and others), The Juilliard Sch., 1995-2015; former trustee Nat. Opera Inst., Brazilian Cultural Found., Collegiate Chorale, Cathedral of St. John the Divine, Animal Med. Ctr., Calamus Found., WNET Channel 13, Manhattan Theatre Club, Lincoln Ctr. for Performing Arts, Am. Composers Orch., N.Y.C., Regenstrief Found.; Founding mem. East Hampton Healthcare Found. and Pianofest; former pres. Alex Hillman Family Found. Served with US Army, 1953—55. Recipient U.S. Presdl. Recognition award, 1986. Mem. Century Assn., Phi Beta Kappa. Republican. Jewish. Home: New York, NY. Died July 5, 2015.

MARCUSE, WILLIAM, technology transfer executive; b. Fairfield, Conn., Aug. 4, 1924; s. Sidney and Jeanette (Holzmasser) M.; m. Shirley Rozinsky; children: Jason C., Steven M. BA, U. Conn., 1947, MA, 1948; PhD, Columbia U., 1956. Cert. cost analyst. Asst. prof. U. Conn., Storrs, 1948-56; analyst OEG of MIT, Washington, 1956-60; assoc. dept. head Mitre Corp., Bedford, Mass., 1960-69; div. head Brookhaven Nat. Lab., Upton, N.Y., 1969-82, office head, from 1983. Detailee Dept. of Energy, Washington, 1980-82. Capt. USAR, 1944-64. Fellow AAAS; mem. Ops. Rsch. Soc. Am., Am. Econ. Assn., Tech. Transfer Soc. Democrat. Avocations: golf, bridge, sailing. Home: Delray Beach, Fla. Died Nov. 4, 2006.

MARINOV, BENJAMIN SIMONOVICH, biophysicist; b. Witebsk, Russia, Feb. 13, 1927; s. Simon Benjaminovich and Rachel Solomonovna (Feigelman) M.; m. Rosa Moiseevna Perskaja; 1 child, Lev Benjaminovich. PhD, Inst. of Biophysics, 1971. Leading engr. Box 17, Frjasino, 1950-62; sr. scientist Inst. of Biophysics, Pushchino, Russia, from 1962. Contbr. articles to profl. jours. Avocations: music, jogging. Home: Pushchino, Russia. Died June 17, 2007.

MARK, MARY ELLEN, photographer; b. Phila., Mar. 20, 1940; d. A. DeRoy and Beatrice (Silverman) M.; m. Frank Anthony Macaoge, 1963 (div. 1964); m. Martin Bell. BFA in Painting and Art History, U. Pa., 1962; MA in Photojournalism, Annenberg Sch. Communication, U. Pa., 1964; DFA (hon.), U. of Arts, Phila., 1992, U. Pa., 1994, Ctr. for Creative Studies, Detroit, 2001, Columbia Coll., Chgo., 2004, Kenyon Coll., Gambier, Ohio, 2004. Lectr., presenter workshops in field. One-woman shows include Photographers Gallery, London, 1976, Castelli Graphics, NYC, 1978, Olympus Gallery, London, 1981, Seson Art Gallery, U. Calif-Santa Cruz, Calif. Mus. Photography, Riverside, Drew U., NJ, 1982, Gallery of Fine Arts, Daytona Beach Community Coll., Fla., Friends of Photography, Carmel, Calif., 1983, Allen Street Gallery, Dallas, 1985, Birmingham (Ala.) Mus. of Art, 1989, numerous others; exhibited in group shows at Photokina, Cologne, 1973, Sidney Janis Gallery, NYC, 1976, Internat. Ctr. of Photography, NYC, 1979, Bibliotheque Nationale, Paris, 1979, Corcoran Gallery of Art and George Eastman House, NY, U. Colo., 1982, Eaton Shoen Gallery, San Francisco, 1983, Barbican Art Gallery, London, 1985, Munich Stadt Mus., 1985, Walker Art Ctr., Mpls., 1986, Portland (Maine) Mus. Art, 1986, Castle Gallery, New Rochelle, NY, Hillwood Art Gallery, Greenvale, NY, UN 40th Anniversary Photography Exhibit, 1985, Paris Opera, 1988, Zeitgenossischen Photography, Frankfurt, 1989, numerous others; author: Passport, 1974, Ward 81, 1979, Falkland Road: Prostitutes of Bombay, 1981, Mother Teresa's Missions of Charity in Calcutta, 1985, Streetwise, 1988, 25 Years, A Retrospective Book, 1992, Mary Ellen Mark: Indian Circus, 1993, A Cry for Help: Stories of Homelessness and Hope, 1996, Mary Ellen Mark: Portraits, 1995, Mary Ellen Mark: American Odyssey, 1999, Twins, 2003, Exposure, 2005, Prom, 2012, Man and Beast, 2014, Tiny: Streetwise Revisited, 2015, others; assoc. prodr. (films) American Heart, 1992; contbr. articles, photographs to profl. publs., mags. Fulbright scholar, 1965-66, Guggenheim fellow, 1994, Erna and Victor Hasselblad Found. grant, 1997; grantee USIA, 1975, NEA, 1977, 79-80, 1990, NY State Coun. for Arts, 1977; recipient Page One award The Newspaper Guild of NY, 1979, First Pl. Feature Picture Stroy U. Mo., 1980, Canon Photo Essayist award Life Mag., 1983, 1st prize Robert F. Kennedy Journalism, 1985, Philippe Halsman award ASMP, Photojournalism award George W. Polk, 1988, Internat. Ctr. Photog. Journalism award, 1997, Cornell Capa award, 2001, Award of Excellence, Commun Arts Photog. Ann., 1998, 1999, Merit award, Art Dirs Club, 1998, Silver award, 1998.; Gold Medal award, Soc. Publ. Designers, 1998, Leadership award, Internat. Photog. Coun., 1999, Award for Excellence in Photojournalism, Photog. Adminstrs. Inc, 1999, Merrill Panitt Citizenship award, Annenberg Sch. Comm., 2000, Lucie award for Documentary Photog, 2003, First Prize in the Arts, World Press Photo Awards, 2004, Photo Vision award, Photog. Ctr. Northwest, 2006, Lifetime Achievement in Photography award, George Eastman House, 2014; named Favorite Woman Photographer of All Time, Am. Photography mag. readers. Mem. Assn. Soc. Mag. Photographers. Died May 25, 2015.

MARKEE, KATHERINE MADIGAN, librarian, educator; b. Cleve., Feb. 24, 1931; d. Arthur Alexis and Margaret Elizabeth (Madigan) M. AB, Trinity Coll., Washington, 1953; MA, Tchr.'s Coll., 1962; MLS, Case Western Res. U., 1968. Employment mgr., br. store tng. supr. The May Co., Cleve., 1965-67; assoc. prof. libr. sci., data bases libr. Purdue U. Libr., West Lafayette, Ind., 1968—96, libr. spl. collections, 1996—2006, oral history libr., 2006—11, prof. emeritus libr. sci. Contbr. articles to profl. jours. Mem. ALA, Sigma Xi (Rsch. Support award 1986, John H Moriarty award 2009, Disting. Hooster award 2011), Oral History Assn., Soc. Am. Archivists. Avocations: photography, sailing, gardening. Home: West Lafayette, Ind. Deceased.

MARKEY, WINSTON ROSCOE, aeronautical engineering educator; b. Buffalo, Sept. 20, 1929; s. Roscoe Irvin and Catherine L. (Higgins) M.; m. Phoebe Anne Sproule, Sept. 10, 1955; children: Karl Richard, Katherine Ilse, Kristina Anne. BS, MIT, 1951, Sc.D., 1956. Engr. MIT, 1951-57, asst. prof., 1957-62, assoc. prof., 1962-66, prof., from 1966, undergrad. officer, 1988-2000, dir. Measurement Systems Lab., 1961-89. Chief scientist USAF, 1964-65, mem. sci. adv. bd., 1966-69 Author: (with J. Hovorka) The Mechanics of Inertial Position and Heading Indication, 1961; Assoc. editor: AIAA Jour, 1963-66. Recipient Exceptional Civilian Service award, USAF, 1965. Mem. Sigma Xi, Tau Beta Pi, Gamma Alpha Rho. Home: Lexington, Mass. Died Jan. 4, 2014.

MARKS, LYNN WILSON, forensic document examiner; b. Dayton, Ohio, Feb. 1, 1955; d. John W. and Beatrice A. (Dorst) Wilson; m. Peter L. Marks, June 19, 1976; children: Erika, Wilson. Student, U. Cen. Fla. Forensic document examiner, owner Lynn Wilson Marks & Assocs., San Antonio, from 1983. Lectr., instr. for academic, legal and forensic disciplines U. Texas Grad. Sch., 1990, U. Texas Health Sci. Ctr. San Antonio, 1988, 90, U. Trier West Germany, 1990, St. Mary's Law Sch., Pan Am. Assn. Forensic Sci.; developer standards in forensic document exam. Editorial asst. Jour. Forensic Document Examination, 1987-91, Forensic Document Examination In Medical Malpractice Cases, AmJur Model Trials, 1992; contbr. articles to profl. jours. Mem. North San Antonio C. of C., Greater Boerne Area C. of C., Assn. Forensic Document Examiners (cert., sec., v.p. 1990, pres. 1991-92), Forgery Investigators Assn. of Tex., Internat. Graphonomics Soc., Zonta Internat. (co-chair internat. rels. com. San Antonio). Avocation: handwriting research. Home: Boerne, Tex. Died July 5, 2007.

MARRETT, MICHAEL MCFARLENE, retired chaplain; b. Greenwich Town, Surrey, Jamaica, Oct. 7, 1935; s. Kenneth Louis and Ivy Lynmae (McFarlane) M.; m. Margery Eva Mugford, Jan. 29, 1984. Cert. gen. ordination, Oxford U., Eng., 1961; cert. edn. in English lang., London U., 1967; MDiv, Gen. Theol. Sem., 1969, STM, 1970, N.Y. Theol. Sem., 1972; postgrad., Princeton Theol. Sem., 1972-73, Columbia U., 1973-75; BA, Fordham U., 1974; postgrad., The Coll. of Preachers, 1979, Yale U., 1979-81; PhD, NYU, 1980; MS, So. Conn. State U., 1982. Lic. pastoral counselor, Md.; cert. profl. mental health clergy, chaplain and fellow of Coll. Chaplains; nat. cert. bereavement facilitator Am. Acad. Bereavement; diplomate Am. Psychotherapy Assn., cert. Assn. profl. Chaplain. Staff chaplain St. Elizabeths Hosp., Washington, 1986-99; ret., 1999. Author: The Lambeth Conferences and Women Priests, 1981. Appointed commissary Diocese of Akoko, West Africa, 1984, appointed hon. canon St. Stephens Cathedral, 1987. Mem. Assn. Clin. Pastoral Edn. (clin.), Am. Assn. Christian Counselors, Am. Assn. Family Counselors. Home: Washington, DC. Died Apr. 9, 2014.

MARSH, BENJAMIN FRANKLIN, lawyer; b. Toledo, Apr. 30, 1927; s. Lester Randall and Alice (Smith) M.; m. Martha Kirkpatrick, July 12, 1952; children: Samuel, Elizabeth. BA, Ohio Wesleyan U., 1950; JD, George Washington U., 1954. Bar: Ohio 1955. Pvt. practice law, Toledo, 1955—88; assoc., ptnr. Doyle, Lewis & Warner, Toledo, 1955—71; ptnr. Ritter, Boesel, Robinson & Marsh, Toledo, 1971—88; mem. Marsh & McAdams, Maumee, 1988—98; pers. officer AEC, 1950—54; asst. atty. gen. State of Ohio, 1969—71; asst. solicitor City of Maumee, 1959—63, solicitor, 1963—92; mem. Marsh McAdams, Ltd., Maumee, 1999—2012; of counsel Marsh Brogan Szozda & Rambo Ltd., from 2012. Mem. U.S. Fgn. Claims Settlement Commn., Washington, 1990-94; counsel N.W. Ohio Mayors and Mgrs. Assn., 1990-2000; regional bd. rev. Indsl. Commn. Ohio, Toledo, 1993-94; mem. Ohio Dental Bd., 1995-2000; trustee Corp. for Effective Govt., 1998-2003; mem. Ohio Elections Commn., 2001-07, chmn. 2003-04 U.S. rep. with rank spl. amb. to 10th Anniversary Independence of Botswana, 1976; past pres. Toledo and Lucas County Tb Soc.; past co-chmn. Citizens for Metro Pks.; past mem. Judges Com. Notaries Pub.; mem. Lucas County Bd. Elections, 1973-78, 2010-11; former chmn. bldg. commn. Riverside Hosp., Toledo; past trustee Com. on Rels. with Toledo, Spain; past chmn. bd. trustee Med. Coll., Ohio; past treas. Coglin Meml. Inst.; chmn. Lucas County Rep. Exec. Com., 1973-74; precinct commiteeman, Maumee, 1959-73; legal counsel, bd. dirs. Nat. Coun. Rep. Workshops, 1960-65; pres. Rep. Workshops, Ohio, 1960-64; alt. del. Rep. Nat. Conv., 1964; candidate 9th dist. U.S. Ho. of Reps., 1968; adminstrv. asst. to Rep. state chmn. Ray C. Bliss, 1954; chmn. Lucas County Bush for Pres., 1980; co-chmn. Reagan-Bush Com. for Northwestern Ohio, 1980, vice chmn. fin. com. Bush-Quayle, 1992; co-chmn. Ohio steering com. Bush for Pres., mem. nat. steering com., 1988; del. Rep. Nat. Conv., 1988; past bd. dirs. Ohio Tb and Respiratory Disease Assn.; apptd. Ohio chmn. UN Day, 1980, 81, 82; adminstrv. asst. Legis. Svc. Commn., Columbus, 1954-55; mem. Lucas County Charter Commn., Toledo, 1959-60; vice-chmn. U.S. Nat. Commn. for UNESCO, mem. legal com., del. 17th gen. conf., Paris, 1972, U.S. observer meeting of nat. commns., Africa, 1974, Addis Ababa, Ethiopia; past mem. industry functional adv. com. on stds. trade policy matters; mem. nat. def. exec. res. Dept. Commerce; active Am. Bicentennial Presdl. Inauguration, Diplomatic Adv. Com. With USNR, 1945-46. Named Outstanding Young Man of Toledo, 1962, Ohio Vet. Hall of Fame, 2011. Mem. ABA, Maumee C. of C. (past pres.), UN Assn., Ohio State Bar Assn., Toledo Bar Assn., Ohio Mun League (past pres.), Am. Legion (past comdr. Toledo Post), Lucas County Maumee Valley Hist. Soc. (past pres.), Internat. Inst. Toledo, Ohio Mcpl. Attys. Assn. (past pres.), Orgn. Security and Cooperation in Europe (registration supr., adjudicator, elections supr. in Bosnia), Western Lake Erie Hist. Soc., Ohio Hist. Soc., Canal Soc. Ohio, Toledo Mus. Art, Ohio Wesleyan U. Alumni Assn. (past pres.), Ohio State Bar Found., Toledo Bar Found., Rotary, Toledo Country Club, Torch Club Toledo (past pres.), Navy League, Omicron Delta Kappa, Delta Sigma Rho, Theta Alpha Phi, Phi Delta Phi, English Speaking Union(Toledo), US5 Grand Canyon Sailors Assn. Presbyterian. Home: Toledo, Ohio. Died May 19, 2014.

MARSH, DANIEL, clothing store executive; b. Bklyn., Apr. 10, 1924; s. Herbert and Ruth (Gesner) M.; m. Zina Renee Feldman, Dec. 31, 1947 (dec. Sept. 1976); children: Joyce Barbara, Helene Myra, Michael Louis; m. Roberta Jacobs, Jan. 9, 1977. Student, Pratt Inst., 1941-42, NYU, 1946-47. Vice pres. Marsh's Men's & Boys' Shop, Huntington, N.Y., from 1945. Author, editor: Keys To Success, 1966 (cert. of distinction Brand Names Found. 1966). Mem. exec. bd. YMCA, Huntington, 1972-78. Sgt. USAAF, 1942-46, ETO. Decorated Bronze Star with two oak leaf clusters). Mem. Huntington Kiwanis (past pres. 1957), Retail Coun. N.Y., Huntington C. of C. (bd. dirs. 1967-69, treas. 1973-75), Huntington Village Mchts. Orgn. (bd. dirs.). Avocations: golf, walking, bicycling, swimming. Home: Huntington, NY. Died Apr. 9, 2007.

MARSHALL, JOSEPHINE PRINCE, retired educator, councilwoman; b. Bellwood, W.Va., May 8, 1931; d. Robert Lee and Mattie Marie (Clinton) Prince; m. Lewis Randolph Marshall, Apr. 20, 1950; children: Timothy LeRoy, Lewis Anthony, Teresa Ellen. BS, Bluefield State Coll., 1950; MEd, U. Va., 1968; cert. in advance grad. studies, Va. Tech., Balcksburg, 1984. Tchr. Mecklenburg Pub. Schs., Clarksville, Va., 1952-68, Halifax County Pub. Schs., South Boston, Va., 1968-71; instr. fgn. langs. Ctrl. Va. C.C., Lynchburg, Va., 1971-75; assoc. prof. Danville (Va.) C.C., 1975-93, ret., 1993; mem. South Boston City Coun., from 1984, chmn. policy com., from 1991. Bd. dirs. Halifax Regional Hosp., South Boston, 1988—. Bd. dirs. Halifax/South Boston C. of C., 1986-88; chmn. Dem. Com., South Boston, 1990—; pres. Habitat for Humanity, South Boston, 1991—; pres. South Boston Devel. Corp., 1991—;

mem. Va. Adv. Com. on Intergovernmental Rels., vice chmn., 1992—. Mem. Va. Mcpl. League (exec. com. 1988—, pres.), Delta Sigma Theta. Democrat. Methodist. Avocations: reading, arts and crafts, cross word puzzles, bowling, travel. Home: South Boston, Va. Died Feb. 5, 2007.

MARTENS, ALEXANDER EUGENE, technical consultant; b. Schemnitz, Slovakia, Czechoslovakia, June 27, 1923; came to U.S., 1960; s. Eugene and Anne (Naumann) M.; m. Rita M. Wenzel, Oct. 16, 1948; children: Anne, Randolph. BSEE, Tech. U., Breslau, Germany, 1942; MSEE, U. Rochester, 1964. V.p. R&D Bausch & Lomb, Rochester, N.Y., 1960-83; tech. cons. Fairport, N.Y., from 1983. Adj. prof. Rochester Inst. Tech., 1977-82; adviser High Tech. of Rochester, 1989—. Contbr. articles to profl. jours.; patentee in field. Bd. dirs. Monroe Community Hosp. Aux., 1991; advisor SCORE, SBA, Rochester, 1988—; With German Army. Recipient 2 awards R&D Mag., 1972, 76. Died May 28, 2007.

MARTIN, DANIEL TUNNIE, academic surgeon; b. Nagpur, Maharastra, India, Nov. 28, 1953; came to U.S. 1972; s. Tunnie and Eloise Madrid (Butler) M.; m. Carolyn S. Campbell, Apr. 2, 1988; children: Joshua Daniel, Caitlyn Campbell. BA, Anderson Coll., 1976; MD, Ohio State U., 1980. Diplomate Am. Bd. Surgery. Clin. instr. surgery (intern and resident) Ohio State U. Hosps., Columbus, 1980-87, rsch. fellow, 1981-83, adminstr. surg. rsch., 1982-88; chmn. dept. surgery Meml. Hosp., Fremont, Ohio, 1988-91; clin. asst. prof. surgery Med. Coll. of Ohio, Toledo, 1988-92; assoc. dir. surg. endoscopy and asst. prof. surgery U. N.Mex., Albuquerque, from 1992. Contbr. articles to profl. jours., chpts. to books. Fellow ACS. Avocations: fly fishing, camping. Home: Albuquerque, N.Mex. Died July 8, 2007.

MARTIN, THERESA H., medical/surgical nurse; b. Savannah, Ga., Oct. 29, 1947; d. Carl Chester and Myrtle Fay (Hannah) Hughes; m. William Wayne Martin, Aug. 31, 1968; children: Cynthia Kay, Evelyn Fay, Jean Ann. Diploma, Meml. Sch. Nursing, Savannah, Ga., 1968; BSN, Bellarmine Coll., Louisville, 1986. Cert. emergency med. tech. instr., Ky., ACLS. DON Breckinridge Meml. Hosp., Hardinsburg, Ky.; nurse mgr. Floyd Meml. Hosp., New Albany, Ind. Tchr. vocat. edn. Mem. Ind. Orgn. Nurse Execs., Sigma Theta Tau. Home: Brandenburg, Ky. Died Nov. 14, 2006.

MARTINEN, JOHN A., travel company executive; b. Sault Ste Marie, Mich., June 26, 1938; s. John Albert and Ina Helia (Jarvi) M. BS with highest honors, Mich. State U., 1960; JD, NYU, 1963. Asst. purser Grace Line Inc., NYC, 1963—65, chief purser, 1965—69; cons. Empresa Turistica Internat., Galapagos Cruises, Quito, Galapagos Islands, Ecuador, 1969—70; regional mgr. Globus & Cosmos (Group Voyagers Inc.), NYC, 1970—73, v.p., 1974—76, exec. v.p., 1977—78, pres., CEO, 1979—92, Littleton, Colo., 1993—98, chmn., 1998; pres., CEO Vista Travel Ventures, Inc., Denver, 1999—2001; pres. Trafalgar Tours, Long Island City, NY, 2002; prin. Safe Passage Internat., Lakewood, Colo., from 2003. Bd. dirs. 366 Broadway Homeowners Assn., NYC, 1983—92, sec., 1987—92; bd. dirs. Edbrooke Homeowners Assn., Denver, 1992—2002, sec., 1994—97, pres., 1997—2002. Named Person of Yr., Travel Agt. Mag., 1996; Root-Tilden Scholar, N.Y.U. Law Sch., 1960—63. Mem. Am. Soc. Travel Agts. (chmn. tour operating program 1995-99), U.S. Tour Operators Assn. (bd. dirs. 1993-99, treas. 1996-97, sec. 1998-99, chmn. travel automation com., 1990-1998), Acad. Travel and Tourism (bd. advisors 1987-92, NY, 1992-01, Denver), Lotos Club NY, Wings Club (NY), Skal Club(bd. dirs.), NY, Am. Tourism Soc., The Travel Inst. Democrat. Achievements include developing and operating the first passenger cruises in the Galapagos islands; providing the first consumer travel insurance plan to be made available to consumers trough travel suppliers; increasing annual tour operator passenger volume from 50,000 to over 280,000; on escorted tours to six continents. Died Dec. 2014.

MARTINEZ, FERNANDO V., civil engineer; b. Blewett, Tex., July 2, 1927; s. Catarino G. and Refugia V. M.; m. Dora Garza, Sept. 27, 1953; children: Fernando G., Karen Martinez Solano, Edward A. BS in Civil Engring, Tex A&M U., 1951. Registered profl. engr., Tex. Field engr. Farnsworth & Chambers Co, Houston, Tex., 1953-54; design engr. Link Belt Co., Houston, 1954, Anderson Clayton & Co., Houston, 1954-59; project engr. Olin Mathieson Chem. Corp., Pasadena, Tex., 1959-80; project mgr. Mobil Oil Corp., Pasadena, from 1980. 1st lt. U.S. Army, 1951-53, Korea. Republican. Roman Catholic. Home: Pasadena, Tex. Died June 12, 2007.

MARTZELL, JOHN ROBERT, lawyer; b. Shreveport, La., Feb. 9, 1937; s. Victor and Catherine (Cloverlee) M. BS in Acctg., U. Notre Dame, 1958, JD, 1961. Law clk. to Hon. J. Kelly Wright U.S. Dist. Ct. (ea. dist.) La., law clk. to Hon. Frank B. Ellis; dir. La. Commn. on Human Relations, Rights and Responsibilities, 1966-72; spl. counsel Gov. John W. McKeithen, 1968-72; ptnr. Martzell & Bickford, New Orleans, from 1973. Lectr. in field; spl. rep. Chiropractic Assn. La.; spl. counsel Bogalusa City Coun. on Civil Rights, 1965, New Orleans City Coun. Pub. Bidding on City Health Ins. Plan, 1980-85; chief counsel pro bono project La. Atty. Gen., 1988. Mem. ABA (com. on acad. freedom, com. on complex bus. crimes), ATLA (mem. admiralty sect., La. Key Man on Legis.ation, spkr. on basic advocacy programs, chmn. dept. pub. affairs 1982-84), La. Bar Assn. (com. on ins., chmn. pub. rels. com., chmn. auto. reparations reform com. 1978, law reform com. 1980, chmn. subcom. on revision of discilplinary procs. of com. on profl. responsibility 1988), La. Trial lawyers Assn. (sec.-treas. 1968-69, 70-71, chmn. legis. com. 1968-70, v.p. 1971-72, pres. 1972-73, bd. govs.), Nat. Assn. Criminal Def. Lawyers, La. Assn. Criminal Def. Lawyers, Am. Coll. Trial Lawyers. Home: New Orleans, La. Died May 23, 2007.

MARVEL, THOMAS STAHL, architect; b. Newburgh, NY, Mar. 15, 1935; s. Gordon Simis and Madelyn Emigh (Jova) M.; m. Lucilla Wellington Fuller, Apr. 19, 1958; children— Deacon Simis, Jonathan Jova, Thomas Stahl AB, Dartmouth Coll., Hanover, NH, 1956; MArch, Harvard U., Cambridge, Mass., 1962. Registered architect, NC, PR, Mass., NY. Designer Synergetics, Inc., Raleigh, NC, 1958; designer IBEC Housing, NYC, 1959; ptnr., architect Torres-Beauchamp-Marvel, San Juan, 1960-85, Marvel-Flores-Cobian, San Juan, 1985-97; ptnr. Thomas S. Marvel Architects, San Juan, 1997—2015. Prof. Sch. Architecture, U. PR, Rio Piedras, 1967-89. Author: Antonin Nechodoma-1877-1928: The Praire School in the Caribbean, 1994; co-author: The Architecture of the Parish Churches of Puerto Rico, 1984. Works include Am. Embassy, Guatemala, 1973, U.S. Courthouse and Fed. Office Bldg., V.I., 1976, City Hall, Bayamon, P.R., 1978, Mcpl. Baseball Stadium, Bayamon, 1975, Am. Embassy, Costa Rica, 1986. Bd. dirs. St. John's Sch., San Juan, 1976-93. Recipient 1st award for regional coll. design U. PR, Utuado, 1983; Harvard Grad. Sch. Design Julia Amory Appleton travelling fellow, 1962, Henry Klumb prize, 1991. Fellow AIA (bd. dirs. 1993-96, Design award for Fla. Caribbean region 1981, 84-85, 90-91); mem. PR Coll. Architects, Acad. Arts and Scis. Clubs: Harvard (NYC). Roman Catholic. Home: San Juan, PR. Died Nov. 3, 2015.

MASON, ANTHONY GEORGE DOUGLAS, professional basketball player; b. Miami, Fla., Dec. 14, 1966; s. Mary Mason; 2 children, Antoine, Anthony, Jr. Grad., Tenn. State U., 1988. Forward Efes Pilsen, 1988—89, N.J. Nets, 1989-90, Tulsa Fast Breakers, 1990-91, Denver Nuggers, 1990, L.I. Surf, 1991, N.Y. Knickerbockers, 1991-96, Charlotte Hornets, 1996—2000, Miami Heat, 2000—01, Milwaukee Bucks, 2001—03. Recipient Miller Genuine Draft NBA 6th Man award, 1995; named to All NBA Third Team, 1997, NBA All-Defense Second Team, 1997; named NBA All Star 2001 Died Feb. 28, 2015.

MASON, DANA, women's mental health nurse; b. Muncie, Ind., Apr. 15, 1951; d. John C. and Gladys G. (Grooms) Hoover; m. H. L. Mason, Sept. 1978; children: Daniel J., Christina L. BSN, U. Wis., 1978; M of Nursing Edn. and Adminstrn., Ball State U., 1983. RN, Wis., Ind. Nurse practitioner Midwest Med. Ctr., Madison, Wis.; prof. nursing Purdue U., W. Lafayette, Ind. Contbr. articles and rsch. to profl. jours. Mem. Am. Nurses AIDS Care, Ind. State Nurses Assn., Soc. for Sci. Study of Sexology, Sigma Theta Tau. Died June 28, 2007.

MASON, RUTH A., home health nurse; b. Paterson, NJ, Oct. 24, 1948; d. Philip Henry and Ruth Mary (Avery) Thornton; m. Harry Mason, Dec. 17, 1976 (dec. Oct. 1985). AAS in Nursing, Bergen C.C., Paramus, NJ, 1978; BSN, Coll. of St. Elizabeth, Convent Station, NJ, 1994. RN, N.J.; cert. operating rm. nurse, Assn. Operating Rm. Nurses. Operating rm. nurse Morristown (N.J.) Meml. Hosp., 1980-87; case coord. N.W. Covenant Hosp., Denville, N.J., 1994-95; home health nurse PSA Healthcare, Lafayette, N.J., 1996, Olsten Health Svcs., Totowa, N.J., from 1997. Contbr. articles to profl. publs. Vol. food drive and home-bound visits St. Peter Roman Cath. Ch., Parsippany, N.J., 1994; vol. Riverside Hosp., Denville, N.J., 1973. Avocations: travel, water and equestrian activities. Home: Zephyrhills, Fla. Died Apr. 23, 2007.

MASSEY, HOWARD CLAYLAND, writer; b. Coolidge, Ga., Oct. 21, 1925; s. Paul Lester and Ruby Dell Massey; m. Hilda Dodson Schroer, June 17, 1966; 1 child, Sondra Gayle Siegel; m. Edna Ann Weller (div.); 1 child, Richard Clayton. M in Plumbing and Heating, Lindsey Hopkins Tech. Edn. Ctr., Miami, 1958. Owner Ctr. Plumbing & Heating Corp., Miami-Dade, 1958—73; plans examiner Met. Bldg. & Zoning Dept., Miami-Dade, 1974—88; author Craftsman Book Co., Hollywood, Fla., 1978—85, Vero Beach, Fla., from 1986. Designer plumbing isometrics State of Fla. Lic. Bd., 1982—84; creator exam. questions Constrn. Industry Lic. Bd., Fla., 1983—85. Author: (tech. book) Plumber's Handbook, 1978, Basic Plumbing With Illustrations, 1980, Estimating Plumbing Costs, 1982, Plumber's Exam Preparation Guide, 1985, Planning Drain, Waste & Vent Systems, 1990, International Plumbing & Fuel Gas Codes, 2003, America's Ragged Edge, 2005, Deep Woods, 2006. Seaman 3d class USN, 1943—45. Mem.: Gideons Internat., Authors Guild. Republican. Home: Vero Beach, Fla. Died Feb. 16, 2015.

MASSIE, WALTER ARTHUR, psychiatrist; b. Pitts., July 21, 1922; s. Arthur Walter and Mathilda V. (Kuhns) M.; m. Anne B. Massie, Aug. 13, 1949; children: Susan, Linda, David, Carol, Nancy, Mark. Student, U. Rochester, 1944; BS, Allegheny Coll., 1948; MD, Temple U., 1948. Diplomate Am. Bd. Psychiatry and Neurology. Intern Allegheny Gen. Hosp., Pitts., 1948-49; resident in psychiatry U.S. Vets. Hosp., Coatesville, Pa., 1950-51, Norwich (Conn.) State Hosp., 1951-52, U. Pitts., 1952-53; pres. Ohio Psychiat. Clinic Dirs., 1956-59; dir. Mansfield (Ohio) Guidance Ctr., 1954-70; practice medicine specializing in psychiatry Mansfield, from 1970. Chief of staff Richland Hosp., 1975—. Class agt. Allegheny Coll., 1984—. Served to lt. USN, 1950-54. Mem. AMA, Ohio Med. Assn., Richland County Med. Soc., Am. Psychiat. Assn., Ohio Psychiat. Assn. Lutheran. Avocations: flying, photography, music. Home: Mansfield, Ohio. Died Feb. 28, 2007.

MASTERS, HILARY THOMAS, writer, educator; b. Kans. City, Feb. 3, 1928; s. Edgar Lee and Ellen Frances (Coyne) Masters; m. Robin Owen Watt, Oct. 1953 (div. Nov. 1954); m. Polly Jo McCulloch, Mar. 5, 1955 (div. May 1985); children: Joellen, Catherine, John; m. Kathleen George, Feb. 25, 1994. BA, Brown U., 1952. Writer-in-residence dept. English U NC, Greensboro, 1973—74, Drake U., 1975—77, Clark U., 1978, Ohio U., 1979, Denver U., 1982, U. NC, Greensboro, 1981, Ohio U., 1982; Fulbright lectr. U. Jyvaskyla, Finland, 1983, Carnegie-Mellon U., Pitts., from 1983. Author: The Common Pasture, 1967, An American Marriage, 1969, Palace of Strangers, 1971, Last Stands: Notes From Memory, 1982, Clemmons, 1984, Hammertown Tales, 1986, Cooper, 1987, Strickland, 1990, Success New and Selected Stories, 1992, Home Is the Exile, 1996; contbr. articles to profl. jours. Advisor NY. State Assembly Spkr., 1967; del. R.F. Kennedy campaign, 1968. With USN, 1947—48. Recipient American Acad. of Arts and Letters award, 2003; Yaddo Corp. fellowship, Saratoga, NY, 1980. Mem.: Am. Soc. Mag. Photographers, PEN Internat., Authors Guild, Beachcombers Club (Provincetown, Mass.), Players Club (NYC). Avocations: skiing, cooking. Home: Pittsburgh, Pa. Died June 14, 2015.

MASTERSON, JOHN HENRY KIRBY, foreign languate educator; b. Montgomery, Ala., Dec. 30, 1923; s. Thomas G. Masterson and Mary Paschal Richardson; m. Kathryn Thurston, Nov. 26, 1948; children: Roger, Mary, Mark, Sara, Bruce, Dale Duff. B of Journalism, U. Mo., 1948; M of Fgn. Study, U. Paris, 1950; MA, So. Meth. U., 1971. Interpretor, translator Ordnance Procurement Ctr. U.S. Dept. of Army, Paris, 1952-54; tchr. French and Spanish University City (Mo.) Sr. H.S., 1955-59; tchr. French Horace Greeley H.S., Chappaqua, N.Y., 1959-65; tchr. French and spanish St. Mark's Sch. of Tex., Dallas, 1965-71; chmn. dept. fgn. lang. Hillsdale Sch., Cin., 1971-73; tchr. ESL Indiana River C.C., Ft. Pierce, Fla., from 1991. Publicity dir. Nat. Music Camp, Interlochen, Mich., summers 1955-57; dir. overseas summer study abroad Ind. Schs., Dallas, 1968. With U.S. Army, 1943-46, ETO. Mem. Am. Assn. Tchrs. of French (pres. 1961-63). Democrat. Episcopalian. Avocations: photography, classical music. Home: Aransas Pass, Tex. Died Feb. 10, 2007.

MASTIN, LYNN P., biology professor; d. Forest Lynn and Martha Hamilton Purdom; m. Nathan Edgar Mastin, Dec. 21, 1974; 1 child, E. Thomas. BA in Biology, U. West Ga., Carrollton, 1971, MS in Biology, 1973. Microbiologist Ctrs. for Disease Control, Atlanta, 1974—76; instr. Oklahoma City Schs., 1979—82, South Okla. City Jr. Coll., Oklahoma City, 1982—84, Mid-Del Christian Sch., Oklahoma City, 1984—89, Life Christian Sch., Oklahoma City, 1989—90, Lee County Schs., Tupelo, Miss., 1992—99, Itawamba C.C., Fulton, Miss., from 1999. Tchr., musician Union Christian Assembly, Tupelo, from 1990. Mem.: Miss. State Tchrs. Assn. Home: Nettleton, Miss. Died June 1, 2007.

MASUR, KURT, conductor, music director; b. Brieg, Silesia, Germany, July 18, 1927; m. Tomoko Sakurai; 1 child, Ken-David; children: Angelika, Carolin, Michael, Matthias. Grad., Nat. Music Schule, Breslau, Germany, 1944, Leipzig Conservatory, 1946-48; degree (hon.), U. Mich., Cleve. Inst. Music, Leipzig U., Westminster Choir Coll., Hamilton Coll. Repetiteur and conductor Halle Nat. Theatre, 1948-51; conductor Erfurt City Theatre, 1951-53, Leipzig City Theatre, 1953-55, Dresden Philharm., 1955-58; gen. music dir. Mecklenburg Staatstheater, 1958-60; mus. dir. Komische Oper Berlin, 1960-64; chief conductor Dresden Philharm., 1967-72; conductor Leipzig Gewandhaus Orch., 1970-96; mus. dir. NY Philharmonic, NYC, 1991—2002; conductor London Philharm. Orch., 1989-92, principal conductor, 2000—07; music dir. Orchestre National de France, Paris, 2002—08; music dir. emeritus Philharmonic Soc. of NY, 2002—15. Prof. Leipzig Acad. Music, from 1975; hon. guest condr. Israel Philharm. Orch., 1992. Musician (tours include): Europe, S.Am., Japan, U.S., Can., Mid. East; musician: (rec. artist) Symphonies by Mendelssohn, Symphonies by Brahms, Symphonies by Bruckner, Symphonies by Beethoven, Symphonies by Schumann, Symphonies by Tchaikovsky, Prokofiev's Piano Concertos, Beethoven's Missa Solemnis. Died Dec. 19, 2015.

MATAS, MYRA DOROTHEA, interior architect, designer, consultant; b. San Francisco, Mar. 21, 1938; d. Arthur Joseph and Marjorie Dorothy (Johnson) Anderson; m. Michael Richard Matas Jr., Mar. 15, 1958; children: Michael Richard III, Kenneth Scott. Cert. interior design, Canada Coll.; cert. interior design, Calif. Owner, operator Miguel's Antiques Co., Millbrae, Calif., 1969-70, Miguel's Antiques & Interiors Co., Burlingame, Calif., 1979-79, Country Elegance Antiques and Interiors Co., Menlo Park, Calif., 1979-84, La France Boutique Co., 1979-84; owner, operator, interior designer, archtl. designer Myra D. Matas Interior Design, San Francisco, 1984-2000, Lafayette, La., from 1994; mgr. LaFrance Imports, Inc., 1982-92; pres., gen. contractor Artisans 3 Inc., Burlingame, 1988-92; gen. contractor Matas Constr., Millbrae, 1993-98; instr. interior design dept. Canada Coll. Contbr. articles in field to profl. jours. Mem. Calif. Coun. Interior or Design. Home: Arnaudville, La. Died Nov. 12, 2006.

MATEO, JULIO CESAR, artist; b. Havana, Cuba, Apr. 16, 1951; came to U.S., 1960; s. Cesar Augusto and Loreto Eulalia (Mirás) M.; m. Raquel Wiltbank, Mar. 17, 1973; 1 child, William Patrick Wiltbank. BFA, U. Fla., 1973; MFA, U. South Fla., 1978. Pub., artist print portfolios The Marriage of Heaven and Earth, 1987, Grace, 19189, Nine Diamonds, 1991; one-man shows Nico Smith Gallery 1985, Stokker-Stikker Gallery 1986, Cathedral Ch. St. John the Divine 1990 (all N.Y.C.); exhibited in group shows Smithsonian Instn., Washington, 1977, Bklyn. Mus., 1985, Mus.

Contemporary Hispanic Art, 1985, 86, 88, Bronx (N.Y.) Mus. Art, 1987, 90, P.S. 1 Mus., N.Y.C., 1990, Artists Space, N.Y.C., 1993; represented in permanent collections N.Y. Pub. Libr., Chase Manhattan Bank, N.Y.C. Fellow Fine Arts Coun. Fla., 1980, Nat. Endowment for Arts, 1989. Home: Truth Or Consequences, N.Mex. Died Dec. 3, 2013.

MATHÉ, LYNDA ANNE PALOMA, educator; b. Hackensack, NJ, Mar. 25, 1948; d. Clarence Eugene and Rose (Heinz) M. BA, Fairleigh Dickinson U., 1969; MA, Columbia U., 1971. Owner, dir. Mathé Dance Studio, Clifton, N.J., 1973-79; program dir., tchr. Meadowlands Area YMCA, Rutherford, N.J., 1979-80; program coord., tchr. Cultural Homestay Inst., Roseville, Calif., 1981-84; tchr. Calif. Youth Authority, Nevada City, 1984-91; program developer, instr. Nevada Union Adult Edn., Grass Valley, Calif., 1984-91; program coord. Mech. Industry Ednl. Found., 1990-92. Adj. prof. Essex Community Coll., Newark, 1972-76, Dutchess Coll., Poughkeepsie, N.Y., 1974-76, Sussex County Coll., Peekskill, N.Y., 1975-76, Sullivan County Coll., 1975-76; publicity dir. Rainbow Theatre Co., Nevada City, 1986-89; publicity dir., instr. Dance Drum Workshop, Grass Valley, 1988-91, organizer, performer STARS (Short Term Artists in Residency), Nevada City, 1987-91; broadcaster Sta. KNCO, Grass Valley, 1988. Columnist Senior Life, 1989. Guest broadcaster Sta. KVMR, Nevada City, and KOBO, Yuba City, Calif., 1984-88. Recipient award Nevada County Arts Coun., 1984, 85, 87, cert. of artistry Nat. Assn. Dance and Assoc. Artists, 1975. Mem. AAUW. Home: Palo Alto, Calif. Died Mar. 4, 2007.

MATHEU, FEDERICO MANUEL, university chancellor; b. Humacao, PR, Mar. 17, 1941; s. Federico Matheu-Baez and Matilde Delgado-Vazquez; m. Myrna Delgado-Miranda, May 30, 1963; children: Federico Antonio, Rosa Myrna, Alfredo Javier, David Reinaldo. BS in Chem. Engring, U. P.R., 1962; PhD in Phys. Chemistry, U. Pitts., 1971. Chem. engr. Commonwealth Oil Refining Co., 1962-63; mem. adminstrv. staff and faculty U. P.R., 1963-78, dir. Humacao Coll., 1976-78; chancellor San German campus Inter Am. U. P.R., 1978-91; exec. dir., gen. coun. on edn. Commonwealth of P.R., Hato Rey, 1991-96; chancellor U. Metropolitana-Ana G. Méndez U. System, from 1996. Cons. in field. Author papers, reports in field. Named Disting. Educator P.R. Jaycees, 1974 Mem. Colegio de Quimicos P.R., Am. Chem. Soc., Sci. Tchrs. Assn. P.R. (pres. 1975-76), P.R. Acad. Arts and Scis., Phi Delta Kappa, Phi Tau Sigma. Home: Guaynabo, PR. Died Nov. 24, 2012.

MATHEWS, KRISTIE RASTATTER, military officer, nurse; b. Erie, Pa., Jan. 24, 1955; d. Herbert F. and Patricia R. (Condon) Rastatter; m. Allen Collier Mathews, Mar. 12, 1983; 1 child, Jacob R. Mathews. BS in Nursing, Fla. State U., 1977; MS in Nursing, U. N.Mex., 1988. Commd. 2d. lt. USAF, 1978, advanced to lt. col., 1992, clin. nurse acute care unit Belleville, Ill., charge nurse, surg. unit Portsmouth, N.H., flight nurse Rhein Main AB, Fed. Republic Germany, nursing evening supr. Albuquerque; nurse mgr. orthopedic unit USAFA Hosp., Colorado Springs, Colo.; asst. chief nurse USAF Acad. Hosp.; ret. USAF, 1995. Air Force Inst. Tech. scholar; named Field Grade Officer of the Yr. USAFA Hosp., 1990. Mem. Sigma Theta Tau (Outstanding Grad. Student 1988), Phi Kappa Phi. Home: Colorado Springs, Colo. Died Aug. 1, 2007.

MATOVICH, MITCHEL JOSEPH, JR., film producer, film company executive; b. Watsonville, Calif., Dec. 16, 1927; s. Mitchel Joseph and Mildred Florence (Ingrom) Matovich; m. Patte Dee Matovich, 1989 (div. 2000); children from previous marriage: Wayne, Mark, Laura. Student, San Jose State U., 1946-49. Mech. designer Stanford Rsch. Inst., Menlo Park, Calif., 1955-59; rsch. specialist Lockheed Missiles & Space Co., Sunnyvale, Calif., 1959-70; mgr. NASA and Dept. of Def. bus. sect. Engineered Sys. divsn. FMC Corp., San Jose, Calif., 1970-77; pres., CEO Morton Co. disvn. Haycor Corp., Hayward, Calif., 1977-82; pres. Concept Devel. Co., Newark, Calif., 1982-89, Matovich Prodns., Hollywood, Calif., from 1987, Stereotronics Inc., Beverly Hills, Calif., from 1988, Movietown Pictures, from 1997. Co-owner Vagabond Theatre, LA, 1990—91. Author: (novels) The Image Machine, Webville, 2001, The Last Discoverer, 2002, The 4th Reich; author, artist: children's book series; prodr.: (films) I Don't Buy Kisses Anymore, 1992 (Best Ind. Feature Houston Internat. Film Festival, Award of Excellence Film Adv. Bd., Angel award Excellence in Media, Top Applause award Santa Clarita Valley Internat. Film Festival, 1994), Lightning in a Bottle, 1993 (Gold award Houston Film Festival, Award of Excellence Film Adv. Bd.); prodr., dir. : Deadly Delusions, 1999; co-prodr.: Social Suicide. Bd. dirs., pres. Interguild Credit Union; chmn. bd. dirs. Santa Clarita Internat. Film Festival, 1995—2001, v.p. With USN, 1945—46, with USN, 1951—52, Korea. Mem.: ASCAP, Prodrs. Guild (bd. dirs.), Dirs. Guild, Soc. Motion Picture and TV Engrs., Acad. TV Arts and Scis., Intertel, Mensa. Avocations: flying, scuba diving, writing, travel, art. Died June 7, 2007.

MATTER, HARRY H., retired wholesale business executive, reflexologist; b. Lykens, PA, May 23, 1914; s. Homer Calvin and Edith Ellen (Seesoltz) Matter; m. Rita M. De Nicholas Matter, July 24, 1949 (dec. Dec. 2004); children: Robert, Tina. Grad., Air War Coll., Maxwell AFB, Maxwell, AL, 1972. Cert. Am. Reflexology Bd., Internat. Inst. of Reflexology, St. Petersburg, FL, 1992, ARCB, PRA. Salesman Baums Sporting Goods, Sunbury, Pa., 1941—48, vice pres. and treas., 1948—64; sales mgr. Coughlanath Mart, Pottstown, Pa., 1965—78; vice pres. Penna Reflexology Assn., Phila., 1984—99; performer, vocals & guitar Western Music Assn. Festival, Tucson, 1991—99; entertainer Am. Fedn. of Musicians, Pocono Mts., 1965—99. Dir. treas., Baums Sporting Goods, Inc., 1948-60, vice pres., Baums Sporting Goods, Inc., 1958-64, sales mgr., Coughlan Athletic Mart, Pottstown, PA, 1965-78, vice pres. (ret.) Penna Reflexology Assn., Phila., PA, 1980-99. Artist, prodr. The Am. Cowboy Legend (cassette, 1981, compact disc, 1991), The Old Rugged Cross (cassette, 1992), Great COuntry Songs (cassette, 1994). Performs, Selinsgrove Ctr. Home for Mentally Challenged, Selinsgrove, PA, 1986-99. Recipient Nat. Commanders Citation, Civil Air Patrol, USAF, 1973, Top Songwriter, Wyo. Country Music Assn., 1981, Meritorious award, Civil Air Patrol, Pa. Wing, 1983, Exceptional Svc. award, Civil Air Patrol, USAF, Pa. Wing, 1984, Pioneer award, Colo. Country Music. Found., 1985—92, Lifetime Achievement Songwriters award, 2001, Artist Trailblazer Kingeagle award, Nashville, Tenn., 2001, Internat. Star award, Lifetime Achievement Songwriters Divsn., London, 2001, King Earle award, Airplay Internat., Nashville, 2001, Artist Trailblazer award, 2001; named to Country Music Hall of Fame, Colo. Country Music. Found., 1985. Mem. BPO Elks Lodge, Loyal Order of Moose, (vice pres.), Penna Reflexology Assn., 1990-99, Country Music Assn., Western Music Assn. (performer), 1991-99, Officer's Club, Indiantown Gap Mil. Res. Republican. Lutheran. Avocations: walking, music, photography, gardening. Home: Shamokin Dam, Pa. Died Aug. 9, 2007.

MATTHEWS, PATRICIA ANNE, writer; b. San Fernando, Calif., July 1, 1927; d. Roy Oliver and Gladys (Gable) Ernst; m. Marvin Owen Brisco, Dec. 3, 1946 (div. 1961); children: Michael A. Brisco, David R. Brisco; m. Clayton Hartley Matthews, Nov. 3, 1971. Student, Pasadena Jr. Coll., 1943-44, Calif. State U., LA, 1960. With Calif. State U., 1959-77. Author: Love's Avenging Heart, 1977, Love's Wildest Promise, 1977, Love, Forever More, 1977, Love's Daring Dream, 1978, Love's Pagan Heart, 1978, Love's Magic Moment, 1979, Love's Golden Destiny, 1979, Love's Raging Tide, 1980, Love's Sweet Agony, 1980, Love's Bold Journey, 1980, Tides of Love, 1981, Embers of Dawn, 1982, Flames of Glory, 1983 (Bronze medal West Coast Rev. Books 1983), Dancer of Dreams, 1984, Gambler in Love, 1985, Tame The Restless Heart, 1986, Destruction at Dawn, 1986, Twister, 1986, Enchanted, 1987 (Best Hist. Gothic award Romantic Times 1986-87), Thursday and The Lady, 1987, Mirrors, 1988, Oasis, 1988, The Night Visitor, 1988, The Dreaming Tree, 1989, Sapphire, 1989, The Death of Love, 1990, The Unquiet, 1991, (poetry) Love's Many Faces, 1979, (with Clayton Matthews) Midnight Whispers, 1981, Empire, 1982 (Silver medal West Coast Rev. Books 1983), Midnight Lavender, 1985, The Scent of Fear, 1992, Vision of Death, 1993, Taste of Evil, 1993, The Sound of Murder, 1994, The Touch of Terror, 1995, (play) Honky Tonk, 1993, (under pseudonym Patty Brisco) Merry's Treasure, 1969, Horror at Gull House, 1973, House of Candles, 1973, The Crystal Window, 1973, The Carnival Mystery, 1974, Mist of Evil, 1976, The Campus Mystery, 1977, Raging Rapids, 1978, Too Much in Love, 1979, (under pseudonym P.A. Brisco) The Other People, 1970, (under pseudonym Laura Wylie) The Night Visitor, 1979 (Silver medal West Coast Rev. Books 1979); contbg. author: Your First Romance, My First Romance, Love's Leading Ladies, Writing the Romance, Writer's Digest, Candlelight, Romance and You, various anthologies; author numerous short stories; contbr. poetry to profl. jours. Recipient (with Clayton Matthews) Team Writing award Romantic Times, 1983. Mem. Mystery Writers Am., Romance Writers Am., Sisters in Crime, Novelists Ink. Avocations: writing and playing music, acting. Died Dec. 7, 2006.

MAU, JACK A., veterinarian; b. Douglas, Wyoming, Aug. 7, 1929; s. Cecil T. and Phyllis M.; m. Martha Jane Moore, Dec. 7, 1952; children: Catherine, Tom, John, Elizabeth, Jim, Bill. DVM, Iowa State U., 1952. Pvt. practice, LeMars, Iowa, 1952-54; ptnr. McIntosh & Mau, La Porte City, Iowa, 1954-71; animal health product mgr. Internat. Multfoods, Mpls., 1971-72, dir. veterinary tech. svcs., from 1975-; dir. mktg. Osborn Lab. Internat. Multfoods, Mpls., 1972-75. Mem. Am. Vet. Med. Assn., Iowa Vet. Med. Assn., Minn. Vet. Med. Assn., Am. Assn. Swine Practitionery, Am. Assn. Bovine Practitionery, Indsl. Veterinarians, Am. Assn. Indsl. Vets. (pres. 1985-86), Am. Feed Ingredient Assn. Republican. Presbyterian. Avocations: golf, fishing, cards. Home: Hopkins, Minn. Died Aug. 14, 2007.

MAXTONE-GRAHAM, JOHN KURTZ, writer; b. East Orange, NJ, Aug. 2, 1929; s. Laurence Patrick Maxtone-Graham and Ellen Taylor; m. Katrina Kanzler, June 4, 1955 (div. 1980); children: Sarah Francois-Poncet, Ian, Emily Maxtone-Graham, Guy; m. Mary Smith Bergeron, 1981. BA, Brown U., 1951. Stage mgr. Broadway, NYC, 1954-68; freelance writer NYC, 1968—2015. Author: The Only Way to Cross, 1972, Dark Brown is the River, 1976, Liners to the Sun, 1985, Olympic & Titanic, 1983, Safe Return Doubtful: The Heroic Age of Polar Exploration, 1988, Cunard: 150 Glorious Years, 1989, Crossing & Cruising, 1992, Titanic Survivor, 1997, Titanic Tragedy: A New Look at the Lost Liner, Queen Mary 2: The Greatest Ocean Liner of Our Time, S.S. United States: Red, White and Blue Riband, Forever, Normandie: France's Legendary Art Deco Ocean Liner and many others; co-author: Under Crown & Anchor, 1995. Trustee Fleming Sch., N.Y.C., 1965-78, Gateway Sch., N.Y.C., 1968-73; trustee Ocean Liner Mus., N.Y.C., 1983-2015, pres., 1996. Capt. USMC, 1952-54, Korea. Avocations: carpentry, needlepoint. Died July 6, 2015.

MAXWELL, MARGARET, retired history and government educator; b. Topeka, Sept. 3, 1913; d. Robert Talmadge and Mary Margaret (Ritchie) Wright; m. Bertram Wayburn Maxwell, June 3, 1936 (dec. 1972). BA, Washburn U., Topeka, 1935; MA, Wellesley Coll., 1936; PhD, NYU, 1952. Instr. history Washburn U., 1936-37; rsch. asst. Kans. State Hist. Soc., Topeka, 1938-41; instr. in history Washington Sq. Coll., NYU, NYC, 1943-52, adj. prof., 1952-68; prof. history and govt. Finch Coll., NYC, 1953-75. Vis. prof. Hunter Coll., Wagner Coll.; ind. rschr., writer, occasional lectr., 1975—. Author: Narodniki Women, 1990; editor, translator: Russian Women's Studies, Sexism in Soviet Society, 1988; contbr. articles and book revs. to Social Sci., Ch. History, The Historian, European Studies Rev., Vyi i Myi, others. Recipient Disting. Svc. award NYU Alumni Fedn., also Disting. Svc. award Grad. Sch. Arts and Scis., 1991. Mem. Wellesley Coll. Alumnae, LWV, NOW, NARAL, Village Ind. Dems., NYU Alumni Fedn. (bd. dirs. 1972—), N.Y. Biography Seminar, N.Y. Society Libr., others. Avocations: walking, swimming. Home: New York, NY. Died Apr. 17, 2007.

MAY, PETER JOSEPH, communications executive; b. Rochester, NY, July 15, 1932; s. Peter George and Florence (Gravelle) M.; m. Ruth Maloney, 1955 (div. 1970); children: Deborah, Lorraine May Palma, Kenneth, Douglas; m. Sue Diringer, 1973 (dec. 1978); stepchildren: Judy Parrons, Donna Pickrell; m. Phyllis Agnes Eicher, Mar. 3, 1979; stepchildren: Steven M., Julie K. Lewis. AB in Math, Niagara U., Niagara Falls, 1954; postgrad., U. Rochester, UCLA, Rochester Inst. Tech. Network synthesis group design engr. to mgr. new sys. tech. Gen. Dynamics/ Stromberg Carlson, Rochester, N.Y., 1956-77; staff cons. to engring. mgr. Anaconda Co., Garden Grove, Calif., 1976-77; dir. engring. Brand Rex Co./Teltronics Co., Lakeland, Fla., 1977-81, San Bar Corp., Garland, Tex., 1981-82; pvt. telephone sys. engring. cons. Rockwall, Tex., 1982-83; network devel. specialist U.S. Tel, Dallas, 1983-85; cons. tech. stds. US Telecom, Kansas City, Mo., 1985-86; mgr. of standards US Sprint, Kansas City, from 1986. Mem. US Sprint voting rep. to ANSI T1 Com. on Telecommunications; rep. Interexchange Carriers Interst Group of the T1 Adv. Grp. of ANSI T1; cons. in field. Contbr. articles to profl. jours.; patentee in field. Mem. IEEE (sr. mem.), IEEE Communications Soc., Overland Park Club, Cosmopolitan Internat. (treas.), Lions, Delta Epsilon Sigma. Roman Catholic. Avocations: reading, investments, music, sports. Home: Lakeland, Fla. Died Mar. 7, 2007.

MAYES, BERNARD DUNCAN, broadcast journalist, educator, dramatist; b. London, Oct. 10, 1929; came to U.S., 1957; s. Reginald Harry and Nellie (Drew) M. BA, Cambridge U., Eng., 1952, MA, 1954. Ordained to ministry Eng. Episc. Ch., 1958. Reporter BBC, London, 1954-79, Hollywood, Calif., 1965-70, ABC, Sydney, 1970-84, CBC, Toronto, Ont., 1970-75, Radio New Zealand, Wellington, 1970-80; mem. summer faculty Stanford (Calif.) U., 1970-84; mgr. Sta. KQED-FM, San Francisco, 1969-71; founding chmn. Nat. Pub. Radio, Washington, 1969-71; exec. v.p. Sta. KQED-TV, San Francisco, 1971-73; pres. Trans Pacific Consortium, San Francisco, 1980-87; mem. faculty U. Va., 1984—99; dir. U. Va. Ctr. Modern Media Studies, Charlottesville, 1987—99, chmn. rhetoric and comms. studies dept., 1993-95. Sr. cons. Corp. for Public Broadcasting, Washington, 1978-84. Author: Getting It Across, 1957, This is Bernard Mayes in San Francisco, 1986, Escaping God's Closet: The Revelations of a Queer Priest, 2001; audio dramatist The Odyssey, Agammemnon and Antigone; actor (audio drama prodns.) The Hobbit, Lord of the Rings; producer documentary USA 200; reader Blackstone Audio Books. Founder Ctr. for Suicide Prevention, San Francisco, 1961-70, The Parsonage Episc. Study Ctr., San Francisco, 1981; chmn. media com. Campaign to End Homophobia, Boston, 1987; bd. dirs. Cerebral Palsy Assn., 1975-77, Heartland Project; mem. Lesbian and Gay Task Force. Recipient Scripts award Nat. Endowment for Arts., Washington, 1985, Jefferson award for Public Svc., 2010 Fellow Brown Coll.; mem. Bay Area Suicide Prevention Assn. (pres. 1975-77). Democrat. Avocation: writing. Home: Charlottesville, Va. Died Oct. 23, 2014.

MAYFIELD, HAROLD FORD, biology educator; b. Mpls., Mar. 25, 1911; s. John Edwin and Ida Mathilda (Thorberg) Blegen; m. Virginia Gaby Duval, June 14, 1936; children: Sigrid Christina, John Eric, Sheryl Melinda, Charles Frederick. BS, Shurtleff Coll., 1933; MA in Math., U. Ill., 1934; DSc (hon.), Occidental Coll., 1968, Bowling Green State U., 1975. Dir. pers. Owens-Illinois Inc., Toledo, 1936-71, ret., 1971; adj. prof. biology U. Toledo, from 1982. Author: The Kirtland's Warbler, 1960; contbr. articles to profl. jours. Coun. mem. President's Com. on Equal Opportunity, Washington, 1962-68; mem. Toledo Bd. Community Rels., 1968-71, Toledo-Lucas County Libr. Bd., 1971, Recovery Team Kirtland's Warbler, Washington, 1975-90. Recipient U.S. Forest Svc. 75th Anniversary award, 1980, Disting. Svc. award Detroit Audubon Soc., 1960, Disting. Svc. award Audubon Soc. Western Pa., 1978, Arthur A. Allen award Cornell U., 1990; named to Ohio Conservation Hall of Fame, 1978. Fellow AAAS, Am. Ornithologists Union (pres. 1966-68); mem. Wilson Ornithol. Soc. (pres. 1961-62), Cooper Ornithol. Soc. (pres. 1974-75). Home: Toledo, Ohio. Died Jan. 27, 2007.

MAYRON, LEWIS WALTER, clinical ecology consultant; b. Chgo., Sept. 20, 1932; s. Max and Florence Minette (Brody) M.; m. Sondra Mayron; children: Leslie Hope Mayron Coff, Eric Brian. BS in Chemistry, Roosevelt U., 1954; MS in Biol. Chemistry, U. Ill., 1955, PhD in Biol. Chemistry, 1959. Rsch. assoc. dept. biochemistry and nutrition U. So. Calif., LA, 1959-61; asst. biochemist dept. biochemistry Presbyn.-St. Luke's Hosp., Chgo., 1961-62; instr. dept. biol. chemistry U. Ill., Chgo., 1961-62; biochemistry group leader Tardanbek Labs., Chgo., 1962-63; sr. devel. chemist Abbott Labs., Chgo., 1963-64; asst. attending physician, mem. spl. staff Michael Reese Hosp. and Med. Ctr., Chgo., 1964-66, rsch. assoc. Dept. Allergy Rsch., 1964-66; asst. prof. in biochemistry and physiology Sch. Dentistry Loyola U., Chgo., 1968-71; guest investigator

Argonne (Ill.) Nat. Lab., 1973-79; rsch. chemist V.A. Hosp., Hines, Ill., 1968-79; chief clin. radiobiochemist nuclear medicine svc. V.A. Wadsworth Hosp. Ctr., LA, 1979-83; cons. in clin. ecology, from 1980. Contbr. articles to profl. jours. Mem. AAAS, Am. Assn. Clin. Chemists, Soc. for Exptl. Biology and Medicine, Sigma Xi. Home: Cedar City, Utah. Died Nov. 2013.

MAYSLES, ALBERT H., filmmaker; b. Boston, Nov. 26, 1926; s. Philip and Ethel (Epstein) M.; m. Gillian Walker, Sept. 14, 1976; children: Rebekah, Philip, Sara; stepchild Auralice Graft BA, Syracuse U., 1949; MA, Boston U., 1953. Rsch. fellow in anesthesia Mass. Gen. Hosp., Boston, 1951-52; instr. social rels. Boston U., 1953-55; pres. Maysles Films, Inc., NYC, 1962—2015. Filmmaker, prodr. Psychiatry in Russia, 1955, (with others) Youth In Poland, 1957, Primary, 1960, Showman, 1963, What's Happening: The Beatles in the USA, 1964, Salesman, 1967, Gimme Shelter, 1970, Christo's Valley Curtain, 1974, (Blue Ribbon award 1975, Acad. award nomination), Grey Gardens, 1976, Running Fence, 1978 (Blue Ribbon award 1978), Ozawa, 1985, Vladimir Horowitz: The Last Romantic, 1985, Islands, 1986 (Blue Ribbon award, Emmy award), Horowitz Plays Mozart, 1987, Christo in Paris, 1990, Soldiers of Music: Rostropovitch Returns to Russia, 1990 (Emmy award), Abortion: Desparate Choices, 1995 (Peabody award), Letting Go, A Hospice Journey, 1996 (Ace Cable award), Concert of Wills: The Making of the Getty Art Center, 1997; LaLee's Kin, 2000, The Gates, 2007, The Reales of Grey Gardens, 2006, Iris, 2014 Served as pvt. U.S. Army, 1944-46. Recipient Career Achievement award, Internat. Documentary Assn., 1994, John Grierson award for Documentary, SMPTE, 1997, Pres.'s award, Am. Soc. Cinematographers, 1998, Vision award, The Boston Film and Video Found., 1998, The Doubletake Career Achievement award, 1998, Lifetime Achievement award, Toronto's Hot Docs, 1999, Flaherty award, 1999, award for documentaries, Sundance Film Festival Cinematography, 2001, Dupont award, 2004, Medal of Honor for Theatre, Nat. Arts Club, 2007, Nat. Medal of Arts, 2014; named one of 100 World's Finest Cinematographers, Eastman Kodak, 1999; Guggenheim fellow, 1965. Mem. The Reality Club (Charter Guggenheim award, 2009). Home: New York, NY. Died Mar. 5, 2015.

MAZER, MILTON, psychiatrist; b. NYC, Mar. 5, 1911; s. Michael and Rose (Orman) M.; m. Virginia O'Leary, 1949; children: Ruth, Mark F. BA, U. Pa., 1932, MD, 1935. Diplomate Am. Bd. Psychiatry and Neurology. Intern Mt. Sinai Hosp., Phila., 1935-36, mem. staff, 1937-39; resident in internal medicine Montefiore Hosp., Bronx, N.Y., 1936-37; physician VA, Washington and Biloxi, Miss., 1939-42, psychiatry NYC, 1946-48; pvt. practice NYC, 1948-61, Marthas Vineyard, Mass., from 1961. Dir. Marthas Vineyard Mental Health Ctr., 1961-83; instr. Harvard Med. Sch., 1962-72, asst. prof. psychiatry, 1972-76, assoc. clin. prof., 1976-81. Author: People and Predicaments, 1976; co-editor: Outline of Psychoanalysis, 1951; contbr. articles to med. jours. Mem. West Tisbury (Mass.) Dem. Town Com., 1962—; moderator West Tisbury Town Meeting, 1967-77. Capt. M.C., USAAF, 1942-45. Fellow Am. Psychiat. Assn. (life). Home: West Tisbury, Mass. Died Jan. 7, 2007.

MAZRUI, ALI AL'AMIN, political science professor, researcher; b. Mombasa, Kenya, Feb. 24, 1933; came to U.S., 1960; s. Al'Amin Ali and Safia (Suleiman) M.; m. Molly Vickerman, 1962 (div. 1982); children: Jamal, Al'Amin, Kim Abubakar; m. Pauline Uti, Oct. 1991; children: Farid Chinedu, Harith Ekenechukwu. BA with distinction, U. Manchester, Eng., 1960; MA, Columbia U., 1961; DPhil, Oxford U., 1966. Lectr. Makerere U., Kampala, Uganda, 1963-65, prof. polit. sci., head dept. polit. sci., 1965-73; dean faculty social scis. Faculty Social Scis., Makerere U., Kampala, Uganda, 1967-69; prof. polit. sci. U. Mich., Ann Arbor, 1974-91, prof. Ctr. Afroam. and African Studies, dept. polit. sci., 1974-91; Andrew D. White prof.-at-large Cornell U., Ithaca, 1986-92; research prof. polit. sci. U. Jos, Nigeria, 1981-86; Albert Schweitzer prof. humanities SUNY, Binghamton, from 1989; sr. scholar, Andrew D. White prof.-at-large emeritus Cornell U, Ithaca, 1992—2014; dir. Inst. Global Cultural Studies SUNY, Binghamton, 1991—2014; chancellor Jomo Kenyatta Univ. Agrl. and Tech., Kenya, 2003—14. Ibn Khaldun prof.-at-large Sch. Islamic and Social Scis., Leesburg, Va., 1997-2000; Reith lectr. BBC, London, 1979; vis. prof. various univs. including U. London, U. Chgo., Oxford U., U. Pa., Ohio State U., Manchester U., Harvard U., Nairobi U., UCLA, Northwestern U., U. Singapore, Colgate Coll., U. Australia, Stanford U., U. Cairo, Sussex U., U. Leeds, Internat. Islamic U., Malaysia; mem. bank's coun. African advisers, World Bank, Washington, 1988-91; Walter Rodney disting. prof. U. Guyana, Georgetown, 1997-98, sr. fellow Prince Alwaleed Bin Talal Ctr. Muslim-Christian Understanding, Georgetown U., 2010 Author: Towards A Pax Africana: A Study of Ideology and Ambition, 1967, The Anglo-African Commonwealth: Political Friction and Cultural Fusion, 1967, On Heroes and Uhuru-Worship: Essays on Independent Africa, 1967, Violence and Thought: Essays on Social Tensions in Africa, 1969, Cultural Engineering and Nation-Building in East Africa, 1972, World Culture and the Black Experience, 1974, The Political Sociology of the English Language: An African Perspective, 1975, Soldiers and Kinsmen in Uganda: The Making of a Military Ethnocracy, 1975, Euro-Jews and Afro-Arabs: The Great Semitic Divergence in World History, Washington, 2008; co-editor: (with Robert I. Rotberg) Protest and Power in Black Africa, 1970, (with Hasu Patel) Africa in World Affairs: The Next Thirty Years, 1973; editor: The Warrior Tradition in Modern Africa, 1978, Africa since 1935 Volume III Unesco General History of Africa, 1973-93, (with Alamin M. Mazrui) The Political Culture of Language: Swahili, Society and the State, 1996—99, (with Alamin M. Mazrui) The Power of Babel: Language and Governance in Africa's Experience, 1998; sr. editor: (with T.K. Levine) The Africans: A Reader, 1986; author: The Trial of Christopher Okigbo, 1971, A World Federation of Cultures: An African Perspective, 1976; Africa's International Relations: The Diplomacy of Dependency and Change, 1977, Political Values and the Educated Class in Africa, 1978, The African Condition: A Political Diagnosis, 1980, (with Michael Tidy) Nationalism and New States in Africa, From About 1935 to the Present, 1984; narrator, presenter: The Africans: A Triple Heritage, 1986, Cultural Forces in World Politics, 1990, A Tale of Two Africas, 2006, Islam Between Globalization and Counterterrorism, 2006; mem. editl. bd. various profl. jours., 1963—, Globalization & Civilization: Are they Forces in Conflict, The Policies of War & Culture of Violence, The African Predicament & The American Experience: A Tale of 2 Edens, African Islamic Experience: History, Culture & Politics, Public Intellectuals and the Politics of Global Africa, DEbating the Africa Condition: Mazroi and His Critics, Race, Gender & Culture Conflict, Vol I, 2003, Governance & Leadership, 2011; contbr. articles to profl. publs. & essays Fellow Ctr for Advanced Study in Behavioral Scis., Palo Alto, Calif., 1972-73; sr. fellow Hoover Instn. on War, Revolution and Peace, Stanford, Calif., 1973-74, Mich. Soc. Fellows, 1978-82; Commander of the Burning Spear award, Kenya, 2005, ECO-WAS award of Living Legend, 2007, South African award of Grand Companion of Oliver Tambo, 2007, Image of Africa prize, Friends Africa Internat., NY, 2008. Fellow Internat. Assn. Mid. Eastern Studies, Ghana Acad. Arts and Scis. (hon.); mem. African Studies Assn. (exec. bd. 1975-80, pres. 1978-79, Disting. Africans award 1995), Internat. Congress African Studies (v.p. 1978-85), Internat. Polit. Sci. Assn. (v.p. 1970-73), World Order Models Project (dir. African sect. 1968-83), Royal African Soc. (v.p.), Royal Commonwealth Soc., United Kenya Club (Nairobi), Athenaeum Club (London), Assn. Muslim Social Scientists (Washington), Assn. Muslim Social Scientists (US & Can-.)(pres. 2009) Home: Vestal, NY. Died Sept. 12, 2014.

MCARDLE, JOSEPH WITHROW, metal products executive; b. Toledo, Apr. 27, 1941; s. Allan Booth and Ann Eliza (Withrow) McArdle; m. Sarah Dallam Toy, Apr. 12, 1969; children: Christopher, Eliza. BS, Yale U., 1963. Adminstrv. asst. Toledo Pressed Steel Co., 1966—72, v.p., 1972—82, pres., 1982—87, Fountain Industries, Fountain Inn, SC, from 1987. Bd. mem. Employees Assn. Toledo, 1981; author computer program. Contbr. articles to mag. Co-founder Friends of the Maumee, 1971; bd. mem. Storer camps YMCA, 1982. Mem.: Am. Metal Stamping Assn. (dist. pres. 1973—74), Precision Metal Forming Assn. (dist. chmn. 1973—74), Rotary, Newcomen Soc. Republican. Episcopalian. Home: Little Switzerland, NC. Died Nov. 10, 2006.

MC AULEY, ROBERT JAMES, JR., pharmacist; b. Trenton, NJ, Mar. 24, 1945; s. Robert James Mc Auley Sr and Elizabeth Mc Auley; m. Joanne Mae Mc Auley, Aug. 31, 1968; children: Robert James III, Angela Mary, Melissa Ann. BS Phamracy, Phila. Coll. Pharmacy, 1968; MS Pharmacy, U. Mich., 1973. Diplomate Am. Bd. Sci. Nuclear Medicine, 1979; lic. pharmacist Md., Pa., N.J., Okla., Tex., Calif., Ark., Mich., Tenn. Intern Cmty Pharmacy Practice, Camden, NJ, 1968—69; resident Brooke Army Med. Ctr., San Antonio, 1974; chief nuclear pharmacy svc. Letterman Army Med. Ctr., San Francisco, 1977—83; chief clin. investigator activity U.S. Army Health Svcs. Commd., San Antonio, 1985—90; chief pharmacy svc. U.S. Army Hosp., Heidelburg, Germany, 1990—93; pharmacy cons. U.S. Army, 1991—93; dir. clin. ops. Maxor, Inc., Balt., 1993—94; clin. edn. cons. Pfizer, Inc., Bel Air, 1994—2001; pharmacist in charge VetCentric, Inc., Annapolis, from 2001. Clin. asst. prof. U. Md. Sch. Pharmacy, from 1997; lectr. Army Med. Dept., Acad. Health Scis., San Antonio, 1986—90; adj. prof. U. Pacific Sch. Pharmacy, Stockton, Calif., 1977—82. Contbr. articles to profl. jours. Col. US Army, 1966—84. Mem.: Md. Soc. Health-System Pharmacists, Assn. Mil. Surgeons U.S., Acad. Managed Care Pharmacy, Am. Pharm. Assn., Am. Soc. Health-System Pharmacists, Am. Coll. Vet. Pharmacists. Republican. Home: Bel Air, Md. Died Jan. 6, 2007.

MCBRIEN, RICHARD PETER, theology educator; b. Hartford, Conn., Aug. 19, 1936; s. Thomas Henry and Catherine Ann (Botticelli) McB. AA, Saint Thomas Sem., Bloomfield, Conn., 1956; BA, Saint John Sem., 1958; MA, Saint John Sem., Brighton, Mass., 1962; STD, Pontifical Gregorian U., Rome, 1967. Ordained priest Archdiocese of Hartford, Conn., 1962; assoc. pastor Our Lady of Victory Ch., West Haven, Conn., 1962-63; prof., dean of studies Pope John XXIII Nat. Sem., Weston, Mass., 1965-70; prof. theology Boston Coll., Newton, Mass., 1970-80, dir. Inst. of Religious Edn. and Pastoral Ministry, 1975-80; prof. theology to Crowley-O'Brien prof. theology U. Notre Dame, Ind., 1980—2013, Crowley-O'Brien prof. theology emeritus Ind., 2013—15, chmn. dept. Ind., 1980-91, pres. faculty senate Ind., 1994—97. Cons. various dioceses and religious communities in the U.S. and Can., 1965-2015; vis. fellow John Fitzgerald Kennedy Sch. of Govt. Harvard U., Cambridge, 1975-76; mem. Council on Theol. Scholarship and Research Assn. of Theol. Schs., 1987-91; invited lectr. in the field Author: The Church In the Thought of Bishop John Robinson, 1966, Do We Need Church?, 1969, What Do We Really Believe?, 1969, rev. edit. 1977, Church: The Continuing Quest, 1970, Who Is A Catholic?, 1971, For the Inquiring Catholic: Questions and Answers for the 1970s, 1973, The Remaking of the Church, 1973, Has the Church Surrendered?. 1974, Roman Catholicism, 1975, In Search of God, 1977, Basic Questions for Christian Educators, 1977, Catholicism, 2 vols., 1980, rev. edit., 1994 (Christopher award 1981), Caesar's Coin: Religion and Politics in America, 1987, Ministry: A Theological, Pastoral Handbook, 1987, Report on the Church: Catholicism after Vatican II, 1992, Inside Catholicism: Rituals and Symbols Revealed, 1995, Responses to 101 Questions on the Church, 1996, Lives of the Popes: The Pontiffs from St. Peter to John Paul II, 1997, Lives of the Saints: from Mary and St. Francis of Assisi to John XXIII and Mother Teresa, 2001, The Pocket Guide to the Popes, 2006, The Pocket Guide to the Saints, 2006, The Church: The Evolution of Catholicism, 2008; assoc. editor: Encyclopedia of Religion, 1987; gen. editor HarperCollins Encyclopedia of Catholicism, 1995; theological cons. for the movie The DaVinci Code; writer (syndicated weekly theology column), Catholic Press, 1996-2015; contbr. of several articles and reviews in various profl. and popular journals; frequent on-air network commentator, cons. for Church-related events, including CBS, NBC, ABC, PBS and several cable stations Bd. overseers Beth Israel Deaconess Med. Ctr., Boston. Recipient Best Syndicated Weekly Column award Cath. Press Assn. of U.S. and Can., 1975, 77, 78, 84. Mem. Cath. Theol. Soc. of Am. (pres. 1973-74, John Courtney Murray award, 1976), Coll. Theology Soc., Am. Acad. Religion. Home: South Bend, Ind. Died Jan. 25, 2015.

MCCAIN, ELMER WAYNE, mechanical engineer; b. Birmingham, Ala., Sept. 17, 1933; s. James Hester and Willie (Herndon) McC.; m. Lynne Anne Palmer, Jan. 24, 1938; children: Kyle Wayne, Kent Michael, Kevin Mark. BSME, MSME, Auburn U. Registered engr., Ala., Miss., La. Engr. McCain Boiler & Engring. Co., Birmingham, Ala., 1959-63; CEO, pres. McCain Engring. Co., Birmingham, Ala., 1963-88, BPS Liquiq Systems, Birmingham, Ala., 1971-88, MISCO, Birmingham, Ala., 1973-88, E. Wayne McCain Engring., Inc., Birmingham, Ala., from 1988. Author: Danger of Combustion Products, 1990. State of Ala. grantee, Montgomery, 1989. Fellow Nat. Acad. Forensic Engring. Avocations: golf, raising dogs. Home: Pelham, Ala. Died Dec. 18, 2006.

MCCALL, BARBARA PARRIS, gerontology nurse; b. St. Albans, NY, Mar. 1, 1955; d. St. Clair and Edna (Mack) Parris; m. Michael G. McCall, Apr. 14, 1981. Diploma, St. Francis Hosp., 1975. Asst. head nurse Newark Beth Israel Med. Ctr., 1981-84; nursing supr. Hospitality Care Ctr., Newark, 1985; patient care coord. Parkway Manor, East Orange, N.J., 1988-89, New Cmty. Extended Care Facility, Newark, N.J., 1990-94; with Correctional Nursing Metro Healthcare Svcs., Edison, N.J., from 1994. Mem. ANA (cert. gerontol. nurse 1990). Home: Keasbey, NJ. Died Oct. 30, 2006.

MCCALL, WILLIAM HUBERT, publishing company executive; b. Montreal, Quebec, Can., Sept. 17, 1917; came to U.S., 1918; s. William Hubert and Anna Veronica (Blemly) McC.; m. Marion Jeanne Partisch, Dec. 21, 1947; children: Marlibeth, Lissa. AB, Brown U., 1940. Pvt. practice, Rye, N.Y., 1950-69; v.p. Judson Roberts Co., Mt. Vernon, N.Y., 1969-78; pres. North Am. Graphics, Inc., Wichita, Kans., from 1978. Dist. leader Republican Party, Rye, 1976-77. Maj. U.S. Army., 1940-45, Italy. Home: West Chester, Pa. Died Jan. 31, 2007.

MCCARTHY, CHARLES FRANCIS, JR., lawyer; b. Springfield, Mass., Dec. 9, 1926; s. Charles Francis and Maude Veronica (Clayton) McC.; m. Dorothy B. Sadosky, June 14, 1952 (dec. June 1987); children: Richard J., Linda A. Moylan, Robert P. AB, St. Michael's Coll., 1949; JD, Boston Coll., 1951. Bar: Mass. 1952, U.S. Dist. Ct. Mass. 1953. Assoc. Ganley, Crook & Smith, Springfield, Mass., 1954-67, Laming, Smith & Auchter, Springfield, 1967-80; of counsel Bacon & Wilson, P.C. and predecessor firms, Springfield, 1980-94; ret., 1994. Clk. Ellis Title Co., Inc., Springfield, 1988—94. Mem.: St. Thomas More Soc. Democrat. Roman Catholic. Home: Springfield, Mass. Died Apr. 21, 2007.

MCCARTHY, MARY A., critical care nurse; b. Worcester, Mass., July 26, 1954; d. Michael Francis and Jennie Josephine (Lelli) McC. BSN, Fitchburg U., Mass., 1977; MSN, Anna Maria Coll., Paxton, Mass., 1985. RN, Mass., Ill. Nurse mgr. Fairlawn Hosp., 1987-88, Leominster Hosp., 1988-90; flight nurse, capt. USAFR, 1988; nurse mgr. Beth Israel Hosp., Boston, from 1990. Mem. AACN, Mass. Coun. Nurse Mgrs. Home: Worcester, Mass. Died Feb. 21, 2007.

MCCARTY, FREDERICK BRIGGS, electrical engineer, consultant; b. Dilley, Tex., Aug. 11, 1926; s. John Frederick Briggs and Olive Ruth (Snell) Briggs McCarty; m. Doris Mary Cox, May 3, 1950 (div. 1970); children: Mark Frederick, David Lambuth, Jackson Clare; m. Nina Lucile Butman, Aug. 17, 1973 (dec. Dec. 31, 2004). BSEE, U. Tex., 1949. Design engr. GE, Schenectady, NY, 1949-51; sr. design engr. Convair, Ft. Worth, 1951-55; sr. engr. Aerojet Gen., Azusa, Calif., 1955-61; sr. engring. specialist Garrett Corp., Torrance, Calif., 1961-91; v.p., founder Patio Pacific, Inc., Torrance, 1973-84; owner, operator Textiger Co., Torrance, 1980-91; cons., 1991—2011. With USNR, 1944—46, PTO. Mem.: IEEE (sr.), Eta Kappa Nu, Tau Beta Pi. Democrat. Achievements include patents in field; design of superconducting acyclic motor for USN and high speed elec. machines for aerospace and transportation; authored computer programs that design and predict performance of generators, motors, permanent magnet couplings, electromagnetic bearings, and sensors; created and supplied word processor for TI 99/4 personal computers. Died June 29, 2014.

MCCAULEY, NORMA ELIZABETH, volunteer, advocate; b. Mpls., June 20, 1905; d. George Arthur Hunt and Mollie Elizabeth Eide; m. Earl Dale McCauley, Nov. 30, 1930; children: Hunt, Mollie. BA, U. Minn., 1923. Pres. YWCA, Sioux City, Iowa; founder Sioux City Planned Parenthood. Recipient 1st Margaret Sanger award in Iowa. Mem. AAUW. Democrat. Congregationalist. Avocations: music, gardening, singing. Home: Kensington, Md. Died Jan. 31, 2007.

MCCLENDON, AUBREY KERR, energy executive; b. Oklahoma City, July 14, 1959; s. Joe Carroll and Carole (Kerr) McClendon; m. Kathleen Upton Byrns, 1981; children: Will, Jack, Callie. BA in History, Trinity Coll. Duke U., 1981. Independent producer of oil & gas, 1982—89; co-founder, chmn., CEO Chesapeake Energy Corp., Okla. City, 1989—2012, CEO, 2012—13; founder American Energy Partners LP, 2014—16. Bd. dirs. Chesapeake Energy Corp., 1989—2013, Chaparral Energy Inc., from 2010, Access Midstream Partners, L.P., 2010—12, Bronco Drilling Co. Inc., from 2011, FTS Internat. Services, LLC, from 2011. Mem. bd. visitors Duke U. Fuqua Sch. Bus. Named Ernst & Young Entrepreneur of the Yr., 2011; named one of The Forbes 400: Richest Americans, from 2006. Mem.: American Natural Gas Alliance. Republican. Home: Saint Joseph, Mich. Died Mar. 2, 2016.

MCCLURE, GORDON, retired electronics company executive; b. Phoenix, Apr. 9, 1922; s. William C. and Maude (Cowden) McC.; m. Eleanor Rosalie Setter, Sept. 22, 1945 (dec. Apr. 1994); children: Mack Patrick, Jeneth Louise, Gary Stuart, Michael Andrew; m. Priscilla Meyer Cole, Nov. 11, 1995. AA, Phoenix Coll., 1942; BSEE, Calif. Inst. Tech., Pasadena, 1947; postgrad., U. Buffalo, 1948-50. Mgr. employment, div. safety engr., gen. foreman Sylvania Electric Products Inc., Buffalo, 1947-51; sr. indsl. engr., mgr. svc. and indsl. rels. Sylvania Electronic Products Inc., Mountain View, Calif., 1952-58, plant mgr., Sylvania Electronic Systems-West mgr. mfg. Santa Cruz, Calif., 1958-66; gen. mgr. Conelco Electronic Products, San Bernardino, Calif., 1966-68; with Bourns Inc., Riverside, Calif., 1968-87, from ops. mgr. precision co., v.p. mfg. and quality control, to corp. v.p., asst. to the pres., ret., 1987. Regional rep. Nat. Assn. Foreman, Buffalo, 1950-51; state bd. dirs. Jr. C. of C., Mountain View, 1956-57; bd. dirs., treas., pres. Variable Resistive Components Inst., Chgo., 1974-78; mem. Pres.' Safety Coun., Washington, 1951. Subject of cover article Factory mag., 1950. Mem. C. of C. founding com. U. Calif., Santa Cruz, 1962-65; founding chmn. Santa Cruz County EEOC, 1964-66; chmn. Bd. Councillors, San Bernardino State Coll., 1977-78, Spl. Gifts II CalTech. Alumni Fund, Pasadena, 1989-92; trustee The Orme Sch., Mayer, Ariz., 1976—; elder various Presbyn. chs., 1960—. Mem. Am. Electronics Assn. (committeeman 1978-83). Democrat. Avocations: theater, science, travel, property mgmt. Home: Pasadena, Calif. Died Aug. 14, 2007.

MCCLUSKEY, JEAN ASHFORD, retired nursing educator; b. Phila., Apr. 27, 1926; d. Charles Robert and Susanna Myers (Smith) Ashford; m. Robert C. McCluskey, June 28, 1947 (dec. Sept. 2000); children: David C., Robert C., Jean Alyce Loux. RN, Jewish Hosp., Phila., 1947; BS in Edn., West Chester U., Pa., 1965; EdM, Temple U., Phila., 1970. Coord. practical nursing prog. North Montco AVTS, Lansdale, Pa., 1967-70; dir. dipl. LPN-RN Sch. Nursing Bucks County Grand View Hosp., Sellersville, Pa., 1970-77; dir. Sch. Practical Nursing Sacred Heart Hosp., Norristown, Pa., 1977-93; nursing edn. cons., 1993-2001. Coord. evening/weekend part time practical nursing program Ea. Ctr. for Arts and Technology, Willow Grove, Pa., 1995-2001; chmn. Healthcare Corp., 1998-2005, mem., 1995-2005; apptd. chair steering com. to achieve Nat. Accreditation Continuing Care Accreditation Coun., 1995, 2000; chmn. Healthcare Corp., 1998-2005, mem.1995-2005. Contbr. articles to profl. jours. Judge of elections Marlborough Twp., Montgomery, Pa., 2001—03; mem. mgmt. bd. Luth. Cmty. at Telford, 1993—99; congl. del. to assembly Southeastern Pa. synod Evang. Luth. Ch. in Am., 1996—2000. Recipient Disting. Svc. award, S.E. Pa. League for Nursing, 1984; named Ky. Col., 1980, others. Mem. Nat. League Nursing (bd. dirs. 1983-87, bd. rvs. CPNP 1987-93). Died Mar. 11, 2007.

MCCULLOCH, STEPHEN A., regional planner; b. Greenfield, Mass., Mar. 4, 1949; s. Alexander Andrew and Lucille (Shaw) McC. M, Villanova U., 1976. Vol. VISTA, Balt. and Richmond, Va., 1970-72; asst. site planner Montgomery County Planning Commn., Norristown, Pa., 1972-76; educator Haverford (Pa.) Sch. Sys., 1976-82; bus. mgr. Mr. Paperback, Ellsworth, Maine, 1982-89; dir. regional planning No. Maine Devel. Commn., Caribou, from 1989. With No. New England chpt. Am. Planning Assn., Maine Assn. Planners; rd. mgmt. specialist Maine Dept. Transp. Author, editor planning related documents, 1989—. Recipient grants fed. and state govts., 1989-97. Mem. Maine Assn. Planners (sec. 1996). Avocations: hunting, fishing, photography, travel, woodworking, writing, reading. Home: Stockholm, Maine. Died Dec. 14, 2006.

MCCULLOUGH, COLLEEN, writer; b. Wellington, N.S.W., Australia, June 1, 1937; m. Ric Robinson, Apr. 13, 1984. Student, U. Sydney, Australia, London U.; LittD (hon.), Macquarie U., Sydney, 1993. Neurophysiologist Yale U. Sch. Medicine, 1967—77, Sydney, 1967—77, London, 1967—77. Author: Tim, 1974, The Thorn Birds, 1977, An Indecent Obsession, 1981, Cooking with Colleen McCullough and Jean Easthope, 1982, A Creed for the Third Millennium, 1985, The Ladies of Missalonghi, 1987, The First Man in Rome, 1990, The Grass Crown, 1991, Fortune's Favorites, 1993, Caesar's Women, 1996, Caesar, 1997, The Song of Troy, 1998, The Courage and the Will: The Life of Roden Cutler, V.C. (The Biography), 1998, Morgan's Run, 2000, The October Horse, 2002, The Touch, 2003, Angel Puss, 2004, On, Off, 2006, Antony and Cleopatra, 2007, The Independence of Miss Mary Bennet, 2008, Too Many Murders, 2009, Naked Cruelty, 2010, The Prodigal Son, 2012, Sins of the Flesh, 2013, Bittersweet, 2014 Fellow: AAAS; mem.: NY Acad. Sciences. Died Jan. 29, 2015.

MCCULLOUGH, SANDRA GAIL, environmental affairs manager; b. Detroit, May 31, 1950; d. Jack Dean and Ethel Mae (Morehead) McC.; m. Kevin Gardner Yost, June 2, 1973; children: Blythe, Gardner, Felicity. BA, U. Mich., 1972; M of Regional Planning, Cornell U., 1974. Staff dir. Broome County Environ. Mgmt. Coun., Binghamton, N.Y., 1974-75; sr. regional planner So. Tier East Regional Planning Bd., Binghamton, N.Y., 1975-77; environ. analyst N.Y. State Dept. of Environ. Conservation, NYC, 1977-79; environ. supr. Port Authority of N.Y. & N.J., NYC, 1979-86, Office of Ferry Transp.-Port Authority, NYC, 1986-90; environ. mgr. Interstate Transp.-Port Authority, NYC, from 1990. Pres. Citizens League for Environ. Action, Millburn, N.J., 1991. Recipient Cert. of Outstanding Achivement award Port Authority of N.Y. & N.J., 1989, Spl. Fellowship for Planners, EPA, 1973. Mem. Air & Waste Mgmt. Assn. Avocations: gardening, local environmental activism. Home: Winnetka, Ill. Died Jan. 4, 2007.

MCDONALD, FORREST, historian, educator; b. Orange, Tex., Jan. 7, 1927; s. John Forrest and Myra (McGill) McD.; m. Ellen Shapiro, Aug. 1, 1963; children from previous marriage: Kathy, Forrest Howard, Marcy Ann, Stephen, Kevin. BA, MA, U. Tex., 1949, PhD, 1955; MA (hon.), Brown U., 1962; LHD (hon.), SUNY, Geneseo, 1989. Exec. sec. Am. History Research Ctr., Madison, Wis., 1953-58; assoc. prof. history Brown U., Providence, 1959-63, prof., 1963-67, Wayne State U., Detroit, 1967-76, U. Ala., Tuscaloosa, 1976-87, disting. univ. rsch. prof., 1987—2002, prof. emeritus, 2002—16. James Pinckney Harrison prof. Coll. of William and Mary, Williamsburg, Va., 1986-87; presdl. appointee Bd. Fgn. Scholarships, Washington, 1985-87; mem. fellowship selection com. Richard M. Weaver Fellowships, Bryn Mawr, Pa., 1980—. Author: We The People, 1958, Insull, 1962, E Pluribus Unum, 1965, Alexander Hamilton, 1979 (Frances Tavern Book award 1980), Novus Ordo Seclorum: The Intellectual Origins of the Constitution, 1985, Requiem, 1988, The American Presidency: An Intellectual History, 1994, States Rights and the Union, 2000, Recovering the Past: A Historian's Memoir, 2004. Trustee Phila. Soc., North Adams, Mich., 1983-86, 87-90, pres. 1988-90; co-chmn. New Eng. for Goldwater, 1964. Served with USN, 1945-46. Recipient George Washington medal Freedom's Found., Valley Forge, Pa., 1980, Best Book award Am. Revolution Round Table, N.Y., 1986, Richard M. Weaver award Ingersoll Found., 1990, First Salvatori award Heritage Found., 1992, Salavatori Book award Intercollegiate Studies Inst., 1994; Guggenheim fellow, N.Y., 1962-63; Jefferson lectr. NEH, 1987. Republican. Avocations: horticulture, tennis. Home: Coker, Ala. Died Jan. 19, 2016.

MCDONALD, ORVILLE LESLIE, public relations consultant; b. Magnolia, Tex., July 27, 1922; s. Leonard Floyd and Edna (Ivey) McDonald; children: Susan, Connie, Kathleen. BS, Abilene Christian U., 1947; LLB, Southern Meth. U., 1965. Bar: Tex. 1966. Pvt. pub. rels. cons. Orville McDonald Assocs., Dallas, from 1947. Mem. Ch. Christ. Col. US Army, 1943—46, MTO. Mem.: Pub. Rels. Soc. America. Republican. Home: Dallas, Tex. Died Dec. 19, 2006.

MCDOUGAL, JEROME R., JR., retired bank executive; b. 1928; m. Rose M. McDougal; children: Linda M., Jerome R. III. Chmn., pres. CEO Apple Bank Services, NYC, 1987—91; pres., CEO Predecessor Bank, 1991—95. Died Aug. 23, 2008.

MCDOWELL, BARBARA, artist; b. Paducah, Ky., Jan. 6, 1921; d. William Bryan Rouse and Mary Marguerite Thomasson; m. William Wells McDowell, Jan. 6, 1944 (dec. 1976). AA, Delmar Coll., Corpus Christi, 1940; BA with hons., Corpus Christi State U., 1986; MA in Studio Art, Tex. A&M U., Corpus Christi, 2003. Artist Davison Paxon, Atlanta, 1944—45; layout artist Tucker Wayne & Co., Atlanta, 1945—46; fashion illustrator Lichtenstein's, Corpus Christi, 1948—49, 1951—52; artist, art dir. Adcraft Advt. Agy., Corpus Christi, 1952—79; owner, artist, writer B. McDowell Graphic Design, Corpus Christi, 1979—2000. One-woman shows include Corpus Christi Mus. Sci. and History, 1973, Bayfront Plz Auditorium, Corpus Christi, 1976, Art Ctr. of Corpus Christi, 1983, 2003, 2006, Tex. A&M U., Kingsville, 1990, Galeria LaVentana, Corpus Christi, 1992—94, Galvan House, 2001, 2002, 2004, exhibited in group shows at S. Tex. Art League, 1972—2006, S.W. Sculpture Soc., 1972—2006, Tex. Watercolor Soc., San Antonio, 1968, 1978, 1982, 1998, Tex. Fine Arts Assn., Austin, 1975, 1979, 1986, Southwestern Watercolor Soc., Dallas, 1985, Hill Country Arts Found., Igram, Tex., 1990, Art Mus. S. Tex., 1990, 2000, 2006, Tex. A&M U. Alumni Show, Corpus Christi, 1992, Upstairs Gallery, 1992, 1996, Third Biennial Gulf of Mex. Symposium, 1995, Gallery Leszarts - Les Cerquex Sous Passavant, France, 1998, Watercolor Art Soc. Houston, 1998, Estelle Stair Art Gallery, Rockport, Tex., 1999, Rockport Ctr. for Arts, 2000, Wilhelmi-Holland Art Gallery, 2000, Watercolor Soc. of S. Texas, Corpus Christi. Donor Art Ctr. Coll. Design, Pasadena, Calif., from 1979, Corpus Christi Botanical Gardens, from 1991, Driscoll Children's Hosp., Corpus Christi, from 1995, Art Mus. S. Tex., 1995, Tex. A & M U., Corpus Christi, from 2000; mem. Rockport Ctr. for Arts; pres. Art Ctr. of Corpus Christi, 2004—05; mem. Art Mus. of S. Tex., Corpus Christi, from 1994, bd. govs., from 2005; mem., com. chair Mcpl. Arts Commn., Corpus Christi, 1986—92. Recipient Nat. Drawing and Sculpture award, Del Mar Coll., 1986, 1993, 1998, Vol. Cert. of Excellence, Caller Times, 1993, prize, NCECA Regional Juried Ceramics Exhibit, Arlington Mus. Art, Ft. Worth, 1995, Purchase award, Tex. A&M U., Corpus Christi, 2002. Mem.: S.W. Sculpture Soc., Watercolor Soc. S. Tex. (pres. from 1977), S. Tex. Art League (chmn. from 1976). Avocations: gardening, ceramics, painting. Home: Corpus Christi, Tex. Died July 4, 2007.

MCDOWELL, RUTH MARIA, retired language educator, real estate company executive; b. Albany, NY, Sept. 11, 1918; d. Pasquale Alexander Pugliese and Blanche Harriet McCammon; m. Arthur Claude McDowell, Oct. 3, 1941 (dec.); 1 child, Walter Schuyler. BA cum laude, Coll. of St. Rose, Albany, NY, 1940. Cert. Tchr. Cert. NY State, 1940, Profl. Real Estate NY State, 1958. English tchr. St. John's H.S., Albany, NY, 1940—42, Miss Quinn's Pvt. Sch., Albany, NY, 1942—44; real estate sales Lucy Rice Realty, Albany, NY, 1958—69, Century 21, Albany, NY, 1963—70; free lance writing Newspapers and mag., Many cities, from 1940. Writing and directing shows Delmar Progress Club, Delmar, NY, 1947—2000; host, writer, dir. Church Women Speak, WABY, Albany, 1949—51. Author: (poetry for periodicals) Ideals, Modern Bride, Scuttlebutt, Genesis; contbr. articles pub. to profl. jour. Bd. mem. & motor corps ARC, Albany, NY, 1942—43; writer and dir. Bethlehem Christmas Festival (Bethlehem is twp. name. Event raises funds for needy.), Delmar, NY, 1945—50; pres. Women of St. Paul's Ch., Albany, NY, 1977—79, Albany Episc. Women's Deanery, 1960; mem. with advanced piloting (ap) cert. US Power Squadron, Albany, NY, 1956—70. Recipient Life membership, Delmar Progress Club, awarded in 1999, Pin for Den Leader, Boy Scouts of Am., 1955. Mem.: Delmar Progress Club (life). Episcopalian. Avocations: quilting, painting, flower arranging, writing. Home: Miami, Fla. Died Dec. 5, 2006.

MCEACHEN, JAMES ALLEN, cardiologist; b. Mar. 14, 1925; s. James A. and Edna Charlotte (Pegler) McE.; m. Eileen Joyce, June 16, 1956; children: James Allen, Brian Paul, Gregory Elwood. BA, U. Nebr., 1946; MD, Western Res. U., 1950. Intern Univ. Hosp., Cleve., 1950-51, asst. resident in medicine, 1951-52; resident Wadsworth VA Hosp., LA, 1952-54; dir. cardiology St. Johns Hosp., Santa Monica, Calif., 1955-78, dir. coronary care, 1968-83, staff cardiologist, 1978-88, hon. staff, from 1988. Part-time physician Borrego Springs (Calif.) Clinic. Recipient Disting. Svc. award Holy Family Adoption Svc., L.A., 1967. Fellow Am. Coll. Cardiology, Soc. for Cardiac Angiography and Intervention. Republican. Avocations: sailing, golf, skiing. Home: Westlake Vlg, Calif. Died Nov. 27, 2006.

MCEACHERN, BEVERLEY C., priest; b. Topeka, Kans., July 12, 1941; d. Melvin A. and Rosalie Conner; m. P. John McEachern, July 29, 1963; children: John, Conner. BS, Fla. State U., Tallahassee, 1962; MDiv, Va. Theol. Sem., Alexandria, 1979. Ordained Episc. Ch., 1980. Pub. sch. tchr. Dougherty County, Albany, Ga., 1965—66; curate St. Thomas Episcopal Ch., Columbus, Ga., 1979—88; pastoral counselor Pastoral Inst., Columbus, 1988—94; assoc. priest Trinity Ch., Columbus, 1994—99; rector, priest St. Nicholas Ch., Hamilton, Ga., from 1999. Chaplain Bradley Ctr., Columbus, 1991—94, Auburn U., 1998—99. Fellow: Am. Assn. Pastoral Counselors; mem.: Kappa Alpha Theta. Republican. Home: Hamilton, Ga. Died May 30, 2007.

MCELROY, JEROME LATHROP, economics professor; b. St. Louis, Sept. 14, 1937; s. King Gerard and Audrey (Lathrop) McE.; m. Birdie Maria Rossow; children: Jacqueline, Christopher. BA, St. Louis U., 1961, PhL, 1962, MA in Econs., 1965; PhD in Econs., U. Colo., 1972. Instr. St. John's Coll., Belize City, Belize, 1962-65; grad. assoc. U. Colo., Boulder, 1971-72; asst. prof. econs. Coll. of V.I., St. Thomas, 1972-75, assoc. prof. econs., 1975-79; dir. planning Govt. of V.I., St. Thomas, 1979-80; assoc. prof. econs. U. Notre Dame, Ind., 1980-82, St. Mary's Coll., South Bend, Ind., 1982-86, prof. econs., from 1986, chmn. dept. bus. and econs., 1990-93. Rsch. fellow Island Resources Found., Washington, 1980—; expert adv. panel Office Tech. Assessment, U.S. Congress, 1985-86; econ. cons. U.S. AID, 1987-89, Govt. V.I., 1974-79, 89; editl. bd. mem. Annals Tourism Rsch.; founding mem. Island Studies Jour. Author: Consumer Expenditure Patterns, 1980, USVI Status Options, 1989, Secret Seams, 2007, Sacred Traces, 2008, Sparks of Eden, 2009, Flashes of Paradise, 2012; numerous poems; contbr. articles to profl. jours. Mem. adv. bd. Ea. Caribbean Ctr., U. V.I., 1993-95. Recipient Maria Pieta Tchr. award, St. Mary's Coll., 1989, Tchr. of the Yr., Coll. of V.I., 1973, Spes Unica Svc. award, 1997. Mem. Am. Econ. Assn., Caribbean Studies Assn., So. Reg. Sci. Assn., Midwest Assn. Latin Americanists, Internat. Small Islands Studies Assn., Internat. Sci. Coun. for Island Devel. (founding mem.), Inst. for Devel. of Insular Economies and Socs. (founding mem.), Island Environ. Inst. (founding mem.). Democrat. Roman Catholic. Avocations: swimming, poetry, fishing. Home: South Bend, Ind. Died Dec. 17, 2014.

MCENTEE, DUCAT, II, retired air force chief master sergeant; b. Honolulu, Mar. 22, 1939; s. Ducat and Janet Frazer (Stoddart) McE.; m. Fumiko Fukuda, Feb. 12, 1965 (div. Oct. 1982); children: Yuki Mullins, Patrick, Chidori; m. Robin Lee Retzloff, Aug. 23, 1988. Student, Community Coll. of Air Force, 1958-82; student, U. Md., Japan, 1961-79. Aircraft armament systems technician USAF, 1958-71; staff munitions maintenance supr. Hqrs. USAF Pacific, Hickam Air Force Base, Hawaii, 1971-75; chief standardization and tng. 318th Fighter Interceptor Squadron, McChord Air Force Base, Wash., 1975-77; weapons maintenance mgr. 18th Tactical Fighter Wing, Kadena Air Base, Japan, 1977-80; aircraft maintenance supt. 18th Aircraft Generation Squadron, Kadena Air Base, 1980-83; prodn. control supr. Lockheed Support Systems, Inc., Eglin Air Force Base, Fla., 1985; postal svc. ctr. project mgr. Fedserv Industries, Inc., Eglin Air Force Base, 1986-87; prodn. control supr. Lockheed Support Systems, Inc., Howard Air Base, Panama, 1987; retired USAF, 1988. Aircraft maintenance cons. various orgns., 1988—. Decorated Disting. Flying Cross, Meritorious Svc. medal, Air medal with oak leaf clusters, Republic of Vietnam Air Svc. medal honor class. Republican. Roman Catholic. Avocations: swimming, camping, model building. Home: Port Saint Joe, Fla. Died Nov. 30, 2007.

MCEVOY, NAN TUCKER (PHYLLIS ANN TUCKER), publishing company executive, olive rancher; b. San Mateo, Calif., July 15, 1919; d. Nion R. and Phyllis (de Young) Tucker; m. Dennis McEvoy, 1948 (div.); 1 child, Nion Tucker McEvoy. Student, Georgetown U., 1975. Newspaper reporter San Francisco Chronicle, 1944-46, N.Y. Herald Tribune, NYC, 1946-47, Washington Post, 1947-48; rep. in pub. rels. John Homes, Inc., Washington, 1959-60; founding mem. U.S. Peace Corps, spl. asst. to dir. Washington, 1961-64; mem. U.S. delegation UNESCO, Washington, 1964-65; dir. Population Coun., Washington, 1965-70; cofounder, dep. dir. Preterm, Inc., Washington, 1970-74; former chmn. bd. Chronicle Pub. Co., San Francisco, 1975-95, dir. emeritus, 1995—2015. Mem. nat. bd. dirs. Smithsonian Instn., Washington, 1994-2015; bd. dirs. Am. Farmland Trust, San Francisco Symphony; mem. coun. Brookings Instn., 1994-2015, Washington; mem. U. Calif. San Francisco Found., 1993-2015; dir. emeritus Nat. Mus. Am. Art; mem. Nat. Coun. Fine Arts Museums; formerly arbitrator Am. Arbitration Assn., Washington. Named Woman of Yr., Washingtonian Mag., 1973. Mem. Am. Art Forum, Burlingame Country Club, The River Club, Commonwealth Club of Calif., World Affairs Coun., Villa Taverna. Home: San Francisco, Calif. Died Mar. 26, 2015.

MCEWAN, GERALDINE, actress; b. Old Windsor, Berkshire, Eng., May 9, 1932; d. Donald and Norah McKeown; m. Hugh Cruttwell McEwan, 1953 (dec. 2002); children: Greg, Claudia. Actor: (1st engagement) Theatre Royal, 1949, (London appearances) Who Goes There?, 1951, Sweet Madness, for Better, for Worse, Summertime, Shakespeare Meml. Theatre, Stratford on Avon, 1956, 1958, 1961, (playing Princess of France) Love's Labours Lost, (playing of Olivia) Twelth Night, (playing of Ophelia) Hamlet, (playing of Marina) Pericles, (playing of Beatrice) Much Ado about Nothing; (plays) School for Scandal, 1962, The Private Ear and the Public Eye, 1963, Love for Love, A Flea in Her Ear, the Dance of Death, Edward II, Home and Beauty, Rites, The Way of the World, The White Devil, Amphitryon 38, Nat. Theatre, 1965—71, Dear Love, 1973, Chez Nous, 1974, The Little Hut, 1974; (plays, musical) Oh Coward, 1975; (plays) On Approval, 1975, Look After Lulu, 1978, The Browning Version, Harlequinade, the Provoked Wife, The Rivals (Evening Std. Darama Best Actress award), You Can't Take It With You, Nat. Theatre, 1980—84, A Lie of the Mind, 1987, Lettice and Lovage, 1988—89, Hamlet, 1992, The Bird Sanctuary, 1994, The Way of the World (Evening Std. Actress award, 1995), The Chairs, 1997; (TV series) The Prime of Miss Jean Brodie, 1978 (TV Critics Best Actress award), L'Elegance, 1982, The Barchester Chronicles, 1983, Come into the Garden, 1982, Mapp and Lucia, 1985—86, Oranges are not the Only Fruit, 1990 (B.A.F.T.A. Best Actress award), Mulberry, 1992—93, Moses, 1996, Thin Ice, 2000, Carrie's War, 2004, Agatha Christies's Marple, 2004—07, Marple: The Body in the Library, 2004, Marple: The Murder at the Vicarage, 2004, Marple: 4:50 from Paddington, 2004, Marple: A Murder is Announced, 2005; (films) Foreign Body, 1986, Henry V, 1989, Robin Hood: Prince of Thieves, 1991; (films, voice) Not Without My Handbag, 1993, Wallace & Gromit: The Curse of the the Were-Rabbit, 2005; (films) The Love Letter, 1999, Titus, 1999, Love's Labour Lost, 2000, The Contaminated Man, 2000, Food of Love, 2002, The Magdalene Sisters, 2002, Pure, 2002, The Lazarus Child, 2004, Vanity Fair, 2004; dir.: As You Like It, 1988, Treats, 1989, Waiting for Sir Larry, 1990, Four Door Saloon, 1991, Keyboard Skills, 1993. Died Jan. 30, 2015.

MC GEE, DAMOUS EMANUEL, minister, educator; b. Fleming, Ky., Sept. 2, 1930; s. Sebastian and Callie (Evans) Mc Gee; m. Shirlene Powell, June 14, 1952; 1 child, Karen Renae. ThM, Bible Baptist Sem., 1952; Diploma, Bible Tng. Inst., 1968; MS, Old Dominion U., 1970; postgrad., Union Theol. Sem., Va., 1966, U. Wis., 1972. Ordained to ministry Ch. of God of Prophecy, 1952, cert. in counseling Bayberry Psychiatric Hosp. Hampton Va. Internat. dir. Youth for Christ, Greenville, SC, Ft. Worth, 1950—52; material releaseman Convair-Vultee Air Craft Co., Ft. Worth, 1950—52; tchr. pub. schs. Norfolk & Virginia Beach, Va., 1956—59; pastor Ch. of God of Prophecy, Richmond, Va., 1952—56, Norfolk, 1956—61, Newport News, Va., 1962—70; pres. Calif. Holding Assn., 1972—76; v.p. West Coast Bible Tng. Inst., Fresno, Calif., 1972—76. Overseer of Wis., 1970—71; overseer of Calif. (English), 1972—76; overseer Ill. Ch. of God of Prophecy, Bartonville, 1976—82, Okla. Ch. of God of Prophecy, Broken Arrow, 1982—87, Md., DC, Lanham, from 1987; organisor & dir. Nat. Pastors Assn., 1967—70; ext. tchr. U. Va., 1968; v.p. East Coast Bible Tng. Inst., 1988; overseer N. NV & N CA, 1991—96; lead organisor GAE, 2004, coord., from 2008. Author: Marriage Booklet, 1968. Mem.: Soc. Pentecostals. Deceased.

MCGEE, JOHN B., pilot, retired; b. Reno, Feb. 26, 1922; s. Charles Bartton and Clara Belle (Henley) M.; m. Carol Anna, Feb. 14, 1946; children: Jack Bart, Diana Lee, Holly Ann. Grad. high sch., Reno. Capt. Am. Airlines, San Francisco, 1956-82. Maj. USMCR, 1944-54. Republican. Home: Reno, Nev. Died Dec. 16, 2006.

MCGEE, LIAM EDWARD, insurance company executive, former bank executive; b. County Donegal, Ireland, Sept. 8, 1954; m. Lori Tomoyasu; children: Stephen Liam, Jordan William Riichi, Aidan Masayoshi, Lauren Margaret Murray Devon. BA, U. San Diego, 1976; MBA, Pepperdine U., Malibu, Calif., 1979; JD, Loyola Marymount U. Law Sch., LA, 1984. With Wells Fargo & Co., Security Pacific Corp.; head Calif. Consumer Bank, corp. tech. & ops. Bank of America Corp., 1990, pres. So. Calif., 1998—2000, pres. Calif., 2000—01, pres. global consumer banking, 2001—04, pres. global consumer & small bus. banking Charlotte, NC, 2004—09; chmn., CEO Hartford Financial Services Group, Inc., Hartford, Conn., 2009—10, chmn., pres., CEO, 2010—14, exec. chmn., 2014—15. Bd. dirs. Hartford Financial Services Group, Inc., 2009—15; prof. in residence, Sch. of Law and Bus. U. San Diego, 2014—15; dir. LA Branch, Fed. Reserve Bank of San Francisco. Bd. trustees Nat. Urban League, Loyola Marymount U., 2003; bd. dirs. Arts & Sci. Coun., Charlotte; chmn. bd. trustees U. San Diego, bd. trustee; chmn. United Way Greater LA; bd. mem. Junior Achievement of So. Calif. Recipient Arthur E. Hughes Career Achievement award, U. San Diego, 2008, Juvenile Diabetes Rsch. Found. Star ofHope, 2012; named to Junior Achievement Bus. Hall of Fame, 2014. Home: West Hartford, Conn. Died Feb. 13, 2015.

MCGEEN, DANIEL SAMUEL, dentist, ornithology and ecology educator; b. Waukesha, Wis., Mar. 30, 1918; s. Norman John and Rhoda Lillian (Eales) McG.; m. Jean Jordan; children: Daniel Thomas, Susan Jean, Donald John, David Norman, Mary Elizabeth. BA summa cum laude, Carroll Coll., Waukesha, Wis., 1942; DDS, U. Detroit, 1947. Grad. tchg. asst. in biology U. Oreg., Eugene, 1942-43; pvt. practice dentistry Pontiac, Mich., 1975-88; pvt. practice dentist Waterford, Mich., 1953-88; base dental officer USCG, Boston, 1951-53; pres. pvt. corp. Waterford, 1976-88; tchr. ornithology and ecology Cranbrook Inst. Sci., Bloomfield Hills, Mich., 1968-74; tchr. ornithology and ecology divsn. continuing edn. Oakland U., Rochester Hills, Mich., 1968-74; pvt. rschr. Auburn Hills, Mich., from 1988. Head oral protection for athletes Pontiac Pub. Schs., 1962-64; ednl. cons. natural history, bird banding Pontiac Sch. Dist., 3 County Sch. Dist., Oakland, Waimo, and Macomb County Sch. Dists., 1953-92. Contbr. articles to profl. publs. Scouter, resource person Boy Scouts Am., 1953-67; founder, past pres. Pontiac, Oakland, Macomb Audubon Soc.; past pres. Eugene (Oreg.) Nat. History Soc.; sr. warden, lay min., cup bearer St. Mary's-in-the Hills Episcopal Ch., Lake Orion, Mich., 1953—. Lt. USPHS, 1951-53. Fellow Royal Soc. Health; mem. AAAS (2 stripes, life mem.), AOU, ADA, Mich. Dental Assn., Oakland County Dental Assn., Wilson Ornithol. Assn., Assn. Field Ornithologists, Sigma Xi, Delta Sigma Nu, Phi Sigma, Beta Beta Beta. Achievements include research in two types of host-cowbird interaction patterns, delineation of habitat--Kirtland's Warbler-Brown-Headed Cowbird cycles; originator of hypothesis that sodium limits the Kirtland's cycle and probably that of other species of animals; that sodium is the deeper invariant of the basic allometric invariant 0.25. Home: Auburn Hills, Mich. Died Feb. 16, 2007.

MCGHEE, DAVID WESSON, financial services executive; b. Blytheville, Ark., Feb. 23, 1945; s. Marion Wesson and Jewel (Maxwell) McG. BS, U. Mo., 1967. Auditor, tax acct. Arthur Andersen & Co., St. Louis, 1967-70; mgr. May Dept. Stores Co., St. Louis, 1970-73, Monsanto Co., St. Louis and London, 1973-80; owner, dir. DWM Investments, St. Louis, 1980-86; mgr. Westinghouse Credit Corp., St. Louis, 1986-88; pres., chief exec. officer, founder Brit.-Am. Forfaiting Co., Inc., St. Louis, from 1988. Founder, The Home Soc., St. Louis, 1988. With U.S. Army, 1967-69. Mem. Assn. Corp. Growth (bd. dirs. 1988—), Regional Commerce and Growth Assn., World Affairs Coun., Internat. Trade Bur., St. Louis World Trade Club, U.S. C. of C. (export fin. task force). Republican. Methodist. Avocation: rowing. Died Nov. 7, 2006.

MCGOVERN, ANN, writer, publisher; b. NYC, May 25, 1930; d. Arthur and Kate (Malatsky) Weinberger; m. Hugh McGovern (div.) m. Martin L. Scheiner, June 6, 1970 (dec. 1992); campanion Ralph Greenberg; children: Peter McGovern, Charles Scheiner, Annie L. Scheiner, James B. Scheiner. Attended, U. New Mexico. Freelance writer, from 1953; writer Little Golden Books; editor Scholastic Books, NYC, 1960-67; pub., editor The Privileged Traveler Mag., Pleaseantville, 1985-87. Lectr. to ednl. and conservation groups. Author 50 books for young people, including Roy Rodgers and the Mountain Lion, 1955, Zoo, Where Are You?, 1964, Little Wolk, 1965, The Runaway Slave: The Story of Harriet Tubman, 1965, Too Much Noise, 1967, The Secret Soldier: The Story of Deborah Sampson, 1975, Shark Lady, 1978, Nicholas Bentley Stoningpot III, 1982, Night Dive, 1984, Stone Soup, 1986, Playing With Penguins: And Other Adventures in Antarctica, 1994; (picture book) Mr. Skinner's Skinney House, 1980; four volumes of poetry for addults; contbr. articles to mags. Fellow Explorers Club; mem. PEN, Soc. Women Geographers, Circumnavigators Club, Internat. Food, Wine and Travel Writers, Am. Soc. Journalists and Authors. Avocations: travel, scuba diving, photography. Died Aug. 8, 2015.

MCGOWAN, SEAN T., lawyer; b. Appleton, Minn., Aug. 19, 1952; s. Martin J. and Elizabeth Nolan McG.; children: Cullen Jay, Courtney. BA, U. Ariz., 1974, JD, 1978. Bar: Ariz. Nev. Law clk. Churchill County, Fallon, Nev., 1978-79; deputy atty. gen. Nev. Atty. Gen., Las Vegas, 1980-84; asst. gen. counsel Del webb Corp., Phoenix, 1984-88; ptnr. McDonald Garano Law Firm, Las Vegas, 1988-93, Schreck Law Firm, Las Vegas, 1993-99; city atty. City North Las Vegas (Nev.), from 2000. Bd. dirs. Clark County Bd. Equalization, Las Vegas, 1996-99. Avocations: childrens activities, travel. Died Jan. 22, 2007.

MCGREW, WAYNE DALE, investment counselor; b. Parkersburg, W.Va., Sept. 12, 1930; s. Wayne D. McGrew and Mary Cathrine (Norris) Boice; m. Kathryn Maxwell, Dec. 12, 1954; children: Ralph Boice, Wayne Dale III, Kathryn Maxwell, Raymond Maxwell. Capt. USMC. Republican. Episcopalian. Died June 9, 2007.

MCGUIRE, PATRICK WILLIAM, sociology educator; b. July 13, 1953; MA, MAT, SUNY, Binghamton, 1977; PhD, SUNY, Stony Brook, 1986. Instr. SUNY, Morrisville, 1978-79; instr. U. N.D., Grand Forks, 1979-81; asst. prof. Mich. Tech. U., Houghton, 1986-87; assoc. prof. U. Toledo, from 1987, dir. univ. urban affairs ctr., from 1999. Author, editor: From the Left Bank to the Mainstream, 1994. Mem. exec. com. electric franchise com. City of Toledo, 1989-99; pres. faculty senate U. Toledo, 1996-97; faculty rep. U. Toledo Bd. Trustees, 1996-98. Recipient Scholarly Achievement award Am. Sociology Assn. Marxist Studies Sect., 1994. Died Mar. 18, 2007.

MCHUGH, ANNETTE S., artist, educator, playwright, writer; b. Greensburg, Pa., May 31, 1926; d. Daniel Karl Shirey and Marian Grabill Kurtz; m. John Edward McHugh Jr., Nov. 24, 1948. Student, Ind. State Tchrs. Coll., Pa., 1945—47, Pa. State U., 1947—49, State Coll. Pa., 1980, student, 1981, Art Alliance Ctrl. Pa., 1981—85, student, 1985—90. File & locate clk. FBI, Washington, 1944—45; sec. to asst. dean edn. Pa. State U., University Park, 1947—49, sec. to exec. dir., 1962, pers. sec. phys. plant; test adminstr. Pa. State Employment Office, Bellefonte, 1962—65; editl. asst. , prodn. sec. Sta. WPSX-TV, 1977—79; tchr. traditional chinese brush painting Art Alliance Ctrl. Pa., Lemont, Pa., 2001—03. Playwright, dir.: Those Were the Days, 1979, We've Come A Long Way Ladies, 1984, Every Night is Opening Night on Broadway, 1989, Madame Pres...Ladies of the Club, 1994, Celebrate State College, 1996. V.p., bd. dirs. Univ. Park Airport, University Park, 1957—62; bd. dirs., flower show chmn. Penn. State Garden Days, University Park, 1957—59; bd. dirs. Art Alliance Ctrl. Pa., 1981—82, pres., 1983, Nittany Coun. Rep. Women, 1961; pres. women's assn. State Coll. Presbyn. Ch., State Coll., Pa., 1971—73, deacon State College, Pa., 1965—71, elder, 1971—74, bd. sec. Recipient State of Pa. award, Pa. Coun. Rep. Women, 1961—62, Pub. Rels. award, Am. Cancer Soc., 1980, 2d pl. art award, Pa. Fedn. Women's Club, 1987. Mem.: Pa. State U. Woman's Club (chair book and play rev., co-editor), State Coll. Woman's Club (pres. 1959—61, past v.p., past pres., art, garden and drama dept. chair). Republican. Presbyterian. Avocations: gardening, photography, reading, golf. Home: State College, Pa. Died Mar. 16, 2007.

MCINNIS, JUDY BREDESON, foreign language educator; b. Roseau, Minn., Sept. 22, 1943; d. Ervin Oliver and Elsie Mae (McFarlane) Bredeson; m. Clay W. McInnis, July 15, 1967; children: Meghan Emily, Clay W., Ian O. BS, Bemidji State U., Minn., 1964; PhD, U. N.C., 1974. Instr. U. Del., Newark, 1971-74, asst. prof., 1975-82, assoc. prof., 1982—2001, prof., from 2001. Author: The Cumaean Sibyl, 1999, Models in Medieval Iberian Literature and Their Modern Reflections, 2002, Gladys Ilarreguís Poemas a medianoche/Poems at Midnight, 2003. NEH fellow, 1979, 95; AAUW scholar, 1963-64, Bemidji State U. scholar, 1961, 62, NDEA scholar, 1966-69. Mem. AAUP, MLA, Mid-Atlantic Coun. on Latin Am., Am. Assn. Tchrs. Spanish and Portuguese (nat. dir. Spanish Exams 1985-91). Avocations: theater, swimming. Home: Elkton, Md. Died Nov. 11, 2006.

MCKENDRY, JOHN H., JR., lawyer; b. Grand Rapids, Mich., Mar. 24, 1950; s. John H. and Lois R. (Brandel) McK.; m. Linda A. Schmalzer, Aug. 11, 1973; children: Heather Lynn, Shannon Dawn, Sean William. BA cum laude, Albion Coll., Mich., 1972; JD cum laude, U. Mich., Ann Arbor, 1975. Bar: Mich. 1975. Assoc., then ptnr. Landman, Latimer, Clink & Robb, Muskegon, Mich., 1976-85; ptnr. Warner, Norcross & Judd, Muskegon, from 1985. Dir. debate Mona Shores High Sch., Muskegon, 1979-90; adj. prof. of taxation (employee benefits), Grand Valley State U., 1988—; debate instr. Muskegon C.C., 1999-2001. Pres. local chpt. Am. Cancer Soc., 1979; bd. dirs. West Shore Symphony, 1993-00, v.p. 1995-97, pres., 1997-99; bd. dirs. Cath. Social Svcs., 1998-04; chair profl. divsn. United Way, 1994, 98; chair bd. dirs. Deaf Hard of Hearing Connection, 2003-09; bd. dirs. Mona Lake Watershed Coun., 2003-05, Hackley Life Counseling, 2007-2010; chair Charter Commn. City of Norton Shores, 2003-06. Recipient Disting. Service award Muskegon Jaycees, 1981; named 1 of 5 Outstanding Young Men in Mich., Mich. Jaycees. 1982; named to Hall of Fame, Mich. Speech Coaches, 1986, Diamond Key Coach Nat. Forensic League, 1987, Friend of Heart Stat award 2015. Mem. ABA, Mich. Bar Assn., Muskegon County Bar Assn. (dir. 1992-98, pres. 1996-97), Muskegon C. of C. (bd. dirs. 1982-88), Mich. Interscholastic Forensic Assn. (treas. 1979-86), Optimists (pres. 1992). Republican. Roman Catholic. Home: Muskegon, Mich. Died Dec. 16, 2015.

MCKENZIE, RICHARD ELVIN, aerospace engineer; b. San Rafael, Calif., Sept. 27, 1951; s. Cecil L. and Estelle B. McKenzie; m. Iris Y. Cavazos, Apr. 28, 1972; children: Jacqueline Nicole, Alexander Scott. BS, U. Tex., 1975, MS, 1976. Consulting engr. Pollak & Skan, Dallas, 1981-85; sr. staff scientist Merit Tech., Inc., Dallas, 1985-89; sr. staff engr. Geodynamics Corp., Denver, from 1989. Co-founder

The Computer Coll., Dallas, 1982-85; cons. System Specialists, Dallas, 1981-85. Patentee for A Terrain Avoidance Algorithm. Pres. Ramshorn Coop., Austin, 1969-70. Sr. mem. AIAA; mem. Assn. Old Crows, Sigma Gamma Tau. Avocations: numerical methods, reading, celestial mechanics, computer applications. Home: Colorado Springs, Colo. Died June 4, 2007.

MCKINLEY, WILLIAM THOMAS, composer, performer, educator; b. New Kensington, Pa., Dec. 9, 1938; s. Daniel Edward and Ellen Lee (Henson) M.; m. Marlene Marie Mildner, Apr. 11, 1956; children: Joseph, Derrick, Jory, Gregory, Elliott. BFA, Carnegie-Mellon U., 1960; MM, MFA, Yale U., 1966. Mem. music faculty SUNY-Albany, 1968-69; prof. music U. Chgo., 1969-73; prof. composition and jazz studies New Eng. Conservatory Music, Boston, 1973-96. Composer numerous works for orch., chamber ensembles, choral works, oratorio, also solo works; commns. include works for Koussevitsky Music Found., 1982, Lincoln Ctr. Chamber Music Soc., 1985, Boston Symphony Pops, 1986, Concert Artist Guild, 1988, Stan Getz, 1988, Am. Symphony, 1988, (2) Fromm Found., John Williams, 1989, NEA Consortium, Rheinische Philharmonie, Fed. Republic Germany, 1990, Queensland Youth Orch., Australia, 1990, Bolshoi Ballet Theatre Orch. USSR, 1990, Pitts. New Music Ensemble, 1991, Quintet Ams., 1992, Md. Bach Aria Group, 1992, Berlin Saxophone Quartet, 1992, 93, Richard Stolzman, 1993, Seattle Symphony, 1993, Absolut Vodka, 1994; performance recs. with Berlin Radio Symphony and Richard Stolzman, Rheinische Philharm., Warsaw Philharm., St. Petersburg Philharm., Slovak Radio Symphony, Seattle Symphony, Krakow Philharm., Silesian Philharm., Prague Radio Symphony, Solati Trio, Manhattan Sinfonia, Cleve. Quartet; founder (record label) MMC (Master Musicians Collective) Recipient Naumberg prize Naumberg Found., 1975; Nat. Endowment Arts composer fellow, 1975-83; Am. Acad. Music award, Am. Acad. and Inst. Arts and Letters, 1983; Guggenheim fellow, 1985; 3 Mass Council fellowships, fellowship Yale U. Sch. of Music, Cert. of Merit, 1998. Mem. Am. Composers Alliance, Am. Music Ctr. Home: Reading, Mass. Died Feb. 3, 2015.

MCKINNEY, JOHN PAUL, performing company executive; b. Birmingham, Ala., Dec. 27, 1956; s. Clifford Littleton and Lisa Michelle (Lankford) McKinney; m. Pamela Elaine Whitaker (div.); 1 child, John Paul II. Cert. in radiological tech., C.C. of the Air Force, 1977; attended, Bethany Bible Coll., 1990; D in biblical studies (hon.), Progressive Life Ch., 1993, D (hon.) in counseling, 1993. Cert. drug and alcohol counseling Alpha & Omega Inc. Pastor, CEO Trinity Cmty. Fellowship, Aptos, Calif., 1987—96; caregiver, adminstr. Trinity Ministries, So. San Francisco, Calif., 1996—2001; min., founder Prepare Ye the Way Ministries, Tuscaloosa, Ala., 2001—04; global relief outreach Solicitor Fund Raiser, Talladega, 2003; writer, dir. Full Moon Inst., Talladega, 2003—04. Pres., founder Trinity Ministries, So. San Francisco, Calif., 1996—2001, Prepare for the Way Ministries, Ala., 2001—04; pres. Full Moon Inst., Talladega, 2003—04. Sgt. USAF, 1976—80. Mem.: Full Moon Insight Soc. Democrat. Baptist. Avocations: chess, reading, golf, hiking. Home: Lincoln, Ala. Died Mar. 12, 2007.

MCKINNON, RONALD IAN, retired economics professor; b. Edmonton, Alta., Can., July 10, 1935; s. Ian Nicholson and Lois Harrison McKinnon; m. Margaret McQueen Learmonth, Sept. 7, 1957; children: Neil Charles, Mary Elizabeth, David Bruce. BA with honors, U. Alta., Edmonton, 1956; PhD, U. Minn., Mpls., 1961. Instr. bus admin U. Minn., Mpls., 1957—59; lectr. economics Syracuse U., NY, 1960—61; asst. prof. Stanford U., Calif., 1961—66, assoc. prof., 1966—69, prof., 1969—2008, prof. emeritus, 2008—14. Rockefeller vis. rsch. prof. internat. economics Brookings Instn., Washington, 1970—71; fellow Ctr. Advanced Study Behavioral Scis., Stanford, 1974—75; Frank D. Graham meml. lectr. Princeton U., NJ, 1977; vis. scholar Hoover Instn., Stanford, 1982—83; cons. IMF and World Bank, Washington. Author: Money and Capital in Economic Development, 1973, Money in International Exchange: The Convertible Currency System, 1979, An International Standard for Monetary Stabilization, 1984, The Order of Economic Liberalization: Financial Control in the Transition to a Market Economy, 1991, The Rules of the Game: International Money and Exchange Rates, 1996, Exchange Rates Under the East Asian Dollar Standard: Living with Conflicted Virtue, 2005, The Unloved Dollar Standard: From Bretton Woods to the Rise of China, 2013; co-author (with Kenichi Ohno): Dollar and Yen: Resolving Economic Conflict Between the United States and Japan, 1997. Home: Stanford, Calif. Died Oct. 1, 2014.

MCKUEN, ROD, poet, composer, author; b. Oakland, Calif., Apr. 29, 1933; s. Clarice Woolever. Pres. Stanyan Records, Discus Records, New Gramaphone Soc., Mr. Kelly Prodns., Montcalm Prodns., Stanyan Books, Cheval Books, Biplane Books, Rod McKuen Enterprises; v.p. Tamarack Books; exec. dir. Am. Guild Variety Artists, NYC. Poetry columnist Cosmopolitan, 1970-71. Appeared in numerous films, TV, concerts; composer motion picture scores, background music for TV, modern classical music; film scores include Joanna, 1968, The Prime of Miss Jean Brodie, 1969, Me, Natalie, 1969, Travels With Charlie, 1969, The Loner, 1969, Say Goodbye, 1970 (Emmy award for Best Musical Score, 1970), A Boy Named Charlie Brown, 1970, Come to Your Senses, 1971, Scandalous John, 1971, Wildflowers, 1971, The Seagull, 1972, Lisa, Bright and Dark, 1973, Big Mo, 1973, The Borrowers, 1973, Hello Again, 1974 (Emmy award for Best Musical Score, 1977), Emily, 1975, The Unknown War, 1979, Man to Himself, 1980, Portrait of Rod McKuen, 1982, Death Rides this Trial, 1983, The Living End, 1983; record prodr. for Frank Sinatra, Sylvia Syms, Kingston Trio, Petula Clark; author: And Autumn Came, 1954, Stanyan Street and Other Sorrows, 1966, Listen to the Warm, 1967, Tweleve Years of Christmas, 1968, Lonesome Cities, 1968, The World of Rod McKuen, 1968, Sea Cycle, 1969, In Someone's Shadow, 1969, Frank Sinatra: A Man Alone, 1969, With Love..., 1970, Caught in the Quiet, 1970, Rod McKuen at Carnegie Hall, 1970, Moment to Moment, 1971, The Carols of Christmas, 1971, So My Sheep Can Safely Graze, 1971, Pastorale: A Collection of Lyrics, 1971, And to Each Season, 1972, Grand Tour, 1972, Beyond the Boardwalk, 1972, Fields of Wonder, 1972, Rod McKuen Calendar and Datebook 1973, 1972, Come to Me in Silence, 1973, Seasons in the Sun, 1974, Celebrations of the Heart, 1975, The Rod McKuen Omnibus, 1975, Alone, 1975, Hand in Hand, 1976, Finding My Father: One Man's Search for Identity, 1976, The Sea Around Me, 1977, Coming Close to the Earth, 1978, We Touch the Sky, 1979, Love's Been Good to Me, 1979, The Power Bright and Shining: Images of My Country, 1980, Looking for a Friend, 1980, An Outstretched Hand: Poems, Prayers, and Meditations, 1980, The Beautiful Strangers, 1981, Too Many Midnights, 1981, Rod McKuen's Book of Days and a Month of Sundays, 1981, Watch for the Wind, 1983, The Sound of Solitude, 1983, Suspension Bridge, 1984, Valentines, 1986, Intervals, 1986, A Safe Place to Land, 2001, Rusting in the Rain, 2004; editor: Henry David Thoreau, The Wind That Blows Is All That Anybody Knows, 1970, The Will to Win, 1971; music collections include New Ballads, 1970, Seasons in the Sun, 1982; songs include Jean, If You Go Away, Seasons in the Sun, I'm Not Afraid, The Lovers, Love's Been Good to Me; compositions include Concerto Number Three for Piano and Orchestra, 1972, The Hains of My Country, 1972, Suite for Narrator and Orchestra: The City, 1973 (Pulitzer Prize nomination for classical music 1973), Ballad of Distances, 1973, Bicentennial Ballet, 1975, Symphony Number Three, 1975; spoken word albums include Lonesome Cities, 1969 (Grammy award for Best Spoken Album, 1969), Pushing the Clouds Away, Time of Desire, The Word, The Yellow Unicorn; vocal albums include After Midnight, Alone, Alone After Dark, Anywhere I Wander, The Beautiful Strangers, The Black Eagle, A Gothic Musical, Blessings in Shade of Green, Cycles, For Friends & Lovers, Global, Goodtime Music, Have a Nice Day, Lonely Summer, McKuen Country, Odyssey, Pastures Green, Road, Rod, There's a Hoot Tonight, Turntable, About Me, In The Beginning, many others. Mem. adv. bd. Market Theatre, Johannesburg, S. Africa, Fund for Animals, Internat. Edn.; mem. bd. dirs. Am. Nat. Theatre of Ballet, Am. Dance Ensemble, Calif. Music Theater, Animal Concern; bd. govs. Nat. Acad. Rec. Arts and Scis.; trustee AGVA Welfare Trust Fund, Freedoms Found., U. Nebr.; pres. Nat. Com. for Prevention of Child Abuse. Recipient Grand Prix du Disc (Paris), 1966, 1974, 1975, 1982, Golden Globe award, 1969, Motion Picture Daily award, 1969, Freedoms Found. medal of honor, 1975, Horatio Alger award, 1975, Humanitarian award First Amendment Soc., 1977, Outstanding Poet award Carl Sandburg Soc., 1978, Literary Trust award Brandeis U., 1981, Sylvester Pat Weaver award for pub. svc. broadcasting, 1981, Freedoms Found. Patriot medal, 1981, Community Svc. award Myasthenia Gravis Found., 1986; named Entertainer of Yr. Shriners Club LA, 1975, Man of Yr. U. Detroit, 1978, Man of Yr. Salvation Army, 1982. Mem. Modern Poetry Assn., ASCAP, Writers Guild, Am. Guild Authors and Composers (dir.), Internat. Platform Assn., AFTRA, AGVA (pres.) Home: Beverly Hills, Calif. Died Jan. 29, 2015.

MCKUSICK, VINCENT LEE, retired state supreme court justice, mediator; b. Parkman, Maine, Oct. 21, 1921; s. Carroll Lee and Ethel (Buzzell) McK.; m. Nancy Elizabeth Green, June 23, 1951; children: Barbara McKusick Liscord, James Emory, Katherine McKusick Ralston, Anne Elizabeth. AB, Bates Coll., 1943; SB, SM, MIT, 1947; LLB, Harvard U., 1950; LLD, Colby Coll., 1976, Nasson Coll., 1978, Bates Coll., 1979, Bowdoin Coll., 1979, Suffolk U., 1983; LHD, U. So. Maine, 1978, Thomas Coll., 1981. Bar: Maine 1952. Law clk. to Hon. Learned Hand US Ct. Appeals (2nd Cir.), 1950-51; law clk. to Justice Felix Frankfurter US Supreme Ct., 1951-52; ptnr. Pierce, Atwood, Scribner, Allen & McKusick and predecessors, Portland, Maine, 1953-77; chief justice Maine Supreme Jud. Ct., 1977-92; of counsel to Pierce Atwood LLP (formerly Pierce, Atwood, Scribner, Allen, Smith, & Lancaster), 1992—2014. Mem. advisory com. rules civil procedure Maine Supreme Jud. Ct., 1957-59, chmn., 1966-75, commr. uniform state laws, 1968-76, sec. nat. conf., 1975-77; mem. Conf. Chief Justices, 1977-92, bd. dirs., 1980-82, 91-92, pres.-elect, 1989-90, pres., 1990-91. standing com. past pres., 1992—; dir. Nat. Ctr. for State Ctrs., 1988-89, chmn.-elect, 1989-90, chmn., 1990-91; spl. master U.S. Supreme Ct. Conn. v. N.H., 1992-93, La. v. Miss., 1994-96, Kans. v. Nebr., 1999-2003; spl. master Mass. S.J.C. Liquidation American Mutual Liability Ins. Co., 1995-96; leader Am. Judges Del. to China, 1983, USSR, 1988, U.S. State Dept. Rule of Law Del. to Republic of Ga., 1992; mem. permanent com. Oliver Wendell Holmes Devise, 1993-2001. Author: Patent Policy of Educational Institutions, 1947, (with Richard H. Field) Maine Civil Practice, 1959, supplements, 1962, 67, (with Richard H. Field and L. Kinvin Wroth) 2d edit., 1970, supplements, 1972, 74, 77; also articles in legal publs. Trustee emeritus Bates Coll.; mem. advisory com. on pvt. internat. law US State Dept., 1980-85, Fed.-State Jurisdiction com., Jud. Conf. of US, 1987-89. With AUS, 1943-46. Recipient The Maine prize U. Maine Sys., 1993, Benjamin E. Mays award Bates Coll., 1994, Big M award Maine State Soc. Washington, 1995, Paul C. Reardon award Nat. Ctr. for State Centers, 1999. Fellow American Bar Found. (bd. dirs. 1977-87), American Philos. Soc. (coun. 1990-96, 97-02, v.p. 2002-05); mem. ABA (chmn. fed. rules com. 1966-71, bd. editors jour. 1971-80, chmn. 1976-77, mem. study group to China 1978, house dels. 1983-87, coun. sr. lawyers divsn. 1997-01), Maine Bar Assn., Cumberland County Bar Assn., American Arbitration Assn. (bd. dirs. 1994-2006), American Judicature Soc. (dir. 1976-78, 92-98), American Law Inst. (coun. 1968—2008), Maine Jud. Coun. (chmn. 1977-92), Inst. Jud. Adminstrn., Supreme Ct. Hist. Soc. (trustee 1994-2006), Rotary Club (hon., past pres. Portland club), Phi Beta Kappa, Sigma Xi, Tau Beta Pi. Republican. Unitarian Universalist. Home: Falmouth, Maine. Died Dec. 4, 2014.

MCLAUGHLIN, BERNARD JOSEPH, bishop emeritus; b. Buffalo, Nov. 19, 1912; s. Michael Henry and Mary Agnes (Curran) McLaughlin. Ordained priest Diocese of Buffalo, NY, 1935; pastor Blessed Sacrament Parish, Buffalo; asst. St. Joseph New Cathedral, 1936—42; sec. diocesan marriage tribunal Diocese of Buffalo, 1942—46, chancellor, 1953—69; founding pastor Coronation of the Blessed Virgin Mary Parish, Buffalo, 1950—61; ordained bishop, 1969; aux. bishop Diocese of Buffalo, 1968—88, aux. bishop emeritus, 1988—2015. Mem. US Conf. Cath. Bishops. Roman Catholic. Died Jan. 5, 2015.

MCMAHON, JOHN KING, employee benefits executive; b. Bridgeport, Conn., July 25, 1933; s. Albert D. and Josephine G. (King) McM.; m. Peggy Anne Dudley, July 6, 1957; children: Patricia, Maura, John, Brian, Meghan. BS, Holy Cross, 1956; LLB, U. Conn., West Hartford, 1965. Bar: Conn. 1965. Pension dir. Travelers Ins. Co., Hartford, Conn., 1960-65; cons. TPF & C, NYC, 1965-66; asst. gen. counsel Wallace Murray Corp., NYC, 1966-70; human resources counselor, gen. mgr. compensation-benefits Continental Group, NYC, 1970-80; dir. employee benefits TRW Inc., Cleve., from 1981. Human resources counsel The Continental Group, 1970-80; chmn. Nat. Healthcare Subcom., Washington, 1983-85. Councilman Town of Trumbull (Conn.), 1970-75. Capt. USAF, 1957-60. Mem. Employers Coun. on Flexible Compensation (bd. dirs. 1989—), Coun. Employee Benefits (trustee, pres. 1991). Home: Medina, Ohio. Died May 16, 2007.

MCMAHON, STEPHANIE MARIE, oncological nurse; b. Pitts., Oct. 16, 1952; d. Harvey L. and Marie (Sekelik) Corba; m. Mark E. McMahon, Mar. 20, 1981; children: William, Brian. ADN, C.C. Allegheny County, Pitts., 1974; lic. funeral dir., Pitts. Inst. Mortuary Sci., 1977; BSN, Pa. State U., 1993; MSN, U. Pitts., 1999. RN, Pa.; cert. oncology nurse specialist, Pa. Staff nurse Allegheny Gen. Hosp., Pitts., 1974-76; funeral dir. Harvey L. Corba Funeral Home, Pitts., 1977-78; staff nurse Presbyn. U. Hosp., Pitts., 1979-82; office nurse Drs. Ellis and Dameshek, Pitts., 1981-88; nurse mgr. outpatient oncology clinic VA Hosp., Pitts., 1988-96; clin. support specialist Amgen, from 1996; vis. staff nurse Interim Health Care, Pitts., 1992-97. Intravenous team staff nurse Presbyn. U. Hosp., Pitts., 1984-93; group leader Teen Fresh Start Program, Am. Cancer Soc., Pitts., 1994. Concessions mgr. Crafton Little Cougars, Pitts., 1989-94. Mem. Oncology Nurse Soc. (ambulatory care spl. interest group 1994, elected dir.-at-large Pitts. chpt. 1996-98, pres.-elect Pitts. chpt. 1999-00). Avocations: reading, cross stitch, crossword puzzles. Died Mar. 28, 2007.

MCMILLAN, WILLIAM WAYNE See ROGERS, WAYNE

MCMURRAY, EARL WILLIAM, psychotherapist, poet; b. Balt., July 15, 1951; s. Earl William and Suzanne Marie McMurray. BA, MacMurray Coll., 1973; MFA, U. Ark., 1985; MSW, Barry U., 1994. Tchg. asst. U. Ark., Fayetteville, 1981—84, instr., 1984—85; vis. creative writer Miss. State U., Starkville, 1985—86; instr. Office Instrnl. Resources U. Fla., Gainesville, 1990; pvt. practice Palm Beach Gardens, Fla., from 1997. Active Poets in the Schs. program Ark. Arts Coun., 1981—84. Author: (chapbook) Perfect Stranger, 1997; contbr. numerous poems to publs. Recipient prize, Acad. Am. Poets, 1985; named winner Ann. Poetry Chapbook Contest, Ledge Press, 1997. Mem.: NASW. Home: West Palm Beach, Fla. Died May 5, 2007.

MCMURTRY, ARTHUR WILLIAM, retired secondary school educator; b. Cambridge, Mass., Jan. 12, 1910; s. Louis Frederick and Selma Florence (Svenson) McM.; m. Erma June Ramsdell, Aug. 15, 1940; children: Selma Joan, Pamela Ann. BA, Mass. Coll. Art, 1932, BS, 1934; postgrad., Boston U., 1939. Supr. art Yarmouth-Dennis-Brewster (Mass.) Sch., 1934-37; head drawing dept. Wethesfield (Conn.) Sch., 1938; curriculum dir. Cambridge (Mass.) Sch. Dept., 1940-75; ret., 1975. Designer Stanley Instrument Corp., Chestnut Hill, Mass., 1941-45; mem. staff Mass. Coll. Art, Harvard U., Tufts U., Cambridge Indsl. Sch., Cape Cod Edn. Found.; lectr. in field. Illustrator for maj. pub. cos. including Macmillan, Prentiss Hall; represented in maj. corps. and pvt. collections in US and abroad. Art dir. for non-profit orgns., hosps. Recipient Valley Forge Freedom Found. award. Mem. Church of England. Home: Dennis, Mass. Died Jan. 24, 2007.

MCNAMARA, A. J. (ABEL JOHN MCNAMARA), federal judge; b. New Orleans, June 9, 1936; s. Henry D. and Ruby (Price) McNamara; m. Alma J. Loisel; children: Nancy(dec.) , Dwight(dec.) , Joni, Price. BS, La. State U., 1959; JD, Loyola U., New Orleans, 1968. Bailiff, law clk. to Hon. Herbert W. Christenberry US Dist. Ct. (eastern dist.) La., New Orleans, 1966-68, sole practice, 1968-72; ptnr. Monton, Roy, Carmouche, Hailey, Bivens & McNamara, New Orleans, 1972-78, Hailey, McNamara, McNamara & Hall, 1978-82; judge US Dist. Ct. (eastern dist.) La., New Orleans, 1982—2001, chief judge, 1999—2001, sr. judge, 2001—14. Mem. La. House of Reps., 1976-80. Served in USN, 1959—62. Republican. Roman Catholic. Died Dec. 2, 2014.

MCQUERRY, ROBERT LEROY, educational administrator; b. Cainsville, Mo., Nov. 7, 1939; s. Eldon and Ella Pauline (Barratt) McQ.; m. Nancy Ann Canaday, June 1, 1973; 1 child, Kevin Patrick. BS, N.W. Mo. State U., 1967; MS, Cen. Mo. State U., 1970, EdS, 1973; EdD, U. Mo., 1979. Counselor, tchr. Santa Fe Sch. Dist., Alma, Mo., 1970-73; supt., elem. prin. Breckenridge (Mo.) R-1 Sch. Dist., 1973-75; supt. schs. Braymer (Mo.) C-4 Sch. Dist., 1975-77, Lakeland R-III Sch. Dist., Deepwater, Mo., 1977-79; dir. trans. and maintenance Grandview (Mo.) C-4 Sch. Dist., 1979-85; area dir. State Schs. for Severly Handicapped, Mo. Dept. Edn., Kansas City, 1985-94; elem. sch. counselor George Washington Latin Grammar Sch., Pitcher Greek, Kansas City, from 1994. Assessor trainer Leadership Acad., Jefferson City, Mo., 1990; assessor Adminstrv. Assessment Ctr., Jefferson City. Deacon, elder, mem. ch. bd. Hickman Mills Cmty. Christian Ch. Sgt. U.S. Army, 1962-65. Mem. U. Mo. Alumni Assn., Masons, Phi Delta Kappa. Home: Raymore, Mo. Died Aug. 18, 2007.

MCSORLEY, DANNY EUGENE, sales executive; b. Huntington, W.Va., Nov. 26, 1960; s. Bernard Eugene and Doris M. (Newman) McS. BBA, Marshall U., Huntington, W.Va., 1983. Mgmt. trainee Lavalette (W.Va.) State Bank, 1980-83; with Profl. Bank Svc., Louisville, 1983-84; territory mgr. Bunzl Paducah (Ky.), 1984-91; sales mgr. Con-Jel Sales, Huntington, W.Va., 1991—2005; pres, CEO McVine Inc., Huntington, W.Va. and Louisville, from 2005. Mem. Marshall Quarterback Club, Marshall Tipoff Club, Big Green Scholarship Club. Democrat. Baptist. Avocations: boating, sports, athletics. Home: Lavalette, W.Va. Died Jan. 27, 2007.

MEADOR, ROY EDWARD, commercial writer; b. Cordell, Okla., Apr. 23, 1929; s. Walter Raymond and Gladys Beatrice (Reed) M. BA, U. So. Calif., 1951; MA, Columbia U., 1972. Advt. mgr. diagnostics divsn. Pfizer, Inc., NYC, 1962-72; advt. mgr. Gelman Scis., Inc., Ann Arbor, Mich., 1972-78; freelance writer Ann Arbor, from 1978. Author: Franklin, Revolutionary Scientist, 1975, Guidelines for Preparing Proposals, 1991, Future Energy Alternatives, 1978, Capital Revenge, 1975, Cogeneration and District Heating, 1981. Mem. adv. bd. Ann Arbor Pub. Libr., 1978-94, mem. pub. rels. com. Democrat. Avocations: rare book collecting, chess, classical music, reading. Died Jan. 16, 2007.

MEADOWS, JAMES WALLACE, chemist, retired; b. Meridian, La., Aug. 16, 1923; s. James Wallace and Mary Jane (Stanley) M.; m. Mary Frances Butler, Dec. 18, 1950; children: Catherine Ann, James Wallace. BS, La. Poly. Inst., 1944; PhD, La. State U., 1950. Tech. assoc. Cyclotron Lab. Harvard U., Cambridge, Mass., 1950-58; chemist Argonne (Ill.) Nat. Lab., 1958-92, ret., 1992. Fellow Am. Nuclear Soc., Am. Phys. Soc.; mem. Am. Chem. Soc. Home: Park Forest, Ill. Died Oct. 24, 2006.

MEARA, ANNE, actress, playwright, writer; b. Bklyn., Sept. 20, 1929; d. Edward Joseph and Mary (Dempsey) M.; m. Gerald Stiller, Sept. 14, 1954; children: Amy, Benjamin. Student, Herbert Berghoff Studio, 1953-54. Apprentice in summer stock, Southold, LI and Woodstock, NY, 1950-53; (off-Broadway appearances) A Month in the Country, 1954, Maedchen in Uniform, 1955 (Show Bus. off-Broadway award), Ulysses in Nightown, 1958, The House of Blue Leaves, 1970, Bosoms and Neglect, 1986, After-Play, 1996, Love, Loss, and What I Wore, 2011; Shakespeare Co., Two Gentlemen of Verona, Ctrl. Park, NYC, 1957, Romeo and Juliet, 1988; (Broadway plays) Spookhouse, 1982, Eastern Standard, 1989, Anna Christie, 1993; (film appearances) The Out-of-Towners, 1968, Lovers and Other Strangers, 1969, The Boys From Brazil, 1978, Fame, 1979, Nasty Habits, 1976, An Open Window, 1990, Mia, 1990, Awakenings, 1991, Reality Bites, 1994, Daytrippers, 1997, The Fish in the Bathtub, 1998, Southie, 1999, The Independent, 2001, Like Mike, 2002, Crooked Lines, 2003, Night at the Museum, 2006, When the Evening Comes, 2009, Another Harvest Moon, 2010, Planes: Fire & Rescue (voice), 2014; comedy act, 1963—; appearances Happy Medium and Medium Rare, Chgo., 1960-61, Village Gate, Phase Two and Blue Angel, NYC, 1963, The Establishment, London, 1963, QE II, 1990; syndicated TV series Take Five with Stiller and Meara, 1977-78; numerous appearances on TV game and talk shows, also spls. and variety shows; rec. numerous commls. for TV and radio (co-recipient Voice of Imagery award Advt. Bur. NY); star TV series Kate McShane, 1975, Archie Bunker's Place, 1979, Alf, 1986-88; (other TV appearances) The Sunset Gang, 1990, Avenue Z Afternoon, 1991, Murphy Brown, 1994, Homicide, 1996, The King of Queens, 1999-2007, Will and Grace, 2002, Sex and the City, 2002-04, Good Morning, Miami, 2003, Gravity, 2010; (TV series) All My Children, 1994-99, (TV films) Jitters, 1997, What Makes a Family, 2001, Rip City, 2011; writer, actress: (TV films) The Other Woman, 1983 (co-recipient Writer's Guild Outstanding Achievement award 1983), Alf, To Make Up to Break Up, The Stiller and Meara pilot; author, actor (play) After-Play, 1996; author: (play) Down the Garden Paths, 2000; video host (with Jerry Stiller) So You Want to Be an Actor? Recipient Outer Critic's Cir. Playwriting award for After-Play, 1995, 4th ann. Alan King award in Jewish Humor, 2003, Productive Aging award Jewish Coun. Aging, 2004, Thalia award (w/ Jerry Stiller) Humbert Coll. Toronto; received joint star with husband on the Hollywood Walk of Fame, 2007. Died May 23, 2015.

MEEK, WALTER BUCHANAN, retired lawyer, director; b. Memphis, Jan. 13, 1926; s. Arthur Maurice and Sarah Christine (Buchanan) Meek; m. Patsy Joyce Hayes, June 26, 1949; children: Christine Thrasher, Buchanan, Joyce Yates. BBA, U. Miss., 1948, LLB, 1950. Bar: Miss. 1950, U.S. Ct. Appeals (5th cir.) 1972. Practice, Eupora, Miss., from 1950; mem. Meek and Meek, Eupora, from 1975. With USAAF, 1943—45. Mem.: ABA, Miss. State Bar. Methodist. Died Nov. 19, 2006.

MEHEARG, CLIFFORD WAYNE, charitable organization executive; b. Wetumpka, Ala., May 25, 1937; s. Dalton George and Madell (Blankenship) M.; m. Jeannine Elizabeth Heath; 1 child, Tracy Jeannine. AB in Sociology, Ga. State U., 1970. With Sears Roebuck and Co., Atlanta, 1959-74, staff advt. asst., 1966-70, mgr. advt. and sales promotions Brunswick, Ga., 1970-74; dir. communications Trident United Way, Charleston, S.C., 1975-76, campaign dir., 1976-77, dir. resources devel., 1977-79; pres. United Way S.W. Ga., United Way S.W. Ga., from 1979. Co. chmn. campaign United Way, Brunswick, 1971; mem. Com. for Brunswick Bicentennial, 1973, Brunswick-Golden Isles C. of C., Brunswick, 1973; co. chmn. U.S. Savs. Bond Drive, Brunswick, 1971, March of Dimes, Brunswick, 1971-73; conv. del. Dorchester County Dems., Summerville, S.C., 1976; county campaign chmn., mem. steering com. Richard Riley for Gov., Summerville, 1978; pres. Deerfield-Windsor Band Parents Assn., Albany, 1985-86. Mem. Ga. Sociol. and Anthrop. Assn., UN Assn. of U.S., Leadership Albany Alumni Assn. (charter), Brunswick Exch. Club, Kiwanis (2d v.p. N.C. chpt. 1976, 1st v.p. 1977, pres. elect N.C. chpt. 1978, Kiwanian of the Yr. 1978), Rotary, Albany C. of C., Phi Eta Sigma, Blue Key, Alpha Delta Kappa. Home: Albany, Ga. Died Jan. 3, 2007.

MEHLING, EMILY, artist; b. Plainfield, NJ, Aug. 28, 1932; d. Hugh and Corlyss Gibson Thompson; m. Harold Mehling, Oct. 8, 1974; children: Daniel Rodriguez, Joshua Rodriguez, Adam Rodriguez. BS, Columbia U., 1962; postgrad., Hunter Coll., 1966—68, Parsons Sch. Design, NYC, 1994—96. Tchr. N.Y.C. Bd. Edn., 1967—71; art dir. Park Row Pubs., NYC, 1972—80; freelance painter and sculptor NYC, from 1980. Mem.: Nat. League Am. PEN Women, Found. for Modern Painters and Sculptors, Am. Soc. Contemporary Artists (treas. 2000—02), Contemporary Artist Guild, Nat. Assn. Women Artists (pres. 2002—04, organizer exhbns.), Amnesty Internat. Avocations: theater, opera. Home: New York, NY. Died June 11, 2007.

MEHNE, PAUL RANDOLPH, consultant, retired medical educator; b. Wilmington, Del., May 27, 1948; s. Paul Herbert and Doris Ruth (Longfritz) M.; m. Carol Ann (Starner), June 12, 1971; children: Meredith Lynn, and Amy Elizabeth. BS in Environ. Sci., SUNY, Syracuse, 1970; PhD, SUNY, 1976, Syracuse Univ., 1976. Asst. prof. East Carolina U. Allied Health, Greenville, NC, 1975-76; assoc. dir. East Carolina U. Ctr. Edn., Devel., and Evaluation, Greenville, NC, 1976-79; coord. of curriculum East Carolina U. Sch. Medicine, Greenville, NC, 1979—81, asst. dean, 1981-85, assoc. dean, 1985—89, assoc. prof., 1988—89, dir. Ctr. Health Sci., Edn., and Info., 1988—89; assoc. dean student and housestaff affairs U. Pa., Phila., 1989—91; assoc. dean acad. and student affairs, assoc. prof. family medicine Robert Wood Johnson Med. Sch., Piscataway, NJ, 1992—2007; chair U. wide tele medicine video com distance learning com. Univ. Medicine and Dentistry N.J., 1995-2000, chmn. acad. info. tech. adv. com., 1996-98, 2005—06. Chmn. exec. bd. dir. MEDCOMP Super Computer Consortium, Athens, Ga., 1986—89; vis. prof. U. N.C., Chapel Hill, 1986, Tulane U., New Orleans, 1988. Contbr. articles to profl. jour. Chmn. Cmty. Appearance Comm., Greenville, NC, 1980—85; ex officio trustee Cooper Univ. Hosp., 2001—07. Grantee NJ Dept. Health and Sr. Svcs., 2003-04; recipient Interactive Video Instrn. Award Digital Equipment Corp., 1985, Med. Edn. Cost Containment award Kate B. Reynolds Health Care Trust, 1985-88, Telemedicine and Med. Informatics Award, 1996-99, US Dept. Commerce NTIA/TIIAP Award for tele-medicine, 1996-98. Mem. IEEE, APHA, Am. Coll. Pers. Assn., Assn. for Med. Edn. and Rsch. on Substance Abuse, Am. Med. Informatics Assn., Am. Edn. Rsch. Assn., Assn. Am. Med. Colls. (chair consortium on student and prof. well being 1993-94, steering com. Clin. Campus Deans 2000—07, chair AAMC Group on Regional Med. Campuses 2005-06, past chmn. 2006—07), Soc. Tchrs. Family Medicine, Alpha Omega Alpha. Died Sept. 14, 2015.

MEINERS, R(OGER) K(EITH), English language educator; b. Forreston, Ill., Dec. 5, 1932; s. John H. and Lillian C. (Buss) M.; m. Lynn E. Dunn, Dec. 12, 1958; children: Katherine Terry, Sally Ann. BA, Wheaton Coll., 1954; BD, Westminster Sem., Phila., 1956; MA, U. Denver, 1957, PhD, 1961. Instr. U. Denver, 1957-59; instr. English Ariz. State U., Tempe, 1959-61, asst. prof., 1961-64; assoc. prof. U. Mo., Columbia, 1964-70; prof. English Mich. State U., East Lansing, from 1970. Editor The Centennial Review, Mich. State U., 1988—. Author: The Last Alternatives, 1963, Everything to be Endured, 1970, Journeying Back to the World, 1975; contbr. essays, poems, book reviews to lit., scholarly jours. Mem. Modern Lang. Assn., Soc. Editors of Learned Jours. Avocations: musical performance, gardening. Home: East Lansing, Mich. Died Dec. 15, 2006.

MEJIA, JORGE MARIA CARDINAL, cardinal, archivist and librarian emeritus of the Holy Roman Church; b. Buenos Aires, Jan. 31, 1923; Attended, Seminary of Villa Devoto, Buenos Aires; Licentiate in Scripture, Pontifical Biblical Institute; ThD, Pontifical U. of Saint Thomas Aquinas (Angelium), Rome, 1948. Ordained priest of Buenos Aires, 1945; prof. Old Testament studies Catholic U., Buenos Aires; dir. Catholic Journal Criterio, 1956—77; sec. Dept. Ecumenism CELAM, 1967—77; sec. Pontifical Commn. for Religious Relations with the Jews, Rome, 1977—86, led the delegation, 2010; peritus Second Vatican Council, 1978; chaplain to His Holiness, 1978; v.p., official Pontifical Council for Justice and Peace, Rome, 1986—94; appointed a Titular Bishop of Apollonia, 1986, ordained, 1986; sec. and raised to archiepiscopal dignity Congregation for Bishops, Rome, 1994—98; sec. College of Cardinals, 1994—98; archivist and librarian of the Holy Roman Church Vatican Secret Archives and Library, Rome, 1998—2003, archivist and librarian of the Holy Roman Church emeritus, from 2003; elevated to cardinal, 2001; cardinal-deacon of San Girolamo della Carita (Saint Jerome of Charity), 2001—11, cardinal-priest, 2011—14. Bd. mem. World Religious Leaders for the Elijah Interfaith Inst., 2013—14. Roman Catholic. Died Dec. 9, 2014.

MELTEBEKE, RENETTE, career counselor; b. Portland, Oreg., Apr. 20, 1948; d. Rene and Gretchen (Hartwig) M. BS in Sociology, Portland State U., 1970; MA in Counseling Psychology, Lewis and Clark Coll., 1985. Lic. profl. counselor, Oreg.; nat. cert. counselor; Veriditas trained labyrinth facilitator. Secondary tchr. Portland Pub. Schs., 1970-80; project coord. Multi-Wash CETA, Hillsboro, Oreg., 1980-81; coop. edn. specialist Portland C.C., 1981-91; pvt. practice career counseling, owner Career Guidance Specialists, Lake Oswego, Oreg., from 1988. Mem. adj. faculty Marylhurst (Oreg.) U., 2003—, Portland State U., 1994-98, Lewis and Clark Coll., 2001—; assoc. Drake Beam Morin Inc., Portland, 1993-96; career cons. Managed Health Network, 1994-98, Career Devel. Svcs., 1990-95, Life Dimensions, Inc., 1994; presenter Internat. Conf., St. Petersburg, Russia, 1995. Rotating columnist Lake Oswego Rev., 1995-99; creator video presentation on work in Am. in 5 langs., 1981; pub. in "Chicken Soup to Inspire a Woman's Soul, 2004. Pres. Citizens for Quality Living, Sherwood, Oreg., 1989; mem. Leadership Roundtable on Sustainability for Sherwood, 1994-95; bd. dirs. Bus. for Social Responsibility for Oreg. and Southwestern Wash., 1999, 2000. Recipient Esther Matthews award for outstanding contbn. to field of career devel., 1998. Mem.: Assn. for Humanistic Psychology (presenter nat. conf. Tacoma 1996), Oreg. Career Devel. Assn. (pres. 1990), Nat. Career Devel. Assn., Willamette Writers. Avocations: walking, swimming, bicycling, cross country skiing, photography. Home: Sherwood, Oreg. Died Mar. 5, 2007.

MELTON, ANDREW JOSEPH, JR., retired investment company executive; b. Bay Shore, NY, Mar. 4, 1920; s. Andrew J. and Alice (Lonergan) M.; m. Mary Ann Shanks, Sept. 18, 1943 (dec. 1999); children: Diana, Andrew, Robert, Karen, Marjorie, Sandra, Michaelle, Edward. BS, Villanova U., 1942. With Smith Barney & Co., NYC, 1946-72, chmn. exec. com., 1968-72; exec. v.p. Dean Witter & Co., Inc., NYC, 1972—78; chmn., CEO Dean Witter Reynolds, Inc., NYC, 1978-82; chmn. bd. Dean Witter Funds, 1982-92. Served with USMC, 1942-46, 51-53. Mem. Investment Bankers Assn. America (pres. 1970), Bond Club of N.Y. (pres. 1982), Knickerbocker Club, Links Club, Dorset Field Club (Vt.), Ekwanok Country Club (Vt.). Home: Jupiter, Fla. Died Oct. 15, 2014.

MELTZER, SANFORD, lawyer, educator; b. Syracuse, NY, July 4, 1933; s. Mose and Gertrude (Hodes) M.; m. Elaine Lois Levine, July 8, 1962; children: Robin Alisa, Marna Denise. BA, Syracuse U., 1957, JD, 1959. Bar: N.Y. 1959, U.S. Dist. Ct. (no. dist.) N.Y. 1959, U.S. Tax Ct. 1960, U.S. Dist. Ct. (so. dist.) N.Y. 1978, U.S. Ct. Appeals (2d cir.) 1978, U.S. Supreme Ct. 1978. Sole practice, Syracuse. Instr. cmty. internship in family law, criminal law and trial practice Syracuse U., 1970—. Mem. coun. N.Y. State Legis. Syracuse, 1968-72; committeeman defending all med. profls. Def. Rsch. Am.; mem. Dewitt Bd. of Assessment Rev., 1982—, chmn., 1989—. Mem. ABA, ATLA, Bar Assn. of Supreme Ct. of. U.S., N.Y. State Bar Assn. (spl. com. on biotech. and the law 1987—), N.Y. State Trial Lawyers Assn., Onondaga County Bar Assn. (bd. dirs. 1981-83), Onondaga County Bar Found., Upstate Trial Lawyers Assn., NRA, Masons, Moose, Shriners. Jewish. Avocations: target pistol shooting, photography, coin collecting/numismatics. Home: Syracuse, NY. Died Feb. 26, 2007.

MENASCHE, LILLI See VERNON, LILLIAN

MENINO, TOM (THOMAS MICHAEL MENINO), former mayor; b. Boston, Dec. 27, 1942; s. Susan & Carl Menino; m. Angela Faletra; children: Susan, Thomas Michael, Jr. AA, Chamberlayne Junior Coll., 1963; BA in Community Planning, U. Mass., 1988; Cert. in State & Local Govt. Program, Harvard U. Mem. Boston City Coun., 1985—93, pres., 1993; acting mayor City of Boston, 1993, mayor, 1993—2014. Sr. rsch. asst. Joint Com. Urban Affairs, 1978-83; pres. U.S. Conf. Mayors, 2002-03. Contbr. articles to historic preservation jours. Regional chmn. Nat. Trust Historic Preservation; bd. dirs. Nat. League Cities, 1985- Democrat. Died Oct. 30, 2014.

MERRELL, JAMES LEE, writer, minister; b. Indpls., Oct. 24, 1930; s. Mark W. and Pauline F. (Tucker) M.; m. Barbara Jean Burch, Dec. 23, 1951; children: Deborah Lea Merrell Griffin, Cynthia Lynn Archer, Stuart Allen. AB, Ind. U., 1952; MDiv, Christian Theol. Sem., 1956; LittD, Culver-Stockton Coll., 1972. Ordained to ministry Christian Ch., 1955; asso. editor World Call, Indpls., 1956-66, editor, 1971-73; pastor Crestview Christian Ch., Indpls., 1966-71; editor The Disciple, St. Louis, 1974-89; sr. v.p. Christian Bd. Publ., 1976-89; sr. minister Affton Christian Ch., St. Louis, 1989-94; interim chaplain Culver-Stockton Coll., Canton, Mo., 1995; interim sr. pastor Friedens United Ch. of Christ, Warrenton, Mo., 1995-98, St. Johns United Ch. of Christ, Mehlville, Mo., 1998—2002, Hamilton Christian Ch., Creve Coeur, 2002—03, Redeemer Evang. Ch., St. Louis, 2003—05, Trinity United Ch. Christ, 2005—11; guest chaplain US Senate, 2009. Bd. dirs. Horizons mag.,

1995-98. Author: They Live Their Faith, 1965, The Power of One, 1976, Discover the Word in Print, 1979, Finding Faith in the Headlines, 1985, We Claim Our Heritage, 1992, Seeing Life: Finding God, 2006. Chmn. bd. Kennedy Meml. Christian Home, Martinsville, Ind., 1971-73; trustee Christian Theol. Sem., 1978-81. Recipient Faith and Freedom award Religious Heritage of Am., 1983; lifetime achievement award Mo. State Sen., 2000. Mem. Associated Ch. Press (award 1973, 79, 80, 81, 82, dir. 1974-75, 78-81, 1st v.p. 1983-85), Christian Theol. Sem. Alumni Assn. (pres. 1966-68), Religious Pub. Rels. Coun. (awards 1979, 80, 84, 87, 90, pres. St. Louis chpt. 1985-86), Sigma Delta Chi (award 1952), Theta Phi, Pi Kappa Alpha. Home: Saint Louis, Mo. *As a religious communicator and as a pastor, I have always believed in applying the same standards in the sacred realm as in the secular. I have tried to pursue the truth, to keep my constituency informed, to celebrate the noble in life, to fight against those who would lie, distort and hide God's truth in the name of some supposed good.* Died Jan. 2015.

MERRICK, TERRY ALLEN, computer repair company executive; b. Kokomo, Ind., June 21, 1950; s. Frank Edward and Virginia Ruth (Brown) M.; m. Terrie Colleen Terhune, Mar. 11, 1967 (div. June 1988); children: Teresa, Terry Jr., Tina, Todd, Ty; m. Lynn Ann Greivelle, July 4, 1992. BA, Ind. U., Kokomo, 1972; DD, Ch. of God, Houston, 1978. Lic. bldg. constrn., electronics technician, computer repair. Mgr. Shell Oil Corp., Kokomo, Ind., 1968-72; inspector Chrysler Corp., Kokomo, 1972-75; owner Merrick Constrn., Tampa, Fla., 1975-77; mgr. Dairy Queen Stores Inc., Houston, 1977-82, Ky. Fried Chicken, Long Beach, Calif., 1982-86; nursing asst. Kimberley Nurses Registry, Los Alamitos, Calif., 1986-89; owner Merrick Electronics, El Monte, Calif., from 1989. Pastor Ch. of God, 1976—. Sgt. U.S. Army, 1970-72, Vietnam. Decorated 3 Purple Hearts, Bronze Star, Air medal. Mem. VFW (sgt. at arms 1974-75), Am. Legion (Outstanding Citizen 1978), Nat. Rifle Assn. Republican. Avocations: reading, gardening, fishing, travel. Died Jan. 25, 2007.

MERRITT, JUDY MILES, retired academic administrator; b. Jacksonville, Ala., Sept. 5, 1943; d. Lawrence and Beatrice (Davis) Miles; m. Thomas E. Merritt (dec.). BS in Secondary Edn., U. Ala., MA in Counseling & Guidance; PhD, in Educational Adminstrn. Counselor admissions Jefferson State Jr. Coll., 1965—75; v.p. student affairs Fla. Internat. U., 1975—79; pres. Jefferson State Community Coll., Birmingham, Ala., 1979—2014. Bd. dirs. Energen Corp., 1993—2014. Mem.: Birmingham Chamber of Commerce (chmn. 1993). Achievements include becoming the first woman to become president of a community college in Alabama, 1979. Died Oct. 19, 2014.

MERTZ, ANNE MORRIS, writer, researcher, journalist, educator; b. Indpls., Sept. 29, 1913; d. Theodore Hatfield and Lisette Susanna (Krauss) Morris; m. Walter Day Mertz, June 29, 1937; children: Suzanne Day Mertz Smalloy, Elizabeth Morris Mertz O'Brien, Walter Day Jr., Theodore Morris. BA cum laude, Randolph-Macon Woman's Coll., Va., 1935. Cert. Tchr. Pa., 1935. Tchr. ch. sch. Germantown Unitarian Ch., Phila., 1935—50; tchr. Yeadon (Pa.) Sch. Dist., 1935—40; religious edn. dir. Unitarian Ch., Wilmington, Del., 1950—60; mus. guide Hagley Mus., Wilmington, 1964-76; travel writer, lectr., from 1965. Author: (booklets) History of Delaware Colonial Dames Headquarters, 1990, 2001, History of Delaware Mayflower Society, 1993, (books) Morris Migration: A Saga of Forbears and Descendants, 1996, 2000, 2001, Windows into Pilgrim Life and Seven Mayflower Ancestors, 1998, Memoirs of Washington in the Eighteen Sixties Including the Witnessing of Lincoln's Assassination, 2001; author: (with others) Reaching the Summit, 1999, America at the Millennium, 2000; contbr., rschr. (articles) many jours., newspapers, mags., Libr. of Congress Archives, Phila. Inquirer, Wayne Suburban, Ardmore Suburban, Greenville Cmty. News, Wilmington News Jour., Sarasota Herald Tribune, Brandenton Herald, Venice Gondolier, Mayflower Quar., Baby Talk Mag., Del. Geneal. Jour., Hockessin Cmty. News, Bank Notes, Dartmouth Coll. and Randolph-Macon Woman's Coll. Mag. Vol. mus. guide Winterthur Mus., Wilmington, 1956—60; active pres.'s adv. bd. Wilmington Trust of Fla., Stuart, 1990—93; bd. dirs. Wilmington Music Sch., 1952—73, Family Svcs. Del.; spkr., dir., hon. bd. dirs. United Fund Planning Com., Wilmington, 1957—65; hon. bd. dirs. Children and Families First, from 1995; hon. bd. mem. Family and Children's Svcs.; profl. womens' adv. bd. mem. Am. Biog. Inst., Inc.; pres. Travelers Aid Soc., Wilmington, 1954—56, Randolph-Macon Woman's Coll. Alumnae of No. Del., 1949—51, 1965—68; nat. v.p. Randolph-Macon Woman's Coll. Alumnae Assn., Lynchburg, Va., 1961—64. Mem.: AAUW (nat. and local life mem., Wilmington Br. chair trustees, 1st v.p. 1970—75, Scholarship-Grant named for her from 1940), Nat. League Am. PEN Women (active Sarasota and Fla.), Del. Colonial Dames (spkr., rschr., oral history interviewer), Del. Hist. Soc., Mayflower Soc. (life; Del. state pres. 1990—93, bd. dirs., gold medal), Del. Geneal. Soc. Avocations: world travel, flowers, gardening, genealogy, embroidery. Died June 25, 2007.

MESQUITA, ROSALYN ANAYA, artist, educator; b. Belen, N.Mex., Aug. 21, 1935; d. Trinidad Jose and Margaret Oliva (Aragon) Anaya; m. Theodore Richard Mesquita, Jan. 14, 1956 (div.); children: John, Richard, Larry, Thresa. BA, Calif. State U., Northridge, 1974; MFA, U. Calif., Irvine, 1976. Cert. community coll. credential, Calif. Curator State of N.Mex., Santa Fe, 1968-72; lectr. L.A. Hist. Soc., from 1978; prof. Pasadena (Calif.) City Coll., from 1981. Lectr. Non.-Govtl. Orgn. UN PLanning Com., Nairobi, Kenya, and N.Y., 1985—; curator, participant Am. Women in Art, UN World Conf., Nairobi, 1985; curator Mus. Natural History, L.A., 1978; planning com. worldwide women's conf. Global Focus, Beijing, 1995; peer panelist Cultural Affairs Dept. City of L.A., 1995—. Lectr. L.A. BiCentennial and 1985 Olympic Com., 1976-84; mem. Santa Monica Art Commn., 1991—. Recipient Col.-Aide-De Camp award Gov. David F. Cargo, 1972; Ford Found. fellow, 1975. Mem. Coll. Art Assn., Nat. Women's Caucus for Art (affirmative action officer 1980-83, honorarium 1983), Hispanic Faculty Assn. (treas. 1980-90), Assn. Latin Am. Artists (pres. 1982-90), L.A. La Raza Faculty Assn. (sec. 1979-85, v.p. 1988-89). Democrat. Roman Catholic. Avocation: travel. Home: Van Nuys, Calif. Died Aug. 20, 2007.

MESSLER, EUNICE CLAIRE, nurse educator; b. Westwood, NJ, Sept. 8, 1930; d. Fred Webb and Eunice Monroe (Pepple) M. AB in Math., Barnard Coll., 1952; M. Nursing, Case-Western Res. U., 1956; EdD in Nursing Edn., Columbia U., 1974. Assoc. prof. Sch. of Nursing Columbia U., NYC, 1973-81, U. Wyo., Laramie, 1982-84; asst. dean Sch. of Nursing East Carolina U., Greenville, N.C., 1984-89; dir. nursing program Westbrook Coll., Portland, Maine, from 1989. Guardian ad litem, Greenville, 1986-89. Mem. AAUW, ANA, Nat. League for Nursing, Altrusa Internat., Sigma Theta Tau. Home: Staunton, Va. Died Aug. 6, 2007.

METIVIER, DONALD ANTHONY, writer; b. Glens Falls, NY, Aug. 2, 1936; s. Anthony Henry and Grace Ann (Usher) MeT.; m. Laraine Helen Martin, Sept. 9, 1961; children: Donna, Richard Kerry, Dianne, Anthony, Stephen, Robert, Laurie. AA, Rider Coll., 1958; BS, Boston U., 1960. Reporter Glens Falls Times, 1961-68; day editor Glens Falls Post-Star, 1968-75, editorial editor, 1975-81; editor, pub. Ski Racing mag., Waitsfield, Vt., 1981-87; pres. Media Matters, Glens Falls, from 1987. Pres. U.S. Ski Writers, 1976-77; bd. dirs. Glens Falls Nat. Bank & Trust. Author: Saturday Morning, 1988, Metivier On, 1990, A Club in the Country, 1990, Iron Clad, 1990; columnist (internat. ski competition) In The Gates, 1996—. Pres. Friends of Crandall Library, Glens Falls, 1988-89, 89-90; chmn. Glens Falls Civic Ctr. Authority, 1981-84, Glens Falls Civic Authority, 1987; trustee Glens Falls Found., Adirondack Community Coll. Found., Crandall Pub. Libr., The Hyde Collection, Glens Falls Symphony. Cpl. U.S. Army, 1960-66, USAR. Mem. Eastern Ski Writers (pres., bd. dirs. 1968-72), N.Y. Turf Writers, Rotary. Republican. Roman Catholic. Avocation: sailing. Home: Lake George, NY. Died Apr. 6, 2007.

METZGER, ERNEST HUGH, aerospace engineer, research scientist; b. Nurnberg, Germany, Oct. 22, 1923; came to U.S., 1939, naturalized, 1943; s. Paul Arthur and Charlotte Babette (Kann) M.; m. Sarah Temple Grinnell, Nov. 19, 1956; children: Lisa Metzger Dunning, Charlotte Bennett (dec.), George Grinnell. BS, CCNY, 1949; MS, Harvard U., 1950. Automatic control engr. Bell Aerospace Co. div. Textron, Buffalo, 1950-54, tech. dir. inertial nav. systems, 1954-60, chief engr., inertial instruments, 1960-70, chief engr., gravity gradiometer systems, 1970-83, dir. gravity sensor systems, 1983-86, exec. dir. engring., 1986-89, cons., 1989-95, Bell Geospace Inc., Buffalo, from 1995. Mem. panel future navigation systems Nat. Acad. Sci., com. on geodesy NRC, 1988-89, accelerator criteria com. NASA, tech. com. navigation guidance and control, AIAA, 1989—; vis. lectr. dept. aernautics and astronautics Stanford U., 1990 Contbr. articles to profl. jours.; patentee in field Served with AUS, 1943-46 Recipient Aerospace Pioneer award Niagara Frontier sect. AIAA, 1977; named to Niagara Frontier Aviation Hall of Fame, 1992. Mem. IEEE, Inst. Navigation (Thurlow award for outstanding contbn. to sci. navigation 1983), AAAS, Air Force Assn., N.Y. Acad. Scis., Explorers Club, Sigma Xi, Tau Beta Pi, Eta Kappa Nu Clubs: Harvard, Buffalo Ski. Home: Williamsville, NY. Died Jan. 17, 2015.

METZGER, EVELYN BORCHARD, artist; b. NYC, June 8, 1911; d. Samuel and Eva (Rose) Borchard; m. H. A. Metzger, June 28, 1934 (dec. 1974); children: James Borchard, Edward Arthur, Eva Metzger Lanier. AB, Vassar Coll., 1932. One-woman shows include Galeria Muller, Buenos Aires, 1950, S.A.G. Gallery, N.Y.C., 1962, Gallerie Bellechasse, Paris, 1963, Vassar Coll. Art Gallery, Poughkeepsie, N.Y., 1963, Everhart Mus., Scranton, Pa., 1963, Frank Partridge Gallery, N.Y.C., 1964, Norfolk (Va.) Mus. Art, 1965, Van Diemen-Lilienfeld Gallery, N.Y., 1966, Columbus Mus., Ga., 1966, Ga. Mus. Fine Arts, Athens, Ga., 1966, Mex.-Am. Cultural Inst., Mexico City, 1967, Telfair Acad. Arts, Savannah, Ga., 1966, U. Maine, Orono, 1967, Slater Meml. Mus., Norwich, Conn., 1967, Albion (Mich.) Coll., 1969, Graham-Eches Sch., Palm Beach, Fla., 1970, Bartholet Gallery, N.Y.C., 1973, Arsenal Gallery, N.Y.C., 1983, Quogue Libr., N.Y., 1988, Nat. Mus. Women in the Arts, Washington 1997, 2002, Joan Whalen Gallery, N.Y.C., 1997, Cornell U., 1998, Washington County Mus. Fine Art, Hagerstown, Md., 1999, Curzen Gallery, Boca Raton, Fla., 2001, AnnNorton Sculpture Garden, Fla., 2001, Am. Norton Sculptur Gardens, West Palm Beach, Fla., 2001, Nat. Mus. Women in Arts, Washington, 2002; represented in permanent collections including Art in Embassies program, U.S. Dept. State. Mem. Artists Equity, Cosmopolitan Club. Avocation: travel. Home: New York, NY. Died Apr. 5, 2007.

METZKER, RAY KRUEGER, photographer; b. Milw., Sept. 10, 1931; s. William Martin and Marian Helen (Krueger) M. BFA, Beloit Coll., 1953; MS, Inst. Design, Ill. Inst. Tech., 1959. Mem. faculty photography-film dept. Phila. Coll. Art, 1962-81, prof., chmn. dept., 1978-79; vis. assoc. prof. U. N.Mex., 1970-72; vis. adj. prof. R.I. Sch. Design, spring 1977; adj. Columbia Coll., Chgo., 1980-83. Smith Disting. vis. prof. art George Washington U., 1987-88. Author: Sand Creatures, 1979; one-man exhbns. include, Art Inst. Chgo., 1959, Mus. Modern Art, N.Y.C., 1967, Milw. Art Ctr., 1970, The Picture Gallery, Zurich, Switzerland, 1974, Marion Locks Gallery, Phila., 1978, 83, Internat. Ctr. Photography, N.Y.C., 1978, Light Gallery, N.Y.C., 1979, Shadai Gallery, Tokyo Inst. Polytechnics, 1992, Turner/Krull Gallery, L.A., 1992, Zola Lieberman Gallery, Chgo., 1995, Lawrence Miller Gallery, 1984, 85, 87, 88, 90, 92, 94; represented in permanent collections, Mus. Modern Art, N.Y.C., Art Inst. Chgo., Smithsonian Inst., Washington, Met. Mus. Art, N.Y.C., Phila. Mus. Art, Bibliotheque Nat., Paris: 25 Yr. Retrospective, Mus. Fine Art, Houston and six other U.S. mus.; subject of monograph: Unknown Territory: Ray K. Metzker, 1984. Served with U.S. Army, 1954-56. Guggenheim fellow, 1966, 79; Nat. Endowment Arts fellow, 1974, 88; residency LaNapoule Art Found., France, 1989. Home: Philadelphia, Pa. Died Oct. 9, 2014.

MEYER, FRANK, journalist; b. Port Chester, NY, Jan. 1, 1936; s. Moses and Jennie (Marcus) M.; m. Michele Jean Landers, Dec. 31, 1980; children: Jana Beth, Ryan Marc. AB in Philosophy, U. Miami, 1959. Acting dir. English programs Israel Broadcasting Authority, Jerusalem, 1971-72; pvt. practice Miami, 1972-74, 81-82; publicity dir. Fla. Philharm., Miami, 1989-81; reporter Variety, NYC, 1974-75, music editor, 1975-80, spl. sects. dir., 1982-83, mng. editor, 1983-88, editor spl. projects, 1988-90; freelance writer-editor, from 1991; exec. dir. Hudson Valley Film Video Office, from 1993. Breeder Lhasa Apsos and West Highland White Teriers, 1992—. With U.S. Army, 1955-58. Democrat. Jewish. Home: Highland, NY. Died Jan. 29, 2007.

MEYER, NANCY JO, law educator; b. Wabash, Ind., Apr. 22, 1942; d. Morris and Eliza Jane (Hawkins) Groverman; m. Roger Eugene Shurr, June 8, 1963 (div. Feb. 1974); children: Laura Marie, Carl Roger; m. Alfred William Meyer, Aug. 6, 1976. AB in Journalism and English, Ind. U., 1964; JD, Valparaiso U., Ind., 1976; LLM in Communications Law, N.Y. Law Sch., 1985. Bar: Ind., N.Y. Reporter, part-time city editor Vidette Messenger, Valparaiso, 1960-64, 73-74; tchr. English Speedway (Ind.) Pub. Schs., 1964-68; staff reporter The Post-Tribune, Gary, Ind., 1974-76; legal asst., judge pro tem Porter County Cir. & Superior Cts., Valparaiso, 1976-77; legal asst. William F. Casler, Atty., St. Petersburg Beach, Fla., 1977-78; assoc. Donald P. Levinson, Atty., Merrillville, Ind., 1978-80; assoc. prof. comms. law Valparaiso U., 1981-92; sr. assoc. dir. comms. Sch. Medicine Ind. U., Indpls., 1992-94; prof. mass comm., dir. grants devel. Coll. of the Desert, Palm Desert, Calif., from 1994. Dir. freshman seminars Valparaiso U., 1989-92; vis. scholar, writing fellow Poynter Inst. for Media Studies, St. Petersburg, Fla., 1988-89; pres. Christian Inst. for Comm. Devel., N.Y.C. and Valparaiso, 1987-93. Mem. Assn. for Edn. in Journalism and Mass Communications, N.Y. State Bar Assn., Ind. Bar Assn., Soc. for Profl. Journalists, Investigative Reporters and Editors, Luth. Acad. Home: Valparaiso, Ind. Died Mar. 17, 2007.

MEYER, ROBERT ALLEN, finance educator; b. Wisconsin Rapids, Wis., May 31, 1943; s. Charles Harold and Viola Bertha (Stoeckmann) M.; 1 child, Timothy Charles. BA, Valparaiso U., Ind., 1966; MA, Mich. State U., 1967, PhD, 1972, postgrad., 1981. Asst. prof. Muskingum Area Tech. Coll., Zanesville, Ohio, 1972-74; adj. prof. U. Fla., Gainesville, 1974-80; dean acad. affairs Santa Fe Community Coll., Gainesville, 1974-80; asst. prof. Purdue U., W. Lafayette, Ind., 1982-84, Ga. State U., Atlanta, 1985-89; assoc. prof., program coord. U. N. Tex., Denton, 1989-91; Fulbright profl. scholar, Bangkok, 1991-92; coord. travel, tourism, hotel, restaurant mgmt. program U. Hawaii Manoa Campus, Honolulu, 1992-97; dir. distance edn., dir. travel, hotel and tourism mgmt. SPC, St. Petersburg, Fla., from 1997. Investor, asst. mgr. LaSiene Restaurant, Ann Arbor, Mich., 1970-72; investor, cons. Cafe Brittany St. Thomas, U.S. V.I., 1974-80, owner, operator, Houston, 1980; pres. RTM Cons., Honolulu, Hawaii, 1989—; educator World Tourism Orgn., 1993—; mem. vis. ind. coun. C. of C., 1993—; club mgr. Assn. Am., 1994—; dir. edn. Am. Assoc. Real Estate License Law Officials; mem. adv. bd. SPC Hospitality Tourism, 2012. Contbr. articles to profl. jours. Founding mem. Fla. Distance Learning Consortium, 1998—; bd. dirs., founder Fla. Virtual Campus, 1998—, dir. hospitality program, 1998—. Recipient White House Commendation for Partnerships with Industry and Higher Edn.,1984, George Washington Medal of Honor for innovations in higher edn., Freedoms Found., 1985, 86, Achievement award in hospitality edn. Coun. of Hotel, Restaurant & Instl. Edn., 1987. Mem. Assn. Real Estate Lic. Law Ofcls. (distance edn. coun. bd. mem. 1999—), Tarrant County Hotel and Motel Assn., Dallas Hotel Assn., Am. Soc. Tng. and Devel., Travel Ind. Assn. Tex., Hotel Sales & Mktg. Assn. (bd. dirs. 1985-89), Coun. of Hotel, Restaurant and Instl. Edn. (grad. com. 1989-90). Home: Vermontville, Mich. Deceased.

MICHAELSON, RUTH LENORE, magazine publishing company executive; b. Arlington Hts., Ill., Jan. 22, 1961; d. Robert Thomas and Lenore Lucille (Simons) M. BA in Communications, Colligiate Inst., London, 1985. Sec. ACBI Architects, Rolling Meadows, Ill., 1985-86; data entry asst. CTi, Carol Stream, Ill., 1986-87, data entry supr., 1987-88, subscription svcs. supr., 1988-89, circulation mgr., from 1989, North Shore Mag., Winnetka, Ill., from 1989. Mem. NAFE. Avocations: travel, creative writing. Home: Genoa, Ill. Died Dec. 4, 2006.

MICHELIN, FRANÇOIS, tire industry executive; b. Clermont-Ferrand, France, July 3, 1926; s. Etienne and Madeleine (Calliès) M.; Bernadette Montagne, July 18, 1951 (dec. 2013); 5 children From co-mgr. to sole mgr. Compagnie Générale des Etablissements Michelin, Michelin SA, 1959-66, co-mgr., from 1966, now mgr. dir.; from co-mgr. to sole mgr. Mfr. Franéaise des Pneumatiques Michelin, Michelin and Co., from 1963; mgr. Compagnie Financière Michelin, from 1968; chmn. Michelin, 1985-99, mng. ptnr. France, 1999—2015. Bd. dirs. Compagnie Financière Michelin, Sociétée Comml. Citroën, Peugot, S.A.; state advisor extraordinary svc., 1989—. Avocation: tennis. Home: Clermont-Ferrand, France. Died Apr. 29, 2015.

MICHELSON, G.G. (GERTRUDE GERALDINE MICHELSON), retired retail executive; b. Jamestown, NY, June 3, 1925; d. Thomas and Celia (Cohen) Rosen; m. Horace Michelson, Mar. 28, 1947 (dec. Apr. 2002); children: Martha Ann (dec.), Barbara Jane. BA, Pa. State U., 1945; LLB, Columbia U., 1947; LLD with honors (hon.), Adelphi U., 1981; DHL with honors (hon.), New Rochelle Coll., 1983; LLD with honors (hon.), Marymount Manhattan Coll., 1988; PhD in Policy Analysis, Rand Grad. Sch., 2002. Mgmt. trainee Macy's NY, 1947-48, various mgmt. positions, v.p. employee personnel, 1963-70, sr. v.p. labor consumer rels., 1970—72; sr. v.p. pers. labor consumer rels. Macy & Co., Inc., 1972-79, sr. v.p. external affairs, 1979-80, R.H. Macy & Co., Inc., 1980-92, sr. advisor, 1992-94; ret., 1995. Bd. dirs. The Quaker Oats Co., 1971—94, Chubb Corp., 1974—98, Gen. Electric Co., 1976—2002, The Stanley Works, 1979—96, The Goodyear Tire & Rubber Co., 1984—96, Markle Found., 1973—88, 1989—97, chmn., 1986—88, 1993—95. Chmn. bd. trustees Columbia U., 1989-92; life trustee Spelman Coll. Recipient Disting. Svc. medal Pa. State U., 1969, Columbia U. Alumni medal, 2011. Mem. NYC Ptnrship. (vice chmn.), Women's Forum, Econ. Club NY Home: New York, NY. Died Jan. 10, 2015.

MICHELSON, ROBERT H., lawyer, judge; b. St. Louis, Dec. 23, 1944; s. Isadore Michelson and Rose (Goldman) M.; m. Carrie R. Wahlen, Aug. 17, 1974; children: Abraham, Noah, Jacob. BA, Beloit Coll., 1967; JD, Duke U., 1972. Bar: Wis. 1972; cert. in consumer bankruptcy law Am. Bd. Bankruptcy. Assoc. Foley, Capwell, Foley & Seehawer, Racine, Wis., 1972-73; ptnr. Goodman and Michelson, Racine, Wis., 1973-83, Hartig, Bjelajac, Michelson & Kivlin, Racine, Wis., 1983-93; prin. Michelson Law Office, Racine, Wis., from 1993. Mcpl. judge City of Racine, 1974—. Contbr. articles to profl. jours. Mem. exec. bd. Racine County dem. Com., Racine, 1973-76. With U.S. Army, 1969-70. Recipient Adv. award Internat. Acad. Trial Lawyers, 1972. Mem. Am. Bankruptcy Inst., Rotary. Jewish. Avocations: travel, reading. Died Mar. 10, 2007.

MIDDLETON, LOIS JEAN, secondary and special education educator; b. Ann Arbor, Mich., Feb. 3, 1930; d. William Jay and Mary Charlette (Mangus) M. BS, U. Mich., 1952; MA, Ea. Mich. U., 1963, EdS, 1964. Cert. tchr., Mich.; tchr. cons.-spl. edn. Tchr. phys. edn. Trenton (Mich.) Pub. Schs., 1952-57, U. Mich., Ann Arbor, 1958-59, Lincoln Park (Mich.) High Sch., 1959-65, counselor, 1965-80, tchr. spl. edn., 1980-93; ret., 1993. Waterfront dir., recreation dir. Interlochen (Mich.) Ctr. for the Arts, summers 1949-57; aquatic dir. City of Lincoln Park, summers 1958-69, coach synchronized swimming, 1959-65, with night sch. aquatics, 1960-70. Author: (manual) Learning Disabled Curriculum, 1985, (handbook) Teen Suicide, 1990. Intermediate Sch. Dist. grantee, 1988, 91, State of Mich. grantee, 1990. Mem. NEA, Mich. Edn. Assn., Mich. Learning Disabilities Educators, Lincoln Park Edn. Assn. (elections com. 1983-92). Methodist. Avocations: reading, ukrainian eggs artist, crossword puzzles. Home: Fort Wayne, Ind. Died May 23, 2007.

MIELE, LUCY F., writer, lecturer; b. St. Paul, Jan. 3, 1935; d. John Colignon and Vera Ruth (Hanawalt) Frohlicher; m. Louis Robert Miele, Dec. 24, 1958 (dec. 1978); children: Margaret Laurel, Vera Ruth; m. Terry Lee Auen, Sept. 5, 1987. BS in Journalism, Northwestern U., Evanston, Ill., 1956. Copy writer Brown & Bigelow, St. Paul, 1952-56; case worker Chgo. Welfare Dept., 1956-58; feature writer Freeport (Ill.) Jour. Standard, 1963-67, Dubuque (Iowa) Telegraph Herald, Rockford (Ill.) Morning Star, 1963-67; columnist Rockford Register Star, from 1967, Moline (Ill.) Daily Dispatch, Ill., from 1980; author, proprietor Hill House Publ., Stockton, Ill., from 1984. Mem. Continuing Edn. Council Highland Community Coll. Freeport Ill., 1965-75. Author, pub.: Absolutely Splendid Cook Book, 1984, Timber 1985, First Person Singular 1986, Green Mountain Meadows 1987, 6-Ingredients, 5-Minutes or 4-get it Cook Book, 1988. Founder Heritage League of No. Ill. Stockton, 1970; Ill. Arts Council; chair exec. com. Media Arts 1979-85. Mem. Internat. Platform Assn., Farm Women of the World, Stockton Woman's Club, AAUW, Women in Communication. Avocations: gardening, cooking, reading, talking, acting. Died July 8, 2007.

MIESOWITZ, JOHN JOSEPH, stock company executive; b. Jersey City, Nov. 12, 1922; s. John E and Josephine (Nowacki) M.; m. Helen R. Kurtz, Aug. 6, 1944; children: Karen, Christina, John, Jyl. BS, Rutgers U., 1951. V.p., mgr. Winslow Cohu & Co., Newark, 1951-69, Weis Voisin & Co, Newark, 1969-73; v.p. Kidder Peabody & Co., Morristown, N.J., from 1973. Bd. trustees N.J. Bond Club, Morristown, N.J., 1984—. Served with USN, 1943-46. Mem.: Rolling Hills Inn; Raritan Valley Country, Elks. Republican. Roman Catholic. Home: Bridgewater, NJ. Died May 15, 2007.

MIGLIACCIO, PATRICK FRANK, salesman; b. Trenton, NJ, Dec. 31, 1942; s. Pasquale Joseph and Marie (Weaver) M.; m. Patricia Ann Opdycke, Oct. 29, 1966; children: Lori, Cara, Ryan. BA, LaSalle U., 1993. Data processing supr. State of N.J., 1960-65; computer operator Edn. Testing Svc., 1965-66; computer operator, programmer RCA, 1966-68; investigator N.J. Mfrs. Ins. Co., Trenton, N.J., 1968-76, spl. rep., from 1976. Bd. dirs. Hamilton Twp. Bd. Edn., N.J., 1987-91, Bd. Social Svcs., Trenton, N.j., 1993-96; dir. bd. sch. Mercer County Spl. Svcs., West Windsor, N.J., 1992-96, Mercer County C.C., 1992—, Mercer County Vocat. Tech. Sch., 1992—; commr. Mercer County Open Space Com., Trenton, 1996—, Mercer County Libr. Commn., Trenton, 1996-97; chmn. Re-Orgn. Bd. Mercer County Improvement Authority, Trenton, 1993-94; mem. Govs. Transition Team, Trenton, 1991-92;dir. Mercer County Parks Commn., Trenton, 1994—. With N.J. Nat. Guard, 1960-66. Mem. N.J. Mfrs. Ins. Co. (spl. rep. 1968—), N.J. Assn. Counties (dir. 1992-95), Lions, Baron Athletic Club. Republican. Roman Catholic. Avocations: computers, fishing, boating, golf. Home: Mercerville, NJ. Died Nov. 12, 2006.

MIHOVICH, MATTHEW FEDELE, export company executive; b. NYC, Dec. 16, 1947; s. Anthony and Providenza (Aiello) M.; m. Eva Gerase, June 28, 1969. BA in English, Boston U., 1969. Direct mail specialist VCR div. Sony Corp., NYC, 1971-75; contbg. editor Computer Dealer, Morristown, N.J., 1981-83; advt. mgr. Hayden Book Co., Rochelle Park, N.J., 1978-81; owner Mi-Ho Stable, Bklyn., from 1974; pres. Direct Mktg. Freelance, Bklyn., from 1981; chief exec. officer, founder Coconuts Exporting Inc., Bklyn., from 1987. Editor: (workbook) Strategic Leadership, 1985; contbg. editor Computer Dealer, Morristown, N.J., 1981-83; contbr. articles to Star Ledger, 1983, N.J. Bus. & Reference, 1983, Venture, 1982, Inc., 1981. Coll. scholar U.S. Army, Ft. Meade, Md., 1967-69. Democrat. Avocation: mountain climbing. Home: Brooklyn, NY. Died Nov. 25, 2006.

MILI, JUDE JOSEPH, priest, religious organization administrator; b. Somerville, Mass., Dec. 27, 1931; s. Spiridione and Gelsomina (Scipione) M. BA, Immaculate Conception Coll., Troy, NY, 1955; MA in Theology, Antonianum, Rome, 1961, STD, 1964; MA in Counselling, W.Va. U., 1972. Joined Order of Friars Minor, 1950, ordained priest Roman Cath. Ch., 1959. Dir. Christian Reneval Ctr., Morgantown, W.Va., from 1972; provincial councilor Franciscan Province of Immaculate Conception-U.S.A., 1980-83. Mem. Nat. Marriage Encounter Bd., 1969-74, Nat. Program Com. for Christian Family Movement in U.S.A., 1973-75, Ea. Regional Bd. of Charismatic Reneval in Cath. Ch.-Ea. U.S.A., 1974-77. Pres. Citizens Concerned for Community Values, Morgantown, 1986—. Died Mar. 9, 2007.

MILLAR, JOHN DONALD, physician, occupational & environmental health services consultant, musician; b. Newport News, Va., Feb. 27, 1934; s. John and Dorothea Virginia (Smith) M.; m. Joan M. Phillips, Aug. 17, 1957; children: John Stuart, Alison Gordon Millar McMillan, Virginia Taylor Millar Helms. BS in Chemistry, U. Richmond, 1956; MD, Med. Coll. Va., 1959; DTPH, London Sch. Hygiene and Tropical Medicine, 1966; D of Pub. Svc. (hon.), Greenville Coll., Ill., 1994. Cert. specialist in Gen. Preventive Medicine 1969. Intern U. Utah Affiliated Hosps., Salt Lake City, 1959-60, asst. resident in medicine, 1960-61; chief Epidemic Intelligence Svc., Ctr. for Disease Control, USPHS, HEW, Atlanta, 1961-63, dep. chief surveillance sect. epidemiology br., 1962-63, chief smallpox unit, 1963-65, dir. smallpox eradication program, 1966-70, dir. Bur. State Svcs., 1970-78, asst. dir. Ctr. for Disease Control for Pub. Health Practice, 1979-80; dir. Nat. Ctr. Environ. Health, Atlanta, 1980-81, Nat. Inst. for Occupation Safety and Health, Atlanta, 1981-93, chmn. exec. com. Nat. Toxicology Program, 1989-93; pres. Don Millar & Assocs., Inc., Atlanta, 1993—2015. Adj. prof. occupl. and environ. health Sch. Pub. Health Emory U., Atlanta, 1988-98; cons. on smallpox, smallpox eradication, immunization programs and occupl. and environ. health WHO; mem. WHO expert adv. panel on occupl. health; bd. dirs. Farm Safety 4 Just Kids, 1993-98; tech. adv. bd. Ctr. Protect Workers' Rights, 1993; disting. fellow, vice chmn. Pub. Health Policy Adv. Bd., Inc., Washington, 1998-2007; mem. bd. dirs. Coll. Pub. Health, U. Ga., 2007-08, mem. Dean's Practice Com., 2008-; mem. string bass sect. DeKalb Symphony Orch., 1982-06, Gainesville (Ga.) Symphony Orch., 2000-04, N.E. Ga. Mountain Chamber Orch., 2001-05, Truett-Macconnell Coll. Wind Symphony, 2002-10, Toccoa Falls Coll. Orch., 2005-, Toccoa Symphony Orch., 2005-11, Piedmont Coll. diameber Orchestra, 2011-. Mem. editl. bd. Am. Jour. Indsl. Medicine, 1985-05, Am. Jour. Occupl. Psychology, 1993-00, Am. Jour. Preventive Medicine, 1993-00; contbr. articles to profl. jours. Recipient Surgeon Gen's. Commendation medal, 1965, Okeke prize London Sch. Hygiene and Tropical Medicine, 1966, Presdl. award for mgmt. improvement, 1972, W.C. Gorgas medal Assn. Mil. Surgeons U.S., 1987, Lucas lectr. Faculty Occupational Medicine Royal Coll. Physicians, London, 1987, Outstanding Med. Alumnus award Med. Coll. Va., 1988; also recipient Equal Employment Opportunity award, 1975, Medal of Excellence, 1977, Joseph W. Mountin lectr. award, 1986, Alexander D. Langmuir MD Meml. lectr. award, 2001, all from Ctrs. for Disease Control, Disting. Svc. medal USPHS, 1983, 89, Exemplary Svc. medal Surgeon Gen. U.S., 1988, Giants in Occupational Medicine lectr. U. Utah, 1989, William S. Knudsen award Am. Coll. Occupational Medicine, 1991, presdl. citation APA, 1991, William Steiger Meml. award Am. Conf. Govtl. Indsl. Hygienists, 1993, Health Watch award for outstanding contbns. toward improving health of minority populations, 1992, Award of Merit Minerva Edn. Inst., 1993, Alumni Disting. Svc. award U. Richmond, 1993, Jeff Lee Mem. Lectr. Am. Indusl. Hygiene Assoc. San Diego, Calif., 2002; named to Order Bifurcated Needle, World Health Orgn., 1978, Faculty Occupational Medicine, Royal Coll. Physicians, London, 1990; elected Safety and Health Hall of Fame Internat., Nat. Safety Coun., 1997. Mem. Am. Indsl. Hygiene Assn. (hon.), Am. Coll. Occupl. and Environ. Medicine, Am. Epidemiol. Soc., Collegium Ramazzini, Am. Assn. Pub. Health Physicians., Assn. Mil. Surgeons U.S., Pub. Health Svc. Commissioned Officers Assn., Alpha Omega Alpha. Died Aug. 30, 2015.

MILLER, ALLAN JOHN, retired lawyer, oil industry executive; b. Beachwood, Ohio, Oct. 17, 1921; s. Carl Frederick and Rhoda (Warren) M.; m. Marjorie Hewitt Pirtle, Aug. 10, 1946; children: James W., Patricia Anne Costas. BBA, Fenn Coll., 1946; LLB, Western Res. U., 1948; D (hon.), Dyke Coll., Cleve., 1986. Bar: Ohio 1948. With Standard Oil Co., Ohio, 1948-77, treas., 1967-77; mem. firm Kiefer, Knecht, Rees, Meyer & Miller, Cleve., 1977-81. Dir. United Screw & Bolt Corp., 1977—97. Pres. South Euclid-Lyndhurst Recreation Com., Ohio, 1953-56; division chair unit plan divsn., United Way Cleve., 1966-69; Chmn. bd. dirs. Luth. Med. Ctr., Cleve., 1967-82; pres. Luth. Med. Ctr. Med. Staff Found., 1979-85; bd. dirs. Christian Residencies Found., 1972-77, St. Luke's Hosp. Assn., 1973-84; chmn. bd. trustees Dyke Coll., Cleve., 1971-86; vol. tax aide AARP, 2005-12. Sgt. Corp. Engrs. US Army, 1943—46, Asiatic Pacific. Named Man of Yr., Cleve. State U. Alumni, 1982, Lutheran Med. Ctr., Cleve., 1984. Presbyterian. Avocations: golf, bridge, music. Home: Venice, Fla. Died Apr. 20, 2014.

MILLER, BELVA IRMA, geriatrics nurse; b. Hot Springs, Ark., Nov. 24, 1933; d. James Earl and Belva Irene (Hardin) Hogue; m. James Chris Miller, Dec. 26, 1953; children: James Chris Miller Jr., Catherine Michelle Miller. Student, U. Tex., 1951-54, Tex. Woman's U., 1969-70, San Antonio Coll., 1975-76; ADN, McLennan Community Coll., Waco, Tex., 1986. RN, Tex. Cert. gerontological nurse, ANA. Staff developer Southland Villa Nursing Home, Temple, Tex., 1986-87; staff nurse Olin Teague Vet.'s Hosp., Temple, from 1987. Home: Flint, Tex. Died Nov. 20, 2006.

MILLER, EUGENE MILO, banker; b. South Lyon, Mich., Sept. 26, 1937; s. Vernon and Loyal Elsie (Bonecutter) M.; m. Kay M. Miller, Aug. 8, 1959; children: Marc, Mathew, Melinda, Michael. BA, Eastern Mich. U., 1960; JD, Notre Dame U., 1964. Cert. trust and fin. analyst. Trust adminstr. First Nat. Bank, Chgo., 1964-67, v.p., trust officer Kenosha, Wis., from 1967. Dir. First Nat. Bank, Kenosha, First Fin. Assocs., Kenosha. Pres. Racine/Kenosha Estate Planning Coun. 1st lt. U.S. Army, 1960-66. Mem. Wis. Trustees Assn. (pres.), Kenosha County Bar Assn. (pres.), Wis. Bar Assn. Republican. Roman Catholic. Avocations: golf, horsehoes, growing roses. Home: Kenosha, Wis. Died Feb. 16, 2007.

MILLER, GARY DOUGLAS, business tax reform consultant, former aerospace company executive; b. Cleve., Dec. 14, 1942; s. Wells Winton and Ruth Alyce (Noreen) M.; m. Julia Ann Walraven, Aug. 7, 1988; children: Eric, Brooke. AA, Moorpark Coll., Calif., 1975; BA in Math. summa cum laude, Calif. State U., Northridge, 1977, MBA in Ops. Rsch. summa cum laude, 1979. Tech. maintenance staff Hughes Aircraft Co., El Segundo, Calif., 1965-72, project dir. tech. pubs., 1972-75, mgr. logistics support, 1975-88, mgr. non-def. initiatives, 1988-94, mgr. internat. studies, 1994-99; urban demographics rschr. City of L.A., 1999—2002; bus. tax reform cons., from 2002. Tech. dir. Sys. Engring. Network, El Segundo, 1993-95; dir. Inst. for Nat. Drug Abuse Rsch., Austin, Tex., 1989-92, Sys. Engring. Adv. Coun., U. So. Calif., L.A., 1993—. Contbr. numerous articles to profl. jours. Sgt. USAF, 1960-64. Mem. AAAS, Am. Def. Preparedness Assn., Nat. Security Indsl. Assn., Internat. Coun. on Sys. Engring., Inst. for Ops. Rsch./Mgmt. Sci., Intertel, Internat. Soc. for Philos. Inquiry, Archaeol. Inst. Am., Mensa, Phi Kappa Phi. Avocations: archaeology, golf. Home: Senoia, Ga. Died Mar. 3, 2007.

MILLER, GERALD LEWIS, computer science educator, electrical engineer; b. Madison, Wis., Mar. 21, 1938; s. Lewis Harrison and Angeline B. (Riley) M.; m. Elizabeth J. Schaeper, July 21, 1962; children: Amy, Alan. BSEE, U. Wis., 1960; MSEE, Ohio State U., 1965; MBA, U. Chgo., 1978. Supr. R&D AT&T Bell Labs., Naperville, Ill., 1960-89; asst. prof. Aurora (Ill.) U., from 1989. Part-time asst. prof. Midwest Coll. of Engring., Lombard, Ill., 1979-87. Mem. Inst. Electronic Engrs., Assn. for Computing Machinery, Am. Assn. Higher Edn. Roman Catholic. Home: Bradenton, Fla. Died Jan. 17, 2007.

MILLER, HARVEY ROBERT, lawyer; b. Bklyn., Mar. 1, 1933; m. Ruth Miller. AB, Bklyn. Coll., 1954; LLB, Columbia U., 1959. Bar: NY 1959, US Supreme Ct., US Ct. Appeals (2nd, 3rd, 4th, 5th and 9th cirs.), US Dist. Ct. (southern and eastern dists. NY). Ptnr. Seligson & Morris, 1963—70, Weil, Gotshal & Manges, LLP, NYC, 1970—2002, sr. ptnr., chair bus. financing & restructuring group, 2007—15; mng. dir., vice chmn. Greenhill & Co., 2002—07. Adj. assoc. prof. law NYU Law Sch., 1974—76, adj. prof. law, from 1976; vis. lectr. Yale Law Sch., 1983—84; lectr. law Columbia U. Sch. Law, from 2000. Bd. visitors Columbia U. Sch. Law. Named a Deal Maker of Yr., The American Lawyer mag., 2009; named one of The Decade's Most Influential Lawyers, The Nat. Law Jour., 2010. Fellow: Am. Bar Found., Am. Coll. Bankruptcy. Died Apr. 27, 2015.

MILLER, JEROME GILBERT, criminologist; b. Wahpeton, ND, Dec. 8, 1931; s. George Ernest and Beatrice Irene (Butts) M.; m. Charlene Elizabeth Coleman, June 9, 1968; 1 child, Patrick. BA in Philosophy, Maryknoll Coll., 1954; MSW, Loyola U., 1957; DSW, Cath. U. Am., 1964. Lic. clin. social worker, Va. Commd. officer USAF, 1957, advanced through grades to capt., psychiat. social work officer Sheppard AFB, Tex., 1957-59, chief social work various locations, U.S., Eng., 1959-68, ret., 1968; assoc. prof. Ohio State Univ., Columbus, 1968-69; commr. Mass.

Dept. Youth Svcs., Boston, 1969-73; dir. Ill. Dept. Children and Family Svcs., Springfield, 1973-75; commr. Pa. Office Children and Youth, Harrisburg, 1975-79; co-founder, pres. Nat. Ctr. on Institutions and Alternatives, 1977—2015; founder Augustus Inst., Alexandria, Va. Author: Last One Over the Wall, 1991; contbr. articles to profl. jours. Named Social Worker of Yr., New Eng. Chpt. NASW, Bostonk, 1972; recipient award in recognition of nat. contbn. to criminal justice adminstrn. Am. Soc. Pub. Adminstrn., 1975, Karl Menninger award Fortune Soc., N.Y., 1977, August Villmer award Am. Soc. Criminology, Montreal, 1987. Home: Woodstock, Va. Died Aug. 7, 2015.

MILLER, JOHN CRATON, insurance company executive; b. Englewood, NJ, Oct. 17, 1939; s. Hugh Lee and Lizzie Adams (Power) M.; m. Bette Carole Boyce, May 19, 1962; children: Elizabeth Anne, David Crawford. BA in History, Va. Mil. Inst., 1961. CPCU, Mo. Commd. 2d lt. U.S. Army, Fed. Republic of Germany, 1961, advanced through grades to capt., resigned, 1963; spl. agt. Aetna Ins. Co., Hartford, Conn., 1963-67, sr. orgn. and systems analyst, 1967-69, regional mgr. Richmond, Va., 1969-71; v.p. Lawton Byrne Bruner, St. Louis, 1971-75; dir. C.J. Thomas Co., St. Louis, 1975-85, mng. dir., from 1985. Cons., lectr. Internat. Risk Mgmt. Inst., Dallas, 1980—; cons. safety Assoc. Gen. Contractors Mo., St. Louis, 1979-82; pres. Rural Housing Reinsurance Co., Hamilton, Bermuda, 1986—; lectr. Washington U., St. Louis, 1980-84. Mem. Soc. CPCU's (bd. dirs. 1973-74, pres. 1975-76), Pine St. Club, Mo. Athletic Club, Town and Country Racquet Club. Presbyterian. Home: Saint Louis, Mo. Died May 24, 2007.

MILLER, JOHN W., retired management and financial consultant; b. Canton, Mo., Aug. 29, 1933; s. Robert Walton and Leona Elizabeth (Bailey) M.; m. Marilyn Jean Peterson, June 26, 1955 (dec. 1982); children: Melanie, Melinda, John II; m. Ruth Kincaid Kitchens, June 4, 1983; stepchildren: Susan, John M., Richard. BS, U.S. Mil. Acad., 1955; postgrad., U.S. Command & Gen. Staff Coll., 1970-71; MPA, U. Mo., Kansas City, 1973. Commd. U.S. Army, 1955-80, inspector gen. Alaska, Vietnam, 1967-70; advisor German Ministry of Def., Bonn, 1973-76; program dir. Ft. Knox, Ky., 1976-77, multiple program dir. Ky., 1977-78, dep. dir. personnel and community activity Ky., 1978-80; exec. dir. Ala. Med. Rev., Inc., Birmingham, 1980-84; chief exec. officer Ala. Quality Assurance Found., Birmingham, 1982-93; mgmt. and fin. cons., pres. MilleVest Co., from 1993. Contbr. articles to profl. jours. Bd. dirs. Birmingham Opera Theater, 1996—. Decorated Legion of Merit; recipient Outstanding Scholarship award, U. Mo., 1973. Mem. AMPRA (legis. com. 1985-87), Green Valley Country Club, The Summit Club, West Point Soc. Ala. (pres. 1993—), Phi Kappa Phi. Avocations: golf, tennis, skiing. Home: Birmingham, Ala. Died Jan. 14, 2007.

MILLER, JOSEPH ARTHUR, manufacturing engineer, consultant, educator; b. Brattleboro, Vt., Aug. 28, 1933; s. Joseph Maynard and Marjorie Antoinette (Hammerberg) Miller; m. Ardene Hedwig Barker, Aug. 19, 1956; children: Stephanie L., Jocelyn A., Shana L., Gregory J. BS in Agrl., Andrews U., Berrien Springs, Mich., 1955; MS in Agrl. Mechs., Mich. State U., 1959; EdD in Vocat. Edn., UCLA, 1973. Constrn. engr. Thornton Bldg. & Supply, Inc., Williamston, Mich., 1959-63, C & B Silo Co., Charlotte, Mich., 1963-64; instr. and dir. retraining Lansing C.C., Mich., 1964-68; asst. prof./prog. coord./coop coord. San Jose State U., 1968-79; mfg. specialist Lockheed Martin Missiles and Space (and predecessor cos.), Sunnyvale, Calif., 1979-81, rsch. specialist, 1981-88, NASA project mgr., 1982-83, staff engr., 1988-96, rsch. staff engr., 1996-98, coord. flexible mfg. system simulation project, 1994-96, team mem. machining outsource initative project, AIMS agile mfg. project, 1995—97, coord. productivity improvement program, 1996—98; engring. and constrn. cons. Berry Creek, Calif., from 1998. Agrl. engring. cons. USDA Poultry Expt. Sta., 1960—62; computer numerical control cons. Dynamechtronics, Inc., Sunnyvale, 1987—90; machining cons. Space Sys. divsn. Lockheed, 1986—96; instr. computer numerical control DeAnza Coll., Cupertino, Calif., 1985—88, Labor Employment Tng. Corp., San Jose, Calif., 1988—93; career counselor Pacific Union Coll., Angwin, Calif., 1985—92; instr. computer-aided mfg. and non traditional machining San Jose State U., 1994—97; team leader pursuit of excellence machine tool project Lockheed Martin Missiles and Space, Sunnyvale, 1990—95, coord. safety award program, 1997—98, quality awareness program screening com., 1998. Author: Student Manual for CNC Lathe, 1990; contbr. articles to profl. jours. UCLA fellow, 1969—73. Mem.: Am. Soc. Indsl. Tech. (pres. 1980—81), Calif. Assn. Indsl. Tech. (pres. 1974—75, 1984—85), Nat. Assn. Indsl. Tech. (mem., chmn. accreditation visitation teams from 1984, pres. industry divsn. 1987—88, bd. cert. 1991—92), Soc. Mfg. Engr. (sr.; chmn. edn. com. local chpt. 1984—85, career guidance counselor 1986—88, fire safe coun. from 2006). Adventist. Avocations: violin, cabinet making, gardening, feeding hummingbirds. Died July 17, 2007.

MILLER, NAIRN LOCKWOOD, small business owner, engineer; b. NYC, Mar. 4, 1922; s. Clyde Kennedy and Leah (Ingraham) M.; m. Evelyn Rickey, Mar. 21, 1948 (div. Ept. 1965); children: Nancy Rickey, Bruce Campbell. BS in Aero. Engring., Renssalaer Poly. Inst., 1943; MBA, Columbia U., 1950. Engr. N.Am. Aviation, Inc., LA, 1944, 46-48; mgr. GE, NYC, Phila., 1950-62; v.p. mktg. Franklin Electric, Co., Bluffton, Ind., 1962-65, Itek Corp., Rochester, N.Y., 1965-68, Baker Industries, NYC, 1968-69; pres. Lockwood Ford Tractor, Inc., Springfield, Mass., 1969-73, N.L. Freedman, Inc., Springfield, from 1973. Inventor 6 component balance system, twin electric circuit breaker. Mem. Better Bus. Bur., Springfield, 1982—, bd. dirs., 1988—. Lt. USN, 1944-46. Mem. C. of C. Republican. Avocations: golf, health, model building, woodworking. Home: Westfield, Mass. Died Jan. 17, 2007.

MILLER, RICHARDS THORN, naval architect, engineer; b. Jan. 31, 1918; s. Herman Geistweit and Helen Buckman (Thorn) M.; m. Jean Corbat Spear, Sept. 13, 1941 (dec.); children: Patricia (Mrs. Charles G. Fishburn), Linda (Mrs. John X. Carrier); m. Alice Johnson Houghton, May 19, 1984. BS in Naval Arch. and Marine Engring., Webb Inst. Naval Arch., Glen Cove, NY, 1940; Naval Engr., MIT, Boston, 1951. Registered profl. engr. Commd. ensign USN, 1940, advanced through grades to capt., 1960; head preliminary design br. Bur. Ships, 1960-63; dir. Mine Def. Lab., Panama City, Fla., 1963-66; dir. ship design Naval Ship Engring. Ctr., 1966-68; specialized work design oceanographic rsch. ships, mine sweepers, torpedo boats, destroyers; ret., 1968. Mgr. ocean engring. Oceanic divsn. Westinghouse Electric Corp., 1969-75, adv. engr., 1975-79; cons. naval arch. and engr., 1968—; arbitrator admiralty and ship bldg. contract cases, 1978—; mem. com. naval arch. Am. Bur. Shipping, 1960-63, mem. tech. com., 1978-92; mem. ship structure com., 1966-68. Author: (with R.G. Henry) Sailing Yacht Design, 1963, (with K.L. Kirkman) Sailing Yacht Design—A New Appreciation, 1990; also sects. in books, articles. Decorated Navy Legion of Merit; recipient William Selkirk Owen award Webb Alumni Assn., 1983. Fellow Soc. Naval Archs. and Marine Engrs. (chmn. S.E. sect. 1965-66, chmn. marine sys. com. 1970-77, chmn. tech. and rsch. steering com. 1977-78, chmn. small craft com. 1983-87, v.p. tech. and rsch. 1979-81, hon. life v.p. 1981—, mem. coun. 1976—, mem. exec. com. 1977-81, Capt. Joseph H. Linnard prize 1964, Disting. Svc. award 1988); mem. Am. Soc. Naval Engrs. (mem. coun. 1976-78), U.S. Naval Inst., Christie Soc., Md. Bd. for Profl. Engrs., N.Y. Yacht Club, Annapolis Yacht Club, Sailing Club of the Chesapeake, (Chesapeake Sailing Yacht Symposia cofounder, 1971), Sigma Xi. Died Dec. 7, 2013.

MILLER, ROBERT NICHOLAS, anesthesiologist; b. St. Louis, Aug. 14, 1935; s. Louis R. and Gladys (Grotjan) M.; m. Dianne Jackson, Aug. 16, 1958; children: Deborah Miller Francois, Melanie Miller Fewell, Dawn, Brett Jackson. AB in Premed., U. Mo., 1957, MD, 1961. Diplomate Am. Bd. Anesthesiology. Resident in anesthesiology U. Mo., Columbia, 1962-64; chief of anesthesia McMillan Hosp., Barnes and Allied Hosps., St. Louis; dir. obstetrical anesthesiology St. John's Mercy Med. Ctr., St. Louis, 1975-82, chmn. dept. anesthesiology, from 1982. Mem. adv. bd. Christian Action Council, St. Louis; bd. dirs. St. Louis Birthright. Capt. U.S. Army, 1964-66. Fellow Am. Coll. Obsterics and Gynecology; mem. St. Louis Soc. Anesthesiology (v.p. 1969, pres. 1970), St. Louis Gynecol. Soc., Soc. Obstet. Anesthesia and Perinatology, Mo. Soc. Anesthesiology (pres. 1989—), Am. Soc. Anesthesiology (del. 1987—), St. Louis Med. Soc. Council (del. 1988—). Died Aug. 16, 2007.

MILLER, RODGER MUCKERMAN, securities management company executive; b. St. Louis, Nov. 13, 1938; m. Ellen McCarthy; children: Mary M., Phoebe E., Rodger Jr., Christopher C. BS, St. Louis U., 1961, MS, 1971. V.p. Am. Money Mgmt. Co. subs. Am. Fin. Corp., Cin., 1976-84, sr. v.p., 1984-87; exec. v.p. Charter Co. subs. Am. Fin. Corp., Cin., from 1987; also bd. dirs. Bd. dirs. Charter Co., Cin., 1987—. Councilman, Terrace Park, Ohio, 1978-83. Republican. Roman Catholic. Avocation: tennis. Died May 8, 2007.

MILLER, WILLIAM CRENSHAW, JR., commercial realtor; b. Brownwood, Tex., Dec. 31, 1905; s. William Crenshaw and Ora Etta (Connell) M.; m. Nell West Bolanz, May 23, 1936; children: Charles Bolanz, William Crenshaw III. BA, So. Meth. U., 1927, JD, 1930. Atty., Dallas, 1930-37; realtor Bolanz & Bolanz, Dallas, 1937-53, Bolanz & W.C. Miller, Dallas, 1953-65, Bolanz & Miller Realtors, Dallas, from 1965. Part-time tchr. So. Meth. Univ. Bus. Sch., Dallas, 1950-54; dir., 1st v.p. Dallas Bd. Realtors; chmn. Tex. Real Estate Commn., 1979-80; bd. dirs. So. Bank & Trust Co., Dallas; chmn. aviation com. for new terminal bldg. and extended runways Love Field. Trustee, chmn. Vickery Ind. Sch. Dist., 1945-52; councilman City of Dallas, 1953-59; dir. State Fair Tex., 1955-80, chmn. horse shows, 1965—; pres. Internat. Arabian Horse Assn., 1957-58; dir., chmn. Greater Dallas Community of Chs., 1960, North Dallas C. of C., 1976; trustee Austin Coll., Sherman, Tex., 1960-80, sr. trustee, 1980—; chmn. bldg. com. Dallas Meml. Auditorium, Downtown Libr. and State Fair Coliseum, 1960-70; chmn. rules com. Am. Horse SHows Assn., 1963-64; and others. Recipient Sam Houston Founders medal Austin Coll., Sherman, Tex., 1987, Toddie Lee Wynn award, 1993, Comty. Builder's award Masonic Lodge, 1993. Mem. Soc. Indsl. Realtors, Cert. Comml. Investment, Nat. Assn. Realtors (cert. property mgr.), Sons of Republic Tex., Sons Confederate Vets., Delta Chi, Delta Theta Phi. Republican. Presbyterian. Avocations: horseman, gardening, all sports. Home: Dallas, Tex. Died Nov. 6, 2006.

MILLER, WILLIAM RUSSELL, oncology educator, researcher; b. Warrington, Lancashire, Eng., Jan. 8, 1944; BSc, U. Leeds, Eng., 1966, PhD, 1969; DSc, U. Edinburgh, Scotland, 1988. Rsch. asst. Leeds U., 1966-69; rsch. fellow Edinburgh U., 1969-80, lectr., 1980-87, reader, 1987-93; dep. dir. Imperial Cancer Rsch. Fund, Edinburgh, from 1988; prof. exptl. oncology Edinburgh U., from 1993. Editor: Brit. Jour. Cancer, The Breast; Expert Opinion on Therapeutic Patents; contbr. articles to sci. jours. Mem. Am. Assn. Cancer Rsch., Brit. Assn. Cancer Rsch. (hon. sec. 1992-95), Imperial Cancer Rsch. Fund (dep. dir. 1988—), Biochem. Soc., Soc. Endocrinology, Brit. Breast Group, Brit. Oncol. Assn. Home: South Queensferry, Scotland. Died Mar. 11, 2007.

MILLIGAN, GLENN EDWARD, poet; b. Detroit, Aug. 21, 1949; s. George Edwin and Doris Ann M. BBA in Econ., Western Mich. U., Kalamazoo, 1984. Disabled american vet., from 1974. Author: Lust, Love, Life, 1986, Nocturnes, 1988, Beyond Bamboo, 1998, Passage, 1999, Lament, 2000. Mem. Disabled Am. Vets., Battle Creek, Mich., 1979—. Home: Battle Creek, Mich. Died Dec. 6, 2006.

MILLMAN, RICHARD MARTIN, lawyer; b. Newark, July 7, 1937; s. Emmanuel and Leona Edith (Schachtel) M.; divorced. BA, Brandeis U., 1957; LLB, Georgetown U., 1960. Bar: D.C. 1961, U.S. Supreme Ct. 1965, Md. 1968. Law clk. to presiding justice U.S. Ct. Appeals (4th cir.), Balt., 1960; practice law Washington, from 1961. Mem. Montgomery County (Md.) Council Fin. Advising, 1967-69, Adminstrn. Justice in D.C., 1967, Md. Gov.'s Com. on Employment of Handicapped, 1967, Nat. Coun. Sr. Citizens Task Force on Housing, 1972, Montgomery County Coun. Task Force on Taxation, 1967, Md. Commn. Jud. Reform, 1974-75; co-chmn. Brandeis U. Annual Givers Fund, greater Washington area, 1971; bd. dirs. Md. div. Am. Trauma Soc., 1974, treas. 1975. Mid-career fellow grad. sch. fgn. svc. Georgetown U., 1981-82. Mem. Md. Bar Assn., D.C. Bar Assn., Phi Delta Phi. Home: Michaels, Md. Died May 21, 2007.

MILLMAN, SIDNEY, physicist, consultant; b. David-Gorodok, Russia, Mar. 15, 1908; came to U.S., 1922; s. Jacob and Nora (Berman) M.; m. Dorothy Rosenfeld, Dec. 26, 1931; 1 child, MIchael G. BS, CCNY, 1931; PhD, Columbia U., 1935; DSc, Lehigh U., 1974. Instr. in physics CCNY, 1939-41, Queens (N.Y.) Coll., 1941-42; radar researcher Columbia Radiation Lab., NYC, 1942-45, Bell Labs, Murray Hill, N.J., 1945-73; exec. dir. rsch., physics Bell Labs., Murray Hill, N.J., 1965-73; sec. Am. Inst. Physics, NYC, 1973-80; sr. fellow Ctr. for Math. Sci. and Computer Edn., Rutgers U., New Brunswick, N.J., 1989-93. Contbr. article to Jour. Applied Physics; contbr. articles to profl. jours. including Phys. Rev. Recipient Townsend Harris medal City Coll. Alumni Assn., 1984. Fellow IEEE, AAAS, APS. Achievements include patents for rising sun magneton, spatial harmonic amplifier. Home: Walnut Creek, Calif. Died Nov. 11, 2006.

MILLS, DON HARPER, pathology and psychiatry educator, lawyer; b. Peking, China, July 29, 1927; came to U.S., 1928; s. Clarence Alonzo and Edith Clarissa (Parrett) M.; m. Lillian Frances Snyder, June 11, 1949; children: Frances Jo, Jon Snyder. BS, U. Cin., 1950, MD, 1953; JD, U. So. Calif., 1958. Diplomate Am. Bd. Legal Medicine. Intern L.A. County Gen. Hosp., 1953-54, admitting physician, 1954-57, attending staff in pathology, from 1959; pathology fellow U. So. Calif., LA, 1954-55, instr. pathology, 1958-62, asst. clin. prof., 1962-65, assoc. clin. prof., 1965-69, clin. prof., from 1969, clin. prof. psychiatry and behavioral sci., from 1986. Asst. in pathology Hosp. Good Samaritan, LA, 1956-65, cons. staff, 1962-72, affiliate staff, 1972-91; dep. med. examiner Office of Los Angeles County Med. Examiner, 1957-61; instr. legal medicine Loma Linda U. Sch. Medicine, Calif., 1960-66, assoc. clin. prof. humanities, 1966-95; cons. HEW, 1972-73, 75-76, Dept. Def., 1975-80; trustee Am. Bd. Legal Medicine, Inc., Chgo., 2004—; med. dir. Profl. Risk Mgmt. Group, 1989-2001, Octagon Risk Svcs., Inc., 2001-07, Sedgwick, 2007—. Column editor Newsletter of the Long Beach Med. Assn., 1960-75, Jour. Am. Osteo. Assn., 1965-77, Ortho Panel, 1970-78; exec. editor Trauma, 1964-88, mem. editl. bd., 1988-2006; mem. editl. bd. Legal Aspects of Med. Practice, 1972-90, Med. Alert Comms., 1973-75, Am. Jour. Forensic Medicine and Pathology, 1979-87, Hosp. Risk Control, 1981-96; contbr. numerous articles to profl. jours. Bd. dirs. Inst. for Med. Risk Studies, 1988—; mem. adv. bd. Pacific Ctr. for Health Policy and Ethics, 1997—2005, chmn., 1999—2005. With USN, 1946—47. Recipient Ritz Heerman award Calif. Hosp. Assn., 1986, Disting. fellow Am. Acad. Forensic Scis., 1993, Genesis award Pacific Ctr. for Health Policy and Ethics, 1993, Founder's award Am. Coll. Med. Quality, 1994. Fellow Am. Coll. Legal Medicine (pres. 1974-76, bd. govs. 1970-78, v.p. 1972-74, chmn. malpractice com. 1973-74, jour. editl. bd. 1984—, gold medal 1999), Am. Acad. Forensic Sci. (gen. program chmn. 1966-67, chmn. jurisprudence sect. 1966-67, 73-74, exec. com. 1971-74, 84-88, v.p. 1984-85, pres. 1986-87, ethics com. 1976-86, 91-2001, chmn. ethics com. 1994-2001, long-term planning com. 1990—2004, jour. editl. bd. 1965-79); mem. AMA (jour. editl. bd. 1973-77), AAAS, ABA, Am. Coll. Med. Quality (hon. life), Los Angeles County Bar Assn., Am. Health Lawyers Assn. Died May 21, 2013.

MILLS, EDGAR COY, telecommunications executive, electrical engineer; b. Peachland, NC, Feb. 6, 1932; s. Edgar Cody and Sarah Emma (Parker) M.; m. Carolyn Erlene Harper, Dec. 17, 1954; children: Sharon M. Sherrer, Lorrie M. Keener, Susan M. Pallares, Edgar C. III, John Parker. BSEE, N.C. State U., 1954; MSEE, Air Force Inst. Tech., Dayton, Ohio, 1959. Assoc. engr. Lockheed Ga., Marietta, Ga., 1954; commd. 2nd lt. USAF, 1954, tactical fighter squadron armament officer Victoria, Tex., 1956-58; missile engring. & flight test pilot Air Force Missile Devel. Ctr., USAF, Holloman Air Force Base, N.M., 1959-63; pilot Air Reconnaissance, USAF, S.E. Asia, 1963-64; fighter requirements test officer Hdqrs. TAC, USAF, Langley Air Force Base, Va., 1964-65; resigned USAF, 1965; advanced devel. engring. & flight test engr. to group engr. Lockheed Ga., Marietta, 1965-74; co-founder, pres. Solid State Systems, Inc., Marietta, Kennesaw, Ga., 1974-88; chief exec. officer, pres. Nat. Telcom Solid State Systems, Kennesaw, from 1988. Cons. Lockheed Ga., Marietta, 1974-75; bd dirs. bus. communications div. Nat. Telecommunications, London, Kennesaw. Inventor, patentee cooperatives sta. keeping system for aircraft, smart remote controlled unit. Mem. Cobb County Republican Party, Marietta, 1975-90. Decorated Air medal with cluster. Mem. Cobb County C. of C., Marietta County Club. Avocations: hunting, fishing. Home: Marietta, Ga. Died July 10, 2007.

MILLS, HAWTHORNE QUINN, international organization executive; b. Beverly Hills, Cal., Mar. 27, 1928; s. Harry Quinn and Ann Mildred (Lamb) M.; m. Diana P. Westacott; children: Nicholas, Alexander, George, Eleni. AB, Colo. Coll., 1950; postgrad., U. Innsbruck, Austria, 1950-51; MA, U. Cal. at Berkeley, 1958; postgrad., Nat. War Coll., 1972-73. Staff announcer Armed Forces Radio Service, Salzburg, Austria, 1951-53; teaching asst. polit. sci. U. Calif., Berkeley, 1956-58; joined Fgn. Service, 1958; 2d sec., polit. officer Am. embassy, Athens, Greece, 1960-63; with Dept. State exec. secretariat, 1963-65; mem. U.S. delegation 19th session UN Gen. Assembly, 1964; 2d sec., econ. officer Am. embassy, The Hague, Netherlands, 1965-67; province sr. adviser Vietnam, 1967-70; 1st sec., mission coordinator Am. embassy, Vietnam, 1970-72; staff dir. bd. examiners fgn. service Dept. State, Washington, 1973-74; counselor of embassy for polit. affairs Tehran, 1974-76; minister, dep. chief of mission Am. Embassy, Athens, 1976-80, chargé d'affaires Kabul, Afghanistan, 1980-82; consul. gen. Amsterdam, 1982-85; dir. gen.'s rep. Multinat. Force and Observers Israel, 1985-90. Bd. dirs., pres. U.S. Ednl. Found. Netherlands. With USN, 1945-46, PTO. Decorated Purple Heart, Gallantry Cross with bronze star Vietnam; recipient Dept. State Heroism award, 1970, Superior Honor award, 1972 Mem. Am. Fgn. Svc. Assn., Bibl. Archaeology Soc., Tau Kappa Alpha, Phi Gamma Delta. Clubs: Royal Selangor Golf and Tennis (Kuala Lumpur, Malaysia), Ft. McNair Officers (Washington), Kabul Golf and Country, Festina Lawn Tennis (Amsterdam), Dan Acadia Tennis (Tel Aviv), Waitangi Golf Club, (Bay of Islands, New Zealand). Died Feb. 3, 2007.

MILLS, WILLIAM HAROLD, mathematician; b. NYC, Nov. 9, 1921; s. Frederick Cecil and Dorothy (Clarke) M.; m. Joan Rounds, July 16, 1949; children: Charles Frederick, James Lawrence, Robert Clarke. BA, Swarthmore Coll., 1943; MA, Princeton U., 1947, PhD, 1949. Instr. Yale U., New Haven, Conn., 1949-52, asst. prof., 1952-58, assoc. prof., 1958-63; mem. tech. staff Inst. Def. Analyses, Princeton, N.J., from 1963, emeritus staff mem. Fellow Inst. Combinatorics; mem. Am. Math. Soc. Democrat. Avocation: square dancing. Home: Newtown, Pa. Died Mar. 7, 2007.

MILLSAP, MARGARET ISRAEL, retired nursing educator; b. Pensacola, Fla., Feb. 4, 1923; d. James Buchanan and Ludia Ann Israel; m. William A. Millsap Jr; children: Cynthia Ann Boykin, Susan Jane. BSN, U. Ala., 1956; MSN, 1958, EdD, 1974. Instr. nursing Bapt. Med. Ctr., Birmingham, 1947—73; prof. nursing Sanford U., Birmingham, 1973—75; dir. nursing U. Ala., Birmingham, 1975—81; chmn. nursing dept. Birmingham So. Coll., 1981—88; ret., 1988. Mem. State Com. Pub. Health, Montgomery, Ala., 1980—83. Author: (book) National League for Nursing, 1976, Community Health Nursing, 1984. Bd. dirs. Children's Aid Soc., Birmingham, from 1983, Assn. Retarded Citizens, Birmingham, from 1983. Recipient Resolution Honor, Ala. Bd. Nursing, 1983, Recognition award, Ala. Commn. Nursing, 1985. Mem.: Ala. League Nurses (pres. 1961—63), Ala. State Nurses Assn. (pres. 1975—76), Order Eastern Star, Sigma Theta Tau (pres. 1958). Republican. Baptist. Avocations: gardening, travel. Home: Jackson, Ala. Died Nov. 3, 2006.

MINICLIER, JOHN CALVIN, JR., purchasing executive; b. Fredericksburg, Va., Dec. 25, 1944; s. John Calvin and Ella L. (Day) M.; m. Judy Leigh Ledford, Apt. 4, 1967; children: John Calvin III, Jeffrey Clark. BS, U. R.I., 1971; MBA, U. North Ala., 1977. Enlisted U.S. Army, 1963, advanced through grades to capt., 1966; assigned to Germany and Vietnam; resigned, 1974; shift foreman Reynolds Metals Co., Sheffield, Ala., 1974-75, indsl. engr., 1975-76, traffic mgr., 1976, buyer, 1976-78, material mgr. Ashville, Ohio, 1978-81, purchasing mgr. Sheffield, 1981-91, prodn., bus. devel. mgr. Sheffield Plant Muscle Shoals, Ala., from 1991. Mem. exec. adv. bd. Ala. Minority Bus. Devel. Coun., 1982—. Decorated Bronze Star. Mem,. Nat. Assn. Purchasing Mgrs. (cert.), Shoals-Florence Area C. of C. (small bus. com.), Rotaryy (chmn. internat. svc. Sheffield). Republican. Baptist. Avocations: golf, racquetball, weightlifting. Died Aug. 14, 2007.

MINNIS, JEAN REYNOLDS, retired secondary educator; b. Iowa, Jan. 15, 1916; d. Harry Elmer and Josephine Erma (DeBooy) Reynolds; m. Roy Barker Minnis, June 28, 1940; children: David Alan, Paul Edward. BA, U. No. Iowa, 1937; postgrad., U. Denver, 1952-53, U. Md., 1964-66; MA, U. Colo., 1970; postgrad., U. Colo., Denver, from 1970. Tchr. high sch. Lamoille (Iowa) Sch. Dist., 1937-38, Paulina (Iowa) Sch. Dist., 1938-40; with Hartford Accident & Indemnity Co., San Francisco, 1943-45; tchr. high sch. Montgomery County (Md.) Sch. Dist., 1964-66, Denver County (Colo.) Sch. Dist., 1960-76. Contbr. poetry to mags. and newspapers. Bass violist Waterloo (Iowa) Symphony Orch., 1933-37, Aurora (Ill.) Symphony Orch., 1940-42; bd. dirs. United Community Campus Ministries in Colo., 1973-76; chmn. fellowship fund, membership dept. Calvary Bapt. Ch., Denver, 1987-90. Mem. AAUW (bd. dirs. 1982-84), Civitan Internat. (bd. dirs. Columbine chpt. 1991—), Am. Bapt. Women (courtesy chmn. 1990—), Amnesty Internat., English-Speaking Union, Kappa Delta Pi, Sigma Tau Delta. Avocations: photography, reading, travel. Home: Adamstown, Md. Died July 9, 2007.

MINSKY, MARVIN LEE, mathematician, educator; b. NYC, Aug. 9, 1927; s. Henry and Fannie (Reyser) M.; m. Gloria Anna Rudisch, July 30, 1952; children: Margaret, Henry, Juliana. BA in Math., Harvard U., 1950; PhD in Math., Princeton U., 1954; PhD (hon.), Free U. of Brussels, 1986, Pine Manor Coll., 1987. Jr. fellow Harvard Soc. Fellows, 1954-57; staff mem. Lincoln Lab., MIT, 1957-58, asst. prof. math., 1958-61, founder, co-dir. artificial intelligence lab., 1959—74, dir., artificial intelligence group MAC project, 1959, prof. elec. engring., 1974, Donner prof. sci., 1974—89; Toshiba prof. media arts and sciences MIT, 1990, prof. emeritus, media arts and sciences. Dir. Info. Internat., Inc., 1961—84; fellow Walt Disney Imagineering; founder Thinking Machines, LOGO Computer Systems, Inc. Author: Computation: Finite and Infinate Machines, 1967, Semantic Information Processing, 1968, Robotics, 1986, The Society of Mind, 1987; co-author (with S. Papert) Perceptrons, 1969, rev. edit., 1988, Artificial Intelligence, 1972, with H. Harrison) The Turning Option, 1992. Served with USN, 1944-45; bd. advisor, Nat. Dance Inst., Planetary Soc.; bd. governor, Nat. Space Soc.; mem. awards coun. Am. Acad. Achievement; mem. League for Programming Freedom. Recipient Turing award Assn. Computing Machinery, 1970, Japan prize Sci. and Tech. Found., Japan, 1990, Rsch. Excellence award Internat. Joint Conf. on Artificial Intelligence, 1991, Joseph Priestley award Dickinson Coll., 1995, Rank prize, Royal Soc. Medicine, 1995, Computer Pioneer award, IEEE Computer Soc., 1995, R.W. Wood prize, Optical Soc. Am., 2001, Benjamin Franklin medal, Franklin Inst, 2001, In Praise of Reason award, World Skeptics Congress, 2002. Fellow IEEE, Am. Acad. Arts & Sciences, Com. for the Scientific Investigation of Claims of the Paranormal; mem. NAE, NAS, Argentine NAS, Am. Assn. for Artificial Intelligence (pres. 1981-82). Achievements include SNARC: First Neural Network Simulator in 1951; Confocal Scanning Microscope in 1955; First head-mounted graphical display in 1963; Concept of Binary-Tree Robotic Manipulator in 1963; Serpentine Hydraulic Robot Arm in 1967; The "Muse" Musical Variations Synthesizer (with E. Fredkin) in 1970; First LOGO "turtle" device (with S. Papert) in 1972. Died Jan. 24, 2016.

MINTZ, ALAN PAUL, radiologist; b. Chgo., May 5, 1938; s. Lee Sol and Ida M.; m. Gloria Porath, Sept. 13, 1959; children: Ari, Steven, Jeffery, Jonathon. BS, U. Chgo., 1959; MD, U. Ill. Med. Sch., 1963. Diplomate Am. Bd. Radiology. Assoc. radiologist St. Therese Hosp., Waukegan, Ill., 1970-74; chmn., dept. med. imaging Mile Square Health Ctr., Chgo., 1974-87; clin. asst. prof. U. Ill. Med. Sch., Chgo., 1975-78; pres., CEO Unimed, Ltd., Highland Park, Ill., 1974-90; chmn. med. imaging dept. North Suburban Clinic, Skokie, Ill., 1984-89; med. imaging dir. MedFirst Clinics, Chgo., 1988-91; staff radiologist Cen. Community Hosp., Chgo., 1974-90, Glendale Heights (Ill.) Community Hosp., 1980-89; various to med. dir. Sch. of Radiol. Tech. So. Chgo. Community Hosp., Chgo., from 1990; pres., CEO MEDICON, Inc., Northbrook, Ill., from 1990; CEO ProActive Med. Mgmt., Northbrook, Ill., from 1992. Numerous positions in field including founder of radiology lectr. series, Hyde Park Hosp., Chgo., 1974—; founder, adminstr. Med. Imaging Provider Networks, Chgo. area 1985—, St. Louis area 1988—, Conn., 1990—; vice-chmn. dept. med. imaging Lincoln West Hosp., Chgo., 1989-91, chmn. dept. med. imaging, Sacred Heart Hosp., Chgo., 1978-91, Mt. Sinai North Hosp., Chgo., 1983-89, Meth. Hosp., Chgo., 1989-91, Edgewater Med. Ctr., Chgo., 1989-91, South Chgo. Community Hosp., 1990—; others in field. Med. adv. Nat. Ski Patrol, Wilmot Mountain, Wis., 1968-86. Lt. USN, 1963-67. Mem. AMA, Ill. State Med. Soc., Chgo. Med. Soc., Radiol. Soc. North Am., Am. Coll. Radiology, Am. Inst. Ultrasound in Medicine, Am. Acad. Sports Physicians, Soc. for Computer Application in Radiology. Jewish. Avocations: skiing, music, latin dancing, piano, ice skating. Home: Las Vegas, Nev. Died June 3, 2007.

MINTZ, SIDNEY WILFRED, anthropologist; b. Dover, NJ, Nov. 16, 1922; s. Solomon and Fromme Leah (Tulchin) M.; m. June Mirken, May 1952 (div. Dec. 1962); children: Eric Daniel, Elizabeth Rachel Nickens; m. Jacqueline Wei, June 6, 1964. BA, Bklyn. Coll., 1943; PhD, Columbia U., 1951; MA, Yale U., 1963. Mem. faculty dept. anthropology Yale U., New Haven, 1951-74, prof., 1963-74; prof. anthropology Johns Hopkins U., Balt., 1974-97, prof. emeritus, 1997—2015. Vis. prof. anthropology MIT, 1964-65, Princeton U., 1975-76; directeur d'études associé E.P.H.E., Paris, 1970-71; professeur associé. Coll. de France, Paris, 1988; editor Yale U. Press Caribbean Series, 1957-74; Lewis Henry Morgan lectr. U. Rochester, 1972; Christian Gauss lectr. Princeton U., 1979; Harry Hoijer lectr. UCLA, 1981; Duijker Found. lectr., Amsterdam, 1988; Rodney lectr. U. Warwick, 1993; W.E.B. DuBois lectr. Harvard U., 2003; Goveia lect. U. W.I., 2003. Author: (with others) People of Puerto Rico, 1956, Worker in the Cane, The Life History of a Puerto Rican Sugar Cane Worker, 1960, Caribbean Transformations, 1974, Sweetness and Power, 1985, (with Richard Price) The Birth of African-American Culture, 1992, Tasting Food, Tasting Freedom: Excursions Into Eating, Culture and the Past, 1996. Served with USAAF, 1943-46. Recipient William Clyde DeVane medal Yale U., 1972, Huxley medalist Royal Anthrop. Inst., 1994, disting. lectr. award Am. Anthrop. Assn., 1996; named Social Sci. Rsch. Coun. Faculty Rsch. fellow, 1958-59, Guggenheim fellow, 1957, Fulbright fellow, 1966-67, 70-71, NEH fellow, 1978-79, Smithsonian Inst. Regents' fellow, 1986-87. Fellow Am. Anthrop. Assn.; mem. Am. Ethnol. Soc. (v.p., pres.-elect 1967-68), Royal Anthrop. Soc. Gt. Britain and Ireland, Am. Acad. Arts and Scis., Sigma Xi. Home: Baltimore, Md. Died Dec. 27, 2015.

MIRVISH, ROBERT FRANKLIN, author; b. Washington, July 17, 1921; s. David and Anna (Kornhauser) M.; m. Lucille A. DeGiglio; children— Anthony David, John Richard. Student, U. Toronto, 1946-47. Producer: play Like Father, Like Fun; author: play A House of Her Own, 1953, The Eternal Voyagers, 1953, Texana, 1954, The Long Watch, 1954, Red Sky at Midnight, 1955, Woman in a Room, 1959, Two Women, Two Worlds, 1960, Dust on the Sea, 1960, Point of Impact, 1961, Cleared Narvik 2000, 1962, The Last Capitalist, 1963, Business is People, 1963, There You Are, But Where Are You?, 1964, Holy Loch, 1964. Served U.S. Mcht. Marine, 1942-45. Mem. Author's Guild Am., Am. Radio Assn. *People have a tendency to confuse Education with Schooling. Schooling is what you get in a classroom. Education is what you get in a poolroom.* Died June 24, 2007.

MISNER, CARL GREGORY, financial planner, insurance association executive; b. Little Falls, NY, Nov. 24, 1946; s. Clarence Paul and Bernice G. (Grzywaczewski) M.; m. Sandra Ann Caruso, Sept. 7, 1969; 1 child, Tracy Lee. Student, SUNY, Albany, 1965-69. Registered rep. Investors Diversified Services, Albany, 1981-84, bus. services account exec., Am. Express, 1983-84; registered rep. Waddell and Reed, Inc., Albany, 1984; ins. agt. various cos., Albany, from 1969; exec. dir. C.G.M.A., Latham, N.Y., from 1984. Cons., tchr., trainer bus. fin. planning, Investers Diversified Services, 1983-84; registered prin. Southmark Fin. Svcs., Inc.; adv. coord. Corp. RIA. Page, U.S. Senate, Washington, 1962; rep. Rep. Nat. Workshop, SUNY, 1970; Rep. candidate N.Y. State Assembly, 1974, County Legislature, 1975; ward leader Albany County Rep. Com., 1975-78; bd. dirs. Kidney Found. NE N.Y., 1986, cons. budget com., 1986; speech and debate coach N. Colonie Sch. System. Named Young Elk of Yr., 1965; recipient Congl. Appreciation award, U.S. Ho. of Reps., 1963, Young Lion award, Prudential Ins. Co., 1971, John F. Kennedy Citizenship award, Presdl. award Nat. Kidney Found., 1988; named Super Starter, Waddell & Reed, Inc., 1984. Mem. Albany County Life Underwriters Assn., Estate Planners Coun. Northeastern N.Y. Roman Catholic. Avocations: golf, work with sr. citizens. Home: Latham, NY. Died Apr. 1, 2007.

MISRA, RAGHUNATH PRASAD, physician, educator; b. Kolkata, West. Bengal, India, Feb. 1, 1928; came to U.S., 1964; s. Guru Prasad and Anandi M.; m. Therese Rettenmund, Sept. 13, 1963; children: Sima, Joya, Maya, Tara. BSc honors, Calcutta U., 1948; MBBS, Med. Coll., Calcutta, 1953; PhD, McGill U., Montreal, Que., 1965. Diplomate Am. Bd. Anat. and Clin. Pathology. Asst. prof., dir. kidney lab. U. Louisville Sch. Medicine, 1964—68; assoc. investigator and dir. kidney lab Mt. Sinai Hosp., Cleve., 1968—73; asst. prof. Case We. Res. Med. Sch., Cleve., 1973—76; asst. prof., dir. kidney lab. Sch. Medicine La. State U., Shreveport, 1976—80, assoc. prof. Sch. Medicine, 1980—86, prof. Sch. Medicine, 1986—98, emeritus prof. Sch. Medicine, from 1998. Cons. VA Med. Ctr., Shreveport, 1977-98, EA Conway Meml. Hosp., Monroe, La., 1980-98; clin. prof. ophthalmology & dir. Ocular Pathology Sch. Medicine La. State U., Shreveport, 1988— Author: Atlas of Skin Biopsy, 1983 Pres. India Assn. of Shreveport, 1979, 81 Tallisman fellow Mt. Sinai Hosp., 1970-73. Fellow Am. Coll. Pathologists, Am. Soc. Clin. Pathologists, Am. Coll. Internat. Physicians, U. Calcutta Med. Alumni Assn. Am. (pres. 1992-93), Sigma Xi (pres. 1987-89) Democrat. Hindu. Avocations: photography, travel. Home: Shreveport, La. Died June 20, 2013.

MITCHELL, ROGER LOWRY, retired agronomy educator; b. Grinnell, Iowa, Sept. 13, 1932; s. Robert T. and and Cecile (Lowry) M.; m. Joyce Elaine Lindgren, June 26, 1955; children: Laura, Susan, Sarah, Martha. BS in Agronomy, Iowa State Coll., 1954; MS, Cornell U., 1958; PhD in Crop Physiology, Iowa State U., 1961. Mem. faculty Iowa State U., 1959-69, prof. agronomy, 1966-69, prof. charge farm operation curriculum, 1962-66; prof. agronomy, chmn. dept. U. Mo., Columbia, 1969-72, 81-83, emeritus prof., from 1998, dean agr., dir. expt. sta., 1983-98, dean extension, 1972-75, emeritus dean, from 1998; v.p. agr. Kans. State U., Manhattan, 1975-80; exec. dir. Mid-Am. Internat. Agrl. Consortium, 1981; ret., 1998. Exec. bd. divsn. agr. Nat. Assn. State Univs. and Land Grant Colls., 1978-80, 85-90, chmn., 1988-89; mem. bd. agr. NRC/NAS, 1983-86. Author: Crop Growth and Culture, 1970; co-author: Physiology of Crop Plants, 1985 Served to 2d lt. USAAF, 1954-56. Danforth fellow, 1956-61; Acad. Adminstrn. fellow Am. Council Edn., 1966-67; recipient Henry A. Wallace award Iowa State U., 1993, Sec.'s Honor award USDA, 1998, Cardinal Key Disting. Alumni award, 2009. Fellow AAAS (chmn. sect. O 1980-81), Am. Soc. Agronomy (pres. 1979-80), Crop Sci. Soc. (pres. 1975-76); mem. Soil Sci. Soc. Am., Coun. Agrl. Sci. and Tech., Sigma Xi, Gamma Sigma Delta, Alpha Zeta, Phi Kappa Phi. Home: Columbia, Mo. Died June 2014.

MIURA, IRENE TAKEI, retired academic administrator; d. Iowa and Jean Abe Takei; m. Neal Isamu Miura, June 26, 1960; children: David Takei, Gregory Ross, Jennifer Miura Yamagishi. BA with honors, U. Calif., Berkeley, 1960; MA in Tchg., Coll. of Notre Dame, Belmont, Calif., 1981; PhD, Stanford U., Calif., 1984. Cert. tchr. Calif. Tchr. St. Matthews Episcopal Day Sch., San Mateo, Calif., 1972—81; prof. child devel. San Jose State U., 1984—2000, exec. asst. to the pres., 2000—04. Trustee St. Matthews Episcopal Sch., San Mateo, 1990—95, U. Calif. Found., 1997—2001; mem. U. Calif. Bd. Regents, Oakland, 1997—2001; pres.

Calif. Alumni Assn., Calif., 1997—99; mem. Berkeley Fellows, from 2003. Mem. editl. bd.: Jour. Ednl. Psychology; contbr. articles to profl. jours., chapters to books. Vestry mem. St. Matthews Episcopal Ch., San Mateo, 1995—98. Mem.: AAAS, Internat. Soc. for the Study of Behavioral Devel., Am. Ednl. Rsch. Assn. (Outstanding Study of Yr. award 1994), Am. Psychol. Soc., Soc. for Rsch. in Child Devel., Phi Kappa Phi (hon.), Delta Phi Epsilon (life). Achievements include research in influence of language on children's understanding of number and mathematics concepts. Home: San Mateo, Calif. Died July 29, 2007.

MOFFETT, CHARLES SIMONTON, JR., museum director, curator, writer; b. Washington, Sept. 19, 1945; s. Charles Simonton M. and Faith Atherton Locke Phelps; m. Jane Pettigrew Daniels, July 28, 1979 (div.); children: Kate Serena, Charles Locke; m. Lucinda Herrick, August, 2011 BA in English, Middlebury Coll., 1967; MA, NYU, 1970. Ford Found. fellow Nelson-Atkins Mus., Kansas City, Mo., 1969-70; expert Sotheby Parke Bernet, NYC, 1970-71; guest asst. curator Met. Mus., NYC, 1974-75, assoc. curator, 1976-81, curator European paintings, 1981-83; curator-in-charge Fine Arts Mus. San Francisco, 1983-87, chief curator, summer 1987; sr. curator paintings Nat. Gallery Art, Washington, 1987-92; dir. The Phillips Collection, Washington, 1992-98; exec. v.p., co-chmn. impressionist, modern, contemporary art world wide Sotheby's, 1998—2014. Organizer mus. exhbns., author catalogues; mem. spl. exhbns. panel Nat. Endowment for Arts, 1987; project dir. publs. grant from J. Paul Getty Trust to Fine Arts Mus. San Francisco, 1987; fellow conf. on econs. of arts, presenter Salzburg (Austria) Conf., 1993; grad. Mus. Mgmt. Inst., 1990, sr. mus. assoc., 1994. Trustee San Francisco Day Sch., 1987, Middlebury Coll., 1987-90, Sterling and Francine Clark Art Inst., 1996-98, Terra Found. for the Arts, 1997-98. Andrew Mellon fellow Met. Mus. Art, 1975; travel grantee Met. Mus. Art, 1980; recipient award for best exhbn. Soho News Arts Awards, 1978; co-recipient Prix Bernier for Manet 1832-1883, 1983, recipient Alumni Achievement award Middlebury Coll., 1985, Kaufman award Nat. Gallery Art, 1989. Episcopalian. Died Dec. 10, 2015.

MOHLER, STANLEY ROSS, preventive medicine physician, educator; b. Amarillo, Tex., Sept. 30, 1927; s. Norton Harrison and Minnie Alice (Ross) M.; m. Ursula Luise Burkhardt, Jan. 24, 1953; children: Susan Luise, Stanley Ross, Mark Hallock. BA, MA, U. Tex., 1953, MD, 1956. Diplomate Am. Bd. Preventive Medicine.; transport pilot and flight instructor certificates. Intern USPHS Hosp., San Francisco, 1956-57; med. officer Center Aging Research, NIH, Bethesda, Md., 1957-61; dir. Civil Aeromedical Rsch. Inst., FAA, Oklahoma City, 1961—65; chief aeromedical applications divsn. FAA, Washington, 1966-78; prof. to prof. emeritus Wright State U. Sch. Medicine, Dayton, Ohio, 1978—2014, vice chmn. dept. community medicine, dir. aerospace medicine residency program, 1978—2004. Rsch. assoc. prof. preventive medicine and pub. health U. Okla. Med. Sch., 1961; vice-chmn. Am. Bd. Preventive Medicine, 1978, sec.-treas., 1980. Co-editor: Space Biology and Medicine (5 vols.), 1995 (Life Scis. Book award Internat. Acad. Astronautics); co-author Wiley Post, His Winnie Mae, and the World's First Pressure Suit; author Medication and Flying: A Pilot's Guide; contbr. articles to profl. jours. Bd. dirs. Sr. Citizens Assn. Oklahoma City, 1962-, Flying Physicians Assn., 1961—. Served with AUS, 1946-48. Recipient Gail Borden Rsch. award, Boothby award Aerospace Med. Assn., 1966, Henry L. Taylor award, 2008, FAA Meritorious Svc. award, 1974, Cecil A. Brownlow Publ. award Flight Safety Found., 1998, Marie Marvingt award French Soc. Aerospace Medicine and Aerospace Med. Assn., 2006; co-recipient Life Scis. Book award in space, biology and medicine Internat. Acad. Astronautics, 1995. Fellow Geriatrics Soc., Aerospace Med. Assn. (pres. 1983, Harry G. Moseley award 1974, Lyster award 1984, Louis H. Bauer Founders award 1998), Am. Coll. Preventive Medicine, Gerontol. Soc.; mem. AMA, Aircraft Owners and Pilots Assn. (Sharples award 1984, Hubertus Strughold award 1991, mem. med. adv. bd.), Experimental Aircraft Assn. (mem. med. adv. panel), Alpha Omega Alpha. Home: Greensburg, Pa. Died Sept. 15, 2014.

MOIZE, JERRY DEE, lawyer, federal official; b. Greensboro, NC, Dec. 19, 1934; s. Dwight Moody and Thelma (Ozment) M.; m. Margaret Ann Wooten, Aug. 13, 1976; 1 child, Jerry Dee Jr. AB cum laude, Elon Coll., NC, 1957; JD, Tulane U., New Orleans, 1960; diploma, Army Command & Gen. Staff Sch., USAR, 1981. Bar: Colo. 1961, US Dist. Ct. Colo. 1961, US Ct. Mil. Appeals 1962, US Supreme Ct. 1965, NC 1965. Legal clk. Air Def. Commd., Colo. Springs, Colo., 1960-61, assistance officer, 1962-63; chief legal assistance divsn. 2nd Army, Ft. Meade, Md., 1964-65; staff JAG, Indiantown Gap Mil. Reservation, 1965; law clk. to hon. Eugen Gordon U.S. Dist. Ct. (mid. dist.) NC, Winston-Salem, 1965-66; dir. Legal Aid Soc. Forsyth County, Winston-Salem, 1966-69; exec. dir. Forsyth Bail Project, Winston-Salem, 1968-69, Lawyer Referral Svc. of Bar of 21st Jud. Dist., Winston-Salem, 1968-69; staff atty. office of gen. counsel FAA, Washington, 1969-70, acting chief admin. & legal resources, 1970-71; staff atty. office of gen. counsel Dept. HUD, Washington, 1971, counsel Jackson area office Miss., 1971-83, chief counsel Jackson field office Miss., 1983-94, acting dir. Jackson field office, 2006, acting sr. advisor to dep. regional dir. Region IV Atlanta, 2006; chief counsel Office Gen. Counsel Miss., Jackson, from 1994; HUD del. Miss. Fed. Exec. Assn., 1997—2000. Lectr. U. W.Va. Conf. on Poverty Law, 1968; HUD program svc. adviser, 2000—. Editor NC Legal Aid Reporter, 1968-69, NC Legal Aid Directory, 1968, Avlex Legal Index (2nd supplement), 1971, developed Miss. low income housing financing mechanism 1975-76; contbr articles to profl. jours., articles to splty. mags. Dem. candidate NC Ho. of Reps., Guilford County, 1964; mem. mil. com. Forsyth County NC Red Cross, 1967-68; pack leader Andrew Jackson coun. Boy Scouts Am., 1986-92; active Project Adv. Group US Office Econ. Opportunity Legal Svc. Program, 1968-69, Adv. Com. on Housing & Urban Devel., Miss., Law Rsch. Inst., 1980-81, Pilot Mountain Preservation & Park Com., Winston-Salem, 1968-70; mem. Race Com. Whitworth Hunt Races, 1973-76; Am. Master of Foxhounds Assn., 1976-79; adv. Order DeMolay, 1997—; sec. Miss Scottish Games, 1999, v.p. 2000, pres. 2001. Capt. AUS, 1960-65; ret. lt. col. USAR, 1966-87. Decorated Meritorous Svc. medal, Army Commendation medal with oak leaf cluster, Army Res. Forces Achievement medal with three oak leaf clusters, Nat. Def. Svc. medal, Armed Forces Res. medal; named Hon. Knight Mason, 1999; recipient Legion of Honor, Order of De Molay, 2000. Mem.: KT, SCV, NRA, Miss. Opera Assn., NC State Bar, Fed. Bar Assn., Caledonian Soc. Miss., The Austin Hunt (joint master of foxhounds 1976—79), Iron Bridge Hunt (v.p. 1964—65), Miss. Hist. Assn., Miss. Track Club, Whitworth Hunt (founder, master of foxhounds 1975—76), Capital Club (Jackson, Miss.), Rosicrucian, Masons (32 degree), Shriners, Order Ea. Star, Pi Gamma Mu. Republican. Episcopal. Avocations: running, book collecting. Home: Ridgeland, Miss. Died Aug. 3, 2007.

MOLINARO, ALBERT FRANCIS, actor; b. Kenosha, Wis., June 24, 1919; s. Ralph Frank and Teresa (Marrone) M.; m. Betty Sydney; 1 child, Michael Martin. Grad. high sch., Kenosha. Appeared in (tv series) as Murray in The Odd Couple, 1970-75, as Al Delvecchio in Happy Days, 1974-84 and Joanie Loves Chachi, 1982-83, as Joe in Family Man, 1990. Died Oct. 30, 2015.

MOLLMAN, JOHN PETER, publishing executive; b. Belleville, Ill., Feb. 8, 1931; s. Kenneth John and Maurine (Farrow) M.; m. Carol J. Piper, Apr. 4, 1998; children: Sarah Chase Underhill, Eric Cleburne. BA, Washington U., St. Louis, 1952; cert. in advanced mgmt. program, Harvard Bus. Sch., 1986. Advt. specialist Gen. Electric Co., Schenectady and Boston, 1952-54, US Army Security Agy., 1954—56; mgr. Enterprise Printing Co., Millstadt, Ill., 1956-66; dir. prodn. Harper & Row Pubs., NYC, 1967-74; pub. Harper's Mag. Press, NYC, 1971-74; v.p. prodn. Random House Inc., NYC, 1974-81; sr. v.p. World Book-Childcraft Inc., Chgo., 1981-88; pres. World Book Pub., 1988-91; pub. cons., 1991-92; dir. intellectual property devel. Multimedia Publishing Microsoft, 1992-96; cons. in electronic pub. Carmel, Calif., from 1996. Mem. vis. com. Washington U.; mem. pub. com. Art Inst. Chgo.; bd. dirs. Yerba Buena Ctr. for the Arts, San Francisco; pres. Internat. ebook Award Found., NY; pres. Carmel Pub.Libr. Found.,Calif. Mem. Golf Club at Quail Lodge, Phi Delta Theta, Sigma Delta Chi, Omicron Delta Kappa. Unitarian Universalist. Home: Carmel, Calif. Died July 30, 2014.

MOLYNEAUX, JAMES HENRY, retired government official; b. Aug. 27, 1920; s. William Molyneaux. Grad., Aldergrove Sch. Vice-chmn. mng. com. Eastern Spl. Care Hosp., Ireland, 1966-73; hon. sec. S. Antrim Unionist Assn., Ireland, 1964-70; v.p. Ulster Unionist Council, 1974; mem. No. Ireland Assembly, 1982-86; leader Ulster Unionist Party House of Commons, 1974-95; M.P. from Antrim South, 1970-83; M.P. from Lagan Valley, 1983-97. Served with Royal Air Force, 1941-46. Decorated Grand Master of Orange Order, Hon. PGM of Can., Sovereign Grand Master. Avocations: gardening, music. Died Mar. 9, 2015.

MOMMSEN, HANS, historian; b. Marburg, Hessen, Fed. Republic of Germany, Nov. 5, 1930; s. Wilhelm and Marie-Therese (Iken) M.; m. Margaretha Reindl, 1966. PhD, U. Tübingen, Fed. Republic Germany, 1958-60. Asst. at hist. seminar U. Tübingen, 1958-60; mem. Inst. for Zeitgeschichte, Munich, 1960-61; asst. at hist. seminar U. Heidelberg, 1962-67; prof. Modern European history Ruhr U. Bochum, 1968—2015, dir. Inst. for History of Labour Movement Fed. Republic of Germany, 1977-83. Vis. prof. Harvard U., Cambridge, Mass., 1974, U. Calif., Berkeley, 1978, Hebrew U. of Jerusalem, 1980, Georgetown U., Washington, 1982; vis. mem. Inst. for Advanced Study, Princeton, N.J., 1974. Author (available in English translation) From Weimar to Auschwitz, 1991, The Rise and Fall of Weimar Democracy, 1996, Alternatives to Hitler: German Resistance Under the Third Reich, 2003, Germans Against Hitler: The Stauffenberg Plot and Resistance Under the Third Reich, 2009; contbr. articles to profl. jours. and chpts. to books. Fellow Inst. for Advanced Study, Berlin, 1983-84. Home: Bochum 1, Germany. Died Nov. 5, 2015.

MONFORTON, GERARD ROLAND, civil engineer, educator; b. Windsor, Ont., Can., July 21, 1938; married, 1960; 4 children. BASc, Assumption U., 1961, MASc, 1962; PhD in Civil Engring., Case Western Reserve U., 1970. Lectr. civil engring. U. Windsor, Ont., Can., 1962-64; rsch. asst. solid mechanics Case Western Reserve U., 1964-68; from asst. prof. to assoc. prof. civil engring. U. Windsor, 1968-76, prof. civil engring., from 1976. Mem. Engring. Inst. Can., Can. Soc. Civil Engrs. Achievements include research in solid mechanics and structural design. Died Nov. 15, 2006.

MONIZE, COLETTE RUTH, correctional education administrator; b. Chicopee, Mass., Apr. 8, 1933; d. Frederic Joseph and Lillian A. (Quenneville) Demers; m. Walter Carl Monize, Aug. 13, 1960. BA, U. New Orleans, 1973; MA, U. Ariz., 1975, PhD, 1988. Assoc. faculty Pima Community Coll., Tucson, 1975-85; career counselor Ariz. State Prison Complex, Tucson, 1981-86, supr. correctional edn., from 1986. Mem. long range planning com. Ariz. Dept. Corrections, 1985—. Writer, editor women's newspaper Source, 1977-80; adv. inmate newspaper Inside the Wire (first class award, 1982). Mem. Ariz. Vocat. Assn. (bd. dirs. 1989-91, vocat. policy fellow 1988-89), Correctional Edn. Assn. (developer constn. and by-laws state chpt., lst pres. Ariz. chpt. 1988), NAFE. Avocation: music. Home: Tucson, Ariz. Died Apr. 22, 2007.

MONROY, THOMAS GERALD, management consulting executive, educator; b. Little Rock, Dec. 11, 1944; s. Martin Jacques and Theresa Antonio (Marchigiano) M.; m. Duane Elizabeth LaVigne; children: Margaret Lang, Thomas Anthony. BBA, St. Leo Coll., 1978; MBA, PhD, Rutgers U. COO Lo Conte Constrn. & Real Estate, Bloomfield, N.J., 1961-65, TJL Media, Inc., NYC, 1978-92; founder, chmn. Tomon Importing, Phu Hiep, Vietnam, 1968-71; officer U.S. Army, 1967-78; pres. Mutual Credit N.J., Bloomfield, 1976-78; CEO Thomas G. Monroy & Assoc. Inc., Cleve., NYC, El Paso, Tex., from 1978; chmn., trustee Monroy Ednl. Systems, Inc., Cleve., from 1992. Adv. bd. Students in Free Enterprise, Berea, Ohio, 1986—; exec. dir.Family/Small Bus. Inst., Berea, 1992—. Author: Activity Guide for Youth Entrepreneurship, 1994; editor: Art & Science of Entrepreneurship Education, vol. I, 1993, vol. II, 1994, vol. III, 1995; contbr. articles to profl. jours. Youth Entrpreneurship mentor Sun Media Group, Cleve., 1992—, Lions Club Internat., Cleve., 1992—. Endowed chairholder in entrepreneurship Figgie Internat./Balwin Wallace Coll. Bera, 1992-94; recipient Best Paper on Entrepreneurship award Coleman Found., Chgo., 1993, 94, Youth Edn. grantee, 1993, 94, 95; recipient Regional Supporter Entrpreneurship Inc. Mag./Ernst & Young, Cleve., 1994. Mem. U.S. Assn. Small Bus. & Entrepreneurs (directorship 1992—, youth entrepreneurship mentor, 1992—, edit. bd. 1994—), U.S. Acad. Mgmt. (entrepreneur divsn., bd. dirs., newsletter editor), Internat. Coun. Small Bus., Assn. Pvt. Entrepreneurship Edn., Family Firm Inst./Family Bus. Rev. (edit. bd., 1994—), Project Excelence in Entrpreneurial Edn. (founder). Republican. Roman Catholic. Avocations: fishing, gardening, power boating, travel. Home: Rainbow City, Ala. Died Aug. 6, 2007.

MOODNICK, RONALD See MOODY, RON

MOODY, RON (RONALD MOODNICK), actor, writer; b. London, Jan. 8, 1924; s. Bernard and Kate (Ogus) Moodnick; m. Therese Blackbourn BSc in Econs., U. London, 1953. Appeared in plays: Intimacy at Eight, 1952, 6 Years Revue, 1959, Candide, 1960, Oliver, as Shylock in Merchant of Venice, 1967, as Polonius in Hamlet, 1972, as Richard in Richard III, 1978, Iago in Othello, 1981, as Harpagon in Moliere's The Miser, Peter Pan, 2000, 05, The Sunshine Boys, 2001, Comedians, 2001, Oliver, 2003, Peter Pan, Malvern, 2005, Scrooge in A Christmas Carol, 2006-07; (films) Davy, 1958, Follow the Star, 1959, Five Golden Hours, 1961, A Pair of Briefs, 1962, Ladies Who Do, 1963, Summer Holiday, 1963, The Mouse on the Moon, 1963, Murder Most Foul, 1964, Seaside Swingers, 1964, San Farry Ann, 1965, The Sandwich Man, 1966, Asterix the Gaul, 1967, Oliver!, 1968, Twelve Chairs, 1970, Flight of the Doves, 1971, Dogpound Shuffle, 1973, Legend of the Werewolf, 1975, Dogpound Shuffle, 1975, Closed Up-Tight, 1975, Dominique, 1979, Unidentified Flying Oddball, 1979, Wrong is Right, 1982, Where is Parsifal?, 1984, Asterix and the Big Fight, 1989, How's Business, 1991, Emily's Ghost, 1992, Kid at King Arthur's Court, 1995, The Three Kings, 2000, Chopsticks, 2000, Steps, 2000, Revelation, 2001, Paradise Grove, 2003, Lost Dogs, 2005, Moussaka and Chips, 2005, The Lizard Boy, 2006, The Legion of Fire, 2007; stage musicals: USA tour HMS Pinafore, 1987, Sherlock Holmes, 1989, Streets of Dublin, 1992, Bertie, 1993, Peter Pan, 1995, The Canterville Ghost, 1998; (TV Series, Mini-Series or films) The Vise, 1958, Alice Through the Looking Box, 1960, The Winter's Tale, 1962, Armchair Mystery Theatre, 1963, Comedy Playhouse, 1963, The Festival, 1963, Thursday Theatre, 1964, ITV Play of the Week, 1964, 1969, The Wednesday Play, 1966, The Avengers, 1966-67, The Harry Secombe Show, 1968, David Copperfield, 1969, Thirty-Minute Theatre, 1970, Shirley's World, 1971, The Edwardians, 1972, Gunsmoke, 1973, Village Hall, 1974, Play for Today, 1976, Starsky and Hutch, 1976, The Strange Case of the End of Civilization as We Know It, 1977, Midnight Is a Place, 1977, The Word, 1978, Tales of the Unexpected, 1980, Nobody's Perfect, 1980, Dial M for Murder, 1981, Into the Labyrinth, 1981, Strike Force, 1981, Tales of the Gold Monkey, 1982, Hart to Hart, 1981-83, Highway to Heaven, 1984, Murder, She Wrote, 1985, Hideaway, 1986, The Telebugs, 1986, Ghost in Monte Carlo, 1990, Mike & Angelo, 1994, Last of the Summer Wine, 1995, The Animals ofFarthing Wood, 1993-95, Noah's Island, 1997, The People's Passion, 1999, EastEnders, 2003, Keen Eddie, 2004, Holby City, 2005-2012, Celebration of Oliver, 2005, The Bill, 2006, Casualty, 2010; dir. (play) Kafka In Love, 1991; author-composer musical comedies Joey, 1966, Saturnalia, 1970, Move Along Sideways, 1971, The Showman, 1976, Nine Lives, 1991; touring Move Along Sideways, 1991, Monologues, 2003; author: (books) The Devil You Don't, 1980, Very Very Slightly Imperfect, Off the Cuff, 1987, The Amazon Box, 1998; writer, composer Moody in Storeland, 1961 Served with RAF, 1943-48. Recipient Golden Globe award, 1968, Moscow Golden Bear award as best actor, 1970, Coco Trophy award, Clowns Internat., 1999; nominated Oscar, 1968. Mem. Am. Acad. Motion Picture Arts and Scis., Variety Club of Great Brit., Actors Equity, Screen Actors Guild, Clowns Internat. (life pres.), Performing Rights Soc. Writers, Soc. Authors. Home: London, England. Died June 11, 2015.

MOOERS, MALCOLM MINTER, retired minister; b. Pleasantville, NJ, Apr. 9, 1924; s. Hadley Victor and Grace Madeline (Price) M.; m. Marjorie Tose, Sept. 13, 1947; children: Richard, Marilyn, John, Deborah. BS in Edn, Boston U., 1945; MDiv, Andover Newton Theol. Sch., 1948. Ordained to ministry United Ch. of Christ, 1948. Pastor Mt. Sinai (N.Y.) Congl. Ch., 1948-52, The Community Ch., Huntington, N.Y., 1952-59, The Congl. Ch. of Huntington, 1959-89, ret., 1989. Dep. chief chaplain Centerport (N.Y.) Fire Dept., 1960-90; moderator Suffolk Assn. N.Y. Conf., 1975-76, N.Y. Conf. United Ch. Christ, 1978-79; del. The Congl. Christian Ch, 1952-56, United Ch. Christ, 1985-87. Bd. dirs. Freedom Ctr., Huntington Station, N.Y., 1961-68, Planned Parenthood, Huntington, 1963-73, Sr. Citizens Housing Com., Huntington, 1981-89; mem. com. Martin L. King Jr. Remembrance, Huntington. Recipient plaques Town of Huntington, 1989, Centerpoint Fire Dept. 1990. Mem. Clergy Assn. Huntington (pres. 1980-85, scroll 1985, treas. 1985-90, citation 1989), Huntington Men's Chorus Club (pres. 1977-79), Kiwanis, Masons. Home: Jupiter, Fla. Died June 10, 2007.

MOORE, ACEL, retired journalist; b. Phila., Oct. 5, 1940; s. Jerry A. and Hura Mae (Harrington) Acel M.; m. Carolyn Weaver, June 1964 (div. 1974); 1 child, Acel Jr.; m. Linda Wright Avery Moore, Aug. 6, 1988; child Mariah Student, Settlement Music Sch., 1958, Charles Morris Price Sch., 1966-67. Copyboy Phila. Inquirer, 1962-64, editorial clk., 1964-68, staff reporter, 1968-80, editorial writer/columnist, 1980-81, assoc. editor, 1981—2005, also mem. edit. bd., 1981. Co-producer Black Perspective on the News (Nat. PBS weekly news program), 1972-78 Served with U.S. Army, 1959-62. Recipient Pulitzer prize, 1977, Robert F. Kennedy Journalism prize, 1977, Heywood Broun prize, 1977, Pa. Prison Soc. award, 1977, Humanitarian award House of Umoja, 1977, Community Service award Youth Devel. Center, 1976, Journalism award Phila. Party, 1977, Phila. Bar Assn. award, 1970, Ann. Paul Robeson award, 1977, Clarion award, 1977, Media award Mental Health Assn., 1977; Nieman fellow Harvard U., 1979-80 Mem. Nat. Assn. Black Journalists (co-founder), Phila. Assn. Black Journalists (pres.), Am. Soc. Newspaper Editors, Sigma Delta Chi (Phila. chpt. Pub. Service awards 1972, 77, Reporting award 1977). Died Feb. 12, 2016.

MOORE, ARCH ALFRED, JR., former Governor of West Virginia; b. Moundsville, W.Va., Apr. 16, 1923; s. Arch Alfred and Genevieve (Jones) M.; m. Shelley S. Riley, 1949 (dec. Sept. 13, 2014); children: Arch Alfred III, Shelley Wellons Moore Capito, Lucy St. Clair Moore Durbin. Student, Lafayette Coll., 1943; AB, W.Va. U., 1948, LL.B., 1951. Bar: W.Va. Pvt. law practice, W.Va., 1951—2015; mem. W.Va. House of Delegates, 1952, US Congress from 1st W.Va. Dist., 1957-69; gov. State of W.Va., 1969-77, 85-89. Republican party candidate for US Senate, 1978. Sergeant US Army, 1943—46. Decorated Bronze star, Purple Heart. Mem. ABA, W.Va. Bar Assn., Nat. Governors Assn. (chmn., 1971-72) Republican. Merthodist. Died Jan. 7, 2015.

MOORE, FREDERICK APPEL, health facility administrator; b. Boston, Apr. 25, 1925; s. Robert Webber and Josephine (Appel) M.; m. Cynthia Newton, June 17, 1950 (dec. June 2000); children: Lucinda Moore Hammett, Joanthan Newton, Stephanie Moore Schulz; m. GeorgeAnn Smith, Mar. 14, 2004. AB, Bowdoin Coll., 1948. CLU. Agt. John Hancock Life Ins. Co., Boston, 1948-56; gen. agy. Mass. Indemnity & Life, Wellesley, 1956-69; 2d v.p. Chubb Life Ins. Co., Concord, NH, 1969-87; owner Moore Ins. & Fin. Svcs., Enfield, 1987-90; dir. gift planning Dartmouth-Hitchcock Med. Ctr., Lebanon, 1990—2004; ret., 2004. Pres. Disability Ins. Tng. Coun., Chgo., 1958-60; treas. Coll. Fin. Planning, Denver, 1973-77; mem. Conn. Valley Estate Planning Coun., Hanover, 1990—. Chmn. planning Bd., Orange, N.H., 1990-2000, Upper Valley Waste Mgmt. Dist., Lebanon, 1990-2000; sr. warden St. Thomas Episcopal. Ch., Hanover, N.H., 1993-95; bd. mem. Upper Valley Planned Giving Coun., 2002-; mem. Phillips Acad. Alumni Coun., Andover, Mass., 2002-04. With USMC, 1943-45. Mem. Social Summit Lodge, Scottish Rite, Shriners. Republican. Episcopalian. Avocations: golf, sailing, tennis, theater, symphony. Home: Ormond Beach, Fla. Died Jan. 30, 2007.

MOORE, JAMES WILLIAM, photographer, television director; b. NYC, Feb. 15, 1936; s. Louis Edward and Evelyn (Seid) M.; m. Linda McMullin (div.); 1 child, Melissa; m. Beate Veronika Schulz, Apr. 24, 1967; children: Nicolai Peter, Vanessa. Student, Bklyn. Coll., 1955-56. Fashion and cosmetic photographer Harpers Bazaar, from 1962; owner James Moore Prodns., NYC. Lectr. Rochester (N.Y.) Inst. Tech., 1970-83, Smithsonian Inst., Washington, 1988; instr. Sch. Visual Arts, N.Y., 1974-81; presenter workshops in field U. Del., Md. Dir. TV commls. Recipient Andy award, Art Dirs. awards. Avocations: tai chi chuan, classical music, guitar, billiards. Home: New York, NY. Died Dec. 27, 2006.

MOORE, JOHN THOMAS, psychologist; b. Middletown, Ohio, July 3, 1950; s. Earl and Mary Francis (Quiett) M.; m. Donna Carolyn Kundtz, Aug. 28, 1971; children: Sarah Elizabeth, Rebecca Anne. BA, Miami U., Oxford, Ohio, 1973; MS, Va. Poly. Inst. and State U., 1975, PhD, 1980. Psychologist Southwestern State Hosp., Marion, Va., 1979-83, Grant Blackford Mental Health Ctr., Marion, Ind., 1983-85; pvt. practice psychology Radford, Va., 1983; psychologist Richmond (Ind.) State Hosp., 1985-86, chief psychologist, from 1986. Cons. clin. psychologist Aurora Chem. Dependency Unit Reid Meml. Hosp., Richmond, 1986—. Mem. Am. Psychol. Assn., Ind. Psychol. Assn., Assn. Advancement of Behavior Therapy. Mem. Soc. Of Friends. Home: Clayton, Ohio. Died Nov. 27, 2006.

MOORE, JUSTIN EDWARD, information technology executive; b. West Hartford, Conn., June 17, 1952; s. Walter Joseph and Victoria Mary (Calcagni) M. BS in Mgmt. Sci., Fla. Inst. Tech., 1974. Systems assoc. Travelers Ins., Hartford, Conn., 1974-77; data processing programmer R.J. Reynolds Industries, Winston-Salem, NC, 1977—78; programmer/analyst Sea-Land Svc., Elizabeth, NJ, 1978-79, mgr. market analysis Oakland, Calif., 1979-82; asst. v.p., dir. application systems Fox Capital Mgmt. Corp., Foster City, Calif., 1982-86; mgr. bus. svcs. mktg. and pricing dept. Am. Pres. Cos., Ltd., Oakland, 1987—88, dir. mktg. and pricing systems, 1988-89; dir. systems devel. The Office Club, Concord, Calif., 1989-91; dir. MIS Revo, Inc., Mountain View, Calif., 1992-93; acct. mgr. Imrex Computer Sys., Inc., South San Francisco, 1993-94; project mgr. Exigent Computer Group, Inc., San Ramon, Calif., 1994—2007, Xerox Corp., San Ramon, Calif., from 2007. Republican. Roman Catholic. Avocations: golf, personal computing, investment mgmt. Home: Concord, Calif. *Personal philosophy: Strive always to do the right things, at the right time, the right way for the right reasons.* Died Dec. 24, 2013.

MOORE, RICHARD, physicist, researcher; b. Hollywood, Calif., Jan. 19, 1927; s. Dennis Albert and Marjorie Jane (Kahn) M.; m. Irene McManus, Apr. 1, 1956 (div. 1965); m. Lillian Elizabeth Karska, Apr. 5, 1969; children: Don Andrew, Ann Marie. Student, Deep Springs Coll., 1944-46; BS in Engring., U. Mo., 1949; PhD in Biophysics, U. Rochester, 1955; DSc in Bioengineering, George Washington U., 1970. Engr. USPHS, Washington, 1955-57; scientist NIH, Bethesda, Md., 1957-60; rsch. scientist Am. Nat. Red Cross Labs., Bethesda, 1960-69; assoc. prof. U. Minn., Mpls., 1969-82; prof., dept. chair U. Witwatersrand, Johannesburg, Republic of South Africa, 1982-87; health physicist U.S. Dept. of Energy, Idaho Falls, Idaho, from 1987. Rsch. assoc. U. Rochester, N.Y., 1950-55; radiol. safety officer Johannesburg Hosp., 1982-87; pres. Svc. and Rsch. Co., Chubbuck, Idaho, 1987—; software coord. Pocatello (Idaho) MacIntosh Users Group, 1988—; consulting physicist Intermountain Cancer Ctr., Bannock Regional Med. Ctr., Pocatello. Editor (jour.) Pattern Recognition, 1968—, Computers in Biology and Medicine, 1968—; contbr. chpts. to 6 books, articles to profl. jours. Mem. spl. study sect. NIH, Bethesda, 1976; mem. cancer com. Minn. Dept. Health, Mpls., 1976; mem. neutron therapy com. Coun. Sci. and Indsl. Rsch., Johannesburg, 1986. Recipient internat. rsch. fellowship Internat. Exchange Com., Prague, Czechoslovakia, 1977, pres.'s award Soc. Radiol. Engring, Chgo., 1977, fellowship German Acad. Exchange Svc., Berlin, 1980, sr. scientist fellowship NATO, Berlin, 1980, study grant U. Witwatersrand, 1987. Fellow AAAS, Soc. Advanced Med. Systems; mem. Am. Heart Assn. (fellow coun. on cardiovascular radiology 1980), Royal Soc. (Republic South Africa), Am. Coll. Med. Physics, Am. Soc. Therapeutic Radiology and Oncology, Health Physics Soc. (nominating com. 1989), Am. Acad. Health Physics, Am. Bd. Health Examiners (panel of examiners). Democrat. Unitarian Universalist. Avocations: music, reading. Home: Chubbuck, Idaho. Died July 31, 2007.

MOORE, ROBERT BYRON, JR., management consultant; b. Houston, Sept. 5, 1957; s. Robert Byron and Mary Frances (Trager) M.; m. Julie Beth Collord, Nov. 21, 1987. BBA, U. Mich., 1979; MBA, U. Ill., 1984. CPA, Ill. Experienced sr. auditor Arthur Andersen & Co., Chgo., 1979-83; research analyst U. Ill., Champaign, 1984; mgr., mgmt. cons. Grant Thornton, Chgo., from 1985. Mem. Am. Inst. CPA's, Ill. CPA Soc., Healthcare Fin. Mgmt. Assn., Beta Alpha Psi. Avocations: golf, photography. Home: Wheaton, Ill. Died Aug. 3, 2007.

MOORE, ROBERT MULLINS, III, chemical company executive; b. Dallas, Sept. 14, 1947; s. Robert Mullins and Mary Nelle (Landrum) M.; m. Carolyn Francis, Mar. 13, 1981; children: Robert Mullins IV, Megan Francis. BA in Chemistry, Tex. Christian U., 1969; MS in Chemistry, U. Tex., Arlington, 1971. Sr. scientist Alcon Labs., Ft. Worth, 1971-76; mgr. product devel. Cooper Vision, Mountain View, Calif., 1977-81; project mgr. Bausch and Lomb, Rochester, N.Y., 1981-83; corp. v.p. Tech. Network, Peoria, Ariz., from 1983, tech. cons., from 1983; mgr. product devel. Carter Glogau Labs., Phoenix, from 1985. Ophthalmic lectr., speaker Cooper Labs., Mountain View, Calif., 1980-81. Contbr. articles to profl. jours.; patentee in field. Advisor explorers Boy Scouts Am., Ft. Worth, 1974-76. Mem. Am. Chem. Soc., Pharm. Mfg. Soc. Methodist. Avocations: tennis, fine ship building, cooking. Home: Glendale, Ariz. Died July 3, 2007.

MOORE, WILLIAM EVAN, corporate executive, consultant, engineer; b. Charleston, W.Va., Sept. 14, 1925; s. Junius Teetzel and Helen Marshall (Pugh) M.; m. Janet Bryce Stocks, June 26, 1954; children: Janet, Katherine, Susan, William. BSME, MIT, 1950, BSCE, 1951; DSc, W.Va. U., 1988. Structural engr. PBI Industries, Pitts., 1951-52, Ferro Products Corp., Charleston, W.Va., from 1953. Pres. Indsl. Constructors, Charleston, 1954-90; exec. v.p. Ferro Products, Charleston, 1972-82, pres., 1982-90; chmn. Nat. Engring. Certification Commn., Clemson, S.C., 1973-75. Mem. pres.'s adv. bd. W.Va. Inst. Tech., 1970-77; mem., sec. W.Va. Bd. Profl. Engrs., Charleston, 1966-80; bd. dirs. Madeira Sch., McLean, Va., 1975-81. Fellow ASCE (pres. Charleston chpt. 1962-63); mem. Nat. Soc. Profl. Engrs., Am. Inst. Steel Construction (com. on specifications 1980—). Republican. Presbyterian. Home: Charleston, W.Va. Died June 1, 2007.

MORAVEC, IVAN, pianist; b. Prague, Nov. 9, 1930; m. Zuzana Moracova; 1 stepchild, Daniel Korte; 1 child from previous marriage, Iva Emmerova. Grad. Prague Conservatory, grad. Prague Acad.; master classes, Arezzo, Italy, 1957—58. Belknap visitor in humanities Princeton U., 2006—07. Pianist (performances) The Cleveland Orch., Severance Hall, 1964, Carnegie Hall, NY Philharmonic, Phila. Orch., Minn. Orch., symphonies, Chgo., Boston, San Francisco, Toronto, Pitts., LA Chamber Orch., Orpheus Chamber Orch., Kennedy Ctr., Washington, DC, Vienna, Amsterdam, Paris, Leipzig, Munich, Oslo, Rome, Milan, Queen Elizabeth Hall, London, Australia, NHK Symphony Orch., Japan, Berlin, (festivals) Tangelwood, Blossom, Ravinia, Hollywood Bowl, Mostly Mozart, Caramoor, Salzburg, Edinburgh, Ruhr, Schleswig-Holstein, Prague, (albums) Dvorak Songs, 1967, 1974, 1983, Dvorak Piano Concerto - Twins, 1983, Ivan Moravec Plays Debussy & Chopin, 1983, Chopin 24 Preludes, Ballade in F Minor, 1988, Mozart Piano Concertos 14, 23, 25, 1990, Brahms Piano Concerto 2, 1990, Chopin: The Four Scherzi And Other Works, 1991, Prokofiev, 1992, Schumann Piano Concerto, Brahms Piano Concerto 1, 1993, Ivan Moravec Plays Beethoven, Vol. 1, 1995, Ivan Moravec Plays Beethoven, Vol. 2, 1995, Ivan Moravec Plays Mozart, Beethoven, and Brahms, 1995, Mozart Piano Concertos 24, 25, 1996, Mozart Piano Concertos 20, 23, 1997 (Cannes Classical award, best solo with orch., 18th Century, 1999), Great Pianists of the 20th Century, 1998, French Keyboard Masterpieces, 1998, Chopin Nocturnes, 1999, Ivan Moravec Plays Schumann and Franck, 2000, Ivan Moravec Plays Czech Music, 2000, Live in Prague, 2001, Ivan Moravec Plays French Music, 2001, Ivan Moravec Plays Chopin, 2001, Ivan Moravec Plays Beethoven, 2001, Ivan Moravec Plays Mozart, 2001, Ivan Moravec/4 CD Collection, 2002, Ivan Moravec/Chopin, 2003, Beethoven Piano Concert 4, Ravel, Franck, 2004, Mozart Piano Concertos 14, 23, 25, 2005, Brahms Piano Concertos, 2006. Recipient Medal of Merit Outstanding Artistic Achievement, Pres. of Czech Republic, 2000, Prize of Charles the Fourth, Czech Republic, 2000, Platinum Disc, Supraphon, 2000, Cannes Classical award lifetime achievement, 2002, Culture award, NY Mag., 2006. Achievements include receiving "Record of the Yr." from High Fidelity, Stereo Review, NY Times, Time Mag., and Newsweek for numerous recordings. Died July 27, 2015.

MORENO-DE-AYALA, OSCAR, research scientist; s. Oscar Moreno-de-Ayala. PhD, U. Calif., Berkley, 1973. CEO, founder NIC.PR, from 1989, Gauss Rsch. Lab. Inc., PR, 2006. PhD thesis advisor UPRM, PR. Contbr. more than 100 articles and sci. papers to profl. publs. Bd. mem. Centro Zen de PR, Gauss Rsch. Found., PR. Grant, NIH, DoD, NSF, NSA. Fellow: IEEE. Buddhist. Achievements include patents for digital watermarking, digital communications; algebraic generator of sequences for communication signals; cryptographic metric for multidimensional arrays. Died July 14, 2015.

MOREY, MARION LOUISE, former quality control chemist; b. Chgo., May 2, 1926; d. Oscar Gilbert and Esther Naomi (Carlson) Engstrom; m. Howard Elmer Morey, Mar. 2, 1957; children: Richard, David. BS summa cum laude, Elmhurst Coll., 1947; postgrad., Northwestern U., Chgo., 1952-54, Loyola U., 1955-56. Quality control chemist Wander Co., Villa Park, Ill., 1947-57. Master gardener vol. U. Ill. Coop. Extension Svc., Amboy, Dixon, 1988—; vol. tchr. ESL, Sauk Valley C.C., Dixon, 1980; sec. Dixon Family YMCA, 1969-79, pres., 1982-84, also bd. dirs. Recipient Lowell Linnes Leadership award YMCA of USA-Midwest Field, 1984. Mem. AAUW (pres. Dixon br. 1980-82), P.E.O. (treas. Ill. AC chpt. 1989-95). Presbyterian. Avocations: choir music, gardening, sewing, reading, travel. Home: Dixon, Ill. Died Nov. 27, 2007.

MORGAN, BEVERLY CARVER, pediatrician, educator; b. NYC, May 29, 1927; d. Jay and Florence (Newkamp) Carver; children: Nancy, Thomas E. III, John E. MD cum laude, Duke U., 1955. Diplomate Am. Bd. Pediat. (oral examiner 1984-90, mem. written examination com. 1990—), Nat. Bd. Med. Examiners. Intern, asst. resident Stanford U. Hosp., San Francisco, 1955-56; clin. fellow pediat., trainee pediatric cardiology Babies Hosp.-Columbia Presbyn. Med. Ctr., NYC, 1956-59; rsch. fellow cardiovasc. diagnostic lab. Columbia-Presbyn. Med. Ctr., NYC, 1959-60; instr. pediat. Coll. Physicians and Surgeons, Columbia U., NYC, 1960; dir. heart sta. Robert B. Green Meml. Hosp., San Antonio, 1960-62; lectr. pediat. U. Tex., 1960-62; spl. rsch. fellow in pediatric cardiology Sch. Medicine, U. Wash., Seattle, 1962-64, from instr. to prof. pediat., 1962-73, chmn. dept. pediat., 1973-80; mem. staff U. Wash. Hosp., chief of staff, 1975-77; mem. staff Harborview Med. Ctr., Children's Orthop. Hosp. and Med. Ctr., dir. dept. medicine, 1974-80; prof., chmn. dept. pediat. U. Calif., Irvine, 1980-88, prof. pediat. and pediatric cardiology, from 1980; pediatrician in chief Children's Hosp. Orange County, 1988. Mem. pulmonary acad. awards panel Nat. Heart and Lung Inst., 1972-75; mem. grad. med. edn. nat. adv. com. to sec. HEW, 1977-80; mem. Coun. on Pediatric Practice; chmn. Task Force on Opportunities for Women in Pediat., 1982; mem. nursing rev. com. NIH, 1987-88. Contbr. articles to profl. jours.; mem. editl. bd. Clin. Pediat., Am. Jour. Diseases of Children, Jour. of Orange County Pediatric Soc., Jour. Am. Acad. Pediat., LA Pediatric Soc. Recipient Women of Achievement award Matrix Table, Seattle, 1974; Disting. Alumnus award Duke U. Med. Sch., 1974; Ann. award Nat. Bd. Med. Coll. Pa., 1977; Career Devel. award USPHS, 1966-71; Moseby scholar, 1955. Mem. Am. Acad. Pediat. (chmn. com. on pediat. manpower 1984-86), Am. Coll. Cardiology, Soc. for Pediat. Rsch., Am. Fedn. Clin.

Rsch., Am. Pediat. Soc., Assn. Med. Sch. Pediat. Dept. Chmn. (sec.-treas. 1981-87), Western Soc. for Pediat. Rsch., Alpha Omega Alpha. Died Jan. 25, 2014.

MORGAN, DONNA BATEMAN, secondary educator; b. Orlando, Fla., Sept. 2, 1956; d. Charles P. and Helen J. (Vaughn) Bateman; m. Charles Thomas Morgan, July 21, 1975; 1 child, William Thomas. BA, U. Cen. Fla., 1977. Cert. math. and sci. tchr., Fla. Paralegal Robert L. Thomas, Apopka, Fla., 1976-88; tchr. math. and sci. Tavares (Fla.) Mid. Sch., from 1989. Republican. Baptist. Avocations: rodeo, Tae Kwon Do. Home: Astatula, Fla. Died Dec. 5, 2006.

MORGAN, JOHN A., corporate director; b. Wichita, Kans., Sept. 4, 1915; s. Leo O. and Maud (Swaim) M.; m. Patricia Crowe, Mar. 31, 1946 (dec. Aug. 1975); children: Eileen, Douglas, Christine, Lisa, Gregory, Deirdre. AB, Wichita State U., 1937; MBA, Harvard U., 1939. Advt. asst. Butler Mfg. Co., Kansas City, Mo., 1939-42, various exec. positions, 1946-51, gen. mgr., exec. v.p., 1951-57, pres., 1957-67, chmn. bd., 1967-74. Chmn. bd. Midwest Research Inst., U. Kansas City, chmn. various non-candidate polit. action campaigns, Kansas City. Served to lt. USNR, 1943-46, PTO. Named Mr. Kansas City, Kansas City C. of C., 1968; recipient Chancellor's medal, U. Mo., Kansas City, 1964; named to Kansas City Bus. Leaders Hall Fame, Jr. Achievement, 1985. Avocation: hiking in the mountains. Home: Kansas City, Mo. Died Jan. 23, 2007.

MORGANTE, LINDA ANN, community health nurse; b. Buffalo, July 12, 1951; d. Prosper and Rosalie (Aquilino) Morgante; m. Joseph Porcelli, Aug. 21, 1982. AAS, SUNY, Syracuse, 1971; BSN, CUNY, 1984, MSN, 1990. Cert. Rehab. Nurse. Assoc. dir. clin. svcs. Multiple Sclerosis Soc., NYC, 1986-90; clin. nurse specialist dept. neurology Maimonides Med. Ctr., Bklyn., from 1988. Adj. clin. instr. NYU Sch. Nursing, 1990-91. Cons. Nat. Multiple Sclerosis Soc., 1993—. Recipient Hunter Bellevue Sch. Nursing Excellence in Clin. Practice award, 1984, Community Leadership award, 1990. Mem. Rehab. Nurses Assn., Sigma Theta Tau. Home: Brooklyn, NY. Died Mar. 26, 2007.

MORITZ, JOHN JOSEPH, JR., waterworks executive; b. Youngstown, Ohio, Mar. 17, 1947; s. John and Ann (Opatich) M.; m. Shirley L. Hapcic, June 16, 1973; 1 child, Jeffrey John. BA, Youngstown State U., 1970, postgrad., 1970-72. With Nat. Engring. & Contracting, Youngstown, 1965-66, Moritz Masonry, Youngstown, 1966-76; with inside sales div. Trumbull Supply, Youngstown, 1976; sales mgr. Victory White Metal Co., Youngstown, 1977-86, v.p., 1986-91, co. ops. mgr., from 1991. Founder Northeastern Ohio Continental Baseball League, 1990 Mem. Eagles. Democrat. Avocations: baseball, golf, olympic pin collector. Home: Youngstown, Ohio. Died Nov. 22, 2006.

MORMINO, AUGUST CHARLES, chiropractor; b. St. Louis, Sept. 2, 1924; s. August Peter and Liboria (Datilo) M.; m. Annette Helen Hogan, June 12, 1952; children: Michael, Anthony, Kathryn. D Chiropractic, Nat. Coll. Chiropractic, Chgo., 1953, cert. in accupuncture, 1977. Minor-league baseball player St. Louis Cardinals orgn., 1946-49; pvt. practice, Decatur, Ill., from 1953. With AUS, 1943-46, ETO. Mem. Am. Chiropractic Assn., Ill. Chiropractic Soc., Nat. Coll. Chiropractic Alumni Assn. (Century Club, President's Club). Democrat. Roman Catholic. Avocations: handball, bicycling, walking. Home: Decatur, Ill. Died Mar. 7, 2007.

MORRILL, BILLIE ALBERTA, librarian; b. Hartford, Conn., Aug. 25, 1942; d. Clifford Kenneth Worland and Alberta Molly Schwartz; m. Richard Melvin Morrill, June 11, 1966; 1 child, Celeste. AS in Gen. Studies, Three Rivers C.C., Norwich, Conn., 1998. Asst. editor Travelers Bull. Travelers Ins. Co., Hartford, 1970—73, head spkrs. bur., 1973—75; copywriter G. Fox & Co., Hartford, 1979—83; freelance writer, 1983—87; circulation clk., 1987—90; reference libr. East Lyme Pub. Libr., Niantic, Conn., from 1987, from 1994, head circulation svcs., 1990—94. Author poetry; contbr. articles to profl. jours. Charter mem., pres. Travelers Toastmistress Club, Hartford, 1970—75. Recipient Trustee's medallion, Three Rivers C.C., 1998. Mem.: Poets of the Sound (facilitator from 1998), Conn. Poetry Soc., LTA Alumni Assn., Phi Theta Kappa. Methodist. Avocations: writing, reading, walking. Home: Niantic, Conn. Died Jan. 5, 2007.

MORRIS, HARRIET R., elementary school educator; b. Springfield, Mass., July 4, 1923; d. Walter Dewitt and Ida Ann (Rome) Bearg; m. Samuel Morris, Oct. 14, 1945 (dec. 1993); children: Robert, Julia, Jonathan, Daniel. BS, Am. Internat. Coll., 1944; MS, Butler U., 1973, EdS, 1985. Cert. tchr. K-12 Ind., mentally retarded, emotionally disturbed, LD/neurol. impaired, reading tchr. Ind., lic. sch. psychologist Ind. Tchr. lang. arts, grades 1-6 Children's Ho., Indpls., 1971—72; tchr. Indpls. Pub. Schs., 1972—89; sch. psychologist Avon Sch. Sys., Ind., 1990. Leader cub scouts Boy Scouts Am., Schenectady, NY, 1955—56; leader brownies Girl Scouts U.S., Schenectady, 1957—58; Sunday sch. tchr. Indpls. Hebrew Congregation, 1964—66; bd. dirs. Indpls. chpt. Hadassah, from 1990; guardian ad litem Ind. Advs. for Children, 1994—95; docent Indpls. Children's Mus., 1996—97; vol. Older Adult Svc. and Info. Sys., 1996—98. Mem.: Mensa. Home: Indianapolis, Ind. Died May 21, 2007.

MORRIS, MARY SUE, real estate investor, developer; b. Wichita Falls, Tex., Oct. 5, 1938; d. William Willard and Ruth (Maxey) Gibson; m. Bill Morris, 1972 (div. 1985). Student, Okla. U., 1956-57; BBA, So. Methodist U., Dallas, 1960; student, NYU, 1981-84. V.p. mktg. Paragon Industries, Inc., Dallas, 1960-64; dir. pub. relations and advt. Haggar Stacks, Dallas, 1964-67; dir. women's sales Am. Airlines, NYC, 1968-72; cons. mgmt. constrn. and mktg. Unit, Inc., Columbus, Ohio, Lexington, Ky., 1972-74; developer The Left Bank, Cin., 1974-81; owner, mgr. Tennis Is My Racket, Cin., 1974-81; owner, developer Amanda, Cin., 1977-81; head of real estate devel. Cumberland, Inc., NYC, 1981-84; pres. founder The Sheridan Group, NYC, from 1984. Bd. dirs. Contemporary Art Council, Cin., 1974; mem. Mayor's Council, Cin., 1981. Mem. Town Tennis Club, West Side Tennis Club, University Club, Pi Beta Phi. Methodist. Avocations: tennis, skiing, reading, travel, architecture. Home: New York, NY. Died Mar. 17, 2007.

MORRIS, OWEN GLENN, engineering corporation executive; b. Shawnee, Okla., Feb. 3, 1927; s. Vestus and Myrtle (Lindsey) M.; m. Joyce Gast; children: Deborah Moree, Janine Inez. BS in Mech. Engring, U. Okla., 1947, M.Aero. Engring., 1948; postgrad., U. Va., 1952-53, Va. Poly. Inst., 1955-56, Coll. William and Mary, 1957-58. Aero., research scientist NASA, Langley Field, Va., 1948-61, mgr. lunar module, 1968—71, mgr. sys. integration space shuttle, 1974—80, mgr. Apollo spacecraft program, 1971—72; pres. Eagle Engring., 1980-86; pres., chief exec. officer Eagle Aerospace, Houston, 1987-90, chmn., chief exec. officer, 1990-93, chmn. bd., from 1992. Served with USNR, 1944-46. Recipient Presdl. Medal of Freedom, 1972, NASA Disting. Svc. medal, 1973, NASA Exceptional Svc. medal, 1969, Outstanding Leadership medal, NASA, 1979. Asso. fellow Am. Inst. Aeros. and Astronautics; mem. Am. Astronautical Soc., Acad. Model Aeros., Tau Beta Pi, Tau Omega. Presbyterian (elder 1964—). Club: Rotary. Home: Houston, Tex. Died Dec. 29, 2014.

MORRISON, CHARLES EDGAR, physician; b. Boston, Sept. 8, 1947; s. James Urban and Mary Elizabeth (Galloway) M.; m. Mary Margaret Boyles, Aug. 16, 1969 (div. Nov. 1984); children: Amanda Michelle, Charles Edgar Jr.; m. Carla Jean Woods, June 21, 1986; 1 child, Macey Lauren. BS, Millsaps Coll., 1969; MD, U. Miss., 1973. Ptnr. Lumberton (N.C.) Urology Clinic, 1978-81, Hinds Urology Clinic, Jackson, Miss., 1981, Columbus (Miss.) Urology Group, from 1981. Chief med. staff Golden Triangle Regional Med. Ctr., Columbus, 1988—; bd. dirs. Golden Triangle Regional Med. Found., Columbus. Deacon First Presbyn. Ch., Columbus, 1988—. Mem. Am. Urological Assn., Am. Assn. Clin. Urologists, AMA, Miss. State Med. Assn., Prairie Med. Soc. Avocations: hunting, fishing, jogging, weight training, bicycling. Home: Columbus, Miss. Died Feb. 11, 2007.

MORRISON, RICHARD DRURY, health policy consultant, medical educator; b. Logan, W.Va., Nov. 14, 1935; s. William Cline Morrison and Gladys Leone Rogers-Morrison-Taylor; m. Carolee Benefico, Oct. 15, 1971 (div.). PhD, Va. Commonwealth U., Richmond, 1988; MA, Coll. of William and Mary in Va., Williamsburg, 1985; BA, Christopher Newport Coll., Newport News, Va., 1976. Adj. asst. prof. Old Dominion U., Norfolk, Va., 1999—2003; cons. in evidence based medicine Ea. Va. Med. Sch., Norfolk, 1999—2003. Cons. and fellow Am. Internat. Health Alliance, Washington, 1996—98, UCSF Ctr. for the Health Professions, Pew Charitable Trusts, San Francisco, 1994—96; dep. dir. Va. Dept. of Health Professions, Richmond, 1984—94; dir. of membership svcs. AVMA, Chgo., 1963—65; asst. dir. Am. Assn. of Dental Schools, Chgo., 1965—69; bd. dirs. Bd. of Certification for Emergency Nurses; standards com. commn. grad. Foreign Nursing Sch.; bd. dirs. Va. Health Quality Ctr.; exec. council health policy AARP/Va. Author (more than 50): (published health policy reviews) On Request. Specialist 5 US Army, 1956—59, Fort Lee, Virginia. Johnataan Duncan McGregor scholar, U. Chgo., 1952—55. Achievements include serving on bd. of dir. Coun. on Licensure, Enforcemenent and Regulation; The Center for Public Affairs, Virginia Commonwealth University; consulting, Bur. of Health Professions, US Department of Health & Human Services; bd. of dr., v.p. , Citizen Advocacy Ctr; cons., Inst. of Medicine, Nat. Acad. of Sciences; cons., The Pew Charitable Trusts; cons., Robert Wood Johnson Found; intern, Va. Joint Legis. Audit and Review Cmmn; intern, The Va. Crime Cmmn; cons. and sr. rsch. fellow, The Williamson Institue, Medical Coll. of Va; mem., Task Force of Pres. Carter's Cmmn.on Mental Health. Avocations: international travel, creative writing. Home: Richmond, Va. Died Mar. 8, 2007.

MORSE, GARY (HAROLD GARY MORSE), construction executive; b. Chgo., Dec. 19, 1936; s. Harold and Mary Louise Schwartz; m. Sharon Dolan (dec. 1999); children: Tracy, Jennifer, Mark; m. Renee Morse; 1 stepchild, Justin. Pres., CEO The Villages, Fla., 1972—2014. Republican. Died Oct. 29, 2014.

MORTON, FREDERIC, author; b. Vienna, Oct. 5, 1924; s. Frank and Rose (Ungvary) M.; m. Marcia Colman, Mar. 28, 1957; 1 dau., Rebecca. BS, Coll. City N.Y., 1947; MA, New Sch. Social Research, 1949. Author: The Hound, 1947, The Darkness Below, 1949, Asphalt and Desire, 1952, The Witching Ship, 1960, The Schatten Affair, 1965, Snow Gods, 1969, An Unknown Woman, 1976, The Forever Street, 1984, Crosstown Sabbath, 1987, (biography) The Rothschilds, 1962, Broadway Musical Version of the Rotuscuizbs, 1970-72, A Nervous Splendor-Vienna 1888-89, 1979, Musical Version of In A Nervous Splendor Produced In Budapest 2007, Tokyo 2008, Vienna, 2009, Solar Southoughts, 1972, Thunder at Twilight-Vienna 1913/14, 1989, Runaway Waltz--A Memoir From Vienna To New York, 2005; books translated into 18 langs.; actor (documentary) Crosstown Sabbath, 1995; contbg. editor: Vanity Fair; contbr. to publs. including Best Am. Short Stories, 1965, Best Am. Essays of 2003, and other anthologies, N.Y. Times, Harper's mag., Atlantic mag., Nation, Playboy, Esquire, N.Y. Mag., Hudson Rev., Wall Street Jour., Vanity Fair, L.A. Times, others; columnist Village Voice, Conde-Nast Traveler, Wall Street Jour.3.2 Recipient Author of Year award Nat. Anti-Defamation League, B'nai B'rith; Hon. Professorship award Republic of Austria, 1980, Tom Osborne Disting. lectureship U. Nebr., 1989; Dodd, Mead Intercollegiate Lit. fellow, 1947; Yaddo residence fellow, 1948, 50; Breadloaf Writers' Conf. fellow, 1947; Columbia U. fellow, 1953; recipient Golden Merit award City of Vienna, 1986, City of Vienna medal of honor in gold, 2001, Cross of Honor for Achievements in Arts, Republic of Austria, 2003. Mem. Author's Guild (exec. coun.), P.E.N. Home: New York, NY. *As a writer I'm trying to tell the truth interestingly.* Died Apr. 20, 2015.

MORTVEDT, JOHN JACOB, soil scientist, researcher; b. Dell Rapids, SD, Jan. 25, 1932; s. Ernest R. and Clara M.; m. Marlene L. Fodness, Jan. 23, 1955; children: Sheryl Mortvedt Jarratt, Lori Mortvedt Klopf, Julie Mortvedt Stride. BS, SD State U., 1953, MS, 1959; PhD, U. Wis., 1962. Soil chemist TVA, Muscle Shoals, Ala., 1962-87, sr. scientist, 1987-92, regional mgr. field programs dept., 1992-93; ext. soils specialist Colo. State U., Ft. Collins, 1994-95, ext. environ. and pesticide edn. specialist, 1996. Agr. cons. U.S. Borax, 1997-2007. Co-author: Fertilizer Technology and Application, 1999; editor: Micronutrients in Agriculture, 1972, 2d edit., 1991; contbr. articles to profl. jours. 1st lt. U.S. Army, 1953-57. Fellow AAAS, Soil Sci. Soc. Am. (pres. 1988-89, editor-in-chief 1982-87, Profl. Svc. award 1991, Disting. Svc. award 1996), Am. Soc. Agronomy (exec. com. 1987-90, Agronomic Svc. award 2003); mem. Internat. Union Soil Sci., Colombian Soil Sci. Soc. (hon.), Exch. Club (pres. Florence, Ala. chpt. 1987-88), Toastmasters (pres. Florence chpt. 1964-65), Phi Kappa Phi. Avocations: photography, golf. Home: Fort Collins, Colo. Died Mar. 13, 2012.

MORUKOV, BORIS VLADIMIROVICH, cosmonaut; b. Moscow, Oct. 1, 1950; s. Vladimir D. Morukov and Lidia F. Khromova; m. Nina M. Morukova; children: Olga, Ivan. MD, Moscow Med. U., 1973; PhD in Space, Aviation and Naval Medicine, 1979; student, Gagarin Cosmonaut Tng. Ctr., 1990—92; grad. advanced course in emergency med. care, 1995, grad. tng. course in endocrinology and hematology, 1996; attended Flight-Surgeon Tng. Course, NASA, Johnson Space Ctr., Houston, 1998—99. Rschr. Inst. for Biomed. Problems, 1978—84, sr. rschr., 1984—88, chief. dept. metabolism and regulation, 1988—89, cosmonaut, rschr., chief lab. metabolism and immunology, 1989—94; cosmonaut, rschr., chief Divsn. of State Rsch. Ctr. RF Inst. for Biomed. Problems, 1995—98; cosmonaut Inst. for Biomed. Problems, 1998—2015; mem. crew STS-106 to Internat. Space Sta., 2000. Med. support for space sta. Salut-6, mem. staff Mission Control Ctr., 1979—80; human life-scis. expts. coord. NASA-Mir Sci. Program, 1995—98. Contbr. over 100 articles to sci. jours. Recipient Leader in Pub. Med. Svc. award, 1989, Medal for Merits to Motherland of 2d degree, 1996. Achievements include patents for 4 inventions; research in calcium metabolism correction; logging 11 days, 19 hours in space. Avocations: reading, movies, cooking. Died Jan. 1, 2015.

MOSHIRI, GERALD ALEXANDER, biology educator; b. Shiraz, Iran, June 1, 1929; came to U.S., 1943; s. Atta and Shams (Mahin) M. BA, Oberlin Coll., 1952, MA, 1954; PhD, U. Pitts., 1968. Postdoct. U. Calif., Davis, 1968-69, Mich. State U., Hickory Corners, 1969; from asst. prof. to prof. U. West Fla., Pensacola, from 1969, dir. Wetlands Rsch. Lab. and Inst. Coastal/Estuarine Rsch., from 1989. Chmn. radioisotope rsch. and control com., U. West Fla., chmn. U. rsch. and creative activities com., 1990-91, chmn. arts and scis. coun., 1983-84, chmn. search com., chmn. community coll. rels. com., chmn. com. to evaluate biology dept. for bd. regents, chmn. coastal zone studies program com., grad. curriculum com., undergrad. curriculum com., adv. com., travel com., student affairs coun., student conduct com., coastal zone adv. com., coll. pers. com., lectr., cons. and presenter in field. Contbr. over 70 articles to profl. jours. Vol. new pride program Escambia County Community Mental Health Ctr.; vice-chmn. Escambia County Resource Recovery Com.; chmn. environ. subcom. Port Pensacola Improvement Task Force; active Pensacola Task Force on Transp.; com. on cons. selections Escambia County, hazardous waste mgmt. com., ad hoc adv. com. pollution control; environ. resources and mgmt. subcom. Escambia/Santa Rosa Coast Resource Planning and Mgmt., land use subcom., archl. and environ. review bd. Santa Rosa Island Authority. Recipient numerous grants for rsch. Mem. AAAS, Am. Soc. Limnology and Oceanography, Freshwater Biol. Assn., Ecol. Soc. Am. (editorial reviewer), Internat. Assn. for Theoretical and Applied Limnology, Assn. Southeastern Biologists, Fla. Acad. Scis., Water Pollution Control Fedn., Fla. Water Pollution Control Assn., Food and Agrl. Orgn. United Nations, Bayou Yexar Assn., Fla. Scientists for the Environment, Sigma Xi (pres.). Democrat. Home: Cantonment, Fla. Died Jan. 23, 2007.

MOSINGER, BEDRICH JOSEPH, biochemist, researcher; b. Otesice, Pilsen, Czech Republic, July 6, 1925; s. Joseph and Anna (Krs) M.; m. Dagmar Brozik, Sept. 23, 1950; children: Bedrich, Jiri. MD, Charles U., Prague, Czech Republic, 1950; PhD, Acad. Scis., Prague, Czech Republic, 1961, DSc, 1966. Dep. chief Physiol. Inst., Charles U., 1951-55; chief biol. dept. Pharmaceutical Inst., Prague, 1956-57; dep. chief physiol. dept. Inst. Human Nutrition, Prague, 1956-80; chief metabolic dept. Inst. Clin. and Exptl. Medicine, Prague, 1980-86, chief lab. cardiovasc. risk factors, 1986-95. Vis. scientist Nat. Inst. Health, Bethesda, Md., 1966-67; vis. prof. McGill U., Montreal, Can., 1967-69, Montreal Gen. Hosp., 1967-69. Author: Handbook of Physiology, 1965, Adipose Tissue, 1970;

contbr. articles to profl. jours. With Terezin Army Hosp., 1950-51. Recipient J.E. Purkinje award Med. Assn., 1967, Ministry Health award Rsch. Coun., 1974. Mem. NIH, N.Y. Acad. Scis. Home: Prague, Czech Republic. Died Jan. 8, 2014.

MOTSINGER, LINDA SUSAN BAUMGARDNER, commercial printing firm owner; b. Chgo., Mar. 14, 1941; d. Bryan Burdette and Chrystal Lucille (Adams) Baumgardner; m. Larry Lee Motsinger, Oct. 2, 1959; 1 child, Eric Lee. Cert. of completion life ins. underwriting Northwestern Mut. Life Ins. Co., Milw., 1962. Bookkeeper Busey Bank Corp., Urbana, Ill., 1959-60, Northwestern Mut. Life Ins. Co., Champaign, Ill., 1960-62, asst. office mgr.-bookkeeper, 1962-65; tech. typist-sec. U. Ill. Coll. Engring., Urbana, 1965-70; entrepreneur pub. rels. L & L Printing Svc., St. Joseph, Ill., from 1975. Co-author, editor, pub.: A Genealogical Record of the Family Baumgardner, 1971; editor, pub.: (reunion handbooks) UHS--20 Years Later, 1979, UHS--30 Years Later, 1989, UHS--Thirty-Five Years Older and Still a Tiger!, 1994; editor, pub. (ann. alumni newsletter) Tiger Pause, 1989—. Organizer, co-chair Reunion Com. UHS, 1959, Urbana, 1978—. Republican. Avocations: genealogy, needlecrafts, photography, fishing, environmental concerns. Home: Saint Joseph, Ill. Died Mar. 24, 2007.

MOULTHROP, ROSCOE EMMETT, lawyer; b. Kansas City, Mo., Apr. 8, 1913; s. Roscoe Emmett and Jennie Jerome (Sullivan) M.; m. Esther Myrtle Burton, Nov. 27, 1937; Esther Joan Muench, Roscoe Emmett III, Jean Kathryn, Wolff, Jeanette Marie Babyok. LLB, Kansas City Sch. Law, 1936. Bar: Mo. 1936. Pvt. practice, Kansas City, 1936-41, Bethany, Mo., from 1941; prosecuting atty. Harrison County, Mo., 1943—44, Mo., 1947—48, Mo., 1951—54, Mo., 1977—80, Mo., 1999—2002. Pros. atty. Harrison County, Bethany, 1943-44, 47-48, 51-54, 77-80. Scout leader Pony Express Coun. Boy Scouts Am., Bethany. Lt. USN, 1944-46, WWII. Mem. ABA, Mo. Bar Assn. (bd. govs. 1964-68). Avocation: farm operation. Home: Chesterfield, Mo. Died July 31, 2007.

MOUNTCASTLE, VERNON BENJAMIN, retired neuroscientist; b. Shelbyville, Ky., July 15, 1918; s. Vernon and Anne-Francis Marguerite (Waugh) Mountcastle; m. Nancy Clayton Pierpont, Sept. 6, 1945; children: Vernon Benjamin III, Anne Clayton, George Earle Pierpont. BS in Chemistry, Roanoke Coll., Salem, Va., 1938, DSc (hon.), 1968; MD, Johns Hopkins U., 1942; DSc (hon.), U. Pa., 1976, Northwestern U., 1985, U. Minn., 1995; MD (hon.), U. Zurich, 1983, U. Siena, 1984, U. Santiago, Spain, 1990. House officer surgery Johns Hopkins Hosp., 1942—43; mem. faculty Johns Hopkins Sch. Medicine, 1946—59, prof. physiology, 1959, dir. dept., 1964—80, prof. neurosci., 1980—92, prof. emeritus, 1992—2015; dir. Bard Labs. Neurophysiology Johns Hopkins U., Balt., 1981—91. Spl. rsch. physiology brain; chmn. physiology study sect., mem. physiology tng. com. NIH, 1958—61; adv. coun. Nat. Eye Inst., 1971—74; vis. prof. Coll. de France, Paris, 1980. Author: Perciptual Neuroscience: The Cerebrel Cortex, 1996, The Sensory Hand: Neural Mechanisms in Somatic Sensation, 2005; editor-in-chief: Jour. Neurophysiology, 1961—64, editor, contbr.: Med. Physiology, 12th edit., 1968, Med. Physiology, 13th edit., 1974, Med. Physiology, 14th edit., 1980; contbr. articles to profl. jours. Lt. (s.g.) M.C. USNR, 1943—46. Recipient Lashley prize, American Philos. Soc., 1974, F.O. Schmitt prize and medal, MIT, 1975, Sherrington prize and Gold medal, Royal Acad. Medicine, London, 1977, Horowitz prize, Columbia U., 1978, Helmholtz prize, 1982, Fyssen Internat. prize, Paris, 1983, Lasker award, 1983, Nat. Medal Sci., The White House, 1986, Zotterman prize and medal, Swedish Physiol. Soc., 1989, Award in Neurosci., Fidia Fedn., 1990, Australia prize, 1993. Mem.: AAAS (McGovern prize and medal 1990), NAS (chmn. sect. on physiology 1971—74, award in neurosci. 1998), Acad. Sci. (Finland, fgn.), Royal Soc. London (fgn.), Acad. Scis. (France, fgn.), Nat. Inst. Medicine, American Philos. Soc. (councillor 1979—82), Soc. Neurosci. (pres. 1970—72, Gerard prize 1980), Harvey Cushing Soc., American Acad. Arts & Sciences, American Physiol. Soc., Physiol. Soc. London (hon.), American Neurol. Assn. (hon. Bennett lectr. 1978), Sigma Xi, Phi Chi, Alpha Omega Alpha, Phi Beta Kappa. Home: Baltimore, Md. Died Jan. 11, 2015.

MOXON, ALVIN LLOYD, chemistry educator; b. Flandreau, SD, July 25, 1909; s. George Harrison and Ada Bertha (Waxdahl) M.; m. Nannette Lorraine Harker, June 11, 1938; 1 child, James Harker Moxon. BS, S.D. State U., 1934, MS, 1937; PhD, U. Wis., 1941. Chemist, head dept. S.D. Agri. Expt. Sta., Brookings, 1940-51; prof. chemistry S.D. State U., Brookings, 1946-51; prof. animal sci. and biochemistry Ohio State U., Columbus, 1951-79, assoc. chmn. dept. animal sci., 1951-67, prof. emeritus, from 1979. Nutrition advisor Punjab (India) Agr. Coll., 1961-62; prof. animal nutrition U. Sao Paulo, Brazil, 1964-66, group leader, 1967-71, vis. prof., 1981-82. Mem. Am. Chem. Soc., Am. Soc. for Biochemistry and Molecular Biology, Kiwanis Club, Sigma Xi. Republican. Episcopalian. Home: Wooster, Ohio. Died May 21, 2007.

MU, XIAO-CHUN, computer company executive; b. Tianjin, China, Mar. 23, 1957; parents Guoguang and Yuanxiang Chi; m. Pei-yang Yan, June 2, 1984; children: Wendy, Kevin. BS, Nankai U., Tianjin, China, 1981; PhD, Pa. State U., 1986. Engr. Dept. mgr. Intel Corp., Santa Clara, Calif., from 1986. Univ. mentor Semiconductor Rsch. Corp., N.C. Contbr. over 50 articles to profl. jours.; patentee in field. Mem. Electrochem. Soc. Avocations: tennis, bicycling. Home: Saratoga, Calif. Died Mar. 10, 2007.

MUCHNICK, RICHARD STUART, ophthalmologist, educator; b. Bklyn., June 21, 1942; s. Max and Rae (Kozinsky) Muchnick; m. Felice Dee Greenberg, Oct. 29, 1978; 1 child, Amanda Michelle. BA with honors, Cornell U., 1963, MD, 1967. Diplomate Am. Bd. Ophthalmology, Nat. Bd. Med. Examiners. Intern in medicine NY Hosp., NYC, 1967—68, resident in ophthalmology, 1970—73, practice medicine, specializing in ophthalmology, notably strabismus & ophthalmic plastic surgery, from 1974. Clin. prof. ophthalmology Cornell U., NYC, from 2009; clin. rschr. strabismus, ophthalmic plastic surgery, from 1973; attending med. staff Lenox Hill Hosp., NYC; attending ophthalmologist NY-Presbyn. Hosp, NYC. With USPHS, 1968—70. Recipient Coryell Prize Surgery, Cornell U. Med. Coll., 1967, McLean Medal in Ophthalmology, Weill Med. Coll. of Cornell U., 2006. Fellow: ACS, Am. Acad. Ophthalmology; mem.: AMA, Manhattan Ophthal. Soc., Greater N.Y. Soc. Pediat. Ophthalmology and Strabismus (pres.), N.Y. Acad. Medicine, N.Y. Soc. Clin. Ophthalmology, Internat. Strabismological Assn., Am. Assn. Pediatric Ophthalmology and Strabismus, Am. Soc. Ophthalmic Plastic and Reconstructive Surgery, 7th Regt. Tennis, Lotos, Alpha Epsilon Delta, Alpha Omega Alpha. Home: New York, NY. Died Mar. 29, 2015.

MUELLER, GEORGE EDWIN, engineer; b. St. Louis, July 16, 1918; s. Edwin and Ella (Bosch) M. m. Maude Rosenbaum (div.); children: Karen Hyvonen, Jean Porter; m. Darla Hix Schwartzman, 1978; stepchildren Wendy Schwartzman, Bill Schwartzman BS in Elec. Engring., Mo. Sch. Mines, 1939; MS in Elec. Engring., Purdue U., 1940; PhD in Physics, Ohio State U., 1951; degree (hon.), Wayne State U., N.Mex. State U., U. Mo., 1964, Purdue U., Ohio State U., 1965. Mem. tech. staff Bell Telephone Labs., 1940-46; prof. elec. engring. Ohio State U., 1946-57; cons. electronics Ramo-Wooldridge, Inc., 1955-57; from dir. electronic lab. to v.p. research and devel. Space Tech. Labs., 1958-62; assoc. adminstr. for manned space flight NASA, 1963-69; corporate officer, sr. v.p. Gen. Dynamics Corp., NYC, 1969-71; chmn., pres. System Devel. Corp., Santa Monica, Calif., 1971-83, chmn., chief exec. officer, 1983; sr. v.p. Burroughs Corp., 1981-83; pres. Jojoba Propagation Labs, from 1981, George E. Mueller Corp., from 1984, Internat. Acad. Astronautics, from 1983; with Kistler Aerospace, Kirkland, Wash. Author: (with E.R. Spangler) Communications Satellites. Recipient 3 Disting. Service medals NASA, 1966, 68, 69; Eugen Sanger award, 1970; Nat. Medal Sci., 1970; Nat. Transp. award, 1979 Fellow AAAS, IEEE, AIAA (Goddard medal 1983, Sperry award 1986), Am. Phys. Soc., Am. Astronautical Soc. (Space Flight award), Am. Geophys. Union, Brit. Interplanetary Soc.; mem. Internat. Acad. Astronautics (pres. 1982—), NAE, N.Y. Acad. Scis. Patentee in field. Home: Santa Barbara, Calif. Died Oct. 12, 2015.

MUI, KAN CHI, investment securities executive; b. May 25, 1917; came to U.S., 1939; m. Phaik-Sim Lim, July 9, 1945; children: Roger Ken, Sui San, Peter Ken, David Ken. BA in Econs., Miami U., 1944; MA in Econs., Princeton U., 1946, PhD in Econs., 1949. Assoc. prof. in fin.-banking Okla. City U., Oklahoma City, 1949-53; pres. Mui Investment Svc., Inc., Oklahoma City, from 1953. Trustee United Presbyterian Found., Synod of the Sun, Denton, Tex., 1979—; dir. Sunbeam Family Svcs., Inc., Oklahoma City, 1986; chmn. emeritus Asia Soc. Okla., 1986—; pres. UN Assn., Oklahoma City chpt., 1987-89, v.p. membership, 1989—. Recipient Sanxay Fellowship, Princeton U., N.J., 1947-49. Mem. Nat. Assn. Security Dealers, Petroleum Club, Men's Dinner Club. Republican. Presbyterian. Avocations: jogging, swimming, reading. Home: Philadelphia, Pa. Died Nov. 28, 2006.

MULCKHUYSE, JACOB JOHN, retired energy conservation consultant; b. Utrecht, The Netherlands, July 21, 1922; arrived in U.S., 1982; s. Lambertus D. and Aagje (Van Geyn) Mulckhuyse; m. Cornelia Jacoba Wentink, Jan. 17, 1953; children: Jacobien, Hans, Dieuwke, Linda, Marlies. MSc, Amsterdam U., Netherlands, 1952, PhD, 1960. Dir. Chemisch-Farmaceutische Fabriek Hamu, the Netherlands, 1951-57; tech. asst. mgr. Polak & Schwarz (now IFF), the Netherlands, 1957-60; asst. tech. mgr. Albatros Superphosphate Fabrieken, the Netherlands, 1960-61; tech. mgr. for overseas subsidiaries Verenigde Kunstmestfabrieken, the Netherlands, 1961-64, gen. mgr. process engring. dept., 1964-70; dept. head process engring. dept. Unie van Kunstmestfabrieken, the Netherlands, 1970-82; sr. chem. engr. World Bank, Washington, 1982-83, sr. cons. chem. engr., 1983-87; ind. cons. environ. engring. World Bank and several cons. firms, 1987-97; ret., 1999. Author (with Heath and Venkataraman): (book) The Potential for Energy Efficiency in the Fertilizer Industry, 1985; author: (with Gamba and Caplin) Industrial Energy Rationalization in Developing Countries and Constraints in Energy Conservation, 1990, Process Safety Analysis: Incenvtive for the Identification of Inherent Process Hazards, 1985, Energy Efficiency and Conservation in the Developing World, 1992; editor: Environmental Balance of the Netherlands, 1972. Mem.: AIChE, N.Y. Acad. Scis., Internat. Inst. for Energy Conservation (bd. dirs. 1990—93), Fertilizer Soc. (pres. 1969—70), Royal Dutch Chem. Soc., Rotary. Avocations: philosophy, tennis, advising developing countries. Died May 25, 2007.

MULDOON, MICHAEL DENNIS, flight instructor; b. Warsaw, NY, June 9, 1941; s. Edward Joseph and Ruth Celeste (Murphy) M.; m. Deborah Jean Stephens, Apr. 1, 1967; children: Michael Dennis II, Caitrin Stephens. BS in Mil. Sci., USAF Acad., 1965. Enlisted USAF, 1959; advanced through grades to maj. U.S. Air Force, ret. 1983, chief ops. and plans procurement analyst budget process Washington, 1981-82, chief ops & plans improvement project analyst budget process, 1982-83; project adminstr. Hughes Missile Electronics Inc., Eufaula, Ala., 1984-85; tech. writer/editor Burnside-Ott, Pensacola, Fla., 1987-88, contract simulator instr., from 1988, cons., 1987. Bd. dirs. Big Bros., Gwinn, Mich., 1971-73; scoutmaster Boy Scouts Am., Pensacola, 1985—; chmn. ways and means com. PTA, Cordova Park Elem. Sch., Pensacola, 1987—; bd. dirs. Ballyshanners, Alexandria, Va., 1982-84. Mem. Ret. Officers Assn., Order of Daedalians, Kiwanis (treas. 1975-76). Roman Catholic. Home: Pensacola, Fla. Died Dec. 2, 2006.

MULHARE, EILEEN MARGARET, social scientist; b. Norwalk, Conn., Jan. 18, 1953; d. Francis Carroll and Mirta Teresita (de la Torre) Mulhare. BA in Anthropology, Carlow Coll., 1972; PhD in Anthropology, U. Pitts., 1986. Instr., researcher U. Pitts., 1972-80; patient accounts supr. Community Home Health Svcs., Phila., 1981-82; sr. devel. assoc. Lawrence Inst. Tech., Southfield, Mich., 1982-87; dir. grants, devel. libraries Wayne State Univ., Detroit, 1988-90; rsch. assoc. Colgate U., Hamilton, N.Y., from 1990. Researcher, translator U. Kans. Biomed. Project, Saltillo, Mexico, 1974; cons. L.P. Campbell Assoc., Pitts., 1976; contract grant writer Social Rsch. Application Corp., Wash., 1977; vis. asst. prof. Hartwick Coll, Oneonta, N.Y., 1991-94. Mem. adv. Allegheny County Indochinese Refugee Resettlement Task force, Pitts., 1975-76. Rsch. fellow Fulbright-Hays, Puebla, Mex., 1978-79, Orgn. Am. States, Puebla, 1979. Fellow Soc. Applied Anthropology, Am. Anthropol. Assn. Home: Hamilton, NY. Died Dec. 23, 2006.

MULLEN, DONNA JO, nursing educator; b. Dubuque, Iowa, June 13, 1951; d. Harold and Darlene (Kieslich) Simmons; m. Ronald Mullen, Sept. 1, 1973; children: Jessie, Sarah, Jacki. Diploma, Finley Hosp. Sch. Nursing, 1972; BSN, U. Dubuque, 1984; MS in Nursing, U. Wis., Madison, 1990. Staff nurse Cuba City Med. Ctr., Cuba City, Wis., 1972-77; office nurse Cuba City Drs. Clinic, 1977-84; nursing instr. S.W. Wis. Tech. Coll., Fennimore, 1985; asst. dir. nursing Orchard Manor, Lancaster, Wis., 1986-87; primary nurse Tri-State Dialysis, Dubuque, 1987-90; adult nurse practitioner Grant Community Clinic, Lancaster, Wis., 1990-91; instr. ADN S.W. Wis. Tech. Coll., Fennimore, from 1991. Mem. ANA, Sigma Theta Tau. Home: Cuba City, Wis. Died May 16, 2007.

MULLER, HERMAN JOSEPH, historian, educator; b. Cleve., Apr. 7, 1909; s. Joseph John and Julia (Zwilling) Muller. LitB, Xavier U., 1932; MA in History, Loyola U., 1935; S.T.L., St. Louis U., 1946; PhD in History, Loyola U., Chgo., 1951; LHD (hon.), U. Detroit Mercy, 2002. Ordained to ministry Roman Cath. Ch., 1941. Tchr. St. Ignatius H.S., Chgo., 1935—38; lectr. Xavier U., Cin., 1943—47; asst. prof. West Baden Coll. (Loyola U.), 1941—43, John Carrol U., Cleve., 1952—56; prof. history U. Detroit, from 1956. Lectr. in History U. Coll., Dublin, 1968—69, Dublin, 1972—73, Cork, Ireland, 1977—78. Author: (History Book) The University of Detroit: 1877-1977, 75 Years of Quality Business Education, 1991, (Hist. Biography) Bishop East of the Rockies, 1994; contbr. articles various profl. jours. Named one of People Who Make a Difference, U. Mercy, 2001. Mem.: Phi Alpha Theta, Alpha Sigma Nu. Roman Catholic. Avocations: fishing, golf, faculty chaplain of Univ. baseball team. Home: Detroit, Mich. Died Apr. 19, 2007.

MULVANIA, WALTER LOWELL, lawyer; b. Rock Port, Mo., Sept. 20, 1905; s. Jesse L. and Eva Viola (Stewart) Mulvania; m. Eunice Mary Umbarger, Jan. 31, 1945 (dec. May 6, 2002); 1 child, Eva Jo Mulvania Van Meter. BA, William Jewell Coll., Liberty, Mo., 1927; JD, U. Mo., 1931. Pvt. practice law, Rock Port, from 1931. Fellow Am. Coll. of Trust and Estate Counsel; mem. ABA, Mo. Bar Assn. (bd. govs. 1965-71), Rotary (pres. 1951-52). Democrat. Baptist. Home: Rock Port, Mo. Died July 24, 2007.

MUNDT, JOHN P., administrative computing executive, consultant; b. Milw., Oct. 28, 1946; s. Peter and Linda Mundt; m. Donna J. Meier, Dec. 18, 1993; children: Katrina, Erica, Jennifer, Heide, James. BA, Northwestern U., 1968. Tchr. Chgo. Bd. Edn., Chgo., 1970-88; head administr. computing Glenview (Ill.) Dist. 34, from 1988. Ptnr. Net Cons., Wilmette, Ill., 1994—; bd. dirs. Net Illinois, Evanston, Ill., 1993—. Republican. Lutheran. Avocation: whitewater boating. Home: Vernon Hills, Ill. Died Feb. 23, 2007.

MUNGER, GEORGE HOWARD, JR., pastor, chaplain; b. Centerville, Iowa, Aug. 10, 1920; s. George Howard and Delia Myra (Swain) M.; m. Leslie Norma Cavanaugh, 1945; children: George Howard III, Leslie N. BS, U. Wis., 1946; BD, Colgate Rochester Div. Sch., 1947, ThM, 1965, D of Ministry, 1984. Ordained to ministry Am. Bapt. Ch., 1945; cert. chaplain Coll. of Chaplains. Various pastorates Am. Bapt. Ch., various, 1946-79; chaplain St. Luke Hosp., St. Louis, 1979-89; interim pastorates Am. Bapt. Chs. Great Rivers Region, Ill., Mo., 1989; min. of care Delmar Bapt. Ch., St. Louis, from 1989. Mem. home mission bds. Am. Bapt. Chs., U.S.A., 1959-68; pres. mins. coun. Am. Bapt. N.Y.S., 1963. Home: Saint Louis, Mo. Died Aug. 27, 2007.

MURASE, JIRO, lawyer; b. NYC, May 16, 1928; BBA, CCNY, 1955; JD, Georgetown U., 1958, LL.D. (hon.), 1982. Bar: DC 1958, NY 1959. Sr. ptnr. Marks & Murase LLP, NYC, 1971-97, Bingham McCutchen Murase, NYC, from 1997. Legal counsel Consulate Gen. of Japan; mem. Pres.'s Adv. Com. Trade Negotiations, 1980-82; mem. Trilateral Commn., 1985—; apptd. mem. World Trade Coun., 1984-94; adv. com. internat. investment, tech. and devel. Dept. State, 1975. Editorial bd.: Law and Policy in Internat. Bus. Trustee Asia Found., 1979-83, Japanese Ednl. Inst. NY; bd. dirs. Japan Soc., Japanese C. of C. in NY, Inc.; hon. bd. regents Georgetown U.; bd. visitors Georgetown

Law Ctr.; adv. coun. Pace U., Internat. House Japan; pres. Japanese-Am. Assn. NY, Inc., 1996-98—, Japan Ctr. Internat. Exch., 2001—. Recipient NY Gov.'s citation for contbns. to internat. trade, 1982; named to Second Order of Sacred Treasure (Japan), 1989. Mem. ABA, Assn. of Bar of City of NY, NY State Bar Assn., NY County Lawyers Assn., Maritime Law Assn., Consular Law Soc., Fed. Bar Coun., Am. Soc. Internat. Law, World Assn. Lawyers, Japanese-Am. Soc. Legal Studies, Am. Arbitration Assn., Lic. Execs. Soc., US C. of C. Clubs: Nippon (dir.); Ardsley Country; NY Athletic; Mid-Ocean (Bermuda). Home: Ardsley On Hudson, NY. Deceased.

MURDOCK, DORIS DEAN, special education educator, program developer; b. Pacific Junction, Iowa, Feb. 7, 1913; m. Myron J. Murdock, June 28, 1933; 1 child, John Timothy. BS in Elem. Edn., So. Oreg. U., 1964; MS in Remedial Edn., U. Oreg., 1968. Primary tchr. Days Creek Elem. Sch., Oreg., 1962—66, Grants Pass Dist., 1966—67, Riddle Elem., Riddle, Oreg., 1968—71; founder, dir. Plowshare Sch., Rogue River, Oreg., 1972—78, Child Life Sanctuary, Rogue River, 1978—88; founder, dir., spl. edn. program developer Ctr. Habilitative Living, Grants Pass, from 1989. Author: No Thank You! No Ritalin for Me Today!, 2003. Vol. Peace Corp., 1978—80. Mem.: Coun. for Exceptional Children (life). Republican. Seventh Day Adventist. Home: Ronan, Mont. Died Sept. 21, 2014.

MURPHY, JAMES RODNEY, playwright; b. Kenton, Ohio, Mar. 23, 1933; m. Teruko Murakami, 1958; children: Cynthia, Laurel. BS in Bus. Adminstrn., U. Tenn., 1962; MS in Edn., U. So. Calif., 1967, MS in Sys. Mgmt., 1983; PhD in Aerospace Studies, Union Inst., Cin., 1990; Air Command and Staff Coll. Diploma, Air U., Maxwell AFB, Ala., 1987, Air War Coll. Diploma, 1988. Enlisted USAF, 1951, advanced through grades to capt., 1968, transp. combat adv., 1968-69; transp. analyst, def. transp. policy coun. advisor Ctr. for Studies and Analyses, Hdqrs. USAF, Washington, 1989-92; hazardous cargo and packaging policy specialist Directorate of Transp., Hdqrs. U.S. Air Force, Washington, 1992-95; ret. USAF, from 1995; playwright/poet, lyricist/librettist Plays Around, Colorado Springs, Colo., from 1995. Author: (musical) Truck Stop, 1994, (opera) Luke and Sarah, (musical) Member of the Team, 1996, (biography) Peon to Pentagon, 1999, also numerous poetry, lyrics and short stories. Founder, chmn. Am. Nat. Opera, 2000. Decorated Meritorious Svc. medal, Bronze Star medal, others. Mem. Nat. Def. Transp. Assn., Coun. Logistics Mgmt., Soc. Logistics Engrs., Nat. Panel Consumer Arbitrators, BBB, Masons, Internat. Soc. Poets, Rockford Writers Guild, Wyo. Players, Opera Am., Dramatists Guild, Writers Guild, Songwriters Assn. Washington, Washington Area Music Assn., Nashville Songwriters Assn. Internat., Am. Soc. Composers, Authors and Pubs., Drama League, Theatre Comms. Group, Colo. Opera Festival Guild, Phi Kappa Phi, Beta Gamma Sigma, Delta Nu Alpha, Delta Sigma Pi. Died Nov. 27, 2006.

MURPHY, RANDALL KENT, writer, educator, consultant; b. Laramie, Wyo., Nov. 8, 1943; s. Robert Joseph and Sally (McConnell) M.; m. Cynthia Laura Hillhouse, Dec. 29, 1978; children: Caroline, Scott, Emily. Student, U. Wyo., 1961—65; MBA, So. Meth. U., 1983. Dir. mktg. Wycoa, Inc., Denver, 1967—70; dir. Comm. Resource Inst., Dallas, 1971—72; account exec. Xerox Learning Sys., Dallas, 1973—74; regional mgr. Systema Corp., Dallas, 1975; pres. Performance Assocs.; pres., dir. Acclivus Corp., Dallas, from 1976; founder, chmn. Acclivus Inst., from 1982. Author: Performance Management, Coaching and Counseling and Performance, 1980, Managing Development and Performance, 1982, Acclivus Performance Planning System, 1983, (with others) BASE For Performance, 1983, Acclivus Coaching, 1984, Acclivus Negotiation, 1985, R3 Service, 1997, BASE for Effective Presentations, 1987, BASE for Strategic Presentations, 1988, The New BASE for Excellence, 1988, Major Account Planning and Strategy, 1989, Strategic Management, 1989, Building on the BASE, 1992, Negotiation Mastery, 1995, R3 Service, 1997, Co-creating R3 Value, 2002, Getting the Meeting, 2004, R3 Interaction, 2005, R3 Negotiation, 2009, R3 Transaction Online, 2010; co-inventor The Randy-Band multi-purpose apparel accessory, 1968. Vice chmn. bd. trustees The Winston Sch., 1994-96, chmn. bd. trustees, 1997-2000; mem. adv. bd. The Women's Ctr. of Dallas, 1995-98. With AUS, 1966. Mem. ASTD, Inst. Mgmt. Scis., Soc. Applied Learning Tech., Assn. Mgmt. Cons., Am. Assn. Higher Edn., World Future Soc., Soc. for Intercultural Edn., Tng. and Rsch., Internat. Fedn. Tng. and Devel. Orgns., Inst. Noetic Scis., Nat. Peace Inst., Amnesty Internat., Acad. Polit. Sci., The Nature Conservancy, Theosophical Soc. Am., So. Meth. U. Alumni Assn., U. Wyo. Alumni Assn, Assn. Humanistic Psychology, Assn. Conflict Resolution. CG Jung Found., NY Hist. Soc., Southern Poverty Law Ctr., Internat. Soc. Performance Improvement, United Nations Assn., Soc. Human Resource Mgmt., Am. Mus. Natural History, Jane Goodall Inst., Human Soc. US, Norman Rockwell Mus., US Holocaust Meml. Mus., Neuroleadership Inst. Home: Dallas, Tex. Died May 17, 2015.

MURPHY, WARREN BURTON, writer, screenwriter; b. Jersey City, Sept. 13, 1933; s. Joseph and Eleanore (Muller) M.; m. Dawn E. Walters, June 25, 1955 (div. 1974); children: Deirdre Lee Abbotts, Megan Patricia Murphy, Warren Brian, Ardath Frances Hering; m. Molly Cochran, Feb. 14, 1984 (div.); 1 child: Devin Miles. Reporter Hudson Dispatch, Union City, N.J., 1950-52, 1956-58, Jersey Jour., Jersey City, 1958-60; editor Kearny (N.J.) Observer, 1960-62; sec. to Mayor Thomas J. Whelan Jersey City, 1962-71; novelist, screenwriter, 1972—2015; commr. N.J. Meadowlands, 1978-81. Founding dir. Am. Crime Writers League. Author of more than 100 books including (novels) Razoni and Jackson series, 1974-76, Digger series, 1977-79, Trace series, 1983-87 (Mystery Writers of Am. Edgar award 1984); (with Richard Ben Sapir) The Destroyer series, 1971-2015, Dead End Street, 1973, One Night Stand, 1973, City in Heat, 1973, Down and Dirty, 1974, Lynch Town, 1974, On the Dead Run, 1975, Leonardo's Law, 1978, Atlantic City, 1979, The Assassin's Handbook, 1982, The Red Moon, (Gold Medal award West Coast Review of Books) 1984, The Ceiling of Hell (Shamus award Pvt. Eye Writers of Am. 1985) 1984, Remo Williams and the Secret of the Sinanju, 1985, Murder in Manhattan, 1986, The Sure Thing, 1988, The Hand of Lazarus, 1988, The Temple Dogs, 1988, The Forever King, 1992, Bloodline, 2015; (with Molly Cochran) Grandmaster, (Mystery Writers of Am. Edgar award 1985) 1984, High Priest, 1987; author screenplay The Eiger Sanction, 1976, (story) Lethal Weapon II, 1989; creator TV series Murphy's Law. Served to sgt. USAF, 1952-56. Recipient Citizenship award Freedoms Found., Valley Forge, Pa., 1955, Pub. Rels. award Nat. League of Cities, 1963. Mem. Private Eye Writers of Am., Mystery Writers of Am., Writers Guild of Am., Mensa. Republican. Methodist. Avocations: chess, math., opera. Died Sept. 4, 2015.

MURRAY, GLADYS MARIE SEYMOUR, medical/surgical and oncological nurse; b. Jackson County, Miss., Aug. 13, 1933; d. James Albert and Rosa Erette (Reeves) Seymour; m. Andrew J. Murray, June 6, 1952; children: Andrew J., James Albert, David P., E. Ann. ADN, Miss. Gulf Coast Jr. Coll., Gulfport, 1983. Cert. for adminstrn. of chemotherapy and mgmt. of vascular access. Staff nurse med. unit Biloxi (Miss.) Regional Med. Ctr.; night charge nurse med.-surg. VA, Biloxi; oncology staff nurse Meml. Hosp. at Gulfport. Mem. ANA, Miss. Nursing Assn., Nat. Oncology Assn., Miss. Oncology Assn. Home: Ocean Springs, Miss. Died Nov. 23, 2006.

MURRAY, JOHN EDWARD, JR., academic administrator, law educator; b. Phila., Dec. 20, 1932; s. John Edward and Mary Catherine (Small) M.; m. Isabelle A. Bogusevich, Apr. 11, 1955 (dec. 2010); children: Bruce, Susan, Timothy, Jacqueline; m. Marjorie Smuts BS, LaSalle U., 1955; JD scholar, Cath. U., 1958; SJD fellow, U. Wis., 1959. Bar: Wis. 1959, Pa. 1986. Assoc. prof. Duquesne U. Sch. Law, Pitts., 1963-64, prof., 1965-67, Villanova U. Sch. Law, 1964-65, U. Pitts. Sch. Law, 1967-84, dean, 1977-84; dean Sch. Law Villanova U., 1984-86; disting. svc. prof. U. Pitts., 1986-88; pres. Duquesne U., Pitts., 1988—2001, chancellor, prof. law, 2001—16. Cons. to law firms; chmn. Pa. Chief Justice's com. on comprehensive jud. and lawyer edn. Author: Murray on Contracts, 1974, 90, Murray, Commercial Transactions, 1975, Murray, Cases & Materials on Contracts, 1969, 76, 83, 91, Purchasing and the Law, 1978, Problems & Materials on Sales, 1982, Murray, Problems & Materials on Secured Transactions, 1987, Sales & Leases: Problems and Materials in National/International Transactions, 1993. Mayor Borough of Pleasant Hills, Pa., 1970-74; chair ComPAC21, Pitts. Intergovenmental Cooperation Authority Mem. Assn. Am. Law Schs. (life, editor Jour. Legal Edn.), mem. Am. Law Inst. Democrat. Roman Catholic. Died Feb. 11, 2015.

MURRAY, SCOTT ALLEN, manufacturing executive; b. Jackson, Mich., Oct. 9, 1946; s. Robert George Jr. and Donna Joan (Hutchinson) M.; m. June Eileen Howard, June 8, 1968; children: Ryan Scott, Steven Robert. BSME, Mich. Tech. U., 1972; MBA, LaGrange Coll., Ga., 1984. Registered profl. engr., Mich., Ga. Product engr. Ford Motor Co., Dearborn, Mich., 1972-74; test engr., design Clark Equipment Co., Benton Harbor, Mich., 1974-79; chief engr. Mastercraft, Tifton, Ga., 1979; plant mgr. Moultrie (Ga.) Mfg., 1980; sr. project engr., engring. mgr. Trackmobile, Inc., La Grange, 1980-85, v.p. engring., 1985-86; pres. Hickory Creek Inc., La Grange, from 1986; chmn. Dunhill Search of La Grange, 1987-89. Pres. Bed-Bud Acquisitions, La Grange, 1987—; sec., treas. Magnolia Aviation, Inc., 1989—; bd. dirs. Aerospec, Inc., Magnolia Aviation, Inc. Bd. dirs. Troup County Airport Authority, La Grange, 1981-87. Served with USN, 1965-69. Mem. Soc. Automotive Engrs., Am. Soc. Metals, ASTM, Am. Assn. Airport Execs. Presbyterian. Home: Madison, Ala. Died Aug. 23, 2007.

MUSETTO, VINCENT ALBERT, JR., retired film critic, writer; b. Morristown, NJ, May 9, 1941; s. Vincent Albert and Jeanne Catherine (Landi) M.; m. Claire Adele Smolensky, May 15, 1965 (div. 1981); 1 child, Carly VanTassell BA in English, Fairleigh Dickinson U., 1964. Copy boy NY Daily Mirror, NYC, 1961; reporter, editor Daily Advance, Dover, NJ, 1962-65; met. editor Star-Ledger, Newark, 1965-73; asst. mng. editor NY Post, NYC, 1973-87, film critic, 1987-90, entertainment editor, 1990—2011, freelance movie critic, 2011—15. Roman Catholic. Avocations: films; ballet. Home: New York, NY. Died June 9, 2015.

MYERSON, BESS, former city official; b. NYC, July 16, 1924; d. Louis and Bella Myerson; m. Allan Wayne, 1946 (div.); 1 child, Barbara Grant; m. Arnold M. Grant, 1962 (div. 1971). BA, Hunter Coll., 1945, LL.D., 1973; D.Pub. Service, Seton Hall U., 1972; L.H.D., Long Island U., 1972; LL.D., Keuka Coll., 1973. Commr. NYC Dept. Consumer Affairs, 1969—74, NYC Dept. Cultural Affairs, 1983—87. Vis. prof. Hunter Coll., 1974; mem. Commn. on Critical Choices, 1975; chmn. Consumer Credit Counseling Svc.; pres. Women United for N.Y.; exec. dir. Fashion Capital of World; piano soloist Carnegie Hall, NYC, 1946; with Sta. WOR-TV, NYC, 1947—51; mistress of ceremonies The Big Payoff, CBS-TV, 1951—59; comml. hostess Philco Playhouse, NBC-TV, 1954—55; TV commentator Miss America Pageant, ABC, 1964—68; co-commentator Tournament of Roses, 1960—68; panelist I've Got a Secret, CBS, 1958—68; news staff CBS Broadcasting Co., 1961—62; hostess Women of Yr., 1974, In the Public Interest, 1975. Author: The Complete Consumer Book, 1979, The I Love N.Y. Diet, 1982. Mem. Pres. Carter's Commn. on Mental Health, Pres. Carter's Commn. on World Hunger, Nat. Alliance to Save Energy; chmn. Hunter Coll. Centennial Fund, NYC, 1965—70; chmn. greater N.Y. Bonds for Israel, 1965—72, hon. chmn., 1972—2014; bd. dirs. Freedom House, PBS, Citizens Union, Anti-Defamation League, Another Mother for Peace, League Sch. for Seriously Disturbed Children, American-Israel Cultural Found., Public Devel. Corp., Com. to Advance Goal Higher Edn. for Disabled in CUNY, Met. Opera. Recipient Outstanding Achievement award, Hunter Coll., 1955, Presdl. Medal of Freedom, The White House, 1970, Clarion award, Women in Comm.; named Miss America, 1945, Woman of the Yr., Anti-Defamation League, 1965. Democrat. Jewish. *To paraphrase the poet Robert Browning, one's reach should exceed one's grasp or what's a life for? That measure of reaching out by each of us without fear or awe of all the unknowns that surround each of us, is the difference between growing or vegetating, emotionally, intellectually, spiritually, and in the blessings that good work done and good friends made can bring to us. If it brings recognition from others, that's one of life's fringe benefits. But with or without recognition, it is the seed from which any personal achievement must spring.* Died Dec. 14, 2014.

NACHMAN, MERTON ROLAND, JR., lawyer; b. Montgomery, Ala., Dec. 21, 1923; s. Merton Roland and Maxine (Mayer) N.; m. Martha Street, June 8, 1968 (div.); children: Nancy Nachman Yardley, Linda Nachman Connelly, Betsy Wild, Amy N. DeRoche, Karen Vann. AB cum laude, Harvard U., 1943, JD, 1948. Bar: Ala. 1949, U.S. Supreme Ct. 1953, U.S. Ct. Appeals (5th and 11th cirs.), U.S. Ct. Claims, U.S. Tax Ct. Asst. atty. gen. State of Ala., 1949-54; ptnr. Knabe & Nachman, Montgomery, 1954-59; adminstrv. asst. to Senator John Sparkman, Ala., 1956; ptnr. Steiner, Crum & Baker, Montgomery, 1959-86, counsel mem., from 2000; from ptnr. to coun. mem. Balch & Bingham, Montgomery, 1986-2000. Chmn. human rights com. Ala. Prison System, 1976-78. With USN, 1943-46. Recipient Merit award Ala. State Bar, 1974;, cert. of appreciation Supreme Ct. of Ala., 1974. Fellow Am. Coll. Trial Lawyers; mem. ABA (com. on fed. judiciary 1982-88, bd. govs. 1978-81), Ala. State Bar (pres. 1973-74), Am. Judicature Soc. (dir. 1976-80, Herbert Lincoln Harley award 1974), Am. Law Inst., Ala. Law Inst., Unity club (Montgomery), Am. Acad. Appellate Lawyers. Episcopalian. Died Nov. 24, 2015.

NAIMARK, GEORGE MODELL, marketing and management consultant; b. NYC, Feb. 5, 1925; s. Myron S. and Mary (Modell) N.; m. Helen Anne Wythes, June 24, 1946; children: Ann, Richard, Jane. BS, Bucknell U., 1947, MS, 1948; PhD, U. Del., 1951. Rsch. biochemist Brush Devel. Co., Cleve., 1951; dir. quality control Strong, Cobb & Co., Inc., Cleve., 1951-54; dir. sci. svcs. White Labs., Inc., Kenilworth, NJ, 1954-60; v.p. Burdick Assocs., Inc., NYC, 1960-66; pres. Rajah Press, Summit, NJ, from 1963, Naimark and Barba, Inc., Florham Park, NJ, from 1966, Naimark & Assocs., Inc., Florham Park, NJ, from 1994; dir. Alteon, Inc., 2000—06. Author: A Patent Manual for Scientists and Engineers, 1961, Communications on Communication, 1971, 3d edit., 1987, A Man Called Skeeter, 1996, How To Be a Truly Rotten Boss, 2006, Cleaning Out My Attic, 2006, Adamant Eve Alias Myrtle Reed, 2006, How to be a Truly Rotten Driver, 2007, The Leadership Disaster, 2014; patentee in field; contbr. articles in profl. jours. With USNR, 1944-46. Fellow AAAS, Am. Inst. Chemists; mem. Am. Chem. Soc., N.Y. Acad. Scis., Am. Mktg. Assn. Deceased.

NAMAN, JAY I., management consultant; b. Waco, Tex., Mar. 28, 1925; s. Wilford W. and Isidora (Levy) N.; m. Virginia Clardy, May 17, 1953; 1 child, William Wilford. BA, Baylor U., 1947, postgrad., 1949, U. Tex., 1948. Cert. meeting profl. Rancher, Valley Mills, Tex., 1949-59; pres. Tex. Farmers Union, Waco, 1960-80, Naman Assocs. Meeting Cons., Waco, from 1980. Mem. exec. bd. Nat. Farmers Union, Denver, 1965-80; del. Internat. Fedn. Agrl. Producers, Rome, 1967, Can., 1968, Austria, 1973, Japan, 1975. Pres. H.O.T. Fair, Waco, 1988; mem. Tex. Gov.'s Older Workers Task Force, 1983-86; bd. dirs. Heart of Tex. Fair, 1986-89; del. Dem. Nat. Conv., N.Y.C., 1980. Lt. (j.g.) USN, 1944-46, PTO. Recipient Outstanding Contbn. to Agr. award Nat. Farmers Union, 1981. Mem. Meeting Planners Internat. Jewish. Avocations: farming, ranching, flying. Home: Waco, Tex. Died Feb. 10, 2007.

NAMBU, YOICHIRO, physics professor; b. Toyko, Jan. 18, 1921; arrived in U.S., 1952; m. Chieko Hida Nambu, Nov. 3, 1945; 1 child, Jun-ichi. BS, U. Tokyo, 1942, DSc, 1952; DSc (hon.), Northwestern U., Evanston, Ill., 1987; degree (hon.), Osaka U., 1996. Research asst. U. Tokyo, 1945—49; prof. physics Osaka City U., Japan, 1950—56; mem. Inst. Advanced Study, Princeton, 1952—54; research assoc. U. Chgo., 1954—56, mem. faculty, 1956—2015, prof. physics, 1958, Henry Pratt Judson disting. svc. prof., 1978—91, Henry Pratt Judson disting. svc. prof. emeritus, 1991—2015, chmn. physics, 1974—77. Contbr. articles to profl. jours. Recipient J. Robert Oppenheimer prize, 1976, Order of Culture, Japan Govt., 1978, US Nat. Medal Sci., 1982, Max Planck medal, German Physical Soc., 1985, Dirac medal, Internat. Centre for Theoretical Physics, 1986, Wolf prize in physics, Wolf Found., Israel, 1994, Gian Carlo Wick Commemorative medal, World Fedn. Scientists, 1995, Bogoliubov prize, Joint Inst. for Nuclear Rsch., 2003, Benjamin Franklin medal in Physics, Franklin Inst., 2005, I Ya. Pomeranchuk prize, Inst. Theoretical and Exptl. Physics, Moscow, 2007; co-recipient Nobel prize in physics, 2008; named one of The World's Most Influential People

TIME mag., 2009. Mem.: NAS, Georgian Acad. Sciences (fgn. fellow 1996), Am. Phys. Soc. (Sakurai prize 1994, Dannie Heineman prize for Math. Physics 1970), Am. Acad. Arts and Scis., Japan Acad. (hon.). Died July 5, 2015.

NAPHTALI, ASHIRAH S., lawyer; b. Kingston, Jamaica, Apr. 6, 1950; came to U.S., 1967; d. Frederick Solomon Cruise and Theresa T. (Spence) Whitter; m. Douglas A. Smith Byroo, June 1, 1978 (div. June 1982); 1 child, Gilah Teshaye Smith Byroo. Cert. Med. Asst., N.Y. Sch. of Dental and Med., Assts., Kew Gardens, NY, 1975; BA, NYU, 1979; M in Bus. Fin., Hofstra U., 1984, JD, 1983. Real estate broker; notary pub. Law asst. Colin A. Moore, Jamaica, N.Y., summer 1983, Michael Laufer, NYC, 1983-85, Reisler and Silverstein, NYC, 1986-87, Barbara Emmanuel and Helen Gregory, Jamaica, 1987-89, Alarid & Naphtali, NYC, 1989-91; pvt. practice Queens, N.Y., from 1992. Cons. NACA, Inc., Jamaica, 1984-89. Sgt. USAF, 1969-74, USAR, 1980-83. Mem. Queens Bar Assn., Nat. Bar Assn., Black Entertainment Sports Lawyers Assn., N.Y. Trial Lawyers Assn., N.Y. State Bar Assn., Kiwanis (pres. Cambria Heights, N.Y. chpt. 1994-95). Democrat. Jewish. Avocations: singing, jogging, tennis. E-mail: aol.naphtali-.com. Home: Laurelton, NY. Died Aug. 3, 2007.

NAPOLEON, MARTY, musician; b. Bklyn., June 2, 1921; s. Matthew Joseph and Jennie (Giampocaro) N.; m. Marie Giordano, May 15, 1921; children: Jeanine Napoleon Goldman, Marty Philip Jr. Educated pub. schs., Bklyn. Jazz pianist (1941-2015) with numerous bands including Chico Marx, Gene Krupa, Charles Barnet, Benny Goodman, Louis Armstrong's All-Stars, 1941-2015, with Bob Crosby's Bob Cats, Hawaii, Red Norvo, Europe, (films) The Glenn Miller Story, All That Jazz, Raging Bull, Tootsie, on record albums with Charles Barnet, Louis Armstrong, Lionel Hampton and several solo albums; appeared on TV variety shows with Dean Martin, Johnny Carson, Dick Cavett, Danny Kaye, Jackie Gleason, (TV series) Soap, Guiding Light; performed at Odessa (Tex.) Jazz Festival, Berne, Switzerland Jazz Festival; Carnegie Hall (with Frank Sinatra show), The White House (with Lionel Hampton Sextet in command performance), JVC Jazz Festival, Nice, France, North Sea Jazz Festival, The Hague, The Netherlands, Downtown Jazz Festival, Toronto, Ont., Can., Jazz Party Festival, Mpls. Mem. ASCAP. Roman Catholic. Avocations: reading, bicycling, writing music, photography, travel. Home: Brooklyn, NY. Died Apr. 27, 2015.

NARAHASHI, TOSHIO, pharmacology educator; b. Fukuoka, Japan, Jan. 30, 1927; arrived in U.S., 1961; s. Asahachi and Itoko (Yamasaki) Ishii; m. Kyoko Narahashi, Apr. 21, 1956; children: Keiko, Taro. BS, U. Tokyo, 1948, PhD, 1960. Instr. U. Tokyo, 1951-65; research assoc. U. Chgo., 1961, asst. prof., 1962, Duke U., Durham, NC, 1962-63, 65-67, assoc. prof., 1967-69, prof., 1969-77, head pharmacology div., 1970-73, vice chmn. dept. physiology and pharmacology, 1973-75; prof., chmn. dept. pharmacology Northwestern U. Med. Sch., Chgo., 1977-94, Alfred Newton Richards prof., 1982—2005; John Evans prof. Northwestern U., Evanston, Ill., from 1986. Mem. pharmacology study sect. NIH, 1976-80; rsch. rev. com. Chgo. Heart Assn., 1977-82, vice chmn. rsch. coun., 1986-87, chmn., 1988-90; mem. Nat. Environ. Health Scis. Coun., 1982-86; rev. com. Nat. Inst. Environ. Health Scis., 1991-95. Editor: Cellular Pharmacology of Insecticides and Pheromones, 1979, Cellular and Molecular Neurotoxicology, 1984, Insecticide Action: From Molecule to Organism, 1989, Ion Channels, 1988—; specific field editor Jour. Pharmacology and Exptl. Therapeutics, 1972-97; assoc. editor Neurotoxicology, 1994—; contbr. articles to profl. jours. Recipient Javits Neurosci. Investigator award, NIH, 1986. Fellow AAAS, Acad. Toxicol. Scis.; mem. Am. Soc. for Pharmacology and Exptl. Therapeutics (Otto Krayer award 2000), Am. Physiol. Soc., Soc. for Neurosci., Biophys. Soc. (Cole award 1981), Soc. Toxicology (DuBois award 1988, Merit award 1991, Disting. Investigator Lifetime Achievement award 2001, Disting. Lifetime Toxicology Scholar award 2008), Agrochem. Divsn. Am. Chem. Soc. (Burdick L. Jackson Internat. award 1989). Home: Chicago, Ill. Died Apr. 21, 2013.

NASH, ALICIA LARDÉ, application developer, physicist; b. San Salvador, Jan. 1, 1933; came to U.S., 1944; d. Carlos Roberto and Alicia (Lopez-Harrison) Larde; m. John Forbes Nash, Jr., Feb. 16, 1957; children: John Charles Martin Nash. BS in Physics, MIT, 1955, postgrad., 1959. Physicist Nuclear Devel. Corp. of Am., White Plains, NY, 1956-57, Tech. Ops., Burlington, Mass., 1957-58; rsch. assoc. MIT Computation Ctr., Cambridge, Mass., 1958-59; physicist, aerospace engr. R.C.A. Astro Divsn., Hightstown, NJ, 1960-66; programmer, analyst Mgmt. Data Processing, NYC, 1972-74, Con Edison, NYC, 1974-80, Blue Cross Blue Shield of N.Y., NYC, 1980-82; systems/analyst programmer specialist N.J. Transit, Newark, from 1983. Mem. AAUW, MIT Club of Princeton (past pres., bd. dirs.), Soc. of Women Engring. Achievements include being the subject for the role of Alicia Nash in the movie "A Beautiful Mind". Home: Princeton Junction, NJ. Died May 23, 2015.

NASH, JOHN FORBES, JR., mathematician, researcher; b. Bluefield, W.Va., June 13, 1928; s. John Nash, Sr. and Margaret; m. Alicia Larde (dec. May 23, 2015); children: John David Stier, John Charles. BS in Math., MS in Math., Carnegie Mellon U., Pitts., 1948; PhD, Princeton U., 1950; DSc (hon.), Carnegie Mellon U., 1999, W.Va. U., 2006, U. Medicine Dentistry NJ, 2008; PhD (hon.), U. Athens, 2000, U. Naples, 2003, U. Charleston, 2003, U. Antwerp, 2007. Rsch. asst., instr. Princeton U., NJ, 1950—51, vis. mem. Inst. Advanced Study, 1956—57, 1961—64, sr. rsch. mathematician, from 1993; Moore instr. MIT, 1951—53, asst. prof., 1953—57, assoc. prof., 1957—59; rschr. Brandeis U., Boston, 1965—67. Cons. RAND Corp., Santa Monica, Calif., 1950, 1952, 1954. Recipient John Von Neumann Theory prize, Inst. Ops. Rsch. & Mgmt. Scis., 1978, Nobel Prize in Economics, The Nobel Found., 1994, Bus. Week award, Erasmus U., Rotterdam, 1998, Leroy P. Steele prize in math., American Math. Soc., 1999, Pres.'s award, Nat. Alliance Mentally Ill, 1999, Herbert Simon award, New Eng. Complex Sys. Inst., 2006, Abel prize, Norwegian Acad. of Sci. and Letters, 2015; Sloan fellow, NSF fellow, Westinghouse scholar. Fellow: Am. Acad. Arts and Scis., Econometric Soc.; mem.: NAS. Home: Princeton Junction, NJ. Died May 23, 2015.

NATHAN, DEBRA, purchasing professional, jazz singer; b. Bklyn., Nov. 28, 1954; d. Matthew and Theda (Kanover) N. Student, Nassau Community Coll., 1973-74, CCNY, Baruch U., 1988. Jazz singer USO, 1974-85; prop house mgr. State Supply, Inc., NYC, 1985-86; mgr. set shop Koenig-Eastern Corp., NYC, 1986-88, dir. purchasing, 1988-89; head purchasing, sales coord. A.I. Friedman, NYC, from 1989. Avocations: singing, piano, billiards, reading. Home: New York, NY. Died Jan. 1, 2007.

NAVON, YITZHAK, deputy prime minister, minister of education and culture, former president of Israel; b. Jerusalem, Apr. 9, 1921; s. Yosef and Miriam Ben-Atar Navon; m. Ofira Reznikov-Erez Navon, 1993; children: Naama, Erez; m. Miri Shafir Navon. Student, Hebrew U., Jerusalem. Formerly tchr. Jerusalem elem. and secondary schs.; dir. Arabic Dept. Hagana, Jerusalem, 1946—49; 2nd sec. Israeli embassy, Argentina and Uruguay, 1949—50; polit. sec. to fgn. minister Israel, 1951—52; head bur. to prime minister, 1952—53; dir. dept. culture, ministry edn. and culture, 1963—65; mem. Knesset, 1965—78; former speaker and chmn. def. and fgn. affairs com.; pres. of Israel, 1978—83; dep. prime minister, minister edn. and culture, 1984—90. Chmn. World Zionist Coun., 1973—78, Wolf Found. Active Mapai Party, 1951—65, Rafi, 1965—68, Israel Labour Party, from 1968. Mem.: Labour Party. Avocations: theater, music. Died Nov. 6, 2015.

NEASE, ALLAN BRUCE, research chemist; b. Wichita, Kans., Dec. 2, 1954; s. Lewis Edward and Margarette (Douglass) N. BS in Chemistry, Wichita State U., 1975; PhD, U. Mo., 1979. Chemist U.S. EPA, Kansas City, Kans., 1976-77; postdoctoral fellow U. S.C., Columbia, 1979-81; sr. rsch. chemist Monsanto Rsch. Corp., Miamisburg, Ohio, 1981-88; rsch. specialist EG&G-Mound Applied Techs., Miamisburg, Ohio, from 1988. Mem. Am. Chem. Soc. (chmn. profl. practices 1983), Soc. Applied Spectroscopy (sect. chmn. 1984-85). Home: Miamisburg, Ohio. Died Dec. 6, 2006.

NEBOLSKY, PEGGY ELLEN, real estate agent; b. Cin., June 28, 1947; d. Mendel Louis and Ida Sarah (Magilsky) Wolf; m. Robert Bruce Nebolsky, Dec. 23, 1967; children: Louis Charles, Joseph, Sheila Irene. Student, Honduras Sch., Cin., 1989, So. Ohio Coll., 1984-86. Acct. Tillie Nebolsky's Cafeteria, Cin., 1968-78; realtor Barnhorn Realtors, Cin., 1984-85, West Shell, Cin., 1985-88, Coldwell Banker, Cin., 1988-91, Woodhouse & Assocs., Cin., from 1992; cashier, trainer, bookkeeper Thriftway, Cin., from 1991. Instr. vols. Everybody Counts, Winton Woods High Sch., 1981—; mem. health and safety com., ways and means coms., rm. mother Finneytown Elem. Sch. PTA, Cin., 1984-87; various offices Finneytown Music Parents, Finneytown High Sch., 1987—; mem. No. Hills Sisterhood, Cin., 1989-92. Avocations: reading, racquetball, family. Home: Cincinnati, Ohio. Died Oct. 23, 2007.

NEEDHAM, PAUL WESLEY, life insurance agent; b. Burleson, Tex., Dec. 12, 1921; s. Raymond Watt and Callie Mae (Bracken) N.; m. Ollie Dale Bransom, June 30, 1951; children: Raymond Wesley, Linda Diane. BA, Tex. Christian, 1950; MS in Fin. Svcs., Am. Coll., 1979. CLU; ChFC. Life underwriter, asst. mgr. Amicable Life Ins. Co., Ft. Worth, 1946-51, dir. tng. and edn. Waco, Tex., 1951-57, dist. mgr. Dallas, 1957-86; gen. agt. Am. Gen. Life Ins. Co. (formerly Am. Amicable Life Ins. Co.), Dallas, from 1986. With USAF, 1941-42. Mem. Am. Soc. CLU and ChFC (regional dir. 1983-85, regional v.p. 1985-86), Nat. Assn. Life Underwriters (Nat. Quality award), Dallas Assn. Life Underwriters, Tex. Assn. Life Underwriters, Dallas Estate Planning Coun., CLU and ChFC (pres. Waco chpt. 1957-58, Dallas chpt. 1975-76), CLU (pres. 1957-58, 75-76). Methodist. Avocations: water sports, fishing. Home: Dallas, Tex. Died Nov. 25, 2006.

NEGLEY, WILLIAM, paint company executive; b. San Antonio, Mar. 28, 1914; s. Richard Van Wyck and Laura (Burleson) N.; m. Carolyn Wells Brown, Nov. 25, 1942 (div. 1958); children: Richard Burleson, James Lutcher, Laura Wells; m. Laura Carrigan, Nov. 25, 1977. BA, U. Tex., 1935. BAR: Tex. 1937. Lawyer Standard Oil Co., various locations, 1937-42; founder, pres. Negley Bag Co., Monroe, La., 1946-55, Paisano Homes, San Antonio, 1959-72; chief exec. officer, chmn. bd. Negley Paint Co., San Antonio, from 1977. Bd. dirs. Pecan Valley Nut Co., Stephenville, Tex. Contbr. articles to mags. Served to 1st lt. with cav. U.S. Army, 1944-46. Mem. Tex. Bar Assn. Clubs: San Antonio Country, Argyle (San Antonio). Lodges: Order of St. Hubertus. Republican. Episcopalian. Avocations: tennis, golf, fishing, hunting. Home: San Antonio, Tex. Died Nov. 7, 2006.

NELSON, BRUCE RICHARD, engineering professional; b. Mpls., July 17, 1953; s. Elof Elander and Lois Julia (Archbold) N.; m. Kathy Marie Harkness, June 12, 1976; children: Stephanie, Karalee. AA, Bismarck State Coll., 1973, postgrad., 1983-85, 96; BSCE, N.D. State U., 1975; postgrad., Colo. State U., 1977-78. Registered profl. engr., Colo., N.D., S.D., Wyoming, Mont. Constrn. engr. U.S. Bur. Reclamation, Pierre, S.D., 1975-76, design and estimate engr. Grand Junction, Colo., 1977, planning engr., 1977-78; div. gas engr. Montana-Dakota Utilities Co., Jamestown, N.D., 1978-81, staff engr. Bismarck, 1981-85, sr. staff engr., 1985-89, gas mktg. mgr., 1989-96, sr. staff engr., 1996, gas distgn. mgr., from 1997. Adviser to project appliance group Gas Rsch. Inst., 1989-96. Grad. mem. Bismarck-Mandan Leadership Program, Bismarck, 1991; neighbor coord. Ch. of Corpus Christi, Bismarck, 1981-84; div. leader United Way, Bismarck, 1986, Boy Scouts of Am., Bismarck, 1983; credit com. Genie-Watt Credit Union, Bismarck, 1985-94. Mem. NSPE (chmn. bd. govs. N.D.), N.D. Soc. Profl. Engrs. (Young Engr. of Yr. 1984, bd. dirs. 1985—, chpt. pres. 1985-86, other offices, nominated State Bd. Reg. Profl. Engrs. & Land Surveyors 1998), Mo. Valley Chpt. Credit Unions (chpt. pres. 1990), Midwest Gas Assn., Toastmasters Internat. (v.p. membership 1997, Competent Toastmaster 1996). Republican. Roman Catholic. Avocations: tennis, swimming, running. Home: Bismarck, ND. Died June 16, 2007.

NELSON, CALVIN RICHARD, osteopathic physician; b. Chgo., Jan. 18, 1927; s. Carl Raymond and Ruth (Seeley) N.; m. Lois Augusta Buck, Apr. 17, 1948 (div. 1977); children: Karen, Mark, Lori; m. Susan Gail Kruger, Sept. 10, 1977; children: Jeffrey, Elizabeth. Student, Aurora U., Ill., 1947, St. Edwards U., Austin, Tex., 1948, U. Tex., 1949-51; DO, Coll. Osteopathic Medicine, Chgo., 1955. Intern Detroit Osteopathic Hosp.; pvt. practice San Antonio, from 1955. With USN, 1945-46, PTO. Mem. Tex. Philatelic Assn. (pres. 1970-72), San Antonio Philatelic Assn. (pres. 1964-66), Alamo Heights Lions Club (pres. 1968, 72), N.W. San Antonio Lions Club (pres. 1984), Dist. Lions Club (dep. dist. gov. 1976, 82), San Antonio Antiques Club (pres. 1989, 90). Republican. Lutheran. Avocations: stamp collecting/philately, antiques, worlds fair collector. Died Mar. 12, 2007.

NELSON, CHARLES A., biochemist; b. Buffalo, June 26, 1936; s. Alvin L. and Josephine L. (Field) N.; m. Rita J. Whitney, Sept. 5, 1964 (dec. Aug. 5, 1985); children: Steven E., Melinda J. BA, Cornell Coll., 1957; MS, U. Iowa, 1960, PhD, 1962. Postdoct. fellow Duke U., Durham, N.C., 1961-64; from asst. to assoc. prof. Sch. Med. Sci. U. Ark., Little Rock, from 1964. Mem. Am. Soc. Molecular Biology and Biochemistry. Home: Little Rock, Ark. Died Dec. 3, 2006.

NELSON, DAVID LEONARD, business executive; b. Omaha, May 8, 1930; s. Leonard A. and Cecelia (Steinert) N.; m. Jacqueline J. Zerbe, Dec. 26, 1952; 1 child, Nancy Jo. BS, Iowa State U., 1952. Mktg. adminstr. Ingersoll Rand, Chgo., 1954-56; with Accuray Corp., Columbus, Ohio, 1956-87, exec. v.p., gen. mgr., 1967, pres., 1967-87, chief exec. officer, 1970-87; pres. process automation bus. unit Combustion Engring., Inc., Columbus, 1987-90; pres. bus. area process automation Asea Brown Boveri, Stamford, Conn., 1990-91, v.p. customer satisfaction Ams. region, 1991-93, v.p. customer support Ams. region, 1994-95; chmn. bd. dirs. Herman Miller Inc., Zeeland, Mich., 1995-2000, counsel, 2000—04. Served to capt. USMCR, 1952-54. Mem. IEEE, Instrument Soc. Am., Newcomen Soc. N.Am., Tau Beta Pi, Phi Kappa Phi, Phi Eta Sigma, Delta Upsilon. Achievements include patents in field. Home: Alexandria, Va. Died Apr. 26, 2015.

NELSON, DAVID SCOTT, lawyer; b. Cedar Rapids, Iowa, Mar. 14, 1953; s. Robert Charles and Bernice Mae (Svoboda) N. BA, Drake U., 1975; JD, U. San Diego, 1978. Bar: Iowa 1978. Ptnr. Nelson Fassler Nelson, Cedar Rapids, from 1978. Mem. ABA, Iowa State Bar Assn., Elks, Masons, El Kahir Shrine. Episcopalian. Died June 9, 2007.

NELSON, JAMES CARMER, JR., writer, editor, advertising executive; b. Denver, Nov. 10, 1921; s. James Carmer and Helen (McClelland) N.; m. Mary-Armour Ransom, Sept. 9, 1950; children: James Carmer III, Marie-Louise Nelson Graves, Jeffrey Armour, Sophia McClelland (dec.), Rebecca McClelland Nelson Sylla. AB, Yale, 1943. Mktg. editor Bus. Week mag., NYC, 1946-48, illustration editor, 1948-52; freelance author Sonoma, Calif., 1952-57; copy chief Hoefer, Dieterich & Brown, Inc., San Francisco, 1957-59, v.p., creative dir., 1959-66, exec. v.p., 1966-76, pres., 1976-79, vice chmn., 1979—80; ptnr. John H. Hoefer & Assocs., 1972—82; vice chmn. Chiat/Day/Hoefer, 1980; pvt. advt. cons., 1980—87. Bd. dir. McKinney, Inc., Phila.; instr. Golden Gate Coll., San Francisco, 1958-59, Nat. Advt. Rev. Bd., 1971-75. Author: The Trouble With Gumballs, 1957, Great Cheap Wines: A Poorperson's Guide, 1977, Great Wines Under $5, 1983, Killing Dave Henderson, etc., 2007, On the Volcano, 2011; contbr. articles and fiction to popular mags. Mem. Harold Brunn Soc. Med. Rsch., Mt. Zion Hosp., San Francisco; bd. assocs. Linus Pauling Inst. Sci. and Medicine, Palo Alto, Calif.; mem. Colony Found., New Haven; trustee Coro Found., 1965-75, Marin Art Complex; bd. mgrs. Marin County YMCA. Served with USNR, 1942-46. Mem. ASCAP. Clubs: Villa Taverna (San Francisco). Home: San Rafael, Calif. Died Jan. 13, 2015.

NELSON, WESLEY JOSEPH, librarian; b. Beloit, Wis., Aug. 13, 1935; s. Joseph Oliver and Grace Helen (Wheeler) N.; m. Jeannette Clara Conrad, Aug. 29, 1959 (div. June 1966); children: Deborah Ruth, Eugene Joseph; m. Annita Marie Palmer, Nov. 28, 1968; 1 child, Michael Lee. BA, Beloit Coll., 1957; ThM, So. Meth. U., 1962; MLS, George Peabody Coll. Tchrs., Nashville, 1967. Pastor United Meth. Ch., Johnson Creek, Wis., 1962-63, Monona, Wis., 1963-66; catalog librn. Joint Univ. Librs., Nashville, 1966-70; assoc. librn. tech. svcs. Stanley Libr. Ferrum (Va.) Coll., from 1970. Bd. dirs. Franklin County United Way, Franklin County Red Cross; 1st lt. Ferrum Rescue Squad, 1987—;

sec., treas. Ferrum Vol. Fire Dept., 1977—. Recipient Cooper Cmty. Svc. award Franklin County C. of C., 1989. Mem. Lions (pres., sec., treas. 1970—, Melvin Jones award 1994). Avocations: sports, woodworking. Home: Ferrum, Va. Died Jan. 21, 2007.

NEU, ARTHUR ALAN, retired state official; b. Carroll, Iowa, Feb. 9, 1933; s. Arthur Nicholas Neu and Martha Margaret Frandsen; m. Mary Naomi Bedwell, Apr. 4, 1964; children: Arthur Eric, Mary Martha, Towle Harold. BSBA, Northwestern U., 1955, JD, 1958; LLM in Taxation, Georgetown U., 1962. Mem. Iowa State Senate, 1967-72; lt. gov. State of Iowa, 1972-79, bd. regents, 1979-85. Served in US Army JAG Corps, 1958—62. Mem. ABA, Ill. State Bar Assn. Republican. Home: Carroll, Iowa. Died Jan. 2, 2015.

NEWCOMB, WALLACE DAMON, lawyer; b. Alameda, Calif., Apr. 11, 1910; s. Guy Houghton and Ruth Burr (Damon) Newcomb; m. Priscilla Cary Newcomb, Feb. 21, 1941; children: Wallace Damon, Peter Cary. BS in Chemistry, Harvard U., 1932; LLB, U. Pa., 1935. Bar: Pa. 1936, US Dist. Ct. (ea. dist.) Pa. 1936, US Ct. Appeals (3d cir.) 1936, US Dist. Ct. (ea. dist.) SC, US Ct. Customs and Patent Appeals 1952, US Ct. Claims 1966, US Supreme Ct. 1939, US Ct. Appeals (Fed. cir.) 1982. Assoc. Paul & Paul, Phila., 1936—37, ptnr., 1937—80, sr. ptnr., from 1980. Bd. dirs. ARC, Phila. Served as lt. USN, 1942—45. Decorated Air medal. Mem.: ABA, Phila. Bar Assn. Rep., Phila. Patent Law Assn., Am. Patent Law Assn., Am. Chem. Soc., Union League Phila. Presbyterian. Home: Bryn Mawr, Pa. Died Dec. 18, 2006.

NEWELL, ROBERT MELVIN, lawyer; b. Anacortes, Wash., Oct. 29, 1918; s. Seymour Melvin and Hildur (Apenese) N.; m. Gertrude A. Brawner, Oct. 31, 1942 (div. Oct. 1954); children: Robert M. Jr., Christine N. Jones, William C.; m. Mary Will, Apr. 2, 1955. AB, Stanford U., 1941, JD, 1946. Bar: Calif., 1946, U.S. Dist. Ct. (cen. dist.) Calif., U.S. Ct. Appeals (9th cir.), U.S. Supreme Ct. Ptnr. Newell & Chester, Los Angeles, 1947-88. Served to lt. USN, 1942-46, PTO. Mem. ABA, Calif. Bar Assn., Los Angeles County Bar Assn. Democrat. Home: San Marino, Calif. Died Oct. 8, 2007.

NEWMAN, JAY, philosopher, philosophy educator; b. Bklyn., Feb. 28, 1948; s. Louis and Kate (Rothbaum) Newman. BA, Bklyn. Coll., 1968; MA, Brown U., 1969; PhD, York U., Toronto, 1971. Lectr. to assoc. prof. U. Guelph, Ont., Canada, 1971—82; prof. philosophy, from 1982; hon. rsch. fellow U. Birmingham, England, 1981; vis. rsch. fellow Calgary Inst. Humanities U. Calgary, 1988—89. Author: Foundations of Religious Tolerance, 1982, The Mental Philosophy of John Henry Newman, 1986, Fanatics and Hypocrites, 1986, The Journalist in Plato's Cave, 1989, Competition in Religious Life, 1989; contbr. articles to profl. jours. Mem.: Phi Beta Kappa, Am. Cath. Philos. Assn., Can. Theol. Soc., Can. Philos. Assn. Home: Guelph, Canada. Died June 17, 2007.

NICHOLAS, WILLADENE LOUISE, artist; b. Streator, Ill., Mar. 21, 1910; d. Almyron Clarence and Etta Helen (Dunbar) Kelly; m. Ray Thomas Nicholas, Dec. 25, 1932 (dec. 1992); children: Sally Jo, Gayle Dene, Ray Thomas Jr. Student, Monmouth Coll., 1926-27, U. Ill., 1928-29. Art tchr. in pvt. practice, Grayslake, Ill., 1945-60; tchr. adult art Grayslake H.S., 1960's. Author (poetry book) Angel Children, 1994, 3d edit. 1999, (non-fiction) Leo & His Rainbow Brush, 1995, Stories of a Railroad Child, 1995, (children's fiction) Minnie the Sunflower, 1995; creator spl. series of wren birdhouses. Charter mem. United Protestant Ch. Grayslake. Named Top Homemaker Grayslake, Grayslake Times, 1962; recipient Blue Ribbon awards State Garden Clubs Ill. Inc., 1996. Mem. Soc. Mayflower Descendants, Grayslake Woman's Club (publicity dir. 1995-97), Grayslake Hist. Soc., Old Plank Rd. Questers, Grayslake Greenery Garden Club (founder, bd. dirs.). Republican. Avocations: experimental research in horticulture, pure translucent watercolorist, ancient chinese art. Home: Ingleside, Ill. Died Aug. 3, 2007.

NICHOLS, HOWARD MELVIN, lawyer; b. Glasgow, Mont., Apr. 25, 1951; s. James Donald and Gertrude Sarah (Rongstad) N.; m. Leslie Ann Downey, July 20, 1974; children: Dylan, Kord. BA in History and Polit. Sci., U. Mont., 1974; JD, Gonzaga U., 1978. Bar: Wash. 1978, U.S. Dist. Ct. (ea. dist.) Wash. 1979, U.S. Dist. Ct. (we. dist.) Wash. 1985. Dep. pros. atty. Spokane County, Wash., 1977-79; assoc. Sharpe, Ganz & Henderson, Spokane, 1979-81, Law Office James J. Workland, Spokane, 1981-84; ptnr. Henderson & Nichols P.S., Spokane, from 1984. Judge pro-tem Spokane County Dist. Ct., 1984—. Bd. dirs. Friends Spokane Airport, 1984—. Mem. ABA, Wash. State Bar Assn. (spl. dist. counsel 1984—), Spokane County Bar Assn., Wash. State Trial Lawyers Assn., Wash. State Assn. Def. Counsel, Legal Services to Armed Com., Def. Research Inst. Clubs: Spokane. Democrat. Lutheran. Avocations: running, golf. Home: Spokane, Wash. Died July 22, 2007.

NICHOLS, MIKE, stage and film director; b. Berlin, Nov. 6, 1931; s. Nicholaievitch and Brigitte (Landauer) Peschowsky; m. Patricia Scott, 1957 (div.); m. Margot Callas, 1974 (div.); 1 child, Daisy; m. Annabel Davis-Goff (div.); children: Max, Jenny; m. Diane Sawyer, Apr. 29, 1988. Student, U. Chgo., 1950-53; student acting, Lee Strasberg. Co-founder, tchr. New Actors Workshop, NYC; contbg. blogger Huffington Post. Ptnr. with Elaine May in comedy act; first appeared at Playwrights Theatre Club, Compass Theatre, Chgo.; NY debut An Evening with Mike Nichols and Elaine May, 1960; acted in A Matter of Position, Phila., 1962; dir.: (plays) Barefoot in the Park, 1963 (Tony award for Best Dir.), The Knack, 1964, Luv, 1964 (Tony award for Best Dir.), The Odd Couple, 1965 (Tony award for Best Director), The Apple Tree, 1966, The Little Foxes, 1967, Plaza Suite, 1968 (Tony award for Best Dir.), The Prisoner of 2d Avenue, 1971 (Tony award for Best Dir.), Uncle Vanya (co-adapted), 1973, Streamers, 1976, Comedians, 1976, The Gin Game, 1977, (LA Drama Critics award), Drink Before Dinner, 1978, Lunch Hour, 1980, Fools, 1981, The Real Thing, 1984 (Tony award 1984), Hurlyburly, 1984, Social Security, 1984, Elliot Loves, 1990, Death and the Maiden, 1992, The Play What I Wrote, 2003, Whoopi, 2004, Spamalot, 2005 (Outer Critic Cir., Outstanding Direction of a Musical, 2005, Julia Hansen award for Excellence in Directing, Drama League, 2005, Tony award for Best Direction of a Musical, 2005, Julia Hansen Award Excellence in Directing, The Drama League, 2005), The Country Girl, 2008, Death of a Salesman, 2012 (Drama Desk award for Outstanding Dir. of A Play, 2012, Tony award for Best Dir.), Betrayal, 2013; (films) Who's Afraid of Virginia Woolf?, 1966, The Graduate, 1967 (Academy award for Best Director, 1968), Catch-22, 1970, Carnal Knowledge, 1971, The Day of the Dolphin, 1973, The Fortune, 1975, Heartburn, 1986, Biloxi Blues, 1987, Working Girl, 1988, Wolf, 1994; dir., prodr.: Silkwood, 1983, Postcards From the Edge, 1990, Regarding Henry, 1991, The Birdcage, 1996, Primary Colors, 1998, What Planet Are You From?, 2000, Closer, 2004, Charlie Wilson's War, 2007; prodr. All the Pretty Horses, 2000; prodr.: (musical) Annie, 1977; dir., exec. prodr. (TV films) Wit, 2001; (mini-series) Angels in America, 2003 (Emmy award Outstanding Directing for a Miniseries, Movie or Dramatic Special, 2004); performed at NY musical Pres. Johnson's Inaugural Gala, 1965. Recipient Nat. Medal Arts, The White House, 2001, Kennedy Ctr. Honors, John F. Kennedy Ctr. for the Performing Arts, 2003, Lifetime Achievement award, American Film Inst., 2009, NY Drama Critics' Cir. award for Contribution to Theater, NY Drama Critics' Cir., 2012. Jewish. Died Nov. 19, 2014.

NICHOLSON, NANCY VIOLA, retired English and American literature educator; b. Lachine, Mich., May 28, 1923; d. John William and Edna Ethel (Mills) Snider; m. Frederick Charles Nicholson, May 24, 1967 (div. Oct. 1968). BA, U. Mich., 1946, MA, 1947, PhD, 1962. English instr. Iowa State Tchrs. Coll., Cedar Falls, 1947-48; instr. Alpena (Mich.) C.C., 1953-54; asst. prof. N.Y. State U., Cortland, 1955-56; instr., supr. Columbia Tchrs. Coll., Kabul, Afghanistan, 1956-57; instr. Tufts U., Medford, Mass., 1957-60; assoc. prof. Clarion (Pa.) State Coll., 1963-66, Wis. State U., LaCrosse, 1966-67; lectr. Ea. Mich. U., Ypsilanti, 1967-69; prof. So. U., Baton Rouge, 1969-71; pvt. rsch. on folklore Lachine, Mich., 1971-74; lectr. U. Isfahan, Iran, 1974-76; assoc. prof. U. Tabriz, Iran, 1977-78; prof. U. Riyadh, Saudi Arabia, 1979-80, Jinan U., Guangzhou, China, 1981-82; lectr. U. Mich., Ann Arbor, 1986. Active Humane Soc., Alpena, Mich., 1979—. Avocations: collecting oriental rugs, gardening. Home: Alpena, Mich. Died Aug. 15, 2007.

NICKERSON, BEE DAVIS, social services administrator, volunteer; b. Balt., Mar. 27, 1933; d. Edward Hollister and Liselotte (Heise) Davis; m. Edward Ashton Nickerson, Sept. 16, 1955; children: Louisa Talcott, Matthew Ashton. BA, Goucher Coll., 1955; M in Social Svcs., Adelphi Coll., 1959; PhD, U. Del., 1981. Caseworker Balt. Dept. Pub. Welfare, 1955-56, Cmty. Svc. Soc., NYC, 1959-61; cons. Barlow Sch., Amenia, N.Y., 1962-64; caseworker Vander Heyden Hall, Troy, N.Y., 1964-67, Family and Children's Svcs., Troy, N.Y., 1967-70; exec. dir. Del. chpt. NASW, Wilmington, 1982-83; assoc. exec. dir. Geriatric Svcs. of Del., Wilmington, 1982-83, exec. dir., 1983-91; ret., 1991. Vol. cons. West Side Model Cities Neighborhood Coun., Wilmington, 1970-72; chair Task Force on Child Protective Svcs., Coun. Family Svcs., 1975-78, Com. on Permanency Planning, Inter-Agy. Child Care Coun., 1980-82; Title XX rev. com. divsn. social svcs. State of Del., 1975-78; vol. cons., v.p. Parents Anonymous of Del., 1980-82. Author: Welfare Handbook, 1972. Rsch. vol. Del. Cmty. Found., Wilmington, 1992; adv. bd. Primary Health Care Network, Sharon, Conn., 1994-95; bd. dirs. Housatonic Ctr. for Mental Health, Lakeville, Conn., 1993-96, Geer Nursing and Rehab. Ctr., Caanan, Conn., 1997-98. Mem.: Litchfield County Univ. Club. Avocations: micro-economics, nonfiction writing, walking, swimming, tai chi. Home: Lakeville, Conn. Died July 10, 2007.

NICKERSON, RICHARD GORHAM, research company executive; b. Harwich, Mass., Nov. 20, 1927; s. Ephriam Gorham and Elizabeth (Wardle) N.; m. Eileen Florence Tressler, June 7, 1957 (dec. Apr. 1994); children: Holly Anne, Wendy Elyse, Susan Denise; m. Barbara Bernice Bagster Harper-Schofield, Aug. 14, 1999. BS cum laude, U. Mass., 1950; PhD, Northwestern U., 1955; postgrad., Poly. Inst. Bklyn., 1955-57; MBA cum laude, Boston U., 1983. Rsch. chemist DuPont, Cellophane Tech. Sect., Richmond, Va., 1954-55; rsch. chemist Dewey & Almy divsn. W.R. Grace Corp., Cambridge, Mass., 1957-60; v.p. R & D Electronautics Corp., Maynard, Mass., 1960-61, pres., 1961-63; project leader Polyco Borden Chem. divsn. Borden, Inc., Leominister, Mass., 1963-65, group leader, 1965-67, devel. mgr., 1967-81, lab. mgr., 1981-87; pres., mng. dir. Boston Profls. Internat., Inc., Hopkinton, Mass., from 1987. Patentee in field; designer, developer of water based polymers to meet specific performance requirement. With Chem. Corps, U.S. Army, 1955-57. Mem. Am. Chem. Soc., Soc. Plastics Engrs., Sigma Xi, Phi Lambda Upsilon, Alpha Chi Sigma. Avocations: sailing, photography, antique autos, classical music, dance. Home: Bellingham, Mass. Died Feb. 25, 2007.

NIDETCH, JEAN (JEAN EVELYN SLUTSKY), health service executive; b. Bklyn., Oct. 12, 1923; d. David and May (Rodin) Slutsky; Martin Nidetch (div. 1971); children—David, Richard (dec. 2006) Co-founder, pres. Weight Watchers Internat., Inc., Manhasset, L.I., until 1973, cons., N.Y. State Assembly Mental Hygiene Com., 1968; adviser Joint Legis. Com. on Child Care Needs, Legislature N.Y.; pres. Weight Watchers Found. Author: Jean Nidetch: Weight Watchers Cookbook, 1966, The Story of Weight Watchers, 1970, Weight Watchers Party & Holiday Cookbook, 1984, The Jean Nidetch Story: An Autobiography, 2010; regular writer for Weight Watchers Mag. column Named Marketing Woman of Yr., Hon. Adm. Gt. Navy Nebr.; Woman of Year, Forest Hills Youth Assn.; recipient Woman of Achievement award, Speakers award Sales Promotion Execs. Assn. Mem. Washington Sq. Bus. and Profl. Womens Club, AFTRA. Died Apr. 29, 2015.

NIELSEN, LEON, animal scientist; b. Viby, Denmark, Apr. 26, 1937; s. Melitha Marie and adopted s. Jens Peter Nielsen; m. Jill Ruth Turcott, Nov. 29, 1985; 1 child, Logan Turcott. Undergrad. in Equine Care, Colo. State U., Ft. Collins, 1973, undergrad. in Care of Captive Wild and Exotic Animals, 1973; undergrad. in Ecology, Atabasca U., Edmonton, Alta., Can., 1976. Cert.: Wis. Dept. Justice (law enforcement standards bd.) 1978. Forestry wildlife officer Alta. Dept. Lands & Forests, High Level, Canada, 1966—70; exec. dir. Calgary Humane Soc., 1970—77, Wis. Humane Soc., Milw., 1977—90; wildlife biologist Safe Capture Internat., Mt. Horeb, Wis., 1990—95; exec. dir. Peninsula Humane Soc., San Mateo, Calif., 1991; dir. St. Maarten Zool. Garden, Phillipsburg, Netherlands Antilles, 1992—93; exec. dir. Conroe Humane Soc., Tex., 1993—95; writer, from 1995. Rschr. (nonfiction) Robert E. Howard - A Collectors Bibliography, Arkham House - A Collector's Guide, Chemical Immobilization of Wild and Exotic Animals, Translocation of Wild Animals, Chemical Immobilization of North American Wildlife; contbr. papers to prof. jours. and pubs. 1st lt. spl. ops. force Danish Army, 1956—67, Denmark. Mem.: Wis. Humane Soc. (bd. dirs., sec. 1980—90). Democrat. Roman Catholic. Achievements include design of radio tracking of rhinoceros with horn implants. Avocations: writing, military history, reading, gardening. Home: Brookfield, Wis. Died July 6, 2007.

NIELSEN, STUART SCOTT, mathematician; b. Denver, Nov. 12, 1959; s. Vernon Stuart and Sandra Sue (Johnson) N.; m. Clara Elizabeth McDonald, May 19, 1990; 1 child, Ashley Heather Courtney. BS in Math., Tex. Tech U., 1987, MS in Math., 1990. Teaching asst. Tex. Tech U., Lubbock, 1987-90; project engr. Bechtel Power Corp., Houston, from 1990. Mem. Am. Math. Soc. Home: Cypress, Tex. Died June 11, 2007.

NIEMAN, RICHARD HOVEY, retired plant physiologist; b. Pasadena, Calif., Nov. 7, 1922; s. Charles Percival and Nancy Leigh (Hovey) N.; m. Mary Owens Hall, Apr. 27, 1946; children: Arthur Hall, Edward Hovey. BA, U. So. Calif., 1949, MS, 1951; PhD, U. Chgo., 1955. Postdoctoral fellow in biochemistry U. Chgo., 1955-56; plant physiologist U.S. Salinity Lab., USDA, Riverside, Calif., 1956-88; ret., 1988. Adj. prof. biochemistry U. Calif., Riverside, 1987-88. Contbr. articles to profl. jours., chpts. to books. Active environmentalist, Riverside, 1980—; vol. feeding the hungry 1st United Meth. Ch., Riverside, 1986—. Staff sgt. USAAF, 1943-46, PTO. Recipient Outstanding Performance award USDA, 1962, award for contbn. to curriculum study Am. Inst. Biol. Scis., 1963; rsch. grantee Agrl. Rsch. Svc., USDA, 1982, 83. Avocations: music, poetry, literature, running. Home: Riverside, Calif. Died July 1, 2007.

NIERENBERG, NORMAN, urban land economist, retired state official; b. Chgo., May 8, 1919; s. Isadore Isaac and Sadie Sarah (Dorfman) N.; m. Nanette Joyce Fortgang, Feb. 9, 1950; children: Andrew Paul, Claudia Robin. AA, U. Chgo., 1939; AB, Calif. State Coll., LA, 1952; MA, U. So. Calif., 1956. Lic. real estate broker, Calif.; cert. supr. and coll. instr., Calif. Right-of-way agt. Calif. Dept. Transp., LA, 1951-61, 85-90, sr. agt. San Francisco, 1988-89; instr. UCLA, 1960-61, 67-75, 81-85; coord. continuing edn. in real estate U. Calif., Berkeley, 1961-64. Coord. econ. benefits study Salton Sea, Calif. Dept. Water Resources, L.A., 1968-69; regional economist L.A. dist. CE, 1970-75, chief economist, 1981-85; regional economist Bd. Engrs. for Rivers and Harbors, Ft. Belvoir, Va., 1975-81; faculty resource person Oakland Project, Ford Found., U. Calif., Berkeley, 1962-64; project reviewer EPA, Washington, 1972-73. Editor: History of 82d Fighter Control Squadron, 1945; assoc. editor Right of Way Nat. Mag., 1952-55. Capt. USAAF, 1942-46, ETO, Lt. Col. USAFR ret. Mem.: Mil. Officers Assn. Am., Omicron Delta Epsilon. Democrat. Jewish. Home: Washington, DC. *Personal philosophy: Strive for excellence. Honorable in all endeavors.* Died Nov. 2, 2006.

NIFONG, GORDON DALE, health physicist; b. Durham, NC, Jan. 21, 1937; s. Samuel Otis and Bessie Lee (Boger) N.; m. Virginia Merle Jones, Nov. 23, 1963. BS, High Point Coll., 1959; PhD, U. Mich., 1970. Diplomate Am. Bd. Indsl. Hygiene. Chemist Union Carbide Co., Oak Ridge, Tenn., 1959-61; indsl. hygienist Fla. Dept. Health, Tampa, 1963-67; supervising chemist Bethlehem (Pa.) Steel Co., 1970-73; indsl. hygiene supr. U.S. Pub. Health Svc., Atlanta, 1973-78; cons. Winter Haven, Fla., 1978-85; dir. rsch. Fla. Inst. Phosphate, Bartow, from 1985. Conf. chmn. Am. Indsl. Hygiene Assn., Atlanta, 1976; councilor Am. Acad. Indsl. Hygiene, 1981-84. Contbr. articles to profl. jours. Sec. Bartow Rotary Club, 1989-91, dir. 1991. Recipient scholarship, pvt. industry, 1955-59, fellowship U.S. Atomic Energy Commn., 1962-63, U.S. Pub. Health Svc., 1967-70. Methodist. Home: Winter Haven, Fla. Died Mar. 5, 2007.

NIGHTENGALE, ROBERT WEBSTER, JR., advertising executive; b. Hampton, Va., Oct. 29, 1936; s. Robert Webster and Alice Virginia (Burleson) N.; m. Sally Ellen Wagener, June 14, 1958; children: Scott Webster, Jennifer Lyn. Student, William and Mary Coll., 1954-56. Pub. relations rep. DuPont de Nemours Co., Wilmington, Del., 1960-64, advt. asst., 1964-68, advt. div. dir., 1981-85, dir. communications, 1985-91; advt. coord. Hercules, Inc., Wilmington, 1968-69; pres. Communications Cons., Inc., Wilmington, 1969-78, MMI Courier, Wilmington, 1969-78; advt. mgr. DuPont Japan, Ltd., Tokyo, 1978-80; pres. Nightengale Assocs., Wilmington, from 1992, Home Furnishings Coun., from 1992, Home Enterprises Inc., from 1997. Co-chmn. Home Furnishings Coun., 1990-91. Trustee Del. Found. for Retarded Children, Wilmington, 1983-87; trustee Sanford Sch., Wilmington, 1983-94, chmn. bd. trustees, 1990-94; bd. dirs. Mary Campbell Ctr., Wilmington, 1981—, Wilmington Zool. Soc., 1991-92, Del. chpt. ARC, 1991-92. 1st lt. USAF, 1956-60. Republican. Baptist. Home: Chadds Ford, Pa. Died Mar. 24, 2007.

NIMOY, LEONARD, actor, director; b. Boston, Mar. 26, 1931; s. Max and Dora (Spinner) N.; m. Sandi Zober, Feb. 21, 1954 (div. 1987); children: Julie, Adam; m. Susan Bay, Jan. 1, 1989. Student (drama scholar), Boston Coll., Pasadena Playhouse, Calif., Jeff Corey, 1960-63; MA, Antioch U., Austin, Tex. Operator drama studio, San Fernando Valley; tchr. Synanon; owner Adajul Music Pub. Co. Actor: (TV appearances) Eleventh Hour, Kraft Theatre, Profiles in Courage, Bonanza, The Twilight Zone, Wagon Train, The Virginian, The Outer Limits, Rawhide, Dr. Kildare, Night Gallery, Columbo, T.J. Hooker, Star Trek: The Next Generation, Fringe, 2009—12; (TV series) Star Trek, 1966—69, Mission: Impossible, 1969—71, Brave New World, 1998; host (TV series) In Search Of..., 1976—80; actor: (films) Rhubarb, 1951, Queen for a Day, 1951, Kid Monk Baroni, 1952, The Brain Eaters, 1958, The Balcony, 1963, Assault on the Wayne, 1971, Catlow, 1971, Baffled!, 1973, The Alpha Caper, 1973, The Missing Are Deadly, 1975, Invasion of the Body Snatchers, 1978, Seizure: The Story of Kathy Morris, 1979, Star Trek: The Motion Picture, 1979, Star Trek II: The Wrath of Khan, 1982, A Woman Called Golda, 1982, The Sun Also Rises, 1984, Star Trek V: The Final Frontier, 1989, Bonanza: Under Attack, 1995, Carpati: 50 Miles, 50 Years, 1996, Star Trek, 2009, Star Trek Into Darkness, 2013; (TV films) Age of Darkness: A Night Gallery Retrospective, 2002; actor, co-prodr. (films) Never Forget, 1991, voice Transformers: The Movie, 1986, The Pagemaster, 1994, A Life Apart: Hasidism in America, 1997, Sinbad: Beyond the Veil of Mists, 2000, Atlantis: The Lost Empire, 2001, Land of the Lost, 2009, Transformers: Dark of the Moon, 2011, Zambezia, 2012, dir., actor Star Trek III: The Search for Spock, 1984, dir., co-writer, actor Star Trek IV: The Voyage Home, 1986, exec. prodr., co-writer, actor Star Trek VI: The Undiscovered Country, 1991; dir.: Three Men and a Baby, 1987, The Good Mother, 1988, Body Wars, 1989, Funny About Love, 1990, Holy Matrimony, 1994; (TV series) Deadly Games, 1995; actor: (stage appearances) Dr. Faustus, Stalag 17, Streetcar Named Desire, Cat on a Hot Tin Roof, Deathwatch, Monserrat, Irma La Douce, Visit to a Small Planet, Fiddler on a Roof, The Man in the Glass Booth, 6 Rms Riv Vu, Equus, Love Letters, others; actor, dir., writer (stage appearances) Vincent; singer: (albums) Leonard Nimoy Presents Mr. Spock's Music From Outer Space, 1967, Two Side of Leonard Nimoy, 1968, The Way I Feel, 1968, The Touch of Leonard Nimoy, 1969, The New World of Leonard Nimoy, 1970; author: (poetry and photography) Will I Think of You, 1974, We Are All Children, 1977, Come Be With Me, 1979, These Words are for You, 1981, Warmed by Love, 1983, A Lifetime of Love: Poems on the Passages of Life, 2002, (bibliography) I Am Not Spock, 1975; narrator Ancient Mysteries, History Channel, 1995—2003. Mem. ACLU; mem. sch. com. adv. bd. Parents for Peace Western LA; del. Dem. Central Com., 1971, 72. Served with AUS, 1954-56. Died Feb. 27, 2015.

NING, XUE-HAN (HSUEH-HAN NING), physiologist, researcher; b. Peng-Lai, Shandong, People's Republic of China, Apr. 15, 1936; came to U.S., 1984; s. Yi-Xing and Liu Ning; m. Jian-Xin Fan, May 28, 1967. MD, Shanghai 1st Med. Coll., People's Republic of China, 1960; post grad., Chinese Traditional Medicine Coll. for Advanced Study, 1960—61; postgrad. in Physiology, U. Mich., 1984—87. Rsch. fellow, rsch. assoc., leader cardiovasc. rsch. group Shanghai Inst. Physiology, Acad. Sinica, 1960—87, head, assoc. prof. cardiovasc. rsch. unit, prof., chair hypoxia dept., 1988-90, vice chairperson academic com., 1988-90; NIH internat. rsch. fellow U. Mich., Ann Arbor, 1984-87; prof. and dir. Key Lab of Hypoxia Physiology Academia Sinica, Shanghai, 1989-90. Acting leader, High Altitude Physiology Group, Chinese mountaineering and sci. expdn. team to Mt. Everest, 1975; leader High Altitude Physiology Group, Dept. Metall. Industry of China and Ry. Engring. Corps, 1979; vis. prof. dept. physiology Mich. State U., East Lansing, U. Mich., U. Wash. Med. Sch., 1989-97; affiliate prof., U. Wash., 1997—; rsch. scientist Children's Hosp. and Regional Med. Ctr., Seattle, 1997—. Author: High Altitude Physiology and Medicine, 1981, Reports on Scientific Expedition to Mt. Qomolungma, High Altitude Physiology, 1980, Environment and Ecology of Qinghai-Xizang (Tibet) Plateau, 1982, Plateau Tin Road Health Line, 2006; mem. editl. bd. Chinese Jour. Applied Physiology, 1984-1992, Acta Physiologica, 1988-90, Chinese Jour. Physiology (Taiwan) 2004-; contbr. articles to profl. jours. Recipient Merit award Shanghai Sci. Congress, 1977, All-China Sci. Congress, Beijing, 1978, Super Class award Academia Sinica, Beijing, 1986, 1st Class award Nat. Natural Scis., Beijing, 1987, 2d Class award Acad. Sinica Sci. and Technol. Achievements, Beijing, 1992, # 1 Best Article award Tzu-Chi Med. Jour., Taiwan, 1995, Shanghai 2006 Excellent Popular Sci. Reading award, 2007. Mem. Am. Physiol. Soc., Am. Heart Assn., Internat. Soc. Heart Rsch., Royal Soc. Medicine, Internat. Soc. for Mountain Medicine. Achievements include first electrocardiography record at summit of Mt. Everest in 1975; research in predictive evaluation of mountaineering performance; characteristics for high altitude adaptation and acclimatization; effect of medicinal herbs on cardiac performance; cardiovascular adaptation and resistance to hypoxia and ischemia; injury threshold of short-cycle-intermittent hypoxia and gene expression in heart; the critical temperature 30 degrees celsius "temperature protection threshold" for modulating myocardial energy, metabolic pathways, and gene expression to resist ischemia and hypoxia; the 29 degrees celsius "temperature injury threshold" for cardiac contractility in the beating heart in vivo; hypothermic cross adaptation protects heart from subsequent ischema and hypoxia by preserving signaling for mitochondrial biogenesis, activateing stress pathways and inactivating apoptosis to maintain myocardial stability and improve functional recovery during reperfusion and reoxygenation; the hypothermia protection has also been proved in human by treated with a hypothermia rescue (32 degrees C Central catheter then 33-35 degrees C for 24 hrs) after his own heart stopped more than 6 mins in 2009. Home: Seattle, Wash. Died Apr. 20, 2015.

NIXON, JOHN HARMON, retired economist; b. Mpls., Apr. 7, 1915; s. Justin Wroe and Ida Elisabeth (Wickenden) N. AB, Swarthmore Coll., 1935; AM, Harvard U., 1949, PhD, 1953. Analyst U.S. R.R. Retirement Bd., Washington, 1938-41; economist U.S. Office of Price Adminstrn., Washington, 1941-46; teaching fellow, sr. tutor Harvard Coll., Cambridge, Mass., 1947-50; asst. prof. econs. CCNY, 1953-56; dir. econ. devel. N.Y. State Dept. Commerce, Albany, 1956-59; dir. area devel. Com. for Econ. Devel., NYC, 1959-65; dir. tech. assistance U.S. Econ. Devel. Adminstrn., Washington, 1966-67; urban economist U.S. AID, Saigon, Vietnam, 1967; economist Ralph M. Parsons Co., Washington, 1968-70, chief economist/systems Pasadena, Calif., 1971-82. Mem. adv. bd. U.S. Area Devel. Adminstrn., Washington, 1963-65. Co-author, editor: Community Economic Development Efforts, 1964, Living Without Water (Cairo), 1980. Dir. Finger Lakes Times, 1958-88; coun. for urban economic evel., 1967-87; vice chmn. Mayor's Com. on Econ. Devel., L.A., 1974-75; pres. Pasadena Devel. Corp., 1982-84 Mem. Plato Soc. UCLA, Phi Beta Kappa. Democrat. Presbyterian. Home: Los Angeles, Calif. Died June 23, 2007.

NOAH, SHERI LYNN, minister; b. LaRochelle, France, Dec. 16, 1954; came to U.S., 1956; d. Grover Carter Noah and Pauline Esther (Takach) Westaby; m. David Hacker, May 25, 1991; stepchildren: Hilary, Corey. AA, Yakima Valley Community Coll., Wash., 1975; BA, Whitworth Coll., 1977; student, Latin Am. Bibl. Sem., San Jose, Costa Rica, 1983; MDiv, McCormick Theol. Seminary, Chgo., 1985. Ordained to ministry Presbyn. Ch. (U.S.A.), 1986. Subsistence worker United Presbyn. Ch. U.S.A./Fedn. of Protestant Chs., Uruguay, 1979-81; minister Trinity Presbyn. Ch., Stockton, Calif., from 1986. Chmn. Stockton Interfaith Sponsoring Com. for Ch.-based Community Organizing, 1989—; mem. Metro Ministries (co-chair Unity in Community Com., 1990-91), Stockton, 1986—, Latin Am. Support Com., Stockton, 1986—; supr. tutoring prog., Trinity Ch., 1989—. Home: Southgate, Mich. Died Mar. 3, 2007.

NOBLE, JULIAN VICTOR, physicist, researcher; b. NYC, June 7, 1940; s. Jacob Barr and Beatrice (Ashbes) N.; m. Harriet Gootnick, Aug. 14, 1960; children; Deborah Jill, Lisa Ann, Benjamin Wolf (dec.). BS, Calif. Inst. Tech., 1962; MA, Princeton U., 1963, PhD, 1966. Rsch. assoc. dept. physics U. Pa., Phila., 1966-68, asst. prof., 1968-71, assoc. prof., 1971-80, prof., from 1980. Program adv. com. Space Radiation Effects Lab., Newport News, Va., 1973-78. Contbr. over 80 articles to profl. jours. Alfred P. Sloan Found. fellow, 1971-74. Mem. Am. Phys. Soc., European Phys. Soc., Soc. Automotive Engrs. Achievements include research in progenitor sum rules in nuclear physics, expansion of nucleons in nucleis, geographic propagation of epidemics. Home: Charlottesville, Va. Died Mar. 11, 2007.

NOEL, JAMES KINGSLEY, III, immunologist, virologist; b. Richmond, Va., Sept. 23, 1937; s. James Kingsley Jr. and Mary Madelin (Bultman) N.; m. Barbara Lynn Edwards, June 29, 1963; children: James IV, Jennifer Eve. BS, Mt. St. Mary's Coll., Emmitsburg, Md., 1959; MS in Microbiology, U. Md., 1961, PhD in Microbiology, 1963. Lab. dir. Flow Labs., Rockville, Md., 1961-80; dir. quality assurance Hazleton Biols., Denver, Pa., 1980-86; sci. dir. Covance Rsch. Products, Denver, Pa., from 1987. Mem. Am. Soc. Microbiology, Am. Assn. Clin. Chemistry, Lions Club (bd. dirs. 1990-95), Sigma Xi. Avocations: golf, gardening, water sports. Home: Ephrata, Pa. Died Dec. 8, 2006.

NOEL, JAMES SHERIDAN, civil engineer, educator; b. Plainview, Tex., June 18, 1930; s. James Simpson and Georgie Pearl (Maxwell) N.; m. Lee Marie Zaleski, Jan. 10, 1953; children: Sharon Kay, Patricia Ann, Jennifer Lee. BSCE, Tex. A&M U., 1952; CE in engr., Columbia U., 1959; PhD, Tex. U., 1965. Registered profl. engr., Tex., N.Y. Structural engr. Grumman Aircraft, Bethpage, N.Y., 1955-60; materials engr. N.Am. Aviation, McGregor, Tex., 1960-74; assoc. prof. Tex. A&M U., College Station, 1974-92, prof. emeritus, from 1992. Patentee in field. Col. C.E., U.S. Army, 1952-55, Korea. Mem. AIAA, ASCE, Aircraft Owners and Pilots Assn., Lions Internat. Avocation: photography. Home: College Station, Tex. Died Dec. 31, 2006.

NOLEN, WILLIAM LAWRENCE, JR., insurance agency owner, real estate investor; b. Austin, Tex., Oct. 3, 1922; s. William Lawrence Sr. and Mary Kate (Smith) N.; m. Joy I. Ingram, Aug. 28, 1946. Grad., Edinburg Jr. Coll., 1942; BBA, U. Tex., 1947. CLU. Active USN, South Pacific, 1942-46; office mgr. John B. Vaught Hardware Co., Austin, 1947-48; acct. def. rsch. lab. U. Tex., Austin, 1948-51; gen. mgr. John B. Vaught Hardware Stores, Austin, 1951-56; agt. Southwestern Life Ins. Co., Austin, 1956-86, William L. Nolen Jr. CLU & Assocs., Austin, from 1986. Bd. dirs. Southwest AutoChlor Corp., Austin. Chair City of Austin Traffic Safety Commn., 1970-91, mem. Airport Adv. Commn., 1971-82; trustee Counseling and Pastoral Care Ctr., Austin, 1988-92; vestry mem., asst. treas. St. Matthew's Episc. Ch., Austin, 1965-68; bd. dirs. Better Bus. Bur. Austin, 1969-70, chmn., 1970-72; U. Tex. Presidents Assn.; pres. Austin Community Found., 1989-90, treas., 1988-89. Lt. comdr. USNR, 1942-45, PTO. Named Boss of Yr. Am. Bus. Womens Assn., 1970, Assoc. of Yr., 1986. Mem. Nat. Sales Achievement award (charter), Tex. Leaders Round Table (life, Outstanding Achievement award 1969-70), Million Dollar Round Table (life), Tex. Assn. Life Underwriters (legis. v.p. 1963-74), Life Underwriters Polit. Action Com. (grantee), Austin Assn. Life Underwriters (past pres.), Austin Chpt. CLU Soc. (bd. dirs. 1986-88), Austin Steam Train Assn. (bd. dirs. 1990-98), Advantage Austin, Austin C. of C. (bd. dirs. 1969-70, v.p. 1970), TIP Club, The Hundred Club (bd. dirs. 1992-98), Headliners Club, Univ. Club (bd. dirs. 1992-94), Kiwanis (bd. dirs. 1960). Episcopalian. Avocations: stamp, coin and wine collecting. Home: Austin, Tex. Died Nov. 1, 2006.

NORMAND, WILLIAM C., psychiatry; b. Aug. 3, 1922; BA, Harvard U., 1943; MD, U. Kansas Med. Sch., 1954. Intern U. Kans. Med. Ctr., 1954-55; resident N.Y. State Psychiatric Inst., 1955-56, Albert Einstein Coll. Medicine, NYC, 1956-58, assoc. clin. prof., from 1974. Contbr. articles to profl. jours. Home: New York, NY. Died Dec. 11, 2006.

NORSKOG, EUGENIA FOLK, retired elementary school educator; b. Staunton, Va., Mar. 23, 1937; d. Ernest and Edna Virginia (Jordan) Folk; m. Russell Carl Norskog, Nov. 25, 1967; children: Cynthia, Carl, Roberta, Eric. BA, King Coll., 1958; MEd, George Mason U., 1977. Cert. tchr., Va. Tchr. elem. Bristol (Va.) Pub. Schs., 1958-61, 62-65, Staunton (Va.) Pub. Schs., 1961-62, Fairfax (Va.) County Pub. Schs., 1965-68; with Project 100,000, USAFI, Fort Ord, Calif., 1969; tchr. elem. Monterey (Calif.) Peninsula Sch. Div., 1970-71, Prince William County Schs., Manassas, Va., 1972-2001, ret., 2001; Va. rehab. sch. Prince William County, Richmond, Va., 1979-82. V.p. Fauquier Gymnastics, Warrenton, Va., 1982-83, pres., 1983-85; coach, bd. dirs., referee Warrenton Soccer Assn., 1980-88; soccer referee Piedmont Referee Assn., Manassas, 1990-95. Mem. NEA, Va. Edn. Assn. Prince William Edn. Assn. (bd. dirs. 1974-77). Home: Warrenton, Va. Died June 3, 2007.

NORTH, DOUGLASS CECIL, economist, educator; b. Cambridge, Mass., Nov. 5, 1920; s. Henry Emerson and Edith (Saitta) North; m. Lois Hiester, 1944 (div.); children: Douglass Alan, Christopher, Malcolm Peter; m. Elisabeth W. Case, Sept. 28, 1972. BA, U. Calif., Berkeley, 1942, PhD, 1952; DSc (hon.), U. Cologne, Germany, 1988, U. Zurich, Switzerland, 1993, Stockholm Sch. Economics, 1994, Prague Sch. Economics, 1995. Asst. prof. economics U. Wash., Seattle, 1950—56, assoc. prof., 1956—60, prof., 1960—83, dir. Inst. Econ. Rsch., 1961—66, chmn. dept. economics, 1967—79; prof. economics and history Washington U., St. Louis, 1983—96, dir. Ctr. Polit. Economy, 1984—90, Spencer T. Olin prof. arts & scis. to emeritus, 1996—2015; dir. Nat. Bur. Econ. Research, 1967—87. Peterkin prof. polit economy Rice U., Houston, 1979; Pitt prof. Am. institutions Cambridge U., 1981—82; fellow Ctr. Advanced Study Behavioral Scis., Stanford U., Calif., 1987—88; Bartlett Burnap sr. fellow Hoover Instn., Stanford, Calif., from 2000. Author: The Economic Growth of the US 1790-1860, 1961, Growth and Welfare in the American Past, 1966, Institutional Change and American Economic Growth, 1971, The Economics of Public Issues (numerous edits.), 1971, The Rise of the Western World, 1973, Structure and Change in Economic History, 1981, Institutions, Institutional Change and Economic Performance, 1990; contbr. articles to profl. jours. Recipient Nobel prize in economics, 1993; grantee, Rockefeller Found., 1960—63, Ford Found., 1961, 1966, Social Sci. Rsch. Coun., 1962, NSF, 1967—73; fellow John Simon Guggenheim Meml. Found., 1972—73. Fellow: Am. Acad. Arts & Scis.; mem.: Econ. History Assn., Brit. Acad. (corr.), Am. Econ. Assn. Home: Saint Louis, Mo. Died Nov. 23, 2015.

NORTON, HENRY W., JR., gas industry executive; b. Ardmore, Okla., July 17, 1946; s. Henry W. and Patty V. (Saxon) N.; m. Carol Anne Becker, Oct. 14, 1974; children: Stacey J., Brett A., Lindsey R., Jenna L., Kelsey A. BSME, U. Okla., 1969. Various engring. and mgmt. positions, U.S., North Sea, Mid. East, 1969-88; mgr. gas processing Mobil Natural Gas Inc., Houston, 1988-90; projects mgr. P.T. Arun Lng Plant, Sumatra, Indonesia, 1990-92; v.p. transp. and mktg. ops. Mobil Natural Gas, Inc., from 1993. Author: (proceeding) Annual Proceeding of SPE, 1984. Soccer coach Kingwood Soccer Assn., 1989, 90, 92, Cherry Creek Soccer Assn., 1985-88; baseball coach Cherry Creek Baseball Assn., 1985-88. Mem. Nat. Gas Transp. Assn., Am. Mgmt. Assn., Gas. Processor's Assn., Assn. Computing Machinery, Soc. Petroleum Engrs. Avocations: golf, woodworking. Died May 3, 2007.

NORWOOD, JANET LIPPE (JANET SONYA LIPPE), economist; b. Newark, Dec. 11, 1923; d. M. Turner and Thelma (Levinson) Lippe; m. Bernard Norwood, June 25,

1943; children: Stephen Harlan, Peter Carlton. BA, NJ Coll. for Women (now Douglass Coll., Part of Rutgers U.), 1945, MA, 1946; PhD, Fletcher Sch. Law and Diplomacy, 1949; LLD (hon.), Fla. Internat. U., 1979, Carnegie Mellon U., Pitts., 1984, Harvard U., Cambridge, Mass., 1997, Rutgers U., 2003; D, State US. Instr., economics Wellesley Coll., 1948-49; economist William L. Clayton Ctr., Tufts U., 1953-58; with Bur. Labor Stats., U.S. Dept. Labor, Washington, 1963-91; dep. commr., then acting commr. Bur. Labor Stats. Dept. Labor, Washington, 1975-79, commr. labor stats., 1979-92; sr. fellow The Urban Inst., Washington, 1992-99; counselor, sr. fellow N.Y. Conf. Bd., 2001—09. Dir. Nat. Opinion Rsch. Ctr., chair adv. coun. unemployment compensation, 1993—96; pres. COSSA, 2001—02; mem. bd. sci. counselors Nat. Ctr. Health Stats., 1975—77; chair panel on offshoring Nat. Acad. Pub. Adminstrn., 2005—07. Author: Organizing to Count: Change in the Federal Statistical System, 1995; contbr. scientific papers in field. Recipient Disting. Achievement award, Dept. Labor, 1972, Spl. Commendation award, 1977, Philip Arnow award, 1979, Elmer Staats award, 1982, Pub. Svc. award, 1984, Presdl. Disting. Exec. Rank, 1988, Elizabeth Scott award, Com. Pres.'s Statis. Assns., 2002; named Hall Disting. Alumni, Rutgers U., 1987. Fellow: AAAS, Nat. Assn. Bus. Economists, Royal Statis. Soc., American Statis. Assn. (pres. 1989, Founder's award 1997); mem.: Nat. Inst. Statis. Sci. (bd. trustees 1991—2000), Nat. Acad. Sci. (assoc.), Nat. Acad. Pub. Adminstrn., Internat. Assn. Ofcls. Stats., Internat. Statis. Inst., Douglass Coll. Soc. Disting. Achievement, Cosmos Club (pres. 1995—96). Home: Austin, Tex. Died Mar. 27, 2015.

NOVAK, ALFREDO ERNEST, bishop emeritus; b. Dwight, Nebr., June 2, 1930; Ordained priest Congregation of the Most Holy Redeemer, 1956; ordained bishop, 1979; aux. bishop Archdiocese of São Paulo, Brazil, 1979—89; bishop Diocese of Paranagua, Brazil, 1989—2006, bishop emeritus, 2006—14. Roman Catholic. Died Dec. 3, 2014.

NOVAK, MICHAEL PAUL, English language educator; b. July 6, 1935; BA, Cath. U. of Am., 1957; MFA, U. Iowa, 1962. Instr. English Ill. State U., Bloomington, 1961-63; assoc. prof. English St. Mary Coll., Leavenworth, Kans., 1963-2001, prof. emeritus, 2001. Home: Leavenworth, Kans. Died Dec. 2, 2006.

NOWLIN, WILLIE CLAIRE SMITH, social services administrator; b. New Orleans, Aug. 11, 1942; d. William Howard and Aura Bessie (McKay) Smith; m. John Henry Nowlin Jr., Nov. 28, 1970; children: Amy Susanne, John Damon (twins). BA in Sociology, Millsaps Coll., 1964; MSW, La. State U., 1967. Lic./cert. social worker. Social worker Child Guidance Clinic, Dallas, 1967-70, Hope Cottage Children's Bur., Dallas, 1971; dir. social svc. The Bapt. Children's Village, Jackson, Miss., from 1971. Foster care review bd. Dept. Human Svc., Jackson, 1986—; peer reviewer and review team chairperson Nat. Assn. of Homes for Children, 1984-88; peer reviewer Coun. on Accreditation of Svc. for Families and Children, N.Y.C., 1988—; foster care, permanency planning task force Gov.'s Commn. for Children and Youth, 1983-88. Mem. NASW (sec., bd. dirs. Miss. chpt. 1990-92), Miss. Assn. Child Care Agencies (pres. 1990-92), Miss. Conf. Social Welfare, DAR (charter Miss. soc.), Acad. Cert. Social Workers. Methodist. Avocations: spectator sports, reading. Home: Jackson, Miss. Died Jan. 10, 2007.

NOYES, JONATHAN HOWARD, investment management executive, rancher; b. Duluth, Minn., Sept. 6, 1920; s. Jonathan A. and Caroline (Clark) N.; m. Earlene Kay Jaster, Oct. 30, 1948; children: Timothy, Joan, Susan, Jonathan C., Margaret. BS, MIT, 1942; JD, U. Tex., 1948. Engr. RCA, Harrison, N.J., 1942-43, Terrell Bartlett Engrs., San Antonio, Tex., 1949-51; broker, sales mgr. Muir Investment Corp., San Antonio, Tex., 1953-58; pres. Porter, Noyes, Inc., Corpus Christi, Tex., 1958-63; v.p., investment rep. Eppler, Guerin & Turner, Corpus Christi, 1963-64, 70-97, Rowles, Winston, Inc., Corpus Christi, 1964-67, Rauscher, Pierce, Corpus Christi, 1967-70; pres. Oxford, Worthington, Inc., Corpus Christi, from 1997. V.p. Gulf Coast Coun. Boy Scouts Am., 1968-73. With U.S. Navy, 1943-46. Mem. Kiwanis Internat. (past pres., bd. dirs. Corpus Christi chpt.). Republican. Avocations: hunting, fishing. Home: Corpus Christi, Tex. Died May 15, 2007.

NUCKLOS, SHIRLEY, health facility administrator, consultant; b. Canton, Ohio, Aug. 30, 1949; D. Boyd Alexander and Julia Lillian (Hood) Curtis; m. William W. Nucklos, Mar. 11, 1972; children: Tuere Tene, Tiombé Nigina, Khari Oji-Lee. BS in Edn., Cen. State U., Wilberforce, Ohio, 1970; MA, Ohio State U., 1971. Cert. elem. tchr., guidance counselor. Guidance counselor Scioto Village High Sch., Powell, Ohio, 1973-78; acad. advisor Franklin U., Columbus, Ohio, 1980-82, acting asst. dir. records, 1982-83, asst. registrar, 1983-90; registrar Ohio Dominican Coll., Columbus, 1990-93; dir. human resources Mid-Am. Phys. Medicine & Exec. Med., Inc., Columbus, Ohio, from 1994; adminstr. Woodland Med. Arts Ctr., Columbus, from 1998. Adminstrv. advisor to Black Student Union, Franklin U., 1982-85; human resource cons. Exec. Med., Inc., Westerville, Ohio, 1989-93, dir. human resources, bus. mgr., 1994—. Vol. tchr. Umoja Sasa Shule, Columbus, 1971-74; booster Mid-west Gymnastic and Cheerleading, Dublin, Ohio, 1988-93; active various com. for minority concerns. Mem. Ohio Assn. Collegiate Registrars and Admissions Officers (sec. 1991-93, Cert. Appreciation 1985, 93), Am. Assn. Collegiate Registrars and Admissions Officers, Nat. Assn. Coll. Deans, Registrars and Admissions Officers, Ohio Assn. Women Deans, Adminstrs. and Counselors, Nat. Assn. Women Deans, Adminstrs. and Counselors, Am. Assn. Univ. Adminstrn., Va. Admissions Counselors for Black Concerns, Ohio Health Info. Mgmt. Assn. Democrat. Mem. Church of God in Christ. Avocations: weight training, bicycling, reading. Home: Powell, Ohio. Died Dec. 24, 2006.

NUGENT, PETER DANIEL, labor and industrial relations educator; b. Kansas City, Mo., Mar. 29, 1938; s. Patrick Henry and Louise Theresa (O'Brien) N.; m. Ashley Baker, June 14, 1969; children: Matthew O'Brien, Megan Bourne. BA, U. Colo., 1969; MA, U. Ill., 1971, PhD, 1975. Lectr. U. Ill., Champaign/Urbana, 1973-75; asst., prof. Stockton State Coll., Pomona, N.J., 1975-76, Cleve. State U., 1976-79; assoc. prof. Rockhurst Coll., Kansas City, Mo., from 1979. Cons. in human resources mgmt. Author: Work in America; contbr. articles to profl. jours. Mem. Indsl. Rels. Rsch. Assn. of Kansas City (pres. 1989-90, bd. dirs.). Home: Kansas City, Mo. Died Mar. 1, 2007.

NYE, GEORGE N, secondary school educator; b. Phila., Aug. 18, 1929; s. Harry S. Nye and Anna (Stoudt) Stopfel. BS, Kutztown State U., 1955; MEd, Pa. State U., 1959, D in Art Edn., DEd in Ednl. Adminstrn., 1969. Tchr. Coatesville (Pa.) Sch., 1955-58; tchr., then prin. of jr. high Southern Cambria Schs., Franklinborough, Pa., 1958-68; asst. supt., then supt. DuBois (Pa.) Area Sch. Dist., 1970-89; curator museum DuBois Area Hist. Soc., from 1995. Bd. dirs., pres. DuBois Hist. Soc., 1970—, Cultural Resources Ins., 1990; mem. sch. bd. DuBois Area Schs., 1994-95. Mem. NEA (life), Pa. State Edn. Assn., Am. Legion, VFW, DAV. Avocations: reading, theater, computers, painting. Home: Du Bois, Pa. Died June 6, 2007.

NYGREN, RUNE LEN, import company executive; b. Stockholm, Nov. 30, 1919; came to U.S., 1979; s. Gustav Anders and Clara (Larsson) N.; children: Anders, Magnus. Grad., Naval Acad., Stockholm, 1944, Tech. Coll., Norrkoping, Sweden, 1948; MBA, Stockholm Bus. Sch., 1952. Export mgr. Eskilstuna (Sweden) Jernbolaget, 1952-57; pres. Näfvegvarns Bruk, Nävekvarn, Sweden, 1958-65, Nävekvarns Maskiner, Malmö, Sweden, 1965-70, Scandi-Ljungbyverken, Ljungby, Sweden, 1970-79; v.p. Interthor, Inc., Broadview, Ill., from 1983. Served to lt. Swedish Navy, 1937-45. Mem. Midamerican Swedish Trade Assn. Lutheran. Avocations: reading, skiing, boxing. Home: Chicago, Ill. Died Apr. 19, 2007.

OAKLEY, ROBERT BIGGER, retired ambassador; b. Dallas, Mar. 12, 1931; s. Robert Newell and Josephine (Bigger) O.; m. Phyllis Elliott, June 8, 1958; children: Mary Bigger, Thomas Elliott. AB, Princeton U., 1948-52; postgrad., Tulane U., 1955-56. Staff mem. US Embassy, Khartoum, Sudan, 1958-60; internat. relations officer US Dept. State, 1960-63; econ. & polit. officer US Embassy, Abidjan, 1963-65, political officer Saigon, 1965-67, Paris, 1967-69, 1969-71, political counselor Beirut, 1971-74, NSC, 1974-77; dep. asst. sec. for East Asia US Dept. State, Washington, 1977-79, US amb. to Zaire, 1979-82, US amb. to Somalia, 1983-84, dir. Office Counter-Terrorism and Emergency Planning, 1984-85, acting amb.-at-large for counter-terrorism, 1985-86; resident assoc. Carnegie Endowment for Internat. Peace, 1986; spl. asst. to Pres., sr. dir. for Near East & South Asia NSC, 1987-88; US amb. to Pakistan US Dept. State, 1988—91, spl. envoy to Somalia, 1993. Served with USN, 1952-55. Recipient Meritorious Honor award US Dept. State, 1963, Disting. Honor award, 1986. Republican. Episcopalian. Died Dec. 10, 2014.

OBERDORFER, DONALD, JR., news correspondent; b. Atlanta, May 28, 1931; s. Donald and Dorothy (Bayersdorfer) O.; m. Laura Klein, Apr. 24, 1955; children: Daniel, Karen. AB in pub. and internat. affairs, Princeton U., 1952. Reporter The Charlotte Observer, NC, 1955-58, Washington corrs. Washington, 1958-61; asst. editor, assoc. editor The Saturday Evening Post, Washington, 1961-65; nat. corrs. Knight Newspaper Bureau, Washington, 1965-68; white house corrs. The Washington Post, Washington, 1968-72, northeast Asia corrs. Tokyo, 1972-75, diplomatic corrs. Washington, 1976-93; journalist-in-residence Johns Hopkins U., Paul H. Nitze Sch. Advanced Internat. Studies, Washington, 1993—2015. Ferris prof. journalism Princeton U., 1977, 82, 86. Author: Tet!, 1971, The Two Koreas: A Contemporary History, The Turn: From the Cold War to a New Era, 1991, Princeton University: The 250 First Years, 1995. Chmn. adv. com. The Asia Soc., Washington, 1986-90, trustee, N.Y.C., 1987-93. With U.S. Army, 1952-54, Korea. Recipient Weintal prize for Diplomatic Corrs. Georgetown U., 1982, 93, Hood award Nat. Press Club, 1981, 88, Nover prize White House Corrs. Assn., 1980. Mem. Coun. Fgn. Rels., Overseas Writers Club (pres. 1994). Home: Washington, DC. Died July 23, 2015.

OBERG, CHARLOTTE HENLEY, English language educator; b. Richmond, Va., Sept. 15, 1936; d. Kenneth Raymond and Elisabeth Wilhelmina (Heusmann) H.; m. Andrew Lewis Oberg, May 1, 1959. BA in English, U. Richmond, 1956, MA in English, 1966; PhD in English, U. Va., 1970. Elem. instr. Hanover County Pub. Schs., Ashland, Va., 1962-63; instr. English Henrico County Pub. Schs., Richmond, Va., 1963-65, Va. Commonwealth U., Richmond, 1966-70; asst. prof. English U. Richmond, 1970-78, assoc. prof. English, from 1978, acting chair English, 1991. Author: A Pagan Prophet: William Morris, 1978. NEH research fellow, 1973-74; research grantee Mednick Fund, 1979, Soc. Cin., 1988. Mem. MLA, William Morris Soc. (exec. com. 1989—), Lychnos Soc. (hon.). Avocations: gardening, collecting arts and crafts movement objects. Home: Richmond, Va. Died Apr. 10, 2007.

OBRAZTOVA, ELENA, mezzo-soprano; b. Leningrad, Russia, July 7, 1937; Grad., Leningrad. Conservatory, 1964. Debut Marina in Boris Godunov, Bolshoi Opera, 1965; prin. roles Russian Opera Reportory, Carmen and Azunena; appearances Amneris in Aida, Delilah in Samson; artistic dir. Mikhailovsky Theater, 2007—08. Recipient Lenin prize, 1976, numerous awards. Died Jan. 12, 2015.

O'BRIEN, CHARLES FRANCIS, historian, educator; b. Danbury, Conn., Mar. 21, 1939; s. Francis Joseph and Edith Rose (McLaughlin) O'B.; children: Terence Charles, Marc Charles, Kristin Marie. AB, St. Michael's Coll., 1960; MA, U. Wyo., 1963; PhD, Brown U., 1967. Instr. English U. Wyo., Laramie, 1963-64; asst. prof. history St. Michael's Coll., Winooski Park, Vt., 1964-68; assoc. prof. history Clarkson U., Potsdam, N.Y., from 1968, chiar dept. social scis., 1976-81. Cons. Ctr. for Can.-Am. Bus. Rels., Potsdam, 1988-92. Author: Sir William Dawson: A Life in Science and Religion, 1971; contbr. articles to profl. jours. Fulbright lectr. Coun. for Internat. Exch. of Scholars, Tunisia 1979, Morocco 1989. Fellow Ctr. for Rsch. on Vt.; mem. Norwood Lake Assn., Cinema 10 Film Soc. (bd. dirs. 1990—). Democrat. Roman Catholic. Avocations: travel, cooking. Home: Ormond Beach, Fla. Died Feb. 10, 2007.

O'BRIEN, MICHAEL JOHN, classics educator; b. NYC, Apr. 27, 1930; emigrated to Can., 1966; s. Michael John and Mary (Collins) O'B.; m. Anne Jordan Webb, July 25, 1959; children— David, Emily. BA, Fordham U., 1951; MA, Princeton, 1953, PhD, 1956. Instr. classics Wesleyan U., Middletown, Conn., 1955-56; from instr. to asso. prof. dept. classics Yale, 1956-66; from asso. prof. to prof. classics Univ. Coll., U. Toronto, Ont., Can., from 1966, chmn. dept., 1973-81. Author: The Socratic Paradoxes and the Greek Mind, 1967; Editor: Twentieth-Century Interpretations of Oedipus Rex, 1968. Morse fellow Yale, Rome, Italy, 1963-64; Guggenheim fellow, 1972-73 Mem. Canadian Assn. U. Tchrs., Am. Philol. Assn., Classical Assn., Classical Assn. Can., Soc. Ancient Greek Philosophy, Classical Soc. of the Am. Acad. (Rome). Roman Catholic. Home: Don Mills, Canada. Died Dec. 28, 2007.

O'BRIEN, ROBERT BROWNELL, JR., banker, consultant, yacht broker; b. NYC, Sept. 6, 1934; s. Robert Brownell and Eloise (Boles) O'B.; m. Sarah Lager, Nov. 28, 1958; children: Robert Brownell III, William Stuart, Jennifer. BA, Lehigh U., 1957; postgrad., NYU, Am. Inst. Banking. Asst. treas., credit officer, br. locations officer Bankers Trust Co., NYC, 1957-63; v.p., dir. bus. devel. George A. Murray Co., gen. contractors, NYC, 1964; also v.p. Bowery Savs. Bank, 1964-69; dir., chief exec. officer Fed. Savs. & Loan Ins. Corp., Washington, 1969-71; chmn. exec. com. Fed. Home Loan Bank Bd., 1969-71; v.p. Bowery Savs. Bank, NYC, 1972; exec. v.p. First Fed. Savs. & Loan Assn., NYC, 1973-75; chmn., chief exec. officer Carteret Savs. Bank, Morristown, 1975-91, also bd. dirs.; mng. dir. Printon Kane Group Inc., Short Hills, NJ, 1991-94; dir., former chief exec. officer Govs. Bank Corp., West Palm Beach, 1992-94; pres., CEO Hubert Johnson Inc., from 1998. Bd. dirs. Fed. Home Loan Bank N.Y., Govs. Bank Corp., Ocean Med. Ctr. Found., Ocean County Atty. Ethics Com.; vice chmn. 1st Mortgage Capital Corp., Vero Beach, Fla.; chmn. Neighborhood Housing Svcs. Am., 1972-91; vice chmn., bd dirs. U.S. League Savs. Instns., Washington, O'Brien Yacht Sales. Contbr. articles to trade mags. Trustee Trinity Pawling Sch., Palm Beach County Housing Partnership, Lehigh U., Ocean Med. Found., Tuckerton Seaport; devel. cons. Ocean County Coll., Toms River, N.J., chair, U. Coun. Georgian Ct. U. Lakewood, 2009; chmn. Housing Opportunities Found.; trustee, pres. Toms River Seaport Soc., N.J. Mus. Boating; trustee, pres., past chmn. Cmty. Found. of N.J., 1987—; trustee, pres. Bay Head Hist. Soc., trustee Ocean Med. Ctr. Found., Brick, NJ; vice chmn., bd. dirs. Dalt Found.; chmn. adv. bd. Palm Beach Maritime Mus., Peanut Island, Fla.; active Nat. Commn. on Neighborhoods, The Kemp Commn.; past chmn., exec. dir. N.J. State Opera. Recipient Barnegat Bay Sailing Hall of Fame. Mem. Nat. Coun. Savs. Instns. (past chmn.), Essex County Savs. and Loan League (past chmn.), NJ Savs. League (past chmn.), NJ Hist. Soc. (past chmn.), Greater Newark C. of C. (bd. dirs.), NJ C. of C. (bd. dirs.), Union League Club, Delray Beach Yacht Club (past commodore), NY Yacht Club, Morris County Golf Club, Somerset Hills Golf Club, Palm Beach Yacht Club, Bay Head Yacht Club (past commodore), Bay Head Fire Co. #1. Republican. Episcopalian. Home: Bay Head, NJ. Died Dec. 4, 2013.

OCHS, STANLEY GILBERT, real estate broker; b. Plainfield, NJ, Oct. 11, 1931; s. Philip and Etta (Porter) O.; m. Arlene Rene Weitzman, Sept. 6, 1953; children: Joseph, Steven. BA, Rutgers U., 1954; MBA, L.I. Univ., 1967. Commd. 2d lt. USAF, 1954, advanced through grades to capt., 1960; asst. project engr. Grumman Aero Space Corp., Bethpage L.I., N.Y., 1963-67, 69-73; pres. Starjo Corp., Smithtown, N.Y., 1973-91, Jericho Sailboats Inc., Smithtown, N.Y., 1973-91, The Proper Yacht, Smithtown, N.Y., 1973-91, AR's Eagle's Nest Homes Inc., Cape Coral, Fla., from 1990. Com. chmn. Boy Scouts Am., Kings Park, N.Y., 1964-73. Mem. Comml. Investors Real Estate, Ft. Myers Bd. Realtors, Cape Coral Assn. Realtors. Avocations: sailing, camping, collect special autos. Home: Cape Coral, Fla. Died Apr. 26, 2007.

O'CONNOR, KEVIN WASHBURN, lawyer; b. Wilmington, Del., Apr. 9, 1955; s. Timothy Edmond and Elizabeth (Clifford) O'C.; m. Ellen Marie Muldoon, Sept. 1, 1984; children: Katherine, Margaret, Anne. Student, Emerson Coll., 1973-75; BA summa cum laude, Macalester Coll., 1977; JD, Am. U., 1984. Bar: Md. 1985. Mem. govtl. affairs staff Am. Speech-Lang.-Hearing Assn., Rockville, Md., 1977-82; assoc. dir. pub. affairs Fedn. Am. Soc. Exptl. Biology, Bethesda, Md., 1982-86; sr. legal analyst, project dir. Office Tech. Assessment U.S. Congress, Washington, 1986-95; exec. dir. Am. Soc. Med. Bio. Engring., Washington, from 1995. Bd. dirs. Cedar Lane Stage, Bethesda, 1986-88. Mem. ABA, Md. Bar Assn. Roman Catholic. Home: Burtonsville, Md. Died Apr. 16, 2007.

O'CONNOR, ROD, chemist, consultant, inventor; b. Cape Girardeau, Mo., July 4, 1934; s. Jay H. and Flora (Winters) O'C.; m. Shirley Ann Sander, Aug. 7, 1955; children: Mark Alan (dec.), Kara Ann, Shanna Suzanne, Timothy Patrick. BS, S.E. Mo. State Coll., 1955; PhD, U. Calif., Berkeley, 1958. Asst. prof. chemistry U. Omaha, 1958-60, Mont. State Coll., 1960-63; assoc. prof. chemistry Mont. State U., Bozeman, 1963-66; assoc. prof., coordinator gen. chemistry Kent (Ohio) State U., 1966-67; prof., dir. 1st year chemistry U. Ariz., Tucson, 1968-72; staff assoc. Adv. Council on Coll. Chemistry Stanford (Calif.) U., 1967-68; vis. prof. Wash. State U., Pullman, 1972-73; prof. chemistry Tex. A&M, College Station, 1973-86; pres. Texas ROMEC Inc., College Station, 1983-98; prof. environ. studies Baylor U., Waco, Tex., 1996-99. Cons. insect venoms Hollister-Stier Labs., Spokane, Wash., 1963-67; lab. separates editor W.H. Freeman Co., 1968-78; ednl. cons. TUCARA-4 Media Resources, Inc., 1971-74; mem. Coll. Chemistry Cons. Service; vis. scientist, tour lectr. Am. Chem. Soc., 1970-86. Author: (with T. Moeller) Ions in Aqueous Systems, 1972, Fundamentals of Chemistry, 1981, (with C. Mickey and A. Hassell) Solving Problems in Chemistry, 1981, (with L. Peck and K. Irgolic) Fundamentals of Chemistry in The Laboratory, 1981, (with T.E. Taylor and P. Glenn) Toward Success in College, 1981, (with A. Hassell and C. Mickey) Advanced Problems in Applied Chemistry, 2000; films Laboratory Safety, 1971; Contbr. articles to profl. jours.; patentee in field Recipient nat. teaching award Mfg. Chemists Assn., 1978; 4 regional teaching awards. Fellow AAAS, Am. Inst. Chemists, Sigma Xi; mem. Internat. Soc. Toxinology, Am. Chem. Soc. Died Aug. 7, 2014.

O'DONNELL, JOSEPH MICHAEL, cable television executive; b. Bronx, NY, Nov. 4, 1944; s. Willobroad Joseph and Florence Rose (Johansmeyer) O'D.; m. Patricia Kathryn Hewson, Apr. 27, 1967; children: Sean Adam, David Alan, Kathryn Elizabeth. BS in Biology, Manhattan Coll., 1966; MBA, Temple U., 1977. Programmer Dubner Computer Systems, NYC, 1971-72; project mgr. Gen. Inst., Hatboro, Pa., 1972-76; system mgr. Group W Teleprompter, Vineland, N.J., 1976-79; chmn., sec. Mullica Cable TV, New Gretna, N.J., from 1989; chmn. Clover Cable Ohio, Las Vegas, Nev., from 1979; sec. Clover Cable Systems, Vineland, N.J., 1989, chief exec. officer, 1981-89; chief exec. Chester Mendham Cable TV, Chester, N.J., from 1985. Bd. dirs. RCH Com. Hopewell Valley, Hopewell, N.J., 1985—. Trainer Vineland High Sch. Swim Team, 1990; mem. Rep. Inner Circle, Washington, 1987—. Manhattan Coll. scholar, 1962. Mem. Soc. Cable TV Engrs., Air Force Assn. Roman Catholic. Avocations: white water rafting, sports, massage, physical training. Home: Vineland, NJ. Died June 8, 2007.

O'FLAHERTY, GERALD NOLAN, secondary school educator, consultant; b. Bradley, Ill., Sept. 24, 1933; s. John Nolan and Dorothy Ann (Toohey) O'F.; m. Marilyn Ann McFarland, July 24, 1955; children: Jeffery Nolan, Mark Edward, Heather Maureen. BS in Edn., Ea. Ill. U., 1961; MS in Biol. Scis., St. Mary's Coll., Winona, Minn., 1965; cert. advanced study in biol. scis., No. Ill. U., 1970; cert. advanced study in ednl. adminstrn., Ill. State U., 1986. Cert. secondary tchr., ednl. adminstr., Ill. Chemist Bradley Roper Co., 1954-56; tchr. St. Anne (Ill.) Elem. Sch., 1958-61; tchr. sci. Kankakee (Ill.) Sch. Dist. 111, 1961-63; tchr. sci., chmn. dept., dir. curriculum mgmt. Bradley-Bourbonnais Community High Sch., from 1963. Rsch. cons. NSF, Washington, 1962-64, spl. seminar participant, New Orleans, 1982; cons. Ill. Office Edn., Springfield, 1965-71, North Cen. Accrediting Assn., Chgo., 1975—, numerous others; presenter in field. With U.S. Army, 1956-58. Recipient Outstanding Tchr. award Bradley-Bourbonnais Community High Sch., 1986; grantee NSF, 1962-75. Mem. NEA, NSTA (secondary curriculum com. 1982-85, spl. seminar participant 1978), Internat. Tissue Culture Assn., Nat. Assn. Biology Tchrs., Ill. Edn. Assn., Sigma Xi. Avocations: target shooting, photography, reading, writing. Home: Bourbonnais, Ill. Died June 27, 2007.

OGDEN, MELVIN J., retire purchaser; b. Richfield, Utah, Jan. 16, 1922; s. Franklin Marsh Ogden and Eleanor Ward; m. Marilyn Fae Hoopes, Apr. 1, 1930 (div. Aug. 1974); children: Tad William, Ward Nash, Janet Lynn, Margaret Ruth, Douglas Colin, Frederick Garn. BA in English, Brigham Young U., 1949; postgrad., U. Calif., Berkeley, 1951, UCLA, 1952. Tchr. S. Sevier H.S., Monroe, Utah, 1950-51, Fresno (Calif.) City Schs., 1952-53; insp. We. Weighinyan and Inspection Bur., Salt Lake City, 1955-56; purchaser Ch. Jesus Christ of Latter-day Saints, Salt Lake City, 1957-66, Granite Sch. Dist., Salt Lake City, 1966-67, Weber State U., Ogden, Utah, 1968-91. Cpl. USAF, 1944-46. Avocations: hiking, swimming, gardening. Home: Ogden, Utah. Died Nov. 2, 2006.

OGIER, ALTON L., lawyer; b. Florence, SC, Aug. 23, 1924; s. James Grayson and Emily Virginia (Sires) O.; m. June 17, 1950; children: Deborah Elizabeth Ogier Barnwell, Cynthia Elaine Ogier. LLB, U. S.C. Law Sch., Columbia, 1951. Claim agent Atlantic Coast Line Railroad, Charleston, 1951-55; lawyer Charleston, 1950-97; asst. state solicitor State S.C., Charleston, 1960-65, magistrate, 1964-83; pres. Home Builders Mortgage Corp., Charleston, 1982-97. Treas. Democratic Party, Charleston, 1954-58. With U.S. Navy, 1943-46. Mem. The Elks. Democratic. Avocations: golf, writing. Home: Charleston, SC. Died Dec. 9, 2006.

OHANNESSIAN, HARRY HAROUTUNE, travel agency executive; b. Jerusalem, Jan. 5, 1919; s. Ohannes and Heripsimeh (Soultanian) C.; m. Eva Hamparsoumian, July 7, 1946 (div. Mar. 1978); children: John, Robert; m. Beatriz Araujo, Dec. 19, 1984. Matriculation, Brit. Govt., 1938; grad., London Sch. of Maths., 1940, London Sch. of Econ. Scis., 1942. Pres. Cedars Travel, Inc., NYC, from 1963; chmn. Wataniyah Corp., NYC, 1973-88; v.p. U.S.-Arab C. of C., NYC, 1973-88; internat. commerce and bus. cons. to the middle east Stony Brook, N.Y., from 1989. Cons. in field. Decorated Knight (Order of St. John). Mem. St. George's Golf and Country Club,. Stony Brook Club. Republican. Mem. Christian Ch. Avocations: tennis, swimming, gardening, music. Home: Stony Brook, NY. Died July 30, 2007.

O'HARA, MAUREEN (MAUREEN FITZSIMONS), actress; b. Dublin, Aug. 17, 1920; d. Charles and Marguerite (Liburn) FitzSimons; m. George Hanley Brown (annulled), Will Price, Dec. 29, 1941 (div. 1952); 1 child, Bronwyn Bridget Fitzsimons; m. Charles Blair, 1967 (dec. 1978) Pres. Antilles Air Boats, St. Croix, V.I., 1978-81, chief exec. officer, 1978-79; owner, columnist The Virgin Islander, 1975-80. Actress in numerous prodns. including: (movies) Jamaica Inn, Hunchback of Notre Dame, 1939, A Bill of Divorcement, Dance, Girls, Dance, 1940, They Met in Argentina, How Green Was My Valley, 1941, To the Shores of Tripoli, 1942, Ten Gentlemen from West Point, 1942, The Black Swan, 1942, This Land is Mine, 1943, Immortal Sergeant, 1943, The Fallen Sparrow, 1943, Buffalo Bill, 1944, The Spanish Main, 1945, Do You Love Me?, 1946, Sinbad the Sailor, 1947, Miracle on 34th St., 1947, Rio Grande, At Sword's Point, 1952, Kangaroo, 1952, Flame of Araby, 1952, The Quiet Man, 1952, Against All Flags, 1952, Redhead from Wyoming, 1953, War Arrow, 1953,Lady Godiva, 1955, Wings of Eagles, 1957, Our Man in Havana, 1960, The Parent Trap, 1961, The Deadly Companions, 1961, Mr. Hobbs Takes a Vacation, 1962, McClintock, 1963, Spencer's Mountain, 1963, The Rare Breed, 1966, The Battle of the Villa Fiorita, 1965, How Do I Love Thee, 1970, Big Jake, 1971, Only the Lonely, 1991; (TV film) The Christmas Box, 1995, Cab to Canada, 1998, The Last Dance, 2000; (play) Christine, 1960; (TV) The Red Pony, Mrs. Miniver, Scarlet Pimpernel, Spellbound, High Button Shoes, Who's Afraid of Mother Goose. Recipient Heritage award, Am. Ireland Fund, 1991. Died Oct. 24, 2015.

O'HERN, THOMAS MONROE, obstetrician/gynecologist; b. Hannibal, Mo., Oct. 4, 1928; s. Alfred Edward and Alma Margaret (Monroe) O'H.; m. Lorraine Rosella Brisky, Oct. 3, 1952; children: Thomas Jr., Mary K., Cynthia M., Janet L. BA, Westminster Coll., Fulton, Mo., 1949; MD, St. Louis U., 1953. Diplomate Am. Bd. Ob-Gyn. Commd. 1st lt. USAF, 1953, advanced through grades to col., 1969, intern Los Angeles County Harbor Gen. Hosp. Torrence, 1953-54, resident in ob-gyn Walter Reed Gen. Hosp. Washington, 1956-59, cons. surgeon gen., 1971-75, ret., 1975; practice medicine specializing in ob-gyn Springfield, Ill., from 1975; clin. asst. prof. ob-gyn sch. medicine So. Ill. U., from 1975. Fellow Am. Coll. Ob/Gyn; mem. AMA. Home: Springfield, Ill. Died Feb. 24, 2007.

OHLSON, THOMAS GUNNAR, social sciences researcher, educator; b. Varberg, Sweden, Feb. 20, 1954; BA, Gothenburg U., MA, 1980; PhD, Uppsala U., 1998. Sr. rsch. fellow, project leader Stockholm Internat. Peace Rsch. Inst., 1980—87, sec. chairperson local trade union, 1981—87; sr. lectr. Inst. Superior de Relações Internacionais, Maputo, 1987—90; chefe dept. estudos estrategicos, prof. associado Ctr. Estudos Africanos, U. Eduardo Mondlane, Maputo, Mozambique, 1987—90; mem., gov. bd. Dept. Peace and Conflict Rsch., Uppsala U., 1996, assoc. prof., 2000—05, prof., from 2005. External reviewer, referee Cambridge U. Press, 1998; editl. & adv. bd. mem. African Jour. Conflict Resolution, 2004. Avocations: sports, reading, music. Died 2012.

OKEKE, NLOGHA ENWELUM, general surgeon; b. Nnewi, Nigeria, Dec. 5, 1926; s. Jeremiah Enwelum and Ona (Odunze) O.; married; children: Emeka, Ona, Nnanyelu, Ifeoma, Nkechi. BSc (cum laude), Bates Coll., 1951; MD, Boston U. Medical Sch., 1955. Diplomate Am. Nat. Bd. Medical Examiners, Am. Bd. Surgery. Intern Boston City Hosp., Boston, 1955-56, jr. asst. resident, sr. asst. resident, chief resident, 1956-60; medical dir., surgeon-in-chief Eastern Nigeria Medical Cen., Enugu, Nigeria, 1961; founder & pres. Enugy C. of C., Enugu, Nigeria, 1963-69; chmn. infection com. St. Luke's Hosp., New Bedford, Mass., 1974-76; chmn. Federal Food & Drugs Adv. Coun., Lagos, Nigeria, 1986-90; pvt.practice New Bedford, Mass., 1970-76. Chmn. U. Nigeria Teaching Hosp., 1966-69; chmn. mng. dir. IFFNA Co. Limited, 1960-69; dir. Industrial Devel. Ctr. Anambra State U. Tech., 1984-93; gov. bd. mem. Nigerian Inst. Policy & Strategic Studies, Kuru, 1984—; chmn. com. on rehabilitationof Oji River Legrosy Hosp., 1984-93; attending surgeon St. Luke's Hosp., Union Hosp., mem. utilazation com. St. Luke's Hosp., medical dir. Our Ladies Haven Nursing Home Bairhave, Mass.; medical adv. New Bedford Urban Coalition, New Bedford, Mass., physician Polariod Co., and others. Author: Anambra State Industrial Information Handbook, 1982, The Nigerian Challenge, 1984. Chmn. Eastern Nigeria Festival of the Arts, 1965-69; trustee Iyi-Enu CMS Hosp, Awo-Omama Hosp., chmn. Food & Drug adv. coun., 1986; chmn. Anambra State Industrial Promotion Coun., 1987, coun. mem. Nigerian Inst. Internat. Affairs, bd. govs., 1988-93; pres. Nigeria/Japan Assn., 1990-94. Fellow Am. Coll. Surgeons, West African Coll. Surgeons, Internat. Coll. Surgeons; mem. Mass. Medical Soc., Nigerian Medical Assn. (vice chmn. 1986), N.Y. Acad. Scis., Medical Coun. of Can. (licenciate), Enugu Rotary Club (pres. 1981-82), Nigerian Assn. C. of C. (2nd deputy nat. pres. 1987-90). Avocations: stamp collecting/philately, collection of african arts & carvings, collection of antiques. Home: Enugu, Nigeria. Died July 18, 2007.

O'LEARY, JOHN JOSEPH, security firm executive; b. St. Paul, Mar. 31, 1934; s. Edward Michael and Gertrude Cecilia (Connell) O'L.; m. Sheila Maria Dudley, May 25, 1957 (div. Aug. 1984); children: Michael Patrick, Mareen Shannon, Kevin Timothy, Patrick John; m. Maria Lourdes Lavalle, Apr. 29, 1990. AA, U. Minn., St. Paul, 1960. Factory rep. U.S. The Lindsay Co., St. Paul, 1955-61; owner Motorette Corp., Reseda, Calif., 1961-68; mgr. nat. accounts The Anderson Co., Gary, Ind., 1968-78; v.p. and ops. mgr. Ameripak, San Dimas, Calif., 1978-80; regional sales mgr. Carter Carburator, LA, 1980-83; regional sales rep. cons. J.S. Paluch Co., Santa Fe Springs, Calif., 1983-93; owner O'Leary Enterprises, San Diego, 1993-97. Inventor: Electric Wheel Chair (sold), Aloud Alarm System, Tops for Turbines. Mayorial bid City of San Diego, 1990; County Sch. Dist. bid City of San Diego, 1992. Sgt. USMC, 1952-55, Korea. Mem. Marine Corp. League (treas.), Ancient Order Hibernians in Am., KC. Republican. Roman Catholic. Avocations: wood working, house repairs and additions, charity volunteer, boating. Died July 3, 2007.

OLEKSY, JÓZEF, former Prime Minister of Poland, economist; b. Nowy Sacz, Poland, June 22, 1946; m. Maria Oleksy; 2 children. B, Warsaw Sch. Econs., 1969, PhD in Economics, 1977. Sci. worker Warsaw Sch. Economics, 1969—78; mem. Coun. Ministers, Warsaw, 1989; dep. to Sejm, 1989—2005; prim. min. Govt. of Poland, 1995—96, minister internal affairs, 2004; chmn. Social-Democratic Party, 1996—98, 2005. Spkr. Parliament, 1993-95, 2004-05; chmn. Democratic Left Alliance, 2004-05 Contbr. articles to profl. jours. Social Democratic Party. Avocations: walking, history, futurology, global challenges. Died Jan. 9, 2015.

OLIVIERI, DONALD HERBERT, architect; b. Chgo., Jan. 14, 1931; s. Joseph J. and Isola (Menconi) O.; m. Gertrude M. Klinkner, Feb. 15, 1958; children: Diane M., Donald H., Janet, John, Teri, Toni. BArch, U. Ill., 1955. Sec. Olivieri Bros., Inc., Chgo., 1963-87, pres. Richton Park, Ill., from 1987, Yates Investment Co., Chgo., 1962-78; prin. Olivieri Assoc. Architects, Chgo., 1958-88; ptnr. Alosi Investments, Chgo., 1959-88. Pres. Prestwick Homeowners, Frankfort, Ill., 1979. Capt. U.S. Army, 1955-57. Mem. AIA, Am. Registered Architects, Lions (v.p. 1988), KC. Roman Catholic. Home: Frankfort, Ill. Died Apr. 17, 2007.

OLSCAMP, PAUL JAMES, retired academic administrator; b. Montreal, Que., Can., Aug. 29, 1937; s. James J. and Luella M. (Brush) O.; m. Ruth I. Pratt, Dec. 2, 1978; children by previous marriage: Rebecca Ann, Adam James. BA, U. Western Ont., 1958, MA, 1960; PhD in Philosophy, U. Rochester, 1962. Instr. Ohio State U., Columbus, 1962, asst. prof., 1963-66, assoc. prof., 1966-69, assoc. dean humanities, 1969; dean faculties, prof. philosophy Roosevelt U., Chgo., 1970-71, v.p. acad. affairs, 1971-72; prof. philosophy Syracuse (N.Y.) U., 1972-75, exec. asst. to chancellor, 1972, vice chancellor student programs, 1972-75; pres. Western Wash. U., Bellingham, 1975-82, Bowling Green State U., Bowling Green, Ohio, 1982—95; interim pres. South Dakota State U., Brookings, SD, 1996—97, Mayville State U., Mayville, ND, 2002—03; interim v.p. instruction North Idaho Coll., Coer d'Alene, Idaho, 2006—07. Grad. fellow in humanities U. Western Ont., 1959 Author: Descartes: The Discourse, Optics, Geometry and Meteorology, 1965, The Moral Philosophy of George Berkeley, 1970, An Introduction to Philosophy, 1971, Malebranche: The Search After Truth, 1980; contbr. articles to profl. jours. Mem. Nat. Coun. on the Humanities, 1988-92, NCAA President's Commn., 1989-91 Recipient Mackintosh Public Speaking and Lecturing award U. Western Ont., 1959-60, Alfred J. Wright award Ohio State U., 1970; Grad. Fellow in Humanities U. Western Ont., 1959, Graduate Studies fellow U. Rochester, 1960, 61-62 Mem. American Assn. State Colleges & Universities (mem. com. undergrad. edn. 1982-90, com. confs. and profl. devel. 1989-92), American Philos. Assn. Died Oct. 14, 2014.

OLSEN, THEODORA EGBERT PECK (MRS. SEVERT ANDREW OLSEN), artist, educator; b. Union, NJ, Sept. 6, 1909; d. Edward Egbert and Theodorea G. (Tucker) Peck; m. Ray Sheldon Wilbur, Sept. 8, 1933 (dec. 1966); m. Severt Andrew Olsen, July 17, 1967 (dec. Feb. 1975); 1 child, Margaret Anne stepchildren: Arlene Christine, Severt Eugene. Student, NY Sch. Design, 1928—2029, Pratt-Phoenix Sch. Design, NYC, 1929—32, Coll. City, NY, 1955, Wagner Coll., 1965. Cons., lectr., pvt. tchr., from 1934; active fund-raising Richmond Meml. Hosp., 1946—54; com. to beautify halls Tottenville HS, S.I., 1958—60; tchr. painting YWCA, S.I., 1968—72. Exhibitions include Contemporary Gallery, Newark, 1932, S.I. Mus., 1947—65, NYC Fedn. Women's Clubs, 1961, Island Art Ctr. Gallery, New Dorp, S.I., 1961, 33d N.J., Montclair Art Mus., 1964, Summit Art Ctr., NJ, 1965, outdoor shows, Sailors Snug Harbour, SI, 1956—63, Greenwich Village, NYC, 1961—64, Southhampton and Westhampton (L.I.) Beach, 1964, Summit Art Ctr., NJ, 1967, Spring Festival Arts, Staten Island, 1968, Represented in permanent collections Wagner Coll., S.I., S.I. Mus., View From Guild Hall, Show Case, Variation on Theme VIII, Long Island Expressway, Seed Pods, Emergence from Chrysalis. Recipient Purchase award, S.I. Mus.-Wagner Coll., from 1958, Julius Weisglass award, S.I. Mus., 1960, 2d prize, 1965, 1st prize and Honorable Mention, NYC Fedn. Women's Clubs Competition, 1961. Mem.: Coast Guard Officer's Wives, Pratt-Phoenix Sch. Design Alumni (pres. 1969—71, Jury awards 1949), Nat. Assn. Mil. Widows, South Shore Artists Group (life; founder, pres. 1946—47, 1949—61, 2nd v.p. 1965—66), Prince Bay Women's, Epsilon Nu Sigma. Home: Staten Island, NY. Died Nov. 17, 2006; Ogdenburg, NY.

OLSEN-FULERO, LYNDA LAVERNE, psychology educator; b. McMinnville, Oreg., Nov. 16, 1947; d. Vernon Hilmar and Eunice Audrey (Evans) Olsen; m. Michael Alex McDonald, Dec. 19, 1969 (div. 1979); 1 child, Ariel Claire; m. Solomon M. Fulero, Jan. 1, 1982; 1 child, David Nathan. BA, Mills Coll., Oakland, Calif., 1970; MA, Portland State U., Oreg., 1973; PhD, U. Oreg., 1979. Lic. psychologist, Ohio. Vis. asst. prof. Wright State U., Dayton, Ohio, 1979-82; asst. prof. Antioch Coll., Yellow Springs, Ohio, 1982-84, Miami U., Hamilton, Ohio, 1984-88, assoc. prof., from 1988. Contbr. articles to profl. jours. Mem. Am. Psychol. Assn., Midwestern Psychol. Assn., Soc. for Rsch. in Child Devel., Phi Beta Kappa. Democrat. Avocations: music, cooking. Died Dec. 29, 2006.

OLSON, FLOYD PALMER, retired service company executive; b. Glencoe, Minn., May 12, 1932; s. Oscar Peter and Hazel Anna (Wolff) O.; m. Sandra Rae Larson, Feb. 5, 1955; children: Douglas, David, Clayton, Sarah. BS, U. Minn., 1954. Mgmt. trainee Wilson Meat Packing Co., Albert Lea, Minn., 1957-60, dept. mgr. Memphis, 1960-62, area mgr. Sao Paulo, Brazil, 1962-69, plant mgr. Oklahoma City, 1969-76; pres. Gol-Pak Corp., Oneida, N.Y., 1976-78; asst. West Coast mgr. Hygrade Food Products, Tacoma, Wash., 1978-79; owner, dir. Servpro, Gig Harbor, Wash., 1979-2000; ret., 2000. Bd. mem. Peninsula Light Co., Gig Harbor, 1992-95; state dir. Servpro Industries, Wash., 1982-2000. Organizer Jr. Achievement, Albert Lea, Minn., 1959; pres. couns. ch., 1975-74. With U.S. Army, 1955-57. Mem. Rotary Internat. (pres. Gig Harbor 1990-91, presdl. citation 1996, dist. gov. 1994-95, zone chmn. 1996-97, dir. elect, Paul Harris fellow 1993). Republican. Avocations: motor-homing, golf, travel. Died Aug. 8, 2007.

OLSON, SANDRA JOANNE, entrepreneur; b. Birmingham, Ala., Oct. 17, 1948; d. Charles Hershel Self and Ruby Virginia Hooper; m. William Wayne Swader, June 11, 1964 (div. Dec. 1970); children: William Brent Swader, Victoria Lynn Journey; m. Richard Charles Olson, July 3, 1995. Cert. R EEG T Am. Bd. Registration of END Technologists, 1974. Dept. mgr. end Med. Ctr. East, Birmingham, Ala., 1991—94; lead eeg technician Gadsden Regional Med. Ctr., Ala., 1994—96; owner END Tech. Svcs., Gadsden, from 1997; dept. mgr. Jacksonville Med. Ctr., Ala., 1999—2004. Author: (tng. booklet) The International 10/20 Electrode Placement System. Founder ENDtechnology.com, Gadsden, 2004—05. Mem.: Ala. Soc. END Technologists (tng., edn. dir. 2005), Am. END Soc. (assoc.). Non-Denominational. Achievements include first to Development of Surgical Monitoring and Seizure Monitoring in Memphis, Tennessee. Avocations: painting (awards won), poetry (awards won), building computers, development of computer programs, needle crafts. Home: Gadsden, Ala. Died Mar. 2, 2007.

O'MALIA, MARY FRANCES, special education educator; d. Horace Emmett Fansler and Frances Fansler Kittle, Robert Blair Kittle (Stepfather); m. William Biff O'Malia, Nov. 8, 1980; children: Nohealani Marie, Shanice Francine. BA, Dominican U. of Calif., San Rafael, 1977; postgrad., Dominican U., 1977—83; postgrad. in Sch. Counseling, U. Nev., from 1998. Lic. tchr. Nev., 1979, cert. alcohol and drug abuse counselor Nev., 1999. Tchg. prin. Mineral County Sch. Dist., Hawthorne, Nev., 1986—88; spl. edn. tchr. Hawaii State Dept. of Edn., Holualoa, 1989—91; HIV/AIDS instr./trainer ARC: Hawaii State Chpt., Honolulu, 1992—97; substance abuse counselor Ctr. Behavioral Health, Reno, 1999—99; grad. tchg. asst. U. Nev., Reno, 1999—2001; spl. edn. diagnostician Washoe County Sch. Dist., Reno, 2001—03; spl. edn. tchr. Silver Stage Mid. Sch., Silver Springs, Nev., from 2003. Contbr. articles to profl. jours. Recipient Vol. of the Quarter, ARC, 1995, Distinquished Svc. award, Mineral County Sch. Dist., 1988. Mem.: Coun. for Exeptional Children. Catholic. Avocations: scuba diving, travel, computers, reading. Home: Fernley, Nev. Died Dec. 18, 2006.

OMER, GEORGE ELBERT, JR., retired orthopaedic surgeon, educator; b. Kansas City, Kans., Dec. 23, 1922; s. George Elbert and Edith May (Hines) O.; m. Wendie Vilven, Nov. 6, 1949; children: George Eric, Michael Lee. BA, Ft. Hays Kans. State U., 1944; MD, Kans. U., 1950; MSc in Orthopaedic Surgery, Baylor U., Waco, Tex., 1955. Diplomate Am. Bd. Orthopaedic Surgery, 1959, (bd. dirs. 1983-92, pres. 1987-88), re-cert. orthopaedics and hand surgery, 1983, cert. surgery of the hand, 1989. 2nd lt. US Army, 1945, advanced through grades to col., 1967, ret., 1970; rotating intern Bethany Hosp., Kansas City, 1950-51; resident in orthopaedic surgery Brooke Army Hosp., San Antonio, 1952-55, William Beaumont Army Hosp., El Paso, Tex., 1955-56; chief surgery Irwin Army Hosp., Ft. Riley, Kans., 1957-59; cons. in orthopaedic surgery 8th Army, chief orthop. surgery 121st Evacuation Hosp. Republic of Korea, 1959-60; asst. chief orthopaedic surgery, chief hand surgeon Fitzsimons Army Med. Center, Denver, 1960-63; dir. orthopaedic residency tng. Armed Forces Inst. Pathology at Walter Reed Army Med. Ctr., Washington, 1963-65; chief orthopaedic surgery and chief Army Hand Surg. Center, Brooke Army Med. Center, 1965-70; cons. in orthopaedic and hand surgery Surgeon Gen. Army, 1967-70; prof. orthopaedics, surgery, and anatomy, chmn. dept. orthopaedic surgery, chief div. hand surgery U. N.Mex., 1970-90, med. dir. phys. therapy, 1972-90, acting asst. dean grad. edn. Sch. Medicine, 1980-81. Mem. active staff U. N.Mex. Hosp., Albuquerque, 1970—2005, chief of med. staff, 1984-86; cons. staff other Albuquerque hosps.; cons. orthopedic surgery USPHS, 1966-85, US Army, 1970-92, USAF, 1970-78, VA, 1970-2000; cons. Carrie Tingley Hosp. for Crippled Children, 1970-99, interim med. dir., 1970-72, 86-87, mem. bd. advisor 1972-76, chair, 1994-96. Mem. bd. editors Clin. Orthopaedics, 1973-90, Jour. AMA, 1973-74, Jour. Hand Surgery, 1976-81; trustee Jour. Bone and Joint Surgery, 1993-99, sec., 1993-96, chmn., 1997-99; contbr. more than 300 articles to profl. jours., numerous chpts. to books. Decorated Legion of Merit, Army Commendation medal with oak leaf cluster; recipient Alumni Achievement award Ft. Hays State U., 1973, Recognition plaque Am. Soc. Surgery Hand, 1989, Recognition plaque N.Mex. Orthopaedic Assn., 1991, Recognition award for hand surgery Am. Osteo. Acad. Orthopaedics, 1982, Pioneer award Internat. Socs. for Surgery Hand, 1995, Rodey award U. N.Mex. Alumni Assn., 1997, Cornerstone award U. N.Mex. Health Scis. Ctr., 1997; recognized with Endowed Professorship U. N.Mex. Sch. Medicine, 1995; recognized with named Annual Orthop. Seminar and Alumni Day Brooke Army Med. Ctr., 1999. Fellow ACS, Am. Orthopaedic Assn. (pres. 1988-89, exec. dir. 1989-93), Am. Acad. Orthopaedic Surgeons, Assn. Orthopaedic Chmn., N.Mex. Orthopaedic Assn. (pres. 1979-81, 1999-2000), La. Orthopaedic Assn. (hon.), Korean Orthopaedic Assn. (hon.), Peru Orthopaedic Soc. (hon.), Caribbean Hand Soc., Am. Soc. Surgery Hand (pres. 1978-79), Am. Assn. Surgery of Trauma, Assn. Bone and Joint Surgeons, Assn. Mil. Surgeons US, Riordan Hand Soc. (pres. 1967-68), Sunderland Soc. (pres. 1981-83), Soc. Mil. Orthopaedic Surgeons, Brazilian Hand Soc. (hon.), S.Am. Hand Soc. (hon.), Groupe D'Etude de la Main, Brit. Hand Soc. (hon.), Venezuela Hand Soc. (hon.), South African Hand Soc. (hon.), Western Orthopaedic Assn. (pres. 1981-82), AAAS, Russell A. Hibbs Soc. (pres. 1977-78), 38th Parallel Med. Soc. (Korea) (sec. 1959-60); mem. AMA, Phi Kappa Phi, Phi Sigma, Alpha Omega Alpha, Phi Beta Pi. Achievements include pioneer work in hand surgery. Home: Spring, Tex. Died Nov. 20, 2014.

ONDRICEK, MIROSLAV, cinematographer; b. Nov. 4, 1934; 1 child, David. Cinematographer: (films) If..., 1969, Slaughterhouse Five, 1971, Taking Off, 1971, O Lucky Man!, 1973, Hair, 1979, Ragtime, 1981 (Academy award nomination best cinematography 1981), The World According to Garp, 1982, Silkwood, 1983, The Divine Emma, 1983, Amadeus, 1984 (Academy award nomination best cinematography 1984), Heaven Help Us, 1985, F/X, 1986, Big Shots, 1987, Funny Farm, 1988, Valmont, 1989, Awakenings, 1990, A League of Their Own, 1992, Let It Be Me, 1995, The Preacher's Wife, 1996, Riding In Cars with Boys, 2001, FX, 2001 Recipient Internat. award, American Soc. of Cinematographers, 2004. Died Mar. 28, 2015.

O'NEILL, JOHN PATRICK, priest, religious educator, counselor; b. Phila., Dec. 13, 1929; s. John Patrick and Marie Basil (Gill) O'N. AB in History, Niagara U., 1954, MS, 1967, Villanova U., 1965. Joined Oblate of St. Francis de Sales, 1950, ordained priest Roman Cath. Ch., 1959. Priest, counselor, from 1959; tchr. secondary Cath. high schs., Pa., Del., NY, Mich., 1960-78; adminstr. De Sales Cath. High Sch., Lockport, N.Y., 1961-69. Pres., chair Diocesan Religious Edn. Adv. Bd., Stockton, Calif., 1981-92. Republican. Avocations: reading, writing, painting, travel, music. Died Feb. 10, 2007.

OREFICE, GASTONE ORTONA, journalist; b. Livorno, Italy, July 18, 1922; came to the U.S., 1973; s. Giorgio and Anna (Castelli) O.; m. Lea Ottolenghi, Oct. 15, 1945; children: Lidia, Laura, Anna. D of Econs., U. Florence, Italy, 1949. Italian profl. journalist. Staff reporter Daily Newspaper, Livorno, 1945-57; corr. Ag Italia, Morocco, 1958, Agy. de Press Italia, Paris, France, 1959-64, RAI Italian Radio TV Syst., Paris, 1966-72, NYC, 1973-87; chief editor RAI Corp., NYC, from 1987. Lectr. in field. Author: A Certain Idea of France, 1971, Reagan The...American Choice, 1981; contbr. articles to profl. jours. Recipient Grand Ofcl., Merit of Italian Republic from the Pres. of the Italian Republic, Rome, 1993. Avocation: tennis. Died Oct. 30, 2006.

OREN, JOHN BIRDSELL, retired coast guard officer; b. Madison, Wis., Dec. 27, 1909; s. Arthur Baker and Lucile Grace (Comfort) O.; m. Harriet Virginia Prentis, Feb. 9, 1934; children— Virginia Joan (Mrs. Luther Warren Strickler II), John Edward. BS, USCG Acad., 1933; MS in Marine Engring, MIT, 1942. Commd. ensign USCG, 1933, advanced through grades to rear adm., 1964; chief engring. div. (11th Coast Guard Dist.), 1957-59, (12th Coast Guard Dist.), 1960-61; dep. chief (Office Engring.), Washington, 1962-63, chief Office of Engring., 1964-68; now ret. Mem. Mcht. Marine Council, 1964— ; chmn. ship structures com. Transp. Dept., 1964— ; exec. dir. Maritime Transp. Research Bd., Nat. Acad. Scis., 1968— ; mem. nat. adv. bd. Am. Security Council Recipient Legion of Merit. Mem. Soc. Am. Mil. Engrs. (pres. 1966, Acad. of Fellows), Am. Soc. Naval Engrs. (pres. 1965), Internat. Inst. Welding (vice chmn. Am. coun. 1964), Ret. Officers Assn. (bd. dirs. 1978), Pan Am. Inst. Naval Engring., Vinson Hall Residents Assn. (v.p. 1998), Masons. Republican. Episcopalian. Home: Mc Lean, Va. Died Dec. 22, 2006.

OROYAN, SUSANNA ELIZABETH, artist, author; b. Portland, Oreg., May 24, 1942; d. Louis B. and Marjorie E. (Hibbert) Scruggs; m. Thomas Oroyan; 1 child, Martin Thomas. BA in English, Calif. State U., Sacramento, 1967; MA in English, U. Oreg., 1971. Tchr. English Eugene (Oreg.) High Sch., 1968-72; artist, owner Fabricat Design, Eugene, from 1979; cons., contbg. editor Doll Artistry Mag., from 1990. Lectr. Original Doll Artist Invitation Seminar, 1977, 78, 80; instr. Search prog. U. Oreg., 1975-76; artist, instr. Jr. League Art in Schs. Progs., 1976, 77, 78, guest instr. sculpture, 1990—; editor: Original Doll Artist Coun. Am. News, 1980—; columnist Dollmaker's Notebook, Doll Rev., 1975-78; author: Dollmaker's Notebook, 1981, Fabric Figures, 1989, Paperclay, 1992, Business and Marketing, Competitions and Critique, Polymer Clay Contracts, 1993, Ideas and Techniques for Dollmaking, 1993; co-author: (with Carol-Lynn Waugh) Contemporary Artist Dolls, 1986; contbr. to various publs. One man shows at Keller Gallery, Salem, Oreg., Contemporary Crafts Gallery, Portland, Springfield (Oreg.) Mus.; exhibited in group shows at Internat. Dollmaker's Assn., 1974-75, United Fedn. Doll Clubs, 1976, 77, 79, 80, Original Doll Artist Coun. Am., 1979-80, Oreg. Art Exhbn., 1975-76, Lane Co., 1975, Wenham Mus., Mass., 1988, Dollmaker's Magic, Houston, N.Y.C., 1988-90, Dolls of 21st Century, Springfield, Oreg., 1990, Artique, Anchorage, 1993, Contemporary Artists Mulvane, Topeka, Kans., 1993. eka; represented in pvt collections. Chmn. Emerald Empire Doll and Toy Festival, 1975, 77, 80. Recipient 1st award Internat. Dollmarker's Assn., 1974, 75, All Oreg. Art Exhibit, 1975, United Fedn. Doll Clubs, 1976. Mem. Original Doll Artist Coun. of Am., Nat. Inst. Am. Doll Artists (pres. 1987—), United Fedn. of Doll Clubs (chmn. region I conf. 1985), Acad. Dollmakers Internat. Died Aug. 22, 2007.

ORTMAN, GEORGE EARL, artist; b. Oakland, Calif., Oct. 17, 1926; s. William Thomas and Anna Katherine (Noll) O.; m. Conni Whidden, Aug. 5, 1960 (dec.); 1 stepson, Roger Graham Whidden; m. Lynn Braswell Student, Calif. Coll. Arts and Crafts, 1947-49, Atelier Stanley William Hayter, 1949, Acad. Andre L'Hote, Paris, 1949-50, Hans Hoffman Sch. Art, 1949-50. Co-founder Tempo Playhouse, NYC, 1954; Instr. painting and drawing NYU, 1962-65; co-chmn. fine arts Sch. Visual Arts NYC, 1963-65; artist-in-residence Princeton U., 1966-69, Honolulu Acad. Art, 1969; head painting dept. Cranbrook Acad. Art, Bloomfield Hills, Mich., 1970-92. One-man exhbns. include Tanager Gallery, 1954, Wittenborn Gallery, 1955, Stable Gallery, 1957, 60, Howard Wise Gallery, 1962, 63, 64, 66, 69, Gimpel-Weitzenhoffer Gallery, 1972 (all N.Y.C.), Swetzoff Gallery, Boston, 1961-62, Fairleigh Dickinson U., 1962, Mirvish Gallery, Toronto, Can., 1964, Walker Art Center, Mpls., 1965, Milw. Art Center, 1966, Dallas Mus. Art, 1966, Portland Mus. Art, 1966, Akron Inst. Art, 1966, U. Chgo., 1967, Princeton U. Art Mus., 1967, Honolulu Acad. Art, 1969, Reed Coll., 1970, Cranbrook Acad. Art, 1970, 92, Indpls. Mus. Art, 1971, J.L. Hudson Gallery, Detroit, 1971, Gimpel-Weitzenhoffer, N.Y.C., 1972, 73, Gertrude Kasle Gallery, Detroit, 1976, Lee Hoffman Gallery, Detroit, 1977, Flint (Mich.) Mus. Art, 1977; other one-man exhbns. include Cranbrook Mus. Art, 1982, Mitchell Algus Gallery, N.Y.C., 2002, 07, 2012, 14; exhibited numerous group shows including Whitney Mus. Am. Art Annual, 1962, 63, 64, 65, 67, 73, Carnegie Internat., Pitts., 1964, 67, 70, Jewish Mus., N.Y.C., 1964, Corcoran Mus., Washington, 1964, others; represented permanent collections, Walker Art Center, Mpls., Mus. Modern Art, Whitney Mus. Am. Art, (both N.Y.C.), Guggenheim Mus., N.Y.C., Albright-Knox Mus., Buffalo, NYU, Christian Theol. Sem., Indpls., Indpls. Mus. Art, Cleve. Mus. Art, Mus. Am. Art, Washington, Honolulu Acad. Art, Newark Mus. Art, Container Corp. Am., Chgo. Ind. U. Music Bldg., Unitarian Ch., Princeton, Mfr. Hanover Trust Bldg., Albert Kahn & Assos., Detroit, Renaissance Center, Detroit, Mich. State Univ. Performing Arts Ctr., East Lansing, Detroit Inst. Arts, Princeton U. Art Mus. Guggenheim fellow, 1965-66; Ford Found. grantee, 1966, Lee Krasner Found. grantee; One of five Am. artists selected for 1965 Japanese Bi-ann.; Sculpture grant Adolph Gottlieb Found.; recipient Gov. NJ's Purchase award 2d ann. exhbn. art, 1967, Krasner Found. award, 2003, Lifetime Achievement award; Best of Show Religion in Art Exhbn., Birmingham, Ala., 1966, purchaser award, Am. Acad. Arts & Letters. Mem. Nat. Acad. of Design. Home: Castine, Maine. Died Dec. 16, 2015.

ORTOLANI, VINCENT, vocational business educator; b. Rochester, NY, July 19, 1941; s. Vincent and Fanny (Micciche) O.; m. Mary Margaret Appel, May 26, 1974; children: Elizabeth, Philip. BS, Niagara U., 1964; MA, The Cath. U. Am., 1968. Tchr. St. John's Mid. Sch., Bronx, N.Y., 1967-71, vice prin., 1970-71, prin., 1971-72; instr. Stratford Sch., Rochester, N.Y., 1977-78; adj. instr. Rochester Inst. of Tech., Nat. Tech. Inst. for Deaf, 1981-88, asst. prof., from 1988. Parent educator Dreikurs Family Edn. Assn. of Rochester (N.Y.), 1980—; cons. pvt. practice, Rochester, 1990—. Bd. dirs. Dreikurs Family Edn. Assn. of Rochester (N.Y.), 1989—. Mem. Nat. Edn. Asn., Nat. Edn. Bus. Assn., Ea. Bus. Edn. Assn. Avocations: art, music. Home: Rochester, NY. Died Apr. 13, 2007.

OSBORNE, MARTHA LEE, facilities manager; b. Fayetteville, NC, May 15, 1938; d. T. Emmett and Mary Omie (Cook) Thomas; m. Stancil Ray Osborne, Feb. 9, 1961 (div. Jan. 1985); children: Sandra Lee Lewis, Sharon Lynn Crane, Steven Ray. BA, U. Maryland, 1959. Tchr. Calvert County Bd. of Edn., Prince Frederick, Md., 1959-60, Fairfax County Bd. of Edn., Springfield, Va., 1960-62; sec. Safeway Stores, Inc., Washington, 1963-65; tchr. Prince Georges County Bd. Edn., Cheverly, Md., 1965-68, 1973-75, Cobb County Bd. Edn., Powder Springs, Ga., 1975-83; mgr. facilities Digital Communications and Assocs., Alpharetta, Ga., from 1983. Pres. The Facility Dept., Inc.; cons. Community Christmas Tree Com., Cumming, Ga., 1987—. Soloist, choir mem. 1st UMC Marietta, Ga., 1975-87; dir. music Children's Community Theater, Marietta, 1983-85; mem. Atlanta Symphony Orch. Chorus, 1975-81; dir., pres. Cumming Chorale, Ga., 1986—; pres. Cobb County Autry PTA, AcWorth, Ga., 1978. Mem. Internat. Facilities Mgmt. Assn. (v.p. Atlanta chpt., pres. 1990), Women in Constrn., NAFE, Forsyth County C. ofC., Airline Owners and Pilots Assn., Panhellenic Assn. (Diamond Honorary 1958), Order of Eastern Star, Sigma Alpha Iota. Republican. Methodist. Avocations: reading, singing, flower arranging, swimming, classes in new fields. Home: Cumming, Ga. Died Aug. 2, 2007.

OSBORNE, WILLIE CARROLL, petroleum geologist, consultant; b. McGehee, Ark., Aug. 16, 1923; s. John Carroll Osborne and Lola Almedia Mangum; m. Dixie Beth Tarver, Nov. 21, 1944; children: Janet Lee, John Carroll II. BS, Centenary Coll. La., 1943. Area geologist Tide Water Assoc. Oil, Midland, Tex., 1946—50, dist. geologist, 1950—51, Union Oil & Gas Corp., Midland, 1951—57; exploration mgr. Am. Trading and Prodn., Midland, 1957—69, gen. mgr., 1969—70; pvt. practice cons. geologist Midland, from 1970. Pres. Apex Oil and Gas Corp., Midland, 1985—90; dir., co-chmn. and chmn. bd. Western State Bank, Midland, 1985—90. Author: Looking Back, 1992, Running High/Looking Good, 1996, Freemasonry & America, 2000. Trustee Scottish Rite Hosp., Dallas, 2000. Lt. USN, 1943—46, PTO. Mem.: West Tex. Geol. Soc., Green Tree Country Club (developer from 1980, pres. 1981), Masons. Republican. Baptist. Avocations: reading, travel. Home: Midland, Tex. Died Jan. 5, 2007.

O'SHEA, HELENE CLAIRE, bookkeeper; b. Springfield, Ill., Dec. 22, 1935; d. David James and Catherine Agnes (Wilson) Eddington; m. David Lawrence O'Shea, July 6, 1957; children: David L. II, Maureen, Linda, Michael. Bookkeeper Harold O'Shea Builders, Springfield, Ill., from 1960. Author: A Handfull of Prisms, 2003. Roman Catholic. Avocation: grandchildren. Home: Springfield, Ill. Died June 22, 2007.

OSWALD, EDWARD THEODORE, vegetation ecologist, researcher; b. Kit Carson, Colo., Nov. 30, 1935; s. Theodore W. and Catherine Helen (Seaman) O.; m. Patricia Emma Pelton, May 27, 1961 (div. 1971); children: Theresa Marie, Vicky Sue, John Kenneth; m. Lorna Grace McCubbing, Apr. 27, 1979. BA, Western State Coll., 1962, MA, 1963; PhD, Mont. State U., 1966. Rsch. scientist Can. Forest Svc., Winnipeg, Man., 1966-70; rsch. officer Forestry Can., Victoria, B.C., from 1970. Mem. nat. site classification working group, 1984-88, nat. vegetation mgmt. working group, 1986-90; field mgr. environ. assessment Alaska Hwy. Pipeline. Contbr. articles to Ecoregions of Yukon Territory, Field Guide to Native Trees of Manitoba, Gabriola Island: A Landscape Analysis, Forest Communities in Lake Laberge Ecoregion, and others. Parks grantee Grand Teton Nat. Pk., Bozeman, Mont., 1964, 65, 66; recipient fellowship Mont. State Univ., Bozeman, 1965, 66. Mem. Can. Soc. Landscape Ecology, Ecol. Soc. Am., Horticulture Soc. Victoria. Achievements include rsch. on land classification, vegetation establishment during five years following wildlife in northern B.C. and southern Yukon Territory. Home: Victoria, Canada. Died Dec. 1, 2006.

OTNES, FRED, JR., (FREDERICK JOSEPH OTNES, JR.), illustrator, collage artist, painter; b. Junction City, Kans., Dec. 3, 1925; s. Frederick Joseph Otnes and Dorthea (Flower); m. Fran McCaughan (dec. 1995). Studied at, Art Inst., Chgo., American Acad. Art. Illustrator Life, Look, McCall's, Sports Illustrated, The Saturday Evening Post, and Collier's, 1950—2015. Instr. Illustrators Workshop. One-man exhbns., 1974, 78, 2015 Served USMC. Recipient numerous awards for nat. exhbns. N.Y. Soc. Illustrators, named to Soc. of Illustrators Hall of Fame, 2011 Home: West Redding, Conn. Died July 28, 2015.

OTNES, JR., FREDERICK JOSEPH See OTNES, FRED JR.

O'TOOLE, ROBERT V., JR., pathologist; b. Albany, NY, Oct. 23, 1931; s. Robert V. Sr and Helen A. (Castello) O'T.; m. Elizabeth Samascott, Sept. 4, 1954 (div. 1965); children: John R., Michael T., Andrew J.; m. Harriet Fowler, Nov. 26, 1965; children: Rovert V. III, Cathleen C. BS in Pre Medicine, Siena Coll., 1953; MD, St. Louis U., 1957. Diplomate Am. Bd. Ob-Gyn, Am. Bd. Pathology. Commd. USAF, 1956, advanced through grades to col.; resident in obgynecolog pathology Albany Med. Ctr., 1958-62; chief ob-gyn USAF, Griffiss AFB, N.Y., 1962-64; fellow in gyn pathology Johns Hopkins U., Balt., 1964-65; chief ob-gyn pathology Wilford Hall USAF, Lockland AFB, Tex., 1965-76, resident in pathology, 1973-74; cons. to surgeon gen. USAF, 1966-76; ret. Wilford Hall USAF, Lockland AFB, Tex., 1976; assoc. prof. pathology and ob-gyn Ohio State U., from 1976, dir. cytology div. dept. pathology, from 1976. Assoc. clin. prof. U. No. Tex., San Antonio, 1973-76. Co-author computer program for cytology mgmt., copyright 1983; contbr. numerous research papers and articles to prof. jours. Fellow Coll. Am. Pathologists, Am. Coll. Ob-Gyn, Air Force Soc. Clin. Surgeons (treas.), Cen. Ohio Soc. Pathologists (pres. 1984-85). Clubs: Quaterback (Worthington, Ohio), (v.p. 1986). Avocation: woodworking. Home: Columbus, Ohio. Died June 17, 2007.

OTSUKA, GEORGE KAZUMI, mechanical engineer, consultant; b. Courtland, Calif., Apr. 3, 1921; s. Kamehachi and Masuye (Otaguro) O. BSME, U. Houston, 1954; postgrad., UCLA, 1954-56, So. Meth. U., 1957-58. Registered engr., Tex., La. Mech. engr. U.S. Naval Test Ctr., Pt. Mugu, Calif., 1954-56, Chance Vought Aircraft, Dallas, 1956-59, Thiokol Chem. Corp., Marshall, Tex., 1959-64; sr. engr. Lockheed Elect. (NASA), Houston, 1965-71; mech. engr. Stewart & Stevenson, Houston, 1971-72; sr. design engr. Pan Am. (NASA), Houston, 1972-78; mech. engr. Channelview, Tex., from 1988. Sgt. U.S. Army, 1943-45. Mem. ASME. Achievements include patent for shape-memory-alloy heat engine. Died Dec. 24, 2006.

OTTO, FREI, architect; b. Siegmar, Saxony, Germany, May 31, 1925; Diploma of Engring., Technical U., Berlin, 1952, ED, 1954. Freelance architect, inventor, author and designer, 1952—72. Prof. Washington U., St. Louis; founder Inst. Lightweight Structures U. Stuttgart, 1964. Exhibitions include Mus. Modern Art, NY, 1971, Natural Design, Mus. Architecture AW Schussew, Moscow, 1981, Shape finding, Villa Stuck, Munich, 1992, German Pavilion, Expo '67 Montreal, Can., 1967, Munich Olympic Stadium, 1972, Ecological Houses, Berlin, 1990, Japanese Pavilion Roof Structure, Expo 2000 Hanover, Germany, 2000. Fighter pilot, World War II. Recipient Thomas Jefferson medal architecture, 1974, Honda prize for architecture and nature, Honda Found., Toyko, 1990, Wolf prize in architecture, Wolf Found., Israel, 1996, Aga Khan award architecture, 1998, Praemium Imperiale (Architecture), Japan Art Assn., 2006, Order of Merit, Fed. Republic Germany, 2006, Pritzker prize, 2015. Mem.: Royal Inst. British Architects (hon. Royal Gold medal 2005), Am. Inst. Architects (hon.). Died Mar. 9, 2015.

OURSEL, LUC, retired energy executive; b. Boulogne-Billancort, France, Sept. 7, 1959; m. Sylvia Delome. Grad., École Nationale Supérieure des Mines de Paris. Head energy and mineral resources divsn. French Regional Dept. Industry and Rsch., Rhone-Alps, 1984—88; head electricity divsn., asst. dir. gas, electricity and coal French Ministry Industry, 1988—91; tech. advisor in charge of indsl. affairs, armament programs and rsch. French Ministry Def., 1991—93; CEO SAE Gardy, CEO Schneider Shanghai Indsl. Control Schneider Electric Group, 1993—98, pres. & mng. dir. Schneider Electric Italia, 1998—2001, indsl. dir., 2001—02; sr. exec. v.p. Sidel Solutions, 2002—04; mgr. Geodis Internat. Subsidiaries, 2004—06; exec. v.p. Sidel Group, 2006—07; pres., CEO AREVA NP, Paris, 2007—10; exec. officer in charge of nuc. ops. AREVA, 2010—11, COO internat., mktg. & projects, 2011, pres., CEO, chmn. exec. bd., 2011—14. Mem. supervisory bd. Souriau Technologies Holding SAS; chmn. Société Française de l'Énergie Nucléaire. Named a Knight Comdr. of the French Legion of Honor, 2010. Died Dec. 3, 2014.

OUTLAW, THOMAS WILLIAM, municipal agency executive; b. Houston, Dec. 21, 1941; s. James Archer and Willeb (Albright) O.; m. Sherry Breakiron, Dec. 31, 1967 (div. Jan. 1993); 1 child, Joel Thomas. BBA, U. Houston, 1970. Staff economist Lockwood, Andrews and Newman, Houston, 1970-79; owner Outlaw Landscaping, Houston, 1979-88; dep. asst. dir. City of Houston, from 1988. Scout Master Boy Scouts of Am., Houston, 1984-89. Staff Sgt. USAF, 1963-68. Avocations: golf, backpacking, fishing, canoeing. Died June 12, 2007.

OUYANG, LIN MIN, surgeon, educator; b. Ouzou, China, May 17, 1921; children: Lucille, Jeanette, Elizabeth, William, David, Benjamin. Student, Talmage Coll., 1933-41; MD, Fujian Med. Coll., 1947; MS, Temple U., 1957. Diplomate Am. Bd. Colon and Rectal Surgery. Intern Holy Cross Hosp., Salt Lake City, 1952-53, resident, 1953-55, Temple U. Med. Ctr., Phila., 1955-57; surgeon Highland Hosp., Rochester, N.Y.; pvt. practice Rochester; retired, 1990. Clin. asst. prof. surgery U. Rochester Sch. Medicine. With Chinese Air Force Med. Corp, 1947-51. Mem. AMA, Am. Coll. Surgeons, Am. Colon and Rectal Surgeons, Soc. Internat. Univ. Colon & Rectal Surgery, N.Y. Med. Assn. Home: Rochester, NY. Died Jan. 25, 2007.

OVERBEEK, JAN THEODOOR GERARD, retired chemistry educator, consultant; b. Groningen, The Netherlands, Jan. 5, 1911; s. Adam Adolf and Johanna Cornelia (Van Rijssel) O.; m. Johanna Clasina Edie, Aug. 18, 1936; children: Reina Elisabeth, Antoinetta Wilhelmina, Marijke, Titia Edie. D in Math. and Scis., U. Utrecht, The Netherlands, 1941; DSc (hon.), Clarkson U., 1967, Bristol U., Eng., 1984. From pvt. to ensign Dutch Mil., 1933-34; rsch. worker Free U., Brussels, 1934-35; asst. U. Ghent, Belgium, 1935-36; asst. in phys. chemistry U. Utrecht, 1936-41, prof. phys. chemistry, 1946-81; rsch. worker N.V. Philips, Eindhoven, The Netherlands, 1941-46. Cons. I.C.I., Manchester, Eng., 1965-83, others; vis. prof. chem. engring. MIT, Cambridge, Mass., 1952-53, 66-67, 68-81, U. So. Calif., 1959-60; lectr. in field. Co-author: (with E.J.W. Verwey and J. Th. G. Overbeek) Theory of the Stability of Lyophobic Colloids, 1948; editor: Chemistry, Physics and Applications of Surface Active Substances, Vol. II, 1964; contbr. over 200 articles to profl. jours., chpts. to books; author, performer 2 video series and study guides. Named Knight Royal Order of the Netherlands Lion, 1971. Fellow Royal Soc. Chemistry (hon.); mem. Royal Netherlands Acad. Scis., Royal Netherlands Chem. Soc. (hon.), Royal Belgian Acad. Scis., Letters and Fine Arts (fgn.), Am. Acad. Arts and Scis. (fgn. hon.), Kolloidgesellschaft (hon., Wolfgang Ostwald prize 1989), Sigma Xi. Home: Bilthoven, Netherlands. Died Feb. 19, 2007.

OWEN, ROBERT HUBERT, lawyer, real estate broker; b. Birmingham, Ala., Aug. 3, 1928; s. Robert Clay and Mattie Lou (Hubert) O.; m. Mary Dane Hicks, Mar. 14, 1954; children: Mary Kathryn, Robert Hubert. BS, U. Ala., 1950; JD, Birmingham Sch. Law, 1956. Bar: Ala. 1957, Ga. 1965. Methods and procedures analyst, supr. Ala. Power Co., Birmingham, 1952-58; assoc. Martin, Vogtle, Balch & Bingham, Birmingham, 1958-63; asst. sec. So. Services, Atlanta, 1963-69; sec. Southern Co. Svcs. Inc., 1969—77, Southern Co., Atlanta, 1969-71, sec., asst. treas., house counsel, 1971—77; exec. v.p., sec., gen. counsel, dir. Proverbs 31 Corp., Atlanta, 1978-81, 90-97; broker Bob Owen Realty, Atlanta, 1990-97; pvt. practice law Marietta, 1978-85; v.p., gen. counsel Hubert Properties, 1985-86. Atlanta area rep. Inst. Basic Life Principles, 1970-80; elder Calvary Bapt. Ch., 1997—. Served to maj. USAF, 1951-52, 61-62. Mem.: Jasons, Phi Eta Sigma, Beta Gamma Sigma, Omicron Delta Kappa, Delta Chi, Delta Sigma Pi. Home: Hoschton, Ga. Died May 12, 2013.

OWENS, GARY (GARY ALTMAN), broadcast personality, entrepreneur, author; b. Mitchell, SD, May 10; s. Bernard and Vennetta O.; m. Arleta Lee Markell, June 26; children: Scott, Christopher. Student (speech and psychology scholar), Dakota Wesleyan U., Mitchell; student, Mpls. Art Inst. Disc jockey Sta. KFWB-AM, LA, 1961—62; with Sta. KMPC, LA, 1962-82, Sta. KPRZ, LA, 1982—86, Sta KFI, LA, 1986-90; pres. Foonman & Sons, Inc., 1987—2015; v.p., creative dir. GoldenWest Broadcasters, 1981-82. V.p., nat. creative dir. Gannett Broadcasting, 1984; TV performer, 1963-2015 Writer Jay Ward Prodns., 1961-62; syndicated radio show The G.O. Spl. Report, from 1969; host: world-wide syndicated show Soundtrack of the 60's, 1981, Biff Owens Sports Exclusive, 1981; USA Today, Mut. Broadcasting System, 1982-83; radio host Gary Owens Music Weekend, Lorimar Telepictures, 1987 performer, writer: world-wide syndicated show Sesame St, 1969-1986, Electric Co, 1969, Dirkniblick (Mathnet) CTW, 1988; performer over 3000 animated cartoons including Dyno-Mutt, ABC-TV, 1975, Roger Ramjet, 1965, Space Ghost, 1966—, Perils of Penelope Pitstop, 1970, Square One, 1987, Godzilla's Power Hour, 1979, Space Heroes, 1981, Mighty Orbots, 1984, World's Greatest Adventures, 1986, Garfield, Cops, Bobby's World, 1990, 96, The 3 Musketeers, Return of Roger Ramjet, Alice in Wonderland, The Count of Monte Cristo, 20,000 Leagues Under the Sea, Godzilla, Mickey Mouse, Donald Duck, Goofy Chip N'Dale, Bill & Ted's Great Adventure, Tom & Jerry Jr., Eek the Cat, Swat Kats, Two Stupid Dogs, Ren & Stimpy, Bonkers, Dirk Niblick, Felix the Cat, numerous others, 1990; appeared: in films The Love Bug, 1968, Prisoner of Second Ave., 1975, Hysterical, 1982, Nat. Lampoon's European Vacation, 1985, I'm Gonna Get You Sucka, 1988, Kill Crazy, 1988, How I Got Into College, 1988, Say Bye Bye, 1989, Green Hornet, 1966-67 Regular on series; performer on camera more than 1000 nat. TV shows; voice or narrator for The Munsters, 1965-66, Space Ghost, 1966, Batman, 1966-67, Scooby's Laff-A Lympics, 1977, Yogi's Space Race, 1978, Yogi's Treasure Hunt, 1985-86, Walt Disney's Wonderful World of Color, 1979-1986, Sledge Hammer!, 1987, Square One TV, 1988-91, Tom & Jerry Kids Show, 1990-93, , The Ren & Stimpy Show, 1992-94, Garfield & Friends, 1988-94, Love & War, 1994, Swat Kats: The Radical Squadron, 1993-94, Space Ghost Coast to Coast, 1996, Nickelodeon #D Movie Maker, 1996, , Eek! The Cat, 1992-97, The New Batman Adventures, 1998, That 70's Show, 1999, Dexter's Laboratory, 1998-2003, Wizards of Waverly Place, 2008, Batman: The Brave and the Bold, 2011, and several others; regular The Rosie O'Donnell Show, 1996; performer: Rowan and Martin's Laugh-in, 1968-73; TV host: Gong Show, ABC-TV, 1976, Monty Pythons Flying Circus, 1975; regular performer: TV Games People Play, 1980-81, Breakaway, 1983; TV spls. include Bob Hope Spls., Like Hep, The Muppets Go Hollywood, Perry Como Visits Hollywood, The Gary Owens All-Nonsense News Network, Jonathan Winters & Friends, NBC's 50 Years, CBS's 50 Years, Battle of Beverly Hills, America's Choice, The American Comedy Awards, 1986, Flip Wilson's Spls., Saturday Night at the Superbowl, Mickey Mouse's 50th Birthday, Mad About You, The Jeff Foxworthy Show, Night Court, Funniest Comedy Duos; author: Elephants, Grapes and Pickles, 1963; 12 printings The Gary Owens What To Do While Your're Holding the Phone Book, revised edit., 1973, A Gary Owens Chrestomathy, 1980; host Encore Pay TV, 1992; author: (screenplay) Three Caraway Seeds and an Agent's Heart, 1979; columnist: Radio and Records newspaper, 1978, Hollywood Citizen-News, 1965-67, Hollywood mag., 1983, The Daily News, 1981; rec. artist MGM, ABC, Epic, Warner Bros., RCA, Reprise, Decca; TV announcer NBC, 1968-80, ABC, 1980-; host many top video's in U.S. including Dinosaurs, More Dinosaurs, Son of Dinosaurs, TV's Greatest Bits; host: How to Collect Comic Books, Aliens, Dragons, Monsters and Me, Gone Fishing, 1993, The Gary Owens All-Nonsense News Network. Chmn. Multiple Sclerosis dr. L.A., 1972; chmn., grand marshall So. Calif. Diabetes Dr., 1974—; mayor City of Encino, Calif., 1972-74; bd. govs. Grammy Awards, 1968—, Emmy Awards, 1972; mem. adv. bd. Pasadena (Calif.) City Coll., 1969—, Sugar Ray Robinson Youth Found., 1971—; mem. nat. miracle com. Juvenile Diabetes Found., 1981—, nat. com. for Carousel Ball Children's Diabetes Found. Denver; radio adv. bd. U. So. Calif., 1980—; hon. chmn. Goodwill Industries Sporting Goods Dr., 1986, chmn., 1986; active telethons Cerebral Palsy, 1980, DARE program, 1985—, S.A.N.E. program, 1985—, comic relief to help U.S. Homeless, 1986. Named outstanding radio personality in U.S., 1965-79, top Radio Personality in World, Internat. Radio Forum, Toronto, 1977, Man of Yr. All-Cities Employees Assn., City of Los Angeles, 1968, Top Radio Broadcaster, Nat. Assn. Broadcasters, 1986, Radio Man of Yr. Nat. Assn. Broadcasters, 1986; recipient Distinguished Service award Hollywood Jaycees, 1966, David award, 1978, Hollywood Hall of Fame award, 1980, Am. award Cypress Coll., 1981, Carbon Mike award Pacific Broadcasters, 1987, 5 Grammy nominations, Emmy award for More Dinosaurs, 1986; Star on Hollywood Walk of Fame, 1981; honored by U.S. Dept. Treasury, 1985, Am. Diabetes Assn., 1990, Variety Clubs Internat., 1990; inducted into Nat. Broadcasters Hall of Fame, 1994, Radio Hall of Fame, 1994, Nat. Assn. Broadcasters Hall of Fame, 1995. Mem. Nat. Cartoonists Soc., So. Calif. Cartoonists Assn., Cartoonists and Artists Profl. Soc. *Without sounding like a coffee break Voltaire, the apothegm that "Everyman is his own Pygmalion" may be correct. I have tried to enrich my life by performing, reading, writing, creating, and helping others whenever possible. I try to stand up for what*

I believe, for it is better to give ulcers than to receive! Humor has helped protect me from the bruises of life, in addition to a daily supply of fantasy and illusion. Died Feb. 12, 2015.

OXLEY, MICHAEL GARVER (MIKE OXLEY), lawyer, former United States Representative from Ohio; b. Findlay, Ohio, Feb. 11, 1944; s. George Garver and Marilyn Maxine (Wolfe) Oxley; m. Patricia Ann Pluguez, Nov. 27, 1971; 1 child, Michael Chadd. BA in Govt., Miami U., Oxford, Ohio, 1966; JD, Ohio State U. Michael E. Moritz Coll. Law, 1969; D (hon.), Miami U., U. Findlay, Pace U. Bar: Ohio 1969, US Supreme Ct. 1986. Agt. FBI, 1969—71; atty. Oxley, Mallone, Fitzgerald & Hollister, 1971—81; mem. Ohio House of Reps., Columbus, 1973-81, US Congress from 4th Ohio Dist., Washington, 1981—2007, US House Energy & Commerce Com., 1983—2001; chmn. US House Commerce, Trade, & Hazardous Materials Subcommittee, 1995—2001, US House Financial Services Com., 2001—07; of counsel Baker & Hostetler LLP, Washington, 2007—16; sr. adv. to bd. NASDAQ OMX Group, Inc., NYC, 2007—16; lobbyist Financial Industry Regulatory Authority (FINRA), Washington, 2011—16. Trustee U. Findlay, Ohio, from 2009. Recipient Taxpayer's Friend award, Nat. Taxpayers Union, Guardian of Small Bus. award, Nat. Fedn. Ind. Bus., Spirit of Enterprise award, US Chamber of Commerce, Award for Mfg. Legis. Excellence, Nat. Assn. Mfrs., Jefferson award, Citizens for Sound Economy, Friend of the Farm Bur. award, Nat. Security award, American Security Coun. Mem. ABA, Ohio Bar Assn., Findlay Bar Assn., Soc. Former Spl. Agts. FBI, Ohio Farm Bur., Sigma Chi., Rotary, Elks. Republican. Lutheran. Died Jan. 1, 2016.

OYAMADA, PAUL HERBERT, dentist, consultant, retired; b. Portland, Oreg., Oct. 19, 1921; m. Alice Yasuko Sono, Nov. 7, 1953; 1 child, Debra Kay. DMD, U. Oreg., 1950. Pvt. practice, Portland, 1952-95; ret., 1995. Dental cons. John Hancock Group, 1974-95, Blue Cross-Blue Shield, 1977-95, Washington Nat. Ins., 1985-95, Prin. Mut. Des Moines, 1985-95. Capt. U.S. Army, 1950-52, Korea. Fellow Am. Coll. Dentists (sect. chmn.), Internat. Coll. Dentists; mem. Oreg. Dental Assn. (pres. 1973-74, del. to ADA 1978-83), Multnomah Dental Soc. (pres. 1969-70), Lions (Roseway pres. 1951), Delta Sigma Delta. Avocation: fishing. Home: Portland, Oreg. Died May 4, 2007.

PACHTER, VICTOR, real estate agent; b. NYC, May 9, 1921; s. Abraham David and Rose Bertha (Deckel) P.; m. Esther Witkoff, July 15, 1943; children: Linda, Barbara, Marsha. BBA, CCNY, 1948. CPA, N.J. Acting contr. Eisen Bros., Inc., Hoboken, N.J.; asst. contr. Lightolier, Inc., Jersey City; chief acct. AA Watts Co., Inc., Belleville, N.J.; sr. auditor Milton N. Hoffman, CPA, NYC; divisional contr. RCA, Cherry Hill, N.J., Plymouth, Mich., NYC; v.p. and compt. Cons. & Designers, Inc. Greyhound Corp., NYC, 1970-75; pvt. practice as CPA, cons., 1975-86; sales assoc. Rosenfeld Inc., Moorestown, N.J., 1986-91, Mertz Corp., Mt. Laurel, N.J., 1991-95; with Fox & Lazo, Inc., Realtors, Cherry Hill, N.J., from 1995. Arbitrator N.Y., Am. Stock Exch. Arbitration Bds., N.Y. Stock Exch., Am. Arbitration Assn. Active Back the Track Com. Garden State Race Track, 1987-89; mem. Camden County Indsl. Devel. Com., 1986-91; commr. Camden County Mcpl. Utilities Authority, 1979-82; chmn. Cherry Hill Planning Bd., 1978-81; treas. Cherry Hill Dem. Party, Inc., 1975-83; pres. Jewish Family Svc., 1981-82; councilman Cherry Hill, 1963-64; mem. Pub. Svc. Electric & Gas Co. Consumer Adv. Panel, So. Div., 1986-88; candidate State Sen., 1977; past treas. and dir. Temple Emanuel, Cherry Hill. With USAF, 1942-45. Decorated D.F.C., Air medal with 4 oak leaf clusters. Mem. N.J. Soc. CPAs. Democrat. Home: Philadelphia, Pa. Died May 24, 2007.

PACKARD, CLAYTON JAMES, towing company official; b. Portland, Oreg., Sept. 3, 1956; s. Dexter Fordyce and Dorothy Maxine (Baker) P.; m. Catherine Jane Packard, Apr. 2, 1977 (div. June 1983); children: Brian James, Jadia Marie; m. Lynnette Kay Cruikshank, Aug. 6, 1988 AS in Bus. Adminstrn., Portland Community Coll., Oreg., 1989. Tow truck driver Nine-T-Nine Towing, Tigard, Oreg., 1984-87, Buck's Towing, Portland, Oreg., 1988, Handy Andy's Towing, Portland, 1988-90, Jim Collins Towing, Beaverton, Oreg., 1990-91, Profl. Towing, Beaverton, from 1991. With USAF, 1974-82. Republican. Avocation: square dancing. Died Dec. 31, 2006.

PACKER, BOYD KENNETH, church official; b. Brigham City, Utah, Sept. 10, 1924; s. Ira Wright and Emma Jenson P.; m. Donna Edith Smith; 10 children BA, Utah State U., 1949, MA, 1953; PhD, Brigham Young U., 1962. Asst. to Twelve Church of Jesus Christ of Latter-Day Saints, 1961—70, Apostle, Quorum of the Twelve, from 1970, former pres. New England Mission, former supr. of Seminaries, acting pres. Quorum of the Twelve, 1994, 1995—2008, pres. Quorum of the Twelve, 2008—15. Pilot, PTO, WWII. Died July 3, 2015.

PACKER, KAREN GILLILAND, cancer patient educator, researcher; b. Washington, Apr. 27, 1940; d. Theodore Redmond and Evelyn Alice (Johnson) Gilliland; m. Allan Richard Packer, Sept. 27, 1962; 1 child, Charles Allan. Student, Duke U., 1957-59, U. Ky., 1959-60, 61-62, U. P.R. Sch. Medicine, 1960-61. Genetics researcher U. Ky., Lexington, 1959-60, 61-62; biologist Melpar Inc., Nat. Cancer Inst., Springfield, Va., 1964-66; rsch. assoc., epidemiology rsch. ctr. U. Iowa Coll. Medicine, Iowa City, 1981-85; founder, dir. Marshalltown (Iowa) Cancer Support Group, from 1987. Mem. County Health Planning Commn., Marshalltown, 1989-96; mem. adv. bd. Cmty. Nursing Svc., Marshalltown, 1990—; v.p. Cmty. Svcs. Coun., Marshalltown, 1992-96, pres. 1996-97; mem. Marshall County Bd. of Health, 1996—2001; mem. dir.'s consumer liaison group Nat. Cancer Inst., 2001-04; mem. Iowa Comprehensive Cancer Control Consortium, 2002—. Editor The Group Gazette, 1988—. Bd. dirs. 1st United Ch. Christ, Hampton, Va., 1973-75; corr. sec. DAR, Marshalltown, 1988-92; chmn. cancer and rsch. aux. VFW, Marshalltown, 1990—; chmn. Marshall County Commn. Aging, 1999—, sec., 2000—03. Recipient Leadership award Marshalltown Area C. of C., 1988, Spl. recognition Nat. Coalition for Cancer Survivorship, 1990, Iowa Senate 1995, 1st place in state award Cmty. Cancer Edn. VFW Aux., 1990-2004, Nat. Vol. Hero of Yr. award Coping Mag., 1995; Genetics Rsch. grantee NSF, 1959-60, NIH, 1961-62. Mem. AAAS, Nat. Guard Bur. Officers Wives Club (publ. editor 1965-68), Iowa Cancer Registrars Assn., N.Y. Acad. Scis. Mem. Congregational Ch. Achievements include establishment of regional orgn. for cancer info. and edn. Died June 5, 2007.

PADBERG, HARRIET ANN, mathematician, educator; b. St. Louis, Nov. 13, 1922; d. Harry J. and Marie L. (Kilgen) P. AB with honors, Maryville Coll., St. Louis, 1943; MMus, U. Cin., 1949; MA, St. Louis U., 1956, PhD, 1964. Cert. Religious of Sacred Heart, Albany, 1946; registered music therapist, cert. tchr. math. and music La., Mo. Tchr. elem. math. and music Kenwood Acad., Albany, N.Y., 1944-46; tchr. secondary math. Acad. of Sacred Heart, Cin., 1946-47; instr. math. and music Acad. and Coll. of Sacred Heart, Grand Coteau, La., 1947-48; secondary tchr. music Acad. Sacred Heart, St. Charles, Mo., 1948-50; instr. math. and music Acad. and Coll. Sacred Heart, Grand Coteau, 1950-55, Maryville Coll., St. Louis, 1955-56; tchr. elem. and secondary math. and music Acad. Sacred Heart, St. Louis, 1956-57; asst. prof. Maryville Coll., St. Louis, 1957-64, assoc. prof., 1964-68, prof. math., 1968-92, prof. emeritus, from 1992; music therapist Emmaus Homes, Marthasville, Mo., from 1992. Recipient Alumni Centennial award Maryville Coll., St. Louis, 1986, Deans award Sch. Health Professions, Alumni Recognition Program Maryville U., St. Louis, 2006, Diana award ESA Mo. State Coun., 2006, Humanitarian award ESA Found., 2006; grantee Danforth Found., Colorado Springs, 1970, Tallahassee, 1970, Edn. Devel. Ctr., Mass., 1975, U. Kans., 1980. Mem. Assn. Women in Math., Am. Math. Soc., Math. Assn. Am., Nat. Coun. Tchr. Math., Mo. Acad. Sci., Delta Epsilon Sigma (sec. local chpt. 1962), Pi Mu Epsilon (sec. local chpt. 1958), Sigma Xi. Avocations: knitting, music. Home: Atherton, Calif. Deceased.

PADEN, ROBERTA L., corporate administrator; b. Colby, Kans., Feb. 15, 1938; d. Homer Ernest and Harriet (McCafferty) P.; m. Gregory Grosbard, Aug. 20, 1963 (div. Feb. 1984); children: Guy Grosbard, Gayle Grosbard; m. Nigel Casserly, June 7, 1987 (dec. Sept. 1989). BA, Wichita State U., 1966; postgrad., U. Tex., El Paso, 1966-69. English lang. educator Santillana Pub. Co., NYC, 1976-79; project editor Curriculum Concepts, NYC, 1979-80; project control adminstr. Drexel Burnham Lambert, NYC, 1980-90; prin. Legin Am. Corp., NYC, from 1990; adminstrv. asst. West Side Campaign Against Hungry, NYC. Project mgmt. cons. DDH&R Consulting, N.Y.C., 1990-91. English lang. editor various text-books, 1977-79; translator: (tchrs. guide) Otras Culturas Series, 1979, (polit. study) Power & Dictatorship, 1981. Democrat. Avocations: reading, music, fine art. Died June 29, 2007.

PAGE, JAKE KENNA, JR., (JAMES K. PAGE JR.), writer, editor; b. Boston, Jan. 24, 1936; s. James Keena Page and Ellen Van Dyke (Gibson) Kunath; m. Aida de Alva Bound, Nov. 28, 1959 (div. 1974); children: Dana de Alva Page, Lea Gibson Page Kuntz, Brooke Bound Page; m. Susanne Calista Stone, Mar. 10, 1974; stepchildren: Lindsey Truitt, Sally Truitt, Kendall Barrett. BA, Princeton U., 1958; MA, NYU, 1959. Asst. sales promotion mgr. Doubleday & Co., 1959-60; editor Doubleday Anchor Books, 1960-62, Natural History Press, Doubleday, NYC, 1962-69; editorial dir. Natural History Mag., NYC, 1966-69; editor-in-chief Walker & Co., NYC, 1969-70; sci. editor Smithsonian Mag., Washington, 1970-76; founder, dir. Smithsonian Books, Washington, 1976-80; start-up editor Smithsonian Air & Space Mag., Washington, 1985; pvt. practice as writer Waterford, Va., Corrales, N.Mex., from 1980; founding editor Live Oak Editions, Placitas, N.Mex., from 2000. Mag. cons. Denver Mus. Nat. History, 1989-90; contract text editor Doubleday, 1992. Author: (with Richard Saltonstall Jr.) Brown Out & Slow Down, 1972, (with Larry R. Collins) Ling-Ling & Hsing Hsing: Year of the Panda, 1973, Shoot the Moon, 1979, (with Wilson Clark) Energy, Vulnerability and War: Alternatives for America, 1981, Blood: River of Life, 1981, (with Susanne Page) Hopi, 1982, Forest, 1983, Arid Lands, 1984, Pastorale: A Natural History of Sorts, 1985, Demon State, 1985, (with Eugene S. Morton) Lords of the Air: The Smithsonian Book of Birds, 1989, Smithsonian's New Zoo, 1990, Zoo: The Modern Ark, 1990, Animal Talk: Science and the Voice of Nature, 1992, The Stolen Gods, 1993, Songs to Birds, 1993 (with Chalres B. Officer) Tales of the Earth, 1993, The Deadly Canyon, 1994 (with David Leeming) Goddess: Mythology of the Female Divine, 1994, The Knotted Strings, 1995, Smithsonian Guides to Natural America: Arizona and New Mexico, 1995, (with Susanne Page) Navajo, 1995, (with David Leeming) God: Mythology of the Male Divine, 1996, The Lethal Partner, 1996, (with Charles Officer) The Great Dinosaur Extinction Controversy, 1996, Operation Shatterhand, 1996, (with Michael Lieder) Wild Justice, 1997, A Certain Malice, 1998, Apacheria, 1998, (with Susanne Page) Field Guide to Southwest Indian Arts and Crafts, 1998, (with David Leeming) The Mythology of Native North America, 1998, Myths, Legends and Folktales of America, 1999, The American Southwest, 1999, (with Charles Officer) Earth and You, 2000, Cavern, 2000; editor: (with Malcolm Baldwin) Law and the Environment, 1970; contbg. editorships Science Mag., 1980-86, Oceans Mag., 1987, Mother Earth News, 1990, National Geographic Traveler, 1990-93, TDC (Destination Discovery), 1991-95, (with J.M. Adovasio) The First Americans: In Pursuit of Archaeology's Greatest Mystery, 2002, In the Hands of the Great Spirit: The 20,000-Year History of American Indians, 2003, The Big One, 2004, Uprising: The Pueblo Indians and the First American War for Religious Freedom, 2013; contbg. author to numerous books and mags. Mem. nat. bd. advisors Futures for Children, Albuquerque, 1980—. Recipient Spur award for short non-fiction Western Writers Am., 1998. Democrat. Avocation: arab horses. Home: Lyons, Colo. Died Feb. 10, 2016.

PAGE, RUTH JOANNE, business educator; b. Knoxville, Tenn., Oct. 31, 1945; d. Richard Dean and Lorraine Virginia (Grant) Faytinger; m. John Thomas Page, June 17, 1966; children: John, Stephen. BS, U. Kans., 1968, MS, 1985. Cert. tchr., Kans. Tchr. bus. Nortonville (Kans.) High Sch., 1968, Desoto (Kans.) High Sch., 1968-70, Shawnee Mission S. High Sch, Overland Pk., Kans., 1970-73; adminstrv. asst. IBM Corp., Mpls., 1974-76; tchr. bus. Trailridge Jr. High Sch., Lenexa, Kans., 1976-85; tchr. bus., div. chmn. Shawnee Mission (Kans.) NW High Sch., from 1985. Drill team dir. Shawnee Mission NW High Sch., 1985—. Presenter Nat. Bus. Edn. Conv., 1984, 85. Mem. NEA, Kans. Bus. Edn. Assn., Superstar Drill Team Dirs. Assn., Kappa Kappa Gamma. Republican. Avocations: aerobic dancing, walking, bridge, cooking, water sports. Home: Shawnee Mission, Kans. Died Mar. 30, 2007.

PALADINO, ALBERT EDWARD, venture capitalist; b. NYC, Aug. 4, 1932; s. Albert E. and Jennie (Fiato) Paladino; m. Dorothy M. Hayes (div. June 1979); children: Thomas A., Robert E., Catherine J., Paul F.; m. Susan Flynn, June 11, 1983. BS in Ceramic Engring., Alfred U., 1954, MS in Ceramic Engring., 1956; ScD in Materials Sci., MIT, 1962. Registered profl. engr., Mass. Staff mem. rsch. divsn. Raytheon Co., Waltham, Mass., 1955-59, mgr. materials and crystal growth lab., 1962-69, mgr. materials and techniques group microwave & power tube divsn., 1969-72, mgr. electronics materials group, 1972-75; program mgr. materials Office of Tech. Assessment US Congress, Washington, 1975-78; asst. dir. tel. ops. tech. ctr. GTE Labs., Waltham, 1978-79; dep. dir. Office Energy Programs US Dept. Commerce, Nat. Inst. Stds. and Tech., Washington, 1979-81; mng. ptnr. Advanced Tech. Ventures, Boston, 1981-98. Bd. dirs. TranSwitch Corp., 1988—2009; chmn. Telaxis Comm. Corp., South Deerfield, Mass., 1988—2003, Electro-Scan Corp., Billerica, Mass., 1990—95, Onex Comm. Corp., 1999—2001, RF Micro Devices, Greensboro, NC, 1992—2009, Paladino & Co., from 2002; telecom. bd. adv. Prism Ventures, 1997—2006, Early Stage Enterprises, 1997—2006; bd. advisers Battelle Ventures, from 2004; bd. adv. Environ. Bus., 2008—11. Contbr. articles to profl. jours. Pres. West Needham Civic Assn., Mass., 1967—69; mem. Needham Town Meeting, 1973—74, Boston Harbor Angels, 2007—09; trustee Alfred U., from 1991. Fellow: Am. Ceramic Soc. (chmn. basic sci. divsn. 1968—69, chmn. New Eng. sect. 1969—70, Disting. New Eng. Ceramic award). Achievements include patents in field. Avocations: painting, music, physical fitness, hiking, reading. Home: Chestnut Hill, Mass. Died Mar. 29, 2014.

PALMER, JEFFRESS GARY, hematologist, educator; b. Bklyn., Oct. 7, 1921; s. William Ware and Margaret Lee (Boswell) P.; m. Jane Ann Cartwright, Feb. 2, 1951; children: Kristin Cartwright, Julie Mitchell. BS, Emory U., 1942, MD, 1944. Intern N.C. Bapt. Hosp., 1944-45; resident in medicine Emory U., Atlanta, 1947-49; fellow hematology U. Utah, Salt Lake City, 1949-52; from asst. prof. to prof. medicine U. N.C., Chapel Hill, from 1952, ret., 1985. Capt. M.C. AUS, 1945-47. Mem. AAAS, AAUP, AMA, Am. Fedn. for Clin. Rsch., So. Soc. for Clin. Investigation, N.Y. Acad. Scis., Am. Soc. Hematology. Died Dec. 19, 2006.

PANETTA, MICHAEL JON, retired state agency administrator, writer; b. Lansing, Mich., Sept. 9, 1949; s. Frank Anthony P. and Elizabeth Virginia Rocchetti; m. Susan Marie Cottrill, May 1, 1971; children: Mary Elizabeth Panetta-Lowe, Michelina Anne Panetta-Cantu, Joseph Andrew. AA, Lansing CC, Mich., 1970; BA, Mich. State U., East Lansing, 1971, MS, 1972, MA equivalency, 1988, DPhil, 2000. Cert. paramedic Mich., lic. emergency med. technician Mich.; pvt. detective Mich. Fed. Manpower adminstr. Manpower Area Planning Coun., Lansing, Mich., 1970—73; spl. agent med. fraud auditor State of Mich., Lansing, 1973—78, supr. fed. food stamp program, 1977—78, emergency med. svcs. program specialist, 1978—89, program specialist Gov.'s Coun. Environ. Quality, 1989—90, departmental policy and procedure specialist, 1990—91, fin. specialist, contract adminstr. child and family health programs, 1991—2002; prof. Spring Arbor U., Lansing, 2001—02; pvt. practice, cons., from 2003. Dir. youth and vet. program Nat. Alliance of Businessmen, Lansing, 1970—73; suggestion award program administr. Mich. Dept. Pub. Health, Lansing, 1990—91. Author: Leader Behavior & Member Response in an Institutional Setting, 1972, Citizens Perceptions of Police & Community Policing, 2000, pamphlets, booklets, guides. Co-founder, pres., v.p. Citizen's to Save Lansing Mich., Lansing, 1992—99; founder Citizens to Save Vets. Civic Ctr., Lansing, 1992—99; co-founder, v.p. Citizens Against the Rain Tax of Lansing, Lansing, 1994—2000. Recipient award, Soc. Study Social Problems Columbia U., 1986; scholar grad. rsch. scholarship, Mich. State U. Bd. Trustees, 1971. Fellow: Am. Lit. Assn.; mem.: Nat. Assn. Welfare Adminstrs., NRA, Mich. State U. Alumni Assn. (life), KC (assoc.; grand knight Richard coun. 1988—90, assoc. mem. Msgr.

John A. Gabriels coun., charter grand knight Msgr. John A. Gabriels coun. 1993—95, Knight of Yr. Richard Coun. 1989, Top Proposer of Yr. Richard Coun. 1990, Knight of Yr. Msgr. John A. Gabriels Coun. 1993—95, Papal medallion 1992, Star Coun. award, Columbian award, Founders award 1993—95), Alpha Kappa Delta (life). Republican. Roman Catholic. Avocations: teaching, writing, travel, bicycling, camping. Home: Lansing, Mich. Died Dec. 22, 2006.

PANGBURN, PATRICIA DILLARD, public relations firm owner; b. Vineland, NJ, Oct. 15, 1933; d. Edgar Pugh and Sue (Atleson) D.; m. Newell Stephen Pangburn, Jr., June 16, 1956; children: Patricia Sue, Bradley. BS, U. Pa., 1955; MA, Western Mich. U., 1981. Sec., tissue lab. Hahnemann Med. Coll., Phila., 1955; educator Yeadon (Pa.) Pub. Schs., 1956, Willistown Twp. Pub. Schs., Paoli, Pa., 1956-57; acctg. technician U.S. Govt., Fort Huachuca, Ariz., 1958-59; pub. rels. dir. Glowing Embers Girl Scout Coun., Kalamazoo, Mich., 1969-73; community rels. dir. Goodwill Industries of S.W. Mich., Kalamazoo, 1976-81; asst. dir. pub. rels. Kalamazoo Coll., 1981-83; owner Pub. Rels. Svcs., Portage, Mich., from 1984. Chair Pvt. Industry Coun., Kalamazoo, 1990; mem. allocation panel United Way, Kalamazoo, 1987—; pres. Kalamazoo Ctr. Ind. Living, 1985-87; bd. dirs. Glowing Embers coun. Girl Scouts U.S.A., 1988-91. Mem. Women In Communication (past pres. 1985-86, Communicator of the Yr. award 1986), Portage Rotary, Kalamazoo C. of C. (bd. dirs. 1988—), Profl. & Exec. Assoc. Kalamazoo (past pres. 1988-89). Died June 14, 2007.

PANSINI, MICHAEL SAMUEL, financial analyst, tax specialist; b. Molfetta, Italy, July 12, 1928; arrived in U.S., 1935; s. Ralph and Isabel (Cirilli) P.; m. Anna D'Angelo, June 5, 1949 (div. 1970); children: Elizabeth, Valerie, Michael; m. Elizabeth Bischoff, Oct. 3, 1970 (div. Feb. 1992); 1 child, Elissa Michelle. BS, NYU, 1950, MBA, 1952, LLM, 1960; LLD, Fordham U., 1956. Bar: NY 1956, US Tax Ct. Tax mgr. Pfizer Corp., NYC, 1951-64; asst. treas. Hooker Chem. Corp., NYC, 1964-69; treas., dir. United Indsl. Corp., NYC, 1969-72; sr. v.p. tax counsel Beker Industries Corp., Greenwich, Conn., 1972-87; pres., dir. Panmer, Inc., from 1987; tax, fin. cons., from 1988; v.p., corp. counsel Champion Energy Corp. and affiliates, 1991-93, Champion Holdings Co. and affiliates, 1993-96. V.p., chmn. various coms. Tax Exec. Inst., NYC, 1963-72; pres., dir. Fed. Tax Forum, Inc., NYC, 1961-72; dir. Intelligent Bus. Communications Corp. Commr., vice chmn. Econ. Devel. Commn., Stamford, Conn., 1994—2011; mem. Rep. Town Com. 19th Dist., Stamford, from 1993; bd. dirs. Stamford Sr. Ctr., 2000—06, treas., 2007—08; bd. dirs., treas. Women's Bus. Devel. Ctr., Inc., 2003—06, chmn. audit com, from 2007; bd. dirs., treas. Food Bank of Lower Fairfield County, 2004—06. Mem.: Sr. Men's Assn. Stamford (bd. dirs., 2d v.p. 2005—06, 1st v.p. 2007—08, pres. from 2008, 1st. v.p. from 2010), North Stamford Assn. (bd. dirs. 1999—2005, v.p. 2000, pres. 2001). Republican. Died Dec. 30, 2014.

PANSKY, EMIL JOHN, entrepreneur; b. Manhattan, NY, June 1, 1921; s. Stanislaus and Anna (Jankovic) P.; m. Billie B. Byrne, May 27, 1955; 1 adopted child, Jimmy. BME, Cooper Union Coll., 1941; MBA, Harvard U., 1949; MADE, NYU, 1950. Registered profl. engr., Mich. Chief insp. flight line Republic Aviation, Farmingdale, L.I., 1941-45, salvage engr., 1946-47; product control supr. to product control mgr. Ford Motor, Detroit, 1949-51; asst. plant mgr. Anderson Brass, Birmingham, Ala., 1951-53; asst. v.p. to v.p. mfg. Cummins Engine, Columbus, Ind., 1953-54; pvt. practice Emil J. Pansky Assoc., San Leandro, Calif., from 1954. Treas. Lane Metal Finishers, 1968-80, Calif. Tech. Metal Finishers, 1988-90; pres. Calif. Mfrs. Tech. Assn., San Francisco, 1978-80; ind. tech. cons. to small bus., 1994—. Patentee die cast auto wheels, 1965. Pres. Menlo Circus Club, Menlo Park, Calif., 1974-81, Home Owners Assn., Kanuela, Hawaii, 1989-99; bd. dirs. No. Calif. Tennis Assn., San Francisco, 1984-87. Mem. ASME (life), Harvard Club San Francisco (bd. dirs. 1986-92), Harvard Bus. Sch. Club San Francisco (bd. dirs. 1970-73, cons. 1994-95). Democrat. Avocations: tennis, chess. Home: Hillsborough, Calif. Died Jan. 20, 2007.

PARDEN, ROBERT JAMES, engineering educator, management consultant; b. Mason City, Iowa, Apr. 17, 1922; s. James Ambrose and Mary Ellen (Fahey) P.; m. Elizabeth Jane Taylor, June 15, 1955; children: Patricia Gale, James A., John R., Nancy Ann. BS in Mech. Engring, State U. Iowa, 1947, MS, 1951, PhD, 1953. Reg. profl. engr. Iowa, Calif.; lic. gen. contractor Calif. Indsl. engr. LaCrosse Rubber Mills, 1947-50; asso. dir. Iowa Mgmt. Course, 1951-53; asso. prof. indsl. engring. Ill. Inst. Tech., 1953-54; prof. engring. mgmt. Santa Clara U., from 1955, dean Sch. Engring., 1955-82; prin. Saratoga Cons. Group (Calif.), from 1982. Mem. Sec. Navy's Survey Bd. Grad. Edn., 1964 Mem. Saratoga Planning Commn., 1959-61. Served to 1st lt., Q.M.C. AUS, 1943-46. Named to Silicon Valley Engring. Hall of Fame Silicon Valley Engring. Coun., 1993. Mem. ASME (chmn. Santa Clara Valley sect. 1958), Am. Soc. Engring. Edn. (chmn. Pacific N.W. sect. 1960), Am. Inst. Indsl. Engrs. (edn. chmn. 1958-63, dir. ASEE-ECPD affairs 1963-68), Nat. Soc. Profl. Engrs., Engrs. Council Profl. Devel. (dir. 1964-65, 66-69), Soc. Advancement Mgmt., ASEM, Sigma Xi, Tau Beta Pi. Roman Catholic. Home: Saratoga, Calif. Died July 20, 2014.

PARIKH, JEKISHAN RATILAL, chemical company executive; b. Bombay, Dec. 21, 1922; came to U.S., 1948; s. Ratilal B. and Ruxmani (Parikh) P.; m. Jean Audrey Fuller, May 1, 1959; children: Jane, Anne, Lynn. BS with honors, U. Bombay, 1943; MS, U. Calif., Berkeley, 1950; PhD, U. Calif., 1953. Rsch. officer U. Va., Charlottesville, 1953-55; postdoctoral rsch. asst. Nat. Inst. Health, Bethesda, Md., 1955-58; rsch. officer Glaxo, U.K., 1958-60, exec. officer India div. Bombay, 1959-64; with UpJohn Co., Kalamazoo, from 1964, dir., from 1980. Mem. Am. Chem. Soc. Democrat. Avocations: tennis, hiking. Home: Kalamazoo, Mich. Died May 30, 2007.

PARIZEAU, JACQUES, former Canadian government official; b. Montréal, Aug. 9, 1930; s. Gérard and Germaine (Biron) P.; m. Alicja Poznanska, Apr. 12, 1956 (dec. 1990); children: Bernard, Isabelle; m. Lisette LaPointe, Dec. 12, 1992. Degree, Inst. d'études politiques, Paris, 1952; PhD in Econs., London Sch. Econs., 1955. Prof. École des Hautes Études commerciales, Montréal, 1955-65, 67-70, 85-89; chmn. Inst. Applied Econs., Montréal, 1970-73; mem. Can. Nat. Assembly, Que., 1976-84 and from 89, pres. Parti Québécois, from 1988; min. fin. Québec Govt., 1976-84, min. revenue, 1976-84, pres. treasury bd., 1976-81, min. fin. instns., 1981-82, chmn. ministerial econ. devel. com., 1981-82, prime min., 1994-95. Econ. and fin. adviser Premiers of Québec: Lesage, Johnson, Bertrand, Que., 1961-69; pres. Que. Fin. Instns. Task Force, 1970-73; chmn. Comm. of Enquiry on Future of Municipalities, Que., 1985. Editor L'Actualité économique, Montréal, 1955-61; chmn. bd. dirs. Daily Le Jour, Montréal, 1974-75; bd. dirs. Daily Le Devoir, Montréal, 1985-87. Bd. dirs. U. Montréal, 1969-74; bd. dirs., bd. govs. Théâtre du Nouveau-Monde, Montréal, 1988-92; pres. No com. Referendum on Charlottetown Accord, Que., 1992. Mem. Club de la Garnison (Que.), Knowlton Golf and Country Club (Lac Brome). Roman Catholic. Avocations: reading, music, gardening. Home: Outremont, Canada. Died June 1, 2015.

PARK, WEE WUONE, architect, concert pianist; b. Seoul, Republic of Korea, Aug. 20, 1931; came to U.S., 1954; s. Yong Kwan and Eun Kyung (Kim) P. BS, U. Wyoming, 1959; MA, Harvard U., 1964; M. Performing Arts, U. Paris, 1970. Registered architect, Colo. Concert pianist, Denver, Paris, from 1950; chief design architect Stapleton Internat. Airport Paul Reddy Architect Group, Denver, 1970-79; pres. Wee Park & Co. Architects, Denver, from 1979. Pres. Wee Park & Co. Architects, Denver, 1979— Pres. Men's Orgn. Denver Symphony, 1975, I Pagliacci opera group, Denver, 1980; bd. dirs. Denver Symphony Assn., 1976; founding bd. mem. Opera Colo., Denver, 1982; v.p. Denver Civic Ballet, 1978-80, bd. dirs., 1980. Capt. Republic of Korea Air Force, 1950-53. Recipient Medal of Honor Republic of Korea, 1950. Mem. Denver Athletic Club, Denver Press Club. Republican. Avocations: skiing, yacht racing, swimming, jogging, mountain climbing, piloting, langs. Died May 8, 2007.

PARKER, BEVERLY ANN, nursing administrator; b. Niagara Falls, NY, Sept. 22, 1941; d. Florentino and Glenora (Garlow) Martinez; m. Donald E. Parker, Sept. 22, 1962; children: Patrick P., Michael William, Mark Daniel. ADS, Niagara County C.C., 1978; BSN, Niagara U., 1986; MS, Buffalo U., 1988. Staff nurse nurse med/surg. and ICU Niagara Falls (N.Y.) Meml. Hosp., 1978-85, nursing supr., 1985-87; v.p. patient svcs. St. Joseph Hosp., Cheektowaga, N.Y., from 1987. Mem. adv. bd. RN program Niagara U., 1986-88; mem. adv. bd. nurse clinician program U. Buffalo, 1988-91; advisor Western N.Y. Coun. Nurse Mgrs., Buffalo, 1991-93. Adv. Bd. Cheektowaga (N.Y.) Sr. Citizens, 1993-94. Roman Catholic. Mem. Am. Orgn. Nurse Execs., Western N.Y. Orgn. Nurse Execs. (pres. 1993-94), N.Y. Orgn. Execs. (bd. dirs. 1993-94), Western N.Y. Health Care Exec. Forum, Greater Buffalo Partnership. Avocations: reading, painting, gardening. Home: Lewiston, NY. Died June 20, 2007.

PARKER, EVERETT CARLTON, clergyman; b. Chgo., Jan. 17, 1913; s. Harry Everett and Lillian (Stern) P.; m. Geneva M. Jones, May 5, 1939 (dec. 2004); children: Ruth A. (Mrs. Peter Weiss), Eunice L. (Mrs. George Kolczun, Jr.), Truman E. AB, U. Chgo., 1935; BD magna cum laude, Chgo. Theol. Sem., 1943, Blatchford fellow, 1944-45, DD, 1964, Catawba Coll., Salisbury, NC, 1958; L.H.D., Fordham U., 1978, Tougaloo Coll., 1987; LLD, Coll. St. Elizabeth, 2000. Pastor Waveland Ave. Congl. Christian Ch., 1943; asst., pub. svc. and war program mgr. navy NBC, 1943—45; founder-dir. Protestant Radio Commn., 1945-50; lectr. communication Yale Div. Sch., 1946-58, dir. communications research project, 1950-54; creator, dir. Public Relations Office for Congregational Christian Churches and Evangelical and Reformed Church, which became the United Church of Christ in 1957, 1954-83; sr. research assoc., adj. prof. Fordham U., 1983—2008, commn. lectr., 1988—2008; founder citizen movement to protect minority rights in media, 1963—2015. Chmn. broadcasting and film commn. Nat. Coun. Chs., 1969-72, gen. bd., 1966-72; chmn. Study Commn. on Theology, Edn. and Electronic Media, 1985-87; founder Found. for Minority Interests in Media, 1985—, treas., 1985-08. Producer-dir.: nat. TV programs including series Off to Adventure, 1956, Tangled World, 1965; originator: series Six American Families, PBS-TV, 1977; Author: Religious Radio, 1948, Film Use in the Church, 1953, The Television-Radio Audience and Religion, 1955, Religious Television, 1961, (with others) Television, Radio, Film for Churchmen, 1969, Fiber Optics to the Home: The Changing Future of Cable, TV and The Telephone, 1989, Social Responsibility of Television in the United States, 1994. Recipient Human Relations award Am. Jewish Com., 1966, Faith and Freedom award Religious Heritage Found., 1966, 77, Alfred I. DuPont-Columbia U. award pub. service in broadcasting, 1969; Roman Cath. Broadcasters Gabriel award pub. service, 1970; Lincoln U. award significant contbn. human relations, 1971; Racial Justice award Com. for Racial Justice, United Ch. Christ, 1973; Ch. Leadership award Coun. for Christian Social Action, 1973; Public Svc. award Black Citizens for a Fair Media, 1979, Pioneer award World Assn. for Christian Comm., 1988, award for Ecumenical Leadership Nat. Coun. Chs., 2000, Ellul award Media Ecology Assn., 2004 Mem.: White Plains Cable TV Commn., Star (NYC). Home: White Plains, NY. Died Sept. 17, 2015.

PARKER, MARGARET DENISE, primary education educator; b. Gadsden, Ala., Apr. 12, 1958; d. Ralph H. Dyer; m. R.L. Parker, Nov. 7, 1981. BS, Jacksonville State U., 1982; MA, U. Ala., 1989. Tchr. J.W. Stewart Head Start, Gadsden, 1980-84, Curtiston Primary Sch., Attalla, Ala., from 1986. Home: Gadsden, Ala. Died Nov. 30, 2006.

PARKER, MARY EVELYN, former state treasurer; b. Fullerton, La., Nov. 8, 1920; d. Racia E. and Addie (Graham) Dickerson; m. William Bryant Parker, Oct. 31, 1954 (dec. 1965); children: Mary Bryant, Ann Graham. BA, Northwestern State U., La., 1941; Diploma in Social Welfare, La. State U., 1943; PhD (hon.), Northwestern State U., La., 1987. Social worker, Allen Parish, La., 1941-42; pers. adminstr. War Dept., Camp Claiborne, La., 1943-47; editor Oakdale, La., 1947-48; exec. dir. La. Dept. Commerce & Industry, Baton Rouge, 1948-52; with Mut. of N.Y., Baton Rouge, 1952-56; chmn. La. Bd. Public Welfare, Baton Rouge, 1950-51; commr. La. Dept. Public Welfare, Baton Rouge, 1956-63; sec. American Public Welfare Assn., 1962-64; commr. La. Divsn. Adminstrn., 1964-67; treas. State of La., 1968-87. Chmn. White House Conf. on Children and Youth, 1960; pres. La. Conf. on Social Welfare, 1959-61; mem. Democratic Nat. Com., 1948-52; bd. dirs. Woman's Hosp., Baton Rouge; trustee Episcopal H.S., Baton Rouge Gen. Hosp. Found.; mem. advisory coun. Coll. Bus., Tulane U., New Orleans. Named Baton Rouge Woman of Yr., 1976 Democrat. Baptist. Home: Baton Rouge, La. Died Jan. 17, 2015.

PARKER, WALLACE CRAWFORD, computer consultant, author; b. Pitts., Apr. 16, 1937; s. Wallace McCullough and Virginia (Crawford) P.; m. Marilyn J. Styrwold Kelly, May 11, 1985; stepchildren: Susan M. Kelly, Ryan W. Kelly. BS in Math., U. Pitts., 1968; BS in Computer Sci., U. Oreg., 1986. Computer instr. Lane C.C., Eugene, Oreg., 1987-90; cons. Eugene, from 1989. Advisor Boston Computer Soc./Macintosh Users Group, 1989-94. Author: Putting MS Works to Work, 2d edit., 1989; manuscript and tech. editors for chpts. to books; contbr. numerous articles to profl. jours. With U.S. Army, 1957-59. Mem. IEEE, Eugene Macintosh Users Group (bd. dirs. 1988-94, editor monthly jour. 1992-94). Avocations: camping, gardening, design. Died Nov. 6, 2006.

PARKINSON, CECIL EDWARD, secretary of state for transport; b. England, Sept. 1, 1931; s. Sidney P.; m. Ann Mary Jarvis, 1957; children Mary, Emma, Joanna; child with Sara Keays, Flora Grad., Royal Lancaster Grammar Sch.; BA, Emmanuel Coll., Cambridge, 1955, MA, 1961. Mgmt. trainee Metal Box Co., 1955; with West, Wake, Price, chartered accts., 1956, ptnr., 1961-71; founder Parkinson Hart Securities Ltd, 1967; dir. of several cos., 1965-79 and from 1984; constituency chmn. Hemel Hempstead Conservative Assn.; chmn. Herts. 100 Cub, 1968-69; Parliamentary pvt. sec. to minister for aerospace and shipping, 1972-74; asst. govt. whip, 1974; opposition whip, 1974-76; opposition spokesman on trade, 1976-79; minister for trade Dept. of Trade, 1979-81; chmn. Conservative Party, 1981-83; paymaster gen., 1982-83; chancellor Duchy of Lancaster, 1982-83; sec. of state for trade and industry, 1983; sec. of state for energy, 1987-89; sec. of state for transport, 1989-90. Sec. Conservative Party Fin. Com., 1971-72; chmn. Anglo-Swiss Party Group, 1979-82; pres. Anglo-Polish Conservative Soc., 1986—. Ran for combined Oxford and Cambridge team against Am. Univs., 1954; ran for Cambridge against Oxford, 1954, 55. Mem.: Beefsteak, Pratts, Hawks (Cambridge). Avocations: reading, golf, skiing. Home: Herts, England. Died Jan. 22, 2016.

PARKMAN, LAURA JEAN, real estate agent, writer; b. LA, Nov. 2, 1948; d. Arthur Jr. Gottlieb; m. Michael David Williamson, Aug. 14, 1965 (div. Jan. 1968); 1 child, Brian Michael Williamson; m. Gordon Wayne Parkman, Dec. 14, 1975. AA, Mesa Coll., 1983; BS, U. Calif., San Diego, 1986. Fashion model, LA, 1969—72; real estate agt. Parkman Realty, San Diego, from 1975. Author: Dreams Don't Last Forever, 2000; inventor: children's game Send Me an Angel, 2001. Mem.: Daus. of the Nile. Democrat. Mem. Assemblies Of God. Avocation: songwriting. Home: Vernal, Utah. Died Apr. 15, 2007.

PARKS, JAMES WILLIAM, insurance company executive; b. Wabash, Ind., Jan. 17, 1929; s. George Lewis and Mildred (Smith) P.; m. Joyce Arlene Lillibridge, June 27, 1949; children: Kimberly Parks Poppa, James W. II, Jeffrey Kent. BS, Ball State U., 1951, MA, 1956. Tchr., prin. pub. schs., Ind., 1954-66; pres., chief exec. officer AAA Hoosier Motor Club, Indpls., from 1966. Pres., chief exec. officer Hoosier Motor Club Ins. Agy., Inc., Indpls., 1966—' sec., chief exec. officer Hoosier Motor Mut. Ins. Co., Indpls., 1973—. Bd. dirs., v.p. Home and Away mag. Sec. bd. trustees Ball State univ.; dir. Ball State Found.; bd. dirs. Indpls. Conv. and Visitors Assn., Ind. Task force to Reduce Driving, Hoosiers for Seat Belts, Inc.; active Indpls. Motorcycle Drill Team. Cpl. U.S. Army, 1952-54. Named one of Outstanding Young Men of Am. U.S. Jaycees, 1965, Sagmore of Wabash Gov. of Ind., 1974, 88, Boss of Yr. Am. Bus. Women's Assn. 1982-83, Admiral in the Great Navy Gov. of Nebr., 1988, Hon. Order Ky. Cols., 1988; recipient Disting. Service award Ball State U., 1972, Benny award Ball State U., 1983. Mem. AAA (found. for traffic safety, midwest and ea. confs.), Midwest Auto Clubs, Inc., Ins. Inst. Ind., Inc., Ind. Soc. Assn. Execs., Ind. Sheriff's Assn. (life),

Indpls. Athletic Club., Service Club Indpls., Am. Legion, Indpls. Press Club, Econ. Club Indpls., Ind. Soc. Chgo., Skyline Club, Elks, Rotary, Sigma Tau Gamma. Methodist. Home: Bloomington, Ind. Died Aug. 23, 2007.

PARRETTE, BERNARD VINCENT, judge; b. Bloomington, Minn., Jan. 2, 1930; s. Mark L. and Theresa Rose (Howard) P.; m. Rosemary Walsh, Apr. 27, 1963; children: Marie Therese, Anne Catherine, Thomas Dominic. Student, U. Vienna, Austria, 1952; BA magna cum laude, St. Thomas U., St. Paul, 1952; JD, U. Minn., 1955; PhB, Dominican House of Studies, River Forest, Ill., 1961; postgrad., Fed. Exec. Inst., 1973, Indsl. Coll. Armed Forces, 1976. Bar: Minn. 1955, D.C. 1968, U.S. Supreme Ct. 1968. Res. divsn. chief adminstrv. divsn., internat. law divsn., mil. justice divsn. Office of Air Force JAG, Washington, 1964-81; chief counsel, dep. chief counsel and legis. atty. Area Redevel. Adminstrn. and Econ. Devel. Adminstrn., Washington, 1962-68; assoc. gen. counsel for property ins. U.S. Dept. Housing, Washington, 1968-71; prin. dep. gen. counsel U.S. Dept. Commerce, Washington, 1974-75; assoc. George K. Bernstein, Washington, 1975-77; ops. sect. chief Amtrak divsn., chief counsel's office Fed. Railway Adminstrn. Dept. Transp., Washington, 1978-80; chief judge Interior Bd. Land Appeals, Arlington, 1980-82; adminstrv. judge Interior Bd. Surface Mining Appeals, Arlington, 1982-83; spl. counsel to dir. Interior Office of Hearings and Appeals, Arlington, 1983; chief adminstrv. judge Interior Bd. Indian Appeals, Arlington, 1983-86; adminstrv. judge Interior Bd. Contract Appeals, Arlington, from 1986. Lt. col. USAF, 1955-81. Roman Catholic. Avocations: classical music, murder mysteries, hiking, motorcycling, indian jewelry and crafts. Home: Mc Lean, Va. Died Nov. 5, 2006.

PARRIGIN, ELIZABETH ELLINGTON, lawyer; b. Colon, Panama, May 23, 1932; d. Jesse Cox and Elizabeth (Roark) Ellington; m. Perry G. Parrigin, Oct. 8, 1975. BA, Agnes Scott Coll., 1954; JD, U. Va., 1959. Bar: Tex. 1959, Mo. 1980. Atty., San Antonio, 1960-69; law libr. U. Mo., Columbia, 1969-77, rsch. assoc., 1977-82; atty. pvt. practice, Columbia, from 1982. Elder, clk. of session First Presbyn. Ch., Columbia; mem. permanent jud. commn. Presbyn. Ch. U.S., 1977-83, mem. advisory com. on constitution, 1983-90. Mem. ABA, Mo. Bar Assn. (chmn. sub-com. revision of Mo. trust law 1988-92), Columbia Kiwanis Club (pres. 1997-98). Democrat. Presbyterian. Avocations: music, gardening, reading. Died July 16, 2007.

PARRIS, PAUL AUGUSTUS, JR., small business owner; b. Paris, Tenn., Oct. 16, 1937; s. Paul A. Sr. and Margret (Platt) P.; m. Doris Fay Farmer, Dec. 21, 1941; children: Vicky Suzanne, Cheryl Ann, Paul Augustus III. Student, U. Extension, Nashville, Tenn., 1958-59, U. Tenn., Nashville. Tool and die designer Fred D. Wright Co., Nashville, 1956-61, Packer Design Svc., Nashville, 1961, Capitol Tool and Die Co., Madison, Ind., 1961-64, White Engring., Nashville, 1964-65; ptnr., owner Parris Tool & Die, Old Hickory, Tenn., from 1965. Deacon Hermitage Hills Baptist Ch., Hermitage, Tenn., 1980-87. Mem. Nat. Tooling and Machine Assn. (pres. 1975-76). Home: Old Hickory, Tenn. Died Nov. 18, 2006.

PARRY, LINDA ENGLISH, management educator; b. Quonsett, RI, Feb. 15, 1949; d. James Edwin and Doris Mae (Maroney) English; children: Patrick Thomas Parry, Peter Michael Parry. BA cum laude, U. Conn., 1970; MBA, SUNY, Albany, 1983, PhD, 1991. Mktg. rsch. asst. Hartford Nat. Corp., Hartford, Conn., 1970-73; mktg. dir. Lab. Microsystems, Troy, N.Y., 1983-85; asst. prof. Russell Sage Coll., Troy, 1985-90, U. Minn., Duluth, from 1990. Cons. State of N.y., 1988-89. Contbr. articles to profl. jours. Bus. rep. Duluth C. of C., 1990—; cons. Albany Red Cross, 1988-90. Mem. AAUW, Acad. Mgmt. Democrat. Roman Catholic. Avocations: running, weightlifting. Home: Bowling Green, Ky. Died Dec. 2, 2006.

PASSMAN, RALPH S., insurance company executive; b. Cleve., Dec. 6, 1924; s. Louis and Anna (Kousin) P.; m. Shirley R. Carr, Apr. 20, 1947; children: Paul A., Suzanne R. Student, U. Calif., Berkeley, 1944-45. Agy. supr. Guardian Life Ins. Co., Kansas City, Mo., 1947-53; assoc. gen. agent Washington Nat. Ins. Co., Kansas City, Mo., 1953-55; v.p. SFO, Inc., Kansas City, 1955-72; pres. Passman & Assoc., Prairie Village, Kans., from 1972. Pres. Acorn Underwriters, Inc. Contbr. articles to profl. jours. Active with Boy Scouts Am., Kansas City,Mo., 1936—. Served as cpl. USMC, 1942-46. Recipient Silver Beaver award Boy Scouts Am., 1976, award of Excellence, Graphic Arts Council, 1969. Mem. Ins. Agts. Assn., Gen. Agts. and Mgrs. Assn., Ind. Ins. Agts. Assn., Accident and Health Underwriters Assn. Greater Kansas City (pres. 1957-58), Greater Kansas City and State of Kans. Health Underwriters Assn. (bd. dirs.), Nat. Assn. Life Underwriters, Nat. Assn. Health Underwriters, B'nai B'rith (pres. Kansas City 1968). Jewish. Avocations: scouting, golf, stamp and coin collecting. Home: Shawnee Mission, Kans. Died May 27, 2007.

PATRICK, MARY KATHLEEN, freelance/self-employed writer, food service executive; b. Daytona Beach, Fla., Aug. 19, 1976; d. William Minor and Mary Kathleen Hawk; m. Mark Andrew Patrick, June 20, 1998. BA in Pub. Adminstrn., U. Ctrl. Fla., 2001, BA in Sociology, 2001. Freelance writer. Poet: www.poetry.com, 2001. Mem.: ASPA, Internat. Soc. of Poets, Nat. Writer's Union. R-Consevative. Avocations: swimming, hiking, reading, writing, cooking. Home: Orlando, Fla. Died May 12, 2007.

PATRONE, JOSEPH S., project engineer; b. Warren, Ohio, Aug. 6, 1935; Student, ATES, Niles, Ohio, 1956-58. Designer Taylor-Winfield, Warren, 1966-76; project engr. Fairfield Machine, Columbiana, Ohio, 1976-92, JB Industries, Warren, from 1992. Democrat. Roman Catholic. Avocations: boating, swimming, gardening. Home: Mineral Ridge, Ohio. Died Dec. 12, 2006.

PATTERSON, ROBERT PORTER, JR., federal judge; b. NYC, July 11, 1923; s. Robert Porter and Margaret (Winchester) P.; m. Bevin C. Daly, Sept. 15, 1956; children: Anne, Robert, Margaret, Paul, Katherine. AB, Harvard U., 1947; LLB, Columbia U., 1950. Bar: N.Y. 1951, D.C. 1966. Law clk. Donovan, Leisure, Newton & Lumbard, NYC, 1950-51; asst. counsel N.Y. State Crime Commn. Waterfront Investigation, 1952-53; asst. U.S. atty. Chief of Narcotics Prosecutions and Investigations, 1953-56; asst. counsel Senate Banking and Currency Com., 1954; assoc. Patterson, Belknap, Webb & Tyler, NYC, 1956-60, ptnr., 1960-88; judge US Dist. Ct. (so. dist.) NY, NY, 1988—98, sr. judge NY, 1998—2015. Counsel to minority select com. pursuant to house resolution no. 1, Washington, 1967; mem. Senator's Jud. Screening Panel, 1974-88, Gov.'s Jud. Screening Panel, 1975-82, Gov.'s Sentencing Com., 1978-79. Contbr. articles to profl. jours. Chmn. Wm. T. Grant Found., 1974-94, Prisoners' Legal Services N.Y., 1976-88; dir. Legal Aid Soc., 1961-88, pres., 1967-71; chmn. Nat. Citizens for Eisenhower, 1959-60, Scranton for Pres., N.Y. State, 1964; bd. mgrs. Havens Relief Fund Soc., 1994—08, Millbrook Sch., 1966-78, Vera Inst. Justice, 1981-99, New Sch. for Social Rsch., 1986-94, George C. Marshall Found., 1987-93; mem. exec. com. Lawyers Com. for Civil Rights Under Law, 1968-88; mem. Goldman Panel for Attica Disturbance, 1972, Temporary Commn. on State Ct. System, 1971-73, Rockefeller U. Council, 1986-88, exec. com. N.Y. Vietnam Vets. Meml. Commn., 1982-85, Mayor's Police Adv. Com., 1985-87. Served to capt. USAAF, 1942-46. Decorated D.F.C. with cluster, Air medal with clusters. Mem. ABA (ho. of dels. 1976-80), N.Y. State Bar Assn. (pres. 1978-79), Assn. Bar City N.Y. (v.p. 1974-75), N.Y. County Lawyers Assn., Am. Law Inst., Am. Judicature Soc. (bd. dirs. 1979). Republican. Episcopalian. Home: Cold Spring, NY. Died Apr. 21, 2015.

PATTERSON, WILLIAM T., writer; b. Findlay, Ohio, July 18, 1933; s. Arthur Dunn Patterson; m. Carol Diane Rockett, Jan. 14, 1968 (div. Mar. 29, 1984); children: Rita, Karen, Sheri. BA, Ohio State U., 1953. Author: (biography) The Farmer's Daughter Remembered. Pres. Pvt. Investigator Assn. Calif., 1967, Guide Dogs of the Desert, 1974—79. Recipient Best Syndicated Pet Column in Newspapers, Dog Writer's Assn. of Am., 1980. Avocation: photography. Home: Las Vegas, Nev. Died Dec. 1, 2007.

PATTON, JOHN THOMAS, judge; b. Cleve., Mar. 2, 1929; m. Patricia J. Keaton, May 26, 1951; 1 child, Kathleen Ann Christyson. Student, Kent State U., 1948-50; BBA in Acctg., Cleve. State U., 1955; JD, Cleveland Marshall Coll. Law, 1958. Bar: Ohio 1958, U.S. Dist. Ct. (no. dist.) Ohio 1963, U.S. Supreme Ct. 1965. Asst. county pros. atty. Cuyahoga County Prosecutor's Office, Cleve., 1959-66, chief asst. county prosecutor, 1963-66, chief appellate divsn., 1965-66; judge Ct. of Common Pleas of Cuyahoga County, Cleve., 1966-76, Ohio Ct. Appeals (8th dist.), Cleve., from 1977, chief justice, 1983, 90, 95. Mem. Gov. of Ohio Criminal Sentencing Commn. Past chmn., mem. bd. overseers Cleveland Marshall Coll. of Law; mem. adv. bd., past chmn. exec. bd. Fenn Ednl. Fund, Cleve. Found. Sgt. U.S. Army Corps Engrs., 1950-53. Mem. ABA, Greater Cleve. Bar Assn., Ohio Bar Assn., Cleve. Bar Assn., Cuyahoga County Bar Assn. (past trustee), Ohio Ct. Appeals Judges Assn. (past chief justice 1994), Ohio Common Pleas Judges Assn. (past pres.), Alumni Assn. Cleve. State U. (past pres., bd. dirs.), Cleveland Marshall Coll. of Law Alumni Assn. (hon. trustee), Am. Legion, VFW, Korean War Vets. Assn., Cuyahoga County Vets Commn. (past pres.), Delta Theta Phi. Roman Catholic. Avocations: golf, theater, reading. Home: Cleveland, Ohio. Died May 16, 2007.

PAUL, WILLIAM ERWIN, immunologist; b. Bklyn., June 12, 1936; s. Jack and Sylvia (Gleicher) Paul; m. Marilyn Heller, Dec. 25, 1958; children: Jonathan M. Carmel, Matthew E. BA summa cum laude, Bklyn. Coll., 1956; MD cum laude, SUNY, Bklyn., 1960, DSc (hon.), 1991; PhD (hon.), Hebrew U., Jerusalem, 2003, Med. U. Cluj-Napoca, Romania, 2003, Nat. U. Athens, Greece, 2007; Laurea hon. causa, U. Rome, 2005; DSc (hon.), Elmezzi Grad. Sch. Molecuilar Medicine, 2010. Intern, asst. resident Mass. Meml. Hosp., Boston Med. Ctr., 1960—62; clin. assoc. Nat. Cancer Inst., NIH, Bethesda, Md., 1962—64; post doctoral fellow, instr. NYU Sch. Medicine, NYC, 1964—68; prin. investigator lab. immunology Nat. Inst. Allergy and Infectious Diseases, NIH, Bethesda, Md., 1968—70, chief lab. immunology, 1970—2015; dir. office of AIDS rsch. NIH, Bethesda, Md., 1993—2015, assoc. dir. AIDS rsch., 1994—97, disting. investigator, 2007—15. Awards jury mem. Albert Lasker Med. Rsch. Awards Program, from 1993; chmn. selection com. Irene Diamond Fund Professorship in Immunology, 1997—2005; Sackler sr. prof. Tel Aviv U., Israel; chair sci. adv. bd. Lupus Rsch. Inst.; mem. Novartis Sci. Bd., 2001—05; adj. prof. U. Pa., from 2002; governing dir. Am. Found. for AIDS Rsch., 2002—05, mem. program adv. bd., from 2006; chair visiting com. assessment of basic biomed. rsch. Israel Acad. Sci. and Humanities, 2007; mem. sci. adv. bd. Trudeau Inst.; chmn., sci. adv. bd. Lupus Research Institute, from 2000; mem. Shaw Prize Com. Life Sci. and Medicine, 2008—12; mem. sci. adv. bd. Inst. Human Virology, from 2013. Adv. editor Jour. Exptl. Medicine, 1974—2006; editor: Ann. Rev. Immunology, Volumes 1-31, 1983—2011, Fundamental Immunology, 1st - 7th edits., from 1984, Immunity, 2003—06; assoc. editor Cell, 1985—96, transmitting editor Internat. Immunology, 1989—96, corr. editor Procs. Royal Soc. Series B, 1989—93, mem. editl. bd. Molecular Biology of Cell, 1990—93; contbg. editor: Procs. NAS U.S.A., 1992—94; mem. editl. bd. Procs. NAS U.S.A., from 2004; contbr. numerous articles to sci. journals. With USPHS, 1962—64, with USPHS, 1975—96. Recipient Founders' prize, Tex. Instruments Found., 1979, Alumni medal, SUNY Downstate Med. Ctr., 1981, DSM, USPHS, 1985, Life Sci. Award, 3M, 1988, Tovi Comet - Wallerstein prize, CAIR Inst., Bar Ilan U., 1992, 6th ann. Excellence Award in Immunologic Rsch., Duke U., 1993, Alumni Honors, Bklyn. Coll., 1994, Abbott Labs. Award in Clin. and Diagnostic Immunology, Am. Acad. Microbiology, 1998, Lifetime Achievement award, Am. Assn. Immunologists, 2002, Sci. Achievement in award, The Irvington Inst., 2002, Rsch. in Action award, Treatment Action Group, 2003, Scientific Leadership award, Lupus Found., 2005, Hon. Lifetime Achievement award, Internat. Cytokine Soc., 2007, Max Delbruck medal, 2008, Clemens von Pirquet medal, 2009, Am. Assn. Immunologists Excellence in Mentoring award, 2014, Lifetime Achievement Award for Sci. Excellence, Inst. Human Virology. Fellow: Am. Acad. Arts and Sci.; mem.: NAS, Internat. Cytokine Soc., Am Assn. Immunologists (pres. 1986—87, Lifetime Achievement award 2002, Mex Delebruck medal 2008), Assn. Am. Physicians, Scandinavian Soc. Immunology (hon.), Am. Soc. Clin. Investigation (pres. 1980—81, 1980—81), Inst. Medicine NAS. Achievements include discovery of interleukin-4 and demonstration of its central role in allergic inflammatory responses; determination of mechanisms of Th2 differentiation; research in cytokine regulation of immunoglobulin class switching; role of MHC molecules in T cell recognition. Home: Washington, DC. Died Sept. 18, 2015.

PAULSON, RAYMOND ARNOLD, science engineering executive; b. Eagle Rock, Calif., Dec. 29, 1921; s. Arnold Edwin and Clara (Martin) P.; m. Beverly Doris, Sept. 21, 1941; children: Larry, Jerry, Celeste. JD, Calif. Coll. Law, 1966; postgrad., Citrus Coll., Nat. U., U. S.C. Law instr. U.S. Armed Forces Inst.; dir., mgr. nat. maj. mfr., prodr. first tactical army missile, first US all weather satelite Howard Highes Corp. The Corporal, 1959; sales mgr., asst. dir. So. Calif. Credit. Bur.; engr., designer radiation and chem. evaluation test labs. USAF; dir., mgr. electro-mech. bus.; JD founder Calif. Coll. Law; pres. chmn. bd. Paulson Internat. Co., 1971-90; ret., hon. chmn. Paulson Internat. Corp., from 1990; pres. World Trust Agy. (div. Paulson Devel. Corp.), 2006; founder Paulson Products Co.; sole proprietor Paulson Co.; established pvt. trust Paulson Trust; established Guatemala Pvt. Sector Country Trust Fund. Devel., instr. exec. leadership tng. program dept. adult edn. Baldwin Pk. Schs.; founder Paulson Zero Emission Energy Rsch. and Devel. Found., mgr., Pacemaker for Medtronics Corp. Talent locator, stage mgr. "I Love Lucy Show"; designer, assoc. dir. World Internat. Air and Space Show, 1995, Sky Harbor and McCarron Airports, Hdqs. World Air and Space Tours; assoc. designer thermal battery and developer 1st semi-perpetual electric vehicle; pioneered color telecasting; 1st color stage mgr. with Carlton Winkler-Ed Wynn on Union Pacific show Sta. CBS-TV; joint originator USMC Christmas program for underprivileged kids Toys for Tots; surveyor, designer congress-approved U.S. Canal, Brownsville, Tex., Nat. City, San Diego; designer Direct Fly by Wire Flight Control Sys.; mfr. 1st all composite single engine bullet proof two place jet spacecraft in world Mach 3 Plus; designer, developer VAC-PAC All Purpose Shipping Container for ship, rail and truck; designer, prodr. semi-perpetual self-contained charging sys. for electric vehicle battery sources, containers and vehicles too way sea level water way; designed concept for US Canal congress-approved Gulfo-Pacific Canal, Mex.; designer-mfr. pacemaker cs. for MedTronics Leadership tng. dir. Boy Scouts Am., Monte Vista dist.; founding mem. Air-Space Mus. Smithsonian Instn., 1994. B-29 radar navaigator pilot US-AAF, 1944—45, WWII,Handicap USAF Vet-Res. AF, Hiroshima Atomic Bombing and Nagaski. Decorated Air Medal and Battle Stars with presdl. citation; recipient Merit award, div. rsch. and sci. guidance LA County Supt. Schs. Mem. TV Acad. Arts and Sci. (co-originator, life assoc.). Achievements include designing and developing the first hybrid-electric jet with semi-perpetual electric charging; development of semi petual charging chip and truth cell; all electric space jet with semi petual charging system design. Died May 2, 2015.

PAULUS, STEPHEN HARRISON, composer; b. Summit, NJ, Aug. 24, 1949; s. Harrison Child and Patricia Jean (Clark) P.; m. Patricia Ann, July 18, 1975; children: Gregory Stephen, Andrew Christopher. Student, Macalester Coll., 1967-69; BA, U. Minn., 1969-71, MA, 1972-74, PhD, 1974-78. Co-founder, fundraiser Minn. Composers Forum, St. Paul, 1973-84; Exxon/Rockefeller composer in residence Minn. Orch., Mpls., 1983-87; composer in residence Santa Fe Chamber Music Festival, summer 1986; Regent's lectr. U. Calif., Santa Barbara, Nov. 1986; composer in residence Atlanta Symphony Orch., 1988-92, Dale Warland Singers, 1991-92. Composer in residence Aspen Festival, summer, 1992. Performances with Tanglewood Festival, 1980, Edinburgh Festival, 1983, Aldeburgh Festival, 1985; composer (orchestral works) Sinfonietta, Concertante, Ordway Overture, Concerto for Orchestra, Seven Short Pieces for Orchestra, Translucent Landscapes, Spectra, Reflections: Four Movements on a Theme of Wallace Stevens, Divertimento for Harp and Chamber Orchestra, Trumpet Concerto, Suite from Harmoonia, Suite from The Postman Always Rings Twice, Ground Breaker--An Overture for Constrn. Instruments and Orch., Symphony in Three Movements, Street Music, Manhattan Sinfonietta, Violin Concerto, Symphony for Strings, Concerto for Violin, Cello & Orch., Organ Concerto, Violin Concerto No. 2, (recordings) Violin Concerto, Concertante and Symphony for Strings, Songs: Bittersuite, All My Pretty Ones, Artsongs, (for orch.) Violin Concerto (Kennedy Ctr. Friedheim award for 3d pl. Am.

Works for Orch., 1988), Symphony for Strings, Street Music, Echoes Between the Silent Peaks, (operas) The Woodlanders, The Postman Always Rings Twice, The Woman At Otowi Crossing, The Village Singer, Harmoonia, The Woman at Otowi Crossing, The Three Hermits; (for chorus and orch.), So Hallow'd Is the Time, (5 carols for chorus and strings) Christmas Tidings, Letters for the Times, North Shore, Canticles: Songs and Rituals for the Easter and the May, Voices, (chamber work) Seven for the Flowers Near the River, Seven Miniatures, Fantasy in Three Parts, Quartessence, Dramatic Suite, others, also numerous works for chamber groups including Partita for Violin and Piano, Music for Contrasts (string Quartet), String Quartet No.2, Quartessence, (for soprano voice, piano, percussion and string quartet) Letters From Colette, American Vignettes (for cello and piano); (for solo voice) All My Pretty Ones, Artsongs, Mad Book, Shadow Book: Michael Morley's Songs, Elizabethan Songs, Bittersuite for baritone and piano, (solo voice/bass-baritone and vn, vc. pf.) The Long Shadow of Lincoln; (for solo instruments) Two Moments for Guitar, (piano) Translucent Landscapes; (for chorus) Madrigali di Michelangelo, Four Preludes on Playthings of The Wind, Peace, Personals, Marginalia, Echoes Between the Silent Peaks, Jesu Carols, Meditations of Li Po, Love's Philosophy, Three Songs for Mixed Chorus, The Earth Sines, The Elixir, God be With Us, Songs from the Japanese, (narrative and chamber orch.) Voices from the Gallery, (chamber) Music of the Night (for violin, voice and percussion), (choral) Visions from Hildegard, Part I (for flute, oboe, timpany, percussion, organ and chorus), Part Two (for brass quintet, percussion and chorus), (for narrator and chamber orch.) Voices from the Gallery, (vocal) Songs of Love and Longing, (chamber/instrumental) Air on Seurat, (chorus) Three Songs for Mixed Chorus, Christ Our Passover, (piano) Preludes, (organ duet) The Triumph of the Saint, Toccata, (chorus and chamber ensemble) Whitman's Dream. Recipient Outstanding Achievement award U. Minn., 1991, Disting. Alumni award, 1991, Lancaster Symphony Orch. Composer's award, 1994, Grammy award for Best Contemporary Classical Composition for "Paulus: Prayers and Remembrances," (posthumously), 2016; Guggenheim fellow, 1982-83, NEA fellow, 1978; NEA Consortium grantee, 1987. Mem. ASCAP (bd. dirs. 1990), American Music Ctr., Minn. Composers Forum (v.p. 1984-87, bd. dirs.). Avocations: tennis, reading. Died Oct. 19, 2014.

PAUSTIAN, FREDERICK FRANZ, retired gastroenterologist; b. Grand Island, Nebr., Nov. 24, 1926; s. Franz Henry and Martha Bertha (Winter) P.; m. Mary Ann Mohrman, June 20, 1953 (dec. May 25, 2007); children: Cheryl Ann, Lynn Carol, James Frederick, John William. BS, U. Nebr., 1949; MD, U. Nebr., Omaha, 1953. Lic. Nebr. Asst. instr. U. Pa. Graduate Sch. Medicine, Phila., 1957-58; instr. U. Nebr. Coll. Medicine, Omaha, 1959-60, asst. prof., 1961—63, assoc. prof., 1963—67, prof., 1967—95, assoc. dean continuing and grad. med. edn., 1980—95. Vice-chmn. Residency Review Com. Internal Medicine, 1975-77, chmn., 1977-79. With U.S. Army, 1945-46, ETO. Master ACP (gov. Nebr. chpt. 1984-88, Laureate award Nebr. chpt. 1989); mem. American Gastroent. Assn., American Soc. Gastroent. Endoscopy, Bockus Internat. Soc. Gastroenterology, Nebr. Med. Assn. (pres. elect 1993-94, pres. 1994-95), Met. Omaha Med. Soc. (pres. 1991-92). Republican. Presbyterian. Avocations: golf, tennis, fishing, upland and water fowl hunting, canoeing. Home: Omaha, Nebr. Died Nov. 2, 2014.

PAVLOSKI, VERONICA THERESA, corporate communications specialist; b. Bklyn., June 23, 1966; d. John W. and Veronica Theresa (Bartelotti) P. BA magna cum laude, Seton Hall U., 1988. Lic. FCC operator. Rsch. analyst Katz Comm., Inc., NYC, 1988; rsch. assoc., multimedia designer CMRA, Emerson, N.J., from 1990. Staff, engr. WSOU-FM, South Orange, N.J., 1986. Computer graphics exhbns. include Images '88 Communication Arts Festival, 1988. Avocations: sketching, videography, claymation, reading, french cooking. Home: Emerson, NJ. Died Nov. 1, 2006.

PAXSON, BUD (LOWELL WHITE PAXSON), retired broadcast executive; b. Rochester, NY, Apr. 17, 1935; s. Donald Earl and Maybelle L. (White) P.; m. Jean Louise Blauvelt, May 2, 1961 (div. Apr. 1977); children: Todd L., Devon W., Julie; m. Barbara Ann Chapman, Nov. 19, 1977 (div. Nov. 1988); children: Thomas, Jennifer; m. Marla J. Bright, Jan. 6, 1990; 1 child, Nicole. BA, Syracuse U., 1956. Pres., owner Sta. WACK-AM, Newark, N.Y., 1957-61, Sta. WKSN-AM/FM, Jamestown, N.Y., 1961-68, Sta. WNYP-TV, Jamestown, 1966-68, Sta. WTBY-AM, Waterbury, Conn., 1968-70, Sta. WYND-AM, Sarasota, Fla., 1968-74, Sta. WAVS-AM, Ft. Lauderdale, Fla., 1973-77, Sta. WWQT-AM, Clearwater, Fla., 1977-83, Sta. WHBS-FM, Holiday, Fla., 1977-83; pres. Full Circle Mktg., Fla., 1968-77; founder, pres emeritus Home Shopping Network, St. Petersburg, Fla., 1982-91; founder, pres. Paxson Broadcasting, St. Petersburg and Clearwater, 1991—2005. Trustee Milligan Coll., Tenn.; bd. dirs. Broadcap, Washington; mem. Coun. of 100 of Pinellas County, St. Petersburg; chmn. City of Sarasota Planning and Zoning Commn., 1970-74. Capt. U.S. Army, 1956-57. Mem. Nat. Assn. Broadcasters, Nat. Cable TV Assn., Direct Mktg. Assn. America, Roebling Soc. Republican. Christian. Avocations: yachting, deep sea fishing. Home: Palm Beach, Fla. Died Jan. 9, 2015.

PAYNE, JOHN HOWARD, university program director; b. Fukuoka, Japan, Aug. 13, 1951; came to U.S., 1951; s. John and Libby Lee (Small) P.; m. Elizabeth gigi Duis, Aug. 26, 1972; children: Nathan, Jessica. BS in Comm., U. No. Colo., 1974, MA in Ednl. Media, 1983. Audio/visual asst. U. No. Colo., Greeley, 1974-79, audio/visual dir., 1979-92; faculty AIMS C.C., Greeley, 1981-82; dir. ednl. and distance learning techs. U. Va., Charlottesville, from 1993. Mem. adv. bd. Sta. WTJU-FM, Charlottesville. Writer, producer, dir. (video) Olgame, Olgame, 1991, Art and Community, 1989, The Turn of Our Century, 1989. Bd. dirs. Greeley Boys Club, 1974; loaned exec. Weld County United Way, Greeley, 1988; mktg. comm. Weld County United Way, Greeley, 1990; bd. dirs. United Way of Weld County, 1991, 92. Mem. Nat. Univ. Continuing Edn. Assn., Assn. Ednl. Comm. Technologists, Internat. TV Assn. (pres.-elect No. Colo. 1991-92, pres. No. Colo. 1992-93). Democrat. Avocations: bicycling, skiing, photography, volunteering. Home: Charlottesvle, Va. Died June 30, 2007.

PEACHEY, VICTOR KENNETH, retired construction executive; b. Fayette, Maine, Dec. 1, 1914; s. George Earle and Dena Victoria (Anderson) Peachey; m. June Louis Savage, Oct. 9, 1978; stepchildren: Wallace D., April, Jason F. Campbell. Student, U. Minn., 1941; BS, U. Maine, 1949. RN. With chemistry lab. Radcliffe Coll., 1932—35; nurse pvt. registry Mayo Clinic, Rochester, Minn., 1940—42; mgr. Cmty. Hosp., Lexington, Nebr., 1943—45; pres. Peachey Builders, Augusta, Maine, 1950—84. Adv. bd. Depositors Trust Co. Mem.: Svc. Corps Ret. Execs. Small Bus. Adminstrn., Small Bus. Assn. New Eng., Assoc. Industries Maine, Augusta Country Club (gov.), Shriners, Masons. Republican. Home: Manchester, Maine. Died Dec. 31, 2006.

PEARSON, RAYMOND MARTIN, SR., educational counseling executive, learning center owner; b. LA, Mar. 21, 1933; s. Dwight Bandy and Evelyn June (Tennis) P.; divorced; children: Kimberly Marie, Amanda Marie, Matthew Long, Raymond Martin Jr., Ryan Martin. BA, Columbia Union Coll., 1968; MA, U. Ctrl. Fla., 1972. Cert. tchr., Fla., reading specialist. Elem. sch. tchr. S.D.A. Ch. Sch., Riverside, Calif., 1960-62, Merced, Calif., 1962-64, Prince Georges, Md., 1965-67; secondary sch. tchr. Mrs. Elizabeth Ann Seese Private Sch., Orlando, Fla., 1967-68; elem. sch. tchr. Orange County Schs., Fla., 1968-70, Seminole County Schs., Fla., 1970-85; reading resources specialist migrant children's program Clermont High Sch., Lake County, Fla., from 1986; owner Family Learning Centre, Altamonte Springs, Fla., from 1991. Substitute tchr. Seminole County, Fla. Active Nat. Audubon Soc., Save the Children; social worker Aid to Dependent Children, Merced, Calif., 1958-60. With USN, 1950-54, Korea. Mem. Internat. Reading Assn., Fla. Reading Assn., Seminole Reading Assn., Orange County Mental Health Assn. Republican. Seventh-Day Adventist. Avocations: canoeing, gardening, folk music festivals, church activities, theater. Home: Altamonte Springs, Fla. Died Jan. 14, 2007.

PECORA, DAVID VICTOR, retired surgeon; b. Yonkers, NY, Oct. 2, 1916; s. Cavaliere Michele and Tulia Pecora; m. Dorothy Edith Beavers, July 22, 1944; children: Ann Pecora Diamond, Michele. BA, Columbia U., 1937; MD, Yale U., 1941. Diplomate Am. Bd. Gen. Surgery, Am. Bd. Thoracic Surgery. Intern Lakeside Hosp., Western Res. U., Cleve., 1941-42; grad. fellow in surgery NY Med. Coll., NYC, 1946-47; asst. resident in surgery Sch. Medicine, Yale U., New Haven, 1947-49, resident surgeon in thoracic surgery Uncas-on-Thames, Conn., 1949-51; chief thoracic surgery, sect. chief second surg. svc. VA Hosp., Providence, 1951-54, McGuire VA Hosp., Richmond, Va., 1967-72; prin. thoracic surgeon Ray Brook State Tb Hosp., NY, 1954-65; chief surgery Sunmount VA Hosp., Tupper Lake, NY, 1964-65, VA Hosp., Altoona, Pa., 1965—67; chief surg. svc. VA Ctr., Wilmington, Del., 1972-82; pvt. practice in thoracic, vascular and gen. surgery Newark, Del.; mem. staff Med. Ctr., Wilmington, Del., Cmty. Hosp., Chester, Pa., Crozer-Chester Hosp., Pa., Union Hosp., Elkton, Md., Riverside Hosp., Wilmington; ret., 1995. Instr. in surgery Boston U., 1953-54; clin. assoc. prof. in surgery SUNY, Syracuse, NY, 1961-70; asst. prof. surgery Med. Coll. Va., Richmond, 1967-70, assoc. prof. surgery, 1970-72; prof. surgery Thomas Jefferson U., Phila., 1972-95; adj. prof. surgery Hahnemann U., Phila., 1988-95; supv. tng. surg. residents numerous hosps. Mem. editl. bd. Del. Med. Jour.; author: Memoir: Between the Raindrops, 1998; contbr. over 130 articles to sci. jours. Capt. med. corps U.S. Army, 1942-46. Fellow ACS (instr. advanved trauma life support); mem. AMA, IEEE, Am. Assn. for Thoracic Surgery, Am. Coll. Chest Physicians, Am. Thoracic Soc., Am. Soc. Microbiology, Am. Med. Writers Assn., Am. Lung Assn. (eastern sect.), Royal Soc. Medicine, Pa. Assn. Thoracic Surgery, Del. Valley Vascular Soc., Md. State Med. Assn., Del. State Med. Assn., Del. Acad. Medicine, Va. Thoracic Soc., New Castle County Med. Assn., Phila. Acad. Surgery, Phila. Coll. Physicians, So. Thoracic Surg. Assn., Soc. Thoracic Surgeons (founder), Soc. Laparoendoscopic Surgeons, Soc. Neurovascular Surgery, Upstate NY Soc. Thoracic Surgery (past pres.), Saranac Lake Med. Soc. (past pres.). Home: Mc Lean, Va. Died July 25, 2014.

PEDERSEN, VAGN MOELLER, engineering company executive; b. Tommerup, Denmark, Mar. 25, 1942; came to U.S., 1971; s. Ejnar M. and Benny M. (Mortensen) P.; m. Hee Jung, Feb. 28, 1981; 1 child, Thomas. MS in Dairy Tech., U. Agr., Copenhagen, 1970. Mgr. research and devel. Charles Hansens Lab., Copenhagen, 1970-71, mgr. prodn. Milw., 1971-79; sales mgr. Far East Danish Turnkey Dairies, Seoul, Korea, 1979-82, mgr. prodn. Muscat, Oman, 1982, Plumrose, Maracaibo, Venezuela, 1982-83; from v.p. to pres. Primodan Tech., Inc., Cedarburg, Wis., 1983-90; pres. Gadan Inc., Mequon, Wis., from 1990. Served to sgt. Civil Def., 1964-66, Denmark. Lutheran. Avocations: hunting, outdoor activities, tennis, gardening. Home: La Mirada, Calif. Died Dec. 24, 2006.

PEETE, CALVIN, retired professional golfer; b. Detroit, July 18, 1943; s. Dennis and Irenia (Bridgeford) P.; m. Christine Sears, Oct. 24, 1974 (div. 1987); children: Charlotte, Calvin, Rickie, Dennis, Kalvanetta; m. Pepper; children Aisha, Aleya Grad. in adult edn., Highland Park Sch., Detroit, 1982; cert. degree hon., Wayne State U., 1983. Profl. golfer, Sawgrass, Fla., 1975-84; winner Greater Milw. Open, 1979, 82, Anheuser-Busch Classic, 1982, Atlanta Classic, 1983, Phoenix Open, 1985, Tournament Players Championship, 1985-86, U.S. F & G, 1986; exhibitionist Ptnrs. for Youth, Miami, Fla., from 1982, Desert Mahie Jr. Golf, Phoenix, from 1983, City of Atlanta Jr. Golf, from 1983, Calvin Peete-Augustus J. Calloway Golf Tournament, Detroit, from 1983. Mem. U.S.A. Team vs. Japan, 1982-83, Ryder Cup Team, 1983, 85. Active supporter Sickle Cell Anemia Found., Palm Beach and Lee Counties (Fla.). Recipient Ben Hogan award, 1983, Good Guy award Gordin Gin, 1983, Jackie Robinson award for athletics Ebony Mag., 1983, Vardon trophy, 1984; named to African American Ethic Sports Hall of Fame, 2002 Mem. Profl. Golfers Assn. Democrat. Baptist. Winner 12 PGA Tournaments, $2.3 million in prize money; led PGA tour in driving accuracy 10 consecutive years, 1981-90. Died Apr. 29, 2015.

PEITHMAN, ROSCOE EDWARD, physicist, educator; b. Hoyleton, Ill., Feb. 26, 1913; s. Edward Henry Peithman and Sarah Jane Smith; m. Laura Jane Davenport, Apr. 3, 1936 (dec. Oct. 13, 1987); children: Ann Davenport, Stephen Edward. BS, So. Ill. U., 1935; MS, U. of Ill., 1939; EdD, Oreg. State U., 1955. Tchr. various HS, Ill., 1935—42; prof. of physics Humboldt State U., Arcata, Calif., 1946—77, chmn. divsn. of phys. scis., 1960—69, dean Sch. Scis., 1969—70, emeritus prof. of physics, from 1977. Academic senator Calif. State U. Sys., Calif., 1963—66. Lt. comdr. USNR, 1942—73. Fellow: Am. Men and Women of Sci. (life); mem.: Am. Assn. of Physics Tchrs. Avocation: amateur radio. Home: Mckinleyville, Calif. Died Feb. 18, 2015.

PELCYGER, ELAINE, retired school psychologist; b. Jersey City, Apr. 13, 1939; d. Maurice C. and Bessie (Schneider) Morley; m. Iran Pelcyger, June 4, 1956; children: Stuart Lawrence, Gwynne Ellice, Wayne Farrol. BA magna cum laude, L.I. U., 1983; MS, St. John's U., Flushing, NY, 1985. Cert. sch. psychologist N.Y., N.Y.C., nat. cert. sch. psychologist, group psychotherapist, N.Y. Sch. psychologist NYC Bd. Edn., 1985—2006; trauma and loss sch. specialist; ret., 2006. Mem. Nat. Assn. Sch. Psychologists, Am. Group Psychotherapists, N.Y. Assn. Sch. Psychologists, Psi Chi. Avocations: handicrafts, reading, old time radio. Home: Smithtown, NY. Died Aug. 4, 2007.

PELOTE, DOROTHY BARNES, retired state legislator; b. Lancaster, SC, Dec. 30, 1929; d. Abraham Barnes & Ethel Green; m. Maceo Pelote; children: Deborah Allen, Miriam Heyward. Ret. sch. tchr. Savannah-Chatham County Sch. Sys.; commr. Chatham County; mem. Dist. 149 Ga. House of Reps., Atlanta, 1992—2002. Active Sr. Citizen Coun., Martin Luther King Jr. Observance Day Assn., Inc., Cmty. Olympic Beautification Com., Phoenix Project, Open Arms for Medically Fragile Infants; bd. dirs. United Way; former pres. Carver hts Mission Improvement Orgn. Mem. NAACP, Order of Eastern Star. Mem. A.M.E. Ch. Home: Savannah, Ga. Died Jan. 18, 2015.

PELS, DONALD ARTHUR, retired broadcast executive; b. New Rochelle, NY, Jan. 23, 1928; s. Herbert and Alice Miriam (Brady) P.; m. Josette Jeanne Bernard, Feb. 11, 1965; children: Juliette, Valerie, Laurence. BS, U. Pa., 1948; JD, NYU, 1953. CPA. With Filene's Dept. Store, Boston, 1948-49, Arthur Young & Co., NYC, 1953-56; bus. mgr. Sta. WABC-TV, NYC, 1956-59; exec. v.p., dir. Capital Cities Communications, NYC, 1959-69; chmn., pres. LIN Broadcasting Corp., NYC, 1969—89. Trustee Barnard Coll.; bd. dirs. U.S. Trust, Philharm. Symphony Soc. N.Y. Mem.: Univ. (N.Y.C.). Home: New York, NY. Died Oct. 16, 2014.

PEMBERTON, JAMES AUBREY, JR., lawyer; b. Kirksville, Mo., Oct. 4, 1939; s. James Aubrey and Marian (Morgan) P.; m. Patricia Anne Sams, Jan. 11, 1975 (dec. Feb. 1979); 1 child, Anne Elizabeth; m. Libby A. Welch, June 15, 1985. AB, U. Mo., 1961, JD, 1963. Bar: Mo. 1963, D.C. 1966. Trial atty. U.S. Dept. Justice, Washington, 1967-71; assoc. King & King, Chartered, Washington, 1971-81, prin., 1981-95, counsel, from 1995. Bd. dirs. Collington Episcopal Life Care Cmty., Inc., Mitchellville, Md., 1991-97; mem. citizen's adv. coun. Fairfax County Police Dept., Fairfax, Va., 1996-97;mem. coun. Washington Diocese Episcopal Ch., 1989-95. Capt. U.S. Army, 1964-67 . Home: Fairfax Station, Va. Died July 30, 2007.

PEMBERTON, LARRY NORVELL, engineer, consultant; b. Slater, Mo., Oct. 31, 1932; s. Lacy E. and Gladys M. (Walker) P.; m. Marilyn D. Howell, Dec. 29, 1951; children: Cynthia L., Lori A. BSME, Finley Engring. Coll., 1958. Layout engr. Gen. Motors, Kansas City, 1959-60, staff engr., 1960-65, plant facilities engr., 1965-68, sr. plant environ. engr., 1978-85; sr. planning engr. Gen. Motors (BOC Div.), Kansas City, 1985-87; project mgr., engr. KC Indsl. Constructors, Kansas City, 1989-93. Bd. dirs. Kansas City Environ. Task Force, 1979-80, Villas Property Owners Assn., 1991; mem. Mo. Water Pollution Control, 1970-80; mem. Rep. Nat. Com.; mem. Friends of Arrow Rock, 1991. With USAF (Korea) 1951-55. Mem. Mo. C. of C. (adv. bd. 1985-87), Kansas City Air Pollution Assn. (bd. dirs. 1970-80), Masons, Shriners, Scottish Rite, Gen. Motors Club. Avocations: boating, skiing, golf, walking, bowling. Home: Kansas City, Mo. Died Nov. 28, 2006.

PEÑA, ELIZABETH, actress; b. Elizabeth, NJ, Sept. 23, 1961; d. Mario Peña and Margarita Toirac; m. Hans Christian Rolla, 1994; children: Fiona, Kaelan. Grad., NYC High Sch. for Performing Arts, 1977. Actor: (plays) Rome and Juliet, Antigone, Blood Wedding, Night of the Assassins, Italian-American Reconciliation, Cinderella, Act One and Only; (films) El Super, 1979, Times Square, 1980, They All Laughed, 1981, Crossover Dreams, 1984, Down and Out in Beverly Hills, 1985, La Bamba, 1986, *batteries not included, 1987, Vibes, 1988, Blue Steel, 1989, Jacob's Ladder, 1990, The Waterdance, 1991, Free Willy II: The Adventure Home, 1994, Dead Funny, 1995, Across the Moon, 1995, Lone Star, 1996 (Independent Spirit award, 1996, Bravo award, 1996), Recon, 1996, The Pass, 1997, Strangeland, 1997, Rush Hour, 1998, Seven Girlfriends, 1999, Imposter, 2000, Things Behind the Sun, 2001, Tortilla Soup, 2001 (ALMA award, 2001), On the Borderline, 2001, Zig-Zag, 2001, Ten Tiny Love Stories, 2001, Keep Your Distance, 2003, Sueño, 2003, (voice only) The Incredibles, 2004, Down in the Valley, 2005, Keep Your Distance, 2005, Transamerica, 2005, Sueño, 2005, How the Garcia Girls Spend Their Summer, 2005, The Lost City, 2005, Goal II: Living the Dream, 2007, Adrift in Manhattan, 2007, Dragon Wars: D-War, 2007, Love Comes Lately, 2007, A Single Woman, 2008, Nothing Like the Holidays, 2008, Mother and Child, 2009, Becoming Eduardo, 2009, Down for LIfe, 2009, The Perfect Family, 2011, Plush, 2013, Blaze You Out, 2013, Girl on the Edge, 2014; (TV films) Shannon's Deal, 1989, Fugitive Among Us, 1992, Roommates, 1994, The Invaders, 1995, It Came From Outer Space II, 1996, Contagious, 1996, The Second Civil War, 1997, Aldrich Ames: America Betrayed, 1998, Border Line, 1999, Hollywood Moms Mystery, 2004, Surburban Madness, 2004, Racing for Time, 2008, King John, 2013, In the Dark, 2013; (TV miniseries) Drug War: The Camarena Story, 1990, (TV appearances) Hillstreet Blues, 1986, T.J. Hooker, 1985, Cagney and Lacey, 1985, Dellaventura, 1997, Dream On, 1993, Dead Man's Gun, 1997, LA Law (4 episodes), 1993—94, The Outer Limits, 1995, Two, 1996, The Eddie Files, 1998, Boston Public (2 episodes), 2002—03, CSI: Miami, 2003, NCIS, 2004, Without a Trace, 2005, Numb3rd, 2005, Minoriteam, 2006, American Dad, 2007, Ghost Whisperer, 2009, Outlaw, 2010, Off the Map, 2011, Charlie's Angels, 2011, Prime Suspect, 2012, Common Law, 2012, Modern Family (2 episodes), 2013; actor, actor: Major Crimes, 2013; (TV series) Tough Cookies, 1986, I Married Dora, 1987—88, Shannon's Deal, 1990—91, (voice only) Maya and Miguel, 2004, Justice League, 2004—05, Matador, 2014; dir.: (plays) Celebrando La Diferencia, 1992; actor, dir.: (TV series) Resurrection Blvd., 2000; (films) The Brothers Garcia, 2002. Mem.: AFTRA, SAG, Hispanic Organization Latin Actors, Directors Guild America, Actors' Equity Assn. Died Oct. 14, 2014.

PENG, YENG KAUNG, electrical engineer; b. Shanghai, Republic of China, Dec. 14, 1948; came to U.S., 1977; s. Shaw Chang and Wei Lun (Lin) P. B in Engring., Coll. Maritime Tech., Taiwan, Republic of China, 1971; MSME, U. Nebr., 1978, PhD in Materials Sci., 1980. Marine engr. Oriental Navigation Co., Hong Kong, 1972-76; from research asst. to research assoc. U. Nebr., Lincoln, 1977-80, postdoctoral researcher, 1981; mem. tech. staff Nitron Corp., Cupertino, Calif., 1981-83; yield enhancement engr., device engr. Monolithic Memories Inc., Santa Clara, Calif., 1983-88, product engring. specialist advanced micro device, from 1988. Contbr. articles to sci. jours. Mem. IEEE, Sigma Xi. Home: Los Altos, Calif. Died Jan. 9, 2007.

PENNER, EUNICE B., religious, educational organization administrator; b. Utica, NY, Aug. 27, 1925; d. Leonard Charles and May (Cummings) Bowles; m. Lloyd Matteson Penner, Jan. 15, 1955; 1 child, Leland M. BBA, Excelsior Sch., 1944. Sec. County Oneida, Utica, 1944-45; sec. to pres. Oneida Nat. Bank & Trust Co., Utica, 1945-55; office mgr. Oneida County Boiler Works Inc., Utica, 1965-88, cons., from 1988; pres. Internat. Order King's Daughters & Sons, Chautauqua, N.Y., from 1990. Contbr. articles to profl. jours. Republican. Presbyterian. Avocations: reading, writing, travel. Home: Washington Mills, NY. Died Feb. 23, 2007.

PEOPLES, DAVID ALEXANDER, writer, speaker; b. Big Rapids, Mich., Aug. 11, 1930; s. Floyd G. and Tressa Z. (Reinhardt) P.; divorced; 1 child, Lisa. BS, U. Tenn., 1955. Mktg. rep. IBM, Chattanooga, 1959-62, sales mgr. Atlanta, 1962-66, br. mgr. Greenville, S.C., 1966-72, industry mgr. Atlanta, 1972-82, cons., from 1982. Profl. speaker, 1985—. Author: Presentations Plus, 1988 (Maeventec award 1988), 2d edit., 1992, Supercharge Your Selling, 1990, Selling to the Top, 1993. 1st lt. USAF, 1956-59. Mem. ASTD, Nat. Assn. Speakers, Ga. Speakers Assn. Avocations: portrait painting, jogger. Died Aug. 16, 2007.

PEPPER, NORMA JEAN, mental health nurse; b. Ellington, Iowa, Nov. 7, 1931; d. Victor F. and Grace Mae (Tate) Shadle; m. Bob Joseph Pepper, Dec. 28, 1956 (dec. Oct. 4, 1985); children: Joseph Victor, Barbara Jean, Susan Claire (dec.). Diploma in Nursing, Broadlawns Polk County Hosp., 1950-53; BSN, U. Iowa, 1953-55; MSN, U. Colo., 1955-60. Cert. mental health nurse. Head nurse Colo. Psychiatric Hosp., Denver, 1956; head nurse, Psychiatry Denver General Hosp., 1958-60; with Nurses Official Registry, Denver, 1960-73; staff nurse VA Med. Ctr., Denver, 1974-94. Counselor VA Hosp. Employee Assistance Com., Denver, 1987-94. Mem. Colo. Nurses Assn. Home: Denver, Colo. Died Feb. 13, 2007.

PEPPERCORN, BERT LEONARD, retired dermatologist; b. Cleve., July 19, 1923; s. Max and Bessie (Auerbach) P.; m. Marjorie Glickman, Mar. 15, 1947; children: Robert Peppercorn, Wendy Peppercorn Grant. BA, Ohio State U., 1944, MD, 1947. Intern City Hosp., Cleve., 1947-48, resident in internal medicine, 1948-50, resident in dermatology, 1950-52; sr. asst. surgeon USPHS, 1952-54; pvt. practice specializing in dermatology Miami, Fla., 1955-88. From clin. instr. to clin. prof. dept. dermatology U. Miami, 1955-88, prof. emeritus. Home: Boca Raton, Fla. Died Apr. 15, 2007.

PEPYNE, EDWARD WALTER, lawyer, psychologist, educator; b. Springfield, Mass., Dec. 27, 1925; s. Walter Henry and Frances A. (Carroll) P.; m. Carol Jean Dutcher, Aug. 2, 1958; children— Deborah, Edward, Jr., Susan, Byron, Shari, Randy, David, Allison, Jennifer, Jaymie Page. BA, Am. Internat. Coll., 1948; MS, U. Mass., 1951, Ed.D., 1968; postgrad., NYU, 1952-55; prof. diploma, U. Conn., 1964; JD, Western New Eng. Coll., 1978. Bar: Mass. 1978, U.S. Supreme Ct. 1981, Vt. 2004. Prin., tchr. Gilbertville Grammar Sch., Hardwick, Mass., 1948-49; sch. counselor West Springfield High Sch., Mass., 1949-53; instr. NYU, 1953-54; supt. schs. New Shoreham, RI, 1954-56; asst. prof. edn. Mich. State U., 1956-58; sch. psychologist, guidance dir. Pub. Sch. System, East Long, Mass., 1958-62; lectr. Westfield State Coll., 1961-65; dir. pupil services Chicopee Pub. Sch., 1965-68; assoc. prof. counselor edn. U. Hartford, West Hartford, Mass., 1968-71, prof., 1971-85, dir. Inst. Coll. Counselors Minority and Low Income Students, 1971-72, dir. Div. Human Services, 1972-77; cons. Aetna Life & Casualty Co., Hartford, 1962-75; hearing officer Conn. State Bd. Edn., 1980-99; exec. dir. Sinapi Assocs., 1959-78; pvt. practice, Ashfield, Mass., 1978—2005, Derby, Vt., from 2004. Co-author: Better Driving, 1958; assoc. editor: Highway Safety and Driver Education, 1954; chmn. editorial com.: Man and the Motor Car, 5th edit., 1954; contbr. numerous articles to profl. jours. Chief welfare svcs. Civil Def., Levittown, NY, 1953-54; chmn. Ashfield Planning Bd., Mass., 1979-83; moderator Town Ashfield, 1980-81, town counsel, Charlemont, Mass., 1983-84; mem. jud. nominating coun. Western Regional Com., 1993-99; mem. Mohawk Regional Sch. Com., 1999-2000; program chmn. Osher Lifelong Learning Inst., 2006-. Mem. ABA, APA, Mass. Bar Assn., Vt. Bar Assn., Mass. Acad. Trial Attys., Am. Pers. and Guidance Assn., New Eng. Pers. and Guidance Assn. (bd. dirs.), New Eng. Ednl. Rsch. Orgn. (pres. 1971), Am. Assn. Sch. Adminstrs., Am. Ednl. Rsch. Assn., Mt. Tom Amateur Radio Assn., Franklin County Amateur Radio Club, Elks, Kiwanis (pres. 1988-89, lt. gov. div. 12, 1991-92), Masons (master 1994-96, sec. 2007—), Shriners, Phi Delta Kappa. Home: Newport, Vt. Died Oct. 4, 2013.

PEREZ, JOSE LUIS, computer scientist, engineer, philosopher; b. Bogota, Colombia, Oct. 31, 1951; came to U.S., 1982; s. Jose Alberto and Elvira Paulina (Restrepo) P.; m. Liliana Maria Pelaez, Nov. 1, 1974 (div. 1981); 1 child, Jose David; m. Debra Helene Dambeck, Nov. 27, 1988; 1 child, Andrew Paul. BA in Philosophy and Lit., Rosario Coll., Bogota, 1968; MSCE, Columbia U., 1978; MS in Computer Sci., Maharishi Internat. U., Fairfield, Iowa, 1986. Registered profl. engr., Colombia. V.p. Jose Perez Ins. Co., Bogota, 1975-78; design engr. Acerias Paz del Rio, Belencito, Colombia, 1978-81; internat. financier Jose L. Perez & Co., LA, 1981-83; dir. engring. lab. Indsl. Electronic Engrs., Van Nuys, Calif., 1983-84; software engr. Planning Rsch. Corp., Washington, 1986-87, Micom Digital Corp., Washington, 1987-88, Glazier Electronics Systems Group (name now Donatech Corp.), Fairfield, from 1988. Cons. Maharishi Global Trading Group, Livingston Manor, N.Y., 1984—, Vision Link, N.Y.C., 1989—; founder Creative Capital Corp., 1990, Cons. Associated, 1996; mem. Radio Tech. Commn. for Aeronautics SC-147. Designer comm. and avionics instrument systems, traffic alert and collision avoidance system for airplanes, test access and control interface software for Boeing 777. Mem. Creating Coherence Program for World Peace, Fairfield, 1984—, Colombian Soc. Friends of Country, Bogota, 1969—; founder, pres. Drug Rehab. Found., Fairfield, 1989. Scholar U. Los Andes, Bogota, 1969, City of L.A., 1983. Mem. Radio Tech. Commn. for Aero. SC-147, U.S. Chess Fedn. (master level), Smithsonian Assocs., Toastmasters. Avocations: chess, bicycling, swimming, volleyball, meditation. Home: Clearwater, Fla. Died Dec. 22, 2006.

PERKINS, LINDA GILLESPIE, real estate executive; b. Albany, Calif., Sept. 17, 1944; d. Leonard Leroy and Cloie Vivian (Howard) Gillespie; m. Harold Michael Morgan, Sept. 18, 1965 (div. Oct. 1978); 1 child, Trisha Leigh Morgan Franz; m. Donald Anthony Perkins, June 1, 1996. BA with honors, N.Mex. State U., 1967, MA in English Lit. with honors, 1972. Social worker N.Mex. Human Svcs., Santa Fe, 1967-78, adoption dir., 1978-81, adolscent crisis counselor, 1978-81; exec. Yablon Real Estate, Santa Fe, 1981-98; CFO, Vista Property Corp., Santa Fe, from 1999. Aerobics instr. Tom Young's Spa, Sante Fe, 1980-85; cons. in field. Author of poems. Foster parent judicial rev. panel Dist. Ct. N.Mex., Santa Fe, 1992-95, permanancy planning project, 1992-95; mem. YMCA. Mem. Planned Parenthood, Mensa, Alpha Chi Omega. Democrat. Methodist. Avocations: reading, travel, foreign languages, snorkeling. Home: Albuquerque, N.Mex. Died Feb. 22, 2007.

PERLMAN, MELVIN L., psychologist, educator; b. Chicago, May 22, 1925; s. Phillip C. and Belle I. (Letchinger) P.; m. Miriam D. Goodman, Dec. 22, 1946; 1 child, Sheri Beth. MA, U. Chgo., 1950, PhD, 1953. Registered psychologist, Ill. Coordinator tng. VA, Downey, Ill., 1953-63; asst. chief psychology Ill. State Psychol. Inst., Chgo., 1963-76, chief psychologist, from 1976. Served with USAF, 1943-46, PTO. Mem. Am. Psychol. Assn., Am. Bd. Profl. Psychologists (dir. exams. 1978-81, bd. examiners 1981—), Ill. Psychol. Assn. Home: Louisville, Ky. Died Nov. 17, 2006.

PERRY, ANTHONY FRANK, entertainment company executive, printing company executive, graphic designer; b. LA, Oct. 23, 1965; s. Frank Guy and Verna Dean Perry. Artist Thunderbird Printing Co., Inc., Reno, Nev., 1983-87; pres., chief exec. officer T-Bird Entertainment, Inc., Reno, 1987-91; mktg. dir. Thunderbird Printing and Screening Inc., Reno, 1991-92; pres., CEO Perri Entertainment Svcs., Inc., Reno, from 1992; pres. Internat. Touring Pers. Assn., from 2001. Tour pass security designer Rolling Stones World Tour, 1989-90, Billy Joel Storm Front Tour, 1990, New Kids on the Block, 1990-91, Jimmy Buffett Chameleon Caravan, 1994, Billy Joel River of Dreams, 1994, ZZ Top Antenna World Tour, 1994; designer credentials for San Francisco 49ers, 1995-2000; founder Knotty Baker Pretzel Co.; promoter Big Bang New Years Party, 1987-91; founder Webcarvers Am. Interactive Devel. Co.; creator StreetMagic web site and products; co-instituted Live Band Karaoke Industry, 2011 Author: The Expert from Out of Town, Sometimes I Forgot to Look Both Ways; lighting designer Sheep Dip Show, Reno Hilton, 1986, 87, 89; designer tour logo Doobie Brothers and Foreigner Tour 1994; designer Michael Jackson History World Tour, 1996-97, U2 World Tour; credential mfr. for Rolling Stones Bridges to Babylon World Tour, 1997-98, Pavarotti Tour 2000, Rolling Stones No Security Tour, 1999; prodr. The First Live Band Karaoke Tour, 2012, Karaoke Rockstarz Mic Time Tour, 2012; founder Nat. Live Karaoke Band Alliance, 2013 Mem. Nev. Repertory Co., 1983-89. Recipient Lifetime Achievement award Reed H.S. Theatre Dept., 1983. Mem. Reno Advt. Club, Rotary Internat. Roman Catholic. Home: Lakeview, Oreg. Died Apr. 14, 2014.

PERRY, JOHN WESLEY, SR., psychotherapist; b. Elleville, Ga., Mar. 30, 1934; s. West Charles and Mary (Willie) P.; m. Alma Perry, Dec 25, 1956; children: Sheranda Pearl, John Wesley Jr., Sheree Denise. AA, Edward Waters Coll., 1955; BS, Paul Quinn Coll., 1962; MEd, Prairie View U., 1967-74; EdD, Calif. Coast U., 1989. Cert. clinical therapist, Tex., counselors tng., U. Ark., U.S. Dept. Labor; lic. profl. counselor Tex. State Bd. Profl. Counselors. Tchr. phys. edn., coach Bremond (Tex.) High Sch., 1962-65; counselor coord. Dept. of Labor, San Marcos, Tex., 1965-70; tchr. hist. Austin (Tex.) I.S.D., 1970-71, 71-72; sch. administr. Pearce Jr. High Sch., Austin, 1971-87; state parole officer Tex. State Parole Bd., Austin, 1987-88; psychotherapist child behavior Killeen, Tex., from 1988. Trustee bd. pro tempo A.M.E. Ch., Austin; active Boy Scouts, Austin. With U.S. Army, 1955-57. Recipient Stewart certificate Grant Chapel A.M.E. Ch., Austin, 1965, Bus. Mgr. award Nat. Alumni Paul Quinn Coll. Alumni, Waco, Tex., 1978, 79, v.p. award, 1980, Outstanding Civic award United Negro Coll. Fund, 1984; grantee Chapel A.M. E. Ch. Home: Austin, Tex. Died July 25, 2007.

PERRY, JOSEPH, office furniture and supplies manufacturing company executive; b. West Warwick, RI, Jan. 1, 1936; s. Joseph B. and Mary R. (Paiva) P.; m. Maureen Jewell, Jan. 3, 1963; children: Raymonde, Joelle Marie. BSBA, U. R.I., 1961. CPA, N.Y., N.J. Mgr. pub. acctg. Arthur Andersen & Co., NYC, 1961-71; treas. Westrans Industries Inc., NYC, 1971-76; v.p. fin. Marline Oil Corp., NYC, 1977-79, also bd. dirs.; controller Newmont Mining Corp., NYC, 1979-84; v.p. fin. Joyce Internat. Inc., Great Neck, N.Y., from 1984. Served with USAF, 1953-57. Mem. Am. Inst. CPA's, N.Y. State Soc. CPA's. Home: Marlboro, NJ. Died Nov. 12, 2006.

PETERS, HANK, retired professional sports team executive; b. St. Louis, Sept. 16, 1924; s. Henry J. and Estelle (Biehl) P.; m. Dorothy Kleimeier, Nov. 21, 1950 (dec. 2010); children: Steven, Sharon. Asst. farm dir. St. Louis Browns, 1946-53; gen. mgr. Burlington (Iowa) Baseball Club, 1954; farm dir. Kansas City A's, 1955-60, asst. gen. mgr., 1962-64, gen. mgr., 1965; farm dir. Cin. Reds, 1961; v.p., dir. player personnel Cleve. Indians, 1966-71; pres. Nat. Assn. Profl. Baseball Leagues, St. Petersburg, Fla., 1972-75; exec. v.p., gen. mgr. Balt. Orioles, 1976-87; pres., COO Cleve. Indians, 1987—91. Served with AUS, 1943-45. Recipient Good Guy award Cleve. chpt. Baseball Writers Assn., 1970, Maj. League Exec. of Yr. award Sporting News-UPI, 1979, 83 Mem.: Elks, St. Petersburg Yacht. Republican. Lutheran. Achievements include being the general manager of the World Series Champion Baltimore Orioles, 1983. Home: Highland Bch, Fla. Died Jan. 4, 2015.

PETERS, MARJORIE M. SCHUSTER, medical nurse; b. Spirit Lake, Iowa, Sept. 22, 1925; d. Gilbert J. and Lila Lydia (Petri) Schuster; m. Clarence Peters, Apr. 12, 1958 (dec.); children: Marie, Paul, Joseph, Nancy, Elaine, Jean, Ruth. Diploma, St. Agnes Sch. Nursing, Fond du Lac, Wis. Staff nurse St. Clare Hosp., Monroe, Wis. Instr. cert. nurse assistance course Voc. Tech. Sch., Fenimore, Wis., Lafayatte County Meml. Hosp. Mem. Wis. Nurses Assn. (bd. dirs. Dist. 2, pub. rels. and mem. com., chair dist. 2 pub. rels. and mem. com.), U.S. Cadet Nurse Corps. Home: Darlington, Wis. Died Jan. 8, 2007.

PETERSEN, WILLIAM LAWRENCE, theology educator; b. Laredo, Tex., Jan. 19, 1950; s. Elizabeth M. Petersen. BA, U. Iowa, 1971; MDiv, Luth. Theol. Sem., Saskatoon, Can., 1975; postgrad., McGill U., 1975-77; D in Theology, Rijksuniversiteit te Utrecht, The Netherlands, 1984. Lectr. Meml. U., St. John's, Newfoundland, Can., 1977; vis. asst. prof. U. Notre Dame, Ind., 1985-86, asst. prof. Ind., 1986-90, Pa. State U., 1990-94, assoc. prof., 1994-99, dir. religious studies, from 1998, prof., from 1999. Author: The Diatessaron and Ephrem Syrus As Sources of Romanos the Melodist, 1985, Tatian's Diatessaron, Its Creation, Dissemination, Significance, and History in Scholarship, 1994; editor: Origin of Alexandria, His World and His Legacy, 1988, Gospel Traditions in the Second Century, Origins,

Recensions, Text and Transmission, 1989, Sayings of Jesus, Canonical and Non-canonical, 1997; mem. editl. bd. New Testament Studies, Vigiliae Christianae, Internat. Greek N.T.; contbr. articles to scholarly jours. Mem. Soc. of Biblical Lit. (mem. editorial bd. The N.T. in the Greek Fathers 1985—), Studiorum Novi Testamenti Soc. Clubs: Alpine Français (Chamonix sect.). Avocations: alpine mountaineering, skiing, music, travel. Died Dec. 20, 2006.

PETERSON, BERTIL L., lawyer; b. Kenosha, Wis., Sept. 25, 1920; s. Bertil L. Sr. and Hilma S. (Carlson) P.; m. Jean Ripton Peterson, July 30, 1949; eight children. BA, Cornell U., 1943, LLB, JD, 1949. Bar: N.Y. 1949, U.S. Ct. Mil. Appeals 1959. Atty. Gibbons, Pottle, Buffalo, 1950-53; ptnr. McDonald & Peterson, Buffalo, 1953-60, Peterson & Peterson, from 1960. Pres. N.Y. State Sch. Attys. Assn., 1965-70; hon. Swedish Consul, 1974-90. Lt. Col. U.S. Army. Mem. N.Y. State Bar Assn., Erie County Bar Assn. Home: Orchard Park, NY. Died May 31, 2007.

PETERSON, E(RIC) C(HRISTOPHER), software engineer, consultant; b. Memphis, Nov. 26, 1957; s. W. A. and M. E. (Blanton) Peterson; m. Patricia A. Connors, Apr. 16, 1983; children: Erik A., Paige D., Haley A. BS, Fla. State U., 1979. Sys. engr. Rockwell Internat., Kennedy Space Ctr., Fla., 1979-84; software engr. Harris Corp., Palm Bay, Fla., 1984-89; cons. Scientific Software Engring., Merritt Island, Fla., 1989-91; software engr. Bell Northern Rsch., Rsch. Triangle Park, N.C., from 1991. Teleco cons. Scientific Software Programming, Raleigh, N.C., 1988-94. Recipient first shuttle flight achievement award Columbia astronauts, 1981. Mem. IEEE, Nature Conservancy, Nat. Trust for Historic Preservation. Died Mar. 16, 2007.

PETERSON, ROBERT AUSTIN, retired manufacturing executive; b. Sioux City, Iowa, July 5, 1925; s. Austen W. and Theresa Peterson; m. Carol May Hudy, May 17, 1952; children: Roberta, Richard., Bruce. BS, U. Minn., 1946, BBA, 1947. Credit mgr. New Holland Machine div. Sperry Rand Corp., Mpls., 1952-61; from credit mgr. to treas. Toro Co., Mpls., 1961-70, v.p., treas. internat. fin., 1970-83; v.p. fin., pres. Toro Credit Co., 1983-93. Chmn. Prior Lake Spring Lake Watershed Dist., 1970-80; chmn., bd. dirs. Prior Lake Bd. Edn., 1965-71; chmn. Scott County Republican Party, 1969-70; bd. dirs. Scott Carver Mental Health Center, 1969-73, Minn. Watershed Assn., 1972-76. Served to ensign USNR, 1943-46. Mem.: Prior Lake Yacht Club (bd. dirs.). Home: Prior Lake, Minn. Died Mar. 5, 2015.

PETRACCHI, ENRIQUE SANTIAGO, judge; b. Buenos Aires, Nov. 16, 1935; s. Enrique Carlos and Lilia Raño; children: Florencia, Enrique Juan, María, Francisco. Justice Supreme Ct., Argentina, 1983—89, chief justice, 1989—90, justice, 1990—2003, pres., 2004—07. Fluent in Spanish, English, French and Italian. Died Oct. 12, 2014.

PETRICONE, JR., ALEXANDER FEDERICO See ROCCO, ALEX

PETRIE, STEWART JUDSON, retired obstetrician, gynecologist; b. New Haven, July 15, 1923; s. Arthur Judson and Emma Robinson Petrie. BS, U. Conn., Storrs, 1943; MD, Temple U., Phila., 1950; postgrad., Yale U., New Haven, 1952—55. Diplomate Nat. Bd. Med. Examiners, Am. Bd. Ob-Gyn. Editor: Conn. Medicine; author: Letters and Journal of a Civil Surgeon, Capital of Libby Prison, Bloody Path to the Shenandoah. Comdr. US Power Squadron. Maj. USAF, 1942—85. Fellow: ACS, ACOG; mem.: New County Med. Assn. Avocations: writing, painting, boating. Home: Branford, Conn. Died Mar. 17, 2007.

PETRZILKA, HENRY See FILIP, HENRY

PEVEC, ANTHONY EDWARD, bishop emeritus; b. Cleve., Apr. 16, 1925; s. Anton and Frances Darovec P.. MA, John Carroll U., Cleve., 1956; PhD, Western Res. U., Cleve., 1964. Ordained priest Diocese of Cleve., Ohio, 1950; assoc. pastor St. Mary Church, Elyria, Ohio, 1950—52, St. Lawrence Ch., Cleve., 1952—53; rector-prin. Borromeo Sem. HS, Wickliffe, Ohio, 1953—75; adminstrv. bd. Nat. Cath. Edn. Assn., 1972—75; pastor St. Vitus Ch., Cleve., 1975—79; rector-pres. Borromeo Coll., Wickliffe, 1979—82; ordained bishop, 1982; aux. bishop Diocese of Cleve., 1982—2001, aux. bishop emeritus, 2001—14. Recipient Honoree, Heritage Found., Cleve., 1982, Alumni medal, John Carroll U., 2004; named Man of Yr., Fedn. Slovenian Nat. Homes, Cleve., 1985, Cath. Man of Yr., KC, 1998, Man of Yr., Pioneer Assn., 2001, Cathedral Latin Alumni Assn., 2003; named to The Hall of Fame, St. Vitus Alumni Assn., 1989, The Wickliffe Hall of Fame, 2000. Mem.: KC (state chaplain 2003—05), Cath. Order Foresters (state chaplain 2000—04), U.S. Cath. Conf. (nat. adv. coun. 1996—97), Nat. Conf. Cath. Bishops (com. on vocations 1984—86, com. on pro-life activities 1990—92, com. on priestly formation 1993—95, com. on sci. and human values 1993—96). Democrat. Roman Catholic. Avocations: reading, music. *Ultimately I must always remember that the Lord is totally in control of my life, no matter how complicated it may seem to be. I am here to do the Lord's will, and wherever I go I come to do His will.* Died Dec. 14, 2014.

PEZZOLI, DOROTHY ANNE, retired medical/surgical nurse; b. Avenel, NJ, Feb. 6, 1927; d. John J. and Emma (Reul) Jayne; m. Richard J. Pezzoli, June 14, 1947; children: Caren, Kathleen, Jayne, Richard, Keith, Maureen. AAS, Suffolk C.C., Selden, NY, 1971; BSN, SUNY, Stony Brook, 1973; MSN, Adelphi U., Garden City, NY, 1977. RN, N.Y.; cert. critical care nurses, cert. clin. nurse specialist. Staff nurse Good Samaritan Hosp., West Islip, N.Y., 1971-72, VA Med. Ctr., Northport, N.Y., 1972-79; clin. nurse specialist Southside Hosp., Bay Shore, N.Y., 1979-81, Northport VA Med. Ctr., 1981-97. Part-time instr. C.W. Post Coll., Westbury, 1983-86; cons. in skin care St. Joseph Infirmary, Maria Regina Infirmary, Brentwood, N.Y. Participant Women's Health Fair; speaker Am. Heart Assn., Bohemia, N.Y. Recipient award for excellence in nursing rsch. Stony Brook Sch Nursing, 1986; named L.I. Nurse of Distinction, State of N.Y., 1993. Mem. ANA, AACN (chpt. sec. 1985), Sigma Theta Tau. Roman Catholic. Avocations: arts and crafts, reading, teaching children, travel. Home: North Babylon, NY. Died Nov. 18, 2006.

PFEIFFER, STEVEN EUGENE, molecular cell biologist, educator; b. Watertown, Wis., Aug. 13, 1940; s. Roy Henry and Doris (Haugen) P.; m. Carol Lee Aldrich, June 24, 1965; children: Julie Kristen, Carin-anna, Shaili Margreta. BA, Carleton Coll., 1962; PhD, Washington U., 1967. Postdoctoral fellow Brandeis U., Waltham, Mass., 1967-69; from asst. prof. to prof. U. Conn. Med. Sch., Farmington, from 1969. Vis. scientist Pasteur Inst., Paris, 1976-77, European Molecular Biology Lab., Heidelberg, Germany, 1984-85, 93; mem. adv. com. on rsch. Nat. Multiple Sclerosis Soc., N.Y.C., 1989-95; mem. com. on space biology and medicine Nat. Rsch. Coun., 1995—. Mem. editl. bd. Jour. Neurosci. Rsch., 1979—, Devel. Neurosci., 1982—, Internat. Jour. Devel. Neurosci., 1991—. Clarinetist Farmington Valley Symphony Orch., 1981—. Josiah Marcy Jr. Faculty scholar, 1976-77; Fulbright fellow, 1983-84; Deutsche Academicer Austausch Dienst fellow, 1993; Jacob Javits Neurosci. Investigator award, 1995—; Rowland Multiple Sclerosis Soc. fellow, 1995-97. Mem. Am. Soc. Neurochemistry, Soc. for Neurosci., Am. Assn. for Cell Biology, Internat. Soc. Devel. Neurosci. (pres. 1996—), Gordon Conf. on Myelin (vice chair 1998). Unitarian Universalist. Avocations: music, camping. Home: Farmington, Conn. Died Aug. 26, 2007.

PHARAON, HASAN MUSA, pediatrician, consultant; b. Jaffa, Palestine, May 1, 1920; arrived in Jordan, 1957; s. Musa Ra'fat Abdel Majid and Badrieh Kheir P; m. Hildur Bech Jensen, Oct. 29, 1935; children: Ali, Omar, Tareq. MD, Am. U., Beirut, Lebanon, 1943; diploma in child health, Fuad U., Cairo, Egypt, 1947; degree in pediat., Paris U., 1957. Clin. asst. Govt. Hosp., Jaffa, Palestine, 1943-45; resident doctor Children's Hosp., Cairo, Egypt, 1945-47, Hadassah Hosp., Tel Aviv, Israel, 1953-55, Hosp. Enfants Malades, Paris, 1955-57; sr. pediatrician Children's Hosp., Amman, Jordan, 1958-72; gen. dir. Univ. Hosp., Amman, Jordan, 1972-73. Dir. study on nutritional status of infants and preschool children in Jordan, 1963-64, study/nutrition survey of Palestinian refugees in Jordan after 1967 war, 1968-69, study on vitamin A in infants in Jordan, in assn. with WHO, 1965-66; establisher First Pediat. Hosp., Ministry of Health, Jordan, 1958; cons. child health World Health Orgn., 1979. Editor Jordan Med. Jour., 1965-75, booklets in pediat. pub. health; contbr. articles to med. jours. Liaison officer Internat. Red Cross Orgn., Jaffa, 1948-53; mem., pres. Save the Children Fund, Jordan, 1960-75. Mem. Jaffa Med. Soc. (sec. gen. 1947-48), Jordan Med. Assn. (asst. gen. sec., v.p. 1957-75), Jordan Pediat. Soc. (establisher 1962), Union of M-E and Med. Pediat. Soc. (asst. gen. sec., treas. 1966-96), Internat. Pediat. Assn. (mem. standing com. 1977-87), Am. U. Beirut Alumni Assn. Muslim. Avocation: archaeology. Home: Amman, Jordan. Died Dec. 2014.

PHERIGO, LINDSEY PRICE, religion educator; b. Miami, Fla., Dec. 29, 1920; s. Ezekiel Lindsey and Dorothy Price (Richardson) P.; m. Viola May Schmitt, Feb. 22, 1942; children: Linda Jane, Stephen Albert, Ruth Armet, Robert Price. BAE, U. Fla., 1942; STB, Boston U., 1945, PhD, 1951. Reader in Biblical history Wellesley (Mass.) Coll., 1947-49; instr. in religion Syracuse (N.Y.) U., 1949-51; asst. prof. religion Scarritt Coll., Nashville, 1951-53, prof. of Bible, 1953-56, Clara Perry prof. Christian life and thought, 1956-59, acad. dean, 1957-59; vis. instr. in New Testament Vanderbilt Divinity Sch., Nashville, 1954-59; prof. New Testament and early ch. history St. Paul Sch. Theology, Kansas City, Mo., 1959-86, prof. emeritus, from 1986. Cons. in Bible and theology The Village Ch., Prairie Village, Kans., 1977-91. Author: The Great Physician, 1983, revised edit. 1991; contbr. articles to profl. publs. Edmund M. Beebe fellow, 1946, Ford Found. fellow, 1952; Lindsey P. Pherigo chair in New Testament named in his honor, 1986. Mem. Soc. Biblical Lit. Democrat. Methodist. Avocations: classical music, photography, stamps, coins, books. Home: Kansas City, Mo. Died Mar. 16, 2007.

PHILLIPS, ANNE LINNEA, writer; d. Carl Oscar and Hanna Tecla Grant; m. Francis Bradbury Phillips, June 8, 1946; children: Katherine, Thomas, Robert. Grad. high sch., Green Bay, Wis. Home: Novato, Calif. Died Mar. 21, 2007.

PHILLIPS, DOROTHY ORMES, elementary school educator; b. Denver, July 26, 1922; d. Jesse Edward and Belle (Noisette) Ormes; m. James Kermit Phillips, Apr. 28, 1945; children: William K., Dorothy E., Valerie A. BBA, Case Western Res. U., 1946, MA, 1959; PhD, U. Akron, 1989. Cert. tchr., adminstr., Ohio. Tchr. Cleve. Pub. Schs., 1955-68, math. cons., 1968-83, adminstrv. intern, 1970-73; grad. asst. U. Akron, Ohio, 1983-85, lectr. elem. edn., supr. student tchrs. Ohio, from 1985. Math. workshop presenter Norton (Ohio) Pub. Schs., 1986, presenter career day, 1997. Bd. dirs. Centerville Mills YMCA Camp, Chagrin Falls, Ohio, chmn., 1996-99. Grantee NDEA, 1960, NSF, 1966. Mem. ASCD, Nat. Coun. Tchrs. Math., Ednl. Computer Consortium Ohio, Cleve. Pub. Schs. Math. Cons. (assoc.), Alpha Kappa Alpha, Pi Lambda Theta. Avocations: swimming, camping, reading. Home: Chagrin Falls, Ohio. Died July 9, 2007.

PHILLIPS, KEITH ANTHONY, professional baseball player; b. Atlanta, Apr. 25, 1959; m. Debi Vosburg; children: Victoria, Selina. Student, N.Mex. Mil. Inst. Infielder Montreal Expos farm sys., 1978—80, San Diego Padres farm sys., 1980—81, Oakland Athletics farm sys., Calif., 1981—82, Oakland Athletics, 1982—89, Detroit Tigers, 1990—94; infielder, outfielder Calif. Angels, Anaheim, Calif., 1995, Chgo. White Sox., 1996—97, Anaheim Angels, 1997, Toronto Blue Jays, 1998, New York Mets, 1998, Oakland Athletics, 1999. Achievements include playing in championship series, Oakland, 1988, 89; playing in World Series, Oakland, 1988, 89; sharing in major league single-game record (9 innings) for most assists by 2d baseman, 1986. Died Feb. 17, 2016.

PHILLIPS, LAWRENCE SEYMOUR, apparel company executive; b. Manhattan, Mar. 20, 1927; s. Seymour J. P.; two marriages that ended in divorce; children David, Laura BA, Princeton U., 1948. With Phillips-Van Heusen Corp., NYC, 1948—2015, v.p. merchandising, 1951-59, exec. v.p., 1959-68, pres., COO, 1968-87, chief exec. officer, dir., 1987, chmn., 1987—91. Co-founder, chmn. American Jewish World Service. Mem. Am. Apparel Mfrs. (dir.) Died Sept. 11, 2015.

PHILLIPS, PHYLLIS CATHERINE, realtor; b. Campbell, Ohio, July 14, 1935; d. Nellie J. Kosko; m. Eugene D. Phillips, Jan. 26, 1957; children: Mark P., Scott M. (dec.). Student, Youngstown U., Ohio, 1952-53, 60-62; BS, Ohio State U., 1956; MEd, St. Francis Coll., Fort Wayne, Ind., 1971. Cert. elem. tchr., Ohio, cert. relocation specialist Employee Relocation Coun.; lic. broker, Ohio, med. technologist, Calif. Med. tech. Children's Hosp., Washington, 1957, Youngstown Hosp. Assn., 1958-62; tchr. Youngstown (Ohio) Pub. Schs., 1962-65, Ayersville Local Schs., Defiance, 1965-74; realtor assoc. Strayer Realty, Inc., Defiance, 1978-80, Yoder's Realty, Defiance, from 1980; broker, realtor assoc. RE/MAX Realty of Defiance, from 1986. Active women's commn. Defiance Coll., Defiance Hosp. Aux. Martha Jennings Found. scholar, 1973-74. Mem. Mut. Improvement Circle, Am. Soc. Clin. Pathologists, Northwest Ohio Bd. Realtors, Nat. Assn. Realtors, Lions, Alpha Delta Kappa. Republican. Roman Catholic. Avocations: golf, crafts, bridge. Died Oct. 24, 2006.

PHILLIPS, ROBIN, director, actor; b. Haslemere, Surrey, Eng., Feb. 28, 1942; arrived in Can., 1973; s. James William and Ellen Ann (Barfoot) P.; life partner Joe Mandel Studied with Duncan Ross, Bristol Old Vic. Theatre Sch. Dir. gen. Citadel Theatre, Edmonton, Alberta, Can. Chmn. and exec. prodr. Theatre Unmasked Ltd. First profl. acting role in The Critic, 1959; TV appearences include: The Forsyte Saga, BBC, The Seagull, BBC; assoc. dir. Bristol Old Vic, 1960; asst. dir. Royal Shakespeare Co., Stratford-upon-Aron, 1965; dir. Two Gentlement of Verona; assoc. dir. Northcott Theatre, 1967-68; dir. The Seagull, Leatherhead, 1969, Tiny 0lice, Royal Shakespeare Co., Aldwych, 1970, Two gentleman of Verona, Abelard and Heloise, London and Broadway, 1970, Caesar and Cleopatra, also Dear Antoine, Chichester, 1971, The Lady's Not for Burning, 1972; artistic dir. Greenwich Theatre, 1973, Stratford Festival Theatre, Can., 1975-80; dir. Virginia Haymarket Theatre, London, 1980-81; world premiere Farther West, Calgary, Alta., 1982, The Jeweller's Shop, Westminster Theatre, London, 1982; artistic dir. Grand Theatre Co., London, Ont., from 1982; dir. Tonight at 8:30, New World, for CentreStage Co., Toronto; dir. A Midsummer Night's Dream, The Crucible, The Philadelphia Story, Citadel Theatre, Edmonton, Alta., 1989-90 season, Jekyll and Hyde; dir. Richard III, N.Y.C., 1990; dir. gen. Citadel Theatre, 1991; actor, dir. numerous others. Active task force on profl. tng. in cultural sector Marcel Masse comm. dept., exec. com. Can. Artists Com. Can. Coun., Ottawa, adv. com. Died July 25, 2015.

PICKETT, JAMES MCPHERSON, speech scientist; b. Clyde, Ohio, Jan. 18, 1921; s. Royce M. and Mattie (Gail) P.; m. Betty Horenstein, Mar. 10, 1952. PhD, Brown U., 1951. Phonetics lab. asst. Oberlin (Ohio) Coll., 1943-47; asst. prof. U. Conn., Storrs, 1950-52; rsch. psychologist USAF, Cambridge, Mass., 1952-61; NIH fellow Royal Inst. Technology, Stockholm, 1961-62; scientist Melpar Inc., Falls Church, Va., 1962-63; prof. Gallaudet U., Washington, 1964-87, prof. emeritus, from 1987. Speech editor Jour. Acoustical Soc. Am., 1978-81; contbr. articles to profl. jours. With USN, 1945-46, WWII, PTO. Named Outstanding Phonetician of Yr., Internat. Soc. Phonetic Scis., 1988. Fellow Acoustical Soc. Am.; mem. Cosmos Club. Achievements include leadership in field of speech processing aids for handicapped. Died July 5, 2007.

PIECH, MARY LOU ROHLING, medical psychotherapist, consultant; b. Elgin, Ill., Jan. 20, 1927; d. Louis Bernard and Charlotte (Wylie) Rohling; m. Raymond C. Piech, Feb. 12, 1950 (dec. Feb. 1985); 1 child, Christine Piech. BA, U. Ill., 1948, MA, 1953; postgrad., Ill. Inst. Tech., 1966-68, Union Inst., 1991-98. Cert. clin. psychologist, Ill.; diplomate Am. Bd. Med. Psychotherapy. Instr. psychology Elmhurst (Ill.) Coll., 1955-61; asst. prof. psychology North Cen. Coll., Naperville, Ill., 1961-67, Elmhurst (Ill.) Coll., 1968-81; med. psychotherapist Shealy Pain & Health Rehab. Ctr., LaCrosse, Wis., 1977-82, Shealy Inst. Comprehensive Health Care, Springfield, Mo., from 1982. Author, editor: (video series) Mental Health, 1982, (audio tape series) Holistic Mental Health, 1983. Recipient award Lilly Found., Elmhurst Coll., Shealy Inst., 1977. Fellow Am. Bd. Med. Psychotherapy; mem. APA, N.Am. Soc. Adlerian Psychology, Assn. Psychol. Type (life), Phi Beta Kappa, Phi Kappa Phi, Mortar Bd. Home: Springfield, Mo. Died Jan. 9, 2007.

PIERCE, CATHERINE MAYNARD, history educator; b. York County, Va., Oct. 11, 1918; d. Edward Walker Jr. and Cassie Cooke (Sheppard) Maynard; m. Frank Marion Pierce Jr., Oct. 4, 1940 (dec. 1974); children: Frank Marion III, Bruce Maynard. BS in Sec. Edn., Longwood Coll., Farmville, Va., 1939; postgrad., Coll. William and Mary, Williamsburg, 1948, 58, 68. Tchr. York County Pub. Schs., Va., 1939-45; instr. Chesapeake (Va.) pub. schs., 1946-49, 57-74; cons. Vol. Svcs., Williamsburg, Va., from 1975. Author audio-visual hist. narratives for use in pub. schs., 1965-86. Organizer The Chapel at Kingsmill on the James, Williamsburg, 1987—, chmn. governing bd., 1987-97. Mem. DAR (regent Williamsburg chpt. 1980-83). Baptist. Avocations: antiques, genealogy, historic research. Home: Elgin, SC. Died July 1, 2007.

PIERRE, JOSEPH HORACE, JR., commercial artist; b. Salem, Oreg., Oct. 3, 1929; s. Joseph Horace and Miriam Elisabeth (Holder) Pierre; m. June Anne Rice, Dec. 20, 1952 (dec. June 2001); children: Joseph Horace III, Thomas E., Laurie E., Mark R., Ruth A.; m. Luverne Melba Starnes, Jan. 9, 2002. Grad., Advt. Art Sch., Portland, Oreg., 1954, Inst. Comml. Art, 1951-52. Lithographic printer Your Town Press, Inc., Salem, Oreg., 1955-58; correctional officer Oreg. State Correctional Instn., 1958-60; owner Illustrators Workshop, Inc., Salem, 1960-61; advt. mgr. North Pacific Lumber Co., Portland, 1961-63; vocat. instr. graphic arts Oreg. Correctional Instn., 1963-70; lithographic printer Lloyd's Printing, Monterey, Calif., 1971-72; illustrator McGraw Hill, 1972-73; owner Publishers Art Svc., Monterey, 1972-81; correctional officer Oreg. State Penitentiary, 1982-90; ret. Owner Northwest Syndicate, 1993—. Editor/publisher: The Pro Cartoonist & Gagwriter; author: The Road to Damascus, 1981, The Descendants of Thomas Pier, 1992, The Origin and History of the Callaway and Holder Families, 1992, Firearms and Freedom, Their Care and Maintenance, 2002; author numerous OpEd cols. in Salem, Oreg. Statesman Jour., others; pub. cartoons nat. mags.; mural Mardi Gras Restaurant, Salem; cartoon strip Fabu, Oreg. Agr. mo. Mem. Rep. Nat. Com., Citizens Com. for Right to Keep and Bear Arms. Served with USN, 1946-51. Decorated victory medal WWII, China svc. medal, Korea medal, Navy occupation medal. Mem. U.S. Power Squadron, Nat. Rifle Assn., Acad. of Model Aeronautics, Oreg. Correctional Officers Assn. (co-founder, hon. mem.), Four Corners Rod and Gun Club. Republican. Avocations: sailing, flying, scuba, model aircraft building and flying. Home: Salem, Oreg. Died Dec. 5, 2006.

PIERSON, NORAH, artist; b. New Haven, June 14, 1940; d. George Wilson and (Mary) Laetitia (Verdery) Pierson; 1 child, (Carl) Ross Palmer. Student, Miss Porter's Sch., Farmington, Conn., 1954—58, Chateau Brillantmont, Lausanne, Switzerland, 1955—56; diploma in graphic design with honors, Sch. Mus. Fine Arts, Boston, 1962. Owner, jeweler Golden Eye, Laguna Beach, Calif., 1971—82, Santa Fe, from 1984. Represented in permanent collections Green & Green, Lambertville, N.J., Squash Blossom, Vale, Colo., Topaz, Atlanta, Spectrum, Willington, N.C.; contbr. articles to publs. Organizer Citizens Nuc. Safety, from 1988. Mem.: Jewelers Bd. Trade, Soc. N.Am. Goldsmiths, Am. Gem Trade Assn. (award 1988). Avocations: painting, gardening, hiking, camping. Home: Lamy, N.Mex. Died May 12, 2007.

PIETRZYK, ZBIGNIEW ADAM, nuclear engineering researcher, consultant; b. Warsaw, Aug. 12, 1935; came to U.S., 1973; s. Czeslaw and Jadwiga (Potembska) P.; m. Maria Elzbieta Budek, Oct. 19, 1963. MS in Aero. Engring., Warsaw Tech. U., 1960; PhD in Applied Physics, Polish Acad. Sci. Inst. Basic Tech. Problems, Warsaw, 1966. Research assoc. Polish Acad. Sci. Inst. Basic Tech. Problems, 1960-66, asst. prof., 1966-68, assoc. prof., 1970-72; postdoctoral fellow NCR Can., Ottawa, Ont., 1968-70; research scientist Ecole Politechnique, Lausanne, Switzerland, 1972-73; research prof. nuclear engring. U. Wash., Seattle, from 1974. Cons. Math. Sci. N.W., Bellevue, Wash., 1975— Co-tech. editor: Laser-Induced Discharge Phenomena, 1976. Recipient Drzewiecki's award Polish Acad. Sci., Warsaw, 1966 Mem. Am. Phys. Soc. Died Dec. 16, 2007.

PIFER, DONALD LEE, owner printing firm; b. Fort Wayne, Ind., July 6, 1933; s. Lloyd D. and Marie C. (Goth) P.; m. Reba Wright, June, 1953 (div. 1961); children: Rhonda, Michael; m. Halyna Buhajenko, Feb. 23, 1963; children: David. Student, Ind. Tech. Sch., 1955, Ind. U., Purdue U., 1983. Press rm. supr. Roberts Assn., Fort Wayne, 1951-58; with sales dept. Western So. Life Ins., Fort Wayne, 1958-60; sales promotion mgr. Platka Export, Fort Wayne, 1960-62; co-owner Ad Kraft Printing, Columbus, Ind., from 1962. Mem. Internat. Club Printing House, Optimist Club (pres. 1966-67, 81-82), Ind. Dist. Optimist (lt. gov. 1985-86). Democrat. Methodist. Home: Columbus, Ind. Died Apr. 22, 2007.

PIKE, SCOTT ALLAN, civil engineer; b. Lisbon, Ohio, Feb. 15, 1964; s. Gary Lee and Judy Anne (Ramsay) P. BSCE, Ohio No. U., 1986. Asst. city engr. City of Marion, Ohio, 1986-87; project engr., cons. Floyd Browne Assoc., Inc., Marion, from 1987-. Official Ohio Spl. Olympics, 1985--. Mem. Am. Soc. Civil Engrs., Ohio Soc. Profl. Engrs. Republican. Presbyterian. Avocations: revolutionary war history, basketball, skiing. Home: Winston Salem, NC. Died Mar. 11, 2007.

PINCKNEY, CLEMENTA CARLOS, state legislator; b. Beaufort, SC, July 30, 1973; s. John and Theopia Aiken Pinckney; m. Jennifer Benjamin, Oct. 23, 1999; children: Eliana, Malana. BA, Allen U., 1995; MPA, U. SC, 1999; attended, Lutheran Theological Southern Seminary, 2008. Pastor Mt. Horry AME Ch., Younges Island, SC, Mother Emanuel African Methodist Episcopal (AME) Church; mem. Dist. 112 SC House of Reps., 1977—2000; mem. Dist. 45 SC State Senate, 2001—15, mem. Banking and Ins. Com., Corrections and Penology Com., Fin. Com., Edn. Com. and Med. Affairs Com. Bd. dirs. Southern Mutual Ins. Company. Rsch. fellow, Princeton U., 1994. Democrat. One of the nine people killed in the brutal massacre at Emanuel AME Church in Charleston, South Carolina on June 17, 2015. Home: Columbia, SC. Died June 17, 2015.

PINCUS, LAURA RHODA, investor, accountant; b. Bklyn., Jan. 19, 1923; d. Sam and Esther (Boimel) Shore; m. William Pincus, Jan. 31, 1942 (dec. Jan. 1994); children: Irene, Stephan. Student, La Salle Inst., NYC, 1940, C.W. Post, LI, NY, 1960-62. Statis. typist Feinberg & Spaulder, NYC, 1939-40, acct., 1948-58; owner Pincus Plumbing, Northport, N.Y., 1958-80; office mgr. James Robinson, NYC, 1960-61; owner Pincus Plumbing, San Diego, 1980-87, Laura's Ltd., Wellington, Fla., from 1987. Youth program dir. Young Men's Hebrew Assn., Bklyn., 1939—41; founder, pres. Thomas Jefferson HS, Bklyn., San Diego, 1982—87; vol. Leukemia Rsch.; active Tifereth Israel Synagogue, San Diego, 1980—87, Temple Beth Torah-Wellington, 1987—96; mem. Palm Beach sect. Nat. Coun. Jewish Women, from 1991; founder, treas. Congregation B'nai Kodesh, Wellington, 1996—2000, advisor to bd. dirs.; bd. dirs. Temple Beth-El, West Palm Beach, from 2000. Mem.: Money Justice Wellington, Cooperfield Assn., Am. Red Mogen David for Israel (life; founder San Diego Tikvah chpt. 1982—87, founder Wellington chpt. 1990, pres. Tikvah chpt. 1982—87, pres. Wellington chpt. from 1990), Wellington Women's Club, Brandeis Club (life; raffle chairperson 1996—2003, auditor Palm Beach East chpt.), B'nai B'rith (pres. Horizon chpt.), Hadassah (life). Avocation: collecting antique glass and crystal. Home: Wellington, Fla. Died May 3, 2007.

PINDLING, LYNDEN OSCAR, former prime minister of The Bahamas; b. Nassau, The Bahamas, Mar. 22, 1930; s. Arnold Franklin and Viola (Bain) P.; m. Marguerite McKenzie, May 5, 1956; children: Lynden Obafemi, Leslie, Michelle, Monique. LLB, London U., 1952; barrister-at-law, Middle Temple, 1953; LLD (hon.), Howard U., 1972; LHD (hon.), U. Miami, 1977; LLD (hon.), Bethune-Cookman Coll., 1978, Fisk U., 1979. Admitted to Eng. and The Bahamas bar, 1953. MP, So. Dist. constituency House of Assembly, The Bahamas, 1956-62, MP, So. Ctrl. Dist. constituency, 1962-67, MP, Kemp's Bay, Andros constituency, 1967—97. Parliamentary leader Progressive Liberal Party, 1956-92; mem. several dels. to former Colonial Office, 1956-66; mem. Constl. Conf., 1963; leader of opposition, 1964-66; mem. del's. spl. com. 24, UN, 1965; premier, min. tourism and devel. Colony of Bahamas Islands, 1967-69; leader Bahamian del. Constl. Conf., London, 1968; prime min. Commonwealth of The Bahamas, 1969-92, min. econ. affairs, 1969-82, 1984-92, min. def., 1983-84; min. fin., 1984-92; leader Independence Conf., London, 1972; privy councillor, 1976; chmn. Fgn. Investment Bd. Home: Nassau, The Bahamas. Died Aug. 26, 2000; Nassau, Bahamas.

PINHEIRO, AILEEN FOLSON, secondary school educator; b. Park River, ND, Oct. 24, 1921; d. Morris Bernard and Clara Christine (Olson) Folson; m. Eugene Arthur Pinheiro, Sept. 9, 1948. BA, Concordia Coll., 1942; MA, Whittier Coll., Calif., 1963. Cert. secondary edn. tchr. Tchr. Kiester (Minn.) High Sch., 1942-44, Wasco (Calif.) Jr. High Sch., 1944-45, Taylors Falls (Minn.) High Sch., 1945-47, Baldwin Park (Calif.) Unified Sch. Dist., 1947-52, 53-73, ret., 1973. Author: (handbook) The Heritage of Baldwin Park, 1981, (pamphlets) The Heritage of Baldwin Park, 1982-88. Volunteer mus. dir. City of Baldwin Park, 1983—. Recipient Older Am. Recognition award L.A. County Bd. Suprs., 1991, Woman of Yr. award San Gabriel Valley District Women's Club, 1997. Mem. AAUW (pres. 1967-69), Baldwin Park Hist. Soc. (bd. dirs. 1981-91, Trophy 1983, chmn. 1985-94), Baldwin Park C. of C. (Golden Heritage award 1983, Citizen of Yr. award 1993), Baldwin Park Women's Club (program chmn. 1990-91, treas. 1991-92, internat. chmn. 1989-96, publicity chmn. 1992-96, Club Woman of Yr. award 1997). Presbyterian. Avocations: arts and crafts, golf, bridge, travel. Home: Baldwin Park, Calif. Died Feb. 1, 2007.

PINKERTON, ALBERT DUANE, II, lawyer; b. Portland, Oreg., Aug. 28, 1942; s. Albert Duane and Barbara Jean Pinkerton; 1 child, Albert Duane III. BA, Willamette U., 1964, JD, 1966. Bar: Oreg. 1966, U.S. Dist. Ct. Oreg. 1966, U.S. Ct. Appeals (9th cir.) 1966, Alaska 1985, Calif. 1986, U.S. Dist. Ct. Calif. 1987. Gen. practice, Springfield, Oreg., 1966-69, Burns, Oreg., 1969-86, Concord, Calif., 1986-88; assoc. Sellar Hazard McNeely & Manning, Walnut Creek, Calif., 1988—2002. Mem. Oreg. State Bar (com. Uniform Jury Instrns. sec. 1972-73, 82-83, chmn. 1973-74, 83-84; com. Procedure and Practice sec. 1985-86, chmn. 1986-87), Am. Judicature Soc., Masons (master 1980-81), Grand Lodge of Oreg. (dist. dep. 1983-86). Home: Walnut Creek, Calif. Died Dec. 29, 2006.

PINKSTON, MOSES SAMUEL, minister; b. Camden, NJ, Jan. 14, 1923; s. William Lincoln and Benena (McDonald) P.; m. Esther Miller, Nov. 18, 1951; children: Moses S. Jr., Steven Alan. BA, Gordon Coll., 1949; MDiv, Temple U., 1952; MSW, Rutgers U., 1968; PhD, Calif. Grad. Sch. Theology, 1977. Ordained to ministry Am. Bapt. Chs. in the U.S.A., 1949. Area min., dir. urban ministries Am. Bapt. Chs., West Oakland, Calif., 1970-74; pastor Antioch Bapt. Ch., San Jose, Calif., 1974-88; ret., 1988. Author: Black Church Development, 1977. Commr. Human Rels. Commn., Santa Clara County, Calif., 1975-77; mem. Urban Task Force, San Jose, 1980-82, San Jose Minority Com., 1984—. Lt. U.S. Army, 1943-46, ETO. Recipient Disting. Citizen award San Jose City, 1981. Mem. NAACP, NASW, Ministerial Alliance Santa Clara (pres. 1981), Masons. Democrat. Home: Santa Clara, Calif. Died Nov. 8, 2006.

PINNIX, ROBERT HENRY, building contractor; b. Greensboro, NC, Feb. 8, 1901; s. Major Henry and Lula (Brooks) P.; m. Jennie Mae Henry, Oct. 21, 1925; 1 dau., Joan Henry (Mrs. Henry Monroe Whitesides). AB, Duke, 1924. Founder, past pres. Robert H. Pinnix, Inc. (bldg. contractors), 1927—, now chmn. bd. Pres. N.C. Indsl. Council, 1964-66, N.C. Bldg. Code Council, 1945-50; former mem. adv. bd. Liberty Mut. Ins. Co., Boston. Bd. mgrs., 3d v.p. Meth. Home for Aged, Charlotte, N.C.; trustee, mem. pres.'s adv. bd. Duke U.; also past chmn. bd. visitors Sch. Engring.; mem. exec. com. Duke U. Nat. Council, 1963-69; past bd. dirs. Ednl. Found. for Commerce and Industry N.C., v.p., 1968— ; trustee, steward 1st United Meth. Ch. Mem. Newcomen Soc., Asso. Gen. Contractors Am. (past nat. dir., past pres. Carolinas br.), N.C. C. of C. (past pres.), Gastonia C. of C. (pres.), Alpha Tau Omega. Clubs: Rotary (past pres.), Charlotte City, Gaston Country (pres.). Home: Gastonia, NC. Died May 1, 1994.

PIONK, RICHARD CLETUS, artist, educator; b. Minn., Apr. 26, 1936; s. Franz E. Spielmann and Esther (Dufrane) Pionk. Cert. in fine arts painting, Art Students League, 1983. Tchr. Art Students League, NYC, from 1991. Mem. bd. control Art Students League, 1983-90. Exhibited in one-man shows Moran Gallery, Tulsa, 1985, Connoisseur Gallery, Rhinebeck, N.Y., 1987, 88, 89, 90, Bklyn. Pub. Libr.; exhibited in group shows Queens Mus., N.Y.C., 1982, Hermitage Found., Norfolk, Va., 1985, Monmouth Mus., Lincroft, N.J., 1985, La Societe des Pastellistes de France, Lille, 1987, Canton (Ohio) Art Inst., 1987, Friends Art Mus., Naples, Fla., 1987, Mel Vin Gallery Southern Coll., Lakeland, Fla., 1987, Wind Borne Gallery, Southport, Conn., 1987, 89, Gregory Gallery, Darien, Conn., 1990, 91, 92, 93, 94, 95, 96, Geary Gallery, Darien, 1997, 98, 99, 2000, 01, 02, The Food Show at Grand Cen. Art Gallery, N.Y.C., 1989, Quincy (Ill.) Art Club, 1989, 90, Jordane Art Gallery, Ft. Myers, Fla., 1990, Pastel Soc., N.Y.C., 1991, Allied Artists, N.Y.C., 1991, Harman-Meek Gallery, Naples, 1992, Butler Inst. Art, 2000, 2003, Nat. Acad. Design, N.Y.C., 2004, others; represented in permanent collections Butler Inst. Art, Ohio, 1st Pastel Mus., China, SalmaGundi Club, N.Y.C., Kidder-Peabody, N.Y., others. Recipient Salzman award, 1999, 2001, Bernhardt Gold medal for pastel, 2002, numerous awards, including medal, Artist's Fellowship, 2002, medal, The Pastel Soc., 2002, 2003. Mem. Pastel Soc. Am. (1st v.p. 1978-91, exhbn. chmn. 1978—, master pastellist, Hall of Fame 1997), Allied Artists Am. (bd. dirs. 1986-91, asst. corr. sec. 1986—), Audubon Artists (juror 1989—), Artists Fellowship Inc. (bd. dirs. 1988—), Nat. Arts Club (Art Spirit Silver medal 2005), Salmagundi Club (mem. curators com., chmn. art com. 1981—, pres. 1994—), Dutch Treat Club. Roman Catholic. Avocation: art. Home: New York, NY. Died June 5, 2007.

PIPPETT, EDWIN BERT, steel company executive; b. Kingsley, Iowa, Aug. 10, 1951; s. Mason Sims Pippett and Mary A. (Aquist) Smyser; m. Bridget O'Shea, June 9, 1984, 1 child, Ashley Nichole. Student, Glendale Coll., Ariz. State U. Owner Pip Properties, Rowlett, Tex., from 1972; pres. Smith Bros. Steel Co., Rowlett, from 1976; ptnr. Pendelton Properties, Nogales, Ariz., from 1974. Mem. Nat. Fedn. Ind. Bus., Rowlett C. of C., Garland (Tex.) C. of C., Big Horn Sheep Soc. Republican. Roman Catholic. Avocations: hunting, fishing, boating, skiing. Home: Rowlett, Tex. Died Nov. 13, 2006.

PIRIE, ROBERT S., investment banker, lawyer; b. Chgo., 1934; m. Deirdre Howard (div. 2000); children John, Sophie Clifton AB, Harvard U., 1956, LLB, 1962. Bar: Mass. 1962, N.Y. 1978. Law clk. to chief justice Mass. Supreme Ct., 1962-63; mem. Gaston, Snow, Motley & Holt, Boston, 1963-73; ptnr. Skadden, Arps, Slate, Meagher & Flom, Boston, 1973-82; pres., CEO Rothschild, Inc., NYC, 1982-92, chmn., CEO, 1992-93; sr. mng. dir. Bear Stearns & Co., Inc., 1993-96; vice chmn. investment banking Soc. Gen. Securities Group, NYC, from 1996. Trustee Aquila Farm, Hamilton, Mass., Asian Cultural Coun., N.Y., The Asia Soc., Rosenbach Mus., Howard Florey Biomed. Found., Am. Acad. in Rome. Fellow AAAS, Am. Antiquarian Soc.; mem. Brook Club, Century Club, Somerset Club, Odd Volumes Club, Roxburghe Club, Saturday Club, Zodiac Club, Manchester Yacht Club. Avocation: collecting books. Died Jan. 15, 2015.

PISAR, SAMUEL, lawyer, writer; b. Bialystok, Poland, Mar. 18, 1929; s. David and Helaina (Suchowolski) P.; m. Judith Frehm, Sept. 2, 1971; 1 child, Leah; children by previous marriage: Helaina Pisar-McKibbin, Alexandra Pisar-Pinto; stepchild Antony J. Blinken LL.B., U. Melbourne, Australia, 1953; LL.M., Harvard U., 1955, D. Juridical Sci., 1959; D.E.S., U. Paris, 1966, LL.D., 1969; L.H.D. (hon.), Dropsie U., 1982, Pepperdine U., 1982. Bar: D.C. 1961, Calif. 1962, N.Y. 1982, Paris Conseil Jurid 1963, London bar Gray's Inn 1966, legal counsel UNESCO 1956-59. Practice internat. law, Paris, Washington and London, from 1959; lectr. U. Paris, 1974. Mem. President J.F. Kennedy Task Force Fgn. Econ. Policy, 1960; adviser Dept. State, 1961; cons. join econ. com. U.S. Congress, 1962; chmn. conf. East-West Trade Mgmt. Center, Europe, 1969-72; lectr. U. Paris. Author: Coexistence and Commerce, 1970, Les Armes de la Paix, 1970, Of Blood and Hope, 1980, La Ressource Humaine, 1983. Named Citizen of Hon., Aix-en-Provence, France, Disting. Fellow Carnegie Mellon U., Pitts., 1982; recipient Sorbonne medal, Paris, 1983, Elie Wiesel Holocaust Remembrance award 1988; honored Samuel Pisar Day, Proclamation, Colo. State U.,

Oct. 13, 1982; named hon. amb., UNESCO, 2012 Mem. ABA, D.C. Bar Assn., Calif. Bar Assn., Am. Judicature Soc., Association Nationale de Conseils Juridiques, Gray's Inn (London). Made U.S. citizen by spl. act of Congress, 1961. Home: Paris 16, France. Died July 27, 2015.

PITTAU, GIUSEPPE, retired archbishop; b. Villacidro, Cagliari, Italy, Oct. 20, 1928; BA in Philosophy, Colegio Máximo, Barcelona, Spain, 1952; MA in Theology, Sophia U., Tokyo, 1960; PhD in Polit. Sci., Harvard U., 1963; LLD (hon.), Loyola U., Chgo., 1987; PhD (hon.), Sogang U., Seoul, Korea, 1996. Ordained priest, Roman Cath. Ch., 1945. Tchg. fellow Harvard U., Cambridge, Mass., 1961-62; asst. prof. Sophia U., 1963-66, prof., 1966-82, acad. dean, 1966-68, chmn. bd. trustees, 1968-75, pres., 1975-81, rector Jesuit comty., 1968-74; provincial of Japanese Province Soc. of Jesus, Tokyo, 1980-81, coadjutor pontifical del. Rome, 1981-83, regional asst. for East Asia and Italy, 1983-92, gen. councillor, from 1983, del. internat. houses of rome, 1988-92; pres. Pontifical Gregorian U., Rome, 1992-98; archbishop Castro di Sardegna, Italy, 1998—2003. Del. Civilta Cattolica jour., Rome, 1995; pres. Roman Ch. Instns. Libr. Network, Rome, 1992; bd. dirs. IFCU. Editor Monumenta Nipponica, Sophia U., 1964-68; author: Political Thought in Early Meiji Japan, 1967, Nihon Rikken Kokka No Seiritsu, 1968, Nippon to Nipponjin, 1979, Nipponjin Eno Atsui Tegami, 1981; editor: Nihon No Shakai Bunkashi, 1974. Recipient Commendatore of the Order of Italian Republic, 1970, Encomienda of Order of Isabel la Católica, Spanish Govt., Order of the Rising Sun, Japanese Govt., 1980, Okano prize Japanese-Italian Assn., 1988, award Japan Found., 1993. Died Dec. 26, 2014.

PITTMAN, PHILIP MCMILLAN, historian; b. Detroit, Apr. 6, 1941; s. Lansing Mizner and Sally Clotilde (Book) P.; m. Julie M. Ducharme, June 22, 1963 (div. 1975); children: Philip McMillan III, Mary Christine Steuart, Noel Ducharme; m. Adele Smith, June 26, 1976 (div. 1989); m. Margaret D. Schlueter, Aug. 26, 1990. AB, Kenyon Coll., 1963; MA, Vanderbilt U., 1964, PhD, 1967. Instr. Vanderbilt U., Nashville, 1966-67; asst. prof. U. Victoria, B.C., Can., 1967-68; assoc. prof. Marshall U., Huntington, W.Va., 1968-80; pres. W.Va. Assn. Coll. English Tchrs., 1978-79; author, historian Cedarville, Mich., from 1980; pub., salesman, v.p., sec., chmn. bd. Les Cheneaux Ventures Inc., from 1985. Adj. prof. W.Va. Coll. Grad. Studies, 1978-80. Author: The Les Cheneaux Chronicles: Anatomy of a Community, 1984, Ripples from the Breezes: A Les Cheneaux Anthology, 1988, North Shore Chinook: Lake Huron Salmon on Light Tackle, 1993, Don't Blame the Treaties: Native American Rights and the Michigan Indian Treaties, 1992; editor, compiler: The Portrayal of Life Stages in English Literature, 1500-1800, 1989, author various scholarly book reviews and articles. Active Les Cheneaux Cmty. Action Com., 1985—, Mich. Nature Conservancy, 1994—, Little Traverse Conservancy, 1990—, bd. dirs., 1994—2006; founding dir. Les Cheneaux Cmty. Found., 1997—; founding mem. Les Cheneaux Econ. Forum, 1997—; active Les Cheneaux Found., 2002. NEH fellow, 1971. Mem. Les Cheneaux Hist. Assn. (pres. 1987-89), Les Cheneaux Islands Assn. (pres. 1982-84, bd. dirs. 1996-2002, historian 1985—), Les Cheneaux Club (sec. 1972-87, 97—), Delta Kappa Epsilon. Republican. Episcopalian. Avocations: fishing, boating, writing, walking. Home: Cedarville, Mich. Died Apr. 20, 2007.

PITTMAN, ROY CLINTON, JR., neurosurgeon, theologian, lawyer, philosopher; b. Florence, SC, Oct. 12, 1931; s. Roy Clinton and Edna Hester (Altman) P.; m. Therese Huguette Lamarche Pittman, Apr. 1958 (div. May 1976); 1 stepdaughter, Michele Lois Young; children: Charlotte Elisabeth, Clinton Christopher, Russell Roy; m. Jeanne Elmore Waters Pittman, Oct. 10, 1976. BS magna cum laude, Wofford Coll., Spartanburg, SC, 1952; MD, Med. U. S.C., Charleston, 1956; JD, Washburn U. Coll. Law, Topeka, Kans., 1991; MDiv with honors, Emory U. Candler Sch. Theology, Atlanta, 1995; DSc (hon.), The London Inst., 1973. Diplomate Am. Bd. Neurol. and Orthopedic Surgery; ordained to ministry Ea. Orthodox Ch., 2000; bar: Fla. 1992, U.S. Dist. Ct. (mid. dist.) Fla. 1992. Intern U.S. Naval Hosp., Newport, RI, 1956-57; resident in neurology U.S. Naval Hosp.-Nat. Naval Med. Ctr., Bethesda, Md., 1957-58; neurologist East Coast Neuropsychiat. Ctr.-U.S. Naval Hosp., Phila., 1958-59, head neurology br., 1959; resident in neurosurgery Jefferson Med. Coll. Hosp., Phila., 1959-61, chief resident, 1961-62; resident in gen. surgery Hahnemann Med. Coll. Hosp., Phila., 1962-63; pvt. practice neurol. surgery Morton Plant and Mease Hosps., Clearwater-Dunedin, Fla., 1963-82, Cmty. Hosp. of New Port Richey, New Port Richey, Fla., 1978-88; pvt. practice legal medicine, med. jurisprudence & bioethics Pittman Profl. Assn., Clearwater, Fla., 1995-98, Tarpon Springs, Fla., 1995-98; pres., gen. counsel The Quintessential Corp., Tarpon Springs, 1998-2000; founder, prior Trinity House Retreat, Greek Orthodox Monastery of the Holy Trinity, from 2001. Protestant chaplain Morton Plant/Mease Countryside Hosp., Clearwater, Fla., 1997-98. Contbr. articles to profl. jours. Pres. St. Petersburg (Fla.) Coll. Alumni Assn., 1973-75. Lt. MC, USN, 1956-59, lt. comdr., 1962. Recipient Top Paper Bioethics and The Law award Washburn U. Coll. Law, Topeka, Kans., 1990, Top paper Comparative Civil Law award Cumberland Sch. Law and U. Heidelberg Germany Faculty of Law, 1990; endowed Jeanne Pittman ann. Bioethics and the Law Top Paper award Washburn U. Coll. Law, Topeka, 1995. Fellow Internat. Coll. Angiology, Royal Soc. Health, Internat. Coll. Surgeons, Am. Coll. Legal Medicine; mem. AMA, Congress Neurol. Surgeons, Fla. Med. Assn., Fla. Bar, Phi Beta Kappa, Phi Delta Phi. Jeffersonian Democrat. Avocations: stamp collecting/philately, anthropology, travel. Died Jan. 20, 2015.

PITTMAN, WILLIAM CLAUDE, JR., retired electrical engineer; b. Pontotoc, Miss., Apr. 22, 1921; s. William Claude and Maude Ella (Bennett) P.; m. Eloise Savage, Apr. 20, 1952 (dec. Oct 13, 2008); children: Patricia A. Pittman Ready, William Claude III, Thomas Allen. BSEE, Miss. State Coll., 1951, MSEE, 1957. Cert. svc. holder US Govt. From electronic engr. to supr. elec. engring. dept. U.S. Army Labs., Redstone Arsenal, Ala., 1951-59; supr. electronic engr. to aero. engring. supr. NASA/Marshall Space Flight Ctr., 1960; electronic engr. Army Missile Labs., 1962-82; program mgr. Army Labs. and R&D Ctr., Redstone Arsenal, 1982-99; vol. cons. Army Aviation and Missile Rsch., Devel. and Engring. Ctr., from 1999. Organizer numerous sci. and tech. confs.; mem. Launch Team First Redstone Missile Cape Canaveral, 1953. Author patents, reports, papers, Flag of United States Flown Over Capitol, 1997. Vol. emeritus US Army, 1999-2012, sgt. USMC, 1940-46, PTO. Recipient Medal of Honor, DAR, Meritorious Civilian Svc. award Dept. Army, 1993, Numerous award & Commendation Letters, award, AMRDEC Medallion, Outreach Program. Fellow AIAA (assoc.; chmn. Miss.-Ala. chpt. 1981-82, Martin Schilling award 1980); mem. IEEE (sr. life; Cert. Svc. Holder), First Marine Div. Assn., DAV, IRE (chmn. Huntsville sect. 1957-58), Madison Hist. Soc., Servic PIN SAR (pres. Tenn. Valley chpt. 1984-85, Ala. Soc. 1990-91, Cert. 1991, Patriot medal), Tau Beta Pi, Phi Kappa Phi, Kappa Mu Epsilon. Avocations: history, genealogy. Home: Huntsville, Ala. Deceased.

PITTS, EDGAR THURLOW, writer, retired educator; b. Rockport, Maine, Sept. 5, 1919; s. George Edgar and Mildred Nettie (Thurlow) Pitts; m. Elizabeth Knowlton, Dec. 21, 1942 (dec. May 1993); 1 child, Nathan Thurlow. BA with hons. in Math., U. Maine, 1942; diploma, U.S. Naval Acad., 1943; MEd in Adminstrn., U. Maine, 1953. Cert. tchr., prin., supt. schs. Maine. Math. tchr./prin. Stonington (Maine) H.S., 1946—53; prin. Ellsworth (Maine) H.S., 1953—70; supervising prin. Five Towns Sch. Dist., Western Hancock County, Maine, 1970—73; pvt. math. tchr. Eastern Maine, 1974—82. Co-author: Deer Isle Remembered, 1989, Stonington Past and Present, 1997; author: Long Ago and Far Away, 1936-45, 2d edit., 2001. Founder, chmn. Acad. Recognition Commn., State of Maine, 1959—63; various ad hoc com. chairs state, regional and local edn., Maine, 1960—98; past pres., exec. com. Main Tchrs. Assn. Lt. USNR, 1942—46. Mem.: NEA, Maine Edn. Assn. (life), Am. Legion (post comdr. 1997—2000), Masons, Phi Beta Kappa. Republican. Avocations: stamp collecting/philately, local and regional history, e-mail. Home: Stonington, Maine. Died Apr. 28, 2007.

PLESS, JORGEN EMIL, plastic surgery consultant; b. Apr. 13, 1934; s. Villy Emanuel and Gerda Frederikke (Bork) P.; m. Eva Festersen, May 21, 1961; children: Thomas, Torsten. MD, Copenhagen U., 1960; DDS, Copenhagen Dental Sch., 1969. Intern Sundby Hosp., 1960-61, Odense U. Hosp., Denmark, 1961, Svendborg Hosp., 1961-62, resident, 1963, asst. registrar surg. dept., 1963—65; registrar Rigshospitalet Copenhagen, 1965-67; sr. registrar Finsen Inst., Copenhagen, 1969-73, Odense U. Hosp., 1973-76, cons. plastic surgery dept., 1976-98, vice-chmn. med. com., 1982-85, chmn. med. com., 1985-89; com. mem. Inst. Exptl. Surgery, Copenhagen, 1970-73; chmn. med. adv. ethics com. Mermaid Clinic Ebeltoft, 1989-95; founder, chmn. TVT Svendborg, 2004—11; shareholder, mem., founder Flexhosp. Ltd., 2011. Ednl. insp. Danish Nat. Bd. Health, 1996—2000; comml. mentor, 2002—04. Contbr. articles to profl. jours. Councillor Coun. Fyn, Denmark, 2001—04, Region So. Denmark, from 2005, mem. vision healthcare policies com., 2009, mem. com. hosp. structure, from 2009; coun. mem. City of Svendburg, 2005—10; founder, vice-chmn. Ind. Citizens Party Funen, Svendborg, 1999—2014. Mem. Danish Soc. Plastic Reconstructive Surgery (pres. 1986-89), Danish Orgn. Plastic Surgery (chmn. 1994-98), Danish Soc. Head Neck Oncology (sec. 1974-85), Danish Soc. Microsurgery (founder, pres. 1974-78), Scandinavian Assn. Plastic Surgeons (pres. 1986-88), Rotary (Paul Harris fellow 1988). Died May 12, 2014.

PLISETSKAYA, MAYA, ballerina; b. Moscow, Nov. 20, 1925; m. Rodion Shchedrin, 1958. Ed., Bolshoi Theatre Ballet Sch. Prin. dancer Bolshoi Theatre, Russia, 1943, prima ballerina, 1962; artistic dir. Rome Opera Ballet, Spanish Nat. Ballet, Madrid; guest artist Paris Opera Ballet, 1961, 1964. Dir. Maya Ann. Internat. Ballet Competitions, 1994. Dancer (ballets) Swan Lake, 1947, Sleeping Beauty, 1961, Carmen Suite, La Rose Malade, Isadora, Ave Maya, 1995; ballerina and choreographer (ballets) Anna Karenina, 1972, Seagull, 1980. Recipient Lenin prize, 1964, Legion of Honor, 1986, Gold Medal of Fine Arts, King Juan Carlos of Spain, 1991, prize, Prince of Astuzias, 2005, Praemium Imperiale award (Theatre/Film), Japan Art Assn., 2006; named People's Artist of USSR, 1958, prima ballerina assoluta, Bolshoi Theatre, 1959. Home: Moscow, Russia. Died May 2, 2015.

PLISKA, EDWARD WILLIAM, lawyer, retired judge; b. Rockville, Conn., Apr. 13, 1935; s. Louis Boleslaw and Constance (Dombrowski) P.; m. Luisa Anne Crotti, Nov. 29, 1958; children: Gregory, John, Thomas, Laura. AB, Princeton U., NJ, 1956; LLB, U. Conn., 1964; LLD (hon.), San Mateo (Calif.) U., 1975. Bar: Calif. 1965. Dep. dist. atty. Santa Barbara (Calif.) County, 1965, San Mateo County Dist. Atty., Redwood City, Calif., 1965-71, chief trial dep., 1970-71; pvt. practice San Mateo, 1971-72; judge San Mateo County Mcpl. Ct., 1973-86; ptnr. Corey, Luzaich, Pliska, DeGhetaldi & Nastari, Millbrae, Calif., from 1986. Officer Am. Judges Assn., 1983-86; prodr. and host (TV and Radio show) Justice Forum, 1973-78; prof. criminal and constitutional law San Mateo Law Sch., 1971-76; leader People to People legal delegations to Europe, India, Nepal, 1985, 87, 91. Editor Ct. Rev., 1981-88. Leader People to People Legal Delegations, Europe, India, Nepal, 1985, 87, 91; trustee Belmont (Calif.) Sch. Dist., 1987-91, pres., 1990; chmn. San Mateo County Cultural Arts Commn., 1987-90; mem. Peninsula Comty. Found. Arts Fund, 1988-99; officer Hillbarn Theatre, 1989-99. With U.S. Army, 1957. NEH grantee, 1975, 80. Mem. Calif. Judges Assn., Calif. State Bar Assn., Nat. Assn. Criminal Def. Lawyers, Calif. Attys. for Criminal Justice, San Mateo County Bar Assn., Calif. Pub. Defenders Assn., Bohemian Club. Democrat. Roman Catholic. Avocations: acting and directing plays, reading, sports spectator. Home: Belmont, Calif. Died Oct. 31, 2006.

PLUMMER, ROBERT EUGENE, educational administrator; b. Ft. Worth, Sept. 7, 1931; s. George G. and Edith (Yates) P.; m. Sandra Sue Cope, Nov. 6, 1959 (div. July 1986); children: David Lee, Steven Paul; m. Mary Beth Maris, Dec. 28, 1987; 1 child, Robert Jones. BBA, U. North Tex., 1958, BS, 1959, MEd, 1963. Tchr. West Covina (Calif.) Unified Sch. Dist., 1963-66, U. North Tex., Denton, 1966-67, Tex. Wesleyan U., Ft. Worth, 1967-68; adminstr., tchr. San Diego Unified Sch. Dist., 1968-70; tchr. Ft. Worth Ind. Sch. Dist., 1970-71, coord. intercultural rels., 1971-74, prin. Oakhurst Elem. Sch., 1974-77, prin. Tanglewood Elem. Sch., 1977-83, coord. elem. magnets/Montessori, 1983-86, prin. South Hi Mount Elem. Sch., 1986-93, prin. Bruce Shulkey Elem. Sch., from 1993. Chmn. bd. dirs. Tarrant County Am. Heart Assn., 1984-85; lifetime mem. PTA; bd. dirs. Am. Heart Assn., Ft. Worth, 1975—, chmn., 1984-85; bd. dirs. Regional XI Blood Bank, Ft. Worth, 1981—, chmn., 1990—; del. to Pisa (Italy) Conf., City of Ft. Worth, 1984. Lt. U.S. Army and USAF, 1951-53, Korea. Recipient svc. plaque March of Dimes, 1975, Key to City, Ft. Worth, 1981, Bd. Mem. of Yr. award Am. Heart Assn., 1977-78, Disting. Svc. award, 1997, rsch. grantee named in hon., 1998, appreciation plaque Carter Blood Bank, appreciation award Optimist Club, 1990, Optimist of Yr. award, 1919, leadership award Ft. Worth Classroom Tchrs., 1990, mayor's cert. of recognition City of Ft. Worth, 1990; Paul Harris fellow Rotary Club Ft. Worth South, 1996. Mem. Colonial Country Club (tennis chair 1973—), Kiwanis (life, pres. Ft. Worth S.W. club 1974-75, lt. gov. internat. 1975-76, Disting. Lt. Gov. award 1976-77, Disting. Svc. award 1976, Appreciation award 1977, others), Phi Delta Kappa (scholar 1982, pres. 1972-73, Svc. Key 1972, Adminstr. of Yr. 1982). Republican. Methodist. Avocations: marathon running, tennis, golf, skydiving. Home: Hurst, Tex. Died Mar. 1, 2007.

POCH, HERBERT EDWARD, retired pediatrician, educator; b. Elizabeth, NJ, Sept. 4, 1927; s. William and Min (Herman) P.; m. Leila Kosberg, Aug. 27, 1952; children: Bruce Jeffrey, Andrea Susan, Lesley Grace. AB, Columbia U., 1949, MD, 1953. Diplomate Am. Bd. Pediatrics. Intern Kings County Hosp. Ctr., Bklyn., 1953-54; resident Babies Hosp., Columbia-Presbyn. Med. Ctr., NYC, 1954-56; pvt. practice medicine specializing in pediatrics Elizabeth, 1956-92. Pres. med. staff, 1989, attending pediatrician Elizabeth Gen. Med. Ctr., 1973, sr. attending pediatrician, 1990, hon. staff, 1993—; attending pediatrician St. Elizabeth Hosp., 1968, chmn. dept. pediatrics, 1971-81, attending pediatrician Monmouth Med. Ctr., 1991-99, emeritus, 1999—, assoc. program dir. pediatrics; instr. pediatrics Columbia U., 1956-72, asst. clin. prof. pediatrics, 1972-91; clin. assoc. prof. pediatrics MCP Hahnemann Sch. Medicine, 1997-99; clin. assoc. prof. pediat. Drexel U., 1999-. With AUS, 1945-46. Fellow Am. Acad. Pediatrics; mem. N.J. Med. Soc., Ambulatory Pediatric Assn. Died Mar. 2014.

PODMOKLY, PATRICIA GAYLE, typesetting company professional; b. Chgo., May 15, 1940; d. Edwin Paul Baker and Frances (Williams) Popiela. Grad., Jones Comml. Sch., Chgo. Bookkeeper, sec. William C. Douglas & Ralph Falk II, Lake Forest, Ill., from 1958; owner Global Graphics, Inc., Elmhurst, Ill., from 1987. Roman Catholic. Died Dec. 30, 2007.

PODOLL, EUGENE VINCENT, grocery store chain executive; b. Hagali Twp., Minn., Nov. 2, 1925; s. Herbert Ferdinand and Alice Elizabeth (Wild) P.; m. Arline Leona Sather, Nov. 2, 1947; children— Dale, Elaine, Deborah Dist. mgr. Safeway Stores, Sacramento, 1970-73, dist. mgr. Hawaii, 1973-76, retail operating mgr. El Paso, Tex., 1976-82, v.p., div. mgr. Sacramento, from 1982. Served to lt. (j.g.) U.S. Mcht. Marines, 1943-47 Mem.: Northridge Country (Sacramento). Avocations: golf; gardening. Died Nov. 4, 2006.

PÖHL, KARL OTTO, retired bank executive; b. Hannover, Germany, Dec. 1, 1929; m. Ulrike Pesch; 4 children. Student, U. Gottingen, 1952-55; degree (hon.), Ruhr U., Tel-Aviv U., Georgetown U., U. Md., U. Buckingham, U. London. Divsn. chief Ifo, Inst. Econ. Research, Munich, 1955-60. Econ. journalist, Bonn, 1961-67; mem. bd. Fed. Assn. German Banks, Cologne, 1968-70; div. chief Fed. Ministry Econs., Bonn, 1970-71; dept. chief Fed. Chancellery, 1971-72; state sec. Fed. Ministry Fin., 1972-77; dep. gov. Deutsche Bundesbank, Frankfurt, 1977-79, pres., chmn. cen. bank coun., 1980-91; gov. Fed. Republic Germany in the IMF, 1980-91; chmn. Group of 10, cen. bank govs., 1983-89. Decorated Grosskreuz des Verdienstordens der Bundesrepublik Deutschland. Died Dec. 9, 2014.

POIROT, JACQUELYN, elementary school educator; b. New Haven, July 1, 1935; d. George and Charlotte (Higgins) P. BS, New Haven State Tchrs. Coll., 1957; postgrad., So. Conn. State Coll., New Haven, 1962. Cert. tchr. early childhood edn., Conn. Libr. Ferguson Libr./Rice Elem. Sch., Stamford, Conn., 1957-58; tchr. 1st grade Brewster Sch., Durham, Conn., 1958-65, reading tchr., 1966-68; primary tchr. Wilson Sch., Lordsburg, N.Mex., 1967-69; tchr. 1st and 2d grades Fair Oaks Schs., Montville, Conn., 1969-92; tchr. 1st grade Charles E. Murphy Elem. Sch., Oakdale, Conn., from 1992. Vol., asst. to dir. Montville High Drama Club, 1977-91; vol. Garde Arts Ctr., New London, Conn., 1987—. Recipient Unsung Hero award New London Rotary Club, 1992, Vol. of Yr. award Garde Arts Ctr., 1994. Mem. Assn. for Childhood Edn. Internat. Avocations: community theater, reading. Home: Hallandale, Fla. Died Apr. 24, 2007.

POKOL, ALBERT RONALD, librarian; b. Donora, Pa., Oct. 15, 1928; s. Alexander and Mary Pokol; m. Gayle M. Sanders, Aug. 12, 1954; children: Bruce Albert, Clifford Albert. BS in Edn., Calif. U., Pa., 1949; MEd, Duquesne U., Pitts., 1966; MLS, U. Pitts., 1969. Cert. in teaching Pa. Dept. Pub. Instrn., 1950. Libr. West Allegheny Sch. Dist., Imperial, Pa., 1952—54, Donora Sch. Dist., 1954—62, Robert Morris U., Pitts., 1962—65; reference libr. Calif. U., 1965—2007, archives/spl. collections libr., from 2008. Pastoral coun. mem. St. Sebastian Ch., Belle Vernon, Pa., 2008. Mem.: Pa. State Coll. & U. Faculties Assn., Calif. U. Pa. Alumni Assn., U. Pitts. Alumni Assn. Democrat. Roman Catholic. Home: Belle Vernon, Pa. Died July 3, 2013.

POLING, KERMIT WILLIAM, minister; b. Elkins, W.Va., Oct. 1, 1941; s. Durward Willis and Della Mae (Boyles) P.; m. Patricia Ann Groves, June 12, 1965; children: David Edward Elson, Mikael Erik. Diploma in Bible, Am. Bible Sch., 1966; BA in Bible, Reed Coll. Religion, 1968; AA, W.Va. U., 1970; ThD, Zion Theol. Sem., 1971; postgrad., Wesley Theol. Sem., 1974; LLD, Geneva Theol. Coll., 1980; DSL (hon.), Berean Christian Coll., 1981; postgrad., Mansfield Coll., U. Oxford, Eng., 1986, Mansfield Coll., U. Oxford, 1990, postgrad., 1991; D Ecumenical Rsch., St. Ephrem's Inst. for Oriental Studies, 1989; BRE, Am. Bible Coll., 1991; M of Herbology, Emerison Coll., 1994. Ordained to ministry United Meth. Ch., 1967. Pastor Parkersburg-Crossroads (W.Va.) Cir., 1967-70; asst. sec. W.Va. Ann. Conf., 1967-69; pastor Hope-Halleck Morgantown Cir., 1970-76, Trinity-Warren Grafton (W.Va.) Charge, 1976-83, 1st Trinity Pennsboro (W.Va.) Charge, 1983-97, South Parkersburg United Meth. Ch., 1997—2004. Editor local ch. news; instr. Bible Bodkin Bible Inst., 1975-75, United Meth. Lay Acad., 1992—2004; mem. staff Taylor County Coop. Parish, 1976-83; coord. Hughes River Coop. Parish, 1983-86; mem. chaplains com. Grafton City Hosp., 1976-82; mem. coun. Ctr. d'Etudes et d'Action Oecumeniques, 1972-74; bishop in Partibus of Tayma. Author: A Crown of Thorns, 1963, A Silver Message, 1964, History of the Halleck Church, 1970, Eastern Rite Catholicism, 1971, From Brahmin to Bishop, 1976, Cult and Occult: Data and Doctrine, 1978, The Value of Religious Education in Ancient Traditional Churches, 1993, Anniversary History of Trinity Church, Pennsboro, 1997; editor: Jane's Heirs; contbr. articles and poems to religious jours. Decorated Royal Afghanistan Order of Crown of Amanullah, Royal Order of the Golden Eagle of Napoca, Byzantine Order of Leo the Armenian, Order of Polonia Resitutia, Mystical Order of St. Peter, knight Grand Cross of the Order of St. Dennis of Zante, companion Naval Order of U.S., Patron and Knight Grand Cross Oder of The Crown of Thorns; recipient Good Citizenship award Doddridge County, 1954, Silver medal Ordre Universel du Merit Humain, Geneva, 1973, Commendation for Outstanding Achievement in Ministry, Ohio Ho. of Reps., 1988; recipient U.S. Heritage award, 2002, St. Eugene Medal of Merit, 2009; named Chief of Dynastic Ho. of Polanie-Patrikios, 1988, Prince of the Holy Roman Empire, 2005. Mem. SAR, Assn. Bible Tchrs. (founder), Internat. Platform Assn., Naval Order U.S., Sovereign Order St. John Jerusalem, Ritchie County Ministerial Assn. (pres. 1984-97), Order Sacred Cup, Knights of Malta, Order of the Crown of Lauriers. Home: Pennsboro, W.Va. Died Mar. 31, 2015.

POLINGER, DAVID HARRIS, broadcast executive; b. NYC, Mar. 16, 1927; s. Elliot Hirsch and Raye Ruth (Newberger) P.; m. Roberta Gilman, Jan. 20, 1951 (div. 1976); children: Yossi Joseph, Doria Lyn; m. Donna Beverly Wheeler, Sept. 10, 1983. BA in Econs., Duke U., 1949; MA in Communications, NYU, 1971. Holder 3d class radio-TV FCC lic. Dir. Latin Am. div. Voice of Am., NYC, 1950-52; v.p., gen. mgr. Sta. WKAQ-TV, San Juan, P.R., 1952-54, Sta. WAPA-TV, San Juan, 1955-56; owner Interp-Am. Prodns., San Juan, 1956-57; v.p., gen. mgr. NTA spot sales Sta. WNTA-AM-FM-TV, NYC, 1958-59; exec. v.p. Lewis & Polinger Advt., Washington, 1959-60; pres. Broadcast div. Friendly Frost Stas. WGLI, WQFM, WTFM, Westbury, N.Y., 1961-69; v.p. ops. Bell TV, NYC, 1970-72; pres. Sta. WSNL-TV/Suburban Broadcasting Corp., Central Islip, N.Y., 1972-76; sr. v.p. WPIX, Inc., NYC, from 1976. Adj. rpof. N.Y. Inst. Tech., Westbury, 1972-75, The Coll. of Ins., N.Y.C., 1975-80, CCNY, 1977-80; mem. Nat. Def. Exec. Reserve, Fed. Emergency, 1960-86. Lt. col. group comdr. Manhattan and Bklyn. group Civil Air Patrol; mem. Adv. Com. CARE, 1965-76; pres. Carcinoid Tumor and Serotonin Rsch. Found., Mt. Sinai Hosp., N.Y.C., 1965—; chmn. L.I. Adv. Com., Office of Civil Def., 1965-78; bd. dirs. Performing Arts Found. L.I., 1968-79, Island Symphony Orch., Inc., 1969-77; dir. adv. com. Borough Pres. Manhattan on Narcotics Addiction Control, 1971-76; mem. Hofstra Coun., Hempstead, N.Y., trustee Dowling Coll., 1978—. With USN, 1944-46, maj. N.Y. Guard, 1989—. Recipient Maj. award Armstrong Meml. Research Found., 1968. Mem. Internat. Radio and TV. Found. (bd. dirs. 1976-78, v.p. 1988—, pres. 1985-86, chmn. 1987-88), Internat. Radio and TV Soc. (v.p. 1977-88), Nat. Assn. Broadcasters (chmn. copyright com. 1978-86, chm;n. FM com. 1967-68), Assn. Ind. TV Stas., Nat. Assn. FM Broadcasters (v.p., bd. dirs. chmn., pres.' adv. com. 1963-69), Am. Mgmt. Assn., Broadcast Pioneers, Nat. Acad. TV Arts and Scis., Advt. Club, Alpha Epsilon Rho. Clubs: Scarsdale Country. Jewish. Avocations: golf, tennis, pvt. pilot. Home: New York, NY. Died July 1, 2007.

POLLACK, ROBERT HARVEY, psychology professor; b. NYC, June 26, 1927; s. Solomon and Bertha (Levy) P.; m. Martha Dee Katz, Aug. 20, 1948; children: Jonathan Keith, Lance Michael, Scott Evan. BS, CCNY, 1948; MS, Clark U., Worcester, Mass., 1950, PhD, 1953. Lectr. U. Sydney, Australia, 1953-61; spl. rsch. fellow Columbia U., NYC, 1960-61; chief div. congitive devel. Inst. Juvenile Rsch., Chgo., 1961-63, dep. dir. rsch., 1963-69; from clin. asst. prof. to clin. assoc. prof. rsch. U. Ill. Coll. Medicine, Chgo., 1962-67; prof. psychology U. Ga., Athens, 1969-96, chair grad. program. exptl. psychology, 1970-78, chair grad. study com., 1978-86; prof. emeritus, from 1996; chair grad. program in life-span psychology U. Ga., Athens, 1988-96. Editor: The Experimental Psychology of Alfred Binet, 1969; contbr. over 100 articles and chpts. to profl. publs. Cpl. U.S. Army, 1945-46. Grantee Nat. Inst. Child Health and Human Devel., 1965, 67, 72, 78. Fellow AAAS, Am. Psychol. Assn.; mem. Am. Assn. Sex Edn., Counsellors and Therapists, Gerontol. Soc. Am., Australian Psychol. Soc., Soc. for Researching Child Devel., Soc. for Sci. Study Sex, Sigma Xi. Democrat. Avocations: travel, stamp collecting/philately, opera, military history. Died Mar. 10, 2015.

POLLOCK, RALPH ERNEST, personnel director; b. Akron, Ohio, Aug. 1, 1925; s. Ralph Emerson and Eunice Ernestine (Walker) P.; m. Reta Ann Parkison, Aug. 30, 1951; children: Gary, Nadine. BS, Ohio No. U., Ada, 1946-50; MA, Ohio State U., 1950-51, postgrad., 1955-64, 68-69. Tchr., Maumee, Ohio, 1951-52, Butler, Ohio, 1952-53; dir. pub., alumni rel. Ohio No. U., 1954-56; supt. Butler (Ohio) Local Schs., 1956-59; field rep., dir. pub. rels. Columbus Heating and Ventilating Co., 1959-65; elem. prin. Westerville (Ohio) Sch., 1965-70, dir. personnel, pub. rels. Ohio, from 1976. Adj. prof., Otterbein Coll, Westerville, 1983-85, U. Dayton, 1988. Bd. Trustee Meth. Ch., Westerville, 1981-85. With U.S. Navy, 1943-47. Mem. Am. Assn. of Sch. Adminstrs., Ohio Assn. Sch. Personnel Adminstrs. (pres. 1976-77), Nat. Sch. Pub. Rels. Assn. (pres. 1976-77), Pub. Rels. Soc. of Am., Rotary (pres. 1972-73). Home: Westerville, Ohio. Died May 27, 2007.

POLOW, BERTRAM, lawyer; b. Irvington, NJ, Apr. 14, 1918; s. Max and Belle (Teiber) P.; m. Betty Ruth Krohn, Mar. 18, 1949; children: David, Sarah, Abigail. LLB, NYU, 1948; LLM, Rutgers U., 1951. Bar: N.J. 1948, U.S. Dist. Ct. N.J. 1948, U.S. Supreme Ct. 1956, Vt. 1987. Ptnr. Polow & Chait, Morristown, N.J., 1949-63; dep. atty. gen. State of N.J., Trenton, 1955; first asst. prosecutor Morris County, Morristown, 1956-63, judge juvenile ct., 1963-73; judge trial div. Superior Ct., N.J., 1973-79, judge appeals div., 1979-83; of counsel Skoloff & Wolfe, Livingston, N.J., from 1983; ptnr. Polow & Polow, Hyde Park, Vt., from 1987. Arbitrator Am. Arbitration Assn., N.J., 1984-86, Nat. Assn. Securities Dealers, Vt. 1988. Editor NYU Law Rev. Pres. Morris County Chest., 1957-58. Served with USAAF, 1941-45, ETO. Fellow Am. Acad. Matrimonial Lawyers; mem. ABA (bd. dirs.), N.J. Bar Assn., Vt. Bar Assn., NYU Law Alumni Assn. (chmn. bd. 1983-87). Avocations: photography, skiing, bicycling. Home: Morrisville, Vt. Died Jan. 30, 2007.

POLUEKTOV, RATMIR, agriculturist, lab administrator; b. Leningrad, Russia, Apr. 14, 1930; s. Alexandr Poluektov and Eugene Tomashevich; m. Ina Stolesnikova, Sept. 13, 1962; children: Andrew, Inna Poluektova. Degree in Engring., Leningrad Poly. Inst., St. Petersburg, Russia, 1954, DSc, 1966; PhD, Leningrad Mil. Aircraft Acad., St. Petersburg, 1958; prof., Agrophys. Rsch. Inst., St. Petersburg, 1969. Engr. Klimov Constrn. Office, St. Petersburg, 1954—61; docent Leningrad Poly. Inst., St. Petersburg, 1961—67; lab. adminstr. Agrophys. Rsch. Inst., St. Petersburg, from 1967. Home: Saint Petersburg, Russia. Died Mar. 27, 2012.

POMEROY, DAVID JAMES, social worker; b. Manistee, Mich., May 5, 1951; s. Edward John and Esther (Stepniewski) P.; m. Lucy Pomeroy, Apr. 25, 1975 (div. Aug. 1991); children: Mary, Alexandria; 1 adopted child, Laura Ann. AA, Muskegon Community Coll., 1972; BS in Social Work, Western Mich. U., 1974. Group leader Adrian (Mich.) Tng. Sch., 1975-79, Camp Shawono, Grayling, Mich., 1979-86, Shawono Ctr. Tng. Sch., Grayling, from 1986, group leader, counselor maximum security detention, from 1994; owner Dave's Mil. Gun Shop, Grayling, from 1990. Group leader Dept. Social Svcs. State of Mich., 1975—; specialist in sex victim and sex offender treatment groups, 1987-94. Recipient Letter of Recognition Osceola County Prosecutor, Reed City, Mich., 1990. Fellow Grayling Karate and Akido Club; mem. AFSME, Grayling War Games Club. Roman Catholic. Avocations: hunting, fishing, canoeing, akido. Home: Grayling, Mich. Died Dec. 30, 2007.

PONTIFLET, ADDIE ROBERSON, nurse, educator; b. Decatur, Ga., Oct. 25, 1943; d. Emory Alexander and Emma Kate (Wilson) Roberson; m. Derrick Mayes, Dec. 12, 1965 (div. Apr. 1966); 1 child, Pamela Denise; m. Theodore Hubert Pontiflet, Nov. 17, 1972. RN diploma, Kings County Hosp. Ctr., Bklyn., 1964, nurse anesthetist diploma, 1973; BS, St. Joseph's Coll., 1975; MSEd, U. So. Maine, 1983. RN, Va.; lic. nurse practitioner, Va. Staff nurse Montifiore Hosp., Bronx, N.Y., 1964-66; head nurse Downstate Med. Ctr., Bklyn., 1967-68; in svc. instr. Kings County Hosp. Ctr., Bklyn., 1968-70; anesthetist Bklyn. Hosp., 1973-74; clin. instr. Ga. Bapt. Med. Ctr., Atlanta, 1976-80; assoc. dir. Mercy Hosp. Sch. of Anesthesia, Portland, Maine, 1980-86; asst. prof. nurse anesthesia Med. Coll. Va., Va. Commonwealth U., Richmond, Va., from 1986. Bd. dirs. YWCA, Portland, 1982-85, Last Stop Gallery, Richmond, 1988-89. Mem. Am. Assn. Nurse Anesthetists (cert.), Va. Assn. Nurse Anesthetists, Phi Delta Kappa. Avocations: music, civic volunteer activities, reading, walking, doll making. Home: Glen Allen, Va. Died July 21, 2007.

PORCELLA, ARTHUR DAVID, lawyer, arbitrator, appellate judge; b. Bklyn., Mar. 25, 1918; s. Quinto John and Pasqualena Louise (Costa) P.; m. Wanda Jane Sprinkel, July 29, 1944; children: Patricia, Pamela, Arthur Jr. AB, Bklyn. Coll., 1941; JD, Case Western Reserve U., 1948. Bar: Ohio 1948, Tex. 1979, U.S. Dist. Ct. (no. dist.) Ohio 1972, U.S. Dist. Ct. (we. dist.) Tex. 1979, U.S. Ct. Appeals (D.C., 5th, 9th and 11th cirs.), U.S. Ct. Claims, U.S. Tax Ct., U.S. Ct. Mil. Appeals, U.S. Army Ct. Mil. Rev., U.S. Supreme Ct. 1956. Enlisted U.S. Army, 1941, commd. 2d lt., 1942, advanced through grades to col., 1965; gen. counsel, assoc. prof. of law U.S. Mil. Acad. U.S. Army, West Point, N.Y., 1964-66; mem. faculty, chief pubs. div. Judge Advocate Gen.'s Sch. U.S. Army, Charlottesville, Va., 1953-57; dep. chief mil. justice U.S. Army, Washington, 1963-64, prosecutor, mil trial judge, dep. gen. counsel Ryukyus, Japan, 1950-53; staff judge adv., gen. counsel Seventh U.S. Army Support Command, Fed. Republic Germany, 1958-61; sr. judge, chief judge U.S. Ct. Mil. Rev. U.S. Army, Washington, 1968-71; sr. trial atty., atty.-in-charge spl. ops. U.S. Dept. Justice, Washington, 1971-78; asst. U.S. atty. U.S. Dist. Ct. (we. dist.) Tex., 1978-82; pvt. practice San Antonio. Arbitrator U.S. Dist. Ct. (we. dist.) Tex., 1982—; arbitrator, mediator Am. Arbitration Assn., 1986—, Forums, Inc.; pvt. judge Pvt. Adjudication Ctr., Duke U. Decorated Legion of Merit, Army Commendation medal with two bronze oak leaf clusters, European Theater Combat star, other medals. Mem. Tex. State Bar Assn., San Antonio Bar Assn., DAV (jr. vice comdr. 1985). Avocations: skiing, golf, racquetball, water sports, aviation. Died Feb. 23, 2007.

PORGES, LOIS HELEN See WEISBERG, LOIS

POSNER, ROY EDWARD, retired finance executive; b. Chgo., Aug. 24, 1933; s. Lew and Julia (Cvetan) P.; m. Donna Lea Williams, June 9, 1956 (div. May 1991); children: Karen Lee, Sheryl Lynn. Student, U. Ill., 1951-53, Internat. Accountants Soc., 1956-59, Loyola U., Chgo., 1959; grad., Advanced Mgmt. Program, Harvard U., 1976. CPA, Ill. Pub. acct. Frank W. Dibble Co., Chgo., 1956-61; supr. Harris, Kerr, Forster & Co. (C.P.A.s), Chgo., 1961-66; with Loews Corp., NYC, 1966-98, v.p. fin. svcs., chief fin. officer, 1973-86, sr. v.p., chief fin. officer, 1986-98, ret. Fin. cons. N.Y. Football Giants, Inc., Rutherford, N.J.; bd. dirs. Bulova Italy S.P.A., Milan, Bulova Systems and Instruments Corp., N.Y.C., Loews Hotels Monaco S.A.M., Monte Carlo, Monaco, Loews Internat. Svcs. S.A., Switzerland, G F Corp., Youngstown, Ohio, Taj Mahal Holding Corp., Atlantic City, CNA Surety Corp., Chgo. Mem. editorial com.: Uniform System of Accounting for Hotels, 7th edit. Pres. No. Regional Valley High Sch. Music Parents Assn., 1978-79; trustee Loews Found., N.Y.C. With U.S. Army, 1953-55. Mem. AICPA, Fin. Execs. Inst., Ins. Acctg. and Stats. Assn., Internat. Hospitality Accts. Assn., Am. Hotel and Motel Assn., Ill. Soc. CPAs, N.Y. State CPAs (chmn. com. on hotel restaurant and club acctg. 1980-82), Tri-County Golf Assn. (treas. 1985-88, v.p. 1988-89), Alpine Country Club (bd. govs. 1982-94, exec. com. 1982-90, pres. 1988-90), Delta Tau Delta. Died Dec. 31, 2006.

POST, GERALD V., business educator; s. Vernon and Doris Post. BA, U. Wis., Eau Claire, 1978; PhD, Iowa State U., 1983. Asst. prof. Oakland U., Rochester Hills, Mich., 1982-89; prof. Western Ky. U., Bowling Green, 1989-99; prof. dept. bus. U. of the Pacific, Stockton, Calif., from 1999. Cons. analyst/programmer The Wala Group, Arden Hills, Minn., 1985-99. Author: Management Information Systems, 2012, Database Management Systems, 2014, Data Mining Business Applications, 2013; contbr. articles to profl. jours. Home: Stockton, Calif. Died Oct. 20, 2014.

POSTERARO, ANTHONY FRANCIS, periodontist; b. NYC, Dec. 5, 1915; s. Vincent and Connie Dora (Iorio) P.; m. Ligia M. Paganelli, June 23, 1943; children: Anthony Francis Jr., Robert, David. AB, Fordham U., 1939; DDS, St. Louis U., 1943; cert. in periodontia, NYU, 1952. Pvt. practice, NYC, from 1947. Dental surgeon Boys Club N.Y., N.Y.C., 1947-50; mem. dental staff N.Y. Eye and Ear Infirmary, N.Y.C., 1952-56; instr. periodontics NYU Coll. Dentistry, N.Y.C., 1952-56, asst. prof. periodontics and oral medicine, 1956-68, assoc. prof., 1969-70, assoc. prof. grad. prosthodontics, 1970-72, assoc. prof. periodontics, 1973-75, clin. assoc. prof., 1976-88; sec. William J. Gies Found. for Advancement Dentistry, Bethesda, Md., 1975-89. Assoc. editor Annals Dentistry, 1963-79. Spl. examiner Mcpl. CSC City N.Y., 1955; mem. adv. com. N.Y. State Edn. Dept., 1970. Capt. AUS, 1943-46, PTO. Recipient Instr. of Yr. award NYU Sr. Class and Student Coun., 1961, 63, 64, 66, sv. citation NYU Coll. Dentistry, 1977, Chmn.'s award Am. Cancer Soc., N.Y.C., 1986, 87, 88, Pierre Fauchard award Pierre Fauchard Acad., 1988. Fellow Am. Coll. Dentists (chmn. 1968-69), N.Y. Acad. Dentistry (chmn. exec. com. 1960, 72, 73, pres. 1973); mem. ADA (del. 1964-77), 1st Dist. Dental Soc. (pres. 1963), Delta Sigma Delta, Omicron Kappa Upsilon. Roman Catholic. Avocations: travel, reading. Home: Larchmont, NY. Died Dec. 31, 2006.

POTTER, DAVID LYNN, retail executive; b. Vincennes, Ind., Sept. 1, 1938; s. Lynn David and Margaret Francis (Gould) P.; m. Katherine Bonner Harris, Feb. 18, 1961; children: Michael, Bradley, Gregory. BS in Bus. with honors, Eastern Ill. U., 1971. Supr. data processing Golden Rule Ins. Co., Lawrenceveille, Ill., 1961-67; instr. data processing Vincennes (Ind.) U., 1967-69; adminstr. Weber Med. Clinic, Olney, Ill., 1971-77; v.p. Harris Supply Co., Inc., Olney, 1977-87, pres., from 1987. Bd. dirs. Weber Med. Found., Olney, 1992—; mem. Richland County Bd., Olney, 1989-90; mem. governing bd. Richland Meml. Hosp., Olney, 1989-90; mem. citizens adv. com. East Richland Sch. Dist., Olney, 1982-83. With U.S. Navy, 1956-59. Mem. Petroleum Club, Elks, Delta Mu Delta. Avocations: tennis, fishing, travel, gardening, gourmet cooking. Home: Olney, Ill. Died Nov. 25, 2006.

PRANGE, SALLY BOWEN, artist, potter; b. Valparaiso, Ind., Aug. 11, 1927; d. Milton Matern and Sarah Louise (Mammen) Bowen; m. A.J. Prange Jr., Feb. 4, 1950 (div. Mar. 1993); children: Christine Anne, Martha Louise, Laura Beth, David Elliott. BA, U. Mich., 1950. One-woman shows at Greenwood Gallery, Washington, 1980, Greenwich House Pottery, N.Y.C., 1983, Olson & Larson Gallery, West Des Moines, Iowa, 1984, Contemporary Crafts Gallery, Portland, Oreg., 1986, Gallery Moderne, Syracuse, N.Y., 1987, Durham (N.C.) Art Guild, 1993, Lee Hansley Gallery, Raleigh, N.C., 1993, Jane Tyndall Gallery, Durham, N.C., 1999, Gallery C., Raleigh, N.C., 2001; exhibited in group shows at N.C. Pottery Ctr., Seagrove, N.C., Grossmont Coll., El Cajon, Calif., Greater Reston (Va.) Arts Ctr., 1984, Kyoto (Japan) Crafts Ctr., 1986, Pewabic Pottery, Detroit, 1990, No. Ariz. U., Flagstaff, 1993, Tyndall Gallery, Durham, 1993, Am. Embassy, Tokyo, 1993; represented in permanent collections at L.A. County Mus., Calif., Renwick Mus., Wash., D.C., Mint Mus. Craft and Design, N.C., So. Progress Corp., Birmingham, Ala., N.C. Mus. History, Raleigh, Everson Mus. Art, Syracuse, N.Y., Victoria & Albert Mus., London, Nat. Mus. Am. Art, Washington, Museo Internazionale della Ceramiche, Faenza, Italy, Glazo Corp, N.C.; TV interview: N.C. People WUNC, 1995; contbr. chpts. in book. Mem. Nat. Coun. Edn. in Ceramic Arts, Am. Craft Coun., Piedmont Crafts, Tri-State Sculptors Guild. Avocations: scuba diving, amateur radio, ballroom dancing. Home: Chapel Hill, NC. Died Aug. 7, 2007.

PRATCHETT, SIR TERRY (TERENCE DAVID JOHN PRATCHETT), writer; b. Beaconsfield, Buckinghamshire, Eng., Apr. 28, 1948; s. David and Eileen P.; m. Lyn Pratchett; 1 child, Rhianna. Student, Wycombe Tech. High Sch.; DLitt (hon.), Univ. Warwick, 1999, Univ. Portsmouth, 2001, Univ. Bristol, 2004; PhD (hon.), Bucks New, 2008; LittD (hon.), U. Dublin, 2008, U. Bradford, 2009. Newspaper reporter, 1965—80; press officer Ctrl. Electricity Generating Bd., 1980—87. Author: (novels) The Carpet People, 1971, The Dark Side of the Sun, 1976, Strata, 1981, The Unadulterated Cat, 1989, Good Omens, 1990 (World Fantasy best novel nominee), (Discworld series-fiction) The Colour of Magic, 1983, The Light Fantastic, 1986, Equal Rites, 1987, Mort, 1987, Sourcery, 1988, Wyrd Sisters, 1988, Pyramids, 1989, Guards!Guards!, 1989, Eric, 1990, Moving Pictures, 19990, Reaper Man, 1991, Witches Abroad, 1991, Small Gods, 1992, Lords and Ladies, 1992, Men at Arms, 1993, Soul Music, 1994, Interesting Times, 1994, Maskerade, 1995, Feet of Clay, 1996, Hogfather, 1996 (Brit. Fantasy Soc. best novel nominee, 1996), Jingo, 1997 (Brit Fantasy Soc. best novel nominee, 1997), The Last Continent, 1998, Carpe Jugulum, 1998, The Fifth Elephant, 1999, The Truth, 2000, Thief of Time, 2001, Night Watch, 2002, Monstrous Regiment, 2003, Going Postal, 2004 (Bollinger Everyman Wodehouse Prize for comic writing nominee, 2005), Thud!, 2005; (Discworld-non-fiction) The Science of Discworld, 1992, Streets of Ankh Morpork, 1993, The Discworld Companion, 1994, The Pratchett Portfolio, 1996, The Science of Discworld III: Darwin's Watch, 2005, I Shall Wear Midnight, 2011, (with Stephen Briggs)Turtle Recall, 2012, The World of Poo, 2012, Raising Stream, 2014, The Shepard's Crown, 2015; (Bromeliad) Truckers, 1988, Diggers, 1990, Wings, 1990; (Discworld childrens) Amazing Maurice and His Educated Rodents, 2001 (Carnegie medal, 2001), The Wee Free Men, 2003, A Hat Full of Sky, 2004; (Johnny Maxwell series) Only You Can Save Mankind, 1992, Johnny and the Dead, 1993, Johnny and the Bomb, 1996 (Smarties Silver award, 1996); co-author (with Neil Galman) Good Omens: The Nice and Accurate Prophecies of Agnes Nutter, Witch, (with Stephen Baxter) The Long Earth, 2012 Recipient BCA Sci. Fiction award, 1993, Writers Guild award for children's books, 1993, Bookseller Services to Bookselling award, Brit. Book awards, 2000; named Best Sci. Fiction Author, SFX Awards, 1996; named an Officer of the Most Excellent Order of British Empire (OBE) for Svc. to Lit., Her Majesty Queen Elizabeth II, 1998, Knight for Svc. to Lit., 2009; named to SFX Hall of Fame for contributions to Sci. Fiction lit., 1996. Avocations: computers, walking. Died Mar. 12, 2015.

PRATHER, WILLIAM C., III, lawyer, writer; b. Toledo, Ill., Feb. 20, 1921; s. Hollie Cartmill and Effie Fern (Deppen) P. BA, U. Ill., 1942, JD, 1947. Bar: Ill. 1947, U.S. Supreme Ct. 1978. Co-pres. student govt. U. Ill., 1942, asst. dean, 1942-43; atty. First Nat. Bank Chgo., 1947-51; asst. gen. counsel U.S. Savs. and Loan League, Chgo., 1951-59; gen. counsel U.S. League of Savs. Instns., Chgo., 1959-82, gen. counsel emeritus, from 1982; sole practice Cumberland County, Ill., from 1981. Sem. lectr. in law, banking. Editor: The Legal Bulletin, 1951-81, The Federal Guide, 1954-81; author: Savings Accounts, 8th edit., 1981; contbr. articles to publs. Founder Civility Found. America Civility Ctr., Toledo, Ill. Served to lt. US Army, ASTP, D-3 mil. govt. France, Germany, 1943—45. Decorated Bronze Star. Mem. ABA, FBA, Internat. Bar Assn., Ill. Bar Assn., Chgo. Bar Assn., Union Internat. des Avocats, Nat. Lawyers Club Washington, Cosmos Club, Univ. Club Chgo., Kiwanis, Mattoon Golf and Country Club, Exeter and County Club (Eng.), Am. Club Riviera (France), Tennis Club de Beaulieu (France), Soc. Colonial Wars, St. Andrew's Soc., Am. Legion, Phi Delta Phi, Phi Gamma Delta, Phi Eta Sigma, Phi Alpha Chi. Home: Toledo, Ill. Died Jan. 16, 2016.

PREAUS, FREDERICK F., lawyer; b. Ruston, La., Oct. 19, 1937; s. Frederick Tidwell and Mona (Gill) P. BBA, Tulane U., 1960, JD, 1962. Bar: La. 1962, Calif. 1990, U.S. Dist. Ct. (ctrl. dist) Calif. 1996, U.S. Dist. (so. dist.) Calif. 1997. Pvt. practice, LA, 1986-97, San Diego, from 1997. Mem. Omicron Delta Kappa. Home: San Diego, Calif. Died Nov. 25, 2006.

PREDMORE, MARIAN CORINNE, retired teacher, volunteer; b. Pittsburg, Kans., July 12, 1923; d. Robert W. and Retta S. Hart; m. William D. Predmore, Oct. 18, 1947; children: Richard L., Robert C. BA, Kans. State Coll., Pitts., 1944; MS, Kans. State U., 1948. Tchr. various secondary schs., Kans., 1944-56, Salina (Kans.) Pub. Schs., 1962-68. Lectr. 1987-90. Editor: Informational Guide to Social Services in Saline County, 1974. Bd. dirs. Saline (Kans.) Girls Home, 1972-75; vol. Salina (Kans.) Day Care Ctr., 1970-72; docent Kans. Mus. of History, 1984—; mission chmn. United Meth. Ch., Silver Lake, Kans., 1988-90; v.p. LWV, Salina, 1970. Mem. AAUW (pres. Norton br. Kans., 1981-82). Home: Wichita, Kans. Died Feb. 23, 2007.

PRESS, ARTHUR I., health services company executive, consultant; b. NYC, July 19, 1934; m. Helen Press; 4 Children. BS, L.I. U., MBA with honors; DPA, NYU. CPA, NY. Acct. various acctg. firms, NY, 1954-60; auditor-in-charge U.S. Army Audit Agy., NY, 1960-63; assoc. adminstr., dep. med. dir. Maimonides Med. Ctr., NY, 1963—68, CEO, 1968—70, CEO, Bronx Lebanon Med Ctr, NY, 1970—77, CEO, Maimonides Med. Ctr., 1977—79; sole owner & CEO Accredited Care Inc., Alpha Health Svc. Corp., N.J., Fla., White Plains, NY, 1979-91; Mainstream Pers. Group Inc., White Plains, 1992—. Cons. Adept Recruiting Corp., N.Y. Corps Under 20,000,000, 1990—; pres. Internat. Specialty Creations, Inc., 1992—; adj. prof. Manhattan Borough of N.Y., 1979-83; preceptor grad. students NYU, 1974-79, Barusch Sch. Bus., 1978, 79; budget, fin. strategic planning com. mem., guest lectr. on mgmt., health economics Am. Med. Assn., 1968-79. Contbr. scientific papers to profl. publs., articles to profl. jours. Chmn. Age As a Barrier to Health Benefits Pub.'s Health Svcs., Ednl. Tasks and Comprehensive Health Planning, 1974—84; bd. dir. Sunrise Condominium, 1984—96, pres., 1986—96; dir. Mahagony Run Condominium, St. Thomas, Va., 1985—92, Austin Condominium, 1989—2006; treas. Hidden Ridge Home Assn., 2006—12; bd. dir. Donnaklein Jewish Acad., from 2012. Recipient Adminstr. Meritorious award Internat. Security Assn., N.Y., 1975; grant NIH, Use of Antimicrobial Agents. Fellow Am. Health Assn. Avocations: bridge, golf, swimming. Home: Boca Raton, Fla. Died Mar. 29, 2015.

PREVILL, ARTHUR ERNEST, retired engineer; b. Rand, W.Va., Oct. 9, 1921; s. Harry Victor and Josephine (Olish) P.; m. Dorothy Martha Beaulieu, Sept. 19, 1952; children: Arthur E. Jr., Victor G., Amanda J., Steven M. BSEE, W.Va. U., 1946. Registered profl. engr., Fla., Md., Va., N.J., Pa., Del., Ga. Layout engr. West Pa. Power Co., Pitts., 1946-48; apllications engr. GE, Lynn, Mass., 1948-49; elec. engr. Johns-Manville Corp., Manville, N.J., 1949-51; design engr. Austin Co., Roselle, N.J., 1951-53; field engr. Rust Co., USAF Testing Lab., Tullahoma, Tenn., 1953-54; design engr. So. Co., Birmingham, Ala., 1954-55; head elc. div. E.J. Sullivan & Assocs., NYC, 1955-58; asst. supr. M.W. Kellogg Co., N.Y., Md., 1958-60; prin. A.E. Previll & Assocs., Silver Spring, Md., 1960-71; engring. mgr., v.p. UPI of Westinghouse and DESC, Balt. and, Va., 1971-84. Mem. Am. Legion, Toastmaster. Home: Silver Spring, Md. Died Dec. 25, 2006.

PRICE, ARNOLD HEREWARD, historian; b. Bonn, Germany, July 1, 1912; arrived in U.S., 1933; s. Hereward Thimbleby and Liese Price; children: Jeffrey Thomas, John Brigham(dec.) , William Frederick Stephen. BA, U. Mich., MA in History, PhD in History, U. Mich. Asst. supt. U. Mich. Arch. Lab. W.P.A., Ann Arbor; analyst Libr. of Congress, Washington; intelligence analyst OSS, Washington; rsch. tchr. U.S. Army, Ft. Eustis, Va.; intelligence State Dept., Washington; spl. historian supr. Libr. of Congress, Washington; chief bibliographer Am. Hist. Assn., Washington. Author: The Evolution of the Zollverein, 1949, Missionary to the Malagasy, 1980, The Germanic Warrior Cubs, 1996, My Twentieth Century, 2003; contbr. articles to profl. jours. Sgt. US Army. Recipient Bronson-Thomas award, U. Mich., 1935, honoree, ABC-Clio Hist. Soc., 1985. Mem.: Assn. for the Bibliography of History, Am. Hist. Assn., OSS Soc. Home: Springfield, Va. Died Dec. 10, 2006.

PRICE, CLEMENT ALEXANDER, historian, educator; b. Washington, 1945; s. James L. Price; m. Mary Sue Sweeney, Dec. 10, 1988. BA, MA, U. Bridgeport; PhD in American History, Rutgers U.; PhD (hon.), William Paterson U.; D (hon.), Rutgers U., 2014. Co-founder Marion Thompson Wright Series, 1981; Bd. Govs. Disting. svc. prof. history Rutgers U., Newark, dir. Inst. on Ethnicity, Culture, and the Modern Experience, 1996—2014. Vice chair President's Advisory Coun. on Historic Preservation, 2011—14. Author: Freedom Not Far Distant: A Documentary History of Afro-Americans in New Jersey, 1980, Many Voices, Many Opportunities: Cultural Pluralism & American Arts Policy, 1994, Slave Culture: A Documentary Collection of the Slave Narratives from the Federal Writers' Project, 2014; co-author: Encyclopedia of the Harlem Renaissance, 2003; contbr. articles to profl. jours. Recipient Lifetime Achievement award, Local Initiatives Support Corp. (LISC) NJ, 2008, Dr. Martin Luther King, Jr. Leadership award, Essex County, 2010, The NJ Nets Basketball Black History Month award, 2011; co-recipient President's Award, Newark Public Libr., 2005; named Prof. of Yr. for NJ, Coun. for Advancement & Support of Edn., 1999; named to The Rutgers U. Hall Disting. Alumni, 2006. Fellow: NJ Hist. Soc.; mem.: Woodrow Wilson Nat. Fellowship Found. (Inaugural Scholar in Residence), NJ Hist. Commn. (Richard J. Hughes award), NJ Coun. on Arts (chmn. 1980—83), Urban League of Essex County, Save Ellis Island Found., Geraldine R. Dodge Found. Died Nov. 5, 2014.

PRICE, EARNEST, JR., religious educator, minister; b. Ellisville, Miss., Mar. 6, 1919; s. Earnest and Vivian (Jordan) P.; m. Catherine Upchurch, May 9, 1941; 1 child, Catherine Elizabeth. BS, Miss. State U., 1940; MA, Columbia U., Union Theol. Sem., 1948; postgrad., Union Theol. Sem., 1945-51. Ordained to ministry, United Ch. of Christ. Assoc. exec. dir. YMCA, Miss. State U., 1940-42, exec. dir., 1943-47; exec. dir. YMCA, coord. religious activities La. State U., Baton Rouge, 1948-53; exec. dir. YMCA, dir. religious life Miss. State U., 1953-56; assoc. exec. dir. Cen. Atlantic Area Coun. YMCA, Newark, 1956-61; assoc. exec. dir. coll. and univ. div. Nat. Coun. YMCA's, NYC, 1961-69, dir. manpower planning, 1969-73, dep. dir. nat. pers. svcs., 1973-77; Kearns prof., dir. human rels. studies High Point (N.C.) Coll., 1977-85; congregational care pastor 1st United Meth. Ch., High Point, 1985-92. Cons. personell adminstrn. S.E. Region Coun. YMCAs, Atlanta, 1977-81, YMCA Greater N.Y., N.Y.C., 1977-78; trustee Am. Humanics, Inc., Kansas City, Mo., 1972—; pres. Nat. Assn. Coll. & Univ. YMCA Dirs., 1953-56. Contbr. articles to profl. jours. Pres. Community Chest, 1960, United Fund, 1961, both Glen Ridge, N.J.; bd. dirs. United Way Greater High Point, 1981-87, High Point Drug Action Coun., 1981-87, Vol. Action Ctr., High Point, 1988-90; bd. dirs., vice-chair Urban Ministry, High Point, 1989—, chair, 1990—; bd. dirs. Habitat for Humanity, High Point, 1990—, vice-chair, 1991—. With U.S. Army, 1942-43. Mem. Kiwanis (bd. dirs. Glen Ridge chpt. 1976-77), Rotary (bd. dirs. Starkville, Miss. chpt. 1955-56), ACLU, Common Cause, Amnesty Internat., People for Am. Way, Clergy and Laity Concerned, Ams. for Dem. Action, Omicron Delta Kappa, Alpha Phi Omega. Democrat. Avocations: golf, classical music, money markets, gardening, travel. Home: Durham, NC. Died June 18, 2007.

PRIDDY, THOMAS WAYNE, brokerage house executive; b. Atlanta, July 8, 1938; s. Robert Thomas Priddy and Ruby Pauline (Dickey) Dobson; m. Gwendolyn Raburn, Sept 26, 1960 (div. 1968); children: Thomas Wayne Jr., Kimberley, Britt, Casey. Student, U. Ga., 1956-57, Ga. State U., 1968. Truck driver Don Swann Sales Corp., Atlanta, 1954-58, salesman, 1958-60, office mgr., 1960-64, v.p., chief exec. officer, 1964-73, owner, chief exec. officer, 1973-88; ptnr. Howard Southern Brokerage, Atlanta, from 1988. Mem. Network Assn. (dir. 1986-88), So. Paper Trade Assn. (dir. 1987-88), Prsche Club Am., Elks, Sigma Nu Alumni. Avocations: art, music, travel. Home: Alpharetta, Ga. Died Mar. 29, 2007.

PRIMAKOV, YEVGENIY MAKSIMOVICH, Russian government official; b. Kiev, Ukraine, Oct. 29, 1929; married; 1 child. Grad., Moscow Inst. Oriental Studies, 1953; PhD in Econ., Moscow State U., 1956. Corr., dep., then editor-in-chief State Com. for TV and Broadcasting, 1953-62; news analyst, dep. editor, corr. for Arab countries Pravda, 1962-70; dep. dir. Inst. World Economy and Internat. Rels. U.S.S.R. (now Russian) Acad. Scis., 1977, dir., 1985-89, dir. Inst. Oriental Studies, 1977-85; head, first main directorate and first dep. chief KGB, 1991; dir. U.S.S.R. (now Russian) Ctrl. Intelligence Svc., 1991, Russian Fgn. Intelligence Svc., 1991-96; min. fgn. affairs Russia, 1996-98; prime minister, 1998-99. Mem. CPSU, 1959-91, mem. ctrl. com., 1989-91; cand. mem. Politburo, 1989-90; elected to Congress of People's Deps. of U.S.S.R., 1989; chmn. Coun. of Unions of Supreme Soviet U.S.S.R., 1989-90; mem. Security Coun. and Presdl. Coun., 1989-90; Pres. Gorbachev's spl. envoy to Gulf, 1990-91. Author: (with I.P. Belyayev) Egypt under Nasser, 1975, The War Which Could Be Avoided, 1991. Died June 26, 2015.

PRIMM, BENY JENE, addiction treatment foundation administrator; b. Williamson, W.Va., May 21, 1928; s. George Oliver and Willie Henrietta (Martin) P.; m. Annie Delphine Evans (dec. 1975); children: Annelle, Martine, Jeanine Primm Jones, Eraka Bath Fortuit. BS, W.Va. State Coll., 1950, DSc (hon.), 1994; cert. fin. studies, MD, U. Geneva, 1959. Lic. physician, Calif., N.Y., N.J., W.Va., Mass. Dir. med. affairs Interfaith Hosp., Jamaica, N.Y., 1965, 66; assoc. anesthesiologist Harlem Hosp. Ctr., NYC, 1966-68, founder, dir. Narcotics Hosp. Orientation Ctr., 1968, 69; founder, exec. dir. Addiction Rsch. and Treatment (now Start Treatment and Recovery Centers), Bklyn., 1969—2013; founder, pres. Urban Resource Inst., Bklyn., 1981—2015; dir. Nat. Ctr. For Substance Abuse Treatment Dept. Health & Human Svcs., Rockville, Md., 1989-93. U.S. speaker U.S. Info. Agy., East and West Africa, 1989; U.S. rep. World Summit on Substance Abuse and AIDS, HHS, London, 1990; presdl. appointee Presdl. Commn. on Human Immunodeficiency Virus, The White House, Washington, 1987-88. Co-author: (memoir) The Healer: A Doctor's Crusade Against Addition and AIDS, 2014. Bd. dirs. Meharry Med. Coll., Nashville, 1988—, W.Va. State Coll. Found., 1993—. 1st lt. U.S. Army, 1950-52. Recipient Cert. of Commendation, HHS, 1988. Mem. Coll. on Problems of

Drug Dependence (bd. dirs. 1989-93, J. Michael Morrison award for sci. adminstrn. 1993), Nat. Med. Assn., Nat. Minority AIDS coun. (bd. dirs. 1994), Black Leadership Commn. on AIDS (bd. dirs. 1989). Avocations: tennis, golf. Home: New Rochelle, NY. Died Oct. 16, 2015.

PRINCE, THOMAS RICHARD, accountant, educator; b. New Albany, Miss., Dec. 7, 1934; s. James Thompson and Callie Florence (Howell) P.; m. Eleanor Carol Polkoff, July 14, 1962; children: Thomas Andrew, John Michael, Adrienne Carol. BS, Miss. State U., 1956, MS, 1957; PhD in Accountancy, U. Ill., 1962. CPA, Ill. Instr. U. Ill., 1960—62; mem. faculty Northwestern U. Kellogg Sch. Mgmt., Evanston, Ill., from 1962, prof. acctg. info. and mgmt., from 1969, chmn. dept. acctg. info. and mgmt., 1968—75, prof. health industry mgmt., from 1990; cons. in field. Dir. Applied Rsch. Sys., Inc. Author: Extension of the Boundaries of Accounting Theory, 1962, Information Systems for Management Planning and Control, 3d edit, 1975, Financial Reporting and Cost Control for Health Care Entities, 1992, Product Life-Cycle Costing and Management of Large-Scale Medical Systems Investments, 1997, Strategic Management for Health Care Entities: Creative Frameworks for Financial and Operational Analysis, 1998. 1st lt. US Army Fin. Corps, 1957—60. Mem. AICPA, INFORMS, AHA, HFMA, HIMMS, AUPHA, Am. Accounting Assn., Am. Econ. Assn., Fin. Execs. Inst., AAAS, Ill. Soc. CPA, Inst. Mgmt. Acct., Alpha Tau Omega, Phi Kappa Phi, Omicron Delta Kappa, Delta Sigma Pi, Beta Alpha Psi. Congregationalist. Home: Kenilworth, Ill. Died Jan. 8, 2015.

PRINCE, WILLIAM TALIAFERRO, retired federal judge; b. Norfolk, Va., Oct. 3, 1929; s. James Edward and Helen Marie (Taliaferro) P.; m. Anne Carroll Hannegan, Apr. 12, 1958; children: Sarah Carroll Prince Pishko, Emily Taliaferro, William Taliaferro, John Hannegan, Anne Martineau Thompson, Robert Harrison. Student, Coll. William and Mary, Norfolk, 1947-48, 49-50; AB, Williamsburg, 1955, BCL, 1957, MLT, 1959. Bar: Va. 1957. Lectr. acctg. Coll. William & Mary, 1955-57; lectr. law Marshall-Wythe Sch. Law, 1957-59; assoc. Williams, Kelly & Greer, Norfolk, 1959-63, ptnr., 1963-90; US magistrate judge US Dist. Ct. (ea. dist.) Va., Norfolk, 1990-2000; ret., 2000; recalled Ct. Appeals 4th Cir., from 2000, Ct. Appeals 10th Cir., 2002, Ct. Appeals 3d Cir., 2002, 2010—11, Ct. Appeals 6th Cir., 2003, Ct. Appeals 5th Cir., 2003, 2009; spl. assignment mem. Southern Dist. NYS, 2006, Eastern Dist. Calif., 2009. Pres. Am. Inn of Ct. XXVII, 1987-89. Bd. editors: The Virginia Lawyer, A Basic Practice Handbook, 1966. Bd. dirs. Madonna Home, Inc., 1978-93, Soc. Alumni of Coll. William and Mary, 1985-88. Fellow Am. Coll. Trial Lawyers, Am. Bar Found., Va. Law found. (bd. dirs. 1976-90); mem. ABA (ho. of dels. 1984-90), Am. Judicature Soc. (bd. dirs. 1984-88), Va. State Bar (coun. 1973-77, exec. com. 1975-80, pres. 1978-79). Roman Catholic. Home: Norfolk, Va. Died Dec. 15, 2014.

PRINGLE, GEORGE OVERTON, real estate developer, business owner, lawyer; b. Oak Park, Ill., Sept. 11, 1923; s. Henry L. and Dorothy (Overton) P.; m. Elisabeth M. Burrell, Nov. 3, 1944; children: George Hale, John Allen, Frank Warren, David Lawrence. LLB, U. Fla., 1948, BSME, 1965. Bar: Fla. 1948, U.S. Dist. Ct. (so. dist.) Fla. 1948. Pvt. practice law, Leesburg, Fla., 1948-55; air conditioning sales rep. The Williamson Co., Cin., 1955-58; pvt. HVAC contractor Leesburg, 1958-64; engr., mgr. Chrysler Corp., Dayton, Ohio, 1965-75; pvt. exporter Dayton, 1975-80; developer, CEO Scottish Highland, Inc. (now Pringle Devel., Inc.), Leesburg, from 1980. Mgr. govt. sales Chrysler Airtemp, Dayton, 1968-75; mgr. OEM Sales, 1970-75, mgr. bldg. system devel., 1972-73. Author: (booklet) "How to Buy Your Home in Florida", 1985; inventor gate latch, hand blower. Mission pilot and angel flight pilot, CAP, Col. Wing comdr., ex. comdr. local squadron and group. Recipient Spl. Recognition award NASA, Cape Kennedy, Fla., 1967, Community Svc. award League Cities, 1993. Mem. Kiwanis (bd. dirs. 1950-52), Leesburg Area C. of C. (bd. dirs. 1991—). Republican. Presbyterian. Avocations: flying, music, ballroom dancing. Home: Leesburg, Fla. Died Dec. 8, 2006.

PRIVITERA, JOSEPH F., retired foreign service official, writer, researcher; b. NYC, Feb. 22, 1914; s. Luigi and Grazia (Paparcuri) Privitera; m. Bettina La Marca, June 30, 1935; children: Joseph Henry, Stephen Louis. BS with honors, NYU, 1935, PhD, 1938; cert. phonetics course, U. Paris, 1936; cert., U. Mex., Mexico City, 1939. Instr. French, NYU, NYC, 1938; asst. prof. Romance langs. St. Louis U., 1939-45; fgn. svcs. officer, dir. Bi-Nat. Cultural Ctr., U.S. Dept. State, Sao Paulo, Brazil, 1945-47; fgn. svc. officer Am. Consulate Gen., Sao Paulo, 1947-50, Am. Embassy, Quito, Ecuador, 1950-52; dir. Italian broadcasts Voice of Am., U.S. Dept. State, NYC, 1955-76; ret., 1976. Author: Charles Chevillet de Chmpmeslé, 1942-1701, 1938, The Latin American Front, 1945, Portrait of America, 1947, Perfil Cultural de America, 1951, Luigi Pirandello, His Plays in Sicilian, 1998, Beginner's Sicilian, 1998; author: (in Italian and English) A Treasury of Italian Cuisine, 1998; author: Faustus in Love, and Other Poems in English and Other Tongues, 1998, Italy, An Illustrated History, 2000, Beginner's Italian, 2000, Sicily, An Illustrated History, 2001; editor (translator): Reference Grammar of Medieval Italian with a Dual Language Edition of the Thirty-One Poems of Dante's Vita Nova, 2001; author: If I Were Minister of Education and Other Poems, Mellen, 2001; author: (with Bettina Privitera) The Mystery of the Sanfratellan Dialect, the Sicilians Legos, 2001; author: Sicilian Dictionary and Phrase Book Hippocrene, 2003, Hippocreue, 2003, The Sicilian Language, 2004, Canti Siciliani, Original Poems in Sicilian and English translation, 2004, Al Qaida, The Early Years, 2004, The Subconscious, Oedipus To Abu Ghraib, 800 B.C.-2004 A.D., 2004, Canti Lidiani, Original Love Poems, 2005, (seri-comic mini opera) EPIC Song of Love and Lust, 2006; co-author: Language as Historical Determinant-The Normans in Sicily, 1060-1200, 1995, Songs of Love and of the Times, 2006. Mem.: Diplomats and Consular Officers Ret. Avocations: salon photographer, amateur flutist. Died Mar. 6, 2007.

PROVDA, LOIS M., psychologist, educator; BS in Social Studies, Boston U., BS in English, 1962; MA in Spl. Edn., NYU, 1964, PhD in Ednl. Psychology, 1983. Cert. marriage, family and child counselor, learning handicapped specialist, reading specialist, advanced study in edn. 1976. Ednl. dir. Payne Whitney Psychiat. Clinic NY Hosp., NYC, 1964—68; dir. reading Buckingham Sch., Bklyn., 1968—73; instr. CUNY, Bklyn., 1973—76, UCLA, 1996—2003; ednl. psychologist LA, from 1976. Ednl. cons. NY Assn. Blind, NYC, 1974—76; ednl. specialist psychol. svcs. dept. Bur. Jewish Edn., LA, from 1982; with Northern LA Select Blue Ribbon Com. on Autism, from 2009; bd. dirs. Kol Hanearim, Inglewood; inventor Pencil Grip Inc., Inglewood, Calif. Fellow: Orthopsychiatric Assn.; mem.: NY Acad. Sci., Internat. Reading Assn., Am. Assn. Sch. Psychology, Assn. Ednl. Therapists. Deceased.

PROVOST, ROY H., registrar; b. Southbridge, Mass., Jan. 11, 1934; s. James Roy and Florence Mabel (Haynes) P.; m. Carolyn Leworah Leigh, July 11, 1956 (div. Oct. 1969); m. Karen Ann Kupstan, Nov. 2, 1969; children: Laura Ann, Deborah Sharon. BS in Indsl. Engring., Ctrl. New England Coll. Tech., 1979. Rsch. technician Am. Optical Co., Southbridge, 1951-65; indsl. engr. Thom McAn Shoes, Worcester, Mass., 1965-79; engring. designer Floor Corp., Irvine, Calif., 1979-86; registration adminstr. Seminole C.C., Sanford, Fla., from 1987. Lt. U.S. Army, 1956-58, Germany. Jehovah'S Witness. Avocation: golf. Home: Orange City, Fla. Died July 2, 2007.

PRUDHOMME, PAUL (GENE AUTRY PRUDHOMME), chef, restaurant owner; b. Opelousas, La., July 13, 1940; m. Kay Hinrichs (dec.); m. Lori Prudhomme. First restaurant Big Daddy's O's Patio, 1957; sold magazines; sous chef Hotel Le Pavillon, 1970; chef Maison Dupuy; cooked for various restaurants; exec. chef Commander's Palace, New Orleans, 1975—79; owner, chef K-Paul's Louisiana Kitchen, New Orleans, 1979—2015. Creator Chef Paul Prudhomme's Magic Seasoning Blends, 1983. Author: (cookbooks) Louisiana Kitchen, 1984, The Prudhomme Family Cookbook, 1987, Louisiana Cajun Magic, 1989, Seasoned America, 1991, Fork in the Road, 1993, Pure Magic, 1995, Fiery Foods That I Love, 1995, Kitchen Expedition, 1997, Louisiana Tastes, 2000, Always Cooking!, 2007, (booklet for Tabasco) Authentic Cajun Cooking, 1984—89, Louisiana Kitchen: Vol. 1: Cajun Blackened Redfish, 1986, Louisiana Kitchen: Vol. 2:Cajun & Creole Classics, 1990; biography Paul Prudhomme; Cajun Sensation, 2009, host (cooking shows for New Orleans, PBS Affiliate WYES) Fork In the Road, 1995, Fiery Foods, 1996, Kitchen Expedition, 1997, Louisiana Kitchen, 1998, Always Cooking, 2007. Vol. Meals on Wheels, Easter Seals, March of Dimes, Big Brothers/Big Sisters, Chef and the Child. Recipient Restaurateur of Yr., La. State Restaurant Assn., 1983, Lifetime Achievement award, Internat. Assn. Culinary Professionals, 2008; named Culinarian of Yr., Culinary Diplomat, Am. Culinary Fedn., 1994; named to Culinary Hall of Fame. Died Oct. 8, 2015.

PRYOR, WILLIAM DANIEL LEE, humanities educator; b. Lakeland, Fla., Oct. 29, 1926; s. Dahl and Lottie Mae (Merchant) P. AB, Fla. So. Coll., 1949; MA, Fla. State U., Tallahassee, 1950, PhD, 1959; postgrad., U. NC, Chapel Hill, 1952—53; pvt. art studies with Florence Wilde; pvt. voice studies with Colin O'More, Anna Kaskas; pvt. piano studies with Waldemar Hille and audited piano master classes of Ernst von Dohnányi. Asst. prof. English, dir. drama Bridgewater Coll., Va., 1950-52; grad. tchg. fellow humanities Fla. State U., Tallahassee, 1953-55, 57-58; instr. English U. Houston, University Park, Houston, 1955-59, asst. prof., 1959-62, assoc. prof., 1962-71, prof., 1971-97, prof. emeritus, 1997. Vis. instr. English, Fla. So. Coll., Lakeland, MacDill Army Air Base, Tampa, Fla., summer 1951, Tex. So. U., 1961-63, humanities, govt. U. Tex. Dental Br., Houston, 1962-63; lectr. The Women's Inst., Houston, 1967-72, humanities series Jewish Cmty. Ctr., Houston, 1972-73; originator, moderator TV and radio program The Arts in Houston Stas. KUHT-TV and KUHF-FM, 1956-57, 58-63. Author: An Examination of the Southern Milieu in Representative Plays by Southern Dramatists, 1963; contbg. author: National Poetry Anthology, 1952, Panorama das Literaturas das Americas, vol. 2, 1958-60, Perspectives on Ernst von Dohnányi, 2005, Dohnányi Evkönyu 2005, 2006; assoc. editor Forum, 1967, editor, 1967-82; contbr. articles to profl. jours.; dir. Murder in the Cathedral (T.S. Elliot), U. Houston, 1965; performed in opera as Sir Edgar in Der Junge Lord (Henze), Houston Grand Opera Assn., 1967; played the title role in Aella (Chatterton), Am. premiere, U. Houston, 1970. Bd. dir., founding mem. Contemporary Music Soc., Houston, 1958-63, Houston Shakespeare Soc., 1964-67; bd. dirs., founding mem., program annotator Houston Chamber Orch. Soc., 1964-76; narrator Houston Symphony Orch., Houston Summer Symphony Orch., Houston Chamber Orch. (with Charles Rosekrans), U. Houston Symphony Orch., St. Stephen's Music Festival Symphony Orch., New Harmony, Ind.; narrator world premier of The Bells (Jerry McCathern), 1969, U. Houston Symphony Orch., 1969, Am. premier Symphony No. Seven, Antartica (Vaughn-Williams), Houston Symphony Orch. (with Andre Previn), 1967, L'Histoire du Soldat (Stravinski), U. Houston Symphony Orch., 1957, Am. premier Babar the Elephant (Poulenc-Francais), Houston Chamber Orch. (with Charles Rosekrans), 1967, Le Roi David (Honegger), 1979, Voice of God in opera Noye's Fludde (Britten), St. Stephen's Music Festival, New Harmony, Ind. 1981; bd. dir., program annotator Music Guild, Houston, 1960-67, v.p., 1963-67, adv. bd., 1967-70; mem.-at-large, bd. dir. Houston Grand Opera Guild, 1966-67; repertory com. Houston Grand Opera Assn., 1967-70; bd. dir. Houston Grand Opera, 1970-75, adv. bd. 1978-79; cultural adv. com. Jewish Cmty. Ctr., 1960-66; bd. dir. Houston Friends Pub. Libr., 1962-67, 73-75, 1st v.p., 1963-67; adv. mem. cultural affairs com. Houston C. of C., 1972-75; adv. bd. dir. The Wilhelm Schole, 1980-98, Buffalo Bayou Support Com., 1985-87, bd. dir. Moores Sch. Music Soc., 1998—, trustee, 2002-04, advisory bd. dir., 2004—; bd. dir. U. Houston Retiree Assn., 1999-2001, 2011-, v.p., 2000-2001; founding bd. dir. Internat. Dohnányi Rsch. Ctr., Inc., 2002-. Recipient Master Tchg. award Coll. Humanities and Fine Arts U., Houston, 1980, Favorite Prof. award Bapt. Student Union, U. Houston, 1991. Mem. MLA, AAUP, Coll. English Assn., L'Alliance Francaise, English-Speaking Union, Alumni Assn. Fla. So. Coll., Fla. State U., South Ctrl. MLA, Conf. Editors Learned Jours., Coll. Conf. Tchrs. English, Nat. Coun. Tchrs. English, Am. Studies Assn., Shepard Soc. Rice U., Nature Conservancy, Nat. Trust for Hist. Preservation, Inst. Internat. Edn., Century Club, Fla. So. Coll., President's Club, James D. Westcott Legacy Soc., Fla. State U., Tex. Ret. Tchrs. Assn., Phi Beta (patron), Phi Mu Alpha Sinfonia, Alpha Psi Omega, Pi Kappa Alpha, Sigma Tau Delta (Outstanding Prof. English U. Houston chpt. 1990), 1927 Soc. U. Houston, Houston Philos. Soc., Caledonian Club (London), Tau Kappa Alpha, Phi Kappa Phi. Episcopalian. Avocations: tennis, racquetball, swimming, travel. Home: West University Place, Tex. *My commitment is to the humanities. I believe that the most important thing that a teacher can do is to help a student to stand on his/her own intellectual hind legs; to help him/her to learn how to aquire facts; to help him/her to learn how to organize and utilize these facts in intelligent, responsible ways.* Died July 14, 2015.

PUNDY, EILEEN MARION, nurse; b. Mpls., Oct. 15, 1937; d. Leonard Inmond and Olga Luella (Stephensen) P. BA, Augsburg Coll., 1959; grad. practical nursing, Mpls. Vocat. Sch., 1978; diploma, Luth. Deaconess Sch. Nursing, 1982. RN, Minn. Mental health worker Andrew Care Home, Mpls., 1977-79; part time LPN Luth. Deaconess Hosp., Mpls., 1980-82; RN Bloomington (Minn.) Maple Manor, 1982-84; RN, LPN, aide Bodin Pool, Mpls., 1984; RN, night supr. Cedar Pines, Mpls., 1984-88; RN David Herman, Mpls., 1988; RN, evening supr. Bloomington (Minn.) Nursing Home, 1988-89; RN Martin Luther Manor, Bloomington, 1990; RN, evening supr. Chateau Health Care, Mpls., 1991-92; home health nurse Becklund Home Health Agy., Golden Valley, Minn., from 1992, Hampton Health Care, Mpls., from 1992; staff nurse Grand Ave. Residence, Mpls., 1992—2004; ret. Sunday sch. tchr. Grace Ch. in Edina, Minn., 1990—. Avocations: music, reading, working with children, mickey mouse collection, cats and dog. Home: Minneapolis, Minn. Died May 4, 2007.

PUNJ, VIKRAM, engineering administrator; b. Lucknow, India, Feb. 13, 1957; came to U.S., 1983. s. Amrik Lal and Prabha P.; m. Taruna Madan, Apr. 18, 1986. BS in Mech. Engr., Birla Inst. Tech., Pilani, India, 1978; MS in Indsl. Engr. with distinction, Nat. Inst. Tng. in Indsl. Engring., Bombay, 1980; MS in MIS with distinction, London Sch. Econs., 1983. Sys. engr. IBM, Bombay, 1980-82; corp. data adminstr. Internat. Tech. Ventures, Dallas, 1983-84; with Hall Fin. Group, Dallas, 1984-86; disting. mem. tech. staff AT&T Bell Labs, Naperville, Ill., 1986-95; sr. dir. engring. Hughes Network Sys., Germantown, Md., from 1995. Cons. Inlaks Inc., N.Y.C., 1983-86. Contbr. articles to profl. jours.; patentee in field, U.S.A., Japan, Europe. Inlaks Found. scholar London U. Sch. Econs., 1982-83. Mem. IEEE (sr. mem, computer communications tech. com., project 802.6, co-contbr. to standard on met. area networks, tech. editor IEEE Communications mag.). Home: San Jose, Calif. Died May 17, 2007.

PUROHIT, SURENDRA NATH, nuclear scientist; b. Jodhpur, Rajasthan, India, Sept. 18, 1925; s. Biejeyraj Hansraj and Agri Devi (Bohra) P.; m. Henriette, Mar. 29, 1959; children: Tara Wojak, Eric Raj. MS in Physics, U. Allahabad, India, 1948, U. Mich., 1955, PhD in Nuclear Sci., 1960. Asst. prof. physics Jaswant Coll., Jodhpur, India, 1948-53; rsch. assoc. Reactor Physics, Brookhaven Nat. Lab., Upton, N.Y., 1960-62; guest physicist AB Atomenergi, Stusvik, Sweden, 1962-65; rsch. assoc. Rensselaer Poly. Inst., Troy, N.Y., 1966-68; physicist Reactor Physics, Brookhaven Nat. Lab., Upton, 1968-70; sr. engr. Nuclear Fuel, Consol. Edison, NYC, 1970-80; mgr. nuclear fuel analysis Consol. Edison, NYC, 1981-92. Adj. prof. in field. Contbr. articles to Nuclear Sci. & Engring., AB Atomenergi, Jour. Physics & Chemistry of Liquids, Proceedings of IAEA Conf. Recipient Gold medal Jaswant Coll., 1946. Mem. Am. Nuclear Soc. (reactor physics div. exec. com. 1975, treas. 1981), N.Y. Acad. Scis. Home: Port Washington, NY. Died Dec. 30, 2006.

PYTLAK, JOHN PAUL, motion-picture engineer; b. Buffalo, July 15, 1948; s. Edward Michael and Bernice Veronica Pytlak; m. Elizabeth Mary van Reuth, Oct. 7, 1972; children: Katherine M., Anne E. BSEE cum laude, SUNY, Buffalo, 1970. Jr. engr. Eastman Kodak Co., Rochester, N.Y., 1970-73, engr., 1974-78, sr. engr., 1979-87, tech. assoc., from 1988. Contbr. articles, papers to profl. jours. Fellow Soc. Motion Picture and TV Engrs. (chmn. theatrical projection tech. com. 1982-85, 96—, Outstanding Svc. citation 1987); mem. Brit. Kinematograph and TV Soc.

(corp.), Internat. Stds. Orgn. (convenor working group U.S. delegation 1991-95). Avocations: vegetable gardening, swimming, cinema, photography. Home: Penfield, NY. Died Aug. 17, 2007.

QUANDT, JOHANNA, automotive executive; b. Berlin, 1926; d. Gunther; m. Herbert Quandt, 1960 (dec. 1982); children: Stefan, Susanne Klatten. Mem. supervisory bd. BMW, 1982—86, dep. bd. chairwoman, 1986—97; co-owner Bayerische Motorenwerke (maker of BMW cars), Altana pharmaceutical firm; shareholder Bayer. Bd. trustees BMW Found. Recipient Germany's nat. order of merit, 2009; named one of World's Richest People, from 1999. Died Aug. 3, 2015.

QUATTLEBAUM, ROBERT BASKIN, urologist; b. Roanoke, Ala., Mar. 6, 1933; s. Robert Baskin and Lucy Mathews Quattlebaum; m. Nelle Fall Binford, Dec. 18, 1959; children: Robyn, Jane, Blake, George, Elizabeth. BS, Vanderbilt U., Nashville, 1955; MD, Med. Coll. Ala., Birmingham, 1961. Diplomate Am. Bd. Urology. Intern Guthrie Clinic, Robert Packer Hosp., Sayre, Pa., 1961—62; resident U. Hosp., Hillnian Clinic, Birmingham, Ala., 1962—67; staff mem. Candler Hosp., St. Joseph Hosp., Meml. Hosp., Savannah, Ga.; pvt. practice urology Savannah, Ga. Contbr. articles to profl. jours. Bd. dirs. Salvation Army, Savannah, 2000—04, Savannah Christian Prep Sch. 2d lt. USAF. Named to, Am. Registry of Outstanding Profs., 2002. Fellow: ACS; mem.: Am. Urol Assn. (past pres. southeastern sect.), Ga. Med. Soc. (past pres.), Rotary (bd. dirs. 1994). Avocations: golf, gardening, fishing. Home: Savannah, Ga. Died Jan. 1, 2007.

QUENTEL, ALBERT DREW, lawyer; b. Miami, Fla., Nov. 27, 1934; s. Charles Edward Jr. and Alberta Amelia (Drew) Q.; m. Paula Staelin Hagar, Feb. 9, 1957 (dec. Mar. 1998); children: Albert D. Jr., Stephen C., Marshall Lee, Paul G., Peter E., Michael J. BA, U. Fla., 1956, LLB with honors, 1959, JD with honors, 1967. Bar: Fla. 1959. Assoc. Mershon, Sawyer, Johnston, Dunwody & Cole, Miami, 1959-64, ptnr., 1965-71; prin., shareholder Greenberg Traurig P.A., Miami, from 1971. Editor-in-chief U. Fla. Law Rev., 1959; contbg. author: Florida Real Property Practice, 1965, Real Estate Partnerships Selected Problems and Solutions, 1991, Commercial Real Estate Finance, 1993. Mem. Gov.'s Growth Mgmt. Adv. Com., Tallahassee, 1985-87; bd. dirs. Nat. Parkinson Found., Miami, 1980-98, v.p., 1985-97. Mem. NRA (life 1989—), Am. Coll. Real Estate Lawyers, Fla. Bar Assn. (chmn. pub. rels. com. 1970-72, chmn. editorial com. jour. 1972-73), Lions (pres. Key Biscayne, Fla. club 1973), Miami Club (pres. 1991-92), Fla. Blue Key, Beta Theta Pi (pres. local chpt. 1954-55), Phi Eta Sigma, Phi Kappa Phi. Republican. Congregationalist. Avocations: reading, shooting, photography. Home: South Miami, Fla. Died Aug. 6, 2015.

QUESTORE, JOSEPH G., telecommunications engineer; b. Bklyn., Oct. 12, 1961; BSEE, Polytech Inst. N.Y., 1983; BS in Journalism, Polytech U., 1986, MS in Mgmt., 1989. Asst. mgr. Radio Shack, Queens, N.Y., 1979-81; clk. N.Y. Telephone Co., NYC, 1979-82; engr. Mini-Circuits Labs., Bklyn., 1983, N.Y. Telephone Co., 1983-88; assoc. dir. NYNEX Svc. Co., White Plains, N.Y., 1988-90; mem. tech. staff Bellcore, Lincroft, N.J., 1990-94, sr. engr., 1995, sr. project mgr., 1996, sr. cons., from 1997. Mem. edn. com. bd. trustees Polytech U., Bklyn., 1984-86. Vol. St. James Cathedral Homeless Shelter, Bklyn., 1986-90, Mobile Meals, Red Bank, N.J., 1996—; Mil. Amateur Radio Svc., Ft. Monmouth, N.J., 1991; bus. cons. Jr. Achievement N.Y.C., 1986-88. Mem. IEEE, N.Y. New Media Assn., Project Mgmt. Inst., Tau Delta Phi. Avocations: creative writing, opera, visual arts, ocean beaches, travel. Died Feb. 11, 2007.

QUINN, PAT (JOHN BRIAN PATRICK QUINN), professional sports team executive, former professional hockey coach; b. Hamilton, Ont., Canada, Jan. 29, 1943; s. John Ernest and Jean (Ireland) Quinn; m. Sandra Georgia Baker, May 1, 1963; children: Valerie, Kathleen. BA in Econs., York U., 1972; LLB, Widener U. Sch. Law, 1987; LLD (hon.), McMaster U., 2008. Defenseman Toronto Maple Leafs, 1968—70, Vancouver Canucks, 1970—72, Atlanta Flames, 1972—77; asst. coach Phila. Flyers, 1977—78, head coach, 1979—82, LA Kings, 1984—86; pres., gen. mgr. Vancouver Canucks, 1987—97, head coach, 1991—95, Toronto Maple Leafs, 1998—2006, Edmonton Oilers, 2009—10, sr. hockey advisor, 2010—14. Player rep. NHL, Atlanta, 1973—77; mem. NHL Bd. Govs., 1987; head coach Team Canada, Olympic Games, Salt Lake City, 2002, Torino, 2006, Team Canada, World Cup of Hockey, 2004, Team Canada, Spengler Cup, 2006, Team Canada, IIHF World 18 & Under Championships, 2008; co-owner Vancouver Giants (Western Hockey League). Recipient Jack Adams Award, 1980, 1992, Coach of Yr., Hockey News, 1980, 1982, Jake Milford Award, 1994, Jack Diamond Award, 1994; named Coach of Yr., Sporting News, 1980, 1992. Roman Catholic. Achievements include being the head coach of gold medal Canadian Hockey Team, Salt Lake City Olympic Games, 2002; being the head coach of World Cup Champion Team Canada, 2004. Avocations: sports, reading. Died Nov. 23, 2014.

RABINOVITCH, BENTON SEYMOUR, chemist, educator emeritus; b. Montreal, Que., Can., Feb. 19, 1919; came to U.S., 1946; s. Samuel and Rachel (Schachter) R.; m. Marilyn Werby, Sept. 18, 1949; children: Peter Samuel, Ruth Anne, Judith Nancy, Frank Benjamin; m. Flora Reitman, 1980. BSc, McGill U., 1939, PhD, 1942; DSc (hon.), Technion Inst., Haifa, 1991. Postdoctoral fellow Harvard, 1946-48; mem. faculty U. Wash., Seattle, from 1948, prof. chemistry, from 1957, prof. chemistry emeritus, from 1985. Cons. and/or mem. sci. adv. panels, coms. NSF, Nat. Acad. Scis.-NRC; adv. com. phys. chemistry Nat. Bur. Standards. Author Antique Silver Servers, 1991, Contemporary Silver, 2000, Contemporary Silver Part II, 2005; co-author: Physical Chemistry, 1964; former editor: Ann. Rev. Phys. Chemistry; mem. editorial bd.: Internat. Jour. Chem. Kinetics, Rev. of Chem. Intermediates, Jour. Phys. Chemistry, Jour. Am. Chem. Soc. Served to capt. Canadian Army, 1942-46, ETO. Nat. Research Council Can. fellow, 1940-42; Royal Soc. Can. Research fellow, 1946-47; Milton Research fellow Harvard, 1948; Guggenheim fellow, 1961; vis. fellow Trinity Coll., Oxford, 1971; recipient Sigma Xi award for original research, Debye award in phys. chemistry, 1984, Polanyi medal Royal Soc. Chemistry; named hon. liveryman Worshipful Co. of Goldsmiths, London, 2000. Fellow Am. Phys. Soc., Am. Acad. Arts and Scis., Royal Soc. London; mem. Am. Chem. Soc. (past chmn. Puget Sound sect., past chmn. phys. chemistry divsn., assoc. editor jour.), Faraday Soc. Achievements include rsch. in Unimolecular gas phase reaction and history and design of silver implements. Home: Seattle, Wash. Died Aug. 2, 2014.

RADEST, HOWARD BERNARD, clergyman, educator; b. NYC, June 29, 1928; s. Louis and Gussie (Permison) R.; m. Rita Stollman, Dec. 22, 1951; children: Robert, Nora, Michael, Karen. AB, Columbia U., 1949, PhD, 1971; MA (Hillman fellow 1950), New Sch. Social Research, 1951. Dir. youth activities N.Y. Soc. Ethical Culture, 1955-56; leader Ethical Culture Soc. Bergen County, Teaneck, N.J., 1956-64; exec. dir. American Ethical Union, NYC, 1964-70; assoc. prof. philosophy Ramapo Coll., 1971-73, prof., 1973-79; dir. Ethical Culture Schools, 1979-91. Author: Understanding Ethical Religion, 1958, On Life and Meaning, 1963, Toward Common Ground, 1969, To Seek a Humane World, 1971, Can We Teach Ethics, 1989, The Devil and Secular Humanism, 1990, Community Service Encounter with Strangers, 1992, Humanism with a Human Face, 1996, Felix Adler: An Ethical Culture, 1998, From Clinic to Classroom, 2000, Biomedical Ethics, 2007, Ethics and Public Health Preparedness in the Time of Terrorism, 2007, Bioethics: Catastrophic Events in a Time of Terror, 2009; also articles; editor: Ramapo Papers, 1976-79, International Humanism 1981-1986; mem. editl. bd. Religious Humanism, Free Inquiry, 1981-2000, The Humanist. Mem. bd. Encampment for Citizenship, 1963-71, Mental Health Assn. Bergen County, Bergen Co. Mental Health Bd., 1964-67, Assn. Moral Edn., 1986-94; mem. bd. past treas., v.p. N.J. Welfare Conf., 1958-64; mem. bd., past pres. Health and Welfare Coun. Bergen County, 1956-64; bd. mgrs. Bergen Pines County Hosp., 1966-70; mem.Bergen County (N.J.) Democratic Com., 1970-71; mem. human svcs. leadership coun. Beaufort County Alliance, 2003—2008, chair, bd. trustees, ethical cmty. charter sch. 2008-12, resident bd. mem. Crane's Mill 2010-12, Ethical Cmty. Charter Schs. Found. Bd., 2013-14 Served with US Army, 1953—55. Recipient Felix Adler Lifetime Svc. award, 2011. Mem. AAUP (treas. N.J. coun. 1973-74), Com. Sane Nuclear Policy (sponsor N.J.), American Assn. UN, American Philos. Assn., Soc. Advancement American Philosophy, North America Com. Humanism, S.C. Philos. Assn., Grad. Faculties Alumni Columbia U. (trustee 1989-91), Network Progressive Educators (steering com. 1988-91), Highlands, Internat. Inst. American Religious Thought, SC Med. Assn., (ethics com., 1997—2008), Phi Beta Kappa; fellow: Ctr.Inquiry. Democrat. Home: West Caldwell, NJ. Died Oct. 11, 2014.

RAFFAY, STEPHEN JOSEPH, manufacturing executive, director; b. McAdoo, Pa., Oct. 25, 1927; s. Stephen John and Stephanie (Severa) R.; m. Audree Eugenia Kuehne, Sept. 12, 1953; children: Andrea, Stephen, Leslie. BA, Columbia U., NYC, 1950, MS, 1951. C.P.A., N.Y. Sr. accountant Arthur Andersen & Co., NYC, 1951-56; asst. controller Emhart Corp., Farmington, Conn., 1956-61, asst. treas., 1961-63, treas., 1963-67, v.p. internat., 1967-72, v.p., group pres., 1972-79, exec. v.p., 1979-84, vice chmn., chief adminstrv. officer, 1984-87, dir., 1980-87; sr. v.p. Dexter Corp., Windsor Locks, Conn., 1987-90. Bd. dirs. United Plumbing Tech., Inc., EDAC Techs. Inc. With US Army, 1946—47. Mem. AICPA, Conn. Soc. CPAs. Home: West Hartford, Conn. Died Nov. 17, 2012.

RAGAN, DENNIS M., mathematics educator; b. Rusville, Nebr., June 1, 1945; s. Joseph E. and Anne M. Ragan. BS in Math., Ill. State U., 1966; MA in Math. (Tchg.), San Diego State U., 1971. Cert. Tchr. Ill. Math. tchr. Shabbona HS, Ill., 1966—70, 1972—81, Elgin Acad., Ill., 1971—72, Kishwaukee Coll., Malta, Ill., from 1981. Village trustee Village of Lee, Ill., from 1991; Diabetes state chair Lions of Ill. Found., Sycamore, from 1998. Recipient Kishwaukee Coll. Bd. Trustees award of excellence, Kishwaukee Coll., Malta, 1993; Melvin Jones fellow, Lions Internat. Mem.: Ill. Math. Assn. Cmty. Colls., Ill. Fedn. Tchrs., Am. Fedn. Tchrs., Nat. Coun. Tchrs. Math. (life). Home: Lee, Ill. Died Apr. 23, 2007.

RAINER, LUISE, actress; b. Vienna, Jan. 12, 1910; d. Heinz and Emmy (Koenigsberger) Rainer; m. Clifford Odets, Jan. 8, 1937 (div. May 14, 1940); m. Robert Knittel, July 12, 1945 (dec. June 15, 1989); 1 child, Francesca. Actress: (films) Ja, der Himmel uber Wien, 1930, Sehnsucht 202, 1932, Heut kommt's drauf an, 1933, Wenn die Musik nicht war, 1935, Escapade, 1935, The Great Ziegfeld, 1936 (Acad. award for Best Actress 1936), The Good Earth, 1937 (Acad. award for Best Actress 1937), The Emperor's Candlesticks, 1937, Big City, 1937, The Toy Wife, 1938, The Great Waltz, 1938, Dramatic School, 1938, Hostages, 1943, La Dolce vita, 1960, The Gambler, 1997; (TV series) Schlitz Playhouse of Stars, 1952, Lux Video Theatre, 1953, Suspense, 1954, Combat!, 1965, The Love Boat, 1983, (TV film) A Dancer, 1988. Recipient George Eastman award, 1982, Star, Hollywood Walk of Fame. Died Dec. 30, 2014.

RAINES, CHARLOTTE AUSTINE BUTLER, artist; b. Sullivan, Ill., July 1, 1922; d. Donald Malone and Charlotte (Wimp) Butler; m. Irving Isaack Raines, Sept. 26, 1941; children: Robin Raines Collison, Kerry Raines Lydon. BA in Studio Arts magna cum laude, U. Md., 1966. One-woman shows at Castle Theatre, 1988, C.T.V. Awards Hall, Md., 1993, Md. Nat. Capital Park and Planning Commn., 2005; numerous group shows including Corcoran Gallery, 1980, Md.'s Best Exhbn., 1986, Md. State House, 1990, four-artist video documentary, 1992, U. Md. Univ.-Coll. Gallery, 1996; artist publ. cover Writers' Ctr., 1997, Md. State House Print Exhbn., 1999, Washington Women Artists Millenium Show, 2001, Md. State Ho. Complex, 2003; represented in various pvt. collections and permanent collection at U. Md. Univ.-Coll.; selected works in U.S. Dept. State Arts in Embassies Program; contbr. poems to lit. publs. Mem. Artists Equity Assn., Writers' Ctr., Phi Kappa Phi. Avocations: piano, gardening. Home: Hyattsville, Md. Died Nov. 19, 2006.

RAINONE, MICHAEL CARMINE, lawyer; b. Phila., Mar. 4, 1918; m. Ledena Tonioni, Apr. 10, 1944; children: Sebastian, Francine. LLB, U. Pa., 1941. Bar: Pa. 1944, U.S. Dist. Ct. Pa. 1944, U.S. Supreme Ct. 1956. Apptd. arbitrator U.S. Dist. Ct. (ea. dist.) Pa., 2003—12. Del. 3d cir. Jud. Conf., 1984—85; mem. Fed. Cts. Com., from 2004. Past pres. Nationalities Svc. Ctr., hon. bd. dirs.; commr. Fellowship Commn., 1973—82; internat. pres. Orphans of Italy, Inc., 1975—83; bd. dirs., mem. govt. rels. com. Mental Health Assn. Southeastern Pa., 1979—91; pres. Columbus Civic Assn. Pa., Inc., 1984—91; regional v.p. Nat. Italian-Am. Found.; pres. Seaview Harbor Civic Assn., 1990—95, pres. emeritus, from 1996; apptd. judge Final Law Sch. Trial Advocacy Program N.E., from 1996; mem. nominating com. NIABA, 1996, bd. dirs., 1996; counsel, v.p. Piccola Opera Com., Phila., from 1997; task force chmn. Mazzei Nat. Constn. Ctr., 2001; trustee Chapel of the Four Chaplains, 2005; bd. dirs. State of Pa., Phila., 1970—85; chmn. lawyers' biog. com. Hist. Soc., U.S. Dist. Ct.; trustee Balch Inst. Ethnic Studies, 1989—92; pres. Grad. Club, bd. dirs., 2000. Recipient Man of the Yr. award, Columbus Civic Assn., 1969, Disting. Svc. award, Nationalities Svc. Ctr., 1975, Legion of Honor, Chapel of Four Chaplains, 1979, Bronze Medallion award, 1982, commendation, Pa. Senate, 1982, Appreciation award, Villanova Law Sch., 1993, Achievement award, Syracuse U., 1994, Hon. Lifetime award, KC, 1997, Resolution of Praise, Pres. City Coun. Phila., 1999, Svc. to Legal Profession and Cmty. award, City Coun. of Phila., 2003, Beccaria award, Phila. Bar Assn., 2006. Mem.: ATLA (supr. judge law sch. trial advocacy competition 2000, Phila. chpt. emeritus chmn. Justice Michael A. Musmanno award 2000, Supervising Judge Advocacy award Phila. region 2000), ABA (chmn. U.S. Supreme Ct. admissions com. 2001), KC (life), Dustnian Soc., Am. Arbitration Assn. (arbitrator 1950—2012), Nat. Itlaian-Am. Bar Assn. (bd. govs. 1986—2012, historian 1987—90, pres. 1991—93, bd. chmn. 1993—95, chmn. Supreme Ct. admissions com. 2000), Phila. Trial Lawyers Assn. (pres. 1982—83, lifetime bd. mem., Disting. Svc. award 2000), Lawyers Club Phila. (pres. 1982—84, chmn. nominating com. 2000—12, chmn. Centennial Celebration 2001, Achievement and Svc. award 2003), Phila. Bar Assn. (bd. dirs. 1980—83, asst. sec. 1983, 1984, chmn. emeritus Beccaria award 1993—2012, Cesare Beccaria award 2006), Pa. Trial Lawyers Assn. (bd. govs. 1982—84), Pa. Bar Assn. (Dist. Svc. award 2006), Justinian Soc. (bd. govs. 1980—83, Sr. Lawyer award 2000), Internat. Acad. Law and Sci., N.Y. Trial Lawyers Assn. (assoc.), Order Sons of Italy (hon. Man of the Yr. award 1995), Grand Lodge Pa. (life). Home: Binghamton, NY. Died Oct. 17, 2012.

RAINS, PATRICIA JANE, learning disabilities educator; b. Portland, Oreg., Mar. 26, 1934; d. Lawrence Marion and Mary Leticia (Roberts) Rains. AB in Edn., Cascade Coll., 1960; BS in Elem. Edn., Portland State U., 1962; diploma, Inst. Children's Lit. Cert. tchr. Tchr. Lynch Sch. Dist. 28, Portland, Oreg., 1960—70, HS Sch. Learning Ctr. Tillamook Edn. Svc. Dist., Oreg., 1970—79, Nehalem Learning Ctr., from 1979, Sch. Dist. 56, Nehalem, 1983—86. Author: Land Series Program, 1957—86. Vol., adult tutor Portland CC, 1969—70; active mem. Sweet Adelines; pres. Wesleyan Fellowship, Tillamook; summer sch. scholar Tillamook Ednl. Svc. and Oreg. State Dept., 1971; chmn., ch., soc. com. mem. Inter-Religious and Ecumenical Concerns, Religion and Race, Status and Role Women. Mem.: NEA, Nat. Assn. Female Execs., Coun. Exceptional Children, Oreg. Ednl. Assn. (del. 1960—86), Tillamook Edn. Tchrs. Assn. (del., pres. 1969—70), Oreg. Sheriff's Assn. (hon.), Internat. Tng. Communication Club (pres., coun. 2 1979). Republican. Avocations: travel, bowling, handicrafts, singing, teaching Sunday Sch. kindergarten. Home: Netarts, Oreg. Died Nov. 18, 2006.

RAINWATER, RICHARD EDWARD, retired investor; b. Ft. Worth, June 15, 1944; m. Karen Rainwater, 1975 (div. 1991); children: Courtney, Todd, Matthew; m. Darla Dee Moore, Dec. 13, 1991. BA in Math., U. Tex., 1966; MBA in Finance & Mktg., Stanford U., 1968. With Goldman, Sachs & Co., NYC, Dallas; chief financial arch. Bass Orgn., Ft. Worth, 1970-86; ind. investor Ft. Worth, 1986-94; founder ENSCO Internat. Inc., 1986; co-founder Columbia Hosp. Corp. (now Columbia/HCA Healthcare Corp.), 1988, Mid Ocean Ltd.; founder, chmn. Crescent Real Estate Equities, Inc., Ft. Worth, 1994. Spkr. Harvard Bus. Sch., Stanford U., U. Tex. Bus. Sch.; ptnr. Texas Rangers franchise Appeared on cover of Bus. Week mag., Oct. 1986; recipient Man of Yr. award, 1989, Kupfer Disting. Exec. award Tex. A&M U., 1991, Golden Plate award American Acad. Achievement, 1992, Ernest C. Arbuckle award Stanford Bus. Sch. Allumni Assn., 2010; named one of The Forbes 400: Richest Americans, 2006-. Died Sept. 27, 2015.

RAMER, JAMES LEROY, civil engineer; b. Marshalltown, Iowa, Dec. 7, 1935; s. LeRoy Frederick and Irene (Wengert) Ramer; m. Jacqueline L. Orr, Dec. 15, 1957; children: Sarah T., Robert H., Eric A., Susan L. Student, U. Iowa, Iowa City, 1953-57; MCE, Washington U., St. Louis, 1976, MA in Polit. Sci., 1978; postgrad., U. Mo., Columbia, from 1984. Registered profl. engr., land surveyor. Civil and constrn. engr. US Army C.E., Tulsa, 1960-63; civil and relocations engr. US State Dept., Del Rio, Tex., 1964; project engr. H.B. Zachary Co., San Antonio, 1965-66; civil and constrn. engr. US Army C.E., St. Louis, 1967-76, tech. advisor for planning and nat. hydropower coord., 1976-78; project mgr. for EPA constrn. grants Milw., 1978-80; chief arch. and engring. HUD, Indpls., 1980-81; civil design and pavements engr. Whiteman AFB, Mo., 1982-86; project mgr. maintenance, from 1993; soil and pavements engr. Hdqrs. Mil. Airlift Command, Scott AFB, Ill., 1986-88; chief design engr. design & hwy. and transp. sys. to accommodate electric vehicles patent design Ramer Innovative Tech., from 2010. Project mgr. AF-1 maintenance hangar; cattle and grain farmer, from 1982; pvt. practice civil-mech. engr., constrn. mgmt., estimating, cost analysis, cash flow, project scheduling, expert witness, profl. land surveying, Fortuna, Mo., 1988—2001; chief constrn. inspector divsn. design and constrn. State of Mo., 1992—93; project engr. Mil. Housing, from 2001; adj. faculty civil engring. Washington U., 1968—78, U. Wis., Milw., 1978—80, Ga. Mil. Coll., Whiteman AFB, Longview Coll., Kansas City; adj. rsch. engr. U. Mo., Columbia, 1985—86; project engr., quality control officer Korte Constrn. Co. Mem.: AAUP, NSPE, ASCE, Soc. Am. Mil. Engrs., Optimists Internat. Lutheran. Achievements include patents for in diverse art, 9 copyrights; development of solar waterstill, deep shaft hydropower concept; design of method of recharging electric vehicle batteries as vehicle is being driven. Died Feb. 27, 2014.

RAMIREZ, RAMON SANTO, professional baseball player; b. Puerto Plata, Dominican Republic, Aug. 31, 1981; Pitcher Colo. Rockies, 2006—08, Kansas City Royals, 2008, Boston Red Sox, 2008—10, San Francisco Giants, 2010—11, 2013, NY Mets, 2012, Balt. Orioles, 2014. Achievements include World Series Champion in 2010. Died Jan. 30, 2016.

RAMSAY, WILLIAM MCDOWELL, retired minister; b. Huntsville, Tex., Aug. 3, 1922; s. Charles Sumner and Catherine (McKay) R.; m. DeVere Maxwell, Apr. 27, 1954; children: William McDowell Jr., John Alston. BA, Rhodes, Memphis, 1946; BDiv, Union Sem., Richmond, Va., 1949; PhD, U. Edinburgh, Scotland, 1954. Ordained to ministry Presbyn. Ch., 1950. Pastor Presbyn. Ch., Knoxville, Paducah, Tenn., Ky., 1950-59; exec. Bd. of Christian Edn., Richmond, Va., 1959-69; prof. King Coll., Bristol, Tenn., 1969-79; Hannibal Seagle prof. Bethel Coll., McKenzie, Tenn., 1979-91. Moderator Bethel Coll. faculty, 1990-91. Author: The Wall of Separation: A Primer on Church and State, Four Modern Prophets: Rauschenbusch, King, Gutierrez, Ruether, Cycles and Renewal: Trends in Protestant Lay Education, The Layman's Guide to the New Testament, The Westminster Guide to The Books of the Bible. With U.S. Army, 1943-46. Mem. Presbytery of Memphis. Avocations: golf, gardening. Home: Cordova, Tenn. Died May 21, 2007.

RAMSEY, GORDON CLARK, English educator; b. Hartford, Conn., May 28, 1941; s. Clark McNary and Virginia Aileen (Childs) R. BA, Yale U., 1963. Instr. English, alumni dir., asst. to headmaster Worcester (Mass.) Acad., 1963-69; sec. bd. alumni fund Yale U., New Haven, Conn., 1969-71, asst. exec. dir. assn. alumni, 1971-77; dir. fin. devel. Avon (Conn.) Old Farms Ssh., 1978-80; devel. cons. Stoneleigh-Burnham Sch., Greenfield, Mass., 1980-82; freelance writer, 1982-85; instr. English U. Hartford (Conn.) Coll. Arts & Scis., from 1985, sec, faculty senate, from 1986, instr. history, from 1992. Speaker in field. Author: Agatha Christie: Mistress of Mystery, 1967, These Fields and Halls, 1974, An Undertaking Sett Forward, 1976, Aspiration and Perseverance, 1984, (cassette tapes) Edwardian organ and vocal music, 1985-92; contbr. articles to profl. jours. Organist 2d Ch. Christ Scientist, Hartford, 1983—; trustee, chmn. pubs. com. Coun. Religion Ind. Schs., 1973-75; trustee mem. exec. com. The Barlow Sch., Amenia, N.Y., 1975-80; pres. Avon, Conn. Hist. Soc., 1988-90, 91-93. Mem. SAR. Republican. Avocations: antiques, antique automobiles, writing. Home: West Hartford, Conn. Died June 21, 2007.

RAND, JONATHAN G., psychophysiologist; b. Detroit, Oct. 20, 1945; m. Donna Rand; children: Collin, Devin, Cassandra, Jillian. BS, USAF Acad., 1968; MS, Brigham Young U., 1975; PhD, Calif. Coast U., 1991. Lic. clin. hypnotherapist, cons. stress mgmt. Dir. Mind Potentials, Walnut Creek, Calif., 1985-87; trainer, instr. Goodlife Experience, Provo, 1985-86; founder, dir. Delta Inst., Inc., West Palm Beach, 1988-91; clin. liaison Inst. Psychiatry and Behavioral Medicine JFK Med. Ctr., West Palm Beach, from 1991. Charter rep. Gulfstream coun. Boy Scouts Am., 1989-91. 2d lt., USAF, 1968-73. Mem. Nat. Guild Hypnotists, Am. Assn. Profl. Hypnotherapists, Assn. Applied Psychophysiology and Biofeedback, Am. Assn. Study Mental Imagery, Assn. Study Subtle Energy. Mem. Lds Ch. Avocations: sports, reading. Home: Aliso Viejo, Calif. Died Jan. 13, 2007.

RANDALL, PETER, retired plastic surgeon; b. Phila., Mar. 29, 1923; s. Alexander and Edith Tilghman (Kneedler) R.; m. Rose Gordon Johnson, May 1, 1948; children: Deborah K., Peter G., Julia B., Susanna T. BA, Princeton U., 1944; MD, Johns Hopkins U., 1946; MS (hon.), U. Pa., 1969. Diplomate Am. Bd. Plastic Surgery. Intern Union Meml. Hosp., Balt., 1946—47; asst. resident in surgery Hosp. of U. of Pa., Phila., 1949—50; fellow in plastic surgery Barnes Hosp.-St. Louis Children's Hosp., 1950—51, resident in plastic surgery, 1951—53; asst. instr. plastic surgery Washington U., St. Louis, 1950—53; from asst. prof. to assoc. prof. plastic surgery U. Pa. Hosp., Phila., 1953—69, prof. plastic surgery, from 1969, emeritus prof. plastic surgery; chief div. plastic surgery sch. medicine U. Pa., Phila., 1979—87; ret., 1994. Sr. surgeon Children's Hosp. Phila., 1965—. Contbr. articles to profl. jours. Pres. Plastic Surgery Edn. Found., 1972-73. Lt. (j.g.) USNR, 1947-49. Recipient Tagliacozzi award, Am. Soc. Maxillofacial Surgeons, 2011. Fellow: ACS (bd. govs., chmn. 1982—84, 1st v.p. 1985—86), Am. Assn. Plastic Surgeons (hon. Clinician of Yr. award 1987, disting. fellow 1994); mem.: AMA, Am. Cleft Palate Assn. (pres. 1965—66, Honors award 1986), Plastic Surgery Rsch. Coun. (founder, chmn. 1964—65), Phila. Acad. Surgery, Phila. County Med. Soc., Northea. Soc. Plastic Surgery (founder), Am. Surg. Assn., Coll. Physicians of Phila., Am. Soc. Plastic Surgeons (pres. 1978—79, Spl. Achievement award 1987), Am. Bd. Plastic Surgery (vice-chmn. 1976—77), Am. Cleft Palate Ednl. Found. (founder, pres. 1972—73), Robert H. Ivy Soc. (founder, pres. 1966—67), Halsted Soc., Sigma Xi. Home: Gwynedd, Pa. Died Nov. 2014.

RANKINE, BAXTER JAMES, aerospace company executive; b. Moncks Corner, SC, June 30, 1936; s. Baxter Grey and Mary DeLellis (Bradley) R.; m. Joyce Marie Lemery, July 24, 1965; children: David James, Julie Dee. BS in Engring., UCLA, 1959. Indsl. engr. GE, 1960-65; material control mgr. Collins Radio Co., Newport Beach, Calif., 1965-67; v.p., mktg. Paco Pumps, Oakland, Calif., 1967-75; dir. corp. devel. Mark Controls Corp., Evanston, Ill., 1975-77; pres. Ctr. Line, Tulsa, Okla., 1977-78, Pacific Valves, Long Beach, Calif., 1978-87, All-Power Mfg. Co., Santa Fe Springs, Calif., from 1987, Kool Mist, Santa Fe Springs, Calif., from 1992. Bd. dirs. Bus. Network, Torrance, Calif. Mem. Kappa Sigma. Republican. Roman Catholic. Home: Palos Verdes Peninsula, Calif. Died Jan. 5, 2007.

RAPHAEL, DANA LOUISE, medical anthropologist; b. New Britain, Conn., Jan. 5, 1926; d. Louis and Naomi (Kaplan) R.; m. Howard Boone Jacobsen (dec. 2013); children: Brett Raphael, Seth, Jessa Murnin. BS, Columbia U., 1956, PhD, 1966. Asst. dir. United Artists TV, NYC, 1973-74; co-founder, dir. Human Lactation Ctr., Westport, Conn., 1974—2016. Asst. adj. prof. Anthropology Ctr. for Lifetime Learning, Fairfield, Conn., 1973-76; lectr. Yale U. Sch. Pub. Health, 1980-; cons. in field; exec. dir., The Eleventh Commandment Found.: Thou Shalt Not Sexually Abuse Children. Author: The Tender Gift: Breastfeeding, 1973, Being Female: Reproduction Power and Change, 1975, Breastfeeding: Food Policy in a Hungry World, 1978; (with Flora Davis) Only Mothers Know, 1985, Global AIDS Policy, ed. Douglas Feldman, 1994; contbr. numerous articles to profl. jours.; appeared on TV shows regarding lactation, weaning and child abuse Geraldo, Sally J. Raphael, Jim Grant; radio stas., Chgo. Cleve., Milw., Rochester, N.Y., India, Japa, Eng., China. Named Outstanding Woman, Nat. Fedn. Bus. and Profl. Women, 1976; Fulbright grantee, Japan, 1989, 91. Mem. Soc. Of Friends. Died Feb. 2, 2016.

RAPOPORT, ANATOL, humanities educator, biophysicist; b. Lozovaya, Russia, May 22, 1911; emigrated to U.S., 1922, naturalized, 1928; s. Boris and Adel (Rapoport) R.; m. Gwen Goodrich, Jan. 29, 1949; children: Anya, Alexander, Charles Anthony. PhD, U. Chgo., 1941; DHL, U. Western Mich., 1971; LLD, U. Toronto, 1986; DS, Royal Mil. Coll. Can., 1995; Ehrendoktor, U. Bern, Switzerland, 1995. Faculty dept. math. Ill. Inst. Tech., 1946-47; com. math. biology U. Chgo., 1947-54; fellow Ctr. Advanced Study Behavioral Scis., Stanford, 1954-55; asso. prof. Mental Health Research Inst., prof. math. biology U. Mich., 1955-70; prof. psychology and math. U. Toronto, 1970-80; dir. Inst. for Advanced Studies, Vienna, 1980-83; prof. peace studies U. Toronto, from 1984. Author: Science and the Goals of Man, 1950, Operational Philosophy, 1953, Fights, Games, and Debates, 1960, Strategy and Conscience, 1964, Prisoner's Dilemma, 1965, Two-Person Game Theory, 1966, N Person Game Theory, 1970, The Big Two, 1971, Conflict in Man Made Environment, 1974, Semantics, 1975, The 2 x 2 Game, 1976, Mathematische Methoden in den Sozialwissenschaften, 1980, Mathematical Models in the Social and Behavioral Sciences, 1983, General System Theory, 1986, The Origins of Violence, 1989, Decision Theory and Decision Behavior, 1989, Canada and the World, 1992, Peace: An Idea Whose Time Has Come, 1992, Gewissheiten and Zweifel, 1994, Uverennost' i Somnenia, 1999, Certainties and Doubts, 2000, Skating on Thin Ice, 2002; editor: General Systems, 1956—77. Served to capt. USAAF, 1942-46. Fellow Am. Acad. Arts and Scis.; mem. Am. Math. Soc., Internat. Soc. Gen. Semantics (pres. 1953-55), Canadian Peace Research and Edn. Assn. (pres. 1972-75), Soc. for Gen. Systems Research (pres. 1965-66), Sci. for Peace (pres. 1984-86) Home: Toronto, Canada. Died Jan. 20, 2007.

RASKY, HARRY, producer, director, writer; b. Toronto, Ont., Can., May 9, 1928; emigrated to U.S., 1955; s. Louis Leib and Pearl (Krazner) R.; m. Ruth Arlene Werkhoven, Mar. 21, 1965; children: Holly Laura, Adam Louis. BA, U. Toronto, 1949, LLD, 1984. Reporter No. Daily News, Kirkland Lake, Ont., 1949; news editor-producer Sta. CHUM, Toronto, 1950, Sta. CKEY, 1951-52; co-founder new documentary dept. CBC, 1952-55; assoc. editor Saturday Night Mag., 1955; producer-dir-writer Columbia Broadcasting Corp., 1955-60, NBC-TV, NYC, 1960-61, ABC-TV, NYC, 1963-69, CBC-TV, Toronto, 1971-78; pres. Harry Rasky Prodns., NYC and Toronto, from 1971, Maragall Prodns., Toronto, from 1978. Guest lectr. film and TV at various univs., colls.; lectr. U. Toronto, York U. Creator (films) Raskymentary (Emmy 1978, 86, San Francisco Film Festival 1978, Grand prize N.Y. TV-Film Festival 1978, Jerusalem medal 1975), Travels Through Life with Leacock, 1976, Arthur Miller on Home Ground, 1979, (TV films) Hall of Kings (Emmy, 1965), prodr., dir., writer (films) Next Year in Jerusalem, 1973, The Wit and World of G. Bernard Shaw, 1974, Tennessee Williams South, 1975, (films) Homage to Chagall-The Colours of Love, 1977 (200 internat. prizes including Oscar nomination Emmy, 1986), Stratasphere, The Mystery of Henry Moore, Karsh: The Searching Eye, (plays) Tiger Tale, 1978, Christopher Plummer: King of Players, 1988, The War Against the Indians, 1992 (Humanities prize, Great Plains Film Festival, Lincoln, Nebr., Golden Hugo award Chgo. Film Festival), Prophecy, 1994 (Golden Angel, honored by Smithsonian, Jerusalem Found.), William Hutt: A Fortunate Man, 1997; author: (memoirs) Nobody Swings on Sunday-The Many Lives of Harry Rasky, 1980, Tennessee Williams a Portrait in Laughter and Lamentation, 1986, Karsh: The Searching Eye, 1986, To Mend the World, 1987, Stratas: An Affectionate Tribute, 1988, Book 2001: The Song of Leonard Cohen, The Great Teacher, 1989, Robertson-Davies-The Magic Season, 1989; author (19 hour retrospective of films including documentaries) Rasky's Gallery: Poets, Painters, Singers and Saints, CBC, 1988, The War Against the Indians, 1993 (12 Internat. awards, adopted Huron Nation title Keeper of the Flame, The Three Harrys, 1999), Modigliani Body & Soul, 2005. Mem. YMCA; mem. adv. coun. Univ. Coll./U. Toronto. Decorated Order of Can.; recipient honors City of Venice, Italy, 1970, Golden Eagle, Grand prize N.Y. Intenat. TV and Film Festival of N.Y., 1977, Cert. of Merit, Acad. Motion Picture Arts and Scis., 1984, Red Ribbon, Am. Assn. Film and Video, N.Y.C., 1988, Blue Ribbon, Am. Film Festival, Emmy award, 1990, Moscow award for cultural contbn. to 20th Century USSR, 1991, Retrospective of Films, 1990, Golden Hugo award Chgo. Film Festival, 1993; named Best Non-Fiction Dir., Dirs. Guild Am., N.Y.C. and L.A., 1988, hon. Mayor N.Y.C., 1977, City of Toronto, 1979; Harry Rasky Day named in his honor, City of Toronto, 1988; Moscow Film Festival honoree, 1991; adopted by Huron Indians, named Keeper of the Spirit, adopted by Ojibway Tribe, named Mountain Eagle; presented to Her Royal Majesty Queen Elizabeth, 2002. Mem. Writers Guild Am. (best non-fiction dir. 1986), Dirs. Guild Am., Writers Union Can., Am., Acad. TV Arts and Scis., Assn. Can. TV and Radio Artists, Producers Assn. Can., Acad. Motion Picture Arts and Scis., Overseas Press Club, Acad. of Can. TV and Film Can. (lifetime achievement award 1992), PEN (Toronto), Nat. Arts Club. Jewish. Avocations: swimming, lecturing. Home: Toronto, Canada. *I have tried to find the positive forces in life and out of them create works of art of a lasting nature with the idea of improving the lives of others. This, plus the adventure of passing on the tradition of my father and his, is my life.* Died Apr. 9, 2007.

RASMUSON, BRENT J., photographer, small business owner; b. Logan, Utah, Nov. 28, 1950; s. Eleroy West and Fae (Jacobsen) Rasmuson; m. Jane Briggs Rasmuson, Nov. 1975 (div. Sept. 1977); 1 child, John; m. Tess Bullen Rasmuson, Sept. 1981 (div. Jan. 2003); children: Mark, Lisa. Grad. auto repair and painting sch., Utah State U.; grad. in Automobile Upholstery & Vehicle Interior Customizing, 1974. Pre-press supr., ptnr. Herald Printing Co., Logan, 1969—80; profl. drummer, 1971-75; owner, builder auto racing engines Valley Automotive Specialties, 1971-76; exec. sec. Herald Printing Co., 1980—89; owner Brent Rasmuson Photography, Logan, from 1986, Temple Picture Classics, Logan, from 1996. Author photo prints of LDS temples: Logan, 1987, 95, 98, 2000, 04, 08, Manti, 1989, 2000, Jordan River, 1989, 96, 98, 2000, Provo, 1990, 2001, Mesa, Ariz., 1990, 96, Boise, Idaho, 1990, 96, 2000, 08, Salt Lake Temple, 1990, 96, 2001, 04, Idaho Falls, 1991, 94, 2000, St. George, 1991, 93, 2000, 11, Portland, Oreg., 1991, 96, 97, 2000, LA, 1991, 96, 97, 2000, Las Vegas, Nev., 1991, 08, Seattle, 1992, Oakland, Calif., 1993, 94, Ogden, 1992, 2001, Bountiful, 2002, Mt. Timpanogos, 2002; author photo prints: Statue of Angel Moroni, 1994, Bryce Canyon with Patterns in Scenery Partially Subdued by Alto Cumulus Clouds, 1990, Tower Above the Fog: Standing on The Golden Gate Bridge in February, 2011; author photos used to make neckties and watch dials of LDS temples: Salt Lake, Manti, Logan, LA, Oakland, Seattle, Las Vegas, Mesa, Portland, St. George, Jordan River, scenic tie Mammoth Hot Springs in Yellowstone Park, 1995; landscape scenic photographs featured in Best of Photography Ann., 1987-89, also in calendars and book covers; author photo print of Harris Rsch., Inc. Internat. Hdqrs. (recipient 1st prize nat. archtl. photo competition); designer several bus. logos. Mem.: Nat. Home Gardening Club, Poetry Found., Internat. Freelance Photographers Orgn., Assoc. Photographers, Internat. Platform Assn., Nat. Air and Space Soc., Nat. Trust Hist. Preservation, Handyman Club America, Sierra Club. Republican. Mem. Lds Ch. Avocations: automobile collecting, travel, reading, coin collecting/numismatics, stamp collecting/philately. Died Dec. 26, 2014.

RAUP, DAVID MALCOLM, paleontology educator; b. Boston, Apr. 24, 1933; s. Hugh Miller and Lucy (Gibson) R.; m. Susan Creer Shepard, Aug. 25, 1956 (div.); 1 son, Mitchell D.; m. Judith T. Yamamoto, May 30, 1987; 1 stepson Mitchell BS, U. Chgo., 1953; MA, Harvard U., 1955, PhD in Geology-, 1957. Instr. Calif. Inst. Tech.,

1956-57; mem. faculty Johns Hopkins U., 1957-65, assoc. prof., 1963-65; mem. faculty U. Rochester, 1965-78, prof. geology, 1966-78, chmn. dept. geol. scis., 1968-71, dir. Center for Evolution and Paleobiology, 1977-78; curator geology, chmn. dept. geology Field Mus. Natural History, Chgo., 1978-80, dean of sci., 1980-82; prof. geophys. sci. U. Chgo., 1980-95, chmn. dept., 1982-85, Sewell L. Avery disting. service prof., 1984-95; prof. emeritus, Sewell L. Avery disting. svc. prof. emeritus, 1995—2015. Geologist U.S. Geol. Survey, part-time, 1959-77; vis. prof. U. Tubingen, Germany, 1965, 72 Author: (with S. Stanley) Principles of Paleontology, 1971, 78, The Nemesis Affair, 1986, 2nd edit., 1999, Extinction: Bad Genes of Bad Luck?, 1991; editor: (with B. Kummel) Handbook of Paleontological Techniques, 1965; contbr. articles to profl. jours. Recipient Best Paper award Jour. Paleontology, 1966; Schuchert award Paleontol. Soc., 1973; grantee Calif. Rsch. Corp., 1955-56, Am. Assn. Petroleum Geologists, 1957, Am. Philos. Soc., 1957, NSF, 1960-66, 75-81, Chem. Soc., 1965-71, NASA, 1983-95. Mem. AAAS, Am. Acad. Arts and Scis., Nat. Acad. Sci., Paleontol. Soc. (pres. 1976-77, medal 1997), Am. Soc. Naturalists (v.p. 1983), Am. Philos. Soc. Home: Washington Island, Wis. Died July 9, 2015.

RAY, PAUL LEO, venture capital and consulting company executive; b. Grinnell, Iowa, Nov. 3, 1946; s. Robert Russell and Julia Barbara (Conrad) R.; children: Cameron Conrad, Jennifer Kirsten. BS in Mktg., Ball State U., Muncie, Ind., 1969. With Dow Corning Corp., 1969-71, V. Mueller div. Am. Hosp. Supply Corp., 1971; co-founder, pres. Gt. Lakes Surg., Inc., Milw., 1978-80; dir. sales Collagen Corp., Palo Alto, Calif., 1980-82, Allergenetics div. Axonics, Inc. (now 3M Diagnostic Systems), Mountain View, Calif., 1982-84; founder, pres., chief exec. officer AllerTech, Inc., Denver, 1984-88; chief exec. officer Alamar Bioscis. Labs., Inc., Napa, Calif., 1988; mng. ptnr. MedCap Venture Ptnrs., Ltd., Englewood, Colo., from 1989, also bd. dirs., 1989-92; acting gen. mgr. Hemotec, Englewood, 1989-90; ptnr. Paradigm Ptnrs., Boulder, Colo., from 1993. Bd. dirs. Primus Corp., Kansas City, Mo., TMJ Implants, Inc., Golden, Colo., Surginetics, Inc., Pixsys, Inc. Bd. dirs. Interplast Inc., nonprofit orgn. providing free plastic surgery to children, 1985-89, mem. adv. coun., 1989—; co-chmn. bd. Colo. Bio/Med. Venture Ctr., Denver, 1990-92. Mem. Rockies Venture Capital Club, Beta Theta Pi. Avocations: sailing, skiing, reading. Home: Boulder, Colo. Died Jan. 4, 2007.

RAY, WILLIAM CARROL, insurance company executive; b. Mobile, Ala., Nov. 10, 1939; s. James Carrol and Helene Marie (Hesselink) R.; m. Bernardina Roos, July 31, 1962; children: Tine B., Michael V., James J. BSCE, U. Wyo., 1968; MS in Engring., U. Calif., Berkeley, 1971. Enlisted USAF, 1958, advanced through grades to capt., 1970, ret., 1978; supr. indsl. hygiene Ariz. State Compensation Fund, Phoenix, 1978-83, mgr. loss prevention, from 1983. Mem. Ariz. Gov's. Task Force of Asbestos in Sch., Phoenix, 1980-83. Fellow Am. Acad. Indsl. Hygiene; mem. Am. Indsl. Hygiene Assn. (pres. Ariz. chpt. 1982-83), Am. Soc. Safety Engrs.(pres. Ariz. chpt. 1986-87, profl.), Bd. cert. Safety Profls., Am. Conf. Govtl. Indsl. Hygienists, S.W. Safety Congress (exec. bd. dirs. 1980—). Republican. Avocations: tennis, jogging. Home: Surprise, Ariz. Died Oct. 23, 2006.

RAYMOND, DAVID WALKER, lawyer; b. Chelsea, Mass., Aug. 23, 1945; s. John Walker and Jane (Beck) R.; m. Sandra Sue Broadwater, Aug. 12, 1967 (div.); m. Margaret Byrd Payne, May 25, 1974; children: Pamela Payne, Russell Wyatt. BA, Gettysburg Coll., 1967; JD, Temple U., 1970. Bar: Pa. 1970, D.C. 1971, Ill. 1975, U.S. Dist. Ct. (no. dist.) Ill. 1981, U.S. Supreme Ct. 1974. Govtl. affairs atty. Sears, Roebuck and Co., Washington, 1970-74, atty. Sears Hdqrs. law dept. Chgo., 1974-80, asst. gen. counsel advt., trademarks and customs, 1981-84, asst. gen. counsel adminstrn., 1984-86, mgr. planning and analysis corp. planning dept., 1986-89, sr. corp. counsel pub. policy corp. law dept., 1989-90; assoc. gen. counsel litigation and adminstrn. law dept. Sears Mdse. Group, 1990-92, dep. gen. counsel, 1992-93, v.p., gen. counsel, 1993-95; v.p. law Sears Roebuck and Co., 1996; of counsel Winston & Strawn, Washington, 1996-2001; v.p., gen. counsel C-NAV Systems, Inc., Gettysburg, Pa., 2001—03. Mem. staff Temple Law Quar., 1968—69; editor: Temple Law Quar., 1969—70. Trustee No. Ill. U., 1996—98; bd. vis. Christopher Newport U., 1999—2003; bd. fellows Gettysburg Coll., 1999—2003; bd. dirs. ATO Chpt. House Corp., from 1997, pres., from 2004; vol. docent Fords Theatre, from 2012. Recipient Patrick Henry award, Va. Gov., 2001. Mem.: ABA, Phi Alpha Delta. Presbyterian. Home: Mc Lean, Va. Died June 21, 2014.

RAYMOND, ROBERT EARL, retired minister; b. Denver, Mar. 12, 1926; s. Elbert Harold and Mary Josephine (Hassan) R.; m. Carol Hathaway, June 9, 1947; children: Michael Leslie, Barbara Lee. BA, U. Denver, 1950; Diplomate in Divinity, McCormick Theol. Seminary, Chgo., 1954; DD, Carroll Coll., 1971. Ordained to ministry Presbyn. Ch., 1954. Minister of edn. First Presbyn. Ch., Kirkwood, Mo., 1954-58, Oklahoma City, Okla., 1958-61; field dir. of ch. edn. Synod of Wis., Waukesha, 1961-70; dir. ecumenical devel. St. Benedict Ctr., Madison, Wis., 1970-73; assoc. synod exec. Synod of Lakes and Prairies, Bloomington, Minn., 1973-91; ret., 1991. Contbr. articles to profl. jours. Bd. dirs. Oklahoma City Community Coun., 1959-60, Okla. Planned Parenthood, 1959-60, various YMCAs, Denver, Oklahoma City, Kirkwood, 1950-61; chief Protestant advisor Boy Scouts of Am., St. Louis, 1954-58. With USN, 1943-46, ETO, ATO. Recipient First prize in Rabbinic Lit., U. Denver, 1950, Farwell Preaching prize McCormick Theol. Seminary, 1954. Mem. World Future Soc. (life), Phi Beta Kappa, Kappa Delta Pi. Home: Green Valley, Ariz. Died Dec. 11, 2006.

RAYNES, MARVIN, legal and social services association administrator; b. NYC, Sept. 9, 1933; s. Abraham and Anna Fanny (Schecter) R.; m. Annette Ruth Karp, Aug. 11, 1957; children: Arnold D., Clifford H., Daniel L., Lawrence E. AAS, N.Y.C. C.C., 1957; BS, Empire State Coll., 1987; JD, CUNY, 1990. Asst. buyer Gimble Bros. Dept. Stores, 1957-59; sr. asst. buyer, dept. mgr. R.H. Macy Dept. Stores, 1959-65; nat. sales mgr. Marvelwood, Inc., 1965-68; merchandise mgr. S. Klein Dept. Stores, 1968-70; mgr. N.Y. br. Keller Industries, Inc., 1970-74; pres. Marvin Raynes Sales, 1975-80, Internat. Carpet Distbrs. Inc., 1980-83; exec. dir. Tracking, Ongoing, Unwavering Care & Help, Inc., from 1990. Bd. dirs. Project L.I.F.E., Inc., Park House, Inc., chmn. adv. bd., 1986— Editor: (monthly newsletter) Parent Alert, 1983-90. Mem. bd. dirs. Nassau Ctr. for Developmentally Disabled, 1985-90; chmn. adv. bd. Prader-Willi N.Y. Assn., Inc., 1980—; chmn., founder Joint Venture, 1983-90, Com. for Community Living, L.I. region, 1985-90, Parents for Sch. Bus Safety, L.I. region, 1985-90; chmn. Friends & Relatives of Suffolk Ctr.'s Residents, 1986-87; pres., founder Rhinebeck (N.Y.) Sch. Assn. of Parents, Inc., 1979-83; gov. bd. mem. Nassau/Suffolk Health Systems Agy., Inc., 1984—, mem. task force mental hygiene, substance & alcohol abuse, 1983-87, program svcs. rev. com., 1985—; active Concerned Citizen for Ctrl Islip, Inc., 1983-87, N.Y. State Task Force on Aging Out, 1983-87, Long Island Task Force on Aging Out, 1987-95, Long Island Respite Network, 1983-89, clearinghouse com. Suffolk Community Coun., 1983—, task force homeless mentally ill Alliance Mentally Ill, 1987-89, ad hoc task force future care & planning CUNY Law Sch., 1993—, mental retardation/devel. disabilities subcom. Suffolk County Health Dept., 1986-95, planning workgroup parents as ptnrs. L.I. region D.D. planning coun., 1990-93, allocations approvals com. Morris Smoller Fund, 1985-86, L.I. respite care network State Regional Devel. Disabilities Svcs. Office, 1981-85, L.I. children Svcs., 1993-95; mem. United Way of L.I. Allocations Com., Youth & Family, 1985-89, Mental Health, 1990-95. With N.Y. Nat. Guard, 1949-52, U.S. Army, 1952-55. Recipient Grad. award North Suffolk Mental Health Ctr., 1974, Cert. of Appreciation award Nassau/Suffolk Health Systems Agy., 1984-93, Allocation Vol. award United Way L.I., 1986, award of appreciation Prader-Willi N.Y. Assn., Inc., 1988, Cert. Appreciation Prader-Willi N.Y. Assn., Inc., 1992, Cert. Achievement award N.Y. State Devel. Disabilities Planning Coun., 1991, Outstanding Achievement award N.Y. State Devel. Disabilities Planning Coun., 1992, numerous letters of commendation, others. Mem. N.Y. State Austistic Soc., N.Y. Assn. Retarded Children, Knights of Pythias (comdr. 1984-85). Avocations: photography, civil war history, hiking, working with disabled children. Home: Coram, NY. Died Dec. 14, 2006.

RAYNOLDS, DAVID ROBERT, buffalo breeder, writer; b. NY, Feb. 15, 1928; s. Robert Frederick and Marguerite Evelyn (Gerdau) R.; m. May (Kean) Raynolds, May 12, 1951; children: Robert, Linda, Martha, Laura, David A.F. AB, Dartmouth Coll., 1949; MA, Wesleyan U., Middletown, Conn., 1955; predoctoral, Johns Hopkins Sch. Advanced Internat. Studies, Washington, 1956; grad., Nat. War Coll., Washington, 1973. Account exec. R.H. Morris Assoc., Newtown, Conn., 1949-50; fgn. svc. officer Dept. of State, Washington, 1956-76; pres. Ranch Rangers, Inc., Lander, Wyo., from 1976. Pres. Nat. Buffalo Assn., Ft. Pierre, S.D., 1987-88. Author: Rapid Development in Small Economies (Praeger); contbr. articles to profl. jours. Trustee, bd. dirs. Liberty Hall Found.; dir. Leader Corp.; mem. steering com. Wyo. Bus. Alliance; chmn. bd. govs. Mus. of the Am. West. With US Army, 1950—53. Recipient Meritorious Svc. Award, Dept. of State, Washington, 1966. Mem. The Explorers Club, Dacor Assn., Fremont County Farm Bur., Fgn. Svc. Assn., Am. Legion, Rotary, Elks. Republican. Episcopalian. Avocation: travel. Home: Lander, Wyo. Died June 19, 2015.

REAGAN, NANCY DAVIS (ANNE FRANCIS ROBBINS), former First Lady of the United States, volunteer; b. NYC, July 6, 1921; d. Kenneth and Edith (Luckett) Robbins, Loyal Davis (Stepfather); m. Ronald Reagan, Mar. 4, 1952 (dec. June 5, 2004); children: Patricia Ann, Ronald Prescott stepchildren: Maureen(dec.) , Michael. BA in Theatre, Smith Coll., 1943; LLD (hon.), Pepperdine U., 1983; LHD (hon.), Georgetown U., 1987. Sales clk. Marshall Fields Dept. Store, Chgo.; First Lady of the US Washington, 1981—89. Contract actress, MGM, 1949-56; films include Portrait of Jennie, 1948, East Side, West Side, 1949, Doctor and the Girl, 1949, Shadow on the Wall, 1950, The Next Voice You Hear, 1950, Night into Morning, 1951, It's a Big Country, 1951, Shadow in the Sky, 1952, Talk About a Stranger, 1952, Donovan's Brain, 1953, Hellcats of the Navy, 1957, Crash Landing, 1958, You Can't Hurry Love, 1988, Lunar: Silver Star Story, 1992; TV credits include Schlitz Playhouse of Stars, 1951, Climax, 1954, General Electric Theater, 1953, Zane Grey Theater, 1956, The Tall Man, 1960, 87th Precint, 1961, Wagon Train, 1957, Different Strokes, 1978, Dynasty, 1981; Broadway: Lute Song, 1946; formerly author syndicated column on prisoner-of-war and missing-in-action soldiers and their families; author: Nancy, 1980; (with Jane Wilkie) To Love a Child, 1982, (with William Novak) My Turn: The Memoirs of Nancy Reagan, 1989. Civic worker, visited wounded Viet Nam vets., sr. citizens, hosps. and schs. for physically and emotionally handicapped children, active in furthering foster grandparents for handicapped children program; hon. nat. chmn. Aid to Adoption of Spl. Kids, 1977; spl. interest in fighting alcohol and drug abuse among youth: hosted first ladies from around the world for 2d Internat. Drug Conf., 1985; hon. chmn. Just Say No Found., Nat. Fedn. of Parents for Drug-Free Youth, Nat. Child Watch Campaign, President's Com. on the Arts and Humanities, Wolf Trap Found. bd. of trustees, Nat. Trust for Historic Preservation, Cystic Fibrosis Found., Nat. Republican Women's Club; hon. pres. Girl Scouts of Am. Named one of Ten Most Admired Am. Women, Good Housekeeping mag., ranking #1 in poll, 1984, 85, 86; Woman of Yr. Los Angeles Times, 1977; permanent mem. Hall of Fame of Ten Best Dressed Women in U.S.; recipient humanitarian awards from Am. Camping Assn., Nat. Council on Alcoholism, United Cerebral Palsy Assn., Internat. Ctr. for Disabled; Boys Town Father Flanagan award; 1986 Kiwanis World Service medal; Variety Clubs Internat. Lifeline award; numerous awards for her role in fight against drug abuse. Republican. Presbyterian. Died Mar. 6, 2016.

REASONER, ELIZABETH DIANE, public relations executive; b. Birmingham, Ala., Nov. 1, 1949; d. George Wilburn and Martha Overton (Eason) Fulmer; m. Richard Merle Reasoner, Feb. 10, 1968; children: Richard Michael, Robert Mark. Diploma in ch. music, Fla. Bapt. Theol. Coll., 1972; AS, Southwest Bapt. U., 1978; BA, Ottawa U., Kans., 1985; MA, Ottawa U., 1994. Substitute tchr. Liberty County Sch. Dist., Bristol, Fla., 1975-76; with dean's office Southwest Bapt. U., Bolivar, Mo., 1977-78; sec., adminstrv. asst. Midwestern Bapt. Theol. Sem., Kansas City, Mo., 1978-87; pub. rels. specialist Ga. Bapt. Conv., Atlanta, 1987-90, assoc. dir. of pub. rels., from 1990. Coord. workshops and musical prodns. Midwestern Bapt. Theol. Sem., Kansas City, 1981-84. Editor: Georgia Baptist Digest, 1990; author, editor publicity material, Ga. Bapt. Conv., 1990—, (newsletter) CenterLines, 1989—. Youth dir. Lake Mystic Bapt. Ch., Bristol, 1974-76; associational music dir. Applachacola Assn., Liberty County, Fla., 1975; music dir. Liberty County Early Learning Ctr., 1974. Recipient Cert. of Merit, The Naval Officers Wives League, Pensacola, 1964, Svc. award Midwestern Singers, Kansas City, Mo., 1987, Award of Excellence Religious Pub. Rels. Coun., 1996, Print Excellence award Industry Assn. Ga., 1996; named one of Outstanding Young Women Am., 1982, Alumnus of Yr., Fla. Bapt. Theol. Coll., 1995. Mem. NAFE, Nat. Orgn. Press Women, Bapt. Pub. Rels. Assn. (v.p. 1994-95), Tau Pi Epsilon (pres. 1972-73). Avocations: conference leader, vocalist, calligraphy. Home: Sugar Hill, Ga. Died Apr. 1, 2007.

RECTOR, EUGENE WALTER, county commissioner, farmer; b. Kalamazoo, Mich., Aug. 18, 1922; s. Walter Lee and Vera (Youngs) R.; m. Eva Louise Garrison, Apr. 10, 1945; children: Phyllis, Nancy, Patricia, Gail. Student, Mich. State U., 1942; assessor degree, Kalamazoo Valley C.C., 1971. Cert. assessor, Mich. Farmer, Kalamazoo area; twp. trustee, then twp. supr. Alamo Twp., Kalamazoo, 1958-89; commr. County of Kalamazoo, Kalamazoo, 1990-93. Dist. rep. State Sen. Jack Welborn, 1986-90; community leader 4-H, Alamo Twp., 1950-56. Mem. Masons, Shriners. Republican. Congregationalist. Avocations: leathercrafting, woodworking, travel. Home: Kalamazoo, Mich. Died Aug. 28, 2007.

RECTOR, ROBERT RUSH, musician, archaeologist, commercial artist, radio station owner; b. Quannah, Tex., Jan. 25, 1947; s. Bill Nat and Hazel Louise (Plyler) R.; m. Paula Marie Clement, Sept. 9, 1972 (div. June 1978); 1 child, Robin Rachael; m. Nancy Gray, June 8, 1985. BS in Comml Art, S.W. Tex. State U., 1978; MA in Anthropology, U. Tex., San Antonio, 1996. Profl. drummer over 30 bands, various locations, from 1962; cartographer H.M. Gousha Co., Comfort, Tex., 1971-73; owner comml. art studio Tripple R. Prodns., Kerrville, Tex., 1977-95; owner P&R Prodns., Kerrville, 1985-95; dir. Rector and Assocs. Archaeol. Cons. Svcs., Kerrville, from 1996, Edwards Plateau Archaeol. Conservation Svcs., Kerrville, from 1996. Art dir. Pony Express Advertiser, Kerrville, 1978-80, art dir. Kerrville Music Found., 1985-86. With U.S. Army, 1969-71. Mem. Musicians Union, Kerrville C. of C., Tex. Archaeol. Soc., So. Tex. Archaeol. Assn., Coun. Tex. Archaeologists, Tex. Hist. Found., Ctr. for Archaeol. Rsch. Friends Archaeology. Republican. Methodist. Home: Kerrville, Tex. Died June 2, 2007.

REDMOUNTAIN, ALEX RODE, psychologist; b. Belgrade, Yugoslavia, Apr. 13, 1934; came to U.S., 1945; s. Zvonko Rosenberger and Nada (Armuth) Rode; m. Meredith Eagon, Aug. 31, 1958 (div. July 1984); children: Jordan Rode, Marnie Rode; m. Carole Sue Light, Nov. 11, 1984; 1 stepchild, Erik Light-Selvey. PhD, George Washington U., 1976. Diplomate Am. Bd. Profl. Psychology. Tchr., dean The Colo. Acad., Denver, 1959-62; tchr. Hawthorne Sch., Washington, 1962-63; headmaster Walden Sch., Washington, 1963-68; psychologist, dir. tng. D.C. Dept. Pub. Health, Washington, 1971-76; pvt. practice D.C., Ga., N.C., from 1976. Bd. dirs. Nat. Alternative Sch. Com., Washington, 1964-70, Runaway House, WAshington, 1971-75, Spl. Approaches to Juvenile Assistance, Washington, 1972-79. Editor: Merit Employment and Civil Rights, 1961; contbr. articles to profl. jours., poetry and fiction to mags., and chpts. to books. Chmn., founder Psychologists for Social Responsibility, Washington, 1981; writer, advisor Robert Kennedy for Pres. campaign, Washington, 1967. With U.S. Army, 1954-56, Korea. Mem. APA, Am. Acad. Psychotherapists, Ga. Psychol. Assn. Mem. Unitarian-Universalist Ch. Died Dec. 15, 2006.

REED, BETTY ANN, lawyer; b. Jacksonville, Ill., Aug. 17, 1943; d. Robert George and Betty Mae Hills; m. Wayne M. Michael, Sept. 13, 1980 (div. 1992); children: Marla Reed

Brandt, Thomas Edward Reed. BA, Douglass Coll., New Brunswick, NJ, 1965. Sole practitioner, Modesto, Calif. Avocation: bird watching. Home: Modesto, Calif. Died Dec. 21, 2007.

REED, KATHLEEN RAND, manufacturer, marketing consultant, sociologist; b. Chgo., Feb. 6, 1947; d. Kirkland James Reed and Johnnie Viola Rand. Student, San Jose State U. Investigator, research cons. Ill. Supreme Ct., Chgo., 1970; account exec. ETA Pub. Relations, Chgo., 1970-72; pub. relations and promotion dir. Sta. WTVS TV, Detroit, 1972; pub. affairs dir. Sta. WJLB Radio, Detroit, 1972-74; pvt. practice bus. resource and research cons. K.H. Arnold, San Francisco, 1974-80; spl. projects coordinator The Hdqrs. Co. subs. United Techs., San Francisco, 1980-81; adminstrn. mgr. Nat. Alliance of Bus.-Region IX, San Francisco, 1981-83; pres. Michael St. Michael/Corp. Leather and Leather Goods Mfr., Menlo Park, Calif., from 1983. Pres. Necronomics, Stanford, Calif., cons. organ transplantation, 1989—. Mem. Am. Sociol. Assn., Pacific Sociol. Assn., Sociologists for Women in Society, Women in Communications, Western Social Sci. Assn., Nat. Assn. Sci. Writers, Acad. Ind. Scholars, Soc. for Study of Women in Legal History, Inst. for Hist. Study, NOW, Women's Inst. for Freedom, Am. Women in Radio and TV Inc., San Francisco C. of C. (com. mem. 1984—), World Trade Assn., Bay Area Purchasing Council (com. mem. 1986—), Urban Coalition West, (bd. dirs. Phoenix chpt. 1986—), San Francisco Convention and Visitors Bur. (bd. dirs. 1986—). Died July 3, 2014.

REED, ROSALIE, horse trainer; b. San Diego, May 5, 1954; d. Lester Woodrow Reed and Pearl (Peterson) Hampton. Trainer Fletcher Hills Ranch, San Diego, 1970-74, Willow Glen Farm, El Cajon, Calif., 1974-77, Moreno Valley Ranch, Lakeside, Calif., 1978-80, Mill Creek Farm, Malibu, Calif., 1980-81, L.A. Equestrian Ctr., from 1981. Judge Appaloosa Horse Club Nat. Show, Syracuse, N.Y., Appaloosa Horse Club. Can. Author: Handbook of Hunter Seat Equitation, 1977, Handbook of Saddle Seat Equitation, 1977; contbr. to profl. publs. Inducted San Diego Hall of Champions, 1978; winner 8 world championships, Appaloosa Horse Club, 1972-76, 7 nat. championships, 1972-76; demonstrator 1984 Summer Olympics, L.A. Mem. ASCAP, Am. Horse Show Assn. (judge), Internat. Arabian Horse Assn. (judge), Pacific Coast Horse Show Assn., Calif. Profl. Horsemen's Assn., Equestrian Trails Internat. Avocations: singing, songwriting, skydiving. Home: Burbank, Calif. Died Nov. 30, 2006.

REED, THOMAS ANDREW, lawyer, judge; b. Yonkers, NY, Feb. 4, 1934; s. John A. and Helen A. Reed; m. Margaret S. Reed, Apr. 20, 1967; children: Danielle S., Jennifer A. BS, Fordham U., 1963; LLB, Cornell U., 1966. Bar: N.Y. 1966. Ptnr. Reed & Reed, Poughkeepsie, N.Y., 1966-97; owner Thomas A. Reed, Esq., Poughkeepsie, from 1998. Town Justice, Town of Pleasant Valley, N.Y., 1972—. Mem. N.Y. State Bar Assn., Dutchess County Bar Assn., N.Y. State Magistrates Assn., Dutchess County Magistrates Assn. (pres. 1977), Pleasant Valley Lions Club (pres., bd. dirs.). Avocation: tennis. Home: Pleasant Valley, NY. Died Dec. 22, 2006.

REED, WALT ARNOLD, artist, art historian, art dealer; b. Big Spring, Tex., July 21, 1917; s. Fay Allen and Edith Anna (Terpening) R.; m. Mary Ines Garavagno, Sept. 14, 1947; children: Stina, Geoffrey, Roger. Student, Grand Rapids Jr. Coll., 1936-38, Pratt Inst., 1938-39, Phoenix Art Inst., 1939-42. Overseas rep. C.A.R.E., NYC, 1948-52, art dir., 1952-54; freelance illustrator Westport, Conn., 1954-57; instr. art Famous Artist Schs., Westport, 1957-72, asst. to dir., 1966-72; mng. editor North Light Publs., Westport, 1972-76; pres. Illustration House Inc., NYC, from 1976. Author: The Illustrator in America 1900-1960s, 1966, Harold Von Schmidt Draws and Paints the Old West, 1972, John Clymer, 1976, The Magic Pen of Joseph Clement Coll, 1978, Great American Illustrators, 1979, The Illustrator in America 1880-1980, 1984; designer U.S. postage stamp series, 50 state flags, 1976. Mem. adv. com. Sanford Low Collection Am. Illustration, New Britain, Conn. Mem. N.Y. Soc. Illustrators (mus. com.). Home: Westport, Conn. Died Mar. 18, 2015.

REEP, EDWARD ARNOLD, artist; b. Bklyn., May 10, 1918; s. Joseph and Elsie (Abramson) R.; m. Karen Patricia Stevens, Dec. 9, 1942; children— Susan Kay, Cristine Elyse, Janine J., Mitchell Jules. Student, Art Center Coll. Design, 1936-41. Instr. painting and drawing Art Center Coll. Design, Los Angeles, 1946-50, Chouinard Art Inst., Los Angeles, 1950-69; prof. painting, chmn. dept., artist in residence E. Carolina U., 1970-85, prof. emeritus, from 1985. Cons. editor Van Nostrand Reinhold Pub. Co.; ofcl. war artist-corr. WWII, Africa and Italy. Author: The Content of Watercolor, 1968, A Combat Artist in World War II, 1987; shows include Whitney Mus. Am. Art Ann., N.Y.C., 1946-48, Los Angeles County Mus. Ann., 1946-60, Corcoran Gallery Art Biennial, Washington, 1949, Nat. Gallery Art, Washington, 1945, They Drew Fire, 2000, Mus. Modern Art, N.Y.C.; represented in permanent collections Los Angeles County Mus., U.S. War Dept., Grunwald Graphic Arts Collection, UCLA, Nat. Mus. Am. Art, Washington, Lytton Collection, Los Angeles, State of Calif. Collection, Sacramento. Guggenheim fellow, 1945-46; Nat. Endowment for Arts grantee, 1975 Mem. AAUP, Nat. Watercolor Soc. (past pres., Lifetime Achievement award 2002), Watercolor USA Honor Soc. (lifetime achievement gold medal 1997). Democrat. Home: Bakersfield, Calif. *I once was consumed by the desire to become an artist. I feel no differently today. There is work ahead. If I had set goals for myself I no longer can recall what they may have been; I go along painting as well or as inventively as I can. Never have I sacrificed living life as I feel I must for my art. My work is a reflection of my life— experiences real and imagined.* Deceased.

REES, ROGER, actor, educator; b. Aberystwyth, Wales, May 5, 1944; s. William John and Doris Louise (Smith) R.; m. Rick Elice, 2011 Educated, Camberwell Sch. Art, Slade Sch. Fine Art. Instr. theatre Columbia U., NYC, 1981-82; Hoffman chair prof. Fla. State U., Tallahassee, 1986; artistic dir. Williamstown Theatre Festival, 2005—07. Made theatre debut in Hindle Wakes, Wimbledon, Eng., 1964; other theatre appearances include The Cherry Orchard, Pitlochry, Scotland, 1965, The Merchant of Venice, Aldwych Theatre, London, also The Island of the Mighty, 1971-72; Candida, Neptune Theatre, Halifax, N.S., 1973; Paradise, Theatre Upstairs, London, also Moving Clocks Go Slow, 1975, The Alchemist, London, 1977, Macbeth, Warehouse Theatre, London, also Factory Birds, 1977, The Way of the World, Aldwych Theatre, 1978, The Suicide, various theatres, London, 1980, The Adventures of Nicholas Nickleby, Aldwych Theatre, London and Plymouth Theatre, N.Y.C., 1981 (Tony award for Best Actor 1982), The Real Thing, Strand Theatre, London, 1983, Cries from the Mammoth House, Royal Court Theatre, London, 1983, Double-Double, Watford Palace and Fortune Theatres, London, 1986, Archangels Don't Play Pinball, Bristol Old Vic Theatre Co., Theatre Royal, London, 1986, Hapgood, Aldwych Theatre, 1988; appeared with Royal Shakespeare Co. in The Taming of the Shrew, 1967, As You Like It, 1967, Julius Caesar, 1968, The Merry Wives of Windsor, 1968, Pericles, 1969, Twelfth Night, 1969, 70, 76, Henry VIII, 1969, The Winter's Tale, 1969, 70, The Plebeians Rehearse the Uprising, 1970, Major Barbara, 1970, Much Ado About Nothing, 1971, Othello, 1971, Romeo and Juliet, 1976, Macbeth, 1976, The Comedy of Errors, 1976, Cymbeline, 1979, Hamlet, 1984, Love's Labours Lost, 1984, Indiscretions, 1995 (Tony nominee - Lead Actor in a Play), The Rehearsal, 1996, Uncle Vanya, 2000, The Addams Family, 2010-2011, Peter and the Starcatcher, 2012-2013, The Winslow Boy, 2013; tour London Assurance, various U.S. cities, 1974-75, tour Is There Honey Still For Tea?, The Three Sisters, Twelfth Night, various U.K. cities, 1978; toured U.K. cities with Cambridge Theatre Co., 1973-74, in Twelfth Night, Aunt Sally or the Triumph of Death, She Stoops to Conquer, Fear and Misery in the Third Reich, Jack and the Beanstalk, 1975, in The Importance of Being Earnest, The Birthday Party, The Visit, 2015; appeared in films Star 80, 1983, Robin Hood: Men in Tights, 1993, Sudden Manhattan, 1996, The Substance of Fire, 1996, Trouble on the Corner, 1997, Next Stop Wonderland, 1998, A Midsummer Night's Dream, 1999, The Bumblebee Flies Anyway, 1999 Black-Male, 2000, 3 A.M., 2001, (voice) Return to Never Land, 2002, The Scorpion King, 2002, Frida, 2002, The Emperor's Club, 2002, The Tulse Luper Suitcases, Part 3: From Sark to the Finish, 2003, Going Under, 2004, Crazy Like a Fox, 2004, Social Grace, 2005, Game 6, 2005, The New World, 2005, The Pink Panther, 2006, Garfield: A Tale of Two Kitties, 2006, Falling for Grace, 2006, The Treatment, 2006, Garfield 2, 2006, The Prestige, 2006, The Invasion, 2007, The Narrows, 2008, Happy Tears, 2009, Almost Perfect, 2011, Affluenza, 2014; appeared in TV films A Christmas Carol, 1984, The Ebony Tower, Great Performances, PBS, 1987, Charles and Diana: Unhappily Ever After, 1992, The Tower, 1993, The Possession of Michael D., 1995, Titanic, 1996, Double Platinum, 1999, The Crossing 2000; (TV series) Cheers, 1989-1993, M.A.N-.T.I.S., 1994-1997 Boston Common, 1997, The West Wing, 2000-2005, Grey's Anatomy, 2007, Warehouse 13, 2009-2013, The Middle, 2013, Elementary 2012-2014, Forever, 2015; (TV miniseries) Bouquet of Barbed Wire, 1976, The Life and Adventures of Nicholas Nickleby, 1982, Imaginary Friends, 1987, Liberty! The American Revolution, 1997, It Could be Worse, 2013. Died July 10, 2015.

REESE, VIRGINIA DAHLENBURG, corporate librarian; b. Erlander, Ky., July 27, 1924; d. Vincent Arnold and Henriette (Feldkamp) Dahlenburg; m. Robert Ralph Reese, Sr., July 31, 1948; children: Janine Schulte, Robert Jr., Miriam Nevitt, Michele Belmont. BA, Thomas More Coll., 1946; MSLS, U. Ky., 1974; postgrad., No. Ky. U., 1980. Cert. tchr. Statis. asst. ANTSCO Greater Cinti. Airport, Boone County, Ky., 1946-48; tchr. pvt. and pub. schs., Kenton County, Ky., 1963-74; sch. libr. Ludlow (Ky.) High Sch., 1974-88; bus. coll. libr., English instr. Ky. Coll. Bus., Florence, 1988-90; corp. libr. Cin. Gas & Electric Co., 1991-95; retired, 1995. Mentor Thomas More Coll., Crestview Hills, Ky., 1982-84; vol. adult reading instr. THomas More Coll. scholar, 1946. Mem. Ky. Retired Tchrs. Assn., Beta Phi Mu. Republican. Roman Catholic. Avocations: reading, travel, golf, tutoring, writing. Home: Crestview Hls, Ky. Died Feb. 7, 2007.

REGAN, EDWARD VAN BUREN (NED REGAN), retired state official; b. Buffalo, May 14, 1930; William & Caroline Van Buren; m. Jennifer Read, 1959 (div. 1988); children: Jane, Julian, Kate' m. Susan Ginsberg, 1991 BA, Hobart Coll., 1952; LLB cum laude, SUNY, Buffalo, 1964. County exec. Erie County, Buffalo, 1972—78; comptr. State of NY, Albany, 1979—93; pres. Baruch Coll., 2000—04; chmn. Erie County Fiscal Stability Authority, 2005—06. Recipient John LaFarge Meml. award for Interracial Justice Cath. Interracial Coun. N.Y., 1981, Public Svc. award SUNY-Buffalo Sch. Law Alumni Assn., 1981, Disting. Leadership award Assn. Govt. Accts., 1981. Republican. Roman Catholic. Avocations: fishing, swimming, skiing. Died Oct. 18, 2014.

REHORN, LOIS M(ARIE) (LOIS MARIE SMITH), nursing administrator; b. Larned, Kans., Apr. 15, 1919; d. Charles and Ethel L. (Canaday) Williamson; m. C. Howard Smith, Feb. 15, 1946 (dec. Aug. 1980); 1 child, Cynthia A. Huddleston; m. Harlan W. Rehorn, Aug. 25, 1981. RN, Bethany Hosp. Sch. Nursing, Kansas City, Kans., 1943; BS, Ft. Hays Kans. State U., Hays, 1968, MS, 1970. RN, N.Mex.; lic. pvt. pilot. Office nurse, surg. asst. Dr. John H. Luke, Kansas City, Kans., 1943-47; supr. nursing unit Larned (Kans.) State Hosp., 1949-68, dir. nursing edn., 1968-71, dir. nursing, 1972-81, ret., 1981. Recipient Order of the Blue Key, 1942-43; named Nurse of Yr. DNA-4, 1986. Mem. Am. Nurses Assn., Kans. Nurses Assn. (dist. treas.), N.Mex. Nurses Assn. (dist. pres. 1982-86, dist. bd. dirs. 1986-88). Avocation: flying (pilot). Home: Larned, Kans. *Keep within you a place where dreams may grow. The fountain of understanding is the willingness to listen.* Died Jan. 21, 2007.

REICH, MERRILL DRURY, intelligence consultant, writer; b. Washington, Aug. 28, 1930; s. Merrill Dale Reich and Evelyn Merle Wright; m. Georgia Ann Ewing, Aug. 28, 1953; 1 child, Alexandra Therese. BA in History, Govt., Rollins Coll., 1954; postgrad., U. Vienna, 1954-55, Naval War Coll., 1973-74; MA in Mgmt., Cen. Mich. U., 1981. Commd. ensign USN, 1956, advanced through grades to capt., ret., 1982; dir. systems mgmt. BDM Corp., Columbia, Md., 1982-92; cons. Crytec, Inc., 1992-95. Fulbright scholar, 1954-55. Mem. SAR, Nat. Trust for Hist. Preservation, U.S. Naval Inst., Naval War Coll. Found., Assn. Former Intelligence Officers, Navy Cryptologic Vets. Assn., Fulbright Assn., New Eng. Hist. Geneal. Soc., Omicron Delta Kappa, Pi Gamma Mu, Phi Kappa Tau. Avocations: genealogy, lapidary, antiques, swimming, sailing. Home: Annapolis, Md. Died June 12, 2007.

REICHMAN, JACK ZEV, mathematician; b. NYC, Dec. 13, 1950; s. Herman and Lillian (Klein) R.; m. Ilene Janice Cohn, June 28, 1977; children: Jonathan Emanuel, Jeffrey. BA, Bklyn. Coll., 1972; PhD, SUNY-Buffalo, 1982. Adj. lectr. Bklyn. Coll., 1972-74; faculty assoc. Wright State U., Dayton, Ohio, 1979-80; asst. prof. U. Dayton, 1980-83; asst. prof. math. Hofstra U., Hempstead, N.Y., 1983-86; actuarial asst. The Equitable Life Assurance Soc., NYC, 1986-89; assoc. actuary Washington Nat. Life Ins. Co. of N.Y., NYC, from 1990. Contbr. articles to profl. jours. U. Dayton summer rsch. fellow, 1983. Mem. Am. Math. Soc., N.Y. Acad. Sci., Assoc. of the Soc. Actuaries. Home: Kew Gardens, NY. Died Dec. 25, 2006.

REID, WILLIAM WATKINS, JR., county commissioner; b. NYC, Nov. 12, 1923; s. William Watkins Sr. and Edith Almond (Fowler) R.; m. Margaret Amelia Latsha, Sept. 7, 1946; children: Philip David, Elizabeth Margaret (Mrs. William Beebe), Thomas William. AB, Oberlin Coll., 1947; MDiv, Yale U., 1950. Ordained elder United Meth. Ch., 1952. Pastor Camptown (Pa.) Meth. Ch., 1950-57, Carverton Meth. Ch., Wyoming, Pa., 1957-67, Ctrl. United Meth. Ch., Wilkes-Barre, Pa., 1967-78; dist. supt. Wilkes-Barre dist. United Meth. Ch., Kingston, Pa., 1978-84; pastor Wyo. (Pa.) United Meth. Ch., 1984-85, Tunkhannock (Pa.) United Meth. Ch., 1985-92; county commr. Wyo. County, Tunkhannock, from 1992. Bd. dirs. Tyler Meml. Hosp., Tunkhannock; chair Wyo. County Rural Health Task Force, Tunkhannock, 1992—, Wyo. County Libr. Bd., Tunkhannock, 1993—; mem. No. Tier Regional Planning and Devel. Coun., Towanda, Pa., 1992—, No. Tier Export Adv. Coun., Towanda, 1994—. Contbg. author: Atlas of Bird Breeding In Pennsylvania, 1992; contbr. articles, hymns to religious and spl. interest jours. Del. gen. conf. United Meth. Ch., 1976, 80, 84, del. N.E. jurisdictional conf., 1972, 76, 80, 84, 88, 92, gen. bd. ch. and soc., 1972-76; active City Coun., Wilkes-Barre, 1972-76; founder, mem. Martin Luther King Jr. Com. for Social Justice, Wilkes-Barre, 1980—; pres. bd. trustees Family Svc. Assn. Wyo. Valley, Wilkes-Barre, 1986—; bd. dirs. Wyo. County United Fund., Tunkhannock, 1987—. With U.S. Army Med. Corp, 1943-45, ETO. Recipient John Frederick Oberlin Outstanding Rural Pastor award Rural Ch. Inst., 1956, Winning Hymn award Nat. Coun. Chs., 1958. Mem. Nat. Assn. Counties (health steering com. 1992—), County Commrs. Assn. Pa. (mem. energy, environment and land use com. 1992—, human svcs. com. 1993—), Wyo. Valley Torch Club (trustee, past pres.). Republican. Avocations: bird study, camping, hymn-writng, drama. Home: Tunkhannock, Pa. Died Mar. 27, 2007.

REILLY, FRANCIS X., lawyer, consultant; b. Westborough, Mass., Sept. 18, 1916; s. Francis Xavier and Blanche Marie (Marshall) R.; m. Beverly E. Blackwell, Oct. 7, 1941 (dec. July 1982); children: Martha J. Reilly Hinchman, John F. AB, Dartmouth Coll., 1938; JD, Harvard U., 1941. Bar: Mass. 1941, Ill. 1954. Atty., treas. Wilson & Co., Inc., Chgo., 1963-67; v.p. LTV Corp., Dallas, 1967-70; v.p., treas. B. F. Goodrich Co., Akron, Ohio, 1970-73, Katy Industries, Inc., Elgin, 1973-76; gen. counsel, v.p. Rollins Burdick Hunter, Chgo., 1976-84; pvt. practice law and cons. Barrington, Ill., 1984-99. Lt. comdr. USNR, 1943-46. Mem. ABA, U. Club of Chgo. Died Nov. 13, 2006.

REINHARDT, JOHN EDWARD, former international affairs specialist; b. Glade Spring, Va., Mar. 8, 1920; s. Edward Vinton and Alice (Miller) R.; m. Carolyn Lillian Daves, Sept. 2, 1947; children: Sharman W. Reinhardt Lancefield, Alice N. (Cicole Reinhardt), Carolyn C. Reinhardt Fenstermaker (Cecile). AB, Knoxville Coll., 1939; MS, U. Wis., 1947, PhD, 1950. Prof. English Va. State Coll., Petersburg, 1950-56; cultural affairs officer USIS, Manila, 1956-58; dir. Am. Cultural Ctr., Kyoto, 1958-63; cultural attache USIS, Tehran, Iran, 1963-66; dep. asst. dir. Office East Asia and Pacific, USIA, Washington, 1966-68, 70-71, asst. dir. Office for Africa, 1968-70; ambassador to Nigeria, 1971-75; asst. sec. state for pub. affairs, 1975-77; dir. USIA, Washington, 1977-78, U.S. Internat. Communication Agy.,

Washington, 1978-81; acting dir. Smithsonian Mus. African Art, Washington, 1981-83; asst. sec. for history and art Smithsonian Instn., Washington, 1983-84, dir. directorate internat. activities, 1984-87; prof. polit. sci. U. Vt., Burlington, 1987-90, prof. emeritus, 1990—2016. Served as officer AUS, 1942-46. Mem. MLA, Am. Fgn. Svc. Assn. (v.p. 1969-71). Clubs: Cosmos. Methodist. Home: Silver Spring, Md. Died Feb. 18, 2016.

REMPEL, ARTHUR GUSTAV, biology professor; b. Marinskaya, Ukraine, Jan. 5, 1910; came to U.S., 1923; s. Gustav Aron and Elisabeth Electra (Dirks) R.; m. Lucile Elma Sommerfield, June 19, 1934; children: Robert Arthur (dec.), Herbert Frank, Paul Leonard (dec.), Margaret Louise, Roland Richard. Cert., Pasadena Jr. Coll., 1931; AB, Oberlin Coll., 1934; PhD, U. Calif., Berkeley, 1938; DSc (hon), Whitman Coll., 1987. Acting curator Mus. Anthropology and Zoology Oberlin (Ohio) Coll., 1931-34; teaching asst. U. Calif., Berkeley, 1934-38; mem. faculty biology Whitman Coll., Walla Walla, Wash., from 1938, prof., 1949-75, prof. emeritus, from 1975. Vis. prof. biology U. Calif., Berkeley, summer 1949, U. Wash., Seattle, summer 1957, 58, 66, 67; rsch. assoc. Wash. State U., Pullman, summer 1956; ranger, historian Nat. Park Svc., summer 1953, 54; ranger, naturalist Nat. Park Svc., Yosemite, Calif., summer 1955. Fellow AAAS; mem. Phi Beta Kappa, Sigma Xi. Avocations: travel, wildlife photography, gardening. Home: Walla Walla, Wash. Died May 1, 2007.

REN, ELIZABETH REBECCA, nurse; b. Elwood, Ind., July 2, 1910; d. Karl Swan and Mayme (Maley) Simison; m. Guilford Abraham Ren, Oct. 7, 1932; children: Mary Katherine, Judith Ann. BS in Nursing, Elmhurst Coll., 1962. Nurse Doctor's Clinic, Villa Park, Ill., 1943-60, Hine's (Ill.) VA Hosp., 1960-68; tchr. Southwest Jr. High Sch., Melbourne, Fla., 1968; asst. dir. nurses Medic Home, Melbourne, 1969-71; dir. nurses Sunny Pines Nursing Home, Rockledge, Fla., 1974-76; adminstr. South Brevard Geriatric Health Ctr., Melbourne, 1979-87, cons., from 1987; chmn. health com. Bay Village Apt. Ctr., Sarasota, from 1987. Indep. researcher Alzheimer's Disease. Author: Fountain of Youth, 1975. Senator Silver Haired Legislature, Tallahassee, 1978-84. Recipient Lily award South Brevard Profl. Women's Network, 1986. Mem. Fla. Nurses Assn. (Nurse of Yr. 1986), Am. Nurses Assn., Am. Assn. Retired Persons (pres. Melbourne chpt. 1980), Nat. Assn. Ret. Fed. Employees (sec. 1981). Republican. Presbyterian. Avocations: travel, poetry. Home: Sarasota, Fla. Died Feb. 24, 2007.

RENAU, DONALD IRWIN, lawyer; b. Louisville, Apr. 28, 1936; m. Lynn Scholl, Dec. 21, 1961. BA, Principia Coll., 1958; JD, U. Louisville, 1967. Bar: Ky. 1968, U.S. Ct. Appeals (6th cir.) 1968. Pvt. practice, Louisville, from 1968. Columnist Am. Agt. & Broker, 1997—. Bd. dirs. Salvation Army Adv. Bd., Louisville, 1990—; past pres. Lions club, 1966—. Avocation: horses. Home: Louisville, Ky. Died Apr. 14, 2007.

RENAUDIN, WILLIAM SUTCLIFFE, obstetrician, gynecologist, educator; b. New Orleans, Aug. 4, 1935; s. George and Pauline (Sutcliffe) R.; m. Janet Elise Boisfontaine, Aug. 16, 1958; children: Elise Renaudin Vincent, William Sutcliffe, George. MD, Tulane U., 1960. Diplomate Am. Bd. Ob-Gyn. Intern So. Bapt. Hosp., New Orleans, 1960-61; resident in ob-gyn Tulane unit Charity Hosp., New Orleans, 1964-66, U.S. Army, 1961-62; med. dir. HealthAmerica La., New Orleans, 1984-87, Equicor, New Orleans, 1987-88; pvt. practice, New Orleans, 1966-84, 87-91; med. dir. Cigna, 1989-91; ptnr. Woman's Clinic, Clarksdale, Miss., 1991—2000; prin. investigator Benchmark Rsch., New Orleans, from 2000. Assoc. prof. Tulane U. Med. Sch., 1978-92; cons. in medicine Travelers Adv., New Orleans, 1988-92. Editor Orleans Parish Med. Jour., 1978-84; contbr. articles to profl. jours. Mem., chmn. Health Edn. Assn. La., New Orleans, 1977-83. Capt. M.C., U.S. Army, 1961-63. Fellow Am. Coll. Obstetrics and Gynecology; mem. Orleans Parish Med. Soc. (pres. 1983-84), Tulane Ob-Gyn. Assn. Soc., Metairie Country Club Avocations: golf, reading. Died May 6, 2007.

RENNER, GLENN DELMAR, retired agricultural products executive; b. Greeneville, Tenn., Nov. 18, 1925; s. Charles Dana and Lula Lucille (Hilton) R.; m. Gladys June Brooks, June 30, 1945; children: Glenna June, Joan Phyllis. BA, Tusculum Coll., 1948; MS, U. Tenn., 1950. Sales trainee Parks Belk Co., Greeneville, 1946—47; tchr., coach Greene County Schs., Greeneville, 1947—48; tchr. City of Greeneville Schs., 1950—54; salesman personal ins. co., Greeneville, 1954—76; real estate owner, pres. Brook Glen Farm Supply, Inc., Greeneville, 1976—98, ret., 1998; farmer, from 1998. Rep. Tenn. Legis., Greeneville, 1965-66; elected commr. Greene County, 1990, 94; participant People to People tour, Russia, Germany, Poland, Austria, Belgium, Switzerland, 1966. Mem. Greeneville Bd. Realtors (bd. dirs., pres. 1964, 71), Greeneville C. of C. (pres. 1986), Kiwanis (pres. Greeneville chpt. 1989—), Shriners (v.p. 1989, pres. 1991). Republican. Methodist. Achievements include 23 day tour sanctioned by USA, Austria, Belgium, Switerland. Avocation: hunting. Home: Greeneville, Tenn. Died Apr. 13, 2014.

RENVALL, JOHAN, ballet dancer; b. Stockholm, July 22, 1959; Studied privately with Alexander Mins. Dancer Royal Swedish Ballet, 1977; with Am. Ballet Theater, NYC, 1978—96, soloist, 1980-87, prin. dancer, 1987-1996. Appeared in numerous ballet co-prodns. including La Bayadere, Coppelia, Etudes, The Rite of Spring, Romeo and Juliet, SinFonietta, The Sleeping Beauty, La Sylphide, Undertow; guest appearances with Royal Swedish Ballet; created role of the Young Fighter in The Informer (Agnes de Mille); appeared in film Dance; choreographer Persnickety, 1987, Tango, Jacob's Pillow Dance Festival, 1990, Romeo and Juliet, 1992, NJ Ballet and Stars of the American Ballet Recipient Silver medal Varna Internat. Ballet Competition, 1978. Died Aug. 24, 2015.

RESIG, JANICE ANNE, correctional facility executive; b. Toledo, Apr. 15, 1950; d. Robert Carl and Margaret Eloise (Ruppel) R. Bachelor in Music, U. Dayton, 1971; postgrad., Ind. State U., 1973-77. Activity therapy aide Dayton (Ohio) Mental Health Ctr., 1970-71; substance abuse counselor Rockville (Ind.) Tng. Ctr., 1977-81; behavioral clinician Westville (Ind.) Correctional Ctr., 1981-83; dir. Westville (Ind.) Work Release Ctr., 1983-90, Westville Transition Unit, from 1990; crisis team cons. Swanson Ctr., Michigan City, 1982-85. Instr. Vincennes U., 1988-89. Mem. Ind. Correctional Assn., Am. Correctional Assn., Sigma Alpha Iota. Avocations: music, needlecrafts, athletics, swimming. Home: Westville, Ind. Died July 11, 2007.

REWCASTLE, NEILL BARRY, neuropathologist; b. Sunderland, Eng., Dec. 12, 1931; arrived in Can., 1955; s. William and Eva R.; m. Eleanor Elizabeth Barton Boyd, Sept. 27, 1958 (dec. Jan. 1999); 4 children. MB, ChB cum laude, U. St. Andrews, Scotland, 1955; MA, U. Toronto, 1962. Licentiate Med. Coun. Can., 1957; cert. in gen. pathology, 1962, cert. in neuropathology, 1968. Rotating intern Vancouver Gen. Hosp., 1955-56; resident in pathology Shaughnessy Hosp., Vancouver, 1956-57, St. Michaels & Toronto Gen. Hosp., Ont., Canada, 1957-60; demonstrator dept. pathology U. Toronto, 1964-65, lectr., acting head divsn. neuropathology, dept. pathology, 1965—69, assoc. prof., 1969-70, prof., head divsn. neuropathology, 1970—81; fellow, pathology Med. Rsch. Coun. Can., U. Toronto & Deutsche Forschungsantalt fur psychiatrie, Munich, 1960-64; prof. & head dept. pathology U. Calgary, 1981-91, prof., 1991—2000, prof. emeritus pathology, lab. medicine, clin. neuroscis., from 2000, mem. neurosci. rsch. group, 1982—2003; sr. pathologist Toronto Gen. Hosp., 1970—81. Dir. dept. histopathology Foothills Hosp., Calgary, 1981-91, pathologist, 1981—2003, cons. neuropathology, 1981-2003; spl. acad. adv. to dean faculty medicine U. Calgary, 1995-97; presenter in field. Contbr. over 147 articles to profl. jour., chpts. to books. Recipient Queen Elizabeth Silver Jubilee medal, 1977. Fellow: Royal Coll. Physicians & Surgeons Can.; mem. Can. Assn. Neuropathologists (ret. mem., sec. 1965-69, pres. 1976-79), Am. Assn. Neuropathologists (sr.), Sunshine Coast Power and Sail Squadron (comdr. 2007-09, past comdr. 2009-), Gibsons Curling Club (bd. dirs. 2006-09) Sunshine Coast Golf and Country Club. Avocations: gardening, philately, golf, curling, sailing. Died Jan. 7, 2014.

REYNOLDS, BRUCE GRAHLMANN, physicist; b. Fort Myers, Fla., Jan. 16, 1937; s. Alva August and Ann (Frantz) R.; m. Dee Ring, Dec. 19, 1961; children: Bruce Jr., Jennifer. BS in Physics, Fla. State U., 1961, MS in Physics, 1963, PhD in Physics, 1966. Asst. prof. physics Fla. State U., Tallahassee, 1966-68, Ohio U., Athens, 1968-71; staff physicist Martin Marietta Corp., Orlando, 1971-74, Argonne (Ill.) Nat. Lab., 1974-81; staff scientist Bell Telephone Labs., Napierville, Ill., 1980-81; CEO Omega Svcs., Mount Dora, Fla., from 1981. Contbr. articles to profl. jours. Mem. Am. Phys. Soc., Sigma Pi Sigma. Home: Mount Dora, Fla. Died Nov. 7, 2006.

REYNOLDS, COLLINS JAMES, III, management consultant; b. NYC, Feb. 28, 1937; s. Collins James and Alta Roberta (Carr) R.; m. Harriet Virginia Blackburn (dec.); children: Collins James IV, Quentin Scott; m. Carol Ann Miller, June 24, 1967; children: Justin Blake, Carson Jonathan (dec.). Student govt. and econs., Harvard U., George Washington U. Data processing supr. missile and space vehicle div. Gen. Electric, Phila., 1961; contract adminstr. Allison div. Gen. Motors, Indpls., 1962-65; country dir. Peace Corps, Mauritania, 1966-67, Sierra Leone, 1971—74; dir. div. ops. Gen. Learning Corp., Time Inc., Washington, 1968-71, trustee, sec., treas., exec. dir. Denver, 1974-79; Carter Presdl. appointee, assoc. dir. Internat. Devel. Coop. Agy., AID, 1980; dir. mktg. Am. TV & Communications Corp., Time Inc., Denver, 1980-81; founder, chmn. bd., pres. Omnicom, Inc., Denver, 1981-87; Bush Presdl. appointee, sr. exec. svc., assoc. dir. mgmt. Peace Corps, 1989-92; dir. comms. divsn. Am. Water Works Assn., 1994-97; trustee The Groundwater Found., 1996—2002; v.p., dir. ops. Internat. Resources Group, Wash., DC, 1999—2002; bd. dirs. Dona Ana County Airport, Mesilla Valley Habitat for Humanity; dir. United Way SW N.Mex. Cons., UN Secretariat, Econ. Devel. Adminstrn., OECD, USAID, USDA, U.S. Dept. Labor, U.S. Dept. Edn., U.S. Dept. Commerce, U.S. Dept. Navy; project dir. Model Cities Edn. Plan, HUD, Gen. Learning, Balt., Dept. Labor/HEW Remedial Edn. and Job Placement Program, Transcentury Corp., Washington; program mgr. Ft. Lincoln New Town Sch. System, Washington; supervising dir. VISTA, Boston, N.Y.C., Atlanta; dir. adminstrn. Job Corps, Kansas City. Founder, editor, pub.: The Bridge; patentee in field. Served as aviator USMCR, 1956-60. Home: Las Cruces, N.Mex. Died Mar. 26, 2015.

REYNOLDS, D. LU, architect; b. Pendleton, Oreg., June 25, 1921; d. Jesse Cyrus and Dorothy Harvey (Wood) Simonsen; m. John Laurin Reynolds, Jan. 25, 1952; 1 child, Heather. BS, U. Oreg., 1946, BArch, 1949. Registered architect, Oreg. Apprentice architect John Laurin Reynolds Architects, Eugene, Oreg., 1946-56; pvt. practice architecture Eugene, Oreg., from 1956. Republican. Lutheran. Avocations: piano, painting, gardening, tennis, swimming. Died Dec. 12, 2006.

REYNOLDS, PATRICIA ELLEN, artist; b. Apr. 6, 1934; d. Edwin and Anna (Pacewicz) Steeg; m. Carlyle Reynolds, Oct. 4, 1953 (div. 1991); children: Clifford, Stephanie. Student, SUNY, Plattsburg, 1951-52, Moon Bus. Sch., NYC, 1953; studied with Robert Whitney, studied with Mario Cooper. Watercolor painter, Willsboro, N.Y. Condr. workshops in field, mem. art juries. One-woman shows include Gallerie Camille Renaud, Paris, 1979, Hollsworthy Gallery, London, 1980, Ctr. Modern Design, Riyadh, Saudi Arabia, 1981-83, 25 Yr. Retro Art Mus., SUNY, Plattsburgh, Remington Mus., 1996, North Country Cultural Ctr., Plattsburgh, NY, 2005; exhibited in group shows at Schenectady Mus., SUNY, Plattsburgh, St. Lawrence U., Canton, N.Y., Ctr. Music, Drama and Arts, Lake Placid, N.Y., 1980, Audubon Artists Ann., 1980, 94, Fleming Mus. Burlington, Vt., Am. Watercolor Soc., 1982, 87 (Traveling Shows awards, Lena Newcastle award), Salmagundi Club (Gold Medal award), 1983, 88-89, 91-92 (awards 1983, 88), Nat. Works Paper, 1982 (award), Nat. Exhbn. Am. Watercolors, 1983-84, 87 (award), Allied Trusts Exhbn., 1987, 91, 93, Watercolor West, 1988, Mid-West Watercolor Soc., 1983, 89, 92, Nat. Watercolor Soc., 1991; permanent collections include Adirondack Mus. Recipient Best of Show arad No. Vt. Artists, 1970-71, 76, 78-79, Adirondack Art Exhbn. award, 1973, Oustanding Woman Artist award Am. Pen Women, 1975, Benedictine Nat. award, 1975, Lena Newcastle award Am. Watercolor Soc., 1987, Travel Exhbn. award Am. Watercolor Soc., 1987, William Kowalsky Meml. award, 1991, Adirondack Pk. Centennial award, 1992, Multi-Focus award, 1992, Adirondack Art Assn. award, 2003 Mem. Transparent Watercolor Soc. Am. (Signature Mem. award 1992, North Country award), Allied Artist Am. (assoc.), Nat. Watercolor Soc. (assoc.), Ctrl. N.Y. Watercolor Soc. (signature), Gallery Des Beaucy Artes Des Ameriques Montreal, Adirondack Art Assn., No Cmty. Cultural Ctr Friends of art, SUNY, Pitts. Died Feb. 4, 2015.

REYNOLDS, PEGGY JEAN, elementary school educator; b. Gaffney, SC, Dec. 28, 1940; d. Floyd and Mary Rebecca (Bratton) R. BA, Limestone Coll., 1963; MA in Teaching, Winthrop Coll., 1973. Cert. elem. tchr., S.C. Sec. Limestone Coll., Gaffney, 1963-68; elem. tchr. Cherokee County Sch. Dist. 1, Gaffney, from 1968. Chmn. sch. improvement coun. Goucher Sch., Gaffney, 1989-91, chmn. spelling bee, 1991—. Mem. Cherokee County Edn. Assn., S.C. Edn. Assn., NEA, Cherokee County Reading Coun. Baptist. Home: Gaffney, SC. Died June 22, 2007.

REYNOLDS, ROBERT BELKNAP, psychiatrist; b. Fenchow, People's Republic of China, Nov. 8, 1922; s. Paul Russell and Charlotte Louise (Belknap) R.; m. M. Jo Hart, Feb. 10, 1951; children: Patricia, Robert Jr., Katheryn. AB, Carleton Coll., 1944; MD, Harvard U., 1947. Intern U. Chgo., 1947-48; resident in psychiatry Malcolm Bliss Hosp., St. Louis, 1948-49, VA Hosp., Jefferson Barracks, Mo., 1949-51, staff psychiatrist, chief intensive treatment service, 1954-56; staff psychiatrist VA Mental Hygiene Clinic, St. Louis, 1951-52; practice medicine specializing in psychiatry St. Louis, from 1956. Clin. instr. to clin. asst. prof. psychiatry, St. Louis U. Med. Sch., 1956—; dir. Child Guidance Clinic City of St. Louis, 1956-68; attending psychiatrist, cons. Cochran VA Hosp., 1956-66; cons. Acid Rescue, Youth Emergency Service, United Meth. Children's Home. Served to capt. U.S. Army Med. Corps, 1952-54. Fellow Am. Psychiat. Assn. (life), Eastern Mo. Psychiat. Soc. (life); founding mem. Greater St. Louis Council for Child Psychiatry (sec. 1971-73, treas. 1975-77). Avocations: gardening, stamp collecting/philately. Home: Glenwood Spgs, Colo. Died Nov. 4, 2006.

REYNOLDS COOCH, NANCY D., sculptor; b. Greenville, Del., Dec. 28, 1919; d. Eugene Eleuthere and Catherine Dulcinea (Moxham) duPont; m. William Glasgow Reynolds, May 18, 1940 (dec. Jan. 1987); children: Katherine Glasgow Reynolds, William Bradford Reynolds, Mary Parminter Reynolds McKeever, Cynthia duPont Reynolds Farris.; m. Edward W. Cooch, Jr., Sept. 6, 2003 (dec. Sept. 23, 2010). Student, Goldey-Beacom Coll., Wilmington, Del., 1938. One-woman shows include Caldwell Inc., 1975, Nat. Museum of Women in Arts, 1998; exhibited in group shows at Corcoran Gallery, Washington, 1943, Soc. Fine Arts, Wilmington, 1937-38, 40-41, 48, 50, 62, 65, Rehoboth Art League, Del., 1963, NAD, NYC, 1964, Pa. Mil. Coll., Chester, 1966, Del. Art Ctr., 1967, Del. Art Mus., Wilmington, Wilmington Art Mus., 1976, Met. Mus. Art, NYC, 1977, Lever House, NYC, 1979, Nat. Mus. Women in the Arts, Washington, 1998; represented in permanent collections Wilmington Trust Co., E.I. duPont de Nemours & Co., Children's Home, Inc., Claymont, Del., Children's Bur., Wilmington, Stephenson Sci. Ctr., Vanderbilt U., Nashville, Lutheran Towers Bldg., Travelers Aid and Family Soc. Bldg., Wilmington, bronze fountain head Longwood Gardens, Kennett Square, Pa., bronze statue Brookgreen Gardens, Murrells Inlet, S.C., bronze sculpture "Veiled Lady", Nat. Mus. Women in Arts, Washington, 1998, bronze sculpture U. Del., Newark, 2001, bronze sculpture Biggs Mus., Dover, Del., 2002; contbr. articles to profl. journals Organizer vol. svc. Del. chpt. ARC, 1938-39, crucifix statue for the Du Pont Chapel, 2011; chmn. Com. for Revision Del. Child Adoption Law, 1950-52; pres., bd. dirs. Children Bur. Del.; pres., trustee Children's Home, Inc.; del., past regent Gunston Hall Plantation, Lorton, Va.; mem. adv. com. Longwood Gardens, Kennett Sq., Pa.; garden and grounds com. Winterthur (Del.) Mus.; mem. rsch. staff Henry Francis DuPont Winterthur Mus., 1955-63; mem. archtl. com. U. Del., Newark. Recipient Confrerie des Chevaliers du Tastevin Clos de Vougeot-Bourgogne France, 1960; Hort. award Garden Club America, 1964, medal of Merit, 1976, Dorothy Platt award Garden Club of Phila., 1980, Alumni medal of merit Westover Sch., Middlebury,

Conn., Medal of Distinction, U. Del., 1999. Mem. Pa. Hort. Soc., Wilmington Soc. Fine Arts, Mayflower Descs., Del. Hist. Soc., Colonial Dames, League American Pen Women, Nat. Trust Hist. Preservation. Garden Club of Wilmington (past pres.), Garden Club of America (past asst. zone 4 chmn.), Vicmead Hunt Club, Greenville Country Club, Chevy Chase Club (Washington), Colony Club (NYC). Episcopalian. Died Jan. 21, 2015.

REZAK, RICHARD, geology and oceanography educator; b. Syracuse, NY, Apr. 26, 1920; s. Habib and Radia (Khoury) R.; m. Hifa Hider, July 1, 1944 (div. Mar. 1965); 1 child, Christine Sara; m. Anna Lucile Nesselrode, Mar. 18, 1965. MA, Washington U., St. Louis, 1949; PhD, Syracuse U., 1957. Geologist U.S. Geol. Survey, Denver, 1952-58; rsch. assoc. Shell Devel. Co., Houston, 1958-67; assoc. prof. oceanography Tex. A&M U., College Station, Tex., 1967-71, prof., 1971-91, prof. emeritus, from 1991. Mem. edit. bd. Geo-MArine Letters, N.Y.C., 1981—; coun. SEPM, Tulsa, Okla., 1968-69; mem. govs. adv. panel Offshore Oil & Chem. Spill Response, Austin, Tex., 1984-85. Co-author: Reefs and Banks of the Northwest Gulf of Mexico, 1985; co-editor: Contributions on the Geological Oceanography of the Gulf of Mexico, 1972, Carbonate Microfabrics, 1993; contbr. articles to profl. jours. Comdr. USNR, 1942-64. Rsch. grantee various fed. agys., 1968-90. Mem. Lions (Melvin Jones fellow). Episcopalian. Home: Bryan, Tex. Died Nov. 10, 2006.

REZNICK, MORRIS MARTIN, lawyer; b. Cleve., Apr. 11, 1923; s. Joseph and Miriam (Baum) R.; children: Martha, Brad. Student, Ill. Inst. Tech., 1944; BS, Ohio U., 1947; JD, Cleve.-Marshal Law Sch., 1951. Bar: Ohio, 1951, U.S. Dist. Ct. (no. dist.) Ohio, 1954, U.S. Ct. Appeals (6th cir.), 1981, U.S. Supreme Ct., 1986. House counsel Midwest Builders Co., University Heights, Ohio, 1958-60; ptnr. Goldfarb and Reznick, Cleve., 1966-96. Served with U.S. Army, 1943-46. Decorated Bronze Star with oak leaf cluster, Purple Heart with oak leaf cluster. Mem. ABA, Ohio Bar Assn., Bar Assn. Greater Cleve. Home: Cleveland, Ohio. Died Nov. 26, 2006.

RHODES, DONALD ROBERT, musicologist, educator, retired electrical engineer; b. Detroit, Dec. 31, 1923; s. Donald Eber and Edna Mae (Fulmer) R.; children: Joyce R. Holbert, Jane E., Roger C., Diane R. Herran. BEE, Ohio State U., 1945, MEE, 1948, PhD, 1953. Research assoc. Ohio State U., Columbus, 1945-54; research engr. Cornell Aero. Lab., Buffalo, 1954-57; head basic research dept. Radiation, Inc., Orlando, Fla., 1957-61, sr. scientist Melbourne, Fla., 1961-66; Univ. prof. N.C. State U., Raleigh, 1966-94, univ. prof. emeritus, from 1994. Author: Introduction to Monopulse, 1959, 2d edit., 1980, Synthesis of Planar Antenna Sources, 1974, A Reactance Theorem, 1977. Co-founder Central Fla. Community Orch., Winter Park, 1961, pres., 1961-62. Recipient Benjamin G. Lamme medal Ohio State U., 1975; Eminent Engr. award Tau Beta Pi, 1976; named to N.C. State U. Acad. Outstanding Tchrs., 1980. Fellow AAAS, IEEE (John T. Bolljahn award 1963, pres. Antennas and Propagation Soc. 1969); mem. Am. Musicological Soc. Home: Kernersville, NC. Died Sept. 10, 2014.

RHUE, NANCY CLIFTON, secondary school educator; b. Milford, Del., Apr. 3, 1948; d. William Carlton and Beatrice Margaret (Hudson) Clifton; m. E. Brent Rhue; children: Michael, Jonathan, Allison. BA, St. Andrew's Presbyn. Coll., 1970. Cert English tchr., Del. Tchr. English Rehoboth Jr. High Sch., Rehoboth Beach, Del., 1970-76, Lewes (Del.) Jr. High Sch., 1976-79, Cape Henlopen High Sch., Lewes, from 1979. Adviser Rehoboth Jr. High cheerleaders, 1970-71, Jr. Honor soc., 1977-78, Nat. Honor Soc. Cape Henlopen High Sch., 1980—, co-adviser Student Leadership Day, 1981—, adviser acad. bowl team, 1984-87; mem. Supt.'s Adv. Council. Mem. Senator Joseph Biden Adv. Council, 1976-82; treas. state rep. campaign, Milford, 1978; mem. H. O. Brittingham Elem. Sch. PTO; ch. pianist Slaughter Neck United Meth. Ch., dir. choir 1981—, worship com. chmn. 1985—, sec. adminstrn. bd. 1972-87, sec., tchr. Sunday sch. 1976-79, dir., music dir., tchr. Vacat. Bible Sch, 1972—, United Methodist Women, 1974— (pres. 1977-78, 1988—), Friends of Milton County Library, 1987—. Named one of Outstanding Young Women Am. Milton Jaycees, 1984. Mem. NEA, Del. State Edn. Assn., Cape Henlopen Edn. Assn., United Meth. Women. Democrat. Avocations: piano, reading, travel, theater. Died Apr. 6, 2007.

RHULE, HOMER ALBERT, insurance association executive, consultant; b. Williamsburg, Pa., Nov. 21, 1921; s. Raymond Albert and Edna Rachael (Greaser) R.; m. Helen Louise Ritchey, Oct. 16, 1950; children: Ann Ritchey, Raymond Albert. BA in Bus. Adminstrn., Am. Univ., 1942; postgrad., Stanford U., 1943; BA in Bus. Adminstrn., Pa. State U., 1947; postgrad., Drexel U., 1968-69. Adjustor, supr. Liberty Mutual Ins. Co., Phila., San Francisco, 1947-51; claims mgr. Transamerica Ins. Co., Harrisburg and Pitts., Pa., 1951-54; owner Rhule Adjustment Co., Altoona, Pa., 1954-55; claims mgr. Crum & Forster Ins. Co.'s, Phila., 1955-69, regional claims mgr. NYC, 1969-78, asst. v.p. Basking Ridge, N.J., 1978-87; exec. dir. Pa. Ins. Guaranty Assn., Phila., from 1987. Pres. Claims Mgrs. Coun., Phila., 1955-62; chmn. Selective Svc. Bd. 107, Bryn Mawr, Pa., 1956-70, Arbitration-Spl., Phila., 1967-69. Commd. Post 355 Am. Legion, Bala Cynwyd, Pa., 1962; dep. commr. 9th Dist. Pa. Am. Legion, Ea. Pa., 1963-64. 2d lt. U.S. Army, 1942-46, ETO. Mem. Masons, F&AM 220, Harrisburg Consistory, Lu Lu Temple. Republican. Presbyterian. Avocations: sailing, hiking, restoration of old houses. Home: Philadelphia, Pa. Died Nov. 2, 2006.

RICE, DOUGLAS ALAN, foreign language professor; b. Concord, NH, Oct. 17, 1949; s. Donald Neal and Mildred Evans (Thomas) R. BA, Bates Coll., 1971; BSEd, U. Idaho, 1975; MA, So. Ill. U., 1989. Asst. prof. English Universidad Nacional de Ancash, Huaraz, Peru, 1982-86; instr. Spanish and English Highland C.C., Freeport, Ill., 1989-91; asst. prof. Spanish and English Pikeville (Ky.) Coll., 1991-93; instr. fgn. lang. Blue Mountain C.C., Pendleton, Oreg., from 1993. Mem. Am. Coun. of Tchrs. of Fgn. Langs., Am. Assn. Tchrs. of Spanish and Portuguese. Avocations: mountain climbing, photography. Died Mar. 27, 2007.

RICE, EDWARD WILLIAM, medical management consultant; b. Great Falls, Mont., July 24, 1911; s. Robert W. and Laura Sebina (Martin) R.; m. Patricia Arnold, July 27, 1940; children: Barbara Beth Rice Wescott, Catherine Marie Rice Green. BS in Econs., U. Kans., 1935; LLB, Kans. U., Lawrence, 1938, JD (hon.), 1953. Bar: Kans. 1938. Collector Internat. Harvester Co., Topeka, Kans., 1941-43; sr. price specialist U.S. Office Price Adminstrn., Boise, Idaho, 1941-43; pres. Profl. Adjustment Co., Boise, Idaho, 1947-84, Drs. Bus. Bur., Boise, Idaho, from 1953. Cons. and lectr. in field. Editorial cons. Physician's Mgmt. mag., 1962—. Mem. city coun. City of Boise, 1954-59, pres., 1959; mem. State of Idaho Ho. of Reps., 1959-67. With USN, 1943-46, PTO, comdr. USNR. Mem. ABA, Idaho Collectors Assn. (pres. 1948-50), Nat. Med.-Dental Hosp. Burs. Am. (pres. 1959-61), Better Bus. Bur., Kiwanis, Shriners, Masons. Republican. Baptist. Avocations: reading, travel, community activities. Home: Boise, Idaho. Died Mar. 30, 2007.

RICE, ELIZABETH F., gerontology nurse, researcher; b. NS, Can., Feb. 8, 1938; d. Kenneth Freeman and Rilla Irene (Morrish) R. Diploma in nursing, U. Wash., 1968; BSN, U. Colo., 1970. RN, Colo., Wash. Nurse, activity dir. Sable Care Ctr., Aurora, Colo.; home care nurse Quality Care Nursing Svcs., Seattle; medication supr. Madison House Retirement Home, Kirkland, Wash.; caregiver Copes program Wash. Dept. Social and Health Svcs., 1991. Rsch. on diabetes type I. Rsch. grantee. Died Jan. 24, 2007.

RICE, ESTHER M., state agency administrator; d. Chauney James and Rosa Kathryn Rice. BA in Edn., Hiram Coll., 1945. Clerical adminstrn. Fed. Pub. Housing, Cleve. and Chgo., 1945—49; placement officer U.S. Dept. Navy, Washington, 1950—56; recruitment officer U.S. Dept. State, Washington, 1956—59, chief field, 1959—61, employee devel. officer, 1961—64, asst., 1964—65. Mem.: Fgn. Svc. Retirees (bd. dirs. 1990—94), Am. Fgn. Svc. Assn., Waterwood Cmty. Assn. (sec. 2000—05). Avocation: golf. Home: Yalaha, Fla. Died Feb. 23, 2007.

RICE, JERRY DALE, artist, educator; b. Durant, Okla., Jan. 10, 1951; s. Felton Jane and Beulah Lorraine (Corley) R.; m. Diane Florence Engles, Nov. 26, 1970 (div. Aug. 1973); m. Karen Viken, 1976 (div. 1987); 1 child, Keith. BA, Southeastern Okla. State U., 1973; postgrad., Adams State Coll., 1974, N.Mex. State U., 1983-84. Layout artist Graphic Arts Inc., Carrollton, Tex., 1974; art tchr. Hi-Plains H.S., Seibert, Colo., 1974-76; art/psychology Navajo C.C., Shiprock, N.Mex., 1978-82, Tohatchi (N.Mex.) H.S., 1976-82; sculptor Self-Studio, Ruidoso, N.Mex., 1982-83; art tchr. Lynn Jr. H.S., Las Cruces, 1983-84; art spl. edn. tchr. Mescalero (N.Mex.) pub. schs., 1984-85; spl. edn. tchr. Kingston (Okla.) Elem. Schs., 1985-87; tchr. art Carrizozo (N.Mex.) H.S., 1987-88, Capitan (N.Mex.) H.S., from 1988. Exhibited in solo shows at Michelena's Italian Restaurant, Ruidoso, 1995-96, Candle Power Gift and Gallery, Ruidoso, 1998; exhibited in group shows at Lincoln County Mus., Lincoln, N.Mex., Fenton's Gallery, Ruidoso, others. Painting judge Gallup Inter-tribal Ceremonial Assn., Gallup, 1979. Democrat. Home: Ruidoso, N.Mex. Died May 18, 2007.

RICE, RICHARD LELAND, bank executive; b. Eustis, Fla., June 20, 1943; s. Wilfred Earnest and Dorothea (Smoak) R.; m. Sally Anne Mowery, Aug. 21, 1966 (div. Oct. 1982); 1 child, Darian Clark; m. Karen L. Oglebay, July 21, 1984. BSBA with honors, U. Fla., 1972. Chartered fin. analyst, Va. Rsch. analyst Southeast Banking Corp., Miami, Fla., 1972-74, 1st Nat. Bank Atlanta, 1974-81; sr. rsch. analyst Capitoline Investment Svcs. subs. Crestar Fin. Corp., Richmond, Va., 1981-88; dir. investment rsch. Signet Asset Mgmt. div. Signet Bank, Richmond, 1988-91; ptnr. Parata Analytics Rsch., Richmond, from 1992. Sgt. U.S. Army, 1963-67, Thailand, Vietnam. Mem. Inst. Chartered Fin. Analysts, Richmond Soc. Fin. Analysts, Assn. Investment Mgmt. Rsch., Beta Gamma Sigma. Republican. Methodist. Avocations: trumpet, flugelhorn, personal computer. Home: Richmond, Va. Died Feb. 7, 2007.

RICH, ALEXANDER, molecular biologist, educator; b. Hartford, Conn., Nov. 15, 1924; s. Max and Bella (Shub) R.; m. Jane Erving King, July 5, 1952; children: Benjamin, Josiah, Rebecca, Jessica. AB magna cum laude in Biochem. Scis, Harvard U., 1947, MD cum laude, 1949; Dr. (hon.), Fed. U. Rio de Janeiro, 1981; PhD honoris causa, Weizmann Inst. Sci., Rehovot, Israel, 1992; DSc (hon.), Eidgenössische Technische Hochschule, Zurich, Switzerland, 1993, Freie U., Berlin, 1996. Rsch. fellow Gates and Crellin Labs., Calif. Inst. Tech., Pasadena, 1949-54; chief sect. phys. chemistry NIMH, Bethesda, Md., 1954-58; vis. scientist Cavendish Lab., Cambridge (Eng.) U., 1955-56; assoc. prof. biophysics MIT, Cambridge, 1958-61, prof. biophysics, 1961—2015, William Thompson Sedgwick prof. biophysics, 1974—2015. Mem. AAAS (coun. mem. 1967-71), com. career devel. awards NIH, 1964-67, postdoctoral fellowship bd., 1955-58; mem. com. exobiology space sci. bd. NAS, 1964-65, adv. bd., acad. forum, 1975-82, nominating com., 1980, exec. com. of council, 1985-88; mem. U.S. nat. com. Internat. Orgn. Pure Applied Biophysics, 1965-67; vis. com. biology dept. Yale U., 1963, Weizmann Inst. Sci., 1965-66, co-chmn. sci. and adv. com. 1987-91; life scis. com. NASA, 1970-75, lunar planetary missions bd., 1968-70; biology team Viking Mars Mission, 1969-80; mem. corp. Marine Biol. Lab., Woods Hole, Mass., 1965-77, 87; sci. rev. com. Howard Hughes Med. Inst., Miami, Fla., 1978-90; vis. com. biology div. Oak Ridge Nat. Lab., 1972-76; chmn. com. on USSR and Ea. Europe Exch. Bd. NAS, 1973-76; mem. Internat. Rsch. and Exchs. Bd. Am. Coun. Learned Socs., N.Y.C., 1973-76, panel judges N.Y. Acad. Sci. ann. book award for children's sci. books, N.Y.C., 1973-90; chmn. nominating com. Am. Acad. Arts and Sci., 1974-77; sci. adv. bd. Stanford Synchrotron Radiation Project, 1976-80, Mass. Gen. Hosp., Boston, 1978-83; mem. U.S. Nat. Sci. Bd., 1976-82; bd. govs. Weizmann Inst. Sci., 1976-; rsch. com. Med. Found., Boston, 1976-80; mem. U.S.-USSR Joint Commn. on Sci. and Tech., Dept. State, Washington, 1977-82; sr. cons. Office of Sci. and Tech. Policy, Exec. Office of Pres., Washington, 1977-81; mem. council Pugwash Confs. on Sci. and World Affairs, Geneva, 1977-82; chmn. basic rsch. com. Nat. Sci. Bd., Washington, 1978-82; mem. U.S. Nat. Com. for Internat. Union for Pure and Applied Biophysics, NAS, 1979-83; bd. dirs. Med. Found., Boston, 1981-90; vis. com. divsn. med. sci. Harvard U., 1981-87; mem. govt.-univ.-industry rsch. round table, 1984-87; chmn. sci. adv. com. dept. molecular biology Mass. Gen. Hosp., Boston, 1983-87; governing bd. NRC, 1985-88; nat. adv. com. Pew Scholars program Pew Meml. Trust, 1986-88; com. on USSR and Eastern Europe Nat. Rsch. Council, Washington, 1986-92; external adv. com. Ctr. for Human Genome Studies, Los Alamos Nat. Lab., N.Mex., 1989-97, Nat. Critical Techs. Panel, Office of Sci. & Tech. Policy, Exec. Office of Pres., Washington, 1990-91; vis. com. NASA Ctr. Exobiology, La Jolla, Calif., 1992-95; vis. prof. Coll. France, Paris, 1987; co-founder, co-chmn. bd. dirs. Repligen Corp., 1981; co-founder Alkermes, dir., 1987; bd. dirs. Profectus Biosciences, Inc. Editor: (with Norman Davidson) Structural Chemistry and Molecular Biology, 1968; mem. editl. bd. Biophys. Jour, 1961-63, Currents Modern Biology, 1966-72, Science, 1963-69, Analytical Biochemistry, 1969-81, Bio-Systems, 1973-86, Molecular Biology Reports, 1974-85, Procs. NAS, 1973-78, Jour. Molecular and Applied Genetics, 1980-84, DNA, 1981-89, EMBO Jour., 1988-90, Jour. Biotech., 1987-2015, Genomics, 1987-2015, Proteins, Structure, Function and Genetics, 1986-91, Jour. Molecular Evolution, 1983—, Springer Series on Molecular Biology, 1980-88; mem. editl. adv. bd. Jour. Molecular Biology, 1959-66, Accounts of Chemical Research, 1980-82, Jour. Biomolecular Structure and Dynamics, 1983-2015, PAABS Revista, 1972-77, Biopolymers, 1963-74, Jour. of Molecular Evolution, 1983-94, others; contbr. over 500 articles to profl. jours. With USN, 1943—46. Fairchild disting. scholar Calif. Inst. Tech., Pasadena, 1976; recipient Skylab Achievement award NASA, 1974, Theodore von Karmin award Viking Mars Mission, 1976, Presdl. award N.Y. Acad. Scis., 1977, Jabotinsky medal Jabotinsky Found., 1980, James R. Killian Faculty Achievement award MIT, 1980, Lewis S. Rosenstiel Basic Biomed. Rsch. award Brandeis U., 1983, Nat. medal Sci. NSF, 1995, Merck award American Soc. Biochemistry and Molecular Biology, Washington, 1998, Bower award in Sci., Franklin Inst., 2000, Proctor prize Sigma Xi, 2001, Passano award, Passano Found., 2002, Welch award in Chemistry, 2008, others; NRC fellow, 1949-51; Guggenheim Found. fellow, 1963; mem. Pontifical Acad. Scis. The Vatican, 1978. Fellow AAAS, American Acad. of Arts and Sciences; mem. NAS (chmn. biotech., program, com. on scholarly comm. with China 1986-93, exec. com. 1985-88, com. on sci. comm. and nat. security 1982), American Chem. Soc. (exec. com. divsn. biol. chemistry 1962, Linus Pauling award 1995), Biophys. Soc. (coun. 1960-69), American Soc. Biol. Chemists, American Crystallographic Soc., Internat. Soc. for Study of Origin of Life (fgn.), French Acad. Sciences, Russian Acad. Sciences. (fgn., Lomonosov Large Gold medal 2002), European Molecular Biology Orgn. (assoc.), Japanese Biochem. Soc. (hon.), Physicians for Social Responsibility (nat. adv. bd. 1983), American Philos. Soc., Inst. of Medicine (sr.), Pontifical Acad. of Sciences, Phi Beta Kappa, Alpha Omega Alpha. Home: Cambridge, Mass. Died Apr. 27, 2015.

RICH, RONALD LEE, chemistry professor; b. Washington, Ill., Mar. 29, 1927; s. Rufus Joseph and Lillian May (Lantz) Rich; m. Elaine Horner Sommers, June 14, 1953; children: Jonathan Joseph, Andrew Forrester, Miriam Sommers, Mark Monroe. BS in Math. and Chemistry, Bluffton Coll., 1948; PhD in Chemistry, U. Chgo., 1953. Rsch. fellow Harvard U., Cambridge, Mass., 1963-64; prof. chemistry Bethel Coll., North Newton, Kans., 1964-66, Internat. Christian U., Tokyo, 1966-79; dean acad. affairs Bluffton (Ohio) Coll., 1979-80, scholar in residence, from 1981. Vis. prof. Stanford (Calif.) U., 1974, U. Ill., Urbana, 1975, U. Oreg., Eugene, 1984; electrochemical engr. N.C. State U., Raleigh, 1989—90. Author: Periodic Correlations, 1965, Inorganic Reactions in Water, 2008; co-author: Chemical English (for Japanese), 1969, 2 vols., 1976; contbr. articles to profl. jours. Named in Henry Taube's Nobel prize, 1983. Achievements include a general way to predict boiling points; a qualitative-analysis scheme whose groups fit in the periodic chart. Died Nov. 28, 2014.

RICH, WALTER GEORGE, railroad transportation executive; b. Oneonta, NY, Jan. 9, 1946; s. George C. and Dorretta (Gregg) R.; m. Karine Schmook, July 14, 1990; children: Derik, Stephanie. BA, Syracuse U., NY, 1968, JD, 1971. Gen. mgr. Delaware Otsego Corp., Oneonta, 1966-68, v.p., gen. mgr., 1968-71, chmn., pres., CEO Cooperstown, NY, from 1971, N.Y. Susquehanna & Western Rwy., Cooperstown, NY, from 1980. Bd. dirs. Delaware Otsego Corp., Cooperstown, Security Mut. Life Ins. Co. of N.Y., Energy

East Corp., Crucible Materials; mem. N.Y. Pub. Transp. Safety Bd., from 1993; chmn. bd. dirs. Am.Shortline and Regional R.R. Assn., 1999—2004; bd. dirs. Crucible Materials, from 2005. Commr. of elections Delaware County, 1971-78; mem. N.Y. Gov. George Pataki's transition team, 1994; bd. dirs. N.Y. Bus. Devel. Corp., 1995—. Mem. Nat. Rwy. Hist. Soc., Lexington Group in Transp., Ft. Orange Club (Albany), Union League Club (Phila.), Met. Club (N.Y.C.), Binghamton (N.Y.) Club. Episcopalian. Republican. Home: Cooperstown, NY. Died Aug. 9, 2007.

RICHARDS, STANLEY HAROLD, financial consultant, lawyer; b. Alton, Ill., Feb. 20, 1922; s. Max Louis and Phoebe (Cohen) Goldberg; m. June Selma Lunensky, May 1, 1949; children: Tracy L. Richards Sachman, Dany C. Richards Fields, John P. BS cum laude, Harvard U., 1944, JD, 1949. Bar: Ill. 1949, Mo. 1949, U.S. Dist. Ct. 1949, U.S. Ct. Appeals (7th cir.) 1951, U.S. Tax Ct. 1950. Ptnr. Lehrer & Richards, Chgo., 1949-56, Foster, Sheppard, Oliver & Richards, Chgo., 1956-60; exec. v.p. Old Kent Bank (formerly Unibanc Trust-Sears Bank & Trust), Chgo., 1960-87; cons. Old Kent Bank (formerly UnibancTrust), Chgo., 1987-92; of counsel Kanter & Mattenson, Chicago, from 1992. Chmn. Arthritis Found. Ill., Chgo., 1963-65; dir. Am. Cancer Soc., Chgo., 1976-82. Mem. Chgo. Bar Assn. (trust law com.), Ill. Bar Assn., Chgo. Estate Planning Soc., Cook County Fiduciary Assn. (past pres.). Jewish. Avocations: bridge, painting. Home: Hallandale, Fla. Died Feb. 26, 2007.

RICHARDSON, MELVIN MARK, retired state legislator, broadcast executive; b. Salt Lake City, Apr. 29, 1928; s. Mark and Mary (Lundquist) R.; m. Dixie Joyce Gordon, 1952; children: Pamela, Mark, Lance, Todd, Kristi. Grad., Radio Operational Engring. Sch., Burbank, Calif., 1951. Radio announcer, program dir. Sta. KBUH, Brigham City, Utah, 1951-54; mgr. Sta. KLGN, Logan, Utah, 1954-58; announcer, sports dir. Sta. KID Radio/TV, Idaho Falls, Idaho, 1958-86; mgr., program dir. Sta. KID-FM/AM, Idaho Falls, 1986; mem. Idaho House of Reps., 1988-92; mem. Dist. 32 Idaho State Senate, Boise, 1992—2008. Cons., dir. INEL Scholastic Tournament, Idaho Nat. Engring. Lab.; speaker in field. Host: Mel's Sports Scene, Thirty Minutes, Channel Three Reports, Probes, Probing America. Dir. Assn. Idaho Cities, Ricks Coll. Booster Club, Bonneville County Crime Stoppers, Idaho Falls Child Devel. Ctr.; active Idaho Centennial Commn., Anti-Lottery Com., Gov.'s Conf. on Children; commr. Bonneville County Parks and Recreation Commn.; mayor City of Ammon, Idaho, 1966-72; candidate from Idaho Dist. # 2 for U.S. Congress. Sgt. USAR, 1951-57. Named Man of Yr., Ricks Coll., 1980. Mem. Idaho Broadcasters Assn. (bd. dirs.). Republican. Mem. Lds Ch. Died Dec. 11, 2014.

RICHARDSON, ROBERT WILLIAM, museum director; b. Rochester, Pa., May 21, 1910; s. Robert Haswell and Anna Pearl (Thomas) R. Mgr. Forge Printshop, Akron, Ohio, 1930-37; editor Linn's Weekly Stamp News, Columbus, Ohio, 1937-41; advt. rep. Seiberling Rubber Co., Akron, 1941-42, 45-47; mgr. Narrow Gauge Motel, Alamosa, Colo., 1948-58, Narrow Gauge Mus., Alamosa, 1953-58; mgr., pres. Colo. R.R. Mus., Golden, 1959-65, exec. dir., from 1965. Sec.-treas. Colo. R.R. Hist. Found., Golden, 1965—. Author: Colo. Rail Annuals, 1972—; contbr. numerous articles on philately to profl. jours. Sgt. Signal Corp., AUS, 1942-45. Mem. Garfield-Perry Stamp Club (life), Ry. and Locomotive Hist. Soc., Manitou and Pikes Peak R.R. Assn., Nat. Narrow Gauge Assn., Collectors Club Denver. Lutheran. Avocations: photography, history, stamp collecting/philately. Home: Golden, Colo. Died Feb. 24, 2007.

RICHELS, JAMES KENNETH, accounting company executive; b. Breckenridge, Minn., Sept. 10, 1944; s. Kenneth Anthony and Lerna Drucilla (Snyder) R.; m. Marlene Ann Lingen, Oct. 18, 1969; children: Wade, Cody, Veeda, Rena. Assoc., N.D. State Sch. Sci., 1964; BBA, U. N.D., 1966. CPA, N.D., Minn. Auditor U.S. Gen. Acctg. Office, Denver, 1966-67, Eide, Helmeke, Boelz & Pasch, Fargo and Bismarck, N.D., 1967-71; ptnr. Richels & Easley, Wahpeton, N.D., from 1971. Treas., dir. Red Youth Activities Assn., Wahpeton, 1981. Mem. Am. Inst. CPA's, N.D. Soc. CPA's. Home: Wahpeton, ND. Died Nov. 6, 2006.

RICHEY, EVERETT ELDON, religious studies educator; b. Claremont, Ill., Nov. 1, 1923; s. Hugh Arthur and Elosia Emma (Longnecker) R.; m. Mary Elizabeth Reynolds, Apr. 9, 1944; children: Eldon Arthur, Clive Everett, Loretta Arlene, Charles Estel. ThB, Anderson U., 1946; MDiv, Sch. Theology, Anderson, Ind., 1956; ThD, Iliff Sch. Theology, Denver, 1960. Pastor Ch. of God, Bremen, Ind., 1946—47, Laurel, Miss., 1947—48, First Ch. of God, Fordyce, Ark., 1948—52; prof. Arlington Coll., Long Beach, Calif., 1961—68; pastor Cherry Ave. Ch. of God, Long Beach, 1964—68; prof. Azusa Pacific U., Calif., 1968—93. Chmn. Commn. on Christian Higher Edn./Ch. of God, 1982-93; pres. Ch. Growth Investors, Inc., 1981-2003, v.p. 2003-. Author: ednl. manual Church Periodical--Curriculum, 1971-83, 97, (book) Faith and the Life, 2002 Mem.: Christian Ministries Tng. Assn., Assn. Profs. and Rschrs. Religious Edn. Republican. Avocation: gardening. Died Nov. 21, 2006.

RICHMOND, ERNEST LEON, retired research engineer, consultant; b. Catskill, NY, Sept. 11, 1914; s. Leon J. and Beulah B. (Garling) R.; m. Constance R. Vroom, Oct. 9, 1943. B of Mech. Engring. cum laude, Clarkson U., Potsdam, NY, 1942; postgrad., N.J. Inst. Tech., Newark, 1950-60, Rutgers U., 1950-60. Registered profl. engr., NJ. Test engr. Mack Trucks, Inc., Plainfield, N.J., 1936-45; from asst chief to chief engr. Worthington Corp., Plainfield Works, 1945-58; rsch. engr. Ethicon, Inc. (div. Johnson & Johnson), Somerville, N.J., 1958-75; ret., 1975. Spkr., cons. in field. Author design papers; patentee in field. Vol. United Fund, Plainfield, 1940-50, Cancer Fund, Plainfield, 1940-50, Heart Fund, Plainfield, 1940-50; coach YMCA Ch. Basketball League, Plainfield, 1960-65, chmn. exec. com., 1964-65. Mem. ASME, NSPE, Am. Electroplaters and Surface Finishers Soc. Republican. Presbyterian. Avocations: civil war history, golf. Home: North Plainfield, NJ. Died May 23, 2007.

RICKMAN, ALAN, actor; b. London, Feb. 21, 1946; Student, Royal Acad. of Dramatic Art. Stage appearances: The Seagull, Mephisto, Les Liaisons Dangereuses, 1985, 87 (Tony nominee Best Actor 1987), Tango at the End of Winter, 1991, Hamlet, 1992, Anthony and Cleopatra, 1998, Private Lives (Tony nominee, Best Stage Actor award Variety Club Show Bus. Awards 2002), Seminar, 2012; dir.: My Name is Rachel Corrie, London & NY, 2005-06; (TV movies) Romeo and Juliet, Masterpiece Theater, 1978, Therese Raquin, 1980, Barchester Chronicles, 1984, Spirit of Man, 1989, Revolutionary Witness, 1989, Victoria Wood's All Day Breakfast, 1992, Fallen Angels, 1993, Rasputin, 1996 (Golden Globe, Emmy and SAG awards for Best Actor), Victoria Wood with All the Trimmings, 2000, We Know Where You Live, 2001, Something The Lord Made (Emmy Nomination Best Actor, 2004); (films) Die Hard, 1988, The January Man, 1989, Robin Hood: Prince of Thieves, 1991, Quigley Down Under, 1990, Truly, Madly, Deeply, 1991, Closet Land, 1991, Close My Eyes, 1991, Bob Roberts, 1992, Mesmer, 1993, An Awfully Big Adventure, 1994, Sense and Sensibility, 1995, Michael Collins, 1996, Judas Kiss, 1998, Dogma, 1998, Dark Harbor, 1998, Galaxy Quest, 1999, Play, 2000, Blow Dry, 2001, Harry Potter and the Sorcerer's Stone, 2001, Search for John Gissing, 2001, Harry Potter and the Chamber of Secrets, 2002, Love Actually, 2003, Harry Potter and the Prisoner of Azkaban, 2004, (voice) The Hitchhiker's Guide to the Galaxy, 2005, Harry Potter and the Goblet of Fire, 2005, Snowcake, 2006, Perfume: The Story of a Murderer, 2006, Nobel Son, 2007, Harry Potter and the Order of the Phoenix, 2007, Sweeney Todd: The Demon Barber of Fleet Street, 2007, Bottle Shock, 2008, Harry Potter and the Half-Blood Prince, 2009, Alice in Wonderland, 2010, Harry Potter and the Deathly Hallows: Part 1, 2010, Harry Potter and the Deathly Hallows: Part II, 2011, Gambit, 2012, Lee Daniels' The Butler, 2013, A Promise, 2013, CBGB, 2013, A Little Chaos, 2014, Eye In the Sky, 2015; writer, dir.: The Winter Guest, 1997 (Best Film award Chgo. Film Festival); dir (theatre) Creditors, London, NY, 2008-, My Name is Rachel Corrie, London, 2005-06. Died Jan. 14, 2016.

RICKS, MAE LOIS, secondary school educator; b. Tyler, Tex., Apr. 21, 1929; d. Roy and Athrea (Thomas) McCauley; m. Robert Earl Ricks, Sept. 12, 1965 (div. July 1977). BS, Tex. Coll., Tyler, 1951; MS, Windsor U., 1975, Pepperdine U., Malibu, Calif., 1985. English tchr. Plano H.S., Tex., 1952-55; subsitute tchr. San Diego Unified Sch. Dist., 1960-61; tchr. third grade Palo Verde Sch. Dist., Blythe, Calif., 1964-67; tchr. kindergarten Baldwin Park Sch. Dist., Calif., 1967-70; tchr. L.A. Unified Sch. Dist., Calif., 1973-83, Compton Unified Sch. Dist., Calif., 1992-96; substitute tchr. Dallas Pub. Schs., from 1997. Author (poetry) There Is No Care In The World, Poetry Parade, 1967, Fellowship in Prayer, 1967, The Lonely Desert, The Guild, 1968, The Loneliness I Choose, It Is Good to Be, Children. Mem. Am. Assn. U. Women, sec., 1994-96, Plano Cmty Forum, sec. 1996—; fundraider L.A. County Rep. Party, 1983-95. Mem. Luth. Women's Missionary League (pres. 1983-85), Assistance League of Stovall Found. (sec. 1979-82), West Side Republican Women (sec.), Tex. Coll. Alumni Assn. (sec.), Delta Sigma Theta Sorority, Inc. Avocations: writing, volunteering, teaching, sewing, painting. Home: Plano, Tex. Died May 12, 2007.

RIDDELL, ROBERT JAMES, JR., retired physicist; b. Peoria, Ill., June 25, 1923; s. Robert James and Hazel (Gwathmey) R.; m. Kathryn Gamble, Aug. 12, 1950; children: Cynthia Riddell Dunham, James Duncan R. BS, Carnegie-Mellon U., 1944; MS, U. Mich., 1947, PhD, 1951. Asst. prof. physics U. Calif., Berkeley, 1951-55; sr. physicist Lawrence Berkeley Lab., 1951-82; ret., 1982. Scientist AEC, Washington, 1958-60; adv. bd. Coll. Nat. Resources, U. Calif. Trustee Pacific Sch. Religion, Berkeley, 1970—, chmn. bd., 1979-84; trustee Grad. Theol. Union, Berkeley, 1982—, chmn. bd., 1990-96; trustee Coll. Prep. Sch., 1998—; pres. Friends U. Calif. Bot. Garden, 1984-95. Lt. (j.g.) USNR, 1944-46. Mem. N.Am. Rock Garden Soc. (pres. Calif. chpt. 1997—). Avocations: gardening, model building. Home: Oakland, Calif. Died Aug. 16, 2007.

RIDENHOUR, MARILYN HOUSEL, retired accountant; b. Madison, Nebr., July 12, 1931; d. Kenneth Virgil Housel and Edna Christina Reese Housel; m. Henry Clifton Ridenhour, Apr. 25, 1954 (dec.); children: Keith James, Susan Marie Ridenhour Redelfs, Jill Housel Ridenhour Cortese. Student, Nebr. Wesleyan U., 1949—50; BS in Bus. Adminstrn. with distinction, U. Nebr., 1953. CPA Mo., 1957. CPA Price Waterhouse & Co., St. Louis, 1953—54, Adolph Kahn, St. Louis, 1954—57; ptnr., CPA Adolph Kahn & Co., St. Louis, 1957—61, Kahn, Ridenhour & Co., St. Louis, 1961—65, Ridenhour Hylton & Co., St. Louis, 1965—91; cons. Baird Kurtz & Dobson, St. Louis, 1991—92, ret., 1992. Citizen leader Chesterfield, Mo. 2d Congl. Dist., 2005. Mem.: Rep. Leadership Found. (founding mem.), Am. Women's Soc. CPA, Am. Soc. Women Accts. (charter pres. 1959), Dawn Hope Soc., Soaring Eagle, Nat. Law Enforcement (founding mem. 2005), Century Soc., U. Nebr. Alumni Assn., St. Labre Indian Sch. Ednl. Assn., Chancellors Club U. Nebr., Beta Gamma Sigma, Phi Chi Theta, Alpha Lambda Delta, Delta Delta Delta. Republican. Methodist. Home: Chesterfield, Mo. Died Dec. 18, 2006.

RIETZ, JOHN THOMAS, investment company executive; b. Evanston, Ill., Mar. 14, 1933; s. Elmer Weber and Ruth (Vanderwicken) R.; m. Jennie Spiro, Sept. 26, 1955; children: Robin, Barry, Jeffrey Dean. Student, Coe Coll., Cedar Rapids, Iowa, 1952. Pres. Hooker Rietz Prodns., Hollywood, Calif., 1958-76, John T. Rietz Co., Inc., Oklahoma City, 1972-89; dir. Rietz Prodns., Ltd., Hollywood, from 1976; pres., chmn. bd. Journeys End Resorts, Inc., Miami, Fla., from 1981; dir. Interfunding Corp., Belize, Cen. Am., from 1990; co-mng. dir. Overseas Trading Corp., Belize, from 1992. Dir. Venture Capital Assn. Belize, 1988—; co-mng. dir. Interfunding Corp. Producer motion pictures, 1959-64. With USMC, 1952-55. Mem. Hotel Devel. Assn. (fin. mgr. Belize 1992), Caribbean Hotel Assn. (rep. P.R. 1982-92), Belize Tourist Assn. Republican. Avocations: fishing, scuba diving, race car driving. Home: Fort Pierce, Fla. Died Nov. 2, 2006.

RILEY, RICHARD LEON, psychiatrist, consultant; b. Omak, Wash., Jan. 31, 1932; s. George Maurer and Lounettie Grace (Chapman) R.; m. Carol Ann Franklin (div. Dec. 1971); children: Kevin, Erin, Brian, Patrick, Michael; m. Renata Karolina Roeber, Dec. 28, 1972; 1 child, Alexandra Elizabeth. Student, El Camino Coll., 1954-56, U. Calif., LA, 1956-57; BS in Medicine, Duke U., 1960; MD, U. So. Calif., LA, 1961. Bd. cert. pediatrics; cert. psychiat. examiner, Calif. Pediatric intern L.A. (Calif.) Children's Hosp., 1961-62, pediatric resident, 1962-64, attending physician, 1964-69; pediatric cons. Gen. Hosp., Peace Corp. APIA, Western Samoa, 1969-70; child psychiatry fellowship Pasadena (Calif.) Guidance Clinic, 1971-73, clin. supr., 1973-75; med. dir., acting exec. dir. San Luis Valley Comp. Cmty. Mental Health Ctr., Alamosa, Colo., 1975-77; chief outpatient dept., cons. Humboldt County Dept. Mental Health, 1977-79; pvt. practice psychotherapy and pharmacotherapy, 1979-86; behavioral pediatrician U.S. Army Exceptional Family Member Program, Stuttgart, Germany, 1986-87, chief EFMP Shape, Belgium, 1987-88, evaluator William Beaumont Army Med. Ctr., 1988-91; cons. Indian Health Svc., Portland, from 1991. Staff Kaiser-Permanente Med. Group, 1964-69, psychiatrist, supr., 1973-75; asst. clin. prof. pediatrics U. Calif., Irvine, 1967-69; pediatric cons. and lectr. Hope Ship Ceylon, Sri Lanka, 1968; presenter in field. Contbr. articles to profl. jours. With USN, 1950-54. Mem. Am. Psychiat. Assn., Am. Acad. Pediatrics, Am. Acad. Child and Adolescent psychiatry, Wash. State Psychiat. Soc. Avocations: golf, gardening, skiing, painting. Home: Spokane, Wash. Died June 23, 2007.

RINEHART, ALICE DAY DUFFY, retired education educator; b. Hartford, Conn., Mar. 2, 1919; d. Ward Everett and Louise Van Ness (Day) Duffy; m. Robert Lloyd Rinehart, 1946 (dec. Apr. 1964); children: Ward E., Janice D. Rinehart Freund, Bradford R. BA, Smith Coll., 1940; MEd, Lehigh U., 1965, EdD, 1969. Cert. social studies tchr. Mass., history and govt. tchr. Pa. Tchr. social studies, guidance counselor Amherst (Mass.) HS, 1940-46; sec. Child Psychology Clinic Stanford U., Palo Alto, Calif., 1946-47; supr. intern tchrs. Lehigh U. Grad. Sch. Edn., Bethlehem, Pa., 1964-84, asst. to and dir. tchr. intern program, ednl. placement dir., 1965-84, prof. sociology of edn., 1965-84, mem. Lehigh U. grad. com., 1978-83, ret., 1984; instr. sociology edn. summer sch. DeSales U. Sch. Nursing, Center Valley, Pa., 1986. Author: Mortals in the Immortal Profession, 1983, One Woman Determined to Make a Difference, 2001; co-author: Early Retirement-Promises and Pitfalls, 1992, Country School Memories, 1999; contbr. chapters to books, articles and book revs. to profl. publs. Pres. Lanark Elem. Sch. PTA, Center Valley, 1957—59, So. Lehigh HS PTA, Center Valley, 1962—63; mem. adv. com. Lehigh County Area Agy. on Aging, 1988—96. Recipient Outstanding Svc. to Edn. award, Lehigh U. Grad. Sch. Edn., 1985. Home: Center Valley, Pa. Died June 22, 2007.

RINEHART, DONALD RAYMOND, psychotherapist; b. Bellingham, Wash., Dec. 14, 1926; s. Jack Edgar and Cecil Kathleen (Stenger) R.; m. Delores Overdorff, June 21, 1952 (div. Mar. 1976); children: Sarah K., Michelle; m. Paula Panting, July 9, 1982. BA, U. Wash., 1951, MSW, 1956; PhD, Columbia Pacific U., 1983. Reg. clin. social worker. Counselor Wash. State Reformatory, Monroe, 1952-54; dir. intake and counseling King County Juvenile Ct., Seattle, 1956-60; dir. tng., probation and parole Wash. State Probation and Parole Div., Seattle, 1960-62; dir. Lane County Youth Project, Eugene, Oreg., 1962-67; assoc. prof. Portland (Oreg.) State U., from 1963, U. Oreg., Eugene, from 1963; pvt. practice counseling, psychotherapy Salem, Oreg., from 1974. Dir. Juvenile Court Summer Sessions U. Oreg., Eugene, 1963-67; advisor Joint Commn. on Correctional Manpower and Tng., Washington, 1970-71. Contbr. articles to profl. jours. Mem. profl. devel. com. Western Correctional Assn., San Jose, Calif., 1969-71; chmn., vice chmn., hospitality and program coms. and planning commn. Nat. Inst. on Crime and Delinquency, 1962-72. Mem. Oreg. Psychol. Assn., Nat. Assn. and Acad. Cert. Social Workers, Jaycees, Sigma Nu (pres. pledge com. council). Home: Salem, Oreg. Died Mar. 30, 2007.

RINTELMANN, RICHARD FREDERICK, consultant; b. Milw., July 1, 1928; s. Ernst Albert and Katherine (Weckmuller) R.; m. Julie Ann Malone, May 20, 1950; children: Jay, Ann, Kathryn, Thomas. BS, Carroll Coll., Waukesha, Wis., 1949; MEP, U. Minn., 1982. Dairy plant fieldman Borden, Chgo., 1949-59; supr. DPF Pure Milk Assn., Chgo., 1959-61; asst. mgr. farm sales Klenzade Div. Ecolab, St. Paul, Minn., 1961-62, mgr. farm sales, 1962-68, asst. v.p. farm sales, 1968-70, div. v.p. nat. accts., 1970-78, div. v.p. mktg., 1978-81, corp. v.p., gen. mgr., 1981-89, cons., from 1989. Chmn. Farm Methods Com. Internat. Sanitarians, Chgo., 1961-68; mem. Excellence Coun., Ecolab, St. Paul, 1985-89. Author: (book) Dairy Farm Sanitation, 1965. Pres. Marengo (Ill.) Jaycees, 1955; sec. Marengo C. of C., 1957-59; chmn. Quest for Excellence in Edn., St. Paul, Minn., 1988-89; trustee Hazelden Found., Center City, Minn., 1975-94, chmn. bd., 1989-91; trustee I.C. Koran Trust, 1991—. Named Man of Yr., Ill. Jaycees, 1956. Mem. Nat. Dairy Plant Field Men. (pres. 1955-61), Town and Country Club, Hastings Country Club, University Park Country Club. Republican. Roman Catholic. Avocations: golf, reading, gardening, travel, racing pigeons, tennis. Home: Bradenton, Fla. Died Apr. 3, 2007.

RITCHEY, TEDDY ALLAN, association executive; b. San Antonio, Sept. 5, 1931; s. Theo Andrew and Eula Mae (Hill) R.; m. Konkordia Ann Helga Kuczynski; children: Kordi Ann (dec.), T. Allan, Robert Scott. BS in Indsl. Edn., Tex. A&M U., 1955; AA in Bus. Mgmt., Cen. Tex. Coll., 1981. Enlisted USNR, 1949; hon. discharge, 1954; commd. 2nd lt. U.S. Army, 1955, advanced through grades to lt. col., 1968, ret., 1975; instr. Cen. Tex. Coll., Killeen, 1976-80; real estate broker Fleming, Nichols & Roley, Killeen, 1981-82; exec. v.p. Cen. Tex. Homebuilders Assn., Harker Heights, from 1982, sec., from 1983, also bd. dirs. Named Realtor of Yr., Ft. Hood Area Bd. Realtors, 1982. Mem. Tex. Real Estate Commn., Tex. Ins. Bd., Tex. A&M U. Alumni Assn. (pres. 1977-79) Avocations: golf, bowling. Home: Harker Hts, Tex. Died Dec. 17, 2006.

RITCHIE, DAVID WAYNE, finance company executive; b. Lexington, Ky., July 22, 1961; s. Ralph Curtis Ritchie and Donna Mae (Thompson) Stone; m. Derinda Sue McConnell, Nov. 7, 1986; children: Ryan Scott Kiefer, Duwayne William, Lance Del Ray. BS, Anderson U., 1983. Asst. storemgr. Camden (Ohio) Iga, 1977-81; dir. fin. Project Ptnr. Inc., Middletown, Ohio, 1983-84; pub. acct. Capin and Crouse Co., Greenwood, Ind., 1984-86; contr. The Exec. Line, Greenwood, 1986-88; with fin. planning IDS Fin. Svcs., Indpls., 1988; instr. Mayflower Transit, Indpls., 1988-89; dir., treas. Elliott 4, Inc., Eaton, Ohio, from 1988; fin. rep. Money Fin. Svcs., Indpls., 1989; acct. Alumax Fabricated Products/Amax Coal, Richmond, Ind., from 1989. Active Big Bros. of Indpls., 1985—. Mem. Nat. Assn. Investors Club, Rotary. Mem. First Church of God. Died Dec. 8, 2006.

RITZ, STEPHEN MARK, lawyer; b. Midland, Mich., Aug. 23, 1962; s. Alvin H. and Patricia M. (Padway) R. BA, Northwestern U., 1985; JD, Ind. U., 1989. Bar: Ill. 1990, U.S. Dist. Ct. (no. dist.) Ill. 1990, Ind. 1996. Atty. Chapman & Cutler, Chgo., 1990-93; CEO Newport Pension Mgmt. LLC, Indpls., 1993—97, atty., from 1997. Home: Carmel, Ind. Died Feb. 13, 2007.

RIVETTE, JACQUES, film director; b. Rouen, France, Mar. 1, 1928; s. André and Andrée (Amiard) R. Student, Lycée Corneille, Rouen. Journalist, critic Cahiers du Cinéma, 1953-82; asst. to Jasques Becker and Jean Renior, 1954. Author, dir. (film) Paris nous appartient, 1958-60; dir. (films.) Aux Quatre Coins, 1950, Le Quadrille, 1950, Le Divertissement, 1952, Le coup du berger, 1956, Suzanne Simenon, La Religieuse de Diderot, 1966, Jean Renoir, Le Patron, 1966, L'Amour fou, 1968, Out One: Spectre, 1973, Céline et Julie vont en bateau, 1974, Le vengeur, Duelle, 1976, Noroit, 1976, Paris S'en Va, 1981, Le pont du Nord, 1982, Merry-go-round, 1983, Wuthering Heights, 1984, L'amour par terre, 1984, The Gang of Four, 1988 (Berlin Film award 1989), La Belle Noiseuse, 1991 (Cannes Grand prize 1991), Jeanne La Pucelle, 1993, Around a Small Mountain, 2009; dir. (play) La religieuse, 1963; dir. writer: Up, Down, Fragile, 1995. Chevalier, Ordre Nat. du Mérite; Grand Prix nat., 1981. Died Jan. 29, 2016.

RIZZO, FRANK ALBERT, physician; b. Detroit, June 7, 1936; MD, U. Mich., 1960. Diplomate Am. Bd. Neurology. Intern Harper Hosp., Detroit, 1960-61; resident Henry Ford Hosp., Detroit, 1963-65; resident in neurology Mt. Sinai Hosp., NYC, 1965-68, fellow in neurology, 1968-70; chief divsn. neurology Jersey City Med. Ctr., 1969-81; pvt. practice NYC, from 1971. Asst. clin. prof., attending neurologist Mt. Sinai Sch. Medicine, N.Y.C., 1971—, chmn. med. records com., 1991-93; attending neurologist Beth Israel Med. Ctr., N.Y.C., 1971—. Lt. USNR, 1961-63. Mem. AMA, AAAS, Am. Acad. Neurology, Med. Soc. N.Y., Tinnitus Soc. Home: Tenafly, NJ. Died Dec. 29, 2006.

ROBBERT, LOUISE BUENGER, retired historian; b. St. Paul, Aug. 18, 1925; d. Albert and Myrtle (Rubbert) Buenger; m. George S. Robbert, Sept. 17, 1960; 1 child, George Harold. BA, Carleton Coll., 1947; MA, U. Cin., 1948, B. Edn., 1949; PhD, U. Wis., 1955. Instr. history Smith Coll., Northampton, Mass., 1954-55, Hunter Coll., NYC, 1957-60; asst. prof. history Tex. Tech U., Lubbock, 1962-63, assoc. prof. history, 1964-75; vis. assoc. prof. history U. Mo., St. Louis, 1978-79, assoc. prof. history, 1979-91, prof. history, 1991—2000, ret., 2001. Author: Venetian Money Market in: Studi Veneziani, 1971, Venice and the Crusades in: The Crusades V., 1985, Il sistema monetario in: Storia di Venezia, Il l'eta del comune, 1995. Officer Wednesday Club, St. Louis, 1981-83, 87-90, 94-96, v.p., 1997—99, pres., 1999-2001. Scholar Fulbright Commn., 1955-57; grantee A.C.L.S., 1960, Gladys Krieble Delmas Found., 1983, 87. Mem. Medieval Acad. Am., Soc. for Study of Crusades & the Latin East, Midwest Medieval History Conf. (pres.). Lutheran. Home: Ballwin, Mo. Died June 11, 2007.

ROBBINS, ANNE FRANCIS See REAGAN, NANCY

ROBEL, RONALD RAY, history educator; b. Oak Park, Ill., Mar. 21, 1934; s. Raymond J. and Mildred A. (Boeche) R. BA, Grinnell Coll., 1956; MA in History, U. Mich., 1957, MA in Far East Lang. and Lit., 1965, PhD in History, 1972. Lectr. U. Md., Far East Div., 1962-64; vis. instr. U. Wis., Madison, 1965-66; instr. history U. Ala., Tuscaloosa, 1966-72, asst. prof. history and Chinese, from 1972, dir. Critical Lang. Ctr., from 1985, dir. Asian studies, from 1989, dir. internat. honors program, from 1997. Mem. Assn. for Asian Studies, Nat. Assn. Self-Instructional Lang. Programs (pres. 1992-94), Ala. Assn. Historians, Ala. Assn. Fgn. Lang. Tchrs., Chinese Lang. Tchrs. Assn. Home: Tuscaloosa, Ala. Died Aug. 24, 2007.

ROBERSON, LINWOOD JOHN, minister; b. Denton, Texas, May 7, 1933; s. Linwood Julius and Leta Brewer R.; m. Eula Bell Enlow, June 28, 1958; children: Holly Ann, Martha Maria. BBA, U. North Tex., 1954; M of Theology, So. Meth. U., 1957, M of Psychology, 1960. Ordained to ministry Meth. Ch., 1956. Min. Lake Highlands Meth. Ch., Dallas, Kirkwood Meth. Ch., Irving, Tex., Gainville (Tex.) Meth. Ch., Blue Mound Meth. Ch., Denton, Tex., Aubrey Meth. Ch., Denton, Tex. Mem. Knights of Pytheon, Sons of Am. Revolution. Avocations: travel, horticulture, fishing, camping, remodeling houses. Died Nov. 20, 2006.

ROBERTS, DONALD EUGENE, minister; b. Marion, Ind., Mar. 28, 1942; s. Frank M. and Nellie Margaret (Hegwood) R.; m. Linda Lou Fultz, Apr. 10, 1965; children: Jacquelyn Ann, Jeffrey Kyle. BS in Edn., Ball State U., 1965, MA in Edn., 1969; MDiv, Bethany Theol. Sem., 1977. Ordained to ministry Ch. of the Brethren, 1977. Elem. sch. tchr. Marion (Ind.) Community Schs., 1965-74; pastor Ch. of the Brethren, Portland, Ind., 1973-74; family life prog. dir. Bethany Union Ch., Chgo., 1974-76; pastor Nettle Creek Ch. of the Brethren, Hagerstown, Ind., 1977-79, Ch. of the Brethren, Lanark, Ill., 1979-84, Topeka, from 1984. Co-founder, bd. dirs. Topeka Peace Resource Ctr., 1985—; co-founder Topeka Religious Leaders Against the Death Penalty, 1987. Co-author: The Death Penalty/Statement of the Ch. of the Brethern, 1987. Democrat. Home: Topeka, Kans. *We are living in a day when it is becoming increasingly clear that what we do individually not only has an impact on the rest of humanity but also on the rest of God's creatures and the whole of God's creation as well. Our survival will depend upon our willingness to base our decisions and our actions on this fact.* Died Aug. 12, 2007.

ROBERTS, NIGRA LEA See SINK, NIGRA LEA

ROBERTS, RALPH JOEL, telecommunications industry and cable broadcast executive; b. NYC, Mar. 13, 1920; s. Robert and Sara (Wahl) Roberts; m. Suzanne Fleisher, Aug. 23, 1942; children: Catherine, Lisa, Ralph Jr., Brian, Douglas (dec. 2011). BS in Econs., U. Pa., 1941; LHD (hon.), Holy Family Coll., 1994; HHD (hon.), Arcadia U., 2004; LLD (hon.), U. Pa., 2005. Account exec. Aitken Kynett Advt., Phila., 1946-48; v.p. Muzak Corp., NYC, 1948-50; pres., chief exec. officer Pioneer Industries, Inc., Darby, Pa., 1950-61; pres. Internat. Equity Corp., Bala Cynwyd, Pa., 1961-83; chmn., chief exec. officer Sural Corp. (merger with Internat. Equity Corp. 1983); chmn. Comcast Corp., Phila., 1997—2002, chmn. exec. com., 2002—09, chmn. emeritus Phila, Pa., 2010—15. Trustee, chmn. conflict interest com. Albert Einstein Med. Ctr.; bd. dirs. Phila. Electric Co., Phila. Nat. Bank, Corestates, Penn Medicine; bd. trustees U. Pa. Health Sys., 2002. Bd. dirs. regional NCCJ; trustee Brandywine Mus. and Conservancy, charter mem. World Bus. Coun.; past mem. mentor program and Benjamin Franklin assocs. U. Pa.; bd. dirs. Phila. Orch., 1993; past v.p. Family Svc. Phila.; past bd. dirs., mem. budget and fees com. State Coll. and Univ. Dirs.; mem. re-regulation and legis. affairs coms. Nat. Cable TV Assn.; past mem. Gov.'s Rev. of Govt. Mgmt., Inc. Lt. USNR, 1942-45. Reipient Americanism award Anti-Defamation League of B'nai B'rith, Brotherhood award NCCJ, 1989, award for outstanding svc. to cable TV industry Walter Kaitz Found., 1990, Acres of Diamonds Entrepreneuriol Excellence award Entrepreneurial Inst. Temple U., 1991, Disting. Vanguard award for leadership Nat. Cable TV Assn., 1993, Golden Plate award Am. Acad. Achievement, 1994, PAL award Police Athletic League Phila., 1995, Edward Powell award for cmty. svc. City of Phila., 1995, Joseph P. Wharton award U. Pa., 1995, Whitney M. Young Jr. Leadership award Urban League Phila., 1997, Disting. Cmty. Leadership award Operation Understanding, 1997, Cable TV Hall of Fame award, 2000, Mensa Achievement award, 2000, Heroes of Liberty award Liberty Mus., 2000, William Penn award Greater Phila. C. of C., 2002, Am. Horizon award for Visionary Leadership, Media Inst., Washington, 2002, Humanitarian award United Jewish Appeal Fedn. of NY, 2003, Trustee award NATAS, 2003, Excellence in Leadership award Temple U., 2005, Partnership for Drug Free Am. hon., 2005; named to Broadcasting and Cable Hall of Fame, 1993. Avocations: tennis, travel. Home: East Fallowfield Township, Pa. Died June 18, 2015.

ROBERTS, WILLIAM ALLAN, engineering company executive; b. NYC, Nov. 16, 1930; s. Israel and Sophie (Steinberg) Rabinovitch; m. Lorrayne Krinsky, July 10, 1954; children: Steven, Susan, Andrea. BChemE, NYU, 1951; MSChemE, Columbia U., 1958; PMD, Harvard U., 1976. Registered profl. engr. N.J., Tex., Mass., Ky., Pa., Mich. Jr. engr. Standard Brands, NYC, 1951-53; project engr. Columbia U., NYC, 1953-56; project mgr. Englehard Industries, Newark, 1956-60; mgr. engring. Chem. Constrn. Corp., NYC, 1960-74; pres. Nichols Engring. and Rsch. Corp., Belle Mead, N.J., 1974-78; mgr. contracts Am. Air Filter, Louisville, 1978-80; project mgr. Lummus Corp., Bloomfield, N.J., 1980-83; pvt. engr. Ramsey, N.J., 1983-88; mgr. contracts Toyo U.S.A., NYC, from 1988. Pres. Parents Assn., The Tng. Sch. at Vineland, N.J., 1987-89; active Assn. for Retarded Citizens, Voice of the Retarded. Mem. Am. Chem. Soc., Harvard Bus. Sch. Club. Avocations: bridge, stamp collecting/philately, coin collecting/numismatics, reading. Home: Goshen, Ky. Died Aug. 25, 2007.

ROBERTS, WILLIAM JOHN ODGERS, investment management company executive; b. Chgo., Nov. 19, 1920; s. William Carrie and Mildred Cook (Klunk) R.; m. Laura Louise Bauer, 1946 (dec. 1956); children: Laura, Anne; m. Ann Elizabeth Vail, 1957; children: Elizabeth, Mary, Michael. AB in Econ. summa cum laude, Brown U., 1942; student, Oxford U., 1978, Cambridge U., 1981. Lic. life ins. broker; registered commodity futures trader. Sales rep., western syndicate mgr., western sales mgr., ptnr Glore, Forgan & Co., 1946-65; sr. v.p. in charge investment rsch. Glore Forgan, Staats, Inc., 1965-68, with investment mgmt. dept., 1968-70; v.p. in charge Mid-Am. investment mgmt. dept. Kidder, Peabody & Co., Inc., 1970-76; investment banker Bacon, Whipple div. subs. Stifel, Nicolaus & Co., Inc., 1976-84; sr. v.p. C.F. Glore, Roberts and Tilden, Loucks & Grannis, 1976-84.; mng. dir. Roberts, Loucks & Co., Chgo., from 1984. Mem. panel of arbitrators N.Y. Stock Exchange and NASD; vis. com. U. Chgo. Oriental Inst., 1961—; guest lectr. Northwestern U., Vanderbilt U., Brown U., U. Chgo. Grad. Sch. Bus., Mich. State U. Grad. Sch. Bus. Adminstrn., U. Colo., Carnegie-Mellon U. Grad. Sch. Indsl. Adminstrn.; expert witness on investment ct. cases Cook County, Ill., Phoenix for Prudential Ins. Co., Ill. Com. for Ill. Bell. Mng. editor Brown Daily Herald. Chmn. Brown U. Bicentennial Fund of Chgo., 1964; alt. del. Nat. Rep. Conv., Chgo., 1952; chmn. Wellesley Coll. Parents Com., 1970-71; officer Order Hosp. St. John Jerusalem; pres. Lake Forest Libr. Bd., 1979. Mem. Investment Bankers Assn. Am. (exec. com. 1961-64), Inst. Chartered Fin. Analysts, Investment Analysts Soc. Chgo. (chmn. investment mgmt. group 1972-74, 78-80, bd. dirs. 1976-78), Brown U. Club Chgo. (past pres.), Onwentsia Club, Chgo. Club, Brown Key, Phi Beta Kappa, Delta Tau Delta. Republican. Presbyterian (elder). Avocations: tennis, travel, archaeology. Home: Lake Forest, Ill. Died Nov. 17, 2006.

ROBERTSON, LAURIE LUISSA, computer scientist; b. Dallas, Feb. 19, 1960; BA, Rice U., 1982; MLS, U. Pitts., 1983; cert. procurement and contracting, U. Va., 1993. Programmer/statistician Galveston (Tex.) Dist. Atty., 1980-82; programmer/analyst Def. Systems Inc., McLean, Va., 1983-85; computer scientist Computer Scis. Corp., Falls Church, Va., 1985-94, Sci. Applications Internat. Corp., Arlington, Va., from 1994. Mem. Computer Soc. of IEEE, Assn. for Computing Machinery, Beta Phi Mu. Home: Arlington, Va. Died Mar. 27, 2007.

ROBINSON, DORIS ANN, secondary school educator; b. New Orleans, Aug. 18, 1947; d. Jesse and Bethel (Finley) R. AA, L.A. C.C., 1968; BA, Calif. State U., LA, 1971. Lic. tchr., Calif. Tchr. L.A. Unified Schs., from 1972. Contbg. writer Martin Luther King Ctr., Atlanta, 1989; contbg. editor Globe Pub. Co., Denver, 1990-91. Contbg. writer: Infusion Model for Teaching Dr. M.L. King's Nonviolent Principles, 1991; contbg. editor: Foundations, 1990. Asst. dir. Girls Club S.W. L.A., 1982-86. Recipient Appreciation for People Who Promote Learning Excellence award Mayor Tom Bradley City of L.A., 1984. Democrat. Baptist. Avocations: singing, sewing, art. Home: Inglewood, Calif. Died Apr. 15, 2007.

ROBINSON, NATHANIEL DAVID, JR., physician, consultant; b. Kans. City, Mar. 6, 1941; s. Nathaniel David Robinson and Dorothy Mae McLaughlin; m. Joanne Marie Kaleida, July 7, 1979; children: Donelle, Nathaniel David Robinson III. BSEE, U. RI, 1963; MD, U. Bologna, 1975. Cert. bd. cert. ins. medicine. Intern Roger Williams Gen. Hosp. Brown U., Providence, 1975—76; resident St. Francis Hosp. and Med. Ctr. U. Conn., Hartford, 1976—77; resident Hamot Med. Ctr., Erie, Pa., 1977—79, Mt. Sinai Med. Ctr., Miami Beach, Fla., 1981—82; med. officer USPHS Hosp., Seattle, 1979—81, VA, Nashville, 1982—85; med. dir. CNA, Nashville, 1985—95, v.p., med. dir., 1997—2004; asst. med. dir. Am. United Life, Indpls., 1995—97; med. cons. AIG Am. Gen., Nashville, from 2005. Cons. in field. Contbr. articles to profl. jours. Mem.: IEEE, AMA, Fla. Med. Assn., Midwest Med. Dirs. Assn., Providence Engring. Soc., Nashville Acad. Medicine, Tenn. Med. Assn., Am. Acad. Ins. Medicine, Am. Radio Relay League. Avocation: amateur radio. Home: Brentwood, Tenn. Died Aug. 30, 2015.

ROBSON, JAMES CLYDE, III, marketing and sales executive; b. Berkeley, Calif., Apr. 24, 1948; s. James Clyde Robson and Lala (Smithwick) Johnson; m. Marsha Gail Hordee, Aug. 15, 1972; children: Yanna Michelle, James Ian Smithwick, Charles Allistair. BS, Appalachian State Coll., 1969; MBA, Pepperdine U., 1990. Leader N.C. Ednl. System, 1969; with sales/mktg. Becton-Dickinson & Co., Rutherford, N.J., 1973-83; mktg. exec. Zimmer/Hall Surg., Santa Barbara, Calif., 1983-91; v.p. mktg. Smith & Neplew Dyonics, Andover, Mass., 1991-93; v.p. sales mktg. AcroMed, Cleve., from 1993. With USMC, 1971-73. Republican. Epsicopalian. Home: Charlotte, NC. Died June 25, 2007.

ROCCO, ALEX (ALEXANDER FEDERICO PETRICONE, JR.), actor; b. Cambridge, Mass., Feb. 29, 1936; s. Alexander Sr. and Mary (Di Biase); m. Sandra (Sadie) Elaine Garrett, Mar. 24, 1966 (dec. 2002); children: Marc Rocco (dec. 2009), Jennifer Rocco, Lucien; m: Shannon Wilcox, 2005; stepchildren Sean Doyle, Kelli Williams Actor all maj. studios, Hollywood, Calif., from 1963. Appearances include (films) Motorpsycho, 1965, The St.

Valentine's Day Massacre, 1967, The Boston Strangler, 1968, Blood Mania, 1970, Wild Riders, 1971, Brute Corps, 1971, The Godfather, 1972, Stanley, 1972, The Outside Man, 1972, Bonnie's Kids, 1973, Slither, 1973, The Friends of Eddie Coyle, 1973, Detroit 9000, 1973, Three the Hard Way, 1974, Freebie and the Bean, 1974, Rafferty and the Gold Dust Twins, 1975, A Women for All Men, 1975, Hearts of the West, 1975, Fire Sale, 1977, Rabbit Test, 1978, Voices, 1979, Herbie Goes Bananas, 1980, The Stunt Man, 1980, Nobody's Perfekt, 1981, The Entity, 1982, Cannonball Run II, 1984, Stick, 1985, Gotcha!, 1985, Stiffs, 1985, P.K. and the Kid, 1987, Return to Horror High, 1987, Scenes from the Goldmine, 1987, Lady in White, 1988, Dream a Little Dream, 1989, Wired, 1989, The Pope Must Diet, 1991, The Flight of the Dove, 1994, That Thing You Do!, 1996, Dead of Night, 1996, Just Write, 1997, Goodbye Lover, 1998, (voice) A Bug's Life, 1998, Dudley Do-Right, 1999, The Last Producer, 2000, The Wedding Planner, 2001, Italian Ties, 2001, The Country Bears, 2002, The Job, 2003, CrazyLove, 2005, Find Me Guilty, 2006, Jam, 2006, Smokin' Aces, 2006, Ready or Not, 2009, Now Here, 2010, And They're Off, 2011, The House Across the Street, 2013, Scammerhead, 2014 (TV films) Legend in Granite, 1973, Hustling, 1975, Twigs, 1975, Husbands and Wives, 1977, A Question of Guilt, 1978, The Grass is Always Greener Over the Septic Tank, 1978, Lily: Sold Out, 1981, The First Time, 1982, Braker, 1985, Badge of the Assasin, 1985, How to Murder a Millionaire, 1990, A Quiet Little Neighborhood, a Perfect Little Murder, 1990, An Inconvenient Woman, 1991, Boris and Natasha, 1992, Love, Honor & Obey: The Last Mafia Marriage, 1993, Harmful Intent, 1993, Sam Churchhill: Search for a Homeless Man, 1999, Big Shot: Confessions of a Campus Bookie, 2002 (TV series) Run for Your Life, 1967, Batman, 1967, Get Smart, 1967, That Girl, 1970-71, The F.B.I., 1972, Mission: Impossible, 1971-73, Circle of Fear, 1973, Losta Luck, 1974, The Rookies, 1974, Get Christie Love!, 1974, Kojak, 1973-75, Cannon, 1972-75, The Blue Knight, 1975, Three for the Road, 1975, Delvecchio, 1976-77, Mary Tyler Moore, 1977, Police Story, 1975-77, The Rockford Files, 1977, Barnaby Jones, 1977, Dog and Cat, 1977, Baretta, 1977, Starsky and Hutch, 1977, What Really Happened to the Class of '65?, 1977, CHiPs, 1980, Small & Frye, 1983, The Best of Times, 1983, Jessie, 1984, Matt Houston, 1984, Hardcastle and McCormick, 1984, St. Elsewhere, 1984, Simon & Simon, 1984, The Love Boat, 1983-84, Hot Pursuit, 1984, Hollywood Beat, 1985, The A-Team, 1985, The Golden Girls, 1985, Murder, She Wrote, 1985-86, T.J. Hooker, 1984-86, CBS Summer Playhouse, 1987, Rags to Riches, 1987, Hotel, 1987, Hunter, 1987, Walt Disney's Wonderful World of Color, 1988, Facts of Life, 1981-88, Murphy Brown, 1989, The Famous Teddy Z, 1989-90 (Emmy award 1990), Carol & Company, 1990, Midnight Caller, 1991, Sibs, 1991-92, Daddy Dearest, 1993, Bonkers, 1993, The George Carlin Show, 1994-95, Can't Hurry Love, 1995, Partners, 1995, Hope & Gloria, 1995, Pinky and the Brain, 1996, Mad About You, 1996, (voice)The Simpsons, 1990-97, Goode Behavior, 1997, Early Edition, 1997, Nick Freno: Licensed Teacher, 1997, Home Improvement, 1997, Michael Hayes, 1998, Silk Stalkings, 1998, Sabrina, The Teenage Witch, 1999, Just Shoot Me!, 1999, Family Law, 1999, The Practice, 2000, Walker, Texas Ranger, 2000, The Angry Beavers, 2000, Family Guy, 1999-2001, Touched By An Angel, 2003, Lucky, 2003, One Life to Live, 2004, The Division, 2001-04, ER, 2005, The Wedding Bells, 2007, Party Down, 2010, The Life & Time of Tim, 2011, Private Practice, 2012, Magic City, 2012-13, Episodes, 2014-15, Maron, 2015 (TV mini-series) Harold Robbins' 79 Park Avenue, 1977 Mem. Baha'i Faith. Avocations: tennis, golf. Home: Malibu, Calif. Died July 18, 2015.

ROCKEFELLER, MARGARETTA LARGE FITLER MURPHY (HAPPY ROCKEFELLER), widow of former vice president of United States; b. Bryn Mawr, Pa., June 9, 1926; d. William Wonderly Fitler Jr. and Margaretta Large Harrison Fitler m. James Slater Murphy (div.) m. Nelson Aldrich Rockefeller on May 4, 1963 (dec. 1979); children: James B. Murphy II, Margaretta H. Bickford, Carol Murphy Lyden, Malinda Murphy Menotti (dec. 2005), Nelson A. Rockefeller, Jr., Mark F. Rockefeller. Volunteer for Nelson Rockefeller's campaign for governor; bd. dirs. ADM Co., Decatur, Ill., 1987; patron of the arts and philanthropist. Died May 19, 2015.

ROCKWELL, ROBERT GOODE, electrical engineer; b. La Junta, Colo., Aug. 20, 1922; s. Leroy Elwood and Laura Belle (Mc Clain) R.; m. Betty Jean Crawford, Dec. 29, 1945 (div. July 1960); children: Laura Amundsen, Melanie Vizenor; m. Norma Jean Fosnaugh, Mar. 25, 1961; children: Michael, Robyn Rockwell-Elkins. BSEE, U. Colo., 1944; MSEE, Stanford U., 1948, Engr., 1949. Mem. tech. staff Hughes Aircraft Corp., Culver City, Calif., 1949-52, Los Angeles, 1969-70; sect. mgr. Varian Assocs., Palo Alto, Calif., 1952-66; mem. tech. staff Fairchild Semiconductor, Palo Alto, 1966-68; mgr. tube tech. Zenith Radio Corp., Glenview, Ill., 1971-82; prin. engr. Rank Electronic Tubes, Scotts Valley, Calif., 1982-86; CRT dispenser cathode cons. Ceradyne Electron Sources, Costa Mesa, Calif., 1986-87; design engr. Electro-Scan, Inc., Garfield, N.J., 1988-89; sr. design engr. Litton Electron Devices, Tempe, Ariz., 1989-90; ret., 1991. Contbr. articles to profl. jours.; patentee in field. Pres. Manakin Huguenots, Calif., 1986-88; mem. Hugenot Soc. of Founders of Manakin in the Colony of Va. (Mayflower descendant). Lt. (J.g.) USNR, 1942-45. Mem. SAR, IEEE (life, sr. Centennial medal 1984), Soc. Info. Display (life), Am. Legion, Colo. Terr. Family, Bucks and Does Sq. Dance Club (Elk Grove Village, Ill., pres. 1979-80), Ahwatukee (Ariz.) Woodworking Club, Ahwatukee Sq. Dance Club, Ahwatukee Lawn Bowling Club (pres. 1993—), Masons, Sigma Xi, Tau Beta Pi, Eta Kappa Nu. Democrat. Christian Ch. Avocations: bicycling, surfing, camping, photography, genealogy. Home: Phoenix, Ariz. Died Jan. 4, 2007.

RODERUCK, CHARLOTTE, retired nutrition educator; b. Walkersville, Md., Dec. 2, 1919; d. George Edgar and Margaret Hazel (Hedges) R. BS in Chemistry, U. Pitts., 1940; MS in Organic Chemistry, Wash. State Coll., 1942; PhD in Biochemistry, U. Iowa, 1949. Rsch. chemist Children's Fund of Mich., Detroit, 1942-46; from asst. to full prof. Iowa State U., Ames, 1948-88, disting. prof., from 1972, prof. emerita, from 1988. Vis. prof. Baroda (India) U., 1964-66; mem. joint rsch. com. Bd. for Internat. Food and Agr. Devel.-Dept. of State, Washington, 1977-83. Contbr. articles to profl. jours. Mem. LWV, Am. Chem. Soc. (emerita), Am. Soc. Nutritional Scis., Am. Home Econs. Assn. Home: Ames, Iowa. Died July 7, 2007.

ROGERS, JOHN MARSHALL, city official; b. San Bernardino, Calif., Jan. 30, 1953; s. Dale Edward and Mary Jane (Prosser) R.; m. Jeneal Bumpus, Oct. 14, 1979; children: Jean Elizabeth, John Paul. BA, Calif. State Coll., 1975; MA, U. Mo., Columbia, 1976. Dir. econ. planning Ozark Foothills Regional Planning Commn., Poplar Bluff, Mo., 1976-79; exec. dir. Emporia-Greensville (Va.) Indsl. Devel. Corp., 1979-81; pres. Grundy County Indsl. Devel. Corp., Morris, Ill., 1981-85, Johnson County Devel. Corp., Clarksville, Ark., 1985-88; exec. v.p. Montgomery County Action Council, Coffeyville, Kans., 1988-95; asst. to city mgr., econ. devel. dir. City of Kirksville, Mo., from 1995; city adminstr. City of Webb City, Mo., from 1997. Chmn. oversite com. Grundy-Livingston-Kankakee Pvt. Industry Coun., Kankakee, Ill., 1983-85; chmn. planning and fin. com. West Ctrl. Ark. Pvt. Industry Coun., Dardanelle, 1985-88; bd. dirs. Indsl. Developers of Ark., Conway, 1986-88; bd. dirs. Mo. TIF Assocs. Mem. Am. Econ. Devel. Council, Am. Planning Assn., Internat. City Mgmt. Assn., C. of C., Kiwanis, Masons. Republican. Methodist. Avocations: tennis, woodworking, bowling. Home: Glenpool, Okla. Died Apr. 4, 2007.

ROGERS, RANDALL LLOYD, mechanical engineer; b. Madison, Ind., Apr. 11, 1923; s. Ernest Ellsworth and Lena Eugenia (Green) R.; m. Jane Coleman, Aug. 16, 1952; children: Susan, Betsy, Gerrit, Carol, Mary. BA in Physics and Math., Hanover Coll., 1951; MEd, Am. Internat. Coll., Springfield, Mass., 1957; cert. in computer tech., Worcester Poly. Inst., 1963; cert. in US explosive saftey laser tech., U. Mich., 1964; cert. in metallurgy, U. Ky. Registered profl. engr.; gen. tel. lic. Radio, tel. & chronograph technician Jefferson Proving Ground, Madison, Ind., 1943-45, test dir. 20mm cannon sect., 1945-52; mech. engr. rsch. & engring. Springfield (Mass.) Armory, 1952-67; mech. engr. Benet Weapons Lab. Watervliet (N.Y.) Arsenal, 1967-94. Math. tchr. evening radio, TV, Springfield, Mass., 1957-67. Coauthor The History of Milton (Ind.) Baptist Church, 1992, (six vols. written for Benet Weapons Lab.) 20mm Gatling Type Guns, 1970; author numerous reports on ammunition acceptance and exptl. tests; editor radar drawings and tests. Mem. ins. commn., Monson, Mass., 1966, Watervliet Arsenal Mus. Soc., N.Y., 1992; pres. Silver St. Chapel, Monson. With USN, 3 mos. Commn. Ky. Col., State of Ky., 1947. Mem. Am. Soc. Metals, Masons, Shriners (Legion of Honor, pres. Hampshire). Baptist. Achievements include utilization of aircraft, police and fixed stations for ammunition testing; graphical method for determining rate of fire of automatic cannons; 120mm plans for rapid fire gun loader. Home: Leicester, Mass. Died Dec. 15, 2006.

ROGERS, RONALD, public relations executive; b. Sept. 19, 1943; Pres., CEO Rodgers & Assocs., LA, 1978—2016. Died Feb. 19, 2016.

ROGERS, STEWART EVAN, retired theater educator; b. Sioux City, Iowa, June 1, 1936; s. Stewart Dwight and Marjorie (Watson) R.; m. Rzella Jane Brass (div. 1965); m. Jeannie F. Griffith, Sept. 3, 1965; children: Scott, Kim. BA, U. Calif., Fullerton, 1962; MS, U. Oreg., 1964. Mem. faculty Golden West Coll., Huntington Beach, Calif., from 1976, coord. TV curriculum, 1976-80, stage dir. dept. theater, 1980-82, now prof. dept. performing arts, from 1968; ret. Freelance film narrator, 1970—; adviser, dir. Theatre of Deaf, Huntington Beach, 1973-78; founder Coast Community Coll. Conservatory, Costa Mesa, Calif., 1984-86. Actor TV prodn. The Navajo, 1971 (Emmy nomination); writer, dir.: Calico, 1968, Red, White & Blue Blackouts, 1976, Orange County Review, 1986, Halloween Haunts, 1988; dir. Bullshot Crummond, 1980; producer, dir. Let Us Entertain You, 1989-90. Bd. dirs. Lake Grove Assn., Garden grove, Calif., 1984, Cedar Slope (Calif.) Water Commn., 1990; v.p. Cedar Slope WaterBoard, prodr., dir., co-host ann. rehab. charity show, 1991-96. Named an Outstanding Art Educator, Huntington Beach, Calif., Extraordinary Educator, Bolsa Grande HS. Democrat. Avocations: astronomy, backpacking, cooking, landscaping. Home: Garden Grove, Calif. Died July 14, 2007.

ROGERS, WAYNE M. (WILLIAM WAYNE MCMILLAN), actor, investor, investment strategist, consultant; b. Birmingham, Ala., Apr. 7, 1933; m. Mitzi McWhorter, 1960 (div. 1983); children Laura, Billy; m. Amy Hirsh, 1988. BA, Princeton U., 1954; student acting, Sanford Meisners Neighborhood Playhouse, Martha Graham. Founder Wayne Rogers & Co. Bd. dirs. Vishay Intertechnology Inc., 2006. Stage appearances in Misalliance, Bus Stop, Under the Yum-Yum Tree; TV series Housecalls, 1979-1982 (also writer, dir.), Stagecoach West, 1960, M*A*S*H, 1972-75, City of Angels, 1976, High Risk, 1988; film debut Odds Against Tomorrow, 1959; other films include The Glory Guys, 1965, Chamber of Horrors, 1966, Cool Hand Luke, 1967, WUSA, 1970, Pocket Money, 1972, The Hot Touch, 1982, The Gig, 1985, The Goodbye Bird, 1993, Ghost of Mississippi, 1996, Love Lies Bleeding, 1999, Frozen with Fear, 2000, Coo Coo Cafe, 2000, 3 Days of Rain, 2000, Miracle Dogs, 2003, Nobody Knows Anything!, 2003 (also prodr.); TV appearances The Top of the Hill, 1980, The Edge of Night, Attack on Terror: The F.B.I. vs Ku Klux Klan, 1975, The November Plan, 1976, Having Babies II, 1977, It Happened One Christmas, 1977, Thou Shalt Not Commit Adultry, 1978, Once in Paris, 1978, (mini series) Chiefs, 1983, He's Fired, She's Hired, 1984, The Lady from Yesterday, 1985, I Dream of Jeannie: 15 Years Later, 1985, One Terrific Guy, 1986, The Girl Who Spelled Freedom, 1986, American Harvest, 1987, The Killing Time, 1987, Drop-Out Mother, 1988, Bluegrass, 1988, Passion and Paradise, 1989, Miracle Landing, 1990; guest appearances include Gunsmoke, 1959, 1962, 1965, Gomer Pyle, U.S.M.C., 1964, The F.B.I. (6 episodes), 1966-73, Barnaby Jones, 1973, Murder, Memories of M*A*S*H, 1991, She Wrote, 1993, 1994, & 1997, Diagnosis Murder, 1997, M*A*S*H: TV Tales, 2002, M*A*S*H 30th Anniversary Reunion, 2002, TV Land Confidential, 2005, The O'Reilly Factor, 2005 and several others; exec. prodr., writer Dr. Sex, 1964, The Astro-Zombies, 1969; exec. prodr. (TV) Perfect Witness, 1989, Night of the Twisters, 1996, Money Plays, 1997; regular contbr., finances and stocks, Fox News Channel. With USN. Named to Hollywood Walk of Fame, 2005. Avocations: basketball, tennis, reading. Died Dec. 31, 2015.

ROLLINS, JACK, motion picture producer; b. 1914; m. Pearl Rose Levine, 1948 (dec. 2012); children: Susan, Hillary, Francesca. Grad., City Coll. of NY, 1937. Cofounder talent mgmt. firm Rollins, Joffe, Morra, Brezner Prodns., NYC. Producer films: (with Charles Joffe) Take The Money and Run, 1969, Bananas, 1971, Everything You Always Wanted to Know...But Were Afraid To Ask, 1972, Sleeper, 1973, Love and Death, 1975, The Front, 1976, Annie Hall, 1977, Interiors, 1978, Manhattan, 1979, Stardust Memories, 1980, Zelig, 1983; producer, actor films: The Purple Rose of Cairo, 1985, Hannah and Her Sisters, 1986, Radio Days, 1986, September, 1987, Another Woman, 1988, New York Stories (Oedipus Wrecks), 1989, Crimes and Misdemeanors, 1989, Shadows and Fog, 1992, Husbands and Wives, 1992, Manhattan Murder Mystery, 1993; TV producer Dick Cavett Show, Late Night with David Letterman, 1982-92; mgmt. firm handles careers of Woody Allen, Mike Nichols, Elaine May, Robin Williams, Robert Klein, Dick Cavett, Lenny Bruce, Billy Crystal. Served US Army. Died June 18, 2015.

RONAN, WILLIAM JOHN, management consultant; b. Buffalo, Nov. 8, 1912; s. William and Charlotte (Ramp) R.; m. Elena Vinadé, May 29, 1939 (dec. 1996); children: Monica, Diana Quasha. AB, Syracuse U., 1934; PhD, NYU, 1940, LLD, 1969; certificate, Geneva Sch. Internat. Studies, 1933. Mus. asst. Buffalo Mus. Sci., 1928-30; with Niagara-Hudson Power Co., 1931; transfer dept. NYC R.R., 1932; Penfield fellow internat. law, diplomacy and belles lettres, 1935; Univ. fellow, 1936; editor Fed. Bank Service, Prentice-Hall, Inc., 1937; instr. govt. NYU, 1938, exec. sec. grad. div. for tng. in pub. services, 1938, asst. dir., 1940, asst. prof. govt., dir. grad. div. for tng. pub. service, 1940, assoc. prof. govt., 1946-47, prof., 1947; dean, grad. sch. public adminstrn. & social service NYU Graduate Sch. Public Adminstrn. & Social Service, 1953-58; Cons. NYC Civil Service Commn., 1938; prin. rev. officer, negotiations officer US Civil Service Commn., 1942; prin. div. asst. US Dept. State, 1943, cons., 1948, US Dept. Def., 1954; dir. studies NY State Coordination Commn., 1951-58; project mgr. NYU-U. Ankara project, 1954-59; cons. ICA, 1955, NY State Welfare Conf.; adminstrv. co-dir. Albany Grad. Program in Pub. Adminstrn.; 1st dep. city adminstr. NYC, 1956-57; exec. dir. NY State Temporary Commn. Constl. Conv., 1956-58; sec. to Gov. Nelson Rockefeller State of NY, Albany, 1959-66; chmn. interdept. com. traffic safety, commr. Port Authority NY & NJ, 1967-90, vice chmn., 1972-74, chmn., 1974-77; with UTDC Corp., West Palm Beach, Fla. Trustee Crosslands Savings Bank; chmn. bd. LI R.R., 1966-74; chmn. Tri-State Transp. Com., NY, NJ, Conn., 1961-67; chmn. interstate com. New Haven R.R., 1960-63; chmn. NY Com. on LI R.R., 1964-65; mem. NY State Commn. Interstate Coop., 1961, NY State Com. Fgn. Ofcl. Visitors, 1961, NY State Coordination Commn., 1960; mem. NY Civil Svc. Commn., Temporary State Commn. on Constl. Conv., 1966-67; chmn. NY State Met. Commuter Transp. Authority, 1965-68, Met. Transp. Authority, 1968-74, Tri-Borough Bridge and Tunnel Authority, 1968-74, NYC Transit Authority, 1968-74, Manhattan and Bronx Surface Transit Operating Authority, 1968-74; chmn. bd., pres. 3d Century Corp., 1974-94; mem. urban transp. adv. com. US Dept. Transp.; sr. adviser Rockefeller family, 1974-80; pres. Nelson Rockefeller Collection, Inc., 1977-80; trustee Power Authority of State of NY, 1974-77; cons. to trustees Penn Ctrl. Transp. Co.; vice chmn. bd. CCX, Inc.; sec.-treas. Sarabam Corp. N.V.; chmn., dir. UTDC (USA) Inc., 1987-88; chmn. UTDC Corp., 1989-94, Transit Svcs. Corp., 1989-94; cons. Herzog Transit Svcs., 1995-99, Dime Savs. Bank, Metal Powder Products Inc., Flomet Inc.; Internat. Mining and Metals Inc., Quadrant Mgmt. Inc., Ohio Highspeed Rail Authority, 1991-93; chmn. NY & NJ Inland Rail Rate Com.; dir. Nat. Mgmt. Coun., 1951. Author: Money Power of States in International Law, 1940, The Board of Regents and the Commissioner, 1948, Our War Economy, 1943, (with others), articles in profl. jours.; adviser: Jour. Inst. Socio-Econ. Studies. Mem. US FOA, American Public Health Assn.; staff relations officer NYC Bd. Edn.; Mem. Nat. Conf. Social Work, Nat. Conf. on Met. Areas, Citizens Com. on Corrections, Council on Social Work Edn.; bd. dirs. World Trade Club; adv. bd. World

Trade Inst.; mem. 42d St. Redevel. Corp., chmn., 1980-94; mem. Assn. for a Better NY; bd. advisers Inst. for Socio-econ. Studies; dir. Nat. Health Council, 1980-86; dep. dir. policy Nelson Rockefeller campaign for Republican presdl. nomination, 1964; mem. NY State Gov.'s Com. on Shoreham Nuclear Plant, 1983-85, Nassau County Indsl. Devel. Authority, 1982-90, US Dept. Transp. Com. on Washington and Capital Dist. Airports, 1985-86; bd. dirs. Ctr. Study Presidency, 1986-90, Alcoholism Council of NY; trustee NY Coll. Osteopathic Medicine, 1986-91; v.p. American Cancer Soc., Palm Beach. Served as lt. USNR, 1943-46. Mem. ASPA, NEA, American Polit. Sci. Assn., American Acad. Pub. Adminstrn., Civil Svc. Assembly of US and Can., Internat. Assn. Met. Rsch. and Devel., Nat. Mcpl. League, Mcpl. Pers. Soc., Citizens Union of NY, Nat. Civil Svc. League, American Acad. Polit. and Social Sci., LI Assn. Commerce and Industry (dir.), Internat. Inst. Adminstrv. Scis., American Fgn. Law Assn., Internat. Union Pub. Transport (mgmt. com., v.p.), American Public Transit Assn. (chmn. 1974-76), Nat. Def. Transp. Assn. (v.p. for Mass transit), English Speaking Union (bd. dirs. Palm Beach), Met. Opera Club, Maidstone Club, Devon Yacht Club, Knickerbocker Club, Hemisphere Club, Harvard Club, Creek Club, Wings Club, Traffic Club, Univ. Club, American Club Riviera, Beach Club (Palm Beach), Everglades Club. Home: West Palm Beach, Fla. Died Oct. 15, 2014.

ROONEY, FRANCIS CHARLES, JR., corporate executive; b. North Brookfield, Mass., Nov. 24, 1921; s. Francis Charles and Evelyn Fullerbrown (Murray) R.; m. Frances Elizabeth Heffernan, June 10, 1950; children: Peter, Michael, Stephen, Jean, William, Carol, Frances, Clare BS in Econs., U. Pa., 1943; D of Comml. Sci. (hon.), Suffolk U., 1968, St. John's U., 1973; PhD (hon.), Boston Coll., 1986. Mem. sales staff John Foote Shoe Co., Brockton, Mass., 1946-48; mem. sales staff Florsheim Shoe Co., Chgo., 1948-53; various positions Melville Shoe Co., NYC, from 1953; pres. Thom McAn div. Melville Shoe Corp., NYC, 1961-64; pres., chief exec. officer Melville Corp., Harrison, NY, 1964-77, NYC, chmn., pres., chief exec. officer Harrison, 1977-80, chmn., chief exec. officer, 1980-86, former chmn. exec. com., 1987; chmn. bd. H.H. Brown Shoe Co., Inc. (acquired by Berkshire Hathaway in 1991), Greenwich, Conn., 1990—2015, CEO, 1990. Dir. Bankers Trust Co., N.Y.C., Crystal Brands Inc., Southport, Conn., N.Y.C., The Neiman Marcus Group, Chestnut Hill, Mass., Collins & Aikman Textile, ADT, AMF, Black and Decker, Dunkin' Donuts Bd. dirs. United Cerebral Palsy, N.Y.C., 1960, Smithsonian Inst., 1975, March of Dimes, Boys and Girls Clubs of America, Wharton Sch., Pace Univ., and Fordham U.; overseers Wharton Sch. U. Pa.; trustee N.Y. Med. Coll. Lt. (j.g.) USN, 1943-46. Mem.: Round Hill (Greenwich); Links (N.Y.C.); Winged Foot (Mamaroneck, N.Y.). Republican. Roman Catholic. Died Mar. 24, 2015.

ROOT, STANLEY WILLIAM, JR., retired lawyer; b. Honolulu, Mar. 2, 1923; s. Stanley William and Henrietta E. (Brown) R.; m. Joan Louise Schimpf, Sept. 3, 1949; children: Henry, Louise. AB, Princeton U., 1947; LLB, U. Pa., 1950. Bar: Pa. 1950, U.S. Ct. Mil. Appeals 1951, U.S. Supreme Ct. 1971. Ptnr. Foley, Schimpf & Steeley, Phila., 1952-69, Ballard, Spahr, Andrews & Ingersoll, Phila., 1970-91, of counsel, 1992-97; ret., 1998. Lectr. Pa. Bar Assn., 1970-80; bd. dirs. Boardman-Hamilton Co., sec. 1980-98. Exec. v.p. Chestnut Hill Cmty. Assn., Phila., 1978; with Whitpain Farm Assn., Blue Bell, Pa., 1987, 90, pres., 1992-94; with St. Paul's Ch. Vestry, Phila., 1969-75; bd. dirs. Lansdale (Pa.) Med. Group, 1972-95, E.B. Spaeth Found. Wills Hosp., Phila., 1975-88, Chevalier Jackson Clinic, Phila., 1965-88; trustee Civil War Libr. and Mus., 1985-93, v.p., 1989, sec., 1992-93, mem. adv. bd., 1993-95; trustee Soc. Protestant Episc. Ch., Pa. Diocese, 1955-95. Lt. col. U.S. Army, 1942-45, ETO, 1950-52, Korea. Decorated Bronze Star; recipient Pa. Commendation medal State of Pa., 1962, French Legion Merit award, 2010. Mem.: Mil. Order Fgn. Wars (comdr. Pa. Commandery 1970), Mil. Order Loyal Legion, Mil. Order World Wars (comdr. Phila. chpt. 1960—61), Union League Phila. (pres. 1983—85), Royal Poinciana Golf Club, Sunnybrook Golf Club. Republican. Episcopalian. Avocations: golf, tennis, fishing. Home: Naples, Fla. Died July 8, 2015.

ROSE, IRWIN ALLEN (ERNIE), biochemist, educator; b. Bklyn., July 16, 1926; s. Harry and Ella Greenwald Royze; m. Zelda Budenstein; children: Howard, Frederic, Robert, Sarah(dec.). BS, U. Chgo., 1948, PhD in Biochemistry, 1952. Faculty dept. biochemistry Yale U., New Haven, 1954—63; rschr. Fox Chase Cancer Ctr., Phila., 1963—95, ret., 1995; disting. prof.-in-residence dept. physiology and biophysics U. Calif., Irvine Sch. Medicine, 1997—2015. Contbr. articles to profl. jour. Served with USN, World War II. Recipient Nobel prize in chemistry, 2004. Mem.: NAS. Achievements include discovery of ubiquitin-mediated protein degradation. Died June 2, 2015.

ROSE, LEONARD EUGENE, retired automotive executive; b. Palestine, Ill., May 22, 1924; s. John Leonard and Martha Emiline (McDade) R.; m. Ella May Williams, Mar. 14, 1953; children: Gina Annette, Barry Eugene. AA, Vincennes U., 1948. Analyst Ford Motor Co., Indpls., 1957-82. Named to Coun. of the Sagamores of the Wabash, Gov. of Ind., 1989; named Hon. Sec. of State, State of Ind., 1990. Mem. Am. Ex-Prisoners of War (nat. dir.). Avocation: veterans affairs. Home: Indianapolis, Ind. Died Nov. 18, 2006.

ROSE, LUCILLE MARIE, retired writer; b. Elysian, Minn., Dec. 20, 1914; d. Oliver Vig Austin and Sarah Rebecca Kiel; 1 child, Raymond. Degree, Northwestern Bible Coll., 1934; BA, Sioux Falls Coll., 1936; BS, San Jose U.; MA, San Francisco Coll., 1958; grad., Hamline U. Conf. spkr.; tutor, lectr., nursing home leader. Author: (book) Christian Women U.S.A., 1958, Not a Fifth Wheel, 1975, God's Kept Woman, 1988; contbr. poetry to anthologies. Mem. various ch. bds.; founder, dir. Christian Women U.S.A.; bd. dirs. PTA. Mem.: Pi Gamma Mu, Delta Kappa Gamma. Republican. Baptist. Home: Dania, Fla. Died Mar. 19, 2007.

ROSEN, ALBERT LEONARD, professional baseball team executive; b. Spartanburg, SC, Feb. 29, 1924; s. Louis and Rose (Levine) R.; m. Rita Kallman, July 24, 1971; children: Robert, Andrew, James, Gail, David. BBA, U. Miami, 1947. Profl. baseball player Cleve. Indians Baseball Team, 1947-56; with Bache & Co., Cleve., 1955-73, 1st Continental Investment Corp., Cleve., 1973-75; br. office mgr. Caesars Palace, Las Vegas, Nev., 1975-77; pres. N.Y. Yankees, NYC, 1977-79; with Bally's Park Pl., Atlantic City, N.J., 1979-80; pres., gen. mgr. Houston Astros Baseball, 1980-85, San Francisco Giants Baseball Club, 1985-93. Served to lt. (j.g.) USNR, 1943-46, PTO. Named Most Valuable Player Am. League, 1953 Mem.: Westwood Country. Jewish. Died Mar. 13, 2015.

ROSEN, ALEXANDER CARL, psychologist, consultant; b. LA, Feb. 2, 1923; s. Benjamin and Pauline (Katz) R.; m. Florence Friedman, Mar. 18, 1951 (div. Nov. 1973); children: Diane, Judith; m. Susan Margaret Gersbacher, Nov. 4, 1973; 1 child, Rebecca. AA, U. Calif., LA, 1943; AB, U. Calif., Berkeley, 1946, PhD, 1953. Diplomate clin. psychology Am. Bd. Profl. Psychology; lic. psychologist. Psychologist Contra Costa County, Martinez, Calif., 1953-56; asst. rsch. psychologist Office Naval Rsch. and San Francisco State Coll., 1953-56, UCLA-Neuropsychiat. Inst., LA, 1956-57; asst. prof. to prof. psychiatry and behavioral sci. UCLA Sch. Medicine, LA, 1956-89; chief psychology UCLA Neuropsychiatric Inst., LA, 1958-89; prof. emeritus UCLA Sch. Medicine, LA, from 1989; pvt. practice psychology cons. LA, from 1973. Instr. San Francisco State Coll., 1955; instr. psychology Calif. Inst. Tech., Pasadena, 1969; staff assoc. Nat. Tng. Lab. Inst. Applied Behavioral Sci., 1962—; cons. tng. U.S. Veteran's Assn., Sepulveda (Calif.) Hosp., 1966—; bd. mem. L.A. Group Psychotherapy Tng. Inst., 1972-75; bd. mem., trustee Calif. Sch. Profl. Psychology, 1974-76, 78; nat. bd., regional bd. Cert. Cons. Internat. Cons. Cons. editor: Jour. Genetic Psychology and Genetic Psychology Monograph, 1984—; contbr. articles to profl. jours. Mem. gov. bd. Hillel Coun., So. Calif.; cons. San Fernando Valley Counseling Ctr., 1991-92, Pacific Ctr. for AIDS, L.A., 1991-94; adv. bd. mem. CSN Valley Youth Orch.; docent Pacific Asia Mus., 1997—; co-chair College-Park Neighborhood Assn., 1997—. Fellow APA, AAAS; mem. Calif. State Psychology Assn. (pres. 1977-78), Western Psychol. Assn. Avocations: photography, music, drama, asian art. Home: Van Nuys, Calif. Died Feb. 28, 2007.

ROSEN, CAROL MENDES, artist; b. NYC, Jan. 15, 1933; d. Bram de Sola and Mildred (Bertuch) Mendes; m. Elliot A. Rosen, June 30, 1957. BA, Hunter Coll., 1954; MA, CUNY, 1962. Tchr. art West Orange (N.J.) Pub. Schs., 1959—85. Co-curator exhibit Printmaking Coun. N.J., Somerville, 1981; exhibit curator 14 Sculptors Gallery, NYC, 1988; guest curator Hunterdon Mus. Art, 2009; collection: Nat. Collection of Fine Arts, Smithsonian Instn., Newark Mus., N.J. State Mus., Bristol-Myers Squibb, AT&T, Noyes Mus., N.Y. Pub. Libr., Zimmerli Art Mus., Mus. of Modern Art, Whitney Mus., Libr. Collection Bklyn. Mus., Victoria & Albert Mus., Nat. Art Gallery, London, Mus. of Tolerance, LA, Hunterdon Mus. Art, Nat. Mus. Women in Arts, Tel Aviv U. and The Jewish Nat. & U. Libr., Jerusalem, Houghton Libr., Harvard U., Yale U., Clark Art Inst., Skidmore, Williams Coll. Mus. Art, Oberlin Coll., William Paterson U., Stanford U., Smith Coll., Wellesley Coll., Tate Britain, Kreitman Rsch. Ctr., Ackland Art Mus., U. NC, U. Wis., Milw., Elias Sourasky Libr., Tel Aviv U., Newark Pub. Libr., Boston Pub. Libr. Contbr. articles to arts mags. Recipient Hudson River Mus. award, Yonkers, 1983; fellow, N.J. State Coun. Arts, 1980, 1983; grant, George& Helen Segal Found., 2012. Jewish. Avocations: gardening, reading. Home: Califon, NJ. Died Apr. 8, 2014.

ROSENBERG, ALEX, mathematician, educator; b. Berlin, Dec. 5, 1926; came to U.S., 1949, naturalized, 1959; s. Theodore and Rela (Banet) R.; m. Beatrice Gershenson, Aug. 24, 1952 (div. Apr. 1985); children: Theodore Joseph, David Michael (dec.), Daniel Alex; m. Brunhilde Angun, June 14, 1985 BA, U. Toronto, 1948, MA, 1949; PhD, U. Chgo., 1951. From instr. to assoc. prof. math. Northwestern U., 1952-61; prof. math. Cornell U., Ithaca, NY, 1961-88, prof. emeritus, from 1988, chmn. dept., 1966-69; prof. U. Calif., Santa Barbara, 1986-94, chmn. dept., 1986-87, prof. emeritus, from 1994; mem. com. undergrad. program math. Math Assn. Am., 1966-76. Mem. Inst. Advanced Study, 1955-57; vis. prof. U. Calif., Berkely, 1961, 1979, U. Calif., Los Angeles, 1969-70, 82, U. London, Queen Mary Coll., 1963-64, U. Munich, 1975-76, E.T.H Zurich, 1976, U. Dortmund, 1984-85; trustee Am. Math Soc., 1973-83. Editor: Proc. Am. Math. Soc., 1960-66, Am. Math. Monthly, 1974-77; Contbr. articles to profl. jours. Recipient Humboldt Stiftung Sr. U.S. Scientist award U. Munich, 1975-76, U. Dortmund, 1981 Home: Schwerte, Germany. Died Oct. 27, 2007.

ROSENBERG, MILTON H., retired chemistry educator; b. NYC, Apr. 16, 1912; s. Julius A. and Rebecca S. (Saltzman) R.; m. Beatrice Nelson, July 1938; children: Carol Ann Rosenberg Marsh, Gerald Nelson. BS, CCNY, 1933, MS in Edn., 1938. Cert. ednl. adminstr., N.Y. Sci. tchr. N.Y.C. High Schs., 1935-51, asst. prin., supr. sci. and math., 1951-72; adj. prof. Pace U., Pleasantville, N.Y., 1972-86. Mem. Ret. Chemists Assn., Three Arrows Coop. Soc., Chemistry Tchrs. Club N.Y. Jewish. Avocations: gardening, tennis, travel, photography, computers. Home: Peekskill, NY. Died Mar. 16, 2007.

ROSENBERG, SELIG, psychologist; b. NYC, Oct. 9, 1914; BA, Bklyn. Coll., 1936; MLitt, U. Pitts., 1944; PhD, NYU, 1952. Staff psychologist VA Clinic, NYC, 1945-58; chief clin. psychologist VA Hosp., Northport, N.Y., 1958-74; chief psychologist L.I. Devel. Ctr., Melville, N.Y., 1974-84; pvt. practice psychology Woodbury, N.Y., from 1984. Lectr. Bkyn. Coll., 1952-65, NYU, N.Y.C., 1965-68; supr. doctoral interns Hofstra U., Uniondale, N.Y., 1965-69, Adelphi U., Garden City, N.Y., 1965-69. Contbr. articles to profl. jours. Sgt. U.S. Army, 1941-45. Died Nov. 15, 2006.

ROSENBLATT, DAVID HIRSCH, chemist, consultant; b. Trenton, NJ, July 24, 1927; s. Samuel and Claire (Woloch) R.; m. Jaclyn Leah Rivkin, Aug. 16, 1949; children: Jonathan, Aaron, Daniel. BA, Johns Hopkins U., 1946; postgrad., U. Md., 1946-47; PhD, U. Conn., 1950. Chemist Balt. Paint and Color Works, 1950-51; rsch. chemist U.S. Army Chem. Warfare Labs., Edgewood, Md., 1951-72, U.S. Army Biomed. Rsch. and Devel. Lab., Ft. Detrick, Md., 1972-89, Argonne (Ill.) Nat. Lab., from 1990; pvt. practice cons. Balt., from 1990. Instr. in organic chemistry Evening Coll., Johns Hopkins U., Balt., 1957-70; mem. Md. Hazardous Substance Adv. Coun., Balt., 1976— Author: Laboratory Course in Organic Chemistry, 1971; editor: Handbook of Chemical Property Estimation Methods, 1982, Environmental Inorganic Chemistry, 1988; contbr. chpts. to books. Mem. Am. Chem. Soc., Soc. Environ. Toxicology and Chemistry. Jewish. Achievements include patents on sterilization of medical material with chloride dioxide; elucidation of mechanisms of reaction of chlorine dioxide with amines and phenols; compilation of methods for estimating psychochemical properties of chemicals in the environment, of physicochemical and toxicological properties of organic explosives and propellents; study of toxic chemical agents in aqueous media; research in environmental contaminants. Died June 16, 2007.

ROSENBLOOM, NOAH HAYYIM, rabbi, educator; b. Sept. 29, 1915; s. Michael and Sarah Leah (Weingelb) R.; m. Pearl Cohen; children: Leah Marion Rosenbloom Kalish, Michaelle Nathanyah Rosenberg. B. Religious Edn., Yeshiva U., 1942, DHL, 1948; MA, Columbia U., 1945; PhD, NYU, 1958. Ordained rabbi, 1942. Rabbi B'nai Israel, Steubenville, Ohio, 1942, Montefiore Hebrew Congregation, NYC, 1943-45, Tikvas Israel, Phila., 1945-48, B'nai Israel Jewish Ctr., Bklyn., from 1949. Author: Luzzatto's Ethico-Psychological Interpretation of Judaism, 1965, Tradition in an Age of Reform, 1976, The Threnody and the Threnodist of the Holocaust, 1980, The Exodus Epic of the Enlightenment and Exegesis, 1983, Malbim: Exegesis Philosophy Science and Mysticism in His Writings, 1988, Studies in Literature and Thought, 1989, others; translator: Luzzatto's Foundations of the Torah, The Song of the Murdered Jewish People, 1980. Recipient Friedman award Histadruth Ivrith of Am., 1983; Horeb award Yeshiva U. Alumni Assn., 1965. Fellow Am. Acad. Jewish Rsch.; mem. Rabbinical Coun. Am. (editorial bd. Tradition). Home: Brooklyn, NY. Died Aug. 9, 2007.

ROSENTHAL, HELEN NAGELBERG, county official, advocate; b. NYC, June 6, 1926; d. Alfred and Esther (Teichholz) Nagelberg; m. Albert S. Rosenthal, Apr. 10, 1949 (dec.); children: Lisa Rosenthal Michaels, Apryl Meredith Rosenthal Stuppler. BS, CUNY, 1948; MA, NYU, 1950; postgrad., Adelphia U., LI U., Lehman Coll., 1975. Cert. early childhood and gifted edn. tchr., NY, NJ, elem. and secondary tchr., Fla. Tchr. gifted students NY Bd Edn., Bklyn., 1949-77, 79-87, Baldwin Pub. Schs., NY, 1977-79; rep. community affairs County of Dade, Fla., 1988-92; ret., 1992; condo dir. Pembroke Pines, from 1999. Author: Criteria for Selection and Curriculum for the Gifted, 1977, Science Experiments for Young Children, 1982, Music in the Air...and in Our Minds. Dir. Condominium, 1989-91. Recipient Departmental award, 1948. Mem. Concerned Citizens for Educating Gifted and Talented (officer NYC chpt.), Assn. Gifted and Talented Edn. (NY chpt.), Am. Inst. Cancer Rsch., Bklyn. Coll. Alumni Assn. (pres. Broward-Dade chpt. 1995-96, v.p. membership 1996—). Died May 5, 2007.

ROSENTHAL, MARILYNN MAE, medical sociology educator; b. Detroit, May 10, 1930; d. Jacob J. and Helen (Link) Waratt; m. Avram Rosenthal, May 21, 1954 (div. 1978); children: Daniel (dec.), Joshua, Helen. BA in Sociology, Wayne State U., 1952; MA in Am. Lit., U. Mich., 1965, PhD in Am. Culture, 1976. Lectr., teaching fellow sociology dept. U. Mich., Ann Arbor, 1973-74, 74-75; instr. dept. community medicine Sch. of Medicine Wayne State U., 1975-76; asst. prof. behavioral scis. dept. U. Mich., Dearborn, 1976-82, assoc. prof. behavioral scis. dept., 1982-88, prof. behavioral scis. dept., from 1988. Vis. scholar Wolfson Coll. Ctr. for Socio-Legal Studies, Oxford (Eng.) U., 1990, 91, 92, 93, SPRI and Swedish Med. Assn., Stockholm, 1990; vis. lectr. dept. health policy and mgmt. Harvard U. Sch. Pub. Health, 1984; dir. program in health policy studies U. Mich., Dearborn, 1980—; cons. Karolinska Hosp. Ctr. for Diabetes Edn. and Tng., Stockholm, 1984-88; assoc. dir. program in soc. and medicine U. Mich. Med. Sch., dir. U. Mich. Forum on Health Policy, 1995—; presenter in field. Mem. editorial bd. Jour. Med. Practice Mgmt., 1984; author: Health Care in the People's Republic of China; Moving Toward Modernization, 1987, Dealing With Medical Malpractice-The British and Swedish Experience, 1987, (with Irene Butter, Mark Field) The Political Dynamics of Physician Manpower Policy, 1990; co-editor: (with Marcel Frenkel) Health Care Systems and Their Patients: An International View, 1992, The Incompetent

Doctor, 1995, (with M. Heirich) Health Policy: Understanding Our Choices from National Reform to Market Forces; contbr. chpts. to books; contbr. articles to profl. jours. Bd. govs. U. Mich. League, 1991-93; chair com. U. Mich., 1991-93; mem. AIDS Task Force, 1988, chair, 1993—; co-chair task force on a smoke-free environment U. Mich., Dearborn, 1991; outside reviewer sociology program divsn. social and econ. sci. NSF, 1988. King Edward Hosp. Trust grantee, 1992-93, Brit. Coun. Travel grantee, 1992, Office of V.P. for Rsch. Small Projects grantee U. Mich., 1991, Fulbright Western European Region Rsch. grantee, 1989-90, U. Mich. Rackham grantee, 1982-83, 89-90, U. Mich.-Dearborn Campus grantee, 1980-83, 90; Swedish Med. Rsch. Coun. Vis. Scientist fellow, 1984-87, Danforth Grad. fellow for women, 1970-75. Mem. APHA, Am. Sociol. Assn., Assn. for Health Svcs. Rsch., Soc. for the Advancement of Scandinavian Studies, Women's Rsch. Club U. Mich. (pres. 1988-89), Sigma Xi. Jewish. Avocations: mountain hiking, biking, reading, film. Home: Ann Arbor, Mich. Died Aug. 9, 2007.

ROSENTHAL, RACHEL, performance artist; b. Paris, Nov. 9, 1926; arrived in US, 1941, naturalized, 1945; d. Leonard and Mara (Jacoubovitch) Rosenthal; m. King Moody (div.). Student, New Sch. Social Rsch., 1945—48, U. Paris, Sorbonne, 1948—49. Mem. Merce Cunningham Co., 1949—50; instr. Pasadena Playhouse, Calif., 1955—56; dir. Instant Theatre, LA, 1956—66, sculptor, 1966—75; instr. Claremont Grad. Sch., Calif., 1979, Otis-Parsons Sch. Design, LA, 1980—81, U. Calif., Irvine, 1982, 1986; creator, condr. DBD Experience, LA, from 1980; dir. Espace DBD, LA, 1981—83; founder, artistic dir. Rachel Rosenthal Co., 1989—2015; vis. artist U. Colo., Boulder, 1983, Calif. State U., Long Beach, 1983—86, NYU, 1985; regents lectr. U. Calif., Santa Barbara, 1991, Calif. State U., LA, 1995—96, Pa. Works include Traps, 1982, Gaia, Mon Amour, 1983, The Others, 1984, Was Black, 1986, Rachel's Brain, 1987, Pangaean Dreams, 1990, (films) Futurfax, 1992, European tour documenta 8, 1987, works presented at L.A. Arts Festival, 1987, 1990, Internat. Theater Festival, Grenada, Spain, 1988, Zagreb, Yugoslavia, 1988, Time Festival, Ghent, Belgium, 1991, Serious Fun, Lincoln Ctr., NYC, 1991, Whitney Mus., 1992, I.C.A., London, 1992, UCLA Ctr. Performing Arts, 1994, Yerba Buena Ctr., Calif., 1995, Calif. State U., LA, 1996; author: (memoir) The DbD Experience: Chance Knows What It's Doing. Co-founder, co-chairperson Womanspace, LA1973, 1973; co-founder Grandview Gallery, LA, 1974, Double X, LA, 1974; tchr. Workshop's & Classes Profl. & Spl. Interest Groups, 1979. Recipient OBIE award, 1989, Artist award, Coll. Arts Assn. America, 1991, Genesis award, 1988; Visual Artist fellow, Nat. Endowment Arts, 1983, Artist fellow, Calif. Arts Coun., 1988, Perfomance fellow, NEA, 1990, 1993—94, Getty Artist fellow, 1990, grantee, Nat. Endowment Arts, 1987—88, US Info. Agy., 1987—98, Tides Found., 1988, Art Matters, 1988, Found. Contemporary Performance, 1993, J. Paul Getty Trust Found., 1995. Mem.: Woman's Bldg. (Vesta award 1983). Home: Los Angeles, Calif. Died May 10, 2015.

ROSETT, LOUIS KENNETH, marketing consultant; b. New Rochelle, NY, Dec. 17, 1920; s. Louis A. and Frieda (Sarasohn) R.; m. Jean Herrmann, July 4, 1943; children: Nancy Ann, John Alan. BS in Bus. Adminstrn. amd Chem. Engring., MIT. Prin. Ken Rosett Assocs., White Plains, N.Y. Trustee Temple Israel New Rochelle, 1954-57, 68-77, hon. trustee, 1977—, v.p., 1970-73; mem. exec. bd. Chgo. Fedn. Reform Synagogues, 1958-63; trustee Union Am. Hebrew Congregations, 1973-77, vice chmn., 1977-81; mem. exec. bd. N.Y. Fedn. Reform Synagogues; v.p. Jewish Nat. Fund, Assn. Reform Zionists Am.; mem bd. dirs. Am. Zionist Fedn., United Israel Appeal; mem. bd. govs. N.Y. MIT Alumni Assn., sec. 1942; life mem. MIT Alumni Council; v.p. Westchester MIT Alumni Assn. Served to col., USAF, World War II, USAFR, Korea. Recipient Bronze Beaver award MIT Alumni Assn., Cambridge, Mass., 1977, Apollo Achievement award NASA, 1987, City of Light award State of Israel Bonds, 1987. Mem. AIAA, Soc. Plastic Engrs., Soc. Plastic Industries (policy com.), Soc. for Metals, Soc. Mfg. Engrs., Suppliers Advanced Composite Materials, Chemists Club N.Y. Clubs: Saxony Golf (Scarsdale, N.Y.). Avocations: photography, golf, baking bread. Home: Clearwater, Fla. Died May 25, 2007.

ROSIE, RONALD DUNCAN, civil engineer; b. Chgo., July 3, 1934; s. John and Mary (Davies) R.; m. Mildren Cutting Thomson, Feb. 13, 1957; children: Jean Campbell, Sheryl Anne. BS, U.S. Coast Guard Acad., New London, Conn., 1958; BCE, Renessalear Poly. Inst., Troy, NY, 1963; ME in Adminstrn., George Washington U., 1969; MBA, U. Puget Sound, 1980. Registered profl. engr., N.Y., La; cert. fin. planner, Colo. Comd. officer USCG, 1958, advanced through grades to capt., 1981; mgr. data buoy program Nat. Oceanic and Atmospheric Adminstrn., Bay St. Louis, Miss., 1972-75; chief civil engr. 13th Coast Guard Dist., Seattle, 1975-79, chief engr., 1979-81; sr. water qualtiy engr. Metro, Seattle, from 1981. Contbr. articles to Naval Engrs. Jour., USCG Engrs. Digest, and confs. Campaign chair Kemp for Pres., 41st Dist., 1988; mem. com. City Centennial Commn., Mercer Island, Wash., 1989; regional chmn. 41st Dist. Rep. Com., Mercer Island, 1990—. Mem. Soc.Am. Mil. Engrs. (bd. dirs. 1979-81), Rotary (Svc. award 1990). Republican. Achievements include research in water environment, lighthouses. Home: Mercer Island, Wash. Died June 25, 2007.

ROSINSKI, EDWIN FRANCIS, medical educator; b. Buffalo, June 25, 1928; s. Theodore Joseph and Josephine M. (Wolski) R.; m. Jeanne C. Hueniger, Oct. 27, 1951; children: John T., Mary E., Sarah J. BS, SUNY, Buffalo, 1950; EdM, U. Buffalo, 1957, EdD, 1959. Prof. health scis. Med. Coll. Va., Richmond, 1959-66; dep. asst. sec. HEW, Washington, 1966-68; exec. vice chancellor U. Calif., San Francisco, 1968-72, prof., 1972-94; prof. emeritus medicine & pharmacy, from 1994. Adv. Rockefeller Found., N.Y.C., 1962-67, WHO, Geneva, 1962-78, Imperial Com. Health, Tehran, Iran, 1974-77; cons. Stanford Research Inst., Menlo Park, Calif., 1975-79. Author: The Assistant Medical Officer, 1965; contbr. over 100 articles to profl. jours. Served with USAF, 1950-54. Recipient spl. citation HEW, 1968, Merrell Flair award, 1991; named disting. prof. Australian Vice Chancellors Office, 1974, disting. vis. prof. Tulane U., New Orleans, 1983, Alumni of Yr. SUNY, Buffalo, 2006. Fellow AAAS; mem. Assn. Am. Med. Colls. (Merrel Flair award), Am. Ednl. Research Assn., Soc. Health and Human Values (founding mem.), Calif. Pharmacists Assn. (hon.), Phi Delta Kappa. Roman Catholic. Avocation: physical fitness. Home: San Francisco, Calif. Deceased.

ROTH, NORMAN GILBERT, microbiologist; b. Chgo., Dec. 11, 1924; s. Joseph and Clara (Schein) R.; m. Rose Marie Klein, Feb. 5, 1950; children: Susan, William. Joseph, Virginia, Sandra, David. BS, U. Chgo., 1947; MS, U. Ill., 1949, PhD, 1951. Rsch. microbiologist U.S. Army Chem. Corps, Frederick, Md., 1951-57, Whirlpool Corp., Benton Harbor, Mich., from 1957, dir., life support space programs, 1960-72, dir. waste mgmt. systems, 1957, 72-77, dir. rsch. engring. svcs., 1977-92; cons., from 1992. Contbr. articles to profl. jours. Recipient NASA awards for achievements in manned space programs. Home: Saint Joseph, Mich. Died Jan. 8, 2007.

ROTH, VELMA DARNELL, nurse consultant; b. Temple, Tex., July 17, 1934; d. Robert Ardal And Velma Irene (Harrison) Thompson; m. Ronald Patrick Roth, Feb. 15, 1958; children: Teresa Ann, Michael Robert. AA, Temple Jr. Coll., 1956; diploma, Scott and White Mem. Hosp. Sch, Temple, Tex., 1956. Cert. CRNI. Staff nurse Scott and White Meml. Hosp., Temple, Tex., 1957-58; I. V. therapy coord. Alexian Bros. Hosp., St. Louis, 1976-80; instr. St. Louis Community Coll., from 1977; I.V. therapy cons. Alexian Bros. Hosp., St. Louis, 1980-87; pres. DR Intravenous Therapy Cons., Inc., St. Louis, from 1987. Pres. Gateway Chpt. INS, St. Louis, Mo., 1979, 85, 88-89, 94-95; LPN I.V. Therapy Task Force Mo. State Bd. Nursing, Jefferson City, Mo., 1984-86. Author: Intravenous Fluid Therapy: A Teaching Guideline, 1995; co-author: Intravenous Fluid Therapy: A Teaching Guideline, 1988; contbg. author Fluid and Electrolyte Balance, Nursing Considerations, 1987, Nurses Handbook of Fluid Balance, 1983; editor: Principles and Practices of I.V. Therapy, 1986. Pres. Resurrection Parrish Mothers Club, St. Louis, 1971-72, sch. bd. mem. Resurrection Parrish, St. Louis, 1972. Mem. League Intravenous Therapy Edn., St. Louis Soc. Hosp. Pharmacists, Intravenous Nurses Soc., Greater St. Louis Soc. Health Manpower, Edn. and Tng., St. Louis Assn. Long Term Care Dirs., Nat. Assn. Vascular Access Networks. Roman Catholic. Avocations: painting, photography, travel. Home: Saint Louis, Mo. Died July 20, 2007.

ROTHENBERG, MIRA KOWARSKI, clinical psychologist, psychotherapist; b. Wilno, Poland; came to U.S., 1938; d. Jacob and Rosa (Joffe) Kowarski; m. Tev Goldsman, Dec. 7, 1960 (div. June 1974); 1 child, Akiva. BA, Bklyn. Coll., 1943; MA, Columbia U., 1957, Yeshiva U., 1959, ABD, 1962. Lic. psychologist, N.Y. Therapist, tchr.ir. Hawthorne (N.Y.) Cedar Knolls, 1952-53, League Sch., Bklyn., 1953-58; founder, clin. dir. Blueberry Treatment Ctrs., Bklyn., 1958-90; staff psychologist L.I. Coll. Hosp., Bklyn., from 1966. Pioneer in working with autistic children; cons. Beachbrook Nursery, Bkyn., 1969-70, San Felipe Del Rio, Santa Fe, 1980-2015, Children's House Montessori Nursery, Bklyn., 1982-89, Austrlia Dept. Edn., Carynia, New South Wales, SOS Village, Vilnius, Lithuania, 1997-2015; adj. prof. L.I. U., Bklyn., 1976-78; internat. speaker in field; worker, lectr. and cons. with psychotic and autistic children, Croatia, 1994, Lithuania, 1994-99, 2007; cons. for movies on foster care, 1990-2015; clin. cons. Sierra Leone project, 2002. Author: Children with Emerald Eyes, 1977, 2003, (with others) Pet Oriented Psychotherapy, 1980, The Outsiders, 1989, The Children of Raquette Lake: One Summer That Helped Change the Course of Treatment for Autism, 2012; contbr. to books and articles to profl. jours. and mags.; documentary movie based on work with autistic children, 1962; Lithuanian play based on book, 1999; Children with Emerald Eyes play based on book, 1999. Bd. dirs. Friends of Island Acad. Mem. APA, World Fedn. Mental Health, N.Y. State Psychol. Assn., Inter. Soc. Child Abuse and Neglect (Hamburg, Germany), Physicians for Social Responsibility, N.Y. Acad. Scis., Amnest Internat., ACLU, NOW, Anti Defamation League, Yivo, Nat. Register Svc. Providers in Psychology. Avocations: writing, painting, sculpture, dance. Died Apr. 16, 2015.

ROUKEMA, MARGE (MARGARET SCAFATI ROUKEMA), former United States Representative from New Jersey; b. West Orange, NJ, Sept. 19, 1929; d. Claude Thomas and Margaret (D'Alessio) Scafati; m. Richard W. Roukema, Aug. 23, 1951; children: Margaret, Todd (dec.), Gregory. BA with honors in History and Polit. Sci, Montclair State Coll., 1951, postgrad. in history and guidance, 1951-53; postgrad. program in city and regional planning, Rutgers U., 1975. Tchr. history, govt., public schools, Livingston and Ridgewood, 1951-55; mem. US Congress from 7th NJ Dist., Washington, 1981—83, US Congress from 5th NJ Dist., Washington, 1983—2003. Vice pres. Ridgewood Bd. Edn., 1970-73 Trustee Spring House, Paramus, N.J.; trustee Leukemia Soc. Northern N.J., Family Counseling Service for Ridgewood and Vicinity; mem. Bergen County (N.J.) Republican Com.; NW Bergen County campaign mgr. for gubernatorial candidate Tom Kean, 1977; bd. mem. Children's Aid & Family Services, The Red Cross, Ramapo Coll. Mem. Bus. and Profl. Women's Orgn. Clubs: Coll. of Ridgewood, Ridgewood Rep. Republican. Home: Pompton Plains, NJ. *I have served in several roles in my life. Wife, mother, teacher, public servant. All are personally rewarding; each affords the opportunity to help others in need and to enrich the lives of those around you. As a member of Congress, I find the most rewards are in the knowledge that I can truly make a difference and improve the lives of thousands of people. The challenges are frequently insurmountable, but the rewards are incalculable.* Died Nov. 12, 2014.

ROULIER, RANDOLPHE G., osteopath; b. Detroit, Nov. 23, 1930; s. Randolphe Edward and Nannie Glenn (Riley) R.; m. Judith A. Corcoran, Sept. 10, 1955; children: Randolphe J., Denise M., Pamela M., David G., Michelle J. BA, Albion Coll., 1952; DO, Chgo. Coll. Osteo. Medicine, 1957. Intern Detroit Osteo. Hosp., Highland Park, Mich., 1957-58, resident general surgery, 1958-61; interim med. dir. med. edn., chmn. nutritional support svc. Mich. Osteo. Med. Ctr., Detroit, 1984-86, acting med. dir., 1985-86; chief of staff (sabbatical) Huron Valley Hosp., 1986-88; chief of staff Parkview Hosp., Toledo, Ohio, 1986-94; osteopath Toledo (Ohio) Surg. Assocs., Mercy Hosp., Toledo, Ohio, from 1994, St. Luke's Hosp., Maumee, Ohio, from 1994, St. Charles Hosp., Oregon, Ohio, from 1995, St. Vincent's Hosp., Toledo, from 1996, Riverside Mercy hosp., Toledo, from 1997, Flower Hosp., Sylvania, Ohio, from 1999. Chmn. staff, chief surgery Med. Ctr. Hosp., Wayne State U., Huron valley Hosp., 1986; sr. surg. com. Detroit Osteo. Hosp., Bicounty Cmty. Hosp., Mich. Osteo. Med. Ctr., Botsford Gen. Osteo. Hosp., Detroit; mem. med. records com. Mich. Osteopathic Med. Ctr., east unit mgmt. com., tissue com., chmn. house staff training com., 1984-86, exec. com. profl. staff., 1978-86, chief of staff, 1978, vice chief of staff, 1979, chmn. dept. surgery, 1974-84; chmn. dept. surgery Palmer Osteo. Hosp., 1963-68, Sturgis (S.D.) Cmty. Hosp., 1961-63; adj. clin. prof. U. Osteo. Medicine and Health Scis., Des Moines, Iowa, 1997—; clin. prof. surgery Ohio U. Coll. Osteo. Medicine, 1998—, adj. clin. faculty, 1978—; clin. prof. surgery, clin. dir. assoc. hosp., Mich. State U. Coll. Osteo. Medicine, 1972; clin. asst. prof. dept. surgery Med. Coll. Ohio, 1994—; clin. assoc. prof. surgery Coll. Osteo. Medicine Pacific, 1984, N.Y. Coll. Osteo. Medicine, 1980; assoc. clin. prof. surgery Kirksville Coll. Osteopathy and Surgery, 1972; clin. faculty Mercy Family Practice Residency Training Program, 1994—; pres. Wayne County Osteo. Assn., mem., bd. dirs. 1983-86, pres. elect 1983-84, chmn. profl. devel. com. 1978, program chmn. 57th Ann. Clin. Assembly Osteo. Specialists, New Orleans, 1984, Am. Coll. Osteo. Surgeons Review Course, Miami, Fla., 1984, Mich. Osteo. Med. Ctr.-Engring. Soc. Detroit, 1980, Am. Coll. Osteo. Physicians, 1980; vice-chmn. dept. surgery, section chief gen. surgery Mercy Hosp., vice chief surgery, mem. cancer com., 1995; mem. exec. com. Parkview Hosp., Toledo, 1993-94, med. records utilization and review com., 1992, physicians quality assurace com., 1992, hysterectomy/endometriosis support group, 1987; mem. sub.com. intern training, 1982-85, com. postdoctoral training, 1987-89; mem. subcom., surg. expert State of Mich. Ins. Bur., 1976—; mem. Program for Affordable Health Care, Southeastern Mich., 1994—, Mercy St. CharlesJoint Instl. Review Bd., 1996; cancer liaison physician ACS; guest spkr. intern grad. dinner Muslegon Gen. Hosp., 1970; guest lectr. Parkview Hosp., 1984-87, montly lectr. series for staff, 1984-86, Flint Osteo. Hosp., 1991, Tex. Coll. Osteo. Medicine, 1976, 77, Ohio State U. Coll. Medicine, 1975, Saginaw (Mich.) Osteo. Hosp., 1975, Mich. Ctr. Continuing Edn., 1974, Ctrl. States Osteo. Soc. Proctology Conv., 1969, Mich. Assn. Osteo. Physicians and Surgeons 85th Ann. Postgrad. Conf. and Sci. Seminar, Grand Rapids, Mich., 1984, postgrad conv., 1979, ann. conf. Dearborn, Mich., 1986, ann. conv., San Francisco, 1982, Phila. Coll. Osteo. Medicine, 1979, postgrad. seminar, 1979, guest spkr., ann. seminar, 1977, practice seminar, 1984, ACOS Ann. Seminars, San Diego, 1985, clin. assembly, 1978, Toronto, 1983, postgrad. course, 1977, Osteo. Student Orgn., Washington, 1986, 94; mem. ACOS com. Ann. Clin. Assembly Program, 1982-87, chmn., 1982, 83, chmn. awards and exhbts. com., 1986, in-depth review com., 1982-83, clin. examiner bd. surgery, 1978, postgrad. edn. com., 1978, chmn. editl. com., 1977, mem. editl. com., 1973, self-evaluation com. # 8; mem. various coms. 1986—. Guest editor Mich. Osteo. Jour., 1972; participant 1st Internat. Symposium Malignancies of Chest, Head and Neck; guest appearance Update of Breast Cancer, Cmty. Care, 1994; guest spkr. WWJ Radio, Detroit, Close Up program, Nat. Osteo. Week, 1983, Channel 62TV panel discussion, 1977; guest Kelly and Co., WXYZ-TV, 1984; contbr. articles to profl. jours. Pres. N.W. Ohio unit Am. Cancer Soc., 1995-96, chmn. profl. edn. com., 1991-93, bd. dirs., v.p. Ohio Divsn., 1993-95; pres. Health Planning Commn., Lucas County, Ohio, 1995; chmn. Spl. Rev. Com. for Health Delivery, N.W. Ohio, 1994—; mem. Physicians Malpractice Arbitration com., 1978, Comprehensive Health Planning coun., Southeast Mich., 1978, Pub. Edn. Com., 1993—, Northwest Ohio Health Planning Com., v.p., 1995, exec. bd. 1992-95, Lucas County rep., 1991-95; bd. govs. Chgo. Coll. Osteo. Medicine, 1969-71; osteo. rep. Mich. Fedn. Physicians; Mich. Ho. Dels. to Am. Osteo. Assn., 1984; chmn. Lucas County Study Com., 1994; mem. instl. review bd. Sisters of Mercy-Northwest Regional, 1997. Recipient Outstanding Faculty award Ohio U. Coll. Osteo. Medicine, 1995, cert. Appreciation, Mich. Kiwanis Club, 1971; named Outstanding Splty. Physician, Ohio U. Osteo. Medicine, 1998. Fellow Am. Coll. Osteo. Surgeons (cert. in gen. surgery,), Acad. Medicine Lucas County; mem. Am. Osteo. Assn. (hosp. examiner 1975-82, 87—, editl. cons. 1987-89, guest spkr. auxiliary), Toledo Acad. Osteo. Physicians (bd. dirs. 1991—), Assn. Surg. Edrs., Am. Trauma Soc. (founding), Detroit Cancer Club (founding), Ohio Osteo. Assn., Toledo Acad. Osteo. Physicians (bd. dirs. 1991—), Mich. Assn. Osteo. Phsicians and Surgeons (mem. health care liason com. 1982, ho. dels. 1978), Roman Catholic. Home: Sylvania, Ohio. Died Dec. 30, 2006.

ROUX, WALTER LELAND, electrical engineer; b. Aug. 31, 1929; s. George Francis and Vinnie Alma (Lanfare) R.; children: Jeanne Elizabeth, Kevin Alan. BS, U. Calif., Berkeley, 1957. Design engr. Westinghouse Electric Co., Emeryville, Calif., 1953-60; with Lockhead Missiles & Space Co., Sunnyvale, Calif., from 1960, rsch. specialist, 1972-81, staff engr., from 1981. Served with USNR, 1948-52. Mem. IEEE, Toastmasters Club (Sunnyvale), Am. Sportsman's Club. Died Dec. 18, 2006.

ROVELL, MICHAEL JAY, lawyer; b. Chgo., Mar. 30, 1949; s. Bernard and Charlotte (Schaefer) R.; m. Laurie Strauss, Sept. 2, 1979; children: Brandon, Kendall, Ryan. BA with honors, U. Ill., Chgo., 1969; JD with honors, U. Ill., 1972. Bar: Ill. 1972, U.S. Dist. Ct. (no. and so. dists.) Ill. 1972, U.S. Ct. Appeals (7th cir.) 1973, U.S. Ct. Appeals (8th cir.) 1981, U.S. Supreme Ct. 1983, U.S. Ct. Appeals (5th cir.) 1986, U.S. Ct. Appeals (1st cir.) 1990, U.S. Dist. Ct. P.R. 1992, U.S. Ct. Appeals (10th cir.) 1992, U.S. Ct. Appeals (3rd cir.) 1993, U.S. Ct. Appeals (2nd cir.) 1996, U.S. Ct. Appeals (9th cir.), 1997, Belgium 1997. Assoc. Jenner & Block, Chgo., 1972-78, ptnr., 1979-90; prin. Law Offices of Michael J. Rovell, Chgo., from 1990. Dir. Cook County Spl. Bail Project, 1972-74; chief exec. officer, bd. dirs. Sunbelt Communications, Colorado Springs, Colo., 1976-78; of counsel Wampler, Buchanan & Breen, Miami, Troncoso & Becker, San Juan, P.R., Law Offices of Robert Bright, Oklahoma City and affiliate offices London, Paris, Brussels; bd. editors U. Ill. Law Forum, 1971-72. Bd. dirs. Steppenwolf Theatre, Chgo., 1979-81. Mem. ABA (coord. litigation seminar on electronic surveillance), Ill. Bar Assn., Hillcrest Country Club (Long Grove, Ill.). Avocations: golf, tennis, bowling. Died May 5, 2007.

ROWAN, HENRY MADISON, JR., electrical engineer; b. Raphine, Va., Dec. 4, 1923; m. Betty Rowan (dec.1997); 2 sons (one dec.), Virginia Smith; m. Lee Edwardson BS in Elec. Engring., MIT. Founder, chmn. Inductotherm Group, Rancocas, NJ, 1953—2015. Patentee in field. Glassboro (N.J.) State Coll. renamed in his honor, 1992. Mem. NAE. Achievements include research in frequency tripler circuit utilizing the third harmonic component of transformers, stabilized controlled rectifyer circuit having inductive load and induction heating systems for efficiently melting metals. Died Dec. 9, 2015.

ROWE, REGINALD, artist; b. Bklyn., Dec. 8, 1920; s. Reginald and Lucia Virginia (Malone) R.; m. Jane Tips, Aug. 3, 1970; children: Michele, Betsy. BA, Princeton U., 1944; MFA, Instituto Allende, San Miguel Allende, Mex., 1958. One-man shows include Wellons Gallery, N.Y.C., 1952, 53, 56, Instituto Allende Mex., 1958, Bianchini, N.Y.C., 1960, Ruth White Gallery, N.Y.C., 1964, 70, U. North Fla., Jacksonville, 1975, Watson DeNagy Gallery, Houston, 1976, McNay Mus., San Antonio, 1977, Wallace Wentworth Gallery, Washington, 1986, Retrospective-McNay Mus., 1996, Ctr. Spirituuality and Arts, San Antonio, 1998, Evanston Art Ctr., Ill., 1999; represented in permanent collections: San Antonio Mus. Art, McNay Mus., Tex., Arts Coun. San Antonio, Exxon Corp., Houston, Galleria Bank, Houston, Gulf Resources, Houston, Hyatt-Regency Hotel, San Antonio, St. Thomas U., Houston, U. Tex. Health Sci. Ctr., San Antonio, Lee Hansley Gallery, Raleigh, N.C., Baylor Un., Waco, Tex. Home: San Antonio, Tex. Died June 15, 2007.

ROWEN, HENRY STANISLAUS, retired economist, former federal agency administrator; b. Boston, Mass., Oct. 11, 1925; s. Henry S. and Margaret ISabelle (Maher) Rowen; m. Beverly Camille Griffiths, Apr. 18, 1951; children: Hilary, Michael, Christopher, Sheila Jennifer, Diana Louise, Nicholas. BS, MIT, 1949; M in Philosophy, Oxford U., Eng., 1955. Economist RAND Corp., Santa Monica, Calif., 1950—53, 1955—60, pres., 1967—72; rsch. assoc. Harvard Ctr. for Internat. Affairs, 1960—61; dep. asst. sec. def. internat. security affairs US Dept. Def., Washington, 1961—64, asst. sec. def. internat. security affairs, 1989—91; asst. dir. US Bur. Budget, 1965—66; prof. pub. policy Stanford U., Calif., 1972—95, prof. emeritus Calif., 1995—2015, dir. pub. policy program Calif., 1972—75, Edwin B. Rust prof. pub. policy and mgmt. Calif., 1986—95, Edwin B. Rust prof. pub. policy and mgmt. emeritus Calif., 1995—2015, dir. Asia/Pacific Rsch. Ctr. Calif., 1997—2001; sr. fellow to sr. fellow emeritus Hoover Inst., Stanford, Calif., 1983—2015. Chmn. nat. intelligence coun. CIA, Washington, 1981—83; chmn. US Dept. Energy Task Force on the Future of Sci. Programs, 2002—03; mem. Commn. on the Intelligence Capabilities of the US Regarding Weapons of Mass Destruction, 2004; sr. fellow emeritus Stanford Inst. for Internat. Studies. Co-author (with R. Imai): Nuclear Energy and Nuclear Proliferation, 1980; co-author: (with C. Wolf Jr.) The Future of the Soviet Empire, 1987; editor: Options for U.S. Energy Policy, 1977, Behind East Asian Growth, 1998; co-editor (with C. Wolf Jr.): The Impoverished Superpower, 1990; co-editor: (with C. Lee, W. Miller, M. Hancock) The Silicon Valley Edge, 2001; contbr. articles to profl. jours. Chmn. chief naval ops. exec. panel USN, Washington, 1972—81, mem. exec. panel, 1983—89, 1991—93; mem. Def. Sci. Bd. US Dept. Def., 1983—89; chmn. Def. Policy Bd., 1991—94. With USN, 1943—46, PTO. Mem.: Internat. Inst. Strategic Studies. Republican. Roman Catholic. Home: Palo Alto, Calif. Died Nov. 12, 2015.

ROYBAL, DAVID D., electrical engineer; b. San Francisco, Sept. 5, 1947; s. Samuel and Gloria R.; m. Mary C. Cleese, June 27, 1970; children: Jennifer K. Roybal Andrews, Deborah L. Roybal Yong, Jonathan D. Roybal. BSEE, Santa Clara U., Calif., 1969. Registered profl. engr., Calif. From sales engr. to fellow application engr. Westinghouse Electric Corp., San Francisco, 1969-90, fellow application engr., 1990-94, Cutler-Hammer, San Francisco, from 1994. Com. chair Boy Scouts of Am., San Mateo, Calif., 1994—. Mem. Internat. Assn. Elec. Inspectors, Nat. Soc. Profl. Engrs., Nat. Fire Protection Assn., Inst. Elec. Electronic Engrs. Democrat. Roman Catholic. Home: San Mateo, Calif. Died Feb. 17, 2007.

ROYCE, ROBERT FARNHAM, manufacturing executive; b. Jersey City, Dec. 9, 1931; s. Farnham Thomas and Virginia Martin (Beattie) R.; m. Dorothy Bailey Dean, Oct. 22, 1960; children: Robert Dean, Susan Virginia, Jennifer Anne. BS in Indsl. Engring., Fairleigh Dickinson U., 1957; MS in Indsl. Engring., Stevens Inst. Tech., 1961. Asst. reg. sales mgr. Union Carbide Corp., Chgo., 1967-68, mgr. mktg. svcs., 1968-70, asst. to gen. mgr. Tarrytown, N.Y., 1970-72, mgr. fin. planning, 1972-74, materials mgr. Florence, S.C., 1974-84, internal cons. mfg. resource planning, just-in-time, 1978-84; mgr. corp. indsl. engring. and ops. systems Viskase Corp., Chgo., 1984-87; dir. materials Application Engring. Corp., Wood Dale, Ill., 1987; sr. cons. Michael Paris Assoc. Ltd., Oak Brook, Ill., 1987-88; v.p. logistics Goodman Mfg. Corp., Houston, 1988-89; dir. customer svc. and distbn. Am. Standard, Inc., New Brunswick, N.J., from 1990. Served as staff sgt. USAF, 1951-55, Korea. Mem. Am. Prodn. and Inventory Control Soc. (pres. chpt. 1984, v.p. edn. chpt. 1983, v.p. programs chpt. 1978, cert. fellow, educator MRP 1982-84). Lodges: Masons (master 1963). Republican. Episcopalian. Avocations: barbershop quartet, community theatre. Home: Powder Springs, Ga. Died July 18, 2007.

ROZUMNYJ, JAROSLAV, literature educator; b. Honcharivka, Ukraine, Sept. 6, 1925; s. Hryhory and Anna (Parubocha) R.; m. Oksana Olha Hrycenko, Mar. 10, 1938; children: Larysa, Roman, Istan, Ruslan. BA with honors, Theol. Sem., Culemborg, Netherlands, 1950; MA, U. Ottawa, Ont., Can., 1958, PhD, 1968. Lectr. Laurentian U., Sudbury, Ont., 1960-63; asst. prof. Western Mich. U., Kalamazoo, 1963-64, U. Man., Winnipeg, Can., 1964-71, head dept., 1976-89, prof. lit., from 1989, sr. scholar, 1997, assoc. prof., 1972—88. Vis. prof. U. Ottawa, 1972, Ukrainian Cath. U., Rome, 1987; dean Faculty of Philosophy, Ukrainian Free U., Munich, Germany, 1995-96; vis. rsch. scholar Macquarie U., Sydney, 1989; mem. internat. adv. bd. U. Kiev-Mohyla Acad., 1992—, hon. prof., 1996. Author: Homeland in the Poetry of Yar Slavutych, 2009; editor: New Soil--Old Roots: The Ukrainian Experience in Canada, 1983, I Was Nineteen... KM Academia, 2001, (compiler/editor) Markian Shashkevych in the West, 2007; editor: Twentieth-Century Ukrainian Literature, 2011; co-editor: To the Source Essays, 2012; editor & co-author: Yesterday, Today, Tomorrow: The Ukrainian Community in Canada, 2004; co-editor: Jubilee Collection of the Ukrainian Academy of Arts and Sciences in Canada, 1976; lit. editor: Anthology of Musical Compositions on the Poems of M. Shashkewych, 1992; editor Can. vol. Ency. of Ukrainian Diaspora, 7 vols.; editor-in-chief: Collection of Scholarly Papers, 1996; mem. editl. bd. Suchasnist, 1984-91. Pres. Ukrainian Cultural and Ednl. Ctr., Winnipeg, 1968-73; pres. Can. Friends of Rukh in Ukraine, Winnipeg, 1990-92; Can. rep. U. Kiev-Mohyla-Acad., 1992—; bd. govs. Man. Mus. Man and Nature, Winnipeg, 1976-80; pres. Markian Shashkevych Ctr., Winnipeg, 1999—. Recipient Outreach Activities award U. Man., 1986, Order of the Eternal Flame in Silver World Conf. Ukranian Scouts, 1994, Taras Shevchenko medal Ukrainian Can. Congress, 1995, Petro Mohyla Silver medal Nat. U. Kyiv Mohyla Acad., 2003; honored Festschrift, Can. Inst. Ukrainian Studies, 2000. Mem. Ukrainian Acad. Arts and Scis. in Can. (pres. 1977-80, v.p. 1995-01, 2010-), Schevchenko Sci. Soc. US, Am. Assn. Ukrainian Studies, Ukrainian Am. Assn. U. Profs. Home: Winnipeg, Canada. Died Dec. 8, 2013.

RUBIN, ALFRED PETER, law educator; b. Bklyn., Oct. 13, 1931; s. Saul and Jeannette (Turberg) R.; m. Susanne Frowein, Sept. 2, 1960; children: Conrad P., Anna F., Naomi E. BA, Columbia U., 1952, LLB, 1957; MLitt, U. Cambridge, Eng., 1963. Bar: N.Y. 1960. Atty. U.S. Dept. of Def., Washington, 1961-66, dir. trade control, 1966-67; prof. of law U. Oreg., Eugene, 1967-73; prof., internat. law Fletcher Sch. Tufts U., Medford, Mass., 1973—2002, disting. prof., 1993, disting. prof. emeritus, from 2000. Stockton chair Naval War Coll., Newport, R.I., 1981-82. Author: International Personality of the Malay Peninsula, 1974, Piracy, Paramountcy and Protectorates, 1974, The Law of Piracy, 1988, Ethics and Authority in International Law, 1997; contbr. articles to profl. jours. and newspapers. Lt. USN, 1952-55. Mem. Am. Soc. Internat. Law (exec. coun. 1982-85, chmn. coms. 1967-98), Internat. Law Assn. (chmn. com. on terrorism and extradition 1981-88, 92-98, exec. com. of Am. br. 1979—, pres. Am. br. 1994-2000). Avocation: bicycling. Home: Belmont, Mass. Died Nov. 30, 2014.

RUBINFELD, ALAN JEFFREY, manufacturing and importing company executive; b. Newark, Feb. 26, 1946; s. Louis and Evelyn (North) R.; m. Sue Ellen Kamler, Apr. 7, 1971. BS, Rider Coll., 1968; MBA, Seton Hall U., 1977. CPA, N.J. Chief operating officer Action Tungsram, Inc., East Brunswick, N.J., from 1977. Commr. East Brunswick (N.J.) Redevel. Agy., 1983-85; councilman Council of Econ. Health, East Brunswick, 1982—. Mem. Am. Inst. CPA's, N.J. Soc. CPA's, Nat. Assn. Accts., Assn. MBA Execs. Jewish. Avocation: sports. Died July 9, 2007.

RUCHMAN, ISAAC, microbiologist; b. NYC, July 2, 1909; s. Nathan Leib and Rose Naomi (Schaffro) R.; m. Marietta Duke, Sept. 6, 1940; 1 child, Reed. BS, CUNY, 1937; MS, U. Cin., 1941, PhD, 1944. Lab technician Rockefeller Inst., NYC, 1930-39; grad. asst. U. Cin., 1939-44; asst. prof. U. Cin. Coll. of Medicine, 1946-55; head microbiology Wm. S. Merrell Co., Cin., 1955-63; prof. U. Ky., Lexington, 1963-74, adj. prof., 1976-86, Transylvania U., Lexington, from 1976. Contbr. articles to profl. jours. Grantee NIH, Lederle. Mem. Optimist, Sigma Xi, Am. Soc. Mircrobiologists, Am. Acad. Microbiologists, Am. Bd. Microbiologists, Am. Assn. Immunologists, Soc. Exptl. Biology & Medicine. Avocations: stamps, environment, overseas travel. Home: Lexington, Ky. Died Jan. 12, 2007.

RUDDY, FRANK, lawyer, retired ambassador; b. NYC, Sept. 15, 1937; s. Francis Stephen and Teresa (O'Neil) Ruddy; children: Neil, David, Stephen. AB, Holy Cross Coll., 1959; MA, NYU, 1962, LLM, 1967; LLB, Loyola U., New Orleans, 1965; PhD, Cambridge U., Eng., 1969. Bar: D.C., N.Y., Tex., U.S. Supreme Ct. Faculty Cambridge U., 1967-69; asst. gen. counsel USIA, Washington, 1969-72, dep. gen. counsel, 1973-74; sr. atty. Office of Telecomm. Policy, White House, Washington, 1972-73; counsel Exxon Corp., Houston, 1974-81; asst. adminstr. AID (with rank asst. sec. state) Dept. State, Washington, 1981-84; U.S. ambassador to Equatorial Guinea, 1984-88; gen. counsel U.S. Dept. Energy, Washington, 1988-89; v.p. Sierra Blanca Devel. Corp., Washington, 1989-92; ptnr. Ruddy & Muir, Washington, 1998—2004; of counsel Sale & Quinn, Washington, from 2004. Vis. scholar Johns Hopkins Sch. Advanced Internat. Studies, 1990—94; dep. chmn. UN Referendum for Western Sahara, 1994. Author: International Law in the Enlightenment, 1975; editor: American International Law Cases (series); editor in chief Internat. Lawyer; contbr. articles to legal jours. Bd. dirs. African Devel. Found., Washington, 1983-84, Human Life Internat., 1999—; mem. Coun. of Am. Ambs., Washington, 1988—. Served with USMCR, 1956-61 Mem.: ABA (chmn. treaty compliance sect. 1991—93), Hague Acad. Internat. Law Alumni Assn., Internat. Law Assn., Am. Soc. Internat. Law, Dacor House, Cosmos Club (Washington), Knights of Malta. Republican. Roman Catholic. Home: Rockville, Md. Died May 7, 2014.

RUDES, GEORGE HARLOW, realtor, insurance agent; b. Genoa, Ohio, Dec. 16, 1923; s. Merrill Basil and Della Matilda (Meyer) R.; m. Marion Helen Bringe, Nov. 12, 1944; children: Randolph Harlow, Connie Joy Moore, Amy Margaret Sutter. Army specialized tng. program, Washington-Jefferson Coll., 1943-44. Ins. agt. Rudes & Reeder Agy., Curtice, Ohio, from 1947; mgr. Nick Stevens Motor Sales, Genoa, 1951-55; prin. George H. Rudes Realtor, Curtice, from 1963. V.p., bd. dirs. Nat. Bank of Oak Harbor (Ohio). Served to staff sgt. C.E., U.S. Army, 1943-46, PTO, ETO. Mem. Nat. Assn. Realtors, Ohio Assn. Realtors, Ottawa County Assn. Realtors, Nat. Assn. Real Estate Appraisers, Nat. Assn. of Rev. Appraisers, Am. Legion, VFW. Lodges: Maccabees. Republican. Methodist. Avocations: fishing, golf. Home: Martin, Ohio. Died May 17, 2007.

RUDOLPH, FREDERICK, history professor; b. Balt., June 19, 1920; s. Charles Frederick and Jennie Hill (Swope) R.; m. Dorothy Dannenbaum, June 18, 1949; children: Marta R., Lisa R. Cushman. BA, Williams Coll., 1942, Litt.D., 1985; MA, Yale U., 1949, PhD, 1953; LHD, U. Rochester, 1994, Wilkes U., 1998. Instr. history Williams Coll., 1946-47; asst. instr. Yale, 1949-50; mem. faculty Williams Coll., from 1951, prof., from 1961, Mark Hopkins prof. history, 1964-82, emeritus, from 1982, chmn. Am. civilization program, 1971-80. Williams Coll. marshal, 1978-87; vis. lectr. history and edn. Harvard U., 1960, 61; vis. prof. Sch. Edn., U. Calif.-Berkeley, 1983; mem. commn. plans and objectives Am. Council Edn., 1963-66; mem. study group on postsecondary edn. Nat. Inst. Edn., 1980-83; mem. com. on baccalaureate degrees Assn. Am. Colls., 1981-85; vis. assoc. Ctr. Studies in Higher Edn., U. Calif.-Berkeley, 1983 Author: Mark Hopkins and the Log, 1956, rev. edit. 1996, The American College and University: A History, 1962, rev. edit., 1990 (Japanese translation, 2003), Curriculum: A History of the American Undergraduate Course of Study Since 1636, 1977, rev. edit., 1993; editor: Essays on Education in the Early Republic, 1965, Perspectives: A Williams Anthology, 1983; exec. editor: Change, 1980-84, cons. editor, 1985-92. Founding mem. Berkshire County Hist. Soc., 1962, v.p., 1962-66, pres., 1966-68, bd. dirs., 1974-76; trustee Hancock-Shaker Cmty. Inc., 1974-91, Wyoming Sem., 1976-79, Bennington Mus., 1985-95; bd. dirs. Armand Hammer United World Coll. Am. West, 1993-2005. Capt. AUS, 1942-46. Guggenheim fellow, 1958-59, 68-69; recipient Frederic W. Ness award Assn. Am. Colls., 1980, Rogerson cup Williams Coll., 1982, Disting. Svc. award Wyo. Seminary, 1986, Bicentennial medal, Williams Coll., 2011; Frederick Rudolph Professorship of Am. Culture established in his honor, Williams Coll., 2007. Mem. AAUP, Nat. Acad. Edn., Mass. Hist. Soc. (fellow), Am. Hist. Assn., Am. Studies Assn., Phi Beta Kappa. Democrat. Home: Williamstown, Mass. Died June 3, 2013.

RUGEN, LLOYD LEONARD, farmer; b. Syracuse, Mo., Mar. 22, 1917; s. August Fred and Grace (Billingsley) R.; m. Anna Lewis Kueffer, Mar. 22, 1947 (dec. Dec. 1984); 1 child, Lewis Leonard. Grad. high sch., Columbia, Mo., 1957. Tractor operator Bur. Reclamation/Dept. of Interior, Heber, Willard, Utah, 1938-40; farmer Pleasant Green, Mo., 1940, Prairie Home, Mo., from 1945. Mem. exec. bd. Concord Bapt. Assn., 1950-57, 59—, com. chmn., 1961-71, sem. extension com., 1972-77; deacon Woldridge Bapt. Ch., 1969. With U.S. Army, 1941-45, ETO/Africa-Middle Eastern Theatre of Ops. Mem. Am. Legion (historian 1954, comdr. 1955, post adjutant 1956—, vice comdr. 8th dist. dept. of Mo. 1956-57, comdr. 8th dist. 1957-58, chaplain 8th dist. 1966—, sgt.-at-arms 1954-56. Baptist. Avocation: hunting. Home: Prairie Home, Mo. Died Apr. 27, 2007.

RUIZ, JOSE, minister; b. Havana, Cuba, May 22, 1925; came to U.S., 1958; s. Jose Ruiz and Conception Reluzco; m. America Alfonso, Dec. 25, 1947; children: Conception, Elda, Teresa. AA, Dade Coll.; BA, Fla. Internat. U.; MEd, U. Miami, New Orleans Bapt., Theol. Seminary; EdD, Calif. Coast U. Ordained to ministry Bapt. Ch., 1960; cert. tchr., Fla. Tchr. Miami (Fla.) High Adult Edn. Ctr., from 1974; pastor Buenas Nuevas Bapt. Ch., from 1979. Prof. New Orleans Bapt. Theol. Seminary, 1980-90. Author: Jesus, The Exorcist, 1974. Republican. Home: Miami, Fla. Died Nov. 8, 2006.

RULE, ANN (ANN RAE STACKHOUSE), author; b. Lowell, Mich., Oct. 22, 1931; d. Chester R. Stackhouse and Sophie (Hansen); m. Bill Rule (div. 1972); children: Leslie, Laura Harris, Michael, Andrew, Bruce Sherles. Degree in Creative Writing, U. Washington, 1953; assoc. degree in criminal justice, Highline Cmty. Coll., Des Moines, Wash.; PhD in Humane Letters, Willamette U., 2004, postgrad. in police sci. Provisional officer, Seattle; spkr. subject of serial killers. Author: (non-fiction books) The Stranger Beside Me, 1980, Lust Killer, 1983, Want-Ad Killer, 1983, Beautiful Seattle, 1984, Small Sacrifices, 1987, The I-5 Killer, 1988, Bitter Harvest, 1998, The End of the Dream, 1999, And Never Let Her Go, 1999, Every Breath You Take, 2001, Green River, Running Red, 2004, Practice to Deceive, 2013, (novels) If You Really Loved Me, 1991, Everything She Ever Wanted, 1992, Possession, 1983, A Rose for Her Grave, 1993, You Belong to Me, 1994, Dead by Sunset, 1995, Perfect Husband, 1996, A Fever in the Heart, 1996, In the Name of Love, 1998, Ann Rule's Omnibus, 1998, A Rage to Kill, 1999, Empty Promises, 2001, Last Dance, Last Chance, 2003, Without Pity, 2003, Heart Full of Lies, 2003, Kiss Me Kill Me, 2004, Worth More Dead, 2005, No Regrets, 2006, Too Late to Say Goodbye, 2007, Smoke, Mirrors, and Murders, 2007, Mortal Danger, 2008, But I Trusted You, 2009, In the Still of the Night, 2010, Don't Look Behind You and Other Truce Cases, 2011, Fatel Friends, Deadly Neighbors and Other True Cases, 2012, Lying in Wait and Other True Crimes, 2014; exec. prodr.: ABC mini-series Small Sacrifices, 1989, NBC mini-series Dead by Sunset, 1995, CBS mini-series And Never Let Her Go, 2000, USA Network mini-series The Stranger Beside Me, 2003; contbr. several articles to newspapers and mags. including True Detective, Cosmopolitan, Ladies' Home Journal, Good Housekeeping and Reader's Digest and others. Vol. Seattle Crisis Clinic. Recipient Washington State Governor's award. Died July 26, 2015.

RUMLER, DIANA GALE, retired geriatrics nurse; b. Manchester, Tenn., Feb. 23, 1943; d. Donald Yale and Thelma Irene (Beach) Miller; m. Herschel Hinkle, Aug. 1961 (div. Jan. 1978); children: David, John, Jody Hinkle West; m. Lester Rumler, Jr. (div. June 1984). AA in Nursing, Ind. U.-Purdue U., Indpls., 1974; BS in Pub. Health-Journalism-Psychology, Ball State U., 1983. RN, Ariz. Psychiat. nurse Meth. Hosp., Indpls., 1974-78; women's infant and children's coord. Cmty. & Family Svcs. Inc., Portland, Ind., 1978-81, Ball Meml. Hosp., Muncie, Ind., 1981-84; pub. health nurse Health & Rehab. Svcs., Ft. Lauderdale, Fla., 1984; med.-surg. nurse Holy Cross Hosp., Ft. Lauderdale, 1985; pre-op-post-op nurse VA Med. Ctr., Nashville, 1986-89, nurse vascular, orthopedics, intensive care, telemetry, tchr. geriat. chart auditing and rsch. data collector, relief staff coord. Tucson, from 1990. WIC advocate hearings/radio show, Ind., 1978-81; health vol. outreach clinic St. Mary's Hosp., Tucson, 1993-94; vol. Hospice Family Care, Tucson, Shalom House, Tucson, 1996-98. Contbr. articles to profl. jours. Mem. Nurses of Vet. Affairs, Ladies' Hermitage Assn. Democrat. Roman Catholic. Avocations: cross stitch, ceramics, crossstitch, health club activities, travel. Died Apr. 24, 2007.

RUNNELS, MIKE LOWELL, former lieutenant governor of New Mexico; b. Magnolia, Ark., Sept. 11, 1945; s. Harold Lowell and Dorothy (Gilland) R.; children— Joshua Lowell, Sean Michael BA, Colo. Coll., 1967; JD, U. Tex., 1981. Vol. with Navajo Nation VISTA, Chinle, Ariz., 1970; lobbyist Central Clearing House, Santa Fe, 1971-72; state dir. Common Cause, N. Mex., 1972-74; mem. Santa Fe City Council, 1976-80; dist. atty. of Judicial Districts of Valencia, Cibola and Sandoval, 1993—2000; lt. gov. State of N.Mex., Santa Fe, 1983—87. Democrat. Died Feb. 5, 2015.

RUNYON, JOHN CHARLES, psychologist; b. Annapolis, Md., Aug. 17, 1944; s. Charles Fredrick and Dorothy (Swift) R.; m. Anna Lee Cox, June 10, 1967 (div. 1987); m. Susan Marie Bard, July 15, 1989; children: Nicole Marie, Christian Fredrick, Aaron Samuel. BS, Murray State U., 1967, MS, 1973. Psychologist-supr. Western Ky. Mental Health/Mental Retardation Bd. Inc., Paducah, 1974-80; psychologist Kelley Psychiat. Clinic, Paducah, 1980-83; psychologist, pres. Psychol. Assocs. Paducah, Inc., from 1983, also chmn. bd. Bd. dirs. Mayfield/Graves County (Ky.) Sr. Citizens, 1976-78, Mayfield-Graves County United Way, 1976-78, Parents Anonymous, Paducah, 1985-87, Childwatch, Paducah, 1987-90; mem. Ky. Post Trauma Response team, 1992—; sec. Ky. Psychol. Assn. Found., 1999. Named Ky. Col. Gov. Ky., 1987, Duke Paducah, Mayor City of Paducah, 1987. Mem. APA (assoc.), Ky. Psychol. Assn. (legis. com. 1990-94, West Ky. rep., bd. dirs. 1994-99, sec. 1999—), Ky. C. of C. (small bus. council 1994—), Psi Chi. Avocations: water sports, private pilot, reading. Home: Paducah, Ky. Died Feb. 24, 2007.

RUPPEL, EDWARD THOMPSON, geologist; b. Fort Morgan, Colo., Oct. 26, 1925; s. Henry George and Gladys Myrtle (Thompson) R.; m. Phyllis Beale Tanner; children: Lisa, David, Douglas, Kristin. BA in Geology, U. Mont., 1948, Doctorate (hon.), 1996; MA in Geology, U. Wyo., 1950; PhD in Geology, Yale U., 1958. Geologist U.S. Geol. Survey, Denver, 1950-68, rsch. geologist, 1968-86; dir., state geologist Mont. Bur. Mines and Geology, Butte, 1986-94; consulting geologist Twin Bridges, Mont., from 1994. Author and co-author more then 50 maps and reports; contbr. articles to profl. jours. Dir., v.p. Virginia City (Mont.) Preservation Alliance, 1997-98. Lt. (j.g.) USNR, 1943-50. Recipient Silver medal, Ted's Montana Grill U., 2013. Fellow Geol. Soc. Am. (sr.), Soc. Econ. Geologists; mem. Am. Inst. Profl. Geologists (cert. profl. geologist), Mont. Geol. Soc., Geol. Soc. Washington, Tobacco Root Geol. Soc. (Excellence in Field Work award 1993). Died June 27, 2014.

RUSSELL, ELIZABETH ANN, graphics artist; b. Salisbury, NC, Aug. 12, 1955; d. Garland Thomas and Mary Elizabeth (Wyatt) R. B Creative Arts, U. N.C., Charlotte, 1977. Tchr. art YMCA, Conover, N.C., 1978-79; picture framer The Finishing Touch, Hickory, N.C., 1982; sr. graphics technician Meredith-Burda Graphics, Hickory, from 1982. Mem. Newton-Conover Rescue Squad. Presbyterian. Avocations: camping, hiking, drawing, exercising, framing pictures. Home: Charlotte, NC. Died Dec. 5, 2007.

RUSSELL, FINDLAY EWING, physician; b. San Francisco, Sept. 1, 1919; s. William and Mary Jane (Findlay) R.; m. Janet Louise Thiel. Feb. 14, 1950; children: Christa Ann, Sharon Jane, Robin Emily, Constance Susan, Mark Findlay. BA, Walla Walla Coll., Wash., 1941; MD, Loma Linda U., Calif., 1950; postgrad. (fellow), Calif. Inst. Tech., 1951-53; postgrad., U. Cambridge, Eng., 1962—63; PhD, U. Santa Barbara, Calif., 1974, LLD (hon.), 1989. Intern White Meml. Hosp., Los Angeles, 1950-51; practice medicine specializing in toxinology and toxicology Los Angeles, from 1953; mem. staff Los Angeles County-U. So. Calif. Med. Center, Loma Linda U. Med. Center, U. Ariz. Med. Ctr.; physiologist Huntington Inst. Med. Research, 1953-55; dir. lab. neurol. research Los Angeles County-U. So. Calif. Med. Center, 1955-80; mem. faculty Loma Linda U. Med. Sch., 1955—2007; prof. neurology, physiology and biology U. So. Calif. Med. Sch., 1966-81; prof. pharmacology and toxicology U. Ariz. Health Scis. Coll. Pharmacy, from 1981. Cons. USPHS, NSF, Office Naval Rsch., WHO, U.S. Army, Walter Reed, USAF, Brooks AFB. Author: Marine Toxins and Venomous and Poisonous Marine Animals, 1965, Poisonous Marine Animals, 1971, Snake Venom Poisoning, 1980; co-author: Bibliography of Snake Venoms and Venomous Snakes, 1964, Animal Toxins, 1967, Poisonous Snakes of The World, 1968, Snake Venom Poisoning, 1983, Bibliography of Venomous and Poisonous Marine Animals and Their Toxins, 1984, Venomous and Poisonous Marine Invertebrates of the Indian Ocean, 1996; editor: Toxicon, 1962-70. Served with AUS, 1942-46. Decorated Purple Heart, Bronze Star; recipient award Los Angeles County Bd. Suprs., 1960; award Acad. Medicine Buenos Aires, 1966; Skylab Achievement award, 1974; Jozef Stefan medal Yugoslavia, 1978; U.S. State Dept. medallion, 2006, Disting. Citizen award, 1992. Fellow A.C.P., Am. Coll. Cardiology, Royal Soc. Tropical Medicine, N.Y. Acad. Scis.; mem. Internat. Soc. Toxinology (pres. 1962-66, Francisco Redi medal 1967), Royal Soc. Medicine, Am. Soc. Physiology, Western Soc. Pharmacology (pres. 1973) Died Apr. 21, 2011.

RUSSELL, JOHN CLARENCE, investment management professional; b. Marlow, Okla., Dec. 22, 1917; s. John Clarence Russell and Effie Lee Howard; m. Betty Lou Rice, Nov. 28, 1943; children: Susan Russell Vivoli, John Robert. BA, U. Tex., 1938; postgrad., U. Okla., 1938-39, Ohio State U., 1968-69. Regional mgr. Am. Optical Co., L.A., Atlanta, 1946-70; broker Sweney Cartwright, Columbus, Ohio, 1970-78; CFO, pres. Tex. Constrn. Assocs., Brownsville, San Antonio, 1978-81; investment counselor E.F. Hutton, Harlingen, Tex., 1981-85, Merrill Lynch, Brownsville, 1985-88; CEO, pres. John C. Russell Investment Mgmt. Inc., Brownsville, from 1988. CEO, pres. Water Purifiers, Inc., Brownsville, 1992—, Russell-Morgan Co., 1994—. Author monthly personal investment letter, 1972-78. Served in U.S. Army Air Corps, 1942-45. Mem. Super Srs. of Brownsville, Nat. Assn. Securities Dealers (bd. arbitrators 1995—). Avocations: tennis, bridge, history. Died June 15, 2007.

RUTLEDGE, ALBERT HENRY, architectural engineer, architect; b. Nashville, June 11, 1928; s. Albert Henry and Emma Jame (Hughes) R.; m. Naomi L. Jenkins, May 9, 1954 (div. July 1965); children: Albert Henry III, Darryl Walker; m. Iva D. Goodwin, Nov. 10, 1965. Student, Cleve. Engring. Inst., 1950-52, John Carrol U., 1954-57; BS in Engring. and Mgmt., Calif. U., Long Beach, 1972. Cert. plant engr. Am. Inst. Plant Engrs.; registered profl. engr., Calif. Piping designer, engr. Fluor Corp., Irvine, Calif., 1966-70; engr. City of Compton, Calif., 1971-73, R.M. Parsons Co., Pasadena, Calif., 1973-76; facilities engr. GE, Mojave, Calif., 1979-87; arch., engr. A.H. Rutledge & Assocs., California City, Calif., from 1987. Mem., deacon First Missionary Bapt. Ch., Ridgecrest, Calif., 1993; mem., usher First Bapt. Ch., Calif., 1994; active Concern Citizens, California City, 1994. Mem. Free and Accepted Masons (worshipful master). Home: California City, Calif. Died Apr. 16, 2007.

RUTLEDGE, WYMAN CY, research physicist; b. Abrahamsville, Pa., Dec. 15, 1924; s. Coe Sanford and Bernice I. (Gregg) R.; Mary Louise Jones, June 6, 1945; Paul, Nancy, Mark. AB in Physics, Math. and Chemistry, Hiram Coll., 1944; MS in Physics, U. Mich., 1948, PhD in Physics, 1952; PhD in Sci. (hon.), Miami U., 1990. Jr. physicist Woods Hole (Mass.) Oceanographic Inst., 1946-47; rsch. assoc. Aero Rsch. Lab. U. Mich., Ann Arbor, 1947-48, rsch. assoc. Nuclear Spectros, 1948-50; rsch. assoc. Argonne Nat. Lab., Lemont, Ill., 1950-52; rsch. physicist Philips Labs., Irvington, N.Y., 1952-56; prin. scientist Mead Cent. Rsch. Labs, Chillicothe, Ohio, 1956-91; cons. Chillicothe, 1991-95; ret., 1995. Cons. measurements Am. Inst. Paper, N.Y.C., 1965—; cons. advanced sensors Dept. Energy, Washington, 1980—; adv. bd. mem. Ohio U., Chillicothe, 1976—, chmn., 1984; trustee Hiram Coll., 1980-86. Contbr. 60 articles to profl. jours. Pres., v.p., treas., bd. dirs. Med. Ctr., Ross County, Ohio, 1968-74; mem., pres. Ross County Hosp. Commn., 1982-92, mem., 1974—; bd. dirs., pres. 4-Coun. Boy Scout Coun., Chillicothe, 1970-71, mem., 1970-92; v.p. 17 County Mid-Ohio Health Planning Fedn., Columbus, Ohio, 1973-75. With U.S. Army, 1944-46. Recipient Phoenix award U. Mich., 1950-51, Garfield Soc. award Hiram Coll., 1980; named Tech. Man of Yr. Inter Soc. Coun., 1975, Layman of Yr. Kiwanis, 1973. Fellow Tech. Assn. Pulp and Paper, Instrument Soc. Am. (nat. v.p. 1974-78, Disting. Svc. award 1982, Golden Achievement award 1988, chmn. admissions com. 1989-91), Symposiarchs Am. (nat. pres. 1970-71, nat. treas. 1991, Symposiarch of Yr. 1952), Sigma Xi. Republican. Achievements include patents infield. Home: Chillicothe, Ohio. Died Jan. 5, 2007.

RUTZ, BETH ILENE, special education educator; b. Battle Creek, Mich., Feb. 1, 1962; d. Layo Judson and Phyllis Ilene Rutz. BS in Spl. Edn., Ea. Mich. U., 1984, MA in Mid. Sch. Math., 1990. Mem. direct care staff Washtenaw Assn. for Retarded Citizens, Ann Arbor, Mich., 1982-87; tchr. expressive arts severly multiply impaired classroom Wayne-Westland (Mich.) Pub. Schs., 1985-89; visually impaired tchr. Monroe, Lenawee County Intermediate Sch. Dists., Mich., from 1990. Tchr. Boston Coll. spl. edn. students, summer 1987. Leader Adoption Identity Movement, Detroit, 1988-90, Adoption Liberty Movement Assn., Ann Arbor, Mich., 1992-93. Mem. So. Mich. Parents of Visually Impaired Students. Avocations: biking, volleyball, windsurfing, skiing, computer technology for special education. Home: Ann Arbor, Mich. Died Mar. 9, 2007.

RUYBALID, LOUIS ARTHUR, social worker, community development consultant; b. Allison, Colo., Apr. 6, 1925; s. Mike Joseph and Helen Mary (Rodriguez) R.; m. Seraphima Alexander, June 12, 1949; children: Mariana, John. BA, U. Denver, 1946-49, MSW, 1951; PhD, U. Calif., Berkeley, 1970; Professor Ad-Honorem (hon.), Nat. U., Caracas, Venezuela, 1964. Social worker, Ariz., Calif., Colo., 1951-62; advisor community devel. Unitarian Service Com., Caracas, 1962-64, U.S. Agy. for Internat. Devel., Rio de Janeiro, Brazil, 1964-66; area coordinator U.S. Office Econ. Opportunity, San Francisco, 1966-68; prof., dept. head U. So. Colo., Pueblo, 1974-80; licensing analyst State of Calif., Campbell, from 1984; prof. sch. of social work Highlands U., Las Vegas, N.Mex., 1988-89. Cons. UN, Caracas, 1978, Brazilian Govt., Brazilia, 1964-66, Venezuelan Govt., Caracas, 1962-64. Author: (books) Favela, 1970, Glossary for Hominology, 1978, (research instrument) The Conglomerate Hom., 1976. Mem. exec. com. Pueblo (Colo.) Regional Planning Com., 1974-79, Nat. Advisory com. The Program Agy. United Presbyn. Ch., 1978-79. Served with USN, 1944-46. Recipient Pro Mundo Beneficio medal Brazilian Acad. Human Sci., Sao Paulo, 1976; United Def. Fund fellow U. Calif., Berkeley, 1961-62, Cert. World Leadership Internat. Leaders of Achievement, 1988-89. Mem. NASW (cert.), Ethnic Minority Commn., IMAGE (nat. edn. chair), Am. Hominol. Assn. (nat. pres. 1975-79), U. Calif. Alumni Assn., AARP (minority spokesperson), Phi Beta Kappa, Phi Sigma Iota. Democrat. Avocations: tennis, boxing history. *Personal philosophy: As a personal credo, I have adopted the philosophy of the Pueblo Indians of New Mexico which is: Amity, not conquest, stability, not strife, conservation, not waste, restraint, not aggression, I embrace the conviction that human energy should be used to care for the primal needs of people!.* Died Mar. 16, 2007.

RYAN, ALICE MARY, import company executive; b. Bay Shore, NY, June 10, 1942; d. James Vincent and Alice Mary (Ryan) Kavanaugh; m. James Anthony Ryan, July 10, 1965; children: Thomas, James, Christopher, Padraig. Diploma, Queen of the Rosary Acad., 1960. Clk. N.Y. Telephone Co., Patchogue, N.Y., 1960-63; receptionist Cantor Bros., Farmingdale, N.Y., 1963-65; owner J.A. Ryan Imports, Babylon, N.Y., from 1981. Pres. Parent Tchr. Group, Babylon, 1975-78; sec. Cub Scout Com., Babylon, 1974-76; active Babylon Varsity Booster Club, Babylon, 1978—. Mem. Nat. Assn. Female Execs., Am. Celtic Pipe Band, Inc., Scottish Tartan Soc., Clan Montgomery Soc., Scottish Clan Assn., Babylon C. of C. Avocations: beach, travel. Home: Lindenhurst, NY. Died July 5, 2007.

RYAN, ELSIE M., medical/surgical nurse; b. College Point, NY, Jan. 14, 1932; d. Robert W. and Mary H. (Turnier) Martin; m. Thomas Ryan, Nov. 11, 1978 (dec.). Diploma, Creedmoor State Hosp., Bellerose, NY, 1953; student, Adelphi Coll., 1953-54. Med. head nurse Luth. Hosp., Bklyn., med. supr., adminstrv. asst.; staff nurse St. Agnes Med. Ctr., Fresno, Calif. Home: Clovis, Calif. Died Jan. 16, 2007.

RYANT, CHARLES JOSEPH, JR., environment executive; b. Chgo., Apr. 1, 1920; BS in Chem. Engring., Armour Inst. Tech., 1940; MS in Chem. Engring., Ill. Inst. Tech., 1941, PhD in Chem. Engring., 1947. Pres. C.J. Ryant, Jr. &

Assocs., Chicago, 1959—70; exec. dir. Midwest Legislative Coun. on the Environment, 1970—80; pres. C.J. Ryant, Maple City, Mich., from 1980. Home: Maple City, Mich. Died Mar. 14, 2007.

RYDOLPH, SIMMIE TOMMY, middle school educator; b. Refugio, Tex., Oct. 25, 1939; s. Simmie T. and Agnes G. Polk. BA, U. Calif., Berkeley, 1969, SUNY, Albany, 1988; MA in Liberal Studies, Wesleyan U., 1988. Cert. tchr., Alaska. Tchr. English Kumasi (Ghana) Secondary Tech. Sch., 1971-73; group counselor Contra Costa County Juvenile Facility, Martinez, Calif., 1970, 73-79; social studies tchr. Gruening Mid. Sch., Eagle River, Alaska, from 1983. Mem. Social Studies Textbook Com., Anchorage, 1992—. Pianist 1st Bapt. Ch., Lualualei, Hawaii, 1963-65; pianist, organist, vocalist 1st Meth. Ch., Wasilla, Alasks, 1985-92; tutor Anchorage Literacy Project, Anchorage, 1990, Concerned Advocates R Everywhere, Anchorage, 1990-93; workshop presenter Anchorage Sch. Dist., Rotary, Ch. Jesus Christ Latter Day Sts., Wasilla. With USN, 1963-65, res. Fulbright-Hayes fellow, 1991; NEH scholar, 1990, 92, 94, Wesleyan U. scholar, 1971-73. Mem. Nat. Coun. Social Studies (mem. acad. freedom, ethics and equity com. 1994-95), Rotary (music dir. 1984—). Died Feb. 24, 2007.

RYLE, HELEN L., medical auditor; b. Wichita Falls, Tex., June 7, 1930; d. Robert E. and Maud Elizabeth (Swarts) R. Diploma in nursing, Wichita Gen. Hosp., Wichita Falls, 1950; student, Harding Coll.; AS, Midwestern U., Wichita Falls, 1950. RN, Pa., Tex. Staff nurse med.-surg. unit St. Luke's Hosp., Bethlehem, Pa.; med.-surg. supr. Garza Meml. Hosp., Post, Tex.; clin. adminstr. critical care Wichita Gen. Hosp.; med. auditor Bus. Office, Wichita Gen. Hosp. Mem. Tex. Med. Auditors Assn. Home: Seymour, Tex. Died Apr. 21, 2007.

SAAD, JOSEPH KANAN, lawyer; b. Clarksdale, Miss., Oct. 28, 1948; s. Joseph Saad and Jeanette (Farris) Chilli. BBA, U. Miss., 1970, JD, 1973. Bar: Miss. 1973, U.S. Dist. Ct. (no. dist.) Miss. 1973. Account exec. Dean Witter & Co., Memphis, 1973-75, Reynolds Securities, Houston, 1974, Lincoln Nat. Life Ins. Co., Houston, 1974-75; claims atty. Fidelity & Deposit Co. Md., Balt., New Orleans, Cleve. and Miami, 1975-80; bond claims atty. Transam Ins. Co., LA, 1980-83, mgr. surety claims, 1983-84, asst. v.p. bonds, 1984-86, v.p. splty. claims, 1986-89; sr. v.p. splty. claims Transam Ins Co., LA, 1989-93; claims counsel Transam Ins. Co., LA, 1988-93; sr. v.p. Assoc. Internat. Ins. Co., 1993-94, exec. v.p., chief adminstrv. officer, from 1994. Asst. v.p. Trans Premier Ins. Co., L.A., 1987-93, Fairmont Ins. Co., L.A., 1987-93, Chilton Ins. Co., Dallas, 1987-93; pres. Rusco Svcs. Inc., 1990-93; exec. v.p. Gryphon Ins. Group, 1996—, Calvert Ins. Co., 1996—. Mem. ABA (fidelity and Surety com. 1976—), Miss. Bar Assn., Fedn. Ins. and Corp. Counsel, Internat. Assn. Def. Counsel, Def. Rsch. Inst., So. Calif. Surety Assn. Home: Los Angeles, Calif. Died Nov. 27, 2006.

SABLE, ARTHUR JUSTIN, electrical and optical engineer; b. Hartford, Conn., Oct. 2, 1924; s. Israel and Tillie (Oliver) S.; m. Barbara Rowe Kinsey, Nov. 3, 1973. BS, U. Chgo., 1949; MA, Boston U., 1965. Sr. engr. Robertshaw-Fulton, Stratford, Conn., 1954-58; engring. mgr. Polaroid Corp., Cambridge, Mass., 1958-63; tech. dir. IBM, Armonk, N.Y., 1963-70; pres. Sable Photo Works, Inc., Boulder, Colo., 1970-74, Sable Instruments, Inc., Boulder, from 1974. Patentee in field. Served as sgt. U.S. Army, 1942-46. Recipient Naval Ordnance Devel. award, 1954. Mem. IEEE, Soc. Photographic Scientists and Engrs., Optical Soc. Am., Sigma Xi. Lodges: Rotary. Democrat. Jewish. Home: Boulder, Colo. Died Mar. 20, 2007.

SACKETT, DAVID LAWRENCE, medical researcher, educator; b. Chgo., Nov. 17, 1934; s. DeForest and Margaret Helen (Ross) S.; m. Barbara Louise Bennett, June 26, 1957; children: David, Charles, Andrew, Robert. BA, Lawrence U., 1956; BSc in Medicine, U. Ill., Chgo., 1958, MD, 1960; MSc., Harvard U., 1967. Chief resident in medicine SUNY, Buffalo, 1965-66; chair dept. clin. epidemology and biostats. McMaster U., Hamilton, Ontario, Can., 1967-73, head internal medicine, 1987-94; physician-in-chief of medicine, head of division of general internal medicine Chedoke Hosp., Hamilton, 1985-87; cons. physician John Radcliffe Hosp., U. Oxford, Oxford U., England, 1994-99; dir. Ctr. for Evidence-Based Medicine, U. Oxford, 1994-99; founder, dir. Kilgore Trout Rsch. & Edn. Centre, Irish Lake, ON, Canada, 1999. Chair steering group Cochrane Collaboration, World-wide, 1993-96, monitoring coms. several internat. randomized trials. Author: (books) Compliance in Health Care, 1979, Clinical Epidemology, 1991, Evidence-Based Medicine, 2000; contbr. several refereed articles to sci. med. jours.; editor Evidence-Based Medicine Jour., London, 1996 Chair Health and Pub. Policy Com., Royal Coll., Ottawa, 1988-92. Surgeon US Pub Health Svc., 1963-65. Recipient Taylor Internat. prize in medicine, 1987, Baxter Internat. Found. Health Svcs. Rsch. Prize, 2005; named Top Clin. Tchr. in N. Am., Am. Assn. Med. Colls., 1990; elected to Can. Med. Hall of Fame, 2000. Fellow Royal Soc. Can., Royal Coll. Physicians, Ottawa, Royal Coll. Physicians, London, Royal Coll. Physicians, Edinburgh. Avocations: hiking, running, squash, singing. Died May 13, 2015.

SACKS, OLIVER WOLF, neurologist, writer; b. London, July 9, 1933; Came to U.S., 1960; s. Samuel and Muriel Elsie (Landau) S.; life partner Bill Hayes BA, U. Oxford, 1954; MA, BM, BCh, Middlesex Hosp., London, 1958; DHL (hon.), Georgetown U., 1990, Coll. Staten Island, CUNY, 1991; DS (hon.), Tufts U., 1991, N.Y. Med. Coll., 1991; DS (hon.), Med. Coll. Pa., 1992, Bard Coll., 1992, U. Turin, 2003. Intern in medicine, surgery and neurology Middlesex Hosp., 1958-60; rotating intern Mt. Zion Hosp., San Francisco, 1961-62; resident in neurology UCLA, 1962-65; I.D. fellow in neuropathology and neurochemistry Albert Einstein Coll. Medicine, NYC, 1965-66, instr. neurology, 1966-75, asst. prof., 1975-78, assoc. prof., 1978-85, clin. prof. neurology, 1985—2007; prof. clin. neurology and clin. psychiatry Columbia U. Med. Ctr., NYC, 2007—15; Columbia Artist Columbia U., NYC, 2007—15. Adj. prof. psychiatry NYU, 1992-2015; sci. advisor Inst. Music and Neurologic Function, Beth Abraham Hosp., 1995-2015; cons. neurologist Comprehensive Epilepsy Ctr., Mt. Sinai Med. Ctr., 1999-2015; cons., speaker, lectr. in field; hon. lectureships in field. Author: Migraine, 1970, Awakenings, 1973, (Hawthornden prize 1975), A Leg To Stand On, 1984, The Man Who Mistook His Wife for a Hat, 1985, Seeing Voices: A Journey into the World of the Deaf, 1989 (Mainichi Pub. Culture award 1996), An Anthropologist on Mars, 1995 (George S. Polk award for mag. reporting 1994, Nat. Assn. Sci. Writers award 1994, Esquire Apple Waterstone's Book of Yr. 1995), The Island of the Color Blind, 1996, Uncle Tungsten: Memories of a Chemical Boyhood, 2001, Oaxaca Journal, 2002, Musicophilia: Tales of Music and the Brain, 2007, The Mind's Eye, 2010, Hallucinations, 2012, On the Move: A Life, 2015 (memoir); compiled several notebooks; published essays in medical journals and magazines, including The New Yorker, The New Review of Books, Antaeus Bd. mem. N.Y. Bot. Garden. Recipient Oskar Pfister award APA, 1988, Harold D. Vursell Meml. award American Acad. & Inst. Arts & Letters, 1989, Communicator of Yr. Royal Nat. Inst. Deaf, 1991, Lewis Thomas prize Rockefeller U., 2002, Sloan Found. award, 2002, Pub. Comm. award NSF, 2004; Guggenheim fellow, 1989, others; named Commander of the British Empire, 2008 Fellow American Acad. Arts & Sciences, American Acad. Arts & Letters, NY Acad. Scis. (hon.); mem. American Acad. Neurology (presdl. citation 1991), American Fern Soc., American Neurological Assn. (hon.), Assn. Brit. Neurologists (hon.), Brit. Pteridological Soc., NY Mineralogical Club, NY Stereoscopic Soc., Soc. Neurosci., NY Inst. Humanities, Alpha Omega Alpha. Died Aug. 30, 2015.

SACULLES, VICTORIA OBEDENCIO, chemist; b. Manila, Philippines, Dec. 23, 1936; d. Casimiro Tangowan Obedencio and Victorina (Marzo) Obedencio; m. Teopilo Saculles, Feb. 27, 1965; children: Faith Ann, Jason Marc. BS in Chemistry, U. Philippines, 1957. Cert. tchr., Calif. Tchr. math. several colls., Philippines, 1957-65; chemist Santee Water Reclamation, Calif., 1969-71; World Environ. Systems, Santee, 1971-73; Teledyn-Ryan Aero, San Diego, 1974-83; sr. chemist, 1983-87; group engr., from 1988. Chemist, cons. Padre Dam Mcpl. Water Dist., Santee, 1972— Recipient Wastewater Cert., Am. Water and Wastewater Assn., 1970. Mem. Nat. Assn. Female Execs., Am. Water and Wasstwater Assn. Roman Catholic. Avocations: chess, sports, reading. Home: Santee, Calif. Died Jan. 30, 2007.

SADD, JOHN ROSWELL, plastic surgeon; b. Chgo., Apr. 18, 1933; s. Sumner Harry and Louise Elizabeth (Beardsley) S.; m. Valerie Crim Lavery; children: Elizabeth, Katherine, Virginia, Dorothy. BS, Purdue U., 1955; MD, U. Rochester, 1959. Diplomate Am. Bd. Plastic Surgery. Resident in plastic surgery U. Wis., 1959-67; attending suregon Toledo Hosp., from 1967, chmn. surgery, 1972-86, trustee. Asst. clin. prof. Med. Coll. Ohio, Toledo, 1972—; bd. dirs. P.I. E. Mus. Ins. Co., Cleve., pres. med. staff, 1989—; trustee Toledo Hosp., Promedica Health Care Systems, Vanguard Health Ins. Co. Contbr. articles to med. jours. Served to lt. USN, 1961-63. Fellow Am. Coll. Surgeons; mem. Am. Soc. Plastic and Reconstructive Surgeons, Ohio Valley Plastic Surgery Soc. Lodges: Rotary. Republican. Episcopalian. Avocations: trout fishing, golf. Home: Sanibel, Fla. Died Nov. 26, 2006.

SADDLER, DONALD EDWARD, choreographer, dancer; b. Van Nuys, Calif., Jan. 24, 1920; s. Elmer Edward and Mary Elizabeth (Roberts) Saddler. Student, Los Angeles City Coll., 1939; dance pupil of, Carmalita Maracci, Anton Dolin, Anthony Tudor, Madame Anderson Ivantzova. Mem. Ballet Theatre, NYC, 1940-43, 46-47; asst. dir., then artistic dir. Harkness Ballet, NYC, 1964-70. Exec. v.p. Rebekah Harkness Found., 1967—69; mem. exec. bd. Internat. Ballet Corp., 1979; prodr. Delacorte Theatre NY Dance Festival; guest artist Valerie Bettis Co. Dancer Grand Canyon Suite, 1937, High Button Shoes, 1947, Dance Me a Song, 1950, Bless You All, 1950, The Song of Norway, 1951, Winesburg, Ohio, 1958, The Golden Round, 1960, The Castle Period, 1961, Happy Birthday, Mr. Abbot!, 1987, with Ballet Theatre, NYC Bluebeard, Billy the Kid, Swan Lake, Aurora's Wedding, Les patineus, Lilac Garden, Gala Performance, Romeo and Juliet, Peter and the Wolf, Follies, 2001; dir.: (TV films) Holiday Hotel, 1950; choreographer theatre Blue Mountain Ballads, 1948, Wish You Were Here, 1952, Wonderful Town, 1952, John Murray Anderson's Almanac, 1953, Tobia la Candida Spia, 1954, La patrona di raddio di luna, 1955, Shangri-La, 1956, Buona notte Bettina, 1956, L'adorabile Giulio, 1957, Winesburg, Ohio, 1958, This Property is Condemned, 1958, Un trapezio per Lisistrata, 1958, When in Rome, 1959, Un manderino per Teo, 1959, Dreams of Glory, 1961, Milk and Honey, 1961, Sophie, 1963, Morning Sun, 1963, To Broadway, With Love, 1964, No, No, Nanette, 1971, Much Ado About Nothing, 1972, Fanfare Gala, 1973, Good News, 1973, Tricks, 1973, The Merry Wives of Windsor, 1974, Miss Moffat, 1974, A Midsummer Night's Dream, 1975, A Doll's House, 1975, A Gala Tribute to Joshua Logan, 1975, Rodgers and Hart, 1975, The Robber Bridegroom, 1975, 1976, Koshare, 1976, Vaudeville, 1976, Dear Friends and Gentle Hearts, 1976, Icedancing, 1978, The Grand Tour, 1979, A Long Way to Boston, 1979, Happy New Year, 1980, Hey Look Me Over!, 1981, Pardon, Monsieur Moliere, 1982, On Your Toes, 1983, The Loves of Anatol, 1985, The Golden Land, 1985, Broadway, 1987, The Student Prince, 1987, Teddy and Alice, 1987, My Fair Lady, 1993, tours The Boys from Syracuse, Aida, La Perichole, The Merry Widow, Tropicana, We Take This Town, 1962, Knickerbocker Holiday, 1971, No, No, Nanette, 1971—73, Good News, 1973—74, Hellzapoppin', 1976—77, On Your Toes, 1984, (films) April in Paris, 1952, By the Light of the Silvery Moon, 1953, Young at Heart, 1954, The Main Attraction, 1963, The Happy Hooker, 1973, Radio Days, 1987, (TV films) Holiday Hotel, 1950, (TV series) The Perry Como Show, 1950, Canozionissima, 1959—60, Bell Telephone Hour, 1961—64, (TV films) Much Ado About Nothing, 1973, (TV miniseries) Tony Award Broadcasts, 1973, 1975—78, 1983, Verna: U.S.O. Girl, 1978; dir., choreographer tour Oh, Kay!, 1978, dir., choreographer theatre Wonderful Town, 1955, A Celebration for Sir Anton Dolin, 1984, 100 Years of Performing Arts at the Met., 1984, Kiss Me Kate, 1989, Am. Ballet Theatre's 40th Anniversary, Tribute to Lucille Lortel, Tribute to Richard Rodgers, Merman-Martin Gala, Tribute to Cy Coleman, An Evening with Kurt Weill, Jo Sullivan in Concert, Tribute to George Abbott, Tribute to Lerner and Loewe, Stratford Shakespeare Festival Gala, Am. Guild of Musical Artists 100th Anniversary Gala, dir., choreographer operas Bitter Sweet, Weiner Blut, Abduction from the Seraglio, Washington Opera Follies; dir.(theatre): Berlin to Broadway with Kurt Weill, 1972, George Abbott...A Celebration, 1976, Life with Father, 1982, I Hear Music...of Frank Loesser and Friends, 1984, State Fair Music Hall, 1957, 1959, Carousel Theatre, 1958, Stratford Shakespeare Festival, 1979; prodr.(theatre): The Sol Hurok Birthday Gala, 1973, The 30th Anniversary of City Center Theatre, 1975, (with Martin Feinstein): The Pre-Inaugural Ballet-Opera Gala, 1981, : The Dance Collection Gala, 1972, The 35th Anniversary of the Am. Ballet Theatre, 1975, The Cynthia Gregory Gala. Recipient Dance Mag. award, 1984, Lifetime Achievement award, Theatre Development Fund, 2001, Living Legend of Dance award, Dance Libr. Israel, 2001, Capezio Dance award, 2006. Home: Englewood, NJ. Died Nov. 1, 2014.

SAETHER, KOLBJORN, structural engineer; b. Trondheim, Norway, July 16, 1925; s. Arne and Beatrice (Thommesen) S.; Barbara Saether; children: Eva, Erik, Linda. MS, Eidgenossische Technische Hochschule, Zurich, 1949. Registered profl. engr., Ill., Calif., Wis., Minn., Ind., Mich., Pa., Mo., Mass. With Norwegian Corps Engrs., 1949-50, Portland Cement Assn., 1955, Case Found. Co., 1956, Kolbjorn Saether & Assocs. Inc., Chgo., from 1956. Bd. dirs. Saether Industries, Inc. Author tech. publs. Patentee MCLS Lift-Slab System, Sky-Fork Loading Tool, C-Lock Air Supported Bldgs., Staircast Precast Stair System. Mem. ASCE, Norwegian Soc. Civil Engrs., Structural Engrs. Assn. Ill. (v.p.), Prestressed Concrete Inst., Am. Concrete Inst. Home: Northfield, Ill. Died May 3, 2007.

SAFFA, SHEILA MARIE MADDEN, marketing professional; b. Sherman, Tex., May 24, 1958; d. Fred Webster and Sarah Francis (Jenkins) Madden; m. Richard Eugene Saffa, Oct. 1, 1979. BS in Home Econs., Tex. Tech. U., 1979; MBA in Marketing, U. North Tex., 1989. Various positions, 1979-87; owner Doc's Daughter, Carrollton, Tex., from 1989. Mem. AAUW (v.p. programs 1991, 92-93, pres. 1994—). Home: Carrollton, Tex. Died Nov. 4, 2006.

SAGAWA, YONEO, horticulturist, educator; b. Olaa, Hawaii, Oct. 11, 1926; s. Chikatada and Mume (Kuno) S.; m. Masayo Yamamoto, May 24, 1962 (dec. Apr. 1988); children: Penelope Toshiko, Irene Teruko. AB, Washington U., St. Louis, 1950, MA, 1952; PhD, U. Conn., Storrs, 1956. Postdoctoral rsch. assoc. biology Brookhaven Nat. Lab., Upton, NY, 1955—57, guest in biology, 1958; asst. prof., then assoc. prof. U. Fla., 1957—64; dir. undergrad. sci. ednl. rsch. participation program NSF, 1964; cons. biosatellite project NASA, 1966—67; prof. horticulture U. Hawaii, 1964—2009; dir. Lyon Arboretum, 1967—91, dir. emeritus, from 2010; rschr. emeritus U. Hawaii, from 2010; assoc. dir. Hawaiian Sci. Fair, 1966—67, dir., 1967—68; rsch. assoc. in biology U. Calif., Berkeley, 1970—71; rsch. assoc. Bot. Rsch. Inst. of Tex., from 1993, Hawaii Tropical Bot. Garden, from 1995; external assessor U. Pertanian, Malaysia, from 1994; rsch. affiliate Bishop Mus., Honolulu, from 2007, assoc. sci., from 2010. Mem. Internat. Orchid Commn. on Classification, Nomenclature and Registration; fellow Inst. voor Toepassing van Atoomenergerie in de Landbouw, U. Agr., Wageningen, The Netherlands, 1979-80; mem. sci. adv. bd. Nat. Tropical Bot. Garden, Kauai, Hawaii; councilor Las Cruces Bot. Garden, Costa Rica; cons. FAO, Singapore, 1971, USAID-Agribus. Assistance Program, Vols. in Overseas Coop. Assistance, UN Devel. Program-UN Internat. Short Term Adv. Resources; dir. Hawaii Tropical Bot. Garden; hon. scientist Rural Devel. Adminstrn., Republic of Korea, 1998—; cons. Fiji-N.Z. Bus. Coun., 1996, 97, 98, 99, 2000; cons. IRETA, Samoa, 1997, 98, 2003, 06, 08; cons. Nat. Hort. Rsch. Inst., Suwon, Republic of Korea, 1998, 2000, UN FAO, Cook Island2007-09, cons., Tonga, 2011-13. Editor: Hawaii Orchid Jour., 1972-99, Pacific Orchid Soc. Bull., 1966-71; mem. editl. bd. Allertonia, 1976; mem. editl. adv. bd. Jour. Orchid Soc. India, 2002—; contbr. numerous articles to profl. jours. Trustee Friends of Honolulu Bot. Gardens, 1973-99. Recipient Disting. Svc. award South Fla. Orchid Soc., 1968, Grand prize for Poster, 1st Nagoya Internat. Orchid Show, 1990, Cert. of Achievement Garden Club Am., 1995, Digest Doer's Profile, 2000, Gold award Hawaii Orchid Growers Assn., 1996; grantee Am. Orchid Soc., Atomic Energy Commn., NIH, HEW, Inst. Mus. Svcs., Stanley Smith Hort. Trust, Honolulu Orchid Soc. Fellow Am. Orchid Soc. (hon. life, Achievement Gold medal 1999); mem. AAAS, Internat.

Assn. Hort. Sci., Hawn Bot. Soc. (past v.p.), Am. Anthurium Soc. (hon. life), Pacific Orchid Soc. (trustee 1994), Kaimuki Orchid Soc. (hon. life), Orchid Growers Hawaii (hon. life), Honolulu Orchid Soc. (hon., life), Lyon Arboretum Assn. (trustee 1974-91), Garden Club Honolulu (hon., life), Aloha Bonsai Club, Sigma Xi, Gamma Sigma Delta, Phi Kappa Phi (past pres., v.p., councillor U. Hawaii chpt.). Democrat. Home: San Diego, Calif. Deceased.

SAKS, GENE (JEAN MICHAEL SAKS), theater and film director, actor; b. NYC, Nov. 8, 1921; s. Morris and Beatrix (Leukowitz); m. Ms. Arthur (div.); children: Matthew, Daniel; m. Keren Ettlinger, 1980; 1 child, Annabelle. Grad., Cornell U. Began career as an actor off-Broadway at Provincetown Playhouse and the Cherry Lane Theatre; played in: Auden's Dog Beneath the Skin, E.E. Cummings' Him, Molière's The Bourgeois Gentilhomme; appeared on Broadway in Mr. Roberts, South Pacific, Middle of the Night, The Tenth Man, A Shot in the Dark, Love and Libel, A Thousand Clowns; debut as dir. on Broadway Enter Laughing, 1963; dir. stage plays Nobody Loves an Albatross, 1964, Half a Sixpence, 1964 (Tony nominee Best Dir. Musical), Generation, 1965, Mame, 1966 (Tony nominee Best Dir. Musical), Same Time, Next Year, 1975 (Tony nominee Best Dir. Play), California Suite, 1972, I Love My Wife (best dir. of Musical award Drama Desk, Tony), 1977, Brighton Beach Memoirs (best dir. award, Tony), 1983, Biloxi Blues (best dir. of play award, Tony), 1985, The Odd Couple (female version), 1985, Broadway Bound, 1986, A Month of Sundays, 1987, Rumors, 1988, Lost in Yonkers, 1991 (Tony nominee Best Dir., Outer Critics Cir. award), Jake's Women, 1992, Barrymore, 1997, Mr. Goldwyn, 2001, Remembering Tennessee, 2001; dir. films Barefoot in the Park, The Odd Couple, Cactus Flower, Last of the Red Hot Lovers, Mame, Brighton Beach Memoirs, A Fine Romance; dir. TV movie Bye, Bye Birdie, 1995; appeared in films including a Thousand Clowns, Prisoner of Second Aveneue, Lovesick, The One and Only, The Goodbye People, 1986, Nobody's Fool, 1994, IQ, 1994. Served with USN. Recipient George Abbott award for lifetime achievement in the theatre, 1990; elected to Theatre Hall of Fame, 1991. Mem. Stage Dirs. and Choreographers (pres.). Died Mar. 28, 2015.

SALIBI, BAHIJ SULAYMAN, neurosurgeon; b. Omdurman, Sudan, May 16, 1922; s. Sleiman Khalil and Salva Ibrahim (Salibi) S.; m. Margaret Elizabeth Beverley, May 16, 1954; children: Lillian Salwa, Charles Khalil, Ernest Kamal. BA, Am. U. Beirut, Lebanon, 1941; MA, 1944; postgrad., U. Mich., 1946; MD, Harvard, 1950. Diplomate Am. Bd. Neurol. Surgery. Intern pathology and clin. pathology Children's Hosp., Boston, 1950—51; intern surgery Barnes Hosp., St. Louis, 1951—52; asst. resident surgery, 1952—53; resident neurosurgery St. Lukes Hosp., Chgo., 1953—54, U. Ill. Neuropsychiat. Inst., Chgo., 1954—56; neurosurgeon Marshfield Clinic, Marshfield, Wis., 1958—86. Mem. staff St. Joseph's Hosp. Contbr. articles to profl. jours. Capt.1958 MC US Army, 1956. Fellow: ACS; mem.: AMA, Internat. Med. Soc. Paraplegia, Am. Assn. Neurol. Surgeons, Central Neurosurg. Soc. (pres. 1968—69), Wis. State Med. Soc. Democrat. Episcopalian. Achievements include invention of artery clamp. Home: North Vancouver, Canada. Died June 25, 2007.

SALTER, EDWIN CARROLL, retired pediatrician; b. Oklahoma City, Jan. 19, 1927; s. Leslie Ernest and Maud (Carroll) S.; m. Ellen Gertrude Malone, June 30, 1962; children: Mary Susanna, David Patrick BA, DePauw U., 1947; MD, Northwestern U., 1951. Intern Cook County Hosp., Chgo., 1951-53; resident in pediatrics Children's Meml. Hosp., Chgo., 1956-58, Cook County Hosp., Chgo., 1956-58; practice medicine specializing in pediatrics Lake Forest, Ill., 1958-97; attending physician Lake Forest Hosp., 1958—97, pres. med. staff, 1981-82. Attending physician Children's Meml. Hosp., Chgo.; clin. faculty mem. dept. pediatrics Northwestern U. Med. Sch. Served to capt. M.C., U.S. Army, 1954-56 Mem. AMA, Ill. State Med. Soc., Lake County Med. Soc. (pres. 1984), Phi Beta Kappa Republican. Methodist. Home: Lake Forest, Ill. Died Nov. 21, 2014.

SALTER, JAMES (JAMES HOROWITZ), writer; b. Passaic, NJ, June 10, 1925; s. L. George Horowitz and Mildred (Scheff); m. Ann Altemus, June 6, 1951 (div. 1976); children: Allan Conard, Nina Tobe, Claude Cray, James Owen; m. Kay Eldredge, 1998; 1 child, Theo Shaw. BS, USMA, 1945; M in Internat. Affairs, Georgetown U., 1950. Author: The Hunters, 1957, The Arm of Flesh, 1961, A Sport and a Pastime, 1967, Light Years, 1975, Solo Faces, 1981, Dusk and Other Stories, 1989 (Pen, Faulkner prize 1989), Burning the Days, 1997, Cassada, 2001, Gods of Tin: The Flying Years, 2004, Last Night, 2005, There and Then: The Travel Writing of James Salter, 2006, All That Is, 2013; Co-Author (with Kay Salter) Life is Meals, 2006, (with Robert Phelps) Memorable Days, 2010. Lt. Col. USAF, 1960. Recipient, Edith Wharton Prize, NY State Author, 1998, English Speaking Union Prize, Pen/West Prize, John Steinbeck Prize., Windham Campbell prize, 2013 Home: Aspen, Colo. Died June 19, 2015.

SALVADOR, VERNON WILLIAM, lawyer; b. Corcoran, Calif., May 25, 1941; s. Antonio Rocha Salvador and Adelaida Rosa Garcia; m. Marilyn Catherine Plevel, Dec. 20, 1964 (div. Feb. 1986); m. Elizabeth Jean Church, Feb. 14, 1998. BA, U. Calif., Berkeley, 1963; JD, U. Calif., San Francisco, 1966. BarL Calif. 1971, U.S. Ct. Appeals (9th cir.) 1971, N.M. 1980, U.S. Dist. Ct. N.M. 1980, U.S. Ct. Appeals (10th cir.) 1989, U.S. Supreme Ct. 1989. Atty. Legal Aide Soc., Oakland, Calif., 1970-75, Albuquerque, N.Mex., 1979-80; academic researcher Agores, Portugal, 1976-78; pvt. practice Albuquerque, from 1981. Photographer: (book) Festas Agoreanas, 1979; contbr. articles to profl. jours. Avocations: photography, history, philosophy. Home: Albuquerque, N.Mex. Died Feb. 13, 2007.

SALVESON, MELVIN ERWIN, management sciences corporation chief executive, educator; b. Brea, Calif., Jan. 16, 1919; s. John T. and Elizabeth (Green) S.; m. Joan Y. Stipek, Aug. 22, 1944; children: Eric C., Kent Erwin BS in Engring., U. Calif. Berkeley, 1941; MS, MIT, Cambridge, 1947; PhD, U. Chgo., 1952. Cons. McKinsey & Co., NYC, 1947—48; asst. prof., dir. Mgmt. Sci. Rsch. Project UCLA, 1948—54; mgr. advanced data sys., cons. strategic planning GE, Louisville and NYC, 1954—57; pres. Mgmt. Scis. Corp., LA, 1957—67; group v.p. Control Data/CEIR, Inc., 1967—68; pres. Electronic Currency Corp., from 1964; chmn. OneCard Internat., Inc., 1983—92, UniCard Sys. Inc., from 1992; founder Inst. Ops. Rsch. & Mgmt. Scis. (formerly Inst. Mgmt. Sci.). Bd. dirs. Diversified Earth Scis., Inc., Eco Rx Inc., Excel Enterprise Inc., Veritas et Justus Inc., Algeran, Inc., Electronic Currency Corp., So. Calif. Econ. Alliance, founder, pres., 1992-96; bd. dirs. Am. Soc. for Edn. and Econ. Devel., founding chair, 1996-98; exec. dir. Am. Found. for Edn. and Econ. Devel.; founder MasterCard Sys., LA, 1966; chmn. Corp. Strategies Internat.; prof. bus. Pepperdine U., founder mgmt. scis. curriculum, 1972-85; adj. prof. U. So. Calif., Webster U., U. Phoenix, 1972-2008; adviser data processing City of LA, 1962-64; futures forecasting IBM, 1957-61; adviser strategic sys. planning USAF, 1961-67; info. sys. Calif. Dept. Human Resources, 1972-73, City of LA Automated Urban Data Base, 1962-67; tech. transfer NASA, 1965-70; mem. bd. trustees, Long Beach City Coll., 1990-95 Contbr. 47 articles to profl. sci. jours. Served to lt. comdr. submarine engring. USN, 1941—46. Named to Long Beach City Coll. Hall of Fame; recipient Dist. Alumnus award Calif. Coll. Sys., 1992 Fellow: AAAS, Inst. Mgmt. Sci. (founder, past pres.), Inst. for Ops. Rsch. and Mgmt. Scis. (founder, fellow, pres. 1956—57); mem.: CSSP Alumnus, Calif. Yacht Club, Founders Club (LA Philharm. Orch.). Republican. Died Sept. 2, 2014.

SALWASSER, HAL (HAROLD J. SALWASSER), forest ecologist; b. Fresno, Calif., Aug. 4, 1945; s. Mervin James and Elizabeth Jean (Thonen) S.; m. Susan Louise Fite, July 12, 1969 (div. 1993); 1 child, James Barrett; m. Linda White Smith, May 28, 1994 (div. 1996); children: Ryan James Smith, Paul Gordon Smith. BA in Biology, Calif. State U., Fresno, 1971; PhD in Wildland Resource Sci., U. Calif., Berkeley, 1979. Cert. wildlife biologist. Rsch. assoc. U. Calif., Berkeley, 1976-79; regional wildlife ecologist US Forest Svc., San Francisco, 1979-82, nat. wildlife ecologist Washington, 1982-85, dep. dir. wildlife & fisheries, 1985-90, dir. new perspectives, 1990-92, regional forester northern region Missoula, Mont., 1995—97, Pacific Southwest rsch. station dir., 1997—2000; Boone & Crockett prof. wildlife conservation U. Mont., 1992-95; dean Oregon. State U. Sch. Forestry, Corvallis, 2000—12, prof. ecosystems & soc., 2012—14. Contbr. articles to profl. jours. With U.S. Army, 1965-68. Mem. Soc. American Foresters, Wildlife Soc. (v.p. 1991-92, pres.-elect 1992-93, pres. 1993-94), Ecol. Soc. America (bd. editors Ecol. Applications 1993-95), Soc. for Conservation Biology (bd. govs. 1985-91). Republican. Avocations: fishing, gardening, golf, hunting. Died Oct. 15, 2014.

SALZBERG, EMMETT RUSSELL, new product developer; b. NYC, Aug. 15, 1924; s. Herman and Freda (Russell) S.; m. Ilene Roslyn Greenhut, Oct. 29, 1960; children: Shelby Russell, Laurie Russell. Grad., Bronx High Sch. of Sci., 1941; student, Columbia U., CCNY. Pres. Dixey Tapes Corp., Stratford, Conn., 1969-85; sr. product mgr. Tuck Tape, New Rochelle, N.Y., 1986-88; pres. Dixey Tapes Corp., Stratford, from 1993. Cons. Tape divsn. Shuford Mills, Hickory, N.C., 1990-92. Patentee telephone answering equipment. Mem. Trumbull Yr.-Round. Edn. Feasibility Study Com.; bd. dirs. Trumbull Librs., 1997. Served with U.S. Army, 1943-45, PTO. Mem. Mensa (pres. So. Conn. chpt. 1996), Inventors Assn. Conn. (co-founder, past mem. exec. bd.). Democrat. Jewish. Avocations: target shooting, photography. Died July 17, 2007.

SAMPUGNA, JOSEPH, chemist, biochemist, educator; b. Brewster, NY, Sept. 27, 1931; s. Anthony and Angela (Agusta) S.; m. Dorothy J. Leduc, June 1, 1957; children: Joseph Anthony, Theresa Ann. BA, U. Conn., 1957, MA, 1962, PhD, 1968. Rsch. assoc. U. Conn., Storrs, 1961-68; asst. prof. U. Md., College Park, 1968-72, assoc. prof., from 1972, dir. undergrad. programs dept. chemistry and biochemistry, from 1995. Treas. Chem. Assn. of Md., University Park, 1980—. Author: Molecules in Living Systems, 1972, 78; contbr. articles to profl. jours. With USAF, 1951-55. Mem. Am. Oil Chem. Soc., Am. Chem. Soc., Am. Inst. Nutrition. Avocation: gardening. Home: Hyattsville, Md. Died Aug. 21, 2007.

SANDERS, CARL EDWARD, lawyer, former Governor of Georgia; b. Augusta, Ga., May 15, 1925; s. Carl T. and Roberta (Ailey) S.; m. Betty Bird Foy, 1947; children: Betty Foy, Carl E. Jr. LLB, Univ. Ga., 1947. Bar: Ga. 1947. Mem. Hammond, Kennedy & Sanders, Augusta, Ga., 1948—52; sr. mem. Sanders, Thurmond, Hester & Jolles, Augusta, Ga., Sanders, Hester, Holley, Ashmore & Boozer; chmn., mem. exec. com. Troutman Sanders LLP (formerly Troutman, Sanders, Lockerman & Ashmore), Atlanta, 1967—2006, chmn. emeritus, 2006—14; mem. Ga. House of Reps., 1954—56, Ga. State Senate, 1957—62, pres. pro tem, 1960—62; gov. State of Ga., Atlanta, 1963—67. Chmn., rules com. Dem. Nat. Conv., 1964; mem., exec. com. Nat. Gov. Conf., 1964—65; chmn. Appalachian Gov. Conf., 1964—65; vice chmn. Southern Gov. Conf., 1965—66; mem. Nat. Commn. on Urban Affairs, 1967; bd. dirs. Pub. Broadcasting Corp., 1968—70; chmn., fin. com. Dem. Party, Ga., 1974—83; bd. dirs. Healthdyne, 1986—96, Matria Healthcare, from 1996, Wachovia Atlanta Adv. Bank Bd.; mem. Atlanta Com., Olympic Games, 1996. Served to 1st lt. (first pilot of B-17 heavy bomber) USAF, WWII. Recipient Order of Sacred Treasure Gold and Silver award, Emperor and Govt. of Japan, 1989; named a Super Lawyer, Atlanta Mag., 2004. Mem.: ABA, Lawyers Club of Atlanta, Atlanta Bar Assn., Phi Delta Phi. Democrat. Achievements include being inducted into Athletic Hall of Fame, 1968, Aviation Hall of Fame, 1997. Died Nov. 16, 2014.

SANDERS, KAY MARIE, writer, editor; b. LaCrosse, Wis., Dec. 13, 1947; d. Ralph Edward and Rose Marie (Schaefer) S. BS, U. Wis., River Falls, 1970; MA, Drake U., 1982. Editor West Bend (Wis.) Co., 1970-72; copywriter advt. Houston Post, 1972-78; copywriter, promotion specialist Better Homes and Gardens, Meredith Corp., Des Moines, 1978-84; editor Better Homes and Gardens, Kitchen and Bath Ideas, Des Moines, 1984-93; dept. head spl. interest publs. Better Homes and Gardens, 1989-93; freelance writer, 1993-94; exec. editor Better Homes and Gardens Book div. Meredith Corp., 1994-95; freelance writer Des Moines, from 1995. Vol. Very Important Ptnrs., Polk County Juvenile Ct., Des Moines, 1991—. Avocations: photography, gardening. Home: Des Moines, Iowa. Died May 17, 2007.

SANDERS, MARLENE, news correspondent, journalism educator; b. Cleve., Jan. 10, 1931; d. Mac and Evelyn (Menitoff) Sanders; m. Jerome Toobin, May 27, 1958 (dec. Jan. 1984); children: Jeff, Mark. Student, Ohio State U., 1948—49. Writer, prodr. Sta. WNEW-TV, NYC, 1955-60, P.M. program Westinghouse Broadcasting Co., NYC, 1961-62; asst. dir. news and pub. affairs Sta. WNEW, NYC, 1962-64; anchor, news program ABC News, NYC, 1964-68, corr., 1968-72, documentary prodr., writer, anchor, 1972-76, v.p., dir. TV documentaries, 1976-78; corr. CBS News, NYC, 1978-87; host Currents Sta. WNET-TV, NYC, 1987-88; host Met. Week in Rev., 1988-90; host Thirteen Live Sta. WNET-TV, 1990-91; prof. dept. journalism NYU, NYC, 1991-93, adj. prof. journalism, 1996—2015; adj. prof. journalism, adminstr. Columbia U. Grad. Sch. Journalism, NYC, 1994-95. Profl.-in-residence Freedom Forum Media Studies Ctr., 1997-2000; freelance broadcaster, narrator; bd. dirs. womensenews.org.; chair RSVP, Inc., 1997-. Co-author: Waiting for Prime Time: The Women of Television News, 1988. Mem. NYC Commn. on Women's Issues, 2003—05. Recipient award NY State Broadcasters Assn., 1976, award Nat. Press Club, 1976, Emmy awards, 1980, 81, others. Mem. Am. Women in Radio and TV (Woman of Yr. award 1975, Silver Satellite award 1977), Women in Comm. (past pres.), Coun. Fgn. Rels. Home: New York, NY. Died July 14, 2015.

SANDERS, PHYLLIS MAY, musician; b. Cleve., Aug. 7, 1922; d. Charles Lester and Marjorie (Roof) Flick; m. Roger Fred Sanders, Aug. 3, 1946 (div. 1986); children: William Paul, Richard Allen, Bruce Edward, Patricia Ann. MusB in Edn., Drake U., Des Moines, 1944. Music tchr. Jefferson (Iowa) jr. high schs., 1944-45, Des Moines jr. high schs., 1945-46; organist, choir dir. Columbia U. Meth. Ch., Columbia Station, Ohio, 1963-83; organist Magyar United Ch. of Christ, Elyria, Ohio, from 1984. Dir. Lorain County Community Messiah Chorus, Elyria, 1981, 88-91; dir., founder Choraliers, Columbia Station, 1975-80, Olmsted Singers, Olmsted Falls, Ohio, 1975-80. Mem. Southwest Chorus, Berea, Ohio, 1988-90, Berea Sr. Ctr. Chorus, 1978—; pres. Columbia Rep. Women, Columbia Station; mem. Columbia Mothersingers, Cleve. Messiah Chorus, 1991—. Mem. Sigma Alpha Iota, Beta Gamma Kappa. Republican. Mem. Christian Ch. (Disciples Of Christ). Avocations: ceramics, needlecrafts. Home: Strongsville, Ohio. Deceased.

SANDLIN, FRED ALLEN, JR., personnel analyst; b. Ft. Benning, Ga., Aug. 24, 1952; s. Fred Allen Sr. and Grace Buren (Strahan) S.; m. Sara Virginia Scott, Oct. 19, 1985. BS, U. Montevallo, 1981. Cert. pub. pers. adminstr. Pers. analyst Pers. Bd. Jefferson County, Birmingham, Ala., 1986-90; pers. analyst II Washoe County Pers. Div., Reno, Nev., from 1990. Mem. Phi Kappa Phi. Avocations: running, weight training, hiking, photography, audio equipment. Home: Joplin, Mo. Died Nov. 20, 2006.

SANDMAN, ALAN GEORGE, sculptor; b. NYC, Nov. 1, 1947; s. Abraham and Helen Mae (Moffett) S.; divorced; 1 child, Rachel. Student, Valencia Community Coll., U. Fla., Santa Fe Community Coll. Sculptor Sandman Sculpture, Atlanta, from 1981; pub. Artlink, Atlanta, from 1989. Cons. in field. Featured in exhbn. catalogs Sculpture Tour, 1986, Sculpture to Touch, 1987. With USN, 1965-68. Exhbn. grantee Atlanta Bur. Cultural Affairs, 1979. Mem. Internat. Sculpture Ctr., On-Line Atlanta Soc., Atlanta Artworks Coalition (pres. 1980-82), Decatur Arts Alliance (co-founder 1987), Individual Visual Artists Coalition (co-founder 1991). Avocations: reading, film, crossword puzzles. Home: Atlanta, Ga. Died July 20, 2007.

SANDS, HARRY, psychologist, health administrator, researcher; b. NYC, Jan. 6, 1917; s. Morris and Lena Sandrowitz; m. Helene Purl, June 24, 1945; children: Jeffrey, Richard. AB, NYU, 1941, PhD in Psychology, 1952. Diplomate Am. Bd. Profl. Psychology; lic. psychologist, N.Y. Rsch. fellow dept neurology Neurol. Inst./Columbia U. Phys. and Surg., NYC, 1941-42, rsch. chief psychophysiologist Head Injury Project, 1942-44; assoc. dir., chief psychologist Baird Found. Clinic for Children with Epilepsy/Beth David Hosp., NYC, 1944-46; instr. Washington Sq. Coll./NYU, 1947-50, Bklyn. Coll., 1950-52; exec. dir. Com. Pub. Understanding of Epilepsy, NYC, 1952-53,

United Epilepsy Assn. Am., NYC, 1953-56; dir. and clin. psychologist Psychol. Lab., Inc., NYC, 1955-61; dir. Epilesy Asn. N.Y., Epilepsy Found. Am., NYC, 1956-68; dir. program planning and evaluation Epilepsy Found. Am., Washington, 1972-74; assoc. staff adult therapy clinic Postgrad. Ctr. for Mental Health, NYC, 1962-66, assoc. staff supervision therapeutic process, 1971-73, assoc. supr., sr. supr. psychoanalysis, psychotherapy, 1974—85, tng. analyst, pyschoanalysis, psychotherapy, 1993-98, exec. v.p., CEO, 1979—87, exec. dir., CEO, 1987—88. Pvt. practice pyschoanalysis and psychotherapy, N.Y.C., 1952-98; cons. divsn. resource devel. Nat. Inst. on Drug Abuse, Rockville, Md., 1978-79, Commn. for Control of Epilepsy and its Consequences, HEW, Washington, 1977, legal and protective svcs. project, Harvard U. Sch. of Pub. Health, Boston, 1974, cons. classification exceptional children, adequacy of classification for physically and sensorially handicapped, Vanderbilt U., Knoxville, 1974, bd. trustees, exec. com., 1988—; bd. dirs. Postgrad. Ctr. Residences, I, II, and III, N.Y.C., 1991-96, sec., 1991-2000, 2002—, pres. Editor: (book) Epilepsy: A Handbook for the Mental Health Professional, 1982 (Book of Yr. award ANA, 1982); co-author: (books) Epilepsy Fact Book, 1979, Education and Training Beyond the Doctoral Degree, 1995, Impact of Managed Care on Psychodynamic Treatment, 1996, The Guide to Pastoral Counseling and Care, 2000; contbr. chpts. in books, articles to profl. jours. Mem. tech. adv. com. on epilepsy N.Y. Dept Health, N.Y.C., 1945, planning com. advisory com on epilepsy, N.Y. State Dept. Mental Hygiene, Albany, 1952, joint legis. com. of State of N.Y. on program of pub. health, medicaid and compulsory health and hosp. ins., Albany, 1953; mem com. on Neurol. Disorders in Industry and com. on Emergency Med. Identification, AMA, Chgo., 1953, com. of info. svcs. and employment com., handicapped sect., Comty. Coun. of Greater N.Y., N.Y.C., 1954, joint legis. com. on mental retardation and physical handicaps, State of N.Y., Albany, 1956. Recipient fellowship Internat. Rehab. Rsch. Program of Social and Rehab. Svcs., HEW, Washington, 1972, Gold medal award for lifetime achievement in practice of psychology, Am. Psychol. Found., Washington, 1995; grantee Social Rehab. Svcs, HEW, Washington, 1968, 78. Fellow APA (bd. govs. coll. profl. practice 1994-99, co-chair nat. conf. on postdoctoral edn. and tng., Washington, 1992-94, bd. govs. coll. profl. practice, 1994-99, coun. reps. 1988-91, 1994, treas. com. for advancement profl. practice, practice directorate, 1992-94, cons. 1995, Karl F. Heiser Presdl. award 1993, Disting. Psychologist award Divsn. Psychotherapy 1995); mem. Am. Acad. Psychology, N.Y. State Psychol. Assn. (pres. 1978-79, 1985-86, coun. of reps. 1957-60, 1986-91, Allen J. Williams Jr. Meml. award 1993), Postgrad. Psychoanalytic Soc., Nat. Acad. of Practices (Disting. Practitioner in Psychology 1995), Psi Chi, Sigma Xi. Democrat. Jewish. Avocations: travel, theater, music, ballet. Died Jan. 3, 2007.

SANTINI, JAMES DAVID, Former United States Representative from Nevada; b. Reno, Aug. 13, 1937; m. Ann Marie Crane; children: David, Lisa, Kerrie, Lorie, Mark, James Danford. Attended, U. Nevada; JD, U. Calif., Hastings Coll., San Francisco. Former mem. Interior & Insular Affairs Com., Energy & Commerce Com., Select Com. on Aging; former ptnr. Jones, Bell, Close & Brown; mem., exec. com. Travel & Tourism Govt. Affairs Coun.; atty. at law; instr. U. Las Vegas, 1967—71; bd. mem. & chmn. Southern New Mus., 1968—74; lectr. Nat. Legal Aid & Defender Assn., 1968, Practicing Law Inst., 1968—70, Am. Acad. Jud. Edn., 1971—74, Nat. Coll. State Judiciary, 1973; owner & lectr. Nev. Bar Review, 1970—74; dep. dist. atty., Clark County Nev., 1968—69; dep. pub. defender to pub. defender, 1968—70; justice of peace, 1970—72; dist. ct. judge, Clark County, 1972—74; US rep. Nev., 1975—82; del. Dem. Nat. Conv., 1976; founder, apptd. mem., adv. bd. Travel & Tourism Caucus, chmn., 1979—82; commr. Nev. Commn. on Tourism, 1983—86; Washington DC rep. Nat. Tour Assn., 1983—2007; mem. Nat. Strategic Materials & Minerals Program Advisor Com., 1984, Nat. Coal Coun., 1985, America Indian Higher Edn. Bd., 1986; apptd. mem. & bd. trustee Inst. America Indian & Alaska Native Culture & Arts Devel., 1988—94; US house rep., 1988—98; mem. & bd. trustee Internat. Econ. Studies Inst. Served in US Army. Recipient Order of Merit of Italian Republic, 1972, Disting. County Svc. award, Nat. Assn. Counties, 1976, Outstanding Congl. Leadership award, 1978, Appreciation award, Travel & Tourism Advisor Coun., 1982, Aviation Leadership award, US Air Tour Assn., 1998; named Watchdog of Treas., Nat. Assn. Businessmen, 1977—80, Man of Yr., Copper Club, 1980, Travel Industry Assn. America, 1981, Man of Yr. in Travel, 1981, Guardian of Small Bus., Nat. Fedn. Ind. Bus. Mem.: Nev. Judges Assn. (pres. 1971). Democrat. Home: Potomac, Md. Died Sept. 22, 2015.

SAPINSLEY, LILA MANFIELD, retired state official; b. Chgo., Sept. 9, 1922; d. Jacob and Doris (Silverman) Manfield; m. John M. Sapinsley, Dec. 23,1 942; children: Jill Sapinsley Mooney, Carol Sapinsley Rubenstein, Joan Sapinsley Lewis, Patricia Sapinsley Levy. BA, Wellesley Coll., 1944; D in Pub. Svc., U. R.I., 1971; D in Pedagogy, R.I. Coll., 1973; LHD, Brown U., 1993. Mem. R.I. State Senate, 1972-84, minority leader, 1974-84; dir. R.I. Dept. Cmty. Affairs, 1985; chmn. R.I. Housing and Mortgage Fin. Corp., 1985-87; commr. R.I. Public Utilities Commn., 1987-93. Pres. bd. trustees Butler Hosp., 1978-84; trustee R.I. State Colls., 1965-70, chmn., 1967-70; trustee U. R.I., R.I. Coll. Found.; bd. dirs. Hamilton House, Trinity Repertory Co., Lincoln Sch., Wellesley Ctr. for Rsch. on Women, 1980, Providence Public Libr. Recipient Alumnae Achievement award Wellesley Coll., 1974, Outstanding Legislator of Yr. award Republican Nat. Legislators Assn., 1984. Republican. Jewish. Home: Providence, RI. Died Dec. 9, 2014.

SAPPER, RICHARD FRANK, industrial designer; b. Munich, May 30, 1932; m. Dorit Polz, 1963; children: Carola, Mathias, Cornelia. Student, U. Munich, 1952-56. Designer Mercedes-Benz, Stuttgart, 1956-57; free-lance designer in studio of Alberto Rosselli and Gio Ponti Milan, 1957-59; free-lance designer in studio of Marco Zanuso, 1959-75; ind. designer Stuttgart, 1970—2016. Design cons. Fiat and Pirelli cos., 1970-76, IBM, 1980—; co-founder Urban Transport Systems Study Group, Milan, 1972; prof. indsl. design Stuttgart Acad. Fine Arts, Vienna (Austria) Hochschule fur Angewandte Kunst, 1986—. Exhibited in group shows at Milan Triennale, 1968, 79, 86, Mus. Modern Art, N.Y.C., 1972, Stadtmuseum, Cologne, 1980, Phila. Mus. Art, 1983, Sala Vincon, Barcelona, 1988; represented in permanent collections Mus. Modern Art, N.Y.C., Phila. Mus. Art. Recipient Compasso d'Oro award, 1960, 62, 64, 67, 79, 86, Gute Form prize, 1969, 83, Premio SMAU, 1969, 81, 86, Gold medal Liubliana Indsl. Design Biennale, 1973, 79; named a hon. royal designer Royal Soc. Arts, 1988. Died Dec. 31, 2015.

SARGENT, JOSEPH DANIEL, film director; b. Jersey City, July 22, 1925; s. Domenico and Maria (Noviello) Sargente; m. Carolyn Nelson, Nov. 22, 1970; children from previous marriage: Athena, Lia. Student in Theatre Arts, New Sch. for Social Rsch., 1946—49. Pres. Joseph Sargent Prodns. Inc. Dir.: (films) Street-Fighter, 1959, The Spy in the Green Hat, 1966, One Spy Too Many, 1966, The Hell with Heroes, 1968, Colossus: The Forbin Project, 1970, The Man, 1972, White Lightning, 1973, The Taking of Pelham One Two Three, 1974 (Best Dir. award San Sebastian Film Festival), MacArthur, 1977, Goldengirl, 1979, Coast to Coast, 1980, Nightmares, 1983, Jaws: The Revenge, 1987; (TV films) The Sunshine Patriot, 1968, The Immortal, 1969, Tribes, 1970 (Outstanding Directorial Achievement award Dirs. Guild Am.), Maybe I'll Come Home in the Spring, 1971, Longstreet, 1971, Man on a String, 1972, The Marcus-Nelson Murders, 1973 (Emmy award, Dirs. Guild Am. award), The Man Who Died Twice, 1973, Wheeler and Murdoch, 1973, Sunshine, 1973, Hustling, 1975, Friendly Persuasion, 1975, The Night That Panicked America, 1975, Amber Waves, 1980, Freedom, 1981, Tomorrow's Child, 1982, Memorial Day, 1983, Choices of the Heart, 1983, Terrible Joe Moran, 1984, Sunday Night Live, 1984, Love Is Never Silent, 1985 (Emmy award), Passion Flower, 1986, The Must Be A Pony, 1986, Of Pure Blood, 1986, The Karen Carpenter Story, 1989, Day One, 1989, The Incident, 1990, Miss Rose White, 1992, Somebody's Daughter, 1992, Skylark, 1993, Abraham, 1994, World War II: When Lions Roared, 1994, My Antonia, 1995, Mandela and de Klerk, 1997, Miss Evers' Boys, 1997, The Long Island Incident, 1998, The Wall, 1998, Crime and Punishment, 1998, A Lesson Before Dying, 1999, Vola Sciusciu, 2000, For Love or Country, 2000, Bojangles, 2001, Out of the Ashes, 2003, Something the Lord Made, 2004, Warm Springs, 2005 (Outstanding Directorial Achievement in Movies for TV Dirs. Guild Am., 2005), Sybil, 2007, Sweet Nothing in My Ear, 2008; (TV series) Gunsmoke, 1962—65, The Man From UNCLE, 1964, The Girl From UNCLE, 1966, Star Trek, 1966, Gallegher Goes West, 1966, The Invaders, 1967, Garrison's Gorillas, 1967, It Takes A Thief, 1968, The Manions of America, 1981, Space, 1985, Streets of Laredo, 1995, Salem Witch Trials, 2002; dir. & actor (TV films) Caroline?, 1990, Ivory Hunters, 1990, The Love She Sought, 1990. With US Army, 1943—46. Mem.: Actors Equity Assn., AFTRA, Screen Actors Guild, Directors Guild America. Home: Malibu, Calif. Died Dec. 22, 2014.

SARKOWSKY, HERMAN, real estate developer, retired professional sports team executive; b. Gera, Germany, June 9, 1925; arrived in US, 1934; m. Faye Sarkowsky; children: Steven, Cathy. BA, U. Wash., 1949. Co-owner Portland Trail Blazers, 1970—75, Seattle Seahawks, 1976—88; chmn. bd. Seattle Art Mus. Bd. dirs. Synetic, 1989—2000, EggHead Inc., 1984—93, WebMD Health Corp., 2009—14, Power Efficiency Corp., 2010—12. Mem.: Nat. Assn. Home Builders (life). Jewish. Died Nov. 2, 2014.

SARNER, HARVEY, lawyer; b. NYC, Feb. 13, 1934; s. Michael and Lillian (Greenblatt) S.; m. Lorisanne C. Jelle, June 9, 1956; children: Kyra, Surah. BS, U. Minn., 1958, LLB, 1959. Atty., advisor Fed. Communications Commn., Washington, 1959-61; assoc. ho. counsel Am. Dental Assn., Chgo., 1961-71; atty. Sarner and Assocs., Chgo., 1971-87. Author: Dental Jurisprudence, 1968, Herman Wouk Checklist, 1994; editor SAA Dr.'s newsletter, 1972-87. Bd. dirs. Jewish Found. for Christian Rescuers, 1985—, Temple Isiah, Palm Springs, 1994—. With USN, 1951-55. Recipient Polish Pres. medal Polish Govt., 1994, Humanitarian award Am. Soc. Oral Surgeons, San Diego, 1993. Jewish. Avocation: book and antiquities collecting. Home: Palm Springs, Calif. Died Feb. 19, 2007.

SARVELA, PAUL D., academic administrator; b. 1959; BA in Psychology, U. Mich., 1981, MS in Ednl. Psychology, 1983, PhD in Health Edn., 1984. With Ford Aerospace & Comm. Corp., 1984—86; from asst. prof. to prof. health edn., family and cmty. medicine U. Ill., Carbondale, Ill., 1986—92, prof. health edn., family & cmty. medicine, 1992—2014, chmn. Dept. Health Care Professions, 1999—2014, interim dean Coll. Applied Sciences & Arts, 2002—14; interim chancellor Northern Ariz. U., 2014. Dir. Ctr. Rural Health and Social Svc. Devel., 1993—2000; cons. in field. Contbr. numerou articles to jours. in field. Mem.: American Coun. Edn., American Coll. Healthcare Executives, American Acad. Health Behavior. Died Nov. 9, 2014.

SATA, MICHAEL CHILUFYA, President of Zambia; b. Mpika, Northern Rhodesia, July 6, 1937; m. Christine Kaseba; 8 children. Sweeper; police officer; mem. United Nat Ind. Party, ward chmn.; MP, Kabwata constituency Zambian Gen. Assembly; dist. gov. City of Lusaka, Zambia; min. state Govt. of Zambia; chmn. local govt. Movement for Multi-party Democracy, nat. sec., 1995—2001; min. local govt. Govt. Zambia, 1991—93, min. labour and social services, 1993—94, min. health, 1994—95, min. without portfolio, 1996—2001; founder, sec. gen. Patriotic Front, Zambia, from 2001, presdl. candidate, 2001, 2006, 2008, 2011; pres. Republic of Zambia, Lusaka, 2011—14. Patriotic Front Party. Died Oct. 28, 2014.

SAUNDERS, FLIP (PHILIP DANIEL SAUNDERS), professional sports team executive, former professional basketball coach; b. Cleve., Feb. 23, 1955; m. Deborah K. Saunders; children: Ryan, Mindy, Rachel, Kimberly Attended, U. Minn. Asst. coach U. Minn. Golden Gophers, 1981—86, U. Tulsa Golden Hurricane, 1986-88; head coach Rapid City Thrillers, Continental Basketball Assn., SD, 1988-89, La Crosse Catbirds, Continental Basketball Assn., Wis., 1989-94, gen. mgr., 1991-93, team pres., 1991-94; head coach Sioux Falls Skyforce, Continental Basketball Assn., SD; gen. mgr., head coach Minn. Timberwolves, 1995—2005, pres. basketball ops., 2013—15, head coach, part owner, 2014—15; head coach Detroit Pistons, 2005—08, Washington Wizards, 2009—12; adv. Boston Celtics, 2012—13. Head coach US Men's Basketball Team Goodwill Games (gold medal), Brisbane, Australia, 2001. Named Continental Basketball Assn. Coach of Yr., 1990, 92. Achievements include head coach of the Continental Basketball Association championship winning La Crosse Catbirds, 1990, 1992. Home: Hamel, Minn. Died Oct. 25, 2015.

SAUNDERS, NORMAN BICKHAM, energy efficiency consultant; b. Cin., Jan. 26, 1916; s. Henery Thomas and Harriet (Seavey) S.; m. Jeanne Roberta Ott, Apr. 12, 1941; children: E.W., Laurence Robert, Holly Weiss, Heather Star. Student, U. Cin., 1933-41. Registered profl. engr., Mass. With Saunders & Co., Chgo., 1939-43, Harvard Underwater Sound Lab., Boston, 1943-51; field engr., mfrs. rep., proprietor Saunders & Co., 1955-68; cons. circuit engring., from 1954. With R&D, Harvard Underwater Sound Lab., Submarine Signal, Ray Theon, Am. Machine and Foundry, Baird Atomic. Contbr. articles to profl. jours.; 20 patents issued relating to solar energy use. Chmn. Bd. Assessors, Weston, Mass., 1991-97; founder Sundry Orgns. for energy efficiencies, 1950—; clk. Kendal Common Corp., Weston, 1965-95. Mem. IEEE, Am. Phys. Soc., Assn. for Computing Machinery, New England Solar Energy Assn., Sigma Xi, Tau Beta Pi, Sigma Pi Sigma. Avocation: gardening. Died Jan. 5, 2007.

SAUNIER, M(ERVIN) KENNETH, financial consultant; b. Fort Morgan, Colo., Mar. 19, 1934; s. Paul C. and Irene (Hizel) S.; m. Maudine Frazier, June 2, 1957; children: Jon Paul, Jeffrey Kenneth, Jason Blake. BA, N.Mex. State U., 1957; BDiv, Southwestern Sem., 1966. With Peace Corp.t-ments, Inc., Washington, 1971-72; asst. to dir. domestic ops. Peace Corp., Washington, 1970-72; v.p. devel. Dag Hammarskjöld Coll., Columbia, Md., 1972-74; chief div. exec. manpower U.S. Dept. Interior, Washington, 1974-78; dean summer sch., dir. planning and devel. Am. U., Cairo, 1978-83; co-founder Am. Bus. Network, Ft. Worth, from 1991. Pres. Aradi Investments, Inc., Ft. Worth, 1983—. Author: What Do I Do Now?, 1992. India desk officer, chief staff recruitment U.S. Peace Corps, Washington, 1970-71, dir. cen. region, India, 1966-70; campus min. U. Tex., 1962-66, Arlington, 1960-62; bd. dirs. Community Assn., Columbia, 1975; pres. Polycultural Inst., Washington, 1975-76; bd. dirs. Cairo (Egypt) Am. Coll., 1981-83. Named one of Outstanding Young Men Am., Jr. C. of C., 1970. Avocations: hiking, fishing, reading. Died Apr. 20, 2007.

SAVAGE, GUS (AUGUSTUS SAVAGE), former congressman; b. Detroit, Oct. 30, 1925; s. Thomas Frederick and Molly (Wilder) S.; m. Eunice King, Aug. 4, 1946 (dec. Feb. 1981); children: Thomas James, Emma Mae Savage-Davis. BA, postgrad., Roosevelt U., 1951, Chgo.-Kent Coll. Law, 1952-53. Editor Am. Negro mag., Chgo., 1954, Woodlawn Booster newspaper, Chgo., 1961-64, The Bulletin, Chgo., 1963-64; asst. editor Ill. Beverage Jour., Chgo., 1955-57; editor, pub. Westside Booster newspaper, Chgo., 1958-60, Citizen newspapers, Chgo., 1965-79, The Chgo. Weekend newspaper, 1973-79; mem. from Ill. Dist. 2 US House of Representatives, 1981—93. Author: (pamphlets) How to Increase the Power of the Negro Vote, 1959, Political Power, 1969. Active civil rights leader; a founder, campaign mgr. Chgo. League Negro Voters, 1958-59; founder, chmn. Protest at the Polls, 1963-64; pres. Orgn. S.W. Communities, 1968-69; founder, 1st chmn. Chgo. Black Pubs. Assn., 1970. Served with USAAF, 1943-46. Named Ind. Journalist of Year Washington Park Improvement Assn., 1965; recipient medal of merit City of Chgo., 1976; award of merit Operation PUSH, 1976; Businessman of Year award Dollars and Sense mag., 1978; Freshman of Year award NAACP, Evanston, Ill., 1981; Presdl. award Cook County Bar Assn., 1981 Home: Chicago, Ill. Died Oct. 31, 2015.

SAVASTANO, EDITH L., critical care nurse; b. New Haven, Jan. 23, 1944; d. Arthur E. and Alice J. (Hannon) S. Diploma, Quincy City Hosp., 1967; postgrad., Bridgewater State Coll., Northeastern U. Staff nurse Quincy (Mass.) City Hosp.; night charge nurse surg. ICU Univ. Hosp., Boston, night charge nurse emergency room. Mem. ANA, Mass. Nurses Assn., Emergency Nurses Assn., Emergency Nurses to Cancel Alcohol-Related Emergencies. Home: Duxbury, Mass. Died Apr. 22, 2007.

SAXONHOUSE, GARY ROGER, economics professor; b. NYC, June 21, 1943; s. Ernest George and Amy (Zweig) S.; m. Arlene Warmbrunn, June 28, 1964; children: Lilly Adaela, Noam Hans, Elena Kathryn. BA, Yale U., 1964, MA, 1966, MPhil, 1968, PhD, 1971. Acting instr. Yale U., New Haven, 1969-70; lectr. U. Mich., Ann Arbor, 1970-71, asst. prof. econs., 1971-75, assoc. prof., 1975-80, prof., from 1980, dir. Commn. on Comparative-Hist. Rsch. on Market Economies, from 1980. Vis. lectr. Harvard U., Cambridge, Mass., 1975; Henry Luce prof. comparative devel. Brown U., Providence, 1980-81; fellow Ctr. Advanced Study in Behavioral Sci., Stanford, Calif., 1984-85, 95-96, 2000; vis. fellow Ctr. Internat. Studies, Princeton U., 2002-03; cons. Coun. Econ. Advisers, Washington, 1989-90; disting. lectr. Assn. for Asian Studies, 1979; mem. adv. bd. Found. Advanced Info.and Rsch., Tokyo, 1987—, Inst. Fiscal and Monetary Policy, Tokyo, Japanese Ministry Fin., Tokyo, 1987—, Rsch. Inst. Internat. Trade and Industry, Tokyo, 1988-98, Japan Found., Tokyo, 1988-98. Author: Comparative Technology Choice, 1988; editor Technique, Spirit and Form in the Making of Modern Economies, 1984, Law and Trade Issues of the Japanese Economy, 1986, Development, Duality and the International Economic Regime, 1999, Finance, Governance and Competiveness, 2000, Japan's Lost Decade, 2004; contbr. articles to profl. jours. Adv. panel on Am. competitiveness Office Tech. Assessment, U.S. Congress, Washington, 1981-82, adv. panel on civilian uses space. 1984-85. Grantee NSF, 1979-81, 84-86, Ford Found., 1981-83; fellow NEH, 2005—, John Simon Guggenheim Meml. Found., 2005— Mem. Am. Econ. Assn., Econ. History Assn. (nominating com. 1988-90, editl. bd. 1990-94, internat. exch. com. 2001-04), Com. on Japanese Econ. Studies (chmn. 1977—) Home: Ann Arbor, Mich. Died Nov. 30, 2006.

SCAASI, ARNOLD MARTIN (ARNOLD ISAACS), fashion designer; b. Montreal, Que., Can., May 8, 1930; came to U.S., 1955; s. Samuel and Elizabeth (Seigler) Isaacs. Student, Cotnoir Capponi Sch. Haute Design, Montreal, 1953, Chambre Syndicale de la Haute Couture Parisienne, Paris, 1954. Apprentice House of Paquin, Paris, 1954; asst. Charles James, NYC, 1955; pres. Arnold Scaasi, Inc., NYC, 1957—2015. Founder made-to-order couture house, 1964-2015; founder Scaasi Boutique, N.Y.C., 1984-2015, Scaasi Sleepware for Warnco, 1991, Scaasi Dress, 1992, Scaasi Accessories for Mark Cross, Scaasi Bride, 1988, Fragrance: Scaasi, 1989, Scaasi Furs for Mohl, Scaasi Mens Suits for Marcraft, Arnold Scaasi for QVC, Scaasi Neckwear, Scaasi Patterns for Vogue, Scaasi Intimate Wear for Exquisite Form, Scaasi Sportswear for Dann Kenney; designer to First Ladies Mamie Eisenhower, Barbara Bush, Hilary Rodham Clinton, and Laura Bush; designer to actresses Joan Crawford, Barbra Streisand, Lauren Bacall, Elizabeth Taylor, Joan Rivers, Diahann Carroll, Catherine Deneuve and Mary Tyler Moore Author: (memoir) Women I Have Dressed (and Undressed!), 2004. Recipient Winnie award City Fashion Critics (also known as Coty American Fashion Critics' award), 1958, Today award NBC TV, 1959, Nieman-Marcus award, 1959, Chgo. Gold Coast Fashion award, 1961, Coun. Fashion Designers award, 1987, Design award Pratt Inst., Spl. award for excellence Coun. Fashion Designers of Am., 1988, Fashion Excellence award Dallas Jr. Apparel Mart, 1992, Lifetime Achievement award, Council of Fashion Designers of America, 1996 Home: New York, NY. Died Aug. 4, 2015.

SCALETTA, HELEN MARGUERITE, volunteer; b. Sioux City, Iowa, Apr. 13, 1927; d. Ralph J. and Ruth Cora (Coyle) Beedle; m. Phillip Jasper Scaletta, May 21(dec. Apr. 24, 2014), 1946; children: Phillip Ralph, Cheryl Diane Kesler. AA in Bus., Edwards Coll. Bus., Sioux City, 1946. Acct. Towners Dept. Store, Iowa City, 1947—48; legal sec. Phillip Scaletta, Sioux City, 1950—74; svc. chmn. Easter Seal Soc., Lafayette, Ind., 1970—88; rec. sec. Home Hosp. Aux., Lafayette, 1989. Danced in Civic Theatre Follies, 1962. Orch. mem. June's All-Girl Ensemble, 1943-50. Pres. Newcomers club YWCA, Lafayette, 1967-68, mem. chmn., bd. dirs., 1979; leader Girl Scouts Am., Ft. Wayne, Ind., 1960-63; chmn. Mental Health Inc., Ft. Wayne, 1960-61, Cancer Crusade, West Lafayette, 1973-74; precinct worker Rep. Cen. Com., West Lafayette, 1974-76; Nat. Missions sec. 1st Presbyn. Ch., 1957. Recipient Citation Easter Seal Soc., 1981, Ernestine Duncan Collins Pearl Ct. award Sigma Kappa, 1997. Mem. Purdue U. Women's Club (pres. 1973-74), Lafayette Country Club (golf chmn. 1971, 90, bowling pres. 1992-93, golf co-chair Battleground 9-hole group 1996), Purdue Women's Bowling League (treas. 1978-79), Cosmopolitan Club, YWCA (Diamond award, 2005), Sigma Kappa (corp. bd., sec., treas. 1971-99), Kappa Kappa Sigma (pres. 1972), Sigma Kappa Lafayette Alumnae (pres. 1970, 1988-93, Ernestine Duncan Collins Pearl Court award 1997). Avocations: collecting dolls, bowling, golf, sports. Home: West Lafayette, Ind. Died Apr. 28, 2014.

SCALIA, ANTONIN GREGORY, United States Supreme Court Justice; b. Trenton, NJ, Mar. 11, 1936; s. Salvatore Eugene and Catherine Louise (Panaro) Scalia; m. Maureen McCarthy, Sept. 10, 1960; children: Ann Forrest, Eugene, John Francis, Catherine Elisabeth, Mary Clare, Paul David, Matthew, Christopher James, Margaret Jane. AB, Georgetown U., 1957; student, U. Fribourg, Switzerland, 1955—56; LLB, Harvard U., 1960. Bar: Ohio 1962, Va. 1970. Assoc. Jones Day Cockley & Reavis, Cleve., 1961—67; assoc. prof. U. Va. Law Sch., 1967—70, prof., 1970—74; gen. counsel Office Telecommunications Policy, Exec. Office of Pres., 1971—72; chmn. Adminstrv. Conf. US, Washington, 1972—74; asst. atty. gen. Office Legal Counsel US Dept. Justice, Washington, 1974—77; prof. law U. Chgo., 1977—82; judge US Ct. Appeals (DC circuit), 1982—86; assoc. justice US Supreme Ct., Washington, 1986—2016. Vis. prof. Georgetown Law Ctr., 1977, Stanford Law Sch., 1980—81; resident scholar American Enterprise Inst. (AEI), 1977. Editor: Regulation mag., 1979—82; author: A Matter of Interpretation: Federal Courts and the Law, 1998; co-author (with Bryan A. Garner): Making Your Case: The Art of Persuading Judges, 2008, Reading Law: The Interpretation of Legal Texts, 2012. Sheldon fellow, Harvard U., 1960—61. Mem.: Va. Bar Assn., Ohio Bar Assn. Republican. Catholic. Died Feb. 13, 2016.

SCARF, HERBERT ELI, economics educator; b. July 25, 1930; s. Louis H. and Lena (Elkman) W.; m. Margaret Klein, June 28, 1953; children: Martha Anne Samuelson, Elizabeth Joan Stone, Susan Margaret Merrell. AB, Temple U., 1951; MA, Princeton U., 1952, PhD, 1954; LHD (hon.), U. Chgo., 1978. With RAND Corp., Santa Monica, Calif., 1954-57; asst., assoc. prof. stats. Stanford U., Calif., 1957-63; prof. econs. Yale U., New Haven, 1963-70, Stanley Resor prof. econs., 1970-78, Sterling prof. economics, 1979—2015. Vis. assoc. prof. Yale U., New Haven, 1959-60; dir. Cowles Found. Rsch. in Econs., Yale U., 1967-71, 1981-84, divsn. social sciences, 1971-72, 1973-74. Author: Studies in the Mathematical Theory of Inventory and Production, 1958, Computation of Economic Equilibria, 1973; editor: Applied General Equilibrium Analysis, 1984. Recipient Lanchester prize Ops. Rsch. Soc. Am., 1974, Von Neumann medal, 1983; named Disting. fellow Am. Econ. Assn., 1991. Fellow: INFORMS, Econometric Soc. (pres. 1983); mem.: NAS, Am. Philos. Soc., Am. Acad. Arts and Scis. Democrat. Jewish. Home: Hamden, Conn. Died Nov. 15, 2015.

SCHAAP, WILLIAM HERMAN, journalist, lawyer; b. NYC, Mar. 1, 1940; s. Maurice William and Leah (Lerner) S.; m. Jill Gerson, Apr. 10, 1964 (div. 1973); m. Ellen Ray, Dec. 1, 1974 (dec. 2015) BA, Cornell U., 1961; JD, U. Chgo., 1964. Bar: N.Y. 1964, D.C. 1977. Pvt. practice, NYC, 1964-72; lawyer Asia Mil. Law Project, Okinawa, Japan, 1972-73, Lawyers Mil. Def. Commn., Heidelberg, Fed. Republic Germany, 1973-74, Ctr. for Constl. Rights, NYC, 1975-76, 81; ptnr. Van Lierop, Burns & Schaap, LLP, NYC, from 1994; editor-in-chief Mil. Law Reporter, Washington, 1976-81; co-founder, co-editor Covert Action Info. Bull., Washington, 1978—2016; co-founder, dir. Sheridan Square Press, NYC, 1981—2016; dir. Inst. for Media Analysis, NYC, 1986—2016. Adj. prof. John Jay Coll., CUNY, N.Y.C., 1987, 88; expert witness U.S. and fgn. courts. Editor: (with others) The CIA in Western Europe, 1978, The CIA in Africa, 1980; mng. editor: Lies of Our Times, 1989-2016; editor numerous books; contbr. articles to profl. jours. and publs. Mem. Nat. Lawyers Guild (pres. D.C. chpt. 1978-79), Internat. Orgn. of Journalists. Democrat. Avocation: stamp collecting/philately. Home: New York, NY. Died Feb. 25, 2016.

SCHALL, STEWART ALLAN, pediatric cardiologist; b. Bklyn., Aug. 13, 1938; s. Jack and Ruth Schall; m. Beatrice Oritsky, Aug. 4, 1971; 1 child, Rachel. BA, Rutgers U., 1960; MD, U. Pa., 1964. Diplomate Am. Bd. Pediats., subspecialty pediat. cardiology. Intern in pediats. Bronx Mcpl. Hosp. Ctr., Albert Einstein Sch. Medicine, 1964-65, jr., sr. resident, 1965-67; fellow Cardiovascular Rsch. Inst. U. Calif. Sch. Medicine, San Francisco, 1969-71; vis. pediat. cardiologist San Francisco Children's Hosp., 1971-72; cons. pediatrician Watts Hosp., Durham, N.C., 1973-76; cons. pediat. cardiologist Wake Meml. Hosp., Raleigh, N.C., 1973-85; attending pediat. cardiologist U. N.C. Hosps., Raleigh, from 1972; attending pediatrician, pediat. cardiologist Moses H. Cone Meml. Hosp., Greensboro, N.C., from 1985; attending pediat. cardiologist Women's Hosp., Greensboro, from 1990; cons. pediat. cardiologist Wesley Long Cmty. Hosp., Greensboro, from 1991. Asst. prof. pediats, U. N.C., 1972-78, assoc. prof., 1978-97, prof., 1997—; mem. pediat. tchg. svc. Moses H. Cone Meml. Hosp., Greensboro, 1985—. Contbr. articles to profl. jours. Fellow Am. Acad. Pediats., Am. Coll. Cardiology; mem. Southeastern Pediat. Cardiology Assn., N.C. Pediat. Soc., N.C. Heart Assn. (bd. dirs. Greensboro divsn.), N.C. Med. Soc., Guilford County Med. Soc. Avocations: travel, wine tasting and collecting, photography. Home: Greensboro, NC. Died May 6, 2007.

SCHANK, BERNARD LYNN, advertising executive; b. Bklyn., Mar. 4, 1921; s. Harry and Esther (Furman) S.; m. Virginia Mary Mangano, Mar. 21, 1952; children: Gary Lynn, Roy Martin, Derrilyn Noelle. BS, Bklyn. Coll., 1946; MS, Yale U., 1947. Pres., chief exec. officer Schank Advt., Inc., NYC, 1948-67, Bernard Schank Assocs., Inc., NYC, 1967-83; cons. Exec. Airport, Ft. Lauderdale, Fla., 1985-87; cons. in advt. Ft. Lauderdale, from 1983. Prof. comm./photography N.Y. Inst. Tech., 1968-75; guest lectr. comm./pub. rels. Dowling Coll., L.I., 1976; active arts and culture coun. City of Lauderhill, Fla. Author: 55-Love: Doubles Strategy for Seniors; contbr. articles/photographs to various tennis mags. Capt. USAAF, 1943-46; ETO. Decorated Air Medal, D.F.C., Presdl. Citation. Avocations: flying, tennis, photography, harmonica. Died Aug. 8, 2007.

SCHAPIRO, DONALD, lawyer; b. NYC, Aug. 8, 1925; s. John Max and Lydia (Chaitkin) S.; m. Ruth Ellen Goldman, June 29, 1952 (dec. Aug. 1991); m. Linda N. Solomon, Oct. 10, 1993; children: Jane G., Robert A. AB, Yale U., 1944, LL.B., 1949. Bar: N.Y. 1949. Assoc. Paul, Weiss, Rifkind, Wharton & Garrison, NYC, 1949-51; asst. chief counsel subcom. ways and means com. on adminstrn. revenue laws US House of Representatives, Washington, 1951-52; assoc. Barrett, Smith, Schapiro, Simon & Armstrong, NYC, 1952-55, partner, 1955-88; ptnr. Chadbourne & Parke, from 1988. Vis. lectr. law Yale U. Law Sch., 1949-78, 94-95, instr. law and econs., 1945-49. Mem. Order of Coif, Phi Beta Kappa, Phi Delta Phi. Home: New York, NY. Died July 2014.

SCHAPIRO, HERB (HERBERT ELLIOTT SCHAPIRO), playwright, educator; b. Bklyn., Jan. 20, 1929; s. Irving & Julie (Neshick) S.; div.; 1 child, Mark Andrew. BA, NYU, 1952, MA, 1956, postgrad., 1968. Instr., prof. English CUNY, Mercer Coll., Rutgers U., 1961-72; project mem. Writer-in-the Schools Project NEA-Arts Council, 1974-78; dir. Prisons and Schools Equity Tour, The Me Nobody Knows, 1973. Author: (musical plays) The Me Nobody Knows, 1970 (Tony nominee for adaption 1970-71), Teddy, 1975, Leading Lady, 1976, Don't Cry, Child, Your Father's in America, 1977-78, (plays) A Little Something Before You Go, 1962 (Stanley drama award), Kid Stuff, 1978, Alinsky and the All-Americans, 1981-82, rev., 1989, Wallenberg, 1985, Opportunities, 1986 (for Nat. Urban League); (with composer Ulf Bjorlin) A Wallenberg Portrait, 1989; (with composer Hale Smith) TraLaLa Lamia, 1991; (with composer Gary William Friedman) Bring in the Morning, 1993; (TV projects) Whatever Happened to the Little Red Schoolhouse?, In the face of Justice, Mary Jemison: An American Life. Served with U.S. Army, 1952-54. Recipient Drama Desk award, 1971, King David award, 1972, Obie award, 1970; N.Y. Council for Humanities grantee, 1977, 80; N.J. Com. for Humanities grantee, 1978, 81, 83, Nat. Endowment for Humanities grantee, 1985; N.Y. State Arts Council Younger Audience Play Commn., 1978, Palm Beach Festival Commn., 1989. Mem. Dramatists Guild, Broadcast Music, Inc. Clubs: Damned Human Race Supper Club Too (N.Y.). Home: New York, NY. Died Oct. 17, 2014.

SCHAPIRO, MIRIAM, artist; b. Toronto, Ont., Can., Nov. 15, 1923; d. Theodore and Fannie (Cohen) S.; married; children Peter BA, State U. Iowa, 1945, MA, 1946, MFA, 1949; doctorate (hon.), Wooster Coll., 1983, Calif. Coll. Arts Crafts, 1989, Mpls. Coll. Art Design, 1994, Miami U., 1995, Moore Coll. Art, Phila., 1995. Co-orginator Womanhouse, Los Angeles, 1972, Heresies mag., N.Y.C., 1975; co-originator feminist art program Calif. Inst. Arts, Valencia, 1971; founding mem. Feminist Art Inst., N.Y.C.; mem. adv. bd. Women's Caucus for Art; assoc. mem. Heresies Collective; lectr. dept. art history U. Mich., 1987. Works in numerous books and catalogues; numerous one-woman shows including, Galerie Liatowitsch, Basel, Switzerland, 1979, Lerner Heller Gallery, N.Y.C., 1979, Barbara Gladstone Gallery, N.Y.C., 1980, Spencer Mus. Art, Lawrence, Kans., 1981, Everson Mus., Syracuse, N.Y., 1981, Galerie Rudolf Zwirner, Cologne, Fed. Republic Germany, 1981, Staatagalerie, Stuttgart, Fed. Republic Germany, 1983, Dart Gallery, Chgo, 1984, Bernice Steinbaum Gallery/Steinbaum Krauss Gallery, N.Y.C., 1986, 88, 90, 91, 94, 97, Brevard Art Ctr. and Mus., Melbourne, Fla., 1991, Guild Hall Mus., East Hampton, N.Y., 1992, ARC Gallery, Chgo., 1993, James Madison U., Harrisburg, Va., 1996, Nat. Mus. Am. Art Smithsonian Inst., Washington, 1997. others; retrospective exhbn., Wooster (Ohio) Coll. Art Mus., 1980; exhibited in numerous group shows, including, Palais de Beaux Arts, Brussels, 1979, Inst. Contemporary Art, Phila., 1979, Delahunty Gallery, Dallas, 1980, Indpls. Mus., 1980, Va. Mus., Richmond, 1980, Laguna Gloria Mus., Austin, Tex., 1980, R.O.S.C., Dublin, Ireland, 1980, Biennale of Sydney, Australia, 1982, Zurich, Switzerland, 1983, Sidney Janis Gallery, N.Y.C., 1984, Am. Acad. Arts and Letters, N.Y.C., 1985, Mus. Modern Art, N.Y.C., 1988, Whyte Mus. Can. Rockies, Banff, Alta., 1991, Nat. Mus. Women in Arts., Wash., 1993, Jane Voorhees Zimmerli art mus. Rutger's U., New Brunswick, N.J., 1994, Mus. of F.A. Boston, 1994, Santa Barbara Mus. of Art, 1994, Hudson River Mus. of Westchester, Yonkers, N.Y., 1995, Mus. of Contemporary Arts, Los Angeles, Calif. Bronx Mus. of the Arts, N.Y., 1995, Columbus (Ga.) Mus., 1996, Parrish Mus., Southampton, N.Y., 1997, Austin (Tex.) Mus., 1997, Whitney Mus., 2000; represented in permanent collections, Hirshhorn Mus., Washington, Bklyn. Mus., Met. Mus. Art, N.Y.C., Mus. Contemporary Art, San Diego, Mpls. Inst. Art, Mulvane Art Center, Topeka, Nat. Gallery Art, Washington, N.Y.U., Peter Ludwig Collection, Aachen, Germany, Stanford U., Palo Alto, Calif., Univ. Art Mus., Berkeley, Calif., Whitney Mus., N.Y.C., Worcester (Mass.) Art Mus., Santa Barbara (Calif.) Mus. Art, Nat. Mus. Am. Art Smithsonian Inst., Washington, also others; author: (books) Women and the Creative Process, 1974, Rondo: An Artists Book, 1988; sculpture Anna and David, Rosslyn, Va., 1987. Guggenheim fellow, 1987, Nat. Endowment for Arts fellow; grantee Ford Found.; recipient numerous other grants and fellowships. Mem. Coll. Art Assn. (past dir.). Home: Wainscott, NY. *Process and ideology in an opulent, multilayered, eccentric and hopeful abstract art: 1. The need for order and stability. 2. The need to destroy order and stability in order to find something else. 3. Finding something else. Pattern, itself an architectural species, reflects order and stability. Then a need to create chaos as though life itself were taking place. Finally the bonding layer by layer, the interpenetration of paint, fabric, photograph, tea towel, ribbon, lace, and glue. A collage: a simultaneity; a visual dazzlement, a multi-layering, a final message for the senses. And the ideology which inspires the work itself? That is feminism, the wish to have the art speak as a woman speaks. To be sensitive to the material used as though there were a responsibility to history to repair the sense of omission and to have each substance in the collage be a reminder of a woman's dreams. All of my works are auto-biographical. They are about the yearnings of a woman who decided a long time ago to become a painter.* Died June 20, 2015.

SCHATZ, IRWIN JACOB, retired cardiologist, educator; b. St. Boniface, Man., Can., Oct. 16, 1931; came to US, 1956, naturalized, 1966; s. Jacob and Reva S.; m. Barbara Jane Binder, Nov. 12, 1967; children: Jacob, Edward, Stephen and Brian (twins). Student, U. Man., Winnipeg, 1951, MD with honors, 1956. Diplomate: Am. Bd. Internal Medicine. Intern Vancouver (B.C.) Gen. Hosp., 1955-56;

resident Hammersmith Hosp., U. London, 1957, Mayo Clinic, Rochester, Minn., 1958-61; head sec. peripheral vascular disease Henry Ford Hosp., Detroit, 1961-68; asso. prof. medicine Wayne State U., 1968-71, chief sect. cardiovascular disease, 1969-71; assoc. prof., asso. dir. sect. cardiology U. Mich., 1972-73, prof. internal medicine, 1973-75; prof. medicine John A. Burns Sch. Medicine, U. Hawaii, 1975—2015, chmn. dept. medicine, 1975-90, interim chmn. dept. medicine, 2003—05. Author: Orthostatic Hypotension, 1986; contbr. numerous articles to med. jour. Mem. jud. coun. State of Hawaii Supreme Ct., from 2000; mem. disciplinary coun. Hawai Supreme Court, from 2010. Rockefeller Found. scholar, 1991. Master ACP (bd. gov. 1984-89, Laureate award Hawaii chpt. 1992, Mayo Clinic Disting Alumni award, 2009); fellow Am. Coll. Cardiology (bd. gov. 1980-84); mem. Am. Heart Assn. (fellow coun. cardiology), Am. Fedn. Clin. Rsch., Asian-Pacific Soc. Cardiology (v.p. 1987-91), Accreditation Coun. for Grad. Med. Edn. (chmn. residence rev. com. internal medicine 1989-95), Hawaii Heart Assn. (pres.), Western Assn. Physicians, Am. Autonomic Soc. (chmn. bd. gov., pres. 1996-98), Pacific Interurban Club. Jewish. Home: Honolulu, Hawaii. Died 2015.

SCHAYES, ADOLF, retired basketball player; b. NYC, May 19, 1928; s. Carl and Tina; m. Naomi Schayes; children: Danny, David, Carrie Gottsch, Debra Ferri. With Syracuse Nationals, 1948-63, Phila. 76ers, 1963-64, coach, 1963-66, Buffalo, 1970-72. Named Rookie of Yr., NBL, 1949, Hall of Fame, 1973, NBA 25th Anniversary All-Time Team, 1970, Coach of Yr., NBA, 1966. Achievements include leading NBA in free throw shooting, 1958, 60, 62; All-Am., 1948; mem. Championship Team, 1955; All-NBA First Team, 1952-55, 57, 58; All-NBA Second Team, 1950, 51, 56, 59-61; twelve-time NBA All-Star game; all-time leading rebounder Phila. 76ers, 1948-64. Home: De Witt, NY. Died Dec. 10, 2015.

SCHELLENBERG, JAMES ARTHUR, sociology educator; b. Vinland, Kans, June 7, 1932; s. Isaac F. and Tena (Franz) S.; m. Diana B. Sadler, July 29, 1956 (div.); children: Robert L. , Franklin M.; m. Christine A. Alberti, Dec. 28, 1974; children: Amy J., Stephen A. AB, Baker U., 1954; MA, U. Kans., 1955, PhD, 1959. Asst. prof. sociology Western Mich. U., Kalamazoo, 1959-63, assoc. prof. sociology, 1963-67, prof. sociology, 1967-76, Ind. State U., Terre Haute, from 1976. Author: An Introduction to Social Psychology, 1970, rev. edit., 1974, Masters of Social Psychology, 1978, The Science of Conflict, 1982, Conflict Between Communities, 1987, Primitive Games, 1990, An Invitation to Social Psychology, 1993, Exploring Social Behavior, 1993, Conflict Resolution, 1996. Mem. AAAS, AAUP, Am. Sociol. Assn. Methodist. Home: Terre Haute, Ind. Died Nov. 6, 2006.

SCHEMEL, DAVID JOSEPH, data processing professional; b. Granite Falls, Minn., Sept. 27, 1951; s. Gordon John and Kathleen Marie (Fisher) S. BS in Computer Sci. and Bus., Mankato State Coll., 1977, BA in Psychology, 1977. Cert. data processor, info. systems auditor. Programmer Sperry Univac, St. Paul, 1977-79; EDP auditor Coopers & Lybrand, Mpls., 1979-83, NYC, 1983-87, Spicer & Oppenheim, NYC, 1987-88, Coopers & Lybrand, Phila., from 1988. Author: (with others) Handbook of EDP Auditing, 1986-90. With USN, 1970-73. Republican. Avocations: music, videos. Died Feb. 23, 2007.

SCHERER, GEORGE ROBERT, retired secondary school educator; b. Marion, Ill., Sept. 2, 1923; s. Herman Albert and Alice Madora (Bulliner) S.; m. Margaret Mary Brzozowski, Dec. 31, 1945; children: Marion, Anne Madora. BS in Piano, Juilliard Sch., NYC, 1948; MMus in Piano, Roosevelt U., 1952; studied with Rudolph Ganz. Cert. elem. and secondary tchr., Ill. Tchr. Chgo. Bd. Edn., 1954-85. Profl. chorister Chgo. Symphony Orch. Chorus, 1965-70; instr. Fenger Jr. Coll., Chgo., 1971-73; Fenger H.S. Choir appeared 4 seasons with Chgo. Civic Symphony Orchestra, 1968-71. Composer music for chorus and piano; author: Scherer "A Genealogy", 1996. Recipient (with choir) 16 superior awards in city and state contests, 1960-75. Mem. Am. Guild of Music Artists, Juilliard Sch. Music Alumni Assn., Roosevelt U. Alumni Assn. Avocations: painting, genealogy, piano. Home: Country Club Hills, Ill. Died May 9, 2007.

SCHIER, ROBERT MORTON, sales executive, consultant; b. Bronx, NY, July 19, 1937; s. Alex and Gertrude (Feinberg) S.; m. Marybelle Rosenberg, Sept. 20, 1976 (div.); m. Donnita Hope DeGoede, June 21, 1986; children: Robin Tidwell, Laura. Assocs. in Bus. Adminstrn., NYU, 1958. Account exec. William, Warren Advt., NYC, 1958-68; sales mgr. Walton Rug Co., Chgo., 1968-74; with exec. sales Phoenix Mut. Life, 1974-76; gen. mgr. King Carpet Co., Phoenix, 1976-80; proprietor Carpet Fashions, Youngstown, Ariz., 1980-87; sales mgr. Carpetime, Phoenix, from 1987. Served to as U.S. Army, 1954-56. Mem.: B'nai Brith (sec. local chpt. 1968, pres. 1969), Elks (pub., editor Glendale, Ariz. chpt.). Democrat. Jewish. Avocations: bowling, tennis. Home: Glendale, Ariz. Died Feb. 19, 2007.

SCHLAMOWITZ, SAMUEL THEODORE, cardiologist; b. NYC, Dec. 23, 1917; s. Albert and Rose (Kirchenbaum) S.; m. Elaine Phyllis Bernstein, July 11, 1943; children: Robert Alan, Kevan Eric, Barbara Irene Gilman, Carol Susan Armon. BS, CCYN, 1938; MD, NYU, 1942. Diplomate Am. Bd. Internal Medicine. Fellow, dept. therapeutics NYU Coll. Medicine, 1946-50; instr., pharmacology N.Y. State U., Syracuse, 1946-57, instr., internal medicine, 1962-80, assoc. prof., internal medicine, 1980-86; attending physician St. Joseph's Hosp. Health Ctr., Syracuse, 1960-86; cardiac cons. N.Y. State Dept. Health, 1948-52. With Army Air Force Med. Corps, 1942-47. Recipient Helen Hayes Whitney Found. fellowship in Rheumatic Fever NYU Sch. Medicine, 1947-49. Fellow ACP, Am. Coll. Cardiology, Am. Coll. Chest Physicians, Am. Coll. Geriat., Am. Coll. Angiology, Cardiology Sect.-Pan Am. Soc., Am. Thoracic Soc., N.Y. Trudeau Soc., N.Y. Acad. Medicine; mem. Am. Heart Assn. (past pres. Indian River chpt.), Sigma Xi. Died Aug. 16, 2007.

SCHLENGER, ROBERT PURNELL, lawyer; b. Balt., Mar. 1, 1932; s. Leo Brennen and Martha (Thompson) S.; m. Gretchen Lausch, Oct. 4, 1958; children: Robert Jr., Carl B., Paul T. BS, U. Va., 1953; LLB, U. Md., 1964. Bar: Md., U.S. Dist. Ct. Md., U.S. Ct. Appeals (4th cir.), U.S. Supreme Ct. Indsl. rels. asst. Bethlehem Steel, Sparrows Point, Md., 1957-62; indsl. rels. assoc. Bendix Radio, Baltimore County, Md., 1962-64, Lord, Whip, Coughlan & Green, Balt., from 1964; ptnr., stockholder Lord & Whip, P.A., Balt., 1964—98, of counsel, from 1998. Pres. Lacross Hall of Fame, Balt., 1970-97. Bd. dirs. U.S. Lacrosse, Balt., 1997—; lacrosse ref. N.C.A.A., 1957-84. Lt. USN, 1953-56. Avocation: improvement and working for the Internat. Lacrosse Fedn. Home: Towson, Md. Died July 16, 2007.

SCHLUSSEL, SEYMOUR, obstetrician, gynecologist; b. NYC, Mar. 22, 1928; s. Albert and Lilian Schlussel; 1 child, Ralph. BA, Johns Hopkins U., Balt., 1946; MD, NY Med. Coll., NYC, 1951. Diplomate Am. Bd. Ob-gyn., Internat. Coll. Surgeons. Clin. prof. ob-gyn. NY Med. Coll., NYC, 1975—2006. Capt. US Army, 1952, Korea. Recipient Medal of Honor, NY Med. Coll., 1978. Fellow: ACS. Home: Bronx, NY. Died Feb. 18, 2007.

SCHMIDT, BARBARA ANN, elementary school educator; b. Evanston, Ill., May 31, 1955; d. Burton J. and Margaret Ann (Bohne) S. BA, Carthage Coll., 1977, MEd, 1983. Cert. phys. edn. and health tchr. Kindergarten thru grade 12, Ill. Tchr. phys. edn., softball, volleyball, basketball coach St. Catherine's High Sch., Racine, Wis., 1977-78; health educator Willow Grove Sch.-Dist. 96, Buffalo Grove, Ill., 1978-83; tchr. phys. edn. Kildeer Countryside Sch., Long Grove, Ill., from 1983. Mem. AAPHERD, Ill. IAHPERD (mem. scholarship com. 1991, 92). Avocations: golf, skiing, racquetball. Home: Libertyville, Ill. Died Apr. 13, 2007.

SCHMIDT, CHARLES LARRY, utility executive; b. Cin., Jan. 6, 1930; s. Charles Henry and Erna Selma (Scholz) S.; m. Mary Jane Heher, Nov. 28, 1953 (div. Oct. 1973); children: Gregory, Robert, Laura, Lisa, David; m. Linda Mae Ferguson, Oct. 15, 1976. BS, U. Cin., 1960, MBA, 1962. V.p. Cin. Gas and Electric Co., from 1949. Trustee Ind. Gas Assn., Ohio Gas Assn., Ky. Gas Assn. Contbr. articles to profl. jours. Mem. Am. Gas Assn. (chmn. operating sect. 1973-75, Disting. Service award 1975), Delta Mu Delta, Alpha Sigma Lambda, Delta Sigma Pi. Clubs: Kenwood Country (Cin.), Cin. Republican. Roman Catholic. Avocations: golf, coin collecting/numismatics. Home: Cincinnati, Ohio. Died Dec. 7, 2006.

SCHMIDT, ROSEMARY CATHERINE, administrative assistant; b. Milw., Nov. 23, 1937; d. Arthur Hugo and Harriet Margaret (Gerlach) Reiff; m. Richard Joseph Schmidt, June 1, 1957; children: Kurt Herbert, Aimee Beth, Kathleen Jo. Grad. parochial high sch., Milw. With corp. records dept. Wis. Electric Power Co., Milw., 1954-57; stenographer Allstate Ins. Co., Milw., 1957-60; freelance pub. stenographer Milw., 1960-67; owner, mgr. Reiff Frame & Moulding, Milw., 1967-77; with steel sales dept. Chgo. Tube & Iron Co., Milw., 1977-87; adminstrv. asst., sec. Marquette U. Sch. Dentistry, Milw., from 1987. Prin. Nat. Bus. Offices, Milw. Recipient 10 yr. svc. award Girl Scouts U.S., Milw., 1977. Mem. Assn. Women in Metals Industry (pres. Milw. 1985-88, past pres. 1988—), Lake Michigan Yachting Assn., Milw. Boat Club (yeoman 1988, sr. pilot 1989), Shamrock Club (editor 1973, sec. 1975). Republican. Roman Catholic. Avocations: reading, golf, travel. Home: West Bend, Wis. Died July 11, 2007.

SCHMIDT, WILLIAM ARTHUR, JR., retired lawyer; s. William and Caroline (Jäger) S.; m. Gerilyn Smith, Sept. 30, 1967; children: Deborah, Dawn, Jennifer. BSBA, Kent State U., 1962; JD, Cleve. State U., 1968. Bar: Ohio 1968, Ill. 1990. Contract specialist NASA-Lewis, Cleve., 1962-66, procurement analyst, 1967-68; atty. Def. Logistics Agy., Alexandria, Va., 1968-73; assoc. counsel Naval Sea Sys. Command, Arlington, Va., 1973-75; procurement policy analyst Energy R & D Adminstrn., Germantown, Md., 1975-76; sr. atty. U.S. Dept. Energy, Germantown, 1976-78, counsel spl. projects Oak Ridge, Tenn., 1978-83; judge Agr. Bd. Contract Appeals, Wash., 1983-87; judge Bd. Contract Appeals HUD, Wash., 1987; chief legal counsel Fermilab, Batavia, Ill., 1987-92; gen. counsel Univ. Rsch. Assn., Inc., Wash., from 1992, Fermi Rsch. Alliance, Wash., 2007—09. Co-author: (NASA handbook) R & D Business Practices, 1968. Founder/dir. DOE Contractor Attys. Assn.; dir. Spotsylvania Crime Solvers. Mem. Fed. Bar (past pres. East Tenn. 1978-83, 25 Yr. Svc. award 1994), Bd. Contract Appeals Judges Assn. (dir.-sec. 1986-88), Sr. Execs. Assn., Delta Theta Phi (dist. chancellor 1978-83), Sigma Chi. Republican. Lutheran. Avocation: classic cars. Home: Spotsylvania, Va. Died June 21, 2015.

SCHNEIDER, DON (CHARLES SCHNEIDER), museum administrator; b. Owosso, Mich., Apr. 15, 1923; s. Gordon Alexander and Kathleen Emily (Skelly) S.; m. Catherine Shuttle, 1944 (dec. 1955); life ptnr. Valerie SoRelle (dec. 1995). Student, Army Air Corps Photo Sch., Denver, 1943, Pasadena Playhouse, 1956-57; cert. in video studio prodn., Valley Cable TV Sta., 1982-83. Developer, negative cutter Technicolor, Hollywood, Calif., 1942-43; printer, timer George W. Colburn Film Lab., Chgo., 1951-54; ind. producer, editor, writer, from 1952; cameraman, dir. Sancho The Homing Steer, Disney Prodns., Burbank, Calif., 1960; film assoc. prodr., dir., editor, mixer, dubbing dir., camerman Fairway Internat., Burbank, 1961-65; lab. supr. Telefilm, Hollywood, 1965-70; Erwin Wasey Advt. Agy., 1970-71; post-prodn. supr., editor Intromedia, Hollywood, 1972; founder, CEO Movie Mus., Mich., from 1979. V.p. Internat. Puppetry Mus., North Hollywood, Calif., 1984—. Editor Titanic Last Survivor Interview, 1974, Movie Museum newsletter, 1979—, writer, House That Found a Home, 1983; prodr.: (bus. film) Majestic Visitor, 1952, (film) How to Use Tools, 1958, (news documentary) Gay Rights Motorcade, 1966, (short) Dancing Lights, Magic Hands of Sculptor Rudy Mercado, 1987, (travel film) Cruise to the Falls, 1953, (musical) Broadway Comes Alive, 1999, Christmas Story, 2009; prodr. Mardi Gras Magic Show, 1999, Haunted Castle Movie Set, 1999; dir.: (film) Four Seasons, 1959, Eegah, The Prehistoric Giant, 1961, (stage prodn.) The Women, 1967; composer: Sonata to a Rose, 1946; set decorator, lights They're Playing Our Song, 1984; actor Let's Do It Again, 1974, Murder at Midnight, 1941, Elks Minstrel Show, 1941, Carmen Opera, 1942, Outlaw Motorcycle Gangs, 1965, Lepke, 1975, Rocky, 1976, Funny Thing Happened On Way To Forum, 2006; film editor Incredible Creatures, 1962, Sadist, 1963, Spies A-Go-Go, 1964, Weekend of Fear, 1965, Man from Clover Grove, 1972, Our Hispanic Heritage, 1977, Norseman, 1978, Mission to Glory, 1979, Players, 1979, Brigham Young, 1984, Forty Days of Musa Dagh, 1987, Christmas Story, 2009; set designer and cast Waltz Dream, 1939; Author (play) Madison, 2008, Army Air Corps Show, 1944, Up In Mabel's Room, 1953. Recipient Award for Saving Demille Barn (Hollywood Bowl), Historic Preservation Soc., 2000. Achievements include establishing Conflict-Resolution Research Libr., 1956; National Endowment for the Arts, 1962; perfecting Eastman color positive/negative process, 1966; founded Separation (church and state) Day 2007 to protect churches 2012, Owosso Historic Commissioner 2012-2014. Died Oct. 27, 2014.

SCHNEIDER, GEORGE WILLIAM, retired aircraft design engineer; b. Riley, Kans., Aug. 17, 1923; s. George William and Helen Juanita (Carey) S.; m. Marguerite Ann Bare, May 7, 1945 (div. Oct. 1977); children: Peggy Diane Schneider Tsolakopolous, Donald Lynn; m. L. Elaine Phillips, Oct. 22, 1977. Student, Wichita State U., 1952-58; BSME in Design, Kans. State U., 1962. Designer Ling Temco Vought, Dallas, 1962-65; lead designer 727 Boeing Airplane Co., Renton, Wash., 1965-66, lead designer 747 Everett, Wash., 1966-72, designer 707, 727, 737, AWACS Renton, 1972-75; designer DeHavilland Dash 7 Boeing Airplane Co., Toronto, Ont., Can., 1975-77; design engr. Boeing Airplane Co., Morgantown, W.Va., 1977-79, lead designer 757 Renton, 1980-81, sr. design engr. Oak Ridge, Tenn., 1981-83; ret., 1983. Vice chmn. Nat. Agenda Bd., 1995-96. Author books, articles, reports in field. Chmn. com. Explorer scouts Boy Scouts Am., Seattle, 1966-68. Mem. ASME (regional chmn. history and heritage 1991, regional nat. agenda bd. 1992-94, sec. nat. agenda bd. 1994-95, editor Dixie News regional news bull., chmn. govtl. rels. Greenville sect. 1990—, chmn. Greenville sect. 1989-93, chmn. awards and hons.), S.C. Coun. of Engring. Soc. (sec., treas. 1992-93, v.p. 1993-94, pres. 1994-95). Avocations: science, photography, travel, woodworking, fishing. Home: Greenville, SC. Died Nov. 17, 2007.

SCHNEIDER, HANS, retired mathematician; b. Vienna, Jan. 24, 1927; came to U.K., 1939, U.S., 1959. s. Hugo and Isabella (Saphir) S.; m. Miriam Wieck, Jan. 6, 1948; children: Barbara Anne, Peter John, Michael Hugo. MA with 1st class honors, Edinburgh U., Scotland, 1948, PhD, 1952. Asst. lectr. Queen's U., Belfast, Northern Ireland, 1952-54, lectr., 1954-59; asst. prof. U. Wis., Madison, 1959-61, assoc. prof., 1961-65, prof. math., 1965—93, James Joseph Sylvester prof., 1988—93. Vis. prof. Wash. State U., Pullman, 1956-57, U. Calif.-Santa Barbara, 1964-65, U. Toronto, 1969-70, U. Tubingen, 1970, Tech. U., Munich, 1972, 74, Centre de Rsch. Math., U. Montreal, 1977, U. Wurzburg, 1980-81; rsch. visitor Unicamp, Campinas, Brazil, 1980; Lady Davis vis. prof. Technion, Haifa, Israel, 1985-86., Birmingham, U. 2005-14 Author: (with F. Brauer and J. Nohel) Linear Mathematics, 1970; (with K. Kapp) Completely O-Simple Semigroups, 1986; (with C. Barker) Linear Algebra and Matrices, 1989; editor-in-chief Linear Algebra and Its Applications, 1972—1992, Linear and Multilinear Algebra, 1972—92; contbr. articles to profl. jours. Mem. Gatlingburg Organizing Com., 1977-2014 Rsch. grantee NSF, 1967—1997, Office Naval Rsch., 1985-86, U.S.-Israel Binat. Sci. Found., 1988—1993. Mem. Internat. Linear Algebra Soc., Soc. Indsl. and Applied Math. (chmn. activities group on linear algebra 1982-84, editor Jour. Algebraic and Discrete Methods 1979-87). Home: Madison, Wis. Died Oct. 28, 2014.

SCHNEIDER, SYLVIA ISAACSON, retired psychological counselor; b. NYC, Dec. 12, 1915; d. Harry and Rebecca Isaacson; m. Aaron David Schneider, Dec. 29, 1934 (dec. Jan. 1973); children: Judith Schneider Wertheimer, Deborah Schneider Poleshuck. BA in English, NYU, 1936; MS in Edn., CUNY, 1963. Rehab. counselor Divsn. Vocat. Rehab.-N.J. State, 1963-83, mgr. Union County, 1977-81, mgr. Passaic County, 1981-83. Past pres. No. N.J. Nat. Rehab. Assn., 1979-83. Vol. bereavement counselor with widowed people We Care of Century Village, Deerfield Beach, Fla., 1984; vol. counselor Ctr. for Group Counseling, Boca Raton, Fla., 1985—. Recipient Cert. Appreciation, N.E. Focal Point Sr. Ctr., Deerfield Beach, 1984, We Care,

Deerfield Beach, 1990, Ctr. for Group Counseling, Boca Raton, 1995; Cert. Achievement, Ctr. for Group Counseling, Boca Raton, 1985. Democrat. Jewish. Home: Deerfield Bch, Fla. Died July 18, 2007.

SCHNELL, GEORGE ADAM, geographer, educator, retired demographer; b. Phila., July 13, 1931; s. Earl Blackwood and Emily (Bernheimer) S.; m. Mary Lou Williams, June 21, 1958; children: David Adam, Douglas Powell, Thomas Earl. BS, West Chester U., 1958; MS, Pa. State U., 1960, PhD, 1965; postdoctoral study, Ohio State U., 1965. Asst. prof. SUNY, New Paltz, 1962-65, assoc. prof., 1965-68, prof. geography, 1968-99, founding chmn. dept., 1968-94, prof. emeritus, from 1999. Adj. prof. SUNY, 2000-05; vis. assoc. prof. U. Hawaii, summer, 1966; cons. cmty. action programming, 1965; manuscript reader, cons. to several pubs., 1967—; founder, founding bd. dirs., investigator Inst. for Devel., Planning and Land Use Studies, 1986-96; cons. Mid-Hudson Pattern for Progress, 1986, Open Space Inst., 1987, Mid-Hudson Regional Econ. Devel. Coun., 1989, Urban Devel. Corp., 1989-90, 93, Tech. Devel. Ctr., 1991, Catskill Ctr., 1991, Ednl. Testing Svc., 1993-94, 96, 97; cons. editor Exams Unltd., Albany, N.Y., 1995-99; ind. contractor and cons. Excelsior U., 2003—05; founding mem. exec. bd. dirs. Hudson Valley Study Ctr., 1995-98; ind. contractor Excelsior U., 2003; cons., presenter in field. Author: (with others) The Local Community: A Handbook for Teachers, 1971, The World's Population, Problems of Growth, 1972; contbr. Pennsylvania Coal: Resources, Technology, Utilization, 1983, West Virginia and Appalachia: Selected Readings, 1977, Hazardous and Toxic Wastes: Technology, Management and Health Effects, 1984, Environmental Radon: Occurrence, Control and Health Hazards, 1990, Natural and Technological Disasters: Causes, Effects and Preventive Measures, 1992, Conservation and Resource Management, 1993, Medicine and Health Care into the 21st Century, 1995, Forests: A Global Perspective, 1996, (with M.S. Monmonier) Ecology of the Wetlands and Associated Systems, 1998, (with M.S. Monmonier) Renewable Energy: Trends and Prospects, 2002; co-author: (with M.S. Monmonier) The Study of Population: Elements, Patterns, Processes, 1983, Map Appreciation, 1988; editor, contbr.: (with with M.S. Monmonier, G.J. Demko, and H.M. Rose) Population Geography: A Reader, 1970; contbr. articles to profl. and scholarly jours. Appt. mem. local bds. and coms. Town and Village New Paltz, New Paltz Ctrl. Sch. Dist., 1965-2007; elder Reformed Ch. New Paltz; Rep. committeeman Town of Gardiner, Ulster County, NY, 2000-01; trustee Gardiner (NY) Pub. Libr., 2005-07. With AUS, 1952-54; bd. mem. River Park Homeowners Assn., 2007—. Recipient Excellence award NY State/United Univ. Professions, 1994, Disting. Alumnus award West Chester U., 1994; named Disting. Tchr. Emeritus, SUNY New Paltz Alumni Assn., 2006. Mem. Assn. Am. Geographers, Pa. Geog. Soc. (mem. editl. bd. Pa. Geographer, Disting. Geographer award 1994), Pa. Acad. Sci. (assoc. editor jour. 1988-2005), Nat. Coun. for Geog. Edn., Geographer Editl. Rev. Bd., Penn. Geog. Soc. (disting. scholar award, 2008). Home: New Paltz, NY. Deceased.

SCHOCH, DAVID EDMUND, minister; b. Pasadena, Calif., Apr. 24, 1920; s. Chester Albert Schoch and Rose (Aurelia) Biedebach; m. Evelyn Audene Ward; children: Rose Ann McKee, Steven Earl. BA in Theology, Living Waters Bible Coll., 1980; DD, Word of Faith Sch. of Theology, 1988. Ordained to ministry Christian Ch., 1953. Assoc. pastor Immanuel Gospel Temple, LA, 1950-52, evangelist, 1952-53; pastor Bethany Chapel, Long Beach, 1953-86; sr. pastor Bethany Missionary Assn., Long Beach, 1953-86; convs. min., counsellor, from 1986. Chmn. Revival Fellowship, Pasadena, 1960-85; mem. Network of Christian Ministries Word of Faith, New Orleans, 1985-90. Author: The Precious Blood, 1964, Sarah, 1952, The Prophetic Ministry, 1978; compiler of scriptures set to music, 1966. Tech. sgt. U.S. Army, 1941-46. Republican. Home: Fort Worth, Tex. Died July 19, 2007.

SCHOFIELD, JAMES ROY, medical consultant, educator; b. July 12, 1923; s. Arthur Monroe and Grace Pearl (West) S. BS, Baylor U., 1945, MD, 1947; LLD (hon.), Queens U., Kingston, Ont., Can., 1988. Instr. to prof. Baylor U. Coll. Medicine, Houston, 1947-71, asst. dean to acad. dean, 1953-71; sec., liaison com. on med. edn. Assn. Am. Med. Colls. and AMA, Washington, 1972-87; ind. cons. on med. edn. Washington, from 1987. Pres. Tex. Acad. Sci., 1961-62; mem. transitional coun. United Arab Emirates U., 1986-89; external auditor Sultan Qaboos Coll. Medicine, Muscat, Oman, 1987-97; vis. disting. prof. history of medicine, univ. cons. on premed. edn. Baylor U., 1992—; faculty Baylor in the British Isles, 1994—; cons. in field. Author: New and Expanded Medical Schools: Midcentury to the 1980's, 1985, Murder in the Medical School, 2000; contbr. articles to profl. jours. Bd. dirs. Am-Polish Found., 1995; leader Md. Boy Scout Jamborie, 1951. Capt. M.C. US Army, 1954—57. Recipient disting. Achievement award Baylor U., 1992, Disting. Alumnus award Baylor Coll. Medicine, 1996. Mem. Sigma Xi, Alpha Omega Alpha. Republican. Baptist. Avocations: woodcarving, cabinet work, collecting old tools, music, writing. Died May 20, 2007.

SCHOOLEY, WARREN CALVIN, evangelist; b. Foster, Mo., Aug. 24, 1923; s. William Ruben and Bessie Mae (Yeokum) S.; m. Ruth Elaine Creel, May 22, 1950; children: Rodney, Rebecca, Charlotte, Milton. Student, York Coll., Nebr., 1963-64, Abilene Christian U., 1966-68, Ala. Christian U., 1988-89, Dept. Christian Ministries, 1990-91. Evangelist Ch. of Christ, Seward, Nebr., 1964-66, Hot Springs, S.D., 1966-78, various cities, 1981-86, from 1986. With U.S. Army, 1942-45. Home: Morris, Ala. Died Aug. 13, 2007.

SCHOONOVER, MELVIN EUGENE, seminary administrator; b. Francesville, Ind., Aug. 22, 1926; s. Charles and Alma Louise (Garrigues) S.; m. Diana Russell Sturgis, May 24, 1957; 1 child, Diana Russell. AB, Wabash Coll., 1951; MDiv, Union Theol. Sem., 1956, STM, 1969; D. Ministry, N.Y. Theol. Sem., 1971; LHD (hon.), Wabash Coll., 1972; DDiv. (hon.), N.Y. Theol. Sem., 1978. Ordained to ministry Am. Bapt. Ch. U.S.A., 1956. Pastor Chambers Meml. Bapt. Ch., NYC, 1958-68, Cen. Bapt. Ch., Wayne, Pa., 1978-83; dean degree programs N.Y. Theol. Sem., NYC, 1969-78, dir. Fla. extention, 1983-85; pres. S. Fla. Ctr. for Theol. Studies, Miami, from 1985. Trustee N.Y. Theol. Sem., 1978-83. Author: Making All Things Human, 1969, Letters to Polly, 1971, What If We Did Follow Jesus, 1978. Home: Miami, Fla. Died July 6, 2007.

SCHORSKE, CARL EMIL, historian, educator; b. NYC, Mar. 15, 1915; s. Theodore A. and Gertrude (Goldschmidt) S.; m. Elizabeth Gilbert Rorke, June 14, 1941 (dec. 2014); children: Carl Theodore, Anne (Mrs. J. L. Edwards), Stephen James (dec. 2013), John Simon, Richard Robert. AB, Columbia U., 1936; MA, Harvard U., 1937, PhD, 1950; DLitt (hon.), Wesleyan U., 1967, Bard Coll., 1982, Clark U., 1983, New Sch. Social Rsch., 1986, Miami U., 1987, Monmouth Coll., 1994, Princeton U., 1997, SUNY, Stony Brook, 1989; DPhil (hon.), U. Salzburg, 1986, U. Graz, 1996. Prof. history Wesleyan U., Middletown, Conn., 1946-60; prof. history U. Calif.-Berkeley, 1960-69, Princeton U., 1969-80, prof. history emeritus, 1980—2015. Author: (with Hoyt Price) The Problem of Germany, 1947, German Social Democracy 1905-1917, 1955, Fin-de-Siècle Vienna, 1980, Thinking with History: Explorations in the Passage to Modernism, 1998. Lt. (j.g.) USNR, 1943-46; with OSS, 1941-46. Recipient Austrian Cross of Honor for arts and scis., 1979, Pulitzer prize gen. nonfiction, 1981, Grand prize cultural edn. City of Vienna, 1985, Harvard Centennial medal, 1999, Wittgenstein prize, Ministry Culture, Austria, 2004, Victor Adler prize, Austria, 2007; named Officer, French Order Arts and Letters, 1987, Great Silver medal of Honor, Austria, 1996, Gold Cross of Honor, City of Vienna, 2000; MacArthur fellow, 1981-86. Fellow Royal Acad. Fine Arts Netherlands (hon.); mem. Am. Acad. Arts and Scis., Austrian Acad. Scis. (corr.), Am. Hist. Assn. (council 1964-68, Disting. Scholar award 1992), Ctr. Advanced Study Behavioral Sci., Inst. Advanced Study., Getty Ctr. Home: Silver Spring, Md. Died Sept. 13, 2015.

SCHRODERHEIM, GORAN, polymer scientist; b. Malmö, Skåne, Sweden, May 7, 1923; s. Johan Elis Schroderheim and Anna Haglund; m. Elisabet Erna Bomhardt, 1958; children: Ann Charlotte. BS, Stockholm U., 1949; M of Chem. Engring., Paris U., 1951; MSc, Akron U., Akron, 1957, MBA, 1964, PhD, 1991. Devel. engr. LM Ericsson, Stockholm, 1950-54; rsch. chemist Polymer Corp., Sarnia, 1954-56; process engr. BF Goodrich, Akron, 1956-60; rsch. chemist Gen. Tire, Akron, 1960-64; lab. mgr. Gislaved Gummi, Sweden, 1964-70; prof. Borås Tech. Coll., Sweden, 1970-89; cons. Gislaved, from 1991. Lectr. Swedish Rubber Group; guest lectr. univs., Sweden and U.S. Contbr. articles to profl. jours. Mem.: SAR, Akron Rubber Group, Swedish Rubber Group, Am. Chem. Soc. (rubber divsn.). Avocations: genealogy, antique furniture. Home: Gislaved, Sweden. Died Oct. 29, 2007.

SCHROEDER, DOUGLAS ROBERT, engineering company executive; b. St. Petersburg, Fla., Mar. 10, 1943; s. Henry Carl and Sarah Frances (Roser) S.; m. Librada Labrador; children: Dawn R. Zimmerman, Teresa D. Pennick, Felicia Y., Douglas R. Jr., Anna Lisa. BSEE, Auburn U., 1968; MSEE, MIT, 1970; grad., USN Test Pilot Sch., 1973. Enlisted USAF, 1962, advanced through grades to maj., 1979, flight test engr. Armament Devel. Test Ctr. Eglin AFB, Fla., 1970-72, instr. test pilot sch. Edwards AFB, Calif., 1973-75, chief engr. combat sage Clark Air Base, Philippines, 1975-81, chief flight test engr. Air Force Wright Aero. Labs. Wright-Patterson AFB, Ohio, 1981-82, dep. program mgr. X-29 program office Flight Dynamics Lab., 1982-83, retired, 1983; sr. engr. Comarco, Ridgecrest, Calif., 1984-85; chief engr. CTA, Inc., Ridgecrest, Calif., 1985-88; pres. Locust Dynamics, Inc., Ridgecrest, from 1988. Author articles, tech. reports. Mem. Ret. Officers Assn., Sigma Xi, Tau Beta Pi, Eta Kappa Nu, Phi Kappa Phi. Avocation: golf. Died Jan. 19, 2007.

SCHULER, RICHARD JOSEPH, priest; b. Mpls., Dec. 30, 1920; s. Otto Henry and Wilhelmine Mary (Hauk) S. BA, Coll. St. Thomas, 1942; MA, U. Rochester, 1950; PhD, U. Minn., 1963. Ordained priest Roman Cath. Ch., 1945. Prof. music Nazareth Hall Seminary, St. Paul, 1945-54; assoc. prof. music Univ. St. Thomas, St. Paul, 1955-69; pastor Ch. St. Agnes, St. Paul, from 1969. Editor: Fourteen Liturgical Works of Giovanni Maria Nanino, 1969, Sacred Music, 1975—. Founder, condr. Twin Cities Cath. Chorale, 1955—. Named Hon. Papal Prelate (monsignor), 1970; recipient Gold Lassus medal Caecilia Soc., Fed. Republic Germany, 1973; Fulbright scholar, 1954-55. Mem. Ch. Music Assn. Am. (gen. sec. 1972-76, pres. 1976—), Consociatio Internat. Musicae Sacrae (v.p. 1967-77). Died Apr. 20, 2007.

SCHULLER, GUNTHER ALEXANDER, composer; b. NYC, Nov. 22, 1925; s. Arthur E. and Elsie (Bernartz) Schuller; m. Marjorie Black, June 8, 1948; children: Edwin Gunther, George Alexander. Student, St. Thomas Choir Sch., NYC; MusD (hon.), Manhattan Sch. Music, 1987, Northeastern U., 1967, U. Ill., 1968, Colby Coll., 1969, Williams Coll., 1975, Cleve. Inst. Music, 1977, New Eng. Conservatory Music, 1978, Rutgers U., 1980, Manhattan Sch. Music, 1987, Oberlin Coll., 1989. Tchr. Manhattan Sch. Music, 1950—63; head composition dept. Tanglewood, 1963—84; pres. New Eng. Conservatory Music, 1967—77; artistic dir. Berkshire Music Ctr., Tanglewood, 1969—84, Festival at Sandpoint, 1985—2000. Founder, pres. Margun Music Inc., 1975, GM Recs., 1980. French horn player Ballet Theatre, 1993, then prin. horn player Cin. Symphony Orch., 1943—45, prin. French horn Met. Opera Orch., 1945—59; author: Horn Technique, 1962, Early Jazz: Its Roots and Development, 1968, Musings: The Musical Worlds of Gunther Schuller, 1985; autobiography Gunther Schuller: A Life in Pursuit of Music and Beauty, 2011; composer: Suite for Woodwind Quintet, 1945, Concerto for Cello and Orchestra, Six Early Songs, 1945, Jumpin' in the Future for jazz ensemble, 1946, Quartet for Four Double Basses, 1947, Perpetuum Mobile for Four Horns & Brass, 1948, Fantasy for Unaccompanied Cello, 1951, Symphony for Brass and Percussion, 1950, Adago for Flute & String Trio, 1952, Recitative and Rondo for Violin and Piano, 1953, Dramatic Overture, N.Y. Philharm., 1956, String Quintet No.1, 1957, Symbiosis, Music for Violin, Piano and Percussion, 1957, Contours, 1958, Woodwind Quintet, 1958, Fantasy Quartet for Four Celli, Seven Studies on Themes of Paul Klee, 1958, Concertino for Jazz Quartet and Orch., Balt. Symphony Orch., 1959, Spectra for Long Orch., 1960, Music for Brass Quintet, 1961, Six Renaissance Lyrics, 1962, String Quartet No. 2, 1965, Symphony, 1965, Concerto No. 1 for Orch., Chgo. Symphony Orch., 1966, Triplum, 1967, Aphorisms for Flute and String Trio, 1967, Capriccio Stravagante, 1972, The Power Within Us, 1972, Tre Invenzioni, 1972, Three Nocturnes, 1973, Four Soundscapes, 1974, Concerto No. 2 for Orch., 1975, Triplum II, 1975, Horn Concerto No. 2, 1976, Violin Concerto, 1976, Diptych for organ, 1976, Sonata Serenata, 1978, Contrabassoon Concerto, 1978, Deaï for 3 orchs., 1978, Trumpet Concerto, 1979, Octet, 1979, Eine Kleine Posaunemusik, 1980, In Praise of Winds (Symphony for Large Wind Orch.), 1981, Symphony for Organ, 1982, Concerto Quaternio, 1983, Concerto for Bassoon and Orch., 1984, On Light Wings (piano quartet), 1984, Duologue for Violin and Piano, 1984, Farbenspiel (Concerto No. 3 for Orch.), 1985, Concerto for Viola and Orch., 1985, String Quartet No. 3, 1986, A Bouquet for Collage for chamber ensemble, 1988, Chimeric Images, 1988, Concerto for String Quartet and Orchestra, 1988, Concerto for Flute and Orchestra, 1988, On Winged Flight: A Divertimento for Band, 1989, Chamber Concerto, 1989, Concerto for Piano Three Hands, 1989, Phantasmata for Violin and Marinba, 1989, 5 Impromptus Eng. Horn and String Quartet, 1989, Impromptus and Cadenzas, 1990, Hommage à Rayechka for 8 cellos/or multiples thereof, 1990, A Trio Setting for clarinet, violin, piano, 1990, Violin Concert No. 2, 1991, Sonata Fantasia for piano, 1992, Ritmica-Melodia-Armonia for orch., 1992, Of Reminiscences and Reflections for orch., 1993 (Pulitzer prize for music, 1994), Brass Quintet No. 2, 1993, The Past is in the Present for orch., 1994, Sextet for left hand piano and woodwind quintet, 1994, Concerto for organ and orch., 1994, Mondrian's Vision, 1994, Magnificat and Nunc Dimittis (choir), 1994, Headin Out, Movin In (jazz ensemble), 1994, Lament for M (jazz ensemble), 1994, Rush Hour an 23d St., 1994, Blue Dawn into White Heat (concert band), 1995, An Arc Ascending, 1996, Bright and Sassy, 1997, Ohio River Reflections for Piano Trio and Horn, 1998, Sonata for Alto Saxophone, 1999, Fantasie Impromptu for Flutet Hpschd, 2000, Quodlibet - Vln, Cello, Oboe, Horn, and Harp, 2001, The Birth of the Cool Suite, 2001, String Quartet No. 4, 2002, Concerto da Camera No. 2, 2002, rev. Duo Concertante for Cello and Piano, 2002, Four Preludes for Harp, 2002, Encounters for Jazz Band and Large Symphony Orch., 2003, String Trio, 2003, Grand Concert for Percussion Ensemble and Three Keyboards, 2005, Nature's Way for Band/Wind Ensemble, 2006, Refrains (for ten euphoniums, twelve tubas), 2006, Where the Word Ends (for orch.), 2006, Three Little Expressions, Cello, Bass Clarinet, 2009, Adagis for Strings: Ode to the Minor Second & Major Seventh, 2007, Three Small Adventures, Marimba, 2008, Piano Trio, 2009, Quintet for Horn & String Quartet, 2009, Sonatima Flute and Piccolo, 2009, Sonata for Piano Four Hands, 2010, Four Soliloquies Piano 4 lands 2 Piano Clar, Cello, 2010, (Operas) The Visitation, 1966, Fisherman and His Wife, 1970. Recipient Creative Arts award, Brandeis U., 1960, Deems Taylor award, ASCAP, 1970, Alice M. Ditson Conducting award, 1970, Rodgers and Hammerstein award, 1971, Friedheim award, 1988, William Schuman award, Columbia U., 1989, Down Beat Lifetime Achievement award, 1993, BMI Lifetime Achievement award, 1994, Gold medal, Am. Acad. Arts and Letters, 1997, Order of Merit Cross, Fed. Republic of Germany, 1997, Max Rudolf award, 1998, Adujog for Strings award, 2007; named Guggenheim fellow, 1962, 1963, MacArthur fellow, 1991, Composer of Yr., Mus. Am., 1995; named to Am. Classical Music Hall of Fame, 1998. Mem.: Am. Acad. Arts and Scis., Nat. Inst. Arts and Letters. Died June 21, 2015.

SCHULLER, ROBERT HAROLD, minister, writer; b. Alton, Iowa, Sept. 16, 1926; s. Anthony and Jennie (Beltman) Schuller; m. Arvella DeHaan, June 15, 1950; children: Sheila, Jeanne, Carol, Gretchen, Robert Anthony. BA, Hope Coll., 1947; BD, Western Theol. Sem., 1950; DD, Hope Coll., 1973; LLD, Azusa Pacific Coll., 1970, Pepperdine U., 1976; LittD, Barrington Coll., 1977; honorary degree, Northwestern Coll., Iowa, Ashland Coll., Ohio, Hanyang U., Korea. Ordained to ministry Reformed Ch. Am., 1950. Pastor Ivanhoe Ref. Ch., Chgo., 1950—55; founder, sr. pastor Garden Grove Cmry. Ch., Calif., from 1955; founder, pres. Hour of Power TV Ministry, 1970—2006; founder, dir. Robert H. Schuller Inst. for Successful Ch. Leadership, from 1970; chmn. nat. religious sponsor program Religion in Am. Life, NYC, from 1975; founding pastor Crystal Cathedral, 1980, retiring as sr. pastor, 2010, chmn. bd. to chmn. emeritus, 2011—12; founded New Hope, 1968. Bd. dirs. Freedoms Found.; founder, hon. chmn. Churches

Uniting in Global Mission. Author: God's Way to the Good Life, 1963, Your Future Is Your Friend, 1964, Move Ahead with Possibility Thinking, 1967, Self Love, the Dynamic Force of Success, 1969, Power Ideas for a Happy Family, 1972, The Greatest Possibiloty Thinker That Ever Lived, 1973, Turn Your Scars into Stars, 1973, You Can Become the Person You Want To Be, 1973, Your Church Has Real Possibilities, 1974, Love or Loneliness - You Decide, 1974, Positive Prayers for Power-Filled Living, 1976, Keep on Believing, 1976, Reach Out for A New Life, 1977, Peace of Mind Through Possibility Thinking, 1977, Turning You Stress Into Strength, 1978, Daily Power Thoughts, 1978, The Peak to Peek Principle, 1981, Living Positively One Day at a Time, 1981, Self Esteen: The New Reformation, 1982, Tough Times Never Last, But, Tough People Do!, 1983, Tough Minded Faith for Tender Hearted People, 1984, The Be-Happy Attitudes, 1985, The Power of Being Debt Free, 1985, Be Happy You Are Loved, 1986, Living Positively One Day At A Time, 1986, Success is Never Ending, Failure is Never Final, 1988, Believe in the God Who Believes in You, 1989, Life's Not Fair, But God Is Good, 1991, Prayer: My Soul's Adventure with God, 1995, My Journey: From An Iowa Farm to a Cathedral of Dreams, 2001, Hours of Power, 2004, Don't Throw Away Tomorrow, 2005; co-author: The Courage of Carol, 1978. Founder Robert H. Schuller Corr. Ctr. Possibility Thinkers, 1976; bd. dirs. Religion in American Life; pres. bd. dirs. Christian Counseling Svcs.; adv. bd. mem. Church Growth Internat., Seoul; bd. counselors YMCA of U.S.A.; adv. bd. mem. Highpoint Cancer Edn. Ctr., Salvation Army; bd. dirs. Horatio Alger Assn. of Disting. Americans. Recipient Ddisting. Alumnus award, Hope Coll., 1970, Prin. award, Freedoms Found., 1974, Freedom award, America's Freedom Festival, Provo, Utah, Horatio Alger award, Horatio Alger Assn. of Disting. Americans, awards of Excellence for Religion in Media, Napoleon Hill Gold medal award for Literacy Achievement, The Golden Plate award, American Acad. Achievement, Outstanding American award, LA Philanthropic Found., Humanitarian of the Yr. award, Nat. Conference of Christians and Jews; co-recipient (with wife) Edith Munger Leadership award, Munger Ctr. for Psychological Services; named Headliner of Yr. in Religion, Orange County, 1977, Clergyman of Yr., Religious Heritage America, 1977. Mem.: AIA (hon.; bd. dirs. from 1986), Religious Guild Architects (hon.), American Acad. of Achievement, Nat. Assn. of Christian Psychotherapists and Counselors, Inc. (hon.), Rotary. Died Apr. 2, 2015.

SCHULTHEISS, EMILY EKONEN, management consultant, writer; b. Oklahoma City, Feb. 6, 1949; d. Tauno Otto and Dorothy Guhlstorf Ekonen; m. Arthur Howard Schultheiss (dec. Aug. 9, 2000). BBA, U. Okla., 1971; MS, LaRoche Coll., 1985. Human resources generalist Westinghouse Electric Corp., Norman, Okla., 1971—77, human resources supr. Boston, 1977—80, human resources mgr. Norman, 1980—81, mgr. orgn. devel. Pitts., 1981—83, mgr. corp. tng., 1983—95; v.p. Impact Strategy Assocs., Pitts., 1996—97; sole proprietor Thriving Sys., Pitts., from 1997. Chair resource team Evang. Luth. Ch. Am. S.W. Pa. Synod, Pitts., from 2003. Author: (Book) Optimizing the Organization, 1988, Day by Day: A Journey Toward Thriving, 1998. V.p. Northland Pub. Libr. Found. Bd., Pitts., 1998—2003. Lutheran. Avocations: music, quilting, reading. Home: Pittsburgh, Pa. Died Mar. 19, 2007.

SCHULTZ, RICHARD DONALD, thoracic, cardiovascular surgeon; b. Schleswig, Iowa, Oct. 7, 1931; s. Shirley V. and Eileen Rosario (Houston) S.; m. Elizabeth Marie Carlin, Aug. 28, 1954; children: Michael John, Sheryl Lee Schultz Whitehouse. BS, Creighton U., 1954, MD, 1958. Diplomate Am. Bd. Surgeons, added qualifications Am. Bd. Thoracic Surgeons. Resident gen. and thoracic surgery U. Wash. Affiliated Hosps., Seattle, 1966; asst. prof. surgery Creighton U. Sch. Medicine, Omaha, Nebr., 1966-74, assoc. prof. surgery, 1974-85, prof., 1985-90, chief thoracic and cardiovascular surgery; col., chief thoracic, cardiovascular surgery Landstuhl (Germany) Regional Med. Ctr. (U.S. Mil.), 1991-94. Cons. U.S. FDA on Duromedic Heart Valve Prostheses, Washington, 1985, on thoracic and cardiovasc. surgery, Mutual of Omaha Ins., 1988-91. Contbr. 86 articles to med. jours., 7 chpts. to med. texts, 1967-87. Mem. 18 nat. and 6 state med. orgns. Col. U.S. mil., 1991-97. Mem. Omaha Happy Hollow Club, Lincoln Univ. Club, Alpha Omega Alpha. Republican. Roman Catholic. Avocations: reading, travel, golf, history, computers. Home: Omaha, Nebr. Died June 12, 2007.

SCHULTZ, STANLEY GEORGE, physiologist, educator, retired dean; b. Bayonne, NJ, Oct. 26, 1931; s. Aaron and Sylvia (Kaplan) S.; m. Harriet Taran, Dec. 25, 1960; children: Jeffrey, Kenneth. AB summa cum laude, Columbia U., NYC, 1952; MD, NYU, 1956. Intern Bellevue Hosp., NYC, 1956-57, resident, 1957-59; research assoc. in biophysics Harvard U., 1959-62, instr. biophysics, 1964-67; assoc. prof. physiology U. Pitts., 1967-70, prof. physiology, 1970-79; prof., chmn. dept. physiology U. Tex. Med. Sch., Houston, 1979-96, prof. dept. internal medicine, 1979—97, prof. dept. integrative biol. pharm. physiology, 1997—2010, vice chmn., 1999—2003, Fondren chair in cell signalling, 1999—2009, dean Sch. Medicine, 2003—06, H. Wayne Hightower Dist. prof. biomed. sci., 2005—07, assoc. dean sch. medicine, 2007—10, emeritus prof., 2010—14. Cons. USPHS, NIH, 1970-2014; mem. physiology test com. Nat. Bd. Med. Examiners, 1974-79, chmn., 1976-79 Editor American Jour. Physiology, Jour. Applied Physiology, 1971-75, Physiol. Revs., 1979-85, Handbook of Physiology: The Gastrointestinal Tract, 1989-91; mem. editl. bd. Jour. Gen. Physiology, 1969-88, Ann. Revs. Physiology, 1974-81, Current Topics in Membranes and Transport, 1975-81, Journal Membrane Biology, Biochim. Biophys. Acta, 1987-89; assoc. editor Ann. Revs. Physiology, 1977-81; assoc. editor News in Physiol. Scis., 1989-94, editor, 1994-2003; contbr. articles to profl. jours. Served to capt. M.C. USAF, 1962-64. Recipient Rsch. Career award NIH, 1969-74, Solomon Berson award NYU, 2003; overseas fellow Churchill Coll., Cambridge U., 1975-76, Prince Mahidol award, Thailand, 2007. Mem. American Heart Assn. (estab. investigator 1964-68), American Physiol. Soc. (councillor 1989-91, pres.-elect 1991-92, pres. 1992-93, past pres. 1993-94, Guyton award 1997, Orr Reynolds award 1999, Daggs award 2003), European Acad. Sci., Fed. American Soc. Exptl. Biology (exec. bd. 1992-95), Internat. Cell Rsch. Orgn., Internat. Union Physiol. Scis. (chmn. internat. com. gastrointestinal physiology 1977-80, chmn. U.S. nat. com. 1992-98), Assn. American Physicians, American Assn. Ob-Gyn. (hon. fellow), Assn. Chmn. Depts. Physiology (pres. 1985-86), Houston Philos. Soc., Phi Beta Kappa, Sigma Xi. Home: Houston, Tex. Died Oct. 23, 2014.

SCHULTZ, WESLEY EDWARD, sales executive; b. Benton Harbor, Mich., June 22, 1927; s. Edward J. and Nettie (Wolverton) S.; m. Delores Joan De Vries, Dec. 30, 1950; children: Suzanne Anderson, Nanette Hamlyn, Kathleen Schultz. BA, Kalamazoo Coll., 1950. From zone svc. adjuster to zone customer rels. mgr. Pontiac (Mich.) Motor Div. GMC, 1950-58; regional sales mgr. Detrex Chem. Industries, Detroit and Northbrook, Ill., 1958-64; dist. sales mgr. Lease Div. Avis Rent A Car, Chgo. and Cleve., 1964-66; dist. mgr. Master Div. Koehring Co., Dayton, Ohio, 1966-74; dist. sales mgr. Turfmaster-OPE Huffy Corp., Dayton, 1974-75, sales mgr. nat. accounts Automotive Products div., 1975-82; sales mgr. nat. accts. KP Industries, Dayton, Mpls., and Olive Branch, Miss., 1982-90. Participant loaned exec. program Dayton United Way, 1981, 82. With USN, 1945-46. Mem. Alpha Sigma Iota Alpha. Home: Dayton, Ohio. Died July 20, 2007.

SCHULWEIS, HAROLD MAURICE, rabbi; b. NYC, Apr. 14, 1925; s. Maurice and Helen (Rezak) S.; m. Malkah Muriel Savod, June 22, 1947; children: Seth, Ethan, Alissa. BA, Yeshiva Coll., 1945; MA, NYU, 1948; MHL, Jewish Theol. Sem., 1950, DD (hon.), 1975; ThD, Pacific Sch. Religion, 1970; HHD (hon.), Hebrew Union Coll., 1983. Rabbi Conservative Jewish Congregation, 1945, Temple Emanuel, Parkchester, N.Y., 1950-52, Temple Beth Abraham, Oakland, Calif., 1952-70, Valley Beth Shalom, Encino, Calif., 1970—2014. Instr. philosophy CCNY, 1948-51; adj. prof. contemporary civilization U. Judaism, L.A.; lectr. Jewish theology Hebrew Union Coll., L.A.; guest of Govt. of Fed. Republic Germany to observe rehab. of German ednl. instns., 1966; mem. nat. rabbinical cabinet Rabbinical Assembly, 1968, sec. assembly, 1978; mem. faculty B'nai B'rith Adult Edn. Commn; founder, dir, Schulweis Inst Author: Evil and the Morality of God, 1983, In God's Mirror: Reflections and Essays, 1990, For Those Who Can't Believe: Overcoming the Obstacles to Faith, 1994, Meditations and Prayers for the Renewal of the Body and the Renewal of the Spirit, 2000, Finding Each Other in Judaism: Meditations on the Rights of Passage from Birth to Immortality, 2001, When You LIe Down and When You Rise Up: Nightstand Meditations, 2001, Conscience: The Duty to Obey, the Duty to Disobey, 2008; co-author: Approaches to the Philosophy of Religion, 1952 Founder Inst. for the Righteous Arts, Judah Magnes Mus., Berkeley, Calif., 1961; founder, chmn. Inst. for Righteous Acts-Documentation and Study Ctr. on Rescuers of Jews in the Nazi Era. Recipient Social Actions award United Synagogue America, 1969, Medal Prime Min. of Israel, 1975; named one of The Top 50 Rabbis in America, Newsweek Mag. 2007. Died Dec. 18, 2014.

SCHULZ, JUERGEN, art historian, educator; b. Kiel, Germany, Aug. 18, 1927; came to U.S., 1938; s. Johannes Martin Askan Schulz and Ilse (Lebenbaum) Hiller; m. Justine Hume, Sept. 1951 (div. 1968); children: Christoph (dec.), Ursula, Catherine; m. Anne Markham, May 19, 1969; 1 child, Jeremy. BA, U. Calif., Berkeley, 1950; PhD in History of Art, U. London, 1958. Reporter San Francisco Chronicle, 1950-51; copy editor UPI, London, 1952-53; from instr. to prof. history of art U. Calif., 1958-68; prof. Brown, Providence, 1968-90, Andrea V. Rosenthal prof. history art and architecture, 1990-95; Samuel H. Kress prof. Nat. Gallery of Art, 2000-2001. Mem. Inst. for Advanced Study, Princeton, N.J., 1971-72. Author: Venetian Painted Ceilings of the Renaissance, 1968, Printed Plans and ...Views of Venice, 1971, La cartografia tra scienza e arte, 1990, The New Palaces of Medieval Venice, 2004; also articles. Staff sgt. U.S. Army, 1945-48. Decorated grande ufficiale Ordine della Stella della Solidarieta della Repubblica Italiana; Guggenheim fellow, 1966-67. Mem. Ateneo Veneto, Centro Internaz. di Studi di Architettura A. Palladio. Home: Providence, RI. Died Nov. 23, 2014.

SCHULZ, OTTO GEORGE, reinsurance broker; b. NYC, July 30, 1930; s. Otto and Rose (Eckstein) S.; m. Catherine O'Donnell, Sept. 3, 1955; children: Kathleen, Gerard, Debbie, Donna. BBA, Pace U., 1959; MBA, St. Johns U., NYC, 1965. Acct. Albert Ullman Marine Agy. Inc., NYC, 1947-59, Transatlantic Reins. Co., NYC, 1959-62; asst. treas. Consol. Mutual Ins. Co., Bklyn., 1962-74; treaty underwriter Am. Re-ins. Co., Princeton, N.J., 1974-86; reins. broker Am-Re Brokers, Inc., Princeton, from 1986. Home: West Milford, NJ. Died Mar. 26, 2007.

SCHULZ, SANDRA E., art educator; b. Dallas, July 2, 1963; d. Lionel Leigh and Ida Maria Johanna Schulz. BS in Art Edn., Tex. Woman's U., 1985, MFA in Sculpture, 1990. Cert. tchr. art all levels Tex. Clk. and advt. Bartos Inc., Dallas, 1982—90; art tchr. 7th and 8th grades Harry Stone Mid. Sch., Dallas, 1990—91; art tchr. 9-12th grades Thomas Jefferson H.S., Dallas, from 1992. Art club sponsor, robotics team sponsor Thomas Jefferson H.S., Dallas. It Is What It Is, Motia, Latitude 32.32. Chair publicity and decoration Tex. Cultural Partnership, Dallas, 1994-2001; publicity chair Am. Czech Culture Soc., Dallas, 1992-2001. Recipient Brookhaven Coll. Pyramid award for tchg., 2001, Tex. Senate Excellence award for outstanding tchrs., Outstanding H.S. Tchr. award, Dallas Rotary Club, 2001—02; named Citizen of the Week, KRLD Radio Sta., 2002. Mem. Nat. Art Educators Assn., Tex. Art Educators Assn., Dallas Art Educators Assn. (publicity chair 1996-98), Sculpture Assn. (sec. 1993-95). Lutheran. Avocations: camping, fishing, gardening, music, electric trains. Home: Royse City, Tex. Died June 10, 2013.

SCHWAGER, KURT HEINZ, business executive; b. Winterthur, Zurich, Switzerland, July 15, 1940; came to U.S., 1969; s. Julius and Marie (Gross) S.; m. Heidi Mathilde Braustein, Mar. 23, 1963; children: Beat, Marcel, Kathy. Service engr. Sulzer Bros., Inc., Winterthur, 1960-72, supr. engring. NYC, 1972-84; pres. Compressor Engring. and Service Cons. Inc., Baldwin, N.Y., from 1984. Avocations: stamp collecting/philately, home bldg. Died Mar. 25, 2007.

SCHWALLER, SHIRLEY FILES, publisher; b. Ft. Worth, Feb. 16, 1946; d. John Thomas and Janette Elizabeth (Hicks) Files; m. Leonard Edward Kowitz, Oct. 6, 1968 (div. Mar. 1979); children: Jeffrey Edward Kowitz, Kendra Denise Kowitz; m. Robert Corbett Schwaller, Sept. 17, 1983; 1 child, Mark Files Schwaller. BBA, U. Tex., 1968; BA in Comm., U. Houston, 1979. Reporter The Mirror, Houston, 1977-78; bus. editor Saudi Rsch. and Mktg., Houston, 1978-79; writer Houston Bus. Jour., 1979-81; v.p. Hart & Assocs., Houston, 1981-82; freelance writer Wall St. Jour. and Houston Bar Jour., Houston, 1982-83; editor Dallas-Ft. Worth Bus. Jour., 1983-85, Dallas Times Herald, 1985-87; co-founder, pub. SR Texas, 1987-93; prin. Horizon Comm., Dallas, from 1994. Contbr. numerous articles to profl. jours.; author 2 corp. histories and 2 ghosted books. Mem. Mayor's Task Force on Employing the Handicapped, Dallas, 1985-87; pres. Shared Housing, City of Dallas; bd. dirs. Metro Dallas YMCA Cmtys. Svc.; mem. adv. bd. Dallas Assistance League; mem. steering com. Safeguards for Srs., 1992-93. Recipient Sr. Affairs award City of Dallas. Mem. Nat. Assn. Women Bus. Owners (bd. dirs. Dallas chpt. 1994—), Nat. Assn. Bus. Editors and Writers, Dallas Press Club (finalist Best Headline Portfolio 1986, finalist Best Splty. Pub. 1986), Soc. Profl. Journalists, Dallas C. of C. (chmn. pub. rels. com. 1985—). Republican. Home: Addison, Tex. Died Jan. 30, 2007.

SCHWARTZ, ANNE SIMMONS, retired sales executive; b. Midlothian, Tex., Dec. 20, 1916; d. John Thomas Simmons and Katherine Maude Dillard; m. Jerome Stephen Schwartz, Feb. 21, 1943; children: John Benjamin, Katherine. BA, Tex. State Coll. Women, 1938; postgrad., U. Mo., 1938—39. Editl. asst. Inst. Propaganda Analysis Tchrs. Coll. Columbia U., NYC, 1939—41; rsch. dir. and editor newsletter Friends of Democracy, NYC, 1941—50; treas. Key Book Svc., Inc., NYC, 1952—79. Founder The Dispute Settlement Ctr., Norwalk, Conn., 1990; Bible tchr. Saugatuck Congl. Ch., Westport, Conn., 1961—78; sec. Norumbega Resident Coun., 2001—03. Died Feb. 1, 2007.

SCHWARTZ, CARL EDWARD, artist, printmaker; b. Detroit, Sept. 20, 1935; s. Carl and Verna (Steiner) S.; m. Kay Joyce Hofmann, June 18, 1955 (div.); children: Dawn Ellen, Cari Leigh; m. Celeste Borah, Jan. 1, 2007. BFA, Art Inst. Chgo. Sch.-U. Chgo., 1957. Past tchr. art Chgo. North Shore Art League, Suburban Fine Arts Ctr., Deerpath Art League; faculty Fla. Gulf Coast U. One-man shows include, South Bend (Ind.) Art Center, Feingarten Gallery, Chgo., 1960, Bernard Horwich Center, Chgo., Covenant Club, Chgo., Barat Coll., Chgo. Pub. Library, Alverno Coll., 1020 Art Center, Rosenberg Gallery, Peoria (Ill.) Art Guild, 1977, Ill. State Mus., 1977 Ill. Inst. Tech., 1978, Miller Gallery, Chgo., 1979, Union League Club, Chgo., 1982, Art Inst. Rental and Sale Gallery, Chgo., 1982, Horwich Gallery, Chgo., 1983, Lake Forest (Ill.) Coll., 1983, Campanile-Capponi Contemporary Gallery, Chgo., 1987, Nagata Gallery, Ft. Myers, Fla., 1988, Jan Cicero Gallery, Chgo., 1990, Neopolitan Gallery, Naples, Fla., 1996, 97; group shows include 9th Ann. Michigana Exhbt, Detroit (Cloetingh and Deman award 1959), Hyde Park Art Center, Chgo., 1960 (prize), Spectrum Exhbn. '63, Chgo. (1st prize), New Horizons Exhbt, Chgo., 1960 (Joseph Shapiro award), Nat. Design Center, Chgo., 1965 (New Horizons in Painting 1st prize), 3d Ann. Chgo. Arts Competition, 1962 (1st prize), Union League Club, Chgo., 1967 (2d prize), North Shore Art League, Chgo., 1965 (1st prize), Artists Guild Chgo., 1965 (prize), McCormack Pl., Chgo., 1965 (1st prize), Detroit Art Inst., 1965 (Commonwealth prize), Park Forest (Ill.) Art Exhbn, 1969 (Best of Show), 14th Ann. Virginia Beach (Va.) Show, 1969 (Best of Show), Suburban Fine Arts Center, Highland Park, Ill., 1970 (prize), 15th Ann. Virginia Beach Show, 1970 (prize), 32d Ann. Artists Guild, Chgo., 1970 (2d prize), North Shore Art League, 1970 (prize), 16th Ann. Virginia Beach Show, 1971 (2d prize), Ill. State Fair, 1972 (prize), Artists Guild Chgo., 1972 (1st prize), 17th Ann. Virginia Beach Exhbt, 1972 (1st prize), Artists Guild 50th Fine Art Exhbn., Chgo., 1973 (prize), Dickinson State U., 1973 (prize), North Shore Art League, 1973 (prize), Lakehurst Exhbt, 1974 (prize), Union League Art Exhbt, 1974 (1st prize), 1976 (prize), Artists Guild Fine Arts Exhbn., 1974 (best of Show), Bluegrass Painting Exhbn, Louisville, 1975 (award Washington, Art Inst. Chgo., K. Van Ella, Chgo., Gardner-Colby Gallery, Naples, Fla., Cape Coral Arts Studio, Van Liebig Art Ctr., 2005, Art League of Bonita Springs (Best of Show, Art Focus award 2007), Alliance for the Arts (award), 2007, 50 yr. Retrospective Show Fla. Gulf Coast U. Art Gallery, 2009. Recipient Logan medal, Art Inst. Chgo., 1958. Home: Fort Myers, Fla. *I am* *a painter of light. I'm intrigued and fascinated with form. To me, there are two worlds-the one we all live in, and the one that I create. Painting is the discipline by which I constantly rediscover both of these worlds.* Died Sept. 21, 2014.

SCHWEIKER, RICHARD SCHULTZ, former trade association administrator, former United States Secretary of Health & Human Services; b. Norristown, Pa., June 1, 1926; s. Malcolm Alderfer and Blanche R. (Schultz) S.; m. Claire Joan Coleman, Sept. 10, 1955 (dec. 2013); children: Malcolm C., Lani Shelton, Kyle Hard, Richard S. Jr., Lara Kristi Carey. BA in Psychology, Pa. State U., 1950; D of Public Svc. (hon.), Temple U., 1970; DSc (hon.), Georgetown U., 1981. Bus. exec. American Olean Tile Company, 1950-60; mem. US Congress from 13th Pa. Dist., 1961—69; US Senator from Pa., 1969—81; sec. US Dept. Health & Human Services (HHS), Washington, 1981—83; pres. American Council Life Ins., Washington, 1983-94. Chmn. Partnership for Prevention, 1991—97. Pres Montgomery County Young Republicans, 1952-54; Alt. del. Nat. Republican Conv., 1952, 56, del., 1972, 80; designated Vice Presdl. Candidate with Ronald Reagan, 1976 Presdl. Election. Served with USNR, World War II, 1944-46 Recipient Disting. Alumnus award Pa. State U., 1970, Dr. Charles H. Best award American Diabetes Assn., 1974, Outstanding Alumnus of Yr. award Phi Kappa Sigma, 1982, Gold medal Pa. Assn. Broadcasters, 1982, Nat. Outstanding Svc. award Headstart, 1983, Public Svc. Gold medal Surgeon Gen. U.S., 1988, Govt. Achievement award Juvenile Diabetes Found., 1990, Disting. Achievement award Nat. Coun. on Aging, 1991, John Newton Russell award Nat. Assn. Life Underwriters, 1992; named Outstanding Young Man of Yr., Jr. Chamber of Commerce, 1960. Mem. Phi Beta Kappa. Republican. Home: Mc Lean, Va. Died July 31, 2015.

SCHWEPPE, JOSEPH LOUIS, control systems consultant; b. Jan. 11, 1921; s. Edward Louis and Dora Vanneta (Jenkins) S.; m. Willa Johnson, Apr. 18, 1942; children: Laura Thorp, Anna Tollison, Mona Depew. BSChE, U. Mo., 1942, MSChE, 1946; PhD, U. Mich., 1950. Lic. profl. engr. Tex. Jr. chem. engr. TVA, Wilson Dam, Ala., 1942-43; chem. engr. du Pont, Orange, Tex., 1949-52; sr. project engr. C.F. Braun, Alhambra, Calif., 1952-58; prof., chmn. dept. mech. engring. U. Houston, 1958-63; pres. Houston Engring. Rsch. Corp., Houston, 1960-90; chmn. bd. JK Control Systems, Inc., Houston, 1991-96. Patentee in field; contbr. articles to profl. jours. Elder St. John's Presbyn. Ch., Houston, 1965-67. Lt. (j.g.) USN, 1943-46, PTO. Decorated Bronze Star; DuPont fellow U. Mich., 1949. Mem. IEEE, ASME, Am. Inst. Chem. Engrs., Sigma Xi, Phi Kappa Phi, Tau Beta Pi. Republican. Avocations: scuba diving, swimming. Home: Houston, Tex. Died Nov. 8, 2006.

SCIUTTO, JOSEPH ARMAND, retired dentist; b. Salinas, Calif., Oct. 19, 1906; s. Charles and Louise (Moiso) S.; M. Dorothy Louise Gale, June 30, 1934; children: Robert James, Barbara Blunden. DDS, U. Calif. Med. Ctr., 1928. Dental surgeon Cowell Meml. Hosp. U. Calif., Berkeley, 1928-37; gen. practice Berkeley, 1928-83; clin. instr. U. Calif. Med. Ctr., San Francisco, 1958-75; ret., 1983. Lectr. continuing dental edn. U. Calif. Sch. of Dentistry, San Francisco, 1955, mem. prosthetic clin. and investigative group, 1970; chmn. 5th Internat. Dental Seminars, Tokyo, Kyoto, Bangkok, Bogota, Lima, Santiago, Buenos Aires, Rio de Janeiro, 14th World Dental Congress, Paris. Named Disting. Alumnus, U. Calif., 1991. Fellow Am. Coll. Dentists, Internat. Coll. Dentists; mem. ADA, Berkeley Dental Soc. (pres.), Calif. Dental Assn. (gen. chmn., ann. meeting), Pacific Dental Conf. (v.p.), U. Calif. San Francisco Dental Alumni Assn. (pres.), Fedn. Dentaire Internat., Am. Prosthodontic Soc., Internat. Prosthodontic Conf., U. Calif. Alumni Assn. (life mem.), Rotary (pres., Paul Harris fellow), Claremont Country Club, Xi Psi Phi. Home: Walnut Creek, Calif. Died Nov. 13, 2006.

SCOLA, ETTORE, film director, script writer; b. Trevico, Italy, May 10, 1931; Journalist humorous mags., 1954; script writer films including Il Sorpasso, 1962, Anni Ruggenti, 1962, I Mostri, 1963, Io la Conoscevo Bene, 1965; dir. films Se permettete Parliamo di Donne, 1964, La Congiuntura, 1964, La Congiontora, 1965, L'Arcidiavolo, 1966, Riusciranno i Nostri Eroi a Ritrovare l'Amico Misteriosamente Scomparso in Africa?, 1968, Il Commissario Pepe, 1969, Dramma della Gelosia, 1970, Permette? Rocco Papaleo, 1971, La più bella Serata della mia Vita, 1972, C'eravamo tanto amati, 1974, Brutti, Sporchi e Cattivi, 1975 (Best Dir., Cannes Internat. Film Festival), Una Giornata Particolare, 1977 (Oscar nomination), I Nuovi Mostri, 1977 (Oscar nomination with title Viva Italia), La Terrazza, 1979, La Nuit de Varennes, La Fuite a Varennes, 1982, Ballando, ballando, 1984 (France's Cesar award 1984, Oscar nomination), Maccheroni, , 1985, La Famiglia, 1987 (Oscar nomination), Splendor, 1988, Che Ora é, 1989, Il Viaggio di Capitan Fracassa, 1990, Mario, Maria e Mario, 1992, Romanzo di un giovane povero, 1994; (documentary) How Strange to Be Names Federico: Scola Narrates Fellini, 2013 Home: Rome, Italy. Died Jan. 19, 2016.

SCOTT, SARAH ANNE, mental health nurse; b. Bluefield, W.Va., May 19, 1957; d. Donald McLean and Jean (Smith) Keesling; m. Glenn Stephen Scott, Feb. 12, 1983; children: Thomas Andrew, Matthew Edward. Nursing degree, Mercer County Vocat. Sch., 1978. LPN, W.Va.; cert. CPR, first aid instr., ARC. Practical nurse Princeton (W.Va.) Cmty. Hosp., 1978, nurse, 1981-82, Bluefield Sanitarium Clinic, 1978; scrub nurse-surgery Bluefield Regional Med. Ctr., 1978-81; nurse Princeton Internists, Inc., Princeton, 1982-86; nurse renal dialysis unit Mercer County Health Ctr., Bluefield, 1986-87; nurse, acting admissions coord. Nova Care So. Hills. Regional Rehab. Hosp., Princeton, 1987-92; nurse So. Highlands Cmty. Mental Health Ctr., Princeton, 1994-99. Poll worker Rep. Party. Republican. Baptist. Avocations: cooking, reading, tennis, swimming, ice skating. Home: Princeton, W.Va. Died June 4, 2007.

SCOTT, STUART, sports commentator; b. Chgo., July 19, 1965; s. O. Ray and Jacqueline Scott; m. Kimberly Scott, 1993 (div. 2007); children: Taelor, Sydni. BA in Speech Comm. & Radio/TV/Film, U. NC, 1987. News reporter, weekend anchor WPDE-TV, Florence, S.C., 1987-88; news reporter WRAL-TV, Raleigh, N.C., 1988-90; sports reporter, sports anchor WESH-TV, Orlando, Fla., 1990-93; sports anchor, sports reporter ESPN, Bristol, Conn., 1993—2015. Anchor reporter SportsNight: College Football Edition, 1995—, co-host SportsNight, 1994. Recipient Jim Valvano award, ESPYs, 2014. Died Jan. 4, 2015.

SCOTT, THOMAS JAMES, environmental services administrator, researcher; b. Providence, Sept. 8, 1920; s. John W. and Ruth (Holbrook) S.; m. Virginia Ranney, Oct. 25, 1941; children: Christopher, Thomas James III, Linell, John, David. Student, Trinity Coll., 1939-41; AM, Harvard U., 1946. Pres. Buckley & Scott Co., Needham, Mass., 1961-75, chmn., 1975-80; pres. Ctr. for Energy Policy, Boston, 1974-80, Ctr. for Policy Negotiation, Boston, from 1980. With USN, 1941-45, PTO. Mem. Ind. Oil Men (pres. New Eng. chpt. 1961-69), Better Home Heat Coun. (chmn. Boston chpt. 1954-56), 25 Yr. Club, Somerset Club, Long Wood Cricket Club. Home: Weston, Mass. Died Mar. 20, 2007.

SEABLOOM, ROBERT WENDELL, civil engineering educator; b. Tacoma, July 18, 1924; s. Oscar Rudolph and Margaret Susan (Anderson) S.; m. Joan Estelle Stapelton, Aug. 9, 1947; children: Wendy, Robert Wendell. BSCE, U. Wash., 1950, MSCE, 1956. Registered profl. engr., Wash., Alaska. Design engr. Seattle Engring. Dept., 1950-51; pub. health engr. Wash. State Health Dept., Seattle, 1952-53; san. engr. U.S. Navy Pub. Works Dept., Seattle, 1953-54; instr. civil engring. U. Wash., Seattle, 1954-56, asst. prof., 1956-59, assoc. prof., 1959-79, prof., from 1979. Home: Seattle, Wash. Died Feb. 12, 2007.

SEARLES, QUENTIN, artist; b. Dunn Center, ND, Feb. 20, 1919; s. Leland Day and Bertha Marie (Schmidt) S.; m. Barbara Hoskins, Nov. 10, 1956; 1 child: Susan Searles Nielsen. BFA, Ctrl. Wash. U., 1948; cert. in secondary tchg., U. Wash., 1949; postgrad., U. Oreg. Social case worker State Dept. Social and Health Svcs., Yakima, Wash., 1953-61; art instr. Yakima Valley (Wash.) C.C., 1964-67; painter Orchard Garden, Naches, Washington, from 1961. With U.S. Army, 1941, CBI. Recipient 1st place Parnassus award U. Wash., 1947, Festival of Arts Columbia Basin Coll., Pasco, Wash., Artists Ctrl. Wash. Larson Gallery: grantee Wash. State Art Commn., 1978. Avocation: book collecting. Home: Naches, Wash. Died May 21, 2007.

SEARS, JOHN WINTHROP, lawyer; b. Boston, Dec. 18, 1930; s. Richard Dudley and Frederica Fulton (Leser) S.; m. Catherine Coolidge, 1965 (div. 1970). AB magna cum laude, Harvard U., Cambridge, Mass., 1952, JD, 1959; MLitt, Oxford U., Eng., 1957; D Polit. Sci. (hon.), Bridgewater State Coll., Mass., 2006. Bar: Mass. 1959, U.S. Dist. Ct. Mass. 1982. Rep. Brown Bros. Harriman, NYC, 1959-63, Boston, 1963-66; mem. Mass. Ho. Reps., 1965-68; sheriff Suffolk County, Mass., 1968-69; chmn. Boston Fin. Commn., 1969-70, Met. Dist. Commn., 1970-75; councilor-at-large Boston City Coun., 1980-82; trustee Sears Office, Boston, from 1975. Contbr. articles to profl. jours.; author: History of the Sears Chapel, 2012, History of the Thursday Evening Club of 1846, 2004. Apptd. bd. dirs. Fulbright Scholarship, 1991-93; trustee Christ's Ch., Longwood, Brookline, Mass., 1965—, Sears Trusts, Boston, 1975—; hon. trustee J.F. Kennedy Libr., 1991—2003; bd. dirs. Am. Mus. Textile Heritage, 1987-97, Shirley-Eustis Assoc., Environ. League, Mass., 1994-97; Rep. candidate Sec. State, Mass., 1978, Gov. of Mass., 1982; vice chmn. Ward 5 Rep. Com., 1965-69, 75-85; chmn. Rep. State Com., 1975-76, mem., 1980-85; del. Rep. Nat. Conv., 1968, 76, State Conv., 1966-92; mem. U.S. Electoral Coll., 1984; bd. dirs. United South End Settlements, 1966—, chmn., 1977-78. Lt. comdr. USNR, 1952-54, 61-62. Recipient Outstanding Pub. Servant award Mass. Legis. Assn., 1975; Rhodes scholar, 1955 Mem. Mass. Bar Assn., New Eng. Hist. and Geneal. Soc. (bd. dirs., councillor 1977-82), Mass. Hist. Soc., Handel and Haydn Soc. (gov. 1982-87), Signet Soc., Boston Athenaeum, Tennis and Racquet Club, Somerset Club, The Country Club (Brookline), St. Botolph Club, Club of Odd Vols., Wednesday Evening Club of 1777, Thursday Evening Club of 1846 (pres. 1999-2004), Spee Club (Cambridge) (pres., trustee), Longwood Cricket Club (hon.), Soc. Colo. Wars (hon. mem. 2013), Phi Beta Kappa, Beacon Hill Seminars. Republican. Home: Tewksbury, Mass. *As the working years come to an end, some of us look for ways to teach, to help neighbors, especially those in need, to build up the beauty and excellence we may have encountered in our own lives, and do our best to pass them on to others.* Died Nov. 4, 2014.

SEARS, MILDRED BRADLEY, environmental and safety scientist; b. New Castle, Pa., Feb. 19, 1933; d. Edward Ellis and Ruth Elaine (Allison) Bradley; m. D. Richard Sears, July 2, 1965 (div. July 1974); 1 child, Margaret Sears Kroen. BA, Coll. of Wooster, 1954; PhD, U. Fla., 1958. Rsch. staff mem. Oak Ridge (Tenn.) Nat. Lab., from 1958. Patentee in field; contbr. 48 articles and tech. reports to profl. publs. Mem. Am. Chem. Soc., Am. Nuclear Soc., Sigma Xi, Phi Beta Kappa, Phi Kappa Phi. Home: Oak Ridge, Tenn. Died Feb. 1, 2007.

SEAWELL, DONALD RAY, lawyer, performing company executive; b. Jonesboro, NC, Aug. 1, 1912; s. Aaron Ashley Flowers and Bertha (Smith) S.; m. Eugenia Rawls, Apr. 5, 1941; children: Brook Ashley, Donald Brockman. AB, U. NC, 1933, JD, 1936, DLitt, 1980; LHD, U. No. Colo., 1978. Bar: NC 1936, NY 1947. With SEC, 1939-41, 45-47, Dept. Justice, 1942-43; chmn. bd., dir., pub., pres. Denver Post, 1966-81; chmn. bd., dir. Gravure West, LA, 1966-81; dir. Swan Prodns., London; of counsel firm Bernstein, Seawell, Kove & Maltin, NYC, 1979—2006; chmn. bd. Denver Ctr. Performing Arts, 1972—2006, chief exec. officer, 1972—2006, chmn. emeritus, 2007—15. Ptnr. Bonfils-Seawell Enterprises, NYC; bd. vis. U. NC Chmn. bd. ANTA, 1965-2015; theatre panel Nat. Coun. Arts, 1970-74; bd. govs. Royal Shakespeare Theatre, Eng.; trustee Am. Acad. Dramatic Arts, 1967-2015, Hofstra U., 1968-69, Cen. City Opera Assn., Denver Symphony; bd. dirs., Air Force Acad. Found., Nat. Ints. Outdoor Drama, Walter Hampden Meml. Library, Hammond Mus.; pres. Helen G. Bonfils Found., 1972-97, pres. emeritus, 1997-2015, Denver Opera Found.; Population Crisis Com., 1982-91; bd. dirs. Family Health Internat., Found. for Internat. Family Health; bd. visitors NC Sch. Arts, 1992-98; pres. Frederick G. Bonfils Found., 1972-92; chmn. Civilian Mil. Inst. Recipient Am. Acad. Achievement award, 1980, Tony award for producing, On Your Toes, 1983, Vocie Rsch. and Awareness award, Voice Found., 1983, Arts and Entertainement Cable Network award, 1987, Third Millennium Leadership award, Am. Diabetes Assn., 1996, Colo. Tourism Hall of Fame award, 1999, Thomas Degaetani award, U.S. Inst. for Theatre Tech., 2000, Benjamin F. Stapleton, Jr. award, 2000, Disting. Svc. award, U. Colo., 2000, Downtown Denver award for Tantalus, 2001, AWARE Honoree award, 2001, Donald Seawell Outstanding Achievement in Theatre award, Colo. Festival World Theatre, 2005, Founders award for Outstanding Contbn. to Am. Theater, Theater Hall Fame, NYC, 2005, Theatre Hall Fame, NYC, 2006; named Officer, Most Excellent Order of the Brit. Empire, 2002. Mem. Bucks Club (London), Dutch Treat Club (NYC), Denver Country Club, Denver Club, Cherry Hills Country Club, Mile High Club (Denver), Garden of Gods Club (Colorado Springs, Colo.). Died Sept. 30, 2015.

SEBASTIAN, JOAN (JOSÉ MANUEL FIGUEROA), musician; b. Juliantla, Mexico, Apr. 8, 1951; m. Maribel Guardia (div.); children: Julián Figueroa, José Manuel Figueroa, Trigo(dec.) , Juan(dec.). Musician: (albums) Rumores, 1985, Oiga, 1987, Ranchero vol. 2, 1987, Mascarada, 1988, Norteno, 1989, Con Banda, 1991, Viva La Vida, 1991, Al Rojo Vivo, 1995, Embustero, 1995, Con Tambora, 1995, Bandido De Amores, 1995, Mis Nuevas Baladas, 1995, Peor de Tus Antojos, 1995, En Vivo en La Arena Mexico, 1995, Tambora Remix, 1995, Me Enamore De Ti, 1995, Con Mariachi, 1995, Tu Y Yo, 1996, Gracias Por Tanto Amor, 1998, Rey del Jaripeo, 1999, Con Norteno, 2000, Secreto de Amor, 2000, Nostalgia y Recuerdos, 2000, Con el Mariachi Vargas de Tecal, 2001, Un Carino Como Tu, 2001, En Vivo: Desde la Plaza el Progreso de Guadalajara, 2001, Lo Dijo el Corazon, 2002 (Grammy award for Best Mexican album, 2002), Afortunado, 2002 (Grammy award for Best Mexican album, 2003), Que Amarren a Cupido, 2004, El Poeta del Pueblo, 2004, Enamorado del Amor, 2004, Frente a Frente: Con Banda, 2004, Mujeres Bonitas, 2004, Inventario, 2005, Rancheras Con Banda, 2005, Canta Para Ti, 2006, Mas Allá del Sol, 2006 (Grammy award for Best Banda Album, 2007), Corridos y Algo Mas, 2007, Siempre Romantico, 2007, No Es de Madera, 2007 (Grammy award for Best Banda Album, 2009), 13 Celebrando el 13, 2013, (songs) Mas Allá del Sol, 2006 (Song of Yr., ASCAP Latin Music awards, 2007, Regional Mex. Album of Yr., Billboard Latin Music awards, 2007), Estos Celos, 2007 (Latin Grammy award for Best Regional Mexican Song, 2008); actor: (films) La Sangre de nuestra raza, 1982, Sangre De Rey, 1997; (TV series) Tu y Yo, 1996. Recipient Silver Pen award, ASCAP, 2000, Golden Note award, 2007, Hall of Fame award, Billboard Latin Music Awards, 2006. Died July 6, 2015.

SECKINGER, GERALD EDWIN, investor; b. Manchester, Mich., May 28, 1925; s. Joseph Edward and Myrta Mae (Weber) S.; widowed; children: Marianne Leitereg, Mark Bernard, Margo Lynn Guzman, Martin Neil, Martha Jean Toffol, Michael John, Matthew Joseph. BA, Mich. State U., 1950. Gen. mgr. Del Mar Hotel, Sault Ste. Marie, Mich., 1950-52; food svc. dir. Montgomery Ward & Co., Chgo., 1952-82; food svc. cons., pres. Seckinger Assocs., Glenview, Ill., 1982-87; pvt. investor Gerald Seckinger, Scottsdale, Ariz., from 1987. Civil def. officer U.S. Govt., Glenview, Ill., 1962-64. 1st lt. U.S. Army Air Corps, 1943-46. Mem. McCormick Ranch POA, Am. Legion, Foodsvcs. Cons. Soc. Internat., KC. Republican. Roman Catholic. Avocations: golf, fishing. Home: Scottsdale, Ariz. Died Dec. 15, 2006.

SEEM, ROBERT PAUL, financial planner; b. Feb. 29, 1932; BS, Davis and Elkins Coll., 1955. CLU, ChFC. Ins./fin. planner, 1961-78; cons. Seem Fin., Orlando, Fla., from 1978. Pilot USAF, 1955-61. Died Jan. 8, 2007.

SEGALL, RALPH SIMON, contractor; b. Shreveport, La., Aug. 5, 1926; s. Bernard E. and Bertha (Simon) S.; m. Betty Lipson Segall, Oct. 30, 1949; 1 child, Susan Lynn Segall Robison. BSME, Tex. A&M Coll., 1949. Registered profl. engr., La. Field supr. B. Segall Co., Shreveport, 1948-49, design engr., 1949-51, chief engr., 1949-60; v.p. B. Segall Co., Inc., Shreveport, 1960-67; pres. The Segall Co., Inc., Shreveport, from 1967. Bd. dirs. Nat. Conf. of Christians and Jews, N.Y.C., 1989—; pres. Shreveport Beautification Soc., 1960-62. With USAF, 1945-47. Mem. Masons (worshipful master), Rotary (pres. Shreveport club 1984-85, dist. conf. chmn. dist. 619, 1987), East Ridge Country Club (v.p. 1973-76), Optimist (life). Avocations: golf, coin collecting/numismatics, walking, reading. Home: Shreveport, La. Died Feb. 16, 2007.

SEHORN, MARSHALL ESTUS, music industry executive, songwriter; b. Concord, NC, June 25, 1934; s. William Thomas and Bertha (Mesmer) S.; m. Barbara Ann Darcy, May 11, 1974. BS in Agr., NC State Coll., 1957. Owner, operator comml. farm Concord, 1957—58; producer, co-owner Fury and Fire Records, NYC, 1958—63; producer EMI, London, 1963—64; pres., co-owner Marsaint/Sansu Enterprises, New Orleans, from 1965. Pres., owner Red Dog Express, Inc., from 1985. Prodr. (recording): Kansas City, 1959 (gold record, 1959); co-prodr.(recording): Lady Marmalade, 1974 (gold record, 1974); prodr.: (song) Southern Nights, 1977 (Broadcast Music, Inc. award, 1977), (album) Elvis Live at La. Hayride, 1983. Recipient Outstanding Svc. award, La. Gov., 1979, 1982, Outstanding Music Contbn. award, Mayor New Orleans, 1982; named Record Man of Yr., Am. Record Mfg. and Distbrs. Assn., 1961. Mem.: Bass Anglers Am. (New Orleans) (life). Republican. Methodist. Avocations: boating, fishing, songwriting, hunting, art collecting. Home: New Orleans, La. Died Dec. 5, 2006.

SEIDEN, SANDRA MAE, artist; b. San Diego, Jan. 26, 1949; d. Edward Irvin and Ruth Margaret (Schmidt) Seiden; 1 child, Shayne Magic McIntyre. Exhibited in numerous shows; artist oil on canvas in Ency. of the Living Artist, 11th edit., 1999. Home: Freedom, Calif. Died July 12, 2007.

SEITZ, JAMES EUGENE, retired college president, freelance writer; b. Columbia, Pa., July 27, 1927; s. Joseph Stoner and Minnie (Frey) S.; m. Florence Arlene Dutcher, Apr. 6, 1950; children: Diane Louise, Ellen Kay, Linda Marie, Karl Steven. BS, Millersville State Coll., 1950; MEd, Pa. State U., 1952; PhD, So. Ill. U., 1971. Tchr. pub. schs., Pa., 1950-56; lectr. Temple U., Phila., 1956-62; asst. prof. engr. tech. Kans. State U., Pitts., 1962-65; dean Mineral Area Coll., Flat River, Mo., 1965-69, Coll. of Lake County, Gravslake, Ill., 1969-73; founding pres. Edison State Community Coll., Piqua, Ohio, 1973-85; freelance writer Sidney, Ohio, from 1985. Founding sec.-treas. Ohio Tech. and C.C. Assn., Columbus, 1976; speaker in field. Author: Woodcarving: A Designer's Notebook, 1989, Country Creations, 1991, Selling What You Make, 1992, Effective Board Participation, 1993, Substance for the Soul, 1999, Practical Woodcarving Design and Application, 2003, Carved Gifts for All Occasions, 2006; contbr. articles to profl. jours. Founding pres. Exch. Club Grayslake, 1970; pres. Epicurian Soc., Sidney, Ohio, 1978-79; mediator Mcpl. Ct., Sidney, 1992-2003; sr. citizens' steering com. Arbor Day Found.; founding pres. Sr. Ctr. of Sidney-Shelby Co., 1996—, choir, 2001—04; trustee Sidney Meml. Bldg., 2003- ; named Outstanding Sr. Citizen, 2001; mem. Ret. Srs. Vol. Program, 2005—. Recipient Leadership and Svc. award, Pa. State U. Alumni Soc., 1990, Disting. Alumni Svc. award, Millersville U., 2007; named to Manor High Sch. Wall of Honor, 2007. Mem. Am. Assn. Ret. Persons (founding chpt. pres. 1990-91), Assn. for Career & Tech. Edn., VFW (charter Post 8757), Am. Legion (scholarship com. and judge Post 217 1996-97, exec. com. 1997—, publicity dir. 1998-2000), Sidney Singing Soldiers (pres., 1998), AmVets, Shelby Woodcarvers Guild (founding pres. 1999), Iota Lambda Sigma. Avocations: woodworking, lecturing. Home: Sidney, Ohio. Died Sept. 4, 2007.

SELEBI, JACKIE (JACOB SELLO SELEBI), former President of Interpol; b. Johannesburg, Mar. 7, 1950; married; 2 children. Rep. World Fedn. Democratic Youth, 1983—87; amb. to UN Govt. of South Africa, NYC, 1995—98, dir.-gen, Dept. Fgn. Affairs, 1998—2000; nat. commr. South African Police Svc., 2000—08; v.p. for Africa Interpol, Lyon, France, 2002—04, pres., 2004—08. Chmn. Human Rights Commn. UN 54th Session; chmn. Anti-Landmine Conference, Oslo; chairperson Justice, Crime Prevention and Security Cluster South African Criminal Justice Sys. Recipient Human Rights award, Internat. Svc. Human Rights, 1997. Died Jan. 23, 2015.

SELFRIDGE, GEORGE DEVER, retired dentist, retired military officer; b. Pitman, NJ, Sept. 24, 1924; s. William John and Edith (Gorman) S.; m. Ruth Motisher, 1948; children: Pamela Ruth, Kimberly Dawn, Cheryl Beth. Student, Gettysburg Coll., 1942-43, Muhlenburg Coll., 1943-45; DDS, U. Buffalo, 1947; MA, George Washington U., 1974. Commd. lt. (j.g.) USN, 1948, advanced through grades to rear adm., 1973; intern Naval Dental Sch., Bethesda, Md., 1948-49, Naval Hosp., St. Albans, NY, 1949-50; asst. dental officer U.S.S. Midway, 1949-51; with USN, 1951-64; sr. dental officer U.S.S. Randolph, 1958-60, U.S.S. Cadmus, 1964-65, U.S.S. Vulcan, 1965-66, Svc. Force, 1964-66, Submarine Force, Atlantic Fleet, 1967-69; from asst. dir. grad. edn. to comdg. officer Navy Grad. Dental Sch., Bethesda, 1969-76; exec. officer Norfolk (Va.) Navy Dental Clinic, 1972-73; ret. USN, 1976; dean Dental Sch., Washington U., St. Louis, 1976-86; dir. dental services Barnes Hosp., St. Louis, 1976—87, Children's Hosp., St. Louis, 1976-87; exec. dir. American Bd. Orthodontics, 1986-97; ret., 1998. Mem. advisory bd. VA Hosp., St. Louis, 1977-79; mem. exec. coun. Cen. Region Testing Svc., 1976-86; adv. com. St. Louis Jr. Coll. Dist., 1976-86. Contbr. articles to med. jours. Decorated Legion of Merit; recipient commendation medals, Greater St. Louis Gold Medallion award, 1995, Spl. Recognition award American Bd. Orthopedics, 1996. Mem. ADA, American Coll. Dentists (past pres.), Internat. Coll. Coll. Dentists (dep. registrar, sec. U.S. sect., Spl. Recognition award), Assn. Mil. Surgeons U.S., Omicron Kappa Upsilon. Republican. Home: O Fallon, Mo. Died Oct. 19, 2014.

SELLARS, GILBERT FITZGERALD, optometrist; b. Balt., May 4, 1932; s. Joseph F. and Rosa Madge (Hicks) S.; m. Gudran Therese Marquand Pederson, Aug. 4, 1957; children: Suzanne Birgite Sellars Hicks, Annette Kirsten. BA, Johns Hopkins U., 1954; OD, New Eng. Coll. Optometry, 1960. Diplomate Nat. Bd. Optometry. Pvt. practice optometry, Henderson, N.C., from 1960. Mem. Vance County Bd. of Edn., 1968-76. Fellow Am. Acad. Optometry; mem. Am. Optometric Assn. (bd. dirs. 1987-93), N.C. Optometric Soc. (trustee 1972), Rotary Club (pres., Henderson 1981). Republican. Methodist. Avocations: reading, travel, dance, politics. Home: Henderson, NC. Died July 3, 2007.

SELLERS, PETER HOADLEY, mathematician, educator; b. Phila., Sept. 12, 1930; s. Lester Hoadley and Therese (Tyler) S.; m. Lucy Bell Newlin, June 21, 1958; children: Mortimer, Therese, Wanja, Lucy Bell. BA, U. Pa., 1953, MA, 1958, PhD, 1965. Math. tchr. Kangaru Sch., Embu, Kenya, 1961-63; programmer U. Pa., Phila., 1958-61; mem. faculty Rockefeller U., NYC, from 1966. Johnson Found. postdoctoral fellow, 1963-65 Mem. editl. bd. Genomics, 1986-97; author: Combinatorial Complexes, 1979; contbr. articles to profl. jours. Trustee Coll. of the Atlantic, Bar Harbor, Maine, 1985-96; curator Rockefeller Hist. Instrument Collection, 1997—. Lt (j.g.) USNR, 1953-55 Mem. Am. Math. Soc., Math. Assn. Am., Soc. Indsl. and Applied Math. Democrat. Episcopalian. Avocations: boat building, sailing. Home: Philadelphia, Pa. Deceased.

SENESE, DANIEL J., electrical engineer, association administrator; b. Chgo., July 7, 1944; s. Anthony J. and Christine S.; m. Joan Cummings, Mar. 20, 1982; children: Margaret D., Amy M. BSEE, U. Ill., 1967, MSEE, 1968. Mem. tech. staff AT&T Bell Labs., Naperville, Ill., 1968-71, supr. Holmdel, N.J., 1971-79, dept. head, 1979-83, Bellcore, Red Bank, N.J., 1984-87, v.p., 1988-95; dir. Ameritech, Chgo., 1987-88; exec. dir. IEEE, Piscataway, N.J., from 1995. Contbr. articles to profl. jours. including IEEE Transactions in Computers. Elder 1st Presbyn. Ch., Red Bank, N.J., 1995-97. Mem. IEEE, IEEE Computer Soc. (Best Paper awards 1974). Achievements include three patents in areas of digital computers. Home: Leonardo, NJ. Died Jan. 6, 2007.

SENFT, JOHN FRANKLIN, forestry educator; b. York, Pa., Apr. 13, 1933; s. Walter Melvin and Rhoda (Garber) S.; m. Kathryn Anna Glatfelter, Jan. 20, 1958; children: Dan (dec.), Nancy. BS, Pa. State U., 1955, MS, 1959; PhD, Purdue U., 1967. Instr. forestry Pa. State U., University Park, 1957-59, Purdue U., West Lafayette, Ind., 1959-67, asst. prof., 1967-72, assoc. prof. forestry, from 1972. Cons. AID, Brazil, 1972, USDA, Madison, Wis., 1980. Contbr. rsch. articles to profl. publs. 1st lt. U.S. Army, 1955-57. Mem. ASTM, Forest Products Rsch. Soc. (sect. pres. 1990-91), Soc. Wood Sci. and Technology. Republican. Lutheran. Home: West Lafayette, Ind. Died Dec. 6, 2006.

SENNER, ROBERT WILLIAM, secondary school educator; b. Freeman, SD, Mar. 19, 1912; s. William Jacob and Elizabeth Pandora (Graber) S.; m. Rachel Bertha Epp, Aug. 15, 1943; children: John William, Rachel Ann, Roberta Ann, Stanley Epp. BA, Bethel Coll., 1942; MusM, Wichita STate U., 1953. Tchr. music Fowler (Kans.) High Sch., 1942-43, Buhler (Kans.) High Sch., 1943-74. Adjudicator Okla. Secondary Sch. Activities, 1960-85. Contbr. articles to profl. jours.; conductor concerts including Handel's Messiah, DuBois' Seven Last Words, Haydn's Creation, 1957-75. Pres. Mennonite Song Festival Soc., Newton, Kans., 1947-50; vol. Mennnonite Disaster svcs., Kans. and Colo. Named to Music Tchrs. Hall of Fame, Kans. Music Edn. Assn., 1978. Mem. Music Educators Nat. Conf., S.D. Music Edn. Assn., Am. Choral Dirs. Assn. (Harry Robert Wilson award 1981), Nature Conservancy S.D., Hawk Mountain Sanctuary Assn. Democrat. Avocations: hunting, fishing, tenor soloist. Died Dec. 17, 2006.

SENSIPER, SAMUEL, electrical engineer; b. Elmira, NY, Apr. 26, 1919; s. Louis and Molly (Pedolsky) S.; m. Elaine Marie Zwick, Sept. 10, 1950; children: Martin, Sylvia, David. BSEE, MIT, 1939, ScD, 1951; EE, Stanford U., 1941. Asst. project engr. to sr. project engr., cons. Sperry Gyroscope, Garden City, Great Neck, NY, 1941-51; sect. head and sr. staff cons. Hughes Aircraft, Culver City, Malibu, Calif., 1951-60; lab. divsn. mgr. Space Gen. Corp., Glendale, Azuza, L.A., 1960—67; lab. mgr. TRW, Redondo Beach, Calif., 1967—70; cons. elec. engr. LA, 1970—73; dir. engring. Transco Products, Venice, Calif., 1973—75; cons. elec. engr. in pvt. practice LA, 1975—95; cons., from 1995. Faculty U. So. Calif., L.A., 1955-56, 79-80. Contbr. articles to profl. jours.; patentee in field. Recipient Cert. of Commendation U.S. Navy, 1946; indsl. electronics fellow MIT, 1947-48. Fellow IEEE (life), AAAS (life); mem. Calif. Soc. Profl. Engrs., MIT Alumni Assn., Stanford Alumni Assn., U. Calif. Alumni Assn., Electromagnetics Acad., Sigma Xi, Eta Kappa Nu, Nat. Soc. Profl. Engr.(life). Home: Davis, Calif. Died May 7, 2014.

SEVERINGHAUS, CHARLES WILLIAM, wildlife biologist; b. Ithaca, NY, Sept. 3, 1916; s. Wilbur Clinton and Jane Margaret (Barden) S.; m. Ethel Long, Dec. 12, 1941 (div. 1971); children: Jane Raena, William Daniel, Charles Long; m. Jacqueline Degraff, Aug. 13, 1971; 1 child, Mark R. BS in Agr., Cornell U., 1939. Conservation laborer N.Y. State Conservation Dept., 1935-41, asst. game rsch. investigator Delmar, 1941, game rsch. investigator, 1941-61, dist. game mgr. Albany, 1941-44, leader deer mgmt. rsch., leader big game mgmt. rsch. Delmar, 1944-61, sr. wildlife biologist, 1961-62, supervising wildlife biologist, 1962-74, prin. wildlife biologist, 1974-77; cons. wildlife biologist Cornell U., Ithaca, N.Y., 1977-86; cons. wildlife biologist in pvt. practice Edinburg, N.Y., from 1986. Discussion leader Big Game session No. Am. Wildlife Conf., 1950; chmn. big game session N.E. Wildlife Conf., 1953, others; co-chmn. N.E. Deer Study Group, 1968. Editorial bd. Jour. Wildlife Mgmt., 1960-67, reviewer, 1972 Active in past numerous civic orgns. including Boy Scouts Am., Meth. Ch. Recipient Conservation award Am. Motors Corp., The Wildlife Soc., 1962, Wildlife Conservationist award Nat. Wildlife Fedn. and Sears Roebuck Found., 1965, Conservation award Sullivan County Sportsmen's Fedn., N.Y., 1966, Outstanding Svc. award Adirondack Deer Forum, 1973, Disting. Svc. award N.Y. State Conservation Coun., 1974, others. Mem. The Wildlife Soc. (founding orgn. mem. 1936, co-chmn. N.E. sect. 1959, awards com. 1962, chmn. 1963, N.Y. state rep. 1962-71, N.Y. chpt. v.p. 1972, pres. 1973-74), Am. Soc. Mammalogists, Am. Wildlife Rsch. Found. (dir. 1991—), Alumni Assn. of N.Y. State Coll. of Agr. and Life Scis., Cornell U. (Outstanding Alumni award 1987), Gamma Sigma Delta (life). Avocations: gardening, fishing, travel. Died July 6, 2007.

SEVERSON, PAUL THOMAS, composer, educator; b. Fargo, ND, Aug. 18, 1928; s. Albert Sherwin and Cora Anetta (Thompson) S.; m. Shirley Jean Thompson (div. June 1986); children: David, Karen; m. Karen Louise Schwankel, Aug. 25, 1951; 1 child, Erin. MusB, Northwestern U., 1950, MusM, 1951. Performed with various orchs. including Stan Kenton, Hal McIntyre, Chgo. Theater, 1951-54; solo trombonist, arranger CBS Studios, Chgo., 1954-62; composer, arranger, producer Dick Marx Assocs., Chgo., 1962-73, also v.p., 1962-73; pres. Severson Enterprises, Grand Junction, Colo and Fargo, N.D., 1975-84; dir. musical industry studies Moorhead (Minn.) State U., 1984-91. Leader, arranger Great Am. Ballroom Band, Fargo, 1980-91; music dir. Red River Dance and Performing Co., 1980-96, Trollwood Sch. Performing Arts; cons. Moorhead State U.; lectr. various schs.; leader, composer, arranger of Mood Indigo, Can./Am. Orch., 1996—, Paul Severson & Friends, Jazz Quintet, 1995—, Internat. Falls Minn. area. Composer, arranger film scores including Poets Return, A Car is Born, Big City Newspaper, Championship Bridge, Restless Spirit, (with others) Last of the Wild Mustangs with Orson Welles), TV and radio commls. including Chevrolet, McDonald's, Sears, Wrigley, Schlitz, Hallmark, indsl. films including Ford Motor Co., United Airlines, Union Oil Co., record albums Hand in Hand, Paul Severson Quartet, Paul Severson Septet, published musical works including 10 popular arrangements (Hal Leonard Publ. Corp.), Brass Quintet (pub. Alphonse LeDuc Paris), Suite for Brass Quintet (Schmidt, Hall & McCreary), 19 Dixieland Folios (76 arrangements) (Hal Leonard Publ. Corp.), Concerto for Trumpet and Trombone (Shawnee Press), Choir arrangements (Bourne Music Co.), numerous standard religious works for brass (Neil Kjos & Co. and Schmidt, Hall & McCreary); composer (rec.) cantata Velvet Thorns, 1991; co-author book Brass/Wind Artistry-Know Your Instrument, Know Your Mind. Recipient Hollywood Advt. Club Grand Slam award, 1965, Silver medal Hollywood Advt. Fedn., 1988, 5 Clio awards. Unitarian Universalist. Avocations: fishing, hiking, playing bridge, tennis. Home: Ranier, Minn. Died May 20, 2007.

SEWARD, GRACE EVANGELINE, retired librarian; b. LA, Feb. 2, 1914; d. William Henry and Maud Leuty (Elphingstone) Seward. BA, Calif. State, LA, 1959; MLS, U. So. Calif., LA, 1961. Cert. tchr. Calif. Page Los Angeles County Pub. Libr., San Gabriel, Calif., 1927-37, asst. branch libr., 1938-40; various clerical positions Zoss Constrn./Consol., San Diego, 1941-42; time keeper Cal Ship Constrn., Wilmington, Calif., 1942-45; turkey ranch mgr. Bagnard Turkey Ranch, Baldwin Park, Calif., 1945-47; filing clk. Union Hardware, LA, 1947-49; libr. asst. Rosemead (Calif.) HS, 1949-60; libr. Anaheim (Calif.) Union HS, 1960-61; catalog head libr. Pasadena (Calif.) City Coll., 1961-79, libr. classifier, 1979-81; ret., 1981. Author: (bibliographies) Man and Environment, 1970, Black America, 1978, (index) American Rose Mag., 1989—90; editor: Bull. Rose Soc. Rose Parade, 1974—87, Bull. Rancho de Duarte Garden Club, Daisy Chain, from 1996. Mem.: Calif. Libr. Assn., Royal Nat. Rose Soc. (life), Pacific Rose Soc. (life Bronze Honor medal 2000, Life Achievement award 2004), L.A. Rose Soc. (life Bronze Honor medal 1994), Am. Rose Soc. (life; life judge, cons. from 1978, elected dist. dir. Pacific S.W. 1985—88, Pacific S.W. Dist. Silver Honor medal 1991, Outstanding Dist. Judge award 1995), Calif. Garden Clubs (life; pres. Rancho de Duarte 1991—96), Beta Phi Mu (hon.). Avocations: rosarian, gardening, book collector. Home: Altadena, Calif. Died June 19, 2007.

SFIKAS, PETER MICHAEL, lawyer, educator; s. Michael E. and Helen (Thureanos) S.; m. Freida Platon, Apr. 24, 1966; children: Ellen M., Pamela C., Sandra N. BS, Ind. U., 1959; JD, Northwestern U., 1962. Bar: Ill. 1962, U.S. Dist. Ct. (no. dist.) Ill. 1963, U.S. Ct. Appeals (7th cir.) 1963, U.S. Supreme Ct. 1970, U.S. Ct. Appeals (9th cir.) 1976, U.S. Ct. Appeals (3d cir.) 1981, U.S. Ct. Appeals (D.C. cir.) 1984, U.S. Ct. Appeals (8th cir.) 1995, U.S. Dist. Ct. (cen. dist.) Ill. 1988. Atty. Legal Aid Bur., United Charities Chgo., 1962-63; sr. ptnr. Peterson & Ross, Chgo., 1970-95; chief counsel, assoc. exec. dir. divsn. legal affairs ADA, Chgo., 1995—2006; ptnr. Bell, Boyd & Lloyd, Chgo., 1996—2009; gen. counsel Chgo. Dental Soc., from 1995; cert. arbitrator and mediator Circuit Court of Cook County, from 2007. Prosecutor Village of LaGrange Park, Ill., 1969-74; mem. rules com. Ill. Supreme Ct., 1975-95, mem. spl. joint com. on discovery rules, 1995; arbitrator Nat. Panel Arbitrators, 1972—; adj. prof. Loyola U. Sch. Law, 1978—2004; guest lectr. U. Ill. Coll. Dentistry, 1988-95; lectr. corp. counsel inst. Northwestern U. Sch. Law, 1984, lectr. Ray Garret Jr. Corp. and Securities Law Inst., 1996. Co-author: Antitrust and Unfair Competition Practice Handbook, 1996; author: Fiduciary Duty of Officers & Directors; contbr. articles to profl. jours. Contrb. to many Dental Law Publ. Mem. Ill. steering com. Ct. Watching Project, LWV, 1975-77; pres. Holy Apostles Greek Orthodox Ch. Parish Coun., 1987-89; co-pres. Oak Sch. PTO, 1989-90; mem. com. to select sch. supr., dist. 86, DuPage County, Ill., 1993-94; mem. Hinsdale Firefighters Bd., Ill., 2011-2012. Recipient Maurice Weigle award, Chgo. Bar Found., 1973, Fones award, Conn. Dental Assn., 1998; named Super Lawyer, Chgo. Mag., 2005, 2006, 2007, 2012, Leading Lawyer, 2005, 2006, 2007. Fellow Am. Bar Found., Am. Coll. Trial Lawyers, Chgo. Bar Found. (life); mem. ABA (editor in chief Forum Law Jour. sect. ins., negligence and compensation law 1972-76), mem. ABA Advisory Panel (2007-present);Ill. Bar Found. (bd. dirs. 1975-77), Northwestern U. Law Alumni Assn. (1st v.p. 1985-86, pres. 1986-87, Svc. award 1990)mem. Law Fund Board (2006-present), Ill. State Bar Assn. (bd. govs. 1970-76, chmn. antitrust law sect. coun. 1986-87), Chgo. Bar Assn. (editl. bd. Chgo. Bar Record 1973-84), Bar Assn. 7th Fed. Cir. (chmn. com. on meetings 1973-75), Ill. Inst. Continuing Legal Edn. (chmn. profl. antitrust problems program 1976, author program on counseling corps., anti-trust and trade regulation), Am. Nat. Standards Inst. (mem. copyright ad hoc group 2004-06), Legal Club Chgo. (sec.-treas, 1984-86, v.p. 1989-90, pres. 1990-91). Mem.,The Lawyers Club Chgo. (2005-present). Home: Hinsdale, Ill. Died Sept. 6, 2014.

SFORZINI, RICHARD HENRY, aerospace engineer, educator; b. Rochester, NY, July 25, 1924; m. Corinne Lorenz, 1947; children: Richard Jr. (dec.), Suzanne Simonelli, Deborah Pugh, Michael, Stephen, Andrew, Mark. Degree of Mech. Engr., MIT, 1954; BS, U.S. Mil. Acad., 1947. Instr. ordnance U.S. Mil. Acad., 1954-56, asst. prof., 1956-57; project dir. anti-tank missile sys. R&D Army Rocket and Guided Missile Agy., Redstone Arsenal, Ala., 1958-59; engr. Huntsville divsn. Thiokol Chem. Corp., Ala., 1959-62, mgr. engring. dept. Ala., 1962-64, dir. engring. space booster divsn. Brunswick, Ga., 1964-66; vis. prof. Auburn (Ala.) U., 1966-67, prof., 1967-85, prof. emeritus aerospace engring., from 1985. Died Jan. 8, 2015.

SHACKELFORD, HELEN METZGER, artist; b. Flagstaff, Ariz., Jan. 16, 1928; d. Harry H. and Gertrude Makin (Perry) Metzger; m. James Gordon Shackelford II, Nov. 25, 1949. Student, Northwestern U., 1945-46, Art Inst. of Chgo., 1945-47, U. Ariz., 1947-48. Ilustrator All Hell Needs Is Water, 1972. Founder, pres. Heard Mus. Guild, Phoenix, 1956-59; bd. dirs. Jr. League of Phoenix, 1957—, Golden Gate Settlement, 1950—, Girls Ranch Samaritan Aux., 1950—, Mental Health Assn., 1950—; founder Orpheum Theatre Found., Phoenix, 1987—; cons. Ariz. exhibit Phoenix Zoo. Mem. We. Art Assn., U. Ariz. Alumni Assn. (Outstanding Alumni 1987). Republican. Episcopalian. Avocations: cattle ranching, tennis, mental health, historic preservation, writing. Home: Phoenix, Ariz. Died June 4, 2007.

SHALHOUB, MICHAEL DEMITRI See **SHARIF, OMAR**

SHALITA, ALAN REMI, dermatologist; b. Bklyn., Mar. 22, 1936; s. Harry and Celia; m. Simone Lea Baum, Sept. 4, 1960; children: Deborah (dec.) and Judith (twins). AB, Brown U., 1957; BS, U. Brussels, 1960; MD, Bowman Gray Sch. Medicine, 1964; DSc (hon.), L.I. U., 1990. Intern Beth Israel Hosp., NYC, 1964-65; resident dept. dermatology NYU Med. Ctr., 1967-68, NIH tng. grant fellow dept. dermatology, 1968-70, instr. dermatology, 1970-71; asst. prof. NYU, 1971-73, Columbia U., 1973-75; assoc. prof. medicine, head divsn. dermatology SUNY Downstate Med. Ctr., Bklyn., 1975-79, prof., from 1979, head divsn. dermatology, 1979-80, chmn. dept. dermatology, from 1980, asst. dean, 1977-83, acting dean Queens campus, 1983-84; assoc. dean clin. affairs SUNY Health Sci. Ctr., Bklyn., 1989-92, assoc. provost for clin. affairs, 1992-93, assoc. v.p. clin. affairs, 1993—2005, assoc. dean grad. med. edn., 1999—2006. Disting. tchg. prof. SUNY Health Sci. Ctr., Bklyn., 1996—; asst. attending in dermatology U. Hosp., NYC, 1970-73, Bellevue Hosp. Ctr., 1970-73, Manhattan VA Hosp., 1971-73, Presbyn. Hosp., 1973-75; bd. dirs. Kings County Hosp. Ctr.; cons. dermatology Bklyn. VA Hosp., 1975—; chief dermatology U. Hosp. Bklyn., 1975—, Brookdale Med. Ctr., 1977-90, Kings County Hosp. Ctr., Bklyn., 1975—, acting med. dir., 1989-92; med. dir. U. Hosp. Bklyn., 1992-96. Pres. Temple Shaaray Tefila, N.Y.C., 1982-86, chmn. bd. trustees, 1987-95. Lt. M.C. USNR, 1965-67. Recipient Torch of Liberty award Anti-Defamation League, 1987, Surg. and Pediat. awards Beth Israel Hosp., NYC, 1965, Leah Dickstein Man of Good Conscience award Women's Med. Assn. NY, 1999, Leadership in Urban Med. Edn. award Arthur Ashe Inst. for Urban Health, 1999; Spl. fellow NIH, 1970-73, Gold medal, Am. Acad. Dermatology, 2013. Mem.: AMA, Venezuelan Dermatology Soc., Argentina Dermatology Soc., Brit. Assn. Dermatologists, N.Y. Dermatol. Soc. (pres. 1989—90), Dermatol. Soc. Greater N.Y. (pres. 1980—81), N.Y. State Dermatol. Soc., N.Y. Acad. Medicine, N.Y. State Med. Soc., N.Y. Acad. Scis., Internat. Soc. Dermatology, Assn. Profs. Dermatology (sec.-treas. 1988—94, pres. 1996—98), Am. Soc. Dermatol. Surgery (past bd. dirs.), Dermatology Found. (past trustee), Soc. Investigative Dermatology, Polish Dermatology Soc. (hon.), Soc. Francaise de Dermatology (hon.), Am. Dermatol. Assn. (hon.; sec.-treas. 1996—2001, pres. 2001—02), Am. Acad. Dermatology (hon.; bd. dirs. 1983—87, v.p. 1995—96), Alpha Omega Alpha. Republican. Home: New York, NY. *Treat others with compassion, dignity and respect, add a little humor to everyone's life. Speak up for what you truly believe, be charitable.* Deceased.

SHANDERA, DOROTHY FRANCES, linguist, educator; b. Sardis, Miss., Nov. 8, 1929; d. George Monroe and Mary Browning (Chamblin) Hammitt; m. Charles Garland Shandera, Apr. 22, 1964; children: Deborah, Cindi. BS, Miss. Women's U., 1951; postgrad. in Criminal Justice, U. Houston, 1971; M.Correctional Edn., Sam Houston State U., 1980. Tchr. high sch. and coll. All Saints Episcopal Coll., Vicksburg, Miss., 1951—52; HS tchr. Tyler (Tex.) Ind. Sch. Dist., 1955—59; probation officer Harris County, 1963—65; tchr. speech and drama Alvin (Tex.) Sch. Dist., 1965—68, Friendswood (Tex.) Sch. Dist., 1968—71; tchr. Spanish and English Round Rock (Tex.) Sch. Dist., 1973—76; bi-lingual instr. Windham Sch. Dist., Tex. Dept. Corrections, Huntsville, 1976—77; life skills instr. Windham Sch. Dist., Tex. Dept. Corrections, Huntsville, 1977—79, bi-lingual specialist, life skills coordinator, from 1979. Participant Adkins Life Skills workshop, 1977; guest lectr. Sam Houston State U., 1979—80, Del., Tex. Women's Meeting, 1977; state del. Nat. Women's Conf., Internat. Women's Yr., Houston, 1977; del. Tex. Democratic Conv., 1980; state steering com. Texans for ERA; bd. dirs. Walker County Bd. Human Resources; mem. Tex. Women's Polit. Caucus; legis. aide for Sarah Weddington, 1973; vol. Green Acres Nursing Home. Contbr. articles to profl. publs. Active PTA. Named one of outstanding career women, Huntsville, 1978. Mem.: NEA, AAUW (chpt. pres. 1974—76, coord. state legis. conf.), Tex. State Ofcl. Ladies, Correctional Edn. Assn., Windham North Assn. (pres., dist. VI legis. chmn.), Tex. State Tchrs. Assn. (state exec. com., pres.-elect), Tex. Corrections Assn. (pres.-elect state orgn. 1981—82), Bus. and Profl. Women., Phi Delta Kappa. Home: Huntsville, Tex. Died Nov. 2, 2007.

SHANE, ELEANOR, executive placement firm executive; b. NYC, July 3, 1932; d. Jack Shane and Gertrude Weise; divorced 1968; children: Susan Herbin, Amy Bysch. BFA, Cornell U., 1954. Designer Richton Internat., NYC, 1968-71; real estate sales agt. William A. White, NYC, 1971-77; mgr. constrn. and engring. placement Allegheny Pers., NYC, from 1977; pres. The Shane Group, NYC, from 1977. Com. mem. Friends of YMHA, N.Y.C.; active Media Educators Assn., Theater Devel. Fund, N.Y.C. Mem. Profl. Women in Constrn., Constrn. Fin. Mgmt. Assn., NAFE, Cornell Club. Democrat. Avocations: painting, tennis, crafts collecting. Home: Boynton Beach, Fla. Died Feb. 19, 2007.

SHANK, WILLIAM HALDEMAN, engineer, publisher; b. Pitts., May 11, 1915; s. Clyde Updegraff and Elizabeth Virginia (Graybill) S.; m. Ruth Adele Hershey; children: Nancy O'Dell, Mary-Ann Moore, J. William. BS in Mech. Engring., Lehigh U., 1937; advanced engring. degree, State U. Iowa, 1944. Registered profl. engr., Pa. Pub. rels. mgr. York (Pa.) Corp., 1937-41; account exec. W.H. Long Co., York, 1946-48; advt. mgr. Hardinge Co., York, 1948-62; pub. rels. mgr. Buchart-Horn, York, 1962-67; account exec. Adams Assocs., York, 1967-70; editor, pub. Am. Canal & Transp. Ctr., York, from 1970. Author: Three Hundred Years with the Pennsylvania Traveler, The Amazing Pennsylvania Canals, Historic Bridges of Pennsylvania, Vanderbilt's Folly, Great Floods of Pennsylvania, Indian Trails to Superhighways, History of the York-Pullman Automobile, York County Historic Sites and Tour Guide. Pres. York Torch Club, 1957-58, York Lehigh Club, 1961-63; supt. Luther Meml. Sunday Sch., 1950-52. With C.E., U.S. Army, 1944-46. Mem. Am. Canal Soc. (pres. 1978-85), Pa. Soc. of Profl. Engrs. (v.p. 1971-73, pres. Lincoln chpt. York, Lancaster, 1964-65, 1978, Engr. of Yr.). Republican. Lutheran. Died Jan. 6, 2007.

SHAPIRO, HOWARD IRWIN, engineering consultant; b. Bklyn., Apr. 16, 1932; s. Charles M. and Rose (Smith) S.; m. Dorothy Arluck, June 20, 1953; children: Jay P., Lawrence K., Gail S., Daniel A. BCE, Poly. Inst. Bklyn., 1953. Registered profl. engr., N.Y., N.J., Ohio, Md., Va., Mo. Engr. Charles M. Shapiro, P.E., Bklyn., 1957-60; ptnr. Charles M. Shapiro & Sons, Bklyn., 1960-74; v.p. Charles M. Shapiro & Sons, P.C., Bklyn., from 1974; pres. Howard I. Shapiro & Assocs. Consulting Engrs., P.C., Bklyn., from 1989. Author: Cranes and Derricks, 1980, 2d edit. (with Jay P. Shapiro and Lawrence K. Shapiro), 1991. 1st lt. CE, U.S. Army, 1953-56. Mem. Nat. Soc. Profl. Engrs., ASCE, Soc. Automotive Engrs., Am. Inst. Steel Constrn., Concrete Industry Bd. Home: Woodmere, NY. Died May 31, 2007.

SHAPIRO, IRVING, lawyer, educator; b. NYC, Aug. 23, 1917; s. Isidor and Bessie (Hecht) Shapiro; m. Rosalind Leonora Roth, Sept. 14, 1941; children: Deanne, Susan, Joyce. JD, 1942; BA, NYU, 1946. Bar: NY 1943. Spl. asst. to adminstrv. judge NY Supreme Ct., Bklyn., 1949—74; prof. St. John's U., Jamaica, NY, from 1974. Dir. programs Ct. Careers, NYC, from 1960; arbitrator Small Claims Ct., NYC, from 1977. Editor: (book) NY Statutes, 1963—73, Dictionary of Legal Terms, 1969, New Dictionary of Legal Terms, 1984; contbr. articles to profl. jours. With US Army, 1943—46. Decorated Army Commendation medal. Fellow: Inst. Ct. Mgmt; mem.: Criminal Justice Educators Assn. Democrat. Jewish. Died Nov. 26, 2006.

SHARF, STEPHAN, automotive executive; b. Berlin, Dec. 30, 1920; arrived in USA, 1947, naturalized, 1952; s. Wilhelm and Martha (Schwartz) S.; m. Rita Schantzer, 1951, (dec. 2001). Degree in Mech. Engring., Tech. U., Berlin, Fed. Republic Germany, 1947; DSc (hon.), Oakland U., Rochester, Mich., 2007; PhD in Humanities (hon.), Oakland U. Tool and die maker Buerk Tool & Die Co., Buffalo, 1947-50; foreman Ford Motor Co., 1950-53, gen. foreman Chgo., 1953-58; with Chrysler Corp., Detroit, 1958-86, master mechanic Twinsburg stamping plant, 1958-63, mfg. engring. mgr., 1963-66, mrg. prodn. Twinsburg stamping plant, 1966-68, plant mgr. Warren stamping plant, 1968-70, plant mgr. Sterling stamping plant, 1970-72, gen. plants mgr. stamping, 1972-78, v.p. Engine and Casting div., 1978-80, v.p. Power Train div., 1980-81, exec. v.p., mfg., dir., 1981-85, exec. v.p. internat., 1985-86, also bd. dirs.; pres. SICA Corp., Bloomfield Hills, Mich., from 1986. Columnist Ward's Auto World Common Sense mag., 1987—. Bd. dirs. Jr. Achievement, Detroit council Boy Scouts Am.; trustee, v.p. Oakland U. Mem. Soc. Auto Engrs., Detroit Engring. Soc. Clubs: Wabeek Country. Avocations: golf, travel, charity. Home: Bloomfield Hills, Mich. Died Aug. 31, 2013.

SHARIF, OMAR (MICHAEL DEMITRI SHALHOUB), actor; b. Alexandria, Egypt, Apr. 10, 1932; s. Joseph and Claire (Saada) Shalhoub; m. Faten Hamama, Feb. 5, 1955 (div. 1966); 1 child, Tarek. Attended, Victoria Coll., Cairo; degree in math. and physics, Cairo U. Actor: (numerous Egyptian, French and Am. films) Ciel d' enfer, 1953, Devil of the Sahara, 1954, Our Best Days, 1955, Land of Peace, 1957, No Fault of My Love, 1958, No Tomorrow, 1958, Hidden Shore, 1958, Goha, 1958, Lady of the Castle, 1959, For the Sake of a Woman, 1959, Struggle on the Nile, 1959, Agony of Love, 1960, There Is a Man in Our House, 1961, I Love My Master, 1961, My Only Love, 1961, The River of Love, 1961, Lawrence of Arabia, 1962 (Golden Globe award for Best Supporting Actor, Most Promising Newcomer-Male), Behold a Pale Horse, 1964, The Fall of the Roman Empire, 1964, Genghis Khan, 1965, The Yellow Rolls Royce, 1965, The Mamelukes, 1965, Marco the Magnificent, 1965, Doctor Zhivago, 1966 (Golden Globe award for Best Actor), Night of the Generals, 1967, More Than a Miracle, 1967, Funny Girl, 1968, Mayerling, 1969, Che!, 1969, MacKenna's Gold, 1969, The Appointment, 1969, The Horsemen, 1970, The Last Valley, 1971, The Burglars, 1972, The Mysterious Island, 1973, The Tamarind Seed, 1974, The Mysterious Island of Captain Nemo, 1974, Juggernaut, 1974, Funny Lady, 1975, Crime and Passion, 1975, Ace Up The Sleeve, The Pink Panther Stikes Again, The Right To Love, Ashanti, 1979, Bloodline, 1979, Oh Heavenly Dog, 1980, The Baltimore Bullet, 1980, Green Ice, 1981, Chanel Solitaire, Top Secret, 1984, Grand Larceny, 1987, Keys to Freedom, 1988, The Rainbow, 1989, The Puppeteer, 1989, Mountains of the Moon, 1990, Journey of Love, 1990, (voice) Umm Kulthum, 1996, Heaven Before I Die, 1997, The 13th Warrior, 1998, Mysteries of Egypt, 1998, The 13th Warrior, 1999, The Parole Officer, 2001, Monsieur Ibrahim, 2003, Hidalgo, 2004, Fire at My Heart, 2006, One Night with the King, 2006, (voice) 10,000 BC, 2008, Hassan wa Marcus, 2008, The Traveller, 2009, I Forgot to Tell You, 2009, Rock the Casbah, 2013, A Castle in Italy, 2013 (as himself); (TV films) Mysteries of the Great Pyramid, 1977, Pleasure Palace, 1980, Anastasia: The Mystery of Anna, 1986, Memories of Midnight, 1991, Mrs. 'Arris Goes to Paris, 1992, Lie Down with Lions, 1994, Red Eagle, 1994, Gulliver's Travels, 1996, Catherine the Great, 1996, Shaka Zulu: The Citadel, 2001, The Search for Eternal Egypt, 2005, Imperium: Saint Peter, 2005, The Ten Commandments, 2006, Kronprinz Rudolf, 2006; (TV miniseries) The Far Pavilions, 1984, Peter the Great, 1986, Le roi de Patagonie, 1990, Mother, 1993; (TV series) Petits mythes urbains, 2003-04; Author: The Eternal Male, 1977, Omar Sharif's Life in Bridge, 1983, Omar Sharif talks Bridge, 2004, (instrn. manual) Bridge Deluxe II play with Omar Sharif. Recipient UNESCO Sergei Eisenstein medal, 2005. Died July 10, 2015.

SHARROW, SHEBA GROSSMAN, artist; b. Bklyn., Apr. 28, 1926; children: Mayda, David. BFA, Art Inst. Chgo.; MFA, Temple U. Speaker in field. Exhibited prin. works in numerous one-woman and group shows including Hunterdon Art Ctr., Clinton, N.J., 1994, N.J. Arts Ann., Trenton, 1994, Moravian Coll., Bethlehem, Pa., 1994, Payne Gallery, 1992, Tremellen Gallery, 1992, 91, 90, Pace Setters, Camden County, N.J., 1992, Cheltenham Art Ctr., 1992, Images of Courage & Compassion Millersville U. Pa., 1991, Noyes Mus. Art; works represented in pub. collections including Steelcase Corp., Armstrong World Industries, Citibank N.Y., Jersey City Mus. Fellow Blue Mountain Art Ctr., 1987, Mishkenot Sha'ananim, 1990, Va. Ctr. for Creative Arts, 1978-79, 81, 83-93; grantee Pa. Coun. on Arts, 1983, N.J. State Coun. Arts, 1997, 2002, Pollock-Krasner Found., 2000. Home: Cherry Hill, NJ. Died Dec. 15, 2006.

SHAW, GAYLORD DEWAYNE, retired publishing executive; b. El Reno, Okla., July 22, 1942; m. Judith Howard, 1960; children: Randall, Kristine (Kristi) Clark, Kelly Martin. Attended, Cameron Coll., 1960-62, U. Okla., 1962-64. Sports writer El Reno American; night police reporter Lawton Constitution Press, Okla., 1960-62; Okla. City bur. night editor, statehouse correspondent AP, 1962-66, Washington bur. night editor, investigative reporter, spl. assignment team editor, White House correspondent, 1966-75; asst. mng. editor to mng. editor/news Dallas Times Herald, 1981-83; editor-in-chief Shaw Comms. Inc., Charlotte, N.C., 1983-85; correspondent Washington, Denver L.A. Times, 1975-81, correspondent, projects coord. Washington bur., 1985-88; Washington bur. chief Newsday, 1988-95, sr. corr. Washington, 1995—2002; ret., 2002. Recipient Pulitzer Prize Nat. Reporting, 1978, Disting. Svc. award for Washington correspondence Sigma Delta Chi/Soc. Profl. Journalists, 1978, Loeb award Disting. Bus. Reporting, 1978, Disting. Reporting award Merriman Smith/White House Correspondents Assn., 1974, Worth Bingham Disting. Reporting award, 1968, Washington Correspondence award Nat. Press Club, 1991. Home: Duncan, Okla. Died Sept. 6, 2015.

SHAW, KENNETH ROGER, vocational rehabilitation counselor; b. Dallas, Dec. 21, 1952; s. Barnie Jonas and Virginia Louise (Akers) S.; m. Terrie Lynn Heatherly, Mar. 12, 1988 (div. June 1990); m. Marianne Albert, Apr. 6, 1996. Student, Mountain View Jr. Coll., Dallas, 1971-73; BS in Psychology, Dallas Bapt. Coll., 1975; MS in Psychology, East Tex. State U., 1977; MDiv, Midwestern Bapt. Theol. Sem., 1986. Ordained to ministry Bapt. Ch., 1986. Mem.

coun. on ministries Preston Hollow Meth. Ch., Dallas, 1977-79, mem. adminstrv. bd., 1977-79, sec. career planning, 1977-78; coll. liaison minister, 1978-79; family counselor Dallas North Counseling Services, 1978-79; internal auditor Cullum Cos., Dallas, 1979-82; chaplain, clin. pastoral orientation Bethany Med. Ctr., Kansas City, Kans., 1986; field chaplain intern Lee's Summit (Mo.) Police Dept., 1985-86; sr. design planner, spl. projects planner Carlton Cards, Dallas, 1987-89; incest counselor Incest Recovery Assn., Dallas, 1989-90; intern Tex. Rehab. Commn., 1995, counselor, clin. cons., from 1995. Profl. portrait photographer, 1979-81. Mem. audio visual dept. inreach/outreach leader singles 25-27 class Prestonwood Bapt. Ch., 1980-83, also photographer and sound technician. Mem. Am. Assn. Christian Counselors (charter), Mt. View Jr. Coll. Bapt. Student Union (program chair 1972-73), Dallas Area Wide Multicultural Youth Summit Task Force (youth participation and registration com., planning com. 1993). Republican. Avocations: music, cultural events, travel, photography, writing. Died Nov. 1, 2006.

SHEDD, FRANCIS WILLIAM, lawyer; b. Niagara Falls, NY, July 29, 1922; s. Will D. and Agnes E. (Choate) S.; m. Barbara Jane Conger, Dec. 10, 1945 (div. 1970); children: Jonathan W., Jennifer Allen, Rebecca Greenberg; m. Audrey Donner, Mar. 24, 1973. LLB, Syracuse U., 1948. Atty., Niagara Falls. Counsel joint legis. com. on regional and area studies, N.Y. Senate and Assembly, 1966-72; rep. plaintiff and co-counsel, Niagara Counsel Charter case/U.S. Supreme Ct., Washington, 1975. Republican candidate for State Assembly, Lewiston and Niagara Falls Dist., 1963. Sgt. U.S. Army, 1943-45, ETO. Decorated Bronze Star (2), Purple Heart. Mem. Niagara Club (pres. 1966, 89), Niagara Falls Country Club (bd. govs. 1991). Methodist. Avocations: travel, gourmet cooking, golf, bowling, cross country skiing. Died Dec. 15, 2006.

SHEELEY, VIRGINIA RUTH, civic volunteer; b. Walker, Mo., Jan. 6, 1936; d. Glenn Monroe and Edna Estella (Thomas) Stevens; m. Charles B. Sheeley, Aug. 3, 1955; children: Steven M., Craig B., Jeffrey A. BS in Edn., S.W. Mo. State U., 1958; postgrad., Drury Coll., Springfield, Mo., 1970. Tchr. Springfield (Mo.) R-12 Schs., 1958-59. Columnist Woodcarving Mag., 1978-85; woodcarver. Mem. dist. com. Boy Scouts Am., Springfield, 1980—; com. mem. S.W. Com. for UNICEF, Springfield, 1980—; regional v.p. Nat. Carvers Mus., 1970-85. Named Outstanding Young Women, Jr. Jaycee Wives, 1970, Silver Beaver award Boy Scouts Am., 1976. Mem. AAUW (hist./program chair), Ozarks Whittlers and Woodcarvers (organizer, pres.). Democrat. Home: Springfield, Mo. Died Aug. 4, 2007.

SHELDON, COURTNEY ROSWELL, freelance/self-employed journalist; b. Schenectady, Mar. 18, 1920; s. Roy Farrar and Ethel May (Flower) S.; m. Elizabeth Yeates, May 28, 1949; children: Eric Yeates, Roy Courtney. BA, Syracuse U., 1942. Diplomatic, Pentagon, White House corr. Washington Bur. Chief, 1947-73; mng. editor The Christian Sci. Monitor, Boston, 1947-73; mem. U.S. delegation, press sec. to ambassadors U.S. Mission to UN, NYC, 1973-77; chief congl. corr. U.S. News and World Report, Washington, 1980-85; corr. Syracuse (N.Y.) Post Standard, 1942, Nat. Pub. Radio, Washington, 1968-73, Economist, London, 1952-57; moderator Voice of Am., Washington, 1970-72; corr. Burlington (Vt.) Free Press, 1946-47, New Delhi Statesman, 1970-72; free lance-journalist Washington, from 1985. Lt. USN, 1943-46, PTO. Mem. AP Mng. Editors Assn. (dir. 1970-72, regent 1972—), Sigma Delta Chi (nat. chmn. Freedom of Info. com. 1972-73). Home: Sykesville, Md. Died May 12, 2007.

SHELEY, KATHY ANN, clinical psychologist; b. Marshall, Tex., Mar. 31, 1951; d. William Arthur and Kathlyn Sunshine (Randle) S.; m. Thomas Ray Urbanek, Dec. 16, 1972 (div. Feb. 1988). BA, U. Tex., 1972; MA, U. Fla., 1975, PhD, 1978. Asst. prof. dept. psychiatry, dept. ob-gyn. U. Tex. Health Sci. Ctr. Med. Sch., San Antonio, 1978-80; coord. psychology svc. Robert B. Green Hosp., San Antonio, 1978-80; coord. inpatient psychiat. unit psychology svc. Bexar County Hosp., San Antonio, 1978-80; co-dir. psychosocial clinic Robert B. Green Hosp., San Antonio, 1978-80; dir. program div. of psychology svcs. Clear Lake Ctr., Austin (Tex.) State Hosp., 1980-82; dir. Austin Counseling Ctr. of Galveston (Tex.) Family Inst., 1982-87; clin. faculty Galveston Family Inst., 1983-87. Adj. asst. prof. dept. psychology Trinity U., San Antonio, 1978-80; adj. faculty Galveston Family Inst., 1980-81; cons. Tex. Dept. Parks & Wildlife, 1984-90, Lago Vista Police Dept., Tex., 1987-91, Georgetown Police Dept., Tex., 1986-92. Mem. Am. Assn. for Marriage and Family Therapy, Am. Psychol. Assn., Internat. Platform Assn. Home: Austin, Tex. Died Feb. 16, 2007.

SHEMA, VIRGINIA KING, lawyer; b. Terre Haute, Ind., Aug. 20, 1957; d. Thomas Frederick and Mary Kathryn (Milner) King; m. Christopher P. Shema, Sept. 17, 1988. BS in Environ. Health Scis., Ind. State U., 1979, BS in English, 1984; JD, Ind. U., Indpls., 1987. Bar: Ind. 1987, U.S. Dist. Ct. (no. and so. dists.) Ind. 1987, Va. 1988, U.S. Dist. Ct. (ea. dist.) Va. 1988, U.S. Ct. Appeals (4th cir.) 1989. Assoc. Breit, Rutter & Montagna, Norfolk, Va., 1987, Breit, Drescher & Breit, Norfolk, 1987-92, Shema & Shema P.C., Norfolk, 1992-95, Anderson & Nichols, Terre Haute, Ind., from 1995. Mem. Ind. Trial Lawyers Assn., Ind. Bar Assn., Va. Bar Assn., Va. Trial Lawyers Assn., Norfolk-Portsmouth (Va.) Bar Assn., Terre Haute Bar Assn. Democrat. Roman Catholic. Home: Terre Haute, Ind. Died Jan. 16, 2007.

SHEN, BENJAMIN CHING-CHUN, physics educator, researcher; b. Shanghai, Jan. 28, 1938; came to U.S., 1956; s. Kuo-Chin and Ding-Cheng (Han) S.; m. Mayling Cheng, Aug. 16, 1963; children: Katherine, Christine. AB, U. Calif., Berkeley, 1959, PhD, 1965. Rsch. assoc. Lawrence Berkeley Lab., 1965-67, Stanford (Calif.) Linear Accelerator Ctr., 1967-69; asst. prof. physics U. Calif., Riverside, 1969-70, assoc. prof., 1970-75, prof., from 1975, chmn. dept., 1988-90, assoc. dir. energy scis. program, 1981-88. Cons. prof. Harbin (People's Republic China) Inst. Tech., 1987—; chmn. Stanford Linear Accelerator Ctr.-Lawrence Berkeley Lab. User Orgn., Palo Alto, 1980-82. Congl. sci. advisor to Rep. George E. Brown, U.S. Ho. of Reps. from 36th dist. Calif., Riverside, 1985—. Mem. Am. Phys. Soc., Sigma Xi. Home: Riverside, Calif. Died July 12, 2007.

SHEPARD, THOMAS ROCKWELL, JR., publishing consultant; b. NYC, Aug. 22, 1918; s. Thomas Rockwell and Marie (Dickinson) S.; m. Nancy Kruidenier, Sept. 20, 1941; children: Sue Shepard Jaques, Molly Shepard Richard, Amy S. Knight, Thomas Rockwell III. BA, Amherst Coll., 1940. Asst. sales promotion mgr. Vick Chemical Co., 1940-41; with Look mag., NYC, 1946-72, advt. sales mgr., 1961-64, advt. dir., 1964-67, pub., 1967-72; cons. Cowles Communications, Inc.; pres. Inst. Outdoor Advt., 1974-76. Co-author: The Disaster Lobby, 1973; contbr. articles to various publs. Pres. Greenwich Community Chest, 1964-65; chmn. Robert A. Taft Inst. Govt., 1978-81, Rep. Roundtable of Greenwich, 1981-85; bd. dirs. Advt. Coun., Lit. Vols. Am., 1989-91, Community Answers, 1988-91; chmn. Amherst Coll. Alumni Fund, 1986; mem. exec. com. alumni coun. Amherst Coll.; hon. pres. Soc. Amherst Coll. Alumni. Lt. comdr. USNR, 1941-45. Recipient George Washington honor medal for pub. address Freedoms Found., 1970, 73, Amherst Coll. medal for eminent svc., 1990. Mem. Princeton Club (N.Y.C.), Bird Key Yacht Club (Fla.), Belle Haven Club, Round Hill Club. Republican. Home: Greenwich, Conn. Died Apr. 29, 2015.

SHEPARDSON, JOHN UPHAM, chemist, consultant; b. Winchendon, Mass., May 4, 1920; s. Donn Clifford and Agnes Gertrude (Upham) S.; m. Camille Jane Comstock, Dec. 25, 1942; children: Ann, Sallie, Roy Michael. BS in Chemistry, U. Mass., 1942; MS in Organic Chemistry, Rensselaer Poly. Inst., 1948, PhD in Analytical Chemistry, 1950. Quality mgr. Mallinckrodt Chem. Works, Weldon Springs, Mo., 1950-64; quality dir. Winthrop Labs., Rensselaer, N.Y., 1964-76; tech. dir. CIS Radiopharmaceuticals, Bedford, Mass., 1976-80; chief chemist Astro Cir. Corp., Lowell, Mass., 1980-84; pvt. practice cons. Lowell, 1984-89; ret., 1989. Contbr. Uranium Production Technology, 1959. Member Ferguson (Mo.) City Coun., 1956-60. Mem. Am. Chem. Soc. Avocations: woodworking, travel. Home: Chelmsford, Mass. Died Dec. 9, 2006.

SHERESKY, NORMAN M., retired lawyer; b. Detroit, June 22, 1928; s. Harry and Rose (Lieberman) Sheresky; m. Elaine B. Lewis, Oct. 30, 1977; 1 child from previous marriage, Brooke Hillary. BA, Syracuse U., NY, 1950; LLB, Harvard U., 1953. Bar: NY 1953. Assoc. Gold & Pollack, NYC, 1954—60; sole practice, 1960—72; ptnr. Sheresky & Kalman, 1972—77, Colton, Hartnick, Yamin & Sheresky, 1977—93, Baer, Marks & Upham, 1993—95, Sheresky, Aronson & Mayefsky, 1995—2010. Adj. prof. matrimonial litig. NY Law Sch., 1979—86. Author: On Trial, 1977; co-author (with Marya Mannes): Uncoupling: The Art of Coming Apart, 1972; contbr., editor: Fairshare mag. Mem.: American Coll. Family Trial Lawyers (founding mem.), Assn. Trial Lawyers America, NY State Bar Assn., American Acad. Matrimonial Lawyers (past pres. NY chpt.), Internat. Acad. Matrimonial Lawyers (mem. com. to examine lawyer conduct in matrimonial actions 1992—95, past treas.). Home: New York, NY. Died Oct. 13, 2013.

SHERMAN, FRED, biochemist, educator; b. Mpls., May 21, 1932; s. Harry and Ann (Kaufman) Sherman; m. Revina Freeman, July 25, 1958 (div.); children: Aaron, Mark, Rhea; m. Elena Rustchenko Bulgac, May 5, 2001. BA, U. Minn., Mpls., 1953; PhD, U. Calif., Berkeley, 1958; PhD (hon.), U. Minn., 2002. Postdoctoral fellow U. Wash., Seattle, 1959—60; 60postdoctoral fellow 61Lab. Genetique Physiol., Gif-sur-Yvette, France, 1960-61; sr. instr. U. Rochester, NY, 1961—62, asst. prof. NY, 1962—66, assoc. prof. NY, 1966—71, prof. dept. biochemistry Sch. Medicine & Dentistry NY, from 1971, chmn. dept. biochemistry NY, 1982—99. Instr. Cold Spring Harbor Lab., NY, 1970—87; Wander Meml. lectr., 1975; Wilson prof. U. Rochester, 1982. Co-author: Cold Spring Harbor Manual on Yeast Genetics and Molecular Biology, 1970—87; assoc. editor: Genetics, 1975—82, Molecular Cell Biology, 1979—88. Grantee NIH, 1963; fellow, 1959—61. Mem.: Am. Soc. Microbiology, Genetic Soc. Am. (bd. dirs. 1983—85), NAS (chmn. genet. sec. 2000—03), AAAS. Home: Rochester, NY. Died Sept. 16, 2013.

SHERMAN, SIGNE LIDFELDT, portfolio manager, former research chemist; b. Rochester, NY, Nov. 11, 1913; d. Carl Leonard Broström and Herta Elvira Maria (Tern) Lidfeldt; m. Joseph V. Sherman, Nov. 18, 1944 (dec. Oct. 1984). BA, U. Rochester, 1935, MS, 1937. Chief chemist Lab. Indsl. Medicine and Toxicology Eastman Kodak Co., Rochester, 1937-43; chief rsch. chemist Chesebrough-Pond's Inc., Clinton, Conn., 1943-44; ptnr. Joseph V. Sherman Cons., NYC, 1944-84; portfolio strategist Sherman Holdings, Troy, Mont., from 1984. Author: The New Fibers, 1946. Fellow Am. Inst. Chemists; mem. AAAS, AAUW (life), Am. Chem. Soc., Am. Econ. Assn., Am. Assn. Ind. Investors (life), Fedn. Am. Scientists (life), Union Concerned Scientists (life), Earthquake Engring. Rsch. Inst., Nat. Ctr. for Earthquake Engring. Rsch., N.Y. Acad. Scis. (life), Cabinet View Country Club. Home: Troy, Mont. Died Nov. 21, 2006.

SHERRILL, BILLY NORRIS, record producer, songwriter; b. Phil Campbell, Ala., Nov. 5, 1936; s. Clyde Rivers and Ora Lucille (Thompson) S.; m. Charlene Evans, Jan. 30, 1961; 1 child, Catherine Eve Sherrill Lale. Recording engr. Sam Phillips Studio, Nashville, 1961-62; studio mgr. Sun Records, 1962—63; staff prodr. Columbia/Epic Records, Nashville, 1963—2015. Songwriter: Almost Persuaded, Stand by Your Man, I Don't Wanna Play House, Your Good Girl's Gonna Go Bad, My Elusive Dreams, He Loves Me All the Way, The Ways to Love a Man, A Picture of Me (Without You), The Grand Tour, The Door, We're Gonna Hold On, We Loved It Away, A Very Special Love Song, The Most Beautiful Girl, Southern California, Two-Story House, numerous others; prodr. Tanya Tucker, Marty Robbins, Johnny Paycheck, Charlie Rich, Johnny Cash, David Allan Coe, Ray Charles, Tammy Wynette, George Jones, Barbara Mandrell. Named to Nat. Songwriter's Assn. Internat. Hall of Fame, 1984, Nashville Songwriters Hall of Fame, 1984, Country Music Hall of Fame, 2010; recipient Nashville Entertainment Assn. Master award, 1986, Nat. Acad. Rec. Arts and Scis. Grammay awards for best songwriter for Best Country and Western Song, Almost Persuaded, 1966, best country song A Very Special Love Song, 1974, Country Music Assn. prodr. awards for albums of the yr. Behind Closed Doors, 1973, A Very Special Love Song, 1974, singles of the yr. Behind Closed Doors, 1973, He Stopped Loving Her Today, 1980, Broadcast Music Inc. Writer Performance awards, 1985, Billboard Mag. Favorite Country Single award, 1966, Top Country Song of Yr. for Most Beautiful Gir, 1974, Ala. Music Hall of Fame Mus. Creator's award, 1985, Acad. Country Music prodr. awards for single record of year Behind Closed Doors, 1973, album of yr. Behind Closed Doors, 1973, single of yr. He Stopped Loving Her Today, 1980, Songwriter of Century award BMI, 1999. Home: Nashville, Tenn. Died Aug. 4, 2015.

SHERWOOD, DONALD, lawyer; b. NYC, July 3, 1928; s. Hally and Jean (Ceecret) S. BA, Bklyn. Coll., 1950; JD, LLB, Columbia U., 1953. Bar: N.Y. Lawyer, Miami, from 1953. Died Jan. 18, 2007.

SHETLAND, MARGARET LOUISE, nursing educator; b. Schenectady, Jan. 9, 1906; d. Andrew J. and Emma (Jones) Shetland. Diploma, U. Hosp. of Good Shepherd, Syracuse, NY, 1926; BS in Pub. Health Nursing, Syracuse U., 1938; MA, Columbia U., NYC, 1942, EdD, 1952. Assoc. dir. nursing Mich. Dept. Health, Lansing, 1945-50; chair, prof. Syracuse U., 1950-56; sr. nursing advisor USOM, Philippines, 1956-58; cons. bachelor and higher degree programs Nat. League Nursing, NYC, 1959-63; dean Coll. Nursing Wayne State U., Detroit, 1964-74; ret., 1974. Short term cons. Pan Am. Health Orgn., WHO, Centa, others, Lebanon, Turkey, Panama, Guatemala, Child, Peru, Venezuela, 1953-75. Fulbright scholar Victoria U., Wellington, New Zealand, 1975. Fellow Nat. League for Nursing; mem. ANA, Am. Pub. Health Assn., Am. Acad. Nursing. Home: Chapel Hill, NC. Died Dec. 1, 2006.

SHI, CHANGXU, materials scientist; b. Xushui; Grad., NW China Inst. of Tech., 1945, Rotterdam U., Netherlands, 1948. Academician Chinese Acad. of Sciences, 1980, rschr., 1994, hon. supt.; acedemician Third World Acad. of Sciences, 1995; academician Chinese Acad. of Engring., 1994, v.p., 2011. Advisor Nat. Natural Sci. Found., China. Recipient State Preeminent Sci. & Technology award, 2010. Died Nov. 10, 2014.

SHIBLES, WARREN ALTON, philosophy educator; b. Hartford, Conn., July 10, 1933; s. Stanley Neal and Jean (Russell) S.; m. Patricia A. Pell (div. 1976); children: Garth, Kirsten, Eric; m. Carolyn Lesley Foster, Jan. 1977. BA, U. Conn., 1958; MA, U. Colo., 1963; postgrad., Ind. U., 1963-67. Instr. North Tex. State U., Denton, 1966; lectr. Parsons Coll., Fairfield, Iowa, 1966-67; prof. philosophy U. Wis., Whitewater, from 1967. Dir. The Lang. Press, Whitewater; lectr. throughout Europe and U.S., including univs. Stockholm, Paris, Munich, Bonn, Basel, Marburg, Utrecht, Leiden. Author more than 20 books; contbr. over 160 articles to profl. jours. With U.S. Army, 1953-55. Home: Whitewater, Wis. Died July 17, 2007.

SHIELDS, EDWARD JOSEPH, chemical engineer, municipal government official; b. Phila., July 30, 1930; s. Edward Joseph and Anna Marie (Hernick) S.; m. Shirley Ann Brown, Apr. 16, 1955; children: Tina Marie, Lisa Rose, Aimee Ann. B in Chem Engring., Villanova U., 1952. Tech. trainee Allied Chem. and Dye Corp., NYC, 1952-53, prodn. supr. Balt., 1953-54, Marcus Hook, Pa., 1958-65; asst. supt. Allied Chem. Corp., Marcus Hook, 1965-67, asst. plant mgr., 1967-69, plant mgr., 1969-73, mgr. pollution control Morristown, N.J., 1973-79; dir. environ. serviced Allied Corp., Morristown, 1979-86; dir. environ. matters Gen. Chem. Corp., Parsippany, N.J., from 1986. Editor: Pollution Control Engineer's Handbook, 1985. Mayor Washington Twp., Morris County, N.J. 1979-87, mem. twp. com., 1977-88, planning bd., 1979-87; chmn. bd. suprs. West Goshen Twp., Chester County, Pa., 1970-73. Served to lt. (j.g.) USCG, 1954-58. Named to Order of Arrow William Penn dist. Boy Scouts Am., 1972. Republican. Roman Catholic. Avocation: collecting historical artifacts. Home: Long Valley, NJ. Died Mar. 12, 2007.

SHIKLER, AARON ABRAHAM, artist; b. Bklyn., Nov. 12, 1922; s. Frank and Annie (Blai) S.; m. Barbara Lurie, Oct. 4, 1947; children: Cathy M., Clifford M. B.F.A., BS in Edn.; M.F.A., Tyler Sch. Fine Arts, Temple U., 1948; student, Barnes Found., Merion, Pa., 1941-43, Hans Hoffmann Sch., NYC, 1949-51. One man shows, Davis Galleries, N.Y.C., 1953, 54, 56, 58, 60, 62, 64, 67, 71, 83, 84, Bklyn. Museum, 1971, Palace of Legion of Honor, San Francisco, 1971, Long Gallery, Houston, 1972, 76, 82, 85,

Davis & Long Co., 1975, 79, Temple U., 1985, Claude Bernard Gallery, Paris, 1988, Davis & Langdale Co., 1987, 90, 93, 2000, 03, Kunsthaus Bühler, Stuttgart, Germany, 2002; represented in permanent collections, Montclair (N.J.) Mus., Hofstra Mus. Art, L.I., Carnegie Inst., Pitts., Met. Mus. Art, Mint Mus. Art, Charlotte, N.C., Parrish Mus. Art, Southampton, L.I., N.A.D., Bklyn. Mus., Hirshorn Mus., Washington, Nat. Art Gallery, Wellington, N.Z., Nat. Gallery, Singapore, New Britain Mus. Am. Art, Sun Rise Mus., Charleston, W.Va., Sheldon Meml. Art Gallery, Lincoln, Nebr., Pa. State U. Gallery, Davis Galleries, 1987, Lyme Acad., 1986 ; executed: portraits Pres. and Mrs. John F. Kennedy for White House, Robert Lehman Pavilion at Met. Mus. Art, Henry F. duPont for Winterthur (Del.) Mus., Robert F. Kennedy for Dept. Justice, Washington, Sec. Carla Hills for HUD, Sec. Carla Hills for Yale Law Sch., Mrs. Lyndon B. Johnson for Johnson Library, Austin, Tex., Senator Mike Mansfield for U.S. Senate, Washington, Dr. Michael DeBakey for Baylor U., Pres.-Elect Ronald Reagan as Man of Yr. for Time mag., James M. Walton for Carnegie Inst., Pitts., Pres. Ronald Reagan and Mrs. Reagan for The White House, Andrew Heiskell for N.Y. Pub. Libr., William S. Paley for Mus. Broadcasting, Dr. Vartan Gregorian, N.Y. Pub. Libr., Dr. Manuel Koehane, Wesley Coll., Mass., Hillary R. Clinton for Time mag., 1999. Served with inf. AUS, 1943-46. Recipient Tiffany award, 1958; Dept. State grantee S.E. Asia and South Pacific, 1976; Temple U. Centennial fellow, 1985. Mem. NAD (Ranger award 1959, Proctor prize 1959, 60, Clarke prize 1961, Altman prize 1976). Clubs: Century Assn. Died Nov. 12, 2015.

SHINOLT, EILEEN THELMA, artist; b. Washington, May 18, 1919; d. Edward Lee and Blanche Addie (Marsh) Bennett; m. John Francis Shinolt, June 14, 1956 (dec. Aug. 1969). Student, Hans Hoffman Sch Art, 1949, Pa. Acad. Arts, 1950, Corcoran Sch. Art, 1945-51, Am. U., 1973-77. Sect. chief Dept. Army, Washington, 1940-73, retired, 1973. One-woman shows include various locations, 1982, 83, 85, 90, 94, 96; group shows include Perlmutter & Co., 1981, Fitch Fox and Brown, 1986, Foundry Gallery, 1987, Ann. Add Arts, 1986, Westminster Gallery, London, 1995; represented in permanent collections Women's Nat. Mus., Washington, Cameo Gallery, Columbia, S.C., Strathmore Hall Arts Ctr., North Bethesda, Md., 1997, 98, 99, 2000, 01, 02, 03, 04. Mem. Woman's Nat. Dem. Club, Washington, 1980—. Mem. Am. Art League (editor newsletter 1985-86, 1st pl. 1987, 2d pl. 1986), Arts Club Washington (exhbn. com. 1985—, admissions com. 1987-88), Miniature Painters, Sculptors & Gravers Soc. (historian 1989-2003, editor newsletter 1986-89), Fine Arts in Miniature. Roman Catholic. Avocations: reading, studying art periodicals, art galleries. Died Jan. 14, 2007.

SHIPP, WILLIAM LEE, deacon; b. Lincoln, Ill., July 31, 1938; s. Floyd Lee and Mary C. (Murray) S.; m. Ann Yong Choe, Sept. 14, 1963; 1 child, Francis Joseph. BS in Math., St. Louis U., 1961; BS in Meteorology, Pa. State U., 1962; MEd, U. Ill., 1971, EdD, 1978. Ordained deacon, Roman Cath. Ch., 1979. Parish asst. St. Malachy, Rantoul, Ill., 1979-84; assoc. chaplain Randolph AFB Chapel, Tex., from 1986; tng. specialist HQ Air Tng. Command, Randolph AFB, from 1984. Faculty Permanent Deacon Program, San Antonio, 1984—; trustee Permanent Deacon Bd. Dirs., 1986—. Contbr. articles to profl. jours. Pres. bd. trustees Randolph Ind. Sch. Dist., 1984—. Lt. col. USAF, 1961-89. Mem. Res. Officers Assn. (pres. 1978, editor newsletter 1976-80), Nat. Soc. for Performance and Instrn. (v.p. Air Force 1988-91), K.C. Home: Rantoul, Ill. Died July 8, 2007.

SHIRLEY, AARON, pediatrician; b. Gluckstadt, Miss., Jan. 3, 1933; married; 4 children. BS, Tougaloo Coll., 1955; MD, McHarry Med. Coll., 1959, U. Miss., 1968. Intern Herbert Hosp., Tenn., 1959—60; gen. practice Vicksburg, 1960—65; project dir. Jackson-Hinds Comprehensive Health Ctr., Jackson, Miss., 1980—96; dir. cmty. health svcs. Jackson (Miss.) Med. Mall, 1996—2014; chmn. Jackson (Miss.) Med. Mall Found., 1996—2014. Mem. faculty medicine Tufts U. Medicine, Mass., 1968—73, U. Miss. Med. Sch., from 1970; head start cons. Am. Acad. Pediat., 1969—74; adv. bd. rural practice project Robert Wood Johnson Found., 1974—78; mem. Select Panel Prom. Child Health, Washington, 1979—81. Recipient Herbert W. Nickens award, 2013. Mem.: Inst. Medicine NAS (mem. coun. from 1988). Died Nov. 26, 2014.

SHULTS, CLIFFORD WALTER, medical researcher; b. Newport, Tenn., Oct. 27, 1950; s. Glen Coile and Ima Love (Gray) S.; m. Ellen Jeanette Koutsky, Sept. 15, 1985; children: Andrew Joseph, Sarah Gray. AB, Brown U., 1973; MD, U. Tenn., Memphis, 1977. Med. staff fellow NIH, Bethesda, Md., 1982-85; neurologist VA Med. Ctr., San Diego, 1985-93, chief neurology svc., from 1993; asst. prof. dept. neuroscis. U. Calif. San Diego, La Jolla, 1985-92, assoc. prof., 1992-97, prof., from 1997. Mem. exec. com. Parkinson Study Group, Rochester, N.Y., 1997—. Author some 70 rsch. articles and book chpts. Mem. Soc. for Neurosci., Am. Neurol. Assn., Am. Acad. Neurology, Movement Disorder Soc. Presbyterian. Died Feb. 6, 2007.

SHUR, EDWARD H., newspaper editor; b. NYC, Apr. 12, 1953; s. Ira Shur and Harriet (Schechter) Steiner. BA, U. R.I., 1978. Night editor Carroll County Times, Westminster, Md., 1983-84; bureau chief The Baltimore (Md.) Sun, 1984-93; exec. editor, gen. mgr. Minn. Sun Publications, Bloomington, Minn., 1993-96; sunday, projects editor Reno (Nev.) Gazette-Journal, from 1996; CEO Shurshots Publishing, Sparks, Nev., from 1978. Recipient Special Section award Suburban Newspapers of Am., 1995, Enterprise award Nev. Press Assn., 1997, Best of Gannett award Gannett Co., Inc., 1997, 98. Mem. Am. Soc. Newspaper Editors, Soc. Profl. Journalists, Newspaper Assn. Am., Investigative Reporters & Editors. Avocations: reading, travel, computers. Home: Sparks, Nev. Died Dec. 27, 2006.

SHUTLER, RICHARD, JR., anthropologist, archaeologist; b. Longmont, Colo., Dec. 8, 1921; s. Richard D. and Tessa Flo (Burnett) S.; m. Jamie Sue Evrard, Mar. 26, 1978; children— Kathryn Allice, John Hall, Richard Burnett. AA, Salinas Jr. Coll., 1942; BA, U. Calif., Berkeley, 1949, MA, 1950; PhD, U. Ariz., 1961. With Nevada State Mus., Carson City, 1959-65; mem. faculty U. Hawaii, 1965-66, San Diego State Coll., 1967-68, U. Victoria, B.C., Can., 1968-72; mem. faculty dept. anthropology U. Iowa, Iowa City, 1972-79, prof., chmn. dept., 1972-79; prof. dept. archaeology Simon Fraser U., Burnaby, B.C., Can., 1979-87, prof. emeritus, 1987. Hon. asso. in anthropology Bernice P. Bishop Mus., 1963— ; hon. curator of archaeology Nat. Mus. of Philippines, 1976— Author: Pleistocene Studies in Southern Nevada, 1967, Oceanic Prehistory, 1975. Served with AUS, 1942-44; Served with USAAF, 1944-46. NSF grantee, 1962, 63, 76 Fellow Am. Anthrop. Assn., AAAS; mem. Soc. Am. Archaeology, Indo-Pacific Prehistory Assn. Died June 28, 2007.

SHUTTLEWORTH, REBECCA SCOTT, English language educator; b. Eupora, Miss., Aug. 18, 1919; d. Thaddeus William and Frances Lucinda (Willingham) Scott; m. Wallace Shuttleworth, June 12, 1943 (dec. Aug. 1961); children: Sally, Rebecca. BA, Miss. U. for Women, 1941, MEd, 1962. Tchr. Okolona (Miss.) High Sch., 1941-42, Indianola (Miss.) High Sch., 1942-43, 45-70, Miss. Delta Community Coll., Moorhead, 1970-89, chmn. lang. arts, 1978-89, tchr. extended learning, 1989-96. Asst. organizer Miss. Community Coll. Creative Writing Assn., 1978. Past pres. Twentieth Century Club, Indianola, 1947-94. Mem. AAUW (Woman of Achievement 1992, Scholarship award 1989), DAR (Am. history chmn. 1990-92, vice-regent 1994-96, regent 1996-98). Republican. Methodist. Avocation: reading. Died Jan. 17, 2007.

SHYLLON, PRINCE E.N., lawyer, educator; b. Freetown, Sierra Leone, Nov. 3, 1943; came to the U.S. s. Henry W.O. and Lois (Johnson) S.; m. Millicent Boutchway, June 8, 1974; children: Nicky H., Selwyn A. BA in Economics, Shaw U., 1972; JD Sch. of Law, N.C. Ctrl. U., Durham, 1975. Bar: N.C. 1977, U.S. Dist. Ct. (ea. dist.), 1978, U.S. Ct. of Appeals (4th cir.), 1978. Ptnr. Shabica, Shyllon & Shyllon, Raleigh, N.C., 1977-79, Shyllon, Shyllon & Ratliff, Raleigh, N.C., 1979-85; prof. Bus. Law and Ins. Saint Augustines Coll., Raleigh, N.C., 1975-91; ptnr. Shyllon & Shyllon, Raleigh, N.C., from 1986. University counsel St. Augustines Coll., 1992—. Mem. ABA, N.C. Acad. of Trial Lawyers. Home: Raleigh, NC. Died Jan. 4, 2007.

SICULAR, GEORGE MYER, civil engineer, educator, consultant; b. NYC, Aug. 15, 1921; s. Theodore and Sophie (Reisner) S.; m. Alice Greene, July 20, 1948; children: Terry, Lawrence. BCE, Cooper Union, 1949; MSCE, Columbia U., 1953; Engrs. degree, Stanford U., 1971. Jr. tool designer Mergen Thaler Linotype Co., NYC, 1941, 42; structural designer Kennedy-VanSaun Engrs., NYC, 1948; asst. prof. CCNY, NYC, 1949-54; part-time cons. engr. Structures and Hydraulics, N.Y., N.J., 1949-54; from asst. prof. to prof. civil engring. San Jose (Calif.) State U., 1954-94, prof. emeritus, from 1994; cons. civil engr. San Francisco Bay area, from 1954. Resident engr. Reconstruction of Grafenwöhr Mil. Base, Bavaria, 1946; civil engring. advisor Project India, U. Roorkee, USAID, 1963-64, Project Singapore, U. Singapore, Ford Found., 1967-69; chmn. mission and goals com. San Jose State U., 1971-72; acad. senator Calif. State U. Sys., 1975-85; conductor feasibility studies, Gilroy, Calif. Reservoir, Upper Llagas Reservoir, Calif., flood studies on various streams, design of energy dissipators, restoration of streams; expert witness in many cases resulting from floods. Contbr. articles to profl. jours. Bd. dirs. Jewish Fedn. San Jose, 1973-77; mem. pub. affairs com. Santa Clara County Med. Assn., 1978; mem. Jewish Pub. Affairs Calif., treas. 1983-84; comdr. post 52 Palo Alto Am. Legion, 1988-89; chmn. adult edn. com. Temple Bethel, Aptos, Calif., 1993-94; mem. tech. adv. com. Pajaro Valley Water Mgmt. Agy., Watsonville, Calif., 1993-94; chair tech. adv. com. Groundwater Guardian Com., Pajaro Valley, Watsonville, Calif., 1994. 2nd Lt. C.E., U.S. Army, 1942-46. Grad. fellow NSF, 1961, 62. Fellow ASCE; mem. United Profs. of Calif. (pres. San Jose State U. chpt. 1973-76, no. v.p. 1980-82). Democrat. Jewish. Avocation: history of german military and its influence on civil govts. Died Feb. 28, 2007.

SIDRAN, MIRIAM, retired physicist; b. Washington, May 25, 1920; d. Morris Samson and Theresa Rena (Gottlieb) S. BA, Bklyn. Coll., 1942; MA, Columbia U., NYC, 1949; PhD, NYU, 1956. Rsch. assoc. dept. physics NYU, NYC, 1950-55, postdoctoral fellow, 1955-57; asst. prof. Staten Island Community Coll., Richmond, NY, 1957-59; rsch. scientist Grumman Aerospace Corp., Bethpage, NY, 1959-67; prof. N.Y. Inst. Tech., NYC, 1967-72; NSF rsch. fellow Nat. Marine Fisheries Svc., Miami, Fla., 1971-72; assoc. prof. then prof. physics Baruch Coll., NYC, 1972-89, chmn. dept. natural scis., 1983-89, prof. emerita, from 1990. V.p. Baruch chpt. Profl. Staff Congress, 1983-89. Contbr. numerous articles to profl. and govtl. publs., chpts. to books. N.Y. State Regents scholar, 1937-41; NSF summer fellow, Miami, 1970. Mem. N.Y. Acad. Scis., Am. Assn. Physics Tchrs., Physics Club N.Y., N.Y. Gilbert and Sullivan Soc., Wynmoor Computer Club, Friends of Mozart, Sigma Xi, Sigma Pi Sigma. Avocations: french and hebrew languages, music, bicycling, poetry, opera. Home: Fairfield, Conn. Died July 23, 2014.

SIEGEL, GARY HOWARD, accountant, sociologist, educator; b. Chgo., Jan. 30, 1944; s. Sam Bernard and Miriam Arlene (Poster) S.; m. Beverly Kolodny, Sept. 14, 1968; children: Adam, Joshua, Sunny, Gabriel, Johanna, Samantha. BA in Acctg. with honors, U. Ill., 1966, PhD in Sociology, 1977; MBA in Acctg., DePaul U., 1967; postgrad., U. Chgo., 1967-68. CPA, Ill. Lectr. U. Ill., Chgo., 1967-70, asst. prof., 1977-80, research asst. Urbana, 1971-73; asst. prof. Ill. Inst. Tech., Chgo., 1974-77; assoc. prof. DePaul U., Chgo., from 1980; pres. Gary Siegel Orgn., Chgo., from 1981. Staff cons. 1st Nat. Bank Chgo., 1968-70; cons. pvt. practice, Chgo., 1975-85; pres. Gary Siegel Orgn., Chgo., 1985—. Co-author: Behavioral Accounting, 1989; assoc. editor Advances in Acctg., 1982-83; referee Decision Scis., 1984—; contbr. articles to profl. jours. Bd. dirs. Yeshiva Migdal Torah, Chgo.; pres. Jewish Burial Soc. Mem. Am. Inst. CPA's, Am. Acctg. Assn. (acctg., behavior and orgns. sect. 1982—), Ill. CPA Soc. (pub. relations council 1973-80, chmn. internal communications subcom. of pub. service and info. com. 1975-77, study team profl. specialization 1976-78), Am. Assn. Pub. Opinion Research, Decision Scis. Inst., Beta Alpha Psi, Delta Mu Delta. Home: Chicago, Ill. Died Nov. 12, 2006.

SIEGEL, SHERMAN HOWARD, aerospace engineer; b. Newark, Oct. 4, 1928; s. Abraham M. and Yetta (Bernstein) S.; m. Barbara Lou King, July 9, 1955; children: Sandra, Karen, Mark. BS, N.J. Inst. Tech., 1950; MEE, Syracuse U., 1963; postgrad., Pa. State U., 1965-68. Registered profl. engr., Pa., N.Y. Design engr. Gen. Electric Co., Binghamton, N.Y., 1953-64, project engr. King of Prussia, Pa., from 1964. Contbr. articles to profl. jours. Served as sgt. U.S. Army, 1946-57. Mem. AIAA, Tau Beta Pi. Democrat. Unitarian Universalist. Home: Kng Of Prussa, Pa. Died Dec. 10, 2006.

SIFFORD, CHARLIE (CHARLES LUTHER SIFFORD), retired professional golfer; b. Charlotte, NC, June 2, 1922; m. Rose Sifford; children: Charles, Craig. LLD (hon.), U. St. Andrews, Scotland, 2006. Profl. golfer, from 1948; mem. PGA Tour, 1960—80, Sr. PGA Tour, from 1980, Super Sr. Tour, from 1991. With 24th Inf. US Army. Recipient Old Tom Morris award, Golf Course Supts. Assn. America, 2007, Golden Tee award, Met. Golf Writers Assn., 2008, Presdl. Medal of Freedom, The White House, 2014; named to The World Golf Hall of Fame (first African American), 2004. Achievements include breaking the color barrier in professional golf as the first African American to compete on the PGA Tour, 1960; winning other notable events including the UGA National Negro Open, 1952-56, 1960, Long Beach Open, 1957, Puerto Rico Open, 1963, Sea Pines, 1971; winning PGA Tour events the Greater Hartford Open, 1967, the Los Angeles Open, 1969; winning the PGA Seniors' Championship, 1975; winning the Champions Tour event, the Suntree Classic, 1980. Died Feb. 3, 2015.

SIKORA, ROBERT GREGORY, pharmacist, consultant; b. Hammond, Ind., Apr. 27, 1949; s. Sylvester J. and Marie Margaret (Herman) S.; m. Nancy Ruth Highsmith, June 24, 1972; children: Robert Anthony, Daniel James. BS in Pharmacy, Purdue U., 1972; MS in Pharmacy, U. Ga., 1980. Registered pharmacist, Tex., Ind. Asst. chief pharmacy svc. U.S. Army Cmty. Hosp., Ft. Knox, Ky., 1977-79; chief inpatient pharmacy Brooke Army Med. Ctr., Ft. Sam Houston, Tex., 1980-84; chief pharmacy svc. U.S. Army Hosp., Berlin, Germany, 1984-88; asst. chief pharmacy svc. Walter Reed Army Med. Ctr., Washington, 1988-91; chief pharmacy svc. Womack Army Med. Ctr., Ft. Bragg, N.C., 1991-94; clin. edn. cons. Pfizer Inc., San Antonio, 1994-95, team mgr., clin. edn., 1995-98, nat. dir. clin. edn., from 1998. Decorated Legion of Merit; recipient Outstanding Achievement in Pharmacy award Merck, Sharp & Dohme, 1992. Mem. Am. Soc. Health System Pharmacists (Pharmacy Practice Rsch. award 1994), Am. Pharm. Assn., Tex. Soc. Health System Pharmacists, Ctrl. Tex. Soc. Health System Pharmacists (bd. dirs. 1995-97), Assn. Mil. Surgeons U.S. Avocations: golf, skiing. Home: Hartsdale, NY. Died Aug. 7, 2007.

SILAS, CECIL JESSE, retired petroleum company executive; b. Miami, Fla., Apr. 15, 1932; s. David Edward and Hilda Videll (Carver) S.; m. Theodosea Hejda, Nov. 27, 1965; children: Karla, Peter, Michael, James. BSChemE, Ga. Inst. Tech., Atlanta, 1953. With Phillips Petroleum Co., Bartlesville, Okla., 1953-94, pres. Europe-Africa, Brussels and London, 1968-74, mng. dir. natural resource group Europe/Africa London, 1974-76, v.p. gas and gas liquids div. natural resources group Bartlesville, 1976-78, sr. v.p. natural resources group, 1978-80, exec. v.p. exploration and prodn., minerals, gas and gas liquids, 1980-82, pres., chief operating officer, 1982-85, chmn., CEO, 1985-94. Bd. dirs. Boys/Girls Clubs Am., Atlanta, parton councillor Atlantic Coun. of the U.S.; bd. dirs. Okla. Found. for Excellence, Ga. Tech. Found.; trustee Frank Phillips Found. Served to 1st lt. Chem. Corps, AUS, 1954-56. Decorated comdr. Order St. Olaf (Norway); inducted into Ga. Inst. Tech. Athletic Hall of Fame, 1959, recipient Former Scholar-Athlete Total Person award, 1988; inducted into Okla. Bus. Hall of Fame, 1989; named CEO of Yr., Internat. TV Assn., 1987. Mem. Am. Petroleum Inst., U.S. C. of C. (past chmn. bd. dirs.), 25 Yr. Club, Phi Delta Theta. Avocations: fishing, golf, hunting. Home: Bartlesville, Okla. Died Dec. 2014.

SILBERBERG, NORMAN ESAU, psychologist, consultant; b. Bklyn., Sept. 12, 1931; s. Hyman L. and Bessie M. (Lasky) S.; m. Margaret Carlson (dec. Nov. 1982); children: Amy, Sarah, Ann. BA, Syracuse U., 1953; MA, U. Minn., 1957; student, U. Paris, 1957-58; PhD, U. Iowa, 1965. Lic. cons. psychologist, Minn. Sch. psychologist North St. Paul Schs., 1963-65; dir. research Sister Kenny Inst., Mpls.,

1967-73, v.p., 1973-77; psychol. cons. Mpls., 1977-85; psychologist Minn. Indian Women's Resource Ctr., Mpls., from 1985. Advisor Red Sch. House, St. Paul, 1973, Nat. Urban League, 1974-75; evaluator AIM Schs., Mpls., St. Paul, 1969-76; mem. Govs. COuncil on Aging, 1973-75; cons. Mpls. Head Start, 1977—. Author: Who Speaks for the Child, 1974; editorial advisor Jour. Learning Disabilities, 1967—; contbr. articles to profl. jours. Bd. dirs. St. Paul Urban League, 1965-74; trustee Northlands Med. Program. 1974-77. Recipient Appreciation awards St. Paul Indian Clinic, 1983, Women's Advocates, 1983, Mpls. Head Start, 1984. Mem. Am. Psychol. Assn. Democrat. Died May 1, 2007.

SILER, OWEN WESLEY, retired military officer, consultant; b. Seattle, Jan. 10, 1922; s. Walter Orlando and Hylda Ruth (Jackson) S.; m. Betty Lilian Walford, Oct. 27, 1945 children: Gregory John, Marsha Joan S. Antista. BS, USCG Acad., 1943; MS, George Washington U., 1968. 2d dist. comdr. USCG, St. Louis, 1971-74, adm. Washington, 1974-78, ret., 1978; mem. bd. dirs. Panama Canal Co., Washington and Panama, 1977-81; v.p. mgmt. Forensic Tech. Internat. Corp., Annapolis, Md., 1980-81; pres. Ann-Bay Trans. Co., Annapolis, 1980-81; chmn. adv. bd. Med. Adv. Systems, Owings, Md., 1981-87. Assoc. Burdeshaw Assocs. Ltd., Bethesda, Md., 1985—. Recipient Gold Medal award Dept. of Transp., 1976, Minute Man of Yr. Res. Officers Assn., 1978. Mem. Propeller of U.S., Navy Leage U.S. (bd. dirs., chmn. resolutions com. 1985—), Ret. Officers Assn. (1st v.p. 1982-84), Rotary (bd. dirs. Washington club 1985-87), Masons. Republican. Avocations: tennis, clock repair. Home: Savannah, Ga. Died July 17, 2007.

SILK, ELEANORE KAHN, retired elementary school educator; b. Salt Lake City, Aug. 2, 1921; d. Edwin Charles and Marion Leopold Kahn; children: Susan Lynne, Barbara Ann. BEd, Nat. Coll. Edn. Tchr., Salt Lake City, 1943—44, Detroit Sch. Sys., 1944—45, 1956—86; ret., 1986. Recipient Freedom award, Southfield, Mich., 1985. Mem.: NEA, Jewish War Vets. Aux. (dept. pres. 1958—59). Democrat. Home: Southfield, Mich. Died Apr. 19, 2007.

SILVERMAN, LEON, lawyer; b. NYC, June 9, 1921; m. Rita Schwartz, 1949; children: Susan, Jane. BA, Bklyn. Coll., 1942; LL.B., Yale U., 1948; postgrad., London Sch. Econs., 1948-49. Bar: N.Y. 1949. Assoc. firm Riegelman, Strasser, Schwartz & Spiegelberg (now known as Fried Frank Harris, Shriver and Jacobson), NYC, 1949-53; asst. U.S. atty. So. Dist. N.Y., 1953—56; asst. dep. atty. gen. Dept. Justice, Washington, 1958-59, spl. prosecutor, 1981-82, ind. counsel investigating Sec. Labor, 1987; ptnr. Fried, Frank, Harris, Shriver & Jacobson, 1956—80, co-chmn. firm NYC, 1960—80, counsel to, 1980—2015. Counsel N.Y. Gov.'s Com. to Rev. N.Y. Laws and Procedure in the Area of Human Rights, 1967-68, Com. to Rev. Legis. and Jud. Salaries, 1972-73; mem. adv. com. on criminal rules to com. on rules of practice and procedure Jud. Conf. U.S.; mem. joint com. to monitor N.Y. drug laws; pres. N.Y. Legal Aid Soc., 1970-72, dir., 1966; pres U.S. Supreme Ct. Hist. Soc., 1980-92, chmn. 1992; spl. master Appellatte divsn. 1st dept. N.Y. Supreme Ct., 1984. Trustee William Nelson Cromwell Found., 1983; chmn. Legal Council for Soviet Jewery, 1987. Recipient Judge Learned Hand Human Relations award, 1981, Emory Buckner Pub. Service medal, 1982, Judge Joseph M. Proskauer award, 1982. Mem. ABA, N.Y. State Bar Assn., Fed. Bar Assn., American Coll. Trial Lawyers (regent 1979, pres. 1982-83), American Law Inst., American Judicature Soc., Practicing Law Inst. (trustee), Assn. Bar City N.Y., Fed. Bar Council, Supreme Ct. Historical Soc. (former pres.) Home: Great Neck, NY. Died Jan. 29, 2015.

SILVERSTEIN, JOSEPH HARRY, conductor, musician; b. Detroit, Mar. 21, 1932; s. Bernard and Ida (Katz) S.; m. Adrienne Shufro, Apr. 27; children: Bernice (Bunny), Deborah, Marc. Student, Curtis Inst. Music, 1945-50; D (hon.), Tufts U., 1971, R.I. U., 1980, Boston Coll., 1981, New Eng. Conservatory, 1986, Susquehanna, 1996, Brigham Young U., 1998. Violinist Houston Symphony Orch., Phila. Orch.; concertmaster Denver Symphony Orch., Boston Symphony Orch.; formerly chmn. string dept. New Eng. Conservatory Music; also chmn. faculty Berkshire Music Sch.; mem. faculty Boston U. Sch. Music, Yale U. Sch. Music; music dir. Boston Symphony Chamber Players, Boston U. Symphony Orch., Chautauqua (N.Y.) Instn., from 1987; interim music dir. Toledo Symphony Orch.; prin. guest condr. Balt. Symphony Orch., 1981; condr. Utah Symphony, music dir., 1983—98, condr. laureate, 1998; acting music dir. Fla. Philharm., 2001. Mem. faculty Longy Sch., Curtis Inst., New England Conservatory, Tanglewood Music Center, also chmn.; artistic advisor Winnepeg and Aartford Symphonies. Recipient Silver medal Queen Elizabeth of Belgium Internat. contest, 1959, Naumburg Found. award, 1960; named one of ten outstanding young men Boston C. of C., 1962. Fellow Am. Acad. Arts and Scis.; mem. Chamber Music Soc. Lincoln Ctr. (artist). Died Nov. 22, 2015.

SIMON, BOB, news correspondent; b. Bronx, NY, May 29, 1941; m. Francoise Simon; 1 child, Tanya. BA in History, Brandeis U., Waltham, Mass., 1962. Fgn. svc. officer US Dept. State, 1964—67; reporter CBS News, NYC, 1967—69, London, 1969—71, 1972—77, Saigon, Vietnam, 1971—72, Tel Aviv, 1977—81, State Dept. corr. Washington, 1981-82, nat. corr. NYC, 1982-87, chief Middle Eastern corr., from 1987, regular contbr. 60 Minutes, 1996—2015, sr. fgn. corr., 2005—15, corr. 60 Minutes II, 1999—2005. Author: Forty Days, 1992. Recipient Overseas Press Club award, 1991, 1996, George Foster Peabody award, 1996, 2000, Edward Weintal prize, Georgetown U. Inst. Study of Diplomacy, 1997, Alfred I. duPont-Columbia U. award, 2001, IRE award, Investigative Reporters & Editors, 2001, 27 Emmy awards, Lifetime Achievement Emmy award, 2003; Fulbright Scholar, Woodrow Wilson scholar. Mem.: Phi Beta Kappa. Died Feb. 11, 2015.

SIMON, KERRY, chef; b. June 17, 1955; Grad., Culinary Inst. Am. Former vegetable cook, saucier La Cote Basque, NYC, La Lavandou, NYC; former chef de partie Lutece, NYC; former personal chef London, NYC; former sous chef, pastry chef Lafayette, NYC; former chef Plaza Hotel, NYC, Blue Star, Miami Beach, Fla., Starfish, Miami Beach, Fla., Max's South Beach, Miami Beach, Fla., Mercury, Miami Beach, Fla.; exec. chef, ptnr. Prime Steakhouse, Las Vegas; exec. chef, proprietor Simon at Palms Restaurant, Las Vegas; owner Simon LA, Los Angeles, Calif., Simon Prime, Atlantic City, KGB and Carson's Kitchen, Las Vegas, Simon Mansion & Supper Club, Hard Rock Hotel and Casino, Punta Cana. Appeared on Iron Chef, 2005, judge Iron Chef America, guest appearances Hell's Kitchen, Fine Living Network's, What Makes It Tick. Achievements include being best known as Rock n' Roll Chef. Avocation: exercise. Died Sept. 11, 2015.

SIMONOWITZ, EVELYN MAY See LIEBERMAN, EVELYN

SIMONS, BARBARA M., lawyer; b. NYC, Feb. 7, 1929; d. Samuel A. and Minnie (Mankes) Malitz; m. Morton L. Simons, Sept. 2, 1951; 1 child, Claudia. BA, U. Mich., 1950, JD, 1952. Bar: N.Y. 1953, U.S. Supreme Ct. 1963, U.S. Ct. Appeals (D.C. cir.) 1971, (5th cir.) 1992, (1st cir.) 1994. Ptnr. Simons & Simons, Washington, from 1962. Pres. Forest Hills Citizens Assn., Washington, 1998-2002; past pres. D.C. chpt. U. Mich. Alumnae, Washington. Alumnae scholar U. Mich., 1946-50. Mem. Washington Coun. Lawyers, Nat. Partnership Women & Families, Sierra Club, Nat. Symphony Orch. Assn., Phi Beta Kappa, Phi Kappa Phi, Alpha Lambda Delta. Home: Washington, DC. Died Feb. 14, 2007.

SIMONSEN, RICHARD SEVERIN, retired aerospace engineer; b. Hollywood, Calif., Nov. 25, 1932; s. Irving P. and Margaret M. (Knox) S.; m. Marilynn Joy Johnson, June 1, 1955; children: Lynda G. Sheasley, Richard R. BS in Engring., UCLA, 1955; postgrad., Harvard U., 1984, U. Calif., Davis, 1980. Engr. Marquardt Aircraft Co., Van Nuys, Calif., 1955-56; engr., program mgr. Aerojet Gen. Corp., Sacramento, 1959-62, mgr. test ops., 1962-78, dir. product and environ. assurance, 1978-80, v.p., gen. mgr. propulsion divsn., 1980-86, pres. solid propulsion co., 1986-90, pres. propulsion co., 1990-93, corp. exec. v.p., 1993-95, ret., 1995. Pres. Sta. KVIE-TV, PBS, Sacremento, 1992-93, bd. dirs. 1987-93; v.p. fin. Boy Scouts Am. for Northern Calif., 1996. Named Engring. Alumnus of Yr. UCLA, 1993. Mem. Soc. Logistics Engrs. AIAA, Assn. U.S. Army, USAF Assn., mem. Boy's Scout of Am., 1996. Republican. Avocations: skiing, hunting, fishing, outdoor activities. Home: Park City, Utah. Died Mar. 26, 2007.

SIMPSON, CHRISTY, critical care nurse, pediatrics nurse; b. Izmir, Turkey, Jan. 28, 1957; came to U.S. d. Roy and Dorothy Ann (Payne) S. BS in Zoology, U. Idaho, 1979; BSN, U. Kans., 1987. RN, Mo.; CCRN cert., BLS, PALS instr. Staff nurse Rsch. Med. Ctr., Kans. City, Mo., Children's Mercy Hosp., Kans. City, Mo., nurse mgr. of Picu. Mem. AACN, Phi Kappa Phi, Sigma Theta Tau. Home: Kansas City, Mo. Died Apr. 28, 2007.

SIMPSON, JACK BENJAMIN, medical technologist, business executive; b. Tompkinsville, Ky., Oct. 30, 1937; s. Benjamin Harrison and Verda Mae (Woods) S.; m. Winona Clara Walden, Mar. 21, 1957; children: Janet Lazann, Richard Benjamin, Randall Walden, Angela Elizabeth. Student, Western Ky. U., 1954-57; grad., Norton Infirmary Sch. Med. Tech., 1958. Asst. chief med. technologist Jackson County Hosp., Seymour, Ind., 1958-61; chief med. technologist, bus. mgr. Mershon Med. Labs., Indpls., 1962-66; founder, dir., officer Am. Monitor Corp., Indpls., 1966-77; founder, pres., dir. Global Data, Inc., Ft. Lauderdale, Fla., from 1986. Mng. ptnr. Astroland Enterprises, Indpls., 1968—2010, 106th St. Assocs., Indpls., 1969-72, Keystones Ltd., Indpls., 1970-82, Delray Rd. Assoc. Ltd., Indpls., 1970-71, Allisonville Assocs. Ltd., Indpls., 1970-82, Grandview Assocs. Ltd., 1977—2010, Rucker Assocs. Ltd., Indpls., 1974—2010; mng. ptnr. Raintree Assocs. Ltd., Indpls., 1978—2010, Westgate Assocs. Ltd., Indpls., 1978—2010; pres., dir. Topps Constrn. Co., Inc., Bradenton, Fla., 1973-91, Acrovest Corp., Asheville, N.C., 1980—; dir. Indpls. Broadcasting, Inc.; founder, bd. dirs. Bank of Bradenton, 1986-92; founder, CFO Biomass Processing Tech., Inc., West Palm Beach, Fla., 1996—2008; also bd. dirs. Mem. Am. Soc. Med. Technologists (cert.), Indpls. Soc. Med. Technologists, Fla. Soc. Med. Technologists, Am. Soc. Clin. Pathologists, Am. Assn. Clin. Chemistry, Royal Soc. Health (London), Internat. Platform Assn., Am. Mus. Natural History, Columbia of Indpls. Club, Harbor Beach Surf Club, Fishing of Am. Club, Marina Bay Club (Ft. Lauderdale), Elks. Republican. Died July 26, 2014.

SIMPSON, JERRY HOWARD, JR., travel company executive; b. Providence, Dec. 11, 1925; s. Jerry Howard Simpson Sr. and Malta Faye (Atkins) Kelly; m. Charlotte Ann Bauserman, June 7, 1947 (div. Feb. 1963); children: Mary Ellen Lehman Jampole, Charles Frederick; m. Jane Coral Augustine, Sept. 4, 1973. Student, Moravian Coll. for Men, 1947-48, Emory & Henry Coll., 1948-50; BA, U. N.C., 1950. Seaman Merchant Marine, 1943-44; writer, dir., producer WSJS-TV, Winston-Salem, N.C., 1962-64; journalist, editor various newspapers and mags., 1965-75; founder, pres., dir. Bike Tour France, Charlotte, N.C., from 1975. Author: Torn Land, 1970, Annals of the Orient, 1987, Cycling France, 1992, Reflections on the French Recolution, 1994, Winter in Paris, 1994, Mille Pensées Impolies Fléches de Ma Cellule, 1996; translator: The Gardens of Villandry (Robert Carvallo), 1986. Sgt. USMC, 1944-46; master sgt. U.S. Army, 1951-58. Decorated Bronze Star; recipient Franco-Am. Friendship medal City of Blois, France, 1984, Tanvier medal J. Tanvier found., 1987. Died Mar. 25, 2007.

SIMPSON, MARY H., retired music educator; b. Fairfield County, Ohio, Oct. 24, 1916; d. Alva Jared and Laura Alberta Hempleman; m. James Frederick Simpson; children: John, Laura. BS in Edn., Ohio State U., 1936; MusM in Music Edn., Converse Coll., Spartanburg, SC, 1968. Tchr. music Fairfield County (Ohio) Pub. Schs., 1936—43; faculty dept. edn. Limestone Coll., SC, 1966—92. Choir dir. Presbyn. Ch., Gaffney, SC, from 1966. Mem.: AAUW, Arts Coun. (v.p.). Home: Gaffney, SC. Died Nov. 26, 2006.

SIMPSON, ROBERT HOMER, meteorologist, consultant; b. Corpus Christi, Tex., Nov. 19, 1912; s. Clyde Robert and Annie Laurie (Rainey) S.; m. Mazie Houston, Dec. 22, 1935 (div. Dec. 1949); m. Joanne Gerould Malkus, Jan. 6, 1965; children: Peggy A., Lynn S.; stepchildren: David Malkus, Steven Malkus, Karen Malkus. BS, Southwestern U., Tex., 1932, DSc (hon.), 1963; MS, Emory U., 1935; PhD, U. Chgo., 1962. Cert. cons. meteorologist. Observer U.s. Weather Bur., Brownsville, Tex., 1940-42, forecaster New Orleans and Miami, Fla., 1942-45, exec. asst. to dep. chief Washington, 1946-48; established Pacific Region of U.S. Weather Bur., Honolulu, 1948-52; rsch. scientist U.S. Weather Bur., Washington, 1952-56, founding dir. Nat. Hurricane Rsch. Project West Palm Beach, Fla., 1956-61, dep. dir. rsch. severe storms Washington, 1961-64; assoc. dir. ops. Nat. Weather Svc., NOAA, Washington, 1964-67, dir. Nat. Hurricane Ctr. Miami, 1967-74; founding dir. Simpson Weather Assoc., Inc., Charlottesville, Va., 1974—2014; rsch. prof. environ. sci. U. Va., Charlottesville, 1974-80. Helped established Mauna Loa Summit Obs., Hawaii, 1951. Author: (with Herbert Riehl) The Hurricane and Its Impact, 1981; chief editor: Hurricane: Coping with Disaster, 2002; contbr. articles to profl. jours. Recipient Gold medal US Dept. Commerce, 1962, Profl. Achievement award U. Chgo. D.C. Alumni Group, 1998, Nona Longtime Acehievement award, 2008. Fellow American Meteorol. Soc. (hon. mem., Cleveland Abbe award 1991), Explorers Club NY; mem. (bd. dir. 2008) Wash. Group. Achievements include (with Herbert Saffir) development and implementation of the Saffir-Simpson scale for hurricane damage potential; pioneering research flight in hurricane, Caribbean Sea, W. Pacific Ocean, first over-the-top flight in hurricane, Atlantic Ocean, 1947; many research penetrations of hurricane eyes. Home: Washington, DC. Died Dec. 18, 2014.

SIMS, ROBERT WARREN, chemistry educator; b. Goliad, Tex., Mar. 14, 1934; s. Alton Lyles and Roberta (Redmond) S.; m. Lana Hughes, Jan. 7, 1939; 1 child, Lydia Sims Derr. BS in Physics, U. Tex., 1962; MS in Chemistry, U. Houston-Cen., 1977, PhD in Chemistry, 1981. Registered profl. engr. Engr. Monsanto Co., Texas City, Tex., 1962-66, sr. inst. engr., 1966-69, specialist, 1969-76, group supr., 1976-80, sr. specialist, 1980-84, sci. fellow, 1984-85; adj. instr. U. Houston-Clear Lake, from 1981; instr. chemistry San Jacinto Coll.-Cen., Pasadena, Tex., from 1986. Cons. in field. Patentee in field; contbr. articles to profl. jours. Chmn. bldg. com. Pasadena Libr. Bd., 1991. With USN, 1951-55. Recipient Monsanto Achievement award, 1976, 86; named Rsch. fellow, 1989. Mem. Am. Chem. Soc. Chem. Educator Div., Tex. Jr. Coll. Tchrs. Assn., Mens Garden Club of Am. Democrat. Unitarian Universalist. Avocations: gardening, old flowers, woodworking, camping. Home: Pasadena, Tex. Died Jan. 9, 2007.

SINGER, IRVING, philosophy educator; b. NYC, Dec. 24, 1925; s. Isidore and Nettie (Stromer) S.; m. Josephine Fisk, June 10, 1949 (dec.); children— Anne, Margaret, Emily, Benjamin. AB summa cum laude, Harvard U., 1948, MA, 1949, PhD, 1952. Instr. philosophy Cornell U., 1953-56; asst. prof. U. Mich., 1956-59; vis. lectr. Johns Hopkins U., 1957-58; mem. faculty M.I.T., from 1958, prof. philosophy, 1969—2013, prof. philosophy emeritus, 2013—15. Author: Santayana's Aesthetics, 1957, The Nature of Love: Plato to Luther, 1966, rev. edit., 1984, The Goals of Human Sexuality, 1973, Mozart and Beethoven, 1977, The Nature of Love: Courtly and Romantic, 1984, The Nature of Love: The Modern World, 1987, Meaning in Life: The Creation of Value, 1992, The Pursuit of Love, 1994, The Creation of Value, 1996, The Harmony of Nature and Spirit, 1996, Reality Transformed: Film as Meaning and Technique, 1998, George Santayana: Literary Philosopher, 2000, Feeling and Imagination: The Vibrant Flux of our Existence, 2001, Sex: A Philosophical Primer, 2001, Explorations in Love and Sex, 2001, Three Philosophical Filmmakers: Hitchcock, Welles, Renoir, 2004, Sex: A Philosophical Primer (expanded edit.), 2004, Modes of Creativity: Philosphical Prospectives, 2011 and others. Served with AUS, 1943-46. Fellow Guggenheim Found., 1965, Rockefeller Found., 1970, Bollingen Found., 1966; grantee Am. Council Learned Socs., 1966; Fulbright fellow, 1955. Mem. Am. Philos. Assn. Home: Boston, Mass. Died Feb. 1, 2015.

SINK, NIGRA LEA (NIGRA LEA ROBERTS), employment specialist; b. Elberfeld, Ind., June 5, 1935; d. Jerrell Wilson and Nigeal Elaine (Besing) Roberts; m. J. Darhl Sink, Aug. 8, 1959 (div. Aug. 1978); 1 child, Karlin Roberts Sink. BS in Edn., Oakland City Coll., Ind., 1957; postgrad., Purdue U., 1959, Ball State U., 1961; MS in Edn., Ind. U., 1963. Cert. tchr., Ind., Ill.; lic. counselor, Ind. Ill. Tchr. pub. schs., Ind., 1957-66, Wis., 1966-67; tchr. Huntley Mid. Sch., DeKalb, Ill., 1967-70; mgr. McDonald's, Jacksonville, Ill., 1972-84; project specialist Lewis & Clark Community Coll., Godfrey, Ill., 1985-90; employment specialist Lincoln

Land Community Coll., from 1990. Instr. part-time MacMurray Coll., Jacksonville, 1985—. Mem. Morgan County Rep. Women, Jacksonville. Gen. Electric Corp. fellow, 1959. Mem. Ill. Adult and Continuing Educators Assn., Ill. Employment and Tng. Assn., Rebeccas (noble grand 1990—), Order of Eastern Star (worthy matron 1979, sec. 1984—), White Shrine of Jerusalem (worthy high priestess 1987, 89, supreme instr. 1988, worthy scribe 1990). Methodist. Home: Springfield, Ill. Died Nov. 7, 2006.

SINNOTT, JOHN PATRICK, lawyer, educator; b. Bklyn., Aug. 17, 1931; s. John Patrick and Elizabeth Muriel (Zinkand) Sinnott; m. Rose Marie Yuppa, May 30, 1959; children: James Alexander, Jessica Michelle. BS, US Naval Acad., 1953; MS, USAF Inst. Tech., 1956; JD, No. Ky. U., Highland Heights, 1960. Bar: Ohio 1961, NY 1963, NJ 1970, Ga 2000, US Patent Office 1963, US Supreme Ct 1977. Assoc. Brumbaugh, Graves, Donohue & Raymond, NYC, 1961-63; patent atty. Bell Tel. Labs., Murray Hill, NJ, 1963-64, Schlumberger Ltd., NYC, 1964-71; asst. chief patent counsel Babcock & Wilcox, NYC, 1971-79; chief patent and trademark counsel Am. Std. Inc., NYC, 1979-92; of counsel Morgan & Finnegan, NYC, 1992-99, Langdale Vallotton, LLP, Valdosta, Ga., from 2000. Adj lectr NJ Inst Technology, Newark, 1974—89; adj prof Seton Hall Univ Sch Law, Newark, 1989—98. Author: Counterfeit Goods Suppression, 1998, World Patent Law and Practice, 1999; co-author: To Paris! August, 1914 and Now-Belgian and Northern French Battlefields, 2006, Document Authentication, 2011; contbr. articles to profl. jours. Mem. local Selective Serv Bd., Plainfield, NJ, 1971; bd dirs New Providence Community Swimming Pool, NJ, 1970. Capt. USAF, 1953—61, col. AUS ret., 1977—91. Decorated Legion of Merit, others. Mem.: Ga. State Bar Assn., Squadron A Assn., Valdosta Country Club, Cosmos Club. Republican. Roman Catholic. Home: Valdosta, Ga. Died Dec. 12, 2012.

SISCHY, INGRID BARBARA, editor, art critic; b. Johannesburg, Republic of South Africa, Mar. 2, 1952; came to U.S., 1967; d. Benjamin and Claire S.; life partner Sandra J. Brant BA, Sarah Lawrence Coll., 1973; PhD (hon.), Moore Coll. Art, 1987. Assoc. editor Print Collector's Newsletter, NYC, 1974-77; dir. Printed Matter, NYC, 1977-78; curatorial intern Mus. Modern Art, NYC, 1978-79; editor Artforum Mag., NYC, 1979-88; cons. editor The New Yorker, NYC, 1988—96; editor-in-chief Interview Mag., NYC, 1989—2008; contributing editor, Vanity Fair Conde Nast, NYC, 1997—2015, internat. editor, Vanity Fair Italy, Vanity Fair Spain, Vanity Fair France, Vogue Germany & Vogue Russia, 2008—15. Band mem. DISBAND, 1978—2015. Home: New York, NY. Died July 24, 2015.

SISLER, HARRY HALL, retired chemistry professor; b. Ironton, Ohio, Mar. 13, 1917; s. Harry C. and Minta A. (Hall) S.; m. Helen E. Shaver, June 29, 1940; children: Elizabeth A., David F., Raymond K., Susan C.; m. Hannelore L. Wass, Apr. 13, 1978. BSc, Ohio State U., 1936; MSc, U. Ill., 1937, PhD, 1939; Doctorate honoris causa, U. Poznan, Poland, 1977. Instr. Chgo. City Colls., 1939-41; from instr. to assoc. prof. chemistry U. Kans., Lawrence, 1941-46; from asst. prof. to prof. chemistry Ohio State U., Columbus, 1946-56; Arthur and Ruth Sloan vis. prof. chemistry Harvard, fall, 1962-63; prof., chmn. dept. chemistry U. Fla., Gainesville, 1956-68, dean Coll. Arts and Scis., 1968-70, exec. v.p., 1970-73, dean grad. sch., 1973-79, dir. divsn. sponsored rsch., 1976-79, Disting. Svc. prof. chemistry, 1979-85, Disting. Svc. prof. chemistry emeritus, from 1985. Indsl. cons. W.R. Grace & Co., Martin Marietta Aerospace, Naval Ordnance Lab., TVA; chemistry adv. panel, also vis. scientists panel NSF, 1959-62; cons. USAF Acad., Battelle Meml. Inst., chmn. interinstl. com. nuclear research, Fla., 1958-64; mem. Fla. Nuclear Devel. Commn. Teaching Sci. and Math., 1958; chemistry adv. panel Oak Ridge Nat. Lab., 1965-69; dir. sponsored rsch. U. Fla., 1976-79. Author: Electronic Structure, Properties, and the Periodic Law, 2d edit, 1973, Starlight-A Book of Poems, 1976, Of Outer and Inner Space—A Book of Poems, 1981, Earth, Air, Fire and Water-A Book of Poems, 1989, (with others) Gen. Chemistry: A Systematic Approach, 2d edit, 1959, Coll. Chemistry: A Systematic Approach, 4th edit, 1980, Essentials of Chemistry, 2d edit, 1959, A Systematic Laboratory Course in Chemistry, 1950, Essentials of Experimental Chemistry, 2d edit, 1959, Semimicro Qualitative Analysis, 1958, rev. edit., 1965, Comprehensive Inorganic Chemistry, Vol. V, 1956, Chemistry in Non-Aqueous Solvents, 1961, The Chloramination Reaction, 1977, Dying-Facing the Facts, 1988, Inorganic Reactions and Methods, Vol. 7, 1988, Encyclopedia of Inorganic Chemistry, Vol. 5, Nitrogen: Inorganic Chemistry, 1994, Autumn Harvest-A Book of Poems, 1996, Perspective-A Book of Poems, 1999; cons. editor: (with others) Dowden, Hutchinson & Ross, 1971-78; series editor: (with others) Phys. and Inorganic Textbook Series, Reinhold Pub. Corp, 1958-70; contbr. (with others) articles to profl. jours.; patentee in field. Decorated Royal Order North Star(Sweden); Named Outstanding Chemist in South, Am. Chem. Soc., 1969, Outstanding Chemist in Southeast, Am. Chem. Soc., 1960, James Flack Norris award Am. Chem. Soc., 1979; recipient Outstanding Centennial Achievement award Ohio State U., 1970. Mem. Am. Chem. Soc. (nat. chmn. div. chem. edn. 1957-58, exec. com. 1957-60, bd. publ. Jour. Chem. Edn. 1956-58), Phi Beta Kappa, Sigma Xi, Phi Delta Kappa, Phi Lambda Upsilon, Phi Kappa Phi, Alpha Chi Sigma. Methodist. Home: Gainesville, Fla. Died Dec. 23, 2006.

SISSON, GEORGE MAYNARD, scientific services administrator; b. Boston, Feb. 3, 1922; s. David and Bessie Sisson; m. Frances Ann Sisson, June 29, 1952 (div. Sept. 1968); children: Barbara Carol, Brenda Harriet, Richard Lewis. BS, Tufts Coll., 1947; PhD, U. Rochester, 1952. Jr. scientist Brookhaven Nat. Lab., Upton, N.Y., 1952; vis. fellow Columbia U. Coll. Phys. and Surg., NYC, 1952-54; group leader Lederle Labs., Pearl Rvr, NY, Stamford, Conn., 1954-59; asst. dir. pharmacology U.S. Vitamin and Pharm. Corp., Yonkers, N.Y., 1959-61; dir. pharm. product info. Mead Johnson Rsch. Ctr., Evansville, Ind., 1961-66; dir. sci. and regulatory affairs Mead Johnson & Co., Evansville, 1966-77, dir. dept. regulatory affairs, from 1979. Cons. Adria Labs., Dublin, Ohio, 1988-91. Co-author: Pharmacological and Biochemical Profiles of Drug Substances, 1979; contbr. articles to profl. jours. Lt. (j.g.) USNR, 1942-47, PTO. Mem. AAAS. Avocations: classical music, the arts and humanities, foreign travel, the theatre, museum activities. Died May 10, 2007.

SISSON, LAURENCE P., artist; b. Boston, Apr. 27, 1928; s. Arthur Foster and Gertrude Davis Sisson; m. Judy Haslee Zimmermann, May 17, 1990; m. Beatrice Bachelder Sisson (div.); children: Mark D., Kerry, David B., Derek Phoenix. Student, Yale U., 1948—49; grad., Worcester Mus. Sch., Mass., 1949; DFA, Maine Coll. Art (formerly Portland Sch. Art), 1992. Artist-in-residence Publick House, Sturbridge, Mass., 1950; guest lectr. Cin. Mus., 1954; instr., dir. Portland Sch. Art, Maine, 1954—58; corporator Worcester Art Mus., Mass., 1972. Artist (cover) Fortune Mag., 1951, artist, actor (film) Maine Harvestors of the Sea, 1969; author: (book) Along Time River, 1975; Represented in permanent collections inclusing Boston U., Berkshire Mus., Bowdin Coll., Clark U., Columbia Mus. Fine Art, Boston Mus. Fine Arts, DeCordova Mus., Darthmouth Coll., and others. With US Army, 1946—47. Recipient 4th Am. prize, Hallmark Internat. Show, 1949, 1st prize, Boston Arts Festival, 1956, 1964, Boston Watercolor Soc., 1957. Avocations: golf, croquet. Home: Albuquerque, N.Mex. Died Aug. 7, 2015.

SISSON, MARY WINIFRED, retired elementary education educator; b. Decatur, Ill., Oct. 8, 1919; d. Leland Eugene and Amy Gertrude (Chaplin) Jayne; m. Lewis Milton Sisson, June 30, 1962 (dec.). BS, Bradley U., 1948. Elem. tchr. Milford (Ill.) Sch., 1941-43, Pekin (Ill.) Douglas Sch., 1943-58, Lake Weston Sch., Orlando, Fla., 1958-60, various, San Jose, Calif., 1960-61, White Sch., Peoria, Ill., 1960-65, Blaine-Sumner Sch., Peoria, 1965-67. Adult tutor Common Place, Peoria, 1985-89, 92-94; leader summer playgrounds, Pekin, Ill., 1954-58. Active Westminster Presbyn. Ch. travel activities. Recipient scholarships Ill. State U., Normal. Mem. DAR, Naomi Cir., Peoria Area Retired Tchrs. Assn., Ill. Retired Tchrs. Assn. Republican. Presbyterian. Avocations: reading, travel. Died July 3, 2007.

SITTON, CLAUDE FOX, newspaper editor; b. Atlanta, Dec. 4, 1925; s. Claude B. and Pauline (Fox) S.; m. Eva McLaurin Whetstone, June 5, 1953; children: Lea Sitton Stanley, Clinton, Suzanna Sitton Greene, McLaurin. AB, Emory U., 1949, L.H.D., 1984. Reporter Internat. News Service, 1949-50; with U.P., 1950-55, writer-editor NYC, 1952-55; information officer USIA, 1955-57; mem. staff New York Times, 1957-68, nat. news dir., 1964-68; editorial dir. The News and Observer Pub. Co., Raleigh, NC, 1968-90, dir., 1969-90, v.p., 1970-90; editor News and Observer, 1970-90; sr. lectr. Emory U., Atlanta, 1991-94. Active Pulitzer Prize Bd., 1985-94, chmn., 1992-93; bd. counselors Oxford Coll. Emory U., 1993-2001. Lay mem. Commn. on Evaluation of Disciplinary Enforcement, Ga. Supreme Ct., 1995-96; mem. Ga. First Amendment Found. Bd., 1994-97. With USNR, 1943-46, PTO. Recipient Pulitzer prize for commentary, 1983. Home: Atlanta, Ga. Died Mar. 10, 2015.

SIZOVA, ALLA IVANOVNA, prima ballerina, educator; b. Moscow, Sept. 22, 1939; d. Ivan Pavlovich and Yekaterina Ivanovna (Morozova) S.; m. Mikhail Serebrennikov (dec. 1980); 1 child, Serebrennikov Ilia (dec. 2004) Student, Acad. Choreography Sch. of Vaganova, 1949-58; diploma, Anna Pavlova Paris Acad. of Dance, 1964. Dancer (ballets) Nutcracker, 1958, Don Quixote, 1958, 70, Giselle, 1958-59, The Stone Flower, 1959-60, Chopeniana, 1959-60, Sleeping Beauty, 1959-60, 61, 63-64, Swan Lake, 1960-61, Seventh Symphony of Shostakovitch, 1960-61, Bakhchisaraiski Fountain, 1962-63, Spartacus, 1962-63, Legend of Konyok Gorbunok, 1963, Cinderella, 1964, A Flying Waltz, 1958-59, Romeo and Juliet, 1964-65, Firebird, 1965, Festival of Flowers, 1969, Hamlet, 1971, The Prince of Pagoda, 1971, Fairy of Rond Mountains, 1971, Pas de Quatre, 1973, Pas de sis, 1978-79, Bronze Horseman, 1983. Recipient Gold medal Festival of Youth, Vienna, 1959, Gold medal Internat. Competition of Dance, Bulgaria, 1964; named Deserved Artist of Russian Fedn., 1966, People's Artist of Russian Fedn., 1972, People's Artist of Soviet Union, 1983. Home: Saint Petersburg, Russia. Died Nov. 23, 2014.

SKLAR, WILFORD NATHANIEL, lawyer, real estate broker; b. Salt Lake City, Dec. 13, 1916; s. Benjamin B. Sklar and Blanche Blau; m. Sarah Cohen, Jan. 16, 1945 (dec. Dec. 2000); children: Beth-Lynn (dec.), Teri Helene. BBA, U. Pitts., 1942; JD, Southwestern Sch. Law, 1960. Bar: Calif. 1960, U.S. Dist. Ct. Calif. 1962, U.S. Supreme Ct. 1965. Pvt. practice, Riverside, Calif., 1960-98; ret., 1998. Co-comdr. mil. affairs com. March AFB, Calif.; active Riverside Family Svcs., 1965-85, Am. Legion. Sgt. USAF, PTO, 1942-46. Mem. B'nai B'rith (Akiba Dist. award 1970, 74), Riverside Jewish War Vets. Democrat. Jewish. Avocations: golf, coin collecting/numismatics, real estate investments. Home: Riverside, Calif. Died May 14, 2007.

SKOGEN, DUANE BLAIR, oil company executive; b. Hettinger, ND, Sept. 4, 1932; m. Henry Joseph Skogen; m. Arlene Kelsey; m. Arliss A. Berg, Dec. 27, 1952; children: Laurie Ann, Nancy Lynn, Connie Kay. BS, SD Sch. Mines, 1956. Registered profl. engr., Mont., Tex. With Conoco Inc., Billings, Mont., 1962—71; mgr. ops. planning divsn. Houston, 1971—73; dir. US mktg. & supply, 1973—74; dir. mfg. Douglas Oil Co., LA, 1974—77; refinery mgr. Conco Ltd., South Killingholme, England, 1977—81, mng. dir. refining London, from 1981, dir. Dir. APT (Immingham) Ltd., South Humberside, HOTT & COT(H), Benzene Mktg. Co., London; v.p., dir. Continental Oil Co., Stamford, Conn., France. Served as sgt. AUS, 1949—52, Korea. Mem.: Wellington Club(London), Brit. Inst. Mgmt. (companion), Inst. Petroleum, Am. Inst. Chem. Engring. Republican. Lutheran. Home: London, England. Died Aug. 23, 2007.

SKOPITZ, LAURENCE MARTIN, rabbi; b. Toronto, Ont., Can., Aug. 26, 1948; came to U.S., 1974; s. Oscar and Ida (Dietchman) S.; children: Shalom, Hyla. BA, York U., 1971; MA in Hebrew Letters, Hebrew Union Coll., 1977; postgrad., Colgate Rochester Div. Sch. Ordained rabbi, 1978. Rabbi Congregation Bnai Israel, Kalamazoo, Mich., 1974-77, Temple Shalom, Louisville, 1978, Temple Beth El, Geneva, N.Y., 1978-81, Temple Beth David, Rochester, N.Y., from 1981; chaplain Rochester Psychiat. Ctr., from 1987. Rabbinic cons. Jewish Family Svc., Rochester, 1987—; instr. Bur. Jewish Edn., Rochester, 1981-91; asst. adj. prof. Alfred (N.Y.) U., 1985-86; bd. mem. Jewish Community Fedn., Rochester, 1986—; v.p. United Empire Region Rabbinic Assembly, 1988—; mem. adv. bd. Jewish Media Rels. Coun.; bd. dirs. Rochester Interfaith Jail Ministry, 1991—. Artist illuminated Jewish marriage contracts; author, illustrator children's books; composer children's music; contbr. articles to profl. jours. Adv. bd. Anti-Drug Coalition, Rochester, 1988—; vol. Vols. Am., Rochester, 1989—. With Can. Army, 1965-66. Recipient Lion of Judah award, Israel Bonds N.Am., 1988. Mem. Cen. Conf. Am. Rabbis, N.Y. State Jewish Chaplains Assn., West Irondequoit Ministerial Assn., Rochester Bd. Rabbis (pres. 1985-87). Home: Rochester, NY. Died Dec. 16, 2006.

SLACK, FREDERICK FORD, retired electronic scientist, writer; b. Lawrence, Mass., June 16, 1917; s. Harold Jay and Grace Regina (Charnley) S.; 1 child, Frederick F., Jr. Grad. high sch. Factory worker J.O. Whitten Co., Winchester, Mass., 1938-40; radio technician Nat. Co., Malden, Mass., 1940-41; electronic technician MIT, Cambridge, Mass., 1941-45; electronic scientist USAF Hanscom Field, Bedford, Mass., 1945-76, ret., 1976. Freelance writer, 1976—. Discoverd universal paradigm that places all mass and energy in the frequency domain, providing physical link to paranormal activity; co-inventor electronic circuitry translator of scanning positions; inventor display earth satellites, light gun; contbr. articles to profl. jours. Avocations: writing, ballroom dancing, poetry. Home: West Newbury, Mass. Died June 30, 2007.

SLADE, TOM, manufacturing executive, political organization worker; b. Albany, Ga., Mar. 13, 1936; s. T.H. and Flora Bell (Jackson) S.; divorced; children: Thomas, Jack, Jeff, Shad. Owner Slade Gas Co., Jacksonville, Fla., 1958-71; pres. Gen. Environ., Jacksonville, 1971-75, Slade & Co., Jacksonville, 1975-80; pres., owner Dozier & Jay Paint Co., Green Cove Springs, 1980—2014; pres. Tidewater Cons., 1998—2014. Mem. Fla. House of Reps., Tallahassee, 1962-64, Fla. State Senate, 1966-70; chmn. Fla. Republican Party, 1993-99; mem. Fla. High Speed Rail Commn., 1991; active in numerous polit. and civic orgns. Republican. Avocations: tennis, boating. Home: Orange Park, Fla. Died Oct. 20, 2014.

SLATER, GRANT GAY, biochemist, consultant; b. Rochester, NY, Jan. 6, 1918; s. Lee Grand and Erma (Gay) S.; m. Roslyn Bernice Alfin, July 30, 1948; children: Robert-,Joanne Catani. BS in Chemistry, U. Miami, Fla., 1940; MS in Biochemistry, U. So. Calif., LA, 1950; PhD in Biochemistry, U. So. Calif., 1954. Chemist Keuffel & Esser, Hoboken, N.J., 1947-48; rsch. assoc. Rsch. Inst. Cedars Lebanon Hosp., LA, 1954-55; instr. biochemistry U. So. Calif., LA, 1954-59; rsch. biochemist Neurobiochemistry Vets. Adminstrn., LA, 1961-68, Gateway Hosp., LA, 1961-68; researcher Sch. Pub. Health, UCLA, 1972-80, researcher biochemist, 1980-83; cons. Slater Cons., LA, from 1988. Mem. nutrition com. Calif. Avocado Nutrition Bd., 1973-95; lectr. in field. Editorial bd. Biochem. Medicine and Metabolic Biology, 1980-93; contbr. articles to profl. jours.; patentee in field. Lt. col. U.S. Army, 1942-78. Grantee, State of Calif./USPHS, 1958-65, GAteways Hosp., 1971, USPHS, 1974, Am. Egg Bd., 1977, Nat. Dairy Coun., 1980. Mem. Am. Chem. Soc., Am. Physiol. Soc., Brain Rsch. Inst., The Endocrine Soc., Soc. of Neurosci., Am. Oil Chemists, Sigma Xi. Avocation: sailing. Home: Santa Barbara, Calif. Died Feb. 11, 2007.

SLATER, HELEN MAE, medical association administrator; b. Pendleton, Oreg., Feb. 27, 1925; d. Clarence Leonard Carson and Nellie (Amy) Chamberlain; m. Darrell Melvin Slater, June 12, 1943; children: Kathleen Sabel, Dennis, Janice, Patrick, Andrew. BA, Portland State U., 1973. Cert. med. transcriber. Med. transcriber Emanuel Hosp., Portland, Oreg., 1974-77; tchr. substitute Cath. Archdiocese, Portland, 1977-78; tchr. John Adams High Sch., Portland, 1976-77; med. transcriber Providence Med. Ctr., Portland, from 1975. Campaign worker Connie McCready for Mayor, Portland, 1972. Mem. AAUW, Multnomah County Assn. Med. Assts. (pres. elect 1958-59, pres. 1959-60) Democrat. Roman Catholic. Avocations: golf, skiing, swimming, bridge, reading. Home: Portland, Oreg. Died Nov. 12, 2006.

SLAWTER, JOHN DAVID, JR., oil industry executive; b. Winston-Salem, May 11, 1917; s. John David and Carrie Wess (Linville) S.; children: Suzanne Marie, Sheila Margaret; m. Joan Margaret Pirek, July 7, 1966. Student, U. N.C., 1935—37, U.N.C., 1938—40. V.p. B&B Gas and Petroleum, Corpus Christi, Tex., 1950-59; exec. v.p. Cal-O-Tex

Oil, Columbus, Ohio, 1959-65; pres. Atlantic Internat. Oil, Charleston, W.Va., 1966-73; CEO Interstate Hotels, Inc., 1975, Pacific Internat. Prodn. Holding Co. for Activated Carbon Corp. Am., Dallas, 1989, Mid-Continent Oil, from 1974, OFG Corp., from 1995, EMTEC, from 1997, HTS, from 1999. Chmn. adv. bd. Cal-O-Tex, 1966—, Atlantic Internat. Oil, 1974—, Pacific Internat., 1974—, Black Diamond Coal Co., 1978—, Southwest Interstate Support Sys., 1985—, Activated Carbon Corp., 1989—; vice chair AIOC Trust, Slawter Trust (lifetime). Author: (patents and copyrights) purification and desalination sys., 1991, pumping unit tech., 1995, oil field gen., 1996, oil field mobile remote control unit, 1998, heat transfer sys., 1999. Mem. Rep. Nat. Nom. Com., Washington, 1994-2000. Maj. Engrs. 1941-45, WWII, PTO. Decorated Purple Heart, Silver Star, Bronze Star with oak leaf cluster, Presdl. Citation, 4 Battle Stars. Mem. internat. petroleum clubs, Geneva Exec. Club (v.p. 1970-78), Chi Phi. Avocations: aviation, golf. Home: Dallas, Tex. Died May 20, 2007.

SLEDGE, PERCY, singer; b. Leighton, Ala., Nov. 25, 1941; Formerly with The Esquires Combo. Singer (solo): (albums) Warm & Tender Soul, 1966, The Percy Sledge Way, 1967, Take Time to Know Her, 1968, I'll Be Your Everything, 1974, Blue Night, 1994 (Best Soul/Blues Album, Blues Music Awards, 1994), Wanted Again, 1998, Shining Through the Rain, 2004, (songs) When A Man Loves a Woman, 1966 (First Gold Record produced by Atlantic Records). Recipient Pioneer award, Rhythm and Blues Found., 1989; named to, Carolina Beach Music Hall of Fame, 2004, Rock and Roll Hall of Fame, 2005, La. Music Hall of Fame, 2007, Ala. Music Hall of Fame, 2010, Delta Music Mus. Died Apr. 14, 2015.

SLOATMAN, ADELAIDE GAIL See ZAPPA, GAIL

SLOCOMBE, DOUGLAS, cinematographer; b. London, Eng., Feb. 10, 1913; m. Muriel Slocombe (dec.); 1 child, Georgina. Cinematographer: (films) (with Wilkie Cooper) The Big Blockade, 1942, (with Ernest Palmer) For Those in Peril, 1944, The Girl on the Canal, 1947, The Loves of Joanna Godden, 1947, Another Shore, 1948, (with Jack Parker) The Captive Heart, 1948, It Always Rains on Sunday, 1949, Kind Hearts and Coronets, 1949, Saraband, 1949, Cage of Gold, 1950, Dance Hall, 1950, (with J. Saeholme) Hue and Cry, 1950, A Run for Your Money, 1950, The Lavender Hill Mob, 1951, Crash of Silence, 1952, His Excellency, 1952, The Man in the White Suit, 1952, The Titfield Thunderbolt, 1953, Lease of Life, 1954, The Love Lottery, 1954, The Light Touch, 1955, Decision Against Time, 1957, Panic in the Parlour, 1957, The Smallest Show on Earth, 1957, All at Sea, 1958, Davy, 1958, Tread Softly Stranger, 1959, The Boy Who Stole a Million, 1960, Circus of Horrors, 1960, The Mark, 1961, Scream of Fear, 1961, Freud, 1962, The L-Shaped Room, 1962, Wonderful to Be Young!, 1962, Guns at Batasi, 1964, The Servant, 1964 (British Academy award best cinematography 1964), The Third Secret, 1964, A High Wind in Jamaica, 1965, The Blue Max, 1966, Promise Her Anything, 1966, Fathom, 1967, The Fearless Vampire Killer; or, Pardon Me but Your Teeth Are in My Neck, 1967, Robbery, 1967, Boom!, 1968, The Lion in Winter, 1968, The Italian Job, 1969, The Buttercup Chain, 1971, Murphy's War, 1971, The Music Lovers, 1971, Travels with My Aunt, 1972 (Academy award nomination best cinematography 1972), Jesus Christ, Superstar, 1973, The Destructors, 1974, The Great Gatsby, 1974 (British Academy award best cinematography 1974), Hedda, 1975, The Maids, 1975, Rollerball, 1975, That Lucky Touch, 1975, The Bawdy Adventures of Tom Jones, 1976, Nasty Habits, 1976, The Sailor Who Fell from Grace with the Sea, 1976, Julia, 1977 (Academy award nomination best cinematography 1977, British Academy award best cinematography 1977), Close Encounters of the Third Kind, 1977, Caravans, 1978, Lost and Found, 1979, The Lady Vanishes, 1980, Nijinsky, 1980, (with Paul Beeson) Raiders of the Lost Ark, 1981 (Academy award nomination best cinematography 1981), Never Say Never Again, 1983, The Pirates of Penzance, 1983, Indiana Jones and the Temple of Doom, 1984, Water, 1985, Lady Jane, 1986, (with Beeson and Robert Stevens) Indiana Jones and the Last Crusade, 1989, (TV movie) The Corn Is Green, 1979; dir. photography: (films) Dead of the Night, 1945, Ludwig II, 1954, Heaven and Earth, 1956; photographer: (TV movie) Love Among the Ruins, 1975, (documentary) Lights Out in Europe. Died Feb. 22, 2016.

SLUTSKY, JEAN EVELYN See NIDETCH, JEAN

SMAIL, ANNETTE KLANG, civic leader, women's rights advocate; b. St. Helena, Calif., July 20, 1920; d. Leon and Victoria Nellie (Hartman) K.; divorced; children: Barry Lee, Karen Smail Poksay. AA, San Francisco Jr. Coll., 1939; AB, U. Calif., Berkeley, 1943; postgrad., U. Chgo., 1945. Cert. adult teaching credential in social studies and English. News reporter Community Newspapers, Chgo., 1945-46; editor textbooks U. Calif., Berkeley, 1948-49; edn. coordinator Econ. Opportunity Council, San Rafael, Calif., 1969-71. Cmty. organizer with Saul Alinsky Back of the Yards. Cmty. organizer, co-founder Novato (Calif.) Human Needs Ctr., 1970-72; founder, leader Older Women's Polit. Caucus, 1977-95, Med. Equality for Dependents, 1977; author various resolutions passed by Calif. legis. on med. rights and women's rights; del. White House Conf. on Aging, Washington, 1981; mem. Calif. Task Force on Feminization of Poverty, Sacramento, 1984. Recipient San Francisco Working Woman Achievement award Working Woman mag., 1983, Women Helping Women award Soroptimists, 1979, Marin Martin Luther King Jr. Humanitarian award, 1991, Calif. Legis. Senate Rules Com. commendation, Eleanor Roosevelt Vision award, 1994; named Disting. Woman of Yr. Novato Advance Newspaper, 1979; inducted into Marin Women's Hall of Fame, 1991. Mem. Nat. Women's Polit. Caucus. Democrat. Initiator and nat. campaign organizer congl. bills: med. rights for former wives, passed 1982; also legis. proposal to create Fed. Council on Women, introduced 1986; leading adv. for passage of gender equity law to cover all govt. apptd. mems. of Calif. bds. and commns., 1989. Home: Novato, Calif. Died Mar. 10, 2007.

SMALL, BERTRICE W. (BERTRICE WILLIAMS), writer; b. NYC, Dec. 9, 1937; d. David Roger Williams, Doris Melissa (Maud) Steen; m. George Sumner Small, Oct. 5, 1963; 1 child, Thomas David. Student, Western Coll. for Women, Oxford, Ohio, Katherine Gibbs Sectl. Sch., NYC, 1959. With Young & Rubicon, NYC, 1959—60, Weed Radio & TV, NYC, 1960—61, Edward Petry & Co., NYC, 1961—63. Author: (Leslie Family Saga Series) The Kadin, 1978, Love Wild and Fair, 1978, (novels) Adora, 1980, Unconquered, 1981, Beloved, 1983, Enchantress Mine, 1987, The Spitfire, 1990, A Moment in Time, 1991, To Love Again, 1993, Hellion, 1996, Betrayed, 1998, Deceived, 1998, The Innocent, 1999, A Memory of Love, 2000, The Dutchess, 2001, The Dragon Lord's Daughters, 2004, (The Border Chronicles) A Dangerous Love, 2006, The Border Lord's Bride, 2007, The Captive Heart, 2008, The Border Lord and Lady, 2009, The Border Vixen, 2010, Bond of Passion, 2011, (O'Malley Family Saga Series) Skye O'Malley, 1981, All the Sweet Tomorrows, 1984, A Love for All Time, 1986, This Heart of Mine, 1988, Lost Love Found, 1989, Wild Jasmine, 1992, (Wyndham Family Saga Series) Blaze Wyndham, 1988, Love, Remember Me, 1994, (Skye's Legacy Series) Darling Jasmine, 1997, Bedazzled, 1999, Besieged, 2001, Intrigued, 2001, Just Beyond Tomorrow, 2002, Vixens, 2003, (Friarsgate Inheritance Saga Series) Rosamund, 2002, Until You, 2003, Philippa, 2004, The Last Heiress, 2005, (Channel Pleasures Series) Private Pleasures, 2004, Forbidden Pleasures, 2006, Sudden Pleasures, 2007, Dangerous Pleasures, 2008, Passionate Pleasures, 2010, Guilty Pleasures, 2011, (World of Hetar Series) Lara, 2005, A Distant Tomorrow, 2006, The Twilight Lord, 2007, The Sorceress of Belmair, 2008, The Shadow Queen, 2009, Crown of Destiny, 2010, (The Silk Merchants Daughter) Bianca, 2012, Francesca, 2013, Lucianna, 2013, Serena, 2014; anthologies in collaboration Ecstasy in Captivated, 1999, Mastering Lady Lucinda in Fascinated, 2000, The Awakening in Delighted, 2002, Zuleika and the Barbarian in I Love Rogues, 2003. Vestrywoman Redeemer Episc. Ch., Mattituck, NY, 1998—2001. Recipient Career Achievement Reviewers Choice award, Romantic Times Mag., 1983, 1988, 1995, 2001. Mem.: L.I. Romance Writers (bd. dirs. 1999—2001), Romance Writers of Am., Authors Guild. Episcopalian. Avocation: gardening. Died Feb. 24, 2015.

SMALLMAN, RAYMOND EDWARD, metallurgist and materials science educator; b. Wolverhampton, W. Midland, Eng., Aug. 4, 1929; s. David and Edith (French) S.; m. Joan Doreen Faulkner, Sept. 6, 1952; children: Lesley Ann Smallman Grimer, Robert Ian. BSc, U. Birmingham, 1950, PhD, 1953, DSc, 1968; DSc (hon.), U. Wales, 1990, U. Novi Sad, Yugoslavia, 1990, Cranfield U., Eng., 2001. Chartered engr. Scientific officer Atomic Energy Rsch. Est., Harwell, Eng., 1953-55, sr. scientific officer, 1955-58; lectr. Univ. Birmingham, 1958-63, sr. lectr., 1963-64, prof. phys. metallurgy, 1964-69, Feeney prof. metallurgy and materials sci., head dept., 1969-93, dean of faculty of sci. and engring., dean of engring., 1984-85, 85-87, vice prin., 1987-92, prof. metallurgy and materials sci., 1993—2000, prof. emeritus metallurgy and materials sci., from 2000. Mem. coun. Sci. and Engring. Rsch. Coun., 1992-93; mem. Materials Commn., 1988-92; mem. coun. Inst. Materials, 1993-99, chmn. internat. affairs com., 1992, v.p., 1995-99; mem. Warden Assay Office, Birmingham, 1994-99. Author: Modern Physical Metallurgy, 1962, 4th edit., 1985; Modern Metallography, 1966, Structure of Metals and Alloys, 1969, Defect Analysis in Electron Microscopy, 1975, Vacancies 76, Metals and Materials: Science, Processes, Applications, 1995, Modern Physical Metallurgy and Materials Engineering, 1999, Physical Metallurgy and Advances Materials, 2009, Modern Physical Metallurgy, 8th edit.; contbr. articles to profl. jours. Decorated Commdr. of Brit. Empire, HM The Queen, 1992; recipient George Beilby Gold medal Inst. of Metals and Inst. of Chemistry, London, 1969,; .Rosenhain medal, 1972,Platinum medal, 1989, Metal Soc. p 1986prize, 1979, Acta Meterialia gold medal, 2004,Fellow Royal Society1986; Fellow Royal Academy Emgineering 1991,Fgn. Assoc. US Nat. Acad. Engring 2005., Hon Fellow Czech Soc. Metal Sci1995., Chinese Ordinance Soc.1993. Fellow Inst. Materials (Platinum medal, 1989, Rosenhain medal, 1972, Acta Materialia Gold Medal prize 2004), Royal Soc., Royal Acad. Engring., China Ordinance Soc.; mem. U.S. NAE (fgn. assoc.), Fedn. of European Materials Socs. (v.p. 1992-94, pres. 1994-96), Birmingham Metall. Soc. (pres. 1972-73), Czech. Soc. Metal Sci. (hon. fgn.). Avocations: writing, travel, golf, bridge. Home: Worcester, England. Died Feb. 25, 2015.

SMEAL, CAROLYN A., retired community health nurse, educator; b. Guilford, NY, Jan. 30, 1930; d. Charles C. and Margaret C. (Wilson) Bloom; m. William C. Smeal, May 28, 1949 (dec. Aug. 1997); children: Dale, Sandra Smeal Barlow, Stacey (dec.), William M. Diploma, Millard Fillmore Hosp., Buffalo, 1950; BS, SUNY, Buffalo, 1967. Cert. community health nurse, sch. nurse-tchr. Staff nurse in oper. rm., emergency rm. Niagara Falls (N.Y.) Meml. Med. Ctr.; staff nurse Niagara Falls Air Base; sch. nurse tchr. Bd. Edn., Niagara Falls; community health nurse Niagara County Health Dept., Niagara Falls; retired, 1995. Bd. dirs. Ctr. for Young Parents, Cerebral Palsy Recreation Group. Mem. Assn. for Retarded Children (bd. dirs., past pres.). Died Dec. 21, 2006.

SMITH, BARBARA RUTHJENA DRUCKER, writer, educator; b. Newport News, Va., June 5, 1936; d. Abraham Louis and Loraine Blechman Drucker; children: Lisa Loraine, Eric Drucker. BA in English, Speech and Journalism, Coll. William and Mary, 1964. Cert. hypnotherapist Ea. Va. Hypnotherapy Inst., 1999, Nat. Assn. Transpersonal Hypnotherapists, 1999. Freelance writer, Newport News, from 1960; pvt. practice hypnotherapy, from 1999; hypnotist Positive Changes Hypnosis Neurolinguistic Programming, Newport News, 2000—04. Workshop leader various pub. schs., Newport News, from 1976; tchr. in English and remedial reading various schs., Newport News, from 1966; mem. adv. bd. Christopher Newport Writer's Conf., Newport News, 1989—2006. Author: Darling Loraine The Story of A. Louis Drucker A Grateful Jewish Immigrant, 2000 (Nominated Best Non-Fiction Book of 2000 award Libr. Va., 2001), A Poetic Journey, 2004 (Nominated Best Poetry Book of 2004 award Libr. Va.), Prose From the Old Century to the New: Vignettes, Petite Petites, Epistles, Points of View, 2006 (Nominated Best Non-Fiction Book of 2006 award Libr. Va.); contbr. Poet's Domain 4 Others, 1987—2000; composer (and pianist): (recordings) Barbarina Piano Impromptus, 2006. Crisis teleph. worker Contact Peninsula, Newport News, 1981—2005; docent Mariner's Mus., Newport News, from 1982. Mem.: Soc. for Historians, Authorship, Reading and Publishing, Nat. Assn. Transpersonal Hypnotherapists, Poetry Soc. Va., Tidewater Writers Assn., Va. Choral Soc., Va. Writers Club. Avocations: bicycling, swimming, piano, travel. Died May 28, 2007.

SMITH, CAROL ESTES, retired councilman; b. Phoenix, Nov. 13, 1934; d. John William and Kathleen (Poynter) Estes; m. David Liles Smith, Jan. 8, 1954 (div. Oct. 1981); children: Kelly Liles, Kevin Estes, Kathleen Marie. BS in Edn., Tex. Christian U., 1957. Ptnr. Waste Control Ariz., N.Mex., Tex., various, 1964-81; mem. city coun. City of Tempe, Ariz., 1986-98; ret., 1998. Bd. dirs., pres. S.W. Ctr. Edn. and Environment, Tempe, from 1988, Papago/Salado Assocs., Tempe, from 1990. Bd. dirs., chmn. Ariz. Recycling Bd., Phoenix, 1991—96; Tempe Gov.'s past pres. Recipient Silver medallion, Boys and Girls Clubs Am., 1991, Spirit of Tempe award, 2002; named Jr. Advisor of the Yr., 1984, Woman of Distinction, Tempe St. Lukes Aux., 1985, Carol Estes Smith Grove in her honor, 1999. Mem.: Rotary, Zonta East Valley (pres. 1998—2000, Don Carlos Humanitarian award 1999). Republican. Presbyterian. Avocations: reading, theater. Home: Tempe, Ariz. Died July 30, 2007.

SMITH, CLARK ROBINSON, lawyer; b. Chgo., Feb. 17, 1938; s. Carlton Robinson and Theda Clark (Peters) S.; m. Trina Helen Hendershot, Jan. 20, 1962; children: Clark Carlton, Luke Owen. BS in Econs., U. Pa., 1961; LLB, U. Wis., 1965. Bar: Mass. 1966, U.S. Surpeme Ct. 1976, U.S. Dist. Ct. Mass. 1976, U.S. Tax Ct. 1976. From law clk. to assoc. Johnson Clapp Ives & King, Boston, 1965-67; pvt. practice Boston, from 1972. Bd. dirs., acting chair Zoning Bd. Appeals, Wenham, Mass., 1982-94; bd. dirs. Menasha Corp., Neenah, Wis., Beverly (Mass.) Nat. Bank. Trustee Beverly Regional YMCA, 1984—; bd. dirs. North Country Sch., Lake Placid, N.Y., 1988-95, Menasha Corp. Found., Neenah, 1994; chmn. bd. Theda C. Smith Found., Neenah, 1980—, United Way Cen. North Shore, Beverly, 1993-94. Fellow Mass. Bar Found. (mem. com., county advisor 1990—); mem. ABA, Mass. Bar Assn., Boston Bar Assn. (coms., vol. civil case appts. 1976—), Boston Bar Found. (life, endowment advisor 1990—). Republican. Episcopalian. Avocations: golf, tennis, skiing. Home: Wenham, Mass. Died Aug. 27, 2007.

SMITH, DAVID BURNELL, state legislator, lawyer; b. Charleston, W.Va., Apr. 8, 1941; s. Ernest Dayton and Nellie Dale (Tyler) S.; m. Rita J. Hughes, Sept. 25, 1967. BA, U. Charleston, 1967; JD, U. Balt., 1972; MJS, U. Nev., 1995. Bar: Colo. 1972, Md. 1972, U.S. Supreme Ct. 1980, Ariz. 1983, U.S. Dist. Ct. Md. 1972, U.S. Dist. Ct. Colo. 1972, U.S. Ct. Appeals (4th Cir.) 1972, U.S. Ct. Appeals (9th cir. 1972, U.S. Ct. Appeals (10th cir.) 1983, state rep., Dist. 7, 2011. Sales rep. Gulf Oil, Washington, 1967-72; pvt. practice Littleton, Colo., 1972-83, Glendale, Ariz., 1983-86, Phoenix, 1986-88, Scottsdale, Ariz., from 1988; mem. Dist. 7 Ariz. House of Reps., from 2011. Pro-tempore judge Wickenburg Mcpl. Ct., 1986—; presiding judge Peoria (Ariz.) Mcpl. Ct., 1987-94, Cave Creek Mcpl. Ct., 1995-98. Appeared as actor in movie Dead Girls Don't Tango, 1990. V.p. South Jefferson County Reps., Lakewood, Colo., 1979, pres., 1990; candidate Dist. 6 for Congress; 2nd vice-chmn. Dist. 7 Rep. Party, pres. Ariz. Rep. Assembly Dist. 28, bd. dirs. Scottsdale (Ariz.) Constitution Commemorative Com., 1995-2003, pres., 2002-; elected Ariz. Ho. of Reps., Dist. 7, 2005-06. With USCG, 1959-66, pres. Scottsland Rep. Forum, 2010-, elect mem. ho. rep., 2010-, rep. District, 2004. Mem. ATLA, ABA (vice-chmn. family law 1983), Nat. Assn. Criminal Lawyers, Am. Judicature Soc., Nat. Assn. Criminal Def. Attys., Ariz. Magistrates Assn., Colo. Bar Assn., Ariz. Bar Assn., Scottsdale (Ariz.) Bar Assn. (sec. 2001-2002, v.p. 2002-2003, pres., 2003-2004), Md. Bar Assn., Colo. Trial Lawyers Assn., Maricopa County Bar Assn., Scottsdale Bar Assn. (bd. dirs., sec. 1996—2005), Masons, Shriners, Elks. Home: Carefree, Ariz. Died Oct. 31, 2014.

SMITH, DAVID HENRIQUE, accountant; b. Picayune, Miss., June 20, 1937; s. Sidney K. and Mattie Evelyn (Spiers) S.; m. Concetta E. D'Antonio, Aug. 19, 1965; children: Shelly, Melissa. BBA, Tulane U. CPA, La. Acct. Raymond Internat., NYC, 1959-64; audit mgr. Arthur

Young and Co., New Orleans, 1964-72; chief fin. officer George Engine Co., Inc., Harvey, La., from 1972. Mem. Am. Inst. CPA's, Fin. Execs. Home: Mandeville, La. Died Mar. 5, 2007.

SMITH, DAVID TODD, publishing company executive; b. Stamford, Conn., Nov. 19, 1953; arrived in Can., 1956; m. Margaret Beryl Starke, Dec. 30, 1978; children: Erik Joseph, Maximilian Peter Starke. BBA in Fin. and Econs., Wilfrid Laurier U., Waterloo, Ont., Can., 1976; MBA in Fin., McMaster U., Hamilton, Ont., 1978. Cert. gen. acct., Ont. Fin. analyst Economical Mut. Ins. Co., Kitchener, Ont., 1976-78; portfolio mgr. Mcht. Trust Co., Toronto, Ont., 1978-80; treasury officer Harlequin Enterprises Ltd., Toronto, 1980-82, asst. treas., 1982-89; treas. Torstar Corp., Toronto, from 1989. Died June 1, 2007.

SMITH, DEAN EDWARDS, retired men's college basketball coach; b. Emporia, Kans., Feb. 28, 1931; s. Alfred Dillon and Vesta Marie (Edwards) S.; m. Ann Cleavinger, 1954 (div. 1973); children: Sharon, Sandy, Scott; m. Linnea Weblemoe, May 21, 1976; children: Kristen, Kelly. BS in Math. & Phys. Edn., U. Kans., 1953. Asst. basketball coach USAF Acad., 1955-58; asst. basketball coach U. N.C., 1958-61, head basketball coach, 1961-97. Mem. U.S. and Canadian Basketball Rules Com., 1967-73; U.S. basketball coach Olympics, Montreal, Que., Can., 1976; lectr. basketball clinics, Germany, Italy. Author: Basketball: Multiple Offense and Defense, 1981, A Coach's Life: My 40 Years in College Basketball, 2002; co-author: The Carolina Way: Leadership Lessons from a Life in Coaching, 2004. With USAF, 1954-58. Recipient Arthur Ashe Courage award, 1998, Joe Lapchick Character award, 2008, Presdl Medal of Freedom The White House, 2013; named Coach of Yr., Atlantic Coast Conf., 1967, 68, 71, 76, 77, 79, Nat. Basketball Coach of Yr., 1977, Nat. Coach of Yr., US Basketball Writers, 1979, named one of The Top 5 Coaches of the 20th Century, ABC-TV and ESPN, Sportman of the Yr., Sports Illustrated, 1997; named to The Naismith Basketball Hall of Fame, 1982, Nat. Collegiate Basketball Hall of Fame, 2006, FIBA Hall of Fame, 2007 Mem. Nat. Assn. Basketball Coaches (Nat. Basketball Coach of Yr. 1976, dir. 1972— , pres. 1981-82), Fellowship Christian Athletes (dir. 1965-70) Democrat. Baptist. Died Feb. 7, 2015.

SMITH, DONALD HAROLD, industrial sales broker; b. Geneva, NY, Sept. 15, 1934; s. Claude Hoster and Mary Elizabeth (Kierst) S.; m. Gladys Margret Jones, June 12, 1954; children: Gregory Howard, Christopher Hilary. AA, Alfred U., 1955. Parts and service mgr. Werres Co., Inc., Rockville, Md., 1957-64; regional sales mgr. Maco Industries, Inc., Chgo., 1964-69, Wil-Mat Corp., Gastonia, N.C., 1969-81; salesman Selectrons, Ltd., Waterbury, Conn., 1983-85; mfg. sales rep. Glen Mills, Pa., 1981-83 and from 85. V.p. sales and mktg. Thorp 211 Aircraft Co., Inc., Pedricktown, N.J. Served with U.S. Army, 1955-57. Mem. Delaco Aviation Assn. (pres. 1978-80). Clubs: Aero (Phila.) (bd. dirs. 1978-82). Died Mar. 18, 2007.

SMITH, GARY DAVID, rehabilitation nurse, charge nurse; b. Tyler, Tex., Dec. 20, 1956; BS in Nursing, U. Tex., 1981. RN, Tex.; cert. rehab. nurse. Staff nurse Brackenridge Hosp., Austin, Tex., 1981-82; gen. duty nurse, emergency dept. St. Luke's Hosp., Duluth, Minn., 1982-84; ICU nurse Brackenridge Hosp., Austin, 1984-85, nurse emergency dept., 1985-87; nurse Tex. Rehab. Inst., Austin, 1987-90; charge nurse orthopedic unit The Rehab. Hosp. of Austin, 1990-92; charge nurse SCI/BI unit St. David's Rehab. Ctr., Austin, from 1992. Mem. Rehab. Nurses Assn. (sec. Ctrl. Tex. chpt.). Home: Dripping Springs, Tex. Died June 26, 2007.

SMITH, GERTRUDE M., artist; b. Collins, Miss., July 25, 1923; d. Leonard and Ida Ella (Coulter) McCarty; m. Percy Lee Smith, Nov. 20, 1943; children: Antje Elizabeth, Eunice Annette, Percy Wayne, Wanda Kay. Exhibits include Mcpl. Art Gallery, Jackson, Miss., 1983, 95, Cottonlandia Mus., Greenwood, Miss., 1984, Coll. Art & Designs, Savannah, Ga., 1985, Edn. TV, Jackson, 1986, Hines Cmty. Coll., Utica, Miss., 1986, Pearl River C.C., Poplarville, Miss., 1994, William Carey Coll., Hattiesburg, Miss., 1997; author: Kaleidoscope, 1992, History of Cold Springs Church, 1995; columnist Hattiesburg (Miss.) Am., 1996—. Pres. Gideon Aux., Collins, Miss., 1995—; chmn. ministry group Women's Missionary Union, Collins, 1995—; Sunday sch. tchr. 1st Bapt. Ch., Collins, 1997—. Mem. Miss. Poetry Soc., Miss. Art Colony, DAR. Republican. Died Apr. 9, 2007.

SMITH, JESSIE ELIZABETH, geriatrics nurse; b. Phila., Dec. 24, 1916; d. William Bilbrough Sr. and Elizabeth Mary (Fowler) Fry; m. Feb. 6, 1943 (dec. Feb. 1981); children: Nancy Smith Aierstok, William E. Jr. LPN, Atlantic City Vocat. Sch., 1958; RN, Atlantic Community Coll., 1969, AAS, 1989. Cert. gerontol. nurse, ANCC. Staff nurse Atlantic City Med. Ctr. (formerly Atlantic City Hosp.), Shore Meml. Hosp., Somens Point, N.J., 1958-76; nurse pvt. duty Nurses Profl. Registry; staff nurse Beachview Nursing Home, Atlantic City, 1976-78, Golden Crest Nursing Home, Atlantic City, 1978-80; charge nurse Eastern Pines Conv. Ctr., Atlantic City, 1978-98; ret., 1998. Presbyterian. Home: Galloway Township, NJ. Died Oct. 30, 2006.

SMITH, JUDITH ANN See KAYE, JUDITH

SMITH, LEONARD GEORGE, JR., accountant; b. Little Rock, Apr. 13, 1936; s. Leonard George Sr. and Agnes (Lebeck) S.; m. Jeannine Louise Embry, July 13, 1956 (div. Jan. 1966); children: Lisa Janice, Laura Louise, Matthew Roy. Student, La. State U., 1954-56; BS in Commerce, Centenary Coll., 1956-58. CPA, La. Credit mgr. Red Barn Chems., Shreveport, La., 1957-60; jr. acct. Heard, McElroy & Vestal, Shreveport, 1960-66; controller Sales Fin., Shreveport, 1966-70; sr. acct. Robert, Cherry & Co., Shreveport, 1971-85; pvt. practice acctg. Shreveport, from 1986. Mem. Am. Inst. CPA's, La. Soc. CPA's, Shreveport Jr. C. of C. (Key Man Cert. 1964, Cert. of Merit 1965). Democrat. Lutheran. Avocations: football, baseball, basketball, horse racing, reading. Home: Shreveport, La. Died Feb. 16, 2007.

SMITH, M(AHLON) BREWSTER, retired psychologist, educator; b. Syracuse, NY, June 26, 1919; s. Mahlon Ellwood and Blanche Alice (Hinman) S.; m. Jean Dresden Schwartz, June 1942 (div. 1945); m. Deborah Anderson, June, 1947; children: Joshua H., T. Daniel, Rebecca M., J. Torquil. Student, Reed Coll., Portland, Oreg., 1935-38; AB, Stanford U., 1939, AM, 1940; PhD, Harvard U., 1947. Jr. analyst Office Coordinator of Info., U.S. Govt., 1941; Rantoul scholar Harvard U., 1940-41, Social Sci. Research Council fellow, 1946-47, asst. prof. social psychology, dept. social rels., 1947-49; prof. psychology, chmn. dept. Vassar Coll., 1949-52; staff Social Sci. Rsch. Coun., 1952-56; prof. psychology NYU, 1956-59, U. Calif. at Berkeley, 1959-68, dir. Inst. Human Devel., 1965-68; prof., chmn. dept. psychology U. Chgo., 1968-70; prof. psychology U. Calif. at Santa Cruz, 1970-88, prof. emeritus, 1988—2011, vice chancellor social scis., 1970-75, ret., 1988. Fellow Ctr. Advanced Studies Behavioral Scis., 1964-65; v.p. Joint Commn. Mental Illness and Health, 1955-61. Author: Social Psychology and Human Values, 1969, Humanizing Social Psychology, 1974, Values, Self and Society, 1991, For a Significant Social Psychology, 2003; co-author: The American Soldier, vol. 2, 1949, Opinions and Personality, 1956; editor: Jour. Social Issues, 1951-55, Jour. Abnormal Soc. Psychology, 1956-61; contbr. articles to profl. jours. Rsch. officer Info. and Edn. divsn. War Dept., 1943-46; rsch. assoc. spl. com. on soldier attitudes Social Sci. Rsch. Coun. 1946. Maj. AUS, 1942-46 Decorated Bronze Star medal; NIMH fellow, 1964-65, NEH fellow, 1975-76; Belding scholar Found. for Child Devel., 1982-83; Gold medal award Am. Psychol. Found., 1992 Fellow AAAS, APA (pres. 1978, Disting. Contbn. to Pub. Interest award 1988, Henry A. Murray award 1993); mem. Soc. Psychol. Study Social Issues (pres. 1959, Kurt Lewin Meml. award 1986, Presdl. citation 2004), Western Psychol. Assn. (pres. 1986, Lifetime Contbn. award 1996), Psychologists for Social Responsibility (pres. 1987-90), Internat. Soc. Polit. Psychology (Harold Lasswell award 1993), Internat. Assn. Applied Psychology (pres. divsn. polit. psychology 1994-98), Soc. Peace, Conflict and Violence (Lifetime Contbn. to Peace Psychology award 1999), Phi Beta Kappa, Sigma Xi. Democrat. Home: Santa Cruz, Calif. Died Aug. 4, 2012.

SMITH, MARTHA VIRGINIA BARNES, retired elementary school educator; b. Camden, Ark., Oct. 12, 1940; d. William Victor and Lillian Louise (Givens) Barnes; m. Basil Loren Smith, Oct. 11, 1975; children: Jennifer Frost, Sean Barnes. BS in Edn., Ouachita Bapt. U., 1963; postgrad., Auburn U., 1974, Henderson State U., 1975. Cert. tchr., Mo. 2d and 1st grade tchr. Brevard County Schs., Titusville and Cocoa, Fla., 1963-65, 69-70; 1st grade tchr. Lakeside Sch. Dist., Hot Springs, Ark., 1965-66, Harmony Grove Sch., Camden, 1972-76; 1st and 5th grade tchr. Cumberland County Schs., Fayetteville, NC, 1966-69; kindergarten tchr. Pulaski County Schs., Ft. Leonard Wood, Mo., 1970-72; 3d grade tchr. Mountain Grove (Mo.) Schs., 1976-99; ret., 1999. Chmn. career ladder com. Mountain Grove Dist., 1991-99. Children's pastor 1st Bapt. Ch., Vanzant, Mo., 1984-88. Mem. NEA (pres.-elect Mountain Grove chpt. 1995-97, pres. Mountain Grove chpt. 1997-99), Kappa Kappa Iota. Avocation: antique and classic cars. Died Oct. 3, 2015.

SMITH, MICHAEL ARTHUR, investment banker; b. Louisville, Nov. 28, 1954; s. Martin Leo and Jean Louise (Hinz) S. BA, U. Wis., 1975; MBA, U. Chgo., 1979. Registered rep., securities prin. Mgr. corp. fin., v.p. Continental Bank, Chgo., 1977-82; mng. dir. investment banking Bear Stearns & Co. Inc., Chgo., 1982-89; founder, sr. mng. dir. BA Ptnrs., Chgo., from 1989; also bd. dirs. Continental Ptnrs. Inc., Chgo. Bd. dirs., chmn. audit com. Zebra Techs. Corp., Vernon Hills, Ill. Mem. Chgo. Club, Chgo. Yacht Club, 1871 Club (at-large), Phi Beta Kappa. Avocation: windsurfing. Home: Chicago, Ill. Died June 30, 2007.

SMITH, PAUL DENNIS, genetics educator; b. Balt., Nov. 14, 1942; s. William P. and Lillian E. (Garrison) S.; m. Ruth L. Dusenbery, Dec. 10, 1982; children: Jennifer, Aimee. BS, Loyola Coll., Balt., 1964; PhD, U. N.C., 1969. Asst. prof. Emory U., Atlanta, 1970-74, assoc. prof., 1974-84; prof., chmn. So. Meth. U., Dallas, 1984-89, Wayne State U., Detroit, from 1989. Cons. Nat. Inst. Environ. Health Sci., 1984, 85, 87, NAS/Inst. Medicine Com., 1988-90. Mem. AAAS, Am. Soc. Microbiology, Environ. Mutagen Soc., Genetics Soc. Am., Sigma Xi (Faculty Rsch. award 1978). Home: Bloomfield Hills, Mich. Died Feb. 11, 2007.

SMITH, REGINALD BRIAN FURNESS, retired anesthesiologist, educator; b. Warrington, Eng., Feb. 7, 1931; s. Reginald and Betty (Bell) S.; m. Margarete Groppe, July 18, 1963; children: Corinne, Malcolm. MB, BS, U. London, 1955; DTM and H, Liverpool Sch. Tropical Medicine, 1959. Intern Poole Gen. Hosp., Dorset, England, 1955-56, Wilson Meml. Hosp., Johnson City, NY, 1962-63; resident in anesthesiology Med. Coll. Va., Richmond, 1963-64, U. Pitts., 1964-65, from clin. instr. to prof., 1965-78, acting chmn. dept. anesthesiology, 1977-78; anesthesiologist in chief Presbyn. Univ. Hosp., Pitts., 1976-78; dir. anesthesiology Eye and Ear Hosp., Pitts., 1971-76; prof., chmn. dept. U. Tex. Health Sci. Ctr., San Antonio, 1978-98, anesthesiologist in chief hosps., 1978-98, clin. prof. anesthesiology, 1999—2007, clin. prof. rehab. medicine, 2003—07, med. dir. hyperbaric medicine and woundcare unit Univ. Hosp., 1993-2000, mem. med. staff Univ. Hosp., 2003—07; ret., 2000. Contbg. editor: Internat. Ophthalmology Clinics, 1973, Internat. Anesthesiology Clinics, 1983; contbr. articles to profl. jours. Served to capt. Brit. Army, 1957—59. Fellow ACP, Am. Coll. Anesthesiologists, Am. Coll. Chest Physicians; mem. AMA, Internat. Anesthesia Rsch. Soc., Am. Soc. Anesthesiologists (pres. Western Pa. 1974-75), Tex. Soc. Anesthesiologists, San Antonio Soc. Anesthesiologists (pres. 1990), Tex. Med. Assn., Bexar County Med. Soc. Home: San Antonio, Tex. Died Dec. 2014.

SMITH, RICHARD HILBERT EDWIN, II, software engineer, business executive; b. Milw., July 25, 1954; s. Richard H. E. and Marilyn R. (Jensen) S.; m. Leah A. Zeldes, Apr. 27, 1985. BA, U. Wis., 1976. Software specialist Digital Equipment Corp., Maynard, Mass., 1977-79; software engr. Bell & Howell Co., Lincolnwood, Ill., 1980-86, Sun Electric Corp., Crystal Lake, Ill., 1986-88; engr. specialist Northrop Corp., Rolling Meadows, Ill., from 1989. Pres. R.H.E. Smith Corp., Wheeling, Ill., 1988—. Mem. Assn. for Computing Machinery, Assn. Old Crows. Avocation: sci. fiction amateur publisher. Home: Prospect Heights, Ill. Died June 5, 2007.

SMITH, ROBERT GILLEN, retired political science consultant; b. Dover, NJ, Oct. 16, 1913; s. John Wesley and Elizabeth Wolfe (Gillen) S.; m. Lois S. Squier, Dec. 23, 1942; children: Robert Logan, Donald Paul. AB summa cum laude, Drew U., 1936, LLD (hon.), 1977; MA in History and Govt., Columbia U., 1939, PhD in History and Govt., 1950. From instr. to Pfeiffer prof., chair Drew U., Madison, N.J., 1940-71, prof. emeritus, from 1977; pvt. cons. intergovernmental policy implementation Arnold, Md., from 1977. Adj. prof. polit. sci. Hunter Coll., 1965-67; vis. prof. NYU, 1966-67; lectr. in field. Author: Public Authorities, Special Districts and Local Government, 1964, Public Authorities in Urban Areas, 1969, Ad Hoc Governments, 1974; contbr. chpt. to (Jerry Mitchell) Public Authorities and Public Policy, 1992; co-author, editor: Military Medical Manual, 1945; contbg. editor: Dictionary of Political Science, 1966; also articles. Mem. evaluation teams Mid. States Commn. Higher Edn., 1962-70; bd. dirs. Coll.-Fed. Agy. Coun., N.Y., 1969-72. With U.S. Army, 1942-46. Decorated Bronze Star; Robert G. Smith scholar established by Drew U. Alumni Assn., 1979; grantee 20th Century Fund, 1967, Eagleton Found., Danforth Found., Ford Found, NSF, Coun. Internat. Urban Liaison, Washington; inducted into Drew U. Athletic Hall of Fame, 1999. Mem. Phi Beta Kappa, Pi Sigma Alpha. Died Dec. 13, 2006.

SMITH, ROBERT JOHN, sales executive; b. Indpls., Feb. 4, 1927; s. Samuel R. and Rosemary (Berry) Smith; m. Arlene Ann Sondgerath, Aug. 19, 1950; children: Pat, Michael, Kathleen, Daniel, Timothy, Robert. BS in Bus., Butler U., 1950; MS, U. Pitts., 1951. Sales agt. Marchant Calculating, Lafayette, Ind., 1951—54; founder, pres Smith Office Equip. Co., Lafayette, from 1955. Mem. St. Thomas Ch. adv. bd., Lafayette, 1960—63; pres. Lafayette Area Parochial Fund dr., 1968. Served US Army, 1945—47. Decorated Army Commendation medal.; recipient Gestetner Outstanding, Dist. Dealer, 1968; named Man Yr., Marchant Calculators, 1953. Mem.: Nat. Office Products Assn., Nat. Office Machine Assn., Lafayette C. of C., Lafayette Country, K.C. Democrat. Roman Catholic. Home: Lafayette, Ind. Died June 23, 2007.

SMITH, ROBERT LOWELL, lawyer; b. St. Peter, Minn., May 7, 1931; m. Lavinia H. Peterson, Aug. 4, 1956; children: Paul R., B. Peter, James E. BA magna cum laude, Gustavus Adolphus Coll., St. Peter, 1953; postgrad., U. Wis., 1954-55; JD, U. Minn, 1959. Bar: Minn. 1959, U.S. Dist. Ct., U.S. Ct. Appeals (8th cir.) 1970. Pvt. practice law, Mpls., from 1959. Chief exec. officer, dir. Cable Systems Mgmt. of Iowa, Inc., Lake Park Cable TV, Inc.; dir., sec., gen. counsel Cable Sys. Svcs., Eagan, Minn., TriCable Inc., Eagan, DuBois Distbg., Forest Lake, others. With U.S. Army, 1954-56. Mem. Kiwanis. Home: Saint Paul, Minn. Died Jan. 27, 2007.

SMITH, ROBERT PEASE, retired physiatrist; b. Burlington, Vt., Apr. 26, 1917; s. Levi Pease and Julia (Pease) S.; m. Caroline Wheelock, July 5, 1947; children: Robert Pease Jr., Cynthia W.S., Julia Smith Wilson Wheelock, Sarah Smith Neagle, Alexander Wheelock, Elizabeth Huntington. AB, Princeton U., 1939; MD, Harvard U., Boston, 1943; postgrad., Harvard U., 1947. Diplomate Am. Bd. Phys. Medicine and Rehab. Intern Mass. Gen. Hosp., Boston, 1943-44; asst. resident in pathology New Eng. Deaconess Hosp., Boston, 1943; resident in medicine Mary Fletcher Hosp., Burlington; rsch. fellow Harvard Med., Boston, Mass., 1955; dir. Vt. Rehab. Ctr., 1956-66; dir. rehab. Louisville (Ky.) Rehab. Ctr., 1969-72, Gaylord Hosp., New Britain (Conn.) Meml. Hosp., 1972-87, Stamford (Conn.) Rehab. Ctr., 1972-76; dir. physical medicine Stamford (Conn.) Hosp., 1972-76; cons. Lawrence Meml. Hosp., New London, Conn. Dir. rehab. Gaylord Hosp., Wallingford, 1969-72; cons. Norwalk Hosp.; asst. prof. Yale U. Sch. Medicine, 1972-80, N.Y. Med. Coll., 1972-83; staff mem. Jewish Meml. Hosp., Ky., Children's Hosp., Louisville Gen. Hosp., Meth. Evangelical Hosp., VA Hosp, Norton Meml. Infirmary; asst., assoc. prof. Coll. Medicine U. Louisville. Contbr. articles to med. jours. Capt. M.C., AUS, 1944-46, ETO. Decorated Bronze Star Combat Med. Badge. Fellow ACP, Am. Acad. Phys. Medicine, Am. Congress Rehab. Medicine; mem. Am. Acad. Phys. Med. and Rehab., Am. Congress Med. Rehab. (past pres. ea. sect.), Am. Soc. for Clin. Evoked Potentials, Chittenden County Med. Soc. (life). Congregationalist. Home: Clermont, Fla. Died Jan. 16, 2007.

SMITH, SIDNEY TED, environmental engineer, retired mechanical engineer; b. Waterloo, Iowa, July 23, 1918; s. Sidney Charles and Maud Katheryn (Fry) S.; m. Dorothy Walton Buckingham, Aug. 17, 1942 (dec. Aug. 1968); children: Karen L. Jones, Sidney Tom, Jonathan Gregg; m. Joyce Lee Smith, June 3, 1972. BS in Mech. Engring., Iowa State U., 1940. Registered profl. engr. Kans., Mo. Owner Sid Smith & Co., Waterloo, 1946-60; profl. engr. Stanley Engring. Co., Muscatine, Iowa, 1960-62, various orgns., Kansas City, Mo., 1962-68; dir. design and projects Burns & McDonnell, Kansas City, 1968-92; cons. Sargent & Lundy, Chgo., 1993-94, Sega, Inc., Overland Park, Kans., from 1994; partially ret. Capt. Air Corps. US Army, 1941—45. Mem. Air and Waste Mgmt. Assn., Am. Legion. Republican. Presbyterian. Achievements include supervision of the design of first limestone flue gas desulfurization system for 500 MW utility boiler that removed 95% sulfur dioxide; supervised the design of first cold side precipitator for 500 MW utility boiler that operated successfully with low sulfur coal flyash. Died Nov. 23, 2006.

SMITH, STEPHEN DEWITT, finance educator; b. Jacksonville, Fla., Apr. 30, 1956; s. Lawrence DeWitt and Ruth Virginia (Miller) S. BA in Bus. Adminstrn., U. South Fla., 1977; PhD in Fin., U. Fla., 1980. Asst. prof. U. Tex., Austin, 1981-85; assoc. prof. Ga. Inst. Tech., Atlanta, 1986-90, Mills B. Lane prof. banking and fin., 1990-91; H. Talmage Dobbs Jr. prof. fin. Ga. State U., Atlanta, from 1992. Vis. scholar 4th dist. Fed. Home Loan Bank Atlanta, 1988-90, 6th dist. Fed. Res. Bank Atlanta, 1991—. Author: Principles of Interest Rates, 1993; contbr. articles to profl. jours. Mem. Am. Fin. Assn., Fin. Mgmt. Assn., Commerce Club. Democrat. Avocations: squash, whitewater rafting, fishing. Died Dec. 7, 2006.

SMITH, STEVEN HAROLD, network administrator; b. Yonkers, NY, Jan. 21, 1954; s. Harold W. and Evelyn D. (Bodnar) S.; m. Anna Violetta Grygo, Dec. 2, 1979 (dec. Dec. 1987). BA, Gettysburg Coll., 1976; MS, Nova U., 1984. Cert. tchr., Fla. Instr. U.S. Peace Corps, Taejon, Republic of Korea, 1977, Hillsborough Dist. Schs., Tampa, Fla., 1980-85; computer instr. Tampa Prep. Sch., 1985-86; microcomputer specialist Citicorp, Tampa, 1986-87; prof. microcomputers Pasco-Hernando Community Coll., Dade City, Fla., 1988-89; computer instr., computer coord. Pasco Dist. Schs., Dade City, 1987-90; network adminstr. Univ. Community Hosp., Tampa, 1990-94; sys. resource mgr. Swanson Inmate Commisry Svcs., Inc., Sarasota, Fla., from 1996. Cons. Wittner & Co., St. Petersburg, Fla., 1986—. Pres. Lake Padgett East Property Owner's Assn., Land O'Lakes, Fla., 1986-88; programmer Smitty's Bull. Bd. Svc., 1984-89. Mem. Fla. Assn. Computers in Edn., Fla. Instrn. Computing Suprs., Netware Users Internat. Democrat. Lutheran. Avocations: playing piano, basketball, camping. Home: Land O'Lakes, Fla. Died Nov. 1, 2006.

SMITH, THOMAS HUGH (T. KILGORE SPLAKE), poet, writer, photographer; b. Three Rivers, Mich., Dec. 8, 1936; s. Emery Crum and Margaret Louise Smith; m. Olga Irma Korzen Muir, July 7, 1977 (div. July 1990); children: Henry Korzen, Heidi Korzen. BA, Western Mich. U., 1959, MA, 1963; postgrad., Mich. State U., 1963—64, U. Maine, 1970. Hs tchr. Comstock (Mich.) Sch., 1959—63; jr. high tchr. Lansing (Mich.) Sch. Sys., 1963—64; prof. Kellogg CC, Battle Creek, Mich., 1964—89, Western Mich. U., Kalamazoo, 1973—74. Photographer (cover) Poesy Mag.; author: numerous poems; contbr. articles and photographs to popular mags.; author: Backwater Graybeard Twilight, 2002. Home: Calumet, Mich. Died May 19, 2007.

SMITH, TWILA LOU, primary educator; b. West Hamlin, W.Va., Nov. 22, 1957; d. Kenneth James and Joyce Renee (Ray) S. BA, Marshall U., 1978, MA, 1981. Cert. profl. tchr., adminstr., W.Va. Day care worker Dept. Human Svcs., Hamlin, W.Va., 1974; primary tchr. Lincoln County Bd. Edn., Hamlin, 1979-85, tchr. kindergarten, from 1985, mem. sch. improvement coun., 1988. Coord. writing to read Hamlin Elem. Sch., 1989-91. Youth leader Hamlin Bapt. Ch., 1978, tchr. Vacation Bible Sch., 1989. Recipient svc. recognition award Hamlin Bapt. Ch., 1989, cert. of honor Lincoln County Bd. Edn., 1991. Mem. Assn. Early Childhood Edn. Internat., W.Va. Edn. Assn., Marshall U. Alumni Assn. Avocations: walking, U.S. travel, flea markets, reading, community interests. Home: Hamlin, W.Va. Died Jan. 16, 2007.

SMITH, WHITMAN DONALD, English language and writing educator; b. NYC, Aug. 25, 1961; s. Clyde Clair and Anne Whitman (Kimball) S.; m. Virginia Susan Stolarski, Aug. 21, 1993. Student, Univ. Coll., London, 1982-83; AB, Dartmouth Coll., 1983; MA, Columbia U., 1985, MA, 1994. Columnist, reporter The Cape Cod Chronicle, Chatham, Mass., 1985-87; chief fin. writer Eaton Vance Corp., Boston, 1987-89; free-lance journalist Chatham and NYC, 1989-91; instr. English and Am. lit. Robert Louis Stevenson Sch., NYC, 1991-94; dean upper sch., chairperson dept. English York Prep. Sch., NYC, 1994-95; chairperson dept. English Hackley Sch., Tarrytown, N.Y., from 1995. Adj. asst. prof. English South Bronx campus Coll. New Rochelle, 1993—; lectr. English and Am. lit. SUNY, Purchase, 1993—. Mem. Eastward Ho! Country Club, Chatham Beach and Tennis Club, Yale Club of N.Y.C., Dartmouth Club of N.Y.C. Democrat. Avocations: cross country running, tennis, golf, theater. Home: Tarrytown, NY. Died Apr. 10, 2007.

SMITH, WILLARD GRANT, psychologist; b. Sidney, NY, June 29, 1934; s. Frank Charles and Myrtle Belle (Empet) S.; m. Ruth Ann Dissly, Sept. 14, 1957; children: Deborah Sue Henri, Cynthia Lynn Koster, Andrea Kay Richards, John Charles. BS, U. Md., 1976; MS, U. Utah, 1978, PhD, 1981. Diplomate Am. Bd. Forensic Examiners, Am. Bd. Psychol. Specialities, cert. forensic cons.; lic. psychologist Utah. Tchg. asst. dept. ednl. psychology U. Utah; rsch. asst. U. Utah Med. Ctr., 1976-78; rsch. cons. Utah Dept. Edn., 1977; program evaluator Salt Lake City Sch. Dist.; program evaluator, auditor Utah State Bd. Edn., 1978; sch. psychologist Jordan Sch. Dist., Sandy, Utah, 1978-82, tchr., 1979-80; exec. dir. Utah Ind. Living Ctr., Salt Lake City, 1982-83; spl. edn. cons. Southeastern Edn. Svc. Ctr., Price, Utah, 1983-85; sch. psychologist Jordan Sch. Dist., Sandy, Utah, 1985—95, asst. prin., 1995—96; assoc. psychologist Don W. McBride & Assocs., Bountiful, Utah, 1989-91; pvt. practice Sandy, Utah, 1991—2012. Master sgt. USAF, 1953-76. Decorated Air Force Commendation medal with 2 clusters. Fellow Am. Coll. Forensic Examiners (life); mem. APA (life), DAV (life), Air Force Assn. (life), Air Force Sgts. Assn. (life), Ret. Enlisted Assn. (life), Am. Legion (life), VFW (life), Phi Kappa Phi (life), Alpha Sigma Lambda. Home: Sandy, Utah. Died Dec. 19, 2014.

SMITH, WREDE HOWARD, food company executive; b. Sioux City, Iowa, Nov. 24, 1921; s. Howard C. and Geneva A. (Chesley) S.; m. Barbara J. Katherman, Aug. 29, 1946; children: Wrede, Roberta, Garrett, Barbara Jeanne. BS, U. Nebr., 1943. V.p. Am. Pop Corn Co., Sioux City, 1946-66, pres., from 1966. Sgt. U.S. Army, 1943-45, World War II. Recipient Watson Rogers award Nat. Food Brokers, 1991. Presbyterian. Home: Sioux City, Iowa. Died July 5, 2007.

SMITHEIMER, LUELLA SUDE, speech and language pathologist; b. NYC, Nov. 19, 1928; d. William and Stella (Meltzer) Sude; m. Aaron Charles Smitheimer, Oct. 19, 1952; children: Roy Jeffrey, Don Lawrence, Eileen Terry. BA, Adelphi Coll., 1950; MS, Adelphi U., 1967; PhD, NYU, 1980. Speech pathologist Adelphi U., Garden City, N.Y., 1965-66, BOCES, Nassau County, Wantagh, N.Y., 1966-70; lectr. St. John's U., Jamaica, N.Y., 1971; pvt. practice pathologist Port Washington, N.Y., from 1971. Adj. assoc. prof. Hofstra U., Hempstead, N.Y., 1971-83, NYU, 1984—. Contbr. articles to profl jours. Co-pres. AFS Port Washington Chpt., 1983—; bd. dirs. Port Children's Ctr., Day Care, 1985—. Mem. Am. Speech, Lang., Hearing Assn., N.Y. State Speech, Lang., Hearing Assn., Assn. for Children with Learning Disabilities. Avocations: choir, knitting, reading, art, music. Home: Port Washington, NY. Died July 16, 2007.

SNAPPER, ERNST, mathematics professor; b. The Netherlands, Dec. 2, 1913; came to U.S., 1938, naturalized, 1942; s. Isidore and Henrietta (Van Buuren) S.; m. Ethel Lillian Klein, June 1941; children: John William, James Robert. MA, Princeton U., 1939, PhD, 1941; MA (hon.), Dartmouth Coll., 1964. Instr. Princeton, 1941-45, vis. asso. prof., 1949-50, vis. prof., 1954-55; asst. prof. U. So. Calif., 1945-48, asso. prof., 1948-53, prof., 1953-55; NSF postdoctoral fellow Harvard, 1953-54; Andrew Jackson Buckingham prof. math. Miami U., Oxford, Ohio, 1955-58; prof. math. Ind. U., 1958-63, Dartmouth, from 1963, Benjamin Pierce Cheney prof. math., 1971—79. Mem. Am. Math. Soc., Math. Assn. Am. (pres. Ind. sect. 1962-63, Carl B. Allendoerfer award 1980), Assn. Princeton Grad. Alumni (governing bd.), Soc. for Preservation Bridges of Konigsburg, Phi Beta Kappa (hon.), Pi Mu Epsilon (hon.). Home: Chapel Hill, NC. Died Feb. 5, 2011.

SNEDDON, TOM (THOMAS WILLIAM SNEDDON JR.), retired prosecutor; b. LA, May 26, 1941; m. Pam Sneddon; 9 children. BA, U. Notre Dame, 1963; JD, UCLA, 1966; Grad., Nat. Dist. Attorneys Sch., U. Houston, 1972, Nat. Homicide Acad., 1977. Dep. dist atty. Santa Barbara County, 1969—77, supr. criminal ops., 1977—82, dist. atty., 1983—2010. Advisor American Prosecutor's Rsch. Ctr.; pres. Calif. Dist. Atty. Assn., 1989—90; co-chair Nat. Dist. Atty. Assn. Nat. Com., 1997. Served in US Army, 1967—69. Recipient Leadership award, Calif. Dept. Social Services, 1993, Director's award, Calif. Family Support Coun., 1995, Disting. Faculty award, Nat. Dist. Atty. Coll., 2000. Died Nov. 1, 2014.

SNEERINGER, ALFRED LAUREN, dentist, retired; b. Ada, Ohio, May 8, 1918; s. Alfred Truman and Grayce Pearle (Hauff) S.; m. Evelyn Alvern Bates, Sept. 5, 1942; children: Sharon Ann Sneeringer Kuntzman, Alfred Lauren, Larry Alan. BA, Ohio State U., 1943, DDS, 1946. Pvt. practice, Shelby, Ohio, 1946-91; ret. Asst. scoutmaster Boy Scouts Am., Shelby, 1960-68; chmn. 164th Bd. Mental Retardation. Lt. USN, 1941-46, PTO. Mem. ADA, Pierre Fauchard Dental Acad., Cen. Ohio Dental Soc. (pres. 1957-58), Ohio Dental Assn., Masons, Shriners, Sertoma (pres. 1958-59, Centurian award), Delta Sigma Delta. Republican. Lutheran. Avocations: photography, woodcarving, cooking. Home: Westerville, Ohio. Died Aug. 21, 2007.

SNELL, RICHARD SAXON, anatomist; b. Richmond, Surrey, Eng., May 3, 1925; came to U.S., 1963; s. Claude Saxon and Daisy Lilian S.; m. Maureen Cashin, June 4, 1949; children: Georgina Sara, Nicola Ann, Melanie Jane, Richard Robin, Charles Edward. MB, BS, Kings Coll., U. London, 1949, PhD, 1955, MD, 1961. House surgeon Sir Cecil P.G. Wakeley, Kings Coll. Hosp. and Belgrave Hosp. for Children, London, 1948-49; lectr. anatomy Kings Coll., U. London, 1949-59, U. Durham, Eng., 1959-63; asst. prof. anatomy and medicine Yale U., 1963-65, assoc. prof., 1965-67, vis. prof. anatomy, 1969; prof., chmn. dept. anatomy N.J. Coll. Medicine and Dentistry, Jersey City, 1967-69; vis. prof. anatomy Harvard U., 1970, 71, 80, 86; prof. anatomy Coll. Medicine, U. Ariz., Tucson, 1970; prof., chmn. dept. anatomy George Washington U. Med. Ctr., Washington, 1972-88, prof. emeritus, from 1988. Author: Clinical Embryology for Medical Students, 1972, 3d edit., 1983, Clinical Anatomy for Medical Students, 1973, 6th edit., 2000, Clinical Anatomy, 7th edit., 2003, Clinical Anatomy By Regions, 9th edit., 2012, Atlas of Normal Radiographic Anatomy, 1976, Atlas of Clinical Anatomy, 1978, Gross Anatomy Dissector, 1978, Clinical Neuroanatomy, 1980, 7th edit., 2009, Student's Aid to Gross Anatomy, 1986, Clinical Anatomy for Anesthesiologists, 1988, Clinical Anatomy of the Eye, 1989, 2d edit., 1997, Gross Anatomy: A Review with Questions and Explanations, 1990, Neuroanatomy: A Review with questions and Explanations, 1992, Clinical Anatomy for Emergency Medicine, 1993, Clinical Neuroanatomy: An Illustrated Review with Questions and Explanations, 3d edit., 2001, Clinical Anatomy: An Illustrated Review with Questions and Explanations, 4th edit., 2003 Clinical Anatomy by Systems, 2006; contbr. articles to med. jours. Med. Rsch. Coun. grantee, 1959; NIH grantee, 1963-65 Mem. Anat. Soc. Gt. Britain, Am. Soc. Anatomists, Am. Assn. Clin. Anatomists Cleave. (Hon. Mem. award, 2009), Alpha Omega Alpha. Home: Madison, Conn. Died Jan. 1, 2015.

SNOW, LEE ERLIN, artist, educator; b. Buffalo, Jan. 2, 1924; d. Edward and MRY (Gaffe) Erlin; m. Herbert Snow, Apr. 2, 1952; 1 child, Dana Alan. BA in Psychology and Sociology, U. Buffalo, 1947; postgrad., Otis Art Inst., LA, 1964-65; ESL accreditation, UCLA, 1980. Instr. multimedia fibre Barnsdall Arts and Crafts Ctr., LA, 1972-76, L.A. County Mus. Art, 1975; instr. adult edn. Santa Barbara (Calif.) City Coll., from 1984, Santa Barbara Art Mus., 1987. Workshop leader non-loom weaving World Crafts Conf., Toronto, Ont., Can., 1974. One-man shows include S.W. Craft Ctr. Gallery, San Antonio, 1975, Front Rm., Dallas, 1976; exhibited in group shows at Galeria de Sol, Santa Barbara, 1976. Art Rental Gallery, L.A. County Mus. Art., 1976-80, Jewish Fedn. Craft Show, L.A., 1983, L.A. Art Assn. Exibit Craft and Folk Art Mus., Santa Barbara Art Assn., 1984—, Juried Weavers Guild, 1984-85, Adult Edn. Fac Shows, 1985—, Gallery 113, Santa Barbara, Santa Barbara Art Walk, 1990-93, 98-99, De Vere Gallery, Mendecino, 1992—, Philip Campbell Assoc. Gallery, Los Olivos, 1993, Cabrillo Gallery, Santa Barbara, 1993, McCormick House, Santa Barbara, 1994; rep. in pub. collections Skirball Mus., L.A., Halls Crown Ctr., Kansas City, Craft and Folk Art Mus., L.A.; co-author: Weaving Off-Loom, 1973, Creative Stitchery with Dona Meilach. Bd. dirs. Adult Edn. Tchrs. Senate, Santa Barbara, 1990-91. UCLA scholar; recipient 3rd Prize Painting award Westwood Art Assn., 1963. Mem. So. Calif. Designer Craftsmen (sr. advisor 1978-80, pres. 1976-78), L.A. Art Assn., Am. Crafts Coun., So. Calif. Weavers Guild, Santa Barbara Art Assn. Gallery 113 (Artist of Month 1990). Avocations: reading, designing necklaces. Died June 26, 2007.

SNOWDEN, JERRY FRANKLIN, broadcast executive; b. Morristown, Tenn., Sept. 18, 1948; s. Estel Noah and Cleo May (Gillette) S.; m.Dixie Lee Croft, Dec. 24, 1966. Cert. in Broadcasting, Internat. Broadcasting Sch., 1975. Staff announcer Sta. KMIS-AM-FM, Portageville, Mo., 1975-77; news anchor, reporter Sta. WCIT, Lima, Ohio, 1977-78; staff announcer Sta. WIMA, Lima, 1978, Sta. WCBL, Benton, Ky., 1978-79; program dir., music dir. Sta. WNGO, Sta. WXID-FM, Mayfield, Ky., from 1979. Committee mem. J.U. Kevil Found., Mayfield, 1986-87. Democrat. Baptist. Avocations: hunting, fishing, four wheelers. Home: Symsonia, Ky. Died Dec. 24, 2006.

SOBOL, THOMAS, education educator; b. Jan. 11, 1932; s. Damasus and Margaret (Moran) m. Harriet Sobol; three children. BA in English, Harvard U., 1953, grad., 1954; PhD, Columbia U., 1969. Head dept. English pub. sch. system, Bedford, NY, 1961-65; dir. instrn., 1965-69; asst. supt. instrn. pub. sch. system Great Neck, NY, 1969-71; supt. sch. systems Scarsdale, NY, 1971-87; commr. N.Y. State edn. Albany, 1987-95; Christian A. Johnson Prof. Columbia Univ. Teacher's College, NYC, 1995—2006, dir. ednl. adminstrs. Author: (memoir) My Life in School, 2013. Died Sept. 3, 2015.

SOCOLOW, SANFORD, media executive; b. NYC, Nov. 11, 1928; s. Adolph and Sarah (Mindich) S.; m. Anne Grace Krulewitch, May 1960 (div. 1977); children: Jonathan Levin, Helen Elisabeth, Michael Joseph. BA in History, CCNY, 1950. News asst. N.Y. Times, NYC, 1949-51; fgn. corr. Internat. News Svc., Tokyo, 1953-56; news script writer Dumont TV Network, NYC, 1956; writer, producer CBS News, NYC, 1956-88; exec. producer CBS Evening News with Walter Cronkite, 1978-81, CBS Evening News with Dan Rather, 1981; bur. chief CBS News, Washington, 1974-78, news dir. Europe, Mid. East, East Europe, bur. chief London, 1982-84; exec. producer, World Monitor Program Christian Science Monitor, Boston, 1988-90; exec. producer Media Access Corp., NYC, 1991-93, Cronkite-Ward Productions, NYC, from 1993. Cons. CS Super Sta., Boston, 1990-92, adv. bd., 1991-92. Producer, writer documentary series Eyewitness to History, 1958-60 (Emmy award 1958, 59, 60), documentary program The Nixon Pardon, 1974 (Emmy award 1975), obituary Harry Truman, 1972; producer Daily TV News, World Monitor Cable TV, 1988-90. 1st lt. U.S. Army, 1951-53, Korea. Poynter Inst. fellow, 1964. Home: New York, NY. Died Jan. 31, 2015.

SOHLIN, DONNELLY ALLEN, diplomat; b. Lakota, ND, Nov. 9, 1926; s. Alfred and Alma Engelive (Simons) S. Student, Oreg. State Coll., 1944; BS, U. Calif., 1950. Supervisory auditor Army and Air Force Exchange Service, Japan, 1950-56; chief audit div. I.C.A. Saigon, 1956-59; dep. controller Vientiane, Laos, 1959-61; controller A.I.D., Conakry, Guinea, 1961-64, area operations officer Washington, 1964-67, dep. asso. dir. financial mgmt. Saigon, 1967-68; asst. dir. finance U.S.O.M., Thailand; also controller A.I.D., Rangoon, Burma, 1969-71; dep. AID affairs officer, controller Am. Embassy, Phnom Penh, Khmer Republic,

1971-74; dep. dir. AID, Khmer Republic, 1974-75; dep. chmn. planning, budgeting, acctg. and reporting Task Force AID, Washington, 1975-76; controller Internat. Narcotics Control Dept. State, 1976-78; pvt. cons. on mgmt. and fin. mgmt., 1978-79; dep. exec. dir. UN Fund Drug Abuse Control, Vienna, from 1979. Served with AUS, 1945-46. Recipient meritorious service award AID, 1964, superior honor award, 1975; Papal medal Pope Paul VI, 1974 Mem. Am. Acad. Polit. and Social Sci., English Speaking Union, Am. Fgn. Service Assn., Asia Soc., Siam Soc., Alliance Francais, Delta Phi Epsilon. Clubs: Royal Bangkok Sports, Saigon Cercle Sportif, Khmer Cercle Sportif. Died Nov. 8, 2006.

SOKOLOFF, LOUIS, retired physiologist, neuroscientist; b. Phila., Oct. 14, 1921; s. Morris and Goldie (Levy); m: Betty (Kaiser) (dec. 2003); children Kenneth (dec. 2007), Ann BA, U. Pa., 1943, MD, 1946; MD (hon.), U. Lund, Sweden, 1980; ScD (hon.), Yeshiva U, NY, 1982, U. Glasgow, UK, 1989, Philipps U. Marburg, Germany, 1990; MD (hon.), U. Rome, 1992; ScD (hon.), Georgetown U., Washington, 1992, Mich. State U., Lansing, 1993, U. Pa., Phila., 1997. Intern Phila. Gen. Hosp., 1946-47; rsch. fellow in physiology U. Pa. Grad. Sch. Medicine, 1949-51, instr., then assoc., 1951-56; assoc. chief, then chief sect. cerebral metabolism NIMH, Bethesda, Md., 1953-68, chief lab. cerebral metabolism, 1968—2004, emeritus scientist, 2004—15. Chief editor Jour. Neurochemistry, 1974-78. Pvt. 1st class US Army, 1943—46, capt. MC US Army, 1947—49. Recipient F.O. Schmitt medal in neurosci., 1980, Albert Lasker clin. med. research award, 1981, Karl Spencer Lashley award Am. Philos. Soc., 1987, Disting. Grad. award U. Pa., 1987, Nat. Acad. Scis. award in Neurosci., 1988, Georg Charles de Hevesy Nuclear Medicine Pioneer award Soc. Nuclear Medicine, 1988, Mihara Cerebrovascular Disorder Rsch. Promotion award, 1988, Ralph Gerard award Soc. Neuroscience, 1996, Lifetime Achievement award Internat. Soc. Cereb and Mental Health, 1999. Mem. NAS, Inst. Medicine (sr.), American Physiol. Soc., Assn. for Rsch. Nervous and Mental Diseases (pres. 1983), American Biophys. Soc., American Neurol. Assn., American Philos. Soc. (Karl Lashley award, 1987), American Acad. Arts & Sciences, American Soc. Biol. Chemists, American Soc. Neurochemistry (pres. 1977-79), Internat. Soc. Neurochemistry, Internat. Soc. Cereb Blood Flow & Metab. Independent. Jewish. Achievements include development of methods for measurement of cerebral blood flow, metabolism and imaging of local functional activity in the brains of animals and man, and application of this for functional imaging in the brains of animals and man. Died July 30, 2015.

SOLARZ, SANFORD, advertising executive; b. Bklyn., Sept. 23, 1927; B in Aero. Engring., NYU, 1948. Engr. Chase Aircraft Co., Trenton, N.J., 1948-50, Avien, Queens, N.Y., 1950-53; advt. mgr. Liquidometer Corp., L.I. City, N.Y., 1953-58, 60-66; copywriter Gray & Rogers, Phila., 1958-60; v.p. Mort Barish Assocs., Princeton, N.J., 1966-73; pres. The Sanford Solarz Co., Trenton, from 1973. Lectr. advt. courses Trenton State Coll. Avocation: aerophilately. Home: Levittown, Pa. Died May 21, 2007.

SOLBERG, RUELL FLOYD, JR., research engineer; b. Clifton, Tex., July 27, 1939; s. Ruel Floyd Sr. and Ruby Mae (Rogstad) S.; m. Laquetta Jane Massey, Oct. 3, 1959; children: Chandra Dawn (Mrs. J. Mark Hamilton), Marla Gaye (Mrs. Daniel Dougherty). Student, Tex. Luth. Coll., 1958-59, U. Tex., Arlington, 1959; BSME, U. Tex., Austin, 1962; MSME, U. Tex., 1967; MBA, Trinity U., San Antonio, 1977. From rsch. engr. to asst. supr. Applied Rsch. Labs., Austin, Tex., 1962-67; from rsch. engr. to sr. rsch. engr. Southwest Rsch. Inst., San Antonio, 1967-87, prin. engr., from 1987. Tech. asst. Applied Mechanics Revs., San Antonio, 1980-83. Co-author: The Solberg Family from Norway to Texas, 1979; co-inventor: Ferrite Core Crossed Spaced Loop Antenna, 1971, Transducer-Reflector System, 1980; contbr. articles to profl. jours. Fellow ASME (Pi Tau Sigma-ASME bd. of awards 1989-93, gen. awards com. 1982-89, commn. on sects. 1991—, vice chmn., 1994—, dir. programs 1991—, advisor 1990—, Charles E. Ballelsen award 1976, 78, Coun. cert. 1977, 79, 80, 81, Centennial award 1980, bd. govs. cert. 1982, 83, 84, 85, 87, 89, 93, Clifford H. Shumaker award 1990); mem. NSPE, Soc. Allied Weight Engrs., Instrument Soc. Am., Order of Engr., Norwegian Am. Mus., Norwegian Soc. Tex., Tau Beta Pi, Pi Tau Sigma, Sigma Xi, Sigma Iota Epsilon. Avocations: genealogy, sports. Died Nov. 25, 2006.

SOLLIEN, FLOYD S., insurance company executive; b. Spring Grove, Minn., Mar. 14, 1929; s. Syver C. and Florence L. (Rauk) S.; m. Mary Lou Schmitt, Mar. 5, 1955; children: Judy, David, Steve. CLU. Asst. mgr. Decorah (Iowa) Newspaper, 1953-59; dist. agt. Northwestern Mutual Life, Decorah, from 1959. Bd. dirs. Decorah Zoning and Adjustment, 1984—, chmn. fin. com. Aase Haugen Homes Inc., Decorah, 1986—. Sgt. U.S. Army, 1950-53, Korea. Named Iowa Tree Farmer of Yr. Am. Tree Farm System, 1988. Mem. Nat. Assn. Life Underwriters (chmn., co-founder 1961-62), Nat. Estate Planning Coun. (chmn., co-founder 1974-75), Nat. Assn. CLU (bd. dirs. 1979-82), Am. Coll. Life Underwriters, Million Dollar Round Table, Rotary Club, Oncota Golf County Club, Masons, Shriners. Republican. Lutheran. Avocations: tree farming, fishing, golf, travel. Home: Decorah, Iowa. Died Aug. 11, 2007.

SOLLINS, SUSAN, curator, television producer; b. 1939; s. Irving V. & Sonya (Peretz) Sollins; m. Earle Brown (dec. 2002) BA, Sarah Lawrence Coll.; postgrad., Columbia U. Dir. studio art program Barnard Coll., U. Columbia, NYC, 1964-66; editor Harry N. Abrams, Inc., NYC, 1967; curator edn. Nat. Mus. American Art, Smithsonian Inst., Washington, 1968-71; producer arts interviews Nat. Public Radio (NPR), 1972-74; exec. dir., co-founder, curator Independent Curators Inc., NYC, 1974—94; exec. prodr., curator Art:21, PBS, from 2001. Dir. Inner City Art Program, Collegiate Sch., NYC, 1965; instr. Art History, NYU, 1965-66; guest curator Balt. Mus. of Art, 1972-73; cons. Balt. Pub. Schs., 1972, San Francisco Mus. Art, 1975, American Assn. Mus., 1975, London (Ontario) Art Gallery, 1976, Neuberger Mus., SUNY Purchase, 1976, Denver Art Mus. 1976, Portland (Oreg.) Art Mus., 1977, Georgetown U., 1988 and numerous other museums, ednl insts. and art galleries; curator contemporary art Art in Landscape, 1975, New Work, NY, 1977, Supershow!, 1979, New Sculpture: Icon and Environment, 1983, Points of View: Four Painters, 1985, Eternal Metaphors: New Art from Italy, 1988, Team Spirit, 1990. Author (tchr. instructional materials on art and art history) Great Ideas, 1976, The City-Project Ideas, 1977, The Decordova Lessons, 1979; (films) You're It, 1971, Learning to Look, 1977; contbr. articles to profl. jours., mags. and newspapers; exec. prodr. and curator: (TV series) Art:21: Art in the Twenty-First Century, 2001, 2003, 2005, 2007; dir., prodr.: (documentaries) William Kentridge: Anything is Possible, 2010 Nat. Jury Awards in the Visual Arts, Southeastern Ctr. for Contemporary Art, 1988; pres. Earl Brown Music Found., Rye, NY, 1996-. Recipient Gov.'s award for Outstanding Service to Artists, Skowhegan, 2008. Mem. Mass. Arts Coun., NY State Arts Coun., Art Table, Inc. (bd. dirs. 1984-87), Ivy Labs. (bd. dirs., chmn. 1991). Died Oct. 13, 2014.

SOLOMON, SARAH ELIZABETH, poultry scientist, emeritus professor; b. Glasgow, Scotland, Apr. 19, 1944; BSc, U. Glasgow, 1968, PhD, 1972. Lectr. U. Glasgow, 1968—90, sr. lectr., 1990—93, reader, 1993—97, prof., 1997—2003; curator Hunterian Mus. Glasgow U., 2003, Art in Sci. Global cons. to poultry industry, from 2007. Recipient Gordon Meml. medal, Brit. Poultry Sci., 1st Tchg. award, World Poultry Sci. Assn. Mem.: World Poultry Sci. Assn. (nominations com. chmn.), Brit. Poultry Sci. (chmn.). Achievements include research in avian eggshell structure and quality and the turtles nesting on the beaches of north cyprus. Avocations: gardening, travel, writing. Home: Brantome, France. Died Feb. 25, 2015.

SOLTERO-HARRINGTON, LUIS RUBÉN, retired surgeon, educator; b. San Juan, Sept. 4, 1925; s. Augusto Rafael Soltero and Anna Lila Harrington; m. Alice Joyce Carpenter, Apr. 24, 1958; children: Luis Ruben, Kathleen Ann, Susan Joyce, Robert Richard, Sharon Theresa. BS in Agr., U. P.R., Rio Piedras, 1945; BM, MD, Northwestern U., Chgo., 1949. Diplomate Am. Bd. Surgery, Nat. Be. Med. Examiners, P.R. Rd. Med. Examiners. Intern Michael Reese Hosp., Chgo., 1949-50; resident in gen. surgery Aguadilla (P.R.) Dist. Hosp., 1950-51; resident in gen. surgery, instr. Baylor U. Coll. Medicine and Affiliated Hosps., Houston, 1954-59; resident in gen. surgery Jefferson Davis, VA and M.D. Anderson Hosps., Houston, 1954-57; resident in pediatric, thoracic and cardiovasc. surgery St. Luke's-Tex. Children's Hosp., Houston, 1957-59; asst. prof. surgery U. P.R. Sch. Medicine, 1960-64, assoc. clin. prof., 1972-73, assoc. clin prof., from 1973, in charge devel. heart surgery program, 1960-64, dir. surgery residency tng. program, 1961-64; pvt. practice San Juan, 1959—2003; ret., 2003; prof. San June Bautisa Sch. Medicine, from 2006. Prof. surgery U. del Caribe Sch. Medicine, Cayey, P.R., 1981—, San Juan Bautista Sch. Med., 2006-; cons. in cardiovasc. and thoracic surgery Med. Examing Bd. P.R., San Juan, 1989; chief thoracic and cardiovasc. surgery Tchrs. Hosp., San Juan, from 1959; dir. surgery residency tng. program Univ. Hosp., Rio Piedras, from 1961-64; cons. in thoracic and cardiovasc. surgery San Juan City Hosp., 1962—, cons. in surgery, 1964—; cons. in surgery Presbyn. Hosp., 1972—, Mimiya's Hosp., 1987—; cons. in thoracic and cardiovasc. surgery Indsl. Hosp., San Juan, 1975—, Hosp. Met., 1982—, Clinic Fernández García, 1983—; chief surgery Ruiz Arnau Hosp., Bayamon, P.R., 1978—; asst. dir. ICU, Hosp. del Maestro, 1987—; bd. dirs. Rsch. Found. Cardiovasc. Surgery Tex., 1984—, Am. Cancer Soc., 1974; mem. Nat. Adv. Cun. Mended Hearts, Inc., 1969. Author: (textbook) The Management of the Acutely Ill Patient, 2002; contbr. articles to med. jours.; patentee partial occlusion vascular clamp to be used in small blood vessels; inventor respirator for infants based on electronic equipment. Capt., M.C., USAF, 1953-54. Recipient award for outstanding work in cardiovasc. surgery Lions Club, Hato Rey, 1961. Fellow Am. Acad. Pediat., Am. Coll. Legal Medicine (assoc.); mem. AMA (physician recognition award 1986); mem. Denton A. Cooley Cardiovasc. Surg. Soc., Michael E. De Bakey Internat. Cardiovasc. Soc., Pan Am. Med. Assn. (coun. pediatric surgery), P.R. Soc. Cardiology, Am. Heart Assn., P.R. Hear Assn., Phi Chi. Avocations: travel, horticulture, bridge. Home: Rio Piedras, PR. Deceased.

SOMMA, THOMAS P., art historian, museum director; b. Somerville, NJ, Sept. 8, 1949; s. Thomas P. and Anne Somma; m. Marie A. Dacchille, Dec. 2, 1983. MA, Rutgers U., 1983; BS, Marietta Coll., Ohio, 1972; PhD, U. Del., 1990. Mus. dir. U. Mary Washington, Fredericksburg, Va., from 1998; adj. prof. Georgetown U., Washington, from 2001; asst. prof., mus. dir. Ithaca Coll., 1991—98, instr. semester Washington program, from 2001. Co-project dir. NEH landmarks of Am. History Summer Workshops, Washington, from 2004. Author: (book) The Apotheosis of Democracy (U. of Del. Am. Manuscript Competition Winner, 1992); co-author: The Library of Congress: The Art and Architecture of the Thomas Jefferson Building, Perspectives on American Sculpture before 1925, 2003; co-editor, contbr.: book American Pantheon; contbr. jour. Recipient U. S. Capitol Hist. Soc. fellowship, 1987, 1991. Mem.: Am. Assn. of Mus., Coll. Art Assn. Avocations: chess, literature, travel. Home: Fredericksburg, Va. Died May 10, 2007.

SOPPELSA, JOHN JOSEPH, decal manufacturing company executive; b. Cleve., Apr. 23, 1948; s. Anthony Joseph and Elizabeth Ann (McCarthy) S.; m. Nikki Lynn Stevens, Sept. 7, 1968. Student, Cleve. State U., 1966-68, Baldwin-Wallace Coll., Berea, Ohio, 1985. Sales rep. Manning Studios, Inc., Cleve., 1967-70, Pitney-Bowes, Inc., Stamford, Conn., 1970-72, Wampole Chem., Stamford, 1972-75; pres. Sun Art Decals Inc., Cleve., from 1975. Home: Olmsted Falls, Ohio. Died Jan. 23, 2007.

SORRELL, MICHAEL E., consulting company and hospitality management executive; b. Pasadena, Calif., Mar. 31, 1944; s. James Hendrick Sorrell and Marie Vivian Bristow. AA, Normandale Coll., Bloomingdale, Minn., 1992; BA, Concordia Coll., St. Paul, Minn., 1994. Pres., CEO, owner Daggers/La. Inc., Metairie, La., 1987-89, Mesa Cons. Svcs./MN/Inc., Mpls., 1989-94, Mesa Cons. Svcs., Inc., Las Vegas, Nev., from 1994; pres., CEO, majority ptnr. S&W Hospitality Group, Inc., Las Vegas, from 1999; dir. S.R. Owl Inc., from 1999; chmn., CEO Bristow-Norwich Group Internat. LLC, Las Vegas, 2000—08; chmn. emeritus Bristow-Norwich Group Internat., from 2008; mgr. Bristow-Sorrell Family Trust, 2008; chmn. Bristow-Sorrell Philanthropies, Inc, 2008; dir. CWA Mfg. Inc., 2010; chmn., exec. dir. Santa Mesa Found., 2010; dir. Liberty Edn. Forum, 2012; founding chmn., pres. Santa Mesa Inst., 2014. With USAF, 1963-69, USN, 1972-89. Mem. VFW, Nat. Assn. Small Bus., Nat. Lic. Beverage Assn., Inst. Mgmt. Cons., Nat. Assn. Corp. Dirs., Soc. Human Resources Mgmt., Soc. Hospitality Cons., Am. Legion, Fleet Res. Assn., Navy League US, U.S. Naval Inst., Amateur Athletic Union of U.S., Marines' Meml. Club, Victory Svcs. Club, LA Athlectic Club. Roman Catholic. Avocations: golf, hiking, tennis. Deceased.

SOTTONG, PHILIPP C., social services consultant, physician, writer, artist, publisher; b. Cattaraugus, NY, Mar. 16, 1920; s. Peter and Grace Marion (Wagner) S.; m. Mary Lou Head, 1944; children: Gary, Geoffrey, Lincoln. Grad., Hamilton Coll., 1941; MD, Rochester U., 1945. Diplomate Nat. Bd. Med. Examiners, Am. Bd. Psychiatry and Neurology. Intern U. Pittsburgh, 1945; fellowship in pathology U. Rochester, 1949, resident in psychiatry, 1949-51; staff mem. Erlanger Children's Meml. Hosp., from 1959; dir. Chatta Guidence Clinic, 1953-59; pvt. practice, from 1959. Rep. Mental Health Execeptional Children Inst., 1955-56; staff psychiatrist Ala. Mental Health Program, 1967-70; cons. Orange Grove Sch, Family Svc., Dept. Voc. Rehab., Depts. Pub. Welfare, VA, Office Hearings and Appeals, John Hancock. Author: Year of Chance, 1989, BZ Art, 1992; 7 one man shows (watercolor); pub.: Songs of Sottongs, 1989. Democratic nominee Dist. 6 Tenn., 1972; chmn. Speakers for McGovern-Shriver Hamilton County, 1972; preservation and restoration Walnut Bridge. Lt. (j.g.) USNR, 1947-48. Honorary fellow and Commonwealth fellow in Anthropology Cornell U., 1951-53. Mem. AMA (life), Am. Psychiat. Assn. (life), Chattanooga and Hamilton County Med. Soc., Tenn. Med. Assn., Tenn. Watercolor Assn., Chattanooga Regional Hist. Assn. Died Dec. 11, 2006.

SOUTHARD, JAMES BRUCE, lecturer, painter; b. Bklyn., Mar. 31, 1921; Student, NAD, 1939-41, Beaux Arts Inst. Design, 1941, Arts Students League, 1946-49, Escuela Pintura Escultura, Mex.; also studied with, Robert Brackman, 1946, Reginald Marsh, 1947, Kenneth Hayes Miller, 1947, Jon Corbino, 1949. With Stockton Mus. Art, San Joaquin, Calif., San Francisco Gen. Hosp.; represented by Maxwell Galleries, San Francisco, Georg Krevsky Art Gallery, San Francisco. Instr. painting. One-man shows include Galleria Arte Moderno, Mexico City, 1951, Galleria Caracalla, Guadalajara, Mex., 1951, Three Arts, Poughkeepsie, N.Y., 1953, Lucian Labault Gallery, San Francisco, 1954, St. Mary's Coll., Moraga, Calif., 1964, San Joaquin Pioneer Mus., Stockton, Calif., 1965, San Francisco Art Commn., 1977; exhibited in group shows at Oakland Mus., 1962-63, John Bolles Gallery, San Francisco, 1976, Calif. State Fair, 1977-78, Kensington Gallery, Calif., 1981, Eleonore Austerer Gallery, San Francisco, 1990, others; represented in permanent collections City and Co. San Francisco, Home Savings, L.A., Health Ctr., San Francisco, Bancroft Libr. Univ. Calif., Berkeley, Palace Legion Honor, San Francisco, San Joaquin Pioneer Mus., Stockton, Calif., San Francisco Dept. Health, Carnegie Art Mus., Oxnard, Calif., 1992; four paintings given to Hudson River Mus. from pvt. collection, Yonkers, N.Y., 1997. Recipient Purchase award Home Savings, San Francisco Arts Commn., Award of Merit, San Francisco Arts Festival. Mem. Artists Equity Assn., Internat. Soc. Artists, Soc. Western Artists, East Bay Watercolor Soc., Duchess County Art Assn. Home: Daly City, Calif. Died July 26, 2007.

SPEAR, SUSAN HOLMES, elementary school educator; b. Norwalk, Conn., Apr. 13, 1934; d. Robert Anderson and Elizabeth (Powell) Holmes; m. George Pitman Spear; children: Susan Elizabeth Spear Sneathen, William David. BS, Cen. Conn. State U., 1956; MA, So. Conn. State U., 1980. Cert. elem. tchr., Conn. Kindergarten tchr. Milford (Conn.) Bd. Edn., 1956-57, 1st grade tchr., 1957-59, Branford (Conn.) Hills Sch., 1982-83; asst. to costume designer Long Wharf Theatre, New Haven, 1965-66; 5th grade tchr. J. B. Sliney Sch., Branford, 1980-82, 4th grade tchr., 1983-91; integrated 3/4 tchr. M.T. Murphy Sch., Branford, from 1991, mentor tchr., from 1992. Coop. tchr. Branford Bd. Edn., 1990—; lang. arts leader Branford Bd. Edn. and Conn. State Bd. Edn., 1991; presenter in field. Mem. Rep. Town Meeting, Branford, 1976-78, mem., 1967-78; trustee Blackstone Meml. Libr., Branford, 1990—. Mem. ASCD, Internat. Reading Assn., Nat. Coun. Tchrs. English, Whole Lang. Umbrella (chmn. Amb. Corps 1992—), Conn. Tchrs. Applying Whole Lang. Mem. United Ch. of Christ. Avocations: fabergé eggery, stitchery, sewing, reading, costume design. Home: Branford, Conn. Died Feb. 16, 2007.

SPEARS, CAROLYN LEE, small business owner; b. Springfield, Ill., June 11, 1944; d. Theodore Leo and Clover Fawn (Notley) Ratterree; m. William Arthur Rowland, May 4, 1963 (div. 1971); 1 child, Kimberly Carol; m. Roger Erwin Spears, Dec. 21, 1979. Grad. high sch., Springfield. Sec. Sangamo Electric Co., Springfield, 1961-63, Nat. Soc. Crippled Children and Adults, Chgo., 1963-65, Regency Life Ins. Co., Springfield, 1965-67; with Prescription Learning Co. (name changed to Jostens Learning Corp. 1989), Phoenix, from 1971; v.p. field ops. Prescription Learning Co., Phoenix, from 1986; owner Picture Perfect Photo Lab, Inc., from 1990; group v.p. edn. svcs. Jostens Learning Corp., Phoenix, 1989-92; rep. Ednl. Svcs. Am., 1993. Died July 1, 2007.

SPELLMAN, ELIZABETH MAY, education administrator; b. Waterbury, Conn., June 23, 1933; d. William Joseph and Beatrice Louella (Hill) Dunn; d. John Franklin Spellman Jr., Aug. 11, 1951 (dec. Mar. 1979); children: John Franklin III, Adam Lyons. BA, U. R.I., 1971; MA, Calif. State U., Northridge, 1972. Instr. Bristol Community Coll., Fall River, Mass., 1972-74, R.I. Sch. for Deaf, Providence, 1972-74, supr., instr., 1974-76, dir. adult svcs., 1977-86, dir. sign lang., 1977—91, transition coord., 1986—91. Mem. R.I. Commn. on Deaf and Hearing Impaired, Providence, 1979-91; mem. adv. bd. Nat. Captioning Inst., Falls Church, Va., 1981-88; facilitator Nat. Conf. on Deaf and Hard of Hearing People, El Paso, Tex., 1988. Editor newsletter Voice, 1990-92; author pamphlet Words From a Deaf Parent, 1973. Named Deaf Woman of yr., 15th Dist. Quota Club, 1978. Mem. Am. Deafness and Rehab. Assn., Nat. Assn. of Deaf, Registry of Interpreters for Deaf Inc. (life, cert.), Nat. Rehab. Assn. Unitarian Universalist. Avocations: needlecrafts, reading. Home: Cranston, RI. Died Dec. 29, 2006.

SPELSON, NICHOLAS JAMES, retired engineering executive; b. Oak Park, Ill., Sept. 10, 1923; s. James and Constance (Rellos) S. BS in Mech. Engring., Ill. Inst. Tech., Chgo., 1947. Mech. engr. pvt. industry, Chgo., 1947-60; mech. engr. USAF, 1960-65, Def. Logistics Agy., Dept. of Def., Chgo., 1965-82; br. chief ops. Def. Logistics Agy.-Def. Contract Adminstrn. Svcs. Region, Chgo., 1982-90; br. chief quality assurance engring. Def. Logistics Agy.-Def. Contracts Dist., Chgo., 1990-94. With US Army, 1943—45. Mem. Am. Legion, Hellenic Profl. Soc. Ill. Greek Orthodox. Avocations: golf, travel. Home: Oak Park, Ill. Died July 29, 2007.

SPENCER, ELDEN A., retired manufacturing company executive; b. Willoughby, Ohio, Mar. 7, 1929; s. Friend Spencer and Edith Mae Prall; m. Imelda E. Mann, Sept. 25, 1949; children: Laura, Lynn, Mark, Micheal, Martin, Lisa, Leslie. Cert. prodn. tech. Pres., CEO ELMAC Corp., Huntington, W.Va., 1977-83; pres. Ohio Rubber Co., Willoughby, Ohio, 1983-90. Mayor Mentor on Lake, Ohio, 1958-62; chmn. Lake County Rep. Party, Painesville, Ohio, 1988—; mem. Lake County Bd. Elections, Painesville, 1989—; commr. Ohio Lottery, Cleve., 1993—; commr. Lake County Jury, Painesville, 1995—. Named to Willoughby H.S. Hall of Fame, 1995. Republican. Avocation: boating. Died June 21, 2007.

SPIEGEL, ALLEN DAVID, medical educator, consultant; b. NYC, June 11, 1927; s. Max and Betty (Silver) S.; m. Lila Spiegel, Apr. 16, 1958; children: Merrill S., Marc B., Andrea M. AB, Bklyn. Coll., 1947; MPH, Columbia U., 1954; PhD, Brandeis U., 1969. Chief radio & TV unit N.Y.C. Health Dept., 1951-61; health edn. assoc. The Med. Found., Inc., Boston, 1961-69; prof. SUNY Downstate Med. Ctr. at Bklyn., from 1969. Cons. in field. Author, editor of numerous books including Strategic Health Planning, 1991, Home Health Care, 2d rev. edit., 1987, Risk Management in Health Care Institutions: A Strategic Approach, 1997, 2d rev. edit., 2003, A. Lincoln, Esquire: A Shrewd Sophisticated Litigator, 2002; mem. editl. adv. bd. Nation's Health; contbr. articles to profl. jours. NEH fellow, 1979, WHO study/travel fellow, 1974, Nat. Ctr. for Health Svcs. Rsch. fellow, 1966-69; recipient of citations from govtl. and pub. agys; seminar leader Profl. Continuing Edn. Programs (overseas), 1988. Mem. Am. Pub. Health Assn. (com. chmn.), Internat. Union for Health Edn., Columbia U. Sch. of Pub. Health Alumni Assn., Community Agy. Pub. Rels. Assn., Coun. on Med. Television, Soc. of Pub. Health Educators, Health Edn. Media Assn., Consumer Commn. on the Accreditation of Health Svcs. Home: Sayreville, NJ. Died Dec. 31, 2006.

SPIEGELBERG, ELDORA HASKELL, retired psychologist, civic worker; b. Philippopolis, Bulgaria, Feb. 6, 1915; d. Edward Bell and Elisabeth (Frohlich) Haskell; m. Herbert Spiegelberg, July 6, 1944 (dec.); children: Gwen Elisabeth (dec.), Lynne Sylvia. BA, Beloit Coll., Wis., 1937; MA, Oberlin Coll., Ohio, 1938; postgrad., U. Pitts., 1940, Pa. State U., 1956. Cert. elem. edn. and tchr. of deaf, Wis., Mo. Tchr., psychologist Western Pa. Sch. for the Deaf, Pitts., 1939-44; psychologist pub. schs. Appleton, Wis., 1949-63; lectr. in clin. psychology Lawrence U., Appleton, 1955-57; sch. and rsch. psychologist pub. schs. University City, Mo., 1964-80; ret., 1980. Mem. parents as tchrs. University City Bd., 1984—; vol., storyteller Reading is Fundamental, St. Louis, 1985—. Pres. Women's Internat. League for Peace and Freedom, St. Louis, 1966-68, 74-79, 89-93, bd. dirs., 1993—; mem. program com. Am. Friends Svc. Com., 1977-83, 89-95; facilitator prison workshops Alternatives To Violence Program, 1994—. Named Ethical Humanist of Yr. Ethical Soc., 1981; recipient Disting. Svc. award Mayor of University City, 1981. Mem. APA (dues-exempt com.). Democratic Socialist. Home: Saint Louis, Mo. Died Aug. 22, 2007.

SPIER, LUISE EMMA, film editor, director; b. Laramie, Wyo., Aug. 22, 1928; d. Louis Constantine Cames and Vina Jane Cochran; m. John Spier, Sept., 1957 (div. 1962). Student, U. Wyo., 1947, U. Calif., Berkeley, 1948-53. Head news film editor Sta. KRON-TV, San Francisco, 1960-70, film editor, from 1980; freelance film editor, director San Francisco, 1970-80 and from 83. Edited and directed numerous news specials and documentaries, including The Lonely Basque, Whaler, The American Way of Eating. Recipient numerous awards for film editing and directing, including Cine Golden Eagle, Best Med. Res. Film award John Muir Med. Found., Chris Statuette, Bronze and Silver Cindy awards Info. Film Producers Am. Died Dec. 2, 2006.

SPIERS, ALEXANDER STEWART D., medical educator; b. Melbourne, Australia, Jan. 31, 1936; came to U.S., 1976; s. Alexander Donaldson and Joan (Patterson) S.; m. Margaret Overend, Dec. 20, 1960; children: Alexander, Ronald, Deborah, Gordon, James. MBBS, U. Melbourne, 1960, PhD, 1968, MD, 1975. Cert. in internal medicine, hematology and oncology. Sr. lectr. in medicine Hammersmith Hosp., London, 1970-75; assoc. prof. Boston U., 1976-80; prof. medicine Albany (N.Y.) Med. Coll., 1980-87, U. South Fla., Tampa, from 1987; ret., 1996. Co-author: Clinical Leukaemia Practice, 1974; editor: Chemotherapy and Urological Malignancy, 1982; contbr.over 400 articles and papers to profl. jours Trustee Leukemia Soc. Am., Albany, 1980-87, Tampa, 1987, chmn. edn. com., 1988. Lt. col. Royal Army M.C., 1987. Recipient Territorial decoration Queen Elizabeth, 1981; traveling fellow The Nuffield Found., 1968, Nat. Svc. medal. Fellow Royal Coll. Pathologists Australasia, Royal Soc. Medicine, ACP, Royal Australasian Coll. Physicians, Royal Coll. Physicians Edinburgh; mem. Brit. Officers Club New Eng., Treasure Island Tennis & Yacht Club. Presbyterian. Avocations: boating, history, travel, antiques, theater, gardening, chess, reading. Home: Maidenhead, England. Died 2014.

SPIKES, DOLORES MARGARET RICHARD, former academic administrator; b. Baton Rouge, Aug. 24, 1936; m. Hermon Spikes (dec. 2008); 1 child, Rhonda Brown (dec.). BS in Math., Southern U., Baton Rouge, 1957; M, U. Ill., Urbana-Champaign; PhD in Math., Louisiana State U., 1971. Asst. prof. math. Southern U., 1961, chancellor New Orleans, 1987—96; pres. U. of Maryland Eastern Shore, Princess Anne, 1996—2001. Bd. mem. Harvard U. Inst. of Educational Mgmt., 1987; mem. of bd. advisors to President Bill Clinton on historically black colleges and universities, 1994; vice-chmn. Kellogg Commission on the Future of State and Land-Grant Universities. Named one of 20 Most Influential Black Women in America, Ebony mag., 1990. Achievements include first African-America woman to earn a PhD in Mathematics from Louisiana State University in 1971; first woman to head a public university in Louisiana when named chancellor of Southern University at New Orleans in 1987; first female president for University of Maryland Eastern Shore. Died June 1, 2015.

SPILLANE, ROBERT RICHARD, school system administrator; b. Lowell, Mass., Oct. 29, 1934; s. John Joseph and Catherine (Barrett) S.; m. Geraldine (Shea); children: Patricia, Robert Jr., Kathleen Orsi, Maura Francis, Patricia McGrath. BS, Ea. Conn. State Coll., 1956; MA, U. Conn., 1959, PhD, 1967. Elem. and secondary tchr., Storrs, Conn., 1956-60, Chaplin, Conn., 1960-62; elem. prin. Trumbull, Conn., 1962-63; secondary prin., 1963-65; asst. supt. Glassboro Pub. Schs., NJ, 1966-68, Roosevelt Schs., Long Island, NY, 1968-70, New Rochelle Pub. Schs., NY, 1970-78; dep. commr. NY State Dept Edn., Albany, NY, 1978-81; supt. Boston Pub. Schs., 1981-85, Fairfax County Pub. Schs., Va., 1985—97; regional officer Office Overseas Schs. US Dept. State, 1997—2006; v.p., dir. Ctr. for Edn. at CAN Corp., Alexandria, Va., 2006—15. Bd. dirs. Council Great City Schs.; mem. adv. bd. Met. Ctr. Ednl. Research, Devel. and Tng. NYU, Instr. Mag.; chmn. pres.' adv. bd. Tchrs. Coll. Columbia U.; co-chmn. adminstrs. com. study on edn. and edn. of tchrs. US Office Edn., Washington; mem. N.Y. State Sch. Officers Resolutions Com. on Legislation, Westchester County Chief Sch. Officers Legis. Com.; bd. dirs. Curriculum Devel. Council So. NJ, Impact II, NYC; adj. prof. sch. edn. Fordham U., NYC, Iona Coll., New Rochelle, Bank St. Coll. Edn., NYC, Glassboro State Coll.; instr. NYU; vis. lectr. U. Bridgeport, Conn. Author: You and Smoking, 1970, Management by Objectives in the Schools, 1978; contbr. articles to profl. jours. Trustee Mus. Fine Arts, Boston; bd. dirs. Jr. Achievement Ea. Mass., Inc.; mem. adv. com. Boston Pub. Library, The Statue of Liberty-Ellis Island Found., Inc., commn. on Bicentennial U.S. Constitution. Recipient Disting. Alumni award Ea. Conn. State Coll., 1969, Disting. Alumni award U. Conn., 1986; named one of Outstanding Young Men of America Mem. American Assn. Sch. Adminstrs. (named Nat. Supt. of Yr., 1995), Mass., Conn., NJ, NY Assns. Sch. Adminstrs., Sch. Mgmt. Study Group (pres. 1971-73, Hall of Fame award 1974), Assn. Supervision and Curriculum Devel., Nat. Sch. Pub. Relations Assn., Phi Delta Kappa. Avocations: swimming, sailing, skiing, theater and the arts, entertaining. Died July 18, 2015.

SPINELLI, ESTHER, school nurse; b. Askov, Minn., Jan. 31, 1921; d. Jens and Johanne (Christensen) Thomsen; m. Louis C. Spinelli, Feb. 8, 1947; children: Lou, Felix, Vana. RN, U. Minn., 1943; BA, Jersey City State Coll., 1981. Pub. health nurse City of Orange (N.J.); sch. nurse Orange Bd. Edn. 1st. lt. U.S. Army Nurse Corps, 1944-47. Mem. Nat. Assn. Sch. Nurses, N.J. Assn. Sch. Nurses, Essex County Sch. Nurses Assn., NEA, Essex County Edn. Assn., N.J. Edn. Assn. Home: N Brunswick, NJ. Died Dec. 1, 2006.

SPINKA, WILLIAM J., art educator; b. Bridgeport, Conn., Oct. 3, 1920; s. Jacob J. Spinka and Anna M. Syrotiak; m. Valerie A. Lauten, June 19, 1943; children: Kenneth W., Caryl V. BS in Edn., CCNY, 1942, MS in Edn., 1945. Tchr., phys. edn. dir. Birch Wathen Sch., NYC, 1942—44; instr. engring. USMcht. Marine Acad., Kings Point, 1944—45; instr. art CCNY, 1946—60, asst. prof. art, 1961—66, assoc. prof., 1967—81, prof., 1981—85, prof. emeritus, 1986, archtl. design rsch. projects structure & color, from 1986. Ednl. affiliate Am. Soc. Interior Design, NYC, 1976—88; profl. mem. Nat. Soc. Interior Designers, 1960—75; sculptor; painter. Exhibitions include Salmagundi Club, Nat. Arts Club, Nat. Acad., NY, 1976—99, Corcoran Gallery, 1946, Lever House Gallery, 1986—95, one-man shows include Canton Artists Guild, Conn., 1979, works pub. in interior mags. Ensign US Maritime Svc., 1944—46. Mem.: Audubon Artists Inc. (v.p. sculpture 1987—93, sr. v.p. 1994—98, Gold medal of honor 1988, Silver medal of honor 1992). Avocations: construction, landscape design, athletics. Died Oct. 12, 2012.

SPIRA, JOEL SOLON, electronics company executive; b. NYC, Mar. 1, 1927; s. Elias and Edna (Shenker) S.; m. Ruth Rodale, Nov. 7, 1954; children: Susan, Lily Housler, Juno. BS in Physics, Purdue U., 1948. Project engr. Reeves Instrument Corp., Paramus, N.J., 1952-59; prin. systems analyst ITT Communications Systems, Paramus, 1959-61; pres., dir. rsch. Lutron Electronics Co., Inc., Coopersburg, Pa., 1961-90, chmn., dir. rsch., 1990—2015. Radar designer USN. Mem. Nat. Acad. Engring., William Oughtred Soc. Achievements include inventing the first lighting dimmer for domestic use; granted first patent for a solid-state dimmer in 1962. Died Apr. 8, 2015.

SPITZER, ROBERT J., academic administrator; BBA, Gonzaga U.; MPhil, St. Louis U.; STB, Gregorian U., Rome; ThM, Weston Sch. Theology, Cambridge, Mass.; PhD in Philosophy, Cath. U. of Am. Tchr. Georgetown U., 1984-90, Seattle U., 1978-80, 90-98; pres. Gonzaga U., from 1998. Co-founder U. Faculty for Life; founder, adv. Life Principles. Died Dec. 25, 2015.

SPLAKE, T. KILGORE See SMITH, THOMAS

SPRAGGINS, ROBERT LEE, organic chemist, research scientist; b. Sedalia, Mo., Feb. 18, 1939; s. William Arthur and Esther Louise (Kurtz) S.; m. Gabriela Solis Pulido, Nov. 25, 1987; children: Robin Lee, William Robert, Leslie Brewton. BS in Chemistry, La. Tech. U., 1963, MS, 1966; PhD, U. Okla., 1970. Chemist Cities Svc. Rsch., Lake Charles, La., 1963—65; rsch. fellow Alza Corp., Palo Alto, Calif., 1970—71; postdoctoral fellow, rsch. scientist Stevens Inst. Tech., Hoboken, NJ, 1971—75; mass spectrometist Tex. A&M U., College Station, 1975—77; sr. scientist, group leader mass spectrometry Radian Corp., Austin, 1978—81; sr. scientist, mgr. analytical chemistry SumX Corp., Austin, 1981—82; prin. chemist Gt. Plains Gasification Assocs., Beulah, ND, 1982—85; sr. rsch. chemist Manville Tech. Ctr., Denver, 1985—91; prin. chemist Sci. Cons. of Colo., Denver, 1991—95, prin. chemist emeritus, from 1995. Mem. N.J. Marine Consortium for Rsch., 1974—75; cons. Sci. Cons.-Glass Phoenix, from 1991. Contbr. articles to profl. jours. Deacon Presbyn. ch., 1988—91; coach Little League Baseball, 1977—80. With USAR, 1962—66. Recipient Seagrant postdoctoral fellow, Stevens Inst. Tech., 1971—72; grantee, N.J. Heart Assn., 1974, NIH, 1975—77. Mem.: Am. Chem. Soc., Phi Lambda Upsilon, Sigma Xi. Presbyterian. Achievements include patents in field; research in pancreatitis and prostaglandins. Home: San Angelo, Tex. Died Apr. 18, 2007.

SPRINGER, GEORGE C., educational association administrator; b. La Boca, Panama, Nov. 9, 1932; came to U.S., 1952; s. Bertley Nimrod and Edna Ethel (Westerman) S.; m. Phyllis Hall, Dec. 17, 1955 (div. 1979); m. Geraldine Brown, Oct. 11, 1980; children: Rosina, Linda, George Jr. Student, Canal Zone Jr. Coll., Panama, 1950-52; BS, Tchrs. Coll. of Conn., 1954; student, Central Conn. State Coll., 1956-62. Cert. tchr., Conn. Indsl. arts tchr. Nathan Hale Jr. High Sch., New Britain, Conn., 1959-67; history tchr. New Britain High Sch., 1967-79; lectr. Central Conn. State Coll., 1975-78; pres. New Britain Fedn. Tchrs., 1971-78, Conn. State Fedn. Tchrs., from 1979; v.p. Am. Fedn. Tchrs., from 1988. Mem. advisory coun. Conn. State U. Ctr. for Edn. Excellence, 1986—; mem. bd. overseers, Regional Lab. for Edn. Improvement in New Eng., Andover, Mass., 1988—; mem. Educational Equity Study Com., Hartford, Conn., 1979-89, Conn. Coalition for Pub. Edn., Conn., 1984—. Vice pres. United Labor Agy., West Hartford, Conn., 1982—; sec. treas. Legis. Electoral Action Program, Hartford, 1982—; co-chair. Sixth Dist. Fed. Priorities Proj., Conn., 1987—; pres. New Britain NAACP, 1982-86; active, AFL-CIO, Conn. AIDS Task Force, Conn. Coalition on Literacy, Conn. Task Force for the Nat. Forum for Youth at Risk, Permanent Task Force on AIDS, Conn. Coun. for Black Students & Profls., Conn. Coalition for Educational Equity. Recipient Educator of Distinction award, Nat. Coalition of 100 Black Woman (Conn. chpt.) 1988, Carl Hurwith award, Legis. Electoral Action Program, Hartford, 1988, Harriet Tubman award, Conn. NOW, 1988, Meritorious Service award, United Negro College Fund, 1987. Democrat. Baptist. Avocations: volleyball, gardening. Home: New Britain, Conn. Died Dec. 19, 2006.

SPROULL, ROBERT LAMB, retired academic administrator, physicist, director; b. Lacon, Ill., Aug. 16, 1918; s. John Steele and Chloe Velma (Lamb) S.; m. Mary Louise Knickerbocker, June 27, 1942; children: Robert F., Nancy

M. Sproull Highbarger. AB, Cornell U., 1940, PhD, 1943; LLD (hon.), Nazareth Coll., 1983; DMusic (hon.), New Eng. Conservatory, 1997. Research physicist RCA labs., 1943-46; faculty mem. Cornell U., 1946-63, 65-68, prof. physics, 1956-63, dir. lab. atomic and solid state physics, 1959-60, dir. materials sci. center, 1960-63, v.p. for acad. affairs, 1965-68; dir. Advanced Research Projects Agy., Dept. Def., Washington, 1963-65; v.p., provost U. Rochester, NY, 1968-70, pres., 1970-84, pres. emeritus, 1984—2014. Prin. physicist Oak Ridge Nat. Lab., 1952; physicist European Rsch. Assoc., Brussels, 1958-59; lectr. NATO, 1958-59; pres. Environ. Literacy Coun., 1997-99; mem. sci. adv. com. GM Corp., 1971-80, chmn., 1973-80; mem. Def. Sci. Bd., 1966-70, chmn., 1968-70; mem. Naval Rsch. Adv. Com., 1974-76, Sloan Commn. Higher Edn., 1977-79, N.Y. Regents Commn. Higher Edn., 1992-93. Author: Modern Physics, 1956, A Scientist's Tools for Business, 1997; Editor: Jour. Applied Physics, 1954-57. Trustee Deep Springs Coll., 1967—75, 1983—87, Cornell U., 1972—77. Ctr. for Advanced Study in Behavioral Scis. fellow, 1973; Meritorious Civilian Svc. medal Sec. of Def., 1970, Telluride Tech Festival award, 2006 Fellow American Acad. Arts & Sciences; mem. Telluride Assn. (pres. 1945-47), Inst. of Def. Analysis (trustee 1984-92). Home: Pittsford, NY. Died Oct. 9, 2014.

SPURGEON, WESLEY C., material handling administrator; b. Clarksville, Ill., Apr. 30, 1937; AD, Louisville Tech. Inst., 1968. Designer Conveyorization, Inc., Louisville, 1988-93; material handling engr. Precision Automation Co., Jeffersonville, Ind., from 1993. Clk., S.E. Ind. Bapt. Assn., 1980—; deacon local ch., 1975—. Baptist. Avocations: assembling model railroad, model airplanes, photography. Home: Clarksville, Ind. Died June 25, 2007.

SQUIRES, NORMA JEAN, artist, writer; b. Toronto, Feb. 15, 1938; d. Ross and Ida (Rolland) S.; m. Gerald Hopman (div. 1996); 1 child, Jessica Hopman. BFA, The Cooper Union, NYC, 1979; MA, Calif. State U., Northridge, 1984. Instr. sculpture Lucinda Art Sch., Tenafly, N.J., 1967-68; artist, freelance writer LA, from 1969; artists' rep. and cons., 1986-88; writer L.A. Artcore, from 1990. Juror Hudson River Mus., Yonkers, N.Y., 1967, Conejo Valley Art Mus., 1999; coord., organizer Thursday's Poets Cultural Affairs Dept. City of L.A., 1994-95; bd. mem. Artists Profl. Exch. Illustrator: children's books I Am a Picture Book, 1977, The Witch Who Whistled, 1977, Mouse in the Magic Forest, 1977; one-woman shows include Palmcrest House, Long Beach, Calif., 1998, Museum Art, LA, 2005, Internat. Art Festival, Seoul, Korea, 2000, Nagasaki (Japan) Mus. Art, 2002, 1st Internat. Art Festival, Jeju Island, Korea, 2004, Internat. Art Festival at Burapha U., Bangkok, Thailand, 2005, 14th Internat. Art Festival, Chonburi, Thailand, 2005, Wind Art Festival, Jeju Island, South Korea, 2005, Gwang Hwa Moon Internat. Art Festival, Seoul, 2006, LELA 15th Internat. Art Festival, L.A., 2006, Represented in permanent collections Sterling Forest Gardens, N.Y.C., Warner Bros. Records, Burbank, Calif., Perkins Bldg. of the City of Glendale, Calif., Siemans Pacesetter Sys., L.A.; curator Quarks to Quasars, 1997, Angels, Ancestors and Spirit Guides, 1997, works rented to numerous movie and TV prodns. including Frasier, 1999; one-woman shows include Internat. Art Exposition, Atelier Gronard, Paris, 2007, one-woman shows include Meet Ararat Internat. Festival, Yerevan Armenia, 2007, one-woman shows include Building Bridges, Intemt. Art Exch., Mex., 2008—10, Internat. Art Festival, Manila, 2009. Named Artist of Month, Artdecollectors Virtual Art Gallery, 2007. Mem.: Artists Profl. Exch. (bd. dirs.). Avocations: reading, flamenco dancing, singing, astronomy, aerobics. Home: North Hills, Calif. Deceased.

SRONCE, WILLIAM CARL, steel wire company executive; b. Rantole, Ill., Jan. 27, 1956; s. Jack Dean and Audrey Ruth (Deines) S.; m. Ariene Marie Howe, May 19, 1980; children: Nicole Marie, Cory Wayne. BA in Metallurgical Engrng., Sch. of Mines & Tech., 1978; Ma in Fin., Webster U., 1985. Metallurgist Armco, Kansas City, Mo., 1978-85; plant metallurgist Nat. Standard, Stillwater, Okla., 1985-90; quality dir. Insteel Inds., Mt. Airy, N.C., from 1990. Mem. Am. Soc. Quality Control, Am. Soc. Marerials (v.p. 1982-83), Wire Assn. Internat. Lutheran. Avocations: racquetball, volleyball, golf. Home: Andrews, SC. Died Mar. 2, 2007.

STABIN, ALICE MARIE, administrative assistant; b. Boston, Mass., May 10, 1932; d. Fred and Martha Annette Stabin. A in Comml. Sci., Boston U., 1951, BS, 1953, student in Pub. Health, 1974—75. Cert. in tchg. Mass., 1954, in human rels. Heidelberg U., Germany, 1960. Exec. med. sec. Harvard Med. Sch., Boston, 1953—55; club dir. Spl. Svcs., Frankfurt, Germany, 1959—61; social security disability claims MA Rehabilitation Commn., Boston; alt. supr., 1974—98; ombudsman, nursing homes, from 1999. Instr. Eastern MA Literacy Coun., Medford, Mass., 2004; mem. Claflin Soc., Boston U., from 1990. Mem.: Coun. on Aging, Am. Soc. U. Women, Sierra Club. Independent. Avocation: travel. Home: Natick, Mass. Died Mar. 19, 2007.

STACK, ANGELA JOHANN, artist; b. St. Louis, Nov. 22, 1946; d. Daniel O'Connell and Angela Elizabeth (Bonn) S. BFA, Washington U., St. Louis, 1969; MFA, Cranbrook Acad., 1972. Dir., gallery, tchr. Florissant Valley Community Coll., St. Louis, 1973-74; tchr., art St. Louis Bd. Edn., 1976; instr., art U. Md., Heidelberg, Germany, 1977-78; graphic artist Cosmetic Speciality Labs. Inc., Lawton, Okla., 1980, 87-88; art specialist Dept. Army, Ft. Sill, Okla., 1983-85; tech. illustrator Mössner Konstrukteur Betriebswirt, Schwäbisch Gmünd, Germany, 1986; instr., art Community Adult Edn. Program, Lawton, 1987-88; tchr. Rite of Passage Sch., Minden, Nev., 1990-92. Master tchr. Adult Basic Edn. Program, St. Louis, 1974-76; interviewer Westat, Rockville, Md., 1988; edn. dir. Yerington Paiute Tribe, Indian counselor Yerington (Nev.) H.S., 1992-1998, acad. specialist, Nev. Dept. Corrections, 1998; caseworker, We. Nev. C. C., 1998-2006. Exhibited in group shows, 1970-86; one-woman shows, 1972, 74, 84, 86, 87, 97. Recipient Tchr. of Yr. award Rite of Passage Schs., 1991; Fulbright fellow, 1972. Democrat. Roman Catholic. Avocations: photography, gardening. Home: Lovelock, Nev. Died Nov. 10, 2006.

STACKHOUSE, ANN RAE See RULE, ANN

STADELMAN, EGON, journalist; b. Berlin, Jan. 31, 1911; came to U.S., 1940; s. Ferdinand and Margarete (Engel) S.; m. Marian Stern, Dec. 19, 1942. Spl. events officer U.S. Office of War Info., also USIA, NYC and Washington, 1944-63; editor New Yorker Staats-Zeitung, NYC, 1963-92, chmn. adv. bd., from 1992. Author, reviewer, critic, reporter. Mem. adv. bd. Help and Reconstrn., N.Y.C., 1960-92. Served with inf. U.S. Army, 1942-44, ETO. Decorated Officers Cross for svcs. helping rebldg. of cultural ties between U.S. and Germany (Fed. Rep. Germany), Merit Great Cross for continued work for improved German-Am. cultural rels.; Grand Cross of Austria. Avocations: classical music, writing, travel, stamp collecting/philately, reading. Home: Riverdale, NY. Died May 27, 2007.

STAFFORD, ELSAN HUGH, novelist, poet, retired deputy sheriff; b. Santa Ana, Calif., Sept. 29, 1913; s. Guy and Elsa (Zimmerman) S.; m. Ann Ruelle (div. May, 1961); children: Mike, Tim, Patrick, Alice. AA in English, L.A. City Coll., 1938. Planner, writer Goodyear Tire Co., LA, 1936-40; police officer L.A. Police Dept., 1945; sherrif's officer L.A. County Police, LA, 1946-51; planner, writer Douglas Aircraft, LA, 1954-58; mgr. Auldin Arms, Torrance, Calif., 1965-68; planner electron industry Torrance, 1969-73; apt. mgr. Goldrich & Kest Co., LA, 1974-83. Bus. cons. Creative Adminstr. Writers, L.A., 1989—; mgr. Lyric Lines Publ., Grants Pass, Oreg., 1998— Author: (poetry) Walk On (finalist 1997), The Star and Rose (finalist 1998). Fund raiser Calif. Rep. Orgn., Reseda, 1980; donor, mem. Audubon Soc., Srs. Coalition. Lt. U.S. Army, 1941-45 Avocations: writing, reading, classical music, chess. Died Jan. 14, 2007.

STAMP, CHARLES LAMONT, farmer, vintner; b. Cumberland, Md., Mar. 25, 1935; s. Frank E. and Lucy (Hillerman) S.; m. Beverly Ann Smith, July 19, 1958; children: Christopher, Michael, David, Teresa. AAS, SUNY, Morrisville, 1957. Owner, mgr. Lakewood Farm, Rock Stream, N.Y., from 1969; pres. Lakewood Vineyards Inc., Watkins Glen, N.Y., from 1989. Fire chief Town of Watkins Glen, 1981-82, dep. fire chief, 1982-83; councilman Town of Reading, Schuyler County, N.Y., 1976-82, supr., 1982—. Named nat. plow champion U.S.A. Plowing Assn., 1958, N.Y. State plowing champion, 1954, 56, 57, 58, 61, Farmer of Yr., Schyuler County, 1990, Grape Grower of Yr., N.Y. Wine and Grape Found., 1991. Mem. Winegrape Growers Am. (pres.), N.Y. State Wine Grape Growers (sec.-treas.). Republican. Died Jan. 1, 2007.

STANCIL, IRENE MACK, family counselor; b. St. Helena Island, Sept. 29, 1938; d. Rufus and Irene (Wilson) Mack; m. Nesby Stancil, Dec. 29, 1968; 1 child, Steve Lamar. BA, Benedict Coll., 1960, CUNY, 1983; MA, New World Bible Coll., 1984; SSD, United Christian Coll., 1985; cert., Mercy Coll., 1993. Supr. City of New York; tchr. local bd. edn., SC; supr, case worker, counselor City of New York. Mem. Am. Ctr. for Law & Justice. Died Dec. 13, 2006.

STANDISH, WILLIAM LLOYD, retired federal judge; b. Pitts., Feb. 16, 1930; s. William Lloyd and Eleanor (McCargo) S.; m. Marguerite Oliver, June 12, 1963; children: Baird M., N. Graham, James H., Constance S. BA, Yale U., 1953; LLB, U. Va., 1956. Bar: Pa. 1957, U.S. Supreme Ct. 1967. Assoc. Reed, Smith, Shaw & McClay, Pitts., 1957—63, ptnr., 1963—80; judge Ct. Common Pleas Allegheny County, Pitts., 1980—87, US Dist. Ct. (western dist.) Pa., Pitts., 1987—2002, sr. judge, 2002—15. Solicitor Edgeworth Borough Sch. Dist., 1963-66. Bd. dirs. Sewickley (Pa.) Cmty. Ctr., 1981-83, Staunton Farms Found., mem., 1984-2002, trustee, 1984-92; corporator Sewickley Cemetery, 1971-87; trustee Mary and Alexander Laughlin Children's Ctr., 1972-90, Leukemia Soc. Am., 1978-80, We. Pa. chpt., 1972-80, We. Pa. Sch. Deaf, 1983—, YMCA of Sewickley, 1996—; bd. trustees Pitts. Theol. Sem., 2001—2010, emeritus, 2011- Recipient Pres. award, Leukemia Soc. Am., 1980. Mem. ABA, Pa. Bar Assn., Allegheny County Bar Assn., Am. Judicature Soc., Acad. Trial Lawyers Allegheny County (treas. 1977-78, bd. dirs. 1979-80), Am. Inn of Ct. (Pitts. chpt. 1993—). Died Jan. 1, 2015.

STAPLEY, EDWARD OLLEY, retired microbiologist, research administrator; b. Bklyn., Sept. 25, 1927; s. Charles Olley and Helen Beulay (Mirrielees) S.; m. Helen Alberta Strang, July 2, 1949; children: Susan Jean, Robin Lynn, Janice Carol. BS, Rutgers U., 1950, MS, 1954, PhD, 1959. Microbiologist Merck & Co., Inc., Rahway, N.J., 1950-58; sr. rsch. microbiologist Merck Sharp & Dohme Rsch. Labs., Rahway, 1959-64, rsch. fellow in microbiology, 1965-68, asst. dir. microbiology, 1969-74, dir. microbiology, 1974-77, sr. dir. microbiology, 1978-83, exec. dir. microbiology, 1984-92. Vis. biologist program speaker Am. Inst. Biol. Scis., 1969-72. Mem. editorial bd. Jour. of Antibiotics, 1974—. Mem. Spotswood (N.J.) Bd. of Edn., 1965, pres., 1967-68. Named to Selman A. Wakeman Lectureship, Theobald Smith Soc., 1990. Fellow Am. Acad. Microbiology, Sigma Xi; mem. Soc. for Indsl. Microbiology (speaker's bur. 1968-71). Republican. Episcopalian. Achievements include 28 patents; discovery of many antibiotics and microbial chemotherapeutics including Fosfomycin, Cephamycin, Thienamycin, Avermectin and Mevinolin. Home: Metuchen, NJ. Died Jan. 23, 2007.

STARKEY, ROBERT ERIC, minister; b. Dunbar, W.Va., July 16, 1939; s. Dorsey Remington and Edith Cora (Nichols) S.; m. Rebecca Joyce McDaniel, Aug. 19, 1960 (div. Oct. 1984); children: Cindy Alice, Lynda Carol; m. Margie Lorraine Farr, July 13, 1985. MusB, W.Va. State Coll., 1961; MEd, Trinity U., 1966; MA, U. Detroit, 1973; D of Ministry, Drew U., 1980. Ordained to ministry Ch. of God (Anderson, Ind.), 1967; lic. psychologist, Mich. Min. 1st Ch. of God, El Paso, 1966-70, Evanswood Ch. of God, Troy, Mich., 1970-83, 1st Congl. Ch., Port Huron, Mich., from 1985. Chmn. gen. assembly Ch. of God, Lansing, Mich., 1980-82; mem. Nat. Inter-Religious Task Force on Criminal Justice, 1990-95; mem. adv. bd. Victim Offender Reconciliation Project, 1997—. Contbr. articles to mags. Adv. bd. Port Huron Area Sch. Dist., 1989; chmn. CROP WALK, Port Huron, 1989—. 1st lt. USAF, 1962-66. Home: Fort Gratiot, Mich. *Henry Drummond echoed the words of the Apostle Paul when he said that love is the greatest thing in the world. Jesus said love would be the identifying mark of His disciples. Ultimately, our love relationships with God and each other determine our success and happiness and our usefulness in God's kingdom.* Died June 8, 2007.

STARKS, FRED WILLIAM, chemicals executive; b. Millford, Ill., Aug. 16, 1921; s. Otis Earl and Evelyn Viola Starks; m. Minnie Jane Reynolds, Sept. 4, 1946; children: David F., Steven J., Daniel J. BS, U. Ill., 1943, MS, 1947; PhD, U. Nebr., 1950. Supr. US Rubber Co., Torrance, Calif., 1943—44, DuPont, Niagara Falls, NY, 1950—57; pres. Starks Assocs., Inc., Buffalo, 1957—89, chmn., from 1989. Spl. lectr. U. Buffalo, 1959—63. Lt. (j.g.) USNR, 1944—46. Avery fellow, 1948—49, USPHS fellow, 1949—50. Mem.: Am. Inst. Chemists, NY Acad. Sci., Am. Chem. Soc., Chemists Club, Buffalo Club, Cosmos, Sigma Xi. Achievements include patents in field. Deceased.

STARNES, PAUL MALVINE, retired state legislator; b. Chattanooga, Dec. 31, 1934; s. James Albert and Helen (Hudgens) S.; m. Mary Grace Feezell, Aug. 1, 1964. AA, Hiwassee Coll., 1955; BA, Tenn. Wesleyan Coll., 1957, LittD, 1981; MEd, U. Chattanooga, 1961. Tchr. McMinn County High Sch., Athens, Tenn., 1957-59, East Ridge High Sch., Chattanooga, 1959-64; dean of students Hiwassee Coll., Madisonville, Tenn., 1964-69; coord. spl. projects Hamilton County Dept. Edn., Chattanooga, 1969-71; asst. prin. East Ridge Jr. High Sch., Chattanooga, 1971-74; mem. Dist. 31 Tenn. House of Reps., 1972—90; community rels. officer Hamilton County Dept. Edn., Chattanooga, 1974-77, asst. to supt., bd. info. officer, 1977-91, dir. div. student svcs. and ednl. devel., 1991—93. Mem. NEA, American Assn. Sch. Adminstrs., Nat. Sch. Public Rels. Assn., Tenn. Assn. Sch. Suprs. & Adminstrs., Tenn. Edn. Assn., East Tenn. Edn. Assn. (pres. twice), Hamilton County Edn. Assn., Phi Delta Kappa. Meth. Home: Chattanooga, Tenn. Died Jan. 9, 2015.

STAUFFER, STANLEY HOWARD, retired newspaper and broadcasting executive; b. Peabody, Kans., Sept. 11, 1920; s. Oscar S. and Ethel L. (Stone) S.; m. Suzanne R. Wallace, Feb. 16, 1945 (div. 1961); children: Peter, Clay, Charles; m. Elizabeth D. Priest, July 14, 1962 (div. 1991); children: Elizabeth, Grant; m. Madeline A. Sargent, Nov. 27, 1992. AB, U. Kans., 1942; DHL (hon.), Washburn U., 2001. Assoc. editor Topeka State Jour., 1946-47; editor, pub. Santa Maria (Calif.) Times, 1948-52; rewrite and copy editor Denver Post, 1953-54; staff mem. AP (Denver bur.), 1954-55; exec. v.p. Stauffer Publs., Inc., 1955-69; gen. mgr. Topeka Capital-Jour., 1957-69; pres. Stauffer Comm., Inc., 1969-86, chmn., 1986-92. Past pres. Topeka YMCA; past chmn. adv. bd. St. Francis Hosp.; past chmn. Met. Topeka Airport Authority; trustee William Allen White Found., Midwest Rsch. Inst., Washburn U. Endowment Assn, Bd. Visitors Menningen Found. With USAAF, 1942-45. Named Chpt. Boss of Yr. Am. Bus. Women's Assn., 1976, Outstanding Kans. Pub. Kappa Tau Alpha, 1980, Legion of Honor De Molay, Topeka Phi of Yr., 1971 Mem. Kans. Press Assn. (past pres.), Inland Daily Press Assn. (past dir.), Air Force Assn. (past pres. Topeka), Kans. U. Alumni Assn. (past dir.), Kans. C. of C. and Industry (past chmn.), Def. Orientation Conf. Assn. (dir.), Topeka Country Club (past dir.), Top of the Tower Club, La Quinta (Calif.) Country Club, Masons (32d deg.), Arab Shrine, Phi Delta Theta (past chpt. pres.), Sigma Delta chi (past chpt. pres.). Episcopalian (past sr. warden). Died Nov. 2, 2006.

STEARNS, ROBERT LELAND, curator; b. LA, Aug. 28, 1947; s. Edward Van Buren and Harriett Ann (Hauck) S.; m. Sheri Roseanne Lucas, Oct. 2, 1982 (div. 1994); children: Marissa Stearns Kuzirian, Caroline Lucas Stearns; m. Richard Kozar, July 11, 2014 Student, U. Calif., San Diego, 1965-68, BFA, 1970; student, Calif. Poly. State U., San Luis Obispo, 1968. Asst. dir. Paula Cooper Gallery, NYC, 1970-72; prodn. asst. Avalanche Mag., NYC, 1972; co-founding dir., founding pres. The Kitchen Ctr. for Video and Music, NYC, 1972-77; dir. Contemporary Arts Ctr., Cin., 1977-82; dir. performing arts Walker Art Ctr., Mpls., 1982-88; founding dir. Wexner Ctr. for Arts, Ohio State U., Columbus, Ohio, 1988-92; mem. Wexner Ctr. Found., Columbus, 1990-92; dir. Stearns & Assocs./Contemporary Exhbn. Svcs., Columbus, Ohio, 1992—2000; sr. prgm. dir. Arts Midwest, Mpls., 1998—2005; cons. curator Franklin Park Conservatory, Columbus, Ohio, 2005—09, Bellevue Arts Mus., Wash., 2008—09; project mgr. Palm Springs Art Mus., 2009. Adj. prof. dept. art, assoc. dean Coll. Art, Ohio State U., Columbus, 1988-92; lectr. Sch. of the Art Inst. Chgo., 2002; cons. McKnight Found., St. Paul, 1978, Jerome Found., 1978-79; chmn. Artists TV Workshop, N.Y.C., 1976-77; bd. dirs., chmn. Minn. Dance Alliance, Mpls., 1983-88; bd. dirs. Haleakala, Inc., N.Y.C.; mem.

various panels Nat. Endowment for Arts, Washington, 1977-91; mem. pub. arts policy Greater Columbus Arts Coun., 1988-90; adv. coun. Bklyn. Acad. Music, 1982-84, Houston Grand Opera, 1991-93; fundraising cons. Art for Life Columbus AIDS Task Force, 2000-2006; mem. Advocacy Com. Ballet Met, Columbus, 2003-2006; former mem. bd. dirs. Architecture and Design Coun. Palm Springs Art Mus., La Quinta Arts Found., Coachella Valley Art Alliance; co-founder, Arts Oasis; former mem., vice-chair Palm Springs Pub. Arts. Comm. Author, editor: Robert Wilson: Theater of Images, 1980, Photography and Beyond in Japan, 1995; author: Mexico Now: Point of Departure, 1997, Robert Wilson: Scenografie e Installazioni, 1997, Illusions of Eden: Visions of the American Heartland, 2000, Aspirations: Toward a Future in the Middle East, 2001, The View from Here: Recent Pictures from Central Europe and the American Midwest, 2002, Russel Wright: Living with Good Design, 2006, Bending Nature, 2008; editor: Dimensions of Black, 1970; exec. editor: Breakthroughs: Avant Garde Art in Europe and America 1950-1990, 1991; author and editor numerous catalogues. Mem. gov.'s residence com. State of Ohio, 2004—06. Decorated chevalier Order of Arts and Letters (France); Travel grantee Jerome Found., 1986, Japan Found., 1991, Can. Cultural Ministry, 2004. Died Dec. 3, 2014.

STEDMAN, MYRTLE LILLIAN, artist; b. Charleston, Ill., Feb. 5, 1908; d. Edward Bullard and Myrtie (Harrell) Kelly; m. Wilfred Henry Stedman, Nov. 15, 1928 (dec. 1950); children: Thomas Wilfred, Wilfred Donald. Student, Mus. Fine Arts, Houston, 1927-34, Art Student's League, NYC, 1979-80. Fine artist, illustrator Stedman Studio, Houston, 1927—34. Designer, builder Tesuque Home Builder, 1952-87. Prin. works include preservation of historic homes Adobe Morada, Taos, N.Mex., 1954, redesign of Tesuque Elem. Playground and Parking Lot, 1974; author, illustrator: The Way Things Are Or Could Be: A New Consciousness, 1996, Ongoing Life, 1993, Artists in Adobe, 1993, A House Not Made With Hands, 1993, Rural Architecture of Southern Colorado and Northern New Mexico, Featuring Barns, Fences, and Corrals, 1990, Of One Mind, 1974, Adobe Architecture, 1936-73, 86, Adobe Remodeling and Fireplaces, 1973, 86, Of Things to Come, 1998, The Ups and Downs of Living Alone in Later Life, 2000. Mem. bd. Las Tres Villas, Tesuque, 1973-83, Santa Fe (N.Mex.) Water Basin, 1970-80, Pojoaque (N.Mex.) Water Bd., 1960's; mem. County Recreational Adv. Com., Santa Fe, 1960's. Recipient Visual and Lit. Arts award N.Mex. Arts Commn., Mayor's award City of Santa Fe, 1994, Old Santa Fe Assn. award, 1993, Watercolor awards Houston Fine Arts Mus., 1933, N.Mex. Gov.'s award for Excellence in the Arts Art/Arch., 1997; named Living Treasure Santa Fe Networks, 1985. Mem. PEN/USA/West, Mus. N.Mex. Found. (life), Inst. Noetic Scis. (charter), Women in the Arts Nat. Mus. (charter), Santa Fe Hist. Found., Old Santa Fe Assn. Avocations: keeping scrapbooks, photography, walking, reading. Died Apr. 21, 2007.

STEFONIC, LARRY EUGENE, food products distribution executive; b. Deadwood, SD, Feb. 9, 1939; s. Martin J. and Reba Lavern (Wallace) S.; m. W. Christine Tranner, Aug. 15, 1964 (div.); children: Reba Dee, Larry Martin; m. Anna Ruth Sue Peterson, Oct. 10, 1979; children: John, Jim, Ann. Sales mgr. Keebler Co., Pocatello, Idaho, 1964-72; pres. Lions Candy Corp., Pocatello, 1972-83, Orawheat Distributorship, Pocatello, 1977-81, Capitol Distbg., Inc., Boise, from 1987-; ind. real estate broker Pocatello, 1983-87. Owner Gooding (Idaho) Trailer Ct., 1974-76, Coll. Market, Pocatello, 1974-76, Jefferson St. Market, Pocatello, 1974-76,Clarks Cookies, Pocatello, 1981-83, Pretzel Factory, Pocatello, 1982-86, Bengel Auto, Pocatello, 1983-84. With USN, 1957-61. Mem. Nat. Candy Wholesaler Assn., Idaho Candy and Tobacco Assn. (v.p.). Roman Catholic. Avocations: fishing, hunting, skiing, motor bikes. Home: Boise, Idaho. Died July 13, 2007.

STEHR, JOHN WILLIAM, minister; b. Lake City, Minn., May 31, 1911; s. John William Stehr and Paulina Sprikes; m. Martha Ann Hass, June 22, 1937; children: Harriet Alice, Phyllis Ann, John William Jr., Richard Allen, Ronald Eugene. Student, Concordia Coll., St. Paul, 1925-31, Concordia Sem., St. Louis, 1931-35; BA in History, Valparaiso U., 1933. Missionary Blackduck Tenstrike (Minn.) Mission, 1936-40; pastor Red Lake Falls, Wylie Plummer, Minn., 1940-48, St. John Luth. Ch., Wood Lake, Minn., 1948-54, Trinity Luth. Ch., Waconia, Minn., 1954-81; part-time pastoral worker Trinity and neighboring congregations, from 1981. Counsellor Carver County Cir., Minn. South Dist., 1968-74; Bible Class Leader Westview Retirement, Waconia, 1985—, Bible Study Leader Trinity Srs. for Christ, 1985—, cir. dir. Luth. Ch. Extension Fund, Minn. South Dist., 1985—. Founder Luth. High Sch., Mayer, Minn., 1962; zone chmn. Luth. Laymens League, 1970-87; Minnetonka rep. to Saints Alive; Growing Ever Serving, 1990; chmn. State Ret. Pastors and Tchrs. Conf., 1990; bd. dirs. Minn. South Dist. Named Outstanding Sr. Citizen Carver County, Minn., 1988. Republican. Home: Waconia, Minn. *I am convinced that the most rewarding activity of my life has been to bring the comfort of the Gospel to young and old, to see them walking in the truth, and to hear an expression of gratitude for this blessing.* Died Feb. 24, 2007.

STEINER, ULRICH ALFRED, chemist; b. Bombay, Mar. 26, 1922; came to the U.S., 1957; s. Jakob Alfred and Mathilde (Gass) S.; m. Ingeborg Maria Lauber, June 2, 1949 (dec. 1959); children: Gabriele Gertsch, Beat Ulrich; m. Claire Beulah Koss, July 15, 1961 (dec. Nov. 2000). Diploma in chemistry, Federal Inst. Tech., Zurich, Switzerland, 1946, Dr. SC, 1948. Rsch. chemist Emser Werke, Domat/Ems, Switzerland, 1948-53, asst. dept. head, 1953-57; rsch. chemist Union Carbide, Boundbrook, N.J., 1957-86; rsch. assoc. Amoco Performance Products, Inc., Boundbrook, N.J., 1986-91; ret. Patentee in field. Recipient Thomas Alva Edison Patent award R&D Coun. N.J., 1992. Home: Boulder, Colo. Died Apr. 8, 2007.

STEINHAUER, GENE DOUGLAS, psychology educator; b. Fresno, Calif., Jan. 1, 1944; s. Wilbert Peter and Rosie Nielsen (Askov) S.; m. Linda Bol, July 7, 1985; children: Christopher William, Karlie Elizabeth. BA, Calif. State U., Fresno, 1972, MA, 1974; PhD, U. Mont., 1977. Asst. prof. SUNY, Oswego, 1977-78; assoc. prof. Calif. State U., Fresno, 1978-86, assoc. prof. psychology Hayward, from 1987. Pres. Artificial Behavior Inc., Fresno, 1985—; cons. Fresno County Schs., 1980—, NIH Council on Children, Media, Mass., 1980-81; grant reviewer NSF, Washington, 1978—. Author: Artificial Behavior, 1986, Computer Assisted Self Observation, 1988, Artificial Behavior II, 1994; contbr. articles to profl. jours., chpts. to books. Served with USAF, 1961-65. NIMH fellow, 1975-77. Mem. Soc. Computer Simulation, Sigma Xi. Home: Brentwood, Calif. Died Apr. 16, 2007.

STEMBERG, THOMAS GEORGE, retail office supply store executive; b. Newark, Jan. 18, 1949; s. Oscar Michael and Erika (Ratzer) Stemberg; m. Maureen Sullivan Stemberg (div. 1987); m. Dola Davis Hamilton, Sept. 24, 1988 (div.); m. Katherine Chapman; children: William, Michael, Clyde, Thomas McDermott, Rylan Hamilton, Darrell Williams stepchildren: Madison Eisler, Meghan O'Gara, MacKenzie O'Gara. Student, Am. Internat. Sch., Vienna, 1962-67; AB, Harvard U., 1971, MBA, 1973. With Jewel Cos., Star Market, Cambridge, Mass., 1973-82, v.p. sales and merchandising, 1982; sr. v.p. sales and merchandising First. Nat. Supermarkets, Hartford, Conn., 1982-83, pres., 1983-84; pres., CEO, co-founder Staples, Inc., Newton, Mass., 1986-88, chmn., CEO Westborough, Mass., 1988-98, CEO Framingham, Mass., 1999—2002, chmn., 1999—2005, chmn. emeritus, 2005—15; co-founder Zoots, 1998—2015, Olly Shoes, 2001—15; venture ptnr. Highland Capital Partners (Highland Consumer Fund), Lexington, Mass., 2005—15. Bd. dirs. PETsMART Inc., from 1988, Polycom Inc, from 2002, NASDAQ Stock Market Inc., from 2002, CarMax Inc., from 2003. Visiting com. Harvard Bus. Sch.; bd. overseers Boston Symphony Orch.; exec. coun. Archdiocese Boston Inner City Scholarship Fund. Baker scholar Harvard Bus. Sch., 1973; R.H. Macy fellow Harvard Bus. Sch., 1973; 1996 Torch of Liberty award, Anti-Defamation League, 1996. Home: Chestnut Hill, Mass. Died Oct. 23, 2015.

STENZEL, FRANZ ROBERT, JR., insurance broker, financial consultant; b. Durham, NC, Apr. 7, 1934; s. Franz R. (dec.) and Marion L. (Mason-Haskell) (dec.) S.; m. Margaret Ellen Manns, July 15, 1967 (div. June 1981); children: Franz III, Laura, Nicholas; m. Cecelia L. Dorminey, Dec. 6, 1997. Grad., Columbia Prep. H.S., Portland, Oreg., 1952. CLU; ChFC. Agt., mgr. Equitable N.Y., LA, 1960-89, ret., 1989; broker, mgr., gen. agt. Trans-Am. Life, LA, 1960-89, ret., 1989; ins. broker, mgr., gen. agt., fin. cons. Stenzel Fin. Svcs., LA, 1960-81, Arroyo Grande, Calif., from 1981. With U.S. Army, 1953-55. Mem. Elks. Republican. Episcopalian. Avocations: travel, reading, tennis, foreign languages. Home: Nipomo, Calif. Died Jan. 25, 2007.

STEPHENS, CHARLES FRANCIS, publishing executive; b. St. Louis, Aug. 19, 1928; s. Charles Frances and Virginia (Smith) S.; m. Barbara Jane Lane; children: Charles Daniel, Christine Lisa, Caroline. BS, Washington U., St. Louis, 1951. V.p. Stephens Bus. Forms, St. Louis, 1950-78; pres. C.F. Stephens Enterprises, St. Louis, from 1978. Mem. Rep. Club, St. Louis. Home: Saint Louis, Mo. Died Dec. 1, 2006.

STEPHENS, JERRY EDWARD, law librarian; b. Dodge City, Kans., June 13, 1945; s. Carl Edward and Mona Grace (McCarty) S.; m. Karen Yvonne Woods, May 27, 1967; children: Shannon Lea, Amy Lyn, Adam Ryan. BA, U. Okla., 1967, MLS, 1968; JD, U. Kans., 1976. Bar: Kans. 1976, U.S. Dist. Ct. Kans. 1976. Libr. North Tex. State U., Denton, 1968-70; law libr. U. Kans. Law Sch., Lawrence, 1970-76; rsch. libr. Kans. Supreme Ct. Law Libr., Topeka, 1976-78; rsch. analyst Kans. Legis. Rsch. Dept., Topeka, 1978-82; sales rep. West Pub. Co., St. Paul, 1982-86; regional dir. Grolier Ednl. Corp., Danbury, Conn., 1986-89; law libr. U.S. Ct. Appeals (10th cir.), Oklahoma City, from 1990. Mem. Am. Assn. Law Librs., Spl. Librs. Assn. Democrat. Unitarian Universalist. Avocations: gardening, sailing, racquetball. Home: Edmond, Okla. Died Jan. 16, 2007.

STEPP, GUSS, JR., human resource executive; b. Detroit, Nov. 25, 1931; s. Guss Earon and Carrie Beatrice (Chapman) S.; m. Gwendolyn Jimmie Bolden, July 5, 1956; 1 child, Ronald. AAS, Devry Tech. Inst., Chgo., 1955; BEE, Syracuse U., 1969, MBA, 1974. With General Electric Co., Syracuse, N.Y., 1956-68, adminstr. equal employment opportunity, 1968-69, mgr. personnel and equal employment opportunity, 1969-72, specialist edn. and tng., 1972-73, specialist salary adminstrn., 1973-74, specialist orgn. and manpower, 1974-76; asst. dir. employee relations Stauffer Chemical Co., Westport, Conn., 1976-86; pres. Stepp, Inc., Wilton, Conn., from 1986; v.p. Derocher Assocs., Ltd., Bridgeport, Conn., 1986-89; pres. Stepp Inc., Wilton, Conn., 1989-90; cons. Pitney Bowes, from 1990, dir. employment, from 1990. Cons. Pitney Bowes, Regional Learning Ctr. Author numerous poems. Pres. The Renaissance Fund, Inc., Norwalk, Conn., 1987—, Renaissance Inc., 1982-86; bd. dirs. Bridgeport Public Edn. Fund; bd. advisors United Negro Coll. Fund. Served to sgt. USAF, 1949-53, Korea. Recipient Scove award State of Conn., 1986. Mem.: U. Coll. of Syracuse U. Alumni (co-founder, 1972-74). Episcopalian. Avocations: poetry, astronomy, marathon running and swimming. Home: Wilton, Conn. Died Aug. 7, 2007.

STERNBERG, JOHN RICHARD, retired minister; b. Chgo., Feb. 12, 1920; s. Max Arthur and Bertha Heneritta (Pretzel) S.; m. Pearl Dorothy Wilshusen, Feb. 4, 1945; children: Richard Nolan, Rhoda Jane Sternberg Becker. AB, Concordia Coll., 1940; BD, Concordia Sem., 1945. Pastor Grace & Trinity Luth. Chs., Neligh and Elgin, Nebr., 1945-50, Meml. Luth. Ch., Vancouver, Wash., 1950-60, St. Peter Luth. Ch., Schaumburg, Ill., 1960-90, ret., 1990. Mem. religion dept. Concordia Coll., Portland, Oreg., 1957-58; chmn. Bd. Christian Edn., Chgo., 1963-90. Mem. Olde Schaumburg Commn., Schaumburg, 1978-90, Hist. Soc., Schaumburg, 1960-90. Mem. Clerge Coun. of Schaumburg, Rotary (Schaumburg chpt.). Home: Portland, Oreg. *Be grateful for your church, community and country in life of service. Whatever your hand finds to do, do with all your might for the welfare of your fellow man and the glory of God.* Died Nov. 23, 2006.

STERNGLASS, ERNEST JOACHIM, physicist, researcher; b. Berlin, Sept. 24, 1923; came to U.S., 1938; s. Joseph and Ella (Jacobsohn) S.; m. Marilyn Seiner, Sept. 21, 1957 (dec. 2004); children—Daniel, Susan. B.E.E., Cornell U., 1944, MS in Engring. Physics (McMullen fellow), 1951, PhD in Engring. Physics, 1953. Research physicist U.S. Naval Ordnance Labs., White Oak, Md., 1946-52; adv. physicist Westinghouse Research Labs., Pitts., 1952-67; prof., dir. radiol. physics Sch. Medicine, U. Pitts., 1967-75, prof. radiol. physics, cons. radiol. imaging div., dept. radiology, 1975-84; prof. emeritus, 1984—2015; adj. prof. dept. history and philosophy of sci. Ind. U., Bloomington, 1979-83. Vis. prof. Inst. Theoretical Physics, U. Paris, 1957-58, Inst. for Theoretical Physics, Stanford U., 1966-67 Author: Low-Level Radiation, 1972, Secret Fallout, 1981; contbr. writings to profl. publs. Served with USN, 1945-46. Westinghouse research fellow, 1957-58 Fellow Am. Phys. Soc.; mem. Radiol. Soc. N.Am., Am. Assn. Physicists in Medicine (com. on diagnostic radiology 1969-71), Fedn. Am. Scientists (chmn. Pitts. chpt. 1962-63), AAAS, Am. Astron. Soc., Philosophy of Sci. Assn., Sigma Xi., Eta Kappa Nu. Democrat. Jewish. Research in field. Died Feb. 12, 2015.

STEVENS, DOROTHY FROST, retired television producer; b. Rockville Centre, NY, June 18, 1924; d. George Sanford Frost and Theodora Barbara Emmanuel; m. Kenneth Hayes Stevens, Aug. 14, 1949 (dec. Apr. 1967). BA, Stanford U., Calif., 1945. Tchr. adult edn., San Jose, Calif., 1945—49; various offices Folk Dance Fedn. Calif., 1945—61; tchr. Los Gatos H.S. Dist., Calif., 1946—51; various positions Calif. State. E.D.D., 1966—82; host, prodr., exec. prodr. Cupertino (Calif) Sr. TV Prodns., 1983—2001; ret., 2001. Prodr.: The Better Part, 1983—2001. Recipient Civic Svc. award, City of Cupertino, 1984, Vol. award, Calif. Parks & Recreation Soc., 1988, Golden Rule award, J.C. Penney, 1993, Outstanding Prodr. award, City of Cupertino, 1997, Ripp King Meml. award, Bay Area Cable Excellence, 1998; named Vol. of Yr., Retired Sr. Vol. Program Santa Clara County, 1994. Presbyterian. Avocations: travel, reading, sewing, gardening. Home: San Jose, Calif. Died Apr. 1, 2007.

STEVENS, RICHARD FRANCIS, retired university official; b. Hammond, Ind., May 19, 1927; s. Richard Morton and Catherine (Dillon) S.; m. Constance Gay, Oct. 15, 1976; children: Richard F., Kathrine H., Patrick D. BFA, Goodman Theatre, 1959; MFA, Carnegie-Melllon U., 1960. Entertainment dir. Dept. U.S. Army, Fed. Republic Germany, 1963-68; Vietnam, 1968-69; Ft. Carson, 1969-70; dir. Richmond (Ind.) Civic Theatre, 1970-71; dir. pub. occasions Ohio U., Athens, 1971-92; ret., 1992. Actor play, Eden on the River, 1987-88; dir. various plays, 1963-76. Cons. Ohio Arts Coun., 1972-80; pres. Hocking Valley Arts Coun., 1973-76. With U.S. Army, 1954-56. Mem. Ohio Regional Assn. Concerts (pres. 1987-89), Assn. Performing Arts Presentors. Avocations: reading, writing, golf. Home: Athens, Ohio. Died Jan. 27, 2007.

STEVERS, WAYNE EUGENE, mathematics educator; b. Olive Branch, Ill., Sept. 26, 1937; s. Loren David and Elva Corlena (McKee) S.; m. Linda Mae Searles, June 30, 1960; children: David Wayne, Katherine Ann. B of Music Edn., So. Ill. U., 1970, MS of Music Edn., 1983. Educator Goreville (Ill.) Elem. Sch., 1960-62, Vienna (Ill.) Elem. Sch., 1962-63, Metropolis (Ill.) City Schs., 1963-74; agt. Prudential Ins. Co., Peducah, Ky., 1974-83; educator Massac County Unit Sch. Dist., Metropolis, from 1983. Choir dir. 1st UnitedMeth. Ch., Metropolis, 1988—; coach basketball JE Jefferson Sch., Metropolis, 1984-89. Mem. NEA, Nat. Coun. Tchrs. Math., Ill. Edn. Assn., Ill. Coun. Tchrs. Math. (presenter, So. Ill. Math. Tchrs. Assn. Methodist. Avocation: golf. Home: Metropolis, Ill. Died June 9, 2007.

STEWART, DALE LYNN, management consultant; b. Indpls., May 13, 1954; s. Paul John and Delores Loretta S.; m. Joy Ann Jenness, June 14, 1986; 1 child, Nicholas Allen. AS, St. Leo Coll., Fla., 1975, BBA, 1981; M. Bus., WEstern Internat., Phoenix, 1983. Lic. project mgmt. profl. Ptnr. S & C Constrn., Virginia Beach, Va., 1973-79; sr. engr. Bechtel Power, Gaithersburg, Md., 1979-80; supr. Ariz. Pub. Svc., Phoenix, 1980-83; owner DLS & Assocs., Loveland, Colo., from 1983. V.p. edn. Project Mgmt. Inst., Denver, 1988-92, chpt. pres., 1992-97, chmn. bd.; assoc. prof. Metro. Coll., Denver, 1988-89. Commr. Planning/Zoning Bd., Loveland, 1991-92; mem. Young Reps., Phoenix, 1981. With USN,

1972—. Mem. Am. Nuclear Soc., Am. Mgmt. Assn. Roman Catholic. Avocations: construction, computer programming, investing, hiking, camping. Home: Loveland, Colo. Died Jan. 22, 2007.

STEWART, JOHN WESTCOTT, physics educator, researcher; b. NYC, Nov. 15, 1926; s. John Quincy and Lilian Vaughan (Westcott) S.; m. Anne Smith, Aug. 26, 1954; 1 child, Christine. AB, Princeton U., NJ, 1949; MA, Harvard U., 1950, PhD, 1954. Rsch. fellow U. Va., Charlottesville, 1954-56, asst. prof., 1956-60, assoc. prof., from 1960, asst. dean, 1970-91. Rsch. fellow U.S. Bur. Standards, Boulder, Colo., 1962-63. Author: The World of High Pressure, 1967; contbr. articles to profl. jours. With U.S. Army, 1945-46. Fellow Am. Phys. Soc.; mem. AAUP, Am. Assn. Physics Tchrs., Sigma Xi. Home: Charlottesville, Va. Died June 20, 2007.

STEWART, JUNE, marketing manager; b. Melrose Park, Ill., Mar. 15, 1931; d. Harry John and Stephanie Gary; m. James Thomas Stewart, Sept. 13, 1953; children: Sue Anna Scribner, Linda, James, John. BA in Journalism, Northeastern U., 1973. Reporter Bugle Publ., Niles, Ill., 1970; editor Reminder Publ., Wheeling, Ill., 1970-73; reporter copy desk Topics Newspapers, Palatine, Ill., from 1975; area rep. Picwick Publs., Park Ridge, Ill., 1976; ad merchandiser Walgreens, Deerfield, Ill., 1976-77; publisher, editor GS Publs., Mt. Prospect, Ill., 1983-84; correspondent Lerner Life Newspapers, Skokie, Ill., 1978-85; acting pres. Gary Stewart HVAC, Mt. Prospect, 1985; editorial dir., mktg. mgr. heating and air conditioning Gary Stewart Advt., from 1984. Reporter Paddock Publs., Arlington Heights, Ill., 1966-69; founder Stewart Cosmetics Co., Wheeling, 1973-76. Editor Nomda mag.; author, editor Hist. Grandma's Recipes, 1984; producer community access TV programming, 1989-91. Chmn. Cub Scouts com., den mother Cub Scouts, Boy Scouts Am., Wheeling; chmn. mental health Bell Ringer March; vol. community producer Community Columnist Series, 1989, 90. With USAF, 1952-54. Mem. Chgo. Computer Soc., Nat. Writer's Union. Home: Wheeling, Ill. Died May 28, 2007.

STEWART, REBEKAH BROOKE, retired small business owner; b. Sycamore, Ga., Oct. 29, 1923; d. Robert Elijah and Ester (Cannon) Brooke; m. Robert E. Stewart (dec. July 1984); children: Richard Lamar, Elizabeth Anne. Student, Armstrong State Coll., Savannah, Ga., 1955-59. Co-owner, asst. mgr. Stewart's Inc., material handling equipment company, Savannah, 1955-95; ret., 1995. Mem. Nat. Assn. Women in Constrn. (past pres. Savannah). Baptist. Home: Lilburn, Ga. Died Oct. 31, 2006.

STEWART, VERNON EDWIN, music minister; b. Pampa, Tex., Sept. 5, 1938; s. Vernon Elias and Amy (Hancock) S.; m. Celia Ann Gomillion, Jan. 11, 1957; children: Timothy Edwin, Charmaine Louise Stewart Smith, Joy Beth Stewart Potts. Student, Frank Phillips Jr. Coll.; grad. sacred music, Bapt. Bible Coll., 1961; BS in Edn., S.W. Mo. State U., 1966; MusM, Pitts. State U., Kans., 1972. Minister music Cherry St. Bapt. Ch., Springfield, Mo., 1959-64, 67-71, Blueridge Bapt. Temple, Kansas City, Mo., 1965-66; prof. music Bapt. Bible Coll., Springfield, Mo., 1966-72, 75-79; headmaster Hollywood (Fla.) Christian Sch., 1972-75; rep., choral cons. Good Life Pub., Scottsdale, Ariz., 1979-86; pres. First Link of Atlanta, Morrow, Ga., 1986-89; minister of music Mt. Zion Bapt. Ch., Jonesboro, Ga., from 1989. Music cons. Good Life Publs., Scottsdale, 1979-86; trainer Leadership Dynamics, Atlanta, 1984—; part-time minister of music Mt. Zion Bapt. Ch., 1982-88. Dep. Mounted Sheriff's Posse, Springfield, 1976-79; staff advisor overcomers outreach Susbstance Abuse Recovery Group, Jonesboro, 1989—. Republican. Baptist. Avocations: hunting, fishing, golf. Home: Morrow, Ga. Died May 26, 2007.

STEWART, VIRGINIA L. CAUDLE, retired cosmetology educator; b. Winston-Salem, NC, Aug. 8, 1925; d. William Henry and Katie (Sullivan) C.; m. Troy Thomas Stewart, June 22, 1946 (dec. Sept. 1991). Diploma, La Mae Beauty Coll., 1945; student, Winston-Salem Tchrs. Coll., 1953-55; BA, Nat. Inst. Cosmetology, 1969, MA, 1973, A doctorate, 1975. Cert. N.C. Dept. Pub. Instruction. Tchr. cosmetology Winston-Salem/Forsyth County Schs., 1976-90. Leader vocat. club Vocat. Indsl. Careeer Ctr., Winston-Salem, 1987-90. Field worker United Fund, Winston-Salem, 1962-70; bd. dirs. YMCA Glade St. Winston-Salem, 1960-68; leader troop 10 Dreamland Ch. Girl Scouts U.S. , Winston-Salem, 1948-52; youth choir dir. Dreamland Bapt. Ch., Winston-Salem, 1946-52, Mars Hill Bapt. Ch., Winston-Salem, 1953-72; clk. Carver Sch. East Ward Precint, Winston-Salem, 1968-70; treas. Carver/Monticello Community Club 1966-68; treas. Mt. Zion Bapt. Handbell Choir, 1989-91; sec. Mt. Zion Bapt. Chancel Choir, 1988-91; trustee Mt. Zion Bapt. Ch., 1993. Recipient plaque Carver/Monticello Community Club, 1986, award Mt. Zion Bapt. Handbell Choir, 1991, Mt. Zion Bapt. Chancel Choir, 1991, Past Matron's lapel pin Sisters of Bivouac Chpt 530, 1949, 6-1st prize ribbons, 3-2d prize ribbons, 1-3d prize ribbon Dixie Classic Fair, 1991, 4-1st prize ribbons, 3-2d prize ribbons Dixie Classic Fair, 1992. Mem. Nat. Beauty Culturists' League (trustee 1960-66, plaque 1966), Winston-Salem Beauticians #2 (pres. 1965-70, Beautician of Yr. trophy 1967, plaque 1970), Best Yet Flower/Garden Club (pres. 1976-80, plaque 1980), Fedn. Garden Clubs N.C. (4th dist. directress 1993, chairperson 4th dist. flower show 1993). Democrat. Avocations: swimming, gardening, basketball, singing, piano. Home: Winston Salem, NC. Died Aug. 6, 2007.

STICKEL, FREDERICK A., retired publishing executive; b. Weehawken, NJ, Nov. 18, 1921; s. Fred and Eva (Madigan) S.; m. Margaret A. Dunne, Dec. 4, 1943 (dec. 2008); children: Fred A., Patrick F., Daisy E. Medici, Geoffrey M., James E., Bridget A. Otto Student, Georgetown U., 1939-42; BS, St. Peter's Coll., 1943. Advt. salesperson Jersey Observer daily, Hoboken, NJ, 1945-51; retail advt. salesperson Jersey Jour., Jersey City, 1951-55, advt. dir., 1955-66, pub., 1966-67; gen. mgr. Oregonian Pub. Co., Portland, Oreg., 1967-72, pres., 1972-86, pub., 1975—2009. Bd. regents U. Portland; adv. bd. Portland State U., St. Vincent's Hosp.; bd. dirs. Portland Rose Festival Assn., United Way Oreg.; chmn. Portland Citizens Crime Commn. Capt. USMC, 1942-45. Mem. Assn. for Portland Progress (dir.), Portland C. of C. (dir.), Oreg. Newspaper Pubs. Assn. (past pres.), Pacific N.W. Newspaper Assn. (past pres.), Newspaper Assn. Am., University Club, Multnomah Athletic Waverley Country Club, Arlington Club, Rotary. Died Sept. 27, 2015.

STIDHAM, DAVID GORDON, energy management consultant; b. Phila., June 17, 1938; s. Amos Cole Jr. and Alma Margaret (Siegmann) S.; m. Gladys Luciele, July 14, 1960 (div. Nov. 1974); m. Sheila Mary Inman, Dec. 3, 1977; children: Scott James, Mark Adam, David Glenn, Bryan Matthew. Student, St. Mary's Coll., Md., 1956-58; ASET, Drexil Inst. Tech., 1964; PhD (hon.), U. Pa., 1965; MBA, Kennedy We. U., 1991. Chmn. Jr. C. of C., Pasco, Fla., 1966-67; v.p. Telesystems Inc., Orlando, Fla., 1970-74, Masterlink Communications, Miami, Fla., 1978-82, Energy Mgmt. Cons., Raleigh, N.C., from 1991; sr. engr. Q.S.I. Space Transport Ops., Santa Maria, Calif., 1982-87; fin. aid cons. Larry Conti Assoc., Inc., Durham, N.C., 1989-90; prin. NSDA, Doluth, Ga., 1990-91; regional sales mgr. Utility Rsch. & Recovery, Greenville, SC, from 1991. Author: (handbook) Testing Telephone Power Sub-Systems, 1986. Mem. Rep. Presdl. Task Force, Washington, 1985-88. Recipient Hon. citation Ford Aerospace, 1986, Citizenship award Kiwanis Internat., 1970. Mem. Ind. Telephone Pioneers Am. Episcopalian. Avocations: sailing, electronics. Home: Pittsboro, NC. Died Apr. 27, 2007.

STIEFEL, VERNON LEO, entomology educator; b. Ft. Carson, Colo., June 8, 1961; s. Werner Konrad and Maria (Frodl) S.; children: Jenna Mae, Clara Marie. BS in Botany, Colo. State U., 1983; MS in Entomology, Kans. State U., 1991, PhD in Insect Ecology, 1995. Lab., field asst. dept. weed sci. Colo. State U., Ft. Collins, 1982-84; agrl. intern Land Inst., Salina, Kans., 1985; grad. rsch. asst. Kans. State U., Manhattan, 1989-91. Cons. botanist Autonomous U. Guadalajara, Jalisco, Mex., 1984. Contbr. articles to profl. publs. Mem. Entomol. Soc. Am. (student), Ctrl. States Entomol. Soc. (student), Kans. State U. Rock Climbing Club (treas./officer 1995), Phi Beta Kappa, Sigma Xi, Phi Kappa Phi. Died Dec. 9, 2006.

STIGWOOD, ROBERT COLIN, film, television, radio and theater producer; b. Adelaide, Australia, Apr. 16, 1934; came to Eng., 1956; s. Gordon and Gwendolyn (Burrows) S. Student, Sacred Heart Coll., Adelaide. Worked as copywriter for advt. agy., Adelaide; opened talent agy. London, 1962; liquidated firm, 1965; became bus. mgr. for group Graham Bond Orgn.; became co-mng. dir. NEMS Enterprises, 1967; prin. Robert Stigwood Orgn., 1967; formed RSO Records, 1973; dir. Polygram, 1976; co-founder (with Rupert Murdoch) R&R Films, 1979. Founder Music for UNICEF. 1st ind. record producer in Eng. with release of single Johnny Remember Me; producer: films, including Jesus Christ Superstar, 1973, Tommy, 1975, Survive, 1976, Saturday Night Fever, 1977, Grease I, 1978, Grease II, 1982, Moment By Moment, 1978, Sergeant Pepper's Lonely Hearts Club Band, The Fan, 1981, Times Square, 1980, Gallipoli, 1980, Staying Alive, 1983, Evita, 1996; stage musicals in Eng. and U.S., including, Hair, Oh! Calcutta, The Dirtiest Show in Town, Sweeney Todd, Pippin, Jesus Christ Superstar, Evita, Grease, Saturday Night Fever; TV producer in Eng. and U.S.; co-prodns. include The Entertainer (dramatic spl.); All in the Family (series), The Prime of Miss Jean Brodie (dramatic series). Recipient Tony award for best musical (Evita); named Internat. Producer of Yr. ABC Interstate Theatres, Inc., 1976. Mem. Royal Bermuda Yacht Club. Clubs: Royal Bermuda Yacht. Avocations: yachting, tennis. Died Jan. 4, 2016.

STILLWAGGON, JAMES GEORGE, maritime consultant, ship pilot; b. NYC, Jan. 25, 1920; s. Walter J. and Sarah (McGrath) S.; m. Rosemary Gronachan, June 7, 1941; children: James M., John W., Eileen M. Diploma, St. Augustine High Sch. Tug capt. Russell Towing/Valentine Transp., NYC, 1941-56; ship pilot, pres. Interport Pilots Agy., Inc., NYC, 1956-90; pres. Pilotage Cons., Inc., NYC, from 1980. Vice chmn. vessel traffic svc. adv. com. USCG, 1970—; mem. N.Y. Harbor Ops. Com., 1975—; lectr., expert witness in field. Mem. Soc. Marine Cons. (exec. com.), Nautical Inst. London, Coun. Am. Master Mariners. Republican. Roman Catholic. Avocations: golf, teaching. Home: New Hyde Park, NY. Died Aug. 4, 2007.

STILWELL, RONALD EDWARD, manufacturing executive; b. Utica, NY, Feb. 20, 1948; s. Elmer Kenneth and Esther Irene (Hunziker) S.; m. Nancy Allyn Rademan, June 6, 1971; children: Carolyn Esther, Kathryn Alexa Rademan. BA in Polit. Sci., U. Rochester, 1970; MS in Adminstrn., Hartford Grad. Ctr., 1979. Field underwriter Mut. of N.Y. Ins., Rochester, 1970-71; credit/collection analyst Marine Midland Bank, Rochester, 1971-72; from credit trainee to v.p. mil. mktg. and adminstrn. Firearms div. Colt Industries, Hartford, Conn., 1972-90; exec. v.p., pres. Colt's Mfg. Co., Inc., Hartford, from 1990. Bd. dirs. Albano Ballet Co., Hartford, 1984—, Big Bros./Big Sisters, Hartford, 1978-85; pres. Waterfront Heights Assn., Coventry, Conn., 1979-81; treas. Oak Grove Assn., Coventry, 1973-80. Mem. Nat. Contract Mgmt. Assn. (pres. 1980-81), Am. Def. Preparedness Assn. (exec. bd. 1986-90, chair small arms 1987-89), Nat. Shooting Sports Found. (bd. dirs. 1990—), Am. Shooting Sports Coalition (bd. dirs. 1990—). Republican. Baptist. Avocations: travel, riding, skiing. Home: Hartford, Conn. Died Mar. 1, 2007.

STIMPSON, RITCHIE PLES, retired military officer; b. Black Mountain, NC, Mar. 22, 1917; s. David Ples and Lydia Hinson Stimpson; m. Marjorie Spruce, May 3, 1942; children: Ritchie P. Jr., David Fleming. BS in Physics, Furman U., 1940. Commd. 2nd lt. USAF, 1941, advanced through grades to col., 1953; squadron comdr. 13th Tactical Reconnaissance Squadron, 1942-44; dir. ops. 24 Composite Wing, Borinquen Field, P.R., 1946-47; liaison officer Armed Forces Spl. Weapons Project to Strategic Air Commd., Offutt AFB, Nebr., 1950-52; dir. plans and negotiations Joint U.S. Asst. Adv. Group, Madrid, 1957-59; staff officer Joint Chiefs of Staff, Washington, 1960-61, Weapons Sys. Evaluation Group/Office of Sec. of Def., 1964-67; comdt. Air Force ROTC detachment Auburn (Ala.) U., 1967-71; ret. USAF, 1971. Owner Ritch Stimpson Co., Inc., College Station, Tex., 1975-82; ind. writer, Dallas, 1982-93. Author: The Protestant Church and Bible Disregard the Truth, 1989, "Is It True?" Answers to Questions About the Bible, 1992. Decorated Commendation medals (2), Identification Badge, Outstanding Unit award. Mem. Air Force Assn., Greater Dallas Ret. Officers Assn., Greater Dallas Ret. Officers Assn. Investment Club, Oakridge Country Club, Furman U. Paladin Club. Republican. Methodist. Avocations: golf, travel, reading, bridge, gardening. Home: Garland, Tex. Died Apr. 8, 2007.

STIMSON, JUDITH NEMETH, lawyer; b. Hammond, Ind., Oct. 30, 1942; d. John G. and Pearl (Lemish) Nemeth; m. Clare M. Stimson, June 5, 1965 (div. Oct. 1981); children: Justin D., Seth C., Sarah L.; m. John R. Conolly, Dec. 30, 1982. BS, St. Mary of the Woods Coll., Terre Haute, Ind., 1964; MS in Clothing and Textiles, Ind. U., 1968; JD, Ind. U., Indpls., 1981. Bar: Ind. 1982. Tchr. pub. schs., Ind., 1964-79; of counsel Buck, Berry, Landau & Breunig, Indpls., 1982-94; with Stimson & Assocs., Indpls., 1994—2004; of counsel Broyles, Kight & Ricafort L.L.P., Inpls., from 2004. Instr. Ind. Continuing Legal Edn. Forum, Indpls., 1983—. Co-editor: Indiana Practitioner Series, Alternative Dispute Resolution, 1995. Named one of Outstanding Young Women in Am., 1974. Fellow: Indpls. Bar Assn. (chmn. family law sect. 1985), Ind. Bar Assn. (assoc.; ADR chmn.1994); mem.: ABA, Ind. State Bar Found., Ind. State Bar Assn. (bd. govs. 1999—2001), Assn. Family and Conciliation Cts. Avocation: travel. Home: Indianapolis, Ind. Died June 24, 2007.

STINGER, KENNETH FRANK, lawyer, professional association executive; b. Trenton, NJ, Apr. 12, 1941; s. Frank and Mary Elisabeth Stinger; m. Eloise V. Czarda, June 8, 1963; children: K. Clinton, Laura Louisa, Emily Elizabeth. BA, Rutgers U., 1963; LLB, George Washington U., 1966. Bar: D.C. 1967, U.S. Supreme Ct. Tax and labor issues mgr. Met. Washington Bd. Trade, 1964-67; exec. mgr. consumer affairs com. C. of C. of U.S.A., Washington, 1967-73; exec. mgr. Am. Movers Conf., Arlington, Va., 1973-76; dir. govt. affairs Am. Trucking Assn., Washington, from 1976; exec. sec. Coalition Against Regressive Taxation, Washington, from 1986. Tchr. Practicing Law Inst., N.Y.C., 1976; mgr. Truck Operators Non-Partisan Com., Washington, 1978-89. Contbr. articles to profl. publs. Recipient Cert. of Appreciation, Practicing Law Inst., 1976. Mem. ABA, D.C. Bar Assn., Transp. Practitioners Assn. (editor Motor Carrier), Nat. Dem. Club, Capitol Hill Club, Pi Sigma Alpha. Episcopalian. Home: Fairfax, Va. Died Jan. 3, 2007.

STOCKER, JOHN EDWARD, federal agency administrator; b. Fairbury, Nebr., Oct. 27, 1924; s. Roy Oscar Stocker and Anna (Augusta) Velebil; m. Gabrielle Erica Gabriel. BS in Fgn. Svc., Georgetown U., 1948; postgrad., London Sch. Econs., 1950-51. Assoc. dir. longshore and harbor workers' compensation U.S. Dept. Labor, Washington, 1970-79; asst. to dir. Office Workers' Compensation Programs, Washington, 1979-85; docent Woodrow Wilson House, Washington, 1986-91. Vol. agy. liaison White House, Washington, 1985-91, vol. comments office, 1993—; vol. Decatur Houst, Washington, 1991-93. Mem. Commonwealth, Nat. Trust. Avocation: history. Home: Arlington, Va. Died Dec. 26, 2006.

STOCKNER, ROBERT DAVID, broadcast executive; b. Memphis, July 21, 1958; s. Aaron Joseph and Jean Lenore (Schiff) S. Student, La. State U., 1977-79. Radio announcer Sta. WAFB-FM, Baton Rouge, 1979-80; program dir. Sta. WHMD-FM, Hammond, La., 1980-81; radio announcer Baton Rouge Broadcasting, 1981-84; pres., chief exec. officer Metro Info. Svc., Inc., Baton Rouge, from 1984, Sound Solutions Inc., Baton Rouge, from 1991. Mem. Baton Rouge Jaycees, 1987, Baton Rouge Concert Band, Rivercity Symphonic Band. Recipient degree of chevalier Order of DeMolay. Mem. Sales & Mktg. Execs. Internat. (Marketer of Yr. 1989), Baton Rouge Bus. Network, Baton Rouge C. of C. Lodges: Demolay (Grand Comdr. in East of La. Ct. 1988-89). Jewish. Avocations: jazz music, pipe and record collecting. Home: Baton Rouge, La. Died Feb. 2, 2007.

STODDARD, ALLAN LEE, writer, musician; b. Perry, Okla., Sept. 1, 1944; s. Leland Luellan and Lena Ethel Stoddard; m. Katherin Ann Gilpen, Apr. 28, 1974; m. Diana Elizabeth Doyle, Apr. 21, 1973 (div. Sept. 1973). Musician The Intruders, Okla., 1959—67; lead guitar The Greenmen,

1965; band leader The Shirelles, 1967—71; prin., owner Cherokee Heart Pub. Co., Shawnee, Okla., from 1967. Musician The Drifters, 1966—67, The Olympics, 1966—67; band leader Mickey Hargitay, 1966—67, 1970, Wolfman Jack, 1966—67; prodr. for Mel Fender and Ashley Fender. Author: Single Pick, 1973 (featured Billboard mag., 1973), Lady You've Been On My Mind, 1973 (featured Billboard mag., 1973), Oklahoma Trade Tokens & Baggage Checks, 2003, Oklahoma Territory and Indian Territory Collectibles, 2003; appearances on (TV program) Danny's Day, Okla. City Channel 4, 1978, featured with Roy Clark, Dub Taylor, and Johnny Gimble (Roy Clark jam) Enid Quail Hunt, 1979; music video writer: Hit and Run Lover, 1990; contbr. articles to profl. jours. including Nat. Treasure Pubs. Vol. Alan Lee Christmas benefit party mentally handicapped children Enid State Sch., 1972; vol. Oklahoma Cystic Fibrosis Found., 2003; musician benefit fundraiser REST Homeless Shelter, Oklahoma City, 2000; mem. Nat. D-Day Mus., New Orleans, 2006; bd. dirs. Washington Irving Mus., Stillwater, Okla., from 2000. With Nat. Guard, 1961—67. Mem.: Philbrook Art Mus., Western Heritage Assn. Republican. Baptist. Avocations: metal detecting, treasure hunting, writing songs, collecting rare indian painting. Home: Shawnee, Okla. Died Nov. 18, 2006.

STODDARD, BRANDON, retired broadcast executive; b. Bridgeport, Conn., Mar. 31, 1937; s. Johnson and Constance (Brandon) S.; married, Feb. 1984; children: Alexandra, Brooke. BA in American Studies, Yale U., 1958; postgrad., Columbia U. Law Sch., 1963. Program asst. Batten, Barton, Durstine and Osborn, NYC, 1960-61; program ops. supr. Grey Advt., NYC, 1962-66, dir. daytime programs, 1966, v.p. in charge of radio and television programs, 1968-70; dir. daytime programs ABC-TV, 1970-72, v.p. daytime programs, 1972-74, v.p. motion pictures for television, 1974-79; pres. ABC Motion Pictures, Los Angeles, 1979-85; sr. v.p. ABC Entertainment, 1979-85, pres., 1985-89, ABC Productions, 1989—95. Served with U.S. Army, 1960-61. Named to The Television of Hall of Fame, 2014. Mem. Hollywood Radio and TV Soc., American Film Inst., Acad. Motion Pictures Arts & Sciences Clubs: Bel Air Bay. Episcopalian. Died Dec. 22, 2014.

STOEBUCK, WILLIAM BREES, law educator; b. Wichita, Mar. 18, 1929; s. William Douglas and Donice Beth (Brees) S.; m. Mary Virginia Fields, Dec. 24, 1951; children: Elizabeth, Catherine, Caroline. BA, Wichita State U., 1951; MA, Ind. U., 1953; JD, U. Wash., 1959; SJD, Harvard U., 1973. Bar: Wash. 1959, US Supreme Ct. 1967. Pvt. practice, Seattle, 1959—64; asst. prof. law U. Denver, 1964—67; assoc. prof. U. Wash., Seattle, 1967—70, prof., 1970—95, Judson Falknor prof., 1995—99, prof. emeritus, from 1999; of counsel Karr, Tuttle, Campbell, Seattle, from 1988. Vis. prof. Hastings Coll. Law, 1987, Wash. & Lee U., 1979—80; guest lectr. U. Tubingen, 1996; spkr., cons. in field. Author: Washington Real Estate: Property Law, 1995, 2d edit., 2004, Washington Real Estate: Transactions, 1995, 2d edit., 2004, Basic Property Law, 1989, Law of Property, 1984, 3d edit., 2000, Nontrespassory Takings, 1977, Contemporary Property, 1996, 3d edit., 2008; contbr. articles to profl. jours. Bd. dirs. Cascade Symphony Orch., 1978-83, Forest Park Libr., 1975-80; ch. elder, congregational pres.; mem. City Lake Forest Pk. Planning Commn., 2008-. 1st lt. USAF, 1951—56. Mem. Pacific Real Estate Inst., Am. Coll. Real Estate Lawyers, Wash. State Bar Assn., Assn. Am. Law Schs., Order of Coif, Seattle Yacht Club. Republican. Presbyterian. Avocations: baroque music, boating, history. Home: Lk Forest Park, Wash. Died Nov. 18, 2012.

STOIANOVICH, MARCELLE SIMONE, artist; b. Paris; d. Charles Caffe and Eugenie Le Nieffe; children: Christian, Diana Revson. Student, Coll. Applied Arts, Paris, 1942-46. Book jacket designer Doubleday Edits., NYC, 1954; archeol. draftsperson Smithsonian Inst., Washington, 1962; window decorator Guerlain Perfumes, Paris, 1975; film creditor Am. Films Festival, Deauville, France, 1975; assoc. editor L'Officiel de la Mode, Paris, 1976-81; jeweler Henri Bendel's, NYC, 1983; free-lance artist NYC and Paris, from 1983. Permanent exhibits Venable/Neslage Galleries, Washington; Lithographs, Original Print Collectors Group, N.Y.C., Bibliotheque Nationale, Paris, Zimmerli Art Mus. NJ, Fernand Braudel, Academie Francaise. Mem. Met. Mus., Nantucket Art Assn. Home: Vanves, France. Died 2015.

STOICHEFF, BORIS PETER, physicist, researcher; b. Bitol, Macedonia, June 1, 1924; s. Peter and Vasilka (Tonna) S.; m. Lillian Joan Ambridge, May 15, 1954; 1 child, Richard Peter. BSc, U. Toronto, 1947, MA, 1948, PhD, 1950, DSc (hon.), 1994, U. Skopje, Macedonia, 1981, York U., 1982, U. Windsor, 1989; DSc (hon.), U. Western Ontario, 2007. McKee-Gilchrist postdoctoral fellow U. Toronto, Ont., Canada, 1950-51; postdoctoral fellow NRC Can., Canada, 1951-53, sr. rsch. officer, 1954-64; vis. scientist MIT, 1963-64; prof. physics U. Toronto, Canada, 1964-89, univ prof., 1977-89, univ. prof. emeritus, from 1989, chmn. engring. sci., 1972-77, H.L. Welsh lectr., 1984; sr. fellow Massey Coll., from 1979; exec. dir. Laser and Lightwave Rsch. Ctr., Ont., Canada, 1988-91. Mem. NRC Can., 1977-83; govt. appointee to coun. Assn. Profl. Engr. Ont., 1985-91; vis. sci. Stanford U., 1978; Walter E. Kaskan lectr. SUNY, Binghamton, 1980; Elizabeth Laird Meml. lectr. U. Western Ont., 1985; UK/Can. Rutherford lectr., 1989; v.p. Internat. Union Pure and Applied Physics, 1994-96. Author: Gerhard Herzberg: An Illustrious Life in Science, 2002; contbr. articles to profl. jours. Decorated officer Order of Can., 1982; I.W. Killam scholar, 1977-79; Geoffrey Frew fellow Australian Acad. Sci., 1980. Fellow Royal Soc. Can. (co-fgn. sec. 1995-2000, Henry Marshall Tory medal 1989), Royal Soc. London, Am. Phys. Soc., Optical Soc. Am. (pres. 1976, William F. Meggers award 1981, Frederic Ives medal 1983, Disting. Svc. award 2002), Indian Acad. Sci. (hon.), Macedonian Acad. Sci. and Arts (hon.), Am. Acad. Arts and Sci. (fgn. hon.); mem. Can. Assn. Physicists (pres. 1984, Gold medal 1974). Achievements include development of techniques for high resolution Raman spectroscopy of gases and determination of geometrical structures many molecules; use of lasers in spectroscopic investigations including Brillouin and Raman scattering and two photon absorption; observation of stimulated Raman absorption and stimulated Brillouin scattering resulting in generation of intense hypersonic waves in solids; use of Brillouin spectra to measure elastic constants of rare gas crystals; generation of tunable coherent VUV radiation for use in atomic and molecular spectroscopy. Home: Toronto, Canada. Died Apr. 15, 2010.

STOKES, LOUIS, lawyer, former United States Representative from Ohio; b. Cleve., Feb. 23, 1925; s. Charles and Louise (Stone) S.; m. Jeanette (Jay) Francis, Aug. 21, 1960; children: Shelley Stokes-Hammond, Louis C., Angela, Lorene (Lori). Student, Case We. Res. U., 1946—48; JD, Cleve. Marshall Law Sch., 1953; 26 Honorary Degree. Bar: Ohio 1953. Mem. US Congress from 11th Ohio Dist., Washington, 1969—93, US Congress from 21st Ohio Dist., Washington, 1993—99; sr. counsel Squire, Sanders & Dempsey LLP, Washington, from 1999. Disting. vis. prof. Mandel Sch. Applied Social Scis. Case Western Res. U., 1999-2015. Served with AUS, 1943-46. Decorated Congl. DSM; recipient numerous awards for civic activities including Disting. Svc. award Cleve. br. NAACP; Certificate of Appreciation US Commn. on Civil Rights. Mem. ABA, ACLU, Cleve. Met. Bar Assn., Urban League, American Legion, Masons, Kappa Alpha Psi. Democrat. Achievements include being the first African-American congressman from Ohio. Died Aug. 18, 2015.

STONE, ALFRED WARD, educator; b. Meadville, Pa., Aug. 13, 1925; s. Clifford Alsworths and Freda (Bruehl) S.; m. Dolores Stone, Dec. 1, 1951 (div.); children: Clifford, John, Bonalyn, David; m. Mary L. Girardat, June 1, 1968; 1 child, 1 Scott. BA in Econs., Allegheny Coll., 1950, MEd, 1957; PhD in Psychology, U. Pitts., 1978; postgrad., U. So. Calif., LA, 1979. Phys. boys sec. YMCA, Meadville, 1952-57, state sec. Harrisburg, Pa., 1957-62, acting exec. sec. Allentown, Pa., 1962-63; exec. dir. War on Poverty, C.A.P., Meadville, 1964-67; prof. emeritus psychology dept., co-dir. gerontology program Edinboro (Pa.) U., 1967—93. Host TV program Understanding People, 1970—; chmn. Regional Cmty. Svcs., Inc.; coord. gerontology programs Edinboro U. Bd. dirs. Westbury Meth. Cmty., West Pa. Health Smart; pres., mem. Profl. Assn. of Specialists of Aging, N.W. Pa., 1978-86; dir. programs for children Milkhaus Found. With U.S. Mcht. Marine, USCG, 1943-46, U.S. Army, 1950-52. Mem. APHA, APA, Gerontol. Soc. Am. Avocations: painting, reading, golf. Home: Edinboro, Pa. Died Aug. 14, 2007.

STONE, BERNY (BERNARD LEONARD STONE), former alderman; b. Chgo., Nov. 24, 1927; s. Sidney and Rebecca (Spinka) S.; m. Lois D. Falk, Aug. 28, 1949 (dec. 1995); children: Holly (dec.), Robin, Jay, Ilana, Lori. JD, John Marshall Law Sch., 1952. Claims adjuster State Farm Mutual Automobile Ins. Co., 1952—54; pvt. practice atty., 1955—71; asst. chief dep. sheriff Cook County, Ill., 1971—73; alderman Ward 50 Chgo. City Coun., 1973—2011; vice mayor City of Chgo., 1998—2011. Chmn. bldgs. com. Chgo. City Coun. Zoning chmn. Hood Ave. Civic Improvement Assn., 1954-58; dist. leader American Cancer Soc., 1959; bd. dirs. Congregation Ezras Israel, 1958—, Bernard Horwich Jewish Cmty. Ctr., 1974-78, campaign chmn. govt. agys. div. Jewish United Fund, 1978-79; commr. Northeastern Ill. Planning Commn., 1977-83; mem. Cook County Commn. on Criminal Justice, 1977-82. Recipient Svc. award, Chgo. & Cook County Criminal Justice Commn., 1982, Pub. Svc. award, Assn. Talmud Torahs, 1982, Spl. Recognition award, Landmark Preservation Coun., 1983, Svc. award, Northeastern Ill. Planning Commn., 1983, Jerusalem award, 1996; named Man of Yr., Shomrin Soc., Ill, 1974. Republican. Jewish. Home: Chicago, Ill. Died Dec. 22, 2014.

STONE, DEANNE COHN, not-for-profit developer; b. Hartford, Conn., May 26, 1939; d. Yale and Janet (Stone) Cohn; m. Harvey S. Stone, June 19, 1961; children: Matthew, Alison. BA, Brandeis U., 1961; MS, Lesley Coll., 1991. Cert. tchr. Tchr., Framingham, Mass., 1975-81; exec. dir. Maimonides Sch., Brookline, Mass., 1978-88, Temple Israel, Boston, 1988-90; exec. dir., cons. Found. for Children's Books, Watertown, Mass., 1990-93; dir. devel. Friends of Yemin Orde, 1994-96; nat. dir. women's dept. Coun. of Jewish Fedns., 1996-99; dir. New Eng. region B'nai B'rith, Brighton, Mass., 1999—2001; NE dir. Am. Com. for Weizmann Instit. of Sci., 2001. Cons./trainer in field. Pres. PTA, Dunning Sch., 1970; v.p. LWV, 1968-72; sec., v.p. Combined Jewish Philanthropies/Women's Divsn.; chmn. Working Group Memorandum of Understanding with U.S. and Israel; bd. dirs. Coun. of Jewish Fedns., nat. chmn. women's divsn., 1987; bd. dirs. United Jewish Appeal/Women's Divsn. Avocations: reading, facilitating and speaking to women's groups. Home: Framingham, Mass. Died Jan. 28, 2007.

STONE, EARL LEWIS, JR., soil scientist; b. Phoenix, NY, July 12, 1915; s. Earl Lewis Sr. and Alison C. (Green) S.; m. Margaret Elizabeth Hodgman, June 7, 1941 (div.); children: Earl III, Jeanne, Nathan; m. Jean LaChance, Jan., 10, 1998. BS, N.Y. State Coll. Forestry, 1938; MS, U. Wis., 1940; PhD, Cornell U., 1948; DS (hon.), SUNY, Syracuse, 1989. Field asst., jr. forester USDA So. Forest Exptl. Sta., New Orleans, 1940-41; from asst. prof. to prof. Cornell U., Ithaca, N.Y., 1948-79, prof. emeritus, from 1979; vis. prof. U. Fla., Gainesville, 1979-82, adj. prof., from 1982. Vis. assoc. prof. U. Philippines, Los Banos, 1958-60; mem. com. scientists USDA, 1977-81; mem. Bikini Atoll Rehab. Com., 1983-89. Sgt. USAAF, 1942-45, PTO. Am. Swiss Found. fellow, 1954, Fulbright Found. fellow, 1962, Bullard fellow Harvard U., 1969-70. Fellow AAAS, Soil Sci. Soc. Am., Am. Soc. Agronomy, Soc. Am. Foresters (Barrington Moore award 1973); mem. Ecol. Soc. Am. Home: Gainesville, Fla. Died July 23, 2007.

STONE, ROBERT ANTHONY, writer; b. NYC, Aug. 21, 1937; s. C. Homer and Gladys Catherine (Grant) S.; m. Janice G. Burr, Dec. 11, 1959; children: Deidre M., Ian A. Student, NYU, 1958-59; Stegner Fellow, Stanford U., 1962. Editorial asst. NY Daily News, NYC, 1958-60; writer Nat. Mirror, NYC, 1965-67. Mem. faculty Johns Hopkins U., Balt., 1993-94; free-lance writer London, Hollywood, Calif., South Vietnam, 1967-71; writer-in-residence Princeton U., 1971-72; faculty Amherst Coll., 1972-75, 77-78, Stanford U., 1979, U. Hawaii-Manoa, 1979-80, Harvard U., 1981, U. Calif.-Irvine, 1982, NYU, 1983, U. Calif.-San Diego, 1985, Princeton U., 1985, endowed chair Tex. State U. San Marcos, 2010-11 Author: (novels) A Hall of Mirrors, 1967, Dog Soldiers, 1974 (Nat. Book award 1975), A Flag for Sunrise, 1981, Images of War, 1986, Children of Light, 1986, Outerbridge Reach, 1992, Bear and His Daughter, 1997, Damascus Gate, 1998, Bay of Souls, 2003, Fun with Problems, 2010, Death of the Black Haired Girl, 2013; (memoir) Prime Green: Remembering the Sixties, 2007; (screenplays) WUSA, 1970, (with Judith Rascoe) Who'll Stop the Rain, 1978; contbg. author: Best American Short-stories, 1970, 88. Served in USN, 1955-58. Recipient William Faulkner prize, 1967, John Dos Passos prize for lit., 1982; Award in Lit. American Acad. & Inst. Arts & Letters, 1982, grantee, 1988-92; Guggenheim fellow, 1971, NEH fellow, 1983. Mem. PEN (exec. bd.) Home: Key West, Fla. Died Jan. 10, 2015.

STONE, ROBERT JOSEPH, public relations executive; b. Kingston, NY, Aug. 23, 1920; s. Morris and Hattie (Mann) S.; m. Shirley S. Siegel, Apr. 11, 1947; children: Barbara, Judith. Student, Rider Coll., 1946-47. Dir. pub. relations Schenectady (N.Y.) Union Star, 1948-50, Trentonian, Trenton, N.J., 1950-51, Civil Def. div. N.J. Dept. Def., Trenton, 1951-52; pub. relations specialist Ford MotorCo., NYC, 1953-58; div. pub. relations dir. ITT, Paramus, 1958-60; dir. fin. pub. relations dept. Ruder & Finn, Inc., NYC, 1960-63; v.p. ops. Monroe B. Scharff & Co., Inc., NYC, 1963-65; sr. v.p., dir. eastern ops. Daniel J. Edelman, Inc., NYC, 1965-70, exec. v.p., 1970-71; pres. Edelman Investor Relations, NYC, 1970-71; pres., chief exec. officer Infoplan Internat., Inc., NYC, 1971; dir. corp. com. Singer Corp., NYC, 1973-75; pres. Bus. Orgns., Inc. subs. Carl Byoir & Assocs., Inc., NYC, 1975-77; v.p. corp. communications and pub. affairs Turbodyne Corp. and Worthington Compressors, Inc., Mpls., 1977-79; dir. communications McGraw-Edison Co., Rolling Meadows, Ill., 1979-81; sr. v.p. Hill and Knowlton, Inc., NYC, 1981-92; prin. Dilenschneider Group Inc., NYC, from 1992. Served with AUS, 1942-46. Mem. Pub. Relations Soc. Am., Internat. Pub. Relations Assn. Clubs: Overseas Press Am. Home: Irvington, NY. Died Dec. 27, 2006.

STONER, MICHAEL C., network specialist; b. San Francisco, Oct. 27, 1967; s. William C. and Lani (Bain) S. Grad., A.A. Stagg H.S., Stockton, Calif., 1986. Cert. CNA. Owner CADS, Stockton, 1989-90; v.p. Accelerated Computer Tng., LA, from 1990. CFO Christopher Street West, L.A., 1994. With USN, 1986-90. IEEE (assoc.). Democrat. Died June 27, 2007.

STOOKEY, STANLEY DONALD, physicist, chemist; b. Hay Springs, Nebr., May 23, 1915; s. Stanley Clarke and Hermie Lucille (Knapp) Stookey; m. Ruth Margaret Watterson, Dec. 26, 1940 (dec.); children: Robert Alan, Margaret Ann, Donald Bruce. BS in Chemistry and Math., magna cum laude, Coe Coll., Cedar Rapids, Iowa, 1936; MS in Chemistry, Lafayette Coll., Easton, Pa., 1937; PhD in Phys. Chemistry, MIT, 1940; LLD (hon.), Coe Coll., 1959, DSc (hon.), 1963, Alfred U., 1984. Mem. rsch. staff Corning Glass Works, Corning, NY, 1940—87, dir. fundamental chem. rsch., 1970—87, ret., 1987. Author: Journey to the Center of the Crystal Ball: An Autobiography, 1985, Explorations in Glass: An Autobiography, 2000; contbr. articles to profl. jours. Recipient John Price Wetherill award, Franklin Inst., Phila., 1953, 1962, Beverly Myers Achievement award, Ednl. Found. Ophthalmic Optics, 1973, Phoenix award for contbn. to glass industry, 1975, Achievement award, Indsl. Rsch. Inst., 1979, Disting. Inventor award, Ctrl. NY Patent Law Assn., 1984, World Materials Congress award, 1988, Nat. Medal Tech., The White House, 1986, 1994, Wilelm Eitel medallion for excellence in silicate sci., 1993; named Inventor of Yr. award, George Wash. U., 1970; named to The Nat. Inventors Hall of Fame, 2010. Fellow: American Inst. Chem. Engineers, American Ceramic Soc. (life Ross Coffin Purdy award 1960, Toledo Glass & Ceramic award 1964, E.C. Sullivan award 1971, Samuel Giejsbeek award 1982); mem.: NAE, Brit. Soc. Glass Tech., American Chem. Soc. (Creative Invention award 1971), Sigma Xi. Republican. Methodist. Achievements include discovery of Fotoform glass which can be photochemically etched into precise and detailed structures and when overheated becomes harder, stronger and higher in electrical resistivity, resulting in the first glass-ceramic; invention of CorningWare, a unique pyroceramic glass cookware resistant to thermal shock that can be used directly on the stovetop; photosensitive glass, a crystal clear glass in which microscopic metallic particles can be formed into a picture or image by exposure to short wave radiations such as ultraviolet light; development of photochromic glass used to make ophthalmic lenses that darken and fade with bright light or lack of. Home: Pittsford, NY. Died Nov. 4, 2014.

STORER, TODD CLEMENT, retired petroleum engineer; b. Pueblo, Colo., Nov. 9, 1922; s. Todd C. and Esther Mathilda (Olson) Storer; m. Jessie Hope Dean, Oct. 24, 1944 (div. June 1978); children: Todd C., Nancy Storer Yang; m. Doris M. McKinney Perry; 1 stepchild, James N. Perry; 1 child, Vivian Storer Shields. Grad. in petroleum engring., Colo. Sch. Mines, 1947. With Amoco Prodn. Co. and predecessors, Chgo., 1947—84, mgr. prodn. sys., 1984. Contbr. articles to profl. jours. Served with C.E. US Army, 1943—46. Mem.: Soc. Petroleum Engrs. of AIME, Data Processing Mgmt. Assn. Republican. Episcopalian. Home: Tulsa, Okla. Died Dec. 19, 2006.

STOTTS, WENDI LE, construction executive; b. Oceanside, Calif., Sept. 29, 1966; d. Daniel Gary and Carla Jean (Byrum) S. AA in Gen. Studies, Palomar Coll., 1989; BA in Bus. Mgmt., U. Phoenix, 1993. Field asst. C.E. Wylie Constrn. Co., San Diego, 1986-87; project coord. Soltek of San Diego, 1987-88; project adminstr. Diversified Turnkey Constrn. Co., National City, Calif., 1988-89, asst. project engr., 1989-90; asst. project mgr. Soltek Gen. Contractor, San Diego, 1990-91; project mgr. Soltek Pacific, San Diego, from 1991, mktg. dir., from 1997. Co-chmn. quality steering com. Soltek Gen. Contractor, 1994-95, chmn. computer com., 1995, strategic planning com., 1996; chmn. mktg. com. Soltek Pacific, 1997. Vol. Feral Cat Coalition, San Diego, 1996-97, H.S. Girls' LaCrosse, San Diego, 1996. Recipient Orchid award AIA, 1994, 96, 97. Mem. Nat. Assn. Women in Constrn., Assoc. Gen. Contractors (edn. com. 1993-94), Soc. Mktg. Profl. Svcs. Avocations: scuba diving, skydiving, travel, jet skiing, reading. Home: San Diego, Calif. Died Apr. 17, 2007.

STOUT, RICHARD ALFRED, insurance executive; b. Long Branch, NJ, Apr. 18, 1927; s. Jones Rutherford and Hannah (Bennett) S.; m. Nancy Anne Brasch, May 1, 1954; children: Richard E., William R., Susan P., David A. BBA, So. Meth. U., 1950. CLU, Pa. Sec. Continental Ins. Co., NYC, 1953-70; v.p. Internat. Group Plans, Inc., Washington, 1970-77; chmn. ConsumersUnited Life Ins. Co., Washington, 1972-77; pres. Protectogon, Inc., Rockville, Md., from 1978. Home: Rockville, Md. Died Jan. 21, 2007.

STRACK, HAROLD ARTHUR, retired electronics executive, military officer, financial consultant, musician, writer; b. San Francisco, Mar. 29, 1923; s. Harold Arthur and Catheryn Jenny (Johnsen) S.; m. Margaret Madeline Decker, July 31, 1945 (dec.); children: Carolyn, Curtis, Tamara (dec.). Student, San Francisco Coll., 1941, Sacramento Coll., 1947, Sacramento State Coll., 1948, U. Md., 1962, Indsl. Coll. Armed Forces, 1963. Commd. 2d lt. USAAF, 1943; advanced through grades to brig. gen. USAF, 1970; comdr. 1st Radar Bomb Scoring Group Carswell AFB, Ft. Worth, 1956-59; vice comdr. 90th Strategic Missile Wing SAC Warren AFB, Cheyenne, Wyo., 1964; chief, strategic nuclear br., spl. studies group Joint Chiefs of Staff, 1965-67, dep. asst. to chmn. JCS for strategic arms negotiations, 1968; comdr. 90th Strategic Missile Wing SAC Warren AFB, Cheyenne, 1969-71; chief Studies, Analysis and Gaming Agy. Joint Chiefs Staff, Washington, 1972-74, ret., 1974; v.p., mgr. MX Peacekeeper Program v.p. strategic planning Northrop Electronics Divsn., Hawthorne, Calif., 1974-88; ret., 1988. 1st clarinetist, Cheyenne Symphony Orch., 1969-71. Mem. Cheyenne Frontier Days Com., 1970-71. Decorated D.S.M., Legion of Merit, D.F.C., Air medal, Purple Heart, Presdl. citation, Army, Air Force and Joint Svc. Commendation medals. Mem. Inst. Nav., Am. Def. Preparedness Assn., Air Force Assn., Aerospace Edn. Found., Am. Fedn. Musicians, Orde Pour le Merite, Cheyenne Frontier Days "Heels", Incline Village Crystal Bay Vets. Group. Home: Incline Village, Nev. *The precepts which have guided me recognize the dignity of the individual and human rights. I believe that living by the Golden Rule contributes to the quality of life by making us better and more useful citizens while favorably influencing others. Integrity, ideals, and high standards reinforce one's own character. While taking pride in accomplishment, show gratitude for opportunity and humility for success. Lead by example and always do your best. Service to humanity and country is the highest calling, and the satisfaction of a job well done, approbation, respect and true friendship are one's greatest rewards.* Died Sept. 15, 2014.

STRAND, MARK, poet; b. Summerside, PEI, Can., Apr. 11, 1934; came to U.S., 1938. s. Robert Joseph and Sonia (Apter) S.; m. Antonia Ratensky, Sept. 14, 1961 (div. June 1973); 1 dau., Jessica; m. Julia Rumsey Garretson, Mar. 15, 1976; 1 son, Thomas Summerfield. BA, Antioch Coll., 1957; BFA, Yale, 1959; MA, U. Iowa, 1962. Instr. English U. Iowa, 1962-65; asst. prof. Mt. Holyoke Coll., 1967; assoc. prof. Bklyn. Coll., 1971-72; Bain-Swiggett lectr. Princeton, 1973; Hurst prof. poetry Brandeis U., 1974-75; prof. U. Utah, 1981-93; U.S. poet laureate Library of Congress, Washington, 1990-91; prof. Johns Hopkins U., 1994—97; Andrew MacLeish Disting. svc. prof. U. Chgo., 1997—2005; prof. English & comparative literature Columbia U., NYC, 2005—14. Fulbright lectr. U. Brazil, Rio de Janeiro, 1965-66; adj. assoc. prof. Columbia U., 1969-72; vis. prof. U. Wash., 1968, 70, U. Va., 1977, Wesleyan U., 1979, Harvard U., 1980; vis. lectr. Yale, 1969-70, U. Va., 1976, Calif. State U., Fresno, 1977, U. Calif., Irvine, 1979. Author: Sleeping with One Eye Open, 1964, Reasons for Moving, 1968, Darker, 1970, The Story of Our Lives, 1973 (Edgar Allan Poe award Acad. Am. Poets 1974), The Sargeantville Notebook, 1974, The Monument, 1978, Elegy for My Father, 1978, The Late Hour, 1978, Selected Poems, 1980, The Planet of Lost Things, 1982, The Night Book, 1983, Mr. and Mrs. Baby and Other Stories, 1985, Rembrandt Takes a Walk, 1986, William Bailey, 1987, The Continuous Life, 1990, Dark Harbor, 1993, Hopper, 1994, Blizzard of One, 2000 (Pulitzer Prize), Man and Camel, 2006; Editor: The Contemporary American Poets, 1968, New Poetry of Mexico, 1970, 18 Poems from Quechua, 1971, The Owl's Insomnia, 1973, The Best American Poetry 1991, The Golden Ecco Anthology, 1994; co-author: 89 Clouds, 1999; co-editor: Another Republic: Seventeen European and South American Writers, 1976, The Art of the Real, 1983, Traveling in the Family, 1987; translator: Souvenir of the Ancient World, 1976. Recipient award American Acad. & Inst. Arts & Letters, 1975, Utah Governor's award in Arts, 1992, Bobbitt Nat. prize for poetry, 1992, Bollingen prize for poetry Yale U. Libr., 1993; Fulbright scholar in Italy, 1960-61; Ingram Merrill Found. grantee, 1966; Nat. Endowment for Arts grantee, 1967-68, 78-79, 86-87; Rockefeller Found. grantee, 1968-69; Guggenheim fellow, 1975-76; Acad. American Poets fellow, 1979; MacArthur Found. fellow, 1987; Pulitzer Prize in Poetry, Blizzard of One, 1999, Wallace Stevens prize, 2004, Gold medal in Poetry Acad. Arts & Letters, 2009 Fellow Acad. American Poets; mem. American Acad. & Inst. Arts & Letters. Home: New York, NY. Died Nov. 29, 2014.

STRANDBERG, JOHN WILLIAM, advertising executive; b. Dagus Mines, Pa., July 4, 1923; s. Sigfred William and Teckla (Swanson) S.; m. Madeline Oates, 1949 (div. 1975); children: Kristin, Keith; m. Karen Clause, June 28, 1975; step-children: Kristin, Susan, Frank. BS in Edn., U. Pa. at Ind., 1949; postgrad., U. Pitts., 1952. Tech. editor Owens-Corning Fiberglas, Toledo, 1951-54; account exec. Fuller & Smith & Ross, Pitts., 1954-57; dir. mktg. Eljer Plumbingware, Pitts., 1957-60; account exec. McCann Erickson, NYC, 1960-63; ptnr., mgr. The Communicators, NYC and Toledo, Ohio, 1963-68; ptnr., v.p. client svcs. Widerschienl Strandberg, 1968-73; pres., owner Widerschienl/Strandberg, Toledo, 1973-81; sr. account supr. Lauerer Markin Gibbs, Inc., Maumee, Ohio, 1981-88, dir. client svcs., 1988-91. Tchr. U. Toledo, 1973-76; cons., free-lance, Toledo, 1983-91; owner John Strandberg Mktg. Comms., Toledo, 1991—. Sgt. USMCR, 1942-45. Mem. Toledo Advt. Club, Inverness Club. Republican. Methodist. Home: Edmond, Okla. Died Nov. 9, 2006.

STRANDBERG, MALCOM WOODROW PERSHING, physicist; b. Box Elder, Mont., Mar. 9, 1919; s. Malcom and Ingeborg (Riestad) S.; m. Harriet Elisabeth Bennett, Aug. 2, 1947 (dec.); children— Josiah R.W., Susan Abby, Elisabeth G., Malcom B. S.B., Harvard Coll., 1941; PhD, M.I.T., 1948. Research asso. M.I.T., Cambridge, 1941-48, asst. prof. physics, 1948-53, asso. prof., 1953-60, prof., 1960-88, prof. emeritus, from 1988. Author: Microwave Spectroscopy, 1954; patentee in field. Fellow Am. Phys. Soc., Am. Acad. Arts and Scis., IEEE, AAAS; mem. Am. Assn. Physics Tchrs. Episcopalian. Died May 3, 2015.

STRANG, JOHN LAWRENCE, human services professional; b. Quincy, Mass., Jan. 31, 1951; s. Wilbur Hyler and Margaret Mary (Knaide) S.; m. Marjorie Frances Corey, Dec. 13, 1975; children: Erin Marie, Jessie Leah, Stacy Ann. AAS, Dutchess Community Coll., Poughkeepsie, NY, 1978; BS, Univ. Maine, 1981; MSW, U. Conn., 1986. Lic. clin. social worker. Dir. chem. dependency recovery prog. V.A. Adminstrn., Portland, Maine, 1987-89, Togus, Maine, from 1989. Cons. Smith House, Portland, 1990—. With U.S. Army, 1971-74, Fed. Republic of Germany. Home: Livermore Falls, Maine. Died June 11, 2007.

STRATTON, ELAINE AUDREY, small business owner, writer; b. Flint, Mich., Apr. 27, 1925; d. Victor William and Eva Jane (Moore) Miller; m. Olin W. Stratton, Dec. 25, 1946 (dec. Sept. 1991); children: Candace, Jeffrey, John. BS in Edn., So. Ill. U., 1946, MS, 1966; cert. in adminstrn., So. Ill. U., Edwardsville, 1976. Cert. sch. adminstrn. Tchr. Coulterville (Ill.) Sch., 1946-47; libr. Highland (Ill.) Cmty. Sch., 1948-80; dir. librs. Highland Cmty. Unit #5, 1970-80; dir. fed. elem. writing program WRITE ON, Highland, 1980-82; book reviewer KMOX, St. Louis, 1986; pub. Swiss Village Book Store, St. Louis, 1985-88, owner, 1978-94. Counselor Svc. Corps. Ret. Execs.-SCORE; cons. Libr. Book Selection Svc., Bloomington, Ill., 1975-82; oral historian, Ill. 1972-77; docent Landmarks, St. Louis; cons. in field. Author, editor, pub.: St. Louis and the River - a "Lite" History, 1988; editor, pub.: Illinois Sketches, 1985. Chmn. Bicentennial Rsch. and Dissemination Com. (developed and produced bicentennial calendar sent to Smithsonian), 1975-76; oral historian, 1975-77; mem. Friends of Louis Latzer Meml. Libr.; program dir., Sch. Vol. Program, 1978-82, Highland, Ill.; vol. St. Louis Visitors and Conv. Ctr., 1995; bd. dirs. Highland Hist. Assn.; sec. bd. dirs. Historyonics Theatre Co., St. Louis, 1992—; vol. Cahokia Internat. Hist. Site, Collinsville, Ill.; program dir. Friends Edwardsville Libr., Ill., 1999—. Recipient Ill. Bicentennial Com. award, 1976; grantee WRITE ON project, 1980-82. Mem. ALA (chair libr. media skills com. 1981-83), Nat. Assn. Women Bus. Owners, Am. Bookman's Assn. Died Apr. 12, 2007.

STRAUBER, RAYMOND JOHN, marketing executive; b. Bklyn., Mar. 16, 1930; s. Milford Irving and Ruth (Buchbinder) S.; m. Bernice Lenore Lefkowitz, Dec. 22, 1952; children: Alan Mark, Pamela Susan Loeb. BS, Hofstra U., 1950, MBA, 1952. Regional sales mgr. tech. divsn. Encyclopedia Britannica Ednl. Corp., N.Y., N.J., Pa., 1966-94; regional sales mgr. PBS Video, N.Y., 1994-95. Trustee John C. Hart Pub. Libr., Shrub Oak, N.Y., 1994—; trustee, v.p. Yorktown (N.Y.) Sch. Bd., 1973-78; trustee, pres., v.p., treas. Yorktown Cmty. & Cultural Ctr., 1979-90. Mem. Masons. Died July 24, 2007.

STRAUSER, ROBERT WAYNE, lawyer; b. Little Rock, Aug. 28, 1943; s. Christopher Columbus and Opal (Orr) S.; m. Atha Maxine Tubbs, June 26, 1971 (div. 1991); children: Robert Benjamin, Ann Kathleen; m. Terri D. Seales, Oct. 17, 1998. BA, Davidson Coll., NC, 1965; postgrad., Vanderbilt U., Nashville, 1965-66; JD, U. Tex., Austin, 1968. Bar: Tex. 1968, U.S. Ct. Mil. Appeals 1971. Staff atty. Tex. Legis. Coun., Austin, 1969-71; counsel Jud. Com., Tex. Ho. of Reps., Austin, 1971-73; chief counsel Jud. Com., Tex. Constl. Conv., Austin, 1974; exec. v.p. and legis. counsel Tex. Assn. Taxpayers, Austin, 1974-85; assoc. Baker Botts, LLP, Austin, 1985-87, ptnr., 1988—2008; pvt. practice, from 2009. Assoc. editor Tex. Internat. Law Jour., 1968. Mem. Tex. Ho. Speakers Econ. Devel. Com., Austin, 1986-87; mem.-at-large McDonald Obs. Bd. Visitors, 1988-; bd. dirs. Tex. Assn. Bus. and C. of C., 2000-2002; bd. dirs. Austin Symphony Orch. Soc., 1985—, v.p., 1993-94, nominating com., 1998-2002. Capt. USNR, ret. Named Rising Star of Tex., Tex. Bus. Mag., 1983. Fellow Tex. Bar Found. (life); mem. State Bar of Tex., Headliners Club (Austin). Died May 21, 2015.

STRAUSS, FRED, producer, communications executive; b. Bielefeld, Westphalia, Germany, Mar. 30, 1925; arrived in U.S., 1938, naturalized, 1944; s. Solly and Fanny (Wertheim) Strauss; m. Barbara Ann Ward, Sept. 1, 1955 (div. 1965); children: Scott, Jonathan, Daniel, Craig. Student, Purdue U., 1944, DePaul U., 1950—51, Western Res. U., 1952—53. Owner, mgr. Fred Strauss Agy., Cleve., 1953—58; personal mgr. Crew Cuts, 1954—58; pres. Talent Corp. of Am., NYC, 1958—60; exec. prodr. Comm. Corp. of Am., Chgo., 1960—67, from 1982; pub. rels. dir. Am. Cancer Soc., Chgo., 1967—82. Exec. dir. Lincoln Park C. of C., Chgo., 1982—89, River North Assn., 1990—97; instr. Roosevelt U., 1980; founder, prodr. Tast of River North, Chgo., 1990—96; guest lectr. Loyola U., Northeastern Ill. U., Columbia Coll., Chgo. Office of Fine Arts, from 1980. Exec. prodr.: (motion pictures) Last Full Measure of Devotion, 1964 (Chris award Columbus Film Festival, N.Y. Film Festival, 1964), Too Personal to Be Private, 1971, (TV prodns.) Teens of the World, 1967—80, Telling a Child About Death, 1965—66; co-prodr.: (motion picture) Impossible Dream Come True, 1967, Medieval Faire in Oz Park; prodr.:, 1985—94 (Lincoln Pk. C. of C.); founder and prodr. Medieval Faire in Oz Park, from 1995 (10-Yr. Achievement award), prodr. numerous TV commls., originator and coord. Chgo.'s Finest Painted Ladies (houses), Chgo. Paint & Coatings Assn., 1987 (nat. award, 1995, 1996), Silver Trumpet, 1997. Pub. info. vol. LWV, Symphony for Survival Com., 1983; coord. TV presentation State of the City, from 1984; coord. TV Prodn. Chgo. Mayoral Debates, 1987—89, Ill. Festival "Hall of Fame", 1994, NARAS, from 1990; mem. adv. bd. St. Joseph Hosp., Chgo., 1982—89, Ill. Masonic Hosp., Chgo., 1984—85, Early Offenders Program, 1985—88; mem. Ill. Arts Coun. Served as intelligence officer US Army, 1944—48, ETO. Recipient Nat. award, Am. Cancer Soc., 1970, Honors Citation, 1977. Mem.: Publicity Club of Chgo. (pres. 1979—80, bd. dirs. 1974—80, from 1996, sch. rels. chmn., internships 1985—86, eligibility from 1988, Disting. Svc. award 1973, 1975), Social Svc. Communicators of Chgo. (bd. dirs. 1974—76, Helen Cody Baker award 1976, 1977). Home: Skokie, Ill. Died Feb. 5, 2016.

STRAUSS, JOHN STEINERT, dermatologist, educator; b. New Haven, July 15, 1926; s. Maurice Jacob and Carolyn Mina (Ullman) Strauss; m. Susan Thalheimer, Aug. 19, 1950; children: Joan Sue, Mary Lynn Strauss-Penka (Gerald)(dec.). BS, Yale U., 1946, MD, 1950. Intern U. Chgo., 1950-51; resident dermatology U. Pa., Phila., 1951-52, 54-55, fellow dermatology, 1955-57, instr., 1956-57; mem. faculty Boston U. Med. Sch., 1958-78, prof., 1966-78; head dept. dermatology U. Iowa Coll. of Medicine, Iowa City, 1978-98, prof. dermatology, 1978-00, prof. emeritus, 2000—14. Mem. editl. bd.: Archives of Dermatology, 1970—79, Jour. Am. Acad. Dermatology, 1979—89, Jour. Investigative Dermatology, 1977—82; contbr. articles to profl. jours. With USNR, 1952—54. Grantee USPHS; fellow James H. Brown Jr., 1947—48, USPHS, 1955—57. Fellow: Am. Acad. Dermatology (pres.); mem.: Internat. Com. Dermatology (pres. 1992—97), Internat. League Dermatol. Socs. (pres. 1992—97), 18th World Congress Dermatology (pres.), Am. Bd. Med. Spltys. (exec. com. 2001—04), Coun. Med. Splty. Socs. (pres.), Am. Fedn. Clin. Rsch., Ctrl. Soc. Clin. Rsch., Assn. Am. Physicians, Am. Dermatol. Assn. (sec., pres.), Am. Bd. Dermatology (bd. dirs., pres., assoc. exec. dir., exec. cons.), Dermatology Found. (pres.), Soc. Investigative Dermatology (sec.-treas., pres.). Achievements include research in sebaceous glands and pathogenesis of acne. Home: Iowa City, Iowa. Died July 28, 2014.

STREET, ROBERT, retired academic administrator, physicist; b. Wakefield, Eng., Dec. 16, 1920; s. Joe and Edith Elizabeth (Jones) S.; m. Joan Marjorie Bere, June 26, 1943; children: Alison Mary, Nicholas Robert. MSc, U. London, 1944, PhD, 1948, DSc, 1966; DSc (hon.), U. Western Australia, 1986, U. Sheffield, Eng., 1987. With Min. Supply, London, 1941-45; lectr. in physics U. Nottingham, Eng., 1945-54; sr. lectr. U. Sheffield, Eng., 1954-60; found. prof. Monash U., Australia, 1960-74; dir. Rsch. Sch. Phys. Sci. Australian Nat. U., Canberra, 1974-78; vice chancellor U. Western Australia, Perth, 1978-86, hon. sr. rsch. fellow, from 1987. Contbr. articles to profl. jours. Decorated officer Order of Australia. Fellow Australian Acad. Sci., Inst. Physics, Australian Inst. Physics; mem. Inst. Elec. Engrs., Weld Club (Perth). Home: Kalamunda, Australia. Died July 4, 2013.

STRICKLER, DOROTHY EVELYN, retired school teacher; b. St. Louis, Oct. 17, 1912; d. William and Lynn Ethel (Gotthelf) Behrens; m. Robert Elsworth Strickler, June 22, 1963 (dec. July, 1964). AB, Harris Teacher's Coll., St. Louis, 1934; MS, Washington U., St. Louis, 1939. Cert. elem. tchr., prin., Mo. (life). Tchr. St. Louis Pub. Schs., 1939-53, prin., 1953-60, elem. supr., 1960-67, elem. prin., 1967-73. Pres. Elementary Tchrs., St. Louis, 1948-50, Tchrs. Coop. Coun., 1951-53; sec. Dept. Elementary Sch. Tchrs. NEA, 1952-54; St. Louis rep Mo. Dept. Elementary Tchrs., Columbia, Mo., 1949-51. Bd. trustees, Retirement System of St. Louis Pub. Schs., 1981—. Mem. Mo. State Tchrs. Assn. (life), NEA (life), Retired Tchrs. of Mo., Kappa Delta Pi, Sigma Zi, Delta Kappa Gamma (charter mem. chpt. treas. 1952), Coll. Club of St. Louis (treas. 1979-83, chmn. hospitality com., 1986-88, chmn. fin. com. 1988-89). Republican. Presbyterian. Died Jan. 6, 2007.

STRINGER, RONALD E., lawyer, educator; b. NYC, Feb. 23, 1934; s. Irving and Mary Stringer; m. Sandra Deutsch, Oct. 30, 1986; children from previous marriage: Scott, David. AB, CCNY, 1954; LLB, Bklyn. Law Sch., 1957, JD, 1968. Bar: N.Y. 1958, U.S. Dist. Ct. (so. and ea. dists.) N.Y., U.S. Supreme Ct. Law sect. to comptroller City of N.Y., 1971-73, counsel to mayor, 1974-77; counsel Balsam Felber & Goldfield, from 1977; asst. prof. John Jay Coll. Criminal Justice, NYC, 1992-99. Hon. consul Dominican Republic, N.Y.C., 1972-74. Recipient Svc. award, Alianza Hispano-Am., 1975. Democrat. Died Apr. 20, 2007.

STROBINO, OTTO P., bank executive, health care administrator; b. Paterson, NJ, Nov. 1, 1926; s. Otto Lewis and Margaret Eleanor (Campbell) S.; m. Agnes T. Gwozdecki, Jan. 2, 1926; children: Charyl Ann, Robert P. BS, Panzer Coll.; MA, NYU. Staff therapist Inst. P.M. & R., NYC, 1952-53; supervising phys. therapist New Britain (Conn.) Meml. Hosp., 1953-55; pres. Cross Health Care, New Britain, from 1955; chmn. bd. dirs., founder Farmington (Conn.) Valley Savs. and Loan, 1979-85, First City Bank, New Britain, from 1988. Mem. Lions (internat. dir. 1992, pres. Conn. Eye Rsch. Found. 1994, Amb. Good Will 1992), YMCA (bd. trustees), Salvation Army (pres.). Home: Cheshire, Conn. Died Mar. 18, 2007.

STROKE, GEORGE WILHELM, physicist, educator, consultant; b. Zagreb, Yugoslavia, July 29, 1924; came to U.S., 1952, naturalized in U.S., 1957; naturalized in Fed. Republic of Germany, 1988; s. Elias and Edith Mechner (Silvers) S.; m. Masako Haraguchi, Feb. 5, 1973. BSc, U. Montpellier, France, 1942; IngDipl, Inst. Optics, U. Paris, 1949; Dr ès Sci. in Physics, Sorbonne U., Paris, 1960. Mem. rsch. staff and def. rsch. staff MIT, 1952-63, lectr. elec. engring., 1960-63; asst. rsch. prof. physics Boston U., 1956-57; NATO rsch. fellow U. Paris, 1959-60; prof. elec. engring., head electro-optical sci. labs. U. Mich., 1963-67; prof. elec. scis. and med. biophysics SUNY, Stony Brook, 1967-79; mem. corp. mgmt. staff Messerschmitt-Bolkow-Blohm GmbH, Munich, W.Ger., 1980-84, chief scientist space divsn., 1984-86, chief scientist corp. hdqrs.-devel., 1986-89; sr. advisor corp. strategy and bus. devel. Daimler-Benz AG/Deutsche Aerospace Corp., 1989-91. Vis. prof. Harvard U. Med. Sch., 1970-73, Tech. U. Munich, 1978-79, Keio U. Med. Sch., Tokyo, 1992-93, faculty sci. and tech., 1993-95; advisor laser task force USAAF Systems Command, 1964; govt. sci. cons. U.S. and abroad, 1964—; cons. NASA Electronics Rsch. Ctr., Cambridge, Mass., 1966—; mem. commn. I, Internat. Radio Sci. Union, Nat. Acad. Scis., 1965—; cons. Am. Cancer Soc., 1972—, RAND Corp., 1978-79; mem. NSF Blue Ribbon Task Force on Ultrasonic Imaging, 1973-74; mem. U.S. Ho. of Reps. Select. Com., photog. evidence panel on Pres. J.F. Kennedy assassination, 1978-79; mem. Max-Planck Soc., 1982-2000, Bavarian Union Bus. Adv. Coun., 1987—; mem. bd. advisors Max-Planck Soc. Inst. Quantum Optics, 1986-95, Inst. Diagnostic and Interventional Radiology, U. Witten/Herdecke, 1993—, Bavarian Acad. Fgn. Trade, 1993—, Soc. German Natural Scientists and Med. Drs., 1995-2000; dir. NATO-AGARD Study Group on Lasers, 1989; invited spkr. in field; advisor to global corps. and govts. Author: An Introduction to Coherent Optics and Holography, 1966, Russian translation, 1967, 2d edit., 1969, Diffraction Gratings, 1967, Optical Engineering, 1980, Influencing and Implementing Corporate Strategy Towards the End of the Twentieth Century, 1990, Risk Prevention: A Structural Problem in World Technology, 1992, The Universalist in the Dilemma between Science, Business and Politics, 1993, Science Versus Pseudo-Science (from Economics to Environment), 1994, There is No CO2 Problem, 1997, Climate Changes are a Natural Phenomenon, 1998, Unlinking CO2 from Global Warming: The Successful Strategy in the Climate Discussion, 2000, How to Avoid Going Astray with Faster-Better-Cheaper Cost Cutting, 2003, Remaining Competetive in the Face of Artificially-Constructed Presumed "Risks" of Products and Services, 2004, Can Strategic Planning Be Made Effective Again?, 2006; co-editor: Ultrasonic Imaging and Holography, 1974; contbr. articles to profl. jours. Recipient Humboldt prize, 1978. Fellow IEEE, Optical Soc. Am., Am. Phys. Soc., Am. Soc. Laser Medicine and Surgery. Died Apr. 21, 2007.

STRONG, GLENN WILLIAM, building contractor, consultant; b. East Orange, NJ, Oct. 26, 1949; s. Harold Thomas and Elaine Elsie (Landgraber) S.; m. Dale Ellen Klieback, June 15, 1980; children: Ashley Jordan, Travis Ryder. Student communications, U. Tex., El Paso, 1967-68. Carpenter Alco Builders, New Providence, N.J., 1968-72; constrn. supr. Sanddollar Constrn. Co., Santa Cruz, Calif., 1973-86; chief exec. officer Sea Hawk Enterprises, Inc., Santa Cruz, from 1986; owner Sea Hawk Constrn. Co., Santa Cruz, from 1986. Industry expert, expert witness Calif. Contractor's State Lic. Bd., Sacramento, 1987—; pres. bd. dirs. Santa Cruz County Builders Exchange, 1988—; disting. expert Nat. Forensics Ctr. Mem. ASTM, Internat. Conf. Bldg. Ofcls. (profl., cert. bldg. insp.), Internat. Assn. Plumbing and Mech. Ofcls. (cert. plumbing and mech. insp.), Constrn. Specifications Inst. (constrn. documents technologists), Western Regional Master Builders, Tech. Adv. Svc. for Attys., Am. Arbitration Assn., Am. Soc. Profl. Estimators, Am. Nat. Standards Inst., Am. Soc. Home Insps., Am. Plywood Assn., Am. Inst. Bldg. Design, Am. Constrn. Insps. Assn. (v.p. No. Calif. chpt.), Am. Concrete Inst., Aptos C. of C., Calif. Bldg. Ofcls., Santa Cruz Bd. Realtors, Calif. Real Estate Inspection Assn., Western Constrn. Cons., Internat. Assn. Elec. Insps. Democrat. Methodist. Avocations: scuba diving, golf, tennis, sky diving, bicycling. Home: Aptos, Calif. Died July 30, 2007.

STRONG, MAURICE FREDERICK, hydro-electric power company executive, former United Nations official; b. Oak Lake, Man., Can., Apr. 29, 1929; s. Frederick Milton and Mary (Fyfe) S.; m. Hanne Marstrand, 1981; children by previous marriage—Frederick, Maurice, Maureen, Louise, Mary Anne, Kenneth, Martin. 35 hon. degrees. Fin. analyst James Richardson & Sons, Winnipeg, Man., and Calgary, 1948-51, asst. to pres., 1951-52; mktg. asst. Caltex (Africa) Ltd., Nairobi, Kenya, 1953-54; v.p., treas. Dome Petroleum Ltd., Calgary, 1955-59; pres. Canadian Indsl. Gas Ltd., Calgary, 1959-64, Power Corp. Can., Montreal, 1962-66, Canadian Internat. Devel. Agy. Ottawa, 1966-70; exec. dir. environment program UN, also sec.-gen. UN Conf. Human Environment, NYC, 1971-75; chmn. bd. Petro-Can., 1975-78; chmn. Internat. Devel. Research Centre, 1977-78, Procor, Inc., AZL Resources, Inc., Phoenix, 1978-83, Internat. Energy Devel. Corp., 1980-83; dir., vice chmn. Can. Devel. Corp., 1981-84, chmn., 1982-84; dir. Massey Ferguson, 1984; exec. coord. UN Office for Emergency Ops. in Africa, 1985-86; pres. World Fedn. UN Assocs., 1987-91; sec.-gen. UN Conf. on Environ. and Devel. (Earth Summit), 1990-92; chmn., CEO Ontario Hydro, 1992-95; spl. advisor UN devel. programme, 1992—2005. Former chmn. Internat. Union for Conservation of Nature and Natural Resources; chmn. Coun. World Econ. Forum, Baca Resources Ltd., Am. Water Devel. Inc., North-South Roundtable, SID, Strovest Holdings; dir. World Soc., First Color. Corp., Baca Corp., Consolidated Press Holdings; chmn. exec. com. Société Générale pour l'Energie et les Ressources; mem. adv. bd. York U., Toronto, 1969-70, vis. prof. govt. adminstrn., 1969; alt. gov. Internat. Bank for Reconstrn. and Devel., Asian Devel. Bank, 1968-70, Caribbean Devel. Bank, 1970; gov. Internat. Devel. Research Centre, 1970-71, 77-78; bd. dirs. Centre D'Etudes Industrielles, Geneva, Switzerland, Aspen Inst. Humanistic Studies; mem. World Com. Environ. and Devel., 1983-87; co-chmn. InterAction Policy Bd. Author: Where on Earth Are We Going?, 2000. Trustee Rockefeller Found., Fitzer Found.; Pres. Nat. Council YMCA's Can., 1967-68; chmn. com. extension and inter-movement aid World Alliance YMCA's, 1963-65; mem. joint com. soc. justice peace World Council Chs., Vatican, 1969-71; Montague Burton prof. Internat. Relations U. Edinburgh, 1973. Decorated officer Order of Can., 1976; recipient Blue Planet Prize, Asahi Glass Foundation, 1995, Pub. Welfare medal NAS, 2003. Fellow Royal Soc. (U.K.), Royal Soc. Can.; mem. Century Assn., Queen's Privy Coun. Can., Yale Club, Univ. Club, Vancouver Club. Died Nov. 28, 2015.

STRZELEC, FRANCIS STANLEY, plant manager; b. Perth Amboy, NJ, Nov. 20, 1949; s. Stanley Valentine and Cecilia (Grabowski) S.; m. Kathleen Marie Waters, May 27, 1972; children: Daniel, Alicia. BSChemE, U. Dayton, 1971; MBA, Rutgers U., 1976. Dept. head Amax Copper Inc., Carteret, N.J., 1971-85; facility mgr. Cylinder Recon Co., Kearny, N.J., 1987-88; plant mgr. C.P. Chemicals, Sewaren, N.J., from 1988. Capt. USAR, 1971—. Mem. AIChE, C. of C. (bd. dirs. 1994-95). Roman Catholic. Avocations: fishing, hunting, camping. Home: Hillsborough, NJ. Died Apr. 13, 2007.

STUHLER, BARBARA JEANNE, university dean; b. Monticello, Iowa, Apr. 18, 1924; d. George Russell and Ethel Mae (Galbraith) S. BA, MacMurray Coll., Jacksonville, Ill., 1945; MA, U. Minn., 1952. Intern Nat. Inst. Pub. Affairs, Washington, 1946-47; research asst. Bur. Pub. Adminstrn., U. Va., Charlottesville, Va., 1947-48; exec. sec. League Women Voters of Minn., Mpls., 1948-50; assoc. dir. World Affairs Ctr., U. Minn., Mpls., 1950-75; exec. assoc. dean continuing edn. and ext. U. Minn., from 1975. Author: Ten Men of Minnesota and American Foreign Policy, 1973; co-editor: Women of Minnesota, 1977; author: No Regrets: Minnesota Women and the Joan Growe Senatorial Campaign, 1986; contbr. articles to profl. jours. Bd. dirs. Minn. Women's Campaign Fund, St. Paul, 1982—; vice chmn. Women's History Ctr. Task Force, St. Paul, 1985—; bd. dirs. Woman Candidate Devel. Coalition, St. Paul, 1985—. Recipient Listing. Alumni award, MacMurray Coll., 1969, Leadership Award in Edn., YWCA, Mpls., 1980. Democrat. Avocations: water and racquet sports, collies. Home: Mendota Hts, Minn. Died Jan. 28, 2007.

STUMP, MIRIAM ELLEN, minister; b. Worcester, Mass., Nov. 16, 1928; d. Robert E. Marston and Irene Ellen (Prairie) Marston Dodd; m. Myron Eugene Stump, Aug. 6, 1949; children: Philip Alan, Paul Marston, Stephen Eugene, Timothy Jon, Lydia Ellen. BS, U. Mass., 1950; MDiv, Sch. of Theology, Claremont, 1982. Ordained deacon United Meth. Ch., 1982, elder, 1984. Chaplain David and Margaret Home, LaVerne, Calif., 1980; assoc. min. West Covina (Calif.) United Meth. Ch., 1982-84, East Whittier (Calif.) United Meth. Ch., 1984-86; min. Crescent Heights United Meth. Ch., West Hollywood, Calif., 1986-88, First United Meth. Ch., Brawley, Calif., from 1988. Mem. rules com., Calif.-Pacific Conf., 1985—; mem. adv. bd. Camp Virginia, Julian, Calif., 1988—. Bd. dirs. Womanhaven, El Centro, Calif. (v.p. 1991); bd. dirs. Neighborhood House, Calexico, Calif., 1988—. Mem. Brawley Ministerial Assn. (pres. 1989—), Kiwanis. Home: Rowland Hghts, Calif. Died Nov. 13, 2006.

STURGIS, JOYCE MARIE, accountant, small business owner; b. St. Louis, Jan. 4, 1941; d. William J. and Mary J. (Van Straat) Sturgis; m. Robert L. Brittingham, Dec. 27, 1969 (div. Jan. 5, 1979); 1 child, Paula Therese. BA, Fontbonne Coll., St. Louis, 1963; MA, St. Louis U., 1970; MBA, St. Ambrose U., Davenport, Iowa, 1983. Cert. tchr., Mo., Iowa. Tchr. St. Joseph's Acad., St. Louis, 1963-70; bus. mgr. Quad City Montessori Assn., Davenport, 1976-79; corp. office mgr. Frank Foundries Corp., Moline, Ill., 1979-81; acct. Normoyle-Berg & Assocs., Rock Island, Ill., 1981-95, Adrian Carriers, Inc., Milan, Ill., from 1996. Owner Joyce Ent., Davenport. Artist jewelry/handpainted silk; exhibited various invitational art fairs. Mem. Friends of Art, Davenport Mus. Art; trustee, corp. sec. Glynn Fellowship Found., Davenport. Fontbonne Coll. scholar, 1959; St. Ambrose U. mktg. rsch. assistantship, 1980. Mem. AAUW (life, bd. dirs., pres. 1988-89, treas. 1984-88), Left Bank Art League. Democrat. Roman Catholic. Avocations: poetry, art needlework, computers. Died Dec. 8, 2006.

STURMAN, GEORGE, poet; b. NY, Oct. 19, 1914; s. Benny and Anna Sturman; m. Mary Kruse, Oct. 18, 1953 (dec. June 27, 1993). Student, C.C. N.Y. Adminstr. officer U.S. Gen. Svc. Adminstrn., Washington, 1935—78. Editl. adv. Truth Seeker; pub. rels. Rancho Bernardo Sun, Poway, Calif. Author: (poetry) A Sonnet to Pavarotti; contbr. articles to profl. jour.; prof. listener (Royal Caribbean cruise line). Vol. Marriott's Remington Ret. Facility, San Diego, from 1998. Recipient Vol. of the Yr., Marriotts Remington Ret. facility., 2002. Died Feb. 23, 2007.

STYRT, JEROME, psychiatrist; b. Chgo., Dec. 12, 1919; m. Mary Avery Onken, Feb. 21, 1946; 2 children. BS in Chemistry, U. Chgo., 1940, MD, 1945; Grad., Balt. Psychoanalytic Inst., 1957. Diplomate Am. Bd. Psychiatry and Neurology. Intern U. Chgo. Clinics, 1945-46; resident in psychiatry Sheppard Pratt Hosp., 1946-48; registrar in psychiatry The Retreat, York, Eng., 1948, Belmont Hosp., Surrey, 1949; fellow in preventive medicine, Commonwealth Fund fellow Johns Hopkins U., Balt., 1949-50; sr. surgeon USPHS, 1950-52; instr. psychiatry U. Md., Balt., 1953-54; pvt. practice psychiatry and psychoanalysis Balt., from 1953; clin. assoc. prof. psychiatry U. Md., from 1970; supr. psychotherapy Sheppard Pratt Hosp., Towson, Md., from 1971; mem. tchg. faculty Balt.-Wash. Psychoanalytic Inst., 1963-93. Cons. in field. Recipient Disting. Teaching award in psychiatry, Sheppard Pratt Hosp., 1989, Outstanding Vol. Tchg. Faculty award U. Md. Sch. Medicine, 1995. Fellow Am. Psychiatric Assn., Am. Orthopsychiatric Assn.; mem. Am. Psychoanalytic Assn., Med. and Chirurgical Faculty of Md., Balt. Wash. Soc. Psychoanalysis, Meadow Mill Athletic Club, Alpha Omega Alpha. Avocations: sports medicine, squash racquets. Home: Baltimore, Md. Died June 10, 2007.

SUAREZ, KENNETH ALFRED, pharmacology educator, college administrator; b. Queens, NY, June 27, 1944; s. Alfred and Louise (Hajek) S.; m. Eileen Lynch, Sept. 29, 1968; 1 child, Christina. BS, U. R.I., 1967, MS, 1970, PhD, 1972. Instr. Chgo. Coll. Osteopathic Medicine, 1972-74, asst. prof., 1974-77, assoc. prof., 1977-82, prof., from 1982, asst. dir. rsch., 1980-82, dir. rsch., 1982-89, assoc. dean rsch., from 1989. Contbr. articles, revs. to profl. jours. Pres. Stonebridge Civic Assn., Hazel Crest, Ill., 1976-77. Lt. col. USAR. Recipient award Am. Fedn. Pharm. Edn., Chgo., 1966, Outstanding Young Men in Am. award Jaycees, 1978; grantee NIH, 1971; fellow Nat. Def. Edn. Act, 1967-70. Mem. AAAS, Soc. Toxicology. Avocations: gardening, woodworking, computers. Home: Naperville, Ill. Died Apr. 12, 2007.

SUISSA, MIREILLE RENEE, company executive, computer consultant; b. Grenoble, France, Feb. 18, 1942; came to U.S., 1965; d. Henri Andre Ptachnik and Cecile (Scheebaum) Lewenszpil; m. Charles Suissa (div. Jan. 1991); 1 child, Henri. Bookkeeper Comgraphix, Inc., El Paso, Tex., 1972-74; acct. El Paso Cancer Treatment Ctr., 1974-80; corp. exec. Chez Carlos, Inc., from 1980. Cons. Econ. Mgmt. Cons., El Paso, 1989—. Mem. Smithsonian Inst. Recipient Outstanding Svc. awards, Special Olympics, Muscular Dystrophy, Missing Children Network, Say No To Drugs, El Paso. Mem. Nat. Sporting Goods Assn., Nat. Fedn. Ind. Bus., U.S. C. of C., El Paso C. of C., Right to Work, B'Nai Zion Congregation Sisterhood. Republican. Jewish. Avocations: needlepoint, cooking, doll collecting, reading. Home: Pompano Beach, Fla. Died Nov. 30, 2006.

SUITS, BERNARD HERBERT, philosophy educator; b. Detroit, Nov. 25, 1925; s. Herbert Arthur and Helen Dorothy (Carlin) S.; m. Nancy Ruth Berr, July 3, 1952; children—Mark, Constance; m. Cheryl Ann Ballantyne, June 14, 1996. BA, U. Chgo., 1944, MA, 1950; PhD, U. Ill., 1958. Investigator venereal disease USPHS, 1950-51; personnel officer Detroit Civil Service Commn., 1952-54; instr. philosophy U. Ill., Urbana, 1958-59; asst. prof. Purdue U., 1959-66; asso. prof. U. Waterloo, Ont., 1966-72, prof. philosophy, chmn. dept., 1971-74, asso. dean arts for grad. affairs, 1981-84. Vis. prof. U. Lethbridge, Alta., Can., 1980, U. Bristol, Eng., 1980, disting. prof. emeritus U. Waterloo, 1995. Author: The Grasshopper: Games, Life, and Utopia, 1978, paper, 1990, 2d edit., 2005; contbr. to profl. jours. and books; featured guest on seven-week TV Ontario series The Academy of Moral Philosophy, 1982. Served with USNR,

1944-46. Recipient Disting. Tchg. award U. Waterloo, 1983. Mem.: Philosphic Soc. Study of Sport (pres. 1973). Home: Orillia, Canada. Died Feb. 5, 2007.

SULLIVAN, JAMES E., religious center administrator, priest; b. NYC, Aug. 10, 1920; s. Patrick J. and Mary G. (Coughlan) S. BA, Immaculate Conception Sem., Huntington, NY, 1942; MS, Iona Coll., 1966. Parish priest Our Lady of Angels Ch., Nativity Ch., St. Marks Ch., Bklyn., 1946-66; dir. Religious Consultation Ctr., Bayside, N.Y., from 1966. Author: My Meditation on the Gospel, 1962, My Meditation on St. Paul, 1967, Journey to Freedom-Path to Self Esteem, 1987. Named Counselor of Yr. Iona Coll., 1986. Mem. APA, AACD. Home: Whitestone, NY. Died Dec. 13, 2006.

SUMMERS, WYMAN DURAND, pharmacist; b. Kingsley, Iowa, June 3, 1925; s. Russell Raymond and Iona Leila (Clark) S.; m. M. Loni Johnson, Mar. 7, 1953; children: Rick Eugene, Steven Craig, Jodi Paige. BS, Oreg. State U. Sec.-treas. CentWise Drug Stores, Inc., Lebanon, Oreg., 1950-88; sec. OK Drug Stores, Portland, Oreg., from 1956. With USN, 1943-46, PTO. Republican. Avocations: hunting, fishing, computers. Home: Lebanon, Oreg. Died July 11, 2007.

SUMNER, DAVID SPURGEON, surgeon, educator; b. Asheboro, NC, Feb. 20, 1933; s. George Herbert and Velna Elizabeth (Welborn) S.; m. Martha Eileen Sypher, July 25, 1959; children: David Vance, Mary Elizabeth, John Franklin. BA, U. N.C., 1954; MD, Johns Hopkins U., 1958. Diplomate Am. Bd. Surgery; cert. spl. qualification gen. vascular surgery. Intern Johns Hopkins Hosp., Balt., 1958-59, resident in gen. surgery, 1960-61, U. Wash. Sch. Medicine, Seattle, 1961-66; clin. investigator in vascular surgery VA Hosp., Seattle, 1967, 70-73; asst. prof. surgery U. Wash. Sch. Medicine, Seattle, 1970-72, assoc. prof. surgery, 1972-75; prof. surgery, chief sect. peripheral vascular surgery So. Ill. U. Sch. Medicine., Springfield, 1975-84, Disting. prof. surgery, chief sect. peripheral vascular surgery, 1984-98, disting. prof. emeritus, 1998. Staff surgeon Seattle VA Hosp., 1973-75, Univ. Hosp., Seattle, 1973-75, St. John's Hosp., Springfield, 1975-98, Meml. Med. Ctr., Springfield, 1975-98; mem. VA Merit Review Bd. Surgery, 1975-78; mem. vascular surgery rsch. award com. The Liebig Found., 1990-95, chmn., 1994; bd. dirs. Am. Venous Forum Found., 1993-95; vis. prof. Cook County Hosp., Chgo., 1971, Washington U., St. Louis, 1976, U. Tex., San Antonio, 1978, Wayne State U., Detroit, 1978, U. Ind., Indpls., 1979, Ea. Va. Med. Sch., Norfolk, 1979, Case-Western Res. U., Cleve., 1980, U. Chgo., 1981, U. Manitoba, Winnipeg, Can., 1983, others; dist. lectr. Yale U., 1982; guest examiner Am. Bd. Surgery, St. Louis, 1982, assoc. examiner, 1989; lectr. in field. Author: (with D.E. Strandness Jr.) Ultrasonic Techniques in Angiology, 1975, Hemodynamics for Surgeons, 1975; (with R.B. Rutherford, V. Bernhard, F. Maddison, W.S. Moore, M.O. Perry) Vascular Surgery, 1977; (with F.B. Hershey, R.W. Barnes) Noninvasive Diagnosis of Vascular Disease, 1984; (with R.B. Rutherford, G. Johnson Jr., R.F. Kempczinski, W.S. Moore, M.O. Perry, G.W. Smith) Vascular Surgery, 3d edit., 1989; (with A.N. Nicolaides) Investigation of Patients With Deep Vein Thrombosis and Chronic Venous Insufficiency, 1991; (with R.B. Rutherford, G. Johnson, K.W. Johnston, R.F. Kempczinski, W.C. Krupski, W.S. Moore, M.O. Perry, A.J. Comerota, R.H. Dean, P. Gloviczki, K.H. Johansen, T.S. Riles, L.M. Taylor Jr.) Vascular Surgery, 4th edit., 1995; (with K.A. Myers, A.N. Nicolaides Lower Limb Ischaemia, 1997; author 150 chpts. to books; mem. editl. bd. Vascular Diagnosis and Therapy, 1980-84, Jour. Soc. Non-Invasive Vascular Tech., 1987—, Jour. Vascular Surgery, 1987-97; series editor Introduction to Vascular Tech., 1990—; mem. exec. editl. com. Phlebology, 1987-91, mem. internat. editl. adv. bd., 1991-2000; mem. editl. com. Internat. Angiology, 1992—; contbr. over 150 articles to profl. jours. Lt. col. U.S. Army, 1967-70. Fellow in surg. rsch. Johns Hopkins U. Sch. Medicine, 1959-60, Am. Cancer Soc., Inc. fellow, 1965-66; Appleton-Century Crofts scholar, 1956, Mosby scholar, 1958. Fellow Am. Coll. Surgeons (Wash. chpt. 1971-75, Ill. chpt. counselor 1981-83), Cyprus Vascular Soc. (hon.); mem. AMA, Soc. Univ. Surgeons, Soc. Vascular Surgery (constn. and by-laws com. 1983, Wiley Fellowship com. 1990), Internat. Soc. Cardiovascular Surgery (N.Am. chpt. program com. 1985-88), Am. Surg. Assn., Am. Heart Assn. (stroke coun., cardiovascular surgery coun. 1978), Soc. Noninvasive Vascular Tech. (hon.), Vascular Surgery Biology Club, Am. Venous Forum (organizing com. 1987, founding mem. 1988, chmn. membership com. 1988-91, treas. 1992-95, pres. elect 1998, pres. 1999-2000), Cardiovascular Sys. Dynamics Soc., Internat. Soc. Surgery, Vascular Soc. So. Africa (hon.), North Pacific Surg. Assn., Ctrl. Surg. Assn., Midwestern Vascular Surg. Soc. (counselor 1977-79, pres.-elect 1980-81, pres. 1981-82), So. Assn. for Vascular Surgery, Ill. Heart Assn., Ill. Med. Soc., Ill. Surg. Soc., Chgo. Surg. Soc., Seattle Surg. Soc., Sangamon County Med. Soc., Henry N. Harkins Surg. Soc., Harbinger Soc., Phi Eta Sigma, Phi Beta Kappa, Sigma Xi, Alpha Omega Alpha. Presbyterian. Achievements include research in surgical hemodynamics and noninvasive methods for diagnosing peripheral vascular disease. Home: Springfield, Ill. Died Nov. 24, 2013.

SUN, ANDREW, business executive; b. Shantung, Ohio, Sept. 6, 1932; s. Tsai-Sheng and Jung-Feng (Wang) Sun; married, Dec. 7, 1964; children: Connie, David. Student, Lang. Sch., Taipei, Taiwan, 1959. Mgr. Topsco. Ltd., Taipei, 1967—71; office mgr. Texmart Ltd., Taipei, 1971—73; pres. Lotus Chem. Co. Ltd., Taipei, 1973; mng. dir. Top Line Enterprises Ltd., Taipei, from 1974; gen. mgr. Vopei Co. Ltd., Taipei, from 1977; dir. Fgn. Textile Co. Ltd. Mem.: Taiwan Constrn. Assn., Taiwan Import & Export Assn. Home: Taiwan, Taiwan. Died Sept. 29, 2007.

SUN, KEUN JENN, physicist; b. Keelung, Taiwan, China, Mar. 5, 1949; came to U.S., 1977; s. Ching-Chuan and Tsai-Hsia (Chiou) S.; m. Hsi Wei, Dec. 19, 1976; children: Bor Jen, Phillip B.R. MS, U. Akron, 1979; PhD, U. Wis., Milw., 1986. Rsch. assoc. Nat. Rsch. Coun., Hampton, Va., 1986-88; rsch. scientist Coll. William and Mary, Williamsburg, Va., from 1988. Co-author: Physical Acoustics, Vol. XX, 1992; contbr. articles to profl. jours. Recipient Langley Rsch. Ctr. cert. of recognition for discovery of method and apparatus for evaluating multilayer objects for imperfections. Mem. IEEE, AAAS, Am. Phys. Soc., Material Rsch. Soc. Achievements include findings of spin-phonon interaction in magnetic superconductors, ultrasonic relaxation attenuation in magnetic superconductors, acoustic waveguide sensors for epoxy curing, and stuctural flaws detection with acoustic plate waves. Home: Yorktown, Va. Died Aug. 11, 2007.

SUNDSTROM, NANCY MARIE, television program director; b. Rapid City, SD, Oct. 5, 1956; d. Ernest Dale and Iola Hope (Erickson) S.; m. David Claude Byington, June 1, 1979; children: Jordan Amanda, Taylor Hope. BS, Western Mich. U., 1977. Social worker Community Mental Health, Traverse City, Mich., 1977-78; pub. relations counselor Third Level Crisis Intervention Ctr., Traverse City, 1978-80; pub. relations program leader Traverse City Friendship Ctr., 1980-81; program dir. Sta. WGTU-TV, Traverse City, from 1981. Producer, dir. (TV show) P.M. Mag., 1983-86; theatre reviewer-critic Traverse City Record Eagle, 1990—; gen. mgr. Mich. Ensemble Theatre, 1991—. Ambassador Nat. Cherry Festival, Traverse City, 1985, 86; bd. dirs. Traverse City Old Town Playhouse, 1986-89, Downtown Devel. Authority, Traverse City, 1986—, Grand Traverse Area Jr. Achievement, 1990—; active Old Town Playhouse, 1986-90. Waldo-Sangren scholar Western Mich. State U., Kalamazoo, 1976-77. Democrat. Avocations: directing and performing theater works, reading, cooking, music, films. Home: Traverse City, Mich. Died Feb. 28, 2007.

SUNKEL, ROBERT JACOB, manufacturing executive; b. Paris, Ill., June 6, 1926; s. Jacob Roy and Mary Elizabeth (Mansfield) S.; divorced; children: Steven Ray, Debra Kay. BS in Music, Ind. U., 1950. Music tchr. Martinsville (Ill.) Schs., 1950-52; sales, owner Men's Shop, 1952-59; sales rep. Midwest Body, Paris, 1959-69, sales mgr., 1969-83, v.p. sales and mktg., from 1983. Active Paris Youth Ctr. Bd., 1965-70. Served as staff sgt. U.S. Army, 1944-46. Mem. Am. Legion, Nat. Truck Equipment Assn., (bd. dirs., trustee 1983-86), Paris C. of C. (pres. 1989—). Clubs: Sycamore Hills Country. Lodges: Elks. Republican. Roman Catholic. Avocations: music, golf. Home: Paris, Ill. Died Oct. 30, 2006.

SUPLIZIO, SAMUEL VICTOR, financial services executive; b. DuBois, Pa., Sept. 14, 1932; Carter, Cynthia Lee, Samuel Paul, Thomas Eugene. BE, U. N.Mex., 1954. Profl. baseball player N.Y. Yankees Orgn., 1953-56; mgr. minor league team Los Angeles Dodgers Baseball Team, Thomasville, GA., 1957; pres. Home Loan & Investment Co., Grand Junction, Colo., 1957-90; scout, instr. Milw. Brewers Baseball Team, from 1975. Bd. dirs. Ctrl. Bank, Grand Junction, Colo. Nat. Bank; pres. Home Loan Indsl. Bank; chmn. Mesa County Econ. Devel. Coun., 1994-95; coach 1982 World Series; vice chmn. Colo. Baseball Com. for Maj. League Baseball to Colo.; speaker in field. Contbr. articles to profl. jours. Chmn. Nat. Jr. Coll. Baseball World Series, Grand Junction, 1959—, Hilltop House Rehab. Ctr., 1963-67, Colo. Easter Seal, 1969; trustee Mesa Jr. Coll., Grand Junction, 1971-74; fin. chmn. Colo. Repub. Com., Denver, 1981-82; mem. Salvation Army Bd., 1967—. Recipient Disting. Svc. award Grand Junction Jaycees, 1963, W.P. "Dutch" Fering award merit U.S. Baseball Fedn., N.Y., 1985; named to All Sports Hall of Fame, DuBois (Pa.) Booster Club, 1968, Baseball Hall of Fame Nat. Jr. Coll. Atheltic Assn., Colorado Springs, 1985; inducted into Colo. Sports Hall of Fame, 1991; named Grand Junction Citizen of Yr., 1989. Mem. Am. Baseball Coaches Assn. (award of merit 1985), Ind. Insurers Colo. (bd. dirs. 1980-87, Outstanding Svc. award 1985-86), Ind. Insurers Colo. (pres. 1986), Club. 20 (pres. 1983), Colo. Basketball Commn. (co-chmn.), U.S. C. of C. (v.p., bd. dirs. 1968-70), Grand Junction C. of C. (bd. dirs. 1969-72), Bookcliffe Knife and Fork Club (pres. 1966), Elks, KC, Kiwanis (pres. Bookcliff chpt. 1973), Fellowship Christian Athletes. Roman Catholic. Avocations: baseball, fishing, handball, jogging. Home: Grnd Junction, Colo. Died Dec. 29, 2006.

SUPRUN, HARRY ZVI, pathologist; b. San Antonio, Aug. 19, 1924; arrived in Israel, 1934; s. Joseph Jacob and Bertha Batya (Payes) S.; m. Hedva Storch-Chassidi, Mar. 26, 1950; children: Ilana Sarah, Leora Oli. BA in Medicine, Am. U. Beirut, 1948; MD, cert. med. studies, U. Lausanne, Switzerland, 1952. Rotating intern Beilinson Med. Ctr., Petah Tikvah, Israel, 1953-54; gen. practice, Affuleh, Israel, 1954-55; resident in pathology Ctrl. Emek Hosp. and Med. Ctr., Affuleh, 1955-58; resident and chief resident in anatomic pathology Tel Aviv U.-Mcpl. Tchg. Med. Ctrs., 1958-62, specialist in anatomic pathology, assoc. attending, 1961; tng. in cytopathology, rsch. fellow Sloan-Kettering Inst., NYC, 1962-63; instr., asst. pathologist Ohio State U. Med. Coll., Columbus, 1963-64; instr. Tel Aviv U. Med. Sch. Tchg. Hosps., 1964-65; dir., founder dept. pathology and cytology Regional Med. Ctr. West Galilee, Nahariyya, Israel, 1965-91; lectr. gynecologic, gastrointestinal, fine needle aspiration cytology and urol. cytopathology Tel Aviv U. Postgrad. Med. Sch., 1987-92; lectr. anatomic pathology, U.S. students Tel Aviv U., 1990-92. Lectr. normal histology Technion Med. Sch., Haifa, Israel, 1977-82; mem. Internat. Bd. Cytopathology, 1986-92; head orgn. com. Israel Soc. Cytology, 1971; fellow Internat. Acad. Cytology, 1971-73. Nat. editor Acta Cytologica, 1971-93, mem. European rev. bd., 1982-93; assoc. editor The Cervix and Lower Female Genital Tract, 1987-90, mem. editl. bd., 1989-91; mem. N.Am. rev. bd. Acta Cytol, 1997--; contbr. more than 100 articles to profl. publs. Rsch. fellow Israel Cancer Rsch. Fund, 1979-82. Fellow Internat. Acad. Cytology (continuing edn. and quality assurance com. 1992—), Israel Soc. Cervical Pathology and Colposcopy (pres. 1986). Achievements include correlative study on incidence of pulmonary cancer and other lung diseases associated with squamous metaplasia of bronchial epithelium. Home: Allentown, Pa. Died Aug. 10, 2007.

SURLAND, AAGE, retired chemical engineer; b. Aalborg, Jutland, Denmark, June 14, 1921; s. Aage Harry Valdemar and Ulla Margrethe (Rasmussen) S.; m. Gudrun Helene Luisita Hansen, Sept. 2, 1944; children: Uffe, Ulla. Student, Tech. U., Copenhagen, 1942-43. Lab. asst. Rørdal Cement Factory, Aalborg, 1938-42, Phys. Lab. Sadolin & Holmblad, Copenhagen, 1951-57; tech. dir. Sadolin's Printing Ink, Helsinki, Finland, 1957-60, Sadolin's Ink, Cali, Colombia, 1960-63; group leader Sinclair & Valentine Rsch., Elmsford, N.Y., 1963-72; tech. mgr. rsch. assoc. Sun Chem., Carlstadt, N.J., 1973-83; ret., 1983. Cons. Sadolin Printing Ink, Copenhagen, 1984, G-Man Printing Ink, Copenhagen, 1985; lectr. in field. Contbr. articles to profl. jours. Active Dansk Samling, Aalborg and Copenhagen, 1940; foreman Dansk Samling Youth, Aalborg, 1945; active Danish Resistance, 1940-45. Comdr. on duty Civil Def., 1943-45. Recipient medal of appreciation Printing Ink Makers Prodn. Club, Phila., 1983; Ednl. grantee Cement Factory Rørdal, Aalborg, 1942. Mem. AAAS, Nat. Geog. Soc., Norwegian Family Hist. Soc. Democrat. Achievements include patentee in field; introduction of testing methods assuring the manufacture of more effective lithographic printing inks, reducing the printed waste in commercial printing. Home: Svenstrup, Denmark. Died Dec. 25, 2006.

SUTTON, DAVID LEROY, research chemist and engineer; b. Harrold, Tex., Oct. 29, 1926; s. Scott Leroy and Maudie (Melton) S.; m. Doris Jean Profitt, Oct. 3, 1955; 1 child, Charlotte LaVaughn Rose. BSChemE, Iowa State U., 1950. Computer profl. S.W. Geophys., Ft. Worth, 1950-51, MidContinental Geophys., Shamrock, Tex., 1952-53; engr. trainee Halliburton Oil Well Cementing Co., Lovington, N.Mex., 1953-55; chemist, div. chemist Halliburton Co., Lovington, 1955-65; regional chemist Halliburton Oil Well Cementing GmbH, Wiesbaden, Fed. Republic Germany, 1965-69; from. sr. chemist to sr. rsch. chemist Halliburton Svcs., Duncan, Okla., from 1965, disting. mem. tech. staff, 1989-91, ret., 1991; cons. Duncan, from 1992. Author 36 tech. papers; patentee in field. Mem. SPE (ASMME). Democrat. Baptist. Home: Duncan, Okla. Died June 10, 2007.

SUZMAN, RICHARD MICHAEL, demography sociologist; b. Johannesburg, Aug. 9, 1942; came to U.S., 1961; s. Arthur and Mary Suzman; m. Janice L. Krupnick, July 21, 1976; children: Daniel, Jessica. AB, Harvard U., 1964, AM, 1969, PhD, 1973; diploma, Oxford U., Eng., 1965. Rsch. assoc., lectr. in sociology Sch. Edn. and Dept. Sociology, Stanford u., Palo Alto, Calif., 1973-75; asst. prof. in residence Dept. Psychiatry U. Calif., San Francisco, 1975-83; health scientist NIH/Nat. Inst. Aging, Bethesda, Md., 1983-87, chief demography and population epidemiology, 1987—2015, assoc. dir. to dir., behavioral and social rsch. divsn., 1998—2015. Former staff dir. Fed. Forum on Aging, Bethesda; former dir. Office of Demography. Editor: Oldest Old, 1992; contbr. articles to profl. jours. Smithsonian Inst. rsch. grantee, 1975, NIH rsch. grantee, 1981-82; Harvard U. scholar, 1961-64. Mem. Population Assn. Am., Gerontol. Soc. Am., Soc. for Epidemiologic Rsch., Am. Sociol. Assn., Am. Pub. Health Assn.; fellow AAAS Home: Bethesda, Md. Died Apr. 16, 2015.

SWADOS, ELIZABETH A., composer, director, writer; b. Buffalo, Feb. 5, 1951; d. Robert O. and Sylvia (Maisel) S.; wife Roz Lichter BA, Bennington Coll., 1972. Composer, mus. dir. Peter Brook's Internat. Theatre Group, Paris, Africa, U.S., 1972-73; composer-in-residence La Mama Exptl. Theater Club, NYC, from 1977. Mem. faculty Carnegie-Mellon U., 1974, Bard Coll., 1976-77, Sarah Lawrence Coll., 1976-77 Author: The Girl With the Incredible Feeling, 1976, Runaways, 1979, Lullaby, 1980, Sky Dance, 1980, Listening Out Loud: Becoming a Composer, 1988, The Four of Us, 1991, The Myth Man, 1994, My Depression: A Picture Book (also a film); composer theatrical scores: Medea, 1969 (Obie award 1972), Elektra, 1970, Fragments of Trilogy, 1974, The Trojan Women, 1974, The Good Women of Setzuan, 1975, The Cherry Orchard, 1977, As You Like It, 1979, The Sea Gull, 1980, Alice in Concert, 1980, (with Garry Trudeau) Doonesbury, 1983, Jacques and His Master, 1984, Don Juan of Seville, 1989, The Tower of Evil, 1990, The Mermaid Wakes, 1991; composer, dir., adapter, mem. cast: Nightclub Cantata, 1977 (Obie award 1977); composer, adapter (with Andrei Serban) Agamemnon, 1976, The Incredible Feeling Show, 1979, Lullaby and Goodnight, 1980; composer, dir., adapter: Wonderland in Concert, N.Y. Shakespeare Festival, 1978, Dispatches, 1979, Haggadah, 1980, The Beautiful Lady, 1984-86, Swing, 1987, Esther: A Vaudeville Megillah, 1988, The Red Sneaks, 1989, Jonah, 1990; author, composer, dir.: Runaways, 1978 (Tony award nominee for best musical, best musical score, best musical book 1978); adapter: Works of Yehuda Amichi, Book of Jeremiah; composer music for films: Step by Step, 1978, Sky Dance, 1979, Too Far to Go, 1979, OHMS, 1980, Four Friends, 1982, Seize the Day, 1986, A Year in the Life, 1986, Family Sins, 1987; composer music CBS Camera Three shows, 1973-74, PBS short stories, 1979, CBS-TV and NBC-TV spls.; composer: Rap Master Ronnie, 1986; composer, dir. Swing, Bklyn. Acad. Music, 1987; performer: Mark Taper Forum, Los Angeles, 1985, Jerusalem Oratorio, Rome, 1985. Recipient Outer Critics Circle award, 1977; Creative Artists Service Program grantee, 1976; N.Y. State Arts Council playwriting grantee, 1977—; Guggenheim fellow. Mem. Broadcast Music Inc., Actors Equity. Jewish. Died Jan. 5, 2016.

SWAINE, HOWARD RALPH, economist, educator, consultant; b. Des Moines, Dec. 21, 1928; s. Alvin Ralph and Sarah (Underhill) S.; m. Suzanne Elise Terrell, Oct, 8, 1952; children: Abigail Ann, Edward Terrell. BA, U. Iowa, 1952, MA, 1956; PhD, UCLA, 1965. Economist Rand Corp., Santa Monica, Calif., 1959-66, Omaha, 1960-61, Washington, 1961-63, Paris, 1965-66; prof. No. Mich. U., Marquette, from 1966, dept. head, 1969—97. Cons. Rand Corp., Santa Monica, 1966-70, CAB, Washington, 1971-72, NSF, Washington, 1975-77. Co-author: (monograph) Navy Cost Model, 1963. Commr. City of Marquette, 1976-81, mayor, 1977-78; bd. dirs. Light & Power Bd., Marquette, 1984-90, Econ. Devel. Bd., Marquette, 1984—. 1st lt. US Army, 1952—54, Korea. Mem. Am. Econ. Assn. Republican. Presbyterian. Home: Marquette, Mich. Died Feb. 2, 2007.

SWALIN, RICHARD ARTHUR, scientist, company executive; b. Mpls., Mar. 18, 1929; s. Arthur and Mae (Hurley) S.; m. Helen Marguerite Van Wagenen, June 28, 1952; children: Karen, Kent, Kristin. BS with distinction, U. Minn., 1951, PhD, 1954. Rsch. assoc. GE, 1954-56; mem. faculty U. Minn., Mpls., 1956-77, prof., head Sch. Mineral and Metall Engring., 1962-68, assoc. dean Inst. Tech., 1968-71, dean Inst. Tech., 1971-77; acting dir. Space Sci. Center, 1965; v.p. tech. Eltra Corp., NYC, 1977-80; v.p. R & D Allied-Signal Corp., Morristown, NJ, 1980-84; dean Coll. Engring. and Mines U. Ariz., Tucson, 1984-87, prof., 1984-94; pres. Ariz. Tech. Devel. Corp., Tucson, 1987; prof. emeritus U. Ariz., Tucson, from 1995. Guest scientist Max Planck Inst. für Phys. Chemie, Göttingen, Fed. Republic Germany, 1963, Lawrence Radiation Lab., Livermore, Calif., 1967; cons. to govt. and industry; bd. dirs. emeritus Medtronic Corp., BMC Industries, Donaldson Corp., Baker Knightseen Corp.; corp. adv. bd. AMP Inc., 1990-93. Author: Thermodynamics of Solids, 2d edit, 1972; Contbr. articles to profl. jours. Dir. div. indsl. coop. U. Ariz. Found., 1985-86; trustee Midwest Research Inst., 1975-78, Sci. Mus. Minn., 1973-77, Nat. Tech. U., 1983-90. Recipient Disting. Teaching award Inst. Tech., U. Minn., 1967, Leadership award U. Minn. Alumni, 1993; NATO sr. fellow in sci., 1971. Mem. Sigma Xi, Tau Beta Pi, Phi Delta Theta, Gamma Alpha. Home: Boise, Idaho. Died Jan. 9, 2015.

SWAN, MARTHA LOUISE, retired educator; b. Chadron, Nebr., May 6, 1912; d. Neal Watterson and Sarrah Abbie (Brower) Cook; m. Earle Jameson Swan; (dec. 1970); children: Judith Louise, Linda Camille, Calvin Lawrence, Noreen Adell. BA, Conn. Coll. for Women, New London, 1937; MEd, Lewis & Clark Coll., Portland, Oreg., 1964. Tchr. Norwich (Conn.) Free Acad., 1937-38; music-art tchr. Milwaukie (Oreg.) Sch. Dist., 1947-48; music tchr. Skyline Elem. Sch., Washington County, Oreg., 1951-52, Vancouver (Wash.) Sch. Dist., 1952-53, 57-58; tchr. Portland (Oreg.) Sch. Dist., 1958-64, French and Spanish tchr., 1965-72; ret., 1972. Pvt. tchr. piano and voice, 1938-92; lectr. on cut glass. Author: (book) American Cut and Engraved Glass: The Brilliant Period in Historical Perspective, 1986, 3d edit., 1998; contbr. articles and poems to numerous pulbs. Winthrop scholar Conn. Coll. for Women, 1936. Mem. AAUW (antiques chpt. Portland), R.I. Honor Soc., Am. Cut Glass Assn., Order Eastern Star (program chair 1938-40), Oreg. Retired Educators Assn. (pres. 1997-98). Avocations: painting, piano, concerts, lectures, antiques. Died Jan. 15, 2007.

SWAN, RICHARD HENRY, secondary school educator; b. Toledo, Aug. 6, 1956; s. Howard Dean and Elizabeth Kathleen (Carpenter) S. B Instrumental Music Edn., Ea. Mich. U., 1979. Tchr. music, dir. Gila River Indian Reservation, Sacaton, Ariz., from 1982. Contbr. to essential skills in edn. State of Ariz., 1988. Avocations: travel, gardening, antiques. Home: Mesa, Ariz. Died Mar. 23, 2007.

SWEENEY, JOHN J(OSEPH), lawyer; b. NYC, Dec. 28, 1924; s. John J. and Rose H. (Galligan) S.; m. Rita V. Colleran, Aug. 27, 1955; children: Jean Maria, John J., Peter F., Thomas P., Michael J., Roseanne. LLB, St. John's U., 1951, BA, 1952. Bar: N.Y., 1951. Vol. lawyer Felony Ct. Legal Aid Soc., NYC, 1951-52; asst. gen. counsel U.S. Trucking Corp., NYC, 1952-55; pvt. practice NYC, 1955-83; editor. N.Y. State Tax Monitor, NYC, 1983-84; mortgage real estate loan officer NYC, 1985-90; tchr. DeWitt Clinton H.S., NYC, 1990-92; pvt. practice Scarsdale, from 1992. Spl. master Supreme Ct., N.Y. County; pre-trial master Civil Ct., N.Y. County; commr., referee, receiver and guardian ad litem Supreme and Surrogate's Ct.; arbitrator Am. Arbitration Assn., Civil Ct., N.Y. County, Better Bus. Bur.; arbitrator, mediator N.Y. State Mediation Bd.; litigator local, state, and fed. cts. Pres. Arthur Manor Assn., Scarsdale, 1970-73, Cath. Big Bros., N.Y.C., 1971-73; mem. nominating com. Village Trustee, Scarsdale, 1970-76, mem. nominating com. sch. bd., 1973-76; mem. Scarsdale Hist. Soc., 1980—. With U.S. Army, 1943-46. Decorated Silver star, two Bronze stars, two Purple Hearts and three Battle stars, Combat Infantry Badge. Mem. Guild Cath. Lawyers (pres. 1969-71), Scarsdale Antiques Running Club (pres. 1984-86). Democrat. Avocations: marathon running, tennis, platform tennis, softball, writing. Died Dec. 23, 2006.

SWEPSTON, GENE FAIN, small business owner; b. Wabbaseka, Ark., July 28, 1919; s. Addison Beleau Sweptston and Thelma Jean Fain; m. India Bracy Hankins, June 17, 1943; children: Carol Swepston Duncan, Gene Jr., Paul. Bachelors, Henderson State U., 1941. V.p. ed. sales Ampro Corp., Chgo., 1946—49; ed. sales Dem. Printing and Litho, Little Rock, 1950—53; pres. Gene Swepston Co., Inc., Little Rock, from 1953. Mem., officer Ark. Bookmen's Assn., Little Rock; mem. Ark. Audio-Visual Assn., Little Rock. Active St. James Meth. Ch., Little Rock, from 1950. Maj. US Army, 1941—45, PTO. Recipient Silver Beaver award, Boy Scouts Am., Little Rock, 1998, Art Auction award, Ark. Repertory Theatre, Little Rock, 2000. Mem.: The Bookfellows (sec.), The Dance Club. Democrat. Avocations: pen and ink drawing, dance, reading, photography. Home: Little Rock, Ark. Died Mar. 14, 2007.

SWINDELL, DOLORES HOLLAND, retired school librarian; b. Indpls., Oct. 20, 1935; d. Earle Rupert and Ada Irene (Rubush) Holland; m. Archie C. Swindell, Dec. 28, 1962; children: Randy Zidick, Matthew Earle. BS in Geology/Geography, So. Meth. U., 1957; MLS, U. N.C., 1970; 6th yr. Edn. Leadership, So. Conn. State U., 1990; M in Computer Edn., Johnson/Wales U., 1995. Cert. media specialist 1-12 Conn., edn. adminstrn. Lab. technician R & D Sun Oil Co., Richardson, Tex., 1957—62; libr. asst. rare books Cornell U. Olin Libr., Ithaca, 1962—64; lab. technician vet. sch. Cornell U. Vet. Virus Rsch. Inst., Ithaca, 1964—66; libr. K-6 Dryden Cent. Sch., 1966—67, Cortland N.Y. Pub. Sch., 1967—68; libr. asst. catalog dept. Wilson Libr., Chapel Hill, NC, 1968—69; dir. Geol./Zoology Librs., Chapel Hill, 1969—70; media specialist K-6 NE Sch. Groton Pub. Sch., Conn., 1970—77, media specialist K-6 Noank Sch. Conn., 1977—88, media specialist grades 6-8 West Side Sch. Conn., 1988—95. Independent. Avocation: reading. Home: Groton, Conn. Died July 5, 2007.

SWOL, STANLEY MATHEW, broadcaster, radio station executive; b. Schongau, Germany, Dec. 28, 1950; came to U.S., 1951; s. Joseph Stanley and Anna (Duda) S. BS in Broadcasting, Brown Inst., 1969. Announcer, account exec. Sta. KEYL, Long Prairie, Minn., 1969-78; mgr. Sta. KMSR-FM, Sauk Centre, Minn., 1978-82; account exec. Sta. KMRS, Morris, Minn., 1982-83; news dir. Sta. KXPO, Grafton, N.D., 1983-84; mgr. Sta. KZZR, Burns, Oreg., from 1984; owner Sta. KZZR Radio, Burns, Oreg., from 1988. Avocations: golf, hunting, professional sports. Home: Burns, Oreg. Died Apr. 2, 2007.

SWOPE, MARJORY MASON, association administrator; b. East Orange, NJ, June 5, 1940; d. Virgil Andrew and Edith Elizabeth (Rae) Mason; m. John Franklin Swope, June 9, 1962; children: Kristin, Kevin Andrew, John Gerard. BA, Mt. Holyoke Coll., 1962. Adminstrv. asst. Yale Law Sch. Capital Fund Dr, New Haven, 1962-63; office mgr. LWV N.H., Concord, 1975-81; state election supr. NBC News, NYC, 1975-81; researcher Bur. Nat. Affairs, Washington, 1978-81, Legislex Assocs., Columbus, Ind., 1980-81; exec. dir. N.H. Assn. Conservation Commns., Concord, from 1981. Mem. N.H. Current Use Bd., Concord, 1981—. Co-author: Guide to Designation of Prime Wetlands in New Hampshire, 1983; author: Handbook for Municipal Conservation Commissions in New Hampshire, 1988. Mem. Concord Sch. Bd., 1976-81, Downtown Concord Revitalization Corp., 1980-84; violinist N.H. Philharmonic Orch., Manchester, 1968—, treas., 1982-89. Mem. LWV (newsletter editor N.H. 1970-75), Concord Conservation Commn. (chmn. 1986—). Avocations: violin, gardening, reading. Home: Concord, NH. Died Apr. 17, 2007.

SWOVICK, MELVIN JOSEPH, forensic chemist; b. Altoona, Pa., Jan. 20, 1926; s. Walter Joseph and Magdalen Mary (Krish) S.; m. Maria Elizabeth Galatz, Nov. 23, 1968; 1 child, Michael Robert Wayne. BS in Chemistry with honors, Detroit Inst. Tech., 1974. Med. tech. VA Hosp., Altoona, 1954-55; lab. asst. Allied Chem. and Dye, Buffalo, 1956-57; lab. tch. Allied Chem. Corp., Buffalo, 1958-60; chemist Nopco Chem. Co., Linden, N.J., 1961-63; analytical chemist Schwarz Bio Rsch., Orangeburg, N.Y., 1964, Reichhold Chems., Inc., Elizabeth, N.J., 1965-79, coatings chemist Ferndale, Mich.; forensic chemist Oakland County Sheriff's Dept., Pontiac, Mich., 1980-91; ret., 1991. Instr. Austin Cath. Preparatory Sch., Detroit, 1975-79. Pres., v.p. Sylvan Glen Homeowners Assn., Troy, Mich., 1978-86, chmn.; instnl. rep. Boy Scouts Am., Grosse Pointe Park, Mich., 1968-74. Mem. Austrian Soc. Detroit, Carpathia Club. Democrat. Roman Catholic. Avocations: hunting, dance, gardening. Home: Troy, Mich. Died June 7, 2007.

SYKES, MATTIE WILDA See DOBBS, MATTIWILDA

SYMONS, BARBARA ADELE SCHALK, academic administrator, counselor; b. Chgo., Jan. 16, 1939; d. Stanley Steven and Adele Mary (Maniak) Schalk; m. Frederick E. Symons, June 17, 1992. BS, Coll. of St. Catherine, St. Paul, 1960; MEd, U. Pitts., 1968. Cert. tchr.; lic. counselor. Camp dir. Mpls. Girl Scout Coun., summers 1960-67; tchr. St. Margaret's Acad., Mpls., 1960-63, Community Sch. Dist., Blue Island, Ill., 1963-67; sch. counselor Shaler Area Sch. Dist., Glenshaw, Pa., 1968-69, guidance counselor, 1970—95, chair guidance dept., 1989—95; ret., 1995. Mem. NEA, Pa. State Edn. Assn., Am. Assn. Counseling and Devel., Am. Sch. Counselors Assn., Allegheny County Counselors Assn. (sec. 1979-93, Counselor of Distinction 1988), Pa. Sch. Counselors Assn. (conf. registrar 1983-92, bd. govs. 1988-91). Avocations: hiking, reading, crossword puzzles, travel, shopping. Home: Hinsdale, Ill. Died Jan. 2014.

SZABO, VALERIE, lawyer; b. Greenville, Mich., Mar. 6, 1956; d. Bernard and Shirley (Fine) S.; m. Glenn Goldenhorn, Sept. 27, 1987. BA, U. S.C., 1977; JD, George Mason U., 1980. Assoc. Ilona Ely Freedman, Alexandria, Va., 1981-83; pvt. practice Arlington, 1984-96; ptnr. Szabo & Angus, PLLC, Arlington, 1996-99, Valerie Szabo, PLLC, from 2000. Mem. ABA, ATLA, Va. Bar Assn., Va. Trial Lawyers Assn., Fairfax County Bar Assn., Arlington County Bar Assn., Delta Theta Phi. Democrat. Died June 23, 2007.

SZENASI, GAIL, educational administrator; b. Portales, N.Mex., Dec. 26, 1946; d. Robert Claude Mersereau and Wanda (Sollock) Sims; m. James Joseph Szenasi, Sept. 2, 1968; children: Clay, Daniel, David. BS, Tex. Tech U., 1969, MEd, 1975; PhD, U. N.Mex., 1989. Cert. tchr., adminstr., N.Mex. Tchr. Denver Pub. Schs., 1969-70, Lubbock (Tex.) Pub. Schs., 1970-76, U. N.Mex. Lab. Sch., Albuquerque, 1981; cons. U. N.Mex., N.Mex., 1984-88; headmistress Sunset Mesa Schs., Albuquerque, from 1988. Cons. Rsch., 1988-94, ETC, Cedar Crest, N.Mex., 1984—, sr. Training cons., Sandia Nat. Labs., Albuquerque, N.Mex. Home: Cedar Crest, N.Mex. Died Mar. 12, 2007.

TAI, PETER YAI-PO, plant geneticist; b. Chutung, Taiwan, Rep. China, July 6, 1937; came to U.S., 1964; s. Yu Shu and Chomay (Liao) T.; m. Rosie Peng, Jan. 30, 1964; children: Robert H., Thomas H. MS, Tex. A&M U., 1966; PhD, Okla. State U., 1972. Rsch. asst. Okla. State U., Stillwater, 1967-72; postdoctoral rsch. assoc. U. Ga. Expt. Sta., Experiment, 1972-75; instr. U. Ga. Coast Plain Sta., Tifton, 1972-77; rsch. geneticist USDA Agrl. Rsch. Svc., Canal Point, Fla., from 1977. Contbr. articles to profl. jours. Mem. AAAS, Am. Soc. Agronomy, Crop Sci. Soc. Am., Am. Soc. Sugarcane Technologists. Achievements include research in development and release of sugarcane varieties, long term sugarcane pollen storage, genetic relationships among three chlorophyll-deficient mutants in peanuts. Home: Canal Point, Fla. Died Feb. 19, 2007.

TALBOT, EMILE JOSEPH, French language educator; b. Brunswick, Maine, Apr. 12, 1941; s. Joseph Emile and Flora Talbot; m. Elizabeth Mullen, Aug. 6, 1966; children: Marc, Paul. BA, St. Francis Coll., Biddeford, Maine, 1963; MA, Brown U., 1965, PhD, 1968. From instr. French to prof. U. Ill., Urbana, 1967—86, prof., 1986—2004, prof. emeritus, from 2004, head dept. French, 1988-94. Editor: (book) La Critique Stendhalienne, 1979; author: Stendhal and Romantic Esthetics, 1985, Stendhal Revisited, 1993, Reading Nelligan, 2002; rev. editor: The French Rev., 1979—82, Quebec Studies, 1988—93, mem. editl. bd.:, 1993—96; mem. editl. bd. Quebec Studies, 2003—05, from 2010; mem. editl. bd.: Nineteenth-Century French Studies, 1986—2003, La Revue Francophone, 1990—96, Etudes Francophones, 1996—2004, Nouvelles Etudes Francophones, 2004—12; editor: Quebec Studies, 2004—09. Decorated chevalier Ordre des Palmes Académiques (France); recipient prize, Quebec, 2006, Alumni Achievement award, U. New Eng., 2008; fellow, Ctr. Advanced Study U. Ill., 1973, Assoc., 1988, NEH, 1973—74, Camargo Found., France, 1976. Mem.: MLA, Am. Coun. Que. Studies (v.p. 1995—97, pres. 1997—99), Assn. Can. Studies in U.S., Am. Assn. Tchrs. French. Roman Catholic. Home: Champaign, Ill. Died Mar. 22, 2014.

TALTON, JAMES RALPH, JR., accountant; b. Wilson, NC, Dec. 4, 1942; s. James Ralph and Victoria (Harrell) T.; m. Myrtle Weaver, Feb. 2, 1964; children: James Ralph III, Elizabeth Paige Johnson. BS, East Carolina U., 1965. CPA, N.C., S.C. Staff acct. Richard M. Hunter & Co., Charlotte, N.C., 1965-66; ptnr. KPMG Peat Marwick LLP, Raleigh, N.C., 1966-69, Greenville, S.C., 1969-86, Raleigh, from 1986. Chmn. Triangle chpt. ARC, Raleigh, 1993-95, East Carolina U. Found., Greenville, 1994-96. Named Boss of Yr. Greenville JC's, 1984. Mem. Nat. Assn. Accts. (past pres. Greater Greenville chpt., Man of Yr. 1986), S.C. Assn. CPAs (past pres.), N.C. Assn. CPAs (legis. com. 1990), Greater Raleigh C. of C. (chmn. 1996-97), Carolina Country Club. Republican. Presbyterian. Avocations: golf, reading. Home: Raleigh, NC. Died Apr. 3, 2007.

TANAY, EMANUEL, psychiatry professor, writer; s. Bunim Tenenwurzel and Betty Kowarski-Tenenwurzel; m. Sandra Jean Eddy, Aug. 13, 1970; children: Elaine Nina Meleski, Anita Hirsch-Tanay, David Emanuel. MD, U. Munich, 1951. Cert. in emanuel tanay State Mich., 1957, diplomate American Bd. Psychiatry and Neurology, 1959, cert. in commendation chmn. task force Occupl. Psychiatry American Psychiat. Assn., 1970, in emanuel tanay American Bd. Forensic Psychiatry, 1979. Assoc. dir. dept. psychiatry Detroit Receiving Hosp., 1958—63; clin. prof. psychiatry Wayne State U. Sch. Medicine, Detroit, 1971—2014; assoc. prof. Wayne State U. Law Sch. Pres. Mich. Psychiat. Soc., Lansing, 1981—82; mem. exec. com. World Psychiat. Assn., Vienna. Author: (books) Murderers: Study of Homicide, 1976, Passport to Life: Reflections of a Holocaust Survivor, 2004, American Legal Injustice: Behind the Scenes with an Expert Witness, 2010. Pres. Jewish Cmty. Coun. Grosse Pointe, Mich.; v.p. Mich. Assn. Marriage, Family and Divorce, Detroit; mem. Internat. Assn. Genocide Scholars. Recipient Flag award, Mich. State Med. Soc., 1969, Exemplary Psychiatrist award, Nat. Alliance Mentally Ill, 1992, Fellowship award, American Coll. Psychiatrists, 1992, Golden Apple award, American Acad. Psychiatry, 1998; Disting. fellow, American Acad. Forensic Sciences, 2008—14, Disting. Life fellow, American Psychiatrics Assn., 2008—14. Mem.: American Psychiatric Assn. Democrat. Achievements include research in psychology of homicide and post traumatic stress disorder. Avocations: sailing, skiing. Home: Ann Arbor, Mich. Died Aug. 5, 2014.

TANNENBAUM, BERNICE SALPETER (BERNICE ANNETTE FRANKLIN), national religious organization executive; b. NYC, Nov. 6, 1913; d. Isidore and May Bisgyer Franklin; m. Hyman Salpeter (dec. 1969); m. Nathan Tannenbaum (dec. 1991); 1 child, Richard Salpeter. BA, Bklyn. coll. Public school tchr.; part-time advertising copy writer; chmn. Comm. on the Status of Women of the

World Jewish Congress; mem. exec. bd. Am. sect. World Jewish Congress; chmn. internat. affairs com.; mem. Zionist Gen. Coun.; active Exec. World Zionist Orgn. Bd. dirs., mem. gen. assembly Jewish Agy.; bd. dirs., v.p. United Israel Appeal; mem. exec. com. Am. Zionist Movement; former chair Hadassah mag.; nat. pres. Hadassah, 1976-80; nat. chmn. Hadassah Internat., 1984-95; liaison Hadassah Found.; sec. Jewish Telegraphic Agy.; bd. govs. Hebrew U. Recipient Henrietta Szold award, 2003. Died Apr. 6, 2015.

TANNENBAUM, JAMES M., nurse anesthetist; b. New Haven, Apr. 13, 1949; s. Sidney Julius and Ruth (Cannon) T. ADN, ADA, Community Coll. R.I.; student, Georgetown U., 1967-70; BSN, Salve Regina U., Newport, RI, 1989-92; cert. in nurse anesthesia, Meml. Hosp. R.I., 1994. RN, R.I. Medication technician Briarcliffe Nursing Home, Johnston, R.I.; staff nurse cardiac stepdown unit ICU Miriam Hosp., Providence; nurse anesthetist R.I. Hosp., Providence. Mem. R.I. Nurses Assn. (membership com.), R.I. Coun. on Alcoholism, Am. Assn. Nurse Anesthetists, Phi Theta Kappa. Home: Cranston, RI. Died Aug. 18, 2007.

TANNENBAUM, RENA MERYL See WOLNER, RENA

TANNER, LAUREL NAN, education educator; b. Detroit, Feb. 16, 1929; d. Howard Nicholas and Celia (Solovich) Jacobson; m. Daniel Tanner, July 11, 1948; m. Kenneth J. Rehage, Nov. 25, 1989. BS in Social Sci, Mich. State U., 1949, MA in Edn., 1953; EdD, Columbia U., 1967. Pub. sch. tchr., 1950-64; instr. tchr. edn. Hunter Coll., 1964-66, asst. prof., 1967-69; supr. Milw. Pub. Schs., 1966-67; mem. faculty Temple U., Phila., from 1969, prof. edn., 1974-89, prof. emerita, from 1993; prof. edn. U. Houston, 1989-96; affiliate prof. U. Washington, from 2009. Vis. professorial scholar U. London Inst. Edn., 1974—75; vis. scholar Stanford U., 1984—85, U. Chgo., 1988—89; curriculum cons., from 1969; disting. vis. prof. San Francisco State U., 1987. Author: Classroom Discipline for Effective Teaching and Learning, 1978, La Disciplina en la enseñanza y el Aprendizaje, 1980, Dewey's Laboratory School: Lessons for Today, 1997; co-author: Classroom Teaching and Learning, 1971, Curriculum Development: Theory into Practice, 1975, 4th edit., 2007, Supervision in Education: Problems and Practices, 1987, (with Daniel Tanner) History of the School Curriculum, 1990; editor Nat. Soc. Study Edn. Critical Issues in Curriculum, 87th yearbook, part 1, 1988. Faculty rsch. fellow Temple U., 1970, 80, 81; recipient John Dewey Rsch. award, 1981-82, Rsch. Excellence award U. Houston, 1992, Outstanding Writing award Am. Assn. Colls. Tchr. Edn., 1998; Spencer Found. rsch. grantee, 1992. Mem. ASCD (dir. 1982-84), Soc. Study Curriculum History (founder, 1st pres. 1978-79), Am. Edn. Rsch. Assn. (com. on role and status of women in ednl. R & D 1994-97, Lifetime Achievement award 2007), Profs. Curriculum Assn. (Factotum 1983-84, chair membership com. 1994-95), Am. Ednl. Studies Assn., John Dewey Soc. (bd. dirs. 1989-91, pres. 2000-01), Alumni Coun. Tchrs. Coll. Columbia U. Home: Wilmette, Ill. *In my view, America has progressed over the years, and the best days are still to come. We have the single necessary resource to solve our most urgent problems and achieve our deepest moral values — human intelligence.* Died 2013.

TANNER, LEONARD R., JR., tire company executive; b. Nashville, Aug. 28, 1915; s. Leonard R. and Lady (Pentecost) T.; m. Anne Brueggeman, Oct. 4, 1941 (dec. 1984); children: Sherry Anne Earnhart, Wendy Leigh Miller, Roscoe Tanner III. BA, U. Chattanooga; JD, Northwestern U. Assoc. Defrees, Buckingham, Fiske & O'Brien, Chgo., 1941-43, Smith, Ristig & Smith, Washington, 1945-46; ptnr. Noone, Tanner & Noone, Chattanooga, 1946-53, Swafford & Tanner, Chattanooga, 1953-55, Tanner, Jahn, Anderson, Bridges & Jahn, Chattanooga, 1955-81; pres., chief exec. officer Mitchell Indsl. Tire Co., Inc., Chattanooga, from 1981, chmn. bd. dirs., from 1981. Dir. Fla. Indsl. tire Co., Inc., 1975—. Served to lt. USN, 1943-45. Mem. ABA, Tenn. Bar Assn., Chattanooga Bar Assn. Clubs: Mountain City (Chattanooga), Walden, Chattanooga Golf and Country; Fairyland Country (Lookout Mountain, Tenn.). Republican. Presbyterian. Home: Lookout Mountain, Ga. Died May 28, 2007.

TANZMAN, MARY, social worker; b. Bialystok, Poland, Sept. 29, 1915; came to U.S., 1920; d. Jacob and Bertha (Cohen) Grodman; m. Jack Tanzman, Feb. 22, 1942; children: Elaine, Edward. BA in Social Work, Wayne State U., 1939; MSW, U. Chgo., 1964. Social worker, dist. supr. Jewish Family and Community Services, Chgo., 1942-49; dir. social work marital dept. Forest Hosp., Des Plaines, Ill., 1959-64; pvt. practice social work Evanston, Ill., from 1955. Cons. in field. Fellow Am. Orthopsychiat. Assn. (life); mem. NASW, Am. Assn. Marital and Family Therapists (clin.). Home: Chicago, Ill. Died Mar. 4, 2007.

TAPLEY, EARL MAYS, retired college dean; b. Marietta, Ga., Nov. 8, 1913; s. Joel David and Emma Melissa (Quarles) T.; m. Ruby Jewell Franklin, June 5, 1935; children: Dwight Lowell, Sharon Roselle, Ruth Annette. AB, Vanderbilt U., 1945; MA, George Peabody Coll., Nashville, 1946; PhD, U. Chgo., 1955; diploma, BTS, 1935. Ordained to ministry, Meth. Ch. Pastor various chs., Ga., Tenn., Ill., 1935-46; dean, academic v.p., interim pres. Lee U., Cleveland, Tenn., 1946—53; assoc. prof., asst. to pres., dir. spl. svcs., head dept. psychology U. Chattanooga, 1953-57; prof., dir. research U. Evansville, Ind., 1957-59, prof., dept. head, 1959-65, dean, grad. sch., 1965-79, grad. dean emeritus, from 1979, dir. internat. studies and travel, 1970—86, creator; assoc. minister First United Meth. Ch., Dunedin, Fla., 1986-90, The Meth. Temple, Evansville, 1980-86. Accreditation cons.; leader comparative edn. study groups USSR, 1969-79, China, 1978-84. Author: Teaching General Education in Junior Colleges, 1955, General Education in the College Curriculum, 1957, The Way It Was, 1994, 2d edit., 2000; contbr. articles to profl. jours. Named to Hall of Fame, Dunedin, 2003. Mem. AAUP (chpt. pres. 1962-64), Ind. Asns. Grad. Schs. (pres. 1972-74), Dunedin Com. Aging, Rotary, Phi Delta Kappa, Phi Kappa Phi. Achievements include a scientific laboratory named after him at Lee University and Multimedia Center at the University of Evansville. Avocations: writing, computers, boating, sport fishing, fishing, astronomy, cosmology. Home: Dunedin, Fla. Died Dec. 23, 2014.

TARKANIAN, JERRY, retired men's college basketball coach; b. Euclid, Ohio, Aug. 8, 1930; m. Lois Huter; children: Pamela, Jodie, Danny, George Attended, Pasadena City Coll., Calif.; B, Calif. State U., Fresno, 1955; M in Ednl. Mgmt., U. Redlands, Calif. Head basketball coach San Joaquin Meml. HS, Fresno, Calif., 1956-57, Antelope Valley HS, Lancaster, Calif., 1958, Redlands HS, Calif., 1959-60, Riverside City Coll. Tigers, Calif., 1961-66, Pasadena City Coll. Lancers, Calif., 1966-68, Calif. State U. Long Beach 49ers, 1968-73, U. Nev. Las Vegas Runnin' Rebels, 1973-92, asst. athletic dir., 1982-92; head coach San Antonio Spurs, 1992; head basketball coach Calif. State U. Fresno Bulldogs, 1995—2002; founder, pres. Tarkanian Basketball Acad., Las Vegas. Co-author (with William E. Warren): Winning Basketball Systems, 1980; co-author: (with Terry Pluto) Tark: College Basketball's Winningest Coach, 1988; co-author: (with Dan Wetzel) Runnin' Rebel: Shark Tales of " Extra Benefits", Frank Sinatra and Winning It All, 2005; author: Winning Basketball: Drills and Fundamentals, 1983; actor: (films) The Fish That Saved Pittsburgh, 1979, Honeymoon in Vegas, 1992, Blue Chips, 1994, The Sixth Man, 1997; (TV series) Caribbean Fantasy, 1995, Arli$$, 1998. Named to Naismith Meml. Basketball Hall of Fame, 2013. Achievements include 12th men's college basketball coach to 700 wins, never had a losing season; lead Long Beach State to NCAA tournament appearances from 1970 to 1973; lead UNLV to the Final Four in 1977, 1987, 1990 and 1991, winning the national title in 1990; lead Fresno State to NCAA tournament appearances in 2000 and 2001. Died Feb. 11, 2015.

TARPLEY, ROY JAMES, retired professional basketball player; b. NYC, Nov. 28, 1964; Student, U. Mich., 1982-86. Forward Dallas Mavericks, 1986—90, 1994—95, Witchita Falls Texans, Continental Basketball Assn., 1991—92; foward Miami Tropics, US Basketball League, 1992; forward Aris, Greece, 1992—93, Olympiacos, Greece, 1993—94, Iraklis, Greece, 1995—96, Apollon Limassol, Cyprus, 1998—99, Ural Great, 1999—2000, Beijing Olympians, 2000—01, Sioux Falls Skyforce, Continental Basketball Assn., SD, 2003—04, Dodge City Legend, US Basketball League, Kans., 2005, Mich. Mayhem, Continental Basketball Assn., 2005—06. Recipient NBA Sixth Man award, 1988; named to The NBA All-Rookie First Team, 1987 Died Jan. 9, 2015.

TARPLEY, WILLIAM BEVERLY, JR., physics and chemistry consultant; b. Richmond, Va., Oct. 12, 1917; s. William B. and Sallie M. (Gatewood) T.; m. Nancy Tarpley, Aug. 10, 1938 (dec. Mar. 1980); 1 child, William B. III; m. Phyllis Malmquist, May 7, 1988. PhD, Columbia U., 1951. R & D chemist Schering Corp., Bloomfield, N.J., 1937-52; sr. phys. scientist U.S. Army Biol. Lab., Frederick, Md., 1952-55; v.p. R & D, Aeroprojects, Inc., West Chester, Pa., 1955-69; dir. materials dept. R & D Labs., Franklin Inst., Phila., 1969-71; v.p. R & D, Fluid Energy Equipment & Processing, Hatfield, N.J., 1971, Organic Recycling subs. UOP, West Chester, 1971-77, Energy & Minerals Rsch., Exton, Pa., 1977-85; ret., 1985; cons. in surface physics and chemistry, Downingtown, Pa., 1985-87. Avocations: reading, photography, travel. Died Oct. 27, 2007.

TARPY, MARTIN LYSTER, beef wholesale executive; b. Central Falls, RI, Aug. 22, 1913; s. Stephen and Mary Frances (Nolan) T.; m. Charlotte Joanna Hosfeld, Oct. 16, 1943; children: Peter, Susan. AB, Brown U., 1937. Pres. Tarpy's Inc., from 1937, West End Land Co, from 1977. Trustee Meml. Hosp., Pawtucket, R.I., 1962—, Hosp. Assn. R.I., Providence, 1985-91, Brown U., Providence, 1969—; bd. dirs. R.I. Renal Inst., Warwick, 1977—; corporator Delta Dental of R.I., Providence, 1974—; mem. Big Bros. Am. (Big Bro. of Yr.), Providence, Boys Club Am. (Keystone award), Pawtucket, R.I. Comdr. USN, 1942-46, PTO. Recipient Silver Beaver award Boy Scouts Am., 1953, Brown Bear award Brown U., 1991, Disting. Svc. award Hosp. Assn. R.I., 1995. Mem. New Eng. Wholesale Meat Dealers Assn. (bd. dirs. 1946—, pres. 1963). Roman Catholic. Home: Pawtucket, RI. Died Feb. 26, 2007.

TARTER, FRED BARRY, advertising executive; b. Bklyn., Aug. 16, 1943; s. Irving and Edna (Kupferberg) T.; m. Lois; children: Scott Andrew, Heather Michelle, Megan Elizabeth. Attended, CCNY, 1962—68. Pres. Jamie Publ. Hootenanny Enterprises, Inc., 1962-65; mdse. dir. Longines Symphonette Soc., 1965-67; with Universal Comm., Inc., NYC, from 1967, pres., CEO, 1969-74; CEO Screenvision Cinema Network, 1972—2000; exec. v.p. Deerfield Comm., Inc., NYC, 1974-87, pres., CEO, 1977-88, pres., 1988—89; pub. S.E.W. mag., NYC, 1977-88; pres. The Rainbow Group Ltd., NYC, from 1988; chmn. Stagebill Mag., 1997-2001; pres., CEO The Lakeside Group of Co., from 2001. Exec. prodr. Joanne Carson's VIP's Miss Am. Teenager Pageant, 1972—73; prodr. Marriage Counselor, 1994, Spenser: Pale Kings & Princes, 1995, Spenser: A Savage Place, 1995, Spenser Judas Goat, 1995, Hearts Adrift, 1995, Ceremony, 1996, Wounded Heart, 1996, Reasons of the Heart, 1996, Lover's Leap, 1996; chmn. Stagebill Enterprises, LLC, 1997—2001; vice-chmn. Affinity Comm., Inc., 1997—2001; pres., CEO The Telephone Co. LLC, 1999—2003; pres. The Programme Exch., U.K. Ltd.; bd. dirs. Boardwalk Entertainment, Ltd., Lakeside Group, Inc., Cinema Events, LLC, Radio Free Europe Found.; bd. mem. Scholar Rescue Fund; mng. dir. Legacy Real Estate Investment Fund, from 2012; CEO The Readers Guild, LLC, 2014. Home: New York, NY. *An integral part of success is the capacity for failure. Persistence, combined with responsibility, has proven to be the winning combination time and again.* Died June 28, 2015.

TARTER, MICHAEL ERNEST, biostatistician, educator; b. Bronx, NY, Dec. 20, 1938; s. William Tarter and Frieda Browdy; m. Orna Benzenburg, Aug. 30, 1975; children: Douglas, Robin. BA in Math., UCLA, 1959, MA in Math., 1961, PhD in Biostats., 1963. Asst. prof. U. Mich., Ann Arbor, 1964-66, assoc. prof., 1967, U. Calif., Irvine, 1968-70, Berkeley, 1970-76, prof., from 1977. Vis. prof. Italian U. Author books and articles; editor: Jour. Am. Statis. Assn. (screening editor for applications 1971-80); co-editor: Proceedings of the Computer Science and Statistics Interface 4th, 6th, 25th edit. Cons. Electric Power Rsch. Inst., Roth Assocs., 1989—91, Precision Data Group, 1993, Failure Analysis Assocs., 1996, Nat. Inst. Occupl. Safety and Health, U. Calif., 1995—98, AIDS Data Safety Monitoring Bd., 1993—97, Pacific Bell, 1996—98, Am. Lung Assn., 1996—97, CalEPA Indoor Air Risk Assessment, 1997—2001, Calif. Environ. Protection Agy., 1995—99, External Adv. Group Uncertainty Analysis Risk Assessment, UC Agrl. Ergonomics Rsch. Ctr., from 1998, Calif. Office Environmental Health Hazards Assessment, from 1999; chair and program chair, sect. risk Am. Statis. Assn.; elected mem. Internat. Inst. Stat. Recipient Disting. Svc. award, UC Divsn. Agr. and Natural Resources, Chptr. Svc. Recognition Award, Nat. Am. Statis. Assn., Honorable Mention award, 20th Anniversary Nat. Meeting of the Assn. Computing Machinery, Fulbright awards, Coun. Internat. Exch. Scholars; fellow, Nat. Am. Statis. Assn. Fellow Am. Statis. Assn. (chmn. com. resources biometrics sect. 1981—, editorial bds. computational stats. and data analysis 1983-86, biometrics 1976-84, stats. 1977-97). Avocation: music. Died May 10, 2014.

TATE, JAMES VINCENT, poet, English educator; b. Kansas City, Mo., Dec. 8, 1943; s. Samuel Vincent Appleby and Betty Jean Whitsitt; m. Dara Wier; stepchildren Emily Pettit, Guy Pettit BA, Kans. State Coll., 1965; MFA, U. Iowa, 1967. Instr. U. Iowa, Iowa City, 1966-67; vis. lectr. U. Calif., Berkeley, 1967-68; asst. prof. English Columbia U., NYC, 1969-71; from assoc. prof. to dist. univ. prof. English U. Mass., Amherst, 1971—2015. Poet-in-residence Emerson Coll., 1970-71; cons. Coord. Coun. Literary Mags., 1971-74, Ky. Arts Commn., 1979; mem. Bollingen Prize Com., 1974-75; poetry editor Dickinson Rev., 1967-76; trustee, assoc. editor Pym-Randall Pr., 1968-80; assoc. editor Barn Dream Pr. Author: (poems) Cages, 1966, The Destination, 1967, The Lost Pilot, 1967 (Yale Younger Poets award 1966), Notes of Woe, 1968, Camping in the Valley, 1968, Mystics in Chicago, 1968, The Torches, 1968, Row with Your Hair, 1969, Is There Anything?, 1969, Shepherds of the Mist, 1969, Amnesia People, 1970, Are You Ready Mary Baker Eddy, 1970, Deaf Girl Playing, 1970, The Oblivion Ha-Ha, 1970, Wrong Songs, 1970, Hints to Pilgrims, 1971, Nobody Goes to Visit the Insane Anymore, 1971, Absences, 1972, Apology for Eating Geoffrey Movius' Hyacinth, 1972, A Dime Found in the Snow, 1973, Hottentot Ossuary, 1974, Marfa, 1974, Suffering Bastards, 1975, Who Gets the Bitterroot?, 1976, Viper Jazz, 1976, Riven Doggeries, 1979, The Rustling of Foliage, the Memory of Caresses, 1979, If It Would All Please Hurray, 1980, Land of Little Sticks, 1981, Constant Defender, 1983, Just Shades, 1985, Reckoner, 1986, Distance from Loved Ones, 1990, Selected Poems, 1991 (Pulitzer Prize for poetry 1992), Worshipful Company of Fletchers, 1993 (Nat. Book Award for Poetry 1994), Shroud of the Gnome, 1997, Return to the City of White Donkeys, 2004, Memoirs of the Hawk, 2005, The Ghost Soldiers, 2008, Dome of the Hidden Pavilion, 2015 (posthumous); (novel) Lucky Darryl, 1977. Named Poet of Yr. by Phi Beta Kappa, 1972; recipient Nat. Inst. Arts and Letters award for poetry, 1974; Mass. Arts and Humanities fellow, 1975, Guggenheim fellow, 1976, Nat. Endowment for the Arts fellow, 1980. Died July 8, 2015.

TAUBMAN, A. ALFRED (ADOLPH ALFRED TAUBMAN), real estate developer; b. Pontiac, Mich., Jan. 31, 1924; s. Philip and Fannie Ester (Blustin) T.; m. Reva Kolodney, Dec. 1, 1949 (div. July 1977); children: Gayle Kalisman, Robert S., William S.; m. Judith Mazor, June 17, 1982. Student, U. Mich., 1945-48, LLD (hon.), 1991; student, Lawrence Inst. Tech., 1948-49, DArch (hon.), 1985; D in Bus. (hon.), Eastern Mich. U., 1984; D in Edn. (hon.), Mich. State U., 1993; HHD (hon.), No. Mich. U., 1995. Chmn. The Taubman Co., Bloomfield Hills, Mich., from 1950, Taubman Ctrs., Inc., Bloomfield Hills, Mich., from 1992. Prin. shareholder Sotheby's Holdings, Inc., N.Y.C., 1983-2001. Author: Threshold Resistance: The Extraordinary Career of a Luxury Retailing Pioneer, 2007. Trustee Ctr. for Creative Studies, Detroit, Harper-Grace Hosps., Detroit; chmn. emeritus Archives Am. Art Smithsonian Inst., Washington, U. Pa. Wharton Real Estate Ctr., Phila.; pres. Arts Commn. of Detroit; mem. nat. bd. Smithsonian Assocs.; established Taubman Ctr. for State and Local Govt. Harvard U., Cambridge, Mass., chmn. Mich. Partnership for New Edn., Program in Am. Instns., U. Mich., Brown U.'s Pub. Policy and Am. Instns. Program; prin. benefactor A. Alfred Taubman Health Care Ctr. and A. Alfred Taubman Med. Libr., U. Mich.; bd. dirs. Detroit Renaissance, Inc., Friends of Art and Preservation in Embassies, Washington; active State of Mich. Gaming Commn.

Recipient Bus. Statesman award Harvard Bus. Sch. Club of Detroit, 1983, Sportsman of Yr. award United Found. Detroit, SE Mich. Chpt. March of Dimes Birth Defects, 1983; named Michiganian of Yr. The Detroit News, 1983; named one of Forbes 400: Richest Americans, 2006-. Mem. Urban Land Inst. (trustee), Nat. Realty Com. (bd. dirs.). Died Apr. 17, 2015.

TAYLOR, ARTHUR ROBERT, former academic administrator, former broadcast executive; b. Elizabeth, NJ, July 6, 1935; s. Arthur Earl and Marion Hilda (Scott) T.; m. Kathryn Pelgrift; children by previous marriage, Martha Josephson, Anne Madden, Sarah Rountree BA magna cum laude, Brown U., 1957, MA in Am. Econ. History, 1961; H.H.D. (hon.), Bucknell U., 1975, Allentown Coll. of St. Francis de Sales; L.H.D. (hon.), Rensselaer Poly. Inst., 1975, Simmons Coll., 1975; LL.D. (hon.), Mt. Scenario Coll., 1975. Asst. dir. admissions Brown U., Providence, 1957-61; with First Boston Corp., NYC, 1961-70, asst. v.p., 1964-66, v.p., 1966-70, also dir.; v.p. fin. Internat. Paper Co., NYC, 1970-71, exec. v.p., dir., 1971-72; pres. CBS Inc., NYC, 1972-76, also dir.; pres. Muhlenberg Coll., Allentown, Pa., 1992—2002. Chmn. Arthur Taylor & Co., Inc., 1977-2015; chmn. The Entertainment Channel, 1980-83; dean faculty of bus. Fordham U., 1985-92; bd. dirs. Nomura Pacific Basin Fund, Pitney Bowes, La. Land & Exploration Co., Jakarta Growth Fund, Japan OTC Equity Fund; mem. adv. com. Toshiba Internat.; founding pres. NYC Partnership; formed Sarabam Corp. Mem. Population Resource Ctr., Nat. Commn. of Civic Renewal; trustee Brown U. Mem. Coun. Fgn. Rels., Trilateral Commn., Phi Beta Kappa. Clubs: Century (N.Y.C.); Met. (Washington); California (L.A.). Congregationalist. Home: Allentown, Pa. Died Dec. 3, 2015.

TAYLOR, FLORIETTA, retired music educator, composer, retired social worker; d. Alfred Leroy and Anna Eliza Diggs; m. John Lawrence Taylor, Dec. 24, 1953; children: Sonja Joy Gore, Rhonna Lynn, Vicki Ann Bass. MusB in Edn., Howard U., Washington, 1952; MS in Edn., Jacksonville State U., 1974. Cert. music tchr. Ala. Organist Quinn Chapel AME Ch., Frederick, Md., 1944—48; pianist Hallelujah Gospel Chorus, Frederick, Md., 1944—48; cottage supr. N.J. State Home for Girls, Trenton, 1955—56; music instr., choral dir. Talladega County Bd. of Edn., Ala., 1957—72; social worker Dept. of Pensions and Security, Talladega, Ala., 1974—88; founder, dir., and organist Mt. Canaan Bapt. Ch. Inspirational Choir, Talladega, Ala., 1975—88; chapel musician, contract worker Fed. Correctional Instn., Talladega, Ala., 1981—82; min. of music First AME Ch., Gaithersburg, Md., 1988—90. 2d trumpet Howard U. Marching and Symphonic Band, Washington, 1948—52; piano instr., Talladega, Ala., from 1957; music dir. of youth choir Mt. Cannan Bapt. Ch., Talladega, Ala., 1959—65; mem. Talladega County Assn. for the Deaf, Blind and Handicapped, Ala., 1976—88, Ala. State Child Abuse and Neglect Bd., Montgomery, 1978—80, Ala. Gerontol. Soc., Montgomery, 1978—88; chmn. Cmty. Housing Resource Bd. of Housing and Urban Devel., Talladega, Ala., 1982—84; mem. Talladega Improvement Assn., Ala., 1984—88; guest spkr. Phyllis Wheatly H.S. All Class Reunion, Childersburg, Ala., 1985—85; mem. Wendell P. Whalum Cmty. Chorus, Atlanta, from 1990, Met. Atlanta Musicians Assn., Inc., from 1990; music dir./organist Sr./Retirees Group of St. Philip African Meth. Episcopal Ch., Atlanta, from 1994; pres. Met. Atlanta Musicians Assn., Inc., Atlanta, 1999—2004; choir participant Brazeal Dennard Choral Ensembles with tDetroit Symphony Civic Orch., 2002—02; music instr. Talladega Coll., 1952—54; pianist (christmas season) South DeKalb Mall. Composer: (four part composition) Hear My Pray'r, O Lord; musician (arranger): (musical compositions) Halleluia, Jesus the Lord is Risen Today; composer: (children's series) Treasure of Inspiration. Musician and advisor Soapstone Sa. Group, Decatur, Ga., 1993—2004; bd. dirs. Chapel Pk. Condominium Assn., Decatur, Ga., 1995—97; celebration participant Met. Atlanta Task Force for Homeless, 1996—96; pres. Taladega County Dem. Conf., Ala., 1980—88; alt. del. Ala. Dem. Party, Talladega Couunty, 1984, del. Talladega County, 1988; music dir. youth choir Mt. Cannan Bapt. Ch., Talladega, Ala., 1959—65; interin choir dir. St. Philip African Meth. Episcopal Ch., Atlanta, 1991—93; mem. choir, European Concert Tour, Ebenezer Bapt. Ch., Atlanta, 2004. Recipient Outstanding Leadership and Svc. award, Talladega County Dem. Conf., 1982, 1983, 1985, 1988, Cmty. Svc. award, Gov. George Wallace, 1983, Office of Sec. of State, Ala., 1983, Lyndon Baines Johnson Leadership award, Ala. Dem. Conf., 1985, Outstanding Leadership and Svc. award, Talladega County Bd. Commrs., 1988, Outstanding Leadership award, Superior Ct. Judge William Sullivan, 1988, Outstanding Cmty. Svc. award, Etowah County Voters League, Ala., 1985, 1988, Talladega Mayor and City Coun., 1988, Office of Lt. Gov., Ala., 1988, Talladega County Dem. Exec. Com., 1988, Speakin' Out Newspaper, Ala., 1988. Mem.: Nat. Assn. of Negro Musicians (exec. bd. dirs. 2002—04), Ga. Music Educators Assn., Star Dusters Social Club (sec., v.p. and pres. 1980—88), Delta Sigma Theta (life). Democrat. Methodist. Avocations: working with humanitarian agencies, traveling, research and writing. Home: Decatur, Ga. Died July 20, 2007.

TAYLOR, KEITH BREDEN, physician, educator; b. Wimbledon, Eng., Apr. 16, 1924; came to U.S., 1963; s. Francis Henry and Florence (Latham) T.; m. Kym Williams, Nov. 24, 1972; children: Matthew (dec.), Sebastian, Nicholas, Daniel, Kate. BA, Magdalen Coll., U. Oxford, 1946, MA, 1949, D.M., 1955. Intern Oxford U. Hosps.; resident Nat. Hosp. Nervous Diseases, London; lectr. in medicine Oxford U. Faculty Medicine, 1954-63; head div. gastroenterology Stanford U. Med. Ctr., Calif., 1963-71, vice chmn. dept. medicine Calif., 1968-78, Barnett prof. medicine Calif., 1966-89, emeritus, 1989.; vice chancellor Sch. Medicine St. George's U., Grenada, W.I., from 1989, new chmn. dept. nutrition. Dir. gen. Health Edn. Coun. Gt. Britain, 1981-82; chief med. svc. Palo Alto (Calif.) VA Hosp., 1968-78; cons. Letterman Army Hosp., San Francisco. Author numerous articles in field; editorial bd. Frontiers Gastrointestinal Rsch. Maj. M.C. Brit. Army, 1951-53. Fellow Rockefeller Found., 1959, Guggenheim Found., 1971; Fogarty sr. internat. fellow NIH, 1979; NIH grantee, 1963-75. Fellow Royal Soc. Medicine, Royal Coll. Physicians (London); mem. Am. Fedn. Clin. Rsch., Am. Gastroenterol. Assn., Am. Soc. Clin. Investigation, Am. Soc. Clin. Nutrition, Assn. Physicians Gt. Britain, Brit. Soc. Gastroenterology, Brit. Soc. Immunology, Western Assn. Physicians. Died Dec. 31, 2006.

TAYLOR, KENNETH DOUGLAS, Canadian diplomat; b. Calgary, Alta., Can., Oct. 5, 1934; s. Richard and Nancy Irene (Wiggins) T.; m. Patricia E. Taylor, Oct. 1, 1960; 1 son, Douglas. BA, U. Toronto, 1957; MBA, U. Calif., Berkeley, 1959; LLD. (hon.), Laurentian U., Ont., Can., 1980. Joined Can. Fgn. Service, 1959; service in Guatemala, Pakistan, U.S. and Eng.; ambassador to Iran, 1977-80; consul gen. NYC, from 1980; commr. to Bermuda, 1981-84; with Nabisco Brands, Inc., NYC, from 1985; sr. v.p. RJR Nabisco Inc, NYC, from 1987; polit. risk cons. Decorated officer Order Can., officer Order Buffalo, Man.; recipient U.S. Congl. Gold Medal, 1980, Haas Internat. award U. Calif., Berkeley, 1980, Detroit-Windsor award Internat. Freedom Festival, 1980, Gold medal Can. Club, N.Y.C., 1980, Gold Plate award Am. Acad. Achievement, 1980; numerous others. Mem. Sigma Chi. Home: New York, NY. Died Oct. 15, 2015.

TAYLOR, RICHARD DOUGLAS, SR., lawyer; b. Nashville, May 31, 1931; s. Carl Douglas and Kathryn Cornelia (Hagerty) T.; m. Caroline Cynthea Braly, Aug. 29, 1953; children: Richard Douglas, Geoffrey Alan, S. Scott, Mary Kathryn. Student, Notre Dame U., 1949-50; BA, Vanderbilt U., 1953, JD, 1955. Bar: Tenn. 1955. Ptnr. Adams Taylor Philbin Pique & Marchetti, Nashville, from 1958. Atty. Cath. Diocese of Tenn., 1972—. Mem. Coun. Metro Govt. Nashville and Davidson County, 1962-71. Lt. USN, 1955-58. Mem. Nashville Bar Assn. (bd. dirs. 1980-84), Tenn. Def. Lawyers Assn. (pres. 1980-81), Fedn. Ins. Counsel. Roman Catholic. Avocations: boating, tennis, reading. Home: Nashville, Tenn. Died Jan. 26, 2007.

TAYLOR, ROD, actor; b. Sydney, Jan. 11, 1930; came to U.S., 1954, naturalized, 1956; s. William Sturt and Mona (Stewart) T.; m. Peggy Williams, 1951 (div. 1954); m. Mary Hilem, June 1, 1962 (div. 1969); 1 child, Felicia Roderica; m. Carol Kikumura, 1982. Student, E. Sydney Art Coll., 1944-48. Pres. Rodlor Pictures Inc., 1960 Actor: (films) Long John Silver, 1954, The Virgin Queen, 1955, Hell on Frisco Bay, 1955, The Catered Affair, 1956, Giant, 1956, Ask Any Girl, 1959, The Time Machine, 1960, 101 Dalmations (voice only, 1961, The Birds, 1964, V.I.P.'s, 1964, Young Cassidy, 1965, Do Not Disturb, 1965, 36 Hours, 1965, Sunday in New York, 1966, Liquidator, 1966, Glass Bottom Boat, 1966, Hotel, 1967, Chuka, 1967, Dark of the Sun, 1968, The Hell with Heroes, 1968, The High Commissioner, 1968, Zabriskie Point, 1969, Man Who Had Power Over Women, 1969, Darker Than Amber, 1970, The Train Robbers, 1973, Trader Horn, 1973, The Deadly Trackers, 1973, Hell River, 1978, On the Run, 1983, Marbella, 1985, Mask for Murder, 1986, Open Season, 1995, Welcome to Woop-Woop, 1997, Kaw, 2007, Inglorious Basterds, 2009; (TV series) Hong Kong, 1960-61, Bearcats, 1971, The Oregon Trail, 1977, A Time to Die, 1983; (TV appearances) Masquerade, 1983-84, Falcon Crest, Outlaws, 1987; (TV films) Powder Keg, 1971, Family Flight, 1972, Oregon Trail, 1976, A Matter of Wife...and Death, 1976, Cry of the Innocent, 1980, Hellinger's Law, 1981, Jacqueline Bouvier Kennedy, 1981, Charles and Diana, 1982, Outlaws, 1987, Palomini, 1991, Grass Roots, 1992. Recipient Golden Globe award, 1960; Motion Picture Exhibitors Golden Laurel award, 1968 Mem. Producers Guild, Motion Picture Acad. Arts & Sciences, Writers Guild. Clubs: Bel Air (Calif.) Country. Died Jan. 7, 2015.

TAYLOR, WILLIAM CARL, communications educator; b. Birmingham, Ala., Nov. 13, 1943; s. Robert Cecil and Vernie (Hunt) T. Student, Samford U., 1962-64; postgrad., U. Ala., 1966-67, 69-70; BA in Spanish, U. Montevallo, 1966; PhD in Linguistics, U. Tex., 1976. Bexar archives translator U. Tex., Austin, 1971-77; assoc. prof. English U. P.R., Río Piedras, 1977-85, Ft. Valley (Ga.) State Coll., 1985-87, Macon (Ga.) Coll., 1987-88; assoc. prof. comms. Talladega (Ala.) Coll., from 1988. Author: Bexar Archives Translations, 40 vols., 1971-77, Bexar Archives Translators' Manual, 1977, Bexar Archives Typists' Manual, 1977; contbr. articles to profl. publs.; composer various works for choir and organ. Trustee, mem. Talladega Cmty. Chorus, 1990—. Grantee Am. Coun. Edn./NEH, 1994-95, Faculty Resource Network, 1993, 96. Mem. Southeastern Conf. on Linguistics, South Atlantic MLA, Am. Assn Tchrs. Spanish and Portuguese (editor chpt. newsletter, exec. com.), Am. Coun. Tchg. Fgn. Langs., Ala. Assn. Fgn. Lang. Tchrs., Ala. Coll. English Tchrs.' Assn., Ala. Conf. Tchrs. English, So. Conf. on Tchg. Fgn. Langs., Am. Dialect Soc., Carolinas symposium on Brit. Studies, Am. Translators Assn. Avocations: historical preservation, musical composition, research in church music. Died Apr. 15, 2007.

TAYLOR, WILLIAM DOUGLAS, college administrator; b. Johnson City, Tenn., Aug. 1, 1948; s. Ben Worley and Frances Nell (Joines) T.; m. Darby Ann O'Neil, Aug. 31, 1973; children: Ashley Elisabeth, Shelby O'Neil. BS, E. Tenn. State U., 1973, MA, 1974; PhD, U. Miss., 1982. Editor, spl. edn. tchr. S.C. Dept. Mental Retardation, Clinton, S.C., 1974-77; counselor U. Miss., Oxford, 1980-82, dir. student counseling ctr., 1982-84; chmn. counseling, developmental studies U. Ga., Athens, 1984-87; dir. career planning Carson-Newman Coll., Jefferson City, Tenn., 1987-90, dir. acad. advising, 1990-92, coord. acad. support, from 1992. Author: College Study Skills, 1982, Home Growed Rebels: History of the 59th Tenn. Inf. REgiment, 1991. Sponsor Boy Scouts Explorer Troop, Jefferson City, 1988-90; mem. vestry, tchr. Episcopal Chs. in S.C., Miss., Tenn., 1975-89. With U.S. Army, 1969-72. Mem. So. Assn. Coll. Student Affairs, Tenn. Coll. Placement Coun., Coll. Placement Coun., 63rd Tenn. Inf. Regiment (re-enactor). Avocations: fishing, civil war study, baseball, football, banjo playing. Home: Morristown, Tenn. Died May 11, 2007.

TAYLOR, WILLIAM MENKE, manufacturing executive; b. Logansport, Ind., May 24, 1918; s. William Thomas and Ethel Mae (Menke) T.; m. Betty Lorraine Flory, May 8, 1945; children: William M. Jr., Alan Richard. BBA, LaSalle Coll., Chgo., 1940. Cost acct. Essex Wire Corp., Logansport, 1935-50, salesman, 1950-55, plant mgr. Phila., 1955-56; sales mgr. Dill Products co., Norristown, Pa., 1960-73; pres. Tay-Mor Industries, Inc., Logansport, from 1973. Pres. BABB Assoc., Logansport, 1972—; v.p. I.B.D. Corp., Logansport, 1972—; pres. Taylor Industries, Inc., Logansport, 1975—. Served with USAF, 1942-46, ETO. Named Ky. Col., Hon. Order Ky. Cols., 1965. Mem. Soc. Automobile Engrs., Ind. State Police Alliance, Ind. Sheriffs Assn. Lodges: Masons, Elks. Republican. Avocation: antique and special interest cars. Home: Logansport, Ind. Died Feb. 15, 2007.

TEETERS, NANCY HAYS, economist; b. Marion, Ind., July 29, 1930; d. S. Edgar and Mabel (Drake) Hays; m. Robert Duane Teeters, June 7, 1952 (dec. 2008); children: Ann, James, John. AB in Econs., Oberlin Coll., 1952, LLD, 1979; MA in Econs., U. Mich., 1954, postgrad., 1956—57, LLD (hon.), 1983, Bates Coll., 1981, Mt. Holyoke Coll., 1983. Tchg. fellow U. Mich., Ann Arbor, 1954—55, instr., 1956—57, U. Md. Overseas, Germany, 1955—56; staff economist govt. fin. sect. Fed. Reserve System, Washington, 1957—66, bd. govs., 1979—84; economist Bur. Budget, 1966—70; economist (on loan) Coun. Econ. Advisers, Exec. Office of the Pres., 1962—63; sr. fellow The Brookings Instn., 1970—73; sr. specialist Congressional Rsch. Svc., Library of Congress, Washington, 1973—74; asst. dir., chief economist US House Budget Com., 1974—78; dir. economics IBM Corp., 1984—86, v.p., chief economist Armonk, NY, 1986—90. Author: (with others) Setting National Priorities: The 1972 Budget, 1971, Setting National Priorities: The 1973 Budget, 1972, Setting National Priorities: The 1974 Budget, 1973; contbr. articles to profl. publs. Recipient Comfort Starr award in econs. Oberlin Coll., 1952; Disting. Alumnus award U. Mich., 1980 Mem. Nat. Economists Club (v.p. 1973-74, pres. 1974-75, chmn. bd. 1975-76, gov. 1976-79), American Econ. Assn. (com. on status of women 1975-78), American Financial Assn. (dir. 1969-71) Democrat. Died Nov. 17, 2014.

TEMPLETON, JOHN MARKS, JR., retired pediatric surgeon, professor, foundation administrator; b. NYC, Feb. 19, 1940; s. John Marks and Judith Dudley (Folk) T.; m. Josephine J. Gargiulo, Aug. 2, 1970; children: Heather Erin, Jennifer Ann. BA, Yale Coll., 1962; MD, Harvard U., 1968; degree (hon.), Beaver Coll., Buena Vista U., Va. Commonwealth U., Alvernia Coll. Intern Med. Coll. Va., Richmond, 1968-69, resident, 1969-73; dir. trauma program U. Pa. and Children's Hosp. Phila., 1989—95, adj. prof. pediat. surgery, 1995. Chmn. bd. Templeton Growth Fund, Ltd. Assoc. editor: Textbook of Pediatric Emergencies, 1993; pub. 6000 Name Geneology, 1997, A Searcher's Life, 1999, Thrift and Generosity, 2004. Chmn. health and safety, exec. bd. Cradle of Liberty coun. Boy Scouts Am.; mem. exec. bd. Eastern U., Fgn. Policy Rsch. Inst., Nat. Recreation Found., Coll. Physicians Phila., Melmark Charitable Found.; nat. bd. dirs., pres. Pa. divsn. Am. Trauma Soc.; bd. dirs. Nat. Bible Assn.; elder Proclamation Presbyn. Ch.; pres., chmn. John Templeton Found. With M.C., USNR, 1975-77; bd. mem. Am. Trauma Soc., Foreign Policy Rsch. Inst., Nat. Bible Assn., EAST Found., John Templeton Found., Session and Proclamation Presbyterian Ch. Barclay fellow Green Templeton Coll., Oxford U., fellow George H. Gallup Internat. Inst. Mem. ACS, Am. Pediat. Surg. Assn., Am. Assn. Surgery Trauma, Ea. Assn. Surgery Trauma, Phila. Coll. Physicians, Union League, Order Charlemagne, Lyford Cay Club, Merion Cricket Club, Athenaeum Club London, Rotary Internat., White's London, United Oxford and Cambridge U. Club (London). Republican. Evangelical. Home: Bryn Mawr, Pa. Died May 16, 2015.

TENNEY, EDWARD JEWETT, II, lawyer; b. Claremont, NH, Jan. 26, 1924; s. Edward Ballou and Rachel Tamson (Demeritt) T.; m. Joan Alberta Kreichbaum, July 11, 1953 (wid. Feb. 8, 1982); children: Cindra Rae Tenney-Fontaine, Edward Ballou II, Jill Kathryn Tenney-Guyer; m. Della Wooten, Feb. 17, 1983; stepchildren: Linda Hughie, Sandra Barnwell, Angela Ailor, Andrew Stilin. BA cum laude, New Eng. Coll., 1949; LLB, Wake Forest U., 1953, JD, 1970. Bar: Vt. 1955, U.S. Supreme Ct. 1962, N.H. 1967, U.S. Ct. Appeals (1st cir.) 1967, U.S. Dist. Ct. Vt. 1955, U.S. Dist. Ct. N.H. 1967, U.S. Ct. Appeals (2d cir.) 1961. Pvt. practice, Claremont, Bellows Falls, N.H., 1955-86; ptnr. Tenney & Tenney, Claremont, 1986-91; ret. Dep. state's atty. Windham County, Vt. 1957-58; acting mcpl. ct. judge Bellow Falls, Vt., 1966-67; county atty. Sullivan County, N.H., 1971-86, dep. sheriff, 1984—. Mem. Claremont Sch. Bd., 1967-73, Claremont Police Commn., 1966-70; chmn. Claremont City Rep. Club, 1966-70. 1st lt. U.S. Army AC, 1942-46, PTO; Col. USAFR, 1978, ret., 1980. Mem. N.H.

Bar Assn., Vt. Bar Assn., Sullivan County Bar Assn. (past sec.-treas., pres.), Masons, Shriners, Am. Legion (judge advocate), Ret. Officers Assn. Avocations: flying, motorcycling, sailing, motor-boating, travel. Home: Claremont, NH. Died June 4, 2007.

TENNOV, DOROTHY, former psychologist, educator; b. Montgomery, Ala., Aug. 29, 1928; d. Daniel Edgar Tennow and Lois Estelle (Moore) Miller; children: Randall (dec.), Russell, Daniel. BA, CUNY, 1950; MA, U. Conn., 1954, PhD, 1964. Prof. U. Bridgeport, Conn., 1964-86; pvt. cons. Millsboro, Del., 1986—92. Pvt. practice cons., Westport, Conn., 1970-74. Author: Psychotherapy: The Hazardous Cure, 1975, Super Self, 1976, Love and Limerence, 1979, reissue, 1999 (2d Press Women award 1980), Mem. AAAS, APA, Am. Psychol. Soc., Authors Guild, Assn. Politics and the Life Scis., Internat. Soc. Human Ethology, Human Behavior and Evolution Soc. Died Feb. 3, 2007.

TEPLY, MARK LAWRENCE, mathematics professor; b. Lincoln, Nebr., Jan. 11, 1942; s. Lawrence Joseph and Gertrude M. (Kupfer) T.; m. Kathleen K. McGrayel, Aug. 1968 (div. 1978); 1 child, David; m. Nancy Lee Wilkowske, Mar. 12, 1983; children: Stephanie, Andrew, Grant. BA, U. Nebr., 1963, MA, 1965, PhD, 1968. Instr. U. So. Calif., LA, 1967—68; asst. prof. U. Fla., Gainesville, 1969—73, assoc. prof., 1973—81, prof., 1981—85, U. Wis., Milw., from 1985. Editor: Communications in Algebra, 1982—; editor 2 book series by Taylor and Francis, 1983—; author: Finiteness Conditions on Torsion Theories, 1984, A History of the Singular Splitting Problem, 1984, Semicocritical Modules, 1987; contbr. more than 80 articles to profl. jours NSF grantee U. Fla., 1973, 77-78, U.S. Dept. Edn. grantee U. Wis., Milw., 1990—2006. Mem. Am. Math. Soc., Math. Assn. Am. Lutheran. Died Nov. 10, 2006.

TERLOUW, JOHN GARY, financial analyst; b. New Brunswick, NJ, May 14, 1945; s. John W. and Jane B. (van Kempen) T.; m. Janet A. Henry, Aug. 1, 1970; children: Janet R., Julie L., Joanne E., John G. Jr. BS in Acctg., Fla. State U., 1971. CPA, Fla. CFO Budget Luxury Inns of Am., Inc., Tallahassee, 1974-75; pres. Mgmt. Cons. Svc., Inc., Tallahassee, 1975-78; staff acct. Givens & Givens, CPA's, Tallahassee, 1979-80; CFO Tallahassee Food Systems Inc., 1980-83, Wenco of El Paso, Tex., 1983-84, Maxxima Corp., Tallahassee, 1984-85; pres. Creative Bu. Concepts, Inc., Tallahassee, 1985-90; sr. mgmt. analyst II Fla. Dept. of Profl. Regulation, Tallahassee, 1990-94, Fla. Agy. for Health Care Adminstrn., Tallahassee, 1994-96; CFO Profl. Emergency Svcs., Inc., Tavernier, Fla., from 1996. With USAF, 1965-69. Home: Key Largo, Fla. Died July 20, 2007.

TERRILL, CHARLES MERLE, transportation executive; b. Mineral Point, Wis., Aug. 16, 1935; s. Merle Willis and Thelma Margaret (Potterton) T.; m. Marilyn Ann Sturdevant, Aug. 31, 1953; children: David, Corinne, Wanda, Kevin, Jill. AS in Bus. Adminstrn., Rockford Bus. Coll., Ill., 1954; A in Bus. Adminstrn. in Sales and Mktg., Am. Inst. Tech., 1961; student, Tri State U., 1979-80; cert. in safety engring., Mich. State U., 1985. Dist. sales mgr. Babson Bros. Co., Chgo., 1953-57, Internat. Mineral and Chem., Chgo., 1957-60; ops. mgr. Terrico, Mineral Point, 1960-69; road driver CW Transport, Milw., 1969-79, safety supr. Fond Du Lac, Wis., 1979-85; v.p. safety Flexible Transport, Milw., from 1985. Bd. dirs. Wis. Decision Driving Ctr., Appleton; past chmn. Truck Driving Championship, Wis., 1983. Treas. Mineral Point Sch. Bd., 1967-68; campaign mem. Washington City Rep. Party, 1979-80. Mem. Wis. Council Safety Suprs. (chmn. 1979, Safety Driver of Yr. award 1984), Am. Trucking Assn. (safety council 1986—), Interstate Carriers Conf. (safety council 1986—), Nat. Safety Council (winter driving league 1984—), Wis. Motor Carriers Assn. (past chmn.), Fox Valley Tech. Inst. (bd. dirs. 1982—). Clubs: West Bend Toastmasters (treas. 1984-85), Long Riders (Milw.). Lodges: Shriners, Odd Fellows (past noble grand master), Masons (past master). Avocations: golf, travel, camping. Home: West Bend, Wis. Died July 23, 2007.

TERRY, CLARK, musician; b. St. Louis, Dec. 14, 1920; m. Pauline Reddon; 2 children. Privately educated. Pres. Etoile Music Prodns., 1955, Pastel Music, 1958; v.p. Creative Jazz Composers, Inc., 1972. Itinerant jazz clinician and educator; exec. dir. Internat. of Jazz; adj. prof. William Paterson U., NJ Leader, Clark Terry Big Bad Band, 1966-2015; albums include: The World of Duke Ellington, Vol. 2, Duke Ellington Such Sweet Thunder, The Terry-Brookmeyer Quintet, Cruisin', Cool Blues, Oscar Peterson Trio with Clark Terry, Clark Terry's Big Bad Band Live on 57th Street, The Happy Horns of Clark Terry, Yes, The Blues, 1981, Paris 1960, 1985, Having Fun, 1990, Second Set, 1990, Live at the Village Gate, 1991, What a Wonderful World: For Lou, 1993, Remember the Time, 1994, Shades of Blue, 1994, Top and Bottom Brass, 1995, Express, 1995, Reunion with Pee Wee Claybrook and Swing Fever, 1995, (with Red Mitchell) Jive at Five, 1993, Best Things in Life (Live), 1996, OW, 1996, Alternate Blues, 1996, Daylight Express, 1998, One on One, 2000, Live on QE2, 2001, Flutin' and Flugin, 2002, Live! At Buddy's Place, 2003, Live at Marian's with the Terry's Young Titans of Jazz, 2005, and several other. Author: Let's Talk Trumpet, 1973, Interpretation of the Jazz Language, 1976, Circular Breathing, 1977, Clark: The Autobiography of Clark Terry, 2011 Served with USN, 1942-45. Recipient numerous awards, including 3 Grammy nominations and 2 Grammy certificates, Pote Distinguished Jazz Artist, Phil., 1989, 2010 Grammy Lifetime Achievement award, NARAS President's Merit award and Died Feb. 21, 2015.

TERRY, ERNEST LEE, clergyman, international evangelist; b. Clovis, N.Mex., Apr. 29, 1932; s. Ernest Lee and Mable Gertrude (Jones) T.; m. Nolie Lee, Dec. 25, 1951; children: Stephen Dennis, Miriam Janice, Ernest Lee III. Student, U. Md., 1951, Am. Bible Sch., Chgo., 1953, Ohio No. U., Ada, 1958-59; DMin, Word of Life, Tampa, Fla., 1975; DD (hon.), Ambassador Coll., Chgo., 1953; PhD (hon.), Hodge Sem., Kansas City, Kans., 1956. Ordained to ministry Ch. of God, Cleveland, Tenn. Min. Pentecostal Ch. of God, Joplin, Mo., 1951-61, Assembly of God, Springfield, Mo., 1963-73; lectr. Duke U., Durham, N.C., 1963, So. U., Houston, 1971, Harvard Coll., Cambridge, Mass., 1972, Golf Coast coll., Panama City, Fla., 1972; pres. Faith Ministries, Internat., Vero Beach, Fla., 1985-93; internat. evangelist Ch. of God, Cleveland, Tenn., from 1973. State youth dir. Pentecostal Ch. of God, Miss. and Ala., 1953-54, sec.-treas., 1954-56; presbyter Pentecostal Ch. of God, Ohio, 1958-60; dist. Christ Amb. dir. Assembly of God, Dallas, 1963-65. Author: Someone Is Coming, 1969, Tongues of Fire, 1972; contbr. articles to profl. jours.; speaker host TV program God Chose Preaching, Madisonville, Ky., 1983-86. Amateur and profl. boxer Golden Gloves and AAU, Wichita Falls, Tex., 1945-51. With U.S. Navy, 1950-51. Named Fighter of Yr., Golden Gloves, 1949, Man of Yr., Vols. of Am., 1958; named Ky. col., 1985. Democrat. Avocations: boxing, racquetball, golf. Died Apr. 14, 2007.

TETRO, CATHERINE ANNE, shop owner; b. Fulton, NY, July 26, 1925; d. Sam and Florence Elizabeth (Corsoneti) Froio; m. John Ralph Tetro, Nov. 29, 1969. Grad. H.S., Fulton, NY, 1942. Clk. U.S. Post Office Substa., Fulton, N.Y., 1941-53; owner, operator Kay's Tot Shop, Fulton, N.Y., 1953-95. Sec. Fulton Merchants Assn., 1982; mem. parish coun., 1982-85, mem. choir. Mem. Fulton Women's Bowling Assn. (treas., mem. Women's Bowling Hall of Fame). Home: Fulton, NY. Died Aug. 15, 2007.

TEZLA, ALBERT, language educator; b. S. Bend, Ind., Dec. 13, 1915; s. Mihály and Lucza (Szénási) Tezla; m. Olive Anna Fox, July 26, 1941; children: Michael William, Kathy Elaine. BA, U. Chgo., 1941, MA, 1947, PhD, 1952. Instr. Ind. U. Ext., S. Bend, 1946-48; from instr. to assoc. prof. U. Minn., Duluth, 1949-61, prof., 1961-82, prof. emeritus, from 1982. Vis. prof. Hungarian lit. Columbia U., N.Y.C., 1966, cons., 1967-71, 77-81, vis. scholar, 1975; cons. U. Minn., Mpls., 1968-83; project reviewer NEH, Washington, 1979-82; vis. prof. Hungarian lit. U. Minn., Duluth, 1998. Author: An Introductory Bibliography to the Study of Hungarian Literature, 1964, Hungarian Authors: A Bibliographical Handbook, 1970, The Hazardous Quest: Hungarian Immigrants in the United States, 1895-1920, 1993; co-author: Academic American Encyclopedia, 1980, World Authors, 1975-1980, 1985, Benét's Readers Encyclopedia, 1987, World Authors, 1980-85, 1991; editor, contbg. translator: Ocean at the Window: Hungarian Prose and Poetry since 1945, 1980, Three Contemporary Hungarian Plays, 1992, contbg. translator: Hungarian Short Stories, 1983, The Kiss: 20th Century Hungarian Short Stories, 1993; translator: God in the Wagon: Ten Short Stories (Ferenc Sánta), 1985 (Hungarian pubs. award, 1985), The Fifth Seal (Ferenc Sánta), 1986 (Hungarian pubs. award, 1986), Somewhere in a Distant Fabled Land: American Hungarians, 1895-1920, 1987, On the Balcony: Selected Short Stories (Iván Mándy), 1988 (Hungarian pubs. award, 1988), Hungary: A Brief History (István Lázár), 1990, An Illustrated History of Hungary (István Lázár), 1992, Memoir of Hungary, 1944-48 (Sándor Máral), 1996, Once There Was a Central Europe: Selected Short Stories and Other Writings (Miklós Máazoly), 1997, A Wartime Memoir, Hungary, 1944-45 (Alaine Polcz), 1998, Authoring, Barbering and Other Occupations, 2002, With One Heart in Two Homelands, 2005; editl. cons. Holmes and Meier Pubs., 1996. Lt. (s.g.) USN, 1942-46, PTO. Recipient Diplome d'honeur, Inst. Cultural Rels., Hungary, 1970, Commemorative medal, 1970, Endre Ady Medallion, Presidium Hungarian PEN Ctr., 1986, Pro Cultura Hungarica award, Rep. Hungary, 1996, Abraham Lincoln award, Am. Hungarian Found., 1998; grantee Rsch. grantee, Am. Coun. Learned Socs., 1961, 1968, NEH, 1978—82; fellow Fulbright Rsch. fellow, Associated Bd. Rsch. Coun., 1959—60, Rsch. fellow, Internat. Co. Traveling Grants, 1963—64, Internat. Rsch. and Exchs. Bd., 1978. Mem. Internat. Assn. Hungarian Studies (mem. exec. com. 1978-83, John Lotz Meml. award 1986), Am. Hungarian Educators' Assn., Fulbright Assn. Democrat. Avocations: gardening, physical fitness, reading, classical films. Home: Duluth, Minn. Died Nov. 26, 2006.

THACHER, BARBARA AUCHINCLOSS, history educator; b. Oyster Bay, NY, July 27, 1918; d. Hugh and Frances Coverdale (Newlands) Auchincloss; m. Thomas Thacher, Aug. 4, 1942; children: Barbara Burrall Thacher Plimpton, Elizabeth Coverdale Thacher Hawn, Thomas Day II, Hugh Auchincloss, Peter Anthony, Andrew. BA cum laude, Bryn Mawr Coll., 1940; MA in History, Columbia U., 1965. Editl. rschr. Newsweek, NYC, 1940-41, 44; writer N.Y. Times Sunday Mag., News of Week Rev., NYC, 1941-43; co-editor Christmas Booklist for Children Harper's Mag., NYC, 1957-59; asst. history dept. Barnard Coll., NYC, 1964-65; rsch. asst. Ctr. Urban Edn., NYC, 1966. Bd. dirs. Bryn Mawr Coll., 1966-88, chair bd. trustees, 1980-87, emeritus, 1988—, City Univ. of N.Y., trustee, 1970-73, WNET-TV-Channel 13, trustee, 1978-88; active Sheltering Arms Children's Svc., Istanbul Women's Coll., Leake & Watts Children's Home Svcs., Yonkers and N.Y.C., 1961-83, emeritus, 1983—, N.Y.C. Park Assn., Riverdale Girls Sch.; trustee Tchrs. Coll. Columbia U. Mem. Cosmopolitan Club (gov.), North Haven Casino. Democrat. Presbyterian. Died Feb. 1, 2007.

THAUNG, AUNG, former government official; b. Myanmar, Dec. 1, 1940; m. Khin Khin Yi Thaung; children: Moe Aung, Nay Aung, Pyi Aung, Khin Ngu Yi Phyo. Grad., Mandalay U. School teacher; dep. commerce min., 1993—96; min. for livestock and fisheries, 1996—97; min. for industry-1 Govt. of Myanmar, 1997—2011; mem. Pyithu Hluttaw, 2011—15. Served and active in Army, 1964—93. Died July 23, 2015.

THAYER, FREDERICK CLIFTON, public policy educator; b. Sept. 6, 1924; m. Carolyn Conn Easley, 1952; children: Jeffrey Lee, Sarah Diane. BS, U.S. Mil. Acad., 1945; MA, Ohio State U., 1954; PhD, U. Denver, 1963. Commd. 2d lt. USAF, 1945, advanced through grades to col., 1965, ret., 1969; assoc. prof. U. Pitts., 1969-83, prof., 1983-91; prof. European div. Troy State U., 1991-94, George Washington U., Washington, 1995-96; prof. public policy, dir. doctoral program So. U., Baton Rouge, 1997-99; vis. prof. U. of the Incarnate Word, San Antonio, 1999-2000, Ctrl. Mich. U., Mt. Pleasant, from 2000. Author: Air Transport Policy and National Security, 1965, An End to Hierarchy and Competition, 1973, 2d edit., 1981, Rebuilding America: The Case for Economic Regulation, 1984; contbr. articles to profl. jours. Home: Pittsburgh, Pa. Died Dec. 23, 2006.

THIBODEAUX, WALTER JOSEPH, town official; b. Church Point, La., July 11, 1922; s. Felix Fed and Marcellet (Boudreaux) T.;m. Edwina Effie Bertrand, July 22, 1945 (Sept. 1977); children: Robert Paul, Danny Karl; m. Hazel Lee Hebert, Sept. 28, 1977. Student, MacNee State Coll., Lake Charles, La., 1946-47, Lamar State Coll., Beaumont, Tex., 1963-64. Owner, mgr. Walter Super Market, Lake Arthur, La., 1947-53; mgr. cattle ranch Angus Cattle, Lake Arthur, 1947-53; asst. mgr. So. Life Ins. Co., Port Arthur, Tex., 1954-58; owner, mgr. Princess Chifs Ware Co., Lafayette, La., 1959-68; broker agt. Bank & Life Ins., Lafayette, 1968-76; maintenance supr. Fed. Housing, Town of Erath (La.), from 1976, Morris Lahasky Nursing Home, Erath, from 1976. Author: Date Sheet for Electric Reading, 1987. Alderman, Town Coun., Lake Arthur, 1948-52. Cpl. USMC, 1942-46, PTO. Decorated Purple Heart. Mem. Am. Legion, DAV, VFW, Dixie Twiler (Abbiville, La.), Fishing Club, Beau Chien (Youngville), Gulf Course. Roman Catholic. Avocations: farming, numismatic investment. Home: Erath, La. Died Mar. 31, 2007.

THIERNAU, ALBERT RICHARD, financial consultant; b. Chgo., June 12, 1927; s. Henry Christopher and Katherine Friedricka (Herzog) T.; m. Hattie Mae Schubert, Feb. 23, 1957 (dec. July 1990); children: H. Suzanne, A. Richard. AB, Cornell Coll., Mt. Vernon, Iowa, 1952; MA, U. Penn., 1954. CLU, Chartered fin. cons. Social worker Jones Community Ctr., Chicago Heights, Ill., 1953-55; sociologist, actuary Ill. Pardon & Parole Bd., Joliet, 1955-57; pvt. fin. practice Homewood, Ill., 1957-87; pres. Thiernau Fin. Svcs., Inc., Homewood, from 1987. Pres. Sch. Dist. 153, Homewood, 1975-77, bd. dirs. Homewood Bd. Edn., 1974-75. Mem. Am. Soc. CLUs, 1965— (dir. Chgo. Chpt. 1973,75,78,80,81,84), Chartered Fin.Consultants. (pres. 1988—), Chgo. Estate Planning Coun., Million Dollar Round Table 1975—, Rotary (pres. Homewood Chpt. 1973-74, dist. gov. 1983-84), Masons (32 degree), Shriners. Republican. Presbyterian. Avocations: travel, bridge. Home: Crete, Ill. *Personal philosophy: Each person needs a guide or standard to assist in decision making, relations with others, and personal conduct. I rely on the 4-Way Test of Rotary International, established by Rotarian Herb Taylor in 1932, as an outcome of prayer in his struggle to prevent his company from going bankrupt. These 4 words are: 1. Is it the truth?, 2. Is it fair to all concerned?, 3. Will it build goodwill and better friendships?, 4. Will it be beneficial to all concerned? It is called "The Four-Way Test" of the things we think, say, or do.* Died July 10, 2007.

THOLE, JEROME LOUIS, food and drug industry executive; b. Cin., Oct. 9, 1930; s. Louis Charles and Hilda Ann (Schneider) T.; m. Mary Jane Fisher; children: Susyn Jayne, Cynthia Lynn, Linda Sue, Jerome Thomas. BS, Xavier U., Cin., 1954; MA, Mich. State U., 1957. From methods supr. to zone mgr. The Kroger Co., Cin., 1957-69, mgr. ops. Ft. Wayne, Ind., 1969-72, dir. ops. Columbus, Ohio, 1972-80; v.p. ops. Kroger/Super X Drugs Div., Cin., 1980-84; div. v.p. The Kroger Co., Fla. div., Orlando, 1984-88; mgmt. cons. Thole & Assocs., Orlando, from 1988. Dir. Affiliated of Fla., Tampa, 1987-88, Fla. Beverage Industry Recycling Program, Orlando, 1986-88. Div. chmn. United Way, Cin., 1961, 82-83. Capt. USAR, 1954-64. Mem. Retail Grocers Fla., Fla. Retail Fedn., Food Mktg. Inst., Nat. Grocers Assn., Orlando C. of C., Heathrow Country Club. Republican. Roman Catholic. Avocations: power boating, golf, fishing. Died Mar. 5, 2007.

THOMAS, ALVA LEE, university administrator; b. Houston, July 23, 1929; d. Young and Luvenia (Dickinson) Lee; m. Aug. 12, 1948 (div. 1964); 1 child, Leiana Thomas Gary. BA in Sociology, Linocln U., Jefferson City, Mo., 1949; MSE, Chgo. State U., Chgo., 1973. Cert. Tchr., Ill., Calif. . Case worker Cook County Dept. Pub. Welfare, Chgo., 1950-56; tchr. Chgo. Pub. Schs., 1956-75; asst. prof. mgmt. Chgo. State U. Coll. Bus. Adminstrn., 1975-80; mgr. job devel. W.L. Dawson Tech. City Coll. Chgo.; dept. chairperson, lectr. Coll. Edn. Kafanchan, Kaduna State, Nigeria, 1981-84; counselor Chgo. Pub. Schs., 1984-86; dir. career planning placement Chgo. State U., from 1986. Coll. cons. Black Collegian Mag., New Orleans 1987--, Cook County Bd. Commrs. Chgo. 1988--, Author, Editor: Training Manuals, Internships, Promotional Lit., Features Newsletters 1979. Pres. Chgo. chpt. Lincoln U. Alumni Assn., 1970-78; bd. dirs. Chgo. State U., 1972-76; mem. Senator Paul E. Simon's Africa Adv. Com., Chgo., 1985—; chairperson

Career Svcs. Adv. Coun., Chgo., 1987—; publicity co-chair Chgo. Alumnae, 1988—; bd. mem. The Jane Addams Conf. Recipient 1st Black History Exhibit award Ahmada Bello U., Zaria Kadunu Nigeria 1983, Women's Devel. Services award Evangelical Ch. Nigeria, Kagaro, Kaduna Nigeria 1984, Recruitment Placement Services award USAF, Chgo. 1987--. Mem. Midwest Coll. Placement Assn., Am. Assn. Coll. U. Personnel, Coll. Placement Assn., Ill. Minority Women's Caucus, Women's Support Ctr., Women in Mgmt., Delta Sigma Theta Inc. Democratic. Avocations: photographer, foreign travel, indoor gardening, writing poetry prose. Died June 25, 2007.

THOMAS, CHARLES EDMUND, anesthesiologist, health facility administrator; b. Balt., Mar. 21, 1933; s. James Clayton and Emily Marie (Shimek) T.; m. Pamela Kay Daniel, May 10, 1986; children: James Philip, Lane Lynn Thomas, Cherylee Karin Bowman, Kevin Charles. DO, U. Health Scis. Coll. Osteo., Kansas City, Mo., 1959. Cert. Am. Osteo. Bd. Anesthesiology. Staff anesthesiologist Redford Receiving Hosp., Detroit, 1962-65, Bi-County Cmty. Hosp., Detroit, 1962-70, Detroit Osteo. Hosp., Detroit, 1962-70; chief dept. ansesthesiology Annie Warner Hosp., Gettysburg, Pa, 1970-72; staff anestheiologist Crippled Children's Hop., 1970-75; chmn. dept. anesthesiology, dir. ICU Hanover (Pa.) Gen. Hosp., 1975-97. Chmn. dept. anesthesiology Gettysburg Gen. Hosp., 1970-72. Mem. AMA, Am. Osteo. Assn., Internat. Anesthesia Rsch. Assn., Pa. Med. Assn., Pa. Osteo. Med. Assn., Pa. Cancer Pain Initiative. Republican. Methodist. Avocation: architecture. Home: Hanover, Pa. Died Nov. 8, 2006.

THOMAS, GWENDOLYN JEANNE (PRAVRAJIKA BHAKTIPRANA), member of religious order; b. San Jose, Calif., Sept. 21, 1922; d. Elmer Willis and Beatrice Genevieve (Johnson) T. BA in Music Edn., Calif. State U., San Jose, 1945; BSc in Violin, Juilliard Sch., NYC, 1947, MSc in Violin, 1949. Ordained to ministry, Vedanta Soc. of So. Calif., Ramakrishna Order of India. Violin tchr. Turtle Bay Music Sch., NYC, 1949-54; novice nun Sarada Convent, Vedanta Soc., Hollywood, Calif., 1954-59, brahmacharini, 1959-65; sannyasini or Pravrajika (Woman Swami), Vedanta Soc., Hollywood, from 1965. Lectr., performer of other ministerial duties, 1977—; dir. women's choir Temple of Vedanta Soc., Hollywood, 1965-77; mem. Hindu-Roman Cath. Dialog Com., L.A., 1990—. Mem. Interreligious Coun. of So. Calif. (del. 1988—). Avocation: spanish. Died Mar. 30, 2007.

THOMAS, MARY ELIZABETH, artist; b. Huntsville, Ohio, Aug. 1, 1937; d. Roe and Bertha Mae (Godwin) Cooke; m. Wilson Woodrow Thomas, Aug. 24, 1957; children: David Gail, Penny Joann, Phyllip Roe, Brent Arthur. Grad. high sch., Belle Ctr., Ohio, 1955. Exhibited in group shows at Ohio Assn. of Family and Cmty. Edn. State Meeting, 1991, (2d pl. award), 95 (1st pl. award), Hardin County Fair, 1992 (Res. Champion), 94 (Grand Champion). Mem. Lawrence Valley Grange Deaf activities (merit for report 1995), Ohio Assn. of Family and Cmty. Edn. (homemakers ext., v.p. local club, 1995), hosp. guild (sewing unit), Women's Assn. United Presbyterian Ch. Democrat. Presbyterian. Avocations: piano, painting and crafts, grandchildren (10), sunday sch. Home: Harrod, Ohio. Died Dec. 6, 2007.

THOMAS, STEPHEN, retired industrial engineer; b. NYC, Aug. 29, 1923; s. Peter and Amelia Thomas; m. Jane Anne Broderick, July 3, 1948; children: Barbara Gail, Jessica Lynne, Susan Amelia. BS in Indsl. Mech. Engring., U. Mich., 1951. From foreman to personnel supr. EI du Pont, Buffalo, Wilmington, Del. and Brevard, NC, 1951—84, personnel supr., 1970—84, ret., 1984. Asst. chem. lab. U. Mich., Ann Arbor, 1948, asst. metalurgical lab., 1948—51; instr. Blue Ridge C.C., Hendersonville, NC, 1970—75; cons. human rels. EI du Pont, Brevard, NC, 1984—91. Chmn. Mayor's Com. for Handicapped, Henderson County, 1980; bd. dirs. Cmty Found. Henderson County, 1986—88; mem. bd. dirs. Laurel Park (NC) Alcohol Beverage Control Bd., 1983—99; mediator Dispute Settlement Ctr. Henderson County, 1984—2002; arbitrator BBB, Asheville, NC, 1986—2002; mem. bd. dirs. Dispute Settlement Ctr. Henderson County, 2001—02; treas. Rep. Party, Henderson County, NC; mem. bd. dirs. Western Carolina Cmty. Action, Henderson County, 1970, Western NC Tomorrow, 1986—94, Margaret R. Pardee Meml. Hosp., Henderson County, 1981—94. 2d lt. transp. corp. US Army, 1945—46. Died July 15, 2007.

THOMMES, TERRY ALLEN, sculptor, educator; b. Plainfield, NJ, Oct. 16, 1953; s. William Burnside and Nancy Jane (Coley) T.; m. Barbara Jackson, June 22, 1953; children: Alexander Randall, Leanna Marie. BFA, U. Western Mich., 1977; MFA, U. Ga., 1980. Sculptor, builder Brooks Bldg., Big Pine Key, Fla., 1980-84; sculptor, contr. North Carribbean, Big Pine Key, 1984-89; sculptor, designer Thommes/Gray & Assocs., Big Pine Key, 1990-94; sculptor Thommes Studio, Big Pine Key, from 1994. Asst. prof. U. Ga., Athens, 1993; adj. instr. Fla. Keys C.C., Key West, Fla., 1997. Ford Found. grantee, 1976, 80, U. Ga., 1979. Mem. Internat. Sculpture Ctr., Coll. Art Assn. Home: Stuart, Fla. Died Jan. 25, 2007.

THOMPSON, ARLENE RITA, nursing educator; b. Yakima, Wash., May 17, 1933; d. Paul James and Esther Margaret (Danroth) T. BS in Nursing, U. Wash., 1966, Masters in Nursing, 1970, postgrad., from 1982. Staff nurse Univ. Teaching Hosp., Seattle, 1966-69; mem. nursing faculty U. Wash. Sch. Nurses, Seattle, 1971-73; critical care nurse Virginia Mason Hosp., Seattle, from 1973; educator Seattle Pacific U. Sch. Nursing, from 1981. Nurse legal cons. nursing edn., critical care nurse. Contbr. articles to profl. jours. USPHS grantee, 1969; nursing scholar Virginia Mason Hosp., 1965. Mem. Am. Assn. Critical Care Nurses (cert.), Am. Nurses Assn., Am. Heart Assn., Nat. League Nursing, Sigma Theta Tau, Alpha Tau Omega. Republican. Presbyterian. Avocations: sewing, swimming, jogging, bicycle riding, hiking. Home: Seattle, Wash. Died Dec. 12, 2006.

THOMPSON, FRED DALTON, actor, former United States Senator from Tennessee; b. Sheffield, Ala., Aug. 19, 1942; s. Fletcher and Ruth Thompson; m. Sarah Elizabeth Lindsey, Sept. 12, 1959; children: Tony, Daniel, Elizabeth Betsy Panici(dec.) ; m. Jeri Kahn, June 29, 2002; 1 child, Hayden Victoria. BS, Memphis State U., 1964; JD, Vanderbilt U., 1967. Asst. U.S. atty. (mid. dist.) Tenn. US Dept. Justice, 1969-72; minority counsel US Senate Select Com. on Presdl. Campaign Activities (Watergate Com.), 1973-74; pvt. practice, 1975-94; spl. counsel to Gov. State of Tenn., 1980; spl. counsel US Senate Fgn. Rels. Coms., 1980—81, US Senate Intelligence Com., 1982; atty. Arent, Fox, Kintner, Plotkin & Kahn, 1991-94; US Senator from Tenn., 1994—2003. Chmn., US Senate Govtl. Affairs Com., 1997-2001, Internat. Security Adv. Bd., US Dept. State, 2005-07; vis. fellow Am. Enterprise Inst., mem. US-China Econ. & Security Review Commn. Actor: (films) Marie: A True Story, 1985, No Way Out, 1987, Feds, 1988, Fat Man and Little Boy, 1989, The Hunt for Red October, 1990, Days of Thunder, 1990, Die Hard 2: Die Harder, 1990, Flight of the Intruder, 1991, Class Action, 1991, Necessary Roughness, 1991, Curly Sue, 1991, Cape Fear, 1991, Aces: Iron Eagle III, 1992, Thunderheart, 1992, White Sands, 1992, Born Yesterday, 1993, In the Line of Fire, 1993, Baby's Day Out, 1994, Download This, 2002, (voice) Racing Stripes, 2005; (TV films) Unholy Matrimony, 1988, Bed of Lies, 1992, Stay the Night, 1992, Day-O, 1992, Keep the Change, 1992, Barbarians at the Gate, 1993,(voice only) Rachel and Andrew Jackson: A Love Story, 2001, Evil Knieval, 2004, Looking for Comedy in the Muslim World, 2005; (TV series) Law & Order, 2002-07; (TV appearances) Wiseguy, 1988, China Beach, 1989, Roseanne, 1989, Matlock, 1989, Sex & the City, 2000, Law & Order: Special Victims Unit, 2003-06, Law & Order: Trial By Jury 2005-06, Law & Order: Criminal Intent, 2005, Conviction 2006; author: At That Point in Time: The Inside Story of the Senate Watergate Committee, 1975. Mem.: Coun. Fgn. Rels. Republican. Died Nov. 1, 2015.

THOMPSON, HOWARD KING, JR., retired physician, educator; b. Boston, May 19, 1928; s. Howard King and Maude Ellen (Short) T.; m. Christine Slotemaker De Bruine, Apr. 11, 1963 (dec. Feb. 1, 1990); children: Ulrike, Friederike, Howard, III. BA, Yale U., 1949; MD, Columbia U., 1953. Diplomate Am. Bd. Internal Medicine. Inter, jr. asst. resident Bellevue Hosp., NYC, 1953-55; sr. asst. resident, chief resident in medicine Duke U. Med. Ctr., Durham, N.C., 1958-59, 60-61; assoc. prof. medicine Duke U., Durham, N.C., 1967-71; prof. medicine Baylor Coll. Medicine, Houston, 1971-78, Albany (N.Y.) Med. Coll., 1978-83; physician in charge Permanente Med. Assoc. Tex., Dallas, 1988-94; retired, 1994. Chmn. biotech. resources rev. com., divsn. rsch. resources NIH, Bethesda, Md., 1981. Contbr. over 50 articles to profl. jours. Capt. USAR, 1956-57, Korea. Avocation: music. Home: East Greenbush, NY. Died Nov. 8, 2007.

THOMPSON, JOHN EDWARD, physician, surgeon; b. Blanchardville, Wis., Dec. 30, 1923; s. Edward Bernard and Mary Rosella (Anderson) T.; m. Germaine Marie Kusnierek, Aug. 23, 1947; children: Vicki, Michael, Rebecca, Nancy, Julie. BA, Augsburg Coll., 1947; MD, U. Wis., 1951. Diplomate Am. Bd. Family Practice, Am. Bd. Geriatric Medicine. Capt. USAF, 1942-52, physician Tex., Fla., 1951-53; surgical resident Gunderson Clinic, Lacrosse, Wis., 1956-57; physician, surgeon Med. Ctr., Nekoosa, Wis., 1957-94; ret., 1994. Med. dir. Wood Co. Home, Port Edwards, Wis., 1960-92; pres. hosp. staff Riverview Hosp., Wisconsin Rapids, Wood Med. Soc., Nekoosa Med. Ctr. Contbr. articles to profl. jours. Decorated Air Medal USAF, 1944, Purple Heart, 1944, Prisoner of War medal, 1988. Mem. VFW, AMA, Wis. State Med. Soc., Air Force Assn., Lions, Elks, Alpha Omega Alpha. Avocations: horticulture, aviation, genealogy, golf. Home: Nekoosa, Wis. Died Apr. 15, 2007.

THOMPSON, MACK EUGENE, historian, educator; b. Burley, Idaho, Feb. 24, 1921; s. Eugene and Nora (McFate) T.; m. Helen Goldhamer, Oct. 30, 1945. AB, Queen's Coll., CUNY, 1948; MA, Brown U., 1951, PhD, 1955. Instr. history Brown U., 1954-55; asst. prof. Calif. Inst. Tech., 1955-56, U. Calif. at Riverside, 1956-62, asso. prof., 1962-66, prof., 1966-77; emeritus prof., from 1977; chmn. div. humanities U. Calif. at Riverside, 1961-63, asso. univ. dean acad. planning, 1965-66, dean, div. undergrad. studies, 1971-74; exec dir. Am. Hist. Assn., Washington, 1974-81. Chmn. editorial bd. Experiment and Innovation: New Directions in Edn., U. Calif., 1966-68 Author: The Ward-Hopkins Controversy and the American Revolution in Rhode Island: An Interpretation, 1959, Moses Brown, Reluctant Reformer, 1962, Causes and Circumstances of the Du Pont Family's Emigration, 1969. Bd. dirs. Harry S. Truman Libr. Inst., 1974-81. With AUS, 1942-45. Home: Oldsmar, Fla. Died Jan. 29, 2014.

THOMPSON, MARY KOLETA, small business owner, not-for-profit developer; b. Portsmouth, Va., Dec. 27, 1938; m. James Burton Thompson, May 5, 1957 (dec. 2006); children: Burt, Suzan, Kate, Jon. BFA, U. Tex., 1982; postgrad., Boston U.; MA in Philanthropy and Devel., St. Mary's U. Minn., 1999. Cert. non-profit mgmt. Pres., CEO The Planning Resource People, Burnet, Tex., from 1990; Tex. fin. devel. specialist ARC Tex., 1994-98; devel. dir. Very Spl. Arts Tex., 1991-92; dir. devel. ARC, Austin, 1992-94; pub. affairs adminstr. Pink Palace Mus. and Memphis Mus. Inc., Memphis, 1998; CEO Lamapasas C. of C., Lampasas, TX, 1998-99; pres., CEO Assn. Non-Profit Orgns., from 1998, Tex. Assn. Bed and Breakfast Innkeepers, 1998; pres. A Little Cottage B&B, 1999—2004; owner Heritage Sta. Antiques, from 1999, Heritage Country Realty, 1999—2006. Dir. Tex. Children's Mus., Fredericksburg, 1987-88, Internat. Hdqrs. SHAPE Command Arts and Crafts Ctr., 1985-86; com. chmn. Symposium for Encouragement Women in Math. and Natural Sci., U. Tex., Austin, 1990; instr. nonprofit mgmt., fin. devel., bd. leadership, grant proposal writing, special event coord., vol. mgmt. Ctrl. Tex. Coll., 2002—. Sculptor portrait busts. Bd. dirs. Teenage Parent Coun., Austin, 1990-92, ARC; lay speaking minister, First United Methodist Ch., 2000-. Named U.S. Vol. of Yr., NATO-Shape Belgium Cmty. Svcs., 1986; grantee, NEA, 1988. Mem.: AAUW (life; pres. 1990—92), Women in Comm. (co-chmn. SW regional conf.), Lometa Lions Club (pub. rels. com. 1999—2003), Heritage Station Antique Vehicle Show (founder), Heritage Station Antiques Show and Sale (founder), Leadership Tex. (life), U. Tex. Ex-Student Assn. (life), Heritage Station Antiques Forum (founder), Raleigh Tavern Soc. (founder), Leadership Tex. Alumnae Assn. (bd. dir.), Tex. Hist. Found (life). Avocations: writing, lecturing, meeting and strategic planning. Home: Burnet, Tex. Died Aug. 5, 2007.

THOMPSON, RICHARD DEANE, entertainment industry consultant; b. Ann Arbor, Mich., Sept. 30, 1933; s. Milton J. and Helen (Frank) T. BFA, U. Tex., 1955; MFA, Yale Drama Sch., 1961. Sales engr. Ward Leonard Electric Co., Mt. Vernon, N.Y., 1961-65; mgr. theater div. Lighting and Electronics, Yonkers, N.Y., 1965-68; dir. planning Imero Fiorentino Assn., NYC, 1968-72; sr. cons. George T. Howard and Assocs., Hollywood, Calif., 1972-75; mgr. staging ops. Worldstage, Hollywood, 1976-79; facilities mgr. Robert Abel and Assocs., Hollywood, 1979-82; mgr. purchasing Cinedco, Inc., Glendale, Calif., 1985-87; prin. Thompson Assocs., Van Nuys, Calif., from 1988. Contbr. articles to profl. jours. Served to pvt. first class U.S. Army, 1956-58. Fellow U.S. Inst. for Theater Tech. (Safety awad 1988); mem. Soc. Motion Picture and TV Engrs., Internat. Alliance of Theatrical Stage Employees, Nat. Fire Protection Assn., Internat. Assn. Elec. Inspectors (as soc. mem.). Avocation: home remodeling. Died Feb. 12, 2007.

THOMPSON, ROBERT SAMUEL, retired lawyer; b. Cleve., Nov. 2, 1930; s. Wayne Charles Thompson and Cornelia Irene (Anderson) Thompson Baker; m. JoAnne Courtney; children: Robert Dale, Richard Wayne. BA, Hamilton Coll., 1953; JD, U. Mich., 1956; postgrad., Air Command and Staff Coll., Montgomery, Ala., 1967-68. Bar: Mich. 1956, Ohio 1962, U.S. Supreme Ct. 1962, Oreg. 1973. Judge advocate USAF, 1956-77; pvt. practice McMinnville, Oreg., 1977—2003; ret., 2003. Judge mcpl. ct. 1977-2003. Mem. Oreg. Soc. SAR (pres. 1989-90), Oreg. Mcpl. Judges Assn. (pres. 1992-93), Rotary (bd. dirs. McMinnville chpt. 1989), Am. Legion, Masons. Died Jan. 30, 2007.

THOMPSON, ROGER JAMES, supermarket business executive; b. Kankakee, Ill., Sept. 2, 1937; s. Paul Melzer and Mary Helen (Bertrand) T.; m. Sally Gail Sutton, Mar. 31, 1956; children: Donald Melzer, Anthony J., Stuart Roger. Student, Kankakee Community Coll., 1974-75. Office staff Commonwealth Edison Co., Harvey, Ill., 1959-68; with mgmt. Spieth's Market Inc., Momence, Ill., from 1968. Dir., sec., treas., co-owner Spieth's Market Inc., Momence, 1982—. With U.S. Army, 1956-59. Republican. Avocations: golf, travel, photography. Home: Momence, Ill. Died Apr. 25, 2007.

THOMPSON, SYDNOR, JR., (CHARLES WILLIAM SYDNOR THOMPSON JR.), lawyer, mediator, arbitrator; b. Balt., Feb. 18, 1924; s. Charles William Sydnor Thompson and Helen Josephine Layne; m. Harriette Line, June 2, 1947; children: Darcy T. Howard, Charles William Sydnor III, Harriet T. Moore, Brenneman L., Mary Katherine Line T. Kelly. AB, Syracuse U., 1947; LLB, Harvard U., 1950; student, St. Andrews U., Scotland, 1945, Manchester U., Eng., 1950, London Sch. Econs., 1951. Cert.: NC Dispute Resolution Commn. (mediator), EEOC, Am. Arbitration Assn. (arbitrator), Fin. Industry Regulatory Authority. Assoc. Davis Polk & Wardwell, NYC, 1951—54; ptnr. Parker Poe Thompson Bernstein Gage & Preston, Charlotte, NC, 1954—94; judge NC Ct. Appeals, Raleigh, NC, 1994; of counsel Parker, Poe, Adams & Bernstein, LLP, Charlotte, from 1995; assoc. Mediation, Inc., Winston-Salem, NC, from 1995. Author: The Sydnor Family Saga, 2000, A Collection of Ad Hominem Verse, 2002, Sydnor Knows the Answer: A Memoir, 2006, Royal Connection-One Family's Odyssey from Tudor England to Colonial America, 2013; contbr. articles to law revs. Pres. Charlotte Symphony Orch., 1958—61, Charlotte Opera Assn., 1971—75; vice chair NC Arts Coun., Raleigh, 1981—84; pres. Mecklenburg Ministries, 1987—89, Wing Haven Found., 2001—02; chmn. Mecklenburg County Dem. Party, 1977—81. With US Army, 1943—46, ETO. Decorated Bronze star; Fulbright scholar, 1950, 1951. Master: William H. Bobbitt Inn of Ct.; mem.: ABA (chmn. circuits subcom. 1977—95), Mecklenburg Bar Assn. (pres. 1990), NC Bar Assn. (chmn. appellate rules study com. 1989—91, chmn. local bar svcs. com. 1991—93), Old Catawba Soc., Horace Williams Philosophy Club, English Speaking Union, Charlotte City Club, Sporadic Book Club, Charlotte Country Club. Avocations: genealogy, writing, tennis, acting. Home: Charlotte, NC. Deceased.

THOMPSON, THEODORE ROBERT, pediatric educator; b. Dayton, Ohio, July 18, 1943; s. Theodore Roosevelt and Helen (Casey) J.; m. Lynette Joanne Shenk; 1 child, S. Beth. BS, Wittenberg U., 1965; MD, U. Pa., 1969. Diplomate Am. Bd. Pediatrics (Neonatal, Perinatal Medicine). Resident in pediat. U. Minn. Hosp., Mpls., 1969—72, chief resident in pediat., 1971—72, fellow neonatal, perinatal, 1974—75, asst. prof., 1975—80, dir. divsn. neonatology and newborn intensive care unit, 1977—91, assoc. prof., 1980—85, prof., from 1985, co-dir. Med. Outreach, 1988—91, med. dir. med. outreach, 1991—2000, assoc. chief pediat. svcs., 1988—2003, assoc. head pediat. edn. and cmty. programs, 2003—04, assoc. head cmty. affairs, 2004—10; med. dir. outreach, bd. dirs. U. Minn. Physicians, 1992—2008; lead acad. advisor U Minn Medical Sch., from 2011; acute patient care placement med. dir. Minn Med. Ctr., Fairview, from 2008; med. dir. NICUs, Fairview Southdale and Fairview Ridges Hosps. Med. exec. com., sec.-treas. U. Minn. Med. Ctr., Fairview, 2002—04, chief of staff elect, 2004—07, chief of staff, 2007—09, past chief staff, 2009—11. Editor: Newborn Intensive Care: A Practical Manual, 1983. Bd. dirs. Life Link III, St. Paul, 1987—; cons. Maternal and Child Health, Minn. Bd. Health, 1975-94; bd. dirs. Minn. Med. Found., 1995-99. With USPHS. 1972-74. Recipient Advocacy award, U. Minn. Med. Sch., Pres.'s award for outstanding svc., U. Minn., Alumni Outstanding Achievements award, Wittenberg U., 2005, Disting. Svc. award, Minn. Chpt. Acad. Pediat., 2009. Fellow: Am. Acad. Pediats.; mem.: Acad. Med. Educators, Gt. Plains Orgn. for Perinatal Health Care (Sioux Falls, SD Kunshe award 1989). Lutheran. Avocation: fly fishing. Home: New Brighton, Minn. Died July 2013.

THOMPSON, WARREN RICHARD, engineering administrator; b. St. Louis, Sept. 8, 1926; s. Wilford Pearl and Nellie (Holler) T.; m. Ruth Anna Scheffing, Sept. 14, 1946; children: Adrienne Marie, Carl Scheffing. BSME, Iowa State U., 1948; MSME, U. Pa., 1959. Registered profl. engr., 11 states. Sr. project mgr. United Engrs. and Constructors Inc., Phila., 1948-86; prin. cons. engr. Warren R. Thompson Profl. Engr., Jenkintown, Pa., 1986-87; dir. engring. Reading Energy Group Inc., Phila., from 1987. Contbr. numerous articles to profl. jours. Vestryman All Hallows Episcopal Ch., Wyncote, Pa., 1975-87. Served with USN, 1943-46, PTO. Mem. ASME (award 1957), Am. Nuclear Soc., Assn. Iron and Steel Engrs., ASTM (past office holder), Afro-Am. Fedn. Inc. (bd. dirs. 1968-78). Republican. Avocations: model railroading, photography. Home: Jenkintown, Pa. Died Mar. 9, 2007.

THOMSON, CARL LOUIS, artist, art appraiser, gallery owner, director; b. Bklyn., Mar. 6, 1913; s. Louis and Hilma (Carlson) T.; m. Dona Lou Morris, Dec. 2, 1944; children: Clara, Carl Jr., Nanci. Student, Pratt Inst., 1932-35. Designer Walter Dorwin Teague Assoc., NYC, 1937-38; advt. mgr. Internat. Projector Corp., NYC, 1939-42; co-owner Weber-Thomson Advt., NYC, 1946-49; owner C. Thomson Advt. Art, NYC, 1949-58; advt. promotion mgr. Am. Home Products, Inc., NYC, 1958-69; owner, pres. Equitable Appraisal Co., Inc., NYC, from 1969; dir. Thomson Gallery, NYC, from 1989. Master sgt. U.S. Army, USAF. Mem. Salamagundi Club (pres. ex officio 1981-83). Republican. Lutheran. Avocations: gardening, fishing, painting, billards. Home: New York, NY. Died Mar. 16, 2007.

THOMSON, GEORGE BREED, retired urban planner; b. Boston, Jan. 10, 1921; s. Malcolm and Helen May (Breed) Thomson; m. Jeanne Goddard Morrison, Aug. 1, 1942 (dec. Nov. 1993); children: Dale Goddard Thomson Milne, Laurie Breed Thomson DiClerico. SB, Harvard Coll., 1942. Design developer various co., Mass., 1949—78; ret., 1978. Chmn., bd. selectmen Swampscott Town Hall, Mass., 1956—64; rep. Met. Boston area Planning Coun., 1964—78; rep. planning com. Upper Valley Regional Planning Commn., NH, from 1979; rep. Mass. Gen. Ct., Boston, 1958—65. Mem.: Lake Sunapee Country Club, Harvard Faculty Club. Republican. Home: New London, NH. Died Nov. 8, 2006.

THOMSON, JAMES ADOLPH, medical group practice administrator; b. Kansas City, Mo., Feb. 25, 1924; s. Edward Wilkins and Gladys Lucile (Opperman) T.; m. Patricia Jane Herron, Jan. 24, 1943; children: Linda Lee Thomson Schwartz, Kenneth Leroy, James Howard. BSBA in Acctg., Rockhurst U., Kansas City, 1950. Cost acct. Std. Brands, Inc., Kansas City, 1950-52; asst. comptr. Menorah Med. Ctr., Kansas City, 1952-56; comptr. Holzer Hosp. and Clinic, Gallipolis, Ohio, 1956-63; adminstr. Oberlin (Ohio) Clinic, Inc., 1963-71; adminstr. and treas. Thompson, Brumm & Knepper Clinic, Inc., St. Joseph, Mo., 1971-80; bus. mgr. Cin. Neurol. Assocs., Inc., 1980-89, ret., 1989. Cons. med. groups, Ohio, 1968-70. V.p. St. Joseph (Mo.) Area C. of C., 1976-78; pres. Oberlin Health Commn., 1968-69; bd. dirs. St. Joseph Sheltered Workshop, 1978-80. Served with M.C. U.S. Army, 1943-46, ETO. Recipient Disting. Svc. award St. Joseph Area C. of C., 1979. Fellow Am. Coll. Med. Group Adminstrs.; mem. Am. Assn. Hosp. Accts. (charter, pres. 1954-56), Mo. Med. Group Mgmt. Assn. (charter, pres. 1978-79), Med. Group Mgmt. Assn., Ohio Med. Group Mgmt. Assn., Cin. Med. Group Mgmt. Assn. (pres. 1983-84), Rotary (pres. Oberlin and St. Joseph), Lions (pres. 1962-63), KC, Masons, Shriners, Am. Legion. Republican. Episcopalian. Avocations: woodworking, gardening, golf. Home: Lees Summit, Mo. Died May 2, 2007.

THOMSON, PHILIP DEPOYSTER, microbiologist; b. San Angelo, Tex., Mar. 13, 1943; s. John Throckmorton and Hazel (Parnell) T.; m. Margaret Jean Hoffmaster, July 29, 1967; 1 child, Philip DePoyster. AA, San Angelo Coll., 1963; BS, Angelo State Coll., San Angelo, 1968; MS, Mont. State U., 1972, PhD in Microbiology/Immunology, 1974. Rsch. asst. in ophthalmology Wilmer Inst., Johns Hopkins U., Balt., 1964-66; grad. fellow Mont. State U., Bozeman, 1968-74; postdoctoral fellow U. Tex. Med. Br., Galveston, 1974-76; chief microbiology divsn. Shriners Burns Inst., Galveston, 1976-83; dir. Burn Ctr. Labs. U. Mich. Hosps., Ann Arbor, 1983-92; asst. dir. technol. planning Mallinckrodt Med., Inc., St. Louis, 1992-94, assoc. dir. technol. planning, from 1994. Chair tissue com. Organ Procurement Agy., Mich., 1988-92; mem. grant rev. com. NIDDR/U.S. Dept. Edn., Washington, 1991—; dir. skin bank U. Mich. Hosps., 1983-92. Editor/co-editor 5 books; contbr. chpts. to books, numerous articles to profl. jours. Mem. Am. Burn Assn., Internat. Soc. Burn Injuries, Wound Healing Soc., N.Am. Burn Soc., Phi Theta Kappa. Avocations: hunting, fishing, photography, graphic art. Home: Pearland, Tex. Died June 23, 2007.

THORNE, RICHARD CHARLES, television producer, director, writer; b. Chgo., Oct. 10, 1925; s. Theodore Charles Thorne and Alta Inez (Brown) Polley; m. Janice Ann Olsen, Apr. 29, 1948; children: Janice Adair, Alynne Lee, Richard Norman, Robin Elizabeth, Lowell Ann. BA in Speech, Columbia Coll., 1948. Writer, producer, announcer TV sta. WGN, Chgo., 1948-52; writer, producer Mut. Broadcasting Systems, Chgo., 1952-54; asst. to county judge, then gov. State of Ill., Chgo., 1955-64; dir. news program Sta. WNUS, Chgo., 1964-69; v.p. Universal Tng. Systems, Northbrook, Ill., from 1969. Author (radio series) Hall of Fantasy, 1952 (CFAC Best Series 1954), The Silver Eagle, 1952, Final Closure, 1989. Exec. dir. Citizens for Kerner, Ill., 1960, 64. Mem. Am. Fedn. of TV and Radio Artists, Screen Actors Guild. Episcopalian. Home: Chicago, Ill. Died Feb. 12, 2007.

THORNTON, JOSEPH SCOTT, research and development company executive, materials scientist; b. Sewickley, Pa., Feb. 6, 1936; s. Joseph Scott and Evelyn (Miller) T.; divorced; children: Joseph Scott III, Chris P. BSME, U. Tex., 1957, PhD, 1969; MSMetE, Carnegie Mellon U., 1962. Engr. Walworth Valve Co., Boston, 1958; metall. engr. Westinghouse Astronuclear Lab., Large, Pa., 1962-64; instr., teaching assoc. U. Tex., Austin, 1964-67; group leader Tracor Inc., Austin, 1967-69, dept. dir., 1973-75; dept. mgr. Horizons Rsch., Inc., Cleve., 1969-73; founder, bd. mem. Tex. Rsch. Internat., Inc. (formerly Tex. Rsch. Inst., Inc.), Austin, from 1975. Contbr. numerous tech. papers to profl. publs.; editor: WANL Materials Manual, 2 vols., 1964; patentee in field. Founder, bd. mem. Cmtys. Recovery 501 (c) Social Profit Corp., Austin, from 2004. Recipient IGS award, 2002; fellow Alcoa, Austin, 1964, RC Baker Found., 1967;Dr. Stewart Nemir Friend of Recovery Recognition Award, 2010; Pres.'s Call to Service Award, Lifetime 2010. Mem.: ASTM, Internat. Geosynthetics Soc. (award 2002), Adhesion Soc., Am. Soc. Metals Internat. (exec. com. 1965—66). Home: Austin, Tex. Died Nov. 23, 2014.

THORPE, LEON FERBER, real estate investment company executive; b. Pitts., May 29, 1940; s. Benjamin and Freda (Ferber) T.; m. Suzanne Rosenthal (div. 1972); children: Joshua Ferber, David Lewis; m. Robin C. Thorpe, 1995. AB, Harvard U., 1961, LLB, 1964. V.p. B. Thorpe & Co., Pitts., 1966-69; pres. Leon Thorpe Realty Co., Pitts., from 1969, Thor Parking Corp., Pitts., from 1992. Mem. com. univ. resources Harvard U., Cambridge, 1983-85; bd. dirs. Chatham Coll., Pitts., 1985-88, investment com. United Jewish Fedn. Western Pa., 1992—; mem. vis. com. Coll. of Harvard U., 1987-92. Mem. Nat. Parking Assn. (bd. dirs. 1978-82, 91-92). Avocations: exercise, travel, piano, reading. Home: Boca Raton, Fla. Died Nov. 7, 2006.

THRALLS, ROBERT KEITH, systems programmer, analyst; b. Ft. Hood, Tex., Dec. 9, 1964; s. Rodney Emil and Anna Lee (Phillips) T.; m. Cynthia Jo Estill, Feb. 14, 1986 (Oct. 5, 1992); children: Robert Keith Jr., Brennan Scott, Katrina Ann, Jeremy Daniel; m. Súsanne Heintke, Oct. 15, 1993. Student, Chadwick U., from 1993. Intelligence analyst Army Security Agy., Ft. Meade, Md., 1984-88; programmer Net Express, Inc., Vienna, Va., 1986-88, syss. programmer, 1989-93; sys. programmer Computer Consoles, Inc., Reston, Va., 1988-89; sys. programmer The Orkand Corp. Ctrs. for Disease Control, Atlanta, 1993-94, sys. programmer Dynamic Resources, Inc., CDC, from 1994. Contbr. poems to anthology, articles to profl. jours. Mem. Task force for Biking and Walking U.S. Dept. Transp., Atlanta, 1995—. Served in U.S. Army Res., 1984-88. Mem. Disting. Soc. Poets. Mem. Wiccan Ch. Avocations: poetry, archery, bicycling, swimming. Home: Pmbk Pines, Fla. Died Mar. 7, 2007.

THRASH, JOHN CURTIS, JR., petroleum engineer, executive; b. Harris County, Tex., Feb. 9, 1925; s. John Curtis and Alicia May (Lindsey) T.; m. Patricia Ruth Francis, Dec. 21, 1949; children: Denise S., John F., Allison E. BS in Petroleum Engring., U. Tex., 1947. Registered profl. engr., Tex. Prodn. engr. Tex. Co., Odessa, 1947-50; dist. engr. Forest Oil Corp., Odessa, Tex., 1950-55, Brit. Am. Oil Co., Dallas, Oklahoma City, 1955-63; cons. profl. engr. Bart De Coat & Assocs., Houston, 1963-65; v.p. Houston Pipe Line Co., Houston, 1965-81; pres. Thrash Oil and Gas Co., Houston, 1979-90, Togco Gas Storage Corp., Houston, 1985-90, e-Corp and Togco Natural Gas Storage Corp., Houston, from 1991. Contbr. articles to profl. jours. Chmn. Houston chpt. Am. Petroleum Inst., 1975-76. Lt. USNR, 1942-47, 51-54, Korea, World War II. Mem. Am. Petroleum Inst. (chmn. Houston chpt. 1975-76), Tex. Ind. Producers Assn., Ind. Producers Assn. of Am., Soc. Petroleum Engrs. Nat. Soc., Am. Gas Assn., Houston C. of C. (air and water conservation com.). Avocations: flying, golf, tennis. Home: Houston, Tex. Died Nov. 4, 2006.

THREADGILL, CECIL RAYMOND, minister, counselor; b. Mt. Vernon, Ala., June 15, 1925; s. Daniel George and Addie Gertrude (Oliver) T.; m. Bonnie Jeanne Wise, June 2, 1946; children: Gloria Jeanne, Gay Dean. AA, Jacksonville Coll., 1949; BA, Baylor U., 1951; postgrad., Tex. Christian U., 1957, U. North Tex., 1960-61, U. Md., 1967-68; MDiv, Southwestern Bapt. Theol. Sem., 1973; postgrad., San Francisco Theol Sem., 1978-79; DEd, New Orleans Bapt. Theol. Sem., 1983; postgrad., U. of Sci. and Arts of Okla., 1987-88, Tex. Women's U., 1991. Ordained to ministry So. Bapt. Conv., 1946; lic. profl. counselor, Okla., Tex. Pastor Bapt. chs., Tex., 1947-54, Plainview Bapt. Ch., Krum, Tex., 1958-59, Calvary Bapt. Ch., Pilot Point, Tex., 1959-61; lt. (j.g.), chaplain USN, 1961, advanced through grades to lt. comdr.; ret., 1982; dir. student affairs and ch.-min. rels. New Orleans Bapt. Sem., 1982-83; dir. Counseling-Edn. Ctr., Grady Bapt. Assn., Chickasha, Okla., 1984-88; pastor Michigan Avenue Bapt. Ch., Chickasha, 1988-90, Antioch Bapt. Ch., Aubrey, Tex., from 1990. Mem. Christian life com. Denton (Tex.) Bapt. Assn., 1990-91. With USMCR, 1944-46, PTO. Decorated Purple Heart. Mem. Am. Assn. for Marriage and Family Therapy (clin.). Republican. *I am deeply grateful to God for the privilege of being a part of His creation that challenges me to keep reaching beyond my grasp as I grow in His likeness in love for and service to others.* Died Aug. 9, 2007.

THRIFT, WILLIAM BOYD, retired lecturer; b. Mosier, Oreg., Nov. 7, 1912; s. Edward Jackson and Lena Mavourneen (McCormick) T.; m. Margaret Wilson, Aug. 2, 1941 (div. Feb. 1954); children: David Edward, Ann Louise, Mardi; m. Suzann Williams, Apr. 30, 1971. BA, Lewis and ClarkU., 1934; MDiv, San Francisco Theol. Sem., 1941; MA, St. Mary's U., 1966. Min. Presbyn. Ch., Morgan Hill, Calif., 1941-42; asst. prof. San Antonio Coll., 1966-69; lectr. English, Speech, Religious U. Md., 1969-95. Lectr. English, Speech, Religion, U. Coll., U. Md. in Greece, Spain, Germany, Eng., Iceland, 1969-95. With USN, 1942-46. With USAF, 1947-66. Avocations: nature study, bird-watching, reading, woodcarving. Died July 22, 2007.

TICKLE, PHYLLIS NATALIE ALEXANDER, writer, publishing executive, poet; b. Johnson City, Tenn., Mar. 12, 1934; d. Philip Wade and Mary Katherine (Porter) Alexander; m. Samuel Milton Tickle, June 17, 1955 (dec.); children: Nora Katherine Cannon, Mary Gammon Ballard, Laura Lee Palermo, John Crockett II, Samuel Milton Jr., Philip Wade, Rebecca Rutledge. BA, E. Tenn. State U., 1955; MA in English, Furman U., 1961; LHD, Yale U., 2004, North Pk. U., 2009. Tchr. Latin, English Memphis City Sch., 1955-57; fellow Furman U., Greenville, SC, 1959-61; lectr. English Rhodes Coll., Memphis, 1961-64; dean humanities Memphis Coll. Art, 1964-71; mng. editor St. Luke's Press, Memphis, 1975-82, sr. editor, 1982-85, Iris Press, Memphis, 1982—85, Peachtree Pubs., Atlanta, 1988-90; dir. trade pub. group The Wimmer Cos., Memphis, 1990-92; founding religion editor Publishers Weekly, 1992-96; contbg. editor Pubs. Weekly, editor-at-large PW's Religion Bookline, 1996—2004. Poet-in-residence Brooks Meml. Gallery, 1981-89; poetry coord. Cumberland Valley Writer's Conf., 1977-83; bd. adv. Servant Publ., 1997-03, Garrett-Medill Ctr. for Religion and the News Media., Christy Awards, Loyola Coll., Md., Religion and Ethics NewsWeekly; exec. bd. Forward Movement Publ.; bd. dirs. Iris Press. Author: Syntactical Patterns in Indo-European Speech, 1968, The Story of Two Johns, It's No Fun to be Sick, 1976, On Beyond Koch, 1981, On Beyond Ais, 1982, The City Essays, 1982, What the Heart Already Knows, Stories for Advent, Christmas and Epiphany, 1985, Final Sanity: Stories of Lent, Easter and the Great Fifty Days, 1987, And Ordinary Time: Stories of the Days Between Ascensiontide and Advent, 1988, The Tickle Papers: Parables and Pandemonium, 1989; (dramas) Figs and Fury, 1976, Tobias and the Angels, 1983, Children of Her Name, 1987; (poetry) American Genesis, 1976, 3d edit., 1984, Selections, 1984; contbg. author: Upper Room devotional, Disciplines, 1989, 365 Meditations for Women, 1990, 365 More Meditations for Women, 1992; gen. editor, contbr.: Confessing Conscience: Church Women on Abortion, 1990, Re-Discovering the Sacred: Spirituality for America, 1995, My Father's Prayer: A Remembrance, 1995; gen. editor: Home Works: An Anthology of Tennessee Writers, 1996; contbr. The Reader's Companion to Crossing the Threshold of Hope, 1996, God-talk in America, 1997, The Divine Hours-Prayers for Summertime (Doubleday-Top Ten Books of Yr.), 2000, The Divine Hours-Prayers for Autumn and Wintertime, 2000, The Divine Hours-Prayers for Springtime, 2001, The Shaping of A Life-A Spiritual Landscape, 2001, A Stitch and A Prayer, 2003, Christmastide-Prayers for Advent through Epiphany from The Divine Hours, 2003, What the Land Already Knows, 2003, Eastertide-Prayers for Lent and Easter from The Divine Hours, 2004, Wisdom in the Waiting, 2004, The Graces We Remember, 2004, Greed, 2004, Prayer is a Place: America's Religious Landscape Observed, 2005, The Night Offices--A Manual for Evening Prayer, 2006, The Pocket Edition of the Divine Hours, 2007, This is What I Pray Today: The Divine Hours for Children, 2007, The Words of Jesus: A Gospel of the Sayings of Our Lord with Reflections, 2008, The Great Emergence, 2008; columnist Dixie Flyer; mem. editl. bd. Episcopal Diocese West Tenn., 1985-99, Parabola Mag., Blueridge Publ.; contbr. articles to popular mags. including Feminist Digest, Newsletter for Ctr. of So. Folklore, Ctr. City, Tenn. Churchman, The Episcopalian, Alive Now!, John Milton mag., others; author numerous poems. Chair lit. panel Tenn. Arts Commn., Nashville, 1991-92, mem. panel, 1978-82, 89-94, past chair artists in edn., 1986-89; exec. bd. Tenn. Humanities Coun., Nashville, 1989-92; vestrywoman St. Anne's Ch., Millington, 1988-95; lay eucharistic min. Episcopal Ch., 1996—; adv. bd. Mary Baker Eddy Libr., D.L. Dykes

Jr. Found. Recipient Alumni award of honor East Tenn. State U., 2006; Ind. Artist fellow Tenn. Arts Commn., Nashville, 1985, Polly Bond award of excellence Episc. Comm., NYC, 1988, Books of Excellence award Body, Mind and Spirit mag., 1996, Book of Yr. 1995 Catholic Press Assn.; named Disting. Alumna of Yr., Shorter Coll., 1997. Mem. Pub. Assn. of the South (bd. dir. 1986—, pres., chair 1985-86, Mays award 1996), Southeastern Booksellers Assn. (bd. dir. 1986-91), Tenn. Lit. Arts Assn. (pres. 1984-86), Religious Newswriters Assn. Died Sept. 22, 2015.

TIERNAN, ROBERT OWENS, former United States Representative from Rhode Island; b. Providence, Feb. 24, 1929; m. Dorothy A. Tiernan, 1953 (dec. 2001); children: Michael M., Robert O., Christopher P. BA, Providence Coll., 1953; JD, Catholic U. Law Sch., 1956. Mem. RI State Senate, 1961—67; del. Democratic Nat Convention, 1968—72; mem. US Congress from 2nd RI Dist., 1967—75; del. Democratic Nat. Mid-Term Conf., 1974; mem. Fed. Election Comm., 1975—78, vice chmn., 1979—84, chmn., 1980—81. Law rev. editor Cath. U. Sch. Law. Mem.: DC Bar Assn., RI Bar Assn., Am. Bar Assn. Democrat. Roman Catholic. Died Oct. 15, 2014.

TIFFT, ELLEN, writer; b. Elmira, NY, June 28, 1916; d. Halsey and Julia (Day) Sayles; m. Bela Crane Tifft, July 16, 1938 (dec. Jan. 1999); children: Wilton, John, Nicol. Student, Elmira Coll., 1935-38. Author: Moon, Moon, Tell Me True, 1996, (chapbooks) A Door in a Wall, 1969, The Kissed Cold Kite, 1972, (poetry) The Live-Long Day, 1972, Carnival Woods, 1973. Bd. dirs. Second Place East, 1950-99; mem. Mark Twain adv. bd. Elmira Coll., 1990-97. Recipient 1st prize Poetry Book mag., 1951, Steele Lib. Poetry Competition, 1998; grantee N.Y. State Coun. for the Arts, Arts of the So. Finger Lakes, among others. Home: Elmira, NY. Died Dec. 17, 2006.

TILL, FRANCES DELEON, history educator; b. Mercedes, Tex., May 15, 1941; d. Raymond Charles and Mary Clovis (Hickman) T. BA, U. Tex., Austin, 1963; MA, U. Tex., 1964. Chmn. history dept. Edinburg (Tex.) Jr. High Sch., 1966-68, Edinburg High Sch., from 1973. Founder Bird Rescue Inc., Weslaco, Tex., 1980; bd. dirs. Frontera Audubon Soc., Weslaco, 1981-83. Recipient Tex. Excellence award for Outstanding High Sch. Tchrs., U. Tex., Austin, 1989; NEH summer fellow, Washington, 1990. Mem. Nat. Coun. Social Studies, Tex. Coun. Social Studies, Tex. Ctr. Ednl. Tech., Tex. Fedn. Tchrs. Roman Catholic. Avocations: wildlife photography, travel, opera and classical music, sports, gardening. Died Feb. 15, 2007.

TINDEMANS, LEO (LEONARD CLEMENCE TINDEMANS), former prime minister of Belgium; b. Zwijndrecht, Apr. 16, 1922; m. Rosa Naesens, 1960; 4 children. Degree, State U. Ghent, Catholic U., Louvain; DLitt (hon.), City U. London. Mem. Belgian Chamber of Deputies, 1961; mayor of Edegem, 1965—76; min. cmty. affairs Govt. of Belgium, Brussels, 1968—71, min. agrl. & middle class affairs, 1972—73, dep. prime minister, minister for budget and instl. problems, 1973—74, prime min., 1974—78, min. fgn. affairs, 1981—89. Pres. European People's Party, 1976—85; mem. European Parliament, 1989—99. Contbr. articles to profl. jours. V.p. European Union of Christian Democrats. Recipient Charlemagne prize, 1976, St. Liborius medaille, Einheit und Frieden, 1977. Christian Democratic. Roman Catholic. Home: Edegem, Belgium. Died Dec. 26, 2014.

TINTURIN, PETER, composer; b. Ekaterinoslav, Russia, June 1, 1910; arrived in U.S., 1929, naturalized; s. Leonid and Elizabeth Tinturin; m. Wela Davies, Sept. 1941 (dec.); children: Leonid, Glenn. Student, Vienna Conservatory Music, 1924—29; BA, U. Vienna, 1929; MusB cum laude, Chapman Coll., 1953. Former v.p. Advanced Pictures Corp., Hollywood; former pres. Fine Arts Recording Co., 1948. Composer, writer various films and plays; author: over 300 works publ.; prodr., writer (musical) Pardon My Ph.D. Pvt. US Army, 1943—44. Mem.: ASCAP (award for outstanding compositions 1934, 1937, 1941). Home: Laguna Hills, Calif. Died Apr. 15, 2007.

TIPPETT, GRACE ESTER See DUKE, ROBIN CHANDLER

TISHMAN, JOHN LOUIS, realty and construction company executive; b. NYC, Jan. 24, 1926; s. Louis and Rose F. (Foreman) T.; m. Suzanne Weisberg (dec. 2005); children: Daniel R., Katherine T. Blacklock BS, U. Michigan, 1946. Taught Math; with Tishman Realty & Constrn. Co., Inc., NYC, 1948—2016. Chmn. New Sch., NY. Co-author: Building Tall: My Life and the Invention of Construction Management, 2011. Mem. bd. execs. Ronald McDonald House, NYU Med. Ctr., Pratt Inst., Carnegie Hall, Central Park Conservancy; chmn. bd. trustees New Sch. Univ., NYC. Served with USN. Home: Bedford, NY. Died Feb. 6, 2016.

TOAFF, ELIO, rabbi; b. Apr. 30, 1915; 1 child, Ariel. Rabbi, Venice, 1947—51; chief Rabbi of Rome, 1951—2002. Recipient Prize Culturae, 2012. Died Apr. 19, 2015.

TOBIN, WALLACE EMMETT, III, paper manufacturing executive; b. NYC, July 23, 1937; s. Wallace Emmett Sr. and Elizabeth (Lovell) T.; m. Eva Britt Dysthe; children by previous marriage: Briggs Lovell, Ashley Manchester, Bliss Radcliffe. BA, Yale U., 1959; MA, Cambridge U., 1961; MBA, U. New Haven, 1980. Dir. devel. Yale U., New Haven, 1967-74; pres. Acigraf Internat. Corp., Branford, Conn., 1974-81; v.p. planning and devel. Dead River Corp., Portland, Maine, 1981-84; sr. v.p. Brant-Allen Industries, Greenwich, Conn., from 1984. Mem. adv. bd. Conn. Bank & Trust, Greenwich, 1985—. Author: Mariner's Pocket Companion; contbr. articles to profl. jours. Mem. Sailing Edn. Assn. Corp., Woods Hole, Mass., 1972—, Fales com. U.S. Naval Acad., Annapolis, Md., 1977—; treas. Am. Friends of Cambridge U., 1988—; treas. Colony Found., New Haven, 1975—. Named Mellon Found. fellow, 1959-61. Mem. Am. Paper Inst., N.Y. Yacht Club, Cruising Club Am., Royal Ocean Racing Club, Indian Harbor Yacht Club, Storm Trysail Club, Off Soundings Club. Avocation: sailing. Died Dec. 31, 2006.

TOMASH, ERWIN, retired computer company executive; b. St. Paul, Nov. 17, 1921; s. Noah and Milka (Ehrlich) T.; m. Adelle Ruben, July 31, 1943; children: Judith Sarada Tomash Diffenbaugh, Barbara Ann Tomash Bussa. BS, U. Minn., Minneapolis, 1943; MS, U. Md., College Park, 1950. Instr. elec. engring. U. Minn., 1946; assoc. dir. computer devel. Univac div. Remington Rand Corp., St. Paul, 1947-51; dir. West Coast ops. Univac div. Sperry Rand Corp., LA, 1953-55; pres. Telemeter Magnetics, Inc., LA, 1956-60; v.p. Ampex Corp., LA, 1961; founder, pres. Dataproducts Corp., LA, 1962-71, chmn. bd., 1971-80, chmn. exec. com., 1980-89; chmn. bd., dir. Newport Corp., Irvine, Calif., 1982-94. Founder, trustee, dir. Charles Babbage Found., U. Minn.; dir. and nat. gov. Coro Found., L.A. Served to capt. Signal Corps AUS, 1943-46. Decorated Bronze Star; recipient Outstanding Grad. award U. Minn., 1983. Mem. IEEE (sr., computer entrepeneur award 1988), Am. Soc. for Technion, History of Sci. Soc., Soc. for History of Tech., Assn. Internationale du Bibliophile. Home: Soquel, Calif. Died Dec. 10, 2012.

TOMPKINS, DOUGLAS RAINSFORD, apparel company executive; b. Ohio, Mar. 20, 1943; m. Susie Tompkins Tompkins, 1964 (div. 1989); children: Quincey, Summer; m. Kristine Tompkins. Founder, owner North Face, North Beach, Calif., 1964—69; with Esprit de Corps Internat., San Francisco, 1969—90. Recipient Design Leadership award, Am. Inst. Graphic Arts, 1987. Died Dec. 8, 2015.

TOPEY, ISHMAEL ALOYSIUS, urban planner; b. Port Henderson, St. Catherine, Jamaica, Nov. 10, 1926; s. Ferdinand Aloysius and Amy (Brown) T.; m. Dulcie Rose Clarke, Feb. 24, 1960; children: Patrick F., Robert I., Amy L., George A. BBA, U. Detroit, 1985; MA in Labor Rels., Wayne State U., Detroit, 1987. Cert. profl. cons./advisor; cert. adminstrv. mgr. Mgr. Sea Food Club, Jamaica, West Indies, 1960-78; tchr. Detroit Pub. Schs., 1986-87; urban renewal asst. City of Detroit, from 1987; founder Inter-Galactic Enterprises, Inc., Detroit, from 1990. Creator of human math.; econ. devel. specialist; cons. in field. Creator Topeyology Sys. of Speedy Learning, 1987, Letter to Stephen Hawking, Debunking the Bell Curve, History of Intelligence. Co-recipient Papal Citation for Social Work, 1985. Mem. AAAS, Am. Planning Assn., Buckminster Fuller Inst., World Future Soc., N.Y. Acad. of Scis., Planetary Soc. Home: Detroit, Mich. Died May 4, 2007.

TOPINKA, JUDY BAAR, state official, former state legislator; b. Riverside, Ill., Jan. 16, 1944; d. William Daniel and Lillian Mary (Shuss) Baar; 1 child, Joseph Baar. BS, Northwestern U., 1966. Features editor, reporter, columnist Life Newspapers, Berwyn and LaGrange, Ill., 1966-77; with Forest Park Rev. & Westchester News, Ill., 1976-77; coord. spl. events dept. fedn. comm. AMA, 1978-80; rsch. analyst to Senator Leonard Becker Ill. State Senate, 1978-79; mem. Dist. 7 Ill. House of Reps., 1980—82, mem. Dist. 43, 1982—84; mem. Dist. 22 Ill. State Senate, 1985—95; treas. State of Ill., Springfield, 1995—2007, comptr., 2011—14; chmn. Ill. State Republican Party, 2002—05. Founder, pres., bd. dirs. West Suburban Exec. Breakfast Club; chmn. Ill. Ethnics for Reagan-Bush, 1984, Bush-Quayle 1988 Recipient Outstanding Civilian Svc. medal, Molly Pitcher award, Abraham Lincoln award, Silver Eagle award U.S. Army and N.G. Republican. Died Dec. 10, 2014.

TOSHACH, CLARICE OVERSBY, real estate developer, retired computer company executive; b. Firbank, Westmoreland, Eng., Nov. 21, 1928; came to U.S., 1955; d. Oliver and Nora (Brown) Oversby; m. Daniel Wilkie Toshach, July 30, 1965 (dec. Aug. 1992); 1 child, Duncan Oversby Toshach (dec.); 1 child from previous marriage, Paul Anthony Beard. Textile designer Storeys of Lancaster, Eng., 1949-55; owner, operator Broadway Lane, Saginaw, Mich., 1956-70; pres., owner Clarissa Jane Inc., Saginaw, 1962-70, Over-Tosh Computers, Inc. dba Computerland, Saginaw and Flint, Mich., 1983-95; mgr., ptnr. Mich. Comml. Devel. L.L.C., Saginaw, from 1995. Trustee Saginaw Gen. Hosp., 1977-83, Home for the Aged, 1978-80; bd. dirs. Vis. Nurse Assn., pres., 1981-83; bd. dirs. Hospice of Saginaw, Inc., v.p., 1981-83; mem. long range planning com. United Way of Saginaw, 1982-83; cmty. advisor Jr. League of Saginaw, 1982-83; pres. Saginaw Gen. Hosp. Aux., 1972-82, pres., 1976-77. Home: Saginaw, Mich. Died June 4, 2014.

TOURNIER, MICHEL EDOUARD, writer; b. Paris, Dec. 19, 1924; s. Alphonse and Marie-Madeleine (Fournier) T. Student, U. Paris, Sorbonne, U. Tubingen; dr honoris causa, London Univ. Coll. In radio and TV prodn., 1949-54. Press attaché, Europe, 1955-58; head lit. services Editions Plon, 1958-68. Author: Vendredi ou les limbes du Pacifique, 1967, Le Roi des Aulnes, 1970, Les meteores, 1975, Le vent paraclet, 1977, Le coq de bruyere, 1978, Des clefs et des serrures, 1979, Gaspard, Melchoir et Balthazar, 1980, La Goutte d'Or, 1986, La Médianoche Amoureux, 1990, Le Crépuscule des Masques, 1992, Le Miroir des Idées Eleazar, 1996. Decorated officier Légion d'Honneur; recipient grand prix du Roma Acad. Française, 1967; prix Goncourt, 1970, Goethe medaille. Mem. Academie Goncourt, Trevio Campiello. Died Jan. 18, 2016.

TOUSSAINT, ALLEN RICHARD, recording studio executive, composer, pianist; b. New Orleans, Jan. 18, 1938; s. Clarence Matthew and Naomi (Neville) Toussaint; children: Naomi Rios, Clarence Reginald, Alison Toussaint-LeBeaux. DFA (hon.), Tulane U., 2013. Pres. Sea-Saint Rec. Studios, Inc., New Orleans; founder NYNO Music, 1998. Lectr. in field. Pianist for: Shirley & Lee, 1957, U.S. Army Soldiers Choir, 1963—65, recorded albums: Tousan-Wild Sounds of New Orleans, 1958, Life, Love & Faith, 1972, Southern Nights, 1975, Motion, 1978, Connected, 1996, A New Orleans Christmas, 1997, A Taste of New Orleans, 1999, Finger Poppin' & Stompin' Feet, 2002, Allen Toussaint's Jazzity Project: Going Places, 2004, The Complete Warner Bros. Recordings, 2005, I Believe To My Soul, 2005, The River in Reverse (with Elvis Costello), 2006, The Bright Mississippi, 2009, founder, v.p. recorded albums: Sansu Enterprises, Inc., from 1965; composer: (songs) Southern Nights (Country Music Assn. Song of Yr., Broadcast Music, Inc. citation of achievement), The Greatest Love, The Optimism Blues, Viva La Money, Whipped Cream, With You In Mind, Working In A Coal Mine, Yes We Can, Can, All These Things (Broadcast Music, Inc. citation of achievement); performer, dir., choreography : (Broadway plays) The High Rollers Social and Pleasure Club, 1992; performer: New Orleans Jazz Festival, annually; writer (songs for films) Ali, 2001, Employee of the Month, 2006, Rachel Getting Married, 2008, Being Flynn, 2012, The Way, Way Back, 2013, numerous other films and TV series. With US Army, 1963—65. Recipient Trustee award, 2009, Nat. Medal of Arts, Nat. Endowments for the Arts, 2012; named to Rock and Roll Hall of Fame, 1998, La. Hall of Fame, 2009, Songwriters Hall of Fame, 2011, Blues Hall of Fame, 2011. Mem.: Contemporary Arts Ctr., Am. Fedn. Musicians, Broadcast Music, Inc. Died Nov. 9, 2015.

TOWNES, CHARLES HARD, physics professor; b. Greenville, SC, July 28, 1915; s. Henry Keith and Ellen Sumter (Hard) Townes; m. Frances H. Brown, May 4, 1941; children: Linda Lewis, Ellen Screven, Carla Keith, Holly Robinson. BS in Physics, BA in Modern Languages, Furman U., Greenville, 1935; MA in Physics, Duke U., Durham, NC, 1937; PhD, Calif. Inst. Tech., 1939. Mem. tech. staff Bell Telephone Lab., 1939—47; assoc. prof. physics Columbia U., NYC, 1948—50, prof. physics, 1950—61, exec. dir. Columbia Radiation Lab., 1950—52, chmn. physics dept., 1952—55; prof. physics, provost MIT, 1961—66, Inst. prof., 1966—67; v.p., dir. rsch. Inst. Def. Analyses, Washington, 1959—61; Univ. prof. physics U. Calif., Berkeley, 1967—86, prof. physics emeritus, 1986—94, prof. Grad. Sch., 1994. Fulbright lectr. U. Paris, 1955—56, U. Tokyo, 1956; dir. Enrico Fermi Internat. Sch. Physics, Italy, 1963; Scott lectr. U. Cambridge, 1963; Centennial lectr. U. Toronto, 1967; Weinberg lectr. Oak Ridge Nat. Lab., Tenn., 1997; Herzberg lectr. U. Toronto, 2010; chmn. sci. & tech. adv. com. for manned space flight NASA, 1964—70; bd. dirs. Perkin-Elmer Corp., 1966—69, GM, 1973—86; mem. Pres.'s Sci. Adv. Com., 1966—69, vice chmn., 1967—69; mem. Pres.'s Com. Sci. & Tech., 1976. Author: How the Laser Happened. Adventures of a Scientist, 1999, Making Waves, 1996; co-author (with A. L. Schawlow): Microwave Spectroscopy, 1955; author, co-editor Quantum Electronics, 1960, Quantum Electronics and Coherent Light, 1964, mem. editl. bd. Rev. Sci. Instruments, 1950—52, Phys. Rev., 1951—53, Jour. Molecular Spectroscopy, 1957—60, Procs. NAS, 1978—84, Can. Jour. Physics, from 1995, contbr. articles to sci. publs. Bd. dirs. Ctr. Theology & Natural Scis., Mount Wilson Inst., Carnegie Instn. Washington. Decorated officier Légion d'Honneur, France; recipient Stuart Ballantine medal, Franklin Inst., 1962, Thomas Young medal and prize, Inst. Physics/Phys. Soc. Eng., 1963, Nobel prize for physics, 1964, Disting. Pub. Svc. medal, NASA, 1969, Wilhelm Exner award, Austria, 1970, Niels Bohr Internat. Gold medal, 1979, Nat. Medal Sci., 1982, Berkeley citation, U. Calif., 1986, CommonWealth award, 1993, ADION medal, Nice Obs., France, 1995, Mendel award, Villanova U., 1999, Frank Annunzio award, Christopher Columbus Fellowship Found., 1999, Rabindranath Tagore Birth Centenary plaque, Asiatic Soc., 1999, Karl Schwarzschild medal, German Astron. Soc., 2002, Drake award, SETI Inst., Mountain View, Calif., 2003, Templeton prize, 2005, Vannevar Bush medal, 2006; named to Nat. Inventors Hall of Fame, 1976, Engring. & Sci. Hall of Fame, 1983. Fellow: IEEE (life Medal of Honor 1967), Calif. Acad. Scis., Indian Nat. Sci. Acad., Optical Soc. America (Mees medal 1968), Am. Phys. Soc. (pres. 1967, Plyler prize 1977, Frederick Ives medal 1996); mem.: NAE (Founders award 2000), NAS (coun. mem. 1968—72, chmn. space sci. bd. 1970—73, coun. mem. 1978—81, Comstock award 1959, Carty medal 1962), NY Acad. Scis., Max-Planck Inst. Physics & Astrophysics (fgn.), Pontifical Acad. Scis., Russian Acad. Scis. (fgn., Lomonosov medal 2000), Royal Soc. (fgn.), Am. Acad. Arts & Scis., Am. Astron. Soc., Am. Philos. Soc. Achievements include patents for masers and lasers. Home: Oakland, Calif. Died Jan. 27, 2015.

TOWNSEND, TIMOTHY JOSEPH, business executive; b. Lima, Ohio, Mar. 30, 1940; s. Francis Upp and Mary Janice (Gorsuch) T.; m. Jacquelyn Ruth Runyan, Feb. 17, 1968; children: Timothy J. II, Amber V. BSEE, Gen. Motors Inst., 1963; MBA, U. Dayton, 1965. Non-auto planning coordinator Delco Products div. Gen. Motors Corp., Dayton, Ohio, 1966-69, staff sales engr., 1969-72, staff planning coordinator, 1972-77; pres., mng. ptnr. Triance Enterprises, Inc., Dayton, from 1977, Gas and Oil Joint Ventures, Dayton, from 1977. Bd. dirs., fin. cons. Beau Townsend Ford, Vandalia, Ohio, 1977—. Fund raiser United Appeals, Dayton, 1973, 74; coach soccer team Springboro, Ohio, 1976-85. Roman Catholic. Avocations: golf, hunting. Home: Springboro, Ohio. Died May 15, 2007.

TOWNSLEY, MARY ELIZABETH, librarian; b. Gainesville, Tex., Dec. 3, 1930; d. Thomas Albin and Oma Letris (Gardner) Hayes; m. Joseph Berkley Townsley, June 29, 1952; children: David Wesley, Louann Townsley Pundt, Thomas Hayes. AA, Cooke County Coll., 1949; BA, Tex. Woman's U., 1950, MLS, 1972. Librarian Gainesville (Tex.) Ind. Sch. Dist., from 1969. Mem. NEA, Tex. State Tchrs. Assn., Tex. Library Assn., Tex. Future Tchrs. Am. (state advisor 1986-87). Republican. Methodist. Avocation: travel. Died Dec. 31, 2006.

TOYNE, DOROTHY JEAN, retired substitute educator, counselor; b. Le Mars, Iowa, Feb. 25, 1932; d. Ralph William and Flora May (MacKinnon) Marcue; m. George W. Toyne, June 26, 1955; children: Lee R., Carol Jean. BA in Edn., Cornell Coll., Mt. Vernon, Iowa, 1953; postgrad., U. Oslo, Norway, 1954; MS in Counseling, Iowa State U., 1968. Cert. clin. mental health counselor. Counselor Muscatine (Iowa) High Sch., 1953-55; core tchr. Aberdeen (Md.) High Sch., 1955-56; jr. high counselor Humboldt (Iowa) Jr. High Sch., 1956-84; high sch. counselor Humboldt High Sch., 1984-85; substitute tchr. Cedar Rapids (Iowa) Sch. System, 1985-86, ret., 1986. V.p. Women's Fellowship, Humboldt, 1991—. Scholar Cornell Coll., 1950, U. Oslo, Norway, 1954. Mem. AAUW (pres. 1981-82), NEA, P.E.O. (internat. chpt., treas. 1991—), Nat. Bd. Cert. Counselors, Nat. Acad. Cert. Clin. Mental Health Counselors, Am. Assn. Counseling and Devel., State Hist. Soc. Iowa, Iowa Ornithological Union, Elks. Avocations: travel, reading, needlepoint, hiking, cross country skiing. Home: Humboldt, Iowa. Died Mar. 4, 2007.

TRACY, MARK LUTHER, minister; b. Portsmouth, Ohio, May 24, 1943; s. W. Luther and Margaret Virginia (Davis) T.; m. Barbara Allen Thompson, July 27, 1969. BA, Ohio U., 1965; MDiv, Andover Newton Theol. Sch., Newton Centre, Mass., 1969; MBA, George Mason U., 1980. Cert. ch. adminstr. Assoc. minister Nat. Bapt. Meml. Ch., Washington, 1969-75; bus. mgr. Bapt. Home of D.C., Washington, 1975-78, Bapt. Home for Children, Bethesda, Md., 1978-81; exec. officer New York Ave. Presbyn. Ch., Washington, 1982-87; bus. mgr. retirement home Culpepper Garden, Arlington, Va., 1987-90; field rep. Am. Bapt. Extension Corp., Valley Forge, Pa., from 1990. Contbr. articles to profl. newsletter. Mem. Ch. Mgmt. Alumni Assn. (pres. Am. Univ. chpt. 1975), Soc. for Religious Orgn. Mgmt. (bd. dirs. 1976-79), Nat. Assn. Ch. Bus. Adminstrn. (nat. conf. chmn. 1988-90), Interfaith Forum on Religion, Art and Architecture. Home: Kng Of Prussa, Pa. Died July 10, 2007.

TRAGER, LILLIAN, anthropologist, educator; b. Princeton, NJ, Apr. 15, 1947; d. William and Ida Trager; m. Richard Ammann, July 9, 1977. AB, Cornell U., 1969; MA, U. Wash., 1971, PhD, 1976. Asst. prof. U. Wis.-Parkside, Kenosha, 1975—83, assoc. prof., 1983—91; asst. rep., program dir. The Ford Found., NYC, 1985—87; prof. U. Wis.-Parkside, from 1991; dir. Ctr. Internat. Studies, from 2003. Cons. The Ford Found., 1988, The World Bank, Washington, 1989. Author: The City Connection, 1988, Yoruba Hometowns, 2001, Migration and Economy, 2005. Bd. dirs. Southside Revitalization, Racine, Wis., from 1993, pres., 2002—03. Recipient Fulbright scholar, Dept. of State, 2000—01, Fulbright Alumni Initiative award, 2004—06; grantee, NIMH, 1978—79, NSF, 1992—96. Fellow: Royal Anthrop. Inst., Am. Anthrop. Assn.; mem.: Soc. Econ. Anthropology (bd. dirs. 1998—2001, pres. 2003—05). Achievements include research on migration, hometown linkages and local development among the Yoruba of Southwestern Nigeria; informal economy of Africa and U.S.; contemporary African art. Home: Racine, Wis. Died Nov. 10, 2006.

TRAHAN, DAVID PAUL, bank counsel; b. Bay City, Mich., Oct. 13, 1950; s. Paul Emmet and Mary Geraldine (Daniels) T.; m. Cathy Ann Hayes, Oct. 16, 1976; children: Kelly Ann, Paul William, Matthew James. BS in BA, Wayne State U., Detroit, 1972; JD, Detroit Coll. Law, 1975. Bar: Mich. 1976. Assoc. Meyering & Trahan, Troy, Mich., 1976-80; gen. counsel Master Lease, Huntington Woods, Mich., 1980-83; assoc. gen. counsel Std. Fed. Bank, Troy, from 1983. Fellow Mich. Bar Assn., Oakland Bar Assn. Home: Troy, Mich. Died Jan. 30, 2007.

TRAINOR, MARY ELLEN, actress; b. San Francisco; m. Robert Zemeckis (div. 2000); 1 child, Alex. Student, San Diego. Prodn. asst. Filmmakers Steven Spielberg & John Milius; exec. in charge of creative affairs Twentieth Century Fox, news editor; station editor KCBS-TV, San Francisco. Film appearances: The Stone Boy, 1984, Romancing the Stone, 1984, The Goonies, 1985, The Monster Squad, 1987, Lethal Weapon, 1987, Die Hard, 1988, Action Jackson, 1988, Lethal Weapon 2, 1989, Ghostbusters II, 1989, Fire Birds, 1990, Ricochet, 1991, Grand Canyon, 1991, Lethal Weapon 3, 1992, Kuffs, 1992, Death Becomes Her, 1992, Little Giants, 1994, Greedy, 1994, Little Giants, 1994, Congo, 1995, Lethal Weapon 4, 1998, Executive Decision, 1996, Anywhere But Here, 1999, Moonlight Mile, 2002, Freaky Friday, 2003, The Music Inside, 2005, Cake: A Wedding Story, 2007; TV appearances: Cheers, 1983, Crazy Like a Fox, 1985, Remington Steele, 1986-87, Amazing Stories, 1987, Tales of the Crypt, 1989, The Outsiders, 1990, Parker Lewis Can't Lose, 1990-93, Relativity, 1996-97, Roswell, 1999-2002; (TV films) Fear Stalk, 1989, Rock Hudson, 1990, Seduced and Betrayed, 1995, A Face to Die For, 1996, Hope, 1997, Someone to Love Me, 1998. McBride:Requiem, 2008 Died May 20, 2015.

TRANSTRÖMER, TOMAS GÖSTA, poet; b. Stockholm, Apr. 15, 1931; m. Monica Bladh, 1958; 2 children. Degree, U. Stockholm, 1956. Psychologist Psychotekniska Instn., Stockholm, 1957-59, Ungdomsanstalten, Roxtuna, Sweden, 1960-65, Parådetin, Västerås, Sweden, from 1966, Arbmarkninst, Västerås, from 1980. Writings include: (verse) 17 dikter (Seventeen Poems), 1954, Hemligheter på vägen, 1958, Den halvfärdiga himlen (The Half-Finished Heaven), 1962, Klanger och spår (Windows and Stones), 1966, Three Poems, 1966, Kvartett, 1967, Mörkerseende (Night Vision), 1970, Twenty Poems, 1970 (English Translation), Windows and Stones (English Translation), 1972, Stigar (Paths), 1973, Elegy, Some October Notes, 1973, Östersjöar (Baltics), 1974, Citoyens, 1974, Friends, You Drank Some Darkness, 1975, Baltics (English Translation), 1975, Sanningsbarriären, 1978, Sikter 1954-1978, 1979, How the Late Autumn Night Novel Begins, 1980, Det vilda torget, 1983, Collected Poems (English Translation), 1987, Selected Poems 1954-1986, 1987, The Blue House/Det blå huset, 1987, För levande och döda (For the Living and the Dead), 1989, Four Swedish Poets: Tranströmer, Sjögren, Espmark, 1990, Minnena Ser Mig (Memories Look At Me), 1993, For the Living and the Dead, 1995, Sorgegondolen (Sorrow Gondola), 1996, New Collected Poems (English Translation), 1997, Samlade dikter, 2001, Air Mail, 1964-90, Tomas Transtrómer—Robert Bly, 2001, The Half-Finished Heaven (English Translation), 2001, The Great Enigma: New Collected Poems, 2003, (English Translation), 2006, The Sorrow Gondola (English Translation), 2010, New Collected Poems (English Translation), 2011. Recipient Aftonbladets prize, 1958, Bellman prize, 1966, Internat. Poetry Forum Swedish award, 1971, Öevralids prize, 1975, Boklotteriets prize, 1981, Petrarca prize, 1981, Pilot Corp. prize, 1988, Nordic Coun. prize, 1990, Swedish Acad. Nordic prize, 1991, Horst Bienek prize Bayerische Akademic des Schönen Künste, 1992, Lifetime Recognition award, Griffin Trust for Excellence in Poetry, 2007, Nobel Prize in Literature, 2011 and several others. Home: Stockholm, Sweden. Died Mar. 26, 2015.

TRAVAGLINI, BARBARA CARLSON (MRS. ALFONSO FREDERICK TRAVAGLINI), retired steel company executive; b. Easton, Pa., Nov. 4, 1925; d. Gunard Oscar and Margaret Bailey (Berry) Carlson; m. Alfonso Frederick Travaglini, June 15, 1946; children: Gunard Carlson, Frederick Carlson, Mark Carlson. Attended, Bryn Mawr Coll., 1943—45, Moore Coll. Art, Phila., 1946—48; B in English, Immaculata U., 1991; HD (hon.), Saint Francis U., 1976. Pilot's License. Vice chmn., sr. v.p. G.O. Carlson, Inc., Thorndale, Pa., 1956—2004, bd. dirs. Author: The Kelly Green Cow, 1949, Henry Hippo, 1972; columnist, As I See It Coatesville Record, 1976—92, columnist Altoona Catholic Register. Pres. Coatesville Hosp. Aux., 1968—73, 1st v.p., 1972; bd. managers, sec. Coatesville Hosp., 1968—74; sec. Chester County Airport Authority; exec. dir., sec., treas. Gunard Berry Carlson Meml. Found.; trustee Saint Francis U., 1973—85, Lafayette Coll., Easton, Pa., 1978—81; bd. mem. Archdiocese of Phila.; mem. bd. managers Catholic Charities, 1987—93; mem. Archbishop's Adv. Com. of Parish Renewal, Pa.; bd. dirs. Saint Martha Manor and Villa Saint Martha, Downingtown; adv. bd. mem. Bishop Shanahan HS Adv. Com. and Bldg. Com.; pres. of the aux. Brandywine Hosp., 2000—04; mem. Brandywine Health Found., 2002—04. Recipient Papal Honor of Pro Ecclesia et Pontifice, 1982, Papal Honor of Lady of the Order of Saint Gregory the Great, 1998, Rebecca Luken award, Graystone Soc. of Coatesville, 2009. Republican. Roman Catholic. Avocations: flying, gardening, sewing, reading, writing, needlepoint. Home: Downingtown, Pa. Died Feb. 14, 2016.

TRAYLOR, WILLIAM ROBERT, publisher; b. Texarkana, Ark., May 21, 1921; s. Clarence Edington and Seba Ann (Talley) T.; m. Elvirez Sigler, Oct. 9, 1945; children: Kenneth Warren, Gary Robert, Mark Daniel, Timothy Ryan. Student, U. Houston, 1945-46, U. Omaha, 1947-48. Div. mgr. Lily-Tulip Cup Corp., NYC, 1948-61; asst. to pres. Johnson & Johnson, New Brunswick, N.J., 1961-63; mgr. western region Rexall Drug & Chem. subs. Dart Industries, LA, 1963-67; pres. Prudential Pub. Co., Diamonds Springs, Calif., from 1967. Cons. to printing industry, 1976-98; syndicated writer (under pseudonym)s. Bill Friday's Bus. Bull., 1989—. Author: Instant Printing, 1976 (transl. into Japanese), Successful Management, 1979, Quick Printing Encyclopedia, 1982, 8th edit., 1998, How to Sell Your Product Through (Not to) Wholesalers, 1980; pubr. Professional Estimator and Management Software for Printing Industry, 1997, Small Press Printing Encyclopedia, 1994. With USCG, 1942-45. Named Man of Yr. Quick Printing Mag., 1987. Mem. Nat. Assn. Quick Printers (hon. lifetime), C. of C., Kiwanis, Toastmasters. Democrat. Avocations: skiing, boating. Home: Carson City, Nev. Died May 26, 2007.

TRIBBLE, RICHARD WALTER, brokerage executive; b. San Diego, Oct. 19, 1948; s. Walter Perrin and Catherine Janet (Miller) T.; m. Joan Catherine Sliter, June 26, 1980. BS, U. Ala., Tuscaloosa, 1968. Grad. Gulf Coast Sch. Drilling Practices, U. Southwestern La., 1976. Registered rep. ITT-Hamilton, Woodridge, Va., 1969-71; stockbroker Shearson, Loeb & Rhoades and Co., Washington, 1971-76; ind. oil and gas investment sales Falls Church, Va., 1976-77; pres. Monroe & Keusink, Inc., Falls Church, Va., 1977-87; instnl. investment officer FCA Asset Mgmt., Columbus, Ohio, 1983-85; fin. cons. Merrill Lynch Pierce Fenner & Smith, Inc., Phoenix, from 1987, cert. fin. mgr., from 1989, sr. fin. cons., from 1992, asst. v.p., 1993—2002, v.p., from 2002, wealth mgmt. advisor, from 2003. Mem. adv. bd. Samaritan Found., 1999—. With USMC, 1969-70. Mem. Ariz. Fiduciary Assn., Ctrl. Ariz. Estate Planning Coun., Ariz. Chpt. Investment Mgmt. Cons. Assn. (dir.). Republican. Methodist. Home: Scottsdale, Ariz. Died Dec. 9, 2006.

TRITES, BEATRICE VIRGINIA, retired secondary school educator; b. Underwood, Minn., Sept. 3, 1917; d. Sylvanus Baughman and Gladys Mary (Shepley) T. BS, U. Minn., 1944; MEd, Mont. State U., 1963; postgrad., Utah State U., 1965. Cert. tchr. Mont., Minn. County club agt. Minn. Extension, Mahnomen, 1944-45, Dodge Center, 1946-47, Redwood Falls, 1947-48; tchr. home econs. Eyota (Minn.) High Sch., 1948-49, Clarissa (Minn.) High Sch., 1949-51, Glasgow (Mont.) High Sch., 1951-85. Mem. Minn. State County Club Agt. Assn. (pres. 1946-47), Mont. Home Econs. Vocat. Assn. (pres. 1962-63), AAUW (treas. 1976, sec. 1989), N.E. Retired Tchrs. Assn. (pres 1988—), N.E. Home Econs. Group (v.p. 1989—), Mont. Edn. Assn., Mont. Edn. Assn., NEA. Avocations: tailoring, gardening, study of the mind, reading. Home: Glasgow, Mont. Died Apr. 18, 2007.

TRITTIPO, JANE KNECHT, publishing executive; b. Rapid City, SD, Oct. 24, 1933; d. Ronald Clem and Ruth Irene (Slocumb) Knecht; m. Thomas Twineham Trittipo, Oct. 6, 1956; children: Karen Ann Trittipo Freedman, Lynn Diane Trittipo Segundo. BS in Med. Tech., U. Colo., 1956. Med. technologist Children's Hosp., Honolulu, 1956-59; pvt. practice med. technologist No. Calif., 1959-88; author, pub., speaker Creative Cookery, Alamo, Calif., from 1988. Bd. dirs. Biovation Corp. Author, pub.: The Everyday Gourmet-Fast and Fabulous Microwave Recipes, 1988, The Marvelous Microwave, 1996. Treasurer Round Hill Property Owners Assn., Alamo, 1983-86; vestry Epsicopal Ch., 1966-90; pres. Lyra chpt. Easter Seals Soc., 1985-86. Mem. AAUW (treas. 1988-89, prse. 1994-95), P.E.O., Am. Soc. Clin. Pathologists, San Francisco Profl. Food Soc., Chi Omega. Republican. Avocations: travel, tennis, music. Home: Goodyear, Ariz. Died Apr. 24, 2007.

TROUTT, ARTHUR ROBERT, artist, arborist; b. Mt. Vernon, Ill., Aug. 26, 1946; s. Arthur Glen and Marry Jewel (Hilt) T.; m. Karen Joice Johnston, May 21, 1976 (div. 1982); m. Leona Sue Troutt Thacker, Feb. 14, 1984; children: Sarah Ann, Travis Ryan. BS in Forestry, So. Ill. U., 1974. Arborist Timber Wolfe Tree Co., Mt. Vernon, 1975-83; artist Gray Wolf Graphics, Mt. Vernon, from 1983. Author various works of art, including murals and illustrations in nat. and internat. publs. Served with Green Berets U.S. Army, 1966-69, Vietnam. Home: Mount Vernon, Ill. Died Aug. 3, 2007.

TSCHIRA, KLAUS ERWIN, retired information technology executive; b. Freiburg, Germany, Dec. 7, 1940; married; 2 children. Diplom, U. Karlsruhe, 1966; PhD (hon.), Klagenfurt U., Austria, 1995. Systems engr. IBM, Mannheim, Germany, 1966—72; co-founder Systemanalyse + Programmentwicklung (later SAP AG-Systems, Applications and Products in Data Processing), 1972, mem. exec. bd., 1972—98, mem. supervisory bd., 1998—2007. Mem. IBM's European Software Vendors' Adv. Coun., 1990—92; mem. GI Praesidium German Informatics Soc., 1991—96; chmn. Friends of the Forschungszentrum für Informatik, Karlsruhe, Germany, from 1992. Founder Klaus Tschira Found., 1995, European Media Lab., 1997. Recipient Deutsche Stifterpreis, Bundesverband Deutscher Stiftungen (Nat. Assn. of German Foundations), 1999; named one of World's Richest People, Forbes mag., from 1999. Mem.: bd. of governors of Ctr. on Philanthropy at IUPUI, Indianapolis, Senate of the Max-Planck Soc. for the advancement of Sci., Honorary Senates of Heidelberg U. Avocation: reading. Died Mar. 31, 2015.

TSIEN, TSUEN-HSUIN, Chinese literature educator emeritus, library science educator emeritus, researcher; b. Dec. 1, 1909; m. Wen-ching Hsu (dec. 2008); children: Ginger (dec.), Gloria, Mary. BA in History, Nanking U., China, 1932; MA, U. Chgo., 1952, PhD, 1957. Asst. libr. Nat. Chiaotung U., Shanghai, 1932-37; mgr. China Libr. Svc., 1936; custodian rare books and other materials, head Nanking and Shanghai offices Nat. Libr. Pelping, 1937-47; curator Far Ea. Libr. U. Chgo., 1947-78, prof. emeritus, East Asian languages and civilizations, curator emeritus, 1979—2015; rsch. fellow Joseph Needham Rsch. Inst., Cambridge, Eng., from 1982; pres. China Pubs. Svc., from 1983. Vis. prof. Asian studies U. Hawaii, 1957; lectr. in field. Author: Written on Bamboo and Silk, 1962, rev. 2004, A History of Writing and Writing Materials in Ancient China, 1975, Paper and Printing, 1985, Chinese-American Cultural Relations, 1998, Collected Writings on Chinese Culture, 2011 and others; past editor, mgr. Quarterly Bull. Chinese Bibliography; contbr. articles to profl. jours. With Chinese Army, 1927. Recipient Disting. Svc. award for shipping some 30,000 vols. Chinese rare books in Shanghai to U.S. Libr. Congress before Japanese bombed Pearl Habour Chinese govt., 1943, 99, Com. E. Asian Librs., 1978, Chinese Am. Librs. Assn., 1985, Profl. Achievement citation U. Chgo. Alumni Assn., 1996, Nat. Libr. Disting. Svc. award 1999, others; named to Sr. Citizen's Hall of Fame City of Chgo.; grantee in field; Festsdrift in honor of his 80th birthday Taipei, 1990, Beijing, 1991. Died Apr. 9, 2015.

TUCKER, FLORENCE RAY, library administrator; b. Henderson, Ky., July 11, 1921; d. Sanford Ray and Nannie Cosby (Moss) T. AB, U. Mich., 1944, ABLS, 1945. Reference librarian Detroit Pub. Library, 1945-59, asst. dept. chief, 1959-66, acting dept. chief, 1966, coordinator major library activities, 1966-77, assoc. dir. support services, from 1978. Adj. instr. Wayne State U., Detroit, 1965-66. Mem. ALA, Mich. Library Assn., Spl. Library Assn., Phi Beta Kappa, Phi Kappa Phi. Home: Royal Oak, Mich. Died Mar. 2, 2007.

TUCKER, GARY JAY, psychiatrist, educator; b. Cleve., Mar. 6, 1934; s. Isadore Martin and Blanche Hanna (Luftig) T.; m. Sharon Ruth Pobby, June 10, 1956; children: Adam, Clare. AB, Oberlin Coll., 1956; MD, Case Western Res. U., 1960; postdoctoral fellow, Yale U., 1961-64; MA (hon.), Dartmouth Coll., 1977. Diplomate Am. Bd. Psychiatry and Neurology. Asst. prof. psychiatry Sch. Medicine Yale U., New Haven, 1967-70, assoc. prof. psychiatry, 1970-71; with Dartmouth Med. Sch., Hanover, N.H., 1971-85, prof. psychiatry, 1974-85, chmn. dept., 1978-85; chmn. psychiatry and behavioral scis. Sch. Med. U. Wash., Seattle, 1985-98; prof. psychiatry U. Wash., Seattle, 1985—99, prof. emeritus, from 1999. Bd. dirs. Am. Bd. Psychiatry and Neurology. Co-author: Rational Hospital Psychiatry, 1974, Behavioral Neurology, 1985; editor: Seminars in Clinical Neuropsychiatry, Jourl. Watch Psychiatry; contbr. articles to profl. jours. Lt. Commdr. USN, 1964-67. Fellow Am. Psychiat. Assn.; mem. W. Coast Coll. Biol. Psychiatry, Sigma Xi, Alpha Omega Alpha. Democrat. Jewish. Avocations: photography, motorcycling. Died Dec. 6, 2006.

TUCKER, PHYLLIS ANN See **MCEVOY, NAN**

TUGGLE, MELVIN, philosophy educator, publishing executive; b. Memphis, Sept. 17, 1948; s. George Jr. and Menola (Hoye) T. BA, LeMoyne-Owen Coll., 1977; MA, Memphis State U., 1988; PhD, So. Ill. U., 1995. Prof. philosophy S.W. Tenn. C.C., Memphis; owner, pub. Tuggle Books. Author: An Analysis of Dr. Martin Luther King's Letter From Birmingham Jail: "Why We Can't Wait", 1996, The Evolution of John Dewey's Conception of Philosophy and His Notion of Truth, 1997. Co-founder, pres. Myers Garden Civic Club, Memphis, 1965-70; guest spkr. 1st Nat. Conf. on Civil/Human Rights of African-Ams., Memphis, 1995; mem., trustee new Philadelphia MB Ch., 1997. Mem. Am. Philos. Soc., Soc. for the Advancement Am. Philosophy, Soc. of Christian Philosophers. Home: Memphis, Tenn. Deceased.

TULLOCK, GORDON, retired economics professor; b. Rockford, Ill., Feb. 13, 1922; s. George and Helen T. JD, U. Chgo., 1947, PhD (hon.), 1994. Fgn. svc. officer, China, 1947-56; postdoctoral fellow U. Va., 1958-59; asst. prof. U. S.C., 1959-60, assoc. prof., 1960-62, U. Va., Charlottesville, 1962-67; prof. economics & polit. sci. Rice U., Houston, 1967-68; prof. economics & public choice Va. Poly. Inst. & State U., Blacksburg, 1968-72, univ. disting. prof. economics & public choice, 1972-83, George Mason U., Fairfax, Va., 1983-87, prof. law & economics Arlington, Va., 1999—2008; prof. U. Ariz., Tucson, 1987-99. Editl. dir. Center for Study of Public Choice, 1968-90; vis. disting. scholar Baruch U., N.Y.C., spring 1987; dir. DHC, Eldora, Iowa; mem. Jour. Social and Biol. Structure; bd. editors Internat. Jour. Law & Economics, Atlantic Econ. Jour., Bioecons. Soc. Author: (with J.M. Buchanan) The Calculus of Consent, 1962, The Politics of Bureaucracy, 1965, The Organization of Inquiry, 1966, Toward a Mathematics of Politics, 1967, Private Wants, Public Means, 1970, The Logic of the Law, 1971, The Social Dilemma, 1974, (with Richard B. McKenzie) The New World of Economics, 1975, (with Richard B. McKenzie) Modern Political Economy, 1978, Trials on Trial, 1980, Toward a Theory of the Rent-Seeking Society, 1980, Economics of Income Redistribution, 1983, The Economics of Wealth and Poverty, 1986, Autocracy, 1987, The Economics of Special Privilege and Rent Seeking, 1989, Economic Hierarchies, Organization and the Structure of Production, 1992, The New Federalist, 1994, On the Trial of Homo Economicus, 1994, On Voting: A Public Choice Approach, 1998, Government Failure: A Primer in Public Choice, 2002, Public Goods, Redistribution, and Rent Seeking, 2005, (with others) The Political Economy of Rent Seeking, 1989. Fellow American Econ. Assn.; mem. American Acad. Arts & Sciences, Southern Econ. Assn. (past pres.), Western Econ. Assn. (pres.), American Polit. Sci. Assn., Pub. Choice Soc., Assn. for Asian Studies, Inst. Econ. Affairs (coun. mem.), Mont Pelerin Soc., Bioecons Soc. (hon. chmn.). Home: Tucson, Ariz. Died Nov. 3, 2014.

TURCOTTE, JEAN-CLAUDE CARDINAL, cardinal, archbishop emeritus; b. Montreal, Canada, June 26, 1936; s. Paul-Émile and Rita (Gravel) Turcotte. Diploma in Theology, Major Seminary of Montreal; Diploma in Social Ministry, Catholic Faculties, Lille, France, 1964—65; DD (hon.), McGill U. Ordained priest of Montreal, 1959, asst. diocesan chaplain for Christian working youth, 1961—64, positions in Office of Clergy, 1967—74, dir. parish pastoral care, 1974—81, vicar gen., gen. co-ordinator of the pastoral programmes, 1981—82, auxiliary bishop, 1982—90, archbishop, 1990—2012, archbishop emeritus, 2012—15; diocesan chaplain JICF and the Movement of Christian Workers, 1965—67; parochial vicar Saint Mathias parish, 1959—61; chaplain Movement of Christian Workers, 1965—67; appointed Titular Bishop of Suas, 1982, ordained, 1982; elevated to cardinal, 1994; cardinal-priest of Nostra Signora del Santissimo Sacramento e Santi Martiri Canadesi (Our Lady of the Blessed Sacrament and the Holy Canadian Martyrs), 1994—2015. Delegate of the Bishops of Quebec to the provincial Govt. for the Holy Father's visit, 1984; pres. Canadian Conf. of Cath. Bishops, 1997—2000; pres. of commission Special Assembly of the Synod of Bishops, 1997; mem. Congregation for the Causes of Saints, Pontifical Council for Social Communications, Special Council for America of the General Secretariat of the Synod of Bishops. Column writer Le Journal de Montreal, 1995—2008. Roman Catholic. Died Apr. 8, 2015.

TURNER, ALICE KENNEDY, editor; b. Mukden, Manchuria, May 29, 1939; d. William Taylor and Florence Bell (Green) T. BA, Bryn Mawr Coll., 1960; advanced degree, NYU. Sr. editor Holiday mag., NYC, 1969-70; assoc. editor Publishers Weekly, NYC, 1972-74; sr. editor Ballantine Books, NYC, 1974-76, New York mag., NYC, 1976-80; fiction editor Playboy mag., Chgo., NYC, 1980—2001, contbg. editor, 2001—15. Author: Yoga for Beginners, 1973, The History of Hell, 1993; co-author: The New York Woman's Guide, 1975; editor: Playboy Stories: The Best of Forty Years of Short Fiction, 1994, The Playboy Book of Science Fiction, 1998, Playboy's College Fiction, 2007; co-editor: Snake's-hands: The Fiction of John Crowley, 2002. Home: New York, NY. Died Jan. 17, 2015.

TURNER, JAMES DANIEL, computer company executive; b. Chevely, Md., Dec. 16, 1950; s. Allen Ephrem and Mary Lynn (Thompson) T.; m. Hari Kertonadi, Nov. 20, 1978; children: Melinda Lee, Imelda Rose. BS in Physics, George Mason U., Fairfax, Va., 1974; ME in Engring. Physics, U. Va., 1976; PhD in Engring. Sci. and Mechanics, Va. Poly. Inst. and State U., Blacksburg, 1980. Dynamics sect. chief Charles Stark Draper Lab., Cambridge, Mass., 1979-84; dynamics and control group leader Photon Rsch. Assocs., Cambridge, 1984-92, divsn. mgr., 1992; v.p. Moldyn (PRA Subs.), Cambridge, 1991-92; pres. Amdyen Systems, Cambridge, from 1992; assoc. dir. NSF Industry & Univ. Coop. Rsch. Ctr. Virtual Proving Ground, Nat. Advanced Driving Simulation, U. Iowa, Iowa City, 1996-2001; adj. prof. mech. engring. U. Iowa, Iowa City, from 2001. Exec. bd. Electricore, Indpls., from 1996; adj. assoc. prof. U. Iowa, 2001; cons. in field. Author: Optimal Spacecraft Rotational Maneuvers, 1986; contbr. chpts. to books. Recipient Rsch. award Sigma Xi, 1981, grants from govt. and industry. Mem. AIAA, Assn. Astronautical Sci., Am. Chem. Soc. Republican. Methodist. Achievements include patents for molecular dynamics simulation method and apparatus, demonstration of applications of advanced multibody dynamics modelling techniques for atomic systems for drug design. Home: Lagrange, Ga. Died Aug. 7, 2007.

TURNIPSEED, BARNWELL RHETT, III, (RHETT TURNER), journalist, broadcaster, public relations consultant; b. Apr. 6, 1929; s. Barnwell Rhett and L. (Rogers) T.; m. Jane Whitley, June 12, 1982. BA in Journalism, U. Ga., 1950, MA in Journalism, 1960. With Sta. WGGA, Gainesville, Ga., 1943-46; prodn. mgr. Sta WGGA, Gainesville, Ga., 1958-60; with Sta. WRFC, Athens, Ga., 1947-50; program dir. Sta. WKYW, Louisville, 1953, Sta. WGBA, Columbus, Ga., 1953-55; broadcasting cons., 1955—60; sr. corr., sci. editor Voice of Am. Worldwide English, 1960-72; coord. radio-TV pub. affairs HEW, 1972-73; mem. staff Ga. Congressman Phil Landrum, 1974-75; dir. solar energy tech. info. Dept. Energy, Washington, 1975-77, spl. asst., 1977-81; pvt. practice, 1981-88 and from 94; instr. West Ga. Coll., Carrollton, 1988-89, 90-94; asst. prof. Brenau Coll., Gainesville, Ga., 1989-90; mgr. WBCX-FM, Gainsville, Ga., 1989—90, WWGC-FM, Carrollton, Ga., 1990-94. Dir. Ga. Broadcasters Annual Awards, 1998—2005. Author: History of Georgia Broadcasting, 1972; prin. corr. Voice of Am. (Peabody award winning space exploration broadcasts, 1969). Symphony Guild rep. Louisville, Columbus, Ga. Jaycees; active symphony and arts devel. Sgt. Korean Army, 1950-52. Recipient Two Meritorious Svc. awards, USIA; named to Ga. Broadcasters Hall of Fame, 2003. Mem. Nat. Assn. Sci. Writers (life), Aircraft Owners and Pilots Assn., Sigma Delta Chi, Kappa Sigma. Democrat. Methodist. Died Jan. 18, 2015.

TURRIZIANI, VINCENT MICHAEL, transportation executive; b. Greensburg, Pa., Jan. 20, 1956; s. Archangel Anthony and Antoinette Rita (D'Itri) T.; m. Barbara Joann Kriek, May 5, 1984; 1 child, Jessica Catherine. BS, St. Vincent Coll., 1978. Asst. to pres. Romco Industries Corp., Greensburg, 1977-79; founder, pres., chief exec. officer Regency Limousine Svc., Inc., Greensburg, from 1980. Chmn. police dept. So. Greensburg Borough, 1982-85, coun. mem., 1982-85; mem. parish coun. mem. St. Bruno Cath. Ch., So. Greensburg, 1978-81, pres. parish coun., 1981-82, eucharistic minister, 1983—; mem. Better Bus. Bur., Dem. Club Westmoreland County. Mem. Nat. Fedn. Ind. Bus., Cen. Westmoreland C. of C. Democrat. Roman Catholic. Avocations: walking, gardening, reading, theater. Home: Greensburg, Pa. Died June 19, 2007.

TYLER, BRENDA KAYE, nurse case manager; b. Kalamazoo, Mich., Oct. 24, 1965; d. Horace Henry Hill and Kaye Arlene Kamps; m. Barry Edward Tyler, Nov. 3, 1990; children: Brandon, Shiana. AS, Mich. Christian Coll., 1986; BSN, Harding U., 1988. RN, Mich. Staff nurse Children's Hosp. Mich., Detroit, 1988-90; home health nurse St. John's Home Health, St. Clair Shores, Mich., 1989-90; clin. nurse newborn nursery Ireland Army Hosp., Ft. Knox, Ky., 1991-93, nurse case mgr. pediats./high risk OB, 1993-95; occupl. health nurse Irwin Army Hosp., Ft. Riley, Kans., 1995-99, nurse cons., case mgr., from 1999. Nurse cons. managed care divsn./IACH, Ft. Riley, 1999. Republican. Baptist. Avocations: cooking, reading. Home: Vine Grove, Ky. Died July 25, 2007.

TYNES, THEODORE ARCHIBALD, former assistant principal; b. Portsmouth, Va., Sept. 24, 1932; s. Theodore Archibald and Mildred Antonette (Lee) T.; m. Bettye Clayton, June, 1955 (div. June 1970); children: Karen A. Culbert, David Lee, Tammy Alecia Simpers; m. Cassandra Washington, Nov. 17, 1989; 1 child, Jordan Alexandria. BS in Edn., W.Va. State Coll., 1954; postgrad., Calif. State U., LA, 1959, Mt. San Antonio Coll, 1962, Chaffey Coll., 1962, Azusa Pacific Coll., 1967; MA in Ednl. Adminstrn., U. Calif., Berkeley, 1969; PhD in Adminstrn. and Mgmt., Columbia Pacific U., 1989. Tchr., athletic dir., coach Walker Grant HS, Fredericksburg, Va., 1958-59; dir. programs and aquatics LA Times Boys Club, LA, 1959-62; tchr., dir. recreation, acting edn. supr. youth tng. sch. Calif. Youth Authority, Chino, 1962-68; tchr., dir. drug abuse program Benjamin Franklin Jr. HS, San Francisco, 1968-70; asst. prin. Pomona HS, Calif., 1970-72; prin. Garey HS, Pomona, 1972-75; adminstrv. asst. to supt. Bd. Edn., East Orange, NJ; asst. to commr. US Dept. Edn., Washington; Rockefeller fellow, supt. adminstrv. intern Rockefeller Found., NYC, 1975-76; supervising state coord. sch. programs Office Essex County Supt. NJ State Dept. Edn., East Orange, 1976-77; rsch. asst., dir. tech. assistance career info. system U. Oreg., Eugene, 1977-79; dir. ednl. placement U. Calif., Irvine, 1979; prin. edn. svcs. Woodrow Wilson Rehab. Ctr., Fisherville, Va., 1980-87; med. courier Urology Inc., Richmond, Va., 1988-90; vice prin. Ithaca HS, NY, 1991-94; asst. prin. Wyandanch Meml. HS, NY, 1996-97. Cons. Fielder and Assocs., Berkeley, 1969-80, Jefferson High Sch., Portland, Oreg., 1970, U. Calif., Berkeley, 1972, U. Calif., Riverside, 1972, Calif. Luth. Coll., 1972, Compton Unified Sch. Dist., 1973, Goleta Unified Schs., 1973, Rialto Sch. Dist., 1973, Grant Union Sch. Dist., Sacramento, Calif., 1973-75, San Mateo Sch. Dist., Tri Dist. Drug Abuse project, 1973, North Ward Cultural Ctr., Newark, NJ, 1976, Nat. Career Conf., Denver, 1978, Opportunities Indulstrialization Ctrs. Am., Phila., Bklyn., Detroit, Poughkeepsie, NY, 1980, Tynes & Assocs., 1988; lectr. seminar San Francisco City Coll., 1968-69. Author various curricula, monitoring procedures, grants. 1965—. City commr. Human Rels., Pomona, Calif., 1972-74; pres. San Antonio League, Calif., 1972-75; exec. bd. dirs. Augusta-Waynesboro Boys and Girls Clubs of Am., 1998-99, corp. v.p. resource & devel., 1998-99. With USAF, 1954-57. Named Coach of Yr. LA Times Boys Club, 1959; fellow Rockefeller Found., 1975; recipient Administrv. award for Excellence Woodrow Wilson Rehab., 1987 Mem. NAACP, Am. Assn. Sch. Adminstrs., Nat. Assn. Secondary Sch. Prins., Nat Alliance Black Sch. Adminstrs., Assn. Supervision and Career Devel., Assn. Ednl. Data Systems., Assn. Calif. Sch. Adminstrs., Va. Govtl. Employees Assn., Va. Rehab. Assn., South Bay Pers. Guidance Assn., Pomona Adminstrs. Assn., Ithaca Prins. Assn., Wyandancg Strategic Planning Assn., Wyandanch Adminstrn. Assn., Fisherville Ruritan, Phi Delta Kappa, Omega Psi Phi (Basilius Pi Rho chpt. 1965). Democrat. Episcopalian. Avocations: video and still photogrpahy, music, art, sports. Home: Waynesboro, Va. Died June 13, 2007.

UBER, DAVID ALBERT, music educator, composer; b. Princeton, Ill., Aug. 5, 1921; s. Thomas Barclay and Rebecca Hartman (Breneman) U.; m. Nancy Sinclair, Jan. 4, 1945; children: David Merrill, Christine Uber Grosse. BA, Carthage Coll., 1944; MA, Columbia U., 1946, EdD, 1965. Solo trombonist N.Y.C. Ballet Co. Orch., 1946-75; dir. ensemble music Nat. Music Camp, Interlochen, Mich., 1960-65; brass instr. Westminster Choir Coll., Princeton, N.J., 1970-76; condr. Princeton U. Band, 1971-78; prof. music Trenton (N.J.) State Coll., from 1959; prof. emeritus Coll. N.J. Cons. Thomas Edison Coll., Trenton, 1968—. Author: Method for Trombone, 1965; composer: 200 mus. compostions (ASCAP award 1959—). Served with USN, 1942-45. Recipient Merit award Trenton State Coll., 1984-86; Released Time grantee Trenton State Coll., 1980-87. Mem. Internat. Trombone Assn., Tubists United Brotherhood Assn., Nat. Assn. Coll. Wind and Percussion Instrs. Republican. Lutheran. Avocation: fishing. Home: Wallingford, Vt. Died June 29, 2007.

UBEROI, MAHINDER SINGH, aerospace engineer, researcher; b. Delhi, India, Mar. 13, 1924; arrived in U.S., 1945, naturalized, 1960; s. Kirpal Singh and Sulaksha (Kochar) Uberoi. BS, Punjab U., Lahore, India, 1944; MS, Calif. Inst. Tech., 1946; DEng, Johns Hopkins U., 1952. Registered profl. engr. Mem. faculty U. Mich., Ann Arbor, 1953-63, prof. aerospace engring., 1959-63, vis. prof., 1963—64; prof. U. Colo., Boulder, 1963—2000, chmn. dept. aerospace engring., 1963-75; fellow F. Joint Inst. Lab. Astrophysics, Boulder, 1963-74; rschr., from 2004. Exch. scientist Soviet Acad. Scis., 1966, U.S. Nat. Acad. Scis.; invited prof. U. Que., Canada, 1972—74; vis. scientist Max Planck Inst. Astrophysics, Munich, 1974; hon. rsch. fellow Harvard U., 1975—76. Contbr. articles to profl. jours.; editor: Cosmic Gas Dynamics, 1974. Coun. mem. Ednl. TV Channel 6, Inc., Denver, 1963—66. Guggenheim fellow, Royal Inst. Tech., Sweden, 1958. Mem.: Am. Phys. Soc., Tau Beta Pi. Home: Boulder, Colo. Died Nov. 25, 2006.

UDEN, DAVID ELLIOTT, cardiologist, educator; b. Montreal, Sept. 7, 1936; s. Reginald and Elsie Ada (Elliott) U.; children: Thomas Elliott, Linda Ann, Christopher Elliott. BSc, McGill U., 1958; MD, McGill U., Quebec, Can., 1962. Diplomate Am. Bd. Internal Medicine; cert. cardiovascular disease, cert. interventional cardiology. Attending cardiologist Toronto We. Hosp., 1972—93, Wellesley Hosp., Toronto, 1990—93; asst. prof. medicine U. Toronto, 1975—93; chief cardiology Oconee Meml. Hosp., Seneca, SC, 1993—97, chief medicine, 1994—96, 2000—02; elected mem. S.C. Med. Discipline Commn., 1996—98, 2000—04; apptd. Discipline Commn., 2000—04. Contbr. articles to profl. jours. With RCAF, 1963-66. Fellow Am. Coll. Cardiology, Am. Heart Assn. Coun. on Clin. Cardiology, Soc. for Cardiac Angiography and Intervention. Avocations: travel, photography. Home: Seneca, SC. Died Jan. 17, 2007.

UGAI, TOSHIYA, banker; b. Kobe, Hyogo Prefecture, Japan, Dec. 25, 1926; s. Keiji and Koshizu (Itoh) U.; m. Mariko Murata, Nov. 26, 1953; children: Yukari Suzuki, Hiroshi Ugai, Junji Murata. B in Econs., Kobe U. Econs., Japan, 1950. Mem. staff Bank Tokyo Ltd., Osaka, NYC, Nagoya, Tokyo, 1950—69, dep. gen. mgr. Singapore office, 1969—74, acting gen. mgr. systems and methods div. Tokyo, 1974—75, gen. mgr. Toa Rd. office Kobe, 1975—78; gen. mgr. fgn. div. The Chiba Kogyo Bank Ltd., Tokyo, 1978—81, dir., gen. mgr. fgn. div., 1981—85, sr. counselor fgn. div., 1985—87, sr. counselor internat. div.,

1987—89; sec. gen. The Hongkong Japanese C. of C., from 1989. With Japanese Navy, 1945. Mem.: Chotaro Country Club (Chiba Prefecture, Japan). Buddhist. Home: Taikoo Shing, Hong Kong. Died Aug. 20, 2007.

ULLMER, JOHN (R. ULLMER), computer company executive, retired educator; b. Chgo., Oct. 16, 1932; s. Ray Joseph and Eleanore (Domagalski) U. BA, St Mary's U., San Antonio, 1955; MA, St. Louis U., 1966, PhD, 1969. Asst. prof. St. Mary's U., San Antonio, 1968-69; prof. San Antonio Coll., 1969-90; ret., 1990. Ptnr. Data Backup Svc., San Antonio, 1989—, DOEL Software Svc., San Antonio, 1990—. Author: (manual) Learning VI in Unix, 1987; designer, programmer: (software) Freshman Eng. Course, 1987, DOEL Writing Skills, 1989, DOEL Reading Skills, 1990. Recipient Chancellor's grant, Alamo Community Coll. Dist., San Antonio, 1989-90, Programming grant, San Antonio Coll., 1989-90. Mem. Assn. of Shareware Profls. Home: San Antonio, Tex. Died Apr. 18, 2007.

UMSCHEID, CHRISTINE, medical surgical and oncological nurse; b. Weiden, West Germany, Jan. 28, 1946; d. Barbara Betty; children; Joyelle, Heidi. AD, Meramec Community Coll., St. Louis, 1969, North Cen. Mich. Coll., Petoskey, 1984. Cert. oncology nurse, renal nurse. Primary nurse No. 3 Mich. Hosp., Inc., Petoskey; primary nurse No. 2 Mich. Hosp., Inc., Petroskey. Contbr. poetry to mags. Home: Petoskey, Mich. Died Mar. 14, 2007.

UNDERWOOD, LARRY DWAINE, education educator, counselor, librarian; b. Delafield, Ill., June 30, 1938; s. Delmah Dwaine and Martha Eleanor (Standerfer) U.; m. Beverly Sue Albert, Nov. 23, 1962; children: Brett Lars, Melissa Anne, Rebeccah Sue. BA, Ea. Ill. U., 1967; MS, So. Ill. U., 1981. Lic. tchr., Ill. Tchr., coach Dahlgren (Ill.) High Sch., 1963-64; tchr., counselor Brussels (Ill.) High Sch., 1964-93; tchr. Lewis and Clark C.C., Godfrey, Ill., from 1987. Textbook cons. Prentice-Hall; social sci. cons. Ill. Rivers Project, So. Ill. U., Edwardsville, 1990—. Author: Butternut Guerillas, 1981, The Custer Fight, 1989, Love and Glory, 1991, Guns, Gold and Glory, 1992, Geronimo: and the Chiricahua Apaches, 1993. With U.S. Army, 1957-60. Mem. Western Writers Am., Nat. Outlaw and Lawmen Assn., Ill. State Hist. Soc., Gallatin County Hist. Soc., Calhoun County Farm Bur., Ea. Ill. U. Alumni Assn. (bd. dirs. 1984-87). Avocation: photography. Home: Meppen, Ill. Died July 30, 2007.

URBAN, DONALD WAYNE, lawyer; b. Belleville, Ill., Oct. 9, 1953; s. Andrew Anthony and Eileen Marie (Tibbitt) U.; m. Mary Beth Evans, June 9, 1979 (div. Oct. 1994); m. Georgianna Dowling, Feb. 2, 1995; 1 child, Andrew Jared. BA, So. Ill. U., 1976; JD, Washington U., 1979. Assoc. Sprague & Sprague, Belleville, 1979-96; ptnr. Sprague & Urban, Belleville, from 1996. Author, lectr. Ill. Inst. for CLE, Springfield. Author: Blasting & Subsidence Illinois Institute for Continuing Legal Education Handbook, 1983, vol. 2, 1986, vol. 3, 1989. Pres. Looking Glass Playhouse, Lebanon, Ill., 1988-90, 95-97, 99-01, 04-05; spokesman St. Clair County Bicentennial, Belleville, 1989. Mem. Gamma Theta Upsilon. Democrat. Avocation: community theatre. Died Oct. 2014.

USHER, HARLAN KING, consulting company executive; b. Superior, Nebr., Apr. 12, 1909; s. Grant and Addra Belle (King) U.; m. Lida Marie Hall, June 17, 1928 (dec. 1961); children: Janet Marie Usher Elliott, Ronald Lee Usher; m. Grace Augusta Brinkman Staton, May 15, 1965. BS in Chemistry, U. Wash., 1930, cert. tchr., 1930. Tchr. scis. Chelan (Wash.) High Sch., 1930-34; chemistry mgr. North Cen. Labs., Inc., Wenatchee, Wash., 1935-39; inspector Boeing Airplane Co., Seattle, 1940-45; tech. sales rep. L.H. Butcher Co., Seattle, 1945-46; sales mgr. Beaver & Bohm Mfg. Co., Mt. Vernon, Wash., 1946-48; sales rep. Balfour, Guthrie & Co., Seattle, 1948-52; supr. engring. and mfg. rsch. The Boeing Co., Seattle, 1953-70; owner, mgr. Acme Pers. Agy., Santa Rosa, Calif., 1970-79; pres., dir. Ell Ell Diversified, Inc., Santa Rosa, 1984-92; co-owner LLD, Santa Rosa, from 1993. Author: How To Get A Job-With No Experience or Not Enough, 1981, Grown Ups Mother Goose, 1982. Counselor Svc. Corps. of Retired Execs., Santa Rosa, 1981-83. Recipient Spl. SCORE award U.S. SBA, 1982. Home: Santa Rosa, Calif. Died Aug. 23, 2007.

USSERY, CALVIN CLIFFORD, minister; b. Denison, Tex., July 17, 1920; s. Garland Hayes and Nellie Lou (Westbrook) U.; m. Juanita Hazel Seabourn, Jan. 21, 1938; children: Joyc Brady, Ronald Wayne. BA, Ouachita Bapt. U., 1948; postgrad., Southwestern Bapt. Theol. Sem. Ordained to ministry Bapt. Ch., 1942. Pastor various chs., Ark., 1947-54, Okla., 1954-89; pastor chs. Sherman, Garland, McKinney, Tex., from 1991. Moderator Hope Assn., Texarkana, 1951—; clk. Frisco Assn., Idabel, Okla., 1956; speaker Bapt. Gen. Conv., Okla., 1956; speaker evangelism conf., Okla., 1966; organizer of four churches and missions, ten ch. bldgs. Pres. Ministerial City Assn., Idabel, 1955-56, Bristow, Okla., 1973. Home: Mc Kinney, Tex. Died Jan. 11, 2007.

UWUJAREN, GILBERT PATRICK, economist, consultant, realtor; b. Oza Agbor, Bendel, Nigeria, May 6, 1945; came to U.S., 1985; s. Jacob Aghahowa and Victoria (Lasila) Uwujaren; m. Ngozi Buzugbe, Aug. 25, 1973; children: Jane, Janice, Jacob, Jo-Anne, Joseph, Jarune. BSc, U. Ibadan, Nigeria, 1971; MA, Columbia U., 1975, MPhil, PhD, Columbia U., 1977. Asst. lectr. U. Ife, Ibadan, 1972-73, sr. lectr. Ile-Ife, Nigeria, 1977-85; economist World Bank, Washington, 1985-89, cons., 1989-95; pres. Econ. Devel. Assocs., Burke, Va., from 1993; realtor Weichert Realtors, Springfield, Va., 1993-95, Fairfax Realty, Inc., Falls Church, Va., 1995-98; cons. African Devel. Bank, Abidjan, Ivory Coast, from 1998. Contbr. articles to profl. jours. Recipient German Acad. award Govt. Fed. Republic Germany, Ibadan, 1970-71, Rockefeller award Rockefeller Found., Ibadan, 1971-73. Mem. Am. Econ. Assn. Died Dec. 22, 2006.

UZAWA, HIROFUMI, retired economics professor; b. Yonago, Tottori, Japan, July 21, 1928; s. Tokio and Toshiko Uzawa; m. Hiroko Aoyoshi, Dec. 1, 1958; children: Tohru, Satoru, Marie. BS in Math, U. Tokyo, 1951; PhD in Econs., Tohoku U., Sendai, Japan, 1963. Rsch. assoc. Stanford U., Palo Alto, Calif., 1956—59, assoc. prof. econs. and stats., 1960—64; prof. econs. U. Chgo., 1964—69; prof. U. Tokyo, 1969—89, dean faculty econs., 1980—82, prof. econs. emeritus, 1989; prof. econs. Niigata U., 1989—94; dir. Rsch. Ctr. of Social Overhead Capital Doshisha U. Sr. advisor Rsch. Inst. Capital Formation Devel. Bank Japan; mem. Japan Acad., 1989. Author: Social Costs of the Automobile, 1974 (Mainichi prize), Reexamination of Modern Economics, 1977, Transformation of Modern Economics, 1986, Towards a Theory of Public Economics, 1987, Preference, Production, and Capital: Selected Papers of Hirofumi Uzawa, 1988, Optimality, Equilibrium, and Growth, 1988, Global Warming: Economic Policy Responses, 1991, Poverty amid 'Prosperity': The Case of Japan, 1989, A History of Economic Thought, 1989; : Economic Analysis, 1990, Beyond the Twentieth Century, 1993, The Collected Writings of Hirofumi Uzawa, 1994, (twelve vols.) Introduction to Mathematics, 1997—2000, Economic Theory and Global Warming, 2003, Economic Analysis of Social Common Capital, 2005; editor: Studies in Linear and Non-Linear Programming, 1958. Recipient prize, Matsunaga Meml. Found., 1969, Yshino prize, Chuo-Koron Sha, 1970, Blue Planet prize, 2009; named A Person of Cultural Merit, Govt. Japan, 1983; named to, Order of Culture, 1997; fellow, Advanced Ctr. for Behavioral Scis., Palto Alto, 1960—61. Fellow: Econometric Soc. (pres. 1976); mem.: Am. Acad. Arts and Scis., Am. Econ. Assn. (fgn. hon.), Royal Econ. Soc. Home: Tokyo, Japan. Deceased.

VACULÍK, LUDVIK, writer, journalist; b. Brumov, Moravia, July 23, 1926; m. Marie Komárková, 1949; 5 children. B in Sociology and Polit. Sci., 1951. With Bata Shoe Factory, Zlin and Zruc, 1941-46; tchr. vocat. sch., until 1949; tutor Ceskoslovenska Kolben-Danek Machine Works, Praque, Czechoslovakia, 1950-51; editor Rude Pravo Pubs., Prague, 1953-57, Beseda venkovské rodiny, Prague, 1957-59, Czechoslovak Radio, Prague, 1959-66, Czechoslovak Writers Union Literární noviny, Prague, 1966-68, Literární listy, Prague, 1968-69; interogated for interview with BBC, 1973. Writings include: (fiction) The Busy House, 1963, The Axe, 1966, English transl., 1973, (manifesto) Two Thousand Words, 1968, The Guinea Pigs, 1970, English transl., 1977, A Czech Dreambook, 1980, English transl., 1983; (other writings) The Youth Farm, 1958, The Relations Between Citizen and Power, 1968, Dear School-Fellows! A Choice of Written Work 1939-1979: 1. Indian Book; 2. A Workers Book, 1986, A Cup of Coffee with My Interrogator: The Prague Chronicles of Ludvik Vaculík, 1987, Spring is Here: Columns from 1981-1987, 1989, The Old Lady is Enjoying Herself, 1990; editor: (with Jiří Gruša and Milan Uhde) Hour of Hope: Anthology of Czech Literature, 1978, Views on the Manuscript of Vaculík's A Czech Dreambook, 1991. Mem. Community Party, 1946-67, expelled, 1967. Served Czechoslovak Armed Forces, 1951-53. Recipient State award, 1964, Ceskoslovensky spisovatel pubs. award, 1967, George Orwell prize, 1976, T.G. Masaryk Order, 1996. Died June 6, 2015.

VADAS, AGNES, musician, writer; b. Budapest, Hungary, Jan. 5, 1929; arrived in U.S., 1966; d. Ignác László Vadas and Margit Rónai. Artist diploma, Ferenc Liszt Music Acad., Budapest, 1950. State soloist, Budapest, 1952—56; asst. to Joseph Gingold Bloomington, Ind., 1966—67; asst. prof. Tex. U. Music Sch., Austin, 1967—71, Ga. U. Music Sch., Athens, 1971—72, Ithaca (N.Y.) Coll., 1972—78; mem. orch. San Francisco Opera, 1980—93. Author: (autobiographical stories) Tales from Hungary, 2002, Truth Betold, 2005. Activist Amnesty Internat., San Francisco, 1990—93, Friday Harbor, Wash., from 1994. Recipient Remènyi prize, Music Acad., Budapest, 1946, 3d prize, Bach Competition, Leipzig, Germany, 1950. Avocations: chess, cards. Home: Friday Harbor, Wash. Died June 3, 2007.

VAIFANUA, MEKIAFA EUTIKA, educational administrator; b. Pago Pago, Am. Samoa, Aug. 2, 1942; s. Eutika Tauiliili Vaifanua and Filoi Siliva (Satele) Tapopo; m. Maraia Tipeni Saelua, Apr. 30, 1971; children: Junior, Jamie, Joey, June, Justin. BS, Okla. Christian Coll., 1966; MEd, U. Hawaii, 1985. Secondary classroom tchr. Am. Samoa Pub. Sch. System, Pago Pago, 1966-71, adminstr. secondary edn., 1972-75, edn. specialist, 1976-80; project dir. Dept. Edn., Pago Pago, 1981-88, staff devel. coord., from 1988. Author: (text book) American Samoa Government, 1983. Group leader ch. youth orgn., Pago Pago, 1970—; mem. Dem. Party, Pago Pago, 1985—; mem. bd. regents Congregational Christian Ch., Am. Samoa, 1990—. Named to Pacific Summer Inst., N.W. Regional Edn. Lab., Honolulu, 1986, East-West Culture Learning Inst., East West Ctr., Honolulu, 1975. Mem. ASCD, nat. Coun. States on Ins. Edn., Commonwealth Coun. Edn. Adminstr. Home: Pago Pago, . Died Mar. 5, 2007.

VAIL, ELIZABETH FORBUS, volunteer; b. July 25, 1918; d. Sample Bouvard and Elizabeth J. (Buchtenkirk) Forbus; children: Judith Ashforth, Suzanne E. Vail Lander. Student, jr. coll., Washington, 1937—39. Copywriter, asst. to Pres. Kastor Chesley, Clifford & Atherton, Inc., NYC; 1st female airport mgr. Lebanon (N.H.) Airport, 1972. Mem. tourism and devel. com. Marathon (Fla.) City Coun., apptd. to City Code Enforcement Bd., apptd. to Marathon Aviation com.; vol. Monroe County Hurricane Ctr.; former mem. Monroe County Tourist Devel. Coun.; vol. Literacy Vols. of Am. Mem.: LWV, Am. Assn. Airport Execs., Internat. Platform Assn., Friends of Marathon Libr., Marathon Yacht Club. Avocation: reading. Home: Marathon, Fla. Died July 11, 2007.

VAILLANCOURT, JEAN-GUY, sociology educator, researcher; b. Chelmsford, Ont., Can., May 24, 1937; s. Royal A. and Marie (Lavallée) V.; m. Pauline Hansen, June 6, 1966 (div. 1983); 1 child, Véronique. BA magna cum laude, U. Sudbury, 1957; licenciate in Philosophy, Faculté des Jésuites, Montreal, Que., Can., 1961; licentiate in Sociology, Gregorian U., Rome, 1964; PhD in Sociology, U. Calif., Berkeley, 1975. Lectr. St. Boniface (Man.) Coll., Canada, 1964-65; asst. prof. U. Montréal, Que., Canada, 1969-76, assoc. prof., 1976-83, prof. sociology, 1983—2007, adj. prof., from 2007, chmn. dept., 1984-87; editor-in-chief Sociologie et Socs., 1978—87; adminstr. U. Montreal, Que., Canada, 1998. Mem. consultative com. Can. amb. for disarmament, Ottawa, Ont., 1984-91, consultative com. on environ. Hydro-Que., 1984-90. Author: Papal Power, 1980, Essais d'écosociologie, 1982; co-editor: Le processus électoral au Québec, 1976, Roots of Peace, 1986, Environnement et développement problèmes socio-politiques, 1991, Gestion de l'environnement, éthique et société, 1992, Instituer le développement durable, 1994, Aspects sociaux des précipitations acides au Québec, 1994, La recherche sociale en environnement, Nouveaux paradigmes, 1996, L'énergie au Québec, Quels sont nos choix? Montréal, Ecosociété, 1998, Environmental sciences sociales, 2007, La gestion écologique des déchets, 2000, Développement durable et participation publique, 2003, Mouvements sociaux et changements institutionnels, 2005; La Mondialisation de la religion, 2007, Religion a l'extreme 2009, Developement durable et responsibilite sociale: de la mobilisation a Institutionnalisation, 2010. Mem. coun. City of Dunham, Que., 1976-80; bd. dirs. Oxfam-Que., 1976-79, Can. Intern. Inst. for Peace and Security, Ottawa, Ont., 1985-91, European Univ. Ctr. for Peace Studies, Burg Schlaining, Burgenland, Austria, 1989-93; pres., v.p. exec. com., bd. dirs., Groupement forestier du Haut-Yamaska, 2007—, Club 2/3, 1995-2005. Trustee Conseil de Recherche en sci. sociale du Canada, 1982, FCAR, 1989-95, 96—, Social Sci. Rsch. Coun., 1983-86, 90—; fellow Can. Coun., 1965-68. Mem. Internat. Sociol. Assn., Assn. Can. des sociologues et anthropologues de langue française, Sci. for Peace, Pugwash, Group 78, ACFAS (Michel Jurdant prize for Environmental science, 2009). Roman Catholic. Avocations: tree farming, writing. Died Aug. 12, 2015.

VAKMAN, DAVID E., physicist; b. Moscow, May 28, 1926; s. Yefim L. and Sima D. (Rabiner) V.; m. Ester Berin, 1954 (dec. Apr. 1988); 1 child, Alex;m. Frida Shambat Ostrora, Oct. 1988. BS, Moscow Aviation U., 1949, M, 1961, PhD, 1970. Prof.,dir. radio engring. dept. Inst. Improvement Qualification, Moscow, 1971-77; sr. rschr. Inst. Mass Measurements, Moscow, 1977-84, Inst. Indsl. Measurements, Moscow, 1984-91. Engr., sr. rschr. Inst. Radio Electronics, Moscow, 1949-71. Author: Asymptotic Methods in Radio-Engineering, 1962, Sophisticated Signals and the Uncertainty Principle in Radar, 1965, English transl., 1968, Problems of Signal Synthesis, 1973; Signals, Oscillations, and Waves: A Modern Approach, 1998; co-author: Frequency Separation in Theory of Oscillations and Waves, 1983; scientist-editor: Signal Theory (Lewis E. Franks), 1974; contbr. articles to profl. jours. Mem. IEEE (sr.), N.Y. Acad. Scis. Home: New York, NY. Died May 1, 2007.

VALDES, LUIS DANIEL, federal agency administrator; b. Las Vegas, Dec. 14, 1966; s. Luis Reinaldo V. and Lourdes (Martinez) Picallo. BA, Bradley U., 1988; Major in Internat. Studies, Granda U., Spain, 1986, La Sorbonne U. Paris, 1987. Admissions counselor Southeastern U., North Miami Beach, Fla., 1988-90, dir. devel., alumni affairs, 1990-92; project offcer U.S. Dept. of Def., Washington, from 1992. Home: APO, . Died Mar. 7, 2007.

VALENTINE, ANDRE GEORGE, retired internist; b. Buzau, Romania, Feb. 14, 1940; s. Marcel and Malvina (Horovitz) V.; m. Helen Rautu, Sept. 26, 1971 (div. 1977); 1 child, Lucia. BMS, U. Geneva Med. Sch., 1960, MD, 1964, PhD, 1965. Lic. physician: Pa., NY, NJ, Nev., Ariz. Intern Maricopa County Gen. Hosp., Phoenix, 1967-68; resident, fellow Downstate Med. Sch. L.I. Coll. Hosp., Bklyn., 1969-70; resident VA Hosp., NYC, 1970, Cornell U., NYC, 1971-72; nephrology fellow Beth Israel Med. Ctr., Newark, 1975-76; pvt. practice, NYC, 1970-87; freelance philosophy applied rsch. NYC, Paris, 1987-97. Internal medicine cons. Albert Einstein Med. sch., Bronx, N.Y., 1973-84, nephrology chief dept., 1976-84; internal medicine nephrology cons. Midwood Med. Ctr., N.Y.C., 1984-87, Glenwood Med. Ctr., N.Y.C., 1984-87. Author: Le Traitement Chirurgical du Sinus Pilonidal, 1966, Herpes Simplex Type One Encephalitis, Case Report, 1978; contbr. articles to profl. jours. Mem. Dem. Club, Woodside, N.Y., 1977-85. Fellow Am. Coll. Medicine; mem. AMA (Physician Recognition award 1971-74, 74-77, 77-81, 81-83, 84-86), Am. Soc. Internal Medicine. Libertarian Democrat. Jewish. Achievements include pioneering research in devastating herpes encephalitis caused by herpes symplex virus type 1 located below the umbilicus, instead herpes simplex virus type 2 located in the genitals below umbilicus; first successful accograft kidney transplant in Bklyn., 1970 (with others). Home: Jamaica, NY. Died Apr. 23, 2007.

VALENTINE, TIM, JR., (ITIMOUS THADDEUS VALENTINE JR.), former United States Representative from North Carolina; b. Nashville, NC, Mar. 15, 1926; s. I.T. and Hazel (Armstrong) V.; m. Elizabeth Salyer Carr, Sept. 6,

1953 (dec. 1981); children: Stephen, Mark, Philip, Beth Dollar; m. Barbara Reynolds, June 27, 1987; stepchildren: Mark, Vaughn Berry-Daniel, Bryan. AB in Polit. Sci., The Citadel, Charleston, SC, 1948; LL.B., U. N.C., 1952. Pvt. practice law, Nashville, 1952-82; mem. US Congress from 2nd N.C. Dist., Washington, 1983—95. Mem. N.C. Gen. Assembly, Raleigh, N.C., 1955-60, chmn. house judiciary com., 1959; legal advisor to Gov., State of NC, Raleigh, 1965; legis. counsel to Gov. 1967. Chmn. N.C. Democratic Exec. Com., Raleigh, 1966-68. Served to Sgt. USAF, 1944-46; PTO Mem. Nash-Edgecombe Bar Assn., N.C. Bar Assn., ABA, N.C. Acad. Trial Lawyers, Nashville Chamber of Commerce, Morning Star Lodge. Democrat. Baptist. Home: Nashville, NC. Died Nov. 10, 2015.

VALLENTYNE, JOHN R. WAY, ecologist, environmental educator; b. Toronto, Ont., Can., July 31, 1926; s. Harold James and Alice Mary (Laurie) V.; m. Ann Vera Tracy, Aug. 30, 1948; children: Peter Lloyd, Stephen Way, Jane Leslie, Anne Marie, Geoffrey Gordon. BA with honors, Queen's U., Kingston, Ont., Can., 1949; PhD, Yale U., 1953; DS (hon.), McMaster U., 1996. Lectr. Queen's U., Kingston, Ont., Can., 1952-55, asst. prof. biology, 1955-58; assoc. prof. zoology Cornell U., Ithaca, N.Y., 1958-62, prof., 1962-66; scientific leader Eutrophication Sect. Fisheries Rsch. Bd. of Can., Freshwater Inst., 1966-72, sr. scientist, 1972-75; adj. prof. U. Manitoba, 1968-72; sr. scientific advisor, ocean and aquatic sci. Fisheries Rsch. Bd. of Can., 1975-77; sr. scientist, Ont. Region Dept. Fisheries and Oceans, 1977-92; scientist emeritus Ont. Region Dept. Fisheries and Oceans, from 1992. Mem. editorial bd. Internat. Joint Commn. on pollution in the lower Great Lakes, 1968-70, Great Lakes Sci. Adv. Bd. Internat. Joint Commn., 1972-81, Can. co-chmn. 1986-91, Tech. Adv. Com. of Lake Winnipeg, Churchill and Nelson Rivers Study Bd., 1972-73, Lake Winnipeg, Churchill and Nelson Rivers Study Bd., 1973-74; chmn. Organizing Com. for the 1974 Congress of the Internat. Assn. Limnology (Can.), 1972-74. Author: The Algal Bowl: Lakes and Man, 1974, The Ecosystem Approach to Environmental Management, 1978. With Can. Army, 1943-45. Sheffield fellow (Yale U.), 1950-51, Carnegie Inst. Wash. DC vis. fellow, 1956-57, Guggenheim Found. fellow, 1964-65; recipient Journal Fund award, 1959, Rachel Carson award Soc. Environ. Toxicology and Chemistry, 1992, Gordin Kaplan award Can. Fedn. Biol. Socs., 1994; named Environmentalist of the Yr. Hamilton and Dist. Conserver Soc., 1989. Fellow AAAS; mem. Am. Soc. Limnology and Oceanography (v.p. 1964-65, editorial bd. 1966-69), Internat. Assn. Limnology (pres. 1974-80), Ecol. Soc. Am., Geochem. Soc. (Organic Group sec. 1962-64, chmn. 1967-68), Internat. Assn. for Great Lakes Rsch., Internat. Assn. for Ecology, Internat. Union of Biol. Sci. (rep. for environ. biology 1979-82), Can. Soc. Environ. Biologists (pres. 1980-82), Rawson Acad. Aquatic Sci. (chmn. 1980-83), World Coun. for the Biosphere (v.p. 1984-92). Achievements include creation of character called "Johnny Biosphere" who plants seeds of ecological wisdom in the minds of children and youth. Home: Hamilton, Canada. Died June 16, 2007.

VALMY, CHRISTINE, small business owner, writer; b. Bucharest, Romania, Oct. 25, 1926; arrived in US, 1961, naturalized, 1966; d. Cristofor J. and Florika (Zamfiratos) Xantopol; m. Henry D. Sterian, June 23, 1972; 1 child from previous marriage, Marina Valmy. Degree in cosmetology, U. Medicine, Bucharest, 1949; grad., Law Sch., Bucharest, 1946—50. Founder, pres. Christine Valmy, Inc., NYC, 1965—2015; dir. Christine Valmy Internat. Sch. Skin Care, 1966—2015. Author: Esthetics, The Keystone Guide to Skin Care, 1978, Christine Valmy's Skin Care and Makeup Book, 1982. Recipient Small Bus. Person of Yr., NJ, SBA, 1976. Mem.: Nat. Cosmetologists Assn., Nat. Coun. Vocat. Edn., Nat. Rep. Heritage Group Coun., Am. Beauty Assn., People to People Internat. (trustee), Cosmetic Career Women, Am. Assn. Esthetics (pres., founder). Died Jan. 18, 2015.

VAN DEN AKKER, KOOS (JACOBUS VAN DEN AKKER), fashion designer; b. The Hague, Netherlands, Mar. 16, 1939; came to U.S., 1968, naturalized, 1982; d. Pieter and Adrana; life ptnr. John Bell (dec. 1991). Student, Royal Acad. Arts, The Hague, 1956-58, Ecole Guerre Lavigne, Paris, 1961; DHL (hon.), San Francisco Acad. of Art Coll., 2002. Apprentice designer Christian Dior Fashion House, Paris, 1963-65; freelance designer, est. custom fashion boutique The Hague, 1965-68; designer Eve Stillman Lingerie Co., NYC, 1969-70; freelance designer, est. boutique, 1971—2015; freelance designer, est. showroom, 1978—2015; owner Koos & Co. Artist in residence and gave masterclass Acad. of Art Univ., San Francisco, 2008; gave masterclass for Vogue Patterns, Canada, 2009; design label for QVC, Koos for the Course!, 1998—2006. Works include: collaged fur coat range, Ben Kahn Furs, 1981, handbag range, Meyers Manufacturing, 1986-88; couture lingerie collections, La Lingerie stores, 1987; collaged upholstery furniture ranges James II Galleries, 1988 Recipient Gold Coast award, 1978, Tommy award Am. Painted Fabrics Coun., 1982. Mem.: Council of Fashion Designers of America. Achievements include being best known for the designer of Bill Cosby's sweaters for The Cosby Show. Died Feb. 3, 2015.

VANDERBEEK, HATTIE BORMAN, retired educator; b. Phila., July 8, 1920; d. Otto and Hattie Viola (Lafferty) Borman; m. Courtland Lake Vanderbeek (dec. Mar. 1979); children: Margaret, Robert, James. BS, East Stroudsburg State Tchrs., 1942; MS, Columbia U., 1947. Cert. phys. edn. and sci. tchr., Pa., N.Y., N.J. Tchr. phys. edn. and sci. pub. schs., Groveland, N.J., 1942-43; tchr. phys. edn. high sch. pub. schs. Somerville, N.J., 1943-45; tchr., coach Presbyn. Hosp. Sch. Nursing, Newark, 1962-67; tchr. high sch. phys. edn. Bd. Edn., Elizabeth, N.J., 1963-71, elem. tchr. aquatics, 1971-90; ret., 1990. Adj. tchr. Kean Coll., Union, N.J., 1966-71; unit counselor Ch. Camp Presbyn., Johnsonburg, N.J., 1956-72; synchronized swimming instr., Mountainside, N.J., 1972-75; drill team-color guard dir. High Sch., Elizabeth, 1963-72. Recipient Profl. Achievement award N.J. Assn. Health, Phys. Edn. and Dance, 1981, Outstanding Tchr. award, 1984, Svc. award ARC, Roselle Park, N.J., 1983, 25 Yr. award Bd. Edn., Elizabeth, N.J., 1986. Mem. NEA, N.J. Edn. Assn., Am. Assn. Health, Physical Edn., Recreation and Dance, N.J. Assn. Health, Physical Edn., Recreation & Dance. Republican. Presbyterian. Avocations: crafts, cooking, gardening, sewing. Home: Roselle Park, NJ. Died Nov. 1, 2006.

VANDERTUIN, VICTORIA ELVA, book seller; b. New Bedford, Mass., Oct. 16, 1933; d. Harry Robinson and Elva Gladys (Ramsay) Belot; m. David Kent Roy, Dec. 13, 1983 (div.); children: Lowell Ramsay, Jewell Pauline. Book seller New Age World Svcs. & Books, Joshua Tree, Calif. Min. Internat. Evangelism Crusades, 1964, Inst. Mentalphysics, 1982. Editor/pub. New Age World Polaris newsletter, 1994; author: My God, The Power and Wisdom of the Universe. Mem. MUFON. Avocation: religious studies. Home: Joshua Tree, Calif. Died June 21, 2007.

VAN DINE, ALAN CHARLES, advertising agency executive, writer; b. Ford City, Pa., Jan. 12, 1933; s. Albert and Helen (Remaley) Van D.; m. Joan Anne Hodges, Jan. 29, 1955 (div. Jan. 1971); children: Lynn, Mark, Barbara, Michael; m. Holly Long Shefler, Apr. 23, 1977. BA, Duquesne U., 1955; postgrad., U. Pitts., 1968—71. Editor Mt. Lebanon News, Pa., 1956-58; editorial dir. Pitts. Suburban Newspapers, 1958-61; writer and assoc. creative dir. Batten, Barton, Durstine & Osborne, Pitts., 1961-70; pres., creative dir. Van Dine, Horton, McNamara, Manges, Inc., Pitts., 1970-89; chmn. Van Dine, Humphrey, Inc., Pitts., 1989-95; cons. in field, from 1996. Mem. adv. coun. Internat. Poetry Forum, Pitts., 1969-80. Author: Can You Imagine?, 1967, Unconventional Builders, 1977, revised edit., 2001, 2007, (humor) The Encyclopedia of Advertising, 1987, Clyde Hare's Pittsburgh, 1994, Light Verse for a Heavy Universe, 2005, Fateful Encounters, 2014; columnist Pitts. mag., 1977-78, Pa. Illustrated, 1979-81; contbr. articles, essays, short stories, and poems to mags. 1st lt. USAF, 1956. Recipient numerous awards Art Dirs. Club NY, 1964—, Bus. and Profl. Advt. Assn., 1964—, Am. Advt. Fedn., 1999. Mem.: Kittanning Country Club. Avocations: golf, tennis, cartooning. Home: Pittsburgh, Pa. Died Sept. 13, 2014.

VAN DUSEN, BETSY ANNE, marriage and family therapist, psychotherapist; b. Ft. Edward, NY, Oct. 28, 1932; d. Clayton Leroy and Bernice (Hamilton) V.; m. Allan Christopher Simon Nov. 10, 1956 (div. 1988); children: Claire Jennifer Simnon, Eric Van Dusen Simon. BA in English with honors, U. Rochester, 1954; MA in Counseling, Fairfield U., Conn., 1978. Sec. Doubleday & Co., NYC, 1954-56; asst. to sales mgr. Rinehart & Co., NYC, 1956-57; asst. editor Henry Holt & Co., NYC, 1957-58; mng. editor Ballantine Books, NYC, 1959-61; freelance editor NYC, 1961-64; therapist Hudson River Counseling, Mt. Kisco, N.Y., 1978-85, Stamford (Conn.) Counseling Ctr., from 1982; site adminstr. Pastoral Counseling Ctr., Trumbull, Conn., from 1986. Adj. prof. psychology Westchester Community Coll. Author: (play) Unitarian Universalist Assn., 1976; editor for books. Mem. Am. Assn. Family and Marriage Therapy, Am. Assn. Pastoral Counseling. Democrat. Unitarian Universalist. Avocations: hiking, canoing, camping. Home: Northville, NY. Died Apr. 13, 2007.

VAN DUSEN, HAROLD ALAN, JR., electrical engineer; b. Bellingham, Wash., Aug. 9, 1922; s. Harold Alan Van Dusen and Eva Marie Kinnie; m. Joyce Hermance, June 18, 1949; children: Randall Dean, Wendy Gay, Shari Lynn. BSEE, Purdue U., 1949. Registered profl. engr., Wis. Engr. Line Material Co./McGraw-Edison, South Milwaukee, Wis., 1949-61; sr. engr. McGraw-Edison, South Milwaukee, Wis., 1961-87; ret.; cons. Lighting Product Design, South Milwaukee, Wis., from 1987. Vol. exec. Internat. Exec. Svc. Corp., Port Said, Egypt, 1990. Contbr. articles to profl. jours. Participant People to People, China, 1984, Roadway Lighting Forum, Europe, 1970. With USAAF, 1942-45. Fellow Illuminating Engring. Soc. Achievements include 17 patents; research on interaction of outdoor lighting equipment with environmental effects such as wind induced vibration, dirt depreciation, optical plastics applications, glassware breakage, etc. Home: Reedsburg, Wis. Died Mar. 3, 2007.

VAN ETTEN, EDYTHE AUGUSTA, retired occupational health nurse; b. Arthur, ND, Oct. 13, 1921; d. Lacy Edward and Emma Erna (Mundt) Roach; m. Robert Scott Van Etten, Feb. 12, 1944 (dec. Jan. 1997); children: Ronald, Cynthia Czernysz, Martin, Roger, Randall, Janet K. Diploma, Mt. Sinai Hosp. Sch. Nursing, Chgo., 1945; AS, Waubonsee Community Coll., Sugar Grove, Ill., 1978; BSN, No. Ill. U., 1981. Cert. occupational health nurse; RN, Ill. Occupation health nurse Barber-Greene Co., Aurora, Ill., 1965-82; occupational health relief nurse No. Ill. Gas Co., Naperville, Ill., 1983-85; supr. or staff nurse Michealsen Health Ctr., Batavia, Ill., 1982-93; occupational health relief nurse The Dial Corp., Montgomery, Ill., 1982-94. Occupational health nurse cons. AT&T Svc. Ctr., West Chicago, Ill., 1988-94. Mem. adminstrv. bd. Ch. of the Good Shepherd Meth., Oswego, Ill., 1988-94; active Fox Bend Ladies Golf League, United Meth. Women; mem. Lyric Opera of Chgo. Mem. Suburban Chgo. Assn. Occupational Health Nurses, Dist. 2 Ill. Nurses Assn. (del. state conv. 1985, Award for Excellence in Nursing Practice 1993, Lifetime membership 1997), Sr. Svcs. Assn. Inc. (adv. 1983-87, Humanitarian award 1985), Oswegoland Women's Civic Club (bd. dirs. 1985-95). Republican. Avocations: piano, baseball. Home: Buckeye, Ariz. Deceased.

VAN HOOSER, JERRY LEE, automobile technician; b. Erie, Pa., Dec. 12, 1950; s. Alex Lee and Doris Elizabeth (Boggs) Van H.; m. Bertha Jean Lemaster, Dec. 21, 1968; 1 child, Michelle Lynn Van Hooser Kennedy. Grad. H.S., East Moline, Ill. Master auto technician Nat. Inst. Automotive Svc. Excellence. Auto technician Reynolds Motor Co., East Moline, Ill., from 1972. Home: East Moline, Ill. Died Feb. 18, 2007.

VANN, JOE ANN, nurse, social worker; b. Conway, Ark., Mar. 3, 1935; d. Louie A. and Ruth (Browning) Smith; m. Ben T. Vann, Oct. 30, 1953; children: Sarah, Delores, Ben T. Jr., Mark, Deborah. Lic. practical nurse, Petit Jean Vocat. Tech., Morrilton, Ark., 1978; lic. social worker, U. Ark., Little Rock, 1981. LPN, Lic. Psychiatric Tech. Nurse, Ark. Employment program adminstr. Cen. Ark. Area Agy. on Aging, North Little Rock, from 1978. Democrat. Baptist. Avocations: reading, knitting, gardening, cross word puzzles. Home: Greenbrier, Ark. Died July 6, 2007.

VAN PATTEN, DICK VINCENT, actor; b. Kew Gardens, NY, Dec. 9, 1928; s. Richard Byron and Josephine (Acerno) Van P.; m. Patricia Poole, Apr. 25, 1954; children: Nels, Jimmy, Vince. Founder Natural Balance, 1989. Broadway debut in Tapestry in Gray, 1935; other stage appearances include Ah, Wilderness!, 1939, 40, Watch on the Rhine, 1942, The Skin of Our Teeth, 1942, Mister Roberts, 1948, 51, 53, The Tender Trap, 1955, Will Success Spoil Rock Hunter?, 1957, Don't Drink the Water, Next, 1969; (Films) Reg'lar Fellers, 1941, Violent Midnight, 1963, Charly, 1968, Zachariah, 1971, Making It, 1971, Beware! The Blob, 1972, Joe Kidd, 1972, Dirty Little Billy, 1972, Snowball Express, 1972, Westworld, 1973, Soylent Green, 1973, Superdad, 1973, The Strongest Man in the World, 1975, Treasure of Matecumbe, 1976, Gus, 1976, Freaky Friday, 1976, High Anxiety, 1977, Spaceballs, 1987, The New Adventures of Pippi Longstocking, 1988, Going to the Chapel, 1988, Body Trouble, 1992, Final Embrace, 1992, Robin Hood: Men in Tights, 1993, A Dangerous Place, 1995, Love is All There Is, 1996, Evasive Action, 1998, Angel on Abbey Street, 1999, Big Brother Trouble, 2000, The Price of Air, 2000, Groom Lake, 2000, Dickie Roberts: Former Child Star, 2003, The Sure Hand of God, 2004, Quiet Kill, 2004, Freezerburn, 2005, Opposite Day, 2009; radio series Young Widder Brown, 1941; (Radio Plays) Kiss and Tell, 1947, State Fair, 1950, 53, Father of the Bride, 1951, Good Housekeeping, 1951; (Regular TV series) Mama, 1949-56, Final Ingredient, 1959, Young Dr. Malone, 1961-62, That Girl, 1970-71, The Partners, 1971-72, The New Dick Van Dyke Show, 1973-74, When Things Were Rotten, 1975, Eight is Enough, 1977-81, The Love Boat, 1978-84, WIOU, 1990-91; (TV guest appearances) Mike Hammer, 1958, The Silent Service, 1958, Rawhide, 1959, The DuPont Show of the Month, 1960, Naked City, 1961, I Dream of Jeannie, 1970, The Governor & J.J., 1970, Arnie, 1970, Great Performances, 1971, Sanford & Son, 1972, The Don Rickles Show, 1972, Hec Ramsey, 1972, Banyon, 1972, The Doris Day Show, 1971-72, McMillan & Wife, 1973, The Brian Keith Show, 1973, Cannon, 1973, The Paul Lynde Show, 1972-73, Thicker Than Water, 1973, Adam's Rib, 1973, Wait Till Your Father Gets Home, 1973, Love, American Sytle, 1971-1973, Banacek, 1974, Chopper One, 1974, The New Dick Van Dyke Show, 1972-74, The Girl With Something Extra, 1974, Sierra, 1974, Kolchak: The Night Stalker, 1974, Adam-12, 1974, Hot L Baltimore, 1975, The Rookies, 1973-75, Medical Center, 1972-75, When Things Were Rotton, 1975, Ellery Queen, 1976, Emergency!, 1972-1976, Barnaby Jones, 1974-76, Phyllis, 1976, The Streets of San Francisco, 1972-76, Maude, 1976, Wonder Woman, 1976, The Six Million Dollar Man, 1975-76, What's Happening!!, 1976, The Tony Randall Show, 1976, Gibbsville, 1977, CPO Sharkey, 1977, One Day at a Time, 1977, Happy Days, 1976-77, CHiPs, 1979, Too Close for Comfort, 1983, Insight, 1973-83, Masquerade, 1984, Finder of the Lost Loves, 1984, The New Mike Hammer, 1984, Hotel, 1983-85, Crazy Like a Fox, 1985, Murder, She Wrote, 1986, War of the Stars, 1987, The Facts of Life, 1987, Rags to Riches, 1987, Growing Pains, 1989, McGee and Me!, 1990, Diagnosis Murder, 1993, Burke's Law, 1994, Baywatch, 1994, Heaven Help Us, 1994, Lois & Clark: The New Adventures of Superman, 1994, Maybe This Time, 1996, Boy Meets World, 1996, The Weird Al Show, 1997, Love Boat: The Next Wave, 1998, Touched By An Angel, 1995, 1998, Family Guy, 1999, 7th Heaven, 2004, Arrested Development, 2005, That '70's Show, 2006, The Sarah Silverman Program, 2008, Hot In Cleveland, 2011; (TV Specials) Grandpa Max, 1975, Drama Ladies of the Corridor, 1975, A Memory of Two Mondays, 1971; (TV Films) Confessions of a Top Crime Buster, 1971, The Crooked Hearts, 1972, Acts of Love and Other Comedies, 1973, Ernie, Madge and Artie, 1974, Young Love, 1974, Grandpa Max, 1975, Ladies of the Corridor, 1975, Ace, 1976, Charo and the Sergeant, 1976, The Love Boat, 1976, With This Ring, 1978, Diary of a Teenage Hitchhiker, 1979, High Powder, 1982, The Hoboken Chicken Emergency, 1984, The Midnight Hour, 1985, Combat High, 1986, Picnic, 1986, Eight is Enough: A Family Reunion, 1987, A Mouse, a Mystery and Me, 1987, 14 Going on 30,1988, An Eight is Enough Wedding, 1989, Jake Spanner: Private Eye, 1989, The Odd Couple: Together Again, 1993, Another Pretty Face, 2002, The Santa Trap, 2002. Mem. SAG, Actors Equity Assn. Achievements include helped establish National Guide Dog Month in 2008. Died June 23, 2015.

VAN PILSUM, JOHN FRANKLIN, biochemist, educator; b. Prairie City, Iowa, Jan. 28, 1922; s. John Peter and Vera Elisabeth (Moore) Van Pilsum; m. Shirley Elaine Newsom, Oct. 14, 1958; children: John Robert, Patricia Mona, Barbara Joyce, Mary Ann, Elizabeth Joan, William Franklin. BS, U. Iowa, 1943, PhD, 1949. Instr. L.I. Coll. Medicine, Bklyn., 1949-51; asst. prof. coll. medicine U. Utah, Salt Lake City, 1951-54; asst. prof. biochemistry U. Minn., Mpls., 1954-63, assoc. prof. biochemistry, 1963-71, prof. biochemistry, 1971—92, prof. biochemistry emeritus, from 1992. Contbr. articles to profl. jours. Lt. USN, 1944-46. Recipient numerous grants NIH. Mem. Am. Soc. Biochemistry and Molecular Biology, Am. Inst. Nutrition, Histochem. Soc. Achievements include work with Guanidinium compound metabolism. Home: Columbia Heights, Minn. Died Nov. 21, 2014.

VAN WAGONER, ROBERT LOUIS, lawyer; b. Lake Orion, Mich., June 4, 1936; s. Ray John and Gladys Elizabeth Van W.; m. Charlotte Robertson, June 10, 1968 (div. 1979); m. Mary Carlin Kaczor, Aug. 10, 1984. BS, Northwestern U., 1958; JD, Calif. We. U., 1966; cert., Nat. Jud. Coll., Reno, Nev., 1981. Bar: Nev. 1967, U.S. Dist. Ct. Nev. 1969, U.S. Supreme Ct. 1973. Commd. ensign USN, 1958; advanced through grades to lt.; retired, 1963; asst. atty. City of Reno, 1967-69, city atty., 1971-78, 83-87; assoc. Law Offices Richard Fray, Reno, 1969-71; judge County of Washoe, Reno, 1979-82; pvt. practice Reno, 1987-88; adminstrv. law judge State of Nev. Bd. Med. Examiners, Reno, from 1996. Adminstrv. atty. Pub. Svc. Commn. Nev., 1988-89, adminstrv. law judge, 1989-95, adminstrv. law judge Nev. State Bd. Med. Examiners, 1996, judicial state leader Nat. Judicial Coll., 1992—. Author: Tort Liability for Firemen, 1986, (bulletin series) Reno Land Use Planning, 1983-87; editor: La Balanza Law Jour., 1963-66. Chmn. Dem. Com. County of Washoe, 1969-71; bd. dirs. Child Runaway Youth Svcs., Reno, 1987—, No. Nev. chpt. Multiple Sclerosis Soc., 1969— (citation of merit 1986); active on Nev. Crime Commn., Carson City, 1971-78; mem. Nat. Assn. of Transp. Practitioners, 1989—, Nat. Conf. State Trans. Specialists, 1990—, Nat. Assn. Administrv. Law Judges, 1992—, The Nat. Trust for Historic Preservation, 1994—; assoc. mem. Am. Mus. Nat. History, 1994—. Mem. ABA, Nev. Bar Assn., Am. Judicature Soc., U.S. Naval Inst., Elks, Masons, Prospectors, Jesters Reno Ct. (bd. dirs. 1984), Am. Legion, The Nat. Trust for Hist. Preservation, Am. Mus. of Nat. History, Nat. Assn. Transp. Practitioners, Nat. Jud. Coll. (state jud. leader 1992—), Nat. Assn. Adminstrv. Law Judges. Avocations: golf, fishing, home repair. Home: Reno, Nev. Died Mar. 5, 2007.

VARNER, RICHARD BRUCE, mental health activist; b. Potsdam, NY, July 3, 1944; s. Richard S. and Shirley Etta (Young) V.; m. Joyce Ruth Chambers; children: Johnathan Lee, Kimberly Lynn, Donna Kay, Richard Bruce Jr., Mark Allen. AA in Psychology, San Jose City Coll., Calif., 1969; postgrad., Fla. State U., 1973-74; BA in Acctg., U. West Fla., Pensacola, 1978; postgrad., So. Bapt. Sem., Tallahassee, Fla., 1989-91. Electronics technician Dept. of the Navy, NAS Moffet Field, Calif., 1968-70; vets. svc. officer DAV, Eastpoint, Fla., 1985-89; pub. spkr. Nat. Alliance for the Mentally Ill, Tallahassee, 1994-97. Spkr. Fla. Consumer Action Coun., Orlando, 1996, Nat. Alliance for the Mentally Ill, Albuquerque, 1997, Fla. Ho. of Reps., 1997, Fla. Senate, 1997. Author: (non-fiction) My Adventure with Schizophrenia, 1994, Ways to Beat Paranoid Schizophrenia, 1997, (video tapes) Overcoming Schizophrenia II, 1996, The Story of Richard Varner, 1996. Mem. Fed. Emergency Mgmt. Act Bd. Franklin County, Apalachicola, Fla., 1987-92. With USN, 1964-68. Named Vol. of Yr., Franklin County Sch. Bd., Apalachicola, 1986. Mem. DAV (comdr., svc. officer). Avocations: fishing, photography, swimming. Home: Eastpoint, Fla. Died Aug. 12, 2007.

VATAVUK, WILLIAM MICHAEL, chemical engineer, writer; b. Sharon, Pa., Jan. 30, 1947; s. William James and Amelia Agnes (Lenarcic) V.; m. Betsy Ann Chandler, Oct. 27, 1973; 1 child, William Chandler. B in Engring., Youngstown State U., Ohio, 1969. Registered profl. engr., NC. Chem. engr. E.I. DuPont de Nemours, Richmond, Va., 1969-70; sr. chem. engr. U.S. EPA, Durham, NC, 1970-99; pres. Vatavuk Engring., from 1999. Author: Dawn of Peace, 1989 (Pulitzer nomination 1990), Estimating Costs of Air Pollution Control, 1990, Marketing Yourself with Technical Writing, 1992; mem. publs. com. Oilfield Jour.; inventor Vatavuk Air Pollution Control Cost Indexes; contbr. articles to profl. jour. Bd. dir. Bennett Pl. Hist. Site Support Fund, Inc., Durham, 1992—; publicity chmn. Hist. Preservation Soc. Durham, 1989-90; bd. dir. NC 4-H Devel. Fund, Raleigh, NC, 1990-93; tchr,. Sunday sch. CCD, 1993. Capt. USPHS, 1970-99. Recipient NC Order of the Long Leaf Pine award, 2006. Mem. NC Farm Bur., Mercer County Hist. Soc. (life), USPHS Commd. Officers Assn. (pres. NC br. 1975-76, 84-85), Mil. Officers Assn. of Am. (life), N.C. Order Long Leaf Pine. Democrat. Roman Catholic. Avocations: reading, writing, jogging, gardening, solving puzzles. Home: Durham, NC. Died May 18, 2007.

VAUGHAN, JOHN H., physician, researcher; b. Richmond, Va., Nov. 7, 1921; s. Warren Taylor and Emma (Heath) V.; m. Marjorie E. Seybold, Mar. 19, 1983; children: John, Nancy, David, Margaret. AB cum laude, Harvard U., 1942, MD, 1945. Diplomate Am. Bd. Internal Medicine, Am. Bd. Allergy and Immunology. Intern in medicine Peter Bent Brigham Hosp., Boston, 1945-46, research fellow, 1948-50, sr. asst. resident in medicine, 1950-51; fellow in research NRC Columbia-Presbyn. Med. Ctr., NYC, 1951-53; asst. prof. medicine Med. Coll. Va., Richmond, 1953-58; assoc. prof. medicine, asst. prof. bacteriology and immunology U. Rochester (N.Y.) Med. Sch., 1958-63, prof. med., head immunology and infectious diseases unit, 1963-70; adj. prof. medicine U. Calif., San Diego, from 1970; chmn. clin. divs. Scripps Clinic and Research Found., La Jolla, Calif., 1970-74, chmn. dept. clin. research, 1974-77, head div. clin. immunology, 1977-87. Editor: Immunological Diseases, 1965, 3d rev. edit., 1978, Dermatology in General Medicine, 1971. Served with AUS, 1946-48. Recipient Resch. Career award NIH, 1966. Mem. Am. Acad. Allergy (pres. 1966-67), Am. Assn. Immunologists, Am. Clin. Climatol. Assn., ACP, Am. Fedn. Clin. Research, Am. Rheumatism Assn. (pres. 1970-71), Am. Soc. Clin. Investigation, Assn. Am. Physicians, Infectious Diseases Soc., San Diego County Med. Soc., Western Assn. Physicians (councillor 1978-81) , Western Soc. Clin. Research, NIH (gen. medicine study sect. 1956-60, allergy and immunology study sect. 1960-64, ad hoc coms. on arthritis ctrs. 1978-80, allergy and clin. immunology research com. 1981, research career award 1966), Nat. Inst. Allergy and Infectious Diseases (bd. councillors for intramural program 1968-72), Yugoslavian Rheumatology Soc. (hon.), Brazilian Soc. Rheumatology (hon.), Alpha Omega Alpha. Home: La Jolla, Calif. Died Nov. 11, 2006.

VAUGHAN, OLIVE ELIZABETH, retired marketing and industrial specialist, educator; b. Bridgeport, Conn., Oct. 23, 1925; d. Joseph Jackson and Olive Elizabeth (Sears) V. BA, Mt. Holyoke Coll., 1947, MA, 1949; PhD in Econs., Columbia U., 1973. Price economist U.S. Bur. Labor Stats., NYC, 1949-50; econ. researcher, chief price sect. The Conf. Bd., NYC, 1951-58; research analyst Gen. Electric Co., NYC, 1958-66; asst. prof. C.W. Post Coll., Greenvale, N.Y., 1967-73, Fordham U., Bronx, N.Y., 1973-76; staff specialist, planning So. New Eng. Telephone, New Haven, Conn., 1977-89. Planning cons. Gen. Electric Co. N.Y.C., 1973-74. Contbr. articles to bus. publs. Mem. Nat. Assn. Bus. Economists, Am. Econ. Assn., Am. Mktg. Assn., Am. Statis. Assn. Died July 27, 2007.

VAUGHAN, STEVIE RAY, guitarist; b. Dallas, Oct. 3, 1956; s. Jim and Martha (Cook) Vaughan; m. Lenny Baile, Dec. 23, 1979 (div.) Albums: (with Double Trouble) Texas Flood, 1983, Couldn't Stand the Weather, 1984, Soul to Soul, 1985, Live Alive!, 1986; (with David Bowie) Let's Dance, 1983; (with Marcia Ball) Soulful Dress, 1984; (with Johnny Copeland) Texas Twister, 1984; (with others) Blues Explosion, 1984; (with Lonnie Mack) Strike Like Lightning, 1985; (with Don Johnson) Heartbeat, 1986; (with Bennie Wallace) Twilight Time, 1986; (with A.C. Reed), I'm in the Wrong Business, 1988; (with Bob Dylan) Under the Red Sky, 1990; (with Jimmie Vaughan) Family Style, 1990 (Grammy award for Best Contemporary Blues Album, 1991); (soundtracks) Back to the Beach, 1987, Bull Durham, 1988. Named to Rock and Roll Hall of Fame (posthumously, with Double Trouble), 2015. Died Aug. 27, 1990.

VÁZQUEZ-RAÑA, MARIO, International Olympic Committee board member; b. Mexico City, June 7, 1932; s. Venancio and Maria (Raña) Vázquez; m. Francisca Ramos Ramos; children: Marisol, Marina, Miriam, Mario, Mauricio. BBA, U. Puebla, Mexico, 1965; PhD (hon.), Moscow State U., 1980, U. Colima, Mexico, 1987. Pres. Hermanos Vazquez Co., Mexico City, 1960—80, Organizacion Editorial Mexicana, Mexico City, 1975, Mexican Radio (ABC Internat.), Mexico City, 1979; chmn., CEO United Press Internat., Washington, 1986-88; mem. exec. bd. Internat. Olympic Com., 2000—12; pres. Cartones Ponderosa, 2001. Pres. Mex. Olympic Com., 1974-2001, Pan Am. Sports Orgn., Mexico City, 1975, Worldwide Assn. Nat. Olympic Committees, Paris, 1979-2012; founder, pres. Benito Juarez Internat. Shooting Tournament, 1972, Am. Shooting Confederation, 1973-79, Organizing Com. of VII Pan Am. Games, 1975, Organizing Com. of Gen. Assembly of Nat. Olympic Coms., 1984; v.p. Mex. Sports Confederation, 1973-76; exec. dir. Nat. Sports Inst., 1976. Mem. Mex. Shooting Fedn. (founder, pres. 1969-74), Am. Shooting Fedn. (founder, pres. 1973-79). Died Feb. 8, 2015.

VENTRESCA, ARNOLD MICHAEL, computer software professional; b. Boston, Oct. 2, 1936; s. Ralph and Phyllis Ann (D'Angelo) V.; m. Dorothy Sidor, May 23, 1964; children: Anthony, Valerie. AS in Electronic Engring., Franklin Inst., 1961; BS in Electronic Tech., Northeastern U., Boston, 1976; BS in Computer Sci., Wentworth Tech. Inst., 1985. Applications engr. Aerovox, New Bedford, Mass., 1961-62; tech. assoc. Sylvania Electric Semi-Conductor, Woburn, Mass., 1962-69; design engr. Viatron Computer, Bedford, Mass., 1969-71; research assoc. Sperry Research Ctr., Sudbury, Mass., 1971-78; layout engr. Digital Equipment Corp., Maynard, Mass., 1978-79, Prime Computer, Natick, Mass., 1979-81, phys. design mgr., 1984-85; layout design supr. Honeywell Systems Div., Billerica, Mass., 1981-84; applications mgr. Computervision, Bedford, 1985; computer designs ops. mgr. Mass. Micro-Electronics Ctr., Westborough, from 1985. Systems cons. Z-Tel, various town govts., 1985—. Chmn. bd. Health, Billerica, 1986—; coach various youth orgns., Billerica, 1975-82; active Town Meeting, Billerica, 1972-85, Fin. Com., Billerica, 1982-85. Democrat. Roman Catholic. Home: Billerica, Mass. Died Aug. 9, 2007.

VERDY, VIOLETTE (NELLY ARMANDE GUILLERM), ballerina; b. Pont-L'Abbe, France, Dec. 1, 1933; d. Renan and Jeanne (Chateaureynaud) Guillerm. Student, Paris.; ArtsD (hon.), Goucher Coll., 1987. Disting. prof., Kathy Ziliak Anderson chair in ballet, Jacob Sch Music Indiana U. With Ballet des Champs Elysees and Ballet de Paris de Roland Petit (1945-51); on tour with London Festival Ballet, U.S.; appeared at La Scala, Milan, 1955-56; appeared with Ballet Rambert Co., Eng., Am. Ballet Theatre, toured, U.S., Europe and Iron Curtain countries, 1957-58, prin. ballerina, N.Y. City Ballet, 1958-77, dir., Paris Opera Ballet, 1977-80, artistic dir., Boston Ballet, 1980-84; now teaching assoc. N.Y.C. Ballet; guest ballerina, Royal Ballet, 1958, guest appearances include: Munich and Stuttgart opera ballets, Jacob's Pillow Festival, others; roles include: Giselle, Miss Julie, Romeo and Juliet, Coppelia, Swan Lake; movie roles in: Ballerina, 1948, The Glass Slipper, 1954; TV appearances in U.S., Eng., France, Belgium, Ger. Recipient Silver Medallion award Annual Dance Mag., 1968; decorated Chevalier Order Arts and Letters France, 1971 Died Feb. 8, 2016.

VERNAVA, ANTHONY MICHAEL, lawyer; b. NYC, May 13, 1937; s. Michel Antonio Vernava and Ana Avellina Guerriero. BS, Georgetown U., 1959; JD, Harvard U., 1962; LLM, NYU, 1965; MA in L.Am. Studies/Internat. Fin., George Washington U., 1999. Bar: N.Y. 1962, U.S. Dist. Ct. (so. and ea. dists.) N.Y. 1963, U.S. Ct. Appeals (2nd cir.) 1963, Mich. 1965, U.S. Dist. Ct. (ea. dist.) Mich. 1966, U.S. Tax Ct. 1966, U.S. Supreme Ct. 1966, Ill. 1973. Atty. Reid & Priest, NYC, 1962-63, IBM Corp., Armonk, N.Y., 1963-65; assoc. prof. Wayne State U., Detroit, 1965-68, prof., 1968-72; pvt. practice law Detroit and Chgo., 1972-75; prof. law So. Meth. U., Dallas, 1975-76; prof. law, consulting atty. U. Detroit Sch. Law, 1976-95; pvt. practice internat. cons. Fairfax, Va., from 1995. Arbitrator Mich. Employment Rels. Commn., Detroit, 1988-95. Contbr. articles to profl. jours. Mem. ABA, N.Y. State Bar. Avocations: international travel, pre-colombian civilizations, boating, hiking. Died Apr. 7, 2007.

VERNON, LILLIAN (LILLI MENASCHE), mail order company executive; b. Leipzig, Germany, Mar. 18, 1927; d. Herman and Erna (Feiner) Menasche; m. Sam Hochberg (div.); children: David C. Hochberg, Fred; m. Robert Katz (div.); m. Paolo Martino, 1998. DCS (hon.), Mercy Coll., Dobbs Ferry, NY, 1984, Coll. New Rochelle; DSc in Bus. Adminstrn. (hon.), Bryant Coll.; LLD (hon.), Baruch Coll.; LHD (hon.), Old Dominion U.; DCS (hon.), Mercy Coll.; DCS Coll. New Rochelle (hon.); D. in Bus. Adminstrn. (hon.), Bryant Coll.; LLD (hon.), Baruch Coll. Founding chmn. Lillian Vernon, Rye, NY, 1951—2015. Chmn. Nat. Women's Bus. Council, 1995; lectr. in field. Contbr. articles to profl. jours. Trustee Coll. Human Svcs., Bryant Coll.; mem. adv. bd. Giraffe Project Girl Scout Coun. Tidewater; mem. adv. bd. Women's News; mem. bd. overseers Columbia U. Bus. Sch., NYU; mem. adv. com. Citizens Amb. Program; mem. bus. com. Met. Mus. Art; bd. govs. The Forum; mem. nat. com. The Kennedy Ctr. for Performing Arts, Washington; active The Ellis Island Reopening Com.; Bd. dirs. Westchester County, Ctr. Preventive Psychiatry, Va. Opera, Children's Mus. Arts, Retinitis Pigmentosa Found. Recipient Disting. Achievement award, Lab. Inst. Merchandising, Entrepreneurial award, Women's Bus. Owners of N.Y., 1983, Bravo award, YWCA, Woman of Achievement award, Woman's NEws, Nat. Hero award, Big. Bros./Big Sisters, Legend in Leadership award, Emory U., A Woman Who Has Made a Differene award, Inter. Womens Forum, medal of honor, Ellis Island, Bus. Leadership award, Gannett Newspapers, Outstanding Bus. Leader award, Northwood Inst., Congl. Record Commendation award, Crystal award, Coll. Human Svcs., City of Peace award, Bonds of Israel, Svc. award, Sr. Placement Bur., Excellence award, Westchester Assn. Women Bus. Owners, Commendation in Cong. Record, Magnificent Seven award, Bus. and Profl. Women, Woman of Distinction award, Birmingham So. Coll.; named Va. Press Women Newsmaker of Yr., woman of Yr., Women's Direct Response Group and Westchester County Fedn. Women's Clubs, Hampton Rds. Woman of Yr., So. New Eng. Entrepreneur of Yr.; named to Acad. Women Achievers, YWCA, Direct Mktg. Assn. Hall of Fame, Conn. Women's Hall of Fame. Mem.: Nat. Retail Fedn. (bd. dirs.), Women's Forum, Com. of 200, Am. Stock Exch. (listed co. adv. com.), Am. Bus. Conf. (dir.), Lotos Club. Home: Greenwich, Conn. Died Dec. 14, 2015.

VERO, RADU, freelance medical and scientific illustrator, educator, writer, consultant; b. Bucharest, Romania, Oct. 20, 1926; came to U.S., 1973; s. Leon and Bella Sylvia (Spiegler) V.; m. Susan Ezpeleta D'Aste. BA, Inst. Architecture, Bucharest, 1951. Freelance illustrator, Bucharest, 1952-61, Israel, 1961-73, NYC, from 1973. Mem. faculty Fashion Inst. Tech., N.Y.C., 1982—; discoverer novel set of curves (cubals) in analytic geometry. Author: Understanding Perspective, 1980, Airbrush, 1982, Airbrush 2, 1984. Recipient illustration award N.Y. Acad. Scis., 1975, Vargas award, 1997. Mem. N.Y. Acad. Scis. Died Feb. 21, 2007.

VICKERS, GEORGE LEE, manufacturing executive; b. Scooba, Miss., Apr. 26, 1946; s. Matthew and Margaret (Beaty) V.; m. Irma Jean Simmons, May 28, 1967; children: George Lee, Gina, Gia, Gennifer. BA, Cartage Coll., Kenosha, Wis., 1974; MBA, Lake Forest Sch. Mgmt., Ill., 1981. With Johnson Motors, Waukegan, Ill., 1964-73; product mgr. to product spr. Abbott Labs., North Chicago, Ill., 1973-80; plant mgr. Graber Ind., Inc., Saginaw, Mich., 1980-82, Foamade Ind., Auburn Hills, Mich., 1982-86; pres. Bell Plastics Inc., Royal Oak, Mich., from 1986. Mem. Am. mgmt. Asns., Soc. Plastics Engrs., Alpha Phi Alpha. Baptist. Avocations: golf, fishing. Home: Drayton Plains, Mich. Died Jan. 12, 2007.

VICKERS, JON, tenor; b. Prince Albert, Sask., Can., 1926; m. Henrietta Outerbridge, 1953 (dec. 1991); children: Allison, William, Jonathan, Kenneth, Wendy; m. Judith Stewart, 1993 Studied with George Lambert; studied with Royal Conservatory of Music, Toronto; doctorate (hon.), U. Sask., 1963, Bishops U., Que., 1965, U. Western Ont., 1970, Brandon U., 1976, Laval U., 1977, U. Guelph, 1978, U. Ill., 1983, Queens U., 1984. Operatic debut Rigoletto, Toronto Opera Festival, 1952; appeared with Stratford (Ont.) Festival, 1956; also Covent Garden, Chgo. Lyric Opera, Vienna State Opera, Bayreuth Festival, Teatro Colón, San Francisco Opera Co., Met. Opera Co., La Scala, Salzburg Festival, numerous others; films include Carmen, Pagliacci, Otello, Norma, Peter Grimes, Tristan and Isolde, Fidelio; recs. include Peter Grimes, Messiah, Otello, Aida, Die Walkure, Samson and Delilah, Fidelio, Italian Arias, Carmen, Les Troyens. Recipient Can. Centennial medal, 1967, Critics' award, London, 1978, Grammy award, 1979; decorated companion Order of Can., 1968 Mem. Royal Acad. Music. Presbyterian. Died July 10, 2015.

VICTORIA, ROGER DALE, minister; b. Cuba, Kans., Aug. 8, 1959; s. Victor Vernon and Mabel Irena (Nash) V. BA in Religious Studies, Macalester Coll., St. Paul, 1981; MDiv, San Francisco Theol. Sem., 1988. Ordained to ministry Presbyn. Ch. (USA), 1989. Vol. in mission Coun. of Chs. of Santa Clara County, San Jose, 1982-84; intern pastor Orick (Calif.) Community Presbyn. Ch., 1986-87; minister of word and sacrament First Presbyn. Ch., St. Paul, Nebr., from 1989. Mem. Coun. of Synod of Lakes & Prariies, 1991—; chmn. peacemaking com. Cen. N.E. presbytery, Nebr., 1990—. Trustee St. Paul Pub. Libr., 1990—. Mem. Howard County Ministerial Assn., Grand Island City Singers, Rotary. Home: Longmont, Colo. Died Apr. 17, 2007.

VIERTEL, GEORGE JOSEPH, lawyer, mediator, arbitrator; b. NYC, June 10, 1912; s. William and Marie Dorothy (Reichert) V.; 1 child, Elise V. Robertson. BSCE, NYU, 1934; LLB, LaSalle U., Chgo., 1952; cert., Old Dominion U., Norfolk, Va., 1963; student, Alliance Francaise, Paris, France, 1971; JD (hon.), Bernadean U., 1973; PhD (hon.), USUA, 1977. Bar: Va. 1954, D.C., 1972, Md., 1981, U.S. Dist. Ct. (ea. dist. Va.) 1954, U.S. Ct. Appeals (4th cir.) 1954, U.S. Tax Ct. 1954, U.S. Supreme Ct. 1957, U.S. Claims Ct. 1961, U.S. Dist. Ct. Hawaii 1962, U.S. Ct. Appeals (9th cir.) 1963, U.S. Dist. Ct. (D.C. dist.) 1972, U.S. Ct. Appeals (7th cir.) 1972, U.S. Ct. Appeals (D.C. cir.) 1973, Ct. Appeals Md. 1981, U.S. Ct. Mil. Appeals 1973, U.S. Dist. Ct. Md. 1981; registered profl. engr. Md., Va., D.C., N.Y., Wis.; cert. expedited dispute settler; cert. arbitrator Superior Ct. D.C.; lic. real estate broker, Md. Freelance constrn. estimator, 1952-57; asst. engr. N.Y.C. Housing Authority, 1934, Bd. Transp. N.Y.C, 1933-34; supr. constrn. M. Shapiro & Son, NYC; engr. N.Y.C. Bd. Water Supply; asst. resident engr. Langley Field Sta., Va.; civil engr. Nat. Adv. Com. for Aeronautics (now known as NASA), Langley Field, 1940-48; assoc. Williams, Coile, Blanchard, Architects and Engrs., Newport News, Va., 1948-50; ptnr., chief engr. Assoc. Architects and Engrs., Newport News, Va., 1950-61; asst. to dir. Office of Constrn. and Facility Mgmt. U.S. Dept. Energy, Wash., 1977-79; pvt. practice Va., from 1954, Washington, from 1972; sole practice law Md., from 1981. Arbitrator, mediator D.C. Superior Ct., Balt. City Cir. Ct., among others. Contbr. articles to profl. jours. Lt. U.S. Army Corps Engrs., 1934-39. Fellow ASCE (life, pres. local chpt. 1965-67); mem. Bar Assn. Montgomery County, Md. Assn. for Conflict Resolution. Died July 3, 2007.

VIGODA, ABE (ABRAHAM CHARLES VIGODA), actor; b. NYC, Feb. 24, 1921; s. Samuel and Lena (Moses) V.; m. Beatrice Schy, Feb. 24, 1968 (dec. 1992); children Carol. Student, Theatre Sch. Dramatic Arts, Am. Theatre Wing. Actor in numerous Broadway prodns. including The Man in The Glass Booth, 1968, Tough to Get Help, 1972, Marat-Sade, 1967, Inquest, 1970, Arsenic and Old Lace, 1986, (off-broadway) Dance of Death, Richard II, Tempest, Mrs. Warren's Profession; film appearances include: The Godfather, 1972, Part II, 1974, The Don is Dead, 1973, Newman's Law, 1973, The Cheap Detective, 1978, Cannonball Run II, 1984, Vasectomy: A Delicate Matter, 1986, Plain Clothes, 1987, Prancer, 1989, Look Who's Talking, 1989, Joe Versus the Volcano, 1990, Keaton's Cop, 1990, Taking Gary Feldman, 1992, Fist of Honor, 1993, Sugar Hill, 1993, Me and the Kid, 1993, (voice) Batman: Mask of the Phantasm, 1993, North, 1994, Home of Angels, 1994, Jury Duty, 1995, The Misery Brothers, 1995, Love is All There Is, 1996, Underworld, 1996, Good Burger, 1997, Farticus, 1997, Me and the Gods, 1997, A Brooklyn State of Mind, 1998, Just the Ticket, 1999, Chump Change, 2000, Tea Cakes or Cannoli, 2000, Crime Spree, 2003, Farce of the Penquins (voice), 2006, Sweet Destiny, 2014; TV appearances include Suspense, 1949, Studio One in Hollywood, 1949, All Star Revue, 1951, As The World Turns, 1956, Dark Shadows, 1969-70, Mannix, 1973, Love American Style, 1973, The Rookies, 1974, Toma, 1973-74, Hawaii Five-O, 1974, Kojak, 1974, Cannon, 1975, Barney Miller 1974-81 (Emmy award nomination 1975-76, 76-77), The Bionic Woman, 1976, Fish, 1977-78, Vega$, 1978, The Rockford Files, 1974-78, The Love Boat, 1979, $weepstake$, 1979, Supertrain, 1979, Eight Is Enough, 1979, Fantasy Island, 1979, B.J. and the Bear, 1979, The Littlest Hobo, 1980, Harper Valley P.T.A., 1981, The New Mike Hammer, 1984, Tales from the Darkside, 1986, Superboy, 1988, B.L. Stryker, 1989, Santa Barbara, 1989, Monsters, 1990, MacGyver, 1990, The New Adventures of the Black Stallion, 1990, Murder She Wrote, 1991, Lucky Luke, 1992, Diagnosis Murder, 1994, Law and Order, 1996, Weird Science, 1996, Wings, 1996, Touched by an Angel, 1997, Promise Land, 1998, Mad About You, 1999, Norm, 1999, Manhattan , AZ, 2000, Deadline, 2001; TV films include The Devil's Daughter, 1973, The Story of Pretty Boy Floyd, 1974, Having Babies, 1976, How To Pick Up Girls!, 1978, The Comedy Company, 1978, Death Car on The Freeway, 1979, Gridlock, 1980, The Big Stuffed Dog, 1981, Witness to the Mob, 1998, High School USA, 2013, others. Mem. Actors Equity Assn., Screen Actors Guild, AFTRA. *When I was a young man I was told success had to come in my youth. I found this to be a myth. My experiences have taught me that if you deeply believe in what you are doing, success can come at any age.* Died Jan. 26, 2016.

VIK, ROLAND KRISTIAN, county government official; b. Akeley, Minn., June 30, 1932; s. Reuben Olaf and Mildred Elizabeth (Waller) V.; m. Marguerite Katherine Cicero, July 3, 1953; children: LaDonne R., Erik E., Brenda L., Vanita K. Vik-Ohlgren. Student, U. Ala., Tuscaloosa, 1952-54. Art editor Air Univ. Quar. Rev., Montgomery, Ala., 1953-55; sec.-treas. Lakes Region Constrn. Co., Inc., Park Rapids, Minn., 1955-57; dep. recorder County of Hubbard, Park Rapids, 1957-59, country treas., 1959-71, county auditor, adminstr., from 1971. Exec. dir. Hubbard County Lic. Bur., 1978—, Hubbard County HRA, 1980—; trustee Hubbard County Law Libr., 1983—; pres. Minn. Assn. County Treas., 1965. Chmn. governing bd. St. Joseph's Hosp., Park Rapids, 1975-76. With U.S. Army, 1950-52, Korea. Mem. Assn. Minn. Counties (del.), Nat. Assn. County Adminstrs., Internat. Pers. Mgmt. Assn., Minn. County Auditors Assn., Minn. Assn. County Officers, Am. Legion, VFW. Republican. Lutheran. Avocations: graphic arts, electronics, boat building, hunting, fishing. Home: Horace, ND. Died May 25, 2007.

VIKRAM, CHANDRA SHEKHAR, optics scientist; b. Payagpur, India, Oct. 31, 1950; came to U.S., 1977; s. Pratap and Kailash Vati Singh; m. Bina Singh, Jan. 15, 1975; children: Preeti, Tushar. BSc in Physics, Chemistry and Math., Agra U., India, 1966; MSc in Physics, Indian Inst. Tech., Kanpur, 1968; M Tech. in Applied Optics, Indian Inst. Tech., New Delhi, 1970, PhD in Optics, 1973. Sr. rsch. fellow Indian Inst. Tech., New Delhi, 1970-75, sci. pool officer, 1975-77; project assoc. Pa. State U., University Park, 1977-80, rsch. assoc., 1980-82, sr. rsch. assoc., 1982-89; sr. rsch. scientist U. Ala., Huntsville, from 1989; rsch. prof., from 1993. Author: Particle Field Holography, 1992; editor: Selected Papers on Holographic Particles Diagnostics, 1990; contbr. numerous articles to profl. jours. Fellow Optical Soc. Am., Internat. Soc. for Optical Engring., Optical Soc. India (life). Home: Huntsville, Ala. Died Aug. 17, 2007.

VILLANUEVA, DANIEL DARIO, former communications executive, investment company executive; b. Tucumcari, N.Mex., Nov. 5, 1937; m. Myrna Schmidt; children: Daniel L. Jr., James. Grad., N.Mex. State U., 1961, PhD (hon.), Calif. Lutheran U. Kicker LA Rams, 1960—64, Dallas Cowboys, 1965—67; station mgr. KMEX-TV, LA, gen. mgr., v.p., pres.; owner, sr. v.p. Spanish Internat. Comm. Corp., 1971—86; co-founder Univision, executive positions, 1986—90; co-founder Bastion Capital Fund, 1990; ptnr. RC Fontis Partners; chmn. Integrated Water Resources. Bd. dirs. Fleetwood Enterprises, Inc., 2003—09. Named to Hall of Fame, Acad. TV Arts & Sciences. Achievements include being one of the first Hispanic-American in the National Football League. Died June 18, 2015.

VINES, SUE ANN, small business owner; b. Cin., July 30, 1946; d. Edward and Frances M.K. (Lamb) Franz; m. Steven Richard Vines, June 8; children: William, Wayne, Jeanny, James, Heather. Registered nat. environ. profl.; registered environ. assessor., Calif. Environ. specialist Gibson Oil Refining Co., Inc., Bakersfield, Calif., 1983-93; owner, mgr. Susieq's Claythings, Bakersfield, from 1993. Bd. dirs. Kern County Sci. Found., Bakersfield; adv. bd. Bur. Land Mgmt., Bakersfield, 1990-93; chmn. steering com. Hazardous Waste Assn. Calif., Bakersfield, 1987-94. Mem. Kern County Household Hazardous Waste Com., Bakersfield, 1990-91, Pauline Larwood's Breakfast Coun., Bakersfield. Recipient Pres. award Hazardous Waste Assn. Calif., Bakersfield, 1991. Mem. Air and Waste Mgmt. Assn., Golden Empire Safety Soc., Kids Saving Earth (leader), Mensa. Home: Vilonia, Ark. Died Feb. 13, 2007.

VOGEL, RICHARD DWIGHT, funeral home director, mortician, grief counselor; b. Hampton, Iowa, Sept. 27, 1956; s. Trent Henry and Judith (Davis) V. Student, N. Iowa Area Community Coll., 1975-76, Wartburg Coll., 1977-78; grad. in mortuary sci. with honors, Dallas Inst. Funeral Services, 1980. Funeral dir. Smith Funeral Home, Grinnel, Iowa, 1980-82, Oppold Funeral Home, Waterloo, Iowa, 1982-85; ptnr. Surls Funeral Homes, Iowa Falls, Alden, Williams, Iowa, from 1985. Mem. adv. bd. mortuary sci. N. Iowa Area Community Coll., 1985-86. Mem. Nat. Funeral Dirs. Assn., Iowa Funeral Dirs. Assn. (dist. lt. gov. 1984—, young funeral dirs. com. 1984—, membership com. 1985—), Iowa Ducks Unltd. (chpt. com.), Iowa Pheasants Forever. Lodges: Rotary (fundraising chair Iowa Falls club 1986—), Elks, Moose. Republican. Methodist. Avocations: skiing, swimming, golf, raquetball, hunting. Home: Alden, Iowa. Died Mar. 22, 2007.

VOGEL, STEVEN, biologist, educator; b. Beacon, NY, Apr. 7, 1940; s. Max and Jeanette Rachel (Zucker) V.; m. Mariette Seeley Booth, June 3, 1963 (div. Jan. 1974); 1 child, Roger Booth; m. Jane Gregory, Dec. 13, 1974. BS, Tufts U., 1961; AM, Harvard U., 1963, PhD in Biology, 1966. Instr. Tufts U., Medford, Mass., 1962; from asst. prof. to prof. Duke U., Durham, NC, 1966-93, James B. Duke prof., 1993—2006, James B. Duke prof. emeritus, 2006—15. Instr. U. Wash., Friday Harbor, summer, 1979, 81, 83; cons. in field. Author: Life in Moving Fluids, 1981, Life's Devices, 1988, Vital Circuits, 1991, Cats' Paws and Catapults, 1998, The Life of a Leaf, 2012, Comparative Biomechanics, 2013; contbr. articles to profl. jours. Jr. fellow Harvard U., 1964; recipient Stone prize for sci. writing L.A. County Museum, 1990. Fellow AAAS. Achievements include findings concerning the interrelationships between the shapes of organisms (from algae to mammals) and the fluid mech. phenomena around and within them. Home: Durham, NC. Died Nov. 24, 2015.

VOGEL, WALTER PAUL, priest, college counselor; b. Encinitas, Calif., Mar. 7, 1935; s. Walter Albert and Ruth Emily (Maurer) V. BA, Villanova U., 1959; MA, Augustinian Coll., Washington, 1963. Ordained priest Roman Cath. Ch., Feb. 9, 1963. Tchr. math. Msgr. Bonner H.S., Phila., 1963-66; tchr. math, ASB moderator St. Augustine H.S., San Diego, 1966-68; tchr., chmn. dept. math. Ctrl. Cath. H.S., Modesto, Calif., 1975-76; asst. headmaster Villanova Prep. Sch., Ojai, Calif., 1968-75, tchr., chmn. dept. math., 1976-78, headmaster, 1979-82; chmn. dept. math., dorm master Woodside Priory, Portola Valley, Calif., 1982-85; tchr. math., counselor St. Augustine H.S., San Diego, 1985-92, coll. counselor, from 1992. Mem. Western Assn. Coll. Counselors, Nat. Assn. Student Coun. Advisors, Nat. Cath. Edn. Assn., Augustinian Ednl. Assn. Roman Catholic. Avocations: cooking, travel, gardening, physical fitness. Home: San Diego, Calif. Died Apr. 28, 2007.

VOGELEY, EVA A., pediatrician; b. Pitts., Jan. 29, 1950; d. Clyde Eicher and Blanche Wormington Vogeley. BS, Muskingum Coll., 1971; MD, U. Pitts., 1975; JD, Duquesne U., 1988. Intern Children's Hosp. Pitts., Gibsonia, pa., 1976-76, resident, 1976-78; pediatrician Agustin and Vogeley, Gibsonia, pa., 1980-96, Children's Cmty. Care, Gibsonia, from 1996. Fellow Am. Acad. Pediats.; mem. Alpha Omega Alpha. Democrat. Avocation: photography. Home: Allison Park, Pa. Died Dec. 27, 2006.

VOGT, ARTHUR C., broadcast engineer; b. Cordell, Okla., May 7, 1923; s. Edwin E. and Bertha (Kosonke) V.; m. Phyllis J. Nichols, June 10, 1946; children: Sandra, Diana, Vincent, Lyndon, Adonna. Student, Okla. State U. Asst. chief engr. WBLR, Dodge City, Ky., 1955-57, chief engr. Goodland, Ks., 1957-59, Elk City, Okla., 1960-63, Yuma, Ariz., 1963-67, Sta. WOOK-TV, Washington, 1968, Sta. WIEX-TV, Lexington, Ky., 1969; owner, operator Vogt Avionics, Lexington, Ky., 1970-85; chief engr. Sta. WCTE-TV, Cookeville, Tenn., from 1985. Served to lt. comdr. USAF, 1943-53. Democrat. So. Baptist. Died Aug. 5, 2007.

VON FURSTENBERG, BETSY (ELIZABETH CAROLINE MARIA AGATHA FELICITAS THERESE FREIIN VON FURSTENBERG-HEDRINGEN), actress, writer; b. Neiheim Heusen, Germany, Aug. 16, 1931; d. Count Franz-Egon and Elizabeth (Johnson) von F.; m. Guy Vincent de la Maisoneuve (div.); 2 children.; m. John J. Reynolds, Mar. 26, 1984. Attended Miss Hewitt's Classes, N.Y. Tutoring Sch.; prepared for stage with Sanford Meisner at Neighborhood Playhouse. Made Broadway stage debut in Second Threshold, N.Y., 1951; appeared in Dear Barbarians, 1952, Oh Men Oh Women, 1954, The Chalk Garden, 1955, Child of Fortune, 1956, Nature's Way, 1957, Much Ado About Nothing, 1959, Mary Mary, 1965, Paisley Convertible, 1967, Avanti, 1968, The Gingerbread Lady, 1970 (toured 1971), Absurd Person Singular, 1976; off Broadway appearances include For Love or Money, 1951; toured in Petrified Forest, Jason and Second Man, 1952; appeared in Josephine, 1953; subsequently toured, 1955; What Every Woman Knows, 1955, The Making of Moo, 1958 (toured 1958), Say Darling, 1959, Wonderful Town, 1959, Season of Choice, 1959, Beyond Desire, 1967, Private Lives, 1968, Does Anyone Here Do the Peabody, 1976; appeared in Along Came a Spider, Theatre in the Park, N.Y.C., 1985; appeared in film Women Without Names, 1950; TV appearances include Robert Montgomery Show, Ed Sullivan Show, Alfred Hitchcock Presents, One Step Beyond, The Mike Wallace Show, Johnny Carson Show, Omnibus, Theatre of the Week, The Secret Storm, As the World Turns, Movie of the Week, Your Money or Your Wife, Another World; writer syndicated column More Than Beauty; contbr. articles to newspapers and mags. including N.Y. Times Sunday Arts and Leisure, Saturday Rev. of Literature, People, Good Housekeeping, Art News, Pan Am Travel; co-author: (novel) Mirror, Mirror, 1988; author, illustrator Grandmothers Surprise, 2004. Avocations: tennis, painting, photography. Home: New York, NY. Died Apr. 21, 2015.

VON HERZEN, RICHARD PIERRE, research scientist, consultant; b. LA, May 21, 1930; s. Constantine Pierre Von Herzen and Elizabeth Martha (Hevener) Hough; m. Janice Elaine Rutter, Mar. 8, 1958 (dec. 2012); children Brian P., Lane BS, Calif. Inst. Tech., 1952; MA in Geological Sciences, Harvard U., 1956; PhD in Geophysics, UCLA, 1960. Asst. rschr. Scripps Inst. Oceanography, LaJolla, Calif., 1960-64, vis. investigator, lectr., 1974-75; dep. dir. Office Oceanography UNESCO, Paris, 1964-66; assoc. to sr. scientist Woods Hole Oceanog. Inst., Mass., 1966-96, emeritus Mass., 1996—2016, chmn. dept. geology and geophysics Mass., 1982-85. Vis. rschr. U. Calif., Santa Cruz, 2001—03. Contbr. articles to profl. jours. With U.S. Army, 1953-55. Served in Army. Fellow Am. Geophys. Union (assoc. editor Jour. Geophys. Rsch. 1969-71, Maurice Ewing Medal 1998). Petterson Medal, Swedish Acad. Scis., 1999. Avocations: travel, sailing, biking. Home: Woods Hole, Mass. Died Jan. 28, 2016.

VON WINKLE, WILLIAM ANTON, electrical engineer, educator; b. Bridgeport, Conn., Nov. 29, 1928; s. William Mathias and Lillian (Wigglesworth) Von W.; m. Arlene McDermott, July 24, 1950; children: Linda, Lee Ellen, Donna, Nancy, William, Karl, Patricia, Eric. B of Engring., Yale U., 1950, M of Engring., 1952; PhD, U. Calif., Berkeley, 1961. Engr. Navy Underwater Sound Lab., New London, Conn., 1952-66, dir. for rsch., 1966-89; chief scientist Old Ironsides, Inc., New London, from 1989; prof. math. and engring. U. New Haven, West Haven, Conn., from 1952, U. Conn., Storrs, from 1953. Editor 2 IEEE spl. issues, 1977, 84. Mem. Water and Pollution Commn., New London, 1990—. Recipient Adm. Martel award Nat. Security Industry Assn., 1988; USN Dept. grad. fellow, 1957-59. Fellow IEEE, Acoustical Soc. Am.; mem. Cosmos Club, Conn. Acad. of Sci. and Engring. (charter), Sigma Xi. Achievements include patents for sonar performance computer and deep integrated virtual array. Home: New London, Conn. Died June 8, 2007.

VORHIES, JACK MCKIM, orthodontist; b. Indpls., Feb. 19, 1923; s. Bacil Jacob and Irene M. (Arbuckle) V.; m. Georgia Thelma Reese, Nov. 2, 1943; children: Lawrence, Brent Carl, Scott, Mark, Joyce, Rhonda. DDS with honors, Ind. U., Indpls., 1950; student, Muskingum Coll., 1943; MS, Ind. U., Indpls., 1953. Diplomate Am. Bd. Orthondontic. Gen. practice dentistry specializing in orthodontics, Greenwood, Ind., 1952-92; ret., 1992. Instr. Ind. U., 1949-53; dental cons. Conn. Gen., Indpls., 1983-84. Bd. dirs. Am. Internat. Charolais Assn., 1965-72, treas. 1969-71. Served to cpl. U.S. Army, 1943-45, ETO. Decorated Bronz Star. Mem. ADA, Am. Assn. Orthodontics, Ind. Soc. Orthodontics (past pres.), Acad. Internat. Dentistry, Orthodontic Edn. and Researce Found., Tweed Found. Orthodontic Research, Edward H. Angle Soc. Orthondotists, Omicron Kappa Upsilon. Lodges: Rotary, Scottish Rite. Republican. Methodist. Avocations: syngraphics, geneology. Home: Greenwood, Ind. Died Mar. 12, 2007.

VORPAGEL, WILBUR CHARLES, historical consultant; b. Milw., Feb. 26, 1926; s. Arthur Fred and Emma (Hintz) V.; Betty J. Hoch, June 19, 1952; stepchildren: Jerry L., Sharon Belveal Sullenberger. Student Army specialized tng. program, U. Ill., 1943-44; BBA, U. Wis., 1949; MBA, U. Denver, 1953. Cert. tchr., Colo. Instr. Montezuma County High Sch., Cortez, Colo., 1949-51; coord. bus. edn. Pueblo (Colo.) Pub. Schs., 1951-56; pvt. practice bus. cons. Pueblo and Denver, from 1956. Tchr. bus. edn. Emily Griffith Opportunity Sch., Denver, 1959-69; various positions with Denver & Rio Grande Western R.R. Co., Denver, 1959-88; cons. in field. Bd. dirs. Colo. Ret. Sch. Employees Assn., Denver, 1988—; rep. Custer Battlefield Hist. & Mus. Assn. Sgt. U.S. Army, 1944-46, ETO. Mem. Augustan Soc., St. John Vol. Corp., S.E. Colo. Geneal. Soc., Rio Grande Vets. Club (bd. dirs. Pueblo chpt.), Biblical Archaeol. Soc. (contbg. writer), Nat. Huguenot Soc., Colo. Huguenot Soc. (organizing pres. 1979-95), 70th Inf. Divsn. Assn., Shriners, Masons. Republican. Mem. Christian Ch. Avocations: archaeology, militaria, coin collecting/numismatics, autographs, incunabula. *Personal philosophy: We really live twice when we can enjoy the past and the present. Born into a world unbidden, assailed by forces beyond our ken, carried out protesting - life is still worth living. The best is yet to come.* Died June 18, 2007.

VORRES, IAN ANDREW, former mayor, museum creator; b. Athens, Sept. 19, 1924; s. Andrew and Stephanie (Chroussakis) V. BA, Queen's U., Kingston, Ont., Can., 1950; MA, U. Toronto, Ont., 1952. Ptnr. John Vorres & Co., Athens, 1964-74; pres. Vorres Mus., Paiania, from 1983; mayor Municipality of Paiania, Greece, 1991-98. Art critic Hamilton Spectator, 1956-60; corr. Southam Press, Greece, 1962-75. Author: The Last Grand Duchess, 1964. Bd. dirs. Athens YMCA. Decorated Order of Finnish Lion, also decorated by Portugal and Austria, Order of Can., 2009, Order of Grand Commander, Hellenic Republic, 2014 Mem. Greek South Africa Assn. (hon. pres.), Hellenic Can. Assn. of Greece (hon. pres.), Fgn. Press Assn. Greece, Soc. Preservation of Greek Heritage (Washington, trustee 1993—). Avocations: swimming, walking, writing, gardening. Home: Paiania, Greece. Died Feb. 27, 2015.

WACHS, ETHEL, retired fine arts educator; b. NYC, Dec. 26, 1933; d. Max and Dora Katzman; m. Paul Philip Wachs, (dec. Nov. 1981); 1 child, Myrna. BA, Bklyn. Coll., 1968, MA, MS, Bklyn. Coll. Tchr. fine art Bd. Edn., NYC, 1959—2004, ret., 2004. Adj. prof. art adult edn. divsn. Bklyn. (N.Y.) Coll., 1968-95. Author: Lesson Plans for Art Teacher, 1967. Recipient Lone Star Industries award Silvermine Guild, New Canaan, 1976, Old Saybrook Spl. award Old Saybrook, Conn., 1980, Audubon medal of honor for aquamedia Audubon Artists, N.Y., 1982, Philip Isenberg award Audubon Artists, 1996, Savoir Faire Paper award Audobon Artists, 1999. Mem. Audubon Artists, Artists Equity, Nat. Assn. Women Artists (Martha Reed Meml. award 1991). Avocation: collecting american art. Home: New York, NY. Died Apr. 1, 2011.

WADEMAN, PATSY ANN, psychiatric, geriatrics nurse; b. Atlantic, Iowa, Nov. 20, 1943; d. Willie Hollesen and Annie Mae (Lewis) Hollesen Bennet; m. Fredrick N. Wademan, Sept. 11, 1966; children: Stephen, Linnea, Bethany. Diploma, Mercy Hosp., Council Bluffs, Iowa, 1966; BGS in Gerontology, U. Nebr., Omaha. Cert. psychiat. mental health nurse, gerontol. nurse. Nurse Nebraska City (Nebr.) Pub. Schs., 1966-68, St. Mary's Hosp., Nebraska City, 1973-74, 76-78; staff nurse Duffs Friendship Villa Nursing Home, Nebraska City, 1986-88; dir. nursing Nebraska City Manor, 1988-89; staff nurse Med. Ctr. U. Nebr. Med. Ctr., Omaha, 1989-97; health coord. Head Start, Tecumseh, Nebr., 1984-86; rsch. nurse intern I U. Nebr. Med. Ctr., Omaha, 1995-96, rsch. nurse intern II, 1996-97, rsch. utilization nurse, from 1997. Instr. Southeast C.C., Lincoln, Nebr., 1976-84; mem. Nat. Coun. on Aging. Mem. Am. Gerontol. Nurses Assn., Nebr. Gerontol. Nurses Assn., Golden Key Nat. Honor Soc. Home: Nebraska City, Nebr. Died June 18, 2007.

WAGNER, DAVID EDWARD, organization development consultant; b. Niagara Falls, NY, Apr. 27, 1938; s. Julius Edward and Emily (Andrews) W.; m. Toby Heidenreich, May 29; children: Eric, Julie; m. Mary Alice Stickney, Apr. 7,; stepchildren: Peter, Rob, Carolyn. BA, Hobart Coll., Geneva, NY, 1961; MS in Pub. Health, U. Mo., 1968. Project mgr. Northern New Eng. Regional Med. Program, Burlinton, Vt., 1968-69; exec. dir. Planned Parenthood of Vt., Burlington, 1969-77; ptnr. New Dynamics, Laconia, N.H., 1977-84 and from 88; dir. ops. Univ. Health Ctr., Burlington, Vt., 1984-88. Co-author: A Male/Female Continuum: Paths to Colleagueship, 1995. Treas. Vt. Dem. Com., 1983-85, Jim Guest for Cong., Vt., 1988; mem. Gov.'s Commn. of Women, Vt., 1985-89; elder, trustee Christ Presbyn. Ch., Burlington, 1986-89, elder Southminster Presby. Ch., 1991-92; del. Presby. of the Cascades, 1991-92. Mem. Orgn. Devel. Network. Home: Hinesburg, Vt. Died May 16, 2007.

WAGNER, FLORENCE ZELEZNIK, retired telecommunications industry executive; b. McKeesport, Pa., Sept. 23, 1926; d. George and Sophia (Petros) Zeleznik; m. Francis Xavier Wagner, June, 18, 1946; children: Deborah Elaine Wagner Franke, Rebecca Susan Wagner Schroettinger, Melissa Catherine Wagner Good, Francis Xavier, Robert Francis. BA magna cum laude, U. Pitts., 1977, MPA, 1981. Sec. to pres. Tube City Iron & Metal Co., Glassport, Pa., 1944-50; cons. Raw Materials, Inc., Pitts., 1955; gen. mgr. Carson Compressed Steel Products, Pitts., 1967-69; ptnr. Universal Steel Products, Pitts., 1970-71; gen. mgr. Josh Steel Co., Braddock, Pa., 1971-78; owner Wagner's Candy Box, Mt. Lebanon, Pa., 1979-80; borough sec./treas. Borough of Pennsbury Village, Allegheny County, Pa., 1980-88; ptnr. Tele-Communications of Am., Burgettstown, Pa., 1984-86; trustee Profit-Sharing Trust, Pension Trust Josh Steel Co., Burgettstown, 1986-88, Consol, Inc., Upper St. Clair, from 1989. Mem. Foster Parents; sec. Sch. Bd. St. Bernard Cath. Elem. Sch., Mt. Lebanon, Pa., 1995—98; vol. Pitts.-Carlow GED Literacy program, 1997—98, Upper St. Clair Libr.; Mem. Jefferson Twp. Planning Commn.; mem. Washington County, Pa. Mem. AAUW, Pitts. Symphony Soc., Pitts. Ballet Theater Guild, Soc. Pub. Adminstrn. (founder U. Pitts. br.), Acad. Polit. Sci., U.S. Strategic Inst., Southwestern Pa. Sec. Assn., Alpha Sigma Lambda (past treas., sec., pres.). Republican. Home: Pittsburgh, Pa. Died Nov. 15, 2006.

WAITE, VERNER STUART, retired surgeon; b. Lindsay, Calif., Aug. 16, 1928; s. Albert Crew Waite and Helen Fowle; m. Elizabeth Souchick, Nov. 5, 1955; children: Peter Stuart, Elizabeth Ruth, Eva Ann, Amelia Catherine, Susan Marie, Alexander Crew. AA, Compton Jr. Coll., 1948; BA, U. Calif., Berkeley, 1950; MD, U. Chgo., 1954. Intern L.A. VA Hosp., 1954-55; resident in surgery St. Louis City Hosp., 1958-61; fellow in surgery Ellis Fischel Cancer Ctr., Colulmbia, Mo., 1961-63; pvt. practice surgery Lynwood and Downey, Calif., 1963-97. Bd. dirs. Downey Hosp., 1994; active Lynwood Sch. Bd., 1967-75; med. exec. com. St. Francis Hosp.; pres. Family Support Ctr. of Downey, 1999-2000. Fellow ACS; mem. Semmelweis Soc. (founder, pres. 1986-97), Lynwood Exch. Club, Downey Exch. Club. Republican. Avocation: stamp collecting/philately. Home: Cypress, Calif. Died Aug. 17, 2007.

WALKER, CHARLES DODSLEY, conductor, organist; b. NYC, Mar. 16, 1920; s. Marshall Starr and Maude Graham (Marriott) Walker; m. Janet Elizabeth Hayes, May 30, 1949 (dec. Feb. 1997); children: Peter Hayes, Susan Starr; m. Elizabeth Ann Phillips, Jan. 14, 2001. BS, Trinity Coll., 1940; AM, Harvard U., 1947. Organist, choirmaster Am. Cathedral, Paris, 1948-50, Ch. of the Heavenly Rest, NYC, 1951-88; music dir. Blue Hill Troupe, Ltd., NYC, 1955-90, Chapin Sch., NYC, 1961-85; mem. organ faculty Union Theol. Sem., NYC, 1962-73, NYU, NYC, 1968-80; dean, music dir. Berkshire Choral Inst., Sheffield, Mass., 1982-91; organist, choirmaster Trinity Episcopal Ch., Southport, Conn., 1988—2007; artist-in-residence St. Luke's Parish, Darien, Conn., from 2007. Contbr. articles to profl. jours. Lt. comdr. USNR, 1942—46. Recipient Disting. Alumnus award, Cathedral Choir Sch., 1988; named Artist of Yr., Fairfield Arts Coun., 2004. Fellow: Am. Guild Organists (nat. pres. 1971—75); mem.: Canterbury Choral Soc. (founder, condr. from 1952), Am. Fedn. Musicians, St. Wilfrid Club, Bohemians. Avocations: travel, photography. Home: New York, NY. Died Jan. 17, 2015.

WALKER, GRACE BAIR, tax consultant; b. Natrona Heights, Pa., Oct. 1, 1926; d. Maurice C. and Rhoda (Culbert) Bair; m. William E. Walker, Dec. 27, 1945; children: Holly Elizabeth, Laurie VanTine, Scott E. Grad. high sch., Natrona Heights. Asst. X-ray technician Alcoa, New Kensington, Pa., 1944-46; geophysics asst. Gulf Rsch., Harmarville, Pa., 1948-52; tax preparer H & R Block, 1976-82, Beneficial Fin., 1983; tax cons. Walkers Tax Svc., from 1984. Vol. Ally Valley Hosp., Natrona Heights, 1985—, Meals on Wheels; elder, deacon Natrona Heights Presbyn. Ch., 1980-85. Mem. Nat. Assn. Enrolled Agts., Nat. Assn. Tax Preparers. Republican. Died June 26, 2007.

WALKER, JOANNE LOURDES, occupational health nurse, educator; b. Oswego, NY, July 18, 1940; d. George Francis and Katherine (Juiffre) Paino; m. H. Edward Walker, Sept. 30, 1961; children: Mark Paul, Lisa Marie. Diploma, St. Joseph Hosp. Sch. Nursing, Syracuse, NY, 1961; BS in Health Edn., Anna Maria Coll., Paxton, Mass., 1985. RN, Mass.; cert. nursing adminstr. Adminstr. Upjohn Health Care, Worcester; occupational health nurse Wright Line, Worcester, U.S. Postal Svc., Worcester; charge nurse occupational health unit Fallon Clinic, Worcester. Emergency med. technician instr.; AIDS educator; instr.-trainer first aid. Chmn. nursing and health, disaster nurse ARC. Recipient Presdl. award of merit. Mem. Worcester County Occupational Nurses Assn. (chmn. Pub. Rels.). Home: Holden, Mass. Died Mar. 8, 2007.

WALKER, KENNETH JOSEPH, judge, lawyer; b. San Antonio, Nov. 20, 1948; s. Joe Aaron and Gwendolyn (Rawls) W.; m. Carol Gillies, Nov. 13, 1994; children: Renée, Laura, Lance, Julie, Carl. BA, U. Tex., 1972; JD, South Tex. Coll. Law, Houston, 1975. Bar: Tex. 1975, U.S. Dist. Ct. (ea. dist.) Tex. 1976, U.S. Dist. Ct. (so. dist.) Tex. 1975. Atty. Simpson, Morgan & Burwell, Texas City, Tex., 1975-76; adminstrv. asst. State Senator A.R. Schwartz, Austin, Tex., 1975-76; asst. dist. atty. Gregg County Dist. Atty.'s Office, Longview, Tex., 1976; atty. Fisher, Patton & Walker, Longview, 1976-78; sole practitioner Longview, from 1978; county judge Gregg County, Longview, 1991-94. Bd. dirs. United Way, Longview, 1990—; chmn. Longview Planning and Zoning Commn., 1988-91. Recipient Cert. of Recognition City of Longview, 1990, Am. Legion, 1992. Mem. Tex. Bar Assn., Tex. Assn. Counties (pres.-elect 1991-92), Masons, Shriners, Am. Bus. Club (bd. dirs. 1992—), Lions Club (bd. dirs. 1990—). Democrat. Episcopalian. Home: Longview, Tex. Died Mar. 21, 2007.

WALKER, OLENE S., former governor; b. Ogden, Utah, Nov. 15, 1930; d. Thomas Ole and Nina Hadley (Smith) W.; m. J. Myron Walker, 1957; children: Stephen Brett, David Walden, Bryan Jesse, Lori, Mylene, Nina, Thomas Myron. BA, Brigham Young U., 1954; MA, Stanford U., 1954; PhD, U. Utah, 1986; HHD (hon.), Weber State U., 1997. V.p. Country Crisp Foods, 1969-92; mem. Utah House of Representatives Dist. 24, 1981—89; lt. gov. State of Utah, 1993—2003, gov., 2003—05. Mem. Salt Lake Edn. Found. bd. dirs. 1983-90; dir. community econ. devel.; mem. Ballet West, Sch. Vol., United Way, Commn. on Youth, Girls Village, Salt Lake Conv. and Tourism Bd.; mem. adv. coun. Weber State U.; established the Olene S. Walker Inst. of Politics and Public Svc., Weber State U., 2012 Mem. Nat. Assn. Secs. of State (Western chmn., nat. lt. gov.'s conf., pres. 1997-98). Republican. Mem. Lds Ch. Achievements include becoming first female elected to office of governor of Utah. Home: Saint George, Utah. Died Nov. 28, 2015.

WALL, FRANCIS JOSEPH, statistical consultant; b. Moss Point, Miss., Mar. 22, 1927; s. Thomas J. and Nina B. (Brewer) W.; m. B. Jean, Apr. 15, 1950; children: David W., Karen S., Leslie J. BS, Sul Ross State U., 1947; MS, U. Colo., 1956; PhD, U. Minn., 1961. Statistician Dow Chem. Co., Boulder, Colo., 1952-57, Sperry Univac, St. Paul, 1957-61, Dikewood Corp., Albuquerque, 1961-69, Lovelace Found., Albuquerque, 1969-71; pvt. practice cons. Albuquerque, from 1972. Author: Statistical Data Analysis Handbook, 1986. Mem. Am. Statis. Assn., Biometric Soc., Sigma Xi. Republican. Mem. United Ch. of Christ. Home: Albuquerque, N.Mex. Died Apr. 25, 2007.

WALLACE, LAWRENCE EUGENE, minister; b. Independence, Mo., July 6, 1940; s. Joe Thomas Patterson and Virginia Lee Kinnemer Rasmuson; m. Mary Ellen Wesson, Oct. 11, 1957; children: Larry Edward, Rhonda Kaye, Rodeny Alan. AA, Tulsa Jr. Coll., 1981; BA, Northeastern State U., 1983; postgrad., Dallas Bapt. U., 1968-69. Ordained to ministry So. Bapt. Conv., 1974. Min. youth 3 So. Bapt. chs., Tehlequah, Okla. and Tulsa area, 1969-77; pastor 3 So. Bapt. chs. Tulsa area, 1978-88, 83-88; min. edn. White City Bapt. Ch., Tulsa, 1980-83; pastor First Bapt. Olive Ch., Drumright, Okla., 1983-88, First Bapt. Ch., Pawhuska, Okla., from 1988. Past bd. dirs. Bapt. Conv. Okla., Oklahoma City, 1985-89; regional sales mgr. fountain sales div. Nat. Dr. Pepper Co., Dallas, 1963-68; sales rep. Andrew Jergens Co., Cin., 1973-74; speaker in field. With U.S. Army, 1957-60. Avocations: fishing, hunting. Home: Tonkawa, Okla. Died Nov. 20, 2006.

WALLACE, MARY ANN, development company executive; b. Reno County, Kans., Feb. 19, 1939; d. Ivan Lewis and Vina Sue (Smith) Newell; m. Alexander Wallace III, Feb. 17, 1968 (div. June 1982); 1 child, Alexander IV. BS, Wichita State U., 1961. Property mgr. 650 S. Grand Bldg. Co., Los Angeles, 1961-68; v.p. Milner Devel., Santa Monica, Calif., 1981-83, chief fin. officer LA, from 1983. Cons. Kitty Prodns., L.A., 1978—; cons., v.p. Am. Mut. Prodns., Redlands, Calif., 1975—. V.p. Sister Servants of Mary Guild, L.A., 1970-77; treas. Hosp. of Good Samaritan Aux., L.A., 1969-75; press sec. Orphanage Guild Jrs., L.A., 1974. Named Downtown Working Angel, Downtown Businessmen's Assn., Best Fund Raiser, Sister Servants of Mary Guild, 1974-76. Mem. L.A. World Affairs Coun., L.A. Women in Bus., Nat. Art Assn. Clubs: L.A. Country (Beverly Hills, Calif.). Republican. Roman Catholic. Avocations: travel, collecting, reading for blind. Home: Scottsdale, Ariz. Died Nov. 4, 2006.

WALLACE, PAUL HARVEY HARVEY, lawyer, educator; b. Fresno, Calif., Oct. 27, 1944; s. Samuel Dunn and Naomi (Hickman) W.; m. Randa Fay Steckler, Mar. 20, 1987; children: Tim, Laura, Christy. BS in Criminology, Calif. State U., Fresno, 1966; JD, U.S. Internat. U., 1974; MPA, Golden Gate U., 1989. Bar: Calif. 1974, U.S. Dist. Ct. (so. dist.) Calif. 1974, U.S. Dist. Ct. (no. dist.) Calif. 1982, U.S. Ct. Appeals (9th cir.) 1985. Dep. dist. atty. San Diego Dist. Atty.'s Office, 1975-79; assoc. Harrison and Watson, San Diego, 1979-81; dep. county counsel Butte County Counsel's Office, Oroville, Calif., 1981-85, county counsel, 1985-87; city atty. City of Fresno, 1987-92; assoc. prof. Calif. State U., Fresno, 1992-96, prof., from 1996. Adj. prof. Nat. U., Fresno, 1987—; bd. dirs. Ctrl. Calaif. Legal Svcs. Corp., 1993-95. Lead author: Fundamentals of Police Administration, 1995, Principles of Criminal Law, 1996; author: Family Violence: Legal, Medical and Social Perspectives, 1996. Asst. coord. San Diego County for U.S. Senator Alan Cranston, 1974. Lt. USMCR, 1967-70, col. Res. Col. United State Marine Corps, 1966—97. Decorated Silver Star, Purple Heart with oak leaf cluster. Mem. State Bar Assn. Calif., Butte County Bar Assn., San Diego Dep. Dist.

Attys. Assn. (sec.-treas. 1976-77, v.p. 1977-78, pres. 1978-79), Am. Legion, VFW, Masons, Shriners. Avocations: photography, jogging. Died June 22, 2007.

WALLEN, JAMES MARSHALL, retail executive; b. Ft. Collins, Colo., Mar. 5, 1948; s. Henry Martenson and Ella Margret (Wehlitz) W.; m. Pamela Jean McGill, Mar. 21, 1969 (div. Feb. 1988); children: Jeremy James, Jennifer Jean. BA, Colo. State U., 1970. Secondary tchr. Wiley (Colo.) Consol. Schs., 1970-72; paint salesman, dealer Kohler McLister Paint Co., Denver, 1972-80; owner Jim's Paint & Paper, Inc., Longmont, Colo.; area mgr. Allen Paint Supply Co., Inc., Denver, 1983-86; ops. mgr., jobber sales, sec.-treas. MFC Allen Paint, Denver, from 1987. Author: Energy Transactions, 1997. Home: Denver, Colo. Died Apr. 16, 2007.

WALLENBERG, PETER, banker, investor; b. Stockholm, May 29, 1926; s. Marcus Wallenberg and Dorothy Mackay; Suzanne Wallenberg (div.); children: Jacob, Peter, Andrea LLM, U. Stockholm; degree (hon.), Stockholm Sch. Econs., Augustana Coll., Upsala Coll., Stockholm, 1984, Georgetown U. Various positions Atlas Copco Group, 1953-67; dep. mng. dir. Atlas Copco AB, 1970-74, chmn., 1974; first vice chmn. Skandiaviska Enskilda Banken, 1974—96; chmn. Investor AB, 1982—97. Avocations: hunting, tennis, sailing. Died Jan. 19, 2015.

WALLER, CHARLOTTE REID, secondary school educator; b. Little Rock, Feb. 19, 1936; d. Charles Willard and Frances Geraldine (Williams) Reid; m. Franklin Wayne Waller, Dec. 30, 1954; 1 child, Franklin Wayne Jr. BSE, U. Ark., Monticello, 1961; ME, U. So. Miss., 1978. Cert. computer sci., math., gen. sci. tchr., secondary sch. adminstr. Tchr. Pine Bluff Pub. Schs., Pine Bluff, Ark., 1960-77; tchr. Hattiesburg Pub. Schs., Hattiesburg, Miss., 1977-78, Forrest City Pub. Schs., Forrest City, Ark., 1978-83, Hattiesburg Pub. Schs., 1983-92, Ctr. for Gifted Studies, U. So. Miss., Hattiesburg, 1989-92; tchr. computer cons. Mission Creek Youth Camp Sch., Belfair, Wash., 1993—97; tchr. Hattiesburg Pub. Schs., Miss., 1998—2003. Mem. adj. faculty Eastern Ark. C.C., Forrest City, 1981-82, William Carey Coll., Hattiesburg, 1988; staff devel. trainer Hattiesburg Pub. Schs., 1986-92. Computer Lit. for Tchrs. grantee, 1988, Shareware Libr. grantee, 1988 Hattiesburg Area Edn. Fund. Mem. Nat. Coun. Tchrs. Math., Miss. Coun. Tchrs. Math. (sec. 1989-91), Miss. Ednl. Computing Assn., Sch., Sci. and Math. Assn., Internat. Soc. Tech. in Edn., Delta Kappa Gamma, Phi Delta Kappa. Episcopalian. Avocations: fishing, reading. Home: Columbia, Miss. Died Mar. 26, 2007.

WALLER, WILLIAM KENNETH, health physicist; b. Yazoo City, Miss., May 28, 1954; s. William Thomas and ruth Inez (Gary) W.; m. Gail Paige Knott, Aug. 11, 1979; children: Enid Michelle, William Charles. AA, Holmes C.C., Goodman, Miss., 1974; BS, Delta State U., Cleveland, Miss., 1976; Cert., Oak Ridge Assoc. U., 1977. Chief radioactive materials sect. Divsn. Radiol. Health, Miss. State Bd. Health, Jackson, 1976-80; from project mgr. to dir. waste mgmt. US Ecology, Inc., Louisville, 1980-90; sr. scientist Battelle Pacific NW Lab., Richland, Wash., 1990-91; tech. dir. environ. restoration and radiation svcs. Law Engring. and Environ. Svcs., Inc., Kennesaw, Ga., from 1991. Co-author: Guidance Manual of REviewing RCRA and CERCLA Documentation, 1989, Comparative Review of U.S. DOE CERCLA Federal Facility Agreements, 1989; contbr. articles to profl. jours. Chmn. ops. stewards Summit Bapt. Ch., Kennesaw, 1994, 95; chmn. pers. stewards Towne View Bapt. Ch., Kennesaw, 1992. Mem. Am. Nuclear Soc., Am. Mgmt. Assn., Health Physics Soc., Internat. Soc. for Decontaimination/Decommissioning Profls. Avocations: golf, fishing, woodworking basketball. Died June 7, 2007.

WALLMARK, JOHN TORKEL, scientist, educator; b. Stockholm, June 4, 1919; s. Gunnar and Vivi (Osterlund) W.; m. Madeline Mihelyi, Apr. 18, 1949; children: John Sigurd, John Torbjorn; m. Gunnel Alsen, Aug. 20, 1975. D Tech., Royal Inst. Tech., Stockholm, 1953. Engr. Standard Radio AB, Stockholm, 1944-45; rsch. asst. Royal Inst. tech., 1945-53; staff mem. RCA Labs., Princeton, N.J., 1947-48, 53-64, 66-68; prof. elec. engring. Chalmers U., Gothenburg, Sweden, 1964-66, 68-83, prof. innovations, 1983-91. Mem. invention com. Fed. Bd. Tech. Devel., 1968-78; rsch. adv. com. Perstorp AB, 1977-85, Fed. Bd. Tech. Devel., 1979-87, Ericsson AB, 1982-85, SKF AB, 1986-89, Frico AB, 1985-90; bd. dirs. Chemtronics AB, 1984-87, Gothenburg Product Devel. Ctr., Inst. Opt. Res.; chmn. idea stipend com. Job Security Coun. SAF-PTK, 1988-92. Author: (with others) Integrated Electronics, 1963, Field-Effect Transistors, 1966, Field-Effect Transistors in Integrated Circuits, 1974, 100 Major Swedish Innovations, 1988. Recipient Polhem award Swedish Engrs. Assn., 1982; H.T. Cedergren medal Royal Inst. Tech., 1984, KTH grand prize, 1989, John Ericsson award Am. Soc. Swedish Engrs., 1994, Chalmers medal Chalmers U. Tech., 1989. Fellow IEEE, AAAS; mem. Royal Swedish Acad. Sci. (L.J. Wallmark award 1954), Royal Swedish Acad. Engring. Sci. (IVA Large Gold medal 1989), Royal Soc. Arts and Sci. Home: Kungsbacka, Sweden. Died Feb. 5, 2007.

WALLSKOG, JOYCE MARIE, nursing educator, retired psychologist; b. Melrose Park, Ill., Apr. 20, 1942; BSN, Alverno Coll., 1977; MSN, U. Wis., Milw., 1982; PhD, Marquette U., Milw., 1992. RN, Wis.; lic. psychologist; diplomate Am. Coll. Forensic Examiners. Staff nurse St. Mary's Hill Hosp., Milw., 1977—78, Waukesha (Wis.) Meml. Hosp., 1978—80, clin. nurse specialist, 1980—87; asst. prof. nursing Marquette U., Milw., 1986—2005; psychotherapist Psychiat. Assocs. Comprehensive Services, Ltd., Milw., 1982—85; nurse psychotherapist Counseling and Wellness Ctr., Waukesha, 1982—2005; adv. practice nurse prescriber, 1995—2005; guest lectr. Concordia U., Milw., 2005. Cons. Alverno Coll., Milw., 1983-84, Health Care Cons., Sussex, Wis., 1985—; coord. Waukesha Premenstrual Syndrome Program, 1980—; nurse psychotherapist Stress Mgmt. and Mental Health Svcs., Waukesha, 1991-94; co-founder Turning Point Mental Health and Cons. Svcs., Waukesha, 1994—; advanced practice nurse prescriber, 1995—. Contbr. articles to profl. jours. Bd. dirs. Waukesha County Mental Health Assn., 1982; mem. Waukesha County Unified Svcs., 1984; adv. bd. Northwest Rehab. Ctr., 1992-94; advisor Resolve Through Sharing, 1986-2001, Women's Health Svcs., 1987-2001; advisor Parish Nurse Program. Mem. APA, ANA (coun. psychiat. and mental health nursing), Wis. Nurses Assn. (rep. Wis. Coalition on Sexual Misconduct by Psychotherapists and Counselors 1988-93), Delta Upsilon Sigma, Phi Lambda Delta. Home: Madison, Wis. Died Dec. 16, 2006.

WALSH, ALAN L., business executive; b. Pasadena, Calif., Sept. 16, 1951; BS in Fin., Calif. State U., Long Beach, 1978; MBA in Fin., Almeda U., 2005. CEO Walsh Enterprises, Bus. Consultancy, from 1991. Home: Placentia, Calif. Deceased.

WALSH, ANDREW JOSEPH, management consultant executive; b. NYC, Jan. 24, 1930; s. Walter Joseph and Mary M. (McCarthy) W.; m. Janet Mary Flood, Nov. 24, 1956; children: Kathleen, Patricia, Jeanne, Thomas, Christopher, Robert, Elizabeth. BS in Mech. Engring., U. Notre Dame, 1951. Sales engr. Gen. Electric Co., Phila., 1954-62, planning mgr., 1962-64, sales mgr., 1964-67, Plainville, Conn., 1967-70, mktg. mgr. Ft. Wayne, Ind., 1970-74, gen. mgr., 1974-75, Gen. Electric Supply Co., Bridgeport, Conn., 1975-83; pres. Economy Electric Supply Co., Manchester, Conn., 1983-87, Andrew Walsh Assocs., Fairfield, Conn., from 1988. Bd. dirs. Northland Electric Supply Co., Mpls., Grand Light and Supply Co., New Haven, Conn.; speaker convs. in field. Contbr. articles to profl. jours. Pres. Forest Ridge Civic Assn., Ft. Wayne, 1972-74. Lt. (j.g.) USN, 1951-54, Atlantic. Recipient scholarship NAVAL ROTC, U. Notre Dame, 1947-51. Mem. Patterson Club (Fairfield, Conn.). Avocations: golf, travel, fin. planning. Home: New Smyrna Beach, Fla. Died Aug. 13, 2007.

WALSH, GERRY O'MALLEY, lawyer; b. Houston, Dec. 22, 1936; d. Frederick Harold and Blanche (O'Malley) W. BS, U. Houston, 1959; JD, South Tex. Coll. Law, 1966. Bar: Tex. 1966, U.S. Dist. Ct. (so. dist.) Tex. 1967, U.S. Dist. Ct. (we. dist.) Tex. 1976; cert. elem. tchr., Tex. Elem. tchr., Houston, 1959-65; instr. bus. law U. Houston, 1966-67; pvt. practice Houston, from 1966. Lectr. legal, jud. and civic orgns. Adviser, den mother Sam Houston coun. Boy Scouts Am.; mem. Mus. Fine Arts. Recipient den mother award Sam Houston coun. Boy Scouts Am. Mem. ABA, Houston Zool. Assn., Houston Archeol. Soc., Bus. and Profl. Women's Assn. (Woman of Yr. 1973), Am. Judicature Soc., Tex. Criminal Lawyers Assn., Harris County Criminal Lawyers Assn., Tex. Trial Lawyers Assn., State Bar Tex., Houston Bar Assn., U. Houston Alumni Assn., So. Tex. Coll. Law Alumni Assn., Nat. Criminal Def. Lawyers Assn., Zeta Tau Alpha (best mem. and rec. sec. 1958), Sigma Chi (award 1958). Died Dec. 23, 2006.

WALSH, SHIRLEY M., nurse consultant; b. Kingston, NY, May 9, 1927; d. Kenneth L. and Mary L. (Straley) Hotaling; m. George E. Walsh, June 29, 1959; children: Mary Quirk, Nathaniel. Grad. RN, Kingston Hosp. Sch. Nursing, 1947; BSN, Boston U., 1967, MSN, 1968. Sch. nursing curriculum coord. Framingham U. Hosp.; asst. dir. edn. Worcester (Mass.) Hahnemann Sch. Nursing; assoc. adminstr. nursing Moline (Ill.) Pub. Hosp.; exec. dir. nursing G. Pierce Wood Meml. Hosp., Arcadia, Fla.; RN cons. G. Price Wood Meml. Hosp., Arcadia, Fla. Mem. Fla. Orgn. Nurse Execs., Nat. League Nursing. Home: Port Charlotte, Fla. Died Dec. 13, 2006.

WALTERS, JOHN LINTON, electronics engineer, consultant; b. Washington, Mar. 8, 1924; s. Francis Marion Jr. and Roma (Crow) W.; m. Grace Elizabeth Piper, June 19, 1948; children: Richard Miller, Gretchen Elizabeth, Christopher Linton, John Michael, Kim Anne. BS, U.S. Naval Acad., 1944; SM, Harvard U., 1949; DrEng, Johns Hopkins U., 1959. Staff mem. Los Alamos (N.Mex.) Sci. Lab., 1949-52; rsch. assoc. Johns Hopkins Nat. U., Balt., 1952-59; assoc. elec. engr. Brookhaven Nat. Lab., Upton, N.Y., 1959-62; rsch. scientist Johns Hopkins U., Balt., 1962-70; electronics engr. Naval Rsch. Lab., Washington, from 1970. Asst. sci. advisor Comdr. 6th Fleet, Gaeta, Italy, 1978-79; lectr. dept. elec. engring. Johns Hopkins U., 1964-65. Lt. (j.g.) USN, 1944-47, PTO. Recipient commendation Dir. of Navy Labs., 1979. Mem. IEEE, Sigma Xi. Achievements include research on electronic countermeasures, refinements to measurement techniques used in particle accelerators, analysis of radar and jamming phenomena, measurement and analysis of anomalous propagation in atmosphere, problems in air traffic control in Navy aircraft carriers and amphibs. Home: Luthvle Timon, Md. Died Apr. 4, 2007.

WALTON, DEWITT TALMAGE, JR., dentist; b. Macon, Ga., May 25, 1937; s. DeWitt T. Sr. and Jimmie (Braswell) W.; m. Joan Robinson, June 11, 1960; children: Jimmie Walton Paschall, Gwen N., Gayle Walton Smith, Joy A. BS, Howard U., 1960, DDS, 1961. Pvt. practice, Macon, from 1963. Chmn. dental adv. com. Ga. Dept. Med. Assistance; dental svcs. adv. com. Dept. Physical Health, Ga. Dept. Human Resources; adv. bd. dirs. Wachovia Bank, Macon-Warner Robins area; bd. dirs. The Ga. Dept. Cmty. Affairs. Fin. chmn. Boy Scouts Am., Piedmont/Creek Dist., 1978-80, exec. bd., 1978-82, v.p. exec. com., 1983-84; apptd. Bibb County Bd. Edn., 1969-73; vice chmn. Macon-Bibb County Transit Authority, 1981-87; dir. exec. com. Devel. Corp. Mid. Ga., 1984-91; sec.-treas. Urban Devel. Authority, Macon-Bibb County, 1984-87; trustee Macon Heritage Found., 1983-87; bd. dirs. Ctrl. Ga. Speech and Hearing Ctr., 1984-87, Boys' Club Macon, Inc., 1986, 87, 88, The Grand Opera House, 1988, 89, 90, Booker T. Washington Ctr., 1993, Pub. Edn. Found., 1995—, Douglass Theater, 1995—; mem. oversight com. Minority Bus. Assistance Program, 1984-91; active Bibb County Commn. on Excellence in Edn., 1984; trustee United Way Macon-Bibb County, 1985, 86, 87; deacon, elder, treas. Washington Ave. Presbyn. Ch.; active Downtown Coun., Coalition for Polit. Awareness, So. Poverty Law Ctr., NAACP; mem. "Cmty. Hero"-torchbearer Olympic Torch Relay for 1996 Olympic games, Atlanta; advisory bd. Wachovia Bank, Macon, Warner-Robins, 1999—; apptd. bd. dirs. Ga. Dept. Cmty. Affairs, 1999—, Cmty. Found. Ctrl. Ga., 2001—. With U.S. Army, 1961-63. Recipient Appreciation cert. State Bar Ga., Citizenship award Bibb County Voter's Registration League, Inc., 1977, Cmty. Svc. award NAACP, 1982, Cmty. Svc. award Alpha Kappa Alpha, 1982, Meritorious Svc. award United Negro Coll. Fund, 1983, Comml. Bldg. of Yr. award Macon Heritage Found., 1983, Faithful Svc. award Bibb County Dept. Family and Children's Svcs., 1983-90, Cmty. Svc. Lifetime Achievement award Boys' and Girls' Clubs, 2002, citation Macon-Bibb County Beautification Clean Cmty. Comm., 1983-84, Appreciation cert. Macon-Bibb County Econ. Opportunity Coun., 1984, Proclamation Mayor George Israel Svc. on Macon-Bibb County Transit Authority, 1984, Outstanding Alumni award Coll. Dentistry Howard U., 1985, Outstanding Svc. award Macon-Bibb County Urban Devel. Authority, 1987, Outstanding Svc. award Macon-Bibb County Transit Authority, 1987, Appreciation cert. Close-Up Found., 1988, Cmty. Svc. award United Way Macon-Bibb County, 1988, Disting. Svc. cert. Devel. Corp. Mid. Ga., 1990, Continuous Corp. Support award Entrepreneurship and Black Youth Program U. Ga., 1990, Appreciation cert. Keep Macon-Bibb Beautiful Commn. and Cherry Blossom Festival, 1990, Appreciation cert. City of Macon, 2002, Bus. of Yr. award After Five Profl. Networking Assn., 2005; named Olympic Torchbearer, 1996. Fellow Acad. Gen. Dentistry (Membership award 1983-85), Acad. Dentistry Internat., Am. Coll. Dentists, Ga. Dental Assn. (hon., Appreciation cert.1988), Internat. Coll. Dentists, Pierre Fauchard Acad.; mem. AAAS, ADA (alt. del. Ga. 1986-91, life mem.), Am. Analgesic Soc., Am. Endodontic Soc., Am. Fund Dental Health, Am. Sch. Health Assn., Am. Soc. Dentistry for Children, Nat. Dental Assn. (Life Membership award 2000), Nat. Rehab. Assn., Ga. Dental Soc. (pres., 1978, Citizenhip award 1979-80, Humanitarian award 1981-82, James E. Carter Jr. award 1993), North Ga. Dental Soc. (pres. 1978-79), Cen. Dist. Dental Soc. (peer rev. com., legis. com., alt. del. to Ga. Dental Assn. 1982, 83, 84, del. 1984, 85, 86, 87), Bibb County Dental Soc. (charter), Acad. Continuing Edn., Fed. Dentaire Internat. (life), So. Poverty Law Ctr. (life, Outstanding Svc. award 1984, Recognition Outstanding Svc. cert. 1990), Am. Dental Assn. (life), Sixth Rong US olympic Com. (charter).Pres'. Club Howard U. (life), Am. Running and Fitness Assn. (life), Greater Macon C. of C. (bd. dirs. 1995-97), Macon Tracks, Sigma Pi Phi, Omega Psi Phi (life), Presbyterian. Achievements include City of Macon, GA declaring February 25 Dr. DeWitt T Walton, Jr. Day (2005); Share-A-Smile Scholarship renamed Dr. DeWitt T. Walton, Jr. Share-A-Smile Scholarship (2005). Avocations: walking, jogging, aerobics, coin collecting/numismatics, real estate. Home: Macon, Ga. Died Jan. 10, 2007.

WALTON, RICHMOND LEE, retired pediatrician; b. Chgo., July 15, 1923; s. William Carlisle and Irma Etta (Neely) W.; m. Barbara Clarke, Oct. 7, 1950; children: Richmond, Joan, James, Nancy, Robert. BA, Drew U., 1944; MD, Harvard U., 1949. Intern R.I. Hosp., Providence, 1949-51; resident SUNY, Syracuse, 1951-53, instr., 1953-54, acting asst. dean, 1953-54; pvt. practice pediatrics Stratford, Conn., 1957-58; maternal and child health pediatrician Ky. State Health Dept., Louisville, 1958-59; pediatrician Davis Clinic, Marion, Ind., 1960-69; pvt. practice pediatrics Marion, 1969-92. Capt. USAF, 1954-56. Avocations: bicycling, photography, music. Home: Marion, Ind. Died Feb. 4, 2007.

WAMBSGANSS, JACOB ROY, accounting educator, small business consultant; b. Hillsboro, Kans., Nov. 9, 1950; s. Eldor Jacob and Betty Maxine (Wait) W.; m. Dona Kay Koby, May 22, 1971; children: Warren Jacob, Jay Roy. BA in History, Wichita State U., 1973; Emporia State U., Emporia State U., Kans., 1981; PhD in Bus. and Acctg., U. Nebr., 1985. CPA, N.D.; cert. govt. fin. mgr. Owner Wagon Wheel Restaurant, Strong City, Kans., 1975-76; mgmt. instr. Minot (N.D.) State U., 1981-83; asst. prof. U. S.D., Vermillion, 1985-88; assoc. prof. Emporia (Kans.) State U., 1988-92; prof. U. N.D., Grand Forks, from 1992. Contbr. articles to profl. jours. Past treas. coun. Pleasant Valley Ch., 1986-88; mem., bell choir dir. Walle Luth. Ch., treas., Greater Grand Forks Sr. Citizens Ctr., Grand Forks Rural Luth. Parish. Grantee Bush Found., 1987; recipient Rsch. award Assn. Govt. Accts., 1990. Mem. Inst. Mgmt. Accts., Am. Acctg. Assn., N.D. Soc. CPAs, Decision Sci. Inst., Midwest Acctg. Soc. (treas. 1991-94, program chair/pres.-elect 1995-96, pres. 1996-97), Assn. Govt. Accts., Midwest Bus. Adminstrn. Assn. (exec. bd. 1996-97). Republican. Lutheran. Avocations: reading, walking, camping, gardening. Home: Fordville, ND. Died Feb. 28, 2007.

WANG, BOARDMAN CHENG, anesthesiology research educator; b. Hwangsien, Shantung, China, Sept. 15, 1913; came to U.S., 1946; s. Ki-Seng and Yu-jung (Chao) W.; m. Mary Dah-Gin Hung, Oct. 11, 1947; children: Mary Hungen, Grace Mu-en, John Ming-en, Philip Sung-en. MD, Cheeloo U., China, 1941. Diplomate Am. Bd. Anesthesiology. Rotating intern Univ. Hosp., Chengtu, China, 1940-41, resident in surgery, 1941-46; resident in anesthesia Bellevue Hosp., NYC, 1946-48; asst. attending anesthesiologist Bellevue Hosp. Ctr., 1956-57, assoc. vis. anesthesiologist, 1967-68, vis. anesthesiologist, 1968-70; asst. prof. clin. anesthesia NYU Sch. Medicine, 1955-56, assoc. prof., 1956-70, clin. prof., from 1971. Asst. attending anesthesiologist Univ. Hosp., N.Y.C., 1950-56, assoc. attending, 1956-65, attending, 1965—; asst. attending Gouverneur Hosp., N.Y.C., 1954-56; lectr., presenter in field. Contbr. articles and abstracts to med. jours. Fellow Am. Coll. Anesthesiologists; mem. AMA, Am. Soc. Anesthesiologists, Am. Soc. Regional Anesthesia, Internat. Anesthesia Rsch. Soc., N.Y. State Med. Soc., N.Y. State Soc. Anesthesiologists, N.Y. County Med. Soc. Home: New York, NY. Died Mar. 28, 2007.

WANZER, ROBERT FRANCIS, retired basketball player; b. NYC, June 4, 1921; m. Nina Wanzer (dec. 2005); children: Mary, Beth, Bobby. Student, Seton Hall. With Rochester Royals, 1947-57, player, coach, 1955—57, coach Cin., 1957-58. With U.S. Marines. Named to Basketball Hall of Fame, 1987. Achievements include All-City selection on two Ben Franklin (N.Y.) H.S. state championship teams, 1940, 41; All-Am., Seton Hall, 1947, All-Time team, number retired Seton Hall; mem. Championship Team, NBA, 1951; All-NBA Second Team selection; five-time All-Star Team selection. Died Jan. 23, 2016.

WARD, RICHARD HURLEY, education educator, writer; b. NYC, Sept. 2, 1939; s. Hurley and Anna C. (Mittasch) W.; children from a previous marriage: Jeanne M., Jonathan B.; m. Michelle Pierczynski, June 15, 1987; 1 child: Michelle Sophia. BS, John Jay Coll., CUNY, 1968; M in Criminology, U. Calif., Berkeley, 1969, D in Criminology, 1971. Detective NYC Police Dept., 1962—70; coord. student activities John Jay Coll., NYC, 1970—71, dean students, 1971—75, v.p., 1975—77, vice chancellor, 1977—93; assoc. chancellor and prof. internat. criminology U. Ill., Chgo., 1993—98; exec. dir. Office Internat. Criminal Justice, 1985—99; exec. v.p. MBF Edn. Group, Malaysia, 1996—97; dean Coll. Criminal Justice, Sam Houston State U., Huntsville, Tex., 1999—2006, assoc. v.p. rsch. and spl. programs, 2006—08; dean Henry C. Lee Coll. Criminal Justice Forensic Scis., U. New Haven, Conn., from 2008. Vis. prof. Zagazig U., Egypt, Egyptian Police Acad., 1986, East China Inst. Politics and Law, Shanghai, 1990-91; lectr., various confs. in China, Egypt, Russia, Italy, Eng., Peru, Germany, Saudi Arabia, Finland, Taiwan, Vietnam, Turkey, Korea, United Arab Emirates and U.S., 1983—. Author: (with others) Police Robbery Control Manual, 1975; Introduction to Criminal Investigation, 1975, (with Robert McCormack) An Anti-Corruption Manual for Administrators in Law Enforcement; Quest for Quality, 1984; gen. editor Foundations of Criminal Justice, 46 vols., 1972-75; editor: (with Austin Fowler) Police and Law Enforcement, Vol. I, 1972; Police and Law Enforcement, Vol. II, 1975; (with Harold Smith) International Terrorism: The Domestic Response, 1982, International Terrorism: Operational Issues, 1988; co-author: (with James Osterburg) Criminal Investigation: A Method for Reconstructing the Past, 1992, 5th edit., 2007, (with K. Kiernan and D. Mabrey) Introduction to Homeland Security, 2006. Mem. Mayor of Chgo.'s Blue Ribbon Pannel on Police Promotion; varsity baseball coach U. Ill., Chgo., 1980-82, John Jay Coll. Criminal Justice, CUNY, 1971-72; chief investigator Mayor's Commn. Police Integrity, 1998; mem. Houston Crime Lab. Com., 2005. Cpl. USMC, 1957-61. Recipient Leonard Reisman award John Jay Coll. Criminal Justice, 1968, Alumni Achievement award, 1978, Richard McGee award U. Calif., Berkeley Sch. Criminology, 1971, Friendship medal Peoples Republic of China, 1994, Hans Mattick award Ill. Acad. Criminology, 1999; Justice Dept. fellow U. Calif., Berkeley, 1971. Mem. ASPA, Acad. Criminal Justice Scis. (pres. 1977-78, Founder's award 1985), Internat. Assn. Chiefs of Police (chmn. edn. and tng. sect. 1974-75), Sigma Delta Chi. Died Feb. 17, 2015.

WARDELL, LYDIA WILHELM, writer; b. St. Johns, Ariz., Aug. 13, 1936; m. David Joseph Wardell. Feature writer Portland Oregonian, 1979—81; distbr. Bamix, Germany, 1981—83; fin. cons. Portland, 1983—84; rschr. Sontag Annis & Assocs., Rockville, Md., 1984—86; children's author Vienna, Va., from 1986. Home: Vienna, Va. Died June 27, 2007.

WARREN, GERALD LEE, retired newspaper editor; b. Hastings, Nebr., Aug. 17, 1930; s. Hie Elias and Linnie (Williamson) W.; m. Euphemia Florence Brownell, Nov. 20, 1965 (div.); children: Gerald Benjamin, Euphemia Brownell; m. Viviane M. Pratt, Apr. 27, 1986. AB, U. Nebr., 1952; M in Theology, Virginia Theological Seminary, 2004. Reporter Lincoln Star, Nebr., 1951-52; reporter, asst. city editor San Diego Union, 1956-61, city editor, 1963-68, asst. mng. editor, 1968-69, editor, 1975-92; bus. rep. Copley News Service, 1961-63; editor San Diego Union-Tribune, 1992-95; ret., editor at large, 1995 (ret.); dep. press sec. to President Gerald Ford, 1974-75. Mem. bd. Pacific coun. internat. policy Eureka Found., Freedoms Found. Lt. (j.g.) USNR, 1952-56.; lay reader Mem. Am. Soc. Newspaper Editors, Coun. Fgn. Rels., Sigma Delta Chi, Sigma Nu Republican. Episcopalian. Died Mar. 20, 2015.

WARREN, TONY EDWIN, internist; b. Macon, Ga., Nov. 13, 1952; s. Willie B. Warren and Lucy M. (Mullis) Woodall; m. Nell Hester Reed, Apr. 2, 1977; children: Alison S., Spencer. MD, Emory U., 1977. Diplomate in pulmonary diseases and critical care Am. Bd. Internal Medicine. Intern Naval Hosp., San Diego, 1977-78, resident, 1978-80, fellow, 1980-82, staff physician, 1982-84; asst. prof. medicine Ebert Sch. of Medicine, Bethesda, Md., 1985-86; pvt. practice physician Harbin Clinic, Rome, Ga., from 1986. Chmn. dept. medicine Redmond Regional Med. Ctr., Rome, 1988-90, pres. med. staff, 1992-93. Comdr. USNR, 1977-86. Fellow Am. Coll. Chest Physicians; mem. ACP, AMA, Am. Thoracic Soc. Home: Rome, Ga. Died June 8, 2007.

WARSINSKE, NORMAN GEORGE, interior designer, sculptor; b. Wichita, Kans., Mar. 4, 1929; s. Norman and Gladys Elmira (Thompson) W.; m. Jackye Lagen, Dec. 20, 1970 (dec. Apr. 1980); children: Marc, Debbie, Brian; m. Sheila Gay Brockway, Mar. 17, 1984; 1 child, Erica. BA in Journalism, U. Mont., 1949; BA in Art, U. Wash., 1959; postgrad., Kunstwerk Sch., Darmstadt, Germany, 1951. Photographer Western Livestock Reporter, Billings, Mont., 1950-55; interior designer, co-owner Miller-Pollard, Seattle, 1959-84; pvt. practice Bellevue, Wash., from 1984. Pres. N.W. Craft Ctr., Seattle, 1965-70, Seattle Art Commn., 1970. Staff sgt. USAF, 1951-54. Recipient 1st pl. sculpture award Bellevue Art Festival, 1960; named Best all Catagories, Henry Art Gallery, 1966. Avocation: gondolier. Home: Bellevue, Wash. Died July 25, 2007.

WASDEN, WINIFRED SAWAYA, English language educator, writer; b. Kemmerer, Wyo., Apr. 15, 1938; d. George Sabeh and Letta Louise (Gerken) Sawaya; m. John Frederic Wasden, Dec. 20, 1960; children: Frederic Keith, Carol Elizabeth. BA with honors, U. Wyo., 1960, MA, 1961. Emergency instr. U. Wyo., Laramie, 1960-61; tchr. English Worland (Wyo.) H.S., 1963; instr. NW C.C., Powell, Wyo., 1964-91, prof., from 1991, English coord., 1990-93. Chair humanities NW C.C., Wyo., 1998—. Author: (oral history) Modern Pioneers, 1998; contbr. articles to profl. jours.; author numerous poems. Mem. Powell Bd. Adjustments, 1974-86; chmn., bd. dirs. Civic Orch. and Chorus, Powell, 1981-88; mem. Wyo. Coun. for the Humanities, 1978-79, coord. Big Horn Basin Project, 1980-85. Mem. Wyo. Oral History and Folklore Assn. (v.p. 1984-85, bd. dirs. 1985-86), Wyo. Assn. Tchrs. English, N.W. Community Coll. Faculty Assn. (pres. 1977-78), AAAUW, Oral History Assn., Am. Folklore Soc., Northwest Oral History Assn., Delta Kappa Gamma (pres. Powell chpt. 1978-80), Phi Rho Pi (hon.). Republican. Roman Catholic. Avocations: travel, reading. Home: Powell, Wyo. Died Feb. 4, 2007.

WASLEY, RICHARD JUNIOR, engineer; b. Oakland, Calif., June 24, 1931; s. Richard John Wasley and Rosaline Sonora (Howell) Previati; m. Margery Louise Ziniker, Oct. 22, 1960; children: Richard, Anne, Pamela. BS, U. Calif., Berkeley, 1954; MS, Stanford U., 1958, PhD, 1961. Registered profl. engr., Calif. Div. leader Lawrence Livermore Nat. Lab., Livermore, Calif., 1972-85, research engr., from 1985. Author: Stress Wave Propagation, 1973; contbr. articles to profl. jours.; patentee in field. Served with AUS, 1953-55. Recipient A. Noble Prize Five Profl. Engring. Orgns., 1961. Fellow ASCE; mem. ASME, Valley Trail Riders (pres. 1984-85). Republican. Lutheran. Avocations: camping, hiking, trail riding. Home: Livermore, Calif. Died Apr. 6, 2007.

WASZKIEWICZ, JOHN CHESTER, III, manufacturing executive; b. Utica, NY, Aug. 24, 1953; s. John Chester Jr. and Joan E. (Potocki) W.; m. Barbara Jane Lawrence, May 1, 1976; children: Carolyn Anne, Katherine Mary, John Chester IV. Salesman Lifesake div. Faster-Form Corp., New Hartford, N.Y., 1975-76; sales mgr. Faster-Form Corp., New Hartford, N.Y., 1976-77, v.p. mktg., 1977-78, pres., from 1978. Mem. Greater Utica Area Small Bus. council. Mem. Wholesale Florist and Flower Suppliers Am., Florists Transworld Delivery (assoc., mem. com.), Eastern Giftware Mfrs. Assn., New Hartford C. of C., Telefolora Assn. (assoc.), Omega Delta Epsilon. Clubs: Lago Mar Beach, Tower (Ft. Lauderdale, Fla.), Atrium (N.Y.C.), Sadaquada Country, Young Presidents (hon.). Lodges: Rotary (Pual Harris fellow). Republican. Roman Catholic. Avocations: boating, cross country, skiing, soccer. Home: New Hartford, NY. Died Oct. 19, 2007.

WATANABE, KYOICHI A(LOYSIUS), pharmacology educator, chemist; b. Amagasaki, Hyogo, Japan, Feb. 28, 1935; s. Yujiro John and Yoshiko Francisca (Hashimoto) W.; m. Krystyna Lesiak; children: Kanna, Kay, Kenneth, Kim, Kelly, Katherine. BA, Hokkaido U., 1958, PhD, 1963. Lectr. Sophia U., Tokyo, 1963; rsch. assoc. Sloan-Kettering Inst., NYC, 1963—66, assoc., 1968—72, assoc. mem., 1972—81, mem., 1981—95; rsch. fellow U. Alta., Edmonton, Canada, 1966—68; assoc. prof. Cornell U., Grad. Sch. Med. Scis., NYC, 1972—81, prof. pharmacology, 1981—98; dir. organic chemistry Codon Pharm., Inc., Gaithersburg, Md., 1996—98; v.p. R&D Pharmasset Inc., Tucker, Ga., 1998—2003; vis. prof. U. Minn., from 2003. Study sect. NIH, Washington, 1981-84. Recipient Szalecki medal, Wojzkowa Akademia Medyczna, 1989, Marie Sklodowka Curie medal, Polish Chem. Soc., 1993, František Šorm Meml. award, Czech Acad. Scis., 2002. Mem. Polish Chem. Soc. (hon.), Russian Acad. Sci. (bd. sci. cons. Engelhardt Inst. Molecular Biology 1994-97), Am. Chem. Soc. (emeritas), Polish Am. Health Assn. Achievements include rsch. in total synthesis of nucleoside antibiotics, novel heterocycle ring transformation, C-nucleoside chemistry, antiviral and anticancer nucleosides, intercalating agents, modified oligonucleotides, triplex DNA for gene repair, inventor of clofaradine clinically used for treatment of children with recurrent leukemia. Home: Stone Mountain, Ga. Died Apr. 7, 2015.

WATANABE, YOSHIO, cardiologist; b. Tokyo, Nov. 8, 1925; s. Yoshisada and Setsuko (Shiga) W.; m. Keiko Ohta, Nov. 18, 1958; children: Mari, Yuri. MD, Keio Gijuku U., 1951, DMS, 1960. Asst. instr. medicine Keio U. Hosp., Tokyo, 1952-60; assoc. prof. medicine, physiology and biophysics Hahnemann Med. Coll., Phila., 1961-72; prof. medicine, dir. cardiovascular inst. Fujita Health U., Toyoake, Japan, 1972-95; hosp. dir. Toyota Regional Med. Ctr., Japan, 1995—99; cons. cardiologist Chiba Tokushukai Hosp., Funabashi, Japan, 1999-2000, Shonan Kamakura Gen. Hosp., Kamakura, Japan, 2001—03, Nagoya Tokushukai Gen. Hosp., Kasugai, Japan, from 2004. Scientific chmn. 5th Internat. Symposium Cardiac Pacing, Tokyo, 1976. Author: Cardiac Arrhythmias, Electrophysiologic Basis for Clinical Interpretation, 1977, Beyond Brain Death, 2000; co-author: International Textbook of Cardiology, 1986, Cardiac Electrophysiology, From Cell to Bedside, 1990; editor: Cardiac Pacing, 1977, Heart and Vessels, 1985-99. Recipient Kato Meml. prize Physiology and Medicine Kato Meml. Found., Tokyo, 1981. Fellow Am. Coll. Cardiology (co-dir. annual program on cardiac arrhythmias 1965-99), Heart Rhythm Soc. (mem. health policy com. 1997-2000); mem. Japanese Soc. Electrocardiology (hon., pres. 1989-90), Brit. Cardiovasc. Soc., Portuguese Soc. Cardiology (hon. mem.), Japanese Circulation Soc. (extraordinary mem.), Japanese Cardiac Arrhythmia Soc. (hon. mem.), Coun. Clin. Cardiology, Am. Heart Assn. (internat. fellow). Buddhist. Avocations: cello, astronomy, hiking. Home: Saint Louis, Mo. Died Oct. 19, 2014.

WATNE, DONALD ARTHUR, retired accountant, educator; b. Gt. Falls, Mont., Jan. 18, 1939; BA with high honors, U. Mont., 1960, MA, 1961; PhD, U. Calif., Berkeley, 1977. CPA, Oreg. Acct. Piquet & Minihan, Eugene, Oreg., 1961-65; mgr. capital investment analysis Weyerhaeuser Co., Tacoma, 1965-68; mktg. rep. IBM Corp., Portland, Oreg., 1968-70; dir. EDP Ctr. in Concejo Mcpl., Barquisimeto, Venezuela, 1971-72; prof. acctg. Portland State U., 1976-2001, prof. emeritus, from 2001. Vis. prof. Xiamen (Fujian, People's Rep. China), 1985-86, U. Otago, Dunedin, New Zealand, 1986, U. Newcastle, Australia, 1986; cons. in field; acctg. qualifications com. Oregon State Bd. Acctg., 1989-98, CPE com., 1998-2001 Author: (with Peter B.B. Turney) Auditing EDP Systems, 2d edit. 1990; contbr. chpts. to books, articles to profl. jours. Del. to Soviet Union citizen amb. program People to People Internat., 1990; active Tng. the Trainers Program, Vilnius, Lithuania, 1993; trustee, treas. First Unitarian Ch. of Portland, 2002-08; mem. bd. stewards First Unitarian Ch. of Portland Found., 2002-07, treas., 2004-07, mem., Audit Ctte bd. dirs., OCHIN, Portland, 2007-13. Mem.: AICPA, Am. Radio Relay League, Oreg. Soc. CPAs, Mensa, Mazamas Mountain Climbing Club. Democrat. Unitarian Universalist. Home: Portland, Oreg. Died Feb. 3, 2015.

WATSEY, STEPHEN, utility company executive; b. Metuchen, NJ, May 1, 1929; s. Stephen and Sophie (Sidorovich) W.; m. Mary Lou Thomson, June 5, 1951 (div. Apr. 1971); children: Stephen T., Kenneth S., Brenda A.; m. Marilyn Storey, Mar. 16, 1974. BS in Engring., U.S. Mil. Acad., 1951. Engr. Fla. Power & Light Co., Miami, 1955-58; sales engr., v.p. Carter-Watsey & Assocs. Inc., Tampa, 1958-76; pres. SW Enterprises, Tampa, 1975-77; mgr. power plant inventory control Fla. Power Corp., St. Petersburg, 1977-79, mgr. power plant stores, 1979-80, mgr. power plant materials, 1980-84, mgr. transmission and distbn. materials, 1984-85, dir. purchasing and stores, 1985-89; v.p. purchasing and stores, from 1989. Mem. Nat. Assn. Purchasing Mgmt. (bd. dirs. Fla. Gulf Coast chpt. 1984—, exec. com. utility purchasing mgmt. group), Edison Elec. Inst. (materials mgmt. and procurement com. 1985—, vice chmn. 1987, chmn. 1988-89, exec. com. 1989). Avocations: flying, golf, walking. Died Aug. 4, 2007.

WATSON, BARBARA K., publishing executive; b. Iowa Falls, Iowa, May 2, 1943; d. Kenneth Scott and Ruth Frances (Beed) Titus; m. Eddie L. Watson, Dec. 27, 1962 (div. Mar. 1984); children: John Lee, Donna Rae. Student, Amarillo Coll., 1960-62, Tex. Women's U., 1962-63. Sec. Phillips Petroleum Co., Amarillo, Tex., 1960-62; exec. sec. Am. Airmotive, Miami, Fla., 1963-64; sec. U.S. Army, Ft. Bragg, N.C., 1965-66, Ft. Sill, Okla., 1967; office mgr. Travel & Meeting Planners, Daytona Beach, Fla., 1971-72; owner, mgr. Creative Crafts, Enterprise, Ala., 1974-79; artist, pub. The Brushworks, Ontario, Calif., from 1980. Judge Orange County (Calif.) Fair, 1985, 86, 87, 88, 89; nationwide art seminar instr., 1979—; product cons. Binney and Smith, Easton, Pa., 1985—, Blair Art Products, Twinsburg, Ohio, 1986-87. Artist, publ. (instrn. book) A Bit of Barb, Vol. I, 1980, Vol. II, 1982, The Color Book, 1986, Our World of Angels, Vol. I, 1986, Vol. II, 1987, Vol. III, 1989, (book) It's Really Acrylic, vol. II, 1988; pub. Birds and Beasts Vol. I, 1983, Vol. II, 1984; contbr. articles to profl. jours. Leader Girl Scouts Am., Enterprise, Ala., 1973-74. Served with USNR, 1960-64. Recipient 2d Place award Coffee County Art Show, Elba, Ala., 1980, 1st Place award Piney Woods Art Festival, Enterprise, 1981. Mem. Nat. Soc. of Tole and Decorative Painters (judge cert. program, 1983, 84, 86, 88, edn. com. 1982-83, founder Barefoot Tolers chpt., 1978, recipient cert. Master Decorative Artist award 1982). Clubs: Luncheon Pilot (pres. 1977-78) (Enterprise). Republican. Avocations: bowling, swimming, reading, archaeology, woodworking. Home: Moreno Valley, Calif. Died Aug. 27, 2007.

WATSON, KERR FRANCIS, management educator; b. Winston-Salem, Jan. 31, 1944; s. Kerr Francis and Mary Lee (Nalley) W.; m. Atalie Carol Marvin, July 31, 1965 (div. 1973); 1 child, David William; m. Carolyn Kay Rambo, July 23, 1974; children: Rebecca Marie, Benjamin Lee. BS in Chemistry, Math., Greensboro Coll., NC, 1967; MBA in Mgmt., East Tenn. State U., 1977; PhD in Bus. Adminstrn., U. Tenn., 1990. Chemist Tenn. Eastman Co., Kingsport, 1967-71; chemist/mgr. Holliston Mills, Kingsport, 1971-74;

chemist Great Lakes Rsch. Corp., Elizabethton, Tenn., 1974-77; economist First Tenn.-Va. Devel. Dist., Johnson City, Tenn., 1977-81; mgr. Johnson City Chem. Co., 1981-82; rsch. and devel. mgr. Strahan Ink Co., Kingsport, Tenn., 1982-83; rsch. and teaching asst. U. Tenn., Knoxville, 1983-85; asst. prof. Western Carolina U., Cullowhee, 1986-88; assoc. prof. mgmt. Tusculum Coll., Greenville, Tenn., 1988-89, Va. Intermont Coll., Bristol, from 1989, faculty sec., 1991-92. Mem. adj. faculty East Tenn. State U., 1983-90, Tusculum Coll., 1984; cons. in field. Contbr. articles to profl. jours. Chmn. long-range planning, head usher Cherokee Meth. Ch., Johnson City, 1989-91; mem. long-range planning com. Va. Intermont Coll., 1991—, mem. orgnl. mgmt. steering com., 1989-92. Recipient Chemistry Achievement award, Greensboro Coll., 1967, Rsch. award, N.C. Acad. Sci., 1965. Mem. Acad. Mgmt., So. Mgmt. Assn., N.Am. Case Rsch. Assn., Am. Mgmt. Assn., Assn. Coll. Bus. Schs. and Programs (program chmn. 1992, sec.-treas. 1993 region II), Greenwood Ruritan (past pres., zone gov.), Beta Gamma Sigma. Methodist. Avocations: water-skiing, skiing, golf. Home: Jonesborough, Tenn. Died Dec. 8, 2006.

WATT, JOHN REID, retired mechanical engineering educator; b. Seattle, Nov. 15, 1914; s. Paul Harris and Roberta Gertrude (Frye) W.; m. Sarah Elizabeth Craven, Oct. 25, 1939 (dec. Jan. 1961); children: John David, Madeleine Megan Watt, Louisa Catherine Kellough (dec.); m. Lillian A. Mann, May 4, 1962. BSME, U. Wash., 1937, MA in Econs., 1942, ME, 1950; MS in Mech. Engring., U. Tex., 1954, PhD in Mech. Engring., 1960; postgrad., Harvard U., 1937-39. Registered profl. engr., Tex. Instr. econs. U. Tex., Austin, 1941-43, instr. mech. engring., 1943-46, asst. prof., 1948-56, assoc. prof., 1956-71; rsch. engr. C.W. Murchison Enterprises, Dallas, 1946-48; vis. prof. indsl. engring. Ga. Inst. Tech., Atlanta, 1971-72, prof. health systems, 1973-75; ret., 1975; chmn. EFC Assocs., Greensboro, N.C., 1977-82; owner Energy Conservation Labs., Inc., Atlanta, 1989-93. Pres. Watt Properties Co., Inc., Atlanta, 1982-93; dir. rsch. in evaporative air cooling U.S. Naval Civil Engring. Rsch. and Evaluation Lab., Port Hueneme, Calif., 1952-53; dir. rsch. Nat. Assn. Home Builders and Nat. Warm Air Assn., Austin, 1954-56. Author: Evaporative Air Conditioning, 1963, Introduction to Typical U.S. General Hospital, 1968, rev. edit., 1975, Evaporative Air Conditioning Handbook, 1986, rev. edit., 1997, Pioneering From Covered Wagons Onward, 1995, also articles, tech. films, TV tapes; patentee for Polar Chips automatic icemaker, others. Fellow ASHRAE (chpt. newsletter editor 1958-59, evaporative cooling com. 1953-60, 84-93, rsch. award 1958); mem. ASME (life), Indsl. Engring. Club (founding pres. Austin, now chpt. Am. Inst. Indsl. Engrs.), Sigma Xi, Pi Tau Sigma. Avocations: writing, research, gardening. Died Apr. 1, 2007.

WATT, NORMAN RAMSAY, chemistry educator, researcher; b. Providence, Oct. 29, 1928; s. Albert Byron and Marie Louise (Turcotte) W. ScB, Brown U., 1951; PhD, U. Conn., 1967. Teaching fellow NYU, NYC, 1951-54; teaching asst. U. Conn., Storrs, 1954-55, asst. instr., 1955-59, instr., 1960-61, 64-67, asst. prof., 1967-82; instr. Danbury (Conn.) State Coll., 1959-60. Home: Cranston, RI. Died Jan. 17, 2007.

WATTENBERG, BEN J. (JOSEPH BEN ZION WATTENBERG), author, commentator; b. NYC, Aug. 26, 1933; s. Judah and Rachel (Gutman) W.; m. Marna Hade, June 24, 1956 (div. Feb. 1981, dec. 1997); children: Ruth, Daniel, Sarah.; m. Diane Abelman, July 10, 1983; 1 child, Rachel BA, Hobart Coll., 1955; LL.D. (hon.), Hobart and William Smith Colls., 1975. Asst. to President Johnson, Washington, 1966-68; aide to Vice President Hubert Humphrey, Mpls., 1970; campaign adviser Senator Henry Jackson, 1972, 76; mem. presdl. adv. bd. on ambassadorial appointments, 1977-80. Eminent scholar, prof.-at-large Mary Washington Coll., 1973-74; disting. vis. prof. U.S. Internat. U., 1978, 79; pub. mem. conf. on human rights U.S. Del. to Madrid, 1980; vice chmn. Bd. Internat. Broadcasting, 1981 and Radio Free Europe/Radio Liberty, Democracy Program, 1982-83; mem. Research Council, Ctr. Strategic and Internat. Studies, 1982—2015; co-founder, chmn. Coalition for a Democratic Majority, 1972—2015. dirs. Reading Is Fundamental; trustee Hudson Inst., 1976—2015; sr. fellow American Enterprise Inst., 1977—2015; mem. U.S. del. UN Population Conf., Mexico City, 1984, pres.'s election observer del., The Philippines, 1986; mem. Commn. U.S. Internat. Broadcasting, Asia, 1990, 91 Host, In Search of Real America, Public Broadcasting Service, 1977-78, Ben Wattenberg's 1980, Public Broadcasting Service, 1980, The Grandchild Gap, America's Number One, What Next?, The Stockholder Society, A Third Choice, Heaven on Earth: The Rise and Fall of Socialism, 2005, The Democrats, The First Measured Century; prodr., host: Ben Wattenberg At Large, PBS, 1981, Think Tank with Ben Wattenberg, 1994-2010; syndicated columnist: United Features, Newspaper Enterprise Assn., 1981-2015; commentator: CBS Spectrum radio broadcast, 1981; author: (with R. Scammon) This U.S.A, 1965, The Real Majority: An Extraordinary Examination of the American Electorate, 1970; The Real America: A Suprising Examination of the State of the Union, 1974, (with Ervin Duggan) Against All Enemies, 1977, (with Richard Whalen) The Wealth Weapon, 1980, The Good News is the Bad News is Wrong, 1984, The Birth Dearth, 1987, The First Universal Nation, 1991, Values Matter Most, 1995, (with Theodore Caplow and Louis Hicks) The First Measured Century: An Illustrated Guide to Trends in America, 1900-2000, 2000, Fewer: How the New Demography of Depopulation Will Shape Our Future, 2004,(memoir) Fighting Words: A Tale of How Liberals Created Neo-Conservatism, 2008; co-editor: Public Opinion Mag., 1977-89, The First Universal Nation, 1990, Values Matter Most, 1995; contbg. editor U.S. News and World Report, 1989-2015; contbr. USA Today, 1997-2015; contbr. articles to mags. Served with USAF, 1956-58. Mem. Council Fgn. Relations Democrat. Jewish. Home: Washington, DC. Died June 28, 2015.

WATTS, ROSS WAKEFIELD, retired school principal, mayor; b. Harrisburg, Pa., Dec. 14, 1926; s. Ralph Ray Sr. and Laura Mae (Wakefield) W.; m. Mildred E. Urich, Jan. 29, 1949; children: Gordon W., Lori L. BS, Pa. State U., 1949, MEd, 1954. Cert. vocat. agr. and gen. sci. tchr., secondary sch. prin., supt. Tchr. vocat. agr. Jersey Shore (Pa.) Area H.S., 1949-59; asst. jr. H.S. prin. Spring Ford Jr. H.S., Royersford, Pa., 1959-60; prin. Palmyra (Pa.) Area H.S., 1960-89, ret., 1989. Contbr. articles to profl. jours. Planning commn. Palmyra Borough, 1965-73, borough councilman, 1974-76, recreation commn., 1975-76, mayor, 1990—. With U.S. Army, 1945-46. Mem. Mid. States Assn. (evaluator, chmn. 1959—), Pa. Assn. Secondary Prins. (pres. 1981-82), Mayors Assn. (pres. 1995-97), VFW, Am. Legion, Brownstone Masonic Lodge, Zembo Shrine, Hershey Shrine Club (pres. 1996, Plaque 1996). Republican. Methodist. Avocations: camping, photography, hiking, golf. Home: Palmyra, Pa. Died Jan. 2, 2007.

WAXMAN, HERBERT JACOB, accountant, poet; b. NYC, Jan. 21, 1913; s. Isadore and Alice (Jacobowitz) W.; m. Vivian S. Krischer, May 28, 1939; children: Jill, Jonathan. Student, NYU, 1929, City Coll. N.Y., 1930-38. CPA, N.Y.C. Jr. acct. Gray, Sheiber Co. CPA, NYC, 1931; office mgr. Breslauer & Fliegler Produce Dealers, NYC, 1932-40; pvt. practice acctg. NYC, 1940-60, 72-75; ptnr. Waxman, Pepper, Gotbetter CPAs, NYC, 1960-72, Waxman & Goldman CPAs, Great Neck, N.Y., 1975-79; pvt. practice CPA Great Neck, from 1979. Treas. N.Y. Quarterly, N.Y.C., 1978-79. Author (poetry) Where the Worm Grows Fat, 1975; contbr. poems, articles to various pubs. Mem. pres.'s council of advisors Hebrew Union Coll. Bd. Govs., 1968, budget adv. com. Great Neck Bd. Edn., 1970-71; pres. Margaret Court Civic Assn., Great Neck, 1952—; trustee Pride of Judea Children's Svcs., N.Y.C., 1965, Library Assn., Great Neck, 1976; founder, trustee, past pres. Temple Emanuel, Great Neck, 1952-89. Named Golden Poet of 1987, 188, World of Poetry, First Prize, Poet in the Community competition, L.I. U., 1988. Mem. N.Y. State Soc. CPA's, Poets and Writers, Inc., L.I. Poetry Collective. Home: Pompano Beach, Fla. Died July 25, 2007.

WEATHERS, LAWRENCE MARTIN, agricultural executive; b. Bowman, SC, Mar. 26, 1924; s. George Whetsell and Gladys (Shuler) W.; m. Frances Fitzhugh Landrum, June 18, 1948; children: Landrum, Virginia, Martin, Hugh. Student, The Citadel, 1941-42. Pres. Weathers Farms, Inc., Bowman, from 1969. Mem exec. com. Dairy div. U.S. Farm Bur., Columbia, S.C., 1968—; bd. dirs. Fed. Land Bank Assn. Orangeburg. Sec., treas. Sunday Sch. Bowman So. Meth. Ch., 1951-84, steward; councilman city of Bowman, 1958-64; mem. Orangeburg (S.C.) County Bd. Edn., 1965-75; commr. Orangeburg County Devel. Commn., 1980—. Served as sgt. U.S. Army, 1942-46, ETO. Named Man of Yr. Co-op, 1968; recipient Dairy Leadership award Clemson U., 1988; named to Dairy Hall of Fame, Clemson U., 1990. Mem. Am. Dairy Assn. (bd. dirs. S.C. chpt. 1968-72, pres. 1972-73), S.C. Council Milk Producers (bd. dirs. 1958—), Palmetto Milk Producers of Carolinas (bd. dirs. 1982—). Home: Bowman, SC. Died Mar. 19, 2007.

WEBBER, EDYTHE MARIE, business consultant, real estate investor/developer; b. Detroit, Nov. 22, 1954; d. Austin Joseph and Ruby Lee (Ennis) McClendon; m. Steven Carl Webber, July 19, 1986; children: Kalese Marie, Steven Carl. AGS, Highland Park Community Coll., Mich., 1977, AS, 1982. Lic. respiratory therapist; registered money broker. Switchboard operator Finney High Sch., Detroit, 1970-73; dishwasher-clothwasher Grosspointe (Mich.) Country Club, 1973-74; med. asst. Detroit Med. and Surg. Ctr., 1976-79; nursing aide St. Anne Nursing Home, Detroit, 1977-80; med. asst. pediatric care Detroit Med. and Surg. Ctr., 1977-80; respiratory therapist Harper-Grace Hosp., Detroit, 1982-84, Binsons Med., Centerline, Mich., 1984-85; charge respiratory therapist intensive care St. Johns Hosp., Grosspointe, 1985-86; pres. K. S. Webber Corp., Southfield, Mich., from 1987. Regional dir. The Hempell Group, Southfield, Mich., 1990—; mem. bd. Mich. State Gov.'s Small Bus. Com. Mem. NAACP, NAFE, CMI, The Kesseler Exchange (outstanding small bus. achievement award 1989), Am. Fin. Coords. Assn., Better Bus. Bur., Southfield C. of C. (membership com. person 1989), Internat. Health Spa, Charles J. Givens Orgn. Avocations: spa exercising, picture taking, travel, park with kids. Died June 14, 2007.

WEBER, BARBARA M., sales executive, consultant; b. Oneonta, NY, Apr. 27, 1945; d. Peter J. and Helen (Bettiol) Macaluso; m. Peter Biddle Weber, July 29, 1972 (div. July 1988). Student, SUNY, Cortland, 1963-67; AAS in Merchandising and Retail Mgmt., SUNY, Mohawk Valley. Service cons. N.Y. Telephone, Albany, N.Y., 1966-68, sr. service advisor, 1970-73; data communications instr. AT & T, nationwide, 1968-70; equipment mgr. Rushmore & Weber, Albany, 1978-82, v.p. ops., 1983-92, gen. mgr., v.p., 1987-88, pres., chief exec. officer, 1988-92, also bd. dirs.; ind. cons. Orange Handling, Inc., Latham, N.Y., 1992-93; owner The Weber Group, Newtonville, N.Y., from 1993. Co-owner The Bistro. Chmn. fin. com. Albany County Rep. Com., 1996-98; bd. dirs. ARC Northeastern N.Y., 1994—. Mem. Schuyler Meadows Country Club. Roman Catholic. Avocations: skiing, tennis, golf, sailing, knitting. Home: Newtonville, NY. Died Jan. 17, 2007.

WECHTER, WILLIAM JULIUS, medical researcher; b. Louisville, Feb. 13, 1932; s. Louis and Elsie (Strauss) W.; m. Roselyn Ann Greenman, May 22, 1956 (div. 1974); children: Laurie Jo, Diane Joy, Julie Lynn; m. Kathryn Elaine Edwards, Apr. 16, 1982. AB, U. Ill., 1953, MS, 1954; PhD, UCLA, 1957. With The Upjohn Co., Kalamazoo, Mich., 1957-78, rsch. mgr., 1978-84; dir. long-range planning Boehringer-Ingelhein Zetralle, Ingelheim, Fed. Republic Germany, 1984; dir. clin. and pharm. rsch. Boots Pharms., Inc., Shreveport, La., 1985-88; rsch. prof. medicine Loma Linda (Calif.) U., from 1988, dir. lab. chem. endocrinology, from 1990. Cons. Sepracor, Inc., Marlborough, Mass., 1988—, Procter and Gamble Pharmaceuticals, 1993—. Editorial bds. J. Clin. Pharm., Jour. of Clinical Trials and Meta-Analysis; patentee over 30 pharm. patents; contbr. to profl. publs. Fellow Am. Coll. Clin. Pharmacology; mem. AAAS, Am. Soc. Pharmacology and Exptl. Therapeutics, Transplantation Soc., Am. Chem. Soc. (sect. pres. 1967), Am. Assn. Immunologists, Am. Rheumatology Assn., Royal Soc. Medicine, Nephrology Soc., Hypertension Soc. Democrat. Jewish. Avocations: film criticism, photography, art collecting, flying, running. Home: Ojai, Calif. Died July 8, 2007.

WEED, LOIS CRON, banker; b. Wilkes-Barre, Pa., May 14, 1927; d. Walter Andrew and Ethel (Gardner) Cron; m. Clarence E. Weed, April 28, 1956 (div. 1980). BA in History, Fordham U., 1988. Sec. Crowell Collier Pub., NYC, 1947-49, Spadea Advt. Co., NYC, 1949; asst. film producer Herbert Kerkow Films, NYC, 1949-68; asst. cashier Chelsea Nat. Bank, NYC, 1969-77; sr. v.p. Union Chelsea Nat. Bank, NYC, from 1977. Gov. Women's Nat. Rep. Club, 1988—. Avocations: travel, cooking, art, architecture, reading. Home: New York, NY. Died Apr. 3, 2007.

WEIDENFELD, ARTHUR GEORGE (BARON OF CHELSEA), publishing company executive; b. Vienna, Sept. 13, 1919; arrived in Eng., 1938, naturalized, 1946; s. Max and Rosa Eisenstein-ish (Horowitz) Weidenfeld; m. Jane Sieff, 1952 (div. 1954); 1 child, Laura; m. Barbara Skelton Connolly, 1956 (div.); m. Sandra Payson Meyer, 1966 (div.); m. Annabelle Whitestone, 1992. Attended in law, U. Vienna, 1938; attended, Konsular Akademie. Head spl. German sect. BBC Overseas Monitoring Svc., 1939—42; diplomatic commentator European affairs BBC Empire, N.Am. Svc., 1942—46; founder Contact mag., 1945—51; founder, chmn. Weidenfeld & Nicolson, NYC, from 1948, Wheatland Corp., NYC, Grove Press, NYC; dir. South Bank, London. Polit. adviser, chef de cabinet to pres. Weizmann of Israel, 1949—50; vice chmn., bd. govs. Ben Gurion U. Negev, Beer-Sheva; gov. U. Tel Aviv, Weizmann Inst. of Sci.; trustee Mishkenot Sha'ananim in Jerusalem, Jerusalem Found. in Britain, Royal Opera House, Covent Garden; chmn. Wheatland Found., NYC; bd. govs. Bezalel Art Acad. Created Knight, 1969, baron, 1976. Died Jan. 20, 2016.

WEIGEL, RICHARD GEORGE, psychologist, educator; b. St. Louis, Feb. 23, 1937; s. George D. and Irene K. (Bretz) W.; Virginia Morris, 1964 (div. 2003); children: Paul K., Laura K.; m. Jean Anderson. BA, DePauw U., 1959; MA, U. Mo., Columbia, 1962, PhD in Psychology, 1968. Diplomate in clin. psychology Am. bd. Profl. Psychology; lic. psychologist Utah. Counselor/asst. prof. psychology Oreg. State U., Corvallis, 1964-67, acting dir. Counseling Ctr., 1967; asst. prof. to prof. and chmn. counseling psychology program Colo. State U., Ft. Collins, 1967-78; sr. cons. psychologist Rohrer, Hibler & Replogle, Inc., Denver, 1978-90, mgr., 1981-86; dir. and adj. prof. psychology Student Counseling Ctr., Ill. State U., Normal, 1990-92; dir. Counseling Ctr. U. Utah, Salt Lake City, from 1992, clin. prof. psychology, ednl. psychology and psychiatry, from 1992, asst. v.p. student devel., 1996-97, interim v.p. for student affairs, 1997-99. Pvt. practice psychology, Ft. Collins, 1970-78; adj. prof. Denver U. Sch. Profl. Psychology, 1977-78, Counseling Psychology Program, Ctr. for Spl. and Advanced Programs of U. No. Colo., Greeley, 1975-78, vis. assoc. prof. counseling psychology program, summer 1975; lectr. continuing edn. for nurses Poudre Valley Meml. Hosp., Ft. Collins, 1975; selection psychologist Peace Corps, 1973-74; asst. prof. psychology divsn. continuing edn. Oreg. State Sys. Higher Edn., Salem, 1965; ind. practice marriage counseling, Corvallis, Oreg., 1965-67; clin. psychologist Mo. Tng. Sch. for Boys, summer 1964; instr. psychology U. Mo., Columbia, 1963-64; counselor Counseling Svc., Stephens Coll., Columbia, 1963-64, Univ. Testing and Counseling Svc., U. Mo., Columbia, 1961-62; instr. psychology, resident advisor George Williams Coll., Lake Geneva, Wis., summer 1961; tchg./rsch. asst. psychology U. Mo., 1960-61; rsch. asst. Purdue U., West Lafayette, Ind., 1960; VA clin. psychology trainee Indpls., 1959-60; vis. scientist/lectr. APA, Drury Coll., 1974; lectr. in field; condr. workshops in field; v.p. Bd. Psychologist Examiners State of Colo., 1973-76. Assoc. editor Cons. Psychology Jour.: Practice and rsch., 1991-93, editl. bd., 1990-97; editl. bd. Jour. Coll. Student Devel., 1970-73, 92—, Profl. Psychology: Rsch. and Practice, 1990-92, Group Dynamics: Theory, Research & Practice, 1999—; reviewer Jour. Counseling Psychology, 1976, 94-96, Counseling Psychologist, 1994-98, Jour. Cons. and Clin. Psychology, 1977; editl. cons. Wadsworth-Brooks/Cole Pub. Co., 1974-78, Univ. Park Press, 1976; contbr. numerous articles to profl. jours.; co-author: Innovative Psychological Therapies, 1975, Innovative Medical-Psychiatric Therapies, 1976. Bd. dirs. Mental Health Assn., Benton County, Oreg., 1966-67; mem. Soc. Indiana Pioneers, 1990—; mem. profl. adv. bd. Denver U. Sch. Profl. Psychology, 1976-78. NIMH grantee, 1977-82, Colo. State U. grantee, 1976-77, Oreg. State U. grantee, 1965-66, 66-67; Paul Harris fellow Rotary, 1981-86. Fellow APA (task force on revision of accreditation criteria 1977-

78, vis. scientist 1974, divsn. cons. psychology pres.-elect 1995-96, pres. 1996-97, past pres. 1997-98, sec. 1993-95, exec. com. 1990-98, com. fellows 1989-93, chair 1991-93, program com. 1990, counseling psychology divsn. awards com. 1993-95, 98, edn. and tng. com. 1975-78, 91-93, coll. counseling interest group 19915, clin. psychology divsn., group psychology and group psychotherapy divsn. com. on fellows 1991-93, 95—, chair 1992-93, pres. 2000—), Am. Psychol. Soc.; mem. AAUP, Assn. Univ. and Coll. Counseling Ctr. Dirs. (governing bd. 1993-95), Rocky Mountain Psychol. Assn. (pres. 1973-74, treas. 1971-72, Disting. Svc. award 1987), Rsch. Consortium of Counseling and Psychol. Svcs. in Higher Edn. (bd. dirs. 1993-95), Internat. Assn. Counseling Svcs. (site visitor 1991-95), Am. Coll. Pers. Assn., Utah Psychol. Assn., Colo. State Bd. Psychologist Examiners (vice chmn. 1974-76, del. to Am. Assn. State Psychology Bds. 1976), Coun. of Counseling Psychology Tng. Programs (bd. dirs. 1974-79, liaison to Am. Assn. State Psychology Bds. 1979), Newcomen Soc. U.S., Sigma Xi, Psi Chi, Phi Gamma Delta, Phi Mu Alpha, Phi Kappa Phi (hon., Golden Key). Avocation: history. Died May 7, 2007.

WEILAND, SCOTT RICHARD (SCOTT RICHARD KLINE), singer; b. Santa Jose, Calif., Oct. 27, 1967; s. Kent Kline and Sharon Williams, Dave Weiland (Stepfather); m. Janina Castaneda, Sept. 17, 1994 (div. Feb. 2000); m. Mary Forsberg, May 20, 2000 (div. 2007); children: Noah Mercer, Lucy Olivia; m. Jamie Wachtel, June 22, 2013. Attended, Orange Coast Coll. Founder, lead singer Mighty Joe Young, 1987—92; lead singer Stone Temple Pilots, 1986—2003, 2008—13, Velvet Revolver, 2003—08, Wildabouts, 2013—15, Art of Anarchy, 2015; founder Softdrive Records, 2006; solo career, 2008—15. Launched clothing line, Weiland for English Laundry, 2009. Singer: (albums) (with Stone Temple Pilots) Core, 1992, Purple, 1994, Tiny Music...Songs From the Vatican Gift Shop, 1996, No. 4, 1999, Shangri-La Dee Da, 2001, Thank You, 2003, Stone Temple Pilots, 2010, (with Velvet Revolver) Contraband, 2004, Libertad, 2007, (with Wildabouts) Blaster, 2015, (with Art of Anarchy) Art of Anarchy, 2015, (solo) 12 Bar Blues, 1998, Happy in Galoshes, 2008, The Most Wonderful Time of the Year, 2011; author: Not Dead & Not for Sale, 2011. Died Dec. 3, 2015.

WEINBERG, ANDREW DAVID, geriatrician, educator; b. NYC, July 10, 1954; BA, Cornell U., 1975; MD, SUNY, Syracuse, 1978; MS, U. Minn., 1981. Diplomate Am. Bd. Internal Medicine. Resident in internal medicine Mayo Clinic, Rochester, Minn., 1978-81; fellow in endocrinology Yale U. Sch. Medicine, New Haven, Conn., 1981-82; attending physician dept. medicine Yale-New Haven Hosp., 1983-92, sect. chief life support edn., 1986-92; acting assoc. chief of staff geriatrics/extended care Brockton (Mass.)/West Roxbury VA Med. Ctr., from 1992. Clin. instr. in medicine Mayo Med. Sch., Rochester, 1980-81, Yale U. Sch. Medicine, 1986-87; asst. clin. prof. medicine Yale U. Sch. Medicine, 1987-92; instr. medicine Harvard Med. Sch., Boston, 1992—; com. on impaired physicians Yale-New Haven Hosp, 1986-88; med. dir. Westrock Health Care Ctr., New Haven, 1987-91, Bentley Gardens Health Care, West Haven, 1989-91, Hamden (Conn.) Health Care Facility, 1989-91, Willows of Woodbridge (Conn.), 1989-91, nursing home care unit Brockton/West Roxbury VA Med. Ctr., 1992—; mem. Joint Commn. on Accreditation of Healthcare Orgns., Profl. and Tech. Adv. Com. on Long Term Care, geriatrics and gerontology adv. com. Dept. Vets. Affairs, Washington, 1988-91, Commn. on Elderly Svcs., Branford, Conn., 1985-92. Author: (with J.L. Paturas) New Standards in Advanced Cardiac Life Support for the Adult Patient: Synopsis and Commentary, 1986, (with others) Quick Reference Guide for Dental Office Emergencies, 1987, The Fifty Most Commonly Asked Questions About Nursing Homes, 1987, (with R. Pies) Quick Reference Guide to Geriatric Psychopharmacology, 1990, (with others) The Most Common Questions About VA Nursing Homes and VA-Contract Community Nursing Homes, 1993; co-editor: Basic Cardiac Life Support: Quick Co-chmn. Sr. Citizen's Com. for 1989 Presdl. Inaugural, Washington, 1989. Rsch. grantee Cornell U., 1972. Fellow Royal Soc. Medicine; mem. AMA (coun. on long range planning and devel. 1981-82), Am. Heart Assn. (chmn. advanced cardiac life support task force Conn. affiliate 1984-89, med. dir. advanced cardiac life support and pediatric advanced cardiac life support programs 1989-92, nat. faculty advanced cardiac life support program 1987-92, affiliate faculty advanced cardiac life support Mass. affiliate 1993—, outstanding program award Conn. affiliate 1988), Am. Coll. Physicians, Am. Geriatrics Soc., Am. Soc. Internal Medicine, Am. Med. Dirs. Assn. (CME adv. panel 1992—), Mass. Med. Soc. (com. on geriatric medicine 1992—), Conn. State Med. Soc. (founder's award com. on geriatrics 1992, com. on state legis. 1983-89, chmn. com. on geriatrics 1987-91, ho. of dels. 1988-92), Gerontol. Soc. Medicine, Alzheimer's Disease and Related Disorders Assn. (bd. dirs. So. Ctrl. Conn. ch. 1990-91) Home: Raynham, Mass. Died Feb. 6, 2007.

WEINBERG, SAMUEL, dermatologist; b. NYC, Jan. 12, 1926; s. Harry and Rose (Stecher) Weinberg; m. Pearl Oksner, Dec. 12, 1948; children: Ronald Andrew, Robin Ann. MB, Chgo. Med. Sch., 1947, MD, 1948. Clin. asst. prof. dermatology Med. Ctr. NYU, NYC, 1961-84, prof. dermatology, from 1984. Author: Color Atlas of Pediatric Dermatology, 1975, 3d rev. edit., 1998. Capt. USAF, 1951—53. Recipient Clark W. Finnerud award, Dermatology Found., 1999. Fellow: ACP, Nassau Acad. Medicine, Am. Acad. Dermatology (chmn. pediat. dermatology sect. 1978—81, mem. task force pediat. dermatology 1981—84, mem. com. dermatol. subspecialties 1984—86), Am. Acad. Pediat. (Alvin Jacobs award 1998); mem.: Soc. Pediat. Dermatology (charter, pres. 1980—81). Home: Great Neck, NY. Died Jan. 26, 2007.

WEINBERG, SAUL ABRAM, psychiatrist; b. Hartford, Conn., Aug. 13, 1925; s. Hyman P. and Rose May (Apter) W.; m. Ethel Schwartz, Aug. 30, 1959; children: David, Diane. BA, Yale U., 1948; MS in Social Svc., Boston U., 1951; MD, U. Pa., 1956. Diplomate, Am. Bd. Psychiatry and Neurology. Pvt. practice, Phila., 1960-80; psychiatric consultation liason dir. Albert Einstein Med. Ctr., Phila., 1980-86; clin. assoc. prof. Sch. Medicine Temple U., Phila., 1984-86; staff psychiatrist Baystate Med. Ctr., Springfield, Mass., 1986-92; pvt. practice Springfield, 1992-96; clin. assoc. prof. Sch. Medicine Sch. Medicine Tufts U., Boston, 1989-94, clin. prof. psychiatry, 1994-96; adj. prof. psychiatry U. N.C., Chapel Hill, from 1997. Lectr. dept. psychiatry U. Pa., Phila., 1976-80. Mem. arts com. Mattoon Arts Festival, Springfield, 1987-90; pres. Mattoon St. Hist. Preservation Assn., Springfield, 1989-91; mem. adv. bd. springfield Fine Arts Mus., 1991—; fin. com. Springfield Libr. and Mus. Assn., 1994—. Mem. AMA, Am. Psychiat. Assn., Mass. Med. Soc., West Mass. Psychiat. Soc., Connecticut Valley Yale Club (sec.), Realty Club, Springfield Cen. (bd. dirs.), Stagewest (bd. dirs.), Phi Beta Kappa. Jewish. Avocations: orchid growing, sailing, theater. Home: Chapel Hill, NC. Died Feb. 1, 2007.

WEINBERGER, ERIC, jewelry importer, fashion accessory designer; b. Vienna, Sept. 7, 1916; came to U.S., 1939; s. Siegfried and Stella (Schein) W.; m. Viola Fischer Lowen, Dec. 1, 1940 (div. 1949); 1 child, Thomas R.; m. Eva Grant, July 16, 1949; children: Peter H., Richard F., William E. M of Bus. Engring., Vienna U., 1938. Pres. Juno, Inc., Cleve., 1944-80; v.p. Atlantic Imports, Inc., Ft. Lauderdale, Fla., from 1951; pres. Nu-Joy, Inc., Ft. Lauderdale, from 1956. Bd. govs. dist. 2 B'nai Brith, Cleve., 1973-75. Democrat. Jewish. Avocations: collecting art, world travel. Home: Boca Raton, Fla. Died July 14, 2007.

WEINSTEIN, ALBERT, ophthalmologist; b. Bridgeport, Conn., June 16, 1932; s. Samuel L. and Jennie (Rome) W.; m. Helen Sue Berger, July 5, 1959; children: Kenneth Louis, Richard Bruce, Jeffrey Paul. BA, Wesleyan U., 1954; MD, Boston U. Sch. Medicine, 1958. Diplomate Am. Bd. Ophthalmology. Cons. ophthalmologist U.S. Pub. Health Svc., Salt Lake City, 1962-64; pvt. practice Bridgeport, from 1964. Mem. Am. Acad. Ophthalmology, Conn. State Med. Soc., Fairfield County Med. Soc. Republican. Jewish. Home: Trumbull, Conn. Died Nov. 26, 2006.

WEINSTEIN, ALLEN, retired archivist; b. NYC, Sept. 1, 1937; s. Samuel and Sarah (Popkoff) W.; m. Adrienne Dominguez, June 14, 1995; children: Andrew Samuel, David Meier; step-children Alex Content BA, CCNY; MA, Yale U., PhD, 1967. Prof. history Smith Coll., Northampton, Mass., 1966-81; editl. staff The Washington Post, 1981; exec. editor, The Washington Quarterly Georgetown Ctr. for Strategic and Internat. Studies, Washington, 1981—83; prof. Georgetown U., Washington, 1981—84; pres. Ctr. for the Study of Democratic Institutions, Santa Barbara, 1984; editor The Ctr. Magazine, 1984; prof. history Boston U., 1985-89; founder, pres. The Ctr. for Democracy, Washington, 1985—2003; sr. adv. for democratic institutions & dir. Internat. Found. for Elections Sys., Washington, from 2003; archivist of the US The Nat. Archives & Records Admin., Washington, 2005—08. Author: Prelude to Populism:Origins of the Silver Issue, 1970, Freedom and Crisis: An American History, 1974, Perjury: The Hiss-Chambers Case, 1978 (NISC award 1978), new edit., 1998, Between the Wars: American Foreign Policy From Versailles to Pearl Harbor, 1978; co-author: The Haunted Wood: Soviet Espionage in America-The Stalin Era, 1999, The Story of America, 2002; editor: American Negro Slavery, 1968, 3d edit., 1981, Harry S Truman and the American Commitment to Israel, 1981. Exec. dir. The Democracy Program, Washington, 1982-83; acting pres. Nat. Endowment for Democracy, Washington, 1983-84; chmn. edn. com. U.S. Inst. Peace, Washington, 1986-2001; mem. U.S. Observer del., Feb., 1986 Philippines election, co-author report; vice chmn. U.S. del. UNESCO World Conf. on Culture, 1982, UNESCO/IPDC meeting, 1983; chmn. Internat. IMPAC/Dublin Lit. award, 1996-2003. Recipient Meade prize in history CCNY, 1960, Egleston prize Yale U., 1967, Binkley-Stephenson prize Orgn. Am. Historians, 1968, UN Peace medal, 1986, Coun. of Europe Silver medal, 1990, 96; Fulbright lectr., Australia, 1968, 71; Commonwealth Fund lectr. U.S. History, U. London, 1981; Fourth of July Orator Fanueil Hall, Boston, 1987. Fellow Woodrow Wilson Ctr., NEH; mem. Soc. Am. Historians, Cosmos Club. Democrat. Jewish. From 1982-84 directed the rsch. study which led to the creation of the Nat. Endowment for Democracy (NED). Home: Bethesda, Md. Died June 18, 2015.

WEINSTEIN, RICHARD NEAL, lawyer; b. Buffalo, June 3, 1948; s. Morris and Sylvia (Lipshultz) W.; m. Marilyn J. Green, June 27, 1970; children: Marc, Steven. BA in History, SUNY, Buffalo, 1969, JD, 1972; LLM in Taxation, NYU, 1976. Bar: N.Y. 1972, U.S. Tax Ct. 1973, Tex. 1978, U.S. Ct. Appeals (2d, 5th and 11th cirs.) 1978; cert. tax planning, probate law, tax law, Tex. Atty. Office Regional Counsel, IRS, Phila., 1972-76; assoc. Saperston, Day & Radler, Buffalo, 1976-78; mem. Oppenheimer, Blend, Harrison & Tate, Inc., San Antonio, from 1978. Mem. editorial adv. bd. The Practical Accountant, 1985—; contbr. articles to profl. jours. Bd. dirs., treas. Golden Manor Home for Aged, 1990—. Mem. ABA (employee benefits com.), Tex. Bar Assn. (chmn. compensation and employee benefits com. 1987-92), Kiwanis (bd. dirs. San Antonio chpt. 1987-92), San Antonio Rotary. Home: San Antonio, Tex. Died Feb. 1, 2007.

WEINTRAUB, JERRY (JEROME CHARLES WEINTRAUB), film producer; b. Bklyn., Sept. 26, 1937; s. Sam and Rose W.; m. Jane Morgan, 1965 (separated); adopted children: Julie, Jamie, Jody; 1 child (from a previous relationship), Michael. Prodr.: (films) Nashville, 1975, Oh God!, 1977, Cruising, 1980, All Night Long, 1981, Diner, 1982, The Karate Kid, 1984, The Karate Kid, Part II, The Karate Kid, Part III, 1989, Pure Country, 1992, The Next Karate Kid, 1994, The Specialist, 1994, The Avengers, 1998, Soldier, 1998, Nancy Drew, 2007, The Karate Kid, 2010; exec. prodr.: (films) The Independent, 2000, (documentaries) 41, 2012, Red Army, 2014 (TV films) Father O Father, 1976, Behind the Candelabra (The David L. Wolper award for Outstanding Prodr. of Long-Form TV, Producers Guild of America, 2014), 2013, (TV series) Years of Living Dangerously, 2014, The Brink, 2015; actor: (films) The Firm, 1993, Full Frontal, 2002, Confessions of a Dangerous Mind, 2002; actor, prodr.: (films) Vegas Vacation, 1997, Ocean's Eleven, 2001, Ocean's Twelve, 2004, Ocean's Thirteen, 2007; co-author: (with Rich Cohen) When I Stop Talking, You'll Know I'm Dead: Useful Stories From a Persuasive Man, 2010. Recipient Star, Hollywood Walk of Fame, 1984, Patron of the Arts award, Screen Actors Guild, 2008. Died July 6, 2015.

WEIR, JAMES ROBERT, metallurgical engineer; b. Middletown, Ohio, Dec. 29, 1932; s. James Robert and Kathleen (Lawson) W.; m. Lois Mattox, Mar. 1951 (dec. 1978); children: James, David, Todd, Pat, Scott. Degree in metallurg. engring., U. Cin., 1955; MS in Metallurgy, U. Tenn., 1961. Registered profl. engr., Ohio. Rsch. mgr. Oak Ridge (Tenn.) Nat. Lab., from 1955. 1st lt. U.S. Army, 1957-59. Named Disting. Alumnus U. Cin., 1974. Fellow Am. Soc. Metals (bd. dirs. 1978-80), AAAS; mem. Internat. Tech. Inst. (bd. dirs. 1985—), Nat. Materials Adv. Bd. Died June 11, 2007.

WEISBERG, LOIS (LOIS HELEN PORGES), arts administrator, city official; b. May 6, 1925; d. Mortimer Porges and Jesse (Berger); m. Leonard Solomon (div.); m. Bernard Weisberg (dec. 1994); children: Jacob, Joseph, Kiki Ellenby, Jerilyn Fyffe(dec.). Grad., Northwestern U. Commr. Chgo. Dept. Cultural Affairs, from 1989. Died Jan. 13, 2016.

WEISMAN, MURRAY, lawyer, counselor; b. Lodz, Poland, Mar. 30, 1930; arrived in U.S., 1950; s. Benjamin Weisman and Sara Brown; m. Marianne Weisman, Aug. 22, 1962; children: Rebecca, Lisa, Neal. BBA, U. Minn., Mpls., 1954, M in Psychology, 1957; JD, U. Chase Coll. Law, Cin., 1962. Bar: Ohio. Exec. dir. Dept. Mental Health, Cin., 1965—75; JAG atty. civil litigation USAF, Dayton, Ohio, 1975—2004. Spkr. in field. Author: The Troubled Generation, 1995; contbr. articles to profl. jours. Presenter to civic and religious orgns. Recipient Outstanding Cmty. Svc. cert., Gov. of Ohio, Excellent Performance cert., JAG, 1986. Mem.: Ohio Fed. Bar Assn. Avocations: tennis, golf, bridge. Home: Delray Beach, Fla. Died Jan. 23, 2014.

WEISS, SAMUEL ABBA, English literature educator; b. Rochester, NY, Oct. 20, 1922; s. Morris and Celia (Salzberg) W.; m. Rana Schima, June 2, 1962. BA cum laude, Bklyn. Coll., 1945; MA, Columbia U., 1946, PhD, 1953. Instr. Bklyn. Coll., 1947, L.I. U., 1949; asst. prof. Knoxville (Tenn.) Coll., 1955-57, U. Ill., Chgo., 1957-62, assoc. prof., 1962-66, prof., 1966—92. Editor: Drama in the Modern World: Plays & Essays, 1964, 1974, Drama in the Western World, 1968, Bernard Shaw's Letters to Siegfried Trebitsch, 1986; author numerous poems and book revs.; contbr. articles to profl. jours. Mem. Shaw Soc. Home: Chicago, Ill. Died Dec. 21, 2006.

WEITZ, DAVID ALLAN, state official; b. Fredric, Wis., Jan. 30, 1944; s. Chauncey Aaron and Mildred Inez (Phillips) W.; m. Christine Carrie DeBoer, May 20, 1978; children: Bekah Victoria, Glynis Allyn. BS, U. Wis., 1966. Reporter Chippewa Falls (Wis.) Herald Telegram, 1966-67; copy editor Davenport (Iowa) Times Dem., 1967-68; reporter The Post Crescent, Appleton, Wis., 1968-79; info. officer Wis. Dept. Natural Resources, Eau Claire, 1979-96, pub. affairs mgr., from 1996. Editor: A Game Warden's Diary, 1981, Leaves from a Game Warden's Diary, 1996. Citizen involvement cons. Wis. Dept. Natural Resources, Eau Claire, 1979—, crisis mgmt. cons., 1984—. Recipient Region V U.S.EPA Communicator of Yr. award Soil Conservation Soc.Am. Mem. Assn. Great Lakes Outdoor Writers, Internat. Assn. Pub. Participation. Home: Mondovi, Wis. Died July 9, 2007.

WEIZSACKER, RICHARD VON, former president of Federal Republic of Germany; b. Stuttgart, Germany, Apr. 15, 1920; m. Marianne von Kretschmann, Oct. 10, 1953; children: Robert, Andreas (dec. 2008), Marianne, Fritz. Student, Oxford U., DCL (hon.), 1988; student, Dr. jur.; Dr. jur. (hon.), D. Weizman Inst. Tel Aviv, Grenoble, Loewen, Belgium, Istanbul, Sucre, Bolivia, Göttingen, Harvard U., Coimbra, Portugal, Oxford.; PhD (hon.), John Hopkins U., 1993; several other honorary degrees. Mem. Christian Democratic Union (CDU), 1954—2015, chmn. commn. on basic policy issues, chmn. regional group Berlin, 1981-83, fed. dep. chmn., 1983-84; mem. German Bundestag, 1969-81, v.p., 1979-81; pres. German Evangelical Church Assembly, 1964—70; mem. Synod and the Coun. of the Evangelical Church, Germany, 1967—84; dep. chmn. Christian Dem. Union/Christian Social Union Parliamentary Py, 1973-79; mem. Ho. of Reps., Berlin, 1979, 81-84; governing mayor City of Berlin, 1981-84; pres. Federal Republic of Germany, 1984-94. Guest prof. Heinrich Heine U., Düsseldorf, Germany, 1996; jury mem., Internat. Nuremberg Human Rights award, 1995-2000; mem. Internat. Commission on the Blakans, 2004-2006 Hon. mem. bd. dirs. Political Science Quarterly; author: From Germany Abroad, German History Continues, From Germany to Europe, Four Times, (memoir) From Weimar to the Wall: My Life in German Politics, 1999. Bd. trustee Robert Bosch Stiftung, Freya von Moltke Found., Hannah Arendt Ctr., U. Oldenburg, Humboldt U. of Berlin, Theodor Heuss Found.; mem. Adv. Council of Transparency Internat., Adv. Commission on the return of cultural property seized as a result of Nazi persecution, 2003—15; chmn. Independent Working Group, Bergedorf Round Table, 1994—2014; adv. bd. mem. Children for Tomorrow, Humboldt-Viadrina Sch. of Governace, Philharmonic Orchestra of Europe, Viktor von Weizsacker Soc.; patron Aktion Deutschland Hilft, 2003—13. Recipient Theodor Heuss prize, 1983, Romano Guardini prize, 1987, Harnack medal, 1990, Heinrich-Heine-Preis, 1991, Nansen Refugee award of the UN High Commissioner for Refugees, 1992, Mercator-Professorship award, 2005, Four Freedoms award, 2008, Henry A. Kissinger prize, American Acad. in Berlin. 2009, Prize for Understanding and Tolerance of the Jewish Mus., Berlin, 2012 and many other honors Mem.: Club of Rome, Club of Budapest (hon.). Died Jan. 31, 2015.

WELGE, MARK ALBERT, mediator, arbitrator; b. NYC, Oct. 13, 1946; s. Albert and Marie Louise Welge; m. Louise Mary Welge, Aug. 8, 1972; 1 child, Caitlin D. BA, Ohio State U., Columbus, 1968; JD, George Washington U., Washington, 1972. Bar: Pa. 1973, US Dist. Ct. (ea. dist.) Pa. 1974, US Dist. Ct. (we. dist.) Mich. 1994, US Dist. Ct. Del. 1994, US Dist. Ct. NJ 1994, US Dist. Ct. (no. dist.) Ala. 1994, US Dist. Ct. (so. dist.) Ind. 1994, US Ct. Appeals (2d cir.) 1995, US Ct. Appeals (3d cir.) 1984, US Ct. Appeals (7th cir.) 1984, US Supreme Ct. 1986. Law clk. to Hon. Thomas Masterson US Dist. Ct. (ea. dist.) Pa., Phila., 1972—73; assoc. Harvey Pennington, Phila., 1973—76, Krusen, Evans & Byrne, Phila., 1976—79; sr. litigator Manta and Welga, Phila., 1979—2001; prin., owner Welge Dispute Solutions LLC, Newtown Sq., Pa., from 2001. Mem. various arbitration panels. Trustee Country Day Sch., Bryn Mawr, Pa., 1991—97; active Pa. Conflict Resolution Initiative. Fellow: Internat. Acad. mediators; mem.: NJ Assn. Profl. Mediators, Assn. Conflict Resolution (pres. Pa. chpt. 2006, pres. NJ chpt. 2006, pres. Del. chpt. 2006, mem. panel, tri-chmn. conf. program com.). Avocation: golf. Died Jan. 9, 2007.

WELTY, QUENTIN REED, music company and advertising executive; b. Apple Creek, Ohio, Mar. 27, 1925; s. Evan E. and Cloyva M. (Blosser) W.; m. Gloria Ash, June 21, 1947; children: Laurel, Sharon, Russell, Dana. BA, Baldwin Wallace Coll., 1948; MA, Northwestern U., 1949, postgrad., 1950. Head radio dept. U. N.D., Grand Forks, 1949-50; mgr. Sta. WMVO, Mt. Vernon, Ohio, 1950-51; sales mgr. Sta. WWST, Wooster, Ohio, 1951-65, mgr., 1965-69; gen. mgr. Jamboree U-S-A Sta. WWVA, Wheeling, W.Va., 1969-71; owner Welty Advt. Agy., Wooster, from 1971, WelDee Music/Red Swan Music, Nashville, from 1971. Co-dir. Miss Ohio Pageant, Wooster, 1954-58; cons. Sta. WHLO, Akron, Ohio, 1972-82, Sta. WDBN, Medina, Ohio, 1982-88, Sta. WQKT, Wooster, Ohio, 1988—; on-board lectr. Princess Cruises, 1997—. Author: Writing and Selling the Popular Song, 1960; producer various nat. country hit records. Past bd. dirs. Wooster Community Hosp., United Found., Wooster. Served as sgt. U.S. Army, 1943-45, PTO. Mem. Nat. Acad. Rec. Arts and Scis. (life), Country Music Assn. (life), Nashville Songwriters Assn. Internat. (life), Ohio Speakers Forum (bd. dirs. 1986-87), Nat. Speakers Assn. Mem. Ch. of the Saviour. Avocation: antiques. Home: Wooster, Ohio. Died Nov. 21, 2006.

WENDTH, ARTHUR JOSEPH, JR., radiologist, consultant; b. Albany, NY, Apr. 28, 1930; s. Arthur Joseph and Mary Ann (Treanor) W.; m. Marcia Eileen Clark, June 23, 1956; children: Arthur J. III, Mary Regina, Jeffrey C., Ann. C., David T. BS, Siena Coll., 1952; MD, Albany Med. Coll., 1956; grad. (honor), USAF Sch Aerospace Medicine, Brook AFB, Tex., 1978. Diplomate Am. Bd. Radiology; lic. N.Y. Gen. med. officer USAF, Dover AFB, Del., 1957-59; radiology resident Albany (N.Y.) Med. Ctr., 1959-65; radiologist, clin. commdr., chief med. officer USAF, Stratton AFB, Scotia, N.Y., 1959-65; staff radiologist St. Francis Hosp., Newcastle, Pa., 1965-69, St. Peter's Hosp., Albany, N.Y., 1969-82, chief radiologist, 1982-91; sr. aviation med. examiner FAA, Albany, 1978-84; staff radiologist VA Med. Ctr., Albany, 1991-97; ret., 1997. Sr. clin. investigator E.R. Squibb & Sons, Inc., Albany, N.Y. and Princeton, N.J., 1963-73, angiographic cons., 1973-91; angiographic evaluator Becton-Dickinson Co., Albany, 1975-76;aerospace clin. commdr. and med. officer US Air Nat. Guard, Stratton AFB, N.Y, 1976-82; adj. assoc. prof. radiology, Albany Med. Coll., 1982—; cons. radiologist Albany County Health Dept., 1992—. Contbr. articles to profl. jours., chpt. to text book. Active in comty. and diocesan projects Diocese of Albany, Town of Bethlehem, City of Albany, 1965—; pre-cana counselor Rensselear Polytech. Inst., Troy, N.Y., 1989—; sustaining mem. N.Y. State Aerospace Mus., Schenectady City Airport, N.Y., 1994. Lt. col. USAF 1957-65. Recipient Pelican award Cath. Scouting Com. Diocese of Albany, 1976, St. George award Nat. Cath. Scouting Com., Washington, 1977. Fellow Am. Coll. of Angiology; mem. Am. Coll. Radiology, Albany Country Club. Achievements include: development of drip infusion pyelography, of intravascular biopsy technique, of percutaneous removal of retained gall stones, of biphasic injector and technique for peripheral angiography, of eye shield for special radiology. Home: Delmar, NY. Died Aug. 15, 2007.

WENNERSTROM, BRUCE KENT, realty executive; b. NYC, Dec. 20, 1926; s. John Edward and Anna Ursula (Thompson) W.; m. Genia Kathrin Walukanis, June 12, 1955 (dec. 2011); children: Nord, Leif, Kirk, Bria. Student, Pa. State U., 1946-48; B.F.A., Pratt Inst., NYC, 1953. Exec. U.S. Publs., NYC, 1953-66, Charter Communications, NYC, 1966-74; pres., pub. Homes Internat., Greenwich, Conn., 1974-84; pres. Previews Inc., Greenwich, 1974-84; chmn., pres., chief exec. officer Sotheby's Internat. Realty, NYC, 1984—2015. Author: The Complete Handbook of Auto Racing, 1968; pub., owner: Motorsport, 1965-74; contbr. articles to mags. Served with U.S. Army, 1944-46. Mem. MENSA Clubs: Madison Ave. Sports Car Driving and Chowder Soc. (N.Y.C.) (co-dir. 1967—2015). Home: Greenwich, Conn. Died Sept. 30, 2015.

WESELY, EDWIN JOSEPH, lawyer; b. NYC, May 16, 1929; s. Joseph and Elizabeth (Bellas) W.; children: Marissa Celeste, Adrienne Lee; m. Marcy Brownson, Sept. 23, 1992. Ed., Deep Springs Coll., 1945-47; AB, Cornell U., 1949; JD, Columbia U., 1954. Bar: NY 1954, DC 1985, US Supreme Ct. 1960, others. Law clk. to judge US Dist. Ct. (so. dist.) NY, 1954-55; asst. US atty. So. Dist. NY, 1955-57; assoc. Winthrop, Stimson, Putnam & Roberts, NYC, 1957-63, ptnr., 1964-2000; sr. counsel Pillsbury Winthrop LLP, NYC, from 2001. Spl. master numerous cases; chmn. spl. com. on effective discovery in civil cases US Dist. Ct. (ea. dist.) NY, 1982-84, com. on civil caseflow, 1985-88, com. on civil litigation, 1988-2002, chmn. emeritus, 2002—, civil justice reform adv. group, 1990-95; com. on pretrial phase civil cases Jud. Coun. 2d Cir., 1984-86, standing com. on improvement civil litigation, 1986-89; ex-officio Civil Justice Reform Act adv. group US Dist. Ct. (so. dist.) NY. Pres. CARE, 1986-89, chmn. 1978-86, bd. dirs. 1989-91; cofounder and bd. dirs. CARE Internat., 1981-90, pres. 1987-90; bd. dirs. Internat. Rescue Com., 1964-2005, bd. overseers, 2005-2014; bd. chmn. Internat. Ctr. NY 1998-2003, bd. mem. 1990-2009; trustee Deep Springs Coll., 1991-2000; vice-chair, 1998-2000. Decorated Order of Civil Merit (Republic of Korea); recipient World Humanitarian award Fgn. Press Assn., 1988, Commendation Bd. Judges US Dist. Ct. (ea. dist.) NY, 1993, Deep Springs Medal, Deep Springs Coll., 2003. Mem. Coun. on Fgn. Rels., Am. Coll. Trial Lawyers, Federal Bar Coun.; mem. ABA (spl. adv. com. on internat. activities 1990-93, litigation sect. chmn. com. on discovery 1977-78, spl. com. study discovery abuse 1977-82, chmn. task force on liaison with internat. profl. assns. on matters of mutual concern 1989-93, Civil Justice Reform Act task force 1991-93, task force on the state of the justice sys. 1993-95, fed. initiatives task force 1995-98, co-chmn. task force on fed. and local rules 1997-98) Internat. Rescue Com. (bd. dirs., 1964-2008, bd. overseers, 2008-14), Deep Springs Coll. (trustee, 1992-2000), UN Assn. USA (bd. dirs. 1991-2004), Assn. of Bar of City of NY (com. chmn., organized demonstration observation panel). Home: New York, NY. Died Feb. 15, 2015.

WESLEY, JAMES PAUL, theoretical physicist, lecturer, consultant; b. St. Louis, July 28, 1921; s. Edgar Bruce and Nanny Fay (Medford) W.; m. Margaret Ellen Martin, June 1943 (div. 1952); 1 child, Martin Medford; m. Dorothy Ree Casey, Aug. 1952 (div. 1963); children: William Casey, David Douglas, Gina Teresa; m. Michele Dudek, June 1963 (div. 1967); 1 child, Sherry Allison; m. Gabriele Beate Modest, July 30, 1975; children: Carl-Eric, Julia Ann, Benjamin Fredrik. BA, U. Minn., 1943; MA, UCLA, 1949, PhD, 1952; postgrad., Scripps Inst. Oceanography, La Jolla, Calif., 1951-52. Various positions, 1943-50; prof. physics U. Idaho, Moscow, 1953-56; rsch. geophysicist Newmont Exploration, Ltd., Jerome, Ariz., 1955-56; rsch. physicist Lawrence Radiation Lab. U. Calif., 1956-61; NIH rsch. fellow, fellow Ctr. Advanced Study Behavioral Sci., Stanford, Calif., 1961-62; rsch. physicist U. Denver, 1962-63, Melpar, Inc., Falls Church, Va., 1963, Roland F. Beers, Inc., Alexandria, Va., 1964; assoc. prof. physics U. Mo., Rolla, 1964-74; lectr., cons. on quantum theory, space-time physics, others Berlin and Blumberg, Germany, from 1974. Author: Ecophysics, 1974, Casual Quantum Theory, 1983, Advanced Fundamental Physics, 1991, Classical Quantum Theory, 1996, To Appreciate Physics, 2000; co-editor: Proc. Internat. Conf. on Space-Time Absoluteness, 1982, Proc. Conf. on Foundations of Mathematics and Physics, 1991, Physics as a Science, 1998, 2d edit., 2001; editor: Progress in Space-Time Physics, 1987, Light & Photon Flux, 2006; contbr. over 100 articles to profl. jours. Rsch. fellow Nat. Bur. Stds., 1950. Mem. Am. Phys. Soc., AAAS. Unitarian Universalist. Avocations: painting, hiking. Died Jan. 20, 2007.

WEST, EULA KIRKPATRICK, retired elementary education educator; b. Fox, Okla., Oct. 16, 1930; d. William B. and Eva (Williams) Kirkpatrick; m. Billy G. West, June 6, 1948 (dec. Apr. 1977); children: William G., Carol Ann West Rushing. Student, Hills Bus. Coll., 1950; BS, U. Southern Miss., 1972. Sec. Social Security Adminstrn., Amarillo, Tex., 1952-61; tchr. Harrison County, Gulfport, Miss., 1968-70, Biloxi (Miss.) Pub. Sch., 1971-96, ret., 1996. Sunday sch. tchr., 1953—. Mem. Miss. Profl. Educators, Eastern Star, Delta Kappa Gamma (sec., treas. pres., fin. com., Women of Distinction 1993). Baptist. Home: Gulfport, Miss. Died Feb. 21, 2007.

WEST, PAUL NODEN, writer, playwright; b. Eckington, Derbyshire, Eng., Feb. 23, 1930; arrived in US, 1961, naturalized, 1971; s. Alfred Massick and Mildred (Noden) W.; m. Diane Ackerman; 1 child Student, Oxford U., 1950-53; MA, Columbia U., 1953. Asst. prof. English Meml. U. Nfld., Canada, 1957-58, assoc. prof., 1958-60; faculty Pa. State U., 1962-95, prof. English and comparative lit., 1968-95, prof. emeritus, 1995—2015. Crawshaw prof. Colgate U., 1972; Melvin Hill disting. vis. prof. Hobart and William Smith Coll., 1973; vis. English prof. Cornell U., 1986; disting. writer in residence Wichita State U., 1982; vis. prof. English Brown U., 1992; fiction judge Creative Artists Pub. Svc. Program, NYC, 1974, 81; writer-in-residence U. Ariz., 1984; judge Katherine Ann Porter Prize for Fiction, 1984, Artists Found. Author: Byron and the Spoiler's Art, 1960, rev. edit., 1990, I Said the Sparrow, 1963, The Snow Leopard, 1965, Tenement of Clay, 1965, The Wine of Absurdity, 1966, Alley Jaggers, 1967, libretta for opera, 1968, Words for a Deaf Daughter, 1969, I'm Expecting to Live Quite Soon, 1970, , Bela Lugosi's White Christmas, 1972, Caliban's Filibuster, 1972, Colonel Mint, 1973, Gala, 1976, The Very Rich Hours of Count von Stauffenberg, 1980, Out of My Depths: A Swimmer in the Universe, 1983, Rat Man of Paris, 1986, theatrical version, 1987, Sheer Fiction, 1987, The Universe and Other Fictions, 1988, The Place in Flowers Where Pollen Rests, 1988, Lord Byron's Doctor, 1989, Portable People, The Women of Whitechapel and Jack the Ripper, 1991, Sheer Fiction: II, 1991, James Ensor, 1991, Love's Mansion, 1992, Tenement of Clay, 2d edit., 1993, Sheer Fiction, III, 1994, A Stroke of Genius, 1995, The Tent of Orange Mist, 1995 (memoir) My Mother's Music, 1996, My Father's War, 2005; (novel) Sporting with Amaryllis, 1996, Terrestrials, 1997, Life With Swan, 1999, O.K.: The Corral, The Earps, and Doc Holliday, 2000, The Dry Danube: A Hitler Forgery, 2000, The Secret Lives of Words, 2000, A Fifth of November, 2001, Master Class, 2001, Oxford Days, 2002, Cheops: A Cupboard for the Sun, 2002, (play) Any Old How, 2002, (radio play) The Sacrifice, 1955, The Immensity of the Here and Now, 2003, Sheer Fiction IV, 2004, Samuel Beckett: Born Astride A Grave, 2004, My Father's War, 2005, Tea with Osiris, 2005, (TV) Sheer Fiction, IV, 2007, The Shadow factory, 2008; contbr. Washington Post and NY Times, 1962-2015, Harper's Mag., Paris Rev., Yale Rev., Parnassus, Agni, Conjunctions, War, Literature and the Arts, First Intensity, Tin Roof; (self-published books) Red in Tooth and Claw, The Ice Lens, The Invisible Riviera; translator Les Romanesques by Rostand, 1954 fiction judge NY Found. for the Arts, Nat. Book award, 1990, Cyclopelic a World Authors, Magills Choice Notable America Novelists. Served RAF, 1954—57. Decorated chevalier de l'Ordre des Arts et des Lettres (France); recipient Aga Khan Fiction prize, 1973, Hazlett Meml. award for Excellence in Arts (lit.), 1981, Lit. award Am. Acad. and Inst. Arts and Letters, 1985, Pushcart prize 1987, 91, 2003, The Best Am. Essays award, 1990, Outstanding Achievement medal Pa. State U., 1991, Grand Prix Halpérine Kaminsky award, 1992, Lannan Fiction award, 1993, Tchg. award Northeastern Assn. Grad. Sch., 1994, Art of Fact prize SUNY, 2000; named Lit. Lion NY Pub. Libr., 1987; Guggenheim fellow, 1963; NEA Creative Writing fellow, 1979, 84; nominated for Médicis, Femina and Meilleur Livre Étranger prizes, France, 1991, Lannan Lit. Videos 35, Nat. Book Critics award for fiction, 1996; named to Honor Roll The Yr. in Fiction, DLB Yearbook, 1996, Conf. on works of West, U. of Tours, France, 2003; manuscript collection at Pattee Libr., Pa. State U. Home: Ithaca, NY. *The unexamined life may not be worth having, but the examined life is endurable only to an open mind, through which life holistically flows, keeping that mind as incomplete as our knowledge of the universe itself.* Died Oct. 18, 2015.

WEXLER, HASKELL, film producer; b. Chgo., Feb. 6, 1922; s. Simon and Lottie Wexler; m. Nancy Ashenhurst (div.); two children; m. Marian Witt (div.); 1 son, Mark; m. Rita Taggart. Ednl. documentaries, Chgo., for eleven years; cinematographer films: The Hoodlum Priest, The Best Man, America America, The Loved One, In the Heat of the Night, Who's Afraid of Virginia Woolf? (Acad. award), The Thomas Crown Affair, American Graffiti, One Flew Over the Cuckoo's Nest, Introduction to the Enemy, Bound for Glory (Acad. award), Coming Home, Colors, Three Fugitives, 1988, Blaze, 1989, Lookin' to Get Out, Matewan, 1987, (Independent Spirit award), Other People's Money, The Babe, Mulholland Falls, 1995, Rich Man's Wife, 1995, (with others) Days of Heaven, (with others) Rolling Stones-IMAX, The Secret of Roan Inish, Canadian Bacon, Limbo, 1999, HBO 1961-2015, 2001, Silver City, 2004; writer, dir., photographer: Medium Cool, 1969; wrote and directed Latino, 1985; feature documentary Bus Riders Union, Five Days in March, Underground, 1976, From Wharf Rats to Lords of the Docks, Who Needs Sleep?, 2006, Four Days In Chicago. Received star on Hollywood's Walk of Fame, 1996. Mem. Acad. Motion Picture Arts and Scis. (bd. govs. cinematographers br.). Died Dec. 27, 2015.

WHARRAN, DAVID LYNN, physician; b. Liberal, Kans., Feb. 5, 1959; s. Ivan Leonard and Mary Lou (Cain) W.; m. Dana Sue French, Aug. 5, 1978; 1 child, Jessica Laynne. BA, Ottawa U., Kans., 1981; D of Chiropractic, Cleve. Chiropractic Coll., 1983. Intern Cleve. Chiropractic Coll., Kansas City, Mo., 1983-84; assoc. dr. Neuman Chiropractic Ctr., Garden City, Kans., 1984-85; head chiropractic physician Wharran Chiropractic Ctr., Chanute, Kans., from 1985. Mem. adminstrv. bd. 1st United Meth. Ch., Chanute, 1988—; co-chmn. Downtown Task Force, Chanute, 1988—. Mem. Kans. Chiropractic Assn. (alt. dir. Topeka chpt. 1988—), Parker Chiropractic Rsch. Found., S.E. Dist. Kans. Chiropractic Assn. (sec., treas. Chanute chpt. 1986-88), Chanute Area C. of C. (bd. dirs. 1987—, fin. chmn. 1987-88), Kans. Jaycees (leadership dir. Kans. chpt. 1984-85, Jaycees Presdl. award 1985, Speakup award 1985, Jaycee of the Yr. 1985). Republican. Methodist. Avocations: body building, golf, woodworking. Home: Pittsburg, Kans. Died May 25, 2007.

WHEELER, SUSIE WEEMS, retired school system administrator; b. Cassville, Ga., Feb. 24, 1917; d. Percy Weems and Cora (Smith) Weems-Canty; m. Dan W. Wheeler Sr., June 7, 1941; 1 child, Dan Jr. BS, Fort Valley State U., Ga., 1945; MEd, Atlanta U., 1947, EdD, 1978; postgrad., U. Ky., 1959-60; EdS, U. Ga., 1977. Tchr. Bartow County Schs., Cartersville (Ga.) City Schs., 1938-44, Jeanes supr., 1946-58; supr., curriculum dir. Paulding Sch. Sys.-Stephens Sch., Calhoun City, 1958-64; summer sch. tchr. Atlanta U., 1961-63; curriculum dir. Bartow County Schs., 1963-79; ret., 1979. Former co-owner Wheeler-Morris Svc. Ctr., 1990—; mem. Ga. Commn. on Student Fin., 1985-95. Coord. Noble Hill-Wheeler Meml. Ctr. Project, 1983—. Recipient Oscar W. Canty Cmty. Svc. award, 1991, Woman in History award Fedn. Bus. and Profl. Women, 1995, New Frontiers Cmty. Svc. award, 1997, Outstanding Achievement for Preserving Georgia Hist., 2000, Life Achievement award Etowah Valley Hist. Soc., 2005; recognized for dedicated svc. on behalf of Bartow County Citizens Comm. Clarence Brown, 2003; named one of Women of Excellence, Star of the Past Bartow Women at Work, 2003. Mem. AAUW (v.p. membership 1989-91, Ga. Achievement award 1993, Edn. Found. award Cartersville-Bartow br.), Ga. Assn. Curriculum and Supervision (pres.-elect 1973-74, pres. 1974-75, Johnnye V. Cox award 1975), Delta Sigma Theta (pres. Rome alumnae chpt. 1978-80, mem. nat. bd. 1984, planning com. 1988—, Dynamic Delta award 1967, 78, Grand Chpt. cert. recognition 2002, recognition 50 plus years, Cartersville Rotary Club (Jean Harris award, 2004), Delta Sigma Theta Sorority, Inc., 2002), Ga. Jeanes Assn. (pres. 1968-70), Delta Kappa Gamma. Home: Birmingham, Ala. Died July 22, 2007.

WHEELING, VIRGINIA MARIE, social services agency administrator; b. Fillmore, Ill., Oct. 9, 1935; d. Robert Homer and Jessie Irene (Grant) Finley; m. Richard Max Wheeling, Oct. 19, 1954 (div. 1964); children: Thomas Richard, Robert Anthony, Theresa Marie, Clarissa Lea. Grad. high sch., Fillmore. County coord. CEFS Econ. Opportunity Corp., Effingham, Ill., 1967-72; exec. dir. Sr. Citizens Montgomery County, Hillsboro, Ill., 1972-87, Sr. Citizens Sangamon County, Inc., Springfield, Ill., from 1988. Mem. Assn. Ill. Sr. Ctrs. (officer), Ill. Gerontology Consortium (officer), Ill. Coalition on Aging (governing bd. 1990-91), Ill. Paratransit Assn. Methodist. Avocations: reading, gardening. Home: Fillmore, Ill. Died Jan. 6, 2007.

WHERRY, PAUL ARTHUR, retired pharmaceutical sales professional, pharmacist; b. Vandergrift, Pa., Jan. 21, 1927; s. Paul Arthur Sr. and Edith (Scott) W.; m. Nancy McGinnis, Sept. 12, 1953; children: Carole Jean, Mark Byron, Thomas Matthew. BS in Pharmacy, Duquesne U., 1952. Lic. pharmacist, Ohio, Pa. Profl. service rep. E.R. Squibb, Cleve. then Columbus, Ohio, 1952-54, hosp. rep. Columbus, 1954-62, full line rep., 1977-82, key acct. rep., 1982-91; pres. Med. Svc. Reps., Worthington, Ohio, from 1958. Pres. Colonial Hills Civic Assn., Worthington, Ohio, 1962. Mem. Am. Pharm. Assn., Ohio Pharm. Assn. (trustee 1983-85), Nat. Assn. Retail Pharmacies, Acad. Pharmacy (pres. cen. Ohio chpt. 1988), Columbus Maennerchor. Republican. Avocations: golf, woodworking. Died Aug. 3, 2007.

WHETTEN, LAWRENCE L., international relations educator; b. Provo, Utah, June 12, 1932; s. Lester B. and Kate (Allred) W.; m. Gabriele Indra, Oct. 28, 1974 (dec. May 1985). BA, Brigham U., 1954, MA, 1955; PhD with honors, NYU, 1963. Sr. polit. analyst Hdqrs. USAFE, Wiesbaden, Fed. Republic Germany, 1963-70; resident dir. grad. program in internat. relations U. So. Calif., Munich, Fed. Republic Germany, 1971-78, dir. studies USC/SIR grad. program in Germany, 1978-86; Erich Voegelin Gast prof. Munich U., 1987-88; lectr. Boston U., from 1988; lectr. Profl. Assoc. Ctr. Def. and Strategic Studies S.W. Mo. State U., Springfield, from 1991. Cons. Fgn. Policy Inst., Phila., 1969-71, 76-79, R & D Assocs., Munich, 1977; prof. Hochschule für Politik, Munich U.; adj. prof., profl. assoc. Ctr. for Def. and Strategic Studies, S.W. Mo. State U., 1991—. Author: Germany's Ostpolitik, 1971, Contemporary American Foreign Policy, 1974, The Canal War: Four Power Conflict, 1974, Germany East and West, 1981. Author, editor: Present State Communist Internationalism, 1983, The Interaction of Political Reforms Within the East Block, 1989. Served to capt. USAF, 1960-63 Penfield fellow NYU, 1957-59; grantee Ford Found., 1970, Royal Inst. Internat. Affairs, London, 1970, Thyssen Found., Cologne, Germany, 1974-82, 89, Volkswagen Found., 1982-85 Mem. Am. Acad. Polit. and Social Scis., Internat. Inst. Strategic Studies, Am. Assn. Advancement of Soviet Studies, Gesellschaft für Auslandskunde, German Am. Assn. Home: Munich, Germany. Died Sept. 27, 2007.

WHITAKER, RUTH REED, state legislator, retired publishing executive; b. Blytheville, Ark., Dec. 13, 1936; d. Lawrence Neill and Ruth Shipton (Weidemeyer) Reed; m. Thomas Jefferson Whitaker, dec. 29, 1961; children: Steven Bryan, Alicia Morrow. BA, Hendrix Coll., 1958. Copywriter, weather person KTVE TV, El Dorado, Ark., 1958-59; nat. bridal cons. Treasure House, El Dorado, 1959; bridal cons. Pfeifers of Ark., Little Rock, 1959-60; dir. of continuity S. M. Brooks Advt. Agy., Little Rock, 1960-61; layout artist C. V. Mosby Co., St. Louis, 1961-62; editor, owner Razorback American Newspaper, Ft. Smith, Ark., 1979-81; ret., 1981; mem. Dist. 3 Ark. State Senate, 2001—13. Host Crawford Conversations TV show; contbr. author indsl. catalog, 1979 (Addy award). State sec. Republican Party of Ark., 1992-94, mem. Ark. Electoral Coll., 1996, del. Republican Nat. Conv., 1996;; mem. Ben Geren Regional Park Commn., Sebastian County, Ark., 1984-89, pres., 1990; past pres. Jr. Civic League; mem. Ft. Smith Orchid Com.; mem. com. of 21 United Way; publicity chmn. Sebastian County Republican Com., 1983-84; state press officer Reagan-Bush Campaign, 1984; exec. dir. Ark. Dole for Pres., 1995-96; pres. Women's Aux. Sebastian County Med. Soc., 1974; mem. Razorback Scholarship Fund; class agt. alumni fund Hendrix Coll., 1990, 91, 92; mem. Sparks Woman's Bd.; 1st vice chmn. 3d Dist. Republican Party; state committeewoman Republican Party Ark.; chmn. Crawford County Republican Com.; apptd. by Gov. of Ark. to Commr. Ark. Ednl. TV Network Commn., sec. 1998-99; mem. city coun. City of Cedarville, Ark., 1998; dist. panelist NOW in Bux., 2003. Recipient Disting. Vol. Leadership award Nat. Found. March of Dimes, 1973, Appreciation award Ft. Smith Advt. Fedn., 1977, 78, Recognition award United Cerebral Palsy, 1980, Hon. Parents of Yr. award U. Ark., 1984, Firekeeper award Sparks Hosp. Women's Ctr., 2003. Mem. AAUW, Alden Soc. America (life), Ft. Smith Chamber of Commerce, Ark. Nature Conservancy, American Legion Aux., Frontier Rschrs. Soc. (pres. 1995-96), Daus. Union Vets. Republican. Presbyterian. Avocations: philanthropy, genealogy, writing, photography, ornithology. Died Nov. 10, 2014.

WHITCOMB, EDGAR DOUD, former governor; b. Hayden, Ind., Nov. 6, 1917; s. John William and Louise Doud Whitcomb; m. Patricia Louise Dolfuss, 1951 (div. 1987); children: Patricia Louise, Alice Elaine, Linda Ann, John Doud, Shelley Jean; m. Mary Evelyn Gayer, 2013. Student, Ind. U., 1936—39, LLB, 1950, LLD (hon.), 1973. Mem. Ind. State Senate, 1951—54; asst. US atty. Justice Dept. (southern dist.) Ind., 1954—56; atty. Seymour, Ind., 1956—83; chmn. Great Lakes Commn., 1965—66; sec. state State of Ind., 1966—68, gov., 1969—73; del. Rep. Nat. Conv., 1972. Author: Escape from Corregidor, 1958, On Celestial Wings, 1996. From flying cadet to maj. USAF, 1940—46, ret. as col. USAF, 1977. Decorated Air medal with Oak Leaf Cluster, Presdl. unit citation with 6 Oak Leaf Clusters. Mem.: Am. Legion, AMVETS (life), Am. Defenders of Battan & Corregidor (life), VFW (life), DAV (life), Phi Delta Phi. Republican. Methodist. Died Feb. 4, 2016.

WHITE, ANN STEWART, language educator, consultant; b. Petersburg, Va., July 24, 1960; d. John Carroll and Agnes Cordelia (Glunt) W. BA in Spanish and internat. studies, Willamette U., 1983; MA in Spanish, lang. and lits., U. Pitts., 1986, PhD Spanish, Linguistics, tchg. methods, 1988. Cert. Latin Am. studies, 1988. Asst. prof. Spanish, tchg. asst. coord. Mich. State U., East Lansing, Mich., 1988-94; asst. prof. Hispanic Studies Conn. Coll., New London, Conn., 1994-97; asst. prof. Spanish Va. Commonwealth Univ., Richmond, from 1997. Adv. coun. mem. Ctrl. States Conf. Fgn. Langs., Indpls., 1991-92; manuscript cons., reviewer McGraw-Hill, Heinle & Heinle, John Wiley Publs., 1989—. Contbr. articles to profl. jours., book reviews. Recipient grants, 1989, 91. Mem. MLA, Fgn. Lang. Assn. of Va., Mich. Fgn. Lang. Assn. (pres. 1992-93), Am. Assn. Tchrs. Spanish & Portuguese, Phi Sigma Iota (pres. 1982-83, officer), Sigma Delta Pi (hon.), Golden Key Nat. Honor. Soc. (hon.). Democrat. Presbyterian. Avocations: painting, photography, calligraphy, travel. Home: Richmond, Va. Died Mar. 3, 2007.

WHITE, DAPHNE MILBANK, writer; b. Vancouver, Can., Apr. 12, 1927; d. Robbins Milbank and Mary Lightfoot; m. Barrie M. White Jr., Sept. 13, 1947 (div. 1966); children: Deborah, Pamela, Ellen, Barrie. BA in Polit. Sci., Smith Coll., 1948; MS in Pub. Affairs, Am. U., 1979; postgrad., George Washington U., 1979—82. Co-mgr. four small bus., 1947—51; br. chief Am. U., Cultural Info. Analysis Ctr., Washington, 1967—68; voters svc. sr. staff specialist League of Women Voters Edn. Fund, Washington, 1969—72; comm. dir. Pub. Affairs Coun., Washington, 1973—74; writer, editor, paralegal, Office Gen. Coun. Nat. Oceanic and Atmospheric Adminstrn., Washington, 1975—78, writer, editor regulations. devel. analyst, Nat. Marine Fisheries Svc., 1979—90, program analyst, Ctr. Ocean Analysis and Prediction Monterey, Calif., 1990—92, program analyst, Monterey Bay Nat. Marine Sanctuary, 1992—93; ret., 1993. Contbr. articles to profl. jours. Enumerator and reviewer Census, 1960; bd. dirs. Youth Citizenship Fund, 1970—72; bd dirs. Memton Fund, Inc., 1981—95, pres., 1989—94; vol. guide Monterey Bay Aquarium, 1993—97; mem. adv. coun. subcom. Monterey Bay Nat. Marine Sanctuary, from 1994; bd. dirs. LWV Monterey Peninsula, 1994—97, Girl Scouts Am. Mem.: LWV, Elkhorn Slough Found., Nonprofit Devel. Ctr., U.N. Assn., Fgn. Policy Assn., Marine Mammal Ctr., Save Our Shores, Cmty. Found., Friends Long Marine Lab, Coyote Point Mus., Monterey History and Art Assn., Environ. Defense, Ocean Conservancy. Home: Peterborough, NH. Died Jan. 1, 2007.

WHITE, GARNETT LEE, psychologist, history educator; b. Newport News, Va., July 30, 1944; s. David F. Sr. and Louise (Atwood) W.; m. Patricia Clifton, June 30, 1967 (div. June 1979); m. Patricia Davis, June 1, 1985; 1 child, Matthew John Pekar. BA, U. Richmond, 1965, MA, 1967, Vanderbilt U., 1970, PhD, 1975; MS in Psychology, Va. Commonwealth U., 1986, PhD in Psychology, 1989. Lic. clin. psychologist, Va. Intern in psychology VA Med. Ctr., Salem, Va., 1987-88; resident in pvt. practice and managed care Behavioral Svcs. Ctr. and Options Mental Health, Midlothian, Va., 1989-90; outpatient treatment coord. Options Mental Health, Richmond, 1989-91, clin. coord., 1992; staff psychologist United Behavioral Systems, Richmond, 1992-93, Nova Care Rehab. Hosp. of Va., from 1993; pvt. practice clin. psychology Petersburg, Va., from 1990, Richmond, from 1992; care mgr. Green Spring of Va., from 1995. Teaching fellow in history Vanderbilt U., 1967-68; assoc. prof. history and philosophy Paul D. Camp C.C., Franklin, Va., 1971-81; adj. assoc. prof. philosophy Old Dominion U., Norfolk, Va., 1975-81; adj. instr. philosophy Va. Wesleyan Coll., 1978-79; adj. asst. prof. history U. Richmond, Va., 1981-82; adj. in history Va. Commonwealth U., Richmond, 1985—; presenter in field. Contbr. articles to profl. jours. Chmn. bicentennial Franklin (Va.)-Southampton Bicentennial Commn., 1974-76; pres. Southampton County (Va.) Hist. Soc., 1979-81. Mem. APA, AAUP (pres. Va. conf. 1979-80), Va. Acad. Clin. Psychology, Va. Psychol. Assn., Richmond Acad. Clin. Psychology (treas.), Phi Alpha Theta. Baptist. Home: Richmond, Va. Died Nov. 10, 2006.

WHITE, HARLAN EDWARD, agronomist, educator; b. Seaford, Del., Nov. 24, 1937; s. James Clarence and Anna Rebecca (Wheatley) W.; m. Jean Fluharty, Sept. 6, 1958; children: Joseph, Robert, Linda Jean. BS, U. Del., 1959; MS, Rutgers U., 1962, PhD, 1964. Prof. Va. Poly. Inst. and State U., Blacksburg, from 1966. Bd. dirs. Am. Forage & Grassland Coun., Lexington, Ky., 1981-84, Forage & Grassland Found., Lexington, 1984-87. Capt., Chem. Corp., U.S. Army, 1964-66. Recipient Geigy award Am. Soc. Agronomy, 1974, Extension Edn. award, 1985, Extension Excellence award Gamma Sigma Delta, 1986. Methodist. Home: Blacksburg, Va. Died June 4, 2007.

WHITE, HELEN FRANCES PEARSON, language educator, real estate broker; b. Bucoda, Mo., Sept. 26, 1925; d. William Sidney and Ella Myrtle Isaccs) Pearson; m. Jewel Porter White, June 21, 1942; children: Sydney LaVergne, Betty Ann, John Patrick. BA, Ark. State U., 1955; postgrad., U. Toulouse, 1965, U. Okla., 1962-64, U. Mex., 1966, Tex. A&M U., 1969; credited study tour on Creole Lang., Tex. A&M, 1969. Life time teaching lic. Mo., Tex., lic. real estate broker, lic. 1st class radio engr., FCC. High sch. English tchr., Manila, Ark., 1955-57; high sch. English, French tchr. New Madrid, Mo., 1958-63; Spanish, French tchr. Hardin Jefferson High Sch., Sour Lake, Tex., 1964-71; cons., instr. Radio Stas. KKAS & KWDX, Silsbee, Tex., from 1969; broker Accent Corner Real Estate, Silsbee, from 1981. Tour dir. Robbins Ednl. Tours, Marquand, Mo., 1957-64, Whites' Tours, Silsbee, 1968—; host family, S.E. Tex. area rep. Youth for Understanding, 1968-75; workshop participant, job tng. instr., Programs for Human Svcs., 1981-84; pvt. lang. tutor, Portageville, Mo., Silsbee. Preservationist Hist. Landmark, 1991 (Tex. Hist. Commn. award for Old Silsbee Ice House); mem. Concept of Care, Kountze, Tex., 1985-88, Hardin County Tourist Bur.; charter commr. S.E. Tex. Women's Commn., 1985-88; coun. mem. County Assn. for Retarded Persons, Silsbee, 1986-89; pres. Silsbee Libr. Adv. Bd., 1986; founder, pres. Hardin County Arts and Ednl. Found., 1987—; mem. First Meth. Ch. Grantee Tex. A&M U., 1969. Mem. AAUW (life, pres. Hardin County br. 1983-86), Hardin County Geneal. Soc., Alpha Delta Kappa. Avocations: philatelist, numismatist, writing, art appreciation. Home: Silsbee, Tex. Died Feb. 4, 2007.

WHITE, JANET MURPHREE, educational administrator; b. Kansas City, Mo., Mar. 14, 1946; d. John Clarence and Ella Emma Mary (Waack) Murphree; m. Harold S. White, July 4, 1970; children: Julia Lee, Alan Edward. BA, William Woods Coll., 1968; MA, U. Mo., 1985; PhD, Kent State U., 1988. Asst. dean admissions William Woods Coll., Fulton, Mo., 1968-70; tchr. Fountain (Colo.)-Ft. Carson Schs., 1971-73, Boone Grove (Ind.) Schs., 1978-79; dir. fin. aid William Woods Coll., 1979-82, v.p. coll. svcs., 1982-85; v.p. instl. advancement Notre Dame Coll., Cleve., 1987-90. Contbr. to edn. periodicals. Episcopalian. Died Nov. 13, 2006.

WHITE, LONNIE JOE, retired history educator; b. Knox City, Tex., Feb. 12, 1931; s. John Alexander and Fannie Coates White; m. Nancy Louella Evans, June 23, 1951; children: John Evans, Brenda Jo White Holman. BA in History, W. Tex. State Coll., 1950; MA in History, Tex. Tech. Coll., 1955; PhD in History, U. Tex., Austin, 1961. Tchg. asst. history U. Tex., Austin, 1957—61; prof. history Memphis State Univ. (now U. Memphis), 1961—89; prof. emeritus U. Memphis, from 1989. Editl. adv. bd. Jour. of the West, Manhattan, Kans., 1963—88; assoc. edit. Military History of Texas and the Southwest, Austin, Tex., 1977—88. Author: Politics on the Southwestern Frontier: Arkansas Territory, 1819-1836, 1964, Panthers to Arrowheads: The 36th (Texas-Oklahoma) Division in World War I, 1984, The 90th Division in World War I: The Texas-Oklahoma Draft Division in the Great War, 1996; co-author: Hostiles and Horse Soldiers: Indian Battles and Campaigns In the West, 1972; co-editor: By Sea to San Francisco, 1849-50: The Journal of Dr. James Morison, 1977, 2nd edit., 2000; editor: Old Mobeetie, 1877-1885: Texas Panhandle News Items from the Dodge City Times, 1967, The Miles Expedition of 1874-1875: An Eyewitness Account of the Red River War, 1971, Chronicle of a Congressional Journey: The Doolittle Committee in the Southwest, 1865, 1975; contbr. more than 45 articles to profl. jour., book reviews over 97 pub. to prof. jour. Sgt. US Army, 1951—53. Grantee Rsch. Grant, Am. Philos. Soc., 1963. Mem.: So. Hist. Assn., Am. Hist. Assn. Republican. Baptist. Avocations: history, writing, travel, flying, genealogy. Home: Texarkana, Tex. Died Feb. 26, 2015.

WHITE, MAURICE, singer, musician; b. Memphis, Dec. 19, 1941; Attended, Chgo. Conservatory Coll. Drummer, formerly session musician, played in local clubs, also with, Ramsey Lewis, 1966-1969; founder, percussionist: musical group Earth Wind and Fire (formally named Salty Peppers), 1971—2016; recorded for, Warner Bros., now, Columbia Records; soundtracks for movies That's the Way of the World, Sweet Sweetback's Baaadaaas Song; songs recorded include Love Is Life, Keep Your Head to the Sky, Shining Star, Can't Hide Love, Getaway, Fantasy; founder, percussionist: albums include Last Days and Time (Gold Album), Head to the Sky, (Gold Album), Open Our Eyes, (Gold

Album), That's the Way of the World, (Gold Album), Gratitude, (Gold Album), Faces. Named to Rock and Roll Hall of Fame, 2000, Songwriters Hall of Fame, 2010. Died Feb. 2016.

WHITE, ROBERT MAYER, meteorologist; b. Boston, Feb. 13, 1923; s. David and Mary (Winkeller) W.; m. Mavis E. Seagle, Apr. 18, 1948; children: Richard Harry, Edwina Janet. BA, Harvard, 1944; MS, Mass. Inst. Tech., 1949, Sc.D., 1950; D.Sc., L.I. U., 1976; D.Sc. (hon.), Rensselaer Poly. Inst., 1977, U. Wis., Milw., 1978; ScD (hon.), U. Bridgeport, 1984, U. R.I., 1986, Clarkson U.; PhD (hon.), Johns Hopkins U., 1982, Drexel U., 1985, Ill. Inst. Tech., 1994. Project scientist Air Force Cambridge Rsch. Ctr., 1950-58, chief meteorol. devel. lab., 1958-59; asso. dir. research dept. Travelers Ins. Co., 1959-60; pres. Travelers Rsch. Ctr., Inc., 1960-63; chief US Weather Bur., 1963-65; adminstr. Environ. Sci. Svcs. Adminstrn., 1965-70, NOAA, 1970-77; pres. Joint Oceanographic Inst., Inc., 1977-79; chmn. Climate Research Bd., exec. officer Nat. Acad. Scis., 1977-79; adminstr. NRC, 1979-80; pres. Univ. Corp. Atmospheric Rsch., 1980-83, Nat. Acad. Eng., 1983-95; Karl T. Compton lectr. MIT, Cambridge, 1995-96; sr. fellow U. Corp. Atmospheric Rsch., 1995—2015. Sr. fellow H. John Heinz III Ctr. for Sci., Econs. and Environment, 1996—2000; pres. Wash. Adv. Group, from 1996. Author: articles in field; mem. editl. bd.: Am. Soc. Engring. Edn. Jour. Bd. overseers Harvard U., 1977—79; mem. vis. com. Kennedy Sch. Govt., Harvard U.; bd. dirs. Resources for the Future, from 1980. Capt. USAF, World War II. Decorated Legion of Honor France; recipient Godfrey L. Cabot award, Aero Club Boston, 1966, Cleveland Abbe award, Am. Meteorol. Soc., 1969, Jesse L. Rosenberger medal, U. Chgo., 1971, Rockefeller Pub. Svc. award, 1974, David B. Stone award, New Eng. Aquarium, 1975, Neptune award, Am. Oceanic Orgn., 1977, Matthew Fontaine Maury award, Smithsonian Instn., 1976, Internat. Conservation award, Nat. Wildlife Fedn., 1976, Internat. Meteorol. Orgn. prize, 1980, Tyler prize for Environ. Achievement, U. Calif., 1992, Vannevar Bush award, Nat. Sci. Bd., 1998, Centenary medal, Australia, 2003, Milennium award, Australian Acad. Engring., 2003. Fellow: Am. Acad. Arts and Scis., Australian Acad. Tech. Scis. and Engring., Am. Geophys. Union, World Acad. Art and Scis., AAAS, UCAR (sr.), Am. Meteorol. Soc. (coun. 1965—67, from 1977, pres. 1980, Charles Franklin Brooks award1978); mem.: Royal Acad. Engring. (U.K.), Russian Acad. Engring., Royal Acad. Engring. (hon.), Engring. Acad. Japan (fgn. assoc.), Am. Philos. Soc., Finnish Acad. Tech. (fgn.), Nat. Action Coun. Minorities in Engring. Inc., Coun. Fgn. Rels., Marine Tech. Soc., NAE (coun. 1977, pres. 1983—95), Cosmos Club (Washington). Home: Bethesda, Md. Died Oct. 14, 2015.

WHITE, VIRGINIA, chemistry educator; b. Cardiff, Wales, June 17, 1939; came to U.S., 1968; d. Stanley Herbert and Thelma Alice (Hansen) Preston; m. Brian White, Feb. 19, 1936 (div.); children: Kathleen Sally, David William. BSc magna cum laude, U. Wales, 1961; MA in Chemistry, Smith Coll., 1978. Tchr. chemistry Highfields Bilateral Sch., Wolverampton, Eng., 1960-61, Newport (Wales) High Sch., 1961-66; geochemist Nova Scotia Rsch. Found., Can., 1966-68; lab. instr. chemistry Smith Coll., Northampton, Mass., 1970-77, lab. dir., instr. chemistry, from 1977. Chair Necuse Lab. Devel., 1988-90. Author: the Outermost Island, 1985, Light and Matter, 1990; contbr. articles to profl. jours. Fellow Sigma Xi; mem. Smith Coll. Amunae Soc. Achievements include research in medicinal bush medicines. Home: Northampton, Mass. Died Nov. 1, 2006.

WHITE, WILLIAM ROY, banker, federal official; b. Kenora, Ont., Can., May 17, 1943; s. Fredrick T. and Helen E. (Mc Cann) W.; m. Margaret Philson, Jan. 2, 1972; children: Matthew J., Katherine L. BA with honors, U. Windsor, Ont., 1965; MSc in Econs., U. Manchester, Eng., 1966; PhD in Econs., U. Manchester, 1969. Economist Bank of England, London, U.K., 1969-72, Bank of Can., Ottawa, 1972-79, chief rsch. dept., 1979-84, adviser to gov., 1984-88, dep. gov., 1988-94. Contbr. articles to profl. jours. Died Nov. 13, 2006.

WHITEHEAD, JOHN CUNNINGHAM, retired bank executive, former federal agency administrator; b. Evanston, Ill., Apr. 2, 1922; s. Eugene C. and Winifred W.; m. Helene E. Shannon, Sept. 28, 1946 (div. Dec. 1971); children: Anne Elizabeth, John Gregory; m. Jaan W. Chartener, Oct. 22, 1972 (div. 1986); 1 child, Sarah; m. Nancy Dickerson, 1989 (dec. 1997); m. Cynthia Matthews, Feb. 7, 2007; 7 step children BA, Haverford Coll., 1943; MBA, Harvard U., 1947; LLD (hon.), Pace. U., Rutgers U., Haverford Coll., Harvard U., Amherst Coll., Seton Hall U.; LLD, Bates Coll., 2004; Gen. Theological Seminary, Berea Coll. With Goldman, Sachs & Co., NYC, 1947-84, ptnr., 1956-76, sr. ptnr., co-chmn., 1976-84; dep. sec. US Dept. State, Washington, 1985-89; chmn. Fed. Res. Bank NY, NYC, 1996—2000, Lower Manhattan Devel. Corp., NYC, 2001—06. Co-owner NJ Devils. Author: A Life in Leadership: From D-Day to Ground Zero, 2005. Trustee Haverford Coll.; past pres. bd. overseers Harvard U.; co-chmn. greater N.Y. coun. Boy Scouts Am.; past chmn. Internat. Rescue Com., UN Assn. U.S.A.; Andrew Mellon Found; founding chmn. World Trade Ctr. Meml. Found., 2005-, former chmn. Brookings Instn., Internat. House, Nat. Gallery of Art; dir. Nature Conservancy, East West Inst., Eisenhower Exch. Fellowship. With USNR, 1943—46. Mem. Coun. on Fgn. Rels., Links Club, Univ. Club, Knickerbocker Club. Republican. Home: New York, NY. Died Feb. 7, 2015.

WHITEHEAD, KENNETH DEAN, writer, translator, retired federal agency administrator, editor; b. Rupert, Idaho, Dec. 14, 1930; s. Clarence Christian and May Bell (Allen) W.; m. Margaret Mary O'Donohue, Aug. 2, 1958; children: Paul Daniel, Steven Francis, Matthew Patrick, David Joseph. BA in French, U. Utah, 1955; postgrad., U. Paris, 1956-57; cert. in Arabic and Middle East studies, Fgn. Service Inst., Beirut, 1962; LittD (hon.), Franciscan U., Steubenville, Oho, 2003. Instr. English U. Utah, Salt Lake City, 1955-56; fgn. service officer Dept. State, Rome, Beirut and Tripoli, Libya, 1957-65; chief Arabic service Voice of Am., Washington, 1965-67; dep. dir. fgn. currency program Smithsonian Instn., Washington, 1967-72; exec. v.p. Caths. United for Faith Inc., New Rochelle, NY, 1972-81; dir. Ctr. for Internat. Edn. U.S. Dept. Edn., Washington, 1982-86, dep. asst. sec. for higher edn. programs, 1986-88, asst. sec. for postsecondary edn., 1988-89. Author: Respectable Killing: The New Abortion Imperative, 1972, Agenda for the Sexual Revolution, 1981, Catholic Colleges and Federal Funding, 1988, DOA: The Ambush of the Universal Catechism, 1993, Political Orphan? The Prolife Cause after 25 Years of Roe v. Wade, 1998, One, Holy, Catholic, and Apostolic: The Early Church Was the Catholic Church, 2000, The New Ecumenism, 2009, Mass Misunderstandings: The Mixed Legacy of the Vatican II Liturgicul Reforms, 2009, The Renewed Church, 2009, Affirming Religious Freedom, 2010; co-author: The Pope, The Council and the Mass, 1981, rev. edit., 2006, Flawed Expectations: The Reception of the Catechism of the Catholic Church, 1996; sr. editor: World Almanac Book of Dates, 1982, Macmillan Concise Dictionary of World History, 1983; editor: Marriage and the Common Good, 2001, Pope John Paul II--Witness to Truth, 2001, The Catholic Imagination, 2003, Voices of the New Springtime, 2004, The Catholic Citizen: Debating the Issues of Justice, 2004, The Church, Marriage, and the Family, 2007, Vatican Council II's Diverse Legacy, 2007, Sacrosanctumn Concilium & the Reform of the Liturgy, 2009, The Idea of the Catholic University, 2009, Conscience, Cooperation And Complicity, 2010, The Thought of Joseph Ratzinger Pope Benedict XVI, 2010; co-editor: The Battle for the Catholic Mind, 2001, The Second Vaticurs Ecumenical Coun., 2010; translator 20 books from French, German, Italian, 1980—. Bd. dir. Notre Dame Inst. for Advanced Study, Arlington, Va., 1986-95, Philosophy Edn. Soc., 1995—, Christas Magister Found., 1997-2001. Fulbright scholar U.S. Dept. State, 1956-57. Mem. Fellowship Cath. Scholars (bd. dir. 1990-2000, 2004-10), Brent Soc. Cath. Profls. (bd. dir. 1992-98), Cath. League for Religious and Civil Rights (bd. dir. 1992—), KC. Republican. Home: Falls Church, Va. Died Apr. 16, 2015.

WHITLATCH, ELBERT EARL, JR., engineering educator, consultant; b. Braddock, Pa., Oct. 29, 1942; s. Elbert Earl and Wanda Louisa (Gibson) W.; m. Janet Kay Baker, June 15, 1974; children: Susan Elizabeth, Brian David. BS in Engring. magna cum laude, Geneva Coll., 1965; BSCE, Carnegie-Mellon U., 1965; MS in Environ. Engring., Johns Hopkins U., 1967, PhD in Environ. Sys. Engring., 1973. Asst. prof. Ohio State U., Columbus, 1973-79, assoc. prof., from 1979; dir. Ohio Water Resources Ctr., Columbus, 1995—2006. Co-author: Civil and Environmental Systems Engineerng, 1997, 2d edit., 2004; contbr. articles to profl. jours. With U.S. Peace Corps., 1967-69. Johns Hopkins fellow, 1965—67, 1969—73. Mem. ASCE (Edn. Rsch. award 1983), Am. Geophys. Union, Am. Water Resources Assn., Am. Water Works Assn., Internat. Water Resources Assn., Inst. for Mgmt. Sci., Water Mgmt. Assn. Ohio, Sierra Club. Avocations: reading, hiking, wildlife conservation, nature observation. Home: Columbus, Ohio. Died Aug. 9, 2007.

WHITMIRE, JOHN LEE, daycare provider; b. Brevard, NC, June 17, 1924; s. John Leander and Betty Burr (Owen) W.; m. Eva Lee Wilson, Aug. 13, 1950; 1 child, Bonita Dawn. Student, Brevard Coll., 1948-49; BS in Acctg., U. Balt., 1960. Asst. tchr. agr. pub. schs., Brevard, 1946-48; office mgr. Peninsula Poultry Co., Balt., 1955-59; auditor accounts receivable Ea. Products Corp., Balt., 1959-62; chief acct. Texize Corp., Mauldin, S.C., 1962-63; contr. Atlas Vending Co., Greenville, S.C., 1966-69; owner, dir. Twinkle Kiddie Kollege & Day Care, Greenville, from 1969. Lobbyist state day care regulation, Columbia, S.C., 1977-81; mem. Adv. Com. on Regulation Child Day Care Facilities, Columbia, 1982-83; field counselor Day Care Child Trend, N.C., S.C., Ga., Ala., Miss., Tenn., Ark. Recipient 100% Dist. Leader Dog award Leader Dogs for the Blind, 1992, 100% Dist. Gov.'s award 1992. Mem. long range planning com. Grove Sch., East Gantt Sch., Greenville; precinct committeeman Greenville Dem. Com., 1970—. Sgt. AUS, 1944-46, ETO; with U.S. Army, 1950-52, Korea. Decorated Purple Heart. Recipient Model Sector Coord. award Campaign Sight First, 1993, Key Leader award, 1993, Leadership award, 1995. Mem. ASCD, Lions (1st v.p. Pleasantburg, L.C. 1985-86, pres. 1987-88, zone chmn. dist. 32-A 1988-89, region chmn. 1989-90, lt. gov. 1990-91, dist. gov. 1991-92, extension chmn., bd. dirs. S.C. Lions Sight Conservation Assn., contbr. Internat. Lions Mag., 1992, Palmetto Lion, 1993-94, Lion of Yr. award 1985, cert. of appreciation from internat. pres. 1989, 91, S.C. Eye Bank Vol. of Yr. award 1992). Baptist. Home: Greenville, SC. Died Dec. 6, 2006.

WHITMORE, FRANK WILLIAM, plant physiologist; b. Ponca City, Okla., May 15, 1932; s. Ralph Wendell and Charlotte Estelle (Cullen) W.; m. Betty Lou Spear, Sept. 14, 1955; children: Susan Adams, David Cullen, Sarah Spear (dec.). BS, Okla. State U., 1954; PhD, U. Mich., 1964. Rsch. forester USDA Forest Svc., Crossett, Ark., 1957-61, plant physiologist Pineville, La., 1964-65; rsch. assoc. U. Mich., Ann Arbor, 1965-67; from asst. prof. to prof. Ohio State U., Wooster, from 1967. Mem. peer review panels U.S. Dept. Agrl., Washington, 1985, 87, Agrl. Biotech. Rsch. Adv. Com., USDA, Washington, 1988—. Contbr. articles to profl. jours. Coun. mem. Wooster City Coun., 1978-85; vice chmn. Wayne Met. Housing Authority, Wooster, 1974-78; del. Dem. Nat. Conv., Miami Beach, Fla., 1972. With U.S. Army, 1955-57. Mem. Am. Soc. Plant Physiologists, Soc. Am. Foresters, Internat. Soc. Plant Molecular Biologists. Democrat. Home: Salisbury, Md. Died Apr. 9, 2007.

WHITNEY, CHARLES LEROY, lawyer; b. Aurora, Nebr., Oct. 1, 1918; s. Charles Leroy and Alta Leona (Entriken) W.; m. Emily Louise Rothman, Nov. 17, 1942; children: Charles Leroy III, Anne Rothman, Mary Elizabeth, William Shafer. AB, York Coll.; LLB, U. Nebr. Bar: Nebr. 1946. Pvt. practice, Aurora, 1946-59; ptnr. Whitney and Newman, Aurora, 1959-73; sr. ptnr. Whitney, Newman, Mersch & Otto, Aurora, 1974-87, of counsel, from 1987. Bd. dirs. Prairie Plains Inst., Aurora. Served to lt. USNR, 1942-46, PTO. Mem. Nebr. State Bar Assn., Aurora C. of C., Am. Legion (past comdr. local post). Democrat. United Methodist. Avocations: fishing, woodworking, photography. Home: Aurora, Nebr. Died July 26, 2007.

WICKERSHAM, ERSKINE BREWSTER, JR., apparel sales company executive; b. Augusta, Ga., Nov. 7, 1943; s. Erskine Brewster and Vivian (Granade) W. BS, Ga. Inst. Tech., 1965. Sales rep. IBM, Atlanta, 1965-67, Honeywell Inc., Atlanta, 1967-69; pres. Lee Kennedy & Assocs., Atlanta, 1969-79; nat. sales mgr. Johnston & Murphy, Nashville, 1979-87; pres. Wickersham Golf Mgmt. Co., Atlanta, from 1987. Mem. Atlanta Country Club, The Farm Golf Club. Avocations: golf, travel. Home: Marietta, Ga. Died July 7, 2007.

WIECKOWSKA, WANDA STEFANIA, retired obstetrician; b. Czestochowa, Poland, Nov. 19, 1920; came to U.S., 1968. d. Edmund Michal and Maria (Bartoszek) Reimschussel; m. Tadeusz Wieckowski, 1940 (dec. 1969); children: John, Anna. MD, U. Poznan, 1948; PhD, Med. Sch., Warsaw, Poland, 1967. Postdoctoral fellow Roswell Pk. Meml. Inst., Buffalo, 1968-70; resident in ob-gyn. Deaconess Hosp./SUNY, Buffalo, 1970-73; pvt. practice, 1973—2001; clin. assoc. prof. SUNY, Buffalo, 1987; ret., 2001. Students program coord. Buffalo Gen. Hosp., 1976-2001 Contbr. articles to profl. jours. Fellow Am. Coll. Ob-Gyn.; mem. AMA, Am. Soc. Colposcopy Cervical Pathology, Am. Fertility Soc., Am. Assn. Gyn. Laparoscopists, N.Y. Acad. Scis., Med. Soc. Erie County, Buffalo Acad. Medicine. Achievements include rsch. in premalignant diseases in gynecological colposcopy. Home: Grand Island, NY. Died Mar. 25, 2007.

WIEDERSPAHN, ALVIN LARAMIE, lawyer, former state senator; b. Cheyenne, Wyo., Jan. 18, 1949; s. John Arling and Edvina (Fahrenbruch) W.; m. Cynthia Marie Lummis, May 30, 1983; 1 child, Annaliese. BS, U. Wyo., 1971; JD, U. Denver, 1976. Bar: Wyo. 1978, US Dist. Ct. Wyo. 1978, US Ct. Appeals (10th cir.) 1985. Assoc. Guy, Williams & White, Cheyenne, 1977-79, Kline & Swainson, Cheyenne, 1979-81, Holland & Hart, Cheyenne, 1981-85; ptnr. Wiederspahn, Lummis & Liepas, P.C., Cheyenne, 1985-94; mem. Wyo. House of Reps., 1979—84, Wyo. State Senate, Cheyenne, 1985—88; chmn. Rocky Mountain Bank F.S.B., Cheyenne, 1988—94, Rocky Mountain Finance Corp., 1990-94. Chmn. Devel. Disabilities Protection and Advocacy System, Cheyenne, 1980-84, S.E. Wyo. Mental Health Ctrs., Cheyenne, 1982-85, Wyo. Gov.'s Task Force on Chronically Mentally Ill, 1984-87, Wyo. Energy Conservation Office, 1980-83, Cheyenne Downtown Devel. Authority, 1984-88; pres. Assn. for Retarded Citizens, Cheyenne, 1979-81, 90-92, Wyo. Taxpayers Assn., 1990-92; bd. dirs. Symphony and Choral Soc., Cheyenne, 1984-86; chmn. COMEA Homeless Shelter, 1992-95, chmn. bldg. com., 1993-95; dir. Cheyenne Downtown Devel. Authority, 1993; bd. dirs. Trinity Luth. Sch., 1991-94. Named Outstanding Vol., Youth Alternatives, 1982; recipient Disting. Svc. award Rocky Mountain Conf. Cmty. Mental Health Ctrs., Outstanding Svc. award Assn. for Retarded Citizens, 1986, Downtown Devel. Authority Mayors award, 1987, Commendation from Sec. of Housing & Urban Devel. for leadership in creating new homeless shelter facility in Cheyenne, 1995. Mem. ABA, Wyo. State Bar, Wyo. Natural Gas Pipeline Authority. Democrat. Lutheran. Avocations: western art, tennis, skiing, lapidary. Home: Cheyenne, Wyo. Died Oct. 24, 2014.

WIENER, THEODORE, rabbi; b. Stettin, Ger., Sept. 28, 1918; s. Max and Toni (Hamburger) W. BA, U. Cin., 1940; MHL, Hebrew Union Coll., Cin., 1943; DD, Hebrew Union Coll., NYC, 1990. Ordained rabbi, 1943. Rabbi Sinai Temple, Sioux City, Iowa, 1943-44, Temple Rodef Shalom, Port Arthur, Tex., 1944-47, Temple Beth Israel, Corsicana, Tex., 1947-48; Hebrew cataloger, later head cataloger Hebrew Union Coll. Libr., Cin., 1950-64; chaplain Home for Jewish Aged, Cin., 1958-64; sr. cataloger in Judaica, Libr. of Congress, Washington, from 1964. Dir. govt. div. United Jewish Appeal, Washington, 1966—; del. Holocaust com. Jewish Community Coun., Washington, 1975—. Contbr. articles to profl. jours. Recipient Claude G. Montefiore Prize, Hebrew Union Coll., Cin., 1941. Mem. Cen. Conf. Am. Rabbis, Assn. Jewish Librs. (life, v.p. 1970-72), Nat. Libr. and Info. Assn. (chmn. coun. 1978-79, 88-89). Home: Arlington, Va. Died Dec. 11, 2006.

WIESNER, YAEL, medical researcher; BA, U. Miami, 1990; MA, SUNY, 1995. Rsch. assoc. U. Miami, Coral Gables, Fla., 1994-96, sr. rsch. assoc. Miami, 1996-2000; res. police officer Homestead Police Dept. Acad., from

2000; police officer Miami Beach (Fla.) Police Dept., from 2001. Avocations: fine scale modeling, sky diving, scuba diving, fencing, reading. Home: Miami, Fla. Died Feb. 28, 2007.

WIGGINS, GLORIA, not-for-profit developer; b. NYC, Jan. 17, 1933; d. John and Gladys (Jones) Pruden; m. Albert Wiggins, Jan. 15, 1954 (dec. Aug. 1982); children: Michael, Teresa. BA, Richmond Coll., SI, NY; MA, SUNY, Albany. Lic. practical nurse. Project dir. Suffolk County Black History Assn., Smithtown, NY, 1982; pres., chair, founder Zamanii Internat. Devel. Corp., Central Islip, NY, from 1983; chair, founder Ikeda Mandela Uhuru Cultural Ctr., Inc., Central Islip, NY, from 1991; LPN, from 1952. Chair Univ. Sons and Daus. of Ethiopia, Deer Park, N.Y., 1990-91. Prodr., artist: pub. access TV Celebration of Kwanzaa, 1993 (grant, 1993); prodr.: Living Arts, 1994 (grant, 1994); prodr.: (exhibit) Adventure to the Homeland, 1995 (grant, 1995), African Women/African Art, 1992 (grant, 1992), 2d Roots Internat. Homecoming Festival, 1998, Women Achievers of 1998, Black History Celebration Senegal, 1999, We Sing America, 2000, International Poets, 2000, Positive Images, 2000, African American Couples in the Arts, 2000, Public Library Exhibits, 2000, TV Public Access, 2001, African Americans in West Africa, Celebration of Black History Month, 2001, (TV pub. access program of Senegalese in N.Y.) A Naming Ceremony, (pub. access TV) 10th Birthday Celebration Pow Wow, 2002, TV Pub. Access programs 100th Birthday Celebration, 2002, African Immigrants in Harlem, 2003, Smithtown Art Exhibit, Sr. Citizen Art Exhibit, Nigerian Art Exhibit, 2003, West African Photography Exhibit, Ikeda Mandela Uhoru Cultural Ctr., 2003, The Art of Romare Bearden, TV Pub. Access, 2004, Exceptional Black Scientist Exhibit, Ikeda Mandela Uhoru Cultural Ctr., Inc., 2005, Nigerian Art Exhibit, photography exhibit, 2005; author (poem) Man of Two Worlds (prize, 2001). Pres. Mariners Harbor Tenant Assn., S.I., N.Y., 1968-70; vol. Peace Corps, 1980, Peace Corps, 1979. Recipient Editors Choice award, Internat. Libr. Photography, 1998, Poet of Yr. medallion and Diamond Homer trophy, Famous Poets Soc., 1999, Internat. Poet Merit award, Internat. Soc. Poets African Woman, 2002, cert. of recognition, L.I. Hall of Fame, 2002, Famous Poets Soc. award Proud to Belong, 2004; named Donor of Yr., Help Hospitalized Vets., 2002; grantee Chase Manhattan Bank, 1996, N.Y. Decentralization Coun. on the Arts, 1987—93, Suffolk County Office of Cultural Affairs, 1987—2002, 2002. Mem.: NAEIR, Smithsonian, Ikeda Mandela Uhucu Cultural Ctr. Inc., Nat. Tree Arbor Found., Zamani Internat. Devel. Corp. (life). Avocations: art, television production, swimming, writing, community service. Home: Central Islip, NY. Died July 15, 2007.

WILDER, ANNE, retired journalist; b. Rochester, NY, Oct. 13, 1913; d. Edward Lyman and Anna Ruth (Johnston) W. BA, Mt. Holyoke Coll., 1935. Press bur. dir. Mt. Holyoke Coll., South Hadley, Mass., 1940-43; news dir. Sta. WIRA, Ft. Pierce, Fla., 1946-61; bur. chief Miami Herald, Ft. Pierce, 1961-80; prof. in journalism Indian River C.C., Ft. Pierce, 1980-87; columnist Miami Herald, Ft. Pierce and Miami, Fla., 1961-91, Ft. Pierce Tribune, Ft. Pierce and Miami, from 1991. Author: Fair and Wilder, 1981. Mem. bd. family self-sufficiency program Ft. Pierce Housing Authority, 1993—; mediator St. Lucie County States Atty. Office, Ft. Pierce, 1991—; bd. dirs. AE (Bean) Backus Art Gallery, Ft. Pierce, 1970—, Sports Hall of Fame, 1992. Lt. (s.g.) USN, 1943-46. Named Woman of Yr., Bus. and Profl. Women's Club, 1961, 73, Dem. Women's Club, 1994, Outstanding Journalist, Ft. Pierce Rotary, 1992; recipient Gold medals for internat. swimming competitions. Democrat. Christian Scientist. Avocation: master swimming. Died June 5, 2007.

WILDER, ELAINE KATHRYN, university official; b. NYC, Apr. 2, 1942; d. Edward Z. and Kathryn A. (Katsaras) Pichler; m. Edward H. Wilder, Jr., June 18, 1983; children: Kathryn Walker Norris, Audrey Walker, David Walker. Grad. in respiratory therapy, Kennebec Valley C.C., Fairfield, Maine, 1983; AS in Gen. Studies, U. Maine, Augusta, 1995; BS in gen. studies, U. Maine, 2000; MA in adult education, U. So. Maine, 2003. Nat. cert. respiratory therapy technician. Physician and clinic asst. ARC, various locations, 1965-77; coord. archives Waterville (Maine) Pub. Libr., 1981; faculty asst., coord. tutoring svcs., tutor U. Maine, Augusta, 1984—99; dir. student svcs., testing and tutoring Maine Home Sch. Inst., from 2003. Bd. dirs. Augusta Area Food Bank,1986—; mem. U. Maine Sys. Disabilities Network, Orono, 1994-98; workshop presenter in field. Bd. dirs. St. Mark's Home, Augusta, 1984—, Belgrade Regional Health Ctr., Belgrade Lakes, Maine, 1995—; mem. planning bd. St. Mark's Home for Women, Augusta, 1994—; vol., mediator Consumer Fraud divsn. Atty. Gen.'s Office, State of Maine. Mem. Am. Assn. for Respiratory Care, Learning Disabilities Assn. Maine, Phi Theta Kappa. Home: Belgrade Lakes, Maine. Died July 25, 2007.

WILDMAN, KENNETH N., professor emeritus of psychology; b. NYC, 1942; s. P. and S. Wildman; married; children: Kevin, Jason. BA in Psychology, Alfred U., 1962; MS in Psychology, Fla. State U., 1965; PhD in Psycho-Biology, Fla. State U., Tallahassee, 1969. Asst. prof. psychology Fla. A & M U., Tallahassee, 1967—71; assoc. prof. psychology Nathaniel Hawthorne Coll., Antrim, NH, 1971—74; prof., chair emeritus psychology Ohio Northern U., Ada, Ohio, 1974—2001. Cons. Monadnock Workshop, Peterborough, NH, 1972—74, Crotched Mountain Rehab. Ctr., Peterborough, 1972—74, State Dept. Edn., Concord, NH, 1973—74, NH. State Hosp., Concord; v.p. Personal HealthCare Sys., Inc., Lima, Ohio, 1978—81; ednl. cons. Timex Computer Corp., 1981—82; mem. Steering Com., Nat. Coun. Undergrad. Psychology Programs, 1988—90; mediator, arbitrator, prin. Positive Negotiations, Ada, from 1997. Contbr. scientific papers. Mem. Drug Abuse Prevention Adv. Coun., Corcord, 1974—74; cons. Area Agy. Aging, Lima, 1976—77; bd. dirs. Tri-Star Cmty. Mental Health Ctr., Lima, 1982—2002; chair Village Planning Commn., Ada, 2007—12; mem. Ceara Brazil Ptnrs. Americas, Concord, NH, 1973—74, Family Resource Ctr. Mental Health Ctr., Lima, 2000—04; reviewer- drug abuse mental health standards Joint Commn. Accreditation Hosps., 1975—75; mem. arbitration com. Nfld. Club Am., from 2008, chair arbitration com., 2010. Recipient Commendation award, Gov. NH., 1973. Mem.: Ohio Mediation Assn. Home: Ada, Ohio. Died July 2013.

WILDSCHUETZ, HARVEY FREDERICK, electric industry executive; b. Independence, Mo., Sept. 3, 1943; s. George Frederick and Dorothy Mae (Knapheide) W.; m. Sharon Kay Eigenmann; children: Holly Dawn, Michael Dean. BSEE, U. Mo., Rolla, 1966. Registered profl. engr., Ill., Mo., N.Mex.; real estate broker, N.Mex. Elec. engr. power div. Burns & McDonnell Engring. Co., Kansas City, Mo., 1966-69; supt. elec. engring. City Water Light & Power, Springfield, Ill., 1969-76; asst. v.p. Plains Electric G&T Corp., Albuquerque, 1976-89; dir. Light and Power Dept., Highland, Ill., 1989-91; mgr. engring. and ops. Ill. Mcpl. Electric Agy., Springfield, 1991-93; utilities dir. City of Lake Worth, Fla., from 1993. Coach Little League. Mem. IEEE, NSPE, N.Mex. Soc. Profl. Engrs., Optimist, Exch. Club. Avocations: camping, fishing, hunting, golf, pool. Home: Lake Worth, Fla. Died July 11, 2007.

WILHELM, ROWENA MAY, psychologist, consultant; b. Independence, Mo., July 17, 1917; d. Alvin Roderick and Clara Bernard (Bradbury) May; m. Ross Johnston, Jan. 23, 1944 (dec. 1983); 1 child, Peter Bradbury. BA, Washburn U., 1939; MA, EdS, U. Mich., PhD, 1970. Occupational therapist The Menninger Clinic, Topeka, 1939-41; dir. recreation, occupational therapist ARC-Midwest, St. Louis, 1941-43; dir. recreation City of St. Petersburg, Fla., 1944; occupational therapist An Arbor (Mich.) Sch., 1945-47, 53-55; asst. psychologist Reading & Learning Skills Ctr., Ann Arbor, 1965-70, dir., 1970-86, cons., from 1986; lab. instr. U. Mich., Washtenaw, from 1990. Mem. reading com. Ann Arbor Sch., 1980-83, U. Mich., Ann Abor, 1980-83; mem. Univ. Com. World Visitors. Contbr. articles to profl. jours. Peer counselor, mem. curriculum com. Diabetic Rsch. Project, Turner Geriatrics, Ann Arbor, 1988—; mem. Rep. Women's Club, Ann Arbor; treas. Ann Arbor Sister Cities. Whiting scholar Washburn U., 1938. Mem. North Cen. Reading Assn. (bd. dirs. 1985, treas. 1986—), Acad. Women's Caucus (chair acad. award com. 1986—), Southeastern Reading Assn. (pres., treas.), The Pipers, Phi Delta Kappa (publicity chair 1986—), Kappa Alpha Theta. Avocations: photography, horseback riding, ping pong/table tennis. Died May 4, 2007.

WILLIAMS, ANNE KINLAW, private security management executive, writer; b. Lumberton, NC, May 11, 1949; d. Juston Troy and Elizabeth (Davis) Kinlaw; m. James Neal Williams, May 17, 1977. Student, Cape Fear Tech. Inst., Wilmington, NC, 1968-78, Southeastern Community Coll., Whiteville, NC, 1973-75, Brunswick Tech. Coll., Supply, NC, 1980-82, Global Training Acad., Myrtle Beach, SC, 1987. Cert. law enforcement, S.C., private security armed officer. Journalist, staff photographer Brunswick Beacon Newspaper, Shallotte, N.C., 1965-69; asst. mgr. Bargain House Discount Store, Shallotte, N.C., 1970-77; prin. operator Squirrel's Nest, Shallotte, N.C., 1977-78; asst. to chief security Day & Night Security, Hickory, N.C., 1979-81; asst. mgr., asst. photographer Williams Photography Studio, Shallotte, N.C., 1981-85; exec. asst. Global Security Specialists, Inc., Myrtle Beach, S.C., 1986-90; staff artist Showcards, Myrtle Beach, S.C., 1988-90; asst. to pres., armed officer Premier Svcs., Inc., Myrtle Beach, S.C., 1990-91, asst. chief of security, CEO, owner, from 1992. Co-founder, pres. Brunswick County Arts Assn., Shallotte, 1975-78; art cons. New Earth Review Mag., Murfreesboro, N.C., 1977-80; exhibit cons. New World Arts Gallery, Shallotte, 1975-77; judge Brunswick County Student Arts Program, 1975-80. Author short stories, human interest, editorials, poetry in regional publs. Fund raiser West Brunswick Lib., Shallotte, 1975-76; pub. rels. County Heart Assn., 1976; vol. arrestor Horry County Am. Cancer Soc., Myrtle Beach, 1990-91. Recipient Governors Apreciation award N.C. Govenors Vols., Raleigh, 1986. Mem. Brunswick County Arts Assn. (sec. 1975-76, pres. 1976-78), Shallotte Camera Club (publicity chmn. 1988), Grandstand Gun Club, Seagate Saddle Club (staff photographer 1981), Muzzleloaders Gun Club. Avocations: rock and gem collecting, horseback riding, gardening. Home: Conway, SC. Died Feb. 14, 2007.

WILLIAMS, ANNETTE POLLY, former state legislator; b. Belzoni, Miss., Jan. 10, 1937; Attended, Milw. Area Tech. Coll.; BS, U. Wis., Milw., 1975. Mem. Dist. 17 Wis. State Assembly, 1981—92, mem. Dist. 10, 1993—2011. Panelist Nat. Conf. State Legislators, 1989; vis. fellow Auckland Inst. Tech., New Zealand, 1993; vis. lectr. Harvard U., Yale U., Marquette U, Stanford U., John Hopkins U., Minn. U. TV appearances include CBS 60 Minutes, NBC Today, ABC World News, PBS MacNeil-Lehrer Report, CNN News, others; contbr. articles to profl. jours. Del. Nat. Dem. Conv., 1984, 1988; Wis. state chair Presdl. campaign Jesse Jackson, 1984, 1988. Recipient President's award for Disting. Svc., Nat. Black Caucus State Legislators, 1990, Outstanding Accomplishment & Svc. award, American Legislative Exch. Coun., 1991, Nat. Human Rights award, Nat. Cath. Ednl. Assn., 1992, Lifetime Achievement award, U. Wis., Milw., 1998; named one of The Thirteen Innovators Who Changed Edn. in 20th Century, The NY Times. Democrat. Died Nov. 9, 2014.

WILLIAMS, BERNADINE, social worker, music educator; b. Harrisburg, Pa., Aug. 28, 1939; d. Edward Augustus and Ida (Kuhnert) Blumenstine; m. H. Robert Williams, Apr. 12, 1991; children: Karen Rosenkilde, Paul Rosenkilde. BA, Gettysburg Coll., Pa., 1961; MA, U. Chgo., 1963; BA, Calif. State U., Hayward, 1986, MA, 1989. Cert. Social Worker. Pvt. practice music tchr., Pleasanton, Calif., from 1982; activity dir. Golden Manor Board and Care Home, Livermore, Calif., 1985-86; social worker VA Hosp., Livermore, 1989, Santa Clara County Social Svcs., San Jose, Calif., 1990-91, VA Med. Ctr. Nursing Home, Livermore, from 1990. Home: Pleasanton, Calif. Died Dec. 24, 2006.

WILLIAMS, BERTRICE See SMALL, BERTRICE

WILLIAMS, CHARLES EDWARD, retail executive; b. Oct. 2, 1915; PhD in Humane letters, Culinary Arts (hon.), Culinary Inst. America, 2005. Founder, chmn. to vice chmn. to dir. emeritus Williams-Sonoma, Inc., 1958—2015. Bd. dirs. Culinary Inst. of America, American Inst. of Wine and Food. Gen. editor Williams-Sonoma Kitchen Library series, New Am. Cooking series, Savoring series, Mastering series. Former bd. dirs. Culinary Inst. of America, Am. Inst. of Wine and Food. Named Who's Who of Food and Beverage, James Beard Found., 1994, Tastemaker of the Yr., Bon Appetit mag., 1999, Lifetime Achievement award, Internat. Assn. of Culinary Professionals, 2001; recipient The Lifetime Achievement award, 1995, Hall of Fame, Culinary Inst. of America, 2002, Humanitarian of the yr., Housewares Found., 2003, guest of honor, annual Chefs, Champagne benefit, The James Beard Found., Sagaponack, NY, 2003, Visionary Retailer, House Beautiful, New York City, 2006, Bernard A. Goldhirsh Lifetime Achievement award, Inc Mag., 2007, Hall of Fame, Direct Mktg. Assn., 2008. Died Dec. 5, 2015.

WILLIAMS, GEORGE PHILLIPS, physician; b. Kansas City, Mo., June 2, 1929; s. Leslie Nathan and Velma Slee (Phillips) S.; m. Loretta Hayes, Nov. 25, 1953; children: Lizabeth Anne, George Thomas, Carol Susan, Laura Ellen, James Homer. AB, U. Mo., 1951, BS in Medicine, 1954; MD, U. Iowa, 1956. Diplomate Am. Bd. Family Practice. Intern Kansas City (Mo.) Gen. Hosp., 1956-57; pvt. practice Kansas City, from 1961. Bd. dirs. bd. edn. Consol. Sch. Dist. No. 1, Hickman Mills, Mo. and Kansas City, 1964-73; chmn. bd. dirs. Bridge Hampton Devel., Kansas City, 1986—; stephen minister leader Hickman Mills Community Christian Ch., Kansas City, 1986—. Capt. m.c. U.S. Army, 1957-60, Europe. Fellow Am. Acad. Family Practice (pres. Mo. chpt. 1984, chmn. bd. 1985), Masons, Shriners. Mem. Christian Ch. (Disciples Of Christ). Avocations: reading, travel, photography, geneology. Died July 5, 2007.

WILLIAMS, JAMES LEE, SR., former banker; b. Portsmouth, Va., Jan. 29, 1939; s. George Eugene and Thelma Lee (Harrell) W.; m. Joan Rae Garthright, June 6, 1959; children: James Lee Jr., Janet Lou. BS in Acctg., U. S.C., 1960; postgrad. in banking, U. Wis., 1976. Mgmt. trainee R.L. Bryan Co., Columbia, S.C., 1960-62; sales rep. NCR Co., Norfolk, Va., 1962-64; acct. Ford Motor Co., Norfolk, 1964-69; dir. budgeting Va. Nat. Bank (now Sovran Fin. Corp.), Norfolk, 1969-83; budget dir. Sovran Fin. Corp., Norfolk, 1984-86, dir. managerial acctg., 1987-88, dir. budget and fin. planning, from 1989. Mem. fin. commn. sch. bd. City of Portsmouth, 1977-80; bd. dirs. Portsmouth Cen. YMCA, 1986-89; mem. baseball com. Old Dominion U., Norfolk, 1987-89; chmn. Portsmouth Invitational Basketball Tournament, 1982-89. Named Sportsman of Yr. Portsmouth Sports Club, 1978, Sports Person of Yr. Downtown Athletic Club, Portsmouth, 1988; U. S.C. athletic scholar football, 1956. Mem. Bank Adminstrn. Inst. (pres. Tidewater chpt. 1983-84, state bd. dirs. 1985,), Hampton Roads C. of C. (Portsmouth div. dir. 1991), Harbor Club, Optimists (life, pres. Norfolk 1974-75), Pi Kappa Alpha. Methodist. Avocations: youth athletics, golf, fishing, travel. Home: Portsmouth, Va. Died July 21, 2007.

WILLIAMS, JOHN ALFRED, educator, author; b. Jackson, Miss., Dec. 5, 1925; m. Lorrain Isaac; 1 son, Adam; children by previous marriage: Gregory, Dennis. Grad., Syracuse U., 1950, Nat. Inst. Arts and Letters, 1962; LLD, U. Mass., Dartmouth, 1978; LittD, Syracuse U., 1995, Southeastern U., SUNY, Old Westbury, 2001, U. Rochester, 2003. With American Com. on Africa, NYC; European correspondent Ebony and Jet Magazines, 1958; reporter for Newsweek from Africa and Middle East; reporter for Europe for Holiday magazine; disting. prof. English La Guardia C.C., 1973-78, Rutgers U., 1979—94, Paul Robeson prof. English, 1990-93; Bard Ctr. fellow Bard Coll., 1994-95. Lectr. CCNY, 1968-69; guest writer Sarah Lawrence Coll., 1972-73; Regents lectr. U. Calif., Santa Barbara, 1972, U. Hawaii, 1974; exam vis. prof., disting. vis. prof. Cooper Union, 1974-75; vis. prof. Boston U., 1978-79, NYU, 1986-87. Started writing poetry during World War II, in Pacific; Author: The Angry Ones, 1960, Night Song, 1961, Sissie, 1963, The Man Who Cried I Am, 1967, Sons of Darkness, Sons of Light, 1969, The King God Didn't Save: Reflections on the Life and Death of Martin Luther King Jr., 1970, Captain Blackman, 1972, Mothersill and the Foxes, 1975, The Junior Bachelor Society, 1976, (play) Last Flight from Ambo Ber, 1981, !Click Song, 1982 (Before Columbus Found. Am. Book award 1983), The Berhama Account, 1985, Jacob's Ladder, 1987, (poems) Safari West, 1998 (Am. Book award), Clifford's Blues, 1999, (opera) Vanqui, 1999, (travel book) This Is My Country Too, 1965, also 11 vols. of non-fiction, 7 anthologies; co-author If I Stop I'll Die: The Comedy and Tragedy of Richard Pryor, 1991; editor Amistad Recipient Centennial medal for outstanding achievement Syracuse U., 1970, award Nat. Endowment Arts, 1977, Lindback award for Disting. Tchg., Rutgers U., 1982; named to Nat. Lit. Hall of Fame, 1998, Lifetime Achievement award, Columbus Found., 2011, Am. Book award, 2011. Home: Teaneck, NJ. *I've tried to adhere to the philosophies of W.E.B. DuBois. He never quit.* Died July 3, 2015.

WILLIAMS, KATHERINE BROWN, human services manager; b. Waco, Tex., Dec. 30, 1944; d. Robert Raymond and Katherine Warwick (Rust) Brown; m. Hollis R. Williams, Feb. 3, 1968; children: Daniell Brodie, Robert Hollis. BA, U. Ark., 1967; MPA, Seattle U., 1993. Supr. Neighborhood Study Ctr., Jacksonville, Little Rock, Ark., 1969-70; libr. Yazoo City (Miss.) Pub. Libr., 1972-73; receptionist Tillery and Lee Vets., Jackson, Miss., 1979-80; vol. dir. Brown Bag Program, Lake Charles, La., 1982-85, Mon. Lunch Program, Everett, Wash., 1986; coord. Partnerships Forum Human Svcs. Coun., Everett, 1988; from vol. youth program to campaign market mgr. United Way of Snohomish County, Everett, 1989-92; devel. officer Everett Gen. Hosp. and Med. Ctr., 1993; dir. endowment Everett Performing Arts Ctr., 1994-95. Commr. Everett Youth Commn., 1994—; chair Ecology br. Everett Woman's Book Club, 1995-96; bd. dirs. Wash. chpt. Nat. Neurofibromatosis Found. Dep. to Grand Conv. of Episcopal Ch., 1985. Democrat. Episcopalian. Avocations: tennis, opera, baseball. Home: Seattle, Wash. Died Mar. 15, 2007.

WILLIAMS, MARILYN CHRISTINE, executive secretary; b. Oklahoma City, Feb. 23, 1960; d. Marion and Lottie Mae (Perry) Jackson; m. Maurice Williams, Apr. 6, 1979; children: Marquise, Maurisha, Maurice, Marcus. Adminstrv. clk. T.G. & Y Hdqrs., Oklahoma City, 1977-87; exec. sec. Organon Teknika, Oklahoma City, from 1987. Mem. Profl. Soc. Internat (rec. sec. 1997—). Democrat. Baptist. Avocations: reading, sewing, knitting, baking. Died Nov. 23, 2006.

WILLIAMS, MARY JANE MONGILLO, nursing educator; b. New Britain, Conn., June 24, 1943; d. Lincoln C. and Alexandrina C. Mongillo; m. Michael J. Williams, Oct. 21, 1978; children: Michael John, Meredith Jane. Diploma, Middlesex Meml. Hosp., Middletown, Conn., 1964; BS, Central Conn. State U., New Britain, 1969; MS in Edn., So. Conn. State U., New Haven, 1976; MS in Nursing, U. Conn., 1982, PhD in Higher Edn. Adminstrn., 1995. Staff/head nurse Middlesex Meml. Hosp., Middletown, 1964-67; office nurse H.A. Kaufman MD, Middletown, 1967-69; head nurse Hosp. St. Raphael, New Haven, 1969-70, insr., 1970-74; rsch. assoc. Yale U., New Haven, 1974-76; asst. prof. Central Conn. State U., New Britain, 1976-81, assoc. prof. nursing, 1981-94, assoc. prof. dept health and human svcs., from 1994. Cons., coord. patient edn. Hartford (Conn.) Hosp., 1986-90. Author: Needs Assessment of RNs, 1983, Pharmacological Knowledge of RNs, 1984, Persistence in RN-BSN Programs, 1989. Mem. ANA, N.E. Orgn. Nursing, Conn. Nurses Assn. (chair cabinet nursing edn. 1988-92, cabinet econs. practice and edn., 1992—), Nat. League Nursing, Conn. League Nursing, Sigma Theta Tau, Phi Kappa Phi, Phi Theta Lambda. Avocations: boating, reading, writing. Home: Southington, Conn. Died Aug. 22, 2007.

WILLIAMS, MARY W., medical/surgical nurse, retired; b. Woodfield, Md., May 15, 1927; d. George P. and Edith Odessa (Burdette) Woodfield; m. Lansdale B. Williams Sr., Sept. 5, 1948; children: Dale, Susan, Mary Lynn, Lisa Kaye. Diploma, Frederick Hosp., Md., 1948. Med.-surg. nurse Montgomery Gen. Hosp., Olney, Md.; office nurse Dr. M.M. Boyer, Damascus, Md., Dr. Thomas P. Sloan, Damascus; ret. Mem. Frederick Meml. Hosp. Alumni Assn. Home: Gaithersburg, Md. Died Feb. 22, 2007.

WILLIAMS, OLIVER ALAN, JR., computer scientist; b. Phila., Feb. 4, 1948; s. Oliver Alan Sr. and Matilda (Minnick) W. BS in Psychology, Temple U., 1968; MS in Computer Sci., Hartford Grad. Ctr., 1977; PhD in Computer Info. Sci., Rensselaer Poly. Inst., 1980. System programmer Hartford-ITT Ins. Co., 1970-74; software analyst Chesebrough Pond, Inc., Greenwich, Conn., 1976-78; system analyst Diversified Tech. Cons., Inc., Waterbury, Conn., 1978-80; auditor security analyst ISQ Assocs., Inc., Waterbury, from 1980. Lt. (j.g.) USNR. Home: Waterbury, Conn. Died Apr. 2, 2007.

WILLIAMS, PAUL THOMAS, banker; b. Stamford, Conn., Aug. 20, 1934; s. Harold T. and Catherine (Fairbanks) W.; m. Harriet Calkins, June 9, 1962; children: David, Matthew, Christopher. BA in Econs., Wesleyan U., Middletown, Conn., 1956. With No. Trust Co., Chgo., 1956-76, No. Trust Bank of Fla. (formerly Security Trust Co.), Miami, from 1976, v.p., sr. trust officer, 1984-89, sr. v.p., sr. trust officer, from 1989, also bd. dirs. Pres., Lake Bluff (Ill.) Park Dist., 1974, Coral Bay Home Owners Assn., Gables by the Sea, Fla., 1986-87. Mem. Riviera Country Club (gov. 1991-95, pres. 1994-95), Rotary (pres. Miami 1990-91). Republican. Episcopalian. Avocation: golf. Home: Kalispell, Mont. Died Jan. 15, 2007.

WILLIAMS, PHYLLIS ELEANOR, retired educator; b. Serene, Colo., Sept. 11, 1920; d. Thomas James and Rebecca Cecilia (Bruce) W. Diploma, Occupational Therapy Sch. U. Pa., 1948; BS in Occupational Therapy with honors, San Jose State U., Calif., 1959, MS in Sociology, 1963. RN, 1942. Dir. occupational therapy for cerebral palsied children St. Christopher's Hosp., Phila., 1948-50; occupational therapist Phila Easter Seal Soc., 1951-55; therapist Chandler Tripp Sch., San Jose, 1955-59; probation officer Santa Clara County Juvenile Probation Dept., San Jose, 1959-63; asst. supt. Juvenile Hall, San Jose, 1963-65; instr. sociology W. Valley Community Coll. Dist., Saratoga, Calif., 1965-78, chair dept. sociology, 1972-73, dir. human svcs., 1974-75, pres. acad. senate, 1975-76; provost Inst. Human Affairs West Valley and Mission Community Coll. Dists., Santa Clara, 1978-83, ret. Saratoga, from 1983. Trustee West Valley and Mission C.C. Dists., 1985-92; lectr. in field. Bd. mem. Saratoga Adult Day Care Ctr., Sr. Info. & Ref. Svcs. Bd., Women's Fund Adv. Bd. With Nurse Corps, USN, 1942-46, 50-51. Mem. LWV, AAUW, U. Calif. Alumni Assn. (life). Democrat. Episcopalian. Home: Moss Landing, Calif. Deceased.

WILLIAMS, RICHARD DWAYNE, physician, educator, urologist; b. Wichita, Kans., Oct. 7, 1944; s. Errol Wayne and Roseanna Jane (Page) W.; m. Beverly Sue Ferguson, Aug. 29, 1964; 1 child, Wendy Elizabeth. BS, Abilene Christian U., 1966; MD, Kans. U., 1970. Diplomate Am. Bd. Urology, Nat. Bd. Med. Examiners. Intern, then resident in gen. surgery U. Minn., Mpls., 1970-72, resident in urology, 1972-76, asst. prof., 1976-79, U. Calif., San Francisco, 1979-84, assoc. prof., 1984; prof., chmn. dept. urology U. Iowa, Iowa City, from 1984. Chief urology VA Med. Ctr., San Francisco, 1979-84, VA Med. Ctr., Iowa City, 1984-88; mem. task force on bd. exams Am. Bd. Urology, 1981-85, guest examiner Oral exams, 1984-, trustee, 1994-2000; Rubin H. Flocks chair in urology U. Iowa, 1994, program com. chair Soc. Internat. Urology (SIU), 2007-09; mem. nat. adv. coun. NIDDK, NIH. Author: (with others) Advances in Urologic Oncology, 1987, Genitourinary Cancer: Basic and Clinical Aspects, 1987, Adult and Pediatric Urology, 1987, General Urology, 1988, Textbook of Medicine, 1988, also others; editor: Advances in Urologic Oncology, 1987; guest editor Seminars in Urology, 1985, Problems in Urology: Prostate Cancer, 1989; bd. editors Jour. Urology, 1980-88; mem. editorial bd. Urology, Jour. Urology; also articles. Bd. dirs. Iowa chpt. Nat. Kidney Found., bd. sci. advisors 1989-92; pres. Am. Found. Urologic Diseases, 2003-05. Maj. USAR, 1971-77. Bordeau scholar Kans. U. Med. Ctr., 1968-69; NIH, VA, Am. Cancer Soc. grantee. Fellow ACS (chmn. urology sect. No. Calif. chpt. 1980-82, chmn. ann. meeting programs 1988, mem. residency rev. com. urology 1993-99, vice chair 1995, chair 1997); mem. AAAS, Iowa Med. Soc., Iowa Urologic Soc., Am. Urologic Assn. (dir. seminar on residency evaluation 1987, bd. editors alt. 1988-, rep. North Ctrl. sect., prodr. slide presentations 1988, recipient prizes 1982, 87, com. mem. 1987-, bd. dirs. 1994, pres.-elect 1997, Hugh Hampion Young award, 2009), Am. Assn. for Cancer Rsch., Am. Soc. Clin. Oncology, Am. Assn. GU Surgeons, Clin. Soc. Genitourinary Surgeons (sec.-treas. 1997-2000), Soc. Internat. D'Urologie (pres. US sect. 2003-, program chair, 2007-), Soc. Univ. Urologists (chmn. com. on residency evaluation 1986-88, councillor 1987-, pres. 1993), Soc. Surg. Oncology, Soc. Urologic Oncology (chmn. membership com. 1987-90, sec. 1990-94, pres.-elect 1995, pres. 1996), Johnson County Med. Soc., Flock's Soc., Western Urologic Forum, Alpha Omega Alpha. Republican. Home: Iowa City, Iowa. Deceased.

WILLIAMS, WALTER BAKER, mortgage banker; b. Seattle, May 12, 1921; s. William Walter and Anna Leland (Baker) W.; m. Marie Davis Wilson, July 6, 1945; children: Kathryn Williams-Mullins, Marcia Frances Williams Swanson, Bruce Wilson, Wendy Susan. BA, U. Wash., 1943; JD, Harvard U., 1948. With Bogle & Gates, Seattle, 1948-63, ptnr., 1960-63; pres. Continental Inc., Seattle, 1963-91, chmn., 1991-97, chmn. emeritus, from 1997. Bd. dirs. United Graphics Inc., Seattle, 1973-86, Fed. Nat. Mortgage Assn., 1976-77; chmn. Continental Savings Bank, 1991-97. Rep. Wash. State Ho. of Reps., Olympia, 1961-63; sen. Wash. State Senate, Olympia, 1963-71; chmn. Econ. Devel. Council of Puget Sound, Seattle, 1981-82; pres. Japan-Am. Soc. of Seattle, 1971-72; chmn. Woodland Park Zoo Commn., Seattle, 1984-85. Served to capt. USMC, 1942-46, PTO. Recipient Brotherhood Citation, NCCJ, Seattle, 1980, First Citizen award Seattle-King County Asn. Realtors, 1997. Mem. Mortgage Bankers Assn. Am. (pres. 1973-74), Wash. Mortgage Bankers Assn. (pres. 1971), Fed. Home Loan Mortgage Corp. (adv. com.), Wash. Savs. League (bd. dirs., chmn. 1991-92), Rotary (pres. local club 1984-85), Rainier Club Seattle (pres. 1987-88). Republican. Congregationalist. Home: Seattle, Wash. Died Nov. 9, 2006.

WILLIAMS, WALTER C. (DUB WILLIAMS), retired state legislator; b. Bogalusa, La., Nov. 16, 1927; m. Kathryn Williams; children: Borde, Neal. Mem. Dist. 56 N.Mex. House of Reps., Santa Fe, 1995—2009. Republican. Died Oct. 27, 2014.

WILLIAMS, WILLIAM BRYANT, JR., director of curriculum; b. Newport News, Va., Mar. 25, 1940; s. William Bryant Sr. and Therease (Clayton) W.; m. Karen Nolan, Nov. 28, 1968; children: Megan Elaine, Erin Blythe, Lauren Ellen. BA, Hampden-Sydney, 1961; MEd, William & Mary Coll., 1968, EdD, 1989. Tchr. Newport News (Va.) Pub. Schs., 1962-67, guidance counselor, 1967-70, prin., 1970-77, dir. of instrn., 1977-86, dir. mid. schs., from 1986. Cons. in field; prof. U. Va., Williamsburg, 1984-89. Author: Teacher Teaming, 1986. Chmn. Sister Cities Commn., Newport News, 1986-91; mem. Hist. Com., Newport News, 1985-91. Mem. Nat. Mid. Sch. Assn., Assn. for Supervision & Curriculum Devel., Phi Delta Kappa, Assembly Club, German Club. Avocations: fitness activities, reading. Home: Newport News, Va. Died May 21, 2007.

WILLIAMS, WILLIAM HENRY, history professor, educational association administrator; b. Port Jervis, NY, June 9, 1936; s. Henry and Esther Marcy (Crocker) W.; m. Helen Garrett, June 28, 1959; children: Dawn, Mark. BA, Drew U., 1958; MS in Edn., Yeshiva U., 1959; PhD, U. Del., 1971. Tchr. social studies Pawling Ctrl. H.S., NY, 1959—63; instr. U. Del., Georgetown, 1967—71, asst. prof., 1971—77, assoc. prof., 1977—86, prof., 1986—2000, prof. emeritus, from 2000, Southern coord. MALS program Georgetown, 1990—2000. Cons. Pa. Hosp., Phila., 1975; mem. bd. archives and history Peninsula Conf. United Meth. Ch., Dover, Del., 1988—; cons. Smith Island Project, State of Md., Annapolis, 1991-93 Author: America's First Hospital, 1976, Garden of American Methodism, 1984, The First State: An Illustrated History of Delaware, 1985, Slavery and Freedom in Delaware, 1996, The Delmarva Chicken Industry, 1998. Chair Del. Humanities Coun., Wilmington, 1976-77, Georgetown Bicentennial Com., 1975-76, Sussex County Magna Carta Com., Georgetown, 1986-87; cons. scholarship com. Del. Heritage Commn., Wilmington, 1985-87, mem. 2001-; trustee Del. Agrl. Mus. U. Del. fellow, 1976, 80, 90-91, Am. Philos. Soc. fellow, 1972, NEH fellow, 1973, 85; recipient Joseph P. del Tufo award Del. Humanities Forum, 1980. Mem. Hist. Soc. Del. (bd. editors 1988—), Soc. History of Early Am. Rep. Methodist. Avocations: travel, sports. Home: Georgetown, Del. Died Apr. 7, 2007.

WILLIAMS, WILLIAM R., finance company executive, consultant; b. Corpus Christi, Tex., Oct. 30, 1948; s. Walter L. and Virgie (Kowen) W.; m. Sandra Kay Stevenson, Dec. 23, 1971; 1 child, Paul. BBA, U. Houston, 1972; MBA, Tex. Tech U., 1974. Bank officer Interfirst, Houston, 1974-78; asst. v.p. U. Houston, 1978-81, treas., 1981-85; pres. Tiger Investment Corp., Houston, from 1985. Bd. dirs. Western Bank, Houston, chmn. audit com. 1984-86; bd. dirs. Preferred Savings Assn. Bd. dirs. Tex. State Treasury Asset Mgmt. Com., 1982—; bd. dirs. Harris County (Tex.) Higher Edn. Authority, 1982—, chmn. 1983—. Served to 1st lt. USAR, 1973-80. Nat. Corp. Cash Mgmt. Assn. (chmn. edn. com.). Home: Houston, Tex. Died Apr. 18, 2007.

WILLIAMSON, BRUCE LOOMIS, writer, retired journalist; b. New London, Conn., Aug. 8, 1921; s. Clyde Loomis Williamson and Gertrude Marion White; m. Leda Bess Palmer, Sept. 4, 1946 (div. 1971); m. Audrey Marie Powell, May 31, 1977; children: Bruce Loomis Jr., Blaine Williamson Kaercher. Student, Brown U. News dir. Radio Sta. WHIM, Providence, 1947-59; v.p., gen. mgr. Radio Sta. WRVM, Rochester, N.Y., 1959-60; news dir., anchor TV Sta. WTEN, Albany, N.Y., 1960-73; news dir. Radio Sta. WABY, Albany, N.Y., 1973-77; media rels. mgr. N.Y. State Sch. Bds. Assn., Albany, N.Y., 1977-88; real estate salesman Welbourne & Purdy, Clifton Park, N.Y., 1988-90. Columnist, politics and media, Albany Knickerbocker News, 1973; legis. corr. N.Y. state govt., Albany, 1960-73. Author: Verse Things I Ever Did, 1994, That Rocky Fella, 1999. Active St. Peter's Episc. Ch., Albany, 39 yrs. Republican. Episcopalian. Avocations: horseback riding, chess, acting. Home: Clifton Park, NY. Died Mar. 24, 2007.

WILLIAMSON, HELEN THORWORTH, clinical psychologist; b. Irvington, NJ, Dec. 15, 1927; d. John Andrew and Hazel Sayre (Tichenor) Thorworth; m. Donald Henry Williamson, Sept. 4, 1948; children: Diane, Steven, Nina, David, Lisa Crane. BA, William Smith Coll., 1949; MA, Fairfield U., 1965; PhD, NYU, 1971; DSc (hon.), Hobart, 1976. Lic. clin. psychologist. Psychologist Lincoln Inst., NYC, 1970-72; prof. psychology Manhattanville Coll., Purchase, N.Y., 1972-80; pvt. practice NYC, from 1971. Cons. in field. Author: Teaching Tolerance for Ambiguity, 1971. Bd. trustees Stamford Hosp., 1960-66; pres. Stamford Hosp. Aux., 1960-66. Recipient Outstanding Civic Leader Stamford Advocate, 1966, Trustee Scholarship, Scholarship Hobart and William Smith Colls., 1945, Founder's Day award NYU, 1971. Mem. APA (mem. clin. div., mem. psychotherapy div.), Psychologists in Ind. Practice, N.Y. Clin. Psychologists, N.Y. State Psychol. Assn., Am. Acad. Psychotherapists, Soc. for Personality Assessment. Presbyterian. Avocations: foreign travel, opera and theatre, ballet, computer. Home: Stamford, Conn. Died Nov. 11, 2006.

WILLIS, HAROLD WENDT, SR., real estate developer; b. Marion, Ala., Oct. 7, 1927; s. Robert James and Della (Wendt) W.; m. Patsy Gay Bacon, Aug. 2, 1947 (div. Jan. 1975); children: Harold Wendt II, Timothy Gay, April Ann, Brian Tad, Suzanne Gail; m. Vernette Jacobson Osborne, Mar. 30, 1980 (div. 1984); m. Ofelia Alvarez, Sept. 23, 1984; children: Ryan Robert, Samantha Ofelia. Student, Loma Linda U., 1950, San Bernardino Valley Coll. Ptnr. Victoria Guernsey, San Bernardino, Calif., 1950-63, co-pres., 1963-74, pres., from 1974. Pres. Energy Delivery Sys., Food and Fuel, Inc. San Bernardino City water commr., 1964-98, pres. bd. water commrs., 1964-98; bd. councillors Loma Linda U., Calif., 1968-85, pres., 1971-74; active So. Calif. Strider's Relay Team (set indoor Am. and World record in 4x800 1992, sec distance medley relay US and World record for 60 yr. old 1992); pres. So. Calif. Striders Track and Field Club, 2001-02. Ensign, US Mcht. Marine, 1945-46. Mem. Calif. Dairy Industries Assn. (pres. 1963, 64), Liga Internat. (2d v.p. 1978, pres. 1982, 83), Socal Striders Masters Track & Field Club (pres. 2001-02). Seventh-day Adventist (deacon 1950-67). Avocation: pvt. pilot. Died Jan. 17, 2016.

WILLIS, SHERRY LYNN, nursing educator; b. Kirksville, Mo., Dec. 24, 1955; d. Robert D. and Mary Louise (Kenepp) Shumaker; m. James W. Willis, Dec. 28, 1985. BS in Nursing, N.E. Mo. State U., 1978, postgrad. Instr. N.E. Mo. State U., Kirksville; cen. coord. insvc. edn. Baylor U. Med. Ctr., Dallas; utilization rev. coord. St. Joseph Mercy Hosp., Centerville, Iowa; coord. practical nursing program Kirksville R-III Schs. Mem. Mo. Voc. Assn., Mo. State Assn. Health Occupational Edn., Mo. Coun. of Practical Nurse Educators, Mo. League Nursing. Home: Kirksville, Mo. Died Apr. 8, 2007.

WILLKE, JOHN CHARLES, physician; b. Maria Stein, Ohio, Apr. 5, 1925; s. Gerard Thomas and Marie Margaret (Wuennemann) W.; m. Barbara Hiltz, June 5, 1948 (dec. 2013); children: Marie, Theresa, Charles, Joseph, Anne, Timothy. MD, U. Cin., 1948; Legum Dr. (hon.), U. Notre Dame, 1983; LHD (hon.), Thomas More Coll., Ky., 1978. Diplomate Am. Bd. Family Practice. Med. resident Good Samaritan Hosp., Cin., 1948-50; pvt. practice Cin., until 1988; sr. attending staff Providence & Good Samaritan Hosps., Cin.; co-chair Cin. Right to Life, 1970-87; pres. Ohio Right to Life, 1975-80, Nat. Right to Life Com., Washington, 1980-83, 84-91, Internat. Right to Life Fedn., Switzerland, 1985-91, Life Issues Inst., Cin., from 1991. Guest participant on radio & TV including Phil Donahue Show, 60 Minutes, Good Morning Am., The Today Show, Crossfire, Larry King, Voice of Am., 700 Club, Geraldo Rivera, and more; author: The Wonder of Sex, 1964, Sex, Should We Wait?, 1969, Sex Education: The How to for Teachers, 1970, Marriage, 1971, Handbook on Abortion, 1971, rev. edits., 1975, 79, How To Teach the Pro-Life Story, 1973, Sex Education, In the Classroom?, 1978, Abortion & Slavery, 1984, Abortion Questions & Answers, 1985, rev., 1991, Sex & Love, 1991; co-author (with wife)(autobiography) Abortion and the Pro-Life Movement: An Inside View, 2014; contbr. to books and articles to profl. jours. Mem. numerous bds. of social action orgns. Capt. USAF, 1952-54. Fellow Am. Bd. Family Physicians; mem. Ohio Acad. Family Physicians, Cin. Acad. Med., Ohio Med. Soc., Am. Assn. Sex Educators, Nat. Alliance for Family Life, Family Life Educators. Home: Cincinnati, Ohio. *Each human life begins as a single cell. That is a scientific fact. Legal abortion is fatal discrimination against an entire class of living humans on the basis of place of residence—still living in the womb. It is a civil rights outrage.* Died Feb. 20, 2015.

WILLOUGHBY, DOROTHY BARNES, nursing administrator, geriatrics nurse; b. Jackson, Miss., Apr. 20, 1931; d. Ira Franklin and Cabbie (Hawkins) Barnes; m. Luther Lee Willoughby, July 27, 1963; children: William, Frank, Jean. Diploma, Miss. Bapt. Hosp., 1952; BS in Edn., Miss. Coll., 1955. RN, La., Miss. Instr. nursing arts Miss. Bapt. Hosp., Jackson; campus nurse Miss. Coll., Clinton; instr. med./surg. nursing Gilfoy Sch. Nursing, Jackson; asst. dir. skilled nursing Baton Rouge Gen. Med. Ctr. Mem. Miss. Bapt. Gilfoy Sch. Nursing Alumnae Assn. Home: Kenner, La. Died Mar. 24, 2007.

WILSON, BEVERLY JEAN, educational administrator; b. Detroit, Apr. 14, 1937; d. Gordon Charles and Dorothy Margaret (Fowler) Anderson; m. David Charles Wilson, Sept. 2, 1961; 1 child, Timothy Reardon. BA in Edn., U. Mich., 1959; postgrad., Mich. State U., 1961; MA in Edn., Fitchburg U., Mass., 1981. Tchr. St. Clair Shores (Mich.) Sch. Dist., 1959-63, various pub. schs., Calif., Colo., N.Y., 1963-65, Dept. Def., Italy and Fed. Republic Germany, 1966-78; asst. v.p. Merchants Nat. Bank, Leominster, Mass., 1979-85; adminstrv. asst. to sr. v.p. Mass. Higher Edn. Assistance Corp., Boston, 1985-87, dir. lender and sch. relations, from 1987. Mem. grad. council Fitchburg State Coll., 1979-81. Author: Computers Made Easy, 1981; contbr. articles to profl. jours. Mem. budget com. United Way, Leominster/Fitchburg, 1983-86. Edn. Policy Program fellow Inst. Ednl. Leadership, 1987. Mem. Mass. Assn. Fin. Aid Adminstrs., Eastern Assn. Fin. Aid Adminstrs., Nat. Assn. Fin. Aid Adminstrs., Nat. Assn. Banking Women (1st v.p. 1986-87), Internat. Officers' Wives Club (pres. 1969-71). Democrat. Lutheran. Avocations: reading, needlepoint, painting, gourmet cooking. Home: Leominster, Mass. Died June 26, 2007.

WILSON, DONALD GREY, engineering management consultant; b. Bridgeport, Conn., Sept. 20, 1917; s. William Gray and Jeannetta McAvoy (Kerr) W.; m. Elizabeth Jean Lanning, Apr. 24, 1943 (div. Mar. 1971, dec. Mar. 2002); children: Kirk Lanning, Craig Gardner, William Grey. BSEE, Rensselaer Poly. Inst., 1938; SM, Harvard U., 1939, MES, 1947, PhD, 1948. Mgr. automatic fire alarm divsn. Sealand Corp., Bridgeport, Conn., 1939-40; instr. elec. engring. Rensselaer Poly. Inst., 1940-42; staff mem. Radiation Lab. MIT, 1942-45; prof. elec. engring. U. Kan., Lawrence, 1947-55, dept. head, 1948-55; dir. Phila. Brass & Bronze, 1962-64, Mallory-Xerox Corp., 1964-65. Cons. U.S. Naval Ordance Test Sta., China Lake, Calif., 1953-54; assoc. dir. rsch. dept. Stromberg-Carlson Co., San Diego, 1955-59, gen. mgr., 1959, asst. v.p., 1959-60; v.p. rsch. P.R. Mallory & Co., Indpls., 1960, v.p. rsch. and engring., 1961-71, v.p. rsch., engring. and environ. affairs, 1971-75; alt. dir. Mallory Metal. Products, Eng., 1967; pres. Contemporary Custom Cabinets, San Diego, 1975-76; v.p. Continental Resources and Minerals Corp., Dayton, Ohio, 1978-79; sr. v.p. Tanzi Mergers/Acquisitions, San Diego, 1983-86; mgmt. cons., 1976—; sr. lectr. U. Rochester, 1956-57; lectr. dept. elec. engring. San Diego State U., 1981-92, asst. dean coll. engring., 1987, prof. emeritus, 1992-96; mng. dir., exec. bd. Nat. Bur. Cert. Cons., 1988-94, sr. adv. counsel, 1994-2001; sr. advisor Nat. Bur. Energy Solutions, 2007—. Contbr. articles to profl. jours. Bd. dirs. Speech and Hearing Clinic, Indpls., 1960-66, Washington Twp. Sch. Dist., 1964-68, pres., 1966-67. Recipient Outstanding Acad. Advisor award San Diego State U., 1992. Fellow AAAS; mem. IEEE (sr. life, exec. com. San Diego sect. 1986-2003, 2004-07, chmn. S.W. area region 6 1999-2000, sec. region 6 2001-02, ethics and mem. conduct com. 2002-03, R&D policy com. 2000—, Third Millennium medal, Region 6 Outstanding Br. Counselor award 1992), Affiliation Profl. Cons. Orgns. (chmn. bd. govs. 1991-93 San Diego Engring. Coun. Outstanding Svc. award 2000), Intertel, Sigma Xi, Sigma Phi Epsilon, Tau Beta Pi, Eta Kappa Nu. Home: Rancho Santa Fe, Calif. Died Dec. 30, 2012.

WILSON, EVELYN SUE, English language educator; b. Decatur, Tex., Nov. 4, 1951; d. Billy George and Laverl (Pearson) W.; m. Mark Allen Cole, Nov. 1, 1974 (div. July 1984). AA, Weatherford Coll., 1971; BS in Edn., North Tex. State U., 1973; MA in English, U. North Tex., 1990. Auditor, biller Allied Electronics, Ft. Worth, Tex., 1973; tchr. high sch. Waxahachie (Tex.) Ind. Sch. Dist., 1973-74; sec. Decibel Products, Dallas, 1974-75; legal sec. Law, Snakard, Brown and Gambill, Ft. Worth, 1975-80; word processor McLean, Sanders, Ft. Worth, 1980; teaching fellow English U. North Tex., Denton, 1990-91; instr. English, Weatherford (Tex.) Coll., from 1992. Mem. Conf. of Coll. Tchrs. of English, North Tex. Writing Ctrs. Assn., Tex. Jr. Coll. Tchrs. Assn., Phi Kappa Phi. Home: Paradise, Tex. Died July 3, 2007.

WILSON, FRANCELIA LATTING, retired elementary school educator; b. Pueblo, Colo., Sept. 28, 1943; d. Trimble Baggett and Patience Sewell Latting; m. Thomas Allen Wilson (dec.); children: Cynthia Anne, Robin Marie. AA, Christian Coll., Columbia, Miss., 1962—63; BA in Elem. Edn., Okla. City U., 1963—67; MEd, Our Lady Lake U., San Antonio, 1969—75. Tchr. Am. Assn. U. Women; ret. Mem.: Am. Assn. U. Women. Died May 21, 2007.

WILSON, GLENN SHAW, quality engineer; b. Pitts., Oct. 25, 1932; s. Claude Weikert and Sarah Dorothy (Shaw) W.; m. Mildred Henrietta Wilson, Dec. 10, 1955 (dec. June 1984); children: Rebecca, Ruth Shidner, Wade; m. Carol Anne Burton, Sept. 28, 1985; 1 stepson, Matthew Elwell. BS in Indsl. Mgmt., Carnegie Mellon U., 1955; postgrad., Alfred U., 1982; MBA, Wilmington Coll., 1988. Cert. quality engr.; cert. quality auditor. Sr. indsl. engr. Wallingford (Conn.) Steel Co., 1957-61; glass plant ind. engr. Hartford divsn. Emhart Corp., Bloomfield, Conn., 1961-69; mgr. finished products Pierce Glass divsn. Indian Head, Port Allegany, Pa., 1969-75; asst. corp. quality mgr. Nat. Bottle Corp., Bala Cynwyd, Pa., 1975-77; dir. quality/productivity improvement Wheaton Glass Co., Millville, N.J., 1977-92; mgr. quality Nat. Refrigerants, Inc., Rosenhayn, N.J., 1994-98. Instr. U. Del., Newark, 1979; adj. mgmt. faculty Rowan U., Glassboro, N.J., 1980—; cons. WingWalker Quality Concepts, Woodstown, N.J., 1989—. Co-author: (pamphlets) Chemical Specialties Manufacturers Assn. Guidelines for Glass Container Aerosol Testing, 1984, Parenteral Drug Assn. Model for Supplier Certification, 1990. Bd. dirs. McKean County Solid Waste Authority, Smethport, Pa., 1965-69; v.p. Port Allegany Sch. Bd., 1965-69; mem. Seneca Highlands Dist. Sch. Bd., Smethport, 1966-69; recycling com. mem. Borough of Woodstown, 1989—. 1st Lt. U.S. Army, 1955-57. Scholar Buhl Found., 1950-51, Carnegie Inst. Tech., 1950-51. Mem. Am. Soc. Quality (sr.; sect. chmn. 1988-90, chmn. examining and auditing com. 1990—, Svc. Appreciation award 1990). Republican. Presbyterian. Avocations: touring, reading, science fiction, bicycling, chess. Home: Cape May C H, NJ. Died June 12, 2007.

WILSON, JAMES LESLIE, JR., artist; b. Sherman, Tex., Dec. 22, 1948; s. James Leslie and Cynthia Lou (Cowling) W.; m. Pamelia Laurence Starnes, Jan. 6, 1972; children: Ashley Laurel, James Leslie III. Student, Tarrant County Jr. Coll., 1969, U. Tex., 1971, East Tex. State U., 1972-73. Mgr., rep. House of Frames, Ft. Worth, from 1976; owner White Field's Gallery, Ft. Worth, 1986-93. Actor Jr. Women's League, Ft. Worth, 1991. Mem. Profl. Picture Framers, Ducks Unltd. (mem. prize com. 1980—, chmn. prize com. 1990, co-chmn. 1991, chmn. 1992). Methodist. Avocations: photography, painting, sculpture, golf, hunting. Home: Burleson, Tex. Died May 27, 2007.

WILSON, JANE, artist; b. Seymour, Iowa, Apr. 29, 1924; d. Wayne and Cleone (Marquis) Wilson; m. John Gruen, Mar. 28, 1948; 1 child, Julia Gruen. BA, U. Iowa, 1945, MA in Painting, 1947. Mem. fine arts faculty Parsons Sch. Design, 1973-83, 89-90. Vis. artist U. Iowa, 1974; adj. assoc. prof. painting and drawing Columbia U., 1975—85, assoc. prof., 1985—86, prof., 1986—88, acting chair, 1986—88; Andrew Mellon vis. prof. painting Cooper Union, 1977—78. One-woman shows include Hansa Gallery, N.Y.C., 1953, 1955, 1957, Stuttman Gallery, 1958, 1959, Tibor de Nagy Gallery, 1960—66, Graham Gallery, 1968, 1969, 1971, 1973, 1975, Fischbach Gallery, 1978, 1981, 1984, 1988, 1990, 1991, 1993, 1995, 1997, Munson-Williams-Proctor Inst., Utica, N.Y., 1980, Cornell U., Ithaca, N.Y., 1982, Compass Rose Gallery, Chgo., 1988, Am. U., Washington, 1989, U. Richmond, Va., 1990, Earl McGrath Gallery, LA, 1990—91, 1993, Dartmouth Coll., Hanover, N.H., 1991, Amot Mus., Elmira, N.Y., 1993—94, Parrish Mus., Southampton, N.Y., 1996, Glenn Horowitz Gallery, East Hampton, N.Y., 1996, D. C. Moore Gallery, N.Y.C., 1999, 2001, 2003, 2004, 2007, Heckscher Mus., Huntington, N.Y., 2001, McKinney Ave. Contemporary, Dallas, 2003, Represented in permanent collections Met. Mus., Mus. Modern Art, Whitney Mus., Wadsworth Athenaeum, Heron Art Mus., NYU Rockefeller Inst., Vassar Coll., Pa. Acad. Fine Arts, Hirsch Horn Mus., Washington, Nelson-Atkins Mus., Kansas City, Mo., San Francisco Mus. Modern Art, Heckscher Mus., L.I. Mus., Stony Brook, others. Recipient Eloise Spaeth award, Guild Hall, East Hampton, N.Y., 1968, Lifetime Achievement award, 2001, Purchase prize, Childe Hassam Fund, 1971, 1973, 1981, Ranger Fund Purchase prize, 1977; Ingram-Merrill grantee, 1963, Louis Comfort Tiffany grantee, 1967. Mem.: Nat. Acad. Design (academician from 1974, pres. 1992—94), American Acad. Arts & Letters (award in Art 1985), Phi Beta Kappa. Home: New York, NY. Died Jan. 13, 2015.

WILSON, JOHN ROBERT, II, property manager; b. San Jose, Calif., Nov. 2, 1959; s. Carter Edward and Betty Bell (Kelly) W.; children: John Robert III, Alexander, Gregory T. Student, Carroll Tech. Inst., Carrollton, Ga., Coll. of San Mateo, Calif. Scientific computing profl. Lockleed Missles and Space, Sunnyvail, Calif., 1978-84; mgr. rental property Carrollton, from 1985; indsl. electronics worker IKKA Tech., Carrollton, from 1990, Flowers Bakery, Carrollton, from 1990, Maplehurst Bakery, Carrollton, from 1990. Owner A Date to Remember Dating Svc., Carrollton, 1986-89, Video Ads Advt. Svcs., Carrollton, 1990, Wilson Agy., Carrollton, 1991—. Bd. dirs. Am. with Disabilities Support Group, Carrollton, 1995-97. Avocations: house renovations, raising children, continuing edn., travel, Tri Chi. Home: Carrollton, Ga. Died Mar. 15, 2007.

WILSON, KAY ARLENE, artist; b. Pemberville, Ohio, Dec. 1, 1937; d. Edwin Thomas and Clarice Kathryn (Reimund) Ridenour; m. David L. Wilson, Aug. 31, 1957; children: Leslie, Julianne, Rhonda. Student, Miami U., Oxford, Ohio, 1956-57; BS in Art Edn., Youngstown State U., Ohio, 1959. Tchr. adult oil painting Butler Inst. Am. Art, Youngstown, Ohio, Trumbull Art Guild, Warren, Ohio, 1970s and 1980s. Owner pvt. home studio, Canfield, Ohio; judge for area shows; speaker, demonstrator for art and civic groups. Exhibited in solo shows at Youngstown Playhouse, 1964, 74, 79, 97, Trumbull br. Kent State U., 1968, Jewish Cmty. Ctr., Youngstown, 1969, Malone Coll., Canton, Ohio, 1970, Trumbull Art Gallery, Warren, Ohio, 1972, 83, 93, Apple Gallery, Boardman, Ohio, 1986, Valley Arts Guild, Sharon, Pa., 1996, Butler Inst. Am. Art, 2001, Valley Art Ctr., Chagrin Falls, Ohio, 2004, Davis Ctr., Fellow Riverside Gardens, 2004, Oakland Ctr. for Performing Arts, 2005; group shows include Butler Inst. Comtemporary Art, 2001, Artist Archives of Western Reserve, Cleve., 2002, 03, 04, Portrait Show invitational Butler Inst. Am. Art, 2004; self portrait in permanent collection Butler Inst. Am. Art, Youngstown, Ohio; digital artwork listed in Adobe Workshop software and Adobe Workshop WOW book; affiliated with galleries in Ohio and Calif. Recipient Boston Mills Invitational Honor awrd, 1974, Women Artists: A Celebration Body of Work award and First Oil, 1989, 92, Margaret Evans award Body of Work, 1994, Margaret Evans award First Oil, 1997, The Artist's Mag. Goldern Gallery of Winners, 1995, Clyde Singer Lifetime Achievement award Butler Inst. Am. Art, 2002 others; named Youngstown's (Ohio) YWCA's Woman of the Year, 1987. Home: Canfield, Ohio. Died May 10, 2007.

WILSON, LORI G., music educator; b. Latrobe, Pa., Dec. 20, 1958; d. James R. and Patricia A. Gamble; m. Jeffrey D. Wilson, Nov. 20, 1982; children: Brian E., Allison M. BS in Edn., U. Findlay, Ohio, 1980; MA in Curriculum and Instrn., Nova Southeastern U., Ft. Lauderdale, Fla., 2005. Lic. in tchg. Dept. Edn., State Ohio. Tchr., band and music Riverdale Local Schs., Mt. Blanchard, 1980—85, Kenton City Schs., Ohio, 1985—91, Ada Exempted Village Schs., Ohio. Mem.: Ohio Music Educators Assn. Home: Dola, Ohio. Died Sept. 6, 2007.

WILSON, MARGARET GIBBONS, social sciences educator; b. Chgo., Nov. 14, 1943; d. Joseph and Florence (Greenberg) Gibbons; m. David Louis Wilson, July 8, 1967; 1 child, Mariah Elizabeth Gibbons Wilson. BA, U. Chgo., 1965, MAT, 1969; MA, U. So. Calif., 1972, PhD, 1978. Instr. dept. social studies Cen. YMCA C.C., Chgo., 1968-69; asst. prof. Coll. of Technology Fla. Internat. U., Miami, 1980-87, dir. rsch. Ctr. for Labor Rsch. & Studies, 1980-91, acting chairperson dept. indsl. systems, 1981-82, acting assoc. dean Coll. of Technology, 1982-83, dir. acad. programs and assoc. dir. Ctr. Labor Rsch. Studies, from 1991. Author: American Women in Transition: The Urban Influence 1876-1920, 1979, Floridans at Work: Yesterday and Today, 1989; editor Florida Labor History Symposium Procs., 1991. Mem. adv. bd. Louis Wolfson II Media History Ctr., Miami, 1986-92, PTSA Carver Mid. Sch., Miami, 1992-95, PTSA Coral Gables H.S., 1995—, Citizens for Open and Safe Streets, 1994—; mem., chmn. rsch. com. Women's Fund of Dade County, Miami, 1993—; mem. Coral Gables Citywide Anti-Crime Com., 1996—. Grantee Fla. Humanities Coun., 1984-85, 86, others. Mem. Univ. and Coll. Labor Edn. Assn. (editor Labor Studies Forum 1987—, editl. bd. Labor Studies Jour., 1987—, chmn. 1996—), Orgn. Am. Historians, Am. Hist. Assn. Democrat. Avocations: bicycling, bird watching, hiking, gardening. Home: Coral Gables, Fla. Died Nov. 8, 2006.

WILSON, MARY ANNE, retired secondary and elementary school educator; b. Pitts., Apr. 21, 1922; d. Herbert Spencer and Helen Buck (Matson) Schiel; m. George Walter Berg, Feb. 21, 1948 (dec. 1969); children: George Berg, Christine Berg Rummer, Marie Berg Lo Parco, James Carl Berg (dec.); m. Joseph Wilson, Aug. 24, 1975 (dec.). BFA, Pratt Inst., 1944; MFA, Columbia U., 1947. Tchr. art Ctr. Moriches (N.Y.) Sch., 1940-41, Bklyn. Pub. Schs., Pub. sch. Jr. High, Corona, N.Y., Bushwick High Sch., Bklyn., 1951-52, Island Trees (N.Y.) Jr. High, 1960, West Islip (N.Y.) Pub. Schs., 1960-80; ret. West Islip Pub. Schs., 1980. Artist water colors. Chmn. Christian edn. com. Presbyn. Ch. Deer Park. Mem. AAUW (past corr. sec.), Assn. Presbyn. Women (rec. sec. 1988-91), Arts Coun. East Islip Libr., South Shore Water Color Soc. Democrat. Presbyterian. Avocations: water color painting, travel, crafts, reading, going to theaters. Died Aug. 8, 2007.

WILSON, PETER MASON, computer programmer; b. NYC, Mar. 14, 1934; s. Kenneth Mason and Priscilla (Nickerson) W.; m. Lois S., July 13, 1957; children: Katherine Rose, Kenneth Mason II. BS, Ga. Inst. Tech., 1960; MS, Fla. State U., 1965, PhD, 1975. Asst. prof. Fla. A&M U., Tallahassee, 1966-77; sys. analyst U. Fla., Tallahassee, 1977-79; instrnl. designer Control Data Corp., Rockville, Md., 1979-85, Booze, Allen & Hamilton, Rockville, 1985-88, Pace Enterprises, Falls Church, Md., 1989-91; sr. tech. trainer Arbitron, Laurel, Md., 1991-94; project mgr., instrnl. designer Bell Atlantic, Balt., from 1994. Chair computer usage in pub. schs. Fairfax (Va.) Bd. of Edn., 1985-88; cons. evaluation spl. edn. Howard County Bd. of Edn., Ellicott City, Md., 1991-93. Active vestry Holy Comforter, Vienna, Va., 1985-89, demographics com. St. John's Ch., Ellicott City, 1992-93. Nat. Urban League fellow, 1969, Atomic Energy Commn. fellow, 1972; recipient Howard County Bd. of Edn. commendation, 1993. Mem. AERA (session chair), SALT (presenter), Math. Assn. Am. (presenter), Theta Chi. Episcopalian. Home: Spotsylvania, Va. Died June 14, 2007.

WILSON, RICHARD DALE, executive training, consulting company; b. LA, July 22, 1933; s. Wayne Merle and June Lillian (Buys) W.; m. Nancy Irene Colby, 1974; children: Christopher, Jennifer, Janie, Matthew, Dixie, Tracey, Mark, Mysti, Tiffany. BA, San Jose Coll., 1964, MTH; LLB, Blackstone Law Sch., 1974; postgrad., Harvard U., 1987; PhD, Kennedy Western U., 1993. Cert. profl. cons. TV news anchor, overseas correspondent, investigative reporter numerous TV stas., 1964-75; legis. services dir. Utah State Legis., Salt Lake City, 1976; pres. Nat. Inst. for Tng. and Consulting, Salt Lake City, from 1977. Sr. cons. The Co. Cons., 1981—; pres. Nat. Inst. for Sales Tng. and Cons. Author: Handwriting 12 Keys to Every Personality, 1968, 10 Basic Habits Superstar Salesperson, 1986, 10 Critical Steps to Building a Powerful and Profitable Sales Organization, 1987, 10 Basic Habits of A Superstar Sales Manager, 1989, Do It Right The First Time: Finding, Assessing and Selecting the Best Sales Force Force For The 90's, 1991; editor, pub. The Co. Cons. Newsletter, 1985—; contbr. articles to profl. jours. Media planner Rep. Conv., N.D., 1972; organizer Rep. Conv., Calif., 1964; del. Utah State Conv., 1976. Sgt. USMC, 195-57, Korea. Recipient Gavel award ABA, 1973; named Regional Dir. Yr. Westworld Services, Inc., 1981. Mem. Soc. Profl. Cons., Am. Handwriting Analysis Found., Nat. Assn. Realtors, Realtors Nat. Mktg. Inst., Nat. Speakers Assn. Mem. Lds Ch. Avocation: certified handwriting expert. Home: Provo, Utah. Died Apr. 21, 2007.

WILSON, SAMUEL ALEXANDER, III, lawyer; b. Charlotte, NC, Apr. 12, 1951; s. Samuel Alexander Jr. and Julia (Hill) W.; m. Harriett Heard, Sept. 28, 1985; children: James W. Knight, Katherine E. Knight, Patricia, Joan, Caroline. BA, U. N.C., 1972, JD, 1975. Bar: U.S. Dist. Ct. (we. dist.) N.C. 1975, U.S. Dist. Ct. (ea. dist.) N.C. 1984, U.S. Dist. Ct. (mid. dist.) N.C. 1991, U.S. Ct. Appeals (4th cir.) 1995. Assoc. Welling and Miller, Charlotte, 1975-77; sole practice Charlotte, 1977-79; ptnr. Jordan, Durham & Wilson, Charlotte, 1979-84, Walker, Palmer & Miller, Charlotte, 1985; legal counsel Gov. Martin, Raleigh, N.C., 1985-87; chmn. N.C. Parole Commn., Raleigh, 1987-89; resident judge Superior Ct., Raleigh, 1989-90; prin. Bush, Thurman & Wilson, P.A., from 1991. Chmn. Mecklenburg Rep., Charlotte, 1984-84; chmn. Mecklenburg County Bd. Elections, 1991-93. Mem. Mecklenburg County Bar Assn. Presbyterian. Home: Charlotte, NC. Died Jan. 26, 2007.

WILSON, WILLIAM PRESTON, retired psychiatrist and seminary professor; b. Fayetteville, NC, Nov. 6, 1922; s. Preston Puckett and Rosa Mae (VanHook) W.; m. Dorothy Elizabeth Taylor, Aug. 21, 1950; children: William Preston, Benjamin V., Karen E., Tammy E., Robert E. BS, Duke U., 1943, MD, 1947; DD, Carolina Grad. Sch. Div., Greensboro, NC, 2012. Diplomate Am. Bd. Psychiatry and Neurology (examiner). Intern Gorgas Hosp., Ancon, Panama; from resident psychiatry to prof. emeritus Duke U. Med. Ctr., Durham, NC, emeritus prof. psychiatry, from 1985; assoc. prof. psychiatry, dir. psychiat. rsch. U. Tex. Med. Br., Galveston, 1958-60; dir. Inst. Christian Growth, Durham, NC, from 1985; dist. prof. counseling Carolina Grad. Sch. Divinity, Greenshore, NC, 1996—2007; ret., 2007. Chief neurophysiol. labs. VA Hosp., Durham, N.C., 1961-76; sec. Am. Bd. Qualification in Electroencephalography, 1971-77; mem. N.C. Gov.'s Task force on Diagnosis and Treatment; mem. med. adv. com. N.C. Found. Mental Health Rsch.; bd. dirs. nat. divsn. Contact Teleminstry USA, also mem. internat. commn. healing; cons. numerous area hosps.; Finch lectr. Fuller Theol. Sem., Pasadena, Calif., 1974; vis. prof. psychiatry Marshall U. Sch. Medicine, Huntington, W.Va., 1985-89. Author: The Nuts and Bolts of discipleship; co-author: The Grace to Grow; editor: Applications of Electroencephalography in Psychiatry; co-editor: EEG and Evoked Potentials in Psychiatry and Behavioral Neurology; contbr. articles to med. jours.; contbr. articles to 166 sci. and religious jours. Mem. ofcl. bd. Asbury United Meth. Ch., Durham; mem. program and curriculum com. United Meth. Ch., 1973-81; trustee Meth. Retirement Home, Durham; pres. United Meth. Renewal Svcs., Inc., 1978-82; scout master BSA. Served with AUS, 1943-46. Recipient Ephraim McDowell award Christian Med. Found., 1982, Pioneer in Christian Psychiatry award Congress on Christian Counseling, 1988; named Educator of Yr., Christian Med. and Dental Assn., 1996, Pres. Heritage award, 2011; EEG Montreal Neurol. Inst. fellow, 1954-55, postdoctoral fellow NIMH. Mem. Am. Psychiat. Assn., So. Psychiat. Assn. (pres. 1977-78), AMA, So. Med. Assn. (chmn. sect. neurology and psychiatry 1970), Med. Soc. N.C., Durham-Orange County Med. Soc. (chmn. student recruitment com. 1965), Soc. Biol. Psychiatry, Am. EEG Soc. (councillor), So. EEG Soc. (pres. 1964), Assn. Rsch. Nervous and Mental Diseases, Am. Epilepsy Soc., AAAS, Am. Acad. Neurology, Sigma Xi, Alpha Omega Alpha, U.S. Power Squadron Club (comdr. Durham 1971), AACC Republican. Methodist. Avocations: fishing, sailing, gardening, camping, hiking, travel. Died Sept. 18, 2013.

WINDHAM, REVISH, poet; b. Panola, Ala., May 31, 1940; s. Ike, Sr. and Lillie (Queen) Windham; m. Janice L. Bowman, Sept. 22, 1985; 1 child, Veronice Wiggins-Windham. BA, Morris Brown Coll., 1962; MPA, NYU, 1989. Cert. mediator N.Y. Case worker N.Y.C. Dept. Social Svcs., 1968—70; youth counselor, group and family counselor, job developer N.Y. State Divsn. Youth, NYC, 1970—90; investigator, unit supr. N.Y. State Divsn. Human Rights, NYC, 1990—99; writer, poet NY, from 1999. Author: Shades of Black, 1970, Shade of Anger, 1972, I Wouldn't Take Nothing for My Journey, 2001, Blues Ain't Nothing but a Tonic, 2005; co-founder Black Forum; poetry editor: Black Forum, editor-in-chief:. Bd. dirs. S.E. Bronx (N.Y.) Neighborhood Ctr., Inc., from 2000, Philipsburg Manor (N.Y.) African Am. Adv. Bd., from 2001. With USN, 1964—68. Mem.: Morris Brown Coll. Alumni Assn., 369th Vets. Assn. (life), Shriners, Pentecost Consistory, Masons, Am. Legion (life), Corinthian, Phi Beta Sigma (life). Democrat. Baptist. Avocations: fishing, travel, reading, gardening. Home: Briarcliff Manor, NY. Died July 6, 2007.

WINE, WILLIAM PHILIP, financial executive, consultant; b. Montreal, Can., June 26, 1944; came to U.S., 1987; s. Abraham Jonah and Rose (Gural) W.; m. Sandra Frema Shuster, Apr. 4, 1967. Degree in Acctg., McGill U., 1967. V.p. fin. Superex Can. Ltd., Toronto, Ont., 1967-82; fin. cons. Leonard, Wine, Waldman & Assocs., Toronto, 1984-85; investment broker various, Toronto, 1982-87, Raymond James & Assocs., Lighthouse Point, Fla., 1987-88; cons. Property Tax Cons. Service, Boca Raton, Fla., 1988; fin. cons. Shearson Lehman Hutton, Pompano Beach, from 1988. Home: Boca Raton, Fla. Died June 18, 2007.

WINICK, CHARLES, sociologist, educator; b. NYC, Aug. 4, 1922; s. David and Sadie (Brussel) W.; m. Mariann Pezzella, July 2, 1961 (dec. 2006); children—Elizabeth, Laura, Raphael. BA, City Coll. N.Y., 1941; MA, N.Y.U., 1949; PhD, 1950. Asst. prof. U. Rochester, 1951-53; research dir. Anti- Defamation League, 1953-55; lectr. Queens Coll., 1953-56; vis. prof. Mass. Inst. Tech., 1956-57, Columbia, 1957-58, 61-63, 75-80, NY U., 1975-76, New Sch., 1974-76; dir. basic research J. Walter Thompson Co., 1959-61; research dir. N.Y. State Narcotics Commn., 1957-59; cons. Am. Social Health Assn., 1961-73; research dir. group therapy dept. Postgrad. Center Mental Health, 1957-66; cons. Central Labor Rehab. Council N.Y., 1977—2015; prof. sociology City Coll. and grad. center of CUNY, 1966—2015; assoc. univ. seminar Columbia U., 1963—2015. Cons. subcom. juvenile delinquency U.S. Senate, 1955-57, Joint Commn. Mental Health Children, 1968-69, Commn. on Obscenity and Pornography, 1969-70, Commn. on Marihuana and Drug Abuse, 1972-73, N.Y. State Commn. on Violence in Criminal Justice, 1986-87. Author: Trends in Human Relation Research, 1955, Dictionary of Anthropology, 1956, Taste and Censor, 1959, Insights into Pricing from Behavioral Science and Operations Research, 1961, For the Young Viewer, 1962, Practicum of Group Psychotherapy, 1963, 2d edit., 1974, Outer Space Humor, 1963, U.S.S.R. Humor, 1964, Group Psychotherapy Today, 1965, The New People: Desexualization in American Life, 1968, The Narcotic Addiction Problem, 1968, The Glue Sniffing Problem, 1968, The Lively Commerce: Prostitution in the United States (with Paul Kinsie), 1971, Children's Television Commercials, 1973, Sociological Aspects of Drug Dependence, 1974, Deviance and Mass Communications, 1978, The Television Experience: What Children See, 1979 (with wife), A Labor Approach to Alcohol Problems, 1982, Starting an Employee Assistance Program, 1984, Desexualization in American Life, 1994; editor: Yearbook of Drug Dependence, 1978—2015, Annual Rev. of Research in Deviance, 1978—2015. Served with AUS, 1942-46. Recipient Flowerman award Postgrad. Center Mental Health, 1960; Edn. Press award Ednl. Press Assn., 1963; Peabody award, 1964; Progressive Architecture award, 1979, Ctrl. Labor Rehab. Coun. of N.Y. award, 1993. Mem. Am. Sociol. Assn., Am. Psychol. Assn., Brit. Soc. Study Addiction, Am. Assn. Pub. Opinion Research, Soc. Study Social Problems, Soc. Psychol. Study Social Issues. Died July 4, 2015.

WINNER, JOHN DENNETT, lawyer; b. Port Washington, Wis., Sept. 10, 1921; s. Paul Chester and Jeanne (Dennett) W.; m. Marcelaine Hobson, Sept. 10, 1949; children: John Randall, Gary Hobson, Scott Paul. BA, U. Wis., 1943, JD, 1949. Bar: Wis. 1949, U.S. Dist. Ct. (we. dist.) Wis. 1950, U.S. Ct. Appeals (7th cir.) 1957, U.S. Supreme Ct. 1957, U.S. Dist. Ct. D.C. 1958, U.S. Dist. Ct. (ea. dist.) Wis. 1983. Assoc. Roberts, Roe & Boardman, Madison, Wis., 1949-56; dist. atty. Dane County, Wis., 1956-57; dep. atty. gen. State of Wis., Madison, 1957-59; ptnr. Winner, Wixson & Pernitz, Madison, 1959-96; ret., 1996. Lectr. law U. Wis., Madison, 1953-56. Served to lt. col. U.S. Army, 1943-46, JAG, 1961-62. Decorated Bronze Star. Fellow Am. Coll. Trial Lawyers, Am. Bar Found.; mem. ABA, State Bar Assn. Wis., Civil Trial Counsel Wis., Dane County Bar Assn. (pres. 1975-76), Def. Research Inst. Home: Madison, Wis. Died July 1, 2007.

WINTER, PHILLIP EMIL, physician; b. Milw., May 28, 1935; s. Emil F. and Emma H. (Brauer) W.; m. Nancy H. Tillberry, June 16, 1956 (dec. 1974); children: Melissa M., Anthony P., Daniel K.; m. Janet L. Beck, Feb. 21, 1976. BA, Carroll Coll., 1956; MD, Washington U., 1960; MPH, U. Calif., Berkeley, 1964. Intern Presbyterian-St. Lukes Hosp., Chgo., 1960-61; resident, fellow infectious diseases Washington U.-Barnes Hosp., St. Louis, 1961-62; resident preventive medicine Walter Reed Army Inst. Rsch., 1964-66; commd. 2d. lt. U.S. Army, 1962, advanced through grades to col., 1974, ret., 1984; sr. med. dir. EER, Inc., Germantown, Md., 1984-86; med. dir. Am. Inst. Biol. Scis., Arlington, Va., 1986-90; dir. Three Rivers Health Dist., Saluda, Va., from 1990. Pres., chmn. Gorgas Meml. Inst., Washington, 1981-83, exec. bd., 1976-90. Fellow ACP, Am. Coll. Preventive Medicine; mem. APHA, Am. Rural Health Assn., Va. Pub. Health Assn. Home: Weems, Va. Died Aug. 6, 2007.

WINTERROWD, SHIRLEY LAWRENCE, banker; b. Taylor, Tex., Oct. 5, 1935; m. Jack C. Winterrowd, Aug. 28, 1954; children: Jack C. Jr., Janet Winterrowd Daniell, Christy Winterrowd Pick, Cass Matthew. Grad. high sch., Thrall, Tex. Teller, customer svc. officer, tng. coord., secrecy officer Bank of West, Taylor, Am. Inst. Banking rep., from 1990. Mem. legis. initiatives for edn. com. Tex. A&M U. System. Sec. Thrall Ind. Sch. Dist. Bd. Edn., 1973-82, also mentor; bd. dirs. Williamson County Youth Fair Assn., 1981—; past chmn. Williamson County Extension Program Com.; leader 4-H Club, 1968—; pres. Williamson County A&M Mothers' Club, 1976-78, 82-83; mem. exec. bd. Fedn. Tex. A&M U. Mothers' Clubs, 1981-90, pres., 1988-89; treas. Bapt. Ch. Recipient Dist. 4-H Leader award Tex. 4-H Vol. Leaders Assn., 1981, Outstanding 4-H Leader award Dist. 10 4-H Leaders Assn., 1987. Mem. VFW Ladies Aux., Williamson County 4-H Adult Leaders Assn. Baptist. Avocations: reading, gourmet cooking, collecting cookbooks and clowns, travel, grandchildren. Home: Thrall, Tex. Died May 7, 2007.

WINTERS, RICHARD ALBERT, retired real estate broker; b. Elmira, NY, Mar. 29, 1928; Installer repairman N.Y. Telephone, Corning, N.Y., 1947-58; PBX installer GTE, St. Petersburg, N.Y., 1958-63; real estate broker Richard Winters Real Estate, Painted Post, N.Y., from 1963. With USN, 1945-46. Mem. Kiwanis (Painted Post Club pres. 1942-43). Avocations: woodworking, target shooting. Died May 6, 2007.

WINTERS, STEPHEN HENRY, health care executive; b. Chattanooga, Sept. 27, 1949; s. Henry Taylor and Connie Marie (Clinard) W.; m. Katherine Lily Harris, Dec. 24, 1978; 1 child, Lesley Marie. BA, Vanderbilt U., 1971. Pres. Ecolodyne Corp., Chattanooga, 1972-79; dir. operational analysis HCA Psychiat. Co., Nashville, 1980-82; v.p. fin. Southwest Health Inc., Arlington, Tex., 1982-83; pres. Medshares Mgmt. Group, Inc., Memphis, from 1984. Active Memphis Arts Coun. Mem. Healthcare Fin. Mgmt. Assn., Memphis Area C. of C. Baptist. Home: Memphis, Tenn. Died Nov. 1, 2006.

WISCH, PAUL JOSEPH, educational consultant; b. Chgo., Nov. 27, 1921; s. Joseph Paul and Martha Barbara (Blazek) W.; children: Paula Jo, Peggy Jane. AB, Ill. Coll., Jacksonville, 1947, LLD, 1971; MS in Ed., Western Ill. U., Macomb, 1951; EdD, No. Colo. U., Greeley, 1962. Tchr., coach, counselor, prin. elem. and jr. high schs., Ill., 1947-61; asst. prof., asst. dir. Edn. Planning Svc. Colo. State Coll., Greeley, 1962-63; prof., dept. head Sch. Adminstrn. and Secondary Edn. Dacca U., Dacca, East Pakistan, 1963-65; asst. prof. Central Mich. U., Mt. Pleasant, 1965-66; mng. assoc., head Div. Planning for Higher Edn. Davis-MacConnell-Ralston and Westinghouse Learning Corp., Palo Alto, Calif., 1966-73; pres. Tasmanian Coll. of Advanced Edn., Hobart, Tasmania, Australia, 1973-77, Rusden State Coll., Melbourne, Victoria, Australia, 1977-82, Capricorn Consulting Corp., Santa Clara, Calif., 1982-83; cons. Roseville, Calif., from 1984-. Cons. in field; lectr. various colls., univs. and assns. Contbr. articles to profl. jours. With USAAC, 1942-46. Mem. NEA (life mem.), Ill. Ed. Assn., Ill. State High Sch. Assn., Assn. of Ill. Guidance Pers. (past pres. Dist. 12,), Coun. of Ednl. Facilities Planners, Soc. of Campus and Univ. Planners, Sch. Bd. of the Am. Sch., Australian Coll. of Edn., Coun. of Commonwealth Ednl. Adminstrn., Australian Conf. of Pres. of Colls. of Advanced Edn., Nat. Com. of Advanced Edn. Statistics, Nat. Com. to Study Attrition in Advanced Edn. (chmn.), State Coll. of Victoria Pres. Assn. (pres.), Phi Delta Kappa. Died Mar. 24, 2007.

WISTRICH, ROBERT SOLOMON, historian, educator; b. Lenger, Kazakhstan, Apr. 7, 1945; arrived in Gt. Britain, 1949, arrived in Israel, 1982; s. Jacob Wistrich and Sabina Silbiger; m. Danielle Paule Boccara, Sept. 12, 1971; children: Anna, Dov, Sonia. BA with honors, U. Cambridge, Eng., 1966, MA, 1969; PhD, Univ. Coll., London, 1974. Dir. rsch. Wiener Libr., London, 1974—81; prof. history Hebrew U., Jerusalem, 1982—2015, chmn. Austrian Studies Ctr., 1999—2015, dir. Vidal Sassoon Internat. Ctr. for the Study of Antisemitism, 2002—15, Neuberger chair for modern European history, 2002—15. Vis. prof. Sch. Higher Studies, Paris, 1990—91, Harvard U., Boston, 1998, Royal Netherlands Acad. Scis., 1999—2000; chair Jewish studies Univ. Coll., 1991—95; sr. advisor London Jewish Cultural Ctr., from 1996; bd. dirs. Leo Baeck Inst., from 1982. Author: Socialism and the Jews, 1982 (James Parkes prize, 1985), The Jews of Vienna in the Age of Franz Joseph, 1991 (Austrian State History prize, 1992), Antisemitism: The Longest Hatred, 1991 (Wingate Non-fiction award U.K., 1992); and several others; editor: (documentaries) The Longest Hatred, 1991, Understanding the Holocaust, 1997 (Best Documentary U.K., 1997). Spl. rapporteur on racism and xenophobia Coun. of Europe, Strasbourg, France, 1993—95; rapporteur com. on human rights UN, Geneva, 1993; mem. Cath.-Jewish Hist. Commn., 1999—2001. Grantee sr. fellow, Shalem Ctr., Jerusalem, 2001. Avocations: theater, tennis, chess, travel, reading. Home: Jerusalem, Israel. Died May 19, 2015.

WISWELL, ALFRED IRVIN, electronics executive; b. Boston, Mass., May 13, 1935; s. Irvin Alfred and Ellen Marie (Hart) W. AB cum laude, Suffolk U., 1965; MBA, Loyola U., Chgo., 1974. Research asst. Harvard U., Cambridge, Mass., 1964-65; mktg. mgr. Perin Products, Randolph, Mass., 1966-69; sales and mktg. mgr. Northwestern

Golf Co., Chgo., 1970-74; v.p. sales TCS Corp., Providence, 1974-76; group product mgr. Sheldahl, Inc., East Providence, 1976-78; v.p. Am. Bus. Cons., Clinton, N.J., 1978-81; gen. mgr. Wells Fargo Alarm Services, Providence, 1982-92; chmn. bd., CEO Ranger Internat. Security, Jensen Beach, Fla., from 1992. Pres. A.I. Wiswell and Assocs. Mgmt. Cons., Pawtucket R.I., 1974—; adj. prof. Stonehill Coll. N. Easton, Mass., 1981; lectr. various colls. Author: Professional Salesmanship, 1979, Distribution Development, 1980, Contact Marking Specialist, 1981, Excel in Management, 1984. Served to capt. AUS, 1953-73. Mem. Am. Mktg. Assn., Am. Soc. of Indsl. Security. Clubs: Westport Yacht (Mass.). Roman Catholic. Avocations: teaching, boating, writing, golf. Died Mar. 14, 2007.

WITOWICH, STEPHEN HENRY, JR., secondary school educator; b. Ambridge, Pa., Sept. 2, 1965; s. Stephen Sr. and Carol L. (McCaffrey) W. BS in Chemistry, Gannon U., 1988, MA in Student Personnel, 1990. Cert. secondary edn. tchr., S.C. Tchr. chemistry Hilton Head (S.C.) H.S., 1990-94, tchr. chemistry, dir. student activities, from 1994. Counselor, officer student svcs. Tech. Coll. of the Low Country, Hilton Head, 1992-93; mem. adv. bd. Beaufort County Sci. Stds., Beaufort, 1994—; mem. com. Sea Island Regional Sci. Fair, 1993—. Mem. Nat. Assn. Sci. Tchrs., S.C. Sci. Coun. (dist. I dir. 1995—), S.C. Assn. Chemistry Tchrs., Nat. Assn. Student Activity Advisers. Avocations: old movies, acting, volleyball. Home: Hilton Head Island, SC. Died Aug. 20, 2007.

WITT, WILLIAM PAXTON, aerospace consultant; b. Carrollton, Ill., June 29, 1948; s. William Paxton and Pauline Elizabeth (Carlton) W.; m. Pamela Rich, Dec. 21, 1970. BS, USAF Acad., 1970; MS, Air Force Inst. Tech., 1977, PhD, 1983. Commd. 2d lt. USAF, 1966, advanced through grades to lt. col., 1986, ret., 1990; prin., dir. CORE Group, Tucson, Ariz., from 1990. Mem. Soviet spacecraft engring. evaluation com. Fgn. Applied Scis. Assessment Ctr., Washington, 1985-86. Contbr. articles to profl. jours. Named one of Outstanding Young Men Am., 1983. Mem. AIAA (mem. structural dynamics tech. com. 1982-84, 1990—, dir. nat. capital sect. 1987-89), Air Force Assn., USAF Acad. Assn. Grads. (dir. 1982-84). Republican. Mem. Lds Ch. Avocations: reading, hiking. Home: Mission Viejo, Calif. Died Dec. 27, 2006.

WITTE, CRAIG HESS, optometrist; b. Chgo., June 25, 1943; s. William Barr and Caroline (Hess) W.; m. Dorothy Mae Blackwell, June 18, 1966; children: Christopher Scott, Adam Douglas. BS, U. Miss., 1966; OD, Ill. Coll. Optometry, 1972. Optometrist State of Ill., Springfield, from 1972. Mem. Ill. Whitehouse Commn. Children, 1980. Served with U.S Army, 1966-68. Mem. Am. Optometrists Assn., Ill. Optometrists Assn., Coll. Optometrists in Vision Devel. (assoc.), Optometric Extension Program (assoc. state dir.). Home: Bloomington, Ill. Died July 3, 2007.

WITTE, LOUISE W., former librarian; b. La Salle, Ill., Oct. 17, 1915; d. Stanley Wujek and Agnes (Olsztynski); m. Michael Witte, Dec. 21, 1940; children: Michael Steven, Janet Louise, Lois Jean, John Craig. BSEd, U. Ill., 1940; MLS, State U. N.J., 1965. Tchr. English and Polish So. Milw. (Wis.) High Sch., 1940-41; libr. Maxson Jr. High Sch., Plainfield, N.J., 1965-67, Westfield (N.J.) Sr. High Sch., 1967-77. Recipient Mayor's Trophy Chatham (N.J.) Pub. Libr., 1984. Home: Lecanto, Fla. Died Apr. 11, 2007.

WITTENBACH, ADOLPH JOHN, JR., retired aeronautical engineer; b. Wichita Falls, Tex., Feb. 14, 1920; s. Adolph John Sr. and Leona Pearl (Stanfield) W.; m. Tacy F. Bowman, Sept. 6, 1941 (div. 1948); m. Martha Isabel Green, June 12, 1949 (div. 1964); children: Mary Martha (dec.), Eric Sanders; m. Billie Irene Trainer, Dec. 26, 1964. BS in Aero. Engring., Tex. A&M U., 1946. Aerodynamicist North Am. Aviation, LA, 1942-46; flight test engr. Convair, Ft. Worth, 1946-48; design engr., phys. testing McDonnell Aircraft, St. Louis, 1948-52; design engr. Selb Mfg. Co., St. Louis, 1952-54, Cessna Aircraft, Wichita, Kans., 1954-67; test engr. Piper Aircraft, Vero Beach, Fla., 1967-69; design engr. Swearingen & Gary A/C, San Antonio, 1969-77, Fairchild Aircraft, San Antonio, 1977-94; ret., 1994. Mem. AIAA, Aircraft Owners and Pilots Assn. Republican. Episcopalian. Home: San Antonio, Tex. Died May 16, 2007.

WITZKE, DAVID JOHN, plastic surgeon, educator; b. Rochester, Minn., Jan. 7, 1951; s. Walton E. and Adeline (Altermatt) W.; m. Barbara-Jo Weko, July 20, 1978; children: Sterling, Mercedes, Beckett, Peyton. BA in Math. summa cum laude, U. Minn., 1973; MD, Mayo Med. Sch., 1977. Diplomate Am. Bd. Surgery, Am. Bd. Plastic Surgery, Nat. Bd. Med. Examiners. Intern gen. surgery Mayo Clinic, 1977-78, resident gen. surgery, 1978-82, resident plastic surgery, 1982-84; rsch. asst. U. Minn., Mpls., 1969-73, Mayo Grad. Sch. Medicine, Rochester, 1973-77; pvt. practice, Sioux Falls, S.D., from 1984. Dir. burn unit McKennan Hosp., Sioux Falls, 1986—; clin. instr. surgery U. S.D. Med. Sch., Sioux Falls, 1986—; presenter in field. Contbg. author: Methods in Cell Biology, 1978, Hypertrophic Cardiomyopathy, 1982; contbr. articles to med. jours. Recipient Donald C. Balfour Alumni award, 1978. Fellow ACS; mem. AMA, Am. Soc. Plastic and Reconstructive Surgeons, Am. Soc. Maxillofacial Surgeons, Am. Burn Assn., Am. Cleft Palate Assn., Am. Assn. for Hand Surgery, Am. Soc. for Reconstructive Microsurgery, Internat. Soc. Craniomaxillofacial Surgery, Internat. Congress Plastic and Reconstructive Surgery, Midwestern Assn. Plastic Surgery, Acad. Plastic Surgeons Minn., S.D. Med. Assn., Mayo Clinic Priestley Surg. Soc., Mayo Alumni Assn., Phi Beta Kappa. Avocations: statistical equity analysis, scuba diving. Home: Sioux Falls, SD. Died Aug. 18, 2007.

WOLF, WILLIAM B., JR., lawyer; b. Washington, Sept. 11, 1927; s. William B. and Ruth (Pack) W.; m. Edna Russell Jacobs, Aug. 8, 1952 (div. Oct. 1976); children: Susan Marcia, William B. III, Victoria Katharine; m. Audrey Ann Riven, Nov. 29, 1980. AB, Princeton, 1948; postgrad., Oxford U., 1950; LLB, Yale U., 1951. Bar: D.C. 1951, U.S. Supreme Ct. 1954, Md. 1963. Ptnr. Wolf & Wolf, Washington, 1951-64 and from 82; sole practice Washington, 1964-72, 75-81; ptnr. Wolf & Rosenblatt, Washington, 1972-75, Wolf, Amram & Hahn, P.C., Washington, 1981-82. Vice chmn. Security Nat. Bank, Washington, 1984-85. Author: Lawyers Are a Dime a Dozen, 1999. Pres. Nat. Capital USO, 1966—67, Jewish Hist. Soc. Greater WAshington, Brotherhood Washington Hebrew Congregation, 1967—68. With USN, 1945, sgt. US Army, 1946—48. Mem.: ABA, Bar Assn. D.C., University (Washington), Nassau (Princeton, N.J.), Edgartown (Mass.) Yacht, Woodmont Country. Republican. Jewish. Home: Washington, DC. Died Aug. 28, 2007.

WOLFSON, PEARL SANDLER, retired pharmacist; b. Bklyn., Jan. 14, 1926; d. Louis Sandler and Minnie Rubinowitz; children: Marc Alan, Gary Robert. Student, Ohio State U., 1944-45; BS in Pharmacy, Rutgers U., 1949. Registered pharmacist, N.J., 1951. Pharmacist various pharmacies, various cities, N.J., 1948-93, Pathmark Pharmacist, 1972-93; ret., 1993. Mem. AAUW, Am. Pharm. Assn., N.J. Pharmacists Assn., Middlesex County Pharm. Soc., Rutgers Coll. Pharmacy Alumni Assn. (pres. 1986-88), Hadassah (newspaper staff), B'nai B'rith, Rutgers Century Club. Democrat. Jewish. Avocations: poetry, reading, theater, concerts, photography, piano. Home: Monroe Twp, NJ. Died Dec. 6, 2006.

WOLLENBERG, MARJORIE See LORD, MARJORIE

WOLNER, RENA MERYL (RENA MERYL TANNENBAUM), publisher; b. Boston, Feb. 22, 1945; d. Samuel and Gertrude (Leaman) Tannenbaum BS, U. Bridgeport, 1967. Spl. asst. to pres. to assoc. publisher Bantam Books, NYC, 1967—77; v.p., publisher Berkley Publishing Corp., NYC, 1977—84, pres., 1984—85, Pocket Books, 1985; pres., pub. Avon Books, NYC, 1985-88; cons. Putnams Berkley Publishing Group., NYC, 1989-94. Bd. dirs. Am. Book Awards, 1981-83. Mem. MS Soc. (bd. dirs. So. N.Y. chpt. 1889—). Home: Delray Beach, Fla. Died Nov. 7, 2015.

WOLTER, ALLAN BERNARD, writer, educator; b. Peoria, Ill., Nov. 24, 1913; s. Bernard Gregory Wolter and Marianne Bernardette Strub. BA, Our Lady of Angels Sem., Cleveland, OH, 1937; MA, Cath. U. of Am., Washington, DC, 1942, PhD, 1947; LG, Franciscan Inst. St. Bonaventure U., Saint Bonaventure, NY, 1952; DSc (hon.), Quincy U., Quincy, IL, 1967. Ordained Roman Catholic Priest Roman Cath. Ch., 1940. Asst. prof. chemistry Our Lady of Angels Franciscan Sem., Cleveland, Ohio, 1943—45, asst. prof. biology, 1943—45, asst. prof. philosophy, 1943—45; assoc. prof. philosophy Franciscan Inst., St. Bonaventure U., Saint Bonaventure, NY, 1946—52; prof., 1952—62, Cath. U. Am., 1952—81; rsch. assoc. Ctr. Medieval and Renaissance Studies, UCLA, 1978—97; Joseph Doino vis. prof. franciscan theology St. Bonaventure U., 1997—2002; prof. emeritus philosophy The Cath. U. Am., 1984—84; vis. lectr. Princeton U., 1965—65; vis. prof. U. Mich., Mich., 1967—67, NYU, NY, 1969—69. Assoc. editor The New Scholasticism, 1949—51; editor Franciscan Studies, 1949—52, Franciscan Inst. Publications, 1946—62. Author books. V.p. Am. Cath. Philos. Assn., 1956—57, pres., 1957—58. Recipient Aquinas Medal, Am. Cath. Philos. Assn., 1998. Fellow: Nat. Endowment Humanities; mem.: Societas Internationalis Scotistica, Soc. for Medieval and Renaissance Studies, Am. Philos. Assn., Phi Beta Kappa. Home: Saint Louis, Mo. Died Nov. 15, 2006.

WOMACK, JOHN W., pharmacist; b. St. Louis, Dec. 6, 1930; s. John Anderson and Della Long Womack; children: Peter Frank, Elin Vera, Brian William, John Anderson, Kimberly Ann. BS in pharmacy, U. Toledo, 1957. Registered Pharmacist Ohio. Chief pharmacist Cunningham Drug Co., Cleve., 1958—73, U. Pharmacy, Cleve., 1973—76, Revco Drug, Cleve., 1976—85, Neon, Cleve., from 1985. Mem. football camp Camp Stonem, Calif., 1953; mem. football team, 1954, AAU Basketball, Cleve., 1959; bd of trustees Free Clinic Greater Cleve., 1968—99; worker Carl Stokes Election, Cleve., 1968. Cpl. US Army, 1952—54, Korea. Mem.: Nat. Pharm. Assn., Ohio State Pharm. Assn., Omega Psi Phi. Episcopalian. Avocations: basketball, football. Home: Bedford, Ohio. Died Nov. 5, 2006.

WOOD, BERENICE HOWLAND, retired secondary school educator; b. Newport, RI, Oct. 21, 1910; d. Horatio Gates and Margaret Lorraine (Doyle) W. AB, Vassar Coll., 1934; MA, Columbia U., 1936; postgrad., U. R.I., 1961-65. Clk. 1st Dist. Ct. R.I., Newport, 1942-50; home service dir. ARC, Newport, 1950-61; tchr. Cranston, R.I., 1961-62, Elmhurst Sch., Portsmouth, R.I., 1962-64, Newport, 1964-82. Sec. to mayor City of Newport, 1941. Pres. Coun. Social Agys., Newport, 1955—57; active Hist. Soc. Newport, Art Mus. Newport, Redwood Libr., Newport, Preservation Soc., Newport, Hill Assn., Newport. Mem. Point Assn. Newport, Nat. Trust Hist. Preservation. Roman Catholic. Avocations: maintaining and preserving antiquities, foreign travel. Home: Newport, RI. Died Oct. 31, 2006.

WOOD, HOWARD JOHN, III, astrophysicist, retired astronomer; b. Balt., July 19, 1938; s. Howard John Jr. and Cara (Loss) W.; m. Austine Barton Read, June 10, 1961 (div. Jan. 1975); children: Cara Loss, Erika Barton; m. Maria Ilona Kovacs, May 22, 1977; 1 child, Andreas M. BA in Astronomy, Swarthmore Coll., 1960; MA, Ind. U., 1962, PhD, 1965. Lectr., asst. prof. then assoc. prof. U. Va., Charlottesville, 1964-70; staff astronomer European So. Obs., Santiago, Chile, 1970-75; Fulbright Rsch. fellow U. Vienna Obs., 1976-78; rsch. assoc. Ind. U., Bloomington, 1978-81; asst. to the dir. Cerro Tololo Inter-Am. Obs., La Serena, Chile, 1982-83; physicist, astronomer NASA/Goddard Space Flight Ctr., Greenbelt, Md., 1984—2012, mgr. instrument synthesis and analysis lab., 2000—08, optics lead engr., Advanced Topographic Laser Altimeter System, 2008—12. Optics lead engr. Mars Observer Laser Altimeter, 1989-90, GSFC Hubble Space Telescope, Greenbelt, 1990—2012; GFC advisor optics and outreach James Webb Space Telescope, Greenbelt, 1996—2012; GFC advisor, participant Hubble Space Telescope Allen Comm., NASA, Danbury, Conn., 1990, Greenbelt; co-chmn. Hubble Space Telescope Ind. Optical Rev. Panel, Columbia, Md., 1990-91; mem. panel The Townes/SAGE Panel-Jet Propulsion Lab., Pasadena, 1991-92. Co-author: (Book) Physics of Ap Stars, 1976; contbr. articles to profl. jours. Grantee NSF (10), 1965-82. Mem. Optical Soc. Am. (chair optical tech. divsn. 1999-2001, co-chair ann. meeting 2002), Am. Astronomical Soc., Sigma Xi. Achievements include discovery of Balmer-Line variability of Ap stars; discovery of magnetic fields in southern Ap stars; alignment testing and delivery of the DIRBE photometric cryogenic telescope on the COBE spacecraft; alignment and optical prescription for Hubble Space Telescope while in orbit. Home: Bowie, Md. Died Oct. 23, 2014.

WOOD, JAMES, retired supermarket executive; b. Newcastle-upon-Tyne, UK, Jan. 19, 1930; came to U.S., 1974; s. Edward and Catherine Wilhelmina (Parker) W.; m. Colleen Margaret Taylor, Aug. 14, 1954; children: Julie, Sarah. Grad., Loughborough Coll., Leicestershire, England; LHD (hon.), St. Peter's Coll., NJ. Chief food chain Newport Coop. Soc., S. Wales, U.K., 1959-62, Grays Food Coop. Soc., Eng., 1962-66; dir., joint dep. mng. dir. charge retailing Cavenham, Ttd., Hayes, Eng., 1966-80; pres. Grand Union Co., Elmwood Park, NJ, 1973-79, CEO, dir., from 1973, chmn. bd., 1979-80; CEO Great Atlantic & Pacific Tea Co., Inc., 1980—98, chmn. bd., 1998—2001. Bd. dirs. Asarco, Inc., Irma Fabrikerne A/S, Denmark, Schering-Plough Corp. Active World USO, UNICEF, United Jersey Bank. With Brit. Army, 1948-50. Mem. Food Mktg. Inst. (bd. dirs.) Roman Catholic. Home: Saddle River, NJ. Died Mar. 26, 2015.

WOOD, JAMES LESLIE, sociology educator; b. Aug. 30, 1941; BA in Sociology, U. Calif., Berkeley, 1963, postgrad., MA in Sociology, 1966, PhD in Sociology, 1973. Asst. prof. San Francisco State U., summer 1972; instr. in sociology Holy Names Coll., 1971-73; lectr. in sociology U. Calif., Riverside, 1973-75, San Diego State U., 1975-76, asst. prof. sociology, 1976-78, assoc. prof. sociology, 1978-81, prof. sociology, from 1981, chmn. sociology, from 1991. SDSU mem. Promotions com., Executive com., Curriculum Com., Methodology com., Syposium com., Post-Tenure review com. (chair), San Diego Poll com., Personnel com., Rsch. Human Subjects com., Applied Social Rsch. Group com., Reappointment Tenure com. (chair), Master's essay com., Graduate com., Master's Degree theory and Methodology Exam com., Colloquium com., Teaching Eval. com.; lectr. in field; resident scholar U. London, Goldsmiths' Coll., 1984. Author: The Sources of American Student Activism, 1974, (co-author) Sociology: Traditional and Radical Perspectives, Adapted for the United Kingdom, 1982, Social Movements: Development, Participation and Dynamics, 1982, 3d printing, 1985, Sociology: Traditional and Radical Perspectives, 2d edit., 1990; author: (monographs) Political Consciousness and Student Activism, New Left Ideology: Its Dimensions and Development, 1975, Aging in America; works presented at profl. organizations; contbr. articles to profl. jours.; chpts. to books in field. U. Calif. grantee, 1969, 73-74, 75, San Diego State U. grantee, 1976, 79, 81, 82, 88, 83, 85, 90, 96. Mem. Am. Sociol. Assn. (collective behavior and social movements sect., polit. sociology sect.), Internat. Soc. Polit. Psychology, Pacific Sociol. Assn., Soc. for the Study of Social Problems, Calif. Sociol. Assn., Phi Beta Delta, Alpha Kappa Delta. Home: Berkeley, Calif. Died Apr. 18, 2007.

WOOD, SCOTT EMERSON, chemistry professor; b. Ft. Collins, Colo., Apr. 9, 1910; s. Jesse Reuben and Maude Louise (Scott) W.; m. Marie Simmons, July 15, 1936; 1 child, Edward Scott. BSChemE, U. Denver, 1930, MS, 1931; PhD, U. Calif., Berkeley, 1935. Rsch. assoc. MIT, Cambridge, Mass., 1935-40; instr. Yale U., New Haven, 1940-43, asst. prof., 1943-48; assoc. prof. Ill. Inst. Technology, Chgo., 1948-54, prof., 1954-75, prof. emeritus, 1975, acting chmn., dept. chmn., 1960-61, adminstrv. officer, 1961, vice chmn., 1961-62, acting assoc. dean rsch., 1962-64. Rsch. assoc. Argonne (Ill.) Nat. Lab., 1953, cons., 1960-80, resident rsch. assoc., 1965; vis. prof. Coll. Dublin (Ireland), 1966-67; cons. in field. Co-author: Thermodynamics-An Introduction, 1968, The Thermodynamics of Chemical Systems, 1990; contbr. articles to profl. jours. Treas. Shepherd of Valley Luth. Ch., El Paso, Tex., 1979-86; adv. bd. Bd. Higher Edn., State of Ill., 1970-71; mem. youth com. YMCA, Oak Pk., Ill., 1953-62, P.T.A. Bd., Riverside Jr. High Sch., 1956-57; audit com. Ames PTA, Riverside, 1951-52; com. mem. Boy Scouts Am., Riverside, 1957-58, Cub Scouts, 1953-54. Fulbright-Hayes grantee, 1966; recipient Outstanding Educator award, 1971. Fellow AAAS; mem. Am. Chem. Soc. Home: Canutillo, Tex. Died June 7, 2007.

WOODARD, WILLIAM AUBREY, computer scientist, company executive; b. Takoma Park, Md., July 25, 1951; s. Aubrey Clyde and Vilma Delores (Hatcher) W.; m. Nancy Liles Gentry, Mar. 20, 1970 (div. Jan. 1979); 1 child, Jennifer Louise; m. Colleen Adair Hoffman, June 25, 1983; step-children: Kristin Elyse, Courtney Alicia-Marre. BS in Econs., U. Md., 1978; MS in Engring., The Johns Hopkins

U., 1988. Computer specialist Export-Import Bank of the U.S., Washington, 1973-78; database cons. Washington, 1978-82; sr. computer scientist Computer Scis. Corp., Falls Church, Va., 1983-85, dir. tech. activity, 1985-88, dir. info. systems ctr., 1988-90, v.p. info. systems, from 1990. Adv. bd. C/A/S/E Outlook Mag., Portland, 1988—; researcher Va. Tech, Falls Church, 1988—. Contbr. articles to profl. publs.; inventor in field. Mem. Computer Soc. IEEE (reviewer 1988—). Republican. Methodist. Home: Fairfax, Va. Died July 4, 2007.

WOODHOUSE, ELIZABETH C., retired government agency administrator; b. Cin., Nov. 10, 1911; d. John Michael Hughes and Katherine Martha Berger; m. Elton Lee Woodhouse, Mar. 25, 1932 (dec. Feb. 8, 1970); children: Allan, Jerry, Carolyn, Margaret. BS, Urbana U., Ohio, 1979; Masters Degree, Cath. Distance U., 2002. Dir. Child Care Ctr., Springfield, Ohio, 1953—82, Mental Health Soc., Springfield, Ohio, 1955—70, USDA Food Svc., Columbus, Ohio, 1977—97. Author: Beginnings, 1987, Johnny Appleseed Poems, 2001. Pres. Child Care Assn., Springfield, 1960—65, Mental Health Assn., Springfield, 1966—70; county chair Ohioana Libr. Assn., Columbus, from 1980; pres. Friends of the Libr. Clark County Pub. Libr., Springfield, Ohio, 2001; pres. Springfield Symphony Orch., 1997—99; pres., sec., treas. Altrusa Internat., 1970, Federated Women's Clubs, 1945—2001. Recipient 3 awards, Clark County and Ohio State Mental Health Assns., Elizabeth Woodhouse award named in her honor, Wittenberg U., Springfield, 1997. Roman Catholic. Avocations: doll collecting, collecting teapots. Home: Springfield, Ohio. Died June 20, 2007.

WOODS, PENDLETON, college director, author; b. Ft. Smith, Ark., Dec. 18, 1923; s. John Powell and Mabel (Hon) W.; m. Lois Robin Freeman, Apr. 3, 1948; children: Margaret, Paul Pendleton, Nancy Cox. BA in Journalism, U. Ark., 1948; D (hon.), Okla. Christian U., Oklahoma City, 2005. Editor, asst. pub. mgr. Okla. Gas & Electric Co., Oklahoma City, 1948—69; dir. Living Legends of Okla., Okla. Christian U., Oklahoma City, 1969—82; dir. project, promotion Enterprise Sq. and Am. Citizenship Ctr., 1982—92, dir. Nat. Edn. Program and Am. Citizenship Ctr., 1992. Arbitrator BBB; leader youth seminars in field; state pub. affairs officer Employer Support Guard and Res. Author: You and Your Company Magazine, 1950, Church of Tomorrow, 1964, Myriad of Sports, 1971, This Was Oklahoma, 1979; recorded Sounds of Scouting, 1969, Born Grown, 1974 (We. Heritage award Nat. Cowboy Hall of Fame), One of a Kind, 1977, Countdown to Statehood, 1982, The Thunderbird Tradition, 1989, A Glimpse at Oklahoma, 1990, Historic Oklahoma County, 2002; editor Libertas. Vol. reader Okla. Libr. for the Blind; past pres. Okla. Assn. Epilepsy, Keep Okla. Beautiful, Okla. City Mental Health Clin.; past pres., hon. lifetime dir. Variety Health Ctr.; pub. rels. chmn. Okla. County chpt. ARC; past chmn. We. Heritage award Nat. Cowboy Hall of Fame; Am. Freedom Coun.; charter dir. Okla. Vets. Med. Rsch. Found.; cons. Exec. Svc. Corps.; ex-state comdr. Am. ex-Prisoners of War; vol. Okla. City VA Hosp.; state historian Okla. N.G.; chmn. Okla. City Independence Day Parade; exec. dir. Okla. City Bicentennial Commn.; v.p. Okla. City chpt. Freedom Found.; v.p. & bd. dirs. Campfire Girls Coun.; bd. dirs. Okla. Jr. Symphony, past pres.; bd. dirs. Zoo Amphitheater of Okla. City, Will Rogers Centennial Commn., Greater Okla. City Tree Bank Found., Boy Scout Am. (life); bd. dirs., co-founder Ctrl. Pk. Neighborhood Assn.; dir. Okla. for Resource Preservation; chmn. State Directional Signage Task Force. With US Army, WWII and Korean War, ret. col. Named Outstanding Young Man of Yr., Oklahoma City Jr. C. of C., 1953; recipient Silver Beaver award Boy Scouts Am., 1963, Wokan award Oklahoma City Coun. Camp Fire Girls, 1968, Silver medal Advt. Fedn. Am., Disting. Cmty. Svc. award Neighborhood Devel. and Conservation Ctr., 2 Commendation awards Am. Assn. for State and Local History, 4 honor medals Freedoms Found., Jefferson Davis medal United Daus. of Confederacy, Okla. Disting. Svc. medal (2), Outstanding Contbn. to Okla. Mus., Okla. Mus. Assn., 1987, Outstanding Contbn. to Okla. Tourism award Okla. Dept. Tourism, 1989, Cmty. Svc. award U. Ark. Alumni Assn., 1992, Citizenship and Patriot awards SAR, 1992, 5 Who Care award KOCO-TV, 1993, Jefferson award Am. Inst. for Pub. Svc., 1993, Mayor's award in Beautification, 1994, George Washington award Youth Leadership Found., St. Augustine, Fla., 1993, Golden Rule award J.C. Penney Found., 1999, Lifetime Achievement award Keep Okla. Beautiful, Pres.'s Vol. Svc. award, 2005, Gold award MetLife Found., 2011; inducted into Okla. Journalism Hall of Fame, 2001, Okla. Mil. Hall of Fame, 2002, Okla. Historians Hall of Fame, 2007, Okla. Outstanding Older Worker award, Washington, DC, 2007, Gold award MetLife Found., Washington, 2011, Nat. Assn. Agy. Aging, 2012. Mem.: DAR (Medal of Honor 2005, Nation's Most Outstanding Ex-prisoner of War 2005, Outstanding Older Worker award for Okla. 2007), VFW, DAV, Okla. Distributive Edn., Okla. Jr. C. of C. (hon. life, past internat. dir.), Ctrl. Okla. Bus. Communicators (past pres., hon. life), Advt. Fedn. Am. (past dist. dir.), Soc. Assoc. Indsl. Editors (past v.p.), Okla. Vets. Coun. (chmn.), Okla. Heritage Assn., Okla. City Beautiful (publ. editor), Okla. Safety Coun. (publ. editor), Okla. County Hist. Soc. (dir., past pres.), 45th Inf. Divsn. Assn. (past pres.), Korean War Vets. Assn., Am. Legion, Mus. Unassigned Lands (chmn.), Mil. Order World Wars (regional comdr., Oklahoma City comdr., Okla. State comdr., nat. staff, Gold and Silver Patrick Henry Patriotism medals), Okla. Hist. Soc. (life; publ. editor,), Words of Jesus Found. (pres.), Okla. Zool. Soc. (past pres.), Okla. Geneal. Soc., Okla. County Sr. Nutrition Found. (sec., bd. dirs.), Freedom's Found. (v.p.), Nat. Eagle Scout Assn. (Okla. chmn.), U. Ark. Alumni Assn. (charter pres. Oklahoma City chpt.), Okla. Lung Assn. (pub. rels. com.), Am. Cancer Soc. (dir. Okla. County chpt.), Okla. Travel Industries Assn., Am. Ex-Prisoners of War (state comdr.), Okla. City Hist. Preservation Commn., Okla. City Clean and Green Coalition, Lincoln Park Country (pres.), Oklahoma City Advt. Club (past pres., hon. life), Kappa Sigma (nat. commr. publs.), Sigma Delta Chi. Home: Oklahoma City, Okla. Deceased.

WOODS, PHILIP WELLS (PHIL WOODS), jazz musician composer; b. Springfield, Mass., Nov. 2, 1931; s. Stanley J. and Clara (Markley) W.; m. Beverly Berg, 1957 (div. 1973); children: Garth Darryl, Aimee Francesca; m. Jill Goodwin, Dec. 20, 1985; stepchildren: Allisen, Tracey Trotter, Kim Parker Student, Juilliard Sch., NYC, 1948-52; LLD (hon.), East Stroudsberg U., 1994. Alto saxophone and clarinet with Dizzy Gillespie and Quincy Jones, alto saxophone with Benny Goodman, Gene Krupa, Thelonious Monk, Buddy Rich, Charlie Barnet, Michel Legrand, many others; leader European Rhythm Machine, 1968-73, Phil Woods Quartet, 1974-84, Phil Woods Quintet, 1984-2015, Phil Woods Little Big Band, 1988-2015, Phil Woods Big Band, 1998-2015; composer Fill the Woods with Light, Rights of Swing, Three Improvisations, Sonata for Alto and Piano (Four Moods), The Sun Suite, I Remember, Deer Head Sketches, numerous others; recs. with own bands include Rights of Swing, 1971, Phil and Quill (3 albums with Gene Quill), Images (with Michel Legrand) (Grammy award 1976), (with Benny Carter) My Man Benny, My Man Phil, I Remember: A Tribute to Some of the Great Jazz Musicians, 1979, More Live (Grammy award 1982), At the Vanguard (Grammy award 1983), (as the Phil Woods Quintet) Astor and Elis, Mile High Jazz, Celebration (Grammy award nomination 1997); played saxophone on many other recs. including Clark Terry and Ben Webster's Happy Faces, Symbiosis by Bill Evans, A New Album with Lena Horne, Just the Way You Are with Billy Joel, Dr. Wu with Steely Dan; also played on motion picture soundtracks The Hustler, 1961, Blow-Up, 1966, Twelve Angry Men, 1957, It's My Turn, 1980, Boy In A Tree. Co-founder, bd. dirs. Delaware Water Gap (Pa.) Celebration of the Arts, 1978-2000, adv. bd., 2000-2015. Named New Star of 1956 Downbeat mag., Nat. Endowment for the Arts Jazz Master, 2007; winner Down Beat Critics' Poll, 1975-79, 81-90, 92-93, 96-98, 2000, Down Beat Readers' Poll, 1975-95, 2000; recipient Golden Feather award for best group Phil Woods Quartet Downbeat Critics' Poll, 1978, Downbeat Readers Poll award for best acoustic group Phil Woods Quintet, 1985, 88-91, Downbeat Critics' Poll award for best acoustic group Phil Woods Quintet, 1998-89, 91-92, 96, Jazz Times Readers Poll award for best alto sax, 1990, 92, Living Jazz Legend award, Kennedy Ctr.; elected to Am. Jazz Hall of Fame, 1994, Beacon Jazz award, 2001. Mem. Am. Fedn. Musicians. Internat. Assn. Jazz Educators. Avocations: reading, cooking, movies, computers. Home: Delaware Water Gap, Pa. Died Sept. 29, 2015.

WOOLF, KAREN HENDRICKSON, education educator; b. Duluth, Minn., Dec. 31, 1944; d. Thomas Christopher Hendrickson; m. Andrew Godfrey, Feb. 1, 1969. BA, U. Wis., 1969; MS, Wheelock U., 1973. Cert. early childhood tchr., Mass. Tchr. Hamilton (Mass.)-Wenham Regional Sch. Dist., 1973-92; instr., tchr.-in-residence U. N.H., Durham, 1992-93. Part-time instr. Gordon Coll., Wenham, Mass., 1987-89, Lesley Coll., Cambridge, Mass., 1992; cons. Portfolios, Storytelling for Tchrs., New Eng., 1989-92; Brain Gym instr. Ednl. Kinesiology Found., Ventura, Calif., 1990-92. Co-author monograph: Speaking Out: Teachers on Teaching, 1986. Horace mann grantee, 1986; Torger Thompson grad. fellow, 1968-69. Mem. ASCD, N.D. Study Group on Evaluation, League for Advancement of New Eng. Tellers (regional rep., storyteller 1986-92). Democrat. Lutheran. Avocations: contra dancing, folk music, weaving, painting, hiking. Home: Brentwood, NH. Died Dec. 19, 2006.

WORMHOUDT, ARTHUR LOUIS, Arabic educator; b. Pella, Iowa, June 17, 1917; s. Cornelius Hendrik and Esther Melissa (Maasdam) W.; m. Pearl Arlene Shinn, Nov. 25, 1948; 1 child, Joda Cornelius. BA with high honors, U. Iowa, 1939; MA, Harvard U., 1940; PhD, U. Iowa, 1942. Grad. asst. U. Iowa, Iowa City, 1941-42, Queens Coll., NYC, 1945; asst. prof. Ctrl. Coll., Pella, 1946; assoc. prof. State U. Minn., St. Cloud, 1949-57, State U. Ill., DeKalb, 1958; prof. lang. and lit. William Penn Coll., Oskaloosa, Iowa, 1958-79, prof. emeritus, from 1979. Author 4 books of lit. explanation, 1949, 53, 56, 61; author Arab Translation series; author: New Book Writing the New Testament, 1994; contbr. articles to mags. With U.S. Army, 1942-45, ETO. Mem. Am. Assn. Tchrs. Arabic, Phi Beta Kappa. Avocations: singing, violin, walking. Home: Ottumwa, Iowa. Died Jan. 15, 2007.

WORMSER, ERIC M(AX), engineering manager, consultant; b. Frankfurt, Fed. Republic of Germany, Apr. 30, 1921; came to U.S., 1938; s. Martin and Anna I. (Meyer) W.; m. Margot Haas, Feb. 15, 1948 (dec. 1987); children: Peter D., Thomas M.; m. Linda Birnbaum, Feb. 20, 1989. BS, MIT, 1942; postgrad., NYU, 1946-48. Registered profl. engr., Conn. Exec. v.p. Barnes Engring., Stamford, Conn., 1952-73; prin. Wormser Sci. Assocs., Stamford, from 1973. Inventor electro optics. Sgt. U.S. Army, 1944-46. Mem. Cosmos Club. Died Apr. 30, 2007.

WRIGHT, EVELYN LOUISE, artist; b. Odessa, Mo., Aug. 2, 1913; d. Elmer Clarence and Anna Bell (Ford) Adams; m. Douglas P. Wright, July 19, 1934 (dec. Dec. 27, 1986); children: Annetta Louise, Judith Elaine, Duane Douglas. Student, Stockton Coll., Calif., 1958—60, U. of Pacific, Stockton, 1960—61, Merced Coll., Calif., 1962—64, Columbia Coll., 1962—64. Graphic artist, Independence, Mo., 1928—34; asst. mgr., bookkeeper Wrights, Stockton, 1945—86; owner, instr. Evelyn's Art Classes and Workshops, Stockton, from 1980; instr. Stockton Sch. Sys., from 1945, Ripona Sch., Calif., 1992—94. Recipient Best of Show award, Richard Yip Art Co., 1980, award, Sonora Nat. Festival, 1982, 1984, Lodi Grape Festival, 1986. Avocation: travel. Died Jan. 27, 2007.

WRIGHT, FRANZ PAUL, poet, writer, translator; b. Vienna, 1953; s. James Wright and Liberty Kardulis; m. Elizabeth Oehlkers. Grad., Oberlin College, 1977; studied postgrad., U. Va. Translator, author of introduction Rainer Maria Rilke, The Unknown Rilke, 1990; translator modern and contemporary French and German poets; author: (poems) Tapping the White Cane of Solitude, 1976, The Earth Without You, 1980, Eight Poems, 1981, The One Whose Eyes Open When You Close Your Eyes, 1982, No Siege Is Absolute, 1983, Going North in Winter, 1986, Entry in an Unknown Hand, 1989, Midnight Postscript, 1990, And Still the Hand Will Sleep in Its Glass Ship, 1990, Rorschach Test, 1995, The Night World and the Word Night, 1993, Knell, 1998, ILL LIT: Selected and New Poems, 1998, The Beforelife, 2001, Walking to Martha's Vineyard, 2003 (Pulitzer Prize for poetry, 2004), God's Silence, 2006, Wheeling Motel, 2009, Kindertotenwald: Prose Poems, 2011, F, 2013; represented in anthologies; contbr. articles to profl. publs. Recipient Witter Bynner prize for Poetry, 1995, PEN/Voelcker award, 1996, Pulitzer prize in Poetry, 2004; NEA fellow, 1985, 92, Guggenheim fellow, 1989, Whiting fellow, 1991. Died May 14, 2015.

WRIGHT, HOWARD LEWIS, financial consultant; b. Detroit, Mar. 31, 1934; s. Asa Howard and Edrie (Albin) W.; m. Audrey Plummer, Apr. 2, 1955; children: Kevin, Lawrence, Sharon. BA, Mich. State U., 1955, MA, 1956. CPA, Mich., D.C. Staff mgr. Arthur Andersen & Co., Detroit, 1956-67, ptnr., 1967-74, Washington, 1974-91; pvt. cons. Mineral, Va., from 1992. Author: (with others) Federal Income Taxation of Banks and Financial Institutions, 1981, A Guide to Bank Taxation, Understanding FIRREA, 1989; editor: Viewpoint Washington newsletter. Pres. Epilepsy Found. Nat. Capital Area, Washington, 1980-82. Fellow Am. Inst. CPA's. Republican. Mem. United Ch. of Christ. Clubs: University (Washington); Westwood Country (Vienna, Va.). Avocations: photography, stamp collecting/philately. Died June 11, 2007.

WRIGHT, JAMES CLAUDE, JR., (JIM WRIGHT), former United States Representative from Texas; b. Ft. Worth, Dec. 22, 1922; s. James C. and Marie (Lyster) W.; m. Mary Ethelyn Lemons, 1942 (div.); children Jimmy, Virginia Sue, Patricia Kay, Alicia Marie; m. Betty Hay, Nov. 12, 1972 Student, Weatherford Coll., U. Tex.; LLD (hon.), Hartwick Coll., 1969, Boston U., 1982, Tex. Christian U., 2002. Ptnr. trade extension and advt. firm; mem. Tex. Legislature, 1947-49; mayor City of Weatherford, Weatherford, Tex., 1950-54; mem. US Congress from 12th Tex. Dist., 1955—89, majority leader, 1977—87, speaker of the House, 1987—89; Disting. lectr. Tex. Christian U., 1991—2003. Mem. exec. com. Dem. Nat. Com.; chmn. Dem. Nat. Conv., Atlanta, 1988. Author: You and Your Congressman, 1965, The Coming Water Famine, 1966, Of Swords and Plowshares, 1968, Reflections of a Public Man, 1984, Worth It All: My War for Peace, 1993, Balance of Power, 1996, The Flying Circus: Pacific War-1943-as Seen Through a Bombsight, 2005; co-author: Congress and Conscience, 1970; columnist Ft. Worth Star Telegram, 1991-2003 Served with USAAF, World War II. Decorated D.F.C., Legion of Merit; named Outstanding Young Man Tex. Jr. C. of C., 1953 Mem. League Tex. Municipalities (pres. 1953) Democrat. Presbyterian. Home: Fort Worth, Tex. Died Apr. 6, 2015.

WUNNICKE, BROOKE, lawyer; b. Dallas, May 9, 1918; d. Rudolph von Falkenstein and Lula Lenore Brooke; m. James M. Wunnicke, Apr. 11, 1940; (dec. 1977); 1 child, Diane B. BA, Stanford U., 1939; JD, U. Colo., 1945. Bar: Wyo. 1946, Colo. 1969, U.S. Dist. Ct. Wyo. 1947, U.S. Dist. Ct. Colo. 1970, U.S. Supreme Ct. 1958, U.S. Ct. Appeals (10th cir.) 1958. Pvt. practice law, 1946—69; ptnr. Williams & Wunnicke, Cheyenne, Wyo., 1956—69; ofcounsel Calkins, Kramer, Grimshaw & Harring, Denver, 1969—73; chief appellate dep. atty. Dist. Atty's Office, Denver, 1973—86; of counsel Hall & Evans LLC, Denver, 1986—2011. Adj. prof. law U. Denver Coll. Law, 1978-97, 1st Frank H. Ricketson Jr. adj. prof., 2003; lectr. Internat. Practicum Inst. Denver, 1976-2003. Author: Ethics Compliance for Business Lawyers, 1987; co-author: Standby Letters of Credit, 1989, Corporate Financial Risk Management, 1992, UCP 500 and Standby Letters of Credit-Special Report, 1994, Standby and Commercial Letters of Credit, 2002, Legal Opinion Letters Formbook, 2010, Annual Supps.; contbr. articles to profl. jours. Pres. Laramie County Bar Assn., Cheyenne, Wyo., 1967-68; Dir. Cheyenne C. of C., 1965-68 Recipient Outstanding Svc. award, Colo. Dist. Attys. Coun., 1979, 1982, 1986, Disting. Alumni awards, U. Colo. Sch. Law, 1986, 1993, William Lee Knous award, 1997, Lathrop Trailblazer award, Colo. Women's Bar Assn., 1992, Eleanor P. Williams award for Disting. Svc. to Legal Profession, 1997, Potter Lifetime Profl. Svc. award, 1999, Nat. award, Def. Rsch. Inst., 1999, Law Star award, Denver Coll. Law, 2003. Fellow Colo. Bar Found., Am. Bar Found.; mem. ABA, Am. Judicature Soc. (hon. mem.), Wyo. State Bar, Denver Bar Assn. (hon. life; trustee 1977-80, award of Merit 2004), Colo. Bar Assn. (hon., life, Award of Merit 1999), CBA-CLE Legal Legend Presentation, William E. Doyle Inn of Ct. (hon.), Order of Coif, Phi Beta Kappa. Independent. Avocations: reading, writing. Home: Denver, Colo. Deceased.

WUNSCH, ANNA CATHERINE MARY O'BRIEN HORTON, artist, consultant; b. Jersey City, Jan. 22, 1921; d. James Joseph and Clara Josephine (Doyle) O'B.; m. Lester William Horton, Mar. 10, 1942 (div. Apr. 17, 1947); children: William Horton, Marianne Horton; m. Alfred Joseph D. Wunsch, July 10, 1948 (dec. Dec. 1989); children: Rosmarie, Irene, Alfred, Kathleen Wunsch. Student, Western Electric AT&T Spec. Mech. Drawing Sch., 1936, St. Paul of the Cross, Jersey City, NJ, 1936, Art Instruction Co., NYC, 1946; GED, Martin Luther King Coll., Jersey City, 1986; child care degree (hon.), Jersey City State Coll., 1989. Emergency cert. ARC, 1965. Comml. artist, engr.'s quality control, design cons. We. Electric Co., Inc./AT&T, Kearney, N.J., 1938-48; prin., owner Handy Hobby House, NJ, 1948—58; timesetter Union City (N.J.) br. Arrow Mfg. Co., 1950; jig artist, box designer Spiedel Watch Bands Co.; art instr. (summer), asst. tchr. head start St. Bridget Sch., 1969; leader, tchr. Mont Gardens Housing, 1970; asst. tchr./Foster Grandparent Act J.C. Med. Cen. Hosp./Cath. Charities, Newark, N.J., 1985, 86; asst. tchr. YHMA JC, Sch. Spl. Child Arts and Crafts/Cath. Charities, Newark, 1985, 86. Prodn. timer (vol.), engr. advisor, cons. bench hand AT&T, Bell Sys., Kearny, South Kearny, Jersey City, West Side, Bayonne, Marion plants, 1938-48. Permanent collections include Jersey City (N.J.) Mus., Jersey City Main Libr., numerous pvt. collections; featured in N.J. Artist, N.Y. State Artist. Den mother Cub Scouts Boys Scouts Am., 1960-69; group mother, leader Girl Scouts USA, 1959; pres. PTO, 1964; soprano J.C. Dollies, 1965-75. Recipient Congl. Medal Honor for vol. work during WWII, Pres. Johnson, 1969, Head Start award, 1969—; subject of personal interview, TV; Draw Me scholar Art Instrn. Sch., N.Y.C., 1944-46. Democrat. Roman Catholic. Avocations: beadwork, knitting, crochet, paper flowers, cooking. Home: Hazlet, NJ. Died Mar. 16, 2007.

WYATT, BRYANT NELSON, education educator, writer; b. Waverly, Va., Sept. 6, 1937; s. Merlin DeWitt and Hazel Lelease Wyatt. BA in English, Va. State U., 1959; MA in English, Boston U., 1960; PhD in English, U. Va., 1970. English tchr. Ctrl. HS, Sussex, Va., 1962—63; prof. English Va. State U., Petersburg, Va., 1963—92, disting. prof. emeritus, from 1992. Vis. prof. English U. Va., 1970, Va. Commonwealth U., 1973. Contbr. articles various profl. jours., poems and stories to lit. publs. Reading tutor Tri-City Reading Coun., Petersburg, Va., 1983—88. Capt. USAR, 1959—68. Decorated Commendation medal U.S. Army; recipient Woodrow Wilson Tchg. Internship, 1965; Woodrow Wilson fellow, 1959, Wemyss Found. Am. Studies fellow, 1964, Ford Found. Advanced Study grantee, 1969. Mem.: Scabbard & Blade, Sigma Tau Delta, Kappa Delta Pi. Avocations: reading, guitar, songwriting, writing. Home: Petersburg, Va. Died Jan. 27, 2007.

WYGAN, DOROTHY CAMILLA, foundation administrator; b. NYC, Apr. 10, 1932; d. Paul and Dorothy Eliza (Grout) Reznikoff; m. Anton Kazimierz Wygan, Nov. 5, 1960 (div. 1974); 1 child, Paul A. BS, Am. U., 1953; MS in Edn., Coll. of New Rochelle, 1973; EdD, Columbia U., 1961. Copywriter J. Walter Thompson, NYC, 1953-58, London, 1958-63; copy chief London Press Exchange, 1963-68; dir. New Rochelle (N.Y.) Day Nursery, 1970-73; devel. learning specialist Wappingers Ctrl. Sch. Dist., Wappingers Falls, N.Y., 1973-76; dir. learning resources ctr. Culinary Inst. Am., Hyde Park, N.Y., 1976-82; dir. fund devel. Dutchess C.C., Poughkeepsie, N.Y., 1982-87; v.p. fund devel. Rockland C.C., Suffern, N.Y., 1987-90; exec. dir. Sarah Wells Girl Scout Coun., Middletown, NY, 1990—97; adj. lectr. Dutchess C.C., 1998—2005. Contbr. articles to profl. jours.; author of TV commls. Den mother Boy Scouts Am., Chelsea, N.Y., 1973-76; v.p. Wappingers Conservation Assn., 1973-82; pres. Leewood Arms Home-owner's Assn., 1977-87; trustee Vassar Temple, 1985-97, treas., 1988-90, 94-97; vol. cook Dutchess Outreach Soup Kitchen, 1985-97; bd. dirs. YWCA in Dutchess County, Poughkeepsie, N.Y., 2000—, treas., 2003, pub. affairs com., Planned Parenthood of the Mid-Hudson Valley, 1998—; mem. County Exec. Affirmative Action Task Force Group, Suffern County, N.Y., 1987-90, N.Y. State Gov.'s Environ. Coun., 1988-91, N.Y. State Gov.'s Adv. Coun. on Women's Issues, 1989-90, County Exec. AIDS Prevention Task Force, Orange County, N.Y., 1994-97; bd. dirs., Stony Kill Environ. Edn. Ctr. Recipient Ann. Grassroots Vol. award, 1st Planned Parenthood, 2003. Mem. Northfield Mt. Hermon Alumni Assn., Older Womens League (leader Hudson Valley chpt. 1999-2001), Mid-Hudson Women's Network. Home: Poughkeepsie, NY. Died June 27, 2007.

WYKER, KENNETH E., lawyer; b. NYC, Apr. 1, 1961; s. Robert Harris and Elin Barbara (Eisner) W. BA, Trinity Coll., 1983; JD, George Washington U., 1986. Bar: Pa. 1987, D.C. 1988. Staff atty. Securities & Exch. Commn., Washington, 1986-87; assoc. gen. counsel Infotech., Fairfax, Va., 1988-90; sr. v.p. legal affairs Clear Channel Comms., San Antonio, from 1993; corp. counsel Greater Media, East Brunswick, N.J., 1990-93; gen. counsel Clear Channel Comms., 2001—06. Bd. charitable giving Children;s Shelter, San Antonio, 1993-95. Mem. Am. Corp. Coun. Assn. (bd. dirs. San Antonio chpt. 1998—). Died Nov. 4, 2006.

WYLER, GRETCHEN, actress; b. Oklahoma City, Feb. 16, 1932; d. Louis and Peggy (Highley) Wienecke; m. Shepard Coleman, June 18, 1956 (div. 1968). Grad. high sch., Bartlesville, Okla. Ballet ensemble Municipal Opera, St. Louis, 1950. Appeared in Broadway plays including Where's Charley, 1951-52, Guys and Dolls, 1952-54, Silk Stockings, 1955-56 (Outer Circle Critics award 1955), Damn Yankees, 1956-57, Rumple, 1957, Bye Bye Birdie, 1961, Applause, 1970-72, Sly Fox, 1976-78, Diamond Lil (Bay Area Theatre Critics Cir. Award); (TV series regular) Bob Crosby Show, 1958, Step This Way, 1966, On Our Own, 1977-78, Dallas, 1981; (films) Devils Brigade, Private Benjamin, Marrying Man; other pub. performances include London's West End, Sweet Charity, 1968-69, Broadway Greats and The Songs That Made Them Famous, N.Y.C., 1976, Town Hall, N.Y.C., 1976, Smithsonian, 1986; performer, producer off-Broadway prodn. Ballad of Johnny Pot, 1972; exec. producer Discovery Channel 5th Ann. Genesis Awards Spl., 1991-97. Vice chmn. Fund for Animals, N.Y.C., 1972-91; founder, pres. The Ark Trust, Inc., 1991—. Recipient Order of Nature award Internat. Soc., France, 1980, St. Francis of Assisi award Los Angeles Dept. of Animal Regulation, 1985, Paloma award L.A. SPCA, 1987. Mem. Women in Film. Democrat. Avocation: animal rights movement. Home: Camarillo, Calif. Died May 27, 2007.

WYMAN, FRANKLIN, JR., management consultant; b. Boston, Mar. 27, 1921; s. Franklin and Madeleine (Cutter) W.; m. Ruth Cheney; children: Franklin III, Janet Cutter Coleman, Sylvia Cheney McKean, Charles Cheney. BS, Harvard U., 1942, postgrad., 1943, MBA in Indsl. Adminstrn., 1946. Export mgr. Genrad Corp., Boston, 1946-50; asst. controller State Mutual Life Assurance Co., Boston, 1950-57; controller mgr. br. stores R.H. Stearns Co., Boston, 1957-64; pres., treas. Bailey's of Boston, Inc., 1964-83, chmn., 1983-87; mgmt. cons. Charles W. O'Conor and Assocs., Boston, 1983-85; chmn., treas. Wright Wyman Inc. (dba O'Conor, Wright Wyman Inc.), Boston, from 1985. Lt. USN, 1943-46, PTO. Home: Brookline, Mass. Died Apr. 19, 2007.

WYNNE-EDWARDS, HUGH ROBERT, geologist, educator, entrepreneur; b. Montreal, Que., Can., Jan. 19, 1934; s. Vero Copner and Jeannie Campbell (Morris) W.-E.; married Janet Elizabeth McGregor; children from previous marriages: Robin Alexander, Katherine Elizabeth, Renée Elizabeth Lortie, Krista Smyth, Jeannie Elizabeth, Alexander Vernon. BSc with 1st class honors, U. Aberdeen, Scotland, 1955; MA, Queen's U., Kingston, Ont., Can., 1957, PhD, 1959; DSc (hon.), Meml. U., 1975. Registered profl. engr., B.C., 1995. With Geol. Survey Can., 1958-59; lectr. Queen's U., 1968-72, asst. prof., then assoc. prof., 1961-68, prof., head dept. geol. scis., 1968-72; prof., then Cominco prof., head dept. geol. scis. U. B.C., Vancouver, Canada, 1972-77; asst. sec. univ. br. Ministry of State for Sci. and Tech., Ottawa, Canada, 1977-79; sci. dir. Alcan Internat. Ltd., Montreal, 1979-80, v.p. R & D, chief sci. officer, 1980-89; CEO Moli Energy Ltd., Vancouver, 1989-90; pres. Terracy Inc., Vancouver, from 1989; sci. advisor Teck Corp., Vancouver, 1989-91; pres., CEO B.C. Rsch. Inc., Vancouver, 1993-97, exec. chmn., pres., 1997-2000. Chmn. Silvagen Inc., 1996-99; advisor Directorate Mining and Geology, Uttar Pradesh, India, 1964, Grenville project Que. Dept. Natural Resources, 1968-72; vis. prof. U. Aberdeen, 1965-66, U. Witwatersrand, Johannesburg, South Africa, 1972; UN cons., India, 1974; pres. SCITEC, 1977-78; mem. sci. adv. com. CBC, 1980-84; mem. Sci. Coun. Can., 1983-89, Nat. Adv. Bd. on Sci. and Tech., 1987-90 indsl. liaison com. UN Ctr. for Sci. and Tech. in Devel., 1982-84; vice chmn. tech. adv. group Bus. Coun. for Sustainable Devel., Geneva, 1991; mem. Nat. Biotech. Adv. Coun., 1995-98; chmn. Neurosci. Can. Partnership, 1999-2003, Azure Dynamics Inc., 2000-01; pres. Silvagen Holdings Inc., 1999-2000; bd. dirs. Welichem Biotech Inc., chmn., 2000-; bd. dirs. Photon Control Inc. Bd. dirs. Royal Victoria Hosp., Montreal, 1984-89. Decorated officer Order of Can., 1991; recipient Spendiarov prize 24th Internat. Geol. Congress, Montreal, 1972. Fellow Can. Acad. Engring., Royal Soc. Can., World Acad. Arts and Scis.; mem. Can. Rsch. Mgmt. Assn. (vice chmn. 1982-84, chmn. 1984-85, Assn. medal 1987), Univ. Club (Montreal). Mem. United Ch. Canada. Avocations: tennis, skiing, carpentry. Home: West Vancouver, Canada. Died 2013.

YABLANS, FRANK, film company executive, film producer; b. NYC, Aug. 27, 1935; s. Morris and Annette Y.; m. Ruth Edelstein, Dec. 21; children: Robert, Sharon, Edward. Student, CCNY, U. Wis. Salesman, Warner Bros., 1956-58; br. mgr. Walt Disney Prodns., 1958-66; v.p. Filmways Prodns., 1966-69; v.p. sales, v.p. marketing, exec. v.p., pres. Paramount Pictures Corp., NYC, 1969-75; pres. Frank Yablans Presentations, Inc., NYC, 1975—83; chmn. bd. MGM/UA Entertainment Co., 1983-85; CEO Promendade Pictures, 2003—14. Prodr.: (films) Silver Streak, 1976, The Other Side of Midnight, 1977, The Fury, 1978, North Dallas Forty, 1979, Mommie Dearest, 1981, Monsignore, 1982, The Star Chamber, 1983, Kid Co, 1983, Boy and Cell, 1989, Lisa, 1990, Congo, 1995, A Dog of Flanders, 1999, The Ten Commandments, 2007, Noah, 2012; co-prodr.: (TV series) Rome, 2005-07 Chmn. entertainment div. Fedn. Jewish Philanthropies; bd. dirs. Boys' Clubs Am., Will Rogers Hosp.; trustee American Film Inst. Served with AUS, 1954-56. Decorated commendatore Repubblica Italiana. Mem. Variety Club Internat. (chmn.), Motion Picture Assn. (dir.) Clubs: Fairview Country. Died Nov. 27, 2014.

YAKUBIK, JOHN, retired pharmaceutical chemist; b. Fords, NJ, Sept. 23, 1928; s. John and Mary (Tarsosky) Y.; m. Ethel R. Kovacs, Nov. 29, 1952; children: Jill Karen, John William. BS in Pharmacy, Rutgers U., 1949; MS in Pharmacy, Purdue U., 1950, PhD in Pharmacy, 1952. Registered pharmacist, N.J. Rsch. assoc. E.R. Squibb, New Brunswick, N.J., 1952-55; mgr. pharm. R&D Schering-Plough Corp., Kenilworth, N.J., 1955-63, dir. sci. liaison, 1963-65, dir. bus. devel., 1975-80, dir. new product devel. internat. divsn., 1980-90, ret., 1991. Fellowship Am. Found. Pharm. Edn., 1949-52. Mem. AAAS, Am. Pharm. Assn. Home: Colonia, NJ. Died July 24, 2007.

YALDEN, MAXWELL FREEMAN, Canadian diplomat; b. Toronto, Ont., Can., Apr. 12, 1930; s. Frederick and Marie (Smith) Y.; m. Janice Shaw, Jan. 28, 1952; children: Robert, Cicely (dec.). BA, Victoria Coll., U. Toronto, 1952; MA, U. Mich., 1954, PhD, 1956; D.U. (hon.), U. Ottawa; LLD (hon.), Carleton U. With Can. Dept. External Affairs, 1956-69, asst. undersec. state, 1969-73, dep. minister communications, 1973-77, commr. ofcl. langs., 1977-84; Can. amb. to Belgium and Luxembourg, 1984-87; chief commr. Can. Human Rights Comms., Ottawa, 1987—96; mem. UN Human Rights Com., 1996—2004. Decorated companion Order of Can. Died Feb. 9, 2015.

YAMAMOTO, TATEKI, marketing executive; b. Kyoto, Dec. 11, 1941; came to U.S., 1967; s. Masaharu and Shigeno (Maki) Y.; m. Kaoru Furukawa, Jan. 15, 1986; 1 child, Erica. BA in Econs., U. Doshisha, Kyoto, 1965; MBA, NYU, 1974. Sales agt. Japan Air Lines, NYC, 1967-70, mktg. mgr., 1971-77; asst. mktg. dir. Newsweek Mag., NYC, 1978-81, mktg. dir. Tokyo, 1981-83; pres. Pacific Mktg. Assn., Irvington, N.Y., 1984-87; dir. mktg. sales Nikkei Bus. Pubs., Inc., NYC, from 1988. Contbr. articles to profl. jours. Mem. Am. Mktg. Assn., Internat. Advt. Assn. Home: Briarcliff Manor, NY. Died Jan. 30, 2007.

YAQUB KHAN, SAHABZADA, former diplomat, United Nation agency official; b. Rampur, Dec. 23, 1920; s. Sahabzada Sir Abdus Samad Khan Bahadur and Sababzadi Aliya Sultan Amir Dulhan Begum Sahiba; m.Begum Tuba; children Samad, Najib Student, Royal Indian Mil. Coll., Indian Mil. Acad., Debra Dun, 1932—40, Pakistan Army Command and Staff Coll., Quatta, Ecole Superieure de Guerre, Paris, 1953—54, Imperial Def. Coll., London. Commd. officer Indian Army, 1940—47, Pakistan Army, 1947, vicechief gen. staff, 1958, advanced through grades to lt. gen., 1969, comdr. armored divsn.; chief gen. staff Parkistan Army, corps. comdr., comdr. Eastern Zone, 1969—71; comdt. Army Staff Coll.; gov., marital law adminstr. of East Pakistan (now Bangladesh); ret., 1971. Pakistan amb. to France, 1972, 1980—82; amb. to Ireland, 1973, to USA, to Jamaica, 1973—77, to Moscow, 1979—80; fgn. min. Govt. Pakistan, Islamabad, 1982—87, 1988—90; spl. rep. of UN sec.-gen. UN Mission for the Referendum in Western Sahara, Laayoune, Western Sahara, from 1993. Founding chmn. bd. trustees Aga Khan U., 1985—2001. Died Feb. 2016.

YATES, ELSIE VICTORIA, retired secondary school educator; b. Newport, RI, Dec. 16, 1916; d. Andrew James and Rachel Agnes (Sousa) Tabb; m. George Herman Yates, July 12, 1941 (div. Apr. 1981); children: Serena, George Jr., Michael, Elsie French, David. AB in English and History, Va. Union U., 1938; postgrad., U. R.I., 1968-73, Salve Regina U., 1968-73. Life cert. in secondary English and reading specialist, R.I. Reading specialist grades 7 and 8 title I Newport (R.I.) Sch., 1971-74, secondary English educator, 1975-87; ret., 1987. Mem. adult com. Young Life, Newport, 1981-93; active Newport (R.I.) Substance Abuse Force, 1989-93; chmn. multicultural curriculum com. New Visions for Newport (R.I.) Schs., 1991-94; mem. edn. com. Swinburne Sch., Newport, 1992-94; active Equity in Edns. Com.-Concerned Citizens Group. Recipient Outstanding Ednl. Contbn. Under Title I award U.S. Office Edn., Bur. Sch. Sys., 1976, Presdl. citation Nat. Edn. Assn. R.I., 1987, Appreciation for Svc. award Cmty. Bapt. Ch., Newport, 1988, Outstanding Svc. award in field of edn. to the youth in cmty. Queen Esther Chpt. 2, Newport, 1992. Mem. NAACP (life), R.I. Ret. Tchrs. Assn., Newport Ret. Tchrs. Assn. Baptist. Avocations: reading, handicrafts, community activities. Died Oct. 30, 2006.

YEE, NANCY W., travel consultant; b. Honolulu, Nov. 6, 1917; d. Sai Ho and Ah Oi Sen Wong; m. Ken Yee, Dec. 2, 1941; children: Roy Jensen, Sylvia Mei-ling McCaffrey, Carolyn Mei-en Lee, Susan Mei-jen. BA in Edn. Music and Dance, U. Hawaii, 1941. Sr. translator U.S. Postal Censorship, Honolulu, 1941-45; pvt. tchr. English and civics Honolulu, 1945-50; radio announcer Chinese KGMB Radio/TV, Honolulu, 1946-56; ptnr. Ken's Electric Motor Svc., Honolulu, 1949-65; travel cons. Royal Adventure/Quality, Honolulu, from 1957; sec., officer mgr. KEMS Inc., Honolulu, 1965-85. Radio announcer Chinese, KAHU, Honolulu, 1956; chmn. Small Bus. Adminstrn. Adv. Bd., Honolulu, 1967-68; advisor Jr. Achievement, Honolulu, 1970-71; pres. Women's Propeller Club U.S., Honolulu, 1977-78. Den mother Cub Scouts, 1948-50; mem., choir mem. First Chinese Ch. of Christ, 1950-99; chmn. fund raiser, den mother Pacific Girl Scouts Am., 1958-68; mem. Honolulu Youth Symphony, 1967-71; sec. Ctrl. Dist. PTA, Honolulu, 1968; vol. Hawaii Heart Assn., Honolulu, 1970-73; vol. tchr. Chinese song and dance Mun Lun Sch., 1970; mem., pres. Mun Lun Sch. PTA, 1970, Palolo Home Aux, Honolulu, 1977-78, Associated Chinese U. Women, 1978. Named Chinese Model Mother of the Yr., United Chinese Soc., Honolulu, 1986, Hawaii Chinese Living Treasure, Chinese Youth Hawaii, Honolulu, 1995. Avocations: playing chinese butterfly harp, singing chinese operas, travel, cruising, volunteer work. Home: Honolulu, Hawaii. Died June 21, 2007.

YEW, LEE KUAN, former prime minister of Singapore; b. Sept. 16, 1923; m. Kwa Geok Choo, 1947 (dec. 2010); children: Lee Hsien Loong, Lee Hsien Yang, Lee Wei Ling. Student, Raffles Coll., Singapore, 1942—45, Ftizwilliam Coll., Cambridge, Eng., 1946-49. Barrister-at-law Mid. Temple, London, 1946—50; practiced law Singapore, 1951—59; legal advisor to trade unions; co-founder People's Action Party (PAP), 1954, sec. gen., 1954-92; MP Singaporean Parliament, 1955—90; rep. Malaysian Parliament, 1963-65; prime min. Govt. of Singapore, Singapore,

1959-90, sr. min., 1990—2004, min. mentor, 2004—11. Author: The Singapore Story: Memoirs of Lee Kuan Yew, 1998, From Third World to First: The Singapore Story, 1965-2000, 2000. Named one of The 100 Most Influential People in the World, TIME mag., 2005, 2010. Died Mar. 23, 2015.

YONTZ, RANDALL EUGENE, lawyer; b. Columbus, Ohio, July 28, 1951; s. E. Eugene and Dorothy L. Keller Y.; m. Deborah Richards, Sept. 29, 1979; children: Brian Randall, Daniel Forrest. BA, Wittenberg U., 1973; JD, Ohio Northern U., 1977. Adminstrv. judge Pub. Utilities Commn., Columbus, 1977-80; asst. pros. atty. Franklin County Prosecuting Attys. Office, Columbus, 1980-84; sole practice Columbus, from 1984; mem. Evans, St. Clair & Kelsey, Columbus, 1986. Mem. ABA, Ohio Bar Assn., Columbus Bar Assn., Assn. Trial Lawyers Am. Died July 26, 2007.

YORKIN, BUD (ALAN DAVID YORKIN), television producer, writer; b. Washington, Pa., Feb. 22, 1926; s. Maurice A. and Jessie (Sachs) Y.; m. Cynthia Sykes, 1989 (div. 2015); children: Nicole, David. BS in Elec. Engring., Carnegie-Mellon U., 1948; postgrad. in English Lit., Columbia U., 1951; LHD, Washington and Jefferson Coll., 1974. Ptnr. Tandem Prodns., Inc., L.A., 1959-74, TOY Prodns. 1976-1979 (acquired by Columbia Pictures TV); owner Bud Yorkin Productions, 1974-76 With engring. staff, NBC, N.Y.C., 1949-50, stage mgr., NBC, 1950-52; assoc. dir. Colgate Comedy Hour, 1952-54; prodr., dir. TV shows including Dinah Shore Show, Tennessee Ernie Ford Show, 1956-61, George Gobel Show, 1954-56, Jack Benny Hour, 1959, Bobby Darrin and Friends, 1961, The Danny Kaye Special, 1961, Henry Fonda and the Family, 1962, Andy Williams Spl. 1962, An Evening with Carol Channing, 1966, The Many Sides of Don Rickles, 1970, Robert Young and Family, 1971; writer, producer, dir. Tony Martin Show, 1954-56, An Evening With Fred Astaire, 1958, Another Evening With Fred Astaire, 1959, Jack Benny spls., 1959; exec. prodr./prodr., dir. The Andy Williams Show, 1963-67; exec. producer TV series All in the Family, 1971-79, Sanford and Son, 1972-77, Maude, 1972-78, Good Times, 1974-79, Diff'rent Strokes, 1978-86, What's Happening, 1976-79, Carter Country, 1977-79 (also dir., writer 1977), Archie Bunker's Place, 1980-83, The Night They Raided Minsky's, Cold Turkey, 1971, Deal of the Century, Blade Runner, also numerous spls.; dir. (films) Come Blow Your Horn, 1963 (also prodr.), Never Too Late, 1965, Divorce, American Style, 1967, Inspector Clouseau, 1968; producer, dir. (films and TV Series/films) The Soldiers, 1955, Start the Revolution Without Me, 1970, The Thief Who Came to Dinner, 1971, Twice in a Lifetime, 1985, Arthur on the Rocks 2, 1988, Love Hurts, 1990; prodr.(films and TV Series/Films) Barnaby, 1965, Duke Ellington...We Love You Madly, 1973, Intersection, 1994; exec. prodr. (TV series/specials) Sanford Arms, 1977, One in a Million, 1980, I Love Liberty, 1982; dir. (TV specials/films) The Spike Jones Show, 1954, P.O.P., 1984 Trustee Am. Film Inst., Mus. Contemporary Art, L.A., Carnegie-Mellon U., Am. Heart Assn., UCLA. Recipient several Emmy awards, Sylvania award, Look award, Dirs. Guild award, Harvard Lampoon's Golden Jester award, Peabody award, Women in Film Lucy award, 1999; named to TV Hall of Fame, 2002 Mem. TV Acad. Arts and Scis. (past gov.), Dirs. Guild Am. (gov.). Died Aug. 18, 2015.

YOST, DEE RENEE, librarian, educator; b. Auburn, Nebr., Apr. 13, 1951; d. Lawrence Welch Wattles and Joyce Arvene Kraft; m. Jonathan Daniel Yost, Sept. 1, 1973; children: Kyle Daniel, Kipp Lawrence. BA, Hastings Coll., 1972; MA in Libr. sci., U. Denver, 1973. Soc. editor Norfolk Daily News, Nebr., 1973—74; media specialist Norfolk Jr. High, 1974—78; music libr. Hastings Coll., Nebr., 1978—79, pub. svcs. libr., assoc. prof. libr. sci., from 2000, prof., from 2005; asst. dir. Hastings Pub. Libr., 1979—89; adminstr. Republican Valley Libr. Sys., Hastings, 1989—2000. Mem. adv. bd. Nebr. Ednl. TV Coun. for Higher Edn., from 2002; mem. del. White Ho. Conf. on Librs., 1990. Bd. dirs., trustee Hastings Pub. Libr., from 2002; bd. dirs. Willa Cather Pioneer Meml. and Ednl. Found., Red Cloud, Nebr., from 2003. Recipient MAX award, Hastings C. of C., 1996. Mem.: AAUP, ALA, Nebr. Libr. Assn. (pres., v.p., past pres., Meritorious Svc. award 1995), Nebr. Ctr. for Book (past pres.,), Sigma Tau Delta, Alpha Chi. Republican. Lutheran. Avocations: reading, gardening, antiques. Home: Hastings, Nebr. Died Mar. 26, 2007.

YOUNG, DAVID LYNN, regulatory consultant; b. Austin, Tex., Apr. 27, 1944; s. Richard Alden and Nell (Wallace) Y.; m. Rebecca Jane Vanemburg, Aug. 24, 1968 (div. Jan. 1980); children: Davy Young, Rebecca Young. BA in Math., U. Tex., 1967; MA in Biblical Studies, Dallas Theol. Sem., 1976. Campus min. Campus Crusade for Christ, San Bernardino, Calif., 1967-74; coll. instr. Dallas Bible Coll., 1975-78; major appliance sales rep. Montgomery Ward, Richardson, Tex., 1978-85; merchandiser GM Warehouse, Seagoville, Tex., 1985; regulator Tex. Dept. of Ins., Austin, 1986-93; regulatory cons. Austin, from 1994. Founder, pres. Scriptural Prayer Emphasis Ministries Internat., Richardson, 1974-79. Author: Prayer God's Way, 1981. Candidate lt. gov. Dem. Primary, Tex., 1986, candidate for railroad commn., 1992, 94; Candidate U.S. Senator Rep. Primary, 1996; chorale mem., tenor Riverbend Ch., Austin, 1990-96, Sunday sch. tchr., 1986-96. Avocations: tennis, golf, reading for knowledge, travel. Home: Austin, Tex. Died Jan. 20, 2007.

YOUNG, JAMES R. (JIM YOUNG), rail transportation executive; b. Omaha, Nebr., 1952; m. Shirley Young; 3 children. Grad., U. Nebr., Omaha. Joined Union Pacific RR Co., 1978, mgmt. finance & ops., asst. v.p. re-engring., 1994—95, v.p. re-engring. & design, 1995—97, v.p. customer svc. planning & quality, 1997—98, v.p. finance & quality, 1998, sr. v.p., corporate treas., 1998—99, sr. v.p. finance, corporate contr., 1999—2004, pres., COO, 2004—07; exec. v.p., CFO Union Pacific Corp., 1999—2005, pres., CEO, 2006—07, chmn., pres., CEO, 2007—12, chmn., 2012—14. Bd. dirs. Union Pacific Corp., from 2005. Bd. mem. Creighton U., Omaha, Joslyn Art Mus., U. Nebr. Med. Ctr.; bd. dirs. Boys Town. Mem.: Assn. American Railroads, Greater Omaha Chamber of Commerce. Died Feb. 15, 2014.

YOUNG, MYRA BETH, psychiatric nurse; b. Malden, Mass., Mar. 8, 1952; d. Stanley and Helayne (Kulvin) Y. BSN, U. Rochester, 1973; MS in Nursing, Boston U., 1980. Cert. clin. specialist adult psychiat. and mental health nursing. Staff nurse Peter Bent Brigham Hosp., Boston, Mt. Auburn Hosp., Cambridge, Mass.; psychiat. nurse New Eng. Deaconess Hosp., Boston; nurse mgr. Lowell (Mass.) Gen. Hosp.; psychiat. nursing program dir. Home Health Vis. Nurse Assn., Haverhill, Mass. Part-time pvt. practice psychotherapy. Mem. Mass. Coun. Nurse Mgrs. Home: Andover, Mass. Died Dec. 19, 2006.

YOUNG, NAOMI BERRY, social worker; b. Tyron, NC, Dec. 26, 1936; d. Roy E. and Odessa L. (Bell) Berry; children: Kyndra, Scott. BA, N.C. Cen. U., 1958; MSW, Simmons Coll., 1974. Lic. social worker. Tchr. Tartt's Day Care, Roxbury, Mass., 1961-67; social worker Mass. Dept. Pub. Welfare, Roxbury, 1967-72; staff clin. social worker Putnam Children's Ctr., Roxbury, 1974-76; staff social worker, supr. Judge Baker Children's Ctr., Boston, 1976-81; founding ptnr., social worker, supr., cons. Thorpe and Young Counseling Assocs., Boston, from 1981; dir. mental health clinic Roxbury Children's Svc., 1982-84. Cons. Alianza Hispana, Roxbury, 1985-86; cons., supr. City Mission Soc., Boston, 1985-86, Brockton (Mass.) Psychiat. Inst., 1985-87, Parenting Program English High Sch., Boston, 1985—. Mem. NASW, Nat. Assn. Black Social Workers, Acad. Cert. Social Workers, Nat. Social Sci. Honor Soc., Pi Gamma Mu. Avocations: physical fitness, reading, music, sports. Home: Walpole, Mass. Died Nov. 18, 2006.

YOUNG, WANDA KAY, nursing educator; b. Peoria, Ill., Jan. 23, 1947; d. William Wayne and Nora Adaline (Cox) Garmon; m. Henry Allen Young Jr., Feb. 6, 1965; children: Glenda Lynnette, Henry Allen III (dec.). ADN, Ill. Cen. Coll., 1977; BSN, West Tex. State U., 1991. RN, Tex.; cert. in inpatient obstet. nursing; cert. BLS instr.-trainer, PALS instr., regional trainer neonatal resuscitation, ACLS; registered beauty culturist. Staff nurse in obstetrics Pekin (Ill.) Meml. Hosp., 1977-81, charge nurse, unit educator obstetrics dept., 1981-82, maternity head nurse, 1982-85; head nurse birthing ctr. Meth. Hosp., Lubbock, Tex., 1985-90, nursing edn. coord., from 1990. Bd. dirs. health occupations edn. Lubbock Ind. Sch. Dist., 1990—; cons. women's wellness conf. Family Therapy and Recovery Ctr., Lubbock, 1993—; mentor for AFDC mother, Tex. Dept. Human Svcs. Sec., health profl. adv. com. March of Dimes, Lubbock, 1989—; Think First coord. Head and Spinal Cord Injury Prevention Programs for Comty. Schs., 1992—; dir. ch. nurseries 1st Ch. of the Nazarene Ch., Lubbock, 1992—. Named Speaker of Yr., Pekin H.S. Vocat. Edn., 1980. Mem. Tex. Nurses Assn. (2d v.p. 1991-92, 1st v.p. 1992-93, pres. 1993-95, Outstanding Svc. and Leadership award 1994), Sigma Theta Tau. Republican. Avocations: reading, boating, travel. Died Apr. 13, 2007.

YU, ANTHONY C., religion and literature educator; b. Hong Kong, Oct. 6, 1938; came to U.S., 1956, naturalized, 1976; s. P.C. and Norma (Au) Y.; m. Priscilla Tang, Sept. 18, 1963; 1 son, Christopher Dietrich. BA in English and History magna cum laude, Houghton Coll., NY, 1960; STB in Theology and Philosophy Religion summa cum laude, Fuller Theol. Sem., Pasadena, Calif., 1963; PhD in Religion and Lit., Divinity Sch., U. Chgo., 1969; DLitt (hon.), Lingnan Coll., Hong Kong, 1996; LHD (hon.), Wittenberg U., Columbus, Ohio, 2006. Instr. U. Ill., Chgo., 1967-68; asst. prof. U. Chgo., 1968-74, assoc. prof., 1974-78, prof., 1978—2005, Carl Darling Buck Disting. Service Prof. emeritus in Humanities and Prof. Emeritus of Religion and Lit. in the Divinity Sch., 2005—15. Assoc. vis. prof. Ind. U., Bloomington, 1975; Whitney J. Oates short-term vis. fellow Princeton U., 1986; disting. vis. prof. Faculty of Arts, U. Alta., Can., 1992; mem. joint com. on study Chinese civilization Am. Coun. Learned Socs., 1980-86, bd. dirs., 1986-94; regional chmn. Mellon Fellowship in Humanities, 1982-92; bd. dirs. Ill. Humanities Coun., 1995-97; vis. prof. dept. religion Chinese U. Hong Kong, 1997; faculty mem. com. social thought U. Chgo., 1978-2015, also departments of Comparative Lit., East Asian Lang. and Civilizations, and English Lang. and Lit.; Siu Lien Ling Wong vis. fellow, Chinese U. Hong Kong, 2006; vis. fellow, Inst. and Sch. Asia and Pacific Studies, 2009 Asst. editor Jour. Asian Studies, 1975-78; co-editor Jour. Religion, 1980—; author, editor: Parnassus Revisited, 1973; editor, translator: The Journey to the West, 4 vols., 1977-83, Essays on The Journey to the West and Other Studies (in Chinese), 1989, The Monkey and the Monk, An Abridgment of the Journey to the West, 2006; co-editor (with Mary Gerhart) Morphologies of Faith: Essays on Religion and Culture in Honor of Nathan A. Scott, Jr., 1990, Rereading the Stone: Desire and the Making of Fiction in Dream of the Red Chamber, 1997, State and Religion in China: Historical and Textual Perspectives, 2005, Dream of the Red Chamber, Journey to the West, and Other Studies, Chinese edit., 2006; author: Comparative Journeys: Essays on Literature and Religion East and West, 2008, Journey to the West, rev. edit., 4 vols., 2012. Recipient Gordon J. Laing prize, 1983, Norman Maclean Faculty award, 2009, Disting. Lectr. award Inst. Chinese Lit. and Philosophy, Acad. Sinica, 2005; Phi Beta Kappa vis. scholar 2001-02. Fellow Am. Acad. Arts and Scis., Acad. Sinicia; mem. Milton Soc. Am., Arts Club. Avocations: amateur radio, cooking. Home: Chicago, Ill. Died May 12, 2015.

ZACHA, CHARLES MICHAEL, JR., motion picture company executive; b. Moberly, Mo., Nov. 12, 1920; s. Charles M. Sr. and Irene (Jasmin) Z.; m. Jan. 11, 1944; children: Charles, Pamela, Paul, Gay Ann, Jeffery, Dawn, Bryan. Diploma, Lincoln Aeronautical Inst., 1941. Registered architect, Mo. Actor TV and films, Los Angeles, 1952-60; facilities engr., asst. studio mgr. MGM and 20th Century Fox Studios, Los Angeles, 1960-66; gen. purchasing agt. Gen. Theaters (now Mann), 1966-68; designer of exhibits, researcher Retlaw Corp., Los Angeles, 1968-70; freelance set designer 20th Century Fox, Aaron Spelling Prodns., MGM, Paramount, Los Angeles, 1971-73; art dir. Universal Studios, Los Angeles, 1974-80; prodn. designer Lorimar, Dallas, 1981-84, Wizan Prodns., CBS, Aaron Spelling Prodns., Los Angeles, 1981-84; founder, developer Charles Michael Prodns., from 1984. Prin. architecture, constrn. and contracting bus., 1945-52. Prodn. designer: (TV) Two Lives of Jenny Logan, Night of the Scarecrow, Pilot of Flamingo Rd., (series) Matt Houston, Dynasty, Columbo, Beretta; set-designer, model maker (films) Hello Dolly, Poseidon Adventure, Cleopatra, Dr. Doolittle; designer of exhibits for Disneyland including Pirates of the Caribbean, Lincoln Memorial, the Matterhorn, the Haunted House; actor appearing on TV shows Perry Mason, Jack Benny Show, Playhouse 90, Red Skelton Show, Passing Parade. Mem. Young Dems. Am. (Nat. Adv. Bd.). Served to capt. with USAF 1941-42. Mem. Motion Picture Producers Qualifications Com., Set Designers and Model Makers Union (pres. 1974-80), Am. Film Inst., Acad. of TV Arts and Scis. Died June 8, 2007.

ZAGURY, CAROLYN S., nurse consultant, management trainer, publisher; b. Camden, NJ, Dec. 14, 1946; d. Harold P. and Rhoda G. Seideman; m. David W. Zagury, Apr. 5, 1975. Diploma, Ann May Sch. Nursing, Neptune, NJ, 1970; BS, St. Josephs Coll., North Windham, Maine, 1985; MS, New Sch. for Social Rsch., NYC, 1989. Head nurse Johns Hopkins Hosp., Balt., 1970-74; nurse Monmouth Med. Ctr., Long Branch, 1974-81, dir. geriatric program, 1981-86, asst. v.p. mktg. and strategic planning, 1986-89; pres. Profl. Healthcare Assocs., Inc., Long Branch, from 1989, Vista Pub., Inc. specializing in nurse authors, Long Branch, from 1991. Named Women of Achievement in Health Monmouth County Adv. Commn. on Status of Women, 1988. Mem. NAFE, Nat. Nurses in Bus. Assn., Acad. Cert. Profl. Cons. and Advisors. Home: Oakhurst, NJ. Died Aug. 5, 2007.

ZALLINGER, JEAN DAY, children's book illustrator; b. Boston, Feb. 15, 1918; d. John Farquharson and Mabel (Soutar) Day; m. Rudolph Franz Zallinger, Sept. 27, 1941; children: Peter Franz, Kristina Lisa. BFA, Yale U., 1942; BFA (hon.), Mass. Coll. Art, 1993. Freelance illustrator, from 1950. Tchr. Saturday classes for young people, New Haven, 1941-42; ret. prof. drawing & illustration Paier Coll. Art, 1967-88; asst. Nat. Youth Adminstrn., 1939-42; asst. designer Yale Press, 1941-43, illustrator, 1942-48; tech. illustrator, draftsman U. Wash., Seattle, 1951-53. Exhbns. include Paint and Clay Club, 1942-43, Yale U. Gallery Fine Arts, 1941-42, Assn. Graphic Arts, 1969, John Slade Ely House, New Haven, 1972, Master Eagle Gallery, N.Y.C., 1984-88, Aetna Gallery, Hartford, Conn., 1987, New Britain Youth Mus., 1987, Nat. Hist. Mus. L.A. traveling show, 1987-91. Recipient Jr. Libr. Guild award, 1993; disting. alumnusMass. Coll. Art, 1992. Home: Branford, Conn. Died Apr. 1, 2007.

ZAPF, HERMANN, book and type designer; b. Nuremberg, Germany, Nov. 8, 1918; s. Hermann and Magdalene (Schlamp) Zapf; m. Gudrun von Hesse, Aug. 18, 1951; 1 child, Christian Ludwig (dec.). D in Fine Arts (hon.), U. Ill., 2003. Freelance designer, from 1938; type dir. D. Stempel AG, type foundry, Frankfurt, Fed. Republic of Germany, 1947-56; design cons. Mergenthaler Linotype Co. (NYC and Frankfurt), 1957-74; cons. Hallmark Internat., Kansas City, Mo., 1966-73; v.p. Design Processing Internat. Inc., NYC, 1977—87; prof. typographic computer programs Rochester (N.Y.) Inst. Tech., 1977-87; chmn. Zapf, Burns & Co., NYC, 1987-91. Instr. lettering Werkkunstschule, Offenbach, Fed. Republic Germany., 1948-50; prof. graphic design Carnegie Inst. Tech., 1960; instr. typography Technische Hochschule, Darmstadt, Fed. Republic Germany, 1972-81. Author: William Morris, 1948, Pen and Graver, 1952, Manuale Typographicum, 1954, 1968, About Alphabets, 1960, 1970, Typographic Variations, 1964, Orbis Typographicus, 1980, Hora fugit/Carpe diem, 1984, Hermann Zapf and His Design Philosophy, 1987, ABC-XYZapf, 1989, Poetry Through Typography, 1993, August Rosenberger, 1996, (film) The Art of Hermann Zapf, German version Die Welt der Buchstaben von Hermann Zapf, (CD-ROM) The World of Alphabets, 2001, Alphabet Stories: A Chronicle of Technical Developments, 2007; designer types Palatino, Melior, Optima, ITC Zapf Chancery, ITC Zapf Internat., Digiset Marconi, Digiset Edison, Digiset Aurelia, Pan-Nigerian, Sequoyah, URW-Roman and San Serif, Renaissance Roman, Linotype, Zapfino Extra, Optima nova, ITC Dingbats, Zapf Essentials, Palatino Sans, Palatino Arabic. Hon. pres. Edward Johnston Found., Ditchling, England. Recipient Silver medal, Brussels, 1962, 1st prize typography, Biennale Brno, Czechoslovakia, 1966, Gold medal, Type Dirs. Club, N.Y., Frederic W. Goudy award, Inst. Tech. Rochester, 1969, Silver medal, Internat. Book Exhbn., Leipzig, 1971, Gold medal, 1989, Johannes Gutenberg prize, Mainz, Fed. German Republic, 1974, Gold medal, Museo Bodoniano, Parma, Italy, 1975, J.H. Merck award, Darmstadt, 1978, Robert Hunter Middleton award, Chgo., 1987, Euro Design award, Oostende, 1994, Wadim

Lazursky award, Acad. of Graphic Arts, Moscow, 1996, SOTA Typography award, Chgo., 2003, Goethe medal, State Hesse, Germany, 2007; named hon. citizen, State of Tex., 1970, hon. Royal Designer for Industry, London, 1985. Mem.: Internat. Gutenberg Gesellschaft, Bund Deutscher Grafik Designer, Alliance Graphique Internat., Am. Math. Soc., Royal Soc. Arts, Dante e.V. (German TEX Group) (hon.), Soc. Scribes N.Y. (hon.), Brno Biennale Assn. (hon.), Goudy Internat. Ctr. (hon.), Alcuin Soc. Can. (hon.), Typographers Internat. Assn. (hon.), Chgo. Calligraphy Collective (hon.), Eesti Kalligraafide Koondis (hon.; Tallinn, Estonia), Wynkyn de Worde Soc. (hon.), Soc. Calligraphy (hon.), Grafiska Inst. (hon.), Bund Deutscher Buchkünstler (hon.), Soc. Graphic Designers Can. (hon.), Soc. Printers (hon.), Soc. Typographic Arts (hon.), Soc. Typographique de France (hon.), Assocs. of Stanford Univ. Librs., Art Dirs. Club Kansas City (hon.), Alpha Beta Club (hon.; Hong Kong), Friends of Calligraphy (hon.), Double Crown Club (hon.), Type Dirs. Club N.Y.C. (hon.), Soc. Scribes and Illuminators (hon.), Typophiles (hon.), Letter Exch. (hon.), Washington Calligrapher's Guild (hon.), Monterey Calligrapher's Guild (hon.), Caxton Club (hon.), Gamma Epsilon Tau (hon.). Home: Darmstadt, Germany. Died June 4, 2015.

ZAPPA, GAIL (ADELAIDE GAIL SLOATMAN), record producer; b. Philadelphia, Jan. 1, 1945; m. Frank Zappa 1967 (dec. 1993); children: Moon Unit, Dweezil, Ahmet, Diva. Created Zappa Family Trust, 2002. Recipient (with Frank Zappa) Best Recording Package-Boxed Grammy award for Frank Zappa's Civilization, Phaze III, 1996. Achievements include being keeper of her husband Frank Zappa's legacy. Died Oct. 7, 2015.

ZARICZNYJ, BASILIUS, orthopedic surgeon; b. Ukraine, Aug. 31, 1924; came to U.S., 1951; m. Stefania Pidburny, Aug. 21, 1954; children: Marta, Stephanie Christine, Andrea Maria, Mark B. MD, U. Bonn, Germany, 1951; MD (hon.), Odessa State Med. U., Ukraine, 1996. Diplomate Am. Bd. Orthopedic Surgery. Resident St. Luke's Hosp., Chgo., 1954-56, Univ. Hosps., Oklahoma City, 1955-56; fellow in orthopedics Northwestern U., Chgo., 1957; asst. prof. Sch. Medicine U. Okla., Oklahoma City, 1957-58; orthopedic surgeon Springfield, Ill., from 1958; clin. prof. Sch. Medicine So. Ill. U., Springfield, Ill., 1973-85, acting chmn. divsn. orthopedic surgery, 1972-75, chief sports medicine sect., 1975-82, program chmn. sports injury symposium, 1977-79, 82, 83. Mem. sports medicine com. Ill. State Med. Soc., 1979-80; chmn. dept. orthopedic surgery St. John's and Meml. Hosps., Springfield, 1970-79; program chmn. Med. Congress of World Fedn. of Ukrainian Med. Assn., Dniepropetrovsk, 1994, Odessa, Ukraine, 1996; presenter Am. Acad. Orthopedic Surgeons, Miami, Fla., 1961, N.Y., 1969, San Francisco, 1971, Washington, 1972, Las Vegas, 1973, 77, Anaheim, Calif., 1983, Chgo. Orthopedic Soc., 1967, 76, O'Donoghue Okla. Orthopedic Alumni Assn., Oklahoma City, 1972, 75, 78, Internat. Soc. for Orthopedic Surgery and Traumatology, XII World Congress, Tel Aviv, 1972, Copenhagen, 1975, Kyoto, Japan, 1978, So. Ill U. Sch. Medicine, Springfield, 1977, 79, 80, 82, Ill. State Orthopedic Soc., Chgo., 1978, ACS, Chgo., 1979, Am. Orthopedic Soc. for Sports Medicine, Atlanta, 1980, Big Sky, Mont., 1980,, Lake Tahoe, Nev., 1981, Clin. Orthopedic Soc., Chgo., 1987, World Fedn. Ukrainian Med. Assn., Kiev, Ukraine, 1990, U. Lviv, Ukraine, 1990, 11th Congress of Orthopedic Surgeons of Ukraine, Kharkiv, 1991, Congress of World Fedn. of Ukrainian Med. Assn., Kharkiv, 1992, Dnipropetrovsk, 1994, Odessa, 1996, Ukraine, among others. Mem. editl. bd. Jour. Ukrainan Med. Assn. N.Am., 1977-95; contbr. articles to profl. jours. and med. textbooks. Fellow Am. Acad. Orthopedic Surgery; mem. AMA, Ill. Orthopedic Soc., Internat. Soc. Orthopedic Surgery and Traumatology, Am. Orthopedic Soc. for Sports Medicine, Internat. Soc. of the Knee, Mid-Am. Orthopedic Assn., Ukrainian Acad. and Profl. Assn. Pres. 1985-89), Sangamon County Med. Soc., Chgo. Orthopedic Soc. Avocations: golf, walking, chess. Died Aug. 28, 2007.

ZARZESKI, MARILYN TAYLOR, accounting educator; b. Youngstown, Ohio, June 28, 1949; d. Anthony J. and Lottie T. (Szabat) Z.; m. Tomas W. Taylor; children: Dean Taylor, Dana Zanezic. BA, Notre Dame Coll., South Euclid, Ohio, 1971; MBA, Youngstown State U., 1976; PhD, U. Fla., 1994. CPA, Fla.; CFP, Fla. Ins. agt. Zarzeski & Daughter Ins. Agy., Youngstown, 1974-76; internal auditor Flagship Bank, Miami, Fla., 1976-78; fin. & retail mgr. Am. Express, NYC, 1978-82; account mgr. CIGNA, Chgo., 1982; assoc. prof. Barry U., Miami Shores, Fla., 1983-93; asst. prof. U. Ctrl. Fla., Orlando, from 1994. Contbr. articles to profl. jours. Bd. dirs. Nat. Assn. Accts., Miami, 1985-87. Mem. AICPA, Am. Acctg. Assn., Acad. Internat. Bus. Democrat. Roman Catholic. Avocations: tennis, piano, hiking, reading, swimming. Home: Oxford, Miss. Died June 24, 2007.

ZATZKIS, HENRY, retired mathematician; b. Holzminden, Germany, Apr. 7, 1915; came to the U.S., 1940; s. Markus and Lifscha (Eber) Z.; m. Natalie Florence Serlin, July 1, 1951; children: Mark, David. BS, Ohio State U., 1941; MS, Ind. U., 1943; PhD, Syracuse U., 1950. Instr. Ind. U., Bloomington, U. N.C., Chapel Hill, Syracuse (N.Y.) U.; asst. prof. U. Conn., Storrs; assoc. prof. N.J. Inst. Tech., Newark, prof., prof. emeritus. Contbr. articles to profl. jours. Mem. Phi Beta Kappa, Sigma Xi. Jewish. Home: Los Angeles, Calif. Died Aug. 15, 2007.

ZAWODNY, ALBERT MICHAEL, manufacturing company executive; b. Balt., Nov. 15, 1927; s. Vincent Paul and Frances Marie (Bialek) Z.; m. Ellen Virginia Derr, June 26, 1948. BS in Acctg., U. Balt., 1954. CPA, Md. Mgr. EDP Holabird Signal Depot, Balt., 1947-51; sr. acct. Deloitte, Haskins & Sells, Balt., 1951-56; asst. controller J. Schoeneman, Inc., Balt., 1957-63; treas. Head Ski Co., Balt., 1963-70; exec. v.p. Lion Bros. Co., Inc., Balt., 1970-82; v.p., treas. Worcester Mfg. Co., Balt., from 1983. Mem. Am. Inst. CPA's, Md. Assn. CPA's, Fin. Execs. Inst. Home: Towson, Md. Died Feb. 18, 2007.

ZEBARAH, DANNY PETER, producer, director, engineer, editor; b. Trenton, Mich., Dec. 31, 1957; s. Albert Peter and Wilma Ruth (Fite) Z.; m. Marla Joy Hillebrandt, Apr. 27, 1985; children: Lisa Michelle, David Peter. BA, U. Detroit, 1980, postgrad. Grip, prodn. asst., Detroit, 1980-85; prodn. mgr. U. Detroit, 1985-93; editor Ameritech, Detroit, 1993; engr. WXYZ-TV, Detroit, from 1994, Ga. Pacific Television, Atlanta, from 1996. Freelance photographer, Detroit, 1977—; freelance producer/dir., Detroit, 1987—. Dir. several TV and radio prodns. including Glad Tidings for the Poor, 1990, Beyond the Ivy Door, 1980, Ask the Professor, 1989; editor MVP Comm., 1996. Mem. NATAS, SMPTE, Detroit Producers Assn., Windsor-Detroit MG Car Club (sec. 1988-92, 95), K.C., Alpha Epsilon Rho (Mem. of Yr. 1980). Democrat. Roman Catholic. Avocations: british sportscars, cub scouts. Home: Brownstwn Township, Mich. Died Aug. 23, 2007.

ZEIGER, DAVID, poet, retired English educator; b. NYC, July 18, 1921; s. Isaac Zeiger and Rose Odessa; m. Lila Anita Leichtling, Nov. 24, 1949; children: Sara, Arnold. BA, Bklyn. Coll., 1943; MA, NYU, 1948. Cert. secondary sch. tchr., N.Y. H.S. sch. tchr. N.Y. pub. schs., 1944-56; English tchr. New Utrecht (N.Y.) H.S., 1944-56; prof. English Fashion Inst. Tech., N.Y., 1956-85; ret., 1985. Vol. instr. English and speech Internat. Ctr., N.Y.C., 1994—. Author: Life On My Breath, 1995. Founder United Coll. Employees, N.Y.C., 1963. Mem. N.Y. State United Tchrs., Poetry Soc. Am. Avocations: dance, chamber music, theater. Died Dec. 14, 2007.

ZEMELKO, JOSEPH ANDREW, addictions and mental health therapist, consultant; b. Gary, Ind., Sept. 12, 1946; s. Joseph John Zemelko and Elizabeth Anne Molik; m. Charlemeine Sandra Zacek, June 3, 1995; adopted children: Andrea, Daniel; m. Joelle Rosalie Pickford, Nov. 20, 1971 (div. June 10, 1993); children: Jennifer, Timothy, Rebecca. BS in Psychology, Calumet Coll. St. Joseph's, Whiting, Ind., 1994; MEd, Purdue Univ. Calumet, Hammond, Ind., 1997. Lic. LCPC Ill., cert. CCBT Nat. Bd. Continue Behavioral Therapists, CADC, registered MISA II, cert. CCJAP. Intake counselor So. Suburban Coun., East Hazel Crest, Ill., 1996; sub. tchr. Merrillville Cmty. Sch., Merrillville, Ind., 1996; counselor intern Porter County Family Counselor, Valpariaso, Ind., 1997; counselor Cmty. Counselor Ctr., Aurora, Ill., 1997—99; sch. counselor, intern Chgo. Internat. Charter Sch., Chgo., 1999; IOP counselor Cmty. Counselors Ctr., Aurora, Ill., 1999—2001; assessment Counselor Sunrise Growth Ctr., Chgo., 2001—03. Contbr. scientific papers. SP4,ER US Army, 1966—69, Germany. Mem.: ACA, Nat. Assn. of Alcohol & Drug Abuse. Roman Cath. Avocations: jogging, piano, music, movies, dine out. Died Feb. 15, 2007.

ZIELIŃSKI, JERZY STANISŁAW, electrical engineering educator, engineering scientist; b. Łódź, Poland, Oct. 27, 1933; s. Jakub and Janina (Bocheńska) Z.; m. Jadwiga Wesołowska, Sept. 1, 1961; 1 child, Wojciech. MSc CEng, Tech. U., Łódź, 1956, PhD, 1964, DSc, 1969. Asst. Tech. U. Łódź, 1956—60, asst. lectr. tech., 1960—64, lectr., 1964—70, asst. prof. engring., 1970—80, Tech. U., Lublin, Poland, 1976—82, assoc. prof., 1982—86, U. Łódź, 1982—90, prof., head dept. informatics, 1988—2004, from 2007, dep. dean mgmt. faculty, 1994—96, prof. emeritus, 2004—06, head dept. informatics and telecomms. Coll. Informatics, 2004—07, head dept. informatics. Cons. Power Inst., Warsaw, 1973, Rsch. Ctr. Automatic, Łódź, 1987-91, Power Co., Zamość, 1988-03, Łódź Region Power Distr. Co., 2003-05; rsch. dir., Rsch. Ctr. Automatic, Łódź, 1991-03; participant in five EU projects; supr. doctoral theses in elec. engring. and computer sci. Author: Trans. Analysis in Electrical Power Systems with Application of the Method of Characteristics, 1975, Overvoltage in Electrical Power Systems Computation with Application of Analog and Digital Computers, 1985; (textbook) Analog and Digital Modeling, 1980, System Engineering, 1984, (editor, co-author) Fifty Years of Jerzy S. Zielinski Scientific Activity, Proceedings, 2004; co-author: Intellegent Knowledge Based Systems in Electrical Power Engineering, 1997; co-author, editor: Intelligent Systems in Management, 1999, Information Society, 2008; editor Acta Universitatis Lodziensis, Folia Informatica; author, co-author more than 280 papers and reports. Decorated Golden Cross of Merit, knight's cross and officer's cross Order of Rebirth of Poland; recipient Long-time Svc. Golden medal, Sci. award Polish Acad. Sci., 1966, Sci. award Minn. Higher Edn., 1965, 76, 2002, Sci. award Polish Soc. Theoretical and Applied Electrotechnics, 1963-68, Sci. award Rectors of Univs., Tech. U., Łódź, 1969, 70, 73, Tech. U. Lublin, 1981-84, U. Łódź, 1985-88, 2011. Mem. IEEE (sr.mem.), Assn. Polish Electricians (expert Disting. Silver and Gold decorations), Polish Soc. Informatics, Polish Soc. Theoretical and Applied Electrotechnics, Łódź Sci. Soc., Sci. Soc., Econ. Informatics (co-founder). Roman Catholic. Avocations: music, bicycling, walking, stamp-collecting. Home: Lodz, Poland. Died Feb. 27, 2011.

ZIGMAN, SEYMOUR, biochemist; b. Rockaway, NY, Nov. 21, 1932; s. David and Sarah (Lutsky) Z.; 1 child, Sheron Fern. BS, Cornell U., 1954; MD, Rutgers U., 1959. Prof. ophthalmology, biochem. U. Rochester (N.Y.), 1962-98; prof. ophthalmology Boston U. Sch. Medicine, from 1998. Cons. in field. Fellow Am. Soc. Ophthalmology. Avocations: golf, fishing, music. Died Dec. 14, 2006.

ZINSSER, WILLIAM KNOWLTON, editor, writer, educator; b. NYC, Oct. 7, 1922; s. William Herman and Joyce (Knowlton) Z.; m. Caroline Fraser, Oct. 10, 1954; children: Amy Fraser, John William. AB, Princeton U., 1944; L.H.D., Rollins Coll., 1984; Litt.D., Ind. State U., 1985, Wesleyan U., 1988. Feature writer N.Y. Herald Tribune, 1946-49, drama editor, 1949-54, film critic, 1955-58, editorial writer, 1958-59; free-lance writer, 1959—1970; commentator on NBC-TV Sunday program, 1964-65; columnist Look mag, 1967, Life mag, 1968-72, N.Y. Times, 1977; faculty Yale U., 1971-79, master Branford Coll., 1973-79; gen. editor, Book-of-the-Month Club, 1979-86. Author: Any Old Place With You, 1957, Seen Any Good Movies Lately?, 1958, Search and Research, 1961, The City Dwellers, 1962, Weekend Guests, 1963, The Haircurl Papers, 1964, Pop Goes America, 1966, The Paradise Bit, 1967, The Lunacy Boom, 1970, On Writing Well, 1976, Writing with a Word Processor, 1983, Mitchell & Ruff: An American Profile in Jazz, 1984, Writing to Learn, 1988, Spring Training, 1989, American Places, 1992, Speaking of Journalism, 1994, Writing About Your Life: A Journey Into the Past, 2004; co-author: Five Boyhoods, 1962; editor Extraordinary Lives, 1986, Inventing the Truth, 1987, Spiritual Quests, 1988, Paths of Resistance, 1989, Worlds of Childhood, 1990, They Went, 1991, Going on Faith, 1999. Bd. dirs. Bklyn. Mus., 1967-72. Served with AUS, 1943-45, MTO. Mem.: Century Assn, Coffee House. Home: New York, NY. Died May 12, 2015.

ZIOMEK, PATRICIA ANN, piano teacher, church organist; b. Oskaloosa, Iowa, Sept. 18, 1932; d. Leonard and Geneva (Kamper) DeMoor; m. Henry Ziomek, Aug. 16, 1956; children: Stanley Ziomek, John Josef Ziomek, Paul Henry Ziomek. BA magna cum laude, Hastings Coll., Nebr., 1954; MusM, Ind. U., 1956. Pvt. piano tchr., Oshkosh, Wis., 1956-60, Athens, Ga., 1966-93; ch. organist Algoma Ave. Meth. Ch., Oshkosh, 1956-58; organist, choir dir. Golden Valley Community Presbyn. Ch., Mpls., 1958-59, Trinity Episcopal Ch., Oshkosh, 1959-60; ch. organist Episcopal Mission Ch., Fort Collins, Colo., 1963-64, Emmanual Episcopal Ch., Athens, Ga., 1966-69, Cen. Presbyn. Ch., Athens, 1980-84; organist, choir dir. First Presbyn. Ch., Winder, Ga., 1984-88; ch. organist St. Stephens Anglican Ch., Athens, 1991-96. Concerto soloist Hastings High Sch. Orch., 1949, Nebr. All-State Orch., 1950, others. Mem. AAUW (pres. 1973-75, officer Athens br. 1968—, Gift honoree 1989), Athens Ladies' Garden Club. Avocations: travel, music, writing. Home: Athens, Ga. Died July 18, 2007.

ZOOK, MERLIN WAYNE, meteorologist, educator; b. Connellsville, Pa., July 2, 1937; s. Ellrose Durr and Frances Adeline (Loucks) Z.; m. Maxine Beatrice Hartzler, May 1, 1965; children: Kevin Ray, Kathleen Joy. BA, Goshen Coll., Ind., 1959; MS, Pa. State U., 1961. Cert. consulting meteorologist. Rsch. assoc. U. Mich., Ann Arbor, 1958; grad. asst. Pa. State U., University Park, 1960-61; audio-visual asst., staff meteorologist Mennonite Cen. Com., Akron, Pa., 1961-63; air quality program specialist Pa. Dept. Environ. Protection, Harrisburg, Pa., 1963-2000; ret., 2000. Book reviewer Sci. Edn. Dept. Boston U., 1990-92, Nat. Weather Assn., Temple Hills, Md., 1983-88, book rev. editor, 1988-92; scientist, participant AAAS-Bell Atlantic Found., Washington, 1989-90; lectr. Goshen (Ind.) Coll., Messiah Coll., Grantham, Pa. Author, contbr.: (chpt.) Behind the Dim Unknown, 1966. Guest lectr. Millersville (Pa.) State U., 1988, 90, Boy Scouts Am., Camp Hill, Pa., 1990, Pa. State U., Middletown, 1990, 91—, Cub Scouts Am., Camp Hill, 1991—. Mem. Am. Meteorol. Soc., Union of Concerned Scientists. Achievements include development of models for the daily prediction of the Air Quality Index of Pa.; collection of cloud type photographs with classifications for study of cloud characteristics/physics; research in mesoscale meteorology and localized forecasting, on the relationship between solar radiation and formation of ozone in urban areas in Pa., research and development of mathematical models for the prediction of ozone episodes in urban areas; on migratory patterns of local birds influenced by meteorological conditions. Home: Camp Hill, Pa. Died Aug. 5, 2007.

ZSIGMOND, VILMOS, cinematographer, film director; b. Szeged, Hungary, June 16, 1930; came to U.S., 1957, naturalized, 1962; s. Vilmos and Bozena (Illichmann) Z.; children: Julia, Susi. MA, U. Film and Theater Arts, Budapest, Hungary, 1955. Free-lance cinematographer for numerous commls., also ednl., documentary and low-budget feature films, 1965-71; now dir., cinematographer on commls. (winner several nat. and internat. awards); feature films, 1971-2016; films include McCabe and Mrs. Miller, 1971; Images, 1972, Deliverance, 1972, The Long Goodbye, 1973, Scarecrow, 1973, Cinderella Liberty, 1973, The Sugarland Express, 1974, Obsession, 1976, Close Encounters of the Third Kind, 1977 (Acad. award 1977), The Last Waltz, 1978, The Rose, 1978, The Deerhunter, 1978 (Acad. award nomination and Brit. Acad. award), Heavens Gate, 1979, The Border, 1980, Blow Out, 1980, Jinxed, 1981, Table for Five, 1982, The River, 1983 (Acad. award nomination), No Small Affair, 1984, Real Genius, 1985, Witches of Eastwick, 1986, Journey to Spirit Island, 1988, Fatman and Little Boy, 1989, Two Jakes, 1989, Bonfire of the Vanities, 1990, Stalin, 1991 (CableAce award, Direction of Photography and/or Lighting Direction in a Dramatic/Theatrical Special/Movie or Miniseries, ASC award, Emmy award), Sliver, 1992; dir. The Long Shadow, 1992, Intersection, 1993, Maverick, 1993, The Crossing Guard, 1994, Assassins, 1995, The Ghost and the Darkness, 1996 (ASC Award nomination), Fantasy for a New Age, 1997, Playing By Heart, 1998, The Body, 1999, The Mists of Avalon, 2000, Life as a House, 2001, (opera film) Bánk

Bán, 2002, Jersey Girl, 2003, Melinda and Melinda, 2004, The Black Dahlia, 2005, Cassandra's Dream, 2007, Torn From the Flag: A Film by Klaudia Kovacs, 2007, You Will Meet a Tall Dark Stranger, 2010, Louis, 2010, Summer Children, 2011, The Maiden Danced to Death, 2011, Compulsion, 2013, God The Father, 2014, Six Dance Lessons in Six Weeks, 2014; (TV series) The Mindy Project, 2012-2014 Recipient lifetime achievement award Worldfest, Flagstaff, 1998. Mem. Acad. Motion Picture Arts and Scis., Dirs. Guild, Am. Soc. Cinematographers (lifetime achievement award 1998). Home: Big Sur, Calif. Died Jan. 1, 2016.

ZUCCOTTI, JOHN EUGENE, real estate company executive; b. NYC, June 23, 1937; m. Susan Sessions; children: Gianna, Andrew, Milena. AB in History, Princeton U., 1959; LLB, Yale U., 1963. Bar: N.Y. 1963, D.C. 1970. Asst. to under sec. and sec. HUD, Washington, 1967-69; sec., counsel Nat. Corp. for Housing Partnerships, Washington, 1969-70; spl. counsel to housing subcom. Banking and Currency Com. US House of Representatives, Washington, 1970-73; ptnr. Tufo, Johnston and Zuccotti, NYC, 1970-72; chmn. N.Y.C. Planning Commn., 1973-75, mem., 1971-73; 1st dep. mayor City of N.Y., 1975-77; sr. ptnr. Tufo, Johnston, Zuccotti and Allegaert, NYC, 1977-86, Brown & Wood, NYC, 1986-89; pres., chief exec. officer Olympia and York Company (U.S.A.), 1989—96; chmn. Brookfield, 1996—2015; of counsel Weil, Gotshal and Manges, 1998—2015. Impartial arbitrator between MTA/TWU, 1981-90. Chmn. Performing Arts Ctr. World Trade Ctr., Downtown-Lower Manhattan Assn., Real Estate Bd. NY Home: Brooklyn, NY. Died Nov. 19, 2015.

ZUERN, THEODORE FRANCIS, priest; b. Milw., Jul 6, 1921; s. Frank John and Margaret Zuern. PhB, Marquette U., 1946. Ordained priest Roman Cath. Ch., 1957. Mem staff St. Francis (S.D.) Mission, 1959-61; asst. dir. Mothe Butler Ctr., Rapid City, S.D., 1961-67, dir., 1967-68, Holy Rosary Mission, Pine Ridge, S.D., 1968-74, Office India Ministry, Archdiocese of St. Paul, 1975-79; legis. dir. Bu Cath. Indian Mission, Washington, from 1979. Author Bread and Freedom, 1991, Call Them Sioux, 1998. Legis dir. Bur. Cath. Indian Missions, Washington, 1979— Home: Washington, DC. Died June 25, 2007.